January 22–24, 2014
San Diego, California, USA



Association for
Computing Machinery

*Advancing Computing as a Science & Profession*

# POPL'14

## Proceedings of the 41st Annual ACM SIGPLAN-SIGACT Symposium on Principles of Programming Languages

*Sponsored by:*

***ACM SIGPLAN***

*In cooperation with:*

***ACM SIGACT***

Association for
Computing Machinery

*Advancing Computing as a Science & Profession*

**The Association for Computing Machinery**
**2 Penn Plaza, Suite 701**
**New York, New York 10121-0701**



**ISBN:** 978-1-4503-2544-8

Additional copies may be ordered prepaid from:

**ACM Order Department**
PO Box 30777
New York, NY 10087-0777, USA

Phone: 1-800-342-6626 (USA and Canada)
+1-212-626-0500 (Global)
Fax: +1-212-944-1318
E-mail: acmhelp@acm.org
Hours of Operation: 8:30 am – 4:30 pm ET

Printed in the USA

# Chairs' Welcome

It is our great pleasure to welcome you to the 41st Annual ACM SIGPLAN-SIGACT Symposium on Principles of Programming Languages – POPL'14, being held in San Diego, CA. POPL was last held here in 1998. We are very pleased that we were able to arrange for a long overdue return, giving an opportunity for our attendees to experience the charm, salubrious weather, and numerous attractions of this vibrant and dynamic city.

POPL 2014 San Diego, CA January 22-24

POPL'14 features the following co-located events:

- The 15th International Conference on Verification, Model-Checking, and Abstract Interpretation (VMCAI)
- The 16th International Symposium on Practical Aspects of Declarative Languages (PADL)
- The Workshop on Partial Evaluation and Program Manipulation (PEPM)
- The Workshop on Programming Languages meets Program Verification (PLPV)
- The Workshop on Program Protection and Reverse Engineering (PPREW)
- The Off the Beaten Track Workshop (OBT)
- The Programming Language Mentoring Workshop (PLMW)
- The Principles in Practice Workshop (PiP) - a new event

Support from corporate sponsors helped tremendously to keep POPL's registration fees modest, and enabled low-cost access to all conference events for students. We are deeply grateful to all of our sponsors for their support and generosity. The POPL'14 organizing committee deserves special thanks for their tireless efforts in helping to (a) coordinate co-located events with the main conference, (b) handle student activities and tutorials, (c) ensure the conference was widely publicized, and (d) manage budgets and financing. The sage advice of the entire POPL steering committee was also invaluable. We are also grateful to the following professionals for their support and contributions: John Lateulere of Integrated Management Solutions; Carole Mann and her team at Registration Systems Labs; Lisa Tolles of Sheridan Printing, and Ashley Cozzi, Adrienne Griscti, Farrah Khan, Maritza Nichols, Stephanie Sabal, and Debra Venedam of ACM SIG services. Our thanks also to the staff at the US Grant hotel for their help in accommodating POPL at their historic venue.

The call for papers attracted 220 submissions. Papers were principally reviewed by a program committee of 27 researchers, who reviewed 21-25 each (typically three PC reviews per paper). The review process did not involve a preselected external review committee. Instead, to try to get the best possible external expert reviews for each paper, reviews were solicited from the community as a whole. One PC member was designated as `guardian' for each paper to take the lead in identifying suitable candidate externals. In all, 273 individials contributed external reviews. The majority of papers (146) received four reviews; 53 received five, 15 received three, and 2 received six (the remaining 4 were withdrawn before the PC meeting). The PC meeting in Cambridge discussed 102 papers over two days, with a first pass in a random order then a second review pass. 51 papers were accepted (23% of the submissions).

A lightweight double-blind review process was used to reduce the effect of first impression biases: authors were asked to anonymise their submissions, but were not restricted from disseminating their work in any of the normal ways. PC members were permitted to de-blind submissions as necessary, e.g. to discuss external reviewers.

PC submissions were allowed but the PC were not involved in any way in the selection process for PC submissions; that was managed by the program and general chairs and involved only external reviewers.

A survey of authors, between the author response period and the PC meeting, gathered their views on the double-blind process and the quality of reviewing. A survey at submission time assessed the current use of mechanised tools such as proof assistants. In all, 1009 individuals were named in the process, including reviewer suggestions; that gives some measure of the size of the POPL community at present. Details of the survey results and the POPL 2014 review process will be available in the Program Chair's report.

We would like to thank the program committee and external reviewers for their sterling work, Eddie Kohler for providing and supporting the HotCRP conference management system, Piete Brooks for managing our HotCRP installation, and Gabriel Kerneis and Dominic Mulligan for their assistance at the PC meeting.

**Suresh Jagannathan**
*POPL'14 General Chair*
*West Lafayette, USA*

**Peter Sewell**
*POPL'14 Program Chair*
*Cambridge, UK*

# Table of Contents

## Session 9b: Functional Programming 2

Session Chair: Neelakantan R. Krishnaswami *(University of Birmingham)*

# POPL 2014 Organization

| | |
|---|---|
| **General Chair** | Suresh Jagannathan (*Purdue University, USA*) |
| **Program Chair** | Peter Sewell (*University of Cambridge, UK*) |
| **Treasurers** | Evan Chang (*University of Colorado, Boulder, USA*)<br>Ross Tate (*Cornell University, USA*) |
| **Publicity Chair** | Viktor Vafeiadis (*MPI-SWS, Germany*) |
| **Co-located Events Chair** | David Van Horn (*Northeastern University, USA*) |
| **Student Activities Chair** | Tobias Wrigstad (*Uppsala University, Sweden*) |
| **Steering Committee** | Radhia Cousot (*ENS, Paris, France*)<br>John Field (*Google, USA*)<br>Roberto Giacobazzi (*University of Verona, Italy*)<br>Jeremy Gibbons (*Oxford University, UK*)<br>Mike Hicks (*University of Maryland, USA*<br>Graham Hutton (*University of Nottingham, UK*)<br>Suresh Jagannathan (*Purdue University, USA*)<br>Peter Sewell (*University of Cambridge, UK*)<br>Jan Vitek (*Purdue University, USA*)<br>Philip Wadler (*University of Edinburgh, UK*) |
| **Program Committee** | Andrew W. Appel (*Princeton University, USA*)<br>Gilles Barthe (*IMDEA Software Institute, Spain*)<br>Nick Benton (*Microsoft Research, Cambridge, UK*)<br>Lars Birkedal (*Aarhus University, Denmark*)<br>Ahmed Bouajjani (*University Paris Diderot, France*)<br>James Cheney (*University of Edinburgh, UK*)<br>Mads Dam (*KTH Royal Institute of Technology, Sweden*)<br>Dino Distefano (*Facebook, USA and Queen Mary, University of London, UK*)<br>Thomas Dillig (*University College London, UK*)<br>Sophia Drossopoulou (*Imperial College London, UK*)<br>Nate Foster (*Cornell University, USA*)<br>Atsushi Igarashi (*Kyoto University, Japan*)<br>Alan Jeffrey (*Alcatel-Lucent Bell Labs, USA*)<br>Neelakantan R. Krishnaswami (*University of Birmingham, UK*)<br>Aditya V. Nori (*Microsoft Research, Bangalore, India*)<br>Noam Rinetzky (*Tel Aviv University, Israel*) |

**Program committee (continued)**

Xavier Rival (*INRIA Paris-Rocquencourt and ENS Paris, CNRS, France*)
Andrey Rybalchenko (*Microsoft Research, Cambridge, UK and Technische Universität München, Germany*)
Jeremy G. Siek (*University of Colorado at Boulder, USA*)
Nikhil Swamy (*Microsoft Research, Redmond, USA*)
Ross Tate (*Cornell University, USA*)
Tayssir Touili (*CNRS Paris, France*)
Aaron J. Turon (*MPI-SWS, Germany*)
Viktor Vafeiadis (*MPI-SWS, Germany*)
Stephanie Weirich (*University of Pennsylvania, USA*)
Thomas Wies (*New York University, USA*)
Elena Zucca (*University of Genoa, Italy*)

**Additional Reviewers**

Andreas Abel
Danel Ahman
Jade Alglave
Davide Ancona
Eugene Asarin
Faouzi Atig
Robert Atkey
Hagit Attiya
Josh Berdine
Martin Berger
Ales Bizjak
Nikolaj Bjorner
Ras Bodik
Hans-J. Boehm
Johannes Borgström
Matko Botincan
John Tang Boyland
Niklas Broberg
James Brotherston
Kim Bruce
Béatrice Bérard
Luís Caires
Brian Campbell
Marco Carbone
Manuel M. T. Chakravarty
Bor-Yuh Evan Chang
Swarat Chaudhuri
Wei Ngan Chin
Adam Chlipala
Ravi Chugh
Albert Cohen
Thomas Colcombet
Roberto Di Cosmo
Patrick Cousot
Karl Crary
Nils Anders Danielsson
Aldric Degorre
Bart van Delft
Mariangiola Dezani
Thomas Dinsdale-Young
Mike Dodds
Nurit Dor
Cezara Dragoi
Roland Ducourneau
Bruno Dutertre
Stephen Edwards
Martin Elsman
Michael Emmi
Constantin Enea
Xinyu Feng
Pietro Ferrara
Andrzej Filinski
Marcelo Fiore
Kathleen Fisher
Matthew Fluet
Cédric Fournet
Song Fu
Marco Gaboardi
Didier Galmiche
Simon Gay

**Additional reviewers (continued)**

Samir Genaim
Colin Gordon
Eric Goubault
Kathryn Gray
Dan Grossman
Arjun Guha
Alexander Gurney
Jurriaan Hage
Kevin Hammond
Sandeep Hans
Nir Hemed
Aquinas Hobor
Lukas Holik
David Van Horn
Chung-Kil Hur
Radu Iosif
Bart Jacobs
Barry Jay
Jonas B. Jensen
Neil Jones
Dejan Jovanović
Max Kanovich
Andrew Kennedy
Vladimir Klebanov
Naoki Kobayashi
Eric Koskinen
Shriram Krishnamurthi
Daniel Kroening
Cesar Kunz
Ugo Dal Lago
Akash Lal
Doug Lea
Xavier Leroy
Paul Blain Levy
Daniel Licata
Francesco Logozzo
Ravichandhran Madhavan
Sergio Maffeis
Pasquale Malacaria
Roman Manevich
Mark Marron
Kenneth McMillan
Ron van der Meyden
Jan Midtgaard
Stefan Milius
Patrice Godefroid
Alexey Gotsman
Bjrn Grathwohl
Timothy G. Griffin
Guy Golan Gueta
Shu-yu Guo
Peter Habermehl
Makoto Hamana
Jad Hamza
Chris Hawblitzel
Fritz Henglein
Martin Hofmann
Florian Horn
Cătălin Hritcu
Martin Hyland
Shachar Itzhaky
Radha Jagadeesan
Wolfgang Jeltsch
Adrian Johnstone
Simon Peyton Jones
Ohad Kammar
Joost-Pieter Katoen
S. Keshav
Gerwin Klein
Ruud Koot
Vasileios Koutavas
Jean Krivine
Markus Kuhn
Orna Kupferman
Shuvendu Lahiri
Dominique Larchey-Wendling
Daan Leijen
Joe Leslie Hurd
Jean-Jacques Levy
Sam Lindley
Hugo Macedo
Anil Madhavapeddy
Rupak Majumdar
Yitzhak Mandelbaum
Luc Maranget
Conor McBride
Paul-André Melliès
Roland Meyer
Matthew Might
Antoine Miné

**Additional reviewers (continued)**

Neil Mitchell
David Monniaux
Simon Moore
J. Garrett Morris
Shin-Cheng Mu
Chunyan Mu
Andrzej S. Murawski
Rasmus Ejlers Møgelberg
Anders Møller
Santosh Nagarakatte
Mayur Naik
David Naumann
Georg Neis
Ryan R. Newton
Kim Nguyễn
Michael Norrish
Peter O'Hearn
Hakjoo Oh
Luke Ong
Vincent van Oostrom
Scott A. Owens
Jens Palsberg
Prakash Panangaden
Matthew Parkinson
Madhusudan Parthasarathy
Étienne Payet
Hila Peleg
Frank Pfenning
David Pichardie
Brigitte Pientka
Benjamin C. Pierce
Keshav Pingali
Nir Piterman
Andrew Pitts
Andreas Podelski
David Pointcheval
Corneliu Popeea
François Pottier
John Power
Shaz Qadeer
Sriram Rajamani
Ganesan Ramalingam
Ulrik Terp Rasmussen
Julian Rathke
Uday Reddy
Laurent Regnier
Jan Reineke
Tom Reps
Ahmed Rezine
Tamara Rezk
Gregor Richards
Tom Ridge
James Riely
Simona Ronchi Della Rocca
Adam Rogalewicz
Andreas Rossberg
Daniel Roy
Alejandro Russo
Didier Rémy
Andrei Sabelfeld
Amr Sabry
Davide Sangiorgi
Arnaud Sangnier
Susmit Sarkar
Gabriel Scherer
Taro Sekiyama
Koushik Sen
Anton Setzer
Jaroslav Ševčík
Paula Severi
Ali Sezgin
Zhong Shao
Marc Shapiro
Filip Sieczkowski
Alexandra Silva
Mihaela Sighireanu
Satnam Singh
Gareth Smith
Ana Sokolova
Armando Solar-Lezama
Christoph Sprenger
Manu Sridharan
Ian Stark
Sam Staton
Thomas Streicher
Pierre-Yves Strub
Aaron Stump
Martin Sulzmann
Kasper Svendsen
Nicolas Tabareau

**Additional reviewers (continued)**

Walid Taha
Jean-Pierre Talpin
Orr Tamir
Serdar Tasiran
Tachio Terauchi
Peter Thiemann
Blaise Thomson
Frank Tip
Hiroshi Unno
Tarmo Uustalu
Vasco Vasconcelos
Martin Vechev
Arnaud Venet
Jules Villard
Janis Voigtläender
Heiko Vogler
Tomas Vojnar
Jérôme Vouillon
Ian Voysey
Daniel Wagner
David Walker
Jingling Xue
Eran Yahav
Hongseok Yang
Kwangkeun Yi
Brent Yorgey
Nobuko Yoshida
Santiago Zanella Beguelin
Francesco Zappa Nardelli
Marek Zawirski
Steve Zdancewic
Noam Zeilberger
Mohammad Zubair
Florian Zuleger

# POPL 2014 Sponsor & Supporters

**Sponsor:** ACM SIGPLAN

**In cooperation with:** SIGACT

**Supporters:**

facebook

Google

IBM Research

Jane Street

Microsoft Research

Oracle Labs

NEC

SAMSUNG

# Modular Reasoning about Concurrent Higher-Order Imperative Programs

Lars Birkedal

Department of Computer Science, Aarhus University

birkedal@cs.au.dk

***Categories and Subject Descriptors*** D.3.1 [*Programming Languages*]: Formal Definitions and Theory – semantics; D.2.4 [*Software Engineering*]: Software/Program Verification

***Keywords*** contextual equivalence; data abstraction; program logics

## 1. Introduction

Modern mainstream programming languages permit a powerful combination of language features: concurrency, higher-order functions, and mutable shared data structures. These features are all very important for programming in practice. However, it is well-known that the combination of them makes it difficult to write correct and secure programs, and it is therefore important to develop mathematically-based techniques for formal reasoning about correctness and security of programs with these features.

To get scalable methods that apply to realistic programs, it is crucial that the mathematical models and logics support *modular* reasoning, meaning that (1) specifications and proofs are compositional wrt. the program structure; and (2) specifications and proofs can concentrate on the resources that a program actually acts upon, instead of its entire state.

In this talk I will give an overview of some of the central developments that my group has worked on when generalizing reasoning techniques for simpler programming languages to concurrent, higher-order, imperative languages. I will consider both relational models and program logics based on higher-order separation logic.

## 2. Kripke Logical Relations

One of the most fundamental notions in formal reasoning about programs is contextual refinement, which expresses when one program fragment may be replaced by another one, without changing the overall behaviour of a complete program. This is the notion of correctness that one is interested in when, e.g., reasoning about data abstraction or proving compiler optimizations correct. It is difficult to reason directly about contextual refinement of programs and thus there has been a lot of work on extending the techniques of (bi)simulations and logical relations from simply-typed purely functional programming languages to programming languages with recursive types, polymorphism, dynamically allocated mutable references, and, lately, also concurrency. For the work on logical relations, the main challenges have been: (1) to develop mathematical techniques that are expressive enough to construct the interpretation of all the types – this is difficult when the programming language includes recursive types and general references, which preclude a definition of the relation by direct induction over the types; (2) to develop models that are sufficiently expressive for reasoning about uses of local state, i.e., to define the logical relations in such a way that one can show that two programs that use local state in very different ways to implement the same functionality are indeed related; and (3) to develop logical relations for concurrent languages which allow one to reason about one thread at a time, while still accounting for the possible interference of other running threads. To address these challenges we have developed new kinds of Kripke logical relations using guarded recursion. The resulting models have been used, e.g., (1) to prove correctness of a parallelization theorem, which expresses when it is sound to evaluate two expressions in parallel instead of sequentially, by giving a relational model for a type-and-effect system; and (2) to show correctness of fine-grained concurrent data structures by showing that they are contextual refinements of their coarse-grained counterparts, so that clients can reason about fine-grained concurrent data structures as if all accessses to them were sequentialized.

## 3. Higher-Order Separation Logics

Instead of specifying a program by relating it to another program, we can specify programs using program logics. Separation logic allows specifications and proofs to concentrate on the resources that a program actually acts upon, instead of its entire state. To allow specifications and proofs to be compositional wrt. the program structure we developed higher-order separation logic. To reason about higher-order imperative programs, we introduced nested triples. These features facilitate modular reasoning about sequential higher-order programs with limited forms of sharing. To also cater for concurrency and sharing, we make use of earlier work that extend rely-guarantee versions of separation logic with protocols governing access to shared mutable state. For modularity, we use higher-order quantification over so-called impredicative protocols. To show soundness of the logic we build a non-trivial model using guarded recursion. The resulting logic can be used, e.g., to give modular specifications of layered and recursive higher-order abstractions, as used ubiquitously in GUI and network applications for implementing asynchronous I/O.



*POPL '14*, January 22–24, 2014, San Diego, CA, USA.

ACM 978-1-4503-2544-8/14/01.
http://dx.doi.org/10.1145/2535838.2537849

# A Galois Connection Calculus for Abstract Interpretation*

Patrick Cousot
CIMS**, NYU, USA pcousot@cims.nyu.edu

Radhia Cousot
CNRS Emeritus, ENS, France rcousot@ens.fr

**Abstract** We introduce a Galois connection calculus for language independent specification of abstract interpretations used in programming language semantics, formal verification, and static analysis. This Galois connection calculus and its type system are typed by abstract interpretation.

***Categories and Subject Descriptors*** D.2.4 [*Software/Program Verification*]
***General Terms*** Algorithms, Languages, Reliability, Security, Theory, Verification.
***Keywords*** Abstract Interpretation, Galois connection, Static Analysis, Verification.

## 1. Galois connections in Abstract Interpretation

In *Abstract interpretation* [3, 4, 6, 7] concrete properties (for example (*e.g.*) of computations) are related to abstract properties (*e.g.* types). The abstract properties are always *sound* approximations of the concrete properties (abstract proofs/static analyzes are always correct in the concrete) and are sometimes *complete* (proofs/analyzes of abstract properties can all be done in the abstract only). *E.g.* types are sound but incomplete [2] while abstract semantics are usually complete [9]. The *concrete domain* $\langle \mathcal{C}, \sqsubseteq\rangle$ and *abstract domain* $\langle \mathcal{A}, \preccurlyeq\rangle$ of properties are posets (partial orders being interpreted as implication). When concrete properties all have a $\preccurlyeq$-most precise abstraction, the correspondence is a *Galois connection (GC)* $\langle \mathcal{C}, \sqsubseteq\rangle \overset{\gamma}{\underset{\alpha}{\leftrightarrows}} \langle \mathcal{A}, \preccurlyeq\rangle$ with *abstraction* $\alpha \in \mathcal{C} \mapsto \mathcal{A}$ and *concretization* $\gamma \in \mathcal{A} \mapsto \mathcal{C}$ satisfying $\forall P \in \mathcal{C} : \forall Q \in \mathcal{A} : \alpha(x) \preccurlyeq y \Leftrightarrow x \sqsubseteq \gamma(y)$ ($\Rightarrow$ expresses soundness and $\Leftarrow$ best abstraction). Each adjoint $\alpha/\gamma$ uniquely determines the other $\gamma/\alpha$. A *Galois retraction* (or *insertion*) has $\alpha$ onto, so $\gamma$ is one-to-one, and $\alpha \circ \gamma$ is the identity. *E.g.* the *interval abstraction* [3, 4] of the power set $\wp(C)$ of complete $\leq$-totally ordered sets $C \cup \{-\infty, \infty\}$ is $\mathcal{S}\llbracket \mathbb{I}[\langle C, \leq\rangle, -\infty, \infty]\rrbracket \triangleq \langle \wp(C), \subseteq\rangle \overset{\gamma^{\mathbb{I}}}{\underset{\alpha^{\mathbb{I}}}{\leftrightarrows}} \langle \mathbb{I}(C\cup\{-\infty,\infty\}, \leq), \Subset\rangle$ with $\alpha^{\mathbb{I}}(X) \triangleq [\min X, \max X]$, $\min \emptyset \triangleq \infty$, $\max \emptyset \triangleq -\infty$, $\gamma^{\mathbb{I}}([a, b]) \triangleq \{x \in C \mid a \leq x \leq b\}$, intervals $\mathcal{S}\llbracket \mathbb{I}(C \cup \{-\infty, \infty\}, \leq)\rrbracket \triangleq \{[a, b] \mid a \in C \cup \{-\infty\} \wedge b \in C \cup \{\infty\} \wedge a \leq b\} \cup \{[\infty, -\infty]\}$, and inclusion $[a, b] \Subset [c, d] \triangleq c \leq a \wedge b \leq d$. A *Galois isomorphism* $\langle \mathcal{C}, \subseteq\rangle \overset{\gamma}{\underset{\alpha}{\leftrightarrows}} \langle \mathcal{A}, \preccurlyeq\rangle$ has both $\alpha$ and $\gamma$ bijective. *E.g.* global and local invariants are isomorphic by the *right image abstraction* $\mathcal{S}\llbracket \curvearrowright[\mathbb{L}, \mathcal{M}]\rrbracket \triangleq \langle \wp(\mathbb{L} \times \mathcal{M}), \subseteq\rangle \overset{\gamma^{\curvearrowright}}{\underset{\alpha^{\curvearrowright}}{\leftrightarrows}} \langle \mathbb{L} \mapsto \wp(\mathcal{M}), \dot{\subseteq}\rangle$ with $\alpha^{\curvearrowright}(P) \triangleq \boldsymbol{\lambda} \ell \bullet \{m \mid \langle \ell, m\rangle \in P\}$, $\gamma^{\curvearrowright}(Q) \triangleq \{\langle \ell, m\rangle \mid m \in Q(\ell)\}$, and $\dot{\subseteq}$ is the pointwise extension of inclusion $\subseteq$.

## 2. Equivalent formalizations of *GC*-based Abstract Interpretation

*GCs* $\langle \mathcal{C}, \sqsubseteq\rangle \overset{\gamma}{\underset{\alpha}{\leftrightarrows}} \langle \mathcal{A}, \preccurlyeq\rangle$ are Galois retracts of/Galois isomorphic to numerous equivalent mathematical structures [6] such as *join-preserving maps* ($\alpha$), *meet-preserving maps* ($\gamma$), *upper-closures* ($\gamma \circ \alpha$), *Moore families* ($\{\gamma(Q) \mid Q \in \mathcal{A}\}$), *Sierpiński topologies* [5] ($\{\neg\gamma(Q) \mid Q \in \mathcal{A}\}$ where $\neg$ is unique complementation in the concrete domain $\mathcal{C}$, if any), *principal downset families* ($\{\downarrow^{\sqsubseteq}\gamma(Q) \mid Q \in \mathcal{A}\}$ where $\downarrow^{\sqsubseteq}x \triangleq \{y \in \mathcal{C} \mid y \sqsubseteq x\}$), *maximal convex congruences* ($\{\{P \in \mathcal{C} \mid \alpha(P) = \alpha(\gamma(Q))\} \mid Q \in \mathcal{A}\}$, *soundness relations* (also called *abstraction relation*, *logical relation*, or *tensor product*, $\alpha \mathbin{⨾} \preccurlyeq\ = \{\langle P, Q\rangle \mid \alpha(P) \preccurlyeq Q\} = \{\langle P, Q\rangle \mid P \sqsubseteq \gamma(Q)\} = \sqsubseteq \mathbin{⨾} \gamma^{-1}$ where $f \equiv \{\langle x, f(x)\rangle \mid x \in \mathsf{dom}(f)\}$, $r \mathbin{⨾} r' = \{\langle x, z\rangle \mid \exists y : \langle x, y\rangle \in r \wedge \langle y, z\rangle \in r'\}$), and, for powersets $\mathcal{C} = \wp(C)$, $\mathcal{A} = \wp(A)$, *polarities* of relations ($\gamma(Q) = \{x \in C \mid \forall y \in Q : R(x, y)\}$ where $R = \{\langle x, y\rangle \mid x \in \gamma(\{y\})\}$).

* See the auxiliary materials. ** Work supported in part by the CMACS NSF award 0926166.



*POPL '14*, January 22–24, 2014, San Diego, CA, USA. Copyright is held by the owner/author(s).
ACM 978-1-4503-2544-8/14/01. http://dx.doi.org/10.1145/2535838.2537850

## 3. Basic *GC* semantics

Basic *GCs* are primitive abstractions of properties. Classical examples are the *identity abstraction* $\mathcal{S}\llbracket \mathbb{1}[\langle \mathcal{C}, \sqsubseteq\rangle]\rrbracket \triangleq \langle \mathcal{C}, \sqsubseteq\rangle \overset{\boldsymbol{\lambda} Q \bullet Q}{\underset{\boldsymbol{\lambda} P \bullet P}{\leftrightarrows}} \langle \mathcal{C}, \sqsubseteq\rangle$, the *top abstraction* $\mathcal{S}\llbracket \top[\langle \mathcal{C}, \sqsubseteq\rangle, \top]\rrbracket \triangleq \langle \mathcal{C}, \sqsubseteq\rangle \overset{\boldsymbol{\lambda} Q \bullet \top}{\underset{\boldsymbol{\lambda} P \bullet \top}{\leftrightarrows}} \langle \mathcal{C}, \sqsubseteq\rangle$, the *join abstraction* $\mathcal{S}\llbracket \cup[C]\rrbracket \triangleq \langle \wp(\wp(C)), \subseteq\rangle \overset{\gamma^{\wp}}{\underset{\alpha^{\wp}}{\leftrightarrows}} \langle \wp(C), \subseteq\rangle$ with $\alpha^{\wp}(P) \triangleq \bigcup P$, $\gamma^{\wp}(Q) \triangleq \wp(Q)$, the *complement abstraction* $\mathcal{S}\llbracket \neg[C]\rrbracket \triangleq \langle \wp(C), \subseteq\rangle \overset{\neg}{\underset{\neg}{\leftrightarrows}} \langle \wp(C), \supseteq\rangle$, the finite/infinite *sequence abstraction* $\mathcal{S}\llbracket \infty[C]\rrbracket \triangleq \langle \wp(C^{\infty}), \subseteq\rangle \overset{\gamma^{\infty}}{\underset{\alpha^{\infty}}{\leftrightarrows}} \langle \wp(C), \subseteq\rangle$ with $\alpha^{\infty}(P) \triangleq \{\sigma_i \mid \sigma \in P \wedge i \in \mathsf{dom}(\sigma)\}$ and $\gamma^{\infty}(Q) \triangleq \{\sigma \in C^{\infty} \mid \forall i \in \mathsf{dom}(\sigma) : \sigma_i \in Q\}$, the *transformer abstraction* $\mathcal{S}\llbracket \rightsquigarrow[C_1, C_2]\rrbracket \triangleq \langle \wp(C_1 \times C_2), \subseteq\rangle \overset{\gamma^{\rightsquigarrow}}{\underset{\alpha^{\rightsquigarrow}}{\leftrightarrows}} \langle \wp(C_1) \overset{\cup}{\longrightarrow} \wp(C_2), \dot{\subseteq}\rangle$ mapping relations to join-preserving transformers with $\alpha^{\rightsquigarrow}(R) \triangleq \boldsymbol{\lambda} X \bullet \{y \mid \exists x \in X : \langle x, y\rangle \in R\}$, $\gamma^{\rightsquigarrow}(g) \triangleq \{\langle x, y\rangle \mid y \in g(\{x\})\}$, the *function abstraction* $\mathcal{S}\llbracket \mapsto[C_1, C_2]\rrbracket \triangleq \langle \wp(C_1 \mapsto C_2), \subseteq\rangle \overset{\gamma^{\mapsto}}{\underset{\alpha^{\mapsto}}{\leftrightarrows}} \langle \wp(C_1) \mapsto \wp(C_2), \dot{\subseteq}\rangle$ with $\alpha^{\mapsto}(P) \triangleq \boldsymbol{\lambda} X \bullet \{f(x) \mid f \in P \wedge x \in X\}$, $\gamma^{\mapsto}(g) \triangleq \{f \in C_1 \mapsto C_2 \mid \forall X \in \wp(C_1) : \forall x \in X : f(x) \in g(X)\}$, the *cartesian abstraction* $\mathcal{S}\llbracket \times[I, C]\rrbracket \triangleq \langle \wp(I \mapsto C), \subseteq\rangle \overset{\gamma^{\times}}{\underset{\alpha^{\times}}{\leftrightarrows}} \langle I \mapsto \wp(C), \dot{\subseteq}\rangle$ with $\alpha^{\times}(X) \triangleq \boldsymbol{\lambda} i \in I \bullet \{x \in C \mid \exists f \in I \mapsto C : f[i \leftarrow x] \in X\}$, $\gamma^{\times}(Y) \triangleq \{f \mid \forall i \in I : f(i) \in Y(i)\}$, and the pointwise extension $\dot{\subseteq}$ of $\subseteq$ to $I$, *etc.*

## 4. Galois connector semantics

*Galois connectors* build a *GC* from *GCs* provided as parameters. Unary Galois connectors include the *reduction connector* $\mathcal{S}\llbracket \mathsf{R}[\langle \mathcal{C}, \sqsubseteq\rangle \overset{\gamma}{\underset{\alpha}{\leftrightarrows}} \langle \mathcal{A}, \preccurlyeq\rangle]\rrbracket \triangleq \langle \mathcal{C}, \sqsubseteq\rangle \overset{\gamma}{\underset{\alpha}{\leftrightarrows}} \langle \{\alpha(P) \mid P \in \mathcal{C}\}, \preccurlyeq\rangle$ and the *pointwise connector* $\mathcal{S}\llbracket X \twoheadrightarrow \langle C, \sqsubseteq\rangle \overset{\gamma}{\underset{\alpha}{\leftrightarrows}} \langle A, \preccurlyeq\rangle\rrbracket \triangleq \langle X \mapsto C, \dot{\sqsubseteq}\rangle \overset{\boldsymbol{\lambda} \overline{\rho} \bullet \gamma \circ \overline{\rho}}{\underset{\boldsymbol{\lambda} \rho \bullet \alpha \circ \rho}{\leftrightarrows}} \langle X \mapsto A, \dot{\preccurlyeq}\rangle$ for the pointwise orderings $\dot{\sqsubseteq}$ and $\dot{\preccurlyeq}$. Binary Galois connectors include the *composition connector* $\mathcal{S}\llbracket \langle \mathcal{C}, \subseteq\rangle \overset{\gamma_1}{\underset{\alpha_1}{\leftrightarrows}} \langle \mathcal{A}_1, \Subset\rangle \mathbin{⨾} \langle \mathcal{A}_2, \sqsubseteq\rangle \overset{\gamma_2}{\underset{\alpha_2}{\leftrightarrows}} \langle \mathcal{A}_3, \preccurlyeq\rangle\rrbracket \triangleq (\!| \langle \mathcal{A}_1, \Subset\rangle = \langle \mathcal{A}_2, \sqsubseteq\rangle \;?\; \langle \mathcal{C}, \subseteq\rangle \overset{\gamma_1 \circ \gamma_2}{\underset{\alpha_2 \circ \alpha_1}{\leftrightarrows}} \langle \mathcal{A}_3, \preccurlyeq\rangle \;:\; \Omega |\!)$ (where $\Omega$ is a static error), the *product connector* $\mathcal{S}\llbracket \langle \mathcal{C}_1, \subseteq\rangle \overset{\gamma_1}{\underset{\alpha_1}{\leftrightarrows}} \langle \mathcal{A}_1, \sqsubseteq\rangle \circledast \langle \mathcal{C}_2, \Subset\rangle \overset{\gamma_2}{\underset{\alpha_2}{\leftrightarrows}} \langle \mathcal{A}_2, \preccurlyeq\rangle\rrbracket \triangleq \langle \mathcal{C}_1 \times \mathcal{C}_2, \subseteq \times \Subset\rangle \overset{\gamma_1 \times \gamma_2}{\underset{\alpha_1 \times \alpha_2}{\leftrightarrows}} \langle \mathcal{A}_1 \times \mathcal{A}_2, \sqsubseteq \times \preccurlyeq\rangle$ (generalizing to tuples), the higher-order *functional connector* $\mathcal{S}\llbracket \langle \mathcal{C}_1, \subseteq\rangle \overset{\gamma_1}{\underset{\alpha_1}{\leftrightarrows}} \langle \mathcal{A}_1, \sqsubseteq\rangle \Longmapsto \langle \mathcal{C}_2, \preccurlyeq\rangle \overset{\gamma_2}{\underset{\alpha_2}{\leftrightarrows}} \langle \mathcal{A}_2, \leqslant\rangle\rrbracket \triangleq \langle \mathcal{C}_1 \overset{\nearrow}{\longrightarrow} \mathcal{C}_2, \dot{\preccurlyeq}\rangle \overset{\boldsymbol{\lambda} g \bullet \gamma_2 \circ g \circ \alpha_1}{\underset{\boldsymbol{\lambda} f \bullet \alpha_2 \circ f \circ \gamma_1}{\leftrightarrows}} \langle \mathcal{A}_1 \overset{\nearrow}{\longrightarrow} \mathcal{A}_2, \dot{\leqslant}\rangle$ for increasing maps and pointwise orderings $\dot{\sqsubseteq}$ and $\dot{\leqslant}$.

## 5. Galois connection calculus

The *GC* calculus $\mathbb{G}$ (to specify verifiers/analyzers compositionally) is $\mathtt{x}, \ldots \in \mathbb{X}$ for program variables, $\ell, \ldots \in \mathbb{L}$ for labels, $e \in \mathbb{E}$ for elements $e ::= \mathsf{true} \mid 1 \mid \infty \mid \mathtt{x} \mid \ell \mid -e \mid \ldots$, $s \in \mathbb{S}$ for sets $s ::= \mathbb{B} \mid \mathbb{Z} \mid \mathbb{X} \mid \mathbb{L} \mid \{e\} \mid [e, e] \mid \mathbb{I}(s, o) \mid s^{\infty} \mid s \cup s \mid s \mapsto s \mid s \times s \mid \wp(s) \mid \ldots$, $o \in \mathbb{O}$ for partial orders $o ::= \Rightarrow \mid \Leftrightarrow \mid \leq \mid \subseteq \mid \Subset \mid = \mid o^{-1} \mid o_1 \times o_2 \mid \dot{o} \mid \ddot{o} \mid \ldots$, $p \in \mathbb{P}$ for posets $p ::= \langle s, o\rangle$, and $g \in \mathbb{G}$ for *GCs* $g ::= \mathbb{1}[p] \mid \top[p, e] \mid \mathbb{I}[p, e, e] \mid \curvearrowright[s, s] \mid \cup[s] \mid \neg[s] \mid \infty[s] \mid \rightsquigarrow[s, s] \mid \mapsto[s, s] \mid \times[s, s] \mid \ldots \mid \mathsf{R}[g] \mid s \twoheadrightarrow g \mid g \mathbin{⨾} g \mid g \circledast g \mid g \Longmapsto g \mid \ldots$. The semantics of interval sets is $\mathcal{S}\llbracket \mathbb{I}(C, \preccurlyeq)\rrbracket \triangleq (\!| \preccurlyeq\ \subseteq C \times C \;?\; \{[a, b]_{\preccurlyeq} \mid a, b \in C\} \;:\; \omega |\!)$ where $\omega$ is a dynamic error (maybe not detectable by typing).

**6. Abstraction** Papers in semantics, verification, and static analysis can be understood by extracting the semantic domain and *GC* which are used. For the interval example [3, 4, p. 247], the semantic domain $\mathcal{S} \triangleq \wp(\Sigma^{\infty})$ is that of (nonempty) sets of nonempty finite or infinite sequences of states in $\Sigma \triangleq \mathbb{L} \times \mathcal{M}$ made of a control state in $\mathbb{L}$ and a memory state in $\mathcal{M} \triangleq \mathbb{X} \mapsto \mathcal{V}$ mapping variables $\mathbb{X}$ to a complete total order $\langle \mathcal{V}, \leq\rangle$ (*e.g.* $\langle \mathbb{Z}, \leqslant\rangle$ or $\langle[\texttt{minint},\texttt{maxint}], \leqslant\rangle$). The *static* (or *collecting*) *semantics* is the *reachability abstraction* of program properties in $\wp(\mathcal{S})$ that is $G^* \triangleq \cup[\Sigma^{\infty}] \,\mathring{,}\, \infty[\Sigma] \,\mathring{,}\, \curvearrowright[\mathbb{L}, \mathcal{M}]$ with abstract domain $\langle \mathbb{L} \mapsto \wp(\mathcal{M}), \dot{\subseteq}\rangle$. The *reduced interval cartesian reachability abstraction* is $G^{\mathfrak{I}^*} \triangleq \mathsf{R}[G^* \,\mathring{,}\, (\mathbb{L} \twoheadrightarrow (\times[\mathbb{X}, \mathcal{V}] \,\mathring{,}\, (\mathbb{X} \twoheadrightarrow \mathbb{I}[\langle \mathcal{V}, \leq\rangle, -\infty, \infty])))]$ that is the abstraction $\langle \wp(\wp((\mathbb{L} \times (\mathbb{X} \mapsto \mathcal{V}))^{\infty})), \subseteq\rangle \xrightarrow[\alpha]{\gamma} \langle \mathbb{L} \mapsto \mathbb{X} \mapsto \mathbb{I}(\mathcal{V} \cup \{-\infty, \infty\}), \ddot{\sqsubseteq}\rangle$ where $\alpha(P) \triangleq \boldsymbol{\lambda}\ell \bullet \mathsf{smash}(\boldsymbol{\lambda}\mathtt{x} \bullet \alpha^{\mathtt{I}}(\alpha^{\times}((\alpha^{\curvearrowright}(\alpha^{\infty}(\alpha^{\wp}(P))))(\ell))(\mathtt{x})))$ and $\mathsf{smash}(\boldsymbol{\lambda}\mathtt{x} \in \mathbb{X} \bullet [a_{\mathtt{x}}, b_{\mathtt{x}}])$ reduces to $\boldsymbol{\lambda}\mathtt{x} \in \mathbb{X} \bullet [\infty, -\infty]$ when some $[a_{\mathtt{x}}, b_{\mathtt{x}}]$ is the empty interval $[\infty, -\infty]$ else to $\boldsymbol{\lambda}\mathtt{x} \in \mathbb{X} \bullet [a_{\mathtt{x}}, b_{\mathtt{x}}]$.

**7. Typing** As usual with syntactic definitions, *GC* expression semantics may be undefined (*i.e.* $\Omega$ or $\omega$). This can be fixed for $\Omega$ by a type system that is an Abstract Interpretation of the properties $\wp(\mathfrak{Gc})$ of the semantics $\mathcal{S}[\![g]\!] \in \mathfrak{Gc}$ of expressions $g \in \mathbb{G}$ belonging to the class $\mathfrak{Gc} \triangleq \{\langle \mathcal{C}, \sqsubseteq\rangle \xrightarrow[\alpha]{\gamma} \langle \mathcal{A}, \preccurlyeq\rangle \mid \mathcal{C}, \mathcal{A}$ are sets $\wedge \sqsubseteq \in \wp(\mathcal{C} \times \mathcal{C}) \wedge \preccurlyeq \in \wp(\mathcal{A} \times \mathcal{A})\} \cup \{\Omega, \omega\}$. Typing is formalized by a *GC* [2] $\langle \wp(\mathfrak{Gc}), \subseteq\rangle \xrightarrow[\alpha^{\mathfrak{T}}]{\gamma^{\mathfrak{T}}} \langle \mathfrak{T}_{/\cong}, \trianglelefteq\rangle$ where the preorder on types is $\mathsf{T} \trianglelefteq \mathsf{T}' \triangleq \gamma^{\mathfrak{T}}(\mathsf{T}) \subseteq \gamma^{\mathfrak{T}}(\mathsf{T}')$ so that types $\mathfrak{T}_{/\cong}$ are considered up to the equivalence $\cong$ for this preorder $\trianglelefteq$ ($\cong$ is $=$ when $\gamma^{\mathfrak{T}}$ is injective). In absence of a $\trianglelefteq$-most precise *i.e.* principal type, hence of a best abstraction $\alpha^{\mathfrak{T}}$, as *e.g.* in [15] for the polyhedral abstraction, only one of $\alpha$ or $\gamma$ is used [7]. A *GC* expression $g \in \mathbb{G}$ has sound types $\mathsf{T} \in \mathfrak{T}$ such that $\{\mathcal{S}[\![g]\!]\} \subseteq \gamma^{\mathfrak{T}}(\mathsf{T})$ *i.e.* $\mathcal{S}[\![g]\!] \in \gamma^{\mathfrak{T}}(\mathsf{T})$ or $\rho^{\mathfrak{Gc}}(\mathcal{S}[\![g]\!], \mathcal{T}[\![g]\!])$ for the soundness relation $\rho^{\mathfrak{Gc}}(S, T) \triangleq S \in \gamma^{\mathfrak{T}}(T)$. For *GCs*, this is equivalent to $\alpha^{\mathfrak{T}}(\{\mathcal{S}[\![g]\!]\}) \trianglelefteq \mathsf{T}$, where $\{\mathcal{S}[\![g]\!]\}$ is the strongest property (collecting semantics) of $g$ and $\alpha^{\mathfrak{T}}(\{\mathcal{S}[\![g]\!]\})$ is the best abstraction of $g$. The type soundness proof is by induction on the structure of the *GC* expressions as in [2] (instead of operational subject reduction *i.e.* induction on program computation steps).

**8. Types** For elements $\mathsf{E} \in \mathfrak{E}$, $\mathsf{E} ::= \textbf{var} \mid \textbf{lab} \mid \textbf{bool} \mid \textbf{int} \mid \textbf{err}$ with $\gamma^{\mathfrak{E}}(\textbf{int}) \triangleq \mathbb{Z} \cup \{-\infty, \infty\}$, $\gamma^{\mathfrak{E}}(\textbf{err}) \triangleq \mathcal{S}(\mathbb{E}) \cup \{\Omega, \omega\}$.

For sets $\mathsf{S} \in \mathfrak{S}$, $\mathsf{S} ::= \mathbf{P}\ \mathsf{E} \mid \mathbf{P}\ \mathsf{S} \mid \textbf{seq}\ \mathsf{S} \mid \mathsf{S} \twoheadrightarrow \mathsf{S} \mid \mathsf{S} * \mathsf{S} \mid \textbf{err}$ with $\gamma^{\mathfrak{S}}(\mathbf{P}\ \mathsf{E}) \triangleq \wp(\gamma^{\mathfrak{E}}(\mathsf{E}))$, $\gamma^{\mathfrak{S}}(\mathbf{P}\ \mathsf{S}) \triangleq \wp(\gamma^{\mathfrak{S}}(\mathsf{S}))$, $\gamma^{\mathfrak{S}}(\textbf{seq}\ \mathsf{S}) \triangleq \{X^{\infty} \mid X \in \gamma^{\mathfrak{S}}(\mathsf{S})\}$, $\gamma^{\mathfrak{S}}(\mathsf{S}_1 \twoheadrightarrow \mathsf{S}_2) \triangleq \{X \mapsto Y \mid X \in \gamma^{\mathfrak{S}}(\mathsf{S}_1) \wedge Y \in \gamma^{\mathfrak{S}}(\mathsf{S}_2)\}$, $\gamma^{\mathfrak{S}}(\mathsf{S}_1 * \mathsf{S}_2) \triangleq \{X \times Y \mid X \in \gamma^{\mathfrak{S}}(\mathsf{S}_1) \wedge Y \in \gamma^{\mathfrak{S}}(\mathsf{S}_2)\}$, $\gamma^{\mathfrak{S}}(\textbf{err}) \triangleq \mathcal{S}(\mathbb{S}) \cup \{\Omega, \omega\}$.

For partial orders $\mathsf{O} \in \mathfrak{O}$, $\mathsf{O} ::= \Rightarrow \mid \Leftrightarrow \mid \leq \mid \subseteq \mid = \mid \mathsf{O}^{-1} \mid \mathsf{O} \star \mathsf{O} \mid \dot{\mathsf{O}} \mid \ldots \mid \textbf{err}$ with $\gamma^{\mathfrak{O}}(\mathsf{O}) \triangleq \{\mathsf{O}\}, \mathsf{O} \in \{\Rightarrow, \Leftrightarrow, \leq, \subseteq, =\}$, $\Rightarrow \triangleq \{\langle \mathsf{false}, \mathsf{false}\rangle, \langle \mathsf{true}, \mathsf{true}\rangle\}$, *etc.*

For posets $\mathsf{P} \in \mathfrak{P}$, $\mathsf{P} ::= \mathsf{S} \circledast \mathsf{O} \mid \textbf{err}$ with componentwise concretization $\gamma^{\mathfrak{P}}(\mathsf{S} \circledast \mathsf{O}) \triangleq \gamma^{\mathfrak{S}}(\mathsf{S}) \times \gamma^{\mathfrak{O}}(\mathsf{O})$.

For *GCs*, $\mathsf{T} \in \mathfrak{T}$, $\mathsf{T} ::= \mathsf{P} \leftrightharpoons \mathsf{P} \mid \mathsf{S} \twoheadrightarrow \mathsf{T} \mid \textbf{err}$ with $\gamma^{\mathfrak{T}}(\mathsf{P} \leftrightharpoons \mathsf{P}') \triangleq \{P \xrightarrow[\alpha]{\gamma} P' \mid P \in \gamma^{\mathfrak{P}}(\mathsf{P}) \wedge P' \in \gamma^{\mathfrak{P}}(\mathsf{P}')\}$ and $\gamma^{\mathfrak{T}}(\mathsf{S} \twoheadrightarrow \mathsf{T}) \triangleq \{\langle X \mapsto \mathcal{C}, \dot{\sqsubseteq}\rangle \xrightarrow[\alpha']{\gamma'} \langle X \mapsto \mathcal{A}, \dot{\preccurlyeq}\rangle \mid X \in \gamma^{\mathfrak{S}}(\mathsf{S}) \wedge \langle \mathcal{C}, \sqsubseteq\rangle \xrightarrow[\alpha]{\gamma} \langle \mathcal{A}, \preccurlyeq\rangle \in \gamma^{\mathfrak{T}}(\mathsf{T})\}$.

**9. Type inference** The type inference algorithm is $\mathscr{E}[\![\mathsf{true}]\!] \triangleq \textbf{bool}, \ldots, \mathscr{E}[\![-e]\!] \triangleq (\!| \mathscr{E}[\![e]\!] = \textbf{bool} \vee \mathscr{E}[\![e]\!] = \textbf{int} \ \text{?}\ \mathscr{E}[\![e]\!] \ \text{:}\ \textbf{err} |\!)$.

For sets $\mathcal{S}[\![\mathbb{B}]\!] \triangleq \mathbf{P}\ \textbf{bool}, \ldots, \mathcal{S}[\![\{e\}]\!] \triangleq (\!| \mathscr{E}[\![e]\!] \neq \textbf{err} \ \text{?}\ \mathbf{P}\ \mathscr{E}[\![e]\!] \ \text{:}\ \textbf{err} |\!), \ldots, \mathcal{S}[\![s_1 \cup s_2]\!] \triangleq (\!| \textbf{err} \neq \mathcal{S}[\![s_1]\!] \cong \mathcal{S}[\![s_2]\!] \neq \textbf{err} \ \text{?}\ \mathcal{S}[\![s_1]\!] \ \text{:}\ \textbf{err} |\!)$ (note the approximation that $s_1$ and $s_2$ must have equivalent types as for alternatives of conditionals in functional languages).

Ignoring error propagation, $\mathcal{S}[\![s^{\infty}]\!] \triangleq \textbf{seq}\ \mathcal{S}[\![s]\!]$, $\mathcal{S}[\![s_1 \mapsto s_2]\!] \triangleq \mathcal{S}[\![s_1]\!] \twoheadrightarrow \mathcal{S}[\![s_2]\!]$, $\mathcal{S}[\![s_1 \times s_2]\!] \triangleq \mathcal{S}[\![s_1]\!] * \mathcal{S}[\![s_2]\!]$, $\mathcal{S}[\![\wp(s)]\!] \triangleq \mathbf{P}\ \mathcal{S}[\![s]\!]$.

For orders and posets, $\mathfrak{O}[\![o]\!] \triangleq o$, $o \in \{\Rightarrow, \Leftrightarrow, \leq, \subseteq, =\}$, $\mathfrak{O}[\![\dot{\sqsubseteq}]\!] \triangleq \subseteq, \ldots, \mathfrak{O}[\![\ddot{o}]\!] \triangleq ((\dot{\mathfrak{O}[\![o]\!]}))$, and $\mathscr{P}[\![\langle s, o\rangle]\!] \triangleq \mathcal{S}[\![s]\!] \circledast \mathfrak{O}[\![o]\!]$.

For *GCs*, $\mathcal{T}[\![\mathbb{1}[p]]\!] \triangleq \mathscr{P}[\![p]\!] \leftrightharpoons \mathscr{P}[\![p]\!]$, $\mathcal{T}[\![\curvearrowright[s_{\mathbb{L}}, s_{\mathcal{M}}]]\!] \triangleq \mathbf{P}(\mathcal{S}[\![s_{\mathbb{L}}]\!] * \mathcal{S}[\![s_{\mathcal{M}}]\!]) \circledast \subseteq \leftrightharpoons \mathcal{S}[\![s_{\mathbb{L}}]\!] \twoheadrightarrow \mathbf{P}\ \mathcal{S}[\![s_{\mathcal{M}}]\!] \circledast \dot{\subseteq}$, $\mathcal{T}[\![\cup[s]]\!] \triangleq \mathbf{P}\ (\mathbf{P}\ \mathcal{S}[\![s]\!]) \circledast \subseteq \leftrightharpoons \mathbf{P}\ \mathcal{S}[\![s]\!] \circledast \subseteq$, $\mathcal{T}[\![\neg[s]]\!] \triangleq \mathbf{P}\ \mathcal{S}[\![s]\!] \circledast \subseteq \leftrightharpoons \mathbf{P}\ \mathcal{S}[\![s]\!] \circledast \subseteq^{-1}$, $\mathcal{T}[\![\infty[s]]\!] \triangleq \mathbf{P}\ (\textbf{seq}\ \mathcal{S}[\![s]\!]) \circledast \subseteq \leftrightharpoons \mathbf{P}\ \mathcal{S}[\![s]\!] \circledast \subseteq$, $\mathcal{T}[\![\rightsquigarrow[s_1, s_2]]\!] \triangleq \mathbf{P}\ (\mathcal{S}[\![s_1]\!] * \mathcal{S}[\![s_2]\!]) \circledast \subseteq \leftrightharpoons \mathbf{P}\ \mathcal{S}[\![s_1]\!] \twoheadrightarrow \mathbf{P}\ \mathcal{S}[\![s_2]\!] \circledast \dot{\subseteq}$, $\mathcal{T}[\![\mapsto[s_1, s_2]]\!] \triangleq \mathbf{P}\ (\mathcal{S}[\![s_1]\!] \twoheadrightarrow \mathcal{S}[\![s_2]\!]) \circledast \subseteq \leftrightharpoons \mathbf{P}\ \mathcal{S}[\![s_1]\!] \twoheadrightarrow \mathbf{P}\ \mathcal{S}[\![s_2]\!] \circledast \dot{\subseteq}$, $\mathcal{T}[\![\times[s_1, s_2]]\!] \triangleq \mathbf{P}\ (\mathcal{S}[\![s_1]\!] \twoheadrightarrow \mathcal{S}[\![s_2]\!]) \circledast \subseteq \leftrightharpoons \mathcal{S}[\![s_1]\!] \twoheadrightarrow \mathbf{P}\ \mathcal{S}[\![s_2]\!] \circledast \dot{\subseteq}$, $\mathcal{T}[\![\mathsf{R}[g]]\!] \triangleq \mathcal{T}[\![g]\!]$, $\mathcal{T}[\![s \twoheadrightarrow g]\!] \triangleq \mathcal{S}[\![s]\!] \twoheadrightarrow \mathcal{T}[\![g]\!], \ldots$

Examples of type errors are $\mathcal{T}[\![\top[p, e]]\!] \triangleq (\!| \mathscr{E}[\![e]\!] \neq \textbf{err} \wedge \exists \mathsf{S} \in \mathfrak{S}, \mathsf{O} \in \mathfrak{O} : \mathscr{P}[\![p]\!] = \mathsf{S} \circledast \mathsf{O} \wedge \mathscr{E}[\![e]\!] \Subset \mathsf{S} \ \text{?}\ \mathscr{P}[\![p]\!] \leftrightharpoons \mathscr{P}[\![p]\!] \ \text{:}\ \textbf{err} |\!)$ or $\mathcal{T}[\![\mathbb{I}[\langle s, o\rangle, b, t]]\!] \triangleq (\!| \textbf{err} \neq \mathscr{E}[\![b]\!] \Subset \mathcal{S}[\![s]\!] \neq \textbf{err} \wedge \textbf{err} \neq \mathscr{E}[\![t]\!] \Subset \mathcal{S}[\![s]\!] \ \text{?}\ (\mathbf{P}\ \mathcal{S}[\![s]\!] \circledast \subseteq) \leftrightharpoons (\mathbf{P}\ \mathcal{S}[\![s]\!] \circledast \subseteq) \ \text{:}\ \textbf{err} |\!)$ where $\Subset$ abstracts set membership $\in$ of top/botton elements to the abstracted set.

This functional presentation is equivalent to a rule-based system *e.g.* $\dfrac{g_1 \vdash \mathsf{P}_1 \leftrightharpoons \mathsf{P}_2,\ g_2 \vdash \mathsf{P}_3 \leftrightharpoons \mathsf{P}_4,\ \mathsf{P}_2 \cong \mathsf{P}_3}{g_1 \mathring{,} g_2 \vdash \mathsf{P}_1 \leftrightharpoons \mathsf{P}_4}$ (where **err** is not derivable), $\dfrac{g_1 \vdash \mathsf{S}_1 \circledast \mathsf{O}_1 \leftrightharpoons \mathsf{S}_2 \circledast \mathsf{O}_2,\ g_2 \vdash \mathsf{S}_3 \circledast \mathsf{O}_3 \leftrightharpoons \mathsf{S}_4 \circledast \mathsf{O}_4}{g_1 \Longrightarrow g_2 \vdash \mathsf{S}_1 \twoheadrightarrow \mathsf{S}_3 \circledast \dot{\mathsf{O}_3} \leftrightharpoons \mathsf{S}_2 \twoheadrightarrow \mathsf{S}_4 \circledast \dot{\mathsf{O}_4}}$, *Id.* for $\circledast$.

For example $\mathcal{T}[\![G^{\mathfrak{I}^*}]\!] = \mathbf{P}\ (\mathbf{P}\ (\textbf{seq}(\mathbf{P}\ \textbf{lab} * (\mathbf{P}\ \textbf{var} \twoheadrightarrow \mathbf{P}\ \textbf{int}))))\ \circledast \subseteq \leftrightharpoons (\mathbf{P}\ \textbf{lab} \twoheadrightarrow \mathbf{P}\ \textbf{var} \twoheadrightarrow \mathbf{P}\ \mathbf{P}\ \textbf{int} \circledast \ddot{\subseteq})$ *i.e.* sets of sets of sequences of states are abstracted to a map of labels to variables to sets of integers (which includes intervals), ordered pointwise.

**10. Type soundness** Typable expressions $g \in \mathbb{G}$ (for which $\mathcal{T}[\![g]\!] \neq \textbf{err}$) cannot go wrong since then $\mathcal{S}[\![g]\!] \in \gamma^{\mathfrak{T}}(\mathcal{T}[\![g]\!]) \cup \{\omega\}$ and $\Omega \notin \gamma^{\mathfrak{T}}(\mathcal{T}[\![g]\!])$. However, dynamic errors ($\mathcal{S}[\![g]\!] = \omega$) cannot be excluded (*e.g.* `int` does not prevent overflows).

**11. Principal type** Arbitrary concrete properties in $\wp(\mathfrak{Gc})$ may have no best abstraction (*e.g.* $\emptyset$ so we add the empty type $\varnothing$). Yet, by considering only semantic properties $P = \{\mathcal{S}[\![g_i]\!] \mid i \in \Delta\}$ of *GC* expressions, the principal type is $\alpha^{\mathfrak{T}}(\emptyset) \triangleq \varnothing$, $\alpha^{\mathfrak{T}}(P) \triangleq [\mathsf{T}]_{\cong}$ when $\forall i \in \Delta \neq \emptyset : \mathcal{T}[\![g_i]\!] \cong \mathsf{T}$ else $\alpha^{\mathfrak{T}}(P) \triangleq \textbf{err}$ so $\langle \wp(\{\mathcal{S}[\![g]\!] \mid g \in \mathbb{G}\}), \subseteq\rangle \xrightarrow[\alpha^{\mathfrak{T}}]{\gamma^{\mathfrak{T}}} \langle (\mathfrak{T} \cup \{\varnothing\})_{/\cong}, \trianglelefteq\rangle$ ($\alpha^{\mathfrak{T}}$ onto).

**12. Types of types** Types $\mathcal{T} \triangleq \{\mathfrak{E}, \mathfrak{S}, \mathfrak{O}, \mathfrak{P}, \mathfrak{T}\}$ have properties $\mathcal{P} \triangleq \wp(\bigcup \mathcal{T})$ can be abstracted to types of types $\overline{\mathfrak{T}} ::= \overline{\varnothing} \mid \overline{\mathfrak{E}} \mid \overline{\mathfrak{S}} \mid \overline{\mathfrak{O}} \mid \overline{\mathfrak{P}} \mid \overline{\mathfrak{T}} \mid \overline{\textbf{err}}$ by $\alpha^{\overline{\mathfrak{T}}}(P) \triangleq (\!| P = \emptyset \ \text{?}\ \overline{\varnothing} \mid P \subseteq \mathsf{T}, \mathsf{T} \in \mathcal{T} \ \text{?}\ \overline{\mathsf{T}} \ \text{:}\ \overline{\textbf{err}} |\!)$.

**13. Static analyzers** In static analyzers [1, 12, 14] *GCs* specify abstract domains modules and Galois connectors their combinations by functors. For scalability, rapid convergence acceleration of infinite fixpoint computations by widening/narrowing abstracting induction and/or their duals for co-induction [3–5] is effective and more precise than finite abstractions [8].

**Acknowledgments** We warmly thank the ACM SIGPLAN Awards Committee for awarding us the 2013 Programming Languages Achievement Award and the programming languages community for its support.

**References**


[1] B. Blanchet, P. Cousot, R. Cousot, J. Feret, L. Mauborgne, A. Miné, D. Monniaux, and X. Rival. A static analyzer for large safety-critical software. *PLDI'03*, 196–207.

[2] P. Cousot. Types as abstract interpretations. *POPL'97*, 316–331.

[3] P. Cousot and R. Cousot. Static determination of dynamic properties of programs. *Proc. 2nd Int. Symp. on Programming*, 106–130, Paris, 1976. Dunod.

[4] P. Cousot and R. Cousot. Abstract interpretation: A unified lattice model for static analysis of programs by construction or approximation of fixpoints. *POPL'77*, 238–252.

[5] P. Cousot and R. Cousot. Static determination of dynamic properties of recursive procedures. *IFIP Conf. on Formal Description of Programming Concepts, St-Andrews, N.B., CN*, 237–277. North-Holland Pub. Co., 1977.

[6] P. Cousot and R. Cousot. Systematic design of program analysis frameworks. *POPL'79*, 269–282.

[7] P. Cousot and R. Cousot. Abstract interpretation frameworks. *J. Logic and Comp.*, 2(4):511–547, 1992.

[8] P. Cousot and R. Cousot. Comparing the Galois connection and widening/narrowing approaches to abstract interpretation. *PLILP'92*, LNCS 631, 269–295.

[9] P. Cousot and R. Cousot. Inductive definitions, semantics and abstract interpretation. *POPL'92*, 83–94.

[10] P. Cousot and R. Cousot. Temporal abstract interpretation. *POPL'00*, 12–25.

[11] P. Cousot and R. Cousot. Systematic design of program transformation frameworks by abstract interpretation. *POPL'02*, 178–190.

[12] P. Cousot and R. Cousot. An abstract interpretation-based framework for software watermarking. *POPL'04*, 173–185.

[13] P. Cousot and R. Cousot. An abstract interpretation framework for termination. *POPL'12*, 245–258.

[14] P. Cousot, R. Cousot, and F. Logozzo. A parametric segmentation functor for fully automatic and scalable array content analysis. *POPL'11*, 105–118.

[15] P. Cousot and N. Halbwachs. Automatic discovery of linear restraints among variables of a program. *POPL'78*, 84–96.

# Polymorphic Functions with Set-Theoretic Types

## Part 1: Syntax, Semantics, and Evaluation

Giuseppe Castagna[1] Kim Nguyễn[2] Zhiwu Xu[1,3] Hyeonseung Im[2] Sergueï Lenglet[4] Luca Padovani[5]

[1]CNRS, PPS, Univ Paris Diderot, Sorbonne Paris Cité, Paris, France [2]LRI, Université Paris-Sud, Orsay, France
[3]State Key Laboratory of Computer Science, Institute of Software, Chinese Academy of Sciences, Beijing, China
[4] LORIA, Université de Lorraine, Nancy, France [5]Dipartimento di Informatica, Università di Torino, Italy

**Abstract.** This article is the first part of a two articles series about a calculus with higher-order polymorphic functions, recursive types with arrow and product type constructors and set-theoretic type connectives (union, intersection, and negation). In this first part we define and study the explicitly-typed version of the calculus in which type instantiation is driven by explicit instantiation annotations. In particular, we define an explicitly-typed $\lambda$-calculus with intersection types and an efficient evaluation model for it. In the second part, presented in a companion paper, we define a local type inference system that allows the programmer to omit explicit instantiation annotations, and a type reconstruction system that allows the programmer to omit explicit type annotations. The work presented in the two articles provides the theoretical foundations and technical machinery needed to design and implement higher-order polymorphic functional languages for semi-structured data.

***Categories and Subject Descriptors*** D.3.3 [*Programming Languages*]: Language Constructs and Features—Polymorphism

***Keywords*** Types, polymorphism, XML, intersection types

## 1. Introduction

The extensible markup language XML is a current standard format for exchanging structured data. Many recent XML processing languages, such as XDuce, ℂDuce, XQuery, OcamlDuce, XHaskell, XAct, are statically-typed functional languages. However, parametric polymorphism, an essential feature of such languages, is still missing, or when present it is in a limited form (no higher-order functions, no polymorphism for XML types, and so on). Polymorphism for XML has repeatedly been requested to and discussed in various working groups of standards (*eg*, RELAX NG [6]) and higher-order functions have been recently proposed in the W3C draft for XQuery 3.0 [9]. Despite all this interest, spurs, and motivations, a comprehensive polymorphic type system for XML was still missing for the simple reason that, until recently, it was deemed unfeasible. A major stumbling block to this research —*ie*, the definition of a subtyping relation for regular tree types with type variables— has been recently lifted by Castagna and Xu [5], who defined and studied a polymorphic subtyping relation for a type system with recursive, product, and arrow types and set-theoretic type connectives (union, intersection, and negation).

In this work we present the next logical step of that research, that is, the definition of a higher-order functional language that takes full advantage of the new capabilities of Castagna and Xu's system.



*POPL '14*, January 22–24 2014, San Diego, CA, USA.

ACM 978-1-4503-2544-8/14/01... $15.00.
http://dx.doi.org/10.1145/2535838.2535840

In other words, we define and study a calculus with higher-order polymorphic functions and recursive types with union, intersection, and negation connectives. The approach is thus general and, as such, goes well beyond the simple application to XML processing languages. As a matter of facts, our motivating example developed all along this paper does not involve XML, but looks like a rather classic display of functional programming specimens:

```
map :: (α->β) -> [α] -> [β]
map f l = case l of
          | [] -> []
          | (x : xs) -> (f x : map f xs)

even :: (Int->Bool) ∧ ((α\Int)->(α\Int))
even x = case x of
          | Int -> (x 'mod' 2) == 0
          |   _ -> x
```

The first function is the classic `map` function defined in Haskell (we just used Greek letters to denote type variables). The second would be an Haskell function were it not for two oddities: its type contains type connectives (type intersection "$\wedge$" and type difference "$\setminus$"); and the pattern in the `case` expression is a type, meaning that it matches all values returned by the matched expression that have that type. So what does the `even` function do? It checks whether its argument is an integer; if it is so it returns whether the integer is even or not, otherwise it returns its argument as it received it (although `even` may be considered as bad programming, it is a perfect minimal example to illustrate all the aspects of our system).

The goal of this work is to define a calculus and a type system that can pass three tests. The first test is that it can define the two functions above. The second, harder, test is that the type system must be able to verify that these functions have the types declared in their signatures. That `map` has the declared type will come as no surprise (in practice, in the second part of this work we show that in the absence of a signature given by the programmer the system can reconstruct a type slightly more precise than this [4]). That `even` was given an intersection type means that it must have all the types that form the intersection. So it must be a function that when applied to an integer it returns a Boolean and that when applied to an argument of a type that does not contain any integer, it returns a result of the same type. In other terms, `even` is a polymorphic (dynamically bounded) overloaded function.

The third test, the hardest one, is that the type system must be able to *infer* the type of the partial application of `map` to `even`, and the inferred type must be equivalent to the following one[1]

```
map even :: ([Int] -> [Bool])  ∧
            ([α\Int] -> [α\Int]) ∧                (1)
            ([α∨Int] -> [(α\Int)∨Bool])
```

since `map even` returns a function that when applied to a list of integers it returns a list of Booleans, when applied to a list that

[1] This type is redundant since the first type of the intersection is an instance (*eg*, for $\alpha$=`Int`) of the third. We included it for the sake of the presentation.

does not contain any integer then it returns a list of the same type (actually, the same list), and when it is applied to a list that may contain some integers (*eg*, a list of reals), then it returns a list of the same type, without the integers but with some Booleans instead (in the case of reals, a list with Booleans and reals that are not integers).

Technically speaking, the definition of such a calculus and its type system is difficult for two distinct reasons. First, for the reasons we explain in the next section, it demands to define an explicitly typed $\lambda$-calculus with intersection types, a task that, despite many attempts in the last 20 years, still lacked a satisfactory definition. Second, even if working with an explicitly typed setting may seem simpler, the system needs to solve "local type inference"[2], namely, the problem of checking whether the types of a function and of its argument can be made compatible and, if so, of inferring the type of their result as we did for (1). The difficulty, once more, mainly resides in the presence of the intersection types: a term can be given different types either by subsumption (the term is coerced into a super-type of its type) or by instantiation (the term is used as a particular instance of its polymorphic type) and it is typed by the intersection of all these types. Therefore, in this setting, the problem is not just to find a substitution that unifies the domain type of the function with the type of its argument but, rather, a *set* of substitutions that produce instances whose intersections are in the right subtyping relation: our `map even` example should already have given a rough idea of how difficult this is.

The presentation of our work is split in two parts, accordingly: in the first part (this paper) we show how to solve the problem of defining an explicitly-typed $\lambda$-calculus with intersection types and how to efficiently evaluate it; in the second part (the companion paper [4]) we will show how to solve the problem of "local type inference" for a calculus with intersection types. In the next section we outline the various problems we met (focusing on those that concern the part of the work presented in this paper) and how they were solved.

## 2. Problems and overview of the solution

The driver of this work is the definition of an XML processing functional language with high-order polymorphic functions, that is, in particular, a polymorphic version of the language ℂDuce [2].

***ℂDuce in a nutshell.*** The essence of ℂDuce is a $\lambda$-calculus with pairs, explicitly-typed recursive functions, and a type-case expression. Types can be recursively defined and include the arrow and product type *constructors* and the intersection, union, and negation type *connectives*. In summary, they are the regular trees coinductively generated by the following productions:

$$t ::= b \mid t \to t \mid t \times t \mid t \wedge t \mid t \vee t \mid \neg t \mid \mathbb{0} \mid \mathbb{1} \qquad (2)$$

where $b$ ranges over basic types (*eg*, `Int`, `Bool`) and $\mathbb{0}$ and $\mathbb{1}$ respectively denote the empty (that types no value) and top (that types all values) types. We use possibly indexed meta-variables $s$ and $t$ to range over types. Coinduction accounts for recursive types. We use the standard convention that infix connectives have a priority higher than constructors and lower than prefix connectives.

From a strictly practical viewpoint, recursive types, products, and type connectives are used to encode regular tree types, which subsume existing XML schema/types while, for what concerns expressions, the type-case is an abstraction of ℂDuce pattern matching (this uses regular expression patterns on types to define powerful and highly optimized capture primitives for XML data). We initially focus on the functional core and disregard products and recursive functions since the results presented here can be easily extended to them (we show it in the electronic appendix available at `http://dl.acm.org`), though we will freely use them for our examples. So we initially consider the following "Coreℂduce" terms:

$$e ::= c \mid x \mid ee \mid \lambda^{\wedge_{i\in I} s_i \to t_i} x.e \mid e{\in}t\, ?\, e : e \qquad (3)$$

where $c$ ranges over constants (*eg*, `true`, `false`, `1`, `2`, ...) which are values of basic types (we use $b_c$ to denote the basic type of the constant $c$); $x$ ranges over expression variables; $e{\in}t\,?\,e_1 : e_2$ denotes the type-case expression that evaluates either $e_1$ or $e_2$ according to whether the value returned by $e$ (if any) is of type $t$ or not; $\lambda^{\wedge_{i\in I} s_i \to t_i} x.e$ is a value of type $\wedge_{i\in I} s_i \to t_i$ that denotes the function of parameter $x$ and body $e$.

In this work we show how to define the polymorphic extension of this calculus, which can then be easily extended to a full-fledged polymorphic functional language for processing XML documents. But before let us explain the two specificities of the terms in (3), namely, why a type-case expression is included and why we explicitly annotate whole $\lambda$-abstractions (with an intersection of arrow types) rather than just their parameters.

The reasons for including a type-case in the terms of the calculus are detailed in [11]: in short, intersection types are used to type overloaded functions, and without a type-case only "coherent overloading" *à la* Forsythe [16] can be defined (which, in our setting, precludes for instance the definition of a non diverging function of type $(\texttt{Int}{\to}\texttt{Bool}) \wedge (\texttt{Bool}{\to}\texttt{Int})$). Also, in our system the relation $s_1{\vee}s_2 \to t_1{\wedge}t_2 \lneq (s_1{\to}t_1){\wedge}(s_2{\to}t_2)$ is, in general, *strict*, and the functions that are in the difference of these two types are those that distinguish non coherent overloading from coherent one. To inhabit this difference we need "real" overloaded functions that execute different code according to the type of their input, whence the need of type-case expressions.

The need of explicitly typed functions is a direct consequence of the introduction of the type-case, because without explicit typing we can run into paradoxes such as $\mu f.\lambda x.f{\in}(\mathbb{1}{\to}\texttt{Int})\,?\,\texttt{true} : 42$, a recursively defined (constant) function that has type $\mathbb{1}{\to}\texttt{Int}$ if and only if it *does not* have type $\mathbb{1}{\to}\texttt{Int}$. In order to decide whether the function above is well-typed or not, we must explicitly give a type to it. For instance, the function is well-typed if it is explicitly assigned the type $\mathbb{1} \to \texttt{Int}{\vee}\texttt{Bool}$. This shows both that functions must be explicitly typed and that specifying not only the type of parameters but also the type of the result is strictly more expressive, as more terms can be typed.

In summary, we need to define an explicitly typed language with intersection types. This is a difficult problem for which no full-fledged solution existed, yet: there exist only few intersection type systems with explicitly typed terms, and none of them is completely satisfactory (see Section 7 on related work). To give an idea of why this is difficult, imagine we adopt for functions a Church-style notation as $\lambda x^t.e$ and consider the following "switch" function $\lambda x^t.(x{\in}\texttt{Int}\,?\,\texttt{true} : 42)$ that when applied to an `Int` returns `true` and returns 42 otherwise. Intuitively, we want to assign to this function the type $(\texttt{Int}{\to}\texttt{Bool}) \wedge (\neg\texttt{Int}{\to}\texttt{Int})$, the type of a function that when applied to an `Int`, returns a `Bool`, and when applied to a value which is not an `Int`, returns an `Int`. For the sake of presentation, let us say that we are happy to deduce for the function above the less precise type $(\texttt{Int}{\to}\texttt{Bool}) \wedge (\texttt{Bool}{\to}\texttt{Int})$ (which is a super-type of the former since if a function maps anything that is not an `Int` into an `Int`—it has type $\neg\texttt{Int}{\to}\texttt{Int}$—, then in particular it maps Booleans to integers —*ie*, it has also type $\texttt{Bool}{\to}\texttt{Int}$). The problem is to determine which type we should use for $t$ in the "switch" function above. If we use, say, $\texttt{Int}{\vee}\texttt{Bool}$, then under the hypothesis that $x : \texttt{Int}{\vee}\texttt{Bool}$ the type deduced for the body of the function is $\texttt{Int}{\vee}\texttt{Bool}$. So the best type we can give to the switch function is $\texttt{Int}{\vee}\texttt{Bool} \to \texttt{Int}{\vee}\texttt{Bool}$ which is far

[2] There are different definitions for *local type inference*. Here we use it with the meaning of finding the type of an expression in which not all type annotations are specified. This is the acceptation used in Scala where type parameters for polymorphic methods can be omitted. In our specific problem, we will omit —and, thus, infer— the annotations that specify how function and argument types can be made compatible.

less precise than the sought intersection type, insofar as it does not make any distinction between arguments of type Int and those of type Bool.

The solution, which was introduced by ℂDuce, is to explicitly type —by an intersection type— whole λ-abstractions instead of just their parameters: $\lambda^{(\texttt{Int}\to\texttt{Bool})\wedge(\texttt{Bool}\to\texttt{Int})}x\,.\,(x{\in}\texttt{Int}\;?\;\texttt{true}:\texttt{42})$ In doing so we also explicitly define the result type of functions which, as we have just seen, increases the expressiveness of the calculus. Thus the general form of λ-abstractions is, as stated by the grammar in (3), $\lambda^{\wedge_{i\in I}s_i\to t_i}x.e$. Such a term is well typed if for all $i \in I$ from the hypothesis that $x$ has type $s_i$ it is possible to deduce that $e$ has type $t_i$. Unfortunately, with polymorphic types, this simple solution introduced by ℂDuce no longer suffices.

***Polymorphic extension.*** The novelty of this work is to allow type variables (ranged over by lower-case Greek letters: $\alpha$, $\beta$, ...) to occur in the types in (2) and, thus, in the types labeling λ-abstractions in (3). It becomes thus possible to define the polymorphic identity function as $\lambda^{\alpha\to\alpha}x.x$, while classic "auto-application" term can be written as $\lambda^{((\alpha\to\beta)\wedge\alpha)\to\beta}x.xx$. The intended meaning of using a type variable, such as $\alpha$, is that a (well-typed) λ-abstraction not only has the type specified in its label (and by subsumption all its super-types) but also all the types obtained by instantiating the type variables occurring in the label. So $\lambda^{\alpha\to\alpha}x.x$ has not only type $\alpha\to\alpha$ but also, for example, by subsumption the types $\mathbb{0}\to\mathbb{1}$ (the type of all functions, which is a super-type of $\alpha\to\alpha$) and $\neg$Int (since every well-typed λ-abstraction is not an integer, then $\neg$Int contains —*ie*, is a super-type of— all function types), and by instantiation the types Int→Int, Bool→Bool, etc.

The use of instantiation in combination with intersection types has nasty consequences, for if a term has two distinct types, then it has also their intersection type (*eg*, $\lambda^{\alpha\to\alpha}x.x$ has type $(\texttt{Int}\to\texttt{Int}) \wedge (\texttt{Bool}\to\texttt{Bool}) \wedge \neg\texttt{Int}$). In the monomorphic case a term can have distinct types only by subsumption and, thus, intersection types are transparently assigned to terms via subsumption. But in the polymorphic case this is no longer possible: a term can be typed by the intersection of two distinct instances of its polymorphic type which, in general, are not in any subtyping relation with the latter: for instance, $\alpha\to\alpha$ is neither a subtype of Int→Int nor vice versa, since the subtyping relation must hold for *all possible* instantiations of $\alpha$ and there are infinitely many instances of $\alpha\to\alpha$ that are neither a subtype nor a super-type of Int→Int.

***Explicit instantiation.*** Concretely, if we want to apply the polymorphic identity $\lambda^{\alpha\to\alpha}x.x$ to, say, 42, then the particular instance obtained by the type-substitution $\{\texttt{Int}/_\alpha\}$ (denoting the replacement of every occurrence of $\alpha$ by Int) must be used, that is $(\lambda^{\texttt{Int}\to\texttt{Int}}x.x)42$. We have thus to *relabel* the type decorations of λ-abstractions before applying them. In implicitly typed languages, such as ML, the relabeling is meaningless (no type decoration is used in terms) while in their explicitly-typed counterparts relabeling can be seen as a logically meaningful but computationally useless operation, insofar as execution takes place on type erasures (*ie*, the terms obtained by erasing all type decorations). In the presence of type-case expressions, however, relabeling is necessary since the label of a λ-abstraction determines its type: testing whether an expression has type, say, Int→Int should succeed for the application of $\lambda^{\alpha\to\alpha\to\alpha}x.\lambda^{\alpha\to\alpha}y.x$ to 42 and fail for its application to true. This means that, in Reynolds' terminology, our terms have an *intrinsic* meaning [17], that is to say, the semantics of a term depends on its typing. If we need to relabel some function, then it may be necessary to relabel also its body as witnessed by the following "daffy" —though well-typed— definition of the identity function:

$$(\lambda^{\alpha\to\alpha}x.(\lambda^{\alpha\to\alpha}y.x)x) \qquad (4)$$

If we want to apply this function to, say, 3, then we have first to relabel it by applying the substitution $\{\texttt{Int}/_\alpha\}$. However, applying the relabeling only to the outer "λ" does not suffice since the application of (4) to 3 reduces to $(\lambda^{\alpha\to\alpha}y.3)3$ which is not well-typed (it is not possible to deduce the type $\alpha\to\alpha$ for $\lambda^{\alpha\to\alpha}y.3$, which is the constant function that always returns 3) although it is the reductum of a well-typed application.[3]

The solution is to apply the relabeling also to the body of the function. Here what "to relabel the body" means is straightforward: apply the same type-substitution $\{\texttt{Int}/_\alpha\}$ to the body. This yields a reductum $(\lambda^{\texttt{Int}\to\texttt{Int}}y.3)3$ which is well typed. In general, however, the way to perform a relabeling of the body of a function is not so straightforward and clearly defined, since two different problems may arise: (*i*) it may be necessary to apply more than a single type-substitution and (*ii*) the relabeling of the body may depend on the dynamic type of the actual argument of the function (both problems are better known as —or are instances of— the problem of determining expansions for intersection type systems [7]). Next, we discuss each problem in detail.

***Multiple substitutions.*** First of all, notice that we may need to relabel/instantiate functions not only when they are applied but also when they are used as arguments. For instance, consider a function that expects arguments of type Int→Int. It is clear that we can apply it to the identity function $\lambda^{\alpha\to\alpha}x.x$, since the identity function *has* type Int→Int (feed it by an integer and it will return an integer). Before, though, we have to relabel the latter by the substitution $\{\texttt{Int}/_\alpha\}$ yielding $\lambda^{\texttt{Int}\to\texttt{Int}}x.x$. As the identity $\lambda^{\alpha\to\alpha}x.x$ has type Int→Int, so it has type Bool→Bool and, therefore, the intersection of the two: $(\texttt{Int}\to\texttt{Int})\wedge(\texttt{Bool}\to\texttt{Bool})$. So we can apply a function that expects an argument of this intersection type to our identity function. The problem is now how to relabel $\lambda^{\alpha\to\alpha}x.x$. Intuitively, we have to apply two distinct type-substitutions $\{\texttt{Int}/_\alpha\}$ and $\{\texttt{Bool}/_\alpha\}$ to the label of the λ-abstraction and replace it by the intersection of the two instances. This corresponds to relabel the polymorphic identity from $\lambda^{\alpha\to\alpha}x.x$ into $\lambda^{(\texttt{Int}\to\texttt{Int})\wedge(\texttt{Bool}\to\texttt{Bool})}x.x$. This is the solution adopted by this work, where we manipulate *sets of type-substitutions* —delimited by square brackets. The application of such a set (*eg*, in the previous example $[\{\texttt{Int}/_\alpha\}, \{\texttt{Bool}/_\alpha\}]$) to a type $t$ returns the intersection of all types obtained by applying each substitution in the set to $t$ (*eg*, in the example $t\{\texttt{Int}/_\alpha\} \wedge t\{\texttt{Bool}/_\alpha\}$). Thus the first problem has an easy solution.

***Relabeling of function bodies.*** The second problem is much harder and concerns the relabeling of the body of a function. While the naive solution consisting of propagating the application of type-substitutions to the bodies of functions works for single type-substitutions, in general, it fails for *sets* of type-substitutions. This can be seen by considering the relabeling via the set of type-substitutions $[\{\texttt{Int}/_\alpha\}, \{\texttt{Bool}/_\alpha\}]$ of the daffy function in (4). If we apply the naive solution, this yields

$$(\lambda^{(\texttt{Int}\to\texttt{Int})\wedge(\texttt{Bool}\to\texttt{Bool})}x.(\lambda^{(\texttt{Int}\to\texttt{Int})\wedge(\texttt{Bool}\to\texttt{Bool})}y.x)x) \qquad (5)$$

which is not well typed. That this term is not well typed is clear if we try applying it to, say, 3: the application of a function of type $(\texttt{Int}\to\texttt{Int})\wedge(\texttt{Bool}\to\texttt{Bool})$ to an Int should have type Int, but here it reduces to $(\lambda^{(\texttt{Int}\to\texttt{Int})\wedge(\texttt{Bool}\to\texttt{Bool})}y.3)3$, and there is no way to deduce the intersection type $(\texttt{Int}\to\texttt{Int}) \wedge (\texttt{Bool}\to\texttt{Bool})$ for the constant function $\lambda y.3$. But we can also directly verify that it is not well typed, by trying typing the function in (5). This corresponds to prove that under the hypothesis $x$ : Int the

[3] By convention a type variable is introduced by the outermost λ in which it occurs and this λ implicitly binds all inner occurrences of the variable. For instance, all the $\alpha$'s in the term (4) are the same while in a term such as $(\lambda^{\alpha\to\alpha}x.x)(\lambda^{\alpha\to\alpha}x.x)$ the variables in the function are distinct from those in its argument and, thus, can be $\alpha$-converted separately, as $(\lambda^{\gamma\to\gamma}x.x)(\lambda^{\delta\to\delta}x.x)$.

term $(\lambda^{(\texttt{Int}\to\texttt{Int})\wedge(\texttt{Bool}\to\texttt{Bool})}y.x)x$ has type Int, and that under the hypothesis $x$ : Bool this same term has type Bool. Both checks fail because, in both cases, $\lambda^{(\texttt{Int}\to\texttt{Int})\wedge(\texttt{Bool}\to\texttt{Bool})}y.x$ is ill-typed (it neither has type Int→Int when $x$:Bool, nor has it type Bool→Bool when $x$:Int). This example shows that in order to ensure that relabeling yields well-typed terms, the relabeling of the body *must change* according to the type of the value the parameter $x$ is bound to. More precisely, $(\lambda^{\alpha\to\alpha}y.x)$ should be relabeled as $\lambda^{\texttt{Int}\to\texttt{Int}}y.x$ when $x$ is of type Int, and as $\lambda^{\texttt{Bool}\to\texttt{Bool}}y.x$ when $x$ is of type Bool. An example of this same problem less artificial than our daffy function is given by the classic apply function $\lambda f.\lambda x.fx$ which, with our polymorphic type annotations, is written as:

$$\lambda^{(\alpha\to\beta)\to\alpha\to\beta}f.\lambda^{\alpha\to\beta}x.fx \tag{6}$$

The apply function in (6) has type (Int→Int)→Int→Int, obtained by instantiating its type annotation by the substitution $\{\texttt{Int}/_{\alpha}, \texttt{Int}/_{\beta}\}$, as well as type (Bool→Bool)→Bool→Bool, obtained by the substitution $\{\texttt{Bool}/_{\alpha}, \texttt{Bool}/_{\beta}\}$. If we want to feed this function to another function that expects arguments whose type is the intersections of these two types, then we have to relabel it by using the set of type-substitutions $[\{\texttt{Int}/_{\alpha}, \texttt{Int}/_{\beta}\}, \{\texttt{Bool}/_{\alpha}, \texttt{Bool}/_{\beta}\}]$. But, once more, it is easy to verify that the naive solution that consists in propagating the application of the set of type-substitutions down to the body of the function yields an ill-typed expression.

This second problem is the showstopper for the definition of an explicitly typed $\lambda$-calculus with intersection types. Most of the solutions found in the literature [3, 13, 18, 21] rely on the duplication of lambda terms and/or typing derivations, while other calculi such as [22] that aim at avoiding such duplication obtain it by adding new expressions and new syntax for types (see related work in Section 7); but none of them is able to produce an explicitly-typed $\lambda$-calculus with intersection types, as we do, by just adding annotations to $\lambda$-abstractions.

***Our solution.*** Here we introduce a new technique that consists in performing a "lazy" relabeling of the bodies. This is obtained by decorating $\lambda$-abstractions by (sets of) type-substitutions. For example, in order to pass our daffy identity function (4) to a function that expects arguments of type (Int→Int) ∧ (Bool→Bool), we first "lazily" relabel it as follows:

$$(\lambda^{\alpha\to\alpha}_{[\{\texttt{Int}/_{\alpha}\},\{\texttt{Bool}/_{\alpha}\}]}x.(\lambda^{\alpha\to\alpha}y.x)x). \tag{7}$$

The new annotation in the outer "$\lambda$" indicates that the function must be relabeled and, therefore, that we are using the particular instance whose type is the one in the interface (*ie*, $\alpha\to\alpha$) to which we apply the set of type-substitutions. The relabeling will be actually propagated to the body of the function at the moment of the reduction, only if and when the function is applied (relabeling is thus lazy). However, the new annotation is statically used by the type system to check soundness. Notice that, unlike existing solutions, we preserve the structure of $\lambda$-terms (at the expenses of some extra annotation that is propagated during the reduction) which is of the uttermost importance in a language-oriented study.

In this paper we focus on the study of the calculus with these "lazy" type-substitutions annotations. We temporarily avoid the problem of local type inference by defining a *calculus with explicit sets of type substitutions*: expressions will be explicitly annotated with appropriate sets of type-substitutions.

***Polymorphic ℂDuce.*** From a practical point of view, however, it is important to stress that, at the end, these annotations will be invisible to the programmer and, as we show in the second part presented in the companion paper [4], all the necessary type-substitutions will be inferred statically. In practice, the programmer will program in the language defined by grammar (3), but where the types that annotate $\lambda$'s may contain type variables, that is, the polymorphic version of ℂDuce. The problem of inferring explicit sets of type-substitutions to annotate the polymorphic version of the expressions in (3) is the topic of the second part of this work presented in the companion paper [4]. For the time being, simply notice that the language defined by (3) and extended with type variables passes our first test inasmuch as the even function can be defined as follows (where $s\backslash t$ is syntactic sugar for $s\wedge\neg t$):

$$\lambda^{(\texttt{Int}\to\texttt{Bool})\wedge(\alpha\backslash\texttt{Int}\to\alpha\backslash\texttt{Int})}x\,.\,x{\in}\texttt{Int}\,?\,(x \bmod 2) = 0 : x \tag{8}$$

while —with the products and recursive functions described in the electronic Appendix— map is defined as (see also discussion in Appendix E)

$$\begin{array}{l}\mu m^{(\alpha\to\beta)\to[\alpha]\to[\beta]}\,f = \\ \quad\lambda^{[\alpha]\to[\beta]}\ell\,.\,\ell{\in}\texttt{nil}\,?\,\texttt{nil} : (f(\pi_1\ell), mf(\pi_2\ell))\end{array} \tag{9}$$

where the type nil tested in the type-case denotes the singleton type that contains just the constant nil, and $[\alpha]$ denotes the regular type that is the (least) solution of $X = (\alpha, X) \vee \texttt{nil}$.

When fed by any expression of this language, the type inference system defined in the companion paper [4] will infer sets of type-substitutions and insert them into the expression to make it well typed (if possible, of course). For example, for the application (of the terms defining) map to even, the inference system of the companion paper [4] infers the following set of type-substitutions $[\{(\alpha\backslash\texttt{Int})/_{\alpha}, (\alpha\backslash\texttt{Int})/_{\beta}\}, \{\alpha\vee\texttt{Int}/_{\alpha}, (\alpha\backslash\texttt{Int})\vee\texttt{Bool}/_{\beta}\}]$ and textually inserts it between the two terms (so that the type-substitutions apply to the type variables of map) yielding the typing in (1). Finally, as we explain in Section 5.3 later on, the compiler will compile the expression into an expression of an intermediate language that can be evaluated as efficiently as the monomorphic calculus.

***Outline.*** The rest of the presentation proceeds as follows. In Section 3 we define and study our calculus with explicit type-substitutions: we define its syntax, its operational semantics, and its type system; we prove that the type system is sound and subsumes classic intersection type systems. In Section 4 we define an algorithm for type inference and prove that it is sound, complete, and terminating. In Section 5 we show that the addition of type-substitutions has in practice no impact on the efficiency of the evaluation since the calculus can be compiled into an intermediate language that executes as efficiently as monomorphic ℂDuce. Section 7 presents related work and in Section 8 we conclude our presentation. In the rest of the presentation we will focus on the intuition and try to avoid as many technical details as possible. We dot the i's and cross the t's in the electronic appendix (available on-line at http://dl.acm.org) where all formal definitions and complete proofs of properties can be found (*n.b.*: references in the text starting by capital letters —*eg*, Definition A.7— refer to this appendix). All these as well as other details can also be found in the third author's PhD thesis manuscript [23].

***Contributions.*** The overall contribution of our work is the definition of a statically-typed core language with $(i)$ polymorphic higher-order functions for a type system with recursive types and union, intersection, and negation type connectives, $(ii)$ an efficient evaluation model, $(iii)$ local type inference for application, and $(iv)$ a limited form of type reconstruction.

The main contribution of this first part of the work is the definition of an *explicitly-typed* $\lambda$-calculus (actually, a family of calculi) with intersection (and union and negation) types and of its efficient evaluation via the compilation into an intermediate language. From a syntactic viewpoint our solution is a minimal extension since it just requires to add annotations to $\lambda$-abstractions of the untyped $\lambda$-calculus (*cf.* Section 3.5). Although this problem has been studied for over 20 years, no existing solution proposes such a minimal extension, which is of paramount importance in a programming language-oriented study (see related works in Section 7).

The technical contributions are the definition of an explicitly typed calculus with intersection types; the proof that it subsumes existing intersection type systems; the soundness of its type system, the definition of a sound, complete and terminating algorithm for type inference (which as byproduct yields an intersection type proof system satisfying the Curry-Howard isomorphism); the definition of a compilation technique into an intermediate language that can be evaluated as efficiently as the monomorphic one; its extension to the so called `let`-polymorphism and the proof of the adequacy of the compilation. Local type inference for application and type reconstruction are studied in the second part of this work presented in the companion paper [4].

## 3. A calculus with explicit type-substitutions

The types of the calculus are those in the grammar (2) to which we add type variables (ranged over by $\alpha$) and, for the sake of presentation, stripped of product types. In summary, types are the regular trees coinductively generated by

$$t ::= \alpha \mid b \mid t \to t \mid t \wedge t \mid t \vee t \mid \neg t \mid \mathbb{0} \mid \mathbb{1} \qquad (10)$$

and such that every infinite branch contains infinitely many occurrences of type constructors. We use $\mathscr{T}$ to denote the set of all types. The condition on infinite branches bars out ill-formed types such as $t = t \vee t$ (which does not carry any information about the set denoted by the type) or $t = \neg t$ (which cannot represent any set). It also ensures that the binary relation $\triangleright \subseteq \mathscr{T}^2$ defined by $t_1 \vee t_2 \triangleright t_i$, $t_1 \wedge t_2 \triangleright t_i$, $\neg t \triangleright t$ is Noetherian (that is, strongly normalizing). This gives an induction principle on $\mathscr{T}$ that we will use without any further explicit reference to the relation. We use $\mathsf{var}(t)$ to denote the *set of type variables* occurring in a type $t$ (see Definition A.2). A type $t$ is said to be *ground* or *closed* if and only if $\mathsf{var}(t)$ is empty.

The subtyping relation for the types in $\mathscr{T}$ is the one defined by Castagna and Xu [5]. For this work it suffices to consider that ground types are interpreted as sets of *values* (*n.b.*, just values, not expressions) that have that type and subtyping is set containment (*ie*, a ground type $s$ is a subtype of a ground type $t$ if and only if $t$ contains all the values of type $s$). In particular, $s{\to}t$ contains all $\lambda$-abstractions that when applied to a value of type $s$, if they return a result, then this result is of type $t$ (so $\mathbb{0}{\to}\mathbb{1}$ is the set of all functions and $\mathbb{1}{\to}\mathbb{0}$ is the set of functions that diverge on all arguments). Type connectives (union, intersection, negation) are interpreted as the corresponding set-theoretic operators and subtyping is set containment. For what concerns non-ground types (*ie*, types with variables occurring in them) all the reader needs to know for this work is that the subtyping relation of Castagna and Xu is preserved by type-substitutions. Namely, if $s \leq t$, then $s\sigma \leq t\sigma$ for every type-substitution $\sigma$ (the converse does not hold in general, while it holds for *semantic* type-substitutions in convex models: see [5]). Two types are equivalent if they denote the same set of values, that is, if they are subtype one of each other (type equivalence is denoted by $\simeq$). An important property of this system we will often use is that every type is equivalent to (and can be effectively transformed into) a type in *disjunctive normal form*, that is, a union of *uniform* intersections of literals. A literal is either an arrow, or a basic type, or a type variable, or their negations. An intersection is uniform if all the literals have the same constructor, that is, either it is an intersection of arrows, type variables, and their negations or it is an intersection of basic types, type variables, and their negations. In summary, a disjunctive normal form is a union of summands whose form is either

$$\bigwedge_{p\in P} b_p \wedge \bigwedge_{n\in N} \neg b_n \wedge \bigwedge_{q\in P'} \alpha_q \wedge \bigwedge_{r\in N'} \neg\alpha_r \qquad (11)$$

or

$$\bigwedge_{p\in P} (s_p{\to}t_p) \wedge \bigwedge_{n\in N} \neg(s_n{\to}t_n) \wedge \bigwedge_{q\in P'} \alpha_q \wedge \bigwedge_{r\in N'} \neg\alpha_r \qquad (12)$$

When either $P'$ or $N'$ is not empty, we call the variables $\alpha_q$'s and $\alpha_r$'s the *top-level variables* of the normal form.

### 3.1 Expressions

Expressions are derived from those of Core$\mathbb{C}$Duce (with type variables in types) with the addition that sets of explicit type-substitutions (ranged over by $[\sigma_j]_{j\in J}$) may be applied to terms and decorate $\lambda$-abstractions

$$e ::= c \mid x \mid ee \mid \lambda^{\wedge_{i\in I} s_i\to t_i}_{[\sigma_j]_{j\in J}} x.e \mid e{\in}t\,?\,e : e \mid e[\sigma_j]_{j\in J} \qquad (13)$$

and with the restriction that the type tested in type-case expressions is closed. Henceforth, given a $\lambda$-abstraction $\lambda^{\wedge_{i\in I} s_i\to t_i}_{[\sigma_j]_{j\in J}} x.e$ we call the type $\bigwedge_{i\in I} s_i{\to}t_i$ the *interface* of the function and the set of type-substitutions $[\sigma_j]_{j\in J}$ the *decoration* of the function. We write $\lambda^{\wedge_{i\in I} t_i\to s_i} x.e$ for short when the decoration is a singleton containing the empty substitution. Let $e$ be an expression. We use $\mathsf{fv}(e)$ and $\mathsf{bv}(e)$ respectively to denote the sets of *free expression variables* and *bound expressions variables* of the expression $e$; we use $\mathsf{tv}(e)$ to denote the set of *type variables* occurring in $e$ (see Definition A.9).

As customary, we assume bound expression variables to be pairwise distinct and distinct from any free expression variable occurring in the expressions under consideration. We equate expressions up to the $\alpha$-renaming of their bound expression variables. In particular, when substituting an expression $e$ for a variable $y$ in an expression $e'$ (see Definition A.11), we assume that the bound variables of $e'$ are distinct from the bound and free variables of $e$, to avoid unwanted captures. For example, $(\lambda^{\alpha\to\alpha}x.x)y$ is $\alpha$-equivalent to $(\lambda^{\alpha\to\alpha}z.z)y$.

The situation is a bit more complex for type variables, as we do not have an explicit binder for them. Intuitively, a type variable can be $\alpha$-converted if it is a *polymorphic* one, that is, if it can be instantiated. For example, $(\lambda^{\alpha\to\alpha}x.x)y$ is $\alpha$-equivalent to $(\lambda^{\beta\to\beta}x.x)y$, and $(\lambda^{\alpha\to\alpha}_{[\{\mathtt{Int}/\alpha\}]}x.x)y$ is $\alpha$-equivalent to $(\lambda^{\beta\to\beta}_{[\{\mathtt{Int}/\beta\}]}x.x)y$. Polymorphic variables can be bound by interfaces, but also by decorations: for example, in $\lambda^{\beta\to\beta}_{[\{\alpha/\beta\}]}x.(\lambda^{\alpha\to\alpha}y.y)x$, the $\alpha$ occurring in the interface of the inner abstraction is "bound" by the decoration $[\{\alpha/\beta\}]$, and the whole expression is $\alpha$-equivalent to $(\lambda^{\beta\to\beta}_{[\{\gamma/\beta\}]}x.(\lambda^{\gamma\to\gamma}y.y)x)$. If a type variable is bound by an outer abstraction, it cannot be instantiated; such a variable is called *monomorphic*. For example, the following expression

$$\lambda^{(\alpha\to\alpha)\to(\alpha\to\alpha)}y.((\lambda^{\alpha\to\alpha}x.x)[\{\mathtt{Int}/\alpha\}]y)$$

is not sound (*ie*, it cannot be typed), because $\alpha$ is bound at the level of the outer abstraction, not at level of the inner one. Consequently, in this expression, $\alpha$ is monomorphic for the inner abstraction, but polymorphic for the outer one (strictly speaking, thus, the monomorphic and polymorphic adjectives apply to occurrences of variables rather than variables themselves). Monomorphic type variables cannot be $\alpha$-converted: $\lambda^{(\alpha\to\alpha)\to(\alpha\to\alpha)}y.(\lambda^{\alpha\to\alpha}x.x)y$ is *not* $\alpha$-equivalent to $\lambda^{(\alpha\to\alpha)\to(\alpha\to\alpha)}y.(\lambda^{\beta\to\beta}x.x)y$ (but it is $\alpha$-equivalent to $\lambda^{(\beta\to\beta)\to(\beta\to\beta)}y.(\lambda^{\beta\to\beta}x.x)y$). Note that the scope of polymorphic variables may include some type-substitutions $[\sigma_i]_{i\in I}$: for example, $((\lambda^{\alpha\to\alpha}x.x)y)[\mathtt{Int}/\alpha]$ is $\alpha$-equivalent to $((\lambda^{\beta\to\beta}x.x)y)[\mathtt{Int}/\beta]$. Finally, we have to be careful when performing expression substitutions and type-substitutions to avoid clashes of polymorphic variable namespaces. For example, substituting $\lambda^{\alpha\to\alpha}z.z$ for $y$ in $\lambda^{\alpha\to\alpha}x.x\ y$ would lead to an unwanted capture of $\alpha$ (assuming $\alpha$ is polymorphic, that is, not bound by a $\lambda$-abstraction placed above these two expressions), so we have to $\alpha$-convert one of them, so that the result of the substitution is, for instance, $\lambda^{\alpha\to\alpha}x.x\ (\lambda^{\beta\to\beta}z.z)$.

To resume, we assume polymorphic variables to be pairwise distinct and distinct from any monomorphic variable in the expres-

$$\textit{(subsum)}\ \frac{\Delta \,\S\, \Gamma \vdash e : t_1 \quad t_1 \leq t_2}{\Delta \,\S\, \Gamma \vdash e : t_2} \qquad \textit{(appl)}\ \frac{\Delta \,\S\, \Gamma \vdash e_1 : t_1 \to t_2 \quad \Delta \,\S\, \Gamma \vdash e_2 : t_1}{\Delta \,\S\, \Gamma \vdash e_1 e_2 : t_2}$$

$$\textit{(abstr)}\ \frac{\Delta \cup \mathsf{var}(\bigwedge_{i\in I, j\in J} t_i\sigma_j \to s_i\sigma_j) \,\S\, \Gamma, (x : t_i\sigma_j) \vdash e@[\sigma_j] : s_i\sigma_j}{\Delta \,\S\, \Gamma \vdash \lambda^{\wedge_{i\in I} t_i \to s_i}_{[\sigma_j]_{j\in J}} x.e : \bigwedge_{i\in I, j\in J} t_i\sigma_j \to s_i\sigma_j} \ \begin{matrix} i \in I \\ j \in J \end{matrix}$$

$$\textit{(var)}\ \frac{}{\Delta \,\S\, \Gamma \vdash x : \Gamma(x)} \qquad \textit{(case)}\ \frac{\Delta \,\S\, \Gamma \vdash e : t' \quad \begin{cases} t' \not\leq \neg t & \Rightarrow \quad \Delta \,\S\, \Gamma \vdash e_1 : s \\ t' \not\leq t & \Rightarrow \quad \Delta \,\S\, \Gamma \vdash e_2 : s \end{cases}}{\Delta \,\S\, \Gamma \vdash (e{\in}t\,?\,e_1 : e_2) : s}$$

$$\textit{(inst)}\ \frac{\Delta \,\S\, \Gamma \vdash e : t \quad \sigma \sharp \Delta}{\Delta \,\S\, \Gamma \vdash e[\sigma] : t\sigma} \qquad \textit{(inter)}\ \frac{\forall j \in J.\ \Delta \,\S\, \Gamma \vdash e[\sigma_j] : t_j}{\Delta \,\S\, \Gamma \vdash e[\sigma_j]_{j\in J} : \bigwedge_{j\in J} t_j} \ |J| > 1$$

**Figure 1.** Static semantics

sions under consideration. We equate expressions up to $\alpha$-renaming of their polymorphic variables. In particular, when substituting an expression $e'$ for a variable $x$ in an expression $e$, we suppose the polymorphic type variables of $e$ to be distinct from the monomorphic and polymorphic type variables of $e'$ thus avoiding unwanted captures. Detailed definitions are given in Appendix A.2.

In order to define both static and dynamic semantics for the expressions above, we need to define the *relabeling* operation "@" which takes an expression $e$ and a set of type-substitutions $[\sigma_j]_{j\in J}$ and pushes $[\sigma_j]_{j\in J}$ to all outermost $\lambda$-abstractions occurring in $e$ (and collects and composes with the sets of type-substitutions it meets). Precisely, $e@[\sigma_j]_{j\in J}$ is defined for $\lambda$-abstractions and (inductively) for applications of type-substitutions as:

$$(\lambda^{\wedge_{i\in I} t_i \to s_i}_{[\sigma_k]_{k\in K}} x.e)@[\sigma_j]_{j\in J} \stackrel{\text{def}}{=} \lambda^{\wedge_{i\in I} t_i \to s_i}_{[\sigma_j]_{j\in J} \circ [\sigma_k]_{k\in K}} x.e$$

$$(e[\sigma_i]_{i\in I})@[\sigma_j]_{j\in J} \stackrel{\text{def}}{=} e@([\sigma_j]_{j\in J} \circ [\sigma_i]_{i\in I})$$

where $\circ$ denotes the pairwise composition of all substitutions of the two sets (see Definition A.7). It erases the set of type-substitutions when $e$ is a variable and it is homomorphically applied on the remaining expressions (see Definition A.12).

## 3.2 Operational semantics

The dynamic semantics is given by the following three notions of reduction (where $v$ ranges over *values*, that is, constants and $\lambda$-abstractions), applied by a leftmost-outermost strategy:

$$e[\sigma_j]_{j\in J} \rightsquigarrow e@[\sigma_j]_{j\in J} \tag{14}$$

$$(\lambda^{\wedge_{i\in I} t_i \to s_i}_{[\sigma_j]_{j\in J}} x.e)v \rightsquigarrow (e@[\sigma_j]_{j\in P})\{v/x\} \tag{15}$$

$$v{\in}t\,?\,e_1 : e_2 \rightsquigarrow \begin{cases} e_1 & \text{if } \vdash v : t \\ e_2 & \text{otherwise} \end{cases} \tag{16}$$

where in (15) we have $P \stackrel{\text{def}}{=} \{j{\in}J \mid \exists i{\in}I, \vdash v : t_i\sigma_j\}$.

The first rule (14) performs relabeling, that is, it propagates the sets of type-substitutions down into the decorations of the outermost $\lambda$-abstractions. The second rule (15) states the semantics of applications: this is standard call-by-value $\beta$-reduction, with the difference that the substitution of the argument for the parameter is performed on the relabeled body of the function. Notice that relabeling depends on the type of the argument and keeps only those substitutions that make the type of the argument $v$ match (at least one of) the input types defined in the interface of the function (*ie*, the set $P$ which contains all substitutions $\sigma_j$ such that the argument $v$ has type $t_i\sigma_j$ for some $i$ in $I$: the type system will ensure that $P$ is never empty). For instance, take the daffy identity function, instantiate it as in (7) by both `Int` and `Bool`, and apply it to 42 —*ie*, $(\lambda^{\alpha\to\alpha}_{[\{\mathtt{Int}/\alpha\},\{\mathtt{Bool}/\alpha\}]} x.(\lambda^{\alpha\to\alpha} y.x)x)42$—, then it reduces to $(\lambda^{\alpha\to\alpha}_{[\{\mathtt{Int}/\alpha\}]} y.42)42$, (which is observationally equivalent to $(\lambda^{\mathtt{Int}\to\mathtt{Int}} y.42)42$) since the reduction discards the $\{\mathtt{Bool}/\alpha\}$ substitution. Finally, the third rule (16) checks whether the value returned by the expression in the type-case matches the specified type and selects the branch accordingly.

The reader may think that defining a functional language in which each $\beta$-reduction must perform an involved relabeling operation, theoretically interesting though it may be, will result in practice too costly and therefore unrealistic. This is not so. In Section 5 we show that this reduction can be implemented as efficiently as in ℂDuce. By a smart definition of closures it is possible to compute relabeling in a lazy way and materialize it only in a very specific case for the reduction of the type-case (*ie*, to perform a type-case reduction (16) where the value $v$ is a function whose interface contains monomorphic type variables and it is the result of the partial application of a polymorphic function) while all other reductions for applications can be implemented as plain classic $\beta$-reduction. For instance, to evaluate the expressions $(\lambda^{\alpha\to\alpha}_{[\{\mathtt{Int}/\alpha\},\{\mathtt{Bool}/\alpha\}]} x.(\lambda^{\alpha\to\alpha} y.x)x)42$ above, we can completely disregard all type annotations and decorations and perform a couple of standard $\beta$ reductions that yield the result 42.

## 3.3 Type system

As expected in a calculus with a type-case expression, the dynamic semantics depends on the static semantics —precisely, on the typing of values. The static semantics of our calculus is defined in Figure 1. The judgments are of the form $\Delta \,\S\, \Gamma \vdash e : t$, where $e$ is an expression, $t$ a type, $\Gamma$ a type environment (*ie*, a finite mapping from expression variables to types), and $\Delta$ a finite set of type variables. The latter is the set of all *monomorphic type variables*, that is, the variables that occur in the type of some outer $\lambda$-abstraction and, as such, cannot be instantiated; it must contain all the type variables occurring in $\Gamma$.

The rules for application and subsumption are standard. In the latter, the subtyping relation is the one defined in [5]. We just omitted the rule for constants (which states that $c$ has type $b_c$).

The rule for abstractions applies each substitution specified in the decoration to each arrow type in the interface, adds all the variables occurring in these types to the set of monomorphic type variables $\Delta$, and checks whether the function has all the resulting types. Namely, it checks that for every possible input type, the (relabeled) body has the corresponding output type. To that end, it applies each substitution $\sigma_j$ in the decoration to each input type $t_i$ of the interface and checks that, under the hypothesis that $x$ has type $t_i\sigma_j$, the function body relabeled with the substitution $\sigma_j$ at issue has type $s_i\sigma_j$ (notice that all these checks are performed under the same updated set of monomorphic type variables, that is, $\Delta \cup \mathsf{var}(\bigwedge_{i\in I,j\in J} t_i\sigma_j \to s_i\sigma_j)$). If the test succeeds, then the rule infers for the function the type obtained by applying the set of substitutions of the decoration to the type of the interface. For example, in the case of the instance of the daffy identity function given in (7), the $\Delta$ is always empty and the rule checks whether under the hypothesis $x : \alpha\{\mathtt{Int}/\alpha\}$ (*ie*, $x$ : `Int`), it is possible to deduce that $(\lambda^{\alpha\to\alpha} y.x)x@[\{\mathtt{Int}/\alpha\}]$ has type $\alpha\{\mathtt{Int}/\alpha\}$ (*ie*, that $(\lambda^{\mathtt{Int}\to\mathtt{Int}} y.x)x$ : `Int`), and similarly for the substitution $\{\mathtt{Bool}/\alpha\}$. The type deduced for the function is then $(\mathtt{Int} \to \mathtt{Int}) \wedge (\mathtt{Bool} \to \mathtt{Bool})$. The relabeling of the body in the premises of the rule (*abstr*) is a key mechanism of the type system: had we used $e[\sigma_j]$ instead of $e@[\sigma_j]$ in the premises of the *(abstr)* rule, the expression (7) could not be typed. The reason is that $e[\sigma_j]$ is more demanding on typing than $e@[\sigma_j]$, since the well typing of $e$ is necessary to the well-typing of the former but not to that of the latter. Indeed while under the hypothesis $x : \texttt{Int}$ we just showed that $((\lambda^{\alpha\to\alpha}y.x)x)@[\{\texttt{Int}/\alpha\}]$ —*ie*, $((\lambda^{\texttt{Int}\to\texttt{Int}}y.x)x)$— is well-typed, the term $((\lambda^{\alpha\to\alpha}y.x)x)[\{\texttt{Int}/\alpha\}]$ is not, for $(\lambda^{\alpha\to\alpha}y.x)$ does not have type $\alpha\to\alpha$. The rule for abstractions also justifies the need for an explicit set $\Delta$ for monomorphic type variables while, for instance, in ML it suffices to consider monomorphic type variables that occur in the image of $\Gamma$ [15]: when checking an arrow of the interface of a function, the variables occurring in the other arrows must be considered monomorphic, too.

To type the applications of a set of type-substitutions to an expression, two different rules are used according to whether the set contains one or more than one substitution. When a single substitution is specified, the rule *(inst)* instantiates the type according to the specified substitution, provided that $\sigma$ does not substitute variables in $\Delta$ (*ie*, $\mathsf{dom}(\sigma) \cap \Delta = \varnothing$, noted $\sigma \sharp \Delta$). If more than one substitution is specified, then the rule *(inter)* composes them by an intersection.

Finally, the *(case)* rule first infers the type $t'$ of the expression whose type is tested. Then the type of each branch $e_i$ is checked only if there is a chance that the branch can be selected. Here the use of "$\not\leq$" is subtle but crucial (it allows us to existentially quantify over type-substitutions). The branch, say, $e_1$ can be selected (and therefore its well-typedness must be checked) only if $e$ can return a value that is in $t$. But in order to cover all possible cases we must also consider the case in which the type of $e$ is instantiated as a consequence of an outer application. A typical usage pattern (followed also by our `even` function) is $\lambda^{\alpha\to\cdots}x.\ x{\in}\texttt{Int}\,?\,e_1 : e_2$: the branch $e_1$ is selected only if the function is applied to a value of type `Int`, that is, if the type $\alpha$ of $x$ is instantiated to `Int` (notice that when typing the body of the function $\Delta$ contains only $\alpha$). More generally, the branch $e_1$ in $e{\in}t\,?\,e_1 : e_2$ can be selected only if $e$ can return a value in $t$, that is to say, if there exists a substitution $\sigma$ for any type variables *even those in* $\Delta$ such as the intersection of $t'\sigma$ and $t$ is not empty ($t$ is a closed, so $t\sigma = t$). Therefore, in order to achieve maximum precision the rule *(case)* must check $\Delta\,\S\,\Gamma \vdash e_1 : s$ only if there exists $\sigma$ such that $t'\sigma \wedge t \neq \mathbb{0}$. Since $t' \leq \neg t$ (strictly) implies that for all substitutions $\sigma$, $t'\sigma \leq \neg t$ (recall that $t$ is a closed type), then by the contrapositive the existence of a substitution $\sigma$ such that $t'\sigma \not\leq \neg t$ implies $t' \not\leq \neg t$. The latter is equivalent to $t' \wedge t \neq \mathbb{0}$: the intersection of $t$ and $t'$ is not empty. So we slightly over-approximate the test of selection and check the type of $e_1$ under the weaker hypothesis $t' \wedge t \neq \mathbb{0}$ which ensures that the typing will hold also under the stronger (and sought) hypothesis that there exists $\sigma$ such that $t'\sigma \wedge t \neq \mathbb{0}$ (the difference only matters with some specific cases involving *indivisible* types: see [5]).

Notice that explicit type-substitutions are only needed to type applications of polymorphic functions. Since no such application occurs in the bodies of `map` and `even` as defined in Section 2 (the $m$ and $f$ inside the body of `map` are abstracted variables and, thus, have monomorphic types), then they can be typed by this system as they are (as long as they are not applied one to the other there is no need to infer any set of type-substitutions). So we can already see that our language passes the second test, namely, that `map` and `even` have the types declared in their signatures. Let us detail just the most interesting case, that is, the typing of the term `even` defined in equation (8) (even though the typing of the type-case in (9), the term defining `map`, is interesting, as well). According to the rule *(abstr)* we have to check that under the hypothesis $x{:}\texttt{Int}$ the expression $x{\in}\texttt{Int}\,?\,(x \bmod 2) = 0 : x$ has type `Bool`, and that under the hypothesis $x : \alpha\backslash\texttt{Int}$ the same expression has type $\alpha\backslash\texttt{Int}$. So we have two distinct applications of the *(case)* rule. In one $x$ is of type `Int`, thus the check $\texttt{Int} \not\leq \texttt{Int}$ fails, and therefore only the first branch, $(x \bmod 2) = 0$, is type checked (the second is skipped). Since under the hypothesis $x : \texttt{Int}$ the expression $(x \bmod 2) = 0$ has type `Bool`, then so has the whole type-case expression. In the other application of *(case)*, $x$ is of type $\alpha\backslash\texttt{Int}$, so the test $\alpha\backslash\texttt{Int} \not\leq \neg\texttt{Int}$ clearly fails, and only the second branch is checked (the first is skipped). Since this second branch is $x$, then the whole type-case expression has type $\alpha\backslash\texttt{Int}$, as expected. This example shows two important aspects of our typing rules. First, it shows the importance of $\Delta$ to record monomorphic variables, since it may contain some variables that do not occur in $\Gamma$. For instance, when typing the first branch of `even`, the type environment contains only $x : \texttt{Int}$ but $\Delta$ is $\{\alpha\}$ and this forbids to consider $\alpha$ as polymorphic (if we allowed to instantiate any variable that does not occur in $\Gamma$, then the term obtained from the `even` function (8) by replacing the first branch by $(\lambda^{\alpha\to\alpha}y.y)[\{\texttt{Bool}/\alpha\}]\texttt{true}$ would be well-typed, which is wrong since $\alpha$ is monomorphic in the body of `even`). Second, this example shows why if in some application of the *(case)* rule a branch is not checked, then the type checking of the whole type-case expression must not necessarily fail: the well-typing of this branch may be checked under different hypothesis (typically when occurring in the body of an overloaded function).[4] The reader can refer to Section 3.3 of [11] for a more detailed discussion on this point.

Finally, notice that the rule *(subsum)* makes the type system dependent on the subtyping relation $\leq$ defined in [5]. It is important not to confuse the subtyping relation $\leq$ of our system, which denotes semantic subtyping (*ie*, set-theoretic inclusion of denotations), with the one typically used in the type reconstruction systems for ML, which stands for type variable instantiation. For example, in ML we have $\alpha \to \alpha \leq \texttt{Int} \to \texttt{Int}$ (because $\texttt{Int} \to \texttt{Int}$ is an instance of $\alpha \to \alpha$). But this is not true in our system, as the relation must hold for *every possible instantiation of* $\alpha$, thus in particular for $\alpha$ equal to `Bool`. In the companion paper [4] we define the preorder $\sqsubseteq_\Delta$ which includes the type variable instantiation of the preorder typically used for ML, so any direct comparison with constraint systems for ML types should focus on $\sqsubseteq_\Delta$ rather than $\leq$ and it can be found in the companion paper [4].

### 3.4 Type soundness

Subject reduction and progress properties hold for this system.

**Theorem 3.1** (Subject Reduction)**.** *For every term e and type t, if* $\Gamma \vdash e : t$ *and* $e \rightsquigarrow e'$, *then* $\Gamma \vdash e' : t$.

**Theorem 3.2** (Progress)**.** *Let e be a well-typed closed term. If e is not a value, then there exists a term* $e'$ *such that* $e \rightsquigarrow e'$.

The proofs of both theorems, though unsurprising, are rather long and technical and can be found in Appendix B.2. They allow us to conclude that the type system is sound.

**Corollary 3.3** (Type soundness)**.** *Let e be a well-typed closed expression, that is,* $\vdash e : t$ *for some t. Then either e diverges or it returns a value of type t.*

### 3.5 Expressing intersection type systems

We can now state the first stand-alone theoretical contribution of our work. Consider the sub-calculus of our calculus in which type-substitutions occur only in decorations and without constants and

[4] From a programming language point of view it is important to check that during type checking every branch of a given type-case expression is checked —*ie*, it can be selected— at least once. This corresponds to checking the absence of redundant cases in pattern matching. We omitted this check since it is not necessary for formal development.

(ALG-VAR)
$$\frac{}{\Delta \fatsemi \Gamma \vdash_{\mathscr{A}} x : \Gamma(x)}$$

(ALG-INST)
$$\frac{\Delta \fatsemi \Gamma \vdash_{\mathscr{A}} e : t}{\Delta \fatsemi \Gamma \vdash_{\mathscr{A}} e[\sigma_j]_{j\in J} : \bigwedge_{j\in J} t\sigma_j}\ \sigma_j \sharp \Delta$$

(ALG-APPL)
$$\frac{\Delta \fatsemi \Gamma \vdash_{\mathscr{A}} e_1 : t \qquad \Delta \fatsemi \Gamma \vdash_{\mathscr{A}} e_2 : s}{\Delta \fatsemi \Gamma \vdash_{\mathscr{A}} e_1 e_2 : t \cdot s}\ \begin{array}{l} t \leq \mathbb{0} \to \mathbb{1} \\ s \leq \mathsf{dom}(t) \end{array}$$

(ALG-ABSTR)
$$\frac{\Delta \cup \Delta' \fatsemi \Gamma, (x : t_i\sigma_j) \vdash_{\mathscr{A}} e@[\sigma_j] : s'_{ij}}{\Delta \fatsemi \Gamma \vdash_{\mathscr{A}} \lambda^{\wedge_{i\in I} t_i \to s_i}_{[\sigma_j]_{j\in J}} x.e : \bigwedge_{i\in I, j\in J} (t_i\sigma_j \to s_i\sigma_j)}\ \begin{array}{l} \Delta' = \mathsf{var}(\wedge_{i\in I, j\in J} t_i\sigma_j \to s_i\sigma_j) \\ s'_{ij} \leq s_i\sigma_j, \quad i\in I, \quad j\in J \end{array}$$

(ALG-CASE-FST)
$$\frac{\Delta \fatsemi \Gamma \vdash_{\mathscr{A}} e : t' \qquad \Delta \fatsemi \Gamma \vdash_{\mathscr{A}} e_1 : s_1}{\Delta \fatsemi \Gamma \vdash_{\mathscr{A}} (e\in t\,?\,e_1 : e_2) : s_1}\ t' \leq t$$

(ALG-CASE-SND)
$$\frac{\Delta \fatsemi \Gamma \vdash_{\mathscr{A}} e : t' \qquad \Delta \fatsemi \Gamma \vdash_{\mathscr{A}} e_2 : s_2}{\Delta \fatsemi \Gamma \vdash_{\mathscr{A}} (e\in t\,?\,e_1 : e_2) : s_2}\ t' \leq \neg t$$

(ALG-CASE-BOTH)
$$\frac{\Delta \fatsemi \Gamma \vdash_{\mathscr{A}} e : t' \qquad \Delta \fatsemi \Gamma \vdash_{\mathscr{A}} e_1 : s_1 \qquad \Delta \fatsemi \Gamma \vdash_{\mathscr{A}} e_2 : s_2}{\Delta \fatsemi \Gamma \vdash_{\mathscr{A}} (e\in t\,?\,e_1 : e_2) : s_1 \vee s_2}\ \begin{array}{l} t' \not\leq \neg t \\ t' \not\leq t \end{array}$$

**Figure 2.** Typing algorithm

type-case expressions, that is,

$$e ::= x \mid ee \mid \lambda^{\wedge_{i\in I} s_i \to t_i}_{[\sigma_j]_{j\in J}} x.e \tag{17}$$

and whose types are *inductively* produced by the grammar

$$t ::= \alpha \mid t \to t \mid t \wedge t$$

This calculus is closed with respect to $\beta$-reduction as defined by the reduction rule (15) (without type-cases, union and negation types are not needed). It constitutes an explicitly-typed $\lambda$-calculus with intersection types whose expressive power subsumes that of classic intersection type systems (without an universal element $\omega$, of course), as expressed by the following theorem.

**Theorem 3.4.** *Let $\vdash_{BCD}$ denote provability in the Barendregt, Coppo, and Dezani system [1], and $\lceil e \rceil$ be the pure $\lambda$-calculus term obtained from e by erasing all types occurring in it.*
*If $\vdash_{BCD} m : t$, then $\exists e$ such that $\vdash e : t$ and $\lceil e \rceil = m$.*

Therefore, this sub-calculus solves a longstanding open problem, that is the definition of explicit type annotations for $\lambda$-terms in intersection type systems, without any further syntactic modification. See Section 7 on related work for an extensive comparison.

The proof of Theorem 3.4 is constructive (*cf.*, Appendix B.3). Therefore we can transpose decidability results of intersection type systems to our system. In particular, type reconstruction for the sub-calculus (17) is undecidable and this implies the undecidability of type reconstruction for the whole calculus *without recursive types* (with recursive types type reconstruction is trivially decidable since every $\lambda$-term can be typed by the recursive type $\mu X.(X \to X) \vee *$). In Section 4 we prove that type inference for our system is decidable. The problem of reconstructing type-substitutions (*ie*, given a term of grammar (3), deciding whether it is possible to add sets of type-substitutions in it so that it becomes a well-typed term of our calculus) is dealt with in the companion paper [4].

To compare with existing intersection type systems, the calculus in (17) includes neither type-cases nor expressions of the form $e[\sigma_j]_{j\in J}$. While it is clear that type-cases increase the expressive power of the calculus, one may wonder whether the same is true for $e[\sigma_j]_{j\in J}$. This is not so as expressions $e[\sigma_j]_{j\in J}$ are redundant. Consider the subcalculus whose terms are

$$e ::= x \mid ee \mid \lambda^{\wedge_{i\in I} s_i \to t_i}_{[\sigma_j]_{j\in J}} x.e \mid e\in t\,?\,e : e \tag{18}$$

that is, the calculus in which sets of type-substitutions appear only in decorations. Consider the embedding $[\![.]\!]$ of our calculus (13) into this subcalculus, defined as $[\![e[\sigma_j]_{j\in J}]\!] = e@[\sigma_j]_{j\in J}$, as the identity for variables, and as its homomorphic propagation for all the other expressions. Then it is easy to prove the following theorem

**Theorem 3.5.** *For every well-typed expression e:*
*1. $e \rightsquigarrow^* v \Rightarrow [\![e]\!] \rightsquigarrow^* [\![v]\!]$,*
*2. $[\![e]\!] \rightsquigarrow^* v \Rightarrow e \rightsquigarrow^* v'$ and $v = [\![v']\!]$*

meaning that the subcalculus defined above is equivalent to the full calculus. Although expressions of the form $e[\sigma_j]_{j\in J}$ do not bring any further expressive power, they play a crucial role in local type inference, which is why we included them in our calculus. As we explain in details in the companion paper, for local type inference we need to reconstruct sets of type-substitutions that are applied to expressions but we *must not* reconstruct sets of type-substitutions that are decorations of $\lambda$-expressions. The reason is pragmatic and can be shown by considering the following two terms: $(\lambda^{\alpha\to\alpha}x.x)3$ and $(\lambda^{\alpha\to\alpha}x.4)3$. Every functional programmer will agree that the first expression must be considered well-typed while the second must not, for the simple reason that the constant function $(\lambda^{\alpha\to\alpha}x.4)$ does not have type $\alpha \to \alpha$. Indeed in the first case it is possible to apply a set of type-substitutions that makes the term well typed, namely $(\lambda^{\alpha\to\alpha}x.x)[\{\mathtt{Int}/_\alpha\}]3$, while no such application exists for the second term. However, if we allowed reconstruction also for decorations, then the second term could be made well typed by adding the following decoration $(\lambda^{\alpha\to\alpha}_{[\{\mathtt{Int}/_\alpha\}]}x.4)3$.

## 4. Typing algorithm

The rules in Figure 1 do not describe a typing algorithm since they are not syntax directed. As customary the problem is the subsumption rule, and the way to go is to eliminate this rule by embedding appropriate checks of the subtyping relation into the rules that need it. This results in the system formed by the rules of Figure 2. This system is algorithmic (as stressed by $\vdash_{\mathscr{A}}$): in every case at most one rule applies, either because of the syntax of the term or because of mutually exclusive side conditions. Subsumption is no longer present and, instead, subtype checking has been pushed in all the remaining rules.

The rule for type-cases has been split in three rules (plus a fourth uninteresting rule we omitted that states that when $e : \mathbb{0}$ —*ie*, it is the provably diverging expression— then the whole type-case expression has type $\mathbb{0}$) according to whether one or both branches can be selected. Here the only modification is in the case where both branches can be selected: in the rule (*case*) in Figure 1 the types of the two branches were subsumed to a common type $s$, while (ALG-CASE-BOTH) returns the least upper bound (*ie*, the union) of the two types.

The rule for abstractions underwent a minor modification with respect to the types returned for the body, which before were subsumed to the type declared in the interface while now the subtyping relation $s'_{ij} \leq s_i\sigma_j$ is explicitly checked.

The elimination of the subsumption yields a simplification in typing the application of type-substitutions, since in the system of Figure 1 without subsumption every premise of an (*inter*) rule is the consequence of an (*inst*) rule. The two rules can thus be merged into a single one, yielding the (ALG-INST) rule (see Appendix C.1 and in particular Theorem C.1).

As expected, the core of the typing algorithm is the rule for application. In the system of Figure 1, in order to apply the (*appl*) rule, the type of the function had to be subsumed to an arrow type, and the type of the argument had to be subsumed to the domain of that arrow type; then the co-domain of the arrow is taken to type the application. In the algorithmic rule (ALG-APPL), this is done by the type meta-operator "$\cdot$" which is formally defined as follows: $t \cdot s \stackrel{\text{def}}{=} \min\{u \mid t \leq s \to u\}$. In words, if $t$ is the type of the function and $s$ the type of the argument, this operator looks for the smallest arrow type larger than $t$ and with domain $s$, and it returns its co-domain. More precisely, when typing $e_1e_2$, the rule (ALG-APPL) checks that the type $t$ of $e_1$ is a functional one (*ie*, $t \leq \mathbb{0} \to \mathbb{1}$). It also checks that the type $s$ of $e_2$ is a subtype of the domain of $t$ (denoted by $\mathsf{dom}(t)$). Because $t$ is not necessarily an arrow type (in general, it is equivalent to a disjunctive normal form like the one of equation (12) in Section 3), the definition of the domain is not immediate. The domain of a function whose type is an intersection of arrows and negation of arrows is the union of the domains of all positive literals. For instance the domain of a function of type $(\texttt{Int}\to\texttt{Int}) \wedge (\texttt{Bool}\to\texttt{Bool})$ is $\texttt{Int} \vee \texttt{Bool}$, since it can be equally applied to integer or Boolean arguments, while the domain of `even` as defined in (8) is $\texttt{Int} \vee (\alpha\backslash\texttt{Int})$, that is $\texttt{Int} \vee \alpha$. The domain of a union of functional types is the intersection of each domain. For instance an expression of type $(s_1\to s_2) \vee (t_1\to t_2)$ will return either a function of type $s_1\to s_2$ or a function of type $t_1\to t_2$, so this expression can be applied only to arguments that fit both cases, that is, to arguments in $s_1 \wedge t_1$. Formally, if $t \leq \mathbb{0}\to\mathbb{1}$, then $t \simeq \bigvee_{i\in I}(\bigwedge_{p\in P_i}(s_p\to t_p) \wedge \bigwedge_{n\in N_i}\neg(s_n\to t_n) \wedge \bigwedge_{q\in Q_i}\alpha_q \wedge \bigwedge_{r\in R_i}\neg\beta_r)$ (with all the $P_i$'s not empty), and therefore $\mathsf{dom}(t) \stackrel{\text{def}}{=} \bigwedge_{i\in I}\bigvee_{p\in P_i} s_p$ (here type variables do not count since they are intersected and universally quantified so the definition of the domain must hold also when their intersection is $\mathbb{1}$). Finally, the type returned in (ALG-APP) is $t \cdot s$, which we recall is the smallest result type that can be obtained by subsuming $t$ to an arrow type compatible with $s$. We can prove that for every type $t$ such that $t \leq \mathbb{0}\to\mathbb{1}$ and type $s$ such that $s \leq \mathsf{dom}(t)$, the type $t \cdot s$ exists and can be effectively computed (see Lemma C.12).

The algorithmic system is sound and complete with respect to the type system of Figure 1 and satisfies the minimum typing property (see Appendix C for the proofs).

**Theorem 4.1** (Soundness). *If* $\Delta \,\S\, \Gamma \vdash_{\mathscr{A}} e : t$*, then* $\Delta \,\S\, \Gamma \vdash e : t$*.*

**Theorem 4.2** (Completeness). *If* $\Delta \,\S\, \Gamma \vdash e : t$*, then there exists a type* $s$ *such that* $\Delta \,\S\, \Gamma \vdash_{\mathscr{A}} e : s$ *and* $s \leq t$*.*

**Corollary 4.3** (Minimum typing). *If* $\Delta \,\S\, \Gamma \vdash_{\mathscr{A}} e : t$*, then* $t = \min\{s \mid \Delta \,\S\, \Gamma \vdash e : s\}$*.*

Finally, it is quite easy to prove that type inference is decidable. It suffices to observe that the algorithmic rules strictly reduce the size of the expressions.

**Theorem 4.4 (Termination).** *Let e be an expression. Then the type inference algorithm for e terminates.*

This system constitutes a further theoretical contribution of our work since with this type system the language defined by grammar (13), the one by grammar (18), and *a fortiori* the one by grammar (17) are intersection type systems that all satisfy the Curry-Howard isomorphism since there is a one-to-one correspondence between terms and proofs of the algorithmic system.

## 5. Evaluation

In this section we define an efficient execution model for the polymorphic calculus as a conservative extension of the execution model of the monomorphic calculus: by "efficient" we mean that monomorphic expressions will be evaluated as efficiently as in the original $\mathbb{C}$Duce runtime. In fact, even polymorphic expressions will be evaluated as efficiently as well (as if type variables were basic monomorphic types) despite the fact that the formal reduction semantics of polymorphic expressions includes a run-time relabeling operation. The key observation that allows us to define an efficient execution model for the polymorphic calculus is that relabeling can be implemented *lazily* so that the only case in which relabeling is computed at run-time will correspond to testing the type of a partial application of a polymorphic function. In practice, this case is so rare —at least in the XML setting— that there is no difference between monomorphic and polymorphic evaluation.

### 5.1 Monomorphic Language

Let us start by recalling the execution model of monomorphic $\mathbb{C}$Duce, which is a classic closure-based evaluation. Expressions and values are defined as

$$e ::= c \mid x \mid \lambda^t x.e \mid ee \mid e \in s\,?\,e : e \qquad v ::= c \mid \langle \lambda^t x.e, \mathscr{E} \rangle$$

where $t$ denotes an intersection of arrow types, $s$ denotes a closed type, and $\mathscr{E}$ denotes an *environment*, that is, a substitution mapping expression variables into values. The big step semantics is:

$$\text{(ME-CONST)}\ \ \mathscr{E} \vdash_{\mathsf{m}} c \Downarrow c \qquad \text{(ME-VAR)}\ \ \mathscr{E} \vdash_{\mathsf{m}} x \Downarrow \mathscr{E}(x) \qquad \text{(ME-CLOSURE)}\ \ \mathscr{E} \vdash_{\mathsf{m}} \lambda^t x.e \Downarrow \langle \lambda^t x.e, \mathscr{E} \rangle$$

$$\text{(ME-APPLY)}\ \ \frac{\mathscr{E} \vdash_{\mathsf{m}} e_1 \Downarrow \langle \lambda^t x.e, \mathscr{E}' \rangle \qquad \mathscr{E} \vdash_{\mathsf{m}} e_2 \Downarrow v_0 \qquad \mathscr{E}', x \mapsto v_0 \vdash_{\mathsf{m}} e \Downarrow v}{\mathscr{E} \vdash_{\mathsf{m}} e_1 e_2 \Downarrow v}$$

$$\text{(ME-TYPE CASE T)}\ \ \frac{\mathscr{E} \vdash_{\mathsf{m}} e_1 \Downarrow v_0 \qquad v_0 \in_{\mathsf{m}} t \qquad \mathscr{E} \vdash_{\mathsf{m}} e_2 \Downarrow v}{\mathscr{E} \vdash_{\mathsf{m}} e_1 \in t\,?\,e_2 : e_3 \Downarrow v}$$

$$\text{(ME-TYPE CASE F)}\ \ \frac{\mathscr{E} \vdash_{\mathsf{m}} e_1 \Downarrow v_0 \qquad v_0 \notin_{\mathsf{m}} t \qquad \mathscr{E} \vdash_{\mathsf{m}} e_3 \Downarrow v}{\mathscr{E} \vdash_{\mathsf{m}} e_1 \in t\,?\,e_2 : e_3 \Downarrow v}$$

To complete the definition we define the relation $v \in_{\mathsf{m}} t$, that is, membership of a (monomorphic) value to a (monomorphic) type:

$$c \in_{\mathsf{m}} t \stackrel{\text{def}}{\iff} b_c \leq t$$
$$\langle \lambda^s x.e, \mathscr{E} \rangle \in_{\mathsf{m}} t \stackrel{\text{def}}{\iff} s \leq t$$

where $\leq$ is the subtyping relation of $\mathbb{C}$Duce [11].

### 5.2 Polymorphic Language

In the naive extension of this semantics to the explicitly-typed polymorphic calculus of Section 3, we deal with type-substitutions as we do for environments, that is, by storing them in closures. This is reflected by the following definition where, for brevity, we write $\sigma_I$ to denote the set of type-substitutions $[\sigma_i]_{i\in I}$:

$$\begin{array}{rcl} e & ::= & c \mid x \mid \lambda^t_{\sigma_I} x.e \mid ee \mid e \in t\,?\,e : e \mid e\sigma_I \\ v & ::= & c \mid \langle \lambda^t_{\sigma_I} x.e, \mathscr{E}, \sigma_I \rangle \end{array}$$

The big-step semantics is then defined as follows, where each expression is evaluated with respect to an environment $\mathscr{E}$ determining the current value substitutions and a set of type-substitutions $\sigma_I$:

$$\text{(PE-CONST)}\ \ \sigma_I; \mathscr{E} \vdash_{\mathsf{p}} c \Downarrow c \qquad \text{(PE-VAR)}\ \ \sigma_I; \mathscr{E} \vdash_{\mathsf{p}} x \Downarrow \mathscr{E}(x)$$

$$\text{(PE-CLOSURE)}\ \ \sigma_I; \mathscr{E} \vdash_{\mathsf{p}} \lambda^t_{\sigma_J} x.e \Downarrow \langle \lambda^t_{\sigma_J} x.e, \mathscr{E}, \sigma_I \rangle \qquad \text{(PE-INSTANCE)}\ \ \frac{\sigma_I \circ \sigma_J; \mathscr{E} \vdash_{\mathsf{p}} e \Downarrow v}{\sigma_I; \mathscr{E} \vdash_{\mathsf{p}} e\sigma_J \Downarrow v}$$

$$\text{(PE-APPLY)}\ \ \frac{\begin{array}{c}\sigma_I; \mathscr{E} \vdash_{\mathsf{p}} e_1 \Downarrow \langle \lambda^{\wedge_{l\in L} s_l \to t_l}_{\sigma_K} x.e, \mathscr{E}', \sigma_H \rangle \qquad \sigma_I; \mathscr{E} \vdash_{\mathsf{p}} e_2 \Downarrow v_0 \\ \sigma_J = \sigma_H \circ \sigma_K \quad P = \{j \in J \mid \exists l \in L : v_0 \in_{\mathsf{p}} s_l\sigma_j\} \\ \sigma_P; \mathscr{E}', x \mapsto v_0 \vdash_{\mathsf{p}} e \Downarrow v\end{array}}{\sigma_I; \mathscr{E} \vdash_{\mathsf{p}} e_1 e_2 \Downarrow v}$$

$$\text{(PE-TYPE CASE T)}\ \ \frac{\sigma_I; \mathscr{E} \vdash_{\mathsf{p}} e_1 \Downarrow v_0 \qquad v_0 \in_{\mathsf{p}} t \qquad \sigma_I; \mathscr{E} \vdash_{\mathsf{p}} e_2 \Downarrow v}{\sigma_I; \mathscr{E} \vdash_{\mathsf{p}} e_1 \in t\,?\,e_2 : e_3 \Downarrow v}$$

$$\text{(PE-TYPE CASE F)}\ \ \frac{\sigma_I; \mathscr{E} \vdash_{\mathsf{p}} e_1 \Downarrow v_0 \qquad v_0 \notin_{\mathsf{p}} t \qquad \sigma_I; \mathscr{E} \vdash_{\mathsf{p}} e_3 \Downarrow v}{\sigma_I; \mathscr{E} \vdash_{\mathsf{p}} e_1 \in t\,?\,e_2 : e_3 \Downarrow v}$$

The membership relation $v \in_{\mathsf{p}} t$ for polymorphic values is inductively defined as:

$$c \in_{\mathsf{p}} t \quad \stackrel{\text{def}}{\iff} \quad b_c \leq t$$
$$\langle \lambda^{s}_{\sigma_J} x.e, \mathscr{E}, \sigma_I \rangle \in_{\mathsf{p}} t \quad \stackrel{\text{def}}{\iff} \quad s(\sigma_I \circ \sigma_J) \leq t$$

where $\leq$ is the subtyping relation of Castagna and Xu [5]. It is not difficult to show that this big-step semantics is equivalent to the small-step one of Section 3. Let $(\!|.|\!)$ be the transformation that maps values of the polymorphic language into corresponding values of the calculus, that is

$$(\!|c|\!) = c \qquad \text{and} \qquad (\!|\langle \lambda^{s}_{\sigma_J} x.e, \mathscr{E}, \sigma_I \rangle|\!) = \lambda^{s}_{\sigma_I \circ \sigma_J} x.(e(\!|\mathscr{E}|\!)) \quad (19)$$

where $(\!|\mathscr{E}|\!)$ applies $(\!|.|\!)$ to all the values in the range of $\mathscr{E}$. Let $\mathbb{I}$ denote the singleton set containing the empty type-substitution $[\{\,\}]$, which is the neutral element of the composition of sets of type-substitutions. Then we have:

**Theorem 5.1.** *Let e be a well-typed closed explicitly-typed expression ($\vdash_{\mathscr{A}} e : t$). Then:* $\mathbb{I}; \varnothing \vdash_{\mathsf{p}} e \Downarrow v \iff e \rightsquigarrow^{*} (\!|v|\!)$.

This implementation has a significant computational burden compared to that of the monomorphic language: first of all, each application of (PE-APPLY) computes the set $P$, which requires to implement several type-substitutions and membership tests; second, each application of (PE-INSTANCE) computes the composition of two sets of type-substitutions. In the next section we describe a different solution consisting in the compilation of the explicitly typed calculus into an intermediate language so that these computations are postponed as much as possible and are performed only if and when they are really necessary.

### 5.3 Intermediate Language

The intermediate language into which we compile the explicitly-typed polymorphic language is very similar to the monomorphic version. The only difference is that $\lambda$-abstractions (both in expressions and closures) may contain type variables in their interface and have an extra decoration $\Sigma$ which is a term *denoting* a set of type-substitutions.

$$\begin{array}{rcl} e & ::= & c \mid x \mid \lambda^{t}_{\Sigma} x.e \mid ee \mid e \in t\,?\,e : e \\ v & ::= & c \mid \langle \lambda^{t}_{\Sigma} x.e, \mathscr{E} \rangle \\ \Sigma & ::= & \sigma_I \mid \mathtt{comp}(\Sigma, \Sigma') \mid \mathtt{sel}(x, t, \Sigma) \end{array}$$

Intuitively, a $\mathtt{comp}(\Sigma, \Sigma')$ term corresponds to an application of the $\circ$ composition operator to the sets of type substitutions denoted by $\Sigma$ and $\Sigma'$, while a $\mathtt{sel}(x, t, \Sigma)$ term selects the subset of type substitutions $\sigma$ denoted by $\Sigma$ that are compatible with the fact that (the value instantiating) $x$ belongs to the domain of $t\sigma$.

The big step semantics for this intermediate language is:

(OE-CONST) $\quad \mathscr{E} \vdash_{\circ} c \Downarrow c$

(OE-VAR) $\quad \mathscr{E} \vdash_{\circ} x \Downarrow \mathscr{E}(x)$

(OE-CLOSURE) $\quad \mathscr{E} \vdash_{\circ} \lambda^{t}_{\Sigma} x.e \Downarrow \langle \lambda^{t}_{\Sigma} x.e, \mathscr{E} \rangle$

(OE-APPLY)

$$\frac{\mathscr{E} \vdash_{\circ} e_1 \Downarrow \langle \lambda^{t}_{\Sigma} x.e, \mathscr{E}' \rangle \qquad \mathscr{E} \vdash_{\circ} e_2 \Downarrow v_0 \qquad \mathscr{E}', x \mapsto v_0 \vdash_{\circ} e \Downarrow v}{\mathscr{E} \vdash_{\circ} e_1 e_2 \Downarrow v}$$

(OE-TYPE CASE T)

$$\frac{\mathscr{E} \vdash_{\circ} e_1 \Downarrow v_0 \qquad v_0 \in_{\circ} t \qquad \mathscr{E} \vdash_{\circ} e_2 \Downarrow v}{\mathscr{E} \vdash_{\circ} e_1 \in t\,?\,e_2 : e_3 \Downarrow v}$$

(OE-TYPE CASE F)

$$\frac{\mathscr{E} \vdash_{\circ} e_1 \Downarrow v_0 \qquad v_0 \notin_{\circ} t \qquad \mathscr{E} \vdash_{\circ} e_3 \Downarrow v}{\mathscr{E} \vdash_{\circ} e_1 \in t\,?\,e_2 : e_3 \Downarrow v}$$

Notice that this semantics is structurally the same as that of the monomorphic language. There are only two minor differences: $(i)$ $\lambda$-abstractions have an extra decoration $\Sigma$ (which has no impact on efficiency since it corresponds in the implementation to manipulate descriptors with an extra field) and $(ii)$ the corresponding (_E-TYPE CASE) rules use a slightly different relation: $\in_{\circ}$ instead of $\in_{\mathsf{m}}$. It is thus easy to see that in terms of steps of reduction the two semantics have the same complexity. What changes is the test of the membership relation ($\in_{\circ}$ rather than $\in_{\mathsf{m}}$) since, when the value to be tested is a closure, we need to materialize relabelings. In other words, we have to evaluate the $\Sigma$ expression decorating the function and apply the resulting set of substitutions to the interface of the function. Formally:

$$c \in_{\circ} t \quad \stackrel{\text{def}}{\iff} \quad b_c \leq t$$
$$\langle \lambda^{s}_{\Sigma} x.e, \mathscr{E} \rangle \in_{\circ} t \quad \stackrel{\text{def}}{\iff} \quad s(\mathsf{eval}(\mathscr{E}, \Sigma)) \leq t$$

where the evaluation of the symbolic set of type-substitutions is inductively defined as

$$\begin{array}{r} \mathsf{eval}(\mathscr{E}, \sigma_I) = \sigma_I \\ \mathsf{eval}(\mathscr{E}, \mathtt{comp}(\Sigma, \Sigma')) = \mathsf{eval}(\mathscr{E}, \Sigma) \circ \mathsf{eval}(\mathscr{E}, \Sigma') \\ \mathsf{eval}(\mathscr{E}, \mathtt{sel}(x, \bigwedge_{i \in I} t_i \to s_i, \Sigma)) = \\ [\, \sigma_j \in \mathsf{eval}(\mathscr{E}, \Sigma) \mid \exists i \in I : \mathscr{E}(x) \in_{\circ} t_i \sigma_j \,] \end{array}$$

Notice in the last rule the crucial role played by $x$ and $\mathscr{E}$: by using an expression variable $x$ in the symbolic representation of type-substitutions and relying on its interpretation through $\mathscr{E}$, we have transposed to type-substitutions the same benefits that closures bring to value substitutions: just as closures allow *value*-substitutions to be materialized only when a formal parameter is used rather than at the moment of the reduction, so our technique allows *type*-substitutions to be materialized only when a type variable is effectively tested, rather than at the moment of the reduction.

It is easy to see that the only case in which the computation of $\in_{\circ}$ is more expensive than that of $\in_{\mathsf{m}}$ is when the value whose type is tested is a closure $\langle \lambda^{t}_{\Sigma} x.e, \mathscr{E} \rangle$ in which $t$ is not closed and $\Sigma$ is not $\mathbb{I}$.[5] The $\Sigma$ decoration is different from $\mathbb{I}$ only if the closure is the result of a partial application of a curried function. The type $t$ is not closed only if such partial application yielded a polymorphic function. In conclusion, the evaluation of an expression in the polymorphic language is more expensive than the evaluation of a similar[6] expression of the monomorphic language only if it tests the type of a polymorphic function resulting from the partial application of a polymorphic curried function. The additional overhead is limited only to this particular test and in all the other cases the evaluation is as efficient as in the monomorphic case. Finally, it is important to stress that this holds true also if we add product types: the test of a pair of values in the polymorphic case is as expensive as in the monomorphic case and so is the rest of the evaluation. Since in the XML setting the vast majority of the computation time is spent in testing products (since they encode sequences, trees, and XML elements), then the overhead brought by adding polymorphism —*ie*, the overhead due to testing the type of a polymorphic partial application of a polymorphic curried function— is negligible in practice.

All that remains to do is to define the compilation of the explicitly-typed language into the intermediate language:

$$\begin{array}{rcl} [\![x]\!]_{\Sigma} & = & x \\ [\![\lambda^{t}_{\sigma_I} x.e]\!]_{\Sigma} & = & \lambda^{t}_{\mathtt{comp}(\Sigma, \sigma_I)} x.[\![e]\!]_{\mathtt{sel}(x, t, \mathtt{comp}(\Sigma, \sigma_I))} \\ [\![e_1 e_2]\!]_{\Sigma} & = & [\![e_1]\!]_{\Sigma} [\![e_2]\!]_{\Sigma} \\ [\![e \sigma_I]\!]_{\Sigma} & = & [\![e]\!]_{\mathtt{comp}(\Sigma, \sigma_I)} \\ [\![e_1 \in t\,?\,e_2 : e_3]\!]_{\Sigma} & = & [\![e_1]\!]_{\Sigma} \in t\,?\,[\![e_2]\!]_{\Sigma} : [\![e_3]\!]_{\Sigma} \end{array}$$

Given a closed program $e$ we compile it in the intermediate language as $[\![e]\!]_{\mathbb{I}}$. In practice, the compilation will be even simpler since we apply it only to expressions generated by local type inference algorithm described in the companion paper where all $\lambda$'s are decorated by $\mathbb{I}$ (*cf.* discussion at the end of Section 3.5).

[5] To be more precise, when there exists a substitution $\sigma \in \mathsf{eval}(\mathscr{E}, \Sigma)$ such that $\mathsf{var}(t) \cap \mathsf{dom}(\sigma) \neq \varnothing$. Notice that the tests of the subtyping relation for monomorphic and polymorphic types have the same complexity [5].

[6] By similar we intend with the same syntax tree but only closed types.

So the second case of the definition simplifies to: $[\![\lambda^t_{\mathbb{I}} x.e]\!]_\Sigma = \lambda^t_\Sigma x.[\![e]\!]_{\texttt{sel}(x,t,\Sigma)}$.

The compilation is adequate:

**Theorem 5.2.** *Let e be a well-typed closed explicitly-typed expression ($\vdash_{\mathscr{A}} e : t$). Then* $\mathbb{I}; \varnothing \vdash_{\mathsf{p}} e \Downarrow v \iff \vdash_{\circ} [\![e]\!]_{\mathbb{I}} \Downarrow v'$ *, with* $(\!|v|\!) = (\!|v'|\!)$.

where $(\!|\langle \lambda^t_\Sigma x.e, \mathscr{E}\rangle|\!)$ evaluates all the symbolic expressions and type-substitutions in the term (see (19)). By combining Theorems 5.1 and 5.2 we obtain the adequacy of the compilation:

**Corollary 5.3.** *Let e be a well-typed closed explicitly-typed expression ($\vdash_{\mathscr{A}} e : t$). Then* $\vdash_{\circ} [\![e]\!]_{\mathbb{I}} \Downarrow v \iff e \rightsquigarrow^* (\!|v|\!)$.

### 5.4 Let-polymorphism

A function is polymorphic if it can be safely applied to arguments of different types. The calculus presented supports a varied palette of different forms of polymorphism: it uses subtype polymorphism (a function can be applied to arguments whose types are subtypes of its domain type), the combination of intersection types and type-case expressions yields "ad hoc" polymorphism (aka overloading), and finally the use of type variables in function interfaces provides parametric polymorphism. Polymorphism is interesting when used with bindings: instead of repeating the definition of a function every time we need to apply it, it is more convenient to define the function once, bind it to an expression variable, and use the variable every time we need to apply the function. In the current system it is possible to combine binding only with the first two kinds of polymorphism: different occurrences of a variable bound to a function can be given different types —thus, be applied to arguments of different types—, either by subsumption (*ie*, by assigning to the variable a super-type of the type of the function it denotes) or by intersection elimination (*ie*, by assigning to a variable one of the types that form the intersection type of the function it denotes). However, as it is well known in the languages of the ML-family, in the current setting it is not possible to combine binding and parametric polymorphism. Distinct occurrences of a variable cannot be given different types by instantiation (*ie*, by assigning to the variable a type which is an instance of the type of the function it denotes). In other terms, all $\lambda$-abstracted variables have monomorphic types (with respect to parametric polymorphism), which is why in ML auto-application $\lambda x.xx$ is not typeable.

The solution is well known and consists in introducing `let` bindings. This amounts to defining a new class of expression variables so that variables introduced by a `let` have polymorphic types, that is, types that have been generalized at the moment of the definition and can be instantiated in the body of the let. To sum up, $\lambda$-abstracted variables have monomorphic types, while `let`-bound variables (may) have polymorphic types and, thus, be given different types obtained by instantiation. For short we call the former $\lambda$-abstracted variables "monomorphic (expression) variables" and the latter `let`-bound variables "polymorphic (expression) variables".

In the explicitly-typed calculi of the previous sections we had just $\lambda$-abstracted variables. That these variables have monomorphic types is clearly witnessed by the fact that, operationally, $x\sigma_I$ is equivalent to (*ie*, reduces to) $x$. Clearly this property must not hold for polymorphic type variables since

$$\texttt{let}\ x = (\lambda^{\alpha\to\alpha} y.y)\ \texttt{in}\ (x[\{\alpha\to\alpha/_\alpha\}])x \qquad (20)$$

is, intuitively, well typed, while the same term obtained by replacing $x[\{\alpha \to \alpha/_\alpha\}]$ with $x$ is not (see the extension of the definition of relabeling for polymorphic variables later on).

To enable the definition of polymorphic functions to our calculus we add a `let` expression. To ease the presentation and to stress that the addition of `let`-bindings is a conservative extension of the previous system, we syntactically distinguish the current monomorphic variables (*ie*, those abstracted by a $\lambda$) from polymorphic variables by underlining the latter ones.

$$e ::= \cdots \mid \underline{x} \mid \texttt{let}\ \underline{x} = e\ \texttt{in}\ e$$

Reduction is as usual:

$$\texttt{let}\ \underline{x} = v\ \texttt{in}\ e \rightsquigarrow e\{v/\underline{x}\}$$

Relabeling is extended by the following definitions

$$\underline{x}@[\sigma_j]_{j\in J} \stackrel{\text{def}}{=} \underline{x}[\sigma_j]_{j\in J}$$
$$(\texttt{let}\ \underline{x}{=}e'\ \texttt{in}\ e)@[\sigma_j]_{j\in J} \stackrel{\text{def}}{=} \texttt{let}\ \underline{x}{=}(e'@[\sigma_j]_{j\in J})\ \texttt{in}\ (e@[\sigma_j]_{j\in J})$$

and the (algorithmic) typing rule is as expected:

$$(let)\ \frac{\Delta\,\S\,\Gamma \vdash_{(\mathscr{A})} e_1 : t_1 \qquad \Delta\,\S\,\Gamma, (\underline{x} : t_1) \vdash_{(\mathscr{A})} e_2 : t_2}{\Delta\,\S\,\Gamma \vdash_{(\mathscr{A})} \texttt{let}\ \underline{x} = e_1\ \texttt{in}\ e_2 : t_2}$$

Type environments $\Gamma$ now map also polymorphic expression variables into types. Notice that for a polymorphic expression variable $\underline{x}$ it is no longer true that $\mathsf{var}(\Gamma(\underline{x})) \subseteq \Delta$ (not adding $\mathsf{var}(\Gamma(\underline{x}))$ to $\Delta$ corresponds to generalizing the type of $\underline{x}$ before typing $e_2$ as in the GEN rule of the Damas-Milner algorithm: *cf.* [15]). As before we assume that polymorphic type variables of a `let`-expression (in particular those generalized for let-polymorphism) are distinct from monomorphic and polymorphic type variables of the context that the `let`-expression occurs in.

Likewise, environments now map both monomorphic and polymorphic expression variables into values so that the rules for evaluation in Section 5.2 are extended with the following ones:

$$(\text{PE-PVAR}_c)\ \frac{\mathscr{E}(\underline{x}) = c}{\sigma_I; \mathscr{E} \vdash_{\mathsf{p}} \underline{x} \Downarrow c} \qquad (\text{PE-PVAR}_f)\ \frac{\mathscr{E}(\underline{x}) = \langle \lambda^t y.e, \mathscr{E}', \sigma_J\rangle}{\sigma_I; \mathscr{E} \vdash_{\mathsf{p}} \underline{x} \Downarrow \langle \lambda^t y.e, \mathscr{E}', \sigma_I \circ \sigma_J\rangle}$$

$$(\text{PE-LET})\ \frac{\sigma_I; \mathscr{E} \vdash_{\mathsf{p}} e_1 \Downarrow v_0 \qquad \sigma_I; \mathscr{E}, \underline{x} \mapsto v_0 \vdash_{\mathsf{p}} e_2 \Downarrow v}{\sigma_I; \mathscr{E} \vdash_{\mathsf{p}} \texttt{let}\ \underline{x} = e_1\ \texttt{in}\ e_2 \Downarrow v}$$

To compile `let`-expressions we have to extend the intermediate language likewise: we will distinguish polymorphic expression variables by decorating them with sets of type-substitution formulæ $\Sigma$ that apply to *that particular occurrence* of the variable. So we add to the productions of Section 5.3 the following ones:

$$e ::= \cdots \mid x_\Sigma \mid \texttt{let}\ \underline{x} = e\ \texttt{in}\ e$$

while the big-step semantics of the new added expressions is

$$(\text{OE-PVAR}_c)\ \frac{\mathscr{E}(\underline{x}) = c}{\mathscr{E} \vdash_{\circ} x_\Sigma \Downarrow c} \qquad (\text{OE-PVAR}_f)\ \frac{\mathscr{E}(\underline{x}) = \langle \lambda^t_{\Sigma'} y.e, \mathscr{E}'\rangle}{\mathscr{E} \vdash_{\circ} x_\Sigma \Downarrow \langle \lambda^t_{\mathsf{comp}(\Sigma,\Sigma')} y.e, \mathscr{E}'\rangle}$$

$$(\text{OE-LET})\ \frac{\mathscr{E} \vdash_{\circ} e_1 \Downarrow v_0 \qquad \mathscr{E}, \underline{x} \mapsto v_0 \vdash_{\circ} e_2 \Downarrow v}{\mathscr{E} \vdash_{\circ} \texttt{let}\ \underline{x} = e_1\ \texttt{in}\ e_2 \Downarrow v}$$

Notice how rule (OE-PVAR$_f$) uses the $\Sigma$ decoration on the variable to construct the closure. The final step is the extension of the compiler for the newly added terms:

$$[\![\underline{x}]\!]_\Sigma = x_\Sigma$$
$$[\![\texttt{let}\ \underline{x} = e_1\ \texttt{in}\ e_2]\!]_\Sigma = \texttt{let}\ \underline{x} = [\![e_1]\!]_\Sigma\ \texttt{in}\ [\![e_2]\!]_\Sigma$$

As an example, the `let`-expression (20) is compiled into

$$\texttt{let}\ \underline{x} = (\lambda^{\alpha\to\alpha} y.y)\ \texttt{in}\ x_{[\{\alpha\to\alpha/_\alpha\}]} x_{\mathbb{I}}$$

where the substitution $[\{\alpha\to\alpha/_\alpha\}]$ that is applied to the leftmost occurrence of $x$ is recorded in the variable and will be used to instantiate the closure associated with $x$ by the environment; the rightmost occurrence of $x$ is decorated by $\mathbb{I}$ and therefore the value bound to it will not be instantiated. Theorems 5.1, 5.2, and Corollary 5.3 hold also for these extensions (see Appendix D for the proofs).

In an actual programming language there will not be any syntactic distinction between the two kinds of expression variables and compilation can be optimized by transforming variables that are let-bound to monomorphic values into monomorphic variables. So, whenever $e_1$ has a monomorphic type $t_1$, the let-expression should be compiled as

$$[\![\mathtt{let}\ \underline{x} = e_1\ \mathtt{in}\ e_2]\!]_\Sigma \quad = \quad [\![(\lambda^{t_1 \to t_2} x.e_2\{x/\underline{x}\})e_1]\!]_\Sigma$$

where $t_2$ is the type deduced for $e_2$ under the hypothesis that $\underline{x}$ has type $t_1$. Notice that this optimization is compositional.

## 6. Design choices and extensions

For the sake of concision we omitted two key features in the presentation: recursive functions and pairs. Recursive functions can be straightforwardly added with minor modifications. In particular, for recursive functions, whose syntax is $\mu f^{\wedge_{i\in I} t_i \to s_i}_{[\sigma_j]_{j\in J}} x.e$, it suffices to add in the type environment $\Gamma$ the recursion variable $f$ associated with the type obtained by applying the decoration to the interface, that is, $f : \wedge_{i\in I, j\in J} t_i\sigma_j \to s_i\sigma_j$: the reader can refer to Section 7.5 in [11] for a discussion on how and why recursion is restricted to functions.

The extension with product types, instead, is less straightforward but can be mostly done by using existing techniques. Syntactically, we add pairs $(e, e)$ and projections $\pi_i e$ (for $i$=1, 2) to terms and the product type constructor $t\times t$ to types. Reduction semantics is standard: two notions of reduction $\pi_i(v_1, v_2) \rightsquigarrow v_i$ (for $i$=1, 2) plus the usual context reduction rules. Typing rules are standard, as well: a pair is typed by the product of the types of its components and if $e$ is of type $t_1\times t_2$, then its $i$-th projection $\pi_i e$ has type $t_i$. The rule for pairs in the algorithmic system $\vdash_{\mathscr{A}}$ is the same as in the static semantics, while the rules for projections $\pi_i e$ become more difficult because the type inferred for $e$ may not be of the form $t_1\times t_2$ but, in general, is (equivalent to) a union of intersections of types. We already met the latter problem for application (where the function type may be different from an arrow) and there we checked that the type deduced for the function in an application is a functional type (*ie*, a subtype of $\mathbb{0}\to\mathbb{1}$). Similarly, for products we must check that the type of $e$ is a product type (*ie*, a subtype of $\mathbb{1}\times\mathbb{1}$). If the constraint is satisfied, then it is possible to define the type of the projection (in a way akin to the definition of the domain dom() for function types) using standard techniques of semantic subtyping (see Section 6.11 in [11]). This is explained in details in Appendix C.

For the semantics of the calculus we made few choices that restrict its generality. One of these, the use of a call-by-value reduction, is directly inherited from $\mathbb{C}$Duce and it is required to ensure subject reduction. If $e$ is an expression of type $\mathtt{Int}\vee\mathtt{Bool}$, then the application $(\lambda^{(\mathtt{Int}\to\mathtt{Int}\times\mathtt{Int})\wedge(\mathtt{Bool}\to\mathtt{Bool}\times\mathtt{Bool})} x.(x, x))e$ has type $(\mathtt{Int}\times\mathtt{Int})\wedge(\mathtt{Bool}\times\mathtt{Bool})$. If we use call-by-name, then this redex reduces to $(e, e)$ whose type $(\mathtt{Int}\vee\mathtt{Bool}\times\mathtt{Int}\vee\mathtt{Bool})$ is larger than the type of the redex. Although the use of call-by-name would not hinder the soundness of the type system (expressed in terms of progress) we preferred to ensure subject reduction since it greatly simplifies the theoretical development.

A second choice, to restrict type-cases to closed types, was made by practical considerations: using open types in a type-case would have been computationally prohibitive insofar as it demands to solve at run-time the problem whether for two given types $s$ and $t$ there exists a type-substitution $\sigma$ such that $s\sigma \leq t\sigma$ (we study this problem, that we call the tallying problems, in the companion paper [4]). Our choice, instead, is compatible with the highly optimized (and provably optimal) pattern matching compilation technique of $\mathbb{C}$Duce. We leave for future work the study of type-cases on types with monomorphic variables (*ie*, those in $\Delta$). This does not require dynamic type tallying resolution and would allow the programmer to test capabilities of arguments bound to polymorphic type variables.

## 7. Related work

We focus on work related to this specific part of our work, namely, existing explicitly-typed calculi with intersection types, and functional languages to process XML data. Comparison with work on local type inference and type reconstruction is done in the second part of this work presented in the companion paper [4].

To compare the differences between the existing explicitly-typed calculi for intersection type systems, we discuss how the term of our daffy identity $(\lambda^{\alpha\to\alpha}_{[\{\mathtt{Int}/\alpha\},\{\mathtt{Bool}/\alpha\}]} x.(\lambda^{\alpha\to\alpha} y.x)x)$ is rendered.

In [18, 21], typing derivations are written as terms: different typed representatives of the same untyped term are joined together with an intersection $\wedge$. In such systems, the function in (4) relabeled with $[\{\mathtt{Int}/\alpha\}, \{\mathtt{Bool}/\alpha\}]$ is written $(\lambda^{\mathtt{Int}\to\mathtt{Int}} x.(\lambda^{\mathtt{Int}\to\mathtt{Int}} y.x)x) \wedge (\lambda^{\mathtt{Bool}\to\mathtt{Bool}} x.(\lambda^{\mathtt{Bool}\to\mathtt{Bool}} y.x)x)$. Type checking verifies that both $\lambda^{\mathtt{Int}\to\mathtt{Int}} x.(\lambda^{\mathtt{Int}\to\mathtt{Int}} y.x)x$ and $\lambda^{\mathtt{Bool}\to\mathtt{Bool}} x.(\lambda^{\mathtt{Bool}\to\mathtt{Bool}} y.x)x$ are well typed separately, which generates two very similar typing derivations. The proposal of [13] follows the same idea, except that a separation is kept between the computational and the logical contents of terms. A term consists in the association of a *marked term* and a *proof term*. The marked term is just an untyped term where term variables are marked with integers. The proof term encodes the structure of the typing derivation and relates marks to types. The aforementioned example is written in this system as $(\lambda x : 0.(\lambda y : 1.x)x)@((\lambda 0^{\mathtt{Int}}.(\lambda 1^{\mathtt{Int}}.0)0) \wedge (\lambda 0^{\mathtt{Bool}}.(\lambda 1^{\mathtt{Bool}}.0)0))$. In general, different occurrences of a same mark can be paired with different types in the proof term. In [3], terms are duplicated (as in [18, 21]), but the type checking of terms does not generate copies of almost identical proofs. The type checking derivation for the term $((\lambda^{\mathtt{Int}\to\mathtt{Int}} x.(\lambda^{\mathtt{Int}\to\mathtt{Int}} y.x)x) \| \lambda^{\mathtt{Bool}\to\mathtt{Bool}} x.(\lambda^{\mathtt{Bool}\to\mathtt{Bool}} y.x)x)$ verifies in parallel that the two copies are well typed.

The duplication of terms and proofs makes the definition of beta reduction (and other transformations on terms) more difficult in the calculi presented so far, because it has to be performed in parallel on all the typed instances that correspond to the same untyped term. *Branching types* have been proposed in [22] to circumvent this issue. The idea is to represent different typing derivations for a same term into a compact piece of syntax. To this end, the branching type which corresponds to a given intersection type $t$ records the *branching shape* (*ie*, the uses of the intersection introduction typing rule) of the typing derivation corresponding to $t$. For example, the type $(\mathtt{Int}\to\mathtt{Int}) \wedge (\mathtt{Bool}\to\mathtt{Bool})$ has only two branches, which is represented in [22] by the branching shape join$\{i{=}*, j{=}*\}$. Our running example is then written as $\Lambda\mathrm{join}\{i{=}*, j{=}*\}.\lambda x^{\{i=\mathtt{Int}, j=\mathtt{Bool}\}}.(\lambda y^{\{i=\mathtt{Int}, j=\mathtt{Bool}\}}.x)x$. Note that the lambda term itself is not copied, and no duplication of proofs happens during type checking either: the branches labeled $i$ and $j$ are verified in parallel.

In [8], the authors propose an expressive refinement type system with intersection, union, but also (a form of) dependent types, making possible to define, *eg*, the type of integer lists of length $n$, written $[\mathtt{Int}]^n$. The variable $n$ can be quantified over either universally or existentially (using respectively $\Pi$ and $\Sigma$). Thanks to this it is possible to consider different instantiations of a dependent type and, thus to type our daffy function by different instances of $[\mathtt{Int}]^n$ (rather than with any type, as for Int and Bool in our example). Type checking requires type annotations to be decidable: to check that $\lambda x.(\lambda y.x)x$ has type $\Pi n.(([\mathtt{Int}]^{2n}\to[\mathtt{Int}]^{2n})\wedge([\mathtt{Int}]^{2n+1}\to[\mathtt{Int}]^{2n+1}))$, the subterm $\lambda y.x$ has to be annotated. This problem is similar to finding appropriate annotations for the daffy function (4) in our language. In [8], terms are annotated with a list of typings: for example, $\lambda y.x$ can be annotated with $A = (x : [\mathtt{Int}]^{2n} \vdash \mathbb{1}\to[\mathtt{Int}]^{2n}, x : [\mathtt{Int}]^{2n+1} \vdash \mathbb{1}\to[\mathtt{Int}]^{2n+1})$, which says that if $x : [\mathtt{Int}]^{2n}$, then $\lambda y.x$ has type $\mathbb{1}\to[\mathtt{Int}]^{2n}$ (and similarly if $x : [\mathtt{Int}]^{2n+1}$). The above annotation $A$ is not sound because when checking that $\lambda x.(\lambda y.x : A)x$ has result type $\Pi n.(([\texttt{Int}]^{2n}\to[\texttt{Int}]^{2n})\wedge([\texttt{Int}]^{2n+1}\to[\texttt{Int}]^{2n+1}))$, one can see that the occurrences of $n$ in $A$ escape their scope: they should be bound by the quantifier $\Pi$ in the result type. To fix this, typing environments in annotations are extended with universally quantified variables, that can be instantiated at type checking. For example, $\lambda y.x : (m : \texttt{Nat}, x : [\texttt{Int}]^m \vdash \mathbb{1} \to [\texttt{Int}]^m)$ means that $\lambda y.x$ has type $\mathbb{1} \to [\texttt{Int}]^m$, assuming $x : [\texttt{Int}]^m$, where $m$ can be instantiated with any natural number. With this annotation, the daffy function can be checked against $\Pi n.(([\texttt{Int}]^{2n}\to[\texttt{Int}]^{2n})\wedge([\texttt{Int}]^{2n+1}\to[\texttt{Int}]^{2n+1}))$, by instantiating $m$ with respectively $2n$ and $2n+1$. It is possible to find a similarity between the annotations of [8] (the lists of typings) and our annotations (*ie*, the combination of interface and decoration) although instantiation in the former is much more harnessed. There is however a fundamental difference between the two systems and it is that [8] does not include a type case. Because of that annotations need not to be propagated at run-time: in [8] they are just used statically to check soundness and then erased at run-time. Without type-cases we could do the same, but it is precisely the presence of type-cases that justifies our formalism.

For what concerns XML programming, let us cite polymorphic XDuce [12] and the work by Vouillon [20]. In both, pattern matching is designed so as not to break polymorphism, but both have to give up something: higher-order functions for [12] and intersection, negation, and local type inference in [20] (the type of function arguments must be explicitly given). Furthermore, Vouillon's work suffers from the original sin of starting from a subtyping relation that is given axiomatically by a deduction system. This makes the intuition underlying subtyping very difficult to grasp (at least, for us). Another route taken is the one of OCamlDuce [10], which juxtaposes OCaml and ℂDuce's type systems in the same language, keeping them separated. This practical approach yields little theoretical problems but forces a value to be of one kind of type or another, preventing the programmer from writing polymorphic XML transformations. Lastly, XHaskell by Sulzmann *et al.* [19] mixes Haskell type classes with XDuce regular expression types but has two main drawbacks. First, every polymorphic variable must be annotated wherever it is instantiated with an XML type. Second, even without inference of explicit annotations (which they do not address), their system requires several restrictions to be decidable (while our system with explicit type-substitutions is decidable).

## 8. Conclusion

The work presented in this and in its companion paper [4] provides the theoretical basis and all the algorithmic tools needed to design and implement polymorphic functional languages for semi-structured data and, more generally, for functional languages with recursive types and set-theoretic unions, intersections, and negations. In particular, our results pave the way to the polymorphic extension of ℂDuce [2] and to the definition of a real type system for XQuery 3.0 [9] (not just one in which all higher-order functions have type "`function()`"). Thanks to local type inference and type reconstruction defined in the second part of this work, these languages can have a syntax and semantics very close to those of OCaml or Haskell, but will include primitives (in particular complex patterns) to exploit the great expressive power of full-fledged set-theoretic types.

Some problems are still open, notably the decidability of type-substitution inference defined in the second part of this work, but these are of theoretical nature and should not have any impact in practice (as a matter of facts people program in Java and Scala even though the decidability of their type systems is still an open question). On the practical side, the most interesting directions of research is to couple the efficient compilation of the polymorphic calculus with techniques of static analysis that would perform partial evaluation of relabeling so as to improve the efficiency of type-case of functional values even in the rare cases in which it is more expensive than in the monomorphic version of ℂDuce.

***Acknowledgments.*** This work was partially supported by the ANR TYPEX project n. ANR-11-BS02-007. Zhiwu Xu was also partially supported by an Eiffel scholarship of French Ministry of Foreign Affairs and by the grant n. 61070038 of the National Natural Science Foundation of China.

## References

[1] H. Barendregt, M. Coppo, and M. Dezani-Ciancaglini. A filter lambda model and the completeness of type assignment. *Journal of Symbolic Logic*, 48(4):931–940, 1983.

[2] V. Benzaken, G. Castagna, and A. Frisch. CDuce: an XML-friendly general purpose language. In *ICFP '03*. ACM Press, 2003.

[3] V. Bono, B. Venneri, and L. Bettini. A typed lambda calculus with intersection types. *Theor. Comput. Sci.*, 398(1-3):95–113, 2008.

[4] G. Castagna, K. Nguyễn, and Z. Xu. Polymorphic functions with set-theoretic types. Part 2: Local type inference and type reconstruction. Unpublished manuscript, available at `http://hal.archives-ouvertes.fr/hal-00880744`, November 2013.

[5] G. Castagna and Z. Xu. Set-theoretic Foundation of Parametric Polymorphism and Subtyping. In *ICFP '11*, 2011.

[6] J. Clark and M. Murata. Relax-NG, 2001. `www.relaxng.org`.

[7] M. Coppo, M. Dezani, and B. Venneri. Principal type schemes and lambda-calculus semantics. In *To H.B. Curry. Essays on Combinatory Logic, Lambda-calculus and Formalism*. Academic Press, 1980.

[8] J. Dunfield and F. Pfenning. Tridirectional typechecking. In *POPL '04*. ACM Press, 2004.

[9] J. Robie et al. Xquery 3.0: An XML query language (working draft 2010/12/14), 2010. `http://www.w3.org/TR/xquery-30/`.

[10] A. Frisch. OCaml + XDuce. In *ICFP '06*, 2006.

[11] A. Frisch, G. Castagna, and V. Benzaken. Semantic subtyping: dealing set-theoretically with function, union, intersection, and negation types. *The Journal of ACM*, 55(4):1–64, 2008.

[12] H. Hosoya, A. Frisch, and G. Castagna. Parametric polymorphism for XML. *ACM TOPLAS*, 32(1):1–56, 2009.

[13] L. Liquori and S. Ronchi Della Rocca. Intersection-types à la Church. *Inf. Comput.*, 205(9):1371–1386, 2007.

[14] B.C. Pierce. *Types and Programming Languages*. MIT Press, 2002.

[15] F. Pottier and D. Rémy. The essence of ML type inference. In B.C. Pierce, editor, *Advanced Topics in Types and Programming Languages*, chapter 10, pages 389–489. MIT Press, 2005.

[16] J.C. Reynolds. Design of the programming language Forsythe. Technical Report CMU-CS-96-146, Carnegie Mellon University, 1996.

[17] J.C. Reynolds. What do types mean?: from intrinsic to extrinsic semantics. In *Programming methodology*. Springer, 2003.

[18] S. Ronchi Della Rocca. Intersection typed lambda-calculus. *Electr. Notes Theor. Comput. Sci.*, 70(1):163–181, 2002.

[19] M. Sulzmann, K. Zhuo, and M. Lu. XHaskell - Adding Regular Expression Types to Haskell. In *IFL*, LNCS n. 5083. Springer, 2007.

[20] J. Vouillon. Polymorphic regular tree types and patterns. In *POPL '06*, pages 103–114, 2006.

[21] J.B. Wells, A. Dimock, R. Muller, and F.A. Turbak. A calculus with polymorphic and polyvariant flow types. *J. Funct. Program.*, 12(3):183–227, 2002.

[22] J.B. Wells and C. Haack. Branching types. In *ESOP '02*, volume 2305 of *LNCS*, pages 115–132. Springer, 2002.

[23] Z. Xu. *Parametric Polymorphism for XML Processing Languages*. PhD thesis, Université Paris Diderot, 2013. Available at `http://tel.archives-ouvertes.fr/tel-00858744`.

# Backpack: Retrofitting Haskell with Interfaces


Scott Kilpatrick
MPI-SWS
skilpat@mpi-sws.org

Derek Dreyer
MPI-SWS
dreyer@mpi-sws.org

Simon Peyton Jones
Microsoft Research
simonpj@microsoft.com

Simon Marlow
Facebook
marlowsd@gmail.com



## Abstract

Module systems like that of Haskell permit only a weak form of modularity in which module implementations depend directly on other implementations and must be processed in dependency order. Module systems like that of ML, on the other hand, permit a stronger form of modularity in which explicit interfaces express assumptions about dependencies, and each module can be typechecked and reasoned about independently.

In this paper, we present Backpack, a new language for building separately-typecheckable *packages* on top of a weak module system like Haskell's. The design of Backpack is inspired by the MixML module calculus of Rossberg and Dreyer, but differs significantly in detail. Like MixML, Backpack supports explicit interfaces and recursive linking. Unlike MixML, Backpack supports a more flexible *applicative* semantics of instantiation. Moreover, its design is motivated less by foundational concerns and more by the *practical* concern of integration into Haskell, which has led us to advocate simplicity—in both the syntax and semantics of Backpack—over raw expressive power. The semantics of Backpack packages is defined by elaboration to sets of Haskell modules and binary interface files, thus showing how Backpack maintains interoperability with Haskell while extending it with separate typechecking. Lastly, although Backpack is geared toward integration into Haskell, its design and semantics are largely agnostic with respect to the details of the underlying core language.



***Categories and Subject Descriptors*** D.3.1 [*Programming Languages*]: Formal Definitions and Theory; D.3.3 [*Programming Languages*]: Language Constructs and Features—Recursion, Abstract data types, Modules; F.3.3 [*Logics and Meanings of Programs*]: Studies of Program Constructs—Type structure

***Keywords*** Type systems; mixin modules; Haskell modules; applicative instantiation; recursive modules; separate modular development; packages; module systems


## 1. Introduction

Suppose an author A wants to write, test, and publish a software component (or "package") P, that needs to call a random-number generator. But A wants each customer C to be able to supply his or her *own* random-number generator. In a typed language, the author A must define the *interface* to the random-number generator, typecheck P with respect to the interface, and publish P. The client C then links P with a particular random-number generator that matches the interface. We refer to this style of development as *separate modular development* (SMD), as distinct from the style of *incremental modular development* (IMD) in which a package can only be typechecked when the implementations of its dependencies are available.

One of the most prominent approaches to SMD is that taken by the ML module system and its many variants [22, 21]. ML provides *functors*, which enable a module M to be *parameterized* over the implementations of its dependencies; the dependencies can then be *instantiated* by functor application in multiple different ways, even within a single program.

An alternative approach is to use *mixin modules* [4, 3, 13, 11]. Instead of relying on parameterization, mixin modules support SMD by combining within their namespaces both *defined* and *undefined* components, the latter specified via interfaces. Unlike functors, mixin modules support *recursive linking*; and since linking is implicitly "by-name", mixins also avoid the propagation of coherence (or "sharing") constraints so common with functor programming. Moreover, recent work by Rossberg and Dreyer on the MixML type system [27] has demonstrated that mixin modules have the capacity to *subsume* the functionality of ML modules.

However, despite their advantages, mixin modules have yet to be adopted by any widely-used statically-typed functional language.[1] In the case of the ML languages, this is understandable: ML already has a powerful module system, and the extra benefit afforded by mixins is arguably not worth the replacement cost.

What about Haskell? Haskell's existing module system was consciously designed as a weak namespace management system without a proper notion of interface [17, Section 8.2], and hence supports only IMD, not SMD. Tools like the Cabal package management system pick up the slack, enabling users to (ab)use version-range dependencies in order to work around the lack of interfaces. But the Haskell community recognizes that this is a makeshift solution and is actively seeking ways to support SMD properly.

In short, Haskell is a prime example of a language that is ripe for extension with interfaces and mixins. The trouble is that the foundational accounts of mixin modules that have appeared in the literature [3, 16, 27] employ a variety of complex and unconventional type systems, and it is not at all clear how to convert any of them into a practical design that could be realistically incorporated into a language like Haskell.

With this in mind, we make the following contributions:

- We present Backpack, a new language for building *mixin-style packages* on top of an existing (weak) module system like Haskell's (Section 2). Like MixML [27], Backpack supports interfaces, recursive linking, abstract data types, and SMD.

[1] We are not counting Scala [24]: it supports mixin composition, but in a way that is integrally tied to its object-oriented mechanisms.




*POPL '14*, January 22–24, 2014, San Diego, CA, USA.



ACM 978-1-4503-2544-8/14/01... $15.00.
http://dx.doi.org/10.1145/2535838.2535884

| | | |
|---|---|---|
| Package Names | $P$ | $\in$ *PkgNames* |
| Module Path Names | $p$ | $\in$ *ModPaths* |
| Package Respositories | $R$ | $::= \overline{D}$ |
| Package Definitions | $D$ | $::=$ **package** $P\ t$ **where** $\overline{B}$ |
| Bindings | $B$ | $::= p = [M] \mid p :: [S] \mid p = p \mid$ **include** $P\ t\ r$ |
| Thinning Specs | $t$ | $::= (\overline{p})$ |
| Renaming Specs | $r$ | $::= \langle \overline{p \mapsto p} \rangle$ |
| Module Expressions | $M$ | $::= \ldots$ |
| Signature Expressions | $S$ | $::= \ldots$ |

**Figure 1.** Backpack syntax.

- Unlike MixML, Backpack supports a more flexible *applicative* (rather than generative) semantics of instantiation [20], thereby extending mixin modules into new territory (Section 2.4). It would be easy to support generativity as well.
- Unlike other strong module systems, Backpack subordinates expressive power to *simplicity*, *practicality*, and *orthogonality* from the core language and its type system. The main technical device that supports this orthogonality is the central notion of *module identity* (Section 3.1), which we can treat largely independently from the type system of the core language. The type system for Backpack is *much* simpler than that of MixML.
- We give a formal description (Sections 3.2–3.4) of how to elaborate a Backpack package into a set of ordinary Haskell modules and module types (the latter corresponding to GHC's existing notion of "binary interface file"). If the package is complete (*i.e.*, fully implemented), it can be compiled and executed. But regardless, the Haskell modules output by elaboration can be *typechecked separately* from their missing dependencies.
- We prove soundness of Backpack's elaboration, which guarantees that a complete package will elaborate to a well-typed set of Haskell modules (Section 3.5). Even *stating* soundness required us to define a formal semantics for separate typechecking of (recursive) Haskell modules, which did not exist previously.

Finally, we conclude the paper in Sections 4 and 5 with a detailed discussion of related and future work. For space reasons, we leave a number of formal details to our accompanying technical appendix, available at `http://plv.mpi-sws.org/backpack/`.

## 2. A Backpack Tour

Figure 1 gives the syntax of Backpack. A *package definition* $D$ gives a package name $P$ to a a sequence of *bindings* $\overline{B}$. The simplest form of binding is a *concrete module binding*, of the form $p = [M]$, which binds the module name $p$ to the implementation $[M]$. For example:

```
package ab-1 where
  A = [x = True]
  B = [import A; y = not x]
```

The code in square brackets represents module *implementations*, whose syntax is just that of a Haskell module (details in the technical appendix; Appendix §5). Indeed, in a practical implementation of Backpack, the term $[M]$ might be realized as the name of a file containing the module's code. However, note that the module lacks a header "module M where ..." because the module's name is given by the Backpack description.[2]

Package ab-1 binds two modules named A and B. The first module, bound to A, imports nothing and defines a core value x, and the second module, bound to B, imports the first module and makes use of that x in its definition of y. The type of this package expresses that it contains a module A which defines `x :: Bool` and a module B which defines `y :: Bool`. (We will more precisely discuss types, at the package and module levels, in Section 3.)

The module bindings in a package are explicitly sequenced: each module can refer only to the modules bound earlier in the sequence. In fact the bindings should be interpreted as iteratively building up a local module context that tracks the name and type of each module encountered. For example, if the order of the two bindings were reversed, then this package would cease to be well-typed, as the module reference A would no longer make sense.

Module bindings do not shadow. Rather, if the same module name is bound twice, the two bindings are *linked*; see Section 2.3.

### 2.1 Top Level and Dependencies

A *package repository* consists of an ordered list of package definitions. Each package in a repository sees only those packages whose definitions occur earlier in the sequence. To make use of those earlier packages — *i.e.*, to depend on them — a package *includes* them using the **include** binding form, thus:

```
package abcd-1 where
  C = [x = False]
  include ab-1
      [import qualified A]
  D = [import qualified C]
      [z = A.x && C.x    ]
```

One should think of an **include** construct as picking up a package and dumping all of its contents into the current namespace. In this case, the modules A and B are inserted into the package abcd-1 as if they were bound between C and D. Consequently the module bound to D can import both A and C. The type of abcd-1 says that it provides four modules: C (which provides `x :: Bool`), D (which provides `z :: Bool`), and the two modules A and B from package ab-1, even though they were defined there and merely included here. (The modules exposed by a package can be controlled with syntax that resembles that of the module level; this feature is discussed as a special case of *thinning* in Section 2.4.)

In this paper, we will treat the example package definitions as the bindings in a single package repository. At this point, that top level includes the definition for ab-1 followed by abcd-1.

### 2.2 Abstraction via Interfaces

Up to this point, the package system appears only to support IMD since each module can only be checked after those that it depends on. For example, abcd-1 could only be developed and checked *after* the package ab-1 had already been developed and checked; otherwise we would not be able to make sense of the import declaration import qualified A and the subsequent usage of A.x as a Bool.

To support SMD as well, Backpack packages may additionally contain *abstract module bindings*, or *holes*. To specify a hole, a developer provides a set of core-language declarations, called a *signature* $S$, and binds a module name $p$ to it by writing $p :: [S]$. One should think of holes as obligations to eventually provide implementing modules; a package is not *complete* until all such obligations are met. Concrete modules, on the other hand, are simply those bound to actual implementations (as in all previous examples). This combination of abstract and concrete components reflects the mixin-module basis of our package system.

As our first example, we simulate how the abcd-1 package might have been developed modularly by specifying holes for the "other" components, A and B:

[2] We still provide syntax for optional "export lists" of core language entities; only the module name disappears.

```
package abcd-holes-1 where
  A :: [x :: Bool]
  B :: [y :: Bool]
  C = [... as before ...]
  D = [... as before ...]
```

By "stubbing out" the other components, the developer of abcd-holes-1 can typecheck her code (in C and D) entirely separately from the developer who provides A and B. In contrast, in the existing Cabal package system, developers cannot typecheck their package code without first choosing particular version instances of their dependencies. Effectively, they test the well-typedness of their code with respect to individual configurations of dependencies which may or may not be the ones their users have installed.

Manually writing the holes for depended-upon components, as above, involves too much duplication. Instead a developer can define a package full of holes that designates the interface of an entire component. A client developer includes that package of holes and thus brings them into her own package without writing all those signatures by hand. The following two packages achieve the same net result (and have the same type) as abcd-holes-1, but without signatures in the client package:

```
package ab-sigs where          package abcd-holes-2 where
  A :: [x :: Bool]               include ab-sigs
  B :: [y :: Bool]               C = [... as before ...]
                                 D = [... as before ...]
```

Holes are included in exactly the same manner as concrete modules, and they retain their status as holes after inclusion. Under the interpretation of holes as obligations, inclusion propagates the obligations into the including package.

In these two examples we have named the packages abcd-holes-1 and abcd-holes-2, which might suggest multiple versions of a single package abcd-holes (*e.g.*, in Cabal). However, while they may convey that informal intuition, in the present work we focus on modularity of packages, leaving a semantic account of versioning for future work.

### 2.3 Linking and Signature Matching

So far, all package examples have contained bindings with distinct names. What has appeared to be mere sequencing of bindings is actually a special case of a more general by-name linking mechanism: linking two mixin modules with strictly distinct names merely concatenates them. Whenever two bindings share the same name, however, the modules to which they are bound must themselves link together. This gives rise to **three cases**: hole-hole, mod-mod, and mod-hole.

**First,** when linking two holes together, we merge their two interfaces into one. This effectively joins together all the core language declarations from their respective signatures. The resulting hole provides exactly the entities that both original holes provided.

```
package yourlib where
  Prelude :: [data List a = ...]
  Yours    = [import Prelude; ...]
package mylib where
  Prelude :: [data Bool = ...]
  include yourlib
  Mine     = [import Prelude; import Yours; ...]
```

The mylib package above declares its own hole for Prelude and also includes the hole for Prelude from yourlib. Before the binding for Mine is checked, the previous bindings of Prelude must have linked together. This module can see both `List` and `Bool` since they are both in the interface of the linked hole, whereas the Yours module could only see the `List` datatype in Prelude. (Swapping the order of the first two bindings of mylib has no effect here.)

This example highlights another aspect of programming with mixin-based packages: each package has the option of writing *precise* interfaces for the other packages (*i.e.*, modules) it depends on. Specifically, yourlib only needs the `List` datatype from the standard library's Prelude module, rather than the entire module's myriad other entities. This results in a stronger type for yourlib since the assumptions it makes about the Prelude module are more precise and focused.

Not all interface merges are valid. For example, if mylib had also declared a `List` datatype, but of a different kind from that in yourlib (*e.g.*, `data List a b = ...`), then the merge would be invalid and the package would be ill-typed.

**Second,** when linking two module implementations together, it intuitively makes no sense to link together two *different* implementations since they define different code and different types. Rather than rejecting all mod-mod linkages, as for instance MixML [27] does, we instead insist that mod-mod linking only succeed if the two implementations are *the same*, in which case the linkage is a no-op. To test this, we require equivalence of their *module identities* (about which see Sections 2.4 and 3.1).

Consider the following classic diamond dependency:

```
package top where          package right where
  Top = [...]                include top
                             Right = [...]
package left where         package bottom where
  include top                include left; include right
  Left = [...]               Bottom = [...]
```

The bottom package of the diamond links together the packages left and right, each of which provides a module named Top that it got from the top package. The linking resulting from the inclusions in bottom is well-typed because left and right provide the *same* module Top from package top.

**Third,** when linking a module with a hole, the module's type must be a subtype of the hole's, and we say that the module "fills," "matches," or "implements" that hole. This form of linking most closely resembles the traditional concept of linking, or of functor application; it also corresponds to how structures match signatures in ML. Roughly, a module implements a hole if it defines all the entities declared in that hole and with the exact same specifications.

The mylib package above has a hole for the Prelude module. As this package is not yet complete, it can be typechecked, but not yet compiled and executed. (Supporting separate *compilation* would require sweeping changes to GHC's existing infrastructure.) We therefore link mylib with a particular implementation of its Prelude hole so that it may now be compiled and used:

```
package mylib-complete-1 where
  include mylib
             [data List a = ...]
  Prelude =  [data Bool = ...  ]
             [null xs = ...    ]
```

The implementation of Prelude provides the two entities declared in the hole (included from mylib) and an additional third entity, the value `null`. This implementation matches the interface of the hole, so the linkage is well-typed.

For simplicity, our definition of when a module matches a hole is based on *width* rather than *depth* subtyping. In other words, a module may provide more entities than specified by the hole it is filling, but the types of any values it provides must be the same as the types declared for those values in the hole's signature. In particular, the match will be invalid if the implemented types are more general than the declared types. For example, a polymorphic

```
package prelude-sig where
  Prelude :: [data List a = Nil | Cons a (List a)]

package arrays-sig where
  include prelude-sig
            ⎡import Prelude                 ⎤
  Array ::  ⎢data Arr (i::*) (e::*)         ⎥
            ⎣something :: List (Arr i e)    ⎦

package structures where
  include arrays-sig
  Set   = [import Prelude; data S ...]
  Graph = [import Prelude; import Array; data G ...]
  Tree  = [import Prelude; import Graph; data T ...]

package arrays-a where
  include prelude-sig
           ⎡import qualified Prelude as P⎤
  Array =  ⎢data Arr i e = MkArr ...     ⎥
           ⎣something = P.Nil            ⎦

package arrays-b where
  include prelude-sig
           ⎡import Prelude               ⎤
  Array =  ⎢data Arr i e = ANil | ...    ⎥
           ⎣something = Cons ANil Nil    ⎦

package graph-a (Graph, Prelude) where
  include arrays-a
  include structures (Graph, Prelude, Array)

package graph-b (Graph, Prelude) where
  include arrays-b
  include structures (Graph, Prelude, Array)

package multinst where
  include graph-a ⟨Graph ↦ GA⟩
  include graph-b ⟨Graph ↦ GB⟩
            ⎡import qualified GA               ⎤
  Client =  ⎢import qualified GB               ⎥
            ⎢export (main, GA.G)               ⎥
            ⎣main = ... GA.G ... GB.G ...      ⎦
```

**Figure 2.** Running example: Data structures library and client.

identity function of type `forall a :: *. a -> a` will not match a hole that declares it as having type `Int -> Int`.

### 2.4 Instantiation and Reuse

Developers can reuse a package's concrete modules in different ways by including the package multiple times and linking it with distinct implementations for its holes; we call each such linkage an *instantiation* of the package. Furthermore, in Backpack, packages can be instantiated multiple times, and those distinct instantiations can even coexist in the same linked result. (In contrast, both Cabal and GHC currently prevent users from ever having two instantiations of a single package in the same program.)

Figure 2 provides an example of multiple instantiations in the multinst package, but this example employs a couple features of Backpack we must first introduce—*thinning* and *renaming*.[3]

[3] In our examples so far, we have omitted thinning specs entirely. But actually, according to Figure 1, all package definitions and inclusions should contain a thinning spec. To infer a thinning spec where one is omitted, one can simply list all module paths provided by the corresponding package. The syntax used in our examples can thus be translated into our formal language with a straightforward (type-directed) rewriting. Moreover, the syntax for package inclusion given in Figure 1 requires that all inclusions additionally contain a renaming. When we omit renaming, it means that one should use the empty renaming, ⟨⟩.

The two packages arrays-a and arrays-b provide two distinct implementations of the Array module described by the hole specification in the earlier arrays-sig package. The next two packages grab the Graph implementation from structures and implement its Array hole with the respective array implementations. Since structures also defines Set and Tree, these (unwanted) modules would naively be included along with Prelude and Array and would thus pollute the namespaces of graph-a and graph-b. Instead, these packages *thin* the structures package upon inclusion so that only the desired modules, Prelude and Array, are added to graph-a and graph-b. (This closely resembles the *import* lists of Haskell modules, which may select specific entities to be imported.) Similarly, implementation details of a package definition can be hidden—rather than provided to clients—by thinning the definition to expose only certain module names. (This closely resembles the *export* lists of Haskell modules.) By thinning their definitions to expose only Prelude and Graph, both packages graph-a and graph-b hide the internal Array modules used to implement their Graph modules.

At this point, graph-a and graph-b provide distinct instantiations of the Graph module from structures, distinct in the sense that they do not have the same *module identity*. The identity of a module—a crucial notion in Backpack's semantics (see Section 3.1)—essentially encodes a dependency graph of the module's source code. Since the Graph modules in graph-a and graph-b import two different module sources for the Array hole—one from arrays-a and the other from arrays-b—they do not share the same dependency graph and hence have distinct identities.

Thus, if the final package multinst were to naively include both graph-a and graph-b, Backpack would complain that multinst was trying to merge two distinct implementations with the same name. To avoid this error, the inclusions of graph-a and graph-b employ *renaming* clauses that rename Graph to GA and GB, respectively, so that the two Graph implementations do not clash.

One may wonder whether it is necessary to track dependency information in module identities: why not just generate fresh module identities to represent each instantiation of a package? To see the motivation for tracking more precise dependency information, consider the example in Figure 3. Both the applic-left and applic-right packages *separately* instantiate the Graph module from structures with the *same* Array implementation from arrays-a—*i.e.*, both instantiations refer to the same identity for Array. Backpack thus treats the two resulting Graph modules (and their G types) as one and the same, which means the code in applic-bot is well-typed. In other words, the identity of Graph inside applic-left is equivalent to that of Graph inside applic-right, and thus the G types mentioned in both packages are compatible.

As this example indicates, our treatment of identity instantiation exhibits sharing behavior. We call this an *applicative* semantics of identity instantiation, as opposed to a potential *generative* semantics in which the two instantiations—even when instantiated with the same identity—would produce distinct identities.

As is well known in the ML modules literature [20, 28], applicativity enables significantly more flexibility regarding when module instantiation must occur in the hierarchy of dependencies. In the previous example, the authors of applic-left and applic-right were free to instantiate Graph *inside* their own packages. Under a generative semantics, on the other hand, in order to get the same Graph instantiation in both packages, it would need to be instantiated in an earlier package (like graph-a from Figure 2) and then included in both applic-left and applic-right; hence, the code as written in Figure 3 would under a generative semantics produce two distinct Graph identities and G types. As Rossberg *et al.* have noted [28], applicative semantics is generally safe only when used in conjunction with purely functional modules. It is thus ideally suited to Haskell, which isolates computational effects monadically.

```
package applic-left (Prelude, Left) where
  include structures
  include arrays-a
  Left = [import Graph; x :: G = ...]

package applic-right (Prelude, Right) where
  include arrays-a
  include structures
  Right = [import Graph; f :: G -> G = ...]

package applic-bot where
  include applic-left
  include applic-right
  Bot = [import Left; import Right; ... f x ...]
```

**Figure 3.** Example of applicativity.

### 2.5 Aliases

Occasionally one wants to link two holes whose names differ. The binding form $p = p$ in Figure 1 allows the programmer to add such aliases, which may be viewed as sharing constraints. For example:

```
package share where
  include foo1 (A, X)
  include foo2 (B, Y)
  X = Y
```

Here, A (from foo1) depends on hole X, and B (from foo2) on hole Y, and we want to require the two holes to be ultimately instantiated by the same module. The binding X = Y expresses this constraint.

### 2.6 Recursive Modules

By using holes as "forward declarations" of implementations, packages can define recursive modules, *i.e.*, modules that transitively import themselves. The Haskell Language Report ostensibly allows recursive modules, but it leaves them almost entirely unspecified, letting Haskell implementations decide how to handle them. Our approach to handling recursive modules follows that of MixML.

The example below defines two modules, A and B, which import each other. By forward-declaring the parts of B that A depends on, the first implementation makes sense—*i.e.*, it knows the names and types of entities it imports from B—and, naturally, the second implementation makes sense after that. This definition is analogous to how these modules would be defined in GHC today.[4]

```
package ab-rec where
  B :: [S_B]
  A = [import B; ...]
  B = [import A; ...]
```

Normal mixin linking ties the recursive knot, ensuring that the import B actually resolves to the B implementation in the end.

GHC allows recursive modules only within a single (Cabal) package. Backpack, on the other hand, allows more flexible recursion. Although packages themselves are not defined recursively, they may be recursively *linked*. Consider the following:

```
package ab-sigs where
  A :: [S_A]
  B :: [S_B]

package a-from-b where
  include ab-sigs
  A = [import B; ...]

package b-from-a where
  include ab-sigs
  B = [import A; ...]

package ab-rec-sep where
  include a-from-b
  include b-from-a
```

[4] In GHC, instead of explicit bindings to a signature and two modules, there would be the two module source files and an additional "boot file" for B that looks exactly like $S_B$. Moreover, the import B within the A module would include a "source pragma" that tells the compiler to import the boot file instead of the full module.

At the level of packages, these definitions do not involve any recursive inclusion, which is good, because that would be illegal! Rather, they form a diamond dependency, like the earlier packages top, left, right, and bottom. There is no recursion *within* the definitions of ab-sigs, a-from-b, and b-from-a either. The recursion instead occurs implicitly, as a result of the mixin linking of modules A and B in the package ab-rec-sep. (Separately typechecked, recursive units may be defined in MixML in roughly the same way.)

Finally, we note that Backpack's semantics (presented in the next section) explicitly addresses one of the key stumbling blocks in supporting recursive linking in the presence of abstract data types, namely the so-called *double vision problem* [6, 8]. In the context of the above example, the problem is that, in ab-sigs, the specification $S_A$ of the hole A may specify an abstract type T, which $S_B$ then depends on in the types of its core-level entities. Subsequently, in a-from-b, when the implementation of A imports B, it will want to know that the type T that it defines is the same as the one mentioned in $S_B$, or else it will suffer from "double vision", seeing two distinct names for the same underlying type. Avoiding double vision is known to be challenging [8, 9, 27], but crucial for enabling common patterns of recursive module programming. Backpack's semantics avoids double vision completely.

## 3. The Semantics of Backpack

The main top-level judgment defining the semantics of Backpack is

$$\Delta \vdash D : \forall\overline{\alpha}.\Xi \rightsquigarrow \lambda\overline{\alpha}.dexp$$

Given a *package definition* $D$, along with a *package environment* $\Delta$ describing the types and elaborations of other packages on which $D$ depends, this judgment ascribes $D$ a *package type* $\forall\overline{\alpha}.\Xi$, and also elaborates $D$ into a *parameterized directory expression* $\lambda\overline{\alpha}.dexp$, which is essentially a set of well-typed Haskell module files.

The above judgment is implemented by a two-pass algorithm.[5] The first pass, called *shaping*, synthesizes a *package shape* $\tilde{\Xi}$ for $D$, which effectively explains the *macro-level* structure of the package, *i.e.*, the modules contained in $D$, the names of all the entities defined in those modules, and how they all depend on one another. The second pass, called *typing*, augments the structural information in $\tilde{\Xi}$ with additional information about the *micro-level* structure of $D$. In particular, it fills in the types of core-language entities, forming a *package type* $\Xi$ and checking that $D$ is well-formed at $\Xi$.

Our goal in the present section is to explain in detail this two-pass typechecking algorithm, as well as the elaboration of Backpack into Haskell. Central to both passes of Backpack typechecking is a notion of *module identity*. Using the multinst package (and its dependencies) from Figure 2 as a running example, we will motivate the role and structure of module identities, and then in subsequent subsections explain the implementation of shaping, typing, and elaboration. Full details are given in Appendix §6.

### 3.1 Module Identities

Figure 5 shows the *shapes* and *types* of multinst and its dependencies. We proceed by explaining Figure 5 in a left-to-right fashion.

The first column of Figure 5 contains the first key component of package types: a mapping from modules' *logical* names $p$ (*i.e.*, their names at the level of Backpack) to their *physical* identities $\nu$ (*i.e.*, the names of the Haskell modules to which they elaborate). The reason for distinguishing between logical names and physical identities is simple: due to aliasing (Section 2.5), there may be

[5] The reason for splitting typechecking into two passes has to do with the *double vision problem* [8], as discussed in Section 2.6. See Section 4 for further discussion, as well as a detailed explanation of how our solution to double vision compares with MixML's.

| | | |
|---|---|---|
| Identity Variables | $\alpha, \beta \in$ | *IdentVars* |
| Identity Constructors | $\mathcal{K} \in$ | *IdentCtors* |
| Identities | $\nu ::= \alpha \mid \mu\alpha.\mathcal{K}\,\overline{\nu}$ | |
| Identity Substitutions | $\phi, \theta ::= \{\overline{\alpha := \nu}\}$ | |

**Figure 4.** Module identities.

multiple logical names for the same physical module. (For further technical justifications for the logical/physical distinction, see the discussion in Section 4.)

In order to motivate the particular logical mappings in Figure 5, let us first explore what physical identities are, which means reviewing how module names work in Haskell.

***Module Names in Haskell*** Modules in Haskell have fixed names, which we call "physical" because they are globally unique in a program, and module definitions may then depend on one another by importing these physical names. Modules serve two related roles: (1) as points of origin for core-level entities, and (2) as syntactic namespaces. Concerning (1), a module may *define* new entities, such as values or abstract data types. Concerning (2), a module may *export* a set of entities, some of which it has defined itself and others of which it has imported from other modules. For example, a module Foo may define a data type named T. A subsequent module Bar may then import Foo.T and re-export it as Bar.T. To ensure that type identity is tracked properly, the Haskell type system models each core-level entity semantically as a pair $[\nu]$T of its core-level name T and its *provenance* $\nu$, *i.e.*, the module that originally defined it (in this example, Foo). Thus, Foo.T and Bar.T will be viewed as equal by Haskell since they are both just different names for the same semantic entity [Foo]T.

To ensure compatibility with Haskell, our semantics for Backpack inherits Haskell's use of physical names to identify abstract types. However, Haskell's flat physical module namespace is not expressive enough to support Backpack's holes, applicative module instantiation, and recursive linking. To account for these features, we enrich the language of physical names with a bit more interesting structure. Figure 4 displays this enriched language of—as we call them—*physical module identities*.[6]

***Variable and Applicative Identities*** Physical module identities $\nu$ are either (1) *variables* $\alpha$, which are used to represent holes; (2) *applications* of identity *constructors* $\mathcal{K}$, which are used to model dependency of modules on one another, as needed to implement applicative instantiation; or (3) *recursive* module identities, defined via $\mu$-constructors. We start by explaining the first two.

Each explicit module expression $[M]$ that occurs in a package definition corresponds (statically) to a globally unique identity constructor $\mathcal{K}$ that encodes it. For example, if a single module source $M$ appears on the right-hand side of three distinct module bindings in a package $P$, then the three distinct identity constructors of those modules are, roughly, $\langle P.M.1\rangle$, $\langle P.M.2\rangle$, and $\langle P.M.3\rangle$.[7]

In the absence of recursive modules, each module identity $\nu$ is then a finite tree term—either a variable $\alpha$, or a constructor $\mathcal{K}$ applied to zero or more subterms, $\overline{\nu}$. The identity of a module is the constructor $\mathcal{K}$ that encodes its source $M$, applied to the $n$ identities to which $M$'s $n$ import statements resolved (in order). For instance, in the very first example from Section 2, ab-1, the identities of A and B are $\mathcal{K}_a$ and $\mathcal{K}_b\ \mathcal{K}_a$, respectively, where $\mathcal{K}_a$ encodes the first module expression and $\mathcal{K}_b$ the second. In a package with holes, each hole gets a fresh variable (within the package definition) as its identity; in abcd-holes-1 the identities of the four modules are, in order, $\alpha_a$, $\alpha_b$, $\mathcal{K}_c$, and $\mathcal{K}_d\ \alpha_a\ \mathcal{K}_c$.

Consider now the module identities in the Graph instantiations in multinst, as shown in Figure 5. In the definition of structures, assume that the variables for Prelude and Array are $\alpha_P$ and $\alpha_A$ respectively, and that $M_G$ is the module source that Graph is bound to. Then the identity of Graph is $\nu_G = \langle\text{structures}.M_G\rangle\ \alpha_P\ \alpha_A$. Similarly, the identities of the two array implementations in Figure 2 are $\nu_{AA} = \langle\text{arrays-a}.M_A\rangle\ \alpha_P$ and $\nu_{AB} = \langle\text{arrays-b}.M_B\rangle\ \alpha_P$.

The package graph-a is more interesting because it *links* the packages arrays-a and structures together, with the implementation of Array from arrays-a *instantiating* the hole Array from structures. This linking is reflected in the identity of the Graph module in graph-a: whereas in structures it was $\nu_G = \langle\text{structures}.M_G\rangle\ \alpha_P\ \alpha_A$, in graph-a it is $\nu_{GA} = \nu_G[\nu_{AA}/\alpha_A] = \langle\text{structures}.M_G\rangle\ \alpha_P\ \nu_{AA}$. Similarly, the identity of Graph in graph-b is $\nu_{GB} = \nu_G[\nu_{AB}/\alpha_A] = \langle\text{structures}.M_G\rangle\ \alpha_P\ \nu_{AB}$. Thus, linking consists of substituting the variable identity of a hole by the concrete identity of the module filling that hole.

Lastly, multinst makes use of both of these Graph modules, under the aliases GA and GB, respectively. Consequently, in the Client module, GA.G and GB.G will be correctly viewed as distinct types since they originate in modules with distinct identities.

As multinst illustrates, module identities effectively encode dependency graphs. The primary motivation for encoding this information in identities is our desire for an *applicative* semantics of instantiation, as needed for instance in the example of Figure 3. In that example, both the packages applic-left and applic-right individually link arrays-a with structures. The client package applic-bot subsequently wishes to use both the Left module from applic-left and the Right module from applic-right, and depends on the fact that both modules operate over the same Graph.G type. This fact will be checked when the packages applic-left and applic-right are both **include**d in the same namespace of applic-bot, and the semantics of mixin linking will insist that their Graph modules have the same identity. Thanks to the dependency tracking in our module identities, we know that the Graph module has identity $\nu_{GA}$ in both packages.

***Recursive Module Identities*** In the presence of recursive modules, module identities are no longer simple finite trees.

Consider again the ab-rec-sep example from the end of Section 2. (Although this example does not concern our current focus, multinst, the careful treatment of recursive module identities deserves explanation.) Suppose that $\nu_A$ and $\nu_B$ are the identities of A and B, and that $M_A$ and $M_B$ are those modules' defining module expressions, respectively. Because $M_A$ imports B and $M_B$ imports A, the two identities should satisfy the recursive equations

$$\nu_A = \langle\text{a-from-b}.M_A\rangle\ \nu_B$$
$$\nu_B = \langle\text{b-from-a}.M_B\rangle\ \nu_A$$

These identity equations have no solution in the domain of finite trees, but they do in the domain of regular, *infinite* trees, which we denote (finitely) as

$$\nu_A = \mu\alpha_A.\langle\text{a-from-b}.M_A\rangle\ (\langle\text{b-from-a}.M_B\rangle\ \alpha_A)$$
$$\nu_B = \mu\alpha_B.\langle\text{b-from-a}.M_B\rangle\ (\langle\text{a-from-b}.M_A\rangle\ \alpha_B)$$

The semantics of Backpack relies on the ability to perform both *unification* and *equivalence* testing on identities. In the presence of recursive identities, however, simple unification and syntactic equivalence of identities no longer suffices since, *e.g.*, the identity $\langle\text{a-from-b}.M_A\rangle\ \nu_B$ represents the exact same module as $\nu_A$, albeit in a syntactically distinct way. Fortunately, we can use Huet's well-known unification algorithm for regular trees instead [18, 14].

[6] To make use of these enriched physical names in our elaboration, we embed them into the space of Haskell's physical names; see Section 3.4.

[7] We write simply $\langle P.M\rangle$, eliding the integer part of the identity constructor, when only one instance of $[M]$ exists in the definition of package P.

| | Logical Mapping | Physical Shapes | Physical Types |
|---|---|---|---|
| prelude-sig | Prelude $\mapsto \alpha_P$ | $\tilde{\Phi}_P$ | $\Phi_P$ |
| arrays-sig | Prelude $\mapsto \alpha_P$<br>Array $\mapsto \alpha_A$ | $\tilde{\Phi}_P, \tilde{\Phi}_A$ | $\Phi_P, \Phi_A$ |
| structures | Prelude $\mapsto \alpha_P$<br>Array $\mapsto \alpha_A$<br>Set $\mapsto \nu_S$<br>Graph $\mapsto \nu_G$<br>Tree $\mapsto \nu_T$ | $\tilde{\Phi}_P, \tilde{\Phi}_A,$<br>$\nu_S{:}\llparenthesis \mathtt{S}(\ldots)\,;[\nu_S]\mathtt{S}(\ldots)\rrparenthesis^+$<br>$\nu_G{:}\llparenthesis \mathtt{G}(\ldots)\,;[\nu_G]\mathtt{G}(\ldots)\rrparenthesis^+$<br>$\nu_T{:}\llparenthesis \mathtt{T}(\ldots)\,;[\nu_T]\mathtt{T}(\ldots)\rrparenthesis^+$ | $\Phi_P, \Phi_A,$<br>$\nu_S{:}\llparenthesis \mathsf{data}\ \mathtt{S}\ \ldots\,;[\nu_S]\mathtt{S}(\ldots)\rrparenthesis^+$<br>$\nu_G{:}\llparenthesis \mathsf{data}\ \mathtt{G}\ \ldots\,;[\nu_G]\mathtt{G}(\ldots)\rrparenthesis^+$<br>$\nu_T{:}\llparenthesis \mathsf{data}\ \mathtt{T}\ \ldots\,;[\nu_T]\mathtt{T}(\ldots)\rrparenthesis^+$ |
| arrays-a | Prelude $\mapsto \alpha_P$<br>Array $\mapsto \nu_{AA}$ | $\tilde{\Phi}_P, \tilde{\Phi}_{AA}$ | $\Phi_P, \Phi_{AA}$ |
| arrays-b | Prelude $\mapsto \alpha_P$<br>Array $\mapsto \nu_{AB}$ | $\tilde{\Phi}_P, \tilde{\Phi}_{AB}$ | $\Phi_P, \Phi_{AB}$ |
| graph-a | Prelude $\mapsto \alpha_P$<br>Graph $\mapsto \nu_{GA}$ | $\tilde{\Phi}_P, \tilde{\Phi}_{AA},$<br>$\nu_{GA}{:}\llparenthesis \mathtt{G}(\ldots)\,;[\nu_{GA}]\mathtt{G}(\ldots)\rrparenthesis^+$ | $\Phi_P, \Phi_{AA},$<br>$\nu_{GA}{:}\llparenthesis \mathsf{data}\ \mathtt{G}\ \ldots\,;[\nu_{GA}]\mathtt{G}(\ldots)\rrparenthesis^+$ |
| graph-b | Prelude $\mapsto \alpha_P$<br>Graph $\mapsto \nu_{GB}$ | $\tilde{\Phi}_P, \tilde{\Phi}_{AB},$<br>$\nu_{GB}{:}\llparenthesis \mathtt{G}(\ldots)\,;[\nu_{GB}]\mathtt{G}(\ldots)\rrparenthesis^+$ | $\Phi_P, \Phi_{AB},$<br>$\nu_{GB}{:}\llparenthesis \mathsf{data}\ \mathtt{G}\ \ldots\,;[\nu_{GB}]\mathtt{G}(\ldots)\rrparenthesis^+$ |
| multinst | Prelude $\mapsto \alpha_P$<br>GA $\mapsto \nu_{GA}$<br>GB $\mapsto \nu_{GB}$<br>Client $\mapsto \nu_C$ | $\tilde{\Phi}_P, \tilde{\Phi}_{AA}, \tilde{\Phi}_{AB},$<br>$\nu_{GA}{:}\llparenthesis \mathtt{G}(\ldots)\,;[\nu_{GA}]\mathtt{G}(\ldots)\rrparenthesis^+$<br>$\nu_{GB}{:}\llparenthesis \mathtt{G}(\ldots)\,;[\nu_{GB}]\mathtt{G}(\ldots)\rrparenthesis^+$<br>$\nu_C{:}\llparenthesis \mathtt{main}\,;[\nu_C]\mathtt{main},\ [\nu_{GA}]\mathtt{G}()\rrparenthesis^+$ | $\Phi_P, \Phi_{AA}, \Phi_{AB},$<br>$\nu_{GA}{:}\llparenthesis \mathsf{data}\ \mathtt{G}\ \ldots\,;[\nu_{GA}]\mathtt{G}(\ldots)\rrparenthesis^+$<br>$\nu_{GB}{:}\llparenthesis \mathsf{data}\ \mathtt{G}\ \ldots\,;[\nu_{GA}]\mathtt{G}(\ldots)\rrparenthesis^+$<br>$\nu_C{:}\llparenthesis \mathtt{main} :: \ldots\,;[\nu_C]\mathtt{main},\ [\nu_{GA}]\mathtt{G}()\rrparenthesis^+$ |

$$\begin{array}{llll}
\nu_{AA} \triangleq \langle \textsf{arrays-a}.M_A\rangle\ \alpha_P & \nu_S \triangleq \langle \textsf{structures}.M_S\rangle\ \alpha_P & \nu_{GA} \triangleq \langle \textsf{structures}.M_G\rangle\ \alpha_P\ \nu_{AA} & \nu_T \triangleq \langle \textsf{structures}.M_T\rangle\ \alpha_P\ \nu_G \\
\nu_{AB} \triangleq \langle \textsf{arrays-b}.M_B\rangle\ \alpha_P & \nu_G \triangleq \langle \textsf{structures}.M_G\rangle\ \alpha_P\ \alpha_A & \nu_{GB} \triangleq \langle \textsf{structures}.M_G\rangle\ \alpha_P\ \nu_{AB} & \nu_C \triangleq \langle \textsf{multinst}.M_C\rangle\ \nu_{GA}\ \nu_{GB}
\end{array}$$

$$\tilde{\Phi}_P \triangleq \begin{pmatrix} \alpha_P{:}\llparenthesis & \emptyset & ;[\beta_{PL}]\mathtt{List(Nil,Cons)}\rrparenthesis^- \\ \beta_{PL}{:}\llparenthesis & \mathtt{List(Nil,Cons)} & ;[\beta_{PL}]\mathtt{List(Nil,Cons)}\rrparenthesis^- \end{pmatrix} \qquad \Phi_P \triangleq \begin{pmatrix} \alpha_P{:}\llparenthesis & \emptyset & ;[\beta_{PL}]\mathtt{List(Nil,Cons)}\rrparenthesis^- \\ \beta_{PL}{:}\llparenthesis & \begin{array}{l}\mathsf{data\ List(a::*)} = \\ \quad \mathtt{Nil} \mid \mathtt{Cons\ a\ ([\beta_{PL}]List\ a)}\end{array} & ;[\beta_{PL}]\mathtt{List(Nil,Cons)}\rrparenthesis^- \end{pmatrix}$$

$$\tilde{\Phi}_A \triangleq \begin{pmatrix} \alpha_A{:}\llparenthesis & \emptyset & ;[\beta_{AA}]\mathtt{Arr}(),\ [\beta_{AS}]\mathtt{something}\rrparenthesis^- \\ \beta_{AA}{:}\llparenthesis & \mathtt{Arr} & ;[\beta_{AA}]\mathtt{Arr}()\rrparenthesis^- \\ \beta_{AS}{:}\llparenthesis & \mathtt{something} & ;[\beta_{AS}]\mathtt{something}\rrparenthesis^- \end{pmatrix}$$

$$\Phi_A \triangleq \begin{pmatrix} \alpha_A{:}\llparenthesis & \emptyset & ;[\beta_{AA}]\mathtt{Arr}(),\ [\beta_{AS}]\mathtt{something}\rrparenthesis^- \\ \beta_{AA}{:}\llparenthesis & \mathsf{data\ Arr\ (i::*)\ (e::*)} & ;[\beta_{AA}]\mathtt{Arr}()\rrparenthesis^- \\ \beta_{AS}{:}\llparenthesis & \mathtt{something} :: [\beta_{PL}]\mathtt{List}\ ([\beta_{AA}]\mathtt{Arr\ i\ e}) & ;[\beta_{AS}]\mathtt{something}\rrparenthesis^- \end{pmatrix}$$

$$\tilde{\Phi}_{AA} \triangleq \nu_{AA}{:}\llparenthesis\ \mathtt{Arr(MkArr),\ something}\ ;\ [\nu_{AA}]\mathtt{Arr(MkArr)},[\nu_{AA}]\mathtt{something}\ \rrparenthesis^+$$

$$\Phi_{AA} \triangleq \nu_{AA}{:}\llparenthesis\ \begin{array}{l}\mathsf{data\ Arr\ (i::*)\ (e::*)} = \mathtt{MkArr}\ldots \\ \mathtt{something} :: [\beta_{PL}]\mathtt{List}\ ([\nu_{AA}]\mathtt{Arr\ i\ e})\end{array}\ ;\ [\nu_{AA}]\mathtt{Arr(MkArr)},\ [\nu_{AA}]\mathtt{something}\ \rrparenthesis^+$$

$$\tilde{\Phi}_{AB} \triangleq \nu_{AB}{:}\llparenthesis\ \mathtt{Arr(ANil,\ldots),\ something}\ ;\ [\nu_{AB}]\mathtt{Arr(ANil,\ldots)},\ [\nu_{AB}]\mathtt{something}\ \rrparenthesis^+$$

$$\Phi_{AB} \triangleq \nu_{AB}{:}\llparenthesis\ \begin{array}{l}\mathsf{data\ Arr\ (i::*)\ (e::*)} = \mathtt{ANil}|\ldots \\ \mathtt{something} :: [\beta_{PL}]\mathtt{List}\ ([\nu_{AB}]\mathtt{Arr\ i\ e})\end{array}\ ;\ [\nu_{AB}]\mathtt{Arr(ANil,\ldots)},\ [\nu_{AB}]\mathtt{something}\ \rrparenthesis^+$$

**Figure 5.** Example package types and shapes for the multinst package and its dependencies.

### 3.2 Shaping

Constructing the mapping from logical names to physical identities is but one part of a larger task we call *shaping*, which constitutes the most unusual and interesting part of Backpack's type system.

The goal of shaping is to compute the shape (*i.e.*, the macro-level structure) of the package. Formally, a package shape $\tilde{\Xi} = (\tilde{\Phi}; \tilde{\mathcal{L}})$ has two parts.[8] The first is a *physical shape context* $\tilde{\Phi} = \overline{\nu{:}\tilde{\tau}^m}$, which, for each module in the package, maps its physical identity $\nu$ to a *polarity* $m$ and a *module shape* $\tilde{\tau}$. The polarity $m$ specifies whether the module $\nu$ is implemented $(+)$ or a hole $(-)$. The module shape $\tilde{\tau} = \llparenthesis \overline{dent}\ ;\ \overline{espc} \rrparenthesis$ enumerates $\nu$'s *defined entities* $\overline{dent}$—*i.e.*, the entities that the module $\nu$ itself defines—as well as *export specs* $\overline{espc}$, which list the names and provenances of the entities that $\nu$ exports. Note that these are not the same thing: a module $\nu$ may import and re-export entities that originated in (*i.e.*, whose provenances are) some other modules $\overline{\nu'}$, and it may also choose *not* to export all of the entities that it defines internally. In our running example in Figure 5, the physical shape contexts $\tilde{\Phi}$ computed for each package are shown in the second column.

The second part of the package shape is a *logical shape context* $\tilde{\mathcal{L}} = \overline{p \mapsto \nu@\tilde{\tau}}$, which, for each module in the package, maps its logical name $p$ to its physical identity $\nu$. (This is the mapping shown in the first column of Figure 5, which we have already discussed in detail in Section 3.1). In addition, $\tilde{\mathcal{L}}$ also maps $p$ to a shape $\tilde{\tau}$, which is required to be a subset of the "principal shape" of $\nu$ (as recorded in the physical shape context $\tilde{\Phi}$). This may seem mysterious: if $\tilde{\mathcal{L}}$ maps $p$ to $\nu$, and $\tilde{\Phi}$ maps $\nu$ to $\tilde{\tau}_0$, say, then why does $\tilde{\mathcal{L}}$ record another $\tilde{\tau}$ as well? The reason is twofold: (1) it is

[8] We write a tilde ($\tilde{\cdot}$) on the metavariables of certain shape objects (*e.g.*, $\tilde{\tau}$) not to denote a meta-level operation, but to highlight these objects' similarity to their corresponding type objects (*e.g.*, $\tau$).

| | |
|---|---|
| Core Level: | |
| Value Names | $x \in \mathit{ValNames}$ |
| Type Names | $T \in \mathit{TypeNames}$ |
| Constructor Names | $K \in \mathit{CtorNames}$ |
| Kind Environments | $\mathit{kenv} ::= \ldots$ |
| Semantic Types | $\mathit{typ} ::= [\nu]T\ \overline{\mathit{typ}} \mid \ldots$ |
| Defined Entity Specs | $\mathit{dspc} ::= \mathtt{data}\ T\ \mathit{kenv} = \overline{K\ \overline{\mathit{typ}}} \mid \mathtt{data}\ T\ \mathit{kenv} \mid x :: \mathit{typ}$ |
| Export Specs | $\mathit{espc} ::= [\nu]\mathit{dent}$ |
| Module Level: | |
| Polarities | $m ::= + \mid -$ |
| Types | $\tau, \sigma ::= \langle\!\vert \overline{\mathit{dspc}}\ ;\ \overline{\mathit{espc}} \vert\!\rangle$ |
| Physical Type Ctxts | $\Phi ::= \overline{\nu{:}\tau^m}$ |
| Logical Type Ctxts | $\mathcal{L} ::= \overline{p \mapsto \nu@\tau}$ |
| Package Level: | |
| Package Types | $\Xi, \Gamma ::= (\Phi; \mathcal{L})$ |
| Package Environments | $\Delta ::= \cdot \mid \Delta,\ P = \lambda\overline{\alpha}.\mathit{dexp} : \forall\overline{\alpha}.\Xi$ |
| Shaping Objects: | |
| Defined Entities | $\mathit{dent} ::= x \mid T \mid T(\overline{K})$ |
| Module Shapes | $\tilde{\tau} ::= \langle\!\vert \overline{\mathit{dent}}\ ;\ \overline{\mathit{espc}} \vert\!\rangle$ |
| Physical Shape Ctxts | $\tilde{\Phi} ::= \overline{\nu{:}\tilde{\tau}^m}$ |
| Logical Shape Ctxts | $\tilde{\mathcal{L}} ::= \overline{p \mapsto \nu@\tilde{\tau}}$ |
| Package Shapes | $\tilde{\Xi}, \tilde{\Gamma} ::= (\tilde{\Phi}; \tilde{\mathcal{L}})$ |

**Figure 6.** Semantic objects for shaping and typing.

convenient in some of the inference rules to be able to look up the shape of a module by merely inspecting the logical shape context $\tilde{\mathcal{L}}$, and (2) it is possible for different logical module names to reflect different restricted subnamespaces of the same underlying module (see the technical appendix for an example of this; Appendix §3). In our running example, however, the reader may ignore this subtlety and assume that all the $\tilde{\tau}$'s associated with $\nu$ in $\tilde{\mathcal{L}}$ and $\tilde{\Phi}$ are equal (which is why we omit them from the first column of Figure 5).

Figure 6 defines the semantic objects for shaping and typing, and Figure 7 gives some of the key rules implementing shaping.

***Shaping Rules*** The main shaping judgment, $\Delta \Vdash \overline{B} \Rightarrow \tilde{\Xi}$, takes as input the body of a package definition, which is just a sequence of bindings $\overline{B}$. Rule SHSEQ synthesizes the shape of $\overline{B}$ by proceeding, in left-to-right order, to synthesize the shape of each individual binding $B$ (via the judgment $\Delta; \tilde{\Gamma} \Vdash B \Rightarrow \tilde{\Xi}$) and then *merge* it with the shapes of the previous bindings (via the judgment $\Vdash \tilde{\Xi}_1 + \tilde{\Xi}_2 \Rightarrow \tilde{\Xi}$).

Let us begin with the judgment that shapes an individual binding. The rule SHALIAS should be self-explanatory.

The rule SHINC is simple as well, choosing fresh identity variables $\overline{\alpha}$ to represent the holes in package $P$ and applying the renaming $r$ to $P$'s shape. (Note that it uses some simple auxiliary definitions: rename, for applying a renaming to the $\mathcal{L}$ part of a shape, and shape, for erasing a package type $\Xi$ to a shape by removing typing information. Moreover, by alpha-varying the type of $P$ we rename its variables to match the freshly chosen $\overline{\alpha}$.)

The rule SHMOD generates the appropriate globally unique identity $\nu_0$ to represent $[M]$, and then calls out to a shaping judgment for Haskell modules, $\tilde{\Gamma}; \nu_0 \Vdash_{\mathsf{c}} M : \tilde{\tau}$ (Appendix §5.1.1), which generates the shape $\tilde{\tau}$ of $M$ assuming that $\nu_0$ is the module's identity. As an example of this, observe the shape generated for the Client module $\nu_C$ in multinst in Figure 5. The shape ascribes provenance $\nu_C$ to the `main` entity, since it is freshly defined in Client, while ascribing provenance $\nu_{GA}$ to the `G` type, since it was imported from GA and is only being re-exported by Client.

The rule SHSIG, for shaping hole declarations, is a bit subtler than the other rules. Perhaps surprisingly, the generated shape declares not only a fresh identity variable $\alpha$ for the hole itself, but also a set of fresh identity variables $\overline{\beta}$, one for each entity speci-

$$\boxed{\Delta; \tilde{\Gamma} \Vdash B \Rightarrow \tilde{\Xi}} \qquad \frac{p' \mapsto \nu@\tilde{\tau} \in \tilde{\Gamma}}{\Delta; \tilde{\Gamma} \Vdash p = p' \Rightarrow (\emptyset; p \mapsto \nu@\tilde{\tau})}\ (\textsc{ShAlias})$$

$$\frac{\nu_0 = \mathsf{mkident}(M; \tilde{\Gamma}) \qquad \tilde{\Gamma}; \nu_0 \Vdash_{\mathsf{c}} M : \tilde{\tau}}{\Delta; \tilde{\Gamma} \Vdash p = [M] \Rightarrow (\nu_0{:}\tilde{\tau}^+; p \mapsto \nu_0@\tilde{\tau})}\ (\textsc{ShMod})$$

$$\frac{\alpha, \overline{\beta}\ \mathsf{fresh} \qquad \tilde{\tau}_0 = \langle\!\vert \emptyset\ ;\ \overline{[\beta]\mathit{dent}} \vert\!\rangle \qquad \tilde{\Gamma}; \tilde{\tau}_0 \Vdash_{\mathsf{c}} S \leadsto \tilde{\tau}; \tilde{\Phi}'}{\Delta; \tilde{\Gamma} \Vdash p :: [S] \Rightarrow ((\alpha{:}\tilde{\tau}^-, \tilde{\Phi}'); p \mapsto \alpha@\tilde{\tau})}\ (\textsc{ShSig})$$

$$\frac{\overline{\alpha}\ \mathsf{fresh} \qquad (P : \forall\overline{\alpha}.\Xi) \in \Delta \qquad \Xi' = \mathsf{rename}(r; \Xi)}{\Delta; \tilde{\Gamma} \Vdash \textbf{include}\ P\ r \Rightarrow \mathsf{shape}(\Xi')}\ (\textsc{ShInc})$$

$$\boxed{\Delta \Vdash \overline{B} \Rightarrow \tilde{\Xi}} \qquad \frac{}{\Delta \Vdash \emptyset \Rightarrow (\emptyset; \emptyset)}\ (\textsc{ShNil})$$

$$\frac{\Delta \Vdash \overline{B_1} \Rightarrow \tilde{\Xi}_1 \qquad \Delta; \tilde{\Xi}_1 \Vdash B_2 \Rightarrow \tilde{\Xi}_2 \qquad \Vdash \tilde{\Xi}_1 + \tilde{\Xi}_2 \Rightarrow \tilde{\Xi}}{\Delta \Vdash \overline{B_1}, B_2 \Rightarrow \tilde{\Xi}}\ (\textsc{ShSeq})$$

**Figure 7.** Shaping rules (ignoring thinning).

fied in the hole signature $S$. (The intermediate $\tilde{\tau}_0$ merely encodes these fresh identities as input to the signature shaping judgment.) The reason for this is simply to maximize flexibility: there is no reason to demand *a priori* that the module that fills in the hole (*i.e.*, the module whose identity $\nu$ will end up getting substituted for $\alpha$) must itself be responsible for *defining* all the entities specified in the hole signature—it need only be responsible for *exporting* those entities, which may very well have been defined in other modules.

The shape $\tilde{\Phi}_A$ in Figure 5 illustrates the output of SHSIG on the Array hole in package arrays-sig. This shape specifies that $\beta_{AA}$ is a module defining an entity called `Arr`, that $\beta_{AS}$ is a module defining an entity called `something`, and that $\alpha_A$ is a module bringing $[\beta_{AA}]$`Arr` and $[\beta_{AS}]$`something` together in its export spec. Of course, when the hole is eventually filled (*e.g.*, in the graph-a package, whose shaping is discussed below), it may indeed be the case that the same module identity $\nu$ is substituted for $\alpha_A$, $\beta_{AA}$, and $\beta_{AS}$—*i.e.*, that $\nu$ both defines *and* exports `Arr` and `something`—but SHSIG does not require this.

Returning now to the merging judgment $\Vdash \tilde{\Xi}_1 + \tilde{\Xi}_2 \Rightarrow \tilde{\Xi}$ that is invoked in the last premise of (SHSEQ): This merging judgment (Appendix §6.6) is where the real "meat" of shaping occurs—in particular, this is where mixin *linking* is performed by *unification* of module identities. If a module with logical name $p$ is mapped by $\tilde{\Xi}_1$ and $\tilde{\Xi}_2$ to physical identities $\nu_1$ and $\nu_2$, respectively, the merging judgment will unify $\nu_1$ and $\nu_2$ together. Moreover, if $\nu_1$ and $\nu_2$ are specified by $\tilde{\Xi}_1$ and $\tilde{\Xi}_2$ as having different module shapes $\tilde{\tau}_1$ and $\tilde{\tau}_2$, respectively, those shapes will be merged as well, with the resulting shape containing all of the components specified in either $\tilde{\tau}_1$ and $\tilde{\tau}_2$. For any entities appearing in both $\tilde{\tau}_1$ and $\tilde{\tau}_2$, their provenances will be unified.

To see a concrete instance of this, consider the merging that occurs during the shaping of the graph-a package in our running example in Figure 5. The graph-a package **include**s two packages defined earlier: arrays-a and structures. As per rule (SHINC), each inclusion will generate fresh identity variables for the packages' holes (say, $\alpha_P$, $\beta_{PL}$, $\alpha_A$, $\beta_{AA}$, $\beta_{AS}$ for structures, and $\alpha'_P$, $\beta'_{PL}$ for arrays-a). Since both packages export Prelude, the merging judgment will unify $\alpha_P$ and $\alpha'_P$, the physical identities associated with Prelude in the shapes of the two packages; consequently, the shape of $\alpha_P$, namely $\langle\!\vert \emptyset\ ;\ [\beta_{PL}]\mathtt{List(Nil,Cons)} \vert\!\rangle$, will be unified with the shape of $\alpha'_P$, namely $\langle\!\vert \emptyset\ ;\ [\beta'_{PL}]\mathtt{List(Nil,Cons)} \vert\!\rangle$, resulting in the unification of $\beta_{PL}$ and $\beta'_{PL}$ as well.

Similarly, since both packages export Array, the merging judgment will link the implementation of Array in arrays-a with the hole for Array in structures by unifying $\alpha_A$, $\beta_{AA}$, and $\beta_{AS}$ with

$\nu_{AA}$. As a result, the occurrences of $\alpha_A$, $\beta_{AA}$, and $\beta_{AS}$ in $\nu_G$ (and its shape) get substituted with $\nu_{AA}$, which explains why the shape of graph-a maps Graph to $\nu_{GA} = \nu_G[\nu_{AA}/\alpha_A]$. Lastly, merging will check that the implementation of Array in arrays-a actually provides all the entities required by the hole specification in structures, *i.e.*, that $\tilde{\Phi}_{AA}$ subsumes $\tilde{\Phi}_A$, which indeed it does.

### 3.3 Typing

In our running example thus far, we have not yet performed any *typechecking* of core-level code, such as the code inside multinst's Client module. There is a good reason for this: before shaping, we don't know whether core-level types such as GA.G and GB.G (imported by Client) are equal, because we don't know what the identities of GA and GB are. But after shaping, we have all the identity information we need to perform typechecking proper.

Thus, as seen in the top-level package rule TyPkg in Figure 8, the output of the shaping judgment—namely, $\tilde{\tilde{\Xi}}_{\mathsf{pkg}}$—is passed as input to the *typing* judgment, $\Delta; \tilde{\tilde{\Xi}}_{\mathsf{pkg}} \vdash \overline{B} : \Xi \rightsquigarrow \mathit{dexp}$. Typing, in turn, produces a *package type* $\Xi$, which enriches the package shape $\tilde{\tilde{\Xi}}_{\mathsf{pkg}}$ with core-level (*i.e.*, Haskell-level) typing information. The final type returned for the package, $\forall\overline{\alpha}.\Xi$, then just quantifies over the variable identities $\overline{\alpha}$ of the holes in $\Xi$, so that they may be instantiated in different ways by subsequent package definitions.

The package types $\Xi$ generated for the packages in our running example appear in the third column of Figure 5. Formally, the only difference between these package types and the package shapes in the second column of Figure 5 lies in the difference between their constituent *module* types $\tau = \langle\!|\, \overline{\mathit{dspc}}\ ;\ \overline{\mathit{espc}} \,|\!\rangle$ and *module* shapes $\tilde{\tau} = \langle\!|\, \overline{\mathit{dent}}\ ;\ \overline{\mathit{espc}} \,|\!\rangle$. Whereas the "defined entities" component $(\overline{\mathit{dent}})$ of $\tilde{\tau}$ only *names* the entities defined by a module, the "defined entity specs" component $(\overline{\mathit{dspc}})$ of $\tau$ additionally specifies their core-level kinds/types. For example, observe the module type ascribed to arrays-a's module $\nu_{AA}$ in $\Phi_{AA}$. This type enriches the pre-computed shape (in $\tilde{\Phi}_{AA}$) with additional information about the kind of `Arr` and the type of `something`.

Let us now explain the typing rules in Figure 8. For the moment, we will ignore the shaded parts of the rules concerning elaboration into Haskell; we will return to them in Section 3.4.

The rules TyNil and TySeq implement typing of a sequence of bindings $\overline{B}$. The procedure is structurally very similar to the one used in the shaping of $\overline{B}$: we process (in left-to-right order) each constituent binding $B$, producing a *type* that we *merge* into the types of the previous bindings. The key difference is that the partial merge operator $\oplus$ does not perform any unification on module identities—it merely performs a mixin merge, which checks that all specifications (kinds or types) assigned to any particular core-level entity are equal. For instance, when typing graph-a, the mixin merge will check that the type of `something` in the Array implementation from arrays-a is equal to the type of `something` in the Array hole from structures, and thus that the implementation satisfies the requirements of the hole.

The remaining rules concern the typing of individual bindings, $\Delta; \Gamma; \tilde{\tilde{\Xi}}_{\mathsf{pkg}} \vdash B : \Xi \rightsquigarrow \mathit{dexp}$. The typing rules TyMod and TySig are structurally very similar to the corresponding shaping rules given in Figure 7. The key difference is that, whereas ShMod and ShSig *generate* appropriate identities for their module/hole, TyMod and TySig instead *look up* the pre-computed identities in the package shape $\tilde{\tilde{\Xi}}_{\mathsf{pkg}}$. As an example of this, observe what happens when we type the Array module in arrays-a using rule TyMod. The package shape $\tilde{\tilde{\Xi}}_{\mathsf{pkg}}$ we pre-computed in the shaping pass tells us that the physical module identity associated with the logical module name Array is $\nu_{AA}$, so we can go ahead and assume $\nu_{AA}$ is the identity of Array when typing its implementation. Note that TyMod and TySig call out to typing judgments for Haskell modules and signatures ($\vdash_{\mathsf{c}}$). Like the analogous shaping judgments, these are defined formally in the appendix (Appendix §5.1.1).

Like TyMod and TySig, the rule TyInc also inspects $\tilde{\tilde{\Xi}}_{\mathsf{pkg}}$ to determine the pre-computed identities of the modules/holes in the package $P$ being **include**d. The only difference is that an **include**d package contains a whole bunch of subcomponents (rather than only one), so looking up their identities is a bit more involved. It is performed by appealing to a "matching" judgment $\vdash \tilde{\tilde{\Xi}}_{\mathsf{pkg}} \leq_{\overline{\alpha}} \Xi' \rightsquigarrow \phi$, similar to the one needed for signature matching in ML module systems [28]. This judgment looks up the instantiations of all the **include**d holes by matching $\Xi'$ (the type of the **include**d package $P$ *after* applying the renaming $r$) against $\tilde{\tilde{\Xi}}_{\mathsf{pkg}}$. This produces a substitution $\phi$ with domain $\overline{\alpha}$, which then gets applied to $\Xi'$ to produce the type of the **include** binding. For example, when typing the package graph-a, we know after shaping that the identity of the Array module is $\nu_{AA}$. When we **include** structures, the matching judgment will glean this information from $\tilde{\tilde{\Xi}}_{\mathsf{pkg}}$, and produce a substitution $\phi$ mapping structures' $\alpha_A$ parameter to the actual Array implementation $\nu_{AA}$.

$$\boxed{\Delta; \Gamma; \tilde{\tilde{\Xi}}_{\mathsf{pkg}} \vdash B : \Xi \rightsquigarrow \mathit{dexp}}$$

$$\frac{p' \mapsto \nu@\tau \in \Gamma}{\Delta; \Gamma; \tilde{\tilde{\Xi}}_{\mathsf{pkg}} \vdash p = p' : (\emptyset; p \mapsto \nu@\tau) \rightsquigarrow \{\}} \ (\textsc{TyAlias})$$

$$\frac{p \mapsto \nu_0@\tilde{\tau}_0 \in \tilde{\tilde{\Xi}}_{\mathsf{pkg}} \qquad \Gamma; \nu_0 \vdash_{\mathsf{c}} M : \tau \rightsquigarrow \mathit{hsmod}}{\Delta; \Gamma; \tilde{\tilde{\Xi}}_{\mathsf{pkg}} \vdash p = [M] : (\nu_0{:}\tau^{+}; p \mapsto \nu_0@\tau) \rightsquigarrow \{\nu_0{}^{\star} \mapsto \mathit{hsmod} : \tau^{\star}\}} \ (\textsc{TyMod})$$

$$\frac{p \mapsto \nu_0@\tilde{\tau}_0 \in \tilde{\tilde{\Xi}}_{\mathsf{pkg}} \qquad \Gamma; \tilde{\tau}_0 \vdash_{\mathsf{c}} S \rightsquigarrow \tau; \Phi' \qquad \Phi'' = \nu_0{:}\tau^{-} \oplus \Phi' \text{ defined}}{\Delta; \Gamma; \tilde{\tilde{\Xi}}_{\mathsf{pkg}} \vdash p :: [S] : (\Phi''; p \mapsto \nu_0@\tau) \rightsquigarrow \{\nu^{\star} \mapsto - : \sigma^{\star} \mid \nu{:}\sigma^{-} \in \Phi''\}} \ (\textsc{TySig})$$

$$\frac{\overline{\alpha} \text{ fresh} \quad (P = \lambda\overline{\alpha}.\mathit{dexp} : \forall\overline{\alpha}.\Xi) \in \Delta \quad \Xi' = \mathsf{rename}(r; \Xi) \quad \vdash \tilde{\tilde{\Xi}}_{\mathsf{pkg}} \leq_{\overline{\alpha}} \Xi' \rightsquigarrow \phi \quad \Xi'' = \mathsf{apply}(\phi; \Xi') \text{ defined}}{\Delta; \Gamma; \tilde{\tilde{\Xi}}_{\mathsf{pkg}} \vdash \textbf{include}\ P\ r : \Xi'' \rightsquigarrow \mathsf{apply}(\phi^{\star}; \mathit{dexp})} \ (\textsc{TyInc})$$

$$\boxed{\Delta; \tilde{\tilde{\Xi}}_{\mathsf{pkg}} \vdash \overline{B} : \Xi \rightsquigarrow \mathit{dexp}} \qquad \frac{}{\Delta; \tilde{\tilde{\Xi}}_{\mathsf{pkg}} \vdash \emptyset : (\emptyset; \emptyset) \rightsquigarrow \{\}} \ (\textsc{TyNil})$$

$$\frac{\Delta; \tilde{\tilde{\Xi}}_{\mathsf{pkg}} \vdash \overline{B_1} : \Xi_1 \rightsquigarrow \mathit{dexp}_1 \qquad \Xi = \Xi_1 \oplus \Xi_2 \text{ defined} \qquad \Delta; \Xi_1; \tilde{\tilde{\Xi}}_{\mathsf{pkg}} \vdash B_2 : \Xi_2 \rightsquigarrow \mathit{dexp}_2}{\Delta; \tilde{\tilde{\Xi}}_{\mathsf{pkg}} \vdash \overline{B_1}, B_2 : \Xi \rightsquigarrow \mathit{dexp}_1 \oplus \mathit{dexp}_2} \ (\textsc{TySeq})$$

$$\boxed{\Delta \vdash D : \forall\overline{\alpha}.\Xi \rightsquigarrow \lambda\overline{\alpha}.\mathit{dexp}}$$

$$\frac{\Delta \Vdash \overline{B} \Rightarrow \tilde{\tilde{\Xi}}_{\mathsf{pkg}} \qquad \Delta; \tilde{\tilde{\Xi}}_{\mathsf{pkg}} \vdash \overline{B} : \Xi \rightsquigarrow \mathit{dexp} \qquad \overline{\alpha} = \mathsf{fv}(\Xi)}{\Delta \vdash \textbf{package}\ P\ \textbf{where}\ \overline{B} : \forall\overline{\alpha}.\Xi \rightsquigarrow \lambda\overline{\alpha}.\mathit{dexp}} \ (\textsc{TyPkg})$$

**Figure 8.** Typing and elaboration rules (ignoring thinning).

### 3.4 Elaborating Backpack to Haskell

We substantiate our claim to retrofit Haskell with SMD through an elaboration of Backpack, our external language (EL), into a model of GHC Haskell, our internal language (IL). The EL, as we have

| | |
|---|---|
| (Module Names) | $f \in \mathit{IlModNames}$ |
| (Module Sources) | $\mathit{hsmod} ::= \ldots$ |
| (File Expressions) | $\mathit{fexp} ::= \underline{\mathit{hsmod}} \mid -$ |
| (File Types) | $\mathit{ftyp} ::= \langle\!\vert\, \overline{\mathit{dspc}^\star}\ ;\ \overline{\mathit{espc}^\star}\, \vert\!\rangle$ |
| (Typed File Expressions) | $\mathit{tfexp} ::= \mathit{fexp} : \mathit{ftyp}$ |
| (Directory Expressions) | $\mathit{dexp} ::= \{\overline{f \mapsto \mathit{tfexp}}\}$ |
| (Identity Translation) | $(-)^\star \in \mathit{Identities}/{\equiv_\mu} \rightarrowtail \mathit{IlModNames}$ |

**Figure 9.** IL syntax. ($dspc^\star$ and $espc^\star$ mention $f$ instead of $\nu$.)

demonstrated so far, extends across the package, module, and core levels, while the IL defines only module and core levels; effectively the outer, package level gets "compiled away" into mere modules in the IL. Figure 9 gives the syntax of the IL; for its semantics, including the typing judgment, see the technical appendix (Appendix §7).

Elaboration translates a Backpack package into a *parameterized directory expression* $\lambda\overline{\alpha}.\mathit{dexp}$, which is a mapping from a set of module names $f$ to typed file expressions $\mathit{tfexp}$, parameterized over the identities $\overline{\alpha}$ of the package's holes. We assume an embedding $(-)^\star$ from module identities into IL module names, which respects the equi-recursive equivalence on module identities that the Backpack type system relies on. However, for readability, we will leave the embedding implicit in the remainder of this section. As for the typed file expressions $\mathit{tfexp}$, they can either be defined file expressions ($\underline{\mathit{hsmod}} : \mathit{ftyp}$), which provide both an implementation of a module along with its type, or undefined file expressions ($- : \mathit{ftyp}$), which describe a hole with type $\mathit{ftyp}$. Thus, all components of a $\mathit{dexp}$ are explicitly-typed. This has the benefit that the modules in a $\mathit{dexp}$ can be typechecked in any order, since all static information about them is specified in their explicit file types.

As a continuation of our running example, Figure 10 displays the elaboration of the multinst package, except with the file types stripped off for brevity. First, note that each module identity $\nu$ in the physical type $\Phi_M$ of multinst (lower-right hand corner of the table in Figure 5) corresponds to one of the Haskell modules in the elaboration of the package, and for each $\nu$, its type in $\Phi_M$ is (modulo the embedding $(-)^\star$) precisely the file type of $\nu$ that we have omitted from Figure 10. The concrete module identities in $\Phi_M$ map to defined file expressions, while the identity variables $\alpha_P$ and $\beta_{PL}$ (representing holes) map to undefined file expressions.

The elaboration of packages (marked with shaded text) is almost entirely straightforward, following the typing rules. More interesting is the elaboration of Haskell *modules*, which is appealed to in the second premise of rule TYMOD (and formalized in the appendix; Appendix §6). Offhand, one might expect module elaboration to be the identity translation, but in fact it is a bit more subtle than that.

Consider the $\nu_C$ entry in the directory, corresponding to the Client module, as a concrete example.

*The module header:* Unlike the original EL implementation of Client, which was anonymous, its elaborated IL version has a module header specifying $\nu_C$ as its fixed physical name, and `main` and GA.`G()` as its exported entities. More generally, the exported entities should reflect those listed in the module's type $\tau$.

*The import statements:* Our elaboration rewrites imports of logical names like GA into imports of physical module identities like $\nu_{GA}$, since the physical identities are the actual names of Haskell modules in the elaborated directory expression. We must therefore take care to preserve the logical module names that the definitions in the module's body expect to be able to refer to. For example, the reference GA.G is seen to have provenance $[\nu_{GA}]$G during Backpack typechecking of Client, so in the elaborated IL version of Client we want GA.G to mean the same thing. We achieve this by means of Haskell's "import aliases", which support renaming of imported module names; *e.g.*, the first import statement in $\nu_C$ imports the

$\lambda\alpha_P\,\beta_{PL}.$

$\alpha_P \mapsto$ ———

$\beta_{PL} \mapsto$ ———

$\nu_{AA} \mapsto$
```
module νAA (Arr(MkArr)) where
  import qualified αP as P (List(Nil,Cons))
  data Arr i e = MkArr ...
  something = P.Nil :: P.List (Arr i e)
```

$\nu_{AB} \mapsto$
```
module νAB (Arr(ANil, ...)) where
  import αP as Prelude (List(Nil, Cons))
  data Arr i e = ANil | ...
  something = Cons ANil Nil
```

$\nu_{GA} \mapsto$
```
module νGA (G(...)) where
  import αP as Prelude (List(Nil, Cons))
  import νAA as Array (Arr(), something)
  data G ...
```

$\nu_{GB} \mapsto$
```
module νGB (G(...)) where
  import αP as Prelude (List(Nil, Cons))
  import νAB as Array (Arr(), something)
  data G ...
```

$\nu_C \mapsto$
```
module νC (main, GA.G()) where
  import qualified νGA as GA (G())
  import qualified νGB as GB (G())
  main = ... GA.G ... GB.G ...
```

**Figure 10.** Elaboration of multinst. (For readability, the translation from identities to module names, $(-)^\star$, and the file type annotation on each module file have been omitted. See Figure 5 for the latter.)

physical name $\nu_{GA}$ but gives it the logical name GA in the body, thus ensuring that the reference GA.G still has (the same) meaning as it did during Backpack typechecking.

*The body:* Thanks to the import aliasing we just described, the entity definitions in the body of $\nu_C$ can remain syntactically identical to those in the original Client module.

*Explicitness of imports and exports:* All imported and exported entities are given as explicitly as the Haskell module syntax allows, even when the original EL modules neglect to make them explicit; *e.g.*, the original code for Graph lists neither its imports nor its exports, but its elaboration (as $\nu_{GA}$ and $\nu_{GB}$) does. The primary reason for this explicitness is that it enables us to prove a "weakening" property on IL modules, which is critical for the proof of soundness of elaboration. If modules are not explicit about which core-level entities they are importing and exporting, their module types will not be stable under weakening.

### 3.5 Formalization of Haskell Modules and Soundness

We have proven the following key soundness theorem about the elaboration: if a package definition $D$ has type $\forall\overline{\alpha}.(\Phi;\mathcal{L})$ and elaborates into a parameterized directory expression $\lambda\overline{\alpha}.\mathit{dexp}$, then every module in $\mathit{dexp}$ is well-typed in the IL, and the identities and types in $\Phi$ directly match those of $\mathit{dexp}$. (For example, soundness means that the identities and EL module types appearing in the type of multinst in Figure 5 correspond precisely to the names and types of the IL modules in Figure 10.)

As part of this effort, our IL constitutes a new formal model of the Haskell module system. This model follows the Haskell Language Report as closely as possible in its definition of well-formed modules—*i.e.*, the processing of module dependencies through import statements and export lists. Unlike previous work on formalizing the Haskell module system [7, 12], our model supports (separately typechecked) recursive modules; furthermore, we have developed some basic metatheory for the IL (*e.g.*, "substitution" and "weakening") in order to prove soundness of elaboration, a non-trivial undertaking given that substitution can result in the merging of module/signature bindings. Full details of the IL are given in the accompanying technical appendix (Appendix §7).

We do not provide any kind of dynamic semantics in Backpack and thus we cannot prove (or even state) any conventional type safety theorem. Instead, the soundness of Backpack's elaboration simply reduces the question of whether Backpack is type-safe to the question of whether Haskell is type-safe.

## 4. Related Work and Technical Discussion

***Detailed Comparison with MixML*** ML modules provide a very expressive and convenient language for programming with abstract data types. However, due to the double vision problem (Section 2.6), functors are fundamentally incompatible with recursive linking [27]. There have therefore been several attempts to synthesize aspects of ML modules and mixin modules in a single system, including Owens and Flatt's typed unit calculus [25] and Duggan's type system for recursive DLLs [10].

Arguably the most advanced system in this space is Rossberg and Dreyer's MixML [27], which aims to be a highly expressive foundational calculus of mixin modules for an ML-like core language. Backpack's design and semantics are inspired by those of MixML, but our design decisions, driven by our goal of retrofitting Haskell with SMD, have led to considerable simplifications.

MixML supports first-class and higher-order *units* (*i.e.*, instantiable mixins), whereas Backpack's units—packages—only exist at the top level. We believe Backpack's units to be sufficient for practical programming, and restricting them to top level streamlines the semantics of applicative identities. MixML also supports hierarchical mixin modules with "deep linking", but Backpack restricts packages to be flat namespaces of modules. Deep linking lets MixML express many different ML constructs (*e.g.*, $n$-ary signatures) using just one form of linking. Since our focus is on practicality rather than expressiveness, we sacrifice features like first-class units and deep linking for simplicity of syntax and semantics, optimizing instead for common usage patterns. In particular, our **include** construct is more straightforward to program with than MixML's binary linking/binding construct, and fits better with the "feel" of the Haskell module language (*e.g.*, its **import** statements). Backpack also provides some features that MixML lacks, such as renaming, thinning, and an applicative semantics of instantiation.

Concerning the double vision problem, MixML solves it through the use of a two-pass algorithm for typechecking linked modules: the first pass computes all information about type components in the modules, and the second pass performs full typechecking. In MixML, these two passes are defined using a single set of inference rules, with the first pass defined by conveniently ignoring certain premises. Backpack adopts the same two-pass idea in order to compute the physical module identities involved in a package before typechecking it. However, Backpack distinguishes the two passes—shaping and typing—using completely separate judgments and rules. Although this leads to a doubling of rules, the rules themselves are (we feel) much easier to understand. In particular, the account of linking given by the sequencing rules SHSEQ and TYSEQ is considerably simpler than MixML's formidable linking rule. Moreover, Backpack stages the shaping pass over a whole package entirely before the typing pass, leading to a clearer conceptual split between the two phases of package typechecking than in MixML, where the two passes are interleaved.

A key reason we can get by with a simpler semantics of linking is that we are deliberately less ambitious than MixML in a certain sense: unlike MixML, we do not aim to completely subsume the functionality of ML modules. MixML does, and this means that its semantics must deal with nested uses of *translucent sealing* (*i.e.*, the ability to define types that are "transparent" inside a module but "opaque" outside), a defining feature of ML modules which compounds the already-tricky double-vision problem. In contrast, Backpack does not attempt to support translucent sealing—and thus does not suffer the attendant complexities—for the simple reason that Haskell, our target of elaboration, cannot support it.

Finally, MixML is defined by elaboration into an internal language, LTG, which was designed specifically to capture all the necessary features of MixML. (LTG is an extension, with linear kinds, of an earlier IL, similarly specialized for recursive ML module systems, called RTG [9].) LTG's unconventional metatheory underscores MixML's status as a foundational calculus rather than a practical language design, in contrast to Backpack, whose IL is a formalization of an existing implementation artifact, the GHC module system. A major benefit of our approach is that the semantics (via elaboration) of a Backpack package may be understood by Haskell programmers essentially in terms of a reshuffling of import and export lists in their Haskell modules. The elaboration in Figure 10 is a case in point.

***Logical Module Names vs. Physical Module Identities*** Module identities, which establish canonical *physical* names for modules (as distinct from program-level *logical* names), serve two important roles in Backpack's semantics: (1) they simplify and regularize the elaboration into Haskell modules (and its soundness proof), and (2) they are the principal component of our solution for how to support applicative mixin linking.

Concerning the first point: The distinction between logical and physical names is a central technical element enabling—and conceptually reinforcing—the elaboration into our Haskell-based IL. In particular, a key invariant of elaboration is that the physical part of a package's EL type gives a precise description of the IL modules that it elaborates to; the logical part of its type is only relevant for namespace management during Backpack-level typechecking.

Concerning the second point: The idea of distinguishing between logical and physical names is not new. A number of prior formalisms for ML-style modules—including the Definition of Standard ML itself—rely on a similar distinction [22, 29, 28]. The key advantage of this approach (as opposed to more direct, syntactic type systems for modules, *e.g.*, [20, 15]) is that physical identities greatly simplify the treatment of type equality in the presence of aliasing: no matter their logical names, two types are equal iff they have the same physical identity. This eliminates the need for fancier mechanisms for handling type sharing, like translucent sums or singleton kinds (see Rossberg *et al.* [28] for further discussion). Moreover, for recursive and mixin module extensions of ML [8, 27], the logical/physical distinction has enabled clean solutions to the double vision problem, as discussed above. (There is some recent work by Im *et al.* [19] on solving double vision "syntactically"—*i.e.*, using only logical names—but it does not account for separate typechecking of mutually recursive modules in general.)

What distinguishes Backpack from these prior systems is its support for *both* separate typechecking of recursive modules *and* an applicative semantics of instantiation, as appropriate for a pure language like Haskell. To handle the combination, we needed to enrich the language of module identities with both (equi-)recursive $\mu$-binders and constructor applications, and employ (standard) unification and equivalence-checking algorithms that work for these recursive identities [18, 14]. To see why, consider the example from Section 2.6, in which the modules A and B in package ab-rec-sep have the recursive identities $\nu_A$ and $\nu_B$ defined on the subsequent page. If one were to define another package ab-rec-sep2 in the same way, the identities of A and B would be exactly the same. In contrast, were we to code up this example in MixML, each distinct package defined like ab-rec-sep would produce modules with "fresh" (distinct) identities, as one would expect given MixML's *generative* semantics of instantiation. Nevertheless, we observe that recursive identities do not complicate the semantics much, a testament to the scalability of the logical/physical approach.

***Separate Compilation for ML*** Setting aside the lack of support for recursive linking, ML functors are not by themselves really a practical mechanism for SMD due to the proliferation of "sharing" constraints that are known to arise when programming in a "fully functorized" style (*i.e.*, in which modules are parameterized explicitly, via the functor mechanism, over all their dependencies). Consequently, a number of systems have been proposed for building a better SMD framework on top of the existing ML module system.

Before discussing these systems in more detail, let us observe two important ways in which they all differ from Backpack. First, unlike Backpack, the separate compilation systems for ML build improved SMD support on top of the already-powerful ML module system, which offers instantiation, reuse, and at least some form of SMD via functors. In contrast, Backpack is built on top of Haskell, which lacks those features, and thus the expressiveness boost it offers over the underlying language is in some sense more significant. Second, we realize this boost not through functors but through mixins; as a result, Backpack supports recursive linking, and avoids the need for any separate notion of sharing constraints.

To address the lack of separate compilation in ML, Cardelli introduced a foundational calculus of *linksets* [5]. However, as a foundational calculus, this framework lacks support for user-defined abstract data types, as well as recursion at the module or core level—two prominent features that drive the complexity of state-of-the-art module systems. Building on Cardelli's linkset foundation, Swasey *et al.* [31] designed a typed language of program fragments, SMLSC, that organizes lists of top-level SML definitions (*e.g.*, modules) into what they call *units*. Linking happens automatically by name when unit definitions are considered in the same linkset. In particular, when multiple units in a linkset have "interface imports" on some common name, those dependencies unify automatically without extra annotations. SMLSC units therefore eliminate the need for sharing constraints on dependencies—as mixin modules do—but they do not permit recursive linking.

In a different vein, targeting "open" modular programming, the Acute language of Sewell *et al.* [30] and the Alice ML language of Rossberg *et al.* [26] support not only separate compilation, but dynamic linking, marshalling/pickling, and (in the case of Acute) versioning of components, all of which are beyond the scope of Backpack. While Acute repurposes modules (with new primitive operations) as a mechanism for compilation units and linking, Alice ML defines "components" by reduction to a simpler construct of "packages" (modules as first-class core values). Linking in Acute consists of (non-recursive) chains of module definitions and imports, whereas Alice ML employs a more flexible and dynamic "component manager" approach based on Java class-loading (rather than linksets). Neither Acute nor Alice ML supports recursive modules.

As part of the OCaml module system [21], the `ocamlc` compilation tool performs separate compilation on files that contain module components. The tool treats the file system rather like a mixin: each component (*i.e.*, a file) can be defined as an implementation (*i.e.*, a `.ml` file) or a hole (*i.e.*, a `.mli` file), and components can be recursively linked. Like SMLSC but unlike Backpack, though, these "mixins" cannot be instantiated and reused: a separately-compiled file cannot be linked with multiple implementations of its dependencies. In essence, `ocamlc` implements something similar to the target IL of Backpack's elaboration, albeit for OCaml (obviously) and extended with full separate compilation rather than just separate typechecking. It does not, however, provide a *language* for building and linking components, as Backpack does.

***Mixin Modules for OO Languages*** Our focus has been on mixin-based SMD in the setting of a typed *functional* language. In the object-oriented community, mixins have already seen significant uptake. Both Scala [24] and J& [23], for instance, incorporate mixin-style composition into the very fabric of their designs. However, as we have explained, we are particularly interested in the question of how to retrofit *existing* languages with mixin-based SMD, and to our knowledge there is relatively little work on that.

The SMARTJAVAMOD/*component* systems of Ancona *et al.* [2] define a new level of mixin modules to encapsulate existing Java classes. A component contains *defined* classes and *deferred* classes, the latter of which are specified as abstract class names with various constraints. The "bind" construct, which performs mixin linking, instantiates components generatively, producing a unique copy of all the classes inside the merged result (and thus fresh abstract types). In contrast, Backpack supports an applicative semantics of instantiation.

The SMARTJAVAMOD/component languages are implemented with a translation into "polymorphic bytecode" [1], essentially an extension of JVM bytecode with markers and constraints for the deferred classes (*i.e.*, holes) in the component. For that reason, their IL resembles Backpack's, although they present no formal definition of their elaboration into this language. Instead, they define a reduction semantics on components that flattens them into fully instantiated Java class definitions. In Backpack, following much work on ML module systems [15, 28, 27], packages do not have a direct reduction semantics—rather, their meaning is given by a formal translation into a typed IL, in our case based on Haskell.

As is the tradition in object-oriented languages, the aforementioned systems emphasize dynamic binding, virtual methods, overriding, etc., and do not consider the issue of the double vision problem. In contrast, Backpack supports only static binding, does not permit overriding, and invests great effort to avoid double vision.

## 5. Future Work

***Type Classes*** Backpack modules only allow data types and values; type classes and type class instances are conspicuously absent. We have left them out of the system deliberately in order to focus attention on the essential features of Backpack that we hope will be broadly applicable, not just to Haskell. That being said, we believe that incorporating type classes into Backpack should be feasible.

In the extension we envision, type classes and instances would both be new kinds of core entities, although the latter would differ from existing entities in that (1) they do not have simple syntactic names and (2) import resolution treats them differently (see below). As with all entities, the export specs (*espc*) listed in a module type would denote which instances a module provides to its clients.

The interaction between instances and signatures poses an interesting challenge: linking an implementation for a hole, or even linking two holes together through aliasing, might result in the existence of two distinct instances for the same type class and type that are visible within a single module. For example, in the bindings

```
P = [class Eq a where ...]
A :: [data T]
B :: [data T]
    [import P                   ]
    [import qualified A         ]
C = [import qualified B         ]
    [instance Eq A.T where ...  ]
    [instance Eq B.T where ...  ]
```

well-typedness of C requires that A.T and B.T be distinct types. But if we then add an alias binding A = B, these two types are unified into a single one, and now C defines two different instances for a single class and type, making it ill-typed.

To prevent this form of error, we would need to amend the definition of merging for sets of export specs ($\overline{espc}$) to prevent two distinct instances for the same class and type from merging together successfully. This would be enough to guarantee that the substitution that links A and B together would not be well defined on the package type for the previous four bindings, thus rejecting the addition of the alias binding A = B.

We would also need to extend the IL in order to maintain a crucial invariant of the elaboration translation, namely that the IL translation of a module only imports the entities that were visible to that module during Backpack-level typechecking (Section 3.4). Naively, this invariant would not be preserved in the presence of type classes because Haskell does not support named instances, so there is no way to explicitly delimit the instances that one module imports from another. For example, suppose a module Y imports a hole X, and then the hole is subsequently filled with an implementation defining an instance that was not in the signature for X. In that case, we do not want the elaboration of Y to suddenly see that new instance, since it might break Y's well-typedness, but there is no way *a priori* to prevent it.

To restore this invariant in the presence of type classes, we would need to introduce—*only in the IL*—the ability to explicitly name instances on import statements. This capability, which would require a minor extension to GHC, would then allow us, when elaborating Y in the above example, to explicitly restrict the import of X to only include those instances that were visible in X's signature.

***Type Synonyms and*** *newtype* We could straightforwardly extend Backpack with both type synonyms and Haskell's `newtype` mechanism for defining abstract data types. Both would be separate entities along with datatypes and values, with accompanying defined entity specs (*dspc*); because they are core entities, they would be imported, exported, and recorded in module types just like datatypes and values. However, for compatibility with GHC, neither would be declarable "abstractly" in signatures (*i.e.*, by omitting the "right-hand sides"), unlike regular data types.

In the case of type synonyms, we would need to treat them as transparently equal to their defining types. To accomplish this, we would simply expand type synonyms as part of Backpack elaboration, ensuring that they never appeared in our semantic objects (the "F-ing modules" approach of Rossberg *et al.* [28] works similarly). Since the synonyms themselves would never appear in any semantic types (*typ*), they would not complicate type equality. In contrast, `newtype`s would not be automatically equated with their defining types; in semantic types (*typ*) they would look and behave essentially like regular data types.

***Versioning*** Lastly, while the support for versioning in Cabal (Haskell's existing package management system) does not obviate interfaces and mixins, neither do interfaces and mixins obviate versioning. An important direction for future work is to investigate how best to integrate versioning into Backpack.

## Acknowledgments

We are grateful for innumerable impromptu whiteboard discussions with Neel Krishnaswami, Joshua Dunfield, Aaron Turon, Beta Ziliani, and Georg Neis; for early design discussions with Claudio Russo, Dimitrios Vytiniotis, and Duncan Coutts; and for detailed technical feedback from Andreas Rossberg.

## References

[1] Davide Ancona, Ferruccio Damiani, Sophia Drossopoulou, and Elena Zucca. Polymorphic bytecode: compositional compilation for Java-like languages. In *POPL '05*.

[2] Davide Ancona, Giovanni Lagorio, and Elena Zucca. Flexible type-safe linking of components for Java-like languages. In *JMLC '06*.

[3] Davide Ancona and Elena Zucca. A calculus of module systems. *JFP*, 12(2), 2002.

[4] Gilad Bracha and Gary Lindstrom. Modularity meets inheritance. In *ICCL '92*.

[5] Luca Cardelli. Program fragments, linking, and modularization. In *POPL '97*.

[6] Karl Crary, Robert Harper, and Sidd Puri. What is a recursive module? In *PLDI '99*.

[7] Iavor S. Diatchki, Mark P. Jones, and Thomas Hallgren. A formal specification of the Haskell 98 module system. In *Haskell '02*.

[8] Derek Dreyer. A type system for recursive modules. In *ICFP '07*.

[9] Derek Dreyer. Recursive type generativity. *JFP*, 17(4&5), 2007.

[10] Dominic Duggan. Type-safe linking with recursive DLLs and shared libraries. *ACM TOPLAS*, 24(6):711–804, 2002.

[11] Dominic Duggan and Constantinos Sourelis. Mixin modules. In *ICFP '96*.

[12] Karl-Filip Faxén. A static semantics for Haskell. *JFP*, 12(5), 2002.

[13] Matthew Flatt and Matthias Felleisen. Units: Cool modules for HOT languages. In *PLDI '98*.

[14] Nadji Gauthier and François Pottier. Numbering matters: First-order canonical forms for second-order recursive types. In *ICFP '04*.

[15] Robert Harper and Chris Stone. A type-theoretic interpretation of Standard ML. In *Proof, Language, and Interaction: Essays in Honor of Robin Milner*. MIT Press, 2000.

[16] Tom Hirschowitz and Xavier Leroy. Mixin modules in a call-by-value setting. *ACM TOPLAS*, 27(5):857–881, 2005.

[17] Paul Hudak, John Hughes, Simon Peyton Jones, and Philip Wadler. A history of Haskell: Being lazy with class. In *HOPL III*, 2007.

[18] Gérard Huet. *Résolution d'équations dans des langages d'ordre* 1, 2, . . ., $\omega$. PhD thesis, Université Paris 7, September 1976.

[19] Hyeonseung Im, Keiko Nakata, Jacques Garrigue, and Sungwoo Park. A syntactic type system for recursive modules. In *OOPSLA '11*.

[20] Xavier Leroy. Applicative functors and fully transparent higher-order modules. In *POPL '95*.

[21] Xavier Leroy. The Objective Caml system: Documentation and user's manual. `http://caml.inria.fr/ocaml/htmlman/`.

[22] Robin Milner, Mads Tofte, Robert Harper, and David MacQueen. *The Definition of Standard ML (Revised)*. MIT Press, 1997.

[23] Nathaniel Nystrom, Xin Qi, and Andrew Myers. J&: Nested intersection for scalable software composition. In *OOPSLA '06*.

[24] Martin Odersky and Matthias Zenger. Scalable component abstractions. In *OOPSLA '05*.

[25] Scott Owens and Matthew Flatt. From structures and functors to modules and units. In *ICFP '06*.

[26] Andreas Rossberg. The missing link – dynamic components for ML. In *ICFP '06*.

[27] Andreas Rossberg and Derek Dreyer. Mixin' up the ML module system. *ACM TOPLAS*, 35(1), 2013.

[28] Andreas Rossberg, Claudio V. Russo, and Derek Dreyer. F-ing modules. In *TLDI '10*. Extended version available from the author's website at: `http://www.mpi-sws.org/~rossberg/f-ing`.

[29] Claudio V. Russo. *Types for Modules*. PhD thesis, University of Edinburgh, 1998.

[30] Peter Sewell, James J. Leifer, Keith Wansbrough, Francesco Zappa Nardelli, Mair Allen-Williams, Pierre Habouzit, and Viktor Vafeiadis. Acute: High-level programming language design for distributed computation. *JFP*, 17(4–5), 2007.

[31] David Swasey, Tom Murphy VII, Karl Crary, and Robert Harper. A separate compilation extension to Standard ML. In *ML '06*.

# Combining Proofs and Programs in a Dependently Typed Language

Chris Casinghino    Vilhelm Sjöberg    Stephanie Weirich

University of Pennsylvania

{ccasin,vilhelm,sweirich}@cis.upenn.edu

## Abstract

Most dependently-typed programming languages either require that all expressions terminate (e.g. Coq, Agda, and Epigram), or allow infinite loops but are inconsistent when viewed as logics (e.g. Haskell, ATS, Ωmega). Here, we combine these two approaches into a single dependently-typed core language. The language is composed of two fragments that share a common syntax and overlapping semantics: a logic that guarantees total correctness, and a call-by-value programming language that guarantees type safety but not termination. The two fragments may interact: logical expressions may be used as programs; the logic may soundly reason about potentially nonterminating programs; programs can require logical proofs as arguments; and "mobile" program values, including proofs computed at runtime, may be used as evidence by the logic. This language allows programmers to work with total and partial functions uniformly, providing a smooth path from functional programming to dependently-typed programming.

***Categories and Subject Descriptors*** D.3.1 [*Programming Languages*]: Formal Definitions and Theory

***Keywords*** Dependent types; Termination; General recursion

## 1. Introduction

Dependently typed languages have developed along two different traditions, distinguished by their attitude towards nonterminating programs. On the one hand, languages like Cayenne [6], ATS [13], Ωmega [33] and Haskell [29] treat dependently-typed programming as an extension of ordinary functional programming. These languages enhance ordinary functional programs, defined by general recursion, with more expressive types. On the other hand, languages like Coq [40], Agda [28] and Epigram [23] treat dependently typed programming as a use-case of constructive theorem proving. These systems disallow nontermination because an infinite loop can be given any type and would therefore make the logic inconsistent.

We would like balance between proving and programming, with neither activity given preferential treatment. Although we are sympathetic to the ideal that all programs should be proven correct, we understand that there are practical reasons not to do so. Instead, we desire a language for heterogeneous verification, allowing programmers to devote their verification budget to critical sections. Such a language must support general recursion as natively as a functional programming language, yet at the same time must provide the expressive reasoning capabilities of a constructive logic proof assistant.

In support of this goal, we propose a novel language that is composed of two fragments: a *logical fragment* where every expression is known to terminate, and a *programmatic fragment* that does not provide this assurance. The key idea of our work is to distinguish between these fragments by indexing the typing judgement with a *consistency classifier* $\theta$ that may be $\mathsf{L}$ ("logic") or $\mathsf{P}$ ("program"), thus

$$\Gamma \vdash^{\theta} a : A$$

When $\theta$ is $\mathsf{L}$, the Curry-Howard Isomorphism applies, and we may consider $a$ a proof of the theorem $A$. When $\theta$ is $\mathsf{P}$, the only interpretation of $a$ is as a functional program. Making this distinction means that one language can subsume both functional programming and constructive logic by embedding each in their respective fragments. However, these activities are not too far apart—the syntax and semantics of the two fragments overlap considerably, because the distinction between them is made through typing.

In this paper, we explore the consequences of this design in the context of a dependently-typed programming language, focusing on the following mechanisms that foster interaction between the two fragments.

- First, we define the logical language as a sublanguage of the programmatic language, so that all logical expressions can be used as programs. (Of course, the programmatic language includes forms that are not available to the logic, including general recursion and the elimination of iso-recursive types.)
- We allow uniform reasoning for logical and programmatic expressions through a heterogenous equality type. Two expressions can be shown to be equal based on their evaluation, which is the same for both fragments. Equality proofs can be used implicitly by the type system.
- We internalize the labeled typing judgment as a new type form $A@\theta$. This type can be used by either fragment to manipulate values belonging to the other.
- We identify a set of "mobile types"—those whose values can freely move between the fragments.

To demonstrate the soundness and consistency of these mechanisms, we define a core dependently-typed language, called $\lambda^{\theta}$, that supports these interactions (see Sections 2 and 3). In addition to the $A@\theta$ type, this language includes dependent functions, products, propositional equality, natural numbers, sums, recursive functions



*POPL '14*, January 22–24, 2014, San Diego, CA, USA.

ACM 978-1-4503-2544-8/14/01...$15.00.
http://dx.doi.org/10.1145/2535838.2535883

and iso-recursive types. We prove that this language is type safe and that the L fragment is normalizing and logically consistent (Section 4). Our normalization proof uses a combination of traditional and step-indexed logical relations. All of our metatheoretic results have been completely machine-checked using the Coq proof assistant and are available online[1].

We also explore how our ideas interact with other programming language features. We have implemented a prototype language, `Zombie`, based on the semantics of $\lambda^\theta$, and discuss that implementation in Section 5. `Zombie` extends $\lambda^\theta$ with features that are convenient for dependently-typed programming: parametric polymorphism, type-level computation, user-defined datatypes, and implicit arguments. We have developed a number of examples using `Zombie`; the implementation is available online[2].

We are not the first to consider the combination of total and partial programming in the setting of dependently-typed languages. Partial types [14] and the coinductive partiality monad [11] embed general recursive programs into constructive logic by modeling nontermination. Alternatively, languages such as Idris [10], Aura [18], and F* [38] identify a restricted sublanguage of pure total functions. However, neither of these approaches provide equal support for total and partial programming. We compare them to our work in Section 6.

### 1.1 Combining Proofs and Programs

Before explaining the semantics of $\lambda^\theta$, we conclude this section with a number of examples to demonstrate the key ideas.

In `Zombie`, declarations must indicate whether they belong to the logical or programmatic fragment of the language. For example, a boolean negation operation is trivially terminating, so it is checkable in the logical fragment, as indicated by the tag **`log`** in its definition:

```
log not : Bool → Bool
not b = if b then False else True
```

Likewise, addition for natural numbers can be shown terminating via natural number induction. In the case expression below, `plus` may be called on any subterm of its argument. The argument `n_eq` is a proof that `n'` is a subterm of `n`.

```
log plus : Nat → Nat → Nat
ind plus n m =
  case n [n_eq] of
    Zero    → m
    Succ n' → Succ (plus n' n_eq m)
```

Alternatively, the following natural number division function diverges when `m` is 0, so it must be tagged with **`prog`**. The **`rec`** keyword indicates that this function is implemented using general recursion.

```
prog div : Nat → Nat → Nat
rec div n m = if lt n m then 0
              else plus 1 (div (minus n m) m)
```

***Subsumption.*** All proofs can be used as programs. In the above example, even though the `plus` operation is logical, we can seamlessly use it (and other logical operations such as `lt` and `minus`) directly in a programmatic term, and call it on an argument whose termination behavior is unknown. Thus, the fact that we know that `plus` terminates does not restrict how it may be used—we do not need to duplicate its definition for it to be available to both fragments.

***Proofs containing programs.*** The @-type allows values to be embedded from one fragment into another. For example, the logical language can safely manipulate programmatic values as long as their types indicate (with `@P`) that they are programmatic. Below, consider the definition of a `Maybe` datatype that could contain arbitrary programs.

```
data Maybe (A : Type) where
  Nothing
  Just of (A @ P)
```

As long as the programmatic component is treated carefully, expressions in the logical fragment can work with this data structure. This includes constructing values of the `Maybe` type, and pattern matching on the data structure.

```
log md3 : Maybe (Nat → Nat)
md3 = Just (\x. div 3 x)

log foo : Maybe (Nat → Nat) → (Nat → Nat @ P)
foo x = case x of
  Just y  → y
  Nothing → \x. x
```

However, if the programmatic component is ever used, then the definition must be marked as programmatic, as an embedded function could cause divergence.

```
prog bar : Maybe (Nat → Nat) → Nat → Maybe Nat
bar x y = case x of
      Just f  → Just (f y)
      Nothing → Nothing

prog boom : Maybe Nat
boom = bar md3 0
```

***Proofs about programs.*** Having defined the programmatic function `div`, we might wish to verify facts about it. As a simple example, we prove that `div 6 3` evaluates to 2. We can state and prove these facts using the logical language, even though the object of study may not terminate.

```
log div63 : div 6 3 = 2
div63 = refl
```

The proof above (**`refl`**) is valid when both sides of an equality proposition evaluate to the same result. (To avoid infinite loops, the typechecker will give up and signal an error if the expression does not reach a normal form within 1000 steps. If more evaluation is required the programmer can write e.g. **`refl 5000`**). In languages like Aura or F*, this theorem cannot even be stated because non-value expressions such as `div 6 3` cannot appear in types. This example illustrates an important property of our language, which we call *freedom of speech*: although proofs cannot themselves use general recursion, they are allowed to *refer* to arbitrary programmatic expressions.

As a more complicated example, we might wish to prove that if the divisor is not zero, then the result is less than the dividend. In other words:

```
log div_le : (n:Nat) → (m:Nat) → (eq m 0 = False)
           → (le (div n m) n = True)
```

Above, `eq` is an equality function for natural numbers and `le m n` determines whether $m \leq n$. We do not show proof of the above theorem here, though it is available with our implementation. The

[1] Proofs available at `http://www.cis.upenn.edu/~ccasin/papers/combining-coq.tgz`

[2] Implementation available at `https://code.google.com/p/trellys` in the branch `branches/zombie-trellys-POPL14/`

proof itself uses strong natural number induction to simultaneously show both that division terminates and that the property above holds for the result.

Note that we can only show properties that are provable via finite reduction sequences. For example, we cannot show that division diverges when the dividend is 0, because that divergence is not finitely observable. (The logic does not have a general principle for reasoning about nonterminating programs, such as fixed-point induction. We return to this issue in Section 6.)

***Programs that return proofs.*** An alternative to writing separate proofs about nonterminating programs is to give the programs themselves more specific types that express their correctness. For example, consider writing a SAT solver that we do not want to prove terminating.

A SAT solver takes a formula of $n$ variables and, if the formula is satisfiable, returns a satisfying assignment for some subset of those variables. We can represent the result of a SAT solver using the following datatype declaration. The result for a given formula is either an assignment together with a proof that that assignment satisfies the formula, or UNSAT when the formula is unsatisfiable.

```
data Ans (n : Nat) (form : Formula n) : Type where
  SAT    of (assign : Vector (Maybe Bool) n)
            (proof  : satisfies assign form =
                      (Just True : Maybe Bool))
  UNSAT
```

The main loop of the solver itself takes a formula and the current assignment and returns whether that assignment can be extended to a satisfying one. If the current assignment is known to be satisfying, then that one is returned. Zombie can automatically fill in the _ below with the proof that assign satisfies the formula. If the assignment is known to invalidate the formula, then the result is UNSAT. Otherwise the algorithm must search for an extension to the assignment using techniques such as unit propagation, pure literal assignment, or merely trying both possibilities for an unassigned variable.

```
prog solver : (n:Nat) → (formula : Formula n)
           → Vector (Maybe Bool) n
           → Ans n formula @ L
solver n formula assign =
  case (satisfies assign formula) of
    Just True  → SAT assign _
    Just False → UNSAT
    Nothing    → ....
```

Since the solver is written in the programmatic fragment, it may not terminate. It also may fail to find an assignment even though the formula was satisfiable. However, the type of this function is more informative than if it had been written in ML or Haskell. The @L in its type indicates that if it *does* return a proof of satisfiability, then that value was type checked in the logical fragment.

When a program contains subexpressions from both fragments, values can be handled more freely than expressions. For example, a logical expression cannot call solver directly because of the possibility of divergence. However, if the result of that call has already been bound to a variable, then the logic has access to that result.

```
let prog f      = (... : Formula n) in
let log  empty = repeat (Nothing : Maybe Bool) n in
let prog isSat = (solver n f empty : Ans n f @L) in
let log  prf    = case isSat of
    SAT assignment pf →
        -- ... use proof of satisfiability ...
    UNSAT  → ...
```

$$
\begin{array}{lcl}
\theta & ::= & \mathsf{L} \mid \mathsf{P} \\
a,\ b,\ A,\ B & ::= & \star \mid (x\!:\!A) \to B \mid a = b \\
& \mid & \mathsf{Nat} \mid A + B \mid \Sigma x\!:\!A.B \mid \mu x.A \mid A@\theta \\
& \mid & x \mid \lambda x.a \mid \mathsf{rec}\ f\ x.a \mid \mathsf{ind}\ f\ x.a \mid a\ b \\
& \mid & \mathsf{refl} \mid \mathsf{inl}\ a \mid \mathsf{inr}\ b \\
& \mid & \mathsf{scase}_z\ a\ \mathsf{of}\ \{\mathsf{inl}\ x \Rightarrow a_1; \mathsf{inr}\ y \Rightarrow a_2\} \\
& \mid & \langle a, b\rangle \mid \mathsf{pcase}_z\ a\ \mathsf{of}\ \{(x,\ y) \Rightarrow b\} \\
& \mid & \mathsf{Z} \mid \mathsf{S}\ a \mid \mathsf{ncase}_z\ a\ \mathsf{of}\ \{Z \Rightarrow a_1; \mathsf{S}\ x \Rightarrow a_2\} \\
& \mid & \mathsf{roll}\ a \mid \mathsf{unroll}\ a \\
\\
v & ::= & \star \mid (x\!:\!A) \to B \mid a = b \\
& \mid & \mathsf{Nat} \mid A + B \mid \Sigma x\!:\!A.B \mid \mu x.A \mid A@\theta \\
& \mid & x \mid \lambda x.a \mid \mathsf{rec}\ f\ x.a \mid \mathsf{ind}\ f\ x.a \mid \mathsf{refl} \\
& \mid & \mathsf{inl}\ v \mid \mathsf{inr}\ v \mid \langle v_1, v_2\rangle \mid \mathsf{Z} \mid \mathsf{S}\ v \mid \mathsf{roll}\ v
\end{array}
$$

$\boxed{a \rightsquigarrow b}$

$$\frac{}{(\lambda x.a)\ v \rightsquigarrow [v/x]a}\ \textsc{SLam}$$

$$\frac{}{(\mathsf{rec}\ f\ x.a)\ v \rightsquigarrow [v/x][\mathsf{rec}\ f\ x.a/f]a}\ \textsc{SFun}$$

$$\frac{}{(\mathsf{ind}\ f\ x.a)\ v \rightsquigarrow [v/x][\lambda y.\lambda z.(\mathsf{ind}\ f\ x.a)\ y/f]a}\ \textsc{SInd}$$

$$\frac{}{\mathsf{scase}_z\ \mathsf{inl}\ v\ \mathsf{of}\ \{\mathsf{inl}\ x \Rightarrow a_1; \mathsf{inr}\ x \Rightarrow a_2\} \rightsquigarrow [\mathsf{refl}/z][v/x]a_1}\ \textsc{SCL}$$

$$\frac{}{\mathsf{scase}_z\ \mathsf{inr}\ v\ \mathsf{of}\ \{\mathsf{inl}\ x \Rightarrow a_1; \mathsf{inr}\ x \Rightarrow a_2\} \rightsquigarrow [\mathsf{refl}/z][v/x]a_2}\ \textsc{SCR}$$

$$\frac{}{\mathsf{pcase}_z\ \langle v_1, v_2\rangle\ \mathsf{of}\ \{(x,\ y) \Rightarrow a\} \rightsquigarrow [\mathsf{refl}/z][v_1/x][v_2/y]a}\ \textsc{SCP}$$

$$\frac{}{\mathsf{unroll}\ (\mathsf{roll}\ v) \rightsquigarrow v}\ \textsc{SUnroll}$$

**Figure 1.** Expressions, values, and operational semantics (excerpt)

***Mobile types*** Finally, some types have the same meaning in both fragments, so they do not benefit from being tagged with a consistency classifier. For example, a value of type Nat can never cause divergence, so it is safe to be used in logical expressions even when not marked as @L. Similarly, the Ans type above is also mobile, so the @L annotation on the type of solver is actually unnecessary. This observation simplifies programming as the only function arguments that must be annotated with their fragment are those that are not mobile.

## 2. The $\lambda^\theta$ language

We begin our technical development with an overview of the formal language, $\lambda^\theta$. This language is based on a call-by-value (CBV) variant of lambda calculus. Its syntax is shown in Figure 1. For uniformity, terms, types and the single kind $\star$ (the "type" of types) are drawn from the same syntactic category, as in pure type systems [7]. The first two lines of the figure list the type forms, the following lines list the terms. By convention, we use lowercase metavariables $a, b$ for expressions that are terms and uppercase metavariables $A, B$ for expressions that are types.

The $\lambda^\theta$ values $v$ and key rules of the operational semantics are also shown in Figure 1. The reduction relation $a \rightsquigarrow b$ defines a small-step call-by-value semantics. The slightly unusual beta rule for natural number induction (SInd) is described in Section 2.1. To save space, most rules have been omitted. The full set of rules can be found in the companion technical report[3].

Values include the standard components of functional programming: recursive functions $\mathsf{rec}\ f\ x.a$, nonrecursive functions $\lambda x.a$, natural numbers (constructed by $\mathsf{Z}$ and $\mathsf{S}\ a$ and eliminated by $\mathsf{ncase}$), disjoint unions (constructed by $\mathsf{inl}\ a$ and $\mathsf{inr}\ a$ and eliminated by $\mathsf{scase}$), dependently typed pairs (constructed by $\langle a, b\rangle$ and eliminated by $\mathsf{pcase}$), and recursive data (introduced by $\mathsf{roll}\ a$ and eliminated by $\mathsf{unroll}\ a$). Values also include $\star$, all type forms, a trivial equality proof $\mathsf{refl}$, and variables. Including variables is safe because CBV evaluation only substitutes values for variables and it is useful because it allows the $\lambda^\theta$ type checker to reduce open terms.

We chose CBV because of its simple cost model, but this choice also affects the interaction between the logical and programmatic fragments. As shown in Sections 2.2 and 3.3, the type system takes advantage of the fact that values cannot induce nontermination. As a result, some typing rules apply only to values.

Note that expressions do not contain type annotations. Types describe terms but do not interfere with equality. We do not want terms with the same runtime behavior to be considered unequal just because they have different annotations.

Due to the lack of annotations, it is not possible to algorithmically compute the type of a $\lambda^\theta$ term. This is not a problem because we do not intend programmers to write these terms directly. Instead, our implementation uses an annotated *surface* language that the type checker elaborates into typing derivations (see Section 5).

The rest of this section describes the specific details of $\lambda^\theta$, including its basic judgements (Section 2.1), and treatment of equality (Section 2.2). In the next section, we introduce the novel features of our language that permit the interaction between the logical and programmatic fragments of the language.

### 2.1 Classifying terminating and nonterminating expressions

The starting point for $\lambda^\theta$ is a dependent type theory where the typing judgment $\Gamma \vdash^\theta a : A$ is indexed by a consistency classifier $\theta$. The judgement is designed so that expressions that type check at $\mathsf{L}$ always terminate.

Figure 2 shows the typing rules for the basic building blocks of the language—variables, functions and various data structures and their types. Because we work with a collapsed syntax, we use the type system to identify which expressions are types: $A$ is a well-formed type if $\Gamma \vdash^\theta A : \star$.

Contexts are lists of assumptions about the types of variables.

$$\Gamma ::= \emptyset \mid \Gamma, x :^\theta A$$

Each variable in the context is tagged with $\theta$ to indicate its fragment, and this tag is checked in the TVAR typing rule. A context is *valid*, written $\vdash \Gamma$, if each type $A$ is valid in the corresponding fragment.

The rules TARR, TSIGMA, TSUM, and TMU check types for well-kindedness. For example, TARR checks a function type by checking the the domain and range. We discuss the premise $\mathsf{Mobile}\,(A)$, which asserts that $A$ is a mobile type, in Section 3.3.

There are three ways to define functions in $\lambda^\theta$. Rule TLAM types non-recursive $\lambda$-expressions in the logical fragment, whereas rule TREC types general recursive rec-expressions and can only be used in the programmatic fragment.

Additionally, terminating recursion over natural numbers is provided in the logical fragment by rule TIND. When typechecking the body of a terminating recursive function ($\mathsf{ind}\ f\ x.b$), the recursive

$\boxed{\vdash \Gamma}$

$$\frac{}{\vdash \cdot}\ \textsc{CNil} \qquad \frac{\vdash \Gamma}{\vdash \Gamma, x :^\theta \star}\ \textsc{CStar} \qquad \frac{\vdash \Gamma \quad \Gamma \vdash^\theta A : \star}{\vdash \Gamma, x :^\theta A}\ \textsc{CType}$$

$\boxed{\Gamma \vdash^\theta a : A}$

$$\frac{(x :^\theta A) \in \Gamma \quad \vdash \Gamma}{\Gamma \vdash^\theta x : A}\ \textsc{TVar} \qquad \frac{\Gamma \vdash^\theta A : \star \quad \mathsf{Mobile}\,(A) \quad \Gamma, x :^\theta A \vdash^\theta B : \star}{\Gamma \vdash^\theta (x\!:\!A) \to B : \star}\ \textsc{TArr}$$

$$\frac{\Gamma \vdash^\theta b : (x\!:\!A) \to B \quad \Gamma \vdash^\theta a : A \quad \Gamma \vdash^\theta [a/x]B : \star}{\Gamma \vdash^\theta b\ a : [a/x]B}\ \textsc{TApp}$$

$$\frac{\Gamma, x :^{\mathsf{L}} A \vdash^{\mathsf{L}} b : B \quad \Gamma \vdash^{\mathsf{L}} (x\!:\!A) \to B : \star}{\Gamma \vdash^{\mathsf{L}} \lambda x.b : (x\!:\!A) \to B}\ \textsc{TLam}$$

$$\frac{\Gamma, f :^{\mathsf{P}} (x\!:\!A) \to B, x :^{\mathsf{P}} A \vdash^{\mathsf{P}} b : B \quad \Gamma \vdash^{\mathsf{P}} (x\!:\!A) \to B : \star}{\Gamma \vdash^{\mathsf{P}} \mathsf{rec}\ f\ x.b : (x\!:\!A) \to B}\ \textsc{TRec}$$

$$\frac{\Gamma, x :^{\mathsf{L}} \mathsf{Nat}, f :^{\mathsf{L}} (y\!:\!\mathsf{Nat}) \to (z\!:\!\mathsf{S}\ y = x) \to B \vdash^{\mathsf{L}} b : B \quad \Gamma \vdash^{\mathsf{L}} (x\!:\!\mathsf{Nat}) \to B : \star}{\Gamma \vdash^{\mathsf{L}} \mathsf{ind}\ f\ x.b : (x\!:\!\mathsf{Nat}) \to B}\ \textsc{TInd}$$

$$\frac{\Gamma \vdash^\theta A : \star \quad \Gamma \vdash^\theta B : \star}{\Gamma \vdash^\theta A + B : \star}\ \textsc{TSum}$$

$$\frac{\Gamma \vdash^\theta a : A \quad \Gamma \vdash^\theta A + B : \star}{\Gamma \vdash^\theta \mathsf{inl}\ a : A + B}\ \textsc{TInl} \qquad \frac{\Gamma \vdash^\theta b : B \quad \Gamma \vdash^\theta A + B : \star}{\Gamma \vdash^\theta \mathsf{inr}\ b : A + B}\ \textsc{TInr}$$

$$\frac{\Gamma \vdash^\theta a : A_1 + A_2 \quad \Gamma \vdash^\theta B : \star \quad \Gamma, x :^\theta A_1, z :^{\mathsf{L}} \mathsf{inl}\ x = a \vdash^\theta b_1 : B \quad \Gamma, x :^\theta A_2, z :^{\mathsf{L}} \mathsf{inr}\ x = a \vdash^\theta b_2 : B}{\Gamma \vdash^\theta \mathsf{scase}_z\ a\ \mathsf{of}\ \{\mathsf{inl}\ x \Rightarrow b_1; \mathsf{inr}\ x \Rightarrow b_2\} : B}\ \textsc{TSCase}$$

$$\frac{\Gamma \vdash^\theta A : \star \quad \mathsf{Mobile}\,(A) \quad \Gamma, x :^\theta A \vdash^\theta B : \star}{\Gamma \vdash^\theta \Sigma x\!:\!A.B : \star}\ \textsc{TSigma} \qquad \frac{\Gamma \vdash^\theta \Sigma x\!:\!A.B : \star \quad \Gamma \vdash^\theta a : A \quad \Gamma \vdash^\theta b : [a/x]B \quad \Gamma \vdash^\theta [a/x]B : \star}{\Gamma \vdash^\theta \langle a, b\rangle : \Sigma x\!:\!A.B}\ \textsc{TPair}$$

$$\frac{\Gamma \vdash^\theta a : \Sigma x\!:\!A_1.A_2 \quad \Gamma \vdash^\theta B : \star \quad \Gamma, x :^\theta A_1, y :^\theta A_2, z :^{\mathsf{L}} \langle x, y\rangle = a \vdash^\theta b : B}{\Gamma \vdash^\theta \mathsf{pcase}_z\ a\ \mathsf{of}\ \{(x,\ y) \Rightarrow b\} : B}\ \textsc{TPCase}$$

$$\frac{\Gamma, x :^{\mathsf{L}} \star \vdash^{\mathsf{L}} A : \star}{\Gamma \vdash^{\mathsf{L}} \mu x.A : \star}\ \textsc{TMu} \qquad \frac{\Gamma \vdash^\theta a : [\mu x.A/x]A \quad \Gamma \vdash^\theta \mu x.A : \star}{\Gamma \vdash^\theta \mathsf{roll}\ a : \mu x.A}\ \textsc{TRoll}$$

$$\frac{\Gamma \vdash^{\mathsf{P}} a : \mu x.A \quad \Gamma \vdash^{\mathsf{P}} [\mu x.A/x]A : \star}{\Gamma \vdash^{\mathsf{P}} \mathsf{unroll}\ a : [\mu x.A/x]A}\ \textsc{TUnroll}$$

**Figure 2.** Typing: variables, functions, and datatypes (rules for Nat omitted)

[3] Available from `http://www.seas.upenn.edu/~ccasin/papers/combining-TR.pdf` and as University of Pennsylvania CIS Technical Report MS-CIS-13-08.

call $f$ takes an extra argument proving that it is being applied to the predecessor of the initial argument $x$. This ensures termination. When beta-reducing such an expression, this argument is ignored by wrapping the function in an extra lambda (rule SIND from Figure 1).

The rule for function application, TAPP, differs from the usual application rule in pure dependently-typed languages in the additional third premise $\Gamma \vdash^\theta [a/x]B : s$, which checks that the result type is well-formed. Some rules of the language (such as $\beta$-reduction) are sensitive to whether terms are values. Because values include variables, substituting an expression $a$ for a value $x$ could cause $B$ to no longer type check.

Any dependently typed language that combines pure and effectful code will likely have to restrict the application rule in some way. Previous work [18, 21, 38] uses a more restrictive typing for applications, by splitting it into two rules: one which permits only *value dependency* and requires the argument to be a value, and one which allows a non-dependent function to be applied to an arbitrary argument. Since substituting a value can never violate a value restriction in $B$, our application rule subsumes the value-dependent version. Likewise, in the case of no dependency, the premise can never fail because the substitution has no effect on $B$.

Being able to call dependent functions with non-value arguments is useful when writing explicit proofs. For example, a programmer may want to first prove a lemma about addition

```
log plus_zero : (n:Nat) → plus n 0 = n
```

and then instantiate the lemma to prove a theorem about a particular expression in the logical fragment.

```
plus_zero (f x) : plus (f x) 0 = (f x)
```

The rules for sum types (TSUM, TINL, TINR, and TSCASE) provide dependent case analysis. The term scase binds the logical variable $z$ inside both branches of the case. This variable provides an equality between the scrutinee and the pattern of the branch so that type checking is flow-sensitive. At runtime, this variable is replaced by refl because the scrutinee must match the pattern for the branch to be taken.

The rules for dependent products (TSIGMA, TPAIR, TPCASE) allow the type of the second component of the pair to depend on the value of the first component. As with function application, the premise $\Gamma \vdash^\theta [a/x]B : \star$ ensures that substituting the expression $a$ does not violate any assumptions made about the value $x$ in the type of the second component. Analogously to sums, the eliminator for pairs makes available a logical proof $z$ that equates the scrutinee to the pattern in the body of the match. The availability of this equality means that the strong elimination forms (projections) for $\Sigma$-types are derivable.

Finally, the rules TMU, TROLL and TUNROLL deal with general recursive types. These are the standard rules for iso-recursive types (see, e.g., [30]). But recursive types with negative occurrences—that is, with the recursive variable appearing to the left of an arrow, such as $\mu x.(x \to \mathsf{Nat})$—are a potential source of nontermination. To ensure normalization, it suffices to restrict the the elimination rule TUNROLL to be in P. The introduction rule TROLL can be used in both fragments. This reflects the fact that it is not dangerous to *construct* negative datatype values; the potential nontermination comes from their elimination.

### 2.2 Reasoning about equivalence

A big benefit of combining termination-checking with dependent types is that it is possible to write proofs *about* programs. For example, in the introduction we showed a proof that when the divisor is not zero, natural number division produces a result less than the dividend. Our rules for propositional equality (Figure 3) are designed to support such reasoning uniformly, based only on the runtime behavior of the expressions being equated, and independent of the fragment that they are defined in.

$\boxed{\Gamma \vdash^\theta a : A}$

$$\frac{\Gamma \vdash^{\mathsf{P}} a : A \quad \Gamma \vdash^{\mathsf{P}} b : B}{\Gamma \vdash^{\mathsf{L}} a = b : \star}\ \text{TEQ}$$

$$\frac{a \Rrightarrow^* c \quad b \Rrightarrow^* c \quad \Gamma \vdash^{\theta_1} a : A \quad \Gamma \vdash^{\theta_2} b : B}{\Gamma \vdash^{\mathsf{L}} \mathsf{refl} : a = b}\ \text{TREFL}$$

$$\frac{\Gamma \vdash^{\mathsf{L}} b : b_1 = b_2 \quad \Gamma \vdash^\theta a : [b_1/x]A \quad \Gamma \vdash^\theta [b_2/x]A : \star}{\Gamma \vdash^\theta a : [b_2/x]A}\ \text{TCONV}$$

**Figure 3.** Typing: equality

Therefore, the rule TEQ shows that the type $a = b$ is well-formed and in the logical fragment even when $a$ and $b$ can be type checked only programmatically. This is freedom of speech: proofs can refer to nonterminating programs.

The term refl is the primitive proof of equality. Rule TREFL says that refl is a proof of $a = b$ just when $a$ and $b$ reduce to a common expression. The notion of reduction used in the rule is *parallel reduction*, denoted $a \Rrightarrow b$. This relation extends the ordinary evaluation $a \rightsquigarrow b$ by allowing reduction under binders, e.g. $(\lambda x.1 + 1) \Rrightarrow (\lambda x.2)$ even though $(\lambda x.1 + 1)$ is already a value. Having this extra flexibility makes equality more expressive and simplifies the proof of preservation.

Proven equalities are used to substitute expressions in types by the elimination rule TCONV. The proof term is checked in L to ensure it is a valid proof. We demand that the equality proof used in conversion type checks in the logical fragment for type safety. All types are inhabited in the programmatic fragment, so if we permitted the user to convert using a programmatic proof of, say, $\mathsf{Nat} = \mathsf{Nat} \to \mathsf{Nat}$, it would be easy to create a stuck term. Similar to TAPP, we need to check that $b_2$ does not violate any value restrictions, so the last premise checks the well-formedness of the type given to the converted term. Rule TCONV is quite general, and may be used to change some small part of $A$ or the entire type by picking $x$ for $A$.

This treatment of equality is a variant of Sjöberg *et al.* [34]. However, that setting did not include a logical sublanguage; instead it enforced soundness by requiring the proof term used in conversion to be a value.

Uses of TCONV are not marked in the term because they are not relevant at runtime. Again, types should describe terms without interfering with equality; we do not want terms with the same runtime behavior to be considered unequal due to uses of conversion.

## 3. Interactions between the fragments

What is interesting about $\lambda^\theta$ is how its two fragments interact. In the introduction, we discussed ways in which logical and programmatic terms work together. Below, we discuss the technical machinery of the type system that supports this interaction.

### 3.1 Subsumption

Every logical expression can be safely used programmatically. We reflect this fact into the type system by the rule TSUB, which says that if a term $a$ type checks logically, then it will also type check programmatically. For example, a logical term can always be supplied to a function expecting a programmatic argument. This rule is useful to avoid code duplication. A function defined in the

$$\boxed{\Gamma \vdash^{\theta} a : A}$$

$$\frac{\Gamma \vdash^{\mathsf{L}} a : A}{\Gamma \vdash^{\mathsf{P}} a : A}\ \textsc{TSub} \qquad \frac{\Gamma \vdash^{\theta'} A : \star}{\Gamma \vdash^{\theta} A@\theta' : \star}\ \textsc{TAt}$$

$$\frac{\Gamma \vdash^{\theta} v : A@\theta' \quad \Gamma \vdash^{\theta'} A : \star}{\Gamma \vdash^{\theta'} v : A}\ \textsc{TUnboxVal} \qquad \frac{\Gamma \vdash^{\theta} a : A \quad \Gamma \vdash^{\theta} A : \star}{\Gamma \vdash^{\mathsf{P}} a : A@\theta}\ \textsc{TBoxP}$$

$$\frac{\Gamma \vdash^{\mathsf{L}} a : A \quad \Gamma \vdash^{\theta} A : \star}{\Gamma \vdash^{\mathsf{L}} a : A@\theta}\ \textsc{TBoxL} \qquad \frac{\Gamma \vdash^{\mathsf{P}} v : A \quad \Gamma \vdash^{\mathsf{P}} A : \star}{\Gamma \vdash^{\mathsf{L}} v : A@\mathsf{P}}\ \textsc{TBoxLV}$$

**Figure 4.** Typing: subsumption and internalized consistency classification

logical fragment can be used without penalty in the programmatic fragment.

Subsumption also eliminates duplication in the design of the language. For example, we need only one type $a = b$ to talk about when two programmatic or two logical terms are equal. In fact, we can also equate logical and programmatic expressions.

### 3.2 Internalized Consistency Classification

To provide a general mechanism for logical expressions to appear in programs and programmatic values to appear in proofs, we introduce a type that internalizes the typing judgment, written $A@\theta$. Nonterminating programs can take logical proofs as preconditions (with functions of type $(x : A@\mathsf{L}) \to B$), return them as postconditions (with functions of type $(x : A) \to (B@\mathsf{L})$), and store them in data structures (with pairs of type $\Sigma x : A.(B@\mathsf{L})$). At the same time, logical lemmas can use @ to manipulate values from the programmatic fragment.

The rules for the $A@\theta$ type appear in Figure 4. Intuitively, the judgment $\Gamma \vdash^{\theta_1} a : A@\theta_2$ holds if the fragment $\theta_1$ may safely observe that $\Gamma \vdash^{\theta_2} a : A$. This intuition is captured by the three introduction rules. The programmatic fragment can internalize any typing judgement (TBoxP), but in the logical fragment (TBoxL and TBoxLV) we sometimes need a restriction to ensure termination. Therefore, rule TBoxLV only applies when the subject of the typing rule is a value. (The rule TBoxL can introduce $A@\theta$ for any $\theta$ since logical terms are also programmatic). Both introduction and elimination of @ is unmarked in the syntax, so the reduction behavior of an expression is unaffected by whether the type system deems it to be provably terminating or not.

For example, a recursive function $f$ can require an argument to be a proof by marking it @L, e.g., $A@\mathsf{L} \to B$, forcing that argument to be checked in fragment L. Similarly, a logical lemma $g$ can be applied to a programmatic value by marking it @P:

$$\frac{\Gamma \vdash^{\mathsf{P}} f : A@\mathsf{L} \to B \quad \dfrac{\Gamma \vdash^{\mathsf{L}} a : A}{\Gamma \vdash^{\mathsf{P}} a : A@\mathsf{L}}\ \textsc{TBoxP}}{\Gamma \vdash^{\mathsf{P}} f\ a : B}\ \textsc{TApp}$$

$$\frac{\Gamma \vdash^{\mathsf{L}} g : A@\mathsf{P} \to B \quad \dfrac{\Gamma \vdash^{\mathsf{P}} v : A}{\Gamma \vdash^{\mathsf{L}} v : A@\mathsf{P}}\ \textsc{TBoxLV}}{\Gamma \vdash^{\mathsf{L}} g\ v : B}\ \textsc{TApp}$$

Of course, $g$ can only be defined in the logical fragment if it is careful to not use its argument in unsafe ways. For example, using TConv we can prove a lemma of type

```
(n: Nat) → (f: (Nat → Nat)@P) → (f (plus n 0) = f n)
```

because reasoning about `f` does not require calling `f` at runtime.

$$\boxed{\mathsf{Mobile}\,(A)} \qquad \frac{}{\mathsf{Mobile}\,(A@\theta)}\ \textsc{MAt}$$

$$\frac{}{\mathsf{Mobile}\,(a = b)}\ \textsc{MEq} \qquad \frac{\mathsf{Mobile}\,(A) \quad \mathsf{Mobile}\,(B)}{\mathsf{Mobile}\,(\Sigma x{:}A.B)}\ \textsc{MSigma}$$

$$\frac{}{\mathsf{Mobile}\,(\mathsf{Nat})}\ \textsc{MNat} \qquad \frac{\mathsf{Mobile}\,(A) \quad \mathsf{Mobile}\,(B)}{\mathsf{Mobile}\,(A + B)}\ \textsc{MSum}$$

$$\boxed{\Gamma \vdash^{\theta} a : A}$$

$$\frac{\Gamma \vdash^{\mathsf{P}} v : A \quad \Gamma \vdash^{\mathsf{L}} A : \star \quad \mathsf{Mobile}\,(A)}{\Gamma \vdash^{\mathsf{L}} v : A}\ \textsc{TMVal}$$

$$\frac{\begin{array}{c}\Gamma \vdash^{\theta} a : (A_1 + A_2)@\theta' \quad \Gamma \vdash^{\theta} B : \star \\ \Gamma, x :^{\theta'} A_1, z :^{\mathsf{L}} \mathsf{inl}\, x = a \vdash^{\theta} b_1 : B \\ \Gamma, x :^{\theta'} A_2, z :^{\mathsf{L}} \mathsf{inr}\, x = a \vdash^{\theta} b_2 : B\end{array}}{\Gamma \vdash^{\theta} \mathsf{scase}_z\ a\ \mathsf{of}\ \{\mathsf{inl}\ x \Rightarrow b_1; \mathsf{inr}\ x \Rightarrow b_2\} : B}\ \textsc{TSCase'}$$

$$\frac{\begin{array}{c}\Gamma \vdash^{\theta} a : (\Sigma x{:}A_1.A_2)@\theta' \quad \Gamma \vdash^{\theta} B : \star \\ \Gamma, x :^{\theta'} A_1, y :^{\theta'} A_2, z :^{\mathsf{L}} \langle x, y\rangle = a \vdash^{\theta} b : B\end{array}}{\Gamma \vdash^{\theta} \mathsf{pcase}_z\ a\ \mathsf{of}\ \{(x,\ y) \Rightarrow b\} : B}\ \textsc{TPCase'}$$

**Figure 5.** Typing: mobile types and cross-fragment case expressions

There is no way to apply a logical lemma to a programmatic *non*-value expression. If an expression `a` may diverge then so may `f a`, so we must not assign it a type in the logical fragment.[4] However, we can work around this restriction by either first evaluating `a` to a value in the programmatic fragment or by thunking.

The @-types are eliminated by the rule TUnboxVal. To preserve termination, the rule is restricted to apply only to values.

Recall the function `solver` of type

```
prog solver : (n:Nat) → (f:Formula n)
         → Vector (Maybe Bool) n → (Ans n f)@L
```

In the introduction, we asserted that the following code type checks.

```
let prog isSat = (solver n f empty : Ans n f @L) in
let log  prf = case isSat of
    SAT a pf → -- ... here pf is logical ...
    UNSAT    → -- ...
```

In this example, the logical program `prf` cannot directly treat `solver n f empty` as a proof because it may diverge. However, once it has been evaluated to a value, it can be safely used by the logical fragment. Above, the let binding forces evaluation of the expression `solver n f empty`, introducing a new programmatic variable `isSat : Ans n f @ L` into the context. Because variables are values, any logical context can freely use the variable through TUnboxVal even though it was computed by the programmatic language.

### 3.3 Mobile types

The consistency classifier tracks which *expressions* are known to come from a normalizing language. For some types of *values*, however, the rules described so far can be unnecessarily conservative. For example, while a programmatic expression of type `Nat` may diverge, a programmatic value of that type is just a number, so we can treat it as if it were logical. On the other hand, we can not treat

[4] This is one drawback of working in a strict rather than a lazy language. If we know that `f` is nonstrict, then this application is indeed safe.

a programmatic function value as logical, since it might cause nontermination when applied.

The rule TMVAL (Figure 5) allows values to be moved from the programmatic to the logical fragment. It relies on an auxiliary judgment Mobile $(A)$.. Intuitively, a type is mobile if the same set of values inhabit the type when $\theta = \mathsf{L}$ and when $\theta = \mathsf{P}$. In particular, these types do not include functions (though any type may be made mobile by tagging its fragment with @).

Concretely, the natural number type Nat is mobile, as is the primitive equality type (which is inhabited by the single constructor refl, as discussed in Section 2.2). Any @-type is mobile, since it fixes a particular $\theta$ independent of the one on the typing judgment. Sum and pair types are mobile if their component types are.

Even if a sum type is not mobile, it is always safe to do one level of pattern matching on one of its values, since such a value must start with a constructor. We reflect that in the rule TSCASE', which generalizes TSCASE from the previous section. This rule allows a scrutinee that type checks in one fragment $\theta'$ to be eliminated in another fragment $\theta$. This lets the logical language reason by case analysis on programmatic values. Similarly, TPCASE' is a more general version of the rule TPCASE. The two rules shown here are the ones actually included in our formalization.

The mobile rule lets the programmer write simpler types, because mobile types never need to be tagged with logical classifiers. For example, without loss of generality we can give a function the type $(a = b) \rightarrow B$ instead of $((a = b)@\mathsf{L}) \rightarrow B$, since when needed, the body of the function can treat the argument as logical through TMVAL. Similarly, multiple @'s have no effect beyond the innermost @ in a type. Values of type $A@\mathsf{P}@\mathsf{L}@\mathsf{P}@\mathsf{L}@\mathsf{P}$ can be used as if they had type $A@\mathsf{P}$.

In fact, the arguments to functions must always have mobile types. This restriction, enforced by rule TARR, means that higher-order functions must use @-types to specify which fragment their arguments belong to. For example, the type $(\mathsf{Nat} \rightarrow \mathsf{Nat}) \rightarrow A$ is not well-formed, so the programmer must choose either $((\mathsf{Nat} \rightarrow \mathsf{Nat})@\mathsf{L}) \rightarrow A$ or $((\mathsf{Nat} \rightarrow \mathsf{Nat})@\mathsf{P}) \rightarrow A$.

In either case, programmers benefit from implicit unboxing. For example, checking well-formedness of a type like

```
(f : (Nat → Nat)@P) → f (plus n 0) = f n
```

implicitly uses TUNBOXVAL. But the equation still talks about the expression `f n`. If we instead had to use explicit unboxing to eliminate the @-type, as in `(unbox f) n`, there would be no way to write a logical lemma proving the original equation. By contrast, mobile arguments do not need nor benefit from tagging.

The reason that function arguments must be mobile is to account for contravariance. Through subsumption, we can introduce a function in the logical fragment and use it in the programmatic:

$$\dfrac{\dfrac{\Gamma, x :^{\mathsf{L}} A \vdash^{\mathsf{L}} b : B}{\Gamma \vdash^{\mathsf{L}} (\lambda x.b) : (x : A) \rightarrow B}\ \text{TLAM}}{\Gamma \vdash^{\mathsf{P}} (\lambda x.b) : (x : A) \rightarrow B}\ \text{TSUB}$$

Here, the definition of $b$ assumed $x$ was logical, yet when the function is called it can be given a programmatic argument. For this derivation to be sound, we need to know that $A$ means the same thing in the two fragments, which is exactly what Mobile $(A)$ checks.

## 4. Metatheory

We now describe the metatheory of $\lambda^\theta$. We are interested in two properties. First, that the entire language is type safe, including both the L and P fragments. Second, that any closed term in the L fragment normalizes, which implies logical consistency.

Type safety is proven using standard progress and preservation theorems. Since the rules TCONV and TCONTRA allow stuck terms to type check given a contradiction, the progress theorem depends on logical consistency. For this reason, we first prove preservation, then normalization and consistency, and finally progress.

The theorems in this paper have been checked in Coq. To prove certain facts about our logical relation we needed a standard axiom of functional extensionality. This axiom is known to be consistent with Coq's logic [41].

### 4.1 Preservation

As usual, the preservation proof relies on weakening, substitution and inversion lemmas. The weakening lemma is standard. Due to the value restrictions in the type system, the substitution lemma is restricted to values:

LEMMA 1 (Substitution). *If* $\Gamma_1, x :^{\theta'} B, \Gamma_2 \vdash^\theta a : A$ *and* $\Gamma_1 \vdash^{\theta'} v : B$, *then* $\Gamma_1, [v/x]\Gamma_2 \vdash^\theta [v/x]a : [v/x]A$.

However, our inversion lemmas are more complicated than usual, because one of the design goals of $\lambda^\theta$ is that typing rules without runtime effects should not require annotation. In particular, uses of TCONV and TBOXP/L/LV are not marked.

For example, consider inversion for $\lambda$-expressions. Usually, it is the case that if $\Gamma \vdash (\lambda x.b) : A$, then $A$ is $\beta$-convertible with some arrow type $(x : B_1) \rightarrow B_2$ and $\Gamma, x : B_1 \vdash b : B_2$. In $\lambda^\theta$ this is not true: if there were a hypothesis $(x :^{\mathsf{L}} (\mathsf{Nat} \rightarrow \mathsf{Nat}) = \mathsf{Nat}) \in \Gamma$, the expression could also have been given type Nat using TCONV. (Restricting preservation to empty contexts would not help, since at this point in the proof—before proving consistency—we cannot rule out that this equality is provable). Alternatively, if the BOX rules were used, $A$ may be an @-type. Taking this into account, our inversion lemma reads:

LEMMA 2 (Inversion for $\lambda$-expressions). *If* $\Gamma \vdash^\theta (\lambda x.b) : B$, *then there is some* $p$ *and* $(x : B_1) \rightarrow B_2$ *such that either*

1. $\Gamma \vdash^{\mathsf{L}} p : B = ((x : B_1) \rightarrow B_2)$ *and* $\Gamma, x :^\theta B_1 \vdash^\theta b : B_2$,
2. *or there are some* $\theta' \ldots \theta''$ *such that* $\Gamma \vdash^{\mathsf{L}} p : B = (((x : B_1) \rightarrow B_2)@\theta' \ldots @\theta'')$ *and* $\Gamma, x :^{\theta'} B_1 \vdash^{\theta'} b : B_2$.

With this and other similar inversion lemmas, we can prove preservation.

THEOREM 3 (Preservation). *If* $\Gamma \vdash^\theta a : A$ *and* $a \rightsquigarrow a'$, *then* $\Gamma \vdash^\theta a' : A$.

The proof of the preservation theorem requires the addition of type constructor discrimination and injectivity rules (Figure 6) to the type system. The discrimination rule TCONTRA eliminates contradictory equalities. If we can prove a contradiction we must be in unreachable code, so we allow giving any typeable expression $a$ any wellformed type $B$ at any $\theta'$.

An equation $B_1 = B_2$ counts as contradictory if the *head forms* of both sides are defined and unequal. The head form of a type is its outermost constructor. For example, the head form of $(x : A) \rightarrow B$ is $\rightarrow$, and the head form of Nat is Nat. The complete definition of $\mathsf{hd}(A)$ appears in the companion technical report.

The injectivity rules invert equality proofs between type forms. For example, from a proof $\Gamma \vdash^{\mathsf{L}} p : ((x : A_1) \rightarrow A_2) = ((x : B_1) \rightarrow B_2)$ we can also derive $\Gamma \vdash^{\mathsf{L}} p : A_1 = B_1$. Similar typing rules are available for @, sum and pair types. These are elided here for space, but included in the technical report.

These rules are necessitated by the weak inversion lemmas. Consider, e.g., the case when a function application beta reduces, $(\lambda x.b)\ v \rightsquigarrow [v/x]b$. From the premises of the rule TAPP we know that $\Gamma \vdash^\theta (\lambda x.b) : (x : A_1) \rightarrow A_2$ and $\Gamma \vdash^\theta v : A_1$, and from

$\boxed{\Gamma \vdash^{\theta} a : A}$

$$\frac{\Gamma \vdash^{\theta} a : ((x{:}A_1) \to A_2) = ((x{:}B_1) \to B_2) \quad \Gamma \vdash^{\theta} A_1 = B_1 : \star}{\Gamma \vdash^{\theta} a : A_1 = B_1}\ \text{TArrInv1}$$

$$\frac{\Gamma \vdash^{\mathsf{L}} a_1 : B_1 = B_2 \quad \mathsf{hd}(B_1) \neq \mathsf{hd}(B_2) \quad \Gamma \vdash^{\theta} a : A \quad \Gamma \vdash^{\theta} A : \star \quad \Gamma \vdash^{\theta'} B : \star}{\Gamma \vdash^{\theta'} a : B}\ \text{TContra}$$

$$\frac{\Gamma \vdash^{\theta} a : ((x{:}A_1) \to A_2) = ((x{:}B_1) \to B_2) \quad \Gamma \vdash^{\theta'} v : A_1 \quad \Gamma \vdash^{\theta} [v/x]A_2 = [v/x]B_2 : \star}{\Gamma \vdash^{\theta} a : [v/x]A_2 = [v/x]B_2}\ \text{TArrInv2}$$

**Figure 6.** Typing: discrimination and injectivity of type constructors (injectivity rules for @-, $\mu$-, pair- and sum-types omitted).

inversion we know either $\Gamma \vdash^{\mathsf{L}} p : ((x : A_1) \to A_2) = ((x : B_1) \to B_2)$ and $\Gamma, x :^{\theta} B_1 \vdash^{\theta} b : B_1$, or else $(x : A_1) \to A_2$ is provably equal to an @-type. In the first case we apply the substitution lemma, using TArrInv1 to prove $A_1 = B_1$, while in the second case we use TContra.

### 4.2 Normalization and Progress

Our proof of normalization builds upon the standard Girard-Tait reducibility method [17, 39] in a CBV-style formulation. The crux of this method is to define a "type interpretation". For each type $A$ we define a set of values $\mathcal{V}_\rho[\![A]\!]^{\theta}_k$ that check in fragment $\theta$ (the additional inputs $\rho$ and $k$ are discussed below). The definition of the type interpretation (Figure 7) is a logical relation and follows the structure of $A$.

Our main theorem is that the interpretation is "sound": any closed logical expression $a$ of type $A$ reduces to a value in $\mathcal{V}_\rho[\![A]\!]^{\mathsf{L}}_k$. The rules TUnboxVal and TmVal can move values from P to L, so for the proof to go through we must generalize the soundness theorem to also characterize expressions in P. For these values we prove a partial correctness property: *if* a closed programmatic expression $a$ of type $A$ reduces to a value, then the value is in $\mathcal{V}_\rho[\![A]\!]^{\mathsf{P}}_k$. These invariants are summarized by a computational type interpretation $\mathcal{C}_\rho[\![A]\!]^{\theta}_k$, which identifies sets of (non-value) expressions, and is defined mutually with $\mathcal{V}_\rho[\![A]\!]^{\theta}_k$.

The type interpretation for programmatic expressions must account for recursive functions and recursive types, which means that it cannot be defined by recursion on $A$. Instead, we use *step-indexing* [1, 5]. The interpretation is indexed by a number $k$. Any value $v$ in $\mathcal{V}_\rho[\![A]\!]^{\mathsf{P}}_k$ will be "well-behaved" for at least $k$ steps of execution. The interpretation is defined by well-founded recursion on the lexicographically ordered triple $(k, A, \mathcal{I})$, where $\mathcal{I}$ is one of $\mathcal{C}$ or $\mathcal{V}$ with $\mathcal{V} < \mathcal{C}$.

However, the usual formulation of a step-indexed type interpretation only lends itself to proving safety properties—it tells us that an expression will not do anything bad for the next $k$ steps. By contrast, normalization is a liveness property: every expression will eventually do something good (namely reduce to a value). In our definition, we take a hybrid approach by only counting steps that happen in the P fragment. The difference can be seen by comparing the definitions of $\mathcal{V}_\rho[\![(x : A) \to B]\!]^{\mathsf{L}}_k$ and $\mathcal{V}_\rho[\![(x : A) \to B]\!]^{\mathsf{P}}_k$, which say "$j \leq k$" and "$j < k$" respectively. If all $\theta$s in a derivation are L, then no inequalities are strict, so the step-count $k$ never needs to decrease.

The input $\rho$ is a substitution mapping free variables of $A$ to values. We use $\rho$ when interpreting equality types. The type $a_1 = a_2$ is interpreted as the singleton set $\{\mathsf{refl}\}$ if $\rho\, a_1$ and $\rho\, a_2$ parallel-reduce to a common expression, and as the empty set otherwise. We inductively define the judgment $\Gamma \models_k \rho$, which asserts that $\rho$ maps to values in the correct interpretation, by

$$\frac{}{\cdot \models_k \emptyset}\ \text{ENil} \qquad \frac{\Gamma \models_k \rho \quad v \in \mathcal{V}_\rho[\![A]\!]^{\theta}_k \quad \Gamma \vdash^{\theta} A : \star}{\Gamma, x :^{\theta} A \models_k \rho[x \mapsto v]}\ \text{ECons}$$

Intuitively, $\Gamma \models_k \rho$ asserts that $\rho$ maps term variables to well-behaved values. Because of the premise $\Gamma \vdash^{\theta} A : \star$ it also asserts that $\Gamma$ does not contain any type variables. This is vacuously true for the empty context, and preserved by each case of the type interpretation.

In a normalization proof for System F or for CC [16], the type interpretation would take an input $\rho$ which specifies the interpretation of type variables in $A$, but not one which specifies the values of term variables. Since we do not have polymorphism in our language, we do not need to account for type variables. But unlike CC, because of the primitive equality type we can not just ignore term variables in types. Our $\rho$ is similar to normalization proofs for systems that have large elimination of datatypes, such as CIC [43].

The soundness theorem relies on a few key lemmas about the interpretation. The first is a standard "downward closure" property for step-indexed relations: it says that requiring values to stay well-behaved for a larger number of steps creates a more precise interpretation.

Lemma 4. *For any $A$, $\theta$ and $\rho$, if $j \leq k$ then $\mathcal{V}_\rho[\![A]\!]^{\theta}_k \subseteq \mathcal{V}_\rho[\![A]\!]^{\theta}_j$.*

The next two lemmas are specific to $\lambda^{\theta}$ because they relate the L and P interpretations of a type. They are used to handle the TSub and TmVal rules, respectively. The first says that the set of logical values is a subset of the corresponding programmatic sets.

Lemma 5. *For any $A$, $k$, $\theta$ and $\rho$, $\mathcal{V}_\rho[\![A]\!]^{\mathsf{L}}_k \subseteq \mathcal{V}_\rho[\![A]\!]^{\mathsf{P}}_k$ and $\mathcal{C}_\rho[\![A]\!]^{\mathsf{L}}_k \subseteq \mathcal{C}_\rho[\![A]\!]^{\mathsf{P}}_k$.*

The second says that for mobile types, the reverse containment also holds. For these types, the interpretations contain the same values in both fragments.

Lemma 6. *For any $k$ and $\rho$, if $\mathsf{Mobile}(A)$ then $\mathcal{V}_\rho[\![A]\!]^{\mathsf{P}}_k \subseteq \mathcal{V}_\rho[\![A]\!]^{\mathsf{L}}_k$.*

Finally, for the TConv rule, we need equal types to have the same interpretation.

Lemma 7. *Suppose $\rho\, B_1 \Rrightarrow^* A$ and $\rho\, B_2 \Rrightarrow^* A$ and $\Gamma \vdash^{\theta} B_1 : \star$ and $\Gamma \vdash^{\theta} B_2 : \star$ and $\Gamma \models_k \rho$. Then $a \in \mathcal{I}_\rho[\![B_1]\!]^{\theta}_k$ iff $a \in \mathcal{I}_\rho[\![B_2]\!]^{\theta}_k$.*

We can now prove soundness by induction on $\Gamma \vdash^{\theta} a : A$. Normalization is an immediate corollary. We also get a characterization of which terms can be proven equal in the empty context. We need such a characterization to prove progress.

Theorem 8 (Soundness). *If $\Gamma \vdash^{\theta} a : A$ and $\Gamma \models_k \rho$, then $\rho\, a \in \mathcal{C}_\rho[\![A]\!]^{\theta}_k$.*

Corollary 9 (Normalization).
*If $\cdot \vdash^{\mathsf{L}} a : A$, then there exists a value $v$ such that $a \leadsto^* v$.*

Corollary 10 (Soundness of propositional equality).
*If $\cdot \vdash^{\mathsf{L}} a : A_1 = A_2$, then there exists some $A$ such that $A_1 \Rrightarrow^* A$ and $A_2 \Rrightarrow^* A$.*

$$
\begin{aligned}
\mathcal{V}_\rho\llbracket\star\rrbracket_k^\theta &= \{v \mid \cdot \vdash^\theta v : \star\}\\
\mathcal{V}_\rho\llbracket\mathsf{Nat}\rrbracket_k^\theta &= \{v \mid\ v \text{ is of the form } \mathsf{S}^n\ \mathsf{Z}\}\\
\mathcal{V}_\rho\llbracket A@\theta'\rrbracket_k^\theta &= \{v \mid \cdot \vdash^{\theta'} \rho\, A : \star \text{ and } v \in \mathcal{V}_\rho\llbracket A\rrbracket_k^{\theta'}\}\\
\mathcal{V}_\rho\llbracket (x\!:\!A) \to B\rrbracket_k^{\mathsf{L}} &= \quad \{\lambda x.b \mid \cdot \vdash^{\mathsf{L}} \lambda x.b : \rho\,((x\!:\!A) \to B)\\
&\qquad\quad \text{and } \forall j \leq k,\ \text{if } v \in \mathcal{V}_\rho\llbracket A\rrbracket_j^{\mathsf{L}} \text{ then } [v/x]b \in \mathcal{C}_{\rho[x\mapsto v]}\llbracket B\rrbracket_j^{\mathsf{L}}\}\\
&\quad \cup \{\mathsf{ind}\ f\ x.b \mid \cdot \vdash^{\mathsf{L}} \mathsf{ind}\ f\ x.b : \rho\,((x\!:\!A) \to B)\\
&\qquad\quad \text{and } \forall j \leq k,\ \text{if } v \in \mathcal{V}_\rho\llbracket A\rrbracket_j^{\mathsf{L}} \text{ then } [v/x][\lambda y.\lambda z.(\mathsf{ind}\ f\ x.b)\ y/f]b \in \mathcal{C}_{\rho[x\mapsto v]}\llbracket B\rrbracket_j^{\mathsf{L}}\}\\
\mathcal{V}_\rho\llbracket (x\!:\!A) \to B\rrbracket_k^{\mathsf{P}} &= \quad \{\lambda x.b \mid \cdot \vdash^{\mathsf{P}} \lambda x.b : \rho\,((x\!:\!A) \to B)\\
&\qquad\quad \text{and } \forall j < k,\ \text{if } v \in \mathcal{V}_\rho\llbracket A\rrbracket_j^{\mathsf{P}} \text{ then } [v/x]b \in \mathcal{C}_{\rho[x\mapsto v]}\llbracket B\rrbracket_j^{\mathsf{P}}\}\\
&\quad \cup \{\mathsf{rec}\ f\ x.b \mid \cdot \vdash^{\mathsf{P}} \mathsf{rec}\ f\ x.b : \rho\,((x\!:\!A) \to B)\\
&\qquad\quad \text{and } \forall j < k,\ \text{if } v \in \mathcal{V}_\rho\llbracket A\rrbracket_j^{\mathsf{P}} \text{ then } [v/x][\mathsf{rec}\ f\ x.b/f]b \in \mathcal{C}_{\rho[x\mapsto v]}\llbracket B\rrbracket_j^{\mathsf{P}}\}\\
&\quad \cup \{\mathsf{ind}\ f\ x.b \mid \cdot \vdash^{\mathsf{P}} \mathsf{ind}\ f\ x.b : \rho\,((x\!:\!A) \to B)\\
&\qquad\quad \text{and } \forall j < k,\ \text{if } v \in \mathcal{V}_\rho\llbracket A\rrbracket_j^{\mathsf{P}} \text{ then } [v/x][\mathsf{ind}\ f\ x.b/f]b \in \mathcal{C}_{\rho[x\mapsto v]}\llbracket B\rrbracket_j^{\mathsf{P}}\}\\
\mathcal{V}_\rho\llbracket A + B\rrbracket_k^\theta &= \quad \{\mathsf{inl}\ v \mid \cdot \vdash^\theta \rho\,(A+B) : \star \text{ and } v \in \mathcal{V}_\rho\llbracket A\rrbracket_k^\theta\}\\
&\quad \cup \{\mathsf{inr}\ v \mid \cdot \vdash^\theta \rho\,(A+B) : \star \text{ and } v \in \mathcal{V}_\rho\llbracket B\rrbracket_k^\theta\}\\
\mathcal{V}_\rho\llbracket \Sigma x\!:\!A.B\rrbracket_k^\theta &= \{\langle v_1, v_2\rangle \mid \cdot \vdash^\theta \rho\,(\Sigma x\!:\!A.B) : \star \text{ and } v_1 \in \mathcal{V}_\rho\llbracket A\rrbracket_k^\theta \text{ and } v_2 \in \mathcal{V}_{\rho[x\mapsto v_1]}\llbracket B\rrbracket_k^\theta\}\\
\mathcal{V}_\rho\llbracket \mu x.A\rrbracket_k^{\theta'} &= \{\mathsf{roll}\ v \mid \cdot \vdash^{\theta'} \mathsf{roll}\ v : \rho\,(\mu x.A) \text{ and } \forall j < k, v \in \mathcal{V}_\rho\llbracket [\mu x.A/x]A\rrbracket_j^\theta\}\\
\mathcal{V}_\rho\llbracket a_1 = a_2\rrbracket_k^\theta &= \{\mathsf{refl} \mid \cdot \vdash^\theta \rho\,(a_1 = a_2) : \star \text{ and } \rho\, a_1 \Rrightarrow^* a \text{ and } \rho\, a_2 \Rrightarrow^* a \text{ for some } a\}\\
\mathcal{V}_\rho\llbracket A\rrbracket_k^\theta &= \emptyset \qquad\qquad \text{otherwise}\\[1em]
\mathcal{C}_\rho\llbracket A\rrbracket_k^{\mathsf{P}} &= \{a \mid \cdot \vdash^{\mathsf{P}} a : \rho\, A \text{ and } \forall j \leq k,\ \text{if } a \leadsto^j v \text{ then } v \in \mathcal{V}_\rho\llbracket A\rrbracket_{(k-j)}^{\mathsf{P}}\}\\
\mathcal{C}_\rho\llbracket A\rrbracket_k^{\mathsf{L}} &= \{a \mid \cdot \vdash^{\mathsf{L}} a : \rho\, A \text{ and } a \leadsto^* v \in \mathcal{V}_\rho\llbracket A\rrbracket_k^{\mathsf{L}}\}
\end{aligned}
$$

**Figure 7.** Type interpretation

Normalization holds only for closed terms. This is a result of the fact that uses of the TCONV rule are unmarked in the syntax. It is possible to assume a contradictory equality and use it to typecheck a non-terminating term in the logical fragment. For example, the following statement is derivable:

$$y :^{\mathsf{L}} \mathsf{Nat} = (\mathsf{Nat} \to \mathsf{Nat}) \vdash^{\mathsf{L}} (\lambda x.x\ x)\ (\lambda x.x\ x) : \mathsf{Nat}$$

This distinguishes $\lambda^\theta$ from intensional type theories like Coq and Agda. In those systems, our rule TCONV arises as the pattern-matching elimination form for a defined equality datatype. Uses of this eliminator would appear in the term above, and their reduction would get "stuck" on the variable $y$, since it does not reduce to the appropriate constructor.

The benefit of giving up normalization of open terms is a more generous equality. Since uses of conversion appear in terms in Coq and Agda, they often get in the way of judging two terms which use such conversions equal. In our system, this can not happen. The drawback is that the typechecker can not automatically normalize expressions (since they may diverge), so uses of `refl` must be explicit and annotated with a maximum step count. However, in a language with general recursion some explicit proofs are unavoidable, since checking a logical term can involve reducing a programmatic term that appears in its type. Since our language must accommodate such proofs in any case, making conversion unmarked is appealing.

The progress theorem relies on a canonical forms lemma (elided). In the TCONV and TCONTRA cases we need to know that there are no proofs of inconsistent equalities such as $(\mathsf{Nat} \to \mathsf{Nat}) = \mathsf{Nat}$. Therefore, this lemma relies on Corollary 10. The progress theorem is then an easy induction on $\cdot \vdash^\theta a : A$.

Surface language (`Zombie`)

⇓ (elaboration)

Annotated language (ZT derivations)

⇓ (erasure)

Core language (ZT)

**Figure 8.** Implementation

THEOREM 11 (Progress). *If* $\cdot \vdash^\theta a : A$, *then either* $a$ *is a value, or there exists* $a'$ *such that* $a \leadsto a'$.

## 5. Implementation

We have implemented a prototype dependently-typed language, called `Zombie`, based on $\lambda^\theta$. We have used this implementation to gain experience with the features described in this paper. Indeed, all of the example code in this paper can be type-checked by our implementation. These, and other examples are available for download.

Our language includes several features which were left out of $\lambda^\theta$ to keep the normalization proof simple. Instead of a single sort $\star$, `Zombie` includes a full predicative hierarchy [22], which allows both polymorphism and type-level functions. We also include a general form for parameterized recursive datatypes, which subsumes $\mathsf{Nat}$, $A + B$, $\Sigma x : A.B$ and $\mu x.A$. Datatypes are always mobile, and `Zombie` provides structural induction for all strictly positive datatypes (not just Nat) following [20]. Finally, Zombie distinguishes between computationally relevant and irrelevant arguments [24], and includes a multiplace conversion operator, called *multiconversion* [34].

Adding these features to $\lambda^\theta$ would complicate the type interpretation, increasing the complexity of our machine-checked proof far beyond its current state. In particular, to add predicative polymorphism and type-level computation we would have to redefine our type interpretation as an induction over typing derivations, which is very painful to do in Coq. However, based on work in progress, we are optimistic that the metatheoretic requirements of these additional features will have little interaction with the fundamental consistency mechanism proposed here.

The general structure of our implementation appears in Figure 8. The part of our implementation that most closely resembles $\lambda^\theta$ is the internal language ZT. This language defines the operational behavior of Zombie expressions. However, like $\lambda^\theta$, type checking is not decidable for ZT expressions. Therefore, the implementation also includes an *annotated* version of ZT that supports syntax-directed type checking, an approach we have explored in previous work [34]. Annotated ZT is a direct representation of ZT typing derivations, marking all uses of conversion, subsumption, cumulativity, and coercion to and from $A@\theta$ types. Furthermore, because reduction may not terminate, annotations on refl control and limit the search for a common reduct when proving that two terms are equal.

Directly working with ZT derivations incurs a considerable annotation burden for programmers. Therefore, the Zombie surface language makes these annotations optional. We are currently experimenting with a number of elaboration strategies to infer these annotations. These include using bidirectional type checking [31] to propagate type information through terms, unification to automatically infer some dependent arguments, and *congruence closure* [27] to automatically infer equality proofs used in conversions.

For example, consider the projection functions (fst and snd) for dependent pairs shown below. These functions pattern match their argument and return its first and second components respectively.

```
data Sigma (A:Type) (B:A → Type) : Type where
  Pair of (x:A) (y : B x)

log fst : [A:Type] ⇒ [B:A → Type] ⇒ Sigma A B → A
fst [A] [B] p = case p of
                  Pair x y → x

log snd : [A:Type] ⇒ [B:A → Type] ⇒ (p:Sigma A B)
           → B (fst p)
snd [A] [B] p = case p of
                  Pair x y → unfold (fst p) in y
```

In the implementation of snd, unification can infer the arguments A and B to fst (which were marked inferable by the fat arrow ⇒ in the declaration of fst). Because not all expressions terminate, the programmer must explicitly ask the type checker to unfold (fst p) by $\beta$-reduction, which introduces the equation (fst p) = x into the context. That equation is then automatically used to convert the type of y from B x to B (fst p).

The examples we have implemented fall into two categories. The first includes the division and SAT-solving programs described in Section 1. These examples illustrate how one can write proofs about general recursive programs, and how general recursive programs can return proofs. Second, we have implemented functions for length-indexed lists (Vectors), finite sets represented as binary search trees, and data compression using run-length encoding, together with proofs of their correctness. Since these functions use simple structural recursion, they can be done entirely in the logical fragment. They show that although our core language requires annotations on refl and conv, the overhead of these annotations is manageable.

## 6. Related Work

In previous work, we introduced the proof technique of hybrid step-indexed/traditional logical relations, but for a simply-typed language [12]. This paper extends the normalization proof to a more expressive type system with dependent function types, an equality type, and conversion. It also improves the treatment of @-types by making them implicit. This change complicates the metatheory (see Lemma 2) but makes the language more expressive and simplifies the application rule.

***Terminating Sublanguage.*** There are other dependently-typed languages which allow general recursion but identify a sublanguage of terminating expressions. Aura [18] and F* [38] do this using the kind system: expressions whose type has kind Prop are checked for normalization. Types can contain values but not non-value expressions, so there is no way to write separate proofs about programs. There also is no facility to treat programmatic values as proofs, e.g. a logical case expression cannot destruct a value from the nonterminating fragment.

ATS [13], GURU [36], and Sep[3] [20] are dependently-typed languages where the logical and programmatic fragments are syntactically separate—in effect rejecting the rule TSub. One of the gains of this separation is that the logical language can be made CBN even though the programmatic one is CBV, avoiding the need for thunking (as discussed in Section 3.3). To do inductive reasoning, the Sep[3] language adds an explicit "terminates" predicate.

Idris [10] is a full-spectrum dependently typed programming language that permits non-total definitions. Internally, it applies a syntactic test to check if function definitions are structurally decreasing, and programmers may ask whether particular definitions have been judged total. The type checker will only reduce expressions that have been proved terminating, again precluding separate equational reasoning about partial programs. Idris' metatheory has not been studied formally.

***Partiality Monad.*** Capretta's partiality monad [11] uses coinductive types to embed general recursion into Type Theory. This approach treats pure functions as the default and nontermination less conveniently. Nonterminating programs must be written using monadic combinators (and are therefore never syntactically equal to pure programs). The partiality monad provides recursive function definitions but not general recursive types.

Furthermore, the coinductive approach requires a separate notion of equivalence to reason about partial programs. In, e.g., Coq, one would compare pure expressions according to the standard operational semantics, but define a coarser equivalence relation for partial terms that ignores the number of steps they take to normalize. Equations like $((\mathsf{rec}\ f\ x.b)\ v) = [v/x][\mathsf{rec}\ f\ x.b/f]b$ do not hold with the usual Coq equality because the step counts differ. Conveniently programming with equivalence relations like this, which are not directly justified by the reduction behavior of expressions, is an active area of research involving topics such as setoids [8], quotient types, and the univalence axiom [42].

***Non-constructive fixpoint semantics.*** The work of Bertot and Komendantsky [9] describes a way to embed general recursive functions into Coq that does not use coinduction. They define a datatype partial $A$ that is isomorphic to the usual Maybe $A$ but is understood as representing a lifted CPO $A_\perp$, and use classical logic axioms to provide a fixpoint combinator fixp. When defining a recursive function the user must prove continuity side-conditions.

Since recursive functions are defined nonconstructively they can not be reduced directly, so instead one must reason about them using the fix-point equation.

***Partial Types.*** Nuprl has at its core an untyped lambda calculus, capable of defining a general fixed point combinator for defining recursive computations. In the core type theory, all expressions must be proven terminating when used. Constable and Smith [14] integrated potentially nonterminating computations through the addition of a type $\overline{A}$ of partial terms of type $A$. The fixpoint operator then has type $(\overline{A} \to \overline{A}) \to \overline{A}$. However, to preserve the consistency of the logic, the type $A$ must be restricted to *admissible*. types. Crary [15] provides an expressive axiomatization of admissible types, but these conditions lead to significant proof obligations, especially when using $\Sigma$-types.

Smith [35] provides an example which shows that Nuprl needs this restriction. Writing $a \downarrow$ for "$a$ terminates", define a $\Sigma$-type $T$ of functions which are not total, and recursively define a $p$ which inhabits $T$.

$$\begin{aligned}
\text{Total}\,(f : \mathbb{N} \to \overline{\mathbb{N}}) &\stackrel{\text{def}}{=} (n : \mathbb{N}) \to (f\ n)\downarrow \\
T &\stackrel{\text{def}}{=} \Sigma(f : \mathbb{N} \to \overline{\mathbb{N}}).\text{Total}\ f \to \text{False} \\
(p : T) &\stackrel{\text{def}}{=} \text{fix}\ (\lambda p.\langle g, \lambda h.\text{—}\rangle) \\
g &\stackrel{\text{def}}{=} \lambda x.\text{if}\ x = 0\ \text{then}\ 0\ \text{else}\ \pi_1(p)(x-1)
\end{aligned}$$

Here the dash is an (elided) proof which sneakily derives a contradiction using $\pi_2(p)$ and the hypothesis $h$ that $g$ is total. On the other hand, a separate induction shows that $\pi_1(p)$ *is* total; it returns 0 for all arguments. This is a contradiction.

$\lambda^\theta$ has almost all the ingredients for this paradox. Instead of a recursively defined pair we can use a recursive function Unit $\to T$, and we can encode $a\downarrow$ as $\Sigma(y : A).a = y$. What saves us is that the proof in the second component of $p$ uses the following reasoning principle: if $\pi_1(p)$ terminates, then $p$ terminates. In Nuprl $a \downarrow$ is a primitive predicate and this inversion principle is built in. But using our encoding, a function $(\pi_1(p)\downarrow) \to (p\downarrow)$ would have to magically guess the second component of a pair knowing only the first component. If we assume this function as an axiom we can encode the paradox and derive inconsistency , so our consistency proof shows that there is no way to write such a function.

***Hoare Type Theory.*** HTT [26, 37] is another embedding of general programs into a type theory like Coq, which goes beyond nontermination to also handle memory effects. Instead of a unary type constructor $\overline{A}$, it adds the indexed type $\{P\}x : A\{Q\}$ representing an effectful computation returning $A$ and with pre- and postconditions $P$ and $Q$. The assertions $P$ and $Q$ can use all of Coq, so the type of a computation can specify its behavior precisely. However, computations can not be evaluated during type checking (the fixpoint combinator and memory access primitives are implemented as Coq axioms with types but no reduction rules).

***Fixpoint induction*** Domain-theory based formalisms provide two basic reasoning principles for proving properties about recursive functions: unfolding a function definition, and *fixpoint induction*. The latter principle (see e.g. [44]) states that to prove a property about a function, one may assume it as an induction hypothesis for the recursive calls of the function. For this to be valid, the property must be "admissible", and it most hold for infinite loops. An equivalent variant [9] is to allow induction on the number of recursive steps an expression takes to normalize.

$\lambda^\theta$ currently provides no such principle. If a theorem can not be proved just from unfolding, there are two ways to proceed. In order to prove `div_le` in Section 1 we used (strong) natural-number induction. For this strategy to work the programmer has to find a termination metric for the function in question, so it only works for functions that are in fact terminating. However, it can still be convenient to give a direct recursive definition of the function. For functions that genuinely do not terminate, one can instead change them to return a $\Sigma$-type asserting the property, so that the property is automatically available for recursive calls. This is what we did for `solver` in Section 1, and it is the only option in Hoare Type Theory.

***Modal types for distributed computation.*** Modal logic reasons about statements whose truth varies in different "possible worlds". Our type system is formally similar, with the possible worlds being L and P. Modal logic has previously been used to design type systems for distributed computation [19, 25]. In particular, $\lambda^\theta$ was inspired by ML5 [25], in which the typing judgment is indexed by what "world" (computer in a distributed system) a program is running on, and which includes a type $A@\theta$ internalizing that judgment. Our rule TMVAL is similar to the GET rule in ML5, and our Mobile$(A)$ is similar to the judgment $A$ mobile in ML5. On the other hand, unlike $\lambda^\theta$, ML5 does not require that the domain of an arrow type be mobile. As we explained in Section 3.1 we make that restriction to accommodate our rule TSUB, a rule which does not make sense in the context of distributed computation.

## 7. Future work

In future work, we hope to extend the metatheory of $\lambda^\theta$ to include more of ZT. We plan to allow polymorphic types and type-level functions in both the L and P fragments, extending our proof using ideas from normalization proofs for the Calculus of Constructions [16]. Following the ideas of Ahn and Sheard [2] and their language Nax [3], we also hope to add combinators to define recursive functions over recursive data to the logical language. Nax places no restriction on what sorts of datatypes can be defined or how they can be constructed. Instead, it limits the analysis of data structures to ensure the soundness of the logic. More generally, we would like to extend our proofs to a general theory of datatype definitions, maybe encoded via recursion, sums, and products as in $\Pi\Sigma$ [4]. One potential worry is that we assume injectivity for all type constructors, which can be used to encode Cantor-like paradoxes. We hope to avoid inconsistency by forbidding impredicative polymorphism and datatypes with "large" indices.

Adding these features will require substantial additional work in the normalization proof, but we do not anticipate any changes to the novel typing rules that connect the L and P fragments.

***Reasoning about general recursive functions*** Currently $\lambda^\theta$ emphasizes lightweight verification. In order to turn it into a tool for full verification of potentially nonterminating programs, we would add stronger reasoning principles.

First, the value restrictions in $\rightsquigarrow$ can get in the way of equational reasoning. If $a$ is an expression in P there is no way to prove an equation like $(\mathsf{let}\ x = a\ \mathsf{in}\ f\ x) = (f\ a)$, even though the two sides are in fact contextually equivalent. To make it provable we could add *termination-case*—a case analysis on whether a programmatic expression evaluates to a value or diverges [20]. Unfortunately, this operator is unimplementable, so we would not want to allow proofs that use this reasoning to be used as programs. One solution is to introduce a new consistency classifier O, for *oracular*, in addition to L and P. By not allowing O expressions to be used as programs, we could control and track the use of termination case.

Second, we would like to investigate whether some (perhaps weakened) form of fixpoint induction can be consistently added. The experience with partial types in Nuprl suggests that this may require a notion of admissible predicates.

## 8. Conclusion

This paper presents a framework for interacting logics and programming languages. The consistency classifiers, $\theta$, describe the set of typing rules that determine the properties of each well-typed expression. At the same time, many standard typing rules are polymorphic in this classifier, leading to uniformity between the systems. Internalizing this judgment as a type and observing that some values can move freely allows the fragments to interact in nontrivial ways, leading to an expressive foundation for dependently-typed programming.

## Acknowledgments

This material is based upon work supported by the National Science Foundation under Grant Nos. 0910500 and 1116620. The `Zombie` implementation was developed with the assistance of the Trellys team, and the ideas in this paper benefitted greatly from that collaboration. This paper was written with the help of the excellent Ott tool [32]. The authors would also like to thank the anonymous reviewers for their considered and helpful comments.

## References

[1] Ahmed, A.: Step-indexed syntactic logical relations for recursive and quantified types. In: ESOP '06: European Symposium on Programming. LNCS, vol. 3924. Springer (2006)

[2] Ahn, K.Y., Sheard, T.: A hierarchy of mendler style recursion combinators: taming inductive datatypes with negative occurrences. In: ICFP '11: International Conference on Functional programming. pp. 234–246. ACM (2011)

[3] Ahn, K.Y., Sheard, T., Fiore, M., Pitts, A.M.: The Nax programming language (work in progress) (2012), talk presented at IFL 2012: the 24th Symposium on Implementation and Application of Functional Languages

[4] Altenkirch, T., Danielsson, N.A., Löh, A., Oury, N.: ΠΣ: Dependent types without the sugar. Functional and Logic Programming pp. 40–55 (2010)

[5] Appel, A.W., McAllester, D.: An indexed model of recursive types for foundational proof-carrying code. ACM Trans. Program. Lang. Syst. 23(5), 657–683 (2001)

[6] Augustsson, L.: Cayenne – a language with dependent types. In: ICFP '98: International Conference on Functional Programming. pp. 239–250. ACM (1998)

[7] Barendregt, H.P.: Lambda calculi with types. In: Abramsky, S., Gabbay, D.M., Maibaum, T.S.E. (eds.) Handbook of Logic in Computer Science. pp. 117–309. Oxford University Press (1992)

[8] Barthe, G., Capretta, V., Pons, O.: Setoids in type theory. Journal of Functional Programming 13(2), 261–293 (2003)

[9] Bertot, Y., Komendantsky, V.: Fixed point semantics and partial recursion in coq. In: PPDP '08: Principles and practice of declarative programming. pp. 89–96. ACM (2008)

[10] Brady, E.C.: Idris—systems programming meets full dependent types. In: PLPV'11: Programming languages meets program verification. pp. 43–54. ACM (2011)

[11] Capretta, V.: General recursion via coinductive types. Logical Methods in Computer Science 1(2), 1–18 (2005)

[12] Casinghino, C., Sjöberg, V., Weirich, S.: Step-indexed normalization for a language with general recursion. In: MSFP '12: Mathematically Structured Functional Programming. EPTCS, vol. 76, pp. 25–39 (2012)

[13] Chen, C., Xi, H.: Combining programming with theorem proving. In: Proceedings of the tenth ACM SIGPLAN international conference on Functional programming. pp. 66–77. ICFP '05, ACM, New York, NY, USA (2005), http://doi.acm.org/10.1145/1086365.1086375

[14] Constable, R.L., Smith, S.F.: Partial objects in constructive type theory. In: Logic in Computer Science (LICS'87). pp. 183–193. IEEE (1987)

[15] Crary, K.: Type Theoretic Methodology for Practical Programming Languages. Ph.D. thesis, Cornell University (1998)

[16] Geuvers, H.: A short and flexible proof of Strong Normalization for the Calculus of Constructions. In: TYPES '94. LNCS, vol. 996, pp. 14–38 (1995)

[17] Girard, J.Y.: Interprétation fonctionelle et élimination des coupures de l'arithmétique d'ordre supérieur. Ph.D. thesis, Université Paris VII (1972)

[18] Jia, L., Vaughan, J.A., Mazurak, K., Zhao, J., Zarko, L., Schorr, J., Zdancewic, S.: AURA: A programming language for authorization and audit. In: ICFP '08: International Conference on Functional Programming). pp. 27–38. ACM (2008)

[19] Jia, L., Walker, D.: Modal proofs as distributed programs (extended abstract). In: ESOP'04: European Symposium on Programming. LNCS, vol. 2986, pp. 219–233. Springer (2004)

[20] Kimmell, G., Stump, A., Eades III, H.D., Fu, P., Sheard, T., Weirich, S., Casinghino, C., Sjöberg, V., Collins, N., Ahn, K.Y.: Equational reasoning about programs with general recursion and call-by-value semantics. In: PLPV '12: Programming languages meets program verification. ACM (2012)

[21] Licata, D.R., Harper, R.: Positively dependent types. In: PLPV '09: Programming languages meets program verification. pp. 3–14. ACM (2008)

[22] Luo, Z.: Computation and Reasoning: A Type Theory for Computer Science. Oxford University Press, USA (1994)

[23] McBride, C., McKinna, J.: The view from the left. J. Funct. Program. 14(1), 69–111 (2004)

[24] Miquel, A.: The implicit calculus of constructions - extending pure type systems with an intersection type binder and subtyping. In: TLCA '01: Proceeding of 5th international conference on Typed Lambda Calculi and Applications. LNCS, vol. 2044, pp. 344–359. Springer (2001)

[25] Murphy, VII, T., Crary, K., Harper, R.: Type-safe distributed programming with ML5. In: Trustworthy Global Computing 2007 (2007)

[26] Nanevski, A., Morrisett, G., Shinnar, A., Govereau, P., Birkedal, L.: Ynot: dependent types for imperative programs. In: ICFP '08: International Conference on Functional Programming. pp. 229–240. ACM (2008)

[27] Nieuwenhuis, R., Oliveras, A.: Fast congruence closure and extensions. Inf. Comput. 205(4), 557–580 (2007)

[28] Norell, U.: Towards a practical programming language based on dependent type theory. Ph.D. thesis, Chalmers University of Technology (2007)

[29] Peyton-Jones, S., Vytiniotis, D., Weirich, S., Washburn, G.: Simple unification-based type inference for GADTs. In: ICFP '06: International Conference on Functional Programming. pp. 50–61. ACM (2006)

[30] Pierce, B.C.: Types and Programming Languages. MIT Press (2002)

[31] Pierce, B.C., Turner, D.N.: Local type inference. In: ACM SIGPLAN–SIGACT Symposium on Principles of Programming Languages (POPL), San Diego, California (1998)

[32] Sewell, P., Nardelli, F., Owens, S., Peskine, G., Ridge, T., Sarkar, S., Strnisa, R.: Ott: Effective tool support for the working semanticist. J. Funct. Program. 20(1), 71–122 (2010)

[33] Sheard, T., Linger, N.: Programming in $\omega$mega. In: Horváth, Z., Plasmeijer, R., Soós, A., Zsók, V. (eds.) 2nd Central European Functional Programming School (CEFP). LNCS, vol. 5161, pp. 158–227. Springer (2007)

[34] Sjöberg, V., Casinghino, C., Ahn, K.Y., Collins, N., Eades III, H.D., Fu, P., Kimmell, G., Sheard, T., Stump, A., Weirich, S.: Irrelevance, heterogeneous equality, and call-by-value dependent type systems. In: MSFP '12: Mathematically Structured Functional Programming. EPTCS, vol. 76, pp. 112–162 (2012)

[35] Smith, S.F.: Partial Objects in Type Theory. Ph.D. thesis, Cornell University (1988)

[36] Stump, A., Deters, M., Petcher, A., Schiller, T., Simpson, T.W.: Verified programming in guru. In: Altenkirch, T., Millstein, T.D. (eds.) PLPV. pp. 49–58. ACM (2009)

[37] Svendsen, K., Birkedal, L., Nanevski, A.: Partiality, state and dependent types. In: Typed lambda calculi and applications (TLCA'11). LNCS, vol. 6690, pp. 198–212. Springer (2011)

[38] Swamy, N., Chen, J., Fournet, C., Strub, P.Y., Bhargavan, K., Yang, J.: Secure Distributed Programming with Value-dependent Types. In: ICFP '11: International Conference on Functional Programming. pp. 285–296. ACM (2011)

[39] Tait, W.W.: Intensional interpretations of functionals of finite type i. The Journal of Symbolic Logic 32(2), pp. 198–212 (1967)

[40] The Coq Development Team: The Coq Proof Assistant Reference Manual, Version 8.3. INRIA (2010), `http://coq.inria.fr/V8.3/refman/`

[41] The Coq Development Team: The Coq Proof Assistant, Frequently Asked Questions. INRIA (2011), `http://coq.inria.fr/faq/`

[42] The Univalent Foundations Program: Homotopy Type Theory: Univalent Foundations of Mathematics (2013), `http://arxiv.org/abs/1308.0729`

[43] Werner, B.: Une Théorie des Constructions Inductives. Ph.D. thesis, Université Paris 7 (1994)

[44] Winskel, G.: The formal semantics of programming languages: an introduction. MIT Press, Cambridge, MA, USA (1993)

# Tracing Compilation by Abstract Interpretation

Stefano Dissegna
Dipartimento di Matematica
University of Padova, Italy

Francesco Logozzo
Microsoft Research
Redmond, WA, USA

Francesco Ranzato
Dipartimento di Matematica
University of Padova, Italy

## Abstract

Tracing just-in-time compilation is a popular compilation schema for the efficient implementation of dynamic languages, which is commonly used for JavaScript, Python, and PHP. It relies on two key ideas. First, it monitors the execution of the program to detect so-called hot paths, *i.e.*, the most frequently executed paths. Then, it uses some store information available at runtime to optimize hot paths. The result is a residual program where the optimized hot paths are guarded by sufficient conditions ensuring the equivalence of the optimized path and the original program. The residual program is persistently mutated during its execution, *e.g.*, to add new optimized paths or to merge existing paths. Tracing compilation is thus fundamentally different than traditional static compilation. Nevertheless, despite the remarkable practical success of tracing compilation, very little is known about its theoretical foundations.

We formalize tracing compilation of programs using abstract interpretation. The monitoring (*viz.*, hot path detection) phase corresponds to an abstraction of the trace semantics that captures the most frequent occurrences of sequences of program points together with an abstraction of their corresponding stores, *e.g.*, a type environment. The optimization (*viz.*, residual program generation) phase corresponds to a transform of the original program that preserves its trace semantics up to a given observation as modeled by some abstraction. We provide a generic framework to express dynamic optimizations and to prove them correct. We instantiate it to prove the correctness of dynamic type specialization. We show that our framework is more general than a recent model of tracing compilation introduced in POPL 2011 by Guo and Palsberg (based on operational bisimulations). In our model we can naturally express hot path reentrance and common optimizations like dead-store elimination, which are either excluded or unsound in Guo and Palsberg's framework.

***Categories and Subject Descriptors*** D.2.4 [*Software Engineering*]: Software/Program Verification – correctness proofs, formal methods; D.3.4 [*Programming Languages*]: Processors – compilers, optimization; F.3.2 [*Logics and Meanings of Programs*]: Semantics of Programming Languages – program analysis

***Keywords*** tracing compilation; abstract interpretation; trace semantics



*POPL '14*, January 22–24, 2014, San Diego, CA, USA.

ACM 978-1-4503-2544-8/14/01...$15.00.
http://dx.doi.org/10.1145/2535838.2535866

## 1. Introduction

Efficient traditional static compilation of popular dynamic languages like JavaScript, Python and PHP is very hard if not impossible. In fact those languages present so many dynamic features which make all traditional static analyses used for program optimization very imprecise. Therefore, practical implementations of dynamic languages should rely on dynamic information in order to produce an optimized version of the program. In particular, tracing just-in-time compilation (TJITC) [1, 3–6, 15, 16, 24] has emerged as a valuable implementation and optimization technique for dynamic languages. For instance, the Facebook HipHop virtual machine for PHP and the V8 JavaScript engine of Google Chrome use some form of tracing compilation [19, 20]. The Mozilla Firefox JavaScript engine used to have a tracing engine, TraceMonkey, which has been later substituted by whole-method just-in-time compilation engines (initially JägerMonkey and then IonMonkey) [13, 14].

### 1.1 The Problem

Tracing JIT compilers leverage runtime profiling of programs to detect and record often executed paths, called hot paths, and then they optimize and compile only these paths at runtime. A path is a linear sequence of instructions through the program. Profiling may also collect information about the values that the program variables may assume during the execution of that path, which is then used to specialize/optimize the code. Of course, this information is not guaranteed to hold for all the subsequent executions of the hot path. Since optimizations rely on that information, the hot path is augmented with guards that check the profiled conditions, such as, for example, variable types. When a guard fails, execution jumps back to the old, non-optimized code. The main hypotheses of tracing compilers, confirmed by the practice, are: (i) loop bodies are the only interesting code to optimize, so they only consider paths inside program loops; and (ii) optimizing straight-line code is easier than a whole-method analysis (involving loops, goto, *etc.*).

Hence, tracing compilers look quite different than traditional compilers. These differences raise some natural questions on trace compilation: (i) what is a viable formal model, which is generic yet realistic enough to capture the behavior of real optimizers? (ii) which optimizations are sound? (iii) how can one prove their soundness? In this paper we answer the above questions.

Our formal model is based on program trace semantics [9] and abstract interpretation [10, 12]. Hot path detection is modeled just as an abstraction of the trace semantics of the program, which only retains: (i) the sequences of program points which are repeated more than some threshold; (ii) an abstraction of the possible program stores, *e.g.*, the type of the variables instead of their concrete values. As a consequence, a hot path does not contain loops nor join points. Furthermore, in the hot path, all the correctness conditions (*i.e.*, guards) are explicit, for instance before performing integer addition, we should check that the operands are integers. If the guard condition is not satisfied then the execution leaves the hot path, reverting to the non-optimized code. Guards are essentially elements of some abstract domain, which is then left as a parameter in our framework. The hot path is then optimized using standard compilation techniques — we only require the optimization to be sound.

We define the correctness of the residual (or extracted) program in terms of abstraction of the trace semantics: the residual program is correct if it is indistinguishable, up to some abstraction of the trace semantics, from the original program. Examples of abstractions are the program store at the exit of a method, or the stores at loop entry and loop exit points.

### 1.2 Main Contributions

This paper puts forward a formal model of TJITC whose key features are as follows:

- We provide the first model of tracing compilation based on abstract interpretation of trace semantics of programs.
- We provide a more general and realistic framework than a recent model of TJITC by Guo and Palsberg [17] based on program bisimulations: we employ a less restrictive correctness criterion that enables the correctness proof of actually implemented optimizations; hot paths can be annotated with runtime information on the stores, notably type information; optimized hot loops can be re-entered.
- We formalize and prove the correctness of type specialization of hot paths.

Our model focusses on source-to-source program transformations and optimizations of a low level imperative language with untyped global variables, which may play the role of intermediate language of some virtual machine. Our starting point is that program optimizations can be seen as transformations that lose some information on the original program, so that optimizations can be viewed as approximations and in turn can be formalized by abstract interpretation. More precisely, we rely on the insight by Cousot and Cousot [12] that a program source can be seen as an abstraction of its trace semantics, *i.e.* the set of all possible execution sequences, so that a source-to-source optimization can be viewed as an abstraction of a transform of the program trace semantics. In our model, soundness of program optimizations is defined as program equivalence w.r.t. an observational abstract interpretation of the program trace semantics. Here, an observational abstraction induces a correctness criterion by describing what is observable about program executions, so that program equivalence means that two programs are indistinguishable by looking only at their observable behaviors.

A crucial part of tracing compilation is the selection of the hot path(s) to optimize. Of course, this choice is made at runtime based on program executions, so it can be seen once again as an abstraction of trace semantics. Here, a simple trace abstraction selects cyclic instruction sequences, *i.e.* loop paths, that appear at least $N$ times within a single execution trace. These instruction sequences are recorded together with some property of the values assumed by program variables at that point, which is represented as a value of a suitable store abstraction, which in general depends on the successive optimization.

A program optimization can be seen as an abstraction of a semantic transformation of program execution traces, as described by the Cousots in [12]. The advantage of this approach is that optimization properties, such as their soundness, are easier to prove at a semantic level. The optimization itself can be defined on the whole program or, as in the case of real tracing JIT compilers, can be restricted to the hot path. This latter restriction is achieved by transforming the original program so that the hot path is extracted, *i.e.* made explicit: the hot path is added to the program as a path with no join points that jumps back to the original code when execution leaves it. A guard is placed before each command in this hot path that checks if the necessary conditions, as selected by the store abstraction, are satisfied. A program optimization can be then confined to the hot path only, making it linear, by ignoring the parts of the program outside it. The guards added to the hot path allows us to retain precision.

We apply our TJITC model to type specialization. Type specialization is definitely the key optimization for dynamic languages such as Javascript [15], as they provide generic operations whose execution depends on the type of run-time values of their operands.

### 1.3 Related Work

A formal model for tracing JIT compilation has been put forward in POPL 2011 by Guo and Palsberg [17]. It is based on operational bisimulation [23] to describe equivalence between source and optimized programs. In Section 11 we show how this model can be expressed within our framework through the following steps: Guo and Palsberg's language is compiled into ours; we then exhibit an observational abstraction which is equivalent to Guo and Palsberg's correctness criterion; finally, after some minor changes that address a few differences in path selection, the transformations performed on the source program turn out to be the same. Our framework overcomes some significant limitations in Guo and Palsberg's model. The bisimulation equivalence model used in [17] implies that the optimized program has to match every change to the store made by the original program, whereas in practice we only need this match to hold in certain program points and for some variables, such as in output instructions. This limits the number of real optimizations that can be modeled in the theoretical framework. For instance, dead store elimination is proven unsound in [17], while it is implemented in actual tracing compilers [15, Section 5.1]. Furthermore, their formalization fails to model some important features of actual TJITC implementation: (i) traces are simple linear paths of instructions, *i.e.*, they cannot be annotated with store properties; (ii) hot path selection is completely non-deterministic, they do not model a selection criterion; and, (iii) once execution leaves an optimized hot path the program will not be able to re-enter it.

It is also worth citing that abstract interpretation of program trace semantics roots at the foundational work by Cousot [8, 9] and has been widely used as a successful technique for defining a range of static program analyses [2, 7, 18, 22, 26–28]. Abstract interpretation has been used to describe static compilation and optimizations. In particular, Rival [25] describes various optimizations as trace abstractions they preserve. In the Cousot and Cousot terminology [12], Rival approach corresponds to offline transformations whereas tracing compilation is an online transformation.

## 2. Language and Concrete Semantics

### 2.1 Syntax

Following [12], we consider a basic low level language with untyped global variables, a kind of elementary dynamic language. Program commands range in $\mathbb{C}$ and consist of a labeled action which specifies a next label (Ł is the undefined label, where the execution becomes stuck).

$$
\begin{array}{rl}
\text{Labels:} & L \in \mathbb{L} \qquad Ł \notin \mathbb{L} \\
\text{Values:} & v \in \text{Value} \\
\text{Variables:} & x \in \text{Var} \\
\text{Expressions:} & \text{Exp} \ni E ::= v \mid x \mid E_1 + E_2 \\
\text{Boolean Expressions:} & \text{BExp} \ni B ::= \text{tt} \mid \text{ff} \mid E_1 \leq E_2 \mid \\
 & \qquad \neg B \mid B_1 \wedge B_2 \\
\text{Actions:} & \mathbb{A} \ni A ::= x := E \mid B \mid \text{skip} \\
\text{Commands:} & \mathbb{C} \ni C ::= L : A \to L' \quad (L' \in \mathbb{L} \cup \{Ł\})
\end{array}
$$

For any command $C \equiv L : A \to L'$, we use the following notation: $lbl(C) \triangleq L$, $act(C) \triangleq A$ and $suc(C) \triangleq L'$. Commands $L : B \to L'$ whose action is a Boolean expression are called conditionals. A program $P \in \wp(\mathbb{C})$ is a (possibly infinite, at least in theory) set of commands, with a distinct initial label $L_{in}$ from which execution starts, so that $P_{in}$ denotes the commands in $P$ labeled by $L_{in}$ ($P_{in}$ consists of two commands when the initial command is a conditional). If a program $P$ includes a conditional $C \equiv L : B \to L'$ then $P$ must also include a unique complement conditional $L : \neg B \to L''$, which is denoted by $cmpl(C)$ or $C^c$, where $\neg\neg B$ is taken to be equal to $B$, so that $cmpl(cmpl(C)) = C$. For simplicity, we consider deterministic programs, *i.e.*, we require that for any $C_1, C_2 \in P$ such that $lbl(C_1) = lbl(C_2)$: (1) if $act(C_1) \neq act(C_2)$ then $C_1 = cmpl(C_2)$; (2) if $act(C_1) = act(C_2)$ then $C_1 = C_2$. The set of well-formed programs is denoted by Program.

### 2.2 Transition Semantics

The language semantics relies on the following type values, where Char is a nonempty set of characters and *undef* represents a generic error.

$$\text{Int} \triangleq \mathbb{Z} \quad \text{Bool} \triangleq \{true, false\}$$
$$\text{String} \triangleq \text{Char}^* \quad \text{Undef} \triangleq \{undef\}$$

In turn, Value and type names in Types are defined as follows:

$$\text{Value} \triangleq \text{Int} \cup \text{String} \cup \text{Undef}$$
$$\text{Types} \triangleq \{\text{Int}, \text{String}, \text{Undef}, \text{Any}, \varnothing\}$$

while $type$ : Value $\to$ Types provides the type of any value. Here, the type name Any plays the role of top type, which is the supertype (*i.e.*, contains) all types, while $\varnothing$ is the bottom type, which is a subtype for all types.

Let $\rho \in \text{Store} \triangleq \text{Var} \to \text{Value}$ denote the set of possible program stores. The semantics of expressions and program actions is standard and goes as defined in Fig. 1. Let us remark that: the binary function $+_{\text{Int}}$ denotes integer addition; $\cdot$ is string concatenation; logical negation and conjunction are extended in order to handle *undef* values, *i.e.*, $\neg undef = undef$ and $undef \wedge b = undef = b \wedge undef$. With a slight abuse of notation we also consider the so-called collecting versions of the semantic functions in Fig. 1:

$$\mathbf{E} : \text{Exp} \to \wp(\text{Store}) \to \wp(\text{Value})$$
$$\mathbf{E}[\![E]\!]S \triangleq \{\mathbf{E}[\![E]\!]\rho \mid \rho \in S\}$$

$$\mathbf{B} : \text{BExp} \to \wp(\text{Store}) \to \wp(\text{Store})$$
$$\mathbf{B}[\![B]\!]S \triangleq \{\rho \in S \mid \mathbf{B}[\![B]\!]\rho = true\}$$

$$\mathbf{A} : \mathbb{A} \to \wp(\text{Store}) \to \wp(\text{Store})$$
$$\mathbf{A}[\![A]\!]S \triangleq \{\mathbf{A}[\![A]\!]\rho \mid \rho \in S, \mathbf{A}[\![A]\!]\rho \notin \{\bot, undef\}\}$$

Program states are pairs of stores and commands: State $\triangleq$ Store $\times \mathbb{C}$. If $P$ is a program then $\text{State}_P \triangleq \text{Store} \times P$. We extend *lbl*, *act* and *suc* to be defined on states, meaning that they are defined on the command component of a state. Also, $store(s)$ returns the store of a state $s$. Given $P \in$ Program, the program transition relation $\mathbf{S}[\![P]\!] : \text{State}_P \to \wp(\text{State}_P)$ between states is defined as follows:

$$\mathbf{S}[\![P]\!]\langle\rho, C\rangle \triangleq \{\langle\rho', C'\rangle \in \text{State}_P \mid \rho' \in \mathbf{A}[\![act(C)]\!]\{\rho\},$$
$$C' \in P,\ suc(C) = lbl(C')\}.$$

It is worth remarking that, according to the above definition, if $C \equiv L : A \to L'$, $C_1 \equiv L' : B \to L''$ and $C_1^c \equiv L' : \neg B \to L'''$ are all commands that belong to $P$ and $\rho' \in \mathbf{A}[\![A]\!]\rho$ then we have that $\mathbf{S}[\![P]\!]\langle\rho, C\rangle = \{\langle\rho', C_1\rangle, \langle\rho', C_1^c\rangle\}$.

#### 2.2.1 Trace Semantics

A partial (forward) trace is a finite sequence of program states which are related by the transition relation $\mathbf{S}$. If $P$ is a program then we define

$$\text{Trace}_P \triangleq \{\sigma \in (\text{State}_P)^* \mid \forall i \in [1, |\sigma|).\ \sigma_i \in \mathbf{S}[\![P]\!]\sigma_{i-1}\}$$

A trace $\sigma \in \text{Trace}_P$ is maximal if for any state $s \in \text{State}_P$, $\sigma s \notin \text{Trace}_P$. Let us note that according to the above definitions, if a trace $\sigma \in \text{Trace}_P$ has a last state $\sigma_{|\sigma|-1} = \langle\rho, L : B \to L'\rangle$ with a conditional command such that $\mathbf{B}[\![B]\!]\rho = false$ then $\sigma$ is maximal. Also, if a trace $\sigma \in \text{Trace}_P$ has a last state $\sigma_{|\sigma|-1} = \langle\rho, L : A \to \text{Ł}\rangle$ whose next label is the undefined label then $\sigma$ is maximal as well.

The trace semantics $\mathbf{T}[\![P]\!]$ is the set of all the partial (including maximal) traces of the program $P$. This set is defined as the least fixed point of a monotonic operator $F[P] : \wp(\text{Trace}_P) \to \wp(\text{Trace}_P)$, called trace transition operator, defined as follows:

$$F[P]X \triangleq \{\langle\rho, C_{in}\rangle \mid \rho \in \text{Store}, C_{in} \in P_{in}\} \cup \{\sigma s s' \in \text{Trace}_P \mid \sigma s \in X,\ s' \in \mathbf{S}[\![P]\!]s\}$$

$$\mathbf{T}[\![P]\!] \triangleq \text{lfp}(F[P]) \in \wp(\text{Trace}_P)$$

The function $F[P]$ is trivially monotone on the complete lattice $\langle\wp(\text{Trace}_P), \subseteq\rangle$, so that its least fixpoint $\mathbf{T}[\![P]\!]$ is well defined.

**Example 2.1.** Let us consider the program below written in some while-language:

> $x := 0$;
> **while** $(x \leq 20)$ **do**
>   $x := x + 1$;
>   **if** $(x\%3 = 0)$ **then** $x := x + 3$;

Its translation in our language is given below, where, with a little abuse, we assume that the syntax of arithmetic and Boolean expression is extended to allow expressions like $x\%3 = 0$.

$$\begin{aligned} P = \{&C_0 \equiv L_0 : x := 0 \to L_1, \\ &C_1 \equiv L_1 : x \leq 20 \to L_2,\ C_1^c \equiv L_1 : \neg(x \leq 20) \to L_5, \\ &C_2 \equiv L_2 : x := x + 1 \to L_3, \\ &C_3 \equiv L_3 : (x\%3 = 0) \to L_4,\ C_3^c \equiv L_3 : \neg(x\%3 = 0) \to L_1 \\ &C_4 \equiv L_4 : x := x + 3 \to L_1, \\ &C_5 \equiv L_5 : \text{skip} \to \text{Ł}\} \end{aligned}$$

The trace semantics $\mathbf{T}[\![P]\!]$ includes the following partial traces, where ? stands for any integer value and stores are denoted within square brackets.

$\langle[x/?], C_0\rangle \quad \in F[P]\varnothing$
$\langle[x/?], C_0\rangle\langle[x/0], C_1\rangle$
$\langle[x/?], C_0\rangle\langle[x/0], C_1^c\rangle$ (maximal)
$\langle[x/?], C_0\rangle\langle[x/0], C_1\rangle\langle[x/0], C_2\rangle$
$\langle[x/?], C_0\rangle\langle[x/0], C_1\rangle\langle[x/0], C_2\rangle\langle[x/1], C_3\rangle$ (maximal)
$\langle[x/?], C_0\rangle\langle[x/0], C_1\rangle\langle[x/0], C_2\rangle\langle[x/1], C_3^c\rangle$
$\langle[x/?], C_0\rangle\langle[x/0], C_1\rangle\langle[x/0], C_2\rangle\langle[x/1], C_3^c\rangle\langle[x/1], C_1\rangle$
$\langle[x/?], C_0\rangle\langle[x/0], C_1\rangle\langle[x/0], C_2\rangle\langle[x/1], C_3^c\rangle\langle[x/1], C_1^c\rangle$ (maximal)
$\langle[x/?], C_0\rangle\langle[x/0], C_1\rangle\langle[x/0], C_2\rangle\langle[x/1], C_3^c\rangle\langle[x/1], C_1\rangle\langle[x/2], C_2\rangle$
$\cdots$
$\cdots$
$\langle[x/?], C_0\rangle \cdots \langle[x/21], C_4\rangle\langle[x/24], C_1\rangle$ (maximal)
$\langle[x/?], C_0\rangle \cdots \langle[x/21], C_4\rangle\langle[x/24], C_1^c\rangle\langle[x/24], C_5\rangle$ (maximal)

□

$$\mathbf{E} : \text{Exp} \to \text{Store} \to \text{Value}$$

$$\mathbf{E}[\![v]\!]\rho \triangleq v \quad \mathbf{E}[\![x]\!]\rho \triangleq \rho(x) \quad \mathbf{E}[\![E_1 + E_2]\!]\rho \triangleq \begin{cases} \mathbf{E}[\![E_1]\!]\rho +_{\text{Int}} \mathbf{E}[\![E_2]\!]\rho & \text{if } \mathit{type}(\mathbf{E}[\![E_i]\!]\rho) = \text{Int} \\ \mathbf{E}[\![E_1]\!]\rho \cdot \mathbf{E}[\![E_2]\!]\rho & \text{if } \mathit{type}(\mathbf{E}[\![E_i]\!]\rho) = \text{String} \\ \mathit{undef} & \text{otherwise} \end{cases}$$

$$\mathbf{B} : \text{BExp} \to \text{Store} \to \{\mathit{true}, \mathit{false}, \mathit{undef}\}$$

$$\mathbf{B}[\![\text{tt}]\!]\rho \triangleq \mathit{true} \quad \mathbf{B}[\![\text{ff}]\!]\rho \triangleq \mathit{false} \quad \mathbf{B}[\![E_1 \leq E_2]\!]\rho \triangleq \begin{cases} \mathbf{E}[\![E_1]\!]\rho \leq \mathbf{E}[\![E_2]\!]\rho & \text{if } \mathit{type}(\mathbf{E}[\![E_i]\!]\rho) = \text{Int} \\ \mathit{undef} & \text{otherwise} \end{cases}$$

$$\mathbf{B}[\![\neg B]\!]\rho \triangleq \neg \mathbf{B}[\![B]\!]\rho \quad \mathbf{B}[\![B_1 \wedge B_2]\!]\rho \triangleq \mathbf{B}[\![B_1]\!]\rho \wedge \mathbf{B}[\![B_2]\!]\rho$$

$$\mathbf{A} : \mathbb{A} \to \text{Store} \to \text{Store} \cup \{\bot, \mathit{undef}\}$$

$$\mathbf{A}[\![x := E]\!]\rho \triangleq \rho[x := \mathbf{E}[\![E]\!]\rho] \quad \mathbf{A}[\![\text{skip}]\!]\rho \triangleq \rho \quad \mathbf{A}[\![B]\!]\rho \triangleq \begin{cases} \rho & \text{if } \mathbf{B}[\![B]\!]\rho = \mathit{true} \\ \bot & \text{if } \mathbf{B}[\![B]\!]\rho = \mathit{false} \\ \mathit{undef} & \text{if } \mathbf{B}[\![B]\!]\rho = \mathit{undef} \end{cases}$$

**Figure 1.** Semantics of program expressions and actions.

## 3. Abstract Interpretation Background

In standard abstract interpretation [10, 11], abstract domains (or abstractions) are specified by Galois connections/insertions (GCs/GIs for short) or, equivalently, adjunctions. Concrete and abstract domains, $\langle C, \leq_C \rangle$ and $\langle A, \leq_A \rangle$, are assumed to be complete lattices which are related by abstraction and concretization maps $\alpha : C \to A$ and $\gamma : A \to C$ that give rise to an adjunction $(\alpha, C, A, \gamma)$, that is, for all $a$ and $c$, $\alpha(c) \leq_A a \Leftrightarrow c \leq_C \gamma(a)$. A GC is a GI when $\alpha \circ \gamma = \lambda x.x$. It is well known that a join-preserving $\alpha$ uniquely determines $\gamma$ as follows: $\gamma(a) = \vee\{c \in C \mid \alpha(c) \leq_A a\}$; conversely, a meet-preserving $\gamma$ uniquely determines $\alpha$ as follows: $\alpha(c) = \wedge\{a \in A \mid c \leq_C \gamma(a)\}$.

Let $f : C \to C$ be some concrete monotone function — for simplicity, we consider 1-ary functions — and let $f^\sharp : A \to A$ be a corresponding monotone abstract function defined on some abstraction $A$ related to $C$ by a GC. Then, $f^\sharp$ is a correct abstract interpretation of $f$ on $A$ when $\alpha \circ f \sqsubseteq f^\sharp \circ \alpha$ holds, where $\sqsubseteq$ denotes the pointwise ordering. Moreover, the abstract function $f^A \triangleq \alpha \circ f \circ \gamma : A \to A$ is called the best correct approximation of $f$ on $A$ because any abstract function $f^\sharp$ is correct iff $f^A \sqsubseteq f^\sharp$. Hence, for any abstraction $A$, $f^A$ plays the role of the best possible approximation of $f$ on the abstract domain $A$.

## 4. Store Abstractions

As usual in abstract interpretation, a store property is modeled by some abstraction $\text{Store}^\sharp$ that we assume to be encoded through a Galois connection

$$(\alpha_{store}, \langle \wp(\text{Store}), \subseteq \rangle, \langle \text{Store}^\sharp, \leq \rangle, \gamma_{store}).$$

For instance, as we will see later, the static types of program variables give rise to a simple store abstraction.

Given a program $P$, a store abstraction $\text{Store}^\sharp$ also induces a corresponding state abstraction $\text{State}^\sharp_P \triangleq \text{Store}^\sharp \times P$ and, in turn, a trace abstraction $\text{Trace}^\sharp_P \triangleq (\text{State}^\sharp_P)^*$.

### 4.1 Nonrelational Abstractions

Nonrelational store abstractions can be easily designed by a standard pointwise lifting of some value abstraction. Let $\text{Value}^\sharp$ be a value abstraction as formalized by a Galois connection

$$(\alpha_{value}, \langle \wp(\text{Value}), \subseteq \rangle, \langle \text{Value}^\sharp, \leq_{\text{Value}^\sharp} \rangle, \gamma_{value}).$$

The abstract domain $\text{Value}^\sharp$ induces a nonrelational store abstraction

$$\text{Store}^\sharp_{value} \triangleq \langle \text{Var} \to \text{Value}^\sharp, \sqsubseteq \rangle$$

where $\sqsubseteq$ is the pointwise ordering induced by $\leq_{\text{Value}^\sharp}$: $\rho_1^\sharp \sqsubseteq \rho_2^\sharp$ iff for all $x \in \text{Var}$, $\rho_1^\sharp(x) \leq_{\text{Value}^\sharp} \rho_2^\sharp(x)$. Here, the bottom and top abstract stores are, respectively, $\lambda x.\bot_{\text{Value}^\sharp}$ and $\lambda x.\top_{\text{Value}^\sharp}$. The abstraction map $\alpha^{\sqsubseteq}_{value} : \wp(\text{Store}) \to \text{Store}^\sharp_{value}$ is thus defined as follows:

$$\alpha^{\sqsubseteq}_{value}(S) \triangleq \lambda x.\alpha_{value}(\{\rho(x) \in \text{Value} \mid \rho \in S\})$$

while the corresponding concretization map $\gamma^{\sqsubseteq}_{value} : \text{Store}^\sharp_{value} \to \wp(\text{Store})$ is defined by adjunction from $\alpha^{\sqsubseteq}_{value}$ as recalled in Section 3 and it is easy to check that it turns out to be defined as follows:

$$\gamma^{\sqsubseteq}_{value}(\rho^\sharp) = \{\rho \in \text{Store} \mid \forall x \in \text{Var}\,.\, \rho(x) \in \gamma_{value}(\rho^\sharp(x))\}.$$

## 5. Hot Path Selection

A loop path is a sequence of program commands which is repeated in some execution of a program loop, together with a store property which is valid at the entry of each command in the path. A loop path becomes *hot* when, during the execution, it is repeated at least a fixed number $N$ of times. In a TJITC, hot path selection is performed by a loop path monitor that also records store properties (see, *e.g.*, [15]). Here, hot path selection is not operationally defined, it is instead modeled as an abstraction map over program traces, *i.e.*, program executions.

We first define a mapping $\mathit{loop} : \text{Trace}_P \to \wp(\text{Trace}_P)$ that returns all the loop paths in some execution trace of a program $P$. Formally, a loop path is a substring (*i.e.*, a segment) $\tau$ of a trace $\sigma$ such that: (1) the successor command in $\sigma$ of the last state in $\tau$ exists and coincides with the command – or its complement, when this is the last loop iteration – of the first state in $\tau$; (2) there is no other such command within $\tau$ (otherwise the sequence $\tau$ would contain multiple iterations); (3) the last state of $\tau$ performs a backward jump in the program $P$. To recognize backward jumps, we consider a topological order on the control flow graph of commands in $P$, here denoted by $\lessdot$:

$$loop(\langle\rho_0, C_0\rangle \cdots \langle\rho_n, C_n\rangle) \triangleq$$
$$\{\langle\rho_i, C_i\rangle\langle\rho_{i+1}, C_{i+1}\rangle \cdots \langle\rho_j, C_j\rangle \mid 0 \le i \le j < n,\ C_i \lessdot C_j,$$
$$lbl(C_{j+1}) = lbl(C_i), \forall k \in (i, j].\ C_k \notin \{C_i, cmpl(C_i)\}\}.$$

Let us remark that a loop path

$$\langle\rho_i, C_i\rangle \cdots \langle\rho_j, C_j\rangle \in loop(\langle\rho_0, C_0\rangle \cdots \langle\rho_n, C_n\rangle)$$

may contain some sub-loop path, namely it may happen that $loop(\langle\rho_i, C_i\rangle \cdots \langle\rho_j, C_j\rangle) \neq \varnothing$ so that some commands $C_k$, with $k \in [i, j]$, occur more than once in $\langle\rho_i, C_i\rangle \cdots \langle\rho_j, C_j\rangle$. We abuse notation by using $\alpha_{store}$ to denote a map $\alpha_{store} : \mathrm{Trace}_P \to \mathrm{Trace}^\sharp_P$ which "abstracts" program traces in $\mathrm{Trace}^\sharp_P$:

$$\alpha_{store}(\langle\rho_0, C_0\rangle \cdots \langle\rho_n, C_n\rangle) \triangleq$$
$$\langle\alpha_{store}(\{\rho_0\}), C_0\rangle \cdots \langle\alpha_{store}(\{\rho_n\}), C_n\rangle.$$

Given a static parameter $N > 0$, we define a function

$$hot^N : \mathrm{Trace}_P \to \wp(\mathrm{Trace}^\sharp_P)$$

which returns the set of $\mathrm{Store}^\sharp$-abstracted loop paths appearing at least $N$ times in some program trace. To count the number of times a loop path appears within a trace we use an auxiliary function $count : \mathrm{Trace}^\sharp_P \times \mathrm{Trace}^\sharp_P \to \mathbb{N}$ such that $count(\sigma, \tau)$ yields the number of times an abstract path $\tau$ occurs in a abstract trace $\sigma$:

$$count(\langle a_0, C_0\rangle \cdots \langle a_n, C_n\rangle, \langle b_0, C'_0\rangle \cdots \langle b_m, C'_m\rangle) \triangleq$$
$$\sum_{i=0}^{n-m} \begin{cases} 1 & \text{if } \langle a_i, C_i\rangle \cdots \langle a_{i+m}, C_{i+m}\rangle = \langle b_0, C'_0\rangle \cdots \langle b_m, C'_m\rangle \\ 0 & \text{otherwise} \end{cases}$$

Hence, $hot^N$ can be defined as follows:

$$hot^N(\sigma \equiv \langle\rho_0, C_0\rangle \cdots \langle\rho_n, C_n\rangle) \triangleq$$
$$\{\langle a_i, C_i\rangle \cdots \langle a_j, C_j\rangle \mid \exists\langle\rho_i, C_i\rangle \cdots \langle\rho_j, C_j\rangle \in loop(\sigma) \text{ s.t.}$$
$$i \le j,\ \alpha_{store}(\langle\rho_i, C_i\rangle \cdots \langle\rho_j, C_j\rangle) = \langle a_i, C_i\rangle \cdots \langle a_j, C_j\rangle,$$
$$count(\alpha_{store}(\sigma), \langle a_i, C_i\rangle \cdots \langle a_j, C_j\rangle) \ge N\}.$$

Finally, an abstraction map $\alpha^N_{hot} : \wp(\mathrm{Trace}_P) \to \wp(\mathrm{Trace}^\sharp_P)$ collects the results of applying $hot^N$ to a set of traces:

$$\alpha^N_{hot}(T) \triangleq \cup_{\sigma\in T}\, hot^N(\sigma).$$

A hot path $hp \in \alpha^N_{hot}(\mathbf{T}[\![P]\!])$ is also called a $N$-hot path and is compactly denoted as $hp = \langle a_0, C_0, ..., a_n, C_n\rangle$. Let us observe that if the hot path is the body of some while loop then its first command $C_0$ is a conditional, namely $C_0$ is the Boolean guard of the while loop. We define the following successor function for indices in hot paths: $next \triangleq \lambda i.\ i = n\,?\,0 : i + 1$. For a $N$-hot path $\langle a_0, C_0, ..., a_n, C_n\rangle \in \alpha^N_{hot}(\mathbf{T}[\![P]\!])$, for any $i \in [0, n]$, if $C_i$ is a conditional command $L_i : B_i \to L_{next(i)}$ then throughout the paper its complement $C^c_i = cmpl(C_i)$ will be also denoted by $L_i : \neg B_i \to L^c_{next(i)}$.

**Example 5.1.** Let us consider the program $P$ in Example 2.1. We consider a trivial one-point store abstraction $\mathrm{Store}^\sharp = \{\top\}$, where all the stores are abstracted to the same abstract store $\top$, *i.e.*, $\alpha_{store} = \lambda S.\top$. Here, we have two 2-hot paths in $P$, that is, it turns out that $\alpha^2_{hot}(\mathbf{T}[\![P]\!]) = \{hp_1, hp_2\}$ where:

$$hp_1 = \langle\top, C_1 \equiv L_1 : x \le 20 \to L_2,$$
$$\top, C_2 \equiv L_2 : x := x + 1 \to L_3,$$
$$\top, C^c_3 \equiv L_3 : \neg(x\%3 = 0) \to L_1\rangle;$$

$$hp_2 = \langle\top, C_1 \equiv L_1 : x \le 20 \to L_2,$$
$$\top, C_2 \equiv L_2 : x := x + 1 \to L_3,$$
$$\top, C_3 \equiv L_3 : (x\%3 = 0) \to L_4,$$
$$\top, C_4 \equiv x := x + 3 \to L_1\rangle.$$

□

## 6. Trace Extraction

For any abstract store $a \in \mathrm{Store}^\sharp$, a corresponding Boolean expression "guard $E_a$" $\in$ BExp is defined (where the notation $E_a$ should hint at an expression which is induced by the abstract store $a$) , whose semantics is as follows: for any $\rho \in$ Store,

$$\mathbf{B}[\![\text{guard } E_a]\!]\rho \triangleq \rho \in \gamma_{store}(a).$$

Thus, in turn, we also have program actions guard $E_a$ such that:

$$\mathbf{A}[\![\text{guard } E_a]\!]\rho \triangleq \begin{cases} \rho & \text{if } \rho \in \gamma_{store}(a) \\ \bot & \text{if } \rho \notin \gamma_{store}(a) \end{cases}$$

Let $P$ be a program and $hp = \langle a_0, C_0, ..., a_n, C_n\rangle \in \alpha^N_{hot}(\mathbf{T}[\![P]\!])$ be a hot path on some store abstraction $\mathrm{Store}^\sharp$. We define a synctatic transform of $P$ where the hot path $hp$ is explicitly extracted from $P$. This is implemented by a suitable relabeling of each command $C_i$ in $hp$ which is in turn preceded by the conditional guard $E_{a_i}$ induced by the store property $a_i$. To this aim, we consider three *injective* relabeling functions

$$\ell : [0, n] \to \mathbb{L}_1$$
$$\mathbb{l} : [1, n] \to \mathbb{L}_2$$
$$\overline{(\cdot)} : \mathbb{L} \to \overline{\mathbb{L}}$$

where $\mathbb{L}_1$, $\mathbb{L}_2$ and $\overline{\mathbb{L}}$ are pairwise disjoint sets of fresh labels, so that $labels(P) \cap (\mathbb{L}_1 \cup \mathbb{L}_2 \cup \overline{\mathbb{L}}) = \varnothing$. The transformed program $extr_{hp}(P)$ for the hot path $hp$ is defined as follows and a graphical example of this transform is depicted in Fig. 2.

**Definition 6.1 (Trace extraction transform).** The *trace extraction transform* of $P$ for the hot path $hp$ is:

$$extr_{hp}(P) \triangleq P \smallsetminus (\{C_0\} \cup \{cmpl(C_0) \mid cmpl(C_0) \in P\})$$
$$\cup \{\overline{L_0} : act(C_0) \to L_1\}$$
$$\cup \{\overline{L_0} : \neg act(C_0) \to L^c_1 \mid cmpl(C_0) \in P\}$$
$$\cup\ stitch_P(hp)$$

where the stitch of $hp$ into $P$ is defined as follows:

$$stitch_P(hp) \triangleq$$
$$\cup \{L_0 : \text{guard } E_{a_0} \to \ell_0,\ L_0 : \neg\text{guard } E_{a_0} \to \overline{L_0}\}$$
$$\cup \{\ell_i : act(C_i) \to \mathbb{l}_{i+1} \mid i \in [0, n-1]\} \cup \{\ell_n : act(C_n) \to L_0\}$$
$$\cup \{\ell_i : \neg act(C_i) \to L^c_{next(i)} \mid i \in [0, n],\ cmpl(C_i) \in P\}$$
$$\cup \{\mathbb{l}_i : \text{guard } E_{a_i} \to \ell_i,\ \mathbb{l}_i : \neg\text{guard } E_{a_i} \to L_i \mid i \in [1, n]\}.$$

□

The new command $L_0$ : guard $E_{a_0} \to \ell_0$ is therefore the entry conditional of the stitched hot path $stitch_P(hp)$, while any command $C \in stitch_P(hp)$ such that $suc(C) \in labels(P) \cup \overline{\mathbb{L}}$ is a potential exit (or bail out) command of $stitch_P(hp)$.

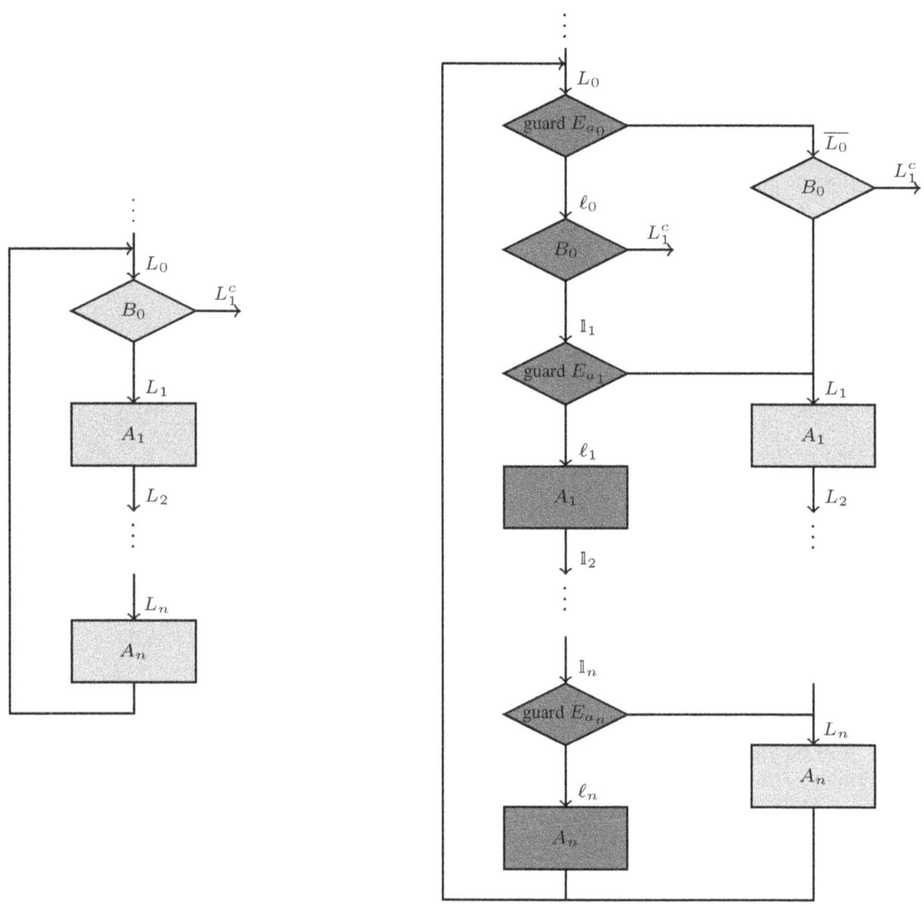


**Figure 2.** An example of trace extraction transform: on the left, a hot path $hp$ with commands in pink (in black/white: loosely dotted) shapes; on the right, the corresponding trace transform $extr_{hp}(P)$ with new commands in blue (in black/white: densely dotted) shapes.

**Lemma 6.2.** *If $P$ is well-formed then, for any hot path $hp$, $extr_{hp}(P)$ is well-formed.*

Let us remark that the stitch of the hot path $hp$ into $P$ is always a linear sequence of different commands, namely, $stitch_P(hp)$ does not contain loops nor join points. Furthermore, this happens even if the hot path $hp$ does contain some inner sub-loop. Technically, this comes as a consequence of the fact that the above relabeling functions are required to be injective. Hence, even if some command $C$ occurs more than once inside $hp$ then these multiple occurrences of $C$ in $hp$ are transformed into differently labeled commands in $stitch_P(hp)$.

**Example 6.3.** Let us consider the program $P$ in Example 2.1 and the hot path $hp_1 = \langle \top, C_1, \top, C_2, \top, C_3^c \rangle$ in Example 5.1, where stores are abstracted to the trivial one-point abstraction $\text{Store}^\sharp = \{\top\}$. Here, we have that for any store $\rho \in \text{Store}$, $\mathbf{B}[\![\text{guard } E_\top]\!]\rho = true$. The trace extraction transform of $P$ w.r.t. $hp$ is therefore as follows:

$$\begin{aligned} extr_{hp}(P) = P \smallsetminus \{C_1, C_1^c\} \\ \cup \{\overline{L_1} : x \leq 20 \to L_2,\ \overline{L_1} : \neg(x \leq 20) \to L_5\} \\ \cup\ stitch_P(hp) \end{aligned}$$

where $stitch_P(hp) =$

$$\begin{aligned} &\{H_0 \equiv L_1 : \text{guard } E_\top \to \ell_0,\ H_0^c \equiv L_1 : \neg\text{guard } E_\top \to \overline{L_1}\} \\ &\cup \{H_1 \equiv \ell_0 : x \leq 20 \to \mathbb{l}_1,\ H_1^c \equiv \ell_0 : \neg(x \leq 20) \to L_5\} \\ &\cup \{H_2 \equiv \mathbb{l}_1 : \text{guard } E_\top \to \ell_1,\ H_2^c \equiv \mathbb{l}_1 : \neg\text{guard } E_\top \to L_2\} \\ &\cup \{H_3 \equiv \ell_1 : x := x + 1 \to \mathbb{l}_2\} \\ &\cup \{H_4 \equiv \mathbb{l}_2 : \text{guard } E_\top \to \ell_2,\ H_4^c \equiv \mathbb{l}_2 : \neg\text{guard } E_\top \to L_3\} \\ &\cup \{H_5 \equiv \ell_2 : \neg(x\%3 = 0) \to L_1,\ H_5^c \equiv \ell_2 : (x\%3 = 0) \to L_4\}. \end{aligned}$$

Hence, $extr_{hp}(P)$ can be rewritten at a high-level representation using while loops and gotos as follows:

$x := 0;$
$L_1$ : **while** guard $E_\top$ **do**
  **if** $\neg(x \leq 20)$ **then goto** $L_5$;
  **if** $\neg$guard $E_\top$ **then goto** $L_2$;
  $x := x + 1$;
  **if** $\neg$guard $E_\top$ **then goto** $L_3$;
  **if** $(x\%3 = 0)$ **then goto** $L_4$;
**if** $\neg(x \leq 20)$ **then goto** $L_5$;
$L_2$ : $x := x + 1$;
$L_3$ : **if** $\neg(x\%3 = 0)$ **then goto** $L_1$;
$L_4$ : $x := x + 3$;
**goto** $L_1$;
$L_5$ : **skip**;

□

## 7. Correctness

As advocated by Cousot and Cousot [12, par. 3.8], correctness of dynamic program transformations and optimizations should be defined with respect to some observational abstraction of program trace semantics: a program transform is correct when, at some level of abstraction, the observation of the execution of the subject program is equivalent to the observation of the execution of the transformed program. The approach by Guo and Palsberg [17] basically relies on a notion of correctness that requires the same *store changes* in both the transformed/optimized program and the original program. This can be easily encoded by an observational abstraction $\alpha_{sc} : \wp(\text{Trace}_P) \to \wp(\text{Store}^*)$ of trace semantics that observes store changes in execution traces of a program $P$:

$$sc : \text{Trace}_P \to \text{Store}^*$$

$$sc(\sigma) \triangleq \begin{cases} \varepsilon & \text{if } \sigma = \varepsilon \\ \rho & \text{if } \sigma = \langle \rho, C \rangle \\ sc(\langle \rho, C_1 \rangle \sigma') & \text{if } \sigma = \langle \rho, C_0 \rangle \langle \rho, C_1 \rangle \sigma' \\ \rho_0\, sc(\langle \rho_1, C_1 \rangle \sigma') & \text{if } \sigma = \langle \rho_0, C_0 \rangle \langle \rho_1, C_1 \rangle \sigma', \rho_0 \neq \rho_1 \end{cases}$$

$$\alpha_{sc}(T) \triangleq \{sc(\sigma) \mid \sigma \in T\}$$

Since $\alpha_{sc}$ obviously preserves arbitrary set unions, it admits a right adjoint $\gamma_{sc} : \wp(\text{Store}^*) \to \wp(\text{Trace}_P)$ defined as $\gamma_{sc}(S) \triangleq \cup\{T \in \wp(\text{Trace}_P) \mid \alpha_{sc}(T) \subseteq S\}$, that gives rise to a GC $(\alpha_{sc}, \langle \wp(\text{Trace}_P), \subseteq \rangle, \langle \wp(\text{Store}^*), \subseteq \rangle, \gamma_{sc})$.

However, the store changes abstraction $\alpha_{sc}$ may be too strong in practice. This condition can be thus relaxed and generalized to an observational abstraction that demands to have the same stores (possibly just for some subset of variables) only at some specific program points. For example, these program points may depend on the language. In a language without output primitives and functions, as that considered in [17], we could be interested just in the final store of the program (when it terminates), or in the entry and exit stores of any loop containing an extracted hot path. If a more general language includes a sort of primitive "put $\mathcal{X}$" that "outputs" the value of program variables ranging in some set $\mathcal{X}$ then we may want to have stores with the same values for variables in $\mathcal{X}$ at each output point. Moreover, the same sequence of outputs should be preserved, *i.e.* optimizations must not modify the order of output instructions.

We therefore consider an additional sort of actions: put $\mathcal{X} \in \mathbb{A}$, where $\mathcal{X} \subseteq$ Var is a set of program variables. The semantics of put $\mathcal{X}$ obviously does not affect program stores, *i.e.*, $\mathbf{A}[\![\text{put } \mathcal{X}]\!]\rho \triangleq \rho$. Correspondingly, an observational abstraction $\alpha_o : \wp(\text{Trace}_P) \to \wp(\text{Store}^*)$ of trace semantics observes program stores at output program points only (we use $\rho_{|\mathcal{X}}$ to denote store restriction to variables in $\mathcal{X}$):

$$out : \text{Trace}_P \to \text{Store}^*$$

$$out(\sigma) \triangleq \begin{cases} \varepsilon & \text{if } \sigma = \varepsilon \\ out(\sigma') & \text{if } \sigma = s\sigma' \wedge act(s) \neq \text{put } \mathcal{X} \\ \rho_{|\mathcal{X}}\, out(\sigma') & \text{if } \sigma = \langle \rho, L : \text{put } \mathcal{X} \to L' \rangle \sigma' \end{cases}$$

$$\alpha_o(T) \triangleq \{out(\sigma) \mid \sigma \in T\}$$

Similarly to $\alpha_{sc}$, here again we have a GC $(\alpha_o, \langle \wp(\text{Trace}_P), \subseteq \rangle, \langle \wp(\text{Store}^*), \subseteq \rangle, \gamma_o)$. This approach is clearly more general because the above store changes abstraction $\alpha_{sc}$ is more precise than $\alpha_o$, *i.e.*, for any set of traces $T$, $\gamma_{sc}(\alpha_{sc}(T)) \subseteq \gamma_o(\alpha_o(T))$, or, equivalently, $\alpha_{sc}(T_1) = \alpha_{sc}(T_2) \Rightarrow \alpha_o(T_1) = \alpha_o(T_2)$.

**Example 7.1 (Dead store elimination).** The above approach based on a generic observational abstraction allows us to prove the correctness of program optimizations that are unsound in Guo and Palsberg [17]'s framework, such as dead store elimination. For example, in a program fragment such as

**while** $(x \leq 0)$ **do**
  $z := 0;$
  $x := x + 1;$
  $z := 1;$

one can extract the hot path

$$hp = \langle x \leq 0, z := 0, x := x + 1, z := 1 \rangle$$

and perform dead store elimination by optimizing $hp$ to $hp' = \langle x \leq 0, x := x+1, z := 1 \rangle$. As observed by Guo and Palsberg [17, Section 4.3], this is clearly unsound in bisimulation-based correctness because this hot path optimization does not output bisimilar code. By contrast, this optimization can be made sound in our framework by choosing an observational abstraction that records store changes at the beginning and at the exit of loops containing extracted hot paths. □

### 7.1 Correctness Proof

It turns out that observational correctness of the hot path extraction transform can be proved w.r.t. the more precise observational abstraction $\alpha_{sc}$.

**Theorem 7.2 (Correctness of trace extraction).** *For any* $P \in$ Program, $hp \in \alpha^N_{hot}(\mathbf{T}[\![P]\!])$, *we have that* $\alpha_{sc}(\mathbf{T}[\![extr_{hp}(P)]\!]) = \alpha_{sc}(\mathbf{T}[\![P]\!])$.

In the rest of this section we outline a proof sketch of this result. Let us fix a hot path $hp = \langle a_0, C_0, ..., a_n, C_n \rangle \in \alpha^N_{hot}(\mathbf{T}[\![P]\!])$ and let $P_{hp} \triangleq extr_{hp}(P)$. The proof relies on a mapping of traces of the program $P$ into corresponding traces of $P_{hp}$ that unfolds the hot path $hp$ (or any its initial fragment) according to the hot path extraction strategy given by Definition 6.1.

We define two functions $\text{tr}^{in}_{hp}, \text{tr}^{out}_{hp} : \text{Trace}_P \to \text{Trace}_{P_{hp}}$ in Fig. 3. The first function, $\text{tr}^{out}_{hp}(s\sigma)$, on the trace $s\sigma$ begins to unfold in $P_{hp}$ the hot path $hp$ when: (i) $s = \langle \rho, C_0 \rangle$ where $C_0$ is the first command of $hp$; and (ii) the condition guard $E_{a_0}$ is satisfied in the store $\rho$. If this unfolding for the trace $s\sigma$ is actually started by applying $\text{tr}^{out}_{hp}(s\sigma)$ then it is carried on by applying $\text{tr}^{in}_{hp}(\sigma)$, *i.e.*, with a *in*-modality. The second function application, $\text{tr}^{in}_{hp}(s\sigma)$, carries on the unfolding of $hp$ in $P_{hp}$ when: (i) $s = \langle \rho, C_i \rangle$ where $i \in [1, n-1]$, namely the command $C_i$ in $hp$ is different from $C_0$ and $C_n$; and (ii) the condition guard $E_{a_i}$ holds for the store $\rho$. If this is not the case then $\text{tr}^{in}_{hp}(\langle \rho, C_i \rangle \sigma)$, after a suitable unfolding step for $\langle \rho, C_i \rangle$, jumps back to the *out*-modality by progressing with $\text{tr}^{out}_{hp}(\sigma)$. It turns out that these two functions are well defined and $\text{tr}^{out}_{hp}$ does not alter store change sequences.

**Lemma 7.3.**

(1) $\text{tr}^{out}_{hp}$ *and* $\text{tr}^{in}_{hp}$ *are well-defined,* i.e., *for any* $\sigma \in \text{Trace}_P$, $\text{tr}^{out}_{hp}(\sigma), \text{tr}^{in}_{hp}(\sigma) \in \text{Trace}_{P_{hp}}$.

(2) *For any* $\sigma \in \text{Trace}_P$, $sc(\text{tr}^{out}_{hp}(\sigma)) = sc(\sigma)$.

**Proof sketch of Theorem 7.2.** Let us define $\text{tr}_{hp} : \wp(\text{Trace}_P) \to \wp(\text{Trace}_{P_{hp}})$ as $\text{tr}_{hp}(T) \triangleq \{\text{tr}^{out}_{hp}(\sigma) \mid \sigma \in T\}$. Technically, the proof consists in showing the following two points.

(A) $\text{tr}_{hp}(\mathbf{T}[\![P]\!]) \subseteq \mathbf{T}[\![P_{hp}]\!]$: this shows that for any execution trace $\sigma$ of $P$, $\text{tr}^{out}_{hp}(\sigma)$ is an execution trace of $P_{hp}$; this is not hard to prove.

(B) $\alpha_{sc}(\mathbf{T}[\![P_{hp}]\!]) \subseteq \alpha_{sc}(\mathbf{T}[\![P]\!])$: this is proved by the following statement: $\sigma \in \mathbf{T}[\![P_{hp}]\!] \smallsetminus \text{tr}_{hp}(\mathbf{T}[\![P]\!]) \Rightarrow F[P_{hp}]\{\sigma\} \in \text{tr}_{hp}(\mathbf{T}[\![P]\!])$. The proof relies on the fact that one such trace $\sigma$ is necessarily of the following shape: $\sigma = \sigma' \langle \rho, C \rangle$ where

$$\mathrm{tr}^{out}_{hp}(\epsilon) \triangleq \epsilon$$

$$\mathrm{tr}^{out}_{hp}(s\sigma) \triangleq \begin{cases} \langle \rho, L_O : \text{guard } E_{a_O} \to \ell_O \rangle \langle \rho, \ell_O : act(C_O) \to \mathbb{l}_1 \rangle\, \mathrm{tr}^{in}_{hp}(\sigma) & \text{if } s = \langle \rho, C_O \rangle,\ \alpha_{store}(\{\rho\}) \leq a_O \\ \langle \rho, L_O : \neg\text{guard } E_{a_O} \to \overline{L_O} \rangle \langle \rho, \overline{L_O} : act(C_O) \to L_1 \rangle\, \mathrm{tr}^{out}_{hp}(\sigma) & \text{if } s = \langle \rho, C_O \rangle,\ \alpha_{store}(\{\rho\}) \not\leq a_O \\ \langle \rho, L_O : \text{guard } E_{a_O} \to \ell_O \rangle \langle \rho, \ell_O : \neg act(C_O) \to L^c_1 \rangle\, \mathrm{tr}^{out}_{hp}(\sigma) & \text{if } s = \langle \rho, cmpl(C_O) \rangle,\ \alpha_{store}(\{\rho\}) \leq a_O \\ \langle \rho, L_O : \neg\text{guard } E_{a_O} \to \overline{L_O} \rangle \langle \rho, \overline{L_O} : \neg act(C_O) \to L^c_1 \rangle\, \mathrm{tr}^{out}_{hp}(\sigma) & \text{if } s = \langle \rho, cmpl(C_O) \rangle,\ \alpha_{store}(\{\rho\}) \not\leq a_O \\ s \cdot \mathrm{tr}^{out}_{hp}(\sigma) & \text{otherwise} \end{cases}$$

$$\mathrm{tr}^{in}_{hp}(\epsilon) \triangleq \epsilon$$

$$\mathrm{tr}^{in}_{hp}(s\sigma) \triangleq \begin{cases} \langle \rho, \mathbb{l}_i : \text{guard } E_{a_i} \to \ell_i \rangle \langle \rho, \ell_i : act(C_i) \to \mathbb{l}_{i+1} \rangle\, \mathrm{tr}^{in}_{hp}(\sigma) & \text{if } s = \langle \rho, C_i \rangle,\ i \in [1, n-1],\ \alpha_{store}(\{\rho\}) \leq a_i \\ \langle \rho, \mathbb{l}_n : \text{guard } E_{a_n} \to \ell_n \rangle \langle \rho, \ell_n : act(C_n) \to L_O \rangle\, \mathrm{tr}^{out}_{hp}(\sigma) & \text{if } s = \langle \rho, C_n \rangle,\ \alpha_{store}(\{\rho\}) \leq a_n \\ \langle \rho, \mathbb{l}_i : \neg\text{guard } E_{a_i} \to L_i \rangle \langle \rho, C_i \rangle\, \mathrm{tr}^{out}_{hp}(\sigma) & \text{if } s = \langle \rho, C_i \rangle,\ i \in [1, n],\ \alpha_{store}(\{\rho\}) \not\leq a_i \\ \langle \rho, \mathbb{l}_i : \text{guard } E_{a_i} \to \ell_i \rangle \langle \rho, \ell_i : \neg act(C_i) \to L^c_{next(i)} \rangle\, \mathrm{tr}^{out}_{hp}(\sigma) & \text{if } s = \langle \rho, cmpl(C_i) \rangle,\ i \in [1, n],\ \alpha_{store}(\{\rho\}) \leq a_i \\ \langle \rho, \mathbb{l}_i : \neg\text{guard } E_{a_i} \to L_i \rangle \langle \rho, cmpl(C_i) \rangle\, \mathrm{tr}^{out}_{hp}(\sigma) & \text{if } s = \langle \rho, cmpl(C_i) \rangle,\ i \in [1, n],\ \alpha_{store}(\{\rho\}) \not\leq a_i \\ s \cdot \mathrm{tr}^{out}_{hp}(\sigma) & \text{otherwise} \end{cases}$$

**Figure 3.** Definition of $\mathrm{tr}^{out}_{hp}$ and $\mathrm{tr}^{in}_{hp}$.

$act(C) \in \{\text{guard } E_{a_i}, \neg\text{guard } E_{a_i}\}$; then, it is not hard to prove that $F[P_{hp}]\{\sigma'\langle \rho, C \rangle\} \in \mathrm{tr}_{hp}(\mathbf{T}[\![P]\!])$. In words, one such trace $\sigma$ of $P_{hp}$ can be extended through an execution step in $P_{hp}$ to a trace in $\mathrm{tr}_{hp}(\mathbf{T}[\![P]\!])$.

We therefore obtain:

$$\begin{aligned} \alpha_{sc}(\mathbf{T}[\![P]\!]) = &\quad [\text{By Lemma 7.3 (2)}, \alpha_{sc} \circ \mathrm{tr}_{hp} = \alpha_{sc}] \\ \alpha_{sc}(\mathrm{tr}_{hp}(\mathbf{T}[\![P]\!])) \subseteq &\quad [\text{By point (A)}] \\ \alpha_{sc}(\mathbf{T}[\![P_{hp}]\!]) \subseteq &\quad [\text{By point (B)}] \\ \alpha_{sc}(\mathbf{T}[\![P]\!]) & \end{aligned}$$

and this closes the proof. □

## 8. Type Specialization

One key optimization for dynamic languages like JavaScript and PHP is type specialization, that is, using type-specific primitives in place of generic untyped operations whose runtime execution can be very costly. As a paradigmatic example, a generic addition operation could be defined on more than one type, so that the execution environment must check the type of its operands and execute a different operation depending on these types: this is the case of the addition operation in JavaScript (see its semantics in the ECMA-262 standard [21, Section 11.6]) and of the semantics of $+$ in our language as given in Section 2.2. Of course, type specialization avoids the overhead of dynamic type checking and dispatch of generic untyped operations. When a type is associated to each variable before the execution of a command in some hot path, this type environment can be used to replace generic operations with type-specific primitives.

### 8.1 Type Abstraction

Let us recall that the set of type names is

$$\text{Types} = \{\text{Int}, \text{String}, \text{Undef}, \text{Any}, \varnothing\}.$$

Type names can be therefore viewed as the following finite lattice $\langle \text{Types}, \subseteq \rangle$:

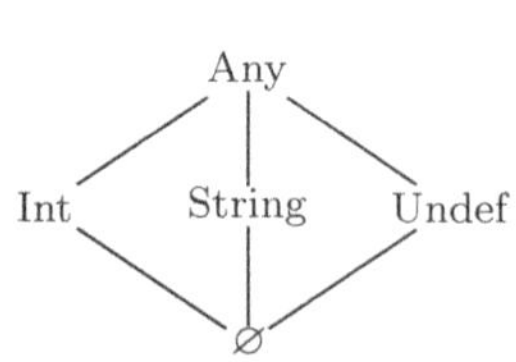


The abstraction map $\alpha_{type} : \wp(\text{Value}) \to \text{Types}$ takes a set of values and returns the smallest type containing it. Since Types viewed as a subset of $\wp(\text{Value})$ is closed under intersections (where Any is interpreted as the top element Value and $\varnothing$ is the bottom element), $\alpha_{type}$ can be indeed defined as a simple closure operator (*i.e.*, a monotonic, increasing and idempotent function) on $\langle \wp(\text{Value}), \subseteq \rangle$:

$$\alpha_{type}(V) \triangleq \cap\{T \in \text{Types} \mid V \subseteq T\}.$$

Given a value $v \in \text{Value}$, $\alpha_{type}(\{v\})$ thus coincides with $type(v)$. Here, the concretization function $\gamma_{type} : \text{Types} \to \wp(\text{Value})$ is simply the identity map (with Any $=$ Value).

Following the general approach described in Section 4.1, we consider a simple nonrelational store abstraction for types

$$\text{Store}^t \triangleq \langle \text{Var} \to \text{Types}, \dot{\subseteq} \rangle$$

where $\dot{\subseteq}$ is the usual pointwise lifting of the ordering $\subseteq$ for Types, so that $\lambda x.\varnothing$ and $\lambda x.\text{Any}$ are, respectively, the bottom and top abstract stores in $\text{Store}^t$. The abstraction and concretization maps $\alpha_{store} : \wp(\text{Store}) \to \text{Store}^t$ and $\gamma_{store} : \text{Store}^t \to \wp(\text{Store})$ are defined as a straight instantiation of the definitions in Section 4.1.

The abstract type semantics $\mathbf{E}^t : \text{Exp} \to \text{Store}^t \to \text{Types}$ of expressions is defined as best correct approximation of the corresponding concrete semantics $\mathbf{E}$ on the type abstractions $\text{Store}^t$ and Types, *i.e.*, $\mathbf{E}^t[\![E]\!]\rho^t \triangleq \alpha_{type}(\mathbf{E}[\![E]\!]\gamma_{store}(\rho^t))$. This definition leads to the following equalities:

$$\mathbf{E}^t[\![v]\!]\rho^t = type(v) \qquad \mathbf{E}^t[\![x]\!]\rho^t = \rho^t(x)$$

$$\mathbf{E}^t[\![E_1 + E_2]\!]\rho^t =$$
$$\begin{cases} \varnothing & \text{if } \exists i.\, \mathbf{E}^t[\![E_i]\!]\rho^t = \varnothing \\ \mathbf{E}^t[\![E_1]\!]\rho^t & \text{else if } \mathbf{E}^t[\![E_1]\!]\rho^t = \mathbf{E}^t[\![E_2]\!]\rho^t \in \{\text{Int}, \text{String}\} \\ \text{Undef} & \text{else if } \forall i.\, \mathbf{E}^t[\![E_i]\!]\rho^t < \text{Any} \\ \text{Any} & \text{otherwise} \end{cases}$$

For instance, we have that:

$$\begin{aligned} &\mathbf{E}^t[\![x + y]\!][x/\text{String}, y/\varnothing] = \varnothing, \\ &\mathbf{E}^t[\![x + y]\!][x/\text{String}, y/\text{String}] = \text{String}, \\ &\mathbf{E}^t[\![x + y]\!][x/\text{Int}, y/\text{String}] = \text{Undef}, \\ &\mathbf{E}^t[\![x + y]\!][x/\text{Int}, y/\text{Any}] = \text{Any}. \end{aligned}$$

According to Section 6, for any abstract type store $[x_i/T_i \mid x_i \in \text{Var}]$ we consider a corresponding Boolean action guard

$$\text{guard } x_0 : T_0 \cdots x_n : T_n \in \text{BExp}$$

whose corresponding program action has the following semantics, which is automatically induced (as defined in Section 6) by the Galois connection $(\alpha_{store}, \wp(\text{Store}), \text{Store}^t, \gamma_{store})$: for any $\rho \in$ Store,

$$\mathbf{A}[\![\text{guard } x_0 : T_0 \cdots x_n : T_n]\!]\rho \triangleq \begin{cases} \rho & \text{if } \forall i.\ \mathit{type}(\rho(x_i)) \subseteq T_i \\ \bot & \exists i.\ \mathit{type}(\rho(x_i)) \not\subseteq T_i \end{cases}$$

### 8.2 Type Specialization of Hot Paths

Let us consider some hot path $hp = \langle \rho_0^t, C_0, \ldots, \rho_n^t, C_n \rangle \in \alpha_{hot}^N(\mathbf{T}[\![P]\!])$ on the type abstraction $\langle \text{Store}^t, \dot{\subseteq} \rangle$, where each $\rho_i^t$ is therefore a type map. The trace extraction transform $extr_{hp}(P)$ of $P$ for $hp$ gives rise to the set $stitch_P(hp)$ of commands that stitches the hot path $hp$ into $P$. Hence, for any $i \in [0, n]$, $stitch_P(hp)$ contains a typed guard that we simply denote as guard $\rho_i^t$. Typed guards allow us to define type specialization of commands in the stitched hot path: this is defined as a program transform that instantiates most type-specific addition operations in place of generic untyped additions by exploiting the type information dynamically recorded by typed guards in $stitch_P(hp)$. Note that if $C \in stitch_P(hp)$ and $act(C) \equiv x := E_1 + E_2$ then $C \equiv \ell_i : x := E_1 + E_2 \to L'$, for some $i \in [0, n]$, where $L' \in \{\mathbb{l}_{i+1}, L_0\}$. Let $\mathbb{C}^t$ denote the set of commands that permits type specific additions $+_{\text{Int}}$ and $+_{\text{String}}$ and, in turn, Program$^t$ denote the possible type specialized programs over $\mathbb{C}^t$. The function $\text{ts}_{hp} : stitch_P(hp) \to \mathbb{C}^t$ is defined as follows:

$$\text{ts}_{hp}(C) \triangleq C \qquad \text{if } act(C) \neq x := E_1 + E_2$$

$$\text{ts}_{hp}(\ell_i : x := E_1 + E_2 \to L') \triangleq$$

$$\begin{cases} \ell_i : x := E_1 +_{\text{Int}} E_2 \to L' & \text{if } \mathbf{E}^t[\![E_1 + E_2]\!]\rho_i^t = \text{Int} \\ \ell_i : x := E_1 +_{\text{String}} E_2 \to L' & \text{if } \mathbf{E}^t[\![E_1 + E_2]\!]\rho_i^t = \text{String} \\ \ell_i : x := E_1 + E_2 \to L' & \text{otherwise} \end{cases}$$

Hence, hot path type specialization TS is defined by

$$\text{TS}(stitch_P(hp)) \triangleq \{\text{ts}_{hp}(C) \mid C \in stitch_P(hp)\} \in \text{Program}^t.$$

The correctness of this program transform is quite straightforward. Let Trace$^t$ be the set of traces for type specialized programs in Program$^t$ and let $tt : \text{Trace}^t \to \text{Trace}$ be defined as follows:

$$tt(\epsilon) \triangleq \epsilon$$

$$tt(s\sigma) \triangleq$$

$$\begin{cases} \langle \rho, L : x := E_1 + E_2 \to L' \rangle tt(\sigma) & \\ \qquad \text{if } s = \langle \rho, L : x := E_1 +_{\text{Type}} E_2 \to L' \rangle \\ s \cdot tt(\sigma) \qquad \text{otherwise} \end{cases}$$

**Theorem 8.1 (Correctness of type specialization).** *For any typed $hp \in \alpha_{hot}^N(\mathbf{T}[\![P]\!])$, we have that $tt(\mathbf{T}[\![\text{TS}(stitch_P(hp))]\!]) = \mathbf{T}[\![stitch_P(hp)]\!]$.*

*Typed trace extraction* $extr_{hp}^t(P)$ consists in extracting and simultaneously type specializing a typed hot path $hp$ in a program $P$, *i.e.*, it can be defined as follows:

$$extr_{hp}^t(P) \triangleq extr_{hp}(P) \smallsetminus stitch_P(hp) \cup \text{TS}(stitch_P(hp)).$$

Correctness of typed trace extraction $extr_{hp}^t$ is a straight consequence of Theorems 7.2 and 8.1.

**Corollary 8.2 (Correctness of typed trace extraction).** *For any typed $hp \in \alpha_{hot}^N(\mathbf{T}[\![P]\!])$, we have that $\alpha_{sc}(\mathbf{T}[\![extr_{hp}^t(P)]\!]) = \alpha_{sc}(\mathbf{T}[\![P]\!])$.*

**Example 8.3.** Let us consider the following sieve of Eratosthenes in a Javascript-like language – this is taken from the running example in [15] – where *primes* is initialized to an array of 100 *true* values. With a slight abuse, we assume that our language is extended with Boolean values and arrays. The semantics of arrays load and stores is as usual: first the index expression is checked to be in bounds, then the value is read or stored into the array. If the index is out of bounds, we assume the program is aborted.

**for** (**var** $i = 2;\ i < 100;\ i = i + 1$) **do**
  **if** (!$primes[i]$) **then continue**;
  **for** (**var** $k = i + i;\ k < 100;\ k = k + i$) **do** $primes[k] = false$;

This program is encoded in our language as follows:

$$\begin{aligned} P = \{ & C_0 \equiv L_0 : i := 2 \to L_1, \\ & C_1 \equiv L_1 : i < 100 \to L_2,\ C_1^c \equiv L_1 : \neg(i < 100) \to L_8, \\ & C_2 \equiv L_2 : primes[i] = \text{tt} \to L_3, \\ & C_2^c \equiv L_2 : \neg(primes[i] = \text{tt}) \to L_7, \\ & C_3 \equiv L_3 : k := i + i \to L_4, \\ & C_4 \equiv L_4 : k < 100 \to L_5,\ C_4^c \equiv L_4 : \neg(k < 100) \to L_7, \\ & C_5 \equiv L_5 : primes[k] := \text{ff} \to L_6, \\ & C_6 \equiv L_6 : k := k + i \to L_4, \\ & C_7 \equiv L_7 : i := i + 1 \to L_1,\ C_8 \equiv L_8 : \text{skip} \to \text{Ł} \}. \end{aligned}$$

Let us consider the type environment $\rho^t$ defined as

$$\rho^t \triangleq \{primes[n]/\text{Bool}, i/\text{Int}, k/\text{Int}\} \in \text{Store}^t$$

where $primes[n]/\text{Bool}$ is a shorthand for $primes[0]/\text{Bool}, \ldots, primes[99]/\text{Bool}$. Then the first traced 2-hot path on the type abstraction Store$^t$ is:

$$hp_1 \triangleq \langle \rho^t, C_4, \rho^t, C_5, \rho^t, C_6 \rangle.$$

As a consequence, the typed transform extraction of $hp_1$ yields:

$$\begin{aligned} P_1 \triangleq extr_{hp_1}^t(P) = & P \smallsetminus \{C_4, C_4^c\} \\ & \cup \{\overline{L_4} : k < 100 \to L_5,\ \overline{L_4} : \neg(k < 100) \to L_7\} \\ & \cup \text{TS}(stitch_P(hp)) \end{aligned}$$

$$\begin{aligned} \text{where } \text{TS}(stitch_P(hp)) = \{ & \\ & H_0 \equiv L_4 : \text{guard } (primes[n] : \text{Bool}, i : \text{Int}, k : \text{Int}) \to \ell_0, \\ & H_0^c \equiv L_4 : \neg\text{guard } (primes[n] : \text{Bool}, i : \text{Int}, k : \text{Int}) \to \overline{L_4}, \\ & H_1 \equiv \ell_0 : k < 100 \to \mathbb{l}_1,\ H_1^c \equiv \ell_0 : \neg(k < 100) \to L_7, \\ & H_2 \equiv \mathbb{l}_1 : \text{guard } (primes[n] : \text{Bool}, i : \text{Int}, k : \text{Int}) \to \ell_1, \\ & H_2^c \equiv \mathbb{l}_1 : \neg\text{guard } (primes[n] : \text{Bool}, i : \text{Int}, k : \text{Int}) \to L_5, \\ & H_3 \equiv \ell_1 : primes[k] := \text{ff} \to \mathbb{l}_2, \\ & H_4 \equiv \mathbb{l}_2 : \text{guard } (primes[n] : \text{Bool}, i : \text{Int}, k : \text{Int}) \to \ell_2, \\ & H_4^c \equiv \mathbb{l}_2 : \neg\text{guard } (primes[n] : \text{Bool}, i : \text{Int}, k : \text{Int}) \to L_6, \\ & H_5 \equiv \ell_2 : k := k +_{\text{Int}} i \to L_4 \}. \quad \square \end{aligned}$$

## 9. A General Correctness Criterion

Abstract interpretation allows us to view type specialization in Section 8 just as a particular *correct* hot path optimization that can be easily generalized. Guarded hot paths are a key feature of our tracing compilation model, where guards are dynamically recorded by the hot path monitor and range over abstract values in some store abstraction. An abstract guard for a command $C$ in some hot path $hp$ thus encodes a store property which is modeled in some abstract domain Store$^\sharp$ and is guaranteed to hold at the entry of $C$. This store information encapsulated by abstract guards can then be used to transform and optimize $hp$, *i.e.*, all the commands in the stitched hot path $stitch_P(hp)$.

This provides a modular approach to proving the correctness of some hot path optimization $O$. In fact, since correctness has to be proved w.r.t. some observational abstraction $\alpha_o$ of trace semantics and Theorem 7.2 ensures that this correctness holds for the store changes abstraction $\alpha_{sc}$ of the unoptimized trace extraction transform, we just need to prove the correctness of the optimization $O$ on the whole stitched hot path $stitch_P(hp)$, which thus includes the abstract guards of the hot path $hp$. Hence, fixing a program $P$, a hot path optimization $O$ is modeled as a program transform

$$O : \{stitch_P(hp) \mid hp \in \alpha^N_{hot}(\mathbf{T}[\![P]\!])\} \to \text{Program}$$

where Program may permit new expressions and/or actions, like the case of type-specific addition operations in type specialization. $O$ is required to be correct according to the following definition.

**Definition 9.1 (Correctness of hot path optimization).** $O$ is *correct* if for any $P \in$ Program and for any $hp \in \alpha^N_{hot}(\mathbf{T}[\![P]\!])$, $\alpha_o(\mathbf{T}[\![O(stitch_P(hp))]\!]) = \alpha_o(\mathbf{T}[\![stitch_P(hp)]\!])$. □

As an example, it would be quite simple to formalize the variable folding optimization of hot paths considered by Guo and Palsberg [17] and to prove it correct in our framework w.r.t. the store changes abstraction $\alpha_{sc}$.

## 10. Nested Hot Paths

Once a first hot path $hp_1$ has been extracted by transforming $P$ to $P_1 \triangleq extr_{hp_1}(P)$, it may well happen that a new hot path $hp_2$ in $P_1$ contains $hp_1$ as a nested sub-path. Following TraceMonkey's trace recording strategy [15], we attempt to nest an inner hot path inside the current trace: during trace recording, an inner hot path is called as a subroutine, this executes a loop to a successful completion and then returns to the trace recorder that may therefore register the inner hot path as part of a new hot path.

To this aim, let us reshape the definitions in Section 5. Let $P$ be the original program and $P'$ be some hot path transform of $P$ so that $P' \smallsetminus P$ contains all the commands (guards included) in the hot path. We define a function $hotcut : \text{Trace}_{P'} \to (\text{State}_{P'})^*$ that cuts from a trace in $P'$ all the states whose commands appear in (some previous) hot path $hp$ except the entry and exit states of $hp$:

$$hotcut(\sigma) \triangleq \begin{cases} \epsilon & \text{if } \sigma = \epsilon \\ hotcut(\langle\rho_1, C_1\rangle\langle\rho_3, C_3\rangle\sigma') & \\ \qquad \text{if } \sigma = \langle\rho_1, C_1\rangle\langle\rho_2, C_2\rangle\langle\rho_3, C_3\rangle\sigma' \;\&\; C_1, C_2, C_3 \notin P \\ \sigma_0\, hotcut(\sigma_1 \cdots \sigma_{|\sigma|-1}) & \text{otherwise} \end{cases}$$

In turn, we define $outerhot^N : \text{Trace}_{P'} \to \wp((\text{State}^\sharp_{P'})^*)$ as follows:

$$\begin{aligned} outerhot^N(\sigma) \triangleq \{&\langle a_i, C_i\rangle \cdots \langle a_j, C_j\rangle \in (\text{State}^\sharp_{P'})^* \mid \\ &\exists\langle\rho_i, C_i\rangle \cdots \langle\rho_j, C_j\rangle \in loop(hotcut(\sigma)) \text{ s.t. } i \le j, \\ &\alpha_{store}(\langle\rho_i, C_i\rangle \cdots \langle\rho_j, C_j\rangle) = \langle a_i, C_i\rangle \cdots \langle a_j, C_j\rangle, \\ &count(\alpha_{store}(hotcut(\sigma)), \langle a_i, C_i\rangle \cdots \langle a_j, C_j\rangle) \ge N\}. \end{aligned}$$

Clearly, when $P' = P$ we have that $hotcut = \lambda\sigma.\sigma$ so that $outerhot^N = hot^N$. Finally, we define the collecting version $\alpha^N_{outerhot} \triangleq \lambda T. \cup_{\sigma \in T}\, outerhot^N(\sigma)$.

**Example 10.1.** Let us consider again Example 6.3, where Store$^\sharp$ is the trivial one-point store abstraction $\{\top\}$. In Example 6.3, we first extracted $hp_1 = \langle\top, C_1, \top, C_2, \top, C_3^c\rangle$ by transforming $P$ to $P_1 \triangleq extr_{hp}(P)$.

We then consider the following trace in $\mathbf{T}[\![P_1]\!]$:

$$\begin{aligned}\sigma = &\langle[x/?], C_0\rangle\langle[x/0], H_0\rangle\langle[x/0], H_1\rangle\langle[x/0], H_2\rangle\langle[x/0], H_3\rangle \\ &\langle[x/1], H_4\rangle\langle[x/1], H_5\rangle \cdots \langle[x/2], H_3\rangle\langle[x/3], H_4\rangle\langle[x/3], H_5^c\rangle \\ &\langle[x/3], C_4\rangle\langle[x/6], H_0\rangle \cdots \langle[x/9], H_5^c\rangle\langle[x/9], C_4\rangle\langle[x/12], H_0\rangle \cdots\end{aligned}$$

Thus, here we have that

$$\begin{aligned} hotcut(\sigma) = &\langle[x/?], C_0\rangle\langle[x/0], H_0\rangle\langle[x/3], H_5^c\rangle\langle[x/3], C_4\rangle \\ &\langle[x/6], H_0\rangle\langle[x/9], H_5^c\rangle\langle[x/9], C_4\rangle \cdots \end{aligned}$$

so that

$$hp_2 = \langle\top, H_0, \top, H_5^c, \top, C_4\rangle \in \alpha^2_{outerhot}(\mathbf{T}[\![P_1]\!])$$

Hence, $hp_2$ contains a nested hot path, which is called at the beginning of $hp_2$ and whose entry and exit commands are, respectively, $H_0$ and $H_5^c$. □

Let $hp = \langle a_0, C_0, \ldots, a_n, C_n\rangle \in \alpha^N_{outerhot}(\mathbf{T}[\![P']\!])$ be a $N$-hot path in $P'$, where, for all $i \in [0, n]$, $C_i \equiv L_i : A_i \to L_{next(i)}$. Let us note that:

- If for all $i \in [0, n]$, $C_i \in P$ then $hp$ actually is a hot path in $P$, *i.e.*, $hp \in \alpha^N_{hot}(\mathbf{T}[\![P]\!])$.
- Otherwise, there exists some $C_k \notin P$. If $C_i \in P$ and $C_{i+1} \notin P$ then $C_{i+1}$ is the entry command of some inner hot path; on the other hand, if $C_i \notin P$ and $C_{i+1} \in P$ then $C_i$ is the exit command of some inner hot path.

The transform of $P'$ for extracting $hp$ is a generalization of Definition 6.1.

**Definition 10.2 (Nested trace extraction transform).** The *nested trace extraction transform* of $P'$ for the hot path $hp$ is:

$$\begin{aligned}
&extr_{hp}(P') \triangleq P \\
(1)\;& \smallsetminus (\{C_0 \mid C_0 \in P\} \cup \{cmpl(C_0) \mid cmpl(C_0) \in P\}) \\
(2)\;& \cup \{\overline{L_0} : act(C_0) \to L_1 \mid C_0 \in P\} \\
& \cup \{\overline{L_0} : \neg act(C_0) \to L_1^c \mid cmpl(C_0) \in P\} \\
(3)\;& \cup \{L_0 : \text{guard } E_{a_0} \to \ell_0,\; L_0 : \neg\text{guard } E_a \to \overline{L_0} \mid C_0 \in P\} \\
(4)\;& \cup \{\ell_i : act(C_i) \to \mathbb{l}_{i+1} \mid i \in [0, n-1], C_i, C_{i+1} \in P\} \\
& \cup \{\ell_n : act(C_n) \to L_0 \mid C_n \in P\} \\
(5)\;& \cup \{\ell_i : \neg act(C_i) \to L^c_{next(i)} \mid i \in [0, n], C_i, cmpl(C_i) \in P\} \\
(6)\;& \cup \{\mathbb{l}_i : \text{guard } E_{a_i} \to \ell_i, \mathbb{l}_i : \neg\text{guard } E_{a_i} \to L_i \mid \\
& \qquad\qquad i \in [1, n], C_i \in P\} \\
(7)\;& \cup \{\ell_i : act(C_i) \to L_{i+1} \mid i \in [0, n-1], C_i \in P, C_{i+1} \notin P\} \\
(8)\;& \smallsetminus \{C_i \mid i \in [0, n-1], C_i \notin P, C_{i+1} \in P\} \\
(9)\;& \cup \{L_i : act(C_i) \to \mathbb{l}_{i+1} \mid i \in [0, n-1], C_i \notin P, C_{i+1} \in P\}
\end{aligned}$$

while $stitch_{P'}(hp) \triangleq (3) \cup (4) \cup (5) \cup (6) \cup (7) \cup (9)$. □

Let us observe that:

- Clauses (1)–(6) are the same clauses of Definition 6.1, with the additional constraints that $C_i$ and $cmpl(C_i)$ are all commands in $P$, conditions which are trivially satisfied in Definition 6.1.
- Clause (7) where $C_i \in P$ and $C_{i+1} \notin P$, namely $next(C_i)$ is the call program point of a nested hot path $nhp$ and $C_{i+1}$ is the entry command of $nhp$, performs a relabeling that allows to correctly nest $nhp$ in $hp$.
- Clauses (8)–(9) where $C_i \notin P$ and $C_{i+1} \in P$, *i.e.*, $C_i$ is the exit command of a nested hot path $nhp$ that returns to the program point $lbl(C_{i+1})$, performs the relabeling of $suc(C_i)$ in $C_i$ in order to return from $nhp$ to $hp$;

- $\overline{L_0}$, $\ell_i$ and $\mathbb{l}_i$ are fresh labels, *i.e.*, they have not been used in $P'$.

**Example 10.3.** Let us go on with Example 10.1. The second traced hot path in $\alpha^2_{outerhot}(\mathbf{T}[\![P_1]\!])$ is:

$$hp_2 = \langle \top, H_0 \equiv L_1 : \text{guard } E_\top \to \ell_0,$$
$$\top, H_5^c \equiv \ell_2 : (x\%3 = 0) \to L_4, \top, C_4 \equiv L_4 : x := x{+}3 \to L_1\rangle.$$

According to Definition 10.2, trace extraction of $hp_2$ in $P_1$ yields the following transform:

$$extr_{hp_2}(P_1) \triangleq$$
$$\text{[by clause (8)]} \quad P_1 \smallsetminus \{H_5^c\}$$
$$\text{[by clause (9)]} \quad \cup \{\ell_2 : (x\%3 = 0) \to \mathbb{h}_2\}$$
$$\text{[by clause (6)]} \quad \cup \{\mathbb{h}_2 : \text{guard } E_\top \to \hbar_2, \mathbb{h}_2 : \neg\text{guard } E_\top \to L_4\}$$
$$\text{[by clause (4)]} \quad \cup \{\hbar_2 : x := x + 3 \to L_1\}$$

where we used additional fresh labels in $\mathbb{h}_2$ and $\hbar_2$. □

**Example 10.4.** Let us consider again Example 8.3. After the trace extraction of $hp_1$ that transforms $P$ to $P_1$, a second traced 2-hot path is the following:

$$hp_2 \triangleq \langle \rho^t, C_1, \rho^t, C_2, \rho^t, C_3, \rho^t, H_0, \rho^t, H_1^c, \rho^t, C_7\rangle$$

where $\rho^t = \{primes[n]/\,\text{Bool}, i/\,\text{Int}, k/\,\text{Int}\} \in \text{Store}^t$. $hp_2$ contains a nested hot path which is called at $suc(C_3) = L_4$ and whose entry and exit commands are, respectively, $H_0$ and $H_1^c$. Here, typed trace extraction according to Definition 10.2 provides the following transform of $P_1$:

$$P_2 \triangleq extr^t_{hp_2}(P_1) \triangleq P_1 \smallsetminus \{C_1, C_1^c\} \cup \{$$
$$\overline{L_1} : i < 100 \to L_2,\ \overline{L_1} : \neg(i < 100) \to L_8,$$
$$H_6 \equiv L_1 : \text{guard } (primes[n] : \text{Bool}, i : \text{Int}, k : \text{Int}) \to \ell_3,$$
$$H_6^c \equiv L_1 : \neg\text{guard } (primes[n] : \text{Bool}, i : \text{Int}, k : \text{Int}) \to \overline{L_1},$$
$$H_7 \equiv \ell_3 : i < 100 \to \mathbb{l}_4,\ H_7^c \equiv \ell_3 : \neg(i < 100) \to L_8,$$
$$H_8 \equiv \mathbb{l}_4 : \text{guard } (primes[n] : \text{Bool}, i : \text{Int}, k : \text{Int}) \to \ell_4,$$
$$H_8^c \equiv \mathbb{l}_4 : \neg\text{guard } (primes[n] : \text{Bool}, i : \text{Int}, k : \text{Int}) \to L_2,$$
$$H_9 \equiv \ell_4 : primes[i] = \text{tt} \to \mathbb{l}_5,$$
$$H_9^c \equiv \ell_4 : \neg(primes[i] = \text{tt}) \to L_7,$$
$$H_{10} \equiv \mathbb{l}_5 : \text{guard } (primes[n] : \text{Bool}, i : \text{Int}, k : \text{Int}) \to \ell_5,$$
$$H_{10}^c \equiv \mathbb{l}_5 : \neg\text{guard } (primes[n] : \text{Bool}, i : \text{Int}, k : \text{Int}) \to L_3,$$
$$H_{11} \equiv \ell_5 : k := i +_{\text{Int}} i \to L_4\}$$
$$\smallsetminus \{H_1^c\} \cup \{(H_1^c)' \equiv \ell_0 : \neg(k < 100) \to \mathbb{l}_6,$$
$$H_{12} \equiv \mathbb{l}_6 : \text{guard } (primes[n] : \text{Bool}, i : \text{Int}, k : \text{Int}) \to \ell_6,$$
$$H_{12}^c \equiv \mathbb{l}_6 : \neg\text{guard } (primes[n] : \text{Bool}, i : \text{Int}, k : \text{Int}) \to L_7,$$
$$H_{13} \equiv \ell_6 : i := i +_{\text{Int}} 1 \to L_1\}.$$

Finally, a third traced 2-hot path in $P_2$ is the following:

$$hp_3 \triangleq \langle \rho^t, H_6, \rho^t, H_9^c, \rho^t, C_7\rangle$$

which contains a nested hot path which is called at the beginning of $hp_3$ and whose entry and exit commands are, respectively, $H_6$ and $H_9^c$. Here, typed trace extraction of $hp_3$ yields:

$$P_3 \triangleq extr_{hp_3}(P_2) \triangleq P_2 \smallsetminus \{H_9^c\} \cup \{$$
$$(H_9^c)' \equiv \ell_4 : \neg(primes[i] = \text{tt}) \to \mathbb{l}_7,$$
$$\mathbb{l}_7 : \text{guard } (primes[n] : \text{Bool}, i : \text{Int}, k : \text{Int}) \to \ell_7,$$
$$\mathbb{l}_7 : \neg\text{guard } (primes[n] : \text{Bool}, i : \text{Int}, k : \text{Int}) \to L_7,$$
$$\ell_7 : i := i +_{\text{Int}} 1 \to L_1\}.$$

We have thus obtained the same three trace extraction steps as described by Gal et al. [15, Section 2]. In particular, in $P_1$ we specialized the typed addition operation $k := k +_{\text{Int}} i$, in $P_2$ we specialized $k := i +_{\text{Int}} i$ and $i := i +_{\text{Int}} 1$, while in $P_3$ we specialized once again $i := i +_{\text{Int}} 1$ in a different hot path. Thus, in $P_3$ all the addition operations have been type specialized. □

## 11. Comparison with Guo and Palsberg's Framework

A formal model for tracing JIT compilation has been put forward in POPL 2011 by Guo and Palsberg [17]. Its main distinctive feature is the use of bisimulation [23] to describe operational equivalence between source and optimized programs. In this section we show how this model can be expressed within our framework.

### 11.1 Language and Semantics

Guo and Palsberg [17] employ a simple imperative language with while loops and a so-called bail construct.

$$E ::= n \mid x + 1$$
$$B ::= x = 0 \mid x \neq 0$$
$$\text{Cmd} \ni c ::= \textbf{skip} \mid x := E \mid \textbf{if } B \textbf{ then } S \mid \textbf{while } B \textbf{ do } S \mid \textbf{bail } B \textbf{ to } S$$
$$\text{Stm} \ni S ::= \epsilon \mid c; S$$

The baseline small-step operational semantics $\to_B \subseteq \text{State} \times \text{State}$, where $\text{State} \triangleq \text{Store} \times \text{Stm}$, is standard. Let us just recall the semantics of bail commands:

$$\langle \rho, (\textbf{bail } B \textbf{ to } S); K\rangle \to_B \langle \rho, K\rangle \quad \text{if } [\![B]\!]\rho = \mathit{false}$$
$$\langle \rho, (\textbf{bail } B \textbf{ to } S); K\rangle \to_B \langle \rho, S\rangle \quad \text{if } [\![B]\!]\rho = \mathit{true}$$

If $\text{Trace}_{GP} \triangleq \{\sigma \in \text{State}^* \mid \forall i \in [0, |\sigma|).\, \sigma_i \to_B \sigma_{i+1}\}$ denotes the set of program traces for Guo and Palsberg's language then given a program $S \in \text{Stm}$, the trace transition operator $GP[S] : \wp(\text{Trace}_{GP}) \to \wp(\text{Trace}_{GP})$ is defined as usual:

$$GP[S](X) \triangleq \{\langle \rho, S\rangle \mid \rho \in \text{Store}\} \cup \{\sigma s s' \mid \sigma s \in X,\ s \to_B s'\}$$

so that the trace semantics of $S$ is $\mathbf{T}_{GP}[\![S]\!] \triangleq \text{lfp}(GP[S]) \in \wp(\text{Trace}_{GP})$.

### 11.2 Language Compilation

Programs in Stm can be easily compiled into Program by resorting to an injective labeling function $\ell : \text{Stm} \to \mathbb{L}$ that assigns different labels to different statements.

**Definition 11.1 (Language compilation).** The compilation function $\mathcal{C} : \text{Stm} \to \wp(\mathbb{C})$ is recursively defined by the following clauses:

$$\mathcal{C}(\epsilon) \triangleq \{\ell(\epsilon) : \textbf{skip} \to \text{Ł}\}$$
$$\mathcal{C}(S \equiv \textbf{skip}; K) \triangleq \{\ell(S) : \textbf{skip} \to \ell(K)\} \cup \mathcal{C}(K)$$
$$\mathcal{C}(S \equiv x := E; K) \triangleq \{\ell(S) : x := E \to \ell(K)\} \cup \mathcal{C}(K)$$
$$\mathcal{C}(S \equiv (\textbf{if } B \textbf{ then } S'); K) \triangleq$$
$$\{\ell(S) : B \to \ell(S'; K),\ \ell(S) : \neg B \to \ell(K)\} \cup \mathcal{C}(S'; K) \cup \mathcal{C}(K)$$
$$\mathcal{C}((\textbf{while } B \textbf{ do } S'); K) \triangleq \mathcal{C}((\textbf{if } B \textbf{ then } (S'; \textbf{while } B \textbf{ do } S')); K)$$
$$\mathcal{C}(S \equiv (\textbf{bail } B \textbf{ to } S'); K) \triangleq$$
$$\{\ell(S) : B \to \ell(S'),\ \ell(S) : \neg B \to \ell(K)\} \cup \mathcal{C}(S') \cup \mathcal{C}(K)$$

□

**Example 11.2.** Consider the following program $S \in \text{Stm}$ in Guo and Palsberg's syntax:

$x := 0;$
**while** $B_1$ **do** $x := 1;$
$x := 2;$
**bail** $B_2$ **to** $x := 3;$
$x := 4;$
$\epsilon$

$S$ is then compiled in our language by $\mathcal{C}$ in Definition 11.1 as follows:

$$\begin{aligned}\mathcal{C}(S) = \{&\ell_0 : x := 0 \to \ell_{\textbf{while}},\\ &\ell_{\textbf{while}} : B_1 \to \ell_1,\ \ell_{\textbf{while}} : \neg B_1 \to \ell_2,\\ &\ell_1 : x := 1 \to \ell_{\textbf{while}},\ \ell_2 : x := 2 \to \ell_{\textbf{bail}},\\ &\ell_{\textbf{bail}} : B_2 \to \ell_3,\ \ell_{\textbf{bail}} : \neg B_2 \to \ell_4,\\ &\ell_3 : x := 3 \to \ell_\epsilon,\ \ell_4 : x := 4 \to \ell_\epsilon,\ \ell_\epsilon : \textbf{skip} \to \text{Ł}\}.\end{aligned}$$

□

Correctness for the above compilation function $\mathcal{C}$ means that for any $S \in \text{Stm}$: (i) $\mathcal{C}(S) \in \text{Program}$ and (ii) program traces of $S$ and $\mathcal{C}(S)$ have the same store sequences. If $st : \text{Trace}_{GP} \cup \text{Trace} \to \text{Store}^*$ returns the store sequence of a trace, *i.e.*, $st(\epsilon) \triangleq \epsilon$ and $st(\langle\rho, S\rangle\sigma) \triangleq \rho \cdot st(\sigma)$, and, for a set $X$ of traces $\alpha_{st}(X) \triangleq \{st(\sigma) \mid \sigma \in X\}$, then correctness goes as follows:

**Theorem 11.3 (Correctness of language compilation).** *For any* $S \in \text{Stm}$, $\mathcal{C}(S) \in \text{Program}$ *and* $\alpha_{st}(\mathbf{T}_{GP}[\![S]\!]) = \alpha_{st}(\mathbf{T}[\![\mathcal{C}(S)]\!])$.

### 11.3 Bisimulation

Correctness of trace extraction in [17] relies on the following notion of bisimulation, which is parameterized by program stores.

**Definition 11.4 ([17]).** A relation $R \subseteq \text{Store} \times \text{Stm} \times \text{Stm}$ is a *bisimulation* when $R(\rho, S_1, S_2)$ implies: (1) if $\langle\rho, S_1\rangle \to_B \langle\rho', S_1'\rangle$ then $\langle\rho, S_2\rangle \to_B^* \langle\rho', S_2'\rangle$, for some $\langle\rho', S_2'\rangle$ such that $R(\rho', S_1', S_2')$; (2) $R(\rho, S_2, S_1)$. □

$S_1$ is bisimilar to $S_2$ for a given store $\rho$, denoted by $S_1 \approx_\rho S_2$, if $R(\rho, S_1, S_2)$ for some bisimulation $R$. It is simple to characterize this program equivalence through an abstraction map of traces that observes store changes (this is analogous to the definition of *sc* in Section 7).

$$stc : \text{Store}^* \to \text{Store}^* \qquad stc(\epsilon) \triangleq \epsilon \qquad stc(\rho) \triangleq \rho$$

$$stc(\rho_1\rho_2\sigma) \triangleq \begin{cases} stc(\rho_2\sigma) & \text{if } \rho_1 = \rho_2 \\ \rho_1 \cdot stc(\rho_2\sigma) & \text{if } \rho_1 \neq \rho_2 \end{cases}$$

Given $\rho \in \text{Store}$, $\alpha^\rho_{stc} : \wp(\text{Trace}_{GP}) \to \wp(\text{Store}^*)$ is defined as follows: $\alpha^\rho_{stc}(X) \triangleq \{stc(\sigma) \mid \sigma \in \alpha_{st}(X),\ \sigma_0 = \rho\}$.

**Theorem 11.5.** *For any* $S_1, S_2 \in \text{Stm}$, $\rho \in \text{Store}$, *we have that* $S_1 \approx_\rho S_2$ *iff* $\alpha^\rho_{stc}(\mathbf{T}_{GP}[\![S_1]\!]) = \alpha^\rho_{stc}(\mathbf{T}_{GP}[\![S_2]\!])$.

### 11.4 Hot Paths and Trace Extraction

In Guo and Palsberg's model [17]: (i) hot paths always begin with an entry while-loop conditional, which is however not included in the hot path; (ii) the store of a hot path is recorded at the end of the first loop iteration and is a concrete store; and (iii) hot paths actually are 1-hot paths according to our definition. Guo and Palsberg's hot loops can be modeled in our framework by relying on a loop selection map $loop_{GP} : \text{Trace} \to \wp(\mathbb{C}^* \times \text{Store})$ defined as follows:

$$\begin{aligned}loop_{GP}(\langle\rho_0, C_0\rangle \cdots \langle\rho_n, C_n\rangle) \triangleq \{&\langle C_iC_{i+1}\cdots C_j, \rho_{j+1}\rangle \mid \\ &0 \le i \le j < n,\ C_i \lessdot C_j,\ lbl(C_{j+1}) = lbl(C_i),\\ &\forall k \in (i, j].\, C_k \notin \{C_i, cmpl(C_i)\}\}.\end{aligned}$$

Notice that, for simplicity, the above definition includes the entry loop conditional in the hot path. The map $\alpha^{GP}_{hot} : \wp(\text{Trace}) \to \wp(\mathbb{C}^* \times \text{Store})$ then lifts $loop_{GP}$ to sets of traces: $\alpha^{GP}_{hot}(T) \triangleq \cup_{\sigma\in T}\, loop_{GP}(\sigma)$.

Let us thus consider a hot path $hp = \langle C_0C_1 \cdots C_n, \rho\rangle \in \alpha^{GP}_{hot}(\mathbf{T}[\![P]\!])$, for some $P \in \text{Program}$ (where $P$ may coincide with a compiled $\mathcal{C}(S)$ for some $S \in \text{Stm}$) and let us follow the same notation used in Section 6. Guo and Palsberg's [17] trace extraction scheme is defined as follows, where the hot path $hp$ cannot be re-entered once execution leaves $hp$.

**Definition 11.6 (GP trace extraction transform).** The *GP trace extraction transform* of $P$ for the hot path $hp$ is:

$$\begin{aligned}extr^{GP}_{hp}(P) \triangleq\ & P \smallsetminus \{C_0\}\\ &\cup \{L_0 : act(C_0) \to \ell_1\}\\ &\cup \{\ell_i : act(C_i) \to \ell_{i+1} \mid i \in [1, n)\} \cup \{\ell_n : act(C_n) \to L_0\}\\ &\cup \{\ell_i : \neg act(C_i) \to L^c_{next(i)} \mid i \in [1, n],\ cmpl(C_i) \in P\}.\end{aligned}$$

□

Clearly, $extr^{GP}_{hp}(P)$ remains a well-formed program. The correctness of this GP trace extraction transform, which is stated and proved in [17, Lemma 3.6], goes as follows.

**Theorem 11.7 (Correctness of GP trace extraction).** *For any* $P \in \text{Program}$, $hp = \langle C_0 \cdots C_n, \rho\rangle \in \alpha^{GP}_{hot}(\mathbf{T}[\![P]\!])$, *we have that* $\alpha^\rho_{stc}(\mathbf{T}[\![extr^{GP}_{hp}(P)]\!]) = \alpha^\rho_{stc}(\mathbf{T}[\![P]\!])$.

**Example 11.8.** Let us consider the program $P$ in Example 2.1 and the GP-hot path

$$hp = \langle C_1C_2C_3^c, \rho = [x/1]\rangle \in \alpha^{GP}_{hot}(\mathbf{T}[\![P]\!]).$$

A corresponding 2-hot path $hp_1$ with the same sequence of commands has been selected in Example 5.1 and extracted in Example 6.3. Here, the GP trace extraction of $hp$ provides the following program transform:

$$\begin{aligned}extr^{GP}_{hp}(P) \triangleq\ & P \smallsetminus \{C_1\}\\ &\cup \{L_1 : x \le 20 \to \ell_1,\ \ell_1 : x := x + 1 \to \ell_2\}\\ &\cup \{\ell_2 : \neg(x\%3 = 0) \to L_1,\ \ell_2 : (x\%3 = 0) \to L_4\}.\end{aligned}$$

□

## 12. Further Work

We have put forward a formal model of tracing compilation and correctness of hot path optimization based on program trace semantics and abstract interpretation. We see a number of interesting avenues for further work on this topic. We aim at making use of this framework to study and relate the foundational differences between traditional static vs dynamic tracing compilation. We then expect to formalize and prove the correctness of most beneficial optimizations employed by tracing compilers of practical dynamic languages like JavaScript, PHP and Python. For example, we plan to cast in our model the allocation removal optimization for Python described in [5] in order to formally prove its correctness. Finally, we plan to adapt our framework in order to provide a model of whole-method just-in-time compilation, as used, e.g., by IonMonkey [14], the current JIT compilation scheme in the Firefox JavaScript engine.

## Acknowledgments

We are grateful to the anonymous referees for their helpful comments. The work of Francesco Ranzato was partially supported by Microsoft Research Software Engineering Innovation Foundation 2013 Award (SEIF 2013) and by the University of Padova under the project BECOM.

## References


[1] V. Bala, E. Duesterwald, and S. Banerjia. Dynamo: a transparent dynamic optimization system. In *Proceedings of the ACM SIGPLAN Conference on Programming Language Design and Implementation (PLDI 2000)*, pages 1–12, New York, NY, USA, 2000. ACM.

[2] R. Barbuti, N. De Francesco, A. Santone, and G. Vaglini. Abstract interpretation of trace semantics for concurrent calculi. *Information Processing Letters*, 70(2):69–78, 1999.

[3] M. Bebenita, F. Brandner, M. Fahndrich, F. Logozzo, W. Schulte, N. Tillmann, and H. Venter. SPUR: a trace-based JIT compiler for CIL. In *Proceedings of the ACM International Conference on Object Oriented Programming Systems Languages and Applications (OOPSLA 2010)*, pages 708–725, New York, NY, USA, 2010. ACM.

[4] I. Böhm, T.J.K. Edler von Koch, S.C. Kyle, B. Franke, and N. Topham. Generalized just-in-time trace compilation using a parallel task farm in a dynamic binary translator. In *Proceedings of the 32nd ACM SIGPLAN Conference on Programming Language Design and Implementation (PLDI 2011)*, pages 74–85, New York, NY, USA, 2011. ACM.

[5] C.F. Bolz, A. Cuni, M. Fijałkowski, M. Leuschel, S. Pedroni, and A. Rigo. Allocation removal by partial evaluation in a tracing JIT. In *Proceedings of the 20th ACM SIGPLAN Workshop on Partial Evaluation and Program Manipulation (PEPM 2011)*, pages 43–52. ACM, 2011.

[6] C.F. Bolz, A. Cuni, M. Fijalkowski, and A. Rigo. Tracing the meta-level: PyPy's tracing JIT compiler. In *Proceedings of the 4th Workshop on the Implementation, Compilation, Optimization of Object-Oriented Languages and Programming Systems (ICOOOLPS 2009)*, pages 18–25, New York, NY, USA, 2009. ACM.

[7] C. Colby and P. Lee. Trace-based program analysis. In *Proceedings of the 23rd ACM SIGACT-SIGPLAN Symposium on Principles of Programming Languages (POPL 1996)*, pages 195–207, New York, NY, USA, 1996. ACM.

[8] P. Cousot. Constructive design of a hierarchy of semantics of a transition system by abstract interpretation (extended abstract). *Electronic Notes in Theoretical Computer Science*, 6(0):77–102, 1997. Proceedings of the 13th Annual Conference on Mathematical Foundations of Progamming Semantics (MFPS XIII).

[9] P. Cousot. Constructive design of a hierarchy of semantics of a transition system by abstract interpretation. *Theoretical Computer Science*, 277(1-2):47–103, 2002.

[10] P. Cousot and R. Cousot. Abstract interpretation: a unified lattice model for static analysis of programs by construction or approximation of fixpoints. In *Proceedings of the 4th ACM SIGACT-SIGPLAN Symposium on Principles of Programming Languages (POPL 1977)*, pages 238–252, New York, NY, USA, 1977. ACM.

[11] P. Cousot and R. Cousot. Systematic design of program analysis frameworks. In *Proceedings of the 6th ACM SIGACT-SIGPLAN Symposium on Principles of Programming Languages (POPL 1979)*, pages 269–282, New York, NY, USA, 1979. ACM.

[12] P. Cousot and R. Cousot. Systematic design of program transformation frameworks by abstract interpretation. In *Proceedings of the 29th ACM SIGACT-SIGPLAN Symposium on Principles of Programming Languages (POPL 2002)*, pages 178–190, New York, NY, USA, 2002. ACM.

[13] Mozilla Foundation. TraceMonkey. `wiki.mozilla.org`, October 2010.

[14] Mozilla Foundation. IonMonkey. `wiki.mozilla.org`, May 2013.

[15] A. Gal, B. Eich, M. Shaver, D. Anderson, D. Mandelin, M.R. Haghighat, B. Kaplan, G. Hoare, B. Zbarsky, J. Orendorff, J. Ruderman, E.W. Smith, R. Reitmaier, M. Bebenita, M. Chang, and M. Franz. Trace-based just-in-time type specialization for dynamic languages. In *Proceedings of the 2009 ACM SIGPLAN Conference on Programming Language Design and Implementation (PLDI 2009)*, pages 465–478, New York, NY, USA, 2009. ACM.

[16] A. Gal, C.W. Probst, and M. Franz. HotPathVM: an effective JIT compiler for resource-constrained devices. In *Proceedings of the 2nd International Conference on Virtual Execution Environments (VEE 2006)*, pages 144–153. ACM, 2006.

[17] S. Guo and J. Palsberg. The essence of compiling with traces. In *Proceedings of the 38th ACM SIGACT-SIGPLAN Symposium on Principles of Programming Languages (POPL 2011)*, pages 563–574, New York, NY, USA, 2011. ACM.

[18] M. Handjieva and S. Tzolovski. Refining static analyses by trace-based partitioning using control flow. In *Proceedings of the 5th International Static Analysis Symposium (SAS 1998)*, volume 1503 of *LNCS*, pages 200–214. Springer, 1998.

[19] Facebook Inc. The HipHop Virtual Machine, Facebook Engineering, December 2011.

[20] Google Inc. A new crankshaft for V8, The Chromium Blog, December 2010.

[21] Ecma International. ECMAScript Language Specification. Standard ECMA-262, Edition 5.1, June 2011.

[22] F. Logozzo. Class invariants as abstract interpretation of trace semantics. *Computer Languages, Systems and Structures*, 35(2):100–142, 2009.

[23] R. Milner. *Communication and Concurrency*. Prentice Hall, 1995.

[24] M. Pall. The LuaJIT Project. `luajit.org`, 2005.

[25] X. Rival. Symbolic transfer function-based approaches to certified compilation. In *Proceedings of the 31st ACM SIGACT-SIGPLAN Symposium on Principles of Programming Languages (POPL 2004)*, New York, NY, USA, 2004. ACM.

[26] X. Rival and L. Mauborgne. The trace partitioning abstract domain. *ACM Trans. Program. Lang. Syst.*, 29(5), 2007.

[27] D.A. Schmidt. Trace-based abstract interpretation of operational semantics. *Lisp Symb. Comput.*, 10(3):237–271, 1998.

[28] F. Spoto and T. Jensen. Class analyses as abstract interpretations of trace semantics. *ACM Trans. Program. Lang. Syst.*, 25(5):578–630, 2003.

# A Type-Directed Abstraction Refinement Approach to Higher-Order Model Checking


Steven J. Ramsay
University of Oxford
steven.ramsay@cs.ox.ac.uk

Robin P. Neatherway
University of Oxford
robin.neatherway@cs.ox.ac.uk

C.-H. Luke Ong
University of Oxford
luke.ong@cs.ox.ac.uk



## Abstract

The trivial-automaton model checking problem for higher-order recursion schemes has become a widely studied object in connection with the automatic verification of higher-order programs. The problem is formidably hard[1]: despite considerable progress in recent years, no decision procedures have been demonstrated to scale robustly beyond recursion schemes that comprise more than a few hundred rewrite rules. We present a new, fixed-parameter polynomial time algorithm, based on a novel, type directed form of abstraction refinement in which behaviours of a scheme are distinguished by the abstraction according to the intersection types that they inhabit (the properties that they satisfy). Unlike other intersection type approaches, our algorithm reasons both about acceptance by the property automaton and acceptance by its dual, simultaneously, in order to minimize the amount of work done by converging on the solution to a problem instance from both sides. We have constructed PREFACE, a prototype implementation of the algorithm, and assembled an extensive body of evidence to demonstrate empirically that the algorithm readily scales to recursion schemes of several thousand rules, well beyond the capabilities of current state-of-the-art higher-order model checkers.



***Categories and Subject Descriptors*** F [3]: 1; D [2]: 4

***Keywords*** higher-order model checking; intersection types; abstraction refinement


## 1. Introduction

*Higher-order model checking*, or the model checking problem for trees generated by higher-order recursion schemes (HORS), is a widely studied decision problem in connection with the theory and practice of the verification of higher-order programs. Since HORS are simultaneously very expressive [21], algorithmically well-behaved [20], and able to accurately model higher-order control flow [8], they are an appealing target for algorithmic verification procedures for functional programs [12, 16, 17, 22, 26]. Indeed, in a precise sense, HORS are the higher-order analogue of Boolean programs, which have played a very successful rôle in the verification of first order, imperative programs [1].




*POPL '14*, January 22–24, 2014, San Diego, CA, USA.



ACM 978-1-4503-2544-8/14/01... $15.00.
http://dx.doi.org/10.1145/2535838.2535873


It is for these reasons, and despite the severe worst-case complexity of the problem[1], that several ingenious algorithms [3, 4, 12, 13, 19] have recently been developed with the aim of solving the higher-order model checking problem for many "practical" instances. However, the state of this effort is summarised well by the authors of [3]:

> "The state-of-the-art model checker TRECS [12] can handle a few hundred lines of HORS generated from various program verification problems. It is, however, not scalable enough to support automated verification of thousands or millions of lines of code. Thus, obtaining a better higher-order model checker is a grand challenge in the field..."

Our main contribution is a new algorithm for higher-order model checking and a large body of evidence to show empirically that it scales well to HORS consisting of several thousand rules. In contrast, the largest instances considered in the literature to date are of the order of several hundred rules. By way of an example, the order-2 benchmark $\mathcal{G}_{2,10000}$ of Kobayashi [12], which consists of 10006 rules, can be processed by our prototype implementation in less than one minute.

Our algorithm, which decides the HORS model checking problem with respect to alternating trivial tree automata, has been designed to be scalable. Since the inherent worst-case complexity of HORS model checking is extreme, to have any chance at all of solving non-trivial instances, one has to work in the belief that those instances that are met in practice are not pathological. Hence, it is essential to ensure that only work that is *relevant* to deciding the particular instance at hand is actually computed. To help achieve this goal, our algorithm is designed in the abstraction refinement paradigm [6]. Initially a relatively cheap but coarse-grained approximation to the problem is processed and, as much as possible, detail is only added by successive iterations where the problem instance necessitates it. Moreover, it can be shown that our algorithm is *fixed-parameter polynomial time* in the size of the scheme; the parameters that are fixed are the order and arity of the scheme, and the size of the tree automaton.

Our algorithm exploits the characterisation of higher-order model checking as an intersection type inference problem [11, 14], representing the state of knowledge about the behaviours of the recursion scheme as a pair of type environments, called the *context*, which assigns intersection types to the non-terminals of the scheme. As the algorithm progresses, the number of types (and hence state of knowledge) in the environments increases, until after some finite number of iterations there will be enough type information to decide the property one way or the other. Furthermore, this limit context will form a certificate of the decision that is independently verifiable by intersection type checking.

[1] $n$-EXPTIME complete for recursion schemes of order $n$ [15, 20]

In order to gain more information and thus populate the context, each iteration consists of constructing a sound abstraction of the configuration graph [12] of the scheme. Since recursion schemes have no facility to inspect the data that they operate over, the behaviours of the scheme arise from the complex interactions between higher-order functions. Hence, we have designed this abstraction around a traditional CFA [10], but with an important twist: in our abstraction, parameters to function calls are distinguished according to the intersection types that they inhabit, in other words, according to the properties that they satisfy. This is, in turn, a function of the context and hence, as the algorithm progresses and the size of the context increases, so the abstractions become more precise, as they are able to distinguish more instances of function calls.

Such an abstract configuration graph is a concise but approximate representation of all the possible reduction sequences of the scheme. Through its analysis, the algorithm can classify certain behaviours that can be seen to generate trees that are accepted by the property automaton and certain other behaviours that can be seen to generate trees that are rejected by the property automaton. From the former it is able to extract new "acceptance" types and from the latter new "rejection" types and both are added to the context ready to proceed with the next iteration. Indeed, a key feature of the algorithm, and a novelty among intersection type based decision procedures, is that it uses types to reason both about property automaton acceptance *and* rejection, simultaneously.

We have implemented the algorithm in a tool, PREFACE, and evaluated its performance over the several hundred problem instances that are now either recorded in the literature or which have resulted from verification tools for higher-order programs. These instances range from a few tens of rules to several thousands and from first order schemes up to fifth order, and a few beyond. The results show very clearly that, whilst PREFACE is sometimes a little slower than other model checkers on examples up to around one hundred rules, its great strength is in solving examples of many hundreds of rules, where it performs consistently better than other model checkers, and several thousands of rules, which are typically instances that it alone can solve.

***Outline*** The rest of the article is structured as follows. In section 2 we fix notation and preliminary definitions. In section 3 we give an informal outline of the algorithm by means of an example. In section 4 the algorithm is defined formally. In section 5 we discuss our prototype implementation and present a digest of the empirical evaluation and associated analysis. In section 6 we discuss related work. All proofs of claims in the text are relegated to the appendix of the long version of this work [24], which also includes a guided run of the algorithm on a second example instance and a full transcript of the empirical evaluation.

## 2. Preliminaries

We assume throughout a denumerable set $(F, G, H \in) \mathcal{F}$ of *function symbols* and a disjoint, denumerable set $(x, y, z \in) \mathcal{V}$ of *variables*.

***Labelled trees*** Let $A$ be a set without restriction. An *$A$-labelled tree* is a partial function $T : \mathbb{N}^* \to A$ whose domain is prefix closed. In case the set $A$ is *ranked*, that is, each symbol $a \in A$ has a specified arity $\mathsf{arity}(a) \in \mathbb{N}$, then the tree $T$ can be said to be *well-ranked* just if, whenever $T(w) = a$ and $\mathsf{arity}(a) = n$ then: $w \cdot i \in \mathsf{dom}(T)$ iff $i \in [1..n]$.

***Simple kinds.*** The *simple kinds*[2] over the kind of trees $o$, denoted $(\kappa \in) \mathbb{S}$, are formed by the grammar $\kappa ::= o \mid \kappa_1 \to \kappa_2$. As usual, we use parentheses to disambiguate the structure of such expressions, observing that the arrow associates to the right. The *arity* and *order* of a simple kind are natural numbers defined as usual. If a simple kind has order 0 (and hence has arity 0) we say that it is *ground*.

***Raw terms.*** Let $(a, b, c \in) \Sigma$ be a set of atomic constants. The set of *raw terms over* $\Sigma$, denoted $(s, t, u, v \in) T_\Sigma(\mathcal{F}, \mathcal{V})$, is defined by the grammar:

$$s, t \quad ::= \quad x \mid F \mid c \mid s\ t$$

The *free variables* of a term $t$, denoted $\mathsf{FV}(t)$, is just the set of variables that occur in $t$. A term $t$ with $\mathsf{FV}(t)$ empty is called *closed* and the set of all closed terms is denoted $T_\Sigma(\mathcal{F})$. We denote the set of closed terms which, moreover, contain no occurrences of function symbols by $T_\Sigma$. In case the atomic constants are said to be *kinded* we assert that there is an associated kinding function kind which maps each constant $c \in \Sigma$ to a first-order kind in $\mathbb{S}$.

***Kinded terms.*** A kind environment $\Delta$, is a finite, partial function from $\mathcal{V} \cup \mathcal{F}$ to $\mathbb{S}$. A *kind judgement* is an expression of the form $\Delta \vdash t : \kappa$. We omit the standard definition of kind assignment to terms, i.e. simple type assignment.

***Recursion Schemes.*** A higher-order recursion scheme (HORS) $\mathcal{G}$ is a tuple $\langle \Sigma, \mathcal{N}, \mathcal{R}, S \rangle$ in which:

- The alphabet of *terminal symbols* $(a, b, c \in) \Sigma$ is a finite set of first-order, kinded constants.
- The alphabet of *non-terminal symbols*, $(F, G, H \in) \mathcal{N}$, is a finite set of kinded function symbols, disjoint from $\Sigma$. We will sometimes view $\mathcal{N}$ as a kind environment mapping non-terminals $F \in \mathcal{N}$ to their kinds $\mathsf{kind}(F)$.
- The *rewrite rules*, $\mathcal{R}$, comprise a function mapping each non-terminal symbol $F$ of kind $\kappa_1 \to \cdots \to \kappa_n \to o$ to an expression $\lambda x_1 \cdots x_n.\, t$, such that:

  $$x_1 : \kappa_1, \cdots, x_n : \kappa_n \vdash t : o$$

  is a provable assignment of kinds to terms. We will often write $(F, \lambda x_1, \ldots, x_n.\, t) \in \mathcal{R}$ as an equation $F = \lambda x_1, \ldots, x_n.\, t$.
- The *start symbol*, $S \in \mathcal{N}$, is a non-terminal symbol of kind $o$.

Each recursion scheme is assigned an *order* which is given by the maximum order of (the kind of) its non-terminal symbols. Recursion schemes have a simple notion of reduction, which is defined as the contextual closure of the following rule:

$$\frac{\mathcal{R}(F) = \lambda x_1 \cdots x_n.\, t}{F\ s_1 \cdots s_n \Rightarrow t[s_1/x_1, \ldots, s_n/x_n]}$$

For the purposes of model checking, we are interested in the trees generated by the scheme. The *value tree* of a scheme $\mathcal{G}$, denoted $\mathsf{Tree}(\mathcal{G})$ is the (possibly infinite) term tree obtained by reducing the start symbol *ad infinitum*. To account for the possibility of infinite, unproductive recursion, the value tree is defined as follows. First, introduce a new symbol of zero arity, $\bot$, into $\Sigma$ and consider the least preordering of $\Sigma$ that asserts $\bot \leq a$ for all $a \in \Sigma$. Next, for each closed term $t$ of ground type, define $t^\bot$ recursively by: (i) $(F\ s_1 \cdots s_n)^\bot = \bot$ and (ii) $(a\ s_1 \cdots s_n)^\bot = a\ s_1^\bot \cdots s_n^\bot$. This mapping sends each term to well-ranked tree in the complete partial order of $\Sigma \cup \bot$-labelled trees, which are ordered by letting $T_1 \sqsubseteq T_2$ just if, for all $\pi \in \mathsf{dom}(T_1)$, $T_1(\pi) \leq T_2(\pi)$. Finally, we set $\mathsf{Tree}(\mathcal{G}) = \bigsqcup\{t^\bot \mid S \Rightarrow^* t\}$.

**Example 1.** Consider the first-order scheme over terminal symbols $a : o \to o \to o$, $b : o \to o$ and $c : o$ in which the non-terminal symbols $S : o$ and $F : o \to o$ are defined by the equations:

[2] These are nothing more than the simple types over the base type $o$, but we prefer to use the word *kind* to avoid conflict with intersection *type* later.

$$S = F\,c$$
$$F = \lambda x.\, a\, x\, (F\,(b\,x))$$

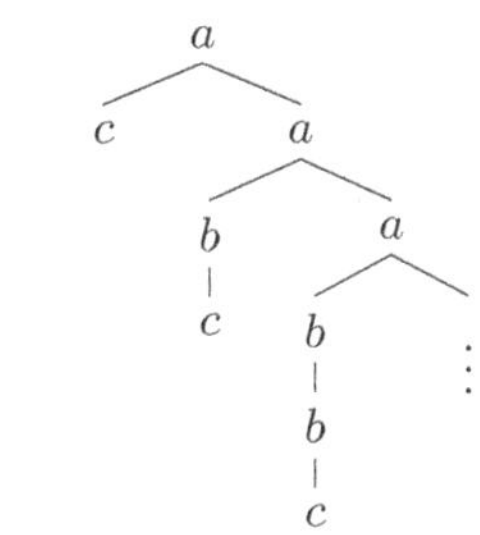

By reducing *ad infinitum*, the start symbol $S$ generates an infinite $a$, $b$ and $c$-labelled tree, a prefix of which is depicted on the right. This tree has no $\bot$-labelled nodes since every redex contraction produces a new terminal symbol in head position.

***Positive Boolean formulae.*** Given a finite set $X$, the *positive Boolean formulas over* $X$, denoted $(\phi \in)\ \mathsf{B}^+(X)$, are defined by the grammar $\phi ::= \mathsf{t} \mid \mathsf{f} \mid x \mid \phi_1 \wedge \phi_2 \mid \phi_1 \vee \phi_2$. Given a positive Boolean formula $\phi$, an *assignment* is a finite subset $S$ of $X$. An assignment $S$ is said to be a *satisfying assignment* for $\phi$, written $S \models \phi$, when assigning $\mathsf{t}$ to elements of $S$ and $\mathsf{f}$ to elements of $X \setminus S$ makes $\phi$ true.

***Alternating (co-)trivial tree automata.*** An alternating (co-)trivial tree automaton (ATT) $\mathcal{A}$ is a tuple $\langle \Sigma,\, Q,\, \delta,\, q_0,\, F\rangle$ in which $\Sigma$, is a finite set of ranked constants, $(q \in)\ Q$, is a finite set of *states*, the *transition function*, $\delta$, is a function in $\Pi_{(q,a)\in Q\times\Sigma} \cdot \mathsf{B}^+([1..\mathsf{arity}(a)] \times Q)$, the *initial state* is $q_0 \in Q$ and the *accepting states*, $F$, are either all of $Q$ or empty. In case $F = Q$, we say that the ATT has a *trivial* acceptance condition, otherwise $F = \emptyset$ and we say that it has a *co-trivial* acceptance condition. More often than not we will simply introduce a given automaton as a trivial or a co-trivial automaton and omit the final component. Furthermore, when specifying particular automata, we will elide clauses of the transition function whose image is $\mathsf{f}$.

Given a $\Sigma$-ranked and labelled tree $T$, a *run tree of* $\mathcal{A}$ *on* $T$ is a $(\mathsf{dom}(T) \times Q)$-labelled, unranked tree $R$ satisfying:

(APT-1) $R(\epsilon) = (\epsilon,\, q_0)$

(APT-2) For all $w \in \mathbb{N}^*$, if $R(w) = (w',\, q)$ then there is some set $S$ that satisfies $\delta(q,\, T(w'))$ and, for all $(i,\, q') \in S$, there exists some $j \in \mathbb{N}$ such that $R(w \cdot j) = (w' \cdot i,\, q')$.

We say that a run tree $R$ is *accepting* just if, on every infinite branch of $R$, there is some state $q \in F$ which occurs infinitely often. The *language* of an ATT $\mathcal{A}$, $\mathcal{L}(\mathcal{A})$, is the set of $\Sigma$-ranked and labelled trees $T$ for which there exists an accepting run-tree on $T$. We define the *complement* of $\mathcal{A}$, denoted $\mathcal{A}^c$, by the standard de Morgan dual construction, which ensures that $\mathcal{L}(\mathcal{A})^c = \mathcal{L}(\mathcal{A}^c)$ [18]. Note, the dual of an ATT with a trivial acceptance condition is an ATT with a co-trivial acceptance condition.

**Example 2.** Consider the ATT over the states $q_0$, $q_1$, $q_2$ and $q_3$, in which the transition function is defined by the following clauses:

$$\begin{aligned}
\delta(q_0,\, a) &= ((1,\, q_1) \wedge (2,\, q_0)) \vee (2,\, q_2)\\
\delta(q_1,\, b) &= (1,\, q_3)\\
\delta(q_1,\, c) &= \mathsf{t}\\
\delta(q_2,\, a) &= (1,\, q_1) \wedge (2,\, q_0)\\
\delta(q_3,\, b) &= (1,\, q_1)
\end{aligned}$$

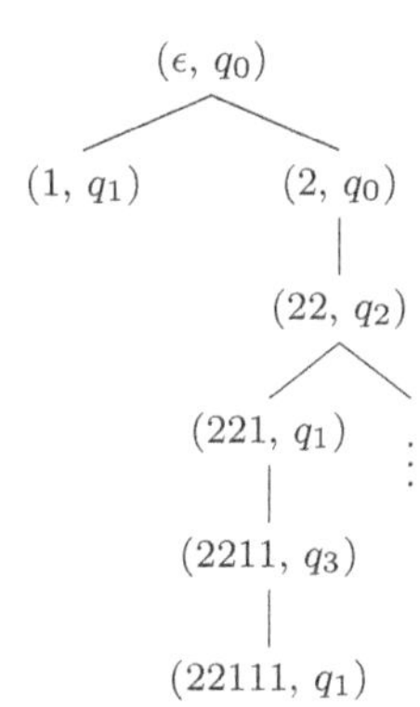

This ATT accepts those trees that have an infinite $a$-labelled spine and of every two consecutive branches off the spine, at least one is required to be labelled by an even number of $b$ nodes terminated by a $c$. A prefix of the run tree over the tree generated by the scheme in Example 1 is depicted to the right.

***Higher-order model checking.*** We define $\mathcal{A}^\bot$ as the ATT $\mathcal{A}$ augmented with extra transitions so as to accept the symbol $\bot$ from every state. The ATT-model checking problem for HORS is, given a HORS $\mathcal{G}$ and an ATT $\mathcal{A}$, to determine the truth of the assertion $\mathsf{Tree}(\mathcal{G}) \in \mathcal{L}(\mathcal{A}^\bot)$.

***Intersection types.*** In what follows fix an ATT $\mathcal{A}$. We consider *intersection types* [7]. As is usual in the higher-order model checking literature, we make a distinction between strict types and intersection types (borrowing the terminology from van Bakel [27]). The *intersection types* over $\mathcal{A}$, denoted $\mathbb{I}_\mathcal{A}$, are defined simultaneously with the *strict types* over $\mathcal{A}$ by the following grammar:

$$\begin{array}{lrcl}
\text{(STRICT TYPES)} & \tau & ::= & q \mid \sigma \to \tau\\
\text{(INTERSECTION TYPES)} & \sigma & ::= & \bigwedge_{i=1}^{n} \tau_i
\end{array}$$

in which $q \in Q$ and $n \geq 0$. We will use $\tau$ and $\sigma$ to denote strict and intersection types respectively. When we are agnostic about whether a particular expression is either a strict type or an intersection type we will say it is simply a *type* and denote it by $\theta$. When no confusion can arise, we will typically write $\top$ for the empty intersection, an intersection containing two elements infix as $\tau_1 \wedge \tau_2$ and an intersection of the singleton set containing $\tau$ simply as $\tau$. Given an intersection $\sigma = \bigwedge_{i=1}^{n} \tau_i$ we will often identify $\sigma$ with its set of conjuncts $\{\tau_1,\, \ldots,\, \tau_n\}$, writing assertions such as $\tau \in \sigma$ and $\sigma_1 \subseteq \sigma_2$ with the obvious interpretation. Finally, we shall have no qualms about constructing the intersection of intersection types, since this can be given naturally as the intersection of the union over their respective strict conjuncts.

***Intersection subtyping.*** There is a natural subtype preorder on intersection types, which was first explicitly considered by Barendregt, Coppo and Dezani-Ciancaglini in [2]. We shall use the following variant, defined inductively by the following clauses.

**(Q-BAS)** $q \leq q$

**(Q-ARR)** if $\sigma_2 \leq \sigma_1$ and $\tau_1 \leq \tau_2$ then $\sigma_1 \to \tau_1 \leq \sigma_2 \to \tau_2$

**(Q-PRJ)** for all $i \in [1..n]$, $\bigwedge_{j=1}^{n} \tau_j \leq \tau_i$

**(Q-GLB)** if, for all $i \in [1..n]$, $\sigma \leq \tau_i$, then $\sigma \leq \bigwedge_{j=1}^{n} \tau_j$

**(Q-TRS)** if $\theta_1 \leq \theta_2$ and $\theta_2 \leq \theta_3$ then $\theta_1 \leq \theta_3$

***Intersection type environment.*** An *intersection type environment* $\Gamma$ is a finite, partial function from $\mathcal{F} \cup \mathcal{V}$ to $\mathbb{I}_\mathcal{A}$. We will often view type environments as total functions assigning $\Gamma(F) = \top$ whenever $F \notin \mathsf{dom}(\Gamma)$. We will write $\Gamma_1 \uplus \Gamma_2$ for the operation sometimes called *type environment multiplication*, which is just the pointwise combination of environments defined by:

$$(\Gamma_1 \uplus \Gamma_2)(F) = \Gamma_1(F) \wedge \Gamma_2(F)$$

and write $\Gamma_1 \Subset \Gamma_2$ just if there is some $\Gamma'$ and $\Gamma_1 \uplus \Gamma' = \Gamma_2$. We will write $\Gamma \upharpoonright X$ for the restriction of $\Gamma$ to only those typings whose subject lies in $X$. Finally, we also extend the subtype relation to environments pointwise, writing $\Gamma_1 \leq \Gamma_2$ just if, $\mathsf{dom}(\Gamma_2) \subseteq \mathsf{dom}(\Gamma_1)$ and, for all $\xi \in \mathsf{dom}(\Gamma_2)$, $\Gamma_1(\xi) \leq \Gamma_2(\xi)$.

***Intersection type assignment.*** An *intersection type judgement* is an expression of the form $\Gamma \vdash t : \tau$ (with $\tau$ a strict type) whose derivations are defined inductively by the system in Figure 1. Note that in that system, we use the notation $S|_i$ to denote the set $\{q \mid (i,\, q) \in S\}$. Given a type environment $\Gamma$ and a term $t$, we define the set of all strict types assignable to $t$ under $\Gamma$ by:

$$\mathbb{T}(\Gamma)(t) = \{\tau \mid \Gamma \vdash t : \tau\}$$

The type system is induced by the property automaton $\mathcal{A}$, which features in the premise to the rule (T-CST). This rule acts to give a meaning to intersection types that can be thought of as follows. Each base type $q$ is the type of all terms $t$ that generate (via infinite

$$\frac{}{\Gamma,\, x : \bigwedge_{i=1}^{n} \tau_i \vdash x : \tau_i}\;(\text{T-VAR})$$

$$\frac{}{\Gamma,\, F : \bigwedge_{i=1}^{n} \tau_i \vdash F : \tau_i}\;(\text{T-FUN})$$

$$\frac{S \models \delta(q,\, c)}{\Gamma \vdash c : \bigwedge(S|_1) \to \cdots \to \bigwedge(S|_n) \to q}\;(\text{T-CST})$$

$$\frac{\Gamma \vdash s : \sigma \to \tau \quad \Gamma \vdash t : \tau'\ [\forall \tau' \in \sigma'] \quad \sigma' \leq \sigma}{\Gamma \vdash s\ t : \tau}\;(\text{T-APP})$$

**Figure 1.** Assignment of types to terms.

$$\frac{}{q :: o}\;(\text{K-BAS})$$

$$\frac{\sigma :: \kappa_1 \qquad \tau :: \kappa_2}{\sigma \to \tau :: \kappa_1 \to \kappa_2}\;(\text{K-ARR})$$

$$\frac{\tau_i :: \kappa\ (i \in [1..n])}{\bigwedge_{i=1}^{n} \tau_i :: \kappa}\;(\text{K-INT})$$

**Figure 2.** Assignment of kinds to types.

reduction) trees that are accepted by the automaton from state $q$. An intersection such as $q_1 \wedge q_2$, is the type of all terms that generate trees that are accepted *both* from state $q_1$ and from state $q_2$. Finally, an arrow such as $q_1 \wedge q_2 \to q$ is the type of those terms which, when applied to a term that generates a tree accepted from $q_1$ and $q_2$, will, as an application, generate a tree accepted from state $q$.

In this work we will be concerned both with type assignment in the intersection type system induced by property automaton $\mathcal{A}$ and type assignment in the intersection type system induced by the dual of this automaton $\mathcal{A}^c$. Hence, whenever needed we will try to disambiguate which notion of type assignment we are referring to by annotating the notation with $\mathcal{A}$ or $\mathcal{A}^c$.

***Intersection refinement types.*** The *intersection refinement types* over $Q$ are those types $\theta$ for which there is some kind $\kappa$ such that $\theta :: \kappa$, pronounced "$\sigma$ refines $\kappa$", is provable in the system of kind assignment below. The *strict refinement types* over $Q$ are defined as the obvious restriction of this system. We lift the refinement relation to environments by writing $\Gamma :: \Delta$ just if, for all $F : \sigma \in \Gamma$, there is a typing $F : \kappa \in \Delta$ and $\sigma :: \kappa$.

***Type environment consistency.*** We say that an intersection type environment $\Gamma$ is $(\mathcal{G},\mathcal{A})$*-consistent* just if, for each typing $F : \sigma \in \Gamma$ such that $F \in \mathsf{dom}(\mathcal{N})$, there is a *possibly infinite* witness, rooted at $\Gamma \triangleright F : \sigma$, and built according to the following system:

$$\frac{\begin{array}{c}\mathcal{R}(F) = \lambda x_1 \ldots x_n.\, t \\ \Gamma,\, x_1 : \sigma_1, \ldots, x_1 : \sigma_n \vdash t : q \\ \Gamma \triangleright G : \sigma\ (\forall G : \sigma \in \Gamma)\end{array}}{\Gamma \triangleright F : \sigma_1 \to \cdots \to \sigma_n \to q} \qquad \frac{\begin{array}{c}\Gamma_1 \Subset \Gamma \quad \Gamma_1 \triangleright F : \tau_1 \\ \cdots \\ \Gamma_n \Subset \Gamma \quad \Gamma_1 \triangleright F : \tau_n\end{array}}{\Gamma \triangleright F : \bigwedge_{i=1}^{n} \tau_i}$$

Similarly, we say that an intersection type environment $\Gamma$ is $(\mathcal{G},\mathcal{A})$*-co-consistent* just if, for each typing $F : \sigma \in \Gamma$ there is a *strictly finite* witness built from the above system. The next theorem follows from Kobayashi and Ong [14].

**Theorem 1.** *Fix a scheme $\mathcal{G}$ and ATT $\mathcal{A}$.*

*(i)* $\mathsf{Tree}(\mathcal{G}) \in \mathcal{L}(\mathcal{A}^{\perp})$ *iff there exists $(\mathcal{G},\, \mathcal{A})$-consistent $\Gamma :: \mathcal{N}$ and $q_0 \in \Gamma(S)$.*

*(ii)* $\mathsf{Tree}(\mathcal{G}) \in \mathcal{L}((\mathcal{A}^{\perp})^c)$ *iff there exists $(\mathcal{G},\, \mathcal{A}^c)$-co-consistent $\Gamma :: \mathcal{N}$ and $q_0 \in \Gamma(S)$.*

## 3. Type directed abstraction refinement

The starting point for the algorithm is the characterisation of the trivial automaton model checking problem for recursion schemes given in Theorem 1. Our algorithm tries to prove (a) $\mathsf{Tree}(\mathcal{G}) \in \mathcal{L}(\mathcal{A}^{\perp})$ and (b) $\mathsf{Tree}(\mathcal{G}) \in \mathcal{L}((\mathcal{A}^{\perp})^c)$ simultaneously, by iteratively constructing two type environments $\Gamma_\exists$ and $\Gamma_\forall$ which are possible witnesses to (a) and (b) respectively. Since an invariant of the algorithm is that $\Gamma_\exists$ is always $(\mathcal{G},\, \mathcal{A})$-consistent and $\Gamma_\forall$ is always $(\mathcal{G},\, \mathcal{A}^c)$-co-consistent, it follows that at most one of the two environments can prove the type assignment $S : q_0$; in fact, upon termination, exactly one of the two will do so. Since the two type systems $\mathcal{A}$ and $\mathcal{A}^c$ share the same underlying set of types, let us call an intersection type an *acceptance type* when we regard it as part of the system $\mathcal{A}$ and let us call it a *rejection type* when we regard it as part of the system $\mathcal{A}^c$.

The algorithm starts with $\Gamma_\exists^0 = \Gamma_\forall^0 = \emptyset$, which is trivially (co-)consistent. On each iteration, new type assignments are inferred which will be added to one or the other of the environments. The way that these new types are inferred is by, on each iteration, constructing and interrogating an auxiliary structure, called the *abstract configuration graph*. As its name suggests, this graph is an abstraction and the precision of the abstraction is a function of the size of the type environments $\Gamma_\exists$ and $\Gamma_\forall$. The more precise the abstraction the more useful the type information that can be deduced by interrogating it. Hence, starting from the empty *context*, $C_0 = \langle \Gamma_\exists^0,\, \Gamma_\forall^0 \rangle$, the abstraction refinement cycle continues as follows. In iteration $i+1$ with context $C_i = \langle \Gamma_\exists^i,\, \Gamma_\forall^i \rangle$, the abstract configuration graph is constructed. Two subgraphs are then carved out called the accepting and rejecting regions. These regions are the parts of the graph from which it is possible to obtain consistent acceptance typings and co-consistent rejection typings respectively. Types are then extracted from the regions and added to context $C_i$ to form a strictly larger context $C_{i+1} = \langle \Gamma_\exists^{i+1},\, \Gamma_\forall^{i+1} \rangle$. If one of these two environments can already type $S : q_0$ then the algorithm terminates. Otherwise the cycle repeats and, since $C_{i+1}$ is strictly larger, the abstract configuration graph constructed in iteration $i+2$ will be strictly more precise, and new type information will be deduced. Since there are only finitely many intersection refinement types associated with a given scheme one of the environments will be eventually become saturated and thus witness the corresponding assertion (a) or (b).

The configuration graph of a model checking problem instance was introduced by Kobayashi and Ong in [12, 14]. It is a kind of product construction, pairing up the reduction relation of the scheme and the transition function of the property automaton and it takes the shape of a rooted, directed graph. Since we are solving the alternating trivial automaton model checking problem for recursion schemes, the configuration graphs that we are interested in are something in between the simple ones of [12], which are appropriate to deterministic trivial automaton properties, and the much more complicated ones of [14], which are appropriate to alternating parity automaton properties. Moreover, we shall not be interested in the configuration graphs themselves, which are in general infinite, but rather in finite abstractions.

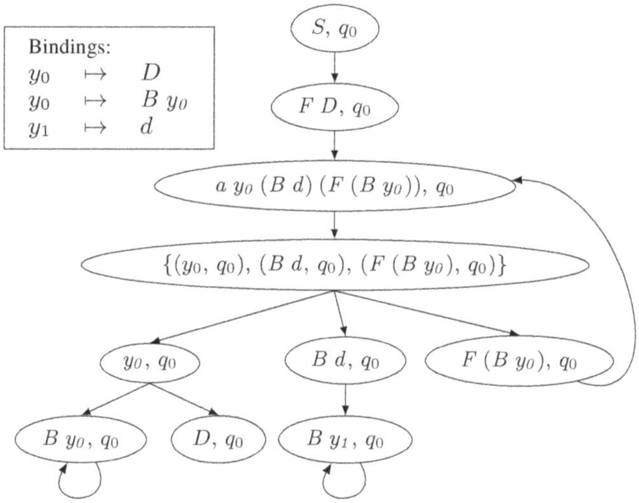


**Figure 3.** An abstract configuration graph.

Consider the following model checking instance, consisting of recursion scheme $\mathcal{G}$ over the terminal symbols $a$ and $d$ and a two-state trivial automaton $\mathcal{A}$:

$$\begin{array}{rcl} S & = & F\ D \\ F & = & \lambda x.\, a\ x\ (B\ d)\ (F\ (B\ x)) \\ B & = & \lambda z.\, B\ z \\ D & = & d \end{array} \qquad \begin{array}{rcl} \delta(q_1,\ d) & = & \mathsf{t} \\ \delta(q_0,\ a) & = & (1,\ q_0) \\ & & \wedge(2,\ q_0) \\ & & \wedge(3,\ q_0) \end{array}$$

As described above, the algorithm begins with the initial context $C_0 = \langle \Gamma^0_\exists,\ \Gamma^0_\forall \rangle$ consisting of $\Gamma^0_\exists = \emptyset$ and $\Gamma^0_\forall = \emptyset$. In order to infer new type assignments it constructs the abstract configuration graph $\mathsf{ACG}(C_0)$, which is given in full in Figure 3. The construction of the graph starts at the root, which is a vertex labelled $(S,\ q_0)$. Every vertex of the graph is either labelled by a pair $(t,\ q)$ of a ground kind term and a state, called a *configuration*, or by a finite set of such configurations. If there is a vertex $(t,\ q)$ in a graph $\mathsf{ACG}(\langle \Gamma_\exists,\ \Gamma_\forall \rangle)$, then it should be read as "neither $\Gamma_\exists \vdash_{\mathcal{A}} t : q$ nor $\Gamma_\forall \vdash_{\mathcal{A}^c} t : q$ is provable". Hence, the starting point for the graph $\mathsf{ACG}(C_0)$ is the fact that $S : q_0$ is not provable in $\emptyset$.

The shape of the successors of a vertex, if it has any, depend upon whether the vertex is a configuration or a set and in case of the former, the syntactic class of which its head symbol is a member. In this case the root of the graph is a configuration and its head symbol is $S$ which is a non-terminal. Hence the term part of this configuration is a redex. In such cases, the vertex has at most one successor and that successor *represents* the contraction of the redex. The contraction of the redex $S$ is $F\ D$ and, because neither $\Gamma^0_\exists \vdash_{\mathcal{A}} F\ D : q_0$ nor $\Gamma^0_\forall \vdash_{\mathcal{A}^c} F\ D : q_0$ is provable, it has a successor, which is labelled by $(F\ D,\ q_0)$. Since this vertex is of the same form, it also has a single successor which represents the contraction of the redex, however the situation is more complicated because this redex involves parameters. It is along such edges that the abstraction happens: rather than substituting actual parameters for formals in the successor, formals are substituted by special variables which are used by the abstraction to represent sets of terms. So we create a new variable $y_0$ and make a note $y_0 \mapsto D$ that one of the possible instantiations of $y_0$ is $D$. In this way, we are always able to recover the real contraction $a\ D\ (B\ d)\ (F\ (B\ D))$ from the abstract one $a\,y_0\,(B\,d)(F(B\,y_0))$ by rewriting occurrences of the variables $y_0$ using the *bindings* $y_0 \mapsto D$. This ensures we are building a *sound* abstraction, in the sense of incorporating all the behaviours of the original. This kind of abstraction is, in essence, a traditional control flow analysis [10], but here we go one step further, which is critical in order to obtain completeness. The extra step that we take is to record the acceptance type and rejection type of the new variable $y_0$. The acceptance type (respectively rejection type) of $y_0$ is just the intersection of types assignable to the term that it has been introduced to represent, in other words, $\bigwedge \mathbb{T}_{\mathcal{A}}(\Gamma^0_\exists)(D) = \top$ (respectively $\bigwedge \mathbb{T}_{\mathcal{A}^c}(\Gamma^0_\forall)(D) = \top$). The types of such variables will later determine when new variables should be created in order to represent actual parameters, as $y_0$ was here, or if variables created previously should be reused.

The frontier of our construction so far consists of a terminal headed configuration. The successors of a configuration of the form $(a\ s_1\ \cdots\ s_n,\ q)$ depend upon the satisfying assignments to $\delta(q,\ a)$. For each satisfying assignment $S$ there is one successor, which is the set of configurations $\{(s_i,\ q') \mid (i,\ q') \in S\}$. In this case, $\delta(q,\ a)$ is satisfied just if the first argument of $a$ is accepted from $q_0$, the second argument is accepted from $q_0$ and the third argument is accepted from $q_0$. Consequently, the set is $\{(y_0,\ q_0),\ (B\ d,\ q_0),\ (F\ (B\ y_0),\ q_0)\}$. Such a set $\{(t_1,\ q_1), \ldots, (t_n,\ q_n)\}$ should be read as "there is some $i$ such that $\Gamma_\exists \vdash_{\mathcal{A}} t_i : q_i$ is not provable". The successors of the set are those configurations $(t,\ q)$ in the set which are not provable in either $\Gamma_\exists$ or $\Gamma_\forall$.

So let us now consider the frontier configuration $(F(B\,y_0),\ q_0)$. Since it is a non-terminal headed configuration, if it has a successor then the successor abstractly represents the contraction in the same way as before. However, since the actual parameter $B\ y_0$ has the same acceptance type and rejection type as the previous one that we considered, $D$ (and is the same kind), we will not create a new variable to represent $B\ y_0$, but we will *reuse* the variable $y_0$ that we used to represent actual parameter $D$. So the abstract contraction is the term $a\ y_0\ (B\ d)\ (F\ (B\ y_0))$ and we form a loop in the graph. To ensure the abstraction remains sound we note that another possible instantiation of $y_0$ is $B\ y_0$, but observe that this merging of vertices resulting from reusing $y_0$ has caused some loss of information. Now the term $a\,y_0\,(B\,d)(F(B\,y_0))$ represents many different concrete instances, including some that are not possible in the original problem, such as $a\ D\ (B\ d)\ (F\ (B\ (B\ D)))$ which results from rewriting the leftmost occurrence of $y_0$ to $D$ and the rightmost occurrence to $B\ D$. The actual parameters $D$ and $B\ y_0$ have become confused because, according to the current context $C_0$, they have the same acceptance and rejection types. In this way, *types direct the abstraction* and refinement will occur because type information in the context increases.

By contrast, the vertex $(B\ d,\ q_0)$ has an actual parameter whose acceptance and rejection types are non-trivial. The terminal $d$ has acceptance type $\bigwedge \mathbb{T}_{\mathcal{A}}(\Gamma^0_\exists)(d) = q_1$ and rejection type $\bigwedge \mathbb{T}_{\mathcal{A}^c}(\Gamma^0_\forall)(d) = q_0$. We have not yet created a new variable with those types, so we do so now, assigning the new variable $y_1$ the acceptance type $q_1$ and the rejection type $q_0$. We record that $d$ is a possible instantiation of $y_1$ and label the successor $(B\ y_1,\ q_0)$. Following the same method, this new vertex has itself as successor. Officially we ought to note that $y_1$ is a possible instance of $y_1$, but such trivial circularities will make no difference to the outcome so we will omit it for brevity.

Let us now consider the frontier vertex $(y_0,\ q_0)$, which is variable headed. At variable headed configurations the consequences of the abstraction are felt. A vertex of the form $(y\ s_1\ \cdots\ s_n,\ q)$ has a successor $(t\ s_1\ \cdots\ s_n,\ q)$ for each binding $y \mapsto t$. For reasons that we have already discussed, its child $(B\ y_0,\ q_0)$ has itself as a successor. Its other child is the vertex $(D,\ q_0)$ whose contraction is $(d,\ q_0)$, however, because $\Gamma^0_\forall \vdash_{\mathcal{A}^c} d : q_0$ we do not add vertex $(d,\ q_0)$ to the graph and so $(D,\ q_0)$ has no successors. We say that $(D,\ q_0)$ is a *rejecting leaf*. This completes the construction of the abstract configuration graph.

We now consider any rejecting leaves in the graph. Rejecting leaves are configurations $(F\,s_1 \cdots s_n,\ q)$ for which the corresponding type assignment $F\ s_1 \cdots s_n : q$ is not provable in either $\Gamma_\exists$ nor $\Gamma_\forall$, yet the type assignment associated with the contraction is provable in $\Gamma_\forall$. This points directly to a weakness in the context. In our example, $\Gamma_\forall^0 \vdash_{\mathcal{A}^c} d : q_0$ is provable, so $d$ is a tree rejected by $\mathcal{A}^\perp$ and $D$ reduces to $d$ in one step, yet $\Gamma_\forall \not\vdash_{\mathcal{A}^c} D : q_0$ is not provable! The rejection environment $\Gamma_\forall$ *ought* to type $D : q_0$, since $D$ generates a tree that is rejected by $\mathcal{A}^\perp$, but it doesn't. Hence, we have discovered a new rejection type assignment. The vertices that we classify as representing typing assignments that ought to have been provable under the rejecting environment are collectively called the *rejecting region* and from this region new rejection types are extracted. Where the rejecting region is, roughly speaking, all the vertices that "definitely" can reach rejecting leaves, the *accepting region* is all the vertices that "definitely" cannot reach rejecting leaves. New acceptance types are extracted from the accepting region. In this case, the rejecting region is the single vertex $(D,\ q_0)$ and the accepting region is all the $B$ headed configurations.

Type extraction from the regions follows a similar approach to that defined in [14]. Briefly, a type is assigned to each prefix $s$ of the term component of each vertex $(s\ t_1 \cdots t_n,\ q)$ in the accepting region. The type assigned to $s$ is constructed by recursively computing the type $\sigma$ assigned to $t_1$ by considering all the ways in which $t_1$ is used within the region (the vertices where $t_1$ is itself a prefix), recursively computing the type $\tau$ assigned to the prefix $s\,t_1$ and then forging the arrow $\sigma \to \tau$. The base case is where the entire term component of the pair, considered as a trivial prefix of itself, is assigned the type $q$. The rejecting region is handled similarly, but care must be taken to only consider uses of $t_1$ in vertices that are strictly closer to the leaves so that a well founded co-consistency argument can be given in the end. The type assignments to prefixes that are themselves non-terminal symbols are extracted and added to the appropriate environments. In this case, there is only one vertex in the rejecting region, so its only prefix is assigned the type $D : q_0$. There are three vertices in the accepting region, of which the prefix $B$ of $(B\ d,\ q_0)$ is assigned acceptance type $q_1 \to q_0$ since $d$ is known to have type $q_0$, prefix $B$ of $(B\,y_0)$ is assigned type $\top \to q_0$ since there are no uses of $y_0$ in the region and, for the same reason, prefix $B$ of $(B\ y_1)$ is assigned the type $\top \to q_0$. The new context is therefore $C_1 = \langle\{B : (\top \to q_0) \wedge (q_1 \to q_0)\},\ \{D : q_0\}\rangle$.

Since the new context neither types $S : q_0$ as accepting nor as rejecting, the process repeats, but this time with more type information, so more of the parameters to calls will be distinguished. In the second iteration the rejecting region is the entire graph. Consequently, $S : q_0$ is added to the rejecting environment and the algorithm terminates, correctly deducing that the input is a no-instance.

## 4. An abstraction refinement algorithm

We now present the algorithm formally. We first give the definition of the key construction, the abstract configuration graph. We then describe how from the graph one can carve out the accepting and rejecting regions and the notion of type extraction appropriate to each. Finally we show how graph construction, regioning and type extraction come together to form a single iteration and we present the algorithm as the repetition of this process.

***Assumption.*** *For the rest of this section, assume a recursion scheme $\mathcal{G} = \langle\Sigma,\ \mathcal{N},\ \mathcal{R},\ S\rangle$ and an alternating trivial automaton $\mathcal{A} = \langle\Sigma,\ Q,\ \delta,\ q_0\rangle$. By an abuse, we will refer to the type system induced by $\mathcal{A}$ simply as $\mathcal{A}$ and the type system induced by $\mathcal{A}^c$ simply as $\mathcal{A}^c$.*

### 4.1 Construction of abstraction

The abstraction is based on a traditional CFA [10], in the sense of over-approximating reduction using an abstract environment. An important twist on the usual formulation is that here every variable in the environment is associated with a kind and a pair of intersection types.

***Typed variables.*** The main mechanism for abstraction will be a set of typed variables. By means of an abstract environment (to be described shortly) each variable represents the set of terms that can be obtained from it by repeated substitution. Each variable has three pieces of associated type information: an acceptance type, a rejection type and a kind. An essential part of the algorithm is in ensuring that type information is invariant across the abstraction, i.e. if a variable abstracts a set of terms, then every term in the set shares the same acceptance type, rejection type and kind as the variable (according to the current context).

**Definition 1.** *Let us say that a kind $\kappa$ is an* argument kind *just if there is some binding $F : \kappa_1 \to \cdots \to \kappa_n \to o \in \mathcal{N}$ and some $i$ such that $\kappa = \kappa_i$. Let* var *be a bijection, mapping the finite set of all triples of the form $(\sigma_\mathsf{A},\ \sigma_\mathsf{R},\ \kappa)$ consisting of kinded types $\sigma_\mathsf{A} :: \kappa$ and $\sigma_\mathsf{R} :: \kappa$ ,where $\kappa$ is an argument kind, to a finite set of term variables $\mathcal{Y} \subseteq \mathcal{V}$. Given such a variable $y \in \mathcal{Y}$, we will write $\mathsf{A}(y)$ for the first component of $\mathsf{var}^{-1}(y)$, $\mathsf{R}(y)$ for the second and $\mathsf{K}(y)$ for the third.*

***Type context.*** The algorithm is ultimately concerned with constructing a pair of type environments $\langle\Gamma_\exists, \Gamma_\forall\rangle$ such that $\Gamma_\exists$ is $(\mathcal{G},\!\mathcal{A})$-consistent and $\Gamma_\forall$ $(\mathcal{G},\!\mathcal{A}^c)$-co-consistent. We will speak of $\Gamma_\exists$ as the "acceptance" type environment and $\Gamma_\forall$ as the "rejection" type environment. Furthermore, we stipulate that every such pair of environments, which we shall call a *type context*, understands the basic assumptions we have made about the typed variables, i.e. the type information contained in A and R (as defined in Definition 1, but viewed as type environments for the typed variables) is also contained in $\Gamma_\exists$ and $\Gamma_\forall$ respectively.

**Definition 2.** *A type context $C = \langle\Gamma_\exists,\ \Gamma_\forall\rangle$ is a pair of intersection type environments for which the following conditions hold:*

*(i)* $\Gamma_\exists :: \mathcal{N} \cup \mathsf{K}$
*(ii)* $\Gamma_\forall :: \mathcal{N} \cup \mathsf{K}$
*(iii) For all $y \in \mathcal{Y}$, $\Gamma_\exists(y) = \mathsf{A}(y)$ and $\Gamma_\forall(y) = \mathsf{R}(y)$*

***Abstract configurations.*** As mentioned in the previous section, the abstraction itself is a finite representation of the possibly infinite *configuration graph*, as defined by [14]. In this *concrete* configuration graph, the configurations are pairs of a *closed* term (a reduct of the start symbol of the scheme) and a state of the automaton, and the edges that connect them must respect the constraints of both the reduction relation of the scheme and of the transition function of the automaton. A configuration $(t,\ q)$ can be read as an assertion: the tree generated by $t$ is accepted by $\mathcal{A}^\perp$ from state $q$. In the *abstract* configuration graph, defined shortly, configurations are still pairs of term and state, but now the term is abstract, which in our setting means that it can contain free occurrences of typed variables.

**Definition 3.** *An abstract configuration is a pair $(t,\ q)$ in which $\mathcal{N} \cup \{y : \mathsf{K}(y) \mid y \in \mathsf{FV}(t)\} \vdash t : o$ is a term and $q \in Q$ is a state. We say that a term $s$ is a* prefix *of a term $t$ just if $t$ has the form $s\ t_1 \cdots t_n$ for some $n \in \mathbb{N}$. A* configuration prefix *is a pair $(c,\ s)$ in which $c$ is a configuration of shape $(t,\ q)$ and $s$ is a prefix of $t$.*

***Abstract typability.*** The central idea of the algorithm is that the type bindings contained in the context constitute a concise summary of all the information that has been gathered about the scheme and its reducts, as far as acceptance by the property automaton is concerned. We will use the type context to judge whether the assertions represented by configurations are true or not, based on the following simple notion of typability.

**Definition 4.** *Let $C = \langle \Gamma_\exists, \Gamma_\forall \rangle$ be a type context and let $(t, q)$ be an abstract configuration. We say that $(t, q)$ is* $C$-accepted *just if $\Gamma_\exists \vdash_{\mathcal{A}} t : q$. We say that $(t, q)$ is* $C$-rejected *just if $\Gamma_\forall \vdash_{\mathcal{A}^c} t : q$. We say that $(t, q)$ is* $C$-unknown *just if it is neither $C$-accepted nor $C$-rejected.*

Until the very last iteration of the algorithm, the configuration $(S, q_0)$, which is the root of the abstract configuration graph, will be $C$-unknown to all the associated contexts $C$, but after the last iteration enough type information will have been contributed to the final context $C'$ in order that $(S, q_0)$ will be seen to be either $C'$-accepting or $C'$-rejecting.

***Abstract configuration graph.*** The vertices of the abstract configuration graph are either abstract configurations or finite sets of abstract configurations. Viewed as an assertion, a vertex which is a finite set of configurations $\{(s_1, q_1), \ldots, (s_n, q_n)\}$ should be interpreted *conjunctively*, i.e. as requiring that for each $i \in [1..n]$, $s_i$ generates a tree that is accepted from state $q_i$.

**Definition 5.** *An* abstract configuration graph *$A$ is a tuple $\langle V, E, B \rangle$ in which $\langle V, E \rangle$ is a directed graph and $B$ is a set of mappings from variables $y \in \mathcal{Y}$ to terms $t \in T_\Sigma(\mathcal{Y}, \mathcal{N})$. Each vertex $v \in V$ is either (i) an abstract configuration or (ii) a finite set of abstract configurations; and edges $E \subseteq V \times V$ are unlabelled. Given a typing context $C$, the* abstract configuration graph of $C$, *denoted* $\mathsf{ACG}(C)$, *is the abstract configuration graph $\langle V_C, E_C, B_C \rangle$ defined inductively by the system in Figure 4.*

The set $B$ of *bindings* acts as the abstract environment for the purposes of defining the abstraction. We consider motivation of each of the rules of the inductive definition in turn. First, the rule (G1) defines the root of the graph. The premise ensures that, if we already know that $S$ generates a tree that is either accepted from $q_0$ or rejected from $q_0$ then we need not do any state space exploration. This kind of premise is common to many of the rules to ensure that work is not done unnecessarily. In fact, one can state an invariant about the abstract typability of the vertices in any abstract configuration graph:

**Lemma 1.** *Let $C$ be a context. For each configuration $c \in V_C$, $c$ is $C$-unknown.*

In case $(S, q_0)$ were $C$-accepting or $C$-rejecting, the graph would be empty and the sequence of contexts will stabilise.

Rule (G2) simulates the contraction of a redex, but it does so in an abstract way. To apply the rule requires that a configuration $(F\ s_1 \cdots s_n,\ q)$ containing a redex occurs in the graph. The consequence is that an abstraction of the contraction of that redex is added as a new configuration. However, it is abstract because, rather than substituting actual parameters for formals, typed variables are substituted for the formals. These typed variables must be appropriate for the actuals that they abstract, hence there is the constraint that, if $y_i$ abstracts actual parameter $s_i$, then it had better be that $y_i = \mathsf{var}(\bigwedge \mathbb{T}_{\mathcal{A}}(\Gamma_\exists)(s_i), \bigwedge \mathbb{T}_{\mathcal{A}^c}(\Gamma_\forall)(s_i), \mathsf{K}(s_i))$. This ensures that type information is invariant across the abstraction, in the following sense:

**Proposition 1.** *Let $C = \langle \Gamma_\exists, \Gamma_\forall \rangle$ be a type context. For all $y \mapsto t \in B_C$, $\bigwedge \mathbb{T}_{\mathcal{A}}(\Gamma_\exists)(y) = \bigwedge \mathbb{T}_{\mathcal{A}}(\Gamma_\exists)(t)$ and $\bigwedge \mathbb{T}_{\mathcal{A}^c}(\Gamma_\forall)(y) = \bigwedge \mathbb{T}_{\mathcal{A}^c}(\Gamma_\forall)(t)$.*

To properly define the abstraction in terms of the new variable $y_i$, a binding is added to $B_C$ with the effect that $y_i \mapsto s_i$. Consequently, we may think that $s_i$ is in the set of terms abstracted by $y_i$.

Rule (G3) simulates a transition of the automaton on reading a terminal symbol: if there is a terminal symbol-headed configuration $(a\ s_1 \cdots s_n,\ q)$ in the graph, then its children comprise all of the possible satisfying assignments to $\delta(q, a)$ expressed as sets of configurations. Recalling that each vertex that is a set of configurations should be thought of conjunctively, the children of $(a\ s_1 \cdots s_n,\ q)$, taken as a whole, should be thought of disjunctively – $a\ s_1 \cdots s_n$ generates a tree accepted from state $q$ just if all the configurations contained in some child (satisfying assignment) are shown to be accepted. Rule (G4) simply decomposes set vertices into their constituent configurations. Therefore, the children of a set vertex should be thought of conjunctively.

(G1) Whenever all the following are true:
  (i) $(S, q_0)$ is $C$-unknown

then all the following are also true:
- $(S, q_0) \in V_C$

(G2) Whenever all the following are true:
  (i) $(F\ s_1 \cdots s_n,\ q) \in V_C$
  (ii) $\mathcal{R}(F) = \lambda x_1 \cdots x_n.\, t$
  (iii) $\mathcal{N}(F) = \kappa_1 \to \cdots \to \kappa_n \to o$
  (iv) $(t[y_1/x_1, \cdots, y_n/x_n],\ q)$ is $C$-unknown
  (v) for each $i \in [1..n]$, $y_i = \mathsf{var}(\bigwedge \mathbb{T}_{\mathcal{A}}(\Gamma_\exists)(s_i), \bigwedge \mathbb{T}_{\mathcal{A}^c}(\Gamma_\forall)(s_i), \kappa_i)$

then all the following are also true:
- $(t[y_1/x_1, \cdots, y_n/x_n],\ q) \in V_C$
- $\langle (F\ s_1 \cdots s_n,\ q), (t[y_1/x_1, \cdots, y_n/x_n],\ q) \rangle \in E_C$
- for each $i \in [1..n]$: $y_i \mapsto s_i \in B_C$

(G3) Whenever all the following are true:
  (i) $(a\ s_1 \cdots s_n,\ q) \in V_C$
  (ii) $S \models \delta(q, a)$
  (iii) for all $(i, q') \in S$, $(s_i, q')$ is not $C$-rejected

then all the following are also true:
- $\{(s_i, q') \mid (i, q') \in S\} \in V_C$
- $\langle (a\ s_1 \cdots s_n,\ q), \{(s_i, q') \mid (i, q') \in S\} \rangle \in E_C$.

(G4) Whenever all the following are true:
  (i) $\{(s_1, q_1), \ldots, (s_n, q_n)\} \in V_C$
  (ii) $i \in [1..n]$
  (iii) $(s_i, q_i)$ is not $C$-accepted

then all the following are also true:
- $(s_i, q_i) \in V_C$
- $\langle \{(s_1, q_1), \ldots, (s_n, q_n)\}, (s_i, q_i) \rangle \in E_C$

(G5) Whenever all the following are true:
  (i) $(y\ s_1 \cdots s_n,\ q) \in V_C$
  (ii) $y \mapsto t \in B_C$

then all the following are also true:
- $(t\ s_1 \cdots s_n,\ q) \in V_C$
- $\langle (y\ s_1 \cdots s_n,\ q), (t\ s_1 \cdots s_n,\ q) \rangle \in E_C$

**Figure 4.** Abstract configuration graph construction.

Finally, rule (G5) ties the knot on the abstraction by considering the case when a typed variable is in head position in a configuration. In this case, the binding set is consulted and a node is added for each binding to the appropriate variable. We will think of the children of such a vertex conjunctively: for $y\ s_1 \cdots s_n$ to generate a tree accepted from state $q$, it had better be that every term that it abstracts generates a tree accepted from state $q$.

Due to the abstraction at the point of contraction in (G2) and the limited substitution (only in head position) in (G5), $\mathsf{ACG}(C)$ is necessarily a finite construction. In fact, we can go further:

**Lemma 2.** *Let $C$ be a type context. Then the size of $V_C$ is bounded by a polynomial function of the size of the scheme.*

***Classification of leaves.*** Let us consider for a moment the leaves of $\mathsf{ACG}(C)$ for some type context $C$. It follows from the definition that the leaves all have a particular form. Every leaf is a configuration headed by a non-terminal symbol, i.e. a redex. Moreover, each such redex, if contracted using rule (G2), would yield a new configuration which is already known to be either $C$-accepting or $C$-rejecting. It is for this reason that such configurations are leaves: (G2) does not apply because the fourth premise would be violated.

**Definition 6.** *Given a type context $C = \langle \Gamma_\exists, \Gamma_\forall \rangle$, the leaves (i.e. those vertices that have no children) of $\mathsf{ACG}(C)$ can be classified into two sets:*

(ACCEPTING LEAVES) *These leaves are configurations of the form $(F\ s_1 \cdots s_n,\ q)$ where $\mathcal{R}(F) = \lambda x_1 \ldots x_n. t$, for each $i \in [1..n]$, there is a typed variable $y_i$ such that $\mathsf{A}(y_i) = \bigwedge \mathbb{T}_{\mathcal{A}}(\Gamma_\exists)(s_i)$ and $\Gamma_\exists \vdash_{\mathcal{A}} t[y_1/x_1, \ldots, y_n/x_n] : q$.*

(REJECTING LEAVES) *These leaves are configurations of the form $(F\ s_1 \cdots s_n,\ q)$ where $\mathcal{R}(F) = \lambda x_1 \ldots x_n. t$, for each $i \in [1..n]$, there is a typed variable $y_i$ such that $\mathsf{R}(y_i) = \bigwedge \mathbb{T}_{\mathcal{A}^c}(\Gamma_\forall)(s_i)$ and $\Gamma_\forall \vdash_{\mathcal{A}^c} t[y_1/x_1, \ldots, y_n/x_n] : q$.*

Note that a rejecting leaf is not itself $C$-rejecting, by Lemma 1 since it is in the graph it is necessarily $C$-unknown, but its contractum is $C$-rejecting. Similarly accepting leaves are not themselves $C$-accepting, but the contractum of an accepting leaf is $C$-accepting.

**Lemma 3.** *Let $C$ be a context. Every leaf in $\mathsf{ACG}(C)$ is accepting or rejecting.*

## 4.2 The rejecting region

***Region of rejection.*** The construction of an ACG from a given type context $C$ is a method for analysing the type context. By constructing the graph it is possible to see where the information in the type context is deficient, and the main tools for identifying and correcting deficiencies are the regions and region type extraction respectively. Consider a rejecting leaf $v$ of the form $(F\ s_1 \cdots s_n,\ q)$. By definition, the contraction of this configuration using (G2) would yield a configuration $(t[y_1/x_1, \ldots, y_n/x_n],\ q)$ which is already $C$-rejecting. In other words, the tree generated by *any* term of the form $t[t_1/y_1, \ldots, t_n/y_n]$ such that $\bigwedge \mathbb{T}_{\mathcal{A}^c}(\Gamma_\forall)(t_i) \leq \bigwedge \mathbb{T}_{\mathcal{A}^c}(\Gamma_\forall)(y_i)$ for each $i$ is sure to be rejected from state $q$. Assuming that $\Gamma_\forall$ is co-consistent, this follows because necessarily $\Gamma_\forall \vdash_{\mathcal{A}^c} t[t_1/y_1, \ldots, t_n/y_n] : q$. Recalling Proposition 1, one such sequence of $t_i$ are the actual parameters of the term component of the rejecting leaf we started with: $v$. Hence, because we know that the contractum of the term part of $v$ generates a tree that is rejected from state $q_0$, necessarily the term part of $v$ itself generates a tree that is rejected from state $q_0$. So we have identified that $v$ should be classified as $C$-rejecting (but is not currently). Through analogous reasoning (and remembering the conjunctive and disjunctive interpretations of the child relation in the graph), it is possible to identify other such vertices which are necessarily rejecting. The collection of all such is called the rejecting region.

**Definition 7.** *Given a context $C$, we define a subset $\mathsf{RR}(C) \subseteq V_C$ of the vertices of $\mathsf{ACG}(C)$, called the* rejecting region, *inductively:*

*(R1) If $c$ is a rejecting leaf then $c \in \mathsf{RR}(C)$.*

*(R2) If $\{(s_1, q_1), \ldots, (s_n, q_n)\} \in V_C$ and there exists $j \in [1..n]$ and $(s_j, q_j) \in \mathsf{RR}(C)$ then $\{(s_1, q_1), \ldots, (s_n, q_n)\} \in \mathsf{RR}(C)$.*

*(R3) If $\langle (F\ s_1 \cdots s_n,\ q),\ (t,\ q) \rangle \in E_C$ and $(t,\ q) \in \mathsf{RR}(C)$ then $(F\ s_1 \cdots s_n,\ q) \in \mathsf{RR}(C)$.*

*(R4) If $(a s_1 \cdots s_n,\ q) \in V_C$ and, for every $v$, $\langle (a s_1 \cdots s_n,\ q),\ v \rangle \in E_C$ implies $v \in \mathsf{RR}(C)$, then $(a\ s_1 \cdots s_n,\ q) \in \mathsf{RR}(C)$.*

*(R5) If $(y\ s_1 \cdots s_n,\ q) \in V_C$ and, for all $y \mapsto t \in B_C$, $(t\ s_1 \cdots s_n,\ q) \in \mathsf{RR}(C)$ then $(y\ s_1 \cdots s_n,\ q) \in \mathsf{RR}(C)$.*

Unless it is the final iteration of the algorithm, the rejecting region will always be non-empty. The fact that an absence of rejecting leaves is an absence of counterexamples in the abstraction is formalised later, in Lemma 6.

***Rejection type extraction.*** The vertices in the rejecting region are those configurations, that we have identified by constructing $\mathsf{ACG}(C)$, which *should* be classified by the context as rejecting, but *are not* – each is necessarily $C$-unknown, since it belongs to the graph. So the rejecting region represents a weakness in the context. To remedy it, from the region we will extract new type information to be added to the context ready for the next iteration.

**Definition 8.** *Let $C = \langle \Gamma_\exists, \Gamma_\forall \rangle$ be a typing context and $v \in \mathsf{RR}(C)$. A witness to the membership of $v$ in $\mathsf{RR}(C)$ is a proof tree $T$ rooted at the statement $v \in \mathsf{RR}(C)$ and constructed according to the rules (R1) – (R5). We describe an assignment of type environments $\mathcal{M}(T)$ to proof trees $T$, inductively on the shape of the proof.*

*(M1) If the proof is by (R1) then $v$ is a configuration of the form $(F\ s_1 \cdots s_n,\ q)$, and we set $\mathcal{M}(T)$ to be the single binding:*

$$F : \bigwedge \mathbb{T}(\Gamma_\forall)(s_1) \to \cdots \to \bigwedge \mathbb{T}(\Gamma_\forall)(s_n) \to q$$

*(M2) If the proof is by (R2) then $v$ is a set $\{(s_1, q_1), \ldots, (s_n, q_n)\}$ and for some $j \in [1..n]$ there is an immediate sub-proof $T'$ of $(s_j, q_j)$. We set $\mathcal{M}(T) = \mathcal{M}(T')$.*

*(M3) If the proof is by (R3) then $v$ is a configuration of the form $(F\ s_1 \cdots s_n,\ q)$ and, necessarily, there is an immediate sub-proof $T'$ of $(t,\ q)$. We take for $\mathcal{M}(T)$ the environment $\mathcal{M}(T')$ augmented by the binding:*

$$F : \bigwedge \mathbb{T}(\Gamma_\forall \uplus \mathcal{M}(T'))(s_1) \to \cdots \to \bigwedge \mathbb{T}(\Gamma_\forall \uplus \mathcal{M}(T'))(s_n) \to q$$

*(M4) If the proof is by (R4) then $v$ is of the form $(a\ s_1 \cdots s_n,\ q)$ with a set $W$ of children. For each $w \in W$, there is a sub-proof $T_w$. We set $\mathcal{M}(T) = \biguplus \{\mathcal{M}(T_w) \mid w \in W\}$.*

*(M5) If the proof is by (R5) then $v$ is a configuration of the form $(y\ s_1 \cdots s_n,\ q)$ and, necessarily, for each $y \mapsto t \in B_C$ there is an immediate sub-proof $T_t$ of $(t\ s_1 \cdots s_n,\ q)$. Let us write $\mathcal{M}(T_y)$ simply as notation for the environment given by $\biguplus \{\mathcal{M}(T_t) \mid y \mapsto t \in B_C\}$. We take for $\mathcal{M}(T)$ the environment:*

$$y : \bigwedge \mathbb{T}(\Gamma_\forall \uplus \mathcal{M}(T_y))(s_1) \to \cdots \to \bigwedge \mathbb{T}(\Gamma_\forall \uplus \mathcal{M}(T_y))(s_n) \to q$$

*Finally, we define a type environment, $\mathsf{env}_{\mathsf{R}}(C)$, whose domain is a subset of $\mathsf{dom}(\mathcal{N})$ and which is extracted from $\mathsf{RR}(C)$ by:*

$$\mathsf{env}_{\mathsf{R}}(C)(F) = \bigwedge \{\mathcal{M}(T)(F) \mid \exists c \in \mathsf{RR}(C) \text{ with witness } T\}$$

So the types are extracted in an inductive fashion, starting from the leaves of each witness with the environment $\Gamma_\forall$ and working backwards, adding new types along with way. It is this well-foundedness that ensures that the types that are extracted are all "correct":

**Lemma 4.** *Let $C = \langle \Gamma_\exists, \Gamma_\forall \rangle$ be a type context. If $\Gamma_\forall$ is $\mathcal{G}$-co-consistent in $\mathcal{A}^c$ then $\Gamma_\forall \uplus \mathsf{env}_\mathsf{R}(C)$ is $\mathcal{G}$-co-consistent in $\mathcal{A}^c$.*

Furthermore, whenever the rejecting region is non-empty, then genuinely new type information will be extracted. Taken together with Lemma 6, the following result is the key measure of progress in the algorithm.

**Lemma 5.** *Let $C = \langle \Gamma_\exists, \Gamma_\forall \rangle$ be a type context and $\mathsf{ACG}(C)$ have some rejecting leaf. Then $\mathsf{env}_\mathsf{R}(C) \setminus \Gamma_\forall \neq \emptyset$.*

### 4.3 The accepting region

***Region of acceptance.*** In a similar way, the accepting region serves to identify those configurations that *should* be classified as accepting by the type context, but which are not. The rules by which vertices can be inferred to be accepting are all complimentary to those that define the rejecting region (except for the case of variable-headed nodes, which are conjunctive in both regions) and, indeed, the construction is coinductive.

**Definition 9.** *Given a typing context $C$, we define a subset $\mathsf{RA}(C) \subseteq V_C$ of the vertices of $\mathsf{ACG}(C)$, called the* accepting region, *coinductively by:*

*(A1) If $(F\ s_1 \cdots s_n,\ q) \in \mathsf{RA}(C)$ with successor $(t,\ q) \in V_C$, then $(t,\ q) \in \mathsf{RA}(C)$.*
*(A2) If $(a\ s_1 \cdots s_n,\ q) \in \mathsf{RA}(C)$, then there is some $S$ such that $S \models \delta(q,\ a)$ and $\{(s_i,\ q') \mid (i,\ q') \in S\} \in \mathsf{RA}(C)$.*
*(A3) If $\{(s_1,\ q_1), \ldots, (s_m,\ q_m)\} \in \mathsf{RA}(C)$ then, for all $i \in [1..m]$, $(s_m,\ q_m) \in \mathsf{RA}(C)$.*
*(A4) If $(y\ s_1 \cdots s_n,\ q) \in \mathsf{RA}(C)$ then, for all $y \mapsto t \in B_C$, $(t\ s_1 \cdots s_n,\ q) \in \mathsf{RA}(C)$.*
*(A5) If $c \in \mathsf{RA}(C)$ is a leaf in $V_C$ then $c$ is an accepting leaf.*

However, unlike the case for rejecting region there is no similar guarantee of non-emptiness on non-final iterations. It is perfectly possible that on any given iteration, the accepting region may be empty. In contrast, the absence of rejecting leaves, and hence emptiness of the rejecting region, leads to termination.

**Lemma 6.** *Let $C$ be a type context and $\mathsf{ACG}(C)$ have no rejecting leaves. Then $\mathsf{ACG}(C) = \mathsf{RA}(C)$.*

Thus, in particular, $\mathsf{RA}(C)$ will contain the root and so $S : q_0$ will be added to the accepting environment, signalling termination.

***Acceptance type extraction.*** To extract new type information from the accepting region we follow the approach of Kobayashi and Ong [12, 14], in which types are assigned to prefixes of configurations recursively based on the kind of the prefix.

**Definition 10.** *Let $C = \langle \Gamma_\exists, \Gamma_\forall \rangle$ be a type context. To each prefix $(c,\ s)$ of each configuration $c \in \mathsf{RA}(C)$, we assign a strict type $\mathsf{extr}(c,\ s)$, which is defined inductively over the structure of the kind of $s$.*

*(i) If $s$ is of base kind, necessarily $c$ is of the form $(s,\ q)$ and set $\mathsf{extr}(c,\ s) = q$.*
*(ii) If $s$ is of arrow kind, necessarily $c$ is of the form $(s\, t_1 \cdots t_n,\ q)$. Let $W$ be the set of accepting region configurations with prefix $t_1$. Set:*

$$\mathsf{extr}(c,\ s) = \bigwedge \mathbb{T}_{\mathsf{A}}(\Gamma_\exists)(t_1) \wedge \bigwedge_{c' \in W} \mathsf{extr}(c',\ t_1) \to \mathsf{extr}(c,\ s\, t_1)$$

*We define a type environment, $\mathsf{env}_\mathsf{A}(C)$, whose domain is a subset of $\mathsf{dom}(\mathcal{N})$ and which is extracted from $\mathsf{RA}(C)$ by:*

$$\mathsf{env}_\mathsf{A}(C)(F) = \bigwedge \{\tau \mid \exists c \in \mathsf{RA}(C) \cdot \mathsf{extr}(c,\ F) = \tau\}$$

The acceptance types extracted in this way are all "correct":

**Lemma 7.** *Let $C = \langle \Gamma_\exists, \Gamma_\forall \rangle$ be a context. If $\Gamma_\exists$ is $(\mathcal{G},\mathcal{A})$-consistent then also $\Gamma_\exists \uplus \mathsf{env}_\mathsf{A}(C)$ is $(\mathcal{G},\mathcal{A})$-consistent.*

### 4.4 Fixed point construction

***Abstraction refinement.*** Finally, we are in a position to describe the overall abstraction refinement loop. Starting from a context $C_0$ that contains only the type assumptions on typed variables used by the abstraction, on each iteration the algorithm analyses the given context, say $C_i$, by constructing $\mathsf{ACG}(C_i)$; it then identifies deficiencies in $C_i$ by constructing regions and attempts to repair those deficiencies by extracting new environments. Eventually, the type $S : q_0$ will be extracted from one of the regions and the algorithm will terminate.

**Definition 11.** *Recall $\mathsf{A}$ and $\mathsf{R}$ in Definition 1. The algorithm consists of constructing an eventually stable sequence of type contexts $(C_i)_{i \in \mathrm{N}}$ as follows:*

$$\begin{array}{lllll} C_0 & = \langle \Gamma_\exists^0,\ \Gamma_\forall^0 \rangle & = \langle \mathsf{A},\ \mathsf{R} \rangle \\ C_{k+1} & = \langle \Gamma_\exists^{k+1},\ \Gamma_\forall^{k+1} \rangle & = \langle \Gamma_\exists^k \uplus \mathsf{env}_\mathsf{A}(C_k),\ \Gamma_\forall^k \uplus \mathsf{env}_\mathsf{R}(C_k) \rangle \end{array}$$

*with limit, say $C = \langle \Gamma_\exists, \Gamma_\forall \rangle$. Then if $q_0 \in \Gamma_\exists(S)$ answer* YES *and otherwise answer* NO.

Since the initial environments $\Gamma_\exists^0$ and $\Gamma_\forall^0$ are trivially $\mathcal{G}$-consistent in $\mathcal{A}$ and $\mathcal{G}$-co-consistent in $\mathcal{A}^c$ respectively and since every extension of these environments by $\mathsf{env}_\mathsf{A}$ and $\mathsf{env}_R$ preserves this property, it follows that the limit of the sequence also enjoys the property and hence can be relied upon to decide the model checking problem. Furthermore, since progress is guaranteed by Lemma 6 and Lemma 5, and the size of rejecting environment $\Gamma_\forall$ is bounded by the number of well-kinded types, we can state the following correctness theorem:

**Theorem 2.** *For any $\mathcal{G}$, $\mathcal{A}$, the algorithm terminates and:*

- *Answer* YES *implies* $\mathsf{Tree}(\mathcal{G}) \in \mathcal{L}(\mathcal{A}^\perp)$.
- *Answer* NO *implies* $\mathsf{Tree}(\mathcal{G}) \notin \mathcal{L}(\mathcal{A}^\perp)$.

Furthermore, since each ACG is, in the worst case, polynomial in the size of the scheme (but in general, hyper-exponential in the order of the scheme) and the amount of work involved in computing the ACG, the regions and type extraction is polynomial in the size of the scheme, it follows that each iteration of the algorithm takes, in the worst case, an amount of time polynomial in the size of the scheme. Since the number of iterations is bounded by the number of well-kinded types, which is also polynomial in the size of the scheme, it follows that the algorithm as a whole is polynomial in the size of the scheme, assuming its order and arity and the size of the automaton are taken to be fixed.

## 5. Implementation and evaluation

We have implemented the algorithm in a prototype tool, called PREFACE, which is written in F# and available to download from `http://mjolnir.cs.ox.ac.uk/web/preface`.

### 5.1 Implementation

To ensure efficiency we have taken a number of decisions about how to code specific aspects of the algorithm which deviate from the presentation. Rather than constructing them as part of initialisation, we build the maps A and R lazily, adding bindings as they are needed by applications of rule (G2). Further, the implementation uses a flow analysis with increased accuracy, distinguishing between instances of arguments using not just the triple of acceptance type, rejection type and kind, but additionally the formal parameter

| Benchmark | Rules | Ord | Dec | PREFACE | HORSAT | HORSATT | C-SHORE | GTRECS2 | TRAVMC | TRECS |
|---|---|---|---|---|---|---|---|---|---|---|
| cfa-psdes | 237 | 7 | A | 0.51 | 0.28 | 1.81 | 3.44 | – | – | – |
| cfa-matrix-1 | 383 | 8 | A | 0.61 | 0.73 | 6.30 | 18.58 | – | – | – |
| cfa-life2 | 898 | 14 | A | 1.46 | 5.94 | – | – | – | – | – |

**Table 2.** Benchmarks of category 2.

| Benchmark | Rules | Ord | Dec | PREFACE | HORSAT | HORSATT | C-SHORE | GTRECS2 | TRAVMC | TRECS |
|---|---|---|---|---|---|---|---|---|---|---|
| exp2-1600 | 1606 | 2 | A | 8.39 | – | – | – | 10.47 | – | – |
| exp2-3200 | 3206 | 2 | A | 17.51 | – | – | – | 59.13 | – | – |
| exp2-6400 | 6406 | 2 | A | 39.58 | – | – | – | – | – | – |
| exp2-12800 | 12806 | 2 | A | 92.19 | – | – | – | – | – | – |
| exp4-400 | 408 | 4 | A | 14.12 | – | 106.53 | – | – | – | – |
| exp4-800 | 808 | 4 | A | 30.55 | – | – | – | – | – | – |
| exp4-1600 | 1608 | 4 | A | 71.06 | – | – | – | – | – | – |
| exp4-3200 | 3208 | 4 | A | – | – | – | – | – | – | – |

**Table 3.** Benchmarks of category 3.

| Benchmark | Rules | Ord | Dec | PREFACE | TRECS |
|---|---|---|---|---|---|
| map_filter-e | 64 | 5 | R | 0.53 | 0.01 |
| fold_left | 65 | 4 | A | 0.39 | 0.03 |
| fold_right | 65 | 4 | A | 0.39 | 0.03 |
| forall_eq_pair | 66 | 4 | A | 0.39 | 0.03 |
| forall_leq | 66 | 4 | A | 0.39 | 0.03 |
| a-cppr | 74 | 3 | R | 0.38 | 0.01 |
| search-e | 96 | 5 | R | 0.90 | 0.01 |
| search | 119 | 4 | A | 0.46 | 1.04 |
| map_filter | 143 | 5 | A | 0.51 | 0.13 |
| risers | 148 | 5 | A | 0.44 | 0.33 |
| r-file | 156 | 2 | A | 0.82 | 1.50 |
| fold_fun_list | 197 | 6 | A | 0.44 | 0.89 |
| zip | 210 | 3 | A | 0.58 | 15.10 |

**Table 1.** Benchmarks of category 1.

and the state component of the calling configuration. Since intersection type checking is frequently invoked as part of the decision procedure, we aim to ensure it is done as efficiently as possible. Hence, we omit subtype checking[3] and hash cons the intersection types. Finally, rather than compute all possible witnessing trees for any given vertex $v \in \mathsf{RR}(C)$, we take one representative, which is a function of the construction of the region.

### 5.2 Evaluation

We have evaluated the tool on the large collection of recursion scheme model checking instances found online and in the related literature. The full listing of results is available in the appendix of the long version of this paper, here we aim to present a very small representative sample in order to describe the general trends.

We have picked a number of benchmarks from three categories, which are displayed in Tables 1, 2 and 3 respectively. The benchmarks were run on an Intel Xeon machine with 12GB of RAM and 4 cores running at 2.4GHz, limiting the run-time of each tool on each benchmark to 2 minutes. In all cases the columns are, respectively, the name of the benchmark, the number of rules (equations), the order of the scheme, whether the tree is accepted (A) or rejected (R) by the property automaton. The remaining columns list the time taken by each tool from start to finish, which is either given in seconds, or marked "–" in case the tool ran out of resources.

[3] Note that this does not affect the soundness or completeness of the decision procedure.

*Category 1.* The first category consists of model checking instances that have arisen from OCaml verification problems via the predicate abstraction tool MoCHi [25]. Although MoCHi can solve many complex examples, the scalability of a full blown predicate abstraction tool for higher-order programs is still an open topic of research. Consequently the problem instances derived from this tool are exclusively quite small and mostly less than 100 rules. MoCHi generates a mild extension of recursion schemes called RSFD [16], which are currently only supported by PREFACE and TRECS. Our tool PREFACE can typically solve each of these instances in less than 0.5 seconds, but this is already roughly an order of magnitude slower than TRECS. However, the overhead incurred by JIT compilation on Mono is a major factor; when compiled ahead of time on Windows, the time taken by PREFACE to solve these instances is typically less than 0.05 seconds, although usually still slower than TRECS. As the benchmarks become slightly larger, towards the bottom of the table, the time taken by TRECS starts to lag behind the time taken by PREFACE, which is the start of a general trend in the data to follow.

*Category 2.* The second category consists of instances arising from a tool for performing exact flow analysis [26]. These examples are significantly larger than those of Category 1 and, indeed, form some of the largest instances on which HORS model checkers have been evaluated in the literature as of the time of writing. Although they have fewer than 1000 rules each, due to the nature of the verification algorithm that produces them, they have high order and very high maximum arity, with `cfa-life2` being order 14 with arity 29 functions. Consequently, many of the tools have difficulty, but among those that are able to solve these instances, the trend observed in the Category 1 examples can be seen to continue.

*Category 3.* The final category consists of instances of a family of schemes due to Kobayashi [13]. This family of instances was designed to be deliberately difficult for bounded model checking style algorithms such as the hybrid algorithm of TRECS, whilst simultaneously being a good indicator of the scalability of Kobayashi's linear time algorithm as implemented in GTRECS. Although these schemes are not "real" in the sense of arising from program analysis problems they seem a good measure of scalability since they generate hyper-exponentially sized trees (and hence use the full power of higher-order schemes), their certificates are proportional to the number of rules and they can push the model checkers much further since the family contains much larger schemes than can be produced by current verification tools. The first half of the table shows instances which are generated with order-2 schemes and the second half shows instances with order-4 schemes. The size of the schemes roughly doubles within each half by row. As expected, GTRECS does a good job at solving even relatively large examples at order-2, though it has some difficulty at higher-orders. PREFACE does even better and, in contrast to the other tools, can be seen to solve these examples in time which is roughly linear in the number of rules.

### 5.3 Analysis

The good performance of our algorithm at scale must be attributed to the abstraction refinement approach that we have adopted. Since recursion schemes cannot destruct the trees that they create, their interesting behaviours are exclusively due to control flow arising from complex uses of higher-order functions. Hence, a CFA-style abstraction in combination with a property directed refinement works well, since this abstraction is particularly well suited to emphasising some of the essential structure of higher-order control flow and the refinement ensures that particular limitations of the CFA with respect to specific problem instances can be compensated for. A good example of this is in the Category 3 examples, whose very regular structure is determined by the analysis quickly and hence all are solved in exactly 3 iterations (independent of the number of rules or the order of the scheme).

However, although the refinement will eventually compensate for these particular limitations of the CFA, it is possible to construct instances in which the number of iterations required is unacceptably large with respect to the characteristics of the instance. Although such examples do not seem to occur in the corpus of instances drawn from the higher-order model checking literature and associated verification tools, we have been able to construct very small and simple schemes which exhibit this bad behaviour. The examples in Table 4 are based on a family of Boolean programs defined in [1]. Each of these instances is first order and consists of a few hundred rules, but the property automaton is strictly alternating. We record the number of iterations (Rnds) and the time (in seconds) taken by PREFACE and an extension, PREFACE$^+$, in the remaining columns.

| | | PREFACE | | PREFACE$^+$ | |
|---|---|---|---|---|---|
| Benchmark | Rules | Rnds | Time | Rnds | Time |
| t100 | 104 | 202 | 45.38 | 8 | 2.17 |
| t200 | 204 | 402 | 178.81 | 8 | 3.99 |
| t400 | 404 | 802 | 732.40 | 8 | 7.97 |
| t800 | 804 | 1602 | 3074.03 | 9 | 18.50 |
| t1600 | 1604 | 3202 | 13561.26 | 9 | 41.02 |

**Table 4.** Bad behaviour.

Each example t$n$ consists of roughly $n$ functions, which make exponentially many calls to each other in sequence, so that function $F1$ calls function $F2$ twice, function $F2$ calls function $F3$ twice and so on. However, what makes the examples expose bad behaviour in PREFACE is not the number of calls (which is hyper-exponentially smaller than the number of calls made by the exp$n$-$m$ examples in Category 3), but the fact that each call is made once with a term that will eventually evaluate to true and once with a term that will eventually evaluate to false and that refutation of the property depends upon distinguishing between the two. On iteration $2i+2$, the flow analysis is only able to distinguish between the true and false variants of the calls made to functions $Fj$ for $j \geq n-i$. Every 2 iterations, enough new information has been discovered in order to distinguish one more level of function calls, and hence each t$n$ is solved after roughly $2n$ iterations.

This analysis suggests that not enough type information is being recovered from the ACG at each iteration and, indeed, by extending our implementation with heuristics for extracting more types, we have solved these examples more quickly. Our extension, labelled PREFACE$^+$ in the table, exploits the *incremental* nature of the algorithm. By this we mean the following characteristics:

(i) The algorithm makes progress on each iteration, in the sense of extracting new types (even if the number of types extracted is perhaps smaller than one would like).

(ii) On each iteration, the provenance of the context is not important, only the fact that it comprises environments that are consistent and co-consistent respectively.

(iii) The larger the context for a given iteration, the more accurate the analysis of that iteration.

Our extension consists of, in a separate thread running in parallel with the main algorithm, taking the ACG that has most recently been computed and, based on the relationships between the vertices, making informed "guesses" at possible new types. In general the guesses may be incorrect, in the sense of leading to the creation of an environment which is unjustifiable, so the new environments are first type-checked according to the rules of (co-)consistency. If they type-check, the new types are then added into the context at the earliest opportunity and the guessing process can be repeated.

This extension appears to work well to solve the examples in Table 4, cutting the time taken to process `t1600` down from almost 3 hours to under one minute! However, it seems unlikely to scale well to higher-orders, where the possible number of types from which to guess is much larger. Consequently, we do not consider this a satisfactory solution and leave to future work a proper treatment of this problem and that of the closely related area of how best to extract counter-example traces.

## 6. Related work

***Higher-order model checking algorithms.*** Exemplified by the tool TRECS [11], the first *practical* algorithms model check HORS with respect to trivial automata, using intersection types as a finite representation of an infinite transition system. They start from the assignment of the automaton initial state to the start non-terminal $S$, and compute the "post-image" in the form of type information required to deduce unreachability of the error configurations. In TRECS, the types of non-terminals are first extracted from a finitely reachable part of the (infinite) configuration graph; the resultant type environment is then expanded and used as an over-approximation of a greatest fixpoint (of *shrink* [12]). PREFACE is similar to TRECS in that it implements a forward algorithm based on intersection types. However, in contrast, PREFACE extracts types from a finite, 0CFA-like abstraction of the configuration graph. Another major difference is that each iteration of PREFACE refines two type environments, one is potentially a certificate of automaton acceptance, and the other of automaton rejection.

Very fast for HORS of up to a few hundred rules, the runtime of TRECS is nonetheless hyper-exponential in the size of the input HORS. The first fixed-parameter polytime (in the size of HORS) algorithm is GTRECS [13] which consists simply of two fixpoint constructions. The key innovation is a game-semantic reading of the intersection types *qua* a pair of expansion relations, modelling the legals moves of the two players of an arena game. The tool TRAVMC [19] is also based on game semantics. The algorithm harvests *variable profiles*, but represented as intersection types, from the *traversals* [20] over the HORS being analysed.

Recently Broadbent et al. [4] have introduced an algorithm based on *collapsible pushdown automata* (CPDA) [8]—which are equi-expressive with HORS—and implemented in the tool C-SHORe [5]. Given an input co-trivial tree automaton, the algorithm uses a generalisation of the saturation algorithm for pushdown automata to compute the "pre-image" of the final error configurations, and checks if it includes the start state. Thus information is propagated in the *backward* direction. Closely related are algorithms HorSat and HorSatT [3]. Though based on saturation (of HORS rather than CPDA), they may be viewed as fixpoint computation of a function over type environments. To accelerate the pre-image computation, these algorithms benefit from a forward flow analysis, which excludes some irrelevant type bindings.

***Abstraction refinement.*** Counterexample-guided abstraction refinement (CEGAR) was introduced by Clarke et al. [6] for symbolic model checking. The CEGAR loop was first applied to higher-order model checking by Ong and Ramsay [22] and by Kobayashi et al. [17]. The former addresses the undecidable problem of verifying safety properties of pattern-matching recursion schemes, using patterns to abstract properties. The latter is used in conjunction with predicate abstraction to verify simply-typed functional programs generated from infinite data domains such as integers. In contrast, Preface builds successively more accurate finite abstractions of the configuration graph of the HORS being analysed, from which potential certificates of acceptance and of rejection are derived.

***Type-based flow analysis.*** Flow analyses were first applied to untyped languages. Jagannathan et al. [9] introduced a type-directed, polyvariant flow analysis for the predicative subset of System F, which can leverage types to analyse programs more precisely. Our algorithm uses an intersection type system for describing automaton definable properties and necessarily works in a situation in which not all type information is known; in contrast theirs uses more standard typing (System F) and starts from a situation in which all types are known. Thus their analysis is comparable to a single iteration of our algorithm where the associated context already contains all the possible correct type information. The property of *respecting types*, which is put forward by the authors as a measure of the appropriateness of a CFA for a typed language is, for us, actually an essential technical requirement in order to extract new, valid type information.

Plevyak and Chien [23] considered a constraint-based type inference for object-oriented programs. Like our algorithm, not all type information is known at the start, and they compute types iteratively based on a flow analysis. However, within a single iteration they do not distinguish based on type information, instead they distinguish based on clashes discovered in the previous iteration. A problem with their approach of distinguishing calls unconditionally is that there may be infinitely many counterexamples which are being distinguished one at a time. Because of possible non-termination, their method cannot handle recursion in general.

## Acknowledgments

We are grateful to Naoki Kobayashi, Hiroshi Unno, Ryosuke Sato, Matthew Hague and Christopher Broadbent for providing their tools and contributing a large number of examples for benchmarking in Section 5. The first author was generously supported in this work by a graduate research grant from Merton College, Oxford.

## References

[1] T. Ball and S. K. Rajamani. Bebop: A symbolic model checker for boolean programs. In *SPIN'00*, volume 1885 of *LNCS*, pages 113–130. Springer, 2000.

[2] H. Barendregt, M. Coppo, and M. Dezani-Ciancaglini. A filter lambda model and the completeness of type assignment. *Journal of Symbolic Logic*, 48(4):931–940, 1983.

[3] C. H. Broadbent and N. Kobayashi. Saturation-based model checking of higher-order recursion schemes. In *CSL'13*, volume 23 of *LIPIcs*, pages 129–148. Schloss Dagstuhl, 2013.

[4] C. H. Broadbent, A. Carayol, M. Hague, and O. Serre. A saturation method for collapsible pushdown systems. In *ICALP'12*, volume 7392 of *Lecture Notes in Computer Science*, pages 165–176. Springer, 2012.

[5] C. H. Broadbent, A. Carayol, M. Hague, and O. Serre. C-SHORe: a collapsible approach to verifying higher-order programs. In *ICFP'13*, pages 13–24. ACM, 2013.

[6] E. M. Clarke, O. Grumberg, S. Jha, Y. Lu, and H. Veith. Counterexample-guided abstraction refinement. In *CAV'00*, pages 154–169. Springer-Verlag, 2000.

[7] M. Coppo and M. Dezani. An extension of the basic functionality theory for the lambda-calculus. *Notre Dame Journal of Formal Logic*, 21(4):685–693, 1980.

[8] M. Hague, A. S. Murawski, C.-H. L. Ong, and O. Serre. Collapsible pushdown automata and recursion schemes. In *LICS'08*, pages 452–461. IEEE Computer Society, 2008.

[9] S. Jagannathan, S. Weeks, and A. K. Wright. Type-directed flow analysis for typed intermediate languages. In *SAS'97*, volume 1302 of *Lecture Notes in Computer Science*, pages 232–249. Springer, 1997.

[10] N. D. Jones. Flow analysis of lambda expressions. In *ICALP'81*, volume 115 of *LNCS*, pages 114–128. Springer, 1981.

[11] N. Kobayashi. Types and higher-order recursion schemes for verification of higher-order programs. In *POPL'09*, pages 416–428. ACM, 2009.

[12] N. Kobayashi. Model-checking higher-order functions. In *PPDP'09*, pages 25–36. ACM, 2009.

[13] N. Kobayashi. A practical linear time algorithm for trivial automata model checking of higher-order recursion schemes. In *FOSSACS 2011*, volume 6604 of *Lecture Notes in Computer Science*, pages 260–274. Springer, 2011.

[14] N. Kobayashi and C.-H. L. Ong. A type system equivalent to the modal mu-calculus model checking of higher-order recursion schemes. In *LICS 2009*, pages 179–188. IEEE Computer Society, 2009.

[15] N. Kobayashi and C.-H. L. Ong. Complexity of model checking recursion schemes for fragments of the modal mu-calculus. *Logical Methods in Computer Science*, 7(4), 2011.

[16] N. Kobayashi, N. Tabuchi, and H. Unno. Higher-order multi-parameter tree transducers and recursion schemes for program verification. In *POPL'10*, pages 495–508, 2010.

[17] N. Kobayashi, R. Sato, and H. Unno. Predicate abstraction and CEGAR for higher-order model checking. In *PLDI'11*, pages 222–233. ACM, 2011.

[18] D. E. Muller and P. E. Schupp. Alternating automata on infinite trees. *Theoretical Compututer Science*, 54(2–3):267–276, 1987.

[19] R. P. Neatherway, C.-H. L. Ong, and S. J. Ramsay. A traversal-based algorithm for higher-order model checking. In *ICFP'12*, pages 353–364. ACM, 2012.

[20] C.-H. L. Ong. On model-checking trees generated by higher-order recursion schemes. In *LICS'06*, pages 81–90. IEEE Comp. Soc., 2006.

[21] C.-H. L. Ong. Models of higher-order computation: Recursion schemes and collapsible pushdown automata. In *LLRS'10*, pages 263–299. 2010.

[22] C.-H. L. Ong and S. J. Ramsay. Verifying higher-order functional programs with pattern-matching algebraic data types. In *POPL'11*, pages 587–598. ACM, 2011.

[23] J. Plevyak and A. A. Chien. Precise concrete type inference for object-oriented languages. In *OOPSLA'94*, pages 324–340. ACM, 1994.

[24] S. J. Ramsay, R. P. Neatherway, and C.-H. L. Ong. A type-directed abstraction refinement approach to higher-order model checking. Long version: `http://mjolnir.cs.ox.ac.uk/papers/preface.pdf`.

[25] R. Sato, H. Unno, and N. Kobayashi. Towards a scalable software model checker for higher-order programs. In *PEPM'13*, pages 53–62. ACM, 2013.

[26] Y. Tobita, T. Tsukada, and N. Kobayashi. Exact flow analysis by higher-order model checking. In *FLOPS'12*, volume 7294 of *LNCS*, pages 275–289. Springer, 2012.

[27] S. van Bakel. Strict intersection types for the lambda calculus. *ACM Computing Surveys*, 43(3):20, 2011.

# Fissile Type Analysis: Modular Checking of Almost Everywhere Invariants

Devin Coughlin  Bor-Yuh Evan Chang
University of Colorado Boulder
{devin.coughlin,evan.chang}@colorado.edu

## Abstract

We present a generic analysis approach to the *imperative relationship update problem*, in which destructive updates temporarily violate a global invariant of interest. Such invariants can be conveniently and concisely specified with dependent refinement types, which are efficient to check flow-insensitively. Unfortunately, while traditional flow-insensitive type checking is fast, it is inapplicable when the desired invariants can be temporarily broken. To overcome this limitation, past works have directly ratcheted up the complexity of the type analysis and associated type invariants, leading to inefficient analysis and verbose specifications. In contrast, we propose a *generic lifting* of modular refinement type analyses with a symbolic analysis to efficiently and effectively check concise invariants that hold *almost everywhere*. The result is an efficient, highly modular flow-insensitive type analysis to *optimistically* check the preservation of global relationship invariants that can fall back to a precise, disjunctive symbolic analysis when the optimistic assumption is violated. This technique permits programmers to temporarily break and then re-establish relationship invariants—a flexibility that is crucial for checking relationships in real-world, imperative languages. A significant challenge is selectively violating the global type consistency invariant over heap locations, which we achieve via *almost type-consistent heaps*. To evaluate our approach, we have encoded the problem of verifying the safety of reflective method calls in dynamic languages as a refinement type checking problem. Our analysis is capable of validating reflective call safety at interactive speeds on commonly-used Objective-C libraries and applications.

***Categories and Subject Descriptors*** F.3.1 [*Logics and Meanings of Programs*]: Specifying and Verifying and Reasoning about Programs

***Keywords*** almost everywhere invariants; dependent refinement types; almost type-consistent heaps; reflection; Objective-C

## 1. Introduction

Modular verification of just about any interesting property of programs requires the specification and inference of invariants. One particularly rich mechanism for specifying such invariants is dependent *refinement types* [38], which have been applied extensively to, for example, checking array bounds [12, 31, 32, 37]. Refinement types are compelling because they permit the specification of *relationships* in a type system framework that naturally admits modular checking. For example, a modular refinement type system can relate an array with an in-bounds index or a memory location with the lock that serializes access to it.

A less well-studied problem that also falls into a refinement type framework is modularly verifying the safety of reflective method call in dynamic languages. Reflective method call is a dynamic language feature that enables programmers to invoke a method via a run-time string value called a *selector*. In many languages, these calls have become commonplace in libraries as a mechanism to decouple client and framework code. Yet while they are powerful and convenient, reflective method calls introduce a new kind of run-time error: the method named by the selector may not exist.

Our key observation about modularly verifying reflective call safety is that the essential property to capture and track through the program is the relationship between a *responder* (the object on which the method is invoked) and a valid selector. In particular, the verifier does not need to determine the actual string value as long as it can ensure that the "responds-to" relationship between the object and the selector holds at the reflective call site. This observation is crucial because the point where this relationship invariant is established and where the selector is known (usually in client code) is likely far removed from the point where the reflective call is performed and at which the invariant is relied upon (usually in framework code).

***The imperative relationship update problem.*** A significant challenge in checking relationship invariants in dynamic, imperative programming languages is reasoning precisely about destructive updates of related storage locations, such as local variables on the stack and object fields on the heap. To illustrate this issue, consider an object `o` with an (object) invariant specifying a relationship between two fields `o.f` and `o.g`. For example, `o.f` could point to an object that should respond to a selector stored in `o.g`. We can then use this invariant to show that a reflective method call on `o.f` using selector `o.g` is safe. Again, there are many other interesting properties that require specification of relationships (e.g., `o.f` is an array with an in-bounds index stored in `o.g`, or `o.f` is a monitor object guarded by the lock stored in `o.g`).

Now consider a call `o.updateRelation(p)` to a simple method `updateRelation` that updates fields `o.f` and `o.g` with the corresponding fields from the argument `p`:

```
def updateRelation(x) = ❶ self.f = x.f; ❷ self.g = x.g; ❸
```

where three program points ❶ to ❸ are marked explicitly. Suppose that fields `p.f` and `p.g` of object `p` have the corresponding relationship with each other as those fields of `o` (e.g., `p.f` responds to `p.g`). Then it is clear that after a call to `o.updateRelation(p)`,


*POPL '14*, January 22–24, 2014, San Diego, CA, USA.

ACM 978-1-4503-2544-8/14/01... $15.00.
http://dx.doi.org/10.1145/2535838.2535855

the relationship invariant between `o.f` and `o.g` should still hold. This property seems obvious, but two issues make it challenging to verify: (1) a standard, flow-insensitive type analysis by itself is insufficient and (2) sound symbolic reasoning about potential aliasing requires an expensive disjunctive analysis.

Issue 1 arises because the first assignment violates the type refinement on **self**.`f`. In our reflective call safety example, after the assignment, the new **self**.`f` (holding the value passed in `x.f`) might not respond to the old **self**.`g`. Switching the order of assignments does not help: then after the first assignment, the old **self**.`f` might not respond to the new **self**.`g`.

Problems arising from imperative relationship updates have been studied in the context of array bounds checking [12, 32, 37]. To deal with Issue 1, these type systems either require simultaneous relationship updates [12] or drop flow-insensitivity altogether and move to a flow-sensitive treatment of typing [32, 37]. In contrast to a flow-insensitive invariant, the type of a location in a flow-sensitive treatment is not fixed globally and is permitted to vary.

We argue that for the relationship update problem, computing new types at every program point is *overly pessimistic*. Although the ideal flow-insensitive type invariant imposed by the refinement on the **self**.`f` field is broken at program point ❷, it is restored almost immediately at point ❸. While the blocks of code between violations and restorations (e.g., points ❶ to ❸) require at least flow-sensitivity, a fast flow-insensitive analysis can still be effective in checking that the relationship invariant is preserved everywhere else.

Issue 2 arises in the above example because we must reason about (potentially) two concrete objects: the object pointed to by **self** and the (possibly same) object pointed to by `x`. While this code satisfies the desired property regardless of whether or not **self** and `x` are aliases, the analysis must consider both cases. Consider a slight variant where, for example, an assignment **self**.`f = null` occurs before point ❶. A sound analysis must detect a bug in this variant (when **self** and `cb` are aliases).

Prior approaches (e.g., [1, 2, 18, 32]) enable strong updates in some situations by reasoning about concrete objects one-at-a-time. While one-at-a-time reasoning is sound, it is insufficiently precise for even this unextraordinary example. In particular, a disjunctive analysis (e.g., a path-sensitive analysis) must reason about two cases: (1) where there is one concrete object—**self** and `x` are aliases—and (2) where there are two objects—**self** and `x` are not aliases.

We also argue that directly augmenting a type system to handle temporary invariant violations or other flow-analysis issues is *overly specific*. The imperative relationship update problem applies to checking just about any property that requires relational invariants. In contrast to the aforementioned works, the essence of our approach is to mix a property-specific refinement type system with a generic, symbolic flow analysis to handle temporary violations of the type invariant. The symbolic analysis performs execution-based reasoning and decouples issues like flow- and path-sensitivity from the particular type abstraction of interest.

***Fissile type analysis.*** We propose flow-insensitive storage location (FISSILE) type analysis—a framework for enriching a dependent refinement type system to tolerate temporary violations via a generic, symbolic, separation logic-based, flow analysis. The result is an analysis that soundly checks a type invariant that holds almost everywhere. When the fast, flow-insensitive analysis detects an invariant violation, FISSILE type analysis *splits* the type environment (which relates storage locations to storage locations) into two components: (1) relationships between symbolic values (i.e., refinement types lifted to values) and (2) the locations where those values are stored (i.e., a symbolic memory). The symbolic analysis permits *bounded violation* of the storage location property and takes over until the type invariant is restored, at which point the fast flow-insensitive analysis resumes. As illustrated in the above example, we must support bounded relationship violations not only among local variables but also among a number of heap locations. Supporting bounded violations of heap locations is a significant challenge.

When applied to relationships that hold almost everywhere, FISSILE type analysis addresses the imperative relationship update problem while still maintaining two key benefits of flow-insensitivity:

1. It is nearly as fast as a flow-insensitive analysis (5,000 to 38,000 lines of code per second—see Section 4), since it begins with the *optimistic* assumption that the invariant holds everywhere and then only has to reason precisely about the relatively few program locations in which any relationships are violated.
2. It permits the vast majority (99.95%) of method type signatures to be flow-insensitive. Flow-insensitive type signatures do not need to specify the effect of the method on the heap. Contrast this to a modular, flow-sensitive analysis that has summaries specifying the effects on all methods, in essence, to rule out the *pessimistic* assumption that any callee could violate the invariant.

In summary, we make the following contributions:

- We describe the FISSILE type analysis framework for intertwined fast type and precise symbolic analysis of almost flow-insensitive storage location properties and instantiate it to check reflective call safety. Our framework is built on the observation that flow-insensitive type invariants on mutable storage locations really serve two roles: specifying facts about the values stored in them and constraining what values are allowed to be stored in them. We define two generic operations to *handoff* between the type and symbolic analyses that essentially either decouples or relinks these roles (Section 3.2).
- We introduce the notion of *almost type-consistent heaps* that (at the concrete level) splits the overall heap into two regions: one explicit region where locations are permitted to be type inconsistent and one implicit region where locations are type consistent up to encountering a location that is potentially inconsistent. We then define type-consistent materialization and summarization operations that permit transitioning an arbitrary number of locations with any connectivity relation between the two regions. With materialized locations, we thus enable strong update reasoning in our disjunctive symbolic analysis. These capabilities are critical for supporting bounded relationship violations among an *arbitrarily* bounded number of heap locations (Sections 2.2, 3.3, and 3.4).
- A key challenge in verifying re-establishment of violated refinement relationships is that the code that breaks a relationship may be in one module while the storage for that relationship is in another. We introduce symbolic summaries that enable programmers to specify encapsulated relationship storage and thus retain modular checking for *cross-module bounded violations* (Sections 2.3 and 3.5).
- We evaluate the effectiveness of our approach to checking reflective call safety on a suite of Objective-C libraries and applications and on code snippets posted by inexperienced developers on public forums (Section 4).

## 2. Overview

In this section, we present an example that illustrates the main challenges in permitting temporary violations of type consistency, particularly with respect to heap-allocated objects. Our examples are drawn from verifying reflective call safety in real-world Objective-C code, which require such temporary violations to be able to use simple, global type invariants. Objective-C, like C++, is an object-oriented layer on top of C that adds classes and methods. We will describe its syntax as needed.

```
1  @interface Button
2  - (void)drawState:(String * ⦇↾in {'Up', 'Down'}⦈ )state {
3    String *m = ...
4    CustomImage *image = ...
5    m = ["draw" append:state];
6    [image setDelegate:self selector:m];
7    [image draw];
8  }
9  - (void)drawUp { ... }
10 - (void)drawDown { ... }
11 @end
12 @interface CustomImage {
13   Object * ⦇↾respondsTo selector()→void⦈ delegate; String *selector;
14 }
15 - (void)setDelegate:(Object * ⦇↾respondsTo s()→void⦈ )d
16            selector:(String *)s {
17   self->delegate = d;
18   self->selector = s;
19 }
20 - (void)draw { [self->delegate performSelector:self->selector]}; }
21 @end
```

**Figure 1.** Verifying reflective call safety requires knowing responds-to relationships between delegates and selectors.

The example in Figure 1, adapted from the ShortcutRecorder library, demonstrates how programmers use reflective method call to avoid boilerplate code and to decouple components. Ignore the annotations in double parentheses ⦇·⦈ for now—these denote our additions to the language of types. The `Button` class (lines 1–11) contains a `drawState:` method (lines 2–8) that draws the button as either up or down, according to whether the caller passes the string `"Up"` or `"Down"` as the `state` argument. A class is defined within `@interface...@end` blocks; an instance method definition begins with `-`. Methods are defined and called using infix notation (Smalltalk-inspired syntax). For example, the code at line 6 calls the `setDelegate:selector:` method on the `image` object with `self` as the first argument and `m` as the second. This call is analogous to `image->setDelegateSelector(self,m)` in C++. Now, a `Button` object draws itself by using the `CustomImage` to call either `drawUp` or `drawDown`. The `CustomImage` sets up a drawing context and *reflectively* calls the passed in selector on the passed in delegate at line 20—the delegate and selector pair form, in essence, a callback. This syntax [$o$ `performSelector:`$s$] for reflective call in Objective-C is analogous to $o$`.send(`$s$`)` in Ruby, `getattr(`$o$`,`$s$`)()` in Python, and $o$`[`$s$`]()` in JavaScript. In this case, the delegate is set to the `Button` object itself, and the selector is constructed by appending the passed in `state` string to the string constant `"draw"` (lines 5–6). Constructing the selector dynamically reduces boilerplate by avoiding, for example, a series of `if` statements inspecting the `state` variable. Using reflection for callbacks also improves decoupling—`CustomImage` is agnostic to the identity of the delegate. This *delegate idiom* is one common way responder-selector pairs arise in Objective-C and other dynamic languages. The use of reflection in this example comes at a cost: while the Objective-C type system statically checks that directly called methods exist, it cannot do so for reflective calls—these are only checked at run time. In this work we present an analysis that enables modular static checking of reflective call safety while still maintaining the benefits of reduced boilerplate. To prove that the program is reflection-safe, we use refinement types [19, 20, 31] to ensure that the responder does, in fact, respond to the selector.

To see how these "responds-to" relationships arise, consider the reflective call at line 20. It will throw a run-time error if the receiver does not have a method with the name specified in the argument—conversely, to be safe, it is sufficient that `self->delegate` responds to `self->selector`. There is an unexpressed invariant that requires that for every instance of `CustomImage`, the object stored in the `delegate` field must respond to the selector stored in the `selector` field. We capture this invariant by applying the **respondsTo** selector()→`void` refinement to the `delegate` field at line 13. This refinement expresses the desired *relationship* between the `delegate` field and the `selector` field. The method signature ()→`void` states that the `selector` field holds the name of a method that takes zero parameters with return type `void`. This expresses an intuitive invariant that, unfortunately, does not quite hold everywhere. Still, our framework is capable of using this *almost* everywhere invariant to check that the required relationships hold when needed—we revisit this point in Section 2.1.

Working backward, we see that the `setDelegate:selector:` method updates the `delegate` and `selector` fields with the values passed as parameters—this demonstrates the need, in a modular analysis, for **respondsTo** refinements to apply to parameters as well as fields. We annotate parameter `d` to require that it responds to `s`. Any time the method is called, the first argument must respond to the second. Thus at the call to `setDelegate:selector:` at line 6, we must ensure that `self` responds to `m`. In the caller (i.e., the client of `CustomImage`), we know a precise type, `Button`, for the first argument (whereas from the callee's point of view it is merely `Object`). This means we know that, from the caller's point of view, the delegate will respond to the selector if the selector is a method on `Button`—so if we limit the values `m` can take on to either `"drawUp"` or `"drawDown"` the **respondsTo** refinement in the callee will be satisfied. We write **in** for the refinement that limits strings to one of a set of string constants (i.e., a union of singletons). For simplicity in presentation, our only refinement for string invariants is **in**, although more complex string reasoning is possible.

### 2.1 Insufficient: Flow-Insensitive Typing of Refinements

Restricting values stored in variables, parameters, and fields with **respondsTo** relationships and **in** refinements captures the essential invariants needed to verify reflective call safety. Here, we show why a flow-insensitive type analysis with these refinements is insufficient in the presence of imperative updates. We focus on the most interesting case: updates to fields of heap-allocated objects.

Refinement types $\{\, v : B \mid R(v) \,\}$ consist of two components: the base type $B$, which comes from the underlying type system, and the (optional) refinement formula $R$, which add restrictions on the value $v$ beyond those imposed by the base type. As a notational convenience, we write them without the bound variable and assume the bound variable is used as the first argument of all atomic relations, writing for example, Int $\restriction \geq 0$ instead of $\{\, v : \text{Int} \mid v \geq 0 \,\}$.

*Subtyping with refinement types.* We assume the refinement type system of interest comes equipped with a subtyping judgment $\Gamma \vdash T_1 <: T_2$ that is a static over-approximation of semantic inclusion (i.e., under a context $\Gamma$, the concretization of type $T_1$ is contained in the concretization of $T_2$). As an example, we consider informally subtyping with the **respondsTo** and the **in** refinements for reflective call safety. For **in** refinements, this is straightforward: an **in**-refined string is a subtype of another string if the possible constant values permitted by the first are a subset of those required by the second. The situation for subtyping the **respondsTo** refinement is complicated by the fact that a relationship refinement can refer to the *contents* of related storage locations. Consider the `Button *` type in the `drawState:` method. The type environment, $\Gamma$, limits the local variable `m` to hold either `"drawUp"` or `"drawDown"`. Since `Button *` is a subtype of `Object *` in the base Objective-C type system and `Button` has both a `drawUp` and a `drawDown` method, `Button *` is a subtype of `Object *` ↾**respondsTo** m *in this environment*. If, for example, $\Gamma$(m) instead had refinement **in** {'Fred'} the above subtyping relationship would not hold. Note that for presentation we have elided the method type on the **respondsTo** here; we do so whenever it is not relevant to the discussion.

*Type checking field assignments.* We check field assignments flow-insensitively with a weakest-preconditions–based approach similar to the Deputy type system [12] (although extended to handle subtyping). Here, we focus on why flow-insensitive typing raises an alarm after the field assignment `self->delegate = d` at line 17 (see Section 3 for more details on how checking proceeds). To check this assignment, we first augment the type environment with fresh locals representing the fields of the assigned-to object and then check the assignment as if it were a local update. Conceptually we *temporarily* bring field storage locations into scope and give them local names. Let this augmented type environment be

$$\Gamma_a \;=\; \Gamma[\mathsf{d} : \texttt{Object} \,*\, \lceil\, \textbf{respondsTo}\, \mathsf{s}\rceil] \\ [\mathsf{delegate} : \texttt{Object} \,*\, \lceil\, \textbf{respondsTo}\, \mathsf{selector}\rceil]$$

for some $\Gamma$ and where we explicitly show the two **respondsTo** refinements (for presentation, we use the field names as the fresh locals). Checking the assignment, we end up with the subtyping check $\Gamma_a \vdash \Gamma_a(\mathsf{d}) <: \Gamma_a(\mathsf{delegate})$, which expresses the invariant that the relationship between delegate and selector should be preserved across this assignment. Note that while this subtyping check is what is prescribed for assignment in a standard, non-dependent type system, the weakest-preconditions–based approach ensures that this same check is also required (and thus also fails) for the next line (line 18) where `selector` is updated. Although these two assignments are each unsafe in isolation, considered in combination, they are safe. The first assignment breaks the invariant that the `delegate` field should respond to `selector`, but the second restores it.

These temporary violations cannot be tolerated by a flow-insensitive type analysis because, in imperative languages, flow-insensitive types on storage locations really perform two duties. First, they express facts about values: any value read from a variable with type **respondsTo** m can be assumed to respond to the value stored in location m. But second, they express constraints on mutable storage: for the fact to universally hold, the type system must disallow any write to that variable of a value that does not respond to m. These constraints are fine for standard types but are problematic for relationships that are established or updated in multiple steps.

## 2.2 Tolerating Violation of Relationship Refinements

As we previewed in Section 1, we argue that moving to a flow-sensitive treatment of typing is *too pessimistic*. A flow-sensitive type analysis drops the global constraints on mutable storage locations that enable concise specification. Instead it focuses on tracking facts on values as they flow through the program, which then require more verbose summaries. Other possible alternatives are to change the programming language to disallow temporary violations (e.g., by requiring simultaneous updates) or to somehow generalize the type invariant to capture the temporary violations of the simpler invariant; we argue that these approaches are *too specific*.

Our work is motivated by the observation that although programmers do sometimes violate refinement relationships, most of the time these relationships hold—they are *almost* flow-insensitive. To set up our notion of *almost type-consistent* heaps, we first make explicit a standard notion of type-consistency.

**Definition 1** (Type-Consistency). A storage location is *type-consistent* if the values stored in it and all locations in its reachable heap conform to the requirements imposed by their flow-insensitive refinement type annotations. Thus, a storage location is *type-inconsistent* if either the value stored in it *immediately* without pointer dereferences violates a type constraint or there is a type-inconsistent location *transitively* in its reachable heap. We distinguish these two cases of *immediately type-inconsistent* versus only *transitively type-inconsistent*.

In this work we rely on two premises about how programmers violate refinement relationships over storage locations on the heap:

**Premise 1** *All* of the heap is type-consistent *most* of the time.

**Premise 2** *Most* of the heap is not immediately type-inconsistent *all* of the time. In other words, only a few locations are responsible for breaking the global type invariant at any time.

Following **Premise 1**, we apply type analysis when the heap is type-consistent and switch to symbolic analysis when the type invariant is violated. Under this premise, these periods of violation are bounded in execution—and short enough that the path explosion from precise symbolic analysis is manageable.

To enable the intertwining of a type and a symbolic analysis, we require two conceptually inverse operations, symbolization and typeification, that are applied when switching between the two kinds of analyses. *Symbolization* splits a type environment $\Gamma$ (which expresses relationship constraints between storage locations) into a symbolic fact map $\widetilde{\Gamma}$ and a symbolic memory $\widetilde{M}$. The fact map expresses relationships between symbolic *values* (i.e., refinement types lifted to the symbolic domain) and the memory indicates where those values are stored (symbolic local variables and heap). So, for example, splitting a type environment $\Gamma$ with $[\mathsf{d} : \texttt{Object} \,*\, \lceil\, \textbf{respondsTo}\, \mathsf{s}\rceil]$ will result in a fact map $\widetilde{\Gamma}$ with fact $[\widetilde{v_1} : \texttt{Object} \,*\, \lceil\, \textbf{respondsTo}\, \widetilde{v_2}\rceil]$ and a memory $\widetilde{M}$ which maps d to $\widetilde{v_1}$ and s to $\widetilde{v_2}$. Here $\widetilde{v_1}$ and $\widetilde{v_2}$ are arbitrary symbolic names for values initially stored in d and s upon symbolization. In order for a symbolization to be sound, the symbolized fact map must be "no stronger" than the original type environment. A type environment $\Gamma$ is not directly comparable to a symbolic fact map $\widetilde{\Gamma}$, so we capture the required relationship with a "subtyping under substitution" judgment $\Gamma <:_{\widetilde{\theta}^{-1}} \widetilde{\Gamma}$ that, in essence, converts the symbolic fact map to a type environment before performing the comparison. We perform this conversion with a substitution $\widetilde{\theta}^{-1}$, constructed from the symbolic memory, that maps symbolic values to the local variables that store them. *Typeification* fuses $\widetilde{\Gamma}$ and $\widetilde{M}$ back into a type environment $\Gamma$. In this case, the type environment under the forward memory substitution must be no stronger than the fact map: $\widetilde{\Gamma} <:_{\widetilde{\theta}} \Gamma$. We describe these relations fully in Section 3.3.

**Premise 2** is at the core of our approach to soundly handling temporary type violations on heap locations. The key idea is a view of the heap as being made up of two separate regions: (a) a small number of individual locations that are allowed to be immediately type-inconsistent and (b) an *almost type-consistent* region consisting of (fully) type-consistent or only transitively type-inconsistent locations, which we illustrate intuitively below:

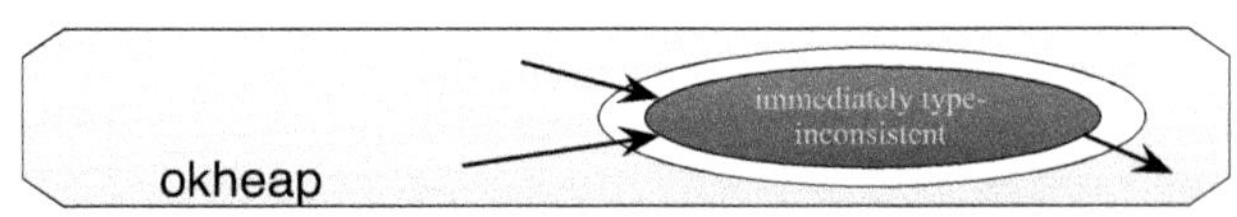


In the illustration, the dark node represents one location that is immediately type-inconsistent, while the light rectangle around it represents the almost type-consistent region. Note that there may be pointers (shown as arrows) to the this location where such objects are not type-consistent but only transitively type-inconsistent. In the analysis, the locations in the almost type-consistent region are summarized and represented by an atomic assertion okheap, while the possibly immediately type-inconsistent locations are materialized and explicitly given in the symbolic memory $\widetilde{M}$.

During symbolic analysis, we can materialize explicit storage locations from the almost type-consistent region okheap and thus update them to hold values that do not match their expected types (i.e., to become immediately type-inconsistent). When the materialized storage is again consistent with its expected types, we can summarize it back into okheap. When the heap consists *entirely* of okheap, we know that the entire heap is fully type-consistent and we can return to type checking. Given this mechanism, we can easily allow for more than one materialization at a time as long as we account for possible aliasing with already materialized locations—Premise 2 suggests that this explosion is also manageable. As an aside, we see okheap as a specialization of separating implication $-\!\!*$ from separation logic [30] for type-consistency. Materializing from okheap corresponds to removing a location from its concretization and introducing an implication awaiting type-consistency of the location (intuitively, the hole in the above illustration). Summarizing into okheap corresponds to putting a location into its concretization and eliminating an implication (see Section 3.3).

### 2.3 Modular Checking and Symbolic Summaries

Flow-insensitive type signatures are effective for achieving method-level modularity, but they do not summarize the effect that a method has on the heap. Such heap effect summaries are needed when the code that breaks and restores a relationship invariant is spread between multiple methods. Consider again the temporary invariant violation at line 17 in Figure 1, but suppose that instead of updating the delegate and selector fields directly, the programmer used the accessor idiom with setDelegate: and setSelector: methods:

```
17 [self setDelegate:d];
18 [self setSelector:s];
```

Each of these methods in isolation break the relationship invariant, but they are safe when used in combination. Flow-insensitive type signatures specify neither alias information nor the effect of the method on the heap—a richer specification is needed to check such cross-method relationship violations.

Rather than complicate the type analysis with flow-sensitive method type signatures or effect annotations, we enrich the symbolic analysis with the ability to summarize methods via pre- and post-conditions describing the structure of the heap (in separation logic [30]). For example, the symbolic summary for the setDelegate: method with a parameter named p would have input heap $\mathsf{self} \mapsto \{\mathsf{delegate} : -\}$ and output heap $\mathsf{self} \mapsto \{\mathsf{delegate} : \mathsf{p}\}$. This summary says that (1) regardless of its contents on method entry, on method exit the delegate field contains the passed in the parameter and (2) the method does not touch any fields other than delegate. When symbolically executing the caller of one of these methods, we can modularly apply the summary, as long we ensure conformance to the summary when checking the method body (Section 3.5).

Uniquely, we need symbolic method summaries only as a rare escape hatch because of an intertwined approach: within symbolic analysis, we can apply a nested type analysis with a different local type invariant. This enables using flow-insensitive method types within symbolic analysis and other ways to leverage symbolic reasoning outside of the type system (see Section 3.5). On one hand, flow-insensitive type signatures are imprecise but simple to express and fast to check. On the other, symbolic method summaries can precisely describe method heap effects but are complex to express and slow to check. We therefore can obtain the same precision as a fully symbolic analysis but still take advantage of the simpler, more efficient type analysis where the global type invariant holds. In contrast to flow-sensitive approaches (e.g., [32]), we do not need heap effect summaries for all methods—but rather only for those very few (0.05%) that leave a relationship invariant violated.

## 3. Storage Type and Symbolic Value Analysis

In this section, we provide an example-driven description of how FISSILE type analysis intertwines flow-insensitive type analysis and path-sensitive symbolic analysis to modularly check refinement relationships between storage locations. For reference, we give the full details of the type and symbolic analyses in our TR [13]; here we focus on the core contributions of our framework and illustrate them via an instantiation to check reflective call safety.

***Preliminaries: Syntax of language and types.*** We describe FISSILE type analysis over a core imperative programming language of expressions $e$ with objects and reflective method call. For presentation purposes, we have only three types of values: unit, strings, and objects. We assume disjoint syntactic classes of identifiers for program variables $x, y, z$, field names $f$, method names $m$, and parameter names $p$, as well as a distinguished identifier 'self' that stands for the receiver object in methods. Program expressions include literals for unit $\langle\rangle$, strings $c$, objects $\{\text{var } f : T = e, \text{def } m(\overline{p : T_p}) : B_{\text{ret}}[S] = e\}$. The 'var' declarations specify mutable fields $f$ of types $T$, and the 'def' declarations describe methods $m$ with parameters $p$ of types $T_p$ and with return type $B_{\text{ret}}$. The return type is a base type, which does not itself have refinements (but could have refinements on its fields in the case of an object base type). An overline stands for a sequence of items. Methods can also be optionally annotated with symbolic summaries $S$, which we revisit in Section 3.5. Objects are heap allocated. Local variable binding 'let $x : T = e_1$ in $e_2$' binds a local variable $x$ of type $T$ initialized to the value of $e_1$ whose scope is $e_2$. We include one string operation for illustration: string append $x_1$ @ $x_2$. Then, we have reads of locals $x$ and fields $x.f$, writes to fields $x.f := y$, basic control structures for sequencing $e_1; e_2$ and branching $e_1 \,[\!]\, e_2$. For presentation, we use non-deterministic branching, as the guard condition of an 'if-then-else' expression has no effect on flow-insensitive type checking and can be reflected in the symbolic analysis in the usual way (i.e., by strengthening the symbolic state with the guard condition). Finally, we have two method call forms: one for direct calls $z.m(\overline{x})$ and one for reflective calls $z.[y](\overline{x})$. A call allocates an activation record for the receiver object $z$ and parameters $\overline{x}$; it then dispatches with the direct name $m$ or the reflective selector $y$. Types $T$ are a base type $B$ for either unit Unit, strings Str, or objects $\{\text{var } f : T_f,\ \text{def } m(\overline{p : T_p}) \to B_{\text{ret}}\}$ with a set of refinements $R$, which are interpreted conjunctively.

The framework is parametrized by the language of refinements $R$ needed to specify the invariants of interest, and refinements should be parametric with respect to the syntactic class of identifiers $\iota$. We decorate with a superscript $R^{\text{L}}$, $R^{\text{F}}$, or $R^{\text{S}}$ when we want to emphasize or make clear over which syntactic class of identifiers the refinement ranges: locals $x$, fields $f$, or symbolic values $\widetilde{v}$ (see Section 3.2), respectively. Because types include refinements, types are parametrized as well, written $T^{\text{L}}$, $T^{\text{F}}$, or $T^{\text{S}}$, as are type environments $\Gamma$.

### 3.1 Instantiation: The Reflection Checking Type Refinement

To verify reflective call safety, we have seen that the key property is the '$\mathsf{respondsTo}\ \iota(\overline{p : T_p}) \to B_{\text{ret}}$' refinement that says an object must respond to the value named by $\iota$ with the given method type. As a symbolic fact, it says that an object must respond to the value named by $\iota$. But as a type invariant on storage locations, the refinement also constrains *both* the storage location on which the refinement is applied and the storage location named by $\iota$ to hold a responder and a correspondingly valid selector for it. We also need some refinements on string values, such as the union of singletons: '$\mathsf{in}\ \{c_1, \ldots, c_n\}$' which says the value is one of the following (string) literals $c_1, \ldots, c_n$.

To type expressions, we use the standard typing judgment form $\Gamma \vdash e : T$ that says in a type environment $\Gamma$, expression $e$ has type $T$. A type environment $\Gamma$ is a finite map from identifiers to types, which we view as the types assigned to program variables (i.e., $\Gamma^{\text{L}} \vdash e : T^{\text{L}}$ for emphasis). The standard typing judgment form emphasizes that $\Gamma$ is a flow-insensitive invariant.

T-REFLECTIVE-METHOD-CALL

$$\frac{\Gamma(z) = \{\cdots\} \restriction \mathsf{respondsTo}\, y(\overline{p : T_p}) \rightarrow B_{\text{ret}} \quad \Gamma <:_{[\overline{p:x},\text{self}:z]} \overline{p : T_p}, \text{self} : \Gamma(z)}{\Gamma \vdash z.[y](\overline{x}) : B_{\text{ret}} \restriction}$$

SUB-OBJ-RESPONDSTO-REFL

$$\frac{\Gamma \vdash \Gamma(x) <: \mathsf{Str} \restriction \mathsf{in}\, \{c_1, \ldots, c_n\} \qquad \forall_{i \in 1..n}\ B \text{ has a method named } c_i \text{ with signature } (\overline{p : T_p}) \rightarrow B_{\text{ret}}}{\Gamma \vdash B \restriction \cdots <: B \restriction \mathsf{respondsTo}\, x(\overline{p : T_p}) \rightarrow B_{\text{ret}}}$$

**Figure 2.** Flow-insensitive typing for reflective method calls. The respondsTo refinement is checked on reflective dispatch.

We provide the full type system for reflective call safety in our TR [13]—here we focus on the rules needed to check reflective calls given the desired type invariant (Figure 2). The T-REFLECTIVE-METHOD-CALL rule for checking a reflective method is itself not complicated: we require that the responder object $z$ has a refinement guaranteeing that it responds to the selector $y$ with method type signature $(\overline{p : T_p}) \rightarrow B_{\text{ret}}$. The arguments to call are checked against the specified types of the parameters via $\Gamma <:_{[\overline{p:x},\text{self}:z]} \overline{p : T_p}, \text{self} : \Gamma(z)$. We write $\Gamma <:_\theta \Gamma'$ as the lifting of subtyping to type environments under a substitution $\theta$ from variables on the right to variables on the left. The type of the call is then the return base type of the method (as expected) without any refinements $B_{\text{ret}} \restriction$.

The respondsTo refinement is introduced via subtyping. The subtyping judgment $\Gamma \vdash T <: T'$ says that in typing environment $\Gamma$, type $T$ implies type $T'$. The SUB-OBJ-RESPONDSTO-REFL subtyping rule combines information from base object types and the environment to introduce respondsTo. This rule says that for any location $x$ that is one of a set of selector strings $c_1, \ldots, c_n$, then any object of base type $B$ with methods of the appropriate signature for all $c_1, \ldots, c_n$ responds to the method named by $x$ with that signature. We also have subtyping rules expressing component-wise implication of refinements, conjunctive weakening of the set of refinements, and disjunctive weakening of in refinements. For our purposes, it does not matter how subtyping is checked as long as it is a sound approximation of semantic subtyping. We could, for example, use an SMT solver as in Liquid Types [31] and also replace the type rules for string operations with an off-the-shelf string solver.

*Another Instantiation: Typing for array refinements.* The FISSILE type analysis framework is parametrized by the language of refinements and a decision procedure for semantic inclusion. To provide context for our approach, we sketch another instantiation that checks array-bounds safety—a property considered by many prior works—with a few refinements and rules. Suppose we augment our programming language to include array allocation and array access and add two refinements: (1) hasLength, which indicates that an array has the specified (non-zero) length and (2) indexedBy, which indicates that the specified index is a valid index for the array—that is, that the index is in bounds. When analyzing an array access $e[x]$, we check that $x$ is a valid index into the array $e$ by requiring that $e$'s type has the refinement indexedBy $x$. We introduce this refinement via subtyping with the following rule, which says that $x$ is a valid index for an array of length $y$ if the environment $\Gamma$ restricts $x$ and $y$ such that $x \geq 0$ and $x < y$:

$$\frac{[\![\Gamma]\!] \vdash_{\text{SMT}} x \geq 0 \wedge x < y}{\Gamma \vdash B \restriction \mathsf{hasLength}\, y <: B \restriction \mathsf{indexedBy}\, x}$$

We verify that this condition holds by encoding the environment into a linear arithmetic formula (written $[\![\Gamma]\!]$) and checking entailment with an SMT solver (written as the judgment $\phi_1 \vdash_{\text{SMT}} \phi_2$ for formulas $\phi_1$ and $\phi_2$). Here we map meta-variables $x$ and $y$ in the typing judgment to logical variables of the same name in the SMT entailment checking judgment.

| | | | |
|---|---|---|---|
| $\widetilde{\Sigma}$ | $::=$ | $(\widetilde{\Gamma}, \widetilde{H})$ | symbolic states |
| $\widetilde{E}$ | $::=$ | $\cdot \mid \widetilde{E}[x : \widetilde{v}]$ | symbolic environments |
| $\widetilde{H}$ | $::=$ | $\mathsf{emp} \mid \widetilde{a} : \tilde{o} \mid \widetilde{H}_1 * \widetilde{H}_2 \mid \mathsf{okheap}$ | symbolic heaps |
| $\widetilde{\Gamma}$ | $::=$ | $\cdot \mid \widetilde{\Gamma}[\widetilde{v} : T^{\text{S}}]$ | symbolic facts |
| $\widetilde{P}$ | $::=$ | $\widetilde{\Sigma} \downarrow \widetilde{v} \mid \widetilde{P}_1 \vee \widetilde{P}_2 \mid \mathsf{false}$ | symbolic paths |
| $\tilde{o}$ | $::=$ | $\mathsf{emp} \mid f : \widetilde{v} \mid \tilde{o}_1 * \tilde{o}_2$ | symbolic objects |
| $\widetilde{v}, \widetilde{a}, \widetilde{x}, \widetilde{y}, \widetilde{z}$ | | | symbolic values |

**Figure 3.** The symbolic analysis state splits type environments into types lifted to values and the locations where values are stored.

### 3.2 Symbolic Analysis State and Handoff

The type analysis is efficient but coarse. It is flow-insensitive—constraining all storage locations to be a fixed type and the heap to be always in a consistent state. When these constraints hold, we get a simple and fast analysis. When they are temporarily violated, our overall analysis can switch to a path-sensitive symbolic analysis that continues until the constraints again hold.

We now walk through a modified version of the example from Section 2 to describe the key components of this switch: (1) we describe our symbolic analysis state and how we convert ("symbolize") a type environment to a symbolic state; (2) we describe type-consistent materialization and summarization from the almost type-consistent heap in Section 3.3; (3) we describe the proofs of soundness for handoff, materialization/summarization, and our overall analysis in Section 3.4; and (4) we explore the interaction between modular symbolic analysis and the almost type-consistent heap in Section 3.5.

***Symbolic analysis state.*** In the symbolic analysis, we split a type environment $\Gamma$ into a symbolic environment $\widetilde{E}$ and a symbolic state $\widetilde{\Sigma}$ (Figure 3). A symbolic environment $\widetilde{E}$ provides variable context: it maps variables to symbolic values $\widetilde{v}$ that represent their values. A symbolic state $\widetilde{\Sigma}$ consists of two components: a symbolic fact context $\widetilde{\Gamma}$, mapping symbolic values to the facts (symbolic types) known about them and a symbolic heap $\widetilde{H}$. A symbolic heap $\widetilde{H}$ contains a partially-materialized sub-heap that maps addresses ($\widetilde{a}$) to symbolic objects ($\tilde{o}$), which are themselves maps from field names ($f$) to symbolic values. We write symbolic objects and heaps using the separating conjunction $*$ notation borrowed from separation logic [30] to state that we refer to disjoint storage locations.

Symbolic values $\widetilde{v}$ correspond to existential, logic variables. For clarity, we often use $\widetilde{a}$ to express a symbolic value that is an address and similarly use $\widetilde{x}, \widetilde{y}, \widetilde{z}$ for values stored in the corresponding program variables $x, y, z$. Relationship refinements in $\widetilde{\Gamma}$ are expressed in terms of types lifted to symbolic values ($T^{\text{S}}$)—that is, the refinements state relationship facts between values and not storage locations (like the refinements in $\Gamma$ for typing). Our overall analysis state is a symbolic path set $\widetilde{P}$, which is a disjunctive set of singleton paths $\widetilde{\Sigma} \downarrow \widetilde{x}$. A singleton path is a pair of a symbolic state and a symbolic value corresponding to the return state and value, respectively.

The symbolic heap $\widetilde{H}$ enables treating heap locations much like stack locations, capturing relationships in the symbolic context $\widetilde{\Gamma}$, though certainly more care is required with the heap due to aliasing. A symbolic heap $\widetilde{H}$ can be empty emp, a single materialized object $\widetilde{a} : \tilde{o}$ with base address $\widetilde{a}$ and fields given by $\tilde{o}$, or a separating conjunction of sub-heaps $\widetilde{H}_1 * \widetilde{H}_2$. Lastly and most importantly, a sub-heap can be okheap, which represents an arbitrary but *almost type-consistent heap*. This formula essentially grants permission to materialize from the almost type-consistent heap and, as discussed in Section 2.2, is the key mechanism for soundly transitioning between the type and symbolic analyses.

***Handoff from type checking to symbolic execution.*** Consider the formal language version of the callback example from Section 2.2:

$$\textsc{T-Sym-Handoff}\quad \frac{\Gamma\ \overrightarrow{\mathsf{symbolize}}\ \widetilde{\Gamma},\widetilde{E} \qquad \widetilde{E} \vdash \{\widetilde{\Gamma},\mathsf{okheap}\}\, e\, \{\bigvee_i (\widetilde{\Gamma}_i,\mathsf{okheap}) \downarrow \widetilde{x}_i\} \qquad \widetilde{\Gamma}_i,\widetilde{E}\ \overrightarrow{\mathsf{typeify}}\ \Gamma \qquad \widetilde{\Gamma}_i \vdash \widetilde{\Gamma}_i(\widetilde{x}_i) <: T[\widetilde{E}] \quad \text{for all } i}{\Gamma \vdash e : T}$$

$$\textsc{C-Stack-Symbolize}\quad \frac{\widetilde{E} \text{ is 1-1} \quad \Gamma <:_{\widetilde{E}^{-1}} \widetilde{\Gamma}}{\Gamma\ \overrightarrow{\mathsf{symbolize}}\ \widetilde{\Gamma},\widetilde{E}} \qquad \textsc{C-Object-Symbolize}\quad \frac{\Gamma^{\mathrm{F}} = \mathrm{fieldtypes(B)} \quad \tilde{o} \text{ is 1-1} \quad \Gamma^{\mathrm{F}} <:_{\tilde{o}^{-1}} \widetilde{\Gamma}}{B\ \overrightarrow{\mathsf{symbolize}}\ \widetilde{\Gamma},\tilde{o}}$$

$$\textsc{M-Materialize}\quad \frac{\widetilde{\Sigma} = \widetilde{\Gamma},\widetilde{H} \qquad \mathsf{okheap} \in \widetilde{H} \qquad \widetilde{a} \notin \mathrm{dom}(\widetilde{H}) \qquad \widetilde{\Gamma}(\widetilde{a}) = B \upharpoonright \cdots \qquad B\ \overrightarrow{\mathsf{symbolize}}\ \widetilde{\Gamma}^{\mathrm{fields}},\tilde{o} \qquad \widetilde{\Gamma}' = \widetilde{\Gamma},\widetilde{\Gamma}^{\mathrm{fields}}}{\widetilde{\Sigma}\ \overrightarrow{\mathsf{materialize}} \left( (\widetilde{\Gamma}',(\widetilde{H} * \widetilde{a} : \tilde{o})) \vee \bigvee_{\widetilde{y} \in \mathrm{mayalias}_{\widetilde{\Sigma}}(\widetilde{a})} \widetilde{\Sigma}|_{\widetilde{a}=\widetilde{y}} \right)}$$

$$\textsc{Sym-Write-Field}\quad \frac{}{\widetilde{E} \vdash \{\widetilde{\Gamma},\widetilde{H}\}\, x.f := y\, \{\widetilde{\Gamma},\widetilde{H}[\widetilde{E}(x) : (\widetilde{H}(\widetilde{E}(x))[f : \widetilde{E}(y)])] \downarrow \widetilde{E}(y)\}}$$

$$\textsc{M-Summarize}\quad \frac{\mathsf{okheap} \in \widetilde{H} \qquad \widetilde{\Gamma}(\widetilde{a}) = B \upharpoonright \cdots \qquad \widetilde{\Gamma},\tilde{o}\ \overrightarrow{\mathsf{typeify}}\ B}{\widetilde{\Gamma},(\widetilde{H} * \widetilde{a} : \tilde{o})\ \overrightarrow{\mathsf{summarize}}\ \widetilde{\Gamma},\widetilde{H}}$$

$$\textsc{C-Object-Typeify}\quad \frac{\widetilde{\Gamma} <:_{\tilde{o}} \mathrm{fieldtypes}(B)}{\widetilde{\Gamma},\tilde{o}\ \overrightarrow{\mathsf{typeify}}\ B} \qquad \textsc{Sub-Types-Facts}\quad \frac{\Gamma \vdash \Gamma(\tilde{\theta}^{-1}(\widetilde{x})) <: T^{\mathrm{S}}[\tilde{\theta}^{-1}] \quad \text{for all } \widetilde{x} : T^{\mathrm{S}} \in \widetilde{\Gamma}}{\Gamma <:_{\tilde{\theta}^{-1}} \widetilde{\Gamma}}$$

$$\textsc{C-Stack-Typeify}\quad \frac{\widetilde{\Gamma} <:_{\widetilde{E}} \Gamma}{\widetilde{\Gamma},\widetilde{E}\ \overrightarrow{\mathsf{typeify}}\ \Gamma} \qquad \textsc{Sub-Facts-Types}\quad \frac{\widetilde{\Gamma} \vdash \widetilde{\Gamma}(\tilde{\theta}(x)) <: T[\tilde{\theta}] \quad \text{for all } x : T \in \Gamma}{\widetilde{\Gamma} <:_{\tilde{\theta}} \Gamma}$$

**Figure 4.** Selected rules demonstrating how FISSILE type analysis switches to a symbolic analysis to tolerate bounded violations.

```
1  { var del: {} ↾ respondsTo sel, var sel: Str,
2    def update(d: {} ↾ respondsTo s, s: Str): Unit =
3      self.del := d;
4      self.sel := s  }
```

Here the `update` method updates the `del` and `sel` fields in sequence. Recall that the assignment at line 3 breaks the type invariant and the assignment at line 4 restores it. We illustrate the core operations (Figure 4) behind FISSILE type analysis by walking through this example. When checking this method, the type analysis will produce a flow-insensitive type error for the assignment at line 3 and so will switch to symbolic execution. To do so, it will (1) "symbolize" a suitable symbolic analysis state from the type environment, (2) symbolically execute the two field writes, and (3) attempt to "typeify" the resultant symbolic analysis state back to the original type environment. If this succeeds, then the type analysis can continue.

The T-SYM-HANDOFF rule formalizes this process. It says the type checker can switch to the symbolic analysis to check an expression $e$ in a type environment $\Gamma$ by creating ("symbolizing") a symbolic state representing $\Gamma$ and symbolically executing $e$ in that state. The judgment form $\widetilde{E} \vdash \{\widetilde{\Sigma}\}\, e\, \{\widetilde{P}\}$ says that in the context of a given symbolic local variable environment $\widetilde{E}$ and with a symbolic state $\widetilde{\Sigma}$ on input, expression $e$ symbolically evaluates to a disjunction of state-value pairs $\widetilde{P}$ on output. Here the input facts and environment are obtained from $\Gamma$ (via the $\Gamma\ \overrightarrow{\mathsf{symbolize}}\ \widetilde{\Gamma},\widetilde{E}$ judgment form), while the input heap is initialized to a fully type-consistent heap okheap. After symbolic execution, the resultant symbolic state must be consistent with ("typeify to") the original $\Gamma$, and the symbolic facts about the resulting symbolic value must be consistent with the inferred type $T$ of the expression. Note that here we lift the subtyping judgment $\cdot \vdash \cdot <: \cdot$ to symbolic types in the expected way. Here $T[\tilde{\theta}]$ converts the standard type $T$ to a symbolic type (fact) $T^{\mathrm{S}}$ with a substitution $\tilde{\theta}$ that replaces all variable references in $T$'s refinements with symbolic values. Both the initially symbolized heap *and* the finally typeified heap must consist solely of okheap—the heap is assumed consistent on entry and must be restored on exit. The key aspect of this handoff is that although the symbolic execution is free to violate any of the flow-insensitive constraints imposed by $\Gamma$, it must restore them to return to type checking. We will discuss restoration in detail later—first we describe symbolization.

***Symbolizing type environments to symbolic states.*** Symbolization splits a type environment $\Gamma$ (which expresses type constraints on local variables) into a symbolic fact map $\widetilde{\Gamma}$ (expressing facts about symbolic values) and a symbolic local variable state $\widetilde{E}$ (expressing where those values are stored). For example, consider the type environment above at line 3, immediately before the first write:

$$\Gamma = [\mathsf{d} : \{\} \upharpoonright \mathsf{respondsTo\ s}][\mathsf{s} : \mathsf{Str}][\mathsf{self} : \mathrm{T}_{\mathrm{Image}}]$$

where $\mathrm{T}_{\mathrm{Image}} = \{\mathsf{var\ del} : \{\} \upharpoonright \mathsf{respondsTo\ sel}, \mathsf{var\ sel} : \mathsf{Str}\}$. We can symbolize this environment to create a symbolic environment where $\widetilde{E} = [\mathsf{d} : \widetilde{\mathsf{d}}][\mathsf{s} : \widetilde{\mathsf{s}}][\mathsf{self} : \widetilde{\mathsf{self}}]$. Here we have created fresh symbolic names to represent the values stored on the stack: $\widetilde{\mathsf{d}}$ is the name of the value stored in local d, $\widetilde{\mathsf{s}}$ in local s, etc. These symbolic values represent concrete values from a type environment in which the storage location refinement relationships hold, so we can safely assume that *values* initially stored in those locations have the equivalent relationships, expressed as lifted types:

$$\widetilde{\Gamma} = [\widetilde{\mathsf{d}} : \{\} \upharpoonright \mathsf{respondsTo}\ \widetilde{\mathsf{s}}][\widetilde{\mathsf{s}} : \mathsf{Str}][\widetilde{\mathsf{self}} : \mathrm{T}_{\mathrm{Image}}]$$

Note that the refinement on $\widetilde{\mathsf{d}}$ refers to symbolic value $\widetilde{\mathsf{s}}$ and not storage location s, but that the refinements on the types of the *fields* of the base type of $\widetilde{\mathsf{self}}$'s fact $\mathrm{T}_{\mathrm{Image}}$ still refer to (field) storage locations. These field refinements on the base object type are, in essence, a "promise" that if any explicit storage for those fields is later materialized, it must be consistent with $\mathrm{T}_{\mathrm{Image}}$ when summarized back into okheap.

We formalize type environment symbolization in rule C-STACK-SYMBOLIZE, which captures the requirement that the symbolized state must over-approximate the original type environment. We note that $\widetilde{E}^{-1}$ forms a substitution map from symbolic values to local variable names and require that the symbolized fact map $\widetilde{\Gamma}$ under that substitution be an over-approximate environment of the original type environment $\Gamma$ (rule SUB-TYPES-FACTS). In essence, any assumptions that the symbolic analysis initially makes about the symbolic facts must also hold in original type environment. That $\widetilde{E}$ is one-to-one ensures that the inverse exists but more importantly encodes the requirement that the newly symbolized environment makes no assumptions about aliasing between values stored on the stack in local variables. Note that when symbolizing a local variable with type $B \upharpoonright R^{\mathrm{L}}$ in a type environment, we do not lift the base type $B$ to the symbolic domain nor do we create storage for any of $B$'s fields. That is, refinements on the *fields* of an object base type remain refinements over fields, expressing both facts about the field contents *and* constraints on those storage locations. This interpretation is what permits materialized, immediately type-inconsistent objects to point back into okheap (i.e., the almost type-consistent region). As we detail next, with this interpretation, our analysis *materializes* storage for objects from okheap *on demand*, which is not only more efficient but is required in the presence of recursion.

### 3.3 Materialization from Type-Consistent Heaps

Returning to the callback example, recall that the analysis has symbolized a state corresponding to the type environment immediately before line 3. A symbolic heap $\widetilde{H}$ consists of two separate regions:

(1) the materialized heap, a precise region with explicit storage that supports strong updates and allows field values to differ from their declared types (i.e., permits immediate type-inconsistency) and (2) the okheap, a summarized region in which all locations are either type-consistent or only transitively type-inconsistent. In a newly symbolized analysis state, $\widetilde{H}$ consists of solely okheap. Before the field write at line 3 can proceed, the analysis must first materialize storage for the $\mathrm{T_{Image}}$ object pointed to by self to get:

$$\widetilde{H} = \mathsf{okheap} * \widetilde{\mathsf{self}} \mapsto \{\mathsf{del} : \widetilde{\mathsf{del}}, \mathsf{sel} : \widetilde{\mathsf{sel}}\}$$

and a new fact map $\widetilde{\Gamma}$ that contains the additional facts: $\widetilde{\mathsf{del}} : \{\} \upharpoonright \mathsf{respondsTo}\ \widetilde{\mathsf{sel}}$ and $\widetilde{\mathsf{sel}} : \mathsf{Str}$.

We formalize type-consistent materialization with the C-OBJECT-SYMBOLIZE and M-MATERIALIZE rules. Creating symbolic storage for an object type is very similar to symbolizing a type environment. As rule C-OBJECT-SYMBOLIZE defines, the analysis can symbolize a type $B$ to a symbolic object $\tilde{o}$ (mapping field names to fresh symbolic values) and a fact map $\widetilde{\Gamma}$ (facts about those values) if the assumed facts about the values are no stronger than those guaranteed by the object's field types. Once the analysis has symbolized an object, it adds the new object storage to the explicit heap and facts about the fresh symbolic values to the fact map in rule M-MATERIALIZE.

For the symbolic analysis to perform strong updates, it must maintain the key invariant that any two objects' storage locations in the explicit heap are definitely separate. When materializing an arbitrary object, the evaluator must consider whether any of the already materialized objects aliases with the newly materialized object and case split on these possibilities. The split is required because any two distinct symbolic values may in fact represent the same concrete value. In M-MATERIALIZE, for any input state $\widetilde{\Sigma}$ in which the heap contains okheap, the symbolic analysis is free to materialize the object stored at a symbolic address $\widetilde{a}$ from the type-consistent heap. For the case where the materialized symbolic address does not alias any address already on the explicit heap, we symbolize a new symbolic object $\tilde{o}$ with fresh symbolic values as described above from the base type of $\widetilde{a}$. In the case where the address may alias some address $\widetilde{y}$ on the materialized heap, we must assert that $\widetilde{a} = \widetilde{y}$. We write $\widetilde{\Sigma}|_{\widetilde{a}=\widetilde{y}}$ for any sound constraining of $\widetilde{\Sigma}$ with the equality (we implement it by substituting one name for the other and applying a meet $\sqcap$ in the symbolic facts $\widetilde{\Gamma}$). We also leave unspecified the $\mathrm{mayalias}_{\widetilde{\Sigma}}(\widetilde{a})$ that should soundly yield the set of addresses that may-alias $\widetilde{a}$; our implementation uses a type-based check to rule out simple non-aliases.

This rule is quite general. It permits an arbitrary number of locations to be immediately type-inconsistent without any constraints on connectivity, ownership, or non-aliasing. To simplify the formalization of type-consistent materialization, we restrict relations expressed by refinements in the heap to be among fields within objects. Relations between fields are captured because all of fields of the object are symbolized at the same time (see C-OBJECT-SYMBOLIZE). Supporting cross-object relations would merely require materializing multiple objects while disjunctively considering all possible aliasing relationships and then symbolizing their fields simultaneously within each configuration. It would also be possible to just materialize the fields corresponding to the specific relationships that we wish to violate by using a field-split model [26, 28] of objects.

***Symbolic execution.*** With the symbolization and materialization complete, the analysis now executes the field writes at lines 3 and 4. The SYM-WRITE-FIELD rule describes symbolic execution of writing the value of a local variable $y$ to a field $f$ of a base address $x$. It requires that the object at the base address $\widetilde{E}(x)$ already be materialized and updates the appropriate field in the symbolic heap $\widetilde{H}$. We give the rest of our symbolic executions rules in our TR [13]—they are as expected. Unlike traditional symbolic analysis, our mixed approach can soundly ensure termination by falling back to type checking. In practice, we switch to types at the end of loop bodies to cut back edges and cut recursion with method summaries.

***Summarizing symbolic objects back into types.*** After execution of the field writes, the symbolic heap at line 4 is:

$$\widetilde{H} = \mathsf{okheap} * \widetilde{\mathsf{self}} \mapsto \{\mathsf{del} : \widetilde{\mathsf{d}}, \mathsf{sel} : \widetilde{\mathsf{s}}\}.$$

That is, the fields now contain the values passed in as parameters. But recall that $\widetilde{\Gamma}(\widetilde{\mathsf{d}}) = \{\} \upharpoonright \mathsf{respondsTo}\ \widetilde{\mathsf{s}}$ and $\widetilde{\Gamma}(\widetilde{\mathsf{self}}) = \mathrm{T_{Image}}$. In this state, the value stored in field del again responds to the value stored in field sel—the flow-insensitive type invariant ($\mathrm{T_{Image}}$) promised by $\widetilde{\Gamma}(\widetilde{\mathsf{self}})$ again holds—and thus the object can be safely summarized back into the okheap. We describe this process in rule M-SUMMARIZE, which says that a symbolic address $\widetilde{a}$ pointing to a materialized object $\tilde{o}$ can be summarized (i.e., removed from the explicit heap) if the object is consistent with (i.e., can be "typeified" to) the base type required of the address in the fact map. Typeifying a symbolic object $\tilde{o}$ to an object type $B$ (rule C-OBJECT-TYPEIFY) is analogous to symbolization except that it goes in the other direction. We require that the symbolic fact map be over-approximated by the field types of $B$, nicely converting it to the symbolic domain using $\tilde{o}$ as the substitution. Note that $\tilde{o}$ does not need to be one-to-one; the observation that this constraint is irrelevant for typeification captures that types are agnostic to aliasing.

Once all materialized objects have been summarized (and thus $\widetilde{H} = \mathsf{okheap}$), the checker can end the handoff to symbolic analysis and resume type checking (back to rule T-SYM-HANDOFF) as long as the symbolic locals are consistent with the original $\Gamma$ for all symbolic paths (rule C-STACK-TYPEIFY) and the returned symbolic values have facts consistent with the return type of the expression.

### 3.4 Concretization and Soundness

An important concern for materialization and summarization is whether information is transferred soundly between the type analysis and the symbolic analysis (i.e., we have a sound reduced product [15]). In particular, materialization "pulls" information from the heap type invariant on demand during symbolic execution and then permits temporary violations of the global heap invariant in some locations. We take an abstract interpretation-based approach [14] to soundness, which is critical for expressing almost type-consistent heaps and connecting the soundness of type checking with the soundness of symbolic analysis. In this section, we describe, via concretization, the different meanings of object types and their associated reachable heaps in the two analyses. Further, we present the properties of these concretizations that are key to proving soundness of handoff and materialization/summarization and also state a theorem of intertwined analysis soundness. We provide complete concretization functions and a full proof of soundness in our TR [13].

***Concretization.*** A concrete state consists of a concrete environment $E$, mapping variables $x$ to values $v$, and a concrete heap $H$, which is a finite map from addresses $a$ to concrete objects $o$ bundled with their allocated base types $B$. We overload $*$ to indicate both the disjoint heap union of two concrete subheaps and the separating conjunction of two static symbolic subheaps.

Concretization functions give meaning to abstract constructs by describing how they constrain the set of possible values and states. As is standard, we write $\gamma$ for concretization and overload it for all constructs, except base types and field types. Object base types and field types, crucially, have different meanings in the type domain and symbolic domain. To disambiguate, we write $\gamma(B)$ for concretization in the type analysis and $\widetilde{\gamma}(B)$ for the symbolic analysis.

*Concretization in the type analysis.* In the type analysis, the concretization of an object type is fairly standard: it constrains

$$\gamma(B) \triangleq \left\{ (H,a) \;\middle|\; \begin{array}{l} \text{exists } o \text{ where } H(a) = \langle o, B\rangle \text{ and} \\ \text{①} \text{ for all methods } m \\ \quad o(m) \in \gamma(B, \overline{(p:T_p)}\to B_{\text{ret}}) \text{ and} \\ \text{②} \text{ for all fields } f \\ \quad (H, o, o(f)) \in \gamma(T_f^{\text{F}}). \end{array} \right\}$$

$$\gamma(B \restriction R_1^{\text{F}}, \cdots, R_n^{\text{F}}) \triangleq \left\{ (H,o,v) \;\middle|\; \begin{array}{l} (H,v) \in \gamma(B) \text{ and} \\ \text{for all refinements } R_i \\ \quad (H,o,v) \in \gamma(R_i^{\text{F}}) \end{array} \right\}$$

(a) Types domain

$$\widetilde{\gamma}(B) \triangleq \left\{ (H^{\text{ok}}, H^{\text{mat}}, a) \;\middle|\; \begin{array}{l} \text{exists } o \text{ where } H^{\text{ok}} * H^{\text{mat}}(a) = \langle o, B\rangle \text{ and} \\ \text{①} \text{ for all methods } m \\ \quad o(m) \in \gamma(B, \overline{(p:T_p)}\to B_{\text{ret}}) \text{ and} \\ \text{②} \text{ for all fields } f \\ \quad f \in \text{dom}(o) \text{ and if } a \in \text{dom}(H^{\text{ok}}) \text{ then} \\ \quad (H, o, o(f)) \in \widetilde{\gamma}(T_f^{\text{F}}). \end{array} \right\}$$

$$\widetilde{\gamma}(B \restriction R_1^{\text{F}}, \cdots, R_n^{\text{F}}) \triangleq \left\{ (H^{\text{ok}}, H^{\text{mat}}, v) \;\middle|\; \begin{array}{l} (H,v) \in \widetilde{\gamma}(B) \text{ and} \\ \text{for all refinements } R_i \\ \quad (H^{\text{ok}} * H^{\text{mat}}, o, v) \in \gamma(R_i^{\text{F}}) \end{array} \right\}$$

(b) Symbolic domain

**Figure 5.** Concretization of an object base type $B = \{\overline{\text{var } f : T_f}, \ \overline{\text{def } m(\overline{p:T_p})\to B_{\text{ret}}}\}$ in the types and symbolic domains. In the symbolic domain, values stored in the fields of an object in $H^{\text{ok}}$ must not be immediately type-inconsistent; values stored in the fields of an object in $H^{\text{mat}}$ are not constrained. The shaded region highlights the key difference between the concretizations.

not only the value but also the entire heap reachable from that object. As we show in Figure 5a, the concretization $\gamma(B)$ of an object type $B = \{\overline{\text{var } f : T_f}, \ \overline{\text{def } m(\overline{p:T_p})\to B_{\text{ret}}}\}$ yields a set of pairs of heaps and values (addresses). The concretization requires that the address point to an object $o$ which ① has suitable method implementations (i.e., constrained by the concretization of the method signature $\overline{(p:T_p)}\to B_{\text{ret}}$ on an object of type $B$) for each method $m$ in the object type and ② has suitable field values for each declared field $f$ of type $T_f^{\text{F}}$. We adorn the type with its storage class, $F$, to make clear that it is a field type dependent on other fields.

The key property of concretization in the type domain is that the concretization of a field type $T^{\text{F}} = B \restriction R_1^{\text{F}}, \cdots, R_n^{\text{F}}$ is mutually inductively defined with that for base types and thus *constrains the entire heap reachable from that field*, in addition to the other fields of the object. This concretization yields a heap-object-value triple where the heap and value are constrained by the concretization of the base type and the entire triple is constrained by the concretization of each of the field refinements $R_i^{\text{F}}$. Because these refinements are dependent refinements, they may constrain *other* fields of the object in addition to the value of the field in question. For example, a heap-object-value triple in the concretization of a field refinement respondsTo $g$ would constrain the $g$ field of the object to store a string with name $m$ that is a valid method for the (potentially different) object pointed to by the value. The concretization of a type environment $\gamma(\Gamma)$ is a set of concrete environment-heap $(E,H)$ pairs where the values stored in local variables are consistent with the declared types and reachable heaps from the type bindings in $\Gamma$.

*Concretization in the symbolic analysis.* In contrast to the type analysis, in the symbolic world part of the heap may be explicitly materialized—and thus immediately type-inconsistent, leaving the rest of the heap almost type-consistent. To capture this difference, the symbolic concretization of an object type yields *two* heaps: $H^{\text{ok}}$ and $H^{\text{mat}}$, corresponding to a non-deterministic choice of which objects are in the almost type-consistent heap and which objects are materialized and thus may have field values differing from their declared types. We write $\widetilde{\gamma}(B)$ here to emphasize concretization of base types in the symbolic domain. The shaded region of Figure 5b illustrates the key difference: in the symbolic domain, an object's fields are only constrained by the concretization of the field types if the object is in $H^{\text{ok}}$. If the object is in $H^{\text{mat}}$, the fields are guaranteed to exist, but the values stored in them are not constrained. Because concretization of object types is defined inductively, the concretization can "opt out" of type constraints for the reachable subheap at each field dereference, depending on the partitioning of the full heap into $H^{\text{ok}}$ and $H^{\text{mat}}$. Crucially, this definition of concretization permits pointers from $H^{\text{ok}}$ to $H^{\text{mat}}$ and vice-versa. Note that regardless of which heap an object resides in, its method implementations are still constrained by their signatures.

The concretization $\gamma(\widetilde{E}, \widetilde{\Sigma})$ of a symbolic state $\widetilde{\Sigma} = (\widetilde{\Gamma}, \widetilde{H})$ with respect to a symbolic environment $\widetilde{E}$ yields a environment-heap pair $(E,H)$. There must exist a valuation $V : \mathsf{SymVal} \to \mathsf{Values}$ mapping symbolic values to concrete values and a partitioning of the heap $H = H^{\text{ok}} * H^{\text{mat}}$ such that the concretizations of $\widetilde{E}$, $\widetilde{\Gamma}$, and $\widetilde{H}$ all agree upon. Symbolic fact maps $\widetilde{\Gamma}$ and heaps $\widetilde{H}$ both concretize to a set of valuation-heap-heap tuples where emp in the symbolic heap requires both $H^{\text{ok}}$ and $H^{\text{mat}}$ be empty whereas okheap requires that $H^{\text{mat}}$ be empty but $H^{\text{ok}}$ can be any heap. The singleton heap formula concretizes to a singleton in $H^{\text{mat}}$ and $*$ is the heap disjoint union in both $H^{\text{ok}}$ and $H^{\text{mat}}$ A symbolic path is a disjunction of singleton paths $\widetilde{P} = \widetilde{\Sigma} \downarrow \widetilde{x}$; its concretization is similar to that of a symbolic state, except that it yields a triple $(E,H,v)$ where $V(\widetilde{x}) = v$.

*Soundness.* The soundness of FISSILE type analysis—and in particular of handoff and materialization/summarization—depends on the following key properties of concretization.

At handoff, the analysis requires that the explicitly materialized heap be empty. The following lemma states that under those conditions (i.e., when the entire heap is $H^{\text{ok}}$), the meaning of base types in the symbolic domain is the same as the meaning of base types in the type domain:

**Lemma 1** (Equivalence of Typed and Symbolic Base Types). $\gamma(B) = \{(H,v) \mid (H,\cdot,v) \in \widetilde{\gamma}(B) \}$

We rely on this result to show that that the T-SYM-HANDOFF and SYM-TYPE-HANDOFF (Section 3.5) rules are sound.

To show soundness of the M-MATERIALIZE rule, we rely on a property about the meaning of base types in the symbolic domain:

**Lemma 2** (Type-Consistent Materialization for Types). If $(H^{\text{ok}} * a : \langle o_a, B_a\rangle, H^{\text{mat}}, v) \in \widetilde{\gamma}(B)$ then $(H^{\text{ok}}, H^{\text{mat}} * a : \langle o_a, B_a\rangle, v) \in \widetilde{\gamma}(B)$.

This lemma considers a value $v$ of type $B$ and a heap containing an object $o_a$ of allocated type $B_a$ stored at address $a$ (informally, $a$ is in $v$'s reachable heap, otherwise it is uninteresting). If there is one concretization of $B$ where $a$ is in the almost type-consistent heap $H^{\text{ok}}$, then the configuration with $a$ moved to the materialized $H^{\text{mat}}$ is also in its concretization. In essence, moving the storage for $a$ to the materialized heap will not cause the type of $v$ to change from the perspective of the symbolic analysis.

$$\textsc{Sym-Type-Handoff}\quad \frac{\widetilde{\Gamma},\widetilde{E}\ \overrightarrow{\mathsf{typeify}}\ \Gamma \qquad \Gamma \vdash e : T \qquad \Gamma\ \overrightarrow{\mathsf{symbolize}}\ \widetilde{\Gamma}',\widetilde{E} \qquad \widetilde{z} \notin \mathrm{dom}(\widetilde{\Gamma}')}{\widetilde{E} \vdash \{\widetilde{\Gamma},\mathsf{okheap}\}\, e\, \{\widetilde{\Gamma}'[\widetilde{z} : T[\widetilde{E}]],\mathsf{okheap} \downarrow \widetilde{z}\}}$$

$$\textsc{Sym-Method-Call-Summary}\quad \frac{\begin{array}{c}(\overline{p})[h/h'] : p^{\mathrm{ret}} = \mathrm{summary}(\widetilde{\Gamma}(\widetilde{E}(x)), m) \\ \widetilde{H} \vdash h \circledast \widetilde{H}^{\mathrm{fr}} \backslash \tilde{\theta}^{\mathrm{h}} \qquad \tilde{\theta} = \tilde{\theta}^{\mathrm{h}} \uplus [\overline{p : \widetilde{E}(y)}]\end{array}}{\widetilde{E} \vdash \{\widetilde{\Gamma},\widetilde{H}\}\, x.m(\overline{y})\, \{\widetilde{\Gamma}, (\widetilde{H}^{\mathrm{fr}} * h'[\tilde{\theta}]) \downarrow \tilde{\theta}(p^{\mathrm{ret}}))\}}$$

**Figure 6.** Symbolic execution rules to switch to the typed analysis and to apply symbolic summaries.

A related lemma describes summarization:

**Lemma 3** (Soundness of Type-Consistent Summarization for States). If $\widetilde{\Gamma},\tilde{o}\ \overrightarrow{\mathsf{typeify}}\ B$ and $\mathsf{okheap} \in \widetilde{H}$ and $\widetilde{\Gamma}(\widetilde{a}) = B \upharpoonright \cdots$ then for all $\widetilde{E}$ we have $\gamma(\widetilde{E},(\widetilde{\Gamma},\widetilde{H} * \widetilde{a} : \tilde{o})) \subseteq \gamma(\widetilde{E},(\widetilde{\Gamma},\widetilde{H}))$ .

That is, if the symbolic execution determines that a materialized symbolic object is not immediately type inconsistent, then it can summarize the symbolic storage for that object back into okheap (rule M-SUMMARIZE) without unsoundly dropping concrete states.

We rely on the above lemmas to prove soundness of the intertwined analysis:

**Theorem 1.** FISSILE *Type Analysis is sound. That is, if* $E \vdash [H]\, e\, [r]$ *then*

1. *If* $\Gamma^{\mathrm{L}} \vdash e : T^{\mathrm{L}}$ *and* $(E,H) \in \gamma(\Gamma^{\mathrm{L}})$ *then* $r = H' \downarrow v'$ *where* $(E,H') \in \gamma(\Gamma^{\mathrm{L}})$ *and* $(E,H',v') \in \gamma(T^{\mathrm{L}})$*; and*
2. *If* $\widetilde{E} \vdash \{\widetilde{\Sigma}\}\, e\, \{\widetilde{P}\}$ *and* $(E,H) \in \gamma(\widetilde{E},\widetilde{\Sigma})$ *then* $r = H' \downarrow v'$ *where* $(E,H',v') \in \gamma(\widetilde{E},\widetilde{P})$.

This is a fairly standard statement of soundness of for both analyses. Here, $E \vdash [H]\, e\, [r]$ says that in a concrete environment $E$ and with a concrete heap $H$, an expression $e$ big-step evaluates to a result $r$. For types, if the initial concrete state is described by the static type environment and the expression type checks, then the expression evaluates to a heap-value pair (that is, not to an error) where the final state still conforms to the type environment and the value conforms to the static type. Similarly, the symbolic analysis soundly over-approximates the concrete execution and rules out a faulting error. The proof proceeds by induction on the derivation of concrete execution and covers an additional judgment form describing generalized path-to-path symbolic analysis—we provide full details in our TR [13].

### 3.5 Fully-Intertwined Type-Symbolic Analysis

As described in Section 3.3, the type analysis can hand off checking of an expression to the symbolic analysis. We also would like to perform the opposite handoff from symbolic to type (i.e., apply type analysis within symbolic analysis). For example, we would like do this handoff when we encounter a method call during symbolic analysis to enable modular analysis with only type specifications.

Fortunately, we can employ the same consistency mechanisms to allow handoff in the other direction, that is, to switch from symbolic analysis to type checking (rule SYM-TYPE-HANDOFF in Figure 6). The key constraint is that the entire heap must be fully type-consistent (okheap). In general, this requirement means summarization should have been applied so that no locations are materialized. The entire state is checked type consistent via "typeify" to $\Gamma$ before type checking, and then symbolic analysis can resume by "symbolize"-ing a new symbolic state from $\Gamma$ and adding an assumption from the type of the expression.

Suppose this symbolic analysis is the context of an outer flow-insensitive type analysis. Observe that type environment $\Gamma$ is derived solely from the current symbolic execution state and could be more precise than the outer flow-insensitive invariant. A common scenario is to leverage symbolic reasoning about guard conditions in an `if` but switch to type analysis inside the `if` body with a stronger invariant without needing to the make any changes to the type analysis (cf. occurrence typing [35]). For the reflective call safety client, the "checked delegate" idiom is quite common where a reflective call is performed after checking if an object responds to a particular string—**`respondsToSelector:`** in Objective-C.

*Symbolic summaries for cross-module bounded violations.* On the other hand, we have seen a handful of cases where a further precision refinement is needed: when programmers break relationship refinements across module boundaries, such as when they abstract the heap with getters and setters. To see how this is a problem, consider the slightly modified version of the update function in which the direct field access is replaced the following setter functions:

```
1   def setDel(d)[del : −/del : d] : − = self.del := d
2   def setSel(s)[sel : −/sel : s] : − = self.sel := s
```

This small change exacerbates the problem of checking relationship refinement safety because now the invariant violation crosses module (function) boundaries and thus cannot go to a fully type-consistent heap on method call. To support this scenario, we enable the programmer to supply additional checked annotations, symbolic method summaries of the form $(\overline{p})[h/h'] : p^{\mathrm{ret}}$, that permit symbolic checking across module boundaries. Here $\overline{p}$ is a sequence of method parameter names, $h$ and $h'$ are summaries of the input heap and output heap respectively, and $p^{\mathrm{ret}}$ specifies the method return value. The input summary gives the form of the part of the heap the method will operate upon (the *footprint*) and gives names to the values stored in the fields of the input heap. The output summary gives the form of the heap after the method has finished executing, in terms of the names given in the input heap and the parameters. For example, the method summary annotation at line 1 says that whatever the `del` field stores before `setDel` is called, after the method is executed the field stores the value from the `d` parameter. Since the method is a setter, the return value is irrelevant. The annotation for `setSel` is analogous. Applying the summary for `setDel` leaves the heap in an inconsistent state, but then the summary for `setSel` restores it.

With these annotations, checking the calls to the setters is analogous to checking the field writes as before, except that rather than applying the symbolic transfer function for field writes, we apply the method summary. We formalize this in the SYM-METHOD-CALL-SUMMARY rule in Figure 6. The auxiliary function $\mathrm{summary}(T,m)$ looks up the summary of a method $m$ on a static type $T$. The judgment $\widetilde{H} \vdash h \circledast \widetilde{H}^{\mathrm{fr}} \backslash \tilde{\theta}^{\mathrm{h}}$ splits the heap $\widetilde{H}$ into a footprint (specified by $h$) and the left-over frame ($\widetilde{H}^{\mathrm{fr}}$) that the method is guaranteed not to touch. This frame inference also produces a symbolic map $\tilde{\theta}^{\mathrm{h}}$ that captures the symbolic variables that the parameters in the $h$ match to during the splitting. We then apply this map (combined with the mapping from parameter names to the symbolic values passed in as parameters) to the output summary $h'$ to get the footprint on method exit and add it back to the frame to get the entire heap on method exit. We also consult this map $\tilde{\theta}$ to look up the value returned as specified by the summary. We write $\uplus$ for disjoint union of maps where the result is undefined if the union is not a map. The frame inference is a simple application of subtraction [3] but makes this rule quite flexible. The developer can choose to refuse access to okheap in a symbolic summary (as above) to provide a stronger guarantee to the method's callers or request it to get a stronger assumption for checking the method implementation.

We note that the particular kind of symbolic summary that we describe above (essentially, standard pre-/post-conditions in separation logic) is not the most interesting point. Other symbolic analysis techniques could be applied, such as context-sensitive, non-modular reasoning. Rather, we argue that the interest lies in that heavier-weight symbolic analysis machinery can be applied when needed without the cost of applying it everywhere, all the time.

*Checking Method Implementations.* For modular checking, we type check each method implementation separately according to its type signature (as is standard). We guarantee that the implementation of a symbolically-summarized method conforms to its summary with our symbolic analysis infrastructure, although the summary checking technique is orthogonal to that for checking relationship refinements. One could substitute a different approach (e.g. abstract interpretation or interactive proofs) if desired.

## 4. Case Study: Checking Reflective Call Safety

We implemented our FISSILE type analysis approach to checking almost flow-insensitive invariants in a prototype method reflection safety checker for Objective-C. We evaluate our prototype, a plugin to the clang static analyzer, by investigating the following questions: What is the increased type annotation cost for checking reflection safety? How much does the mixed FISSILE approach improve precision? Do our premises about how programmers violate relationships hold in practice? Is our intertwined "almost type" analysis as fast as we hope? We also discuss a bug found by our tool—surprising in a mature application. The bug fix that we proposed was accepted by the application developer.

Table 1 describes our prototype's performance on a benchmark suite of 6 libraries and 3 large applications. The OmniFrwks are noteworthy because they are very large and have been in continuous development since 1997. The fact that our tool can run on them provides evidence for the kind of real world Objective-C that we can handle—something that would be challenging for a purely symbolic analysis. We discuss these results throughout the rest of this section.

***The developer cost to add modular reflection checking.*** To seed potential type errors, we first annotated the reflection requirements on 76 system library functions (i.e., with **respondsTo** refinements). These are requirements imposed by the system API enriched to check for method reflection errors. Then, for each benchmark we report the total number of developer annotations required, as well as the average number required per reflective call site, to give an indication of how much work it would be for developers to modularly check their use of reflection (column "Total Annotations"). All annotations are *checked*—they emit a static type error if their requirements are not met. Based on this column, we observe that our benchmarks fall into three categories, depending on how they use reflection. *Clients* of reflective APIs, such as Sparkle and ZipKit, have a very low (essentially zero) annotation burden. In contrast, benchmarks that *expose* reflective interfaces, such as SCRecorder and OAuth have a higher annotation burden. This is perhaps not surprising, since annotations are the mechanism through which interfaces expose requirements to clients. In the middle are those that use reflection in both ways: parts of OmniFrwks do expose a reflective API, but they also use internal reflection quite significantly. Our application benchmarks also fall in this category: they are structured into modular application frameworks and a core application client.

Over our entire benchmark suite we find that we need 0.10 annotations and 0.01 symbolic summaries per reflective callsite (row "Combined," columns "Total Annotations" and "Symbolic Annotations"). In other words, on average, the programmer should expect to write one annotation for every 10 uses of reflection and a single symbolic heap effect summary for every 100 uses of reflection. Importantly, note that almost all of annotations are extremely lightweight refinement annotations, like **respondsTo**—only 0.05% of methods required a symbolic summary. Even there, the summaries were very simple because they were on leaf methods, such as setters. This overall low annotation burden highlights a key benefit of our optimistic mostly flow-insensitive approach: whenever the reflection relationship is preserved flow-insensitively, no method summary is needed. Contrast this to a modular flow-sensitive approach where a summary is needed on all methods to describe their potential effects on reflection-related fields.

***Improved precision.*** We verified reflection safety on our benchmarks using two configurations: a completely flow-insensitive analysis (no switching) and our mixed FISSILE approach. We then compared the number of static type errors reported by each (columns "FI Type Errors" and "FISSILE Type Errors"). FISSILE type analysis sometimes significantly reduces the number of static type alarms (e.g., ASIHTTP)—and by 29% in our combined benchmark suite.

The number of FISSILE static type alarms ranges from 0 (for SCRecorder and ZipKit) to 74 (for OmniFrwks, our most challenging benchmark). Pessimistically viewing our tool as a post-development analysis, we manually triaged all the reported static type errors to determine if they could manifest at run-time as true bugs (see discussion on bugs below) or otherwise are false alarms due to static over-approximation. The single biggest source of false alarms were reflection calls on objects pulled from collection classes. Retrofitting Objective-C's underlying type system for parametric polymorphism (like, what has been for Java with generics) would directly improve precision for this case. At the same time, as discussed below, the efficiency of FISSILE makes it feasible to instead consider it as a development-time type checker where a small number code rewritings or cast insertions are not unreasonable (especially if most casts would go away altogether with generic types).

***Premises.*** We designed FISSILE type analysis around two core premises (Section 2.2): (1) that most of the program can be checked flow-insensitively and (2) that even when a flow-insensitive relationship between heap storage locations is violated, most other relationships on the heap remain intact. As Table 1 shows, the number of times the analysis switches to symbolic execution and back (column "Successful Symbolic Sections") is quite low, even for large programs—Premise 1 appears to hold empirically. The maximum number of simultaneous materializations (column "Max. Mats.) is also low—Premise 2 holds as well empirically. Note that we need more than the single materialization that would be possible with a non-disjunctive flow-sensitive analysis.

***Modular reflection checking at interactive speeds.*** Our two core premises hold, enabling FISSILE type analysis to soundly verify "almost everywhere" invariants quickly. Analysis times range from less than a second for our smaller (around 1,000 lines of code) benchmarks to around 9 seconds (for our largest, about 180,000 lines of code). These results (column "Analysis Time") include only the time to run our analysis: they do not include parsing or clang's base type checker. Our goal with these measurements is to determine the additional compile-time penalty a developer would incur when adding our analysis to her existing work-flow. Expressed as a rate (thousands of lines of code per second), our analysis ranges from about 5 kloc/s to around 38 kloc/s, with a weighted average of 23.0 kloc/s. In general, the larger benchmarks show a faster rate because they amortize the high cost of checking system headers (which are typically more than 100 kloc) over larger compilation units.

***Finding bugs.*** When running our tool on the Vienna benchmark, we found a real reflection bug in a mature application:

```
NSNotificationCenter *nc = [NSNotificationCenter defaultCenter];
[nc addObserver:self selector:"autoCollapseFolder"
         name:"MA_Notify_AutoCollapseFolder" object:nil];
```

Here an object registers interest in being notified whenever any code in the project auto-collapses a folder. This notification takes the form of a reflective callback: the `autoCollapseFolder` method of `self` will be called. Unfortunately, `self` has no such method. Our

| Benchmark | Lines of Code | Refl. Call Sites | Methods | Total Annotations / Per Refl. Site | Symbolic Annotations / Per Refl. Site | Check Sites | FI Type Errors | FISSILE Type Errors (% Reduced) | Successful Symbolic Sections | Max. Mats. | Analysis Time (Rate) |
|---|---|---|---|---|---|---|---|---|---|---|---|
| OAuth | 1248 | 7 | 92 | 5 / 0.71 | 0 / 0.00 | 11 | 7 | 2 (- 71%) | 7 | 1 | 0.24s ( 5.3 kloc/s) |
| SCRecorder | 2716 | 12 | 200 | 9 / 0.75 | 4 / 0.33 | 15 | 2 | 0 (-100%) | 2 | 2 | 0.28s (10.8 kloc/s) |
| ZipKit | 3301 | 28 | 165 | 0 / 0.00 | 0 / 0.00 | 28 | 0 | 0 (–) | 0 | 0 | 0.10s (33.0 kloc/s) |
| Sparkle | 5290 | 40 | 320 | 0 / 0.00 | 0 / 0.00 | 40 | 4 | 1 (- 75%) | 3 | 1 | 0.67s ( 7.9 kloc/s) |
| ASIHTTP | 13565 | 68 | 707 | 2 / 0.03 | 2 / 0.03 | 68 | 50 | 10 (- 80%) | 59 | 2 | 0.50s (27.2 kloc/s) |
| OmniFrwks | 160769 | 192 | 7611 | 49 / 0.26 | 2 / 0.01 | 259 | 82 | 74 (- 10%) | 9 | 1 | 4.25s (37.8 kloc/s) |
| Vienna | 37348 | 186 | 2261 | 24 / 0.13 | 4 / 0.02 | 207 | 59 | 38 (- 36%) | 28 | 2 | 2.79s (13.4 kloc/s) |
| Skim | 60211 | 207 | 3010 | 7 / 0.03 | 0 / 0.00 | 212 | 43 | 43 (- 0%) | 0 | 0 | 2.49s (24.1 kloc/s) |
| Adium | 176632 | 587 | 8723 | 40 / 0.07 | 0 / 0.00 | 648 | 87 | 70 (- 20%) | 17 | 1 | 8.79s (20.1 kloc/s) |
| Combined | 461080 | 1327 | 23089 | 136 / 0.10 | 12 / 0.01 | 1488 | 334 | 238 (- 29%) | 125 | 2 | 20.09s (23.0 kloc/s) |

**Table 1.** The "Lines of Code" count includes project headers but excludes comments and whitespace; "Methods" indicates the total number of methods; "Refl. Call Sites" gives the number of calls to system library methods that perform reflection, either directly or as part of some other operation; "Total Annotations" lists the total number of annotations and the average number of annotations required per reflective callsite; "Symbolic Annotations" lists gives the number of symbolic summaries required; "Check Sites" gives the number of program sites where some annotation was checked; "FI Type Errors" indicates the number of check sites where a flow-insensitive type analysis produces a type error; "FISSILE Type Errors" indicates the number of check sites where we emit a static type error and the corresponding percent reduction from the flow-insensitive approach; "Successful Symbolic Sections" gives the number of times our analysis successfully switched from type checking to symbolic execution and back again; "Max. Mats." gives the maximum number of materialized objects ever present in the explicit heap (this includes unsuccessful symbolic sections); and "Analysis Time" indicates the speed of our analysis on each benchmark, in both absolute terms and in lines of code per second. Our benchmarks include OAuth, which performs OAuth Consumer authentication; SCRecorder, which records custom keyboard shortcuts and is the source of our motivating example in Section 2; ZipKit, which reads and writes compressed archives; Sparkle, a widely-used automatic updater; ASIHTTP, which performs web services calls; and the OmniFrwks, which provide base functionality to the widely used OmniGraffle application; Vienna, an RSS newsreader; Skim, a PDF reader; and Adium, an instant message chat client. The "Combined" row treats all of the benchmarks together as a combined workload. Experiments were performed on a 4-core 2.6 GHz Intel Core i7 laptop with 16GB of RAM running OS X 10.8.2. We used clang 3.2 (trunk 165236) compiled in "Release+Asserts" mode to perform the analysis and xcodebuild 4.6/4H127 to drive the build.

analysis detects this error and issues an alarm. We reported the bug to the developers; they acknowledged it as a bug and fixed it (see `https://github.com/ViennaRSS/vienna-rss/pull/85`).

Our tool was also useful in finding bugs in beginner Objective-C code. We used it to statically detect run-time errors in 12 code snippets culled from mailing lists and discussion forums. These novice reflective errors fell into three different categories: (1) typos in selector names, (2) intending to reflectively call a method with a selector stored in a variable but instead passing in a constant selector with the *name* of the variable, and (3) passing the wrong responder into a reflective call, typically a field of self instead of self itself. These results show that our tool can statically detect a common class of novice errors; they provide evidence in favor of including reflective call checking with FISSILE type analysis in the compiler.

## 5. Related Work

Dependent refinement types [20, 38] enable programmers to restrict types based on the value of program expressions and thus rule out certain classes of run-time errors, such as out-of-bounds array accesses. Extending dependent types to imperative languages [34, 37] has generally led to flow-sensitive type systems because mutation may change the value of a variable referred to in a type. The high burden that flow-sensitive type annotations impose on the programmer motivates sophisticated inference schemes [31], of which CSOLVE [32] is perhaps the closest work to ours. In contrast to CSOLVE, which performs flow-sensitive checking of inferred flow-sensitive types with at most one materialization, we use path-sensitive checking of flow-insensitive annotations [12] and support arbitrary materialization with a disjunctive symbolic analysis, as opposed to proving non-aliasing for one materialization (e.g., [1, 2, 18]). DJS [11] checks dependent refinements in JavaScript, including the safety of dynamic field accesses—a problem similar to reflective method call safety—but supports only single materialization and employs a flow-sensitive heap.

There has been a recent explosion in techniques (e.g., [7, 22]) that have significantly improved the effectiveness of symbolic execution. The SMPP approach [24] leverages SMT technology combined with abstract interpretation on path programs to lift a symbolic-execution–based technique to exhaustive verification. This technique can be seen as applying a fixed one level of analysis switching between a top-level symbolic executor and an abstract interpreter for loops. Our approach of switching between type checking and symbolic execution is similar to the MIX system [25] for simple types. A significant difference is that our approach enables the symbolic executor to leverage the heap-consistency invariant enforced by the type analysis through a type-consistent materialization operation, which is critical for our rich refinement relationship invariants, whereas the symbolic and type analyses in MIX interact minimally with respect to the heap. The notion of temporary violations of an invariant is also reminiscent of the large body of work on object invariants (see [17] for an overview). We remark on two perspective differences that make FISSILE complementary to this work. First, the points where the invariant is assumed and where they may be violated is not based on the program structure (e.g., inside a method or not) but instead is based on the analysis being applied (i.e., type or symbolic). Second, the symbolic analysis takes a more global view of the heap and decides specifically which objects may violate the global type invariant. Issues like reentrancy and multi-object invariants are not as salient in FISSILE, but are possible at the cost of separate symbolic summaries or more expensive, disjunctive analysis in certain complex situations.

On materialized heap locations, our symbolic analysis works over separation logic [3, 30] formulas. We define an on-demand materialization [33] that is universal in separation-logic–based analyzers [4, 9, 16]. However, our materialization operator pulls out heap cells that are summarized and validated *independently* using a refinement type analysis. Bi-abductive shape analyses [8, 23] are modular analyses that try to infer a symbolic summary for each method. Our analysis is modular using a fast, flow-insensitive type analysis with few uses of symbolic summaries. Bi-abduction and our technique could complement each other nicely in that (1) we do not require symbolic summaries on all methods—only those that violate type consistency across method boundaries—and (2) bi-abduction could be applied to generate candidate symbolic summaries.

Most prior work on reflection analysis has focused on whole-program *resolution*: determining, at a reflective site, what method is called (either statically [6, 10, 36] or dynamically [5, 21]).

We address the problem of modular static checking of reflective call safety: ensuring that the receiver responds to the selector, in languages with imperative update. Politz et al. [29] describe a type system that modularly checks reflection safety by combining occurrence typing [35] with first-class member names specified by string patterns. In contrast, we treat the "responds-to" *relationship* as first-class (i.e., we permit the user to specify it with a dependent refinement), allowing us to (1) check relationships between mutable fields and (2) express that an object responds to two completely unknown (i.e. potentially identical) selectors. Livshits et al. [27] *assume* reflection safety and leverage this assumption to improve precision of callgraph construction.

## 6. Conclusion

We have described FISSILE type analysis, which intertwines fast type analysis over storage locations and precise symbolic analysis over values to efficiently, effectively, and modularly prove relationship properties. We have evaluated FISSILE using an interesting safety property—reflective method call safety. The key technical enabler for our analysis is *materialization from an almost type-consistent heap*. On a benchmark suite consisting of commonly-used Objective-C libraries (6) and applications (3), we find that our approach is capable of finding confirmed bugs in both production and beginner code. It has a balanced annotation burden that is negligible for clients of reflection and moderate (up to 0.75 annotations per reflective call site) for reflective interfaces.

FISSILE type analysis starts with the optimistic assumption that global flow-insensitive relationship invariants hold almost everywhere—it only has to use precise and expensive reasoning for those few program locations that violate a relationship. Contrast this to traditional modular flow-sensitive analyses, which require *all* methods to specify their effect on the heap to rule out the pessimistic assumption that relationship invariants could be violated anywhere. Our approach permits the vast majority (99.95%) of methods to avoid any annotations related to heap effects. Checking most of the program flow-insensitively allows FISSILE to validate reflective method call safety at interactive speeds (5 to 38 kloc/s with an overall rate of 23.0 kloc/s over our benchmark suite).

## Acknowledgments

We thank Sriram Sankaranarayanan, Amer Diwan, Jeremy Siek, the CUPLV group, and Ranjit Jhala for insightful discussions, as well as the anonymous reviewers for their helpful comments. This material is based upon work supported by the National Science Foundation under Grant Nos. CCF-1218208 and CCF-1055066.

## References


[1] A. Ahmed, M. Fluet, and G. Morrisett. $L^3$: A linear language with locations. *Fundam. Inform.*, 77(4), 2007.

[2] A. Aiken, J. S. Foster, J. Kodumal, and T. Terauchi. Checking and inferring local non-aliasing. In *PLDI*, 2003.

[3] J. Berdine, C. Calcagno, and P. W. O'Hearn. Symbolic execution with separation logic. In *APLAS*, 2005.

[4] J. Berdine, C. Calcagno, B. Cook, D. Distefano, P. W. O'Hearn, T. Wies, and H. Yang. Shape analysis for composite data structures. In *CAV*, 2007.

[5] E. Bodden, A. Sewe, J. Sinschek, H. Oueslati, and M. Mezini. Taming Reflection: Aiding static analysis in the presence of reflection and custom class loaders. In *ICSE*, 2011.

[6] M. Braux and J. Noyé. Towards partially evaluating reflection in Java. In *PEPM*, 2000.

[7] C. Cadar, D. Dunbar, and D. R. Engler. KLEE: Unassisted and automatic generation of high-coverage tests for complex systems programs. In *OSDI*, 2008.

[8] C. Calcagno, D. Distefano, P. W. O'Hearn, and H. Yang. Compositional shape analysis by means of bi-abduction. In *POPL*, 2009.

[9] B.-Y. E. Chang and X. Rival. Relational inductive shape analysis. In *POPL*, 2008.

[10] A. S. Christensen, A. Møller, and M. I. Schwartzbach. Precise analysis of string expressions. In *SAS*, 2003.

[11] R. Chugh, D. Herman, and R. Jhala. Dependent types for JavaScript. In *OOPSLA*, 2012.

[12] J. Condit, M. Harren, Z. R. Anderson, D. Gay, and G. C. Necula. Dependent types for low-level programming. In *ESOP*, 2007.

[13] D. Coughlin and B.-Y. E. Chang. Fissile Type Analysis: Modular checking of almost everywhere invariants (extended version), 2013.

[14] P. Cousot and R. Cousot. Abstract interpretation: A unified lattice model for static analysis of programs by construction or approximation of fixpoints. In *POPL*, 1977.

[15] P. Cousot and R. Cousot. Systematic design of program analysis frameworks. In *POPL*, 1979.

[16] D. Distefano, P. W. O'Hearn, and H. Yang. A local shape analysis based on separation logic. In *TACAS*, 2006.

[17] S. Drossopoulou, A. Francalanza, P. Müller, and A. J. Summers. A unified framework for verification techniques for object invariants. In *ECOOP*, 2008.

[18] M. Fähndrich and R. DeLine. Adoption and focus: Practical linear types for imperative programming. In *PLDI*, 2002.

[19] C. Flanagan. Hybrid type checking. In *POPL*, 2006.

[20] T. Freeman and F. Pfenning. Refinement types for ML. In *PLDI*, 1991.

[21] M. Furr, J.-h. D. An, and J. S. Foster. Profile-guided static typing for dynamic scripting languages. In *OOPSLA*, 2009.

[22] P. Godefroid, N. Klarlund, and K. Sen. DART: Directed automated random testing. In *PLDI*, 2005.

[23] B. S. Gulavani, S. Chakraborty, G. Ramalingam, and A. V. Nori. Bottom-up shape analysis. In *SAS*, 2009.

[24] W. R. Harris, S. Sankaranarayanan, F. Ivancic, and A. Gupta. Program analysis via satisfiability modulo path programs. In *POPL*, 2010.

[25] Y. P. Khoo, B.-Y. E. Chang, and J. S. Foster. Mixing type checking and symbolic execution. In *PLDI*, 2010.

[26] V. Laviron, B.-Y. E. Chang, and X. Rival. Separating shape graphs. In *ESOP*, 2010.

[27] B. Livshits, J. Whaley, and M. S. Lam. Reflection analysis for Java. In *APLAS*, 2005.

[28] M. J. Parkinson. *Local Reasoning for Java*. PhD thesis, University of Cambridge, Computer Laboratory, 2005.

[29] J. G. Politz, A. Guha, and S. Krishnamurthi. Semantics and types for objects with first-class member names. In *FOOL*, 2012.

[30] J. C. Reynolds. Separation logic: A logic for shared mutable data structures. In *LICS*, 2002.

[31] P. M. Rondon, M. Kawaguchi, and R. Jhala. Liquid types. In *PLDI*, 2008.

[32] P. M. Rondon, M. Kawaguchi, and R. Jhala. Low-level liquid types. In *POPL*, 2010.

[33] M. Sagiv, T. Reps, and R. Wilhelm. Solving shape-analysis problems in languages with destructive updating. *ACM Trans. Program. Lang. Syst.*, 20(1), 1998.

[34] R. Tate, J. Chen, and C. Hawblitzel. Inferable object-oriented typed assembly language. In *PLDI*, 2010.

[35] S. Tobin-Hochstadt and M. Felleisen. The design and implementation of Typed Scheme. In *POPL*, 2008.

[36] O. Tripp, M. Pistoia, S. J. Fink, M. Sridharan, and O. Weisman. TAJ: Effective taint analysis of web applications. In *PLDI*, 2009.

[37] H. Xi. Imperative programming with dependent types. In *LICS*, 2000.

[38] H. Xi and F. Pfenning. Dependent types in practical programming. In *POPL*, 1999.

# A Trusted Mechanised JavaScript Specification


Martin Bodin
Inria & ENS Lyon
martin.bodin@inria.fr

Arthur Charguéraud
Inria & LRI, Université Paris Sud, CNRS
arthur.chargueraud@inria.fr

Daniele Filaretti
Imperial College London
d.filaretti11@imperial.ac.uk

Philippa Gardner
Imperial College London
philippa.gardner@imperial.ac.uk

Sergio Maffeis
Imperial College London
sergio.maffeis@imperial.ac.uk

Daiva Naudžiūnienė
Imperial College London
d.naudziuniene11@imperial.ac.uk

Alan Schmitt
Inria
alan.schmitt@inria.fr

Gareth Smith
Imperial College London
gareth.smith05@imperial.ac.uk



## Abstract

JavaScript is the most widely used web language for client-side applications. Whilst the development of JavaScript was initially just led by implementation, there is now increasing momentum behind the ECMA standardisation process. The time is ripe for a formal, mechanised specification of JavaScript, to clarify ambiguities in the ECMA standards, to serve as a trusted reference for high-level language compilation and JavaScript implementations, and to provide a platform for high-assurance proofs of language properties.

We present JSCert, a formalisation of the current ECMA standard in the Coq proof assistant, and JSRef, a reference interpreter for JavaScript extracted from Coq to OCaml. We give a Coq proof that JSRef is correct with respect to JSCert and assess JSRef using test262, the ECMA conformance test suite. Our methodology ensures that JSCert is a comparatively accurate formulation of the English standard, which will only improve as time goes on. We have demonstrated that modern techniques of mechanised specification can handle the complexity of JavaScript.



***Categories and Subject Descriptors*** D.3.1 [*Programming Languages*]: Formal Definitions and Theory

***Keywords*** JavaScript, mechanised semantics, Coq


## 1. Introduction

JavaScript is by far the most widely used web language for client-side applications. Initially, JavaScript development was entirely led by implementation, with Netscape releasing the first JavaScript implementation in 1996 and Microsoft responding with their own version in the same year. Netscape quickly realised that standardisation was crucial. Client code that works on some of the main browsers, and not others, is not useful. The first official standard appeared in 1997. Now we have ECMAScript 3 (ES3, 1999) and ECMAScript 5 (ES5, 2009), supported by all browsers. There is increasing momentum behind the ECMA standardisation process, with plans for ES6 and 7 well under way.

JavaScript is the only language supported natively by all major web browsers. Programs written for the browser are either written directly in JavaScript, or in other languages which compile to JavaScript. This fundamental role seems unlikely to change. However, JavaScript is very complex. The ECMAScript standards, by necessity, are large and full of corner cases. Despite the best efforts of their editors, these documents are sometimes unclear and, in some isolated cases, even inconsistent. We believe the time is ripe for a formal, mechanised specification of JavaScript, to clarify ambiguities in the ECMA standards, to serve as a trusted reference for high-level language compilation and JavaScript implementations, and to provide a platform for high-assurance proofs of language properties.

We introduce JSCert, a mechanised specification of ES5 written in the interactive proof assistant Coq. We also introduce JSRef, an executable reference interpreter extracted from Coq to OCaml. We give a Coq proof that JSRef is correct with respect to JSCert. The correctness proof ensures that we can have full confidence that a JSRef program has the behaviour specified by JSCert. All our Coq code is available at `http://www.jscert.org`. We believe that both JSCert and JSRef are necessary: JSCert, unlike JSRef, is well-suited for developing inductive proofs about the semantics of JavaScript; JSRef, unlike JSCert, can be used to run JavaScript programs.

Our challenge is to convince ourselves and others that JSCert is indeed an accurate formulation of the ES5 English specification. We designed JSCert to follow the structure of the ES5 English standard as much as possible. Whenever we found parts of ES5 English prose to be ambiguous, we checked the browser implementations and were active on discussion groups such as `es-discuss`. We also ran JSRef on the official ECMA test suite, test262. Since JSRef is correct with respect to JSCert, failed tests meant discrepancies between ES5, JSCert, and the tests. Using this methodology, we were able to correct several bugs in JSCert and JSRef. We




*POPL '14*, January 22–24, 2014, San Diego, CA, USA.



ACM 978-1-4503-2544-8/14/01... $15.00.
http://dx.doi.org/10.1145/2535838.2535876

also discovered, and reported [58, 60], a number of bugs in all the browser implementations, the ECMA standards, and test262. We have demonstrated that modern techniques of mechanised specification can handle the complexity of JavaScript.

***JSCert.*** We introduce JSCert, a mechanised Coq specification of ES5. In 2008, Maffeis, with Mitchell and Taly from Stanford, developed a hand-written, small-step operational semantics for formally describing the full behaviour of JavaScript [36, 37], faithfully following ES3 except when the English standard was incorrect or ambiguous. Apart from moving to ES5, we also differ from [36] in that we use a big-step semantics to be closer to the style of the English prose. However, the traditional big-step approach would lead to many duplicated rules, since the JavaScript control flow is quite complex. We use a pretty-big-step semantics, an approach recently developed by Charguéraudfor a simple ML dialect [11]. Our work here demonstrates that the technique scales to a real-world standard, and yields a close connection between ES5 and JSCert.

Note that we are not trying to usurp ES5, which has an ease of readability that would be difficult to match with a mechanised specification. We are aiming for an accurate, mechanised specification of ES5 which can be used for clarification when the ES5 prose is unclear. By gathering a team of Coq and JavaScript experts, we have been able to handle the size and the complexity of the JavaScript semantics.

As with most large specification projects, a significant question is when to stop. We have formally specified the core language, where we believe most of the interest for our project lies. We have not specified the for-in command, because in trying to do so we discovered that ES5 and ES6 are broken in this respect.[1] We have not specified the parsing of JavaScript source code, which would be a challenging, orthogonal task. Also, our formalisation of native libraries is partial. We have formalised nearly all of the library functions that expose internal features of JavaScript, with the exception of functions involving arrays which is future work. In particular, we have formalised most of the functions from libraries `Object`, `Function`, `Boolean`, `Number`, and `Errors`. We are not planning to formalise the other native libraries. They contain hundreds of library functions that do not interact with internal JavaScript features, in the sense that they could be implemented as plain JavaScript code.

***JSRef.*** We introduce JSRef, an executable reference interpreter, which we have proved correct with respect to JSCert and tested using the ECMAScript conformance test suite, test262. By design, JSCert is not directly executable. It is presented as an inductive definition, essential for developing safety proofs, and it matches the looseness of ES5's "implementation-dependent" features. We therefore developed a computable Coq specification and, from this, automatically extracted the corresponding OCaml code, obtaining the executable reference interpreter JSRef. Our computable Coq specification follows the ES5 pseudo-code as much as possible. Where the implementation details were left unspecified, we made arbitrary but natural choices.

In fact, we developed JSCert and JSRef in parallel. This approach was invaluable when understanding an unclear part of ES5: we sometimes needed the specifier's broad intuition; sometimes the implementer's pragmatic intuition about what was really meant. Recall that JSCert specifies the core language of ES5, but does not specify the parser nor many of the native libraries. The same restrictions apply for JSRef. In particular, we rely on an off-the-shelf JavaScript parser, taken from the Google Closure Compiler [25], for parsing the initial source code and for implementing `eval`.

[1] We have filed a bug report (n. 1444 of [58]) for ES6.

***Trust.*** Our methodology for obtaining trust in our mechanised semantics can be summarised as follows:

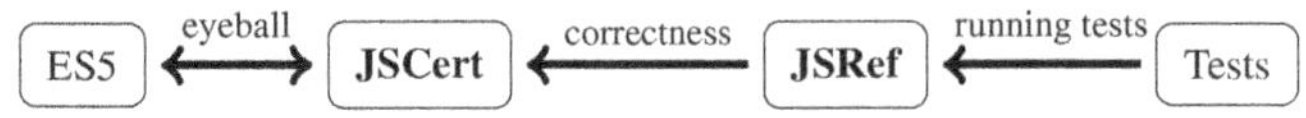


For JSCert, trust arises from the 'eyeball closeness' of JSCert to ES5. We can place the English prose and the formal rules side-by-side, and compare the two: one line of ES5 pseudo-code corresponds to one or two rules in JSCert. If commands need changing, as inevitably they will for future standards, it is relatively straightforward to see which part of JSCert needs changing.

For JSRef, we have a machine-checked correctness proof that it satisfies JSCert. More precisely, we prove in Coq that, if the execution of a JavaScript program in JSRef returns a result, then there exists a reduction derivation in JSCert relating this program to this result. Because of the looseness of ES5, our interpreter cannot be proved complete. Nevertheless, we believe that, on the deterministic subset of ES5, our interpreter is complete. We trust the extraction mechanism of Coq, used to obtain the OCaml code of JSRef, since it is standard and widely-used (e.g., in [8]).

We also test JSRef using test262 [18]. JSRef successfully executes all the tests that we expect to pass given our coverage of JSRef. There are 2782 tests associated with the core language (chapters 8–14): we pass 1796 tests; the others fail due to for-in, calls to libraries we have not specified, or the parser. We also use the OCaml bisect tool [14] to investigate the coverage of these tests. Our emphasis on testing provides a different level of trust from that usually found in Coq development (see related work), which is perhaps more accessible to JavaScript implementers and programmers. It also provides a first step in the analysis of what it means to trust test262.

As we were developing the proof of correctness and running the tests, we inevitably found bugs in JSCert and JSRef. It was necessary to go around the loop many times, fixing inaccuracies, continuing with the correctness proof and testing, and so on. Our correctness proof guarantees that JSRef is an accurate reference interpreter for JSCert (up to our trust of the Coq extraction process). However, despite our principled development of JSCert and JSRef, we cannot yet guarantee that JSCert is bug free in the sense that there may well be mismatches with ES5. A few mismatches will be due to the ambiguity of ES5. The ECMA authors have been very responsive to our queries on es-discuss and it has always been possible to reach consensus. Other mismatches, however, will be due to inaccuracies in JSCert. We do believe that, over time, with more proof reading and testing by ourselves, and with help from others, we will be able to eliminate all the bugs.

***Applications.*** There are many potential applications of JSCert and JSRef. For example, we can investigate properties of fragments of JavaScript used for secure sandboxing by companies such as Yahoo!, Google, and Facebook. Several high-level languages are compiled to JavaScript. JSCert provides a formal target to verify the correctness of the compilation. A natural first language to explore in this respect is Microsoft's F* compilation to JavaScript (and back for full abstraction, see related work). JavaScript implementers can compare their implementation with JSRef. For example, a direct extension of our work would be to characterise the differences between Firefox and JSRef by running the Firefox test suite on JSRef. A dream is that our mechanised specification might even be used as part of the creation of future ECMA standards: ES6 is already taking shape, but ES7 is only just being planned. This paper demonstrates that it is feasible to provide a Coq specification of ES5 together with a reference interpreter passing the ES5 tests. We are impacting on ES6 with bug reports. It may not be beyond reach to provide a mechanised specification for ES7 as part of the official standard.

## 2. Related work

A real-world language specification can come in many forms: an implementation of the compiler/VM as specification (e.g., PHP); an English definition with varying degrees of rigour (e.g., the C standard [10] and ES5 are fairly precise and complete); a formal mathematical specification (e.g., Standard ML [41]); and mechanised specification. Our work on JavaScript is part of the established tradition to mechanise existing, real-world programming language specifications. In this section, we survey related work on the large-scale mechanisations of programming languages in general, and on various formalisations of JavaScript in particular.

### 2.1 Large-scale mechanised specifications

One of the most prominent, fully formalised presentations of a programming language is Standard ML by Milner, Tofte, Harper, and Macqueen [41]. A mechanised specification was given by Lee, Crary, and Harper [34] in the Twelf theorem prover [48]. Unlike ML, many real-world languages are designed without formalism in mind. Such languages provide a considerable challenge to mechanisation.

There has been a wide body of work on mechanised language specifications in HOL. For example, Norrish [44] specifies a small-step operational semantics of C in HOL [43], and proves substantial meta-properties of the semantics. Norrish's formalism has not been tested for conformance with implementations. Another example is Sewell *et al.*'s work [7] on formalising transmission control protocols (TCP) in Isabelle/HOL [43]. They created a post-hoc specification of TCP from several prominent implementations, an enterprise not so far off the creation of the original ECMA standard for JavaScript. Although not focusing on language specification, their work is notable in the context of our work as it validates the specification against several thousand test traces captured from implementations, using a special-purpose symbolic model checker programmed above HOL.

In the CompCert project [15], Blazy and Leroy [8] built a verified optimising compiler for CLight, a significant fragment of C, with a Coq proof that the generated compiled code behaves exactly as prescribed by the semantics of the source program. The CompCert project initiated major technological breakthroughs in Coq mechanisation, some of which we substantially use in this project. The aims of the projects are different. CLight was not intended to capture precisely the C specification. Also, CLight is not directly executable, although it would be possible to obtain an interpreter without too much additional effort, by leveraging the Coq code extraction mechanism. Several substantial projects build on CompCert: Appel's verified software tool chain [3] combining program verification with verified compilation; Shao's project to certify an OS kernel; Zhao *et al.*'s verified LLVM which extracts an interpreter from Coq code that is tested using the LLVM regression suite (134 out of 145 runnable tests); and Sewell's CompCertTSO [61], verifying compilation the x86 weak memory model [1].

The use of proof assistants such as HOL and Coq requires quite a substantial learning curve. Researchers are beginning to explore how to make mechanised specification easier. The $\mathbb{K}$ framework is designed specifically for writing and analysing language definitions using a rewrite logic [19]. In particular, Ellison and Rosu [19] have defined an executable formal semantics of C in $\mathbb{K}$ [53]. Their formalisation has been extensively tested against the GCC torture suite [22]. Besides being executable, their semantics also comes with an explicit-state model checker. Their aim is to define an accurate reference interpreter, justified by testing, rather than provide a full semantics of the C standard. Their work is analogous to JSRef. In addition, the Ott tool [55] provides a lightweight environment using ASCII notation for writing definitions of programming languages and calculi, which automatically translate to HOL, Isabelle, and Coq. Owens *et al.* have developed a mechanised semantics of OCaml Light using Ott.

For space reasons, we cannot detail all the interesting examples of mechanised specifications of programming languages. Inevitably, there is a wide body of work on mechanised specifications of Java and C#: e.g., Syme's HOL semantics [56] of Drossopoulou and Eisenbach's formal Java semantics [17]; the executable formalisation of the C# standard by Börger *et al.* [9] using Abstract State Machines [29]; and the executable formal semantics of Java 1.4 in rewrite logic by Farzan *et al.* [20]. We should also mention the formal semantics of Batty *et al.* on C++ concurrency [4, 5], which is currently having real impact on the C11 standard [10]. The work is currently not mechanised but, considering the research group, it will surely happen soon.

Our mechanised specification of ES5 shares many of the difficult challenges faced by the work described above, and involves many new ones due to the complex dynamic nature of JavaScript. They are detailed in § 4. We now provide a more detailed survey on formalising and mechanising the JavaScript semantics.

### 2.2 Formal JavaScript specifications

In 2005, Anderson *et al.* [2] and Thiemann [59] were the first to propose formal type systems for subsets of JavaScript. To prove type-soundness, they formalised idealised cores of the language that abstracted away features not crucial for the type analysis at hand, focusing instead on the challenges addressed by their analyses. Since then, researchers have studied various typed JavaScript subsets and static analyses, including [12, 13, 26, 27, 30, 32, 33, 45–47]. For example, Jensen *et al.* [33] used abstract interpretation to develop a tool to infer abstract types for the full language, although the formal theory only works for subsets. Others have studied information flow [13], with [30] proving their results in Coq.

All these techniques have been helpful for addressing specific safety problems. None provide general-purpose analyses, most do not work with the full language and, of those that prove soundness, all do so with respect to their abstract models rather than the ECMA semantics or an actual concrete implementation. The security issues identified in [35, 38, 39] demonstrate that the semantic subtleties of corner cases of the language matter crucially. Moreover, the empirical analysis by Richards *et al.* [52] confirms that some of the language features, excluded by construction from the work mentioned so far, are in fact important for actual web programmers.

In 2007, Herman and Flanagan [31] proposed a formalisation of the JavaScript semantics as a definitional interpreter written in ML. Their interpreter was the first executable formal semantics for a non-trivial subset of JavaScript. The advantages of their approach were the ability to test their interpreter and the familiarity of their work to functional programmers. The drawbacks were a loose correspondence with the specification and implementation details that sometimes obscured the semantics of the language features.

In 2008, Maffeis, Mitchell, and Taly [37] defined the first full operational semantics for the ES3 language. They covered the whole language, apart from a few corner cases such as regular expressions, dates, and machine arithmetic. The formalisation consists of a large set of small-step operational semantics rules and some theorems about the determinacy and well-definedness of the language. This work has been useful to prove soundness of security-related JavaScript subsets [35, 38, 39], and influenced the definition of further JavaScript formalisations. For example, the semantics of Secure ECMAScript underlying [57], and the big-step operational semantics of core JavaScript, proposed in [24] and used in [6], is based on this work. This formal semantics differentiates itself from the work described above because its goals were to cover the entire language, without excluding "uncomfortable" features, to serve as a basis for formal proofs of real language properties. The main shortcomings of this work is that, since the rules are not mechanised, the proof of language properties is labour intensive, the maintenance and extension of the semantics is not easy, and a comparison with implementations is impossible.

In 2010, Guha *et al.* [28] came up with a completely different approach to developing language semantics. They provide a translation from JavaScript to a Scheme-like, executable language, called $\lambda_{JS}$, which has as its core a simple $\lambda$-calculus with references. Their aim was to develop provably sound type systems to reason about the safety of client-side web applications. They target the Firefox implementation of ES3, and validate their semantics by testing it against the test262 and Mozilla test suites [18, 42]. More recently, $\lambda_{JS}$ has been extended to model the strict mode of ES5 [50], and an unpublished, small-scale Coq formalisation of $\lambda_{JS}$ has been announced on the Brown PLT blog [51].

The work on $\lambda_{JS}$ has been influential in proving properties of well-behaved JavaScript typed subsets, where the programmer accepts restrictions on full JavaScript in exchange for safety guarantees. For example, Politz *et al.* [49] define a type system for $\lambda_{JS}$ that captures the informal restrictions enforced by Crockford's ADSafe [16], a subset of JavaScript for sandboxing web advertising. Fournet *et al.* [21] define a translation between F*, a subset of Microsoft F# with refinement types, and $\lambda_{JS}$. They show that their encoding is fully abstract, hence the safety properties enjoyed by a source F* program are preserved when it is translated to JavaScript and run on a *trusted* web page. The $\lambda_{JS}$work has also been a significant source of inspiration for our development of our executable semantics, JSRef, and our focus on testing. We have tested JSRef using the test262 conformance tests, and in future will use the Firefox test suite to compare JSRef with the Firefox implementation.

Our work is not the first to give a formal and/or executable semantics to JavaScript. However, JSCert is the first semantics for the entire language, closely reflecting the official standard, which is both executable and formalised in a proof assistant. Working with the source language itself, and reflecting the structure of the specification has several advantages over a translational approach: the JavaScript programmer intuition is better reflected; the semantics is robust to local changes of the standard, such as those anticipated for ECMAScript 6 and 7; and the correctness of the semantics does not rely on possibly unknown assumptions associated with translation.[2]

Throughout this project, it has been important for us to establish *trust* in our mechanised semantics. As JSCert and JSRef are explored by ourselves and other formalists, by people compiling to JavaScript, by JavaScript implementers, and maybe even by ECMA authors, so our trust will increase. If someone questions our interpretation of ES5 or if a test fails, we know which part of JSCert to check and alter. Building on much of the work detailed above, we believe we have developed a methodology for providing a trusted mechanised specification of an English language standard. We do just wonder if this methodology has been fully demonstrated before.

## 3. The JavaScript standard

We give an overview of the semantics of JavaScript, as described in the ECMAScript 5 standard and implemented in current browsers (§ 3.1). We introduce our running example (§ 3.2), and identify the parts of the standard that have not been included in our mechanised specification (§ 3.3).

### 3.1 ECMAScript 5

ECMAScript 5 (ES5) is the current standard for JavaScript. Existing browsers largely implement ES5, but sometimes introduce custom extensions or make different choices in how to implement certain cases that the specification defines as "implementation dependent". In addition to the language, ES5 also describes a collection of native libraries, which provide convenient functionality (e.g., handling of regular expressions, date formats) as well as a few extra language features (useful for reflection). In this paper, we focus on the language itself, only specifying the native libraries necessary for the extra language features.

The grammar of JavaScript is divided into three main categories: expressions, statements, and programs. A JavaScript program consists of a list of statements. The body of a function definition is a JavaScript program. Similarly, the argument of the notorious `eval` statement, once parsed, is a JavaScript program. The result of the evaluation of an expression, statement, or program is a *completion triple*. A completion triple is composed of a type, a value, and a label. The type is one of `Normal`, `Return`, `Break`, `Continue`, or `Throw`, corresponding to the termination mode of the evaluation. The value, which can be empty, describes the result of an expression or statement (if the type is `Normal`), the value carried by a return statement (if the type is `Return`), or the object describing the exception being thrown (if the type is `Throw`). The label, which can also be empty, is only used for `Break` and `Continue` types, in order to divert the execution flow to the instruction annotated with the target label.

One of the reasons we were attracted to study ES5 is that it has not been defined with mechanised specification in mind. The standard is not optimised for conciseness and reuse. It has a lot of copy/paste which increases the workload of our formalisation. The standard uses representations that are practical for e.g., VM implementers, but less helpful for reasoning. For example, completion triples have implicit invariants that for our purposes would be better captured with an inductive definitions. Also, the standard becomes very particular when describing browser-specific extensions, and is not explicit about whether under-specified functions should have deterministic behaviours.

Apart from this determinism issue, we have found ES5 to be precise and non-ambiguous, with two exceptions. First, the specification of *data attributes*, used to represent parameters of properties (object fields) such as writable and enumerable flags, has two different representations in different parts of the specification. We give both representations in our specification and prove that they are equivalent, so that we can follow ES5 as closely as possible. Second, the specification of `for-in` suffers from major issues related to the loose specification of the order of enumeration of the property names [58].

### 3.2 Running example: the `while` statement

There are many interesting features in the semantics of JavaScript. These include prototype-based inheritance, return value propagation through "empty" statements, implicit type conversion (which may result in arbitrary side effects), the unique JavaScript approach to variable resolution, and the notorious `with` and `eval` statements. All of these features are properly described by our JSCert semantics. Since space is limited, we chose just one language feature to demonstrate our approach, and at least *some* of the subtleties of the JavaScript language. Our running example will be the `while` statement.

[2] In order to prove the correctness of such a translation, one needs a formal semantics for the source language in the first place. In this sense, our work will make it possible to prove the correctness of the encoding of JavaScript in $\lambda_{JS}$, increasing confidence in the validity of $\lambda_{JS}$ or F* safety properties on actual JavaScript programs.

"`while` ( *Expression* ) *Statement*" is evaluated as follows:

1. Let $V$ = `empty`.
2. Repeat
   a. Let *exprRef* be the result of evaluating *Expression*.
   b. If `ToBoolean`(`GetValue`(*exprRef*)) is `false`, return (`normal`, $V$, `empty`).
   c. Let *stmt* be the result of evaluating *Statement*.
   d. If *stmt*.value is not empty, let V = *stmt*.value.
   e. If *stmt*.type is not `continue` || *stmt*.target is not in the current label set, then
      i. If *stmt*.type is `break` and *stmt*.target is in the current label set, then return (`normal`, $V$, `empty`).
      ii. If *stmt* is an abrupt completion, return *stmt*.

**Figure 1.** ECMAScript 5 semantics of while loops

Fig. 1 shows the English specification of while exactly as it appears in the ES5 standard. The text should be interpreted as pseudo-code, executing each statement in order. The ES5 specification of while is relatively short in comparison with other constructs, such as `switch`, whose specification spans more than one full page. This ES5 pseudo-code, like a traditional imperative programming language, leaves completely implicit three major aspects of the semantics. The first aspect is divergence; ES5 never talks explicitly about diverging programs, but it should be understood that if the evaluation of a sub-expression diverges, then the parent expression will also diverge. The second aspect is the threading of the mutable state; ES5 assumes that there is one global heap storing objects, and that the instructions in the pseudo-code can modify such heap. The third is the propagation of exceptions through expressions; ES5 describes the semantics of expressions in terms of the result of the sub-expressions, but does not recall every time that exceptions propagate outwards from expressions.[3] Unlike ES5, our JSCert specification is fully explicit about divergence, mutation, and exceptions.

We describe the pseudo-code from Fig. 1 in more detail. The basic skeleton is standard: repeat the loop body until the loop condition becomes false, or until the body of the loop produces a break, a return, or an exception. Step 2b is non-standard, illustrating one of the mechanisms necessary to interact with JavaScript's variable store. The result of an expression is not necessarily ready to be used, but may be a *reference* to a variable stored as a field of an object. The internal `GetValue` function is used to de-reference it. In addition, JavaScript uses the internal function `ToBoolean` to implicitly coerce the loop guard to a boolean before attempting to test it. A further complication comes from the fact that JavaScript allows labelled break and continue statements that may refer to an outer loop. A current loop may be interrupted by such labelled break and continue operations, just like it would be interrupted if an exception was thrown. In Fig. 1, the "current label set" refers to the set of labels that are associated with the current loop (since a loop might have several labels as in e.g., `a:b:c:while(1){break b;}`). Finally, notice that while loops have a return value in JavaScript. The definition of the JavaScript syntax forbids us from writing statements like `1+while(x>3){x--}`, however it does allow `1+eval("while(x>3){x--}")`. The assignments to the internal pseudo-code variable $V$ in Fig. 1 are aimed at maintaining the value that will serve as the "result" of the current while loop. The value $V$ is used in one of two cases: a break or a continue has been issued for this loop, or a break or a continue has been issued for an outer loop and does not yet carry a non-empty value.

Without further details, the reader may appreciate the complexity of JavaScript semantics with respect to output values of statements by looking at the following while loop examples, which return the last value that was produced by a statement in their body (if any):

```
eval("a: while(1){ while(1){ break a; }}")
==> undefined
eval("a: while(1){ while(1){ y=2; break a; }}")
==> 2
eval("a: while(1){ x=3; while(1){ y=2; break a; }}")
==> 2
eval("a: while(1){ x=3; while(1){ break a; }}")
==> 3
```

The most surprising example is the fourth one: 3 is returned because the statement `x=3` has completion value 3 and the statement `while(1){ break a; }` has an empty completion value.

### 3.3 What we do not specify

The ES5 standard is a document of 16 chapters, ranging over 209 pages, plus some additional annexes. It consists largely of pseudo-code in the style of Fig. 1, with clarifications in English. The document includes: the specification of parsing; the specification of the syntax (e.g., objects, heaps, environment records); the pseudo-code describing the semantics of expressions, statements, programs, and internal properties; and the pseudo-code describing the semantics of native library functions.

We have given a mechanised Coq specification for the important part of the language: the syntax (as an abstract syntax tree); the semantics of expressions, statements and programs; and most native library functions that expose internal features of JavaScript. In particular, we have specified the `Object`, `Function` and `Errors` libraries, with the only exception being functions involving the manipulation of arrays. We also have specifications for the constructors and most functions from the libraries `Boolean` and `Number`. For floating-point numbers, we rely on the Coq formalisation of IEEE 754 standard provided by the Flocq library [40].

We have not formalised other standard libraries, such as `Array`, `String` and `Date`. These libraries involve hundreds of functions. The vast majority of them do not interact with any internal feature of JavaScript, and could be implemented as plain JavaScript code [54]. The specification of these JavaScript standard library functions is orthogonal to the formalisation of the JavaScript programming language *per se*.

We also have not specified the parsing of JavaScript programs. Parsing is important because of JavaScript's `eval` statement, which requires parsing source code at runtime. The normalisation of the formal grammar of a programming language is more complicated than one might expect. The parsing of JavaScript programs is made particularly tricky by the treatment of implicit semi-colons, as it involves a one token look-ahead. We therefore leave the specification of parsing to future work, and use the parser of the Google Closure Compiler [25] in our reference interpreter JSRef.

## 4. JSCert: JavaScript specification in Coq

Our formal development in Coq, available from our project's webpage `http://www.jscert.org`, consists of five main parts:

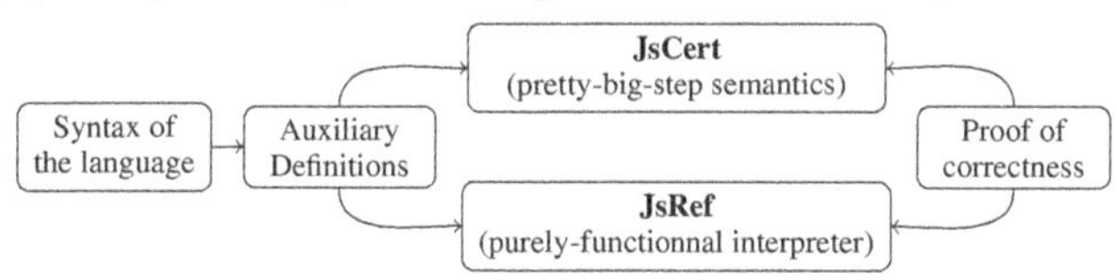


[3] In ES5, the propagation of exceptions out of expressions is implicit, whereas the propagation of exceptions out of statements is explicit. This asymmetry is not only awkward, it is also a potential source of ambiguities. This issue has been resolved in ES6, where, like in our formalisation, the propagation of exceptions is always explicitly specified.

```
Inductive restype := (* result type *)
  | restype_normal
  | restype_break
  | restype_continue
  | restype_return
  | restype_throw.

Inductive resvalue := (* result value *)
  | resvalue_empty : resvalue
  | resvalue_value : value → resvalue
  | resvalue_ref : ref → resvalue.

Inductive reslabel := (* result label *)
  | reslabel_empty : reslabel
  | reslabel_string : string → reslabel.

Record res := { (* completion triple *)
  res_type : restype;
  res_value : resvalue;
  res_label : reslabel }.
```

**Figure 2.** JSCert completion triples

The first part describes the syntax and data structures, such as heaps and scopes, that are used to describe the formal semantics. The second part contains a collection of auxiliary definitions, such as functions used to convert a primitive value (a value that is not object) into a boolean, a number, or a string. These first two parts are described in § 4.1. The next two parts correspond to JSCert (§ 4.2) and JSRef (§ 5). The last part contains the correctness proof, that any result computed by JSRef is correct with respect to the semantics from JSCert (§ 6).

### 4.1 Syntax and auxiliary definitions

We give a simple summary of the syntax and auxiliary definitions shared by JSCert and JSRef. The full Coq specifications are given in the file `JsPreliminary.v`.

***Abstract syntax tree.*** Following common practice, we do not model the parsing of language source code. Instead we work directly on the AST (abstract syntax tree). We obtain the AST by running the parser of the Google Closure Compiler [25], extended with some additional interface code defined by us.

The grammar of JavaScript expressions and statements is defined, in file `JsSyntax.v`, through a conventional inductive definition that represents the abstract syntax tree. This definition is relatively short, since there are only 13 kinds of expressions and 17 kinds of statements. We should note that we have factorised similar forms of if-statements and try-statements using option types, and that the definition of expressions depends on the grammar of literals (null, bool, number, string), the grammar of the 11 unary operators, and the grammar of the 24 binary operators. A JavaScript program consists of a list of statements, plus a strictness flag which stipulates the evaluation order of the list of statements. The body of a function definition is itself a JavaScript program. The argument of a call to `eval`, once parsed, is also a JavaScript program.

***Completions.*** As we noted in § 3, the result of the evaluation of an expression, a statement or a program produces a *completion triple*, as given in Fig. 2. A completion triple (type `res`) is made of a type, an optional value (or reference, if the expression is a variable name), and an optional label. The type is one of `Normal`, `Return`, `Break`, `Continue`, or `Throw`, corresponding to the control flow directive obtained from an evaluation. The value, if any, is either a primitive value (a literal or `undefined`) or the location of an allocated object. This value describes the result of a `Normal` expression or statement, the value carried by a `Return` statement, or the exception being thrown in a `Throw` result. The optional label of a completion triple is only used for `Break` and `Continue` types, in order to implement the `break label` and `continue label` instructions.

A number of invariants apply to completion triples. For example, if a completion triple carries a non-empty label, then it must be of type `Break` or `Continue`. In order to better capture all the invariants on completion triples, we were tempted to use a clean inductive definition with one constructor per type, and different arguments for each type. However, recall that one of our goals is a direct correspondence between our JSCert specification and the ES5 standard. A change in the representation of something as fundamental as completion triples would put considerable distance between the English prose of the ES5 and our formalisation of it. Forced to choose between a more elegant Coq representation and a more direct correspondence with the ECMA standard, we chose the latter.

***Program execution.*** A JavaScript program is always executed in a given *state* and in a given *execution context*. The state consists of the set of allocated objects (the *heap*), plus the set of allocated *environment records*.

***The heap.*** The JavaScript object heap is represented as a finite map from locations to objects. An object is represented as a record with 25 fields, including the `prototype` object, the `class` name, a boolean `extensible` property, an optional `primitive value` (for objects of class `Boolean`, `Number` or `String`), the *property map*, as well as internal methods such as `get` or `put`, optional fields such as `body` and `scope` for functions, and optional internal methods such as `call` or `construct`. Each internal method may have a small number of different behaviours depending on the object on which it is called (Arguments objects, for instance, have a different implementation of `[[Get]]`). We distinguish these different behaviours using a tag that describes how the internal method should be processed.

***Object properties.*** The property map binds field names to *property attributes*, rather than directly to values. A property attribute is a record that contains a number of fields. There are two kinds of property attributes: *data property attributes* which have a `value` field, a `writable` field, an `enumerable` field, and a `configurable` field; and *data accessor attributes* which have a `get` field, a `set` field, an `enumerable` field, and a `configurable` field.

The ES5 standard suggests that property attributes should be represented as a record with 6 optional fields. In particular, the specification of the function `DefineOwnProperty` involves the construction of a property attribute, which explicitly manipulates records using arbitrary subsets of the 6 optional fields. At the same time, in many other places, the standard uses exactly 4 fields, (loosely) making the assumption that particular fields are present and implicitly exploiting the fact that the property attribute is known to be either a data property or a data accessor attribute from the context and implicit invariants.

Since we wanted to be faithful to the standard everywhere, we chose to provide two distinct representations of data properties: the first consists of a record with 6 optional fields; and the second consists of an inductive type with two cases, one for data property attributes and one for data accessor attributes, both represented as records with exactly 4 mandatory fields. The overhead of defining conversion functions between the two forms was negligible compared to the benefits of avoiding the pollution of many rules with accesses to optional fields.

***Environment records.*** Recall that the JavaScript state consists of the heap and the set of allocated environment records. We store environment records in a similar data structure to that used for the object heap, using a pointer to refer to a given environment record. An environment record can take one of two forms: a *declarative environment record*, which maps variable names to values (and to mutability flags); or an *object environment record*, which consists of the location of a JavaScript object (and some "provide-this" flags). Declarative environment records provide the local scoping associated with function calls, while object environment records provide the dynamic scoping associated with the `with` construct. In addition, there is always at least one object environment record which points to *the global object*. To properly model function closures, a given function object represents the environment it closes over as a *lexical environment* stored in one of its internal fields.

***Execution context.*** The execution context is represented as a triple that consists of the scope (both the *lexical environment* and the *variable environment*, as specified by ES5), the current "this" object, and the current strictness flag. We represent both lexical environments and variable environments as a stack (a list) of pointers to environment records.

### 4.2 JSCert

Based on the syntax and auxiliary definitions described above, the main JSCert rules are defined in the file `JsPrettyRules.v`. We formalise the semantics of JavaScript statements using a judgement of the form $t/S/C \Downarrow_s o$, where: $t$ denotes a statement; $S$ denotes the state comprising the object heap and the environment record heap; $C$ denotes the context comprising the lexical and variable environment, the ES5 "this" object, and the strictness flag; and $o$ denotes the *output*. We have similar judgements $\Downarrow_e$, $\Downarrow_i$ and $\Downarrow_p$ for expressions, internal reductions, and full programs.

For terminating computations, the output is a pair made of the final state and the completion triple produced by the evaluation. Our JSCert semantics, expressed in pretty-big-step style [11], also captures diverging computations, using a coinductive interpretation of the same set of evaluation rules. We discuss this further below. One key ingredient to the factorisation of the evaluation rules is the definition of the output of an evaluation as a sum type, shown below, that describes either termination in a given state with a given result, or divergence:

```
Inductive out :=
| out_ter : state → res → out
| out_div : out.
```

Internal reductions, however, return results of many different types. Some, for instance, return property descriptors. We thus use a more general return type, `specret T`, that is parameterised by the type `T` of what is returned. To add further complexity, internal reductions may call arbitrary user code which may terminate with an abrupt termination, such as throwing an exception, or which may diverge. Their return type is, thus, not uniform: it returns a modified state and a term of type `T` when the computation is successful; it returns a term of type `out` when the computation diverges or results in an abrupt termination. This behaviour is captured by the following type:

```
Inductive specret T :=
  | specret_val : state → T → specret T
  | specret_out : out → specret T.
```

***Pretty-big-step semantics.*** We express the JSCert semantics using the *pretty-big-step* operational semantics recently developed by Charguéraud [11]. The key difference between the traditional big-step semantics and Charguéraud's pretty-big-step semantics is that we can decompose the evaluation of a single program construct using *intermediate forms* (defined in `JsPrettyInterm.v`), which extend the grammar of program statements and can be evaluated just like any other program. This style of semantics allows us to more effectively match the modularity of the ES5 standard.

The advantages of the *pretty-big-step* semantics have been described in [11]. Here, we only recall the arguments applicable to large existing language standards such as ES5. Nearly all English standards for industrial programming languages, including ES5, use sentences of the form "let $R$ be the result of evaluating $t$". These sentences relate a term directly to its result, just as a big-step judgement would do. Because we want to be close to ES5, we cannot work with a small-step presentation, as in [37], with rules of the form "to evaluate `if e then t1 else t2`, execute one step to reduce `e` into `e1`, and then evaluate `if e1 then t1 else t2`."

If we attempt to use traditional big-step semantics, we quickly find that we have to duplicate a significant amount of material across several rules. For example, consider the loop `while(e){ t }`. In big-step, we need a rule to handle the case where $e$ evaluates to an exception, another rule for the case where $e$ evaluates to a value converted to the boolean false, yet another rule for the case where $e$ evaluates to a value converted to the boolean true and the body of the loop evaluates to an exception, and so on.

The problem here is that the steps made by a big-step semantics are "too big" to cleanly correspond to ES5. As suggested by our example, if we attempt to shoehorn ES5 into a big-step presentation, our repetition of premises will lead to a quadratic explosion in the size of our rule set. For an idealised research programming language, this sort of duplication may not present much of a problem. However, we soon realised that formalising ES5 in this way would quickly become unmanageable. This observation motivated the development of the pretty-big-step semantics, which has enabled us to write rules which very closely follow the structure of ES5.

***Pretty-big-step semantics for while loops.*** Consider the ES5 description of while loops given in Fig. 1. The corresponding JSCert semantics is given in Fig. 3. Notice the close correspondence between the steps of the ES5 pseudo-code and the JSCert rules. Step 1 of the ES5 pseudo-code says "Let V=empty". The corresponding rule red_while_1 uses the notation `stat_while L e1 t2` to refer to a `while` construct with guard `e1`, body `t2` and label set `L` (used for managing `break` and `continue` statements). The rule says that in a given state, the loop may evaluate to the output $o$ if the *intermediate form*

```
stat_while_1 L e1 t2 resvalue_empty
```

also evaluates to $o$. This intermediate form carries all the information of the original `while` construct, and also carries the additional information that the value of "V" is `resvalue_empty`, which is our Coq representation of the ES5 "empty" value.

Step 2 of Fig. 1 begins the loop in the ES5 pseudo-code. In our JSCert rules, we may loop back to this point at any time, by using the `stat_while_1` intermediate form as a premise of a rule.

Now let us consider Steps 2a and 2b. These steps represent a pattern which is very common in ES5. First we evaluate some sub-expression, then we perform a `GetValue` *and* a type conversion on the result of that evaluation. In this case, we are converting to a boolean. Notice that a great deal is left implicit in the ES5 pseudo-code, which we wish to make explicit in our rules: the sub-expression or statement could diverge or throw an exception; the type conversion could diverge or throw an exception;[4] and both the sub-evaluation *and* the type conversion could have side effects on the program state. This pattern occurs so frequently that we introduced a special intermediate form to handle

[4] This is actually not the case for conversions to booleans, but it may happen in conversions to other types, such as String or Number.

red_while_1

$$\frac{\texttt{stat\_while\_1 L e1 t2 resvalue\_empty}/S/C \Downarrow_s o}{\texttt{stat\_while L e1 t2}/S/C \Downarrow_s o}$$

red_while_2b'_false

$$\frac{}{\texttt{stat\_while\_2 L e1 t2 rv (vret } S \texttt{ false)}/\_/C \Downarrow_s \texttt{out\_ter } S \texttt{ rv}}$$

red_while_2d

$$\frac{\begin{array}{l}\texttt{rv}' = \left(\begin{array}{l}\texttt{If res\_value R} \neq \texttt{resvalue\_empty} \\ \texttt{then res\_value R else rv}\end{array}\right) \\ \texttt{stat\_while\_4 L e1 t2 rv' R}/S/C \Downarrow_s o\end{array}}{\texttt{stat\_while\_3 L e1 t2 rv (out\_ter } S \texttt{ R)}/\_/C \Downarrow_s o}$$

red_while_2e_true

$$\frac{\begin{array}{l}\neg(\texttt{res\_type R} = \texttt{restype\_continue} \wedge \texttt{res\_label\_in R L}) \\ \texttt{stat\_while\_5 L e1 t2 rv R}/S/C \Downarrow_s o\end{array}}{\texttt{stat\_while\_4 L e1 t2 rv R}/S/C \Downarrow_s o}$$

red_while_2e_i_true

$$\frac{\texttt{res\_type R} = \texttt{restype\_break} \wedge \texttt{res\_label\_in R L}}{\texttt{stat\_while\_5 L e1 t2 rv R}/S/C \Downarrow_s \texttt{out\_ter } S \texttt{ rv}}$$

red_while_2e_ii_true

$$\frac{\texttt{res\_type R} \neq \texttt{restype\_normal}}{\texttt{stat\_while\_6 L e1 t2 rv R}/S/C \Downarrow_s \texttt{out\_ter } S \texttt{ R}}$$

red_while_2a_2b

$$\frac{\begin{array}{l}\texttt{spec\_expr\_get\_value\_conv spec\_to\_boolean e1}/S/C \Downarrow_i \texttt{y1} \\ \texttt{stat\_while\_2 L e1 t2 rv y1}/S/C \Downarrow_s o\end{array}}{\texttt{stat\_while\_1 L e1 t2 rv}/S/C \Downarrow_s o}$$

red_while_2b'_true_2c

$$\frac{\texttt{t2}/S/C \Downarrow_s o1 \qquad \texttt{stat\_while\_3 L e1 t2 rv o1}/S/C \Downarrow_s o}{\texttt{stat\_while\_2 L e1 t2 rv (vret } S \texttt{ true)}/\_/C \Downarrow_s o}$$

red_while_2e_false

$$\frac{\begin{array}{l}\texttt{res\_type R} = \texttt{restype\_continue} \wedge \texttt{res\_label\_in R L} \\ \texttt{stat\_while\_1 L e1 t2 rv}/S/C \Downarrow_s o\end{array}}{\texttt{stat\_while\_4 L e1 t2 rv R}/S/C \Downarrow_s o}$$

red_stat_exception

$$\frac{\begin{array}{l}\texttt{out\_of\_ext\_stat t} = \texttt{Some } o \qquad \texttt{abort } o \\ \neg(\texttt{abort\_intercepted\_stat t})\end{array}}{\texttt{t}/S/C \Downarrow_s o}$$

red_while_2e_i_false

$$\frac{\begin{array}{l}\neg(\texttt{res\_type R} = \texttt{restype\_break} \wedge \texttt{res\_label\_in R L}) \\ \texttt{stat\_while\_6 L e1 t2 rv R}/S/C \Downarrow_s o\end{array}}{\texttt{stat\_while\_5 L e1 t2 rv R}/S/C \Downarrow_s o}$$

red_while_2e_ii_false

$$\frac{\begin{array}{l}\texttt{res\_type R} = \texttt{restype\_normal} \\ \texttt{stat\_while\_1 L e1 t2 rv}/S/C \Downarrow_s o\end{array}}{\texttt{stat\_while\_6 L e1 t2 rv R}/S/C \Downarrow_s o}$$

**Figure 3.** JSCert semantics of while loops

it, while making these side effects, divergence, and exception propagation clear. The reader may see this special intermediate form at work in the rule red_while_2a_2b. Here, the intermediate form `spec_expr_get_value_conv` takes care of the evaluation of `e1`, its `GetValue`, and its type conversion. In this case, we specify which type to convert to using the flag `spec_to_boolean`. The remaining work of Step 2b is performed by rule red_while_2b'_false. Notice that since the type-conversion may have side effects, the rule red_while_2b'_false takes its initial state $S$ from the result of the type conversion as given by the intermediate form. Rule red_while_2b'_false is a terminating rule, since the corresponding ES5 step says to "return (normal, V, empty)". In our formalisation, the pseudo-code variable V corresponds to the variable `rv`. Since we do not mention a completion type, our formalism assumes the completion type "normal", and since we do not mention a label set, our formalism assumes the label set "empty". This is done in Coq using a type coercion:

```
Coercion res_normal rv := { res_type = restype_normal;
    res_value = rv; res_label = label_empty }
```

Step 2c (which corresponds to rule red_while_2b'_true_2c) follows the pretty-big-step pattern: evaluate some sub-expression or statement (in this case `t2`), and store the result in some pseudo-code variable. Each new pseudo-code variable becomes a parameter of a new intermediate form – in this case the `o1` parameter of `stat_while_3`. Notice that the rules red_while_2b'_false and red_while_2b'_true_2c both assume that the result of the type-conversion performed by rule red_while_2a_2b was successful. In the event that the type conversion diverges, or throws an exception, that "aborting computation" will be propagated by the general rule red_stat_exception[5]. We handle divergence and exceptional termination of the loop body (*Statement* in ES5 and `t2` in our formalism) in exactly the same way. The rule red_stat_exception uses the `out_of_ext_stat` function to extract the output from any intermediate form, checks that this output is an aborting one, and checks that this aborting computation should not be intercepted by a more specific rule. For example, in a while loop computation, if an exception or divergence happens in Step 2c, instead of always propagating the exception/divergence, in some cases we want to intercept it. That is, the part of the definition of `abort_intercepted_stat t` is the case where `t` can be pattern-matched with `stat_while_3 L e1 t2 rv (out_ter S R)`. In this case the value of `abort_intercepted_stat t` is:

$$\begin{array}{l}\texttt{res\_label\_in R L} \wedge \\ \left(\begin{array}{l}\texttt{res\_type R} = \texttt{restype\_continue} \vee \\ \texttt{res\_type R} = \texttt{restype\_break}\end{array}\right)\end{array}$$

This condition checks for exceptional terminations caused by `continue` and `break` statements that target the particular loop that we are currently evaluating, and should be properly handled by Step 2e (below).

Step 2d is another conditional assignment, which we handle with a condition of our own in rule red_while_2d. Notice that we insist that we will only proceed with step 2d if our previous steps terminated. This insistence is encoded in our pattern matching for `out_ter S R` — which is the result of a terminating computation. The case in which the previous computation did not terminate is handled also by the abort rule which propagates diverging results.

Step 2e begins a nested conditional expression. It is simplest to describe the "false" case first, since this results in simply looping back to the beginning of Step 2. This case is handled by rule red_while_2e_false, the first premise of which is the negation of the guard written in Fig. 1. The second premise of this rule begins the next iteration of the loop by re-using the intermediate form

[5] We have similar "aborting computation" rules for expressions, internal reductions, and full programs.

`stat_while_1`. In the "true" case, rule red_while_2e_true continues with a new intermediate form.

Step 2e(i) is another conditional expression, which we describe with two simple rules. The "true" case which describes the terminating computation breaking out of the loop corresponds to rule red_while_2e_i_true. The "false" case, which continues to step 2e(ii) corresponds to rule red_while_2e_i_false.

Finally, we come to step 2e(ii): another conditional, modelled with a pair of rules. The "abrupt completion" case, which terminates the computation corresponds to rule red_while_2e_ii_true. The "normal" case, which loops back to the beginning of Step 2 using the `stat_while_1` intermediate form corresponds to rule red_while_2e_ii_false.

It is a simple matter to express the rules given above as Coq definitions.[6] For example the rule red_while_2e_ii_false can be written in Coq as follows.

```
| red_while_2e_ii_false : ∀S C labs e1 t2 rv R o,
    res_type R = restype_normal →
    red_stat S C (stat_while_1 labs e1 t2 rv) o →
    red_stat S C (stat_while_6 labs e1 t2 rv R) o
```

***JavaScript formalisation challenges.*** The first challenge with formalising ES5 is the size of the definition. ES5 consists of 16 chapters (209 pages, plus some additional annexes) of English language and pseudo-code description. While we do not aim to formalise the parsing of concrete JavaScript syntax (most of chapters 1-7), JSCert and JSRef cover, and have a correctness proof for, all of chapters 8-14 and 16, except for the `for-in` statement (chapter 12), array initialisation (chapter 11) and some type conversions (chapter 9). See `http://www.jscert.org` for the current state of our JSCert specification, which will grow over time. We choose not to formalise `for-in` at this stage because it is loosely specified and broken: based on the ES5 standard and conversations with ES5 authors and browser implementors, we filed bugs in the current draft of the upcoming ES6 standard (bugs 1444 and 1443 of [58]). Still, it is an interesting challenge to give a more precise description of the semantics of `for-in` and we leave it for future work. Chapter 15 contains the native libraries, and would be considerable work to specify in full. We have JSCert rules and JSRef code (but no correctness proof) for those parts of chapter 15 where the libraries expose important JavaScript features.

The inductive definition of JSCert is sometimes a little verbose, as illustrated by the rules for `while`. This verbosity is due to the fact that we closely follow ES5, which is itself quite verbose, and we are being fully explicit about the evolution of the state and the context. In contrast, we shall see that the JSRef fix-point presentation is significantly more compact (§ 5). Despite its verbosity, the inductive presentation of JSCert is ideally suited to conducting formal proofs, because it gives a fine-grained view of the different steps, allowing modular reasoning about the evaluation of a given JavaScript language construct. Moreover, as we have experienced with the verification of the code of JSRef with respect to JSCert, the regularity of the pretty-big-step rules (which never have more than two evaluation premises), significantly eases the development of specialised tactics that help automate formal proofs.

The second main challenge with formalising ES5 is the high complexity of the behaviour of a few features such as the representation of scopes and variable lookup, the non-obvious representation of data attributes, the treatment of function calls and arguments object, and the aforementioned evaluation of `for-in`. Several features introduced in ES5, such as execution contexts and strict mode, are spread throughout the specification and hence are non-trivial to capture.

Finally, JavaScript "internal methods" can return types not allowed to user code, and yet may call user code. We thus had to devise a definition that was flexible, yet allowed for proofs to be automated as much as possible. The next section on JSRef illustrates how such an effort enabled us to factorise much of the presentation using a monadic approach.

***Semantics of diverging programs.*** ES5 never explicitly mentions diverging programs — a program diverges as soon as the evaluation of any subprogram diverges. Even though we have not conducted so far any formal reasoning related to divergence, we could formally capture the semantics of diverging JavaScript programs without requiring additional work. The constant `out_div`, which we introduced in the grammar of outputs $o$, materialises divergence. This constant is propagated through the evaluation rules, just as exceptions are propagated. We derive the judgement capturing the semantics of diverging programs by considering a *coinductive* interpretation (greatest fixed-point) of the exact same set of evaluation rules as we have for terminating programs. Additional details may be found in [11].

## 5. JSRef: a reference interpreter for JavaScript

Our goal in defining JSRef is to obtain an executable JavaScript interpreter, whose definition closely follows ES5 and can be proved correct with respect to JSCert. Note that JSRef does not need to be fast. It simply needs to be efficient enough to interpret programs such as those found in the JavaScript test suites.

***Host language for JSRef.*** We have chosen to write JSRef directly in Coq: that is, in a core, purely-functional language that admits only total functions. We could have chosen to use an imperative language with implicit state in the hope that this would make translating ES5 pseudo-code easier. However, this would have made the correspondence between our interpreter and our formal specification much more difficult to establish. By using Coq as a programming language, we make JavaScript's state and exception propagation explicit (which we consider an advantage), and make the formal statement and proof that our interpreter is sound comparatively straightforward, as described in § 6.

***Structure of JSRef.*** The interpreter consists of a record that contains functions for evaluating programs, statements, expressions, function calls, and so forth. The record type, slightly simplified for clarity, appears below:

```
Record runs_type : Type := runs_type_intro {
    runs_type_expr : state → execution_ctx → expr → result;
    runs_type_stat : state → execution_ctx → stat → result;
    runs_type_prog : state → execution_ctx → prog → result;
    runs_type_stat_while : state → execution_ctx → resvalue
        → label_set → expr → stat → result; ...}.
```

Since our Coq implementation must consist only of terminating functions, we bound the number of steps that JSRef may take in any given run, a standard technique in ACL2 and Coq. This is similar to decide in advance "If it hasn't finished in 30 days, I'll hit Control-C". The token `result_bottom` is the result of a computation that was interrupted in this way. In practice, it is rare to observe `result_bottom`, because we can specify a very large bound on the number of steps. We thus define our `runs` function as a fixpoint which takes an integer as an argument and returns a record of functions with the type of the record above:

[6] In our Coq development, we use a slightly different naming convention for the evaluation rules, which we believe will be easier to maintain when migrating from one version of the ECMA standard to the next. That said, for pseudo-code involving more than 5 steps, we left a comment next to each evaluation rule indicating its corresponding ES5 step number.

```
Fixpoint runs max_step : runs_type := match max_step with
 | O ⇒
  { runs_type_expr := fun S _ _ ⇒result_bottom S;
    runs_type_stat := fun S _ _ ⇒result_bottom S;
    runs_type_prog := fun S _ _ ⇒result_bottom S;
    runs_type_stat_while := fun S _ _ _ _ _ ⇒result_bottom S;
   ...}
 | S max_step' ⇒(* max_step = 1 + max_step' *)
  { runs_type_expr := fun S ⇒run_expr (runs max_step') S;
    runs_type_stat := fun S ⇒run_stat (runs max_step') S;
    runs_type_prog := fun S ⇒run_prog (runs max_step') S;
    runs_type_stat_while := fun S ⇒
      run_stat_while (runs max_step') S;
   ...}
 end.
```

Each function in the record takes the record itself as its first parameter, instantiated with one fewer step, and all recursive calls are routed through the record. For example, `run_stat runs S C s` evaluates the statement `s` in the *state* `S` (heap of objects and environment records) and in the *evaluation context* `C` (used for variable lookups), so long as the record `runs` contains functions for running any kind of term (programs, statements, expressions, etc.). As a first approximation, the reader may simply think of the projections `runs.runs_type_expr` as a direct recursive call to the function for evaluating expressions.

The function `run_javascript` below uses a record `runs` built with a sufficiently large number to serve as a bound on our recursive calls. Since the bound is handled by this record, it does not pollute our main development.

```
Definition run_javascript runs p : result :=
  runs.runs_type_prog state_init execution_ctx_init p.
```

An evaluation using a function from JSRef returns a *result*, which is either a completed computation, or a special token that states the interpreter has reached an impossible state or that the computation did not terminate in the allocated time. As with JSCert, the type of the result may depend on what is being evaluated (typically for internal reductions); we thus define the following polymorphic `resultof` type:

```
Inductive resultof T :=
| result_some : T → resultof T
| result_impossible
| result_bottom : state → resultof T.
```

The token `result_impossible` is returned by the interpreter if an invariant of the JavaScript language is violated: e.g., if the ES5 internal `GetOwnProperty` method is somehow called on a primitive value. We claim that starting from a well-formed initial state, the interpreter will never return `result_impossible` because we conjecture than all invariants are preserved by execution.

As first approximation, terminating programs have a result of type `resultof out` (as defined in § 4.2, except that `out_div` is never used), whereas internal reduction have a result of type `resultof ( specret T)` for some `T`. In fact, for purpose of better code factorisation, terminating programs have the following `result` type, which is isomorphic to `resultof out`:

```
Inductive nothing : Type :=. (* uninhabited *)
Definition result := resultof (specret nothing).
```

Since there is no inhabitant of the `nothing` type, the only way to obtain a `result_some` of the `result` type is through `specret_out`, which carries a value of type `out`. This approach guarantees that every result type is an instance of `specres T = resultof (specret T)`, greatly simplifying the definition of monadic operators.

***Monadic-style programming in JSRef.*** In order to avoid clutter, JSRef is programmed in a *monadic style*. For example, say

```
Definition if_result_some (A B : Type)
  (W : resultof A) (K : A → resultof B) : resultof B :=
  match W with
  | result_some a ⇒K a
  | result_impossible S ⇒result_impossible S
  | result_bottom S ⇒result_bottom S end.

Definition if_spec (A B : Type)
  (W : specres A) (K : state → A → specres B) : specres B :=
  if_result_some W (fun sp ⇒
    match sp with
    | specret_val S0 a ⇒K S0 a
    | specret_out o ⇒
        if_abort o (fun _ ⇒result_some (specret_out o))
    end).
```

**Figure 4.** Two JSRef monadic operators

```
Definition run_stat_while runs S C rv labs e1 t2 : result :=
  if_spec (run_expr_get_value runs S C e1) (fun S1 v1 ⇒
    Let b := convert_value_to_boolean v1 in
    if b then
      if_ter (runs.runs_type_stat S1 C t2) (fun S2 R ⇒
        Let rv' := ifb res_value R ≠resvalue_empty
                 then res_value R else rv in
        Let loop := fun _ ⇒runs.runs_type_stat_while S2 C rv'
              labs e1 t2 in
        ifb res_type R ≠restype_continue
              ∨ res_label_in R labs
        then (ifb res_type R = restype_break
                ∧ res_label_in R labs
                then res_ter S2 rv'
             else (ifb res_type R ≠restype_normal
                   then res_ter S2 R else loop tt))
        else loop tt)
    else res_ter S1 rv).

Definition run_stat runs S C t : result :=
  match t with
  | stat_while ls e1 t2 ⇒
    runs.runs_type_stat_while S C ls e1 t2 resvalue_empty ...
```

**Figure 5.** JSRef semantics of while loops

we want to evaluate a composite expression $e$ which contains subexpression $e_1$. First we evaluate $e_1$. If this evaluation terminates with a completion triple of type normal, then we want to use the value produced by $e_1$. However, if the evaluation of $e_1$ produces either `result_bottom` or `result_impossible`, we want to propagate this result immediately, without executing the rest of the code for processing $e$. In JSRef, this pattern requires a simple use of the `if_spec` monadic operator: `if_spec (runs.run_expr_get_value S C e1)(fun S' v1 → ...)`, where the "..." contains the code for processing the result value `v1` of `e1` in the updated state `S1`. Fig. 4 shows the definition of `if_spec`. It depends on `if_result_some` which first filters out the cases where the computation failed. Otherwise, the continuation `K` is called on the result. The `if_spec` function constructs such a continuation (`fun sp ⇒...`), which ensures that the result of the computation is not an abrupt termination (a result of the form `specret_out o` where `o` satisfies the predicate `abort`).

***JSRef function for while loops.*** Fig. 5 shows the function `run_stat_while` used to interpret while statements. The three first arguments have been described before. Arguments `e1` and `t2` are respectively the condition and body of the while loop. Argument `labs` is a set of labels annotating the loop (to deal with `break` and `continue` statements). Finally, `rv` is the current value to return in the completion triple. It corresponds to the $V$ of Fig. 1. Intuitively, calling this function amounts to executing the JavaScript statement `labs:while(e1){t2}` starting from heap `S` and execution context `C`. As we reuse this function for the next step of the loop, we also need to carry around the last computed value `rv`. As shown in the extract from `run_stat`, `rv` is initially set to the empty value.

We now detail the code of the loop. We first evaluate the condition `e1` and capture its result using the continuation (`fun S1 v1 ⇒...`). Remember that this continuation runs only if the result of the computation is successful and if it is not an abrupt termination. The value `v1` is then converted to a boolean to choose which branch of the `if` to execute. If it is `false`, the `else` branch is taken (Line 17), and the current state is returned alongside with the last computed value `rv` (coerced to the triple (`normal,rv',empty`)). Otherwise, the statement `t2` is evaluated using the monadic operator `if_ter`. This operator is very similar to `if_spec`, except that it applies the continuation even if the result is an abrupt termination. This allows us to check for a `break` or `continue` result from running the statement. Lines 6 and 7 update `rv` if the result value of the statement was not empty. We then inspect the termination type of the result to proceed. Line 16 is taken if it is a `continue` with its label in `labs`. Otherwise, if the result is a `break` with its label in `labs`, then the computation terminates as a normal result (Line 13). If the result is not normal (e.g., a `return` or a `break` with a different label), then it is returned as such (Line 15, then branch). Finally, if the result is normal, then the next iteration of the while loop is run (else branch).

Note how the while loop code in JSRef is more concise than that in JSCert. This observation applies in general to most parts of the definitions. Overall, the full definition of JSCert is ~3,000 lines of Coq, whereas the corresponding definition of JSRef is ~2,000 lines.

***Running the interpreter.*** The Coq system provides a way to automatically extract OCaml code from the definition of computable functions. This is crucial to our ability to run our interpreter and test it against existing test suites. There are experimental tools that allow the extraction of OCaml code directly from an inductive definition, such as the one of JSCert. We did not pursue this approach for the following reasons: these tools are not yet mature; the development of JSRef is independently interesting; and, this way, we could make natural choices when ES5 was underspecified.

At the expense of some trust, Coq provides the ability to locally override the default mapping from Coq values and types to OCaml values and types. Of course, this feature should be used sparingly. We use it in two ways. First, as previously explained, we rely on an untrusted parser. More precisely, our development assumes the existence of a parser returning either *some* AST or *none* in case of a parse error: `Axiom run_parse : string → option prog` In order to run tests and execute the `eval` operator, we provide an OCaml function that implements `run_parse` by calling an existing JavaScript parser [25] and then translating the output to the OCaml representation of our AST for JavaScript code. The second customisation regards numbers. In JavaScript, all numbers are IEEE 754 double precision floating-point numbers. In our formalisation, we use the Flocq library [40] to precisely model IEEE 754 floating-point numbers and their operations. Since the OCaml type `float` corresponds to IEEE 754, it is safe for us to extract JavaScript numbers directly to OCaml `float`. Similarly, we provide direct OCaml implementations for other operations on numbers mentioned in ES5, such as conversion to and from `Int32` types.

# 6. Evaluation: establishing trust

An important aim for us was to design JSCert and JSRef in such a way that they could be evaluated, and hence eventually trusted, by e.g., ECMA authors, implementors of JavaScript virtual machines, designers of secure subsets or compilers targeting JavaScript, and developers of JavaScript analysis tools. In this section, we describe our methodology for establishing trust, how to extend our results in future to strengthen such trust, and the bugs that we have found in ES5 and ES6, test262, and several major browsers.

Our methodology for establishing trust involves four components: the English standard ES5 and the ECMA conformance test suite, test 262, pre-existed our work; the mechanised specification, JSCert, and the certified interpreter, JSRef, are introduced in this paper. We establish connections between ES5, JSCert, JSRef and test 262, to justify our claim that JSCert and JSRef have been designed in such a way that they can be evaluated and trusted. We also explore ways of establishing further connections in future.

We have constructed JSCert to be as close as possible to ES5, and have proved JSRef correct with respect to JSCert. Independently, engineers have developed test 262 to cover as many aspects of ES5 as they reasonably could. We have been able to check that JSRef behaves as expected on all the appropriate tests, given our coverage of ES5. JSCert and JSRef can therefore be challenged through two distinct paths: through the eyeball correspondence with ES5; and through the execution of tests by our reference interpreter. Having these two *independent* paths significantly decreases the likelihood of bugs remaining in JSCert.

## 6.1 Connections to establish trust

***Eyeball closeness.*** As discussed in § 4, we have designed JSCert to be as close to ES5 as we can. We follow the ES5 data structures precisely. Every line of pseudocode in ES5 corresponds to one or two rules in JSCert, and our code is commented to make these correspondences explicit. Anyone with basic training in reading Coq specifications should be able to check the correspondence between the ES5 prose and our JSCert definitions.

We have intentionally chosen to differ from ES5 at a few places. We make explicit several constructs that are left implicit in ES5, to help with the eyeball assessment that JSCert is a correct formalisation of ES5. Unlike ES5, we treat the state, exceptions, and divergence explicitly. We always mention the current evaluation context and strictness flag, whereas ES5 only describes places where they are modified. Moreover, contrary to ES5 pseudo-code, in JSCert we do not use a "repeat" statement but rely instead on an explicit control-flow jump. We did experiment with an higher-order intermediate form to capture "repeat" loops in the inductive semantics. However, we concluded that it obfuscated the definitions and added technicalities for very limited benefit. Setting aside these differences in the style of presentation, we believe that JSCert is close enough to ES5 that (at least several) ECMA authors should be able to proof read our definitions

***Correctness.*** We have formally proved in Coq that JSRef is correct with respect to JSCert. More precisely, if the JSRef interpreter evaluates program $p$ to output $o$, in a finite number of steps bounded by $n$, then it must be the case that the program $p$ is related to the output $o$ by the inductive semantics of JSCert. More formally, the Coq statement of the theorem is

```
Theorem run_javascript_correct : ∀(n:nat) (p:prog) (o:out),
  run_javascript (runs n) p = result_some (specret_out o) →
  red_javascript p o.
```

where `red_javascript` corresponds to the evaluation judgement $\Downarrow_p$ specialised to the initial state. The proof of this theorem consists of 3500 lines of Coq and is relatively straightforward. We inspect the code of JSRef line by line, following the case analyses and the function call performed and showing that each of these operations corresponds to the application of one or two pretty-big-step evaluation rules from JSCert.

More precisely, recall from § 5 that JSRef is written in a monadic style. To step through the code of JSRef, we need to reason about the behaviour of the monadic operators. To do this, we prove, for each monadic operator, a lemma specifying its behaviour. We then define a custom Coq tactic that looks at the head monadic operator of the JSRef piece of code at hand, and automatically applies the corresponding lemma. Thanks to this tactic, we are able to automate the reasoning on the abrupt termination cases. As a result, our proof script basically consists of case analyses and calls to our custom tactic with the names of the evaluation rules to be applied given as arguments.

As we were proving correctness, we were able to detect and correct many typos, and also a small number of more serious misinterpretations of ES5. JSCert and JSRef were intentionally developed by different researchers. Despite close interaction between researchers, there were inevitable discrepancies in interpretation between JSCert and JSRef, which were picked up during the course of proving correctness. This proof is a cornerstone of our work, as it enables us directly to validate our JSCert specification with testing.

***Tests.*** We ran JSRef against test262, the ES5 conformance test suite. JSRef successfully executed all the tests that we expected it to pass, given our coverage of ES5. In test262, there are 11746 tests, organised by chapters. There are no tests for chapters 1–5. Chapters 6 and 7 relate to the parser rather than the language, chapter 15 corresponds to native libraries, and there are some additional test directories (e.g. "best practice" and "intl402") which we do not study. There are 2782 main tests associated with chapters 8–14. Our of these, we pass 1796. We have been able to check (with the help of search tools) that all the remaining tests fail because: either they use for-in; or they use chapter 15 library functionalities which we have not implemented; or they fail due to the Google Closure parser being slightly more permissive than ES5 and hence not failing where expected.

Running JSRef over thousands of tests has been very useful, as it allowed us to detect and fix several bugs in JSRef and JSCert. Most of these bugs were simple typos, but a few of them were more serious: e.g., converting a record to a data property instead of a data accessor.

### 6.2 Increasing trust in JSCert and JSRef

Since we are discussing trust, we ought to also recall that, by design, the correctness of our development relies on the formal tools, formal libraries, parsers, compilers and glue code involved in our tool chain. More precisely, trust in JSCert and JSRef requires trust in Coq, Coq's extraction mechanism, the OCaml compiler, the Google Closure parser, our glue code for linking the parser to the extracted code of JSRef, and our glue code for binding boolean and floating-point JavaScript values to their OCaml counterparts.

There are three main ways in which we may further increase our trust in JSCert and JSRef: by establishing determinacy for most of the evaluation rules for JSCert; by establishing the completeness of JSRef with respect to JSCert; and by using a code-coverage analysis of JSRef to help us complete existing test suites so as to cover all aspects of ES5. The last two correspond to the dotted arrows in the following diagram:

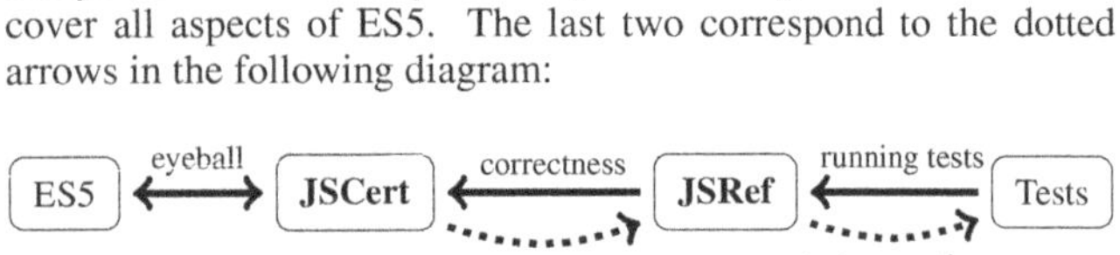


ES5 does not explicitly say that the semantics of JavaScript is deterministic. Yet, it turns out that, with the exception of the loosely-specified "for-in" statement and "implementation-dependent" constructs, the standard only describes deterministic behaviour. We should be able to prove this. Conducting such a proof would ensure that JSCert does not contain errors leading to more behaviours being accepted by JSCert than ES5. If JSCert was erroneous in this way, it could compromise e.g. the verification of tools that compile other programming languages into JavaScript. In future, we would like to prove in Coq that JSCert is deterministic. We have not attempted to do this proof yet due to a limitation of the case-analysis tactic of Coq. This tactic leads to an (unnecessary) quadratic explosion of the size of the proof-term when performing a nested case analysis on two derivations, precisely what is necessary for proving determinacy. We are waiting for the release of the new case-analysis tactic, under development, which should enable us to build proof terms of size linear in that of the proof.

We would also like to prove the completeness of JSRef with respect to JSCert. Currently, when executing a JavaScript program that terminates within a reasonable amount of time, our interpreter might, in theory, return `result_impossible` or `result_bottom` instead of the expected result. (Note that, as established by the correctness result, if JSRef produces some result then it must be the right result.) In practice, on all the tests that we considered, we never obtained `result_impossible` or `result_bottom`. This situation is very unlikely to happen because, from looking at the source code of JSRef, it appears obvious that we never return `result_bottom` except when the bound on the number of steps is reached, and it is relatively straightforward to check we would only return `result_impossible` if the invariants on the state (e.g., there are no dandling pointers) were to be broken. That said, it would be more satisfying to prove in Coq that if a program is related to some output using JSCert, then executing this program using JSRef would produce the same output. The reason we have not done it yet is because the invariants on the states involved are numerous and quite arduous to define, and because completeness is not critical to safety.

Another way to increase the trust in JSCert and JSRef would be to extend existing test suites so as to include sufficiently many tests to cover all the paths of ES5. With such full coverage, we would significantly increase the degree of confidence in the correctness of JSRef through the testing path. The ECMAScript community acknowledges that the test262 coverage needs improvement, and in fact has a long-standing open bug on the test262 bugzilla entitled "Need academic-like review of existing test coverage versus ES5.1" [23]. Using JSRef in combination with a coverage analysis tool for OCaml programs, called the *Bisect* tool [14], we have been able to visualise the lines of JSRef that are never executed by any test program. We therefore have at least some technology for investigating the coverage of JSRef, and hence of ES5 (provided that JSRef does not miss entire pieces of ES5). We need more manpower to extend test262 with the missing tests.

An alternative approach to producing tests manually would be to generate them automatically, by using automated theorem provers to exhibit tests whose execution is able to reach a particular line of JSRef code. As these tests would be generated from JSRef, they would certainly not trigger bugs in JSRef. However, if these tests were to fail on other JavaScript virtual machines, then we would know that there is either a bug in JSRef or in the virtual machines. This alternative approach to producing tests would increase our trust in JSRef, by showing that it mainly behaves like existing JavaScript implementations on tests that cover all of its source code and by highlighting where it diverges from particular implementations.

### 6.3 Bugs discovered

Through our work, we have been trying to understand and express in Coq the semantics of JavaScript, including its darkest corners. To understand the semantics intended by ECMA authors and the semantics intended by implementers of JavaScript virtual machines, we looked not only at ES5, but also at the next version of ECMAScript (ES6), at several test suites, and at the behaviour of the major browsers. We spotted bugs in all of these places, obtaining confirmation from ECMA authors and JavaScript implementers that they were indeed bugs.

In ES6, we discovered three bugs, ranging from simple typos to an "informative algorithm" which did not correctly implement the behaviour it was claiming. In test262, we discovered three bugs, the most interesting being a test which contains code that seems to do nothing and whose purpose is unknown to the current maintainers. V8 and Webkit incorrectly implement enumeration in the presence of shadowing, as used by `for-in`. This was discovered by Miller [60] and strengthened by ourselves. All browser implementations give (different) incorrect completion values for `try`...`catch` ...`finally`, also discovered in part by Bargull [60]. In addition, we observed in V8 that dead code after a `try`...`catch`...`finally` block may incorrectly change the value that is returned by the block [60].

Finding bugs in browsers, standards and industry tests was not the main motivation for the work presented here. The bugs mentioned are simply a side effect of attempting to understand ES5 well enough to build JSCert and JSRef. In future, we hope to use JSRef to construct more complete test suites, for potentially detecting unknown bugs in existing browsers.

## 7. Conclusions and future work

This paper investigates a scientific method for developing a trusted, mechanised specification of a programming language. We focused on JavaScript because the language is and will continue to be used by many people, the standards are quite mature and still evolving, and, for many applications, JavaScript programs need to be secure. There are a few key tools used to support large-scale language formalisations; see related work. We used the Coq theorem prover, because it supports large-scale mechanised proof as well as specification, and it has a well-used mechanism for extracting executable OCaml code.

We have introduced JSCert, a Coq specification of ES5, and JSRef, an executable reference interpreter which is provably correct with respect to JSCert. JSCert closely corresponds to ES5, following its natural modularity. JSRef is tested against industrial test suites. Our design methodology means that (assuming you trust Coq), if you trust either the eyeball connection to ES5 or the industrial tests, you can trust *both* JSCert and JSRef.

It remains to be seen what impact might be possible with the ECMA standards. For ES6, which is nearing the end of its development, we have filed bug reports and are having on-going discussions with some of its authors. For ES7, our work demonstrates that it might be feasible for a Coq specification to evolve at nearly the same time as the English standard. One key question is what might we be able to offer the ECMA standards. It is not our role to make key design decisions for ECMAScript. We do, however, believe that providing an official mechanised specification alongside the English prose standard would add significant value for tool developers and language analysts. Moreover, an executable reference interpreter that provably complies with the Coq specification and passes the ECMA tests can help validate language implementations or optimisations, by providing an oracle to define the expected results of new tests.

We have many future plans. To begin with, we would like to increase as much as possible the trust in our definitions, as explained in § 6, by formalising determinacy and completeness in Coq, by running additional test suites (e.g., Firefox tests), and by designing new tests towards achieving full coverage of ES5. Then, we would also like to extend our formalisation. First, it could be interesting to investigate the formalisation of parsing. Second, we may want to formalise browser-specific behaviours. Third, we would be interested in extending our work to ES6 and ES7. We are, of course, also interested in many of the practical applications of our work, as discussed in § 1.

***Acknowledgements.*** We are grateful to the POPL'14 reviewers for their insightful comments and suggestions. We would like to thank our interns Lorenz Breidenbach for help with testing and debugging, and Benjamin Farinier for his help in setting up the code coverage tool. Bodin and Schmitt are partially supported by the French ANR-10-LABX-07-01 Laboratoire d'excellence CominLabs. Filaretti and Maffeis are supported by EPSRC grant EP/I004246/1. Gardner and Smith are partially supported by EPSRC grant EP/K032089/1 and EPSRC programme grant EP/H008373. Naudziuniene is supported by an EPSRC DTA award.

## References

[1] J. Alglave, L. Maranget, S. Sarkar, and P. Sewell. Fences in weak memory models. In *Proc. CAV: 22nd International Conference on Computer Aided Verification, LNCS 6174*, pages 258–272, 2010.

[2] C. Anderson, P. Giannini, and S. Drossopoulou. Towards type inference for JavaScript. In *ECOOP'05*, pages 428–452. Springer, 2005.

[3] A. W. Appel. Verified software toolchain - (invited talk). In *ESOP*, pages 1–17, 2011.

[4] M. Batty, S. Owens, S. Sarkar, P. Sewell, and T. Weber. Mathematizing C++ concurrency. In *POPL*, pages 55–66, 2011.

[5] M. Batty, M. Dodds, and A. Gotsman. Library abstraction for C/C++ concurrency. In *POPL*, 2013.

[6] K. Bhargavan, A. Delignat-Lavaud, and S. Maffeis. Language-based defenses against untrusted browser origins. In *USENIX Security Symposium*, 2013.

[7] S. Bishop, M. Fairbairn, M. Norrish, P. Sewell, M. Smith, and K. Wansbrough. Engineering with logic: HOL specification and symbolic-evaluation testing for TCP implementations. In *POPL*, pages 55–66, 2006.

[8] S. Blazy and X. Leroy. Mechanized semantics for the Clight subset of the C language. *J. Autom. Reasoning*, 43(3):263–288, 2009.

[9] E. Börger, N. G. Fruja, V. Gervasi, and R. F. Stärk. A high-level modular definition of the semantics of C#. *Theor. Comput. Sci.*, 336 (2-3):235–284, 2005.

[10] C11. ISO/IEC 9899:2011. `http://www.iso.org/iso/iso_catalogue/catalogue_tc/catalogue_detail.htm?csnumber=57853`, 2011.

[11] A. Charguéraud. Pretty-big-step semantics. In *ESOP*, pages 41–60, 2013.

[12] R. Chugh and R. Jhala. Dependent types for JavaScript. *CoRR*, abs/1112.4106, 2011.

[13] R. Chugh, J. A. Meister, R. Jhala, and S. Lerner. Staged information flow for JavaScript. In *PLDI'09*, pages 50–62. ACM, 2009.

[14] X. Clerc. Bisect. `http://bisect.x9c.fr/`, 2012.

[15] Compcert Team. Compcert. `http://compcert.inria.fr/`, 2013.

[16] D. Crockford. ADSafe: Making JavaScript safe for advertising. `http://adsafe.org/`, 2007.

[17] S. Drossopoulou and S. Eisenbach. Is the Java type system sound? In *FOOL4*, 1997.

[18] ECMA International. Test262. `http://test262.ecmascript.org/`, 2010.

[19] C. Ellison and G. Rosu. An executable formal semantics of C with applications. In *POPL*, pages 533–544, 2012.

[20] A. Farzan, F. Chen, J. Meseguer, and G. Rosu. Formal analysis of Java programs in JavaFAN. In *CAV*, pages 501–505, 2004.

[21] C. Fournet, N. Swamy, J. Chen, P.-É. Dagand, P.-Y. Strub, and B. Livshits. Fully abstract compilation to JavaScript. In *POPL*, pages 371–384, 2013.

[22] Free Software Foundation. C language testsuites: "C-torture" version 4.4.2. http://gcc.gnu.org/onlinedocs/gccint/C-Tests.html, 2010.

[23] D. Fugate. Test262 bug 56. https://bugs.ecmascript.org/show_bug.cgi?id=56, 2011.

[24] P. Gardner, S. Maffeis, and G. D. Smith. Towards a program logic for JavaScript. In *POPL'12*, pages 31–44. ACM, 2012.

[25] Google Inc. The Closure Compiler. https://developers.google.com/closure/compiler/, 2009.

[26] S. Guarnieri and V. B. Livshits. GATEKEEPER: Mostly static enforcement of security and reliability policies for JavaScript code. In *USENIX Security Symposium*, pages 151–168, 2009.

[27] S. Guarnieri, M. Pistoia, O. Tripp, J. Dolby, S. Teilhet, and R. Berg. Saving the world wide web from vulnerable JavaScript. In *ISSTA*, pages 177–187, 2011.

[28] A. Guha, C. Saftoiu, and S. Krishnamurthi. The essence of JavaScript. *ECOOP 2010*, pages 126–150, 2010.

[29] Y. Gurevich. Evolving algebras. In *IFIP Congress (1)*, pages 423–427, 1994.

[30] D. Hedin and A. Sabelfeld. Information-flow security for a core of JavaScript. In *CSF'12*, pages 3–18. IEEE, 2012.

[31] D. Herman and C. Flanagan. Status report: specifying JavaScript with ML. In *ML*, pages 47–52, 2007.

[32] D. Jang and K. Choe. Points-to analysis for JavaScript. *Proc. of SAC '09*, page 1930, 2009.

[33] S. H. Jensen, A. Møller, and P. Thiemann. Type analysis for JavaScript. In *SAS '09*. Springer, 2009.

[34] D. K. Lee, K. Crary, and R. Harper. Towards a mechanized metatheory of Standard ML. In *POPL*, pages 173–184, 2007.

[35] S. Maffeis and A. Taly. Language-based isolation of untrusted JavaScript. In *CSF'09*. IEEE, 2009.

[36] S. Maffeis, J. Mitchell, and A. Taly. ECMA 262-3 operational semantics. http://jssec.net/semantics/, 2007.

[37] S. Maffeis, J. Mitchell, and A. Taly. An operational semantics for JavaScript. In *APLAS'08*, pages 307–325. Springer, 2008.

[38] S. Maffeis, J. Mitchell, and A. Taly. Isolating JavaScript with filters, rewriting, and wrappers. In *ESORICS'09*. Springer, 2009.

[39] S. Maffeis, J. C. Mitchell, and A. Taly. Object capabilities and isolation of untrusted web applications. In *Security and Privacy (SP)*, pages 125–140. IEEE, 2010.

[40] G. Melquiond. Floats for Coq 2.1.0. http://flocq.gforge.inria.fr/, 2012.

[41] R. Milner, M. Tofte, and D. Macqueen. *The Definition of Standard ML*. MIT Press, Cambridge, MA, USA, 1997. ISBN 0262631814.

[42] Mozilla. Mozilla automated JavaScript tests. https://developer.mozilla.org/en-US/docs/SpiderMonkey/Running_Automated_JavaScript_Tests, 2013.

[43] T. Nipkow, L. C. Paulson, and M. Wenzel. *Isabelle/HOL - A Proof Assistant for Higher-Order Logic*, volume 2283 of *Lecture Notes in Computer Science*. Springer, 2002.

[44] M. Norrish. *Formalising C in HOL*. PhD thesis, Computer Lab., University of Cambridge, 1998.

[45] D. S. P. Phung and A. Chudnov. Lightweight self protecting JavaScript. In *ASIACCS 2009*. ACM Press, 2009.

[46] C. Park, H. Lee, and S. Ryu. An empirical study on the rewritability of the with statement in JavaScript. In *FOOL*, 2011.

[47] C. Park, H. Lee, and S. Ryu. SAFE: Formal specification and implementation of a scalable analysis framewrok for ECMAscript. In *FOOL*, 2012.

[48] F. Pfenning and C. Schürmann. System description: Twelf - a meta-logical framework for deductive systems. In *CADE*, pages 202–206, 1999.

[49] J. G. Politz, S. A. Eliopoulos, A. Guha, and S. Krishnamurthi. ADsafety: Type-based verification of JavaScript sandboxing. In *USENIX Security Symposium*, 2011.

[50] J. G. Politz, M. J. Carroll, B. S. Lerner, J. Pombrio, and S. Krishnamurthi. A tested semantics for getters, setters, and eval in JavaScript. *SIGPLAN Not.*, 48(2):1–16, Oct. 2012.

[51] J. G. Politz, B. S. Lerner, H. Q. de la Vallee, T. Nelson, A. Guha, M. Carroll, and S. Krishnamurthi. Mechanized $\lambda_{JS}$. http://blog.brownplt.org/2012/06/04/lambdajs-coq.html, 2012.

[52] G. Richards, C. Hammer, B. Burg, and J. Vitek. The eval that men do - A large-scale study of the use of eval in JavaScript applications. In *ECOOP'11*, pages 52–78. Springer, 2011.

[53] G. Roşu and T. F. Şerbănuţă. An overview of the K semantic framework. *Journal of Logic and Algebraic Programming*, 79(6):397–434, 2010.

[54] T. Schneidereit. Convert some array extras to self-hosted js implementations. https://hg.mozilla.org/mozilla-central/rev/5593cd83590e, 2012.

[55] P. Sewell, F. Z. Nardelli, S. Owens, G. Peskine, T. Ridge, S. Sarkar, and R. Strnisa. Ott: Effective tool support for the working semanticist. *J. Funct. Program.*, 20(1):71–122, 2010.

[56] D. Syme. Proving Java type soundness. In *Formal Syntax and Semantics of Java*, pages 83–118, 1999.

[57] A. Taly, Ú. Erlingsson, J. C. Mitchell, M. S. Miller, and J. Nagra. Automated analysis of security-critical JavaScript APIs. In *IEEE Symposium on Security and Privacy*, pages 363–378, 2011.

[58] The JSCert Team. Mozilla Bug 862771, V8 Issue 2529, ES6 Bugs 1442-1444, Test262 Bug 1445, 1450, 1600. https://bugzilla.mozilla.org/show_bug.cgi?id=862771, http://code.google.com/p/v8/issues/detail?id=2529, https://bugs.ecmascript.org/show_bug.cgi?id={1442-1445,1450,1600}, 2013.

[59] P. Thiemann. Towards a type system for analyzing JavaScript programs. In *ESOP'05*, pages 140–140. Springer, 2005.

[60] Various developers. Bugs in ES6, Test262 and browsers. https://bugs.webkit.org/show_bug.cgi?id={38970,104309} http://code.google.com/p/v8/issues/detail?id={705,2446} https://bugzilla.mozilla.org/show_bug.cgi?id=819125, 2010–2012.

[61] J. Ševčík, V. Vafeiadis, F. Zappa Nardelli, S. Jagannathan, and P. Sewell. Relaxed-memory concurrency and verified compilation. In *Proc. POPL*, 2011.

# An Operational and Axiomatic Semantics for Non-determinism and Sequence Points in C

Robbert Krebbers *

ICIS, Radboud University Nijmegen, The Netherlands

mail@robbertkrebbers.nl

## Abstract

The C11 standard of the C programming language does not specify the execution order of expressions. Besides, to make more effective optimizations possible (*e.g.* delaying of side-effects and interleaving), it gives compilers in certain cases the freedom to use even more behaviors than just those of all execution orders.

Widely used C compilers actually exploit this freedom given by the C standard for optimizations, so it should be taken seriously in formal verification. This paper presents an operational and axiomatic semantics (based on separation logic) for non-determinism and sequence points in C. We prove soundness of our axiomatic semantics with respect to our operational semantics. This proof has been fully formalized using the Coq proof assistant.

***Categories and Subject Descriptors*** D.3.1 [*Programming Languages*]: Formal Definitions and Theory; F.3.1 [*Logics and Meanings of Programs*]: Specifying and Verifying and Reasoning about Programs

***Keywords*** Operational Semantics, Separation Logic, C Verification, Interactive Theorem Proving, Coq

## 1. Introduction

The C programming language [16, 17] is not only among the most popular programming languages in the world, but it is also among the most dangerous programming languages. Due to weak static typing and the absence of runtime checks, it is extremely easy for C programs to have bugs that make the program crash or behave badly in other ways. NULL-pointers can be dereferenced, arrays can be accessed outside their bounds, memory can be used after it is freed, *etc.* Furthermore, C programs can be developed with a too specific interpretation of the language in mind, giving portability and maintenance problems later.

Instead of forcing compilers to use a predefined execution order for expressions (*e.g.* left to right), the C standard does not specify it. This is a common cause of portability and maintenance problems, as a compiler may use an arbitrary execution order for each expression. Hence, to prove the correctness of a C program with respect to an arbitrary compiler, one has to verify that each possible execution order is legal and gives the correct result. To make more effective optimizations possible (*e.g.* delaying of side-effects and interleaving), the C standard requires the programmer to ensure that all execution orders satisfy certain conditions. If these conditions are not met, the program may do anything. Let us take a look at an example where one of those conditions is not met.

```
int main() {
  int x; int y = (x = 3) + (x = 4);
  printf("%d %d\n", x, y);
}
```

By considering all possible execution orders, one would naively expect this program to print `4 7` or `3 7`, depending on whether the assignment `x = 3` or `x = 4` is executed first. However, the *sequence point restriction* does not allow an object to be modified more than once (or being read after being modified) between two *sequence points* [16, 6.5p2]. A sequence point occurs for example at the end `;` of a full expression, before a function call, and after the first operand of the conditional `? :` operator [16, Annex C]. Hence, both execution orders lead to a sequence point violation, and are thus illegal. As a result, the execution of this program exhibits *undefined behavior*, meaning it may do literally anything.

The C standard uses a "garbage in, garbage out" principle for undefined behavior so that compilers do not have to generate (possibly expensive) runtime checks to handle corner cases. A compiler therefore does not have to generate code to test whether a sequence point violation occurs, but instead is allowed to assume no sequence point violations will occur and can use this information to perform more effective optimizations. Indeed, when compiled with `gcc -O1` (version 4.7.2), the above program prints `4 8`, which does not correspond to any of the execution orders.

Non-determinism in C is even more unrestrained than some may think. That the execution order in `e1 + e2` is unspecified, does not mean that either `e1` or `e2` will be executed entirely before the other. Instead, it means that execution can be interleaved; first a part of `e1`, then a part of `e2`, then another part of `e1`, and so on... Hence, the following expression is also allowed to print `bac`.

```
printf("a") + (printf("b") + printf("c"));
```

Many existing tools for C verification determinize the target program in one of their first phases, and let the user verify the correctness of the determinized version. When targeting a specific compiler for which the execution order is known, and which does not perform optimizations based on the sequence point restriction, this approach works. But to prove the correctness of a program with respect to an arbitrary compiler, this approach is insufficient even if all possible execution orders are considered (see the counterexample in `gcc` above).

* Part of this research has been done while the author was visiting INRIA-Paris Rocquencourt, France.



*POPL '14*, January 22–24, 2014, San Diego, CA, USA.

ACM 978-1-4503-2544-8/14/01.
http://dx.doi.org/10.1145/2535838.2535878

Some verification tools perform syntactical checks to exclude sequence points violations. However, as it is undecidable whether a sequence point violation may occur [12], determinization combined with such checks is either unsound (slides 13 and 15 of Ellison and Rosu's POPL 2012 talk [13] present some examples in existing tools), or will exclude valid C programs.

***Approach.*** As a step towards taking non-determinism and the sequence point restriction seriously in C verification, we extend the small step operational and separation logic for non-local control flow by Krebbers and Wiedijk [21] with non-deterministic expressions with side-effects and the sequence point restriction. Soundness of the axiomatic semantics is proved with respect to the operational semantics using the Coq proof assistant.

The straightforward approach to verification of programs with non-determinism is to consider all possible execution orders. However, naively this may result in a combinatorial explosion, and also it is not entirely clear how to use this approach in an axiomatic semantics that also handles the sequence point restriction. Hence, we take a different approach: we extend the axiomatic semantics with a Hoare judgment $\{P\}\, e\, \{Q\}$ for expressions. As usual, $P$ is an assertion called the precondition. Like Von Oheimb [29], we let the postcondition $Q$ be a function from values to assertions, because expressions not only have side-effects but primarily yield a value. Intuitively, the judgment $\{P\}\, e\, \{Q\}$ means that if $P$ holds for the memory beforehand, and execution of $e$ yields a value $v$, then $Q\, v$ holds for the resulting memory afterwards.

Besides partial program correctness, the judgment $\{P\}\, e\, \{Q\}$ ensures that $e$ exhibits no undefined behavior due to the sequence point restriction. To deal with the unrestrained non-determinism in C, we observe that non-determinism in expressions corresponds to a form of concurrency, which separation logic is well capable of dealing with. Inspired by the rule for the parallel composition of separation logic (see [27]), we propose the following kind of rules for each operator $\circledcirc$.

$$\frac{\{P_l\}\, e_l\, \{Q_l\} \qquad \{P_r\}\, e_r\, \{Q_r\}}{\{P_l * Q_l\}\, e_l \circledcirc e_r\, \{P_r * Q_r\}}$$

The idea is that, if the memory can be split up into two disjoint parts (using the separating conjunction $*$), in which the subexpressions $e_l$ respectively $e_r$ can be executed safely, then the full expression $e_l \circledcirc e_r$ can be executed safely in the whole memory.

The actual rules of the axiomatic semantics (see Section 5) are more complicated. We have to deal with the return value, and have to account for undefined behavior due to integer overflow. To ensure no sequence point violations occur, we use separation logic with permission accounting. Like in ordinary separation logic with permissions [6], the singleton assertion becomes $e_1 \overset{\gamma}{\mapsto} e_2$ where $\gamma$ is the permission of the object $e_2$ at address $e_1$, but we introduce a special class of *locked* permissions.

The inference rules of our axiomatic semantics are set up in such a way that reads and writes are only allowed for objects that are not locked, and moreover such that objects become locked after they have been written to. At constructs that contain a sequence point, the inference rules ensure that these locks are released. Fractional permissions [7] are used to allow memory that will not be written to be shared by multiple subexpressions.

Our approach to handling non-determinism and sequence points at the level of the operational semantics is inspired by Ellison and Rosu [12] and Norrish [25]. We annotate each object in memory with a permission, that is changed into a locked variant whenever a write occurs. This permission is changed back into the unlocked variant at the subsequent sequence point. Furthermore, we have a special state `undef` for undefined behavior that is used for example whenever a write to a locked object occurs.

To bring the operational semantics closer to our axiomatic semantics, we make locks local to the subexpression where they were created. That means, at a sequence point we only unlock objects that have been locked by that particular subexpression, instead of unlocking all objects. This modification lets some artificial programs that were legal by the C standard exhibit undefined behavior (see page 5), but is not unsound for program verification.

An important part of both the operational and axiomatic semantics is the underlying permission system. We give an abstract specification of it (as an extension of permission algebras [8]), and give various instances of this abstraction.

***Related work.*** Non-determinism, side-effects in expressions, and sequence points have been treated numerous times in formal treatments of C, but to our surprise, there is little evidence of work on program verification and program logics for these concepts.

The first formalization of a significant part of C is due to Norrish [25] using the proof assistant HOL4. An important part of his work was to accurately formalize non-determinism and sequence points as described by the C89 standard. He proved various Hoare rules for statements to facilitate reasoning about C programs. To reason about non-deterministic expressions, he proved that execution of sequence point free expressions is confluent [26]. This result is also useful for more efficient symbolic execution. Reasoning about arbitrary C expressions was left as an open problem.

Papaspyrou [30] has given a denotational semantics for a part of C89, including non-determinism and sequence points. He has implemented his semantics in Haskell to obtain a tool that can be used to explore all behaviors of a C program. Papaspyrou did not consider an axiomatic semantics.

More recently, Ellison and Rosu [12] have defined an executable semantics of the C11 standard using the $\mathbb{K}$-framework. Their semantics is very comprehensive and also describes non-determinism and the sequence point restriction. Moreover, since their semantics is effectively executable, it can be used as a debugger and an interpreter to explore all behaviors of a C program. It has been thoroughly tested against C test suites, and has been used by Regehr *et al.* to find bugs in widely used C compilers [31].

CompCert, a verified compiler C compiler by Leroy *et al.* written in Coq [23], supports non-determinism in expressions in the semantics of its source language. The interpreter by Campbell [9] can be used to explore this non-determinism. Krebbers [18] has extended CompCert's source language and interpreter with the sequence point restriction in the style of Ellison and Rosu [12].

There have been various efforts to verify programs in CompCert C. Appel and Blazy's axiomatic semantics for CompCert [2] operates on an intermediate language in which expressions have been determinized and side-effects have been removed. Their axiomatic semantics is thus limited to verification of programs compiled with CompCert, and will not work for arbitrary compilers. Herms [15] has formalized a verification condition generator based on the Why platform in Coq that can be used as a standalone tool via Coq's extraction mechanism. He proved the tool's soundness with respect to an intermediate language of CompCert, and it thus suffers from the same limitations as Appel and Blazy's work.

Black and Windley [5] have developed an axiomatic semantics for C. They define inference rules to factor out side-effects of expressions by translating these into semantically equivalent versions. Their axiomatic semantics seems rather limited, and soundness has not been proven with respect to an operational semantics.

Extending an axiomatic semantics with a judgment for expressions is not new, and has been done for example by Von Oheimb [29] for Java in the proof assistant Isabelle. His judgments for expressions are quite similar to ours, but his inference rules are not. Since he considered Java, he was able to use that the execution order of expressions is fully defined, which is not the case for C.

***Contribution.*** Our contribution is fourfold:

- We define an abstract interface for permissions on top of which the memory model is defined, and present an algebraic method to reason about disjoint memories (Section 2).
- We define a small step operational semantics that handles non-determinism and sequence points (Section 3 and 4).
- We give an axiomatic semantics that allows reasoning about programs with non-determinism. This axiomatic semantics ensures that no undefined behavior (*e.g.* sequence point violations and integer overflow) occurs (Section 5).
- We prove the soundness of our axiomatic semantics (Section 6). This proof, together with some extensions (Section 7), has been fully formalized using Coq (Section 8).

As this paper describes a large formalization effort, we often omit details and proofs. The interested reader can find all details online as part of our Coq formalization.

## 2. The memory and permissions

We model memories as finite partial functions from some countable set of *memory indices* ($b \in \mathsf{index}$) to pairs of values and permissions. A value is either indet (which is used for uninitialized memory and the return value of functions without explicit return), a bounded integer, a pointer, or a NULL-pointer. Values are untyped (apart from integer values) and intentionally kept simple to focus on the issues of the paper.

DEFINITION 2.1. *A* partial function *from $A$ to $B$ is a (total) function from $A$ to $B^{\mathsf{opt}}$, where $B^{\mathsf{opt}}$ is the* option type, *defined as containing either $\bot$ or $x$ for some $x \in B$. A partial function is called* finite *if its domain is finite. The operation $f[x := y]$ stores the value $y$ at index $x$, and $f[x := \bot]$ deletes the value at index $x$.*

DEFINITION 2.2. Integer types *and* values *are defined as:*

$$\tau \in \mathsf{inttype} ::= \mathsf{signed\ char} \mid \mathsf{unsigned\ char} \mid \mathsf{signed\ int} \mid \ldots$$
$$v \in \mathsf{val} ::= \mathsf{indet} \mid \mathsf{int}_\tau\, n \mid \mathsf{ptr}\, b \mid \mathsf{NULL}$$

*For an integer value $\mathsf{int}_\tau\, n$, the mathematical integer $n \in \mathbb{Z}$ should be within the bounds of $\tau$. A value $v$ is* true, *notation* $\mathsf{istrue}\ v$, *if it is of the shape $\mathsf{int}_\tau\, n$ with $n \neq 0$, or $\mathsf{ptr}\, b$. It is* false, *notation* $\mathsf{isfalse}\ v$, *if it is of the shape $\mathsf{int}_\tau\, 0$ or* NULL.

Notice that indet is neither true nor false, because at an actual machine uninitialized memory has arbitrary contents.

In order to abstract from a concrete choice for a permission system (no permissions, simple read/write/free permissions, fractional permissions, *etc.*) in the definition of the memory, we define an abstract interface for permissions. We organize permissions using four different *permission kinds* (pkind):

- Free, which allows all operations (read, write, free),
- Write, which allows just reading and writing,
- Read, which allows solely reading, and
- Locked, which is temporarily used to lock an object between a write to it and a subsequent sequence point.

This organization is inspired by Leroy *et al.* [24], but differs by the fact that we abstract away from a concrete implementation and allow much more complex permission systems (*e.g.* those based on fractional permissions). These are needed for our separation logic.

We define a partial order on permission kinds as the reflexive-transitive closure of $\mathsf{Read} \subseteq \mathsf{Write}$, $\mathsf{Locked} \subseteq \mathsf{Write}$ and $\mathsf{Write} \subseteq \mathsf{Free}$. Since read-only memory cannot be used for writing, and therefore cannot be locked, the kinds Locked and Read are incomparable on purpose.

DEFINITION 2.3. *A* permission system *consists of a set $P$, binary relations $\subseteq$ and $\bot$, binary operations $\cup$ and $\setminus$, and functions* $\mathsf{kind} : P \to \mathsf{pkind}$ *and* $\mathsf{lock}, \mathsf{unlock} : P \to P$, *satisfying:*

1. *$(P, \subseteq)$ is a partial order*
2. *$\bot$ is symmetric*
3. *$(P, \cup)$ is a commutative semigroup*
4. *If $x \subseteq y$, then $\mathsf{kind}\ x \subseteq \mathsf{kind}\ y$*
5. *If $x \perp y$, then $\mathsf{kind}\ x = \mathsf{Read}$*
6. *If $\mathsf{Write} \subseteq \mathsf{kind}\ x$, then $\mathsf{unlock}\ (\mathsf{lock}\ x) = x$*
7. *If $\mathsf{kind}\ x \neq \mathsf{Locked}$, then $\mathsf{unlock}\ x = x$*
8. *$\mathsf{kind}\ (\mathsf{unlock}\ x) \neq \mathsf{Locked}$*
9. *If $x \perp y$ and $x' \subseteq x$, then $x' \perp y$*
10. *If $x \cup y \perp z$, then $x \perp z$ and $x \perp y \cup z$*
11. *If $x \perp y$, then $x \subset x \cup y$*
12. *If $x \subseteq y$, then $z \cup x \subseteq z \cup y$*
13. *If $z \perp x$, $z \perp y$, and $z \cup x \subseteq z \cup y$, then $x \subseteq y$*
14. *If $x \subset y$, then $x \perp y \setminus x$ and $x \cup y \setminus x = y$*

Permission systems extend *permission algebras* by Calcagno *et al.* [8] by organizing permissions using kinds, and by having operations for locking and unlocking. Whereas $\cup$ is a partial function in a permission algebra, we require it to be a total function, and account for partiality using a relation $\perp$ to describe that two permissions are disjoint and may be joined. For permissions that are not disjoint, the result of $\cup$ is not specified in the definition of a permission system. This relieves us from dealing with partial functions in Coq. Lastly, we require $\setminus$ to be a primitive so we can lift it to an operation on memories (see Definition 2.9) that is an actual Coq function.

Dockins *et al.* [11] remedy the issue of partially by defining $\cup$ as a relation instead of a function. But as for the operation $\setminus$, we prefer to use functions to ease reasoning about memories.

Rule 5 ensures that only permissions whose kind is Read are disjoint. This is to ensure that only readable parts of disjoint memories may overlap.

Before we define memories, we define three instances of permission systems. We begin with fractional permissions [7].

DEFINITION 2.4. Fractional permissions *($z \in \mathsf{frac}$) are rational numbers within $(0, 1]$. We let $z_1 \subseteq z_2$ iff $z_1 \leq z_2$, and $z_1 \perp z_2$ iff $z_1 + z_2 \leq 1$. The operations are defined as:*

$$z_1 \cup z_2 := \begin{cases} z_1 + z_2 & \text{if } z_1 + z_2 \leq 1 \\ 1 & \text{otherwise} \end{cases} \qquad \mathsf{kind}\ z := \begin{cases} \mathsf{Write} & \text{if } z = 1 \\ \mathsf{Read} & \text{otherwise} \end{cases}$$

$$z_1 \setminus z_2 := \begin{cases} z_1 - z_2 & \text{if } 0 < z_1 - z_2 \\ 1 & \text{otherwise} \end{cases} \qquad \mathsf{lock}\ z := \mathsf{unlock}\ z := z$$

Notice that in the above definition we yield the dummy value 1 for $z_1 \cup z_2$ if $z_1 \not\perp z_2$, and $z_1 \setminus z_2$ if $z_2 \not\subseteq z_1$.

To account for locks due to the sequence point restriction, we extend fractional permissions with a special permission Seq.

DEFINITION 2.5. Sequenceable permissions *are defined as:*

$$\gamma_s \in \mathsf{seqfrac} ::= \mathsf{Seq} \mid \mathsf{UnSeq}\ z$$

*Disjointness $\perp$ is inductively defined as:*

1. *if $z_1 \perp z_2$ then $\mathsf{UnSeq}\ z_1 \perp \mathsf{UnSeq}\ z_2$*

*The order $\subseteq$ is inductively defined as:*

1. $\mathsf{Seq} \subseteq \mathsf{Seq}$
2. *if $z_1 \subseteq z_2$, then $\mathsf{UnSeq}\ z_1 \subseteq \mathsf{UnSeq}\ z_2$*

*The operations $\cup$ and $\setminus$ are defined point-wise, and:*

$$\begin{array}{ll} \mathsf{kind\ Seq} := \mathsf{Locked} & \mathsf{kind}\ (\mathsf{UnSeq}\ z) := \mathsf{kind}\ z \\ \mathsf{lock\ Seq} := \mathsf{Seq} & \mathsf{lock}\ (\mathsf{UnSeq}\ z) := \mathsf{Seq} \\ \mathsf{unlock\ Seq} := \mathsf{UnSeq}\ 1 & \mathsf{unlock}\ (\mathsf{UnSeq}\ z) := \mathsf{UnSeq}\ z \end{array}$$

We extend sequenceable permissions to account for some subtleties of C. First of all, we need to deal with objects that are declared using the `const` qualifier (those are read-only). Secondly, whereas dynamically allocated memory obtained via `alloc` can be freed manually using `free`, memory of block scope variables cannot be freed using `free`. Freeing it should therefore be prohibited by the permission system.

DEFINITION 2.6. Full permissions *are defined as:*

$$\gamma \in \mathsf{perm} ::= \mathsf{Freeable}\ \gamma_s \mid \mathsf{Writable}\ \gamma_s \mid \mathsf{ReadOnly}\ z$$

*Here, all relations and operations are defined point-wise by lifting those on fractional and sequenceable permissions. We use the abbreviations* F, W *and* R *for the permissions* Freeable (UnSeq 1), Writable (UnSeq 1) *and* ReadOnly 1*, respectively.*

Given an arbitrary permission system with carrier $P$, the definition of the memory is now straightforward.

DEFINITION 2.7. Memories *($m \in \mathsf{mem}$) are finite partial functions from memory indices to pairs $(v, x)$ with $v \in \mathsf{val}$ and $x \in P$.*

First we define the operations that are used by the operational semantics (Section 4) to interact with the memory.

DEFINITION 2.8. *The* memory operations *are defined as:*

$$\mathsf{perm}\ b\ m := \begin{cases} x & \text{if } m\,b = (v,\,x) \\ \bot & \text{otherwise} \end{cases}$$

$$m\ !!\ b := \begin{cases} v & \text{if } m\,b = (v,\,x) \text{ and } \mathsf{kind}\ x \neq \mathsf{Locked} \\ \bot & \text{otherwise} \end{cases}$$

$$m[b := v] := \begin{cases} m[b := (v,\,x)] & \text{if } m\,b = (v',\,x) \\ m & \text{otherwise} \end{cases}$$

$$\mathsf{alloc}\ b\ v\ x\ m := m[b := (v,\,x)]$$

$$\mathsf{free}\ b\ m := m[b := \bot]$$

$$\mathsf{locks}\ m := \{b \mid m\,b = (v,\,x) \wedge \mathsf{kind}\ x = \mathsf{Locked}\}$$

$$\mathsf{lock}\ b\ m := \begin{cases} m[b := (v,\,\mathsf{lock}\ x)] & \text{if } m\,b = (v,\,x) \\ m & \text{otherwise} \end{cases}$$

$$\mathsf{unlock}\ \Omega\ m := \{(b, (v, \mathsf{unlock}\ x)) \mid b \in \Omega \wedge m\,b = (v,\,x)\} \cup \{(b, (v, x)) \mid b \notin \Omega \wedge m\,b = (v,\,x)\}$$

*Here, we have* $\Omega \subseteq_{\mathsf{fin}} \mathsf{index}$.

The function perm is used to obtain the permission of an object. Allocation alloc $b\ v\ x\ m$ of an object with value $v$ and permission $x$ should only be used with unused indices $b$ in $m$ (*i.e.* with perm $b\ m = \bot$). Likewise, a store $\_[\_ := \_]$ and deallocation using free, should only be used when the permissions are appropriate. We will take care of these side-conditionals in the rules of the operational semantics. Next, we define the memory operations that are used by the axiomatic semantics (Section 5).

DEFINITION 2.9. *The* separation memory relations *are defined as:*

- *We let $m_1 \perp m_2$ iff for all $b$, $v_1$, $x_1$, $v_2$ and $x_2$ with $m_1\,b = (v_1,\,x_2)$ and $m_2\,b = (v_2,\,x_2)$ we have $v_1 = v_2$ and $x_1 \perp x_2$.*
- *We let $m_1 \subseteq m_2$ iff for all $b$, $v_1$ and $x_1$ with $m_1\,b = (v,\,x_1)$ there exists an $x_2 \subseteq x_1$ with $m_2\,b = (v,\,x_2)$.*

*The* separation memory operations *are defined as:*

$$\begin{aligned} m_1 \cup m_2 := {} & \{(b, (v_1, x_1 \cup x_2)) \mid m_1\,b = (v_1,\,x_1) \wedge m_2\,b = (v_2,\,x_2)\} \\ & \cup \{(b, (v_1, x_1)) \mid m_1\,b = (v_1,\,x_1) \wedge m_2\,b = \bot\} \\ & \cup \{(b, (v_2, x_2)) \mid m_1\,b = \bot \wedge m_2\,b = (v_2,\,x_2)\} \end{aligned}$$

$$\begin{aligned} m_1 \setminus m_2 := {} & \{(b, (v_1, x_1 \setminus x_2)) \mid m_1\,b = (v_1,\,x_1) \wedge m_2\,b = (v_2,\,x_2) \wedge x_2 \subset x_1\} \\ & \cup \{(b, (v_1, x_1)) \mid m_1\,b = (v_1,\,x_1) \wedge m_2\,b = \bot\} \end{aligned}$$

The union $\cup$ and empty memory $\emptyset$ form a monoid that is commutative and cancellative for disjoint memories.

For the soundness proof of our axiomatic semantics (Section 6) we often need to reason about preservation of disjointness under memory operations. To ease that kind of reasoning, we define a relation $\vec{m}_1 \equiv_\perp \vec{m}_2$ that describes that the memories $\vec{m}_1$ and $\vec{m}_2$ behave equivalently with respect to disjointness.

DEFINITION 2.10. Disjointness of a list of memories $\vec{m}$, *notation* $\perp \vec{m}$*, is inductively defined as:*

1. $\perp [\,]$
2. *If* $m \perp \bigcup \vec{m}$ *and* $\perp \vec{m}$*, then* $\perp (m :: \vec{m})$

Notice that $\perp \vec{m}$ is stronger than merely having $m_i \perp m_j$ for each $i \neq j$. For example, using fractional permissions, we do not have $\perp [\{(b, (v, 0.5))\}, \{(b, (v, 0.5))\}, \{(b, (v, 0.5))\}]$, whereas we clearly do have $\{(b, (v, 0.5))\} \perp \{(b, (v, 0.5))\}$.

DEFINITION 2.11. Equivalence of $\vec{m}_1$ and $\vec{m}_2$ with respect to disjointness, *notation* $\vec{m}_1 \equiv_\perp \vec{m}_2$*, is defined as:*

$$\vec{m}_1 \leq_\perp \vec{m}_2 := \forall m\,.\perp (m :: \vec{m}_1) \to \perp (m :: \vec{m}_2)$$

$$\vec{m}_1 \equiv_\perp \vec{m}_2 := \vec{m}_1 \leq_\perp \vec{m}_2 \wedge \vec{m}_2 \leq_\perp \vec{m}_1$$

It is straightforward to show that $\leq_\perp$ is reflexive and transitive, being respected by concatenation of sequences, and is being preserved by list containment. Hence, $\equiv_\perp$ is an equivalence relation, a congruence with respect to concatenation of sequences, and also being preserved by permutations. The following results allow us to reason algebraically about disjoint memories.

FACT 2.12. *If* $\vec{m}_1 \leq_\perp \vec{m}_2$ *and* $\perp \vec{m}_1$*, then* $\perp \vec{m}_2$*.*

THEOREM 2.13. *We have the following algebraic properties:*

1. $\emptyset :: \vec{m} \equiv_\perp \vec{m}$
2. $(m_1 \cup m_2) :: \vec{m} \equiv_\perp m_1 :: m_2 :: \vec{m}$ *provided that* $m_1 \perp m_2$
3. $\bigcup \vec{m}_1 :: \vec{m}_2 \equiv_\perp \vec{m}_1 +\!\!+ \vec{m}_2$ *provided that* $\perp \vec{m}_1$
4. $m[b := v] :: \vec{m} \equiv_\perp m :: \vec{m}$ *provided that* perm $b\ m = x$ *for some $x$ that is not a fragment*
5. $\{(b, (v_1, x))\} :: \vec{m} \equiv_\perp \{(b, (v_2, x))\} :: \vec{m}$ *provided $x$ is not a fragment*
6. $m_2 :: \vec{m} \equiv_\perp m_1 :: (m_2 \setminus m_1) :: \vec{m}$ *provided that* $m_1 \subseteq m_2$
7. $m :: \vec{m} \leq_\perp \mathsf{lock}\ b\ m :: \vec{m}$ *provided that* perm $b\ m = x$ *for some $x$ that is not a fragment*
8. $m :: \vec{m} \leq_\perp \mathsf{unlock}\ \Omega\ m :: \vec{m}$

*Here, a permission $x$ is a* fragment *if there is a $y$ such that $x \perp y$.*

## 3. The language

In this section we define the syntax of expressions and statements.

DEFINITION 3.1. Expressions *are defined as:*

$$\circledcirc \in \mathsf{binop} ::= \texttt{==} \mid \texttt{<=} \mid \texttt{+} \mid \texttt{-} \mid \texttt{*} \mid \texttt{/} \mid \texttt{\%} \mid \ldots$$

$$e \in \mathsf{expr} ::= x_i \mid [v]_\Omega \mid e_1 := e_2 \mid f(\vec{e}) \mid \texttt{load}\ e \mid \texttt{alloc} \mid \texttt{free}\ e \mid e_1 \circledcirc e_2 \mid e_1\ ?\ e_2 : e_3 \mid (\tau)\,e$$

*Instead of* $[v]_\emptyset$*, we just write* $v$*.*

Expressions may contain side-effects: assignments $e_1 := e_2$, function calls $f(\vec{e})$, and allocation `alloc` and deallocation `free` $e$ of dynamic memory. Unary operators, prefix and postfix increment and decrement, assignment operators, and the comma operator, are omitted in this paper, but are included in the Coq formalization. The logical operators are defined in terms of the conditional.

Values $[v]_\Omega$ are annotated with a finite set $\Omega$ of *locked* memory indices. This set is initially empty, but whenever a write is performed, the written object is locked in memory and its memory index is added to $\Omega$ (see Section 4). Whenever a sequence point occurs, the locked objects in $\Omega$ will be unlocked in memory. The operation $\mathsf{locks}\ e$ collects the annotated locks in $e$.

*Stacks* ($\rho \in \mathsf{stack}$) are lists of memory indices. Variables are De Bruijn indices, *i.e.* the variable $x_i$ refers to the $i$th memory index on the stack. De Bruijn indices avoid us from having to deal with shadowing due to block scope variables. Especially in the axiomatic semantics this is useful, as we do not want to lose information by a local variable shadowing an already existing one. The stack contains references to the value of each variable instead of the values itself so as to treat pointers to both local and allocated storage in a uniform way. Execution of a variable $x_i$ thus consists of looking up its address $b$ at position $i$ in the stack, and returning a pointer $\mathsf{ptr}\, b$ to that address. Execution of `load` $e$ consists of evaluating $e$ to $\mathsf{ptr}\, b$ and looking up $b$ in the memory.

DEFINITION 3.2. Statements *are defined as:*

$$s \in \mathsf{stmt} ::= e \mid \texttt{skip} \mid \texttt{goto}\ l \mid \texttt{return}\ e \mid \texttt{block}\ c\ s \mid s_1\, ; s_2$$
$$\mid l : s \mid \texttt{while}(e)\ s \mid \texttt{if}\ (e)\ s_1\ \texttt{else}\ s_2$$

The statement syntax is adapted from Krebbers and Wiedijk [21], but we treat assignments and function calls as expression constructs instead of statements constructs. Hence, assignments and function calls can be nested, and can occur in the expressions of a return, while, and conditional statement.

The construct `block` $c\ s$ opens a block scope with one local variable, where the boolean $c$ specifies whether the variable is `const`-qualified or not. The permission $\mathsf{blockperm}\ c$ is defined as: $\mathsf{blockperm\ True} := \mathsf{R}$ and $\mathsf{blockperm\ False} := \mathsf{W}$. Since we use De Bruijn indices, the construct `block` $c\ s$ is nameless.

## 4. Operational semantics

We define the semantics of expressions and statements by a small step operational semantics. That means, computation is defined by the reflexive transitive closure of a reduction relation $\twoheadrightarrow$ on *program states*. To define this reduction, we first define head reduction of expressions, and then use *evaluation contexts* (as introduced by Felleisen *et al.* [14]) to define reduction of whole programs. In the remainder of this paper, we will use a memory instantiated with full permissions (Definition 2.6).

DEFINITION 4.1. *Given a stack $\rho$,* head reduction *of expressions* $(e_1, m_1) \twoheadrightarrow_{\mathsf{h}} (e_2, m_2)$ *is inductively defined as:*

1. $(x_i, m) \twoheadrightarrow_{\mathsf{h}} (\mathsf{ptr}\, b, m)$, *in case* $\rho\, i = b$
2. $([\mathsf{ptr}\, b]_{\Omega_1} := [v]_{\Omega_2}, m) \twoheadrightarrow_{\mathsf{h}} ([v]_{\{b\}\cup\Omega_1\cup\Omega_2}, \mathsf{lock}\ b\ (m[b{:=}v]))$, *in case* $\mathsf{perm}\ b\ m = \gamma$ *and* $\mathsf{Write} \subseteq \mathsf{kind}\ \gamma$
3. $(\texttt{load}\ [\mathsf{ptr}\, b]_\Omega, m) \twoheadrightarrow_{\mathsf{h}} ([v]_\Omega, m)$, *for any* $v$ *with* $m\ !!\ b = v$
4. $(\texttt{alloc}, m) \twoheadrightarrow_{\mathsf{h}} (\mathsf{ptr}\, b, \mathsf{alloc}\ b\ \mathsf{indet\ F}\ m)$, *for any* $b$ *with* $\mathsf{perm}\ b\ m = \bot$
5. $(\texttt{free}\ [\mathsf{ptr}\, b]_\Omega, m) \twoheadrightarrow_{\mathsf{h}} ([\mathsf{indet}]_\Omega, \mathsf{free}\ b\ m)$, *in case* $\mathsf{perm}\ b\ m = \gamma$ *and* $\mathsf{kind}\ \gamma = \mathsf{Free}$
6. $([v_1]_{\Omega_1} \circledcirc [v_2]_{\Omega_2}, m) \twoheadrightarrow_{\mathsf{h}} ([v']_{\Omega_1\cup\Omega_2}, m)$, *in case* $v_1 \circledcirc v_2 = v'$
7. $([v]_\Omega\ ?\ e_2 : e_3, m) \twoheadrightarrow_{\mathsf{h}} (e_2, \mathsf{unlock}\ \Omega\ m)$, *in case* $\mathsf{istrue}\ v$
8. $([v]_\Omega\ ?\ e_2 : e_3, m) \twoheadrightarrow_{\mathsf{h}} (e_3, \mathsf{unlock}\ \Omega\ m)$, *in case* $\mathsf{isfalse}\ v$
9. $((\tau)\ [v]_\Omega, m) \twoheadrightarrow_{\mathsf{h}} ([v']_\Omega, m)$, *in case* $(\tau)\, v = v'$

*If the stack $\rho$ is not clear from the context, we write* $\rho \vdash (e_1, m_1) \twoheadrightarrow_{\mathsf{h}} (e_2, m_2)$. *Note that picking an unused index for allocation in Rule 4 is non-deterministic.*

In Rules 6 and 9, $v_1 \circledcirc v_2$ and $(\tau)\, v$ are partial functions that evaluate a binary operation on values and integer cast on values respectively. These functions fail in case of integer overflow, or if an operation is used wrongly (*e.g.* division by zero).

An assignment $[\mathsf{ptr}\, b]_{\Omega_1} := [v]_{\Omega_2}$ (Rule 2) not only stores the value $v$ at index $b$, but also locks $b$ in the memory. Locking $b$ enforces the sequence point restriction, because consecutive reads and writes to $b$ will fail (as ensured by the side-condition of the assignment rule, and Definition 2.8 of the $\_\ !!\ \_$ operation). In order to keep track of the lock of $b$, we add $b$ to the set $\{b\}\cup\Omega_1\cup\Omega_2$. Rules 7 and 8 for the conditional $[v]_\Omega\ ?\ e_2 : e_3$ model a sequence point by unlocking the indices $\Omega$ in the memory, making future reads and writes possible again. Other constructs with a sequence point will be given a similar semantics (see Definition 4.10).

Like Ellison and Rosu [12], we implicitly use non-determinism to capture undefined behavior due to sequence point violations. For example, in `x + (x = 10)` only one execution order (performing the read after the assignment) leads to a sequence point violation. In Norrish's semantics [25] both execution orders lead to a sequence point violation as he also keeps track of reads.

Our treatment of sequence points assigns undefined behavior to more programs than the C standard, and Ellison and Rosu do. Ellison and Rosu release the locks of all objects at a sequence point, whereas we just release the locks that have been created by the subexpression where the sequence point occurred. For example, we assign undefined behavior to the following program of Ellison.

```
int x, y, *p = &y;
int f() { if (x) { p = &x; } return 0; }
int main() {
  return (x = 1) + (*p = 2) + f();
}
```

The execution order that leads to undefined behavior is (a) `x = 1`, (b) call `f` which changes `p` to `&x`, (c) `*p = 2`. Here, the lock of `&x` survives the function call. In the semantics of Ellison and Rosu, this program has defined behavior, as the sequence point before the function call releases all locks, so also the lock of `&x`.

We believe that this is a reasonable trade-off, because dealing with sequence points *locally* instead of *globally* brings the operational semantics closer to the axiomatic semantics as separation logic only talks about a local part of the memory. We believe only artificial programs become illegal, because different function calls in the same expression can still write to a shared part of the memory (which is useful for memoization). For example, given

```
int f(int y) {
  static int map[MAP_SIZE];
  if (map[y]) { return map[y]; }
  return map[y] = expensive_function(y);
}
```

the expression `f(3) + f(3)` has defined behavior according to our semantics of sequence points.

Since the C standard does not allow interleaved execution of function calls [16, 6.5.2.2p10], these are not described by the head reduction $\twoheadrightarrow_{\mathsf{h}}$. Instead, a function call changes the whole program state to a state in which its body is executed. When execution of the function body is finished, the result will be plugged back into the whole expression. To describe this behavior, and to select a head redex in an expression, we define *expression contexts*.

DEFINITION 4.2. Singular expression contexts *are defined as:*

$$\mathcal{E}_{\mathsf{s}} \in \mathsf{ectx_s} ::= \square := e \mid e := \square \mid f(\vec{e}_1, \square, \vec{e}_2) \mid \texttt{load}\ \square \mid \texttt{free}\ \square$$
$$\mid \square \circledcirc e_2 \mid e_1 \circledcirc \square \mid \square\ ?\ e_2 : e_3 \mid (\tau)\, \square$$

Expression contexts *($\mathcal{E} \in$ ectx) are lists of singular contexts. Given an expression context $\mathcal{E}$ and an expression e, the* substitution of $e$ for $\square$ in $\mathcal{E}$, *notation* $\mathcal{E}[\,e\,]$, *is defined as usual.*

In the reduction of whole programs (Definition 4.10), we allow $\mathcal{E}[\,e_1\,]$ to reduce to $\mathcal{E}[\,e_2\,]$ provided that $(e_1, m_1) \twoheadrightarrow_{\mathsf{h}} (e_2, m_2)$. To enforce that the first operand of the conditional $e_1\ ?\ e_2 : e_3$ is executed entirely before the others, it is essential that we omit the contexts $e_1\ ?\ \square : e_3$ and $e_1\ ?\ e_2 : \square$.

The reduction of whole programs uses a *zipper*-like data structure, called a *program context* [21], to store the location of the substatement that is being executed. Execution of the program occurs by traversal through the program context in the direction *down* $\searrow$, *up* $\nearrow$, *jump* $\curvearrowright$, or *top* $\Uparrow$. When a `goto` $l$ statement is executed, the direction is changed to $\curvearrowright l$, and the semantics performs a small step traversal through the program context until the label $l$ has been reached. Program contexts extend the zipper by annotating each block scope variable with its associated memory index, and furthermore contain the full call stack of the program.

Program contexts can also be seen as a generalization of continuations (as for example being used in CompCert [2, 23]). However, there are some notable differences.

- Program contexts implicitly contain the stack, whereas a continuation semantics typically stores the stack separately.
- Program contexts also contain the part of the program that has been executed, whereas continuations only contain the part that remains to be done.
- Since the complete program is preserved, looping constructs like the while statement do not have to duplicate code.

The fact that program contexts do not throw away the parts of the statement that have been executed is essential for the treatment of goto. Upon an invocation of a goto, the semantics traverses through the program context until the corresponding label has been found. During this traversal it passes all block scope variables that go out of scope, allowing it to perform required allocations and deallocations in a natural way. Hence, the point of this traversal is not so much to *search* for the label, but much more to incrementally *calculate* the required allocations and deallocations.

DEFINITION 4.3. Singular statement contexts *are defined as:*

$$\begin{aligned}\mathcal{S}_{\mathsf{s}} \in \mathsf{sctx_s} ::= {} & \square\,;s_2 \mid s_1\,;\square \mid l : \square \mid \mathtt{while}(e)\ \square \\ & \mid \mathtt{if}\ (e)\ \square\ \mathtt{else}\ s_2 \mid \mathtt{if}\ (e)\ s_1\ \mathtt{else}\ \square\end{aligned}$$

*Given a singular statement context $\mathcal{S}_{\mathsf{s}}$ and a statement s,* substitution of $s$ for $\square$ in $\mathcal{S}_{\mathsf{s}}$, *notation* $\mathcal{S}_{\mathsf{s}}[\,s\,]$, *is defined as usual.*

A pair $(\vec{\mathcal{S}_{\mathsf{s}}},\ s)$ consisting of a list $\vec{\mathcal{S}_{\mathsf{s}}}$ of singular statement contexts and a statement $s$ forms a zipper for statements without block scope variables. That means, $\vec{\mathcal{S}_{\mathsf{s}}}$ is a statement turned inside-out that represents a path from the focused substatement $s$ to the top of the whole statement.

DEFINITION 4.4. Expression statement contexts *and* singular program contexts *are defined as:*

$$\mathcal{S}_{\mathsf{e}} \in \mathsf{sctx_e} ::= \square \mid \mathtt{return}\ \square \mid \mathtt{while}(\square)\ s \mid \mathtt{if}\ (\square)\ s_1\ \mathtt{else}\ s_2$$

$$\mathcal{P}_{\mathsf{s}} \in \mathsf{ctx_s} ::= \mathcal{S}_{\mathsf{s}} \mid \mathtt{block}_b\ c\ \square \mid (\mathcal{S}_{\mathsf{e}}, e) \mid \mathsf{resume}\ \mathcal{E} \mid \mathsf{params}\ \vec{b}$$

Program contexts *($k \in$ ctx) are lists of singular program contexts. Given an expression statement context $\mathcal{S}_{\mathsf{e}}$ and an expression e,* substitution of $e$ for $\square$ in $\mathcal{S}_{\mathsf{e}}$, *notation* $\mathcal{S}_{\mathsf{e}}[\,e\,]$, *is defined as usual.*

The previously defined program contexts will be used as follows in the operational semantics.

- When entering a block scope `block` $c\ s$, the singular context $\mathtt{block}_b\ c\ \square$ is appended to the head of the program context. It associates the block scope with its memory index $b$.
- When executing a statement construct $\mathcal{S}_{\mathsf{e}}[\,e\,]$ that contains an expression $e$, the singular context $(\mathcal{S}_{\mathsf{e}}, e)$ is appended to the head of the program context to keep track of the statement. We need to keep track of the expression $e$ as well so that it can be restored when execution of the expression is finished.
- When executing a function call $\mathcal{E}[\,f(\vec{v})\,]$, the singular context resume $\mathcal{E}$ is appended to the head of the program context. When the function returns with value $v$, execution of the expression $\mathcal{E}[\,v\,]$ with the return value $v$ plugged in, is continued.
- When a function body is entered, the singular context params $\vec{b}$ is appended to the head of the program context. It contains a list $\vec{b}$ of memory indices of the function parameters.

As program contexts implicitly contain the stack, we define a function to extract it from them.

DEFINITION 4.5. *The* corresponding stack $\mathsf{getstack}\,k$ *of a program context k is defined as:*

$$\begin{aligned}\mathsf{getstack}\,(\mathcal{S}_{\mathsf{s}} :: k) &:= \mathsf{getstack}\,k\\ \mathsf{getstack}\,(\mathtt{block}_b\ c\ \square :: k) &:= b :: \mathsf{getstack}\,k\\ \mathsf{getstack}\,((\mathcal{S}_{\mathsf{e}}, e) :: k) &:= \mathsf{getstack}\,k\\ \mathsf{getstack}\,(\mathsf{resume}\ \mathcal{E} :: k) &:= [\,]\\ \mathsf{getstack}\,(\mathsf{params}\ \vec{b} :: k) &:= \vec{b} \mathbin{+\!\!+} \mathsf{getstack}\,k\end{aligned}$$

We define $\mathsf{getstack}\,(\mathsf{resume}\ \mathcal{E} :: k)$ as $[\,]$ instead of $\mathsf{getstack}\,k$, as otherwise it would be possible to refer to the local variables of the calling function.

DEFINITION 4.6. Directions, focuses *and* program states *are defined as:*

$$\begin{aligned}d \in \mathsf{direction} &::= \searrow \mid \nearrow \mid \curvearrowright l \mid \Uparrow v\\ \phi \in \mathsf{focus} &::= (d,\ s) \mid e \mid \overline{\mathsf{call}\,f\,\vec{v}} \mid \overline{\mathsf{return}\,v} \mid \overline{\mathsf{undef}}\\ S \in \mathsf{state} &::= \mathbf{S}(k,\ \phi,\ m)\end{aligned}$$

A program state $\mathbf{S}(k,\ \phi,\ m)$ consists of a program context $k$, the part of the program $\phi$ that is focused, and the memory $m$. Similar to Leroy's Cmedium [23], we have five kinds of states:

- $(d,\ s)$ for execution of a statement $s$ in direction $d$,
- $e$ for execution of an expression $e$,
- $\overline{\mathsf{call}\,f\,\vec{v}}$ for calling a function $f$ with arguments $v$,
- $\overline{\mathsf{return}}\ v$ for returning from a function with return value $v$, and
- $\overline{\mathsf{undef}}$ to capture undefined behavior.

We have additional states for execution of expressions and undefined behavior. The semantics of Leroy's Cminor [22], and the semantics of Krebbers and Wiedijk [21], do not have such states, because their expressions are deterministic and side-effect free. They capture undefined behavior by letting the reduction get stuck, whereas that will not work in the presence of non-determinism.

DEFINITION 4.7. *The relation* $\mathsf{allocparams}\ \gamma\ m_1\ \vec{b}\ \vec{v}\ m_2$ allocates fresh blocks $\vec{b}$ for function parameters $\vec{v}$ *with permission* $\gamma$ *(non-deterministically). It is inductively defined as:*

1. $\mathsf{allocparams}\ \gamma\ m\ [\,]\ [\,]\ m$
2. *If* $\mathsf{allocparams}\ \gamma\ m_1\ \vec{b}\ \vec{v}\ m_2$ *and* $\mathsf{perm}\ b\ m_2 = \bot$, *then* $\mathsf{allocparams}\ \gamma\ m_1\ (b :: \vec{b})\ (v :: \vec{v})\ (\mathsf{alloc}\ b\ v\ \gamma\ m_2)$

DEFINITION 4.8. *An expression is a* redex *if it is of the following shape: (a)* $x_i$, *(b)* $[v_1]_{\Omega_1} := [v_2]_{\Omega_2}$, *(c)* $f([v_1]_{\Omega_1}, \dots, [v_2]_{\Omega_2})$, *(d)* $\texttt{load}\ [v]_\Omega$, *(e)* $\texttt{alloc}$ *(f)* $\texttt{free}\ [v]_\Omega$, *(g)* $[v_1]_{\Omega_1} \circledcirc [v_2]_{\Omega_2}$, *(h)* $[v]_\Omega\ ?\ e_2 : e_3$, *or (i)* $(\tau)\ [v]_\Omega$.

DEFINITION 4.9. *An expression is* safe *in stack* $\rho$ *and memory* $m$ *if: (a) it is of the shape* $f(\vec{e})$, *or (b) there is an expression* $e'$ *and memory* $m'$ *such that* $\rho \vdash (e, m) \to_{\mathsf{h}} (e', m')$.

DEFINITION 4.10. *Given a finite partial function* $\delta$ *mapping function names to statements, the* small step reduction $S_1 \to S_2$ *is inductively defined as:*

1. For simple statements:
   - *(a)* $\mathbf{S}(k,\ (\searrow,\ \texttt{skip}),\ m) \to \mathbf{S}(k,\ (\nearrow,\ \texttt{skip}),\ m)$
   - *(b)* $\mathbf{S}(k,\ (\searrow,\ \texttt{goto}\ l),\ m) \to \mathbf{S}(k,\ (\curvearrowright l,\ \texttt{goto}\ l),\ m)$
   - *(c)* $\mathbf{S}(k,\ (\searrow,\ \mathcal{S}_{\mathsf{e}}[e]),\ m) \to \mathbf{S}((\mathcal{S}_{\mathsf{e}}, e) :: k,\ e,\ m)$
2. For expressions:
   - *(a)* $\mathbf{S}(k,\ \mathcal{E}[e_1],\ m_1) \to \mathbf{S}(k,\ \mathcal{E}[e_2],\ m_2)$ *for any* $e_2$ *and* $m_2$ *s.t.* $\mathsf{getstack}\ k \vdash (e_1, m_1) \to_{\mathsf{h}} (e_2, m_2)$
   - *(b)* $\mathbf{S}(k,\ (\searrow,\ \mathcal{E}[f([v_0]_{\Omega_0}, \dots, [v_n]_{\Omega_n})]),\ m) \to \mathbf{S}(\mathsf{resume}\ \mathcal{E} :: k,\ \overline{\mathsf{call}}\ f\ \vec{v},\ \mathsf{unlock}\ (\bigcup \vec{\Omega})\ m)$
   - *(c)* $\mathbf{S}(k,\ (\searrow,\ \mathcal{E}[e]),\ m) \to \mathbf{S}(k,\ \overline{\mathsf{undef}},\ m)$, *provided that* $e$ *is an unsafe redex*
3. For finished expressions:
   - *(a)* $\mathbf{S}((\square, e) :: k,\ [v]_\Omega,\ m) \to \mathbf{S}(k,\ (\nearrow,\ e),\ \mathsf{unlock}\ \Omega\ m)$
   - *(b)* $\mathbf{S}((\texttt{return}\ \square, e) :: k,\ [v]_\Omega,\ m) \to \mathbf{S}(k,\ (\Uparrow v,\ \texttt{return}\ e),\ \mathsf{unlock}\ \Omega\ m)$
   - *(c)* $\mathbf{S}((\texttt{while}(\square)\ s, e) :: k,\ [v]_\Omega,\ m) \to \mathbf{S}(\texttt{while}(e)\ \square :: k,\ (\searrow,\ s),\ \mathsf{unlock}\ \Omega\ m)$ *provided that* $\mathsf{istrue}\ v$
   - *(d)* $\mathbf{S}((\texttt{while}(\square)\ s, e) :: k,\ [v]_\Omega,\ m) \to \mathbf{S}(k,\ (\nearrow,\ \texttt{while}(e)\ s),\ \mathsf{unlock}\ \Omega\ m)$ *provided that* $\mathsf{isfalse}\ v$
   - *(e)* $\mathbf{S}((\texttt{if}\ (\square)\ s_1\ \texttt{else}\ s_2, e) :: k,\ [v]_\Omega,\ m) \to \mathbf{S}(\texttt{if}\ (e)\ \square\ \texttt{else}\ s_2 :: k,\ (\searrow,\ s_1),\ \mathsf{unlock}\ \Omega\ m)$ *provided that* $\mathsf{istrue}\ v$
   - *(f)* $\mathbf{S}((\texttt{if}\ (\square)\ s_1\ \texttt{else}\ s_2, e) :: k,\ [v]_\Omega,\ m) \to \mathbf{S}(\texttt{if}\ (e)\ s_1\ \texttt{else}\ \square :: k,\ (\searrow,\ s_2),\ \mathsf{unlock}\ \Omega\ m)$ *provided that* $\mathsf{isfalse}\ v$
4. For compound statements:
   - *(a)* $\mathbf{S}(k,\ (\searrow,\ \texttt{block}\ c\ s),\ m) \to \mathbf{S}((\texttt{block}_b\ c\ \square) :: k,\ (\searrow,\ s),\ \mathsf{alloc}\ b\ \mathsf{indet}\ (\mathsf{blockperm}\ c)\ m)$ *for any* $b$ *such that* $\mathsf{perm}\ b\ m = \bot$
   - *(b)* $\mathbf{S}(k,\ (\searrow,\ s_1\, ;s_2),\ m) \to \mathbf{S}((\square\, ;s_2) :: k,\ (\searrow,\ s_1),\ m)$
   - *(c)* $\mathbf{S}(k,\ (\searrow,\ l : s),\ m) \to \mathbf{S}((l : \square) :: k,\ (\searrow,\ s),\ m)$
   - *(d)* $\mathbf{S}((\texttt{block}_b\ c\ \square) :: k,\ (\nearrow,\ s),\ m) \to \mathbf{S}(k,\ (\nearrow,\ \texttt{block}\ c\ s),\ \mathsf{free}\ b\ m)$
   - *(e)* $\mathbf{S}((\square\, ;s_2) :: k,\ (\nearrow,\ s_1),\ m) \to \mathbf{S}((s_1\, ;\square) :: k,\ (\searrow,\ s_2),\ m)$
   - *(f)* $\mathbf{S}((s_1\, ;\square) :: k,\ (\nearrow,\ s_2),\ m) \to \mathbf{S}(k,\ (\nearrow,\ s_1\, ;s_2),\ m)$
   - *(g)* $\mathbf{S}(\texttt{while}(e)\ \square :: k,\ (\nearrow,\ s),\ m) \to \mathbf{S}(k,\ (\searrow,\ \texttt{while}(e)\ s),\ m)$
   - *(h)* $\mathbf{S}((\texttt{if}\ (e)\ \square\ \texttt{else}\ s_2) :: k,\ (\nearrow,\ s_1),\ m) \to \mathbf{S}(k,\ (\nearrow,\ \texttt{if}\ (e)\ s_1\ \texttt{else}\ s_2),\ m)$
   - *(i)* $\mathbf{S}((\texttt{if}\ (e)\ s_1\ \texttt{else}\ \square) :: k,\ (\nearrow,\ s_2),\ m) \to \mathbf{S}(k,\ (\nearrow,\ \texttt{if}\ (e)\ s_1\ \texttt{else}\ s_2),\ m)$
   - *(j)* $\mathbf{S}((l : \square) :: k,\ (\nearrow,\ s),\ m) \to \mathbf{S}(k,\ (\nearrow,\ l : s),\ m)$
5. For function calls:
   - *(a)* $\mathbf{S}(k,\ \overline{\mathsf{call}}\ f\ \vec{v},\ m_1) \to \mathbf{S}(\mathsf{params}\ \vec{b} :: k,\ (\searrow,\ s),\ m_2)$ *for any* $s$, $\vec{b}$ *and* $m_2$ *s.t.* $\delta\ f = s$ *and* $\mathsf{allocparams}\ \mathsf{W}\ m_1\ \vec{b}\ \vec{v}\ m_2$
   - *(b)* $\mathbf{S}(\mathsf{params}\ \vec{b} :: k,\ (\nearrow,\ s),\ m) \to \mathbf{S}(k,\ \overline{\mathsf{return}}\ \mathsf{indet},\ \mathsf{free}\ \vec{b}\ m)$
   - *(c)* $\mathbf{S}(\mathsf{params}\ \vec{b} :: k,\ (\Uparrow v,\ s),\ m) \to \mathbf{S}(k,\ \overline{\mathsf{return}}\ v,\ \mathsf{free}\ \vec{b}\ m)$
   - *(d)* $\mathbf{S}(\mathsf{resume}\ \mathcal{E} :: k,\ \overline{\mathsf{return}}\ v,\ m) \to \mathbf{S}(k,\ \mathcal{E}[v],\ m)$
6. For non-local control flow:
   - *(a)* $\mathbf{S}((\texttt{block}_b\ c\ \square) :: k,\ (\Uparrow v,\ s),\ m) \to \mathbf{S}(k,\ (\Uparrow v,\ \texttt{block}\ c\ s),\ \mathsf{free}\ b\ m)$
   - *(b)* $\mathbf{S}(\mathcal{S}_{\mathsf{s}} :: k,\ (\Uparrow v,\ s),\ m) \to \mathbf{S}(k,\ (\Uparrow v,\ \mathcal{S}_{\mathsf{s}}[s]),\ m)$
   - *(c)* $\mathbf{S}(k,\ (\curvearrowright l,\ l : s),\ m) \to \mathbf{S}((l : \square) :: k,\ (\searrow,\ s),\ m)$
   - *(d)* $\mathbf{S}(k,\ (\curvearrowright l,\ \texttt{block}\ c\ s),\ m) \to \mathbf{S}((\texttt{block}_b\ c\ \square) :: k,\ (\curvearrowright l,\ s),\ \mathsf{alloc}\ b\ \mathsf{indet}\ (\mathsf{blockperm}\ c)\ m)$ *for any* $b$ *such that* $\mathsf{perm}\ b\ m = \bot$, *and provided that* $l \in \mathsf{labels}\ s$
   - *(e)* $\mathbf{S}(\texttt{block}_b\ c\ \square :: k,\ (\curvearrowright l,\ s),\ m) \to \mathbf{S}(k,\ (\curvearrowright l,\ \texttt{block}\ c\ s),\ \mathsf{free}\ b\ m)$ *provided that* $l \notin \mathsf{labels}\ s$
   - *(f)* $\mathbf{S}(k,\ (\curvearrowright l,\ \mathcal{S}_{\mathsf{s}}[s]),\ m) \to \mathbf{S}(\mathcal{S}_{\mathsf{s}} :: k,\ (\curvearrowright l,\ s),\ m)$ *provided that* $l \in \mathsf{labels}\ s$
   - *(g)* $\mathbf{S}(\mathcal{S}_{\mathsf{s}} :: k,\ (\curvearrowright l,\ s),\ m) \to \mathbf{S}(k,\ (\curvearrowright l,\ \mathcal{S}_{\mathsf{s}}[s]),\ m)$ *provided that* $l \notin \mathsf{labels}\ s$

*Note that the selection of redexes in Rule 2a, 2b, and 2c is non-deterministic. Moreover, note that the rules 6c and 6f overlap, and that the splitting into* $\mathcal{S}_{\mathsf{s}}$ *and* $s$ *in rule 6f is non-deterministic.*

DEFINITION 4.11. *We let* $\to^*$ *denote the reflexive-transitive closure of* $\to$, *and let* $\to^n$ *denote paths of* $\leq n$ $\to$*-reduction steps.*

Execution of a statement $\mathbf{S}(k,\ (d,\ s),\ m)$ is performed by traversing through the program context $k$ and statement $s$ in direction $d$. The direction *down* $\searrow$ (respectively *up* $\nearrow$) is used to traverse downwards (respectively upwards) to the next substatement that has to be executed. When a substatement $\mathcal{S}_{\mathsf{e}}[e]$ containing an expression $e$ has been reached (Rule 1c), the location of the expression $\mathcal{S}_{\mathsf{e}}$ is stored on the program context, and execution is continued in $\mathbf{S}((\mathcal{S}_{\mathsf{e}}, e) :: k,\ e,\ m)$.

Execution of an expression $\mathbf{S}(k,\ e,\ m)$ is performed by non-deterministically decomposing $e$ into $\mathcal{E}[e']$. Rule 2a allows $e'$ to perform a $\to_{\mathsf{h}}$-step, and Rule 2b allows $e'$ to perform a function call. If the redex $e'$ is unsafe and thereby cannot be contracted (*e.g.* because of a sequence violation or integer overflow), Rule 2c ensures that the whole program reduces to the $\overline{\mathsf{undef}}$ state. When execution of an expression has resulted in a value $[v]_\Omega$, we model a sequence point by unlocking $\Omega$ in memory (Rule 3a-3f).

For a function call $\mathbf{S}(k,\ \mathcal{E}[f([v_0]_{\Omega_0}, \dots, [v_n]_{\Omega_n})],\ m)$, two reductions occur before the function body will be executed. The first to $\mathbf{S}(\mathsf{resume}\ \mathcal{E} :: k,\ \overline{\mathsf{call}}\ f\ \vec{v},\ \mathsf{unlock}\ (\bigcup \vec{\Omega})\ m)$ (Rule 2b) stores the location of the caller on the program context and takes care of the sequence point before the function call. The subsequent reduction to $\mathbf{S}(\mathsf{params}\ \vec{b} :: \mathsf{resume}\ \mathcal{E} :: k,\ (\searrow,\ s),\ m')$ (Rule 5a) looks up the callee's body $s$, allocates the parameters $\vec{v}$, and then performs a transition to execute the function body $s$.

We consider two directions for non-local control flow: *jump* $\curvearrowright l$ and *top* $\Uparrow v$. After a $\texttt{goto}\ l$ (Rule 1b), the direction $\curvearrowright l$ is used to traverse to the substatement labeled $l$ (Rule 6c-6g). Although this traversal is non-deterministic (in the case of duplicate labels), there are some side-conditions in order to ensure that the reduction is not going back and forth between the same locations. This is required because we may otherwise impose non-terminating behavior on terminating programs. The non-determinism could be removed entirely by adding additional side-conditions. However, as we already have other sources of non-determinism, we omitted doing so to ease formalization.

When execution of the expression $e$ of a $\texttt{return}\ e$ statement has resulted in a value $v$ (Rule 3b), the direction $\Uparrow v$ is used to traverse to the *top* of the whole statement (Rule 6a and 6b). When this traversal reaches the top of the statement, there are two reductions to give the return value $v$ to the caller. The first reduction, from $\mathbf{S}(\mathsf{params}\ \vec{b} :: \mathsf{resume}\ \mathcal{E} :: k,\ (\Uparrow v,\ s),\ m)$ to $\mathbf{S}(\mathsf{resume}\ \mathcal{E} :: k,\ \overline{\mathsf{return}}\ v,\ \mathsf{free}\ \vec{b}\ m)$ (Rule 5c), deallocates the function parameters, and the second reduction, to $\mathbf{S}(k,\ \mathcal{E}[v],\ \mathsf{free}\ \vec{b}\ m)$ (Rule 5d), resumes execution of the expression $\mathcal{E}[v]$ at the caller.

## 5. Axiomatic semantics

Judgments of Hoare logic are triples $\{P\}\,s\,\{Q\}$, where $s$ is a statement, and $P$ and $Q$ are *assertions* called the pre- and postcondition. The intuitive reading of such a triple is: if $P$ holds for the memory before executing $s$, and execution of $s$ terminates, then $Q$ holds afterwards. For our language, we have two such judgments: one for expressions and one for statements.

Our expression judgments are quadruples $\Delta \vdash \{P\}\,e\,\{Q\}$. As usual, $P$ and $Q$ are the pre- and postcondition of $e$ respectively, but whereas $P$ is just an assertion, $Q$ is a function from values to assertions. It ensures that if execution of $e$ yields a value $v$, then $Q\,v$ holds afterwards. The environment $\Delta$ is a finite function from function names to their pre- and postconditions that is used to cope with (mutually) recursive functions.

As in Krebbers and Wiedijk [21], our judgments for statements are sextuples $\Delta;\ R;\ J \vdash \{P\}\,s\,\{Q\}$, where $R$ is a function from values to assertions, and $J$ is a function from labels to assertions. The assertion $R\,v$ has to hold when executing a `return` $e$ (for each value $v$ obtained by execution of $e$), and $J\,l$ is the jumping condition that has to hold when executing a `goto` $l$.

We use a shallow embedding to represent assertions. This treatment is similar to that of Appel and Blazy [2], Von Oheimb [29], Krebbers and Wiedijk [21], *etc.* In order to talk about expressions without side-effects (assignments, allocation and deallocation, and function calls) in assertions (we need this for various rules of our axiomatic semantics, see Definition 5.9), we define an evaluation function for *pure* expressions.

DEFINITION 5.1. Evaluation $[\![\, e \,]\!]_{\rho,m}$ of an expression $e$ *in a stack* $\rho$ *and memory* $m$ *is a partial function that is defined as:*

$$
\begin{aligned}
[\![\, x_i \,]\!]_{\rho,m} &:= \mathsf{ptr}\, b && \text{if } \rho\, i = b\\
[\![\, v \,]\!]_{\rho,m} &:= v\\
[\![\, \mathtt{load}\ e \,]\!]_{\rho,m} &:= m \mathbin{!!} b && \text{if } [\![\, e \,]\!]_{\rho,m} = \mathsf{ptr}\, b\\
[\![\, e_1 \circledcirc e_2 \,]\!]_{\rho,m} &:= [\![\, e_1 \,]\!]_{\rho,m} \circledcirc [\![\, e_2 \,]\!]_{\rho,m}\\
[\![\, e_1 \mathbin{?} e_2 : e_3 \,]\!]_{\rho,m} &:= \begin{cases} [\![\, e_2 \,]\!]_{\rho,m} & \text{if } [\![\, e_1 \,]\!]_{\rho,m} = v \text{ and } \mathsf{istrue}\ v\\ [\![\, e_3 \,]\!]_{\rho,m} & \text{if } [\![\, e_1 \,]\!]_{\rho,m} = v \text{ and } \mathsf{isfalse}\ v\end{cases}\\
[\![\, (\tau)\, e \,]\!]_{\rho,m} &:= (\tau)\, [\![\, e \,]\!]_{\rho,m}
\end{aligned}
$$

DEFINITION 5.2. Assertions *are predicates over the the stack and the memory. We define the following connectives on assertions.*

$$
\begin{aligned}
P \to Q &:= \lambda \rho\, m \,.\, P\,\rho\, m \to Q\,\rho\, m & \forall x \,.\, P\, x &:= \lambda \rho\, m \,.\, \forall x \,.\, P\, x\, \rho\, m\\
P \wedge Q &:= \lambda \rho\, m \,.\, P\,\rho\, m \wedge Q\,\rho\, m & \exists x \,.\, P\, x &:= \lambda \rho\, m \,.\, \exists x \,.\, P\, x\, \rho\, m\\
P \vee Q &:= \lambda \rho\, m \,.\, P\,\rho\, m \vee Q\,\rho\, m & \ulcorner P \urcorner &:= \lambda \rho\, m \,.\, P\\
\neg P &:= \lambda \rho\, m \,.\, \neg P\,\rho\, m & e \Downarrow v &:= \lambda \rho\, m \,.\, [\![ e ]\!]_{\rho,m} = v
\end{aligned}
$$

*We treat* $\ulcorner \_ \urcorner$ *as an implicit coercion, e.g. we write* True *instead of* $\ulcorner$True$\urcorner$. *Also, we often lift these connectives to functions to assertions, e.g. we write* $P \wedge Q$ *instead of* $\lambda v \,.\, P\, v \wedge Q\, v$.

DEFINITION 5.3. *We let* $P \models Q$ *denote that for all stacks* $\rho$ *and memories* $m$ *we have* $P\,\rho\, m$ *implies* $Q\,\rho\, m$.

DEFINITION 5.4. *An assertion* $P$ *is called* stack independent *if for all* $\rho_1, \rho_2 \in \mathsf{stack}$ *and* $m \in \mathsf{mem}$ *with* $P\,\rho_1\, m$ *we have* $P\,\rho_2\, m$. *Similarly,* $P$ *is called* unlock independent *if for all* $\rho \in \mathsf{stack}$, $m \in \mathsf{mem}$ *and* $\Omega \subseteq \mathsf{index}$ *with* $P\,\rho\, m$ *we have* $P\,\rho\,(\mathsf{unlock}\ \Omega\ m)$.

Next, we define the assertions of separation logic [28]. The *separating conjunction* $P * Q$ asserts that the memory can be split into two disjoint parts such that $P$ holds in the one part, and $Q$ in the other (due to the use of fractional permissions, these parts may overlap as long as their permissions are disjoint and their values agree). Finally, $e_1 \overset{\gamma}{\mapsto} e_2$ asserts that the memory consists of exactly one object at $e_1$ with contents $e_2$ and permission $\gamma$.

DEFINITION 5.5. *The* connectives of separation logic *are:*

$$
\begin{aligned}
\mathsf{emp} &:= \lambda \rho\, m \,.\, m = \emptyset\\
P * Q &:= \lambda \rho\, m \,.\, \exists m_1\, m_2 \,.\, m = m_1 \cup m_2 \wedge\\
&\qquad m_1 \perp m_2 \wedge P\,\rho\, m_1 \wedge Q\,\rho\, m_2\\
e_1 \overset{\gamma}{\mapsto} e_2 &:= \lambda \rho\, m \,.\, \exists b\, v \,.\, [\![\, e_1 \,]\!]_{\rho,m} = \mathsf{ptr}\, b \wedge\\
&\qquad [\![\, e_2 \,]\!]_{\rho,m} = v \wedge m = \{(b, (v, \gamma))\}\\
e_1 \overset{\gamma}{\mapsto} - &:= \exists e_2 \,.\, e_1 \overset{\gamma}{\mapsto} e_2
\end{aligned}
$$

To enforce the sequence point restriction, the rule for assignment changes the permission $\gamma$ of $e_1 \overset{\gamma}{\mapsto} e_2$ into $\mathsf{lock}\ \gamma$. Subsequent reads and writes are therefore no longer possible. At constructs that have a sequence point, we use the assertion $P \rhd$ to release these locks, and to make future reads and writes possible again.

DEFINITION 5.6. *The* unlocking assertion $P \rhd$ *is defined as:*

$$P \rhd := \lambda \rho\, m \,.\, P\,\rho\,(\mathsf{unlock}\ (\mathsf{locks}\ m)\ m).$$

We proved properties as $P \rhd * Q \rhd \models (P * Q) \rhd$ to push the $\rhd$-connective through an assertion.

Similar to Krebbers and Wiedijk [21], we need to lift an assertion such that the De Bruijn indices of its variables are increased so as to deal with block scope variables. The lifting $P \uparrow$ of $P$ is defined semantically, and we prove that it behaves as expected.

DEFINITION 5.7. *The* lifting assertion $P \uparrow$ *is defined as:*

$$P \uparrow := \lambda \rho\, m \,.\, P\,(\mathsf{tail}\ \rho)\ m.$$

LEMMA 5.8. *The operation* $(\_) \uparrow$ *distributes over the connectives* $\to$, $\wedge$, $\vee$, $\neg$, $\forall$, $\exists$, *and* $*$. *We have* $(e \Downarrow v) \uparrow\ =\ (e\uparrow) \Downarrow v$ *and* $(e_1 \overset{\gamma}{\mapsto} e_2) \uparrow = (e_1 \uparrow) \overset{\gamma}{\mapsto} (e_2 \uparrow)$, *where the operation* $e\uparrow$ *replaces each variable* $x_i$ *in* $e$ *by* $x_{i+1}$.

The specification of a function with parameters $\vec{v}$ consists of an assertion $P\,\vec{y}\,\vec{v}$ called the precondition, and a function $Q\,\vec{y}\,\vec{v}$ from (return) values to assertions called the postcondition. We allow universal quantification over arbitrary logical variables $\vec{y}$ in order to relate the pre- and postcondition. The pre- and postcondition should moreover be stack independent because local variables will have a different meaning at the caller than at callee. We denote such a specification as $\forall \vec{y}\, \forall \vec{v} \,.\, \{P\,\vec{y}\,\vec{v}\}\ \{Q\,\vec{y}\,\vec{v}\}$.

DEFINITION 5.9. *Given a finite partial function* $\delta$ *mapping function names to statements, the expression judgment* $\Delta \vdash \{P\}\,e\,\{Q\}$ *and statement judgment* $\Delta;\ R;\ J \vdash \{P\}\,s\,\{Q\}$ *of* the axiomatic semantics *are mutually inductively defined as shown in Figure 1.*

We have a frame, weaken, and exist rule for both the expression and statement judgments. The traditional frame rule of separation logic [28] includes a side-condition $\mathsf{modifies}\ s \cap \mathsf{free}\ A = \emptyset$. Like Krebbers and Wiedijk [21], we do not need this side-condition as our local variables are (immutable) references into the memory. Since the return and goto statements leave the normal control flow, the postconditions of the (goto) and (return) rules are arbitrary.

The rules for function calls are based on those by Krebbers and Wiedijk [21]. The (e-call) rule is used to call a function $f(\vec{e})$ that is already in $\Delta$. The assertion $B\,\vec{v}$ is used to frame a part of the memory that is used by $\vec{e}$ but not by the $f$ itself.

The (add funs) rule can be used to add an arbitrary family $\Delta'$ of specifications of (possibly mutually recursive) functions to $\Delta$. For each function $f$ in $\Delta'$ with precondition $P'$ and postcondition $Q'$, it has to be verified that the function body $\delta\, f$ is correct for all instantiations of the logical variables $\vec{y}$ and input values $\vec{v}$. The precondition $\Pi_*[\, x_i \overset{\mathsf{W}}{\mapsto} v_i \,] * P'\vec{y}\,\vec{v}$, where $\Pi_*[\, e_i \overset{\gamma_i}{\mapsto} e_i' \,]$ denotes the

$$\frac{\Delta \vdash \{P\}\, e\, \{Q\}}{\Delta \vdash \{A * P\}\, e\, \{A * Q\}}\ \text{(e-frame)} \qquad \frac{\forall x\,.\,(\Delta \vdash \{P\,x\}\, e\, \{Q\})}{\Delta \vdash \{\exists x\,.\,P\,x\}\, e\, \{Q\}}\ \text{(e-exists)} \qquad \frac{P' \models P \quad \Delta \vdash \{P\}\, e\, \{Q\} \quad (\forall v\,.\,Q\,v \models Q'\,v)}{\Delta \vdash \{P'\}\, e\, \{Q'\}}\ \text{(e-weaken)}$$

$$\frac{P \models e \Downarrow v}{\Delta \vdash \{P\}\, e\, \{\lambda v'\,.\,v = v' \wedge P\}}\ \text{(e-base)} \qquad \frac{}{\Delta \vdash \{\mathsf{emp}\}\, \mathtt{alloc}\, \{\lambda a\,.\,a \overset{\mathsf{F}}{\mapsto} -\}}\ \text{(e-alloc)} \qquad \frac{\Delta \vdash \{P\}\, e\, \{\lambda a\,.\,Q * a \overset{\mathsf{F}}{\mapsto} -\}}{\Delta \vdash \{P\}\, \mathtt{free}\, e\, \{\lambda \_\,.\,Q\}}\ \text{(e-free)}$$

$$\frac{\mathsf{kind}\,\gamma \neq \mathsf{Locked} \quad \Delta \vdash \{P\}\, e\, \{\lambda a\,.\,\exists v\,.\,Q\,a\,v * a \overset{\gamma}{\mapsto} v\}}{\Delta \vdash \{P\}\, \mathtt{load}\, e\, \{\lambda v\,.\,\exists a\,.\,Q\,a\,v * a \overset{\gamma}{\mapsto} v\}}\ \text{(e-load)}$$

$$\frac{\mathsf{Write} \subseteq \mathsf{kind}\,\gamma \quad \Delta \vdash \{P_1\}\, e_1\, \{Q_1\} \quad \Delta \vdash \{P_2\}\, e_2\, \{Q_2\} \quad \forall a v\,.\,(Q_1\,a * Q_2\,v \models a \overset{\gamma}{\mapsto} - * R\,a\,v)}{\Delta \vdash \{P_1 * P_2\}\, e_1 := e_2\, \{\lambda v\,.\,\exists a\,.\,a \overset{\gamma}{\mapsto} v * R\,a\,v\}}\ \text{(e-assign)}$$

$$\frac{\Delta \vdash \{P_1\}\, e_1\, \{Q_1\} \quad \Delta \vdash \{P_2\}\, e_2\, \{Q_2\} \quad \forall v_1\, v_2\,.\,(Q_1\,v_1 * Q_2\,v_2 \models \exists v\,.\,R\,v\,v_1\,v_2 \wedge v_1 \circledcirc v_2 \Downarrow v)}{\Delta \vdash \{P_1 * P_2\}\, e_1 \circledcirc e_2\, \{\lambda v\,.\,\exists v_1\, v_2\,.\,R\,v\,v_1\,v_2\}}\ \text{(e-binop)}$$

$$\frac{\Delta\,f = (\forall \vec{z}\,\forall \vec{w}\,.\,\{P'\,\vec{z}\,\vec{w}\}\,\{Q'\,\vec{z}\,\vec{w}\}) \quad \forall i\,.\,(\Delta \vdash \{P_i\}\, e_i\, \{Q_i\}) \quad \forall \vec{v}\,.\,(\Pi_*[\,Q_i\,v_i\,] \models P'\,\vec{y}\,\vec{v} * A\,\vec{v}) \quad \forall \vec{v}\,v\,.\,(Q'\,\vec{y}\,\vec{v}\,v * A\,\vec{v} \models R\,v)}{\Delta \vdash \{\Pi_*[\,\vec{P}\,]\}\, f(\vec{e})\, \{R\}}\ \text{(e-call)}$$

$$\frac{\Delta \vdash \{P\}\, e_1\, \{\lambda v\,.\,v \neq \mathsf{indet} \wedge P'\,v \triangleright\} \quad \Delta \vdash \{\exists v\,.\,\mathsf{istrue}\,v \wedge P'\,v\}\, e_2\, \{Q\} \quad \Delta \vdash \{\exists v\,.\,\mathsf{isfalse}\,v \wedge P'\,v\}\, e_2\, \{Q\}}{\Delta \vdash \{P\}\, e_1\ ?\ e_2 : e_3\, \{Q\}}\ \text{(e-if)}$$

$$\frac{\Delta;\, R;\, J \vdash \{P\}\, s\, \{Q\}}{\Delta;\, A * R;\, A * J \vdash \{A * P\}\, s\, \{A * Q\}}\ \text{(frame)} \qquad \frac{\forall x\,.\,(\Delta;\, R;\, J \vdash \{P\,x\}\, s\, \{Q\})}{\Delta;\, R;\, J \vdash \{\exists x\,.\,P\,x\}\, s\, \{Q\}}\ \text{(exists)}$$

$$\frac{\forall v\,.\,(R\,v \models R'\,v) \quad \forall l \in \mathsf{labels}\,s\,.\,(J'\,l \models J\,l) \quad \forall l \notin \mathsf{labels}\,s\,.\,(J\,l \models J'\,l) \quad P' \models P \quad \Delta;\, R;\, J \vdash \{P\}\, s\, \{Q\} \quad Q \models Q'}{\Delta;\, R';\, J' \vdash \{P'\}\, s\, \{Q'\}}\ \text{(weaken)}$$

$$\frac{\Delta \vdash \{P\}\, e\, \{\lambda \_\,.\,Q \triangleright\}}{\Delta;\, R;\, J \vdash \{P\}\, e\, \{Q\}}\ \text{(expr)} \qquad \frac{}{\Delta;\, R;\, J \vdash \{P\}\, \mathtt{skip}\, \{P\}}\ \text{(skip)} \qquad \frac{\Delta;\, R;\, J \vdash \{P\}\, s_1\, \{P'\} \quad \Delta;\, R;\, J \vdash \{P'\}\, s_2\, \{Q\}}{\Delta;\, R;\, J \vdash \{P\}\, s_1\, ;\, s_2\, \{Q\}}\ \text{(comp)}$$

$$\frac{\Delta \vdash \{P\}\, e\, \{R \triangleright\}}{\Delta;\, R;\, J \vdash \{P\}\, \mathtt{return}\, e\, \{Q\}}\ \text{(return)} \qquad \frac{\Delta;\, R;\, J \vdash \{J\,l\}\, s\, \{Q\}}{\Delta;\, R;\, J \vdash \{J\,l\}\, l : s\, \{Q\}}\ \text{(label)} \qquad \frac{}{\Delta;\, R;\, J \vdash \{J\,l\}\, \mathtt{goto}\, l\, \{Q\}}\ \text{(goto)}$$

$$\frac{\gamma = \mathsf{blockperm}\,c \quad \Delta;\, x_0 \overset{\gamma}{\mapsto} - * J \uparrow;\, x_0 \overset{\gamma}{\mapsto} - * R \uparrow \vdash \{x_0 \overset{\gamma}{\mapsto} - * P \uparrow\}\, s\, \{x_0 \overset{\gamma}{\mapsto} - * Q \uparrow\}}{\Delta;\, R;\, J \vdash \{P\}\, \mathtt{block}\, c\, s\, \{Q\}}\ \text{(block)}$$

$$\frac{\Delta \vdash \{P\}\, e\, \{\lambda v\,.\,v \neq \mathsf{indet} \wedge Q\,v \triangleright\} \quad \Delta;\, R;\, J \vdash \{\exists v\,.\,\mathsf{istrue}\,v \wedge Q\,v\}\, s\, \{P\}}{\Delta;\, R;\, J \vdash \{P\}\, \mathtt{while}(e)\ s\, \{\exists v\,.\,\mathsf{isfalse}\,v \wedge Q\,v\}}\ \text{(while)}$$

$$\frac{\Delta \vdash \{P\}\, e\, \{\lambda v\,.\,v \neq \mathsf{indet} \wedge P'\,v \triangleright\} \quad \Delta;\, R;\, J \vdash \{\exists v\,.\,\mathsf{istrue}\,v \wedge P'\,v\}\, s_1\, \{Q\} \quad \Delta;\, R;\, J \vdash \{\exists v\,.\,\mathsf{isfalse}\,v \wedge P'\,v\}\, s_1\, \{Q\}}{\Delta;\, R;\, J \vdash \{P\}\, \mathtt{if}\ (e)\ s_1\ \mathtt{else}\ s_2\, \{Q\}}\ \text{(if)}$$

$$\frac{\begin{array}{l}\forall f\,P'\,Q'\,.\,\Delta'\,f = (\forall \vec{z}\,\forall \vec{w}\,.\,\{P'\,\vec{z}\,\vec{w}\}\,\{Q'\,\vec{z}\,\vec{w}\}) \to \forall \vec{y}\,\vec{v} \\ \quad (\Delta' \cup \Delta;\, \lambda l\,.\,\mathsf{False};\, \lambda v\,.\,\Pi_*[\,x_i \overset{\mathsf{W}}{\mapsto} -\,] * Q'\,\vec{y}\,\vec{v}\,v \vdash \{\Pi_*[\,x_i \overset{\mathsf{W}}{\mapsto} v_i\,] * P'\,\vec{y}\,\vec{v}\}\, \delta\,f\, \{\Pi_*[\,x_i \overset{\mathsf{W}}{\mapsto} -\,] * Q'\,\vec{y}\,\vec{v}\,\mathsf{indet}\}) \\ \Delta' \cup \Delta;\, R;\, J \vdash \{P\}\, s\, \{Q\} \qquad\qquad \mathsf{dom}\,\Delta' \subseteq \mathsf{dom}\,\delta\end{array}}{\Delta;\, R;\, J \vdash \{P\}\, s\, \{Q\}}\ \text{(add funs)}$$

**Figure 1.** The rules of the axiomatic semantics.

assertion $e_0 \overset{\gamma_0}{\mapsto} e_0' * \cdots * e_n \overset{\gamma_n}{\mapsto} e_n'$, states that the function parameters $\vec{x}$ are allocated with values $\vec{v}$ for which the precondition $P'$ of the function holds. The postcondition $\Pi_*[\,x_i \overset{\mathsf{W}}{\mapsto} -\,] * Q'\,\vec{y}\,\vec{v}\,\mathsf{indet}$ and returning condition $\lambda v\,.\,\Pi_*[\,x_i \overset{\mathsf{W}}{\mapsto} -\,] * Q'\,\vec{y}\,\vec{v}\,v$ ensure that the parameters have not been deallocated during the execution of the function and that the postcondition $Q'$ holds for the return value. The jumping condition $\lambda l\,.\,\mathsf{False}$ ensures that all gotos jump to a label that occurs in the function body.

Our axiomatic semantics is at least as powerful as an ordinary separation logic for C because not only variants of the ordinary inference rules can be derived, but also derived rules for more complex constructs. For example

$$\frac{e_1 \overset{\gamma_1}{\mapsto} - * e_2 \overset{\gamma_2}{\mapsto} - * P \models e_3 \Downarrow v}{\{e_1 \overset{\gamma_1}{\mapsto} - * e_2 \overset{\gamma_2}{\mapsto} - * P\}\, e_1 := e_2 := e_3\, \{e_1 \overset{\gamma_1}{\mapsto} v * e_2 \overset{\gamma_2}{\mapsto} v * P\}}$$

provided that $e_1$ and $e_2$ are $\mathtt{load}$-free, $P$ is unlock independent and $\mathsf{Write} \subseteq \mathsf{kind}\,\gamma_1, \mathsf{kind}\,\gamma_2$.

## 6. Soundness of the axiomatic semantics

We will define judgments $\Delta \models \{P\}\, e\, \{Q\}$ (Definition 6.6) and $\Delta;\, J;\, R \models \{P\}\, s\, \{Q\}$ (Definition 6.7) to describe partial program correctness. The judgment $\Delta \models \{P\}\, e\, \{Q\}$ guaranties that if the precondition $P$ holds in $m$ and $\mathbf{S}([\,],\, e,\, m) \rightarrow\!\!\triangleright^* \mathbf{S}([\,],\, [v]_\Omega,\, m')$, then the postcondition $Q\,v$ holds in $m'$. Also, it ensures no undefined behavior occurs for each possible execution order. Soundness of the axiomatic semantics means that $\Delta \vdash \{P\}\, e\, \{Q\}$ implies $\Delta \models \{P\}\, e\, \{Q\}$ (and likewise for $\Delta;\, J;\, R \models \{P\}\, s\, \{Q\}$).

We prove soundness (Theorem 6.8) by mutual induction on the derivations of $\Delta \vdash \{P\}\, e\, \{Q\}$ and $\Delta;\, J;\, R \vdash \{P\}\, s\, \{Q\}$. Hence, $\Delta \models \{P\}\, e\, \{Q\}$ and $\Delta;\, J;\, R \models \{P\}\, s\, \{Q\}$ should be sufficiently strong so that we get appropriate induction hypotheses. The main difficulty is that the subexpressions $e_l$ and $e_r$ in $e_l \circledcirc e_r$ can do interleaved reduction steps. A simple minded definition of $\Delta \vDash \{P\}\,e\,\{Q\}$ that only talks about the end result of executing $e$ does not work, because we also need to have information about states in between. Since the definitions of $\Delta \vDash \{P\}\,e\,\{Q\}$ and $\Delta;\ J;\ R \vDash \{P\}\,s\,\{Q\}$ have a lot in common, we define a more general notion to factor out similarities.

Like Krebbers and Wiedijk [21], we have to enforce the reduction $\mathbf{S}(k,\ \phi,\ m) \twoheadrightarrow^* \mathbf{S}(k',\ \phi',\ m')$ to remain below a certain program context.

DEFINITION 6.1. *The $k$-restricted reduction $S_1 \twoheadrightarrow_k S_2$ is defined as $S_1 \twoheadrightarrow S_2$ provided $k$ is a suffix of the program context of $S_2$.*

DEFINITION 6.2. *Given a predicate $\bar{P} \subseteq \mathsf{stack} \times \mathsf{mem} \times \mathsf{focus}$, the judgment $\bar{P} \vDash^n_l \hat{\mathbf{S}}(k,\ \phi,\ m)$ is inductively defined as:*

1. $\bar{P} \vDash^0_l \hat{\mathbf{S}}(k,\ \phi,\ m)$
2. *If $\bar{P}\,(\mathsf{getstack}\,l)\,m\,\phi$, then $\bar{P} \vDash^n_l \hat{\mathbf{S}}(l,\ \phi,\ m)$.*
3. *If for all $m_f$ with $m \perp m_f$ we have*
   *(a) $\mathbf{S}(k,\ \phi,\ m \cup m_f)$ is $\twoheadrightarrow_l$-reducible, and*
   *(b) if $\mathbf{S}(k,\ \phi,\ m \cup m_f) \twoheadrightarrow_l S_2$, then the state $S_2$ is of the shape $\mathbf{S}(k_2,\ \phi_2,\ m_2 \cup m_f)$ with $m_2 \perp m_f$, $\phi \neq \overline{\mathsf{undef}}$, $\mathsf{locks}\ \phi_2 \subseteq \mathsf{locks}\ m_2$, and $\bar{P} \vDash^n_l \hat{\mathbf{S}}(k_2,\ \phi_2,\ m_2)$,*

   *then $\bar{P} \vDash^{1+n}_l \hat{\mathbf{S}}(k,\ \phi,\ m)$.*

The intuitive meaning of $\bar{P} \vDash^n_l \hat{\mathbf{S}}(k,\ \phi,\ m)$ is that all $\twoheadrightarrow_l$-reductions paths of at most $n$ steps starting at $\mathbf{S}(k,\ \phi,\ m \cup m_f)$:

- do not get stuck, and do not end up in the $\overline{\mathsf{undef}}$ state,
- always satisfy $\mathsf{locks}\ \phi \subseteq \mathsf{locks}\ m$ during the execution, and
- the end-state satisfies $\bar{P}$ and has program context $l$.

To handle interleaving of expressions, we allow the framing memory $m_f$ to change at each step during the execution. Hence, instead of defining $\bar{P} \vDash^n_l \hat{\mathbf{S}}(k,\ \phi,\ m)$ using the reflexive transitive closure of $\twoheadrightarrow_l$, we defined it inductively using single steps. The condition $\mathsf{locks}\ \phi_2 \subseteq \mathsf{locks}\ m_2$ on the annotated locks with respect to the locks in the memory is used to separate the locks of subexpressions. We use a step-indexed approach to handle function calls.

The judgment $\bar{P} \vDash^n_l \hat{\mathbf{S}}(k,\ \phi,\ m)$ enjoys a nice composition property, and satisfies an abstract version of the weakening and frame rule of separation logic.

LEMMA 6.3. *Given contexts $k_1$, $k_2$ and $k_3$ with $k_2$ a suffix of $k_1$ and $k_3$ a suffix of $k_2$. If (a) $\bar{P} \vDash^n_{k_2} \hat{\mathbf{S}}(k_1,\ \phi,\ m)$, and (b) for all $m'$ and $\phi'$ with $\bar{P}\,(\mathsf{getstack}\,k_2)\,m'\,\phi'$ we have $\bar{Q} \vDash^n_{k_3} \hat{\mathbf{S}}(k_2,\ \phi',\ m')$, then finally we have $\bar{Q} \vDash^n_{k_3} \hat{\mathbf{S}}(k_1,\ \phi',\ m)$.*

LEMMA 6.4. *Given memories $m$ and $m_2$ such that $m \perp m_2$. If (a) $\bar{P} \vDash^n_l \hat{\mathbf{S}}(k,\ \phi,\ m)$, and (b) for all $m'$ and $\phi'$ with $m' \perp m_2$ and $\bar{P}\,(\mathsf{getstack}\,l)\,m'\ \phi'$ we have $\bar{Q}\,(\mathsf{getstack}\,l)\,(m' \cup m_2)\,\phi$, then finally we have $\bar{Q} \vDash^n_l \hat{\mathbf{S}}(k,\ \phi,\ m \cup m_2)$.*

DEFINITION 6.5. Validity of the environment $\Delta$, *notation $\vDash_n \Delta$ is defined as: for all $f$ with $\Delta\,f = (\forall \vec{y}\,.\,\forall \vec{v}\,.\,\{P\,\vec{y}\,\vec{v}\}\,\{Q\,\vec{y}\,\vec{v}\})$ and $P\,\vec{y}\,\vec{v}\,(\mathsf{getstack}\,k)\,m$ we have $\bar{Q}_{\vec{y},\vec{v}} \vDash^n_k \hat{\mathbf{S}}(\overline{\mathsf{call}}\,f\,\vec{v},\ k,\ m)$. Here, $\bar{Q}_{\vec{y},\vec{v}}$ is defined as:*

$$\bar{Q}_{\vec{y},\vec{v}} := \lambda \rho\,\phi\,m'\,.\,\exists v\,.\,\phi = \overline{\mathsf{return}}\,v \wedge \mathsf{locks}\ m = \emptyset \wedge Q\,\vec{y}\,\vec{v}\,v\,\rho\,m'.$$

DEFINITION 6.6. Partial correctness of an expression $e$, *notation $\Delta \vDash \{P\}\,e\,\{Q\}$ is defined as: if $\vDash_n \Delta$, $\mathsf{locks}\ e = \mathsf{locks}\ m = \emptyset$ and $P\,d\,(\mathsf{getstack}\,k)\,m$, then $\bar{Q} \vDash^n_k \hat{\mathbf{S}}(e,\ k,\ m)$. Here $\bar{Q}$ is defined as:*

$$\bar{Q} := \lambda \rho\,\phi\,m'\,.\,\exists v\,\Omega\,.\,\phi = [v]_\Omega \wedge \mathsf{locks}\ m = \Omega \wedge Q\,v\,\rho\,m'.$$

Krebbers and Wiedijk [21] noticed that the assertions $P$, $Q$, $J$ and $R$ in $\Delta;\ J;\ R \vDash \{P\}\,s\,\{Q\}$ correspond to the four directions $\searrow$, $\nearrow$, $\curvearrowright$ and $\upuparrows$ in which traversal through a statement is performed. Hence, we treat $\Delta;\ J;\ R \vDash \{P\}\,s\,\{Q\}$ as a triple $\Delta;\ \vec{P} \vDash s$, where $\vec{P}$ is a function from directions to assertions such that $\vec{P}\searrow\ = P$, $\vec{P}\nearrow\ = Q$, $\vec{P}\,(\curvearrowright l) = J\,l$ and $\vec{P}\,(\upuparrows v) = R\,v$.

DEFINITION 6.7. Partial correctness of a statement $s$, *notation* $\Delta;\ \vec{P} \vDash s$ *is defined as: if $\vDash_n \Delta$, $\mathsf{down}\ d\,s$, $\mathsf{locks}\ s = \mathsf{locks}\ m = \emptyset$ and $\vec{P}\,d\,(\mathsf{getstack}\,k)\,m$, then $\bar{P}_s \vDash^n_k \hat{\mathbf{S}}((d,\ s),\ k,\ m)$. Here, $\mathsf{down}$ holds if $\mathsf{down}\ \searrow s'$ or $\mathsf{down}\ (\curvearrowright l)\,s'$ with $l \in \mathsf{labels}\ s'$, and $\bar{P}_s$ is defined as:*

$$\bar{P}_s := \lambda \rho\,\phi\,m'\,.\,\exists d'\ s'\,.$$
$$\phi = (d',\ s') \wedge \neg\mathsf{down}\ d'\ s' \wedge \mathsf{locks}\ m = \emptyset \wedge \vec{P}\,d'\,\rho\,m'.$$

THEOREM 6.8 (Soundness). *We have:*

1. *$\Delta \vdash \{P\}\,e\,\{Q\}$ implies $\Delta \vDash \{P\}\,e\,\{Q\}$, and*
2. *$\Delta;\ J;\ R \vdash \{P\}\,s\,\{Q\}$ implies $\Delta;\ J;\ R \vDash \{P\}\,s\,\{Q\}$.*

This theorem is proven by mutual induction on the derivation of $\Delta \vdash \{P\}\,e\,\{Q\}$ and $\Delta;\ J;\ R \vdash \{P\}\,s\,\{Q\}$. Thus, for each rule of the axiomatic semantics, we have to show that it holds in the model. In order to prove the (e-base) case, we need to show that the expression evaluation $[\![\, e \,]\!]_{\rho,m}$ is sound with respect to the operational semantics. To prove the cases of the other expressions constructs, we use the following generic lemma that deals with the subtleties of interleaving subexpressions.

LEMMA 6.9. *Given a singular expression context $\mathcal{E}$ with $u$ holes and $\mathsf{locks}\ E = \emptyset$, memories $\vec{m}$ with $\perp \vec{m}$, expressions $\vec{e}$ with $\mathsf{locks}\ e_i \subseteq \mathsf{locks}\ m_i$ for each $i < u$, and functions of values to assertions $\vec{P}$ and $Q$. Now, if*

1. *$\bar{P}_i \vDash^n_k \hat{\mathbf{S}}(k,\ e_i,\ m_i)$ for each $i < u$, and*
2. *for all $\vec{\Omega}$, $\vec{v}$ and $\vec{m}'$ with $\perp \vec{m}'$,*
   *(a) $\mathsf{locks}\ m_i = \Omega_i$ for each $i < u$, and*
   *(b) $P_i\,v_i\,k, m'_i$ for each $i < u$,*
   *we have $\bar{Q} \vDash^n_k \hat{\mathbf{S}}(k,\ E[\,[v_0]_{\Omega_0} \ldots [v_n]_{\Omega_n}\,],\ \bigcup \vec{m}')$,*

*then $\bar{Q} \vDash^n_k \hat{\mathbf{S}}(k,\ E[\,\vec{e}\,],\ \bigcup \vec{m})$.*

The previous lemma is proven by induction on the number of steps $n$. Theorem 2.13 is used to reason about disjoint memories. The proofs of the cases for the statement judgments are quite similar to those by Krebbers and Wiedijk [21]; they involve chasing all possible reduction paths and use Lemma 6.3. We refer to the Coq formalization for the actual proofs.

## 7. Extensions

In this section we describe two extensions of our axiomatic semantics that improve handling of function calls. The first extension makes it easier to deal with pure functions (*i.e.* functions that have no side-effects), whereas the second extension enables different function calls in the same expression to have access to a shared writable part of the memory. These extensions do not change the memory model or the operational semantics.

We make it possible to associate a mathematical function to a pure function. For example, this can be used to smoothly use Coq's `gcd` function to reason about its counterpart in C. We extend the environment $\Delta$ to map function names to:

1. Specifications of pure functions by partial Coq functions, or,
2. Specifications of impure functions using their pre- and postcondition $\forall \vec{y}\,\forall \vec{v}\,.\,\{P\,\vec{y}\,\vec{v}\}\,\{Q\,\vec{y}\,\vec{v}\}$.

The (add funs) rule is extended so that a pure function $f$ with corresponding Coq function $F$ : $\mathsf{list\ val} \to \mathsf{val}^{\mathsf{opt}}$ can be added to $\Delta$ by proving $\forall \vec{v}\,.\,\{\mathsf{emp} \wedge F\,\vec{v} \neq \bot\}\,\{\lambda v\,.\,\mathsf{emp} \wedge F\,\vec{v} = v\}$. Assertions are made parametric with respect to the environment $\Delta$ so that pure functions can be given an interpretation by $[\![\, e \,]\!]_{\rho,m}$. The (e-base) rule becomes:

$$\frac{P \models_{\Delta} e \Downarrow v}{\Delta \vdash \{P\}\, e\, \{\lambda v'\,.\, v = v' \wedge P\}}$$

Apart from the parametrization by $\Delta$, most rules of the axiomatic semantics remain unchanged. To prove soundness of the (e-base) rule, we now also have to deal with pure function calls.

The rules for expressions of our axiomatic semantics require the memory to be separated into disjoint parts for the subexpressions $e_l$ and $e_r$ at each operator $e_l \circledcirc e_r$. Hence, only read-only memory can be shared by function calls that appear in both $e_l$ and $e_r$. This is not very satisfactory, as functions (even when used in the same expression) often need to have access to shared data structures (*e.g.* a buffer or hash-table). To that end, we extend the expression judgment $\Delta;\, B \vdash \{P\}\, e\, \{Q\}$ with an assertion $B$ that can be used to describe the invariant of shared memory by all function calls in $e$. The following frame rule can be used to move the memory out of the pre- and postcondition into the assertion $B$.

$$\frac{\Delta;\, A * B \vdash \{P\}\, e\, \{Q\}}{\Delta;\, B \vdash \{P * A\}\, e\, \{Q * A\}}$$

The rule (e-call) for function calls is changed so that $B$ can be used to prove the precondition, and so that $B$ has to be reobtained from the postcondition when the function call is finished.

For the soundness proof, we need to generalize Definition 6.2 so that the memory of $B$ is part of the framing memory $m_f$ during execution of the expression, and so that is will be transferred to the active memory at a function call. This extension still does not give completeness of the axiomatic semantics though. Consider:

```
int x = 0;
int f(int y) { return (x = y); }
int main() { f(3) + f(4); return x; }
```

Since the invariant $B$ should hold before, after, and in between the function calls in the expression `f(3) + f(4)`, the best choice for it is $\mathtt{x} \overset{\mathsf{W}}{\mapsto} 0 \vee \mathtt{x} \overset{\mathsf{W}}{\mapsto} 3 \vee \mathtt{x} \overset{\mathsf{W}}{\mapsto} 4$. Hence, one can only prove that the program returns 0, 3 or 4 in the end, whereas it actually returns 3 or 4. We believe programs as the above are artificial, and such non-determinism is not frequent in actual C programs.

## 8. Formalization in Coq

All proofs in this paper have been fully formalized using the Coq proof assistant. Formalization has been of great help in order to develop and debug the semantics. We used Coq's notation mechanism combined with unicode symbols and type classes for overloading to let the Coq development correspond as well as possible to the definitions in this paper. However, in this paper, we presented the axiomatic semantics as an inference system, and showed that it has a model. Since we did not consider completeness, we directly proved all rules to be derivable with respect to the model.

We used Coq's type classes to provide abstract interfaces for commonly used structures like finite sets and finite partial functions, so that we were able to prove theory and implement automation in an abstract way. Our approach is greatly inspired by the *unbundled* approach of Spitters and van der Weegen [33]. However, whereas their work heavily relies on *setoids* (types equipped with an equivalence relation), we tried to avoid that by using Leibniz equality as much as possible.

In particular, our interface for finite partial functions requires *extensionality* with respect to Leibniz equality, *i.e.* $m_1 = m_2$ iff $\forall x\,.\, m_1\, x = m_2\, x$. Extensional equality of finite partial functions is particularly useful for dealing with assertions, which are defined as predicates on the stack and memory (Definition 5.2). Due to extensionality, we did not have to equip assertions with a proof that they respect extensional equality on memories.

Although intensional type theories like Coq do not satisfy extensionality, finite functions indexed by a countable type can still be implemented in a way that extensionality holds. This is achieved by representing finite functions as trees in canonical form.

Coq's support for dependent types has been particularly useful to formulate Lemma 6.9 where we have to deal with expression contexts with multiple holes. We represented these expression contexts using a type indexed by the number of holes.

Because the semantics described in this paper is rather big, it is quite cumbersome to prove properties about it without automation. In particular, the reduction $\twoheadrightarrow$ (Definition 4.10) is defined as an inductive type consisting of 33 constructors. To this end, we have automated many steps of the proofs. For example, we implemented a tactic `do_cstep` to automatically perform reduction steps and to solve the required side-conditions, a tactic `inv_cstep` to perform case analyzes on reductions and to automatically discharge impossible cases, and a tactic `solve_mem_disjoint` to automatically prove disjointness of memories using the algebraic method described in Section 2. Ongoing experiments show that this approach is successful, as the semantics can be extended easily without having to redo many proofs.

Our Coq code, available at `http://robbertkrebbers.nl/research/ch2o`, is about 10 000 lines of code including comments and white space. Apart from that, our library on general purpose theory (finite sets, finite functions, lists, *etc.*) is about 9 000 lines.

## 9. Conclusions and further research

The further reaching goal of this work is to develop an operational and axiomatic semantics for a large part of the C11 programming language [20]. Formal treatment of non-determinism and sequence points in expressions with side-effects is a necessary step towards this goal. Our next step is to integrate the work of Krebbers [19] on the C memory model and type system into our formalization, and make the language typed. Once integrated, we intend to develop a verified type checker and interpreter so we can test the semantics using actual C programs.

Extending our operational semantics to deal with concurrency is also an interesting topic for future research. For example, it would be useful to investigate whether our semantics can be extended to weak memories in the same way as CompCert has been extended to CompCert TSO [32].

In order to turn the theory presented in this paper into an actual tool for verification of C programs, we need to develop a verification condition generator. A verification condition generator takes a program with logical annotations and generates a set of verification conditions that need to be verified. For ordinary Hoare logic, the most common approach is to use a variant of Dijkstra's weakest precondition calculus. For separation logic, one typically uses symbolic execution (see for example Berdine *et al.* [4]). In case of our axiomatic semantics, it is not directly clear whether any of these two approaches can be applied. The problematic part is that in the rules for binary operations, one has to split the memory in two parts using the separating conjunction $*$. It would be interesting to investigate how this can be automated.

Another challenge to use our axiomatic semantics for program verification is strong automation for separation logic. Specific to the Coq proof assistant there has been work on this by for example Appel [1], Chlipala [10], and Bengtson *et al.* [3].

As shown in Section 7, our axiomatic semantics is not complete with respect to the operational semantics. Nonetheless, as demonstrated in Section 5, we can derive the ordinary rules of separation logic, and rules specifically tailored for certain constructs. It would be useful to investigate whether it is complete for another variant of the operational semantics.

Due to our *local* treatment of locks to model the sequence point restriction, our operational semantics assigns undefined behavior to more programs than the C11 standard does (see page 5). We believe that this is a reasonable trade-off, because it brings the operational semantics closer to the axiomatic semantics, and only makes artificial programs illegal. Moreover, this treatment of locks may enable some useful optimizations that are not allowed by the C11 standard.

A particular optimization that is not justified by the C11 standard is CompCert [23]'s passing by reference of struct and union values through expressions. In CompCert, copies of struct and union values are made only at function calls and assignments. Let us take a look at the following example.

```
struct S { int x; } s1 = { 1 }, s2 = { 2 };
int f() {
  if (s1.x == 2) { s2.x = 40; } return 0;
}
int main() { return (s1 = s2).x + f(); }
```

The execution order where the CompCert semantics deviates from the C11 standard is: (a) perform the assignment `s1 = s2` whose result is a reference to `s2` instead of a copy of `s2`, (b) call `f`, which uses an `if (s1.x == 2)` to detect that the assignment `s1 = s2` has been executed, and finally (c) the field `x` of the struct that has been modified by `f` is taken. The return value for this execution order is 40, which cannot be obtained from any execution order if structs were passed by value.

Using a global treatment of sequence points (as in Ellison and Rosu [12] or Norrish [26]), no execution order of this program leads to a sequence point violation. However, with our local treatment of sequence points, the execution order described above will exhibit a sequence point violation, and hence our treatment would justify by reference passing of struct values for this program. It would be interesting to investigate whether our semantics of sequence points justifies by reference passing of struct and union values through expressions for arbitrary programs.

## Acknowledgments

I thank my advisors Freek Wiedijk and Herman Geuvers, and the anonymous referees for their helpful suggestions. I am indebted to Xavier Leroy for many useful discussions. This work is financed by the Netherlands Organisation for Scientific Research (NWO).

## References

[1] A. W. Appel. Tactics for Separation Logic, 2006. Available at `http://www.cs.princeton.edu/~appel/papers/septacs.pdf`.

[2] A. W. Appel and S. Blazy. Separation Logic for Small-Step Cminor. In *TPHOLs*, volume 4732 of *LNCS*, pages 5–21, 2007.

[3] J. Bengtson, J. B. Jensen, and L. Birkedal. Charge! - A Framework for Higher-Order Separation Logic in Coq. In *ITP*, volume 7406 of *LNCS*, pages 315–331, 2012.

[4] J. Berdine, C. Calcagno, and P. W. O'Hearn. Symbolic Execution with Separation Logic. In *APLAS*, volume 3780 of *LNCS*, pages 52–68, 2005.

[5] P. E. Black and P. J. Windley. Inference Rules for Programming Languages with Side Effects in Expressions. In *TPHOLs*, volume 1125 of *LNCS*, pages 51–60, 1996.

[6] R. Bornat, C. Calcagno, P. W. O'Hearn, and M. J. Parkinson. Permission Accounting in Separation Logic. In *POPL*, pages 259–270, 2005.

[7] J. Boyland. Checking Interference with Fractional Permissions. In *SAS*, volume 2694 of *LNCS*, pages 55–72, 2003.

[8] C. Calcagno, P. W. O'Hearn, and H. Yang. Local Action and Abstract Separation Logic. In *LICS*, pages 366–378, 2007.

[9] B. Campbell. An Executable Semantics for CompCert C. In *CPP*, volume 7679 of *LNCS*, pages 60–75, 2012.

[10] A. Chlipala. Mostly-automated verification of low-level programs in computational separation logic. In *PLDI*, pages 234–245. ACM, 2011.

[11] R. Dockins, A. Hobor, and A. W. Appel. A Fresh Look at Separation Algebras and Share Accounting. In *APLAS*, volume 5904 of *LNCS*, pages 161–177, 2009.

[12] C. Ellison and G. Rosu. An executable formal semantics of C with applications. In *POPL*, pages 533–544, 2012.

[13] C. Ellison and G. Rosu. Slides of [12], 2012. `http://fsl.cs.uiuc.edu/pubs/ellison-rosu-2012-popl-slides.pdf`.

[14] M. Felleisen, D. P. Friedman, E. E. Kohlbecker, and B. F. Duba. A syntactic theory of sequential control. *Theoretical Computer Science*, 52:205–237, 1987.

[15] P. Herms. *Certification of a Tool Chain for Deductive Program Verification*. PhD thesis, l'Université Paris-Sud, 2013.

[16] International Organization for Standardization. *ISO/IEC 9899-2011: Programming languages – C*. ISO Working Group 14, 2012.

[17] B. W. Kernighan and D. M. Ritchie. *The C Programming Language*. Prentice Hall, 2nd edition, 1988.

[18] R. Krebbers. Non-determinism and sequence points in C (blog post), 2013. Available at `http://gallium.inria.fr/blog/non-determinism-and-sequence-points-in-c/`.

[19] R. Krebbers. Aliasing restrictions of C11 formalized in Coq. In *CPP*, volume 8307 of *LNCS*, 2013.

[20] R. Krebbers and F. Wiedijk. A Formalization of the C99 Standard in HOL, Isabelle and Coq. In *CICM*, volume 6824 of *LNAI*, pages 297–299, 2011.

[21] R. Krebbers and F. Wiedijk. Separation Logic for Non-local Control Flow and Block Scope Variables. In *FoSSaCS*, volume 7794 of *LNCS*, pages 257–272, 2013.

[22] X. Leroy. A formally verified compiler back-end. *Journal of Automated Reasoning*, 43(4):363–446, 2009.

[23] X. Leroy. The CompCert verified compiler, software and commented proof. Available at `http://compcert.inria.fr/`, 2012.

[24] X. Leroy, A. W. Appel, S. Blazy, and G. Stewart. The CompCert Memory Model, Version 2. Research report RR-7987, INRIA, 2012.

[25] M. Norrish. *C formalised in HOL*. PhD thesis, University of Cambridge, 1998.

[26] M. Norrish. Deterministic Expressions in C. In *ESOP*, volume 1576 of *LNCS*, pages 147–161, 1999.

[27] P. W. O'Hearn. Resources, Concurrency and Local Reasoning. In *CONCUR*, volume 3170 of *LNCS*, pages 49–67, 2004.

[28] P. W. O'Hearn, J. C. Reynolds, and H. Yang. Local Reasoning about Programs that Alter Data Structures. In *CSL*, volume 2142 of *LNCS*, pages 1–19, 2001.

[29] D. v. Oheimb. Hoare logic for Java in Isabelle/HOL. *Concurrency and Computation: Practice and Experience*, 13(13):1173–1214, 2001.

[30] N. Papaspyrou. *A Formal Semantics for the C Programming Language*. PhD thesis, National Technical University of Athens, 1998.

[31] J. Regehr, Y. Chen, P. Cuoq, E. Eide, C. Ellison, and X. Yang. Test-case reduction for C compiler bugs. In *PLDI*, pages 335–346, 2012.

[32] J. Sevcík, V. Vafeiadis, F. Z. Nardelli, S. Jagannathan, and P. Sewell. CompCertTSO: A Verified Compiler for Relaxed-Memory Concurrency. *Journal of the ACM*, 60(3):22, 2013.

[33] B. Spitters and E. van der Weegen. Type classes for mathematics in type theory. *Mathematical Structures in Computer Science*, 21(4): 795–825, 2011.

# NetKAT: Semantic Foundations for Networks

Carolyn Jane Anderson
Swarthmore College *

Nate Foster
Cornell University

Arjun Guha
University of Massachusetts Amherst *

Jean-Baptiste Jeannin
Carnegie Mellon University *

Dexter Kozen
Cornell University

Cole Schlesinger
Princeton University

David Walker
Princeton University

## Abstract

Recent years have seen growing interest in high-level languages for programming networks. But the design of these languages has been largely ad hoc, driven more by the needs of applications and the capabilities of network hardware than by foundational principles. The lack of a semantic foundation has left language designers with little guidance in determining how to incorporate new features, and programmers without a means to reason precisely about their code.

This paper presents NetKAT, a new network programming language that is based on a solid mathematical foundation and comes equipped with a sound and complete equational theory. We describe the design of NetKAT, including primitives for filtering, modifying, and transmitting packets; union and sequential composition operators; and a Kleene star operator that iterates programs. We show that NetKAT is an instance of a canonical and well-studied mathematical structure called a Kleene algebra with tests (KAT) and prove that its equational theory is sound and complete with respect to its denotational semantics. Finally, we present practical applications of the equational theory including syntactic techniques for checking reachability, proving non-interference properties that ensure isolation between programs, and establishing the correctness of compilation algorithms.

***Categories and Subject Descriptors*** D.3.2 [*Programming Languages*]: Language Classifications—Specialized application languages

***Keywords*** Software-defined networking, Frenetic, Network programming languages, Domain-specific languages, Kleene algebra with tests, NetKAT.

## 1. Introduction

Traditional network devices have been called "the last bastion of mainframe computing" [9]. Unlike modern computers, which are implemented with commodity hardware and programmed using standard interfaces, networks have been built the same way since the 1970s: out of special-purpose devices such as routers, switches, firewalls, load balancers, and middle-boxes, each implemented with custom hardware and programmed using proprietary interfaces. This design makes it difficult to extend networks with new functionality and effectively impossible to reason precisely about their behavior.

However, a revolution has taken place with the recent rise of *software-defined networking* (SDN). In SDN, a general-purpose *controller machine* manages a collection of *programmable switches*. The controller responds to network events such as new connections from hosts, topology changes, and shifts in traffic load by re-programming the switches accordingly. Because the controller has a global view of the network, it is easy to use SDN to implement a wide variety of standard applications such as shortest-path routing, traffic monitoring, and access control, as well as more sophisticated applications such as load balancing, intrusion detection, and fault-tolerance.

A major appeal of SDN is that it defines open standards that any vendor can implement. For example, the OpenFlow API [21] clearly specifies the capabilities and behavior of switch hardware and defines a low-level language for manipulating their configurations. However, programs written directly for SDN platforms such as OpenFlow are akin to assembly: easy for hardware to implement, but difficult for humans to write.

***Network programming languages.*** In recent years, several different research groups have proposed domain-specific languages for SDN [5–7, 23–25, 31, 32]. The goal of these *network programming languages* is to raise the level of abstraction of network programs above hardware-oriented APIs such as OpenFlow, thereby making it easier to build sophisticated and reliable SDN applications. For example, the languages developed in the Frenetic project [30] support a two-phase programming model: (i) a general-purpose program responds to network events by generating a static forwarding policy; and (ii) the static policy is compiled and passed to a run-time system that configures the switches using OpenFlow messages. This model balances expressiveness—dynamic policies can be expressed by having the general-purpose program generate a sequence of static policies—and simplicity—forwarding policies are written in a simple domain-specific language with a clear semantics, so programs can be analyzed and even verified using automated tools [7, 26].

Still, it has never been clear what features a static policy language should support. The initial version of Frenetic [6] used simple lists of predicate-action rules as policies, where the actions in-

* This work performed at Cornell University.


*POPL '14*, January 22–24, 2014, San Diego, CA, USA.

http://dx.doi.org/10.1145/2535838.2535862

cluded constructs for filtering, forwarding, duplicating, and modifying packets. Subsequent versions of the language added (and later removed) the ability to embed arbitrary packet-processing functions in policies [23], as well as constructs for composing policies in parallel and sequence [24]. As Frenetic evolved, its designers added, removed, and modified the meaning of primitives as dictated by the needs of applications. Without principles or metatheory to guide its development, its evolution has lacked clear direction and foresight. The ad hoc semantics has not made clear which primitives are essential and which ones can be derived, and when new constructs have been added to the language, it has not been clear how they should interact with existing constructs and what behavioral laws they should obey.

An even more pressing issue is that these static policy languages only specify the forwarding behavior of the switches in the network. However, when a network program is actually executed, end-to-end functionality is determined both by the behavior of the switches and by the structure of the network topology. To answer almost any interesting question about the network such as *"Can X connect to Y?"*, *"Is traffic from A to B routed through Z?"*, or *"Is there a loop involving S?"*, the programmer must step outside the confines of the linguistic model and the abstractions it provides.

To summarize, we believe that a foundational model for network programming languages is essential. Such a model should (i) identify the essential constructs for programming networks, (ii) provide guidelines for incorporating new features, and (iii) unify reasoning about switches, topology and end-to-end behavior.

***Semantic foundations.*** This paper presents the first network programming language that meets these criteria. To begin, we focus on the global behavior of the network, unlike previous network programming languages, which have focused on the local behavior of individual switches. Abstractly, a network can be seen as an automaton that moves packets from node to node along the links in its topology. Hence, from a linguistic perspective, it is natural to use regular expressions, the language of finite automata. Regular expressions are a standard way to specify the packet-processing behavior of a network: a path is encoded as a concatenation of processing steps ($p \cdot q \cdot \cdots$), a set of paths is encoded as a union of paths ($p + q + \cdots$), and iterated processing is encoded using Kleene star. Moreover, by modeling the network in this way, we get a ready-made theory for reasoning about formal properties: *Kleene algebra* (KA), a decades-old sound and complete equational theory of regular expressions.

With Kleene algebra as the choice for representing global network structure, we can turn our attention to specifying local switch-processing functionality. Fundamentally, a switch implements *predicates* to match packets and *actions* that transform and forward matching packets. Existing languages build various abstractions atop the predicates and actions supplied by the hardware, but predicates and actions are essential. As a consequence, a foundational model for SDN must incorporate both *Kleene algebra* for reasoning about network structure and *Boolean algebra* for reasoning about the predicates that define switch behavior. Fortunately, these classic mathematical structures have already been unified in previous work on *Kleene algebra with tests* (KAT) [14].

By now KAT has a well-developed metatheory, including an extensive model theory and results on expressiveness, deductive completeness, and complexity. The axioms of KAT are sound and complete over a variety of popular semantic models, including language, relational, and trace models, and KAT has been applied successfully in a number of application areas, including compiler, device driver, and communication protocol verification [3, 15, 16, 22]. Moreover, equivalence in KAT has a PSPACE decision procedure. This paper applies this theory to a new domain: networks.

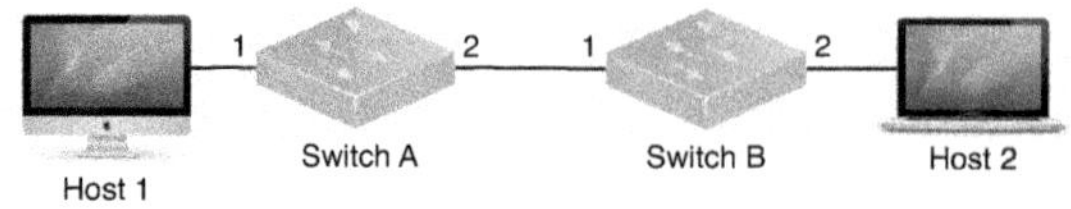


**Figure 1.** Example network.

***NetKAT.*** NetKAT is a new framework for specifying, programming, and reasoning about networks based on Kleene algebra with tests. As a programming language, NetKAT has a simple denotational semantics inspired by NetCore [23], but modified and extended in key ways to make it sound for KAT (which NetCore is not). In this respect, the semantic foundation provided by KAT has delivered true guidance: the axioms of KAT dictate the interactions between primitive program actions, predicates, and other operators. Moreover, any future proposed primitive that violates a KAT axiom can be summarily rejected for breaking the equations that allow us to reason effectively about the network. NetKAT thus provides a foundational structure and consistent reasoning principles that other network programming languages lack.

For specification and reasoning, NetKAT also provides a finite set of equations that capture equivalences between NetKAT programs. The equational theory includes the axioms of KAT, as well as domain-specific axioms that capture transformations on packets. This set of axioms enables reasoning about local switch processing functionality (needed in compilation and optimization) as well as global network behavior (needed to check reachability and traffic isolation properties). We prove that the equational theory is sound and complete with respect to the denotational semantics. While the soundness proof is straightforward, our proof of completeness is novel: we construct an alternate language model for NetKAT and leverage the completeness of KA.

To evaluate the practical utility of our theory and the expressive power of NetKAT, we demonstrate how it can be used to reason about a diverse collection of applications. First, we show that NetKAT can answer a variety of interesting reachability queries useful to network operators. Next, we state and prove a non-interference property for networks that provides a strong form of isolation between NetKAT programs. Finally, we prove that NetKAT can be correctly compiled to a low-level form analogous to switch flow tables.

In summary, the contributions of this paper are as follows:

- We develop a new semantic foundation for network programming languages based on Kleene algebra with tests (KAT).
- We formalize the NetKAT language in terms of a denotational semantics and an axiomatic semantics based on KAT; we prove the equational axioms sound and complete with respect to the denotational semantics.
- We apply the equational theory in several diverse domains including reasoning about reachability, traffic isolation, and compiler correctness.

The next section presents a simple example to motivate NetKAT and introduces the key elements of its design. The subsequent sections define the language formally, develop its main theoretical properties, and present applications.

## 2. Overview

This section introduces the syntax and semantics of NetKAT using a simple example. Consider the network shown in Figure 1. It consists of switches $A$ and $B$, each with ports labeled 1 and 2, and two hosts. The switches and hosts are connected together in series. Suppose we want to configure the network to implement the following policies:

- *Forwarding:* transfer packets between hosts, but
- *Access control:* block SSH packets.

The forwarding component is straightforward—configure both switches to forward packets destined for host 1 out port 1, and likewise for host 2—but there are several ways to implement the access control component. We will develop two implementations and prove them equivalent using NetKAT's equational theory.

***Forwarding.*** To warm up, let us define a simple NetKAT policy that implements the forwarding component. To a first approximation, a NetKAT policy can be thought of as a function from packets to sets of packets. (In the next section we will generalize this type to functions from lists of packets to sets of lists of packets, where the lists encode packet-processing histories, to support reasoning about network-wide properties.) We represent a packet as a record with fields for standard headers such as source address (src), destination address (dst), and protocol type (typ), as well as two fields, switch (sw) and port (pt), that identify the current location of the packet in the network.

Atomic NetKAT policies filter and modify packets. A filter ($f = n$) takes any input packet $pk$ and yields the singleton set $\{pk\}$ if field $f$ of $pk$ equals $n$, and $\{\}$ otherwise. A modification ($f \leftarrow n$) takes any input packet $pk$ and yields the singleton set $\{pk'\}$, where $pk'$ is the packet obtained from $pk$ by setting $f$ to $n$.

To allow programmers to express more sophisticated policies, NetKAT also has policy combinators that build bigger policies out of smaller ones. The union combinator ($p + q$) generates the union of the sets produced by applying each of $p$ and $q$ to the input packet, while the sequential composition combinator ($p \cdot q$) first applies $p$ to the input packet, then applies $q$ to each packet in the resulting set, and finally takes the union of all of the resulting sets. With these operators, we can implement the forwarding policy as follows:

$$p \triangleq (\mathsf{dst} = H_1 \cdot \mathsf{pt} \leftarrow 1) + (\mathsf{dst} = H_2 \cdot \mathsf{pt} \leftarrow 2)$$

At the top level, this policy is the union of two sub-policies. The first updates the pt field of all packets destined for $H_1$ to 1 and drops all other packets, while the second updates the pt field of all packets destined for $H_2$ to 2. The union of the two generates the union of their behaviors—in other words, the policy forwards packets across switches $A$ and $B$ in both directions.

***Access control.*** Next, we extend the policy with access control. The simplest way to do this is to compose a filter that blocks SSH traffic with the forwarding policy in sequence:

$$p_{AC} \triangleq \neg(\mathsf{typ} = \mathrm{SSH}) \cdot p$$

This policy drops the input packet if its typ field is SSH and otherwise forwards it using $p$. Of course, a quick inspection of the network topology shows that it is not necessary to test *all* packets at *all* locations in the network to block SSH traffic—packets traveling between host 1 and host 2 must traverse both switches, so it is sufficient to filter only at switch $A$,

$$p_A \triangleq (\mathsf{sw} = A \cdot \neg(\mathsf{typ} = \mathrm{SSH}) \cdot p) + (\mathsf{sw} = B \cdot p)$$

or at switch $B$:

$$p_B \triangleq (\mathsf{sw} = A \cdot p) + (\mathsf{sw} = B \cdot \neg(\mathsf{typ} = \mathrm{SSH}) \cdot p)$$

Both of these policies are more complicated than the original policy, but more efficient because they avoid having to store and enforce the access control policy at both switches. Naturally, we would prefer one of the optimized policies. In addition, we would like to be able to answer the following questions:

- *"Are non-SSH packets forwarded?"*
- *"Are SSH packets dropped?"*
- *"Are $p_{AC}$, $p_A$, and $p_B$ equivalent?"*

Network administrators ask these sorts of questions whenever they write a network policy. However, note that we cannot answer them by inspecting the policies alone—the answers depend fundamentally on the network topology. We will see how to incorporate topology information into a NetKAT program next.

***Topology.*** A network topology is a directed graph with hosts and switches as nodes and links as edges. We can model the topology as the union of smaller policies that encode the behavior of each link. To model an internal link, we use the sequential composition of a filter that retains packets located at one end of the link and a modification that updates the sw and pt fields to the location at the other end of the link, thereby capturing the effect of sending a packet across the link. To model a link at the perimeter of the network, we simply use a filter that retains packets located at the ingress port. We assume that links are uni-directional, and encode bi-directional links using pairs of uni-directional links. For example, the following policy models the internal links between switches $A$ and $B$, and the links at the perimeter to hosts 1 and 2:

$$\begin{aligned} t = {} & (\mathsf{sw} = A \cdot \mathsf{pt} = 2 \cdot \mathsf{sw} \leftarrow B \cdot \mathsf{pt} \leftarrow 1) + \\ & (\mathsf{sw} = B \cdot \mathsf{pt} = 1 \cdot \mathsf{sw} \leftarrow A \cdot \mathsf{pt} \leftarrow 2) + \\ & (\mathsf{sw} = A \cdot \mathsf{pt} = 1) + \\ & (\mathsf{sw} = B \cdot \mathsf{pt} = 2) \end{aligned}$$

Note that although we represent the links as policies, unlike switch policies, these link policies cannot actually be controlled programmatically—they must be consistent with the structure of the underlying physical topology.

***Switches meet topology.*** A packet traverses the network in interleaved steps of processing by the switches and topology. In our example, if host 1 sends a non-SSH packet to host 2, it is first processed by switch $A$, then the link between $A$ and $B$, and finally by switch $B$. This can be encoded by the NetKAT term $p_{AC} \cdot t \cdot p_{AC}$. More generally, a packet may require an arbitrary number of steps—in particular, if the topology has a cycle. Using the Kleene star operator, which iterates a policy zero or more times, we can encode the overall behavior of the network:

$$(p_{AC} \cdot t)^*$$

Note however that this policy processes packets that enter and exit the network at arbitrary locations, including at internal locations such as on the link between switches $A$ and $B$. It is often useful to restrict attention to packets that enter and exit the network at specified external locations $e$:

$$e \triangleq (\mathsf{sw} = A \cdot \mathsf{pt} = 1) + (\mathsf{sw} = B \cdot \mathsf{pt} = 2)$$

Using this predicate, we can restrict the policy to packets sent or received by one of the hosts:

$$p_{net} \triangleq e \cdot (p_{AC} \cdot t)^* \cdot e$$

More generally, the input and output predicates may be distinct:

$$in \cdot (p \cdot t)^* \cdot out$$

This encoding is inspired by the model used in Header Space Analysis [10]. We call a network modeled in this way a *logical crossbar* [20], since it encodes end-to-end processing behavior (and elides internal processing steps). Section 3 discusses a more refined model that encodes hop-by-hop processing.

***Formal reasoning.*** We now turn to formal reasoning and investigate whether the logical crossbar correctly implements the specified forwarding and access control policies. It turns out that these

**Syntax**

$$
\begin{array}{rrll}
\text{Fields} & f ::= & f_1 \mid \cdots \mid f_k & \\
\text{Packets} & pk ::= & \{f_1 = v_1, \cdots, f_k = v_k\} & \\
\text{Histories} & h ::= & pk::\langle\rangle \mid pk::h & \\
\text{Predicates} & a, b ::= & 1 & \textit{Identity} \\
 & \mid & 0 & \textit{Drop} \\
 & \mid & f = n & \textit{Test} \\
 & \mid & a + b & \textit{Disjunction} \\
 & \mid & a \cdot b & \textit{Conjunction} \\
 & \mid & \neg a & \textit{Negation} \\
\text{Policies} & p, q ::= & a & \textit{Filter} \\
 & \mid & f \leftarrow n & \textit{Modification} \\
 & \mid & p + q & \textit{Union} \\
 & \mid & p \cdot q & \textit{Sequential composition} \\
 & \mid & p^* & \textit{Kleene star} \\
 & \mid & \mathsf{dup} & \textit{Duplication}
\end{array}
$$

**Semantics**

$$
\begin{array}{rl}
[\![p]\!] \in \mathsf{H} \rightarrow \mathcal{P}(\mathsf{H}) & \\
[\![1]\!]\ h \triangleq \{h\} & \\
[\![0]\!]\ h \triangleq \{\} & \\
[\![f = n]\!]\ (pk::h) \triangleq \begin{cases} \{pk::h\} & \text{if } pk.f = n \\ \{\} & \text{otherwise} \end{cases} & \\
[\![\neg a]\!]\ h \triangleq \{h\} \setminus ([\![a]\!]\ h) & \\
[\![f \leftarrow n]\!]\ (pk::h) \triangleq \{pk[f := n]::h\} & \\
[\![p + q]\!]\ h \triangleq [\![p]\!]\ h \cup [\![q]\!]\ h & \\
[\![p \cdot q]\!]\ h \triangleq ([\![p]\!] \bullet [\![q]\!])\ h & \\
[\![p^*]\!]\ h \triangleq \bigcup_{i \in \mathbb{N}} F^i\ h & \\
\text{where } F^0\ h \triangleq \{h\} \text{ and } F^{i+1}\ h \triangleq ([\![p]\!] \bullet F^i)\ h & \\
[\![\mathsf{dup}]\!]\ (pk::h) \triangleq \{pk::(pk::h)\} &
\end{array}
$$

**Kleene Algebra Axioms**

| | |
|---|---|
| $p + (q + r) \equiv (p + q) + r$ | KA-PLUS-ASSOC |
| $p + q \equiv q + p$ | KA-PLUS-COMM |
| $p + 0 \equiv p$ | KA-PLUS-ZERO |
| $p + p \equiv p$ | KA-PLUS-IDEM |
| $p \cdot (q \cdot r) \equiv (p \cdot q) \cdot r$ | KA-SEQ-ASSOC |
| $1 \cdot p \equiv p$ | KA-ONE-SEQ |
| $p \cdot 1 \equiv p$ | KA-SEQ-ONE |
| $p \cdot (q + r) \equiv p \cdot q + p \cdot r$ | KA-SEQ-DIST-L |
| $(p + q) \cdot r \equiv p \cdot r + q \cdot r$ | KA-SEQ-DIST-R |
| $0 \cdot p \equiv 0$ | KA-ZERO-SEQ |
| $p \cdot 0 \equiv 0$ | KA-SEQ-ZERO |
| $1 + p \cdot p^* \equiv p^*$ | KA-UNROLL-L |
| $q + p \cdot r \leq r \Rightarrow p^* \cdot q \leq r$ | KA-LFP-L |
| $1 + p^* \cdot p \equiv p^*$ | KA-UNROLL-R |
| $p + q \cdot r \leq q \Rightarrow p \cdot r^* \leq q$ | KA-LFP-R |

**Additional Boolean Algebra Axioms**

| | |
|---|---|
| $a + (b \cdot c) \equiv (a + b) \cdot (a + c)$ | BA-PLUS-DIST |
| $a + 1 \equiv 1$ | BA-PLUS-ONE |
| $a + \neg a \equiv 1$ | BA-EXCL-MID |
| $a \cdot b \equiv b \cdot a$ | BA-SEQ-COMM |
| $a \cdot \neg a \equiv 0$ | BA-CONTRA |
| $a \cdot a \equiv a$ | BA-SEQ-IDEM |

**Packet Algebra Axioms**

| | |
|---|---|
| $f \leftarrow n \cdot f' \leftarrow n' \equiv f' \leftarrow n' \cdot f \leftarrow n$, if $f \neq f'$ | PA-MOD-MOD-COMM |
| $f \leftarrow n \cdot f' = n' \equiv f' = n' \cdot f \leftarrow n$, if $f \neq f'$ | PA-MOD-FILTER-COMM |
| $\mathsf{dup} \cdot f = n \equiv f = n \cdot \mathsf{dup}$ | PA-DUP-FILTER-COMM |
| $f \leftarrow n \cdot f = n \equiv f \leftarrow n$ | PA-MOD-FILTER |
| $f = n \cdot f \leftarrow n \equiv f = n$ | PA-FILTER-MOD |
| $f \leftarrow n \cdot f \leftarrow n' \equiv f \leftarrow n'$ | PA-MOD-MOD |
| $f = n \cdot f = n' \equiv 0$, if $n \neq n'$ | PA-CONTRA |
| $\sum_i f = i \equiv 1$ | PA-MATCH-ALL |

**Figure 2.** NetKAT: syntax, semantics, and equational axioms.

questions, and many others, can be reduced to policy equivalence. We write $p \equiv q$ when $p$ and $q$ return the same set of packets on all inputs, and $p \leq q$ when $p$ returns a subset of the packets returned by $q$ on all inputs. (Note that $p \leq q$ can be treated as an abbreviation for $p + q \equiv q$.) To establish that $p_{net}$ correctly filters all SSH packets going from port 1 on switch $A$ to port 2 on switch $B$, we check the following equivalence, where 0 is the filtering policy that drops all packets:

$$
\left(\begin{array}{l} \mathsf{typ} = \mathsf{SSH} \cdot \mathsf{sw} = A \cdot \mathsf{pt} = 1 \cdot \\ (p_{AC} \cdot t)^* \cdot \\ \mathsf{sw} = B \cdot \mathsf{pt} = 2 \end{array}\right) \equiv 0
$$

To establish that the optimized policies $p_A$ and $p_B$ correctly filter SSH packets going from port 1 on switch $A$ to port 2 on switch $B$, we check the following equivalences,

$$
\left(\begin{array}{l} \mathsf{typ} = \mathsf{SSH} \cdot \mathsf{sw} = A \cdot \mathsf{pt} = 1 \cdot \\ (p_A \cdot t)^* \cdot \\ \mathsf{sw} = B \cdot \mathsf{pt} = 2 \end{array}\right) \equiv 0
$$

and:

$$
\left(\begin{array}{l} \mathsf{typ} = \mathsf{SSH} \cdot \mathsf{sw} = A \cdot \mathsf{pt} = 1 \cdot \\ (p_B \cdot t)^* \cdot \\ \mathsf{sw} = B \cdot \mathsf{pt} = 2 \end{array}\right) \equiv 0
$$

Finally, to establish that $p_{AC}$ correctly forwards non-SSH packets from $H_1$ to $H_2$, we check the following inclusion:

$$
\begin{array}{l} (\neg(\mathsf{typ} = \mathsf{SSH}) \cdot \mathsf{sw} = A \cdot \mathsf{pt} = 1 \cdot \mathsf{sw} \leftarrow B \cdot \mathsf{pt} \leftarrow 2) \\ \leq (p_{AC} \cdot t)^* \end{array}
$$

and similarly for non-SSH packets $H_2$ to $H_1$.

Of course, to actually check these equivalences formally, we need a proof system. NetKAT is designed to not only be an expressive programming language, but also one that satisfies the axioms of a Kleene algebra with tests (KAT). Moreover, by extending KAT with additional axioms that capture the domain-specific features of networks, the equational theory is complete—*i.e.*, it can answer all the questions posed in this section, and many more. The following sections present the syntax, semantics, and equational theory of NetKAT formally (Section 3); prove that the equational theory is sound and complete with respect to the semantics (Section 4); and illustrate its effectiveness on a broad range of questions including additional reachability properties (Section 5), program isolation (Section 6) and compiler correctness (Section 7).

## 3. NetKAT

This section defines the syntax and semantics of NetKAT formally.

***Preliminaries.*** A packet $pk$ is a record with fields $f_1, \ldots, f_k$ mapping to fixed-width integers $n$. We assume a finite set of *packet* *headers*, including Ethernet source and destination addresses, VLAN tag, IP source and destination addresses, TCP and UDP source and destination ports, along with special fields for the switch (sw), port (pt), and payload. For simplicity, we assume that every packet contains the same fields. We write $pk.f$ for the value in field $f$ of $pk$, and $pk[f := n]$ for the packet obtained from $pk$ by updating field $f$ to $n$.

To facilitate reasoning about the paths a packet takes through the network, we maintain a *packet history* that records the state of each packet as it travels from switch to switch. Formally, a packet history $h$ is a non-empty sequence of packets. We write $pk::\langle\rangle$ to denote a history with one element, $pk::h$ to denote the history constructed by prepending $pk$ on to $h$, and $\langle pk_1, \ldots, pk_n\rangle$ for the history with elements $pk_1$ to $pk_n$. By convention, the first element of a history is the current packet; other elements represent previously-processed packets. We write H for the set of all histories, and $\mathcal{P}(\mathsf{H})$ for the powerset of H.

***Syntax.*** Syntactically, NetKAT expressions are divided into two categories: predicates $(a, b)$ and policies $(p, q)$. Predicates include constants true (1) and false (0), tests $(f = n)$, and negation $(\neg a)$, disjunction $(a+b)$, and conjunction $(a \cdot b)$ operators. Policies include predicates, modifications $(f \leftarrow n)$, union $(p + q)$ and sequential composition $(p \cdot q)$, iteration $(p^*)$, and a special policy that records the current packet in the history (dup). The complete syntax of NetKAT is given in Figure 2. By convention, $(^*)$ binds tighter than $(\cdot)$, which binds tighter than $(+)$. Hence, $a \cdot b + c \cdot d^*$ is the same as $(a \cdot b) + (c \cdot (d^*))$.

***Semantics.*** Semantically, every NetKAT predicate and policy denotes a function that takes a history $h$ and produces a (possibly empty) set of histories $\{h_1, \ldots, h_n\}$. Producing the empty set models dropping the packet (and its history); producing a singleton set models modifying or forwarding the packet to a single location; and producing a set with multiple histories models modifying the packet in several ways or forwarding the packet to multiple locations. Note that policies only ever inspect or modify the first (current) packet in the history. This means that an implementation need not actually record histories—they are only needed for reasoning.

Figure 2 defines the denotational semantics of NetKAT. Note that there is no separate definition for predicates—every predicate is a policy, and the semantics of $(\cdot)$ and $(+)$ are the same whether they are composing policies or predicates. The syntactic distinction between policies and predicates arises solely to ensure that negation is only applied to a predicate, and not, for example, to a policy such as $p^*$. Formally, a predicate denotes a function that returns either the singleton $\{h\}$ or the empty set $\{\}$ when applied to a history $h$. Hence, predicates behave like filters. A modification $(f \leftarrow n)$ denotes a function that returns a singleton history in which the field $f$ of the current packet has been updated to $n$. The union operator $(p + q)$ denotes a function that produces the union of the sets generated by $p$ and $q$, and sequential composition $(p \cdot q)$ denotes the Kleisli composition $(\bullet)$ of the functions $p$ and $q$, where the Kleisli composition of functions of type $\mathsf{H} \rightarrow \mathcal{P}(\mathsf{H})$ is defined as:

$$(f \bullet g)\, x \triangleq \bigcup \{g\, y \mid y \in f\, x\}\,.$$

Policy iteration $p^*$ is interpreted as a union of semantic functions $F_i$ of $h$, where each $F_i$ is the Kleisli composition of function denoted by $p$ $i$ times. Finally, dup denotes a function that duplicates the current packet and adds it to the history. Since modification updates the packet at the head of the history, dup "freezes" the current state of the packet and makes it observable.

Readers familiar with Frenetic and NetCore may notice some differences between the syntax used in previous network programming languages. This paper focuses on theoretical foundations, so we use the traditional "algebraic" syntax for KAT, which conflates

| Algebraic syntax | Surface syntax |
|---|---|
| $a, b ::= 1$ | `a,b ::= true` |
| $\mid\ 0$ | `\| false` |
| $\mid\ f = n$ | `\| f = n` |
| $\mid\ a + b$ | `\| a or b` |
| $\mid\ a \cdot b$ | `\| a and b` |
| $\mid\ \neg a$ | `\| not a` |
| $p, q ::= a$ | `p,q ::= filter a` |
| $\mid\ f \leftarrow n$ | `\| f := n` |
| $\mid\ p + q$ | `\| p \| q` |
| $\mid\ p \cdot q$ | `\| p ; q` |
| $\mid\ p^*$ | `\| p*` |
| $\mid$ dup | `\| dup` |

**Figure 3.** NetKAT algebraic and surface syntax.

the $(\cdot)$ and $(+)$ operators for predicates and programs and has constants 0 and 1. Figure 3 shows the relationship between this algebraic syntax and the surface syntax we use in programs.

***Equational theory.*** As its name suggests, NetKAT is a Kleene algebra with tests. Formally, a *Kleene algebra* (KA) is an algebraic structure,

$$(K, +, \cdot, ^*, 0, 1)$$

where $K$ is an idempotent semiring under $(+, \cdot, 0, 1)$, and $p^* \cdot q$ (respectively $q \cdot p^*$) is the least solution of the affine linear inequality $p \cdot r + q \leq r$ (respectively $r \cdot p + q \leq r$), where $p \leq q$ is an abbreviation for $p + q = q$. The axioms of KA are listed in Figure 2. A *Kleene algebra with tests* (KAT) is a two-sorted algebraic structure,

$$(K, B, +, \cdot, ^*, 0, 1, \neg)$$

where $\neg$ is a unary operator defined only on $B$, such that

- $(K, +, \cdot, ^*, 0, 1)$ is a Kleene algebra,
- $(B, +, \cdot, \neg, 0, 1)$ is a Boolean algebra, and
- $(B, +, \cdot, 0, 1)$ is a subalgebra of $(K, +, \cdot, 0, 1)$.

The axioms of Boolean algebra consist of the axioms of idempotent semirings (already listed as KA axioms) and the additional axioms listed in Figure 2. In previous work on KAT, the elements of $B$ and $K$ have usually been called *tests* and *actions* respectively; in this paper we will refer to them as predicates and policies.

It is easy to see that NetKAT has the required syntactic structure to be a KAT. However, the KAT axioms are not complete for the underlying NetKAT packet model. To establish completeness, we also need the packet algebra axioms listed in Figure 2. The first three axioms specify commutativity conditions. For example, the axiom PA-MOD-MOD-COMM states that assignments $\mathsf{src} \leftarrow X$ and $\mathsf{dst} \leftarrow Y$ can be applied in either order, as src and dst are different:

$$\mathsf{src} \leftarrow X \cdot \mathsf{dst} \leftarrow Y \equiv \mathsf{dst} \leftarrow Y \cdot \mathsf{src} \leftarrow X$$

Similarly, axiom PA-MOD-FILTER-COMM states that the assignment $\mathsf{src} \leftarrow X$ and predicate $\mathsf{sw} = A$ can be applied in either order. The axiom PA-DUP-FILTER-COMM states that every predicate commutes with dup. Interestingly, only this single axiom is needed to characterize dup in the equational theory. The next few axioms characterize modifications. The PA-MOD-FILTER axiom states that modifying a field $f$ to $n$ and then filtering on packets with $f$ equal to $n$ is equivalent to the modification alone. Similarly, the axiom PA-FILTER-MOD states that filtering on packets with field $f$ equal to $n$ and then modifying that field to $n$ is equivalent to just the filter. PA-MOD-MOD states that only the last assignment in a sequence of assignments to the same $f$ has any effect. The final two axioms characterize filters. The axiom PA-CONTRA states that a field cannot be equal to two different values at the same time, while the axiom

| | | |
|---|---|---|
| KAT-INVARIANT | If $a \cdot p \equiv p \cdot a$ then $a \cdot p^* \equiv a \cdot (p \cdot a)^*$ | Lemma 2.3.2 in [14] |
| KAT-SLIDING | $p \cdot (q \cdot p)^* \equiv (p \cdot q)^* \cdot p$ | Identity 19 in [14] |
| KAT-DENESTING | $p^* \cdot (q \cdot p^*)^* \equiv (p + q)^*$ | Identity 20 in [14] |
| KAT-COMMUTE | If for all atomic $x$ in $q$, $x \cdot p \equiv p \cdot x$ then $q \cdot p \equiv p \cdot q$ | Corollary of Lemma 4.4 in [2] |

**Figure 4.** KAT theorems.

PA-MATCH-ALL states that the sum of filters on every possible value is equivalent to the identity. This implies packet values are drawn from a finite domain, such as fixed-width integers.

***Example: access control.*** To illustrate the NetKAT equational theory, we prove a simple equivalence in Figure 5 using the policies from Section 2. Recall that the policy $p_A$ filters SSH packets on switch $A$ while $p_B$ filters SSH packets on switch $B$. We prove that these programs are equivalent on SSH traffic going from left to right across the network topology shown in Figure 1. This can be seen as a simple form of code motion—relocating the filter from switch $A$ to switch $B$. We use the logical crossbar encoding with the following input and output predicates:

$$in \triangleq (\mathsf{sw} = A \cdot \mathsf{pt} = 1)$$
$$out \triangleq (\mathsf{sw} = B \cdot \mathsf{pt} = 2)$$

As a warm up, we first prove two simpler lemmas that will be useful for the main code motion proof. The proofs of these lemmas are straightforward calculations using the NetKAT axioms and some standard KAT theorems (given in Figure 4). We shade the term(s) on each line that will be changed on the next step of the proof. To lighten the notation, we elide uses of axioms related to associativity, and use the following abbreviations:

$$a_A \triangleq (\mathsf{sw} = A) \qquad a_1 \triangleq (\mathsf{pt} = 1)$$
$$a_B \triangleq (\mathsf{sw} = B) \qquad a_2 \triangleq (\mathsf{pt} = 2)$$
$$m_A \triangleq (\mathsf{sw} \leftarrow A) \qquad m_1 \triangleq (\mathsf{pt} \leftarrow 1)$$
$$m_B \triangleq (\mathsf{sw} \leftarrow B) \qquad m_2 \triangleq (\mathsf{pt} \leftarrow 2)$$
$$\textsc{ssh} \triangleq (\mathsf{typ} = \textsc{ssh})$$

Lemma 1 states that the sequential composition of the input predicate, the predicate $a_B$, and an arbitrary policy $q$ is equivalent to the policy that drops all packets. Intuitively this holds because the input predicate matches packets on switch $A$ and $a_B$ matches packets on switch $B$. Lemma 2 states that the sequential composition of an arbitrary policy $q$, the predicate $a_A$, the topology $t$ from Section 2, and the output predicate is equivalent to the policy that drops all packets. Intuitively this holds because the topology does not forward packets located on any port of switch $A$ to port 2 of switch $B$. The proof is essentially a case analysis on the links in the topology. Using these lemmas, we then prove Lemma 3, which states that $p_A$ and $p_B$ both drop SSH traffic going from host 1 to host 2. Formal statements of these lemmas and proofs using the NetKAT equational axioms can be found in Figure 5.

## 4. Soundness, Completeness, and Decidability

This section proves the soundness and completeness of the NetKAT axioms with respect to the denotational semantics defined in Section 3. More formally, these results state that every equivalence provable using the NetKAT axioms also holds in the denotational model (Theorem 1), and that every equivalence which holds in the denotational model is provable using the axioms (Theorem 2). We also prove the decidability of NetKAT equivalence, and show that the problem is PSPACE-complete.

To obtain these results, we prove theorems that are stronger and more enlightening from a theoretical point of view. For soundness, we prove that the packet-history model used in the denotational semantics is isomorphic to a model based on binary relations, and appeal to the soundness of KAT over binary relation models. For completeness, we develop a language model for NetKAT that plays the same role as regular sets of strings and guarded strings do for KA and KAT respectively. We then relate the packet-history and language models, which allows us to leverage the completeness of KA to prove the completeness of the NetKAT axioms.

### 4.1 Soundness

To prove soundness, we begin by reformulating the standard packet-history semantics introduced in Section 3 in terms of binary relations. In the standard semantics, policies and predicates are modeled as functions $[\![p]\!] \in \mathsf{H} \to \mathcal{P}(\mathsf{H})$. This semantics is isomorphic to a relational semantics $[\cdot]$ in which each policy and predicate is interpreted as a binary relation $[p] \subseteq \mathsf{H} \times \mathsf{H}$:

$$(h_1, h_2) \in [p] \;\Leftrightarrow\; h_2 \in [\![p]\!]\,(h_1).$$

Intuitively, $[p]$ is the set of input-output pairs of the policy $p$.

Formally, the maps $[\![p]\!] \in \mathsf{H} \to \mathcal{P}(\mathsf{H})$ are morphisms of type $\mathsf{H} \to \mathsf{H}$ in $\mathsf{Kl}\,\mathcal{P}$, the Kleisli category of the powerset monad. It is well known that the Kleisli category $\mathsf{Kl}\,\mathcal{P}$ is isomorphic to the category $\mathsf{Rel}$ of sets and binary relations, as witnessed by currying:

$$X \to \mathcal{P}(Y) \cong X \to Y \to \mathbf{2} \cong X \times Y \to \mathbf{2} \cong \mathcal{P}(X \times Y).$$

In the relational model $[\cdot]$, product is interpreted as ordinary relational composition, and the remaining KAT operations translate under the isomorphism to the usual KAT operations on binary relations. Since the relational model with these distinguished operations satisfies the axioms of KAT (see *e.g.* [14, 17]), so do NetKAT models with the packet-history semantics of Section 3.

Let $\vdash$ denote provability in NetKAT. The following Theorem states the soundness of the NetKAT axioms.

**Theorem 1** (Soundness). *The* KAT *axioms and packet algebra axioms listed in Figure 2 are sound with respect to the semantics of Section 3. That is, if* $\vdash p \equiv q$, *then* $[\![p]\!] = [\![q]\!]$.

*Proof sketch.* We have already argued that the packet-history semantics is isomorphic to a relational KAT, and therefore satisfies the KAT axioms listed in Figure 2. It remains to show that the additional packet algebra axioms on the right-hand side of Figure 2 are also satisfied. These can all be verified by elementary arguments in relational algebra (see *e.g.* [28]). Some are special cases of [2, Equations (6)–(11)], whose soundness is proved in [2, Theorem 4.3]. See the long version of this paper for the full proof. □

### 4.2 Completeness

The proof of completeness proceeds in four steps:

1. We first define *reduced* NetKAT, a subset of NetKAT where policies are regular expressions over *complete tests* (a normal form for sequences of tests), *complete assignments* (a normal form for sequences of modifications), and dup. We show that every NetKAT policy is provably equivalent to a reduced NetKAT policy and that reduced terms have a simplified set of axioms pertaining to assignments and tests.
2. Inspired by past proofs of completeness for KA and KAT, we then develop a *language model* for reduced NetKAT. This language model gives semantics to policies via sets of guarded

**Lemma 1.** $in \cdot a_B \cdot q \equiv 0$

*Proof.*

$$
\begin{array}{l}
\quad in \cdot a_B \cdot q \\
\equiv \{ \text{ definition } in \ \} \\
\quad a_A \cdot a_1 \cdot a_B \cdot q \\
\equiv \{ \text{ KAT-COMMUTE } \} \\
\quad a_A \cdot a_B \cdot a_1 \cdot q \\
\equiv \{ \text{ PA-CONTRA } \} \\
\quad 0 \cdot a_1 \cdot q \\
\equiv \{ \text{ KA-ZERO-SEQ } \} \\
\quad 0 \qquad \square
\end{array}
$$

**Lemma 2.** $q \cdot a_A \cdot t \cdot out \equiv 0$

*Proof.*

$$
\begin{array}{l}
\quad q \cdot a_A \cdot t \cdot out \\
\equiv \{ \text{ definition } t \ \} \\
\quad q \cdot a_A \cdot (a_A \cdot a_2 \cdot m_B \cdot m_1 + \\
\qquad a_B \cdot a_1 \cdot m_A \cdot m_2 + \\
\qquad a_A \cdot a_1 + \\
\qquad a_B \cdot a_2) \cdot out \\
\equiv \{ \text{ KA-SEQ-DIST-L, KA-SEQ-DIST-R } \} \\
\quad q \cdot a_A \cdot a_A \cdot a_2 \cdot m_B \cdot m_1 \cdot out + \\
\quad q \cdot a_A \cdot a_B \cdot a_1 \cdot m_A \cdot m_2 \cdot out + \\
\quad q \cdot a_A \cdot a_A \cdot a_1 \cdot out + \\
\quad q \cdot a_A \cdot a_B \cdot a_2 \cdot out \\
\equiv \{ \text{ definition } out \ \} \\
\quad q \cdot a_A \cdot a_A \cdot a_2 \cdot m_B \cdot m_1 \cdot a_B \cdot a_2 + \\
\quad q \cdot a_A \cdot a_B \cdot a_1 \cdot m_A \cdot m_2 \cdot a_B \cdot a_2 + \\
\quad q \cdot a_A \cdot a_A \cdot a_1 \cdot a_B \cdot a_2 + \\
\quad q \cdot a_A \cdot a_B \cdot a_2 \cdot a_B \cdot a_2 \\
\equiv \{ \text{ PA-MOD-FILTER } \} \\
\quad q \cdot a_A \cdot a_A \cdot a_2 \cdot m_B \cdot m_1 \cdot a_1 \cdot a_B \cdot a_2 + \\
\quad q \cdot a_A \cdot a_B \cdot a_1 \cdot m_A \cdot a_A \cdot m_2 \cdot a_B \cdot a_2 + \\
\quad q \cdot a_A \cdot a_A \cdot a_1 \cdot a_B \cdot a_2 + \\
\quad q \cdot a_A \cdot a_B \cdot a_2 \cdot a_B \cdot a_2 \\
\equiv \{ \text{ KAT-COMMUTE } \} \\
\quad q \cdot a_A \cdot a_A \cdot a_2 \cdot m_B \cdot m_1 \cdot a_B \cdot a_1 \cdot a_2 + \\
\quad q \cdot a_A \cdot a_B \cdot a_1 \cdot m_A \cdot m_2 \cdot a_A \cdot a_B \cdot a_2 + \\
\quad q \cdot a_A \cdot a_A \cdot a_B \cdot a_1 \cdot a_2 + \\
\quad q \cdot a_A \cdot a_B \cdot a_2 \cdot a_B \cdot a_2 \\
\equiv \{ \text{ PA-CONTRA } \} \\
\quad q \cdot a_A \cdot a_A \cdot a_2 \cdot m_B \cdot m_1 \cdot a_B \cdot 0 + \\
\quad q \cdot a_A \cdot a_B \cdot a_1 \cdot m_A \cdot m_2 \cdot 0 \cdot a_2 + \\
\quad q \cdot a_A \cdot a_A \cdot a_B \cdot 0 + \\
\quad q \cdot 0 \cdot a_2 \cdot a_B \cdot a_2 \\
\equiv \{ \text{ KA-SEQ-ZERO, KA-ZERO-SEQ } \} \\
\quad 0 + 0 + 0 + 0 \\
\equiv \{ \text{ KA-PLUS-IDEM } \} \\
\quad 0 \qquad \square
\end{array}
$$

**Lemma 3.** $in \cdot \text{SSH} \cdot (p_A \cdot t)^* \cdot out \equiv in \cdot \text{SSH} \cdot (p_B \cdot t)^* \cdot out$

*Proof.*

$$
\begin{array}{l}
\quad in \cdot \text{SSH} \cdot (p_A \cdot t)^* \cdot out \\
\equiv \{ \text{ KAT-INVARIANT, definition } p_A \ \} \\
\quad in \cdot \text{SSH} \cdot ((a_A \cdot \neg\text{SSH} \cdot p + a_B \cdot p) \cdot t \cdot \text{SSH})^* \cdot out \\
\equiv \{ \text{ KA-SEQ-DIST-R } \} \\
\quad in \cdot \text{SSH} \cdot (a_A \cdot \neg\text{SSH} \cdot p \cdot t \cdot \text{SSH} + a_B \cdot p \cdot t \cdot \text{SSH})^* \cdot out \\
\equiv \{ \text{ KAT-COMMUTE } \} \\
\quad in \cdot \text{SSH} \cdot (a_A \cdot \neg\text{SSH} \cdot \text{SSH} \cdot p \cdot t + a_B \cdot p \cdot t \cdot \text{SSH})^* \cdot out \\
\equiv \{ \text{ BA-CONTRA } \} \\
\quad in \cdot \text{SSH} \cdot (a_A \cdot 0 \cdot p \cdot t + a_B \cdot p \cdot t \cdot \text{SSH})^* \cdot out \\
\equiv \{ \text{ KA-SEQ-ZERO/ZERO-SEQ, KA-PLUS-COMM, KA-PLUS-ZERO } \} \\
\quad in \cdot \text{SSH} \cdot (a_B \cdot p \cdot t \cdot \text{SSH})^* \cdot out \\
\equiv \{ \text{ KA-UNROLL-L } \} \\
\quad in \cdot \text{SSH} \cdot (1 + (a_B \cdot p \cdot t \cdot \text{SSH}) \cdot (a_B \cdot p \cdot t \cdot \text{SSH})^*) \cdot out \\
\equiv \{ \text{ KA-SEQ-DIST-L, KA-SEQ-DIST-R, definition } out \ \} \\
\quad in \cdot \text{SSH} \cdot a_B \cdot a_2 + \\
\quad in \cdot \text{SSH} \cdot a_B \cdot p \cdot t \cdot \text{SSH} \cdot (a_B \cdot p \cdot t \cdot \text{SSH})^* \cdot a_B \cdot a_2 \\
\equiv \{ \text{ KAT-COMMUTE } \} \\
\quad in \cdot a_B \cdot \text{SSH} \cdot a_2 + \\
\quad in \cdot a_B \cdot \text{SSH} \cdot p \cdot t \cdot \text{SSH} \cdot (a_B \cdot p \cdot t \cdot \text{SSH})^* \cdot a_B \cdot a_2 \\
\equiv \{ \text{ Lemma 1 } \} \\
\quad 0 + 0 \\
\equiv \{ \text{ KA-PLUS-IDEM } \} \\
\quad 0 \\
\equiv \{ \text{ KA-PLUS-IDEM } \} \\
\quad 0 + 0 \\
\equiv \{ \text{ Lemma 1, Lemma 2 } \} \\
\quad in \cdot a_B \cdot \text{SSH} \cdot a_2 + \\
\quad in \cdot \text{SSH} \cdot (a_A \cdot p \cdot t \cdot \text{SSH})^* \cdot p \cdot \text{SSH} \cdot a_A \cdot t \cdot out \\
\equiv \{ \text{ KAT-COMMUTE, definition } out \ \} \\
\quad in \cdot \text{SSH} \cdot out + \\
\quad in \cdot \text{SSH} \cdot (a_A \cdot p \cdot t \cdot \text{SSH})^* \cdot a_A \cdot p \cdot t \cdot \text{SSH} \cdot out \\
\equiv \{ \text{ KA-SEQ-DIST-L, KA-SEQ-DIST-R } \} \\
\quad in \cdot \text{SSH} \cdot (1 + (a_A \cdot p \cdot t \cdot \text{SSH})^* \cdot (a_A \cdot p \cdot t \cdot \text{SSH})) \cdot out \\
\equiv \{ \text{ KA-UNROLL-R } \} \\
\quad in \cdot \text{SSH} \cdot (a_A \cdot p \cdot t \cdot \text{SSH})^* \cdot out \\
\equiv \{ \text{ KA-SEQ-ZERO/ZERO-SEQ, KA-PLUS-ZERO } \} \\
\quad in \cdot \text{SSH} \cdot (a_A \cdot p \cdot t \cdot \text{SSH} + a_B \cdot 0 \cdot p \cdot t)^* \cdot out \\
\equiv \{ \text{ BA-CONTRA } \} \\
\quad in \cdot \text{SSH} \cdot (a_A \cdot p \cdot t \cdot \text{SSH} + a_B \cdot \neg\text{SSH} \cdot \text{SSH} \cdot p \cdot t)^* \cdot out \\
\equiv \{ \text{ KAT-COMMUTE } \} \\
\quad in \cdot \text{SSH} \cdot (a_A \cdot p \cdot t \cdot \text{SSH} + a_B \cdot \neg\text{SSH} \cdot p \cdot t \cdot \text{SSH})^* \cdot out \\
\equiv \{ \text{ KA-SEQ-DIST-R } \} \\
\quad in \cdot \text{SSH} \cdot ((a_A \cdot p + a_B \cdot \neg\text{SSH} \cdot p) \cdot t \cdot \text{SSH})^* \cdot out \\
\equiv \{ \text{ KAT-INVARIANT, definition } p_B \ \} \\
\quad in \cdot \text{SSH} \cdot (p_B \cdot t)^* \cdot out \qquad \square
\end{array}
$$

**Figure 5.** Code motion proofs.

strings. We prove the language model and the standard model of NetKAT given by the denotational semantics are isomorphic.

3. We then define a normal form for NetKAT policies, and show that every policy is provably equivalent to its normal form.
4. Finally, we relate NetKAT normal forms to regular sets of guarded strings, and obtain the completeness of NetKAT from the completeness of KA.

The rest of this section outlines the key steps of this proof. The long version of this paper gives further details.

***Step 1: Reduced NetKAT.*** Let $f_1, \ldots, f_k$ be a list of all fields of a packet in some (fixed) order. For each tuple $\bar{n} = n_1, \ldots, n_k$ of values, let $\bar{f} = \bar{n}$ and $\bar{f} \leftarrow \bar{n}$ denote the expressions

$$f_1 = n_1 \cdots f_k = n_k \qquad f_1 \leftarrow n_1 \cdots f_k \leftarrow n_k,$$

**Reduced NetKAT syntax**

| | | | |
|---|---|---|---|
| Complete assignments | $\pi \triangleq$ | $f_1 \leftarrow n_1 \cdots f_k \leftarrow n_k$ | |
| Complete tests | $\alpha, \beta \triangleq$ | $f_1 = n_1 \cdots f_k = n_k$ | |
| Reduced terms | $p, q ::= \alpha$ | | *Complete test* |
| | $\mid \pi$ | | *Complete assignment* |
| | $\mid p + q$ | | *Union* |
| | $\mid p \cdot q$ | | *Sequence* |
| | $\mid p^*$ | | *Kleene star* |
| | $\mid \mathsf{dup}$ | | *Duplication* |

**Simplified axioms for $A$ and $P$**

$$\pi \equiv \pi \cdot \alpha_\pi \qquad \alpha \cdot \mathsf{dup} \equiv \mathsf{dup} \cdot \alpha \qquad \sum_\alpha \alpha \equiv 1,$$

$$\alpha \equiv \alpha \cdot \pi_\alpha \qquad \pi \cdot \pi' \equiv \pi' \qquad \alpha \cdot \beta \equiv 0,\ \alpha \neq \beta$$

**Regular interpretation:** $R(p) \subseteq (\Pi + A + \mathsf{dup})^*$

$$\begin{aligned} R(\pi) &= \{\pi\} \\ R(p+q) &= R(p) \cup R(q) \\ R(\alpha) &= \{\alpha\} \\ R(p \cdot q) &= \{xy \mid x \in R(p), y \in R(q)\} \\ R(\mathsf{dup}) &= \{\mathsf{dup}\} \\ R(p^*) &= \bigcup_{n \geq 0} R(p^n) \end{aligned}$$

**Figure 6.** Reduced NetKAT.

**Language model:** $G(p) \subseteq I = A \cdot (\Pi \cdot \mathsf{dup})^* \cdot \Pi$

$$\begin{aligned} G(\pi) &= \{\alpha \cdot \pi \mid \alpha \in A\} \\ G(p+q) &= G(p) \cup G(q) \\ G(\alpha) &= \{\alpha \cdot \pi_\alpha\} \\ G(p \cdot q) &= G(p) \diamond G(q) \\ G(\mathsf{dup}) &= \{\alpha \cdot \pi_\alpha \cdot \mathsf{dup} \cdot \pi_\alpha \mid \alpha \in A\} \\ G(p^*) &= \bigcup_{n \geq 0} G(p^n) \end{aligned}$$

**Guarded concatenation**

$$\alpha \cdot p \cdot \pi \diamond \beta \cdot q \cdot \pi' = \begin{cases} \alpha \cdot p \cdot q \cdot \pi' & \text{if } \beta = \alpha_\pi \\ \text{undefined} & \text{if } \beta \neq \alpha_\pi \end{cases}$$

$$A \diamond B = \{p \diamond q \mid p \in A,\ q \in B\} \subseteq I$$

**Figure 7.** NetKAT language model.

respectively. We call these expressions *complete tests* and *complete assignments* respectively. We often call complete tests *atoms* because they are atoms (minimal nonzero elements) of the Boolean algebra generated by the tests. Note that complete tests and complete assignments are in one-to-one correspondence according to the values $\bar{n}$. Hence, if $\alpha$ is an atom, we denote the corresponding complete assignment by $\pi_\alpha$, and if $\pi$ is a complete assignment, we denote the corresponding atom by $\alpha_\pi$. We let $A$ denote the set of atoms and $\Pi$ the set of complete assignments.

Now that we have defined atoms and complete assignments, we investigate their properties. Figure 6 gives a collection of simple axioms for reduced policies that are easily provable using the full NetKAT axioms. One useful consequence of these axioms is

$$\textstyle\sum_{\alpha \in A} \alpha \cdot \pi_\alpha \equiv 1.$$

Any policy is provably equivalent to a policy in which all atomic assignments $f \leftarrow n$ appear in the context of a complete assignment. The proof of this fact is straightforward.

$$\begin{aligned} f \leftarrow n &\equiv 1 \cdot f \leftarrow n \\ &\equiv (\textstyle\sum_{\alpha \in A} \alpha \cdot \pi_\alpha) \cdot (f \leftarrow n) \\ &\equiv \textstyle\sum_{\alpha \in A} \alpha \cdot \pi'_\alpha \end{aligned}$$

where $\pi'_\alpha$ is $\pi_\alpha$ with the assignment to $f$ replaced by $f \leftarrow n$. Similarly, every test is equivalent to a sum of complete tests:

$$b \equiv \textstyle\sum_{\alpha \leq b} \alpha$$

Since all modifications can be replaced by complete assignments and all tests by atoms, any NetKAT policy $p$ can be viewed as a regular expression over the alphabet $\Pi \cup A \cup \{\mathsf{dup}\}$. The bottom of Figure 6 shows this by defining a mapping $R$ from reduced NetKAT to regular sets over this alphabet. We assume for the remainder of this section that all NetKAT policies are in reduced form.

***Step 2: Language model.*** Both KA and KAT have language models in which expressions are interpreted as regular sets of minimal nonzero terms (often called join-irreducible terms). For KA, the language model is the regular sets of strings, and for KAT, it is the regular sets of guarded strings [17]. NetKAT also has a language model. It consists of regular subsets of a restricted class of guarded strings $I = A \cdot (\Pi \cdot \mathsf{dup})^* \cdot \Pi$. Each string in this set has the form

$$\alpha \cdot \pi_0 \cdot \mathsf{dup} \cdot \pi_1 \cdot \mathsf{dup} \cdots \mathsf{dup} \cdot \pi_n$$

for some $n \geq 0$. These strings represent the minimal nonzero elements of the standard model of NetKAT.

Figure 7 defines the language model as a mapping $G$ from reduced NetKAT expressions to regular subsets of $I$. The case for sequential composition makes use of the concatenation operator ($\diamond$) over strings from $I$, which we lift to concatenation of sets of guarded strings from $I$. Both definitions appear at the bottom of Figure 7. Note that $\diamond$ is a partial function on strings but a total function on sets of strings. Using the simplified axioms of Figure 6, it is easy to show that $\diamond$ is associative on strings and sets, distributes over union, and has two-sided identity $\{\alpha \cdot \pi_\alpha \mid \alpha \in A\}$. Also note that if

$$\alpha \cdot p \cdot \pi \diamond \beta \cdot q \cdot \pi'$$

exists, then

$$\vdash \alpha \cdot p \cdot \pi \cdot \beta \cdot q \cdot \pi' \equiv \alpha \cdot p \cdot \pi \diamond \beta \cdot q \cdot \pi' \in I$$

and otherwise:

$$\vdash \alpha \cdot p \cdot \pi \cdot \beta \cdot q \cdot \pi' \equiv 0$$

Having defined the language model, we now show that it is isomorphic to the standard packet model presented in Section 3. We first show that the standard semantics of every NetKAT expression is equal to the union of its minimal nonzero terms.[1] The proof is straightforward by induction on $p$.

**Lemma 4.** *For all policies $p$, we have $[\![p]\!] = \bigcup_{x \in G(p)} [\![x]\!]$.*

Next we prove that every $x$ in $I$ is completely determined by $[\![x]\!]$.

**Lemma 5.** *If $x, y \in I$, then $[\![x]\!] = [\![y]\!]$ if and only if $x = y$.*

Finally, using Lemmas 4 and 5, we conclude that the language model is isomorphic to the denotational model presented earlier.

**Lemma 6.** *For all policies $p$ and $q$, we have $[\![p]\!] = [\![q]\!]$ if and only if $G(p) = G(q)$.*

[1] We abuse notation slightly here by applying the union operator $\bigcup$ to functions $\mathsf{H} \to \mathcal{P}(\mathsf{H})$. This is interpreted pointwise: $\bigcup [\![p]\!] = \lambda s. \bigcup [\![p]\!](s)$.

***Step 3: Normal forms.*** Next we define a normal form for NetKAT policies and prove that every policy is provably equivalent to one in normal form.

**Definition 1.** *A NetKAT policy $p$ is in* normal form *if $R(p) \subseteq I$. A policy is* normalizable *if it is provably equivalent to a policy in normal form.*

**Lemma 7.** *Every policy $p$ is normalizable.*

*Proof.* The inductive proof requires a slightly strengthened inductive hypothesis. Let us say that a policy is in *strong normal form* if it is in normal form and is a sum of zero or more guarded policies, where a policy is *guarded* if it is of the form either $\alpha \cdot \pi \cdot x \cdot \pi'$ or $\alpha \cdot \pi$. We show by induction on $p$ that every policy is equivalent to a policy in strong normal form.

The cases for atomic policies are straightforward:

$$\begin{array}{lcl} h \leftarrow n & \equiv & \sum_{\alpha \in A} \alpha \cdot \pi'_\alpha \\ \mathsf{dup} & \equiv & \sum_{\alpha \in A} \alpha \cdot \pi_\alpha \cdot \mathsf{dup} \cdot \pi_\alpha \\ b & \equiv & \sum_{\alpha \leq b} \alpha \cdot \pi_\alpha \end{array}$$

The case for union is trivial, and the case for sequential composition follows by a simple argument:

$$\left(\sum_i s_i\right) \cdot \left(\sum_j t_j\right) \equiv \sum_i \sum_j s_i \cdot t_j \equiv \sum_i \sum_j s_i \diamond t_j.$$

The most interesting case is for Kleene star. Consider an expression $p^*$, where $p$ is in strong normal form. We first prove the uniform case: when all guarded terms in $p$ have the same initial atom $\alpha$, that is, $p = \alpha \cdot t$ where $t$ is a union of terms each with a leading and trailing $\pi$, and $R(t) \subseteq \Pi \cdot (\mathsf{dup} \cdot \Pi)^*$. Let $u$ be $t$ with all terms whose trailing $\pi$ is not $\pi_\alpha$ deleted and with the trailing $\pi_\alpha$ deleted from all remaining terms. By the simplified axioms of Figure 6, we have $t \cdot \alpha \cdot t \equiv u \cdot t$, therefore $t \cdot \alpha \cdot t \cdot \alpha \equiv u \cdot t \cdot \alpha$. Using KAT-COMMUTE [2, Lemma 4.4],

$$\begin{array}{lcl} (t \cdot \alpha)^* \cdot t & \equiv & t + t \cdot \alpha \cdot (t \cdot \alpha)^* \cdot t \\ & \equiv & t + u^* \cdot t \cdot \alpha \cdot t \\ & \equiv & t + u^* \cdot u \cdot t \\ & \equiv & u^* \cdot t, \end{array}$$

and hence

$$\begin{array}{lcl} p^* & \equiv & 1 + p^* \cdot p \\ & \equiv & 1 + (\alpha \cdot t)^* \cdot \alpha \cdot t \\ & \equiv & 1 + \alpha \cdot (t \cdot \alpha)^* \cdot t \\ & \equiv & 1 + \alpha \cdot u^* \cdot t \\ & \equiv & 1 + \alpha \cdot t + \alpha \cdot u \cdot u^* \cdot t, \end{array}$$

which after normalizing the 1 is in strong normal form. For the case $p^*$ where the initial tests in $p$ are not uniform, the argument is by induction on the number of terms in the union. If $p = \alpha \cdot x + q$, then by the inductive hypothesis, $q^*$ has an equivalent strong normal form $\hat{q}^*$. Using KAT-DENESTING (Figure 4), we obtain

$$p^* \equiv (\alpha \cdot x + q)^* \equiv q^* \cdot (\alpha \cdot x \cdot q^*)^* \equiv \hat{q}^* \cdot (\alpha \cdot x \cdot \hat{q}^*)^*,$$

then proceed as in the previous case. □

***Step 4: Completeness.*** We need just one more lemma before delivering the completeness result, which says that the regular interpretation and language model coincide for NetKAT policies in normal form.

**Lemma 8.** *If $R(p) \subseteq I$, then $R(p) = G(p)$.*

*Proof.* Suppose $R(p) \subseteq I$. It is straightforward to show that $G(p)$ is equal to the union of the elements of $R(p)$, by induction on $p$:

$$G(p) = \bigcup_{x \in R(p)} G(x).$$

Then, since $G(x) = \{x\}$ for $x \in I$, we have

$$G(p) = \bigcup_{x \in R(p)} \{x\} = R(p). \qquad \square$$

The proof of completeness for NetKAT now follows from the completeness of KA [12].

**Theorem 2** (Completeness). *Every semantically equivalent pair of NetKAT expressions is provably equivalent using the NetKAT axioms. That is, if $[\![p]\!] = [\![q]\!]$, then $\vdash p \equiv q$.*

*Proof.* Let $\hat{p}$ and $\hat{q}$ be the normal forms of $p$ and $q$. By Lemma 7, we can prove that each is equivalent to its normal form: $\vdash p \equiv \hat{p}$ and $\vdash q \equiv \hat{q}$. By soundness we have $[\![p]\!] = [\![\hat{p}]\!]$ and $[\![q]\!] = [\![\hat{q}]\!]$, hence $[\![\hat{p}]\!] = [\![\hat{q}]\!]$. By Lemma 6, we have $G(\hat{p}) = G(\hat{q})$. Moreover, by Lemma 8, we have $G(\hat{p}) = R(\hat{p})$ and $G(\hat{q}) = R(\hat{q})$, thus $R(\hat{p}) = R(\hat{q})$. Since $R(\hat{p})$ and $R(\hat{q})$ are regular sets, we have $\vdash \hat{p} \equiv \hat{q}$ by the completeness of KA. Finally, as $\vdash p \equiv \hat{p}$ and $\vdash q \equiv \hat{q}$ and $\vdash \hat{p} \equiv \hat{q}$, we conclude that $\vdash p \equiv q$. □

### 4.3 Decidability

The final theorem presented in this section shows that deciding the equational theory of NetKAT is no more nor less difficult than for KA or KAT.

**Theorem 3.** *The equational theory of NetKAT is PSPACE-complete.*

*Proof sketch.* To show PSPACE-hardness, reduce KA to NetKAT as follows. Let $\Sigma$ be a finite alphabet. For a regular expression $e$ over $\Sigma$, let $R(e)$ be the regular set of strings over $\Sigma$ as defined in §4. Transform $e$ to a NetKAT expression $e'$ by replacing each occurrence in $e$ of a symbol $p \in \Sigma$ with $(p \cdot \mathsf{dup})$ and prepending with an arbitrary but fixed atom $\alpha$. It follows from Lemmas 6 and 8 that $R(e_1) = R(e_2)$ if and only if $R(e'_1) = R(e'_2)$ if and only if $G(e'_1) = G(e'_2)$ if and only if $[\![e'_1]\!] = [\![e'_2]\!]$.

To show that the problem is in PSPACE, given two NetKAT expressions $e_1$ and $e_2$, we know that $[\![e_1]\!] \neq [\![e_2]\!]$ if and only if there is a packet $pk$ and packet history $h$ such that $h \in [\![e_1]\!]\,(pk) \setminus [\![e_2]\!]\,(pk)$ or $h \in [\![e_2]\!]\,(pk) \setminus [\![e_1]\!]\,(pk)$; let us say the former without loss of generality. We guess $pk$ nondeterministically and follow a nondeterministically-guessed trajectory through $e_1$ that produces some $h \in [\![e_1]\!]\,(pk)$. At the same time, we trace all possible trajectories through $e_2$ that could generate a prefix of $h$, ensuring that none of these produce $h \in [\![e_2]\!]$. It takes only polynomial space to represent the current values of the fields of the head packet and the possible positions in $e_2$ for the current prefix of $h$. The algorithm is nondeterministic, but can be made deterministic using Savitch's theorem. □

## 5. Reachability Properties

Network administrators often ask questions such as, *"Can all hosts talk to each other?"*, or *"Are managed hosts kept separate from unmanaged hosts?"*, or *"Does all untrusted traffic traverse the intrusion detection system?"*, and so on. Automated tools for answering these and other questions about *reachability properties* have been the focus of several recent research projects [10, 11, 19]. Most existing tools work by encoding the topology and policy as a logical structure, and then translating the reachability property into a formula whose satisfiability can be checked using a SAT solver or other tool. This section presents a different approach: we show how to encode two important classes of reachability properties as NetKAT equations. We then prove the equations are sound and complete with respect to intuitive, semantic definitions of reachability using the language model developed in Section 4.

***Reachability.*** The simplest reachability properties answer questions such as, *"Can host A send packets to host B?"* If $A$ can send packets to $B$, then the denotational model of the network must include a packet history that starts from host $A$ and ends at host $B$: $\langle pk_B, \cdots, pk_A\rangle$. More generally, we can ask if packets satisfying some predicate $a$ can be transformed so that they satisfy some predicate $b$. These predicates may denote single hosts, groups of hosts, or even arbitrary classes of traffic, such as Web traffic.

To reason about reachability, we use a small generalization of the logical crossbar model introduced in Section 2. In the logical crossbar model, we model the end-to-end behavior of the network using the following NetKAT expression,

$$in \cdot (p \cdot t)^* \cdot out$$

where $p$ and $t$ define the behavior of switches and links as dup-free NetKAT policies. Because the policy does not contain dup, it does not record the individual "hops" that packets take as they go through the network. To do this, we must augment the logical crossbar to record the state of the packet at each intermediate hop:

$$in \cdot \mathsf{dup} \cdot (p \cdot t \cdot \mathsf{dup})^* \cdot out$$

Using this encoding, we can define reachability as follows:

**Definition 2** (Reachability). *We say $b$ is reachable from $a$ if and only if there exists a trace*

$$\langle pk_1, \cdots, pk_n\rangle \in rng([\![\mathsf{dup} \cdot (p \cdot t \cdot \mathsf{dup})^*]\!])$$

*such that* $[\![a]\!]\,\langle pk_n\rangle = \{\langle pk_n\rangle\}$ *and* $[\![b]\!]\,\langle pk_1\rangle = \{\langle pk_1\rangle\}$.

To decide whether $b$ is reachable from $a$ we check the following NetKAT equivalence:

$$a \cdot \mathsf{dup} \cdot (p \cdot t \cdot \mathsf{dup})^* \cdot b \not\equiv 0$$

Intuitively, the prefix predicate, $a$, filters the policy to only include histories that begin with packets satisfying $a$. Similarly, the postfix predicate, $b$, filters the policy to only include histories that end with packets satisfying $b$. We do need to prove that this equation holds if and only if $b$ is reachable from $a$. The key to the proof is to translate both the denotational definition of reachability and the reachability equation to the language model, where they are easy to relate.

**Theorem 4** (Reachability Correctness). *For predicates $a$ and $b$, policy $p$, and topology $t$, $a \cdot \mathsf{dup} \cdot (p \cdot t \cdot \mathsf{dup})^* \cdot b \not\equiv 0$, if and only if $b$ is reachable from $a$.*

*Proof.* We translate the NetKAT equation into the language model:

$$\begin{aligned} & a \cdot \mathsf{dup} \cdot (p \cdot t \cdot \mathsf{dup})^* \cdot b \not\equiv 0 \\ \Rightarrow\ & \exists \alpha, \pi_n, \cdots, \pi_1. \\ & \quad \alpha \cdot \pi_n \cdot \mathsf{dup} \cdots \mathsf{dup} \cdot \pi_1 \in G(a \cdot \mathsf{dup} \cdot (p \cdot t \cdot \mathsf{dup})^* \cdot b) \end{aligned}$$

We also translate each term in the semantic definition of reachability into the language model:

$$\begin{aligned} & \exists pk_1, \cdots, pk_n. \\ & \quad \langle pk_1, \cdots, pk_n\rangle \in \mathsf{rng}(\,[\![\mathsf{dup} \cdot (p \cdot t \cdot \mathsf{dup})^*]\!]), \\ & \quad [\![a]\!]\,\langle pk_n\rangle = \{\langle pk_n\rangle\} \text{ and} \\ & \quad [\![b]\!]\,\langle pk_1\rangle = \{\langle pk_1\rangle\} \\ \Rightarrow\ & \exists \pi'_1, \cdots, \pi'_m. \\ & \quad \alpha_{\pi'_m} \cdot \pi'_m \cdot \mathsf{dup} \cdots \mathsf{dup} \cdot \pi'_1 \in G(\mathsf{dup} \cdot (p \cdot t \cdot \mathsf{dup})^*), \\ & \quad \alpha_{\pi'_m} \cdot \pi'_m \in G(a) \text{ and} \\ & \quad \alpha_{\pi'_1} \cdot \pi'_1 \in G(b) \end{aligned}$$

To prove soundness we let $\alpha = \alpha_{\pi_n}$ and $m = n$ to show that if

$$\alpha \cdot \pi_n \cdot \mathsf{dup} \cdots \mathsf{dup} \cdot \pi_1 \in G(a \cdot \mathsf{dup} \cdot (p \cdot t \cdot \mathsf{dup})^* \cdot b)$$

then,

$$\alpha_{\pi'_m} \cdot \pi'_m \cdot \mathsf{dup} \cdots \mathsf{dup} \cdot \pi'_1 \in G(\mathsf{dup} \cdot (p \cdot t \cdot \mathsf{dup})^*)$$

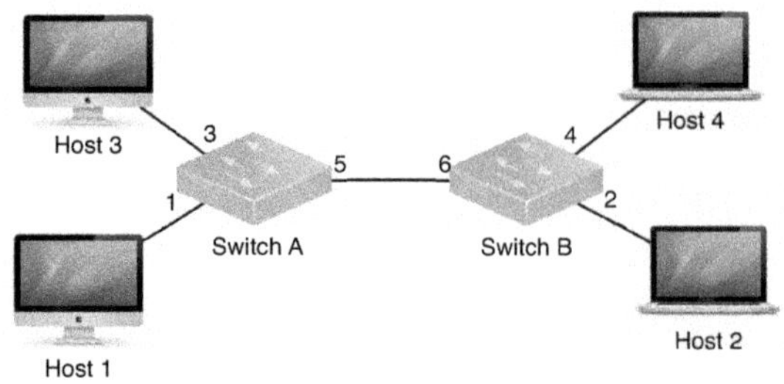


**Figure 8.** A simple network controlled by two parties.

which holds by definition of $\diamond$. The proof of completeness follows by a similar argument. □

***Waypointing.*** A *waypoint*, $w$, from $a$ to $b$ is a location that all packets traverse en route from $a$ to $b$. For example, a network operator might want to ensure that all traffic from untrusted hosts to trusted hosts traverses a firewall.

**Definition 3** (Waypoint). *We say $w$ is a waypoint from $a$ to $b$, if and only if, for all histories $\langle pk_1 \cdots pk_n\rangle \in rng(\,[\![\mathsf{dup} \cdot (p \cdot t \cdot \mathsf{dup})^*]\!])$ where $[\![a]\!]\,\langle pk_n\rangle = \{\langle pk_n\rangle\}$ and $[\![b]\!]\,\langle pk_1\rangle = \{\langle pk_1\rangle\}$, there exists a $pk_x \in \langle pk_1 \cdots pk_n\rangle$ such that:*

- $[\![w]\!]\,\langle pk_x\rangle = \{\langle pk_x\rangle\}$,
- $[\![b]\!]\ pk_i = \{\}$ *for all* $1 < i < x$, *and*
- $[\![a]\!]\ pk_j = \{\}$ *for all* $x < j < n$.

To decide whether $w$ is a waypoint from $a$ to $b$, we check the following NetKAT inequality:

$$\begin{aligned} & a \cdot \mathsf{dup} \cdot (p \cdot t \cdot \mathsf{dup})^* \cdot b \\ & \leq a \cdot \mathsf{dup} \cdot (\neg b \cdot p \cdot t \cdot \mathsf{dup})^* \cdot w \cdot (\neg a \cdot p \cdot t \cdot \mathsf{dup})^* \cdot b \end{aligned}$$

The left-hand side is exactly hop-by-hop reachability from $a$ to $b$. The right-hand side is also a hop-by-hop expression, but it has a predicate to check that packets traverse $w$. Furthermore, it tests that packets do not prematurely visit $b$ before $w$ or return to $a$ after reaching $w$.

**Theorem 5** (Waypoint Correctness). *For predicates $a$, $b$, and $w$,*

$$\begin{aligned} & a \cdot \mathsf{dup} \cdot (p \cdot t \cdot \mathsf{dup})^* \cdot b \\ & \leq a \cdot \mathsf{dup} \cdot (\neg b \cdot p \cdot t \cdot \mathsf{dup})^* \cdot w \cdot (\neg a \cdot p \cdot t \cdot \mathsf{dup})^* \cdot b \end{aligned}$$

*if and only if all packets from $a$ to $b$ are waypointed through $w$.*

*Proof.* Similar to the proof of reachability correctness above. See the long version of this paper for the full proofs. □

Using these encodings and theorems as building blocks, we can develop techniques for checking other reachability properties as well. For example, we can check for self-loops, test whether a firewall policy is correctly implemented, and string together multiple waypoints into composite tests.

## 6. Traffic Isolation

NetKAT's policy combinators help programmers construct complex network policies out of simple parts. The most basic combinator is union, which combines two policies by taking the union of the results generated by the sub-policies. However, naive use of union can lead to undesirable results, because each sub-policy may receive and modify packets intended for the other sub-policy.

***Example.*** Consider the network in Figure 8. Suppose the task of routing traffic between hosts 1 and 2 has been assigned to one programmer, while the task of routing traffic between hosts 3 and 4 has been assigned to another programmer. The first programmer might produce the following policy for switch $B$,

$$p_{B1} \triangleq \mathsf{sw} = B \cdot (\mathsf{pt} = 6 \cdot \mathsf{pt} \leftarrow 2 + \mathsf{pt} = 2 \cdot \mathsf{pt} \leftarrow 6)$$

and the second programmer might produce a similar switch policy for $B$. This second policy differs from the first only by sending traffic from port 6 out port 4 rather than port 2:

$$p_{B2} \triangleq \mathsf{sw} = B \cdot (\mathsf{pt} = 6 \cdot \mathsf{pt} \leftarrow 4 + \mathsf{pt} = 4 \cdot \mathsf{pt} \leftarrow 6)$$

Similar policies $p_{A1}$ and $p_{A2}$ define the behavior at switch $A$. Now, if we assume $t$ captures the topology of the network properly, then

$$((p_{A1} + p_{B1}) \cdot t)^*$$

correctly sends traffic from host 1 to host 2. However, when the second policy is added in,

$$(((p_{A1} + p_{B1}) + (p_{A2} + p_{B2})) \cdot t)^*$$

packets sent from host 1 will be copied to host 4 as well as host 2. In this instance, union actually produces *too many behaviors.* In the best case, sending additional packets to host 4 from host 1 leads to unnecessary congestion. In the worst case, it may violate the security policy for host 1. Either alternative demonstrates the need for better ways of composing forwarding policies.

***Slices.*** A *network slice* [8] is a lightweight abstraction that facilitates modular construction of policies. Intuitively, a slice defines a piece of the network that can be programmed independently of the rest of the network. The boundaries of a slice are defined by ingress ($in$) and egress ($out$) predicates, while the behavior in the slice is determined by the internal policy $p$. Each slice also has a unique identifier ($w$) to differentiate it from other slices.[2]

Packets that match $in$ are injected into the slice. Once in a slice, packets stay in the slice and obey $p$ until they match the predicate $out$, at which point they are ejected. We write slices as follows:

$$\{in\}\ w : (p)\ \{out\}$$

where $in$ and $out$ are the ingress and egress predicates and $p$ defines the internal policy.

To define slices in NetKAT, we begin by picking a header field, for example, $\mathsf{tag}$, to record the packet's current slice.[3] In order for our elaboration to have the desired properties, however, the $\mathsf{tag}$ field must not be used elsewhere in the policy or in the ingress or egress predicates. We call a predicate *tag-free* if it commutes with any modification of the $\mathsf{tag}$ field, and a policy *tag-free* if it commutes with any test of the $\mathsf{tag}$ field.

Given tag-free predicates $in$, $out$ and policy $p$, and a tag $w_0$ representing packets not in any slice, we can compile a slice into NetKAT as follows:

$$\begin{aligned}&(\!|\{in\}\ w : (p)\ \{out\}|\!)^{w_0} \triangleq\\ &\quad \mathsf{let}\ pre = (\mathsf{tag} = w_0 \cdot in \cdot \mathsf{tag} \leftarrow w + \mathsf{tag} = w)\ \mathsf{in}\\ &\quad \mathsf{let}\ post = (out \cdot \mathsf{tag} \leftarrow w_0 + \neg out)\ \mathsf{in}\\ &\quad (pre \cdot p \cdot post)\end{aligned}$$

Compilation wraps the slice policy with pre- and post-processing policies, $pre$ and $post$. The $pre$ policy tests whether a packet (i) is outside the slice (tagged with $w_0$) and matches the ingress predicate, in which case it is injected by tagging it with $w$, or (ii) has already been injected (already tagged with $w$). Once injected, packets are processed by $p$. If $p$ emits a packet that matches the egress predicate $out$, then $post$ strips the tag, restoring $w_0$. Otherwise, the packet remains in the slice and is left unmodified.

[2] The unique identifier $w$ may be defined by the compiler and need not appear in the surface syntax.

[3] In practice, the vlan field is often used to differentiate different classes of network traffic [34].

***Isolation.*** A key property of slices is that once a packet enters a slice, it is processed solely by the policy of that one slice until it is ejected, even across multiple hops in the topology. The following theorem captures this idea more precisely.

**Theorem 6** (Slice Composition). *For all* tag*-free slice ingress and egress predicates in and out, identifiers $w$, policies $s, q$,* tag*-free policies $p$, and topologies $t$, if*

- $s = (\!|\{in\}\ w : (p)\ \{out\}|\!)^{w_0}$,
- $w \neq w_0$,
- $out \cdot t \cdot \mathsf{dup} \cdot q \equiv 0$,
- $q \cdot t \cdot \mathsf{dup} \cdot in \equiv 0$,
- *$q$ drops $w$-tagged traffic,*

*then*

$$((s + q) \cdot t \cdot \mathsf{dup})^* \equiv (s \cdot t \cdot \mathsf{dup})^* + (q \cdot t \cdot \mathsf{dup})^*.$$

In a nutshell, this theorem says that executing the union of $s$ and $q$ is the same as sending packets through two separate copies of the network, one containing the slice and the other containing $q$. The proof of the theorem is by equational reasoning and makes use of the KAT-DENESTING theorem from Figure 4.

An interesting corollary of the result above is that when the ingress slice boundary of $s$ and the domain of $q$ do not overlap, for traffic destined for the ingress of $s$, the union of $s$ and $q$ is equivalent to $s$ alone.

**Corollary 1.** *For all* tag*-free slice ingress and egress predicates in and out, identifiers $w$, policies $s, q$, and topologies $t$, such that*

- $s = (\!|\{in\}\ w : (p)\ \{out\}|\!)^{w_0}$,
- $w \neq w_0$,
- $out \cdot t \cdot \mathsf{dup} \cdot q \equiv 0$,
- $q \cdot t \cdot \mathsf{dup} \cdot in \equiv 0$,
- $in \cdot q \equiv 0$, *then*

$$\begin{aligned}&in \cdot \mathsf{tag} = w_0 \cdot ((s + q) \cdot t \cdot \mathsf{dup})^*\\ &\equiv in \cdot \mathsf{tag} = w_0 \cdot (s \cdot t \cdot \mathsf{dup})^*\end{aligned}$$

Corollary 1 connects to traditional language-based information flow properties [27]. If $s$ defines public, low-security data and $q$ defines private, high security data, the corollary implies that the observable behavior of the network remains unchanged regardless of whether the high-security data ($q$) is present, absent, or replaced by some alternate high security data ($q'$).

***Example, redux.*** Slices provide a solution to the scenario described in the example at the beginning of the section. We can assign each programmer a unique slice with boundaries that correspond to the locations of the end hosts under control of that slice. For instance, the first programmer's $in$ and $out$ predicates include the network access points for hosts 1 and 2, while the second programmer's $in$ and $out$ predicates include the network access points for hosts 3 and 4.

$$\begin{aligned}in_1 &\triangleq \mathsf{sw} = A \cdot \mathsf{pt} = 1 + \mathsf{sw} = B \cdot \mathsf{pt} = 2\\ out_1 &\triangleq \mathsf{sw} = A \cdot \mathsf{pt} = 1 + \mathsf{sw} = B \cdot \mathsf{pt} = 2\\ s_1 &\triangleq \{in_1\}\ w_1 : (p_{A1} + p_{B1})\ \{out_1\}\\ in_2 &\triangleq \mathsf{sw} = A \cdot \mathsf{pt} = 3 + \mathsf{sw} = B \cdot \mathsf{pt} = 4\\ out_2 &\triangleq \mathsf{sw} = A \cdot \mathsf{pt} = 3 + \mathsf{sw} = B \cdot \mathsf{pt} = 4\\ s_2 &\triangleq \{in_2\}\ w_2 : (p_{A2} + p_{B2})\ \{out_2\}\end{aligned}$$

| Pattern | Action |
|---|---|
| typ=SSH | Drop |
| port=1 | Output 2 |
| port=2 | Output 1 |
| * | Drop |

if typ=SSH then 0
else if pt=1 then pt:=2
else if pt=2 then pt:=1
else 0

**Figure 9.** A flow table and an equivalent NetKAT policy.

| | | | |
|---|---|---|---|
| ONF Action Sequence | $a$ | $::=$ | $1 \mid f \leftarrow n \cdot a$ |
| ONF Action Sum | $as$ | $::=$ | $0 \mid a + as$ |
| ONF Predicate | $b$ | $::=$ | $1 \mid f = n \cdot b$ |
| ONF Local | $\ell$ | $::=$ | $as \mid \text{if } b \text{ then } as \text{ else } \ell$ |
| ONF | $p$ | $::=$ | $0 \mid (\mathsf{sw} = sw \cdot \ell) + p$ |

**Figure 10.** OpenFlow Normal Form.

The original difficulty with this example was caused by packet duplication when, for example, a packet was sent from host 1 to host 2. Corollary 1 proves that we can use slices to solve the problem: host 1 is connected to slice 1, and restricting the input to that of slice 1 implies that the behavior of the entire program is precisely that of slice 1 alone.

## 7. Compilation

In order to execute a NetKAT program on an OpenFlow switch, we must compile it to a *flow table*, the low-level programming abstraction that OpenFlow supports. A flow table is a prioritized list of rules, where each rule consists of a pattern to match packet headers and actions to apply to matching packets. When a packet arrives at a switch, the actions associated with the highest priority matching rule are applied to it.

For example, the flow table on the left-hand side of figure 9 blocks SSH packets, but forwards all other traffic between ports 1 and 2. Alongside the flow table is an equivalent NetKAT policy. To make the connection between these two equivalent representations obvious, we introduce a conditional construct as shorthand:

$$\text{if } b \text{ then } as \text{ else } \ell \stackrel{\text{def}}{=} (b \cdot as) + (\neg b \cdot \ell)$$

Logically, a flow table pattern is a conjunction of positive literals, and each action is a combination of modifications. We can interpret prioritized rules as cascades of conditional expressions. In this section we describe the design of a compiler based on this idea.

The input to the compiler is NetKAT without dup or $\mathsf{sw} := n$ terms. These constructs are necessary to model network topology, but the output produced by the compiler is meant to execute on switches. Therefore, it is reasonable to exclude these features. The output of the compiler is a stylized subset of NetKAT called *OpenFlow Normal Form* (ONF). An ONF policy is a sum of conditional cascades, where each cascade is guarded by a test for a switch:

$$(\mathsf{sw} = sw_1 \cdot \ell_1) + \cdots + (\mathsf{sw} = sw_n \cdot \ell_n)$$

Each term can be interpreted as a complete flow table for a given switch. Figure 10 presents the full grammar for ONF. Mapping ONF to flow tables, is mostly straightforward, and many of the low-level details have been addressed in previous work [7].

The rest of this section outlines the major steps required to compile NetKAT to ONF. Each step eliminates or restricts an element of NetKAT syntax. In other words, each step translates from one intermediate representation to another until we arrive at ONF. We write NetKAT$^{-(op)}$ to denote NetKAT expressions that do not use the *op* operator. For example, if:

$$p \in \text{NetKAT}^{-(\mathsf{dup},\mathsf{sw}\leftarrow)}$$

then $p$ does not contain dup and does not modify the sw field. This is the source language for the compiler, as described above.

***Step 1: Star elimination.*** The first step is to eliminate Kleene star from the input policy. This step is critical as switches do not support iterated processing of packets—indeed, many switches only support a single phase of processing by a table! Formally, we prove that any program without dup, or, less importantly, assignment to sw, is equivalent to a Kleene star-free program (again without the dup primitive or assignments to sw).

**Lemma 9** (Star Elimination). *If* $p \in$ *NetKAT*$^{-(\mathsf{dup},\mathsf{sw}\leftarrow)}$, *then there exists* $p' \in$ *NetKAT*$^{-(\mathsf{dup},\mathsf{sw}\leftarrow,*)}$ *where* $p \equiv p'$.

*Proof.* We show that $p'$ can be obtained from the normal form used in the completeness theorem. More specifically, let $p''$ be the policy obtained from $p$ by the normalization construction of Lemma 7. By construction, dup can only appear in the normal form of an expression already containing dup, so $p''$ cannot contain dup. $R(p'') \subseteq I$ and $p''$ does not contain dup, so $R(p'') \subseteq At \cdot P$. Therefore, $p''$ does not contain Kleene star.

Let us now prove that any assignment of the form $\mathsf{sw} \leftarrow sw_i$ in $p''$ is preceded in the same term by the corresponding test $\mathsf{sw} = sw_i$. Because $p$ does not contain any assignment of the form $\mathsf{sw} \leftarrow sw_i$, it commutes with any test of the form $\mathsf{sw} = sw_i$. Therefore $p''$ also commutes with any test of the form $\mathsf{sw} = sw_i$. It follows that $p''$ can be written as a sum of $\alpha \cdot p$ for some atom $\alpha$ and complete assignment $p$. Suppose for a contradiction that term, $\alpha$ contains a test $\mathsf{sw} = sw_i$, and $p$ contains an assignment $\mathsf{sw} \leftarrow sw_j$, with $sw_i \neq sw_j$. Then

$$\alpha \cdot (\mathsf{sw} = sw_i) \cdot p'' \cdot (\mathsf{sw} = sw_j) \geq \alpha \cdot p \neq 0$$
$$\alpha \cdot (\mathsf{sw} = sw_j) \cdot p'' \cdot (\mathsf{sw} = sw_i) = 0$$

but those two terms are also equal, which is a contradiction.

Therefore any assignment of the form $\mathsf{sw} \leftarrow sw_i$ in $p''$ is preceded, in the same term, by the corresponding test $\mathsf{sw} = sw_i$, and can be removed using axiom PA-FILTER-MOD to produce the desired $p'$. Tests and assignments to other fields than sw could appear in between, but we can use the commutativity axioms PA-MOD-MOD-COMM and PA-MOD-FILTER-COMM to move the assignment $\mathsf{sw} \leftarrow sw_i$ to just after the test $\mathsf{sw} = sw_i$. □

***Step 2: Switch specialization.*** Next, we show that every star-free policy can be specialized for the switches in the network. This transformation allows us to remove nested tests of the sw field and put the policy into a form where it can easily be compiled into a flow table for each switch.

**Lemma 10** (Switch Specialization). *If* $p \in$ *NetKAT*$^{-(\mathsf{dup},\mathsf{sw}\leftarrow,*)}$, *then for all switches* $sw_i$, *there exists* $p' \in$ *NetKAT*$^{-(\mathsf{dup},\mathsf{sw}\leftarrow,*,\mathsf{sw})}$ *such that* $\mathsf{sw} = sw_i \cdot p \equiv \mathsf{sw} = sw_i \cdot p'$.

*Proof.* Let $g$ be the unique homomorphism of NetKAT defined on primitive programs by:

$$g(\mathsf{sw} = sw) \triangleq \begin{cases} 1 & \text{if } sw = sw_i \\ 0 & \text{otherwise} \end{cases}$$
$$g(f \leftarrow v) \triangleq f \leftarrow v$$
$$g(\mathsf{dup}) \triangleq \mathsf{dup}$$

For every primitive program element $x$ of NetKAT$^{-(\mathsf{dup},\mathsf{sw}\leftarrow,*)}$, we have both:

$$\mathsf{sw} = sw_i \cdot x \equiv g(x) \cdot \mathsf{sw} = sw_i$$
$$g(x) \cdot \mathsf{sw} = sw_i \equiv \mathsf{sw} = sw_i \cdot g(x)$$

$$\begin{array}{rl} & (\text{if dst} = A \text{ then pt} := 1 \text{ else } 0) + \\ & (\text{if src} = B \text{ then pt} := 2 \text{ else } 0) \\ = & \text{if dst} = A \cdot \text{src} = B \text{ then pt} := 1 + \text{pt} := 2 \\ & \text{else if dst} = A \text{ then pt} := 1 \\ & \text{else if src} = B \text{ then pt} := 2 \\ & \text{else } 0 \end{array}$$

**Figure 11.** Compiling ONF policy union.

$$\begin{array}{rl} & (\text{if typ} = \text{SSH then vlan} := W \text{ else } 1) \cdot \\ & (\text{if dst} = A \text{ then pt} := 1 \text{ else if dst} = B \text{ then pt} := 2 \text{ else } 0) \\ = & \text{if dst} = A \cdot \text{typ} = \text{SSH then vlan} := W \cdot \text{pt} := 1 \\ & \text{else if dst} = A \text{ then pt} := 1 \\ & \text{else if dst} = B \cdot \text{typ} = \text{SSH then vlan} := W \cdot \text{pt} := 2 \\ & \text{else if dst} = B \text{ then pt} := 2 \\ & \text{else } 0 \end{array}$$

**Figure 12.** Compiling ONF policy sequence.

Hence, applying KAT-COMMUTE [2, Lemma 4.4] twice shows:

$$\mathsf{sw} = sw_i \cdot p \equiv g(p) \cdot \mathsf{sw} = sw_i$$
$$g(p) \cdot \mathsf{sw} = sw_i \equiv \mathsf{sw} = sw_i \cdot g(p)$$

By the definition of $g$, any occurrence of $\mathsf{sw} = v$ in $p$ is replaced by either 1 or 0 in $g(p)$. Moreover, since $p \in \text{NetKAT}^{-(\text{dup},\text{sw}\leftarrow,*)}$, it follows that $g(p)$ does not contain any occurrence of $\mathsf{sw} = v$ and since $p' = g(p) \in \text{NetKAT}^{-(\text{dup},\text{sw}\leftarrow,*,\text{sw})}$ we also have

$$\mathsf{sw} = sw_i \cdot p \equiv \mathsf{sw} = sw_i \cdot p' \qquad \square$$

***Step 3: Converting to* ONF.** The third step is to compile policies in $\text{NetKAT}^{-(\text{dup},\text{sw}\leftarrow,*,\text{sw})}$ to ONF. This is a recursive procedure that first compiles sub-policies to ONF.

To calculate the union of two ONF policies, we take the cross-product of the predicates and actions. This procedure is based on earlier work [23], but we present a purely syntactic proof of correctness. Figure 11 shows an example of compiling policy union, which illustrates why the cross-product construction is necessary.

Calculating the sequence of two ONF policies is more involved, since we have to commute the modifications in the first policy with the tests in the second policy to produce a single if-then-else cascade, as illustrated in figure 12. As the NetKAT axiom PA-MOD-FILTER-COMM shows, modifications and tests commute naively only if they affect distinct fields. The compiler has several transformations to ensure that various kinds of overlapping tests and modifications do commute.

**Lemma 11** (Switch-local Compilation). *If $p \in \text{NetKAT}^{-(\text{dup},\text{sw}\leftarrow,*,\text{sw})}$ then there exists a policy $p'$ such that $p \equiv p'$ and $p' \in$ ONF.*

The proof goes by induction on the structure of $p$.

***Step 4: Combining results.*** Lemmas 9, 10 and 11 suffice to prove any policy $p$ in $\text{NetKAT}^{-(\text{dup},\text{sw}\leftarrow)}$ may be converted to OpenFlow normal form.

**Theorem 7** (ONF). *If $p_{in} \in \text{NetKAT}^{-(\text{dup},\text{sw}\leftarrow)}$ then there exists $p_{out} \equiv p_{in}$ such that $p_{out} \in$ ONF.*

***Optimizations.*** Naive compilation of network programs can produce flow tables that are unmanageably large [23]. Hence, existing systems implement optimizations to generate smaller tables. For example, the following lemma describes a common optimization called fall-through elimination, which removes unnecessary rules from the table.

**Lemma 12** (Fall-through Elimination). *If $b_1 \leq b_2$ then*

$$\text{if } b_1 \text{ then } as \text{ else if } b_2 \text{ then } as \text{ else } \ell \equiv \text{if } b_2 \text{ then } as \text{ else } \ell$$

We plan to study further optimizations in future work.

# 8. Related Work

Kleene algebra is named for its inventor, Stephen Cole Kleene. Much of the basic algebraic theory of KA was developed by John Horton Conway [4]. Kleene algebra with tests was introduced by Kozen [13, 14]. KA and KAT have been successfully applied in many practical verification tasks, including verification of compiler optimizations [16], pointer analysis [22], concurrency control [3], and device drivers [15]. This is the first time KA has been used as a network programming language or applied to verification of networks. The proof of the main result in this paper—completeness of the equational axioms—is based on a novel model of KAT.

While many other systems have been proposed for analyzing networks, we believe ours is the first to provide a complete, high-level algebra for reasoning about network programs *as they are written*. Systems such as Anteater [19], FlowChecker [1], Header Space Analysis [10], VeriFlow [11], and Formally Verifiable Networking [33], encode information about network topology and forwarding policies into SAT formulae (Anteater), graph-based representations (VeriFlow, Header Space Analysis), or higher-order logic (Formally Verifiable Networking). These systems then define custom algorithms over these models to check specific properties such as reachability or packet loss. Such systems can check for violations of important network invariants, but do not provide sound and complete systems for reasoning *directly* about programs. Moreover, although these systems have expressive languages for encoding properties, they do not connect these encodings back to denotational or operational models of the network. In contrast, in section 5, we show how to encode a reachability property as a NetKAT equation and then prove that the reachability equation is equivalent to a semantic definition of reachability.

As a programming language, NetKAT is most similar to NetCore [7, 23] and Pyretic [24], which both stemmed from earlier work on Frenetic [6]. NetCore defined the fragment of NetKAT with filters, modification and union, and Pyretic extended NetCore with sequential composition (although Pyretic has neither a formal semantics nor a compiler). Neither language defined an equational theory for reasoning about programs, nor did they include Kleene star—unlike these previous languages, NetKAT programs can describe potentially infinite behaviors.

NDLog [18] is a logic programming language with an explicit notion of location and a distributed execution model. In contrast to NDLog, NetKAT and NetCore are designed for programming centralized (not distributed) SDN controllers. Because NDLog is based around Datalog (with general recursion and pragmatic extensions that complicate its semantics), equivalence of NDLog programs is undecidable [29]. NetKAT's Kleene star is able to model network behavior, but has decidable (PSPACE-complete) equivalence.

# 9. Conclusion

This paper presents NetKAT, a new language for SDN programming and reasoning that is based on a solid semantic foundation—Kleene algebra with tests. NetKAT's denotational semantics describes network programs as functions from packet histories to sets of packets histories and its equational theory is sound and complete with respect to this model. The language enables programmers to create expressive, compositional network programs and reason effectively about their semantics. We demonstrate the power of our framework on a range of practical applications including reachability, traffic isolation, access control, and compiler correctness.

***Acknowledgments*** The authors wish to thank Timothy Griffin, Shriram Krishnamurthi, Nick McKeown, Jennifer Rexford, the members of the Cornell PLDG, and the POPL reviewers for helpful comments, as well as Alec Story and Stephen Gutz for work on a preliminary version of slices. This work is supported in part by the NSF under grants CNS-1111698, CNS-0931985, CNS-1111520, and SHF-1016937, the ONR under award N00014-12-1-0757, a Sloan Research Fellowship, and a Google Research Award.

## References


[1] Ehab Al-Shaer and Saeed Al-Haj. FlowChecker: Configuration analysis and verification of federated OpenFlow infrastructures. In *SafeConfig*, 2010.

[2] Allegra Angus and Dexter Kozen. Kleene algebra with tests and program schematology. Technical Report TR2001-1844, Computer Science Department, Cornell University, July 2001.

[3] Ernie Cohen. Using Kleene algebra to reason about concurrency control. Technical report, Telcordia, Morristown, N.J., 1994.

[4] John Horton Conway. *Regular Algebra and Finite Machines*. Chapman and Hall, London, 1971.

[5] Andrew D. Ferguson, Arjun Guha, Chen Liang, Rodrigo Fonseca, and Shriram Krishnamurthi. Participatory networking: An API for application control of SDNs. In *SIGCOMM*, 2013.

[6] Nate Foster, Rob Harrison, Michael J. Freedman, Christopher Monsanto, Jennifer Rexford, Alec Story, and David Walker. Frenetic: A network programming language. In *ICFP*, September 2011.

[7] Arjun Guha, Mark Reitblatt, and Nate Foster. Machine-verified network controllers. In *PLDI*, June 2013.

[8] Stephen Gutz, Alec Story, Cole Schlesinger, and Nate Foster. Splendid isolation: A slice abstraction for software-defined networks. In *HotSDN*, 2012.

[9] James Hamilton. Networking: The last bastion of mainframe computing, December 2009. Available at `http://tinyurl.com/y9uz64e`.

[10] Peyman Kazemian, George Varghese, and Nick McKeown. Header space analysis: Static checking for networks. In *NSDI*, 2012.

[11] Ahmed Khurshid, Xuan Zou, Wenxuan Zhou, Matthew Caesar, and P. Brighten Godfrey. VeriFlow: Verifying network-wide invariants in real time. In *NSDI*, 2013.

[12] Dexter Kozen. A completeness theorem for Kleene algebras and the algebra of regular events. *I&C*, 110(2):366–390, May 1994.

[13] Dexter Kozen. Kleene algebra with tests and commutativity conditions. In *TACAS*, pages 14–33, Passau, Germany, March 1996.

[14] Dexter Kozen. Kleene algebra with tests. *Transactions on Programming Languages and Systems*, 19(3):427–443, May 1997.

[15] Dexter Kozen. Kleene algebras with tests and the static analysis of programs. Technical Report TR2003-1915, Computer Science Department, Cornell University, November 2003.

[16] Dexter Kozen and Maria-Cristina Patron. Certification of compiler optimizations using Kleene algebra with tests. In *CL*, July 2000.

[17] Dexter Kozen and Frederick Smith. Kleene algebra with tests: Completeness and decidability. In *CSL*, September 1996.

[18] Boon Thau Loo, Joseph M. Hellerstein, Ion Stoica, and Raghu Ramakrishnan. Declarative routing: Extensible routing with declarative queries. In *SIGCOMM*, 2005.

[19] Haohui Mai, Ahmed Khurshid, Raghit Agarwal, Matthew Caesar, P. Brighten Godfrey, and Samuel Talmadge King. Debugging the data plane with Anteater. In *SIGCOMM*, 2011.

[20] James McCauley, Aurojit Panda, Martin Casado, Teemu Koponen, and Scott Shenker. Extending SDN to large-scale networks. In *ONS*, 2013.

[21] Nick McKeown, Tom Anderson, Hari Balakrishnan, Guru Parulkar, Larry Peterson, Jennifer Rexford, Scott Shenker, and Jonathan Turner. OpenFlow: Enabling innovation in campus networks. *SIGCOMM Computing Communications Review*, 38(2):69–74, 2008.

[22] B. Möller. Calculating with pointer structures. In *Algorithmic Languages and Calculi. Proc. IFIP TC2/WG2.1 Working Conference*, February 1997.

[23] Christopher Monsanto, Nate Foster, Rob Harrison, and David Walker. A compiler and run-time system for network programming languages. In *POPL*, January 2012.

[24] Christopher Monsanto, Joshua Reich, Nate Foster, Jennifer Rexford, and David Walker. Composing software-defined networks. In *NSDI*, April 2013.

[25] Tim Nelson, Arjun Guha, Daniel J. Dougherty, Kathi Fisler, and Shriram Krishnamurthi. A balance of power: Expressive, analyzable controller programming. In *HotSDN*, 2013.

[26] Mark Reitblatt, Nate Foster, Jennifer Rexford, Cole Schlesinger, and David Walker. Abstractions for network update. In *SIGCOMM*, 2012.

[27] Andrei Sabelfeld and Andrew C. Myers. Language-based information-flow security. *IEEE Journal on Selected Areas in Communications*, 21(1):5–19, 2003.

[28] Gunther Schmidt. *Relational Mathematics*. Cambridge University Press, 2010.

[29] O. Shmueli. Decidability and expressiveness aspects of logic queries. In *PODS*, pages 237–249, 1987.

[30] The Frenetic Project, 2013. See `http://frenetic-lang.org`.

[31] Andreas Voellmy and Paul Hudak. Nettle: Functional reactive programming of OpenFlow networks. In *PADL*, 2011.

[32] Andreas Voellmy, Junchang Wang, Y. Richard Yang, Bryan Ford, and Paul Hudak. Maple: Simplifying SDN programming using algorithmic policies. In *SIGCOMM*, 2013.

[33] Anduo Wang, Limin Jia, Changbin Liu, Boon Thau Loo, Oleg Sokolsky, and Prithwish Basu. Formally veriable networking. In *HotNets*, 2009.

[34] Minlan Yu, Jennifer Rexford, Xin Sun, Sanjay G. Rao, and Nick Feamster. A survey of virtual LAN usage in campus networks. *IEEE Communications Magazine*, 49(7):98–103, 2011.

# Bias-Variance Tradeoffs in Program Analysis

Rahul Sharma
Stanford University
sharmar@cs.stanford.edu

Aditya V. Nori
Microsoft Research
adityan@microsoft.com

Alex Aiken
Stanford University
aiken@cs.stanford.edu

## Abstract

It is often the case that increasing the precision of a program analysis leads to worse results. It is our thesis that this phenomenon is the result of fundamental limits on the ability to use precise abstract domains as the basis for inferring strong invariants of programs. We show that *bias-variance tradeoffs*, an idea from learning theory, can be used to explain why more precise abstractions do not necessarily lead to better results and also provides practical techniques for coping with such limitations. Learning theory captures precision using a combinatorial quantity called the *VC dimension*. We compute the VC dimension for different abstractions and report on its usefulness as a precision metric for program analyses. We evaluate *cross validation*, a technique for addressing bias-variance tradeoffs, on an industrial strength program verification tool called YOGI. The tool produced using cross validation has significantly better running time, finds new defects, and has fewer time-outs than the current production version. Finally, we make some recommendations for tackling bias-variance tradeoffs in program analysis.

***Categories and Subject Descriptors*** D.2.4 [*Program Verification*]: Statistical methods; F.3.2 [*Semantics of Programming Languages*]: Program analysis; I.2.6 [*Learning*]: Parameter learning

***Keywords*** Program Analysis; Machine Learning; Verification

## 1. Introduction

In program analysis, it is well understood that imprecise abstractions can lead to inferior results. However, what is not so well understood is that precise abstractions can also produce inferior results, in some cases even worse than very imprecise abstractions. We show that *bias-variance tradeoffs*, an idea from learning theory, can be used to explain how the quality of analysis results changes with precision. Learning theory quantifies precision using a combinatorial quantity called *Vapnik-Chervonenkis dimension* or *VC dimension*; we use VC dimension to analyze the behavior of a number of commonly used program analysis abstractions. In addition, using *cross validation*, a technique routinely applied in machine learning to address bias-variance tradeoffs, we are able to improve the performance of YOGI, an industrial strength program verification tool.

How can better precision adversely affect an analysis? Note that we are not talking about cost or efficiency—the question only concerns the quality of the results. The class of static analysis systems to which our results apply have two distinguishing characteristics. First, there is some domain of facts (e.g., an abstract domain) over which the analysis computes. Second, there is some step in the analysis that takes such facts and attempts to generalize them (e.g., to an invariant of the program). Many analysis frameworks such as abstract interpretation [17], counter-example guided abstraction refinement (CEGAR) [13], and various other inference techniques [10, 28, 49] have this structure. For example, abstract interpretation can use *widening* (Section 4.1) and CEGAR can use *interpolants* (Section 4.2) as a generalization step. There are also static analyses that do not have this structure and our results do not apply to them (see Section 6). Using results on bias-variance tradeoffs we show that increasing the precision of the underlying domain, at some point, may lead to worse results from the generalization step.

Consider the program in Figure 1, which we analyze using different program analyses with increasing precision. Each program analysis is a basic abstract interpreter over a different abstract domain. First, consider an interval analysis [16], which infers upper and lower bounds for numeric variables. Using intervals to analyze the program in Figure 1, we obtain the loop invariant $1 \le i \le 5 \wedge j \ge 0$ [36]. This result is perhaps the best invariant that one could expect with intervals. Intervals can only express facts about single variables, and hence the invariant has no details on any relationship between $i$ and $j$. The problem is lack of precision: the abstract domain is not precise enough to express certain behaviors. We increase the precision to octagons [39], which can infer bounds on the sum or difference of pairs of variables. We obtain the following loop invariant [36]:

$$1 \le i \le 5 \wedge i - j \le 1 \wedge i + j \ge 1 \wedge j \ge 0$$

This result is quite good, providing a useful relationship between $i$ and $j$ and good bounds. Next, we use the even more precise domain of polyhedra [19] which can express bounds on arbitrary linear combinations of program variables. We obtain the weak invariant $i \le 5$ [36]. This result is not only worse than octagons, it is even worse than intervals. Increasing the precision of the analysis results in a decrease in the quality of the results.

Let us examine this outcome in some detail. The abstract interpreter generates some abstract states and then tries to generalize via joins and widening [17]. However, because polyhedra are so expressive, there are many incomparable polyhedra that perfectly describe any finite set of abstract states. It is difficult for the generalization step to pick the best one for this particular program from such a large candidate pool. For this example, we start with $i = 1 \wedge j = 0$ as the initial abstract state and we show the fixpoint iterations [17] published in [41]. First, we fit on $i = 1, j = 0$ and $i = 2, j = 1$ to obtain the polyhedra $-i + j \ge -1 \wedge i \ge 1$. Next, we obtain $i + j \ge -1 \wedge 7i - 4j \ge 7$ that fits $i = 1, j = 0$, $i = 2, j = 1$, and $i = 5, j = 7$. Note that there are an unbounded number of polyhedra, including the one discovered by octagons,


*POPL '14*, January 22–24, 2014, San Diego, CA, USA.

http://dx.doi.org/10.1145/2535838.2535853

```
int i = 1, j = 0;
while (i<=5) {
  j = j+i ;
  i = i+1;
}
```

**Figure 1.** Example program from [41].

that can fit these states. The domain of polyhedra is so precise that the generalization step has many valid choices and hence it can pick a hypothesis that fits these specific abstract states but does not hold in general. In the next iteration, we obtain $-i + j \geq -1$, and, finally, *true*. Using the loop guard and narrowing [17], we terminate with $i \leq 5$ as the invariant. One might be tempted to blame specific choices made in this analysis run for the result, but that misses the point that the phenomenon is general: any method that attempts to select the best generalization from a large set of equally viable but different candidates will run into the same problem on many programs. For example, other analyses such as [3] meet a similar fate on this example [41].

Very abstractly, a program has some behaviors, and if an analysis is not expressive enough to capture these behaviors, then we have *underfitting* and the results are poor. If the analysis engine is too expressive, then it can *overfit* the specific behaviors and fail to generalize. Currently, program analysis designers apply folk knowledge to avoid underfitting and overfitting. Our aim is to give a formal framework to understand these rules of thumb and use the foundations to obtain better tools.

In learning theory [34], underfitting is characterized by *bias* and overfitting is characterized by *variance* [21], and by varying the precision, one gets a bias-variance tradeoff. Low precision leads to high bias and low variance, while high precision leads to low bias but high variance. With an appropriate choice of precision, one can balance bias and variance and obtain good results. As an example, consider Figure 2. YOGI is a verification engine in Microsoft Windows SDV (Static Driver Verifier) toolkit that checks safety properties of Windows device drivers [25]. In Figure 2, increasing values on the $x$-axis indicate increasing precision (for details see [43] and Section 5). The $y$-axis shows the time taken by YOGI on 2490 verification tasks (a superset of the tasks reported in [25]). Higher analysis times are indicative of more time-outs and poorer quality of results. One observes the bias-variance tradeoff in Figure 2. At low precision the performance of the tool is poor. With increasing precision, the bias decreases and the performance of the tool improves. However, after a certain point, the variance starts increasing and the performance starts to degrade.

To develop a theory that can explain these empirical observations, we need a formal definition of generalization. Unfortunately, even though the term generalization frequently occurs in the program analysis literature, defining generalization precisely is difficult and there is no widely accepted definition. Just as complexity theory works with a model of machines and generates qualitative (as opposed to quantitative) results for comparing the efficiency of algorithms, we want a useful theory, perhaps working with a model, that generates useful qualitative feedback about bias-variance tradeoffs.

In a recent work, [47] applied the definition of generalization given by the PAC (*probably approximately correct*) learning framework [48] to prove that a verification algorithm for checking safety properties generalizes. According to this definition (which we give formally in Section 2), an algorithm generalizes if given enough samples of program states as input, it is likely to generate predicates that separate almost all the program's safe reachable states from erroneous program states. In this paper, we explore an alternative use of this framework, namely modeling bias-variance tradeoffs. We

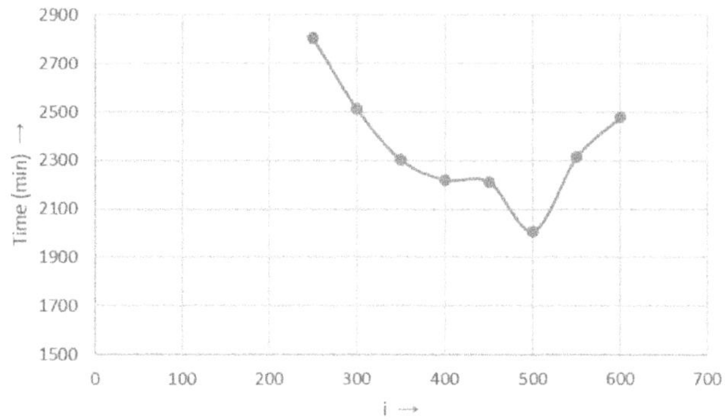


**Figure 2.** Result of running YOGI on 2490 driver-properties pairs. The best performance is achieved at $i = 500$.

do not claim that this definition is *the* correct definition of generalization. However, the motivation for our work is largely practical, and we show that this existing framework yields some immediately useful results. In the future, different definitions of generalization might be available and the framework developed here can be instantiated with the alternative definitions to derive other useful conclusions for the benefit of program analysis tools.

We believe that if program analysis tool designers are explicitly made aware of bias-variance tradeoffs and have mathematical tools to qualitatively reason about generalization, they can make better informed design decisions. In our framework, variance is proportional to VC dimension (Theorem 2.2). Hence, a high VC dimension is indicative of overfitting. We calculate the VC dimension of several abstractions used in program analysis (Section 3), including abstractions for numerical programs, array manipulating programs, and heap manipulating programs. We observe that more precise abstractions, that is, the abstractions with higher variance, have higher VC dimension. These proofs increase our confidence in the applicability of our framework to program analyses and provide evidence that VC dimension is a useful qualitative metric for characterizing the precision of abstractions.

Since our definition of generalization has been borrowed from learning theory, we can build on well-known techniques in the machine learning community for addressing bias-variance tradeoffs. Cross validation [2] is one of the simplest techniques for this purpose. Consider a fully automatic analysis tool that has a number of configuration parameters. How to set these parameters optimally is usually unclear, and the typical case is that such an optimal configuration might not even exist, although clearly some configurations are better than others. One logical candidate configuration is the one that performs best on a benchmark suite. However, we demonstrate that this strategy can overfit on the particular benchmark suite and significantly degrade the quality of the tool on new inputs (Section 5). Cross validation avoids overfitting, and we show that by applying cross validation to tune the configuration parameters of YOGI [25], we are able to significantly improve YOGI's running time while also reducing the number of timeouts and finding new defects.

Thus, overfitting can adversely impact program analysis in at least two ways. First, overly precise abstract domains can overfit and lead to poor generalization and hence inferior invariants. Second, tools can overfit their benchmark suite resulting in poor performance on new analysis tasks. We show that these seemingly different problems are both instances of bias-variance tradeoffs and hence the same principles (Theorem 2.2) apply to both. Learning

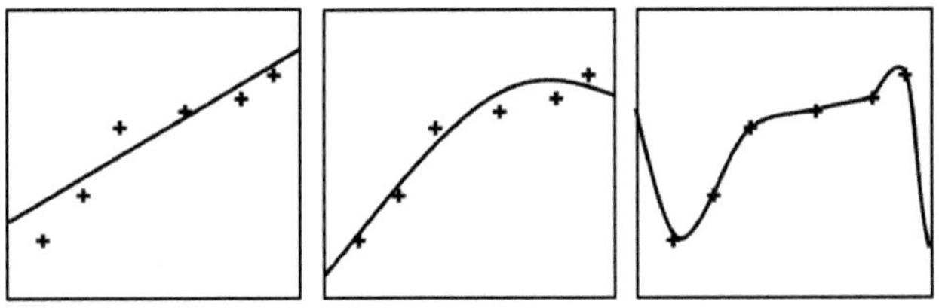

(a) (b) (c)

**Figure 3.** Regression example: underfit (a), good fit (b), overfit (c).

theory addresses bias-variance tradeoffs in general and can provide techniques to tackle both these problems.

To summarize, our contributions are as follows:

- We observe that improving precision does not necessarily lead to better results in program analysis. We connect this phenomenon to bias-variance tradeoffs in learning theory (Section 2).
- We show that VC dimension captures the precision of abstract domains used in program analysis. We calculate the VC dimension of a number of abstractions relevant to program analysis, including formulas over arrays and separation logic (Section 3).
- We explain several empirical observations in program analysis using bias-variance tradeoffs. For example, by incrementally increasing precision, one can balance bias and variance (Section 2), a strategy that is employed in several existing program analyses [32, 41, 49] (Section 4).
- Using bias-variance tradeoffs we show how overfitting to benchmark suites can result in unnecessarily poor performance on new inputs. Using cross validation to guide precision tuning, we are able to improve the performance of YOGI, a fully automatic, production quality program verification tool (Section 5).
- We make some specific recommendations for tackling bias-variance tradeoffs in program analysis (Section 6).

## 2. Preliminaries

We first review concepts from learning theory used in subsequent sections; readers already familiar with learning theory may safely skip this section. For more details, the reader is referred to the excellent textbook by Kearns and Vazirani [34].

### 2.1 Bias-Variance Tradeoffs in Regression

Bias-variance tradeoffs have been well-studied in machine learning and before introducing the formal definitions it is instructive to look at a machine learning example.

Consider the problem of regression [6]. We are given a set of input-output pairs (observations) $(x_1, y_1), \ldots (x_n, y_n)$ and we want to predict the output $y$ for additional but unknown input values $x$. In other words, we want to learn a function $f$, such that $y_i = f(x_i), 1 \leq i \leq n$. The standard way to solve this problem is to consider a template for $f$ (a restricted class of functions from which the solution is chosen) and then fit the template to these observations.

Figure 3 fits three different templates to the same set of six observations. In Figure 3(a), we show the best fit line. Even though we have chosen the best of all possible lines, the fit is quite poor (meaning there are large errors even for the observed data points) and we do not expect the predictions obtained to be good. Figure 3(a) illustrates *underfitting*: lines are too imprecise to represent our observations. Next, we fit a quadratic curve (Figure 3(b)) and it seems to be a good fit: we expect it to produce good predictions. Figure 3(c) shows the fit of a polynomial of degree five: a fifth degree polynomial can interpolate between the six observations. The fit is extremely good for the actual observations, but there seems little reason for confidence in the predictions for very large or very small values of $x$ given by this particular choice of function. Figure 3(c) illustrates *overfitting*.

The nature of the underfitting and the overfitting for the examples in Figure 1 and Figure 3 have similarities and differences. We observe that both excess precision and limited precision lead to bad results. But there are some obvious differences. The program analysis example in Figure 1 looks cleaner: the abstractions are over-approximating some of the loop behaviors, whereas in Figure 3(b) the quadratic model does not even agree with the observations. The difference is due to noise. In machine learning, the data is typically noisy, whereas programs are precise descriptions. Therefore, the definition of generalization we use and the development in this paper are for the noise-free case. Of course, programs can have bugs and these can be thought of as noise and learning theory has mechanisms for incorporating noise in generalization [34]. Defining and handling noise in program analysis is interesting future work.

### 2.2 Learning Theory Primer

Consider an *instance space* $\chi$ which is the set of all instances. Suppose each $x_i \in \chi$ is associated with a *label* $\ell(x_i)$ that belongs to a *label set* $\gamma$. Let $\mathcal{H}$ be a *hypothesis class*, that is, the set of all functions $h : \chi \to \gamma$ considered by the learning algorithm. The goal of a learning algorithm is to choose an $h \in \mathcal{H}$ such that for each $x_i \in \chi$, $h(x_i)$ is a good estimate of the label $\ell(x_i)$. For the example in Section 2.1, $\chi = \mathbb{R}$, $\gamma = \mathbb{R}$, and $\mathcal{H}$ is a set of polynomials. We are given a set $S = \{(x_i, y_i) : i = 1, \ldots, m\} \subseteq \chi \times \gamma$ called the *training set*, and we want to find a hypothesis $h \in \mathcal{H}$ which generalizes over the whole instance space, that is, for all $x \in \chi$, $|h(x) - \ell(x)|$ is small.

The notion of instance space is general and can capture program states: it can be the collection of points in $\mathbb{R}^n$ for numerical programs, a collection of stack and heap pairs for heap manipulating programs, or a valuation of some numerical variables and arrays for array manipulating programs. One example of labels can be whether a state is reachable or unreachable and we might want our hypothesis to be a predicate which predicts for each state a label *true* (denoting reachable) or *false* (denoting unreachable), given some known reachable and unreachable states. For program analysis, we are interested in predicates as hypothesis classes. Hence, there are only two labels, *true* and *false*, and we limit our discussion to binary labels $\gamma = \{true, false\}$ unless stated otherwise.

Given a set of labeled instances called the training set $S \subseteq \chi \times \gamma$, one natural method to perform learning is *empirical risk minimization* (ERM): find a hypothesis $h \in \mathcal{H}$ such that the number of labeled instances $(x_i, y_i) \in S$ for which $h(x_i) \neq y_i$ is minimized. By finding a hypothesis that works well on the training set, we hope to find a hypothesis which works for the whole instance space $\chi$.

However, it is not clear whether such an $h$ generalizes. Next, we formally define the notion of generalization that we use. PAC learning [48] assumes that the training set $S$ consists of $m$ independent and identically distributed (iid) labeled instances drawn from an arbitrary but fixed distribution $D$ over the instance and label space. If we draw a new labeled iid sample from $D$, then we are interested in the probability that the actual label agrees with the predicted label: if $(x, y) \sim D$ then what is $Pr[h(x) = y]$? So first we *train*, that is, generate a hypothesis using a training set, and then we *test*, that is, evaluate the performance of the hypothesis on the new samples. A *PAC learner* takes some samples from $D$ as input and with high probability outputs a hypothesis that is approximately correct—if one were to draw a new sample from $D$, then with high probability the predicted and the actual label agree. Since the output of the PAC learner predicts the labels for instances that it has not seen, we say that it *generalizes*.

**Definition 2.1.** *A learner* ***generalizes*** *if given $m$ samples (determined by parameters $\delta$, $\epsilon$ and the hypothesis space $\mathcal{H}$) from a distribution D, with probability $1-\delta$ it outputs a hypothesis $h \in \mathcal{H}$, such that $(x, y) \sim D \Rightarrow Pr[h(x) \neq y] \leq \epsilon$.*

Now, why does this definition make sense? Suppose the learner wants to convince an adversary that it can produce hypotheses that generalize. If an adversary controls the training set, then she can generate a very bad training set with no information about the structure of the problem. For example, the adversary can just duplicate a labeled instance an unbounded number of times and can claim to have generated a large or even an unbounded training set. Or she can generate samples in the training set that are related to some particular behaviors, and when testing the generalization properties of the generated hypothesis use completely different behaviors. The poor hypothesis generated using certain behaviors is bound to perform poorly on behaviors that it has no idea about. An algorithm that can succeed against such a powerful adversary seems unlikely and so it seems reasonable to weaken the adversary. First, to define generalization, the training set should have some guarantee of having a good coverage of behaviors; by selecting training inputs randomly, we ensure formally that our training set is not adversarially generated. In testing, the adversary might defeat the generated hypothesis by testing on very skewed inputs. By testing on iid samples, we also take this power away from the adversary.

### 2.2.1 Bias and Variance

First, we formally define ERM. The learner finds a hypothesis that minimizes the empirical error $\hat{\varepsilon}$ over a training set $S = \{(x_i, y_i) : 1 \leq i \leq n\}$:

$$\hat{\varepsilon}(h) = \frac{1}{m}\sum_{i=1}^{m} \mathbf{1}\{h(x_i) \neq y_i\} \qquad (1)$$

where $\mathbf{1}$ is the indicator function: $\mathbf{1}\{b\} = 1$ if $b$ is *true* and 0 if $b$ is *false*. In *empirical risk minimization*, we try to find a hypothesis $h$ that minimizes the empirical error $\hat{\varepsilon}(h)$ and hope that it generalizes. The generalization error $\varepsilon(h)$ for a hypothesis $h$ is defined as follows:

$$\varepsilon(h) = Pr_{(x,y)\sim D}\left[h(x) \neq y\right] \qquad (2)$$

The objective of a learning algorithm is to compute a hypothesis with low generalization error. By minimizing the empirical error, we hope to achieve this objective.

One of the fundamental theorems in machine learning is the following [34]:

**Theorem 2.2.** *For a hypothesis space $\mathcal{H}$, let $d = VC(\mathcal{H})$ (defined in Section 2.3). Then, given $m$ samples, empirical risk minimization with high probability produces $\hat{h} \in \mathcal{H}$ such that:*

$$\varepsilon(\hat{h}) \leq \hat{\varepsilon}(\hat{h}) + \mathcal{O}\left(\sqrt{\frac{d}{m}}\right)$$

*and also*

$$\varepsilon(\hat{h}) \leq \varepsilon(h^*) + \mathcal{O}\left(\sqrt{\frac{d}{m}}\right)$$

*where $h^*$ is a hypothesis with the minimum generalization error in $\mathcal{H}$.*

This theorem gives us a bound on the generalization error. In particular, the first part of the theorem bounds the generalization error using the empirical error. To generalize well or to have a low generalization error we want the bound to be small. This theorem says that we can produce a large generalization error for two reasons:

1. The term $\varepsilon(h^*)$, the *bias*, is the generalization error of the best hypothesis in $\mathcal{H}$, i.e., the one that minimizes the generalization error. If this value is large then the hypothesis class underfits: even if we select the best available hypothesis, we still have generalization errors.
2. The term $\mathcal{O}\left(\sqrt{\frac{d}{m}}\right)$, the *variance*, grows with the VC dimension or precision of the hypothesis class. If this value is large generalization errors occur from overfitting the training data.

Therefore, low precision causes generalization error due to bias and high precision causes generalization error due to variance, and this leads to the bias-variance tradeoff. A corollary of this theorem has been used by [47] for an alternative purpose: for a specific hypothesis class $\mathcal{H}$, using $VC(\mathcal{H})$ to bound the number of samples required to ensure that the generalization error is below a user-specified tolerance.

By trying multiple hypothesis classes in order of increasing precision, one can address bias-variance tradeoffs. One starts with an imprecise hypothesis class and gradually increases precision until the bounds start degrading. In the extreme, when we have an empty hypothesis class, then the bias is high and the variance is zero. At the other extreme, for very expressive classes, the bias can become zero and the variance is high. When the size of the hypothesis class increases, so that successive hypothesis classes include the previous hypothesis classes, then bias decreases monotonically and variance increases monotonically. By gradually increasing precision, we can find a "sweet spot" and achieve low bounds on generalization error [24].

## 2.3 VC dimension

The *Vapnik-Chervonenkis* or *VC dimension* [34] is a purely combinatorial quantity that measures the capacity of a hypothesis class.

**Definition 2.3.** *A hypothesis $h$ satisfies a set of labeled instances $(X, \ell)$, iff $\forall x \in X$, $h(x) = \ell(x)$.*

**Definition 2.4.** *Given a set $X$ of instances, a hypothesis class $\mathcal{H}$ shatters $X$ if for any labeling $\ell$ there exists an $h \in \mathcal{H}$ s.t. $h$ satisfies $(X, \ell)$.*

**Definition 2.5.** *$VC(\mathcal{H})$ is the cardinality of the largest set that $\mathcal{H}$ can shatter.*

In our setting, when a hypothesis satisfies a set of labeled instances, some of the instances are labeled $true$ and others are labeled $false$, and the hypothesis is a predicate containing all the points labeled $true$ and excluding the points labeled $false$. If a class is able to shatter large sets, then it has high precision, and it is precisely able to separate instances with different labels. The VC dimension is the largest number of points that one can shatter. If the VC dimension is too high then we can overfit, and ERM does not produce a hypothesis that generalizes. In the extreme case, if the VC dimension of a hypothesis class is infinite, then we cannot bound its generalization error (Theorem 2.2).

To prove that the VC dimension of a hypothesis class $\mathcal{H}$ is at least $d$, we need to show a set of $d$ points in the instance space $\chi$ that $\mathcal{H}$ can shatter. To prove an upper bound $u$ on VC dimension, we need to show that for *any* possible selection of $u$ points from $\chi$, $\mathcal{H}$ cannot shatter the $u$ points. Since we want an upper bound on generalization error, it is generally sufficient to find upper bounds on VC dimension.

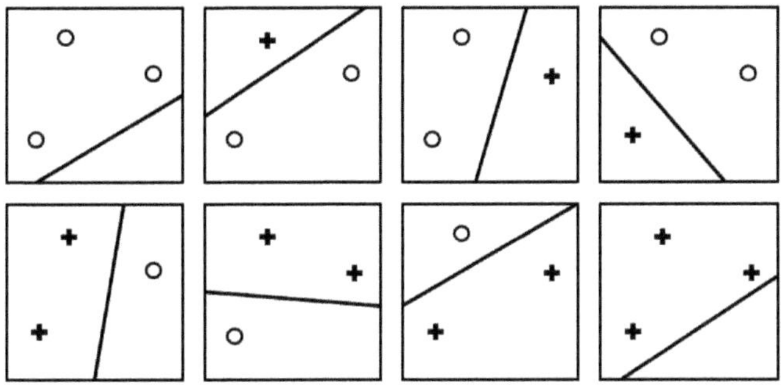

**Figure 4.** Shattering three points in two dimensions using one inequality.

## 3. Abstract Domains

In this section, we calculate the VC dimension for several popular abstract domains and show that the VC dimension gives results which match our expectations. Our goal is not to calculate the VC dimension of every possible abstract domain. We consider some simple abstract domains and the techniques we develop are useful (but might not be sufficient) for computing the VC dimension of other more complicated abstract domains as well. The VC dimensions of the numerical domains we consider (Section 3.1, Section 3.2, and Section 3.3) follow from standard results in learning theory. We also consider predicates over arrays (Section 3.4) and separation logic (Section 3.5). We are unaware of any previous study of VC dimensions of these domains.

### 3.1 Standard numerical domains

Our main idea is to compute the VC dimension of different abstract domains in order to capture their precision. The formal proofs for the numerical domains discussed in this section are standard textbook material in machine learning [34]. The instance space $\chi$ we first consider is $\mathbb{R}^n$, which can represent the state of $n$-variable numerical programs with no arrays and no data structures. Arrays and data structures are discussed in Sections 3.4 and 3.5.

#### 3.1.1 Single Inequality

First, let us consider the hypothesis class consisting of single linear inequalities. We select this class as it is one of the simplest hypothesis classes. The following result is known:

**Theorem 3.1.** *The VC dimension of the set of single inequalities in $n$ dimensions is $n + 1$.*

Consider the 2-dimensional space $\mathbb{R}^2$. This theorem states that the VC dimension of the class of inequalities of the form $ax + by + c \geq 0$ is three. Figure 4 shows a set of three points that can be shattered using this hypothesis class. Circles are the points labeled *false* and crosses are the points labeled *true*.

Note that we cannot shatter some configurations of three points, but that does not matter for VC dimension (Definition 2.5). For instance, as shown in Figure 5, if the points are collinear, then there is a labeling that cannot be satisfied by a single inequality: there is no inequality that can include the two crosses and exclude the circle.

We cannot shatter any configuration of four points using a single inequality, and the canonical configurations that cannot be shattered are shown in Figure 6. In the first configuration of four points, we cannot satisfy the inner point with label *false* and the other three with label *true*. In the second configuration, we cannot satisfy the labeling in which diagonally opposite points have the same label and adjacent points have different labels.

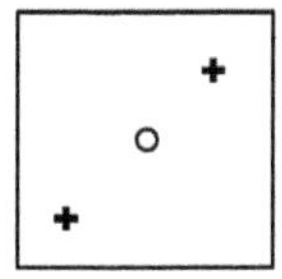

**Figure 5.** One inequality cannot shatter 3 collinear points.

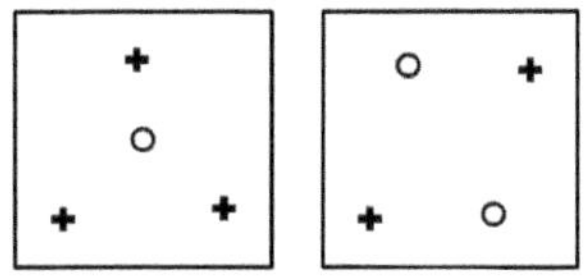

**Figure 6.** One inequality cannot shatter four points.

To prove Theorem 3.1, observe that an inequality in $n - 1$ dimensions can be looked upon as $f(x) \geq 0$, where $f(x)$ is a plane in $n$ dimensions passing through the origin. It is easy to see that we can shatter $n$ points with such inequalities. Consider a set $X$ of $n$ points where the $i^{th}$ point has the coordinate 1 in the $i^{th}$ dimension and 0 otherwise. If $Z \subseteq X$ is the set of examples labeled *true*, then the inequality $f(x) \geq 0$, where $f(x)$ has the $i^{th}$ coordinate 1 if $x_i \in Z$ and $-1$ otherwise, satisfies $X$. So the VC dimension of an inequality in $n$ dimensions is at least $n + 1$. To get the upper bound, we instantiate the following generalized lemma:

**Lemma 3.2.** *Let $\mathcal{F}$ be a function class containing functions $f : \chi \mapsto \mathbb{R}$, and let $\mathcal{A} = \{\{x : f(x) \geq 0\} : f \in F\}$, then $VC(\mathcal{A}) \leq dimension(\mathcal{F})$.*

Since planes in $n$ dimensions passing through the origin are generated from $n$ basis vectors, we conclude that the dimension of such planes is $n$, and Theorem 3.1 follows.

From this simple example of a VC dimension calculation, one can observe that computing the VC dimension of a hypothesis class can be a non-trivial task and can require reasoning about the mathematical structures underlying the instance space and the hypothesis class. Now we proceed to some of the more complicated hypothesis classes that are relevant for program analyses.

#### 3.1.2 Intervals

Intervals or conjunctions of inequalities of the form $\pm x \geq c$ is a well-studied abstract domain [16]. It is also known for underfitting, as useful invariants often require relationships between multiple variables.

**Theorem 3.3.** *The VC dimension of intervals in $n$ dimensions is $2n$.*

*Proof.* Consider the $2n$ points $X = \{x_{-n}, \ldots, x_{-1}, x_1, \ldots, x_n\}$, where $x_i$ has $sign(i)$ as coordinate $|i|$ and the rest of the coordinates zero. We can shatter these $2n$ points using a construction that is a generalization of Figure 7. Moreover, intervals cannot shatter $2n + 1$ points. Any collection of $2n + 1$ points has at most $2n$ extreme points: an extreme point of a collection of points has the highest or the lowest coordinate along some dimension among the points in the collection. There is at least one non-extreme point as there are $2n$ extremes and $2n + 1$ total points. Since intervals are convex, if we consider any set of $2n + 1$ points, and assign the extreme points the label *true* and the non-extreme point(s) the label *false* then no interval can include all the *true* and exclude the *false* point(s). For example, if we consider $2n + 1$ points consisting of $X$ and the origin, then the points in $X$ are extreme points and an interval cannot satisfy the labeling, where points in $X$ are labeled *true* and the origin is labeled *false*. □

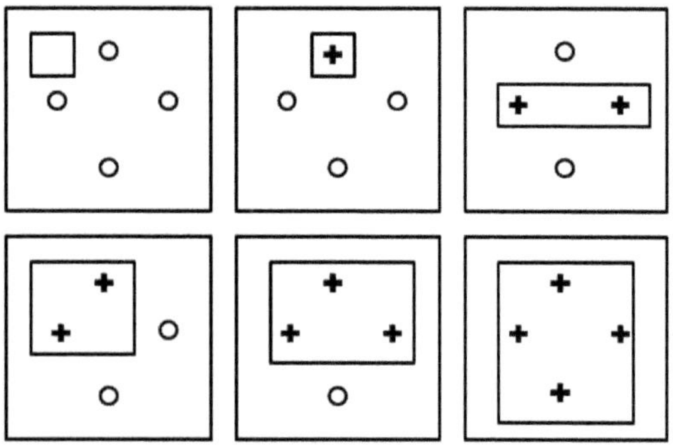

**Figure 7.** Shattering four points using intervals in 2 dimensions. Symmetric labelings have been omitted.

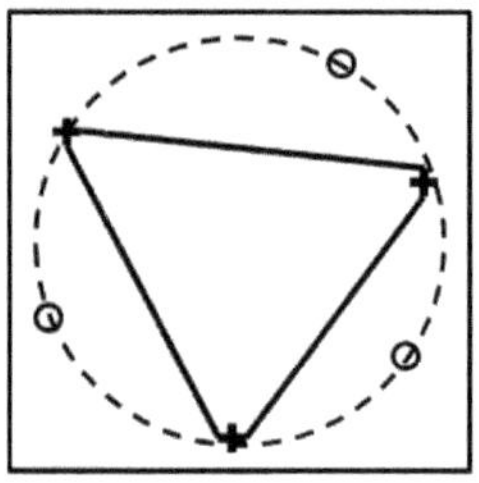

**Figure 8.** Using a polyhedron to satisfy a labeling.

We now move on to more expressive abstract domains and show that these have higher VC dimension than intervals.

### 3.1.3 Polyhedra

Given an arbitrary number of points on a circle, with arbitrary labelings, using convex hulls, polyhedra can separate the points labeled *true* from points labeled *false*. An example is shown in Figure 8. As a consequence, we have the following theorem:

**Theorem 3.4.** *The VC dimension of polyhedra is infinite.*

Using Theorem 2.2, we can conclude that when using polyhedra, it is not possible to bound the generalization error in our framework. However, many useful invariants require general inequalities. The fact that the VC dimension of polyhedra is infinite does not prevent us from handling general inequalities and these are addressed in the next section.

## 3.2 Templates

If we restrict polyhedra to $k$ inequalities, then it turns out that the VC dimension is bounded above by $\mathcal{O}(kn\log(k))$. The proof of this fact relies on general composition theorems [8, 9] that relate how the VC dimension composes when complex hypothesis classes are obtained by composition of more primitive classes. Here we are composing $k$ inequalities to generate a polyhedra and these theorems are applicable. To state these theorems, we require additional technical machinery that does not add to the development of the ideas in this paper and therefore we omit them.

In this case, as expected, the VC dimension is higher than intervals but seems manageable. If one can perform program analysis while keeping the number of inequalities fixed, then the generalization error is bounded in our framework and one might be able to combat overfitting. Template-based invariant inference engines perform analysis assuming the number of inequalities to be a fixed user-provided constant [15, 27, 28].

Now consider a given boolean combination instead of just conjunctions of inequalities. Approaches for performing abstract interpretation with a given fixed number of disjunctions are known [46]. In the case of template-based invariant inference, the recipe for finding the invariant is the same—one constructs a template and solves constraints to instantiate template parameters. The template can have only conjunctions [15] or a given boolean combination of inequalities [27]. Indeed, the VC dimension of a given boolean combination of $k$ inequalities in $n$ dimensions is also bounded by $\mathcal{O}(kn\log(k))$, which is the same as the VC dimension of conjunctions of $k$ inequalities [9]. This observation suggests that one does not expect results to degrade significantly due to higher variance when using this more expressive template.

TCM (template constrained matrix) domains [45] provide a knob to vary precision. In TCM, one can provide linear expressions, and abstract interpretation infers lower and upper bounds for them. Intervals and octagons are special cases of TCM. As we increase the number of linear expressions, the VC dimension increases. In the limit, when we have an infinite number of linear expressions, TCM becomes polyhedra and the VC dimension is infinite. Here is an example of a family of abstract domains that can combat bias-variance tradeoffs. An intelligent template choice ensures that we neither underfit nor overfit and therefore leads to better results.

Moreover, by calculating the VC dimension, one can observe how the precision increases if additional linear expressions are added and thus can help an abstract interpretation designer make systematic decisions for choosing linear expressions by answering questions such as the expected increase in precision from adding a new linear expression.

## 3.3 Non-linear arithmetic

First, we compute an upper bound on the VC dimension of the hypothesis classes composed of polynomial inequalities. Recall that an upper bound on the VC dimension suffices for bounding the generalization error (see Theorem 2.2). We show that the bound depends on the degree of the polynomial. Suppose we are given that the invariant is composed of quadratic inequalities. Conceptually, we can create a new variable for every monomial up to degree two [1]. The quadratic invariant in the old set of variables becomes a linear invariant over the new set of variables. The calculations done above carry over, just with an increased dimension. Since the number of monomials increases with the degree under consideration, the bound also increases with the increasing polynomial degree.

In the extreme, when the degree is unbounded, we cannot bound the VC dimension. If there are other sources of non-linearities, similar arguments apply and we can add new variables so that non-linear invariants are reduced to linear invariants [26].

## 3.4 Arrays

Consider an array manipulating program. The program state is the valuation of integer variables and potentially unbounded arrays. The examples of useful invariants over arrays that occur in the program analysis literature are generally universally quantified predicates involving a small number (1 to 3) of arrays [7]. Likewise, if we consider the predicates of the form $\forall i \,.\, \pm a[i] \geq c$ as the hypothesis class $\mathcal{H}$, and the instance space $\chi$ as the valuation of an array denoted by $a$, then the VC dimension is 2, which is the same as an interval in one variable. Thus, such predicates can suffer from the same problem of underfitting as intervals.

**Theorem 3.5.** *The VC dimension of predicates* $\forall i \,.\, \pm a[i] \geq c$ *is 2.*

*Proof.* Consider three states, and let $v_i$ denote the smallest value stored in the array of the $i^{th}$ state. Among the eight labelings that need to be satisfied, consider the configuration in which the states with the smallest and largest $v_i$ are labeled *true* and the third state is labeled *false*. This labeling cannot be satisfied by this class of predicates. Also, two distinct states, each consisting of only a single element in the array, are shattered by the predicates of the form $x \geq \pm c$. $\square$

We can extend the above result to a more general statement. Consider the instance space $\chi$ of points in $n+1$ dimensions, $\chi = \mathbb{R}^{n+1}$, that represents the values of $n+1$ numerical variables. Also consider the instance space $\chi^a$ that represents the values of an array $a$ of unbounded size and $n$ numerical variables, $\chi^a = \mathbb{R}^\omega \times \mathbb{R}^n$. We define three maps. The map $\mathcal{M}$ maps each predicate over $\chi$ to a predicate over $\chi^a$, $\mathcal{M}(P(x, x_1, \ldots, x_n)) = \forall j.P(a[j], x_1, \ldots, x_n)$ and $j \notin \{x_1, \ldots, x_n\}$. We also use $\mathcal{M}$ to denote pointwise extension of this map to a set of predicates. Next, $f : \chi \rightarrow \chi^a$, is a map such that $f(c, c_1, \ldots, c_n)$ is an instance in $\chi^a$ where the array $a$ has all elements equal to $c$ and the $i^{th}$ numerical variable of $\chi^a$ is assigned $c_i$. Finally, $g : \chi^a \rightarrow \chi$ is a map where $g(a, c_1, \ldots, c_n)$ assigns the first numerical variable of $\chi$ an arbitrary element of $a$ and the rest of the $n$ variables are assigned values $c_1, \ldots, c_n$. If $\mathcal{H}$ is an arbitrary hypothesis class of predicates over $\chi$ then the following result holds:

**Theorem 3.6.** $VC(\mathcal{H}) = VC(\mathcal{M}(\mathcal{H}))$.

*Proof.* To prove $VC(\mathcal{H}) \leq VC(\mathcal{M}(\mathcal{H}))$, observe that if $\mathcal{H}$ can shatter $m$ points $p_1, \ldots, p_m$ using predicates $P_1, \ldots P_{2^m}$ then $\mathcal{M}(\mathcal{H})$ can shatter $f(p_1), \ldots, f(p_m)$ using $\mathcal{M}(P_1), \ldots, \mathcal{M}(P_{2^m})$. The proof for the reverse inclusion, that is, $VC(\mathcal{H}) \geq VC(\mathcal{M}(\mathcal{H}))$ is similar and uses $g$ and $\mathcal{M}^{-1}$ (which exists since $\mathcal{M}$ is one to one). $\square$

This result allows us to compute the VC dimension of richer hypothesis classes and boolean combinations of the same. For example, if we have a numerical variable $z$ and an array $a$ as our program variables, then by the results in Section 3.1 and Theorem 3.6 the VC dimension of the class of predicates $\forall j.a[j] + c_1 z \leq \pm c_2$ is three and for the class of conjunctions of predicates of the form $\forall j.a[j] \geq \pm c$ and $z \geq \pm c$ is four.

### 3.5 Separation Logic

For heap manipulating programs, separation logic has emerged as a successful approach [44]. We do not review all the details of separation logic here and keep the discussion at an abstract level. The predicates or the elements of the hypothesis class are formulas written in separation logic and elements of the instance space or the program states are pairs of a store $s$ and a heap $h$. Since we focus on the heap, we keep the store fixed. Our instance space is composed of program states in which the store maps a single variable $z$ to a heap location $l$.

In [10], a heuristic algorithm for inference with lists has been described. The related fragment shown below has an infinite VC dimension.

$$\begin{array}{lcl} e & ::= & x \mid X \mid c \\ p & ::= & \texttt{emp} \mid e_1 \mapsto e_2, e_3 \mid p * q \mid \mathit{list}\ e \end{array}$$

An expression is either a variable $x$, or a logical variable $X$, or a constant $c$ (e.g. `nil`) and an assertion says that the heap is either empty, or it contains one cons cell and $e_1$ is the address of the cons cell with contents $e_2$ and $e_3$, or the assertion has a separating conjunction $(p*q)$ that decomposes the heap into two disjoint parts, one where $p$ is true and one where $q$ is true. A *list* denotes a `nil` terminated singly linked list. The logical variables in the assertions are implicitly existentially quantified.

**Theorem 3.7.** *VC dimension of the above class of predicates is infinite.*

| Bench | PK/OCT | | | PK/BOX | | | OCT/BOX | | |
|---|---|---|---|---|---|---|---|---|---|
| | $\subsetneq$ | $\supsetneq$ | unc. | $\subsetneq$ | $\supsetneq$ | unc. | $\subsetneq$ | $\supsetneq$ | unc. |
| a2ps | 12.74 | 0.78 | 0 | 21.64 | 0 | 2.13 | 18.94 | 0 | 0.93 |
| gawk | 21.34 | 0 | 0 | 26.96 | 0 | 0 | 17.97 | 0 | 0 |
| chess | 5.99 | 5.78 | 2.47 | 12.67 | 3.68 | 2.24 | 14.87 | 0 | 0 |
| gnugo | 18.75 | 2.08 | 2.08 | 22.50 | 1.66 | 1.11 | 10.86 | 0 | 1.12 |
| grep | 3.30 | 0 | 0 | 8.26 | 0 | 0 | 8.26 | 0 | 0 |
| gzip | 21.16 | 2.18 | 0 | 32.84 | 0.72 | 1.45 | 26.27 | 0 | 0 |
| lapack | 11.84 | 5.67 | 0.85 | 78.96 | 2.16 | 2.99 | 85.03 | 0 | 0 |
| make | 6.50 | 4.00 | 5.50 | 6.52 | 4.34 | 5.97 | 11.94 | 0 | 0 |
| tar | 5.17 | 4.20 | 0 | 9.70 | 3.23 | 0.97 | 9.38 | 0 | 0 |

**Figure 9.** Results of comparing abstract domains published in [29].

*Proof.* We need to show that given any $n$, we can construct $n$ heaps and shatter them using the predicates of our logic. We give a proof sketch. The intuition is that we can introduce an unbounded number of logical variables in the heap and lists can encode a boolean choice. Therefore, we can make an unbounded number of boolean choices and shatter unbounded sets. Suppose $n$ is two. The construction below can be generalized to arbitrary $n$. Recall, the store maps $z$ to $l$. Consider two heaps, $h_1 = [l \mapsto (l_1, \texttt{nil}), l_1 \mapsto (\texttt{nil}, \texttt{nil})]$ and $h_2 = [l \mapsto (\texttt{nil}, l_1), l_1 \mapsto (\texttt{nil}, \texttt{nil})]$. The predicates $z \mapsto (X, Y)$, $z \mapsto (X, Y) * \mathit{list}(X)$, $z \mapsto (X, Y) * \mathit{list}(Y)$, and $z \mapsto (X, Y) * \mathit{list}(X) * \mathit{list}(Y)$ shatter the four labelings, $(\mathit{false}, \mathit{false}), (\mathit{true}, \mathit{false}), (\mathit{false}, \mathit{true}), (\mathit{true}, \mathit{true})$, of $(h_1, h_2)$ repectively. In general, by introducing $n$ logical variables we can shatter $n$ heaps obtained using this construction. $\square$

Similar to Section 3.2, we can restrict the size of the predicates to bound the VC dimension and hence the generalization error. We are unaware of any template-based analysis that restricts the structure of the predicates in separation logic, but given the success of template-based invariant inference for numerical programs, it seems to be a useful research direction to pursue in the future.

## 4. Discussion

In this section, we consider empirical results from various papers on program analysis and try to interpret these results using bias-variance tradeoffs. We do not claim to be exhaustive; the goal here is to show that a variety of useful techniques can be justified using our framework.

### 4.1 Abstract Interpretation

Consider the subset of results (Figure 9) obtained from the PAGAI static analyzer that were published in [29]. The columns in the table of Figure 9 compare the quality of invariants found by polyhedra (PK) and octagons (OCT), polyhedra (PK) and intervals (BOX), and octagons (OCT) and intervals (BOX) respectively. In each comparison there are three values: the first value is the percentage of invariants for which the results of the first abstract domain are logically stronger than the second; the second value is the percentage of invariants for which the results of the second domain are stronger than the first; the third is the percentage of incomparable invariants; the remaining percentage of invariants are logically identical.

It can be seen from Figure 9 that as precision increases the quality of the inferred invariants gets better: this result is expected as richer abstract domains can express invariants that weaker domains cannot. We share the observation with the authors that for a non-negligible percentage of invariants, polyhedra perform worse than intervals and octagons. Other evaluations in [29] (not studied here) show that the basic forward analysis of [19] can produce better results than the "path-focused" approach of [30, 40], even though the latter can produce more precise intermediate results. The authors explain these observation using the non-monotonicity of the

| Outcome | SATABS | MAGIC | BLAST | BLAST (new) |
|---|---|---|---|---|
| Verified | 0 | 0 | 8 | 12 |
| Refinement failed | 13 | 13 | 0 | 0 |
| Did not finish | 0 | 0 | 5 | 1 |

**Figure 10.** Results for interpolation with incremental increase of precision published in [32]. SATABS [14] and MAGIC [12] are based on weakest preconditions and BLAST [31] uses interpolants.

widening operator. In abstract interpretation, the widening operator is responsible for generalization [17]. Widening is usually non-monotonic because widening more precise information can lead to worse generalizations [18]. For example, $[0, 1]\nabla[0, 2] = [0, \infty]$ and $[0, 2]\nabla[0, 2] = [0, 2]$. In this example, widening more precise intervals leads to less precise results.

Non-monotonicity of the widening operator is related to bias-variance tradeoffs. Intuitively, if there were a monotonic widening operator, then improving the precision of the underlying abstract domain would lead to better generalizations, consequently, there would be no bias-variance tradeoff. The tradeoff seems to be a fundamental limit on generalization, and therefore monotonic widening operators for sophisticated abstract domains seem unlikely.

### 4.2 Interpolants

Interpolant-based engines [31, 38] find simple proofs of infeasibility of a finite number of spurious counterexample paths and hope that because the proofs are simple the predicates used in the proof will generalize and refute all possible spurious counterexamples. Inability to find good predicates can result in divergence in CEGAR. We motivate the usefulness of simple proofs using bias-variance tradeoffs.

An interpolant is required to prove the infeasibility of a spurious counterexample. This requirement ensures that the interpolant is not too weak—it must be strong enough to prove a potentially useful fact. This requirement can also be seen as a means to tackle underfitting: we are imposing a lower bound on the precision of the language of interpolants. To avoid overfitting, we want the interpolant to be simple. The hope is that simple predicates will not overfit to a specific path and hence can avoid high variance. The definition of an interpolant ensures simplicity by restricting the variables that can occur in an interpolant, which corresponds to lowering the dimension of the instance space, and consequently the VC dimension as well.

However, it has been observed that only restricting the variables is not enough to avoid divergence. In [32], the language of interpolants or the hypothesis class is restricted to a finite set and this set is expanded gradually. If the hypothesis class is finite, then in our framework the following result is known:

**Theorem 4.1.** *If $\hat{h}$ is obtained from an ERM algorithm, $|\mathcal{H}| = k$, $m$ is the size of the sample set, and $\delta$ is fixed, then with probability at least $1 - \delta$ we have*

$$\varepsilon(\hat{h}) \leq (min_{h \in \mathcal{H}} \varepsilon(h)) + 2\sqrt{\frac{1}{2m} log \frac{2k}{\delta}}$$

This theorem states that when the language is inexpressive, we have high bias, and as we increase the expressiveness of the language under consideration, $|\mathcal{H}|$ increases, and so does the variance. Similar to Theorem 2.2, by gradually increasing the size of the hypothesis class, the bounds on the generalization error can be minimized.

Consider the empirical results of Jhala and McMillan published in [32] and shown in Figure 10. SATABS, MAGIC, and BLAST are predicate abstraction based tools that use CEGAR [13] and add predicates during their analysis to perform refinement. A poor choice of refinement predicates can cause divergence. These predicates are obtained by refuting spurious counterexample paths. If the predicates overfit the paths, then they are typically not useful for finding an invariant. The last column shows the results obtained from the following strategy for generating predicates: use interpolants as refinement predicates and first restrict the interpolants to a finite language $L_0$. For example, $L_0$ can be the language of predicates that have their numeric constants restricted to either zero or $c \pm 0$ where $c$ is a numerical constant statically occurring in the program. The language is incrementally expanded to $L_1$, $L_2$, and so on. The penultimate column just uses the interpolants in the language $L_\infty$. We observe that by incrementally increasing the expressiveness of the language of interpolants, one can avoid the overfitting present in $L_\infty$ and obtain better results, verifying 12 instead of 8 programs from the benchmark suite of 13 programs.

### 4.3 Incrementally Increasing Precision

In recent years, there has been a growing interest in exploring optimal abstractions [37, 49]. These papers argue for the most imprecise abstraction that is sufficient to prove the desired property of a program. (This line of work is different from the techniques that aim to compute the least fixed point [22, 23].) Generally, an increase in precision is associated with a decrease in efficiency. Imprecise abstractions are computationally cheap and hence are desirable. Liang et al. [37] show that quite imprecise abstractions can be sufficient to prove most properties of interest. Zhang et al. [49] have an abstraction refinement algorithm that successively tries abstractions of increasing cost. Stratified analysis [41] is another technique that incrementally increases precision: abstract interpretation is performed in a stratified fashion, running successive analyses of increasing precision by incrementally increasing the number of program variables under consideration. The later analyses use the results of the previous analyses and heuristics based on dataflow dependencies. By performing the stratified analysis, the authors obtain the same or better invariants than classical [19] or alternative widening schemes [3] for all the cases of their study [41]. All of these, including [32] (discussed in Section 4.2), can be seen as examples of addressing bias-variance tradeoffs by starting with low precision and moving to high precision. It is also possible to achieve the same effect by starting from high precision and moving towards lower precision (e.g., as done in [5]). In the next section, we explore whether the techniques for combating bias-variance tradeoffs in machine learning can also benefit program analysis tools.

## 5. Cross Validation

In this section, we describe our experience with applying techniques for addressing bias-variance tradeoffs to program analysis tools. In particular, we discuss the application of cross validation to YOGI, a verification engine in Windows SDV [25].

Machine learning tools generally have a number of precision knobs and finding a configuration of these knobs that does not overfit the training set is recognized as a problem [11, 21]. One widely used solution is cross validation [2]. While providing formal guarantees for cross validation algorithms is a topic of current research [2, 33], cross validation has been found to be extremely useful empirically and is standard practice in machine learning [21]. We study the simplest cross validation algorithm here. Evaluation of more sophisticated variants such as k-fold cross validation [2] is left as future work.

Cross validation partitions the training set into *training data* and *test data*. Next, multiple learning algorithms, called *learners*, are trained on the training data and tested on the test data. The learner that generates the hypothesis performing best on the test data is selected. For example, for the regression example of Section 2.1, we would consider a subset of the observations as training data and the rest as test data (say a 70-30 split). Now consider different learning algorithms where each algorithm fits a polynomial of a different degree on the training data. We find the best fit line, quadratic, cubic, etc., for the training data and pick the degree which corresponds to the hypothesis that performs the best on our test data.

We observe that the learner obtained from cross validation generates a hypothesis using training data that generalizes to test data. If we train a learner on the full training set without performing cross validation, then we might overfit. In Figure 3, the curve that corresponds to the fifth degree polynomial curve best fits the observations (among linear, quadratic, and fifth degree polynomials) and thus performs the best on the observed data. During cross validation, the fifth degree polynomial overfits on the training data and shows large deviations from the observations in the test data. Thus, cross validation can serve as a guide which rejects fifth degree polynomials for this example and prevents overfitting.

Here is a full description of cross validation:

1. Randomly split the training set $S$ into $S_{train}$ and $S_{test}$.
2. For each learner $M_i$, train it on $S_{train}$ to get a hypothesis $h_i$. Training can be just ERM over $S_{train}$.
3. Pick the learner $M_k$ corresponding to $h_k$ with smallest error on $S_{test}$. Train $M_k$ on $S$ to obtain the output hypothesis $h$.

Note that once we have selected the learner $M_k$ that generalizes best to the test data, the final hypothesis is computed by training $M_k$ on all of the available data. We remark that cross validation is not a silver bullet and if used improperly can itself start to overfit [42].

YOGI is an industrial strength tool for checking Windows device driver properties. YOGI has a benchmark suite of 2490 driver-property pairs and in the current production version its precision knobs have been tuned to perform the best on these benchmarks [43]. As discussed above, this process can lead to overfitting; in fact, we show that simply by using cross validation we can significantly improve YOGI's performance.

In our setting, the instances are input programs that YOGI analyzes and the hypothesis class consists of all the versions of Yogi that can be created by different choices of configuration parameters. We are given some benchmarks and these constitute our training set. The labels for these benchmarks, correct or buggy, are known. The goal of the learner is to find a hypothesis (which is a tool) that generalizes well, that is, even for new programs it has not seen, we want it to assign the correct label. For YOGI, the learner is simply ERM, which selects the best parameter configuration for YOGI on the training set.

We consider a sequence of tools $Yogi_i$ where $i$, the number of *test steps*, is one of the most important parameters in YOGI (see [43] for details). The actual details of how YOGI works are unimportant; what is pertinent here is that a higher $i$ corresponds to increased precision. In Figure 2, the timing results are shown where each $Yogi_i$ has been trained on the full benchmark set: the parameters (other than $i$) have been tuned to obtain the best results. We observe the expected bias-variance tradeoff curve. As $i$ is increasing, the precision is increasing, and the results first improve with increasing precision and then they degrade. From Figure 2, the best value of $i$ for all 2490 driver-property pairs is 500. Note that [43] uses the total runtime as a performance metric. Hence, we also use total runtime for comparing performance of different configurations during cross validation. However, more general performance metrics are certainly possible. We observe that the authors of [43] have discovered a good configuration of the tool, which we call the old YOGI; old YOGI is $Yogi_{500}$ trained on the full set of 2490 driver-property pairs and is the current production version.

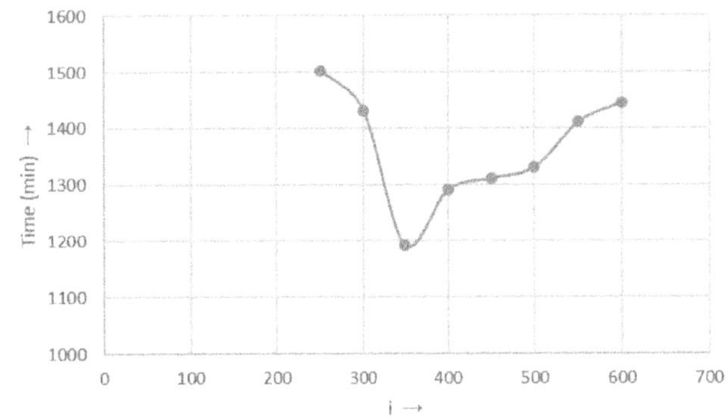


**Figure 11.** Result of running Yogi on 747 driver-properties test pairs with $i \in [250, 600]$.

| Tool | Time (min) | #defects | #time-outs |
|---|---|---|---|
| $Yogi_{350}$ | 4704 | 189 | 21 |
| $Yogi_{500}$ | 8279 | 183 | 66 |

**Table 1.** Performance of $Yogi_{350}$ and $Yogi_{500}$ on 2106 new driver-property pairs. The time-out was set to 30 minutes.

Now we consider the alternative, performing cross validation on YOGI. We split the 2490 driver-property pairs into 70% training data (consisting of 1743 driver-property pairs), and 30% test data (consisting of 747 driver-property pairs). We train each $Yogi_i$ (finding values for the parameters other than $i$) so that it performs as well as possible on the training data. Next, we pick the $Yogi_k$ that performs best on the test data (shown in Figure 11). From Figure 11, this best value occurs for $i = 350$. Next we train $Yogi_{350}$ on all 2490 driver-property pairs to obtain the new YOGI.

When verification is performed on new verification tasks (in this case, a new set of 2106 driver-property pairs), we observe that the new YOGI (with $i = 350$) shows better generalization properties than the old YOGI (with $i = 500$). Even though the new YOGI performs worse on the 2490 driver-property pairs (the old YOGI was the best configuration), it actually performs better on the new verification tasks, as shown in Table 1. We conclude that old YOGI was overfitted to the benchmarks. Here we have been able to reduce the run time by more than 40%, find new defects, and decrease the number of time-outs simply by using cross validation to set configuration parameters.

Here are some additional details about Table 1. The new YOGI and the old YOGI find 182 defects in common. The new YOGI timed out on one defect which the old YOGI could find. Also, there are 19 time-outs that are common between the old and the new YOGI. Such a result is expected as there is no best configuration. Using cross validation we are trying to find a configuration that avoids overfitting and is expected to work well in most cases.

To summarize, we empirically validate that YOGI has been overfitted to its benchmark suite and we remove this overfitting by cross validation to obtain a better tool. We believe other existing tools could be similarly improved with the straightforward application of cross validation.

## 6. Recommendations and Limitations

In this section, we consider the implications of bias-variance tradeoffs in the design of automatic program analyses. We also discuss some limitations of our approach and make a number of specific recommendations.

Bias-variance tradeoffs can help in the selection of an abstract domain. One should avoid abstract domains with infinite VC dimension, otherwise we cannot bound the generalization error in our framework (Theorem 2.2) and we expect it to be large in practice. Ideally, one should use domains with finite VC dimension while ensuring the domain is rich enough to express the invariants of interest (to avoid large generalization error due to bias). One natural way to achieve this goal is to start with an imprecise domain and increase precision by gradually expanding the hypothesis class (Section 4).

We now discuss how bias-variance tradeoffs apply to fully automatic verification. Most practical tools have benchmarks and some parameters to tune. Take for instance the Astrée tool [20], which has more than a hundred parameters governing the abstract domains to enable, widening strategies, and so on. The best choice for the parameters is not usually clear. If one aims for a fully automatic tool like YOGI [25], then before shipping the tool one generally performs ERM: the parameters are tuned to give best results on a benchmark suite [43]. But if bias-variance tradeoffs exists, then this strategy is suboptimal. One can overfit to the benchmarks and unknowingly hamper the performance of the tool on new inputs (Section 5).

A common practice in the program analysis community is to tune to a benchmark suite and then report results [25, 43]. Given the results in this paper, it is clear that this approach provides no protection against overfitting and is therefore methodologically weak. As an extreme example, one can build a tool for any benchmark suite by simply creating a lookup table with the correct answer for each benchmark. This tool works perfectly in the reported experimental results and fails completely in practice. A more realistic scenario is that a tool builder discovers her tool gives poor results on some program $P$ in her benchmark suite. She makes a change and as a result the tool works better on $P$. But has the tool really improved in general, or has the tool designer overfit to $P$? It might be that the tool's users were better off without the change. A tool that performs poorly on some of its benchmarks is not a bad thing if the alternative is overfitting.

The goal, of course, should be to build tools that work on previously unseen examples, not just on the benchmark suite. An experimental methodology that divides inputs into a training set that can influence the design of the tool and a separate test set that cannot inform the design of the tool is one way to validate that tools generalize beyond the benchmarks used to design them. Some researchers may be doing this already, but we are unaware of anyone mentioning this point explicitly in the literature. Note that this recommendation might not be directly applicable to tools that are not designed to be fully automatic. For example, Astrée [20] relies on user interaction to select the appropriate parameters for the program under analysis.

Despite our general critique of overfitting static analysis tools to benchmarks, there are situations in which that may be the right thing to do. When the goal is to analyze a specific program (e.g., the verification of seL4 [35]) rather than to build a tool that works for any program, it might make sense to overfit to the one important benchmark. The situation is also different for analysis algorithms that can be proven analytically to give an optimal or best result, such as certain classes of type inference, dataflow analysis, abstract interpretation over finite lattices, and the analysis of loop-free and recursion-free programs. Here the setting is sufficiently tractable that the generalization strategy is provably the best possible (or generalization is not needed at all) and reporting how well the algorithm works on a single full benchmark suite is a reasonable practice. Finally, if one had some guarantee that a benchmark suite was representative of all possible inputs there would be no need for a separate test suite—in this case improving performance on the training set guarantees improvement in general. However, it seems difficult to obtain or prove that a benchmark suite is representative, even for a particular domain. The drivers we consider as the training set in Section 5 are a superset of the benchmarks of [25] and from our results we can conclude that they are not representative.

The competition on software verification [4] was introduced as a common platform to compare tools. However, the current structure of the competition does not avoid overfitting. The benchmarks and the expected results of the competition are public and the benchmarks used to compare tools are a *subset* of the publicly released benchmarks. This contest design addresses a real concern, which is that because the semantics of C is underspecified and the benchmarks are C programs, publishing all benchmarks in advance helps ensure that the organizers and participants agree on the intended meaning of the programs. Our recommendation to organizers of competitions to evaluate software tools is that they should always evaluate the tools on some new, unseen programs as a check on overfitting. These unseen programs must be chosen carefully to ensure that any possible variations in interpretation are irrelevant to the verification task.

## 7. Conclusion

Because of bias-variance tradeoffs, increasing the precision of a program analysis can lead to a decrease in the quality of results. We have adapted the PAC learning framework to explain bias-variance tradeoffs in program analysis and used VC dimension as a measure of the precision of abstract domains. We have computed the VC dimension for some popular abstractions for numerical, array manipulating, and heap manipulating programs and we observe that more precise abstractions have higher VC dimension. We have also shown that standard techniques for addressing bias-variance tradeoffs, such as incrementally increasing precision and using cross validation in tuning parameters, are applicable to program analysis tools.

## Acknowledgments

We thank Saurabh Gupta, Bharath Hariharan, Sriram Rajamani, and the anonymous reviewers for their constructive comments. This work was supported by NSF grant CCF-1160904. This material is also based on research sponsored by the Air Force Research Laboratory, under agreement number FA8750-12-2-0020. The U.S. Government is authorized to reproduce and distribute reprints for Governmental purposes notwithstanding any copyright notation thereon.

## References

[1] G. Amato, M. Parton, and F. Scozzari. Discovering invariants via simple component analysis. *J. Symb. Comput.*, 47(12):1533–1560, 2012.

[2] S. Arlot and A. Celisse. A survey of cross-validation procedures for model selection. *Statistics Surveys*, 4:40–79, 2010.

[3] R. Bagnara, P. M. Hill, E. Ricci, and E. Zaffanella. Precise widening operators for convex polyhedra. *Sci. Comput. Program.*, 58(1-2):28–56, 2005.

[4] D. Beyer. Second competition on software verification - (summary of SV-COMP 2013). In *TACAS*, pages 594–609, 2013.

[5] D. Beyer, T. A. Henzinger, and G. Théoduloz. Program analysis with dynamic precision adjustment. In *ASE*, pages 29–38, 2008.

[6] C. M. Bishop. *Pattern Recognition and Machine Learning (Information Science and Statistics)*. Springer-Verlag New York, Inc., 2006. ISBN 0387310738.

[7] N. Bjørner, K. L. McMillan, and A. Rybalchenko. On solving universally quantified horn clauses. In *SAS*, pages 105–125, 2013.

[8] A. Blumer, A. Ehrenfeucht, D. Haussler, and M. K. Warmuth. Learnability and the Vapnik-Chervonenkis dimension. *J. ACM*, 36(4):929–965, 1989.

[9] N. H. Bshouty, S. A. Goldman, H. D. Mathias, S. Suri, and H. Tamaki. Noise-tolerant distribution-free learning of general geometric concepts. *J. ACM*, 45(5):863–890, 1998.

[10] C. Calcagno, D. Distefano, P. W. O'Hearn, and H. Yang. Compositional shape analysis by means of bi-abduction. In *POPL*, pages 289–300, 2009.

[11] G. C. Cawley and N. L. C. Talbot. On over-fitting in model selection and subsequent selection bias in performance evaluation. *Journal of Machine Learning Research*, 11:2079–2107, 2010.

[12] S. Chaki, E. M. Clarke, A. Groce, and O. Strichman. Predicate abstraction with minimum predicates. In *CHARME*, pages 19–34, 2003.

[13] E. M. Clarke, O. Grumberg, S. Jha, Y. Lu, and H. Veith. Counterexample-guided abstraction refinement. In *CAV*, pages 154–169, 2000.

[14] E. M. Clarke, D. Kroening, N. Sharygina, and K. Yorav. Predicate abstraction of ansi-c programs using sat. *Formal Methods in System Design*, 25(2-3):105–127, 2004.

[15] M. Colón, S. Sankaranarayanan, and H. Sipma. Linear invariant generation using non-linear constraint solving. In *CAV*, pages 420–432, 2003.

[16] P. Cousot and R. Cousot. Static determination of dynamic properties of programs. In *ISOP*, pages 106–130, 1976.

[17] P. Cousot and R. Cousot. Abstract interpretation: A unified lattice model for static analysis of programs by construction or approximation of fixpoints. In *POPL*, pages 238–252, 1977.

[18] P. Cousot and R. Cousot. Comparing the Galois connection and widening/narrowing approaches to abstract interpretation. In *PLILP*, pages 269–295, 1992.

[19] P. Cousot and N. Halbwachs. Automatic discovery of linear restraints among variables of a program. In *POPL*, pages 84–96, 1978.

[20] P. Cousot, R. Cousot, J. Feret, L. Mauborgne, A. Miné, and X. Rival. Why does Astrée scale up? *Formal Methods in System Design*, 35(3): 229–264, 2009.

[21] P. Domingos. A few useful things to know about machine learning. *Commun. ACM*, 55(10):78–87, 2012.

[22] T. Gawlitza and H. Seidl. Precise fixpoint computation through strategy iteration. In *ESOP*, pages 300–315, 2007.

[23] T. Gawlitza and H. Seidl. Precise relational invariants through strategy iteration. In *CSL*, pages 23–40, 2007.

[24] S. Geman, E. Bienenstock, and R. Doursat. Neural networks and the bias/variance dilemma. *Neural Computation*, 4(1):1–58, 1992.

[25] P. Godefroid, A. V. Nori, S. K. Rajamani, and S. Tetali. Compositional may-must program analysis: unleashing the power of alternation. In *POPL*, pages 43–56, 2010.

[26] B. S. Gulavani and S. Gulwani. A numerical abstract domain based on expression abstraction and max operator with application in timing analysis. In *CAV*, pages 370–384, 2008.

[27] S. Gulwani, S. Srivastava, and R. Venkatesan. Program analysis as constraint solving. In *PLDI*, pages 281–292, 2008.

[28] A. Gupta, R. Majumdar, and A. Rybalchenko. From tests to proofs. In *TACAS*, pages 262–276, 2009.

[29] J. Henry, D. Monniaux, and M. Moy. Pagai: A path sensitive static analyser. *Electr. Notes Theor. Comput. Sci.*, 289:15–25, 2012.

[30] J. Henry, D. Monniaux, and M. Moy. Succinct representations for abstract interpretation - combined analysis algorithms and experimental evaluation. In *SAS*, pages 283–299, 2012.

[31] T. A. Henzinger, R. Jhala, R. Majumdar, and K. L. McMillan. Abstractions from proofs. In *POPL*, pages 232–244, 2004.

[32] R. Jhala and K. L. McMillan. A practical and complete approach to predicate refinement. In *TACAS*, pages 459–473, 2006.

[33] M. Kearns and D. Ron. Algorithmic stability and sanity-check bounds for leave-one-out cross-validation. *Neural Computation*, 11:152–162, 1997.

[34] M. J. Kearns and U. V. Vazirani. *An introduction to computational learning theory*. MIT Press, Cambridge, MA, USA, 1994. ISBN 0-262-11193-4.

[35] G. Klein, J. Andronick, K. Elphinstone, G. Heiser, D. Cock, P. Derrin, D. Elkaduwe, K. Engelhardt, R. Kolanski, M. Norrish, T. Sewell, H. Tuch, and S. Winwood. seL4: formal verification of an operating-system kernel. *Commun. ACM*, 53(6):107–115, 2010.

[36] G. Lalire, M. Argoud, and B. Jeannet. The Interproc Analyzer. http://pop-art.inrialpes.fr/people/bjeannet/bjeannet-forge/interproc/index.html.

[37] P. Liang, O. Tripp, and M. Naik. Learning minimal abstractions. In *POPL*, pages 31–42, 2011.

[38] K. L. McMillan. An interpolating theorem prover. *Theoretical Computer Science*, 345(1):101–121, 2005.

[39] A. Miné. The octagon abstract domain. *Higher-Order and Symbolic Computation*, 19(1):31–100, 2006.

[40] D. Monniaux and L. Gonnord. Using bounded model checking to focus fixpoint iterations. In *SAS*, pages 369–385, 2011.

[41] D. Monniaux and J. L. Guen. Stratified static analysis based on variable dependencies. *Electr. Notes Theor. Comput. Sci.*, 288:61–74, 2012.

[42] A. Y. Ng. Preventing "overfitting" of cross-validation data. In *ICML*, pages 245–253, 1997.

[43] A. V. Nori and S. K. Rajamani. An empirical study of optimizations in YOGI. In *ICSE (1)*, pages 355–364, 2010.

[44] J. C. Reynolds. Separation logic: A logic for shared mutable data structures. In *LICS*, pages 55–74, 2002.

[45] S. Sankaranarayanan, H. B. Sipma, and Z. Manna. Scalable analysis of linear systems using mathematical programming. In *VMCAI*, pages 25–41, 2005.

[46] S. Sankaranarayanan, F. Ivancic, I. Shlyakhter, and A. Gupta. Static analysis in disjunctive numerical domains. In *SAS*, pages 3–17, 2006.

[47] R. Sharma, S. Gupta, B. Hariharan, A. Aiken, and A. V. Nori. Verification as learning geometric concepts. In *SAS*, pages 388–411, 2013.

[48] L. G. Valiant. A theory of the learnable. *Commun. ACM*, 27(11): 1134–1142, 1984.

[49] X. Zhang, M. Naik, and H. Yang. Finding optimum abstractions in parametric dataflow analysis. In *PLDI*, pages 365–376, 2013.

# Abstract Satisfaction


Vijay D'Silva
Department of Computer Science
University of California, Berkeley
vijayd@eecs.berkeley.edu

Leopold Haller
Department of Computer Science
University of Oxford
leopold.haller@cs.ox.ac.uk

Daniel Kroening
Department of Computer Science
University of Oxford
daniel.kroening@cs.ox.ac.uk



## Abstract

This article introduces an abstract interpretation framework that codifies the operations in SAT and SMT solvers in terms of lattices, transformers and fixed points. We develop the idea that a formula denotes a set of models in a universe of structures. This set of models has characterizations as fixed points of deduction, abduction and quantification transformers. A wide range of satisfiability procedures can be understood as computing and refining approximations of such fixed points. These include procedures in the DPLL family, those for preprocessing and inprocessing in SAT solvers, decision procedures for equality logics, weak arithmetics, and procedures for approximate quantification. Our framework provides a unified, mathematical basis for studying and combining program analysis and satisfiability procedures. A practical benefit of our work is a new, logic-agnostic architecture for implementing solvers.



***Categories and Subject Descriptors*** F.4.1 [*Mathematical Logic*]: Mechanical Theorem Proving; I.2.3 [*Deduction and Theorem Proving*]: Deduction

***Keywords*** Abstract interpretation; Logic; Decision Procedures


## 1. Reasoning and Abstraction

Static analyzers and satisfiability solvers represent practical triumphs of computer science in the face of theoretical hardness results. Static analysis problems are typically undecidable yet analyzers compute information that is indispensable in compiler optimization and program verification. The satisfiability problem for several logics and theories is NP-hard but SAT and SMT solvers handle large problem instances arising in practice. In this paper, we introduce an abstract interpretation framework that makes explicit some fundamental similarities between the way undecidable and NP-hard problems are solved in practice. This framework has several applications including lattice-theoretic characterizations of satisfiability algorithms [18, 19], the development of SMT solvers based on abstract interpretation [26], and the generalization of satisfiability algorithms to static analysis [3, 20].

Abstract interpretation is a lattice-theoretic framework for reasoning about fixed points [10, 13]. The idiomatic approach to applying abstract interpretation to a problem is to characterise solutions to the problem by fixed points, identify a space of fixed point approximations, and design an algorithm to compute these approximations. The application of abstract interpretation to static analysis can be understood in terms of the schema below. The box on the left is called an *abstract domain*. It consists of a lattice $(A, \sqsubseteq, \sqcap, \sqcup, \bot, \top)$ with each element $a$ of $A$ representing a set of program states. Each statement $s$ in the programming language defines four transformers. The predecessor transformer $pre_s$ maps $a$ to states the program *may* have come from before executing $s$, while the successor transformer $post_s$ maps $a$ to states the program *may* reach after executing $s$. The transformers $\widetilde{pre}_s$ and $\widetilde{post}_s$ capture *must* behaviour. Properties of programs are specified as fixed points of such transformers.

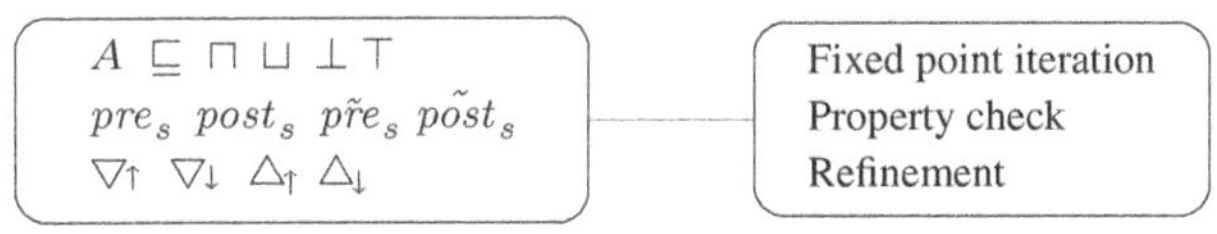


The box on the right represents procedures that use components of the abstract domain to reason about fixed points. Iterative procedures are used to compute fixed points. These procedures may use a widening ($\nabla_\uparrow$) or dual widening ($\nabla_\downarrow$) operator to accelerate convergence. If the result is not precise enough, a narrowing ($\triangle_\downarrow$) or dual narrowing ($\triangle_\uparrow$) operator is used to refine the result. The architecture above achieves a valuable separation of concerns by allowing the design and implementation of an abstract domain to be independent of the fixed point approximation procedures.

Abstract satisfaction is a framework for applying fixed point approximation to logical reasoning in the same manner that abstract interpretation was first applied to static analysis [10]. Consider the satisfiability problem for a logic. An SMT solver typically works in a fragment $T$ of the logic. Elements of $T$ are represented using data structures such as sets, partial functions, graphs, or matrices. These elements are manipulated using techniques called constraint propagation, decisions, learning and subsumption.

We show that a solver can be understood in terms of the schema below, which closely resembles the structure of a static analyzer. Elements of $T$, ordered by implication, form a lattice of approximations $(T, \Rightarrow, \sqcap, \sqcup, \mathsf{false}, \mathsf{true})$. A solver can use *deduction* to compute facts implied by $\varphi$, or use *abduction* to compute facts that imply $\varphi$. These operations define deduction and abduction transformers ($ded_\varphi$ and $abd_\varphi$), and their counterparts ($cded_\varphi$ and $cabd_\varphi$) for contrapositive reasoning.

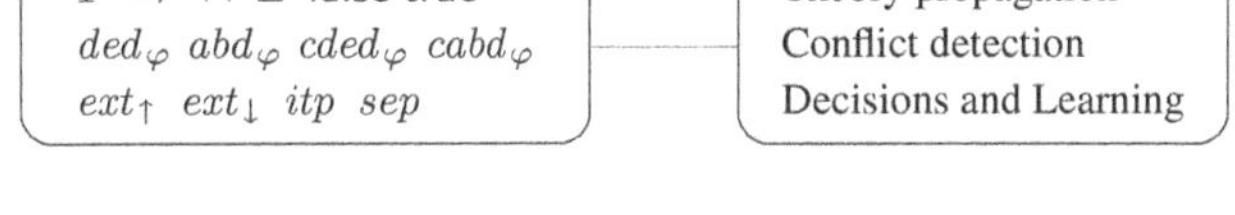





*POPL '14*, January 22–24, 2014, San Diego, CA, USA.
Copyright is held by the owner/author(s).
ACM 978-1-4503-2544-8/14/01.
http://dx.doi.org/10.1145/2535838.2535868

Propagation and learning in solvers can be viewed as the application of these transformers. Techniques like decisions, used by a solver to improve precision, correspond to a relaxation of widening called *extrapolation* (denoted $ext_\uparrow$ and $ext_\downarrow$), while techniques like subsumption and clause minimization correspond to a relaxation of narrowing, which we call *interpolation* (denoted $int_\uparrow$ and $int_\downarrow$). Thus, despite external differences, there are fundamental similarities between the internals of SAT and SMT solvers and static analyzers. We believe that making these similarities explicit has several consequences that we discuss below.

***Abstract Interpretation to* SMT** One consequence is a transfer of techniques from abstract interpretation to SMT solvers. Solvers have been extended with abstractions [4, 30] and joins [1] to improve time and memory efficiency, and with widening [33] to aid in guessing loop invariants. We show that the internal data structures of SMT solvers are lattices, which means that these data structures also support joins and widening. Crucially, we show that quantifiers are transformers, which means that abstract quantifiers and best abstract quantifiers are well defined notions. Thus, an abstract interpretation perspective suggests a new, approximate approach to deduction and quantifier elimination.

**SMT *to Static Analysis*** The main conclusion of our work is that SMT solvers, like static analyzers, operate on imprecise abstractions. However, SMT solvers return precise results, which means their algorithms can be understood as techniques for refining an imprecise analysis. These techniques are based on properties of lattices and can be used to refine static analyses. SMT solvers for decidable logics implement refinement procedures that are guaranteed to terminate (though termination proofs can be non-trivial). The fundamental undecidability of static analysis problems precludes the existence of terminating refinement procedures.

An insight we present in Section 4 is that deduction and abduction in a logic coincide with reasoning about the postconditions and preconditions of conditional statements. Improvements in deduction should lead to an improved handling of conditionals in static analyzers. Moreover, preprocessing and inprocessing techniques, which are responsible for recent performance improvements in solvers can be lifted to static analysis constraints.

***A Grand Unification*** A lofty goal, towards which this work is an early step, is to achieve a uniform theoretical and practical treatment of static analysis and SMT solving. Specifically, if both technologies can be understood in terms of lattices and transformers, their similarities and differences can be studied using lattice theoretic techniques. The three different problems of combining static analyzers, combining SMT solvers, and combining a static analyzer with an SMT solver can be reduced to the single problem of combining fixed point approximation procedures. Existing procedures such as the reduced product, Nelson-Oppen, and DPLL(T), which are now understood to be combination procedures [2, 11, 14], can all be applied to the same task.

We anticipate practical benefits from carrying out a unification programme. Decomposing a complex piece of software like a static analyzer or an SMT solver into smaller blocks consisting of lattice elements, transformers, and an iteration engine leads to a mathematically justified modular design. We expect this modularity to contribute to the development of extensible and programmable solvers and analyzers, and reduce the performance and development overheads involved in integrating different technologies.

## 2. Mathematical Preliminaries

We denote the complement of a set $S$ as $\neg S$, and the set of all subsets of $S$, as the *powerset* $\mathcal{P}(S)$. The function from $x$ to $f(g(x))$ is denoted $f \circ g$, and a function $f$ is treated as a set $\{a \mapsto f(a), \ldots\}$ when convenient.

***Sequences*** We use sequences to simplify presentation. An *$m$-termed $A$-sequence* is a function $\bar{s} : \{0, \ldots, m-1\} \to A$, whose length $m$ is denoted $len(\bar{s})$. We write $f(\bar{s})$ for the application $f(s_0, \ldots, s_{n-1})$ and leave implicit that $\bar{s}$ has length $n$. Given a function $g : A \to C$, we write $g[a \mapsto c]$ for the function that maps $a$ to $c$ and $x$ distinct from $a$ to $g(x)$. We write a sequence of substitutions $g[a_0 \mapsto c_0][a_1 \mapsto c_1] \cdots$ with pairwise distinct elements $a_i$ as $g[\bar{a} \Mapsto \bar{c}]$.

***Lattices*** A *transformer* is a monotone function on a lattice. A lattice is *bounded* if it has a greatest element, called *top* and denoted $\top$, and has a least element called *bottom* and denoted $\bot$. A function $f$ on a lattice is *reductive* if $f(x) \sqsubseteq x$ for all $x$ and is *extensive* if $f(x) \sqsupseteq x$ for all $x$. A function is *idempotent* if $f(f(x)) = f(x)$ for all $x$. An *upper closure* is an idempotent and extensive transformer, and a *lower closure* is an idempotent and reductive transformer. The *pointwise order* $f \sqsubseteq g$ between functions from a set to a poset holds if $f(x) \sqsubseteq g(x)$ holds for all $x$. The *pointwise meet* of $f$ and $g$, denoted $f \sqcap g$, where both functions map into a lattice is defined as $\lambda x.\ f(x) \sqcap g(x)$. The pointwise join is similarly defined. The set of transformers on a complete lattice form a complete lattice under the pointwise order.

A lattice is *distributive* if every $x, y$ and $z$ satisfy $x \sqcap (y \sqcup z) = (x \sqcap y) \sqcup (x \sqcap z)$, which is equivalent to the identity obtained by interchanging meets and joins. An element $y$ on a bounded lattice is the *complement* of $x$ if $x \sqcap y = \bot$ and $x \sqcup y = \top$. Complements may not exist and when they do, may not be unique. We use the notation $\neg x$ or $\sim x$ for unique complements. Complements in a distributive lattice are unique. A *Boolean lattice* is complemented and distributive. The *De Morgan dual* of a function $f$ on a Boolean lattice is $\tilde{f} \mathrel{\hat{=}} \neg \circ f \circ \neg$. The *powerset lifting* of $f : A \to B$ is the function $f : \mathcal{P}(A) \to \mathcal{P}(B)$ that maps a set to its image under $f$.

The least and greatest fixed points of a monotone function $f$ on a complete lattice are denoted $\mathsf{gfp}(f)$ and $\mathsf{lfp}(f)$.

***Galois Connections*** Let $(L, \sqsubseteq)$ and $(M, \preccurlyeq)$ be posets. Two functions $\alpha : L \to M$ and $\gamma : M \to L$ form a *Galois connection* if for all $x \in L$ and $y \in M$, $\alpha(x) \preccurlyeq y$ if and only if $x \sqsubseteq \gamma(y)$. A Galois connection is written as $L \underset{\alpha}{\overset{\gamma}{\leftrightarrows}} M$ or $(L, \alpha, \gamma, M)$. The function $\alpha$ is called the *left adjoint* and $\gamma$ is called the *right adjoint* of the Galois connection. In a Galois insertion, $\alpha$ is a surjection.

## 3. A Collecting Semantics for First-Order Logic

The phrase *collecting semantics* in abstract interpretation refers to associating meaning to an object in terms of its properties. For example, a trace property is a set of sequences of states and the collecting trace semantics of a program, which is also the strongest trace property the program satisfies, is the set of all program executions. In this section, we introduce a compositional, collecting semantics for quantified first-order formulae. Our semantics allows us to interpret a formula as an element of a lattice, so that abstract interpretation of formulae, and of properties of formulae, is well defined. The collecting semantics of a term is defined by lifting the standard evaluation semantics of terms to sets of environments. The collecting semantics of a formula is the set of models of the formula. The Boolean operations of conjunction, disjunction and negation have their standard interpretation as intersection, union and set complement. Quantifiers are interpreted as transformers between structures over different sets of variables.

Of several lattice-theoretic semantics for quantified first-order logics [38], we use a category-theoretic treatment due to Pitts [40]. A key feature of this treatment is to make the set of free variables part of the syntax of a formula. The structure of the lattices over which a formula is interpreted are then determined by the syntax of formula. Quantifiers define transformers between lattices over different sets of free variables. See [38] for a discussion of the challenges in giving a lattice-theoretic semantics to quantifiers.

***Structural Rules*** We recall the structural rules for forming terms and formulae. The signature of a first-order logic $(Sig, ar)$ consists of disjoint sets $Sig = Pred \cup Fun$ of predicate and function symbols whose arity is $ar : Sig \to \mathbb{N}$. A nullary function symbol is called a *constant*. We use $P, Q, R$ to range over predicate symbols and $F, G, H$ to range over function symbols.

Let $Vars$ be a set of variables and $x, y, z$ range over variables. A *first-order context* $\Gamma$ is a finite sequence of variables in which each variable occurs exactly once. We write $[]$ for the empty sequence, $\Gamma, \Gamma'$ for sequence concatenation, and $var(\Gamma)$ for the set of variables in a context. In the case of many-sorted logic, a context is a sequence of pairs, where each pair consists of a variable and a sort. A context $\Gamma'$ is a *subcontext* of $\Gamma$ if $var(\Gamma') \subseteq var(\Gamma)$.

The rules from [40] for forming terms-in-context are given below. Henceforth, we abbreviate 'terms-in-context' to 'terms' for convenience. In addition to standard rules for variable introduction (VAR) and function composition (FUN), we use a rule (SEQ) for forming a sequence of terms. The rule for function composition has the side condition that $ar(F)$ is $len(\bar{t})$. We leave such side conditions implicit in the remaining rules.

$$\text{VAR}\ \frac{}{x : \Gamma, x, \Gamma'} \qquad \text{FUN}\ \frac{\bar{t} : \Gamma}{F(\bar{t}) : \Gamma} \qquad \text{SEQ}\ \frac{t_0 : \Gamma \cdots t_{n-1} : \Gamma}{\bar{t} : \Gamma}$$

From these rules, we can derive the rules for complete substitution (CSUB) and weakening (WEAK) given below.

$$\text{CSUB}\ \frac{t : \bar{x} \qquad r_0 : \Gamma' \cdots r_{n-1} : \Gamma'}{t[\bar{x} \mapsto \bar{r}] : \Gamma'} \qquad \text{WEAK}\ \frac{t : \Gamma}{t : \Gamma, \Gamma'}$$

Terms-in-context are composed with predicate symbols and Boolean operations to obtain *formulae-in-context*. We henceforth abbreviate 'formula-in-context' to 'formula'. In the Boolean operator rule below, *op* is one of $\mathsf{true}$, $\mathsf{false}$, $\vee$, $\wedge$ or $\neg$ applied to the appropriate number of arguments.

$$\text{PRED}\ \frac{\bar{t} : \Gamma}{P(\bar{t}) : \Gamma} \qquad \text{OP}\ \frac{\varphi : \Gamma \qquad \psi : \Gamma}{\varphi\ op\ \psi : \Gamma}$$

The weakening rule for formulae is similar to that for terms. Quantification changes the set of free variables in a formula and causes contraction of a context.

$$\exists\text{-Q}\ \frac{\varphi : \Gamma, x, \Gamma'}{\exists x.\varphi : \Gamma, \Gamma'} \qquad \forall\text{-Q}\ \frac{\varphi : \Gamma, x, \Gamma'}{\forall x.\varphi : \Gamma, \Gamma'}$$

The sets of terms and formulae in a context $\Gamma$ are denoted $Term_\Gamma$ and $Form_\Gamma$, respectively. An *atomic predicate* is the composition of a predicate symbol with terms and a *literal* is an atomic predicate or its negation. A *clause* is a disjunction of literals and a *cube* is a conjunction of literals. A formula in *Conjunctive Normal Form* (CNF) is a conjunction of clauses and one in *Disjunctive Normal Form* (DNF) is a disjunction of cubes. The sets containing these formulae are denoted $Lit_\Gamma$, $Clause_\Gamma$, $Cube_\Gamma$, $CNF_\Gamma$, and $DNF_\Gamma$, respectively. If not specified, the formulae we deal with are quantifier-free.

***Semantic Structures*** We now introduce a lattice-theoretic structure in which to interpret formulae. This structure consists of a lattice and transformers and provides a template for implementing SMT solvers based on abstract interpretation. Recall that the classical semantics of first-order logic is given by a $Sig$-interpretation $\mathcal{M} = (Val, int)$, which consists of a universe $Val$ and an interpretation that maps each function symbol $F$ to a function $int(F) : Val^{ar(F)} \to Val$ and each predicate symbol $P$ to a relation $int(P) \subseteq Val^{ar(P)}$.

An *environment* over $\Gamma$ maps variables in $\Gamma$ to values. Let $Env_\Gamma \mathrel{\hat{=}} var(\Gamma) \to Val$ be the set of environments over $\Gamma$. The classical semantics of first-order logic is given by a relation $\mathcal{M}, \varepsilon \models \varphi$ specifying when an environment satisfies a formula.

Categorical logic does away with environments by observing that $Env_\Gamma \to Val$ is isomorphic to $Val^{len(\Gamma)}$. First-order hyperdoctrines significantly extend this observation to provide a category-theoretic semantics for first-order logic [32, 40]. In Definition 1 below, we adapt the definition of a first-order hyperdoctrine to powersets of environments. The reader may rightly baulk at the length of the definition. One can view the classical and algebraic definitions of semantics as making different tradeoffs. In the classical semantics, first-order structures have a succinct definition but the definition of $\models$ is verbose. In algebraic semantics, the definition of a structure may appear involved, but (in our opinion) leads to a succinctly defined semantics.

Each item in Definition 1 is required to provide semantics for some aspect of first-order logic. The lattices of tuples $\mathcal{P}(Val^n)$ represent the domains over which function symbols are interpreted. The lattices of environments $\mathcal{P}(Env_\Gamma)$ represent the domains over which terms-in-context are interpreted. We use the function $v\text{-}to\text{-}e_\Gamma$ that maps values to environments to deal with substitution into a term, and the function $e\text{-}to\text{-}v_\Gamma$ to deal with substitution into a predicate. The existential and universal projection functions ($epr$ and $upr$) give a concrete transformer semantics to quantifiers.

**Definition 1.** *A collecting $Sig$-structure defined by a first-order structure $\mathcal{M} = (Val, int)$ consists of the items below.*

1. *The lattices of tuples* $\{(\mathcal{P}(Val^n), \subseteq) \mid n \in \mathbb{N}\}$.
2. *The lattices of environments* $(\mathcal{P}(Env_\Gamma), \subseteq)$ *for every context* $\Gamma$.
3. *For every context $\Gamma = (x_0, \ldots, x_{n-1})$ of length $n$, there are two translation functions for mapping between tuples and environments.*
$$v\text{-}to\text{-}e_\Gamma : \mathcal{P}(Val^n) \to \mathcal{P}(Env_\Gamma)$$
$$v\text{-}to\text{-}e_\Gamma \mathrel{\hat{=}} V \mapsto \{x_i \mapsto v_i \mid \bar{v} \in V\}$$
$$e\text{-}to\text{-}v_\Gamma : \mathcal{P}(Env_\Gamma) \to \mathcal{P}(Val^n)$$
$$e\text{-}to\text{-}v_\Gamma \mathrel{\hat{=}} E \mapsto \{\{i \mapsto v_i \mid \varepsilon(x_i) = v_i\} \mid \varepsilon \in E\}$$
4. *There is a weakening function for mapping environments from a subcontext $\Gamma$ of $\Gamma'$ to environments over $\Gamma'$.*
$$wk_{\Gamma,\Gamma'} : \mathcal{P}(Env_\Gamma) \to \mathcal{P}(Env_{\Gamma'})$$
$$wk_{\Gamma,\Gamma'} \mathrel{\hat{=}} E \mapsto \{\varepsilon' \mid \varepsilon \in E, \text{ for all } x \text{ in } \Gamma, \varepsilon(x) = \varepsilon'(x)\}$$
5. *For every subcontext $\Gamma$ of $\Gamma'$ an existential projection $epr_{\Gamma',\Gamma}$ and a universal projection $upr_{\Gamma',\Gamma}$, in $\mathcal{P}(Env_{\Gamma'}) \to \mathcal{P}(Env_\Gamma)$.*
$$epr_{\Gamma',\Gamma} \mathrel{\hat{=}} E \mapsto \{\varepsilon \mid wk_{\Gamma',\Gamma}(\varepsilon) \cap E \neq \emptyset\}$$
$$upr_{\Gamma',\Gamma} \mathrel{\hat{=}} E \mapsto \{\varepsilon \mid wk_{\Gamma',\Gamma}(\varepsilon) \subseteq E\}$$
6. *A lifting of the interpretation of function symbols to sets.*
$$cint(F) : \mathcal{P}(Val^{ar(F)}) \to \mathcal{P}(Val)$$
$$cint(F) \mathrel{\hat{=}} V \mapsto \{int(F)(\bar{v}) \mid \bar{v} \in V\}$$
7. *The relation $int(P)$ for each predicate symbol.*

The existential and universal projection functions as defined above eliminate arbitrary subcontexts. We only use them to eliminate single variables and use the following abbreviations. We write $epr_x$ and $upr_x$ for projections that extract a single variable by mapping environments over the context $\Gamma, x$ to those over $x$. Conversely, we write $some_x$ and $all_x$ for projections that eliminate a single variable by mapping environments over $\Gamma, x$ to environments over $\Gamma$. We also write $wk_x$ for the weakening function from environments over $\Gamma$ to those over $\Gamma, x$.

***Collecting Semantics*** The collecting semantics of terms and sequences of terms with respect to a classical interpretation $\mathcal{M}$ follows. We drop the subscript $\mathcal{M}$ when no ambiguity arises.

$$[\![\cdot]\!]_{\mathcal{M}} : Term^n_\Gamma \to (\mathcal{P}(Env_\Gamma) \to \mathcal{P}(Val^n))$$

The semantics function is defined inductively below. The semantics of a term $t$ with respect to a set of environments $E$ is given by evaluating $t$ in each environment in $E$. The semantics of a sequence of terms is a set of sequences of values. Substitution constructs a sequence of values and lifts it to an environment.

$$\begin{aligned}
[\![x : \Gamma]\!] &\hat{=} E \mapsto \{\varepsilon(x) \mid \varepsilon \in E\}\\
[\![\bar{t} : \Gamma]\!] &\hat{=} E \mapsto \{\bar{v} \in Val^{len(\bar{t})} \mid \text{for some } \varepsilon \in E,\\
&\qquad v_i \in [\![t_i : \Gamma]\!](\varepsilon) \text{ for all } 0 \leq i < len(\bar{t})\}\\
[\![F(\bar{t}) : \Gamma]\!] &\hat{=} cint(F) \circ [\![\bar{t} : \Gamma]\!]\\
[\![t[\bar{x} \mapsto \bar{r}] : \Gamma]\!] &\hat{=} [\![t : \Gamma']\!] \circ v\text{-}to\text{-}e_{\Gamma'} \circ [\![\bar{r} : \Gamma]\!]
\end{aligned}$$

Example 1 below demonstrates how to calculate the semantics of a term in the presence of substitution. Observe that the term does not have to be rewritten before being evaluated.

Example 1. Consider the term $t \hat{=} x + 2y[y \mapsto 2x]$ derived below.

$$\dfrac{\dfrac{\dfrac{\dfrac{\dfrac{}{x : x}\text{VAR}}{x : x, y}\text{WEAK} \quad \dfrac{\dfrac{}{y : y}\text{VAR}}{y : x, y}\text{WEAK}}{x + 2y : x, y}\text{FUN}}{} \quad \dfrac{\dfrac{}{x : x}\text{VAR}}{2x : x}\text{FUN}}{x + 2y[x \mapsto x, y \mapsto 2x] : x}\text{CSUB}$$

We interpret variables as natural numbers and $+$ as addition. The semantics of the term above is a function in $\mathcal{P}(Env_x) \to \mathcal{P}(\mathbb{N})$.

$$\begin{aligned}
&[\![x + 2y[x \mapsto x, y \mapsto 2x] : x]\!]\\
&= [\![x + 2y : x, y]\!] \circ v\text{-}to\text{-}e_{x,y} \circ [\![(x, 2x) : x]\!]\\
&= [\![x + 2y : x, y]\!] \circ v\text{-}to\text{-}e_{x,y} \circ \lambda E.\, \{(\varepsilon(x), 2\varepsilon(x)) \mid \varepsilon \in E)\}\\
&= [\![x + 2y : x, y]\!] \circ \lambda E.\, \{\{x \mapsto \varepsilon(x), y \mapsto 2\varepsilon(x)\} \mid \varepsilon \in E\}\\
&= [\![x + 2y : x, y]\!] \circ \lambda E.\, \{\varepsilon(x) + 4\varepsilon(x) \mid \varepsilon \in E\}\\
&= \lambda E.\, \{5\varepsilon(x) \mid \varepsilon \in E\}
\end{aligned}$$

In short, a set of environments is mapped to values obtained by multiplying the value of $x$ by 5. $\triangleleft$

The collecting semantics of terms is the standard evaluation semantics (also called 'forward interpretation') implemented in program analyzers. The semantics of quantifier-free formulae given next is a 'backward interpretation' and is known [9] but is less standard. The inverse $[\![\bar{t} : \Gamma]\!]^{-1} : \mathcal{P}(Val^{len(\bar{t})}) \to \mathcal{P}(Env_\Gamma)$ is defined as follows.

$$[\![\bar{t} : \Gamma]\!]^{-1} \hat{=} V \mapsto \{\varepsilon \in Env_\Gamma \mid [\![\bar{t}]\!](\varepsilon) \cap V \neq \emptyset\}$$

The semantics of a formula is given by a function $[\![\cdot]\!]_{\mathcal{M}} : Form_\Gamma \to \mathcal{P}(Env_\Gamma)$ defined inductively below. Boolean operators have their standard set-theoretic interpretation.

$$\begin{aligned}
[\![P(\bar{t}) : \Gamma]\!] &\hat{=} [\![\bar{t} : \Gamma]\!]^{-1}(int(P)) & [\![\mathsf{true} : \Gamma]\!] &\hat{=} Env_\Gamma\\
[\![\varphi \vee \psi : \Gamma]\!] &\hat{=} [\![\varphi : \Gamma]\!] \cup [\![\psi : \Gamma]\!] & [\![\mathsf{false} : \Gamma]\!] &\hat{=} \emptyset\\
[\![\varphi \wedge \psi : \Gamma]\!] &\hat{=} [\![\varphi : \Gamma]\!] \cap [\![\psi : \Gamma]\!] & [\![\neg\varphi : \Gamma]\!] &\hat{=} \neg[\![\varphi : \Gamma]\!]
\end{aligned}$$

Quantifiers are interpreted using projection functions.

$$[\![\exists x.\varphi : \Gamma]\!] \hat{=} some_x([\![\varphi : \Gamma, x]\!]) \quad [\![\forall x.\varphi : \Gamma]\!] \hat{=} all_x([\![\varphi : \Gamma, x]\!])$$

Example 2. We extend Example 1 to illustrate the semantics of quantification. Consider the formula

$$\varphi \hat{=} \exists x.x + 2y[y \mapsto 2x] = z$$

with $=$ interpreted as equality over the natural numbers. The relation $cint(=)$ is $\{(n, n) \mid n \in \mathbb{N}\}$ and the semantics of the formula is a set of environments over $z$.

$$\begin{aligned}
&[\![\exists x.x + 2y[x \mapsto x, y \mapsto 2x] = z : z]\!]\\
&= some_x \circ [\![(x + 2y[x \mapsto x, y \mapsto 2x], z)]\!]^{-1}(cint(=))\\
&= some_x \circ (\lambda E.\, \{(5\varepsilon(x), \varepsilon(z)) \mid \varepsilon \in E\})^{-1}(cint(=))\\
&= some_x(\{\varepsilon \mid \varepsilon(z) = 5(\varepsilon(x))\})\\
&= \{\{z \mapsto 5n\} \mid n \in \mathbb{N}\}
\end{aligned}$$

As expected, $z$ maps to multiples of 5. This example shows that the semantics of a quantified formula can be calculated mechanically by applying the appropriate transformers. If the concrete transformers are replaced with abstract transformers, we can similarly calculate an abstract semantics. $\triangleleft$

The collecting semantics we have defined is consistent with the classical semantics of first-order logic.

**Theorem 2.** *For each formula $\varphi : \Gamma$ in non-empty context $\Gamma$, classical, first-order interpretation $\mathcal{M}$ and environment $\varepsilon \in Env_\Gamma$, $\mathcal{M}, \varepsilon \models \varphi$ exactly if $\varepsilon \in [\![\varphi : \Gamma]\!]_{\mathcal{M}}$.*

We also refer to environments as *structures*. Let $\Gamma$ be a non-empty context. A structure $\varepsilon$ is a *model* of $\varphi$ if $\varepsilon \in [\![\varphi : \Gamma]\!]$. A formula $\varphi$ is *unsatisfiable in* $\mathcal{M}$ if $[\![\varphi : \Gamma]\!]_{\mathcal{M}}$ is the empty set and is *satisfiable in* $\mathcal{M}$ otherwise. We refer to satisfiability in a structure as satisfiability for the rest of the paper.

A *sentence* is a formula in an empty context. The set of environments over the empty context is the empty set. If $[\![\varphi : []]\!]_{\mathcal{M}}$ is $\{\emptyset\}$, we say that $\varphi$ is *true in* $\mathcal{M}$, and otherwise, $\varphi$ is *false in* $\mathcal{M}$.

## 4. Concrete Reasoning

The basic operations in logical reasoning can be viewed as giving a dynamic interpretation to an implication $\varphi \Rightarrow \psi$. Deduction is the process of deriving $\psi$ from $\varphi$. Abduction is the process of deriving $\varphi$ from $\psi$. In classical logic, these processes have contrapositive formulations: we can start with $\neg\psi$ and attempt to deduce $\neg\varphi$, a process we call *contradeduction*, or start with $\neg\varphi$ and attempt to abduce $\neg\psi$, a process we call *contraabduction*. In this section, we model these processes using transformers and characterize properties of formulae as fixed points of these transformers. As with fixed point characterisations of program correctness, these fixed points are not meant to be computed but will be used to design fixed point approximation algorithms.

The set of formulae that can be derived from a set of formulae $\Phi$ using a set of rules $R$ forms the *deductive closure* of $\Phi$ with respect to $R$. Deductive closure and automated reasoning procedures have characterizations in terms of Tarski's consequence operator, or as the transitive closure of a set of rewrite rules. An important difference between these characterizations and ours is that we operate on sets of structures, so our notions of deduction and abduction are semantic. Existing characterizations can be derived from ours by abstract interpretation but we can also derive abstractions of deduction that operate on objects other than formulae.

### 4.1 Structure Transformers

A *structure transformer* for formulae in $Form_\Gamma$ is a function $T_\varphi : \mathcal{P}(Env_\Gamma) \to \mathcal{P}(Env_\Gamma)$. Structure transformers encode reasoning about the models and countermodels of a formula. The *deduction transformer* $ded_\varphi$ which encodes reasoning about models of $\varphi$. In the definition below, we assume that the set-theoretic operations are lifted pointwise to functions.

$$ded_{P(\bar{t})}(X) \mathrel{\hat{=}} X \cap [\![P(\bar{t}) : \Gamma]\!] \qquad ded_{\varphi \wedge \psi} \mathrel{\hat{=}} ded_\varphi \cap ded_\psi$$
$$ded_{\neg\varphi} \mathrel{\hat{=}} \neg[\![\varphi : \Gamma]\!] \qquad ded_{\varphi \vee \psi} \mathrel{\hat{=}} ded_\varphi \cup ded_\psi$$

The use of negation in defining $ded_{\neg\varphi}$ is problematic in general because lifting such a definition to abstractions requires a structure that supports Boolean reasoning. We discuss this issue in greater detail shortly.

The *contradeduction* transformer $cded_\varphi$ encodes contrapositive reasoning and manipulates countermodels of $\varphi$. If $ded_\varphi$ is used for satisfiability checking, $cded_\varphi$ can be used for validity checking.

$$cded_{P(\bar{t})}(X) \mathrel{\hat{=}} X \cap \neg[\![P(\bar{t}) : \Gamma]\!] \qquad cded_{\varphi \wedge \psi} \mathrel{\hat{=}} cded_\varphi \cup cded_\psi$$
$$cded_{\neg\varphi} \mathrel{\hat{=}} \neg cded_\varphi \qquad cded_{\varphi \vee \psi} \mathrel{\hat{=}} cded_\varphi \cap cded_\psi$$

The two transformers above reason forwards in that they start from hypotheses and attempt to derive conclusions. The dual notion to deduction is abduction, where we start from a conclusion and derive the hypotheses under which that conclusion holds. For example if we can abduce true from a formula $\varphi$, we know that $\varphi$ is valid with respect to a set of structures.

$$abd_{P(\bar{t})}(X) \mathrel{\hat{=}} X \cup \neg[\![P(\bar{t}) : \Gamma]\!] \qquad abd_{\varphi \wedge \psi} \mathrel{\hat{=}} abd_\varphi \cup abd_\psi$$
$$abd_{\neg\varphi} \mathrel{\hat{=}} cabd_\varphi \qquad abd_{\varphi \vee \psi} \mathrel{\hat{=}} abd_\varphi \cap abd_\psi$$

Finally, we have a contraabduction transformer which models starting from a conclusion and deriving the fallacies: hypotheses from which that conclusion surely does not follow. A contraabduction transformer can be used to prune the space of abductions.

$$cabd_{P(\bar{t})}(X) \mathrel{\hat{=}} X \cup [\![P(\bar{t}) : \Gamma]\!] \qquad cabd_{\varphi \wedge \psi} \mathrel{\hat{=}} cabd_\varphi \cap cabd_\psi$$
$$cabd_{\neg\varphi} \mathrel{\hat{=}} abd_\varphi \qquad cabd_{\varphi \vee \psi} \mathrel{\hat{=}} cabd_\varphi \cup cabd_\psi$$

In addition to deduction and abduction, quantifier elimination is fundamental to logical reasoning. The transformers $some_x$ and $all_x$ model quantifier elimination and will henceforth be called *quantification transformers*.

There are several symmetries between deduction and abduction, which are preserved in our formulation. We make these properties explicit in Theorem 3, below. The set-theoretic identities are not necessarily satisfied by abstract transformers, which is why they are not used as a definition. The characterizations of deduction and abduction as closures extend the existing characterization of logical consequence as a closure. The characterization of existential quantification ($wk_x \circ some_x$) as an upper closure, and of universal quantification ($wk_x \circ all_x$) as a lower closure, when combined with the view of closure operators as abstractions [11], reiterates the connection between quantification and abstraction used in model checking [5]. The Galois connection between weakening and quantification was first observed by Lawvere [32] and indicates that even domains that do not support negation will support both existential and universal quantification.

**Theorem 3.** *Structure transformers have the following properties.*

1. *The transformers satisfy the identities below.*

$$ded_\varphi(X) = (X \cap [\![\varphi : \Gamma]\!]) \qquad cded_\varphi(X) = (X \cap \neg[\![\varphi : \Gamma]\!])$$
$$cabd_\varphi(X) = (X \cup [\![\varphi : \Gamma]\!]) \qquad abd_\varphi(X) = (X \cup \neg[\![\varphi : \Gamma]\!])$$

2. *The transformers $ded_\varphi$ and $cded_\varphi$ are lower closures.*
3. *The transformers $cabd_\varphi$ and $abd_\varphi$ are upper closures.*
4. *The composition $wk_x \circ some_x$ is an upper closure and $wk_x \circ all_x$ is a lower closure.*
5. *The pairs of transformers $(ded_\varphi, abd_\varphi)$, $(cded_\varphi, cabd_\varphi)$ and $(all_x, some_x)$ are De Morgan duals.*
6. *The pairs of transformers $(ded_\varphi, abd_\varphi)$ $(cded_\varphi, cabd_\varphi)$ form a Galois connection on $(\mathcal{P}(Env), \subseteq)$.*
7. *The quantification transformers are related to weakening by the following Galois connections.*

$$(\mathcal{P}(Env_\Gamma), \subseteq) \underset{wk_x}{\overset{all_x}{\leftrightarrows}} (\mathcal{P}(Env_{\Gamma,x}), \subseteq), \textit{ and}$$
$$(\mathcal{P}(Env_{\Gamma,x}), \subseteq) \underset{some_x}{\overset{wk_x}{\leftrightarrows}} (\mathcal{P}(Env_\Gamma), \subseteq)$$

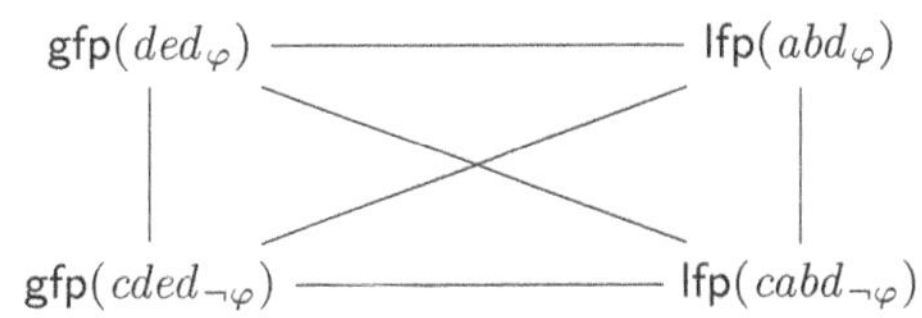


**Figure 1.** The vertices represent deduction or abduction procedures for checking satisfiability of $\varphi$ or validity of $\neg\varphi$. The edges represent combinations of deduction and abduction procedures.

The Galois connections are useful for deriving equivalent formulations of properties of a formula. For example, the models of $\varphi$ are $ded_\varphi(Env)$. A formula is unsatisfiable exactly if $ded_\varphi(Env) \subseteq \emptyset$, which by the Galois connection, is equivalent to $Env \subseteq abd_\varphi(\emptyset)$. In words, we can determine if a formula is unsatisfiable by trying to deduce false from $\varphi$ or trying to abduce $\varphi$ from false. Similarly, a formula is valid exactly if $cded_\varphi(Env) \subseteq \emptyset$, or equivalently $Env \subseteq cabd_\varphi(\emptyset)$.

Since satisfiability corresponds to existence of a model, we can equivalently define it in terms of existential quantification. Treating quantifiers as transformers allows us to formalise techniques that combine variable elimination and deduction.

### 4.2 Fixed Points for Satisfiability

We now show that properties of a formula can be characterized by fixed points of structure transformers. Consider the process of computing consequences of $\varphi$. We initially know nothing about $\varphi$, which we can express as $\varphi \Rightarrow \mathsf{true}$. A single step of a reasoning algorithm may indicate that $\varphi \Rightarrow \psi_1$. After $k$ steps, the algorithm may deduce that $\varphi \wedge \cdots \psi_1 \wedge \psi_{k-1} \Rightarrow \psi_k$. What we know about the models of $\varphi$ can be represented by the sequence $[\![\mathsf{t}]\!]$, $[\![\psi_1]\!]$, $\ldots$, $[\![\psi_1 \wedge \cdots \psi_k]\!]$. The process of deduction can thus be viewed as a greatest fixed point computation, whose limit expresses the maximal information we can derive about models of $\varphi$.

Fixed points of structure transformers represent brute force algorithms. The greatest fixed point $\mathsf{gfp}(ded_\varphi)$ represents the semantics of a solver that initially assumes that every structure is a model of $\varphi$ and then eliminates countermodels of $\varphi$. The fixed point $\mathsf{gfp}(cded_\varphi)$ represents a procedure that progresses by eliminating countermodels of $\varphi$. The fixed point $\mathsf{lfp}(abd_\varphi)$ represents a procedure that initially assumes $\varphi$ has no countermodels and progresses by finding countermodels of $\varphi$, while $\mathsf{lfp}(cabd_\varphi)$ does the same for models of $\varphi$. The characterisation below first appeared in [18] and is included here to include validity as the dual of satisfiability.

**Theorem 4.** *The following statements are equivalent.*

1. *The formula $\varphi$ is unsatisfiable.*
2. *The greatest fixed point $\mathsf{gfp}(ded_\varphi)$ is empty.*
3. *The least fixed point $\mathsf{lfp}(abd_\varphi)$ has all structures.*
4. *The formula $\neg\varphi$ is valid.*
5. *The least fixed point $\mathsf{lfp}(cabd_{\neg\varphi})$ has all structures.*
6. *The greatest fixed point $\mathsf{gfp}(cded_{\neg\varphi})$ is empty.*

In program analysis and model checking, combinations of forward and backward analysis have advantages over a single method [9, 28]. In logical reasoning, we can similarly combine the benefits of deduction and abduction. For instance, as shown in [19], Conflict Driven Clause Learning (CDCL) combines deduction and abduction. The original Davis and Putnam algorithm [16] combined deduction via ordered resolution and variable elimination with the pure literal rule. CDCL solvers that use the pure literal rule for pre-/in-processing combine all three [21].

We define combinations of deduction and abduction transformers below. The transformers are defined on $\mathcal{P}(Env) \times \mathcal{P}(Env)$ with the lattice order shown alongside. For intuition about these combinations, consider a greatest fixed point iteration with the transformer $da_\varphi$, which combines deduction and abduction. The first element is $(Env, \emptyset)$, representing that every structure is a potential model and no structure is a potential countermodel. A single application of $da_\varphi$ yields $(ded_\varphi(Env), abd_\varphi(\emptyset))$, which is a fixed point. If $\varphi$ is unsatisfiable, this fixed point is $(\emptyset, Env)$, representing that there are no models and every structure is a countermodel. When using abstract transformers, a fixed point may not be reached in a single step so iteration allows information to be transferred between deduction and abduction.

$$dcd_\varphi(X,Y) \mathrel{\hat{=}} (ded_\varphi(X \cap Y), cded_{\neg\varphi}(X \cap Y)) \qquad \subseteq \times \subseteq$$
$$da_\varphi(X,Y) \mathrel{\hat{=}} (ded_\varphi(X \cap \neg Y), abd_\varphi(\neg X \cup Y)) \qquad \subseteq \times \supseteq$$
$$dca_\varphi(X,Y) \mathrel{\hat{=}} (ded_\varphi(X \cup Y), cabd_{\neg\varphi}(\neg X \cup Y)) \qquad \subseteq \times \supseteq$$
$$cda_\varphi(X,Y) \mathrel{\hat{=}} (cded_{\neg\varphi}(X \cap \neg Y), abd_\varphi(\neg X \cup Y)) \qquad \subseteq \times \supseteq$$
$$cdca_\varphi(X,Y) \mathrel{\hat{=}} (cded_{\neg\varphi}(X \cap \neg Y), cabd_{\neg\varphi}(\neg X \cup Y)) \qquad \subseteq \times \supseteq$$
$$aca_\varphi(X,Y) \mathrel{\hat{=}} (abd_\varphi(X \cup Y), cabd_{\neg\varphi}(X \cup Y)) \qquad \supseteq \times \supseteq$$

The $dcd_\varphi$ transformer is based on Cousot's forward-backward iteration [9], but the other combinations are, to the best of our knowledge, new. An additional possibility for reasoning about satisfiability is to combine deduction with existential quantification ($ds_\varphi$) and abduction with universal quantification ($aa_\varphi$). These are only two of many possible combinations.

$$ds_\varphi(X,Y) \mathrel{\hat{=}} (ded_\varphi(X \cap Y), wk_x \circ some_x(X \cap Y)) \qquad \subseteq \times \subseteq$$
$$aa_\varphi(X,Y) \mathrel{\hat{=}} (abd_\varphi(X \cup Y), wk_x \circ all_x(X \cup Y)) \qquad \supseteq \times \supseteq$$

The application of these transformers to satisfiability is below.

**Theorem 5.** *The following statements are equivalent.*

1. *The formula $\varphi$ is unsatisfiable.*
2. *The fixed point $\mathsf{gfp}(da_\varphi)$ is $(\emptyset, Env)$.*
3. *The fixed point $\mathsf{gfp}(dcd_\varphi)$ is $(\emptyset, \emptyset)$.*
4. *The fixed point $\mathsf{gfp}(dca_\varphi)$ is $(\emptyset, Env)$.*
5. *The fixed point $\mathsf{gfp}(cda_\varphi)$ is $(\emptyset, Env)$.*
6. *The fixed point $\mathsf{gfp}(cdca_\varphi)$ is $(\emptyset, Env)$.*
7. *The fixed point $\mathsf{gfp}(aca_\varphi)$ is $(Env, Env)$.*
8. *The fixed point $\mathsf{gfp}(ds_\varphi)$ is $(\emptyset, \emptyset)$.*
9. *The fixed point $\mathsf{gfp}(aa_\varphi)$ is $(Env, Env)$.*

### 4.3 Connection to Programs

We now relate deduction and abduction transformers to transformers generated by programs. Assume a first-order signature $Sig$ and variables $Vars$ as before. We write $\mathsf{assume(b)}$, abbreviated to $[\mathsf{b}]$, for an assumption statement with a quantifier-free formula $\mathsf{b}$. The operational semantics of the statement is below.

$$rel([\mathsf{b}]) \mathrel{\hat{=}} \{(\varepsilon, \varepsilon) \mid \varepsilon \in [\![b]\!]\}$$

The *context* for a program is the set of variables in the program. The operational semantics defines the four transformers below, which are related to deduction and abduction in Theorem 6.

$$post_{[\mathsf{b}]} \mathrel{\hat{=}} X \mapsto X \cap [\![\mathsf{b}]\!] \qquad \widetilde{post}_{[\mathsf{b}]} \mathrel{\hat{=}} \neg \circ post_{[\mathsf{b}]} \circ \neg$$
$$pre_{[\mathsf{b}]} \mathrel{\hat{=}} X \mapsto X \cap [\![\mathsf{b}]\!] \qquad \widetilde{pre}_{[\mathsf{b}]} \mathrel{\hat{=}} \neg \circ pre_{[\mathsf{b}]} \circ \neg$$

**Theorem 6.** *For a quantifier-free test $[\varphi]$ we have that $ded_\varphi = post_{[\varphi]}$ and $abd_\varphi = \widetilde{pre}_{[\varphi]}$.*

The consequence of Theorem 6 is that the same transformers can be used for deduction and abduction in an SMT solver or for reasoning about conditionals in program analysis. Improvements in solvers lead to improved reasoning about conditionals and vice versa. Moreover, the Galois connection between deduction and abduction is a special case of the classic Galois connection between postcondition and precondition transformers [7].

What of assignments? A beautiful result of categorical logic shows that substitution defines a transformer that has two adjoints, which generalise universal and existential quantification [32]. Transformers for assignments are closely related to transformers for quantification. Consequently, assignment transformers, which are ubiquitous in program analysis, define approximate quantification procedures. Improvements in quantifier elimination procedures should lead to better transformers for assignments. Due to space restrictions, we do discuss this connection further.

## 5. Abstract Reasoning

This section presents three ideas. The first is a standard application of abstract interpretation to the collecting semantics of formulae: if concrete transformers are replaced by abstract transformers, we obtain sound but incomplete conclusions about the properties of a formula. The second is the notion of an *abstract reasoning domain*, which provides the building blocks for SMT solvers based on abstract interpretation in the same way that traditional abstract domains are building blocks of program analyzers. The third idea is that standard logical notions such as definability or completeness are properties of a Galois connection between lattices of structures and lattices of formulae.

***Abstract Interpretation*** We recall essential notions of abstract interpretation. Assume two posets $C$ and $A$ related by a Galois connection between an abstraction function $\alpha : C \to A$ and a concretisation function $\gamma : A \to C$. The fundamental fixed point approximation theorem of abstract interpretation is below, with $aF$ representing the abstract transformer corresponding to $F$.

**Theorem 7** ([7]). *Let $(C, \alpha, \gamma, A)$ be a Galois connection between two complete lattices and $F : C \to C$ and $aF : A \to A$ be transformers satisfying $\alpha \circ F \sqsubseteq aF \circ \alpha$. Then, $\alpha(\mathsf{lfp}(F)) \sqsubseteq \mathsf{lfp}(aF)$ and $\alpha(\mathsf{gfp}(F)) \sqsubseteq \mathsf{gfp}(aF)$.*

In the case that $C$ is a powerset lattice $\mathcal{P}(S)$, we call $A$ *overapproximating* if $X \subseteq \gamma(\alpha(X))$ for all $X \subseteq S$ and *underapproximating* if $\gamma(\alpha(X)) \subseteq X$ for all $X \subseteq S$. An abstract transformer $aF : A \to A$ is a *sound overapproximation* of a concrete transformer $F : \mathcal{P}(S) \to \mathcal{P}(S)$ if $F \circ \gamma \subseteq \gamma \circ aF$ and is a *sound underapproximation* if $F \circ \gamma \supseteq \gamma \circ aF$.

An abstract transformer $aF$ is *$\alpha$-complete for $F$ at $c$* if it satisfies $\alpha(F(c)) = aF(\alpha(c))$ and is *$\alpha$-complete* if $\alpha \circ F = aF \circ \alpha$. We say that $f$ is *$\alpha$-fixed point complete* if $\alpha(\mathsf{lfp}(F)) = \mathsf{lfp}(aF)$. An abstract transformer $aF$ is *$\gamma$-complete for $F$ at $a$* if $\gamma(aF(a)) = F(\gamma(a))$ and is *$\gamma$-complete* if $\gamma \circ aF = F \circ \gamma$.

### 5.1 Abstract Interpretation of Formulae

We introduce *abstract $Sig$-structures* which are derived from collecting $Sig$-structures by replacing concrete transformers with abstract transformers. Evaluating a formula with respect to an abstract $Sig$-structure allows us to approximate the semantics of a formula in a predictable manner.

**Definition 8.** *An abstract $Sig$-structure $\mathcal{A}$ consists of the following complete lattices and transformers.*

1. *Abstract value lattices $(aVal_n, \sqsubseteq, \sqcap, \sqcup)$ for each $n \in \mathbb{N}$.*
2. *Abstract environment lattices $(aEnv_\Gamma, \sqsubseteq, \sqcap, \sqcup)$ for each $\Gamma$.*

3. *Abstract translation functions* $av\text{-}to\text{-}e_\Gamma : aVal_n \to aEnv_\Gamma$ *and* $ae\text{-}to\text{-}v_\Gamma : aEnv_\Gamma \to aVal_n$ *whenever* $len(\Gamma) = n$.
4. *An abstract weakening function* $awk_{\Gamma,\Gamma'} : aEnv_\Gamma \to aEnv_{\Gamma'}$ *for each context* $\Gamma'$ *and subcontext* $\Gamma$.
5. *Projection functions* $aepr_{\Gamma',\Gamma}, aupr_{\Gamma',\Gamma} : aEnv_{\Gamma'} \to aEnv_\Gamma$, *for every subcontext* $\Gamma$ *of* $\Gamma'$.
6. *An abstract interpretation* $aint(F) : aVal_{ar(F)} \to aVal_1$ *and its inverse* $ainv(F) : aVal_1 \to aVal_{ar(F)}$ *for every function symbol* $F \in Sig$.
7. *An abstract interpretation* $aint(P) \in aVal_{ar(P)}$ *of every predicate symbol* $P \in Sig$.

*Every abstract lattice above is related to the corresponding concrete lattice by a Galois connection* $(C, \alpha, \gamma, A)$. *We extend the convention for collecting structures and write* $asome_x$ *and* $aall_x$ *for elimination of a single variable.*

The abstract semantics of terms and of formulae with respect to an abstract $Sig$-structure is given by the functions below.

$$[\![\cdot]\!]_{\mathcal{A}} : Term^n_\Gamma \to aEnv_\Gamma \to aVal_n \qquad [\![\cdot]\!]_{\mathcal{A}} : Form_\Gamma \to aEnv_\Gamma$$

We obtain these by replacing concrete transformers and semantics by their abstract counterparts in the definition $[\![]\!]_C$ given earlier. Existing abstract domains already implement several components of Definition 8. These domains have abstract value and environment domains. The abstract semantics of terms is called 'forward abstract interpretation of expressions' and the abstract semantics of a quantifier-free formula is called 'backward abstract interpretation of expressions' in [8].

The abstract semantics of a quantifier-free $\varphi$ *overapproximates the concrete semantics* if $[\![\varphi : \Gamma]\!]_C \subseteq \gamma([\![\varphi : \Gamma]\!]_{\mathcal{A}})$. Underapproximation is dually defined. Abstract domains in program analysis need not have a representation of the empty set. For example, the one-element abstraction is a sound overapproximation [10]. When dealing with satisfiability, a representation of the empty set is necessary to express that a formula is unsatisfiable. Soundness, as defined below, includes this condition. The one-element abstraction is not necessarily sound in the sense below.

**Definition 9.** *An abstract Sig-structure* $\mathcal{A}$ *soundly overapproximates a collecting Sig-structure* $\mathcal{C}$ *if every lattice in* $\mathcal{A}$ *satisfies* $\gamma(\bot) = \emptyset$ *and concrete and abstract transformers satisfy* $F \circ \gamma \subseteq \gamma \circ aF$. *An abstract transformer* $aF$ *is the best abstract transformer if* $aF = \alpha \circ F \circ \gamma$.

When dealing with underapproximations, these definitions are dualised. The soundness of abstraction for negation-free formulae is given below. We discuss negation is more detail shortly.

**Theorem 10.** *If* $\mathcal{A}$ *is a sound overapproximation of* $\mathcal{C}$ *and* $\varphi$ *is negation-free* $[\![\varphi : \Gamma]\!]_C \subseteq \gamma([\![\varphi : \Gamma]\!]_{\mathcal{A}})$.

***The Interval Domain*** We present an extended example of abstractly interpreting quantified formulae over intervals. It is known that interval propagation can be used reason about terms, but the example we present shows that it also supports sound but incomplete reasoning about quantifiers. The example also exhibits a difference between abstract quantifiers and best abstract quantifiers.

The complete lattice of intervals $(Intv, \sqsubseteq, \sqcap, \sqcup)$ is defined over the set $Intv \mathrel{\hat{=}} \{[a,b] \mid a \leq b, a, b \in \mathbb{Z} \cup \{-\infty, \infty\}\}$, with $\bot$ representing the empty interval and $\top$ being $[-\infty, \infty]$. The interval structure $\mathcal{I}$ contains the items below.

1. The value lattices $aVal_n$ are product lattices $Intv^n$.
2. The interval environments $aEnv_\Gamma$ are $var(\Gamma) \to Intv$.
3. The weakening function extends an interval with the new variable going to $\top$.

$$awk_{\Gamma,\Gamma'} \mathrel{\hat{=}} \varepsilon \mapsto \varepsilon \cup \{y \mapsto \top \mid y \in var(\Gamma) \setminus var(\Gamma')\}$$

4. The projection functions are given below.

$$aepr_{\Gamma,\Gamma'} \mathrel{\hat{=}} \varepsilon \mapsto \{x \mapsto \varepsilon(x) \mid x \in var(\Gamma')\}$$

$$aupr_{\Gamma,\Gamma'} \mathrel{\hat{=}} \varepsilon \mapsto \begin{cases} \{x \mapsto \varepsilon(x) \mid x \in var(\Gamma')\} \text{ if} \\ \quad \varepsilon(y) = \top \text{ for all } y \in var(\Gamma) \setminus var(\Gamma') \\ \bot \text{ otherwise} \end{cases}$$

Existential projection drops certain variables and universal projection is not $\bot$ only if the variables being dropped are all $\top$.

The interpretation of functions and predicates depends on the signature of the theory considered.

Example 3. We compute the abstract semantics $[\![\varphi]\!]_{Intv}$ of the formula $\varphi \mathrel{\hat{=}} x \geq 5 \wedge x \leq 10 \wedge y = 2$ using the interval domain.

$$[\![x \geq 5]\!] \sqcap [\![x \leq 10]\!] \sqcap [\![y = 2]\!] = \{x \mapsto [5, 10], y \mapsto [2, 2]\}$$

The domain also supports abstract quantification.

$$[\![\exists y.\varphi]\!] = asome_y([\![\varphi]\!]) = \{x \mapsto [5, 10]\}$$
$$[\![\forall y.\varphi]\!] = aall_y([\![\varphi]\!]) = \bot$$

Now consider $\psi \mathrel{\hat{=}} \varphi \wedge y = 3$ whose semantics is $[\![\psi]\!]_{Intv} = \{x \mapsto [5, 10], y \mapsto \bot\}$. We have that

$$asome_y([\![\psi]\!]_{Intv}) = \{x \mapsto [5, 10]\}\,, \text{ but}$$
$$\alpha(some_y(\gamma([\![\psi]\!]_{Intv}))) = \alpha(some_y(\emptyset)) = \bot$$

showing that the existential projection transformer we have defined is not the best possible. $\lhd$

***Negation*** Theorem 10 only applies to negation-free formulae. Example 4 illustrates the problem of formulae with negation.

Example 4. Consider a logic with unary predicates of the form $x = k$ interpreted over the integers. Consider the parity lattice $Par \mathrel{\hat{=}} (\{\bot, \mathsf{E}, \mathsf{O}, \top\}, \sqsubseteq)$, which represents even and odd numbers. Let $[\![x = k]\!]_{Par}$ be $\mathsf{E}$ if $k$ is even and be $\mathsf{O}$ otherwise. The complement $\sim$ in this lattice *cannot be used* to approximate negation. To see why, consider evaluating $\neg(x = 2)$ as $\sim[\![x = 2]\!]_{Par}$, which is $\sim\mathsf{E} = \mathsf{O}$ but $\gamma(\mathsf{O})$ does not include all models of $\neg(x = 2)$. The only sound abstraction of negation is to map every element to $\top$. $\lhd$

More generally, in domains that allow for strict overapproximation of the semantics of a formula, the only sound abstract negation will map every element to $\top$. This problem only exists if the syntax of formulae have arbitrary negation. If negation is limited to atomic predicates, Definition 8 can be extended to include an abstract interpretation $aint(\neg P)$ of the negation of every predicate, Definition 9 can be extended to require sound overapproximation of negation of predicates, and Theorem 10 can be extended to formulae in negation normal form. A similar restriction is applied when model checking is combined with abstraction [5].

### 5.2 Abstract Reasoning Domains

We now identify the structure of an abstract domain for logical reasoning. In addition to a lattice that provides approximate semantics of formulae and abstract transformers that provide approximate semantics for logical operators, the domain includes operators for inductive reasoning (in the sense of philosophical logic). Unlike deductive and abductive reasoning, which are both sound with respect to implication, inductive reasoning models generalization or specialization which are not necessarily sound.

Widening and dual-widening operators implement inductive reasoning in program analyzers. Craig interpolation is another technique used for generalisation [34]. Narrowing is a restricted form of interpolation in a lattice because it maps a pair satisfying $A \sqsubseteq B$ to an element $I$ satisfying $A \sqsubseteq I$ and $I \sqsubseteq B$. Narrowing does not have the syntactic constraints of Craig interpolation because the lattice is not necessarily constructed from formulae. McMillan's notion of interpolation, which we call *separation*, maps a pair satisfying $A \sqcap B \sqsubseteq \bot$ to an $I$ satisfying $A \sqsubseteq I$ and $I \sqcap B \sqsubseteq \bot$. While interpolation and separation are inter-derivable on Boolean lattices they are not in general, hence have distinct definitions.

**Definition 11.** *A reasoning domain is an extension of an abstract Sig structure with the following operations.*

1. *Abstract transformers* $aded_\varphi$, $acded_\varphi$, $aabd_\varphi$ *and* $acabd_\varphi$ *for deduction and abduction.*
2. *A unary, extensive function* $ext_\uparrow : L \to L$ *called upwards extrapolation and its dual* $ext_\downarrow : L \to L$ *called downwards extrapolation.*
3. *A partial, interpolation function* $itp : L \times L \to L$, *satisfying* $x \sqsubseteq itp(x,y) \sqsubseteq y$ *whenever* $x \sqsubseteq y$. *The element* $itp(x,y)$ *is called an interpolant.*
4. *A partial, separation function* $sep : L \times L \to L$, *satisfying* $x \sqsubseteq sep(x,y)$ *and* $sep(x,y) \sqcap y \sqsubseteq \bot$ *whenever* $x \sqcap y \sqsubseteq \bot$. *The element* $sep(x,y)$ *is called a separator.*

We use the word 'function' and not 'transformers' above because the operations need not be monotone, as with widening [9].

Example 5. We apply abstract, interval deduction by computing $\mathsf{gfp}(aded_\varphi)$ with $\varphi \mathrel{\hat{=}} x \geq 5 \land x \leq 10 \land y = 2x$ and $E_0 = \top$.

$$\begin{aligned} E_1 &= aded_\varphi(E_0) \\ &= [\![x \geq 5]\!](\top) \sqcap [\![x \leq 10]\!](\top) \sqcap [\![y = 2x]\!](\top) \\ &= \{x \in [5,10], y \mapsto [-\infty, \infty]\} \\ E_2 &= aded_\varphi(E_1) \\ &= [\![x \geq 5]\!](E_1) \sqcap [\![x \leq 10]\!](E_1) \sqcap [\![y = 2x]\!](E_1) \\ &= \{x \in [5,10], y \mapsto [10,20]\} = \mathsf{gfp}(aded_\varphi) \end{aligned}$$

The fixed point is superfluous in the concrete but yields more information in the abstract than one transformer application. $\lhd$

The overapproximation and underapproximation conditions given earlier provide the following abstract satisfaction theorem.

**Theorem 12.** *Let* $\mathcal{O}$ *be an overapproximate reasoning domain and* $\mathcal{U}$ *be an underapproximate one.*

1. *If* $\gamma(\mathsf{gfp}(aded_\varphi)) = \emptyset$ *in* $\mathcal{O}$ *then* $\varphi$ *is unsatisfiable.*
2. *If* $\gamma(\mathsf{lfp}(aabd_\varphi)) = Env_\Gamma$ *in* $\mathcal{U}$ *then* $\varphi$ *is unsatisfiable.*

### 5.3 Galois Connection of Syntax and Semantics

The first abstraction we identify is between syntax and semantics. The Galois connection below has been observed in different settings in the literature [32, 42]. We are not aware of this connection being identified in the setting that we use.

***Theories and Definability*** A *theory* is a set of formulae, each called an *axiom*. A *complete theory* is a set of formulae closed under implication. The theory of a set of structures $S$ consists of formulae which are true in every structure in $S$. A set of structures $S$ is *definable* if there exists a formula $\varphi$ such that $S = [\![\varphi]\!]$. These notions lead to a Galois connection.

$$th : \mathcal{P}(Env_\Gamma) \to \mathcal{P}(Form_\Gamma) \qquad st : \mathcal{P}(Form_\Gamma) \to \mathcal{P}(Env_\Gamma)$$

$$th \mathrel{\hat{=}} S \mapsto \{\varphi \mid S \subseteq [\![\varphi]\!]\} \qquad st \mathrel{\hat{=}} \Phi \mapsto \bigcap_{\varphi \in \Phi} [\![\varphi]\!]$$

**Theorem 13.** *There is a Galois connection* $(\mathcal{P}(Env), \subseteq) \underset{th}{\overset{st}{\leftrightarrows}} (\mathcal{P}(Form), \supseteq)$ *between structures and formulae.*

The superset order is chosen because we interpret a set of formulae as their conjunction. The Galois connection allows us to view formulae as abstractions of structures and is appropriate for our goal of studying satisfiability. In a proof-theoretic investigation, one may prefer to accord primacy to formulae and view structures as abstractions. By the Galois connection, a *complete theory* $\Phi$ is one satisfying $th(st(\Phi))$ and a set of structures $S$ is *definable* if $st(th(S)) = S$.

***Proof Systems*** The Galois connection of syntax and semantics allows us to view proof rules as transformers on an abstract domain of formulae and logical soundness and completeness as soundness and completeness in the sense of abstract interpretation.

A *proof rule* is a relation between formulae. In a rule containing $(\varphi_0, \ldots, \varphi_{n-1}, \varphi_n)$ the formulae $\varphi_0, \ldots, \varphi_{n-1}$ are called *antecedents* and $\varphi_n$ is the *consequent*. A *proof system* is a collection of proof rules of possibly different arities. A unary rule is a set of formulae, which are also called the *hypotheses*.

A formula $\psi$ is *derived from* a set of formulae $\Phi$ using a proof system, written $\Phi \vdash \psi$, if $\psi$ occurs in $\Phi$ or if $\psi$ is derived from $\varphi_0, \ldots, \varphi_{n-1}$ by applying an $n$-ary inference rule and the formulae $\varphi_1, \ldots, \varphi_n$ are derived from $\Phi$. The *deductive closure* of a set of axioms $\Phi$ with respect to a proof system $\vdash$ is the set of all formulae that can be derived from $\Phi$ with $\vdash$. A proof system is *deductively sound* if every $\psi$ derived from $\Phi$ is in the theory of $\Phi$. A proof system is *deductively complete* if every $\psi$ in the theory of $\Phi$ can be derived from $\Phi$. A *refutation* is a derivation of $\mathsf{false}$.

A proof system $\vdash$ defines a transformer $aded_\varphi : \mathcal{P}(Form) \to \mathcal{P}(Form)$ from a set of formulae to its immediate consequences.

$$\begin{aligned} aded_\varphi \mathrel{\hat{=}} \Phi \mapsto \{\psi \mid &\text{ there exist } \varphi_i \in \Phi \cup \{\varphi\} \\ &(\varphi_0, \ldots, \varphi_{n-1}, \psi) \text{ is in a proof rule }\} \end{aligned}$$

The fixed point $\mathsf{gfp}(aded_\varphi)$ (with respect to the superset order) contains all formulae derivable from $\varphi$. Since multiple applications of proof rules are required to derive a conclusion, $aded_\varphi$ is not usually a closure operator. Properties of proof systems become properties of the abstract transformer.

**Lemma 14.** *A proof system* $\vdash$ *is deductively sound exactly if* $ded_\varphi \circ st \supseteq aded_\varphi \circ th$ *and is deductively complete exactly if* $th \circ ded_\varphi \circ st = \mathsf{gfp}(aded_\varphi)$.

While deductive soundness corresponds to soundness in abstract interpretation, deductive completeness is fixed point completeness, which is only one of several completeness notions [24].

## 6. Abstract Satisfaction Procedures

The framework in the previous section has already been applied to characterize satisfiability procedures for propositional and first-order logics in terms of the lattices and transformers. The method of truth tables, propositional resolution, and Boolean Constraint Propagation were formalized as greatest fixed points in [18]. The classic DPLL algorithm was shown to be a fixed point refinement procedure in [18], and CDCL was formalized as a combination of deduction and abduction in [19]. The congruence closure algorithm for the theory of equality with uninterpreted functions is a fixed point in a lattice of partitions, and the application of the Bellman-Ford algorithm for deciding difference logic is a fixed point in a lattice of weighted graphs [2]. The DPLL(T) algorithm used in SMT solvers was characterized as an approximate, reduced product construction in [2]. Though different frameworks were used to give a lattice-theoretic characterization of the Nelson-Oppen procedure [14] and Stålmarck's method [44], those procedures can also be formulated in the language of this paper.

This section introduces a simple and systematic formulation of the abstractions above. We introduce lattice-theoretic generalizations of CNF and DNF formulae. A wide range of lattices used in practice, such as partial assignments, equality graphs, the intervals, and binary implication graphs, admit such a representation. We exhibit Galois connections showing that CNF and DNF and their generalizations define semantic abstractions. Moreover, these lattices support logical notions such as resolution, the pure literal rule, and subsumption. We demonstrate that pre- and in-processing techniques used in SAT solvers can be understood as abstract quantification procedures. Thus, these procedures have a semantic justification, abstract interpretation-based soundness proofs, and generalize to program analysis.

***Upwards and Downwards Closure*** We will use the notions of upward and downward closure to generalise CNF and DNF formulae to logics defined over posets.

A subset $Q$ of a poset $A$ is *downwards closed* if for every $x$ in $Q$ and $y$ in $A$, $y \sqsubseteq x$ implies that $y$ is in $Q$. A downwards-closed set is called a *downset*. The smallest downset containing $Q$ is denoted $Q{\downharpoonleft}$, and the downset of a singleton set $\{x\}$ is denoted $x{\downharpoonleft}$. In examples, we denote a downset as the set of its maximal elements. The *downset lattice* over $A$, written $(\mathcal{D}(A), \subseteq, \cap, \cup)$, is the set of downsets of $A$ ordered by inclusion. Downsets strictly generalise powersets because the downset lattice with respect to the identity relation is isomorphic to $\mathcal{P}(S)$. The dual notion to downset is *up-sets*. The smallest up-set containing $Q$ is $Q{\upharpoonleft}$, and $(\mathcal{U}(A), \supseteq)$ is the *up-set* lattice with intersection as join and union as meet. Let $min(Q)$ and $max(Q)$ denote the minimal and maximal elements of a poset $Q$. These sets form antichains. When convenient, we assume that up-sets are represented by minimal elements and downsets by maximal elements.

An abstraction $A$ of a powerset lattice *is disjunctive* if $\gamma(a \sqcup b) = \gamma(a) \cup \gamma(b)$. Downset completion is an operation that enriches an abstraction with disjunction [12]. The *downset completion* of $A$ is the lattice $\mathcal{D}(A)$ with the abstraction and concretisation functions below. Unlike the standard treatment, we use downsets as underapproximating abstractions.

$$\begin{aligned} \gamma_{\mathcal{D}(A)} &: \mathcal{D}(A) \to \mathcal{P}(S) & \gamma_{\mathcal{D}(A)}(Q) &\triangleq \bigcup \{\gamma(x) \mid x \in Q\} \\ \alpha_{\mathcal{D}(A)} &: \mathcal{P}(S) \to \mathcal{D}(A) & \alpha_{\mathcal{D}(A)}(P) &\triangleq \{x \mid \gamma(x) \subseteq P\} \\ \gamma_{\mathcal{U}(A)} &: \mathcal{U}(A) \to \mathcal{P}(S) & \gamma_{\mathcal{U}(A)}(Q) &\triangleq \bigcap \{\gamma(x) \mid x \in Q\} \\ \alpha_{\mathcal{U}(A)} &: \mathcal{P}(S) \to \mathcal{U}(A) & \alpha_{\mathcal{U}(A)}(P) &\triangleq \{x \mid \gamma(x) \supseteq P\} \end{aligned}$$

Consult [12] for proofs that the pairs of functions above form Galois connections and that the domains are disjunctive. We can dually define the *up-set completion* of a lattice. If a lattice $A$ overapproximates $\mathcal{P}(S)$, the downset completion overapproximates $\mathcal{P}(S)$ and the up-set completion *underapproximates* $\mathcal{P}(S)$.

### 6.1 Generalised Cube Abstract Domains

There is some debate about whether the use of CNF representations is beneficial or detrimental to solvers [43]. We believe that CNF is advantageous for solvers because it leads to simple and efficient data structures. We also believe there must be deeper, algebraic properties of CNF that are advantageous to solvers. One reason is because, as we observed earlier, CNF leads to a simpler treatment of negation. Another is that several domains used in practice have generalized CNF representations.

Consider a poset $(gLit, \sqsubseteq)$ of *generalised literals*. One may think of $gLit$ as a set of semantically distinct formulae. We define generalised cubes, clauses, CNF and DNF formulae by using up-sets to form conjunctions and downsets to form disjunctions.

$$\begin{aligned} gClause &\triangleq (\mathcal{D}(gLit), \subseteq) & gCube &\triangleq (\mathcal{U}(gLit), \supseteq) \\ gCNF &\triangleq (\mathcal{U}(gClause), \supseteq) & gDNF &\triangleq (\mathcal{D}(gCube), \subseteq) \end{aligned}$$

Since up- and downsets become powersets if the identity relation is used as the order, standard cubes and clauses are special cases of this definition. If $gLit$ contains formulae, the concretisation function for the poset $A$ is the function $st : gLit \to \mathcal{P}(Env_\Gamma)$ from formulae to models. If $a$ is a generalized literal, we write $\sim a$ for a literal that satisfies $\gamma(a) \cup \gamma(\sim a) = \top$.

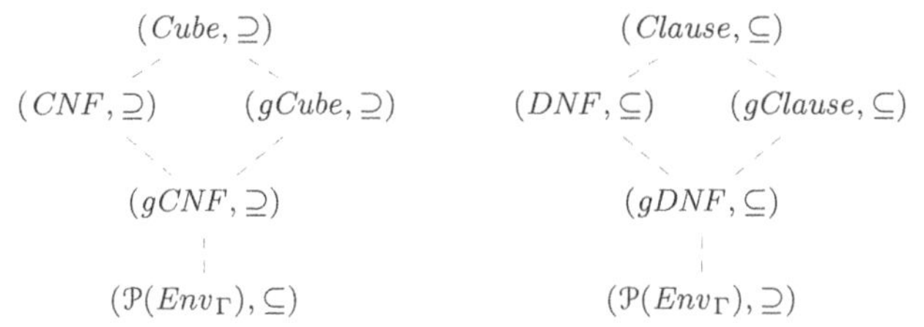


**Figure 2.** Refinement order between the generalised CNF domains.

| $gLit$ | $gCube$ |
|---|---|
| $(\{p, \neg p \mid p \in Prop\}, =)$ | Partial assignments |
| $(\{x = y, x \neq y \mid x \in Vars\}, =)$ | Equality graphs |
| $(\{x <= y, x < y \mid x \in Vars\}, =)$ | Difference graphs |
| $(\{x \leq k, x \geq k \mid k \in \mathbb{N}\}, \Rightarrow)$ | Interval cubes |
| $(\{m \vee n \mid m, n \in Lit\}, =)$ | Binary Implication Graphs |

**Table 1.** Domains viewed as generalised clauses, cubes and CNF

The relationship between these domains is depicted in the Hasse diagram in Figure 2, where an upward line denotes an abstraction relationship. Cubes constructed by powerset operations are overapproximations of generalised cubes and CNF formulae, which are in turn overapproximations of generalised CNF, which are overapproximations of environments. On the other hand, the dual constructions give us underapproximating domains of clauses, generalised clauses, DNF and generalised DNF respectively.

Another property of this construction is that all domains obtained are distributive because up-set and downset lattices are distributive [15]. As we show shortly, these domains are distributive lattices but do not express disjunction. Table 1 lists domains that have generalized cube descriptions.

***Partial Assignments*** Consider a set of Boolean variables $Prop$, a set of literals $Lit$ and the identity relation. The lattice $gCube$ is isomorphic to the lattice of partial assignments, the main data structure in solvers based on DPLL. This domain was studied in [18].

***Equality Graphs*** Consider generalized clauses over the literals $ELit = \{x = y, x \neq y\}$ with the identity relation on literals. (Caution! Identity between literals is different from the equality between variables.) Cubes over equality literals define equality graphs, which are used in several solvers [36, 47]. Figure 3 depicts a graph with elements representing literals highlighted at the top. Two important operations in equality logic decision procedures are transitive closure and cycle detection. We formalize transitive closure by the transformer $trans : \mathcal{U}(ELit) \to \mathcal{U}(ELit)$.

$$trans \triangleq G \mapsto G \cup \{x = y \mid x = z, z = y \in G\}$$

Recall that a reduction operator is an abstract transformer $\rho$ satisfying that $\gamma(a) = \gamma(\rho(a))$ for all $a$. Observe that transitive closure is a reduction operator and the saturation of a graph with transitive edges is a greatest fixed point.

A *conflicting cycle* in an equality graph contains only equalities and exactly one disequality edge [36]. A graph with a conflicting

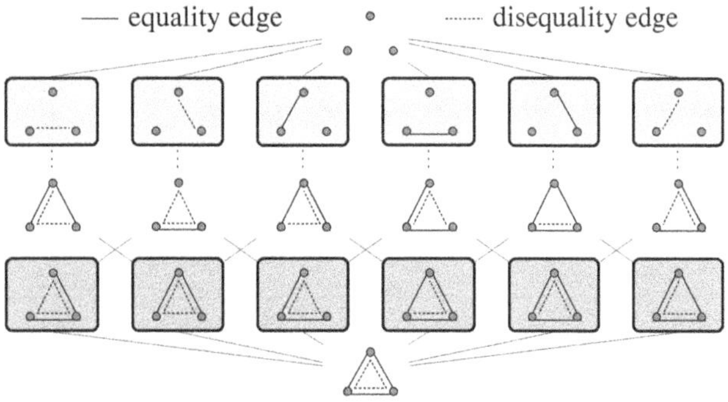


**Figure 3.** Equality graphs over three variables. The shaded elements at the top are literals and the shaded elements at the bottom all concretise to the empty set.

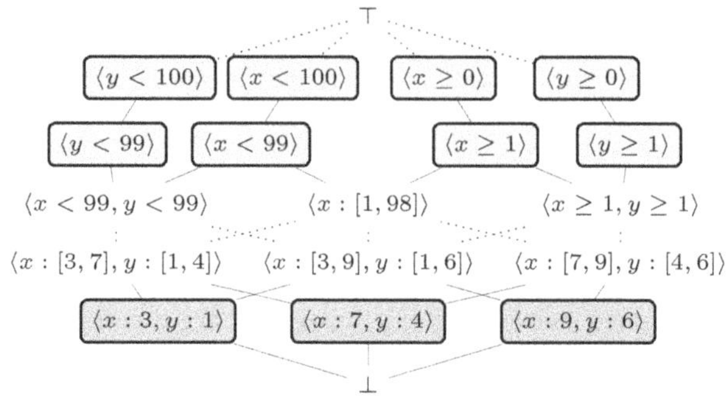


**Figure 4.** The lattice of interval environments over two variables. The shaded elements at the top represent the poset of literals while elements at the bottom represent singleton values.

cycle satisfies $\gamma(G) = \emptyset$. The shaded elements at the bottom of Figure 3 all contain conflicting cycles and concretise to the empty set. A similar abstract domain and reduction operation appear in the logic of order and directed graphs in [31].

***Interval Cubes*** Consider the set of single variable inequalities $(BLit = \{x \leq k, x \geq k \mid k \in \mathbb{Z}\}, \Rightarrow)$. which form a poset under implication. The elements of $BLit$ are light grey in Figure 4. By representing intervals as cubes instead of pairs, we obtain a set-based representation that supports proof rules such as resolution and other algorithms in solvers that target clauses and cubes. Example 6 illustrates how intervals can be manipulated using up-sets.

Example 6. The interval domain as defined in Section 5 is not distributive because identities such as the one below fail.

$$([0, 1] \sqcup [6, 7]) \sqcap [3, 4] = [3, 4]$$
$$\neq ([0, 1] \sqcap [3, 4]) \sqcup ([6, 7] \sqcap [3, 4]) = \bot$$

Now consider intervals represented as up-sets. The meet in this lattice is union and join is intersection, so it is trivially distributive. We represent up-sets by their minimal elements.

$$(\{x \geq 0, x \leq 1\} \upharpoonright \cap \{x \geq 6, x \leq 7\} \upharpoonright) \cup \{x \geq 3, x \leq 4\} \upharpoonright$$
$$= \{x \geq 0, x \leq 7\} \upharpoonright \cup \{x \geq 3, x \leq 4\} \upharpoonright = \{x \geq 3, x \leq 4\} \upharpoonright$$

A similar calculation yields the expected interval for the other interval expression. The cube representation expresses the same concrete elements as the classic pair representation of intervals but contains more redundancy. $\lhd$

***Binary Implication Graphs*** If the set of generalised literals contains clauses of length 2 (such as $\{p, \neg q\}$) ordered by equality, each generalised literal represents two implications $q \Rightarrow p$ and $\neg p \Rightarrow q$, which can be viewed as edges in a directed graph. The resulting *Binary Implication Graph* abstract domain is used for preprocessing in SAT solvers [29]. Though a lattice-based analysis has not been previously applied to Binary Implication Graphs, we need not explicitly define Galois connections or their approximation properties, as these follow from the cube representation. As with equality graphs, transitive closure is a reduction.

***The CNF Domains*** The generalized CNF domains show that CNF formulae have a lattice structure that is usually not recognized. To see the difference between $gCNF$ and $CNF$, consider $BLit$. The set $\{x \geq 2, x \leq 5, x \leq 7\}$ represents a clause but not a generalized clause, while $\{x \geq 2, x \leq 5\} \downharpoonleft$ is a generalised clause.

Solvers use a variety of subsumption techniques to minimize formulae without explicitly checking implication. The inclusion orders in Figure 2 correspond to subsumption notions and also underapproximate implication. For instance, $\{\{p\}, \{p, q\}\}$ and $\{\{p\}\}$ are logically equivalent but we can only show $\{\{p\}\} \subseteq \{\{p\}, \{p, q\}\}$ using the lattice order. From the abstract interpretation perspective, subsumption is not a substitute for implication but is fundamental to the lattice structure of CNF and DNF domains.

### 6.2 Abstract Transformers in Solvers

***Generalized Unit Rule*** The unit rule in SAT solvers asserts that if a cube represents a region of the search space and the cube falsifies all but one literal in a clause, the remaining literal can be added to the clause. The Abstract Conflict Driven Learning algorithm (ACDCL) of [19] generalises the unit rule to abstract domains based on the notion of complementable meet irreducibles. The unit rule can be viewed as a technique for refining generalized cubes using generalized clauses.

$$gunit : gClause \rightarrow (gCube \rightarrow gCube)$$
$$gunit_\theta \mathrel{\hat{=}} \pi \mapsto \pi \cup \{a\}, \text{ where } a \in \theta, \gamma(\pi) \cap \gamma(a) \neq \emptyset, \text{ and}$$
$$\text{for all } b \in \theta \setminus \{a\}, \gamma(\pi) \cap \gamma(b) = \emptyset$$

We write $\mathsf{gfp}_x(f)$ for the function that maps elements $a$ to fixed points $\mathsf{gfp}(f(a, x))$ of a function $f(y, x)$. The main observation of [18] was that Boolean Constraint Propagation (BCP) is a fixed point $bcp(\varphi, x) \mathrel{\hat{=}} \mathsf{gfp}_x(\bigsqcap_{\theta \in \varphi} gunit_\theta)$ defined pointwise over unit rules. The generalized cubes in Table 1, when combined with the generalized clauses, also support the unit rule and BCP.

***Failed Literal Probing*** Failed literal probing [21, 22] is a preprocessing technique in SAT solvers. The technique chooses literal $a$, computes $bcp(a, \varphi)$ and if the result is $\bot$, adds the singleton clause $\{b\}$ to $\varphi$, where $b$ satisfies that $\gamma(a) \cup \gamma(b) = \top$. No action is taken if the result is not bottom. Note that we have not only described failed literal probing, but also its generalization to CNF domains.

***Clause Dropping*** Variable elimination is a fundamental operation underlying quantifier elimination, deduction and syntactic simplification of formulae. The simplest form of sound variable elimination is to drop clauses from a CNF formula in which the target variable occurs. This idea lifts directly to generalized CNF domains if we drop constraints based on the literals they contain.

$$drop : gLit \times gCNF \rightarrow gCNF$$
$$drop_p(\varphi) \mathrel{\hat{=}} \{C \mid \{p, {\sim}p\} \cap C = \emptyset, C \in \varphi\}$$

In general, $drop_p$ is an overapproximation of the deduction transformer. If $p$ is a Boolean variable, $drop_p$ also overapproximates existential quantification with respect to $p$.

***Resolution*** The resolution principle asserts that if $C \vee p$ and $\neg p \vee D$ are both satisfiable, so is $C \vee D$. The variable $p$ is the *pivot* and $C \vee D$ is the *resolvent*. Generalised CNF domains support a generalization of resolution $res : gLit \times gCNF \to gCNF$.

$$res(p, \varphi) \hat{=} \{C \cup D \mid C \cup \{p\}, D \cup \{q\} \in \varphi, \gamma(p) \cap \gamma(q) = \emptyset\}$$

Generalized CNF domains that apply this transformer can produce resolution-style proofs, which is a first step towards combining existing abstract domains with proof-theoretic techniques.

Example 7. The generalised CNF element

$$\varphi \hat{=} \{\{x \geq 10, x \leq 5\} \downarrow, \{x \geq 7, x \leq 13\} \downarrow\}$$

represents a conjunction of disjunctions of bounds. Standard interval propagation will lose precision in the clauses, while standard resolution does not apply because no constraint is the negation of another. The result of generalized resolution with respect to the literal $x \geq 7$ is $res(x \geq 7, \varphi) = \{\{x \geq 10, x \leq 13\}\}$. Though arithmetic techniques methods can deduce the same information, generalised resolution is simple and suffices in this case. ◁

***The Pure Literal Rule*** Clause dropping is a sound but incomplete simplification technique because a formula $\varphi$ that is unsatisfiable might become satisfiable after clause dropping. The pure literal rule, introduced in the original algorithm of Davis and Putnam [16] can be understood as an application of clause dropping only in situations where it does not change the satisfiability of a formula. We formalize the pure literal rule for generalized CNF domains.

Recall that $gLit$ is the set of generalized literals. We say that a set of literals $A$ is *pure* if for each $a$ in $A$, no $b$ satisfying $\gamma(a) \cap \gamma(b) = \emptyset$ is also in $A$. We assume that $gLit$ is the disjoint union of two pure sets $P$ and $N$ such that for each $a$ in $P$, there exists a $b$ in $N$ satisfying that $\gamma(a) \cap \gamma(b) = \emptyset$ and vice-versa. The elements of $P$ are positive literals and of $N$ are negative literals. Define a set $\{+, -\}$ of *polarities*, a lattice of polarities $\mathcal{P}(\{+, -\})$, and a lattice of polarity maps $P \to \mathcal{P}(\{+, -\})$.

*Polarity analysis* of a generalized CNF formula $\varphi$ computes a polarity map $\rho$. such that $\rho(\ell)$ is $\{+\}$ or $\{-\}$ if the generalized literal $\ell$ only occurs positively or only negatively in $\varphi$, and is $\emptyset$ if $\ell$ does not occur in $\varphi$, and is $\{+, -\}$ if $\ell$ occurs both positively and negatively in $\varphi$. The polarity of a literal $\ell$ is $\{+\}$ if $a$ is in $P$, and is $\{-\}$ if $\ell$ is in $N$. The polarity map for a literal $\ell$ sends $\ell$ to its polarity and sends all literals $b \neq a$ to the empty set. The polarity map for a generalized clause is the pointwise join of of polarity maps of its literals. The polarity map of a generalized CNF element is the pointwise join of of polarity maps of its clauses. Note that the join is used in both cases.

The pure literal rule for a generalized CNF formula, applies $drop_\ell$ to a formula $\varphi$ only if the polarity map for $\varphi$ does not send the literal $\ell$ to $\{+, -\}$. The pure literal rule is a sound overapproximation of the deduction transformer and is a refinement of clause dropping. In propositional logic, the pure literal rule applied to a variable $p$ is also a sound abstraction of the existential quantification transformer $(wk_p \circ some_p)$.

## 7. Discussion and Related Work

This paper contributes to a research programme that seeks to close the gap between abstract interpretation techniques and deduction algorithms, both in theory and practice. One direction of this program is to use deduction algorithms to refine static analyses. Precision loss due to joins was reduced by boosting a static analysis with unification [46], DPLL(T) [27], or CDCL [20]. Best abstract transformers have been synthesized using satisfiability solvers [41], and Stålmarck's method [45], while [37] applied satisfiability techniques to reduce precision loss in fixed point iteration.

Another direction in this programme is to characterize satisfiability procedures as abstract interpretations. Boolean constraint propagation was shown to be an abstract interpretation in [18], and CDCL was generalized to combine deduction and abduction over lattices in [19]. Stålmarck's method was characterized as a technique for refining abstract transformers in [44]. The Nelson-Oppen method for theory combination implemented in SMT solvers was shown to be a special case of the reduced product of abstract domains [14]. The DPLL(T) technique for reasoning about a theory by combining a SAT solver with a theory solver was also shown to be a special case of the reduced product in [2].

In addition to static analysis applications, these characterizations provide a new way for lifting solver algorithms to new logics. For example, Stålmarck's method was lifted to arithmetic in [45], while CDCL was lifted to floating point logic in [26]. Note that the Nelson-Oppen combination was lifted to abstract domains [25] prior to the reduced product characterization.

Abstract satisfaction is lattice-theoretic in an attempt to align with static analysis. If static analysis is ignored, the DPLL(T) framework provides one generic approach to implementing decision procedures [23]. The separation of Boolean and theory reasoning in DPLL(T) can be detrimental to performance and has driven the search for other frameworks. Abstract DPLL [39], natural domain SMT [6], generalized DPLL [35], and the model construction calculus [17] are attempts in this direction.

## 8. Conclusion

Abstraction is fundamental to practical reasoning about computationally intractable problems. Abstract interpretation has traditionally been applied to reason about undecidable problems such as checking semantic properties of programs. This paper introduced a framework for applying abstract interpretation to problems that are NP-hard but decidable, such as satisfiability.

This framework allows for novel perspectives of SMT algorithms. Solvers can be viewed as abstract interpretation portfolios, which combine several different, weak abstractions to achieve a conclusive result. Moreover, while solvers use incomplete abstractions they produce complete results. This is not due to brute-force enumerations but clever, semantics-based refinement techniques. Our framework makes some of these techniques explicit, but more importantly provides a general vocabulary for studying a wide range of satisfiability procedures.

While the focus of this paper has been theoretical, our goal is to contribute to the practical state of the art. The original abstract interpretation framework provided a simple recipe for constructing static analyzers. Abstract satisfaction plays a similar role and provides a foundation for the development of programmable, lattice-based SMT solvers.

There are three different axes for future work. One is to apply abstract interpretation to the implementation of SMT solvers by constructing sound but incomplete solvers and abstract quantification procedures from existing abstract domains. The second axis is to lift techniques in SMT solvers to improve the precision and efficiency of program analysis. The classic DPLL, DPLL(T), CDCL and Stålmarck's method have each been lifted to a single static analysis problem, but more applications and evaluation are required to understand their strengths in a static analysis context. Preprocessing, subsumption, and sparsity techniques have all been integral to improving the performance of solvers, and the connections in this paper indicate that such techniques should lift to program analysis as well. The final axis is to investigate new implementations of abstract domains with interfaces rich enough to support SMT solving, static analysis, implication graph construction, and domain and theory combinations. We look forward to these developments.

## Acknowledgments

This work was supported by the Toyota Motor Corporation, ERC project 280053, EPSRC project EP/H017585/1, and the FP7 STREP PINCETTE. The research reported in this paper was conducted between 2011 and 2013. In 2011, Vijay D'Silva was supported by a Microsoft Research scholarship.

## References

[1] N. Bjørner, B. Duterte, and L. de Moura. Accelerating lemma learning using joins - DPLL(⊔). In *LPAR*, 2008.

[2] M. Brain, V. D'Silva, L. Haller, A. Griggio, and D. Kroening. An abstract interpretation of DPLL(T). In *VMCAI*, 2012.

[3] M. Brain, V. D'Silva, L. Haller, A. Griggio, and D. Kroening. Interpolation-based verification of floating-point programs with abstract CDCL. In *SAS*, 2013.

[4] R. E. Bryant, D. Kroening, J. Ouaknine, S. A. Seshia, O. Strichman, and B. Brady. Deciding bit-vector arithmetic with abstraction. In *TACAS*, pages 358–372. Springer, 2007.

[5] E. M. Clarke, O. Grumberg, and D. E. Long. Model checking and abstraction. *ACM TOPLAS*, 16(5):1512–1542, Sept. 1994.

[6] S. Cotton. Natural domain SMT: A preliminary assessment. In *FORMATS*, pages 77–91, 2010.

[7] P. Cousot. Semantic foundations of program analysis. In S. Muchnick and N. Jones, editors, *Program Flow Analysis: Theory and Applications*, chapter 10, pages 303–342. Prentice-Hall, Inc., 1981.

[8] P. Cousot. The calculational design of a generic abstract interpreter. In M. Broy and R. Steinbrüggen, editors, *Calculational System Design*. NATO ASI Series F. IOS Press, Amsterdam, 1999.

[9] P. Cousot. Abstract interpretation. MIT course 16.399, 2005.

[10] P. Cousot and R. Cousot. Abstract interpretation: a unified lattice model for static analysis of programs by construction or approximation of fixpoints. In *POPL*, pages 238–252. ACM Press, 1977.

[11] P. Cousot and R. Cousot. Systematic design of program analysis frameworks. In *POPL*, pages 269–282. ACM Press, 1979.

[12] P. Cousot and R. Cousot. Abstract interpretation and application to logic programs. *Journal of Logic Programming*, 13(2–3):103–179, 1992.

[13] P. Cousot and R. Cousot. Abstract interpretation frameworks. *Journal of Logic and Computation*, 2(4):511–547, Aug. 1992.

[14] P. Cousot, R. Cousot, and L. Mauborgne. Theories, solvers and static analysis by abstract interpretation. *JACM*, 59(6):31:1–31:56, Jan. 2013.

[15] B. A. Davey and H. A. Priestley. *Introduction to lattices and order*. Cambridge University Press, Cambridge, UK, 1990.

[16] M. Davis and H. Putnam. A computing procedure for quantification theory. *JACM*, 7:201–215, July 1960.

[17] L. M. de Moura and D. Jovanovic. A model-constructing satisfiability calculus. In *VMCAI*, pages 1–12, 2013.

[18] V. D'Silva, L. Haller, and D. Kroening. Satisfiability solvers are static analysers. In *SAS*, pages 317–333. Springer, 2012.

[19] V. D'Silva, L. Haller, and D. Kroening. Abstract conflict driven learning. In *POPL*, pages 143–154, New York, NY, USA, 2013. ACM Press.

[20] V. D'Silva, L. Haller, D. Kroening, and M. Tautschnig. Numeric bounds analysis with conflict-driven learning. In *TACAS*, pages 48–63. Springer, 2012.

[21] N. Eén and A. Biere. Effective preprocessing in SAT through variable and clause elimination. In *SAT*, pages 61–75, Munich, Germany, 2005. Springer.

[22] J. W. Freeman. Failed literals in the Davis-Putnam procedure for SAT. Technical report, Rutgers University, 1993.

[23] H. Ganzinger, G. Hagen, R. Nieuwenhuis, A. Oliveras, and C. Tinelli. DPLL(T): Fast decision procedures. In *CAV*, pages 175–188, 2004.

[24] R. Giacobazzi, F. Ranzato, and F. Scozzari. Making abstract interpretations complete. *JACM*, 47(2):361–416, 2000.

[25] S. Gulwani and A. Tiwari. Combining abstract interpreters. In *PLDI*, pages 376–386. ACM Press, 2006.

[26] L. Haller, A. Griggio, M. Brain, and D. Kroening. Deciding floating-point logic with systematic abstraction. In *FMCAD*, pages 131–140, 2012.

[27] W. R. Harris, S. Sankaranarayanan, F. Ivančić, and A. Gupta. Program analysis via satisfiability modulo path programs. In *POPL*, pages 71–82, 2010.

[28] T. A. Henzinger, O. Kupferman, and S. Qadeer. From pre-historic to post-modern symbolic model checking. *FMSD*, 23(3):303–327, Nov. 2003.

[29] M. J. H. Heule, M. Järvisalo, and A. Biere. Efficient CNF simplification based on binary implication graphs. In *SAT*, pages 201–215, 2011.

[30] D. Kroening, J. Ouaknine, S. A. Seshia, and O. Strichman. Abstraction-based satisfiability solving of Presburger arithmetic. In *CAV*, pages 308–320, July 2004.

[31] D. Kroening and G. Weissenbacher. An interpolating decision procedure for transitive relations with uninterpreted functions. In *HVC*, pages 150–168, 2011.

[32] W. Lawvere. Adjointness in foundations. *Dialectica*, 23:281–296, 1969.

[33] K. R. M. Leino and F. Logozzo. Using widenings to infer loop invariants inside an SMT solver, or: A theorem prover as abstract domain. In *Workshop on Invariant Generation*, pages 70–84. RISC Report 07-07, 2007.

[34] K. L. McMillan. Interpolation and SAT-based model checking. In *CAV*, pages 1–13, 2003.

[35] K. L. McMillan, A. Kuehlmann, and M. Sagiv. Generalizing DPLL to richer logics. In *CAV*, pages 462–476, 2009.

[36] O. Meir and O. Strichman. Yet another decision procedure for equality logic. In *CAV*, pages 307–320, 2005.

[37] D. Monniaux and L. Gonnord. Using bounded model checking to focus fixpoint iterations. In *SAS*, pages 369–385, 2011.

[38] I. Németi. Algebraization of quantifier logics, an introductory overview. *Studia Logica: An International Journal for Symbolic Logic*, 50(3/4):485–569, 1991.

[39] R. Nieuwenhuis, A. Oliveras, and C. Tinelli. Solving SAT and SAT modulo theories: From an abstract Davis–Putnam–Logemann–Loveland procedure to DPLL(T). *JACM*, 53:937–977, 2006.

[40] A. M. Pitts. Categorical logic. In S. Abramsky, D. M. Gabbay, and T. S. E. Maibaum, editors, *Handbook of Logic in Computer Science, Volume 5. Algebraic and Logical Structures*, chapter 2, pages 39–128. Oxford University Press, 2000.

[41] T. W. Reps, S. Sagiv, and G. Yorsh. Symbolic implementation of the best transformer. In *VMCAI*, pages 252–266, 2004.

[42] P. Smith. The Galois connection of syntax and semantics. Technical report, Cambridge University, 2010.

[43] P. J. Stuckey. There are no CNF problems. SAT, pages 19–21, 2013.

[44] A. Thakur and T. Reps. A generalization of Stålmarck's method. In *SAS*. Springer, 2012.

[45] A. V. Thakur and T. W. Reps. A method for symbolic computation of abstract operations. In *CAV*, 2012.

[46] A. Tiwari and S. Gulwani. Logical interpretation: Static program analysis using theorem proving. In *CADE*, pages 147–166, 2007.

[47] O. Tveretina. DPLL-based procedure for equality logic with uninterpreted functions. In *IJCAR Doctoral Programme*, volume 106 of *CEUR Workshop Proceedings*. CEUR-WS.org, 2004.

# Proofs That Count

Azadeh Farzan Zachary Kincaid
University of Toronto

Andreas Podelski
University of Freiburg

## Abstract

Counting arguments are among the most basic proof methods in mathematics. Within the field of formal verification, they are useful for reasoning about programs with *infinite control*, such as programs with an unbounded number of threads, or (concurrent) programs with recursive procedures. While counting arguments are common in informal, hand-written proofs of such programs, there are no fully *automated* techniques to construct counting arguments. The key questions involved in automating counting arguments are: *how to decide what should be counted?*, and *how to decide when a counting argument is valid?* In this paper, we present a technique for automatically constructing and checking counting arguments, which includes novel solutions to these questions.

***Categories and Subject Descriptors*** D.2.4 [*Software/Program Verification*]: Correctness Proofs; F.3.1 [*Logics and Meanings of Programs*]: Specifying, Verifying and Reasoning about Programs

***General Terms*** Languages, Verification

***Keywords*** Concurrency, Verification, Static Analysis

## 1. Introduction

A *counting argument* (in the context of formal methods) is a program proof that makes use of one or more *counters*, which are not part of the program itself, but which are useful for abstracting program behaviour. For example it may be useful to refer to the number of threads that have requested access to a shared resource, or the number of times a recursive procedure has been called. Despite the usefulness of counting arguments in hand-written proofs, the problem of constructing such arguments automatically is little explored. This paper presents one such approach.

The main intellectual challenge of constructing counting arguments automatically is that we must design an algorithm which can choose what to count. This is a task that, when carried out by humans, seems to require genuine creativity. The question of whether machines are capable of simulating this type of creativity is a challenging problem in formal verification. It is also a *fundamental* one: counters may be viewed as a class of *auxiliary variables* (*á la* Owicki-Gries [41]), in the sense that they remember useful information about the program history that can be used in a formal argument. The problem of "choosing what to count" can be viewed as one incarnation of the well-known (and yet under-explored) problem of auxiliary variable synthesis.

This paper presents a strategy for automatically constructing counting arguments for program verification. This strategy is outlined in Figure 1. The input to our algorithm is a program $\mathcal{P}$ and a pre/postcondition specification $\psi_{\mathsf{pre}}/\psi_{\mathsf{post}}$. The algorithm can be viewed as a kind of language inference algorithm. The program $\mathcal{P}$ is treated as a black box: we can sample traces from $\mathcal{P}$, but we may not inspect its internal structure (so effectively, we identify $\mathcal{P}$ with a language of traces). The goal of our algorithm is to learn a *counting proof* $\langle A, \varphi \rangle$ for $\mathcal{P}$. A counting proof consists of a *counting automaton* $A$, which determines a language of traces, and an annotation $\varphi$, which is a proof that all traces in the language of $A$ satisfy the specification $\psi_{\mathsf{pre}}/\psi_{\mathsf{post}}$. If our algorithm can learn a counting proof $\langle A, \varphi \rangle$ such that $A$ recognizes all the traces from $\mathcal{P}$, then $\mathcal{P}$ is correct with respect to the specification $\psi_{\mathsf{pre}}/\psi_{\mathsf{post}}$.

The algorithm in Figure 1 operates as follows. We start by (a) constructing a counting proof $\langle A, \varphi \rangle$ for set of sample traces $Tr$. We then (b) check if every program trace in $\mathcal{P}$ is recognized by the counting automaton $A$. If the check succeeds, the algorithm has learned a counting proof for $\mathcal{P}$. If it fails, it produces a counterexample $\tau$ (a program trace that is not recognized by $A$). We then (c) check whether $\tau$ satisfies the specification $\psi_{\mathsf{pre}}/\psi_{\mathsf{post}}$. If not, we are done: $\tau$ is a counterexample which shows that $\mathcal{P}$ is incorrect. If yes, then (d) we add $\tau$ to the set of sample traces $Tr$, and repeat. Note that in the first iteration (since initially $Tr$ is empty) the language of $A$ is empty, so $\tau$ is any program trace.

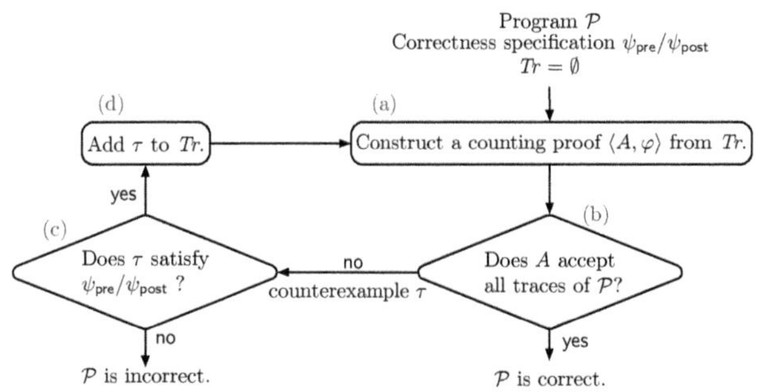


**Figure 1.** Counting proof inference.

Before we explain counting proofs further, we remark on the important distinction between *discovery* and *synthesis* of auxiliary variables (and counters in particular). Counter discovery is essentially a white-box technique: the goal is to expose existing counters in a program which are relevant for a proof (for example, discovery of relevant program counters for Owicki-Gries proofs, as in [23]). Counter synthesis is a black-box technique: the goal is to discover new counters which are useful for a proof, which do not necessarily correspond to anything in the program. This paper addresses the latter problem. This is the motivation behind our


*POPL '14,* January 22–24, 2014, San Diego, CA, USA.

http://dx.doi.org/10.1145/2535838.2535885

language-theoretic model of program correctness: by treating the $\mathcal{P}$ as a language of traces, we are forced to synthesize counting arguments from scratch. Our interest in counter synthesis stems from the fact that the internal control structure of $\mathcal{P}$ may be very complicated. Counter synthesis gives a strategy for constructing proofs for $\mathcal{P}$ that avoids reasoning about its control and data simultaneously.

We will explain counting proofs and our proof inference algorithm by way of an example. Consider the program that consists of an arbitrary number of threads whose control flow graph is pictured to the right. The (global) integer variables $s$ and $t$ are initially 0. The task is to automatically construct a proof that the error location $\ell_{error}$ is unreachable (i.e., the program satisfies the specification $s = t = 0$/*false*). The task is complicated by the fact that the seemingly simple program has a complex control structure, since it must retain the control location for every thread (of which there are unboundedly many).

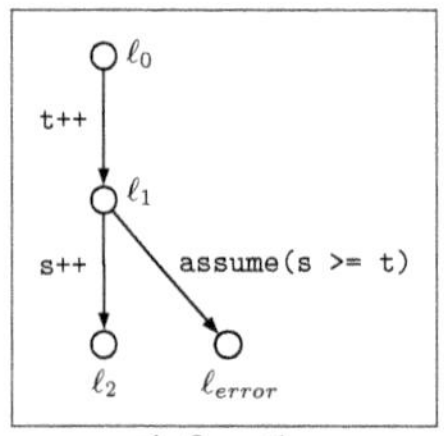


We begin by sampling an error trace from this program, say

$$\tau = \texttt{t++; t++; s++; assume(s >= t)}$$

A correctness proof for $\tau$ is a sequence of intermediate assertions, shown below in Figure 2(a). This proof can be generalized to a proof for a whole language of program traces. This is done by constructing a finite automaton annotated with a Floyd/Hoare proof (with one state for each distinct assertion) as pictured in Figure 2(b). It is easy to see that any trace accepted by this automaton satisfies the given specification.

$\{0 = t - s\}$ t++ $\{1 = t - s\}$ t++ $\{2 = t - s\}$ s++ $\{1 = t - s\}$ assume(s<t) $\{false\}$

(a)

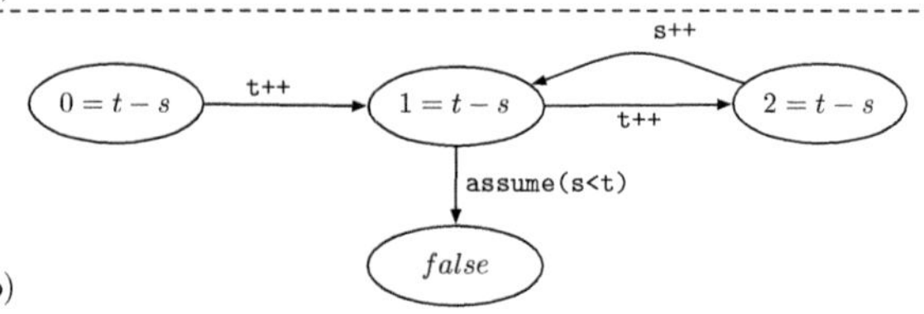


(b)

**Figure 2.** Proof for the sample trace $\tau$.

Unfortunately, this automaton does not accept every trace of the program. We could continue by sampling a new trace, for instance

$$\tau' = \texttt{t++; t++; t++; s++; assume(s >= t)},$$

but it is already clear that this strategy is doomed to fail. There is no regular language which contains all the program traces and which does not contain incorrect traces.

Our solution to this problem is pictured to the right. This *counting proof* consists of a counting automaton $A$ (a kind of restricted counter machine) paired with an annotation $\varphi$ mapping the states of $A$ to assertions. The counting automaton $A$ is a finite automaton equipped with a $\mathbb{N}$-valued counter denoted $k$ (initially 0). Each transition of the automaton is equipped with an action for $k$, which may be `inc` (increment the counter), `dec` (decrement, but block unless the counter is $\geq 1$), `tst` (block unless the counter is $\geq 1$), or `nop` (do nothing). The annotation $\varphi$ associates with each state of this automaton a formula over the program variables and the counter variable $k$. This annotation is *inductive* in the sense that each transition is associated with a valid Hoare triple: for example,

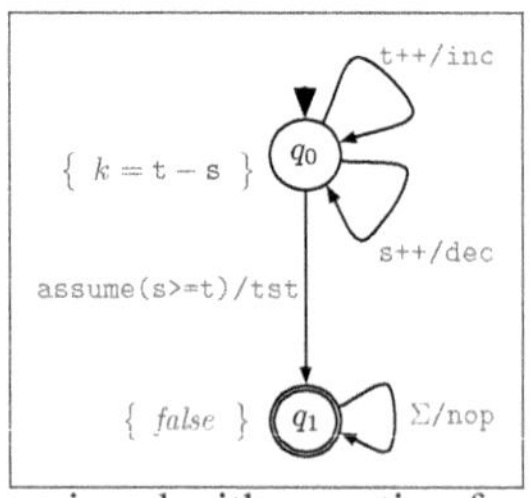


| | | |
|---|---|---|
| $\{k = t - s\}$ | `t++; k++` | $\{k = t - s\}$ |
| $\{k = t - s\}$ | `s++; k--` | $\{k = t - s\}$ |
| $\{k = t - s\}$ | `assume(t<s); assume(k≥1)` | $\{false\}$ |

A trace is accepted by $A$ if it labels a path from $q_0$ (the initial state) to $q_1$ (the final state), and none of the counter actions block. Every trace which is accepted by $A$ is associated with a sequence of intermediate assertions which prove its correctness. This sequence is obtained from the accepting run of $A$ by taking, for each position in the run, the assertion at the current state with $k$ replaced by its current value. For example, the proof for the trace $\tau$ above is as follows:

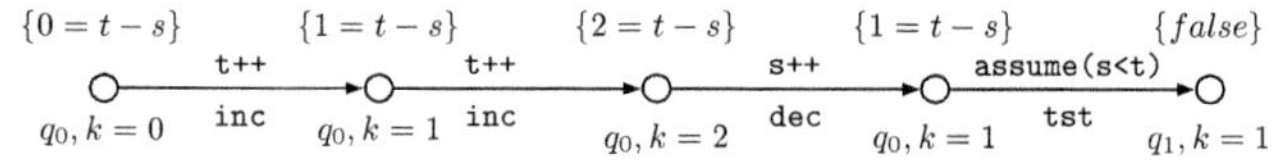


This counting proof works not only for the trace $\tau$, but for *every* trace of the program (that is, the proof is enough to show that $\ell_{error}$ is unreachable). The key to this proof is the use of the counter variable $k$, which intuitively counts the number of `t++` statements in excess of `s++` statements along a trace. Using this auxiliary counter allows us to make a simple, succinct argument for the correctness of this program.

There are two algorithmic problems associated with our proof inference strategy: (1) how to construct a counting proof for a set of sample traces (Figure 1 (a)), and (2) how to prove that a counting proof recognizes all program traces (Figure 1 (b)).

The essential idea for our solution to (1) is to encode the proof construction problem as an SMT query. Our encoding requires us to specify the "size" of the candidate proof to find (e.g., the number of states that may be used), and will always succeed if a proof of that size exists. The main insight behind our proof construction procedure is that by looking for *small* proofs, we can force an SMT solver to synthesize nontrivial counting arguments. For example, we can force an SMT solver to "discover" the need to count the number of `t++` statements in excess of `s++` statements in the proof above completely automatically, simply by asking for a proof with 2 states.

Our solution to (2) is based on the observation that counting automata can be converted into a kind of labelled Petri nets. To enable our language inclusion checking procedure we use *control flow nets* as our program model. A control flow net is a hybrid of a control flow graph and a Petri net. As in a control flow graph, a transition is labelled with an imperative program statement (over infinite data domains). As in a Petri net, tokens can be used to model infinite control, such as (parametrized) concurrency. Once we have modelled a program with a control flow net, problem (2) reduces to a Petri net language inclusion problem which is known to be decidable.

## 2. Motivating Example

We will formalize the verification problem for an industrially motivated example [46] through a control flow net and then present a counting proof.

Figure 3(a) presents a simplified version of the bluetooth device driver code (similar to the one that appears in [46]). The program consists of an arbitrary number of *work threads*, which all execute `Add`, and one *stop thread*, which executes `Stop`. The global variables are the integer variable `pendingIo` (initially 1), and the Boolean flags `stopped`, `stoppingEvent`, and `stoppingFlag`, (initially *false*).

We want to show that the statement `assert(!stopped)` never fails, which means that no configuration is reachable where one of the work threads is still working after the stop thread has ex-

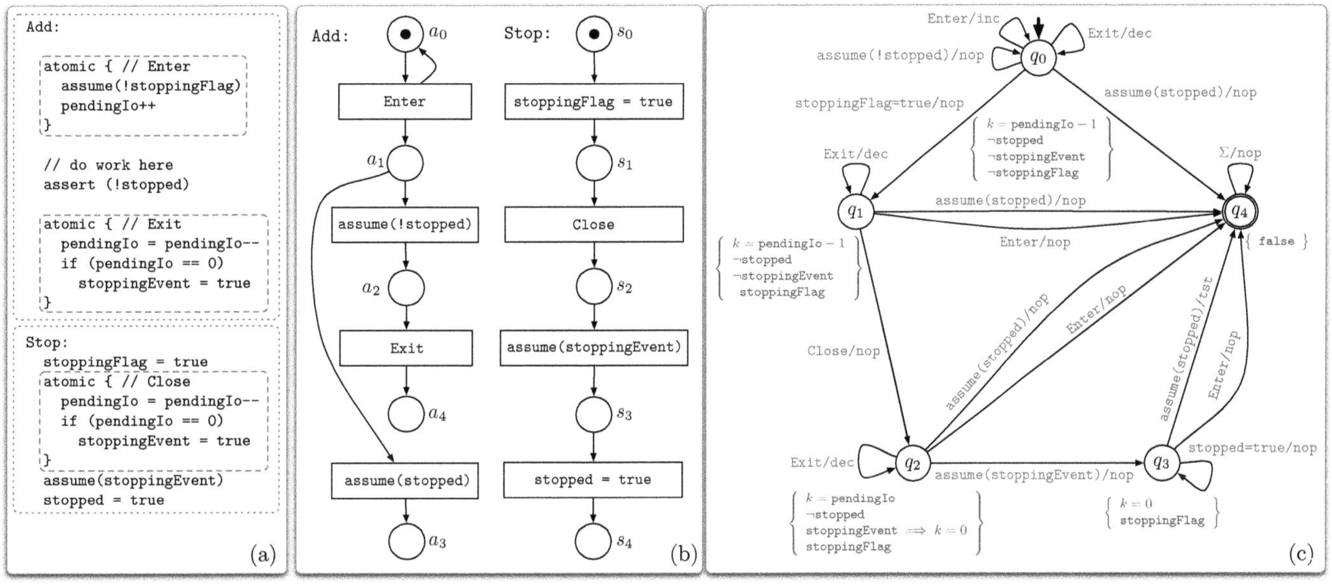


**Figure 3.** (a) Bluetooth device driver code. (b) Control flow net for Bluetooth. The initial marking is as shown (no token other than on $a_0$ and on $s_0$). The final markings are those where at least $a_3$ has at least one token. (c) Bluetooth counting proof.

ecuted the statement `stopped = true`. The correctness relies on the atomicity of the three statements `Enter`, `Exit`, and `Close`. The bug detected in the version from [46] has been fixed by making `Enter` atomic.

***Control Flow Net.*** The control flow net in Figure 3(b) models that an arbitrary number of work threads and one stop threads run in parallel. To model the fact that unboundedly many work threads can be active simultaneously, the initial `Add` transition `Enter` puts a token back on $a_0$, so that `Enter` remains enabled (just as if yet another work thread was spawned). The number of tokens on $a_i$ models the number of work threads in the corresponding control location (there is always one token in `Stop` half of the net, since there is only one stop thread). A *final marking* is any marking where there is at least one token on the error location $a_3$. Each sequence of transitions (a *firing sequence*) of the net that reaches such a final marking corresponds to a thread interleaving that violates the assertion. The goal is to prove that the corresponding sequence of statements is infeasible (has the postcondition *false*).

***Counting Proof.*** The counting automaton in Figure 3(c) is a finite state automaton augmented with a counter $k$. Transitions are labelled by letters of the alphabet of program statements and corresponding counter actions (the same letters are used to label the transitions in the control flow net). The counting proof consists of this automaton and the inductive annotation which maps the automaton states to assertions (blue terms in the figure).

Intuitively, at any moment while reading a trace $\tau$ (i.e., a sequence of statements), the value of the counter $k$ records by how much the `Enter` transitions outnumber the `Exit` transitions (initially by 0).

The automaton states $q_0, \ldots, q_3$ records what *statements of the stop thread* have appeared so far, in sequence: none (recorded by $q_0$), `stoppingFlag = true` (transition from $q_0$ into $q_1$), `Close` (transition from $q_1$ into $q_2$), `assume(stoppingEvent)` (transition from $q_2$ into $q_3$).

The automaton state $q_4$ is reached if: (1) the statement `assume(stopped)` of the work thread has appeared, or (2) the statement `Enter` of the work thread has appeared after the statement `stoppingFlag = true` of the stop thread has appeared.

It is easy to see that the annotation is inductive. Initially, the flags `stopped`, `stoppingEvent`, and `stoppingFlag` have the value *false*, `pendingIo` is 1, and $k$ is 0, and thus, the assertion for the initial state $q_0$ is satisfied. One can check that for every transition, the corresponding Hoare triple holds.

The check of the trace inclusion between a control flow net and a counter automaton is decidable (as we will show in Section 6). To obtain an intuition why the inclusion here holds, consider the (informal) invariants: $s_0 = q_0$, $s_1 = q_1$, $s_2 = q_2$, $s_3 + s_4 = q_3$, and $a_1 + a_2 = k$.

The annotation of the final state $q_4$ with the assertion *false* means that every trace accepted by the counter automaton has postcondition *false*. Since every trace of the control flow net is accepted by the counter automaton, this means that the execution of the statement `assume(stopped)` is never feasible, i.e., the statement `assert(!stopped)` never fails, which is what we wanted to show.

## 3. Proofs That Count

One of the key contributions of this paper is a new formalism for proving program correctness, which we call *counting proofs*. A counting proof consists of a *counting automaton* and an *inductive annotation*. The automaton defines a set of traces and determines *what to count* (by associating counter actions to transitions in the automaton). The inductive annotation is a "correctness proof" for the counting automaton, which shows that every trace accepted by the automaton satisfies a given specification. Thus, we may prove the correctness of a program $\mathcal{P}$ by exhibiting a counting proof such that all traces of $\mathcal{P}$ belong to the counting automaton associated with the proof. In this section, we give a formal definition of our notion of counting proof.

### Preliminaries

First, we define some terminology for our program model. We fix a (possibly infinite) set $S$ of *memory states* (usually defined as valuations assigning values to a finite set of global and local variables), a set $\Sigma$ of *program statements*, and a *semantic function* $[\![\cdot]\!] : \Sigma \to 2^{S \times S}$ which interprets each program statement as a relation between memory states. A *trace* is a sequence of statements (i.e., a word in $\Sigma^*$). Intuitively, we will think of a program as a set of traces; this allows us to abstract away from the control structure of the program, which may be complicated.

We fix a set of *program assertions*, which is denoted $\Phi$, as well as an *entailment relation* $\models \subseteq S \times \Phi$. For $s \in S$ and $\varphi \in \Phi$, $s \models \varphi$ indicates that the assertion $\varphi$ holds in state $s$. A *(pre/post) specification* for $\mathcal{P}$ consists of a pair $\psi_{\mathsf{pre}}/\psi_{\mathsf{post}} \in \Phi$ indicating a *precondition* and *postcondition*. In the following, it will frequently be convenient to consider program assertions over an extended vocabulary that includes a fresh set of $\mathbb{N}$-sorted variable symbols $V$ (depending on the application at hand, such a variable symbol may be interpreted as the values of some counter variables, or as the number of tokens on a place of a Petri net (Section 7)). The set of such *extended program assertions* will be denoted $\Phi^V$.

For a statement $\sigma \in \Sigma$ and assertions $\varphi, \varphi'$, we use the typical Hoare notation $\{\varphi\}\ \sigma\ \{\varphi'\}$ to denote that for every $s, s'$ such that $s \models \varphi$ and $\langle s, s'\rangle \in [\![\sigma]\!]$, we have $s' \models \varphi'$. We extend this notation to sequences of statements in the obvious way.

### Counting proofs

We may now introduce the definition of counting proofs. We start by defining counting automata, which are finite automata augmented with zero or more counter variables which can be incremented, decremented, and tested.

**Definition 3.1** (Counting automaton) A (deterministic) *counting automaton* is a 6-tuple $A = \langle Q, n, q_0, \mathbf{k}_0, \delta, \Omega\rangle$ where $Q$ is a finite set of states, $n \in \mathbb{N}$ is the *dimension* of the automaton (i.e., the number of counters used by the automaton), $q_0 \in Q$ is an initial state, $\mathbf{k}_0 \in \mathbb{N}^n$ is an initial vector, $\Omega : Q \to 2^{\mathbb{N}^n}$ is a mapping that takes each state to an upwards closed[1] set of final (accepting) vectors, and $\delta : Q \times \Sigma \rightharpoonup Q \times \mathsf{Act}^n$ is a partial function which maps (state, program statement) pairs to pairs consisting of a successor state and an action for each counter, where $\mathsf{Act} = \{\mathsf{inc}, \mathsf{dec}, \mathsf{nop}, \mathsf{tst}\}$. Note that since $\delta$ is partial, not every state is associated with a transition for each program statement. ⌟

**Remark 3.2** A special case of particular interest is when the acceptance condition of a counting automaton $A = \langle Q, n, q_0, \mathbf{k}_0, \delta, \Omega\rangle$ is specified by a set of final states $F \subseteq Q$ (rather than a mapping $\Omega$ from states to upwards-closed sets of final vectors). This case is accommodated by setting $\Omega(q) = \mathbb{N}^n$ for every final state $q \in F$ and $\Omega(q') = \emptyset$ for every non-final state $q' \notin F$. This special case is used frequently in this paper, and in diagrams of counting automata we will use double circles to denote final states.

We also remark that nondeterministic finite automata are a special case of counting automata, where the dimension of the counting automaton is 0. Note that $\mathbb{N}^0$ is a singleton set, and so for any state $q$, the only choices for $\Omega(q)$ are $\mathbb{N}^0$ and $\emptyset$ (i.e., 0-dimensional counting automata always fall into the case described above, where the acceptance condition is determined by a set of final states). ⌟

We now introduce some additional terminology for counting automata. Let $A = \langle Q, n, q_0, \mathbf{k}_0, \delta, \Omega\rangle$ be a counting automaton. A *configuration* of $A$ consists of a pair $\langle q, \mathbf{k}\rangle$, where $q \in Q$ is a state and $\mathbf{k} \in \mathbb{N}^n$ is a valuation for each counter. The *initial configuration* is $\langle q_0, \mathbf{k}_0\rangle$, and any configuration $\langle q, \mathbf{k}\rangle$ where $\mathbf{k} \in \Omega(q)$ is a *final configuration*. We lift $\delta$ to a partial transition function on configurations as follows:

$$\delta(\langle q, (k_1, k_2, ..., k_n)\rangle, c) \triangleq \langle q', (k_1', k_2', ..., k_n')\rangle$$

if $\delta(q, (k_1, k_2, ..., k_n)) = \langle q', (\alpha_1, \alpha_2, ..., \alpha_n)\rangle$ and each $k_i'$ is defined as

$$k_i' \triangleq \begin{cases} k_i + 1 & \text{if } \alpha_i = \mathsf{inc} \\ k_i - 1 & \text{if } \alpha_i = \mathsf{dec} \wedge k_i > 0 \\ k_i & \text{if } \alpha_i = \mathsf{nop} \\ k_i & \text{if } \alpha_i = \mathsf{tst} \wedge k_i > 0 \\ \text{undefined} & \text{otherwise} \end{cases}$$

We lift $\delta$ to a partial transition function $\delta^*$ on statement sequences in the obvious way. A trace $w \in \Sigma^*$ is *accepted* by $A$ if $\delta^*(\langle q_0, \mathbf{k}_0\rangle, w)$ is a final configuration. The set of all traces accepted by $A$ is denoted $\mathcal{L}(A)$.

We may now move on to our definition of an inductive annotation. In essence, an inductive annotation is a Floyd/Hoare proof.

**Definition 3.3** (Annotation) Let $A = \langle Q, n, q_0, \mathbf{k}_0, \delta, \Omega\rangle$ be a counting automaton. Let $\mathtt{K} = \{\mathtt{k}_1, ..., \mathtt{k}_n\}$ be a set of distinguished $\mathbb{N}$-sorted variable symbols. An *annotation* is a map $\varphi : Q \to \Phi^{\mathtt{K}}$. We say $\varphi$ is *inductive* if for all $q, q' \in Q$, $\sigma \in \Sigma$, and $\mathbf{k}, \mathbf{k}' \in \mathbb{N}^n$ such that $\delta(\langle q, \mathbf{k}\rangle, \sigma) = \langle q', \mathbf{k}'\rangle$ the Hoare triple

$$\{\varphi(q)[\mathbf{k}]\}\ \sigma\ \{\varphi(q')[\mathbf{k}']\}$$

holds (where for an assertion $\psi$ and vector $\mathbf{k} = (k_1, ..., k_n) \in \mathbb{N}^n$, $\psi[\mathbf{k}]$ denotes the formula obtained by replacing each $\mathtt{k}_i$ with the corresponding element $k_i$ of the vector $\mathbf{k}$). ⌟

Finally, we may define a counting proof as a pair consisting of a counting automaton and an inductive annotation for it.

**Definition 3.4** (Counting proof) A *counting proof* is a pair $\langle A, \varphi\rangle$ consisting of a counting automaton $A = \langle Q, n, q_0, \mathbf{k}_0, \delta, \Omega\rangle$ and an inductive annotation $\varphi$ for $A$.

We say that $\langle A, \varphi\rangle$ *satisfies* a given specification $\psi_{\mathsf{pre}}/\psi_{\mathsf{post}}$ if the following two conditions hold:

(i) $\psi_{\mathsf{pre}} \models \varphi(q_0)[\mathbf{k}_0]$
(ii) For all $q \in Q$ and all $\mathbf{k}_f \in \Omega(q)$, we have $\varphi(q)[\mathbf{k}_f] \models \psi_{\mathsf{post}}$.

⌟

We now justify using counting proofs as proof objects. Recall that our use of counting proofs is the following (informal) proof rule: *Suppose that $\mathcal{P}$ is a program, $\langle A, \varphi\rangle$ is a counting proof which satisfies the specification $\psi_{\mathsf{pre}}/\psi_{\mathsf{post}}$, and that every trace of $\mathcal{P}$ is accepted by $A$. Then $\mathcal{P}$ satisfies the specification $\psi_{\mathsf{pre}}/\psi_{\mathsf{post}}$.* For this proof rule to be sound, we must show that every trace in $\mathcal{L}(A)$ satisfies the specification $\psi_{\mathsf{pre}}/\psi_{\mathsf{post}}$. With this goal in mind, we first prove a lemma.

**Lemma 3.5** Let $A = \langle Q, n, q_0, \mathbf{k}_0, \delta, \Omega\rangle$ be a counting automaton, and let $\varphi$ be an inductive annotation for $A$. Let $\tau \in \Sigma^*$. If $q, q', \mathbf{k}, \mathbf{k}'$ are such that $\delta^*(\langle q, \mathbf{k}\rangle, \tau) = \langle q', \mathbf{k}'\rangle$, then the following Hoare triple holds:

$$\{\varphi(q)[\mathbf{k}]\}\ \tau\ \{\varphi(q')[\mathbf{k}']\}$$

⌟

*Proof.* By induction on $\tau$. The base case ($\tau$ is empty) is trivial. The induction step follows from Definition 3.3 and the sequential composition rule for Hoare logic.

□

We may now state the main result of this section: a soundness theorem which justifies our proof rule.

**Theorem 3.6** Let $\langle A, \varphi\rangle$ be a counting proof with $A = \langle Q, n, q_0, \mathbf{k}_0, \delta, \Omega\rangle$, and let $\psi_{\mathsf{pre}}$ and $\psi_{\mathsf{post}}$ be assertions such that

[1] Recall that a set of vectors $V$ is upwards closed if for all $\mathbf{v} \in V$ and all $\mathbf{v}'$ such that $\mathbf{v} \leq \mathbf{v}'$, we have $\mathbf{v}' \in V$.

$\langle A, \varphi \rangle$ satisfies $\psi_{\mathsf{pre}}/\psi_{\mathsf{post}}$. Then for any $\tau \in \mathcal{L}(A)$, $\tau$ satisfies the Hoare triple $\{\psi_{\mathsf{pre}}\}\ \tau\ \{\psi_{\mathsf{post}}\}$. ⌟

*Proof.* Follows from Lemma 3.5, Definition 3.4, the definition of $\mathcal{L}(A)$, and the consequence rule of Hoare logic. □

## 4. Constructing Counting Proofs

We now consider the problem of automatically synthesizing a counting proof which certifies that a given (finite) set of traces $Tr \subseteq \Sigma^*$ is correct with respect to a given specification $\psi_{\mathsf{pre}}/\psi_{\mathsf{post}}$. Our algorithm for constructing counting proofs is divided into two parts. The first part is a decision procedure which determines whether a counting proof of a given "size" exists for a given set of traces and specification (here "size" should be understood informally). The second part is a search procedure, which repeatedly calls the decision procedure on different candidate sizes until a proof is found, and attempts to find the smallest proof possible. We start by describing the decision procedure, and then discuss the search procedure.

The idea behind our proof construction procedure is to encode the proof construction problem as a formula $\Psi$ and use an off-the-shelf SMT solver to find a model for $\Psi$. From any such model, we may extract a counting proof $\langle A, \varphi \rangle$ which satisfies $\psi_{\mathsf{pre}}/\psi_{\mathsf{post}}$ and such that $Tr \subseteq \mathcal{L}(A)$.

Since the goal is to develop a decision procedure for proof construction, we must limit the program statement language and the language of program assertions to a decidable logic. A *convex linear real formula* is a conjunction of a finite number of linear inequalities over a set of real variables with real coefficients. The number of inequalities appearing in a convex linear real formula $\psi$ will be called the *size* of $\psi$, and denoted $|\psi|$.

In this section we fix a set of traces $Tr$ and a pre/post specification $\psi_{\mathsf{pre}}/\psi_{\mathsf{post}}$. We will assume that $\psi_{\mathsf{pre}}$ and $\psi_{\mathsf{post}}$ are convex linear real formulae, and that every program statement can be expressed as a convex linear real formula. For simplicity, we will also assume that $Tr$ consists of a single trace $\tau = \sigma_1 \cdots \sigma_{|\tau|}$ (the generalization to multiple traces is straightforward).

Let $\langle A, \varphi \rangle$ be a counting proof, with $A = \langle Q, n, q_0, \mathbf{k}_0, \delta, \Omega \rangle$. The "size" of $\langle A, \varphi \rangle$ is determined by four numbers:

1. The number of states, $\#\mathsf{States}(A, \varphi) \triangleq |Q|$
2. The dimension of $A$, $\mathsf{dim}(A, \varphi) \triangleq n$
3. The size of the assertions used in the annotation $\varphi$,
$$\#\mathsf{Atoms}(A, \varphi) \triangleq \sum_{q \in Q} |\varphi(q)|$$
4. The number of minimal final vectors:
$$\#\mathsf{Min}(A, \varphi) \triangleq \sum_{q \in Q} |\{\mathbf{v} : \nexists \mathbf{v}' \in \Omega(q).\mathbf{v}' < \mathbf{v}\}|$$

Our decision procedure will take four additional parameters as input $\overline{Q}, \overline{N}, \overline{K}, \overline{M} \in \mathbb{N}$, corresponding (in order) to the four components of counting proof size described above. The idea behind this algorithm is to construct a QF_UFNRA[2] formula which is satisfiable iff there exists a counting proof $\langle A, \varphi \rangle$ such that $A$ accepts $\tau$, $A$ satisfies $\psi_{\mathsf{pre}}/\psi_{\mathsf{post}}$, $\#\mathsf{States}(A, \varphi) = \overline{Q}$, $\mathsf{dim}(A, \varphi) = \overline{N}$, $\#\mathsf{Assert}(A, \varphi) = \overline{K}$, and $\#\mathsf{Min}(A, \varphi) = \overline{M}$.

For presentation purposes, we assume that $\overline{N} = \overline{M} = 1$ and that we are searching for a proof with $\overline{K} = \overline{Q}$ with one atom per state (but that $\overline{Q}$ is arbitrary). The generalization of the construction to arbitrary values of the parameters $\overline{N}$, $\overline{M}$, and $\overline{K}$ is straightforward. The construction of the QF_UFNRA formula follows.

[2] Quantifier-free non-linear real arithmetic formulae with uninterpreted function symbols

**Automaton constraints** Without loss of generality, we may construct a counting proof with state space $Q = \{1, ..., \overline{Q}\}$. Recall that the transition function of a 1-dimensional counting automaton over the state space $Q$ is a partial function

$$\delta : Q \times \Sigma \rightharpoonup Q \times \mathsf{Act},$$

where $\mathsf{Act} = \{\mathsf{inc}, \mathsf{dec}, \mathsf{nop}, \mathsf{tst}\}$ is a set of counter actions. For our encoding, we introduce for each $\sigma \in \Sigma(\tau) \triangleq \{\sigma_1, ..., \sigma_{|\tau|}\}$ a pair of uninterpreted function symbols

$$\delta_\sigma : Q \to Q$$
$$\alpha_\sigma : Q \to \mathsf{Act}$$

We now encode the constraint that the counting automaton accepts the trace $\tau$. We introduce a set of integer variables $q_0, ..., q_{|\tau|}, k_0, ..., k_{|\tau|}$; the interpretation of these variables is that, after reading the prefix $\sigma_1\sigma_2 \cdots \sigma_i$ of the trace $\tau$, the state of the counter automaton is $q_i$, and the value of the counter is $k_i$ ($q_0$ and $k_0$ represent the initial state and initial value of the counter). This interpretation is encoded by the following constraints:

$$\Psi_{\delta\text{-state}} \triangleq \bigwedge_{i=1}^{|\tau|} \delta_{\sigma_i}(q_{i-1}) = q_i$$

$$\Psi_{\delta\text{-counter}} \triangleq k_0 \geq 0 \wedge \bigwedge_{i=1}^{|\tau|} k_i = k_{i-1} + \mathsf{incr}(\alpha_{\sigma_i}(q_{i-1}))$$

where

$$\mathsf{incr}(\alpha) \triangleq \begin{cases} 1 & \text{if } \alpha = \mathsf{inc} \\ -1 & \text{if } \alpha = \mathsf{dec} \\ 0 & \text{otherwise} \end{cases}$$

The preceding constraints ensure that $\tau$ labels a path through the counting automaton and that at each step along this path $k_i$ is updated appropriately. Another constraint is required for $\tau$ to be accepted by the counting automaton, which is that none of the transitions that label the accepting path may block (recall that the dec and tst counter actions block when the counter is 0). This non-blocking condition is enforced by the following constraint:

$$\Psi_{\delta\text{-block}} \triangleq \bigwedge_{i=1}^{|\tau|} \left(\alpha_{\sigma_i}(q_{i-1}) \in \{\mathsf{dec}, \mathsf{tst}\} \Rightarrow k_{i-1} \geq 1\right)$$

The last requirement to ensure that $\tau$ is accepted by the counting automaton is that we must synthesize an upwards closed set of final vectors for the state $q_{|\tau|}$. For the case of 1-dimensional counting automata, an upwards closed set is completely determined by a single natural number, which is the lower bound on the set. Thus, we introduce an integer variable $k_{\mathit{final}}$ and create a constraint that the value of the counter after reading $\tau$ is greater than or equal to $k_{\mathit{final}}$:

$$\Psi_{\mathsf{accept}} \triangleq k_{\mathit{final}} \leq k_{|\tau|}$$

Collecting these constraints, we have

$$\Psi_A \triangleq \Psi_{\delta\text{-state}} \wedge \Psi_{\delta\text{-counter}} \wedge \Psi_{\delta\text{-block}} \wedge \Psi_{\mathsf{accept}}$$

Models of $\Psi_A$ correspond to $\overline{Q}$-state, 1-dimensional counting automata which accepts the trace $\tau$.

**Annotation constraints** We now consider the constraints used to construct the inductive annotation of the counting automaton. We use a constraint-based technique to synthesize linear invariants, as described in [15].

Fix a set of program variables $X = \{x_1, ..., x_{|X|}\}$. For each program variable $x_i$, we introduce an uninterpreted function symbol $C_{x_i}$ of sort $Q \to \mathbb{R}$. We also introduce two additional uninterpreted function symbols $C_k, C_1$ of sort $Q \to \mathbb{R}$. For a given state $q \in Q$, $C_{x_i}(q)$ will be the coefficient of $x_i$, $C_{\mathtt{k}}(q)$ will be the coefficient of $\mathtt{k}$, $C_1(q)$ will be the constant coefficient in the linear inequality assigned to $q$. That is, for $q \in Q$, the annotation at $q$ will be:

$$\mathsf{inv}(q) \triangleq \Big(\sum_{i=1}^{|X|} C_{x_i}(q) \cdot x_i\Big) + C_{\mathtt{k}}(q) \cdot \mathtt{k} + C_1(q) \leq 0$$

For any statement $\sigma \in \Sigma$, we use $\mathsf{tf}(\sigma)$ to denote the *transition formula* of $\sigma$, which is a formula over the variables $x_1, ..., x_{|X|}$ and their "primed" copies $x'_1, ..., x'_{|X|}$ that represents the meaning of the statement $\sigma$. For a counter machine action $\alpha \in \mathsf{Act}$, we use $\mathsf{tf}(\alpha)$ to denote the transition formula corresponding to $\alpha$, defined below as:

$$\mathsf{tf}(\alpha) \triangleq \begin{cases} \mathtt{k}' = \mathtt{k} + 1 & \text{if } \alpha = \mathsf{inc} \\ \mathtt{k} \geq 1 \land \mathtt{k}' = \mathtt{k} - 1 & \text{if } \alpha = \mathsf{dec} \\ \mathtt{k} \geq 1 \land \mathtt{k}' = \mathtt{k} & \text{if } \alpha = \mathsf{tst} \\ \mathtt{k}' = \mathtt{k} & \text{if } \alpha = \mathsf{nop} \end{cases}$$

We may now define the consecution constraints, which ensure that the annotation is inductive. We define a consecution constraint for each $i \in \{1, ..., |\tau|\}$ as follows:

$$\Psi_i \triangleq (\forall \mathtt{k}, \mathtt{k}', X, X')(\mathsf{inv}(q_{i-1}) \land \mathsf{tf}(\sigma_i) \land \mathsf{tf}(\alpha_{\sigma_i}(q_{i-1})) \Rightarrow \mathsf{inv}(q_i)')$$

where $\mathsf{inv}(q_i)'$ denotes the formula obtained from $\mathsf{inv}(q_i)$ by replacing each variable $x_i$ with its primed copy $x'_i$ and $k$ with $k'$.

The last annotation constraints ensure that the counting proof satisfies the specification $\psi_{\mathsf{pre}}/\psi_{\mathsf{post}}$:

$$\Psi_{\mathsf{init}} \triangleq (\forall \mathtt{k}, X)(\psi_{\mathsf{pre}} \Rightarrow \mathsf{inv}(q_0))$$

$$\Psi_{\mathsf{final}} \triangleq (\forall \mathtt{k}, X)(\mathsf{inv}(q_{|\tau|}) \land \mathtt{k} \geq k_{\mathit{final}} \Rightarrow \psi_{\mathsf{post}})$$

The annotation constraints defined in this section all feature universal quantification. However, all the formulae defined in this section belong to a class of formulae for which the universal quantifiers can be replaced by existential quantifiers by applying Farkas' lemma (see [15] for details). We will use $\Psi_i^{\exists}$, $\Psi_{\mathsf{init}}^{\exists}$ and $\Psi_{\mathsf{final}}^{\exists}$ to denote the corresponding transformed formulae.

Finally, we collect the annotation constraints into a single formula $\Psi_\varphi$:

$$\Psi_\varphi \triangleq \Psi_{\mathsf{init}}^{\exists} \land \Psi_{\mathsf{final}}^{\exists} \land \Big(\bigwedge_{i=1}^{|\tau|} \Psi_i^{\exists}\Big)$$

**Counting proof extraction** We conjoin the automaton and annotation constraints to arrive at a formula $\Psi$ whose models correspond to counting proofs:

$$\Psi \triangleq \Psi_A \land \Psi_\varphi$$

Suppose that $\mathcal{M}$ is a model of $\Psi$. For a term *term*, we use $\mathit{term}^{\mathcal{M}}$ to denote the interpretation of *term* in the model $\mathcal{M}$. A counting proof can be constructed as follows:

$$Q \triangleq \{1, ..., \overline{Q}\}$$

$$q_0 \triangleq q_0^{\mathcal{M}}$$

$$\mathbf{k}_0 \triangleq k_0^{\mathcal{M}}$$

$$\Omega \triangleq \lambda q. \begin{cases} \{k : k \geq k_{\mathit{final}}\} & \text{if } q = q_{n+1}^{\mathcal{M}} \\ \emptyset & \text{otherwise} \end{cases}$$

$$\delta \triangleq \lambda \langle q, \sigma \rangle . \begin{cases} \langle \delta_\sigma(q)^{\mathcal{M}}, \alpha_\sigma(q)^{\mathcal{M}} \rangle & \text{if } \exists i. q = q_i \land \sigma = \sigma_{i-1} \\ \text{undefined} & \text{otherwise} \end{cases}$$

$$\varphi \triangleq \lambda q. \Big(\sum_{i=1}^{|X|} C_{x_i}(q)^{\mathcal{M}} \cdot x_i\Big) + C_{\mathtt{k}}(q)^{\mathcal{M}} \cdot \mathtt{k} + C_1(q)^{\mathcal{M}} \leq 0$$

The following proposition states that our encoding is, in a sense, complete.

**Proposition 4.1** Let *Tr* be a finite set of traces (such that each command is expressible as a convex linear real formula) and let $\psi_{\mathsf{pre}}/\psi_{\mathsf{post}}$ be a (convex linear real) specification. Let $\overline{N}, \overline{Q}, \overline{K}, \overline{M} \in \mathbb{N}$. The problem of *determining whether there exists a counting proof* $\langle A, \varphi \rangle$ *that satisfies the specification* $\psi_{\mathsf{pre}}/\psi_{\mathsf{post}}$*, such that* $Tr \subseteq \mathcal{L}(A)$*, and such that* $\#\mathit{States}(A, \varphi) = \overline{Q}$*,* $\mathit{dim}(A, \varphi) = \overline{N}$*,* $\#\mathit{Assert}(A, \varphi) = \overline{K}$*, and* $\#\mathit{Min}(A, \varphi) = \overline{M}$*, is decidable.* ⌟

### 4.1 Searching for Small Counting Proofs

The decision procedure presented in the preceding section suggests a simple algorithm for constructing a counting proof. Suppose we are given a set of traces *Tr* and a specification $\psi_{\mathsf{pre}}/\psi_{\mathsf{post}}$. First, we check whether some $\tau \in Tr$ violates the specification $\psi_{\mathsf{pre}}/\psi_{\mathsf{post}}$ (this can be accomplished with an SMT query). If such a $\tau$ exists, we are done: no proof exists. Otherwise, enumerate the space of parameters $\langle \overline{N}, \overline{Q}, \overline{K}, \overline{M} \rangle \in \mathbb{N}^4$, applying the decision procedure described in the previous section until a counting proof is found.

The termination of this simple algorithm relies on the following observation:

**Observation 4.2** Let $Tr$ be a set of traces and let $\psi_{\mathsf{pre}}/\psi_{\mathsf{post}}$ be a specification such that for each $\tau \in Tr$, $\{\psi_{\mathsf{pre}}\}\ \tau\ \{\psi_{\mathsf{post}}\}$. Then there is a counting proof $\langle A, \varphi \rangle$ which satisfies $\psi_{\mathsf{pre}}/\psi_{\mathsf{post}}$ and which accepts every trace in *Tr*. ⌟

The intuition behind this observation is that we can always find a counting proof where the counting automaton is 0-dimensional (i.e., a counting automaton that does not use counters) and shaped like a prefix tree. The existence of an inductive annotation for such an automaton is a consequence of Farkas' lemma.

While this observation is enough to prove termination of our proof synthesis procedure, it is not very satisfying: it says that in the worst case, we can always construct a counting proof that does not, in fact, count. The key insight behind our counting proof synthesis procedure is that we can constrain the parameters given to the decision problem to force an SMT solver to discover a non-trivial counting argument. For example, consider the sample trace $\tau$ from Section 1. Setting $\overline{Q} = 2, \overline{K} = 2, \overline{N} = \overline{M} = 1$, we can force the SMT to synthesize a non-trivial counter, simply because there is no 0-dimensional counting proof for these traces that only uses 2 states (so, by virtue of the fact that our decision procedure *will* find a 2-state proof if one exists, it must find a proof that uses a non-trivial counting argument).

In the remainder of this section, we present a refinement on the simple algorithm discussed above, which fixes a particular way of enumerating the parameter space. The intuition behind this refinement is that we want to synthesize a counting proof that minimizes the sum of the number of states ($\overline{Q}$) and the number of assertions ($\overline{K}$).[3] Our aim in presenting this algorithm is not to present a practical proof construction procedure, but rather a theoretical algorithm capable of synthesizing proofs that are (in a sense) optimal. In practice, one would expect a heuristic-based method for exploring the

[3] This algorithm can be adapted to minimize any objective function which is strictly increasing in $\overline{Q}$ and $\overline{K}$.

parameter space (which cannot necessarily guarantee optimality) would be more effective.

Observation 4.2 yields a coarse upper bound on the sum of the number of states and atoms used in a counting proof for a given set of traces *Tr* of $2 \cdot \sum_{\tau \in Tr} |\tau|$. Since we have an upper bound on $\overline{Q} + \overline{K}$, the parameter space $\overline{Q}, \overline{K} \in \mathbb{N} \times \mathbb{N}$ can be searched efficiently using binary search. The termination of this algorithm relies on the following proposition:

**Proposition 4.3** Let *Tr* be a finite set of traces, $\psi_{\mathsf{pre}}/\psi_{\mathsf{post}}$ be a specification, and $Z \in \mathbb{N}$. The problem of determining whether there exists a counting proof $\langle A, \varphi\rangle$ that satisfies $\psi_{\mathsf{pre}}/\psi_{\mathsf{post}}$ such that $Tr \subseteq \mathcal{L}(A)$, and such that $\#\mathsf{Atoms}(A,\varphi) + \#\mathsf{States}(A,\varphi) = Z$ is decidable. ⌟

This proposition is not trivial, because even though fixing the size of $\#\mathsf{Atoms}(A,\varphi) + \#\mathsf{States}(A,\varphi)$ implies finitely many choices for $\overline{Q}$ and $\overline{K}$, the space for the remaining parameters $\overline{N}$ and $\overline{M}$ is infinite and cannot be searched exhaustively. The following two lemmas imply that we may place a finite upper bound on $\overline{N}$ and $\overline{M}$ once *Tr* and $\overline{Q}$ are fixed.

**Lemma 4.4** Let $A = \langle Q, n, q_0, \mathbf{k}_0, \delta, \Omega\rangle$ be a counting automaton, and let $Tr$ be a finite set of traces which are accepted by $A$. There exists a mapping $\Omega' : Q \to 2^{\mathbb{N}^n}$ such that the counting proof $\langle A', \varphi\rangle$ with $A' = \langle Q, n, q_0, \mathbf{k}_0, \delta, \Omega'\rangle$ satisfies

$$\#\mathsf{Min}(A', \varphi) \leq |Tr|$$

and $Tr \subseteq \mathcal{L}(A')$. ⌟

*Proof.* Intuitively, we define $\Omega'$ to be the upwards closure of the set of configurations that result from reading the traces in $Tr$. Formally, for any $q \in Q$, define

$$\Omega'(q) \triangleq \{\mathbf{k}' \in \mathbb{N}^n : (\exists \tau \in Tr, \exists \mathbf{k} \in \mathbb{N}^n)(\mathbf{k} \leq \mathbf{k}' \wedge \delta^*(\langle q_0, \mathbf{k}_0\rangle, \tau) = \langle q, \mathbf{k}\rangle)\}$$

□

**Lemma 4.5** Let $\langle \varphi, A\rangle$ be a counting proof, with $A = \langle Q, n, q_0, \mathbf{k}_0, \delta, \Omega\rangle$. There exists a counting proof $\langle \varphi', A'\rangle$ such that $A'$ recognizes the same language as $A$, and $A'$ has dimension at most $3^{|\mathsf{dom}(\delta)|}$ (where $|\mathsf{dom}(\delta)|$ indicates the cardinality of the domain of the partial transition function $\delta$). ⌟

*Proof.* Suppose that $n > 3^{|\mathsf{dom}(\delta)|}$. By the pigeonhole principle, there exists distinct counters $s, t \in \{1, ..., n\}$ which agree on all their actions. That is, for any $q \in Q, \sigma \in \Sigma$, if $\delta(q, \sigma) = (\alpha_1, ..., \alpha_n)$, then $\alpha_s = \alpha_t$. Without loss of generality, we can assume that $s = 1$ and $t = 2$.

Letting $(k_1, ..., k_n) = \mathbf{k}_0$, we define $\Delta \triangleq k_1 - k_2$. Without loss of generality, we may assume that $\Delta \geq 0$. We construct an $(n-1)$-dimensional counting automaton $A' = \langle Q, n-1, q_0, \mathbf{k}_0', \delta', \Omega'\rangle$ and an inductive annotation $\varphi'$ as follows:

- $\mathbf{k}_0' \triangleq (k_2, ..., k_n)$, where $(k_1, ..., k_n) = \mathbf{k}_0$
- For any $q, \sigma$ such that $\delta(q, \sigma) = \langle q', (\alpha_1, ..., \alpha_n)\rangle$, we define

$$\delta'(q, \sigma) \triangleq \langle q', (\alpha_2, ..., \alpha_n)\rangle$$

- For any $q \in Q$, we define

$$\Omega'(q) \triangleq \{(\min\{k_1 - \Delta, k_2\}, k_3, ..., k_n) : (k_1, ..., k_n) \in \Omega(q)\}$$

- For any $q \in Q$, we define

$$\varphi'(q) \triangleq (\exists \mathrm{k}_1)(\mathrm{k}_2 - \Delta = \mathrm{k}_1 \wedge \varphi(q))$$

(the quantifier $(\exists \mathrm{k}_1)$ can be eliminated to yield a convex linear real formula). □

The proof of Proposition 4.3 follows easily from the preceding two lemmata.

We conclude this section with an algorithm summarizing the search procedure described above. In this algorithm, we use constraints(...) to denote the formula constructed in the previous section, and extract-proof)$(\Psi)$ to denote the counting proof extracted from a model of a formula $\Psi$.

**Input**: $Tr, \psi_{\mathsf{pre}}, \psi_{\mathsf{post}}$ such that for all $\tau \in Tr$, $\{\psi_{\mathsf{pre}}\}\ \tau\ \{\psi_{\mathsf{post}}\}$
**Output**: A counting proof $\langle A, \varphi\rangle$ which satisfies $\psi_{\mathsf{pre}}/\psi_{\mathsf{post}}$ and with $Tr \subseteq \mathcal{L}(A)$
$min \leftarrow 2$;
$max \leftarrow 2 \cdot \sum_{\tau \in |Tr} |\tau|$;
$\overline{M} = |Tr|$;
/* Binary search for minimal proof */
**while** $max \neq min$ **do**
  $mid \leftarrow (max + min)/2$;
  $\overline{Q} \leftarrow mid - 1$;
  $\overline{K} \leftarrow 1$;
  $\overline{N} \leftarrow 3^{|\Sigma(Tr)| \cdot \overline{Q}}$; // $\Sigma(Tr) = \bigcup\{\Sigma(\tau) : \tau \in Tr\}$
  $\Psi \leftarrow \mathsf{constraints}(Tr, \psi_{\mathsf{pre}}, \psi_{\mathsf{post}}, \overline{N}, \overline{Q}, \overline{K}, \overline{M})$;
  /* Search for proof of size $\overline{Q} + \overline{K}$ */
  **while** $\Psi$ *is unsatisfiable and* $\overline{Q} \geq 1$ **do**
    $(\overline{K}, \overline{Q}) \leftarrow (\overline{K} + 1, \overline{Q} - 1)$;
    $\overline{N} \leftarrow 3^{|\Sigma(Tr)| \cdot \overline{Q}}$;
    $\Psi \leftarrow \mathsf{constraints}(Tr, \psi_{\mathsf{pre}}, \psi_{\mathsf{post}}, \overline{N}, \overline{Q}, \overline{K}, \overline{M})$;
  **end**
  **if** $\Psi$ *is satisfiable* **then**
    $\langle A, \varphi\rangle \leftarrow \mathsf{extract\text{-}proof}(\Psi)$;
    $max \leftarrow mid$;
  **end**
  $min \leftarrow mid + 1$;
**end**
**return** $\langle A, \varphi\rangle$

**Algorithm 1:** Counting proof construction

## 5. Control Flow Nets

In the preceding, we have considered the control structure of a program to be a black box. In order to implement the algorithm outlined in Figure 1, we need an effective procedure for checking whether a given counting automaton accepts all the traces of a given program. In this section, we introduce *control flow nets*, an expressive program model that features infinite control, but for which the inclusion check is decidable (Section 6).

We begin by introducing some notions from Petri net theory, which form the basis of control flow nets.

**Definition 5.1** (Petri net structure) A *Petri net structure* is a tuple $N = \langle P, T, \mathcal{E}\rangle$, where $P$ is a finite set of *places*, $T$ is a finite set of *transitions*, and $\mathcal{E} \subseteq (P \times T) \cup (T \times P)$ is an *incidence relation* connecting places to transitions and vice-versa. ⌟

We now recall some standard definitions for Petri nets. Let $N = \langle P, T, \mathcal{E}\rangle$ be a Petri net structure. Given a transition $t \in T$, we define its *pre-set*, ${}^\bullet t$, and *post-set*, $t^\bullet$, as the set of places with incoming/outgoing arcs to $t$:

$${}^\bullet t \triangleq \{p : \langle p, t\rangle \in \mathcal{E}\} \qquad t^\bullet \triangleq \{p : \langle t, p\rangle \in \mathcal{E}\}$$

A *marking* of $N$ is a map $m : P \to \mathbb{N}$. Given a marking $m$ and a transition $t \in T$, we say that $t$ is *enabled in* $m$ if for all $p \in {}^\bullet t$,

$m(p) \geq 1$. We write $m \xrightarrow{t} m'$ to denote that $t$ is enabled in $m$ and that for all $p$,

$$m'(p) = m(p) - |\{p\} \cap {}^{\bullet}t| + |\{p\} \cap t^{\bullet}|$$

For markings $m, m'$ we write $m \preceq m'$ if for all $p$, $m(p) \leq m'(p)$. A set of markings $M$ is *upwards closed* if for all $m \in M$ and all $m'$ such that $m \preceq m'$, we have $m' \in M$. Any upwards closed set of markings can be represented by its set of minimal elements, which is always finite.

We may now introduce our program model, *control flow nets*. Control flow nets are programs which have Petri nets as control structures. We may think of them as an infinite analogue of control flow graphs: just as a control flow graph is a finite automaton labelled by program statements, a control flow net is a Petri net structure with transitions labelled by program statements. A slightly unusual feature (although not without precedent [25]) is that we also include acceptance conditions for control flow nets – this enables us to view control flow nets as language recognition devices. Formally,

**Definition 5.2** (Control flow net) A *control flow net* is a tuple $\mathcal{P} = \langle P, T, \mathcal{E}, \ell, m_0, F\rangle$, where $\langle P, T, \mathcal{E}\rangle$ is a Petri net structure, $\ell : T \to \Sigma$ is an injective map which labels transitions with program statements, $m_0$ is an initial marking and $F$ is an upwards closed set of final markings. ⌟

Control flow nets are a very expressive program model. For example, Figure 3(b) depicts a control flow net for a concurrent program with arbitrarily many threads. With their foundations on Petri nets, modelling concurrency is a particularly strong suit for control flow nets, but they can also be useful for representing other control features. For example, Figure 4 depicts a control flow net where tokens are used to count the number of stack frames in a recursive program.

In view of our black-box strategy for counting proof synthesis, we conclude this section with a definition of the traces and correctness of a control flow net.

**Definition 5.3** (Correctness) A *trace* of a control flow net $\mathcal{P} = \langle P, T, \mathcal{E}, \ell, m_0, F\rangle$ is a sequence of statements $\tau = \sigma_1 ... \sigma_n \in \Sigma^*$ such that there exists transitions $t_1, ..., t_n$ where $\ell(t_1) = \sigma_1, \ldots, \ell(t_n) = \sigma_n$, and markings $m_1, ..., m_n$ where $m_n \in F$ such that

$$m_0 \xrightarrow{t_1} m_1 \xrightarrow{t_1} \cdots \xrightarrow{t_n} m_n \ .$$

The set of all traces of $\mathcal{P}$ is denoted $\mathcal{L}(\mathcal{P})$. Given a pre/postcondition pair $\psi_{\mathsf{pre}}/\psi_{\mathsf{post}}$, the control flow net $\mathcal{P}$ is *correct* if all of its traces are correct, i.e., if the Hoare triple $\{\psi_{\mathsf{pre}}\}\ \tau\ \{\psi_{\mathsf{post}}\}$ holds for all $\tau \in \mathcal{L}(\mathcal{P})$. ⌟

## 6. Proof Checking

A counting proof $\langle A, \varphi\rangle$ which satisfies a specification $\psi_{\mathsf{pre}}/\psi_{\mathsf{post}}$ represents a set of correct behaviours which are correct with respect to that specification. If every trace of a given program $\mathcal{P}$ is represented by $A$, this implies that $\mathcal{P}$ is correct. Thus, in order to check a counting proof, we must check the inclusion of the language of traces of a control flow net $\mathcal{P}$ inside the language of a counting automaton. In this section, we prove that this check is decidable and give a characterization of the computational complexity of proof checking.

First, we state our decidability result. The essence of the proof of this theorem is that counting proof checking can be reduced to Petri net reachability, which is known to be decidable [35].

**Theorem 6.1** Let $\mathcal{P} = \langle P, T, \mathcal{E}, \ell, m_0, F\rangle$ be a control flow net and let $A = \langle Q, n, q_0, \mathbf{k}_0, \delta, \Omega\rangle$ be a counting automaton. The problem of checking the inclusion $\mathcal{L}(\mathcal{P}) \subseteq \mathcal{L}(A)$ is decidable.

This result still holds even if we relax the accepting sets for control flow nets and/or counting automata to be semi-linear rather than upwards closed. ⌟

*Proof.* The proof proceeds by reduction to an inclusion problem for Petri net languages, a problem known to be reducible to Petri net reachability. It is sufficient to show that for any counting automaton we may construct a control flow net which recognizes the same language, which is a *deterministic* Petri net (by construction). From the point of view of language recognition, control flow nets are equivalent to $L$-type labelled Petri nets.[4] In [42] it is show that deterministic $L$-type Petri net languages are closed under compliment, and in [26], it is shown that the problem of checking the inclusion of an $L$-type Petri net language in a deterministic $L$-type Petri net language is decidable.

An example illustrating the construction of a control flow net from a counting automaton in the figure below, which depicts the control flow net associated with the counting automaton for the example in Section 1. Note that in this picture, the transition labelled $\Sigma$ represents three (parallel) transitions, one for each letter in $\Sigma = \{$`t++`, `s++`, `assume(s >= t)`$\}$. In the rest of this proof, we make the construction formal.

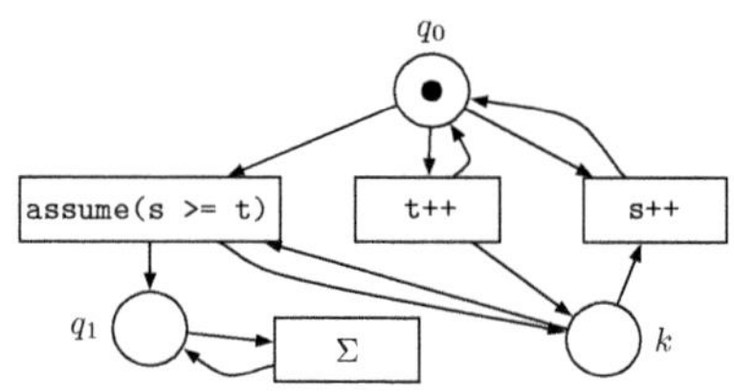


Let $A = \langle Q, n, q_0, \mathbf{k}_0, \delta, \Omega\rangle$ be a counting automaton. We define a control flow net $\mathcal{P}_A = \langle P, T, \mathcal{E}, \ell, m_0, F\rangle$ as follows. The places of $\mathcal{P}_A$ are defined to be the disjoint union of the set of states of $A$ and a set of $n$ distinguished "counter" places $p_1, ..., p_n$:

$$P = Q + \{p_1, ..., p_n\}$$

The transitions correspond to points in the domain of $\delta$:

$$T = \{\langle q, \sigma\rangle \in Q \times \Sigma : \delta(q, \sigma) \text{ is defined}\}$$

We define the incidence relation $\mathcal{E}$ indirectly, by defining the pre-set and post-set of every transition. Let $\langle q, \sigma\rangle \in T$ and suppose that $\delta(q, \sigma) = \langle q', (\alpha_1, ..., \alpha_n)\rangle$. Then we may define:

$${}^{\bullet}\langle q, \sigma\rangle = \{q\} \cup \{p_i : \alpha_i = \mathsf{dec} \lor \alpha_i = \mathsf{tst}\}$$

$$\langle q, \sigma\rangle^{\bullet} = \{q'\} \cup \{p_i : \alpha_i = \mathsf{inc} \lor \alpha_i = \mathsf{tst}\}$$

We define a map $\zeta$ from configurations of $A$ to markings of $\mathcal{P}_A$. For a given configuration $\langle q, (k_1, ..., k_n)\rangle$, we define

$$\zeta(q, (k_1, ..., k_n)) = \lambda p. \begin{cases} 1 & \text{if } p = q \\ k_i & \text{if } p = p_i \\ 0 & \text{otherwise} \end{cases}$$

We define the initial marking $m_0$ to be $\zeta(q_0, \mathbf{k}_0)$ and we define the (upwards closed) set of final markings $F$ by taking the image of the accepting configurations of $A$ under $\zeta$. The labelling function $\ell$ is defined by $\ell(q, \sigma) = \sigma$.

It is easy to prove that this mapping $\zeta$ from configurations of $A$ to markings of $\mathcal{P}_A$ is an isomorphism when restricted to the reachable configurations of $A$ and the reachable markings of $\mathcal{P}_A$. Lastly, it is clear to see that $\delta(q, \mathbf{k}) = \langle q', \mathbf{k}'\rangle$ iff $\zeta(q, \mathbf{k}) \to \zeta(q', \mathbf{k}')$, which completes the proof of equivalence. □

[4] There is a slight technical difference: the labelling function for labelled Petri nets is not required to be injective. We will, in fact, ignore the injectivity restriction in our construction.

### 6.1 Complexity of Proof Checking

The decidability of this language inclusion problem is of fundamental importance, because it justifies calling counting proofs "proofs." A desirable result would be that checking proofs is not only decidable but *efficiently* so. Theorem 6.1 relies on a reduction to Petri net reachability. This problem is at least EXPSPACE-hard, but the best known upper bound for its complexity is NONELEMENTARY. So, a natural question is: *can we do better than reducing to Petri net reachability*? The following theorem states that we can not in general: Petri net reachability and counting proof checking are equivalent from the perspective of computational complexity.

**Theorem 6.2** The Petri net reachability problem is polytime inter-reducible with the counting proof checking problem. ⌟

*Proof.* One direction of the proof is given in the proof of Theorem 6.1 (it is easy to prove that the reduction to reachability is polytime). For the other direction, we give a polytime reduction from the single-place zero-reachability problem to proof checking. This implies the result due to Lemma 4.1 in [24]. In fact, [24] states a slightly weaker result: that reachability is recursively reducible to single-place zero-reachability. However, it is easy to see that the reduction from the proof of [24] is polytime.

Consider a Petri net $G = \langle P, T, \mathcal{E}\rangle$, a marking $m$ of $G$, and a place $p \in P$. Given an initial marking $m_0$, we say that a place $p$ is zero-reachable if there exists a marking $m'$ which is reachable from $m_0$ and such that $m'(p) = 0$. We reduce the problem of checking zero-reachability of $p$ to counting proof checking by constructing a control flow net $\mathcal{P}$ and a counting automaton $A$ such that $A$ accepts all the traces of $\mathcal{P}$ iff $p$ is zero-reachable.

We suppose that $\mathsf{zr}$ is a new transition which does not belong to $T$. We take $\mathcal{P} = \langle P, T', \mathcal{E}, m_0, \ell, F\rangle$, where $T' = T \cup \{\mathsf{zr}\}$, $\ell$ is an arbitrary injective labelling, and $F$ is the set of all markings ($P$, $\mathcal{E}$, and $m$ are as above). Intuitively, $\mathcal{P}$ is just $G$ extended with a "do nothing" transition $\mathsf{zr}$, which can always fire.

We define a counting automaton $A = \langle \{q\}, n, q, \mathbf{k}_0, \delta, \Omega\rangle$ from $G$ as follows. Define $n \triangleq |P|$, and let $\mathit{place} : \{1, ..., n\} \to P$ be a bijection. The initial vector is defined to be $\mathbf{k}_0 \triangleq (k_1, ..., k_n)$, where for each $i$,

$$k_i = m_0(\mathit{place(i)})$$

The transition function is defined, for any $c \in \Sigma$ such that there is some $t \in T$ with $\ell(t) = c$, by

$$\delta(q, c) \triangleq \langle q, (\alpha_1, ..., \alpha_i)\rangle$$

where for each $i$

$$\alpha_i = \begin{cases} \mathsf{tst} & \text{if } \mathit{place}(i) \in {}^\bullet t \cap t^\bullet \\ \mathsf{dec} & \text{if } \mathit{place}(i) \in {}^\bullet t \\ \mathsf{inc} & \text{if } \mathit{place}(i) \in t^\bullet \\ \mathsf{nop} & \text{otherwise} \end{cases}$$

We also add another transition to $\delta$ for the distinguished "do nothing" transition $\mathsf{zr}$, except that instead of doing nothing, we check that $p$ is non-zero: with one exception: we define

$$\delta(q, \ell(\mathsf{zr})) \triangleq \langle q, (\alpha_1, ..., \alpha_n)\rangle$$

$$\alpha_i = \begin{cases} \mathsf{tst} & \text{if } \mathit{place}(i) = p \\ \mathsf{nop} & \text{otherwise} \end{cases}$$

Last, we define $\Omega$ by

$$\Omega(q) \triangleq \{(k_1, ..., k_n) \in \mathbb{N}^n : \exists m \in F. \forall i. k_i = m(\mathit{place(i)})\}.$$

We define an annotation $\varphi$ for $A$ that is trivially inductive by taking $\varphi(q) \triangleq \mathit{true}$. We have that $\langle \varphi, A\rangle$ is a counting proof.

It is easy to see that the control flow net $\mathcal{P}$ and the counting automaton $A$ act exactly the same, except at markings where $\mathcal{P}$ can fire $\mathsf{zr}$, but $A$ cannot. Such a marking is reachable from $m$ (in $\mathcal{P}$ and $A$) iff $p$ is zero reachable $m$ (in $G$), thus completing the proof. □

While the decision problem for proof checking has high computational complexity, from the standpoint of certifying the correctness of a program we may be satisfied with a faster semi-decision procedure. For example, acceleration has proved to be an effective technique in practice for Petri net reachability [7]. We also note a recent result by Leroux [35]: if a given marking of a Petri net is not reachable, there exists a Presburger-definable inductive invariant for the Petri net. This allows for the possibility of using well-known reachability algorithms for (sequential) integer programs (e.g., [12, 39]) to be used for counting proof checking.

## 7. Completeness

We now show the (relative) completeness of our counting proof method, when programs are modelled as control flow nets. First, we observe that proving that a control flow net $\mathcal{P}$ satisfies a given specification $\psi_{\mathsf{pre}}/\psi_{\mathsf{post}}$ is equivalent to proving that a particular *flattened* program $\mathcal{P}^\flat$ satisfies $\psi_{\mathsf{pre}}/\psi_{\mathsf{post}}$. The flattened program is a sequential program with extra natural-typed variables which are used to represent a marking. We then show that any inductive assertion for $\mathcal{P}^\flat$ can be (trivially) transformed into a counting proof. The relative completeness of counting proofs thus follows from the relative completeness of the inductive assertion method. We now formalize this argument.

Let $\mathcal{P} = \langle P, T, \mathcal{E}, \ell, m_0, F\rangle$ be a control flow net. A *configuration* of $\mathcal{P}$ is a pair $\langle m, s\rangle$, where $m$ is a marking and $s \in S$ is a memory state. The *flattened program* $\mathcal{P}^\flat$ is a transition system where the state space is the set of configurations of $\mathcal{P}$ and the transition relation is

$$\langle m, s\rangle \to \langle m', s'\rangle \iff \exists t \in T. m \xrightarrow{t} m' \text{ and } \langle s, s'\rangle \in [\![\ell(t)]\!]$$

A *flattened assertion* is a formula in $\Phi^P$ (assertions over an extended vocabulary that includes an additional variable symbol $\mathsf{p}$ of sort $\mathbb{N}$ for each place $p \in P$). A configuration $\langle m, s\rangle$ of $\mathcal{P}$ can be viewed as a structure for this vocabulary (in the model-theoretic sense) by interpreting each new variable symbol $\mathsf{p}$ as $m(p)$.

For flattened assertions $\psi, \psi'$ and a transition $t \in T$, we write

$$\{\psi\}\ t\ \{\psi'\}$$

if for all configurations $\langle m, s\rangle$ and $\langle m', s'\rangle$ such that $\langle m, s\rangle \models \psi$ and $\langle m, s\rangle \xrightarrow{t} \langle m', s'\rangle$, we have $\langle m', s'\rangle \models \psi'$.

**Definition 7.1** Let $\mathcal{P} = \langle P, T, \mathcal{E}, \ell, m_0, F\rangle$ be a control flow net and let $\psi_{\mathsf{pre}}/\psi_{\mathsf{post}}$ be a specification. A *global inductive assertion* is a flattened assertion $\psi$ for which the following hold:

- $\psi_{\mathsf{pre}} \wedge \varphi_{m_0} \models \psi$
- $\psi \wedge \varphi_F \models \psi_{\mathsf{post}}$
- For all $t \in T$, $\{\psi\}\ t\ \{\psi\}$

where $\varphi_{m_0}$ is a formula defining the initial marking $m_0$ and $\varphi_F$ is a formula defining the set of final markings $F$. ⌟

**Theorem 7.2** Let $\mathcal{P} = \langle P, T, \mathcal{E}, \ell, m_0, F\rangle$ be a control flow net and let $\psi_{\mathsf{pre}}/\psi_{\mathsf{post}}$ be a specification. If there exists a global inductive proof that $\mathcal{P}$ satisfies the specification $\psi_{\mathsf{pre}}/\psi_{\mathsf{post}}$, then there exists a counting proof. ⌟

*Proof.* Let $\mathcal{P} = \langle P, T, \mathcal{E}, \ell, m_0, F\rangle$ be a control flow net and let $\psi_{\mathsf{pre}}/\psi_{\mathsf{post}}$ be a specification. Suppose that $\psi$ is a global inductive assertion for $\mathcal{P}^\flat$ that proves that $\mathcal{P}$ satisfies the specification $\psi_{\mathsf{pre}}/\psi_{\mathsf{post}}$.

We construct a counting automaton $A$ that is equivalent to $\mathcal{P}$ as in the proof of Theorem 6.2. Consider the formula $\psi'$ obtained by replacing each place variable $\mathbf{p}$ with its associated counter variable $\mathtt{k}_i$. It is easy to check that $\langle A, \lambda q.\psi' \rangle$ is a counting proof that proves that $\mathcal{P}$ satisfies the specification $\psi_{\mathsf{pre}}/\psi_{\mathsf{post}}$. □

## 8. Discussion Through Examples

In this section, we use examples to have a more in-depth discussion about a few points about the counting proofs framework. These points include:

- Control flow nets are a very general mechanism for representing programs with infinite control, no matter what the source of infinity of the control may be (Section 8.1).
- The structure of counting proof is in some sense independent of the control flow structure of the original program (Section 8.1).
- Control flow nets encode a verification problem. That is, they represent an integration of the control flow of the program and the correctness property. An adequate representation of program and property by a control flow net may not exist, and if it does, it may be difficult to build (Section 8.2).

### 8.1 Tree Traversal Example

```
Traverse(node) {
   if (node == null)
      return;
   visit(node);
   Traverse(node.left);
   Traverse(node.right);
}
```

On the right is a recursive (pre-order) tree traversal routine. We will give two implementations of this program, one a sequential recursive program and the other a parallel recursive program, to illustrate two important features of the counting proofs framework: first, control flow nets are a very general mechanism for representing programs with infinite control; and second, counting proofs are in some sense independent of the control flow structure of the original program.

We will use two different implementations of the generic traversal template from above: (i) a sequential recursive implementation, and (ii) a parallel and recursive implementation, to demonstrate the generality of the control flow nets, and the independence of counting proofs' structure from that of the program. We diverge slightly from the presentation of counting proofs and control flow nets from the preceding sections by using an acceptance condition based on linear arithmetic formulae rather than upwards closed sets (i.e., the set of accepting vectors of a counting proof and the set of accepting markings of a control flow net can be described by a QF_LRA formula rather than just an upwards closed set). As noted in Section 6, proof checking is decidable for this class (and in fact, the more general class of semi-linear sets). It is easy to see that the proof synthesis procedure from Section 4 can be adapted to this more general setting as well.

#### Recursive Traverse

We first look at a variation of the code above which is a sequential recursive program to demonstrate how recursive programs (which have non-regular trace languages) can be modelled using control flow nets. It is known that Petri net languages are incomparable with context free languages. However, they do properly include (and the inclusion is proper) the set of bounded context free languages, which is the most general class for which decidability results have been proved [21].

Figure 4 includes a simplified implementation of `Traverse` which abstracts away the heap manipulation operations, but keeps the relevant control information. We introduce two global counters to count the number of `leaves` and internal `nodes` that are visited by the `Traverse()` routine. If `nodes` and `leaves` are initially

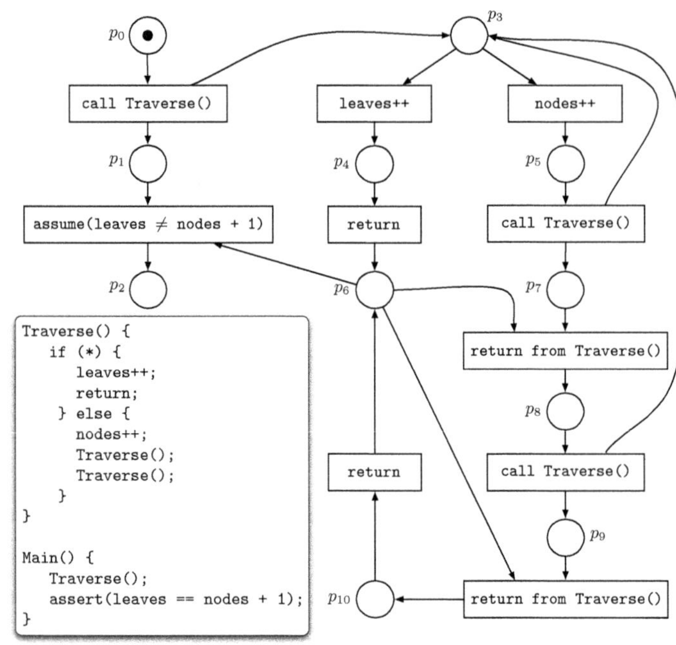


**Figure 4.** Sequential `Traverse` code and control flow net. The control flow net accepts when a token is at $p_2$ and there are no other tokens.

set to 0, then after `Traverse` is finished, for any binary tree the property `leaves = nodes + 1` is true.

Figure 4 also illustrates the control flow net for this program. A call statement is modelled by two transitions: a `call` transition and a `return from call` transition. The call adds a token at the place $p_3$ (the entry location of `Traverse`), to trigger another execution of the method body. However, the current execution is blocked from progressing (note the incoming edge from place $p_6$ to the `return from call` statement) until a return token is provided through $p_6$. The erroneous traces (and therefore those in the language of the control flow net) are those that put a token at place $p_2$ (i.e. when the assertion is violated), and all other places contain zero tokens. The latter ensures that the all executions of all pending frames of `Traverse` are completed before the property is checked to hold. The control flow model allows several partial executions of different frames to co-exist, and the property does not hold until they all finish.

#### Proof of Correctness for Traverse

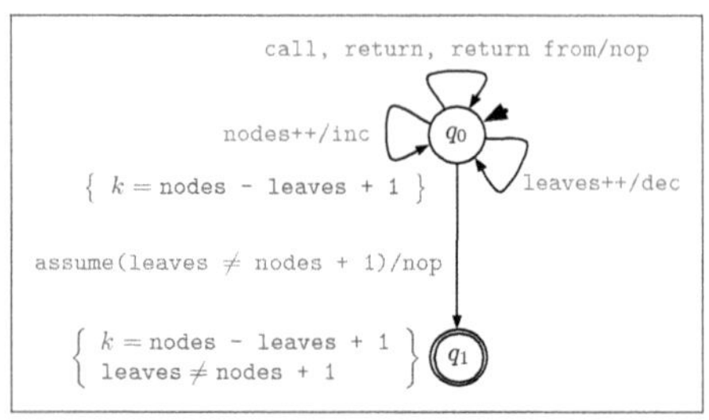


The proof of the correctness of the recursive `Traverse` appears on the right. It is a counting automaton with an additional counter variable $k$, which counts the difference between `nodes+1` and `leaves`. Note that the initial value of this counter is 1 (rather than 0, as we have seen in previous examples). When `Traverse` returns to the `Main` procedure and we check the assertion condition `count` and proceed to error location (i.e., we execute `assume(leaves != nodes + 1)`), we move to the state $q_1$ and stop reading additional statements. The automaton accepts when the final value of the counter $k$ is 0, which implies that $0 = k = nodes - leaves + 1$, contradicting the assumption $leaves \neq nodes + 1$.

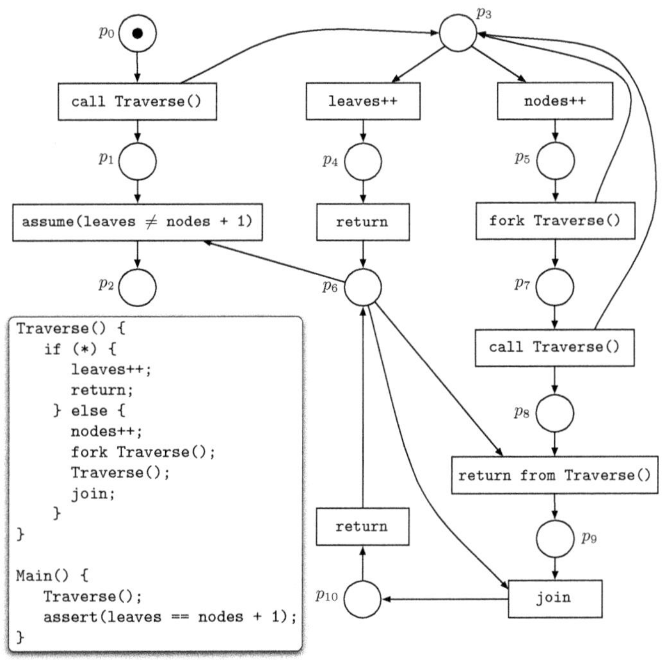


**Figure 5.** Parallel `Traverse` code and control flow net. The control flow net accepts when a token is at $p_2$ and there are no other tokens.

### Recursive and Parallel Traverse

Figure 5 presents a variation of the traverse implementation from Figure 4 in which the two recursive calls to `Traverse` are executed in parallel by forking a new thread for one of them. This program is both concurrent and recursive with both unbounded recursion and unbounded parallelism, which puts it in a class of very difficult programs to verify.

The control flow net for the parallel version is also depicted in Figure 5. Note that the join statement expects a token provided after the completion of the execution of the forked thread to continue, as with `return from call` in the recursive case.

A remarkable fact is that the proof of correctness of this version of `Traverse` is still the same proof that was presented in the previous section for the recursive version (with the minor addition of the `join` action to the set of actions `call, return, return from` that are labelling the self loop on $q_0$). Despite the fact that the two programs have substantially different control flow structure, the counting arguments for the correctness of their set of traces are the same. This is due to the fact that the proof is constructed based on a set of program traces, and independent of the control structure. Basically, in both cases the same counting argument applies for the correctness of program traces. It is a rather interesting feature to be able to *reuse* a proof of correctness when a program is changed, for example, for performance reasons (as is the case when we parallelize `Traverse`).

## 8.2 Ticket Algorithm

Our approach assumes that the alphabet of program statements is finite. If an unbounded number of threads execute a program over local variables, we need an infinite alphabet of statements (each program statement that manipulates a local variable, must be copies for each thread). However, our approach may still be applicable by using a *symmetry* argument. This section gives an example of such an argument.

We consider a well-known mutual exclusion protocol for an unbounded number of processes, namely the *ticket algorithm*. At each instant, a ticket counter $t$ contains the value for the next available ticket, and a service counter $s$ contains the number of already serviced clients. A client can acquire a ticket by setting its own local ticket number $m$ to the current value of the ticket counter $t$, after which $t$ is incremented by 1 to reflect the available ticket for the next client (`t++`). When a local ticket number $m$ is equal to or smaller than the service number $s$, the client can enter the *critical* section (`assume(m <= s)`). When this customer exits the critical section, the service number $s$ is incremented by 1 (`s++`).

The `Ticket` program consists of an arbitrary number of threads which each execute the same code, pictured to the right.

| | |
|---|---|
| `idle:` | `m = t++` |
| `wait:` | `assume(m <= s)` |
| `crit:` | `s++` |

The variables $s$ and $t$ are global (initially, $s = t = 0$). The variable $m$ is local to each thread. The mutual exclusion property is that at most one thread can be at `crit`, or equivalently, while some thread $T_1$ is still at `crit`, another thread $T_2$ cannot enter `crit`.

Interestingly, it does not seem possible to encode the verification problem for mutual exclusion by a control flow net (even after using a symmetry argument). Instead of mutual exclusion, we will consider a stronger correctness property (i.e., a property that implies mutual exclusion): if a thread $T_2$ has requested a ticket after another thread $T_1$, then $T_2$ cannot enter `crit` while $T_1$ is still at `wait` or `crit`. For brevity we refer to this property as FCFS, First Come First Serve.

Our encoding of the FCFS property relies on the notion of *minimal error traces*. Consider an error trace $\tau$ which violates FCFS. We call $\tau$ *minimal* if no proper prefix of $\tau$ already violates FCFS. To prove correctness, it is sufficient to show that every minimal error trace is infeasible.

We can decompose every minimal error trace as follows (we mark a statement by the thread that executes it):

$$\tau; [T_1\colon \texttt{m}_2\texttt{=t++}]; \tau'; [T_2\colon \texttt{m}_1\texttt{=t++}]; \tau''; [T_2\colon \texttt{assume(m}_1\texttt{<=s)}]$$

where $[T_1\colon \texttt{s++}]$ does not occur in $\tau$, in $\tau'$, or in $\tau''$. That is, every minimal error trace contains, in order, the request of $T_1$, the request of $T_2$, and, at the last position, the enter of $T_2$, and thread $T_1$ may or may not enter after its request, but if it does, it cannot not exit.

In the setting above, the thread $T_2$ is the *bad thread*. We now use a symmetry argument: without loss of generality, we may assume that the bad thread is thread 0. The reason that this is no loss of generality, is due to the symmetry of `Ticket`. For any minimal error trace where the bad thread is some thread other than thread 0, we may simply swap that thread and thread 0 and arrive at another minimal error trace, one where the bad thread is thread 0. Thanks to this symmetry, it is sufficient to show that all such 0-distinguished minimal error traces are infeasible.

We finitize the alphabet of program statements by "forgetting" the local variables of every *environment thread* (i.e., a thread other than thread 0). The statement `m = t++` of an environment thread becomes `_ = t++` (which is semantically the same as `t++`), and likewise `assume(m <= s)` becomes `assume(_ <= s)` (which is semantically the same as `assume(true)`). It is sufficient to show that every 0-distinguished minimal error trace over the finite alphabet of program statements is infeasible (since forgetting local variables can only make more traces feasible).

The set of traces of the control flow net in Figure 6(a) contains all 0-distinguished minimal error traces over the finite alphabet of program statements (incidentally, it contains also some non-minimal ones). The transitions and places are arranged in three columns. The left most column corresponds to environment threads that acquire their ticket before thread 0, the second column corresponds to the distinguished thread 0, and the last column corresponds to environment threads that acquire their ticket after thread 0.

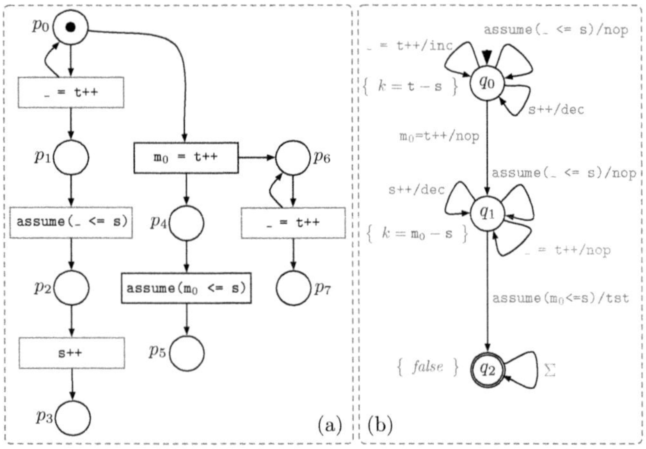


**Figure 6.** `Ticket`: (a) Control flow net. The set of final markings is defined by $p_1 + p_2 \geq 1 \wedge p_5 \geq 1$. (b) Counting proof.

***Counting Proof of Ticket*** The counting automaton shown in Figure 6 has three states. The initial state is $q_0$, its only final state is $q_2$. The initial value of the counter $k$ is 0. While in state $q_0$, the automaton counts the request statements (positively) and the exit statements of environment threads (negatively); it does not count enter statements. While in state $q_1$, it counts the exit statements of environment threads (negatively); it counts neither request statements nor enter statements. The request statement of the distinguished thread leads from $q_0$ to $q_1$. The enter statement of the distinguished thread leads from $q_1$ to $q_2$ if the `tst` operation succeeds, i.e., if $k \geq 1$.

$$\begin{aligned} p_1 + p_2 &\leq k \\ p_0 &\leq q_0 \\ p_4 &\leq q_1 \\ p_5 &\leq q_2 \vee k \leq 0 \end{aligned}$$

***Proof Checking*** We use this example to convey our intuition that proving the inclusion of the language of a control flow net in the language of a counting automaton often involves a set of very simple invariants. The formula pictured to the right is a linear arithmetic formula which relates configurations of the control flow net with configurations of the counting proof (two configurations are related if they satisfy the formula to the right; the control flow net configuration is used to interpret $p$ variables and the counting automaton configuration is used to interpret $k$ and the $q$ variables; the value of $q$ is 1 or 0). One may check that this relation is a kind of simulation: whenever the control flow net may take a step, the counting automaton may take a corresponding step *or* the control flow net is in a "dead" configuration that cannot reach a final marking. Moreover, the initial and final configurations of the control flow net and counting automaton are related. Thus, this formula shows that the traces of the control flow net are accepted by the counting automaton.

## 9. Related Work

Extensive research has been done about verification of parameterized systems. Apt and Kozen [4] argued that with little capabilities granted to individual processes, the verification problem becomes undecidable. There has since been a great deal of study of decidability/undecidability of subclasses of parameterized systems [32, 38]. There is a good survey [49] that covers a lot of the existing techniques for verification of parameterized systems. We emphasize here that our goal is not to verify parameterized distributed protocols, but programs; and therefore, we do not mention a lot of related work that is focused on the intricacies of verifying these protocols.

***Deductive techniques*** We are aware of two proof systems that are applicable to parameterized systems: (1) a parameterized Owicki-Gries type proof system [40], in which if the assertions (and the auxiliary variables) are provided by the user as annotations, then the proof checking is done mostly automatically, and (2) The QED [17] system that is based on the Lipton's reduction by inferring atomic blocks, which works independently of how many threads are running in parallel. Both of these systems need (partial or total) user-provided annotations to prove programs correct.

***Induction-based techniques*** There are techniques based on induction (on the number of processes) [33, 36], that rely on finding an abstraction and approximation of *network invariants* [13, 14, 31].

The method of *invisible invariants* [5, 44] automatically generates inductive assertions for the verification of safety properties of parameterized systems. First, the symmetry of parameterized systems is exploited to *guess* a universally quantified assertion that over-approximate the set of reachable states. then, a *small model theorem* establishes when the assertions over parameterized systems can be model checked on small instantiations (whose size depend on the system and the assertions) to derive the validity over any instantiation. This method is limited, however, to systems with finite data, and the application of it in some contexts is far from trivial.

***Regular model checking*** The idea, which was introduced in [48], is to represent the set of reachable states of a parameterized system using a regular language. Processes are assumed to be finite-state to give rise to a finite alphabet (alphabet letters correspond to processes' states). Transducers are used to approximate (through acceleration) the transitive closure of transition relation, and hence compute all reachable configurations of the systems. A lot of research has been done in improving the laborious problem of computing the meta transitions [1, 11, 36, 43] (including techniques based on acceleration, transitive closure, and widening), and even going beyond regular languages in [20]. The restriction that processes need to be finite state persists in all these extensions. The focus of this line of research has been on the verification of protocols, and hence, they often have much richer input languages (than the one we use in this paper) that are beyond our scope of parameterized programs; e.g. the use of existentially or universally quantified guards, which is not normally found in software systems.

***Abstraction-based techniques*** In [27], a system of $N$ processes communicating through finite-domain shared variables is abstracted by mapping the state systems into tuples where each dimension (having the values, 0, 1, or many) corresponds to the number of processes at a given local state, and additional dimensions are used to capture the value of global variables (finitely many possibilities). The resulting finite-state system was then verified by model checking (finite-state verification). In this and other *counter abstraction* techniques, a concrete state is counter abstracted by counting the number of processes in each local state [37, 45] limiting the counter to at most 2. Counter abstraction is simple to apply and when applicable works well. Its shortcoming is that it is only applicable to systems where each process has a small number of individual local states. More recently, in [28] symbolic techniques are used to overcome this problem and allow verification processes with larger number of local states. A new form of counter abstraction is discussed in [28] using parametric interval abstraction that facilitates verification of fault-tolerant distributed algorithms.

There is a class of techniques that are not strictly counter abstraction in the above sense (since the resulting abstract system is not finite), but have a similar flavour since they use the same counters, but untruncated. In [22], German and Sistla consider a parameterized system of processes that communicate synchronously, and show how to verify single-index properties. They achieve this by encoding the problem as a Petri net safety property and using Karp-Miller's coverability tree construction [30]. Similar abstraction-based techniques have been applied to verification of multi-threaded C [6], and Java [16] programs. In all these instances, processes are abstracted into finite-state processes, and the only source of infinity remains the existence of unboundedly many of these finite-state processes.

In [2], a CEGAR algorithm for parameterized systems is presented. The program model in this paper is very similar to ours (although the technique proposed in [2] is focused on proving safety for Petri net programs where the data variables are integers). The reachability algorithm employed by [2] is a fairly standard backward coverability algorithm - the insight of this paper is that the well quasi-order used for this algorithm can be refined using counter examples. The authors do not approach the problem of automatically synthesizing auxiliary variables.

In [8], it is shown how to represent a parameterized system of finite-state processes in the decidable logic WS1S, i.e. the current state of the system is modelled as a fixed number of finite subsets of natural numbers and the transitions of processes are described in WS1S formulae. Later, in [9], they extend the method, using a combination of theorem proving and the algorithmic techniques from [8], so that each process can have an unbounded state space. The theorem proving side helps prove a simulation relation between the original system and a so-called doubly-parametric system which is restricted enough to be expressible and checkable within the original framework from [8].

The problem of proving data structure invariants for programs with unboundedly many threads is attacked in [10] and [47]. [10] aims to exploit thread-modularity in their proofs, which restricts the ways in which thread-local variables may be correlated (for the practical gain of a faster analysis). Additional correlations can be captured using the technique of [47], in which a universally quantified *environment assertion* is used to keep track of relationships between a distinguished thread and all other threads. [18] is another technique that, like [10, 47], loses variable correlations in the interests of speed. Unlike [10] and [47], [18] is designed to compute numerical invariants rather than data structure invariants.

The conditions that need to be satisfied by the abstraction are restrictive enough that, as an example, the ticket example discussed here cannot be handled by the method.

The technique of trace abstraction has previously been discussed in [25] and in [19]. There, the sets of traces of sequential programs respectively concurrent (non-parameterized) programs were abstracted by regular languages. The issue of auxiliary variable synthesis was not investigated in that work, although it is potentially interesting also for sequential and concurrent (non-parameterized) programs.

***Cut-off detection*** There is a strong belief (backed by empirical evidence) that parameterized systems often enjoy a small model property. This belief has given rise to a collection of techniques for verification of parameterized concurrent systems [3, 29, 34]. More precisely, analyzing a small number of processes (the so-called *cut-off* points) and their interactions is sufficient to determine the reachability of any bad states. In [29, 34], parameterized Boolean programs (more specifically the result of predicate abstraction of device drivers) are analyzed. The technique in [29] is complete with respect to Boolean programs (note that this does not carry over to the original infinite-state C programs), while the one in [34] is even incomplete for Boolean programs. More recently, in [3], communication protocols are the focus, and an abstraction scheme is used that attempts to detect the cut-off points dynamically during the verification procedure to stop the search. Here, also, the processes are assumed to be finite state.

## 10. Conclusion

In this paper, we introduced *counting proofs*, a new system for proving safety properties for programs with infinite control. We believe that counting proofs have independent interest, outside of the software verification algorithm presented here. For example, we believe it may have applications to analysis of black-box systems, where the proof checking problem cannot be done, but we may be able to make other guarantees (e.g., testing coverage). Another potential direction for future work is application is white-box verification where the proof checking problem is undecidable in general, but an incomplete semi-test can be used for proof checking.

This paper shows that a particular class of auxiliary variables – counters – can be synthesized automatically. A natural question is to ask what other classes of auxiliary variables admit synthesis procedures. Another question is whether basic ideas introduced in this paper can be applied to auxiliary variable synthesis in other proof systems, such as Owicki-Gries [41]. The problem of auxiliary variable synthesis is largely unexplored, and this paper takes a step in the direction.

## References


[1] P. A. Abdulla, A. Bouajjani, B. Jonsson, and M. Nilsson. Handling global conditions in parameterized system verification. In *CAV*, pages 134–145, 1999.

[2] P. A. Abdulla, Y.-F. Chen, G. Delzanno, F. Haziza, C.-D. Hong, and A. Rezine. Constrained monotonic abstraction: a cegar for parameterized verification. In *CONCUR*, pages 86–101, 2010.

[3] P. A. Abdulla, F. Haziza, and L. Holík. All for the price of few. In *VMCAI*, pages 476–495, 2013.

[4] K. R. Apt and D. Kozen. Limits for automatic verification of finite-state concurrent systems. *Inf. Process. Lett.*, 22(6):307–309, 1986.

[5] T. Arons, A. Pnueli, S. Ruah, J. Xu, and L. D. Zuck. Parameterized verification with automatically computed inductive assertions. In *CAV*, pages 221–234, 2001.

[6] T. Ball, S. Chaki, and S. K. Rajamani. Parameterized verification of multithreaded software libraries. In *TACAS*, pages 158–173, 2001.

[7] S. Bardin, A. Finkel, J. Leroux, and L. Petrucci. Fast: acceleration from theory to practice. *Int. J. Softw. Tools Technol. Transf.*, 10(5): 401–424, Sept. 2008.

[8] K. Baukus, S. Bensalem, Y. Lakhnech, and K. Stahl. Abstracting WS1S systems to verify parameterized networks. In *TACAS*, pages 188–203, 2000.

[9] K. Baukus, K. Stahl, S. Bensalem, and Y. Lakhnech. Networks of processes with parameterized state space. *Electr. Notes Theor. Comput. Sci.*, 50(4):386–400, 2001.

[10] J. Berdine, T. Lev-Ami, R. Manevich, G. Ramalingam, and M. Sagiv. Thread quantification for concurrent shape analysis. In *CAV*, pages 399–413, 2008.

[11] A. Bouajjani, B. Jonsson, M. Nilsson, and T. Touili. Regular model checking. In *CAV*, pages 403–418, 2000.

[12] A. R. Bradley. Sat-based model checking without unrolling. In *VMCAI*, pages 70–87, 2011.

[13] E. M. Clarke, O. Grumberg, and M. C. Browne. Reasoning about networks with many identical finite-state processes. In *PODC*, pages 240–248, 1986.

[14] E. M. Clarke, O. Grumberg, and S. Jha. Veryfying parameterized networks using abstraction and regular languages. In *CONCUR*, pages 395–407, 1995.

[15] M. A. Colón, S. Sankaranarayanan, and H. B. Sipma. Linear invariant generation using non-linear constraint solving. In *Computer Aided Verification*, pages 420–432, 2003.

[16] G. Delzanno, J.-F. Raskin, and L. V. Begin. Towards the automated verification of multithreaded java programs. In *TACAS*, pages 173–187, 2002.

[17] T. Elmas, S. Qadeer, and S. Tasiran. A calculus of atomic actions. In *POPL*, pages 2–15, 2009.

[18] A. Farzan and Z. Kincaid. Verification of parameterized concurrent programs by modular reasoning about data and control. In *POPL*, pages 297–308, 2012.

[19] A. Farzan, Z. Kincaid, and A. Podelski. Inductive data flow graphs. In *POPL*, pages 129–142, 2013.

[20] D. Fisman and A. Pnueli. Beyond regular model checking. In *FSTTCS*, pages 156–170, 2001.

[21] P. Ganty, R. Majumdar, and B. Monmege. Bounded underapproximations. *Formal Methods in System Design*, 40(2):206–231, 2012.

[22] S. M. German and A. P. Sistla. Reasoning about systems with many processes. *J. ACM*, 39(3):675–735, 1992.

[23] A. Gupta, C. Popeea, and A. Rybalchenko. Predicate abstraction and refinement for verifying multi-threaded programs. In *POPL*, pages 331–344, 2011.

[24] M. Hack. *Decidability questions for Petri nets*. PhD thesis, MIT, June 1976.

[25] M. Heizmann, J. Hoenicke, and A. Podelski. Refinement of trace abstraction. In *SAS*, pages 69–85, 2009.

[26] L. E. Holloway, B. H. Krogh, and A. Giua. A survey of petri net methods for controlled discrete eventsystems. *Discrete Event Dynamic Systems*, 7(2):151–190, Apr. 1997.

[27] C. N. Ip and D. L. Dill. Verifying systems with replicated components in mur$\varphi$. *Formal Methods in System Design*, 14(3):273–310, 1999.

[28] A. John, I. Konnov, U. Schmid, H. Veith, and J. Widder. Parameterized model checking of fault-tolerant distributed algorithms by abstraction. In *FMCAD*, pages 201–209, 2013.

[29] A. Kaiser, D. Kroening, and T. Wahl. Dynamic cutoff detection in parameterized concurrent programs. In *CAV*, pages 645–659, 2010.

[30] R. M. Karp and R. E. Miller. Parallel program schemata. *J. Comput. Syst. Sci.*, 3(2):147–195, 1969.

[31] Y. Kesten, A. Pnueli, E. Shahar, and L. D. Zuck. Network invariants in action. In *CONCUR*, pages 101–115, 2002.

[32] S. R. Kosaraju. Decidability of reachability in vector addition systems (preliminary version). In *STOC*, pages 267–281, 1982.

[33] R. P. Kurshan and K. L. McMillan. A structural induction theorem for processes. *Inf. Comput.*, 117(1):1–11, 1995.

[34] S. La Torre, P. Madhusudan, and G. Parlato. Model-checking parameterized concurrent programs using linear interfaces. In *CAV*, pages 629–644, 2010.

[35] J. Leroux. Vector addition system reachability problem: a short self-contained proof. In *POPL*, pages 307–316, 2011.

[36] D. Lesens, N. Halbwachs, and P. Raymond. Automatic verification of parameterized linear networks of processes. In *POPL*, pages 346–357, 1997.

[37] B. D. Lubachevsky. An approach to automating the verification of compact parallel coordination programs i. *Acta Inf.*, 21:125–169, 1984.

[38] M. Maidl. A unifying model checking approach for safety properties of parameterized systems. In *CAV*, pages 311–323, 2001.

[39] K. L. McMillan. Lazy abstraction with interpolants. In *CAV*, pages 123–136, 2006.

[40] L. P. Nieto. Completeness of the Owicki-Gries system for parameterized parallel programs. In *IPDPS*, page 150, 2001.

[41] S. Owicki and D. Gries. Verifying properties of parallel programs: an axiomatic approach. *Commun. ACM*, 19:279–285, May 1976. ISSN 0001-0782.

[42] E. Pelz. Closure properties of deterministic petri nets. In *STACS*, pages 371–382, 1987.

[43] A. Pnueli and E. Shahar. Liveness and acceleration in parameterized verification. In *CAV*, pages 328–343, 2000.

[44] A. Pnueli, S. Ruah, and L. D. Zuck. Automatic deductive verification with invisible invariants. In *TACAS*, pages 82–97, 2001.

[45] A. Pnueli, J. Xu, and L. D. Zuck. Liveness with (0, 1, $\infty$)-counter abstraction. In *CAV*, pages 107–122, 2002.

[46] S. Qadeer and D. Wu. Kiss: keep it simple and sequential. In *PLDI*, pages 14–24, 2004.

[47] M. Segalov, T. Lev-Ami, R. Manevich, R. Ganesan, and M. Sagiv. Abstract transformers for thread correlation analysis. In *APLAS*, pages 30–46, 2009.

[48] P. Wolper and B. Boigelot. Verifying systems with infinite but regular state spaces. In *CAV*, pages 88–97, 1998.

[49] L. Zuck and A. Pnueli. Model checking and abstraction to the aid of parameterized systems (a survey). *Comput. Lang. Syst. Struct.*, 30 (3-4):139–169, Oct. 2004.

# A Verified Information-Flow Architecture

Arthur Azevedo de Amorim[1] Nathan Collins[2] André DeHon[1] Delphine Demange[1]
Cătălin Hriţcu[1,3] David Pichardie[3,4] Benjamin C. Pierce[1] Randy Pollack[4] Andrew Tolmach[2]

[1]University of Pennsylvania [2]Portland State University [3]INRIA [4]Harvard University

## Abstract

SAFE is a clean-slate design for a highly secure computer system, with pervasive mechanisms for tracking and limiting information flows. At the lowest level, the SAFE hardware supports fine-grained programmable tags, with efficient and flexible propagation and combination of tags as instructions are executed. The operating system virtualizes these generic facilities to present an information-flow abstract machine that allows user programs to label sensitive data with rich confidentiality policies. We present a formal, machine-checked model of the key hardware and software mechanisms used to control information flow in SAFE and an end-to-end proof of noninterference for this model.

***Categories and Subject Descriptors*** D.4.6 [*Security and Protection*]: Information flow controls; D.2.4 [*Software Engineering*]: Software/Program Verification

***Keywords*** security; clean-slate design; tagged architecture; information-flow control; formal verification; refinement

## 1. Introduction

The SAFE design is motivated by the conviction that the insecurity of present-day computer systems is due in large part to legacy design decisions left over from an era of scarce hardware resources. The time is ripe for a complete rethink of the entire system stack with security as the central focus. In particular, designers should be willing to spend more of the abundant processing power available on today's chips to improve security.

A key feature of SAFE is that every piece of data, down to the word level, is annotated with a *tag* representing policies that govern its use. While the tagging mechanism is very general, one particularly interesting use of tags is for representing *information-flow control (IFC)* policies. For example, an individual record might be tagged "This information should only be seen by principals `Alice` or `Bob`," a function pointer might be tagged "This code is trusted to work with `Carol`'s secrets," or a string might be tagged "This came from the network and has not been sanitized yet." Such tags representing IFC policies can involve arbitrary sets of principals, and principals themselves can be dynamically allocated to represent an unbounded number of entities within and outside the system.

At the programming-language level, rich IFC policies have been extensively explored, with many proposed designs for static [19, 40, etc.] and dynamic [3, 20, 39, 44, etc.] enforcement mechanisms and a huge literature on their formal properties [19, 40, etc.]. Similarly, operating systems with information-flow tracking have been a staple of the OS literature for over a decade [28, etc.]. But progress at the hardware level has been more limited, with most proposals concentrating on hardware acceleration for taint-tracking schemes [12, 15, 45, 47, etc.]. SAFE extends the state of the art in two significant ways. First, the SAFE machine offers hardware support for sound and efficient purely-dynamic tracking of both explicit and implicit flows (i.e., information leaks through both data and control flow) for *arbitrary* machine code programs—not just programs accepted by static analysis, or produced by translation or transformation. Moreover, rather than using just a few "taint bits," SAFE associates a word-sized tag to every word of data in the machine—both memory and registers. In particular, SAFE tags can be pointers to arbitrary data structures in memory. The interpretation of these tags is left entirely to software: the hardware just propagates tags from operands to results as each instruction is executed, following software-defined rules. Second, the SAFE design has been informed from the start by an intensive effort to formalize critical properties of its key mechanisms and produce machine-checked proofs, in parallel with the design and implementation of its hardware and system software. Though some prior work (surveyed in §12) shares some of these aims, to the best of our knowledge no project has attempted this combination of innovations.

Abstractly, the tag propagation rules in SAFE can be viewed as a partial function from argument tuples of the form (*opcode*, *pc tag*, *argument*$_1$ *tag*, *argument*$_2$ *tag*, ...) to result tuples of the form (*new pc tag*, *result tag*), meaning "if the next instruction to be executed is *opcode*, the current tag of the program counter (PC) is *pc tag*, and the arguments expected by this opcode are tagged *argument*$_1$ *tag*, etc., then executing the instruction is allowed and, in the new state of the machine, the PC should be tagged *new pc tag* and any new data created by the instruction should be tagged *result tag*." (The individual argument-result pairs in this function's graph are called *rule instances*, to distinguish them from the symbolic *rules* used at the software level.) In general, the graph of this function *in extenso* will be huge; so, concretely, the hardware maintains a *cache* of recently-used rule instances. On each instruction dispatch (in parallel with the logic implementing the usual behavior of the instruction—e.g., addition), the hardware forms an argument tuple as described above and looks it up in the rule cache. If the lookup is successful, the result tuple includes a new tag for the PC and a tag for the result of the instruction (if any); these are combined with the ordinary results of instruction execution to yield the next machine state. Otherwise, if the lookup is unsuccessful, the hardware invokes a *cache fault handler*—a trusted piece of system software with the job of checking whether the faulting combination of tags corresponds to a policy violation or whether it should be allowed. In the latter case, an appropriate rule instance specifying tags for the instruction's results is added to the cache, and the faulting instruction is restarted. Thus, the hardware is generic and the interpretation of policies (e.g., IFC, memory safety or control


*POPL '14*, January 22–24, 2014, San Diego, CA, USA.

ACM 978-1-4503-2544-8/14/01.
`http://dx.doi.org/10.1145/2535838.2535839`

flow integrity) is programmed in software, with the results cached in hardware for common-case efficiency.

The first contribution of this paper is to explain and formalize, in Coq, the key ideas in this design via a simplified model of the SAFE machine, embodying its tagging mechanisms in a distilled form and focusing on enforcing IFC using these general mechanisms. In §2, we outline the features of the full SAFE system and enumerate the most significant simplifications in our model. To streamline the exposition, most of the paper describes a further-simplified version of the system, deferring to §11 the discussion of the more sophisticated memory model and IFC label representation that we have actually formalized in Coq. We begin by defining a very simple *abstract IFC machine* with a built-in, purely dynamic IFC enforcement mechanism and an abstract lattice of IFC labels (§3). We then show, in three steps, how this abstract machine can be implemented using the low-level mechanisms we propose. The first step introduces a *symbolic IFC rule machine* that reorganizes the semantics of the abstract machine, splitting out the IFC enforcement mechanism into a separate judgment parameterized by a *symbolic IFC rule table* (§4). The second step defines a generic *concrete machine* (§5) that provides low-level support for efficiently implementing many different high-level policies (IFC and others) with a combination of a hardware *rule cache* and a software *fault handler*. The final step instantiates the concrete machine with a concrete fault handler enforcing IFC. We do this using an *IFC fault handler generator* (§6), which compiles the symbolic IFC rule table into a sequence of machine instructions implementing the IFC enforcement judgment.

Our second contribution is a machine-checked proof that this simplified SAFE system is *correct* and *secure*, in the sense that user code running on the concrete machine equipped with the IFC fault handler behaves the same way as on the abstract machine and enjoys the standard *noninterference* property that "high inputs do not influence low outputs." The interplay of the concrete machine and fault handler is complex, so some proof abstraction is essential. In our proof architecture, a first abstraction layer is based on *refinement*. This allows us to reason in terms of a high-level view of memory, ignoring the concrete implementation of IFC labels, while setting up the intricate indistinguishability relation used in the noninterference proof. A second layer of abstraction is required for reasoning about the correctness of the fault handler. Here, we rely on a verified custom Hoare logic that abstracts from low-level machine instructions into a reusable set of verified structured code generators.

In §7 we prove that the IFC fault handler generator correctly compiles a symbolic IFC rule table and a concrete representation of an abstract label lattice into an appropriate sequence of machine instructions. We then introduce a standard notion of refinement (§8) and show that the concrete machine running the generated IFC fault handler refines the abstract IFC machine and vice-versa, using the symbolic IFC rule machine as an intermediate refinement point in each direction of the proof (§9). In our deterministic setting, showing refinement in both directions guarantees that the concrete machine does not diverge or get stuck when handling a fault. We next introduce a standard *termination-insensitive noninterference (TINI)* property (§10) and show that it holds for the abstract machine. Since deterministic TINI is preserved by refinement, we conclude that the concrete machine running the generated IFC fault handler also satisfies TINI. Finally, we explain how to accommodate two important features that are handled by our Coq development but elided from the foregoing sections: dynamic memory allocation and tags representing sets of principals (§11). We close with a survey of related work (§12) and a discussion of future directions (§13). We omit proofs and some parts of longer definitions; a long version and a Coq script formalizing the entire development are available at `http://www.crash-safe.org`.

## 2. Overview of SAFE

To establish context, we begin with a brief overview of the full SAFE system, concentrating on its OS- and hardware-level features. More detailed descriptions can be found elsewhere [14, 16, 17, 21, 22, 29, 34].

SAFE's system software performs process scheduling, stream-based interprocess communication, storage allocation and garbage collection, and management of the low-level tagging hardware (the focus of this paper). The goal is to organize these services as a collection of mutually suspicious compartments following the principle of least privilege (a *zero-kernel OS* [43]), so that an attacker would need to compromise multiple compartments to gain complete control of the machine. It is programmed in a combination of assembly and *Tempest*, a new low-level programming language.

The SAFE hardware integrates a number of mechanisms for eliminating common vulnerabilities and supporting higher-level security primitives. To begin with, SAFE is (dynamically) typed at the hardware level: each data word is indelibly marked as a number, an instruction, a pointer, etc. Next, the hardware is memory safe: every pointer consists of a triple of base, bounds, and offset (compactly encoded into 64 bits [17, 29]), and every pointer operation includes a hardware bounds check [29]. Finally, the hardware associates each word in the registers and memory, as well as the PC, with a large (59-bit) tag. The hardware rule cache, enabling software-specified propagation of tags from operands to result on each machine step, is implemented using a combination of multiple hash functions to approximate a fully-associative cache [16].

An unusual feature of the SAFE design is that formal modeling and verification of its core mechanisms have played a central role in the design process since the beginning. The long-term goal—formally specifying and verifying the entire set of critical runtime services—is still some ways in the future, but key properties of simplified models have been verified both at the level of *Breeze* [21] (a mostly functional, security-oriented, dynamic language used for user-level programming on SAFE) and, in the present work, at the hardware and abstract machine level. Experiments are also underway to use random testing of properties like noninterference as a means to speed the design process [22].

Our goal in this paper is to develop a clear, precise, and mathematically tractable model of one of the main innovations in the SAFE design: its scheme for efficiently supporting high-level data use policies using a combination of hardware and low-level system software. To make the model easy to work with, we simplify away many important facets of the real SAFE system. In particular, (i) we focus only on IFC and noninterference, although the tagging facilities of the SAFE machine are generic and can be applied to other policies (we return to this point in §13); (ii) we ignore the Breeze and Tempest programming languages and concentrate on the hardware and runtime services; (iii) we use a stack instead of registers, and we distill the instruction set to just a handful of opcodes; (iv) we drop SAFE's fine-grained privilege separation in favor of a more conventional user-mode / kernel-mode dichotomy; (v) we shrink the rule cache to a single entry (avoiding issues of replacement and eviction) and maintain it in kernel memory, accessed by ordinary loads and stores, rather than in specialized cache hardware; (vi) we omit a large number of IFC-related concepts (dynamic principals, downgrading, public labels, integrity, clearance, etc.); (vii) we handle exceptional conditions, including potential security violations, by simply halting the whole machine; and (viii) most importantly, we ignore concurrency, process scheduling, and interprocess communication, assuming instead that the whole machine has a single, deterministic thread of control. The absence

| | | | |
|---|---|---|---|
| *instr* | ::= | | Basic instruction set |
| | \| | Add | addition |
| | \| | Output | output top of stack |
| | \| | Push $n$ | push integer constant |
| | \| | Load | indirect load from data memory |
| | \| | Store | indirect store to data memory |
| | \| | Jump | unconditional indirect jump |
| | \| | Bnz $n$ | conditional relative jump |
| | \| | Call | indirect call |
| | \| | Ret | return |

**Figure 1.** Instruction set

of concurrency is a particularly significant simplification, given that we are talking about an operating system that offers IFC as a service. However, we conjecture that it may be possible to add concurrency to our formalization, while maintaining a high degree of determinism, by adapting the approach used in the proof of noninterference for the seL4 microkernel [35, 36]. We return to this point in §13.

## 3. Abstract IFC Machine

We begin the technical development by defining a very simple stack-and-pointer machine with "hard-wired" dynamic IFC. This machine concisely embodies the IFC mechanism we want to provide to higher-level software and serves as a specification for the symbolic IFC rule machine (§4) and for the concrete machine (§5) running our IFC fault handler (§6). The three machines share a tiny instruction set (Fig. 1) designed to be a convenient target for compiling the symbolic IFC rule table (the Coq development formalizes several other instructions). All three machines use a fixed *instruction memory* $\iota$, a partial function from addresses to instructions.

The machine manipulates integers (ranged over by $n$, $m$, and $p$); unlike the real SAFE machine, we make no distinction between raw integers and pointers (we re-introduce this distinction in §11). Each integer is protected by an individual IFC *label* (ranged over by $L$). We assume an arbitrary set of labels $\mathcal{L}$ equipped with a partial order ($\leq$), a least upper bound operation ($\vee$), and a bottom element ($\bot$). For instance we might take $\mathcal{L}$ to be the set of levels $\{\bot, \top\}$ with $\bot \leq \top$ and $\bot \vee \top = \top$. We call a pair of an integer $n$ and its protecting label $L$ an *atom*, written $n@L$ and ranged over by $a$.

An *abstract machine state* $\langle \mu\ [\sigma]\ pc \rangle$ consists of a data memory $\mu$, a stack $\sigma$, and a program counter $pc$. (We sometimes drop the outer brackets.) The *data memory* $\mu$ is a partial function from integer addresses to atoms. We write $\mu(p) \leftarrow a$ for the memory that coincides with $\mu$ everywhere except at $p$, where its value is $a$. The *stack* $\sigma$ is essentially a list of atoms, but we distinguish stacks beginning with return addresses (written $pc;\sigma$) from ones beginning with regular atoms (written $a,\sigma$). The *program counter* (PC) $pc$ is an atom whose label is used to track implicit flows, as explained below.

The step relation of the abstract machine, written $\iota \vdash \mu_1\ [\sigma_1]\ pc_1 \xrightarrow{\alpha} \mu_2\ [\sigma_2]\ pc_2$, is a partial function taking a machine state to a machine state plus an output action $\alpha$, which can be either an atom or the silent action $\tau$. We generally omit $\iota$ from transitions because it is fixed. Throughout the paper we study other, similar relations, and consistently refer to non-silent actions as *events* (ranged over by $e$).

The stepping rules in Fig. 2 adapt a standard purely dynamic IFC enforcement mechanism [3, 39] to a low-level machine, following recent work by Hriţcu et al. [22]. The rule for Add joins ($\vee$) the labels of the two operands to produce the label of the result, which ensures that the result is at least as classified as each of the operands. The rule for Push labels the integer constant added to the stack as public ($\bot$). The rule for Jump uses join to raise the label

$$\frac{\iota(n) = \mathsf{Add}}{\begin{array}{l}\mu \quad [n_1@L_1, n_2@L_2, \sigma]\ n@L_{pc} \quad \xrightarrow{\tau} \\ \mu\ [(n_1{+}n_2)@(L_1 \vee L_2), \sigma]\ (n{+}1)@L_{pc}\end{array}}$$

$$\frac{\iota(n) = \mathsf{Output}}{\mu\ [m@L_1, \sigma]\ n@L_{pc} \xrightarrow{m@(L_1 \vee L_{pc})} \mu\ [\sigma]\ (n{+}1)@L_{pc}}$$

$$\frac{\iota(n) = \mathsf{Push}\ m}{\mu\ [\sigma]\ n@L_{pc} \xrightarrow{\tau} \mu\ [m@\bot, \sigma]\ (n{+}1)@L_{pc}}$$

$$\frac{\iota(n) = \mathsf{Load} \qquad \mu(p) = m@L_2}{\mu\ [p@L_1, \sigma]\ n@L_{pc} \xrightarrow{\tau} \mu\ [m@(L_1 \vee L_2), \sigma]\ (n{+}1)@L_{pc}}$$

$$\frac{\begin{array}{l}\iota(n) = \mathsf{Store} \qquad \mu(p) = k@L_3 \qquad L_1 \vee L_{pc} \leq L_3 \\ \mu(p) \leftarrow (m@L_1 \vee L_2 \vee L_{pc}) = \mu'\end{array}}{\mu\ [p@L_1, m@L_2, \sigma]\ n@L_{pc} \xrightarrow{\tau} \mu'\ [\sigma]\ (n{+}1)@L_{pc}}$$

$$\frac{\iota(n) = \mathsf{Jump}}{\mu\ [n'@L_1, \sigma]\ n@L_{pc} \xrightarrow{\tau} \mu\ [\sigma]\ n'@(L_1 \vee L_{pc})}$$

$$\frac{\iota(n) = \mathsf{Bnz}\ k \qquad n' = n{+}((m = 0)?1 : k)}{\mu\ [m@L_1, \sigma]\ n@L_{pc} \xrightarrow{\tau} \mu\ [\sigma]\ n'@(L_1 \vee L_{pc})}$$

$$\frac{\iota(n) = \mathsf{Call}}{\mu\ [n'@L_1, a, \sigma]\ n@L_{pc} \xrightarrow{\tau} \mu\ [a, (n{+}1)@L_{pc}; \sigma]\ n'@(L_1 \vee L_{pc})}$$

$$\frac{\iota(n) = \mathsf{Ret}}{\mu\ [n'@L_1; \sigma]\ n@L_{pc} \xrightarrow{\tau} \mu\ [\sigma]\ n'@L_1}$$

**Figure 2.** Semantics of IFC abstract machine

of the PC by the label of the target address of the jump. Similarly, Bnz raises the label of the PC by the label of the tested integer. In both cases the value of the PC after the instruction depends on data that could be secret, and we use the label of the PC to track the label of data that has influenced control flow. In order to prevent *implicit flows* (leaks exploiting the control flow of the program), the Store rule joins the PC label with the original label of the written integer and with the label of the pointer through which the write happens. Additionally, since the labels of memory locations are allowed to vary during execution, we prevent leaking information via labels using a "no-sensitive-upgrade" check [3, 48] (the $\leq$ precondition in the rule for Store). This check prevents memory locations labeled public from being overwritten when either the PC or the pointer through which the store happens have been influenced by secrets. The Output rule labels the emitted integer with the join of its original label and the current PC label.[1] Finally, because of the structured control flow imposed by the stack discipline, the rule for Ret can soundly restore the PC label to whatever it was at the time of the Call. (Readers less familiar with the intricacies of dynamic IFC may find some of these side conditions a bit mysterious. A longer explanation can be found in [22], but the details are not critical for present purposes.)

All data in the machine's initial state are labelled (as in all machine states), and the simple machine manages labels to ensure noninterference as defined and proved in §10. There are no instructions that explicitly raise the label (classification) of an atom. Such an instruction, joinP, is added to the machine in §11.

[1] We assume the observer of the events generated by Output is constrained by the rules of information flow—i.e., cannot freely "look inside" bare events. In the real SAFE machine, atoms being sent to the outside world need to be protected cryptographically; we are abstracting this away.

| *opcode* | *allow* | $e_{rpc}$ | $e_r$ |
|---|---|---|---|
| add | TRUE | $\mathtt{LAB}_{pc}$ | $\mathtt{LAB}_1 \sqcup \mathtt{LAB}_2$ |
| output | TRUE | $\mathtt{LAB}_{pc}$ | $\mathtt{LAB}_1 \sqcup \mathtt{LAB}_{pc}$ |
| push | TRUE | $\mathtt{LAB}_{pc}$ | BOT |
| load | TRUE | $\mathtt{LAB}_{pc}$ | $\mathtt{LAB}_1 \sqcup \mathtt{LAB}_2$ |
| store | $\mathtt{LAB}_1 \sqcup \mathtt{LAB}_{pc} \sqsubseteq \mathtt{LAB}_3$ | $\mathtt{LAB}_{pc}$ | $\mathtt{LAB}_1 \sqcup \mathtt{LAB}_2 \sqcup \mathtt{LAB}_{pc}$ |
| jump | TRUE | $\mathtt{LAB}_1 \sqcup \mathtt{LAB}_{pc}$ | -- |
| bnz | TRUE | $\mathtt{LAB}_1 \sqcup \mathtt{LAB}_{pc}$ | -- |
| call | TRUE | $\mathtt{LAB}_1 \sqcup \mathtt{LAB}_{pc}$ | $\mathtt{LAB}_{pc}$ |
| ret | TRUE | $\mathtt{LAB}_1$ | -- |

**Figure 3.** Rule table $\mathcal{R}^{\mathsf{abs}}$ corresponding to abstract IFC machine

## 4. Symbolic IFC Rule Machine

In the abstract machine described above, IFC is tightly integrated into the step relation in the form of side conditions on each instruction. In contrast, the concrete machine (i.e., the "hardware") described in §5 is generic, designed to support a wide range of software-defined policies (IFC and other). The machine introduced in this section serves as a bridge between these two models. It is closer to the abstract machine—indeed, its machine states and the behavior of the step relation are identical. The important difference lies in the *definition* of the step relation, where all the IFC-related aspects are factored out into a separate judgment. While factoring out IFC enforcement into a separate reference monitor is commonplace [2, 39, 41], our approach goes further. We define a small DSL for describing symbolic IFC rules and obtain actual monitors by interpreting this DSL (in this section) and by compiling it into machine instructions using verified structured code generators (in §6 and §7).

More formally, each stepping rule of the new machine includes a uniform call to an *IFC enforcement* relation, which itself is parameterized by a *symbolic IFC rule table* $\mathcal{R}$. Given the labels of the values relevant to an instruction, the IFC enforcement relation (i) checks whether the execution of that instruction is allowed in the current configuration, and (ii) if so, yields the labels to put on the resulting PC and on any resulting value. This judgment has the form $\vdash_{\mathcal{R}} (L_{pc}, \ell_1, \ell_2, \ell_3) \leadsto_{opcode} L_{rpc}, L_r$, where $\mathcal{R}$ is the rule table and *opcode* is the kind of instruction currently executing.

For example, the stepping rule for Add

$$\frac{\iota(n) = \mathsf{Add} \qquad \vdash_{\mathcal{R}} (L_{pc}, L_1, L_2, \_) \leadsto_{\mathsf{add}} L_{rpc}, L_r}{\begin{array}{l}\mu\ [n_1@L_1, n_2@L_2, \sigma]\ n@L_{pc} \quad \xrightarrow{\tau} \\ \mu\ \ [(n_1{+}n_2)@L_r, \sigma]\ (n{+}1)@L_{rpc}\end{array}}$$

passes three inputs to the IFC enforcement judgment: $L_{pc}$, the label of the current PC, and $L_1$ and $L_2$, the labels of the two operands at the top of the stack. (The fourth element of the input tuple is written as _ because it is not needed for Add.) The IFC enforcement judgment produces two labels: $L_{rpc}$ is used to label the next program counter $(n + 1)$ and $L_r$ is used to label the result value. All the other stepping rules follow a similar scheme. (The one for Store uses all four input labels.)

A symbolic IFC rule table $\mathcal{R}$ describes a particular IFC enforcement mechanism. For instance, the rule table $\mathcal{R}^{\mathsf{abs}}$ corresponding to the IFC mechanism of the abstract machine is shown in Fig. 3. In general, a table $\mathcal{R}$ associates a *symbolic IFC rule* to each instruction opcode (formally, $\mathcal{R}$ is a total function). Each of these rules is formed of three symbolic expressions: (i) a boolean expression indicating whether the execution of the instruction is allowed or not (i.e., whether it violates the IFC enforcement mechanism); (ii) a label-valued expression for $L_{rpc}$, the label of the next PC; and (iii) a label-valued expression for $L_r$, the label of the result value, if there is one.

These symbolic expressions are written in a simple domain-specific language (DSL) of operations over an IFC lattice. The grammar of this DSL includes label variables $\mathtt{LAB}_{pc}, \ldots, \mathtt{LAB}_3$, which correspond to the input labels $L_{pc}, \ldots, L_3$; the constant BOT; and the lattice operators $\sqcup$ (join) and $\sqsubseteq$ (flows).

The IFC enforcement judgment looks up the corresponding symbolic IFC rule in the table and directly *evaluates* the symbolic expressions in terms of the corresponding lattice operations. The definition of this interpreter is completely straightforward; we omit it for brevity. In contrast, in §6 we *compile* this rule table into the IFC fault handler for the concrete machine.

## 5. Concrete Machine

The concrete machine provides low-level support for efficiently implementing many different high-level policies (IFC and others) with a combination of a hardware rule cache and a software cache fault handler. In this section we focus on the concrete machine's hardware, which is completely generic, while in §6 we describe a specific fault handler corresponding to the IFC rules of the symbolic rule machine.

The concrete machine has the same general structure as the more abstract ones, but differs in several important respects. One is that it annotates data values with integer *tags* T, rather than with *labels* $L$ from an abstract lattice; thus, the *concrete atoms* $a$ in the data memories and the stack have the form $n@\mathtt{T}$. Similarly, a *concrete action* $\alpha$ is either a concrete atom or the silent action $\tau$. Using plain integers as tags allows us to delegate their interpretation entirely to software. In this paper we focus solely on using tags to implement IFC labels, although they could also be used for enforcing other policies, such as type and memory safety or control-flow integrity. For instance, to implement the two-point abstract lattice with $\bot \leq \top$, we could use 0 to represent $\bot$ and 1 to represent $\top$, making the operations $\vee$ and $\leq$ easy to implement (see §6). For richer abstract lattices, a more complex concrete representation might be needed; for example, a label containing an arbitrary set of principals might be represented concretely by a pointer to an array data structure (see §11). In places where a tag is needed but its value is irrelevant, the concrete machine uses a specific but arbitrary *default tag* value (e.g., -1), which we write $\mathtt{T}_{\mathtt{D}}$.

A second important difference is that the concrete machine has two modes: *user mode* (u), for executing the ordinary user program, and *kernel mode* (k), for handling rule cache faults. To support these two modes, the concrete machine's state contains a *privilege bit* $\pi$, a separate *kernel instruction memory* $\phi$, and a separate *kernel data memory* $\kappa$, in addition to the user instruction memory $\iota$, the user data memory $\mu$, the stack $\sigma$, and the PC. When the machine is operating in user mode ($\pi = \mathsf{u}$), instructions are looked up using the PC as an index into $\iota$, and loads and stores use $\mu$; when in kernel mode ($\pi = \mathsf{k}$), the PC is treated as an index into $\phi$, and loads and stores use $\kappa$. As before, since $\iota$ and $\phi$ are fixed, we normally leave them implicit.

The concrete machine has the same instruction set as the previous ones, allowing user programs to be run on all three machines unchanged. But the tag-related semantics of instructions depends on the privilege mode, and in user mode the semantics further depends on the state of the *rule cache*. In the real SAFE machine, the rule cache may contain thousands of entries and is implemented as a separate near-associative memory [16] accessed by special instructions. Here, for simplicity, we use a cache with just one entry, located at the start of kernel memory, and use Load and Store instructions to manipulate it; indeed, until §11, it constitutes the entirety of $\kappa$.

The rule cache holds a single rule instance, represented graphically like this: | *opcode* | $\mathtt{T}_{pc}$ | $\mathtt{T}_1$ | $\mathtt{T}_2$ | $\mathtt{T}_3$ || $\mathtt{T}_{rpc}$ | $\mathtt{T}_r$ |. Location 0 holds an integer representing an opcode. Location 1 holds the PC tag. Locations 2 to 4 hold the tags of any other arguments needed by this particular opcode. Location 5 holds the tag that should go on the PC after this instruction executes, and location 6 holds the tag for the instruction's result value, if needed. For example, suppose the cache contains | add | 0 | 1 | 1 | -1 || 0 | 1 |. (Note that we are showing just the "payload" part of these seven atoms; by convention, the tag part is always $T_D$, and we do not display it.) If 0 is the tag representing the label $\bot$, 1 represents $\top$, and -1 is the default tag $T_D$, this can be interpreted abstractly as follows: "If the next instruction is Add, the PC is labeled $\bot$, and the two relevant arguments are both labeled $\top$, then the instruction should be allowed, the label on the new PC should be $\bot$, and the label on the result of the operation is $\top$."

There are two sets of stepping rules for the concrete machine in user mode; which set applies depends on whether the current machine state matches the current contents of the rule cache. In the "cache hit" case the instruction executes normally, with the cache's output determining the new PC tag and result tag (if any). In the "cache miss" case, the relevant parts of the current state (opcode, PC tag, argument tags) are stored into the input part of the single cache line and the machine simulates a Call to the fault handler.

To see how this works in more detail, consider the two user-mode stepping rules for the Add instruction.

$$\frac{\iota(n) = \mathsf{Add} \qquad \kappa = \boxed{\mathsf{add} \mid T_{pc} \mid T_1 \mid T_2 \mid T_D \,\|\, T_{rpc} \mid T_r}}{\mathsf{u}\ \kappa\ \mu\ [n_1@T_1, n_2@T_2, \sigma]\ n@T_{pc} \xrightarrow{\tau} \mathsf{u}\ \kappa\ \mu\ [(n_1{+}n_2)@T_r, \sigma]\ n{+}1@T_{rpc}}$$

$$\frac{\iota(n) = \mathsf{Add} \qquad \kappa_i \neq \boxed{\mathsf{add} \mid T_{pc} \mid T_1 \mid T_2 \mid T_D} = \kappa_j}{\mathsf{u}\ [\kappa_i, \kappa_o]\ \mu\ [n_1@T_1, n_2@T_2, \sigma]\ n@T_{pc} \xrightarrow{\tau} \mathsf{k}\ [\kappa_j, \kappa_D]\ \mu\ [(n@T_{pc}, \mathsf{u}); n_1@T_1, n_2@T_2, \sigma]\ 0@T_D}$$

In the first rule (cache hit), the side condition demands that the input part of the current cache contents have form | add | $T_{pc}$ | $T_1$ | $T_2$ | $T_D$ |, where $T_{pc}$ is the tag on the current PC, $T_1$ and $T_2$ are the tags on the top two atoms on the stack, and the fourth element is the default tag. In this case, the output part of the rule, | $T_{rpc}$ | $T_r$ |, determines the tag $T_{rpc}$ on the PC and the tag $T_r$ on the new atom pushed onto the stack in the next machine state.

In the second rule (cache miss), the notation $[\kappa_i, \kappa_o]$ means "let $\kappa_i$ be the input part of the current rule cache and $\kappa_o$ be the output part." The side condition says that the current input part $\kappa_i$ does not have the desired form | add | $T_{pc}$ | $T_1$ | $T_2$ | $T_D$ |, so the machine needs to enter the fault handler. The next machine state is formed as follows: (i) the input part of the cache is set to the desired form $\kappa_j$ and the output part is set to $\kappa_D \triangleq$ | $T_D$ | $T_D$ |; (ii) a new return frame is pushed on top of the stack to remember the current PC and privilege bit (u); (iii) the privilege bit is set to k (which will cause the next instruction to be read from the kernel instruction memory); and (iv) the PC is set to 0, the location in the kernel instruction memory where the fault handler routine begins.

What happens next is up to the fault handler code. Its job is to examine the contents of the first five kernel memory locations and either (i) write appropriate tags for the result and new PC into the sixth and seventh kernel memory locations and then perform a Ret to go back to user mode and restart the faulting instruction, or (ii) stop the machine by jumping to an invalid PC (-1) to signal that the attempted combination of opcode and argument tags is illegal. This mechanism is general and can be used to implement many different high-level policies (IFC and others).

In kernel mode, the treatment of tags is almost completely degenerate: to avoid infinite regress, the concrete machine does not consult the rule cache while in kernel mode. For most instructions, tags read from the current machine state are ignored (indicated by _) and tags written to the new state are set to $T_D$. This can be seen for instance in the kernel-mode step rule for addition

$$\frac{\phi(n) = \mathsf{Add}}{\mathsf{k}\ \kappa\ \mu\ [n_1@\_, n_2@\_, \sigma]\ n@\_ \xrightarrow{\tau} \mathsf{k}\ \kappa\ \mu\ [(n_1{+}n_2)@T_D, \sigma]\ n{+}1@T_D}$$

The only significant exception to this pattern is Ret, which takes both the privilege bit and the new PC (including its tag!) from the return frame at the top of the stack. This is critical, since a Ret instruction is used to return from kernel to user mode when the fault handler has finished executing.

$$\frac{\phi(n) = \mathsf{Ret}}{\mathsf{k}\ \kappa\ \mu\ [(n'@T_1, \pi); \sigma]\ n@\_ \xrightarrow{\tau} \pi\ \kappa\ \mu\ [\sigma]\ n'@T_1}$$

A final point is that Output is not permitted in kernel mode, which guarantees that kernel actions are always the silent action $\tau$.

## 6. Fault Handler for IFC

Now we assemble the pieces. A concrete IFC machine implementing the symbolic rule machine defined in §4 can be obtained by installing appropriate fault handler code in the kernel instruction memory of the concrete machine presented in §5. In essence, this handler must emulate how the symbolic rule machine looks up and evaluates the DSL expressions in a given IFC rule table. We choose to generate the handler code by compiling the lookup and DSL evaluation relations directly into machine code. (An alternative would be to represent the rule table as abstract syntax in the kernel memory and write an interpreter in machine code for the DSL, but the compilation approach seems to lead to simpler code and proofs.)

The handler compilation scheme is given (in part) in Fig. 4. Each gen$*$ function generates a list of concrete machine instructions; the sequence generated by the top-level genFaultHandler is intended to be installed starting at location 0 in the concrete machine's kernel instruction memory. The implicit addr$*$ parameters are symbolic names for the locations of the opcode and various tags in the concrete machine's rule cache, as described in §5. The entire generator is parameterized by an arbitrary rule table $\mathcal{R}$. We make heavy use of the (obvious) encoding of booleans where false is represented by 0 and true by any non-zero value. We omit the straightforward definitions of some of the leaf generators.

The top-level handler works in three phases. The first phase, genComputeResults, does most of the work: it consists of a large nested if-then-else chain, built using genIndexedCases, that compares the opcode of the faulting instruction against each possible opcode and, on a match, executes the code generated for the corresponding symbolic IFC rule. The code generated for each symbolic IFC rule (by genApplyRule) pushes its results onto the stack: a flag indicating whether the instruction is allowed and, if so, the result-PC and result-value tags. This first phase never writes to memory or transfers control outside the handler; this makes it fairly easy to prove correct.

The second phase, genStoreResults, reads the computed results off the stack and updates the rule cache appropriately. If the result indicates that the instruction is allowed, the result PC and value tags are written to the cache, and true is pushed on the stack; otherwise, nothing is written to the cache, and false is pushed on the stack.

The third and final phase of the top-level handler tests the boolean just pushed onto the stack and either returns to user code (instruction is allowed) or jumps to address -1 (disallowed).

The code for symbolic rule compilation is built by straightforward recursive traversal of the rule DSL syntax for label-valued expressions (genELab) and boolean-valued expressions (genBool). These functions are (implicitly) parameterized by lattice-specific generators genBot, genJoin, and genFlows. To implement these

$$
\begin{array}{l}
\mathsf{genFaultHandler}\ \mathcal{R} = \mathsf{genComputeResults}\ \mathcal{R} \mathbin{+\!\!+} \\
\qquad\qquad\qquad\qquad\quad \mathsf{genStoreResults} \mathbin{+\!\!+} \\
\qquad\qquad\qquad\qquad\quad \mathsf{genIf}\ [\mathsf{Ret}]\ [\mathsf{Push}\ (\text{-}1);\ \mathsf{Jump}]
\end{array}
$$

$$
\begin{array}{l}
\mathsf{genComputeResults}\ \mathcal{R} = \\
\quad \mathsf{genIndexedCases}\ []\ \mathsf{genMatchOp}\ (\mathsf{genApplyRule} \circ \mathit{Rule}_{\mathcal{R}})\ \mathsf{opcodes}
\end{array}
$$

$$
\begin{array}{l}
\mathsf{genMatchOp}\ op = \\
\quad [\mathsf{Push}\ op] \mathbin{+\!\!+} \mathsf{genLoadFrom}\ \mathsf{addrOpLabel} \mathbin{+\!\!+} \mathsf{genEqual}
\end{array}
$$

$$
\begin{array}{l}
\mathsf{genApplyRule}\ \langle allow, e_{rpc}, e_r\rangle = \mathsf{genBool}\ allow \mathbin{+\!\!+} \\
\quad \mathsf{genIf}\ (\mathsf{genSome}\ (\mathsf{genELab}\ e_{rpc} \mathbin{+\!\!+} \mathsf{genELab}\ e_r))\ \mathsf{genNone}
\end{array}
$$

$$
\begin{array}{lll}
\mathsf{genELab}\ \mathtt{BOT} & = & \mathsf{genBot} \\
\qquad\quad \mathtt{LAB}_i & = & \mathsf{genLoadFrom}\ \mathsf{addrTag}_i \\
\qquad\quad LE_1 \sqcup LE_2 & = & \mathsf{genELab}\ LE_2 \mathbin{+\!\!+} \mathsf{genELab}\ LE_1 \mathbin{+\!\!+} \mathsf{genJoin}
\end{array}
$$

$$
\begin{array}{lll}
\mathsf{genBool}\ \mathtt{TRUE} & = & \mathsf{genTrue} \\
\qquad\quad LE_1 \sqsubseteq LE_2 & = & \mathsf{genELab}\ LE_2 \mathbin{+\!\!+} \mathsf{genELab}\ LE_1 \mathbin{+\!\!+} \mathsf{genFlows}
\end{array}
$$

$$
\begin{array}{l}
\mathsf{genStoreResults} = \\
\quad \mathsf{genIf}\ (\mathsf{genStoreAt}\ \mathsf{addrTag}_r \mathbin{+\!\!+} \mathsf{genStoreAt}\ \mathsf{addrTag}_{rpc} \mathbin{+\!\!+} \mathsf{genTrue}) \\
\qquad \mathsf{genFalse}
\end{array}
$$

$$
\begin{array}{l}
\mathsf{genIndexedCases}\ \mathit{genDefault}\ \mathit{genGuard}\ \mathit{genBody} = g \\
\quad \text{where } g\ \mathsf{nil} \qquad\ \, = \mathit{genDefault} \\
\qquad\quad\ g\ (n :: ns) = \mathit{genGuard}\ n \mathbin{+\!\!+} \mathsf{genIf}\ (\mathit{genBody}\ n)\ (g\ ns)
\end{array}
$$

$$
\begin{array}{lll}
\mathsf{genIf}\ t\ f & = & \mathsf{genSkipIf}\ (\mathsf{length}\ f') \mathbin{+\!\!+} f' \mathbin{+\!\!+} t \\
 & & \text{where } f' = f \mathbin{+\!\!+} \mathsf{genSkip}(\mathsf{length}\ t) \\
\mathsf{genSkip}\ n & = & \mathsf{genTrue} \mathbin{+\!\!+} \mathsf{genSkipIf}\ n \\
\mathsf{genSkipIf}\ n & = & [\mathsf{Bnz}\ (n{+}1)]
\end{array}
$$

$$
\mathsf{opcodes} = \mathsf{add} :: \mathsf{output} :: \ldots :: \mathsf{ret} :: \mathsf{nil}
$$

**Figure 4.** Generation of fault handler from IFC rule table.

generators for a particular lattice, we first need to choose how to represent abstract labels as integer tags, and then determine a sequence of instructions that encodes each operation. We call such an encoding scheme a *concrete lattice*. For example, the abstract labels in the two-point lattice can be encoded like booleans, representing $\bot$ by 0, $\top$ by non-0, and instantiating genBot, genJoin, and genFlows with code for computing false, disjunction, and implication, respectively. A simple concrete lattice like this can be formalized as a tuple $CL = (\mathsf{Tag}, \mathsf{Lab}, \mathsf{genBot}, \mathsf{genJoin}, \mathsf{genFlows})$, where the encoding and decoding functions Lab and Tag satisfy $\mathsf{Lab} \circ \mathsf{Tag} = id$; to streamline the exposition, we assume this form of concrete lattice for most of the paper. The more realistic encoding in §11 will require a more complex treatment.

To raise the level of abstraction of the handler code, we make heavy use of structured code generators; this makes it easier both to understand the code and to prove it correct using a custom Hoare logic that follows the structure of the generators (see §7). For example, the genIf function takes two code sequences, representing the "then" and "else" branches of a conditional, and generates code to test the top of the stack and dispatch control appropriately. The higher-order generator genIndexedCases takes a list of integer indices (e.g., opcodes) and functions for generating guards and branch bodies from an index, and generates code that will run the guards in order until one of them computes true, at which point the corresponding branch body is run.

## 7. Correctness of the Fault Handler Generator

We now turn our attention to verification, beginning with the fault handler. We must show that the generated fault handler emulates the IFC enforcement judgment $\vdash_{\mathcal{R}} (L_{pc}, \ell_1, \ell_2, \ell_3) \leadsto_{opcode} L_{rpc}, L_r$ of the symbolic rule machine. The statement and proof of correctness are parametric over the symbolic IFC rule table $\mathcal{R}$ and concrete lattice, and hence over correctness lemmas for the lattice operations.

***Correctness statement*** Let $\mathcal{R}$ be an arbitrary rule table and $\phi_{\mathcal{R}} \triangleq$ genFaultHandler $\mathcal{R}$ be the corresponding generated fault handler. We specify how $\phi_{\mathcal{R}}$ behaves as a whole—as a relation between initial state on entry and final state on completion—using the relation $\phi \vdash cs_1 \rightarrow^{\star}_{\mathsf{k}} cs_2$, defined as the reflexive transitive closure of the concrete step relation, with the constraints that the fault handler code is $\phi$ and all intermediate states (i.e., strictly preceding $cs_2$) have privilege bit k.

The correctness statement is captured by the following two lemmas. Intuitively, if the symbolic IFC enforcement judgment allows some given user instruction, then executing $\phi_{\mathcal{R}}$ (stored at kernel mode location 0) updates the cache to contain the tag encoding of the appropriate result labels and returns to user-mode; otherwise, $\phi_{\mathcal{R}}$ halts the machine ($pc$ = -1).

**Lemma 7.1** (Fault handler correctness, allowed case)**.** Suppose that $\vdash_{\mathcal{R}} (L_{pc}, \ell_1, \ell_2, \ell_3) \leadsto_{opcode} L_{rpc}, L_r$ and

$$\kappa_i = \boxed{opcode \mid \mathsf{Tag}(L_{pc}) \mid \mathsf{Tag}(\ell_1) \mid \mathsf{Tag}(\ell_2) \mid \mathsf{Tag}(\ell_3)}\ .$$

$$
\begin{array}{lllll}
\text{Then } \phi_{\mathcal{R}} \vdash & \langle \mathsf{k}\ [\kappa_i, \kappa_o]\ \mu\ [(pc, \mathsf{u}); \sigma] & 0@\mathrm{T_D}\rangle & \rightarrow^{\star}_{\mathsf{k}} \\
 & \langle \mathsf{u}\ [\kappa_i, \kappa'_o]\ \mu\ [\sigma] & pc\rangle &
\end{array}
$$

with output cache $\kappa'_o = (\mathsf{Tag}\ (L_{rpc}), \mathsf{Tag}\ (L_r))$ .

**Lemma 7.2** (Fault handler correctness, disallowed case)**.** Suppose that $\vdash_{\mathcal{R}} (L_{pc}, \ell_1, \ell_2, \ell_3) \not\leadsto_{opcode}$, and

$$\kappa_i = \boxed{opcode \mid \mathsf{Tag}(L_{pc}) \mid \mathsf{Tag}(\ell_1) \mid \mathsf{Tag}(\ell_2) \mid \mathsf{Tag}(\ell_3)}\ .$$

Then, for some final stack $\sigma'$,

$$
\begin{array}{lll}
\phi_{\mathcal{R}} \vdash & \langle \mathsf{k}\ [\kappa_i, \kappa_o]\ \mu\ [(pc, \mathsf{u}); \sigma] \quad 0@\mathrm{T_D}\rangle & \rightarrow^{\star}_{\mathsf{k}} \\
 & \langle \mathsf{k}\ [\kappa_i, \kappa_o]\ \mu\ [\sigma'] \qquad\quad\ \text{-}1@\mathrm{T_D}\rangle . &
\end{array}
$$

***Proof methodology*** The fault handler is compiled by composing generators (Fig. 4); accordingly, the proofs of these two lemmas reduce to correctness proofs for the generators. We employ a custom Hoare logic for specifying the generators themselves, which makes the code generation proof simple, reusable, and scalable. This is where defining a DSL for IFC rules and a *structured* compiler proves to be very useful approach, e.g., compared to symbolic interpretation of hand-written code.

Our logic comprises two notions of Hoare triple. The generated code mostly consists of self-contained instruction sequences that terminate by "falling off the end"—i.e., that never return or jump outside themselves, although they may contain internal jumps (e.g., to implement conditionals). The only exception is the final step of the handler (third line of genFaultHandler in Fig. 4). We therefore define a standard Hoare triple $\{P\}\ c\ \{Q\}$, suitable for reasoning about self-contained code, and use it for the bulk of the proof. To specify the final handler step, we define a non-standard triple $\{P\}\ c\ \{Q\}^{O}_{pc}$ for reasoning about escaping code.

***Self-contained-code Hoare triples*** The triple $\{P\}\ c\ \{Q\}$, where $P$ and $Q$ are predicates on $\kappa \times \sigma$, says that, if the kernel instruction memory $\phi$ contains the code sequence $c$ starting at the current PC, and if the current memory and stack satisfy $P$, then the machine will run (in kernel mode) until the PC points to the instruction immediately following the sequence $c$, with a resulting memory and stack satisfying $Q$. Note that the instruction memory $\phi$ is unconstrained outside of $c$, so if $c$ is not self-contained, no triple about it will be provable; thus, these triples obey the usual composition laws. Also, because the concrete machine is deterministic, these triples express total, rather than partial, correctness, which is essential for proving termination in lemmas 7.1 and 7.2. To aid automation of proofs about code sequences, we give triples in weakest-precondition style.

We build proofs by composing atomic specifications of individual instructions, such as

$$\frac{\begin{array}{r}P(\kappa,\sigma) := \exists\, n_1\, \mathtt{T}_1\, n_2\, \mathtt{T}_2\, \sigma'. \quad \sigma = n_1 @ \mathtt{T}_1, n_2 @ \mathtt{T}_2, \sigma' \\ \wedge\, Q(\kappa, ((n_1{+}n_2) @ \mathtt{T}_\mathtt{D}, \sigma'))\end{array}}{\{P\}\ [\mathsf{Add}]\ \{Q\}},$$

with specifications for structured code generators, such as

$$\frac{\begin{array}{l}P(\kappa,\sigma) := \exists\, n\, \mathtt{T}\, \sigma'.\ \sigma = n @ \mathtt{T}, \sigma' \wedge (n \neq 0 \Longrightarrow P_1(\kappa,\sigma')) \\ \qquad\qquad\qquad \wedge (n = 0 \Longrightarrow P_2(\kappa,\sigma')) \\ \{P_1\}\ c_1\ \{Q\} \qquad \{P_2\}\ c_2\ \{Q\}\end{array}}{\{P\}\ \mathsf{genIf}\ c_1\ c_2\ \{Q\}}.$$

(We emphasize that all such specifications are *verified*, not *axiomatized* as the inference rule notation might suggest.)

The concrete implementations of the lattice operations are also specified using triples in this style.

$$\frac{P(\kappa,\sigma) := Q(\kappa, (\mathsf{Tag}\,(\bot) @ \mathtt{T}_\mathtt{D}, \sigma))}{\{P\}\ \mathsf{genBot}\ \{Q\}}$$

$$\frac{\begin{array}{r}P(\kappa,\sigma) := \exists\, L\, L'\, \sigma'. \quad \sigma = \mathsf{Tag}\,(L) @ \mathtt{T}_\mathtt{D}, \mathsf{Tag}\,(L') @ \mathtt{T}_\mathtt{D}, \sigma' \\ \wedge\, Q(\kappa, \mathsf{Tag}\,(L \vee L') @ \mathtt{T}_\mathtt{D}, \sigma')\end{array}}{\{P\}\ \mathsf{genJoin}\ \{Q\}}$$

$$\frac{\begin{array}{r}P(\kappa,\sigma) := \exists\, L\, L'\, \sigma. \quad \sigma = \mathsf{Tag}\,(L) @ \mathtt{T}_\mathtt{D}, \mathsf{Tag}\,(L') @ \mathtt{T}_\mathtt{D}, \sigma' \\ \wedge\, Q(\kappa, (\text{if } L \leq L' \text{ then } 1 \text{ else } 0) @ \mathtt{T}_\mathtt{D}, \sigma')\end{array}}{\{P\}\ \mathsf{genFlows}\ \{Q\}}$$

For the two-point lattice, it is easy to prove that the implemented operators satisfy these specifications; §11 describes an analogous result for a lattice of sets of principals.

***Escaping-code Hoare triples*** To be able to specify the entire code of the generated fault handler, we also define a second form of triple, $\{P\}\ c\ \{Q\}^O_{pc}$, which specifies mostly self-contained, total code $c$ that either makes *exactly one* jump outside of $c$ or returns out of kernel mode. More precisely, if $P$ and $Q$ are predicates on $\kappa \times \sigma$ and $O$ is a function from $\kappa \times \sigma$ to outcomes (the constants `Success` and `Failure`), then $\{P\}\ c\ \{Q\}^O_{pc}$ holds if, whenever the kernel instruction memory $\phi$ contains the sequence $c$ starting at the current PC, the current cache and stack satisfy $P$, and

- if $O$ computes `Success` then the machine runs (in kernel mode) until it returns to user code at $pc$, and $Q$ is satisfied.
- if $O$ computes `Failure` then the machine runs (in kernel mode) until it halts ($pc = -1$ in kernel mode), and $Q$ is satisfied.

To compose self-contained code with escaping code, we prove two composition laws for these triples, one for pre-composing with specified self-contained code and another for post-composing with arbitrary (unreachable) code:

$$\frac{\{P_1\}\ c_1\ \{P_2\} \qquad \{P_2\}\ c_2\ \{P_3\}^O_{pc}}{\{P_1\}\ c_1{+\!\!+}c_2\ \{P_3\}^O_{pc}} \qquad \frac{\{P\}\ c_1\ \{Q\}^O_{pc}}{\{P\}\ c_1{+\!\!+}c_2\ \{Q\}^O_{pc}}$$

We use these new triples to specify the $\mathsf{Ret}$ and $\mathsf{Jump}$ instructions, which could not be given useful specifications using the self-contained-code triples, e.g.

$$\frac{\begin{array}{l}P(\kappa,\sigma) := \exists \sigma'.\ Q(\kappa,\sigma') \wedge \sigma = (pc, \mathsf{u}); \sigma' \\ O(\kappa,\sigma) := \mathtt{Success}\end{array}}{\{P\}\ [\mathsf{Ret}]\ \{Q\}^O_{pc}}$$

Everything comes together in verifying the fault handler. We use contained-code triples to specify everything except for $[\mathsf{Ret}]$, $[\mathsf{Jump}]$, and the final $\mathsf{genIf}$, and then use the escaping-code triple composition laws to connect the non-returning part of the fault handler to the final $\mathsf{genIf}$.

## 8. Refinement

We have two remaining verification goals. First, we want to show that the concrete machine of §5 (running the fault handler of §6 compiled from $\mathcal{R}^{\mathsf{abs}}$) enjoys TINI. Proving this directly for the concrete machine would be dauntingly complex, so instead we show that the concrete machine is an implementation of the abstract machine, for which noninterference will be much easier to prove (§10). Second, since a trivial always-diverging machine also has TINI, we want to show that the concrete machine is a *faithful* implementation of the abstract machine that emulates all its behaviors.

We phrase these two results using the notion of *machine refinement*, which we develop in this section, and which we prove in §10 to be TINI preserving. In §9, we prove a two-way refinement (one direction for each goal), between the abstract and concrete machines, via the symbolic rule machine in both directions.

From here on we sometimes mention different machines (abstract, symbolic rule, or concrete) in the same statement (e.g., when discussing refinement), and sometimes talk about machines generically (e.g., when defining TINI for all our machines); for these purposes, it is useful to define a generic notion of machine.

**Definition 8.1.** A *generic machine* (or just *machine*) is a 5-tuple $M = (S, E, I, \cdot \xrightarrow{\cdot} \cdot, \mathit{Init})$, where $S$ is a set of *states* (ranged over by $s$), $E$ is a set of *events* (ranged over by $e$), $\cdot \xrightarrow{\cdot} \cdot \subseteq S \times (E + \{\tau\}) \times S$ is a step relation, and $I$ is a set of *input data* (ranged over by $i$) that can be used to build *initial states* of the machine with the function $\mathit{Init} \in I \to S$. We call $E + \{\tau\}$ the set of *actions* of $M$ (ranged over by $\alpha$).

Conceptually, a machine's program is included in its input data and gets "loaded" by the function *Init*, which also initializes the machine memory, stack, and PC. The notion of generic machine abstracts all these details, allowing uniform definitions of refinement and TINI that apply to all three of our IFC machines. To avoid stating it several times below, we stipulate that when we instantiate Definition 8.1 to any of our IFC machines, *Init* must produce an initial stack with no return frames.

A generic step $s_1 \xrightarrow{e} s_2$ or $s_1 \xrightarrow{\tau} s_2$ produces event $e$ or is silent. The reflexive-transitive closure of such steps, omitting silent steps (written $s_1 \xrightarrow{t}{}^{\star} s_2$) produces *traces*—i.e., lists, $t$, of events. When the end state of a step starting in state $s$ is not relevant we write $s \xrightarrow{e}$, and similarly $s \xrightarrow{t}{}^{\star}$ for traces.

When relating executions of two different machines through a refinement, we establish a correspondence between their traces. This relation is usually derived from an elementary relation on events, $\triangleright \subseteq E_1 \times E_2$, which is lifted to actions and traces:

$$\begin{array}{rcl}\alpha_1\ [\triangleright]\ \alpha_2 & \triangleq & (\alpha_1 = \tau = \alpha_2\ \vee\ \alpha_1 = e_1 \triangleright e_2 = \alpha_2) \\ \vec{x}\ [\triangleright]\ \vec{y} & \triangleq & \mathsf{length}(\vec{x}) = \mathsf{length}(\vec{y}) \wedge \forall i.\ x_i \triangleright y_i.\end{array}$$

**Definition 8.2** (Refinement). Let $M_1 = (S_1, E_1, I_1, \cdot \xrightarrow{\cdot}_1 \cdot, \mathit{Init}_1)$ and $M_2 = (S_2, E_2, I_2, \cdot \xrightarrow{\cdot}_2 \cdot, \mathit{Init}_2)$ be two machines. A *refinement* of $M_1$ into $M_2$ is a pair of relations $(\triangleright_i, \triangleright_e)$, where $\triangleright_i \subseteq I_1 \times I_2$ and $\triangleright_e \subseteq E_1 \times E_2$, such that whenever $i_1 \triangleright_i i_2$ and $\mathit{Init}_2(i_2) \xrightarrow{t_2}{}^{\star}$, there exists a trace $t_1$ such that $\mathit{Init}_1(i_1) \xrightarrow{t_1}{}^{\star}$ and $t_1\ [\triangleright_e]\ t_2$. We also say that $M_2$ *refines* $M_1$. Graphically:

$$\begin{array}{lll} i_1 & \mathit{Init}_1(i_1) \overset{t_1}{\dashrightarrow}{}^{*} & \\ \triangleright_i \mid & & [\triangleright_e] \\ i_2 & \mathit{Init}_2(i_2) \underset{t_2}{\longrightarrow}{}^{*} & \end{array}$$

(Plain lines denote premises, dashed ones conclusions.)

In order to prove refinement, we need a variant that considers executions starting at arbitrary related states.

**Definition 8.3** (Refinement via states). Let $M_1, M_2$ be as above. A *state refinement* of $M_1$ into $M_2$ is a pair of relations $(\triangleright_s, \triangleright_e)$, where $\triangleright_s \subseteq S_1 \times S_2$ and $\triangleright_e \subseteq E_1 \times E_2$, such that, whenever $s_1 \triangleright_s s_2$ and $s_2 \xrightarrow{t_2}{}^{\star}$, there exists $t_1$ such that $s_1 \xrightarrow{t_1}{}^{\star}$ and $t_1 \; [\triangleright_e] \; t_2$.

If the relation on inputs is compatible with the one on states, we can use state refinement to prove refinement.

**Lemma 8.4.** Suppose $i_1 \triangleright_i i_2 \Rightarrow \mathit{Init}_1(i_1) \triangleright_s \mathit{Init}_2(i_2)$, for all $i_1$ and $i_2$. If $(\triangleright_s, \triangleright_e)$ is a state refinement then $(\triangleright_i, \triangleright_e)$ is a refinement.

## 9. Refinements Between Concrete and Abstract

In this section, we show that (1) the concrete machine refines the symbolic rule machine, and (2) vice versa. Using (1) we will be able to show in §10 that the concrete machine is noninterfering. From (2) we know that the concrete machine faithfully implements the abstract one, exactly reflecting its execution traces.

***Abstract and symbolic rule machines*** The symbolic rule machine (with the rule table $\mathcal{R}^{\mathsf{abs}}$) is a simple reformulation of the abstract machine. Their step relations are (extensionally) equal, and started from the same input data they emit the same traces.

**Definition 9.1** (Abstract and symbolic rule machines as generic machines). For both abstract and symbolic rule machines, input data is a 4-tuple $(p, \mathit{args}, n, L)$ where $p$ is a program, $\mathit{args}$ is a list of atoms (the initial stack), and $n$ is the size of the memory, initialized with $n$ copies of $0@L$. The initial PC is $0@L$.

**Lemma 9.2.** The symbolic rule machine instantiated with the rule table $\mathcal{R}^{\mathsf{abs}}$ refines the abstract machine through $(=, =)$.

***Concrete machine refines symbolic rule machine*** We prove this refinement using a fixed but arbitrary rule table, $\mathcal{R}$, an abstract lattice of labels, and a concrete lattice of tags. The proof uses the correctness of the fault handler (§7), so we assume that the fault handler of the concrete machine corresponds to the rule table of the symbolic rule machine ($\phi = \phi_{\mathcal{R}}$) and that the encoding of abstract labels as integer tags is correct.

**Definition 9.3** (Concrete machine as generic machine). The input data of the concrete machine is a 4-tuple $(p, \mathit{args}, n, \mathtt{T})$ where $p$ is a program, $\mathit{args}$ is a list of concrete atoms (the initial stack), and the initial memory is $n$ copies of $0@\mathtt{T}$. The initial PC is $0@\mathtt{T}$. The machine starts in user mode, the cache is initialized with an illegal opcode so that the first instruction always faults, and the fault handler code parameterizing the machine is installed in the initial privileged instruction memory $\phi$.

The input data and events of the symbolic rule and concrete machines are of different kinds; they are matched using relations ($\triangleright_i^{\mathsf{c}}$ and $\triangleright_e^{\mathsf{c}}$ respectively) stipulating that payload values should be equal and that labels should correspond to tags modulo the function $\mathsf{Tag}$ of the concrete lattice.

$$\frac{\mathit{args}' = \mathsf{map}\;(\lambda(n@L).\; n@\mathsf{Tag}(L))\;\mathit{args}}{(p, \mathit{args}, n, L) \triangleright_i^{\mathsf{c}} (p, \mathit{args}', n, \mathsf{Tag}(L))} \qquad \frac{}{n@L \triangleright_e^{\mathsf{c}} n@\mathsf{Tag}(L)}$$

**Theorem 9.4.** The concrete IFC machine refines the symbolic rule machine, through $(\triangleright_i^{\mathsf{c}}, \triangleright_e^{\mathsf{c}})$.

We prove this theorem by a refinement via states (Lemma 9.7); this, in turn, relies on two technical lemmas (9.5 and 9.6).

The matching relation $\triangleright_s^{\mathsf{c}}$ between the states of the concrete and symbolic rule machines is defined as

$$\frac{\mathcal{R} \vdash \kappa \qquad \sigma_q \triangleright_\sigma \sigma_c \qquad \mu_q \triangleright_m \mu_c}{\mu_q, [\sigma_q], n@L \;\triangleright_s^{\mathsf{c}}\; \mathsf{u}, \kappa, \mu_c, [\sigma_c], n@\mathsf{Tag}(L)}$$

where the new notations are defined as follows. The relation $\triangleright_m$ demands that the memories be equal up to the conversion of labels to concrete tags. The relation $\triangleright_\sigma$ on stacks is similar, but additionally requires that return frames in the concrete stack have their privilege bit set to $\mathsf{u}$. The basic idea is to match, in $\triangleright_s^{\mathsf{c}}$, only concrete states that are in user mode. We also need to track an extra invariant, $\mathcal{R} \vdash \kappa$, which means that the cache $\kappa$ is consistent with the table $\mathcal{R}$—i.e., $\kappa$ never lies. More precisely, the output part of $\kappa$ represents the result of applying the symbolic rule judgment of $\mathcal{R}$ to the opcode and labels represented in the input part of $\kappa$.

$$\begin{array}{l} \mathcal{R} \vdash [\kappa_i, \kappa_o] \triangleq \forall \mathit{opcode}\; L_1\; L_2\; L_3\; L_{pc}, \\ \quad \kappa_i = \boxed{\mathit{opcode} \mid \mathsf{Tag}(L_{pc}) \mid \mathsf{Tag}(L_1) \mid \mathsf{Tag}(L_2) \mid \mathsf{Tag}(L_3)} \Rightarrow \\ \quad \exists L_{rpc}\; L_r, \quad \vdash_{\mathcal{R}} (L_{pc}, L_1, L_2, L_3) \leadsto_{\mathit{opcode}} L_{rpc}, L_r \\ \qquad\qquad \wedge\; \kappa_o = (\mathsf{Tag}\,(L_{rpc}), \mathsf{Tag}\,(L_r)) \end{array}$$

To prove refinement via states, we must account for two situations. First, suppose the concrete machine can take a user step. In this case, we match that step with a single symbolic rule machine step. We write $cs^{\pi}$ to denote a concrete state $cs$ whose privilege bit is $\pi$.

**Lemma 9.5** (Refinement, non-faulting concrete step). Let $cs_1^{\mathsf{u}}$ be a concrete state and suppose that $cs_1^{\mathsf{u}} \xrightarrow{\alpha_c} cs_2^{\mathsf{u}}$. Let $qs_1$ be a symbolic rule machine state with $qs_1 \triangleright_s^{\mathsf{c}} cs_1^{\mathsf{u}}$. Then there exist $qs_2$ and $\alpha_a$ such that $qs_1 \xrightarrow{\alpha_a} qs_2$, with $qs_2 \triangleright_s^{\mathsf{c}} cs_2^{\mathsf{u}}$, and $\alpha_a \; [\triangleright_e^{\mathsf{c}}] \; \alpha_c$.

Since the concrete machine is able to make a user step, the input part of the cache must match the opcode and data of the current state. But the invariant $\mathcal{R} \vdash \kappa$ says that the corresponding symbolic rule judgment holds. Hence the symbolic rule machine can also make a step from $qs_2$, as required.

The second case is when the concrete machine faults into kernel mode and returns to user mode after some number of steps.

**Lemma 9.6** (Refinement, faulting concrete step). Let $cs_0^{\mathsf{u}}$ be a concrete state, and suppose that the concrete machine does a faulting step to $cs_1^{\mathsf{k}}$, stays in kernel mode until $cs_n^{\mathsf{k}}$, and then exits kernel mode by stepping to $cs_{n+1}^{\mathsf{u}}$. Let $qs_0$ be a state of the symbolic rule machine that matches $cs_0^{\mathsf{u}}$. Then $qs_0 \triangleright_s^{\mathsf{c}} cs_{n+1}^{\mathsf{u}}$.

To prove this lemma, we must consider two cases. If the corresponding symbolic rule judgment holds, then we apply Lemma 7.1 to conclude directly—i.e., the machine exits kernel code into user mode. Otherwise, we apply Lemma 7.2 and derive a contradiction that the fault handler ends in a failing state in kernel mode.

Lemmas 9.5 and 9.6 can be summarized graphically by:

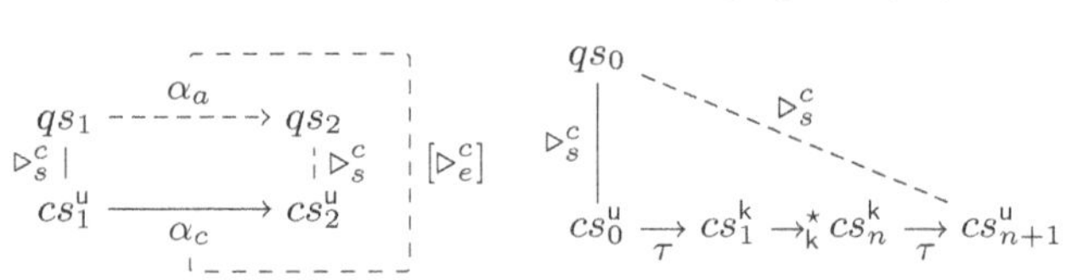


Given two matching states of the concrete and symbolic rule machines, and a concrete execution starting at that concrete state, these two lemmas can be applied repeatedly to build a matching execution of the symbolic rule machine. There is just one last case to consider, namely when the execution ends with a fault into kernel mode and never returns to user mode. However, no output is produced in this case, guaranteeing that the full trace is matched. We thus derive the following refinement via states, of which Theorem 9.4 is a corollary.

**Lemma 9.7.** The pair $(\triangleright_s^{\mathsf{c}}, \triangleright_e^{\mathsf{c}})$ defines a refinement via states between the symbolic rule machine and the concrete machine.

***Concrete machine refines abstract machine*** By composing the refinement of Lemma 9.2 and the refinement of Theorem 9.4 instantiated to the concrete machine running $\phi_{\mathcal{R}^{\mathsf{abs}}}$, we can conclude that the concrete machine refines the abstract one.

***Abstract machine refines concrete machine*** The previous refinement, $(\triangleright_s^c, \triangleright_e^c)$, would also hold if the fault handler never returned when called. So, to ensure the concrete machine reflects the behaviors of the abstract machine, we next prove an inverse refinement:

**Theorem 9.8.** The abstract IFC machine refines the concrete IFC machine via $(\triangleright_i^{-c}, \triangleright_e^{-c})$, where $\triangleright_i^{-c}$ and $\triangleright_e^{-c}$ are the relational inverses of $\triangleright_i^c$ and $\triangleright_e^c$.

This guarantees that traces of the abstract machine are also emitted by the concrete machine. As above we use the symbolic rule machine as an intermediate step and show a state refinement of the concrete into the symbolic rule machine. We rely on the following lemma, where $\triangleright_s^{-c}$ is the inverse of $\triangleright_s^c$.

**Lemma 9.9** (Forward refinement). Let $qs_0$ and $cs_0$ be two states with $cs_0 \triangleright_s^{-c} qs_0$. Suppose that the symbolic rule machine takes a step $qs_0 \xrightarrow{\alpha_a} qs_1$. Then there exist concrete state $cs_1$ and action $\alpha_c$ such that $cs_0 \xrightarrow{\alpha_c}{}^\star cs_1$, with $cs_1 \triangleright_s^{-c} qs_1$ and $\alpha_c \; [\triangleright_e^{-c}] \; \alpha_a$.

To prove this lemma, we consider two cases. If the cache input of $cs_0$ matches the opcode and data of $cs_0$, then the concrete machine can take a step $cs_0 \xrightarrow{\alpha_c} cs_1$. Moreover, $\mathcal{R} \vdash \kappa$ in $cs_0$ says the cache output is consistent with the symbolic rule judgment, so the tags in $\alpha_c$ and $cs_1$ are properly related to the labels in $\alpha_a$ and $qs_1$. Otherwise, a cache fault occurs, loading the cache input and calling the fault handler. By Lemma 7.1 and the fact that $qs_0 \xrightarrow{\alpha_a} qs_1$, the cache output is computed to be consistent with $\mathcal{R}$, and this allows the concrete step as claimed.

***Discussion*** The two top-level refinement properties (9.4 and 9.8) share the same notion of matching relations but they have been proved independently in our Coq development. In the context of compiler verification [30, 42], another proof methodology has been favored: a backward simulation proof can be obtained from a proof of forward simulation under the assumption that the lower-level machine is deterministic. (CompCertTSO [42] also requires a *receptiveness* hypothesis that trivially holds in our context.) Since our concrete machine is deterministic, we could apply a similar technique. However, unlike in compiler verification where it is common to assume that the source program has a well-defined semantics (i.e. it does not get stuck), we would have to consider the possibility that the high-level semantics (the symbolic rule machine) might block and prove that in this case either the IFC enforcement judgment is stuck (and Lemma 9.6 applies) or the current symbolic rule machine state and matching concrete state are both ill-formed.

## 10. Noninterference

In this section we define TINI [1, 19] for generic machines, show that the abstract machine of §3 satisfies TINI (Theorem 10.4), that TINI is preserved by refinement (Theorem 10.5), and finally, using the fact that the concrete IFC machine refines the abstract one (Theorem 9.4), that the concrete machine satisfies TINI (Theorem 10.7).

***Termination-insensitive noninterference (TINI)*** To define noninterference, we need to talk about what can be observed about the output trace produced by a run of a machine.

**Definition 10.1** (Observation). A *notion of observation* for a generic machine is a 3-tuple $(\Omega, \lfloor\cdot\rfloor_\cdot, \cdot \approx_\cdot \cdot)$. $\Omega$ is a set of *observers* (i.e., different degrees of power to observe), ranged over by $o$. For each $o \in \Omega$, $\lfloor\cdot\rfloor_o \subseteq E$ is a predicate of *observability of events for observer* $o$, and $\cdot \approx_o \cdot \subseteq I \times I$ is a relation of *indistinguishability of input data for observer* $o$.

We write $\lfloor t \rfloor_o$ for the trace in which all unobservable events in $t$ are filtered out using $\lfloor\cdot\rfloor_o$. We write $t_1 \approx t_2$ to say that traces $t_1$ and $t_2$ are *indistinguishable*; this truncates the longer trace to the same length as the shorter and then demands that the remaining elements be pairwise identical.

**Definition 10.2** (TINI). A machine $(S, E, I, \cdot \xrightarrow{\cdot} \cdot, Init)$ with a notion of observation $(\Omega, \lfloor\cdot\rfloor_\cdot, \cdot \approx_\cdot \cdot)$ satisfies TINI if, for any observer $o \in \Omega$, pair of indistinguishable initial data $i_1 \approx_o i_2$, and pair of executions $Init(i_1) \xrightarrow{t_1}{}^\star$ and $Init(i_2) \xrightarrow{t_2}{}^\star$, we have $\lfloor t_1 \rfloor_o \approx \lfloor t_2 \rfloor_o$.

Since a machine's program is part of its input data, this definition of TINI, quantified over all observers and input data, is conceptually quantified over all programs too. Because of the truncation of traces, the observer cannot detect the absence of output, i.e., it cannot distinguish between successful termination, failure with an error, or entering an infinite loop with no observable output. This TINI property is standard for a machine with output [1, 19].[2]

***TINI for abstract machine***

**Definition 10.3** (Observation for abstract machine). Let $\mathcal{L}$ be a lattice, with partial order $\leq$. Define indistinguishability of atoms, $a_1 \approx_o^a a_2$ by

$$\frac{}{a \approx_o^a a} \qquad \frac{\neg\lfloor a_1 \rfloor_o \quad \neg\lfloor a_2 \rfloor_o}{a_1 \approx_o^a a_2}. \tag{1}$$

The notion of observation is $(\mathcal{L}, \lfloor\cdot\rfloor_\cdot^a, \cdot \approx_\cdot^a \cdot)$, where

$$\lfloor n@L \rfloor_o^a \triangleq L \leq o$$

$$(p, args_1, n, L) \approx_o^a (p, args_2, n, L) \triangleq args_1 \; [\approx_o^a] \; args_2.$$

(On the right-hand side of the second equation, $[\approx_o^a]$ is indistinguishability of atoms, lifted to lists.)

We prove TINI for the abstract machine using a set of standard *unwinding conditions* [18, 22]. For this we need to define indistinguishability on states, and thus also indistinguishability of stacks; this is where we encounter one subtlety. Indistinguishability of stacks is defined pointwise when the label of the PC is observable ($L_{pc} \leq o$). When the PC label is not observable, however, we only require that the stacks are pointwise related below the most recent Call from an observable state. This is necessary because the two machines run in lock step only when their PC labels are observable; they can execute completely different instructions otherwise.

**Theorem 10.4.** The abstract IFC machine enjoys TINI.

***TINI preserved by refinement***

**Theorem 10.5** (TINI preservation). Suppose that generic machine $M_2$ refines $M_1$ by refinement $(\triangleright_i, \triangleright_e)$ and that each machine is equipped with a notion of observation. Suppose that, for all observers $o_2$ of $M_2$, there exists an observer $o_1$ of $M_1$ such that the following compatibility conditions hold for all $e_1, e_1' \in E_1$, all $e_2, e_2' \in E_2$, and all $i_2, i_2' \in I_2$. (i) $e_1 \triangleright_e e_2 \Rightarrow (\lfloor e_1 \rfloor_{o_1} \Leftrightarrow \lfloor e_2 \rfloor_{o_2})$; (ii) $i_2 \approx_{o_2} i_2' \Rightarrow \exists i_1 \approx_{o_1} i_1'. \; (i_1 \triangleright_i i_2 \;\wedge\; i_1' \triangleright_i i_2')$; (iii) $(e_1 \approx_{o_1} e_1' \;\wedge\; e_1 \triangleright_e e_2 \;\wedge\; e_1' \triangleright_e e_2') \Rightarrow e_2 \approx_{o_2} e_2'$. Then, if $M_1$ has TINI, $M_2$ also has TINI.

Some formulations of noninterference are subject to the *refinement paradox* [23], in which refinements of a noninterferent system may violate noninterference. We avoid this issue by employing a strong notion of noninterference that restricts the amount of nondeterminism in the system and is thus preserved by *any* refinement (Theorem 10.5).[3] Since our abstract machine is deterministic, it is easy to show this strong notion of noninterference for it. In §13 we discuss a possible technique for generalizing to the concurrent setting while preserving a high degree of determinism.

[2] It is called "progress-insensitive noninterference" in a recent survey [19].

[3] The recent noninterference proof for the seL4 microkernel [35, 36] works similarly (see §12).

| | | | |
|---|---|---|---|
| *instr* | ::= | | extensions to instruction set |
| | \| | ... | |
| | \| | Alloc | allocate a new frame |
| | \| | SizeOf | fetch frame size |
| | \| | Eq | value equality |
| | \| | SysCall $id$ | system call |
| | \| | GetOff | extract pointer offset |
| | \| | Pack | atom from payload and tag |
| | \| | Unpack | atom into payload and tag |
| | \| | PushCachePtr | push cache address on stack |
| | \| | Dup $n$ | duplicate atom on stack |
| | \| | Swap $n$ | swap two data atoms on stack |

**Figure 5.** Additional instructions for extensions

$$\frac{\iota(n) = \mathsf{Alloc} \qquad \mathsf{alloc}\, k\, (L \vee L_{pc})\, a\, \mu = (id, \mu')}{\begin{array}{l}\mu \quad [(\mathsf{Int}\, k)@L, a, \sigma] \;\; n@L_{pc} \xrightarrow{\tau} \\ \mu' \;\; [(\mathsf{Ptr}\,(id, 0))@L, \sigma] \;\; (n{+}1)@L_{pc}\end{array}}$$

$$\frac{\iota(n) = \mathsf{SizeOf} \qquad \mathsf{length}\,(\mu(id)) = k}{\mu\; [(\mathsf{Ptr}\,(id, o))@L, \sigma]\; n@L_{pc} \xrightarrow{\tau} \mu\; [(\mathsf{Int}\, k)@L, \sigma]\; (n{+}1)@L_{pc}}$$

$$\frac{\iota(n) = \mathsf{GetOff}}{\mu\; [(\mathsf{Ptr}\,(id, o))@L, \sigma]\; n@L_{pc} \xrightarrow{\tau} \mu\; [(\mathsf{Int}\, o)@L, \sigma]\; (n{+}1)@L_{pc}}$$

$$\frac{\iota(n) = \mathsf{Eq}}{\begin{array}{l}\mu \quad [v_1@L_1, v_2@L_2, \sigma] \;\; n@L_{pc} \xrightarrow{\tau} \\ \mu \;\; [(\mathsf{Int}\,(v_1 == v_2))@(L_1 \vee L_2), \sigma] \;\; (n{+}1)@L_{pc}\end{array}}$$

$$\frac{\begin{array}{ll}\iota(n) = \mathsf{SysCall}\; id & T(id) = (k, f) \\ f(\sigma_1) = v@L & \mathsf{length}\,(\sigma_1) = k\end{array}}{\mu\; [\sigma_1 {+\!\!+} \sigma_2]\; n@L_{pc} \xrightarrow{\tau} \mu\; [v@L, \sigma_2]\; (n{+}1)@L_{pc}}$$

**Figure 6.** Semantics of selected new abstract machine instructions

***TINI for concrete machine with IFC fault handler*** It remains to define a notion of observation on the concrete machine, instantiating the definition of TINI for this machine. This definition refers to a concrete lattice $CL$, which must be a correct encoding of an abstract lattice $\mathcal{L}$: the lattice operators genBot, genJoin, and genFlows must satisfy the specifications in §7.

**Definition 10.6** (Observation for the concrete machine). Let $\mathcal{L}$ be an abstract lattice, and $CL$ be correct with respect to $\mathcal{L}$. The observation for the concrete machine is $(\mathcal{L}, \lfloor\cdot\rfloor^{c}_{\cdot}, \cdot \approx^{c}_{\cdot} \cdot)$, where

$$\lfloor n@\mathrm{T} \rfloor^{c}_{o} \triangleq \mathsf{Lab}(\mathrm{T}) \leq o,$$

$$(p, args'_1, n, \mathrm{T}) \approx^{c}_{o} (p, args'_2, n, \mathrm{T}) \triangleq args_1\; [\approx^{a}_{o}]\; args_2,$$

and $args'_i = \mathsf{map}\;(\mathsf{fun}\; n@L \rightarrow n@\mathsf{Tag}(L))\; args_i$.

Finally, we prove that the backward refinement proved in §9 satisfies the compatibility constraints of Theorem 10.5, so we derive:

**Theorem 10.7.** The concrete IFC machine running the fault handler $\phi_{\mathcal{R}^{\mathrm{abs}}}$ satisfies TINI.

## 11. An Extended System

Thus far we have described our model and proof results only for a simple machine architecture and IFC discipline. Our Coq development actually works with a significantly more sophisticated model, extending the basic machine architecture with a *frame-based* memory model supporting *dynamic allocation* and a *system call* mechanism for adding special-purpose primitives. Building on these features, we define an abstract IFC machine that uses *sets of principals* as its labels and a corresponding concrete machine implementation

$$\frac{\begin{array}{l}\iota(n) = \mathsf{Alloc} \qquad \mathsf{alloc}\, k\, \mathsf{u}\, a\, \mu = (id, \mu') \\ \mu(cache) = \boxed{\mathsf{alloc} \mid \mathrm{T}_{pc} \mid \mathrm{T}_1 \mid \mathrm{T}_{\mathrm{D}} \mid \mathrm{T}_{\mathrm{D}} \,\|\, \mathrm{T}_{rpc} \mid \mathrm{T}_r}\end{array}}{\begin{array}{l}\mathsf{u}\;\; \mu \;\; [(\mathsf{Int}\, k)@\mathrm{T}_1, a, \sigma] \qquad n@\mathrm{T}_{pc} \xrightarrow{\tau} \\ \mathsf{u}\;\; \mu' \;\; [(\mathsf{Ptr}\,(id, 0))@\mathrm{T}_r, \sigma] \;\; (n{+}1)@\mathrm{T}_{rpc}\end{array}}$$

$$\frac{\phi(n) = \mathsf{Alloc} \qquad \mathsf{alloc}\, k\, \mathsf{k}\, a\, \mu = (id, \mu')}{\begin{array}{l}\mathsf{k}\;\; \mu \;\; [(\mathsf{Int}\, k)@\_, a, \sigma] \qquad n@\_ \xrightarrow{\tau} \\ \mathsf{k}\;\; \mu' \;\; [(\mathsf{Ptr}\,(id, 0))@\mathrm{T}_{\mathrm{D}}, \sigma] \;\; (n{+}1)@\mathrm{T}_{\mathrm{D}}\end{array}}$$

$$\frac{\phi(n) = \mathsf{PushCachePtr}}{\mathsf{k}\; \mu\; [\sigma]\; n@\_ \xrightarrow{\tau} \mathsf{k}\; \mu\; [(\mathsf{Ptr}\,(cache, 0))@\mathrm{T}_{\mathrm{D}}, \sigma]\; (n{+}1)@\mathrm{T}_{\mathrm{D}}}$$

$$\frac{\phi(n) = \mathsf{Unpack}}{\mathsf{k}\; \mu\; [v_1@v_2, \sigma]\; n@\_ \xrightarrow{\tau} \mathsf{k}\; \mu\; [v_2@\mathrm{T}_{\mathrm{D}}, v_1@\mathrm{T}_{\mathrm{D}}, \sigma]\; (n{+}1)@\mathrm{T}_{\mathrm{D}}}$$

$$\frac{\phi(n) = \mathsf{Pack}}{\mathsf{k}\; \mu\; [v_2@\_, v_1@\_, \sigma]\; n@\_ \xrightarrow{\tau} \mathsf{k}\; \mu\; [v_1@v_2, \sigma]\; (n{+}1)@\mathrm{T}_{\mathrm{D}}}$$

$$\frac{\iota(n) = \mathsf{SysCall}\; id \qquad T(id) = (k, n') \qquad \mathsf{length}\,(\sigma_1) = k}{\mathsf{u}\; \mu\; [\sigma_1 {+\!\!+} \sigma_2]\; n@\mathrm{T} \xrightarrow{\tau} \mathsf{k}\; \mu\; [\sigma_1 {+\!\!+} (n{+}1@\mathrm{T}, \mathsf{u}); \sigma_2]\; n'@\mathrm{T}_{\mathrm{D}}}$$

**Figure 7.** Semantics of selected new concrete machine instructions

where tags are pointers to dynamically allocated representations of these sets. While still much less complex than the real SAFE system, this extended model shows how our basic approach can be incrementally scaled up to more realistic designs. Verifying these extensions requires no major changes to the proof architecture of the basic system, serving as evidence of its robustness.

Fig. 5 shows the new instructions supported by the extended model. Instruction PushCachePtr, Unpack, and Pack are used only by the concrete machine, for the compiled fault handler (hence they only have a kernel-mode stepping rule; they simply get stuck if executed outside kernel mode, or on an abstract machine). We also add two stack-manipulation instructions, Dup and Swap, to make programming the kernel routines more convenient. It remains true that any program for the abstract machine makes sense to run on the abstract rule machine and the concrete machine. For brevity, we detail stepping rules only for the extended abstract IFC machine (Fig. 6) and concrete machine (Fig. 7); corresponding extensions to the symbolic IFC rule machine are straightforward (we also omit rules for Dup and Swap). Individual rules are explained below.

***Dynamic memory allocation*** High-level programming languages usually assume a structured memory model, in which independently allocated *frames* are disjoint by construction and programs cannot depend on the relative placement of frames in memory. The SAFE hardware enforces this abstraction by attaching explicit runtime types to all values, distinguishing pointers from other data. Only data marked as pointers can be used to access memory. To obtain a pointer, one must either call the (privileged) memory manager to allocate a fresh *frame* or else offset an existing pointer. In particular, it is not possible to "forge" a pointer from an integer. Each pointer also carries information about its base and bounds, and the hardware prevents it from being used to access memory outside of its frame.

*Frame-based memory model* In our extended system, we model the user-level view of SAFE's memory system by adding a frame-structured memory, distinguished pointers (so *values*, the payload field of atoms and the tag field of concrete atoms, can now either be an integer (Int $n$) or a pointer (Ptr $p$)), and an allocation instruction to our basic machines. We do this (nearly) uniformly at all levels of abstraction.[4] A *pointer* is a pair $p = (id, o)$ of a frame identifier $id$ and an offset $o$ into that frame. In the machine state, the data memory $\mu$ is a partial function from pointers to individual storage cells that is undefined on out-of-frame pointers. By abuse of notation, $\mu$ is also a partial function from frame identifiers to frames, which are just lists of atoms.

The most important new rule of the extended abstract machine is Alloc (Fig. 6). In this machine there is a separate memory region (assumed infinite) corresponding to each label. The auxiliary function alloc in the rule for Alloc takes a size $k$, the label (region) at which to allocate, and a default atom $a$; it extends $\mu$ with a fresh frame of size $k$, initializing its contents to $a$. It returns the id of the new frame and the extended memory $\mu'$.

*IFC and memory allocation* We require that the frame identifiers produced by allocation at one label not be affected by allocations at other labels; e.g., alloc might allocate sequentially in each region. Thus, indistinguishability of low atoms is just syntactic equality, preserving Definition 10.3 from the simple abstract machine, which is convenient for proving noninterference, as we explain below. We allow a program to observe frame sizes using a new SizeOf instruction, which requires tainting the result of Alloc with $L$, the label of the size argument. There are also new instructions Eq, for comparing two values (including pointers) for equality, and GetOff, for extracting the offset field of a pointer into an integer. However, frame ids are intuitively *abstract*: the concrete representation of frame ids is not accessible, and pointers cannot be forged or output. The extended concrete machine stepping rules for these new instructions are analogous to the abstract machine rules, with the important exception of Alloc, which is discussed below.

A few small modifications to existing instructions in the basic machine (Fig. 2) are needed to handle pointers properly. In particular: (i) Load and Store require pointer arguments and get stuck if the pointer's offset is out of range for its frame. (ii) Add takes either two integers or an integer and a pointer, where $\mathsf{Int}\, n + \mathsf{Int}\, m = \mathsf{Int}\,(n{+}m)$ and $\mathsf{Ptr}\,(id, o_1) + \mathsf{Int}\, o_2 = \mathsf{Ptr}\,(id, o_1{+}o_2)$. (iii) Output works only on integers, not pointers. Analogous modifications are needed in the concrete machine semantic rules.

*Concrete allocator* The extended concrete machine's semantics for Alloc differ from those of the abstract machine in one key respect. Using one region per tag would not be a realistic strategy for a concrete implementation; e.g., the number of different tags might be extremely large. Instead, we use a single region for all user-mode allocations at the concrete level. We also collapse the separate user and kernel memories from the basic concrete machine into a single memory. Since we still want to be able to distinguish user and kernel frames, we mark each frame with a privilege mode (i.e., we use two allocation regions). Fig. 7 shows the corresponding concrete stepping rule for Alloc for two cases: non-faulting user mode and kernel mode. The concrete Load and Store rules prevent dereferencing kernel pointers in user mode. The rule cache is now just a distinguished kernel frame *cache*; to access it, the fault handler uses the (privileged) PushCachePtr instruction.

*Proof by refinement* As before, we prove noninterference for the concrete machine by combining a proof of noninterference of the abstract machine with a two-stage proof that the concrete machine refines the abstract machine. By using this approach we avoid some well-known difficulties in proving noninterference directly for the concrete machine. In particular, when frames allocated in low and high contexts share the same region, allocations in high contexts can cause variations in the precise pointer values returned for allocations in low contexts, and these variations must be taken into account when defining the indistinguishability relation. For example, Banerjee and Naumann [4] prove noninterference by parameterizing their indistinguishability relation with a partial bijection that keeps track of indistinguishable memory addresses. Our approach, by contrast, defines pointer indistinguishability only at the abstract level, where indistinguishable low pointers are identical. This proof strategy still requires relating memory addresses when showing refinement, but this relation does not appear in the noninterference proof at the abstract level. The refinement proof itself uses a simplified form of *memory injections* [31]. The differences in the memory region structure of both machines are significant, but invisible to programs, since no information about frame ids is revealed to programs beyond what can be obtained by comparing pointers for equality. This restriction allows the refinement proof to go through straightforwardly.

***System calls*** To support the implementation of policy-specific primitives on top of the concrete machine, we provide a new *system call* instruction. The SysCall $id$ instruction is parameterized by a system call identifier. The step relation of each machine is now parameterized by a table $T$ that maps system call identifiers to their implementations.

In the abstract and symbolic rule machines, a system call implementation is an arbitrary Coq function that removes a list of atoms from the top of the stack and either puts a result on top of the stack or fails, halting the machine. The system call implementation is responsible for computing the label of the result and performing any checks that are needed to ensure noninterference.

In the concrete machine, system calls are implemented by kernel routines and the call table contains the entry points of these routines in the kernel instruction memory. Executing a system call involves inserting the return address on the stack (underneath the call arguments) and jumping to the corresponding entry point. The kernel code terminates either by returning a result to the user program or by halting the machine.

This feature has no major impact on the proofs of noninterference and refinement. For noninterference, we must show that all the abstract system calls preserve indistinguishability of abstract machine states; for refinement, we show that each concrete system call correctly implements the abstract one using the machinery of §7.

***Labeling with sets of principals*** The full SAFE machine supports dynamic creation of security principals. In the extended model, we make a first step toward dynamic principal creation by taking principals to be integers and instantiating the (parametric) lattice of labels with the lattice of finite sets of integers.[5] In this lattice, $\bot$ is $\emptyset$, $\vee$ is $\cup$, and $\leq$ is $\subseteq$. We enrich our IFC model by adding a new *classification* primitive joinP that adds a principal to an atom's label, encoded using the system call mechanism described above. The operation of joinP is given by the following derived rule, which is an instance of the SysCall rule from Fig. 6.

$$\frac{\iota(n) = \mathsf{SysCall\,joinP}}{\begin{array}{ll}\mu\ [v@L_1, (\mathsf{Int}\ m)@L_2, \sigma]\ \ n@L_{pc} & \xrightarrow{\tau} \\ \mu\ [v@(L_1 \vee L_2 \vee \{m\}), \sigma]\ \ (n{+}1)@L_{pc} & \end{array}}$$

At the concrete level, a tag is now a pointer to an array of principals (integers) stored in kernel memory. To keep the fault handler code simple, we do not maintain canonical representations of sets: one set may be represented by different arrays, and a given array may have duplicate elements. (As a consequence, the mapping from abstract labels to tags is no longer a function; we return

[4] It would be interesting to describe an *implementation* of the memory manager in a still-lower-level concrete machine with no built-in Alloc instruction, but we leave this as future work.

[5] This lattice is statically known, but models dynamic creation by supporting unbounded labels and having no top element.

to this point below.) Since the fault handler generator in the basic system is parametric in the underlying lattice, it doesn't require any modification. All we must do is provide concrete implementations for the appropriate lattice operations: genJoin just allocates a fresh array and concatenates both argument arrays into it; genFlows checks for array inclusion by iterating through one array and testing whether each element appears in the other; and genBot allocates a new empty array. Finally, we provide kernel code to implement joinP, which requires two new privileged instructions, Pack and Unpack (Fig. 7), to manipulate the payload and tag fields of atoms; otherwise, the implementation is similar to that of genJoin.

A more realistic system would keep canonical representations of sets and avoid unnecessary allocation in order to improve its memory footprint and tag cache usage. But even with the present simplistic approach, both the code for the lattice operations and their proofs of correctness are significantly more elaborate than for the trivial two-point lattice. In particular, we need an additional code generator to build counted loops, e.g., for computing the join of two tags.

$$\begin{array}{l} \mathsf{genFor}\ c\ = \\ \quad [\mathsf{Dup}] \mathbin{+\!\!+} \mathsf{genIf}\ (\mathsf{genLoop}(c \mathbin{+\!\!+} [\mathsf{Push}\ (-1), \mathsf{Add}]))\ [] \\ \quad \text{where } \mathsf{genLoop}\ c\ =\ c \mathbin{+\!\!+} [\mathsf{Dup}, \mathsf{Bnz}\ (-(\mathsf{length}\ c + 1))] \end{array}$$

Here, $c$ is a code sequence representing the loop body, which is expected to preserve an index value on top of the stack; the generator builds code to execute that body repeatedly, decrementing the index each time until it reaches 0. The corresponding specification is

$$\frac{\begin{array}{l} P_n(\kappa,\sigma) := \exists\, \mathrm{T}\, \sigma'.\ \sigma = n@\mathrm{T}, \sigma' \wedge Inv(\kappa,\sigma) \\ Q_n(\kappa,\sigma) := \exists\, \mathrm{T}\, \sigma'.\quad \sigma = n@\mathrm{T}, \sigma' \\ \qquad\qquad\qquad\qquad \wedge\, \forall\, \mathrm{T}'.\ Inv(\kappa, ((n-1)@\mathrm{T}', \sigma')) \\ \forall\, n.\ 0 < n \Longrightarrow \{P_n\}\ c\ \{Q_n\} \\ P(\kappa,\sigma) := \exists\, n\, \mathrm{T}\, \sigma'.\ 0 \le n \wedge \sigma = n@\mathrm{T}, \sigma' \wedge Inv(\kappa,\sigma) \\ Q(\kappa,\sigma) := \exists\, \mathrm{T}\, \sigma'.\ \sigma = 0@\mathrm{T}, \sigma' \wedge Inv(\kappa,\sigma) \end{array}}{\{P\}\ \mathsf{genFor}\ c\ \{Q\}}$$

To avoid reasoning about memory updates as far as possible, we code in a style where all local context is stored on the stack and manipulated using Dup and Swap. Although the resulting code is lengthy, it is relatively easy to automate the corresponding proofs.

***Stateful encoding of labels*** Changing the representation of tags from integers to pointers requires modifying one small part of the basic system proof. Recall that in §6 we described the encoding of labels into tags as a *pure* function Lab. To deal with the memory-dependent and non-canonical representation of sets described above, the extended system instead uses a *relation* between an abstract label, a concrete tag that encodes it, and a memory in which this tag should be interpreted.

If tags are pointers to data structures, it is crucial that these data structures remain intact as long as the tags appear in the machine state. We guarantee this by maintaining the very strong invariant that each execution of the fault handler only allocates new frames, and never modifies the contents of existing ones, except for the *cache* frame (which tags never point into). A more realistic implementation might use mutable kernel memory for other purposes and garbage collect unused tags; this would require a more complicated memory invariant.

The TINI formulation is similar in essence to the one in §10, but some subtleties arise for concrete output events, since tags in events cannot be interpreted on their own anymore. We wish to (i) keep the semantics of the concrete machine independent of high-level policies such as IFC and (ii) give a statement of noninterference that does not refer to pointers. To achieve these seemingly contradictory aims, we model an event of the concrete machine as a pair of a concrete atom plus the whole state of the kernel memory. The resulting trace of concrete events is abstracted (i.e., interpreted in terms of abstract labels) only when stating and proving TINI. This is an idealization of what happens in the real SAFE machine, where communication of labeled data with the outside world involves cryptography. Modeling this is left as future work.

## 12. Related Work

The SAFE design spans a number of research areas, and a comprehensive overview of related work would be huge. We focus here on a small set of especially relevant points of comparison. The long version discusses additional related work.

***Language-based IFC*** Static approaches to IFC have generally dominated language-based security research [40, etc.]; however, statically enforcing IFC at the lowest level of a real system is challenging. Soundly analyzing native binaries with reasonable precision is hard, even more so without the compiler's cooperation (e.g., for stripped or obfuscated binaries). Proof-carrying code [5, etc.] and typed assembly language [33, etc.] have been used for enforcing IFC on low-level code without low-level analysis or adding the compiler to the TCB. In SAFE [14, 17] we follow a different approach, enforcing noninterference using purely dynamic checks, for arbitrary binaries in a custom-designed instruction set. The mechanisms we use for this are similar to those found in recent work on purely dynamic IFC for high-level languages [3, 20, 21, 39, 44, etc.]; however, as far as we know, we are the first to push these ideas to the lowest level.

***seL4*** Murray et al. [35] recently demonstrated a machine-checked noninterference proof for the implementation of the seL4 microkernel. This proof is carried out by refinement and reuses the specification and most of the existing functional correctness proof of seL4 [27]. Like the TINI property in this paper, the variant of intransitive noninterference used by Murray et al. is preserved by refinement because it implies a high degree of determinism [36]. This organization of their proof was responsible for a significant saving in effort, even when factoring in the additional work required to remove all observable non-determinism from the seL4 specification. Beyond these similarities, SAFE and seL4 rely on completely different mechanisms to achieve different notions of noninterference. Whereas, in SAFE, each word of data has an IFC label and labels are propagated on each instruction, the seL4 kernel maintains separation between several large partitions (e.g., one partition can run an unmodified version of Linux) and ensures that information is conveyed between such partitions only in accordance with a fixed access control policy.

***PROSPER*** In parallel work, Dam et al. [13, 26, etc.] verified information flow security for a tiny proof-of-concept separation kernel running on ARMv7 and using a Memory Management Unit for physical protection of memory regions belonging to different partitions. The authors argue that noninterference is not well suited for systems in which components are supposed to communicate with each other. Instead, they use the bisimulation proof method to show trace equivalence between the real system and an ideal top-level specification that is secure by construction. As in seL4 [35], the proof methodology precludes an abstract treatment of scheduling, but the authors contend this is to be expected when information flow is to be taken into account.

***TIARA and ARIES*** The SAFE architecture embodies a number of innovations from earlier paper designs. In particular, the TIARA design [43] first proposed the idea of a zero-kernel operating system and sketched a concrete architecture, while the ARIES project proposed using a hardware rule cache to speed up information-flow tracking [7]. In TIARA and ARIES, tags had a fixed set of fields and were of limited length, whereas, in SAFE, tags are pointers to arbitrary data structures, allowing them to represent complex IFC labels encoding sophisticated security policies [34]. Moreover, unlike TIARA and ARIES, which made no formal soundness claims, SAFE proposes a set of IFC rules aimed at achieving noninterference; the proof we present in this paper, though for a simplified model, provides evidence that this goal is within reach.

***RIFLE and other binary-rewriting-based IFC systems*** RIFLE [46] enforces user-specified information-flow policies for x86 binaries using binary rewriting, static analysis, and augmented hardware. Binary rewriting is used to make implicit flows explicit; it heavily relies on static analysis for reconstructing the program's control-flow graph and performing reaching-definitions and alias analysis. The augmented hardware architecture associates labels with registers and memory and updates these labels on each instruction to track explicit flows. Additional security registers are used by the binary translation mechanism to help track implicit flows. Beringer [6] recently proved (in Coq) that the main ideas in RIFLE can be used to achieve noninterference for a simple While language. Unlike RIFLE, SAFE achieves noninterference purely dynamically and does not rely on binary rewriting or heroic static analysis of binaries. Moreover, the SAFE hardware is generic, simply caching instances of software-managed rules.

While many other information flow tracking systems based on binary rewriting have been proposed, few are concerned with soundly handling implicit flows [11, 32], and even these do so only to the extent they can statically analyze binaries. Since, unlike RIFLE (and SAFE), these systems use unmodified hardware, the overhead for tracking implicit flows can be large. To reduce this overhead, recent systems track implicit flows selectively [25] or not at all—arguably a reasonable tradeoff in settings such as malware analysis or attack detection, where speed and precision are more important than soundness.

***Hardware taint tracking*** The last decade has seen significant progress in specialized hardware for accelerating taint tracking [12, 15, 45, 47, etc.]. Most commonly, a single tag bit is associated with each word to specify if it is tainted or not. Initially aimed at mitigating low-level memory corruption attacks by preventing the use of tainted pointers and the execution of tainted instructions [45, etc.], hardware-based taint tracking has also been used to prevent high-level attacks such as SQL injection and cross-site scripting [12]. In contrast to SAFE, these systems prioritize efficiency and overall helpfulness over the soundness of the analysis, striking a heuristic balance between false positives and false negatives (missed attacks). As a consequence, these systems ignore implicit flows and often don't even track all explicit flows. While early systems supported a single hard-coded taint propagation policy, recent ones allow the policy to be defined in software [12, 15, 47] and support monitoring policies that go beyond taint tracking [8, 15, etc.]. Harmoni [15], for example, provides a pair of caches that are quite similar to the SAFE rule cache. Possibly these could even be adapted to enforcing noninterference, in which case we expect the proof methodology introduced here to apply.

***Verification of low-level code*** The distinctive challenge in verifying machine code is coping with unstructured control flow. Our approach using structured generators to build the fault handler is similar to the mechanisms used in Chlipala's Bedrock system [9, 10] and by Jensen et al. [24], but there are several points of difference. These systems each build macros on top of a powerful low-level program logic for machine code (Ni and Shao's XCAP [38], in the case of Bedrock), whereas we take a simpler, ad-hoc approach, building directly on our stack machine's relatively high-level semantics. Both these systems are based on separation logic, which we can do without since (at least in the present simplified model) we have very few memory operations to reason about. We have instead focused on developing a simple Hoare logic specifically suited to verifying structured runtime-system code; e.g., we omit support for arbitrary code pointers, but add support for reasoning about termination. We use total-correctness Hoare triples (similar to Myreen and Gordon [37]) and weakest preconditions to guarantee progress, not just safety, for our handler code. Finally, our level of automation is much more modest than Bedrock's, though still adequate to discharge most verification conditions on straight-line stack manipulation code rapidly and often automatically.

## 13. Conclusions and Future Work

We have presented a formal model of the key IFC mechanisms of the SAFE system: propagating and checking tags to enforce security, using a hardware cache for common-case efficiency and a software fault handler for maximum flexibility. To formalize and prove properties at such a low level (including features such as dynamic memory allocation and labels represented by pointers to in-memory data structures), we first construct a high-level abstract specification of the system, then refine it in two steps into a realistic concrete machine. A bidirectional refinement methodology allows us to prove (i) that the concrete machine, loaded with the right fault handler (i.e. correctly implementing the IFC enforcement of the abstract specification) satisfies a traditional notion of termination-insensitive noninterference, and (ii) that the concrete machine reflects all the behaviours of the abstract specification. Our formalization reflects the programmability of the fault handling mechanism, in that the fault handler code is compiled from a rule table written in a small DSL. We set up a custom Hoare logic to specify and verify the corresponding machine code, following the structure of a simple compiler for this DSL.

The development in this paper concerns three *deterministic* machines and simplifies away concurrency. While the lack of concurrency is a significant current limitation that we would like to remove as soon as possible by moving to a multithreading single-core model, we still want to maintain the abstraction layers of a proof-by-refinement architecture. This requires some care so as not to run afoul of the refinement paradox [23] since some standard notions of noninterference (for example possibilistic noninterference) are not preserved by refinement in the presence of non-determinism. One promising path toward this objective is inspired by the recent noninterference proof for seL4 [35, 36]. If we manage to share a common thread scheduler between the abstract and concrete machines, we could still prove a strong double refinement property (concrete refines abstract and vice versa) and hence preserve a strong notion of noninterference (such as the TINI notion from this work) or a possibilistic variation.

Although this paper focuses on IFC and noninterference, the tagging facilities of the concrete machine are completely generic. In current follow-on work, we aim to show that the same hardware can be used to efficiently support completely different policies targeting memory safety and control-flow integrity. Moreover, although the rule cache / fault handler design arose in the context of SAFE, we believe that this mechanism can also be ported to more traditional architectures. In the future, we plan to reuse and extend the formal development in this paper both to a larger set of high-level properties and to more conventional architectures. For instance, we expect the infrastructure for compiling DSLs to fault handler software using verified structured code generators to extend to runtime-system components (e.g. garbage collectors, device drivers, etc.), beyond IFC and SAFE.

***Acknowledgments*** We are grateful to Maxime Dénès, Deepak Garg, Greg Morrisett, Toby Murray, Jeremy Planul, Alejandro Russo, Howie Shrobe, Jonathan M. Smith, Deian Stefan, and Greg Sullivan for useful discussions and helpful feedback on early drafts.

We also thank the anonymous reviewers for their insightful comments. This material is based upon work supported by the DARPA CRASH program through the US Air Force Research Laboratory (AFRL) under Contract No. FA8650-10-C-7090. The views expressed are those of the authors and do not reflect the official policy or position of the Department of Defense or the U.S. Government.

## References

[1] A. Askarov, S. Hunt, A. Sabelfeld, and D. Sands. Termination-insensitive noninterference leaks more than just a bit. *ESORICS*. 2008.

[2] A. Askarov and A. Sabelfeld. Tight enforcement of information-release policies for dynamic languages. *CSF*. 2009.

[3] T. H. Austin and C. Flanagan. Efficient purely-dynamic information flow analysis. *PLAS*. 2009.

[4] A. Banerjee and D. A. Naumann. Stack-based access control and secure information flow. *JFP*, 15(2):131–177, 2005.

[5] G. Barthe, D. Pichardie, and T. Rezk. A certified lightweight non-interference Java bytecode verifier. *ESOP*. 2007.

[6] L. Beringer. End-to-end multilevel hybrid information flow control. *APLAS*. 2012.

[7] J. Brown and T. F. Knight, Jr. A minimally trusted computing base for dynamically ensuring secure information flow. Technical Report 5, MIT CSAIL, 2001. Aries Memo No. 15.

[8] S. Chen, M. Kozuch, T. Strigkos, B. Falsafi, P. B. Gibbons, T. C. Mowry, V. Ramachandran, O. Ruwase, M. P. Ryan, and E. Vlachos. Flexible hardware acceleration for instruction-grain program monitoring. *ISCA*. 2008.

[9] A. Chlipala. Mostly-automated verification of low-level programs in computational separation logic. *PLDI*, 2011.

[10] A. Chlipala. The Bedrock structured programming system: Combining generative metaprogramming and Hoare logic in an extensible program verifier. *ICFP*. 2013.

[11] J. A. Clause, W. Li, and A. Orso. Dytan: a generic dynamic taint analysis framework. *ISSTA*. 2007.

[12] M. Dalton, H. Kannan, and C. Kozyrakis. Raksha: a flexible information flow architecture for software security. *ISCA*, 2007.

[13] M. Dam, R. Guanciale, N. Khakpour, H. Nemati, and O. Schwarz. Formal verification of information flow security for a simple ARM-based separation kernel. *CCS*, 2013. To appear.

[14] A. DeHon, B. Karel, T. F. Knight, Jr., G. Malecha, B. Montagu, R. Morisset, G. Morrisett, B. C. Pierce, R. Pollack, S. Ray, O. Shivers, J. M. Smith, and G. Sullivan. Preliminary design of the SAFE platform. *PLOS*, 2011.

[15] D. Y. Deng and G. E. Suh. High-performance parallel accelerator for flexible and efficient run-time monitoring. *DSN*. 2012.

[16] U. Dhawan and A. DeHon. Area-efficient near-associative memories on FPGAs. In *International Symposium on Field-Programmable Gate Arrays, (FPGA2013)*, 2013.

[17] U. Dhawan, A. Kwon, E. Kadric, C. Hriţcu, B. C. Pierce, J. M. Smith, A. DeHon, G. Malecha, G. Morrisett, T. F. Knight, Jr., A. Sutherland, T. Hawkins, A. Zyxnfryx, D. Wittenberg, P. Trei, S. Ray, and G. Sullivan. Hardware support for safety interlocks and introspection. *AHNS*, 2012.

[18] J. A. Goguen and J. Meseguer. Unwinding and inference control. *IEEE S&P*. 1984.

[19] D. Hedin and A. Sabelfeld. A perspective on information-flow control. Marktoberdorf Summer School. IOS Press, 2011.

[20] D. Hedin and A. Sabelfeld. Information-flow security for a core of JavaScript. *CSF*. 2012.

[21] C. Hriţcu, M. Greenberg, B. Karel, B. C. Pierce, and G. Morrisett. All your IFCException are belong to us. *IEEE S&P*. 2013.

[22] C. Hriţcu, J. Hughes, B. C. Pierce, A. Spector-Zabusky, D. Vytiniotis, A. Azevedo de Amorim, and L. Lampropoulos. Testing noninterference, quickly. *ICFP*, 2013.

[23] J. Jacob. On the derivation of secure components. *IEEE S&P*. 1989.

[24] J. B. Jensen, N. Benton, and A. Kennedy. High-level separation logic for low-level code. *POPL*. 2013.

[25] M. G. Kang, S. McCamant, P. Poosankam, and D. Song. DTA++: Dynamic taint analysis with targeted control-flow propagation. *NDSS*. 2011.

[26] N. Khakpour, O. Schwarz, and M. Dam. Machine assisted proof of ARMv7 instruction level isolation properties. *CPP*, 2013. To appear.

[27] G. Klein, K. Elphinstone, G. Heiser, J. Andronick, D. Cock, P. Derrin, D. Elkaduwe, K. Engelhardt, R. Kolanski, M. Norrish, T. Sewell, H. Tuch, and S. Winwood. seL4: Formal verification of an OS kernel. *SOSP*. 2009.

[28] M. N. Krohn and E. Tromer. Noninterference for a practical DIFC-based operating system. *IEEE S&P*. 2009.

[29] A. Kwon, U. Dhawan, J. M. Smith, T. F. Knight, Jr., and A. DeHon. Low-fat pointers: compact encoding and efficient gate-level implementation of fat pointers for spatial safety and capability-based security. *CCS*. 2013.

[30] X. Leroy. A formally verified compiler back-end. *Journal of Automated Reasoning*, 43(4):363–446, 2009.

[31] X. Leroy and S. Blazy. Formal verification of a C-like memory model and its uses for verifying program transformations. *JAR*, 41(1):1–31, 2008.

[32] W. Masri, A. Podgurski, and D. Leon. Detecting and debugging insecure information flows. *ISSRE*. 2004.

[33] R. Medel, A. B. Compagnoni, and E. Bonelli. A typed assembly language for non-interference. *ICTCS*. 2005.

[34] B. Montagu, B. C. Pierce, and R. Pollack. A theory of information-flow labels. *CSF*. 2013.

[35] T. C. Murray, D. Matichuk, M. Brassil, P. Gammie, T. Bourke, S. Seefried, C. Lewis, X. Gao, and G. Klein. seL4: from general purpose to a proof of information flow enforcement. *IEEE S&P*. 2013.

[36] T. C. Murray, D. Matichuk, M. Brassil, P. Gammie, and G. Klein. Noninterference for operating system kernels. *CPP*. 2012.

[37] M. O. Myreen and M. J. C. Gordon. Hoare logic for realistically modelled machine code. *TACAS*. 2007.

[38] Z. Ni and Z. Shao. Certified assembly programming with embedded code pointers. *POPL*. 2006.

[39] A. Russo and A. Sabelfeld. Dynamic vs. static flow-sensitive security analysis. *CSF*. 2010.

[40] A. Sabelfeld and A. Myers. Language-based information-flow security. *JSAC*, 21(1):5–19, 2003.

[41] A. Sabelfeld and A. Russo. From dynamic to static and back: Riding the roller coaster of information-flow control research. In *Ershov Memorial Conference*. 2009.

[42] J. Sevcík, V. Vafeiadis, F. Z. Nardelli, S. Jagannathan, and P. Sewell. Relaxed-memory concurrency and verified compilation. *POPL*. 2011.

[43] H. Shrobe, A. DeHon, and T. F. Knight, Jr. Trust-management, intrusion-tolerance, accountability, and reconstitution architecture (TIARA), 2009.

[44] D. Stefan, A. Russo, J. C. Mitchell, and D. Mazières. Flexible dynamic information flow control in Haskell. *Haskell*. 2011.

[45] G. E. Suh, J. W. Lee, D. Zhang, and S. Devadas. Secure program execution via dynamic information flow tracking. *ASPLOS*, 2004.

[46] N. Vachharajani, M. J. Bridges, J. Chang, R. Rangan, G. Ottoni, J. A. Blome, G. A. Reis, M. Vachharajani, and D. I. August. RIFLE: An architectural framework for user-centric information-flow security. *MICRO*, 2004.

[47] G. Venkataramani, I. Doudalis, Y. Solihin, and M. Prvulovic. FlexiTaint: A programmable accelerator for dynamic taint propagation. *HPCA*, 2008.

[48] S. A. Zdancewic. *Programming Languages for Information Security*. PhD thesis, Cornell University, 2002.

# CakeML: A Verified Implementation of ML

Ramana Kumar * [1] Magnus O. Myreen † [1] Michael Norrish [2] Scott Owens [3]

[1] Computer Laboratory, University of Cambridge, UK
[2] Canberra Research Lab, NICTA, Australia ‡
[3] School of Computing, University of Kent, UK

## Abstract

We have developed and mechanically verified an ML system called CakeML, which supports a substantial subset of Standard ML. CakeML is implemented as an interactive read-eval-print loop (REPL) in x86-64 machine code. Our correctness theorem ensures that this REPL implementation prints only those results permitted by the semantics of CakeML. Our verification effort touches on a breadth of topics including lexing, parsing, type checking, incremental and dynamic compilation, garbage collection, arbitrary-precision arithmetic, and compiler bootstrapping.

Our contributions are twofold. The first is simply in building a system that is end-to-end verified, demonstrating that each piece of such a verification effort can in practice be composed with the others, and ensuring that none of the pieces rely on any over-simplifying assumptions. The second is developing novel approaches to some of the more challenging aspects of the verification. In particular, our formally verified compiler can bootstrap itself: we apply the verified compiler to itself to produce a verified machine-code implementation of the compiler. Additionally, our compiler proof handles diverging input programs with a lightweight approach based on logical timeout exceptions. The entire development was carried out in the HOL4 theorem prover.

***Categories and Subject Descriptors*** D.2.4 [*Software Engineering*]: Software/Program Verification—Correctness proofs, Formal methods; F.3.1 [*Logics and meanings of programs*]: Specifying and Verifying and Reasoning about Programs—Mechanical verification, Specification techniques, Invariants

***Keywords*** Compiler verification; compiler bootstrapping; ML; machine code verification; read-eval-print loop; verified parsing; verified type checking; verified garbage collection.

* supported by the Gates Cambridge Trust

† supported by the Royal Society, UK

‡ NICTA is funded by the Australian Government through the Department of Communications and the Australian Research Council through the ICT Centre of Excellence Program.



*POPL '14*, January 22–24, 2014, San Diego, CA, USA..
Copyright is held by the owner/author(s). Publication rights licensed to ACM.
ACM 978-1-4503-2544-8/14/01...$15.00.
http://dx.doi.org/10.1145/2535838.2535841

## 1. Introduction

The last decade has seen a strong interest in verified compilation; and there have been significant, high-profile results, many based on the CompCert compiler for C [1, 14, 16, 29]. This interest is easy to justify: in the context of program verification, an unverified compiler forms a large and complex part of the trusted computing base. However, to our knowledge, none of the existing work on verified compilers for general-purpose languages has addressed all aspects of a compiler along two dimensions: one, the compilation algorithm for converting a program from a source string to a list of numbers representing machine code, and two, the execution of that algorithm as implemented in machine code.

Our purpose in this paper is to explain how we have verified a compiler along the full scope of both of these dimensions for a practical, general-purpose programming language. Our language is called CakeML, and it is a strongly typed, impure, strict functional language based on Standard ML and OCaml. By verified, we mean that the CakeML system is ultimately x86-64 machine code alongside a mechanically checked theorem in higher-order logic saying that running that machine code causes an input program to yield output or diverge as specified by the semantics of CakeML.

We did not write the CakeML compiler and platform directly in machine code. Instead we write it in higher-order logic and synthesise CakeML from that using our previous technique [22], which puts the compiler on equal footing with other CakeML programs. We then apply the compiler to itself, *i.e.*, we *bootstrap* it. This avoids a tedious manual refinement proof relating the compilation algorithm to its implementation, as well as providing a moderately large example program. More specifically,

- we write, and can run, the compiler as a function in the logic, and we synthesise a CakeML implementation of the compiler inside the logic;
- we bootstrap the compiler to get a machine-code implementation inside the logic; and
- the compiler correctness theorem thereby applies to the machine-code implementation of the compiler.

Another consequence of bootstrapping is that we can include the compiler implementation as part of the runtime system to form an interactive read-eval-print loop (REPL). A verified REPL enables high-assurance applications that provide interactivity, an important feature for interactive theorem provers in the LCF tradition, which were the original motivation for ML.

***Contributions***

- Semantics that are carefully designed to be simultaneously suitable for proving meta-theoretic language properties and for supporting a verified implementation. (Section 3)
- An extension of a proof-producing synthesis pathway [22] originally from logic to ML, now to machine code (via verified compilation). (Sections 4–6, 10)

- A lightweight method for proving divergence-preservation using a clock and timeout exceptions — these only appear in the proof, not in the implementation. It allows us to do all of our compiler proofs by induction and in the direction of compilation. (Section 7)
- To the best of our knowledge, this is the first bootstrapping of a formally verified compiler. The bootstrapping is done within the logic so that the compiler correctness theorem can be instantiated to apply directly to the compiler's output. (Section 9)

***Result*** The result of this work is an end-to-end verified REPL implementation in 64-bit x86, including lexing, parsing, type inference, compilation, garbage collection, printing, and arbitrary-precision integer arithmetic. The entire formal development was carried out in the HOL4 theorem prover [8]. All of our definitions and proofs are available at **https://cakeml.org**.

## 2. Approach

The CakeML system and verification divides into three layers.

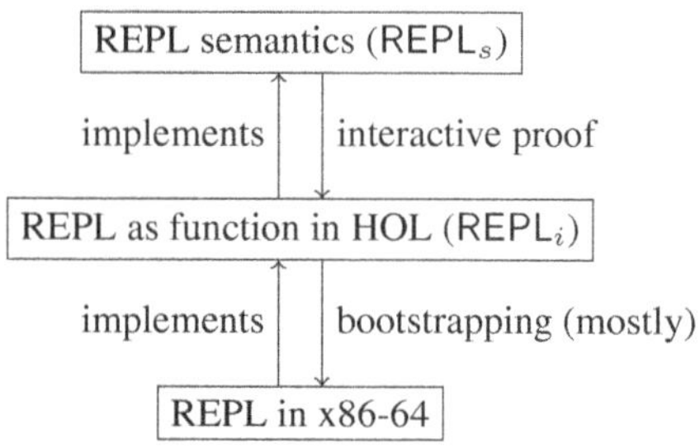


At the top is the semantic specification of the REPL. At the bottom is machine code implementing the REPL. In between is an implementation of the REPL as a function in logic. We describe the components of each layer in more detail below, then give an overview of the proof that each layer implements the one above it.

***The REPL Specification*** The semantics for the CakeML REPL is given by a relation

$$\mathsf{REPL}_s : \mathsf{bool\ list} \to \mathsf{string} \to \mathsf{repl\_result} \to \mathsf{bool}$$

between a string representing the read input and a repl_result, which is a list of strings representing the printed output, ending in a nil value that indicates whether the REPL has terminated or diverged. The bool list argument indicates which input declarations have type errors (needed because we have not yet verified completeness for the type inferencer; see Section 5).

The input string is treated as a series of declarations separated by semicolons. Each declaration might yield an output string describing a result value or reporting a lex, parse, or type error; or it might diverge.

In the definition of REPL$_s$, we apply an executable lexer specification to the entire input string and split the resulting list of tokens at top-level semicolons, yielding a list of possibly invalid declarations.[1] For each declaration, we pick a valid parse tree according to the CakeML grammar, if one exists. If none exists, the result for that declaration is a parse error. We then translate away some syntactic sugar, and resolve the scoping of types and datatype constructors.

CakeML has a declarative (non-algorithmic) typing relation in the standard style. If the declaration has a type, we move on to the operational semantics. If it does not have a type, then the semantics gets stuck or signals a type error depending on the corresponding value in the bool list.

[1] We use an executable specification instead of a regular expression-based one because ML comments are not expressible with regular expressions.

The operational semantics is given as a big-step relation, on which our compiler correctness proofs can all proceed by induction since both the compiler and big-step semantics are defined inductively over CakeML abstract syntax. To precisely define divergence, and to support a syntactic type-soundness proof [31], we also give a small-step semantics for expressions as a CEK machine [5], and prove that it is equivalent to the big-step relation.

If the declaration diverges, REPL$_s$ relates it to the repl_result divergence-nil value. If it terminates normally or with an unhandled exception, or if a parse or type error occurred, REPL$_s$ updates its state, converts the result to a string and conses it to the result of evaluating the rest of the input.

***The REPL Implementation*** The REPL$_s$ specification is implemented by a HOL function

$$\mathsf{REPL}_i : \mathsf{string} \to \mathsf{repl\_result}$$

from an input string to a list of result strings ending in either termination or divergence (as above). The function is total; however, it is not computable, since it correctly ends the output list with divergence when necessary: being a function in the logic, it is able to ask whether there exist a number of steps in which execution of code for the next declaration would terminate.

We define REPL$_i$ as a loop that consumes the input string while transforming the state of a low-level virtual machine for CakeML Bytecode (Section 6.3) and accumulating results. The loop is split into three parts:

1. (REPL$_i$_step: Read and compile) The first part reads and lexes the input until the next semicolon, parses the resulting tokens, performs type inference on the resulting syntax and then compiles it to produce bytecode.
2. (Evaluate) The second part returns the result, if it exists, of executing the bytecode simulator on the bytecode, or else signals divergence.
3. (Print and Loop) If the simulator terminates, the last part continues the loop with the new machine state after accumulating the results from the new state. If the simulator diverges, or if all input has been read, the loop ends. If any step fails, the loop continues after accumulating the error message.

***The REPL in Machine-Code*** The bottom layer is a machine-code implementation of the REPL, created mostly by bootstrapping. Specifically, we translate the HOL function, REPL$_i$_step, the main part of REPL$_i$, into CakeML declarations using proof-producing synthesis [22]. We then evaluate the compiler in the logic on those declarations to produce a verified bytecode implementation of REPL$_i$_step. This bytecode is mapped via a verified translation into x86-64 machine code.

To implement the other parts of REPL$_i$, we separately synthesise a small amount of x86-64 machine code to jump to the code produced by the compiler, and to tie the loop together. We also synthesise verified machine code for the lexer, printer, garbage collector and arbitrary-precision integer package, which complete the verified implementation.

### 2.1 Correctness and Verification

The correctness of the x86-64 machine-code implementation of the CakeML REPL is stated with respect to our machine model for x86-64. The theorem (which appears in more detail as Theorem 25) can informally be read as follows:

**Theorem 1.** If the machine is loaded with the CakeML REPL code and started with accessible memory for the data and code heaps, and provided with a finite input character stream $i$, then one of the following happens.

- The machine terminates successfully with an output stream $output$, and there exist $l$ and $o$ such that REPL$_s$ $l$ $i$ $o$ holds, $o$

ends with termination, and out $o = output$. (Here out converts a repl_result to a string by joining the results.)

- The machine diverges after producing a finite output stream $output$, and there exist $l$ and $o$ such that $\mathsf{REPL}_s\ l\ i\ o$ holds, $o$ ends with divergence, and out $o = output$.
- The machine terminates with an out-of-memory error. The output stream is terminated with an error message.

We prove the correctness theorem using two methods: interactive proof, to establish a connection between $\mathsf{REPL}_s$ and $\mathsf{REPL}_i$ and to put the final result together, and a combination of interactive proof and proof-producing synthesis (including bootstrapping) to construct verified machine code that implements $\mathsf{REPL}_i$.

The main lemma proved interactively is that for every $input$, there is an $l$ such that $\mathsf{REPL}_s\ l\ input\ (\mathsf{REPL}_i\ input)$ holds. We prove this (Section 8) by composing proofs that relate each of the components of $\mathsf{REPL}_i$ to the corresponding component of $\mathsf{REPL}_s$.

Since $\mathsf{REPL}_i$ reads its input one character at a time, whereas $\mathsf{REPL}_s$ splits the whole input string up front, we first prove, for the lexer, that the resulting list of declarations is the same either way. We then prove our parser sound and complete with respect to CakeML's grammar (Section 4), which means the results of parsing in $\mathsf{REPL}_i$ match the choice of valid parse tree made by $\mathsf{REPL}_s$.

We prove soundness for the type inference algorithm: if a type is inferred, the type system allows that type. We verify the rest of the loop in $\mathsf{REPL}_i$ under the assumption that type inference succeeded, and hence the operational semantics does not encounter a type error. Internally, $\mathsf{REPL}_s$ is defined by inductive relations parameterised by an environment and store. We maintain an invariant between these semantic objects, the state of the compiler, and the bytecode machine state.

Our first compiler correctness theorem (Section 6) is for when $\mathsf{REPL}_s$ says the declaration yields a new environment and output string. We carry our invariant around an iteration of the $\mathsf{REPL}_i$ loop with this theorem, which says running the compiled code for the declaration leads the virtual machine to produce the same output string and to terminate in a state that satisfies the invariant updated with the new environment.

In the case of divergence, we have a second compiler correctness theorem (Section 7) that says that if $\mathsf{REPL}_s$ says a declaration diverges, then a run of the compiled code for that declaration also diverges, causing the entire REPL to diverge.

The x86-64 machine-code implementation is constructed using forward proof, most of which is automated. The bulk of the verified machine code, *i.e.* that implementing $\mathsf{REPL}_i$_step, is produced via compiler bootstrapping:

1. We start by translating the HOL function $\mathsf{REPL}_i$_step into CakeML abstract syntax, a list of CakeML declarations (ml_repl_step_decls). The translation is automatic and proof-producing: it proves that the generated CakeML declarations implement the HOL functions.

2. Once we have the $\mathsf{REPL}_i$_step in CakeML abstract syntax, we evaluate the verified compiler on this abstract syntax. The evaluation happens *inside the logic* and proves a theorem:

   compile_decs init ml_repl_step_decls = (bytecode, cstate)

   By the compiler correctness theorems, we prove that the generated code, *i.e.* bytecode, accurately implements the CakeML declarations produced in the previous step.

3. In order to construct verified and executable machine code from bytecode, we apply a verified translation from bytecode instructions to x86-64 machine code.

The steps outlined above produced verified x86-64 code for part of $\mathsf{REPL}_i$, namely $\mathsf{REPL}_i$_step. We construct the machine code for all other parts, including garbage collector and bignum library, using a different form of proof-producing synthesis of machine code [23]. The top-level theorem is proved interactively by plugging together theorems describing the behaviour of the components.

```
id   ::=  x | Mn.x
cid  ::=  Cn | M.Cn
t    ::=  int | bool | unit | α | id | t id | (t(,t)*)id
       |  t * t | t -> t | t ref | (t)
l    ::=  i | true | false | () | []
p    ::=  x | l | cid | cid p | ref p | _ | (p(,p)*) | [p (,p)*]
       |  p :: p
e    ::=  l | id | cid | cid e | (e,e (,e)*) | [e (,e)*]
       |  raise e | e handle p => e (| p => e)*
       |  fn x => e | e e | ((e ;)* e) | uop e | e op e
       |  if e then e else e | case e of p => e (| p => e)*
       |  let (ld|;)* in (e ;)* e end
ld   ::=  val x = e | fun x y+ = e (and x y+ = e)*
uop  ::=  ref | ! | ~
op   ::=  = | := | + | - | * | div | mod | < | <= | > | >= | <> | ::
       |  before | andalso | orelse
c    ::=  Cn | Cn of t
tyd  ::=  tyn = c (| c)*
tyn  ::=  (α(,α)*) x | α x | x
d    ::=  datatype tyd (and tyd)* | val p = e
       |  fun x y+ = e (and x y+ = e)*
       |  exception c
sig  ::=  :> sig (sl |;)* end
sl   ::=  val x : t | type tyn | datatype tyd (and tyd)*
top  ::=  structure Mn sig? = struct (d |;)* end; | d; | e;
```

where $x$ and $y$ range over identifiers (must not start with a capital letter), $\alpha$ over SML-style type variables (*e.g.*, 'a), $Cn$ over constructor names (must start with a capital letter), $Mn$ over module names, and $i$ over integers.

**Figure 1.** CakeML source grammar

## 3. The Specification of CakeML

CakeML (Figure 1) is a subset of Standard ML (SML) [18], including datatypes and pattern-matching, higher-order functions, references, exceptions, polymorphism, and modules and signatures. CakeML integers are arbitrary precision. The main features not included are records, input/output, and functors.

All CakeML programs should run on an off-the-shelf SML implementation with the same result;[2] however, we have not proved that fact with respect to the *Definition of Standard ML*. Thus, any formal reasoning about CakeML programs must be carried out with respect to the CakeML semantics, rather than SML's. We chose to be faithful to SML so that potential CakeML users do not have to learn a new programming language from scratch, but our main focus is not on SML *per se*, but rather on a call-by-value, impure, strongly typed, functional language. We choose SML over OCaml for technical reasons (Section 12); on our subset, the difference is mostly in the syntax.

Section 2 summarises the specification: as a lexer, context-free grammar, de-sugarer, elaborator, type system, and big-step operational semantics wrapped in a REPL. Most of these are typical, so here we focus on their properties, and on our design decisions.

CakeML's concrete syntax is specified by a context-free grammar similar to Figure 1's, but that unambiguously encodes the various parsing precedences and resolves the "dangling case" ambiguity. The transformation to abstract syntax removes syntactic sugar.

[2] CakeML does not enforce equality types, so an SML implementation will statically reject some programs that CakeML accepts. Our implementation of equality raises an exception if one of its arguments contains a closure.

For example, a Let expression with multiple val bindings is desugared into nested Lets, each with one binding.

Our abstract syntax uses a first-order representation of binding where variables, constructors, etc. are represented as strings. This straightforward representation fits well with our semantics, which uses closures rather than substitutions, and it also enables bootstrapping, because the AST closely corresponds to a CakeML datatype (CakeML does not support strings, but they become lists of integers during synthesis).

The elaborator walks the AST and replaces uses of types and constructors in patterns and expressions with fully qualified names, *i.e.*, with the full module path to the constructor. Thus, each constructor is canonically named, and the type system and operational semantics do not have to generate unique stamps at datatype declarations in order for a type preservation lemma to hold.

A key design principle for the operational semantics is for it to raise a distinguished exception Rtype_error whenever something goes wrong, instead of getting stuck or continuing on anyway. By raising Rtype_error instead of getting stuck, the big-step semantics has a precise correspondence between divergence and failure of an expression to relate to a result. This is a key part of our technique for verifying the compiler for diverging input programs (Section 7).

The Rtype_error behaviour of the semantics forms the interface between the type soundness proof and the compiler proof, as the compiler proof assumes that programs do not raise Rtype_error, and type soundness theorem guarantees this. Even though these choices only affect programs that do not type check, they are how the compiler proof can use the fact that these situations do not arise. For example, when evaluating a pattern match, the value's constructor might be from a different type than the first pattern's, as in `case true of None => 0 | true => 1`. The semantics could just move on to the next pattern since the value's and first-pattern's constructors are not equal. Instead the semantics detects this case and raises Rtype_error.

The semantics relies on the following definitions of values $v$; environments for variables $envE$, constructors $envC$, and modules $envM$; stores $s$; and results $r$. The constructor environment records the arity of the constructor and what type of values it constructs.

$$
\begin{array}{lll}
v & ::= & loc \mid l \mid cid \mid cid\ v \mid (v,v(,v)^*) \mid \mathsf{Closure}\langle E,x,e\rangle \\
 & \mid & \mathsf{RecClosure}\langle E,(\mathtt{fun}\ x\ y = e\ (\mathtt{and}\ x\ y = e)^*),x\rangle \\
loc & ::= & \mathsf{num} \\
envE, E & = & (x,v)\ \mathsf{list} \\
envC, C & = & (cid, \mathsf{num}{*}id)\ \mathsf{list} \\
envM, M & = & (id, E)\ \mathsf{list} \\
s & = & loc\ \mathsf{list} \\
r & ::= & \langle s, C, \langle M, E\rangle\rangle \mid \langle s, C, ex\rangle \mid \langle s, C, \mathsf{Rtype\_error}\rangle
\end{array}
$$

The type system relies on typing contexts for variables $tE$, constructors $tC$, modules $tM$, and stores $tS$. We then have relations for evaluation, divergence, and typing for top-level declarations.

$$
\begin{array}{l}
\mathsf{evaluate\_top} : M \to C \to s \to E \to top \to r \to \mathsf{bool} \\
\mathsf{top\_diverges} : M \to C \to s \to E \to top \to \mathsf{bool} \\
\mathsf{type\_top} : tM \to tC \to tE \to top \to tM \to tC \to tE \to \mathsf{bool}
\end{array}
$$

We use closures for function values, rather than performing substitutions at function applications, to keep a close connection between the semantics of functions and their implementation strategy.

The REPL repeatedly calls evaluate_top, and must update its state between each call, installing new bindings, using the new store, etc. After completing a module declaration, the REPL updates the type system's state with the module's bindings according to its signature, since future declarations must not refer to hidden bindings or constructors. However, the operational semantics' state must be updated because references to the hidden constructors will generally be reachable from the environment or from the store.

The last remaining subtlety lies in module declarations that raise an un-handled exception part-way through. When any declaration raises an exception, its bindings do not take effect, and so the type environments are not updated. However, the operational semantics might need its constructor information updated, since the module might have placed a locally defined constructor in the store first before raising the exception.

We have two options, either updating the constructor environment with just the constructors seen, or with all of the constructors from the module body. Both are sound, and neither affect the programmer, since they are not in the type environments. We choose the latter, to match how the compiler implements modules.

### *Metatheory*

**Theorem 2** (Determinism). If evaluate_top $M\ C\ s\ E\ top\ r_1$ and evaluate_top $M\ C\ s\ E\ top\ r_2$ then $r_1 = r_2$.

*Proof sketch.* By induction on the big-step relation. □

**Theorem 3** (Totality). ($\exists r.$ evaluate_top $M\ C\ s\ E\ top\ r$) iff $\neg$top_diverges $M\ C\ s\ E\ top$.

*Proof sketch.* First, we establish, by induction along a small step trace, that the small-step semantics cannot get stuck. Then we use the big-step/small-step equivalence theorem to transfer the result to the big-step semantics. □

The invariant of the type soundness theorem existentially quantifies constructor and module type environments that represent the declarations that are hidden by module signatures. The update_type_sound_inv function updates the state depending on whether the result is an exception or not following the discussion above.

type_sound_inv$(tM, tC, tE, M, C, E, s)$ =
 $\exists\ tS\ tM\_no\_sig\ tC\_no\_sig.$
 the environments are well-formed and consistent with each other,
 MAP FST $tM\_no\_sig$ = MAP FST $tM$,
 $tM\_no\_sig$ weakens $tM$,
 $tC\_no\_sig$ weakens $tC$, and
 the constructors in $tC\_no\_sig$ but not $tC$ are all in modules in the domain of $tM$.

**Theorem 4** (Type soundness).
Let $state = \langle tM, tC, tE, M, C, E, s\rangle$ be given.
For all $top$, if type_sound_inv $state$ and
type_top $tM\ tC\ tE\ top\ tM'\ tC'\ tE'$ then either
top_diverges $M\ C\ s\ E\ top$ or there exists $s'$, $C'$, and $r$ such that
$r \neq$ Rtype_error,
evaluate_top $M\ C\ s\ E\ top\ \langle s', C', r\rangle$, and
type_sound_inv
 (update_type_sound_inv $top\ state\ tM'\ tC'\ tE'\ s'\ C'\ r$)

*Proof sketch.* We prove the usual preservation and progress lemmas along a small-step trace. Then we use the big-step/small-step equivalence theorem to transfer the result to the big-step semantics. We then reason about declarations entirely with the big-step semantics. This poses no problem because declarations cannot diverge apart from their sub-expressions diverging. The preservation and progress lemmas were proved directly on our CEK-style small-step semantics, which uses closures and a context stack. To our knowledge no such proof appears in the literature. The main impact on the proof is to flatten out its structure (*e.g.*, no substitution lemma), and instead to require an invariant that types the continuation stack. The usual subtleties about type substitution and weakening were unchanged; we use de Bruijn indices for type variables. □

# Part II: Verification and Implementation

We now turn to the implementation and verification of each part of the compiler. Afterward, we include a high-level discussion of CakeML's design and significance (Section 12).

## 4. Parsing

We implement the first phase of parsing with a Parsing Expression Grammar (PEG), following Koprowski and Binsztok's mechanisation in Coq [11]. We have a general inductive relation peg_eval, which takes a grammar, an input sequence of tokens, a PEG expression, and returns a verdict of either failure, or success with a returned value and the remaining input. We prove the results from Koprowski and Binsztok that the peg_eval relation always has a value when the PEG is well-formed, and that it is deterministic. Thus, on well-formed PEGs (we prove the CakeML PEG is one such), peg_eval specifies a function.

PEG expressions are accompanied by "semantic actions" that can transform the values associated with sub-parses into a combined return value. Our semantic actions, in HOL, cannot be dependently typed, as can be done in Coq where it is pleasant to have parses of different non-terminals return values of different types. Instead, all our PEG-expressions have semantic actions that simply return lists of CFG-parse-trees. In this way, the first phase of parsing concentrates on turning a linear sequence of tokens into a tree; later phases map different parts of these trees into different types.

Even though peg_eval specifies a function, its definition is not well-suited to computation. Rather, we define a general PEG interpreter peg_exec that is tail-recursive, written in a continuation-passing style. Whenever its PEG argument is well-formed, we prove the interpreter has a well-defined result, and one that is equal to the result demanded by the peg_eval relation. It is this definition that is compiled into the bytecode that is eventually executed.

**Theorem 5** (Parser Soundness). Whenever the PEG successfully parses a non-terminal $N$, its result is a single CFG parse-tree with $N$ at its head and whose fringe of tokens corresponds to the input consumed by the execution of the PEG.

*Proof sketch.* Induction on the lexicographic combination of the length of the input given to peg_eval, and the *rank* of the non-terminal. Each non-terminal is given a natural number rank such that if executing the PEG on non-terminal $N$ can result in needing to execute non-terminal $M$ without having consumed any input, then $N$'s rank is greater than $M$'s. The fact that this ranking is possible stems from the same argument that gives the well-formedness of the PEG. □

**Theorem 6** (Parser Completeness). If a parse tree exists for a given input, then the PEG implementation will find it.

*Proof sketch.* Induction on the lexicographic combination of the length of the parse tree's fringe, and the rank of the tree's head non-terminal. □

As PEG execution is deterministic, this also implies that our CFG is unambiguous.

## 5. Type Inference

Type inference is based on Milner's algorithm $\mathcal{J}$ (and hence $\mathcal{W}$) [17]. We represent unification variables as numbers, and increment a counter to generate fresh variables. Since the inferencer is written in higher-order logic (in a state-and-exception monad), we cannot use the common technique of doing substitutions by updating pointers in the types. Instead we re-use our previous formalisation (from the HOL4 examples directory) of *triangular* substitutions, which are not idempotent, but are instead designed to maintain sharing for greater efficiency in a pure functional setting [12].

**Theorem 7** (Type Inferencer Soundness).
If infer_top $tM$ $tC$ $tE$ $top$ $state$ =
(Success($tM'$, $tC'$, $tE'$), $state'$) and $tM$, $tC$, $tE$ contain no unification variables, then type_top $tM$ $tC$ $tE$ $top$ $tM'$ $tC'$ $tE'$.

*Proof sketch.* The soundness proof is long and tedious, but not particularly surprising. A large part of the proof is devoted to establishing invariants on the usage of type variables in the various environments and state components of the algorithm. □

There are two ways in which our inferencer verification falls short of what could be seen as an ideal for SML, but neither directly affects our end-to-end correctness theorem. First, the types of let-bound variables are not generalised, restricting polymorphism to top-level and module-top-level declarations;[3] and second, we have not verified completeness of the inferencer. In both cases, the potential for the CakeML system to behave badly is limited to signalling a type error on a declaration that the programmer expected to pass type checking. In particular, there is no possibility for the programmer to be deceived by the system appearing to returning an erroneous result of executing the definition.

We gave proving inferencer completeness low priority because, in practice, we find the inferencer does not fail on the programs we expect to have types. If it did, a completeness theorem would tell us that the bug is in CakeML's declarative type system, rather than possibly also in the inferencer.

## 6. Compilation

We now turn to translation from abstract syntax to CakeML Bytecode, our assembly language for a virtual stack machine, which is the final language before translation to x86-64 machine code. We describe the bytecode in detail in Section 6.3, but first take a high-level look at the compiler and its verification.

The main function is compile_top which takes a top-level declaration and the compiler's state, including environments mapping variables to bytecode stack offsets, and returns code and two new compiler states. One is used if the code runs successfully and the other if it raises an un-handled exception. For the verification, we define a relation

compiler_inv $envM$ $envC$ $s$ $envE$ $rs$ $z$ $rd$ $bs$

between the semantic context (the module, constructor, and value environments, and the store), the compiler's state $rs$, the bytecode machine state $bs$, and additional context indicating the size, $z$, of the stack before the last complete declaration, and information about references and closures in $rd$.

We explain the compiler along with its verification, beginning with the statement of the correctness theorem for terminating programs (for diverging programs see Section 7).

**Theorem 8** (Compiler Correctness). If
 $top$ is well-typed, evaluate_top $m$ $c$ $s$ $e$ $top$ $res$,
 compile_top $rs$ $top$ = ($rss$, $rsf$, $code$), and,
 compiler_inv $m$ $c$ $s$ $e$ $rs$ $|bs$.stack$|$ $rd$ $bs$,
then a run of $bs$ with $code$ terminates with a new state $bs'$, satisfying the following condition, depending on $res$:
If $res$ is a successful result with new environments $m'$, $c'$, and $e'$, and new store $s'$, then there exists $rd'$ such that
 $bs'$ has reached the end of $code$ (no next instruction),
 compiler_inv $m'$ $c'$ $s'$ $e'$ $rss$ $|bs'$.stack$|$ $rd'$ $bs'$, and,
 $bs'$ has the result of printing the new bindings in its output.

[3] Vytiniotis et al. [30, Section 4.3] provide evidence that generalisation for let expressions is rarely used in practice.

Otherwise if *res* is an exception *exc* with a new store $s'$, then there exists $rd'$ and $bv$ such that
the next instruction for $bs'$ is Stop,
$bs'$.stack $= bv :: bs$.stack,
$bv$ is a refinement of *exc*, and,
compiler_inv $m\ c'\ s'\ e\ rsf\ |bs.\mathsf{stack}|\ rd'\ bs''$,
where $bs''$ is $bs'$ with $bv$ popped. (The printing and popping of $bv$ is done by the main REPL loop after the Stop instruction is reached.)

*Proof sketch.* The compile_top function is implemented using functions for compiling declarations and expressions, mirroring the structure of the big-step semantics. The proof for each layer is by induction on the appropriate big-step relation. □

Our compilation strategy has three phases: translation to an intermediate language, analysis for the purpose of compiling functions, and finally translation to bytecode. We proceed with a description of the implementation and verification of each phase.

### 6.1 Translation to Intermediate Language

The intermediate language (IL) simplifies the source language in the following ways:

- Pattern-matching is replaced by conditional expressions and constructor-tag equality tests.
- Named variables are replaced by de Bruijn indices. Constructor names are replaced by numeric tags.
- All functions are syntactically recursive, and may have zero or more arguments.
- The set of primitive operations is smaller (*e.g.* no greater-than, only less-than).

The translation to IL expressions is a straightforward recursion on the abstract syntax of CakeML. We also define a translation from CakeML values to IL values, which makes use of the expression translation since closures are amongst the values.

***Verification*** We give a big-step operational semantics for the intermediate language, similar to the one for the source language. The correctness theorem for the translation to IL says whenever the CakeML semantics gives a program $p$ a result $r$, the IL semantics gives the translated program $[p]$ a result $r'$ that is related to $[r]$. The proof is by induction on the CakeML big-step evaluation relation.

We cannot prove identity between the translated CakeML result and the result produced by the IL semantics, because closure environments may differ. The translation to IL sometimes introduces fresh variables that will appear in an IL closure's environment but not in the translation of the source closure's. We need a coarser relation on IL closures, allowing their environments to differ.

For this purpose, we define a relation $\approx$ on IL expressions, values, and environments. The relation $V \vdash (z_1, e_1) \approx (z_2, e_2)$ relates an IL expression together with the size of its environment to another such pair. It is parameterised by a relation $V\,v_1\,v_2$ indicating variables that are assumed to be bound to equivalent values. To relate values, the relation $v_1 \approx v_2$ needs no sizes or parameters, since closures carry their environments so the size can be computed.

We have proved $\approx$ reflexive and transitive (symmetry fails as explained in the next section) and the following two theorems.

**Theorem 9.** If the IL semantics says $e_1$ evaluates in environment $env_1$ to a result $r_1$; whenever $V\ v_1\ v_2$ holds, $env_1(v_1) \approx env_2(v_2)$ does also; and, $V \vdash (|env_1|, e_1) \approx (|env_2|, e_2)$; then there is a result $r_2$ to which $e_2$ evaluates in $env_2$ and $r_1 \approx r_2$.

*Proof sketch.* By induction on the IL evaluation relation. □

The main purpose of the $\approx$ relation is to enable closure environments to be manipulated. The second theorem supports the renumbering of variables that is required in a closure's body when its environment is changed.

**Theorem 10.** Let $e'$ be the result of renumbering variables in $e$ and suppose $V$ relates indices under the same renumbering scheme, then $V \vdash e \approx e'$.

*Proof sketch.* By induction on syntax-directed renumbering. □

We use these theorems for verifying the translation to IL including the removal of pattern matching. We also use $\approx$ to relate IL function bodies to annotated IL closure bodies, described below.

### 6.2 Intermediate Language Closure Annotation

For every function body, we compute how to compile each occurrence of a variable, and how to build the closure environment. We use flat closure environments that only have bindings for variables that actually occur free in the function's body.

As an example, consider the following IL expression (written in concrete syntax with named variables, but recall that the IL actually uses de Bruijn indices):

```
let val a = e1 val b = e2 val c = e3
    fun f h x =
       if x = 6 then h 7 else (g x) + (f (x - a))
    and g x = f (fn y => x + y - b) (a - c)
in e4 end
```

Analysis of the bodies records this about the free variables:

| for f: | for g: | for λ: |
|---|---|---|
| x -> arg 0 | f -> rec 0 | x -> env 0 |
| h -> arg 1 | b -> env 0 | y -> arg 0 |
| g -> rec 1 | a -> env 1 | b -> env 1 |
| f -> self | c -> env 2 | cl env = [0,2] |
| a -> env 0 | cl env = [1,2,0] | |
| cl env = [2] | | |

The `env` annotation gives an index into the closure environment, which is itself a list of indices into the enclosing environment (so in the anonymous function's closure environment, 0 refers to g's argument, and 2 refers to the first element of g's environment, since 1 would refer to g itself).

We update the variables in function bodies so that they refer to the closure environment instead of the enclosing environment. For example, in the body of `f`, the de Bruijn index for `a` is decremented twice, because the intervening variables in the enclosing environment are omitted in the closure environment. CakeML's operational semantics also uses closures, making the proof of correspondence conceptually straightforward, but closures in the semantics contain the whole enclosing environment.

We generate, for each function body, a unique label that is used (Section 6.4) as a code pointer to bytecode implementing the body.

***Verification*** We store the closure environment information as annotations on the function bodies within the expression. The IL semantics uses the closure (rather than enclosing) environment to evaluate a call when such an annotation exists. Similarly, the relation $V, U \vdash (z_1, bs_1) \approx (z_2, bs_2)$ allows the bodies in $bs_1$ and $bs_2$ to be annotated, and uses the closure environment rather than $V$ and $z$ as appropriate. The relation is directed (hence not symmetric): if a body in $bs_1$ is annotated, then the corresponding body in $bs_2$ must have the same annotation; however an unannotated body in $bs_1$ may be related to an annotated body in $bs_2$.

**Theorem 11.** If $e'$ is the result of annotating $e$, and $e$ is unannotated and has free variables all less than $z$, then $(=) \vdash (z, e) \approx (z, e')$, and $e'$ is fully annotated with environments that cover the free variables of its bodies.

*Proof sketch.* By induction on syntax-directed annotation. □

| | | |
|---|---|---|
| *bc_inst* | ::= | Stack *bc_stack_op* \| PushExc \| PopExc |
| | \| | Return \| CallPtr \| Call *loc* |
| | \| | PushPtr *loc* \| Jump *loc* \| JumpIf *loc* |
| | \| | Ref \| Deref \| Update \| Print \| PrintC char |
| | \| | Label $n$ \| Tick \| Stop |
| *bc_stack_op* | ::= | Pop \| Pops $n$ \| Shift $n$ $n$ \| PushInt int |
| | \| | Cons $n$ $n$ \| El $n$ \| TagEq $n$ \| IsBlock $n$ |
| | \| | Load $n$ \| Store $n$ \| LoadRev $n$ |
| | \| | Equal \| Less \| Add \| Sub \| Mult \| Div \| Mod |
| *loc* | ::= | Lab $n$ \| Addr $n$ |
| $n$ | = | num |
| *bc_value* | ::= | Number int \| RefPtr $n$ \| Block $n$ $bc\_value^*$ |
| | \| | CodePtr $n$ \| StackPtr $n$ |
| *bc_state* | ::= { | stack : $bc\_value^*$; refs : $n \mapsto bc\_value$; code : $bc\_inst^*$; pc : $n$; handler : $n$; output : string; names : $n \mapsto$ string; clock : $n^?$ } |

**Figure 2.** CakeML Bytecode syntax, values, and machine state

$$\frac{\mathsf{fetch}(bs) = \mathsf{Stack}\ (\mathsf{Cons}\ t\ n) \quad bs.\mathsf{stack} = vs \,@\, xs \quad |vs| = n}{bs \rightarrow (\mathsf{bump}\ bs)\{\mathsf{stack} = \mathsf{Block}\ t\ (\mathsf{rev}\ vs) :: xs\}}$$

$$\frac{\mathsf{fetch}(bs) = \mathsf{Return} \quad bs.\mathsf{stack} = x :: \mathsf{CodePtr}\ ptr :: xs}{bs \rightarrow bs\{\mathsf{stack} = x :: xs;\ \mathsf{pc} = ptr\}}$$

$$\frac{\mathsf{fetch}(bs) = \mathsf{CallPtr} \quad bs.\mathsf{stack} = x :: \mathsf{CodePtr}\ ptr :: xs}{bs \rightarrow bs\{\mathsf{stack} = x :: \mathsf{CodePtr}\ (\mathsf{bump}\ bs).\mathsf{pc} :: xs;\ \mathsf{pc} = ptr\}}$$

$$\frac{\mathsf{fetch}(bs) = \mathsf{PushExc} \quad bs.\mathsf{stack} = xs \quad bs' = \mathsf{bump}\ bs}{bs \rightarrow bs'\{\mathsf{stack} = \mathsf{StackPtr}\ (bs.\mathsf{handler}) :: xs;\ \mathsf{handler} = |xs|\}}$$

$$\frac{\mathsf{fetch}(bs) = \mathsf{PopExc} \quad bs.\mathsf{handler} = |ys| \quad bs.\mathsf{stack} = x :: xs \,@\, \mathsf{StackPtr}\ h :: ys}{bs \rightarrow (\mathsf{bump}\ bs)\{\mathsf{stack} = x :: ys;\ \mathsf{handler} = h\}}$$

**Figure 3.** CakeML Bytecode semantics (selection). The helper function fetch calculates the next instruction using the pc and code, and bump updates the pc to the next instruction.

### 6.3 CakeML Bytecode

The target language of the compiler is CakeML Bytecode (Figure 2), a low-level assembly language for a virtual machine with a single random-access[4] stack.

CakeML Bytecode was designed with three separate goals: to be (i) conveniently abstract as a target for the compiler and its proofs, and (ii) easy to map into reasonably efficient machine code that is (iii) possible to reason about and verify w.r.t. an operational semantics for x86-64 machine code. To support (i), the bytecode has no notion of pointers to the heap, and provides structured data (Cons packs multiple bytecode values into a Block) on the stack instead. Also, the bytecode Number values are mathematical integers; the x86-64 implementation includes a bignum library to implement the arithmetic instructions. For (ii), we ensure that most bytecode instructions map to one or two x86-64 machine instructions; and for (iii), the bytecode essentially only operates over a single 'stack', the x86-64 stack which we access using the normal stack and base pointers, `rsp` and `rbp` registers. (See Section 10 for the implementation of the bytecode in x86-64.)

The bytecode semantics is a deterministic state transition system: the relation $bs_1 \rightarrow bs_2$ fetches from code the instruction indicated by pc and executes it to produce the next machine state. We give some example clauses in Figure 3.

Our data refinement relation $l, r, Cv \models bv$ says $bv$ is a bytecode value representing the IL value $Cv$. It is parameterised by two functions: $l$ to translate labels to bytecode addresses, and $r$ providing extra information about code pointers for closures.

The refinement of closures is most interesting. There are two components to a closure: its body expression, and its environment which may refer to other closures in mutual recursion. We use a correspondence of labels to link a code pointer to an annotated IL body, and for the environment, we assume the IL annotations correctly specify the closure environment. In the IL, a closure looks like CRecClos *env defs n*, where *env* is the enclosing[5] environment, and the body is the $n$th element of the bundle of recursive definitions *defs*. We say

$$l, r, \mathsf{CRecClos}\ env\ defs\ n \models \mathsf{Block}\ \mathsf{c}\ [\mathsf{CodePtr}\ a;\ \mathsf{Block}\ \mathsf{e}\ bvs]$$

holds (c and e are tags indicating closure and environment Blocks) when:

- $defs[n]$ has label *lab* and annotations *ann*, $l(lab) = a$, and $|ann| = |bvs|$;
- for every variable $x$ with an `env` annotation in *ann*, the corresponding bytecode value $bv$ in $bvs$ satisfies $l, r, env(x) \models bv$; and,
- for every variable with a `rec` $i$ annotation in *ann*, the corresponding bytecode value in $bvs$ is RefPtr $p$, for some $p$, and there are $env'$, $defs'$, and $j$ such that $r(p) = (env', defs', j)$ and CRecClos $env\ defs\ i \approx$ CRecClos $env'\ defs'\ j$.

Thus, for a function in mutual recursion we assume it is behind the indirection of a RefPtr; the function $r$ acts as an oracle indicating the closure that should be pointed to. To tie the knot, the inductive hypothesis in our compilation proof says whenever $r(p) = (env', defs', j)$ the bytecode machine refs binds $p$ to a value $bv$ satisfying $l, r$, CRecClos $env\ defs\ j \models bv$.

### 6.4 Translation to Bytecode

The main compilation algorithm takes an IL expression as input and produces bytecode instructions. Additional context for the compiler includes an environment binding IL variables to stack offsets, and a return context indicating the number of variables that need to be discarded before a jump if the expression is in tail position.

The correctness theorem for this phase is similar to Theorem 8 (whose proof uses this one as a lemma), assuming evaluation in the IL semantics rather than the source semantics. In particular, we have a relation called IL_inv that captures an invariant between the IL environment and store, the compiler state, the bytecode machine state, and proof information like the $l$ and $r$ functions. This relation is used in the definition of compiler_inv, which crosses the three languages (CakeML, IL, Bytecode). The theorem below depends only on the IL and the bytecode.

**Theorem 12.** If the IL semantics says *Cexp* evaluates in environment *Cenv* and store *Cs* to a new store *Cs'* and result *Cres*, and all the values in the context are fully annotated, then for all bytecode machine states $bs$ satisfying IL_inv with *Cenv* and *Cs* (and proof information including $l$ and $r$), then

- If *Cres* is a value, *Cv*, then
  - Running $bs$ with code from compiling *Cexp* in non-tail position leads the bytecode machine to terminate in a new state $bs'$ such that IL_inv holds of *Cenv*, *Cs'*, and $bs'$, and $bs'.\mathsf{stack} = bv :: bs.\mathsf{stack}$ with $l, r', Cv \models bv$; and,

[4] Most operations work on the top of the stack, but Load $n$ and Store $n$ read/write the cell $n$ places below the top, and LoadRev takes an index from the bottom.

[5] Annotations on $defs[n]$ build the closure environment from *env*.

- Assuming $bs$.stack $= lvs$ @ CodePtr $ret$ :: $args$ @ $st$, running $bs$ with code from compiling $Cexp$ in tail position ready to discard $|lvs|$ and $|args|$ leads the machine to a state $bs'$ satisfying the invariant as above, and also $bs'$.pc $= ret$ and $bs'$.stack $= bv :: st$, with $l, r', Cv \models bv$.
- Otherwise, if $Cres$ is an exception value $Cx$, and if $bs$.stack $= vs$ @ StackPtr $h$ :: CodePtr $hdl$ :: $st$, and $bs$.handler $= |st| + 1$, then running $bs$ with code for compiling $Cexp$ (in either call context) leads the machine to a state $bs'$ satisfying the invariant, and with $bs'$.pc $= hdl$, $bs'$.stack $= bv :: st$, $l, r', Cx \models bv$, and $bs'$.handler $= h$.
- Finally, if $Cres$ is a timeout exception, then a run of $bs$ on code for $Cexp$ causes the machine to time out. (See Section 7 for details.)

*Proof sketch.* By induction on the big-step semantics for the IL. The invariant includes a condition on $bs$.code: it must already contain code resulting from compiling all the function bodies appearing in $Cexp$ and for closures in $Cs$ and $Cenv$. This assumption is justified by the compilation of function bodies described below. □

***Function Bodies*** Before compiling the main expression, we compile the functions. For each body, the compilation environment is the closure environment and the return context is tail position (ready to discard just the arguments to the function but no local variables). We lay the resulting stretches of bytecode in sequence each preceded by the label annotating the closure's body.

***Closure Creation*** As we saw in the definition of $l, r, Cv \models bv$, we represent a closure using a Cons block containing a code pointer and an environment block, which is built following the annotations on the closure body. For mutually recursive closures (the `rec` annotation), we build the closure environment using references, and update them with the appropriate closures once all the closures are created, thereby ensuring mutually recursive functions appear as RefPtrs in the closure environment.

***Function Calls and Proper Tail Calls*** The generated code for a function call depends on whether it is tail position or not. In both cases, we first evaluate the closure and its arguments, and extract the code pointer from the closure. For a non-tail call, we use the CallPtr instruction, which generates a return pointer and jumps. For a tail call, since we are assuming a return pointer is already on the stack, we reorganise the stack, discarding the local variables and arguments, then use the Return instruction to make the call.

The key lemma enabling our proof by induction for the function call case says that if $bs$.stack $= benv$ :: CodePtr $ret$ :: $bvs$ @ Block c $[p; benv]$ and $l, r,$ CRecClos $env\ defs\ n \models$ Block c $[p; benv]$, then we can establish IL_inv for $bs$ with the closure environment made from $env$ and the annotations on $defs[n]$. Thus we can use the inductive hypothesis on the closure body even though it is not a subexpression of the original $Cexp$ in the theorem statement.

***Declarations*** So far we have looked at the compilation of IL expressions. A CakeML program, however, is a sequence of declarations of types, values, or structures. Our IL does not have declarations, so to compile a value declaration `val` $p$ `=` $e$, we construct the CakeML expression `case` $e$ `of` $p$ `=>` $vs$, where $vs$ is a tuple of the variables appearing in $p$, translate this expression to the IL and compile it, and generate a bit of additional code to extract the new bindings from the tuple. For type declarations, we need not generate any code at all and simply update the compiler's state component mapping constructor names to bytecode block tags.

***Modules*** Structure declarations are, from the compiler's perspective, just a sequence of type and value declarations. But they must be treated as a single unit, so there is a subtlety: if any of the declarations within a structure raises an un-handled exception, the bindings for the whole structure need to be discarded. Therefore, we must set up an exception handler around the whole sequence of declarations, enabling unwinding of the stack before proceeding to the next top-level declaration. If the sequence of declarations finishes successfully, we pop the exception handler and hence need to shift the stack offsets for the new bindings in the compiler's environment. We reuse this machinery and its proof for top-level declarations (treating them as unnamed structures with one declaration).

## 7. Diverging Programs

So far we have seen our compilation algorithm and how we prove that if a source declaration terminates then the bytecode terminates with the same result. By assuming termination, we might appear to admit a compiler that causes programs that should diverge to do anything at all, including returning a wrong result. Here we show how to establish that our compiler in fact preserves divergence.

The proofs of the previous section are all performed in the direction of compilation by induction on the big-step semantics. We would like to handle diverging programs in the same way, to avoid establishing a simulation from a small-step bytecode trace to a small-step source trace against the direction of compilation, and to avoid introducing a co-inductive big-step semantics [15]. Because the bytecode semantics is deterministic, all we have to do is show that the compiler maps diverging source expressions to diverging bytecode expressions.

First, we add optional clocks to the source big-step semantics and to the bytecode machine state. In the big-step semantics, the clock is decremented by 1 on each function call, and a timeout exception is raised if a function is called when the clock is 0. In the bytecode, the `Tick` instruction decrements the clock, and the semantics gets stuck if the clock is 0. The compiler emits a `Tick` instruction for each source function call, and we prove that if a program times out in the semantics with a certain clock, then the compiled version times out in the bytecode with the same clock. This is the core of the compiler proof for divergence, and it follows the same inductive approach as the rest of the compiler proof. The conclusion of Theorem 12 handles the case of a timeout exception, and thereby supports an analogue of Theorem 8 for diverging programs.

It remains to show how to establish our main divergence result when the source semantics ignores the clock and the `Tick` instruction is implemented as a no-op (and thus produces no x86-64 instructions). We sketch the proofs here with a simplified notation. We will write $c \vdash e \Downarrow v$ for convergence in the source language with clock $c$ to a value (or non-timeout exception), and $c \vdash e \Downarrow \emptyset$ for a timeout exception. We use a clock of $\infty$ to indicate the version that ignores the clock.

**Lemma** (Big-step Clocked Totality)**.** For all clocks $c$ and expressions $e$, either $c \vdash e \Downarrow \emptyset$ or $\exists v.\ c \vdash e \Downarrow v$.

*Proof sketch.* By well-founded induction on the lexicographic ordering of the clock and size of the expression. In all but one case, the applicable big-step rules have inductive premises that have the same or smaller clocks (because the clock is monotonically non-increasing) and smaller sub-expressions. Thus, by induction the results for the sub-expressions combine to give a result for the expression. (It is important here that all mis-applied primitives evaluate to an exceptional result.) The only case where the expression might be bigger is function application, but it decrements the clock first. □

**Lemma** (Big-step Clock/Unclock)**.** $c \vdash e \Downarrow v$ implies $\infty \vdash e \Downarrow v$ and, $\infty \vdash e \Downarrow v$ implies $\exists c.\ c \vdash e \Downarrow v$.

*Proof sketch.* Straightforward induction. □

The bytecode's operational semantics is small-step, so we define an evaluation relation in the standard way:

$$c \vdash bs \Downarrow_{bc} bs' \equiv bs\{\texttt{clock} = c\} \rightarrow^* bs' \wedge \forall bs''. \neg(bs' \rightarrow bs'')$$

We say the machine has timed out if it evaluates to a state with $\texttt{clock} = 0$ and next instruction `Tick`. A bytecode machine state diverges if it can always take another step.

**Lemma** (Bytecode Clock/Unclock). $c \vdash bs \Downarrow_{\text{bc}} bs'$ implies $bs\{\texttt{clock} = \infty\} \rightarrow^* bs'\{\texttt{clock} = \infty\}$, and $\infty \vdash bs \Downarrow_{\text{bc}} bs'$ implies $\exists c.\ c \vdash bs \Downarrow_{\text{bc}} bs'\{\texttt{clock} = 0\}$.

*Proof sketch.* Straightforward induction. □

**Lemma** (Clocked Bytecode Determinism). $c \vdash bs \Downarrow_{\text{bc}} bs'$ and $c \vdash bs \Downarrow_{\text{bc}} bs''$ implies $bs' = bs''$.

*Proof sketch.* The small-step relation is deterministic by inspection of the rules; the main result follows by induction on $\rightarrow^*$. □

**Theorem 13.** Evaluation of $e$ diverges in the un-clocked semantics iff the compilation of $e$ (loaded into a bytecode state $bs$) diverges in the un-clocked bytecode semantics.

*Proof.* For the forwards direction, we have $c \vdash e \Downarrow \emptyset$, for all clocks $c$, by the source language's determinism, and the totality and clock/unclock lemmas. Therefore by the compiler correctness result, we know for all clocks $c$ there is a $bs'$ such that $c \vdash bs \Downarrow_{\text{bc}} bs'$ and $bs'$ is timed out. Now we must show that $bs\{\texttt{clock} = \infty\}$ diverges. Suppose, for a contradiction, there is some $bs''$ with $\infty \vdash bs \Downarrow_{\text{bc}} bs''$. Let $c$ be one more than the number of `Tick` instructions on the trace from $bs$ to $bs''$, which is unique by determinism. This contradicts the existence of a $bs'$ above: if evaluation stops before reaching $bs''$, it will not have passed enough `Ticks` to deplete the clock, and if it reaches $bs''$ it stops without timing out.

The backwards direction follows easily from Theorem 8 and the clock/unclock lemmas. □

## 8. Read-Eval-Print Loop

To interact with our compiler, we build a REPL. We define this first as a logic function, $\mathsf{REPL}_i$, that implements $\mathsf{REPL}_s$. (In later sections, we describe how we produce an x86-64 machine code implementation of the REPL.)

```
loop (bs, b) input =
  case lex_until_toplevel_semicolon input of
  | None → Terminate
  | Some (tokens, rest_of_input) →
    case REPL_i_step(tokens, s) of
    | Failure error_msg →
        Result error_msg
          (loop (bs, s) rest_of_input)
    | Success (code, s, s_exc) →
        let bs = install_code s.cstate code bs in
          case bc_eval bs of
          | None → Diverge
          | Some bs →
              let s = if success bs then s else s_exc in
                Result bs.output
                  (loop (bs, s) rest_of_input)

REPL_i input = loop initial_state input
```

On each iteration of its main loop $\mathsf{REPL}_i$ lexes part of the input string up until the first top-level semicolon; it then calls the $\mathsf{REPL}_i$_step function, which performs parsing, elaboration, type inference and then compilation to bytecode. Once the input has been turned into code, it installs the code into a bytecode state and starts execution (bc_eval) of the new bytecode state. If the generated code terminates, then it loops back to the top and starts again.

Here bc_eval is a non-computable function which describes the small-step execution of the bytecode semantics. This function is total and returns None if the bytecode fails to terminate, otherwise it returns the resulting state inside Some.[6]

**Theorem 14** ($\mathsf{REPL}_i$ Correct). For all inputs $i$ and outputs $o$, if $\mathsf{REPL}_i\ i = o$ then $\mathsf{REPL}_s$ (get_type_error_mask $o$) $i$ $o$. Where $\mathsf{REPL}_s$ is the REPL semantics described in Section 2 and get_type_error_mask picks out the inputs that output `"<type error>"`, to let the REPL semantics know where the type system should fail.

*Proof sketch.* By induction on the length of $i$. This theorem pulls together the parser soundness and completeness theorems, the inference soundness theorem, the type soundness theorem and the compiler correctness theorem. Most of the proof is devoted to showing that the various invariants required by the theorems are maintained across the iterations of loop. □

The verified $\mathsf{REPL}_i$ function is well suited for simulating the implementation in the theorem prover: we can evaluate $\mathsf{REPL}_i$ using the HOL4 prover's `EVAL` mechanism. For example,

```
EVAL ``REPL_i "fun f x = x + 3; f 2;"``
```

automatically derives a theorem:

```
REPL_i "fun f x = x + 3; f 2;" =
Result "val f = <fn>" (Result "val it = 5" Terminate)
```

Note that this evaluation of $\mathsf{REPL}_i$ inside the logic by inference does not terminate if the bc_eval fails to terminate, *i.e.*, this evaluation won't return Diverge.

## 9. Bootstrapping

Most of the complexity in the definition of $\mathsf{REPL}_i$ is contained within the definition of $\mathsf{REPL}_i$_step, a function that combines parsing, elaboration, type inference and compilation to bytecode. The next section describes how we construct a verified x86-64 machine-code implementation of $\mathsf{REPL}_i$, and therefore of $\mathsf{REPL}_s$. In order to make the construction of x86-64 for $\mathsf{REPL}_i$ an easier task, we use the verified compiler to compile $\mathsf{REPL}_i$_step to bytecode. The $\mathsf{REPL}_i$_step function contains the compiler itself, which means that this application of compilation amounts to *bootstrapping* the compiler. This section explains the bootstrapping method; the next section explains how we use the result.

Our starting point is $\mathsf{REPL}_i$_step. We want to have bytecode which is proved to implement the $\mathsf{REPL}_i$_step function. The $\mathsf{REPL}_i$_step is defined in logic (HOL), where functions are specified using equations, *e.g.* it is easy to define a HOL constant, fac, that is characterised by the equations:

$$\begin{aligned} \mathsf{fac}\ 0 &= 1 \\ \mathsf{fac}\ (n+1) &= (n+1) \times \mathsf{fac}\ n \end{aligned}$$

In order to apply the verified compiler to functions defined in HOL, we need these equations to exists as CakeML abstract syntax for function definitions, *i.e.*, we need CakeML declarations defining $\mathsf{REPL}_i$_step.

A previously developed proof-producing tool [22], implements exactly this kind of translation. Given a constant from HOL with equations that look sufficiently ML-like, the tool generates CakeML abstract syntax and proves that the generated CakeML implements the constant described by equations in HOL. When applied to $\mathsf{REPL}_i$_step, this translation produces a long list of

[6] bc_eval is the $\Downarrow_{bc}$ relation from Section 7.

CakeML declarations:

$$\begin{array}{l}\mathsf{ml\_repl\_step\_decls} \;=\\ \;[\texttt{datatype ..., datatype ...,}\\ \;\;\texttt{fun ..., fun ..., ..., fun repl\_step x = ...}]\end{array}$$

The tool also proves two relevant theorems:

**Theorem 15** (Evaluating ml_repl_step_decls)**.** Evaluation of the declaration list succeeds and produces a semantic environment, *i.e.*, a mapping from names to values. We will refer to this environment as ml_repl_step_env.

**Theorem 16** (Evaluating `repl_step`)**.** The value associated with the name `repl_step` in ml_repl_step_env, is a closure which implements $\mathsf{REPL}_i$_step w.r.t. refinement invariants input and output (relations between abstract values and CakeML semantic values). In the notation of Myreen and Owens [22]:

$$\begin{array}{c}\mathsf{Eval\ ml\_repl\_step\_env\ "repl\_step"}\\ ((\mathsf{input} \to \mathsf{output})\ \mathsf{REPL}_i\mathsf{\_step})\end{array}$$

*Proof sketch.* By algorithm from Myreen and Owens [22] □

The CakeML-to-bytecode compiler is then applied to the declaration list. The result is a theorem produced by evaluation.

**Theorem 17** (Compiling ml_repl_step_decls)**.** Given an initial compiler state init and the declaration list, the compiler produces bytecode and a new compiler state cstate.

$$\mathsf{compile\_decs\ init\ ml\_repl\_step\_decls} = (\mathsf{bytecode}, \mathsf{cstate})$$

*Proof sketch.* By evaluation in the logic (`EVAL` from above). □

Next, we instantiate the compiler correctness theorem (the compile_decs version of Theorem 8) for use with Theorems 15 and 16. Two further theorems are outlined below. We omit the definition of run_inv.

**Theorem 18** (Running bytecode)**.** Executing the compiler generated bytecode terminates in some state $bs$ such that this state contains ml_repl_step_env and run_inv $bs\ v$ is true, for some $v$.

*Proof sketch.* By instantiation of a lemma supporting Theorem 8. □

**Theorem 19** (Calling `repl_step`)**.** For any bytecode state $bs$, semantics value $v$ and $x$ such that run_inv $bs\ v$ and input $x\ v$, running a snippet of bytecode which calls the code for `repl_step`, terminates in a new bytecode state $bs'$ and $v'$ such that run_inv $bs'\ v'$ and output ($\mathsf{REPL}_i$_step $x$) $v'$. In other words, calling the code for `repl_step` computes $\mathsf{REPL}_i$_step.

*Proof sketch.* By instantiation of Theorem 12 and other lemmas supporting Theorem 8. □

## 10. Implementation in x86-64

The verified x86-64 implementation is constructed so that it exactly implements the in-logic-defined $\mathsf{REPL}_i$ function from above. Thanks to the bootstrapping, large parts of $\mathsf{REPL}_i$, namely $\mathsf{REPL}_i$_step, exist in the form of verified bytecode. In other words, much of the effort involved in constructing the x86-64 implementation of $\mathsf{REPL}_i$ boils down to producing an implementation of the bytecode that the compiler targets.

In order to verify the x86-64 code we need a semantics, a programming logic and proof automation for x86-64 machine code. For these, we build on previous work.

***Semantics of x86-64*** We use a conventional small-step operational semantics for x86 machine code. This semantics originates in a definition for 32-bit x86 that Sarkar et al. [28] validated against real hardware. The semantics was extended in Myreen [19] to handle self-modifying code and used in our previous work on a verified implementation of a REPL for Lisp [21]. The current semantics has a small coverage of the user-mode x86-64 instruction set. However, it tries to be as accurate as possible for the subset it describes.

***Programming Logic*** For most proofs (manual and automatic), we use the machine-code Hoare logic for our previous work on self-modifying code [19]. However, for the current work, we had to define a new more expressive programming logic in order to state and prove the top-level theorem. The top-level theorem must be able to specify that the machine code diverges. Our previously developed Hoare logic is only able to specify that a state satisfying the postcondition is eventually reached (termination).

The new programming logic (also embedded in HOL), makes statements, using temporal logic, about the sequence of all possible executions of the underlying x86-64 machine. This new programming logic makes judgements of the form temporal $code\ \phi$. It is strictly more expressive than the Hoare triple.

**Theorem 20** (Hoare Triple Instance of temporal)**.** The machine-code Hoare triple, $\{p\}\ code\ \{q\}$, is an instance of temporal:

$$\{p\}\ code\ \{q\} \iff \mathsf{temporal}\ code\ ((\mathsf{now}\ p) \Rightarrow \Diamond(\mathsf{now}\ q))$$

*Proof sketch.* Follows immediately from the definitions. □

We define temporal, now, $\Rightarrow$, $\Diamond$, *etc.* as follows. The definitions below take a few concepts from Myreen [19], in particular x86_seq $s\ t$ is true if $t$ is a valid x86-64 trace starting from state $s$, and $p \preceq s$ is true if $p$ holds for a copy of a state $s$ with a less precise instruction cache [19]; for most purposes, simply read $p \preceq s$ as $p\ s$.

$$\begin{array}{l}\mathsf{temporal}\ code\ \phi \;=\\ \quad \forall s\ t\ r.\\ \quad\quad \mathsf{x86\_seq}\ s\ t \implies \phi\ (\lambda p\ s.\ (p * \mathsf{code}\ code * r) \preceq s)\ t\end{array}$$

$$\begin{array}{rcl}\mathsf{now}\ p &=& \lambda assert\ t.\ assert\ p\ (t\ 0)\\ \Box\,\phi &=& \lambda assert\ t.\ \forall k.\ \phi\ assert\ p\ (\lambda n.\ t\ (n+k))\\ \Diamond\,\phi &=& \lambda assert\ t.\ \exists k.\ \phi\ assert\ p\ (\lambda n.\ t\ (n+k))\\ \mathsf{later}\ \phi &=& \lambda assert\ t.\ \exists k.\ \phi\ assert\ p\ (\lambda n.\ t\ (n+k+1))\\ \phi \vee \psi &=& \lambda assert\ t.\ \phi\ assert\ t \vee \psi\ assert\ t\\ \phi \Rightarrow \psi &=& \lambda assert\ t.\ \phi\ assert\ t \implies \psi\ assert\ t\end{array}$$

Using these, we can specify divergence of a machine-code program. For example, from initial configuration $p$, $code$ will always, at some some later point, reach a state satisfying $q$. In other words, $q$ will be true infinitely many times.

$$\mathsf{temporal}\ code\ ((\mathsf{now}\ p) \Rightarrow \Box\Diamond(\mathsf{now}\ q))$$

In our theorems, we instantiate $q$ to say that the compiled bytecode is still running. Divergence means that the program runs bytecode forever.

***Bytecode Heap Invariant*** Central to our proofs is the invariant which specifies how bytecode states are concretely represented in the x86-64 machine state. This invariant is formalised as a state assertion bc_heap $bs\ aux\ s$, which relates bytecode state $bs$ and auxiliary state $aux$ to (part of) machine state $s$.

The formal definition of bc_heap is not shown due to its length. However, informally, this invariant states that:

- memory is split into two data heaps (of which only one is in use at any point in time, enabling stop-and-copy garbage collection), a code heap, the normal x86-64 stack and a separate global state record;
- registers `rax–rdx` hold bytecode values – in the case of a Block, a large (bignum) Number, or a RefPtr, this means they contain a pointer into the data heap;
- the top of the bytecode stack is stored in register `rax`,

- the rest of the bytecode stack is kept in the x86-64 stack, *i.e.*, all values in the x86-64 stack are roots for the garbage collector,
- the stack is accessed through the normal stack and base pointers, registers `rsp` and `rbp`;
- other registers and state keep track of temporary values, the state of the allocator and system configuration.
- output is produced via calls to a special code pointer, for which we have an assumption that each call to this code pointer puts a character onto some external stream (in practice we link to C's `putc` routine). Input is handled similarly (using `getc`).
- memory contains code for supporting routines: the verified garbage collector, arbitrary-precision arithmetic library *etc.*

The garbage collector updates the heap and the stack (*i.e.*, the roots for the heap), both of which can contain code pointers and stack pointers. In order for the garbage collector to distinguish between data pointers and code/stack pointers all code/stack pointers must have zero as the least significant bit (*i.e.*, appear to be small integers). We ensure that all code pointers end with zero as the least significant bit by making sure that each bytecode instruction is mapped into x86-64 machine code that is of even length.

***Implementation of CakeML Bytecode*** Having formalised the representation of bytecode states, we define a function that maps CakeML Bytecode instructions into concrete x86-64 machine instructions (*i.e.* lists of bytes). Here $i$ is the index of the instruction that is to be translated ($i$ is used for the translation of branch instructions, such as Jump).

$$\begin{array}{rcl} \mathsf{x64}\ i\ (\mathsf{Stack\ Pop}) & = & [\mathtt{0x48}, \mathtt{0x58}] \\ \mathsf{x64}\ i\ (\mathsf{Stack\ Add}) & = & [\mathtt{0x48}, \ldots] \\ & \vdots & \end{array}$$

Entire bytecode programs are translated by x64_code:

$$\begin{array}{rcl} \mathsf{x64\_code}\ i\ [\,] & = & [\,] \\ \mathsf{x64\_code}\ i\ (x :: xs) & = & \mathsf{let}\ c = \mathsf{x64}\ i\ x\ \mathsf{in} \\ & & \quad c \mathbin{@} \mathsf{x64\_code}\ (i + \mathsf{length}\ c)\ xs \end{array}$$

We prove a few key lemmas about the execution of the generated x86-64 machine code.

**Theorem 21** (x64_code Implements Bytecode Steps)**.** The code generated by x64_code is faithful to the execution of each of the CakeML Bytecode instructions. Each instruction executes at least one x86-64 instruction (hence later). Note that execution must either reach the target state or resort to an error (out_of_memory_error).

$$\begin{array}{l} bs \rightarrow bs' \implies \\ \mathsf{temporal}\ \{(base, \mathsf{x64\_code}\ 0\ bs.\mathsf{code})\} \\ \quad (\mathsf{now}\ (\mathsf{bc\_heap}\ bs\ (base, aux)) \Rightarrow \\ \quad\quad \mathsf{later}\ (\mathsf{now}\ (\mathsf{bc\_heap}\ bs'\ (base, aux)) \\ \quad\quad\quad\quad \vee\ \mathsf{now}\ (\mathsf{out\_of\_memory\_error}\ aux))) \end{array}$$

*Proof sketch.* For simple cases of the bytecode step relation ($\rightarrow$), the proof was manual using the programming logic from Myreen [19]. More complex instruction snippets (such as the supporting routines) were produced using a combination of manual proof and proof-producing synthesis (*e.g.* [20]). □

**Theorem 22** (x64_code Implements Terminating Bytecode Executions)**.** Same as the theorem above, but with $\Downarrow_{\mathsf{bc}}$ instead of $\rightarrow$.

*Proof sketch.* Induction on the number of steps. □

**Theorem 23** (x86-64 Implementation of $\mathsf{REPL}_i$_step)**.** Executing the x64_code-generated code for the result of the bootstrapping (*i.e.* bytecode) and the bytecode snippet that calls `repl_step` has the desired effect w.r.t. bc_heap.

*Proof sketch.* Follows from theorems 18, 19 and 22. □

The only source of possible divergence in our x86-64 implementation of $\mathsf{REPL}_i$ is the execution performed by bc_eval. When the logic function bc_eval returns None, we want to know that the underlying machine gets stuck in an infinite loop and that the output stays the same. (Only the top-level loop is able to print output.)

$$\begin{array}{l} \mathsf{repl\_diverged}\ out\ aux\ = \\ \quad \Box \Diamond (\mathsf{now}\ (\exists bs.\ \mathsf{bc\_heap}\ bs\ aux * (bs.\mathsf{output} = out))) \end{array}$$

**Theorem 24** (x86-64 Divergence)**.** For any $bs$, such that $\mathsf{bc\_eval}\ bs = \mathsf{None}$, we have:

$$\begin{array}{l} (\forall bs'.\ bs \rightarrow^* bs' \implies bs.\mathsf{output} = bs'.\mathsf{output}) \implies \\ \mathsf{temporal}\ \{(base, \mathsf{x64\_code}\ 0\ bs.\mathsf{code})\} \\ \quad (\mathsf{now}\ (\mathsf{bc\_heap}\ bs\ (base, aux)) \Rightarrow \\ \quad\quad \mathsf{later}\ (\mathsf{repl\_diverged}\ bs.\mathsf{output}\ aux) \\ \quad\quad\quad\quad \vee\ \mathsf{now}\ (\mathsf{out\_of\_memory\_error}\ aux))) \end{array}$$

*Proof sketch.* Theorem 21 and temporal logic. □

***Top-level Correctness Theorem*** The top-level theorem for the entire x86-64 implementation is stated as follows.

**Theorem 25** (x86-64 Implementation of $\mathsf{REPL}_s$)**.** If the state starts from a good initial state (init), then execution behaves according to $\mathsf{REPL}_s\ l$ for some list $l$ of type inference failures.

$$\begin{array}{l} \mathsf{temporal\ entire\_machine\_code\_implementation} \\ \quad (\mathsf{now}\ (\mathsf{init}\ inp\ aux) \Rightarrow \\ \quad\quad \mathsf{later}\ ((\exists l\ res.\ \mathsf{repl\_returns}\ (\mathsf{out}\ res)\ aux\ \wedge \\ \quad\quad\quad\quad\quad\quad (\mathsf{REPL}_s\ l\ inp\ res \wedge \mathsf{terminates}\ res)) \\ \quad\quad\quad\quad \vee \\ \quad\quad\quad\quad (\exists l\ res.\ \mathsf{repl\_diverged}\ (\mathsf{out}\ res)\ aux\ \wedge \\ \quad\quad\quad\quad\quad\quad (\mathsf{REPL}_s\ l\ inp\ res \wedge \neg\mathsf{terminates}\ res)) \\ \quad\quad\quad\quad \vee \\ \quad\quad\quad\quad \mathsf{now}\ (\mathsf{out\_of\_memory\_error}\ aux))) \end{array}$$

Here repl_returns states that control is returned to the return pointer of $aux$, and out and terminates are defined as follows.

$$\begin{array}{l} \mathsf{out\ Terminate}\ =\ \texttt{""} \\ \mathsf{out\ Diverge}\ =\ \texttt{""} \\ \mathsf{out}\ (\mathsf{Result}\ str\ rest)\ =\ str \mathbin{@} \mathsf{out}\ rest \end{array}$$

$$\begin{array}{l} \mathsf{terminates\ Terminate}\ =\ \mathsf{true} \\ \mathsf{terminates\ Diverge}\ =\ \mathsf{false} \\ \mathsf{terminates}\ (\mathsf{Result}\ str\ rest)\ =\ \mathsf{terminates}\ rest \end{array}$$

*Proof sketch.* The execution of bytecode is verified as sketched above. The other parts of the x86-64 implementation (the setup code, the lexer and the code that ties together the top-level loop) was verified, again, using a combination of manual Hoare logic reasoning and proof-producing synthesis. Theorem 14 was used to replace $\mathsf{REPL}_i$ by the top-level specification $\mathsf{REPL}_s$. □

## 11. Small Benchmarks

To run the verified x86-64 machine code, we inline the code into a 30-line C program, which essentially just allocates memory (with execute permissions enabled) then runs it (passing in function pointers for `getc` and `putc`).

The result of running a few benchmarks is shown below. Execution times are compared with interpreted OCaml: CakeML runs the Fibonacci example 2.2 times faster than interpreted OCaml.

| | compiled OCaml | Poly/ML | CakeML |
|---|---|---|---|
| Fibonacci | 7.9 | 4.6 | 2.2 |
| Quicksort | 3.1 | 10.0 | 0.6 |
| Batched queue | 2.0 | 12.9 | 0.4 |
| Binary tree | 4.3 | 5.6 | 0.6 |

The Fibonacci benchmark computes the 31st Fibonacci number

using the naïve recursive definition; the second benchmark applies Quicksort to a list of length 2,000; the batched queue benchmark performs enqueue-enqueue-dequeue 1,000,000 times on a purely functional implementation of queues; the last benchmark constructs a 2,000-element binary tree and then flattens it. We used OCaml version 4.01 and Poly/ML 5.4.1.

## 12. Design and Context

Our overall goal for CakeML is to provide the most secure system possible for running verified software and other programs that require a high-assurance platform. Thus, our primary focus has been on reducing the trusted computing base, rather than on compiler optimisations or exotic language features.

### 12.1 Trusted Computing Base

Our correctness theorem relies on a machine code semantics for x86-64 and on a semantics for CakeML. If the machine code semantics does not soundly reflect actual processor behaviour, then the program might not behave as verified. Having a machine code semantics in the trusted computing base is intrinsic to the problem. The only alternative is to restrict execution to a verified processor, severely limiting the usefulness of the verified compiler compared to one that targets off-the-shelf hardware. However, the target machine code semantics only needs to cover, and be tested on, the instructions that the compiler actually generates, which in our case is significantly smaller than the entire x86-64 ISA.

If a programmer wants to understand what their CakeML program does, they currently have two strategies: one, is to reason about it relative to the CakeML semantics, and the other is to synthesise verified CakeML from higher-order logic (*e.g.*, using the same technique [22] that we use for bootstrapping). In the latter case, the CakeML semantics is not part of the trusted computing base, because the synthesised CakeML is verified with respect to the CakeML semantics. In this sense, the CakeML semantics is just the interface between the compiler, and the user's chosen verification approach. In the future, we hope to implement further (verified) ways to verify CakeML code, in the spirit of the Princeton "verified software toolchain" [1], which takes the same viewpoint, but for a C-like source language.

We also trust a small amount of code to set up the initial execution environment with functions to get a character from standard input and to write a character to standard output, because our machine model does not include these features.

A theorem prover or checker is also intrinsically part of the trusted computing base. In practice, our proofs can only be checked by automated means: too much of their content is in the minute details. Furthermore, the bootstrapping and machine code synthesis steps use verified computation in the prover itself to create the verified code: the proofs generated here are not human readable. One could apply a separate proof checking tool (*e.g.*, OpenTheory [9]), or simply trust HOL4 which follows the LCF approach and relies for its own soundness only on a small ($\approx$1000 lines) trusted kernel.

Lastly, we note that we do not rely on the correctness of another compiler in our trusted computing base (except perhaps as part of the proof checker or theorem prover).

### 12.2 Other Targets, Other Sources

CakeML currently translates from an SML-like language to x86-64 machine code; however, neither of those choices are mandated by our approach. In the future, we hope to extend CakeML to generate ARM machine code as well. Because CakeML compiles to a low-level, machine independent bytecode, and then to machine code, retargeting it only requires introducing a new bytecode to machine code level. This means that the amount of effort required to get a verified compiler for a second platform is much smaller than the effort required to build the system in the first place. Even though going through a machine-independent bytecode can potentially limit the compiler's ability to generate optimal code, we consider it well worth it in this context.

It would take more effort to adapt CakeML to new source languages: any of the lexer, parser, type checker and compilation to intermediate language (or even bytecode, if the source language is different enough) might have to change. However, this work would not be of a different character – it would just be in re-doing proofs of different parsing/typechecking/etc. algorithms following the strategy laid out here. In particular, the use of clocks (Section 7) to handle divergence and maintaining equivalent small-step and big-step semantics will be helpful in building a verified compiler for any similar language.

***What about OCaml?*** For the features that CakeML supports, SML and OCaml are very similar, and CakeML follows OCaml in several ways including the capitalisation restrictions on variables and constructors, and our lack of equality types and overloading. However, OCaml lacks two things that are important to our development: deterministic evaluation order and an equality function that always terminates (OCaml's follows reference cells into their contents, instead of just comparing them for identity). Thus, in order to be a semantic subset of an existing language, SML is our only choice. However, retargeting CakeML to an OCaml-like syntax (albeit with these small differences) would just be a matter of providing a new lexer and parser.

## 13. Related Work

The Jitawa verified Lisp implementation [21] has a similar goal of end-to-end verification about the compiler running as machine code. However, the source language of Jitawa is simpler than ours, with much simpler parsing, no type system, no modules, no handleable exceptions, no pattern matching, and no higher-order functions. Thus, CakeML demonstrates a substantial scaling-up of the kind of language that can be supported in a very high assurance setting. Furthermore, Jitawa does not bootstrap itself, and its top-level correctness theorem assumes that every input program terminates.

The CompCert compiler [14] and projects based on it, including CompcertTSO [29] and the Princeton "verified software toolchain" [1], focus on a C-like source language in contrast to our ML-like language. The emphasis is variously on optimisations, concurrency and program logics. Whereas our emphasis is on end-to-end correctness and a very small trusted computing base.

The VLISP project [7], which produced a *rigorously* – not formally – verified implementation of Scheme, emphasised end-to-end verification and did bootstrap their Scheme compiler to produce a verified implementation of their compiler.

Chlipala [4] is the most closely related work on verification of compiling impure functional programs with higher-order functions. Chlipala's compiler has simpler source and target languages, and its proofs do not address divergence. He emphasises the use of parametric higher-order abstract syntax (PHOAS) instead of the more conventional substitution semantics. For CakeML, we made the closure environments explicit in order to keep things simple.

Turning to the front end, there has been significant focus on mechanised meta-theory for language researchers (*e.g.*, POPLMark [2]), but it has not typically focussed on fitting into the overall context of a verified compiler. For type inference, Naraschewski and Nipkow [25] verify algorithm $\mathcal{W}$ for a basic typed $\lambda$-calculus plus let expressions. Our overall approach is similar to theirs, but they verify completeness and generalise nested lets, whereas we have a much richer language. Our approach to type soundness is similar to OCaml light [26], which also uses a concrete representation for ordinary variables and de Bruijn indices for type variables. The languages supported are also similar, except that they support type abbreviations whereas we support a module system. They also use a substitution-based semantics. Two other notable formalisations of ML metatheory by Lee at al. [13] and by Garrigue [6] focus on sophisticated type system features (functors and structural polymorphism, respectively).

Verified parsing has been a productive area recently. Our work distinguishes itself in its combination of soundness, completeness, guaranteed termination, and relative efficiency. Jourdan *et al.* [10] validate LR automata generated from a CFG, proving soundness and completeness. However, they have to provide a "fuel" parameter in order to ensure that the automata's execution terminates. Ridge [27] verifies a sound, complete and terminating parsing algorithm for arbitrary CFGs. As the input grammars may be ambiguous, Ridge's algorithm returns a list of parses. It is also rather inefficient, potentially $O(n^5)$. Earlier still, work by Barthwal and Norrish [3] achieves soundness and completeness, but is again missing termination. The big difference between these approaches and our own is that our approach is not *generic* as theirs are. Our PEG was hand-crafted, and its proofs of soundness and completeness with respect to the CFG were done manually.

## 14. Conclusion

The primary aim of CakeML is to provide an implementation of a practical programming language running on off-the-shelf hardware with the highest-levels of security and trustworthiness. We hope that it will be used as a platform for the development and deployment of programs where their correctness is the most important concern. Thus the trade-offs we have made in the design of the project differ from other efforts along the same lines. In particular, our focus has been on minimising the trusted computing base, not on optimisation or on breadth of source language features. In this sense, we believe that CakeML complements the verification efforts based around CompCert, which *are* focussed on optimisation and mainstream programming languages.

However, the design of CakeML does not rule out source- or IL-level optimisations, such as good support for multiple argument functions, inlining, constant propagation, and lambda lifting; the interesting question will be how to integrate them into the existing verification without requiring unreasonable effort. Furthermore, it does not appear difficult to add lower level optimisations with only modest changes to CakeML Bytecode, for example, the addition of registers and some form of register allocation.

Lastly, a verified compiler is most important in the context of verified applications to run on it. We are already working toward one example — a theorem prover using CakeML as its execution environment [24] — and hope that others will join in with applications drawn from a variety of domains.

## References


[1] A. W. Appel. Verified software toolchain (invited talk). In *ESOP*, volume 6602 of *LNCS*, 2011.

[2] B. E. Aydemir, A. Bohannon, M. Fairbairn, J. N. Foster, B. C. Pierce, P. Sewell, D. Vytiniotis, G. Washburn, S. Weirich, and S. Zdancewic. Mechanized metatheory for the masses: The POPLMark challenge. In *TPHOLs*, volume 3603 of *LNCS*, 2005.

[3] A. Barthwal and M. Norrish. Verified, executable parsing. In *ESOP*, volume 5502 of *LNCS*, 2009.

[4] A. Chlipala. A verified compiler for an impure functional language. In *POPL*, 2010.

[5] M. Felleisen, R. B. Findler, and M. Flatt. *Semantics Engineering with PLT Redex*. MIT Press, 2009.

[6] J. Garrigue. A certified implementation of ML with structural polymorphism. In *APLAS*, volume 6461 of *LNCS*, 2010.

[7] J. Guttman, J. Ramsdell, and M. Wand. VLISP: A verified implementation of Scheme. *Lisp and Symbolic Computation*, 8(1/2):5–32, 1995.

[8] HOL4. `http://hol.sourceforge.net`.

[9] J. Hurd. The OpenTheory standard theory library. In *NASA Formal Methods*, volume 6617 of *LNCS*, 2011.

[10] J.-H. Jourdan, F. Pottier, and X. Leroy. Validating LR(1) parsers. In *ESOP*, volume 7211 of *LNCS*, 2012.

[11] A. Koprowski and H. Binsztok. TRX: A formally verified parser interpreter. *Logical Methods in Computer Science*, 7(2), 2011.

[12] R. Kumar and M. Norrish. (Nominal) Unification by recursive descent with triangular substitutions. In *ITP*, volume 6172 of *LNCS*, 2010.

[13] D. K. Lee, K. Crary, and R. Harper. Towards a mechanized metatheory of Standard ML. In *POPL*, 2007.

[14] X. Leroy. Formal verification of a realistic compiler. *Commun. ACM*, 52(7), 2009.

[15] X. Leroy and H. Grall. Coinductive big-step operational semantics. *Inf. Comput.*, 207(2), 2009.

[16] A. McCreight, T. Chevalier, and A. P. Tolmach. A certified framework for compiling and executing garbage-collected languages. In *ICFP*, 2010.

[17] R. Milner. A theory of type polymorphism in programming. *J. Comput. Syst. Sci.*, 17(3), 1978.

[18] R. Milner, M. Tofte, R. Harper, and D. MacQueen. *The Definition of Standard ML (Revised)*. MIT Press, 1997.

[19] M. O. Myreen. Verified just-in-time compiler on x86. In *POPL*, 2010.

[20] M. O. Myreen and G. Curello. Proof pearl: A verified bignum implementation in x86-64 machine code. In *CPP*, volume 8307 of *LNCS*, 2013.

[21] M. O. Myreen and J. Davis. A verified runtime for a verified theorem prover. In *ITP*, volume 6898 of *LNCS*, 2011.

[22] M. O. Myreen and S. Owens. Proof-producing synthesis of ML from higher-order logic. In *ICFP*, 2012.

[23] M. O. Myreen, K. Slind, and M. J. C. Gordon. Extensible proof-producing compilation. In *CC*, volume 5501 of *LNCS*, 2009.

[24] M. O. Myreen, S. Owens, and R. Kumar. Steps towards verified implementations of HOL Light. In *ITP*, volume 7998 of *LNCS*, 2013.

[25] W. Naraschewski and T. Nipkow. Type inference verified: Algorithm W in Isabelle/HOL. *J. Autom. Reasoning*, 23(3-4), 1999.

[26] S. Owens. A sound semantics for OCaml light. In *ESOP*, volume 4960 of *LNCS*, 2008.

[27] T. Ridge. Simple, functional, sound and complete parsing for all context-free grammars. In *CPP*, volume 7086 of *LNCS*, 2011.

[28] S. Sarkar, P. Sewell, F. Zappa Nardelli, S. Owens, T. Ridge, T. Braibant, M. O. Myreen, and J. Alglave. The semantics of x86-CC multiprocessor machine code. In *POPL*, 2009.

[29] J. Ševčík, V. Vafeiadis, F. Zappa Nardelli, S. Jagannathan, and P. Sewell. Relaxed-memory concurrency and verified compilation. In *POPL*, 2011.

[30] D. Vytiniotis, S. L. Peyton Jones, T. Schrijvers, and M. Sulzmann. OutsideIn(X) Modular type inference with local assumptions. *J. Funct. Program.*, 21(4-5), 2011.

[31] A. K. Wright and M. Felleisen. A syntactic approach to type soundness. *Inf. Comput.*, 115(1), 1994.

# Probabilistic Relational Verification for Cryptographic Implementations

Gilles Barthe[1] Cédric Fournet[2] Benjamin Grégoire[3]
Pierre-Yves Strub[1] Nikhil Swamy[2] Santiago Zanella-Béguelin[2]
IMDEA Software Institute[1] Microsoft Research[2] INRIA[3]
{gilles.barthe,pierreyves.strub}@imdea.org, {fournet,nswamy,santiago}@microsoft.com, benjamin.gregoire@sophia.inria.fr

## Abstract

Relational program logics have been used for mechanizing formal proofs of various cryptographic constructions. With an eye towards scaling these successes towards end-to-end security proofs for implementations of distributed systems, we present RF$^\star$, a relational extension of F$^\star$, a general-purpose higher-order stateful programming language with a verification system based on refinement types. The distinguishing feature of RF$^\star$ is a relational Hoare logic for a higher-order, stateful, probabilistic language. Through careful language design, we adapt the F$^\star$ typechecker to generate both classic and relational verification conditions, and to automatically discharge their proofs using an SMT solver. Thus, we are able to benefit from the existing features of F$^\star$, including its abstraction facilities for modular reasoning about program fragments. We evaluate RF$^\star$ experimentally by programming a series of cryptographic constructions and protocols, and by verifying their security properties, ranging from information flow to unlinkability, integrity, and privacy. Moreover, we validate the design of RF$^\star$ by formalizing in Coq a core probabilistic $\lambda$-calculus and a relational refinement type system and proving the soundness of the latter against a denotational semantics of the probabilistic $\lambda$-calculus.

***Categories and Subject Descriptors*** D.3.1 [*Programming Languages*]: Formal Definitions and Theory—Semantics; D.2.4 [*Software Engineering*]: Software/Program Verification.

***Keywords*** program logics; probabilistic programming

## 1. Introduction

Many fundamental notions of security go beyond what is expressible as a property of a single execution of a program. For example, non-interference [25], the property underlying information-flow security, relates the observable behaviors of two program executions. Recognizing the importance to computer security of such *hyperproperties* [20], researchers have developed a range of program analyses and verification tools for proving relations between two or more programs, or two or more executions of the same program. For instance, Benton's relational Hoare logic [11] generalizes Hoare logic to reason about properties of two programs.

In addition, security properties must often account for probabilistic behaviors. For instance, in cryptography, simulation- and indistinguishability-based notions of security are specified in terms of the probability that an adversary wins in some probabilistic experiment. Starting from Kozen's seminal work [30], many logics for reasoning about probabilistic programs have been developed.

Recently, these two lines of work have been combined into a relational program logic called pRHL for reasoning about probabilistic imperative programs [7]. This logic can justify common patterns of probabilistic reasoning about hyperproperties used in cryptographic proofs, including observational equivalence, equivalence up to failure and reductionist arguments. pRHL forms the backbone of EasyCrypt [8], a tool-assisted framework which has been used for verifying the security of encryption and signature schemes, modes of operation for block-ciphers, and hash function designs in the computational model. These advances, among others, raise the prospect of a new class of verifiably secure systems: those that are proven secure based on standard computational assumptions (such as the existence of one-way functions) and whose verification encompasses all aspects of the system implementation.

**RF$^\star$*: end-to-end security of cryptographic implementations*** In an effort to scale logics like pRHL towards end-to-end security proofs of system implementations, this article presents a new language called RF$^\star$, building on F$^\star$ [45], a dependently typed dialect of ML. F$^\star$, and its predecessor F7 [12], make use of refinement types to verify implementations scaling to tens of thousands of lines of code, including the Transport Layer Security Internet standard (TLS) [13], multi-party sessions, web-browser extensions, zero-knowledge protocols, and the F$^\star$ typechecker itself.

RF$^\star$ integrates within F$^\star$ an expressive system of *relational* refinements to support fine-grained reasoning about *probabilistic* computations. Through careful language design, we are able to use the relational features of RF$^\star$ in smooth conjunction with the existing features of F$^\star$, allowing the large corpus of already-verified F$^\star$ code to be reasoned about effectively when used in a relational context. As such, our work opens the door to semi-automated security verification through relational refinement types, instead of a somewhat inflexible combination of parametricity and type safety (as in F7), or through detailed tactic-based interactive proofs (as in EasyCrypt), as a basis for certifying the security of critical pieces of Internet infrastructure, such as a reference implementation of TLS.

Technically, this paper makes three broad contributions:

This work has been partially supported by the Amarout European Program.


*POPL '14*, January 22–24, 2014, San Diego, CA, USA.
Copyright is held by the owner/author(s). Publication rights licensed to ACM.
ACM 978-1-4503-2544-8/14/01...$15.00.
http://dx.doi.org/10.1145/2535838.2535847

1. *A relational logic for higher-order stateful probabilistic programs:* we formalize in the Coq proof assistant $\lambda_p$, a lambda calculus with references, random sampling, and unbounded recursion. We develop a relational refinement type system for $\lambda_p$ and prove it sound with respect to a denotational interpretation of judgments as relations over pairs of store-passing probabilistic functions. To our best knowledge, $\lambda_p$ is the first relational logic for higher-order stateful probabilistic programs. (§3)
2. *The design and implementation of* RF*: $\lambda_p$ forms the basis of the design of RF*, an extension of F*. We show how to encode relational refinement types within a new relational state monad, RDST. We provide a type inference algorithm for RDST, in the form of a weakest pre-condition calculus that computes relational verification conditions. Proofs of these verification conditions can be discharged automatically by the RF* typechecker and the Z3 [21] SMT solver. (§4)
3. *An experimental evaluation of* RF*: we demonstrate the expressiveness of RF* through a representative set of examples, starting from simple (non-probabilistic) information flow, and gradually moving towards more advanced cryptographic models and systems. To date, we have used RF* to automatically verify a total of around 1,400 lines of code for a variety of relational properties, ranging from termination-insensitive non-interference to various indistinguishability-based properties for encryption, besides others. Several examples make essential use of higher-order and stateful features of RF*, emphasizing the utility of the $\lambda_p$ logic for practical security verification. (§2 and §5)

The $\lambda_p$ theory formalized in Coq, the RF* compiler, and all the example programs mentioned in this paper are available online from `http://research.microsoft.com/fstar`.

## 2. Programming with relational refinements

We start by describing RF* informally through a series of examples, beginning with a brief introduction to F* itself, and then focusing on the main new feature in RF*, i.e., relational refinement types.

**2.1 From classic to relational refinements.** F* is a call-by-value higher-order programming language with primitive state and exceptions, similar to ML, but with a more expressive type system based on dependent refinement types. Refinement types are written x:t{$\phi$} where $\phi$ is a logical formula. For instance, the code fragment below defines a refined type for non-negative integers, then for integers modulo some number p:

```
type nat = n:int { 0 ≤ n }
type mod p = n:nat { n < p }
let p = 97
let n : mod p = 73
```

Typechecking F* programs involves logical proof obligations, which are delegated to the Z3 SMT solver. For instance, to check that n has type mod p, the F* typechecker emits the proof obligation p = 97 $\Longrightarrow$ 0 $\leq$ 73 < p, which is easily discharged by Z3. Type safety means that, whenever an expression $e$ with type x:t{$\phi$} reduces to a value $v$, this value $v$ satisfies the formula $\phi$[x := $v$]. The type system provides structural subtyping. For instance, nat is a subtype of int, and mod p is a subtype of mod q when $p \leq q$. These subtyping relations are automatically proved and applied by F*.

Refinements can be combined with dependent function types, written x:t $\to$ t', where the formal parameter x:t is in scope in the result type t'. We also use dependent pairs, written x:t $*$ t', where the variable x of the first component is in scope in the type t' of the second component. For instance, we may write and typecheck addition modulo as follows (where the refinement braces bind tighter than the arrow):

```
val add: p:nat → x:mod p → y:mod p → z:mod p { z = (x + y) % p }
let add p x y = let s = x + y in if s < p then s else s − p
```

F* also provides primitive support for programming with state. For example, one may write **let** incr i = i := !i + 1. By combining refinements with references, one can express invariants on the program state, e.g., **ref** nat is the type of mutable locations that contain non-negative integers. To describe more precise properties of effectful programs, F* provides more advanced mechanisms, including a monadic mode [46], where one can reason about programs using variants of the Hoare state monad of Nanevski et al. [34] together with McCarthy's select/update theory for modeling the heap [32]. For example, one can give incr a specification of the form i:**ref** nat $\to$ ST ($\lambda$h.True) unit ($\lambda$ h () h'.h'=Upd h i (1 + Sel h i)), where ST pre t post can be understood as the state-passing function type h:heap{pre h} $\to$ (x:t $*$ h':heap{post h x h'}) although, in reality, F* provides primitive support for state. That is, the type of incr states a trivial pre-condition on the input heap h, and a post-condition indicating that the final heap h' differs from h at the location i, which is incremented. F* provides type inference in the form of a higher-order weakest pre-condition calculus to help ease the burden of writing such precise specifications [46].

RF* extends F* with *relational refinements*: a type can (also) be decorated with a relational formula, placed within double braces {|...|}, that specifies a joint property on pairs of values. Relational formulas can independently refer to the *left* and *right* values of every program variable in scope, using the projections L and R, respectively; projections extend naturally to arbitrary formulas. Intuitively, for deterministic programs, type safety means that, whenever we obtain two results $v_L$ and $v_R$ by evaluating an expression $e$: x:t{|$\phi$|} in two contexts that provide well-typed substitutions for $e$'s free variables, then the formula $\phi$[L x := $v_L$][R x := $v_R$] is valid. More generally, instead of considering two executions of the same program $e$, RF* allows proving relations between the results of two programs, i.e., we relate $e_0$ and $e_1$ at a (relationally refined) type using $e_0 \sim e_1$ : t. We write $e$ : t as a shorthand for $e \sim e$ : t.

We start with a few simple examples. Take the expression $e$ to be z − z; we can give $e$ the type x:int{|L x = R x|}, meaning that for any pair of substitutions $\sigma_L$ and $\sigma_R$, evaluating $\sigma_L e$ yields the same result as evaluating $\sigma_R e$. Similarly, we have x + x $\sim$ 2$*$x : z:int {| L x = R x $\Longrightarrow$ L z = R z |}, stating a simple equivalence between two integer expressions evaluated with the same value for $x$.

Relational refinements can also be used to describe properties beyond equivalence. For example, we can express the type of monotonic integer functions as x:int $\to$ y:int {| L x $\leq$ R x $\Longrightarrow$ L y $\leq$ R y |} and the type of $k$-sensitive integer functions, for some metric dist, as x:int $\to$ y:int {| dist (L y) (R y) $\leq$ k $*$ dist (L x) (R x) |}. RF* can automatically check (by subtyping) that a function such as **fun** x $\to$ k $*$ x is both monotonic and $k$-sensitive for any $k \geq 0$.

Relational refinements are strictly more expressive than plain refinements: one can encode any plain refinement { $\phi$ } as the relational refinement {| L $\phi$ $\wedge$ R $\phi$ |} that independently specifies *left* and *right* properties. For instance, the type nat above is automatically desugared to n:int {| 0 $\leq$ L n $\wedge$ 0 $\leq$ R n |}. Pragmatically, this enables us to mix property refinements and relational refinements in our concrete syntax, and to import any refinement-typed F* library in *relational mode* by applying the encoding. When authoring programs with specific relational properties in mind, one need issue only a single compiler directive (aka a pragma) to switch the verifier to relational mode. We contend that the resulting language, RF*, brings relational program verification out of the domain of tools applied to small fragments of pseudocode with interactive proofs, to a practical programming language suitable for small- to medium-scale systems implementations.

**2.2 Information flow.** Relational refinements can be systematically used to give a semantic characterization of termination-insensitive non-interference [41]. Whereas standard type-based information flow controls resort to security labels and ad hoc syntactic mechanisms to conservatively determine when the observable outputs of a program may depend on its secret inputs, RF* can directly verify the corresponding equivalences, as illustrated below.

Recall that non-interference means that public results do not depend on secrets. If an expression $e$ with base type $a$ that computes over some secret information can be given the type **type** eq a = x:a{|L x = R x|}, then its result can be safely published, since the execution of $e$ reveals no information about the secrets.

Capturing the intuition from labelled information flow type systems with "high" and "low" confidentiality levels, we use the type eq a (the type of values that are "equal on both sides") for low-confidentiality values, also written low a. In contrast, we use the type a (the type of unrelated left and right values) for high-confidentiality values, writing hi a as an alias for a. As usual, low a is a subtype of hi a, meaning that public values can be treated as secret, but not the converse.

Using these type abbreviations, we can write programs such as **fun** (x,y) → (x + y, y + 1) and give them information flow types such as hi int ∗ low int → hi int ∗ low int. More interestingly, we can supplement these types with relational refinements that capture more flexible information-flow policies. For example, a plausible confidentiality policy for credit card numbers conceals all but their last four digits, as specified and implemented below.

```
val last4: n:hi int→ s:string{|(L n%10000 = R n%10000)⟹ L s = R s|}
let last4 n = "********" ^ int2string (n % 10000)
```

Tracking leaks via control dependencies (aka implicit flows) is a characteristic feature of information flow type systems. To illustrate how RF* reasons about implicit flows, consider the program **fun** b → **if** b **then** $e$ **else** $e'$. Assuming that b is secret, flow-insensitive type systems would conservatively give this program the type hi bool → hi a. To give this program the more precise type hi bool → low a, we need to analyze four cases that arise from applying this function twice to arbitrary boolean arguments L b and R b, and prove that the results in all cases are the same. The four typechecking goals are

- $e$:low a, assuming L b = R b = true;
- $e'$:low a, assuming L b = R b = false;
- $e \sim e'$:low a, assuming L b = true and R b = false; and
- $e' \sim e$:low a, assuming L b = false and R b = true.

Anticipating on the next section, our proof rules for relating two values $v_0$ and $v_1$ are relatively simple. Proving $v_0 \sim v_1$ : x:t{| $\phi$ |} involves first proving $v_0 \sim v_1$ : t (which for base types involves simply showing that both $v_0$ and $v_1$ have type t), and then proving $\phi$[L x, R x := $v_0, v_1$]. So, RF* can easily prove, for instance,

```
(fun b → if b then 0 else 0) : hi bool → low int  and
(fun x → if x=0 then x else 0) : hi int → low int
```

even though, syntactically, those functions branch on confidential values. For expressions, particularly those that have side effects, the problem is more complex. Our strategy is to adapt the Hoare monad ST pre t post provided by F* to a relational version called RST, where RST pre t post can be seen as the type shown below:

```
h:heap{| pre (L h) (R h) |}
→ (x:t ∗ h':heap{| post (L h) (R h) (L x) (R x) (L h') (R h')|})
```

This is the type of pairs of functions that, when run in a pair of input heaps L h and R h satisfying the 2-place relational pre-condition predicate pre, may diverge, but if they both converge, yield results L x and R x and output heaps L h' and R h' that satisfy the 6-place relational post-condition predicate post.

Using the RST monad and its associated weakest pre-condition calculus, we can type the following program, which branches on a confidential value and then performs matching public side-effects:

```
val f: x:ref int → b:bool → RST (λ_ _. True) unit post
      where post h0 h1 _ _ h0' h1' = L x=R x ∧ h0=h1⟹ h0'=h1'
let f x b = if b then x := 1 else x := 1
```

RF* infers a weakest pre-condition predicate transformer for this program, then checks that it is consistent with any programmer supplied annotation (the annotation is optional for loop-free programs). In our example, the pre-condition of f states that it can be run in any pair of heaps, while its post-condition ensures that, if f is applied twice to the same references in the same heaps, then regardless of its boolean argument, the resulting heaps are also the same, i.e., the type reveals that f does not leak information despite having side-effects guarded by a secret boolean.

More complex programs, for example those that may leak information via side-effects based on aliasing, can be verified similarly:

```
val g: x:ref int → y:ref int → b:bool → RST (λ_ _. True) unit post
     where post h0 h1 _ _ h0' h1' = L x≠L y ∧ R x≠R y
                                 ⟹ Sel h0' (L y)=Sel h1' (R y)
let g x y b = if b then x := 1; y := 1 else y := 1; x := 0
```

The type of g states that, if x and y are not aliased, then the final contents of the reference y are the same.

Thus, the expressiveness of RF*, combined with its ability to use Z3 to discharge proof obligations, enables automated reasoning in the style of a relational Hoare logic for proving non-interference properties of higher-order stateful programs.

**2.3 Sampling, chosen-plaintext security, and one-time pads.** We introduce probabilistic relational reasoning in RF* using symmetric encryption schemes. Our goal is to communicate encrypted messages between a sender and a receiver without leaking any information about their content. (From an information flow viewpoint, ciphertexts are public, whereas plaintexts are secret.) For simplicity, we assume that messages range over byte arrays with a fixed size $n$ (called blocks) and we do not consider active attackers. Padding and authentication against chosen-ciphertext attacks can be easily added, but would complicate our presentation (see §5 for a description of our model for chosen-ciphertext security).

We assume that the sender and the receiver share a secret key $k$ (also a block), sampled uniformly at random by calling the primitive function sample. We model this assumption by writing a single program where both parties are within the scope of this key. The simplest secure encryption scheme is the one-time pad, implemented, for instance, using bitwise XOR: to encrypt the message $p$, compute $c = k \oplus p$; to decrypt $c$, compute $p = k \oplus c$.

```
type block = b:bytes { Length b = n }
let encrypt k p = xor k p
let decrypt k c = xor k c
```

Next, we explain how to specify and prove that an encryption scheme is secure. In cryptography, confidentiality is usually stated as resistance against chosen-plaintext attacks (CPA) and encoded as a decisional game in which an adversary chooses two plaintexts, receives the encryption of one of them under a fresh key, and must guess which of the two plaintexts was encrypted. (Decryption plays no role in this simple game; still, we may typecheck that it undoes encryption using classical refinements and properties of XOR.) This game may be coded in RF* as follows:

```
let cpa b p0 p1 = let p = if b then p0 else p1 in encrypt (sample n) p
```

where b is private and p0, p1, and the result are public. We thus express (perfect) CPA security relationally with the following type:

```
val cpa: b:bool → eq block → eq block → eq block
```

stating that the encryption of one of the two chosen-plaintext blocks p0 or p1 depending on b does not leak any information about b, hence does not help the adversary to win the game.

In fact, viewing CPA security from an information flow perspective, a simpler formulation is possible. Instead of reasoning about two messages selected by b, we just need to show that the function **let** cpa' p = encrypt (sample $n$) p has the type block → eq block. This is the best type we can hope for encryption, treating the plaintext as private and the ciphertext as public. This more compact typing property subsumes the first one.

To prove secrecy for the one-time pad, some probabilistic reasoning is called for. Indeed, operationally, calling sample $n$ twice does not usually return the same value. However, relying on our formal semantics, we show that it is permissible to give sample $n$ a more specific relational type that allows us to complete the proof. In particular, as explained below, we can type the call to sample $n$ in a way that depends on the plaintext p and give it the type

```
m:block {| xor (L p) (L m) = xor (R p) (R m) |}
```

From this type, RF$^\star$ automatically proves cpa': block → eq block. Intuitively, this relational refinement is sound inasmuch as the distribution of the resulting ciphertext is independent of the plaintext.

In programs that contain sample, the interpretation of assertions in the RST monad becomes probabilistic. We formalize this in §3, but provide some intuition for their meaning here. If we can give the type RST (λ_ _. True) t Q to $e_0 \sim e_1$, then our logic guarantees that if Q is an equivalence relation partitioning t in a set of equivalence classes $\overline{S}$, and if running $e_0$ in a heap $h_0$ reduces to $v_0$ and $e_1$ in $h_1$ reduces to $v_1$, then for any $S \in \overline{S}$, the probability that $v_0 \in S$ is equal to the probability that $v_1 \in S$. Similar conclusions can be drawn in general. For example, if Q h0 h1 x0 x1 h0' h1' implies P0 x0 ⟹ P1 x1, then the validity of the above assertion implies that Pr[P0 $v_0$] ≤ Pr[P1 $v_1$].

From this interpretation, one should be able to see that the relational refinement on the result of sample in RF$^\star$ is not specific to XOR. More generally, sample can be given a specification to state that any two calls to it return a pair of values related by *any* given one-to-one function on its range. Intuitively, relational refinements in RF$^\star$ capture relations between the *distribution over values* generated by probabilistic programs, rather than between values obtained in specific executions. The relational typing of sample is valid since applying a one-to-one function to a value uniformly chosen from a discrete set does not change its distribution.

To reflect these general properties of uniform sampling, our library provides a polymorphic, typed variant of sample, that takes as additional ghost parameter F, a binary predicate on sampled values of type block, whose refinement states that it must be an injective function (or, equivalently, a bijection). This parameter has kind block ⇒ block ⇒ E, where E is the kind of ghost refinements in F$^\star$ (types in E are erased at runtime). In the RF$^\star$ standard library, sample is typed as follows

```
type Function F = ∀a.∃ b.F a b ∧ ∀a b1 b2.F a b1 ∧ F a b2 ⟹ b1=b2
type Injective F = Function F ∧ ∀a1 a2 b. F a1 b ∧ F a2 b ⟹ a1=a2
val sample: ∀F. len:nat{Injective F} → b:block len{| F (L b) (R b) |}
```

In our one-time pad example, when calling sample $n$ in cpa', we instantiate F to λ b0 b1. xor (L p) b0 = xor (R p) b1, which is indeed injective. In §5, we describe security proofs of more realistic encryption schemes based on variants of the above typing for sample.

**2.4 Implicit flows and passport linkability.** Before justifying our typing rules, notably for sample, we present a concrete protocol for RFID-equipped passports, implemented in RF$^\star$, and we discuss a linkability attack against this protocol recently uncovered by Chothia and Smirnov [19]. We refer to their work for a detailed discussion. This attack is representative of common weaknesses in cryptographic implementations due to implicit flows in the handling of errors while processing decrypted data.

| **Passport Tag** | (physically sharing $k$) | **Reader** |
|---|---|---|
| sample $nt$ | $\longrightarrow nt \longrightarrow$ | |
| decrypt<br>verify MAC<br>verify $nt$ | $\longleftarrow \{nt \parallel nr \parallel kr\}_k$ — | sample $nr, kr$ |
| sample $kt$ | — $\{nr \parallel nt \parallel kt\}_k \longrightarrow$ | decrypt<br>verify MAC<br>verify $nr$ |
| $s = kt \oplus kr$ | ⟵ exchange data ⟶ | $s = kt \oplus kr$ |

**Figure 1.** Basic Access Control protocol for passports

Following the ICAO specification for machine-readable travel documents, all recent European passports embed RFID tags featuring the Basic Access Control protocol, outlined in Fig. 1. The protocol has two roles, a passport tag and a reader, exchanging messages using short-distance wireless communications. The goal of the protocol is to establish a shared session key for accessing biometric data on the passport. Each passport tag has a unique key $k$; the reader derives this key from information obtained by scanning the passport. (In reality, there is a negligible chance of two passports having the same key, because the key is derived from a hash of this information.)

The passport first samples a 64-bit nonce $nt$ and sends it as a challenge to the reader. The reader samples its own nonce $nr$ and some keying materials $kr$, then encrypts the concatenation of these three values using $k$. Concretely, the protocol implements authenticated encryption as triple-DES encryption concatenated with a plaintext Message Authentication Code (MAC). The passport decrypts, recomputes and checks the MAC to ensure that the message has not been tampered with, then compares the received nonce $nt$ with the challenge, to confirm that the reader responded correctly. If both checks succeed, it generates its own keying materials $kt$, appends them to the concatenation of the two nonces (in a different order than before), and computes the session key $s = kt \oplus kr$. The reader then similarly decrypts the received ciphertext, checks the MAC, and computes $s$.

The code the tag uses for handling the encrypted message of the reader is shown below; encrypt and decrypt provide authenticated encryption; concat and split convert between triples of 64-bit values and their concatenation.

```
let tag1 k nt c = match decrypt k c with
  | Some p → let (nt',nr,kr) = split p in
               if nt = nt' then encrypt k (concat nr nt (sample_kt()))
               else nonceError
  | None → decryptError
```

The code either produces an encrypted message, or it returns an error code. As written, it enables the following linkability attack:

1. The attacker eavesdrops any run of the protocol between a target passport and an honest reader, and records their second message.
2. Later, to test the local presence of this passport, the attacker runs the protocol (as the reader), replays the recorded message, and observes the response: although the protocol always fails to establish a key, the tag returns a nonceError if the two passports are the same, and a decryptError otherwise.

Experimentally, French passports reliably return different error messages, whereas other European passports return the same error message, but with measurably different timings. Although our approach does not directly catch timing attacks, those attacks can be conservatively analyzed by treating error codes produced at different code locations as distinct.

We interpret the above attack as an implicit flow of information from the key used to decrypt to the error message. Indeed, if we type the key k as high confidentiality and the nonce nt and the cipher c with eq refinements (since they are exchanged on a public network), relational typechecking fails on the body of tag1. The result of the decryption is (a priori) not the same on both sides, so the cross-cases involve proving, for instance that when decryption returns Some p on the left and None on the right, the two resulting expressions are equal, which fails on the proof obligation nonceError = decryptError.

By ensuring that the same error messages are returned in both cases (i.e., by requiring that nonceError = decryptError) this case is prevented, but this alone is not sufficient for verifying the code. Naïvely, the cross-cases that arise when verifying the nested conditionals require proving, under a suitable relational path condition, that the encryption on the third line is indistinguishable from the error messages—which is patently false. However, by reflecting several cryptographic assumptions into detailed typing invariants in the protocol implementation, we can prove that such problematic cross-cases never actually arise (i.e., the path conditions guarding these cases are infeasible) and we can verify that this code preserves unlinkability. Specifically, we assume that the encryption is CPA, key-hiding, and CTXT (all specified by typing) and that there are no nonce collisions (the probability of a collision is less than $q^2 2^{-64}$ where $q$ is the number of sessions observed by the adversary). Arapinis et al. [5] also analyze the corrected protocol, using the applied $\pi$-calculus, essentially proving unlinkability in a more abstract, symbolic model of cryptography. Please refer to our online materials for a full listing and further discussion of the specification and implementation of tag1.

## 3. Formal development

We formalize a core of RF$^\star$ in the Coq proof assistant by developing $\lambda_p$, a minimal higher-order language with (statically allocated) references, probabilistic assignments, and unbounded recursion. The formalization is based on the SSREFLECT extension [26], and on the ALEA library for distributions [6]. Overall, the formalization comprises over 2,500 lines of code excluding the aforementioned libraries.

The formalization is built in two steps. First, we consider a simply typed system $G \vdash_{e} e : \mathbf{T}$ for $\lambda_p$. Simple types $\mathbf{T}$ are extended to *relational refinement types* $\mathcal{C}$ where one can add relational pre- and post-conditions to function types. This allows us to define a relational type system $\mathcal{G} \vdash e_0 \sim e_1 : \mathcal{C}$ that relates a pair of expressions $e_0$ and $e_1$ in the type $\mathcal{C}$ under the *relational context* $\mathcal{G}$.

We then give a denotational semantics for well-typed judgments. Simple types are given a cpo interpretation $[\![\mathbf{T}]\!]$ in the standard way. Judgments $G \vdash_{e} e : \mathbf{T}$ are interpreted as the elements of the form $(\!|e|\!)_I$, where $I$ is any valuation for the context $G$. Taking into account that $\lambda_p$ is a language with references and probabilistic assignments, the denotation $(\!|e|\!)_I$ of $e$ is defined as a function from memories (equivalently, states or heaps) to distributions over pairs composed of a memory and an element of $[\![\mathbf{T}]\!]$; we denote by $\mathsf{M}([\![\mathbf{T}]\!])$ this function space. Relational types $\mathcal{C}$ are interpreted as a binary relation $\langle\!|\mathcal{C}|\!\rangle$ over $\mathsf{M}([\![\mathbf{T}]\!])$, where $\mathbf{T}$ is the simple type derived from $\mathcal{C}$ by erasing all refinements. This allows us to interpret (Theorem 1) a valid judgment $\mathcal{G} \vdash e_0 \sim e_1 : \mathcal{C}$ by all the pairs of the form $((\!|e|\!)_{I_\mathcal{L}}, (\!|e|\!)_{I_\mathcal{R}}) \in \langle\!|\mathcal{C}|\!\rangle$ for any pair of valuations $(I_\mathcal{L}, I_\mathcal{R})$ for the erasure $G$ of $\mathcal{G}$.

$$\frac{x : \mathbf{T} \in G \quad \tau \in \{\mathcal{L}, \mathcal{R}\}}{G \mid G' \vdash x_\tau : \mathbf{T}} \qquad \frac{x : \mathbf{T} \in G'}{G \mid G' \vdash x : \mathbf{T}}$$

$$\frac{r : \mathsf{ref}\,\mathbf{B} \quad \tau \in \{\mathcal{L}, \mathcal{R}\}}{G \mid G' \vdash r_\tau : \mathbf{B}} \qquad \frac{G \mid G' \vdash v_i : \mathbf{T}}{G \mid G' \vdash v_1 = v_2}$$

$$\frac{G \mid G', y : \mathbf{B} \vdash \phi}{G \mid G' \vdash \forall y : \mathbf{B}.\, \phi}$$

**Figure 2.** Well-formed relational formulas (excerpt)

**3.1 $\lambda_p$: syntax.** $\lambda_p$ is a simply typed $\lambda$-calculus with references and probabilistic assignments. For simplicity, we only consider two forms of probabilistic assignments: assigning a uniformly sampled boolean to a boolean variable (flip), and assigning an integer value sampled uniformly in a non-empty interval $[i, j]$ to an integer variable ($\mathsf{pick}_i^j$). Formally, the sets of types, contexts, values and expressions are given by the following grammars:

$$\begin{array}{llll}
\text{type} & \mathbf{T} & ::= & \mathbf{B} \mid \mathbf{T} \to \mathbf{T} \\
\text{ctxt.} & G & ::= & [] \mid G, [x : \mathbf{T}] \\
\text{value} & v, u & ::= & c \mid x \mid o(v_1, \ldots, v_n) \mid \mathsf{fun}\ x : \mathbf{T} \to e \\
\text{expr.} & e & ::= & v \mid e\ v \mid\ !r \mid r := v \mid \mathsf{flip} \mid \mathsf{pick}_i^j \mid \mathsf{let}\ x = e_1\ \mathsf{in}\ e_2 \\
 & & \mid & \mathsf{letrec}\ f\ x = e_1\ \mathsf{in}\ e_2 \mid \mathsf{if}\ v\ \mathsf{then}\ e_1\ \mathsf{else}\ e_2
\end{array}$$

where $x$ ranges over a set var of variables, $r$ ranges over a set ref of references and $o$ ranges over a set $\mathcal{O}$ of $\mathbf{B}$-sorted operators, whose signature is of the form $\mathbf{B}_1 \times \cdots \times \mathbf{B}_n \to \mathbf{B}_0$. We assume that $\mathbf{B}$ contains the unit type (**unit**) along with the types of Booleans (**bool**) and integers (**int**). Their associated constructors are $\bullet$, true, false and $\mathbf{n}$ for $n \in \mathbb{N}$. We implicitly assume that each reference has an ambient base type, and write $r : \mathsf{ref}\,\mathbf{B}$ to denote that $r$ is a reference with base type $\mathbf{B}$. The dynamic semantics is defined in the standard way as the compatible closure (for a call-by-value convention) of the $\beta\iota\mu\delta$-contraction.

**3.2 $\lambda_p$: typing.** As usual, a typing context is a sequence of bindings $x : \mathbf{T}$ such that the bound variables are pairwise distinct. The typing rules for deriving valid judgments $G \vdash_{v} v : \mathbf{T}$ and $G \vdash_{e} e : \mathbf{T}$, in a simply typed setting, are standard and omitted.

RELATIONAL REFINEMENT TYPES. Relational assertions are formulas over tagged variables $x_\mathcal{L}$ or $x_\mathcal{R}$ and tagged references $r_\mathcal{L}$ or $r_\mathcal{R}$; informally, tags determine whether the interpretation of $x$ or $r$ will be taken w.r.t. the left or right projection of a relational valuation. In order to interface with automated first-order provers, relational assertions are first-order $\mathbf{B}$-sorted formulas built from operators in $\mathcal{O}$ and predicates taken from a set of $\mathbf{B}$-sorted predicates that includes at least the equality predicates for all the base types. Note that tagged variables always occur free in assertions, and only logical variables can be bound. For instance, the relational assertion $\forall y : \mathbf{int}.\, x_\mathcal{L} \leq y \Rightarrow x_\mathcal{R} \leq y + r_\mathcal{R}$ is well-formed under any context $G$ such that $x : \mathbf{int} \in G$, assuming that $r : \mathsf{ref}\,\mathbf{int}$.

Formally, relational assertions are defined using a first-order type system with judgments of the form $G \mid G' \vdash \Phi$ for formulas (resp. $G \mid G' \vdash v : \mathbf{T}$ for values) where $G$ (resp. $G'$) is a context for relational variables (resp. for non-relational variables introduced by quantifiers). Figure 2 shows the typing rules for variables, references, equality, and universal quantification. We say that an assertion $\Phi$ is well-formed in context $G$ iff $G \mid \emptyset \vdash \Phi$ (written $G \vdash \Phi$).

*Refinement types* are either *relational types* (denoted by $\mathcal{T}, \mathcal{U}, \mathcal{V}$), which will be used for relational typing of values, or *computation types* (denoted by $\mathcal{C}$), used for relational typing of expressions.

They are defined by the following grammar:

$$\mathcal{T},\mathcal{U},\mathcal{V} \;:=\; \mathbf{B} \mid (x:\mathcal{T}) \rightarrow \mathcal{C} \qquad \mathcal{C} \;:=\; \{\Phi\}x:\mathcal{T}\{\Psi\}$$

where $\Phi$ and $\Psi$ are relational assertions. By convention, $x$ is bound in $(x : \mathcal{T}) \rightarrow \mathcal{C}$ and $\{\Phi\}x : \mathcal{T}\{\Psi\}$, and can be free in $\mathcal{C}$ or $\Psi$. However, the type system enforces that $x$ occurs in $\mathcal{C}$ and $\Psi$ only if $\mathcal{T}$ is a base type. In other cases, we write $\mathcal{T} \rightarrow \mathcal{C}$ and $\{\Phi\}\mathcal{T}\{\Psi\}$.

A *relational context* $\mathcal{G}$ is a sequence of bindings $x : \mathcal{T}$ such that the bound variables are pairwise distinct. The refinement type $\mathcal{T}$ is a refinement of $T$ under $G$, written $G \vdash \mathcal{T} \lhd T$, if $T$ is the result of erasing all pre- and post-conditions occurring in $\mathcal{T}$ and if any assertion $\Phi$ that appears in $\mathcal{T}$ is well-formed in $G$ augmented by the local context of $\Phi$ in $\mathcal{T}$. This relation is extended to relational contexts: $\mathcal{G} \lhd G$ is the smallest relation such that $[] \lhd []$ and if $\mathcal{G} \lhd G$ and $G \vdash \mathcal{T} \lhd T$ then $\mathcal{G}, x : \mathcal{T} \lhd G, x : T$.

RELATIONAL TYPING. Figure 3 gives a significant subset of the rules that define the relational typing judgments $\mathcal{G} \vdash v_1 \sim v_2 : \mathcal{T}$ for values and $\mathcal{G} \vdash e_1 \sim e_2 : \mathcal{C}$ for expressions. In the figure, $e[x := e_0, e_1]$ stands for $e[x_{\mathcal{L}} := e_0][x_{\mathcal{R}} := e_1]$. The full set of rules appear in the accompanying Coq formalization.

A judgment of the form $\mathcal{G} \vdash e_1 \sim e_2 : \{\Phi\}x : \mathcal{T}\{\Psi\}$ is valid when, for any pair of valuations $I_{\mathcal{L}}, I_{\mathcal{R}}$ for $\mathcal{G}$ and any pair of *states* $m_1, m_2$ satisfying the pre-condition $\Phi$, the distributions over values and states obtained by executing $e_1$ in $I_{\mathcal{L}}, m_1$ and $e_2$ in $I_{\mathcal{R}}, m_2$ are related by the lifting of the post-condition $\Psi$ to distributions.

The formal notion of lifting a relation to distributions is given below. We anticipate that although assertions in relational refinements are first-order formulas that do not mention probabilities, the definition of lifting is such that valid typing judgments can be used to prove relations between probability quantities. For instance, when $\Psi$ denotes an equivalence relation on $\mathcal{T}$, $[] \vDash e_1 \sim e_2 : \{\mathsf{true}\}x : \mathcal{T}\{\Psi\}$ implies that $\Pr[e_1 \in S] = \Pr[e_2 \in S]$, for any equivalence class $S$ of $\Psi$. Intuitively, observing to which equivalence class the results belong does not help in distinguishing the two expressions. As sketched in §2.3, we are not limited to simply proving probabilistic equivalences; other kinds of probabilistic assertions (e.g., inequalities) can also be expressed.

The rules come in two flavors: double-sided or single-sided. Double-sided rules allow us to relate programs with the same head symbol. For instance, rules [LET] and [APP] are double-sided. They work by relating sub-expressions pairwise, composing pre- and post-conditions using the implicit order of evaluation. Rule [LET] emphasizes this, with the post-condition of the let-bound expression being the pre-condition of the body.

It is not always possible to progress using double-sided rules. For instance, one may want to show that the two expressions (if $b$ then $v$ else $v$) and $v$ are related by a suitable post-condition. The two expressions having different head symbol, no double-sided rule can apply. Single-sided rules allow us to overcome this limitation. Rule [IF-LEFT], which permits to relate an if-expression to an arbitrary expression, is an example of a single-sided rule.

All the single-sided rules come in pairs: one variant (tagged [*-LEFT]) where the progression is done on the left expression, and one (tagged [*-RIGHT]) where the progression is on the right. Instead of showing both cases explicitly, we give a general rule [SYM] that transforms any [*-LEFT] rule into its [*-RIGHT] counterpart.

Rules for reference assignment ([REF], [REF-LEFT]), which come in two flavors too, make use of the ability to write assertions about the resulting memory. For example, the two expressions $r := v_0$ and $r := v_1$ are related by a post-condition $\Psi$ when $\Psi$, after replacing all occurrences of $r_{\mathcal{L}}$ (resp. $r_{\mathcal{R}}$) with $v_0$ (resp. $v_1$), holds as a pre-condition.

So far, we only considered rules for expressions headed by non-probabilistic constructions. Rules for random sampling ([FLIP] and [SAMPLE]) are double-sided and require the existence of a bijection $f$ between the support of the two distributions, ensuring a one-to-one correspondence between related values. In the case of [FLIP], we explicitly give the only two existing bijections from **bool** to **bool**.

### 3.3 $\lambda_p$: denotational semantics.

BACKGROUND. The denotational semantics of well-typed expressions is based on the sub-probability monad over sets [6, 37] and its generalization to complete partial orders (cpos); recall that a cpo is a partial order in which every ascending chain has a supremum. The unit interval $[0, 1]$ has a cpo structure w.r.t. the natural order on reals; moreover, every set can be lifted to a flat cpo by adding a bottom element, and the set of functions $A \rightarrow B$ between a set $A$ and a cpo $B$ can be given the structure of a cpo. A function between two cpos is monotonic if it is order-preserving, and it is continuous if it is monotonic and preserves suprema. Given two cpos $A$ and $B$, we let $A \stackrel{m}{\rightarrow} B$ and $A \stackrel{c}{\rightarrow} B$ denote the set of monotonic and continuous functions from $A$ to $B$ respectively. By Kleene's fixed point theorem, every continuous function $f$ on a cpo has a least fixed point fix $f$. A discrete sub-distribution over a set $X$ is a continuous functional $\mu : (X \stackrel{c}{\rightarrow} [0,1]) \stackrel{c}{\rightarrow} [0,1]$ that satisfies axioms of linearity, compatibility with inverse, and discreteness. In particular, the latter axiom states that the support $\mathsf{supp}(\mu)$ of $\mu$, consisting of all elements $x \in X$ such that $\mu\ \delta_x > 0$, is discrete—where $\delta_x$ denotes the Dirac function for $x$: i.e., $\delta_x(x) = 1$ and $\delta_x(y) = 0$ if $x \neq y$. We let $\mathcal{D}(X)$ be the set of discrete sub-distributions over $X$. $\mathcal{D}(X)$ has the structure of an $\omega$-complete partial order. Moreover, sub-distributions can be given the structure of a monad; the unit and composition operators are denoted by unit and bind respectively.

The relational interpretation of types rests on an operator $\cdot^\sharp$ that lifts relations over $A \times B$ into relations over $\mathcal{D}(A) \times \mathcal{D}(B)$; the operator is inspired from early works on probabilistic bisimulations [28], and is used in CertiCrypt [7] and EasyCrypt [9] to interpret relational judgments. Formally, let $\mu_1 \in \mathcal{D}(A)$ and $\mu_2 \in \mathcal{D}(B)$; then $R^\sharp\ \mu_1\ \mu_2$ iff:

$$\exists \mu : \mathcal{D}(A \times B).\ \pi_1(\mu) = \mu_1 \wedge \pi_2(\mu) = \mu_2 \wedge \mathsf{supp}(\mu) \subseteq R$$

where $\pi_1$ and $\pi_2$ are the projections for distributions over pairs, i.e.

$$\pi_1(\mu) = \mathsf{bind}\ \mu\ (\lambda(x,y).\ \mathsf{unit}\ x)$$
$$\pi_2(\mu) = \mathsf{bind}\ \mu\ (\lambda(x,y).\ \mathsf{unit}\ y)$$

A fundamental property of this lifting operator is that given $f : A \stackrel{c}{\rightarrow} [0,1]$ and $g : B \stackrel{c}{\rightarrow} [0,1]$ such that

$$\forall a \in A, b \in B.\ R\ a\ b \Rightarrow f\ a = g\ b$$

then $R^\sharp\ \mu_1\ \mu_2$ implies that $\mu_1\ f = \mu_2\ g$, i.e., the expected values of $f$ in $\mu_1$ and $g$ in $\mu_2$ coincide. Note that events can be viewed as $\{0,1\}$-valued functions, and in this case expectation coincides with probability.

INTERPRETATION. We first provide a non-relational interpretation of valid judgments. We assume each base type $\mathbf{B}$ is interpreted as a (flat) cpo $[\![B]\!]$, and that each constructor $c$ belonging to the base type $\mathbf{B}$ is given a denotation $\mathcal{B}(c) \in [\![B]\!]$. We define the set of semantical values as $\bigcup_{\mathbf{B}} [\![B]\!]$, and then the set $\mathcal{M}$ of *states* as the set of well-typed mappings from references to semantical values.

$$\mathcal{M} = \{m : \mathsf{ref} \rightarrow \bigcup_{\mathbf{B}} [\![B]\!] \mid \forall r : \mathsf{ref}\ \mathbf{B}.\ m(r) \in [\![B]\!]\}$$

Then we extend the interpretation to functional types by setting

$$[\![T_1 \rightarrow T_2]\!] = [\![T_1]\!] \stackrel{c}{\rightarrow} \mathsf{M}([\![T_2]\!])$$

where $\mathsf{M}(X) \triangleq \mathcal{M} \rightarrow \mathcal{D}(X \times \mathcal{M})$.

A valuation $I$ is a function that maps every declaration $x : \mathbf{T}$ to a semantical value. A valuation $I$ is well-formed for $G$, written $I \vDash G$, if $I$ maps every declaration $x : \mathbf{T}$ in $G$ to an element of $[\![\mathbf{T}]\!]$.

$$[\textsc{Constr}]\ \frac{G \vdash_{\mathsf{v}} v_0 : \mathbf{B} \qquad G \vdash_{\mathsf{v}} v_1 : \mathbf{B} \qquad \mathcal{G} \lhd G}{\mathcal{G} \vdash v_0 \sim v_1 : \mathbf{B}} \qquad [\textsc{Var}]\ \frac{\mathcal{G} \lhd G \qquad x \in \mathrm{dom}(\mathcal{G})}{\mathcal{G} \vdash x \sim x : \mathcal{G}(x)}$$

$$[\textsc{Fun-Base}]\ \frac{\mathcal{G}, x : \mathbf{B} \vdash e_0 \sim e_1 : \mathcal{C} \qquad \mathcal{G} \lhd G}{\mathcal{G} \vdash \mathsf{fun}\ x : \mathbf{B} \to e_0 \sim \mathsf{fun}\ x : \mathbf{B} \to e_1 : (x : \mathbf{B}) \to \mathcal{C}} \qquad [\textsc{Fun}]\ \frac{\mathcal{G}, x : \mathcal{T} \vdash e_0 \sim e_1 : \mathcal{C} \qquad \mathcal{G} \lhd G \qquad x \notin \mathcal{C}}{\mathcal{G} \vdash \mathsf{fun}\ x : \mathcal{T} \to e_0 \sim \mathsf{fun}\ x : \mathcal{T} \to e_1 : \mathcal{T} \to \mathcal{C}}$$

$$[\textsc{Base-Value}]\ \frac{\mathcal{G} \vdash v_0 \sim v_1 : \mathbf{B} \qquad \mathcal{G} \lhd G \qquad G, x{:}\mathbf{B} \vdash \Phi}{\mathcal{G} \vdash v_0 \sim v_1 : \{\Phi[x := v_0, v_1]\}x : \mathbf{B}\{\Phi\}} \qquad [\textsc{Value}]\ \frac{\mathcal{G} \vdash v_0 \sim v_1 : \mathcal{T} \qquad \mathcal{G} \lhd G \qquad G \vdash \Phi}{\mathcal{G} \vdash v_0 \sim v_1 : \{\Phi\}\mathcal{T}\{\Phi\}}$$

$$[\textsc{Ref}]\ \frac{r : \mathsf{ref}\,\mathbf{B} \in \mathcal{G} \qquad \mathcal{G} \vdash v_0 \sim v_1 : \mathbf{B} \qquad \mathcal{G} \lhd G \qquad G, x{:}\mathbf{B} \vdash \Phi}{\mathcal{G} \vdash r := v_0 \sim r := v_1 : \{\Phi[x := v_0, v_1]\}\mathbf{unit}\{\Phi[x := r]\}} \qquad [\textsc{Ref-Left}]\ \frac{\begin{array}{c} r : \mathsf{ref}\,\mathbf{B} \in \mathcal{G} \qquad \mathcal{G} \lhd G \qquad G \vdash_{\mathsf{v}} v : \mathbf{B} \\ \mathcal{G} \vdash e_0 \sim e_1 : \mathcal{C}[x_{\mathcal{L}} := v] \end{array}}{\mathcal{G} \vdash r := v; e_0 \sim e_1 : \mathcal{C}[x_{\mathcal{L}} := r_{\mathcal{L}}]}$$

$$[\textsc{App-Base}]\ \frac{\mathcal{G} \vdash e_0 \sim e_1 : (x : \mathbf{B}) \to \mathcal{C} \qquad \mathcal{G} \vdash v_0 \sim v_1 : \mathbf{B}}{\mathcal{G} \vdash e_0\, v_0 \sim e_1\, v_1 : \mathcal{C}[x := v_0, v_1]} \qquad [\textsc{App}]\ \frac{\mathcal{G} \vdash e_0 \sim e_1 : \mathcal{T} \to \mathcal{C} \qquad \mathcal{G} \vdash v_0 \sim v_1 : \mathcal{T}}{\mathcal{G} \vdash e_0\, v_0 \sim e_1\, v_1 : \mathcal{C}}$$

$$[\textsc{Let}]\ \frac{\mathcal{G} \vdash e_0 \sim e_1 : \{\Phi\}x : \mathcal{T}\{\Xi\} \qquad \mathcal{G}, x : \mathcal{T} \vdash e_0' \sim e_1' : \{\Xi\}y : \mathcal{U}\{\Psi\} \qquad x \notin \mathrm{FV}(\mathcal{U}, \Psi)}{\mathcal{G} \vdash \mathsf{let}\ x = e_0\ \mathsf{in}\ e_0' \sim \mathsf{let}\ x = e_1\ \mathsf{in}\ e_1' : \{\Phi\}y : \mathcal{U}\{\Psi\}}$$

$$[\textsc{Let-Left}]\ \frac{\mathcal{G} \lhd G \qquad G \vdash \mathcal{T} \lhd \mathbf{T} \qquad \mathcal{G} \vdash e \sim e : \mathcal{T} \qquad \mathcal{G}, x : \mathcal{T} \vdash e_0 \sim e_1 : \{\Phi\}y : \mathcal{U}\{\Psi\} \qquad x \notin \mathrm{FV}(\mathcal{U}, e_1, \Psi)}{\mathcal{G} \vdash \mathsf{let}\ x = e\ \mathsf{in}\ e_0 \sim e_1 : \{\Phi\}y : \mathcal{U}\{\Psi\}}$$

$$[\textsc{LetRec}]\ \frac{\begin{array}{c} f, x \notin \mathrm{FV}(\mathcal{V}, \Psi) \\ \mathcal{G}, f : (x : \mathcal{T}) \to \{\Phi\}\mathcal{U}\{\Phi\}, x : \mathcal{T} \vdash e_0 \sim e_1 : \{\Phi\}\mathcal{U}\{\Phi\} \qquad \mathcal{G}, f : (x : \mathcal{T}) \to \{\Phi\}\mathcal{U}\{\Phi\} \vdash e_0' \sim e_1' : \{\Xi\}y : \mathcal{V}\{\Psi\} \end{array}}{\mathcal{G} \vdash \mathsf{letrec}\ f\ x = e_0\ \mathsf{in}\ e_0' \sim \mathsf{letrec}\ f\ x = e_1\ \mathsf{in}\ e_1' : \{\Xi\}y : \mathcal{V}\{\Psi\}}$$

$$[\textsc{If-Left}]\ \frac{\mathcal{G} \lhd G \qquad G \vdash_{\mathsf{v}} v : \mathbf{bool} \qquad \mathcal{G} \vdash e_1 \sim e : \{\Phi_1\}x : \mathcal{T}\{\Psi\} \qquad \mathcal{G} \vdash e_2 \sim e : \{\Phi_2\}x : \mathcal{T}\{\Psi\}}{\mathcal{G} \vdash \mathsf{if}\ v\ \mathsf{then}\ e_1\ \mathsf{else}\ e_2 \sim e : \{(v_{\mathcal{L}} \Rightarrow \Phi_1) \wedge (\neg v_{\mathcal{L}} \Rightarrow \Phi_2)\}x : \mathcal{T}\{\Psi\}}$$

$$[\textsc{If}]\ \frac{\mathcal{G} \lhd G \qquad G \vdash_{\mathsf{v}} v : \mathbf{bool} \qquad \mathcal{G} \vdash e_1 \sim e_1' : \{\Phi_1\}x : \mathcal{T}\{\Psi\} \qquad \mathcal{G} \vdash e_2 \sim e_2' : \{\Phi_2\}x : \mathcal{T}\{\Psi\}}{\mathcal{G} \vdash \mathsf{if}\ v\ \mathsf{then}\ e_1\ \mathsf{else}\ e_2 \sim \mathsf{if}\ v\ \mathsf{then}\ e_1'\ \mathsf{else}\ e_2' : \{(v_{\mathcal{L}} \iff v_{\mathcal{R}}) \wedge (v_{\mathcal{L}} \Rightarrow \Phi_1) \wedge (\neg v_{\mathcal{L}} \Rightarrow \Phi_2)\}x : \mathcal{T}\{\Psi\}}$$

$$[\textsc{Flip}]\ \frac{\begin{array}{c} \mathcal{G} \lhd G \qquad G, x{:}\mathbf{bool} \vdash \Phi \\ f = x \mapsto x \text{ or } f = x \mapsto \neg x \end{array}}{\mathcal{G} \vdash \mathsf{flip} \sim \mathsf{flip} : \{\forall y : \mathbf{bool}.\, \Phi[x := y, f(y)]\}x : \mathbf{bool}\{\Phi\}} \qquad [\textsc{Sample}]\ \frac{\begin{array}{c} \mathcal{G} \lhd G \qquad G, x{:}\mathbf{int} \vdash \Phi \\ f \in \mathbb{N} \to \mathbb{N}, \text{ bijective from } [i..j] \text{ to } [i..j] \end{array}}{\mathcal{G} \vdash \mathsf{pick}_i^j \sim \mathsf{pick}_i^j : \{\Phi[x := y, f(y)]\}x : \mathbf{int}\{\Phi\}}$$

$$[\textsc{Red-Left}]\ \frac{e_1 \xrightarrow{\beta\iota\mu\delta} e_2 \qquad \mathcal{G} \vdash e_1 \sim e : \mathcal{C}}{\mathcal{G} \vdash e_2 \sim e : \mathcal{C}} \qquad [\textsc{Sym}]\ \frac{\begin{array}{c} \mathcal{G} \vdash e_1 \sim e_2 : \mathcal{C} \\ \cdot^* \text{ is the operator swapping } \cdot_{\mathcal{L}} \text{ and } \cdot_{\mathcal{R}} \end{array}}{\mathcal{G}^* \vdash e_2 \sim e_1 : \mathcal{C}^*}$$

**Figure 3.** Relational typing rules

Let $I$ be a valuation and $m$ be a memory. The interpretations $(\!|v|\!)_I$ of a value $v$ and $(\!|e|\!)_I^m$ of an expression $e$ are defined in Figure 4. If $I$ is a well-formed valuation for $G$, and $G \vdash_{\mathsf{v}} v : \mathbf{T}$ is derivable, then $(\!|v|\!)_I \in [\![\mathbf{T}]\!]$. Likewise, if $G \vdash_{\mathsf{e}} e : \mathbf{T}$ is derivable then $\lambda m.\, (\!|e|\!)_I^m \in \mathsf{M}([\![\mathbf{T}]\!])$.

We now turn to giving a relational interpretation of valid judgments. A well-formed *relational valuation* $\mathcal{I}$ for $G$, written $\mathcal{I} \models G$, is a pair of well-formed valuations for $G$. If $\mathcal{I} = (I_{\mathcal{L}}, I_{\mathcal{R}})$, we write $\pi_1(\mathcal{I})$ (resp. $\pi_2(\mathcal{I})$) for $I_{\mathcal{L}}$ (resp. $I_{\mathcal{R}}$), and $\mathcal{I}(x)$ for $(I_{\mathcal{L}}(x), I_{\mathcal{R}}(x))$. We assume given a relational interpretation for formulas, written $(\!|\Phi|\!)_{\mathcal{I}}$, such that for any formula $\Phi$ well-formed under $G$, for any relation valuation $\mathcal{I} \models G$, $(\!|\Phi|\!)_{\mathcal{I}}$ is a binary relation on $\mathcal{M}$. This relation is defined as usual, using the left/right valuation (resp. left/right memory argument) for interpreting variables on the left/right (resp. references on the left/right). Figure 5 defines the interpretation of relational types, written $(\!|G \vdash \mathcal{T} \lhd \mathbf{T}|\!)_{\mathcal{I}}$, and computation types, written $(\!|G \vdash \mathcal{C} \lhd \mathbf{T}|\!)_{\mathcal{I}}$, w.r.t. a relational valuation $\mathcal{I}$. A relational valuation $\mathcal{I}$ is well-formed w.r.t a relational context $\mathcal{G}$, written $\mathcal{I} \models \mathcal{G}$, if for any context $G$ such that $\mathcal{G} \lhd G$, and every variable $x$ declared in $G$, $\mathcal{I}(x) \in (\!|G \vdash \mathcal{G}(x) \lhd G(x)|\!)_{\mathcal{I}}$.

Finally, we define the semantic validity of judgments: we say that two values $v_1$ and $v_2$ are semantically related in $\mathcal{T}$ under $\mathcal{G}$, written $\mathcal{G} \models v_1 \sim v_2 : \mathcal{T}$, if $\mathcal{G} \lhd G$, and $G \vdash \mathcal{T} \lhd T$, and

$$\forall \mathcal{I} \models \mathcal{G},\ ((\!|v_1|\!)_{\pi_1(\mathcal{I})}, (\!|v_2|\!)_{\pi_2(\mathcal{I})}) \in (\!|G \vdash \mathcal{T} \lhd \mathbf{T}|\!)_{\mathcal{I}}$$

We say that two expressions $e_1$ and $e_2$ are semantically related in $\mathcal{C}$ under $\mathcal{G}$, written $\mathcal{G} \models e_1 \sim e_2 : \mathcal{C}$, if $\mathcal{G} \lhd G$, and $G \vdash \mathcal{T} \lhd T$, and

$$\forall \mathcal{I} \models \mathcal{G},\ (\lambda m.\, (\!|e_1|\!)_{\pi_1(\mathcal{I})}^m, \lambda m.\, (\!|e_2|\!)_{\pi_2(\mathcal{I})}^m) \in (\!|G \vdash \mathcal{C} \lhd \mathbf{T}|\!)_{\mathcal{I}}$$

The following theorem states that all judgments of the logic are sound w.r.t. their interpretation; it implies that typing can be used to verify probabilistic claims, thanks to the properties of lifting.

**Theorem 1** (Soundness)**.**

- *If* $\mathcal{G} \vdash v_1 \sim v_2 : \mathcal{T}$, *then* $\mathcal{G} \models v_1 \sim v_2 : \mathcal{T}$,
- *If* $\mathcal{G} \vdash e_1 \sim e_2 : \mathcal{C}$, *then* $\mathcal{G} \models e_1 \sim e_2 : \mathcal{C}$.

$$
\begin{aligned}
(\!|c|\!)_I &= \mathcal{B}(c)\\
(\!|x|\!)_I &= I(x)\\
(\!|\mathsf{fun}\ x : \mathbf{T} \to e|\!)_I &= \lambda d.\ \lambda m.\ (\!|e|\!)^m_{I[x:=d]}\\
(\!|v|\!)^m_I &= \mathsf{unit}\ ((\!|v|\!)_I, m)\\
(\!|e\ v|\!)^m_I &= \mathsf{bind}\ (\!|e|\!)^m_I\ (\lambda f.\ \lambda m.\ f\ (\!|v|\!)_I m)\\
(\!|\mathsf{let}\ x = e_1\ \mathsf{in}\ e_2|\!)^m_I &= \mathsf{bind}\ (\!|e_1|\!)^m_I\ (\lambda d.\ \lambda m.\ (\!|e_2|\!)^m_{I[x:=d]})\\
(\!|\mathsf{letrec}\ f\ x = e_1\ \mathsf{in}\ e_2|\!)^m_I &\\
&= \mathsf{bind}\ (\mathsf{fix}\ F)\ (\lambda d.\ \lambda m.\ (\!|e_2|\!)^m_{I[f:=d]})\\
(\!|!r|\!)^m_I &= \mathsf{unit}\ (m(r), m)\\
(\!|r := e|\!)^m_I &= \mathsf{bind}\ (\!|e|\!)^m_I\ (\lambda d.\ \lambda m.\ (\bullet, m[r := d]))\\
(\!|\mathsf{flip}|\!)^m_I &= \mathsf{bind}\ \mathcal{U}_{\mathbb{B}}\ (\lambda b.\ (b, m))\\
(\!|\mathsf{pick}^j_i|\!)^m_I &= \mathsf{bind}\ \mathcal{U}_{[i,j]}\ (\lambda n.\ (n, m))
\end{aligned}
$$

where $F = \lambda d_f.\ \lambda d_x.\ \lambda m.\ (\!|M|\!)^m_{I[f:=d_f][x:=d_x]}$

**Figure 4.** Interpretation of values and expressions

Technically, we prove the soundness of each rule as a lemma, directly from the semantics. It allows us to fall back to the full generality of Coq whenever reasoning outside of the logic is required.

# 4. Encoding $\lambda_p$ in RF*

We now discuss our language design and implementation. There are two key ideas behind our encoding of $\lambda_p$ in RF*. First, as shown in §2.3, we introduce probabilistic computations into F* axiomatically, by providing a sample primitive at the appropriate type. Programmers can instantiate sample at runtime by providing a suitable source of randomness. Next, as discussed in §2.2, we adapt the Hoare state monad ST to a monad RST for computations with relational pre- and post-conditions. We provide here more details about our encodings, in particular the style we adopt to compute relational VCs for the RST monad, and the manner in which we reuse classical specifications.

**4.1 Representing $\lambda_p$ types.** To implement $\lambda_p$, we begin with a translation of its types into F* augmented with a relational state monad. To stay close to $\lambda_p$, our translation uses a monad RST0, which we then adapt to the monad RST of §2. Like in $\lambda_p$, post-conditions in RST0 only relate the output values and heaps, not the initial heaps. Specifically, the type RST0 pre a post can be interpreted in RF* as a store-passing function (over a primitive heap) with the signature shown below:

```
RST0 pre a post = h:heap{|pre (L h) (R h)|}
        → (x:a * h':heap{| post (L x) (R x) (L h') (R h') |})
```

The type translation is homomorphic on most of $\lambda_p$'s typing constructs, with the interesting cases mainly on the computation types, where $[\{\Phi\}y{:}\mathcal{T}\{\Psi\}]$ is RST0 $[\Phi]$ $[\mathcal{T}]$ $(\lambda y_0 y_1.[\Psi])$.

**4.2 A monad of predicate transformers for VC generation.** Next, to provide type inference for RF*, rather than writing relational Hoare triples in RST0, we write specifications using predicate transformers. This style is adapted from the *Dijkstra state monad*, previously introduced for inferring classical (non-relational) verification conditions for stateful F* programs [46]. In particular, we introduce the *relational* Dijkstra state monad, RDST, and show its signature below. (We write polymorphic types implicitly assuming their free type variables are prenex quantified.)

```
type RDST a wp = ∀p. RST0 (wp p) a p
val return : x:a → RDST a (Λp. p (L x) (R x))
val bind: RDST a wp1 → (x:a → RDST b (wp2 x))
  → RDST b (Λp.λh0 h1. wp1 (λx0 x1 h0' h1'.
              (∀ x. L x=x0 ∧ R x=x1 ⟹ wp2 x p h0' h1')) h0 h1)
```

The type RDST t wp is an abbreviation for the RST0 monad that is polymorphic in its post-condition. Specifically, RDST t wp is the type of computation which for any relational post-condition p on ts and heaps, the pre-condition on the input heaps is given by wp p.

Unlike the Hoare-style RST0 monad, the RDST monad yields a weakest pre-condition calculus by construction. As indicated by the signature of bind, when composing computations in the RDST monad, we simply compute a pre-condition for the computation by composing the predicate transformers of each component. A slight complication arises from the need to constrain the formal parameter x:a of wp2 relationally. In general, wp2 will have free occurrences of L x and R x. We relate these to the result of the first computation using the guard L x=x0 and R x=x1, before composing wp1 and wp2.

Additionally, by exploiting the post-condition parametricity of RDST, we can recover the expressiveness of a 6-place post-condition relation in the RST monad that we use in our examples. We show the definition of RST below.

```
type RST pre a post = RDST a (Λp.λh0 h1. pre h0 h1
        ∧ ∀x0 x1 h0' h1'. post h0 h1 x0 x1 h0' h1' ⟹ p x0 x1 h0' h1')
```

**4.3 Lifting classical specifications.** To promote reuse of existing verified F* code in RF*, we provide combinators to lift specifications written with classical predicate transformers into the RDST monad. To illustrate our approach, we show the RF* specifications of primitive operations on references—the same combinators apply to arbitrary classically verified code.

```
type lift wp0 wp1 p h0 h1 =
      wp0 (λx0 h0'. wp1 (λx1 h1'. p x0 x1 h0' h1') h1) h0

type Rd x p h = p (Sel h x) h
val (!) : x:ref a → RDST a (lift (Rd (L x)) (Rd (R x)))

type W x v p h = p () (Upd h x v)
val (:=): x:ref 'a→ v:'a→ RDST unit (lift (W (L x) (L v)) (W (R x) (R v)))
```

The combinator lift takes two classical predicate transformers wp0 and wp1 and composes them by, in effect, "running" them separately on the heaps h0 and h1 and relating the results and heaps using the relational post-condition p. The types given to dereference and assignment should be evident—these are simply the relational liftings of the standard, classical weakest pre-condition rules for these constructs (Rd and W, respectively).

**4.4 Computing relational VCs.** We repurpose the bulk of F*'s type-checking algorithm to RF*. Although the relational typing rules of Fig. 3 generally analyze a pair of programs $e_0 \sim e_1$, for the most part, we are concerned with proving relational properties of multiple executions of a single program. Thus, in the special symmetric case where we are analyzing $e \sim e$, the two-sided rules of Fig. 3 degenerate into the standard typing rules for monadic F* (which is parametric in the choice of monad, so configuring it to use RDST is easy).

The main subtlety in computing relational VCs arises when analyzing the cross-cases of conditional expressions—for this we implement the single-sided rules in the judgment, and we attempt to revert to the symmetric case as soon as we detect that the program fragments are indeed the same. For example, the rule [IF] allows us to relate **if** b **then** $e$ **else** $e' \sim e$, by generating subgoals for $e \sim e$ and $e' \sim e$, where at least the former can be handled once again by the symmetric rules.

The rules [RED-LEFT] and [RED-RIGHT] of Fig. 3 are impossible to implement in full generality—they permit reasoning about stateful programs after arbitrary reductions of open terms. Instead, these rules are approximated by the RF* typechecker for terms that can be given classical predicate transformer specifications. In particular, when trying to relate $e_0 \sim e_1$, if we can use the symmetric judgments and type $e_0 \sim e_0$ : RDST t (lift wp0 _), and $e_1 \sim e_1$ : RDST t (lift _ wp1), then we type $e_0 \sim e_1$ at type

$$\frac{f_1, f_2 \in [\![\mathbf{T}]\!] \to \mathcal{M} \to \mathcal{D}([\![\mathbf{U}]\!] \times \mathcal{M}) \qquad \forall t_1, t_2 \in (\!|G \vdash \mathcal{T} \lhd \mathbf{T}|\!)_{\mathcal{I}}.\, (f_1\, t_1, f_2\, t_2) \in (\!|G \vdash \mathcal{C} \lhd \mathbf{U}|\!)_{I[x:=(t_1,t_2)]}}{(f_1, f_2) \in (\!|G \vdash (x : \mathcal{T}) \to \mathcal{C} \lhd \mathbf{T} \to \mathbf{U}|\!)_{\mathcal{I}}}$$

$$\frac{(d_1, d_2) \in [\![\mathbf{B}]\!]^2}{(d_1, d_2) \in (\!|G \vdash \mathbf{B} \lhd \mathbf{B}|\!)_{\mathcal{I}}} \qquad \frac{\mu_1, \mu_2 \in \mathcal{M} \to \mathcal{D}([\![\mathbf{U}]\!] \times \mathcal{M}) \qquad \forall m_1, m_2 \in \mathcal{M}.\, (\!|\Phi|\!)_{\mathcal{I}}(m_1, m_2) \Rightarrow P^{\sharp}\, (\mu_1\, m_1)\, (\mu_2\, m_2)}{(\mu_1, \mu_2) \in (\!|G \vdash \{\Phi\} y : \mathcal{U}\{\Psi\} \lhd \mathbf{U}|\!)_{\mathcal{I}}}$$

where $P = \lambda((u_1, m_1'), (u_2, m_2')).\, (u_1, u_2) \in (\!|G \vdash \mathcal{U} \lhd \mathbf{U}|\!)_{\mathcal{I}} \wedge (\!|\Psi|\!)_{\mathcal{I}[y:=(u_1,u_2)]}(m_1', m_2')$

**Figure 5.** Interpretation of relational refinement types

RDST t (lift wp0 wp1). In effect, by making use of classical predicate transformers on either side, we approximate the reduction relation for stateful terms used by [RED-LEFT] and [RED-RIGHT].

All these measures for handling the asymmetric cases are still incomplete. When trying to prove a relation between $f\ v_0 \sim g\ v_1$ in a context $\mathcal{G}$ with relational types for $f$ and $g$ that cannot be decomposed into a pair of classical specifications, it becomes impossible to complete the derivation. In such cases, RF$^\star$ emits False as the VC (guarded by a relational path condition). Nevertheless, it may still be possible to discharge the VC, if the path condition is infeasible. This is the case, for example, when trying to relate the result of encrypt with errorNonce in the passport example of §2.4.

**4.5 Proving VCs using Z3.** Once a VC has been computed, we ride on an existing encoding of VCs for the classic Dijkstra monad within Z3. We rely on a theorem from Swamy et al. [46] which guarantees that, despite the use of higher-order logic when computing VCs, once a predicate transformer is applied to a specific first-order post-condition, so long as there is no inherent use of higher-order axioms in the context, a first-order normal form for the VC can always be computed.

## 5. Applications

Table 5 summarizes our experimental evaluation of RF$^\star$. For each program, we give the Makefile target name in the F$^\star$ distribution, the number of lines of code and type annotations (excluding comments), and the typechecking time in seconds, which is mostly dominated by the time spent solving VCs in Z3. All experiments were conducted on a 3GHz HP Z820 32-core workstation with 32GB of RAM (although the verifier makes use of only one core). For lack of space, most of these examples are only briefly described, with a more detailed discussion of the last two programs, counter in §5.1 (a cryptographic construction) and meter in §5.2 (a privacy protocol).

INFORMATION FLOW. The first five programs provide many information flow examples, such as those of §2.2, and test cases for single-sided rules using several variations of the RDST monad construction of §4.

PASSPORT UNLINKABILITY. The sixth program, passport illustrates the verification of the Basic Access Control protocol for RFID-equipped passports, presented in §2.4. It establishes passport unlinkability for the modified protocol that returns the same error message in all failure cases. (As can be expected, the original protocol yields a typechecking error.) Its verification illustrates the use of single-sided rules for nested tests (see tag1 in §2.4) and also involves modelling key-hiding symmetric encryption.

RANDOM ORACLES. The program ro provides an idealized implementation of a cryptographic hash function in the random oracle model. In this model, widely used in applied cryptography, the hash function is assumed to be indistinguishable from a uniformly random function. Thus, knowledge of the hash function values on a subset of its domain yields no *a priori* information about its values outside this subset, and protocols that share the hash function with an adversary can treat those values as secret as long as they use disjoint subsets of its domain. The purpose of ro is to capture this reasoning pattern in a library that enables type-based verification of protocols in the random oracle model.

Our implementation lazily samples (and memoizes) the random function, using a mutable reference holding a table mapping hash queries made by both honest participants $H$ and adversaries $A$. To verify the program, this table carries several invariants, including that the tables grow monotonically; that in every pair of executions, the tables agree on the fragments corresponding to queries made by $A$; and that on the fragments corresponding to queries by $H$, the sampled entries are related by an injective function that ensures they have indistinguishable distributions. The interface of ro is designed to allow the full use of relational sample on the $H$ fragment, and to account for failure events (e.g., returning a value to $A$ that collides with one that was already provided to $H$), allowing for its modular use in a context that must bound their probability.

CCA2 ENCRYPTION. Resistance to adaptive chosen-plaintext and chosen-ciphertext attacks (CCA2) is a standard cryptographic security assumption for public key encryption schemes. To verify protocols relying on this assumption, we program an ideal, stateful functionality for CCA2 encryption that maintains a log of prior oracle encryptions, similar to those proposed by Fournet et al. [24], but with a more convenient relational interface. Using the F7 type system with only classic refinements, they require that all code that operates on secrets be placed in a separate module that exports plaintexts as an abstract type. Using instead relational types for secrets, in the style of §2.3, we lift this restriction, enabling us to verify protocol code that uses encryption without restructuring. Our code is essentially higher-order; it simulates ML functors using a dependently typed record of functions.

NONCE-BASED AUTHENTICATION. Exploiting the modularity of our CCA2 implementation, we program and verify simplenonce, a protocol that illustrates a common authentication pattern based on fresh random values, or nonces, formalizing the intuition that, if $A$ encrypts a fresh nonce using the public key of $B$, and later decrypts a response containing that nonce, then the whole response must have been sent by $B$.

PRIVATE AUTHENTICATION. Further extending simplenonce, and relying on a key-hiding variant of CCA2, we implement a protocol for private authentication, proposed by Abadi and Fournet [1], that allows two parties to authenticate one another and to initiate private communications without disclosing their presence and identities to third parties. Although the protocol has been studied symbolically in the applied pi calculus, to our knowledge we provide its first verification in a computational model of cryptography.

ELGAMAL ENCRYPTION. The chosen-plaintext security (CPA) of ElGamal encryption by reduction to the decisional Diffie-Hellman assumption is a classic example of cryptographic proof. We verify it in RF$^\star$, building on an axiomatic theory of cyclic groups.

SECURITY "UP TO BAD". The program uptobad illustrates a common pattern to prove refinement formulas of the form $\varphi \vee$ Bad where $\varphi$ is the property we are interested in and Bad captures conditions that may cause the program to 'fail', usually with a small probability (e.g. when the adversary guesses a private key). To

| NAME | LOC | TC(S) | DESCRIPTION |
|---|---|---|---|
| arith | 43 | 4.5 | Information flow with arithmetic |
| pure1 | 35 | 1.7 | Information flow & inference |
| pure2 | 33 | 1.7 | Information flow & inference (variant) |
| st | 52 | 3.6 | Information flow with state |
| singlesided | 111 | 14.2 | Information flow using single-sided rules |
| passport | 97 | 44.2 | Unlinkability for RFID passport protocol |
| ro | 73 | 21.2 | Random-Oracle hash function |
| cca2 | 88 | 6.5 | Idealized CCA2 encryption |
| simplenonce | 108 | 42.5 | Nonce-based Authentication protocol |
| privateauth | 175 | 81.4 | Private authentication protocol |
| elg | 217 | 124.5 | ElGamal encryption |
| uptobad | 15 | 1.4 | Up-to-failure reasoning |
| counter | 106 | 24.1 | Counter mode encryptions using AES |
| meter | 182 | 79.8 | Commitments & smart meter protocol |
| Total | 1,378 | 451.3 | |

**Table 1.** Summary of experiments

avoid polluting all our specifications with this disjunction, we define an up-to-bad variant of the RDST monad, where all pre- and post-conditions, and all heap invariants, are enforced only as long as a distinguished boolean memory reference is false. Intuitively, this adds an implicit '∨ Bad' to every refinement.

Our encoding proceeds in two steps. First, we define mref a p, the type of monotonic references r to an a-value whose contents can be updated only when the update condition p holds. That is, when p is a reflexive transitive binary $a$-predicate, given two heaps h and h', if h' is a successor of h then p (Sel h r) (Sel h' r) holds. We give below the resulting specification of mwrite, requiring the update condition $p$ as a pre-condition.

```
private type mref a (p:a ⇒ a ⇒ E ) = ref a
val mwrite: a::⋆ → p::a⇒ a⇒ E → r:mref a p → v:'a
  → RST (λh0 h1. p (Sel h0 (L r)) (L v) ∧ p (Sel h1 (R r)) (R v)) unit
        (λh0 h1 () () h0' h1'. h0'=Upd h0 (L r) (L v)
                               ∧ h1'=Upd h1 (R r) (R v))
```

Next, we define UpTo bad requires a ensures as an alias for the RST monad, with pre-condition requires, result type a, and post-condition ensures, unless the reference bad is set to true in the left or right heap, in which case both pre- and post-conditions are trivial:

```
type Bad b h0 h1 = Sel h0 (L b)=true ∨ Sel h1 (R b)=true
type UpTo (bad:mref bool (λb b'. b=true ⟹ b'=true))
          (requires:heap ⇒ heap ⇒ E) (a::⋆ )
          (ensures::heap ⇒ heap ⇒ a ⇒ a ⇒ heap ⇒ heap ⇒ E) =
    RST (λh0 h1. requires h0 h1 ∨ Bad bad h0 h1) a
        (λh0 h1 x0 x1 h0' h1'. ensures h0 h1 x0 x1 h0' h1'
        ∨ Bad bad h0 h1)
```

Independently, we can compute (or bound) the probability of bad being set to true; for passport, for instance, we set bad to true as we detect a collision between two sampled nonces, and bound its probability with $q^2/2^{64}$ where $q$ is the number of sessions.

**5.1 Pseudo-random functions and counter-mode.** Resuming from the one-time pad example (§2.3), we implement a more useful symmetric encryption scheme based on a block cipher, such as triple-DES or AES. Blocks are just fixed-sized byte arrays, e.g. 16 bytes for AES. Block ciphers take a key and a plaintext block, and produce a ciphertext block. A common cryptographic security assumption is that the block cipher is a *pseudo-random function* (PRF): for a fixed key, generated uniformly at random, and used only as input to the cipher, the cipher is computationally indistinguishable from a uniformly random function from blocks to blocks. We first present our sample scheme, then formalize the pseudo-random assumption, and finally explain how we verify it by relational typing.

ENCRYPTING IN COUNTER MODE. The purpose of symmetric encryption modes is to apply the block cipher keyed with a single, short secret in order to encrypt many blocks of plaintexts. In counter mode, to encrypt a sequence of plaintext blocks $p_i$, we use a sequence of index blocks $i_i$, obtained for instance by incrementing a counter. We independently apply the block cipher to each $i_i$ to obtain a mask $m_i$; and compute the ciphertext block $c_i$ as $p_i \oplus m_i$, effectively using the masks as one-time pads. A practical advantage of this construction is that both encryption and decryption are fully parallelizable, and that the sequence of masks can be pre-computed. The blocks i need not be secret, but they must be pairwise-distinct. Otherwise, from the two ciphertexts $p \oplus m_i$ and $p' \oplus m_i$, one trivially obtains $p \oplus p'$, which leaks a full block of information.

For simplicity, we keep the block cipher key implicit, writing f for the resulting pseudo-random function; we focus on the functions for processing individual plaintext blocks, rather than lists of blocks; and we attach the (public) index to every ciphertext block. First, assume there is a single encryptor, that counts using an integer reference and uses toBytes to format the integer as a block.

```
let n = ref 0;
let encrypt (p:block) = let i = toBytes !n in n := !n + 1; (i, xor (f i) p)
let decrypt i c = xor (f i) c
```

To enable independent encryptions of plaintext blocks, we can remove the global counter and instead sample a block i for each encryption, as follows. This random block i is called the initialization vector (IV) for the encryption.

```
let encrypt'(p:block) = let i = sample 16 in (i, xor (f i) p)
```

Much as for the one-time pad, we show that encrypt and encrypt' can be typed as block → eq (block ∗ block), the type of functions from (private) blocks to pairs of public blocks, under suitable cryptographic assumptions. More general combinations of sampling and incrementing can also be used for independent multi-block encryptions; for instance, the usual counter mode is programmed as:

```
let encrypt_counter_mode (ps:list block) =
  let iv = sample 16 in let i = ref iv in
  iv::List.map (fun p → incrBytes i; xor (f !i)) ps
```

PSEUDO-RANDOM FUNCTIONS. To study the security of protocols using a block cipher, we program and type it as a random function from blocks to blocks. (To test our encryption, we also implement it concretely by just calling AES.) If we can prove the security of a protocol using this ideal random-function implementation, then the same protocol using the concrete block cipher is also secure under the pseudo-random-function assumption (with a probability loss bounded by the probability of distinguishing between the two ciphers). We implement the function f using lazy sampling: when called, f first looks up for a previously-sampled mask in its log; otherwise, f samples a fresh mask. As for the one-time pad, we pass the plaintext block p as a ghost parameter, and take advantage of sampling to generate a mask with a relational refinement to specifically hide p. Of course, this fails if the mask has already been sampled, so we type f for encryption with a pre-condition that depends on the current log and requires that i does not occur in the log yet. (We use the same code with a different type for decryption, requesting that $i$ occurs in the log.)

```
val f: i:index → p:block → iRST pre block post
where pre h0 h1 = (∗ Requires: i not in the log yet ∗)
      not (In (L i) (Domain (Sel h0 (L log))))
    ∧ (L i = R i) ∧ (Seqn (L i) < Sel h0 (L n))
  and post h0 h1 m0 m1 h0' h1' = (∗ Ensures: log extended with (i,p,m) ∗)
      Mask (L p) (R p) m0 m1 (∗ and sampled m's related by injectivity ∗)
    ∧ h0' = Upd h0 (L log) ((Entry (L i) (L p) m0)::Sel h0 (L log))
    ∧ h1' = Upd h1 (R log) ((Entry (R i) (R p) m1)::Sel h1 (R log))
let f p i = match assoc i !log with
  | Some(_,m) → m (∗ unreachable ∗)
  | None → let m = sample p in
           log := (Entry i p m)::!log; m
```

When using a single counter (function encrypt), typechecking relies on a joint invariant on the counter n and the content of the log that states that all entries in the log have an index block i formatted from some n' < n. It also involves excluding counter overflows and assuming that toBytes is injective. This enables us to prove that our encryption is secure with no loss in the reduction: the advantage of a CPA adversary against our code is the same as the advantage of some adversary against the PRF assumption.

When using instead a fresh random block (function encrypt'), the situation is more complex, as there is a non-null probability that two different encryptions sample the same index i. Our construction is secure as long as no such collisions happen. We capture this event using the 'up to bad' approach presented above, for a Fresh module that silently detects collisions and sets the bad flag accordingly. Concretely, the probability of having a collision when sampling $q$ blocks of 16 bytes each is bounded by $q^2/2^{128}$. By typing, we prove that encryption, and any program that may use it, leaks information only once *bad* is true. Thus, we prove the concrete security of encrypt' with a loss of $q^2/2^{128}$ in the reduction to PRF.

**5.2 Privacy-preserving smart metering & billing.** We finally implement and verify the "fast billing" protocol of Rial and Danezis [40], which involves recursive data structures and homomorphic commitments. The protocol has three roles:

- a certified meter that issues private, signed, fine-grained electricity readings (say one reading every 10 minutes);
- a utility company that issues public, signed rates (for the same time intervals, depending on some public policy); and
- a user, who receives both inputs at the end of the month to compute (and presumably pay) his electricity bill.

The two security goals of the protocol are to guarantee (1) integrity of the monthly fee paid to the utility company; and (2) privacy of the detailed readings, which otherwise leak much information on the user's lifestyle. The protocol relies on Pedersen commitments [36] and public-key signatures. Next, we explain how we prove perfect, information-theoretic privacy (entirely by relational typing) and computational integrity by reduction to the discrete log problem (by typing using 'up-to-bad').

HOMOMORPHIC PEDERSEN COMMITMENTS. We first implement typed commitments, parameterized by some multiplicative group of prime order $p$. We outline their interface and review their main security properties.

```
type pparams = eq public_param
type opening (pp:pparams) (x:text) =
  o:opng {| Eq ((trap (L pp) * L x) + L o) ((trap (R pp) * R x) + R o) |}

val sample: pp:pparams → x:text → opening pp x
val commit: pp:pparams → x:text → r:opening pp x →
  c:eq elt { c = Commit pp x r }
let commit pp x r = pp.g ^ x * pp.h ^ r
let verify pp x r c = (c = pp.g ^ x * pp.h ^ r)
```

The public parameters pp consist of the prime $p$ and two distinct group generators $g$ and $h$ (possibly chosen by the utility). Texts and openings range over integers modulo $p$. A *commitment* to $x$ with opening $o$ is a group element $c = g^x h^o$. Although assumed hard to compute, there exists $\alpha$ (known as the *trapdoor* for these parameters) such that $g = h^\alpha$. Accordingly, we use $\alpha =$ trap pp for specification purposes, in refinement formulas but not in the protocol code. We use $\alpha$ in particular to specify an injective function for randomly sampling the opening $o$ (modulo $p$) so that it perfectly hides $x$: the relational refinement type opening in the post-condition of sample records that $\alpha$*(L $x$) + (L $o$) = $\alpha$*(R $x$) + (R $o$), which implies $g^{Lx}h^{Lo} = g^{Rx}h^{Ro}$ and enables us to type the result of commit as public (eq elt). Intuitively, every commitment can be opened to any $x'$, for some hard-to-compute $o'$, so the commitment itself does not leak any information about $x$ as long as $o$ is randomly sampled and kept secret. At the same time, given $x$ and $o$, it is computationally hard to open the commitment to any $x' \neq x$.

Commitments can be multiplied: $g^x h^o * g^{x'} h^{o'} = g^{x+x'} h^{o+o'}$ and exponentiated: $(g^x h^o)^p = g^{xp} h^{op}$ to compute commitments to linear combinations of their exponents without necessarily knowing them. These operations are used below to compute the bill; their (omitted) types show that they preserve eq and opening relational refinements.

Next, we show some typed code for each role of the protocol.

METER. We have abstract predicates Readings and Rates to specify authentic lists of readings and rates. We rely on a signature scheme to sign a list of commitments to private readings; this scheme is assumed resistant against existential forgery attacks; as explained in [24], we express this property using (non-relational) refinements. For simplicity, we keep the signing and verification keys implicit.

```
type Signed (pp:pparams) (cs:list elt) =
    ∃xrs. Readings (fsts xrs) ∧ cs = Commits pp xrs
val sign: pp:pparams → cs:eq (list elt){Signed pp cs} → eq dsig
val verify_meter_signature: pp:pparams
  → cs:eq (list elt) → eq dsig → b:eq bool{ b=true ⟹ Signed pp cs }
```

The Signed predicate above states that the commitments have been computed from authentic readings; it is a pre-condition for signing (at the meter) and a post-condition of signature verification (at the utility). It uses a specification function fsts that takes a list of pairs and returns the list of their first projections.

Given authentic readings xs, the meter function below calls commits, a recursive function that maps sample and commit (specified above) to every element of xs and returns both a list of pairs of readings and openings $x_t, o_t$ for the user and a public list of commitments $c_t$ for the utility. These commitments are then signed, yielding a public signature. From their eq types, we can already conclude that the data passed from the meter to the utility (that is, the list of commitments and its signature) does not convey any information about the readings.

```
val meter: pp:pparams → xs:list int{ Readings xs } →
  xrs:(list (x:int * opening pp x)) { xs = fsts xrs } *
  cs:eq list elt * eq dsig{ Commits pp xrs = cs }
let meter pp xs = let xrs,cs = commits pp xs in (xrs, cs, sign pp cs)
```

USER. Given a list of pairs $x_t, o_t$ from the meter and a list of rates $p_t$ from the utility, the user calls make_payment to compute two scalar products: the fee $\sum_t x_t p_t$, and a fee opening $\sum_t o_t p_t$, and pass them to the utility.

```
val make_payment: pp:pparams
  → xrs: (list (x:text * opening pp x)) { Readings (fsts xrs) }
  → ps:eq (list text){| Rates (L ps) ∧ Rates (R ps) ∧
              SP (fsts (L xrs)) (L ps) = SP (fsts (R xrs)) (R ps) |}
  → (eq text * eq opng)
let make_payment pp xrs ps = let x,r = sums xrs ps in (x,r)
```

The relational pre-condition on the 4th line (SP...) is a *declassification condition*, capturing the user's intent to publish the fee, computed as the scalar product SP of the detailed readings and rates, by requiring that the 'left' and 'right' fees be equal. By typing the code of the double scalar product sums, we get the same equation for the openings, showing that the fee opening is then also public. The result type of make_payment tells us that those two scalars reveal no further information on any readings leading to the same fee.

More explicitly, we can use the types of the meter and the user to typecheck a 'privacy game' whereby the adversary chooses a list of rates and two lists of readings leading to the same fee; obtains the list of commitments, its signature, the fee, and the fee opening computed by the meter and user code for one of the two readings (each selected at random with probability $1/2$); and attempts to guess which of the two readings was used. Typing guarantees that the adversary guess does not depend on the random selection of readings, hence that the guess is correct with probability $1/2$. Interestingly, this privacy property is information-theoretic, and does not rely on any computational assumption.

UTILITY. The utility verifies the signature on the commitments $c_t$; uses the rates $p_t$ to compute the product of exponentials

$$\prod_t c_t{}^{p_t} = \prod_t (g^{x_t} h^{o_t})^{p_t} = \prod_t g^{x_t p_t} h^{o_t p_t} = g^{\sum_t x_t p_t} h^{\sum_t o_t p_t}$$

and compares it to the commitment $g^x h^o$ computed from the fee $x$ and fee opening $o$ presented by the user. Unless the user can open a commitment to several values $x$ (which can be further reduced to the discrete log problem), this confirms that $x$ is the correct payment. To type the verifier code, we write classic (but non-trivial) refinements, using ghost scalar products to keep track of its computation.

```
val verify_payment: pp:pparams
  → ps:eq (list int){Rates ps}
  → cs:eq (list elt) → s:eq dsig (* from the meter *)
  → x:eq text → r:eq opng (* from the user *)
  → b:eq bool{ b=true ⟹ ∃xs. Readings xs ∧ x=SP xs ps }
let verify_payment pp ps cs s x r =
  verify_meter_signature pp cs s ∧
  verify_commit pp x r (scalarExp pp cs ps)
```

## 6. Related work and conclusions

Our work spans semantics of higher-order probabilistic programs, relational program verification, and cryptographic protocol verification, enabling us to verify the security of protocol implementations under computational assumptions by relational typing.

REASONING ABOUT PROBABILISTIC PROGRAMS. The semantics of RF* is based on the monadic representation of probabilities used in [6, 37]. Our semantics is confined to discrete sub-distributions; for some applications, such as robotics and machine learning, it is however essential to support continuous distributions. Higher-order programs over continuous distributions are considered in [15, 35]. An alternative approach is to embed probabilistic programming in a general purpose language, as done e.g. by Kiselyov and Shan [29].

Reif [38], Kozen [30], and Feldman and Harel [23] were among the first to develop logics for reasoning about probabilistic programs. Similar logics were later developed by McIver and Morgan [33] and more recently by Chadha et al. [17]. Hurd [27] provides a formalization of the framework of McIver and Morgan in the HOL proof assistant. All these logics are non-relational, and do not allow directly proving relations between probabilities.

RELATIONAL PROGRAM VERIFICATION. Relational Hoare Logic was first introduced for a core imperative program to reason about the correctness of program optimizations and information flow properties [11]. It was later extended to probabilistic procedural programs with adversarial code, and used to formally verify reductionist security proofs of cryptographic constructions [7] and differential privacy of randomized algorithms [10]. Relational Hoare Type Theory (RHTT) is an extension of Hoare Type Theory, used to reason interactively about advanced information flow policies of higher-order stateful programs with real world data structures [42]; RHTT does not consider probabilistic computations, which are essential to reason about cryptographic protocols. RHTT is fully formalized as a shallow embedding in the Coq proof assistant. The formalization is restricted to programs with first-order store, but in principle it could be extended to programs with higher-order store using an axiomatic extension of Coq [44]. In contrast, we formalize in Coq a core fragment of RF*, and rest on the F* infrastructure to verify large programs. Our formalization is restricted to programs with first-order store; as we adopt a deep embedding, our formalization could in principle be extended to higher-order store using recent developments in step-indexed semantics [4]. Beyond RHTT and HTT, there have been many efforts to develop and sometimes machine-check program logics for higher-order stateful programs; see [39] for an account of the field.

Relational logics can also be used to reason about continuity [18]. Naturally, numerous program analyses and specialized relational logics enforce 2-properties of programs.

COMPARISON WITH EASYCRYPT. EasyCrypt [8] is a framework for proving the security of cryptographic constructions in the computational model. The core of EasyCrypt is a probabilistic Relational Hoare Logic (pRHL) that is able to capture common patterns of reasoning in cryptographic proofs, including observational equivalence, equivalence up to failure, and reductionist arguments. The relational refinement type system of RF* is inspired from pRHL, but it also incorporates concerns of compatibility with F* and automation. In contrast to EasyCrypt, RF* offers only limited support to carry relational reasoning about structurally different programs, and to reason about probabilities of postconditions—the latter is achieved in EasyCrypt using a probabilistic (but non-relational) Hoare Logic, which has no counterpart in RF*. As a consequence, some cryptographic constructions whose formalization in EasyCrypt requires interactive game-based proofs and complex probabilistic arguments cannot be verified in RF*; on the other hand, verification in RF* is fully automatic.

Moreover, EasyCrypt is not primarily designed for building, verifying and deploying large systems. Recent work [3] explores how EasyCrypt can be used to verify C implementations of well-known cryptographic constructions, and through verified compilation derive guarantees about x86 executables. However, this approach does not scale to verifying detailed protocol implementations. In contrast, RF* allows programmers to combine relational and non-relational refinements freely, so that relational reasoning steps can take advantage of program invariants embedded in non-relational refinements. This distinctive ability of RF* is essential to verify system implementations that rely on cryptography.

PROTOCOL VERIFICATION. Blanchet's recent account of the field of protocol verification provides a panorama of existing tools and major achievements [14]. Most of the literature focuses on verifying protocol specifications, or protocol implementations through model extractors [2]; alternatives include generating implementations from verified models [16]. Our work is most closely related to approaches that reason directly about implementations in the symbolic [12, 22] or computational models [13, 24, 31].

MODULAR TYPE-BASED CRYPTOGRAPHIC VERIFICATION [24]. Type systems usefully apply to many notions of security. In the context of computational cryptography, Fournet et al. rely on F7 typed interfaces to encode classic game-based security definitions, such as CPA and CCA2, using a combination of type refinements for authenticity and type abstraction for integrity and confidentiality.

In comparison, RF* enables both probabilistic and relational reasoning, letting us typecheck constructions previously out of reach. In their reference implementation of TLS [13], for example, the security of several intricate cryptographic constructions is specified by typing, but justified by handwritten proofs; the corresponding code is trusted, rather than typechecked. (This is the case, e.g. for the MAC-Encode-then-Encrypt construction in the record layer, somewhat similar to our counter mode encryption example in §5.1.) We intend to carry over their 7,000 lines of code to RF*, reusing their detailed, classic refinements unchanged, and making use of relational typing to verify additional cryptographic libraries.

CONCLUSIONS AND PROSPECTS. Our work on RF* represents a significant first step towards our goal of building software whose security has been verified down to core cryptographic assumptions. On the theory side, we have shown how to generalize prior probabilistic relational logics to a higher-order language, which provides a formal basis for the use of high-level abstractions in system implementations. Practically, through careful language design, our extension of F* towards RF* paves the way for carrying out probabilistic relational verification in a semi-automated manner using refinement types and SMT solvers. Still, much remains to be done. As immediate next steps, we anticipate extending our theory to account for dynamic allocation and local state. Toward improving our tools, on the empirical side, we plan to port an existing reference implementation of TLS [13] to RF*. We expect that RF*'s more flexible idioms, better support for type inference, and its self-certified kernel [43] will ease verification and allow us to push towards obtaining a high-performance implementation of the Internet standard with certified security.

## References


[1] M. Abadi and C. Fournet. Private authentication. *Theor. Comput. Sci.*, 322(3):427–476, 2004.

[2] M. Aizatulin, A. D. Gordon, and J. Jürjens. Computational verification of C protocol implementations by symbolic execution. In *CCS 2012*, pages 712–723. ACM, 2012.

[3] J. B. Almeida, M. Barbosa, G. Barthe, and F. Dupressoir. Certified computer-aided cryptography: efficient provably secure machine code from high-level implementations. In *CCS 2013*. ACM, 2013. Also appears as Cryptology ePrint Archive, Report 2013/316.

[4] A. W. Appel and D. A. McAllester. An indexed model of recursive types for foundational proof-carrying code. *ACM Trans. Program. Lang. Syst.*, 23(5):657–683, 2001.

[5] M. Arapinis, T. Chothia, E. Ritter, and M. Ryan. Analysing unlinkability and anonymity using the applied Pi calculus. In *CSF 2010*, pages 107–121. IEEE Computer Society, 2010.

[6] P. Audebaud and C. Paulin-Mohring. Proofs of randomized algorithms in Coq. *Sci. Comput. Program.*, 74(8):568–589, 2009.

[7] G. Barthe, B. Grégoire, and S. Zanella-Béguelin. Formal certification of code-based cryptographic proofs. In *POPL 2009*, pages 90–101. ACM, 2009.

[8] G. Barthe, B. Grégoire, S. Heraud, and S. Zanella-Béguelin. Computer-aided security proofs for the working cryptographer. In *CRYPTO 2011*, volume 6841 of *Lecture Notes in Computer Science*, pages 71–90. Springer, 2011.

[9] G. Barthe, B. Grégoire, Y. Lakhnech, and S. Zanella-Béguelin. Beyond provable security. Verifiable IND-CCA security of OAEP. In *CT-RSA 2011*, volume 6558 of *Lecture Notes in Computer Science*, pages 180–196. Springer, 2011.

[10] G. Barthe, B. Köpf, F. Olmedo, and S. Zanella-Béguelin. Probabilistic relational reasoning for differential privacy. In *POPL 2012*, pages 97–110. ACM, 2012.

[11] N. Benton. Simple relational correctness proofs for static analyses and program transformations. In *POPL 2004*, pages 14–25. ACM, 2004.

[12] K. Bhargavan, C. Fournet, and A. D. Gordon. Modular verification of security protocol code by typing. In *POPL 2010*, pages 445–456. ACM, 2010.

[13] K. Bhargavan, C. Fournet, M. Kohlweiss, A. Pironti, and P.-Y. Strub. Implementing TLS with verified cryptographic security. In *S&P 2013*, pages 445–459. IEEE Computer Society, 2013.

[14] B. Blanchet. Security protocol verification: Symbolic and computational models. In *POST 2012*, volume 7215 of *Lecture Notes in Computer Science*, pages 3–29. Springer, 2012.

[15] J. Borgström, A. D. Gordon, M. Greenberg, J. Margetson, and J. V. Gael. Measure transformer semantics for bayesian machine learning. In *ESOP 2011*, volume 6602 of *Lecture Notes in Computer Science*, pages 77–96. Springer, 2011.

[16] D. Cadé and B. Blanchet. From computationally-proved protocol specifications to implementations. In *ARES 2012*, pages 65–74. IEEE Computer Society, 2012.

[17] R. Chadha, L. Cruz-Filipe, P. Mateus, and A. Sernadas. Reasoning about probabilistic sequential programs. *Theor. Comput. Sci.*, 379(1-2):142–165, 2007.

[18] S. Chaudhuri, S. Gulwani, and R. Lublinerman. Continuity and robustness of programs. *Commun. ACM*, 55(8):107–115, 2012.

[19] T. Chothia and V. Smirnov. A traceability attack against e-passports. In *FC 2010*, volume 6052 of *Lecture Notes in Computer Science*, pages 20–34. Springer, 2010.

[20] M. R. Clarkson and F. B. Schneider. Hyperproperties. *J. of Comput. Sec.*, 18(6):1157–1210, 2010.

[21] L. M. de Moura and N. Bjørner. Z3: An efficient SMT solver. In *TACAS 2008*, volume 4963 of *Lecture Notes in Computer Science*, pages 337–340. Springer, 2008.

[22] F. Dupressoir, A. D. Gordon, J. Jürjens, and D. A. Naumann. Guiding a general-purpose C verifier to prove cryptographic protocols. In *CSF 2011*, pages 3–17. IEEE Computer Society, 2011.

[23] Y. A. Feldman and D. Harel. A probabilistic dynamic logic. *J. Comput. Syst. Sci.*, 28(2):193–215, 1984.

[24] C. Fournet, M. Kohlweiss, and P.-Y. Strub. Modular code-based cryptographic verification. In *CCS 2011*, pages 341–350. ACM, 2011.

[25] J. A. Goguen and J. Meseguer. Security policies and security models. In *S&P 1982*, pages 11–20. IEEE Computer Society, 1982.

[26] G. Gonthier, A. Mahboubi, and E. Tassi. A small scale reflection extension for the Coq system. Technical Report RR-6455, INRIA, 2008.

[27] J. Hurd, A. McIver, and C. Morgan. Probabilistic guarded commands mechanized in HOL. *Theor. Comput. Sci.*, 346(1):96–112, 2005.

[28] B. Jonsson, W. Yi, and K. G. Larsen. Probabilistic extensions of process algebras. In *Handbook of Process Algebra*, pages 685–710. Elsevier, 2001.

[29] O. Kiselyov and C.-c. Shan. Embedded probabilistic programming. In *DSL 2009*, volume 5658 of *Lecture Notes in Computer Science*, pages 360–384. Springer, 2009.

[30] D. Kozen. A probabilistic PDL. *J. Comput. Syst. Sci.*, 30(2):162–178, 1985.

[31] R. Küsters, T. Truderung, and J. Graf. A framework for the cryptographic verification of Java-like programs. In *CSF 2012*, pages 198–212. IEEE Computer Society, 2012.

[32] J. McCarthy. Towards a mathematical science of computation. In *IFIP Congress*, pages 21–28, 1962.

[33] A. McIver and C. Morgan. *Abstraction, Refinement, and Proof for Probabilistic Systems*. Monographs in Computer Science. Springer, 2005.

[34] A. Nanevski, G. Morrisett, A. Shinnar, P. Govereau, and L. Birkedal. Ynot: dependent types for imperative programs. In *ICFP 2008*, pages 229–240. ACM, 2008.

[35] S. Park, F. Pfenning, and S. Thrun. A probabilistic language based upon sampling functions. In *POPL 2005*, pages 171–182. ACM, 2005.

[36] T. P. Pedersen. Non-interactive and information-theoretic secure verifiable secret sharing. In *CRYPTO '91*, volume 576 of *Lecture Notes in Computer Science*, pages 129–140. Springer, 1991.

[37] N. Ramsey and A. Pfeffer. Stochastic lambda calculus and monads of probability distributions. In *POPL 2002*, pages 154–165. ACM, 2002.

[38] J. H. Reif. Logics for probabilistic programming (extended abstract). In *STOC 1980*, pages 8–13. ACM, 1980.

[39] B. Reus and N. Charlton. A guide to program logics for higher-order store, 2012. Unpublished manuscript.

[40] A. Rial and G. Danezis. Privacy-preserving smart metering. In *WPES 2011*, pages 49–60. ACM, 2011.

[41] A. Sabelfeld and A. C. Myers. Language-based information-flow security. *IEEE Journal on Selected Areas in Communications*, 21(1): 5–19, 2003.

[42] G. Stewart, A. Banerjee, and A. Nanevski. Dependent types for enforcement of information flow and erasure policies in heterogeneous data structures. In *PPDP 2013*, pages 145–156. ACM, 2013.

[43] P.-Y. Strub, N. Swamy, C. Fournet, and J. Chen. Self-certification: Bootstrapping certified typecheckers in F* with Coq. In *POPL 2012*, pages 571–584. ACM, 2012.

[44] K. Svendsen, L. Birkedal, and A. Nanevski. Partiality, state and dependent types. In *TLCA 2011*, pages 198–212. Springer, 2011.

[45] N. Swamy, J. Chen, C. Fournet, P.-Y. Strub, K. Bhargavan, and J. Yang. Secure distributed programming with value-dependent types. In *ICFP 2011*, pages 266–278. ACM, 2011.

[46] N. Swamy, J. Weinberger, C. Schlesinger, J. Chen, and B. Livshits. Verifying higher-order programs with the Dijkstra monad. In *PLDI 2013*, pages 387–398. ACM, 2013.

# Bridging Boolean and Quantitative Synthesis Using Smoothed Proof Search *

Swarat Chaudhuri
Rice University
swarat@rice.edu

Martin Clochard
ENS Paris &
Université Paris-Sud (LRI & Inria Saclay)
martin.clochard@lri.fr

Armando Solar-Lezama
MIT
asolar@csail.mit.edu

## Abstract

We present a new technique for parameter synthesis under boolean and quantitative objectives. The input to the technique is a "sketch" — a program with missing numerical parameters — and a probabilistic assumption about the program's inputs. The goal is to automatically synthesize values for the parameters such that the resulting program satisfies: (1) a boolean specification, which states that the program must meet certain assertions, and (2) a quantitative specification, which assigns a real valued rating to every program and which the synthesizer is expected to optimize.

Our method — called *smoothed proof search* — reduces this task to a sequence of unconstrained smooth optimization problems that are then solved numerically. By iteratively solving these problems, we obtain parameter values that get closer and closer to meeting the boolean specification; at the limit, we obtain values that provably meet the specification. The approximations are computed using a new notion of *smoothing* for program abstractions, where an abstract transformer is approximated by a function that is continuous according to a metric over abstract states.

We present a prototype implementation of our synthesis procedure, and experimental results on two benchmarks from the embedded control domain. The experiments demonstrate the benefits of smoothed proof search over an approach that does not meet the boolean and quantitative synthesis goals simultaneously.

***Categories and Subject Descriptors*** D.2.4 [*Software/Program Verification*]: Correctness proofs; F.3.2 [*Semantics of Programming Languages*]: Program analysis; I.2.2 [*Automatic Programming*]: Program synthesis; I.2.3 [*Deduction and Theorem Proving*]: Uncertainty, "fuzzy,", and probabilistic reasoning

***Keywords*** Synthesis; Probabilistic Verification; Probabilistic Programs; Program Smoothing; Abstract Interpretation

* The authors are ordered alphabetically. This work was supported by NSF Award #1162076.



*POPL '14*, January 22–24, 2014, San Diego, CA, USA.

ACM 978-1-4503-2544-8/14/01... $15.00.
http://dx.doi.org/10.1145/2535838.2535859

## 1. Introduction

Traditional reasoning tasks in formal methods are *boolean*: we are asked to prove that a program satisfies a set of boolean properties (program verification), or to realize a given logical specification in the form of an implementation (program synthesis). However, in many applications, boolean reasoning alone is not enough — we also need *quantitative reasoning*.

The need for combined boolean and quantitative reasoning is especially prominent in program synthesis. Here, a boolean specification is naturally used to set a "lower bound" on the desirability of the synthesized implementation: "the program should *at least* meet the following safety properties." However, there can be many implementations that meet these properties, and some of them are more desirable than others. Given this, it is appropriate to consider synthesis tasks where the synthesized implementation must not only meet a boolean specification, but also be optimal with respect to a *quantitative objective* [3, 6].

A plausible approach to solve such synthesis problems is to separately handle the boolean and quantitative goals, for example by searching for candidates that are locally optimal with respect to the quantitative criterion and then attempting to verify them against the boolean specification. The disadvantage of this approach is that if the search for a function that is good with respect to the quantitative objective happens without regards to the subsequent verification phase it may take a long time to find a solution that can be verified. This suggests that a procedure for quantitative synthesis should aim to meet its boolean and quantitative objectives *simultaneously*. The benefits of such an approach are corroborated by prior work on (boolean) synthesis [28, 34], which combines synthesis and verification to make the overall process more tractable. In this paper, we offer such a combined verification and synthesis procedure for the problem of synthesizing values for unknown program parameters.

Specifically, we introduce *smoothed proof search* as a new technique to combine quantitative synthesis and verification. The key idea here is to reduce the synthesis problem to a *sequence of unconstrained optimization problems* where the objective function for each problem is a continuous approximation of the boolean and quantitative objectives. As the sequence progresses, the approximate objective gets closer to the original objective, and in the limit the method finds parameters that provably meet the boolean specification. At the same time, the continuity of the approximations lets us optimize them effectively using local numerical techniques, which rely heavily on smoothness assumptions, and do poorly on the discontinuous functions that programs often represent.

We clarify these ideas with a simple example. Suppose our goal is to find the value of the parameter $c$ in the procedure

```
double P (double x) {
  c := ??;
  if (x > c) { y := x + 1; } else { y := 10; }
  return y
}
```

while satisfying the safety invariant $B : (c - 10 \leq y \leq c + 10)$, and a quantitative specification that states that the return value of the procedure should be as low as possible. This is an example of a *verified parameter synthesis* problem [25, 30, 32, 33]. The programmer has provided an implementation with missing numerical parameters —also known as a "sketch" [30]— and the synthesis problem is to find values for these parameters such that the resulting program satisfies the combined Boolean and quantitative specification.

The problem described above is not yet well defined, as there are different ways to interpret the optimality requirement. One interpretation is that the programmer wishes to minimize the *worst-case* behavior of the system; alternatively, Chatterjee et al. [6] have argued that a more natural goal is to optimize the expected value of the output. This is potentially a harder problem, because it requires knowledge of the distribution of its inputs, and it requires an analysis capable of deriving the distribution of the outputs from this input distribution. In this paper, we focus on this probabilistic view of the problem; specifically, we focus on problems where the input, say $x$, is drawn from a given probability distribution $\mu_x$, and the quantitative specification is that "The *expected* return value of $P$ on input $x$ is minimal." Because the analysis is probabilistic, the boolean assertion can also be generalized to a probabilistic one. This new assertion (call it $\varphi$) is "$(c - 10 \leq x \leq c + 10)$ with probability greater than or equal to a certain threshold $\theta$."

Our approach to this problem is a refinement of the following idea. Using existing ideas on probabilistic abstract interpretation [20], we can symbolically represent the input distribution $\mu_x$ of $x$, then compute an approximation $\widetilde{P}_c(\mu_x)$ of the actual distribution of outputs $P_c(x)$ of the program on input $x$ drawn from the distribution $\mu_x$ (these outputs depend on $c$; hence the subscript $c$ in $P_c$). From $\widetilde{P}(\mu_x, c)$, we can compute a *sound* upper bound $p$ on the probability with which $P_c(x)$ violates the assertion $B$ and a real interval $I$ such that the expectation of $P_c(x)$ is guaranteed to fall within $I$. Given this mapping from $c \mapsto (p, I)$, our goal is to find a value of $c$ that leads to low values of $p$ as well as $I$. We can frame this as a single-objective optimization problem where the goal is to find a $c$ that minimizes $\sup(I) + Penalty(p, \theta)$, where $\sup(I)$ is the least upper bound on $I$, $Penalty(p, \theta)$ is a penalty function that is zero when $p \leq \theta$, and a large positive value (larger than any upper bound on $I$) when $p$ is larger than $\theta$. Minimizing this function gives us a value of $c$ that is desirable according to the quantitative criterion while satisfying the probabilistic assertion $\varphi$.

Numerical search techniques like gradient descent or Nelder-Mead search [22] seem like the natural choice for solving this optimization problem, because even though they do not provide any guarantees on the optimality of the result, they are known to work well in practice when the function to optimize satisfies certain continuity requirements. These techniques cannot be applied directly, though, because the results of abstract interpretation are highly discontinuous. To understand the source of the discontinuities, consider our example program from before. Let us consider an abstract interpretation where, following prior work [20], probability distributions are approximated by structures that are essentially histograms: disjunctions of pairs $(E_i, w_i)$, where each $E_i$ is a set of possible values for a random variable (a bin in the histogram), and $w_i$ is an upper bound on the measure concentrated in $E_i$ (*i.e.* the probability that the value will fall in that bin). Fig. 1 depicts an example abstraction of a continuous distribution by such a structure.

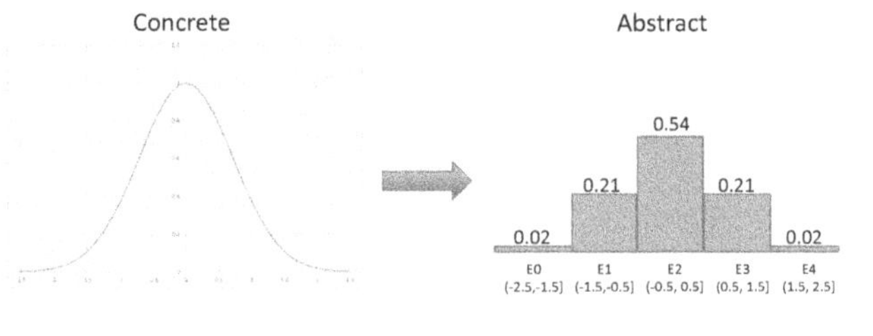


**Figure 1.** Example of probabilistic abstraction

Now suppose the abstract state of $x$, right before the conditional "`if (x > c)`" in our example program, is as in Fig. 1. Note that if $c$ is exactly $0.5$, the probability that $x > c$ will be bounded from below by $0.23$, but for any $\epsilon > 0$, making $c = 0.5 + \epsilon$ will change the lower bound on the probability to $0.02$. This is because the abstract state tells us that the probability of falling in the range $(0.5, 1.5]$ is $0.21$, but the abstract state has lost the information about the exact probability of falling between $0.5$ and $0.5 + \epsilon$. This property of the abstract domain makes the function $c \mapsto (p, I)$ highly discontinuous.

Our approach overcomes this difficulty via a novel notion of *smoothing* for abstract interpretations. Instead of using the abstract transformer $\widetilde{P}_c(\mu_x)$ to generate a target for optimization, we use a series of *approximations* to the abstract transformer that are continuous in the analytical sense. Because of the continuity of these approximations, numerical optimization can be used to compute high-quality minima in objectives generated from them.

We define these approximations by first defining "smooth" analogs of the classic operators of abstract interpretation, such as join and widening. The approximations are neither abstractions or refinements of the sound abstraction $\widetilde{P}_c$ — in fact, they bear no resemblance to operations on abstract interpreters studied in the literature. Notably, each of them is an unsound abstraction. While this may sound like a violation of our stated goals, it is not so. Each of our approximations is parameterized by a real value $\beta$; in the limit as $\beta$ approaches zero, the approximations converge to $\widetilde{P}_c$. Therefore, by iteratively finding local minima on objectives generated from approximations parameterized by lower and lower values of $\beta$, we can find parameters that are satisfy our boolean specification with maximal probability. We call the above strategy for meeting a combination of boolean and quantitative synthesis goals *smoothed proof search*.

We have implemented our algorithm in the form of a tool called FERMAT, built on top of the SKETCH program synthesizer. We have used FERMAT to do verified parameter synthesis on two benchmarks from the embedded control domain: a model of a thermostat and a model of an aircraft controller. Our experiments show that smoothing significantly improves the quality of parameters synthesized through search, and that searching simultaneously with respect to the boolean and quantitative objectives gives better results than applying the two kinds of search in sequence.

In summary, this paper makes the following contributions:

- We introduce *smoothed proof search*, a new way to reconcile boolean and quantitative reasoning in program synthesis. The essence of the idea is to reduce a combination of proof and optimization tasks to a sequence of smooth optimization problems.
- We present a concrete smoothed proof search algorithm for verified parameter synthesis in programs with probabilistic inputs. We prove several properties of our algorithm, including

(a) soundness; and (b) the smoothness of the objectives that we generate for numerical optimization.

- We present a prototype implementation of our algorithm, called FERMAT, and perform case studies on two benchmarks from the embedded control domain.

The rest of the paper is organized as follows. In Section 2, we formulate our synthesis problem. In Section 3, we present smoothed proof search as well as a concrete algorithm based on this strategy. Section 4 presents the FERMAT system and experimental results. Section 5 discusses related work; we conclude with some discussion in Section 6. Finally, we had to omit proofs for most of our theorems due to lack of space; these can be found in an online technical report [7].

## 2. Problem formulation

In this section, we formalize the verified parameter synthesis problem. As outlined earlier, we will be focusing on the probabilistic version of the problem where the goal is to meet the optimality criterion on the average input. The key technical task of this section is the definition of the probabilistic semantics.

***Measures*** To define the semantics of our programs rigorously, we need some definitions from probability theory. For brevity, we only give the most essential of these definitions. A more thorough treatment of this background material can be found in a textbook such as Billingsley's [2].

**Definition 1** (Borel sets)**.** A *$\sigma$-algebra* $\sigma$ over $\mathbb{R}^n$ is a set of subsets of $\mathbb{R}^n$ that contains $\emptyset$, and is closed under complementation and countable union. The collection of *Borel sets*, denoted $\mathscr{B}$, is the smallest $\sigma$-algebra over $\mathbb{R}^n$ containing the open sets.

Examples of Borel sets include the set $\mathbb{R}^n$, the set of all rational vectors, and the sets of real vectors satisfying conjunctions or disjunctions of polynomial inequalities (in practice, all subsets of the reals of interest in program analysis).

**Definition 2** (Measure)**.** A *(finite, nonnegative) measure* $\mu$ (over $\mathbb{R}^n$) is a function $\mu : \mathscr{B} \to [0, +\infty)$ such that: (1) $\mu(\emptyset) = 0$, and (2) If $(A_n)_{n\in\mathbb{N}}$ is a countable collection of disjoint subsets of $\mathbb{R}^n$, then $\mu(\bigcup_{n\in\mathbb{N}} A_n) = \sum_{n\in\mathbb{N}} \mu(A_n)$.

The *total weight* of $\mu$ is $\|\mu\| = \mu(\mathbb{R}^n)$. If $\|\mu\| = 1$, then $\mu$ is a *probability measure*; if $\|\mu\| \leq 1$, then $\mu$ is a *subprobability measure*. A measure $\mu$ over $\mathbb{R}^n$ is *concentrated* over a subset $Y \subseteq \mathbb{R}^n$ if $\mu(\mathbb{R}^n \setminus Y) = 0$. The *support* $supp(\mu)$ of a measure $\mu$ is the least closed set $Y \subseteq \mathbb{R}^n$ such that $\mu$ is concentrated on $Y$.

Intuitively, if $\mu$ is a probability measure associated with a random variable $x$, then $\mu(Y)$ is the probability that $x \in Y$. Non-probability measures $\mu$ formalize "unnormalized" probability distributions, where the probability of the "certain" event does not have to be 1.

A function $f : \mathbb{R}^n \to \mathbb{R}^n$ is a *measurable function* if for all Borel sets $Y \subseteq \mathbb{R}^n$, $f^{-1}(Y)$ is also a Borel set. For measurable functions $f : \mathbb{R}^n \to \mathbb{R}^n$ and random variables $x$ with measure $\mu$, we can define the *expectation* $\mathbb{E}_\mu[f(x)]$ of $f(x)$ by the standard *Lebesgue integral*: $\mathbb{E}_\mu[f(x)] = \int f\, d\mu$. All the functions that we consider in this paper are measurable.

***Programs*** Now we define the language (call it IMP) of programs that we want to synthesize. IMP is a core imperative language with standard control constructs. Programs here are allowed to update $n$ memory locations containing real values for a fixed but arbitrary constant $n$; hence, the state of a program is described by a real vector of length $n$. Assignments in the program correspond to affine transformations applied to this vector.

Let us fix a single variable $x$, ranging over $\mathbb{R}^n$, that stores the state of a program. The syntax of Boolean expressions $B$ and programs $S$ in IMP are given by:

$$\begin{array}{rcl} B & ::= & {}^t b_v \cdot x + b_0 > 0 \\ S & ::= & \texttt{skip} \mid x := M \cdot x + c \mid \\ & & \texttt{if } B \texttt{ then } S_1 \texttt{ else } S_2 \mid \\ & & \texttt{while } B \texttt{ do } S_1 \mid S_1; S_2 \end{array}$$

where $b_v, c \in \mathbb{R}^n$, $b_0 \in \mathbb{R}$, $M$ is a real matrix, and ${}^t b_v$ denotes the transpose of $b_v$.

We assign a probabilistic concrete semantics $[\![S]\!]$ to each IMP program $S$ (we use $[\![S]\!]_{det}$ whenever we need to refer to the standard non-probabilistic semantics). This semantics is defined as a transformation on finite measures $\mu$ (*i.e.* measures with $\|\mu\| < \infty$). Specifically, $[\![S]\!](\mu)$ is the output probability measure of $S$ when applied to an input probability measure $\mu$. The semantics of a boolean expression $b$ is a function $[\![b]\!]$ that maps the state vector to a Boolean, but abusing notation, we also use $[\![b]\!]$ to denote the set of vectors $v$ that satisfy $b$.

We need some more notation. Given a matrix $M$ and a set of vectors $U \subseteq R^n$, we define $M^{-1}U = \{v | Mv \in U\}$ to be the set of vectors that when multiplied times $M$ produce a vector in $U$. Note that this operation is well defined even for non-invertible matrices. We also abuse notation by using $(U - a)$ to refer to the set $\{y - a | y \in U\}$. The probabilistic semantics of loop-free programs is now given by the following rules:

$$\begin{array}{rcl} [\![\texttt{skip}]\!](\mu) & = & \mu \\ [\![{}^t b_v \cdot x + b_0 > 0]\!] & = & \{x \in \mathbb{R}^n | {}^t b_v \cdot x + b_0 > 0\} \\ [\![x := Mx + c]\!](\mu) & = & \lambda U.\mu(M^{-1}(U - c)) \\ [\![S_1; S_2]\!](\mu) & = & [\![S_2]\!]([\![S_1]\!](\mu)) \\ [\![\texttt{if } b \texttt{ then } S_1 \texttt{ else } S_2]\!](\mu) & = & [\![S_1]\!](\lambda U.\mu(U \cap [\![b]\!])) \\ & & +[\![S_2]\!](\lambda U.\mu(U \setminus [\![b]\!])) \end{array}$$

To give semantics to loops, let us define an operation $steps_{S,b}(\mu) = [\![S]\!](\lambda U.\mu(U \cap [\![b]\!]))$. We use the notation $step^n_{S,b}$ to refer to the composition of $steps_{S,b}$ $n$ times, with $step^0_{S,b}$ being the identity function. Now we define:

$$[\![\texttt{while } b \texttt{ do } S]\!](\mu)(U) = \sum_{n=0}^{\infty} step^n_{S,b}(\mu)(U \setminus [\![b]\!]).$$

The quantity $step^n_{S,b}(\mu)(U \setminus [\![b]\!])$ corresponds to the probability that some initial state $x$ will cause the loop to iterate exactly $n$ times and after those $n$ iterations, the resulting state belongs to the set $U$. For simplicity, in this paper we only consider programs $S$ that terminate on *almost every input* — i.e., the set of inputs on which the program does not terminate is of measure 0.

**Example 1.** Suppose we are trying to analyze the program from the introduction after having replaced c with 0.5.

```
if (x > 0.5) { y := x + 1; } else { y := 10; }
```

Now, suppose the input $x$ is uniformly distributed over the range $[0, 10)$. The distribution can be represented by a probability measure $\mu(A)$ which for any set $A$ produces the probability that $x \in A$. In particular, for any interval $(a, b)$ with $0 < a < b < 10$,

$$\mu((a, b)) = \frac{b - a}{10}.$$

For any set $A$ that does not intersect $[0, 10)$, $\mu(A) = 0$.

According to the semantic rules, the distribution of the output $y$ is given by the following function:

$$\begin{array}{rl} \mu_{out} = \lambda U.\, & \mu(M_1^{-1}(U - 1) \cap [0.5, \infty)) + \\ & \mu(M_2^{-1}(U - 10) \cap (-\infty, 0.5)). \end{array}$$

Now $M_1^{-1}(A) = A$ for any $A$, and since $M_2$ is the zero matrix, $M_2^{-1}(A) = \mathbb{R}$ if $0 \in A$, and is the empty set otherwise. Thus, on the range $(1.5, 2)$, we have

$$\mu_{out}((1.5,2)) = \mu((0.5,1.0) \cap [0.5,\infty)) + \mu(\emptyset \cap (-\infty,0.5)) \\ = \mu((0.5,1.0)) = 0.05$$

and on the range $(9, 12)$, we have

$$\mu_{out}((9,12)) = \mu((8,11) \cap [0.5,\infty)) + \mu(\mathbb{R} \cap (-\infty,0.5)) \\ = \mu((8,11)) + \mu((-\infty,0.5)) = 0.25$$

*i.e.* the probability of the output being between 9 and 12 is 0.25, while the probability of the output being between 1.5 and 2.0 is 0.05.

**Lemma 1** (Properties of concrete semantics)**.** The concrete semantics of IMP satisfies the following properties. For all programs $S$,

$$[\![S]\!](\mu_1 + \mu_2) = [\![S]\!](\mu_1) + [\![S]\!](\mu_2)$$
$$\|\mu_1\| = \|[\![S]\!](\mu_1)\|$$

Moreover, $[\![S]\!](\mu)(U) = \mu([\![S]\!]^{-1}_{det}(U))$, where $[\![\cdot]\!]_{det}$ stands for the usual deterministic semantics of programs.

***Sketches*** A sketch is an IMP program with missing parameters. Formally, let $H$ be a special name for a variable storing an $n$-tuple of (missing) *control parameters*. We define an *implementation sketch* (or simply a *sketch*) to be a term $S_H$ with the syntax

$$\begin{array}{lll} B & ::= & {}^t b_v \cdot x + {}^t b'_v \cdot H + b_0 > 0 \\ S_H & ::= & \texttt{skip} \mid \\ & & x := M \cdot x + M' \cdot H + c \mid \\ & & \texttt{if } B \texttt{ then } S_{1H} \texttt{ else } S_{2H} \mid \\ & & \texttt{while } B \texttt{ do } S_{1H} \mid S_{1H}; S_{2H} \end{array}$$

where $b_v, c, b'_v \in \mathbb{R}^n$, $b_0 \in \mathbb{R}$, and $M, M'$ are real matrices. By substituting $H$ by a constant vector $c$ in $S_H$, we obtain an IMP program. We denote this program by $S_H[H \mapsto c]$ or $S_c$. Note that as the sketch performs only linear operations in $H$, we can treat the concatenation of $H$ and $x$ as a state vector; the sketch then becomes a standard IMP program $S(x : H)$ on that extended vector.

***Assertions*** A *(probabilistic) assertion* for a program $S$ is a pair $\varphi = (B; \theta)$, where $B$ is a boolean expression in IMP and $0 \leq \theta \leq 1$ is a constant.

**Definition 3** (Satisfaction)**.** A measure $\mu$ satisfies $\varphi = (B; \theta)$ if $\mu([\![B]\!]) \geq \theta$. A program $S$ satisfies $\varphi$ on the input $\mu$ if $\mu' = [\![S]\!](\mu)$ satisfies $\varphi$. Intuitively, if $S$ satisfies $\varphi$ under $\mu$, then the probability that the assertion $B$ will hold on termination of $S$ is greater than or equal to $\theta$. Also, note that if $\theta = 1$, then $\varphi$ is a non-probabilistic assertion that is expected to be true for all inputs allowed by the distribution.

For simpler notation, we only allow assertions as postconditions in the formal exposition of our method. However, our method easily extends to requirements asserted at intermediate labels within a program, and such assertions are permitted in our implementation.

***Error value*** Our programs compute an error value, *i.e.* a real value reflecting how close the behavior was to the ideal. In general, we assume that there is an error function $Err(x)$ that computes the error value from the final state of the program. Usually, the error value will just be stored as one of the components of the state vector; for example, if the program is storing the error value in the first component of the state vector, $Err(x) = \delta_0 \cdot x$, where $\delta_0$ is the Kronecker delta.

***Parameter synthesis*** Now we define the parameter synthesis problem that we solve.

**Problem 1** (Verified parameter synthesis)**.** Given an implementation sketch $P$, an input measure $\mu$ (assumed to be of bounded support for technical convenience), and a boolean requirement $\varphi$, find a vector $c \in \mathbb{R}^n$ such that:

1. **[Boolean goal]** $S_c = S_H[H \mapsto c]$ satisfies $\varphi$ on input $\mu$.
2. **[Quantitative goal]** The expected error value produced by $S_c$ is minimal. Formally, $c = \text{argmin}_c\, \Phi(c)$, where $\Phi(c) = \mathbb{E}_{[\![S_c]\!](\mu)}[Err(x)]$ is the expected value of component zero of $x$ according to the *output* distribution of $S_c$.

If we use $S_c(x)$ as a shorthand for $Err([\![S_c]\!]_{det}(x))$, *i.e.* the function that maps an input to its error value, then it is easy to prove that $\mathbb{E}_{[\![S_c]\!](\mu)}[Err(x)] = \mathbb{E}_\mu[S_c(x)]$, so we will use the two notations interchangeably.

**Example 2.** Let us go back to th e example in the introduction:

```
if (x > c) { y := x + 1; } else { y := 10; }
```

The Boolean goal can be expressed as $\varphi : ((c - 10 \leq y \leq c + 10); 1.0)$. As in Example 1, let us assume that the input $x$ is distributed uniformly within $[0, 10)$.

The probability of passing the assertion at the end of the program is equal to $\mu_{out}([c - 10, c + 10])$, and the expected final value of $y$ is $\mathbb{E}_{\mu_{out}}[y]$ (because our stated goal is to minimize the output $y$, $Err(y)$ is just the identity function). For this simple program, both of these functions can be computed from the definition of $\mu_{out}$.

Using Lebesgue integration, we see that when $0 \leq c \leq 10$ the expected value as a function of $c$ is:

$$\int y \, d\mu_{out} = 5.05 + (c+1) - \frac{(c+1)^2}{20}$$

So, for example, when $c = 1$, the expected value is 6.85, and when $c = 9$, the expected value is 10.05.

From this, we can see that in order to minimize the output $y$ while preserving the invariant, we need to set $c = 1$. Any value of $c$ lower than 1 will reduce the probability of satisfying the invariant below 1. On the other hand, any value of $c$ in $(1, 10]$ will lead to a higher expected value of $y$ by the above calculation, and if $c > 10$, then the output will be the constant 10.

**Example 3** (Thermostat)**.** Let us now understand our problem statement using a "real" example — a controller for a thermostat. The thermostat has two inputs: a *target temperature* $l_{target}$ for the room, and the value $l_{in}$ of the outside temperature. These two inputs are probabilistic, because while we do not know what the outside or the target temperatures will be at a given time, we can collect statistics from the local weather and user's preferences to determine an expected distribution of these input values. The joint distribution $\mu$ on $l_{in}$ and $l_{target}$ is assumed to be given.

The output of the program is the difference between the real temperature and the target temperature over a period of time, and the goal is to design a thermostat that will minimize the expected value of this error.

A natural partial implementation for our controller[1] is in Fig. 2. Here the placeholders `??(`$c_1$`,`$c_2$`)` stand for missing real-valued parameters; by using a placeholder like the above, the programmer communicates the additional insight that the parameter is likely to lie in the interval $[c_1, c_2]$. The code captures the simple high-level insight that a thermostat is a system with two discrete modes: one where the heater it controls is off and one where the heater is on. When the temperature goes above a certain threshold `tOff`, it is appropriate to turn off the heater; when the room temperature is below a certain `tOn`, the heater must come back on.

[1] This code is written in SKETCH [30]—the language used in our implementation—but is easily translated to IMP.

```
double thermostat(double lin, double ltarget) {
  double h = ??(0,10);
  double tOn = ltarget + ??(-10,0);
  double tOff = ltarget + ??(0,10);
  double isOn = 0.0; double K = 0.1; double curL = lin;
  assert(tOn < tOff; 0.9);  assert(h > 0; 0.9);
  assert(h < 20; 0.9);
  for(int i = 0; i < 40; i = i + 1) {
    if(isOn > 0.5) {
      curL = curL + (h - K * (curL - lin));
      if(curL > tOff) {  isOn = 0.0; }
    } else {
      curL = curL - K * (curL - lin);
      if(curL < tOn) {  isOn = 1.0;  } }
    assert(curL < 120; 0.9); }
  Error = abs(curL - ltarget);
  return Error;
}
```

**Figure 2.** Sketch of a thermostat. abs is the absolute value function.

The synthesis problem is to find values for tOn and tOff, as well the heat h given off by the heater in each time step, such that the following two conditions are satisfied. First, after 40 steps the temperature of the room should be as close to the target as possible; this is the Error value computed by the sketch. Second, the values of the parameters must be such that if the inputs follow a distribution $\mu$, then the controller *provably* satisfies each probabilistic assertion in the sketch—e.g., the property that the temperature curL should be below 120° with probability $> 0.9$.

## 3. Smoothed proof search

In this section, we describe the smoothed proof search approach to verified parameter synthesis. Of the two goals in the statement of the problem, we view the boolean requirement as a minimum requirement on the solutions, and guarantee that every solution satisfies it. However, the quantitative goal is met approximately using local optimization, and substantiated empirically. This choice is akin to how in most program analyses, one guarantees soundness but leaves completeness as an empirical consideration.

Formally, suppose we are given an instance of an optimal synthesis problem $\langle S_H, \varphi, \mu\rangle$, where the components of the tuple have meanings as before. Let $\varphi = (B, \theta)$, and for any $c \in \mathbb{R}^n$, let $S_c = S_H[H \mapsto c]$.

Now, suppose we have a way to compute both the expected error value at the end of the execution as well as the probability that the execution value satisfies $B$, both as a function of $c$.

$$\Phi(c) = \mathbb{E}_{[\![S_c]\!](\mu)}[Err(x)] \qquad \Delta(c) = \mathbb{P}[[\![S_c]\!](\mu) \text{ satisfies } B]$$

The goal is to find a $c$ that minimizes $\Phi(c)$ under the constraint that $\Delta(c) < \theta$. We can also frame this as an unconstrained, single-objective optimization problem by introducing a penalty term when $\Delta(c) \geq \theta$. Specifically, such a problem can have the form:

$$\min_c \left(\Phi(c) + Penalty(\Delta(c), \theta)\right).$$

where $Penalty(p, \theta)$ is 0 for $p \leq \theta$ and an arbitrarily large positive value for $p > \theta$.

Our smoothed proof search algorithm addresses two challenges faced in solving the optimization problem above. The first challenge is that computing the true values of $\Phi$ and $\Delta$ is prohibitively expensive, so we need to have *sound* approximations that can be computed efficiently but can still guarantee that the result does indeed satisfy the probability bound. Second, while local numerical search algorithms — such as Nelder-Mead simplex search — are the only reasonable way of solving the problem, these algorithms rely very strongly on the continuity of the objective function. Due to the presence of braching control constructs, this assumption does not hold in our setting.

**Algorithm 1** Smoothed proof search

1. Initialize $In_c$ to a random value.
2. Let $\beta_0, \beta_1, \ldots, \beta_m$ be a series of values where $\beta_0$ is a heuristically chosen real constant and $\beta_i = \beta_0 * \kappa^i$ for a constant $0 < \kappa < 1$, and $\beta_m$ is the first $\beta_i$ below a certain threshold $\epsilon_\beta$
3. For $\beta$ in $\beta_0, \beta_1, \ldots, \beta_m$:

(a) Obtain representations of $\Phi^\#_\beta(c)$ and $\Delta^\#_\beta(c)$. Let $I^\Phi_\beta = \Phi^\#_\beta(c)$ and $I^\Delta_\beta = \Delta^\#_\beta(c)$.

(b) Set $G := \lambda(c).(\sup(I^\Phi_\beta) + Penalty^\#_\beta(max(I^\Delta_\beta), \theta))$.

(c) Minimize $G$ using local numerical search, starting from the initial point $In_c$. Let $c^* = \text{argmin}_c\, G(c)$

(d) Set $In_c := c^*$

4. Verify that $S_{c^*}$ satisfies $\varphi$. If this fact can be proved, then terminate; report $c^*$ as the optimal parameter value. Otherwise, go to step 1.

The key idea behind our algorithm is to derive a set of continuous approximations to $\Phi(c)$ and $\Delta(c)$. The approximations $\Phi^\#_\beta(c)$ and $\Delta^\#_\beta(c)$ are continuous but unsound approximations of $\Phi(c)$ and $\Delta(c)$ parameterized by value $\beta$ that controls the degree of approximation. Specifically, $\Phi^\#_\beta$ maps each control parameter value to an interval $I^\Phi_\beta$, and $\Delta^\#_\beta$ maps each control parameter value to an interval $I^\Delta_\beta$. For values of $\beta > 0$, the mappings $\Phi^\#_\beta$ and $\Delta^\#_\beta$ are continuous, and bigger values of $\beta$ will lead to "smoother" functions that are easier to optimize numerically. In the limit as $\beta$ goes to zero, on the other hand, the intervals returned by the approximations converge to sound bounds over the original functions $\Phi$ and $\Delta$. In other words:

- Let $\lim_{\beta\to 0} \Phi^\#_\beta(c) = I^\Phi_0$. Then $\Phi(c) \in I^\Phi_0$.
- Let $\lim_{\beta\to 0} \Delta^\#_\beta(c) = I^\Delta_0$. Then $\Delta(c) \in I^\Delta_0$.

Thus, bigger values of $\beta$ make numerical optimization easier, while small values of $\beta$ make the function closer to the sound but discontinuous approximation we would like to optimize.

Finally, the function $Penalty(p, \theta)$ is also a source of discontinuity, so it is approximated by a smooth function $Penalty^\#_\beta(p, \theta)$. In particular, we use an approximation of the form $Penalty^\#_\beta(p, \theta) = sigmoid(p, \theta, \beta)$, where $sigmoid(p, \theta, \beta)$ is a smooth sigmoid (S-shaped) function that monotonically increases in value with $p$, has a single inflection point at $p = \theta$, and smoothly approaches the function $Penalty(p, \theta)$ as $\beta \to 0$.

We exploit these properties in our smoothed proof search algorithm (Algorithm 1). Note that, while the abstraction of the error function returns an interval, the algorithm optimizes the *supremum* or least upper bound on this interval (i.e., if $I^\Phi_\beta = (l^\Phi_\beta, h^\Phi_\beta)$, then we optimize $h^\Phi_\beta$). However, in principle we could have also chosen to optimize a different real objective derived from the interval. On the other hand, it is important that we optimize the upper bound $\sup I^\Delta_\beta$ on the probability of assertion failure, because our goal is to guarantee that the probability of error is below the threshold.

The check in step 4 of our algorithm is important because the bounds computed by approximation $G$ in Step 3 are not sound approximations: the interval $I^\Phi_{\beta_m}$ may not bound the value of $\Phi(c)$, and the interval $I^{\Delta}_{\beta_m}$ may not bound the the value of $\Delta(c)$. However, we can show that as $\beta$ approaches zero, the approximation converges to sound bounds. Thus, step 4 can be seen to be a "limit" of the iteration in Step 3.

Now we show how to compute $\Phi^{\#}_{\beta}$ and $\Delta^{\#}_{\beta}$ using abstract interpretation. In Section 3.1, we give a method to compute sound bounds for the expected value of a function on an input measure. The procedure that computes sound bounds is discontinuous, so the parameter $\beta$ does not play a role here. (However, the soundness of the procedure means that we can use it in the verification step — Step 4 — in the algorithm.) Subsequently, in Section 3.2, we present our method for smooth approximation of programs.

### 3.1 Sound but discontinuous domain

Our abstract interpretation for computing sound (but discontinuous) bounds on the expected output of a program builds on the work of Monniaux [20]. We improve upon this work by leveraging an assumption of structured control flow to handle conditionals more precisely.

***Abstract states*** An abstract state in our domain is a tuple of the form $\mathcal{A} = (I, \{w_i\}, \{p_i\}, \{E_i\})$. Here $I$ is a set of indices; for each index $i \in I$ there is exactly one weight $w_i$, one fraction $p_i$ and one subset $E_i$ of $\mathbb{R}^n$.

The meaning of each of these components is best understood by defining the concretization function $\gamma$, which maps abstract states to sets of sub-probability measures over $\mathbb{R}^n$:

$$\begin{aligned}&\gamma((I, \{w_i\}, \{p_i\}, \{E_i\})) = \\ &\quad \{\mu \mid \mu = \textstyle\sum_{i \in I} \mu_i \wedge \forall i \in I:\ supp(\mu_i) \subseteq E_i \wedge ||\mu_i|| \leq w_i \\ &\qquad \wedge p_i = 0 \Rightarrow \mu_i = 0 \wedge p_i = 1 \Rightarrow ||\mu_i|| = w_i\}\end{aligned}$$

In other words, the measure can be decomposed into a sum of component measures $\mu_i$, where each of these components is concentrated in the set $E_i$. The values $p_i$ carry information about abstraction precision and are one of the distinguishing features of our abstract domain compared to that of Monniaux. Each $p_i$ lies between 0 and 1; when $p_i$ is 0 or 1, we know that the total weight of the corresponding component $\mu_i$ is respectively 0 and the full weight ($w_i$). An intermediate value means that we don't know the precise value of $||\mu_i||$ but we have a bound on it.

As we saw in the introduction, when $n = 1$ and each $E_i$ is an interval, the abstract state is essentially a histogram; each $E_i$ corresponds to a bucket in the histogram, and the value $w_i$ bounds the total area of the $i^{th}$ bar in the histogram—or if $p = 1$, $w_i$ gives the exact area of that bar. The abstract domain allows us to symbolically propagate this "histogram" through the program. As this histogram passes through branches, we lose certainty about the weight in any given bucket $E_i$. To see why, suppose the branch condition $b$ has an intersection with $E_i$. Given that we do not know how the measure on $E_i$ is distributed, we do not know if the weight on $b \cap E_i$ is the total initial weight on $E_i$.

However, note that by the time the abstract interpretation reaches the end of the branch, this lost certainty is once again regained. This is because, by this point, all the paths into which $E_i$ could have been split within the branch-statement have been joined. Thus, we know that the total weight on $E_i$ at this point is the same as the initial weight on $E_i$.

Formally, the partial order $\sqsubseteq$ over the abstract states is defined as follows:

$$\begin{aligned}(I, \{w_i\}\{p_i\}, \{E_i\}) \sqsubseteq (I, \{w_i\}, \{q_i\}, \{F_i\}) \ &\Leftrightarrow \\ \forall i \in I:\ p_i \sqsubseteq_p q_i \wedge E_i \subseteq F_i&\end{aligned}$$

where the relation $\sqsubseteq_p$ is defined as

$$a \sqsubseteq_p b = \begin{cases} true & \text{if } a = b \\ true & \text{if } b \notin \{0, 1\} \\ false & \text{otherwise.} \end{cases}$$

It is important to note a few properties about the partial order. First, note that the partial order is only defined when the abstract states share the same sets $I$ and $w_i$. In principle, it is possible to provide a more general partial order that also relates abstract states with different index sets and weights, but for the purpose of our analysis, this partial order will suffice. The second point to note is the rationale behind the definition of $\sqsubseteq_p$. The main idea is that when $p_i \in \{0, 1\}$, it restricts the set of measures in the concretization, but if $p_i$ has a fractional value, it is inconsequential.

**Example 4.** Consider abstract states A and B below:

| | | | |
|---|---|---|---|
| A: | $I^A = \{0\}$<br>$w_0^A = 0.5$<br>$p_0^A = 1/2$<br>$E_0^A = [0, 2.5]$ | B: | $I^B = \{0\}$<br>$w_0^B = 0.5$<br>$p_0^B = 1/4$<br>$E_0^B = [0, 2.5]$ |

In this case, both $p_0^A$ and $p_0^B$ are fractional, so the concretization of both abstract states is the same and hence $A \sqsubseteq_p B$ even though they have different values of $p_i$. If $p_0^A$ were equal to 1, the concretization of $A$ would be a subset of the concretization of $B$, so $A \sqsubseteq_p B$ would still hold. However, if $p_0^B$ was to equal 1 or 0, the partial order would only hold if $p_0^A$ was also made equal to $p_0^B$.

***Abstraction of loop-free programs*** The abstract semantics of loop-free programs is given by the following rules:

- $[\![x := Mx + c]\!](I, \{w_i\}, \{p_i\}, \{E_i\})$
  $= (I, \{w_i\}, \{p_i\}, \{ME_i + c\})$
- $[\![S_1; S_2]\!](I, \{w_i\}, \{p_i\}, \{E_i\})$
  $= [\![S_2]\!]([\![S_1]\!](I, \{w_i\}, \{p_i\}, \{E_i\}).$
- $[\![\texttt{if}\ b\ \texttt{then}\ S_1 \texttt{else}\ S_2]\!](I, \{w_i\}, \{p_i\}, \{E_i\})$
  $= [\![S_1]\!](I, \{w_i\}, \{p_i^b\}, \{E_i^b\}) \sqcup$
  $[\![S_2]\!](I, \{w_i\}, \{p_i^{\neg b}\}, \{E_i^{\neg b}\}).$

Here

$$p_i^b = \begin{cases} 0 & \text{if } [\![b]\!] \cap E_i = \emptyset \\ p_i & \text{if } E_i \subseteq [\![b]\!] \\ p_i/2 & \text{otherwise} \end{cases}$$

and $p_i^{\neg b}$ is defined in an analogous way. The set $E_i^b$ is some superset of $E_i \cap [\![b]\!]$. The operator $\sqcup$ on abstract states is defined as follows:

$$\begin{aligned}&(I, \{w_i\}, \{p_i^a\}, \{E_i^a\}) \sqcup (I, \{w_i\}, \{p_i^b\}, \{E_i^b\}) = \\ &\qquad (I, \{w_i\}, \{p_i^a + p_i^b\}, \{join(p_i^a, E_i^a, p_i^b, E_i^b)\})\end{aligned}$$

where

$$\begin{aligned}&join(p_i^a, E_i^a, p_i^b, E_i^b) = \\ &\quad \{x \mid (x \in E_i^a \wedge p_i^a > 0) \vee (x \in E_i^b \wedge p_i^b > 0)\}.\end{aligned}$$

Finally, the notation $ME_i + c$ is used to describe the set of points $\{Mx + c \mid x \in E_i\}$.

Note how the propagation of abstract states through a branch (say with condition $b$) tracks precision information. If $[\![b]\!] \cap E_i$ is either empty or equal to $E_i$, we have not lost any precision by propagation through the branch condition. However, if these conditions not hold, then we have lost precision, and this is tracked by shrinking $p_i$ by half. Note also that the $\sqcup$ operator ensures that we will regain this lost precision at the end of the branch.

We observe that $\sqcup$ is not actually a join operation in the traditional sense, because $p_i^b + p_i^{\neg b} = p_i$ and we could have $p_i \sqsubseteq_p p_i^b$.

We refer to this operation as a *subjoin* because it produces a more precise result than the join. However, the result is still sound because of the relationship between the distributions from the two branches as we prove in the appendix. The use of a sub-join operation and the use of the values $p_i$ to help track the precision of the approximation are the main distinguishing features between our method and prior work on probabilistic abstract interpretation by Monniaux [20].

We also observe that $\sqcup$ is defined only when for all $i$, $p_i^a + p_i^b \leq 1$. It so happens that at any step where the $\sqcup$ operation is applied, this condition holds. Specifically, $\sqcup$ is used only on abstract states computed from two conditional branches. As abstract interpretation of assignments preserves the values of $\{p_i\}$, the $\{p_i\}$ resulting from both branches will sum to the ones before the branch, which was already lower than 1. The rationale behind the definition of the subjoin is illustrated by the following example.

**Example 5.** Consider a simple code fragment:

```
if (x >= 0.5) { x = x + 10; }
```

Now, suppose the abstract state before the **if** statement is

$$(I = \{0\}, w_0 = 1.0, p_0 = 1, E_0 = [0, 1])$$

That means that $x$ will fall between 0 and 1, but the abstract state has no information about the exact distribution of $x$ in that range. Now, inside the conditional, the abstract state is

$$(I = \{0\}, w_0 = 1.0, p_0 = 1/2, E_0 = [0.5, 1])$$

*i.e.* x is now between 0.5 and 1, but we don't know the probability that the branch was taken; all we know is that it is bounded by 1. This uncertainty is reflected by the fractional value of $p_0$. After the branch, the new abstract state will be:

$$(I = \{0\}, w_0 = 1.0, p_0 = 1, E_0 = [0, 0.5) \cup [10.5, 11])$$

Note that $p_0$ is again 1, because even though the probability of taking each side of the conditional is unknown, we do know that the probabilities add up to $w_0$, so after the two branches merge, we know that the probability of $x \in E_0$ is exactly $w_0$.

***While loops.*** Let us now define the abstract semantics of while-loops. First we define an abstract *step* operation:

$$step((I, w_i, p_i, E_i)) = [\![S]\!](I, w_i, p_i^b, E_i^b).$$

The transformations $(step^n)_{n\in\mathbb{N}}$ generate a sequence of abstract states, $((I, \{w_i\}, \{p_{i,n}\}, \{E_{i,n}\}))$, that are visited in succession in an abstract execution. Now we have:

$$[\![\texttt{while}\ b\ \texttt{do}\ S]\!](I, \{w_i\}, \{p_i\}, \{E_i\}) = (I, \{w_i\}, \{p_i\}, \{\nabla((E_{i,n}^{\neg b})_{n\in\mathbb{N}})\})$$

where $\nabla((E_{i,n}^{\neg b})_{n\in\mathbb{N}})$ is a superset of $\bigcup_{n\in\mathbb{N}} E_{i,n} \cap [\![\neg b]\!]$. The concrete definition of $\nabla$ relies on a widening policy (see Section 3.2).

We can prove the following properties of the abstract domain. (For proofs, see the technical report version of the paper [7].)

**Theorem 1.** *Let $S$ be any* IMP *program. For each abstract state $\mathcal{A}$ and for $\mu \in \gamma(\mathcal{A})$, we have $[\![S]\!](\mu) \in \gamma([\![S]\!](\mathcal{A}))$.*

**Theorem 2.** *Consider an abstract state $(I, \{w_i\}, \{p_i\}, \{E_i\})$ such that for all $i \in I$ we have $p_i = 1$, and $\mu$ is a probability measure in the abstract state's concretization. Then $\mathbb{E}_\mu[x_k] \leq \sum_{i\in I} \sup(\delta_k E_i) w_i$, where $\delta_k$ is the function mapping $x$ to its $k^{th}$ component $x_k$, and $\sup(\delta_k E_i)$ is the supremum of the $k^{th}$ component over the set $E_i$.*

**Theorem 3.** *Let $A$ be an event, and $\mu$ a probability measure in the concretization of an abstract state $(I, \{w_i\}, \{p_i\}, \{E_i\})$. Then $\mathbb{P}_\mu[A] \leq \sum_{i\in IA} w_i$, where $IA = \{i \mid E_i \cap A \neq \emptyset\}$.*

The above theorems lead to a strategy for sound verification of probabilistic assertions $\varphi = (B, \theta)$. Given an input measure $\mu$, let us abstract $\mu$ into an abstract state $\mathcal{A}_\mu$, then use abstract interpretation to compute $[\![S]\!](\mathcal{A}_\mu) = (I, \{w_i\}, \{p_i\}, \{E_i\})$. Let us certify the program as satisfying $\varphi$ if $\sum_{i\in ID} w_i \leq \theta$, where $ID = \{i \mid E_i \cap [\![B]\!] \neq \emptyset\}$. From the above theorems, this strategy is sound — i.e., a program certified as satisfying $\varphi$ does, in fact, satisfy $\varphi$.

This strategy is used to implement Step 4 of the smoothed proof search algorithm (Algorithm 1). By the argument given above, we have:

**Theorem 4** (Soundness). *If Algorithm 1 returns a value $c^*$ of the missing parameters, then the implementation $S_{c^*}$ satisfies the assertion $\varphi$.*

***Ellipsoid Domain: Representing sets of points.*** The abstract domain described above assumes we have a representation of the sets $E_i$ that can be manipulated efficiently. Our algorithm represents these sets as *ellipsoids*, or $n$-dimensional generalizations of ellipses. This choice is a matter of pragmatics rather than fundamentals. The reason we use ellipsoids — as opposed to other natural choices like polytopes — is that they offer an attractive tradeoff between efficiency and precision. For instance, with ellipsoids, computing volumes (an essential step for us) is inexpensive, whereas for polytopes, volume computations are #P-hard. We note that efficiency considerations are especially important in our setting, where an abstract interpretation is performed on every query from the top-level numerical search routine, and the total number of calls to the abstract interpreter can be in the hundreds/thousands.

Formally, we represent each set $E_i$ as a collection of $N$-dimensional open ellipsoids $E_i = \{O_{i,j}\}$. Each ellipsoid is represented by a pair $O = \langle M, t\rangle$ of an invertible matrix and a vector. The pair represents a set of points defined as follows:

$$\langle M, t\rangle = \{x \mid \exists r.\ x = Mr + t \wedge \|r\| \leq 1\}.$$

We also have a special non-ellipsoid element $\top$, standing for $\mathbb{R}^n$.

The abstract semantics requires the following operations on the sets $E_i$: (1) computing the image of set under an affine transformation; (2) checking whether the intersection $E_i \cap [\![b]\!]$ for boolean tests $b$ is empty, and computing the sets $E_i^b$ and $E_i^{\neg b}$, (3) the subjoin operation, and (4) the $\nabla$ operator for loops.

Of these, affine transformations of ellipsoids can be performed exactly in most cases. The one exception is non-invertible assignments, which generate "flat" ellipsoids whose axes along some dimensions equal zero. Our algorithm overapproximates such ellipsoids by ones where each axis is nonzero. For the special case when an ellipsoid equals $\top$, the transformation returns $\top$.

For testing intersections, suppose $b$ equals ${}^t b_v \cdot x + b_o > 0$. Therefore, $[\![b]\!] \cap \langle M, t\rangle$ is nonempty iff $\exists r\ s.t.\ {}^t b_v(Mr+t)+b_o > 0 \wedge \|r\| = 1$. A solution for $r$ in the above equation will exist if and only if we have $\|{}^t M b_v\| + ({}^t b_v \cdot t + b_o) > 0$. By running this check, we can determine if the intersection is empty or not.

As for the sets $E_i^b$ and $E_i^{\neg b}$, we could retain soundness by setting them both to $E_i$. However, in practice, we achieve higher precision by setting $E_i^b$ and $E_i^{\neg b}$ to the *minimum-volume enclosing ellipsoids* (MVEEs) of the sets $E_i \cap [\![b]\!]$ and $E_i \cap [\![\neg b]\!]$, respectively. We can compute these MVEEs by symbolically transforming $E_i$ — we skip the details.

The subjoin operation is accomplished by simply concatenating the lists of ellipsoids from the two abstract states. If one of the arguments is $\top$, then it returns $\top$. Finally, the $\nabla$ operator for loops is defined via loop unrolling. We define the $\nabla$ operator in such a way that it is equivalent to replacing the loop by the unrolling of its $n_0$ first iterations, and to return $\top$ in the abstract for the branch corresponding to non-termination in $n_0$ iterations.

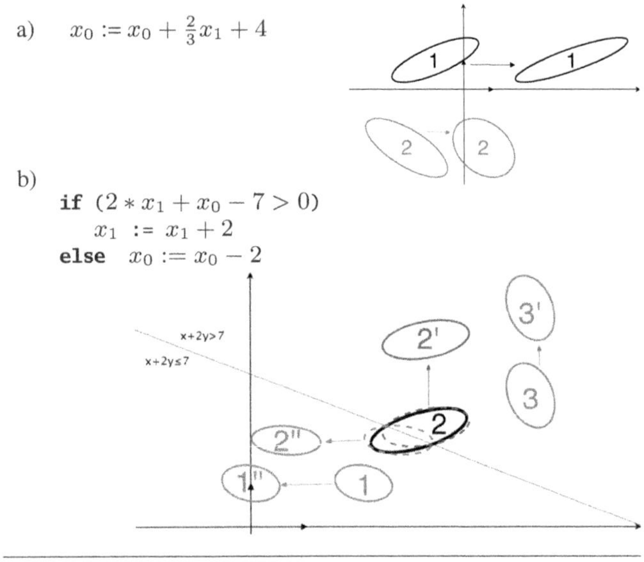


**Figure 3.** Effect of different statements on ellipsoid domain

Fig. 3 illustrates abstract interpretation using the above domain. Part (a) shows the way an assignment transforms an abstract state with two ellipsoids. Fig. 3-(b) shows the effect of an if-statement. The ellipsoid $E_2$ that straddles the boundary is split into two parts, with each part translated by the assignment in the corresponding branch. This means that at the join point, the set $E_2$ now comprises two ellipsoids, while the sets $E_1$ and $E_3$ still have one each.

### 3.2 Continuous approximation

The abstract domain described so far is sound but discontinuous: small changes to a program's inputs could lead to an arbitrarily large change to the expected output. Discontinuities mostly come from ellipsoids appearing and disappearing from the sets $E_i$. For example, in program (b) on figure Fig. 3, a small change to $x_0$ that caused ellipsoid 2 to fall entirely below the $x + 2y > 7$ line will cause ellipsoid $2'$ to suddenly vanish from final abstract state. This will result in a discontinuity of $\sup(\delta_0 E_2)$ relative to $x_0$ and therefore also in the bound computed for $\mathbb{E}[x_0]$. This is the same effect that was illustrated in the introduction with a one dimensional example where the ellipsoids become intervals.

Now we give a domain called *smooth ellipsoids* that provides a continuous, unsound approximation of the above domain. We call the abstract semantics under the smooth ellipsoids domain the *smooth semantics* $[\![\cdot]\!]_\beta$. As stated earlier, the approximation is parameterized by a value $\beta$ that controls the degree of smoothing. As $\beta$ approaches zero, the domain converges to the sound domain of Section 3.1.

Compared to the original domain, the smooth ellipsoids domain now associates with each ellipsoid in the set $E_i$ a measure $\alpha_{i,j} \in [0, 1]$ that reflects how close each ellipsoid is from disappearing. Specifically, each $E_i$ now corresponds to a multiset $E_i = \{(O_{i,j}, \alpha_{i,j})\}$. The smooth semantics $[\![\cdot]\!]_\beta$ will modify $O_{i,j}$ as before; the $\alpha_{i,j}$ will be initialized to one for all ellipsoids and will be unaffected by assignments but modified by branches. For example, the rule for if-statements will now be as follows:

$$\begin{aligned}&[\![\texttt{if}\ b\ \texttt{then}\ S_1 \texttt{else}\ S_2]\!]_\beta(I, \{w_i\}, \{p_i\}, \{(O_{i,j}, \alpha_{i,j})\}) = \\ &\quad [\![S_1]\!]_\beta(I, \{w_i\}, \{p_i^b\}, \{(O_{i,j}, \rho_\beta(O_{i,j}, b) * \alpha_{i,j})\}) \\ &\quad\quad \sqcup [\![S_2]\!]_\beta(I, \{w_i\}, \{p_i^{\neg b}\}, \{(O_{i,j}, \rho_\beta(O_{i,j}, \neg b) * \alpha_{i,j})\}).\end{aligned}$$

The $\sqcup$ operation at the end of the if-statement will be computed as before, by taking the union of the sets of ellipsoids for each $E_i$ for which $p_i$ is not zero. As for $\rho_\beta$, it is a special continuous function. Because the arguments of $\rho_\beta$ are sets, its continuity needs to be defined with respect to a metric on sets. We choose this metric to be the *Hausdorff metric*, defined below:

**Definition 4** (Hausdorff distance)**.** Let $A$ and $B$ be two non-empty subsets of $\mathbb{R}^n$. The Hausdorff distance $D_H(A, B)$ between $A$ and $B$ is defined by

$$D_H(A, B) = \inf_{r \in \mathbb{R}^+} \{A \subseteq B_r \wedge B \subseteq A_r\}$$

where $A_r$ is defined as $\{x | \exists y \in A : ||x - y|| \leq r\}$. In other words, the distance between $A$ and $B$ is the smallest $r$ such that if we draw a halo of width $r$ around $A$, the halo will contain $B$, and if we draw a halo of width $r$ around $B$, the halo will contain $A$.

Formally, the function $\rho_\beta$ is a function with the following properties:

- $\rho_\beta$ is continuous with respect to the Hausdorff distance.
- $\rho_\beta(O_{i,j}, b) = \begin{cases} 0 & \text{if } O_{i,j} \cap [\![b]\!] = \emptyset \\ 1 & \text{if } O_{i,j} \subseteq [\![b]\!]. \end{cases}$
- As $\beta$ approaches zero, $\rho_\beta$ should smoothly approximate the following function:

$$\rho_0(O_{i,j}, b) = \begin{cases} 0 & \text{if } O_{i,j} \cap [\![b]\!] = \emptyset \\ 1 & \text{otherwise.} \end{cases}$$

- $O_x \cap [\![b]\!] \subseteq O_y \cap [\![b]\!] \Rightarrow \rho_\beta(O_x, b) \leq \rho_\beta(O_y, b)$
- For all invertible affine transformations $f$,

$$\rho_\beta(f(O_x), b \circ f^{-1}) = \rho_\beta(O_x, b).$$

In other words, $\rho_\beta$ is stable under affine transformation.

(The last requirement is not needed by our proofs, but expresses the fact that we do not want our abstraction to behave differently over programs that are affine transformations of each other.)

The properties imply that if $p_x$ is equal to zero in an abstract state $(I, \{w_i\}, \{p_i\}, \{(O_{i,j}, \alpha_{i,j})\})$, then all the $\alpha_{x,j}$ will be equal to zero as well because the condition under which $p_i$ becomes zero are the same as those under which $\rho_\beta$ becomes zero.

There are many functions that satisfy the above criteria for $\rho_\beta$. A natural choice, which we use in practice, is

$$\rho_\beta(O, b) = \begin{cases} \min(1, \frac{V(O \cap [\![b]\!])}{f(\beta)V(O)}) & \text{if } O \text{ is finite} \\ 1 - f(\beta) & \text{if } O \text{ is the universal set} \end{cases}$$

where $f(\beta) = \min(1/2, \lambda\beta)$ and $\lambda$ is a constant parameter. Here, $V(S)$ stands for the $n$-dimensional volume of a subset $S$ of $\mathbb{R}^n$.

***Initial distribution*** A sketch $S_c(x)$ takes two different kinds of inputs: $x$ and $c$. The initial distribution for inputs $x$ is known and is given as part of the problem definition, but $c$ is unknown. Previous work on smooth interpretation [8] showed that as the search algorithms tries different values $c^i$ for parameter $c$, it can get better information about the function to be optimized by executing on a distribution centered at $c^i$. In our context, this means that the initial distribution must be a product between the initial input distribution $\mu$ and a distribution $\mu_{(c_i,\beta)}$ centered at $c_i$ and with variance proportional to $\beta$. Since we are interested in an abstraction of $\mu \times \mu_{(c_i,\beta)}$, we need a sound product operation over abstract states. In general, this is defined as

$$\begin{aligned}\mathcal{A}_\mu \times \mathcal{A}_{\mu_{(c_i,\beta)}} &= (I, w_i^a, p_i^a, E_i^a) \times (J, w_j^b, p_j^b, E_j^b) = \\ &\quad (I \times J, w_i^a w_j^b, p_i^a p_j^b, E_i^a \times E_j^b).\end{aligned}$$

However, ellipsoids are not closed under cross product; *e.g.* in the one dimensional case, the product of two ellipsoids $[-a, a]$ and $[-b, b]$ is a rectangle. Instead of overapproximating this rectangle with a bigger ellipsoid, we actually underapproximate it by the largest ellipsoid enclosed by the rectangle. This is unsound in general, but it becomes sound in the limit as $\beta$ approaches zero.

As for $\mathcal{A}_{\mu_{(c_i,\beta)}}$, for our experiments, we use

$$\mathcal{A}_{\mu_{(c_i,\beta)}} = (\{0\}, \{w_0 = 1\}, \{p_0 = 1\}, \{E_0^{(c_i,\beta)}\})$$

where $E_0^{(c_i,\beta)}$ is the sphere centered at $c_i$ with radius $\beta$.

***Continuity of*** $[\![\cdot]\!]_\beta$ Now we establish the continuity of our domain. For space reasons, we only offer a proof sketch of the central theorem behind this property. Full proofs are available in the technical report version of the paper [7].

In order to prove continuity, we first need to define a distance metric $D(\mathcal{A}^a, \mathcal{A}^b)$ between two abstract states $\mathcal{A}^a = (I^a, \{w_i^a\}, \{p_i^a\}, \{E_i^a\})$ and $\mathcal{A}^b = (I^b, \{w_j^b\}, \{p_j^b\}, \{E_i^b\})$, where the sets $E$ are represented as weighted sets of ellipsoids $E_i^x = \{(O_{i,j}^x, \alpha_{i,j}^x)\}$ as discussed earlier.

**Definition 5** (Distance)**.** We define the distance to be $\infty$ between two abstract states with different index sets or different $w_i^x$. When index sets and $w_i^x$ are identical, the distance $D(\mathcal{A}^a, \mathcal{A}^b)$ between two abstract states is defined by the following equation:

$$\max_i \min_{\sigma_i} \sum_j D((O_{i,j}^a, \alpha_{i,j}^a), (O_{i,\sigma_i(j)}^b, \alpha_{i,\sigma_i(j)}^b))$$

where the $\sigma_i$-s are bijective functions. The distance between two weighted ellipsoids is defined in terms of the Hausdorff distance $D_H$ between ellipsoids.

$$D((O^a, \alpha^a), (O^b, \alpha^b)) = \min(D_H(O^a, O^b) + |\alpha^a - \alpha^b|, \max(\alpha^a, \alpha^b)).$$

The definition assumes without loss of generality that matching $E_i$ are represented by the same number of ellipsoids. If this is not the case, we pad with extra ellipsoids with $\alpha = 0$. The choice of the extra ellipsoid does not affect the distance measure because when one of the alphas, say $\alpha^a$ equals zero, the distance $D((O^a, \alpha^a), (O^b, \alpha^b))$ always equals the other alpha $\alpha^b$ irrespective of $O^a$.

At a high-level, given two abstract states with matching index sets, the definition above computes the distance for each index independently and returns the minimum over all of them. For a given index, the distance function tries to produce the best match between ellipsoids in one state and ellipsoids in the other. For each pair of ellipsoids and their alphas, the distance is dictated by the magnitude of the alphas when the ellipsoids are far apart, and by the distance between the ellipsoids when the ellipsoids are very close together.

Our continuity theorem requires the introduction of an additional technical condition known as *boundedness*.

**Definition 6** (Bounded states)**.** Let $B$ be an Euclidean ball; an abstract state is $B$-bounded if $O_{i,j} \subseteq B$ for all finite ellipsoids $O_{i,j}$ with non-zero measure $\alpha_{i,j}$ that are part of the abstract state. A set of abstract states is bounded if all the abstract states in the set are $B$-bounded for some Euclidian ball $B$.

The boundedness condition in the definition of continuity is there because of the previously mentioned property that when distances between ellipsoids are large, the distance metric is dominated by alpha. This means that for any $\epsilon$ it is possible to find states that are $\epsilon$-close to $\mathcal{A}^E$ but whose ellipsoids are arbitrarily far and such states could violate the continuity property. Such states, lying outside the $B$-ball, however, are not relevant from the point of view of smoothed proof search, so this definition of continuity is sufficient for us.

Now we establish that the abstract semantic function $[\![\cdot]\!]_\beta$ is continuous over bounded sets.

**Theorem 5.** *For any ball $B$, any $\epsilon$ and any $B$-bounded $\mathcal{A}^E$ there exists a $\delta$ such that for all $B$-bounded $\mathcal{A}^F$,*

$$D(\mathcal{A}^E, \mathcal{A}^F) < \delta \Rightarrow D([\![S]\!]_\beta(\mathcal{A}^E), [\![S]\!]_\beta(\mathcal{A}^F)) < \epsilon.$$

*Also, the abstract semantics maps bounded sets to bounded sets.*

*Proof.* (Sketch). We only prove the theorem for loop-free programs. The proof is by induction on the execution of the abstract interpretation. The base case corresponds to assignments; as assignments are linear, the property clearly holds for them.

The interesting inductive case corresponds to conditionals. Let $B$ be any euclidean ball, $\epsilon$ any positive real, and $(I, \{w_i\}, \{p_i\}, \{E_i\})$ be any $B$-bounded abstract state. We have

$$\begin{aligned}[\![\texttt{if } b \texttt{ then } S_1 \texttt{ else } S_2]\!]_\beta(I, \{w_i\}, \{p_i\}, \{E_i\}) = \\ [\![S_1]\!]_\beta(I, \{w_i\}, \{p_i^b\}, \{E_i^b\}) \sqcup \\ [\![S_2]\!]_\beta(I, \{w_i\}, \{p_i^{\neg b}\}, \{E^{\neg b}\})\end{aligned}$$

where $E_i^b$ is defined as $\{((O_{i,j}^E)^b, \rho_\beta(O_{i,j}, b) * \alpha_{i,j}^E)\}$ from $E_i = \{(0_{i,j}^E, \alpha_{i,j}^E)\}$.

By the induction hypothesis, $[\![S_1]\!]_\beta$ and $[\![S_2]\!]_\beta$ are continuous maps from bounded sets to bounded sets. So we only need prove this property for $\sqcup$ and the functions $(I, \{w_i\}, \{p_i\}, \{E_i\}) \rightarrow (I, \{w_i\}, \{p_i^{b'}\}, \{E_i^{b'}\})$, where $b' \in \{b, \neg b\}$.

Let us first focus on $\sqcup$. The only possible source of discontinuity comes from the fact that we only merge components with $p_i \neq 0$. However, when $p_i = 0$, every $\alpha_{i,j} = 0$, so distance between union with and without this component is 0. So it is equivalent to componentwise multiset union, which is obviously continuous over the pairs of abstract states. Moreover, if both abstract states are $B_1$-bounded and $B_2$-bounded, then resulting abstract states is $B$-bounded for any ball $B$ enclosing both $B_1$ and $B_2$. Since such a ball exists those properties are true for $\sqcup$.

Thus, we only need to prove that the transformation $(I, \{w_i\}, \{p_i\}, \{E_i\}) \mapsto (I, \{w_i\}, \{p_i^b\}, \{E_i^b\})$ maps bounded sets to bounded sets and is continuous over them. The `else` branch case is symmetrical.

The first property directly follows from properties of Minimum Volume Enclosing Ellipsoids (MVEEs). For a full-dimensional convex set $S$, $\frac{1}{n} MVEE(S) \subseteq S \subseteq MVEE(S)$. Since our resulting ellipsoids are MVEEs of subsets of a common ball, they are included inside this ball scaled by a factor $n$ around its center.

As for the second property, we note that the intersection operation between a convex-set and a half-space is continuous with respect to the Hausdorff distance. Moreover, one can show that the function that computes MVEEs is continuous with respect to Hausdorff distance on full-dimensional sets, so $O_{i,j} \rightarrow O_{i,j}^b$ is continuous on ellipsoids intersecting $[\![b]\!]$.

Now, let us restrict to a distance $\delta$ small enough such that any ellipsoid $\delta$-close to some $O_{i,j}^E$ that intersects $[\![b]\!]$, also intersects $[\![b]\!]$. A value $\delta$ satisfies this property if for every $O_{i,j} \cap [\![b]\!]$, the furthest point of $b$ hyperplane is at least $\delta$ far from it, so such a $\delta$ exists. We then restrict this distance to be lower than one so index sets and weights must be identical.

Let $(I, \{w_i\}, \{q_i\}, \{F_i\})$ be any $B$-bounded abstract state with distance lower than $\delta$ from $(I, \{w_i\}, \{p_i\}, \{E_i\})$. By definition of distance, we have

$$\begin{aligned}D((I, \{w_i\}, \{p_i\}, \{E_i\}), (I, \{w_i\}, \{q_i\}, \{F_i\})) = \\ \max_i \sum_j D((O_{i,j}^E, \alpha_{i,j}^E), (O_{i,j}^F, \alpha_{i,j}^F)).\end{aligned}$$

Here we assume, without loss of generality, an indexing for sets $E_i$ and $F_i$ such that minimum over bijective functions are reached at identity maps. Then

$$D((I,\{w_i\},\{p_i^b\},\{E_i^b\}),(I,\{w_i\},\{q_i^b\},\{F_i^b\})) \leq \max_i \sum_j D(((O_{i,j}^E)^b, \alpha_{i,j}^E * \rho_\beta(O_{i,j}^E,b)), ((O_{i,j}^F)^b, \alpha_{i,j}^F * \rho_\beta(O_{i,j}^F,b)).$$

In the above, in order to simplify notation, $(O_{i,j}^E)^b$ is defined as any padding ellipsoid when $O_{i,j}^E$ do not intersect $[\![b]\!]$. This is justified by corresponding $\alpha_{i,j}^E * \rho_\beta(O_{i,j}^E, b)$ being zero.

To complete the proof (for the loop-free case), we only need to show how to construct a $\delta_g$ such that for any such $B$-bounded $(I,\{w_i\},\{q_i\},\{F_i\})$,

$$D((I,\{w_i\},\{p_i\},\{E_i\}),(I,\{w_i\},\{q_i\},\{F_i\})) < \delta_g \Rightarrow D((I,\{w_i\},\{p_i^b\},\{E_i^b\}),(I,\{w_i\},\{q_i^b\},\{F_i^b\})) < \epsilon.$$

This construction is somewhat involved and hence we skip it. Interested readers will find the details in the technical report version of the paper [7]. □

***Smooth expectation and probability*** The measures $\alpha_{i,j}$ are used to compute a smooth approximation of the expected value. Recall that a sound upper approximation of the expected error can be computed as follows:

$$\mathbb{E}[x_k] \leq \sum_{i\in I}(\sup(\delta_k E_i))w_i.$$

In the smooth approximation of this expression, we use the following expression in place of $\sup((\delta_k E_i))$:

$$\mathbb{E}_\beta^\#(k,(I,\{w_i\},\{p_i\},\{E_i\})) = \sum_{i\in I} wsup_\beta(k,\{(O_{i,j},\alpha_{i,j})\})w_i$$

The function $wsup_\beta$ is defined as follows. First, let $S_i = [(b_{i,l}, \alpha_{i,\lfloor \frac{l}{2}\rfloor})]$ be a list that contains the supremums and infimums of every $\delta_k O_{i,j}$ with their respective measures; *i.e.*, $b_{i,2*j}$ is the supremum and $b_{i,2*j+1}$ the infimum of coordinate $k$ of ellipsoid $O_{i,j}$ and they are both associated with $\alpha_{i,j}$.

The function $wsup_\beta$ is defined in terms of $S_i$ as follows.

$$wsup_\beta(k,E_i) = \frac{\sum_l \alpha_{i,\lfloor \frac{l}{2}\rfloor} * b_{i,l} * e^{\frac{b_{i,l}}{\beta}}}{\sum_l \alpha_{i,\lfloor \frac{l}{2}\rfloor} * e^{\frac{b_{i,l}}{\beta}}}$$

Note that as $\beta$ approaches $\infty$, the function reduces to a weighted average of ellipsoid centers weighted by $\alpha_i$. In the limit as $\beta$ approaches zero, on the other hand, the function converges to the supremum. This can be seen by considering the equivalent formula

$$wsup_\beta(k,E_i) = \frac{\sum_l \alpha_{i,\lfloor \frac{l}{2}\rfloor} * b_{i,l} * e^{\frac{b_{i,l}-b_{max}}{\beta}}}{\sum_l \alpha_{i,\lfloor \frac{l}{2}\rfloor} * e^{\frac{b_{i,l}-b_{max}}{\beta}}}$$

where $b_{max}$ is the maximum of the $b_{i,l}$, i.e the actual supremum. When $\beta$ is close to 0, all the exponential coefficients will converge to zero except for the ones where $b_{i,l} = b_{max}$, so the result will converge to $b_{max}$.

Note that the universals elements should have special handling here. Instead of using $b_{i,l} * e^{\frac{b_{i,l}}{\beta}}$ factors as for other ellipsoids on the numerator, we use $f(\alpha_{i,l})$, where $f$ is an increasing continuous function with the properties that $f(0) = 0$ and $f(1) = \infty$. On the denominator, $e^{\frac{b_{i,l}}{\beta}}$ are removed for universal elements.

A smooth approximation to an upper bound on the probability of an event, specified as an affine boolean expression $b$, is defined in a similar way:

$$\mathbb{P}_\beta^\#([\![b]\!]) = \sum_{i\in I} w_i * \sum_j \alpha_{i,j} * \rho_\beta(O_{i,j},b)$$

From the definition of these bounds and from Theorem 5, we have:

**Theorem 6.** *For each $\beta > 0$, the expressions $\mathbb{E}_\beta^\#$ and $\mathbb{P}_\beta^\#$ are continuous over bounded sets of abstract states.*

This in turn implies the continuity requirement that we demanded in Section 3:

**Theorem 7** (Continuity of $\Phi_\beta^\#$ and $\Delta_\beta^\#$). *Assuming programs are abstracted using smooth ellipsoids and that the abstraction of the initial distribution is $B$-bounded for some $B$, the functions $\Phi_\beta^\#(c)$ and $\Delta_\beta^\#(c)$ in Algorithm 1 are continuous.*

**Example 6.** To illustrate the effect of $\alpha$, consider the following 1D example where ellipsoids become intervals. Consider two abstract states that are relatively close to each other

$$A_1 = (I = \{0,1\}, \{w_0 = 0.4, w_1 = 0.6\}, \{p_0 = 1.0, p_1 = 1.0\}, \{E_0 = ([0,1], 1.0), E_1 = ([2,3], 1.0)\})$$
$$A_2 = (I = \{0,1\}, \{w_0 = 0.4, w_1 = 0.6\}, \{p_0 = 1.0, p_1 = 1.0\}, \{E_0 = ([0,0.99], 1.0), E_1 = ([2,3], 1.0)\})$$

Now, consider the following code

```
if (x > 0.99) { x = x + 5; } else { x = x - 5; }
```

In the original discontinuous domain, the state at the end of the conditional would be:

$$[\![P]\!](A_1) = (I = \{0,1\}, \{w_0 = 0.4, w_1 = 0.6\}, \{p_0 = 1.0, p_1 = 1.0\}, \{E_0 = [-5,-4.01] \cup (5.99, 6], E_1 = [7,8]\})$$
$$[\![P]\!](A_2) = (I = \{0,1\}, \{w_0 = 0.4, w_1 = 0.6\}, \{p_0 = 1.0, p_1 = 1.0\}, \{E_0 = [-5,-4.01], E_1 = [7,8]\})$$

That means that under $A_1$, the upper bound on the expected value will be $0.4 * 6 + 0.6 * 8 = 7.2$, whereas the under the slightly different $A_2$, the upper bound on the expected value is now $0.4 * -4.1 + 0.6 * 8 = 3.16$.

By contrast, under the continuous domain using $\beta = 10$, the abstract states at the end of the program will be:

$$[\![P]\!](A_1) = (I = \{0,1\}, \{w_0 = 0.4, w_1 = 0.6\}, \{p_0 = 1.0, p_1 = 1.0\}, \{E_0 = \{([-5,-4.01],1), ((5.99,6], 0.01)\}, E_1 = ([7,8], 1.0)\})$$
$$[\![P]\!](A_2) = (I = \{0,1\}, \{w_0 = 0.4, w_1 = 0.6\}, \{p_0 = 1.0, p_1 = 1.0\}, \{E_0 = ([-5,-4.01], 1.0), E_1 = ([7,8], 1.0)\})$$

This means that the smooth upper bound over the expected value for $[\![P]\!](A_1)$ will now be

$$0.4 * \frac{1.0 * -5 * e^{-0.5} + 1.0 * -4.01 * e^{-0.401} + 0.01 * 5.99 * e^{0.599} + 0.01 * 6 * e^{0.6}}{1.0 * e^{-0.5} + 1.0 * e^{-0.401} + 0.01 * e^{0.599} + 0.01 * e^{0.6}} + 0.6 * \frac{7 * e^{0.7} + 8 * e^{0.8}}{e^{0.7} + e^{0.8}} = 2.87$$

and for $[\![P]\!](A_2)$ it will now be

$$0.4 * \frac{-5 * e^{-0.5} + -4.01 * e^{-0.401}}{e^{-0.5} + e^{-0.401}} + 0.6 * \frac{7 * e^{0.7} + 8 * e^{0.8}}{e^{0.7} + e^{0.8}} = 2.76$$

so whereas the original sound approximation was discontinuous, the smoothed approximation changes only slightly when we make a small change to the input distribution. As $\beta$ decreases, however, the smooth approximation approaches the sound bound, so for example, with $\beta = 1$, the approximate bounds will be 7.02 and 2.92 respectively.

***Conservative merges and widening*** One problem with the domain presented so far is that the representation of each $E_i$ as a set of ellipsoids can potentially double in size after every `if`-statement. The partial order in the discontinuous domain gives us some leeway to define less precise merge functions that prevent some of this blowup. For example, multiple ellipsoids can be replaced by a single one that cover all of them without losing soundness. In the case of the smooth domain, however, such an operation can potentially introduce discontinuity. Our approach described in this section follows the same strategy we followed to achieve continuity in the original semantics. Namely, we introduce a smooth join operation, and show that the abstract semantics using the parameterized join are continuous. Moreover, as $\beta$ goes to zero (and every $\alpha$ converges to one), the operation converges to a sound join operation.

In order to define join, we define an operation $wcover(\{(O_i, \alpha_i)\})$. The function's input is a non-empty multiset of weighted ellipsoids. Each ellipsoid $O_i = \langle M_i, c_i\rangle$ is represented by a matrix-vector pair as described earlier. The output $(O_{out}, \alpha_{out})$ is a single weighted ellipsoid with the following properties :

$$\alpha_{out} = min(\sum_i \alpha_i, 1)$$
$$\alpha_i = 1 \Rightarrow O_i \subseteq O_{out}.$$

In order to define $wcover$, we first define a function $wadjust$ which adjust the size and position of each ellipsoid based on its weight. The output $O_i'$ is defined as follows. Let $c_{out} = \frac{\sum_i \alpha_i c_i}{\sum_i \alpha_i}$ be the center of gravity of ellipsoid centers. Then,

$$O_i' = (\alpha_i' * M_i, \alpha_i' * c_i + (1 - \alpha_i') * c_{out})$$

where $\alpha_i' = \frac{\alpha_i}{\max \alpha_i}$. Note that the uniform center of gravity of resulting center is now $c_{out}$. The ellipsoid $O_{out}$ produced by $wcover$ is then the Minimum Volume Enclosing Ellipsoid (MVEE) of the ellipsoids $O_i'$. The computation of MVEE is performed using an adaptation of an algorithm by Jambawalikar and Kumar [15].

Fig. 4 illustrates the merge process. Here, consider the ellipsoids labeled 2, $2'$, and $2''$. For ellipsoids $2'$ and $2''$, $\alpha < 1$; therefore, during the merge they are "shrunk" to the small, purple ellipsoids. Ellipsoid 2 does not shrink as $\alpha = 1$ for it. Now we compute the MVEE of 2, $2'$, and $2''$, leading to the dashed red ellipsoid. This is the output of the merge. A similar process applies to ellipsoids 1, $1'$, and $1''$.

The universal elements are handled differently: they are combined in a single universal element, with $\alpha_i$ combined as before.

Now, let us add to our language a statement $ABSTRACT$, whose concrete semantics are equivalent to $skip$ and whose abstract semantics is defined as follows:

$$[\![ABSTRACT]\!]((I, \{w_i\}, \{p_i\}, \{E_i\})) = (I, \{w_i\}, \{p_i\}, \{wcover(E_i)\}).$$

We can prove that $[\![ABSTRACT]\!]$ satisfies the inductive hypothesis of Theorem 5. Furthermore, this is obviously sound on the discontinuous domain.

**Theorem 8** (Continuity of conservative merge). *$[\![ABSTRACT]\!]$ maps bounded set of abstract states to bounded sets and is continuous over bounded set of abstract states.*

In that case, Theorem 5 is preserved even if we add the conservative merge operation $ABSTRACT$ to our language. Now we do the same for loops. To get loops to converge, we need a widening strategy. Our strategy is very simple. After a constant number of iterations, we widen our representation to the universal element, then apply $[\![ABSTRACT]\!]$. To be precise, we replace every ellipsoid representation by the universal element before applying $[\![ABSTRACT]\!]$.

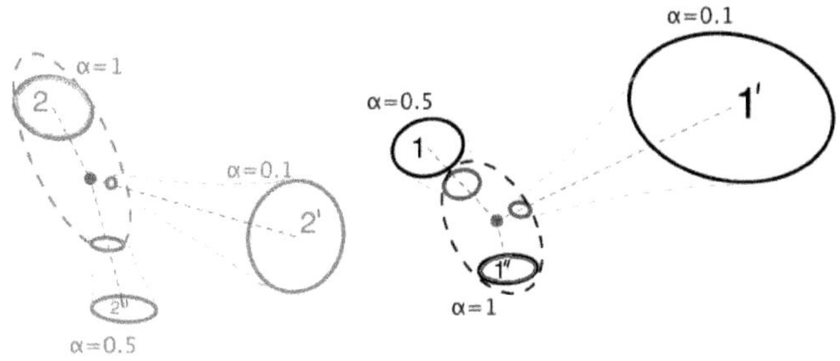


**Figure 4.** Merge process

Note that this strategy is equivalent to peeling the first $k$ iterations of the loop and then replacing the rest of the loop with the statement $WIDEN$(`while` $b$ `do` $S$) followed by $ABSTRACT$. This transformation preserves the concrete semantics and is sound for the discontinuous abstract semantics. We show that it does not break the continuity of the smooth semantics by showing that:

**Theorem 9** (Continuity of widening). *$[\![WIDEN(\texttt{while}\ b\ \texttt{do}\ S)]\!]$ is continuous over abstract states and maps bounded sets to bounded sets.*

## 4. Implementation and evaluation

We conducted two case studies using our implementation of FERMAT. The case studies both come from the embedded control domain, and include the thermostat controller introduced in Section 2, and a model of an aircraft collision avoidance maneuver [24].

FERMAT uses the SKETCH program synthesis infrastructure [31] to parse sketches into an AST which is then translated into a C++ program that implements the smooth abstract semantics described earlier. For numerical search, FERMAT uses the Nelder-Mead simplex search [22] available in GNU Scientific Library (GSL) as the underlying local optimization method.

Our two case studies were designed to help answer the following questions:

1. *Does our algorithm really compute better-quality parameters (i.e., parameters that lead to a lower upper bounds on average-case error) than those computed by regular numerical search?* Note that the outcome of any local search routine depends on the starting point of the search, and we cannot expect our algorithm to perform better than the competing approach on *all* starting points. Instead, it is the *distribution* of the expected error value, across starting points, that should interest us. The question is whether this distribution skews to lower expected error values.
2. *In practice, what are the "highest-quality" proofs that the algorithm can find?*

   Consider a probabilistic assertion $(B; 1 - \theta)$, which states that "$B$ is violated with probability $< \theta$". As $\theta$ becomes smaller, one would expect the task of finding parameters that provably satisfy this assertion to get harder. The question is to find the lowest value of $\theta$ (an "upper bound on the probability of assertion failure") for which different synthesis algorithms can find a parameter meeting this proof goal. Naturally, this bound depends on the start point of the search. The question is whether the distribution of the bounds computed using our algorithm is better than the distribution one would get running a less sophisticated technique.
3. *In our method, a search for optimal parameters is interleaved with a search for a boolean proof. Is this really needed, or could*

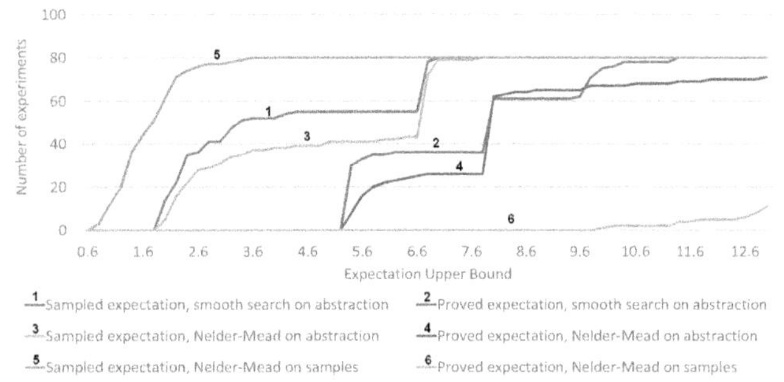


**Figure 5.** CDF for upper bound on the expected value of the fitness function for the Thermostat experiment.

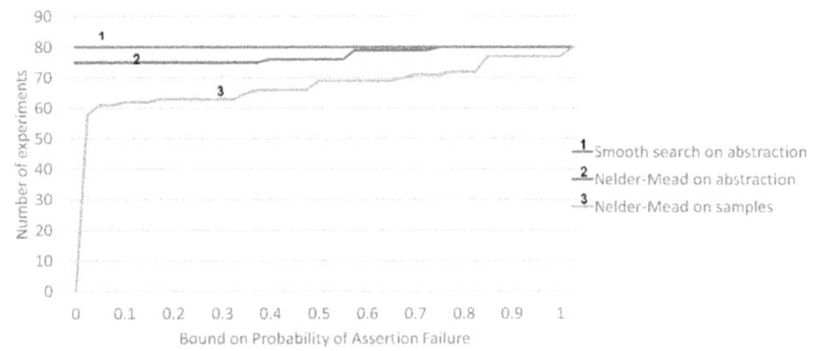


**Figure 6.** CDF for upper bound on the probability of assertion failure for the Thermostat experiment.

*we first find optimal program parameters* and then *establish the boolean goal for these parameters?*

For each of the two case studies, we compared three different approaches for parameter synthesis:

- **Smoothed Proof Search** is the algorithm described in this paper, where the synthesizer is using smoothed numerical search to find parameters that allow it to jointly optimize the expected fitness and the probability of assertion failure.
- **Nelder-Mead with Abstract Interpretation** uses a standard Nelder-Mead numerical search to jointly optimize the expected fitness and the probability of assertion failure as computed by the non-smoothed abstract interpretation presented earlier.
- **Nelder-Mead with Sampling** also tries to jointly optimize the expected fitness and the probability of assertion failure, but computes these by running the program on a fixed sample of inputs drawn from the input distribution.

Using each of these approaches, we solved the parameter synthesis problem for the two problems 80 different times from different random starting points in order to get a representative sample of the distribution of solutions that each of these three methods can produce. The results of these experiments are summarized in Figures 5, 6, 7 and 8. The rest of this section describes each of the benchmarks individually and discusses the results.

### Thermostat

Recall our thermostat example, where the goal is to shift the temperature of a room from an initial temperature `lin` to a target temperature `ltarget`, and the sketch to be completed is as in Fig. 2. Here, `lin` and `target` are both probabilistic inputs. The distribution of `lin` is trimodal and bell-shaped with modes centered at 30, 35, and 50 and spread $\pm 3$. The distribution of `ltarget` is unimodal and bell-shaped, with mean 75 and spread $\pm 1$. The parameters to be synthesized are the temperatures `tOn` and `tOff` at which the heater respectively switches off and on, and the heat h released in a time step. Our safety property states that `tOn` is lower than `tOff` with high probability, and sets limits on the temperature of the room.

Note that the code in the figure permits variables of discrete types. This is syntactic sugar. When such a variable depends on the inputs, we just cast it to a real. Otherwise, the compiler encodes it using control flow—for example, the variable `i` in Fig. 2 is eliminated by unrolling the main loop to a depth of 40.

Fig. 5 shows the cumulative distribution function for the expected value of the fitness function for the thermostat example for each of the three methods above. For each of these methods, we computed the expected value in two ways: a) for the lines labeled "Sampled expectation" we computed the expected fitness by running the synthesized algorithms on a random sample of inputs. And b) for the lines labeled "Proved expectation" we plotted the upper bound of the expected value as computed with abstract interpretation. Fig. 6, shows the probability of assertion failure as proved by abstract interpretation for the solutions generated by the three methods. Together these two graphs allow us to answer the three questions as they apply to the thermostat benchmark.

The results are surprising at first sight; Fig. 5 shows that Nelder-Mead with sampling is able to produce parameters with better average fitness than any of the methods that rely on abstract interpretation, whether smoothed or not. However, while the parameters led to good behavior in practice, the resulting implementations were difficult to analyze, leading to the huge gap between their empirically observed behavior and the probabilities that can be proved for these implementations. This is reinforced by Fig. 6; for the methods where the search used abstract interpretation, the proved probability of assertion failure was close to zero for most instances; by contrast, of the implementations generated by Nelder-Mead there were 60 that had probabilities of failure greater than 2.5%, and a full 10 that had probabilities of failure higher than 50

Of the two methods that use the results of abstract interpretation, we find that smoothed numerical proof was able to produce better results both in terms of their empirically evaluated fitness as well as in the bounds on the expected fitness can prove. The differences are not very big, but they are statistically significant. Using the Wilcoxon signed-rank test, we computed a p-value of 0.027 for the for the expectation upper bound determined empirically and a p-value of less than 0.01 for the proved bounds respectively, supporting the hypothesis that smoothing helped us find better parameters. In the case of the probability of assertion failure, the difference between smooth and non-smooth search was not statistically significant (p-value of 0.25). So in short, we were able to find good bounds for the probability of failure (Question 2), and the use of smoothing had an effect on the fitness of the solutions we got, but not on the probability of assertion failure (Question 1).

### Aircraft collision avoidance

In this problem, we want to synthesize parameters for an airplane that performs maneuvers to avoid a collision with a second plane [24]. The controller has four control states called *CRUISE*, *LEFT*, *STRAIGHT*, and *RIGHT*. Normally, our plane flies in the *CRUISE* control state. If it gets within a distance $\delta(\texttt{x1}, \texttt{y1}, \texttt{x2}, \texttt{y2}) < \texttt{criticalDist}$ of the other plane, then it starts flying left (in the *LEFT* state) at an angle of 45°, continuing for `delay` number of timesteps. Then it flies *STRAIGHT* for a while. After `delay2` steps it turns *RIGHT*, comes back to its original course, and changes state back to *CRUISE* (see Fig. 10).

Our error value here is the total delay, as in an idealized setting, our airplane returns to its course immediately. Our safety assertions set a minimum distance between the two planes, and ensure that the plane does not start the maneuver too early or too late.

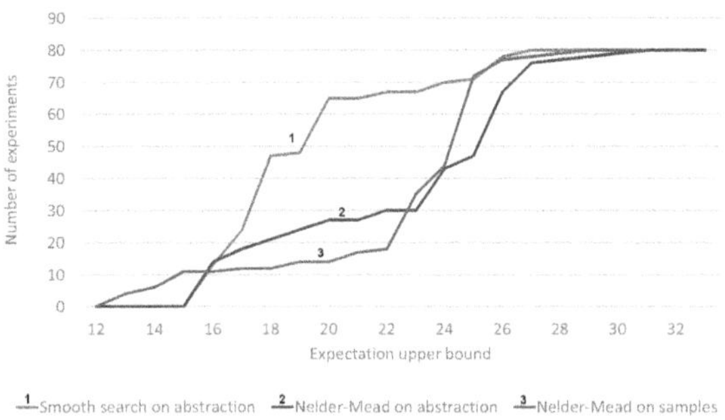


**Figure 7.** CDF for upper bound on the fitness function for the Aircraft experiment.

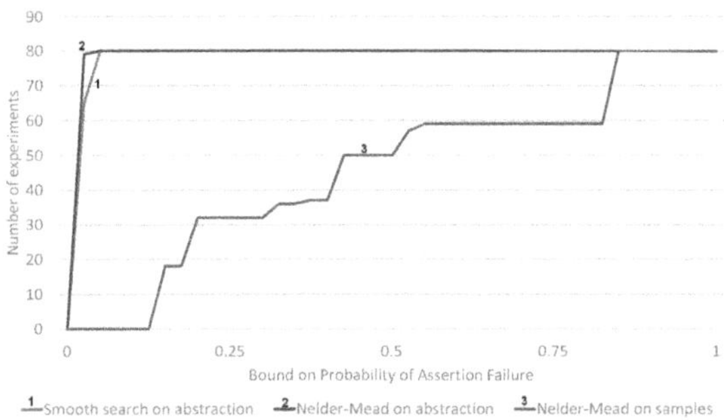


**Figure 8.** CDF for upper bound on the probability of assertion failure Aircraft experiment.

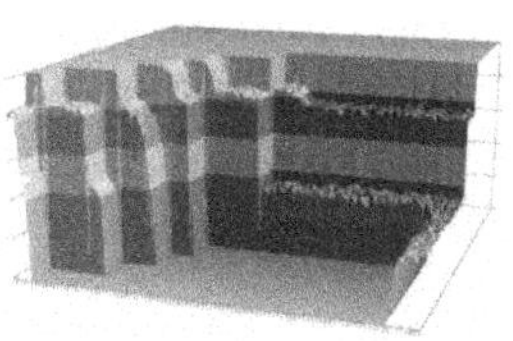

**Figure 9.** Landscape of safe and unsafe states (lower values imply lower probability of assertion failure)

A sketch of this controller is provided in Fig. 10. Here, the probabilistic inputs are the initial velocities of the two planes. The distribution of the velocity `v1` of our plane is unimodal with mean 8 and spread $\pm 0.1$; that of the other plane is trimodal with modes centered at 7, 8, and 8.5 and spreads 0.3, 0.4, and 0.2 respectively. Our goal is to synthesize values for the optimal distance from the other plane at which our program's plane should embark on this maneuver, as well as the amount of time that this plane should spend in control states *LEFT*, *RIGHT* and *STRAIGHT*.

The landscape of expected error turns out to be fairly regular in this benchmark. Nonetheless, the presence of assertions leads to a discontinuous search landscape for an optimizer that aims to find "safe" program parameters. Fig. 9 plots the probability of assertion failures at various points in the space of parameter values, as estimated by a sampling of the input space. Note that this probability changes in an highly discontinuous manner.

Because the fitness function is a very simple linear function of the unknown values, so the proved bound is the same as the empirically determined bound for all methods, which is why we only show one line per method in Fig. 7. However, we can see that for this benchmark, smoothing had a big effect on the quality of the parameters we were able to obtain. In terms of the probability of assertion failure, using abstract interpretation as part of the search had a big effect in allowing us to find parameters for which we could prove good bounds for assertion failures, but again, the difference between search with smoothing and without smoothing were not statistically significant.

```
double aircraft(double v1,double v2) {
  ...
  double criticalDist = ??(6,9); double safetyDist = 3.0;
  double delay = ??(10,15); double delay2 = ??(9,14);
  assert(delay > 0.0; θ); assert(delay2 > 0.0; θ);
  assert(criticalDist > safetyDist; θ);
  assert(criticalDist < 10; θ);
  for(int i = 0; i < 50; i = i+1) {
    if (stage == CRUISE) {
      move_straight (x1, y1, x2, y2, v1, v2);
      if(δ(x1, y1, x2, y2) < criticalDist) {
        stage = LEFT; assert(!haveLooped; θ); steps = 0; }
    }
    if(stage == LEFT) {
     move_left (x1, y1, x2, y2, v1, v2); steps = steps + 1;
     if (delay - steps < 0) {
       stage = STRAIGHT; steps = 0; }
    }
    if (stage == STRAIGHT) {
     move_straight (x1, y1, x2, y2, v1, v2); steps = steps + 1;
     if(delay2 - steps < 0) {
       stage = 3; steps = 0; }
    }
    if(stage == RIGHT) {
      move_right (x1, y1, x2, y2, v1, v2);
      steps = steps + 1;
      if(delay - steps < 0) {
        stage = CRUISE;
        haveLooped = 1; }
    }
    assert
    (δ(x1, y1, x2,y2) < safetyDist; θ);
  }
  return(2 * delay + delay2);
}
```

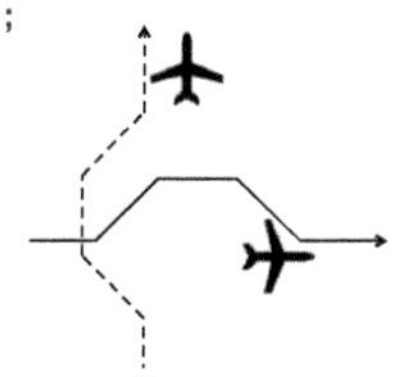

**Figure 10.** Sketch of collision-avoiding controller

## 5. Related work

Symbolic smoothing of programs was previously studied by Chaudhuri and Solar-Lezama [8–10]. Unlike the present paper, these prior approaches did not allow any boolean requirement. Also, goal of those papers was to find program parameters that are optimal for a *fixed* set of input values — this question reduces to a function minimization problem of the form $\min_c P(c)$. In contrast, our present approach allows the program inputs to vary, and this leads to a harder optimization problem.

Quantitative synthesis has been studied in the past by the automata-theoretic synthesis community [3–6]. Specifically, the statement for our problem is derived from prior work by Chatterjee et al [6]. However, the solutions provided by these papers are restricted to finite-state systems, whereas our programs and specifications are infinite-state.

Also related is an emerging literature at the interface of machine learning and program analysis. In probabilistic programming [11, 19, 35], the goal is to do probabilistic inference on statistical models written as programs, and synthesis of missing parameters can be viewed as a form of probabilistic inference on programs. However, unlike our paper, prior work on probabilistic programming is not concerned with proving satisfaction of boolean properties. On the other hand, machine learning techniques have also been used recently to prove program correctness [23, 26, 27]. However, the goal there is verification with respect to a boolean objective, as opposed to synthesis with respect to boolean and quantitative goals.

Another thread of related work comes from the embedded software community. The closest match to this paper is Jha et al's work on optimal switching logic synthesis for hybrid systems [17] and synthesis of fixed-point code from floating-point designs [16]. Unlike our work, both these approaches focus on non-stochastic systems, and do not reason about average-case system behavior. Earlier efforts on parameter synthesis in these areas include [13, 14]. However, these papers do not consider stochastic system models and do not have optimality as a goal. While there is an emerging literature on stochastic hybrid systems, researchers here do not appear to have studied the synthesis problem of interest to us.

Smoothed proof search assumes a procedure for sound analysis of probabilistic programs. The particular abstract domain we use for this purpose builds on Monniaux's work on probabilistic abstract interpretation [20, 21]. However, sound analysis of probabilistic systems has also been explored by other researchers [1, 12, 18, 29], and it is plausible that our smoothing technique could be combined with these other abstractions.

## 6. Conclusion

We have presented a new approach to combined boolean and quantitative reasoning in parameter synthesis. Our method has demonstrated that both reasoning tasks can be accomplished using numerical optimization. The discrete task of finding a proof can be "smoothed" into a continuous optimization task. While this process is unsound, we have offered a way to make it sound in the limit.

Although our approach has used abstract interpretation for proof search, the idea of smoothing can apply to other proof search strategies as well. We are especially interested in applying smoothing to constraint-based approaches to verification and synthesis.

Finally, we are keen on exploring connections between the ideas of this paper and probabilistic programming [19, 35]. Probabilistic programming aims to allow Bayesian inference on models written in a general-purpose programming language; this is accomplished using a combination of machine learning techniques that do the inference, and program analysis techniqes that generate auxiliary information about how probabilities propagate through programs. It is possible that the probabilistic abstraction and symbolic smoothing techniques introduced in this paper can be adapted to this end.

## References


[1] A. Adje, O. Bouisseau, J. Goubault-Larrecq, E. Goubault, and S. Putot. Static analysis of programs with imprecise probabilistic inputs. In *VSTTE*, 2013.

[2] Patrick Billingsley. *Probability and measure*. John Wiley & Sons, 2008.

[3] R. Bloem, K. Chatterjee, T. Henzinger, and B. Jobstmann. Better quality in synthesis through quantitative objectives. In *CAV*, pages 140–156, 2009.

[4] P. Cerný, K. Chatterjee, T. Henzinger, A. Radhakrishna, and R. Singh. Quantitative synthesis for concurrent programs. In *CAV*, pages 243–259, 2011.

[5] P. Cerný and T. Henzinger. From boolean to quantitative synthesis. In *EMSOFT*, 2011.

[6] K. Chatterjee, T. Henzinger, B. Jobstmann, and R. Singh. Measuring and synthesizing systems in probabilistic environments. In *CAV*, pages 380–395, 2010.

[7] S. Chaudhuri, M. Clochard, and A. Solar-Lezama. Bridging boolean and quantitative synthesis using smoothed proof search. Technical report, Rice University, 2014.

[8] S. Chaudhuri and A. Solar-Lezama. Smooth interpretation. In *PLDI*, pages 279–291, 2010.

[9] S. Chaudhuri and A. Solar-Lezama. Smoothing a program soundly and robustly. In *CAV*, pages 277–292, 2011.

[10] S. Chaudhuri and A. Solar-Lezama. Euler: A system for numerical optimization of programs. In *CAV*, 2012.

[11] G. Claret, S. Rajamani, A. Nori, A. Gordon, and J. Borgström. Bayesian inference using data flow analysis. In *ESEC/SIGSOFT FSE*, pages 92–102, 2013.

[12] P. Cousot and M. Monerau. Probabilistic abstract interpretation. In *ESOP*, pages 169–193, 2012.

[13] A. Donzé, B. Krogh, and A. Rajhans. Parameter synthesis for hybrid systems with an application to Simulink models. In *HSCC*, 2009.

[14] T. Henzinger and H. Wong-Toi. Using HyTech to synthesize control parameters for a steam boiler. In *Formal Methods for Industrial Applications*, pages 265–282, 1995.

[15] S. Jambawalikar and P. Kumar. A note on approximate minimum volume enclosing ellipsoid of ellipsoids. In *ICCSA*, pages 478–487, 2008.

[16] S. Jha and S. Seshia. Synthesis of optimal fixed-point implementations of numerical software routines. In *NSV*, 2013.

[17] S. Jha, S. Seshia, and A. Tiwari. Synthesis of optimal switching logic for hybrid systems. In *EMSOFT*, pages 107–116, 2011.

[18] J. Katoen, A. McIver, L. Meinicke, and C. Morgan. Linear-invariant generation for probabilistic programs: Automated support for proof-based methods. In *SAS*, pages 390–406, 2010.

[19] A. McCallum, K. Schultz, and S. Singh. Factorie: Probabilistic programming via imperatively defined factor graphs. In *NIPS*, pages 1249–1257, 2009.

[20] D. Monniaux. Abstract interpretation of probabilistic semantics. In *SAS*, pages 322–339, 2000.

[21] D. Monniaux. Backwards abstract interpretation of probabilistic programs. In *ESOP*, 2001.

[22] J.A. Nelder and R. Mead. A simplex method for function minimization. *The computer journal*, 7(4):308, 1965.

[23] A. Nori and R. Sharma. Termination proofs from tests. In *ESEC/SIGSOFT FSE*, pages 246–256, 2013.

[24] A. Platzer. *Logical Analysis of Hybrid Systems: Proving Theorems for Complex Dynamics*. Springer-Verlag, 2010.

[25] S. Seshia. Sciduction: combining induction, deduction, and structure for verification and synthesis. In *DAC*, pages 356–365, 2012.

[26] R. Sharma, S. Gupta, B. Hariharan, A. Aiken, P. Liang, and A. Nori. A data driven approach for algebraic loop invariants. In *ESOP*, pages 574–592, 2013.

[27] R. Sharma, S. Gupta, B. Hariharan, A. Aiken, and A. Nori. Verification as learning geometric concepts. In *SAS*, pages 388–411, 2013.

[28] R. Singh and A. Solar-Lezama. Synthesizing data structure manipulations from storyboards. In *SIGSOFT FSE*, pages 289–299, 2011.

[29] M. Smith. Probabilistic abstract interpretation of imperative programs using truncated normal distributions. *Electron. Notes Theor. Comput. Sci.*, 220(3):43–59, 2008.

[30] A. Solar-Lezama. *Program Synthesis by Sketching*. PhD thesis, UC Berkeley, 2008.

[31] Armando Solar-Lezama. Program sketching. *STTT*, 15(5-6):475–495, 2013.

[32] S. Srivastava, S. Gulwani, and J. Foster. From program verification to program synthesis. In *POPL*, pages 313–326, 2010.

[33] M. Vechev and E. Yahav. Deriving linearizable fine-grained concurrent objects. In *PLDI*, pages 125–135, 2008.

[34] M. Vechev, E. Yahav, and G. Yorsh. Abstraction-guided synthesis of synchronization. In *POPL*, pages 327–338, 2010.

[35] J. Winn and T. Minka. Probabilistic programming with infer .NET. *Machine Learning Summer School lecture notes, available at http://research.microsoft.com/~minka/papers/mlss2009*, 2009.

# A Constraint-Based Approach to Solving Games on Infinite Graphs

Tewodros A. Beyene
Technische Universtität München

Swarat Chaudhuri
Rice University

Corneliu Popeea
Technische Universtität München

Andrey Rybalchenko
Microsoft Research Cambridge and
Technische Universtität München

## Abstract

We present a constraint-based approach to computing winning strategies in two-player graph games over the state space of infinite-state programs. Such games have numerous applications in program verification and synthesis, including the synthesis of infinite-state reactive programs and branching-time verification of infinite-state programs. Our method handles games with winning conditions given by safety, reachability, and general Linear Temporal Logic (LTL) properties. For each property class, we give a deductive proof rule that — provided a symbolic representation of the game players — describes a winning strategy for a particular player. Our rules are sound and relatively complete. We show that these rules can be automated by using an off-the-shelf Horn constraint solver that supports existential quantification in clause heads. The practical promise of the rules is demonstrated through several case studies, including a challenging "Cinderella-Stepmother game" that allows infinite alternation of discrete and continuous choices by two players, as well as examples derived from prior work on program repair and synthesis.

***Categories and Subject Descriptors*** D.2.4 [*Software Engineering*]: Software/Program Verification; F.3.1 [*Logics and Meanings of Programs*]: Specifying and Verifying and Reasoning about Programs

***Keywords*** program synthesis; games; reactive synthesis; proof rules; static analysis; Horn clauses

## 1. Introduction

Many fundamental questions in formal methods reduce to computing winning strategies in *turn-based graph games* [18], i.e., games where two players take turns in moving a token along the edges of a graph, and a player wins if the sequence of nodes visited by the token satisfies a certain $\omega$-regular *winning condition*. For example:

- To synthesize a reactive system from a temporal specification [7, 38, 43], one constructs a graph game where the goal of one player is to satisfy the specification and the goal of the other is to violate it. The desired system is realizable if and only if the first player has a winning strategy in this game.
- The problem of verifying a branching-time property of a system is naturally framed as a graph game [14]. Here, one player models the existential path quantifiers in the property; the other player models the universal quantifiers. The system satisfies the property if and only if the existential player has a winning strategy.
- Graph games are a natural model for "open" systems [32] that explicitly model interactions between a controller (one player) and its environment (the other player). To prove such a system correct, we show that the controller has a strategy to enforce its requirements no matter how the environment behaves.

There is a rich literature on algorithmic approaches to graph games motivated by applications in formal methods [10, 12, 30, 47]. The majority of these approaches focus on decidable classes of games, such as games on finite graphs. This focus limits the applications of these techniques. For example, an algorithm that requires a finite game graph can only be applied to the verification and synthesis of finite-state systems. To use games in the analysis and synthesis of infinite-state programs, we need symbolic, abstraction-based algorithms for solving games on the state spaces of such programs. While a few such algorithms exist in the literature [12, 26], much more remains to be done on this topic.

This paper presents a new approach to this problem space. Our contribution is an algorithmic technique based on automated deduction for solving (turn-based) games over infinite-state symbolic transition systems.

Specifically, we target three classes of games over infinite graphs: *safety games*, *reachability games*, and *Linear Temporal Logic (LTL) games* [18]. These games differ in the winning condition for the player for whom we are computing a winning strategy (call this player Eve; the other player is called Adam). In a safety game, Eve wins a play (an infinite sequence of nodes visited by the game token) if and only if the play avoids a certain "unsafe" set of nodes. In a reachability game, a play is winning for Eve if and only if it reaches a certain target set of nodes. In LTL games, Eve


*POPL '14*, January 22–24, 2014, San Diego, CA, USA.

http://dx.doi.org/10.1145/2535838.2535860

wins a play if and only if the play satisfies an LTL property. We note that, LTL games subsume parity games, an important class of games where each node of the game graph is labeled with a "color" from the set $\{1, \ldots, N\}$, and a play is winning for Eve if and only if the minimum color seen infinitely often in the play is odd.

The importance of solving the above types of games to formal methods is well-established in the literature. For instance, the problem of solving a parity game over a program's state space is equivalent to that of verifying program properties written in the modal $\mu$-calculus [14, 18] (note that the $\mu$-calculus subsumes popular temporal logics like LTL, CTL, and CTL*). The solution of LTL games is also at the core of reactive synthesis from temporal specifications. Reachability and safety games are important special cases of LTL games that are sufficient for many applications, including program repair [21, 29], program synthesis [41], synthesis of interface specifications [1], and verification of the fragment of the $\mu$-calculus without alternation of fixpoint quantifiers.

For each of the above types of games, we give a deductive proof rule that, given a symbolic representation of the game graph, symbolically represents a winning strategy in the game using quantified Horn constraints. The rule is then automated by applying the EHSF engine for automated deduction [3].

To understand how our rules work, consider a safety game where the objective of Eve is to satisfy the state property $p$ at all points in all plays. To find a winning strategy for Eve, our rule for safety games computes an invariant $inv$ that describes the set of states from which Eve can win the game. This invariant needs to satisfy the following criteria: (a) the initial condition of the game implies $inv$; (b) $inv$ implies $p$; and (c) for all Adam transitions out of $inv$ (let us say to a destination state $\sigma$), $\sigma$ satisfies $p$ and there is a Eve transition from $\sigma$ back to $inv$.

Strategy computation in reachability games relies on well-founded transition invariants [39] to guarantee that a target state is reached after a finite number of rounds of the game. We solve LTL games with temporal objective $\varphi$ by converting $\neg\varphi$ into a nondeterministic Büchi automaton, then performing a fair termination check on the product of this automaton and the game graph.

All of our rules are sound, meaning that if they derive a strategy for a player, then the player actually wins under the strategy, as well as relatively complete, meaning that they can always derive a winning strategy when one exists, assuming a suitably powerful assertion language.

From a practical point of view, the appeal of our rules is that they leverage the most recent developments in SMT-solving, invariant generation, and termination verification [3, 20]. Specifically, our implementation CONSYNTH feeds our proof rules to the EHSF engine in the form of Horn-like clauses (in some cases with existential quantifiers in clause heads). Solving the game now amounts to resolving these clauses to a bounded depth, proving the unsatisfiability of the resolvent, repeating the process and generalizing from proofs of unsatisfiability to a solution for the original clauses. EHSF does so using a combination of counterexample-guided abstraction-refinement (CEGAR), interpolation, and SMT solving, and with help from user-provided templates that capture high-level intuitions about the strategy.

We evaluate CONSYNTH using several challenging case studies, including the "Cinderella-Stepmother game" — an existing challenge problem for infinite-state graph games that allows infinite alternation of discrete and continuous choices by the two players — and games arising out of prior work on program repair [29] and synthesis [45].

Now we summarize the main contributions of the paper:

- We take on the problem of solving games over state spaces of infinite-state programs using the power of modern automated software analysis technology.
- We present three deductive proof rules for solving such games under the safety, reachability, and LTL winning conditions. Our rules are sound and relatively complete, and our automata-theoretic rule for LTL games avoids the need to determinize a Büchi automaton.
- We offer a prototype implementation of our rules on top of an existing automated deduction engine. We illustrate the promise of the system through several case studies using examples posed in prior work.

This paper is organized as follows. In Section 2, we describe the Cinderella-Stepmother game as a motivating example. Section 3 formally defines graph games and the strategy computation problem. Section 4 gives our proof rules for solving games and proves them correct, i.e., sound and relatively complete. Section 5 revisits the example from Section 2 and applies our rules to variants of it; Section 6 presents applications of our rules to repair and synthesis problems from prior work. Section 7 presents concrete experimental results. Related work is described in Section 8; we conclude with some discussion in Section 9.

## 2. The Cinderella-Stepmother game

In this section, we describe a synthesis problem that motivated this work, and that we use in a case study later in the paper. A version of the problem was previously posed by Rajeev Alur as a challenge problem for the software synthesis community (see Bodlaender et al. [4] and Hurkens et al. [28] for more on the problem).

The problem involves a turn-based game between the mythical Cinderella, and her nemesis, the Stepmother. The game setup involves five buckets arranged in a circle. Each bucket can hold up to $c$ (a constant) units of water; initially, all buckets are empty. In each round of the game, Stepmother brings 1 unit of additional water and splits it among the five buckets. If any of the buckets overflow, Stepmother wins. If not, Cinderella empties two *adjacent* buckets. Cinderella wins if the game goes on forever.

We can model the Cinderella-Stepmother game using the following symbolic transition system. Let $v$ be a set of system variables that represent the amount of water in the five buckets, $v = (b_1, b_2, b_3, b_4, b_5)$. All the buckets are initially empty — this fact is specified as the initial condition

$$init(v) = (b_1 = 0 \land \cdots \land b_5 = 0).$$

The transition relation of Stepmother represents a non-deterministic choice of buckets in which 1 unit of additional water is added:

$$\begin{aligned} stepmother(v, v') = (&b'_1 + \cdots + b'_5 = b_1 + \cdots + b_5 + 1 \\ &\land b'_1 \geq b_1 \land \cdots \land b'_5 \geq b_5). \end{aligned}$$

The transition relation of the Cinderella player represents a non-deterministic choice of two consecutive buckets that are emptied.

$$cinderella(v, v') = \bigvee_{i \in \{1 \ldots 5\}} \left( \begin{array}{l} b'_i = 0 \land b'_{(i+1)\%5} = 0 \\ \land \left( \bigwedge_{j \in \{1..5\}} \left( \begin{array}{c} j \neq i \land j \neq (i+1)\%5 \\ \rightarrow b'_j = b_j \end{array} \right) \right) \end{array} \right).$$

The condition that one of the buckets overflows is described by the assertion

$$overflow(v) = (b_1 > c \lor \cdots \lor b_5 > c).$$

***Safety game*** We observe that in the above game, Cinderella wants to enforce a *safety property* — specifically, the property $G(\neg overflow(v))$ — in every play of the game. This property is Cinderella's *winning condition*. Games are classified according to the winning condition of the player for whom we want to compute a strategy. Specifically, suppose we want to compute a strategy for Cinderella. In that case, we are trying to solve a *safety game*.

***Reachability game*** Now suppose we want to compute a strategy for Stepmother instead. We note that the winning condition for Stepmother is the reachability property $F\ \mathit{overflow}(v)$. The game is a *reachability game*.

***LTL and parity games*** It is easy to define generalizations of the game where the winning condition for a player is a general Linear Temporal Logic (LTL) property. Such a game is called an *LTL game*. LTL games are an extremely challenging class of games — the problem of solving such games on finite game graphs is 2EXPTIME-complete [38]. The intuitive reason for this hardness is that it requires a conversion from an LTL formula to a nondeterministic Büchi automaton (an exponential blowup) and then the determinization of this automaton (another exponential blowup).

An important special case of LTL games is *parity games* [18]. Here, each state of the transition system is assigned a color (a number in $\{1, \ldots, N\}$), and the winning condition for a play is that the minimum color seen infinitely often in the play is odd. (The condition can be stated in LTL in an obvious way.) In Section 7, we use CONSYNTH on a parity game generalizing our original game.

***Discussion*** From the determinacy of the classes of graph games that we study [35], it follows that for every value of $c$, either Cinderella or Stepmother has a winning strategy in each of the above games. Now we give some intuitions about what such a winning strategy would look like in the game as originally stated. The discussion of how to automatically solve the problem using CONSYNTH is postponed until Section 5.

First note that if $c < 1.5$ units, then Stepmother wins. Her strategy is as follows: in the first round, she divides 1 unit into two non-adjacent buckets. Then no matter what Cinderella does, there will be a bucket with $0.5$ units at the end of the round, and Stepmother can cause a spill in second round by adding 1 unit in that bucket. If $c \geq 3$ units, Cinderella wins: she can just select the buckets in a round-robin order, emptying two buckets in each round, and this strategy is winning no matter what Stepmother does.

The problem becomes more challenging for $1.5 \leq c < 3$. We leave this case as a challenge for the reader — it will soon be apparent that it is highly nontrivial. In such cases, fully automated strategy synthesis seems unrealistic, and computer-*assisted* proofs driven by user-provided hints or templates are more plausible. This is the strategy that our approach takes.

## 3. Preliminaries

In this section we formally define games and strategies, and also sketch the deduction framework used to automate them.

### 3.1 Games

***Syntax*** A *(two-player, turn-based, graph) game* is a pair consisting of a symbolic transition system and a *winning condition*:

- We consider symbolic transition systems that are composed from two players, Adam and Eve. Let $v$ be a tuple of variables. We assume that valuations of $v$ describe states of the system under consideration. (For simplicity, we do not distinguish between variables controlled by Eve and Adam.)

  We represent the initial states of the transition system by an assertion $\mathit{init}(v)$. The transition relations of Adam and Eve are given by assertions $\mathit{adam}(v, v')$ and $\mathit{eve}(v, v')$, respectively.

- A *winning condition obj* for a game is given by a set of infinite sequences of system states. A game is said to be a safety game, a reachability game, and an LTL game respectively when its winning condition is a safety property, a reachability property, and a general LTL property.

***Semantics*** We present the semantics of games in two steps. First, we define strategies of the individual players. A *strategy* $\sigma$ for Eve is a set of infinite trees over the states of the system that satisfies the following conditions:

- The roots of trees in $\sigma$ coincide with the set of initial states, and are considered to be on the first level of the tree. (Here, the level of a node is the length of the path to the root plus one.)
- The set of successors of each tree node $s$ at an odd level consists of the following set of states.
  $$\{s' \mid (s, s') \models \mathit{adam}(v, v')\}$$
- The set of successors of each tree node $s$ at an even level consists of a non-empty subset of the following set of states.
  $$\{s' \mid (s, s') \models \mathit{eve}(v, v')\}$$

Thus, a strategy for Eve alternates between universal choices of Adam and existential choices of Eve. We call each infinite sequence of system states that starts at a root of a strategy $\sigma$ and follows some branch a *play* $\pi$ determined by $\sigma$.

A strategy $\sigma$ for Eve is *winning* if every play determined by $\sigma$ is included in the winning condition.

For the given system and a formula $\varphi$ that describes a winning condition in some temporal logic, we write
$$(\mathit{init}(v), \mathit{eve}(v, v'), \mathit{adam}(v, v')) \models \varphi$$
when Eve has a winning strategy.

We also consider Adam's perspective. A strategy $\sigma$ for Adam is defined in a similar way. The roots of $\sigma$ represent a non-empty subset of $\mathit{init}(v)$. $\sigma$ alternates between existential choices of Adam and universal choices of Eve. If a tree node $s$ is on an odd level, then its successors form a non-empty subset of $\{s' \mid (s, s') \models \mathit{adam}(v, v')\}$. Otherwise, the set of successors is $\{s' \mid (s, s') \models \mathit{eve}(v, v')\}$.

### 3.2 The EHSF engine

Our proof rules are automated using the EHSF [3] engine for resolving forall-exists Horn-like clauses extended with well-foundedness criteria.

We skip the syntax and semantics of the clauses targeted by this system — see [3] for more details. Instead, we illustrate these clauses with the following example:

$$x \geq 0 \rightarrow \exists y : x \geq y \wedge \mathit{rank}(x, y), \qquad \mathit{rank}(x, y) \rightarrow \mathit{ti}(x, y),$$
$$\mathit{ti}(x, y) \wedge \mathit{rank}(y, z) \rightarrow \mathit{ti}(x, z), \qquad \mathit{dwf}(\mathit{ti}).$$

Intuitively, these clauses represent an assertion over the interpretation of "query symbols" $\mathit{rank}$ and $\mathit{ti}$ (the predicate $\mathit{dwf}$ represents disjunctive well-foundedness, and is not a query symbol). The semantics of these clauses maps each predicate symbol occurring in them into a constraint over $v$.

Specifically, the above set of clauses has a solution that maps both $\mathit{rank}(x, y)$ and $\mathit{ti}(x, y)$ to the constraint $(x \geq 0 \wedge y \geq x - 1)$.

EHSF resolves clauses like the above using a CEGAR scheme to discover witnesses for existentially quantified variables. The refinement loop collects a global constraint that declaratively determines which witnesses can be chosen. The chosen witnesses are used to replace existential quantification, and then the resulting universally quantified clauses are passed to a solver for such clauses. At this step, we can benefit from emergent tools in the area of solving Horn clauses over decidable theories, e.g., HSF [19] or $\mu Z$ [27]. Such a solver either finds a solution, i.e., a model for uninterpreted relations constrained by the clauses, or returns a counterexample, which is a resolution tree (or DAG) representing a contradiction. EHSF turns the counterexample into an additional constraint on the set of witness candidates, and continues with the next iteration of the refinement loop. Notably, this refinement loop conjoins constraints that are obtained for all discovered counterexamples. This way EHSF guarantees that previously handled counterexamples are not rediscovered and that a wrong choice of witnesses can be mended.

For the existential clause above, EHSF introduces a witness/Skolem relation $sk$ over variables $x$ and $y$, i.e., $x \geq 0 \wedge sk(x, y) \rightarrow x \geq y \wedge rank(x, y)$. In addition, since for each $x$ such that $x \geq 0$ holds we need a value $y$, we require that such $x$ is in the domain of the Skolem relation using an additional clause $x \geq 0 \rightarrow \exists y : sk(x, y)$. In the EHSF approach, the search space of a skolem relation $sk(x, y)$ is restricted by a template function TEMPL$(sk)(x, y)$. In general, a template is required for both the Skolem relation as well as for its guard. For this paper, templates for the guards can be derived automatically as the projection from the template of the corresponding Skolem relation, therefore we omit them from our presentation.

## 4. Proof rules for games

In this section, we present proof rules for three kind of games: safety, reachability and parity/LTL games. These proof rules conclude that Eve has a winning strategy by imposing implication and well-foundedness conditions on auxiliary assertions over system variables. For each proof rule we prove its soundness, i.e., a winning strategy exists if the premises are satisfied by some auxiliary assertions, and relative completeness, i.e., if a winning strategy exists then auxiliary assertions satisfying the premises exist under an assumption that the assertion language of our choice is sufficiently expressive. Such correctness criteria are standard for temporal proof rules [33].

### 4.1 Safety games

We consider a safety game for which Eve has a winning strategy if only states from $safe(v)$ are visited by all plays.

We present the corresponding proof rule in Figure 1. The proof rule relies on an invariant assertion $inv(v)$ that represents a set of states reached by Eve in a winning strategy. We connect the invariant assertion with the reachable states by resorting to reasoning by induction on the number of steps to reach a state. The condition S1 requires that the initial state of the game are considered in $inv(v)$. S2 represent the induction step. Here, we require that for every step from $inv(v)$ executed by Adam there exist a step by Eve that leads back to $inv(v)$. Of course, since the winning condition requires that all states of a play need to satisfy $safe(v)$, we require that all states reached after Adam made a step as well as $inv(v)$ satisfy the assertion $safe(v)$. The former condition is enforced by a conjunct $safe(v')$ in the head of S2. The later condition is guaranteed by S3.

**Theorem 1** (Correctness of rule RULESAFE). *The proof rule RULESAFE is sound and relatively complete.*

*Proof.* We split the proof into two parts: soundness and completeness.

***Soundness*** We prove the soundness by contradiction. Assume that there exists an assertion $inv(v)$ that satisfies the premises of RULESAFE, yet the conclusion of RULESAFE does not hold. That is, there is no winning strategy for Eve. Hence, there exists a strategy $\sigma$ for Adam in which each play reaches a state that violates $safe(v)$. This strategy $\sigma$ alternates between existential choices of Adam and universal choices of Eve. Let $aux(v)$ be a set of states for which $\sigma$ provides existentially chosen successors wrt. Adam.

We derive a contradiction by relying on a certain play $\pi$ that is determined by $\sigma$. The play $\pi$ is constructed iteratively. We start from some root state $s_1$ of $\sigma$, which also satisfies the initial condition $init(v)$. Note that $s_1 \models inv(v)$, due to S1, and $s_1 \models aux(v)$ due to $\sigma$. Each iteration round extends the play obtained so far by two states, say $s'$ and $s''$. We maintain a condition that each such $s''$ satisfies $inv(v)$ and $aux(v)$. Let $s$ be the last state of the play $\pi$ constructed so far. Due to our condition, we have $s \models inv(v) \wedge aux(v)$. Then, $\sigma$ determines a successor state $s'$ such that $(s, s') \models adam(v, v')$, and S2 guarantees that there exists a state $s''$ such that $(s', s'') \models eve(v, v')$ and $s'' \models inv(v)$. Furthermore, $s''$ satisfies $aux(v)$ due to $\sigma$. Finally, from S2 and S3 follows that $s' \models safe(v)$ and $s'' \models safe(v)$, respectively.

By iteratively constructing $\pi$ using the above step we obtain a play that satisfies the strategy $\sigma$. Thus, we obtain a contradiction, since according to our construction all states in $\pi$ satisfies $safe(v)$, however $\sigma$ guarantees that each play eventually reaches a state that violates $safe(v)$.

***Completeness*** Assume that Eve has a winning strategy, say $\sigma$, i.e., the conclusion of RULESAFE holds. We prove the completeness claim by showing how to construct $inv(v)$ that satisfies the premises of RULESAFE.

This strategy $\sigma$ alternates between universal choices of Adam and existential choices of Eve. Let $inv(v)$ be a set of states for which $\sigma$ provides universally chosen successors wrt. Adam. Since $\sigma$ is a winning strategy, all states satisfying $inv(v)$ also satisfy $safe(v)$, i.e., $inv(v)$ satisfies S3. $inv(v)$ satisfies S1, since $\sigma$ guarantees that Eve wins from every initial state. Now we consider an arbitrary state $s$ that satisfies $inv(v)$. $\sigma$ guarantees that for every successor $s'$ of $s$ wrt. Adam there exists a successor $s''$ wrt. Eve such that $s'' \models inv(v)$. Furthermore, since $\sigma$ is winning, we have $s' \models safe(v)$. Thus we conclude that $inv(v)$ satisfies the condition S2 as well. □

### 4.2 Reachability games

In contrast to safety games, the winning condition of reachability games ensures that a certain set of states called $dst(v)$ is eventually reached by each play. Reasoning about such eventuality properties demands the use of well-founded orders.

We present a rule RULEREACH for proving that Eve has a winning strategy for a reachability property given by an LTL formula $F\,dst(v)$ in Figure 2. RULEREACH requires an invariant assertion $inv(v)$ together with a binary relation $round(v, v')$. Similarly to RULESAFE, we use $inv(v)$ to keep track of states that are reached by Eve. This is captured by R1 and a part of R2. To ensure that Adam makes progress when aiming at the set $dst(v)$ we keep track of pairs of states towards reaching it in $round(v, v')$, see the last conjunct in R2. We note that the proof rule only imposes conditions when $dst(v)$ is not yet reached, as encoded by the second conjunct in R2. Finally, to ensure that $dst(v)$ is eventually reached by each play we require that $round(v, v')$ represents a well-founded relation. Thus, it is impossible to return to $inv(v) \wedge \neg dst(v)$ infinitely many times.

**Theorem 2** (Correctness of rule RULEREACH). *The proof rule RULEREACH is sound and relatively complete.*

*Proof.* We split the proof into two parts: soundness and completeness.

***Soundness*** We prove the soundness by contradiction. Assume that there exist assertions $inv(v)$ and $round(v, v')$ that satisfy the premises of RULEREACH, yet the conclusion of RULEREACH does not hold. That is, there is no winning strategy for Eve. Hence, there exists a strategy $\sigma$ for Adam in which each play never reaches a

Find assertion $inv(v)$ such that:

$$\begin{array}{lll} \text{S1}: & init(v) & \rightarrow inv(v) \\ \text{S2}: & inv(v) \wedge adam(v,v') & \rightarrow safe(v') \wedge \exists v'' : eve(v',v'') \wedge inv(v'') \\ \text{S3}: & inv(v) & \rightarrow safe(v) \end{array}$$

---

$$(init(v), eve(v,v'), adam(v,v')) \models G\ safe(v)$$

**Figure 1.** Proof rule RULESAFE for a safety game, i.e., the winning condition is given by a formula $G\ safe(v)$.

Find assertions $inv(v)$ and $round(v,v')$ such that:

$$\begin{array}{lll} \text{R1}: & init(v) & \rightarrow inv(v) \\ \text{R2}: & inv(v) \wedge \neg dst(v) \wedge adam(v,v') \wedge \neg dst(v') & \rightarrow \exists v'' : eve(v',v'') \wedge inv(v'') \wedge round(v,v'') \\ \text{R3}: & well\text{-}founded(round(v,v')) & \end{array}$$

---

$$(init(v), eve(v,v'), adam(v,v')) \models F\ dst(v)$$

**Figure 2.** Proof rule RULEREACH for a reachability game, i.e., the winning condition is given by a formula $F\ dst(v)$.

state that satisfies $dst(v)$. This strategy $\sigma$ alternates between existential choices of Adam and universal choices of Eve. Let $aux(v)$ be a set of states for which $\sigma$ provides existentially chosen successors wrt. Adam. Note that the implication $aux(v) \rightarrow \neg dst(v)$ is valid, since no play determined by $\sigma$ visits $dst(v)$.

We derive a contradiction by relying on a certain play $\pi$ that is determined by $\sigma$. The play $\pi$ is constructed iteratively, in a similar way as done in the proof of Theorem 1. We start from some root state $s_1$ of $\sigma$, which satisfies the initial condition $init(v)$. Note that $s_1 \models inv(v)$, due to R1, and $s_1 \models aux(v)$ due to $\sigma$. Each iteration round extends the play obtained so far by two states, say $s'$ and $s''$. We maintain a condition that each such $s''$ satisfies $inv(v)$ and $aux(v)$. Let $s$ be the last state of the play $\pi$ constructed so far. Due to our condition, we have $s \models inv(v) \wedge aux(v)$. Then, $\sigma$ determines a successor state $s'$ such that $(s,s') \models adam(v,v')$, and R2 guarantees that there exists a state $s''$ such that $(s',s'') \models eve(v,v')$ and $s'' \models inv(v)$. Furthermore, $s''$ satisfies $aux(v)$ due to $\sigma$. Finally, from R2 also follows that $s' \models \neg dst(v)$ and $(s,s'') \models round(v,v')$.

By iteratively constructing $\pi = s_1, s_2, \dots$ using the above step we obtain a play that satisfies the strategy $\sigma$. Thus, there is an infinite sequence of states $s_1, s_3, s_5, \dots$ that takes states occurring at odd positions in $\pi$ such that each pair of consecutive states $s_{2i-1}$ and $s_{2i+1}$ is connected by $round(v,v')$, for $i \geq 1$. The existence of such an infinite sequence contradicts the well-foundedness condition imposed by R3.

***Completeness*** Assume that Eve has a winning strategy, say $\sigma$, i.e., the conclusion of RULEREACH holds. We prove the completeness claim by showing how to construct $inv(v)$ and $round(v,v')$ that satisfy the premises of RULEREACH.

The strategy $\sigma$ alternates between universal choices of Adam and existential choices of Eve. Each play $\pi = s_1, s_2, s_3, \dots$ contributes elements to $inv(v)$ and $round(v,v')$ as follows. Let $k$ be the position of the first occurrence of a state in $\pi$ that satisfies $dst(v)$, i.e., we have $s_k \models dst(v)$ and $s_i \not\models dst(v)$ for each $i \in 1..k-1$. Such position exists, since the play satisfies $F dst(v)$. Then, for each $i \geq 1$ such that $2i-1 \leq k$ we add the state $s_{2i-1}$ to $inv(v)$. Furthermore, for each $i \geq 1$ such that $2i+1 \leq k$ we add the pair of states $s_{2i-1}$ and $s_{2i+1}$ to $round(v,v')$.

We note that the above construction ensures that for each pair of states $s$ and $s''$ such that $(s,s'') \models round(v,v'')$ holds: i) we have $s \not\models dst(v)$, and ii) there exists a state $s'$ such that $s' \not\models dst(v)$, $(s,s') \models adam(v,v')$, and $(s',s'') \models eve(v,v')$.

We observe that $inv(v)$ satisfies R1, since $\sigma$ guarantees that Eve wins from every initial state. Now we consider each pair of states $s$ and $s'$ that satisfies the left hand side of R2. $\sigma$ guarantees that there exists a successor $s''$ wrt. Eve. Regardless whether $s'' \models dst(v)$ the above construction guarantees that the right-hand side of R2 is satisfied by assigning $s$, $s'$, and $s''$ to $v$, $v'$, and $v''$, respectively.

Now we show by contradiction that $round(v,v')$ is well-founded. Assume otherwise, i.e., there exists an infinite sequence of states $s_1, s_2, \dots$ induced by $round(v,v')$. As noted previously, for each pair of consecutive states $s_i$ and $s_{i+1}$ there exists an intermediate state $s'_i$ such that the sequence $s_1, s'_1, s_2, \dots, s_i, s'_i, s_{i+1}, \dots$ is a play. Since this play does not visit any state that satisfies $dst(v)$, we obtain a contradiction to the assumption that Eve has a winning strategy. Hence, we conclude that R3 is satisfied. □

### 4.3 LTL and parity games

Now we show how to solve LTL games and, as a special case, parity games. To state the parity winning condition we assume that the set of all states is partitioned into $N$ subsets that are denoted by the assertions $p_1(v), \dots, p_N(v)$. Thus, $p_1(v) \vee \dots \vee p_N(v)$ is valid and for each $1 \leq i < j \leq N$ we have that $p_i(v) \wedge p_j(v)$ is unsatisfiable. Without loss of generality we assume that $N$ is an odd number.

The parity condition states that the system wins the game for a given computation if among the subsets $p_{i_1}(v), \dots, p_{i_K}(v)$ that are visited infinitely many times by the computation the minimal identifier is odd, i.e., $\min\{i_1, \dots, i_K\}$ is odd. We can represent the parity condition by the following LTL formula $\varphi$.

$$\begin{aligned}\varphi = \ & GFp_1(v) \\ & \vee GFp_3(v) \wedge FG\neg(p_1(v) \vee p_2(v)) \\ & \dots \\ & \vee GFp_N(v) \wedge FG\neg(p_1(v) \vee \dots \vee p_{N-1}(v))\end{aligned}$$

The first disjunct states that $p_1(v)$ is visited infinitely often, while the second disjunct states that $p_3(v)$ is visited infinitely often and there exists a suffix that neither visits $p_1(v)$ nor $p_2(v)$. The last disjunct states that $p_N(v)$ is visited infinitely often and there is a suffix that visits no other subset.

To solve games where the winning condition is an LTL formula $\varphi$, we negate $\varphi$ and apply a standard technique, e.g., [17], for translating LTL formulas to Büchi automata on the resulting $\neg\varphi$. Let $\mathcal{B}$ be the obtained automaton. We represent $\mathcal{B}$ using assertions over the program counter of the automaton $pc_{\mathcal{B}}$ and the system variables $v$. Let the initial condition of the automaton be given by $init_{\mathcal{B}}(pc_{\mathcal{B}})$. We represent the transition relation of $\mathcal{B}$ by $next_{\mathcal{B}}(pc_{\mathcal{B}}, v, pc'_{\mathcal{B}})$. This transition relation evolves the value of the program counter of the automaton while taking into consideration the current state of the system given by a valuation of $v$. Finally, we assume that $acc_{\mathcal{B}}(pc_{\mathcal{B}})$ represents the accepting states of the automaton.

Given a sequence of states $\pi = s_1, s_2, \dots$ we define a run of $\mathcal{B}$ on $\pi$ to be an infinite sequence of automaton states $q_0, q_1, q_2, \dots$ such that $q_0 \models init_{\mathcal{B}}(pc_{\mathcal{B}})$ and $(q_{i-1}, s_i, q_i) \models next_{\mathcal{B}}(pc_{\mathcal{B}}, v, pc'_{\mathcal{B}})$ for each $i \geq 1$. A run is accepting wrt. the Büchi acceptance condition if it contains infinitely many states that satisfy $acc_{\mathcal{B}}(pc_{\mathcal{B}})$. The automaton $\mathcal{B}$ accepts a play $\pi$ if there exists an accepting run on $\pi$. Note that our construction ensures that if $\mathcal{B}$ accepts $\pi$ then $\pi \not\models \varphi$.

A proof rule BÜCHITERM for LTL games based on the above automata-theoretic approach [44] is presented in Figure 3. BÜCHITERM requires that the negation of the winning condition is translated into a Büchi automaton $\mathcal{B}$, which together with the system description appears in the proof rule. An interesting property of this proof rule is that it relies on a non-deterministic Büchi automaton representation of the negated winning condition, and does not require any determinization via Rabin, Muller, or Streett acceptance conditions.

We consider a synchronous parallel product of the transition relations of the players and the transition relation of the Büchi automaton, which is expressed in the proof rule by appropriate conjunctions. We use $w = (v, pc_{\mathcal{B}})$ to refer to the vector of the system variables and the program counter of the automaton.

The existence of a winning strategy for Eve depends on the identification of auxiliary assertions $inv(w)$, $aux(w, w', v'')$, $round(w, w', w'')$, and $fair(w, w')$ as follows. $inv(w)$ keeps track of the system states reached by Adam, similarly to RULESAFE and RULEREACH. To deal with the non-determinism in the transition relation of the automaton, we introduce an intermediate bookkeeping assertion $aux(w, w', v'')$, which allows us to decouple the treatment of the automaton state $q''$ from the selection of $s''$. $round(w, w', w'')$ contains all triples of adjacent program states occurring in plays. Here, it is more fine-grained than the counterpart in RULEREACH, as we keep track of intermediate states visited by Eve instead of only considering the combined steps (visited by Adam). For keeping track of acceptance $fair(w, w')$ contains all pairs of program states that describe play segments visiting Büchi accepting states at least once. We derive $fair(w, w')$ from $round(w, w', w'')$ using transitive closure-like conditions B4 and B5. Finally, the well-foundedness condition B6 shows that accepting states cannot be visited infinitely many times.

**Theorem 3** (Correctness of rule BÜCHITERM). *The proof rule* BÜCHITERM *is sound and relatively complete.*

*Proof.* We split the proof into two parts: soundness and completeness.

***Soundness*** We prove the soundness by contradiction. Assume that there exist assertions $inv(w)$, $aux(w, w', v'')$, $round(w, w', w'')$, and $fair(w, w')$ that satisfy the premises of BÜCHITERM, yet the conclusion of BÜCHITERM does not hold. That is, there is no winning strategy for Eve. Hence, there exists a strategy $\sigma$ for Adam in which each play violates $\varphi$. This strategy $\sigma$ alternates between existential choices of Adam and universal choices of Eve. We derive a contradiction by relying on a certain set of trees whose branches are sequences $(s_1, q_1), (s_2, q_2), \dots$ that are jointly determined by $\sigma$ and the assumed assertions (via BÜCHITERM).

The requisite branches are constructed iteratively, in a similar way as the play construction is done in the proof of Theorem 1. We start from some root state $s_1$ of $\sigma$, which satisfies the initial condition $init(v)$. Then the play is extended from a state $s$ by considering an existential choice $s'$ offered by $\sigma$ that is followed by an existential choice $s''$ offered by B2. We obtain appropriate runs $q_0, q_1, \dots$ by applying B1, B2, and B3 for values of $v$, $v'$, and $v''$ determined by currently considered $s$, $s'$, and $s''$, respectively. Since the automaton $\mathcal{B}$ is non-deterministic, for each $s$, $s'$, and $s''$ there is a set of appropriate automaton states. Considering each choice leads to a tree construction, as described below.

First, we consider $s_1$ and B1, and for each $q_1$ such that there exists $q_0$ with $init(s_1) \wedge init_{\mathcal{B}}(q_0) \wedge next_{\mathcal{B}}(q_0, s_1, q_1)$ we add a $(s_1, q_1)$ as a root to our tree. We remember the state $q_0$ that was used to create each $(s_1, q_1)$. Then, for each tree leaf $(s, q)$ we perform the following tree expansion. First, we consider the state $s'$ that $\sigma$ provides as a successor of $s$. Then, we rely on B2, and for each $q'$ such that $next_{\mathcal{B}}(q, s', q')$ holds we add $(s', q')$ as a child node of $(s, q)$. Furthermore, for given $s$ and $q$, and each $s'$ and $q'$ we take $s''$ such that $eve(s', s'') \wedge aux(s, q, s', q', s'')$. Now we rely on B3, and for each $q''$ such that $next_{\mathcal{B}}(q', s'', q'')$ holds we add $(s'', q'')$ as a child node of the corresponding $(s', q')$.

By applying the above tree expansion steps we construct a set of trees where every branch is a sequence $(s_1, q_1), (s_2, q_2), \dots$ that comes with the corresponding initial automaton state $q_0$. Note that $s_1, s_2, \dots$ is a play determined by $\sigma$, hence it violates $\varphi$. Thus, there exists a branch for which the sequence $q_0, q_1, \dots$ is an accepting run of $\mathcal{B}$ for the corresponding play determined by the branch. Let $(s_{i_1}, q_{i_1}), (s_{i_2}, q_{i_2}), \dots$ be a subsequence such that $q_{i_j} \models acc_{\mathcal{B}}(pc_{\mathcal{B}})$ for each $j \geq 1$. Then, each pair $(s_{i_j}, q_{i_j})$ contributes

$$((s_{i_j}, q_{i_j}), (s_{i_{j+1}}, q_{i_{j+1}}))$$

(or its closest neighbour visited by Adam) to $fair(w, w')$. Thus, the condition B6 is violated.

***Completeness*** Assume that Eve has a winning strategy, say $\sigma$, i.e., the conclusion of BÜCHITERM holds. We prove the completeness claim by showing how to construct $inv(w)$, $aux(v, w', v'')$, $round(v, w', w'')$, and $fair(w, w')$ that satisfy the premises of BÜCHITERM.

The strategy $\sigma$ alternates between universal choices of Adam and existential choices of Eve. Each play $\pi = s_1, s_2, s_3, \dots$ contributes elements to $inv(w)$, $aux(v, w', v'')$, and $round(w, w', w'')$ in the following way through an appropriate sequence of automaton states $q_0, q_1, q_2, \dots$. Since $\pi \models \varphi$, we note that $\pi$ is not accepted by $\mathcal{B}$. Hence, either there is an infinite run $q_0, q_1, q_2, \dots$ that is not accepting, or the exists a finite run $q_0, \dots, q_n$ that cannot be extended (i.e., there is no automaton

Find assertions $inv(w)$, $aux(w, w', v'')$, $round(w, w', w'')$, and $fair(w, w')$ where $w = (v, pc_{\mathcal{B}})$ such that:

$$
\begin{array}{lll}
\text{B1}: & init(v) \wedge init_{\mathcal{B}}(pc_{\mathcal{B}}) \wedge next_{\mathcal{B}}(pc_{\mathcal{B}}, v, pc'_{\mathcal{B}}) & \rightarrow inv(v, pc'_{\mathcal{B}}) \\
\text{B2}: & inv(w) \wedge adam(v, v') \wedge next_{\mathcal{B}}(pc_{\mathcal{B}}, v', pc'_{\mathcal{B}}) & \rightarrow \exists v'' : eve(v', v'') \wedge aux(w, w', v'') \\
\text{B3}: & aux(w, w', v'') \wedge next_{\mathcal{B}}(pc'_{\mathcal{B}}, v'', pc''_{\mathcal{B}}) & \rightarrow inv(w'') \wedge round(w, w', w'') \\
\text{B4}: & round(w, w', w'') \wedge (acc_{\mathcal{B}}(pc_{\mathcal{B}}) \vee acc_{\mathcal{B}}(pc'_{\mathcal{B}})) & \rightarrow fair(w, w'') \\
\text{B5}: & fair(w, w') \wedge round(w', w'', w''') & \rightarrow fair(w, w''') \\
\text{B6}: & well\text{-}founded(fair(w, w')) &
\end{array}
$$

---

$$(init(v), eve(v, v'), adam(v, v')) \models \varphi$$

**Figure 3.** Proof rule BÜCHITERM for an LTL game, i.e., the winning condition is given by an LTL formula $\varphi$. From $\neg\varphi$ we obtain a Büchi automaton $\mathcal{B}$ with an initial condition $init_{\mathcal{B}}(pc_{\mathcal{B}})$, a transition relation $next_{\mathcal{B}}(pc_{\mathcal{B}}, v, pc'_{\mathcal{B}})$, and accepting states $acc_{\mathcal{B}}(pc_{\mathcal{B}})$.

state $q_{n+1}$ such that $next_{\mathcal{B}}(q_n, s_n, s_{n+1})$). In either case, for each $i \geq 0$ (and $2i + 1 \leq n$ if the run is finite) we let $(s_{2i-1}, q_{2i-1})$ be an element of $inv(w)$, $(s_{2i-1}, q_{2i-1}, s_{2i}, q_{2i}, s_{2i+1})$ be an element of $aux(w, w', v'')$, and $(s_{2i-1}, q_{2i-1}, s_{2i}, q_{2i}, s_{2i+1}, q_{2i+1})$ be an element of $round(w, w', w'')$. Then we define $fair(w, w')$ for the obtained $round(w, w', w'')$ as the least solution of B4 and B5.

Since the run is not accepting, it visits accepting states only finitely many times. Hence, $fair(w, w')$ is well-founded. □

## 5. Case study: Cinderella-Stepmother games

In this section we illustrate our constraint-based approach to solving games applying it to the Cinderella-Stepmother game introduced in Section 2. We consider five variants of this game corresponding to different winning conditions. In Section 7 we report on running times required for solving these games using CONSYNTH.

### 5.1 Games with Cinderella's safety objective

In these games, we attempt to obtain winning strategies for Cinderella in her attempt to keep the buckets from overflowing. The winning condition for Cinderella is $G\ \neg overflow(v)$. As mentioned in Section 2, the Cinderella player has simple winning strategies for bucket capacity $c \geq 3$. For values $2 \leq c \leq 3$, the strategies are more involved. (For values $c \leq 2$ there are no strategies for the player Cinderella to win the game).

***Round strategy*** We define the first game using the value $c = 3$ for the bucket capacity. A winning strategy might follow an alternation of consecutive buckets that are emptied. Accordingly, we use an auxiliary variable $r$ for a pair of buckets to be emptied, to remember the previous choice made by the Cinderella player. The tuple of game variables contains the five bucket variables from $v$ and is extended with the round variable $r$ as follows: $w = (b_1, b_2, b_3, b_4, b_5, r)$. The initial states assertion sets the round variable to $r = 1$. We let Adam play the role of Stepmother and therefore the transition relation of Adam is based on the assertion $stepmother(v, v')$, while the transition relation of Eve is given by $cinderella(v, v')$. (Both constraints are given in Section 2.)

$$
\begin{aligned}
init(w) &= (b_1 = 0 \wedge \cdots \wedge b_5 = 0 \wedge r = 1) \\
eve(w, w') &= cinderella(v, v') \\
adam(w, w') &= (stepmother(v, v') \wedge r' = r)
\end{aligned}
$$

Considering the safety condition $obj(w) = G(\neg overflow(v))$, we instantiate the proof rule from Figure 1 as follows.

$$(init(w), adam(w, w'), eve(w, w')) \models obj(w)$$

There exists a strategy for Eve provided that the premises of the proof rule are satisfied. These premises are Horn clauses over the auxiliary assertion $inv(w)$. We apply a solver, e.g., CONSYNTH, to find a solution for the auxiliary assertion. The clauses S1 and S3 are universally quantified over the game variables, while the existentially quantified clause S2 is skolemized in the CONSYNTH approach. We use the skolem relation $sk(w, w', w'')$ to denote the witness constraint corresponding to the existentially quantified variables $w''$.

$$
\begin{aligned}
&inv(w) \wedge stepmother(v, v') \wedge r' = r \wedge sk(w, w', w'') \rightarrow \\
&\qquad\qquad cinderella(v', v'') \wedge inv(w'')
\end{aligned}
$$

CONSYNTH requires a template for the skolem relation and we present below the intuition behind this constraint. For each of the five disjuncts from $cinderella(v, v')$ transition relation, we add guards (one guard exclusive to the others) and update the value of the round variable. We use $c_1(v, v')$ to $c_5(v, v')$ to denote the five disjuncts from the transition relation of the Cinderella player introduced in Section 2. We obtain the following template constraint.

$$
\begin{aligned}
\text{TEMPL}(sk)(w, w', w'') = (&r' = 1 \wedge r'' = ?_1 \wedge c_1(v', v'') \vee \\
&r' = 2 \wedge r'' = ?_2 \wedge c_2(v', v'') \vee \\
&r' = 3 \wedge r'' = ?_3 \wedge c_3(v', v'') \vee \\
&r' = 4 \wedge r'' = ?_4 \wedge c_4(v', v'') \vee \\
&r' = 5 \wedge r'' = ?_5 \wedge c_5(v', v''))
\end{aligned}
$$

The template parameters are denoted by "?"-variables and different subscripts indicate distinct template parameters.

Our approach is able to synthesize automatically the values used to update the round and implicitly the order in which the Cinderella player should alternate emptying the buckets. CONSYNTH returns the solution $?_1 = 4, ?_2 = 1, ?_3 = 1, ?_4 = 3, ?_5 = 1$. Corresponding to this solution, the strategy for the Cinderella player consists of a repeating sequence of three player moves:

1. Since initially $r = 1$ and the first disjunct is enabled, decide to empty buckets 1 and 2 and update the round variable $r'' = 4$.
2. Since the disjunct $r' = 4 \wedge r'' = ?_4$ is enabled, decide to empty buckets 4 and 5 and update the round variable to $r'' = 3$.
3. Since the disjunct $r' = 3 \wedge r'' = ?_3$ is enabled, decide to empty buckets 3 and 4 and update the round variable to $r'' = 1$.

After these three moves, $r$ has value 1, the first disjunct is again enabled and the strategy will continue with the first move/decision above. This strategy ensures that the Cinderella player empties often enough all the buckets and therefore the Stepmother player cannot enforce an overflow. This game is won by the Cinderella player based on the round strategy described above.

***Second strategy*** We show how our approach can be used to obtain a strategy for the case of the game that is more difficult for Cinderella to win, i.e., $c = 2$.

We fix the roles of the two players similar to the previous paragraph: $eve(v, v') = cinderella(v, v')$ and $adam(v, v') = stepmother(v, v')$. To explain the rationale behind the Cinderella's decisions for this case, we refer to the proof rule from Figure 1. We repeat the second clause S2 instantiated for the two players of the C-S game:

$$inv(v) \land stepmother(v, v') \to safe(v') \land \exists v'' : cinderella(v', v'') \land inv(v'')$$

To change the state of the system from $v'$ to $v''$, the strategy for the Cinderella player takes into consideration her previous move (reflected in variables $v$) and the reply by Stepmother (reflected in variables $v'$). Therefore the template for the strategy considers five cases depending on which buckets the Cinderella player may have emptied in the previous turn:

$$\begin{aligned}\textsc{Templ}(sk)(v, v', v'') = (&b_1 = 0 \land b_2 = 0 \land T_{12}(v', v'') \lor \\ &b_2 = 0 \land b_3 = 0 \land T_{23}(v', v'') \lor \\ &b_3 = 0 \land b_4 = 0 \land T_{34}(v', v'') \lor \\ &b_4 = 0 \land b_5 = 0 \land T_{45}(v', v'') \lor \\ &b_5 = 0 \land b_1 = 0 \land T_{51}(v', v'')).\end{aligned}$$

The $T_{ij}$ conjuncts refer to non-obvious knowledge and relate to an invariant stating that each pair of non-adjacent buckets should have total contents at most 1 [28]. The first part of the template, i.e., $T_{12}$, is based on the intuition that if in the previous round Cinderella emptied buckets 1 and 2 ($b_1 = 0 \land b_2 = 0$), then during the next round she will decide to empty another pair of buckets. That is, either the pair of buckets 3 and 4 ($b''_3 = 0 \land b''_4 = 0$) or the pair of buckets 4 and 5 ($b''_4 = 0 \land b''_5 = 0$) will be emptied. However, the condition on which to decide if to empty buckets 3 and 4 or buckets 4 and 5 is not straightforward. We use template parameters and leave the decision to be automated by our game solving approach. The formula $T_{12}$ is provided as follows.

$$\begin{aligned}T_{12}(v', v'') = (&?_5 * b'_5 + ?_2 * b'_2 \le 1 \land b''_3 = 0 \land b''_4 = 0 \lor \\ &?_1 * b'_1 + ?_3 * b'_3 \le 1 \land b''_4 = 0 \land b''_5 = 0)\end{aligned}$$

Following a similar argument, we obtain the formulas that complete the definition of the template $\textsc{Templ}(sk)(v, v', v'')$:

$$\begin{aligned}T_{23}(v', v'') = (&?_1 * b'_1 + ?_3 * b'_3 \le 1 \land b''_4 = 0 \land b''_5 = 0 \lor \\ &?_2 * b'_2 + ?_4 * b'_4 \le 1 \land b''_5 = 0 \land b''_1 = 0) \\ T_{34}(v', v'') = (&?_2 * b'_2 + ?_4 * b'_4 \le 1 \land b''_5 = 0 \land b''_1 = 0 \lor \\ &?_3 * b'_3 + ?_5 * b'_5 \le 1 \land b''_1 = 0 \land b''_2 = 0) \\ T_{45}(v', v'') = (&?_3 * b'_3 + ?_5 * b'_5 \le 1 \land b''_1 = 0 \land b''_2 = 0 \lor \\ &?_4 * b'_4 + ?_1 * b'_1 \le 1 \land b''_2 = 0 \land b''_3 = 0) \\ T_{51}(v', v'') = (&?_4 * b'_4 + ?_1 * b'_1 \le 1 \land b''_2 = 0 \land b''_3 = 0 \lor \\ &?_5 * b'_5 + ?_2 * b'_2 \le 1 \land b''_3 = 0 \land b''_4 = 0).\end{aligned}$$

The template parameters are marked as before by "?"-variables and we aim to obtain solutions for the five template parameters $?_1, ?_2, ?_3, ?_4, ?_5$. Our approach is indeed able to synthesize automatically values for these parameters. The tool ConSynth returns the solutions $?_1 = 1, ?_2 = 1, ?_3 = 1, ?_4 = 1, ?_5 = 1$. The resulting strategy for the Cinderella player guarantees that no state with overflow can be reached. For a different perspective, we refer the interested reader to an article on (non-automated) reasoning and invariants needed to establish strategies for the Cinderella-Stepmother game similar to the ones we synthesize [28].

### 5.2 Game with Stepmother's reachability objective

We continue illustrating our approach with the Cinderella-Stepmother game, this time based on a reachability objective: the winning condition for the Stepmother player requires that a state with overflow is reached, $obj(v) = F\ overflow(v)$. For this game, we use the bucket capacity $c = 1.4$, a value for which the Stepmother has indeed a winning strategy. To derive this strategy, we instantiate the proof rule for the reachability game as follows.

$$\begin{aligned}init(v) &= (b_1 = 0 \land \cdots \land b_5 = 0) \\ eve(v, v') &= stepmother(v, v') \\ adam(v, v') &= cinderella(v, v')\end{aligned}$$

Next we provide a template corresponding to the existentially quantified clause. The insight behind the template is that the quantity of water from each bucket increases during the turn of Stepmother, but without specifying the amount, i.e., ($b''_i = b'_i + ?_i \land ?_i \ge 0$).

$$\textsc{Templ}(sk)(v, v', v'') = (?_1 + \cdots + ?_5 = 1 \land \bigwedge_{i \in \{1..5\}} (b''_i = b'_i + ?_i \land ?_i \ge 0)$$

Our approach computes the auxiliary assertions that are required by the reachability proof rule and a witness for the existential quantifier. The witness instantiates the template parameters and represents the Stepmother's strategy to ensure that the buckets eventually overflow no matter what moves are made by the Cinderella player.

$$\begin{aligned}sk(v, v') = (&b'_1 = b_1 + 0.8 \land b'_2 = b_2 \\ &\land b'_3 = b_3 + 0.1 \land b'_4 = b_4 \land b'_5 = b_5 + 0.1)\end{aligned}$$

In this case, since the addition of water is done in non-adjacent buckets, e.g., $b_1$ and $b_3$, eventually the game reaches an overflow state, and the Stepmother is the player to win this game.

### 5.3 Games with Cinderella's LTL objectives

Apart from games with safety and reachability objectives, our approach is able to handle games with more general LTL objectives. For this game, we use the following player roles.

$$\begin{aligned}init(v) &= (b_1 = 0 \land \cdots \land b_5 = 0) \\ eve(v, v') &= cinderella(v, v') \\ adam(v, v') &= stepmother(v, v')\end{aligned}$$

We use the value $c = 1.4$ for the bucket capacity, similar to Section 5.2. As already explained, with this value Stepmother has a strategy to win the game with the objective $\varphi(v) = F overflow(v)$. Consequently, Cinderella does not have a strategy to win the game with the objective set to the complement formula, i.e., $\neg\varphi(v) = G\ \neg overflow(v)$. For this section, we formalize a winning condition that is a weaker logical formula than $\neg\varphi(v)$ for which Cinderella has a winning strategy. The objective constraint $GF\ \neg overflow(v)$ states that an overflow state does not occur infinitely often in the plays of the game.

More generally, we use *color* to indicate the most significant bucket for which an overflow occurs.

- A state without overflow: $(color = 0)$.
- A state with overflow such that $i$ is the smallest index of those that correspond to buckets that have overflown: $(color = i)$.

We group the states of the system based on the truth value of the predicates $color = i$ as follows.

$$p_0(v) = (color = 0) = (b_1 \leq 1.4 \wedge \cdots \wedge b_5 \leq 1.4)$$
$$p_1(v) = (color = 1) = (b_1 > 1.4)$$
$$p_2(v) = (color = 2) = (b_1 \leq 1.4 \wedge b_2 > 1.4)$$
$$p_3(v) = (color = 3 \vee color = 4 \vee color = 5) = \ldots$$

A winning condition corresponding to a value $i$ ensures that states from $p_i(v)$ occur infinitely often in the plays of the system, and that $i$ is the smallest value for which states occur infinitely often.

$$win(v, i) = (GF\ p_i(v) \wedge \bigwedge_{j \in \{0,..,i-1\}} FG\ \neg p_j(v))$$

Our approach for solving games with LTL objectives proceeds in three steps: 1) complement the LTL formula $\varphi$ representing the winning condition; 2) construct a Büchi automaton corresponding to the complemented formula $\neg\varphi$; 3) instantiate the proof rule from Figure 3 using the Büchi automaton representation.

***LTL game 1*** For the first LTL game, we define the objective for the Cinderella player $obj(v) = win(v, 0) = GF\ p_0(v)$. We complement the objective formula to obtain $FG\ \neg p_0(v) = FG\ overflow(v)$, then construct the Büchi automaton corresponding to the complemented formula as follows.

$$init_{\mathcal{B}}(pc_{\mathcal{B}}) = (pc_{\mathcal{B}} = 0)$$
$$next_{\mathcal{B}}(pc_{\mathcal{B}}, v, pc'_{\mathcal{B}}) = (pc_{\mathcal{B}} = 0 \wedge pc'_{\mathcal{B}} = 0 \vee pc_{\mathcal{B}} = 0 \wedge pc'_{\mathcal{B}} = 1 \wedge overflow(v) \vee pc_{\mathcal{B}} = 1 \wedge pc'_{\mathcal{B}} = 1 \wedge overflow(v))$$
$$acc_{\mathcal{B}}(pc_{\mathcal{B}}) = (pc_{\mathcal{B}} = 1)$$

We instantiate the proof rule from Figure 3 as follows.

$$(init(v), adam(v, v'), eve(v, v')) \models obj(v)$$

There exists a strategy for Eve provided that the premises of the proof rule are satisfied. These premises are Horn clauses over the auxiliary assertion $inv(w)$, $aux(w, w', v'')$, $round(w, w', w'')$, and $fair(w, w')$. We apply ConSynth to find a solution for the auxiliary assertions. The clause B2 is an existentially quantified clause. By skolemization of the existential clause B2 we obtain the following.

$$inv(w) \wedge stepmother(v, v') \wedge next_{\mathcal{B}}(pc_{\mathcal{B}}, v, pc'_{\mathcal{B}}) \wedge sk(w, w', v'') \rightarrow cinderella(v', v'') \wedge aux(w, w', v'')$$

Using the template described in the paragraph "Second strategy" from Section 5.1, our approach is able to derive solutions for the auxiliary assertions and the following template parameters $?_1 = ?_2 = ?_3 = ?_4 = ?_5 = 1$. We conclude that Cinderella is the player to win this game, and that her strategy ensures that states without overflow occur infinitely often in the plays of the game.

***LTL game 2*** For the second LTL game, we define the objective for the Cinderella player $win(v, 0) \vee win(v, 2)$. The objective for the Stepmother player is $win(v, 1) \vee win(v, 3)$. The formula corresponding to the Cinderella's objective:

$$\varphi = (GF\ p_0(v) \vee (GF\ p_2(v) \wedge FG\ \neg p_1(v) \wedge FG\ \neg p_0(v))).$$

The complemented formula is

$$\neg\varphi = (FG\ \neg p_0(v) \wedge (FG\ \neg p_2(v) \vee GF\ p_1(v) \vee GF\ p_0(v))).$$

The Büchi automaton corresponding to the complemented formula contains 10 distinct control states, from which two are accepting states. Using our proof rule, we are able to compute automatically auxiliary assertions and obtain that the same second strategy is winning for the Cinderella player.

Note that for the player Cinderella, the LTL game 2 (with objective $win(v, 0) \vee win(v, 2)$) is easier to win than the LTL game 1 (with objective $win(v, 0)$). However, the relation between the two objectives is not immediately usable in a deductive approach like ours. We presented both LTL games 1 and 2, since our approach based on the proof rule from Figure 3 constructs different Buechi automata and different auxiliary assertions for the two objectives.

## 6. Case study: program repair/synthesis games

In this section we illustrate how our constraint-based approach to solving games applies to the synthesis of reactive programs from temporal specifications. We consider synthesis problems obtained from program repair questions, see Section 6.1 and Section 6.2, as well as inference of thread synchronization, see Section 6.3. In Section 7 we report on running times required for solving these games using ConSynth.

### 6.1 Program repair game with safety objective

We model program repair as a game following [29]. That is, given a set of suspect statements, we look for a modification of those program statements such that the modified program satisfies its specification. For the first repair game, we assume that a program is given by a tuple $(init(v), next(v, v'), error(v))$ that represents initial states, a transition relation, and error states, respectively.

As an example we consider the program shown in Figure 3 in [29]. The program has three program variables $v = (l, gl, pc)$. The variable $l$ models a lock, the variable $gl$ is used to keep track of the status of the lock, while the variable $pc$ is the program counter variable. The initial states of the program are

$$init(v) = (gl = 0 \wedge l = 0 \wedge pc = \ell_0).$$

We show the control-flow graph of the program below.

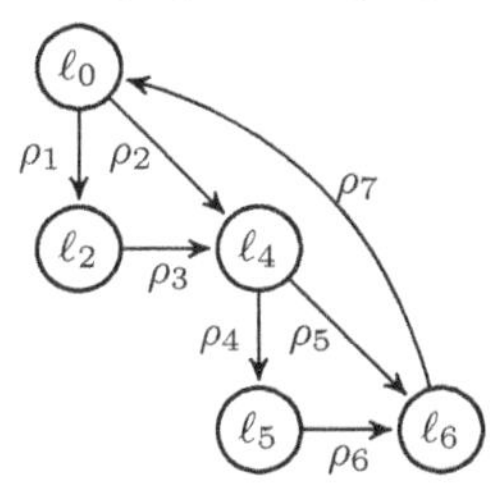


The transition relation is defined as follows.

$$\begin{aligned}
\rho_1(v, v') &= (pc = \ell_0 \wedge pc' = \ell_2 \wedge l' = l \wedge gl' = gl)\\
\rho_2(v, v') &= (pc = \ell_0 \wedge pc' = \ell_4 \wedge l' = l \wedge gl' = gl)\\
\rho_3(v, v') &= (pc = \ell_2 \wedge pc' = \ell_4 \wedge l \leq 0 \wedge l' = 1)\\
\rho_4(v, v') &= (pc = \ell_4 \wedge pc' = \ell_5 \wedge gl \neq 0 \wedge l' = l \wedge gl' = gl)\\
\rho_5(v, v') &= (pc = \ell_4 \wedge pc' = \ell_6 \wedge gl = 0 \wedge l' = l \wedge gl' = gl)\\
\rho_6(v, v') &= (pc = \ell_5 \wedge pc' = \ell_6 \wedge l \geq 1 \wedge l' = 0 \wedge gl' = gl)\\
\rho_7(v, v') &= (pc = \ell_6 \wedge pc' = \ell_0 \wedge l' = l)\\
next(v, v') &= (\rho_1(v, v') \vee \cdots \vee \rho_7(v, v'))
\end{aligned}$$

Note that in $\rho_3(v, v')$ and $\rho_7(v, v')$ the variable $gl$ is assigned a non-deterministic value, since it is not constrained by the corresponding assertions. The execution of the program enters an error state at location $\ell_2$ if the lock variable $l$ is held, and at location $\ell_5$ if the lock variable $l$ is not held, i.e., we have

$$error(v) = (pc = \ell_2 \wedge l = 1 \vee pc = \ell_5 \wedge l = 0).$$

We instantiate the safety game proof rule such that the system role is played by the program transition relation and the environment role is to provide inputs to the program (in this case, the program does not expect any inputs).

$$\begin{aligned} eve(v, v') &= next(v, v') \\ adam(v, v') &= skip(v, v') \\ obj(v) &= G\ \neg error(v) \end{aligned}$$

A repair of the program restricts the transition relation of the program such that $G\ \neg error(v)$ holds. To this end, we provide a template corresponding to the existentially quantified clause of the proof rule:

$$\begin{aligned} \text{TEMPL}(sk)(v, v', v'') = (&pc' = \ell_2 \wedge pc'' = \ell_4 \wedge gl'' = ?_1 \\ \vee\ &pc' = \ell_6 \wedge pc'' = \ell_0 \wedge gl'' = ?_2) \end{aligned}$$

Our algorithm returns the witness for the existential quantifier clause that instantiates the template parameters $?_1 = 1$ and $?_2 = 0$. This corresponds to a repaired program that assigns the value 1 to $gl$ at location $\ell_2$, and assigns the value 0 to $gl$ at location $\ell_6$. We obtain the same program repair as the solution originally presented in [29].

### 6.2 Concurrent program repair games with safety and response objectives

We illustrate how our approach can be applied to concurrent program repair problems, and in particular to repair problems under fairness assumptions. We use the CRITICAL SECTION example from Figure 5 in [29] for this purpose. In this example, the assignment $turn1B = false$ at location $\ell_2$ is faulty. The goal is to repair this assignment, and hence, the entire program by checking if there exists an assignment to the variable $turn1B$ from its domain $\{true,\ false\}$ such that the resulting program satisfies certain temporal properties. These properties are used in directing the repair process towards the correct version of the program.

Let $(f1a, f1b, t1b, f2a, f2b, t2b)$ be abbreviations of original variable names $(flag1A,\ flag1B,\ turn1B,\ flag2A,\ flag2B,\ turn2B)$. We encode the original program over variables $v = (pc_1, pc_2, x, y, f1a, f1b, t1b, f2a, f2b, t2b)$ using an initial condition $init(v)$ such that

$$\begin{aligned} init(v) = (&f1a = 0 \wedge f1b = 0 \wedge t1b = 0 \wedge f2a = 0 \\ &\wedge f2b = 0 \wedge t2b = 0 \wedge pc_1 = \ell_1 \wedge pc_2 = \ell_1), \end{aligned}$$

and a transition relation $next(v, v')$. Since the program is multi-threaded with two threads, we give $next(v, v')$ as a disjunction of transition relations of individual threads

$$next_1(v, v') \wedge pc_2' = pc_2 \vee next_2(v, v') \wedge pc_1' = pc_1.$$

For the first thread we define (note that we explicate assignments of a non-deterministic value to a variable $z$ by $z' = ND$ and we omit equalities for variables that do not change, hence, each variable $z$ that does not appear in $z' = \ldots$ is constrained by $z' = z$):

$$\begin{aligned} next_1(v, v') = (&pc_1 = \ell_1 \wedge pc_1' = \ell_2 \wedge f1a' = 1 \vee \\ &pc_1 = \ell_2 \wedge pc_1' = \ell_3 \wedge t1b' = ND \vee \\ &pc_1 = \ell_3 \wedge f1b = 1 \wedge t1b = 1 \wedge pc_1' = \ell_3 \vee \\ &pc_1 = \ell_3 \wedge (f1b = 0 \vee t1b = 0) \wedge pc_1' = \ell_4 \vee \\ &pc_1 = \ell_4 \wedge pc_1' = \ell_5 \wedge f1a' = 0 \vee \\ &pc_1 = \ell_5 \wedge t1b = 1 \wedge pc_1' = \ell_6 \wedge f2a' = 1 \vee \\ &pc_1 = \ell_5 \wedge t1b = 1 \wedge pc_1' = \ell_9 \vee \\ &pc_1 = \ell_6 \wedge pc_1' = \ell_7 \wedge t2b' = 1 \vee \\ &pc_1 = \ell_7 \wedge f2b = 1 \wedge t2b = 1 \wedge pc_1' = \ell_7 \vee \\ &pc_1 = \ell_7 \wedge (f2b = 0 \vee t2b = 0) \wedge pc_1' = \ell_8 \vee \\ &pc_1 = \ell_8 \wedge pc_1' = \ell_9 \wedge f2a' = 0 \vee \\ &pc_1 = \ell_9 \wedge pc_1' = \ell_1). \end{aligned}$$

Note that the second disjunct above leaves the value of $t1b$ unrestricted, as denoted by $t1b' = ND$. For the second thread we define:

$$\begin{aligned} next_2(v, v') = (&pc_2 = \ell_1 \wedge pc_2' = \ell_2 \wedge f1b' = 1 \vee \\ &pc_2 = \ell_2 \wedge pc_2' = \ell_3 \wedge t1b' = 0 \vee \\ &pc_2 = \ell_3 \wedge f1a = 1 \wedge t1b = 0 \wedge pc_2' = \ell_3 \vee \\ &pc_2 = \ell_3 \wedge (f1a = 0 \vee t1b = 1) \wedge pc_2' = \ell_4 \vee \\ &pc_2 = \ell_4 \wedge pc_2' = \ell_5 \wedge f2b' = 1 \vee \\ &pc_2 = \ell_5 \wedge pc_2' = \ell_6 \wedge t2b' = 0 \vee \\ &pc_2 = \ell_6 \wedge f2a = 1 \wedge t2b = 0 \wedge pc_2' = \ell_6 \vee \\ &pc_2 = \ell_6 \wedge (f2a = 0 \vee t2b = 1) \wedge pc_2' = \ell_7 \vee \\ &pc_2 = \ell_7 \wedge pc_2' = \ell_8 \wedge f2b' = 0 \vee \\ &pc_2 = \ell_8 \wedge pc_2' = \ell_9 \wedge f1b' = 0 \vee \\ &pc_2 = \ell_9 \wedge pc_2' = \ell_1). \end{aligned}$$

In the original problem there are two properties directed by which the program should be repaired. The first property requires that the two threads do not enter their critical sections at the same time. This property is specified with the following LTL formula.

$$\begin{aligned} \varphi_1(v) = G\ (&(pc_1 = \ell_4 \rightarrow pc_2 \neq \ell_4) \wedge \\ &(pc_1 = \ell_8 \rightarrow pc_2 \neq \ell_7)) \end{aligned}$$

The second property requires that neither of the threads can be in a deadlock state. This property is specified as follows.

$$\begin{aligned} \varphi_2(v) = G\ (&(pc_1 = \ell_3 \rightarrow F\ (pc_1 = \ell_4)) \wedge \\ &(pc_1 = \ell_7 \rightarrow F\ (pc_1 = \ell_8)) \wedge \\ &(pc_2 = \ell_3 \rightarrow F\ (pc_2 = \ell_4)) \wedge \\ &(pc_2 = \ell_6 \rightarrow F\ (pc_2 = \ell_7))) \end{aligned}$$

***Safety game*** Doing the program repair using the first property amounts to applying the safety proof rule from Figure 1 to find $inv(v)$. Since there is no interaction with the environment, $adam(v, v')$ will simply be equivalent with $skip(v, v')$. To apply our proof rule, we use $next(v, v')$ for $eve(v, v')$ and $\varphi_1(v)$ as the winning condition $obj$. We use the following template for the existential clause:

$$\text{TEMPL}(sk)(v, v', v'') = (t1b'' = ?_1).$$

CONSYNTH computes the solution $?_1 = 1$, and correspondingly we obtain a modified version of $next_1(v, v')$ where the non-deterministic assignment $t1b' = ND$ from the second disjunct is replaced by $t1b' = 1$.

***Fair LTL game*** The second property relies on fairness assumptions. To deal with the fairness, we apply a transformation technique from [36] that reduces fair parallelism semantics to the usual parallelism semantics. The idea is to use the equivalence $P \models_{fair} \Phi$ if and only $T_{fair}(P) \models \Phi$, where $P$ is the original program, $T_{fair}$ is the fair transformation function, $T_{fair}(P)$ is the transformed program with embedded tracking of fairness, and $\Phi$ is the property to check. The transformation does not change the initial states of the program, but it significantly modifies the semantics of the transition relation of the program. A counter variable is introduced for each thread from the program, and the first statement of each loop is strengthened by adding a guard and an update involving the counter variables. See [36] for details. For our example program, the transformation:

- introduces the counters $k_1$ and $k_2$,
- adds the guard $k_1 \leq k_2$ and the update constraint $(k_1' = ND \wedge k_2' = k_2 - 1)$ to the first, third and ninth disjunct from $next_1(v, v')$,

- adds the guard $k_2 \leq k_1$ and the update constraint $(k_1' = k_1 - 1 \wedge k_2' = ND)$ to the first, third and sixth disjunct in $next_2(v, v')$.

Let $initT(v, k_1, k_2) = init(v)$ be the initial condition of the transformed program. We refer to the transformed transition relations as $nextT_1(v, k_1, k_2, v', k_1', k_2')$ and $nextT_2(v, k_1, k_2, v', k_1', k_2')$, and present them below.

$$\begin{aligned}
&nextT_1(v, k_1, k_2, v', k_1', k_2') = \\
&\quad (pc_1 = \ell_1 \wedge pc_1' = \ell_2 \wedge f1a' = 1 \\
&\quad \wedge k_1 \leq k_2 \wedge k_1' = ND \wedge k_2' = k_2 - 1 \vee \\
&\quad \ldots \vee \\
&\quad pc_1 = \ell_3 \wedge f1b = 1 \wedge t1b = 1 \wedge pc_1' = \ell_3 \\
&\quad \wedge k_1 \leq k_2 \wedge k_1' = ND \wedge k_2' = k_2 - 1 \vee \\
&\quad \ldots \vee \\
&\quad pc_1 = \ell_7 \wedge f2b = 1 \wedge t2b = 1 \wedge pc_1' = \ell_7 \\
&\quad \wedge k_1 \leq k_2 \wedge k_1' = ND \wedge k_2' = k_2 - 1 \vee \\
&\quad \ldots)
\end{aligned}$$

$$\begin{aligned}
&nextT_2(v, k_1, k_2, v', k_1', k_2') = \\
&\quad (pc_2 = \ell_1 \wedge pc_2' = \ell_2 \wedge f1b' = 1 \\
&\quad \wedge k_2 \leq k_1 \wedge k_1' = k_1 - 1 \wedge k_2' = ND \vee \\
&\quad \ldots \vee \\
&\quad pc_2 = \ell_3 \wedge f1a = 1 \wedge t1b = 0 \wedge pc_2' = \ell_3 \\
&\quad \wedge k_2 \leq k_1 \wedge k_1' = k_1 - 1 \wedge k_2' = ND \vee \\
&\quad \ldots \vee \\
&\quad pc_2 = \ell_6 \wedge f2a = 1 \wedge t2b = 0 \wedge pc_2' = \ell_6 \\
&\quad \wedge k_2 \leq k_1 \wedge k_1' = k_1 - 1 \wedge k_2' = ND \vee \\
&\quad \ldots)
\end{aligned}$$

The second property is more complicated than the first property since it involves nesting of temporal operators. Like the case for the first property, we assume $adam(v, v')$ to be equivalent with $skip(v, v')$. We make $nextT(v, v')$ to play the role of $eve(v, v')$, and $G\ ((pc_1 = \ell_3 \rightarrow F\ pc_1 = \ell_4) \wedge (pc_1 = \ell_7 \rightarrow F\ pc_1 = \ell_8) \wedge (pc_2 = \ell_3 \rightarrow F\ pc_2 = \ell_4) \wedge (pc_2 = \ell_6 \rightarrow F\ pc_2 = \ell_7))$ is now a winning condition $obj$.

We reuse the template used for the previous game and we get exactly the same solution. That is, we determine $t1b' = ND$ to $t1b' = 1$ in the second disjunct of $nextT_1(v, k_1, k_2, v', k_1', k_2')$.

### 6.3 Synthesis of synchronization game with safety objective

Synthesis of synchronization in multi-threaded programs [45] can be automated using our approach. For illustration, we use the example program from Figure 1 in [45] and represent it using a tuple $(init(v), next(v, v'), error(v))$ for the case when three threads are involved in computation. The program variables are $v = (x, y_1, y_2, z, pc_1, pc_2, pc_3)$, the initial states are described by $init(v) = (x = 0 \wedge z = 0 \wedge pc_1 = \ell_1 \wedge pc_2 = \ell_1 \wedge pc_3 = \ell_1)$. The transition relation of the program is

$$\begin{aligned}
next(v, v') = (&next_1(v, v') \wedge pc_2' = pc_2 \wedge pc_3' = pc_3 \vee \\
&next_2(v, v') \wedge pc_1' = pc_1 \wedge pc_3' = pc_3 \vee \\
&next_3(v, v') \wedge pc_1' = pc_1 \wedge pc_2' = pc_2)
\end{aligned}$$

such that

$$\begin{aligned}
&next_1(v, v') = \\
&\quad (pc_1 = \ell_1 \wedge pc_1' = \ell_2 \wedge x' = x + z \wedge skip(y_1, y_2, z) \vee \\
&\quad\ pc_1 = \ell_2 \wedge pc_1' = \ell_3 \wedge x' = x + z \wedge skip(y_1, y_2, z)) \\
&next_2(v, v') = \\
&\quad (pc_2 = \ell_1 \wedge pc_2' = \ell_2 \wedge z' = z + 1 \wedge skip(x, y_1, y_2) \vee \\
&\quad\ pc_2 = \ell_2 \wedge pc_2' = \ell_3 \wedge z' = z + 1 \wedge skip(x, y_1, y_2))
\end{aligned}$$

$$\begin{aligned}
&next_3(v, v') = \\
&\quad (pc_3 = \ell_1 \wedge pc_3' = \ell_2 \wedge x = 1 \wedge y_1' = 3 \wedge skip(x, y_2, z) \vee \\
&\quad\ pc_3 = \ell_1 \wedge pc_3' = \ell_2 \wedge x = 2 \wedge y_1' = 6 \wedge skip(x, y_2, z) \vee \\
&\quad\ pc_3 = \ell_1 \wedge pc_3' = \ell_2 \wedge (x \leq 0 \vee x \geq 3) \wedge y_1' = 5 \wedge \\
&\quad\ skip(x, y_2, z) \vee \\
&\quad\ pc_3 = \ell_2 \wedge pc_3' = \ell_3 \wedge y_2' = x \wedge skip(x, y_1, z) \vee \\
&\quad\ pc_3 = \ell_3 \wedge pc_3' = \ell_4 \wedge y_1 \neq y_2 \wedge skip(x, y_1, y_2, z)).
\end{aligned}$$

Different interleavings of the three threads lead to different values of $y_1$ and $y_2$. An assertion in the third thread at location $\ell_3$ requires that the values given to $y_1$ and $y_2$ are not equal, i.e., we have

$$error(v) = (pc_3 = \ell_3 \wedge y_1 = y_2).$$

For the given program, some interleavings lead to the values of $y_1$ and $y_2$ being equal, while other interleavings lead to distinct values for the two variables. The goal of [45] is to add synchronization to the program such that the assertion holds on all executions. To apply our proof rule to this problem, we encode the choice between executing a single step and executing an atomic section using auxiliary variables. The transition relation of the program is augmented with guards deciding a single step or an atomic section based on the values of the auxiliary variables. For our example, we use four auxiliary variables $(c_{11}, c_{21}, c_{31}, c_{32})$. We obtain an extended tuple of variables $w = (v, c_{11}, c_{21}, c_{31}, c_{32})$. A constraint $c_{ij} = \ell$ is used in thread $i$ to decide that the control flows from location $\ell_j$ to location $\ell$. Correspondingly, the transition relation of the first thread is augmented to:

$$\begin{aligned}
&next_1(w, w') = \\
&(pc_1 = \ell_1 \wedge c_{11} = \ell_2 \wedge pc_1' = \ell_2 \wedge x' = x + z \wedge skip(\ldots) \vee \\
&\ pc_1 = \ell_1 \wedge c_{11} = \ell_3 \wedge pc_1' = \ell_3 \wedge x' = x + 2 * z \wedge skip(\ldots) \vee \\
&\ pc_1 = \ell_2 \wedge pc_1' = \ell_3 \wedge x' = x + z \wedge skip(\ldots))
\end{aligned}$$

The transition relations of the second and third thread are instrumented similarly. We instantiate the safety game proof rule such that the system role is played by the instrumented program transition relation and the environment role is to provide inputs to the program (similar to the previous case, this example program does not expect any inputs).

$$\begin{aligned}
init(w) &= init(v) \\
eve(w, w') &= (next_1(w, w') \vee next_2(w, w') \vee next_3(w, w')) \\
adam(w, w') &= skip(w, w')
\end{aligned}$$

Furthermore, we represent the search of initial parameter values using a strengthening of the original initial condition with an assertion $mid(w, t)$ such that:

$$\begin{aligned}
&init(w) \rightarrow \exists t : mid(w, t) \\
&(mid(w, t), eve(w, w'), adam(w, w')) \models G\ \neg error(w)
\end{aligned}$$

We use ConSynth and provide the following template for the existential clause involving the initial states.

$$\begin{aligned}
\text{Templ}(sk)(w, t) = (&c_{11} = ?_{11} \wedge c_{21} = ?_{21} \\
&\wedge c_{31} = ?_{31} \wedge c_{32} = ?_{32}).
\end{aligned}$$

| Name | Game | Player $p$ | Objective for player $p$ | Result | Time (z3) | Time (Barcelogic) |
|---|---|---|---|---|---|---|
| G1 | Cinderella ($c = 3$) | Cinderella | $G\ \neg overflow$ | ✓ | 3.2s | **1.2s** |
| G2 | Cinderella ($c = 2$) | Cinderella | $G\ \neg overflow$ | ✓ | **1m52s** | **1m52s** |
| G3 | Cinderella ($c = 1.4$) | Stepmother | $F\ overflow$ | ✓ | **18s** | 1m14s |
| G4 | Cinderella ($c = 1.4$) | Cinderella | $win(0)$ | ✓ | **7m16s** | SysError |
| G5 | Cinderella ($c = 1.4$) | Cinderella | $win(0) \vee win(2)$ | ✓ | **4.7s** | **4.7s** |
| G6 | Repair-Lock | Program | $G\ \neg error$ | ✓ | **0.3s** | **0.3s** |
| G7 | Repair-Critical | Program | $G\ \neg error$ | ✓ | 17.7s | **16.9s** |
| G8 | Repair-Critical | Program | $G\ (at\_p \rightarrow F\ \neg at\_p)$ | ✓ | **53.3s** | 3m6s |
| G9 | Synth-Synchronization | Program | $G\ \neg error$ | ✓ | T/O | **1s** |

**Table 1.** Statistics for case studies. A T/O-mark stands for time out after 15 minutes.

A solution to $mid(w, t)$ sets the auxiliary variables to target program locations so that the objective of the game is satisfied, i.e., the error states are not reachable. ConSynth returns the following witness for the existential quantifier clause:

$$sk(w, t) = (c_{11} = 3 \wedge c_{21} = 3 \wedge c_{31} = 4 \wedge c_{32} = 3).$$

We note that our proof rule does not represent an optimization problem. The solutions we obtain correspond to a synthesized program that is not necessarily the most efficient one, i.e., the longest atomic sections may be picked instead of smaller steps. Dealing with optimality is a subject for future work.

## 7. Experimental results

In this section we describe how we used ConSynth as a proof-of-concept implementation of our proposed approach to solving infinite-state games. ConSynth is implemented in SICStus Prolog and is a solver for Horn clauses over linear inequalities. The implementation uses two SMT solvers for handling non-linear constraints: the Z3 solver [13] and the Barcelogic solver [5, 6].

For our experiments we used a computer with an Intel Core 2 Duo 2.53 GHz CPU and 4 GB of RAM. Table 1 shows the results corresponding to the case studies described in the paper: Cinderella-Stepmother games with safety objectives (G1 and G2), with reachability objectives (G3) and with more general LTL objectives (G4 and G5). Lastly, we show results on the program repair/synthesis games (G6, G7, G8 and G9).

For each game we report the player and the objective for which we synthesize strategies (see Columns 3 and 4). Column 5 shows the result obtained from our tool: an ✓-mark stands for a strategy successfully synthesized by our tool using either Z3 or Barcelogic as solving back-ends. In one case (G5), due to the general LTL objective we obtain a large Büchi automaton. Our normal encoding times-out for both Z3 and Barcelogic. However, ConSynth can synthesize a winning strategy quickly if we exploit an optimization where we treat infinite datatypes symbolically using a decision procedure, and finite domain datatypes explicitly without abstraction. Because the control locations of the Büchi automaton $pc_{\mathcal{B}}$ range over a finite domain, this optimization allows the tool to track the states of $pc_{\mathcal{B}}$ explicitly, and this simplifies the proof obligations.

We believe our approach will benefit from future improvements in constraint solving. The cases when either Z3 or Barcelogic times out are challenging SMT problems and of potential interest to the SMT-solving community.

## 8. Related work

There is a rich literature on decision procedures for graph games with application to formal methods [14, 32, 38, 43]. In particular, many techniques, both explicit-state [43] and symbolic [25, 37], are known for games on finite graphs. Decidability results are also known for games on certain restricted classes of infinite graphs, such as pushdown graphs [8, 46] and prefix-recognizable graphs [9].

Known approaches to games on graphs that represent state spaces of general infinite-state programs can be divided into two categories: those based on symbolic execution and those based on abstraction-refinement. De Alfaro et al [12] offer an example of the first kind of approach. In this work, a symbolic semi-algorithm is used to explore the state space of the game directly. In contrast, we reduce the problem of solving a game to Horn constraint solving, leaving the constraints to be solved by a dedicated solver relying on CEGAR and interpolation.

The second category of methods [2, 15, 16, 22–24] lift predicate abstraction and CEGAR, originally proposed for safety verification, to games. The core idea here is the use of abstract transition systems where overapproximate ("may") and underapproximate ("must") transitions are permitted, and which are model-checked against properties with 3-valued semantics. In contrast to existing approaches of this sort, we do not directly construct a program abstraction with must-transitions or 3-valued semantics. Instead, we use a Skolem relation that is iteratively refined. Moreover, our backend solver uses disjunctively well-founded transition invariants [39] to resolve liveness goals for players, which (so far as we are aware) existing approaches do not do. This algorithmic difference has a significant impact in practice.

Our approach is perhaps more closely related to a recent paper by Cook and Koskinen [11], which uses a combination of CEGAR with a form of Skolemization for verification of branching-time properties of programs. However, this method only studies verification of CTL — the class of properties that we handle is significantly larger (e.g., it includes the full $\mu$-calculus).

Games have a particularly close connection to program synthesis and repair, areas that have seen a flurry of activity in the last few years. However, in recent as well as classical algorithms in these areas, the focus is tends to be either on finite-state systems [29, 38, 41], or on functional, rather than reactive, programs [31, 42, 45]. In contrast, the natural application of our approach is in the repair and synthesis of infinite-state reactive programs.

Finally, our work here was inspired by the rich tradition of on deductive program synthesis [34, 38, 40]. The main difference between this line of work and ours lies in our focus on automation. For example, Slanina [40] also offers a deductive rule for games with response objectives. However, the proof rule demands global ranking functions and justice and compassion assumptions, which are known to be difficult to discharge automatically.

## 9. Conclusion

We have presented a constraint based approach to computing winning strategies in infinite-state games. The approach consists of: (1) a set of sound and relatively complete proof rules for solving such games, and (2) automation of the rules on top of an existing automated deduction engine. We demonstrate the practical promise of our approach through several case studies using examples derived from prior work on program repair and synthesis.

Many avenues for future work remain open. The system we have presented is a prototype. Much more remains to be done on engineering it for greater scalability. In particular, we are especially interested in applying the system to reactive synthesis questions arising out of embedded systems and robotics. On the theoretical end, exploring opportunities of synergy between our approach and abstraction-based [22, 24] and automata-theoretic approaches to games [43] remains a fascinating open question.


### Acknowledgements

This research was supported in part by the ERC project 308125, by the DFG Graduiertenkolleg 1480 (PUMA), and by NSF Awards #1162076 and #1156059.


## References


[1] R. Alur, P. Cerný, P. Madhusudan, and W. Nam. Synthesis of interface specifications for java classes. In *POPL*, pages 98–109, 2005.

[2] T. Ball and O. Kupferman. An abstraction-refinement framework for multi-agent systems. In *LICS*, pages 379–388. IEEE, 2006.

[3] T. Beyene, C. Popeea, and A. Rybalchenko. Solving existentially quantified Horn clauses. In *CAV*, 2013.

[4] M. Bodlaender, C. Hurkens, V. Kusters, F. Staals, G. Woeginger, and H. Zantema. Cinderella versus the Wicked Stepmother. In *IFIP TCS*, pages 57–71, 2012.

[5] M. Bofill, R. Nieuwenhuis, A. Oliveras, E. Rodríguez-Carbonell, and A. Rubio. The Barcelogic SMT solver. In *CAV*, pages 294–298, 2008.

[6] C. Borralleras, S. Lucas, A. Oliveras, E. Rodríguez-Carbonell, and A. Rubio. SAT modulo linear arithmetic for solving polynomial constraints. *J. Autom. Reasoning*, 48(1):107–131, 2012.

[7] J. R. Büchi and L. Landweber. Solving sequential conditions by finite-state strategies. *Trans. Amer. Math. Soc.*, 138:295–311, 1969.

[8] T. Cachat. Symbolic strategy synthesis for games on pushdown graphs. In *ICALP*, pages 704–715. 2002.

[9] T. Cachat. Uniform solution of parity games on prefix-recognizable graphs. *Electronic Notes in Theoretical Computer Science*, 68(6):71–84, 2003.

[10] K. Chatterjee and L. Doyen. Energy parity games. *TCS*, 2012.

[11] B. Cook and E. Koskinen. Reasoning about nondeterminism in programs. In *PLDI*, 2013.

[12] L. De Alfaro, T. Henzinger, and R. Majumdar. Symbolic algorithms for infinite-state games. In *CONCUR*, pages 536–550. Springer, 2001.

[13] L. M. de Moura and N. Bjørner. Z3: An efficient SMT solver. In *TACAS*, 2008.

[14] E. A. Emerson and C. Jutla. Tree automata, mu-calculus and determinacy. In *FOCS*, pages 368–377. IEEE, 1991.

[15] H. Fecher and M. Huth. Ranked predicate abstraction for branching time: Complete, incremental, and precise. In *ATVA*, pages 322–336. Springer, 2006.

[16] H. Fecher and S. Shoham. Local abstraction–refinement for the $\mu$-calculus. *STTT*, 13(4):289–306, 2011.

[17] P. Gastin and D. Oddoux. Fast LTL to Büchi automata translation. In *CAV*, pages 53–65, 2001.

[18] E. Grädel, W. Thomas, and T. Wilke, editors. *Automata, Logics, and Infinite Games: A Guide to Current Research*, 2002.

[19] S. Grebenshchikov, A. Gupta, N. P. Lopes, C. Popeea, and A. Rybalchenko. HSF(C): A software verifier based on Horn clauses - (competition contribution). In *TACAS*, 2012.

[20] S. Grebenshchikov, N. P. Lopes, C. Popeea, and A. Rybalchenko. Synthesizing software verifiers from proof rules. In *PLDI*, 2012.

[21] A. Griesmayer, R. Bloem, and B. Cook. Repair of boolean programs with an application to C. In *CAV*, pages 358–371. Springer, 2006.

[22] O. Grumberg, M. Lange, M. Leucker, and S. Shoham. Dont know in the $\mu$-calculus. In *VMCAI*, pages 233–249, 2005.

[23] O. Grumberg, M. Lange, M. Leucker, and S. Shoham. When not losing is better than winning: Abstraction and refinement for the full $\mu$-calculus. *Information and Computation*, 205(8):1130–1148, 2007.

[24] A. Gurfinkel and M. Chechik. Why waste a perfectly good abstraction? In *TACAS*, pages 212–226. 2006.

[25] A. Harding, M. Ryan, and P.-Y. Schobbens. A new algorithm for strategy synthesis in ltl games. In *TACASs*, pages 477–492. Springer, 2005.

[26] T. A. Henzinger, R. Jhala, and R. Majumdar. Counterexample-guided control. In *ICALP*, pages 886–902, 2003.

[27] K. Hoder, N. Bjørner, and L. M. de Moura. *Z*- an efficient engine for fixed points with constraints. In *CAV*, pages 457–462, 2011.

[28] A. J. C. Hurkens, C. A. J. Hurkens, and G. J. Woeginger. How Cinderella won the bucket game (and lived happily ever after). *Mathematics Magazine*, 84(4):pp. 278–283, 2011.

[29] B. Jobstmann, A. Griesmayer, and R. Bloem. Program repair as a game. In *CAV*, pages 226–238, 2005.

[30] M. Jurdziński. Small progress measures for solving parity games. In *STACS*, pages 290–301, 2000.

[31] V. Kuncak, M. Mayer, R. Piskac, and P. Suter. Complete functional synthesis. In *PLDI*, 2010.

[32] O. Kupferman and M. Y. Vardi. Robust satisfaction. In *CONCUR*, pages 383–398, 1999.

[33] Z. Manna and A. Pnueli. Completing the temporal picture. *Theor. Comput. Sci.*, 83(1):91–130, 1991.

[34] Z. Manna and R. Waldinger. A deductive approach to program synthesis. *TOPLAS*, 2(1):90–121, 1980.

[35] D. Martin. Borel determinacy. *The Annals of Mathematics*, 102(2): 363–371, 1975.

[36] E.-R. Olderog and K. R. Apt. Fairness in parallel programs: The transformational approach. *TOPLAS*, 10(3), 1988.

[37] N. Piterman, A. Pnueli, and Y. Saar. Synthesis of reactive(1) designs. In *VMCAI*, pages 364–380, 2006.

[38] A. Pnueli and R. Rosner. On the synthesis of a reactive module. In *POPL*, pages 179–190. ACM, 1989.

[39] A. Podelski and A. Rybalchenko. Transition invariants. In *LICS*, 2004.

[40] M. Slanina. Control rules for reactive system games. In *AAAI Spring Symposium on Logic-Based Program Synthesis*, 2002.

[41] A. Solar-Lezama, L. Tancau, R. Bodík, S. A. Seshia, and V. A. Saraswat. Combinatorial sketching for finite programs. In *ASPLOS*, pages 404–415, 2006.

[42] S. Srivastava, S. Gulwani, and J. S. Foster. From program verification to program synthesis. In *POPL*, pages 313–326, 2010.

[43] W. Thomas. On the synthesis of strategies in infinite games. In *STACS*, pages 1–13, 1995.

[44] M. Y. Vardi. Verification of concurrent programs: The automata-theoretic framework. *Ann. Pure Appl. Logic*, 51(1-2):79–98, 1991.

[45] M. T. Vechev, E. Yahav, and G. Yorsh. Abstraction-guided synthesis of synchronization. In *POPL*, 2010.

[46] I. Walukiewicz. Pushdown processes: Games and model-checking. *Information and computation*, 164(2):234–263, 2001.

[47] W. Zielonka. Infinite games on finitely coloured graphs with applications to automata on infinite trees. *Theoretical Computer Science*, 200 (1):135–183, 1998.

# Sound Compilation of Reals

Eva Darulova
EPFL
eva.darulova@epfl.ch

Viktor Kuncak
EPFL
viktor.kuncak@epfl.ch

## Abstract

Writing accurate numerical software is hard because of many sources of unavoidable uncertainties, including finite numerical precision of implementations. We present a programming model where the user writes a program in a real-valued implementation and specification language that explicitly includes different types of uncertainties. We then present a compilation algorithm that generates a finite-precision implementation that is guaranteed to meet the desired precision with respect to real numbers. Our compilation performs a number of verification steps for different candidate precisions. It generates verification conditions that treat all sources of uncertainties in a unified way and encode reasoning about finite-precision roundoff errors into reasoning about real numbers. Such verification conditions can be used as a standardized format for verifying the precision and the correctness of numerical programs. Due to their non-linear nature, precise reasoning about these verification conditions remains difficult and cannot be handled using state-of-the art SMT solvers alone. We therefore propose a new procedure that combines exact SMT solving over reals with approximate and sound affine and interval arithmetic. We show that this approach overcomes scalability limitations of SMT solvers while providing improved precision over affine and interval arithmetic. Our implementation gives promising results on several numerical models, including dynamical systems, transcendental functions, and controller implementations.

***Categories and Subject Descriptors*** D.2.4 [*Software Engineering*]: Program Verification

***Keywords*** roundoff error; floating-point arithmetic; fixed-point arithmetic; verification; compilation; embedded systems; numerical approximation; scientific computing; sensitivity analysis

## 1. Introduction

Writing numerical programs is difficult, in part because the programmer needs to deal not only with the correctness of the algorithm but also with different forms of uncertainties. Program inputs may not be exactly known because they come from physical experiments or were measured by an embedded sensor. The computation itself suffers from roundoff errors at each step, because of the use of finite-precision arithmetic. In addition, resources like energy may be scarce so that only a certain number of bits are available for the numerical data type.

At the same time, the computed results in these domains can have far-reaching consequences if used to control, for example, a vehicle or a nuclear power plant. It is therefore becoming increasingly urgent to develop tools that improve confidence in numerical code [38]. One of the first challenges in doing this is that most of our automated reasoning tools work with real arithmetic, whereas the code is implemented with finite-precision. Many current approaches to verify numerical programs start with the finite-precision implementation and then try to verify the absence of (run-time) errors. Not only are such verification results specific to a given representation of numbers, but the absence of run-time errors does not guarantee that program behavior matches the desired specification expressed using real numbers. Fundamentally, the source code semantics is currently expressed in terms of low-level data types such as floating-points. This is problematic not only for developers but also for compiler optimizations, because, e.g., the associativity law is unsound with respect to such source code semantics.

In this paper we advocate a natural but ambitious alternative: source code programs should be expressed in terms of mathematical real numbers. In our system, the programmer writes a program using a **Real** data type, states the desired postconditions, and specifies explicitly the uncertainties as well as the desired target precision. It is then up to our trustworthy compiler to check, taking into account all uncertainties and their propagation, that the desired precision can be soundly realized in a finite-precision implementation. If so, the compiler chooses and emits one such implementation, selecting from a range of (software or hardware) floating-point or fixed-point arithmetic representations.

A key question that such a compiler needs to answer is whether a given finite-precision representation remains close enough to an ideal implementation in terms of real numbers. To answer this question, we present a method to generate verification conditions that encode reasoning about finite-precision roundoff errors into reasoning about real numbers. Our verification conditions explicitly model the *ideal* program without external uncertainties and roundoffs, the *actual* program, which is executed in finite precision with possibly noisy inputs, and the relationship between the two. Solving such verification conditions is one of the key tasks of a sound compiler for reals.

Our approach is parametric in the bitwidth of the representations and can thus be used on different platforms, from embedded controllers without floating-point units (where fixed-point implementations are needed), to platforms that expose high-precision floating-point arithmetic in their instruction set architecture. Using libraries we can also emit code that uses precision twice or four times that of the ubiquitous 'double' data type. When multiple representations are available, the compiler can select, e.g., the smallest representation needed to deliver the desired number of trusted significant digits.



*POPL '14*, January 22–24, 2014, San Diego, CA, USA.

http://dx.doi.org/10.1145/2535838.2535874

To summarize, viewing source code as operating on real numbers has many advantages:

- Programmers can reason about correctness using real arithmetic instead of finite-precision arithmetic. We achieve separation of the design of algorithms (which may still be approximate for other reasons) from their realization using finite-precision computations.
- We can verify the ideal meaning of programs using techniques developed to reason over real numbers, which are more scalable and better understood than techniques that directly deal with finite-precision arithmetic.
- The approach allows us to quantify the deviation of implementation outputs from ideal ones, instead of merely proving e.g. range bounds of floating-point variables which is used in simpler static analyses.
- The compiler for reals is free to do optimizations as long as they preserve the precision requirements. This allows the compiler to apply, for example, associativity of arithmetic [17], or even select different approximation schemes for transcendental functions.
- In addition to roundoff errors, the approach also allows the developer to quantify program behavior in the face of external uncertainties such as input measurement errors.

Using our verification conditions, the correctness and the precision of compilation for small programs can, in principle, be directly verified using an SMT solver such as Z3 [20] (see Section 5.3). The capabilities of such solvers are likely continue to improve as the solvers advance, benefiting our approach. However, the complexity of the generated verification conditions for larger programs is currently out of reach of such solvers and we believe that specialized techniques are and will continue to be necessary for this task. This paper presents two specialized techniques that improve the feasibility of the verification task. The first technique performs local approximation and is effective even in benchmarks containing nonlinear arithmetic. The second technique specifically handles conditional expressions.

### 1.1 Solving Non-Linear Constraints. Forward Propagation

Nonlinear arithmetic poses a significant challenge for verification because it cannot directly be handled using Simplex-like algorithms embedded inside SMT solvers. Although interesting relevant fragments are decidable and are supported by modern solvers, the complexity of solving such constraints is much higher, in terms of both worst-case complexity and the experience in practice. Unfortunately, non-linear arithmetic is ubiquitous in numerical software. Furthermore, our verification conditions add roundoff error terms to arithmetic expressions, so the resulting constraints grow further in complexity, often becoming out of reach of solvers. An alternative to encoding into SMT solver input is to use a sound and over-approximating arithmetic model such as interval or affine arithmetic [19]. However, when used by itself on non-linear code, these approaches yield too pessimistic results, failing to establish any bounds on precision in a number of useful benchmarks.

We show that we can combine range arithmetic computation with SMT solving to overcome the limitations of each of the individual techniques. From the point of view of the logical encoding of the problem, range arithmetic becomes a specialized method to perform approximate quantifier elimination of bounded variables that describe the uncertainties. We obtain a sound, precise, and somewhat scalable procedure. During range computation, our technique also checks for common problems such as overflow, division by zero or square root of a negative number, emitting the corresponding warnings. Because the procedure is a forward computation, it is suitable for automatically generating function summaries containing output ranges and errors of a function. This is a feature that SMT solvers do not solve by themselves, because their primary functionality is answering formula satisfiability questions.

### 1.2 Sound Compilation of Conditionals

In the presence of uncertainties, conditional branches become another verification challenge. Namely, the ideal execution may follow one branch, but, because of input or roundoff errors, the actual execution follows another. This behavior may be acceptable, however, if we can show that the error on the output remains within required bounds. Our approach could benefit from modular automated analysis of continuity, which was advocated previously [53]. Because we are interested in concrete bounds, we present a new method to check that different paths taken by real-valued and finite-precision versions of the program still preserve the desired precision specification. Our check does not require continuity (which can be difficult to prove for non-linear code). Instead, it directly checks that the difference between the two values on different branches meets the required precision. This technique extends our method for handling non-linear arithmetic, so it benefits from the combination of range arithmetic and SMT solving.

### 1.3 Implementation and Evaluation

We have implemented our compilation and verification procedure, including the verification condition generation, analysis of possibly non-linear expressions, and the handling of conditionals. Our system is implemented as an extension of the Leon verifier for functional Scala programs [7]. The implementation relies on a range arithmetic implementation [15] for Scala as well as on the Z3 SMT solver [20]. We have evaluated the system on a number of diverse benchmarks, obtaining promising results. Our implementation and the benchmarks are available from

`http://lara.epfl.ch/w/rosa`

To support programming of larger code fragments, our system also supports a basic modular verification technique, which handles functions by replacing calls with function postconditions or by inlining bodies of called functions. We thus expect that our technique is applicable to larger code bases as well, possibly through refactoring code into multiple smaller and annotated functions. Even on the benchmarks that we release, we are aware of no other available system that would provide the same guarantees with our level of automation.

### 1.4 Summary of Contributions

Our overall contribution is an approach for sound compilation of real numbers into finite-precision representation. Specifically:

- We present a real-valued implementation and specification language for numerical programs with uncertainties; we define its semantics in terms of verification constraints that they induce. We believe that such verification conditions can be used as a standardized format for verifying the precision and the correctness of numerical programs.
- We develop an approximation procedure for computing precise range and error bounds for nonlinear expressions which combines SMT solving with interval arithmetic. We show that such an approach significantly improves computed range and error bounds compared to standard interval arithmetic, and scales better than SMT solving alone. Our procedure can also be used independently as a more precise alternative to interval arithmetic, and thus can perform forward computation without requiring function postconditions to be provided.

- We describe an approach for soundly computing error bounds in the presence of branches and uncertainties, which ensures soundness of compilation in case the function defined by a program with conditionals.
- We have implemented our framework and report our experience on a set of diverse benchmarks, including benchmarks from physics, biology, chemistry, and control systems. The results show that our technique is effective and that it achieves a synergy of the techniques on which it relies.

## 2. Example

We demonstrate some aspects of our system on the example written in the Scala programming language [45] in Figure 1. The methods triangle and triangleSorted compute the area of a triangle with side lengths $a, b$ and $c$. We consider a particular application where the user may have two side lengths given, and may vary the third. She has two functions available to do the computation and wants to determine whether either or both satisfy the precision requirement of 1e−11 on line 8. **require** and **ensuring** give the pre- and postconditions of functions, which are written in Scala. Notation res +/− 1e−11 denotes that the return value res should have an absolute error of at most 1e−11 compared to the ideal computation over reals. Our tool determines that such requirement needs at least double floating-point precision and emits the corresponding code. In general, the challenge is to establish that this precision is sufficient to ensure the required bounds, given that errors in finite-precision code accumulate and grow without an *a priori* bound.

Our tool verifies fully automatically that the method triangleSorted indeed satisfies the postcondition and generates the source code with the Double data type which also includes a more precise and complete postcondition on main:

$$0.01955760940017617 \leq \text{res} \wedge \text{res} \leq 12.51998402556971 \wedge$$
$$\text{res} +/- 8.578997409317759e{-}12$$

To achieve this result, our tool first checks that the precondition of the function call is satisfied using the Z3 solver. Then, it inlines the body of the function triangleSorted and computes a sound bound on the result's uncertainty with our approximation procedure. It uses the computed bounds to show that the postcondition of main is satisfied. The error computation takes into account in a sound way the input uncertainty (here: an initial roundoff error on the inputs), its propagation, and roundoff errors committed at each arithmetic operation. Additionally, due to the roundoff error, the comparison on line 21 may give a different truth value in boundary cases. Certain floating-point computations will therefore take a different branch than their corresponding real-valued computation. More precisely, the total error when computing the condition is $2e-15$, as computed by our tool. That is, floating-point values that satisfy $a < b + 2e - 15$ may take the **else** branch, even though the corresponding real values would follow the then branch, and similarly in the opposite direction. Our tool verifies that, despite this phenomenon, the difference in the computed result in two branches remains within the precision requirement. Intuitively, the values of computed branches are close for the interval where the truth value of the condition changes, and these values in real-valued and finite-precision implementation are close to each other. Finally, our tool uses our novel range computation procedure to also find a more precise output range than we could have obtained in, e.g., interval arithmetic or any static analysis method that does not differentiate roundoff error variations from the fact that a program can be ran over an interval of inputs. Our tool computes the range $[0.0195, 12.52]$ for both methods, but shows a difference in the absolute error of the computation. For the method triangle, the verification fails, because the computed error $(2.3e-11)$ exceeds the

```
   def main(a: Real, b: Real, c: Real): Real = {
2    require(4.500005 ≤ a && a ≤ 6.5)
     val b = 4.0
4    val c = 8.5
     //val area = triangle(a, b, c)
6    val area = triangleSorted(a, b, c)
     area
8  } ensuring(res ⇒ res +/− 1e−11)

10 def triangle(a: Real, b: Real, c: Real): Real = {
     require(1 < a && a < 9 && 1 < b && b < 9 && 1 < c && c < 9 &&
12     a + b > c + 1e−6 && a + c > b + 1e−6 && b + c > a + 1e−6)
     val s = (a + b + c)/2.0
14   sqrt(s ∗ (s − a) ∗ (s − b) ∗ (s − c))
   }
16
   def triangleSorted(a: Real, b: Real, c: Real): Real = {
18   require(1 < a && a < 9 && 1 < b && b < 9 && 1 < c && c < 9 &&
       a + b > c + 1e−6 && a + c > b + 1e−6 && b + c > a + 1e−6 &&
20     a < c && b < c)
     if (a < b) {
22     sqrt((c+(b+a)) ∗ (a−(c−b)) ∗ (a+(c−b)) ∗ (c+(b−a)))/4.0
     } else {
24     sqrt((c+(a+b)) ∗ (b−(c−a)) ∗ (b+(c−a)) ∗ (c+(a−b))) / 4.0
     }
26 }
```

**Figure 1.** Computing the area of a triangle with a given precision.

required precision bound. This result is expected—the textbook formula for triangles is known to suffer from imprecision for flat triangles [35], which is somewhat rectified in the method triangleSorted. On the other hand, our tool proves that using triangleSorted delivers the desired precision of $10^{-11}$ on the result.

## 3. Programs with Reals

Each program to be compiled consists of one top-level object with methods written in a functional subset of the Scala programming language [45]. All methods are functions over the **Real** data type and the user annotates them with pre- and postconditions that explicitly talk about uncertainties. **Real** represents ideal real numbers without any uncertainty. We allow arithmetic expressions over **Real**s with the standard arithmetic operators $\{+, -, *, /, \sqrt{}\}$, and together with conditionals and function calls they form the body of methods. Our tool also supports immutable variable declarations as **val** x = .... This language allows the user to define a computation over real numbers. Note that this specification language is not executable.

The precondition allows the user to provide a specification of the environment. A complete environment specification consists of lower and upper bounds for all method parameters and an upper bound on the uncertainty or noise. Range bounds are expressed with regular comparison operators. Uncertainty is expressed with a predicate such as x +/− 1e−6, which denotes that the variable $x$ is only known up to $1e-6$. Alternatively, the programmer can specify the relative error as x +/− 1e−7 ∗ x. If no noise except for roundoff is present, roundoff errors are automatically added to input variables.

The postcondition can specify constraints on the output, and in particular the range and the maximum accepted uncertainty. In addition to the language allowed in the precondition, the postcondition may reference the errors on inputs directly in the following way: res +/− 3.5 ∗ !x, which says that the maximum acceptable error on the output variable $res$ is bounded from above by 3.5 times the initial error on $x$. Whereas the precondition may only talk about the ideal values, the postcondition can also reference the actual value directly via ∼x. This allows us to assert that runtime values will not exceed a certain range, for instance.

***Floating-point arithmetic*** Our tool and technique support in the generated target code any floating-point precision and in particular, single and double floating-point precision as defined by the IEEE 754 floating-point standard [51]. We assume rounding-to-nearest rounding mode and that basic arithmetic operations $\{+, -, *, /, \sqrt{}\}$ are rounded correctly, which means that the result from any such operation must be the closest representable floating-point number. Hence, provided there is no overflow and the numbers are not in denormal range, the result of a binary operation $\circ_F$ satisfies

$$x \circ_F y = (x \circ_R y)(1 + \delta), \quad |\delta| \leq \epsilon_M, \quad \circ \in \{+, -, *, /\} \quad (1)$$

where $\circ_R$ is the ideal operation in real numbers and $\epsilon_M$ is the machine epsilon that determines the upper bound on the relative error. This model provides a basis for our roundoff error estimates. When there is a possibility of an overflow or denormal values, our analysis reports an error. An extension of the analysis to handle denormals is straightforward, by adding an additional error term in Equation 1.

***Fixed-point arithmetic*** Our tool and technique also support standard fixed-point arithmetic; for more details see [3]. Our precision analysis supports any bit-width. Our code generator generates code for 16 and 32 bit fixed-point arithmetic, which are the most common choices, using integers and bit-shifts.

***Other finite-precision representations of rationals*** The techniques described in this paper are general in that they are also applicable to other arithmetic representations, as long as roundoff errors can be computed at each computation step from the ranges of variables. Examples include floating-point implementations with a different number of bits for the exponent and mantissa, or redundant arithmetic.

## 4. Compiling Reals to Finite Precision

Given a specification or program over reals and possible target data type(s), our tool generates code over floating-point or fixed-point numbers that satisfy the given pre- and postconditions (and thus meet the target precision). Figure 2 presents a high-level view of our compilation algorithm. Our tool first analyses the entire specification and generates one verification condition for each postcondition to be proven. To obtain a modular algorithm, the tool also generates verification conditions that check that at each function call the precondition of the called function is satisfied. The methods are then sorted by occurring function calls. This allows us to reuse already computed postconditions of function calls in a modular analysis. If the user specifies one target data type, the remaining part of the compilation process is performed with respect to this data type's precision. If not or in the case the user specified several possible types, our tool will perform a binary search over the possible types to find the least in the list that satisfies all specifications. The user of our tool can provide the list of possible data types manually and sort them by her individual preference. Currently, the analysis is performed separately for each data type, which is not a big issue due to the relatively small number of alternatives. We did identify certain shared computations between iterations; we can exploit them in the future for more efficient compilation. In order for the compilation process to succeed, the specification has to be met with respect to a given finite-precision arithmetic, thus the principal part of our algorithm is spent in verification, which we describe in Section 5.

We envision that in the future the compilation task will also include automatic precision-preserving code optimizations, but in

```
Input: spec: specification over Reals, prec: candidate precisions
for fnc ← spec.fncs
  fnc.vcs = generateVCs(fnc)

spec.fncs.sortBy((f1, f2) => f1 ⊆ f2.fncCalls)

while prec ≠ ∅ and notProven(spec.fncs)
  precision = prec.nextPrecise
  for fnc ← spec.fncs
    for vc ← fnc.vcs
      while vc.hasNextApproximation ∧ notProven(vc)
        approx = getNextApproximation(vc, precision)
        vc.status = checkWithZ3(approx)
  generateSpec(fnc)
generateCode(spec)

Output: floating−point or fixed−point code
```

**Figure 2.** Compilation algorithm.

this paper we concentrate on the challenging groundwork of verifying the precision of code.

Our tool can currently generate Scala code over

- fixed-point arithmetic with a 16 or 32 bit width, or
- floating-point arithmetic in single (32 bit), double (64 bit), double-double (128 bit) and quad-double (256 bit) precision.

We currently do not support mixing of data types in one program, but plan to explore this avenue in the future. For double-double and quad-double precision, which were implemented in software by [5], we provide a Scala interface to the library with the generated code. In case the verification part of compilation fails, our tool prints a failure report with the best postconditions our tool was able to compute. The user can then use the generated specifications to gain insight why and where her program does not satisfy the requirements.

While we have implemented our tool to accept specifications in a domain specific language embedded in Scala and generate code in Scala, all our techniques apply equally to all programming languages and hardware that follow the floating-point abstraction we assume (Equation 1).

## 5. Verifying Real Programs

We will now describe the verification part of our compilation algorithm. In the following we will call the *ideal* computation the computation in the absence of any uncertainties and implemented in a real arithmetic, and the *actual* computation the computation that will finally be executed in finite-precision and with potentially uncertain inputs.

### 5.1 Verification Conditions for Loop-Free Programs

For each method with a precondition $P$ and a postcondition $Q$ our approach considers the following verification condition:

$$\forall \vec{x}, \vec{res}, \vec{y}.\ P(\vec{x}) \wedge body(\vec{x}, \vec{y}, \vec{res}) \rightarrow Q(\vec{x}, \vec{res}) \quad (*)$$

where $\vec{x}, \vec{res}, \vec{y}$ denote the input, output and local variables respectively. Table 1 summarizes how verification constraints are generated from our specification language for floating-point arithmetic. Each variable x in the specification corresponds to two real-valued variables $x, x_\circ$, the ideal one in the absence of uncertainties and roundoff errors and the actual one, computed by the compiled program. Note that the ideal and actual variables are related only through the error bounds in the pre- and postconditions, which al-

| | |
|---|---|
| a <= x && x <= b | $x \in [a,b]$ |
| x +/− k | $x_\circ = x + err_x \wedge err_x \in [-k, k]$ |
| x +/− m ∗ x | $x_\circ = x + err_x \wedge err_x \in [-\lvert mx\rvert, \lvert mx\rvert]$ |
| ∼x | $x_\circ$ |
| !x | $err_x$ |
| x ⋄ y (ideal part) | $(x \diamond y)$ |
| x ⋄ y (actual part) | $(x_\circ \diamond y_\circ)(1+\delta_1)$ |
| sqrt(x) (ideal part) | $sqrt(x)$ |
| sqrt(x) (actual part) | $sqrt(x_\circ)(1+\delta_2)$ |
| **val** z = x | $z = x \wedge z_\circ = x_\circ$ |
| **if** (c(x)) e1(x) | $((c(x) \wedge e_1(x)) \vee (\neg c(x) \wedge e_2(x)))\wedge$ |
| **else** e2(x) | $((c_\circ(x_\circ) \wedge e_{1\circ}(x_\circ)) \vee (\neg c_\circ(x_\circ) \wedge e_{2\circ}(x_\circ)))$ |
| g(x) | $g(x) \wedge g_\circ(x_\circ)$ |

$\diamond \in \{+, -, *, /\}$

$-\epsilon_m \leq \delta_i \wedge \delta_i \leq \epsilon_m$, all $\delta$ are fresh

$cond_\circ$ and $e_\circ$ denote functions with roundoff errors at each step

**Table 1.** Semantics of our specification language.

lows for the ideal and actual executions to take different paths. In the method body we have to take into account roundoff errors from arithmetic operations and the propagation of existing errors. Our system currently supports operations $\{+, -, *, /, \sqrt{}\}$, but these can be in principle extended to elementary functions, for instance by encoding them via Taylor expansions [41]. Note that the resulting verification conditions are parametric in the machine epsilon.

For fixed-point arithmetic constraints such as above can also be generated, although the translation is more complex due to the fact that fixed-point formats have to be statically determined. Roundoff error can thus no longer be encoded by a formula such as Equation 1. One possible translation is to speculatively assign fixed-point formats (including the position of the fixed point) based on real-valued ranges, and then verify that the resulting constraint with the assigned formats still holds in the presence of roundoff errors. However, because a direct attempt to solve verification conditions using an off-the-shelf solver alone is not satisfactory (see Section 5.3), our tool directly uses the approximation procedure from Section 5.4 and computes sound ranges for fixed-point implementation, allocating fixed-point formats on the fly.

### 5.2 Specification Generation

In order to give feedback to developers and to facilitate automatic modular analysis, our tool also provides automatic specification generation. By this we mean that the programmer still needs to provide the environment specification in form of preconditions, but our tool automatically computes a precise postcondition.

Formally, we can rewrite the constraint (*) as

$$\forall \vec{x}, res.\ (\exists \vec{y}.\ P(\vec{x}) \wedge body(\vec{x}, \vec{y}, res)) \rightarrow Q(\vec{x}, res)$$

where $Q$ is now unknown. We obtain the most precise postcondition $Q$ by applying quantifier elimination (QE) to $P(\vec{x}) \wedge body(\vec{x}, \vec{y}, res)$ and eliminate $\vec{y}$. The theory of arithmetic over reals admits QE so it is theoretically possible to use this approach.
We do not currently use a full QE procedure for specification generation, as it is expensive and it is not clear whether the returned expressions would be of a suitable format. Instead, we use our approximation approach which computes ranges and maximum errors in a forward fashion and computes an (over) approximation of a postcondition of the form $res \in [a, b] \wedge res \pm u$. When proving a postcondition, our tool automatically generates these specifications and provides them as feedback to the user.

**def** getNextApproximation(vc, precision):

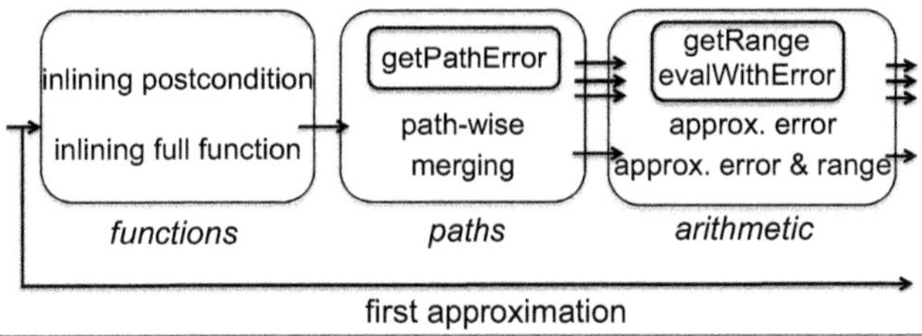


**Figure 3.** Approximation pipeline.

### 5.3 Difficulty of Simple Encoding into SMT solvers

For small functions we can already prove interesting properties by using the exact encoding of the problem just described and discharging the verification constraints with Z3. Consider the following code a programmer may write to implement the third B-spline basic function which is commonly used in signal processing [33].

```
def bspline3(u: Real): Real = {
  require(0 ≤ u && u ≤ 1 && u +/− 1e−13)
  −u∗u∗u / 6.0
} ensuring (res ⇒ −0.17 ≤ res && res ≤ 0.05 && res +/− 1e−11)
```

Functions and the corresponding verification conditions of this complexity are already within the possibilities of the nonlinear solver within Z3. For more complex functions however, Z3 does not (yet) provide an answer in a reasonable time, or returns unknown. Whether alternative techniques in SMT solvers can help in such cases remains to be seen [10, 34]. We here provide an approach based on step-wise approximation that addresses the difficulty of general-purpose constraint solving.

### 5.4 Verification with Approximations

To soundly compile more interesting programs, we have developed an approximation procedure that computes a sound over-approximation of the range of an expression and of the uncertainty on the output. This procedure is a forward computation and we also use it to generate specifications automatically. We describe the approximation procedure in detail in Section 6, for now we will assume that it exists and, given a precondition $P$ and an expression $expr$, computes a sound bound on the output range and its associated uncertainty:

$$([a,b], err) = \text{evalWithError}(P, expr) \Rightarrow$$
$$\forall \vec{x}, \vec{x}_\circ, res, res_\circ. P(\vec{x}, \vec{x_\circ}) \wedge res = expr(\vec{x}) \wedge res_\circ = expr_\circ(\vec{x}_\circ)$$
$$\rightarrow (a \leq res \vee res \leq b) \wedge |res - res_\circ| < err$$

We have identified three possibilities for approximation: nonlinear arithmetic, function calls, and paths due to conditionals and each can be approximated at different levels. We have observed in our experiments, that "one size does not fit all" and a combination of different approximations is most successful in proving the verification conditions we encountered. For each verification condition we thus construct approximations until Z3 is able to prove one, or until we run out of approximations where we report the verification as failed. We can thus view verification as a stream of approximations to be proven. We illustrate the pipeline that computes the different approximations in Figure 3. The routines getPathError, getRange and evalWithError are described in the following sections in more detail.

The first approximation (indicated by the long arrow in Figure 3) is to use Z3 alone on the entire constraint constructed by the rules in Table 1. This is indeed an approximation, as all function calls are treated as uninterpreted functions in this case. As noted before, this approach only works in very simple cases or when no uncertainties and no functions are present. Then, taking all possible combinations of subcomponents in our pipeline we obtain the other approximations, which are filtered accordingly depending on whether the constraint contains function calls or conditional branches.

***Function calls*** If the verification constraint contains function calls and the first approximation failed, our tool will attempt to inline postconditions and pass on the resulting constraint down the approximation pipeline. We support inlining of both user-provided postconditions and postconditions computed by our own specification generation procedure. If this still is not precise enough, we inline the entire function body.

Postcondition inlining is implemented by replacing the function call with a fresh variable and constraining it with the postcondition. Thus, if verification succeeds with inlining the postcondition, we avoid having to consider each path of the inlined function separately and can perform modular verification avoiding a potential path explosion problem. Such modular verification is not feasible when postconditions are too imprecise and we plan to explore the generation of more precise postconditions in the future. One step in this direction is to allow postconditions that are parametric in the initial errors, for example with the operator $!x$ introduced in Section 3. While our tool currently supports postcondition inlining with such postconditions, we do not yet generate these automatically.

***Arithmetic*** The arithmetic part of the verification constraints generated by Table 1 can be essentially divided into the ideal part and the actual part, which includes roundoff errors at each computation step. The ideal part determines whether the ideal range constraints in the postcondition are satisfied and the actual part determines whether the uncertainty part of the postcondition is satisfied. We can use our procedure presented in Section 6 to compute a sound approximation of both the result's range as well as its uncertainty.

Based on this, our tool first constructs an approximation which leaves the ideal part unchanged, but replaces the actual part of the constraint by the computed uncertainty bound. This effectively removes a large number of variables and is many times a sufficient simplification for Z3 to succeed in verifying the entire constraint. If Z3 is still not able to prove the constraint, our tool constructs the next approximation by also replacing the ideal part, this time with a constraint of the result's range which has been computed by our approximation procedure previously. Note that this second approximation may not have enough information to prove a more complex postcondition, as correlation information is lost. We note that the computation of ranges and errors is the same for both approximations and thus trying both does not affect efficiency significantly. In our experiments, Z3 is able to prove the ideal, real-valued part in most cases, so this second approximation is rarely used.

***Paths*** In the case of several paths through the program, we have the option to consider each path separately or to merge results at each join in the control flow graph. This introduces a tradeoff between efficiency and precision, since on one hand, considering each path separately leads to an exponential number of paths to consider. On the other hand, merging at each join looses correlation information between variables which may be necessary to prove certain properties. Our approximation pipeline chooses merging first, before resorting to a path-by-path verification in case of failure. We believe that other techniques for exploring the path space could also

```
def comparisonValid(x: Real): Real = {
  require(−2.0 < x && x < 2.0)
  val z1 = sineTaylor(x)
  val z2 = sineOrder3(x)
  z1 − z2
} ensuring(res ⇒ res <= 0.1 && res +/− 5e−14)

def comparisonInvalid(x: Real): Real = {
  require(−2.0 < x && x < 2.0)
  val z1 = sineTaylor(x)
  val z2 = sineOrder3(x)
  z1 − z2
} ensuring(res ⇒ res <= 0.01 && res +/− 5e−14)

def sineTaylor(x: Real): Real = {
  require(−2.0 < x && x < 2.0)
  x − (x*x*x)/6.0 + (x*x*x*x*x)/120.0 − (x*x*x*x*x*x*x)/5040.0
} ensuring(res => −1.0 < res && res < 1.0 && res +/− 1e−14)

def sineOrder3(x: Real): Real = {
  require(−2.0 < x && x < 2.0)
  0.954929658551372 * x − 0.12900613773279798*(x*x*x)
} ensuring(res ⇒ −1.0 < res && res < 1.0 && res +/− 1e−14)
```

**Figure 4.** Different polynomial approximations of sine.

be integrated into our tool [12, 36]. Another possible improvement are heuristics that select a different order of approximations depending on particular characteristics of the verification condition.

***Example*** We illustrate the verification algorithm on the example in Figure 4, using double floating-point precision as the target. The functions sineTaylor and sineOrder3 are verified first since they do not contain function calls. Verification with the full verification constraint fails. Next, our tool computes the errors on the output and Z3 succeeds to prove the resulting constraint with the ideal part untouched. From this approximation our tool directly computes a new, more precise postcondition, in particular it can narrow the resulting errors to `1.63e-15` and `1.11e-15` respectively. Next, our tool considers the comparisonValid function. Inlining only the postcondition is not enough in this case, but computing the error approximation on the inlined functions succeeds in verifying the postcondition. Note that our tool does not approximate the real-valued portion of the constraint, i.e. Z3 is used directly to verify the constraint $z1 - z2 \leq 0.1$. This illustrates our separation of the real reasoning from the finite-precision implementation: with our separation we can use a real arithmetic solver to deal with algorithmic reasoning and verify with our error computation that the results are still valid (within the error bounds) in the implementation. Finally, the tool verifies that the preconditions of the function calls are satisfied by using Z3 alone. Verification of the function comparisonInvalid fails with all approximations. Our tool is able to determine that the ideal real-valued constraint alone ($z1 - z2 \leq 0.01$) is not valid, reports a counterexample ($x = 1.875$) and returns invalid as the verification result.

### 5.5 Soundness

Our procedure is sound because our constraints over-approximate the actual errors. Furthermore, even in the full constraint as generated from Table 1, roundoff errors are over-approximated since we assume the worst-case error bound at each step. While this ensures soundness, it also introduces incompleteness, as we may fail to validate a specification because our over-approximation is too large. This implies that counterexamples reported by Z3 are in general only valid, if they disprove the ideal real-valued part of the verification constraint. Our tool checks whether this is the case by constructing a constraint with only the real-valued part, and reports the counterexamples, if such are returned from Z3.

### 5.6 Loops and Recursion

In principle, our techniques can be applied to programs with loops via recursion, however, because of accumulation of roundoff errors only self-stabilizing systems can be expected to have simple inductive invariants, and such systems can to some extent also be addressed using runtime verification techniques [16]. For non-self-stabilizing systems the uncertainties depend on the number of iterations, which makes specifications of such functions very complex. Note that, for ensuring the stability of certain embedded control systems, it has been shown that it is sufficient to consider the body of the control loop only [3].

## 6. Solving Nonlinear Constraints

Having given an overview of the approximation pipeline, we now describe the computation of the approximation for nonlinear arithmetic, which corresponds to the last box in Figure 3. For completeness of presentation, we first review interval and affine arithmetic which are common choices for performing sound arithmetic computations and which we also use as part of our technique. We then present our novel procedure for computing the output range of a nonlinear expression given ranges for its inputs that can be a more precise substitute for interval or affine arithmetic. Finally, we continue with a procedure that computes a sound over-approximation of the uncertainty on the result of a nonlinear expression.

One possibility to perform guaranteed computations is to use standard interval arithmetic [43]. Interval arithmetic computes a bounding interval for each basic operation as

$$x \circ y = [min(x \circ y), max(x \circ y)] \qquad \circ \in \{+, -, *, /\}$$

and analogously for square root.

Affine arithmetic was originally introduced in [19] and addresses the difficulty of interval arithmetic in handling correlations between variables. Affine arithmetic represents possible values of variables as affine forms

$$\hat{x} = x_0 + \sum_{i=1}^{n} x_i \epsilon_i$$

where $x_0$ denotes the *central value* (of the represented interval) and each *noise symbol* $\epsilon_i$ is a formal variable denoting a deviation from the central value, intended to range over $[-1, 1]$. The maximum magnitude of each *noise term* is given by the corresponding $x_i$. Note that the sign of $x_i$ does not matter in isolation, it does, however, reflect the relative dependence between values. E.g., take $x = x_0 + x_1\epsilon_1$, then

$$\begin{aligned} x - x &= x_0 + x_1\epsilon_1 - (x_0 + x_1\epsilon_1) \\ &= x_0 - x_0 + x_1\epsilon_1 - x_1\epsilon_1 = 0 \end{aligned}$$

If we subtracted $x' = x_0 - x_1\epsilon_1$ instead, the resulting interval would have width $2 * x_1$ and not zero.

The range represented by an affine form is computed as

$$[\hat{x}] = [x_0 - rad(\hat{x}), x_0 + rad(\hat{x})], \qquad rad(\hat{x}) = \sum_{i=1}^{n} |x_i|$$

A general affine operation $\alpha\hat{x} + \beta\hat{y} + \zeta$ consists of addition, subtraction, addition of a constant ($\zeta$) or multiplication by a constant ($\alpha, \beta$). Expanding the affine forms $\hat{x}$ and $\hat{y}$ we get

$$\alpha\hat{x} + \beta\hat{y} + \zeta = (\alpha x_0 + \beta y_0 + \zeta) + \sum_{i=1}^{n} (\alpha x_i + \beta y_i)\epsilon_i$$

```
def getRange(expr, precondition, precision, maxIterations):
  z3.assertConstraint(precondition)
  [aInit, bInit] = evalInterval(expr, precondition.ranges);

  //lower bound
  if z3.checkSat(expr < a + precision) == UNSAT
    a = aInit
    b = bInit
    numIterations = 0
    while (b−a) < precision ∧ numIterations < maxIterations
      mid = a + (b − a) / 2
      numIterations++
      z3.checkSat(expr < mid) match
        case SAT ⇒ b = mid
        case UNSAT ⇒ a = mid
        case Unknown ⇒ break
    aNew = a
  else
    aNew = aInit

  //upper bound symmetrically
  bNew = ...
  return: [aNew, bNew]
```

**Figure 5.** Algorithm for computing the range of an expression.

An additional motivation for using affine arithmetic is that different contributions to the range it represents remain, at least partly, separated. This information can be used for instance to help identify the major contributor of a result's uncertainty or to separate contributions from external uncertainties from roundoff errors.

### 6.1 Range Computation

The goal of this procedure is to perform a forward-computation to determine the real-valued range of a nonlinear arithmetic expression given ranges for its inputs. Two common possibilities are interval and affine arithmetic, but they tend to over-approximate the resulting range, especially if the input intervals are not sufficiently small (order 1). Affine arithmetic improves over interval arithmetic somewhat by tracking linear correlations, but in the case of nonlinear expressions the results can become actually worse than for interval arithmetic (e.g. $x * y$, where $x = [-5, 3], y = [-3, 1]$ gives $[-13, 15]$ in affine arithmetic and $[-9, 15]$ in interval arithmetic).

***Observation:*** A nonlinear theorem prover such as the one that comes with Z3 can decide with fairly good precision whether a given bound is sound or not. That is we can check with a prover whether for an expression $e$ the range $[a, b]$ is a sound interval enclosure. This observation is the basis of our range computation.

The input to our algorithm is a nonlinear expression $expr$ and a precondition $P$ on its inputs, which specifies, among possibly other constraints, ranges on all input variables $\vec{x}$. The output is an interval $[a, b]$ which satisfies the following:

$$\begin{aligned} &[a, b] = \text{getRange}(P, expr) \Rightarrow \\ &\qquad \forall \vec{x}, res. P(\vec{x}) \wedge res = expr(\vec{x}) \rightarrow (a \leq res \vee res \leq b) \end{aligned}$$

***The algorithm*** for computing the lower bound of a range is given in Figure 5. The computation for the upper bound is symmetric. For each range to be computed, our tool first computes an initial sound estimate of the range with interval arithmetic. It then performs an initial quick check to test whether the computed first approximation bounds are already tight. If not, it uses the first approximation as the starting point and then narrows down the lower and upper bounds using a binary search. At each step of the binary search our tool uses Z3 to confirm or reject the newly proposed bound.

The search stops when either Z3 fails, i.e. returns unknown for a query or cannot answer within a given timeout, the difference between subsequent bounds is smaller than a precision threshold, or the maximum number of iterations is reached. This stopping criterion can be set dynamically.

***Additional constraints*** In addition to the input ranges, the precondition may also contain further constraints on the variables. For example consider again the method triangle in Figure 1. The precondition bounds the inputs as $a, b, c \in [1, 9]$, but the formula is useful only for valid triangles, i.e. when every two sides together are longer than the third. If not, we will get an error at the latest when we try to take the square root of a negative number. In interval-based approaches we can only consider input intervals that satisfy this constraint for all values, and thus have to check several (and possibly many) cases. In our approach, since we are using Z3 to check the soundness of bounds, we can assert the additional constraints up-front and then all subsequent checks are performed with respect to all additional and initial constraints. This allows us to avoid interval subdivisions due to imprecisions or problem specific constraints such as those in the triangle example. This becomes especially valuable in the presence of multiple variables, where we may otherwise need an exponential number of subdivisions.

### 6.2 Error Approximation

We now describe our approximation procedure which, for a given expression $expr$ and a precondition $P$ on the inputs, computes the range and error on the output. More formally, our procedure satisfies the following:

$$([a, b], err) = \text{evalWithError}(P, expr) \Rightarrow$$
$$\forall \vec{x}, \vec{x_\circ}, res, res_\circ . P(\vec{x}, \vec{x_\circ}) \wedge res = expr(\vec{x}) \wedge res_\circ = expr_\circ(\vec{x_\circ})$$
$$\rightarrow (a \leq res \vee res \leq b) \wedge |res - res_\circ| < err$$

where $expr_\circ$ represents the expression evaluated in finite-precision arithmetic and $\vec{x}, \vec{x_\circ}$ are the ideal and actual variables. The precondition specifies the ranges and uncertainties of initial variables and other additional constraints on the ideal variables. The uncertainty specification is necessary, as it relates the ideal and actual variables.

The idea of our procedure is to "execute" a computation while keeping track of the output range of the current expression and its associated errors. At each arithmetic operation, we propagate existing errors, compute an upper bound on the roundoff error and add it to the overall errors. Since the roundoff error depends proportionally on the range of values, we need to keep track of the ranges as precisely as possible.

Our procedure is build on the abstraction that a computation is an ideal computation plus or minus some uncertainty. The abstraction of floating-point roundoff errors that we choose also follows this separation:

$$fl(x \diamond y) = (x \diamond y)(1 + \delta) = (x \diamond y) + (x \diamond y)\delta$$

for $\delta \in [-\epsilon_m, \epsilon_m]$ and $\diamond \in \{+, -, *, /\}$. This allows us to treat all uncertainties in a unified manner. For fixed-point arithmetic the situation is similar, but we first determine the fixed-point format from the current range, and only from this compute the roundoff error.

Our procedure builds on the idea of the SmartFloat data type [15], which uses affine arithmetic to track both the range and the errors. For nonlinear operations, however, the so computed ranges become quickly very pessimistic and the error computation may also suffer from this imprecision. We observed that since the errors tend to be relatively small, this imprecision does not affect the error propagation itself to such an extent. If the initial errors are small (less than one), multiplied nonlinear terms tend to be even smaller, whereas if the affine terms are larger than one, the nonlinear terms grow. We thus concentrate on improving the ideal range of values and use our novel range computation procedure for this part and leave the error propagation with affine arithmetic as in [15].

In our adaptation, we represent every variable and intermediate computation result as a datatype with the following components:

$$x : (range : Interval, \hat{err} : AffineForm)$$

where $range$ is the range of this variable, computed as described in Section 6.1 and $\hat{err}$ is the affine form representing the errors. The (over-approximation) of the actual range including all uncertainties is then given by $totalRange = range + [\hat{err}]$, where $\hat{err}$ denotes the interval represented by the affine form.

***Roundoff error computation*** Roundoff errors for floating-point arithmetic are computed at each computation step as

$$\rho = \delta * maxAbs(totalRange)$$

where $\delta$ is the machine epsilon, and added to $\hat{err}$ as a fresh noise term. Note that this roundoff error computation makes our error computation parametric in the floating-point precision. For fixed-point arithmetic, roundoff errors are computed as

$$\rho = getFormat(totalRange, bitWidth).quantizationError$$

where the $getFormat$ function returns the best fixed-point format [3] that can accommodate the range. This computation is also parametric in the bit-width.

***Error propagation*** For affine operations addition, subtraction, and multiplication by a constant factor the propagated errors are computed term-wise and thus as for standard affine arithmetic. We refer the reader to [15, 19] for further details and describe here only the propagation for nonlinear arithmetic. For multiplication, division and square root, the magnitude of errors also depends on the ranges of variables. Since our ranges are not affine terms themselves, propagation has to be adjusted. In the following, we denote the range of a variable $x$ by $[x]$ and its associated error by the affine form $\hat{err}_x$. When we write $[x] * \hat{err}_y$ we mean that the interval $[x]$ is converted into an affine form and the multiplication is performed in affine arithmetic.

Multiplication is computed as

$$\begin{aligned} x * y &= ([x] + \hat{err}_x)([y] + \hat{err}_y) \\ &= [x] * [y] + [x] * \hat{err}_y + [y] * \hat{err}_x + \hat{err}_x * \hat{err}_y + \rho \end{aligned}$$

where $\rho$ is the new roundoff error. Thus the first term contributes to the ideal range and the remaining three to the error affine form. The larger the factors $[x]$ and $[y]$ are, the larger the finally computed errors will be. In order to keep the over-approximation as small as possible, we evaluate $[x]$ and $[y]$ with our new range computation.

Division is computed as

$$\begin{aligned} \frac{x}{y} &= x * \frac{1}{y} = ([x] + \hat{err}_x)([1/y] + \hat{err}_{1/y}) \\ &= [x] * [\frac{1}{y}] + [x] * \hat{err}_{\frac{1}{y}} + [\frac{1}{y}] * \hat{err}_x + \hat{err}_x * \hat{err}_{\frac{1}{y}} + \rho \end{aligned}$$

For square root, we first compute an affine approximation of square root as in [15]: $\sqrt{x} = \alpha * x + \zeta + \theta$, and then perform the affine multiplication term wise.

***Overflows and NaN*** Our procedure allows us to detect potential overflows, division by zero and square root of a negative value, as our tool computes ranges of all intermediate values. We currently report these issues as warnings to the user.

### 6.3 Limitations

The limitation of this approach is clearly the ability of Z3 to check our constraints. We found its capabilities satisfactory, although we expect the performance to still significantly improve. To emphasize the difference to the constraints that are defined by Table 1, the constraints we use here do not add errors at each step and thus the number of variables is reduced significantly. We also found several transformations helpful, such as rewriting powers (e.g. $x * x * x$ to $x^3$), multiplying out products and avoiding non-strict comparisons in the precondition, although the benefits were not entirely consistent. Note that at each step of our error computation, our tool computes the current range. Thus, even if Z3 fails to tighten the bound for some expressions, we still compute more precise bounds than interval arithmetic overall in most cases, as the ranges of the remaining subexpressions have already been computed more precisely.

## 7. Conditional Statements

In this Section we consider the difference between the ideal and actual computation due to uncertainties on computing branch conditions and the resulting different paths taken. We note that the full constraint constructed according to Section 3 automatically includes this error. Recall that the ideal and actual computations are independent except for the initial conditions, so that it is possible that they follow different paths through the program.

In the case of using approximation, however, we compute the error on individual paths and have to consider the error due to diverging paths separately. We propose the following algorithm to explicitly compute the difference between the ideal and the actual computation across paths. Note that we do not assume continuity, i.e. the algorithm allows us to compute error bounds even in the case of non-continuous functions.

For simplicity, we present here the algorithm for the case of one conditional statement: **if** (c(x)<0) f1(x) **else** f2(x).
It generalizes readily to more complex expressions. W.l.o.g. we assume that the condition is of the form $c(x) < 0$. Indeed, any conditional of the form $c(x) == 0$ would yield different results for the ideal and actual computation for nearly any input, so we do not allow it in our specification language.

The actual computation commits a certain error when computing the condition of the branch and it is this error that causes some executions to follow a different branch than the corresponding ideal one would take. Consider the case where the ideal computation evaluates f1, but the actual one evaluates f2. The algorithm in Figure 6 gives the computation of the *path error* in this case. The idea is to compute the ranges of f1 and f2, but only for the inputs that could be diverging. The final error is then the maximum difference of these value. The algorithm extends naturally to several variables. In the case of several paths through the program, this error has to be, in principle, computed for each pair of paths. We use Z3 to rule out infeasible paths up front so that the path error computation is only performed for those paths that are actually feasible.

Our tool implements a refined version of this approach, which merges paths to avoid having to consider an exponential number of path combinations. It also uses a higher default precision and number of iterations threshold during the binary search in the range computation as this computation requires in general very tight intervals for each path.

We identify two challenges for performing this computation:

1. As soon as the program has multiple variables, the inputs for the different branches are not two-dimensional intervals anymore, which makes an accurate evaluation of the individual paths difficult.

```
   def getPathError:
2  Input: pre: (x ∈ [a,b] ∧ x ± n)
          program: (if (cond(x) < 0) f1(x) else f2(x))
4
     val pathError1 = computePathError(pre, cond, f1, f2)
6    val pathError2 = computePathError(pre, ¬ cond, f2, f1)
     return max (pathError1, pathError2)
8
   def computePathError(pre, c, f1, f2):
10   ([c], err_c) = evalWithError(pre, c)

12   ([f2]_float, err_float) =
       evalWithError(pre ∧ c(x) ∈ [0, err_c], f2)
14   [f1]_real =
       getRange(pre ∧ c(x) ∈ [−err_c, 0], f1)
16   return: max |[f1]_real − ([f2]_float + err_float)|
```

**Figure 6.** Computing error due to diverging paths. Quantities denotes by [x] are intervals.

2. The inputs for the two branches are inter-dependent. Thus, simply evaluating the two branches with inputs that are in the correct ranges, but are not correlated, yields pessimistic results when computing the final difference (line 16).

We overcome the first challenge with our range computation which takes into account additional constraints. For the second challenge, we use our range computation as well. Unfortunately, Z3 fails to tighten the final range to a satisfactory precision due to timeouts. We still obtain much better error estimates than with interval arithmetic alone, as the ranges of values for the individual paths are already computed much more precisely. We report in Section 8 on the type of programs whose verification is within our reach today.

## 8. Experiments

The examples in Figure 1 and 4 and Section 5.3 provide an idea of the type of programs our tool is currently able to verify fully automatically. The B-spline example from Section 5.3 is the largest meaningful example we were able to find that Z3 alone could verify in the presence of uncertainties. For all other cases, it was necessary to use our approximation methods.

We have chosen several nonlinear expressions commonly used in physics, biology and chemistry [44, 48, 54] as benchmark functions, as well as benchmarks used in control systems [2] and suitable benchmarks from [22]. Experiments were performed on a desktop computer running Ubuntu 12.04.1 with a 3.5GHz i7 processor and 16GB of RAM.

### 8.1 Compiling Programs

Which data type is suitable for a given program depends on the parameter ranges, the code itself but also the precision required by the application using the code. For example, take the functions in Figure 7. Depending on which precision on the output the user needs, our tool will select different data types. For the requirement res +/− 1e−12, as specified, Double is be a suitable choice for doppler and turbine, however for the jetEngine example this is not sufficient, and thus DoubleDouble would be selected by our tool. The user can influence which data types are preferred by supplying a list to our tool which is ordered by her preference.

Figure 8 illustrates the tradeoff between the precision achieved by different data types against the runtime of the compiled code generated by our tool. We used the Caliper [1] framework for benchmarking the running times.

| Benchmark | Our range | interval arithmetic | Simulated range |
|---|---|---|---|
| doppler1 | [-137.639, -0.033951] | [-158.720, -0.029442] | [-136.346, -0.035273] |
| doppler2 | [-230.991, -0.022729] | [-276.077, -0.019017] | [-227.841,-0.023235] |
| doppler3 | [-83.066, -0.50744] | [-96.295, -0.43773] | [-82.624, -0.51570] |
| rigidBody1 | [-705.0, 705.0] | [-705.0, 705.0] | [-697.132, 694.508] |
| rigidBody2 | [-56010.1, 58740.0] | [-58740.0, 58740.0] | [-54997.635, 57938.052] |
| jetEngine | [-1997.037, 5109.338] | $[-\infty, \infty]$ | [-1779.551, 4813.564] |
| turbine1 | [-18.526, -1.9916] | [-58.330, -1.5505] | [-18.284, -1.9946] |
| turbine2 | [-28.555, 3.8223] | [-29.437, 80.993] | [-28.528, 3.8107] |
| turbine3 | [0.57172, 11.428] | [0.46610, 40.376] | [0.61170, 11.380] |
| verhulst | [0.31489, 1.1009] | [0.31489, 1.1009] | [0.36685,0.94492] |
| predatorPrey | [0.039677, 0.33550] | [0.037277, 0.35711] | [0.039669,0.33558] |
| carbonGas | [4.3032 e6, 1.6740 e7] | [2.0974 e6, 3.4344 e7] | [4.1508 e6, 1.69074 e7] |
| Sine | [-0.9999, 0.9999] | [-2.3012, 2.3012] | [-1.0093, 1.0093] |
| Sqrt | [1.0, 1.3985] | [0.83593, 1.5625] | [1.0, 1.3985] |
| Sine (order 3 approx.) | [-1.0001, 1.0001] | [-2.9420, 2.9420] | [-1.0, 1.0] |

**Table 2.** Comparison of ranges computed with out procedure against interval arithmetic and simulation. Simulations were performed with $10^7$ random inputs. Ranges are rounded outwards. Affine arithmetic does not provide better results than interval arithmetic.

```
def doppler(u: Real, v: Real, T: Real): Real = {
  require(−100 < u && u < 100 && 20 < v && v < 20000 &&
          −30 < T && T < 50)

  val t1 = 331.4 + 0.6 ∗ T
  (− (t1) ∗v) / ((t1 + u)∗(t1 + u))
} ensuring(res ⇒ res +/− 1e−12)

def jetEngine(x1: Real, x2: Real): Real = {
  require(−5 < x1 && x1 < 5 && −20 < x2 && x2 < 5)

  val t = (3∗x1∗x1 + 2∗x2 − x1)
  x1 + ((2∗x1∗(t/(x1∗x1 + 1))∗
  (t/(x1∗x1 + 1) − 3) + x1∗x1∗(4∗(t/(x1∗x1 + 1))−6))∗
  (x1∗x1 + 1) + 3∗x1∗x1∗(t/(x1∗x1 + 1)) + x1∗x1∗x1 + x1 +
  3∗((3∗x1∗x1 + 2∗x2 −x1)/(x1∗x1 + 1)))
} ensuring(res ⇒ res +/− 1e−12)

def turbine(v: Real, w: Real, r: Real): Real = {
  require(−4.5 < v && v < −0.3 && 0.4 < w && w < 0.9 &&
          3.8 < r && r < 7.8)

  3 + 2/(r∗r) − 0.125∗(3−2∗v)∗(w∗w∗r∗r)/(1−v) − 4.5
} ensuring(res ⇒ res +/− 1e−12)
```

**Figure 7.** Benchmark functions from physics and control systems.

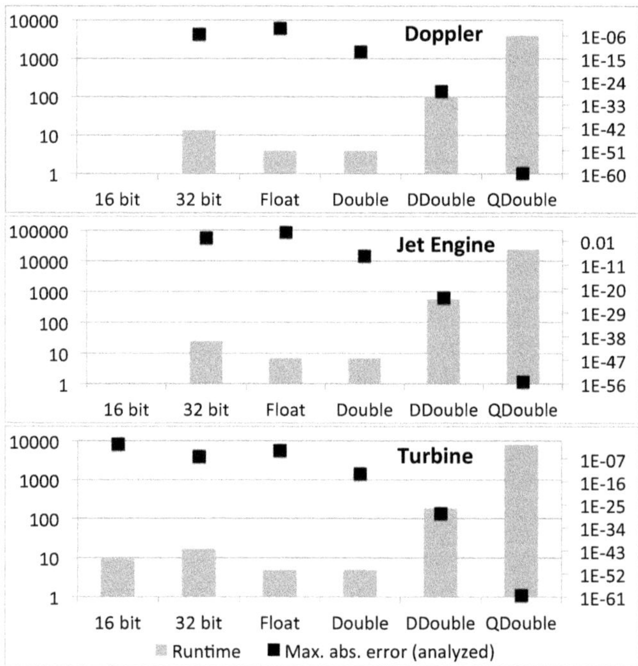


**Figure 8.** Runtimes of benchmarks compiled for different precisions in nanoseconds (left) vs. abs. error bounds computed for that precision by our tool (right).

For our benchmarks with their limited input ranges, 32 bit fixed-point implementations provide better precision than single floating-point precision because single precision has to accommodate a larger dynamic range which reduces the number of bits available for the mantissa. That said, fixed-point implementations run slower, at least on the JVM, than the more precise double floating-point arithmetic with its dedicated hardware support. However, the choice for fixed-point rather than floating-point may be also due to this hardware being unavailable. Our tool can thus support a wide variety of applications with different requirements. We also note that across the three (not specially selected) benchmarks, the results are very consistent and we expect similar behavior for other applications as well.

### 8.2 Evaluating Effectiveness on Nonlinear Expressions

***Range computation*** Stepwise estimation of errors crucially depends on the estimate of the ranges of variables. The strength of using a constraint solver such as Z3 is that it can perform such estimation while taking into account the precise dependencies between variables in preconditions and path conditions. Table 2 compares results of our range computation procedure described in Section 6 against ranges obtained with standard interval arithmetic. Interval arithmetic is one of the methods used for step-wise range estimation; an alternative being affine arithmetic, which we found to give more pessimistic results in our experiments. We believe that this is due to imprecision in computing nonlinear operations. Note, however, that we still use affine arithmetic to estimate errors given the computed ranges.

For our range computation, we set the default precision threshold to 1e−10 and maximum number of iterations for the binary search to 50. To obtain an idea about the true ranges of our functions, we have also computed a lower bound on the range using simulations with $10^7$ random inputs and with exact rational arithmetic evaluation of expressions. We observe that our range computation can significantly improve over standard interval bounds. The jetEngine benchmark is a notable example, where interval arithmetic yields the bound $[-\infty, \infty]$, but our procedure can still provide bounds that are quite close to the true range.

***Error computation*** Table 3 compares uncertainties computed by our tool against maximum uncertainties obtained through extensive simulation with $10^7$ random inputs for different precisions. To obtain (under-approximations of) error bounds, we ran the simulation in parallel with rational and their corresponding floating-point or fixed-point values and obtained the error by taking the difference in the result. Selected benchmarks, marked with (*), also have added uncertainties on the input parameters. To our knowledge this is the first quantitative comparison of an error computation precision with (an approximation) of the true errors on such benchmarks. Our computed uncertainties are mostly within about an order and many times even closer to the under-approximation of the true errors provided by simulation. In the case of the jetEngine* benchmark, we believe that the imprecision is mainly due to its complexity and subsequent failures of Z3 in the range computation. The values in parentheses in the second column indicate errors computed if ranges at each arithmetic operation are computed using interval arithmetic alone. While we have not attempted to improve the affine arithmetic-based error computation from [15], we can see that in some cases a more precise range computation can gain us improvements. The full effect of the imprecision of standard range computation appears when, due to this imprecision, we obtain possible errors such as division-by-zero or square root of a negative number errors. The first case happens in the case of the non-linear jetEngine benchmark, so with interval arithmetic alone we would therefore not obtain any meaningful result. Similarly, for the triangle example from Section 2, without being able to constrain the inputs to form valid triangles, we cannot compute any error bound, because the radicand becomes possibly negative.

Table 4 presents another relevant experiment, evaluating the ability to use additional constraints during our range computation. For this experiment, we use double precision and the triangle example from Section 2 with additional constraints allowing increasingly flat triangles by setting the threshold on line 12 (a + b > c + 1e−6) to the different values given in the first column. As the triangles become flatter, we observe an expected increase in uncertainty on the output since the formula becomes more prone to roundoff errors. At threshold 1e−10 our range computation fails to provide the necessary precision and the radicand becomes possibly negative. Using our tool, the developer can therefore go beyond rules of thumb and informal estimates and be confident that the computed area is accurate up to seven decimal digits even for triangles that whose difference $a + b - c$ is as small as $10^{-9}$.

***Compilation Running Time*** Running times for compilation are below seven seconds for all benchmarks from Table 3 and for the sine example from Figure 4, except for jetEngine which runs in about two minutes due to timeouts from Z3 for some intermediate ranges. Examples that require computation of the path error are much more computationally challenging: verifying the postcondi-

| Benchmark | Our error (IA only) | Simulated error |
|---|---|---|
| doppler1* (dbl) | 2.36e-6 | 5.97e-7 |
| doppler1 (dbl) | 4.92e-13 (4.95e-13) | 7.11e-14 |
| doppler2 (dbl) | 1.29e-12 | 1.14e-13 |
| doppler2 (32bit) | 8.67e-6 (8.79e-6) | 1.57e-6 |
| doppler3 (dbl) | 2.03e-13 (2.05e-13) | 4.27e-14 |
| rigidBody1* (dbl) | 9.21e-7 | 8.24e-7 |
| rigidBody1 (dbl) | 5.08e-13 | 2.28e-13 |
| rigidBody2 (dbl) | 6.48e-11 | 2.19e-11 |
| jetEngine* (dbl) | 0.15 (-) | 3.58e-5 |
| jetEngine (dbl) | 1.62e-8 (-) | 5.46e-12 |
| jetEngine (32bit) | 0.0972 (-) | 1.77e-4 |
| turbine1* (dbl) | 4.86e-6 | 3.71e-7 |
| turbine1 (dbl) | 1.25e-13 (1.38e-13) | 1.07e-14 |
| turbine1 (16bit) | 0.0487 (0.0522) | 0.00623 |
| turbine2 (dbl) | 1.76e-13 (1.96e-13) | 1.43e-14 |
| turbine3 (dbl) | 8.50e-14 (9.47e-14) | 5.33e-15 |
| verhulst* (dbl) | 2.82e-4 | 2.40e-4 |
| verhulst (dbl) | 6.82e-16 | 2.23e-16 |
| predatorPrey* (dbl) | 9.22e-5 | 8.61e-5 |
| predatorPrey (dbl) | 2.94e-16 (2.96e-16) | 1.12e-16 |
| carbonGas* (dbl) | 2114297.84 | 168874.70 |
| carbonGas (dbl) | 4.64e-8 (5.04e-8) | 3.73e-9 |
| Sine (dbl) | 9.57e-16 (1.46e-15) | 4.45e-16 |
| Sine (fl) | 1.03e-6 (1.57e-6) | 1.79e-7 |
| Sine (16bit) | 2.87e-4 (6.79e-4) | 1.55e-4 |
| Sqrt (dbl) | 8.41e-16 (8.87e-16) | 4.45e-16 |
| Sqrt (fl) | 9.03e-7 (9.52e-7) | 2.45e-7 |
| Sqrt (16bit) | 5.97e-4 | 1.58e-4 |
| Sine, order 3 (fl) | 1.19e-6 (1.55e-6) | 2.12e-7 |
| Sine, order 3 (dbl) | 1.11e-15 (1.44e-15) | 3.34e-16 |

**Table 3.** Comparison of errors computed with our procedure against simulated errors. Simulations were performed with $10^7$ random inputs. (*) indicates that inputs have external uncertainties associated. dbl and fl denotes double and single floating-point precision respectively, 32 or 16 bit is the bit-width of the fixed-point implementation.

| Benchmark | Area | Max. abs. error |
|---|---|---|
| triangle1 (0.1) | [0.29432, 35.0741] | 2.72e-11 |
| triangle2 (1e-2) | [0.099375, 35.0741] | 8.04e-11 |
| triangle3 (1e-3) | [3.16031e-2, 35.0741] | 2.53e-10 |
| triangle4 (1e-4) | [9.9993e-3, 35.0741] | 7.99e-10 |
| triangle5 (1e-5) | [3.1622e-3, 35.0741] | 2.53e-9 |
| triangle6 (1e-6) | [9.9988e-4, 35.0741] | 7.99e-9 |
| triangle7 (1e-7) | [3.1567e-4, 35.0741] | 2.54e-8 |
| triangle8 (1e-8) | [9.8888e-5, 35.0741] | 8.08e-8 |
| triangle9 (1e-9) | [3.0517e-5, 35.0741] | 2.62e-7 |
| triangle10 (1e-10) | - | - |

**Table 4.** Area computed and error on the result for increasingly flat triangles. All values are rounded outwards. Interval arithmetic alone fails to provide any result.

```
   def cav10(x: Real): Real = {
2    require(0 < x && x < 10)
     if (x*x − x >= 0)
4      x/10
     else
6      x*x + 2
   } ensuring(res => 0 <= res && res <= 3.0 && res +/− 3.0)
8
   def squareRoot3(x: Real): Real = {
10   require(0 < x && x < 10 && x +/− 1e−10 )
     if (x < 1e−5)
12     1 + 0.5 * x
     else
14     sqrt(1 + x)
   } ensuring(res => res +/− 1e−10)
16
   def smartRoot(a: Real, b: Real, c: Real): Real = {
18   require(3 <= a && a <= 3 && 3.5 <= b && b <= 3.5 &&
       −2 < c && c < 2 && b*b − a * c * 4.0 > 0.1)
20
     val discr = b*b − a * c * 4.0
22   if(b*b − a*c > 10.0) {
       if(b > 0.0) c * 2.0 /(−b − sqrt(discr))
24     else if(b < 0.0) (−b + sqrt(discr))/(a * 2.0)
       else (−b + sqrt(discr))/(a * 2.0)
26   } else {
       (−b + sqrt(discr))/(a * 2.0)
28   }
   } ensuring(res => res +/− 6e−15)
```

**Figure 9.** Path error computation examples.

tion on the main function from the initial example takes about one minute. Running times depend highly on whether Z3 fails to tighten intermediate ranges and the timeout used for Z3. Our default setting is one second; we did not find much improvement in the success rate above this threshold.

### 8.3 Evaluating Errors across Program Paths

Figure 9 presents several examples to evaluate our error computation procedure across different paths from Section 7. The first method cav10 [26] has been used before as a benchmark function for computing the output range. Our tool can verify the given postcondition immediately. Note that the error on the result is actually as large as the result itself, since the method is non-continuous, an aspect that has been ignored in previous work, but that our tool detects automatically. The method squareRoot3 is also a non-continuous function that computes the square root of $1+x$ using an approximation for small values and the regular library method otherwise. Note the additional uncertainty on the input, which could occur for instance if this method is used in an embedded controller. Our tool can verify the given specification. If we change the condition on line 10 to x < 1e−4 however, verification fails. In this fashion, we can use our tool to determine the appropriate branch condition to meet the precision requirement. These two examples verify in under 5 seconds. Finally, the smartRoot method computes one root of a quadratic equation using the well-known more precise method from [27]. Our tool compares the values error across different paths in real and finite-precision implementation and succeeds in verifying the postcondition under 25s.

## 9. Related work

Current approaches for verifying finite-precision code include abstract interpretation, interactive theorem proving and decision procedures, which we survey in this section. We are not aware of work that would automatically integrate reasoning about uncertainties into a programming model.

***Abstract interpretation (AI)*** Abstract domains that are sound with respect to floating-point computations can prove bounds on the ranges of variables [8, 14, 24, 32, 42]. The only work in this area that can also quantify roundoff errors is the tool Fluctuat [21, 28]. These techniques use interval or affine arithmetic and together with the required join and meet operations may yield too pessimistic results. [47] improves the precision of Fluctuat by refining the input domains with a constraint solver. Our approach can be viewed as approaching the problem from a different end, starting with an exact constraint and then using approximation until the solver succeeds. Unlike AI tools in general, our system currently does not perform widening to ensure convergence. If the user can provide inductive postconditions, then we can still prove the code correct, but we do not in general discover these postconditions ourselves. Our focus is on proving precise bounds on the ranges in the presence of nonlinear computations and the quantification of roundoff errors and other uncertainties.

***Theorem proving*** The Gappa tool [18, 39] generates a proof checkable by the interactive theorem prover Coq from source code with specifications. It can reason about properties that can be reduced to reasoning about ranges and errors, but targets very precise properties of specialized functions, such as software implementations of elementary functions. The specification itself requires expertize and the proofs human intervention. A similar approach is taken by [4] which generate verification conditions that are discharged by various theorem provers. Harisson has also done significant work on proving floating-point programs in the HOL Light theorem prover [30]. Our approach makes a different compromise on the precision vs. automation tradeoff, by being less precise, but automatic. The Gappa and interactive theorem provers can be used as complements to our tool: if our tool detects that more precision is needed, interactive tools can be employed by an expert user on selected methods; the results can then used by our tool in the context of the overall program.

***Range computation*** The Gappa tool and most constraint solvers internally use interval arithmetic for sound range computations, whose limitations are well-known. [23] describes an arithmetic based on function enclosures and [41] use an arithmetic based on taylor series as an alternative. This approach is useful when checking a constraint, but is not suitable for a *forward computation* of ranges and errors.

***Decision procedures*** An alternative approach to verification via range computation are floating-point decision procedures. Bit-precise constraints, however, become very large quickly. [11] addresses this problem by using a combination of over- and under-approximations. [29] present an alternative approach in combining interval constraint solving with a CDCL algorithm and [25] is a decision procedure for nonlinear real arithmetic combining interval constraint solving with an SMT solver for linear arithmetic.[49] formalizes the floating-points for the SMT-LIB format. While these approach can check ranges on numeric variables, they do not handle roundoff errors or other uncertainties and cannot compute specifications automatically. [46] use a floating-point decision procedure to detect stability issues and while their approach provides witnesses of instability if such exist, it is not able to prove sound error bounds with respect to a real-valued semantics. [3] prove fixed-point constraints with a combination of bit vectors and reals, but such an encoding is only possible for fixed-points and less efficient than reals alone. An alternative to our approach is using linear approximations to solve polynomial constraints [10]. We believe that such advances are largely orthogonal to our use of range arithmetic and complement each other.

***Testing*** Symbolic execution is a well-known technique for generating test inputs. [9] use a combination of meta-heuristic search and interval constraint solving to solve the floating-point constraints that arise, whereas [37] combine random search and evolutionary techniques. [52] test numerical code for precision by perturbing low-order bits of values and rewriting expressions. The idea is to exaggerate initial errors and thus make imprecisions more visible. Probabilistic arithmetic [50] is a similar approach but it does the perturbation by using different rounding modes. [6] also propose a testing produce to detect accuracy problems by instrumenting code to perform a higher-precision computation side by side with the regular computations. While these approaches are sound with respect to floating-point arithmetic, they only generate or can check individual inputs and are thus not able to verify or compute output ranges or their roundoff errors.

***Robustness analysis*** [31] combines abstract interpretation with model checking to check programs for stability by tracking the evolution of the width of the interval representing a single input. [40] use concolic execution to find inputs which, given maximum deviations on inputs, maximize the deviation on the outputs. These two works however, use a testing approach and cannot provide sound guarantees. [12] presents a framework for continuity analysis of programs along the mathematical $\epsilon - \delta$ definition of continuity and [13] builds on this work and presents a sound robustness analysis. This framework provides a syntactic proof of robustness for programs over reals and thus does not consider floating-points. Our approach describes a quantitative measure of robustness for nonlinear programs with floating-point numbers and other uncertainties, and we believe that it can complement the cited framework.

## 10. Conclusion

We have presented a programming model for numerical programs that decouples the mathematical problem description from its realization in finite precision. The model uses a **Real** data type that corresponds to mathematical real numbers. The developer specifies the program using reals and indicates the target precision; the compiler chooses a finite-precision representation while checking that the desired precision targets are met. We have described the soundness criteria by translating programs with precision requirements into verification conditions over mathematical reals. The resulting verification conditions, while a natural description of the problem being solved, are difficult to solve using a state-of-the art SMT solver Z3. We therefore developed an algorithm that combines SMT solving with range computation. Our notion of soundness incorporates full input/output behavior of functions, taking into account that, due to conditionals, small differences in values can lead to different paths being taken in the program. For such cases our approach estimates a sound upper bound on the total error of the computation.

We have evaluated our techniques on a number of benchmarks from the literature, including benchmarks from physics, biology, chemistry, and control systems. We have found that invocation of an SMT solver alone is not sufficient to handle these benchmarks due to scalability issues, whereas the use of range arithmetic by itself is not precise enough. By combining these two techniques we were able to show that a finite-precision version of the code conforms to the real-valued version with reasonable precision requirements.

We believe that our results indicate that it is reasonable to introduce **Real**s as a data type, following a list of previously introduced mathematical abstractions in programming languages, such as unbounded integers, rationals, and algebraic data types. The feasibility of verified compilation of our benchmarks suggests that it is realistic to decouple the verification of executable mathematical models over reals from their sound compilation. We therefore expect that this methodology will help advance rigorous formal verification of numerical software and enable us to focus more on high-level correctness properties as opposed to run-time errors alone. Furthermore, we expect that having real numbers as a data type facilitates automatic reordering of finite-precision computations [17] as well as high-level optimizations such as replacing one version of a numerical algorithm with another to achieve the desired combination of efficiency and rigorous worst-case bounds on precision.

## References


[1] Caliper open source framework. http://code.google.com/p/caliper/.

[2] A. Anta and P. Tabuada. To Sample or not to Sample: Self-Triggered Control for Nonlinear Systems. *IEEE Transactions on Automatic Control*, 55(9), 2010.

[3] A. Anta, R. Majumdar, I. Saha, and P. Tabuada. Automatic Verification of Control System Implementations. In *EMSOFT*, 2010.

[4] A. Ayad and C. Marché. Multi-prover verification of floating-point programs. In *IJCAR*, 2010.

[5] D. H. Bailey, Y. Hida, X. S. Li, and B. Thompson. C++/Fortran-90 double-double and quad-double package. http://crd-legacy.lbl.gov/~dhbailey/mpdist/, 2013.

[6] F. Benz, A. Hildebrandt, and S. Hack. A dynamic program analysis to find floating-point accuracy problems. In *PLDI*, 2012.

[7] R. Blanc, E. Kneuss, V. Kuncak, and P. Suter. An Overview of the Leon Verification System: Verification by Translation to Recursive Functions. In *Scala Workshop*, 2013.

[8] B. Blanchet, P. Cousot, R. Cousot, J. Feret, L. Mauborgne, A. Miné, D. Monniaux, and X. Rival. A static analyzer for large safety-critical software. In *PLDI*, pages 196–207, 2003.

[9] M. Borges, M. d'Amorim, S. Anand, D. Bushnell, and C. S. Pasareanu. Symbolic Execution with Interval Solving and Meta-heuristic Search. In *ICST*, 2012.

[10] C. Borralleras, S. Lucas, A. Oliveras, E. Rodríguez-Carbonell, and A. Rubio. Sat modulo linear arithmetic for solving polynomial constraints. *J. Automated Reasoning*, 48(1), 2012.

[11] A. Brillout, D. Kroening, and T. Wahl. Mixed abstractions for floating-point arithmetic. In *FMCAD*, pages 69–76, 2009.

[12] S. Chaudhuri, S. Gulwani, and R. Lublinerman. Continuity analysis of programs. In *POPL*, 2010.

[13] S. Chaudhuri, S. Gulwani, R. Lublinerman, and S. Navidpour. Proving Programs Robust. In *ESEC/FSE*, 2011.

[14] L. Chen, A. Miné, J. Wang, and P. Cousot. Interval Polyhedra: An Abstract Domain to Infer Interval Linear Relationships. In *SAS*, 2009.

[15] E. Darulova and V. Kuncak. Trustworthy Numerical Computation in Scala. In *OOPSLA*, 2011.

[16] E. Darulova and V. Kuncak. Certifying Solutions for Numerical Constraints. In *RV*, 2012.

[17] E. Darulova, V. Kuncak, R. Majumdar, and I. Saha. Synthesis of Fixed-Point Programs. In *EMSOFT*, 2013.

[18] F. de Dinechin, C. Lauter, and G. Melquiond. Certifying the Floating-Point Implementation of an Elementary Function Using Gappa. *IEEE Trans. Comput.*, 2011.

[19] L. H. de Figueiredo and J. Stolfi. *Self-Validated Numerical Methods and Applications*. IMPA/CNPq, Brazil, 1997.

[20] L. De Moura and N. Bjørner. Z3: an efficient SMT solver. In *TACAS*, 2008.

[21] D. Delmas, E. Goubault, S. Putot, J. Souyris, K. Tekkal, and F. Vedrine. Towards an industrial use of FLUCTUAT on safety-critical avionics software. In *FMICS*, 2009.

[22] V. D'Silva, L. Haller, D. Kroening, and M. Tautschnig. Numeric Bounds Analysis with Conflict-driven Learning. In *TACAS*, 2012.

[23] J. A. Duracz and M. Konecny. Polynomial function enclosures and floating point software verification. In *CFV/IJCAR*, 2008.

[24] J. Feret. Static Analysis of Digital Filters. In *ESOP*, 2004.

[25] S. Gao, M. Ganai, F. Ivancic, A. Gupta, S. Sankaranarayanan, and E. Clarke. Integrating ICP and LRA solvers for deciding nonlinear real arithmetic problems. In *FMCAD*, 2010.

[26] K. Ghorbal, E. Goubault, and S. Putot. A Logical Product Approach to Zonotope Intersection. In *CAV*, 2010.

[27] D. Goldberg. What every computer scientist should know about floating-point arithmetic. *ACM Comput. Surv.*, 23(1), 1991.

[28] E. Goubault, S. Putot, and F. Védrine. Modular static analysis with zonotopes. In *SAS*, 2012.

[29] L. Haller, A. Griggio, M. Brain, and D. Kroening. Deciding floating-point logic with systematic abstraction. In *FMCAD*, 2012.

[30] J. Harrison. Floating-Point Verification using Theorem Proving. In *Formal Methods for Hardware Verification, SFM*, 2006.

[31] F. Ivancic, M. Ganai, S. Sankaranarayanan, and A. Gupta. Numerical stability analysis of floating-point computations using software model checking. In *MEMOCODE*, 2010.

[32] B. Jeannet and A. Miné. Apron: A Library of Numerical Abstract Domains for Static Analysis. In *CAV*, 2009.

[33] J. Jiang, W. Luk, and D. Rueckert. FPGA-Based Computation of Free-Form Deformations. In *FPL*, 2003.

[34] D. Jovanović and L. de Moura. Solving Non-linear Arithmetic. In *IJCAR 2012*, 2012.

[35] W. Kahan. Miscalculating Area and Angles of a Needle-like Triangle. Technical report, University of California Berkeley, 2000.

[36] V. Kuznetsov, J. Kinder, S. Bucur, and G. Candea. Efficient State Merging in Symbolic Execution. In *PLDI*, 2012.

[37] K. Lakhotia, N. Tillmann, M. Harman, and J. de Halleux. FloPSy - Search-Based Floating Point Constraint Solving for Symbolic Execution. In *Testing Software and Systems*. Springer Berlin / Heidelberg, 2010.

[38] X. Leroy. Verified squared: does critical software deserve verified tools? In *POPL*, 2011.

[39] M. D. Linderman, M. Ho, D. L. Dill, T. H. Meng, and G. P. Nolan. Towards program optimization through automated analysis of numerical precision. In *CGO*, 2010.

[40] R. Majumdar, I. Saha, and Z. Wang. Systematic Testing for Control Applications. In *MEMOCODE*, 2010.

[41] K. Makino and M. Berz. Taylor Models and Other Validated Functional Inclusion Methods. *International Journal of Pure and Applied Mathematics*, 4, 2003.

[42] A. Miné. Relational Abstract Domains for the Detection of Floating-Point Run-Time Errors. In *ESOP*, 2004.

[43] R. Moore. *Interval Analysis*. Prentice-Hall, 1966.

[44] J. D. Murray. *Mathematical Biology*. Springer, 2002.

[45] M. Odersky, L. Spoon, and B. Venners. *Programming in Scala: A Comprehensive Step-by-step Guide*. Artima Incorporation, 2008.

[46] G. Paganelli and W. Ahrendt. Verifying (In-)Stability in Floating-point Programs by Increasing Precision, using SMT Solving. In *SYNASC*, 2013.

[47] O. Ponsini, C. Michel, and M. Rueher. Refining Abstract Interpretation Based Value Analysis with Constraint Programming Techniques. In *CP*, 2012.

[48] A. Quarteroni, F. Saleri, and P. Gervasio. *Scientific Computing with MATLAB and Octave*. Springer, 3rd edition, 2010.

[49] P. Rümmer and T. Wahl. An SMT-LIB Theory of Binary Floating-Point Arithmetic. In *Informal proceedings of SMT at FLoC*, 2010.

[50] N. Scott, F. Jézéquel, C. Denis, and J.-M. Chesneaux. Numerical 'health check' for scientific codes: the CADNA approach. *Computer Physics Communications*, 2007.

[51] I. C. Society. IEEE Standard for Floating-Point Arithmetic. *IEEE Std 754-2008*, 2008.

[52] E. Tang, E. Barr, X. Li, and Z. Su. Perturbing numerical calculations for statistical analysis of floating-point program (in)stability. In *ISSTA*, 2010.

[53] E. M. Westbrook and S. Chaudhuri. A Semantics for Approximate Program Transformations. *CoRR*, 2013.

[54] C. Woodford and C. Phillips. *Numerical Methods with Worked Examples*, volume 2nd. Springer, 2012.

# 30 Years of Research and Development around Coq

Gérard Huet
INRIA Paris – Rocquencourt, France
Gerard.Huet@inria.fr

Hugo Herbelin
INRIA Paris – Rocquencourt, France
Hugo.Herbelin@inria.fr

The Coq Proof Assistant is an interactive software system based on higher-order type theory, designed and implemented by a team of French researchers as a continuous effort over the last 30 years. It implements a logical framework, called the Calculus of Inductive Constructions, endowed with notational facilities and a modular structure, allowing its use as a high-level language fit for the development of compositional mathematical components. Explicit potential proof structures are built by execution of ML tactics and tacticals, along a choice of proof schemes combinators. This allows a wide spectrum of inference granularity, from step-by-step inference, to full decision procedures and reflection principles. The validity of such a potential proof is verified by an independent core proof checker, whose meta-theory has been itself formally justified.

Coq proofs may be seen as programs in a high-level functional notation, decorated by correctness assertions, and translators into existing programming languages such as OCaml and Haskell are available. Conversely, specialized subsystems allow the development of algorithms with logical assertions, whose validity is checked by Coq. The Coq Proof Assistant, an open-source software development, is in use by a large community of users. Some notable successes have been achieved, in formalized mathematics (the 4 color theorem, the odd order theorem in group theory), as well as in software certification (a Java Card processing environment, the CompCert certified C compiling project).

The talk will have two parts. First, Gérard Huet will evoke the genesis of Coq, its roots in early type theory, through the influence of Per Martin-Löf's dependent type theory, Jean-Yves Girard's polymorphic $\lambda$-calculi $F$ and $F_\omega$, Nicolaas de Bruijn's Automath languages and type-checkers, and the ML-LCF-Hope effort of Robin Milner and colleagues at the University of Edinburgh. He will discuss the rationale behind a few design decisions, and briefly evoke the historical contributors in the 80s and 90's. Hugo Herbelin will then address a couple of contemporary issues related to the logical status of equality, the proof methods, the high-level specification language, the user interfaces.



*POPL '14*, January 22–24, 2014, San Diego, CA, USA.

ACM 978-1-4503-2544-8/14/01.
http://dx.doi.org/10.1145/2535838.2537848

# The Essence of Reynolds

Stephen Brookes
Carnegie Mellon University

Peter W. O'Hearn
Facebook

Uday Reddy
University of Birmingham

## Abstract

John Reynolds (1935-2013) was a pioneer of programming languages research. In this paper we pay tribute to the man, his ideas, and his influence.

***Categories and Subject Descriptors*** D.3 [*Programming Languages*]; F.3 [*Logics and Meanings of Programs*]

***Keywords*** Polymorphic λ-calculus, Separation Logic, Parametricity, Data Abstraction, Subtypes, Defunctionalization, Substructural Logic and Typing, Possible World Semantics

## 1. Introduction

John Reynolds died on April 28, 2013. He will be remembered for his fundamental and far-sighted research on programming languages: semantics, specifications, language design, logics and proof methodology.

John was born on June 1, 1935, and was raised in Glen Ellyn, Illinois, a suburb of Chicago. He attended Purdue University as an undergraduate, graduating in 1956. His Ph.D. thesis in Theoretical Physics (Harvard University, 1961) was titled "Surface Properties of Nuclear Matter". In later years, with typical modesty and humility, John would describe this, one of his earliest experiences in computer science, as a "big number-crunching program" designed to produce "an uninteresting computation of an unimportant quantity in a bad approximation". At Harvard John met Mary A. Allen, and they married in 1960. John is survived by Mary and their sons, Edward (born 1963) and Matthew (born 1965).

After Harvard, with a burgeoning interest in computer science, John worked as a physicist at Argonne National Laboratory. While at Argonne, he developed a compiler for compilers, called COGENT (1965), and he designed the language GEDANKEN (1969). In 1970 he left Argonne for academia, moving to Syracuse University as a Professor of Computer and Information Science. After a long and fruitful period at Syracuse he moved to Carnegie Mellon University in 1986, where he stayed until retirement at the end of 2012. Over the years he enjoyed sabbaticals and visiting positions at many universities and institutions, including Stanford University, INRIA (Rocquencourt and Sophia Antipolis), Imperial College (University of London), Lucent Technologies, Queen Mary (University of London), Edinburgh University, Aarhus University, and Microsoft Research (Cambridge, England). He forged long-lasting ties with many researchers and was highly valued as a colleague. He was an invited speaker at conferences and symposia spanning the world.

John was an active member of the Association for Computing Machinery (ACM) for many years, including a long stint as editor of the Communications of the ACM and the Journal of the ACM. He became an ACM Fellow in 2001, and received the ACM SIGPLAN Programming Language Achievement Award in 2003. He was a prominent member of IFIP Working Group 2.3. (Programming Methodology), which he joined in 1969, and IFIP Working Group 2.2 (Formal Language Definition), in which he participated from 1977 to 1991. The British Computer Society awarded him the Lovelace Medal in 2011. He was a proud recipient of an Honorary D. Sc. degree conferred by Queen Mary, University of London, in July 2007. Carnegie Mellon University honored him with the Dana Scott Distinguished Research Award in April 2006. In November 2013 ACM SIGPLAN honoured John's memory by renaming their Outstanding Doctoral Dissertation Award to the John C. Reynolds Doctoral Dissertation Award.

John laid the foundations for the work of many of us in the programming languages research community. The influence of his more widely known work – on parametric polymorphism and on Separation Logic – is very plain to see, for example by browsing the pages of recent POPL conferences. What is less well known, and perhaps even more striking, is the sheer number of absolutely first-rate contributions made by John across a broad range, all of which display his characteristic deep insight. In remembering him, and what he was like as a researcher and colleague, there is no better place to start than with a simple recollection of these results.

## 2. Main works.

***Early Works.*** While working at Argonne John became interested in both programming languages and in automatic theorem proving. He produced COGENT, an early compiler-compiler. He then produced a very significant, yet somewhat overlooked, paper:

- **Automatic computation of data set definitions.** IFIP Congress (1) 1968: 456-461

In modern terminology, this paper computed an over-approximation of the kinds of data structures reached in a program, where the data was constructed using Lisp-style operations (car, cdr, etc).

There is a story associated with this paper. Years later, people were pursuing automatic shape analysis based on Separation Logic, as represented in tools such as SPACE INVADER, SLAYER, THOR and INFER. Reynolds wanted to pursue proofs of full functional correctness, beyond the reach of mere program analysis, leading to many good-natured arguments and discussions. In arguing his position, John seemed to be eerily skilled at pinpointing the limitations of the techniques in these tools, even though he could see and appreciate the excitement. It turns out that the people working on these tools were not aware that "Automatic Computation of Data Set Definitions" could be regarded as an early shape analysis.



*POPL '14*, January 22–24, 2014, San Diego, CA, USA.

ACM 978-1-4503-2544-8/14/01. . . $15.00.
http://dx.doi.org/10.1145/10.1145/2535838.2537851

You can find yourself at a disadvantage when your opponent just happens to be the source of the founding works underpinning the position you are defending!

This story is typical. Again and again during his career Reynolds was seen to be years ahead of the field, and it became a kind of joke amongst friends that John had gotten there 10 years or more before everyone else. Once, when hearing a talk on types, Reynolds complimented the speaker on one of the ideas he explained, and the speaker said that the idea was taken from a Reynolds paper. At this point a round of jokes began on the theme of Reynolds being 10 years ahead of himself; John joined in, teasing himself gleefully.

The next important paper was in the direction of John's other early interest, theorem proving.

- **Transformational systems and the algebraic structure of atomic formulas**. Machine Intelligence 5, pages 135151. 1969.

This paper developed an anti-unification algorithm, which solves the dual problem to unification: it seeks the most specific common generalization of two terms. This is a fundamental idea that forms part of the basis of the field of inductive logic programming.

These two papers, which are probably not so well known in the PL community, would already have given a very respectable career. But it was now that John entered a kind of golden of period, an extended run of high productivity and extreme quality.

***Golden Period. 1970-1984.*** There are so many top-flight papers here that we simply list them with brief comments, a kind of annotated bibliography.

- **GEDANKEN - a simple typeless language based on the principle of completeness and the reference concept**. CACM 13(5): 308-319 (1970)

  This was an untyped call-by-value programming language whose way of mixing imperative features and functions is similar to the core of ML. This paper won the 1971 ACM Annual Programming Systems and Languages Paper Award, 1971

- **Definitional Interpreters for Higher-Order Programming Languages**, Proceedings, 25th National ACM Conference (August 1972), pp. 717-740. Reprinted in Higher-Order and Symbolic Computation, 11 (1998), pp. 363-397.

  This paper showed how to transform a series of interpreters, eventually ending up with a compiler. This work helped to popularize continuations as a tool in language implementation, and introduced the concept of *defunctionalization* where functions in the interpreter are replaced by their representations (such as closures) in more concrete data structures.

- **On the Relation between Direct and Continuation Semantics**. ICALP 1974 : 141-156

  At the time the power of continuations was becoming apparent, and John asked the simple question of whether continuation and direct semantics can be connected by a precise theorem. The question was non-trivial because, as the abstract states, 'The heart of the problem is the construction of a relation which must be a fixed-point of a non-monotonic 'relational functor".' The paper introduced a general technique for constructing relations between recursively-defined domains.

- **Towards a theory of type structure**. Symposium on Programming 1974: 408-423

  Introduced the Polymorphic $\lambda$-calculus, the first type theory of polymorphic functions. Reynolds's work on Poly$\lambda$ as well as his later work on parametricity influenced the designs of generics in Java and in .Net (Phil Wadler and Andrew Kennedy, personal communication). The polymorphic lambda calculus is beautiful as well as powerful. It consists of just five constructs, yet it can define many of the data structures of central importance in programming. Like many timeless scientific discoveries, this calculus was invented twice, in this case by Reynolds and by the logician Jean-Yves Girard (who called it System F).

  In this paper John attempted, not for the last time, to make a model of the polymorphic calculus. This was difficult because of the impredicative (circular) nature of the calculus, which made it seem to be skirting Russell's paradox. He almost got there, but stated: "we must admit a serious lacuna in our chain of argument". Later, John said (jokingly) that the lacuna admission was one of the most fortunate phrases he had ever included in a paper.

- **User-Defined Types and Procedural Data Structures as Complementary Approaches to Data Abstraction**, New Directions in Algorithmic Languages 1975

  This paper was ahead of its time in pinpointing the essential difference between object-oriented approaches to data abstraction and abstract data types... a topic often revisited decades later. Essentially, procedural approaches are easy to extend because their data representations are decentralized, ADT's provide for binary and multi-nary operations because they are centralized, and the strengths of one are the limitations of the other.

- **Syntactic Control of Interference**. POPL 1978: 39-46

  A strikingly original paper on using what is now called an affine $\lambda$-calculus to control aliasing and other forms of interference between program parts. Possibly the first use of substructural type theory to control resources, 9 years before the appearance of linear logic.

- **Programming with Transition Diagrams**. Programming Methodology, A Collection of Papers by Members of IFIP WG 2.3, ed. D. Gries, Springer-Verlag, 1978, pp. 153–165.

  In this paper, Reynolds goes against the grain, demonstrating how well-designed programs with goto statements can be easy to prove correct.

- **Reasoning about Arrays**, CACM 22(5): 290–299 (1979)

  An early application of *separation* principles for reasoning about arrays using a notation called partition diagrams that Reynolds invented for this purpose. The material is also covered in Chapter 2 of *Craft of Programming*. A technique that Reynolds often used for motivating this material was to ask students to write a binary search program and let them discover for themselves how it is hard it is to get it right. With Reynolds's technique, it is almost impossible to get it wrong.

- **Using category theory to design implicit conversions and generic operators**, Semantics-Directed Compiler Generation 1980: 211-258

  A generalization of many-sorted algebras, category-sorted algebras, is defined and used to account for generic operators applied to different types in the presence of implicit conversions between types, ensuring that the order of applying the conversions does not affect the final result.

- **The Essence of Algol**, Algorithmic Languages, ed. J. W. de Bakker and J. C. van Vliet, North-Holland, 1981, pp. 345-372.

  In this highly influential and oft cited paper, Reynolds contended that Algol should be considered as an applied call-by-name $\lambda$-calculus, and described Idealized Algol to illustrate a number of principles of language design that he proposed as constituting Algol's essence. This paper made significant technical inventions that go far beyond Idealized Algol.

  - Explained how types encapsulate effects naturally in the call-by-name design, and consequently full $\beta\eta$ laws are valid. This idea was echoed in the use of types to control effects in Haskell, which used similar principles to insulate functions from effects and went beyond Algol's monoid of commands to monads (a sort of parameterized commands).

- Possible world (functor category) semantics of local state, which is still influencing technical developments at the edge of programming language theory, as in recent POPL papers of Ahmed, Dreyer, Birkedal and others on reasoning about local state with Kripke relations.
- Typed $\lambda$-calculus with subtypes, which has been used significantly in the foundations of object-oriented languages and elsewhere.

Typically, John did not make a big deal about any of these specific contributions, or single out any one for special attention; it was as if they were mere intellectual tools used in crafting his larger points about language design. But what tools! One wonders in retrospect how he managed to cram so many significant and original ideas into a single paper.

- **The Craft of Programming**. Prentice Hall International series in computer science, Prentice Hall 1981, ISBN 978-0-13-188862-3, pp. I-XIII, 1-434
  and
  **Idealized Algol and its Specification Logic**, Tools and Notions for Program Construction, ed. D. Neel, Cambridge University Press (1982), pp. 121-161.

  In this book and paper Reynolds's ideas about program proving are developing. There is a significant focus on abstraction and refinement in "craft", and on controlling interference as an aid to modular reasoning.
- **Types, Abstraction and Parametric Polymorphism**. IFIP Congress 1983: 513-523

  Perhaps the only computer science paper in which the phrase 'moral turpitude' features, in a not-to-be-missed fable involving Bessel and Descartes. Arguably the best article ever written on the point and purpose of types, exploring the idea that types enforce abstraction. Written as a counterpoint to the prevailing attitude at the time, in which types (only) classify values and rule out errors; while the conventional view emphasized one laudable aspect, Reynolds was convinced that there was more to types and makes a compelling case.

  Technically, the paper is notable for formalizing the Abstraction Theorem and for introducing Relational Parametricity.
- **Polymorphism is not Set-Theoretic**. Semantics of Data Types 1984: 145-156

  Reynolds had been convinced that the polymorphic $\lambda$-calculus should have a set-theoretic model, because "types are not limited to computation", and he set out to find a set-theoretic model. Instead, he ended up showing that there actually is no non-trivial model of the polymorphic $\lambda$-calculus in which types denote sets and where the function type denotes the collection of all set-theoretic functions from one type to another. Interestingly, this was done assuming *classical* set theory, and observations of Hyland, Moggi, Pitts and others later demonstrated the possibility of set-theoretic models assuming *intuitionistic* set theory. Nowadays there are many models of the polymorphic calculus.

  Although he did not question the truth of his result, John was never satisfied with the models of polymorphism that have been obtained, and upon questioning he would become fidgety: it was as if he felt there was something missing in his own insight (if not that of others).

***1985-2000.*** In this period John continued producing high-quality work, but not at quite the same pace as in the golden period. Some of the key works are the following.

- **Syntactic Control of Interference, Part 2**, ICALP'89
- **On Functors Expressible in the Polymorphic Typed Lambda Calculus**. Inf. Comput. 105(1): 1-29, 1993 (with Plotkin)
- **Using Functor Categories to Generate Intermediate Code**. POPL 1995: 25-36
- **Theories of programming languages**. Cambridge University Press 1998, ISBN 978-0-521-59414-1, pp. I-XII, 1-500
- **From Algol to polymorphic linear lambda-calculus**. J. ACM 47(1): 167-223, 2000. (with O'Hearn)

The JACM'00 paper connected up his interests on Algol and on polymorphism; more on that in the next section.

The POPL'95 paper is remarkable for connecting category theory to compilation. John used category theory, and semantics in general, as a tool for guiding design (of a language or a compiler), and not just for after-the-fact study. This attitude is summed up neatly in his remark:

> *Programming language semanticists should be the obstetricians of programming languages, not their coroners.*
> John C. Reynolds

***Separation Logic.*** In 1999, at age 64, John produced one of his most stunning papers.

- **Intuitionistic Reasoning about Shared Mutable Data Structure**, Millennial Perspectives in Computer Science: Proceedings of the 1999 Oxford-Microsoft Symposium in Honour of Sir Tony Hoare, Palgrave, 2000.

This paper came like a bolt from the blue. In it, John showed proofs of heap-mutating programs that were almost as simple as those for purely-functional programs. The key insight was how linked data structures could be described using inductive definitions and a connective which we now call the separating conjunction. One could fold and unfold the definitions, and work in isolation on components of the separating conjunction.

John's paper built on an early work of Burstall (Some techniques for proving programs which alter data structures. Machine Intelligence, 1972). Reynolds extended it by using a form of substructural logic, which turned out to be an instance of the Bunched Logic of O'Hearn and Pym. After a POPL'01 paper by O'Hearn and Ishtiaq detailing this connection, there was one further paper.

- **Local Reasoning about Programs that Alter Data Structures**. CSL 2001: 1-19 (with O'Hearn and Yang)

This paper described the canonical semantics and proof theory of Separation Logic as it is now understood. It used a boolean rather than an intuitionistic form of logic and it worked for a low-level programming language closer to assembly, whereas the 1999 paper was formulated for a language without memory deallocation or address arithmetic.

Although Reynolds was a proponent of influential ideas, he never regarded the positions he adopted as cast in stone. Indeed, it might seem strange that John Reynolds, one of the leading proponents of safe programming languages, would advance a logic for an unsafe language in his work. Here was the inventor of GEDANKEN, Idealized Algol, and the Polymorphic $\lambda$-calculus, working with a language with 'dirty' features. But, armed with program logic, safety could be achieved. Reynolds proved a number of low-level programs to test his ideas, such as for a form of doubly-linked lists which save space by storing the xor of forward and back pointers rather than each separately, and the inductive definition in Separation Logic and the proof came out surprisingly easily.

Next, John wrote an influential survey article covering these papers and others on Separation Logic up to 2002.

- **Separation Logic: A Logic for Shared Mutable Data Structures**. LICS 2002: 55-74

This paper was associated with an invited talk by John at the LICS'02 conference. At the end of his talk John started to try to sum up where we had got to and then stopped, looked at the audience, and simply said: 'a growing number of people are working on this formalism and... well... we think we're on to something'. John Reynolds was humble and not prone to overstatement, and coming from him this was a strong statement.

The next section will provide more context for this work on Separation Logic.

***Later Papers.*** After the founding of Separation Logic, John produced several further papers.

- **Separation and information hiding**. POPL 2004: 268-280 (with O'Hearn and Yang)
- **Local reasoning about a copying garbage collector**. POPL 2004: 220-231 (with Birkedal and Torp-Smith)
- **Towards a Grainless Semantics for Shared Variable Concurrency**, FSTTCS 2004: Foundations of Software Technology and Theoretical Computer Science, LNCS 3328, pp. 35-48, 2004
- **Syntactic Control of interference for Separation Logic**. POPL 2012: 323-336 (with Reddy)

The paper on grainless semantics picks up an old bugbear of his, influenced by Dijkstra's idea that the understanding of concurrent programs should not be dependent on a particular 'grain to time'. His final paper, with Reddy, fittingly brings together two of his major contributions.

## 3. State and abstraction

The issues of state and abstraction were central themes in Reynolds's research, especially during the time of his "golden period." *State* is of the kind represented in imperative "Algol-like" languages, with Algol W being his favorite. This preference was because the effects are concentrated in the base types of "expressions" and "commands," and the function types remain "pure," subject to full $\beta\eta$ equivalence. Thus, "Algol-like" meant an integration of "imperative" and "functional" aspects, preserving both of their fundamental properties without any corruption. *Abstraction* is represented in strong type systems, semantically based, as well as in how the store is viewed in Algol-like languages. Reynolds saw intimate connections between these two views of abstraction and sought to build bridges so that the ideas could be carried back and forth between them. In addition to the abstraction inherent in the store, Reynolds also wanted additional *modularity* in the management of store, going beyond what is representable in conventional language designs. This desire led him to new proposals for type systems, logics and semantic frameworks, as represented in *syntactic control of interference*, *Separation Logic* and *grainless semantics*.

Reynolds's golden period coincides with his teaching of a graduate course on programming at Syracuse. The material he developed for this course is published as *The Craft of Programming* (1981). It contains a wealth of information about

- what imperative programming *means*,
- how to *develop* imperative programs rigorously,
- the *type structure* of imperative programs,
- *reasoning principles* (both *practical*, *e.g.*, arrays, and *abstract*, *e.g.*, Specification Logic), and
- how to reason about *data abstraction* (or *information hiding*).

His analysis of this material gave rise to a series of insightful papers, the most prominent of which are *The Essence of Algol* (1981), and *Idealized Algol and its Specification Logic* (1982). However, the most novel material of the book, the chapter on *Data representation structuring*, is not directly represented in these papers. So, one must go to the source to understand these ideas. However, we believe that these insights influenced Reynolds's papers on types: *A theory of type structure* (1974) and *Types, abstraction and parametric polymorphism* (1983). These are the "bridges" we speak of.

Reynolds always thought of the store in imperative programs as an "abstract type," whose full information is hidden from the program. Soon after defining the polymorphic lambda calculus in 1974, he worked on a project titled *A polymorphic model of Algol*. We have a copy of his handwritten notes, dated "9–23–75," which contain these key equations

$$\begin{aligned} B_{\mathbf{sta}}[S] &= S \xrightarrow{\sim} S \\ B_{w_1 \to w_2}[S] &= \forall S'.\, B_{w_1}[S \times S'] \to B_{w_2}[S \times S'] \end{aligned}$$

We see here that Reynolds thinks of the (Idealized) Algol types for statements (**sta**) and procedures ($w_1 \to w_2$) as *type constructors* $B_{\mathbf{sta}}$ and $B_{w_1 \to w_2}$. These type constructors are parametrized by a type variable $S$ representing the set of states for a store. This is in marked contrast to Strachey's denotational semantics where the store is fixed and *global*. Here the store is a *type variable*. In essence, this means that the program can work with whatever "type" of store we supply, as long as it has all the required data variables. An intuitive interpretation of parametric polymorphism immediately implies that the program will act *the same way* for all these different "types" of stores.

This model of Algol could not be finished in 1975 because it did not satisfy the $\beta$ equivalence of Algol. In 1981, Reynolds moved from type constructors to functors in the *Essence of Algol* model, which depend on the postulation of morphisms between store types. We suspect that he was never fully satisfied with functors. In 2000, he returned to the original equations in the joint paper with O'Hearn, *From Algol to polymorphic linear lambda calculus*, where these equations appear again, adapted to the linear context. So, what happened to the problem with $\beta$ equivalence? It is still open! Linearity rules out the obvious counterexamples and enough evidence is gathered to show that the model is worthy even if it does not satisfy $\beta$ equivalence.

This is one direction of the "bridge." We expect that the other direction was implicit in Reynolds's thinking. The chapter on *Data representation structuring* contains programming examples where graph algorithms are treated (including Tarjan's algorithm for strong components, posed as a challenge problem by Knuth for program correctness) using data refinement. An initial algorithm expressed in terms of sets of nodes and edges is gradually refined to an algorithm involving concrete data objects within Algol W. The relationship between the two sets of data structures is captured using a technique that Reynolds invents for this purpose: *general invariants*, which are true throughout a particular region of the program (as opposed to Floyd-Hoare invariants that are true at particular points in the program). Transporting these ideas back across the bridge, we notice that the programs are operating on two independent state spaces $S_A$ and $S_C$, and the general invariants are relations $R \subseteq S_A \times S_C$ that are maintained by the two slices of the program without any observable difference. Here, we see the principles of relational parametricity taking shape, not in an abstract theoretical setting, but in concrete programming examples involving data abstraction.

The essence of relational parametricity is that, if a program term is parametrized by a type variable (or an *opaque* type), then the information about the type is hidden from the term, and the term behaves *the same way* for all possible instantiations of the type variable. Hence, if we consider two instantiations $A$ and $A'$ of the type variable and allow ourselves the freedom to substitute particular elements $x \in A$ by elements $x' \in A'$ then the results produced by the program term should be the same, modulo the substitution we have made. What kind of substitutions can one make? In early years of modern mathematics, isomorphisms, *i.e.*, structure-preserving *one-to-one* correspondences, were allowed. After the advent of category theory, homomorphisms, *i.e.*, *many-to-one* correspondences, were allowed. But, if $A$ and $A'$ are two *arbitrary* instantiations, there is no intuitive reason why the allowed correspondences should be asymmetric. Hence, logical relations, *i.e.*, structure-preserving *many-to-many* correspondences, are the only intuitively appealing answer to the question for programming applications. They form the basis of *relational parametricity*. In a good theory of parametricity, both "isomorphism parametricity" and "homomorphism parametricity" (natural transformations) become special cases of relational parametricity.

While we mentioned "program terms" above for the sake of explanation, these ideas are by no means limited to programs. Any mathematical formula, any algorithmic process or any mechanism in which output quantities are causally derived from input quantities, whether discrete or continuous, can have the notion of being parametrized by types and, if so, we might expect it to be parametric. Bob Atkey makes a beginning with this line of enquiry in the present POPL. He shows that the symmetries of physical system as required for the "Noether's theorem" in classical mechanics can be viewed as instances of parametricity. This should pave the way for broader applications of the relational parametricity principle in mathematics and science.

With the formulation of relational parametricity, the "bridge" is completed. The reasoning principles of *Data representation structuring* are translated into the parametricity principles of the polymorphic lambda calculus, via the translation of the 1975 notes (or the 2000 paper employing polymorphic linear lambda calculus).

Imperative programs are complicated for a variety of reasons and those complications do not go away just by defining semantics. Reynolds repeatedly sought to create intellectual tools to control and master the complications. A key idea was that the state should not be treated as a monolithic entity; rather it should be partitioned into *separate* portions and distributed to different parts of the program to operate on independently. In *Syntactic Control of Interference* (1978), he proposed a system of rules that allows program terms to be viewed as "owning" portions of the store, based on their free identifiers, and only terms that own separate portions can be combined using the procedure mechanism. This is roughly the meaning of saying that a procedure and its argument "should not interfere." Specification logic (1982) involves subtler notions of non-interference, which were investigated in a novel semantics of Tennent (*Semantical Analysis of Specification Logic*, Inform. Comput. 1985) and in O'Hearn's 1991 Ph.D. thesis. In *Reasoning about Arrays* (1979), Reynolds applied the separation principle to arrays, inventing a powerful notation called "partition diagrams" to document such separation.

All of this was perhaps only setting the stage for the powerful *Separation Logic* for dynamic data structures to come in 1999-2001 which came as a surprising *tour de force* even to those of us that had thought about the problem and knew all the technical tools that Reynolds, O'Hearn and others deployed in solving it. Separation Logic represents a giant intellectual leap in recognizing that ownership (what can be accessed) and separation (divisions of the state) are not static, spanning all states, but can vary from state to state.

In his 2000 paper *Intuitionistic Reasoning about Shared Mutable Data Structure*, Reynolds introduced the separating conjunction, which allows the *pre-conditions* of operations to break the state into components. Reynolds demonstrated that this allowed for simple proofs of heap-mutating programs and, more deeply enabled a new spatial dimension to modular reasoning which complements that of abstraction. In a sense, the pre-conditions not only specify what is *true* in a state but also describe the *structure of the store* (mainly the heap). This idea has far-reaching consequences, and it is extremely fortunate that Reynolds made this step forward at the time he did, because he opened the flood gates for new ideas.

The foremost of the new ideas was the resolution of the frame problem by O'Hearn. In *Local reasoning about programs that alter data structures* (2001, by Reynolds jointly with O'Hearn and Yang), pre-conditions specify not merely what portion of the store *can be* used from a program point, but *only* that portion of the store that will be so used. This has the remarkable consequence that specifications need to talk about only the portion of the store actually manipulated by program fragments, referred to as their "footprint". A general rule called the *frame rule* allows such local specifications to be extended to larger contexts as needed; and, using the separating conjunction, this passage from smaller to larger contexts can be described extremely directly and compactly.

Separation Logic, as represented in the 'Local Reasoning' paper and finally in Reynolds's LICS'02 paper, can be seen as the culmination of his theme of *making the structure of the store explicit* in programming language theories (be they semantics or logics). In the end, Separation Logic derives much of its power from the interplay between dynamic separation and framing. And, the passage from local specifications to larger contexts by framing can be seen as a logical analogue of Reynolds's idea of expanding a store shape in his work on possible world semantics, going back as far as the 1975 notes mentioned above, but with the separating conjunction providing a more flexible form of extension.

Today, Separation Logic is a thriving research direction with a tremendous investment in building automated tools and solving a variety of reasoning problems that have been perceived as too difficult or impossible for a long time. It represents a major force for taming the looming problem of concurrent software to be run on multi-core processors.

## 4. Conclusion

John Reynolds was one of the greatest minds programming research has seen. What was his secret? What was the essence of Reynolds?

Certainly, he had great talent, and he also had great determination. But his way of working and interacting with others, conveying what was important to him, was special and inspiring to those who knew him. John Reynolds was as pure a scientist as you would ever meet, and this is what made him tick. It was not academic politics, or funding, or fame, it was just the ideas.

It was not uncommon for John to talk to someone about their own ideas for hours at a time. Not only 20 minutes, or one hour, but three, four or five hours. This was especially true for students and junior faculty, but also held for more senior people as well. He would set everything else aside, his own time included, in his desire to get to the heart of the matter. These were intense sessions of deep concentration and back-and-forth discussion, and while John would argue vigorously and ask probing questions he always managed to be patient and pleasant with whoever he was talking to. It was as if programming and programming languages held wonderful treasures waiting to be uncovered, and he wanted to see them. John Reynolds just wanted to understand.

And he came to understand a lot. In the course of his career he discovered numerous deep ideas of lasting value – anti-unification, defunctionalization, theory of subtypes, possible world semantics of state, polymorphic $\lambda$-calculus, relational parametricity, Separation Logic, and others – and we are much the richer for it.

# Freeze After Writing

## Quasi-Deterministic Parallel Programming with LVars

Lindsey Kuper
Indiana University
lkuper@cs.indiana.edu

Aaron Turon
MPI-SWS
turon@mpi-sws.org

Neelakantan R. Krishnaswami
University of Birmingham
N.Krishnaswami@cs.bham.ac.uk

Ryan R. Newton
Indiana University
rrnewton@cs.indiana.edu

## Abstract

Deterministic-by-construction parallel programming models offer the advantages of parallel speedup while avoiding the nondeterministic, hard-to-reproduce bugs that plague fully concurrent code. A principled approach to deterministic-by-construction parallel programming with shared state is offered by *LVars*: shared memory locations whose semantics are defined in terms of an application-specific lattice. Writes to an LVar take the least upper bound of the old and new values with respect to the lattice, while reads from an LVar can observe only that its contents have crossed a specified threshold in the lattice. Although it guarantees determinism, this interface is quite limited.

We extend LVars in two ways. First, we add the ability to "freeze" and then read the contents of an LVar directly. Second, we add the ability to attach event handlers to an LVar, triggering a callback when the LVar's value changes. Together, handlers and freezing enable an expressive and useful style of parallel programming. We prove that in a language where communication takes place through these extended LVars, programs are at worst *quasi-deterministic*: on every run, they either produce the same answer or raise an error. We demonstrate the viability of our approach by implementing a library for Haskell supporting a variety of LVar-based data structures, together with a case study that illustrates the programming model and yields promising parallel speedup.

***Categories and Subject Descriptors*** D.3.3 [*Language Constructs and Features*]: Concurrent programming structures; D.1.3 [*Concurrent Programming*]: Parallel programming; D.3.1 [*Formal Definitions and Theory*]: Semantics; D.3.2 [*Language Classifications*]: Concurrent, distributed, and parallel languages

***Keywords*** Deterministic parallelism; lattices; quasi-determinism

## 1. Introduction

Flexible parallelism requires tasks to be scheduled dynamically, in response to the vagaries of an execution. But if the resulting schedule nondeterminism is *observable* within a program, it becomes much more difficult for programmers to discover and correct bugs by testing, let alone to reason about their code in the first place.

While much work has focused on identifying methods of deterministic parallel programming [5, 7, 18, 21, 22, 32], *guaranteed* determinism in real parallel programs remains a lofty and rarely achieved goal. It places stringent constraints on the programming model: concurrent tasks must communicate in restricted ways that prevent them from observing the effects of scheduling, a restriction that must be enforced at the language or runtime level.

The simplest strategy is to allow *no* communication, forcing concurrent tasks to produce values independently. Pure data-parallel languages follow this strategy [28], as do languages that force references to be either task-unique or immutable [5]. But some algorithms are more naturally or efficiently written using shared state or message passing. A variety of deterministic-by-construction models allow limited communication along these lines, but they tend to be narrow in scope and permit communication through only a single data structure: for instance, FIFO queues in Kahn process networks [18] and StreamIt [16], or shared write-only tables in Intel Concurrent Collections [7].

***Big-tent deterministic parallelism*** Our goal is to create a broader, general-purpose deterministic-by-construction programming environment to increase the appeal and applicability of the method. We seek an approach that is not tied to a particular data structure and that supports familiar idioms from both functional and imperative programming styles. Our starting point is the idea of *monotonic* data structures, in which (1) information can only be added, never removed, and (2) the order in which information is added is not observable. A paradigmatic example is a set that supports insertion but not removal, but there are many others.

Our recently proposed *LVars* programming model [19] makes an initial foray into programming with monotonic data structures. In this model (which we review in Section 2), all shared data structures (called LVars) are monotonic, and the states that an LVar can take on form a *lattice*. Writes to an LVar must correspond to a *join* (least upper bound) in the lattice, which means that they monotonically increase the information in the LVar, and that they commute with one another. But commuting writes are not enough to guarantee determinism: if a read can observe whether or not a concurrent write has happened, then it can observe differences in scheduling. So in the LVars model, the answer to the question "has a write occurred?" (*i.e.*, is the LVar above a certain lattice value?) is always *yes*; the reading thread will block until the LVar's contents reach a desired threshold. In a monotonic data structure, the absence of information is transient—another thread could add that information at any time—but the presence of information is forever.

The LVars model guarantees determinism, supports an unlimited variety of data structures (anything viewable as a lattice), and


*POPL '14*, January 22–24, 2014, San Diego, CA, USA.

ACM 978-1-4503-2544-8/14/01...$15.00.
http://dx.doi.org/10.1145/2535838.2535842

provides a familiar API, so it already achieves several of our goals. Unfortunately, it is not as general-purpose as one might hope.

Consider an unordered graph traversal. A typical implementation involves a monotonically growing set of "seen nodes"; neighbors of seen nodes are fed back into the set until it reaches a fixed point. Such fixpoint computations are ubiquitous, and would seem to be a perfect match for the LVars model due to their use of monotonicity. But they are not expressible using the threshold read and least-upper-bound write operations described above.

The problem is that these computations rely on *negative* information about a monotonic data structure, *i.e.*, on the *absence* of certain writes to the data structure. In a graph traversal, for example, neighboring nodes should only be explored if the current node is *not yet* in the set; a fixpoint is reached only if no new neighbors are found; and, of course, at the end of the computation it must be possible to learn exactly which nodes were reachable (which entails learning that certain nodes were not). But in the LVars model, asking whether a node is in a set means waiting until the node *is* in the set, and it is not clear how to lift this restriction while retaining determinism.

***Monotonic data structures that can say "no"*** In this paper, we propose two additions to the LVars model that significantly extend its reach.

First, we add *event handlers*, a mechanism for attaching a callback function to an LVar that runs, asynchronously, whenever events arrive (in the form of monotonic updates to the LVar). Ordinary LVar reads encourage a synchronous, *pull* model of programming in which threads ask specific questions of an LVar, potentially blocking until the answer is "yes". Handlers, by contrast, support an asynchronous, *push* model of programming. Crucially, it is possible to check for *quiescence* of a handler, discovering that no callbacks are currently enabled—a transient, negative property. Since quiescence means that there are no further changes to respond to, it can be used to tell that a fixpoint has been reached.

Second, we add a primitive for *freezing* an LVar, which comes with the following tradeoff: once an LVar is frozen, any further writes that would change its value instead throw an exception; on the other hand, it becomes possible to discover the exact value of the LVar, learning both positive and negative information about it, without blocking.[1]

Putting these features together, we can write a parallel graph traversal algorithm in the following simple fashion:

```
traverse :: Graph → NodeLabel → Par (Set NodeLabel)
traverse g startV = do
  seen ← newEmptySet
  putInSet seen startV
  let handle node = parMapM (putInSet seen) (nbrs g node)
  freezeSetAfter seen handle
```

This code, written using our Haskell implementation (described in Section 6),[2] discovers (in parallel) the set of nodes in a graph g reachable from a given node `startV`, and is guaranteed to produce a deterministic result. It works by creating a fresh `Set` LVar (corresponding to a lattice whose elements are sets, with set union as least upper bound), and seeding it with the starting node. The `freezeSetAfter` function combines the constructs proposed above. First, it installs the callback `handle` as a handler for the `seen` set, which will asynchronously put the neighbors of each visited node into the set, possibly triggering further callbacks, recursively. Second, when no further callbacks are ready to run—*i.e.*, when the `seen` set has reached a fixpoint—`freezeSetAfter` will freeze the set and return its exact value.

[1] Our original work on LVars [19] included a brief sketch of a similar proposal for a "consume" operation on LVars, but did not study it in detail. Here, we include freezing in our model, prove quasi-determinism for it, and show how to program with it in conjunction with our other proposal, handlers.

[2] The `Par` type constructor is the monad in which LVar computations live.

***Quasi-determinism*** Unfortunately, freezing does not commute with writes that change an LVar.[3] If a freeze is interleaved before such a write, the write will raise an exception; if it is interleaved afterwards, the program will proceed normally. It would appear that the price of negative information is the loss of determinism!

Fortunately, the loss is not total. Although LVar programs with freezing are not guaranteed to be deterministic, they do satisfy a related property that we call *quasi-determinism*: all executions that produce a final value produce the *same* final value. To put it another way, a quasi-deterministic program can be trusted to never change its answer due to nondeterminism; at worst, it might raise an exception on some runs. In our proposed model, this exception can in principle pinpoint the exact pair of freeze and write operations that are racing, greatly easing debugging.

Our general observation is that *pushing towards full-featured, general monotonic data structures leads to flirtation with nondeterminism*; perhaps the best way of ultimately getting deterministic outcomes is to traipse a small distance into nondeterminism, and make our way back. The identification of quasi-deterministic programs as a useful intermediate class is a contribution of this paper. That said, in many cases our freezing construct is only used as the very final step of a computation: after a global barrier, freezing is used to extract an answer. In this common case, we can guarantee determinism, since no writes can subsequently occur.

***Contributions*** The technical contributions of this paper are:

- We introduce *LVish*, a quasi-deterministic parallel programming model that extends LVars to incorporate freezing and event handlers (Section 3). In addition to our high-level design, we present a core calculus for LVish (Section 4), formalizing its semantics, and include a runnable version, implemented in PLT Redex (Section 4.7), for interactive experimentation.
- We give a proof of quasi-determinism for the LVish calculus (Section 5). The key lemma, Independence, gives a kind of *frame property* for LVish computations: very roughly, if a computation takes an LVar from state $p$ to $p'$, then it would take the same LVar from the state $p \sqcup p_F$ to $p' \sqcup p_F$. The Independence lemma captures the commutative effects of LVish computations.
- We describe a Haskell library for practical quasi-deterministic parallel programming based on LVish (Section 6). Our library comes with a number of monotonic data structures, including sets, maps, counters, and single-assignment variables. Further, it can be extended with new data structures, all of which can be used compositionally within the same program. Adding a new data structure typically involves porting an existing scalable (*e.g.*, *lock-free*) data structure to Haskell, then wrapping it to expose a (quasi-)deterministic LVar interface. Our library exposes a monad that is *indexed* by a determinism level: fully deterministic or quasi-deterministic. Thus, the *static type* of an LVish computation reflects its guarantee, and in particular the freeze-last idiom allows freezing to be used safely with a fully-deterministic index.
- In Section 7, we evaluate our library with a case study: parallelizing control flow analysis. The case study begins with an existing implementation of $k$-CFA [26] written in a purely functional style. We show how this code can easily and safely be parallelized by adapting it to the LVish model—an adaptation that

[3] The same is true for quiescence detection; see Section 3.2.

yields promising parallel speedup, and also turns out to have benefits even in the sequential case.

## 2. Background: the LVars Model

*IVars* [1, 7, 24, 27] are a well-known mechanism for deterministic parallel programming. An IVar is a *single-assignment* variable [32] with a blocking read semantics: an attempt to read an empty IVar will block until the IVar has been filled with a value. We recently proposed *LVars* [19] as a generalization of IVars: unlike IVars, which can only be written to once, LVars allow multiple writes, so long as those writes are monotonically increasing with respect to an application-specific lattice of states.

Consider a program in which two parallel computations write to an LVar $lv$, with one thread writing the value 2 and the other writing 3:

$$\begin{aligned} &\texttt{let par}\ \_ = \texttt{put}\ lv\ 3 \\ &\qquad\quad \_ = \texttt{put}\ lv\ 2 \\ &\texttt{in get}\ lv \end{aligned} \qquad \text{(Example 1)}$$

Here, put and get are operations that write and read LVars, respectively, and the expression

$$\texttt{let par}\ x_1 = e_1;\ x_2 = e_2;\ \ldots\ \texttt{in}\ body$$

has *fork-join* semantics: it launches concurrent subcomputations $e_1, e_2, \ldots$ whose executions arbitrarily interleave, but must all complete before *body* runs. The put operation is defined in terms of the application-specific lattice of LVar states: it updates the LVar to the *least upper bound* of its current state and the new state being written.

If $lv$'s lattice is the $\leq$ ordering on positive integers, as shown in Figure 1(a), then $lv$'s state will always be $\max(3, 2) = 3$ by the time get $lv$ runs, since the least upper bound of two positive integers $n_1$ and $n_2$ is $\max(n_1, n_2)$. Therefore Example 1 will deterministically evaluate to 3, regardless of the order in which the two put operations occurred.

On the other hand, if $lv$'s lattice is that shown in Figure 1(b), in which the least upper bound of any two distinct positive integers is $\top$, then Example 1 will deterministically raise an exception, indicating that conflicting writes to $lv$ have occurred. This exception is analogous to the "multiple put" error raised upon multiple writes to an IVar. Unlike with a traditional IVar, though, multiple writes of the *same* value (say, put $lv$ 3 and put $lv$ 3) will *not* raise an exception, because the least upper bound of any positive integer and itself is that integer—corresponding to the fact that multiple writes of the same value do not allow any nondeterminism to be observed.

***Threshold reads*** However, merely ensuring that writes to an LVar are monotonically increasing is not enough to ensure that programs behave deterministically. Consider again the lattice of Figure 1(a) for $lv$, but suppose we change Example 1 to allow the get operation to be interleaved with the two puts:

$$\begin{aligned} &\texttt{let par}\ \_ = \texttt{put}\ lv\ 3 \\ &\qquad\quad \_ = \texttt{put}\ lv\ 2 \\ &\qquad\quad x = \texttt{get}\ lv \\ &\texttt{in}\ x \end{aligned} \qquad \text{(Example 2)}$$

Since the two puts and the get can be scheduled in any order, Example 2 is nondeterministic: $x$ might be either 2 or 3, depending on the order in which the LVar effects occur. Therefore, to maintain determinism, LVars put an extra restriction on the get operation. Rather than allowing get to observe the exact value of the LVar, it can only observe that the LVar has reached one of a specified set of *lower bound* states. This set of lower bounds, which we provide as an extra argument to get, is called a *threshold set* because the values in it form a "threshold" that the state of the LVar must cross before the call to get is allowed to unblock and return. When the threshold has been reached, get unblocks and returns *not* the exact value of the LVar, but instead, the (unique) element of the threshold set that has been reached or surpassed.

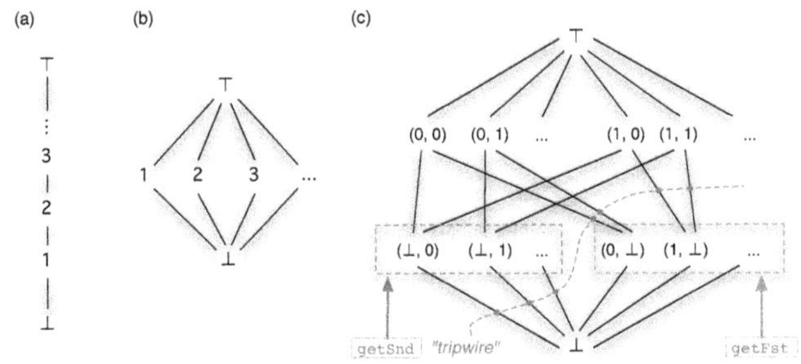


**Figure 1.** Example LVar lattices: (a) positive integers ordered by $\leq$; (b) IVar containing a positive integer; (c) pair of natural-number-valued IVars, annotated with example threshold sets that would correspond to a blocking read of the first or second element of the pair. Any state transition crossing the "tripwire" for getSnd causes it to unblock and return a result.

We can make Example 2 behave deterministically by passing a threshold set argument to get. For instance, suppose we choose the singleton set $\{3\}$ as the threshold set. Since $lv$'s value can only increase with time, we know that once it is at least 3, it will remain at or above 3 forever; therefore the program will deterministically evaluate to 3. Had we chosen $\{2\}$ as the threshold set, the program would deterministically evaluate to 2; had we chosen $\{4\}$, it would deterministically block forever.

As long as we only access LVars with put and (thresholded) get, we can arbitrarily share them between threads without introducing nondeterminism. That is, the put and get operations in a given program can happen in any order, without changing the value to which the program evaluates.

***Incompatibility of threshold sets*** While the LVar interface just described is deterministic, it is only useful for synchronization, not for communicating data: we must specify in advance the single answer we expect to be returned from the call to get. In general, though, threshold sets do not have to be singleton sets. For example, consider an LVar $lv$ whose states form a lattice of *pairs* of natural-number-valued IVars; that is, $lv$ is a pair $(m, n)$, where $m$ and $n$ both start as $\bot$ and may each be updated once with a non-$\bot$ value, which must be some natural number. This lattice is shown in Figure 1(c).

We can then define getFst and getSnd operations for reading from the first and second entries of $lv$:

$$\texttt{getFst}\ p \triangleq \texttt{get}\ p\ \{(m, \bot) \mid m \in \mathbb{N}\}$$

$$\texttt{getSnd}\ p \triangleq \texttt{get}\ p\ \{(\bot, n) \mid n \in \mathbb{N}\}$$

This allows us to write programs like the following:

$$\begin{aligned} &\texttt{let par}\ \_ = \texttt{put}\ lv\ (\bot, 4) \\ &\qquad\quad \_ = \texttt{put}\ lv\ (3, \bot) \\ &\qquad\quad x = \texttt{getSnd}\ lv \\ &\texttt{in}\ x \end{aligned} \qquad \text{(Example 3)}$$

In the call getSnd $lv$, the threshold set is $\{(\bot, 0), (\bot, 1), \ldots\}$, an infinite set. There is no risk of nondeterminism because the elements of the threshold set are *pairwise incompatible* with respect to $lv$'s lattice: informally, since the second entry of $lv$ can only be written once, no more than one state from the set

$\{(\bot, 0), (\bot, 1), \ldots\}$ can ever be reached. (We formalize this incompatibility requirement in Section 4.5.)

In the case of Example 3, `getSnd` $lv$ may unblock and return $(\bot, 4)$ any time after the second entry of $lv$ has been written, regardless of whether the first entry has been written yet. It is therefore possible to use LVars to safely read parts of an incomplete data structure—say, an object that is in the process of being initialized by a constructor.

***The model versus reality*** The use of explicit threshold sets in the above LVars model should be understood as a mathematical modeling technique, *not* an implementation approach or practical API. Our library (discussed in Section 6) provides an unsafe `getLV` operation to the authors of LVar data structure libraries, who can then make operations like `getFst` and `getSnd` available as a safe interface for application writers, implicitly baking in the particular threshold sets that make sense for a given data structure without ever explicitly constructing them.

To put it another way, operations on a data structure exposed as an LVar must have the *semantic effect* of a least upper bound for writes or a threshold for reads, but none of this need be visible to clients (or even written explicitly in the code). Any data structure API that provides such a semantics is guaranteed to provide deterministic concurrent communication.

## 3. LVish, Informally

As we explained in Section 1, while LVars offer a deterministic programming model that allows communication through a wide variety of data structures, they are not powerful enough to express common algorithmic patterns, like fixpoint computations, that require both positive and negative queries. In this section, we explain our extensions to the LVar model at a high level; Section 4 then formalizes them, while Section 6 shows how to implement them.

### 3.1 Asynchrony through Event Handlers

Our first extension to LVars is the ability to do asynchronous, event-driven programming through event handlers. An *event* for an LVar can be represented by a lattice element; the event *occurs* when the LVar's current value reaches a point at or above that lattice element. An *event handler* ties together an LVar with a callback function that is asynchronously invoked whenever some events of interest occur. For example, if $lv$ is an LVar whose lattice is that of Figure 1(a), the expression

$$\texttt{addHandler}\ lv\ \{1, 3, 5, \ldots\}\ (\lambda x.\, \texttt{put}\ lv\ x + 1) \qquad \text{(Example 4)}$$

registers a handler for $lv$ that executes the callback function $\lambda x.\, \texttt{put}\ lv\ x + 1$ for each odd number that $lv$ is at or above. When Example 4 is finished evaluating, $lv$ will contain the smallest even number that is at or above what its original value was. For instance, if $lv$ originally contains 4, the callback function will be invoked twice, once with 1 as its argument and once with 3. These calls will respectively write $1 + 1 = 2$ and $3 + 1 = 4$ into $lv$; since both writes are $\leq 4$, $lv$ will remain 4. On the other hand, if $lv$ originally contains 5, then the callback will run three times, with 1, 3, and 5 as its respective arguments, and with the latter of these calls writing $5 + 1 = 6$ into $lv$, leaving $lv$ as 6.

In general, the second argument to `addHandler` is an arbitrary subset $Q$ of the LVar's lattice, specifying which events should be handled. Like threshold sets, these *event sets* are a mathematical modeling tool only; they have no explicit existence in the implementation.

Event handlers in LVish are somewhat unusual in that they invoke their callback for *all* events in their event set $Q$ that have taken place (*i.e.*, all values in $Q$ less than or equal to the current LVar value), even if those events occurred prior to the handler being registered. To see why this semantics is necessary, consider the following, more subtle example:

$$\begin{aligned}&\texttt{let par}\ \_ = \texttt{put}\ lv\ 0\\ &\qquad\quad \_ = \texttt{put}\ lv\ 1\\ &\qquad\quad \_ = \texttt{addHandler}\ lv\ \{0, 1\}\ (\lambda x.\, \texttt{if}\ x = 0\ \texttt{then put}\ lv\ 2)\\ &\ \ \texttt{in get}\ lv\ \{2\}\end{aligned}$$

(Example 5)

Can Example 5 ever block? If a callback only executed for events that arrived after its handler was registered, or only for the largest event in its handler set that had occurred, then the example would be nondeterministic: it would block, or not, depending on how the handler registration was interleaved with the `puts`. By instead executing a handler's callback once for *each and every* element in its event set below or at the LVar's value, we guarantee quasi-determinism—and, for Example 5, guarantee the result of 2.

The power of event handlers is most evident for lattices that model collections, such as sets. For example, if we are working with lattices of sets of natural numbers, ordered by subset inclusion, then we can write the following function:

$$\texttt{forEach} = \lambda lv.\, \lambda f.\, \texttt{addHandler}\ lv\ \{\{0\}, \{1\}, \{2\}, \ldots\}\ f$$

Unlike the usual `forEach` function found in functional programming languages, this function sets up a *permanent*, asynchronous flow of data from $lv$ into the callback $f$. Functions like `forEach` can be used to set up complex, cyclic data-flow networks, as we will see in Section 7.

In writing `forEach`, we consider only the singleton sets to be events of interest, which means that if the value of $lv$ is some set like $\{2, 3, 5\}$ then $f$ will be executed once for each singleton subset ($\{2\}, \{3\}, \{5\}$)—that is, once for each element. In Section 6.2, we will see that this kind of handler set can be specified in a lattice-generic way, and in Section 6 we will see that it corresponds closely to our implementation strategy.

### 3.2 Quiescence through Handler Pools

Because event handlers are asynchronous, we need a separate mechanism to determine when they have reached a *quiescent* state, *i.e.*, when all callbacks for the events that have occurred have finished running. As we discussed in Section 1, detecting quiescence is crucial for implementing fixpoint computations. To build flexible data-flow networks, it is also helpful to be able to detect quiescence of multiple handlers simultaneously. Thus, our design includes *handler pools*, which are groups of event handlers whose collective quiescence can be tested.

The simplest way to use a handler pool is the following:

$$\begin{aligned}&\texttt{let}\ h\ =\ \texttt{newPool}\\ &\ \ \texttt{in addInPool}\ h\ lv\ Q\ f;\\ &\qquad \texttt{quiesce}\ h\end{aligned}$$

where $lv$ is an LVar, $Q$ is an event set, and $f$ is a callback. Handler pools are created with the `newPool` function, and handlers are registered with `addInPool`, a variant of `addHandler` that takes a handler pool as an additional argument. Finally, `quiesce` blocks until a pool of handlers has reached a quiescent state.

Of course, whether or not a handler is quiescent is a non-monotonic property: we can move in and out of quiescence as more `puts` to an LVar occur, and even if all states at or below the current state have been handled, there is no way to know that more `puts` will not arrive to increase the state and trigger more callbacks. There is no risk to quasi-determinism, however, because `quiesce` does not yield any information about *which* events have been handled—any such questions must be asked through LVar functions like `get`. In practice, `quiesce` is almost always used together with freezing, which we explain next.

### 3.3 Freezing and the Freeze-After Pattern

Our final addition to the LVar model is the ability to *freeze* an LVar, which forbids further changes to it, but in return allows its exact value to be read. We expose freezing through the function `freeze`, which takes an LVar as its sole argument, and returns the exact value of the LVar as its result. As we explained in Section 1, `puts` that would change the value of a frozen LVar instead raise an exception, and it is the potential for races between such `puts` and `freeze` that makes LVish quasi-deterministic, rather than fully deterministic.

Putting all the above pieces together, we arrive at a particularly common pattern of programming in LVish:

$$\texttt{freezeAfter} = \lambda lv.\, \lambda Q.\, \lambda f.\ \texttt{let}\ h = \texttt{newPool}\ \texttt{in}\ \texttt{addInPool}\ h\ lv\ Q\ f;\ \texttt{quiesce}\ h;\ \texttt{freeze}\ lv$$

In this pattern, an event handler is registered for an LVar, subsequently quiesced, and then the LVar is frozen and its exact value is returned. A set-specific variant of this pattern, `freezeSetAfter`, was used in the graph traversal example in Section 1.

## 4. LVish, Formally

In this section, we present a core calculus for LVish—in particular, a quasi-deterministic, parallel, call-by-value $\lambda$-calculus extended with a store containing LVars. It extends the original LVar formalism to support event handlers and freezing. In comparison to the informal description given in the last two sections, we make two simplifications to keep the model lightweight:

- We parameterize the definition of the LVish calculus by a *single* application-specific lattice, representing the set of states that LVars in the calculus can take on. Therefore LVish is really a *family* of calculi, varying by choice of lattice. Multiple lattices can in principle be encoded using a sum construction, so this modeling choice is just to keep the presentation simple; in any case, our Haskell implementation supports multiple lattices natively.
- Rather than modeling the full ensemble of event handlers, handler pools, quiescence, and freezing as separate primitives, we instead formalize the "freeze-after" pattern—which combined them—directly as a primitive. This greatly simplifies the calculus, while still capturing the essence of our programming model.

In this section we cover the most important aspects of the LVish core calculus. Complete details, including the proof of Lemma 1, are given in the companion technical report [20].

### 4.1 Lattices

The application-specific lattice is given as a 4-tuple $(D, \sqsubseteq, \bot, \top)$ where $D$ is a set, $\sqsubseteq$ is a partial order on the elements of $D$, $\bot$ is the least element of $D$ according to $\sqsubseteq$ and $\top$ is the greatest. The $\bot$ element represents the initial "empty" state of every LVar, while $\top$ represents the "error" state that would result from conflicting updates to an LVar. The partial order $\sqsubseteq$ represents the order in which an LVar may take on states. It induces a binary *least upper bound* (lub) operation $\sqcup$ on the elements of $D$. We require that every two elements of $D$ have a least upper bound in $D$. Intuitively, the existence of a lub for every two elements of $D$ means that it is possible for two subcomputations to independently update an LVar, and then deterministically merge the results by taking the lub of the resulting two states. Formally, this makes $(D, \sqsubseteq, \bot, \top)$ a *bounded join-semilattice* with a designated greatest element ($\top$). For brevity, we use the term "lattice" as shorthand for "bounded join-semilattice with a designated greatest element" in the rest of this paper. We also occasionally use $D$ as a shorthand for the entire 4-tuple $(D, \sqsubseteq, \bot, \top)$ when its meaning is clear from the context.

### 4.2 Freezing

To model freezing, we need to generalize the notion of the state of an LVar to include information about whether it is "frozen" or not. Thus, in our model an LVar's *state* is a pair $(d, frz)$, where $d$ is an element of the application-specific set $D$ and $frz$ is a "status bit" of either true or false. We can define an ordering $\sqsubseteq_p$ on LVar states $(d, frz)$ in terms of the application-specific ordering $\sqsubseteq$ on elements of $D$. Every element of $D$ is "freezable" except $\top$. Informally:

- Two unfrozen states are ordered according to the application-specific $\sqsubseteq$; that is, $(d, \mathsf{false}) \sqsubseteq_p (d', \mathsf{false})$ exactly when $d \sqsubseteq d'$.
- Two frozen states do not have an order, unless they are equal: $(d, \mathsf{true}) \sqsubseteq_p (d', \mathsf{true})$ exactly when $d = d'$.
- An unfrozen state $(d, \mathsf{false})$ is less than or equal to a frozen state $(d', \mathsf{true})$ exactly when $d \sqsubseteq d'$.
- The only situation in which a frozen state is less than an unfrozen state is if the unfrozen state is $\top$; that is, $(d, \mathsf{true}) \sqsubseteq_p (d', \mathsf{false})$ exactly when $d' = \top$.

The addition of status bits to the application-specific lattice results in a new lattice $(D_p, \sqsubseteq_p, \bot_p, \top_p)$, and we write $\sqcup_p$ for the least upper bound operation that $\sqsubseteq_p$ induces. Definition 1 and Lemma 1 formalize this notion.

**Definition 1** (Lattice freezing). Suppose $(D, \sqsubseteq, \bot, \top)$ is a lattice. We define an operation $\text{Freeze}(D, \sqsubseteq, \bot, \top) \triangleq (D_p, \sqsubseteq_p, \bot_p, \top_p)$ as follows:

1. $D_p$ is a set defined as follows:
$$D_p \triangleq \{(d, frz) \mid d \in (D - \{\top\}) \wedge frz \in \{\mathsf{true}, \mathsf{false}\}\} \cup \{(\top, \mathsf{false})\}$$
2. $\sqsubseteq_p \in \mathcal{P}(D_p \times D_p)$ is a binary relation defined as follows:
$$\begin{array}{lclcl} (d, \mathsf{false}) & \sqsubseteq_p & (d', \mathsf{false}) & \iff & d \sqsubseteq d' \\ (d, \mathsf{true}) & \sqsubseteq_p & (d', \mathsf{true}) & \iff & d = d' \\ (d, \mathsf{false}) & \sqsubseteq_p & (d', \mathsf{true}) & \iff & d \sqsubseteq d' \\ (d, \mathsf{true}) & \sqsubseteq_p & (d', \mathsf{false}) & \iff & d' = \top \end{array}$$
3. $\bot_p \triangleq (\bot, \mathsf{false})$.
4. $\top_p \triangleq (\top, \mathsf{false})$.

**Lemma 1** (Lattice structure). *If $(D, \sqsubseteq, \bot, \top)$ is a lattice then $\text{Freeze}(D, \sqsubseteq, \bot, \top)$ is as well.*

### 4.3 Stores

During the evaluation of LVish programs, a *store* $S$ keeps track of the states of LVars. Each LVar is represented by a binding from a location $l$, drawn from a set *Loc*, to its state, which is some pair $(d, frz)$ from the set $D_p$.

**Definition 2.** A *store* is either a finite partial mapping $S : Loc \overset{\text{fin}}{\rightarrow} (D_p - \{\top_p\})$, or the distinguished element $\top_S$.

We use the notation $S[l \mapsto (d, frz)]$ to denote extending $S$ with a binding from $l$ to $(d, frz)$. If $l \in dom(S)$, then $S[l \mapsto (d, frz)]$ denotes an update to the existing binding for $l$, rather than an extension. We can also denote a store by explicitly writing out all its bindings, using the notation $[l_1 \mapsto (d_1, frz_1), l_2 \mapsto (d_2, frz_2), \ldots]$.

It is straightforward to lift the $\sqsubseteq_p$ operations defined on elements of $D_p$ to the level of stores:

Given a lattice $(D, \sqsubseteq, \bot, \top)$ with elements $d \in D$:

$$
\begin{array}{rcl}
\text{configurations } \sigma & ::= & \langle S;\, e\rangle \mid \textbf{error} \\
\text{expressions } e & ::= & x \mid v \mid e\, e \mid \texttt{get}\ e\ e \mid \texttt{put}\ e\ e \mid \texttt{new} \mid \texttt{freeze}\ e \\
& \mid & \texttt{freeze}\ e\ \texttt{after}\ e\ \texttt{with}\ e \\
& \mid & \texttt{freeze}\ l\ \texttt{after}\ Q\ \texttt{with}\ \lambda x.\, e, \{e, \ldots\}, H \\
\text{stores } S & ::= & [l_1 \mapsto p_1, \ldots, l_n \mapsto p_n] \mid \top_S \\
\text{values } v & ::= & () \mid d \mid p \mid l \mid P \mid Q \mid \lambda x.\, e \\
\text{eval contexts } E & ::= & [\,] \mid E\, e \mid e\, E \mid \texttt{get}\ E\ e \mid \texttt{get}\ e\ E \mid \texttt{put}\ E\ e \\
& \mid & \texttt{put}\ e\ E \mid \texttt{freeze}\ E \mid \texttt{freeze}\ E\ \texttt{after}\ e\ \texttt{with}\ e \\
& \mid & \texttt{freeze}\ e\ \texttt{after}\ E\ \texttt{with}\ e \mid \texttt{freeze}\ e\ \texttt{after}\ e\ \texttt{with}\ E \\
& \mid & \texttt{freeze}\ v\ \texttt{after}\ v\ \texttt{with}\ v, \{e \ldots\ E\, e \ldots\}, H
\end{array}
$$

$$
\begin{array}{rcl}
\text{"handled" sets } H & ::= & \{d_1, \ldots, d_n\} \\
\text{threshold sets } P & ::= & \{p_1, p_2, \ldots\} \\
\text{event sets } Q & ::= & \{d_1, d_2, \ldots\}
\end{array}
\qquad
\begin{array}{rcl}
\text{states } p & ::= & (d, \mathit{frz}) \\
\text{status bits } \mathit{frz} & ::= & \mathsf{true} \mid \mathsf{false}
\end{array}
$$

**Figure 2.** Syntax for LVish.

**Definition 3.** A store $S$ is *less than or equal to* a store $S'$ (written $S \sqsubseteq_S S'$) iff:

- $S' = \top_S$, or
- $dom(S) \subseteq dom(S')$ and for all $l \in dom(S)$, $S(l) \sqsubseteq_p S'(l)$.

Stores ordered by $\sqsubseteq_S$ also form a lattice (with bottom element $\emptyset$ and top element $\top_S$); we write $\sqcup_S$ for the induced lub operation (concretely defined in [20]). If, for example,

$$(d_1, \mathit{frz}_1) \sqcup_p (d_2, \mathit{frz}_2) = \top_p,$$

then

$$[l \mapsto (d_1, \mathit{frz}_1)] \sqcup_S [l \mapsto (d_2, \mathit{frz}_2)] = \top_S.$$

A store containing a binding $l \mapsto (\top, \mathit{frz})$ can never arise during the execution of an LVish program, because, as we will see in Section 4.5, an attempted `put` that would take the value of $l$ to $\top$ will raise an error.

### 4.4 The LVish Calculus

The syntax and operational semantics of the LVish calculus appear in Figures 2 and 3, respectively. As we have noted, both the syntax and semantics are parameterized by the lattice $(D, \sqsubseteq, \bot, \top)$. The reduction relation $\hookrightarrow$ is defined on *configurations* $\langle S;\, e\rangle$ comprising a store and an expression. The *error configuration*, written **error**, is a unique element added to the set of configurations, but we consider $\langle \top_S;\, e\rangle$ to be equal to **error** for all expressions $e$. The metavariable $\sigma$ ranges over configurations.

LVish uses a reduction semantics based on evaluation contexts. The E-EVAL-CTXT rule is a standard context rule, allowing us to apply reductions within a context. The choice of context determines where evaluation can occur; in LVish, the order of evaluation is nondeterministic (that is, a given expression can generally reduce in various ways), and so it is generally *not* the case that an expression has a unique decomposition into redex and context. For example, in an application $e_1\, e_2$, either $e_1$ or $e_2$ might reduce first. The nondeterminism in choice of evaluation context reflects the nondeterminism of scheduling between concurrent threads, and in LVish, the arguments to `get`, `put`, `freeze`, and application expressions are *implicitly* evaluated concurrently.[4]

Arguments must be fully evaluated, however, before function application ($\beta$-reduction, modeled by the E-BETA rule) can occur. We can exploit this property to define `let par` as syntactic sugar:

$$\texttt{let par}\ x = e_1;\ y = e_2\ \texttt{in}\ e_3 \ \triangleq\ ((\lambda x.\, (\lambda y.\, e_3))\ e_1)\ e_2$$

[4] This is in contrast to the original LVars formalism given in [19], which models parallelism with explicitly simultaneous reductions.

Because we do not reduce under $\lambda$-terms, we can sequentially compose $e_1$ before $e_2$ by writing $\texttt{let}\ \_ = e_1\ \texttt{in}\ e_2$, which desugars to $(\lambda\_.\, e_2)\ e_1$. Sequential composition is useful, for instance, when allocating a new LVar before beginning a set of side-effecting `put`/`get`/`freeze` operations on it.

### 4.5 Semantics of `new`, `put`, and `get`

In LVish, the `new`, `put`, and `get` operations respectively create, write to, and read from LVars in the store:

- `new` (implemented by the E-NEW rule) extends the store with a binding for a new LVar whose initial state is $(\bot, \mathsf{false})$, and returns the location $l$ of that LVar (*i.e.*, a pointer to the LVar).
- `put` (implemented by the E-PUT and E-PUT-ERR rules) takes a pointer to an LVar and a new lattice element $d_2$ and updates the LVar's state to the *least upper bound* of the current state and $(d_2, \mathsf{false})$, potentially pushing the state of the LVar upward in the lattice. Any update that would take the state of an LVar to $\top_p$ results in the program immediately stepping to **error**.
- `get` (implemented by the E-GET rule) performs a blocking threshold read. It takes a pointer to an LVar and a *threshold set* $P$, which is a non-empty set of LVar states that must be *pairwise incompatible*, expressed by the premise $incomp(P)$. A threshold set $P$ is pairwise incompatible iff the lub of any two distinct elements in $P$ is $\top_p$. If the LVar's state $p_1$ in the lattice is *at or above* some $p_2 \in P$, the `get` operation unblocks and returns $p_2$. Note that $p_2$ is a unique element of $P$, for if there is another $p_2' \neq p_2$ in the threshold set such that $p_2' \sqsubseteq_p p_1$, it would follow that $p_2 \sqcup_p p_2' = p_1 \neq \top_p$, which contradicts the requirement that $P$ be pairwise incompatible.[5]

Is the `get` operation deterministic? Consider two lattice elements $p_1$ and $p_2$ that have no ordering and have $\top_p$ as their lub, and suppose that `put`s of $p_1$ and $p_2$ and a `get` with $\{p_1, p_2\}$ as its threshold set all race for access to an LVar $lv$. Eventually, the program is guaranteed to fault, because $p_1 \sqcup_p p_2 = \top_p$, but in the meantime, `get` $lv$ $\{p_1, p_2\}$ could return either $p_1$ or $p_2$. Therefore, `get` *can* behave nondeterministically—but this behavior is not observable in the final answer of the program, which is guaranteed to subsequently fault.

### 4.6 The `freeze` – `after` – `with` Primitive

The LVish calculus includes a simple form of `freeze` that immediately freezes an LVar (see E-FREEZE-SIMPLE). More interesting is the `freeze` – `after` – `with` primitive, which models the "freeze-after" pattern described in Section 3.3. The expression `freeze` $e_{\mathrm{lv}}$ `after` $e_{\mathrm{events}}$ `with` $e_{\mathrm{cb}}$ has the following semantics:

- It attaches the callback $e_{\mathrm{cb}}$ to the LVar $e_{\mathrm{lv}}$. The expression $e_{\mathrm{events}}$ must evaluate to a event set $Q$; the callback will be executed, once, for each lattice element in $Q$ that the LVar's state reaches or surpasses. The callback $e_{\mathrm{cb}}$ is a function that takes a lattice element as its argument. Its return value is ignored, so it runs solely for effect. For instance, a callback might itself do a `put` to the LVar to which it is attached, triggering yet more callbacks.
- If the handler reaches a quiescent state, the LVar $e_{\mathrm{lv}}$ is frozen, and its *exact* state is returned (rather than an underapproximation of the state, as with `get`).

[5] We stress that, although $incomp(P)$ is given as a premise of the E-GET reduction rule (suggesting that it is checked at runtime), in our real implementation threshold sets are not written explicitly, and it is the data structure author's responsibility to ensure that any provided read operations have threshold semantics; see Section 6.

Given a lattice $(D, \sqsubseteq, \bot, \top)$ with elements $d \in D$:

$$incomp(P) \triangleq \forall p_1, p_2 \in P.\ (p_1 \neq p_2 \implies p_1 \sqcup_p p_2 = \top_p) \qquad \boxed{\sigma \hookrightarrow \sigma'}$$

E-EVAL-CTXT
$$\frac{\langle S;\ e\rangle \hookrightarrow \langle S';\ e'\rangle}{\langle S;\ E[e]\rangle \hookrightarrow \langle S';\ E[e']\rangle}$$

E-BETA
$$\frac{}{\langle S;\ (\lambda x.\, e)\ v\rangle \hookrightarrow \langle S;\ e[x := v]\rangle}$$

E-NEW
$$\frac{}{\langle S;\ \texttt{new}\rangle \hookrightarrow \langle S[l \mapsto (\bot, \mathsf{false})];\ l\rangle}\ (l \notin dom(S))$$

E-PUT
$$\frac{S(l) = p_1 \qquad p_2 = p_1 \sqcup_p (d_2, \mathsf{false}) \qquad p_2 \neq \top_p}{\langle S;\ \texttt{put}\ l\ d_2\rangle \hookrightarrow \langle S[l \mapsto p_2];\ ()\rangle}$$

E-PUT-ERR
$$\frac{S(l) = p_1 \qquad p_1 \sqcup_p (d_2, \mathsf{false}) = \top_p}{\langle S;\ \texttt{put}\ l\ d_2\rangle \hookrightarrow \mathbf{error}}$$

E-GET
$$\frac{S(l) = p_1 \qquad incomp(P) \qquad p_2 \in P \qquad p_2 \sqsubseteq_p p_1}{\langle S;\ \texttt{get}\ l\ P\rangle \hookrightarrow \langle S;\ p_2\rangle}$$

E-FREEZE-INIT
$$\frac{}{\langle S;\ \texttt{freeze}\ l\ \texttt{after}\ Q\ \texttt{with}\ \lambda x.\, e\rangle \hookrightarrow \langle S;\ \texttt{freeze}\ l\ \texttt{after}\ Q\ \texttt{with}\ \lambda x.\, e, \{\}, \{\}\rangle}$$

E-SPAWN-HANDLER
$$\frac{S(l) = (d_1, frz_1) \qquad d_2 \sqsubseteq d_1 \qquad d_2 \notin H \qquad d_2 \in Q}{\langle S;\ \texttt{freeze}\ l\ \texttt{after}\ Q\ \texttt{with}\ \lambda x.\, e_0, \{e, \dots\}, H\rangle \hookrightarrow \langle S;\ \texttt{freeze}\ l\ \texttt{after}\ Q\ \texttt{with}\ \lambda x.\, e_0, \{e_0[x := d_2], e, \dots\}, \{d_2\} \cup H\rangle}$$

E-FREEZE-FINAL
$$\frac{S(l) = (d_1, frz_1) \qquad \forall d_2\ .\ (d_2 \sqsubseteq d_1 \wedge d_2 \in Q \Rightarrow d_2 \in H)}{\langle S;\ \texttt{freeze}\ l\ \texttt{after}\ Q\ \texttt{with}\ v, \{v \dots\}, H\rangle \hookrightarrow \langle S[l \mapsto (d_1, \mathsf{true})];\ d_1\rangle}$$

E-FREEZE-SIMPLE
$$\frac{S(l) = (d_1, frz_1)}{\langle S;\ \texttt{freeze}\ l\rangle \hookrightarrow \langle S[l \mapsto (d_1, \mathsf{true})];\ d_1\rangle}$$

**Figure 3.** An operational semantics for LVish.

To keep track of the running callbacks, LVish includes an auxiliary form,

$$\texttt{freeze}\ l\ \texttt{after}\ Q\ \texttt{with}\ \lambda x.\, e_0, \{e, \dots\}, H$$

where:

- The value $l$ is the LVar being handled/frozen;
- The set $Q$ (a subset of the lattice $D$) is the event set;
- The value $\lambda x.\, e_0$ is the callback function;
- The set of expressions $\{e, \dots\}$ are the running callbacks; and
- The set $H$ (a subset of the lattice $D$) represents those values in $Q$ for which callbacks have already been launched.

Due to our use of evaluation contexts, any running callback can execute at any time, as if each is running in its own thread.

The rule E-SPAWN-HANDLER launches a new callback thread any time the LVar's current value is at or above some element in $Q$ that has not already been handled. This step can be taken nondeterministically at any time after the relevant `put` has been performed.

The rule E-FREEZE-FINAL detects quiescence by checking that two properties hold. First, every event of interest (lattice element in $Q$) that has occurred (is bounded by the current LVar state) must be handled (be in $H$). Second, all existing callback threads must have terminated with a value. In other words, every enabled callback has completed. When such a quiescent state is detected, E-FREEZE-FINAL freezes the LVar's state. Like E-SPAWN-HANDLER, the rule can fire at any time, nondeterministically, that the handler appears quiescent—a transient property! But after being frozen, any further `put`s that would have enabled additional callbacks will instead fault, raising **error** by way of the E-PUT-ERR rule.

Therefore, freezing is a way of "betting" that once a collection of callbacks have completed, no further `put`s that change the LVar's value will occur. For a given run of a program, either all `put`s to an LVar arrive before it has been frozen, in which case the value returned by `freeze – after – with` is the lub of those values, or some `put` arrives after the LVar has been frozen, in which case the program will fault. And thus we have arrived at *quasi-determinism*: a program will always either evaluate to the same answer or it will fault.

To ensure that we will win our bet, we need to guarantee that quiescence is a *permanent* state, rather than a transient one—that is, we need to perform all `put`s either prior to `freeze – after – with`, or by the callback function within it (as will be the case for fixpoint computations). In practice, freezing is usually the very last step of an algorithm, permitting its result to be extracted. Our implementation provides a special `runParThenFreeze` function that does so, and thereby guarantees full determinism.

### 4.7 Modeling Lattice Parameterization in Redex

We have developed a runnable version of the LVish calculus[6] using the PLT Redex semantics engineering toolkit [14]. In the Redex of today, it is not possible to directly parameterize a language definition by a lattice.[7] Instead, taking advantage of Racket's syntactic abstraction capabilities, we define a Racket macro, `define-LVish-language`, that wraps a template implementing the lattice-agnostic semantics of Figure 3, and takes the following arguments:

- a *name*, which becomes the *lang-name* passed to Redex's `define-language` form;
- a *"downset" operation*, a Racket-level procedure that takes a lattice element and returns the (finite) set of all lattice elements that are below that element (this operation is used to implement the semantics of `freeze – after – with`, in particular, to determine when the E-FREEZE-FINAL rule can fire);
- a *lub operation*, a Racket-level procedure that takes two lattice elements and returns a lattice element; and
- a (possibly infinite) set of *lattice elements* represented as Redex *patterns*.

Given these arguments, `define-LVish-language` generates a Redex model specialized to the application-specific lattice in ques-

[6] Available at `http://github.com/iu-parfunc/lvars`.

[7] See discussion at `http://lists.racket-lang.org/users/archive/2013-April/057075.html`.

tion. For instance, to instantiate a model called `nat`, where the application-specific lattice is the natural numbers with `max` as the least upper bound, one writes:

```
(define-LVish-language nat downset-op max natural)
```

where `downset-op` is separately defined. Here, `downset-op` and `max` are Racket procedures. `natural` is a Redex pattern that has no meaning to Racket proper, but because `define-LVish-language` is a macro, `natural` is not evaluated until it is in the context of Redex.

## 5. Quasi-Determinism for LVish

Our proof of quasi-determinism for LVish formalizes the claim we make in Section 1: that, for a given program, although some executions may raise exceptions, all executions that produce a final result will produce the same final result.

In this section, we give the statements of the main quasi-determinism theorem and the two most important supporting lemmas. The statements of the remaining lemmas, and proofs of all our theorems and lemmas, are included in the companion technical report [20].

### 5.1 Quasi-Determinism and Quasi-Confluence

Our main result, Theorem 1, says that if two executions starting from a configuration $\sigma$ terminate in configurations $\sigma'$ and $\sigma''$, then $\sigma'$ and $\sigma''$ are the same configuration, or one of them is **error**.

**Theorem 1** (Quasi-Determinism). *If $\sigma \hookrightarrow^* \sigma'$ and $\sigma \hookrightarrow^* \sigma''$, and neither $\sigma'$ nor $\sigma''$ can take a step, then either:*

1. *$\sigma' = \sigma''$ up to a permutation on locations $\pi$, or*
2. *$\sigma' =$ **error** or $\sigma'' =$ **error**.*

Theorem 1 follows from a series of *quasi-confluence* lemmas. The most important of these, Strong Local Quasi-Confluence (Lemma 2), says that if a configuration steps to two different configurations, then either there exists a single third configuration to which they both step (in at most one step), or one of them steps to **error**. Additional lemmas generalize Lemma 2's result to multiple steps by induction on the number of steps, eventually building up to Theorem 1.

**Lemma 2** (Strong Local Quasi-Confluence). *If $\sigma \equiv \langle S;\, e\rangle \hookrightarrow \sigma_a$ and $\sigma \hookrightarrow \sigma_b$, then either:*

1. *there exist $\pi, i, j$ and $\sigma_c$ such that $\sigma_a \hookrightarrow^i \sigma_c$ and $\sigma_b \hookrightarrow^j \pi(\sigma_c)$ and $i \leq 1$ and $j \leq 1$, or*
2. *$\sigma_a \hookrightarrow$ **error** or $\sigma_b \hookrightarrow$ **error**.*

### 5.2 Independence

In order to show Lemma 2, we need a "frame property" for LVish that captures the idea that independent effects commute with each other. Lemma 3, the Independence lemma, establishes this property. Consider an expression $e$ that runs starting in store $S$ and steps to $e'$, updating the store to $S'$. The Independence lemma allows us to make a double-edged guarantee about what will happen if we run $e$ starting from a larger store $S \sqcup_S S''$: first, it will update the store to $S' \sqcup_S S''$; second, it will step to $e'$ as it did before. Here $S \sqcup_S S''$ is the least upper bound of the original $S$ and some other store $S''$ that is "framed on" to $S$; intuitively, $S''$ is the store resulting from some other independently-running computation.

**Lemma 3** (Independence). *If $\langle S;\, e\rangle \hookrightarrow \langle S';\, e'\rangle$ (where $\langle S';\, e'\rangle \neq$ **error**), then we have that:*
*$\langle S \sqcup_S S'';\, e\rangle \hookrightarrow \langle S' \sqcup_S S'';\, e'\rangle$,*
*where $S''$ is any store meeting the following conditions:*

- *$S''$ is non-conflicting with $\langle S;\, e\rangle \hookrightarrow \langle S';\, e'\rangle$,*
- *$S' \sqcup_S S'' =_{frz} S$, and*
- *$S' \sqcup_S S'' \neq \top_S$.*

Lemma 3 requires as a precondition that the stores $S' \sqcup_S S''$ and $S$ are *equal in status*—that, for all the locations shared between them, the status bits of those locations agree. This assumption rules out interference from freezing. Finally, the store $S''$ must be *non-conflicting* with the original transition from $\langle S;\, e\rangle$ to $\langle S';\, e'\rangle$, meaning that locations in $S''$ cannot share names with locations newly allocated during the transition; this rules out location name conflicts caused by allocation.

**Definition 4.** Two stores $S$ and $S'$ are *equal in status* (written $S =_{frz} S'$) iff for all $l \in (dom(S) \cap dom(S'))$, if $S(l) = (d, frz)$ and $S'(l) = (d', frz')$, then $frz = frz'$.

**Definition 5.** A store $S''$ is *non-conflicting* with the transition $\langle S;\, e\rangle \hookrightarrow \langle S';\, e'\rangle$ iff $(dom(S') - dom(S)) \cap dom(S'') = \emptyset$.

## 6. Implementation

We have constructed a prototype implementation of LVish as a monadic library in Haskell, which is available at

`http://hackage.haskell.org/package/lvish`

Our library adopts the basic approach of the `Par` monad [24], enabling us to employ our own notion of lightweight, library-level threads with a custom scheduler. It supports the programming model laid out in Section 3 in full, including explicit handler pools. It differs from our formal model in following Haskell's by-need evaluation strategy, which also means that concurrency in the library is *explicitly marked*, either through uses of a `fork` function or through asynchronous callbacks, which run in their own lightweight thread.

Implementing LVish as a Haskell library makes it possible to provide compile-time guarantees about determinism and quasi-determinism, because programs written using our library run in our `Par` monad and can therefore only perform LVish-sanctioned side effects. We take advantage of this fact by indexing `Par` computations with a phantom type that indicates their *determinism level*:

```
data Determinism = Det | QuasiDet
```

The `Par` type constructor has the following kind:[8]

```
Par :: Determinism → * → *
```

together with the following suite of `run` functions:

```
runPar   :: Par Det a → a
runParIO :: Par lvl a → IO a
runParThenFreeze :: DeepFrz a ⇒ Par Det a → FrzType a
```

The public library API ensures that if code uses `freeze`, it is marked as `QuasiDet`; thus, code that types as `Det` is guaranteed to be fully deterministic. While LVish code with an arbitrary determinism level `lvl` can be executed in the `IO` monad using `runParIO`, only `Det` code can be executed as if it were pure, since it is guaranteed to be free of visible side effects of nondeterminism. In the common case that `freeze` is only needed at the end of an otherwise-deterministic computation, `runParThenFreeze` runs the computation to completion, and then freezes the returned LVar, returning its exact value—and is guaranteed to be deterministic.[9]

[8] We are here using the `DataKinds` extension to Haskell to treat `Determinism` as a kind. In the full implementation, we include a second phantom type parameter to ensure that LVars cannot be used in multiple runs of the `Par` monad, in a manner analogous to how the `ST` monad prevents an `STRef` from being returned from `runST`.

[9] The `DeepFrz` typeclass is used to perform freezing of nested LVars, producing values of frozen type (as given by the `FrzType` type function).

### 6.1 The Big Picture

We envision two parties interacting with our library. First, there are data structure authors, who use the library directly to implement a specific monotonic data structure (*e.g.*, a monotonically growing finite map). Second, there are application writers, who are clients of these data structures. Only the application writers receive a (quasi-)determinism guarantee; an author of a data structure is responsible for ensuring that the states their data structure can take on correspond to the elements of a lattice, and that the exposed interface to it corresponds to some use of `put`, `get`, `freeze`, and event handlers.

Thus, our library is focused primarily on *lattice-generic* infrastructure: the `Par` monad itself, a thread scheduler, support for blocking and signaling threads, handler pools, and event handlers. Since this infrastructure is unsafe (does not guarantee quasi-determinism), only data structure authors should import it, subsequently exporting a *limited* interface specific to their data structure. For finite maps, for instance, this interface might include key/value insertion, lookup, event handlers and pools, and freezing—along with higher-level abstractions built on top of these.

For this approach to scale well with available parallel resources, it is essential that the data structures themselves support efficient parallel access; a finite map that was simply protected by a global lock would force all parallel threads to sequentialize their access. Thus, we expect data structure authors to draw from the extensive literature on scalable parallel data structures, employing techniques like fine-grained locking and lock-free data structures [17]. Data structures that fit into the LVish model have a special advantage: because all updates must commute, it may be possible to avoid the expensive synchronization which *must* be used for non-commutative operations [2]. And in any case, monotonic data structures are usually much simpler to represent and implement than general ones.

### 6.2 Two Key Ideas

***Leveraging atoms*** Monotonic data structures acquire "pieces of information" over time. In a lattice, the smallest such pieces are called the *atoms* of the lattice: they are elements not equal to $\bot$, but for which the only smaller element is $\bot$. Lattices for which every element is the lub of some set of atoms are called *atomistic*, and in practice most application-specific lattices used by LVish programs have this property—especially those whose elements represent collections.

In general, the LVish primitives allow arbitrarily large queries and updates to an LVar. But for an atomistic lattice, the corresponding data structure usually exposes operations that work at the atom level, semantically limiting `puts` to atoms, `gets` to threshold sets of atoms, and event sets to sets of atoms. For example, the lattice of finite maps is atomistic, with atoms consisting of all singleton maps (*i.e.*, all key/value pairs). The interface to a finite map usually works at the atom level, allowing addition of a new key/value pair, querying of a single key, or traversals (which we model as handlers) that walk over one key/value pair at a time.

Our implementation is designed to facilitate good performance for atomistic lattices by associating LVars with a set of *deltas* (changes), as well as a lattice. For atomistic lattices, the deltas are essentially just the atoms—for a set lattice, a delta is an element; for a map, a key/value pair. Deltas provide a compact way to represent a change to the lattice, allowing us to easily and efficiently communicate such changes between `puts` and `gets`/handlers.

***Leveraging idempotence*** While we have emphasized the commutativity of least upper bounds, they also provide another important property: *idempotence*, meaning that $d \sqcup d = d$ for any element $d$. In LVish terms, repeated `puts` or `freezes` have no effect, and since these are the only way to modify the store, the result is that $e; e$ behaves the same as $e$ for any LVish expression $e$. Idempotence has already been recognized as a useful property for work-stealing scheduling [25]: if the scheduler is allowed to occasionally duplicate work, it is possible to substantially save on synchronization costs. Since LVish computations are guaranteed to be idempotent, we could use such a scheduler (for now we use the standard Chase-Lev deque [10]). But idempotence also helps us deal with races between `put` and `get/addHandler`, as we explain below.

### 6.3 Representation Choices

Our library uses the following generic representation for LVars:

```
data LVar a d =
     LVar { state :: a,  status :: IORef (Status d) }
```

where the type parameter `a` is the (mutable) data structure representing the lattice, and `d` is the type of deltas for the lattice.[10] The `status` field is a mutable reference that represents the status bit:

```
data Status d = Frozen | Active (B.Bag (Listener d))
```

The status bit of an LVar is tied together with a bag of waiting *listeners*, which include blocked `gets` and handlers; once the LVar is frozen, there can be no further events to listen for.[11] The bag module (imported as `B`) supports atomic insertion and removal, and *concurrent* traversal:

```
put     :: Bag a → a → IO (Token a)
remove  :: Token a → IO ()
foreach :: Bag a → (a → Token a → IO ()) → IO ()
```

Removal of elements is done via abstract *tokens*, which are acquired by insertion or traversal. Updates may occur concurrently with a traversal, but are not guaranteed to be visible to it.

A listener for an LVar is a pair of callbacks, one called when the LVar's lattice value changes, and the other when the LVar is frozen:

```
data Listener d = Listener {
  onUpd :: d → Token (Listener d) → SchedQ → IO (),
  onFrz ::     Token (Listener d) → SchedQ → IO () }
```

The listener is given access to its own token in the listener bag, which it can use to deregister from future events (useful for a `get` whose threshold has been passed). It is also given access to the CPU-local scheduler queue, which it can use to spawn threads.

### 6.4 The Core Implementation

Internally, the `Par` monad represents computations in continuation-passing style, in terms of their interpretation in the `IO` monad:

```
type ClosedPar = SchedQ → IO ()
type ParCont a = a → ClosedPar
mkPar :: (ParCont a → ClosedPar) → Par lvl a
```

The `ClosedPar` type represents ready-to-run `Par` computations, which are given direct access to the CPU-local scheduler queue. Rather than returning a final result, a completed `ClosedPar` computation must call the scheduler, `sched`, on the queue. A `Par` computation, on the other hand, completes by passing its intended result to its continuation—yielding a `ClosedPar` computation.

Figure 4 gives the implementation for three core lattice-generic functions: `getLV`, `putLV`, and `freezeLV`, which we explain next.

***Threshold reading*** The `getLV` function assists data structure authors in writing operations with `get` semantics. In addition to an LVar, it takes two *threshold functions*, one for global state and one for deltas. The *global threshold* `gThresh` is used to initially check whether the LVar is above some lattice value(s) by global inspection; the extra boolean argument gives the frozen status of the LVar. The *delta threshold* `dThresh` checks whether a particular update

[10] For non-atomistic lattices, we take `a` and `d` to be the same type.

[11] In particular, with one atomic update of the flag we both mark the LVar as frozen and allow the bag to be garbage-collected.

```
getLV :: (LVar a d) → (a → Bool → IO (Maybe b))
                    → (d → IO (Maybe b)) → Par lvl b
getLV (LVar{state, status}) gThresh dThresh =
  mkPar $λk q →
    let onUpd d = unblockWhen (dThresh d)
        onFrz   = unblockWhen (gThresh state True)
        unblockWhen thresh tok q = do
          tripped ← thresh
          whenJust tripped $ λb → do
            B.remove tok
            Sched.pushWork q (k b)
    in do
      curStat ← readIORef status
      case curStat of
        Frozen → do   -- no further deltas can arrive!
          tripped ← gThresh state True
          case tripped of
            Just b  → exec (k b) q
            Nothing → sched q
        Active ls → do
          tok ← B.put ls (Listener onUpd onFrz)
          frz ← isFrozen status -- must recheck after
                                -- enrolling listener
          tripped ← gThresh state frz
          case tripped of
            Just b  → do
              B.remove tok  -- remove the listener
              k b q         -- execute our continuation
            Nothing → sched q

putLV :: LVar a d → (a → IO (Maybe d)) → Par lvl ()
putLV (LVar{state, status}) doPut = mkPar $ λk q → do
  Sched.mark q  -- publish our intent to modify the LVar
  delta   ← doPut state       -- possibly modify LVar
  curStat ← readIORef status -- read while q is marked
  Sched.clearMark q           -- retract our intent
  whenJust delta $ λd → do
    case curStat of
      Frozen → error "Attempt␣to␣change␣a␣frozen␣LVar"
      Active listeners → B.foreach listeners $
        λ(Listener onUpd _) tok → onUpd d tok q
  k () q

freezeLV :: LVar a d → Par QuasiDet ()
freezeLV (LVar {status}) = mkPar $ λk q → do
  Sched.awaitClear q
  oldStat ← atomicModifyIORef status $ λs→(Frozen, s)
  case oldStat of
    Frozen → return ()
    Active listeners → B.foreach listeners $
      λ(Listener _ onFrz) tok → onFrz tok q
  k () q
```

**Figure 4.** Implementation of key lattice-generic functions.

takes the state of the LVar above some lattice state(s). Both functions return `Just r` if the threshold has been passed, where `r` is the result of the read. To continue our running example of finite maps with key/value pair deltas, we can use `getLV` internally to build the following `getKey` function that is exposed to application writers:

```
-- Wait for the map to contain a key; return its value
getKey key mapLV = getLV mapLV gThresh dThresh where
  gThresh m frozen = lookup key m
  dThresh (k,v) | k == key  = return (Just v)
                | otherwise = return Nothing
```

where `lookup` imperatively looks up a key in the underlying map.

The challenge in implementing `getLV` is the possibility that a *concurrent* `put` will push the LVar over the threshold. To cope with such races, `getLV` employs a somewhat pessimistic strategy: before doing anything else, it enrolls a listener on the LVar that will be triggered on any subsequent updates. If an update passes the delta threshold, the listener is removed, and the continuation of the `get` is invoked, with the result, in a new lightweight thread. *After* enrolling the listener, `getLV` checks the *global* threshold, in case the LVar is already above the threshold. If it is, the listener is removed, and the continuation is launched immediately; otherwise, `getLV` invokes the scheduler, effectively treating its continuation as a blocked thread.

By doing the global check only after enrolling a listener, `getLV` is sure not to miss any threshold-passing updates. It does *not* need to synchronize between the delta and global thresholds: if the threshold is passed just as `getLV` runs, it might launch the continuation twice (once via the global check, once via delta), but by idempotence this does no harm. This is a performance tradeoff: we avoid imposing extra synchronization on *all* uses of `getLV` at the cost of some duplicated work in a rare case. We can easily provide a second version of `getLV` that makes the alternative tradeoff, but as we will see below, idempotence plays an *essential* role in the analogous situation for handlers.

***Putting and freezing*** On the other hand, we have the `putLV` function, used to build operations with `put` semantics. It takes an LVar and an *update function* `doPut` that performs the `put` on the underlying data structure, returning a delta if the `put` actually changed the data structure. If there is such a delta, `putLV` subsequently invokes all currently-enrolled listeners on it.

The implementation of `putLV` is complicated by another race, this time with freezing. If the `put` is nontrivial (*i.e.*, it changes the value of the LVar), the race can be resolved in two ways. Either the freeze takes effect first, in which case the `put` must fault, or else the `put` takes effect first, in which case both succeed. Unfortunately, we have no means to both check the frozen status *and* attempt an update in a single atomic step.[12]

Our basic approach is to ask forgiveness, rather than permission: we eagerly perform the `put`, and only afterwards check whether the LVar is frozen. Intuitively, this is allowed because *if* the LVar is frozen, the `Par` computation is going to terminate with an exception—so the effect of the `put` cannot be observed!

Unfortunately, it is not enough to *just* check the status bit for frozenness afterward, for a rather subtle reason: suppose the `put` is executing concurrently with a `get` which it causes to unblock, and that the `get`ting thread subsequently freezes the LVar. In this case, we *must* treat the `freeze` as if it happened after the `put`, because the `freeze` could not have occurred had it not been for the `put`. But, by the time `putLV` reads the status bit, it may already be set, which naively would cause `putLV` to fault.

To guarantee that such confusion cannot occur, we add a *marked* bit to each CPU scheduler state. The bit is set (using `Sched.mark`) prior to a `put` being performed, and cleared (using `Sched.clear`) only *after* `putLV` has subsequently checked the frozen status. On the other hand, `freezeLV` waits until it has observed a (transient!) clear mark bit on every CPU (using `Sched.awaitClear`) before actually freezing the LVar. This guarantees that any `puts` that *caused* the freeze to take place check the frozen status *before* the freeze takes place; additional `puts` that arrive concurrently may, of course, set a mark bit again after `freezeLV` has observed a clear status.

The proposed approach requires no barriers or synchronization instructions (assuming that the `put` on the underlying data structure acts as a memory barrier). Since the mark bits are per-CPU flags, they can generally be held in a core-local cache line in exclusive mode—meaning that marking and clearing them is extremely

[12] While we could require the underlying data structure to support such transactions, doing so would preclude the use of existing lock-free data structures, which tend to use a single-word compare-and-set operation to perform atomic updates. Lock-free data structures routinely outperform transaction-based data structures [15].

cheap. The only time that the busy flags can create cross-core communication is during `freezeLV`, which should only occur once per LVar computation.

One final point: unlike `getLV` and `putLV`, which are polymorphic in their determinism level, `freezeLV` is statically `QuasiDet`.

***Handlers, pools and quiescence*** Given the above infrastructure, the implementation of handlers is relatively straightforward. We represent handler pools as follows:

```
data HandlerPool = HandlerPool {
  numCallbacks :: Counter,  blocked :: B.Bag ClosedPar }
```

where `Counter` is a simple counter supporting atomic increment, decrement, and checks for equality with zero.[13] We use the counter to track the number of currently-executing callbacks, which we can use to implement `quiesce`. A handler pool also keeps a bag of threads that are blocked waiting for the pool to reach a quiescent state.

We create a pool using `newPool` (of type `Par lvl HandlerPool`), and implement quiescence testing as follows:

```
quiesce :: HandlerPool → Par lvl ()
quiesce hp@(HandlerPool cnt bag) = mkPar $ λk q → do
  tok ← B.put bag (k ())
  quiescent ← poll cnt
  if quiescent then do B.remove tok; k () q
               else sched q
```

where the `poll` function indicates whether `cnt` is (transiently) zero. Note that we are following the same listener-enrollment strategy as in `getLV`, but with `blocked` acting as the bag of listeners.

Finally, `addHandler` has the following interface:

```
addHandler ::
     Maybe HandlerPool               -- Pool to enroll in
  → LVar a d                         -- LVar to listen to
  → (a → IO (Maybe (Par lvl ()))) -- Global callback
  → (d → IO (Maybe (Par lvl ()))) -- Delta callback
  → Par lvl ()
```

As with `getLV`, handlers are specified using both global and delta threshold functions. Rather than returning results, however, these threshold functions return computations to run in a fresh lightweight thread if the threshold has been passed. Each time a callback is launched, the callback count is incremented; when it is finished, the count is decremented, and if zero, all threads blocked on its quiescence are resumed.

The implementation of `addHandler` is very similar to `getLV`, but there is one important difference: handler callbacks must be invoked for *all* events of interest, not just a single threshold. Thus, the `Par` computation returned by the global threshold function should execute its callback on, *e.g.*, all available atoms. Likewise, we do not remove a handler from the bag of listeners when a single delta threshold is passed; handlers listen continuously to an LVar until it is frozen. We might, for example, expose the following `foreach` function for a finite map:

```
foreach mh mapLV cb = addHandler mh lv gThresh dThresh
  where
    dThresh (k,v) = return (Just (cb k v))
    gThresh mp    = traverse mp (λ(k,v) → cb k v) mp
```

Here, idempotence really pays off: without it, we would have to synchronize to ensure that no callbacks are duplicated between the global threshold (which may or may not see concurrent additions to the map) and the delta threshold (which will catch all concurrent additions). We expect such duplications to be rare, since they can only arise when a handler is added concurrently with updates to an LVar.[14]

## 7. Evaluation: $k$-CFA Case Study

We now evaluate the expressiveness and performance of our Haskell LVish implementation. We expect LVish to particularly shine for: (1) parallelizing complicated algorithms on structured data that pose challenges for other deterministic paradigms, and (2) composing pipeline-parallel stages of computation (each of which may be internally parallelized). In this section, we focus on a case study that fits this mold: *parallelized control-flow analysis*. We discuss the process of porting a sequential implementation of $k$-CFA to a parallel implementation using LVish. In the companion technical report [20], we also give benchmarking results for LVish implementations of two graph-algorithm microbenchmarks: breadth-first search and maximal independent set.

### 7.1 $k$-CFA

The $k$-*CFA* analyses provide a hierarchy of increasingly precise methods to compute the flow of values to expressions in a higher-order language. For this case study, we began with a simple, sequential implementation of $k$-CFA translated to Haskell from a version by Might [26].[15] The algorithm processes expressions written in a continuation-passing-style $\lambda$-calculus. It resembles a nondeterministic abstract interpreter in which stores map addresses to *sets* of abstract values, and function application entails a cartesian product between the operator and operand sets. Further, an address models not just a static variable, but includes a fixed $k$-size window of the calling history to get to that point (the $k$ in $k$-CFA). Taken together, the current redex, environment, store, and call history make up the abstract state of the program, and the goal is to explore a graph of these abstract states. This graph-exploration phase is followed by a second, summarization phase that combines all the information discovered into one store.

***Phase 1: breadth-first exploration*** The following function from the original, sequential version of the algorithm expresses the heart of the search process:

```
explore :: Set State → [State] → Set State
explore seen [] = seen
explore seen (todo:todos)
  | todo ∈ seen = explore seen todos
  | otherwise   = explore (insert todo seen)
                          (toList (next todo) ++ todos)
```

This code uses idiomatic Haskell data types like `Data.Set` and lists. However, it presents a dilemma with respect to exposing parallelism. Consider attempting to parallelize `explore` using purely functional parallelism with futures—for instance, using the Strategies library [23]. An attempt to compute the next states in parallel would seem to be thwarted by the the main thread rapidly forcing each new state to perform the seen-before check, `todo ∈ seen`. There is no way for independent threads to "keep going" further into the graph; rather, they check in with `seen` after one step.

We confirmed this prediction by adding a parallelism annotation: `withStrategy (parBuffer 8 rseq) (next todo)`. The GHC runtime reported that 100% of created futures were "duds"—that is, the main thread forced them before any helper thread could assist. Changing `rseq` to `rdeepseq` exposed a small amount

[13] One can use a high-performance *scalable non-zero indicator* [13] to implement `Counter`, but we have not yet done so.

[14] That said, it is possible to avoid all duplication by adding further synchronization, and in ongoing research, we are exploring various locking and timestamp schemes to do just that.

[15] Haskell port by Max Bolingbroke: `https://github.com/batterseapower/haskell-kata/blob/master/0CFA.hs`.

of parallelism—238/5000 futures were successfully executed in parallel—yielding no actual speedup.

***Phase 2: summarization*** The first phase of the algorithm produces a large set of states, with stores that need to be joined together in the summarization phase. When one phase of a computation produces a large data structure that is immediately processed by the next phase, lazy languages can often achieve a form of pipelining "for free". This outcome is most obvious with *lists*, where the head element can be consumed before the tail is computed, offering cache-locality benefits. Unfortunately, when processing a pure `Set` or `Map` in Haskell, such pipelining is not possible, since the data structure is internally represented by a balanced tree whose structure is not known until all elements are present. Thus phase 1 and phase 2 cannot overlap in the purely functional version—but they will in the LVish version, as we will see. In fact, in LVish we will be able to achieve partial deforestation in addition to pipelining. Full deforestation in this application is impossible, because the `Sets` in the implementation serve a memoization purpose: they prevent repeated computations as we traverse the graph of states.

### 7.2 Porting to the LVish Library

Our first step was a *verbatim* port to LVish. We changed the original, purely functional program to allocate a new LVar for each new set or map value in the original code. This was done simply by changing two types, `Set` and `Map`, to their monotonic LVar counterparts, `ISet` and `IMap`. In particular, a store maps a program location (with context) onto a set of abstract values:

```
import Data.LVar.Map as IM
import Data.LVar.Set as IS
type Store s = IMap Addr s (ISet s Value)
```

Next, we replaced allocations of containers, and `map`/`fold` operations over them, with the analogous operations on their LVar counterparts. The `explore` function above was replaced by the simple graph traversal function from Section 1! These changes to the program were mechanical, including converting pure to monadic code. Indeed, the key insight in doing the verbatim port to LVish was to consume LVars as if they were pure values, ignoring the fact that an LVar's contents are spread out over space and time and are modified through effects.

In some places the style of the ported code is functional, while in others it is imperative. For example, the `summarize` function uses nested `forEach` invocations to accumulate data into a store map:

```
summarize :: ISet s (State s) → Par d s (Store s)
summarize states = do
  storeFin ← newEmptyMap
  IS.forEach states   $ λ (State _ _ store _) →
    IM.forEach store  $ λ key vals →
      IS.forEach vals $ λ elmt   →
        IM.modify storeFin key (putInSet elmt)
  return storeFin
```

While this code can be read in terms of traditional parallel nested loops, it in fact creates a network of handlers that convey incremental updates from one LVar to another, in the style of data-flow networks. That means, in particular, that computations in a pipeline can *immediately* begin reading results from containers (*e.g.*, `storeFin`), long before their contents are final.

The LVish version of $k$-CFA contains 11 occurrences of `forEach`, as well as a few *cartesian-product* operations. The cartesian products serve to apply functions to combinations of all possible values that arguments may take on, greatly increasing the number of handler events in circulation. Moreover, chains of handlers registered with `forEach` result in cascades of events through six or more handlers. The runtime behavior of these would be difficult to reason about. Fortunately, the programmer can largely ignore the temporal behavior of their program, since all LVish effects commute—rather

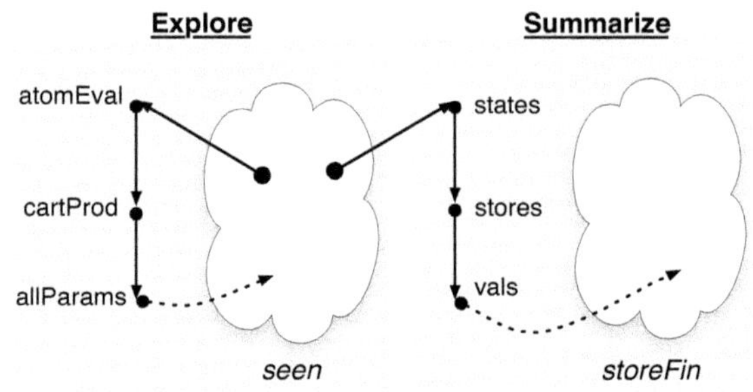


**Figure 5.** Simplified handler network for $k$-CFA. Exploration and summarization processes are driven by the same LVar. The triply-nested `forEach` calls in `summarize` become a chain of three handlers.

like the way in which a lazy functional programmer typically need not think about the order in which thunks are forced at runtime.

Finally, there is an optimization benefit to using handlers. Normally, to flatten a nested data structure such as `[[[Int]]]` in a functional language, we would need to flatten one layer at a time and allocate a series of temporary structures. The LVish version avoids this; for example, in the code for `summarize` above, three `forEach` invocations are used to traverse a triply-nested structure, and yet the side effect in the innermost handler directly updates the final accumulator, `storeFin`.

***Flipping the switch*** The verbatim port uses LVars poorly: copying them repeatedly and discarding them without modification. This effect overwhelms the benefits of partial deforestation and pipelining, and the *verbatim* LVish port has a small performance overhead relative to the original. But not for long! The most clearly unnecessary operation in the verbatim port is in the `next` function. Like the pure code, it creates a fresh store to extend with new bindings as we take each step through the state space graph:

```
store' ← IM.copy store
```

Of course, a "copy" for an LVar is persistent: it is just a handler that forces the copy to receive everything the original does. But in LVish, it is also trivial to *entangle* the parallel branches of the search, allowing them to share information about bindings, simply by *not* creating a copy:

```
let store' = store
```

This one-line change speeds up execution by up to 25× on a single thread, and the asynchronous, `ISet`-driven parallelism enables subsequent parallel speedup as well (up to 202× total improvement over the purely functional version).

Figure 6 shows performance data for the "blur" benchmark drawn from a recent paper on $k$-CFA [12]. (We use $k = 2$ for the benchmarks in this section.) In general, it proved difficult to generate example inputs to $k$-CFA that took long enough to be candidates for parallel speedup. We were, however, able to "scale up" the blur benchmark by replicating the code $N$ times, feeding one into the continuation argument for the next. Figure 6 also shows the results for one synthetic benchmark that managed to negate the benefits of our sharing approach, which is simply a long chain of 300 "not" functions (using a CPS conversion of the Church encoding for booleans). It has a small state space of large states with many variables (600 states and 1211 variables).

***The role of lock-free data structures*** As part of our library, we provide lock-free implementations of finite maps and sets based on concurrent skip lists [17].[16] We also provide reference implementations that use a nondestructive `Data.Set` inside a mutable container.

[16] In fact, this project is the first to incorporate *any* lock-free data structures in Haskell, which required solving some unique problems pertaining

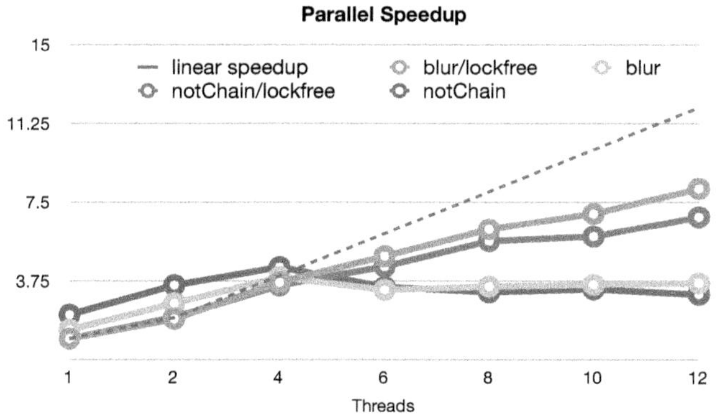


**Figure 6.** Parallel speedup for the "blur" and "notChain" benchmarks. Speedup is normalized to the sequential times for the *lock-free* versions (5.21s and 9.83s, respectively). The normalized speedups are remarkably consistent for the lock-free version between the two benchmarks. But the relationship to the original, purely functional version is quite different: at 12 cores, the lock-free LVish version of "blur" is 202× faster than the original, while "notChain" is only 1.6× faster, not gaining anything from sharing rather than copying stores due to a lack of fan-out in the state graph.

Our scalable implementation is not yet carefully optimized, and at one and two cores, our lock-free $k$-CFA is 38% to 43% slower than the reference implementation on the "blur" benchmark. But the effect of scalable data structures is quite visible on a 12-core machine.[17] Without them, "blur" (replicated 8×) stops scaling and begins slowing down slightly after four cores. Even at four cores, variance is high in the reference implementation (min/max 0.96s / 1.71s over 7 runs). With lock-free structures, by contrast, performance steadily improves to a speedup of 8.14× on 12 cores (0.64s at 67% GC productivity). Part of the benefit of LVish is to allow purely functional programs to make use of lock-free structures, in much the same way that the `ST` monad allows access to efficient in-place array computations.

## 8. Related Work

***Monotonic data structures: traditional approaches*** LVish builds on two long traditions of work on parallel programming models based on monotonically-growing shared data structures:

- In *Kahn process networks* (KPNs) [18], as well as in the more restricted *synchronous data flow* systems [21], a network of processes communicate with each other through blocking FIFO channels with ever-growing *channel histories*. Each process computes a sequential, monotonic function from the history of its inputs to the history of its outputs, enabling pipeline parallelism. KPNs are the basis for deterministic stream-processing languages such as StreamIt [16].
- In parallel *single-assignment languages* [32], "full/empty" bits are associated with heap locations so that they may be written to at most once. Single-assignment locations with blocking read semantics—that is, *IVars* [1]—have appeared in Concurrent ML as `SyncVars` [30]; in the Intel Concurrent Collections system [7]; in languages and libraries for high-performance computing, such as Chapel [9] and the Qthreads library [33]; and have even been implemented in hardware in Cray MTA machines [3]. Although most of these uses incorporate IVars into already-nondeterministic programming environments, Haskell's `Par` monad [24]—on which our LVish implementation is based—uses IVars in a deterministic-by-construction setting, allowing user-created threads to communicate through IVars without requiring `IO`, so that such communication can occur anywhere inside pure programs.

LVars are general enough to subsume both IVars and KPNs: a lattice of channel histories with a prefix ordering allows LVars to represent FIFO channels that implement a Kahn process network, whereas an LVar with "empty" and "full" states (where $empty < full$) behaves like an IVar, as we described in Section 2. Hence LVars provide a framework for generalizing and unifying these two existing approaches to deterministic parallelism.

***Deterministic Parallel Java (DPJ)*** DPJ [4, 5] is a deterministic language consisting of a system of annotations for Java code. A sophisticated region-based type system ensures that a mutable region of the heap is, essentially, passed linearly to an exclusive writer, thereby ensuring that the state accessed by concurrent threads is disjoint. DPJ does, however, provide a way to unsafely assert that operations commute with one another (using the `commuteswith` form) to enable concurrent mutation.

LVish differs from DPJ in that it allows overlapping shared state between threads as the default. Moreover, since LVar effects are already commutative, we avoid the need for `commuteswith` annotations. Finally, it is worth noting that while in DPJ, commutativity annotations have to appear in application-level code, in LVish only the data-structure author needs to write trusted code. The application programmer can run untrusted code that still enjoys a (quasi-)determinism guarantee, because only (quasi-)deterministic programs can be expressed as LVish `Par` computations.

More recently, Bocchino *et al.* [6] proposed a type and effect system that allows for the incorporation of nondeterministic sections of code in DPJ. The goal here is different from ours: while they aim to support *intentionally* nondeterministic computations such as those arising from optimization problems like branch-and-bound search, LVish's quasi-determinism arises as a result of schedule nondeterminism.

***FlowPools*** Prokopec *et al.* [29] recently proposed a data structure with an API closely related to ideas in LVish: a FlowPool is a bag that allows concurrent insertions but forbids removals, a `seal` operation that forbids further updates, and combinators like `foreach` that invoke callbacks as data arrives in the pool. To retain determinism, the `seal` operation requires explicitly passing the expected bag *size* as an argument, and the program will raise an exception if the bag goes over the expected size.

While this interface has a flavor similar to LVish, it lacks the ability to detect quiescence, which is crucial for supporting examples like graph traversal, and the `seal` operation is awkward to use when the structure of data is not known in advance. By contrast, our `freeze` operation is more expressive and convenient, but moves the model into the realm of quasi-determinism. Another important difference is the fact that LVish is *data structure-generic*: both our formalism and our library support an unlimited collection of data structures, whereas FlowPools are specialized to bags. Nevertheless, FlowPools represent a "sweet spot" in the deterministic parallel design space: by allowing handlers but not general freezing, they retain determinism while improving on the expressivity of the original LVars model. We claim that, with our addition of handlers, LVish generalizes FlowPools to add support for arbitrary lattice-based data structures.

to Haskell's laziness and the GHC compiler's assumptions regarding referential transparency. But we lack the space to detail these improvements.

[17] Intel Xeon 5660; full machine details available at `https://portal.futuregrid.org/hardware/delta`.

***Concurrent Revisions*** The Concurrent Revisions (CR) [22] programming model uses isolation types to distinguish regions of the heap shared by multiple mutators. Rather than enforcing exclusive access, CR clones a copy of the state for each mutator, using a deterministic "merge function" for resolving conflicts in local copies at join points. Unlike LVish's least-upper-bound writes, CR merge functions are *not* necessarily commutative; the default CR merge function is "joiner wins". Still, semilattices turn up in the metatheory of CR: in particular, Burckhardt and Leijen [8] show that, for any two vertices in a CR revision diagram, there exists a *greatest common ancestor* state which can be used to determine what changes each side has made—an interesting duality with our model (in which any two LVar states have a lub).

While CR could be used to model similar types of data structures to LVish—if versioned variables used least upper bound as their merge function for conflicts—effects would only become visible at the end of parallel regions, rather than LVish's asynchronous communication within parallel regions. This precludes the use of traditional lock-free data structures as a representation.

***Conflict-free replicated data types*** In the distributed systems literature, *eventually consistent* systems based on *conflict-free replicated data types* (CRDTs) [31] leverage lattice properties to guarantee that replicas in a distributed database eventually agree. Unlike LVars, CRDTs allow intermediate states to be observed: if two replicas are updated independently, reads of those replicas may disagree until a (least-upper-bound) merge operation takes place. Various data-structure-specific techniques can ensure that non-monotonic updates (such as removal of elements from a set) are not lost.

The Bloom$^L$ language for distributed database programming [11] combines CRDTs with *monotonic logic*, resulting in a lattice-parameterized, confluent language that is a close relative of LVish. A monotonicity analysis pass rules out programs that would perform non-monotonic operations on distributed data collections, whereas in LVish, monotonicity is enforced by the LVar API.

Future work will further explore the relationship between LVars and CRDTs: in one direction, we will investigate LVar-based data structures inspired by CRDTs that support non-monotonic operations; in the other direction, we will investigate the feasibility and usefulness of LVar threshold reads in a distributed setting.

## Acknowledgments

Lindsey Kuper and Ryan Newton's work on this paper was funded by NSF grant CCF-1218375.

## References

[1] Arvind, R. S. Nikhil, and K. K. Pingali. I-structures: data structures for parallel computing. *ACM Trans. Program. Lang. Syst.*, 11, October 1989.

[2] H. Attiya, R. Guerraoui, D. Hendler, P. Kuznetsov, M. M. Michael, and M. Vechev. Laws of order: expensive synchronization in concurrent algorithms cannot be eliminated. In *POPL*, 2011.

[3] D. A. Bader and K. Madduri. Designing multithreaded algorithms for breadth-first search and st-connectivity on the Cray MTA-2. In *ICPP*, 2006.

[4] R. L. Bocchino, Jr., V. S. Adve, S. V. Adve, and M. Snir. Parallel programming must be deterministic by default. In *HotPar*, 2009.

[5] R. L. Bocchino, Jr., V. S. Adve, D. Dig, S. V. Adve, S. Heumann, R. Komuravelli, J. Overbey, P. Simmons, H. Sung, and M. Vakilian. A type and effect system for deterministic parallel Java. In *OOPSLA*, 2009.

[6] R. L. Bocchino, Jr. et al. Safe nondeterminism in a deterministic-by-default parallel language. In *POPL*, 2011.

[7] Z. Budimlić, M. Burke, V. Cavé, K. Knobe, G. Lowney, R. Newton, J. Palsberg, D. Peixotto, V. Sarkar, F. Schlimbach, and S. Taşirlar. Concurrent Collections. *Sci. Program.*, 18, August 2010.

[8] S. Burckhardt and D. Leijen. Semantics of concurrent revisions. In *ESOP*, 2011.

[9] B. L. Chamberlain, D. Callahan, and H. P. Zima. Parallel programmability and the Chapel language. *International Journal of High Performance Computing Applications*, 21(3), 2007.

[10] D. Chase and Y. Lev. Dynamic circular work-stealing deque. In *SPAA*, 2005.

[11] N. Conway, W. Marczak, P. Alvaro, J. M. Hellerstein, and D. Maier. Logic and lattices for distributed programming. In *SOCC*, 2012.

[12] C. Earl, I. Sergey, M. Might, and D. Van Horn. Introspective pushdown analysis of higher-order programs. In *ICFP*, 2012.

[13] F. Ellen, Y. Lev, V. Luchangco, and M. Moir. SNZI: Scalable NonZero Indicators. In *PODC*, 2007.

[14] M. Felleisen, R. B. Findler, and M. Flatt. *Semantics Engineering with PLT Redex*. The MIT Press, 1st edition, 2009.

[15] K. Fraser. *Practical lock-freedom*. PhD thesis, 2004.

[16] M. I. Gordon, W. Thies, M. Karczmarek, J. Lin, A. S. Meli, C. Leger, A. A. Lamb, J. Wong, H. Hoffman, D. Z. Maze, and S. Amarasinghe. A stream compiler for communication-exposed architectures. In *ASPLOS*, 2002.

[17] M. Herlihy and N. Shavit. *The Art of Multiprocessor Programming*. Morgan Kaufmann, 2008.

[18] G. Kahn. The semantics of a simple language for parallel programming. In J. L. Rosenfeld, editor, *Information processing*. North Holland, Amsterdam, Aug 1974.

[19] L. Kuper and R. R. Newton. LVars: lattice-based data structures for deterministic parallelism. In *FHPC*, 2013.

[20] L. Kuper, A. Turon, N. R. Krishnaswami, and R. R. Newton. Freeze after writing: Quasi-deterministic parallel programming with LVars. Technical Report TR710, Indiana University, November 2013. URL `http://www.cs.indiana.edu/cgi-bin/techreports/TRNNN.cgi?trnum=TR710`.

[21] E. Lee and D. Messerschmitt. Synchronous data flow. *Proceedings of the IEEE*, 75(9):1235–1245, 1987.

[22] D. Leijen, M. Fahndrich, and S. Burckhardt. Prettier concurrency: purely functional concurrent revisions. In *Haskell*, 2011.

[23] S. Marlow, P. Maier, H.-W. Loidl, M. K. Aswad, and P. Trinder. Seq no more: better strategies for parallel Haskell. In *Haskell*, 2010.

[24] S. Marlow, R. Newton, and S. Peyton Jones. A monad for deterministic parallelism. In *Haskell*, 2011.

[25] M. M. Michael, M. T. Vechev, and V. A. Saraswat. Idempotent work stealing. In *PPoPP*, 2009.

[26] M. Might. $k$-CFA: Determining types and/or control-flow in languages like Python, Java and Scheme. http://matt.might.net/articles/implementation-of-kcfa-and-0cfa/.

[27] R. S. Nikhil. Id language reference manual, 1991.

[28] S. L. Peyton Jones, R. Leshchinskiy, G. Keller, and M. M. T. Chakravarty. Harnessing the multicores: Nested data parallelism in Haskell. In *FSTTCS*, 2008.

[29] A. Prokopec, H. Miller, T. Schlatter, P. Haller, and M. Odersky. FlowPools: a lock-free deterministic concurrent dataflow abstraction. In *LCPC*, 2012.

[30] J. H. Reppy. *Concurrent Programming in ML*. Cambridge University Press, Cambridge, England, 1999.

[31] M. Shapiro, N. Preguiça, C. Baquero, and M. Zawirski. Conflict-free replicated data types. In *SSS*, 2011.

[32] L. G. Tesler and H. J. Enea. A language design for concurrent processes. In *AFIPS*, 1968 (Spring).

[33] K. B. Wheeler, R. C. Murphy, and D. Thain. Qthreads: An API for programming with millions of lightweight threads, 2008.

# Replicated Data Types: Specification, Verification, Optimality

Sebastian Burckhardt
Microsoft Research

Alexey Gotsman
IMDEA Software Institute

Hongseok Yang
University of Oxford

Marek Zawirski
INRIA & UPMC-LIP6

## Abstract

Geographically distributed systems often rely on replicated eventually consistent data stores to achieve availability and performance. To resolve conflicting updates at different replicas, researchers and practitioners have proposed specialized consistency protocols, called replicated data types, that implement objects such as registers, counters, sets or lists. Reasoning about replicated data types has however not been on par with comparable work on abstract data types and concurrent data types, lacking specifications, correctness proofs, and optimality results.

To fill in this gap, we propose a framework for specifying replicated data types using relations over events and verifying their implementations using replication-aware simulations. We apply it to 7 existing implementations of 4 data types with nontrivial conflict-resolution strategies and optimizations (last-writer-wins register, counter, multi-value register and observed-remove set). We also present a novel technique for obtaining lower bounds on the worst-case space overhead of data type implementations and use it to prove optimality of 4 implementations. Finally, we show how to specify consistency of replicated stores with multiple objects axiomatically, in analogy to prior work on weak memory models. Overall, our work provides foundational reasoning tools to support research on replicated eventually consistent stores.

**Categories and Subject Descriptors** D.2.4 [*Software Engineering*]: Software/Program Verification; F.3.1 [*Logics and Meanings of Programs*]: Specifying and Verifying and Reasoning about Programs

**Keywords** Replication; eventual consistency; weak memory

## 1. Introduction

To achieve availability and scalability, many networked computing systems rely on *replicated stores*, allowing multiple clients to issue operations on shared data on a number of *replicas*, which communicate changes to each other using message passing. For example, large-scale Internet services rely on *geo-replication*, which places data replicas in geographically distinct locations, and applications for mobile devices store replicas locally to support offline use. One benefit of such architectures is that the replicas remain locally available to clients even when network connections fail. Unfortunately, the famous CAP theorem [19] shows that such high **A**vailability and tolerance to network **P**artitions are incompatible with *strong* **C***onsistency*, i.e., the illusion of a single centralized replica handling all operations. For this reason, modern replicated stores often provide weaker forms of consistency, commonly dubbed *eventual consistency* [36]. 'Eventual' usually refers to the guarantee that

> if clients stop issuing update requests, then the replicas will eventually reach a consistent state. (1)

Eventual consistency is a hot research area, and new replicated stores implementing it appear every year [1, 13, 16, 18, 23, 27, 33, 34, 37]. Unfortunately, their semantics is poorly understood: the very term eventual consistency is a catch-all buzzword, and different stores claiming to be eventually consistent actually provide subtly different guarantees. The property (1), which is a form of *quiescent consistency*, is too weak to capture these. Although it requires the replicas to converge to the same state eventually, it doesn't say which one it will be. Furthermore, (1) does not provide any guarantees in realistic scenarios when updates never stop arriving. The difficulty of reasoning about the behavior of eventually consistent stores comes from a multitude of choices to be made in their design, some of which we now explain.

Allowing the replicas to be temporarily inconsistent enables eventually consistent stores to satisfy clients' requests from the local replica immediately, and broadcast the changes to the other replicas only after the fact, when the network connection permits this. However, this means that clients can concurrently issue conflicting operations on the same data item at different replicas; furthermore, if the replicas are out-of-sync, these operations will be applied to its copies in different states. For example, two users sharing an online store account can write two different zip codes into the delivery address; the same users connected to replicas with different views of the shopping cart can also add and concurrently remove the same product. In such situations the store needs to ensure that, after the replicas exchange updates, the changes by different clients will be merged and all conflicts will be resolved in a meaningful way. Furthermore, to ensure eventual consistency (1), the conflict resolution has to be uniform across replicas, so that, in the end, they converge to the same state.

The protocols achieving this are commonly encapsulated within *replicated data types* [1, 10, 16, 18, 31, 33, 34] that implement *objects*, such as registers, counters, sets or lists, with various conflict-resolution strategies. The strategies can be as simple as establishing a total order on all operations using timestamps and letting the last writer win, but can also be much more subtle. Thus, a data type can detect the presence of a conflict and let the client deal with it: e.g., the *multi-value register* used in Amazon's Dynamo key-value store [18] would return both conflicting zip codes in the above example. A data type can also resolve the conflict in an application-specific way. For example, the *observed-remove set* [7, 32] processes concurrent operations trying to add and remove the same element so that an add always wins, an outcome that may be appropriate for a shopping cart.

Replicated data type implementations are often nontrivial, since they have to maintain not only client-observable object state, but also *metadata* needed to detect and resolve conflicts and to handle network failures. This makes reasoning about their behavior challenging. The situation gets only worse if we consider multi-



*POPL '14*, January 22–24, 2014, San Diego, CA, USA.

http://dx.doi.org/10.1145/2535838.2535848

ple replicated objects: in this case, asynchronous propagation of updates between replicas may lead to counterintuitive behaviors—*anomalies*, in database terminology. The following code illustrates an anomaly happening in real replicated stores [1, 18]:

$$\begin{array}{r|l} \text{Replica } r_1 \rightarrow x.\mathtt{wr}(\textit{post}) & i = y.\mathtt{rd} \text{ // } \textit{comment} \leftarrow \text{Replica } r_2 \\ y.\mathtt{wr}(\textit{comment}) & j = x.\mathtt{rd} \text{ // } \textit{empty} \end{array} \quad (2)$$

We have two clients reading from and writing to register objects $x$ and $y$ at two different replicas; $i$ and $j$ are client-local variables. The first client makes a post by writing to $x$ at replica $r_1$ and then comments on the post by writing to $y$. After every write, replica $r_1$ might send a message with the update to replica $r_2$. If the messages carrying the writes of *post* to $x$ and *comment* to $y$ arrive to replica $r_2$ out of the order they were issued in, the second client can see the comment, but not the post. Different replicated stores may allow such an anomaly or not, and this has to be taken into account when reasoning about them.

In this paper, we propose techniques for reasoning about eventually consistent replicated stores in the following three areas.

**1. Specification.** We propose a comprehensive framework for specifying the semantics of replicated stores. Its key novel component is *replicated data type specifications* (§3), which provide the first way of specifying the semantics of replicated objects with advanced conflict resolution declaratively, like abstract data types [25]. We achieve this by defining the result of a data type operation not by a function of states, but of *operation contexts*—sets of events affecting the result of the operation, together with some relationships between them. We show that our specifications are sufficiently flexible to handle data types representing a variety of conflict-resolution strategies: last-write-wins register, counter, multi-value register and observed-remove set.

We then specify the semantics of a whole store with multiple objects, possibly of different types, by *consistency axioms* (§7), which constrain the way the store processes incoming requests in the style of weak shared-memory models [2] and thus define the anomalies allowed. As an illustration, we define consistency models used in existing replicated stores, including a weak form of eventual consistency [1, 18] and different kinds of causal consistency [23, 27, 33, 34]. We find that, when specialized to last-writer-wins registers, these specifications are very close to fragments of the C/C++ memory model [5]. Thus, our specification framework generalizes axiomatic shared-memory models to replicated stores with nontrivial conflict resolution.

**2. Verification.** We propose a method for proving the correctness of replicated data type implementations with respect to our specifications and apply it to seven existing implementations of the four data types mentioned above, including those with nontrivial optimizations. Reasoning about the implementations is difficult due to the highly concurrent nature of a replicated store, with multiple replicas simultaneously updating their object copies and exchanging messages. We address this challenge by proposing *replication-aware simulations* (§5). Like classical simulations from data refinement [21], these associate a concrete state of an implementation with its abstract description—structures on events, in our case. To combat the complexity of replication, they consider the state of an object at a single replica or a message in transit separately and associate it with abstract descriptions of only those events that led to it. Verifying an implementation then requires only reasoning about an instance of its code running at a single replica.

Here, however, we have to deal with another challenge: code at a single replica can access both the state of an object and a message at the same time, e.g., when updating the former upon receiving the latter. To reason about such code, we often need to rely on certain *agreement properties* correlating the abstract descriptions of the message and the object state. Establishing these properties requires global reasoning. Fortunately, we find that agreement properties needed to prove realistic implementations depend only on basic facts about their messaging behavior and can thus be established once for broad classes of data types. Then a particular implementation within such a class can be verified by reasoning purely locally.

By carefully structuring reasoning in this way, we achieve easy and intuitive proofs of single data type implementations. We then lift these results to stores with multiple objects of different types by showing how consistency axioms can be proved given properties of the transport layer and data type implementations (§7).

**3. Optimality.** Replicated data type designers strive to optimize their implementations; knowing that one is optimal can help guide such efforts in the most promising direction. However, proving optimality is challengingly broad as it requires quantifying over all possible implementations satisfying the same specification.

For most data types we studied, the primary optimization target is the size of the metadata needed to resolve conflicts or handle network failures. To establish optimality of metadata size, we present a novel method for proving lower bounds on the *worst-case metadata overhead* of replicated data types—the proportion of metadata relative to the client-observable content. The main idea is to find a large family of executions of an arbitrary correct implementation such that, given the results of data type operations from a certain fixed point in any of the executions, we can recover the previous execution history. This implies that, across executions, the states at this point are distinct and thus must have some minimal size.

Using our method, we prove that four of the implementations we verified have an optimal worst-case metadata overhead among all implementations satisfying the same specification. Two of these (counter, last-writer-wins register) are well-known; one (optimized observed-remove set [6]) is a recently proposed nontrivial optimization; and one (optimized multi-value register) is a small improvement of a known implementation [33] that we discovered during a failed attempt to prove optimality of the latter. We summarize all the bounds we proved in Fig. 10.

We hope that the theoretical foundations we develop will help in exploring the design space of replicated data types and replicated eventually consistent stores in a systematic way.

## 2. Replicated Data Types

We now describe our formal model for replicated stores and introduce *replicated data type implementations*, which implement operations on a single object at a replica and the protocol used by replicas to exchange updates to this object. Our formalism follows closely the models used by replicated data type designers [33].

A replicated store is organized as a collection of named ***objects*** $\mathsf{Obj} = \{x, y, z, \ldots\}$. Each object is hosted at all ***replicas*** $r, s \in \mathsf{ReplicaID}$. The sets of objects and replicas may be infinite, to model their dynamic creation. Clients interact with the store by performing ***operations*** on objects at a specified replica. Each object $x \in \mathsf{Obj}$ has a ***type*** $\tau = \mathsf{type}(x) \in \mathsf{Type}$, whose ***type signature*** $(\mathsf{Op}_\tau, \mathsf{Val}_\tau)$ determines the set of supported operations $\mathsf{Op}_\tau$ (ranged over by $o$) and the set of their return values $\mathsf{Val}_\tau$ (ranged over by $a, b, c, d$). We assume that a special value $\bot \in \mathsf{Val}_\tau$ belongs to all sets $\mathsf{Val}_\tau$ and is used for operations that return no value. For example, we can define a counter data type $\mathtt{ctr}$ and an integer register type $\mathtt{intreg}$ with operations for reading, incrementing or writing an integer $a$: $\mathsf{Val}_{\mathtt{ctr}} = \mathsf{Val}_{\mathtt{intreg}} = \mathbb{Z} \cup \{\bot\}$, $\mathsf{Op}_{\mathtt{ctr}} = \{\mathtt{rd}, \mathtt{inc}\}$ and $\mathsf{Op}_{\mathtt{intreg}} = \{\mathtt{rd}\} \cup \{\mathtt{wr}(a) \mid a \in \mathbb{Z}\}$.

We also assume sets $\mathsf{Message}$ of messages (ranged over by $m$) and timestamps $\mathsf{Timestamp}$ (ranged over by $t$). For simplicity, we let timestamps be positive integers: $\mathsf{Timestamp} = \mathbb{N}_1$.

DEFINITION 1. *A **replicated data type implementation** for a data type $\tau$ is a tuple $\mathcal{D}_\tau = (\Sigma, \vec{\sigma}_0, M, \mathsf{do}, \mathsf{send}, \mathsf{receive})$, where $\vec{\sigma}_0$ :*

**Figure 1.** Illustrations of a concrete (a) and two abstract executions (b, c)

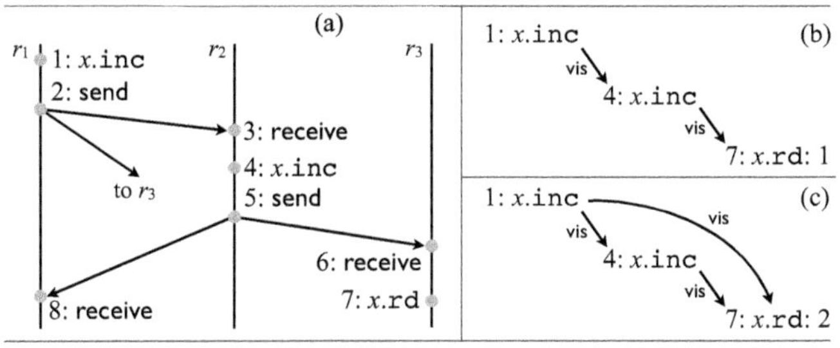


**Figure 2.** Three replicated data type implementations

(a) Op-based counter (`ctr`)

| | | | |
|---|---|---|---|
| $\Sigma = \mathbb{N}_0 \times \mathbb{N}_0$ | $\mathsf{do}(\mathtt{rd}, \langle a, d \rangle, t)$ | $=$ | $(\langle a, d \rangle, a)$ |
| $M = \mathbb{N}_0$ | $\mathsf{do}(\mathtt{inc}, \langle a, d \rangle, t)$ | $=$ | $(\langle a+1, d+1 \rangle, \bot)$ |
| $\vec{\sigma}_0 = \lambda r.\, \langle 0, 0 \rangle$ | $\mathsf{send}(\langle a, d \rangle)$ | $=$ | $(\langle a, 0 \rangle, d)$ |
| | $\mathsf{receive}(\langle a, d \rangle, d')$ | $=$ | $\langle a + d', d \rangle$ |

(b) State-based counter (`ctr`)

| | | |
|---|---|---|
| $\Sigma$ | $=$ | $\mathsf{ReplicaID} \times (\mathsf{ReplicaID} \to \mathbb{N}_0)$ |
| $\sigma_0$ | $=$ | $\lambda r.\, \langle r, \lambda s.\, 0 \rangle$ |
| $M$ | $=$ | $\mathsf{ReplicaID} \to \mathbb{N}_0$ |
| $\mathsf{do}(\mathtt{rd}, \langle r, v \rangle, t)$ | $=$ | $(\langle r, v \rangle, \sum\{v(s) \mid s \in \mathsf{ReplicaID}\})$ |
| $\mathsf{do}(\mathtt{inc}, \langle r, v \rangle, t)$ | $=$ | $(\langle r, v[r \mapsto v(r) + 1] \rangle, \bot)$ |
| $\mathsf{send}(\langle r, v \rangle)$ | $=$ | $(\langle r, v \rangle, v)$ |
| $\mathsf{receive}(\langle r, v \rangle, v')$ | $=$ | $\langle r, (\lambda s.\, \max\{v(s), v'(s)\}) \rangle$ |

(c) State-based last-writer-wins register (`intreg`)

| | | |
|---|---|---|
| $\Sigma$ | $=$ | $\mathbb{Z} \times (\mathsf{Timestamp} \uplus \{0\})$ |
| $\vec{\sigma}_0$ | $=$ | $\lambda r.\, \langle 0, 0 \rangle$ |
| $M$ | $=$ | $\Sigma$ |
| $\mathsf{do}(\mathtt{rd}, \langle a, t \rangle, t')$ | $=$ | $(\langle a, t \rangle, a)$ |
| $\mathsf{do}(\mathtt{wr}(a'), \langle a, t \rangle, t')$ | $=$ | if $t < t'$ then $(\langle a', t' \rangle, \bot)$ else $(\langle a, t \rangle, \bot)$ |
| $\mathsf{send}(\langle a, t \rangle)$ | $=$ | $(\langle a, t \rangle, \langle a, t \rangle)$ |
| $\mathsf{receive}(\langle a, t \rangle, \langle a', t' \rangle)$ | $=$ | if $t < t'$ then $\langle a', t' \rangle$ else $\langle a, t \rangle$ |

$\mathsf{ReplicaID} \to \Sigma$, $M \subseteq \mathsf{Message}$ *and*

$$\mathsf{do} : \mathsf{Op}_\tau \times \Sigma \times \mathsf{Timestamp} \to \Sigma \times \mathsf{Val}_\tau;$$
$$\mathsf{send} : \Sigma \to \Sigma \times M; \qquad \mathsf{receive} : \Sigma \times M \to \Sigma.$$

We denote a component of $\mathcal{D}_\tau$, such as do, by $\mathcal{D}_\tau$.do. A tuple $\mathcal{D}_\tau$ defines the class of implementations of objects with type $\tau$, meant to be instantiated for every such object in the store. $\Sigma$ is the set of states (ranged over by $\sigma$) used to represent the current state of the object, including metadata, at a single replica. The initial state at every replica is given by $\vec{\sigma}_0$.

$\mathcal{D}_\tau$ provides three methods that the rest of the store implementation can call at a given replica; we assume that these methods execute atomically. We visualize store executions resulting from repeated calls to the methods as in Fig. 1(a), by arranging the calls on several vertical timelines corresponding to replicas at which they occur and denoting the delivery of messages by diagonal arrows. In §4, we formalize them as sequences of transitions called *concrete executions* and define the store semantics by their sets; the intuition given by Fig. 1(a) should suffice for the following discussion.

A client request to perform an operation $o \in \mathsf{Op}_\tau$ triggers the call $\mathsf{do}(o, \sigma, t)$ (e.g., event 1 in Fig. 1(a)). This takes the current state $\sigma \in \Sigma$ of the object at the replica where the request is issued and a timestamp $t \in \mathsf{Timestamp}$ provided by the rest of the store implementation and produces the updated object state and the return value of the operation. The data type implementation can use the timestamp provided, e.g., to implement the last-writer-wins conflict-resolution strategy mentioned in §1, but is free to ignore it.

Nondeterministically, in moments when the network is able to accept messages, a replica calls send. Given the current state of the object at the replica, send produces a message in $M$ to broadcast to all other replicas (event 2 in Fig. 1(a)); sometimes send also alters the state of the object. Using broadcast rather than point-to-point communication does not limit generality, since we can always tag messages with the intended receiver. Another replica that receives the message generated by send calls receive to merge the enclosed update into its copy of the object state (event 3 in Fig. 1(a)).

We now reproduce three replicated data type implementations due to Shapiro et al. [33].They fall into two categories: in ***op-based*** implementations, each message carries a description of the latest operations that the sender has performed, and in ***state-based*** implementations, a description of *all* operations it knows about.

**Op-based counter (`ctr`).** Fig. 2(a) shows an implementation of the `ctr` data type. A replica stores a pair $\langle a, d \rangle$, where $a$ is the current value of the counter, and $d$ is the number of increments performed since the last broadcast (we use angle brackets for tuples representing states and messages). The send method returns $d$ and resets it; the receive method adds the content of the message to $a$. This implementation is correct, as long as each message is delivered exactly once (we show how to prove this in §5). Since `inc` operations commute, they never conflict: applying them in different orders at different replicas yields the same final state.

**State-based counter (`ctr`).** The implementation in Fig. 2(b) summarizes the currently known history by recording the contribution of every replica to the counter value separately (reminiscent of vector clocks [29]). A replica stores its identifier $r$ and a vector $v$ such that for each replica $s$ the entry $v(s)$ gives the number of increments made by clients at $s$ that have been received by $r$. A `rd` operation returns the sum of all entries in the vector. An `inc` operation increments the entry for the current replica. We denote by $v[i \mapsto j]$ the function that has the same value as $v$ everywhere, except for $i$, where it has the value $j$. The send method returns the vector, and the receive method takes the maximum of each entry in the vectors $v$ and $v'$ given to it. This is correct because an entry for $s$ in either vector reflects a prefix of the sequence of increments done at replica $s$. Hence, we know that $\min\{v(s), v'(s)\}$ increments by $s$ are taken into account both in $v(s)$ and in $v'(s)$.

**State-based last-writer-wins (LWW) register (`intreg`).** Unlike counters, registers have update operations that are not commutative. To resolve conflicts, the implementation in Fig. 2 uses the last-writer-wins strategy, creating a total order on writes by associating a unique timestamp with each of them. A state contains the current value, returned by `rd`, and the timestamp at which it was written (initially, we have 0 instead of a timestamp). A $\mathtt{wr}(a')$ compares its timestamp $t'$ with the timestamp $t$ of the current value $a$ and sets the value to the one with the highest timestamp. Note that here we have to allow for $t' < t$, since we do not make any assumptions about timestamps apart from uniqueness: e.g., the rest of the store implementation can compute them using physical or Lamport clocks [22]. We show how to state assumptions about timestamps in §4. The send method just returns the state, and the receive method chooses the winning value by comparing the timestamps in the current state and the message, like `wr`.

**State-based vs. op-based.** State-based implementations converge to a consistent state faster than op-based implementations because they are ***transitively delivering***, meaning that they can propagate updates indirectly. For example, when using the counter in Fig. 2(b), in the execution in Fig. 1(a) the read at $r_3$ (event 7) returns 2, even though the message from $r_1$ has not arrived yet, because $r_3$ learns about $r_1$'s update via $r_2$. State-based implementations are also resilient against transport failures like message *loss, reordering, or duplication.* Op-based implementations require the replicated store using them to mask such failures (e.g., using message sequence numbers, retransmission buffers, or reorder buffers).

The potential weakness of state-based implementations is the size of states and messages, which motivates our examination of space optimality in §6. For example, we show that the counter in Fig. 2(b) is optimal, meaning that no counter implementation satisfying the same requirements (transitive delivery and resilience against message loss, reordering, and duplication) can do better.

## 3. Specifying Replicated Data Types and Stores

Consider the concrete execution in Fig. 1(a). What are valid return values for the read in event 7? Intuitively, 1 or 2 can be justifiable, but not 100. We now present a framework for specifying the expected outcome declaratively, without referring to implementation details. For example, we give a specification of a replicated counter that is satisfied by both implementations in Fig. 2(a, b).

In presenting the framework, we rely on the intuitive understanding of the way a replicated store executes given in §2. Later we define the store semantics formally (§4), which lets us state what it means for a store to satisfy our specifications (§4 and §7).

### 3.1 Abstract Executions and Specification Structure

We define our specifications on *abstract executions*, which include only user-visible events (corresponding to do calls) and describe the other information about the store processing in an implementation-independent form. Informally, we consider a concrete execution correct if it can be justified by an abstract execution satisfying the specifications that is "similar" to it and, in particular, has the same operations and return values.

Abstract executions are inspired by axiomatic definitions of weak shared-memory models [2]. In particular, we use their previously proposed reformulation with visibility and arbitration relations [13], which are similar to the reads-from and coherence relations from weak shared-memory models. We provide a comparison with shared-memory models in §7 and with [13] in §8.

DEFINITION 2. *An* ***abstract execution*** *is a tuple* $A = (E, \mathsf{repl}, \mathsf{obj}, \mathsf{oper}, \mathsf{rval}, \mathsf{ro}, \mathsf{vis}, \mathsf{ar})$, *where*

- $E \subseteq \mathsf{Event}$ *is a set of events from a countable universe* $\mathsf{Event}$;
- *each event* $e \in E$ *describes a replica* $\mathsf{repl}(e) \in \mathsf{ReplicaID}$ *performing an operation* $\mathsf{oper}(e) \in \mathsf{Op}_{\mathsf{type}(\mathsf{obj}(e))}$ *on an object* $\mathsf{obj}(e) \in \mathsf{Obj}$, *which returns the value* $\mathsf{rval}(e) \in \mathsf{Val}_{\mathsf{type}(\mathsf{obj}(e))}$;
- $\mathsf{ro} \subseteq E \times E$ *is a* ***replica order****, which is a union of transitive, irreflexive and total orders on events at each replica;*
- $\mathsf{vis} \subseteq E \times E$ *is an acyclic* ***visibility relation*** *such that* $\forall e, f \in E.\, e \xrightarrow{\mathsf{vis}} f \implies \mathsf{obj}(e) = \mathsf{obj}(f)$;
- $\mathsf{ar} \subseteq E \times E$ *is an* ***arbitration relation****, which is a union of transitive, irreflexive and total orders on events on each object.*

*We also require that* ro, vis *and* ar *be well-founded.*

In the following, we denote components of $A$ and similar structures as in $A$.repl. We also use $(e, f) \in \mathsf{r}$ and $e \xrightarrow{\mathsf{r}} f$ interchangeably.

Informally, $e \xrightarrow{\mathsf{vis}} f$ means that $f$ is aware of $e$ and thus $e$'s effect can influence $f$'s return value. In implementation terms, this may be the case if the update performed by $e$ has been delivered to the replica performing $f$ before $f$ is issued. The exact meaning of "delivered", however, depends on how much information messages carry in the implementation. For example, as we explain in §3.2, the return value of a read from a counter is equal to the number of inc operations visible to it. Then, as we formalize in §4, the abstract execution illustrated in Fig. 1(b) justifies the op-based implementation in Fig. 2(a) reading 1 in the concrete execution in Fig. 1(a). The abstract execution in Fig. 1(c) justifies the state-based implementation in Fig. 2(b) reading 2 due to transitive delivery (§2). There is no abstract execution that would justify reading 100.

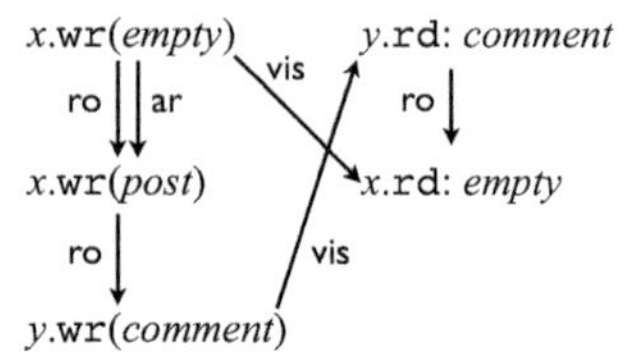


The ar relation represents the ordering information provided by the store, e.g., via timestamps. On the right we show an abstract execution corresponding to a variant of the anomaly (2). The ar edge means that any replica that sees both writes to $x$ should assume that *post* overwrites *empty*.

We give a store specification by two components, constraining abstract executions:

1. ***Replicated data type specifications*** determine return values of operations in an abstract execution in terms of its vis and ar relations, and thus define conflict-resolution policies for individual objects in the store. The specifications are the key novel component of our framework, and we discuss them next.
2. ***Consistency axioms*** constrain vis and ar and thereby disallow anomalies and extend the semantics of individual objects to that of the entire store. We defer their discussion to §7. See Fig. 13 for their flavor; in particular, COCV prohibits the anomaly above.

Each of these components can be varied separately, and our specifications will define the semantics of any possible combination. Given a specification of a store, we can determine whether a set of events can be observed by its users by checking if there is an abstract execution with this set of events satisfying the data type specifications and consistency axioms.

### 3.2 Replicated Data Type Specifications

In a sequential setting, the semantics of a data type $\tau$ can be specified by a function $\mathcal{S}_\tau : \mathsf{Op}_\tau^+ \to \mathsf{Val}_\tau$, which, given a non-empty sequence of operations performed on an object, specifies the return value of the last operation. For a register, read operations return the value of the last preceding write, or zero if there is no prior write. For a counter, read operations return the number of preceding increments. Thus, for any sequence of operations $\xi$:

$$\begin{aligned} \mathcal{S}_{\mathtt{intreg}}(\xi\,\mathtt{rd}) &= a, \text{ if } \mathtt{wr}(0)\,\xi = \xi_1\,\mathtt{wr}(a)\,\xi_2 \text{ and} \\ &\qquad \xi_2 \text{ does not contain } \mathtt{wr} \text{ operations;} \\ \mathcal{S}_{\mathtt{ctr}}(\xi\,\mathtt{rd}) &= \text{(the number of } \mathtt{inc} \text{ operations in } \xi\text{);} \\ \mathcal{S}_{\mathtt{intreg}}(\xi\,\mathtt{inc}) &= \mathcal{S}_{\mathtt{ctr}}(\xi\,\mathtt{wr}(a)) \;=\; \bot. \end{aligned}$$

In a replicated store, the story is more interesting. We specify a data type $\tau$ by a function $\mathcal{F}_\tau$, generalizing $\mathcal{S}_\tau$. Just like $\mathcal{S}_\tau$, this determines the return value of an operation based on prior operations performed on the object. However, $\mathcal{F}_\tau$ takes as a parameter not a sequence, but an *operation context*, which includes all we need to know about a store execution to determine the return value of a given operation $o$—the set $E$ of all events that are visible to $o$, together with the operations performed by the events and visibility and arbitration relations on them.

DEFINITION 3. *An* ***operation context*** *for a data type* $\tau$ *is a tuple* $L = (o, E, \mathsf{oper}, \mathsf{vis}, \mathsf{ar})$, *where* $o \in \mathsf{Op}_\tau$, $E$ *is a finite subset of* Event, $\mathsf{oper} : E \to \mathsf{Op}_\tau$, $\mathsf{vis} \subseteq E \times E$ *is acyclic and* $\mathsf{ar} \subseteq E \times E$ *is transitive, irreflexive and total.*

We can extract the context of an event $e \in A.E$ in an abstract execution $A$ by selecting all events visible to it according to $A$.vis:

$$\mathsf{ctxt}(A, e) = (A.\mathsf{oper}(e), G, (A.\mathsf{oper})|_G, (A.\mathsf{vis})|_G, (A.\mathsf{ar})|_G),$$

where $G = (A.\mathsf{vis})^{-1}(e)$ and $\cdot|_G$ is the restriction to events in $G$. Thus, in the abstract execution in Fig. 1(b), the operation context of the read from $x$ includes only one increment event; in the execution in Fig. 1(c) it includes two.

DEFINITION 4. *A* ***replicated data type specification*** *for a type* $\tau$ *is a function* $\mathcal{F}_\tau$ *that, given an operation context* $L$ *for* $\tau$, *specifies a return value* $\mathcal{F}_\tau(L) \in \mathsf{Val}_\tau$.

Note that $\mathcal{F}_\tau(o, \emptyset, \ldots)$ returns the value resulting from performing $o$ on the initial state for the data type (e.g., 0 for the LWW-register).

We specify multiple data types used in a replicated store by a partial function $\mathbb{F}$ mapping them to data type specifications.

DEFINITION 5. *An abstract execution $A$ **satisfies** $\mathbb{F}$, written $A \models \mathbb{F}$, if the return value of every event in $A$ is computed on its context by the specification for the type of the object the event accesses:*

$$\forall e \in A.E.\ (A.\mathsf{rval}(e) = \mathbb{F}(\mathsf{type}(A.\mathsf{obj}(e)))(\mathsf{ctxt}(A, e))).$$

We specify a whole store by $\mathbb{F}$ and a set of consistency axioms (§7). This lets us determine if its users can observe a given set of events by checking if there is an abstract execution with these events that satisfies $\mathbb{F}$ according to the above definition, as well as the axioms.

Note that $\mathcal{F}_\tau$ is deterministic. This does not mean that so is an outcome of an operation on a store; rather, that all the non-determinism arising due to its distributed nature is resolved by vis and ar in the context passed to $\mathcal{F}_\tau$. These relations are chosen arbitrarily subject to consistency axioms. Due to the determinacy property, two events that perform the same operation and see the same set of events produce the same return values. As we show in §7, this property ensures that our specifications can formalize eventual consistency in the sense of (1).

We now give four examples of data type specifications, corresponding to the four conflict-resolution strategies mentioned in §1 and §2: (1) operations commute, so no conflicts arise; (2) last writer wins; (3) all conflicting values are returned; and (4) conflicts are resolved in an application-specific way. We start by specifying the data types whose implementations we presented in §2.

**1. Counter (ctr)** is defined by

$$\begin{aligned} \mathcal{F}_{\mathtt{ctr}}(\mathtt{inc}, E, \mathsf{oper}, \mathsf{vis}, \mathsf{ar}) &= \bot; \\ \mathcal{F}_{\mathtt{ctr}}(\mathtt{rd}, E, \mathsf{oper}, \mathsf{vis}, \mathsf{ar}) &= \big|\{e \in E \mid \mathsf{oper}(e) = \mathtt{inc}\}\big|. \end{aligned} \quad (3)$$

Thus, according to Def. 5 the executions in Fig. 1(b) and 1(c) satisfy the counter specification: both 1 and 2 are valid return values for the read from $x$ when there are two concurrent increments.

**2. LWW-register (intreg)** is defined by

$$\mathcal{F}_{\mathtt{intreg}}(o, E, \mathsf{oper}, \mathsf{vis}, \mathsf{ar}) = \mathcal{S}_{\mathtt{intreg}}(E^{\mathsf{ar}} o), \quad (4)$$

where $E^{\mathsf{ar}}$ denotes the sequence obtained by ordering the operations performed by the events in $E$ according to ar. Thus, the return value is determined by establishing a total order of the visible operations and applying the regular sequential semantics. For example, by Def. 5 in the example execution from §3.1 the read from $x$ has to return *empty*; if we had a vis edge from the write of *post* to the read from $x$, then the read would have to return *post*. As we show in §7, weak shared-memory models are obtained by specializing our framework to stores with only LWW-registers.

We can obtain a concurrent semantics $\mathcal{F}_\tau$ of any data type $\tau$ based on its sequential semantics $\mathcal{S}_\tau$ similarly to (4). For example, $\mathcal{F}_{\mathtt{ctr}}$ defined above is equivalent to what we obtain using this generic construction. The next two examples go beyond this.

**3. Multi-value register (mvr).** This register [1, 18] has the same operations as the LWW-register, but its reads return a set of values:

$$\begin{aligned} \mathcal{F}_{\mathtt{mvr}}(\mathtt{rd}, E, \mathsf{oper}, \mathsf{vis}, \mathsf{ar}) = \{a \mid \exists e \in E.\, \mathsf{oper}(e) = \mathtt{wr}(a) \\ \wedge \neg\exists f \in E.\, \mathsf{oper}(f) = \mathtt{wr}(\_) \wedge e \xrightarrow{\mathsf{vis}} f\}. \end{aligned}$$

(We write _ for an expression whose value is irrelevant.) A read returns the values written by currently conflicting writes, defined as those that are not superseded in vis by later writes; ar is not used. For example, a rd would return $\{2, 3\}$ in the context on the right.

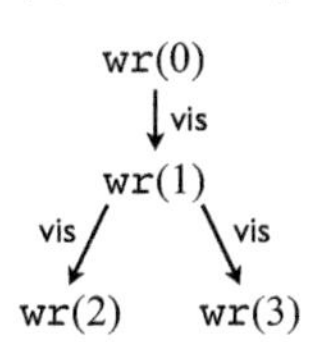


**Figure 3.** The set of configurations Config and the transition relation $\longrightarrow_{\mathbb{D}}$: Config × Event × Config for a data type library $\mathbb{D}$. We use $e : \{h_1 = u_1, h_2 = u_2\}$ to abbreviate $h_1(e) = u_1$ and $h_2(e) = u_2$. We uncurry $R \in$ RState where convenient.

$$\begin{aligned} \mathsf{Obj}_\tau &= \{x \in \mathsf{Obj} \mid \mathsf{type}(x) = \tau\} \\ \mathsf{RState} &= \textstyle\bigcup_{X \subseteq \mathsf{Obj}} \prod_{x \in X} (\mathsf{ReplicaID} \to \mathbb{D}(\mathsf{type}(x)).\Sigma) \\ \mathsf{TState} &= \mathsf{MessageID} \rightharpoonup \textstyle\bigcup_{\tau \in \mathsf{Type}} (\mathsf{ReplicaID} \times \mathsf{Obj}_\tau \times \mathbb{D}(\tau).M) \\ \mathsf{Config} &= \mathsf{RState} \times \mathsf{TState} \end{aligned}$$

$$\frac{\begin{array}{c}\mathbb{D}(\mathsf{type}(x)).\mathsf{do}(o, \sigma, t) = (\sigma', a) \\ e : \{\mathsf{act} = \mathsf{do},\ \mathsf{obj} = x,\ \mathsf{repl} = r,\ \mathsf{oper} = o,\ \mathsf{time} = t,\ \mathsf{rval} = a\}\end{array}}{(R[(x, r) \mapsto \sigma],\ T) \xrightarrow{e}_{\mathbb{D}} (R[(x, r) \mapsto \sigma'],\ T)}$$

$$\frac{\begin{array}{c}\mathbb{D}(\mathsf{type}(x)).\mathsf{send}(\sigma) = (\sigma', m) \qquad mid \notin \mathsf{dom}(T) \\ e : \{\mathsf{act} = \mathsf{send},\ \mathsf{obj} = x,\ \mathsf{repl} = r,\ \mathsf{msg} = mid\}\end{array}}{(R[(x, r) \mapsto \sigma],\ T) \xrightarrow{e}_{\mathbb{D}} (R[(x, r) \mapsto \sigma'],\ T[mid \mapsto (r, x, m)])}$$

$$\frac{\begin{array}{c}\mathbb{D}(\mathsf{type}(x)).\mathsf{receive}(\sigma, m) = \sigma' \qquad r \neq r' \\ e : \{\mathsf{act} = \mathsf{receive},\ \mathsf{obj} = x,\ \mathsf{repl} = r,\ \mathsf{srepl} = r',\ \mathsf{msg} = mid\}\end{array}}{\begin{array}{l}(R[(x, r) \mapsto \sigma],\ T[mid \mapsto (r', x, m)]) \xrightarrow{e}_{\mathbb{D}} \\ \qquad (R[(x, r) \mapsto \sigma'],\ T[mid \mapsto (r', x, m)])\end{array}}$$

**4. Observed-remove set (orset).** How do we specify a replicated set of integers? The operations of adding and removing different elements commute and thus do not conflict. Conflicts arise from concurrently adding and removing the same element. For example, we need to decide what rd will return as the contents of the set in the context $(\mathtt{rd}, \{e, f\}, \mathsf{oper}, \mathsf{vis}, \mathsf{ar})$, where $\mathsf{oper}(e) = \mathtt{add}(42)$ and $\mathsf{oper}(f) = \mathtt{remove}(42)$. If we use the generic construction from the LWW-register, the result will depend on the arbitration relation: $\emptyset$ if $e \xrightarrow{\mathsf{ar}} f$, and $\{42\}$ otherwise. An application may require a more consistent behavior, e.g., that an add operation always win against concurrent remove operations. Observed-remove (OR) set [7, 32] achieves this by mandating that remove operations cancel only the add operations that are visible to them:

$$\begin{aligned} \mathcal{F}_{\mathtt{orset}}(\mathtt{rd}, E, \mathsf{oper}, \mathsf{vis}, \mathsf{ar}) = \{a \mid \exists e \in E.\, \mathsf{oper}(e) = \mathtt{add}(a) \\ \wedge \neg\exists f \in E.\, \mathsf{oper}(f) = \mathtt{remove}(a) \wedge e \xrightarrow{\mathsf{vis}} f\}, \end{aligned} \quad (5)$$

In the above operation context rd will return $\emptyset$ if $e \xrightarrow{\mathsf{vis}} f$, and $\{42\}$ otherwise. The rationale is that, in the former case, add(42) and remove(42) are not concurrent: the user who issued the remove knew that 42 was in the set and thus meant to remove it. In the latter case, the two operations are concurrent and thus add wins.

As the above examples illustrate, our specifications can describe the semantics of data types and their conflict-resolution policies declaratively, without referring to the internals of their implementations. In this sense the specifications generalize the concept of an *abstract data type* [25] to the replicated setting.

# 4. Store Semantics and Data Type Correctness

A ***data type library*** $\mathbb{D}$ is a partial mapping from types $\tau$ to data type implementations $\mathbb{D}(\tau)$ from Def. 1. We now define the semantics of a replicated store with a data type library $\mathbb{D}$ as a set of its *concrete executions*, previously introduced informally by Fig. 1(a). We then state what it means for data type implementations of §2 to satisfy their specifications of §3.2 by requiring their concrete executions to be justified by abstract ones. In §7 we generalize this to the correctness of the whole store with multiple object with respect to both data type specifications and consistency axioms.

**Semantics.** We define the semantics using the relation $\longrightarrow_{\mathbb{D}}$: Config × Event × Config in Fig. 3, which describes a single step of the store execution. The relation transforms ***configurations*** $(R, T) \in \mathsf{Config}$ describing the store state: $R$ gives the object state at each replica, and $T$ the set of messages in transit between them, each identified by a message identifier $mid \in \mathsf{MessageID}$. A message is annotated by the origin replica and the object to which it pertains. We allow the store to contain only some objects from Obj and thus allow $R$ to be partial on them. We use a number of functions on events, such as act, obj, etc., to record the information about the corresponding transitions, so that $\longrightarrow_{\mathbb{D}}$ is implicitly parameterized by them; we give their full list in Def. 6 below.

The first rule in Fig. 3 describes a replica $r$ performing an operation $o$ on an object $x$ using the do method of the corresponding data type implementation. We record the return value using the function rval. To communicate the change to other replicas, we can at any time perform a transition defined by the second rule, which puts a new message $m$ created by a call to send into the set of messages in transit. The third rule describes the delivery of such a message to a replica $r$ other than the origin replica $r'$, which triggers a call to receive. Note that the relation $\longrightarrow_{\mathbb{D}}$ does not make any assumptions about message delivery: messages can be delivered in any order, multiple times, or not at all. These assumptions can be introduced separately, as we show later in this section. A concrete execution can be thought of as a finite or infinite sequence of transitions:

$$(R_0, T_0) \xrightarrow{e_1} (R_1, T_1) \xrightarrow{e_2} \ldots \xrightarrow{e_n} (R_n, T_n) \ldots,$$

where all events $e_i$ are distinct. To ease mapping between concrete and abstract executions in the future, we formalize it as a structure on events, similarly to Def. 2.

DEFINITION 6. *A* ***concrete execution*** *of a store with a data type library* $\mathbb{D}$ *is a tuple*

$$C = (E, \mathsf{eo}, \mathsf{pre}, \mathsf{post}, \mathsf{act}, \mathsf{obj}, \mathsf{repl}, \mathsf{oper}, \mathsf{time}, \mathsf{rval}, \mathsf{msg}, \mathsf{srepl}).$$

*Here* $E \subseteq \mathsf{Event}$, *the* ***execution order*** eo *is a well-founded, transitive, irreflexive and total order on* $E$, *relating the events according to the order of the transitions they describe,* time *is injective and* pre, post : $E \to \mathsf{Config}$ *form a valid sequence of transitions:*

$$(\forall e \in E.\, \mathsf{pre}(e) \xrightarrow{e}_{\mathbb{D}} \mathsf{post}(e)) \wedge$$
$$(\forall e, f \in E.\, e \xrightarrow{\mathsf{eo}} f \wedge \neg\exists g.\, e \xrightarrow{\mathsf{eo}} g \xrightarrow{\mathsf{eo}} f \implies \mathsf{post}(e) = \mathsf{pre}(f)).$$

We have omitted the types of functions on events, which are easily inferred from Fig. 3: e.g., act : $E \to \{\mathsf{do}, \mathsf{send}, \mathsf{receive}\}$ and time : $E \rightharpoonup \mathsf{Timestamp}$, defined only on $e$ with $\mathsf{act}(e) = \mathsf{do}$.

We denote the initial configuration of $C$ by $\mathsf{init}(C) = C.\mathsf{pre}(e_0)$, where $e_0$ is the minimal event in $C$.eo. If $C.E$ is finite, we denote the final configuration of $C$ by $\mathsf{final}(C) = C.\mathsf{post}(e_{\mathsf{f}})$, where $e_{\mathsf{f}}$ is the maximal event in $C$.eo. The ***semantics*** $[\![\mathbb{D}]\!]$ of $\mathbb{D}$ is the set of all its concrete executions $C$ that start in a configuration with an empty set of messages and all objects in initial states, i.e.,

$$\exists X \subseteq \mathsf{Obj}.\, \mathsf{init}(C) = ((\lambda x \in X.\, \mathbb{D}(\mathsf{type}(x)).\vec{\sigma}_0), [\,]),$$

where $[\,]$ is the everywhere-undefined function.

**Transport layer specifications.** Data type implementations such as the op-based counter in Fig. 2(a) can rely on some guarantees concerning the delivery of messages ensured by the rest of the store implementation. They may similarly assume certain properties of timestamps other than uniqueness (guaranteed by the injectivity of time in Def. 6). We take such assumptions into account by admitting only a subset of executions from $[\![\mathbb{D}]\!]$ that satisfy a ***transport layer specification*** $\mathcal{T}$, which is a predicate on concrete executions. Thus, we consider a ***replicated store*** to be defined by a pair $(\mathbb{D}, \mathcal{T})$ and the set of its executions be $[\![\mathbb{D}]\!] \cap \mathcal{T}$.

Even though our definition of $\mathcal{T}$ lets it potentially restrict data type implementation internals, the particular instantiations we use only restrict message delivery and timestamps. For technical reasons, we assume that $\mathcal{T}$ always satisfies certain closure properties: for every $C \in \mathcal{T}$, the projection of $C$ onto events on a given object or a subset of events forming a prefix in the eo order is also in $\mathcal{T}$.

As an example, we define a transport layer specification ensuring that a message is delivered to any single replica at most once, as required by the implementation in Fig. 2(a). Let the ***delivery relation*** $\mathsf{del}(C) \in C.E \times C.E$ pair events sending and receiving the same message:

$$e \xrightarrow{\mathsf{del}(C)} f \iff e \xrightarrow{C.\mathsf{eo}} f \wedge C.\mathsf{act}(e) = \mathsf{send} \wedge$$
$$C.\mathsf{act}(f) = \mathsf{receive} \wedge C.\mathsf{msg}(e) = C.\mathsf{msg}(f).$$

Then the desired condition on concrete executions $C$ is

$$\forall e, f, g \in C.E.\, e \xrightarrow{\mathsf{del}(C)} f \wedge e \xrightarrow{\mathsf{del}(C)} g \wedge$$
$$C.\mathsf{repl}(f) = C.\mathsf{repl}(g) \implies f = g. \quad \text{(T-Unique)}$$

**Data type implementation correctness.** We now state what it means for an implementation $\mathcal{D}_\tau$ of type $\tau$ from Def. 1 to satisfy a specification $\mathcal{F}_\tau$ from Def. 4. To this end, we consider the behavior of $\mathcal{D}_\tau$ under the "most general" client and transport layer, performing all possible operations and message deliveries. Formally, let $[\![\mathcal{D}_\tau]\!]$ be the set of executions $C \in [\![[\tau \mapsto \mathcal{D}_\tau]]\!]$ of a store containing a single object $x$ of a type $\tau$ with the implementation $\mathcal{D}_\tau$, i.e., $\mathsf{init}(C) = (R, [\,])$ for some $R$ such that $\mathsf{dom}(R) = \{x\}$.

Then $\mathcal{D}_\tau$ should satisfy $\mathcal{F}_\tau$ under a transport specification $\mathcal{T}$ if for every concrete execution $C \in [\![\mathcal{D}_\tau]\!] \cap \mathcal{T}$ we can find a "similar" abstract execution satisfying $\mathcal{F}_\tau$ and, in particular, having the same operations and return values. As it happens, all components of the abstract execution except visibility are straightforwardly determined by $C$; as explained in §3.1, we have some freedom in choosing visibility. We define the choice using a ***visibility witness*** $\mathcal{V}$, which maps a concrete execution $C \in [\![\mathcal{D}_\tau]\!]$ to an acyclic relation on $(C.E)|_{\mathsf{do}}$ defining visibility (here $\cdot|_{\mathsf{do}}$ is the restriction to events $e$ with $C.\mathsf{act}(e) = \mathsf{do}$). Let

$$e \xrightarrow{\mathsf{ro}(C)} f \iff e \xrightarrow{C.\mathsf{eo}} f \wedge C.\mathsf{repl}(e) = C.\mathsf{repl}(f);$$
$$e \xrightarrow{\mathsf{ar}(C)} f \iff e, f \in (C.E)|_{\mathsf{do}} \wedge$$
$$C.\mathsf{obj}(e) = C.\mathsf{obj}(f) \wedge C.\mathsf{time}(e) < C.\mathsf{time}(f).$$

Then the abstract execution justifying $C \in [\![\mathcal{D}_\tau]\!]$ is defined by

$$\mathsf{abs}(C, \mathcal{V}) = (C.E|_{\mathsf{do}}, E.\mathsf{repl}|_{\mathsf{do}}, E.\mathsf{obj}|_{\mathsf{do}}, E.\mathsf{oper}|_{\mathsf{do}}, E.\mathsf{rval}|_{\mathsf{do}},$$
$$\mathsf{ro}(C)|_{\mathsf{do}}, \mathcal{V}(C), \mathsf{ar}(C)).$$

DEFINITION 7. *A data type implementation* $\mathcal{D}_\tau$ ***satisfies*** *a specification* $\mathcal{F}_\tau$ *with respect to* $\mathcal{V}$ *and* $\mathcal{T}$, *written* $\mathcal{D}_\tau\ \mathsf{sat}[\mathcal{V}, \mathcal{T}]\ \mathcal{F}_\tau$, *if* $\forall C \in [\![\mathcal{D}_\tau]\!] \cap \mathcal{T}.\, (\mathsf{abs}(C, \mathcal{V}) \models [\tau \mapsto \mathcal{F}_\tau])$, *where* $\models$ *is defined in Def. 5.*

As we explained informally in §3.1, the visibility witness depends on how much information the implementation puts into messages. Since state-based implementations, such as the ones in Fig. 2(b, c), are transitively delivering (§2), for them we use the witness $\mathcal{V}^{\mathsf{state}}(C) = (\mathsf{ro}(C) \cup \mathsf{del}(C))^+|_{\mathsf{do}}$. By the definition of $\mathsf{ro}(C)$ and $\mathsf{del}(C)$, $(\mathsf{ro}(C) \cup \mathsf{del}(C))$ is acyclic, so $\mathcal{V}^{\mathsf{state}}$ is well-defined. State-based implementations do not make any assumptions about the transport layer: in this case we write $\mathcal{T} = \mathsf{T\text{-}Any}$. In contrast, op-based implementations, such as the one in Fig. 2(a), require $\mathcal{T} = \mathsf{T\text{-}Unique}$. Since such implementations are not transitively delivering, the witness $\mathcal{V}^{\mathsf{state}}$ is not appropriate for them. We could attempt to define a witness for them by straightforwardly lifting the delivery relation:

$$\mathcal{V}^{\mathsf{op}}(C) = \mathsf{ro}(C)|_{\mathsf{do}} \cup \{(e, f) \mid e, f \in (C.E)|_{\mathsf{do}} \wedge$$
$$\exists e', f'.\, e \xrightarrow{\mathsf{ro}(C)} e' \xrightarrow{\mathsf{del}(C)} f' \xrightarrow{\mathsf{ro}(C)} f\}.$$

However, we need to be more careful, since for op-based implementations $e \xrightarrow{\mathsf{ro}(C)} e' \xrightarrow{\mathsf{del}(C)} f' \xrightarrow{\mathsf{ro}(C)} f$ does not ensure that the update of $e$ is taken into account by $f$: if there is another send event $e''$ in between $e$ and $e'$, then $e''$ will capture the update of $e$ and $e'$ will not. Hence, we define the witness as:

$$\begin{aligned}\mathcal{V}^{\mathsf{op}}(C) = \mathsf{ro}(C)|_{\mathsf{do}} \cup \{(e,f) \mid e,f \in (C.E)|_{\mathsf{do}} \\ \wedge \exists e', f'.\, e \xrightarrow{\mathsf{ro}(C)} e' \xrightarrow{\mathsf{del}(C)} f' \xrightarrow{\mathsf{ro}(C)} f \\ \wedge \neg\exists e''.\, e \xrightarrow{\mathsf{ro}(C)} e'' \xrightarrow{\mathsf{ro}(C)} e' \wedge C.\mathsf{act}(e'') = \mathsf{send}\}.\end{aligned}$$

We next present a method for proving data type implementation correctness in the sense of Def. 7. In §7 we lift this to stores with multiple objects and take into account consistency axioms.

## 5. Proving Data Type Implementations Correct

The straightforward approach to proving correctness in the sense of Def. 7 would require us to consider global store configurations in executions $C$, including object states at all replicas and all messages in transit, making the reasoning non-modular and unintuitive. To deal with this challenge, we focus on a single component of a store configuration using *replication-aware simulation relations* $\mathcal{R}_r$ and $\mathcal{M}$, analogous to simulation (aka coupling) relations used in data refinement [21]. The $\mathcal{R}_r$ relation associates the object state at a replica $r$ with an abstract execution that describes *only those events that led to this state*; $\mathcal{M}$ does the same for a message. For example, when proving $\mathcal{D}_{\mathtt{ctr}}$ in Fig. 2(b) with respect to $\mathcal{F}_{\mathtt{ctr}}$ in (3), $\mathcal{M}$ associates a message carrying a vector $v$ with executions in which each replica $s$ makes $v(s)$ increments. As part of a proof of $\mathcal{D}_\tau$, we require checking that the effect of its methods, such as $\mathcal{D}_\tau$.do, can be simulated by appropriately transforming related abstract executions while preserving the relations. We define these transformations using *abstract methods* $\mathsf{do}^\sharp$, $\mathsf{send}^\sharp$ and $\mathsf{receive}^\sharp$ as illustrated in Fig. 4(a, b). For example, if a replica $r$ executes $\mathcal{D}_\tau$.do from a state $\sigma$ related by $\mathcal{R}_r$ to an abstract execution $I$ (we explain the use of $I$ instead of $A$ later), we need to find an $I'$ related by $\mathcal{R}_r$ to the resulting state $\sigma'$. We also need to check that the value returned by $\mathcal{D}_\tau$.do on $\sigma$ is equal to that returned by $\mathcal{F}_\tau$ on $I$.

These conditions consider the behavior of an implementation method on a single state and/or message and its effect on only the relevant part of the abstract execution. However, by localizing the reasoning in this way, we lose some global information that is actually required to verify realistic implementations. In particular, this occurs when discharging the obligation for receive in Fig. 4(b). Taking a global view, $\sigma$ and $m$ there are meant to come from the same configuration in a concrete execution $C$; correspondingly, $I$ and $J$ are meant to be fragments of the same abstract execution $\mathsf{abs}(C, \mathcal{V})$. In this context we may know certain ***agreement properties*** correlating $I$ and $J$, e.g., that the union of their visibility relations is itself a well-formed visibility relation and is thus acyclic. Establishing them requires global reasoning about whole executions $C$ and $\mathsf{abs}(C, \mathcal{V})$. Fortunately, we find that this can be done knowing only the abstract methods, not the implementation $\mathcal{D}_\tau$. Furthermore, these methods state basic facts about the messaging behavior of implementations and are thus common to broad classes of them, such as state-based or op-based. This allows us to establish agreement properties using global reasoning once for a given class of implementations; at this stage we can also benefit from the transport layer specification $\mathcal{T}$ and check that the abstract methods construct visibility according to the given witness $\mathcal{V}$. Then a particular implementation within the class can be verified by discharging local obligations, such as those in Fig. 4(a, b), while assuming agreement properties. This yields easy and intuitive proofs.

To summarize, we deal with the challenge posed by a distributed data type implementation by decomposing reasoning about it into global reasoning done once for a broad class of implementations and local implementation-specific reasoning. We start by presenting the general form of obligations to be discharged for a single implementation within a certain class (§5.1) and the particular form they take for the class of state-based implementations (§5.2), together with some examples (§5.3). We then formulate the obligations to be discharged for a class of implementations (§5.4), which in particular, establish the agreement properties assumed in the per-implementation obligations. In [12, §B], we give the obligations for op-based implementations, together with a proof of the counter in Fig. 2(a). An impatient reader can move on to §6 after finishing §5.3, and come back to §5.4 later.

**Figure 4.** Diagrams illustrating replication-aware simulations

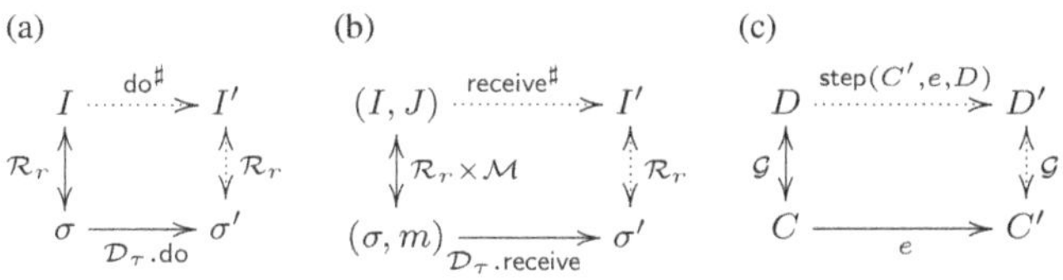


Since Def. 7 considers only single-object executions, we fix an object $x$ of type $\tau$ and consider only concrete and abstract executions over $x$, whose sets we denote by $\mathsf{CEx}[x]$ and $\mathsf{AEx}[x]$.

### 5.1 Replication-Aware Simulations

As is typical for simulation-based proofs, we need to use auxiliary state to record information about the computation history. For this reason, actually our simulation relations associate a state or a message with an ***instrumented execution***—a pair $(A, \mathsf{info}) \in \mathsf{IEx}$ of an abstract execution $A \in \mathsf{AEx}[x]$ and a function $\mathsf{info} : A.E \to \mathsf{AInfo}$, tagging events with auxiliary information from a set AInfo. As we show below, AInfo can be chosen once for a class of data type implementations: e.g., AInfo = Timestamp for state-based ones (§5.2). We use $I$ and $J$ to range over instrumented executions and shorten, e.g., $I.A.E$ to $I.E$. For a partial function $h$ we write $h(x)\downarrow$ for $x \in \mathsf{dom}(h)$, and adopt the convention that $h(x) = y$ implies $h(x)\downarrow$.

DEFINITION 8. *A* ***replication-aware simulation*** *between $\mathcal{D}_\tau$ and $\mathcal{F}_\tau$ with respect to* info *and* ***abstract methods*** $\mathsf{do}^\sharp$, $\mathsf{send}^\sharp$ *and* $\mathsf{receive}^\sharp$ *is a collection of relations $\{\mathcal{R}_r, \mathcal{M} \mid r \in \mathsf{ReplicaID}\}$ satisfying the conditions in Fig. 5.*

Here info and abstract methods are meant to be fixed for a given class of implementations, such as state or op-based. To prove a particular implementation within this class, one needs to find simulation relations satisfying the conditions in Fig. 5. For example, as we show in §5.3, the following relation lets us prove the correctness of the counter in Fig. 2(b) with respect to info and abstract methods appropriate for state-based implementations:

$$\begin{aligned}&\langle s, v\rangle\ [\mathcal{R}_r]\ I \iff (r = s) \wedge (v\ [\mathcal{M}]\ I);\\ &v\ [\mathcal{M}]\ ((E, \mathsf{repl}, \mathsf{obj}, \mathsf{oper}, \mathsf{rval}, \mathsf{ro}, \mathsf{vis}, \mathsf{ar}), \mathsf{info}) \iff \\ &\qquad \forall s.\, v(s) = \big|\{e \in E \mid \mathsf{oper}(e) = \mathtt{inc} \wedge \mathsf{repl}(e) = s\}\big|.\end{aligned} \tag{6}$$

INIT in Fig. 5 associates the initial state at a replica $r$ with the execution having an empty set of events. DO, SEND and RECEIVE formalize the obligations illustrated in Fig. 4(a, b). Note that $\mathsf{do}^\sharp$ is parameterized by an event $e$ (required to be fresh in instantiations) and the information about the operation performed.

The abstract methods are partial and the obligations in Fig. 5 *assume* that their applications are defined. When instantiating $\mathsf{receive}^\sharp$ for a given class of implementations, we let it be defined only when its arguments satisfy the agreement property for this class, which we establish separately (§5.4). While doing this, we can also establish some ***execution invariants***, holding of single ex-

**Figure 5.** Definition of a replication-aware simulation $\{\mathcal{R}_r, \mathcal{M}\}$ between $\mathcal{D}_\tau$ and $\mathcal{F}_\tau$. All free variables in each condition are implicitly universally quantified and have the following types: $\sigma, \sigma' \in \Sigma$, $m \in M$, $I, I', J \in \mathsf{IEx}$, $e \in \mathsf{Event}$, $r \in \mathsf{ReplicaID}$, $o \in \mathsf{Op}_\tau$, $a \in \mathsf{Val}_\tau$, $t \in \mathsf{Timestamp}$.

$$\mathcal{R}_r \subseteq \Sigma \times \mathsf{IEx},\ r \in \mathsf{ReplicaID}; \qquad \mathcal{M} \subseteq M \times \mathsf{IEx}$$

$$\mathsf{do}^\sharp : \mathsf{IEx} \times \mathsf{Event} \times \mathsf{ReplicaID} \times \mathsf{Op}_\tau \times \mathsf{Val}_\tau \times \mathsf{Timestamp} \rightharpoonup \mathsf{IEx}$$

$$\mathsf{send}^\sharp : \mathsf{IEx} \rightharpoonup \mathsf{IEx} \times \mathsf{IEx}; \qquad \mathsf{receive}^\sharp : \mathsf{IEx} \times \mathsf{IEx} \rightharpoonup \mathsf{IEx}$$

INIT: $\mathcal{D}_\tau.\vec{\sigma}_0(r)\ [\mathcal{R}_r]\ I_\emptyset$, where $I_\emptyset.E = \emptyset$

DO: $(\mathsf{do}^\sharp(I, e, r, o, a, t) = I' \wedge \mathcal{D}_\tau.\mathsf{do}(o, \sigma, t) = (\sigma', a) \wedge \sigma\ [\mathcal{R}_r]\ I) \implies (\sigma'\ [\mathcal{R}_r]\ I' \wedge a = \mathcal{F}_\tau(\mathsf{ctxt}(I'.A, e)))$

SEND: $(\mathsf{send}^\sharp(I) = (I', J) \wedge \mathcal{D}_\tau.\mathsf{send}(\sigma) = (\sigma', m) \wedge \sigma\ [\mathcal{R}_r]\ I) \implies (\sigma'\ [\mathcal{R}_r]\ I' \wedge m\ [\mathcal{M}]\ J)$

RECEIVE: $(\mathsf{receive}^\sharp(I, J){\downarrow} \wedge \sigma\ [\mathcal{R}_r]\ I \wedge m\ [\mathcal{M}]\ J) \implies (\mathcal{D}_\tau.\mathsf{receive}(\sigma, m)\ [\mathcal{R}_r]\ \mathsf{receive}^\sharp(I, J))$

ecutions supplied as parameters to $\mathsf{do}^\sharp$ and $\mathsf{send}^\sharp$. We similarly assume them in Fig. 5 via the definedness of these abstract methods.

### 5.2 Instantiation for State-Based Implementations

Fig. 6 defines the domain AInfo and abstract methods appropriate for state-based implementations. In §5.4 we show that the existence of a simulation of Def. 8 with respect to these parameters implies $\mathcal{D}_\tau\ \mathsf{sat}[\mathcal{V}^{\mathsf{state}}, \mathsf{T\text{-}Any}]\ \mathcal{F}_\tau$ (Theorems 9 and 10). The $\mathsf{do}^\sharp$ method adds a fresh event $e$ with the given attributes to $I$; its timestamp $t$ is recorded in info. In the resulting execution $I'$, the event $e$ is the last one by its replica, observes all events in $I$ and occupies the place in arbitration consistent with $t$. The $\mathsf{send}^\sharp$ method just returns $I$, which formalizes the intuition that, in state-based implementations, send returns a message capturing all the information about the object available at the replica. The $\mathsf{receive}^\sharp$ method takes the component-wise union $I \sqcup J$ of executions $I$ related to the current state and $J$ related to the message, applied recursively to the components of $I.A$ and $J.A$. We also assume that $I \sqcup J$ recomputes the arbitration relation in the resulting execution from the timestamps. This is the reason for recording them in info: we would not be able to construct $\mathsf{receive}^\sharp(I, J).\mathsf{ar}$ solely from $I.\mathsf{ar}$ and $J.\mathsf{ar}$.

The agreement property $\mathsf{agree}(I, J)$ guarantees that $I \sqcup J$ is well-formed (e.g., its visibility relation is acyclic) and that, for each replica, $I$ describes a computation extending $J$ or vice versa. The latter follows from the observation we made when explaining the state-based counter in §2: a message or a state in a state-based implementation reflects a prefix of the sequence of events performed at a given replica. The first conjunct of the execution invariant inv requires arbitration to be consistent with event timestamps; the second conjunct follows from the definition of $\mathcal{V}^{\mathsf{state}}$ (§4). When discharging the obligations in Fig. 5 with respect to the parameters in Fig. 6 for a particular implementation, we can rely on the agreement property and the execution invariant.

### 5.3 Examples

We illustrate the use of the instantiation from §5.2 on the state-based counter, LWW-register and OR-set. In [12, §A] we also give proofs of two multi-value register implementations.

**Counter:** $\mathcal{D}_{\mathtt{ctr}}$ in Fig. 2(b) and $\mathcal{F}_{\mathtt{ctr}}$ in (3). Discharging the obligations in Fig. 5 for the simulation (6) is easy. The key case is RECEIVE, where the first conjunct of agree in Fig. 6 ensures that $\min\{v(s), v'(s)\}$ increments by a replica $s$ are taken into account both in $v(s)$ and in $v'(s)$:

$$(\langle r, v\rangle\ [\mathcal{R}_r]\ I) \wedge (v'\ [\mathcal{M}]\ J) \implies (\forall s.\ \min\{v(s), v'(s)\} = |\{e \in I.E \cap J.E \mid I.\mathsf{oper}(e) = \mathtt{inc} \wedge I.\mathsf{repl}(e) = s\}|).$$

**Figure 6.** Instantiation for state-based data type implementations. In $\mathsf{do}^\sharp$ we omit the straightforward definition of $\mathsf{ar}'$ in terms of $I.\mathsf{info}$ and $t$.

$$\mathsf{AInfo} = \mathsf{Timestamp}$$

$$\mathsf{agree}(I, J) \iff \forall r.\ ((\{e \in I.E \mid I.\mathsf{repl}(e) = r\}, I.\mathsf{ro}) \text{ is a prefix of } (\{e \in J.E \mid J.\mathsf{repl}(e) = r\}, J.\mathsf{ro}) \text{ or vice versa}) \wedge (I \sqcup J \in \mathsf{IEx})$$

$$\mathsf{inv}(I) \iff (\forall e, f \in I.E.\ (e, f) \in I.\mathsf{ar} \iff I.\mathsf{info}(e) < I.\mathsf{info}(f)) \wedge ((I.\mathsf{vis} \cup I.\mathsf{ro})^+ \subseteq I.\mathsf{vis})$$

$$\mathsf{do}^\sharp(I, e, r, o, a, t) = I', \quad \text{if } \mathsf{inv}(I) \wedge e \notin I.E \wedge I' \in \mathsf{IEx}$$

where $I' = ((I.E \cup \{e\},\ I.\mathsf{repl}[e \mapsto r],\ I.\mathsf{obj}[e \mapsto x],\ I.\mathsf{oper}[e \mapsto o],\ I.\mathsf{rval}[e \mapsto a],\ I.\mathsf{ro} \cup \{(f, e) \mid f \in I.E \wedge I.\mathsf{repl}(f) = r\},\ I.\mathsf{vis} \cup \{(f, e) \mid f \in I.E\}, \mathsf{ar}'),\ I.\mathsf{info}[e \mapsto t])$

$$\mathsf{send}^\sharp(I) = (I, I), \quad \text{if } \mathsf{inv}(I)$$

$$\mathsf{receive}^\sharp(I, J) = I \sqcup J, \quad \text{if } \mathsf{inv}(I) \wedge \mathsf{inv}(J) \wedge \mathsf{agree}(I, J)$$

This allows establishing $\mathsf{receive}(\langle r, v\rangle, v')\ [\mathcal{R}_r]\ (I \sqcup J)$, thus formalizing the informal justification of correctness we gave in §2.

**LWW-register:** $\mathcal{D}_{\mathtt{intreg}}$ in Fig. 2(c) and $\mathcal{F}_{\mathtt{intreg}}$ in (4). We associate a state or a message $\langle a, t\rangle$ with any execution that contains a $\mathtt{wr}(a)$ event with the timestamp $t$ maximal among all other $\mathtt{wr}$ events (as per info). By inv in Fig. 6, this event is maximal in arbitration, which implies that $\mathtt{rd}$ returns the correct value; the other obligations are also discharged easily. Formally, $\forall r.\ \mathcal{R}_r = \mathcal{M}$ and

$$\langle a, t\rangle\ [\mathcal{M}]\ ((E, \mathsf{repl}, \mathsf{obj}, \mathsf{oper}, \mathsf{rval}, \mathsf{ro}, \mathsf{vis}, \mathsf{ar}), \mathsf{info}) \iff (t = 0 \wedge a = 0 \wedge (\neg\exists e \in E.\ \mathsf{oper}(e) = \mathtt{wr}(\_))) \vee (t > 0 \wedge (\exists e \in E.\ \mathsf{oper}(e) = \mathtt{wr}(a) \wedge \mathsf{info}(e) = t) \wedge (\forall f \in E.\ \mathsf{oper}(f) = \mathtt{wr}(\_) \implies \mathsf{info}(f) \leq t)).$$

**Optimized OR-set:** $\mathcal{D}_{\mathtt{orset}}$ in Fig. 7 and $\mathcal{F}_{\mathtt{orset}}$ in (5). A problem with implementing a replicated set is that we often cannot discard the information about an element from a replica state after it has been removed: if another replica unaware of the removal sends us a snapshot of its state containing this element, the semantics of the set may require our receive to keep the element out of the set. As we prove in §6, for the OR-set keeping track of information about removed elements cannot be fully avoided, which makes its space-efficient implementation very challenging. Here we consider a recently-proposed OR-set implementation [6] that, as we show in §6, has an optimal space complexity. It improves on the original implementation [32], whose complexity was suboptimal (we have proved the correctness of the latter as well; see [12, §A]).

An additional challenge posed by the OR-set is that, according to $\mathcal{F}_{\mathtt{orset}}$, a $\mathtt{remove}$ operation may behave differently with respect to different events adding the same element to the set, depending on whether it sees them or not. This causes the implementation to treat internally each add operation as generating a unique *instance* of the *element* being added, further increasing the space required. To combat this, the implementation concisely summarizes information about instances. An instance is represented by a unique *instance identifier* that is generated when a replica performs an add and consists of the replica identifier and the number of adds (of any elements) performed at the replica until then. In a state $\langle r, V, w\rangle$, the vector $w$ determines the identifiers of all instances that the current replica $r$ has ever observed: for any replica $s$, the replica $r$ has seen $w(s)$ successive identifiers $(s, 1), (s, 2), \ldots, (s, w(s))$ generated at $s$. To generate a new identifier in $\mathsf{do}(\mathsf{add}(a'))$, the replica $r$ increments $w(r)$. The connection between the vector $w$ in a state or a message and add events $e_{s,k}$ in corresponding executions is formalized in lines 1-3 of the simulation relation, also shown in Fig. 7. In receive we take the pointwise maximum of the two vectors $w$ and $w'$. Like for the counter, the first conjunct of agree implies that this preserves the clauses in lines 1-3.

**Figure 7.** Optimized OR-set implementation [6] and its simulation

$$\Sigma = \mathsf{ReplicaID} \times ((\mathbb{Z} \times \mathsf{ReplicaID}) \to \mathbb{N}_0) \times (\mathsf{ReplicaID} \to \mathbb{N}_0)$$
$$\vec{\sigma}_0 = \lambda r.\, \langle r, (\lambda a, s.\, 0), (\lambda s.\, 0) \rangle$$
$$M = ((\mathbb{Z} \times \mathsf{ReplicaID}) \to \mathbb{N}_0) \times (\mathsf{ReplicaID} \to \mathbb{N}_0)$$
$$\mathsf{do}(\mathtt{add}(a'), \langle r, V, w \rangle, t) = (\langle r, (\lambda a, s.\, \text{if } a = a' \wedge s = r \text{ then } w(r) + 1 \text{ else } V(a, s)), w[r \mapsto w(r) + 1] \rangle, \bot)$$
$$\mathsf{do}(\mathtt{remove}(a'), \langle r, V, w \rangle, t) = (\langle r, (\lambda a, s.\, \text{if } a = a' \text{ then } 0 \text{ else } V(a, s)), w \rangle, \bot)$$
$$\mathsf{do}(\mathtt{rd}, \langle r, V, w \rangle, t) = (\langle r, V, w \rangle, \{a \mid \exists s.\, V(a, s) > 0\})$$
$$\mathsf{send}(\langle r, V, w \rangle) = (\langle r, V, w \rangle, \langle V, w \rangle)$$
$$\mathsf{receive}(\langle r, V, w \rangle, \langle V', w' \rangle) = \langle r, (\lambda a, s.\, \text{if } (V(a, s) = 0 \wedge w(s) \geq V'(a, s)) \vee (V'(a, s) = 0 \wedge w'(s) \geq V(a, s)) \text{ then } 0 \text{ else } \max\{V(a, s), V'(a, s)\}), (\lambda s.\, \max\{w(s), w'(s)\}) \rangle$$

---

$$\langle s, V, w \rangle \; [\mathcal{R}_r] \; I \iff (r = s) \wedge (\langle V, w \rangle \; [\mathcal{M}] \; I)$$

$\langle V, w \rangle \; [\mathcal{M}] \; ((E, \mathsf{repl}, \mathsf{obj}, \mathsf{oper}, \mathsf{rval}, \mathsf{ro}, \mathsf{vis}, \mathsf{ar}), \mathsf{info}) \iff$

1: $\exists$ distinct $e_{s,k}$. $(\{e_{s,k} \mid s \in \mathsf{ReplicaID} \wedge 1 \leq k \leq w(s)\} =$
2: $\{e \in E \mid \mathsf{oper}(e) = \mathtt{add}(\_)\}) \wedge$
3: $(\forall s, k, j.\, (\mathsf{repl}(e_{s,k}) = s) \wedge (e_{s,j} \xrightarrow{\mathsf{ro}} e_{s,k} \iff j < k)) \wedge$
4: $(\forall a, s.\, (V(a, s) \leq w(s)) \wedge (V(a, s) \neq 0 \implies$
5: $(\mathsf{oper}(e_{s,V(a,s)}) = \mathtt{add}(a)) \wedge$
6: $(\neg \exists k.\, V(a, s) < k \leq w(s) \wedge \mathsf{oper}(e_{s,k}) = \mathtt{add}(a)) \wedge$
7: $(\neg \exists f \in E.\, \mathsf{oper}(f) = \mathtt{remove}(a) \wedge e_{s,V(a,s)} \xrightarrow{\mathsf{vis}} f))) \wedge$
8: $(\forall a, s, k.\, e_{s,k} \in E \wedge \mathsf{oper}(e_{s,k}) = \mathtt{add}(a) \implies$
9: $(k \leq V(a, s) \vee \exists f \in E.\, \mathsf{oper}(f) = \mathtt{remove}(a) \wedge e_{s,k} \xrightarrow{\mathsf{vis}} f))$

---

The component $w$ in $\langle r, V, w \rangle$ records identifiers of both of those instances that have been removed and those that are still in the set (are *active*). The component $V$ serves to distinguish the latter. As it happens, we do not need to store all active instances of an element $a$: for every replica $s$, it is enough to keep the last active instance identifier generated by an $\mathtt{add}(a)$ at this replica. If $V(a, s) \neq 0$, this identifier is $(s, V(a, s))$; if $V(a, s) = 0$, all instances of $a$ generated at $s$ that the current replica knows about are inactive. The meaning of $V$ is formalized in the simulation: each instance identifier given by $V$ is covered by $w$ (line 4) and, if $V(a, s) \neq 0$, then the event $e_{s,V(a,s)}$ performs $\mathtt{add}(a)$ (line 5), is the last $\mathtt{add}(a)$ by replica $s$ (line 6) and has not been observed by a $\mathtt{remove}(a)$ (line 7). Finally, the $\mathtt{add}(a)$ events that are not seen by a $\mathtt{remove}(a)$ in the execution are either the events $e_{s,V(a,s)}$ or those superseded by them (lines 8-9). This ensures that returning all elements with an active instance in $\mathtt{rd}$ matches $\mathcal{F}_{\mathtt{orset}}$.

When a replica $r$ performs $\mathsf{do}(\mathtt{add}(a'))$, we update $V(a', r)$ to correspond to the new instance identifier. Conversely, in $\mathsf{do}(\mathtt{remove}(a'))$, we clear all entries in $V(a')$, thereby deactivating all instances of $a'$. However, after this their identifiers are still recorded in $w$, and so we know that they have been previously removed. This allows us to address the problem with implementing receive we mentioned above: if we receive a message with an active instance $(s, V'(a, s))$ of an element $a$ that is not in the set at our replica ($V(a, s) = 0$), but previously existed ($w(s) \geq V'(a, s)$), this means that the instance has been removed and should not be active in the resulting state (the entry for $(a, s)$ should be 0). We also do the same check with the state and the message swapped.

As the above explanation shows, our simulation relations are useful not only for proving correctness of data type implementations, but also for explaining their designs. Discharging obligations in Fig. 5 requires some work for the OR-set; due to space constraints, we defer this to [12, §A].

**Figure 8.** Function step that mirrors the effect of an event $e \in C'.E$ from $C' \in \mathsf{CEx}[x]$ in $D \in \mathsf{DEx}$, defined when so is the abstract method used

$$\mathsf{step}(C', e, D) = D[r \mapsto \mathsf{do}^\sharp(D(r), e, r, C'.\mathsf{oper}(e), C'.\mathsf{rval}(e), C'.\mathsf{time}(e))], \text{ if } C'.\mathsf{act}(e) = \mathsf{do} \wedge C'.\mathsf{repl}(e) = r$$
$$\mathsf{step}(C', e, D) = D[r \mapsto I, C'.\mathsf{msg}(e) \mapsto J], \text{ if } C'.\mathsf{act}(e) = \mathsf{send} \wedge C'.\mathsf{repl}(e) = r \wedge C'.\mathsf{msg}(e) \notin \mathsf{dom}(D) \wedge \mathsf{send}^\sharp(D(r)) = (I, J)$$
$$\mathsf{step}(C', e, D) = D[r \mapsto \mathsf{receive}^\sharp(D(r), D(C'.\mathsf{msg}(e)))], \text{ if } C'.\mathsf{act}(e) = \mathsf{receive} \wedge C'.\mathsf{repl}(e) = r$$

### 5.4 Soundness and Establishing Agreement Properties

We present conditions on $\mathsf{AInfo}$ and abstract methods ensuring the soundness of replication-aware simulations over them and, in particular, establishing the agreement property and execution invariants assumed via the definedness of abstract operations in Fig. 5.

THEOREM 9 (Soundness). *Assume* $\mathsf{AInfo}$, $\mathsf{do}^\sharp$, $\mathsf{send}^\sharp$, $\mathsf{receive}^\sharp$, $\mathcal{V}$ *and* $\mathcal{T}$ *that satisfy the conditions in Fig. 9 for some* $\mathcal{G}$. *If there exists a replication-aware simulation between* $\mathcal{D}_\tau$ *and* $\mathcal{F}_\tau$ *with respect to these parameters, then* $\mathcal{D}_\tau \; \mathsf{sat}[\mathcal{V}, \mathcal{T}] \; \mathcal{F}_\tau$.

Conditions in Fig. 9 require global reasoning, but can be discharged once for a class of data types. For example, they hold of the instantiation for state-based implementations from §5.2, as well as one for op-based implementations presented in [12, §B].

THEOREM 10. *There exists* $\mathcal{G}$ *such that, for all* $\mathcal{D}_\tau$, *the parameters in Fig. 6 satisfy the conditions in Fig. 9 with respect to this* $\mathcal{G}$, $\mathcal{V} = \mathcal{V}^{\mathsf{state}}$, $\mathcal{T} = \mathsf{T\text{-}Any}$.

The proofs of Theorems 9 and 10 are given in [12, §B]. To explain the conditions in Fig. 9, here we consider the proof strategy for Theorem 9. To establish $\mathcal{D}_\tau \; \mathsf{sat}[\mathcal{V}, \mathcal{T}] \; \mathcal{F}_\tau$, for any $C \in [\![\mathcal{D}_\tau]\!] \cap \mathcal{T}$ we need to show $\mathsf{abs}(C, \mathcal{V}) \models [\tau \mapsto \mathcal{F}_\tau]$. We prove this by induction on the length of $C$. To use the localized conditions in Fig. 5, we require a relation $\mathcal{G}$ associating $C$ with a ***decomposed execution***—a partial function $D : (\mathsf{ReplicaID} \cup \mathsf{MessageID}) \rightharpoonup \mathsf{IEx}$ that gives fragments of $\mathsf{abs}(C, \mathcal{V})$ corresponding to replica states and messages in the final configuration of $C$. We write $\mathsf{DEx}$ for the set of all decomposed executions, so that $\mathcal{G} \subseteq \mathsf{CEx}[x] \times \mathsf{DEx}$. The existence of a decomposed execution $D$ such that $C \; [\mathcal{G}] \; D$ forms the core of our induction hypothesis. G-CTXT in Fig. 9 checks that the abstract methods construct visibility according to $\mathcal{V}$: it requires the context of any event $e$ by a replica $r$ to be the same in $D(r)$ and $\mathsf{abs}(C, \mathcal{V})$. Together with DO in Fig. 5, this ensures $\mathsf{abs}(C, \mathcal{V}) \models [\tau \mapsto \mathcal{F}_\tau]$.

We write $C' \sim (C \xrightarrow{e} (R, T))$ when $C'$ is an extension of $C$ in the following sense: $C'.E = C.E \uplus \{e\}$, the other components of $C$ are those of $C'$ restricted to $C.E$, $e$ is last in $C'.\mathsf{eo}$ and $C'.\mathsf{post}(e) = (R, T)$. For the induction step, assume $C \; [\mathcal{G}] \; D$ and $C' \sim (C \xrightarrow{e} (R, T))$; see Fig. 4(c). Then the decomposed execution $D'$ corresponding to $C'$ is given by $\mathsf{step}(C', e, D)$, where the function $\mathsf{step}$ in Fig. 8 mirrors the effect of the event $e$ from $C'$ in $D$ using the abstract methods. G-STEP ensures that it preserves the relation $\mathcal{G}$. Crucially, G-STEP also requires us to establish the definedness of $\mathsf{step}$ and thus the corresponding abstract method. This justifies the agreement property and execution invariants encoded by the definedness and allows us to use the conditions in Fig. 5 to complete the induction. We also require G-INIT, which establishes the base case, and G-VIS, which formulates a technical restriction on $\mathcal{V}$. Finally, the conditions in Fig. 9 allow us to use the transport specification $\mathcal{T}$ by considering only executions $C$ satisfying it.

## 6. Space Bounds and Implementation Optimality

Object states in replicated data type implementations include not only the current client-observable content, but also metadata

**Figure 9.** Proof obligations for abstract methods. Free variables are implicitly universally quantified and have the following types: $C, C' \in \mathsf{CEx}[x] \cap \mathcal{T}$, $D \in \mathsf{DEx}$, $r \in \mathsf{ReplicaID}$, $e \in \mathsf{Event}$, $(R, T) \in \mathsf{Config}$.

G-CTXT: $(C\ [\mathcal{G}]\ D\ \wedge\ e \in \mathsf{abs}(C, \mathcal{V}).E\ \wedge\ \mathsf{abs}(C, \mathcal{V}).\mathsf{repl}(e) = r)$
$\implies \mathsf{ctxt}(D(r).A, e) = \mathsf{ctxt}(\mathsf{abs}(C, \mathcal{V}), e)$

G-STEP: $(C' \sim (C \xrightarrow{e} (R, T))\ \wedge\ (C\ [\mathcal{G}]\ D))$
$\implies (\mathsf{step}(C', e, D)\!\downarrow\ \wedge\ C'\ [\mathcal{G}]\ \mathsf{step}(C', e, D))$

G-INIT: $(C.E = \{e\}\ \wedge\ C.\mathsf{pre}(e) = (\_, []))$
$\implies (\mathsf{step}(C, e, D_\emptyset)\!\downarrow\ \wedge\ C\ [\mathcal{G}]\ \mathsf{step}(C, e, D_\emptyset))$,
where $D_\emptyset$ is such that $\mathsf{dom}(D_\emptyset) = \mathsf{ReplicaID}\ \wedge$
$\forall r \in \mathsf{ReplicaID}.\ D_\emptyset(r).E = \emptyset$

G-VIS: $(e \in \mathsf{abs}(C, \mathcal{V}).E\ \wedge\ (C$ is a prefix of $C'$ under $C'.\mathsf{eo}))$
$\implies \mathsf{ctxt}(\mathsf{abs}(C, \mathcal{V}), e) = \mathsf{ctxt}(\mathsf{abs}(C', \mathcal{V}), e)$

needed for conflict resolution or masking network failures. Space taken by this metadata is a major factor determining their efficiency and feasibility. As illustrated by the OR-set in §5.3, this is especially so for state-based implementations, i.e., those that satisfy their data type specifications with respect to the visibility witness $\mathcal{V}^{\mathsf{state}}$ and the transport layer specification T-Any. We now present a general technique for proving lower bounds on this space overhead, which we use to prove optimality of four state-based implementations (we leave other implementation classes for future work; see §9). As in §5, we only consider executions over a fixed object $x$ of type $\tau$.

### 6.1 Metadata Overhead

To measure space, we need to consider how data are represented. An ***encoding*** of a set $S$ is an injective function $\mathsf{enc} : S \to \Lambda^+$, where $\Lambda$ is some suitably chosen fixed finite set of characters (left unspecified). Sometimes, we clarify the domain being encoded using a subscript: e.g., $\mathsf{enc}_{\mathbb{N}_0}(1)$. For $s \in S$, we let $\mathsf{len}_S(s)$ be the length of $\mathsf{enc}_S(s)$. The length can vary: e.g., for an integer $k$, $\mathsf{len}_{\mathbb{N}_0}(k) \in \Theta(\lg k)$. We use standard encodings (listed in [12, §C]) for return values $\mathsf{enc}_{\mathsf{Val}_\tau}$ of the data types $\tau$ we consider and assume an arbitrary but fixed encoding of object states $\mathsf{enc}_{\mathcal{D}_\tau.\Sigma}$.

To distinguish metadata from the client-observable content of the object, we assume that each data type has a special `rd` operation that returns the latter, as is the case in the examples considered so far. For a concrete execution $C \in [\![\mathcal{D}_\tau]\!]$ over the object $x$ and a read event $e \in (C.E)|_{\mathtt{rd}}$, we define $\mathsf{state}(e)$ to be the state of the object accessed at $e$: $\mathsf{state}(e) = R(x, C.\mathsf{repl}(e))$ for $(R, \_) = C.\mathsf{pre}(e)$.

We now define the metadata overhead as a ratio, by dividing the size of the object state by the size of the observable state. We then quantify the worst-case overhead by taking the maximum of this ratio over all read operations in all executions with given numbers of replicas $n$ and update operations $m$. To define the latter, we assume that each data type $\tau$ specifies a set $\mathsf{Upd}_\tau \subset \mathsf{Op}_\tau$ of update operations; for all examples in this paper $\mathsf{Upd}_\tau = \mathsf{Op}_\tau \setminus \{\mathtt{rd}\}$.

DEFINITION 11. *The **maximum metadata overhead** of an execution $C \in [\![\mathcal{D}_\tau]\!]$ of an implementation $\mathcal{D}_\tau$ is*

$$\mathsf{mmo}(\mathcal{D}_\tau, C) = \max \left\{ \frac{\mathsf{len}_{\mathcal{D}_\tau.\Sigma}(\mathsf{state}(e))}{\mathsf{len}_{\mathsf{Val}_\tau}(C.\mathsf{rval}(e))} \mid e \in (C.E)|_{\mathtt{rd}} \right\}.$$

*The **worst-case metadata overhead** of an implementation $\mathcal{D}_\tau$ over all executions with $n$ replicas and $m$ updates ($2 \le n \le m$) is*

$$\begin{aligned}\mathsf{wcmo}(\mathcal{D}_\tau, n, m) = \max\{&\mathsf{mmo}(\mathcal{D}_\tau, C) \mid C \in [\![\mathcal{D}_\tau]\!]\ \wedge \\ &n = |\{C.\mathsf{repl}(e) \mid e \in C.E\}|\ \wedge \\ &m = |\{e \in C.E \mid C.\mathsf{oper}(e) \in \mathsf{Upd}_\tau\}|\}.\end{aligned}$$

We consider only executions with $m \ge n$, since we are interested in the asymptotic overhead of executions where all replicas are mutated (i.e., perform at least one update operation).

**Figure 10.** Summary of bounds on metadata overhead for stated-based implementations, as functions of the number of replicas $n$ and updates $m$

| Type | Existing implementation | | | Any implementation |
|---|---|---|---|---|
| | algorithm | ref. | overhead | overhead |
| `ctr` | Fig. 2(b) | [32] | $\widehat{\Theta}(n)$ | $\widehat{\Omega}(n)$ |
| `orset` | Fig. 7 | [6] | $\widehat{\Theta}(n \lg m)$ | $\widehat{\Omega}(n \lg m)$ |
| | Fig. 15, [12, §A] | [32] | $\widehat{\Theta}(m \lg m)$ | |
| `intreg` | Fig. 2(c) | [32] | $\widehat{\Theta}(\lg m)^\dagger$ | $\widehat{\Omega}(\lg m)$ |
| `mvr` | Fig. 17, [12, §A] | new$^\ddagger$ | $\widehat{\Theta}(n \lg m)$ | $\widehat{\Omega}(n \lg m)$ |
| | Fig. 16, [12, §A] | [32] | $\widehat{\Theta}(n^2 \lg m)$ | |

† Assuming timestamp encoding is $O(\lg m)$, satisfied by Lamport clocks.
‡ An optimization of [32] discovered during the optimality proof.

DEFINITION 12. *Assume $\mathcal{D}_\tau$ and a positive function $f(n, m)$.*

- *$f$ is an **asymptotic upper bound** ($\mathcal{D}_\tau \in \widehat{O}(f(n, m))$) if $\sup_{n,m\to\infty}(\mathsf{wcmo}(\mathcal{D}_\tau, n, m)/f(n, m)) < \infty$, i.e.,*
$$\exists K > 0.\, \forall m \ge n \ge 2.\, \mathsf{wcmo}(\mathcal{D}_\tau, n, m) < K f(n, m);$$
- *$f$ is an **asymptotic lower bound** ($\mathcal{D}_\tau \in \widehat{\Omega}(f(n, m))$) if $\lim_{n,m\to\infty}(\mathsf{wcmo}(\mathcal{D}_\tau, n, m)/f(n, m)) \ne 0$, i.e.,*
$$\exists K > 0.\, \forall m_0 \ge n_0 \ge 2.\, \exists n \ge n_0, m \ge n_0.\ \mathsf{wcmo}(\mathcal{D}_\tau, n, m) > K f(n, m);$$
- *$f$ is an **asymptotically tight bound** ($\mathcal{D}_\tau \in \widehat{\Theta}(f(n, m))$) if it is both an upper and a lower asymptotic bound.*

Fig. 10 summarizes our results; as described in §5, we have proved all the implementations correct. Matching lower and upper bounds indicate worst-case optimality of an implementation (note that this is different from optimality in all cases). The derivation of upper bounds relies on standard techniques and is deferred to [12, §C]. We now proceed to the main challenge: how to derive lower bounds that apply to *any* implementation of $\tau$. We present proofs for `ctr` and `orset`; `intreg` and `mvr` are covered in [12, §C].

### 6.2 Experiment Families

The goal is to show that for any correct implementation $\mathcal{D}_\tau$ (i.e., such that $\mathcal{D}_\tau\ \mathsf{sat}[\mathcal{V}^{\mathsf{state}}, \mathsf{T\text{-}Any}]\ \mathcal{F}_\tau$), the object state must store some minimum amount of information. We achieve this by constructing an *experiment family*, which is a collection of executions $\mathbb{C}_\alpha$, where $\alpha \in Q$ for some index set $Q$. Each experiment contains a distinguished read event $\mathsf{e}_\alpha$. The experiments are designed in such a way that the object states $\mathsf{state}(\mathsf{e}_\alpha)$ must be distinct, which then implies a lower bound $\lg_{|\Lambda|} |Q|$ on the size of their encoding. To prove that they are distinct, we construct black-box tests that execute the methods of $\mathcal{D}_\tau$ on the states and show that the tests must produce different results for each $\mathsf{state}(\mathsf{e}_\alpha)$ provided $\mathcal{D}_\tau$ is correct. Formally, the tests induce a read-back function $\mathsf{rb}$ that satisfies $\mathsf{rb}(\mathsf{state}(\mathsf{e}_\alpha)) = \alpha$. We encapsulate the core argument in the following lemma.

DEFINITION 13. *An **experiment family** for an implementation $\mathcal{D}_\tau$ is a tuple $(Q, n, m, \mathbb{C}, \mathsf{e}, \mathsf{rb})$ where $Q$ is a finite set, $2 \le n \le m$, and for each $\alpha \in Q$, $\mathbb{C}_\alpha \in [\![\mathcal{D}_\tau]\!]$ is an execution with $n$ replicas and $m$ updates, $\mathsf{e}_\alpha \in (\mathbb{C}_\alpha.E)|_{\mathtt{rd}}$ and $\mathsf{rb} : \mathcal{D}_\tau.\Sigma \to Q$ is a function satisfying $\mathsf{rb}(\mathsf{state}(\mathsf{e}_\alpha)) = \alpha$.*

LEMMA 14. *If $(Q, n, m, \mathbb{C}, \mathsf{e}, \mathsf{rb})$ is an experiment family, then*

$$\mathsf{wcmo}(\mathcal{D}_\tau, n, m) \ge \lfloor \lg_{|\Lambda|} |Q| \rfloor \,/\, (\max_{\alpha \in Q} \mathsf{len}(\mathbb{C}_\alpha.\mathsf{rval}(\mathsf{e}_\alpha))).$$

PROOF. Since $\mathsf{rb}(\mathsf{state}(\mathsf{e}_\alpha)) = \alpha$, the states $\mathsf{state}(\mathsf{e}_\alpha)$ are pairwise distinct and so are their encodings $\mathsf{enc}(\mathsf{state}(\mathsf{e}_\alpha))$. Since there are fewer than $|Q|$ strings of length strictly less than $\lfloor \lg_{|\Lambda|} |Q| \rfloor$, for some $\alpha \in Q$ we have $\mathsf{len}(\mathsf{enc}(\mathsf{state}(\mathbf{e}_\alpha))) \geq \lfloor \lg_{|\Lambda|} |Q| \rfloor$. Then

$$\mathsf{wcmo}(\mathcal{D}_\tau, n, m) \geq \mathsf{mmo}(\mathcal{D}_\tau, \mathbb{C}_\alpha) \geq \frac{\mathsf{len}(\mathsf{state}(\mathbf{e}_\alpha))}{\mathsf{len}(\mathbb{C}_\alpha.\mathsf{rval}(\mathbf{e}_\alpha))} \geq \frac{\lfloor \lg_{|\Lambda|} |Q| \rfloor}{\max_{\alpha' \in Q} \mathsf{len}(\mathbb{C}_{\alpha'}.\mathsf{rval}(\mathbf{e}_{\alpha'}))}. \quad \square$$

To apply this lemma to the best effect, we need to find experiment families with $|Q|$ as large as possible and $\mathsf{len}(\mathbb{C}_{\alpha'}.\mathsf{rval}(\mathbf{e}_{\alpha'}))$ as small as possible. Finding such families is challenging, as there is no systematic way to derive them. We relied on intuitions about "which situations force replicas to store a lot of information" when searching for experiment families.

**Driver programs.** We define experiment families using ***driver programs*** (e.g., see Fig. 11). These are written in imperative pseudocode and use traditional constructs like loops and conditionals. As they execute, they construct concrete executions of the data type library $[\tau \mapsto \mathcal{D}_\tau]$ by means of the following instructions, each of which triggers a uniquely-determined transition from Fig. 3:

| | |
|---|---|
| $\mathsf{do}_r\ o\ ^t$ | do operation $o$ on $x$ at replica $r$ with timestamp $t$ |
| $u \leftarrow \mathsf{do}_r\ o\ ^t$ | same, but assign the return value to $u$ |
| $\mathsf{send}_r(mid)$ | send a message for $x$ with identifier $mid$ at $r$ |
| $\mathsf{receive}_r(mid)$ | receive the message $mid$ at replica $r$ |

Programs explicitly supply timestamps for do and message identifiers for send and receive. We require that they do this correctly, e.g., respect uniqueness of timestamps. When a driver program terminates, it may produce a return value. For a program $P$, an implementation $\mathcal{D}_\tau$, and a configuration $(R, T)$, we let $\mathsf{exec}(\mathcal{D}_\tau, (R, T), P)$ be the concrete execution of the data type library $[\tau \mapsto \mathcal{D}_\tau]$ starting in $(R, T)$ that results from running $P$; we define $\mathsf{result}(\mathcal{D}_\tau, (R, T), P)$ as the return value of $P$ in this run.

### 6.3 Lower Bound for State-Based Counter (ctr)

THEOREM 15. *If* $\mathcal{D}_{\mathtt{ctr}}$ $\mathsf{sat}[\mathcal{V}^{\mathsf{state}}, \mathsf{T\text{-}Any}]$ $\mathcal{F}_{\mathtt{ctr}}$, *then* $\mathcal{D}_{\mathtt{ctr}}$ *is* $\widehat{\Omega}(n)$.

We start by formulating a suitable experiment family.

LEMMA 16. *If* $\mathcal{D}_{\mathtt{ctr}}$ $\mathsf{sat}[\mathcal{V}^{\mathsf{state}}, \mathsf{T\text{-}Any}]$ $\mathcal{F}_{\mathtt{ctr}}$, $n \geq 2$ *and* $m \geq n$ *is a multiple of* $(n-1)$, *then tuple* $(Q, n, m, \mathbb{C}, \mathsf{e}, \mathsf{rb})$ *as defined in the left column of Fig. 11 is an experiment family.*

The idea of the experiments is to force replica 1 to remember one number for each of the other replicas in the system, which then introduces an overhead proportional to $n$; cf. the implementation in Fig. 2(b). We show one experiment in Fig. 12. All experiments start with a common initialization phase, defined by $init$, where each of the replicas $2..n$ performs $m/(n-1)$ increments and sends a message after each increment. All messages remain undelivered until the second phase, defined by $exp(\alpha)$. There replica 1 receives exactly one message from each replica $r = 2..n$, selected using $\alpha(r)$. An experiment concludes with the read $\mathbf{e}_\alpha$ on the first replica.

The read-back works by performing separate tests for each of the replicas $r = 2..n$, defined by $test(r)$. For example, to determine which message was sent by replica 2 during the experiment in Fig. 12, the program $test(2)$: reads the counter value at replica 1, getting 12; delivers the final message by replica 2 to it; and reads the counter value at replica 1 again, getting 14. By observing the difference, the program can determine the message sent during the experiment: $\alpha(2) = 5 - (14 - 12) = 3$.

PROOF OF LEMMA 16. The only nontrivial obligation is to prove $\mathsf{rb}(\mathsf{state}(\mathbf{e}_\alpha)) = \alpha$. Let $(R_\alpha, T_\alpha) = \mathsf{final}(\mathbb{C}_\alpha)$. Then

$$\begin{aligned} \alpha(r) &\overset{(i)}{=} \mathsf{result}(\mathcal{D}_{\mathtt{ctr}}, (R_0, T_0), (init; exp(\alpha); test(r))) \\ &= \mathsf{result}(\mathcal{D}_{\mathtt{ctr}}, (R_\alpha, T_\alpha), test(r)) \\ &\overset{(ii)}{=} \mathsf{result}(\mathcal{D}_{\mathtt{ctr}}, (R_{init}[(x,1) \mapsto R_\alpha(x,1)], T_{init}), test(r)) \\ &= \mathsf{rb}(R_\alpha(x,1))(r) = \mathsf{rb}(\mathsf{state}(\mathbf{e}_\alpha))(r), \end{aligned}$$

**Figure 11.** Experiment families $(Q, n, m, \mathbb{C}, \mathbf{e}, \mathsf{rb})$ used in the proofs of Theorem 15 (`ctr`) and Theorem 17 (`orset`)

| `ctr` | `orset` |
|---|---|
| Conditions on $n, m$ (number of replicas/updates) | |
| $m \geq n \geq 2$<br>$m \mod (n-1) = 0$ | $m \geq n \geq 2$<br>$(m-1) \mod (n-1) = 0$ |
| Index set $Q$ | |
| $Q = ([2..n] \to [1..\frac{m}{n-1}])$ | $Q = ([2..n] \to [1..\frac{m-1}{n-1}])$ |
| Family size $\|Q\|$ | |
| $\|Q\| = (\frac{m}{n-1})^{n-1}$ | $\|Q\| = (\frac{m-1}{n-1})^{n-1}$ |
| Driver programs | |
| **procedure** $init$<br>**for all** $r \in [2..n]$<br>**for all** $i \in [1..\frac{m}{n-1}]$<br>$\mathsf{do}_r$ `inc` $^{rm+i}$<br>$\mathsf{send}_r(mid_{r,i})$<br>**procedure** $exp(\alpha)$<br>**for all** $r \in [2..n]$<br>$\mathsf{receive}_1(mid_{r,\alpha(r)})$<br>$\mathsf{do}_1$ `rd` $^{(n+2)m}$ // read $\mathbf{e}_\alpha$<br>**procedure** $test(r)$<br>$u \leftarrow \mathsf{do}_1$ `rd` $^{(n+3)m}$<br>$\mathsf{receive}_1(mid_{r,\frac{m}{n-1}})$<br>$u' \leftarrow \mathsf{do}_1$ `rd` $^{(n+4)m}$<br>**return** $\frac{m}{n-1} - (u' - u)$ | **procedure** $init$<br>**for all** $r \in [2..n]$<br>**for all** $i \in [1..\frac{m-1}{n-1}]$<br>$\mathsf{do}_r$ `add(0)` $^{rm+i}$<br>$\mathsf{send}_r(mid_{r,i})$<br>**procedure** $exp(\alpha)$<br>**for all** $r \in [2..n]$<br>$\mathsf{receive}_1(mid_{r,\alpha(r)})$<br>$\mathsf{do}_1$ `remove(0)` $^{(n+2)m}$<br>$\mathsf{do}_1$ `rd` $^{(n+3)m}$ // read $\mathbf{e}_\alpha$<br>**procedure** $test(r)$<br>**for all** $i \in [1..(\frac{m-1}{n-1})]$<br>$\mathsf{receive}_1(mid_{r,i})$<br>$u \leftarrow \mathsf{do}_1$ `rd` $^{(n+4)m+i}$<br>**if** $0 \in u$<br>**return** $i - 1$<br>**return** $\frac{m-1}{n-1}$ |
| Definition of executions $\mathbb{C}_\alpha$ | |
| $\mathbb{C}_\alpha = \mathsf{exec}(\mathcal{D}_\tau, (R_0, T_0), init; exp(\alpha))$<br>where $(R_0, T_0) = ([x \mapsto \mathcal{D}_\tau.\vec{\sigma}_0], \emptyset)$ | |
| Definition of read-back function $\mathsf{rb} : \mathcal{D}_\tau.\Sigma \to Q$ | |
| $\mathsf{rb}(\sigma) = \lambda r : [2..n].\mathsf{result}(\mathcal{D}_\tau, (R_{init}[(x,1) \mapsto \sigma], T_{init}), test(r))$<br>where $(R_{init}, T_{init}) = \mathsf{post}(\mathsf{exec}(\mathcal{D}_\tau, (R_0, T_0), init))$ | |

**Figure 12.** Example experiment ($n = 4$ and $m = 15$) and test for `ctr`. Gray dashed lines represent the configuration $(R_{init}[(x,1) \mapsto R_\alpha(x,1)], T_{init})$ where the $test$ driver program is applied.

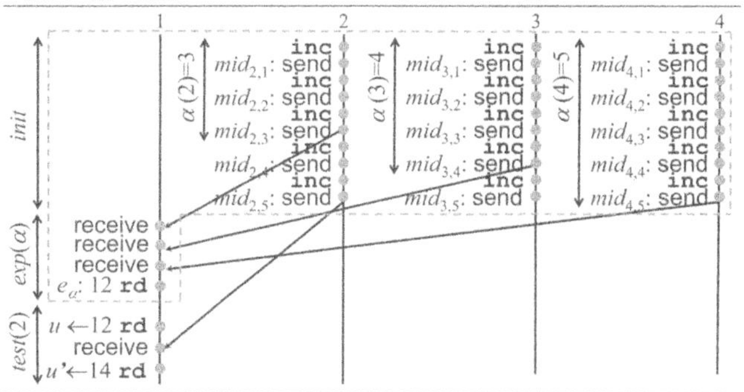


where:

(i) This is due to $\mathcal{D}_{\mathtt{ctr}}$ $\mathsf{sat}[\mathcal{V}^{\mathsf{state}}, \mathsf{T\text{-}Any}]$ $\mathcal{F}_{\mathtt{ctr}}$, as we explained informally above. Let

$$C'_\alpha = \mathsf{exec}(\mathcal{D}_{\mathtt{ctr}}, (R_0, T_0), (init; exp(\alpha); test(r))).$$

Then the operation context in $\mathsf{abs}(C'_\alpha, \mathcal{V}^{\mathsf{state}})$ of the first read in $test(r)$ contains $\sum_{r=2}^{n} \alpha(r)$ increments, while that of the second read contains $(m/(n-1)) - \alpha(r)$ more increments.

(ii) We have $T_\alpha = T_{init}$ because $exp(\alpha)$ does not send any messages. Also, $R_\alpha$ and $R_{init}[(x,1) \mapsto R_\alpha(x,1)]$ can differ only in the states of the replicas $2..n$. These cannot influence the run of $test(r)$, since it performs events on replica 1 only. □

PROOF OF THEOREM 15. Given $n_0, m_0$, we pick $n = n_0$ and some $m \geq n_0$ such that $m$ is a multiple of $(n-1)$ and $m \geq n^2$. Take the experiment family $(Q, n, m, \mathbb{C}, \mathsf{e}, \mathsf{rb})$ given by Lemma 16. Then for any $\alpha$, $\mathbb{C}_\alpha.\mathsf{rval}(\mathsf{e}_\alpha)$ is at most the total number of increments $m$ in $\mathbb{C}_\alpha$. Using Lemma 14 and $m \geq n^2$, for some constants $K_1, K_2, K_3, K$ independent from $n_0, m_0$ we get:

$$\mathsf{wcmo}(\mathcal{D}_{\mathtt{ctr}}, n, m) \geq \lfloor \lg_{|\Lambda|} |Q| \rfloor / (\max_{\alpha \in Q} \mathsf{len}(\mathbb{C}_\alpha.\mathsf{rval}(\mathsf{e}_\alpha))) \geq$$

$$K_1 \frac{\lg_{|\Lambda|} (\frac{m}{n-1})^{n-1}}{\mathsf{len}_{\mathbb{N}_0}(m)} \geq K_2 \frac{n \lg(m/n)}{\lg m} \geq K_3 \frac{n \lg \sqrt{m}}{\lg m} \geq Kn. \quad \square$$

### 6.4 Lower Bound for State-Based OR-Set (orset)

THEOREM 17. *If* $\mathcal{D}_{\mathtt{orset}}$ $\mathsf{sat}[\mathcal{V}^{\mathsf{state}}, \mathsf{T\text{-}Any}]$ $\mathcal{F}_{\mathtt{orset}}$*, then* $\mathcal{D}_{\mathtt{orset}}$ *is* $\widehat{\Omega}(n \lg m)$.

LEMMA 18. *If* $\mathcal{D}_{\mathtt{orset}}$ $\mathsf{sat}[\mathcal{V}^{\mathsf{state}}, \mathsf{T\text{-}Any}]$ $\mathcal{F}_{\mathtt{orset}}$, $n \geq 2$ *and* $m \geq n$ *is such that* $(m-1)$ *is a multiple of* $(n-1)$*, then the tuple* $(Q, n, m, \mathbb{C}, \mathsf{e}, \mathsf{rb})$ *on the right in Fig. 11 is an experiment family.*

The proof is the same as that of Lemma 16, except for obligation (i). We therefore give only informal explanations.

The main idea of the experiments defined in the lemma is to force replica 1 to remember element instances even after they have been removed at that replica; cf. our explanation of the challenges of implementing the OR-set from §5.3. The experiments follow a similar pattern to those for `ctr`, but use different operations. In the common $init$ phase, each replica $2..n$ performs $\frac{m-1}{n-1}$ operations adding a designated element 0, which are interleaved with sending messages. In the experiment phase $exp(\alpha)$, one message from each replica $r = 2..n$, selected by $\alpha(r)$, is delivered to replica 1. At the end of execution, replica 1 removes 0 from the set and performs the read $\mathsf{e}_\alpha$. The return value of this read is always the empty set.

To perform the read-back of $\alpha(r)$ for $r = 2..n$, $test(r)$ delivers all messages by replica $r$ to replica 1 in the order they were sent and, after each such delivery, checks if replica 1 now reports the element 0 as part of the set. From $\mathcal{D}_{\mathtt{orset}}$ $\mathsf{sat}[\mathcal{V}^{\mathsf{state}}, \mathsf{T\text{-}Any}]$ $\mathcal{F}_{\mathtt{orset}}$ and the definition (5) of $\mathcal{F}_{\mathtt{orset}}$, we get that exactly the first $\alpha(r)$ such deliveries will have no effect on the contents of the set: the respective add operations have already been observed by the remove operation that replica 1 performed in the experiment phase. Thus, if 0 appears in the set right after delivering the $i$-th message of replica $r$, then $\alpha(r) = i-1$, and if 0 does not appear by the time the loop is finished, then $\alpha(r) = (m-1)/(n-1)$.

PROOF OF THEOREM 17. Given $n_0, m_0$, we pick $n = n_0$ and some $m \geq n_0$ such that $(m-1)$ is a multiple of $(n-1)$ and $m \geq n^2$. Take the experiment family $(Q, n, m, \mathbb{C}, \mathsf{e}, \mathsf{rb})$ given by Lemma 18. For any $\alpha \in Q$, $\mathbb{C}_\alpha.\mathsf{rval}(\mathsf{e}_\alpha) = \emptyset$, which can be encoded with a constant length. Using Lemma 14 and $m \geq n^2$, for some constants $K_1, K_2, K$ we get:

$$\mathsf{wcmo}(\mathcal{D}_{\mathtt{orset}}, n, m) \geq \lfloor \lg_{|\Lambda|} |Q| \rfloor \, / \, (\max_{\alpha \in Q} \mathsf{len}(\mathbb{C}_\alpha.\mathsf{rval}(\mathsf{e}_\alpha)))$$

$$\geq K_1 n \lg(m/n) \geq K_2 n \lg \sqrt{m} \geq K n \lg m. \quad \square$$

## 7. Store Correctness and Consistency Axioms

Recall that we define a replicated store by a data type library $\mathbb{D}$ and a transport layer specification $\mathcal{T}$ (§4), and we specify its behavior by a function $\mathbb{F}$ from types $\tau \in \mathsf{dom}(\mathbb{D})$ to data type specifications and a set of consistency axioms (§3). The axioms are just constraints over abstract executions, such as those shown in Fig. 13; from now on we denote their sets by $\mathsf{X}$. So far we have concentrated on single data type specifications $\mathbb{F}(\tau)$ and their correspondence to implementations $\mathbb{D}(\tau)$, as stated by Def. 7. In this section we consider consistency axioms and formulate the notion of correctness of the whole store $(\mathbb{D}, \mathcal{T})$ with respect to its specification $(\mathbb{F}, \mathsf{X})$.

Our first goal is to lift the statement of correctness given by Def. 7 to a store $(\mathbb{D}, \mathcal{T})$ with multiple objects of different data types. To this end, we assume a function $\mathbb{V}$ mapping each type $\tau \in \mathsf{dom}(\mathbb{D})$ to its visibility witness $\mathcal{V}$. This allows us to construct the visibility relation for a concrete execution $C \in [\![\mathbb{D}]\!] \cap \mathcal{T}$ by applying $\mathbb{V}(\tau)$ to its projection onto the events on every object of type $\tau$:

$$\mathsf{witness}(\mathbb{V}) \;=\; \lambda C. \bigcup \{\mathbb{V}(\mathsf{type}(x))(C|_x) \mid x \in \mathsf{Obj}\},$$

where $\cdot|_x$ projects to events over $x$. Then the correctness of every separate data type $\tau$ in the store with respect to $\mathbb{F}(\tau)$ according to Def. 7 automatically ensures that the behavior of the whole store is consistent with $\mathbb{F}$ in the sense of Def. 5.

PROPOSITION 19. $(\forall \tau \in \mathsf{dom}(\mathbb{D}).\ \mathbb{D}(\tau)\ \mathsf{sat}[\mathbb{V}(\tau), \mathcal{T}]\ \mathbb{F}(\tau)) \implies (\forall C \in [\![\mathbb{D}]\!] \cap \mathcal{T}.\ \mathsf{abs}(C, \mathsf{witness}(\mathbb{V})) \models \mathbb{F})$.

This motivates the following definition of store correctness. Let us write $A \models \mathsf{X}$ when the abstract execution $A$ satisfies the axioms $\mathsf{X}$.

DEFINITION 20. *A store* $(\mathbb{D}, \mathcal{T})$ *is* ***correct*** *with respect to a specification* $(\mathbb{F}, \mathsf{X})$*, if for some* $\mathbb{V}$:

*(i)* $\forall \tau \in \mathsf{dom}(\mathbb{D}).\ (\mathbb{D}(\tau)\ \mathsf{sat}[\mathbb{V}(\tau), \mathcal{T}]\ \mathbb{F}(\tau))$*; and*
*(ii)* $\forall C \in [\![\mathbb{D}]\!] \cap \mathcal{T}.\ (\mathsf{abs}(C, \mathsf{witness}(\mathbb{V})) \models \mathsf{X})$.

We showed how to discharge (i) in §5. The validity of axioms $\mathsf{X}$ required by (ii) most often depends on the transport layer specification $\mathcal{T}$: e.g., to disallow the anomaly (2) from §1, $\mathcal{T}$ needs to provide guarantees on how messages pertaining to different objects are delivered. However, data type implementations can also enforce axioms by putting enough information into messages: e.g., implementations correct with respect to $\mathcal{V}^{\mathsf{state}}$ from §4 ensure that $\mathsf{vis}$ is transitive regardless of the behavior of the transport layer. Fortunately, to establish (ii) in practice, we do not need to consider the internals of data type implementations in $\mathbb{D}$—just knowing the visibility witnesses used in the statements of their correctness is enough, as formulated in the following definition.

DEFINITION 21. *A set* $W$ *of visibility witnesses and a transport layer specification* $\mathcal{T}$ ***validate*** *axioms* $\mathsf{X}$*, if*

$$\forall C, \mathbb{V}.\ (C \in \mathcal{T}) \wedge (\{\mathbb{V}(\tau) \mid \tau \in \mathsf{dom}(\mathbb{V})\} \subseteq W) \implies (\mathsf{abs}(C, \mathsf{witness}(\mathbb{V})) \models \mathsf{X}).$$

Since visibility witnesses are common to wide classes of data types (e.g., state- or op-based), our proofs of the validity of axioms will not have to be redone if we add new data type implementations to the store from a class already considered.

We next present axioms formalizing several variants of eventual consistency used in replicated stores (Fig. 13 and 14) and $W$ and $\mathcal{T}$ that validate them. We then use this as a basis for discussing connections with weak shared-memory models. Due to space constraints, we defer technical details and proofs to [12, §D].

**Basic eventual consistency.** EVENTUAL and THINAIR define a weak form of eventual consistency. EVENTUAL ensures that an event cannot be invisible to infinitely many other events on the same object and thus implies (1) from §1: informally, if updates stop, then reads at all replicas will eventually see all updates and will return the same values (§3.2). However, EVENTUAL is stronger than quiescent consistency: the latter does not provide any guarantees at all for executions with infinitely many updates to the store, whereas our specification implies that the return values are computed according to $\mathbb{F}(\tau)$ using increasingly up-to-date view of the store state. We formalize these relationships in [12, §D].

THINAIR prohibits values from appearing "out-of-thin-air" [28], like 42 in Fig. 14(a) (recall that registers are initialized to 0). Cycles in $\mathsf{ro} \cup \mathsf{vis}$ that lead to out-of-thin-airs usually arise

**Figure 13.** A selection of consistency axioms over an execution $(E, \mathsf{repl}, \mathsf{obj}, \mathsf{oper}, \mathsf{rval}, \mathsf{ro}, \mathsf{vis}, \mathsf{ar})$

**Auxiliary relations**

$\mathsf{sameobj}(e, f) \iff \mathsf{obj}(e) = \mathsf{obj}(f)$

Per-object causality (aka happens-before) order:
$\mathsf{hbo} = ((\mathsf{ro} \cap \mathsf{sameobj}) \cup \mathsf{vis})^+$

Causality (aka happens-before) order: $\mathsf{hb} = (\mathsf{ro} \cup \mathsf{vis})^+$

**Axioms**

EVENTUAL:
$\forall e \in E. \neg(\exists \text{ infinitely many } f \in E. \mathsf{sameobj}(e, f) \wedge \neg(e \xrightarrow{\mathsf{vis}} f))$

THINAIR: $\mathsf{ro} \cup \mathsf{vis}$ is acyclic

POCV (Per-Object Causal Visibility): $\mathsf{hbo} \subseteq \mathsf{vis}$

POCA (Per-Object Causal Arbitration): $\mathsf{hbo} \subseteq \mathsf{ar}$

COCV (Cross-Object Causal Visibility): $(\mathsf{hb} \cap \mathsf{sameobj}) \subseteq \mathsf{vis}$

COCA (Cross-Object Causal Arbitration): $\mathsf{hb} \cup \mathsf{ar}$ is acyclic

**Figure 14.** Anomalies allowed or disallowed by different axioms

(a) Disallowed by THINAIR:

$x, y$ : `intreg`

| | |
|---|---|
| $i = x$.`rd` | $j = y$.`rd` |
| $y$.`wr`$(i)$ | $x$.`wr`$(j)$ |

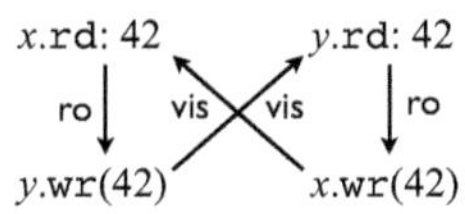


(b) Disallowed by POCV:

$x$ : `orset`

| | | |
|---|---|---|
| $x$.`add`(1) | $i = x$.`rd` | $j = x$.`rd` |
| $x$.`add`(2) | $x$.`add`(3) | |

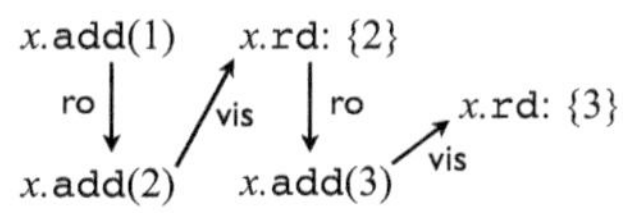


(c) Allowed by COCV and COCA:

$x, y$ : `intreg`

| | |
|---|---|
| $x$.`wr`(1) | $y$.`wr`(1) |
| $i = y$.`rd` | $j = x$.`rd` |

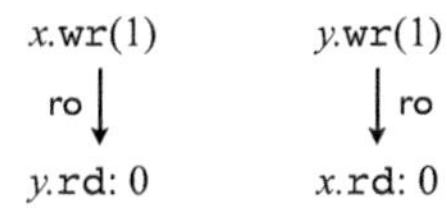


from effects of speculative computations, which are done by some older replicated stores [36].

THINAIR is validated by $\{\mathcal{V}^{\mathsf{state}}, \mathcal{V}^{\mathsf{op}}\}$ and T-Any, and EVENTUAL by $\{\mathcal{V}^{\mathsf{state}}, \mathcal{V}^{\mathsf{op}}\}$ and the following condition on $C$ ensuring that every message is eventually delivered to all other replicas and every operation is followed by a message generation:

$$(\forall e \in C.E. \forall r, r'. C.\mathsf{act}(e) = \mathsf{send} \wedge C.\mathsf{repl}(e) = r \wedge r \neq r' \implies \exists f. C.\mathsf{repl}(f) = r' \wedge e \xrightarrow{\mathsf{del}(C)} f) \wedge$$
$$(\forall e \in C.E. C.\mathsf{act}(e) = \mathsf{do} \implies \exists f. \mathsf{act}(f) = \mathsf{send} \wedge e \xrightarrow{\mathsf{roo}(C)} f),$$

where $\mathsf{roo}(C)$ is $\mathsf{ro}(C)$ projected to events on the same object.

**Causality guarantees.** Many replicated stores achieve availability and partition tolerance while providing stronger guarantees, which we formalize by the other axioms in Fig. 13. We call an execution ***per-object***, respectively, ***cross-object causally consistent***, if it is eventually consistent (as per above) and satisfies the axioms POCV and POCA, respectively, COCV and COCA. POCV guarantees that an operation sees all operations connected to it by a causal chain of events on the same object; COCV also considers causal chains via different objects. Thus, POCV disallows the execution in Fig. 14(b), and COCV the one in §3.1, corresponding to (2) from §1. POCA and COCA similarly require arbitration to be consistent with causality. The axioms highlight the principle of formalizing stronger consistency models: including more edges into vis and ar, so that clients have more up-to-date information.

Cross-object causal consistency is implemented by, e.g., COPS [27] and Gemini [23]. It is weaker than strong consistency, as it allows reading stale data. For example, it allows the execution in Fig. 14(c), where both reads fetch the initial value of the register, despite writes to it by the other replica. It is easy to check that this outcome cannot be produced by any interleaving of the events at the two replicas, and is thus not strongly consistent.

An interesting feature of per-object causal consistency is that state-based data types ensure most of it just by the definition of $\mathcal{V}^{\mathsf{state}}$: POCV is validated by $\{\mathcal{V}^{\mathsf{state}}\}$ and T-Any. If the witness set is $\{\mathcal{V}^{\mathsf{state}}, \mathcal{V}^{\mathsf{op}}\}$, then we need $\mathcal{T}$ to guarantee the following: informally, if a send event $e$ and another event $f$ are connected by a causal chain of events on the same object, then the message created by $e$ is delivered to $C.\mathsf{repl}(f)$ by the time $f$ is done. POCA is validated by $\{\mathcal{V}^{\mathsf{state}}, \mathcal{V}^{\mathsf{op}}\}$ and the transport layer specification $(\mathsf{roo}(C) \cup \mathsf{del}(C))^+|_{\mathsf{do}} \subseteq \mathsf{ar}(C)$. This states that timestamps of events on every object behave like a Lamport clock [22]. Conditions for COCV and COCA are similar.

There also exist consistency levels in between basic eventual consistency and per-object causal consistency, defined using so-called ***session guarantees*** [35]. We cover them in [12, §D].

**Comparison with shared-memory consistency models.** Interestingly, the specializations of the consistency levels defined by the axioms in Fig. 13 to the type `intreg` of LWW-registers are very close to those adopted by the memory model in the 2011 C and C++ standards [5]. Thus, POCA and POCV define the semantics of the fragment of C/C++ restricted to so-called *relaxed* operations; there this semantics is defined using *coherence* axioms, which are analogous to session guarantees [35]. COCV and COCA are close to the semantics of C/C++ restricted to *release-acquire* operations. However, C/C++ does not have an analog of EVENTUAL and does not validate THINAIR, since it makes the effects of speculations visible to the programmer [4]. We formalize the correspondence to C/C++ in [12, §D]. In the future, this correspondence may open the door to applying technology developed for shared-memory models to eventually consistent systems; promising directions include model checking [3, 9], automatic inference of required consistency levels [26] and compositional reasoning [4].

## 8. Related Work

For a comprehensive overview of replicated data type research we refer the reader to Shapiro et al. [32]. Most papers proposing new data type implementations [6, 31–33] do not provide their formal declarative specifications, save for the expected property (1) of quiescent consistency or first specification attempts for sets [6, 7]. Formalizations of eventual consistency have either expressed quiescent consistency [8] or gave low-level operational specifications [17].

An exception is the work of Burckhardt et al. [10, 13], who proposed an axiomatic model of causal eventual consistency based on visibility and arbitration relations and an operational model based on revision diagrams. Their store specification does not provide customizable consistency guarantees, and their data type specifications are limited to the sequential $\mathcal{S}$ construction from §3.2, which cannot express advanced conflict resolution used by the multi-value register, the OR-set and many other data types [32]. More significantly, their operational model does not support general op- or state-based implementations, and is thus not suited for studying the correctness or optimality of these commonly used patterns.

Simulation relations have been applied to verify the correctness of sequential [25] and shared-memory concurrent data type implementations [24]. We take this approach to the more complex setting of a replicated store, where the simulation needs to take into account multiple object copies and messages and associate them with structures on events, rather than single abstract states. This poses technical challenges not considered by prior work, which we address by our novel notion of replication-aware simulations.

The distributed computing community has established a number of asymptotic lower bounds on the complexity of implementing certain distributed or concurrent abstractions, including one-shot timestamp objects [20] and counting protocols [15, 30]. These works have considered either programming models or metrics significantly different from ours. An exception is the work of Charron-Bost [14], who proved that the size of vector clocks [29] is optimal to represent the happens-before relation of a computation (similar to the visibility relation in our model). Specifications of `mvr` and `orset` rely on visibility; however, Charron-Bost's result does not directly translate into a lower bound on their implementation complexity, since a specification may not require complete knowledge about the relation and an implementation may represent it in an arbitrary manner, not necessarily using a vector.

## 9. Conclusion and Future Work

We have presented a comprehensive theoretical toolkit to advance the study of replicated eventually consistent stores, by proposing methods for (1) specifying the semantics of replicated data types and stores abstractly, (2) verifying implementations of replicated data types, and (3) proving that such implementations have optimal metadata overhead. By proving both correctness and optimality of four nontrivial data type implementations, we have demonstrated that our methods can indeed be productively applied to the kinds of patterns used by practitioners and researchers in this area.

Although our work marks a big step forward, it is only a beginning, and creates plenty of opportunities for future research. We have already made the first steps in extending our specification framework with more features, such as mixtures of consistency levels [23] and transactions [34, 37]; see [11]. In the future we would also like to study more data types, such as lists used for collaborative editing [32], and to investigate metadata bounds for data type implementations other than state-based ones, including more detailed overhead metrics capturing optimizations invisible to the worst-case overhead analysis. Even though our execution model for replicated stores follows the one used by replicated data type designers [33], there are opportunities for bringing it closer to actual implementations. Thus, we would like to verify the algorithms used by store implementations [27, 34, 37] that our semantics abstracts from. This includes fail-over and session migration protocols, which permit clients to interact with multiple physical replicas, while being provided the illusion of a single virtual replica.

Finally, by bringing together prior work on shared-memory models and data replication, we wish to promote an exchange of ideas and results between the research communities of programming languages and verification on one side and distributed systems on the other.

**Acknowledgements.** We thank Hagit Attiya, Anindya Banerjee, Carlos Baquero, Lindsey Kuper and Marc Shapiro for comments that helped improve the paper. Gotsman was supported by the EU FET project ADVENT, and Yang by EPSRC.

## References

[1] Riak key-value store. http://basho.com/products/riak-overview/.

[2] S. V. Adve and K. Gharachorloo. Shared memory consistency models: A tutorial. *Computer*, 29(12), 1996.

[3] J. Alglave, D. Kroening, V. Nimal, and M. Tautschnig. Software verification for weak memory via program transformation. In *ESOP*, 2013.

[4] M. Batty, M. Dodds, and A. Gotsman. Library abstraction for C/C++ concurrency. In *POPL*, 2013.

[5] M. Batty, S. Owens, S. Sarkar, P. Sewell, and T. Weber. Mathematizing C++ concurrency. In *POPL*, 2011.

[6] A. Bieniusa, M. Zawirski, N. Preguiça, M. Shapiro, C. Baquero, V. Balegas, and S. Duarte. An optimized conflict-free replicated set. Technical Report 8083, INRIA, 2012.

[7] A. Bieniusa, M. Zawirski, N. M. Preguiça, M. Shapiro, C. Baquero, V. Balegas, and S. Duarte. Brief announcement: Semantics of eventually consistent replicated sets. In *DISC*, 2012.

[8] A.-M. Bosneag and M. Brockmeyer. A formal model for eventual consistency semantics. In *IASTED PDCS*, 2002.

[9] S. Burckhardt, R. Alur, and M. M. K. Martin. Checkfence: checking consistency of concurrent data types on relaxed memory models. In *PLDI*, 2007.

[10] S. Burckhardt, M. Fähndrich, D. Leijen, and B. P. Wood. Cloud types for eventual consistency. In *ECOOP*, 2012.

[11] S. Burckhardt, A. Gotsman, and H. Yang. Understanding eventual consistency. Technical Report MSR-TR-2013-39, Microsoft Research, 2013.

[12] S. Burckhardt, A. Gotsman, H. Yang, and M. Zawirski. Replicated data types: specification, verification, optimality (extended version), 2013. http://research.microsoft.com/apps/pubs/?id=201602.

[13] S. Burckhardt, D. Leijen, M. Fähndrich, and M. Sagiv. Eventually consistent transactions. In *ESOP*, 2012.

[14] B. Charron-Bost. Concerning the size of logical clocks in distributed systems. *Information Processing Letters*, 39(1), 1991.

[15] J.-Y. Chen and G. Pandurangan. Optimal gossip-based aggregate computation. In *SPAA*, 2010.

[16] N. Conway, R. Marczak, P. Alvaro, J. M. Hellerstein, and D. Maier. Logic and lattices for distributed programming. In *SOCC*, 2012.

[17] A. Fekete, D. Gupta, V. Luchangco, N. Lynch, and A. Shvartsman. Eventually-serializable data services. In *PODC*, 1996.

[18] G. DeCandia et al. Dynamo: Amazon's highly available key-value store. In *SOSP*, 2007.

[19] S. Gilbert and N. Lynch. Brewer's conjecture and the feasibility of consistent, available, partition-tolerant web services. *SIGACT News*, 33(2), 2002.

[20] M. Helmi, L. Higham, E. Pacheco, and P. Woelfel. The space complexity of long-lived and one-shot timestamp implementations. In *PODC*, 2011.

[21] C. A. R. Hoare. Proof of correctness of data representations. *Acta Inf.*, 1, 1972.

[22] L. Lamport. Time, clocks, and the ordering of events in a distributed system. *Commun. ACM*, 21(7), 1978.

[23] C. Li, D. Porto, A. Clement, R. Rodrigues, N. Preguiça, and J. Gehrke. Making geo-replicated systems fast if possible, consistent when necessary. In *OSDI*, 2012.

[24] H. Liang, X. Feng, and M. Fu. A rely-guarantee-based simulation for verifying concurrent program transformations. In *POPL*, 2012.

[25] B. Liskov and S. Zilles. Programming with abstract data types. In *ACM Symposium on Very High Level Languages*, 1974.

[26] F. Liu, N. Nedev, N. Prisadnikov, M. T. Vechev, and E. Yahav. Dynamic synthesis for relaxed memory models. In *PLDI*, 2012.

[27] W. Lloyd, M. J. Freedman, M. Kaminsky, and D. G. Andersen. Don't settle for eventual: scalable causal consistency for wide-area storage with COPS. In *SOSP*, 2011.

[28] J. Manson, W. Pugh, and S. V. Adve. The Java memory model. In *POPL*, 2005.

[29] F. Mattern. Virtual time and global states of distributed systems. *Parallel and Distributed Algorithms*, 1989.

[30] S. Moran, G. Taubenfeld, and I. Yadin. Concurrent counting. In *PODC*, 1992.

[31] H.-G. Roh, M. Jeon, J.-S. Kim, and J. Lee. Replicated abstract data types: Building blocks for collaborative applications. *J. Parallel Distrib. Comput.*, 71(3), 2011.

[32] M. Shapiro, N. Preguiça, C. Baquero, and M. Zawirski. A comprehensive study of Convergent and Commutative Replicated Data Types. Technical Report 7506, INRIA, 2011.

[33] M. Shapiro, N. M. Preguiça, C. Baquero, and M. Zawirski. Conflict-free replicated data types. In *SSS*, 2011.

[34] Y. Sovran, R. Power, M. K. Aguilera, and J. Li. Transactional storage for geo-replicated systems. In *SOSP*, 2011.

[35] D. B. Terry, A. J. Demers, K. Petersen, M. Spreitzer, M. Theimer, and B. W. Welch. Session guarantees for weakly consistent replicated data. In *PDIS*, 1994.

[36] D. B. Terry, M. M. Theimer, K. Petersen, A. J. Demers, M. J. Spreitzer, and C. H. Hauser. Managing update conflicts in Bayou, a weakly connected replicated storage system. In *SOSP*, 1995.

[37] M. Zawirski, A. Bieniusa, V. Balegas, S. Duarte, C. Baquero, M. Shapiro, and N. Preguiça. SwiftCloud: Fault-tolerant geo-replication integrated all the way to the client machine. Technical Report 8347, INRIA, 2013.

# Verifying Eventual Consistency of Optimistic Replication Systems

Ahmed Bouajjani Constantin Enea Jad Hamza
LIAFA, Univ Paris Diderot, Sorbonne Paris Cité, Paris, France.
{abou,cenea,jhamza}@liafa.univ-paris-diderot.fr

## Abstract

We address the verification problem of eventual consistency of optimistic replication systems. Such systems are typically used to implement distributed data structures over large scale networks. We introduce a formal definition of eventual consistency that applies to a wide class of existing implementations, including the ones using speculative executions. Then, we reduce the problem of checking eventual consistency to reachability and model checking problems. This reduction enables the use of existing verification tools for message-passing programs in the context of verifying optimistic replication systems. Furthermore, we derive from these reductions decision procedures for checking eventual consistency of systems implemented as finite-state programs communicating through unbounded unordered channels.

***Categories and Subject Descriptors*** Theory of Computation [*Logics and meanings of programs*]: General

***Keywords*** message passing concurrency, model checking, static program analysis

## 1. Introduction

Optimistic data replication is a key technology for achieving high availability and performance in distributed systems. It consists of a set of techniques for maintaining multiple copies of the same data, called *replicas*, on different sites in a large-scale network. Many interactive collaborative applications, ranging from social networks to collaborative spaces and online shops, use this technology, in order to increase the quality of their services. In fact, they use this technology even though the latter lets replicas temporarily diverge, and thus users may see inconsistent data from time to time. This is due to the fact that ensuring strong consistency (i.e., making all replicas always consistent) – which can only be achieved by synchronizing all replicas after each update – is practically infeasible, and therefore users generally prefer high responsiveness and availability to strong consistency. In fact, systems implementing optimistic data replication, called *optimistic replication systems* (ORS), can only ensure weak consistency notions, and one of the important issues in this context is to determine what are precisely these notions. By the CAP theorem [10], ensuring sequential consistency or linearizability together with availability and partition tolerance is not possible, and thus, the correctness criteria adopted for ORS must in general be weaker than these ones (that are more suitable for shared memory systems). One of the most popular correctness criteria for ORS (and which is in some sense the weakest that can be accepted) is *eventual consistency*. Many ORS that are widely used in practical applications, e.g., Amazon Simple Storage Service and Google App Engine Datastore, (are supposed to) satisfy eventual consistency.

Optimistic replication systems, such as those mentioned above, are extremely complex and hard to get right, and therefore, there is a real need in developing automated formal methods for reasoning about their behaviors and verifying their correctness w.r.t. criteria such as eventual consistency. However, the first issue to be addressed to achieve that is defining precisely and formally these criteria that are still not well understood in general. For instance, many works adopt different variants of what is called eventual consistency. Then, the second issue to address is (1) investigating the limits of decidability and complexity bounds for checking these criteria, and (2) designing effective algorithmic methods for their verification. In this paper, we address both of these semantical and algorithmic issues for eventual consistency. We introduce a formal definition of eventual consistency that is applicable to a wide class of ORS, including systems with speculative executions and roll-backs, and we provide an approach for its automatic verification based on effective reductions to reachability and model-checking queries.

In the following, we explain in more details the context and the nature of our contributions.

**Optimistic replication systems:** Many variants of ORS have been defined, e.g., [2, 7, 15–18, 20, 23]. In general, they are based on the following scenario: (1) users submit operations (i.e., self-contained updates or queries) to one of the sites, (2) operations are immediately applied to the local replica to let users continue working based on the effect of those operations, and (3) in the background, sites exchange and apply remote operations. Actually, this is the scenario used by *operation transfer systems*. There also exist *state transfer systems*, where the sites exchange the contents of their replicas. Although they may use different techniques, state transfer systems can be emulated by operation transfer systems, where the allowed operations are only to read and overwrite an entire object [20]. Therefore, we focus in this paper on operation transfer systems.

The communication between sites is usually based on *epidemic propagation*, which allows every operation to be communicated to all sites independently of the communication topology. When applying remote operations several critical components come into play (see Saito and Shapiro [19] for a survey):

- *scheduling policies*, used to order operations in a way expected by users, and to make sites eventually agree on some ordering, (a generic scheduling policy is to label operations by timestamps and execute them in the order of their timestamps),


*POPL '14*, January 22–24, 2014, San Diego, CA, USA.

http://dx.doi.org/10.1145/2535838.2535877

- *conflict detection*, used to detect operations that are submitted concurrently by users to different sites and touch the same data (e.g., two requests to a room-booking system that concern the same room and the same time slot),
- *conflict resolution*, used to define the effect of a set of conflicting operations (e.g., in the room-booking system, the system might require that each request comes with some alternative time slots, and in the case of two conflicting requests, one will get an alternative time slot),
- *commitment protocols*, used to make sites agree about the order in which they execute the operations.

In particular, a large class of ORS, e.g., Bayou [23], C-Praxis [18], IceCube [16], Telex [2], use *speculative executions*, i.e., operations are tentatively applied as they are received from the user or from the other sites. In such systems, the sites may receive the operations in different orders and thus, they may have to repeatedly roll-back some operations as they gradually converge towards a final order (for example, in the case of Bayou, the final order is decided by a designated primary site).

**Eventual consistency:** In its simplest formulation[1], eventual consistency requires that if the users stop submitting operations, then all the sites will eventually reach a consistent state (i.e., they agree on the way operations should be executed). However, as mentioned in Burckhardt et al. [6], this formulation is too loose and the reason is twofold. First, this definition does not impose some notion of correctness for the operations executed by the system, i.e., the fact that they should satisfy some well-defined specification. Second, this property offers no guarantees when the system never stops, i.e., when the users continuously submit new operations. For that, eventual consistency should take into account infinite executions of the system involving infinitely many operations.

In fact, works investigating the formal definition of eventual consistency (and correctness criteria for distributed data structures in general) are still very rare. To our knowledge, Burckhardt et al. [6] is the first attempt to provide a formal framework for reasoning about eventual consistency. However, the proposed formalization in that paper does not allow to reason about ORS, that use speculative executions and roll-backs (as the authors of that paper mention). So, the first issue that we address in this paper is providing a general formal definition of eventual consistency, that is applicable to a wider class of ORS.

We define eventual consistency as a property over *traces*. A trace models the view of an external observer of the system; it is a set of sequences of operations, where one sequence consists of all the operations submitted to one site. It abstracts away implementation details such as the messages exchanged between sites.

Eventual consistency is defined as the composition of a safety property that specifies the correct effects of the operations, and a liveness property guaranteeing that sites will eventually agree on the order in which the operations should be executed. Let us look closer to each of these components.

*Safety:* Following the scenario described earlier, the return value of an operation $o$ submitted to some site $N$ depends on (1) the operations received and scheduled by $N$ before $o$, and the order in which these operations are executed, (2) the conflict detection and conflict resolution policies applied by $N$, and (3) the behavior of the executed operations[2].

A trace is called *safe* iff the return values of all its operations are correct in a sense described hereafter. First, the correctness is defined with respect to a *specification* that, roughly, models the expected outcome of executing a poset of operations on a single site. Concretely, a poset of operations models a schedule, where incomparable elements are considered to be in conflict (i.e., submitted concurrently to different sites) and executing a poset of operations involves the actual implementations of the operations together with the conflict resolution policy (that defines the effect of concurrently submitted operations). A specification $S$ associates return values of operations with posets of operations. Intuitively, the return value $r$ of an operation $o$ is associated with some poset $\rho$ if $o$ returns $r$ whenever it is executed after the poset of operations $\rho$.

More precisely, a trace $\tau$ is safe w.r.t a specification $S$ iff for each operation $o$, there exists a poset $li[o]$ of operations in $\tau$, which is associated by $S$ with the return value of $o$. The poset $li[o]$ is called the *local interpretation* of $o$. Additionally, because of physical constraints, we define an *executed-before* relation $eb$ over the operations in the trace such that $(o', o) \in eb$ iff $o'$ belongs to the local interpretation of $o$, and we require that the union of $eb$ with the program order relation is an acyclic relation. Concretely, $(o', o) \in eb$ iff $o$ is an operation submitted to some site $N$ and $o'$ is scheduled by $N$ before $o$ while the local interpretation $li[o]$ models the result of applying the scheduling and conflict detection policies.

Note that, for ORS that use speculative executions and roll-backs, the local interpretations associated with two operations are arbitrarily different, even if the two operations are submitted to the same site. (The issue of convergence is left to the liveness part.)

*Liveness:* The liveness part of eventual consistency requires that there exists some partial order relation $gi$ (for global interpretation) over all the operations in an infinite trace, such that it is possible to choose some local interpretations satisfying the safety property, which *converge* towards $gi$. The convergence is formally stated as follows: for any prefix $P$ of $gi$ (a prefix of a poset is a restriction of the poset to a downward closed subset) there exists only finitely many local interpretations for which $P$ is not a prefix. This corresponds to the informal definition given in Saito and Shapiro [19].

**Verifying eventual consistency:** After providing a formal and general definition of eventual consistency, we address the problem of checking whether a given ORS satisfies eventual consistency w.r.t some given specification. Our aim is twofold. First, we investigate the question of defining a generic algorithmic verification method for eventual consistency which is independent from the class of programs used for the implementation. This is actually a hard problem since, regardless of the complexity of the implementation, eventual consistency requires reasoning about nested quantifiers over (infinite) partial orders. Then, our second goal is to derive from the generic verification method decidability and complexity results for particular, as large as possible, classes of implementations. Let us then examine each of these points.

*From eventual consistency to model-checking problems:* We show that the static verification of (the safety and liveness parts of) eventual consistency can be reduced to reachability and model checking problems. This reduction allows to use any existing tools for exact/approximate verification of concurrent (message-passing) programs in the context of verifying eventual consistency. The reduction is done by defining a monitor which, when composed in parallel with the system, reaches some specific error state or violates some temporal logic formula (in LTL extended with Presburger predicates) if and only if there exists an execution of the system that violates eventual consistency. The monitor is a sequential program that observes, in a centralized way, the operations submitted to all the sites in the network. Therefore, its observations are interleavings of operations performed by the ORS. Reasoning about such centralized observations is possible since we are concerned with the static (offline) verification of ORS. The monitor is the parallel composition of two monitors, one for checking the safety part in eventual consistency and one for checking the liveness part. These monitors

[1] Also called, quiescent consistency [12]

[2] In this paper, we make the simplifying assumption that replicas are copies of the same object. In general, a replica may be composed of copies of multiple objects but most replication systems manage each object independently.

are abstractly defined as state transition systems that take a step each time an operation is executed in the system. Actually, they can be seen as a way of instrumenting every operation performed by the system in order to obtain a program on which the reachability and model-checking queries mentioned above are applied.

For these reductions, we assume that the operations are instances of a finite set of *methods* with a finite set of possible input/return values. However, system implementations can still be very complex: users are allowed to submit unboundedly many operations, and systems can use unbounded domains for timestamps or unbounded channels for communication.

The constructions we provide are based on subtle arguments. Indeed, one of the issues is that return values of operations depend on arbitrarily large sets of prior operations, and unbounded number of possible orders between these operations. The effect of each operation depends on the local view of the site $N$ to which it is submitted. The local view consists of the set of operations known by $N$ and the order in which $N$ *believes* they were executed by other sites. In fact, when considering the safety part, we only need to check that, for each operation, such a local view exists and it is consistent with the return value of the operation. Unlike for the liveness part, we do not need to check the convergence of the local views toward a global view – which is a partial order over the infinite set of operations in the trace. In order to know if such local views exist, it is sufficient to count the number of *methods* previously issued. A careful analysis of the definition allows to show that it is possible to count only up to some finite bound, and thus only consider the minimal posets in the specification. Therefore, the problem of finding a violation for the safety property can be reduced to some bounded counting argument where the monitor counts the number of times the system executes each of the methods and then compares the counter values to the number of methods in the minimal posets of the specifications. This raises the problem of computing the number of methods in the minimal posets of the specification. In order to address this problem, we need to consider some concrete formalism for describing the specifications.

Therefore, we introduce a class of automata for describing specifications of ORS. Essentially, each poset of operations in the specification is abstracted into a sequence of multisets of methods (each method in these multisets corresponds to the method instantiated by an operation in the poset) which is then recognized by an automaton, called *multiset automaton*, where the transitions, instead of being labeled by symbols as in the case of automata over words, are labeled by Presburger formulas. The sequence of multisets corresponds to a decomposition of the poset in *levels*, used in algorithms for parallel tasks scheduling [22], where a level is a set of elements for which the length of the longest path to a maximal element is the same. These automata offer a good compromise between tractability and expressive power. In particular, they allow to define a wide-class of specifications, e.g., specifications of replication systems that use the Last Writer Wins conflict resolution policy [15] or commutative conflict resolution policies like in the case of the CRDTs [7, 20]. We then prove that for specifications recognized by multiset automata, it is possible to effectively compute the number of methods in the minimal posets.

For the liveness part of eventual consistency, we consider again a parallel composition between the system and a monitor that counts the number of times the system executes each of the methods. We show that the problem of finding a violation can be reduced to the problem of checking that the monitor reaches a state where its counters satisfy some specific property, and from there on, the methods executed by the system return only some particular set of values. The property that the counters should satisfy is quite complex; it characterizes the number of methods occurring finitely-often in the limit of an infinite sequence of posets belonging to the specification. However, we show that for specifications recognized by multiset automata, this property is definable by a Presburger formula, which can be effectively computed.

*Decidability and complexity:* Based on these reductions, we define decision procedures for checking eventual consistency of ORS, which are defined as the parallel composition of a fixed set of boolean programs communicating through unbounded unordered channels. Indeed, we consider that it is natural in our context to assume that channels are unordered since in general large-scale networks offer no guarantees on the order in which messages arrive even if they are sent by the same site. These decidability results are based on the fact that (1) this class of systems can be modeled by Vector Addition Systems with States (VASS, for short), since unbounded channels can be encoded as counters, and (2) the problems to which we reduce checking the safety, resp., the liveness, part of eventual consistency are decidable for VASS.

## 2. Preliminaries

**Sets, relations:** For a set $A$, $\mathcal{P}(A)$ denotes the set of all subsets of $A$. Let $R \subseteq A \times B$ be a relation. For any $y \in B$, $R^{-1}(y)$ denotes the set of elements $x \in A$ such that $(x, y) \in R$. The notation is extended to subsets of $B$ as usual.

**Sequences:** Let $\Sigma$ be a finite alphabet. The set of all finite, resp., infinite, sequences over $\Sigma$ is denoted by $\Sigma^*$, resp., $\Sigma^\omega$. Also, $\Sigma^\infty = \Sigma^* \cup \Sigma^\omega$. A set of sequences is called prefix-closed if the prefix of any sequence in the set is also in the set.

**Posets:** Let $(A, \leq)$ be a possibly infinite partially-ordered set (poset, for short). A path of length $n$ in $(A, \leq)$ is a sequence of elements $x_0, x_1, \ldots, x_n$ such that for all $0 \leq i \leq n-1$, $x_i \leq x_{i+1}$.

The downward closure of $B \subseteq A$ w.r.t. $\leq$, denoted by $\downarrow^{\leq} B$, is the set of all elements in $A$ smaller than $B$, i.e., $\downarrow^{\leq} B = \leq^{-1}(B)$. Similarly, the upward closure of $B \subseteq A$ w.r.t. $\leq$, denoted by $\uparrow^{\leq} B$, is the set of all elements in $x \in A$ such that $y \leq x$, for some $y \in B$. The superscript may be omitted when the partial order $\leq$ is clear from the context. We say that $B$ is downward closed, resp., upward closed, w.r.t. $\leq$ iff $B = \downarrow B$, resp., $B = \uparrow B$.

The poset $(A_1, \leq_1)$ is called a *prefix* of $(A_2, \leq_2)$, denoted by $(A_1, \leq_1) \preceq (A_2, \leq_2)$, iff $A_1 \subseteq A_2$, $\leq_1$ is the intersection of $\leq_2$ and $A_1 \times A_1$, and $A_1$ is downward closed w.r.t. $\leq_2$.

We say that a poset $(A, \leq)$ is *prefix-founded* iff for all finite sets $B \subseteq A$, $\downarrow B$ is finite.

**Labeled posets:** A $\Sigma$*-labeled poset* is a triple $(A, \leq, \ell)$, where $(A, \leq)$ is a poset and $\ell : A \to \Sigma$ is a function that labels each element of $A$ with a symbol in $\Sigma$. The set of all $\Sigma$-labeled posets is denoted by $\mathsf{PoSet}_\Sigma$.

Given $\Sigma' \subseteq \Sigma$, the *projection* of a $\Sigma$-labeled poset $(A, \leq, \ell)$ over $\Sigma'$ is the $\Sigma'$-labeled poset $(B, \leq', \ell')$, where $B$ is the subset of $A$ containing all the elements labeled by symbols in $\Sigma'$, i.e., $B = \{a \mid \ell(a) \in \Sigma'\}$, and $\leq'$, resp., $\ell'$ are the projections of $\leq$, resp., $\ell$ over $B \times B$, resp., $B$.

The Parikh image of a possibly infinite $\Sigma$-labeled poset $\rho = (A, \leq, \ell)$ is the multiset $\Pi_\Sigma(\rho) : \Sigma \to \mathbb{N} \cup \{\omega\}$ mapping each symbol $a \in \Sigma$ to the number of elements $x$ of $A$ such that $\ell(x) = a$. If some symbol $a$ occurs infinitely often then $\Pi_\Sigma(\sigma)(a) = \omega$. Note that the Parikh image of a labeled poset $\rho$ can be also interpreted as the multiset of symbols in $\rho$. The notion is extended to sets of labeled posets as usual.

A labeled poset $\rho_1 = (A_1, \leq_1, \ell_1)$ is called a prefix of $\rho_2 = (A_2, \leq_2, \ell_2)$ iff the poset $(A_1, \leq_2)$ is a prefix of $(A_2, \leq_2)$ and $\ell_1(y) = \ell_2(y)$, for all $y \in A_1$. We also say that $\rho_2$ is a *completion* of $\rho_1$. This is denoted by $\rho_1 \preceq \rho_2$. Moreoever, if $\ell_2(A_2 \setminus A_1) \subseteq \Sigma'$ where $\Sigma' \subseteq \Sigma$, we say that $\rho_2$ is a $\Sigma'$-completion of $\rho_1$.

Two labeled posets $(A_1, \leq_1, \ell_1)$ and $(A_2, \leq_2, \ell_2)$ are isomorphic iff there exists a bijection $h : A_1 \to A_2$ such that for all

$x, y \in A_1$, $x \leq_1 y$ iff $h(x) \leq_2 h(y)$ and $\ell_1(x) = \ell_2(h(x))$. A set of labeled posets $\mathcal{A}$ is called *isomorphism-closed* iff any labeled poset isomorphic to some labeled poset in $\mathcal{A}$ belongs also to $\mathcal{A}$.

**Functions:** Let $A$ and $B$ be two sets. We denote by $A \to B$ the set of functions from $A$ to $B$. For a function $f \in A \to B$, and $a \in A$, $b \in B$, $f[a \mapsto b]$ is the function which maps all elements $a' \neq a$ to $f(a')$, and which maps $a$ to $b$. If $A = \{a_1, \ldots, a_n\}$, and $b_1, \ldots, b_n$ are (possibly equal) elements of $B$, we denote by $(a_1 \mapsto b_1, \ldots, a_n \mapsto b_n)$ the function $f \in A \to B$ which maps $a_i$ to $b_i$ for all $1 \leq i \leq n$. Likewise, for $b \in B$, we denote by $(a \in A \mapsto b)$ the function which maps every $a \in A$ to $b$.

For functions $f : A \to \mathbb{N}$, and $g : A' \to \mathbb{N}$ with $A' \subseteq A$, $f + g : A \to \mathbb{N}$ maps each $a' \in A'$ to $(f+g)(a') = f(a') + g(a')$ and each $a \in A \setminus A'$ to $(f+g)(a) = f(a)$.

## 3. Modeling optimistic replication systems

A concrete execution of an ORS is modeled as a trace, that abstracts away many implementation details. A trace is a poset of operations, where all the operations submitted to the same site are totally ordered. We suppose that operations are instances of a fixed set of *methods*. For static verification of eventual consistency, an ORS is viewed as a prefix-closed set of *sequential observations*. These are sequences of pairs of the form $(N, o)$, where $N$ is a site name and $o$ is an operation. Such a pair denotes an operation $o$ submitted to site $N$. The trace represented by a sequential observation $\eta$ contains all the operations in $\eta$ such that any two operations submitted to different sites are incomparable and the order between any two operations submitted to the same site is consistent with the order in which these two operations appear in the sequence $\eta$.

Let $\mathbb{M}$ be the set of method names and $\mathbb{D}$ the domain of return values. For simplicity, we suppose that input parameters are encoded in the method names. A *method synopsis* is a pair $m \triangleright r$, where $m \in \mathbb{M}$ and $r \in \mathbb{D}$. We denote by $\mathbb{M} \triangleright \mathbb{D}$ the set of all method synopses. An *operation* $o$ is a pair $(i, a)$ formed of an identity $i \in \mathbb{N}$ and a method synopsis $a \in \mathbb{M} \triangleright \mathbb{D}$. We denote by $\mathbb{O}$ the set of all operations. Given a method synopsis $a = m \triangleright r$, we let $\mathsf{meth}(a) = m$, $\mathsf{rval}(a) = r$, and given an operation $o = (i, m \triangleright r)$, we let $\mathsf{id}(o) = i$, $\mathsf{meth}(o) = m$, $\mathsf{rval}(o) = r$, and $\mathsf{syn}(o) = m \triangleright r$. An operation $o = (i, m \triangleright r)$ may be called an *$m$-operation* or an *$m \triangleright r$-operation*. Also, given a set of method names $M \subseteq \mathbb{M}$ (resp., a set of method synopses $Y \subseteq \mathbb{M} \triangleright \mathbb{D}$) $o$ is called an *$M$-operation* (resp., *$Y$-operation*) iff $m \in M$ (resp., $m \triangleright r \in Y$).

A *trace* $\tau$ is a (possibly infinite) poset $(O, po)$, where $O \subseteq \mathbb{O}$ and $po$, called the *program order*, is a disjoint union of a set of prefix-founded irreflexive total orders over $O$. We assume that a trace does not contain two operations with the same identity. The set of operations, resp., the program order, in a trace $\tau$ are denoted by $O_\tau$, resp., $po_\tau$.

Given a fixed set $\mathcal{N}$ of site names, a *sequential observation* (observation, for short) of an ORS is a possibly infinite sequence over $\mathbb{O}_\mathcal{N} = \mathcal{N} \times \mathbb{O}$ (we assume that such a sequence does not contain two operations with the same identity). A sequential observation models the view of a centralized sequential observer over the concrete executions of the replication system. Then, an *optimistic replication system* $\mathcal{I}$ is a state machine that produces a prefix-closed subset of $(\mathbb{O}_\mathcal{N})^\infty$. By an abuse of notation, the set of sequences produced by $\mathcal{I}$ is denoted also by $\mathcal{I}$.

Given an observation $\eta$, let $O_\eta$ denote the set of operations that occur in $\eta$, i.e., the set of operations $o$ for which there exists $N \in \mathcal{N}$ such that $(N, o)$ occurs in $\eta$. Given an observation $\eta \in (\mathbb{O}_\mathcal{N})^\infty$, the *trace of* $\eta$ is defined by $trace(\eta) = (O, po)$, where

- $O = O_\eta$ and
- $po = \{(o, o') \mid \exists N \in \mathcal{N}$ s.t. $(N, o)$ occurs before $(N, o')$ in $\eta\}$

Next, we give examples of ORS that we use throughout the paper.

**Example 1** (One-value Register). The One-Value Register (Register) maintains an integer register and supports the set of methods $\mathbb{M}_\mathsf{R} = \{\mathtt{wr}(i) \mid i \in \mathbb{N}\} \cup \{\mathtt{rd}\}$, where $\mathtt{wr}(i)$ assigns value $i$ to the register and $\mathtt{rd}$ reads the current value of the register. A method $\mathtt{rd}$ can return any value from $\mathbb{N}$ while the methods $\mathtt{wr}(i)$ return some special value $\top$, i.e., the domain of return values is $\mathbb{D}_\mathsf{R} = \mathbb{N} \cup \{\top\}$. We thus have $\mathbb{M} \triangleright \mathbb{D}_\mathsf{R} = \{\mathtt{wr}(i) \triangleright \top, \mathtt{rd} \triangleright i \mid i \in \mathbb{N}\}$.

**Example 2** (Multi-Value Register). The Multi-Value Register [7, 14] (MV-Register) maintains an integer register and supports the same set of methods as the Register. A method $\mathtt{rd}$ can return any *set* of values from $\mathbb{N}$. Thus, the domain of return values of the MV-Register is $\mathbb{D}_{\mathsf{MV\text{-}R}} = \mathcal{P}(\mathbb{N}) \cup \{\top\}$ and its set of method synopses is $\mathbb{M} \triangleright \mathbb{D}_{\mathsf{MV\text{-}R}} = \{\mathtt{wr}(i) \triangleright \top, \mathtt{rd} \triangleright I \mid i \in \mathbb{N} \text{ and } I \subseteq \mathbb{N}\}$.

**Example 3** (Observed-Remove Set). The Observed-Remove Set [20] (OR-Set) maintains a set of integers over which one can apply the set of methods $\mathbb{M}_{\mathsf{OR\text{-}S}} = \{\mathtt{add}(i), \mathtt{rem}(i), \mathtt{lookup}(i) \mid i \in \mathbb{N}\}$, where $\mathtt{add}(i)$ adds the integer $i$ to the set, $\mathtt{rem}(i)$ removes $i$ from the set, and $\mathtt{lookup}(i)$ tests if the integer $i$ is in the set. We assume that the methods $\mathtt{add}$ and $\mathtt{rem}$ return some fixed value $\top$, while $\mathtt{lookup}(i)$ can return 1 or 0. Thus, the set of return values is $\mathbb{D}_{\mathsf{OR\text{-}S}} = \{1, 0, \top\}$ and $\mathbb{M} \triangleright \mathbb{D}_{\mathsf{OR\text{-}S}} = \{\mathtt{add}(i) \triangleright \top, \mathtt{rem}(i) \triangleright \top, \mathtt{lookup}(i) \triangleright 1, \mathtt{lookup}(i) \triangleright 0 \mid i \in \mathbb{N}\}$.

## 4. Eventual consistency

In this section, we introduce a formal definition for eventual consistency, whose main artifacts are presented hereafter.

**Specification:** In the context of shared-memory, resp., ORS, the correctness of the operations associated to some object usually involves some mechanism of conflict resolution in order to define the effect of a set of operations executed by different threads, resp., submitted concurrently at different sites. In the case of shared-memory systems, the conflict resolution mechanism is usually specified by the notion of *linearizability* [13], which requires that the effect of a set of concurrent operations (that overlap in time) is the same as the one of a sequential execution of the same set of operations. In the context of ORS, where each site maintains its own copy of the object, some more general mechanisms of conflict resolution are required.

To specify both the sequential semantics of the operations and the conflict resolution mechanisms we use posets of operations instead of sequences of operations, as in the case of linearizable objects. We don't use a total order because, in general, it is unfeasible that all sites agree on a total order of operations, and sometimes even unnecessary, in case of commutative operations for instance. Moreover, the mechanisms used to detect conflicting (causally unrelated) operations are not always precise.

We assume that the specification can't distinguish between two posets that are identical (i.e., isomorphic) when ignoring the identities and the return values of the operations. The insensitivity to return values is motivated by the fact that, in real implementations, the sites exchange operations without their return values (in such systems, it is not expected that an operation returns the same value when executed at different sites).

A specification associates to each method synopsis $m \triangleright r$ an isomorphism-closed set of $\mathbb{M}$-labeled posets. The closure under isomorphism and the fact that we use labeled posets model the fact that the specification doesn't observe identities and return values. The fact that a poset $\rho$ is associated to $m \triangleright r$ means that any site that sees the set of operations in $\rho$ in that order reaches a state where the call to $m$ produces the value $r$.

**Definition 1** (Specification). A *specification* is a function $S : \mathbb{M} \triangleright \mathbb{D} \to \mathcal{P}(\mathsf{PoSet}_\mathbb{M})$, where for each method synopsis $a \in \mathbb{M} \triangleright \mathbb{D}$, $S(a)$ is an isomorphism-closed set of $\mathbb{M}$-labeled posets.

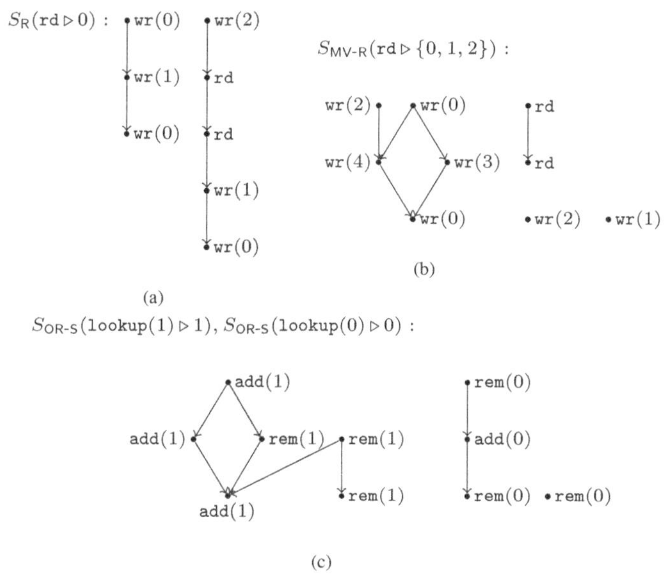


Figure 1: Examples of labeled posets belonging to (a) the specification of the Register (b) the specification of the MV-Register, and (c) the specification of the OR-Set. The order relations are defined by arrows: an arrow from an element $x$ to some element $y$ means that $x$ is ordered before $y$. We omit arrows implied by transitivity.

We give several examples of specifications for the replication systems mentioned in the previous section.

**Example 4** (Register specification)**.** The specification $S_R$ of the Register is given by: (1) for every $a = \mathtt{wr}(i) \triangleright \top$, $S_R(a)$ is the set of all $\mathbb{M}_R$-labeled totally-ordered sets, and (2) for every $a = \mathtt{rd} \triangleright i$, $S_R(a)$ is the set of all $\mathbb{M}_R$-labeled totally-ordered sets where the maximal element labeled by a write is labeled by $\mathtt{wr}(i)$. Figure 1a contains two examples of totally-ordered sets in $S_R(\mathtt{rd} \triangleright 0)$.

**Example 5.** [MV-Register specification] The specification $S_{MV\text{-}R}$ of the MV-Register is defined by: (1) for any $a = \mathtt{wr}(i) \triangleright \top$, $S_{MV\text{-}R}(a)$ is the set of all $\mathbb{M}_R$-labeled posets and (2) for any $a = \mathtt{rd} \triangleright I$, $S_{MV\text{-}R}(a)$ is the set of all $\mathbb{M}_R$-labeled posets $\rho$ such that $i \in I$ iff there exists a maximal element labeled by $\mathtt{wr}(i)$ in the projection of $\rho$ over the elements labeled by write methods $\{\mathtt{wr}(i) \mid i \in \mathbb{N}\}$. Figure 1b contains an $\mathbb{M}_R$-labeled poset in $S_R(\mathtt{rd} \triangleright \{0,1,2\})$.

**Example 6.** [OR-Set specification] The specification $S_{OR\text{-}S}$ is given by: (1) for any $a = \mathtt{add}(i) \triangleright \top$ or $a = \mathtt{rem}(i) \triangleright \top$, $S_{OR\text{-}S}(a)$ is the set of all $\mathbb{M}_{OR\text{-}S}$-labeled posets, and (2) for any $a = \mathtt{lookup}(i) \triangleright 1$, resp., $a = \mathtt{lookup}(i) \triangleright 0$, $S_{OR\text{-}S}(a)$ is the set of all $\mathbb{M}_{OR\text{-}S}$-labeled posets $\rho$ such that the projection of $\rho$ over the elements labeled by $\mathtt{add}(i)$ or $\mathtt{rem}(i)$ contains a maximal element labeled by $\mathtt{add}(i)$, resp., contains no maximal element labeled by $\mathtt{add}(i)$. Figure 1c contains an example of a labeled poset that belongs to both $S_{OR\text{-}S}(\mathtt{lookup}(1) \triangleright 1)$ and $S_{OR\text{-}S}(\mathtt{lookup}(0) \triangleright 0)$.

**Local interpretation:** The return value of some operation $o$ submitted to some site $N$ depends on the set of operations applied at $N$ before $o$ and on the the effect of applying the scheduling and conflict detection policies over this set of operations. Taken together they can be represented by a poset of operations, called the *local interpretation* of $o$ and denoted by $li[o]$. Because of speculative executions, one has to consider a local interpretation for each operation $o$ in the trace (the order in which known operations are executed can change at any time).

The local interpretations define another relation over the operations in the trace, called *executed-before* and denoted by *eb*. We say that some operation $o'$ is executed before another operation $o$, i.e., $(o', o) \in eb$, iff $o'$ belongs to the local interpretation of $o$. For example, Figure 2a pictures a trace of the Register, where the arrows define a possible *eb* relation. Note that the $\mathtt{wr}(1)$-operation is executed before the first occurrence of $\mathtt{rd} \triangleright 0$ but not before the second occurrence of $\mathtt{rd} \triangleright 0$.

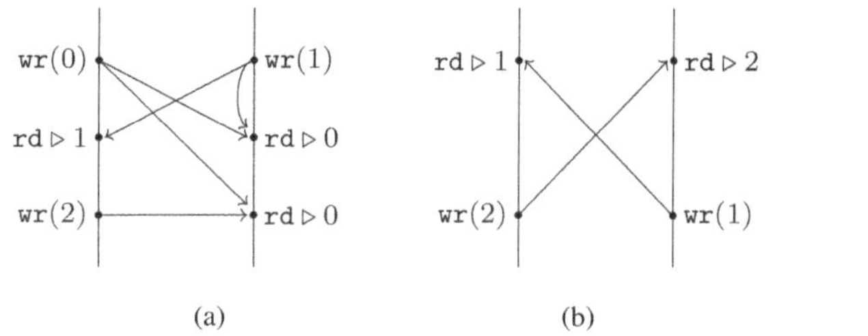


Figure 2: Traces of the Register. For simplicity, the return values of the wr operations and the ids of each operation are omitted. The program order is defined by the vertical lines, from top to bottom.

We say that the return value of some operation $o$ is *correct* iff the labeled poset defined by $li[o]$, where every operation $o'$ is labeled by $\mathsf{meth}(o')$, belongs to $S(\mathsf{syn}(o))$. Then, a trace $\tau$ is *safe* iff the return values of all operations in $\tau$ are correct.

For example, in the case of the first $\mathtt{rd} \triangleright 0$-operation in Figure 2a, one can choose to order the $\mathtt{wr}(1)$-operation before the $\mathtt{wr}(0)$-operation. This local interpretation defines an $\mathbb{M}_R$-labeled poset, which belongs to the specification of the Register, $S_R(\mathtt{rd} \triangleright 0)$. Similarly, one can show that all return values in Figure 2a are correct.

Because of physical constraints, *eb* must not create cycles together with the program order. For example, the trace in Figure 2b could be one of the Register if the relation *eb* is defined by the arrows in the figure (we assume that the initial value of the register is 0). However, this means that the site executing the operations in the left received a message from the other site containing the $\mathtt{wr}(1)$ operation and this message was created after $\mathtt{rd} \triangleright 2$ has finished. Thus, in real time, $\mathtt{rd} \triangleright 2$ has happened before the $\mathtt{wr}(2)$-operation, which contradicts the *eb* relation.

**Global interpretation:** The fact that the sites will eventually agree on the way operations should be executed is defined as a liveness property over infinite traces of the system. Given an infinite trace $\tau$, we consider a partial-order over all the operations in $\tau$, called the *global interpretation* and denoted by $gi$. The liveness property requires that the local interpretations defined for the operations in $\tau$ *converge* towards $gi$. More precisely, for any finite prefix $P$ of $gi$, the number of local interpretations for which $P$ *is not* a prefix is finite. Note that this implies that any operation $o$ in the trace is executed before all operations in $\tau$, except some finite set. A system that satisfies only this property will be called *weak eventually consistent*.

We will require that $gi$ satisfies some sanity condition, i.e., that it is prefix-founded, which basically, means that every operation can be executed after only finitely many other operations.

For example, let us consider the infinite trace in Figure 3. We consider a global interpretation $gi$, which in this case is a total order, that arranges the write operations in a sequence of the form $(\mathtt{wr}(0)\,\mathtt{wr}(1))^\omega$, and keeps the same order as in the trace for the $\mathtt{wr}(0)$ operations (resp., the $\mathtt{wr}(1)$ operations). In the following, we ignore the order between the rd-operations because they are not important for justifying the correctness of the return values. We show that it is possible to choose local interpretations for the $\mathtt{rd} \triangleright 0$ operations such that the return values are correct, and such that the orders converge towards $gi$. In a similar way, this can be shown for all the other operations in the trace.

For each $\mathtt{rd} \triangleright 0$-operation $o$, the local interpretation $li[o]$ is the poset that consists of all the write operations that occur before $o$ (i.e., if $o$ is the $i$th occurrence of $\mathtt{rd} \triangleright 0$ then the poset $li[o]$ contains

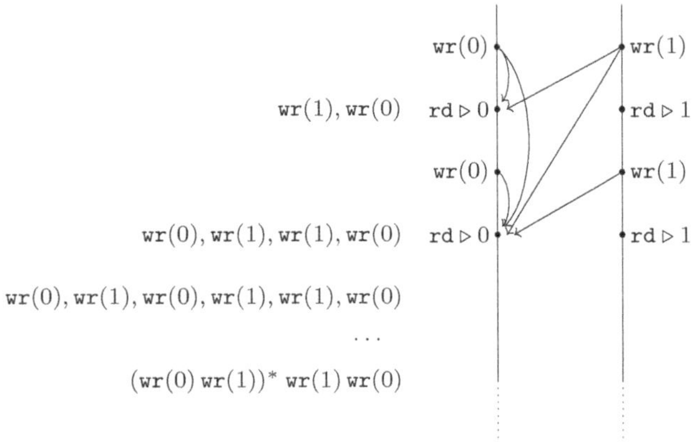


Figure 3: An infinite trace of Register, where one site executes ( $\mathtt{wr}(0)\ \mathtt{rd} \triangleright 0$ )$^\omega$ and another site executes ( $\mathtt{wr}(1)\ \mathtt{rd} \triangleright 1$ )$^\omega$.

the $j$th occurrence of $\mathtt{wr}(1)$ and $\mathtt{wr}(0)$, for all $j < i$), totally ordered in a sequence of the form $(\mathtt{wr}(0)\,\mathtt{wr}(1))^*\ \mathtt{wr}(1)\,\mathtt{wr}(0)$ consistent with the program order. The relation *eb* is pictured by arrows in Figure 3. Defined as such, the local interpretations converge towards the global interpretation $gi$.

We now give the definition of eventual consistency. For any poset $li[o] = (A, \leq)$ as above, $li_{\mathbb{M}}[o]$ denotes the labeled poset $li[o]$ where every operation is labeled by the corresponding method name in $\mathbb{M}$, i.e., $li_{\mathbb{M}}[o] = (A, \leq, \mathsf{meth})$.

**Definition 2.** [Safety, (Weak) Eventual consistency] A trace $\tau = (O, po)$ is called *eventually consistent* w.r.t. a specification $S$ iff:

$$\begin{array}{l}\exists\, gi \text{ an irreflexive partial order over } O\\ \quad \forall\, o \in O\ \exists\, li[o] \text{ an irreflexive poset.}\\ \qquad \textsc{GIpf} \wedge \textsc{ThinAir} \wedge \textsc{RVal} \wedge \textsc{Eventual}\end{array}$$

It is said to be *weak eventually consistent* w.r.t $S$ iff EVENTUAL is replaced by WEAKEVENTUAL in the condition above (thus, $gi$ and GIPF can be removed). Finally, it is said to be *safe* w.r.t $S$ iff only the axioms THINAIR and RVAL are satisfied, i.e.,

$$\begin{array}{l}\forall\, o \in O\ \exists\, li[o] \text{ an irreflexive poset.}\\ \qquad \textsc{ThinAir} \wedge \textsc{RVal}\end{array}$$

The relation *eb* is defined by: $(o', o) \in eb$ iff $o' \in li[o]$

| | |
|---|---|
| THINAIR | $eb \cup po$ is acyclic |
| RVAL | for all $o = (i, a) \in O$, $li_{\mathbb{M}}[o] \in S(a)$ |
| GIPF | $gi$ is prefix-founded |
| WEAKEVENTUAL | for all $o \in O$, $\{o' \mid (o, o') \notin eb\}$ is finite |
| EVENTUAL | for any finite prefix $P$ of the poset $(O, gi)$, $\{o \mid P \not\leq li[o]\}$ is finite |

Table 1: The list of axioms used in Definition 2.

Axioms THINAIR and RVAL are thus safety conditions, and ensure that the operations respect the specification $S$. Axiom WEAKEVENTUAL is a liveness condition, which ensures that eventually, every operation will be executed before all the other operations in the system. Axiom EVENTUAL is a stronger liveness condition which ensures that all nodes eventually agree on a (possibly partial) order in which to execute all the operations.

An ORS $\mathcal{I}$ is said to be (weak) eventually consistent, resp., safe, iff for every observation $\eta$ of $\mathcal{I}$, $trace(\eta)$ is (weak) eventually consistent, resp., safe.

In the next sections, we consider the problem of verifying eventual consistency and **we assume that $\mathbb{M} \triangleright \mathbb{D}$ is finite**.

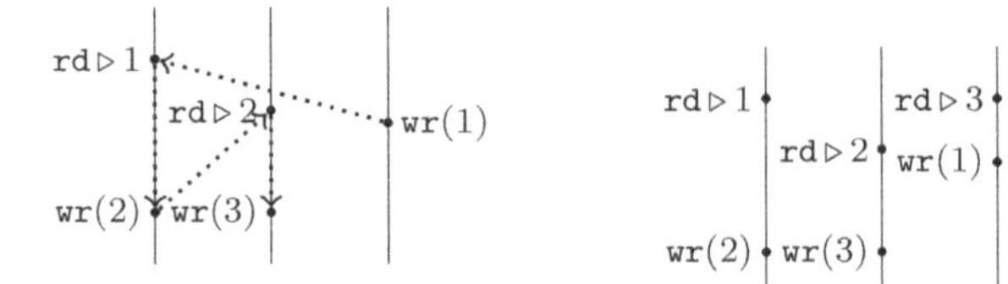


(a) A safe trace, with one possible total order $e$ depicted with arrows

(b) An unsafe trace

Figure 4: Examples of traces of the Register

## 5. Safety

We consider the problem of checking that an ORS is safe and we prove that it can be reduced to a reachability problem. First, we show that in any total ordering over the operations of an *unsafe* trace $\tau$, consistent with the program order, one can find an operation $o$ such that there are not sufficiently many operations before $o$ (in this total ordering) to construct a labeled poset belonging to its specification (i.e., $S(\mathsf{syn}(o))$). For example, for an unsafe trace of the Register, e.g., the trace in Figure 4b, with read and write operations, this means that, no matter in which order – consistent with the program order – it is read, there will always exist a read that returns a value not written by a previous write.

This allows us to define a monitor for checking the safety of a replication system $\mathcal{I}$, that records all the operations executed by $\mathcal{I}$, and stops with a negative answer at any time that it detects an operation $o$ for which, with the recorded set of operations, it cann't build a labeled poset belonging to the specification of $o$. Actually, we prove that it is sufficient that the monitor only counts the number of times the system executes each of the methods in $\mathbb{M}$ (until some bound) and then, compare the counter values with the minimal vectors in the Parikh image of the specification.

The next lemma states the characterization of (un)safe traces.

**Lemma 1.** *A trace $\tau$ is safe w.r.t $S$ iff there exists a prefix-founded total order* e *– called the* issue order *– on $O_\tau$, consistent with po, such that for every operation $o$ of $\tau$, there exists a poset $(V_o, \leq_o)$, where $V_o$ is a subset of $\mathrm{e}^{-1}(o)$ and $(V_o, \leq_o, \mathsf{meth}) \in S(\mathsf{syn}(o))$.*

*Proof.* ($\Leftarrow$) For each $o$, define $li[o] = (V_o, \leq_o)$. This ensures that axiom RVAL holds. Moreover, the relations *eb* and *po* are both consistent with e, which implies that axiom THINAIR holds.

($\Rightarrow$) Conversely, assume that for each operation $o$, there exists $li[o]$ such that THINAIR and RVAL hold. Let $e$ be any total order compatible with *eb* and *po*, which exists since $eb \cup po$ has no cycle. Figure 4a illustrates one such total order on a safe trace. Then, for each operation $o$, define $(V_o, \leq_o)$ as the poset $li[o]$. □

Lemma 1 implies that if $\tau$ is the trace of an observation $\eta$ and it is unsafe, then there exists a prefix of $\eta$ which ends in an operation whose return value is not correct, i.e., it is not possible to define a labeled poset that contains only operations in this prefix that belongs to the specification of $o$. This is stated in the following lemma.

**Lemma 2.** *Given an ORS $\mathcal{I}$, the following are equivalent:*

1. *there exists an observation $\eta \in \mathcal{I}$ such that $trace(\eta)$ is not safe*
2. *there exists an observation $\eta = \eta'(N, (\mathsf{id}, a)) \in \mathcal{I}$ such that there exists no poset $(V_o, \leq_o)$ whose elements are a subset of $O_{\eta'}$, such that $(V_o, \leq_o, \mathsf{meth}) \in S(a)$.*

*Proof.* Assume that (2) holds for $\eta = \eta'(N, (\mathsf{id}, a))$. Let $o = (\mathsf{id}, a)$ be the last operation of $\eta$. If $\eta$ was safe, we would have a local interpretation $li[o]$ such that $li_{\mathbb{M}}[o] \in S(a)$. Note that the operations in $li[o]$ belong to $O_{\eta'}$, which contradicts (2). Thus, $\eta$ is not safe and (2) implies (1).

Conversely, if we have an observation $\eta$ such that $trace(\eta)$ is not safe, then by Lemma 1, there exists a prefix $\eta_p$ of $\eta$ such that $\eta_p$ satisfies (2). Indeed, if there were no such prefix, the total order on $O_\eta$ induced by $\eta$ would satisfy the condition of Lemma 1, which would contradict the fact that $trace(\eta)$ is not safe. □

The following corollary is a reformulation of Lemma 2 in terms of Parikh images. For any finite observation $\eta$, the $\mathbb{M}$-Parikh image of $\eta$ is a function $\Pi_{\mathbb{M}}(\eta) : \mathbb{M} \to \mathbb{N}$, that maps each $m \in \mathbb{M}$ to the number of operations $o$ in $\eta$ with $m = \mathsf{meth}(o)$. The $\mathbb{M}$-Parikh image of a finite trace $\tau$, denoted by $\Pi_{\mathbb{M}}(\tau)$, is defined similarly.

**Corollary 1.** *An optimistic replication system $\mathcal{I}$ is not safe iff there exists $\eta'(N, (\mathsf{id}, a)) \in \mathcal{I}$ such that $\Pi_{\mathbb{M}}(\eta') \notin \uparrow \Pi_{\mathbb{M}}(S(a))$.*

Given an observation $\eta$ and an integer $i$, $\Pi^i_{\mathbb{M}}(\eta)$ is the Parikh image of $\eta$, where all the components larger than $i$ are set to $i$, that is $\Pi^i_{\mathbb{M}}(\eta) = (m \in \mathbb{M} \mapsto min(i, \Pi_{\mathbb{M}}(\eta)(m)))$.

For each $a \in \mathbb{M} \rhd \mathbb{D}$, let $V_a$ be the set of minimal elements of $\Pi_{\mathbb{M}}(S(a))$ (w.r.t. the ordering relation over vectors of natural numbers), so that $\uparrow \Pi_{\mathbb{M}}(S(a)) = \uparrow V_a$, and let $i_a$ be the maximum value appearing in the vectors of $V_a$. Let $i = \max\{i_a \mid a \in \mathbb{M} \rhd \mathbb{D}\}$.

We remark that $\Pi_{\mathbb{M}}(\eta') \notin \uparrow \Pi_{\mathbb{M}}(S(a))$ is equivalent to the fact that $\Pi_{\mathbb{M}}(\eta')$ is *not* greater than one of the minimal elements $v_a \in V_a$. Moreover, since all the components of the vectors of $V_a$ are smaller than $i$, $\Pi_{\mathbb{M}}(\eta') \notin \uparrow \Pi_{\mathbb{M}}(S(a))$ is equivalent to $\bigwedge_{v_a \in V_a} \Pi^i_{\mathbb{M}}(\eta') \ngeq v_a$.

In general, the sets $V_a$ cannot be computed, but in Section 7, we give a class of specifications for which they can. We define a monitor $\mathcal{M}_{\mathtt{safe}}$, which counts all the methods it sees up to the bound $i$, and every time it reads a symbol $(N, (\mathsf{id}, a))$, it goes to an error state $q_{\mathtt{err}}$ iff the vector of methods seen is not larger than some $v_a \in V_a$.

Formally, $\mathcal{M}_{\mathtt{safe}}$ is a deterministic finite-state transition system $(Q, Q_0, \delta)$, where

- $Q = (\mathbb{M} \to \{0, \ldots, i\}) \cup \{q_{\mathtt{err}}\}$ is the finite set of states
- $Q_0$, the set of initial states, only contains $q_0 = (m \in \mathbb{M} \mapsto 0)$
- $\delta \subseteq Q \times \mathbb{O}_{\mathcal{N}} \times Q$ with
  - $(q, (N, (\mathsf{id}, a)), q_{\mathtt{err}}) \in \delta$ iff $\bigwedge_{v_a \in V_a} q \ngeq v_a$
  - $(q_1, (N, (\mathsf{id}, a)), q_2) \in \delta$ iff $\bigvee_{v_a \in V_a} q \geq v_a$ and $q_2 = q_1[\mathsf{meth}(a) \mapsto \min(q_1(\mathsf{meth}(a)) + 1, i)]$

**Theorem 1** (Safety Monitoring). *An optimistic replication system $\mathcal{I}$ is not safe if and only if the parallel composition $\mathcal{I} \| \mathcal{M}_{\mathtt{safe}}$ can reach the error state $q_{\mathtt{err}}$.*

## 6. Liveness

In this section, we give properties which characterize (weak) eventually consistent traces that will be used to define reductions of deciding (weak) eventual consistency to LTL model checking.

### 6.1 Weak Eventual Consistency

We first consider the case of weak eventual consistency because it is simpler while already showing some of the difficulties we have to solve. Moreover, for some systems, weak eventual consistency implies eventual consistency, for instance, when all the operations are commutative.

For an infinite trace $\tau$ to be weak eventually consistent there must exist some local interpretations which show that $\tau$ is safe but also, which ensure that each operation $o \in O_\tau$ is executed-before all the other operations, except for some finite set. The latter implies that any finite set of operations is executed-before every operation after some finite prefix. Thus, for any $a \in \mathbb{M} \rhd \mathbb{D}$, if there are infinitely many $a$-operations in $\tau$, then $S(a)$, the specification of $a$, must contain arbitrarily large posets. This property of $S(a)$ can be stated as a property of the Parikh image of $S(a)$ and this allows us to define a reduction of checking if some replication system $\mathcal{I}$ is weak eventually consistent to checking if $\mathcal{I}$ is safe and if the parallel composition of $\mathcal{I}$ with a monitor that counts the methods executed by $\mathcal{I}$ satisfies some LTL formula. Mainly, the temporal operators in this formula are used to identify the infinitely occurring method synopses in some execution.

In the following lemma, we characterize weak eventually consistent traces. To identify the infinitely occurring method synopses in some trace $\tau$ we use the following notation. Given $B \subseteq \mathbb{M} \rhd \mathbb{D}$ and a finite trace $\tau_p$, let $\tau_p B^\omega$ be the set of all traces $\tau$ which extend $\tau_p$ (i.e., $\tau_p$ is a prefix of $\tau$) by an infinite set of $B$-operations such that there are infinitely many $a$-operations in $\tau$, for each $a \in B$.

**Lemma 3.** *[Characterization of Weak Eventual Consistency] Given $B \subseteq \mathbb{M} \rhd \mathbb{D}$ such that $\mathsf{meth}(B) = \{m_1, \ldots, m_k\}$, a trace $\tau \in \tau_p B^\omega$ is weak eventually consistent w.r.t. $S$ if and only if*

- *$\tau$ is safe and*
- *$\forall a \in B. \forall n \in \mathbb{N}. \exists n_1, \ldots, n_k \geq n.$*
  *$\Pi_{\mathbb{M}}(\tau_p) + (m_1 \to n_1, \ldots, m_k \to n_k) \in \Pi_{\mathbb{M}}(S(a))$*

*Proof.* ($\Rightarrow$) If $\tau$ is eventually consistent, then for each operation $o \in O_\tau$, there exists a local interpretation $li[o]$ such that the axioms ThinAir, RVal, and WeakEventual hold.

Let $a \in B$, and $n \in \mathbb{N}$. Since there are infinitely many $a$-operations in $\tau$, we deduce from axiom WeakEventual that there exists one, noted $o$, such that $li[o]$ (or equivalently, $eb^{-1}(o)$) contains the operations of $\tau_p$ and at least $n$ additional $m$-operations for each $m \in \mathsf{meth}(B)$. From axiom RVal, we know that $li_{\mathbb{M}}[o] \in S(a)$, which shows that there exists $n_1, \ldots, n_k \geq n$ such that $\Pi_{\mathbb{M}}(\tau_p) + (m_1 \to n_1, \ldots, m_k \to n_k) \in \Pi_{\mathbb{M}}(S(a))$.

($\Leftarrow$) Since $\tau$ is safe, there exists an issue order $e$ over $O_\tau$ that satisfies the conditions in Lemma 1. In the following, we consider that the operations in $\tau$ are totally ordered according to $e$.

For each $n \in \mathbb{N}^*$, let $o_n$ be the last operation in $\tau$, which occurs after at most $n$ $m_i$-operations for each $m_i \in \mathsf{meth}(B)$. For each $a \in B$ and $n \in \mathbb{N}^*$, let $n^a_1, \ldots, n^a_k \geq n$ such that

$$\Pi_{\mathbb{M}}(\tau_p) + (m_1 \to n^a_1, \ldots, m_k \to n^a_k) \in \Pi_{\mathbb{M}}(S(a))$$

and let $o^a_n$ be the first operation in $\tau$ such that the prefix $\tau'$ of $\tau$ that ends in $o^a_n$, satisfies

$$\Pi_{\mathbb{M}}(\tau') \geq \Pi_{\mathbb{M}}(\tau_p) + (m_1 \to n^a_1, \ldots, m_k \to n^a_k). \quad (1)$$

The existence of $o^a_n$ is ensured by the fact that $\tau$ contains infinitely many $a$-operations, for each $a \in B$.

For all $n \in \mathbb{N}^*$ and $a$-operation $o$ in $\tau$ between $o^a_n$ and $o^a_{n+1}$, the local interpretation $li[o] = (V_o, \leq_o)$ is defined as follows. The set $V_o$ consists of all the operations of $\tau_p$, all the $m_i$-operations before $o_n$, and some $m_i$-operations before $o$ s.t.

$$\Pi_{\mathbb{M}}(V_o) = \Pi_{\mathbb{M}}(\tau_p) + (m_1 \to n^a_1, \ldots, m_k \to n^a_k).$$

This is possible because, for each $m_i \in \mathsf{meth}(B)$, there are at most $n$ $m_i$-operations before $o_n$, and $o$ occurs after $o^a_n$, that satisfies (1).

Now, since $\Pi_{\mathbb{M}}(V_o) \in \Pi_{\mathbb{M}}(S(a))$, there exists a partial order $\leq_o$ over the set $V_o$ such that $(V_o, \leq_o, \mathsf{meth}) \in S(a)$. For the finite number of $a$-operations $o$ that occur in $\tau$ before $o^a_1$, we use the local interpretations whose existence is ensured by the safety of $\tau$.

Since both $eb$ and $po$ are consistent with the total order $e$, axiom ThinAir holds. For each operation, we have chosen $li[o]$ so that axiom RVal holds. Moreover, for all $n \in \mathbb{N}^*$, each operation $o$ that occurs before $o_n$ is executed-before all operations, except for a finite set – those that precede some $o^a_n$ with $a \in B$. Thus, $eb$ satisfies axiom WeakEventual, which concludes the proof. □

By Lemma 3, an ORS $\mathcal{I}$ violates weak eventual consistency iff it violates safety or if it produces a trace in $\tau_p B^\omega$, for some $\tau_p$ and $B \subseteq \mathbb{M} \rhd \mathbb{D}$ with $\{m_1, \ldots, m_k\} = \mathsf{meth}(B)$, such that there exists a method synopsis $a \in B$ satisfying:

$$\exists n \in \mathbb{N}. \forall n_1, \ldots, n_k \geq n.$$
$$\Pi_{\mathbb{M}}(\tau_p) + (m_1 \to n_1, \ldots, m_k \to n_k) \notin \Pi_{\mathbb{M}}(S(a)) \quad (2)$$

Given $B \subseteq \mathbb{M} \triangleright \mathbb{D}$ and $a \in B$, let

$$\Pi_{\mathsf{notWEC}}(S, B, a) = \{v \mid \exists n \in \mathbb{N}. \forall n_1, \ldots, n_k \geq n. \\ v + (m_1 \to n_1, \ldots, m_k \to n_k) \notin \Pi_{\mathbb{M}}(S(a))\}.$$

Then, (2) can be rewritten as $\Pi_{\mathbb{M}}(\tau_p) \in \Pi_{\mathsf{notWEC}}(S, B, a)$.

Like for safety, we construct a monitor $\mathcal{M}_{\mathtt{live}}$, which counts the methods executed by the ORS, but this time without any bound. Finding a violation of weak eventual consistency reduces to finding a $B \subseteq \mathbb{M} \triangleright \mathbb{D}$ and a finite execution $\eta_p$ in the monitored system $\mathcal{I}\|\mathcal{M}_{\mathtt{live}}$, such that $\bigvee_{a \in B} \Pi_{\mathbb{M}}(\eta_p) \in \Pi_{\mathsf{notWEC}}(S, B, a)$ and $\eta_p$ can be extended by only using $B$-operations as well as infinitely many $a$-operations, for each $a \in B$. The latter can be checked using LTL model checking by adding to each state of the monitor, a register recording the method synopsis of the last transition.

Formally, $\mathcal{M}_{\mathtt{live}}$ is a transition system $(Q, Q_0, \delta)$, where

- $Q = (\mathbb{M} \to \mathbb{N}) \times \mathbb{M} \triangleright \mathbb{D}$,
- $I$ is the set of initial states: $(q_0, a) \in I$ iff $q_0 = (m \in \mathbb{M} \mapsto 0)$ and $a \in \mathbb{M} \triangleright \mathbb{D}$,
- $\delta \subseteq Q \times \mathbb{O}_{\mathcal{N}} \times Q$ where $((q_1, b), (N, (\mathsf{id}, a)), (q_2, a)) \in \delta$ iff $q_2 = q_1[\mathsf{meth}(a) \mapsto q_1(\mathsf{meth}(a)) + 1]$ and $a, b \in \mathbb{M} \triangleright \mathbb{D}$.

Now, given a replication system $\mathcal{I}$, we consider the monitored system $\mathcal{I}\|\mathcal{M}_{\mathtt{live}}$ defined as the parallel composition of $\mathcal{I}$ and $\mathcal{M}_{\mathtt{live}}$. Define the following LTL formula:

$$\varphi_{\mathsf{notWEC}} = \bigvee_{B \subseteq \mathbb{M} \triangleright \mathbb{D}} \bigvee_{a \in B} \Diamond(\Pi_{\mathsf{notWEC}}(S, B, a) \wedge \bigcirc \Box B \wedge \bigwedge_{b \in B} \Box \Diamond b).$$

By an abuse of notation, $\Pi_{\mathsf{notWEC}}(S, B, a)$ denotes also an atomic proposition, which holds in a state of the monitored system iff the vector formed by the counters of $\mathcal{M}_{\mathtt{live}}$ is in $\Pi_{\mathsf{notWEC}}(S, B, a)$. As for the minimal elements used in monitoring safety, the sets $\Pi_{\mathsf{notWEC}}(S, B, a)$ cannot be computed in general. In Section 7, we give a class of specifications for which they can. For each $B \subseteq \mathbb{M} \triangleright \mathbb{D}$ (resp., $b \in \mathbb{M} \triangleright \mathbb{D}$), $B$ (resp., $b$) is an atomic proposition which holds in a state iff the second part of the state of $\mathcal{M}_{\mathtt{live}}$ is in $B$ (resp., is $b$). Also, $\Diamond$, $\bigcirc$, and $\Box$ denote the temporal operators of LTL eventually, next, and always, respectively.

**Theorem 2** (Weak Eventual Consistency Monitoring). *An optimistic replication system $\mathcal{I}$ is weak eventually consistent if and only if $\mathcal{I}\|\mathcal{M}_{\mathtt{safe}}$ cannot reach $q_{\mathtt{err}}$ and $\mathcal{I}\|\mathcal{M}_{\mathtt{live}} \models \neg\varphi_{\mathsf{notWEC}}$.*

### 6.2 Eventual Consistency

By following the same line of reasoning as the one used for weak eventual consistency, we first derive a necessary and sufficient condition for a trace to be eventually consistent.

In the case of an eventually consistent infinite trace $\tau$, axiom EVENTUAL ensures that, for every finite prefix $P$ of the global interpretation order $gi$, after some finite prefix of $\tau$, all the operations have $P$ as a prefix of their local interpretations.

If $B \subseteq \mathbb{M} \triangleright \mathbb{D}$ is the set of all $a$ such that $\tau$ contains infinitely many $a$-operations, then the specification of each $a \in B$ must contain an infinite sequence of $\mathbb{M}$-labeled posets such that any prefix $P$ of $gi$ is a prefix of all these posets, except for some finite set. Thus, any prefix $P$ of $gi$ can be extended in order to belong to each of the $S(a)$ with $a \in B$. Moreover, if $P$ contains all the finitely occurring operations in $\tau$, then the extension can only add elements labeled by methods in $\mathsf{meth}(B)$. The set of labeled posets which can be extended in such a way is denoted by $Quot(S, B)$. This implies that an infinite sequence of increasing prefixes of $gi$ must belong to $Quot(S, B)$, which, by extending a classical definition of limit from words to labeled posets, can be stated as the poset defined by $gi$ is in the *limit* of $Quot(S, B)$. Now, since $gi$ is a reordering of $\tau$, this is equivalent to the fact that the multiset of methods that occur in $\tau$ is the same as the multiset of methods that occur in some infinite labeled poset belonging to the limit of $Quot(S, B)$. Thus, the eventual consistency of a trace $\tau$ can also be characterized in terms of Parikh images. We show in the following that the same monitor $\mathcal{M}_{\mathtt{live}}$ defined previously can be used to reduce the problem of checking eventual consistency to LTL model checking.

Next, we formally define $Quot(S, B)$ and the notion of limit.

**Definition 3** (Quotient). Given a specification $S$, $B \subseteq \mathbb{M} \triangleright \mathbb{D}$, and $a \in B$, let $S(a)\mathsf{meth}(B)^{-1}$ – the *quotient* of $S$ by $\mathsf{meth}(B)$ – be the set of labeled posets for which there exists an $\mathsf{meth}(B)$-completion in $S(a)$. Then, let

$$Quot(S, B) = \bigcap_{a \in B} S(a)\mathsf{meth}(B)^{-1}.$$

**Definition 4** (Limit). Given a set $\mathcal{A}$ of finite labeled posets, we denote by $lim(\mathcal{A})$ the set of infinite labeled posets $(A, \leq, \ell)$ which have an infinite sequence of increasing prefixes in $\mathcal{A}$ such that every element in $A$ is in a prefix (and all greater ones).

**Remark 1.** In the context of totally-ordered sets, the condition that every element in $A$ is in a prefix is already implied by the rest of the definition. However, this is not true in the general case. For instance, let $(A, \leq, \ell)$ be an infinite labeled poset, where $A = \{a_i \mid i \in \mathbb{N}\} \cup \{b_i \mid i \in \mathbb{N}\}$, $\ell(a_i) = a$, $\ell(b_i) = b$ for all $i \geq 0$, $a_0 \leq a_1 \leq \ldots$, and $b_0 \leq b_1 \leq \ldots$. This poset is not in the limit of $\mathcal{A}$, the set of all finite totally-ordered sets where all elements are labeled by $a$, even though it has an infinite increasing sequence of prefixes which are in $\mathcal{A}$. This is due to the fact that the prefixes don't contain all the elements of $(A, \leq, \ell)$.

This leads us to the following necessary and sufficient condition for eventual consistency.

**Lemma 4** (Characterization of Eventual Consistency). *Let $\tau = (O_\tau, po)$ be an infinite in $\tau_p B^\omega$. The trace $\tau$ is eventually consistent iff it is safe and $\Pi_{\mathbb{M}}(\tau) \in \Pi_{\mathbb{M}}(lim(Quot(S, B)))$.*

*Proof.* ($\Rightarrow$) If $\tau$ is eventually consistent, then there exist $gi \subseteq O_\tau \times O_\tau$, and for each operation $o \in O_\tau$, $li[o] \subseteq O_\tau \times O_\tau$ satisfying the axioms GIPF, THINAIR, RVAL, EVENTUAL.

It is enough to show that $(\mathbb{O}_\tau, gi, \mathsf{meth}) \in lim(Quot(S, B))$. Let $P$ be a finite prefix of $(\mathbb{O}_\tau, gi, \mathsf{meth})$ containing at least the operations of $\tau_p$. For any $a \in B$, by axiom EVENTUAL, since there are infinitely many $a$-operations, there exists at least one, $o$, such that $P$ is a prefix of $li_{\mathbb{M}}[o]$. By RVAL, $li_{\mathbb{M}}[o]$ belongs to $S(a)$, and by the fact that $P$ contains all operations in $\tau_p$, $li_{\mathbb{M}}[o]$ is a $\mathsf{meth}(B)$-completion of $P$. Thus, $P \in Quot(S, B)$. Since we can find an infinite increasing sequence of such prefixes $P$ containing every operation of $O_\tau$, we have $(\mathbb{O}_\tau, gi, \mathsf{meth}) \in lim(Quot(S, B))$.

($\Leftarrow$) This part of the proof is illustrated on Figure 5. Let $(A, \leq, \ell)$ be an $\mathbb{M}$-labeled poset in $\Pi_{\mathbb{M}}(lim(Quot(S, B)))$ with $\Pi_{\mathbb{M}}(\tau) = \Pi_{\mathbb{M}}(A)$. Define $gi$ such that $(\mathbb{O}_\tau, gi, \mathsf{meth})$ is isomorphic to $(A, \leq, \ell)$ and let $f$ be an isomorphism from $A$ to $O_\tau$.

There exists an infinite sequence of increasing prefixes $A_1, A_2, \ldots$ of $A$ such that every $f(A_i)$ contains the operations of $\tau_p$ and such that, for all $a \in B$, and for all $n \in \mathbb{N}^*$, $A_n \in S(a)\mathsf{meth}(B)^{-1}$. Moreover, each operation of $O_\tau$ appears in at least one $f(A_i)$, for some $i$ (and in every $f(A_j)$ with $j \geq i$).

Since $\tau$ is safe, there exists an issue order $e$ over $O_\tau$ that satisfies the conditions in Lemma 1. In the following, we consider that the operations in $\tau$ are totally ordered according to $e$.

The properties on $A_1, A_2, \ldots$ imply that, for every $a \in B$ and every $n \in \mathbb{N}^*$, there exists an $\mathsf{meth}(B)$-completion $A_n^a$ of $f(A_n)$ such that $A_n^a \in S(a)$. We assume that the elements added to $f(A_n)$ to obtain $A_n^a$ come from $O_\tau$ and that they occur after the operations in $f(A_n)$. This is possible because $\tau$ contains infinitely many $a$-

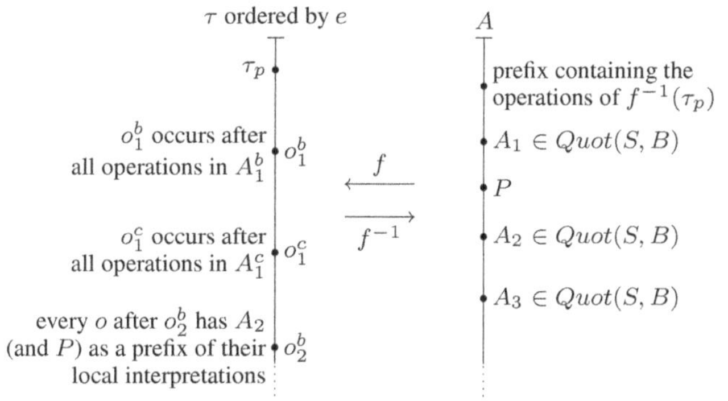


Figure 5: Illustration of the proof of the second part of Lemma 4 for $B = \{b, c\}$

operations, for each $a \in B$. For every $a \in B$ and $n \in \mathbb{N}^*$, let $o_n^a$ be the first operation that occurs in $\tau$ after all the operations in $A_n^a$.

In the following, we define $li[o]$, for every $o$, such that all the axioms of eventual consistency hold:

- for every $a \in B$, for the finite number of $a$-operations $o$, that occur in $\tau$ before $o_1^a$, we use the local interpretations whose existence is ensured by the fact that $\tau$ is safe. Similarly, for every $a' \in \mathbb{M} \triangleright \mathbb{D}$ such that $\tau$ contains finitely many $a'$-operations.
- for every $n \in \mathbb{N}^*$, $a \in B$, and for every $a$-operation $o$ between $o_n^a$ and $o_{n+1}^a$, we define $li[o] = A_n^a$. Note that this implies that $f(A_n) \preceq li_{\mathbb{M}}[o]$ and that $li_{\mathbb{M}}[o] \in S(a)$.

Axioms THINAIR and RVAL hold for the same reasons given in the proof of Lemma 3. Axiom GIPF holds because of the way we have defined the limit of a set of labeled posets. It remains to show that axiom EVENTUAL holds. Let $P$ be a prefix of $(O_\tau, gi)$. Let $A_n$ be one of the previously defined prefixes such that $P \preceq f(A_n)$. For every $a \in B$ and for every $a$-operation $o$ that occurs after $o_n^a$, $P$ is a prefix of $li[o]$. Thus, there are only finitely many operations which do not have $P$ as a prefix of their local interpretations, which concludes the proof. □

Monitoring for eventual consistency is similar to the monitoring used for weak eventual consistency. Let $\Pi_{\mathsf{notEC}}(S, B)$ be the set

$$\Pi_{\mathsf{notEC}}(S, B) = \{v \in \mathbb{M} \to \mathbb{N} \mid v + (m \in \mathsf{meth}(B) \mapsto \omega) \notin \Pi_{\mathbb{M}}(lim(Quot(S, B)))\}$$

According to Lemma 4, in order to find a trace which is not eventually consistent, it is enough to look for a trace in $\tau_p B^\omega$ for some $\tau_p$ and some $B \subseteq \mathbb{M} \triangleright \mathbb{D}$ such that $\Pi_{\mathbb{M}}(\tau_p) \in \Pi_{\mathsf{notEC}}(S, B)$. This problem can be again reduced to LTL model checking over the parallel composition of $\mathcal{I}$ and the same monitor $\mathcal{M}_{\mathtt{live}}$. In this case, the LTL formula to be checked is:

$$\varphi_{\mathsf{notEC}} = \bigvee_{B \subseteq \mathbb{M} \triangleright \mathbb{D}} \Diamond(\Pi_{\mathsf{notEC}}(S, B) \wedge \bigcirc \Box B \wedge \bigwedge_{b \in B} \Box \Diamond b)$$

As previously, for any $B \subseteq \mathbb{M} \triangleright \mathbb{D}$, $\Pi_{\mathsf{notEC}}(S, B)$ holds in a state of the monitored system if and only if the vector formed by the counters of $\mathcal{M}_{\mathtt{live}}$ is in $\Pi_{\mathsf{notEC}}(S, B)$.

**Theorem 3** (Eventual Consistency Monitoring). *An optimistic replication system $\mathcal{I}$ is eventually consistent if and only if $\mathcal{I} \| \mathcal{M}_{\mathtt{safe}}$ cannot reach $q_{\mathtt{err}}$ and $\mathcal{I} \| \mathcal{M}_{\mathtt{live}} \models \neg\varphi_{\mathsf{notEC}}$.*

## 7. Specifications of finite-state optimistic replication systems

The reductions of eventual consistency to reachability and LTL model checking are effective if one can compute the set of minimal elements in the Parikh image of the specification and effective representations for the sets of vectors $\Pi_{\mathsf{notWEC}}(S, B, a)$ and $\Pi_{\mathsf{notEC}}(S, B)$ defined in Section 6.1 and 6.2. In the following, we introduce automata-based representations for specifications of finite-state optimistic replication systems, for which this is possible.

Essentially, each $\Sigma$-labeled poset is abstracted as a sequence of multisets of symbols in $\Sigma$ which is then recognized by a finite-state automaton where the transitions, instead of being labeled by symbols as in the case of automata over words, are labeled by Presburger constraints. By viewing multisets of symbols as vectors of integers, a sequence of multisets is recognized by an automaton if there exists a run such that the sequence satisfies the constraints imposed by the transitions of this run at each step. The abstraction of a poset as a sequence of multisets is defined based on its decomposition in *levels*, used in algorithms for parallel tasks scheduling [22].

These automata offer a good compromise between simplicity and expressiveness. Since they can recognize words over an alphabet $\Sigma$, they can represent specifications, that contain only totally-ordered sets, required by ORS based on the Last Writer Wins conflict resolution policy [15]. They are also able to represent specifications of ORS with commutative conflict resolution policies (i.e., the effect of a set of conflicting operations does not depend on the order in which they are read) such as the CRDTs [7, 20] (see Example 8). For the latter case, the specifications represented by multiset automata are not exactly the ones introduced by the designers of these systems. However, we can prove that eventual consistency w.r.t the original specification is equivalent to eventual consistency w.r.t. the specification recognized by the multiset automaton. In the following, we give a precise statement of this result.

Let $S : \mathbb{M} \triangleright \mathbb{D} \to \mathcal{P}(\mathsf{PoSet}_{\mathbb{M}})$ be a specification and $\sim$ a symmetric binary relation over $\mathbb{M}$, called *commutativity relation*. We say that an $\mathbb{M}$-labeled poset $(A, \leq, \ell)$ is *canonical w.r.t.* $\sim$ iff any two elements labeled by symbols, that are in the relation $\sim$, are incomparable, i.e., for any $x, y \in A$, $\ell(x) \sim \ell(y)$ implies that $x \not\leq y$ and $y \not\leq x$. Then, the specification $S$ is called *$\sim$-closed* iff, for every $a \in \mathbb{M} \triangleright \mathbb{D}$, if $S(a)$ contains a labeled poset $\rho = (A, \leq, \ell)$, then $S(a)$ also contains a labeled poset $\rho' = (A, \leq', \ell)$, which is canonical w.r.t. $\sim$ and such that $\leq' \subseteq \leq$. Furthermore, let $S_\sim$ be a specification s.t. for every $a \in \mathbb{M} \triangleright \mathbb{D}$, $S_\sim(a)$ is the set of posets in $S(a)$, that are canonical w.r.t. $\sim$.

For example, the labeled poset in Figure 1c, belonging to the OR-Set specification, is canonical w.r.t the relation $\sim_O$ that consists of any pair of methods having different arguments (e.g., $\mathtt{add}(i)$ and $\mathtt{rem}(j)$ with $i \neq j$), and any pair formed of an add or a remove and respectively, a lookup (e.g., $\mathtt{add}(i)$ and $\mathtt{lookup}(i)$). The OR-Set specification in Example 6 is $\sim_O$-closed. Also, the MV-Register specification in Example 5 is $\sim_M$-closed, where $\sim_M$ contains any pair of a $\mathtt{wr}(i)$ method and a $\mathtt{rd}$ method.

The following result follows from the fact that eventual consistency imposes rather weak constraints on the local interpretations associated to the operations in a trace.

**Proposition 1.** *Let $\mathcal{I}$ be an ORS, $\sim$ a symmetric binary relation over $\mathbb{M}$, and $S$ a $\sim$-closed specification. Then, $\mathcal{I}$ is eventually consistent w.r.t $S$ iff $\mathcal{I}$ is eventually consistent w.r.t $S_\sim$.*

A specification $S$ is called *canonical w.r.t.* $\sim$ iff for every $a \in \mathbb{M} \triangleright \mathbb{D}$, $S(a)$ contains only posets, that are canonical w.r.t. $\sim$. Proposition 1 shows that, for ORS like the MV-Register and the OR-Set, it is enough to consider canonical specifications. In the following, we define multiset automata and show how they can be used to represent canonical specifications.

Let $\rho = (A, \leq, \ell)$ be a $\Sigma$-labeled poset. The $i$th level of $\rho$ is the set of elements $x$ in $A$ such that the length of the longest path starting in $x$ is $i$. A *decomposition* of $\rho$ is a sequence $A_{n-1}, \ldots, A_0$, where $n - 1$ is the length of the longest path in $\rho$ and, for all $0 \leq i \leq n - 1$, $A_i$ is the $i$th level of $\rho$. Note that the decomposition of a labeled poset is unique. The *$\Sigma$-decomposition* of $\rho$ is the

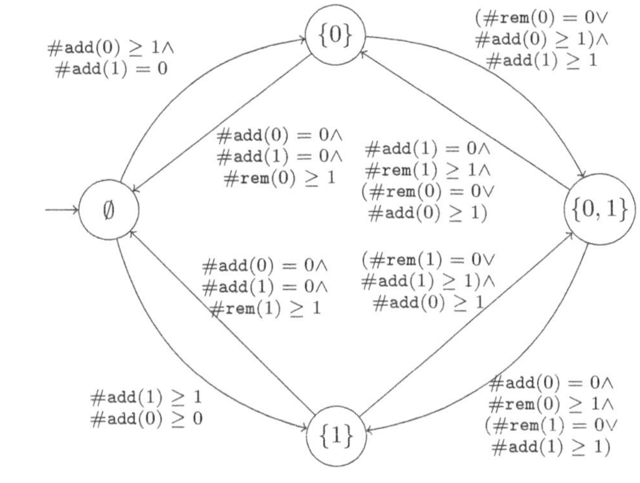


Figure 6: Some transitions of a multiset automaton that recognizes a specification of an OR-Set with at most two elements. The method synopsis $\texttt{lookup}(0) \triangleright 0$ labels the states $\emptyset$ and $\{1\}$, $\texttt{lookup}(0) \triangleright 1$ labels the states $\{0\}$ and $\{0,1\}$, and so on.

sequence $\Gamma_{n-1}, \ldots, \Gamma_0$, where for all $0 \leq i \leq n-1$, $\Gamma_i$ is the Parikh image of $A_i$. By definition, the length of $\Gamma_{n-1}, \ldots, \Gamma_0$ is $n$.

**Example 7.** [$\Sigma$-decomposition] Consider the $\mathbb{M}_{\text{OR-S}}$-labeled poset in Figure 1c. The $\mathbb{M}_{\text{OR-S}}$-decomposition of this labeled poset is:

$$\Gamma_2 = \{\texttt{add}(1), \texttt{rem}(1)\},$$
$$\Gamma_1 = \{\texttt{add}(1), \texttt{rem}(1), \texttt{rem}(1), \texttt{add}(0)\},$$
$$\Gamma_0 = \{\texttt{add}(1), \texttt{rem}(1), \texttt{rem}(0), \texttt{rem}(0)\}.$$

We define an effective representation for isomorphism-closed sets of $\mathbb{M}$-labeled posets by finite automata that recognize their $\mathbb{M}$-decompositions, i.e., sequences of *non-empty* multisets of symbols from $\mathbb{M}$. In order to represent multisets of symbols from $\mathbb{M}$, we consider Presburger formulas $\varphi$ over a set of free variables $\{\#m \mid m \in \mathbb{M}\}$, where $\#m$ denotes the number of occurrences of the symbol $m$. Let $\mathcal{F}_{\mathbb{M}}$ denote the set of all such formulas. Also, for any Presburger formula $\varphi$, let $[\varphi]$ denote the set of models of $\varphi$.

**Definition 5** (Multiset Automata). A *multiset automaton* over $\mathbb{M}$ and $\mathbb{M} \triangleright \mathbb{D}$ is a tuple

$$\mathcal{A} = (Q, \delta, Q_0, (Q_a \mid a \in \mathbb{M} \triangleright \mathbb{D})),$$

where $Q$ is a finite set of states, $\delta \subseteq Q \times \mathcal{F}_{\mathbb{M}} \times Q$ is the transition relation, $Q_0 \subseteq Q$ is the set of initial states, and, for any $a \in \mathbb{M} \triangleright \mathbb{D}$, $Q_a \subseteq Q$ (we say that the states in $Q_a$ are labeled by $a$).

Intuitively, an $\mathbb{M}$-labeled poset is recognized by $\mathcal{A}$ iff there exists a run in $\mathcal{A}$ starting in the initial state such that the transitions are labeled by formulas that are satisfied successively by the Parikh images of the $n-1$th level, $n-2$th level, etc. (where $n-1$ is the length of the longest path). For example, the multiset automaton in Figure 6 recognizes the labeled poset in Figure 1c because there exists a run starting in the initial state that goes through the states labeled by $\emptyset$, $\{1\}$, $\{0,1\}$, $\{1\}$ such that the associated sequence of formulas describe the $\mathbb{M}_{\text{OR-S}}$-decomposition in Example 7.

A run of a multiset automaton $\mathcal{A}$ is a sequence $q_0 \overset{\varphi_0}{\to} q_1 \overset{\varphi_1}{\to} \ldots \overset{\varphi_{n-1}}{\to} q_n$, s.t. for every $0 \leq i \leq n-1$, $(q_i, \varphi_i, q_{i+1}) \in \delta$. Such a run *recognizes* an $\mathbb{M}$-labeled poset $\rho$ iff the $\mathbb{M}$-decomposition of $\rho$ is $\Gamma_{n-1}\Gamma_{n-2}\ldots\Gamma_0$ and for every $0 \leq i \leq n-1$, $\Gamma_{n-1-i} \in [\varphi_i]$. We say that the length of this run is $n$.

Given $q \in Q$, the set of all $\mathbb{M}$-labeled posets recognized by a run of a $\mathcal{A}$, that ends in $q$, is denoted by $\mathcal{L}(\mathcal{A}, q)$. The labeled posets in $\mathcal{L}(\mathcal{A}, q)$ are said to be *interpreted to* $q$. Given a set of states $F \subseteq Q$, $\mathcal{L}(\mathcal{A}, F)$ denotes the union of $\mathcal{L}(\mathcal{A}, q)$ with $q \in F$.

**Definition 6** (Canonical specifications and multiset automata). A specification $S$ canonical w.r.t $\sim$ is *recognized* by a multiset automaton $\mathcal{A}$ iff for every $a \in \mathbb{M} \triangleright \mathbb{D}$, $S(a)$ is the set of posets in $\mathcal{L}(\mathcal{A}, Q_a)$, that are canonical w.r.t. $\sim$.

**Example 8.** [A multiset automaton for the OR-Set] Let $S^2_{\text{OR-S}}$ be a finite-state restriction of the OR-Set specification in Example 6 s.t. (1) the set object contains at most two elements 0 and 1 and (2) $S^2_{\text{OR-S}}$ contains only posets canonical w.r.t $\sim_O$. This specification is defined over the set of methods $\texttt{add}$, $\texttt{rem}$, and $\texttt{lookup}$ with arguments 0 and 1, denoted by $\mathbb{M}^2_{\text{OR-S}}$. The automaton in Figure 6 recognizes $S^2_{\text{OR-S}}$.

The following theorem is a direct consequence of the fact that, for any multiset automaton $\mathcal{A}$, one can construct a finite-automaton over sequences whose language has exactly the same Parikh image as the set of labeled posets recognized by $\mathcal{A}$.

**Theorem 4.** *Let $S$ be a specification recognized by a multiset automaton $\mathcal{A}$. Then, for every $a \in \mathbb{M} \triangleright \mathbb{D}$, there exists an effectively computable Presburger formula $\psi_a$ s.t. $\Pi(S(a)) = [\psi_a]$.*

Theorem 4 implies that, for every $a \in \mathbb{M} \triangleright \mathbb{D}$, the set of minimal elements in $\Pi(S(a))$ is effectively computable and that there exists a computable Presburger formula describing $\Pi_{\text{notWEC}}(S, B, a)$.

Given $B \subseteq \mathbb{M} \triangleright \mathbb{D}$, we show that $\Pi_{\text{notEC}}(S, B)$ defined in Section 6.2 is definable as an effectively computable Presburger formula provided that the specification $S$ is recognized by a multiset automaton $\mathcal{A}$ satisfying some conditions.

First, $\mathcal{A}$ must recognize a prefix-closed set of labeled posets, i.e., $\bigcup_q \mathcal{L}(\mathcal{A}, q)$ is prefix-closed. This is quite natural since the set of all posets in some specification, i.e., $\bigcup_a S(a)$, is usually prefix-closed. Another condition that $\mathcal{A}$ must satisfy can be roughly stated as follows: given a set of methods $M$ and a labeled poset $\rho$ interpreted to some state $q$, the fact that there exists an $M$-completion of $\rho$ interpreted to $q'$ depends only on the states $q$, $q'$, and the set of methods $M$. Formally, for all $q, q' \in Q$, $M \subseteq \mathbb{M}$, and $\rho_1, \rho_2 \in \mathcal{L}(\mathcal{A}, q)$, $\rho_1 \in \mathcal{L}(\mathcal{A}, q')M^{-1}$ iff $\rho_2 \in \mathcal{L}(\mathcal{A}, q')M^{-1}$. For example, if we consider the automaton in Figure 6, for any labeled poset interpreted to the state labeled by $\{1\}$ there exists an $\{\texttt{add}(0)\}$-completion interpreted to the state labeled by $\{0, 1\}$. In the case of the poset in Figure 1c this completion contains one more element labeled by $\texttt{add}(0)$, which is greater than all the elements labeled by $\texttt{rem}(0)$. Finally, we require that either $\mathcal{A}$ is a *word automaton*, i.e., the transitions are labeled by Presburger formulas that describe singleton multisets, or that for all $q$, if the limit of $\mathcal{L}(\mathcal{A}, q)$ contains an infinite poset $\rho$, then it also contains an infinite poset $\rho'$ with the same Parikh image as $\rho$ and such that the decomposition of $\rho'$ has at most $|Q|$ levels. This last condition is satisfied by the automaton in Figure 6 (and an automaton representing an MV-Register specification). Actually, the bound $|Q|$ can be replaced by the constant 2. It is satisfied also by an automaton that describes a specification for the MV-Register. An automaton $\mathcal{A}$ satisfying all these conditions is called *completion-bounded*.

**Theorem 5.** *Let $S$ be a specification recognized by a completion-bounded multiset automaton $\mathcal{A}$. Then, for every $B \subseteq \Sigma$, there exists an effectively computable Presburger formula $\varphi_B$ such that $[\varphi_B] = \Pi_{\text{notEC}}(S, B)$.*

*Proof sketch.* Given $a \in \mathbb{M} \triangleright \mathbb{D}$ and $M \subseteq \mathbb{M}$, we can prove that there exists a maximal set of states $F_{M,a}$ such that $S(a)M^{-1} = \mathcal{L}(\mathcal{A}, F_{M,a})$. To decide if a state $q$ belongs to $F_{M,a}$, one has to consider a minimal labeled poset interpreted to $q$ and search for an $M$-completion interpreted to a state in $Q_a$. It can be proved that if there exists such a completion there also exists one of bounded size.

Let $B \subseteq \mathbb{M} \triangleright \mathbb{D}$, $\mathbb{M}_B = \mathsf{meth}(B)$ and $F_B = \bigcap_{a \in B} F_{\mathbb{M}_B, a}$. If $F_B = \emptyset$ then $\varphi_B = \mathit{true}$. Otherwise, we compute a Presburger formula $\varphi$ that describes the complement of $\Pi_{\text{notEC}}(S, B)$, i.e., the set of vectors $v \in \mathbb{M} \to \mathbb{N}$ such that $v + (m \in \mathsf{meth}(B) \mapsto \omega) \in \Pi_{\mathbb{M}}(lim(Quot(S, B)))$. By definition, $Quot(S, B) = \mathcal{L}(\mathcal{A}, F_B)$.

First, we prove that $lim(\mathcal{L}(\mathcal{A}, F_B))$ is the union of $lim(\mathcal{L}(\mathcal{A}, q))$ with $q \in F_B$. Let $\rho$ be an infinite labeled poset, which has an infinite set of increasing prefixes $\rho_0, \rho_1, \ldots$ in $\mathcal{L}(\mathcal{A}, F_B)$. Also, let $\theta_0, \theta_1, \ldots$ be an infinite sequence of runs in $\mathcal{A}$ such that, for all $i$, $\theta_i$ is a run that recognizes $\rho_i$. By Ramsey's theorem, there exist infinitely many runs $\theta_{j_1}, \theta_{j_2}, \ldots$, that end in the same state $q \in F_B$. Thus, the infinitely many posets $\rho_{j_1}, \rho_{j_2}, \ldots$ belong to $\mathcal{L}(\mathcal{A}, q)$, which shows that $\rho \in lim(\mathcal{L}(\mathcal{A}, q))$. Next, we compute for each $q \in F_B$, a formula $\varphi_q$ that describes the set of vectors $v \in \mathbb{M} \to \mathbb{N}$ such that $v + (m \in \mathsf{meth}(B) \mapsto \omega) \in \Pi_{\mathbb{M}}(lim(\mathcal{L}(\mathcal{A}, q)))$. If $\mathcal{A}$ is a word automaton, then $\varphi_q$ describes the Parikh image of all the sequences accepted by a run of $\mathcal{A}$ that ends in a cycle on $q$ with at least one transition for each symbol in $\mathbb{M}_B$ and only transitions labeled by symbols in $\mathbb{M}_B$. Thus, $\varphi_q$ is effectively computable. Otherwise, we enumerate all the runs $q_0 \overset{\varphi_0}{\to} q_1 \overset{\varphi_1}{\to} \ldots \overset{\varphi_{n-1}}{\to} q_n = q$ of $\mathcal{A}$ of length at most $|Q|$. For every such run $\theta$, every index $0 \leq i \leq n-1$, and every surjective mapping $f : \mathbb{M}_B \to \{i, \ldots, n-1\}$, we define a run $\theta_f$ as follows. For each $i \leq j \leq n-1$, let $\varphi'_j$ be a formula describing the set of all multisets $v$ of symbols from $\mathbb{M} \setminus \mathbb{M}_B$ s.t. for every integer $L$, there exists a multiset modeled by $\varphi_j$, that consists of $v$, at least $L$ symbols $m$, for all $m \in f^{-1}(j)$, and possibly other symbols from $\mathbb{M}_B$. The run $\theta_f$ is obtained from $\theta$ by replacing $\varphi_j$ with $\varphi_j \wedge \varphi'_j$, for all $i \leq j \leq n-1$. The models of $\varphi_q$ are the Parikh images of all the posets, which are recognized by a run $\theta_f$ as above. To prove that the formula $\varphi_q$ is effectively computable, one can use the same reasoning as in the proof of Theorem 4. Finally, $\varphi$ is the disjunction of $\varphi_q$ with $q \in F_B$ and $\varphi_B = \neg\varphi$.

## 8. Decidability Results

We give decidability results for the case where the specifications are given by multiset automata, and where the optimistic replication system is composed of a fixed number of boolean programs communicating through uni-directional unbounded unordered channels. Each boolean program has instructions $\texttt{send}(\mathsf{msg}, j)$ that can be used to send a message $\mathsf{msg}$, which belongs to a finite set of messages, to the site identified by $j$. When a message is sent from a site $i$ to a site $j$, it is put in an unbounded unordered channel $ch_{i,j}$ from which site $j$ can read by using an instruction $\texttt{receive}(\mathsf{msg}, i)$. Such systems are called *finite-state optimistic replication systems*.

In order to define an operational model for finite-state optimistic replication systems, we use *Vector Addition Systems with States* (VASSs for short). Formally, a VASS $\mathcal{V}$ is a tuple $(Q, d, \delta)$ where $Q$ is a finite set of states, $d \in \mathbb{N}$ is the number of counter variables in the VASS, and $\delta \subseteq Q \times \mathbb{N}^d \times Q$ is the transition relation. The transition system induced by $\mathcal{V}$ is defined in the usual way. A configuration of $\mathcal{V}$ is a pair $(q, \boldsymbol{v})$ where $q \in Q$ and $\boldsymbol{v} \in \mathbb{N}^d$. There is a transition from a configuration $(q, \boldsymbol{v})$ to a configuration $(q', \boldsymbol{v}')$ iff there exists a transition $(q, \boldsymbol{u}, q')$ such that $\boldsymbol{v}' = \boldsymbol{v} + \boldsymbol{u}$.

We briefly describe how to model a finite-state optimistic replication system $\mathcal{I}$ using a VASS $\mathcal{V}$. A configuration of $\mathcal{I}$ is composed of two parts: the first part is a tuple where each component describes the state of a boolean program; the second part is a function, describing the content of each channel. In $\mathcal{V}$, the first part can be encoded in the finite set of states $Q$. Moreover, if Msg denotes the set of messages exchanged by the sites, the content of an unbounded unordered channel $ch$ of an optimistic replication system can be modeled by $|\mathsf{Msg}|$ counters $ch_1, \ldots, ch_{|\mathsf{Msg}|}$ used to count how many of each kind of messages there are in $ch$.

We are given a finite-state optimistic replication system $\mathcal{I}$ and a specification $S$ described by a multiset automaton $\mathcal{A}$. As a direct consequence of Theorem 4, given $a \in \mathbb{M} \triangleright \mathbb{D}$, the set of minimal elements in $\Pi(S(a))$ is effectively computable. This implies that also the safety monitor $\mathcal{M}_{\mathtt{safe}}$ can be effectively constructed. Moreover, if $\mathcal{V}$ is a VASS modeling $\mathcal{I}$, we can construct the parallel composition $\mathcal{V} \| \mathcal{M}_{\mathtt{safe}}$ of $\mathcal{V}$ with $\mathcal{M}_{\mathtt{safe}}$. We get a VASS $\mathcal{V}_{\mathtt{safe}}$, on which we can solve the problem of control state reachability, in order to know if it is possible to reach the error state $q_{\mathtt{err}}$ of the monitor. The bound $i$ for the minimal vectors $V_a$ used to construct $\mathcal{M}_{\mathtt{safe}}$ is exponential in $|A|$ and thus, the number of states in $\mathcal{M}_{\mathtt{safe}}$ (and in $\mathcal{V} \| \mathcal{M}_{\mathtt{safe}}$) is also exponential in $|A|$. Moreover solving control-state reachability in VASS is known to be EXPSPACE-complete, which leads to the following theorem.

**Theorem 6** (Decidability of Safety). *For a finite-state optimistic replication system $\mathcal{I}$ (given as a VASS), and a specification $S$ described by a multiset automaton, the problem of checking the safety of $\mathcal{I}$ w.r.t. $S$ is decidable, and in 2-EXPSPACE.*

The following lemma is used for proving the decidability of both weak eventual consistency and eventual consistency.

**Lemma 5.** *Let $\mathcal{V} = (Q, d, \delta)$ be a VASS where the states are labeled with atomic propositions coming from a finite set $AP$. Let $\varphi$ be a Presburger formula with d free variables, and $P \subseteq AP$. The problem of checking the LTL formula*

$$\mathcal{V} \models \neg\Diamond(\varphi \wedge \bigcirc\Box P \wedge \bigwedge_{p \in P} \Box\Diamond p)$$

*is decidable, and can be reduced to reachability in VASS.*

*Proof.* For the formula to be satisfied, there must exist an infinite execution in $\mathcal{V}$ of the form $(q_0, \boldsymbol{v}_0) \ldots (q_i, \boldsymbol{v}_i) \ldots$ where (1) the valuation of the counters in $\boldsymbol{v}_i$ satisfies $\varphi$, (2) for all $j > i$, $q_j$ is labeled by a proposition in $P$, and (3) for each $p \in P$, there are infinitely many $q_j$ labeled by $p$.

First, Th. 2.14 in Valk and Jantzen [24] shows that it is possible to compute the minimal elements of the upward-closed set of configurations $U_P$ from which there exists an infinite execution visiting only states labeled by a proposition in $P$ and infinitely many states labeled by $p$, for each $p \in P$. Then, we construct a Presburger formula $\varphi'$ representing the intersection of $[\varphi]$ and $U_P$. The problem of checking if there exists a reachable configuration in $\mathcal{V}$ satisfying $\varphi'$ can be reduced to (configuration) reachability in VASS [4]. □

**Theorem 7** (Decidability of (Weak) Eventual Consistency). *Given a finite-state optimistic replication system $\mathcal{I}$, and a specification $S$ described by a multiset automaton, the problem of checking the (weak) eventual consistency of $\mathcal{I}$ w.r.t. $S$ is decidable.*

## 9. Related Work

Our definition of eventual consistency is inspired by the one given in Burckhardt et al. [6] but it differs from it on several points. In that paper, eventual consistency is defined over traces that are also posets of operations, but the partial order, called *session order*, is defined such that all the operations performed by an user in a session are totally ordered and operations from different sessions are incomparable. Then, a trace is eventually consistent iff there exist two relations over the operations in the trace, called arbitration and resp., visibility relation (denoted by ar and resp., vis), such that (1) the union of vis with the session order is acyclic, (2) for every operation $o$, the return value of $o$ is associated by the specification to the pair formed of the $\mathbb{M}$-labeled poset $(\mathsf{vis}^{-1}(o), \mathsf{vis}, \mathsf{meth})$ and the projection of ar over the operations in $\mathsf{vis}^{-1}(o)$, (3) ar is a total order, and (4) every operation $o$ is not visible only to some finite set of operations, i.e., for every $o$, $\{o' \mid (o, o') \notin \mathsf{vis}\}$ is finite.

First, the partial orders over operations that define a trace have different meanings. The operations in a session can be submitted to multiple sites and thus, an infinite extension of the execution in Fig. 2b, where each operation appearing in the figure is executed in a different session, is declared to be eventually consistent although the union of vis with the session order is acyclic. Then, the definition of a specification in Burckhardt et al. [6] is different because it contains labeled posets augmented with a total order. With our understanding of ORS we think that it is not necessary to add such total orders. A specification should model only the semantics of the operations and some abstraction of the conflict resolution policy. The formalization of the fact that sites will eventually see a consistent state is also different. In fact, the formalization in Burckhardt et al. [6] does not apply to systems that perform speculative executions (this is remarked also by the authors). Intuitively, the order in which two operations are executed cann't change once they are visible. For example, two operations $o_1$, $o_2$ with $\mathsf{vis}^{-1}(o_1) = \mathsf{vis}^{-1}(o_2)$, which are instances of the same method, must return the same value. But, for this class of systems, it is possible that the order in which the operations in $\mathsf{vis}^{-1}(o_1)$ are executed changes in between the execution of $o_1$ and the execution of $o_2$ and thus, it is possible that the two operations return different values. Another difference is that in our case the local interpretations may converge toward a *partial* order over the operations in the trace, while in Burckhardt et al. [6] they can converge only toward a total order. For instance, this allows that the sites don't have to agree on the order between two conflicting operations, which are commutative.

There are other works that provide formal definitions for eventual consistency, e.g., [3, 9, 20, 21], but they either consider its weaker form, i.e., quiescent consistency, or they use a particular model for the ORS. In general, there exist ORS that guarantee stronger criteria than eventual consistency, e.g., strong eventual consistency [20] or causal+ consistency [17]. Stronger notions for the safety part of eventual consistency, e.g., causal consistency or session guarantees, are formalized in Burckhardt et al. [6] by adding more requirements on the session order and the relation vis. With slight modifications, such requirements can be also added to our definition.

There are works that define decision procedures for the verification of correctness criteria like sequential consistency or linearizability, e.g., [1, 5, 8, 11]. The techniques used in these cases are different from the ones introduced in this paper for eventual consistency, in particular because they are defined over finite traces.

## 10. Conclusion

We provide an algorithmic approach for verifying eventual consistency of ORS. Our approach is based on reducing the problem of checking eventual consistency to reachability and model-checking problems. This connection is a fundamental result which opens the doors to using existing – exact or approximate – verification tools for message-passing programs (depending on the considered class of systems for the implementation) in the context of verifying ORS.

Our reduction is defined for a general, formally defined, notion of eventual consistency, allowing to reason about a wide class of systems, including those using speculative executions and roll-backs such as Bayou [23] or Telex [2]. In fact, one of the contributions of our paper is to provide such a definition of eventual consistency, as well as a new class of automata that is expressive enough to capture usual specifications of distributed data structures, and which has the needed properties for use in algorithmic verification.

We have in addition shown that when implementations are defined as communicating boolean programs through unbounded unordered channels, the problem of verifying eventual consistency is decidable. As for complexity, our algorithm for checking the safety part of eventual consistency is in 2EXPSPACE, but the problem is EXPSPACE-hard (it is at least as hard as state reachability in VASS). Therefore, an interesting question is whether it is possible to match the two bounds in this case. For the general case of eventual consistency (with liveness), we know that the problem is also EXPSPACE-hard, and that it can be solved using configuration reachability in VASS, which is decidable but with an unknown upper-bound. Then, an interesting question is whether configuration reachability in VASS is needed. We believe that this is the case.

## References


[1] R. Alur, K. L. McMillan, and D. Peled. Model-checking of correctness conditions for concurrent objects. *Inf. Comput.*, 160(1-2):167–188, 2000.

[2] L. Benmouffok, J.-M. Busca, J. M. Marquès, M. Shapiro, P. Sutra, and G. Tsoukalas. Telex: A semantic platform for cooperative application development. In *CFSE*, Toulouse, France, 2009.

[3] A.-M. Bosneag and M. Brockmeyer. A formal model for eventual consistency semantics. In *IASTED PDCS*, pages 204–209, 2002.

[4] A. Bouajjani and P. Habermehl. Constrained properties, semilinear systems, and petri nets. In *CONCUR*, pages 481–497, 1996.

[5] A. Bouajjani, M. Emmi, C. Enea, and J. Hamza. Verifying concurrent programs against sequential specifications. In *ESOP*, 2013.

[6] S. Burckhardt, A. Gotsman, and H. Yang. Understanding eventual consistency. Technical Report MSR-TR-2013-39, Microsoft Research.

[7] G. DeCandia, D. Hastorun, M. Jampani, G. Kakulapati, A. Lakshman, A. Pilchin, S. Sivasubramanian, P. Vosshall, and W. Vogels. Dynamo: amazon's highly available key-value store. In *SOSP*, 2007.

[8] A. Farzan and P. Madhusudan. Monitoring atomicity in concurrent programs. In *CAV 2008*, pages 52–65. Springer.

[9] A. Fekete, D. Gupta, V. Luchangco, N. A. Lynch, and A. A. Shvartsman. Eventually-serializable data services. In *PODC*, pages 300–309, 1996.

[10] S. Gilbert and N. A. Lynch. Brewer's conjecture and the feasibility of consistent, available, partition-tolerant web services. *SIGACT News*, 33(2):51–59, 2002.

[11] T. A. Henzinger, S. Qadeer, and S. K. Rajamani. Verifying sequential consistency on shared-memory multiprocessor systems. In *CAV*, volume 1633 of *LNCS*, pages 301–315, 1999.

[12] M. Herlihy and N. Shavit. *The art of multiprocessor programming*.

[13] M. Herlihy and J. M. Wing. Linearizability: A correctness condition for concurrent objects. *ACM Trans. Program. Lang. Syst.*, 12(3):463–492, 1990.

[14] J. H. Howard, M. L. Kazar, S. G. Menees, D. A. Nichols, M. Satyanarayanan, R. N. Sidebotham, and M. J. West. Scale and performance in a distributed file system. *ACM Trans. Comput. Syst.*, 6(1):51–81, 1988.

[15] P. R. Johnson and R. H. Thomas. The maintenance of duplicate databases. Technical Report Internet Request for Comments RFC 677, Information Sciences Institute, January 1976.

[16] A.-M. Kermarrec, A. I. T. Rowstron, M. Shapiro, and P. Druschel. The icecube approach to the reconciliation of divergent replicas. In *PODC*, pages 210–218, 2001.

[17] W. Lloyd, M. J. Freedman, M. Kaminsky, and D. G. Andersen. Don't settle for eventual: scalable causal consistency for wide-area storage with COPS. In *SOSP*, pages 401–416, 2011.

[18] J. Michaux, X. Blanc, M. Shapiro, and P. Sutra. A semantically rich approach for collaborative model edition. In *SAC*, pages 1470–1475, 2011.

[19] Y. Saito and M. Shapiro. Optimistic replication. *ACM Comput. Surv.*, 37(1):42–81, 2005.

[20] M. Shapiro, N. Preguiça, C. Baquero, and M. Zawirski. A comprehensive study of Convergent and Commutative Replicated Data Types. Rapport de recherche RR-7506, INRIA, Jan. 2011.

[21] M. Shapiro, N. M. Preguiça, C. Baquero, and M. Zawirski. Conflict-free replicated data types. In *SSS*, pages 386–400, 2011.

[22] O. Sinnen. *Task Scheduling for Parallel Systems*. 2007.

[23] D. B. Terry, M. M. Theimer, K. Petersen, A. J. Demers, M. J. Spreitzer, and C. H. Hauser. Managing update conflicts in bayou, a weakly connected replicated storage system. *SIGOPS Oper. Syst. Rev.*, 29(5): 172–182, Dec. 1995.

[24] R. Valk and M. Jantzen. The residue of vector sets with applications to decidability problems in petri nets. *Acta Inf.*, 21:643–674, 1985.

# On Coinductive Equivalences for Higher-Order Probabilistic Functional Programs

Ugo Dal Lago  Davide Sangiorgi
Università di Bologna & INRIA
{dallago,sangio}@cs.unibo.it

Michele Alberti
Institut de Mathématiques de Luminy
CNRS & Université d'Aix-Marseille
michele.alberti@univ-amu.fr

## Abstract

We study bisimulation and context equivalence in a probabilistic $\lambda$-calculus. The contributions of this paper are threefold. Firstly we show a technique for proving congruence of *probabilistic applicative bisimilarity*. While the technique follows Howe's method, some of the technicalities are quite different, relying on non-trivial "disentangling" properties for sets of real numbers. Secondly we show that, while bisimilarity is in general strictly finer than context equivalence, coincidence between the two relations is attained on pure $\lambda$-terms. The resulting equality is that induced by *Levy-Longo trees*, generally accepted as the finest extensional equivalence on pure $\lambda$-terms under a lazy regime. Finally, we derive a coinductive characterisation of context equivalence on the whole probabilistic language, via an extension in which terms akin to distributions may appear in redex position. Another motivation for the extension is that its operational semantics allows us to experiment with a different congruence technique, namely that of *logical bisimilarity*.

***Categories and Subject Descriptors*** F.3.1 [*Logics and Meaning of Programs*]: Specifying and Verifying and Reasoning about Programs—logics of programs; F.3.2 [*Logics and Meaning of Programs*]: Semantics of Programming Languages—operational semantics.

***General Terms*** Theory

***Keywords*** Bisimulation; Probabilistic Lambda Calculus; Coinduction; Howe's Technique.

## 1. Introduction

Probabilistic models are more and more pervasive. Not only are they a formidable tool when dealing with uncertainty and incomplete information, but they sometimes are a *necessity* rather than an option, like in computational cryptography (where, e.g., secure public key encryption schemes need to be probabilistic [17]). A nice way to deal computationally with probabilistic models is to allow probabilistic choice as a primitive when designing algorithms, this way switching from usual, deterministic computation to a new paradigm, called probabilistic computation. Examples of application areas in which probabilistic computation has proved to be useful include natural language processing [29], robotics [44], computer vision [8], and machine learning [33].

This new form of computation, of course, needs to be available to programmers to be accessible. And indeed, various probabilistic programming languages have been introduced in the last years, spanning from abstract ones [24, 32, 37] to more concrete ones [18, 34], being inspired by various programming paradigms like imperative, functional or even object oriented. A quite common scheme consists in endowing any deterministic language with one or more primitives for probabilistic choice, like binary probabilistic choice or primitives for distributions.

One class of languages that cope well with probabilistic computation are functional languages. Indeed, viewing algorithms as functions allows a smooth integration of distributions into the playground, itself nicely reflected at the level of types through monads [20, 37]. As a matter of fact, many existing probabilistic programming languages [18, 34] are designed around the $\lambda$-calculus or one of its incarnations, like Scheme.

The focus of this paper are operational techniques for understanding and reasoning about program equality in higher-order probabilistic languages. Checking computer programs for equivalence is a crucial, but challenging, problem. Equivalence between two programs generally means that the programs should behave "in the same manner" under any context. Specifically, two $\lambda$-terms are *context equivalent* if they have the same convergence behavior (i.e., they do or do not terminate) in any possible context. Finding effective methods for context equivalence proofs is particularly challenging in higher-order languages.

*Bisimulation* has emerged as a very powerful operational method for proving equivalence of programs in various kinds of languages, due to the associated coinductive proof method. To be useful, the behavioral relation resulting from bisimulation — *bisimilarity* — should be a *congruence*, and should also be sound with respect to context equivalence. Bisimulation has been transplanted onto higher-order languages by Abramsky [1]. This version of bisimulation, called *applicative bisimulation* has received considerable attention [19, 27, 28, 35, 36, 39]. In short, two functions $M$ and $N$ are applicative bisimilar when their applications $MP$ and $NP$ are applicative bisimilar for any argument $P$.

Often, checking a given notion of bisimulation to be a congruence in higher-order languages is nontrivial. In the case of applicative bisimilarity, congruence proofs usually rely on Howe's method [22]. Other forms of bisimulation have been proposed, such as environmental bisimulation and logical bisimulation [25, 41, 42], with the goal of relieving the burden of the proof of congruence, and of accommodating language extensions.

In this work, we consider the pure $\lambda$-calculus extended with a probabilistic choice operator. Context equivalence of two terms



*POPL '14*, January 22–24, 2014, San Diego, CA, USA.

http://dx.doi.org/10.1145/2535838.2535872

means that they have the same *probability of convergence* in all contexts. The objective of the paper is to understand context equivalence and bisimulation in this paradigmatic probabilistic higher-order language, called $\Lambda_\oplus$.

The paper contains three main technical contributions. The first is a proof of congruence for probabilistic applicative bisimilarity along the lines of Howe's method. This technique consists in defining, for every relation on terms $\mathcal{R}$, its Howe's lifting $\mathcal{R}^H$. The construction, essentially by definition, ensures that the relation obtained by lifting bisimilarity is a congruence; the latter is then proved to be itself a bisimulation, therefore coinciding with applicative bisimilarity. Definitionally, probabilistic applicative bisimulation is obtained by setting up a labelled Markov chain on top of $\lambda$-terms, then adapting to it the coinductive scheme introduced by Larsen and Skou in a first-order setting [26]. In the proof of congruence, the construction $(\cdot)^H$ closely reflects analogous constructions for nondeterministic extensions of the $\lambda$-calculus. The novelties are in the technical details for proving that the resulting relation is a bisimulation: in particular our proof of the so-called Key Lemma — an essential ingredient in Howe's method — relies on non-trivial "disentangling" properties for sets of real numbers, these properties themselves proved by modeling the problem as a flow network and then apply the Max-flow Min-cut Theorem. The congruence of applicative bisimilarity yields soundness with respect to context equivalence as an easy corollary. Completeness, however, fails: applicative bisimilarity is proved to be finer. A subtle aspect is also the late vs. early formulation of bisimilarity; with a choice operator the two versions are semantically different; our construction crucially relies on the late style.

In our second main technical contribution we show that the presence of higher-order functions and probabilistic choice in contexts gives context equivalence and applicative bisimilarity maximal discriminating power on pure $\lambda$-terms. We do so by proving that, on pure $\lambda$-terms, both context equivalence and applicative bisimilarity coincide with the *Levy-Longo tree equality*, which equates terms with the same Levy-Longo tree (briefly LLT), and is generally accepted as the finest extensional equivalence on pure $\lambda$-terms under a *lazy* regime. The result is in sharp contrast with what happens under a nondeterministic interpretation of choice (or in the absence of choice), where context equivalence is coarser than LLT equality.

Our third main contribution is a coinductive characterisation of probabilistic context equivalence on the whole language $\Lambda_\oplus$ (as opposed to the subset of pure $\lambda$-terms). We obtain this result by setting a bisimulation game on an extension of $\Lambda_\oplus$ in which weighted formal sums — terms akin to distributions — may appear in redex position. Thinking of distributions as sets of terms, the construction reminds us of the reduction of nondeterministic to deterministic automata. The technical details are however quite different, because we are in a higher-order language and therefore — once more — we are faced with the congruence problem for bisimulation, and because formal sums may contain an *infinite* number of terms. For the proof of congruence of bisimulation in this extended language, we have experimented the technique of logical bisimulation. In this method (and in the related method of environmental bisimulation), the clauses of applicative bisimulation are modified so to allow the standard congruence argument for bisimulations in first-order languages, where the bisimulation method itself is exploited to establish that the closure of the bisimilarity under contexts is again a bisimulation. Logical bisimilarities have two key elements. First, bisimilar functions may be tested with *bisimilar* (rather than identical) arguments (more precisely, the arguments should be in the context closure of the bisimulation; the use of contexts is necessary for soundness). Secondly, the transition system should be small-step, deterministic (or at least confluent), and the bisimulation game should also be played on internal moves. In our probabilistic setting, the ordinary logical bisimulation game has to be modified substantially. Formal sums represent possible evolutions of running terms, hence they should appear in redex position only (allowing them anywhere would complicate matters considerably). The obligation of redex position for certain terms is in contrast with the basic schema of logical bisimulation, in which related terms can be used as arguments to bisimilar functions and can therefore end up in arbitrary positions. We solve this problem by moving to *coupled logical bisimulations*, where a bisimulation is formed by a pair of relations, one on $\Lambda_\oplus$-terms, the other on terms extended with formal sums. The bisimulation game is played on both relations, but only the first relation is used to assemble input arguments for functions.

Another delicate point is the meaning of internal transitions for formal sums. In logical bisimilarity the transition system should be small-step; and formal sums should evolve into values in a finite number of steps, even if the number of terms composing the formal sum is infinite. We satisfy these requirements by defining the transition system for extended terms on top of that for $\Lambda_\oplus$-terms. The proof of congruence of coupled logical bisimilarity also exploits an "up-to distribution" bisimulation proof technique.

In the paper we adopt call-by-name evaluation. The results on applicative bisimilarity can be transported onto call-by-value; in contrast, transporting the other results is more problematic, and we leave it for future work. See Section 6 for more details.

An extended version of this paper is available [10].

### 1.1 Further Related Work

Research on (higher-order) probabilistic functional languages have, so far, mainly focused on either new programming constructs, or denotational semantics, or applications. The underlying operational theory, which in the ordinary $\lambda$-calculus is known to be very rich, has remained so far largely unexplored. In this section, we give some pointers to the relevant literature on probabilistic $\lambda$-calculi, without any hope of being exhaustive.

Various probabilistic $\lambda$-calculi have been proposed, starting from the pioneering work by Saheb-Djahromi [38], followed by more advanced studies by Jones and Plotkin [24]. Both these works are mainly focused on denotational semantics. More recently, there has been a revamp on this line of work, with the introduction of adequate (and sometimes also fully-abstract) denotational models for probabilistic variations of PCF [11, 16]. There is also another thread of research in which various languages derived from the $\lambda$-calculus are given types in monadic style, allowing this way to nicely model concrete problems like Bayesian inference and probability models arising in robotics [20, 32, 37]; these works however, do not study operationally based theories of program equivalence.

Nondeterministic extensions of the $\lambda$-calculus have been analysed in typed calculi [3, 27, 43] as well as in untyped calculi [6, 13, 23, 30]. The emphasis in all these works is mainly domain-theoretic. Apart from [30], all cited authors closely follow the testing theory [12], in its modalities *may* or *must*, separately or together. Ong's approach [30] inherits both testing and bisimulation elements.

Our definition of applicative bisimulation follows Larsen and Skou's scheme [26] for fully-probabilistic systems. Many other forms of probabilistic bisimulation have been introduced in the literature, but their greater complexity is usually due to the presence of *both* nondeterministic and probabilistic behaviors, or to continuous probability distributions. See surveys such as [5, 21, 31].

Contextual characterisations of LLT equality include [7], in a $\lambda$-calculus with multiplicities in which deadlock is observable, and [15], in a $\lambda$-calculus with choice, parallel composition, and both call-by-name and call-by-value applications. See [14] for a survey on observational characterisations of $\lambda$-calculus trees.

## 2. Preliminaries

### 2.1 A Pure, Untyped, Probabilistic Lambda Calculus

Let $\mathsf{X} = \{x, y, \ldots\}$ be a denumerable set of variables. The set $\Lambda_\oplus$ of *term expressions*, or *terms* is defined as follows:

$$M, N, L ::= x \;\big|\; \lambda x.M \;\big|\; MN \;\big|\; M \oplus N,$$

where $x \in \mathsf{X}$. The only non-standard operator in $\Lambda_\oplus$ is probabilistic choice: $M \oplus N$ is a term which is meant to behave as either $M$ or $N$, each with probability $\frac{1}{2}$. A more general construct $M \oplus_p N$ where $p$ is any (computable) real number from $[0, 1]$, is derivable, given the universality of the $\lambda$-calculus (see, e.g., [9]). The set of free variables of a term $M$ is indicated as $\mathsf{FV}(M)$ and is defined as usual. Given a finite set of variables $\overline{x} \subseteq \mathsf{X}$, $\Lambda_\oplus(\overline{x})$ denotes the set of terms whose free variables are among the ones in $\overline{x}$. A term $M$ is *closed* if $\mathsf{FV}(M) = \emptyset$ or, equivalently, if $M \in \Lambda_\oplus(\emptyset)$. The (capture-avoiding) substitution of $N$ for the free occurrences of $x$ in $M$ is denoted $M\{^N/x\}$. We sometimes use the identity term $I \stackrel{\text{def}}{=} \lambda x.x$, the projector $K \stackrel{\text{def}}{=} \lambda x.\lambda y.x$, and the purely divergent term $\Omega \stackrel{\text{def}}{=} (\lambda x.xx)(\lambda x.xx)$.

Terms are now given a call-by-name semantics following [9]. A term is a *value* if it is a closed $\lambda$-abstraction. We call $\mathsf{V}\Lambda_\oplus$ the set of all values. Values are ranged over by metavariables like $V, W, X$. Closed terms evaluates not to a single value, but to a *(partial) value distribution*, that is, a function $\mathscr{D} : \mathsf{V}\Lambda_\oplus \to \mathbb{R}_{[0,1]}$ such that $\sum_{V \in \mathsf{V}\Lambda_\oplus} \mathscr{D}(V) \le 1$. Distributions do not necessarily sum to 1, so to model the possibility of (probabilistic) divergence. Given a value distribution $\mathscr{D}$, its *support* $\mathsf{S}(\mathscr{D})$ is the subset of $\mathsf{V}\Lambda_\oplus$ whose elements are values to which $\mathscr{D}$ attributes positive probability. Value distributions ordered pointwise form both a lower semilattice and an $\omega\mathbf{CPO}$: limits of $\omega$-chains always exist. Given a value distribution $\mathscr{D}$, its *sum* $\sum \mathscr{D}$ is $\sum_{V \in \mathsf{V}\Lambda_\oplus} \mathscr{D}(V)$.

The call-by-name semantics of a closed term $M$ is a value distribution $[\![M]\!]$ defined in one of the ways explained in [9]. We recall this now, though only briefly for lack of space. The first step consists in defining a formal system deriving finite *lower approximations* to the semantics of $M$. Big-step approximation semantics, as an example, derives judgments in the form $M \Downarrow \mathscr{D}$, where $M$ is a term and $\mathscr{D}$ is a value distribution of finite support (see Figure 1). Small-step approximation semantics can be defined similarly, and derives judgments in the form $M \Rightarrow \mathscr{D}$. Noticeably, big-step and small-step can simulate each other, i.e. if $M \Downarrow \mathscr{D}$, then $M \Rightarrow \mathscr{E}$ where $\mathscr{E} \ge \mathscr{D}$, and *vice versa* [9]. In the second step, $[\![M]\!]$, called the *semantics* of $M$, is set as the least upper bound of distributions obtained in either of the two ways:

$$[\![M]\!] \stackrel{\text{def}}{=} \sup_{M \Downarrow \mathscr{D}} \mathscr{D} = \sup_{M \Rightarrow \mathscr{D}} \mathscr{D}.$$

Notice that the above is well-defined because for every $M$, the set of all distributions $\mathscr{D}$ such that $M \Downarrow \mathscr{D}$ is directed, and thus its least upper bound is a value distribution because of $\omega$-completeness.

EXAMPLE 2.1. *Consider the term $M \stackrel{\text{def}}{=} I \oplus (K \oplus \Omega)$. We have $M \Downarrow \mathscr{D}$, where $\mathscr{D}(I) = \frac{1}{2}$ and $\mathscr{D}(V)$ is 0 elsewhere, as well as $M \Downarrow \emptyset$, where $\emptyset$ is the empty distribution. The distribution $[\![M]\!]$ assigns $\frac{1}{2}$ to $I$ and $\frac{1}{4}$ to $K$.*

The semantics of terms satisfies some useful equations, such as:

LEMMA 2.2. $[\![M \oplus N]\!] = \frac{1}{2}[\![M]\!] + \frac{1}{2}[\![N]\!]$.

We are interested in context equivalence in this probabilistic setting. Typically, in a qualitative scenario as the (non)deterministic one, terms are considered context equivalent if they both converge or diverge. Here, we need to take into account quantitative information.

```
expone f n = (f n) (+) (expone f n+1)
exptwo f = (\x -> f x) (+) (exptwo (\x -> f (x+1)))
expthree k f n = foldp k n f (expthree (expone id k) f)

foldp 0 n f g = g n
foldp m n f g = (f n) (+) (foldp (m-1) (n+1) f g)
```

**Figure 2.** Three Higher-Order Functions

DEFINITION 2.3 (Context Preorder and Equivalence). *The expression $M \Downarrow_p$ stands for $\sum [\![M]\!] = p$, i.e., the term $M$ converges with probability $p$. The* context preorder *$\le_\oplus$ stipulates $M \le_\oplus N$ if $C[M]\Downarrow_p$ implies $C[N]\Downarrow_q$ with $p \le q$, for every closing context $C$. The equivalence induced by $\le_\oplus$ is* probabilistic context equivalence, *denoted as $\simeq_\oplus$.*

REMARK 2.4 (Types, Open Terms). *The results in this paper are stated for an untyped language. Adapting them to a simply-typed language is straightforward; we use integers, booleans and recursion in examples. Moreover, while the results are often stated for closed terms only, they can be generalized to open terms in the expected manner. In the paper, context equivalences and preorders are defined on open terms; (bi)similarities are defined on closed terms and it is then intended that they are extended to open terms by requiring the usual closure under substitutions.*

EXAMPLE 2.5. *We give some basic examples of higher-order probabilistic programs, which we will analyse using the coinductive techniques we introduce later in this paper. Consider the functions* `expone`, `exptwo`, *and* `expthree` *from Figure 2. They are written in a* Haskell*-like language extended with probabilistic choice, but can also be seen as terms in a (typed) probabilistic $\lambda$-calculus with integers and recursion akin to $\Lambda_\oplus$. Term* `expone` *takes a function* `f` *and a natural number* `n` *in input, then it proceeds by tossing a fair coin (captured here by the binary infix operator* `(+)`*) and, depending on the outcome of the toss, either calls* `f` *on* `n`*, or recursively calls itself on* `f` *and* `n+1`*. When fed with, e.g., the identity and the natural number* `1`*, the program* `expone` *evaluates to the geometric distribution assigning probability $\frac{1}{2^n}$ to any positive natural number $n$. A similar effect can be obtained by* `exptwo`*, which only takes* `f` *in input, then "modifying" it along the evaluation. The function* `expthree` *is more complicated, at least apparently. To understand its behavior, one should first look at the auxiliary function* `foldp`*. If* `m` *and* `n` *are two natural numbers and* `f` *and* `g` *are two functions,* `foldp m n f g` *call-by-name reduces to the following expression:*

```
(f n) (+) ((f n+1) (+) ... ((f n+m-1) (+) (g n+m))).
```

*The term* `expthree` *works by forwarding its three arguments to* `foldp`*. The fourth argument is a recursive call to* `expthree` *where, however,* `k` *is replaced by any number greater or equal to it, chosen according to a geometric distribution. The functions above can all be expressed in $\Lambda_\oplus$, using fixed-point combinators. As we will see soon,* `expone`, `exptwo`, *and* `expthree k` *are context equivalent whenever* `k` *is a natural number.*

### 2.2 Probabilistic Bisimulation

In this section we recall the definition and a few basic notions of bisimulation for labelled Markov chains, following Larsen and Skou [26]. In Section 3 we will then adapt this form of bisimilarity to the probabilistic $\lambda$-calculus $\Lambda_\oplus$ by combining it with Abramsky's applicative bisimilarity.

DEFINITION 2.6. *A* labelled Markov chain *is a triple $(\mathcal{S}, \mathcal{L}, \mathcal{P})$ such that:*

- *$\mathcal{S}$ is a countable set of* states*;*
- *$\mathcal{L}$ is set of* labels*;*

$$\frac{}{M \Downarrow \emptyset}\ \mathsf{bt} \qquad \frac{}{V \Downarrow \{V\}}\ \mathsf{bv} \qquad \frac{M \Downarrow \mathscr{D} \quad \{P\{^N/x\} \Downarrow \mathscr{E}_{P,N}\}_{\lambda x.P \in \mathsf{S}(\mathscr{D})}}{MN \Downarrow \sum_{\lambda x.P \in \mathsf{S}(\mathscr{D})} \mathscr{D}(\lambda x.P) \cdot \mathscr{E}_{P,N}}\ \mathsf{ba} \qquad \frac{M \Downarrow \mathscr{D} \quad N \Downarrow \mathscr{E}}{M \oplus N \Downarrow \frac{1}{2} \cdot \mathscr{D} + \frac{1}{2} \cdot \mathscr{E}}\ \mathsf{bs}$$

**Figure 1.** Big-step call-by-name approximation semantics for $\Lambda_\oplus$.

- $\mathcal{P}$ *is a* transition probability matrix, *i.e. a function*

  $$\mathcal{P} : \mathcal{S} \times \mathcal{L} \times \mathcal{S} \to \mathbb{R}_{[0,1]}$$

  *such that the following normalization condition holds:*

  $$\forall \ell \in \mathcal{L}. \forall s \in \mathcal{S}. \mathcal{P}(s, \ell, \mathcal{S}) \leq 1$$

  *where, as usual* $\mathcal{P}(s, \ell, X)$ *stands for* $\sum_{t \in X} \mathcal{P}(s, \ell, t)$ *whenever* $X \subseteq \mathcal{S}$.

If $\mathcal{R}$ is an equivalence relation on $\mathcal{S}$, $\mathcal{S}/\mathcal{R}$ denotes the *quotient* of $\mathcal{S}$ modulo $\mathcal{R}$, i.e., the set of all equivalence classes of $\mathcal{S}$ modulo $\mathcal{R}$. Given any binary relation $\mathcal{R}$, its reflexive and transitive closure is denoted as $\mathcal{R}^*$.

DEFINITION 2.7. *Given a labelled Markov chain* $(\mathcal{S}, \mathcal{L}, \mathcal{P})$, *a* probabilistic bisimulation *is an equivalence relation* $\mathcal{R}$ *on* $\mathcal{S}$ *such that* $(s, t) \in \mathcal{R}$ *implies that for every* $\ell \in \mathcal{L}$ *and for every* $\mathrm{E} \in \mathcal{S}/\mathcal{R}$, $\mathcal{P}(s, \ell, \mathrm{E}) = \mathcal{P}(t, \ell, \mathrm{E})$.

Note that a probabilistic bisimulation has to be, by definition, an *equivalence relation*. This means that, in principle, we are not allowed to define probabilistic bisimilarity simply as the union of all probabilistic bisimulations. As a matter of fact, given $\mathcal{R}, \mathcal{T}$ two equivalence relations, $\mathcal{R} \cup \mathcal{T}$ is not necessarily an equivalence relation. The following is a standard way to overcome the problem:

LEMMA 2.8. *If* $\{\mathcal{R}_i\}_{i \in I}$, *is a collection of probabilistic bisimulations, then also their reflexive and transitive closure* $(\bigcup_{i \in I} \mathcal{R}_i)^*$ *is a probabilistic bisimulation.*

Lemma 2.8 allows us to define the largest probabilistic bisimulation, called *probabilistic bisimilarity*. It is $\sim \stackrel{\text{def}}{=} \bigcup\{\mathcal{R} \mid \mathcal{R}$ is a probabilistic bisimulation$\}$. Indeed, by Lemma 2.8, $(\sim)^*$ is a probabilistic bisimulation too; we now claim that $\sim = (\sim)^*$. The inclusion $\sim \subseteq (\sim)^*$ is obvious. The other way around, $\sim \supseteq (\sim)^*$, follows by $(\sim)^*$ being a probabilistic bisimulation and hence included in $\sim$.

In the notion of a probabilistic simulation, preorders play the role of equivalence relations: given a labelled Markov chain $(\mathcal{S}, \mathcal{L}, \mathcal{P})$, a *probabilistic simulation* is a preorder relation $\mathcal{R}$ on $\mathcal{S}$ such that $(s, t) \in \mathcal{R}$ implies that for every $\ell \in \mathcal{L}$ and for every $X \subseteq \mathcal{S}$, $\mathcal{P}(s, \ell, X) \leq \mathcal{P}(t, \ell, \mathcal{R}(X))$, where as usual $\mathcal{R}(X)$ stands for the $\mathcal{R}$*-closure* of $X$, namely the set $\{y \in \mathcal{S} \mid \exists x \in X.\ x \ \mathcal{R}\ y\}$. Lemma 2.8 holds for probabilistic simulations, and as a consequence, we are allowed to define *similarity* simply as $\lesssim \stackrel{\text{def}}{=} \bigcup\{\mathcal{R} \mid \mathcal{R}$ is a probabilistic simulation$\}$.

Any symmetric probabilistic simulation is a probabilistic bisimulation. Contrary to the nondeterministic case, however, simulation equivalence coincides with bisimulation:

PROPOSITION 2.9. $\sim$ *coincides with* $\lesssim \cap \lesssim^{op}$.

For technical reasons that will become apparent soon, it is convenient to consider Markov chains in which the state space is partitioned into disjoint sets, in such a way that comparing states coming from different components is not possible. Remember that the disjoint union $\biguplus_{i \in I} X_i$ of a family of sets $\{X_i\}_{i \in I}$ is defined as $\{(a, i) \mid i \in I \wedge a \in X_i\}$. If the set of states $\mathcal{S}$ of a labelled Markov chain is a disjoint union $\biguplus_{i \in I} X_i$, one wants that (bi)simulation relations only compare elements coming from the same $X_i$, i.e. $(a, i)\mathcal{R}(b, j)$ implies $i = j$. In this case, we say that the underlying labelled Markov chain is *multisorted*.

## 3. Probabilistic Applicative Bisimulation and Howe's technique

In this section, notions of similarity and bisimilarity for $\Lambda_\oplus$ are introduced, in the spirit of Abramsky's work on applicative bisimulation [1]. Definitionally, this consists in seeing $\Lambda_\oplus$'s operational semantics as a labelled Markov chain, then giving the Larsen and Skou's notion of (bi)simulation for it. States will be terms, while labels will be of two kinds: one can either *evaluate* a term, obtaining (a distribution of) values, or *apply* a term to a value.

The resulting bisimulation (probabilistic applicative bisimulation) will be shown to be a congruence, thus included in probabilistic context equivalence. This will be done by a non-trivial generalization of Howe's technique [22], which is a well-known methodology to get congruence results in presence of higher-order functions, but which has not been applied to probabilistic calculi so far.

Formalizing probabilistic applicative bisimulation requires some care. As usual, two values $\lambda x.M$ and $\lambda x.N$ are defined to be bisimilar if for every $L$, $M\{^L/x\}$ and $N\{^L/x\}$ are themselves bisimilar. But how if we rather want to compare two arbitrary closed terms $M$ and $N$? The simplest solution consists in following Larsen and Skou and stipulate that every equivalence class of $\mathsf{V}\Lambda_\oplus$ modulo bisimulation is attributed the same measure by both $[\![M]\!]$ and $[\![N]\!]$. Values are thus treated in two different ways (they are both terms and values), and this is the reason why each of them corresponds to *two* states in the underlying Markov chain.

DEFINITION 3.1. $\Lambda_\oplus$ *can be seen as a multisorted labelled Markov chain* $(\Lambda_\oplus(\emptyset) \uplus \mathsf{V}\Lambda_\oplus, \Lambda_\oplus(\emptyset) \uplus \{\tau\}, \mathcal{P}_\oplus)$ *that we denote with* $\Lambda_\oplus$. *Labels are either closed terms, which model parameter passing, or* $\tau$, *that models evaluation. Please observe that the states of the labelled Markov chain we have just defined are elements of the disjoint union* $\Lambda_\oplus(\emptyset) \uplus \mathsf{V}\Lambda_\oplus$. *Two distinct states correspond to the same value* $V$, *and to avoid ambiguities, we call the second one (i.e. the one coming from* $\mathsf{V}\Lambda_\oplus$*) a* distinguished value. *When we want to insist on the fact that a value* $\lambda x.M$ *is distinguished, we indicate it with* $\nu x.M$. *We define the transition probability matrix* $\mathcal{P}_\oplus$ *as follows:*

- *For every term* $M$ *and for every distinguished value* $\nu x.N$,

  $$\mathcal{P}_\oplus(M, \tau, \nu x.N) \stackrel{\text{def}}{=} [\![M]\!](\nu x.N);$$

- *For every term* $M$ *and for every distinguished value* $\nu x.N$,

  $$\mathcal{P}_\oplus(\nu x.N, M, N\{^M/x\}) \stackrel{\text{def}}{=} 1;$$

- *In all other cases,* $\mathcal{P}_\oplus$ *returns* 0.

Terms seen as states only interact with the environment by performing $\tau$, while distinguished values only take other closed terms as parameters.

Simulation and bisimulation relations can be defined for $\Lambda_\oplus$ as for any labelled Markov chain. Even if, strictly speaking, these are binary relations on $\Lambda_\oplus(\emptyset) \uplus \mathsf{V}\Lambda_\oplus$, we often see them just as their restrictions to $\Lambda_\oplus(\emptyset)$. Formally, a *probabilistic applicative bisimulation* (a PAB) is simply a probabilistic bisimulation on $\Lambda_\oplus$. This way one can define *probabilistic applicative bisimilarity*, which is denoted $\sim$. Similarly for *probabilistic applicative simulation* (PAS) and *probabilistic applicative similarity*, denoted $\lesssim$.

REMARK 3.2 (Early vs. Late). *Technically, the distinction between terms and values in Definition 3.1 means that our bisimulation is in* late *style. In bisimulations for value-passing concurrent languages, "late" indicates the explicit manipulation of functions in the clause for input actions: functions are chosen first, and only later, the input value received is taken into account [40]. Late-style is used in contraposition to* early *style, where the order of quantifiers is exchanged, so that the choice of functions may depend on the specific input value received. In our setting, adopting an early style would mean having transitions such as* $\lambda x.M \xrightarrow{N} M\{N/x\}$, *and then setting up a probabilistic bisimulation on top of the resulting transition system. We leave for future work a study of the comparison between the two styles. In this paper, we stick to the late style because easier to deal with, especially under Howe's technique. Previous works on applicative bisimulation for nondeterministic functions also focus on the late approach [30, 36].*

REMARK 3.3. *Defining applicative bisimulation in terms of multisorted labelled Markov chains has the advantage of recasting the definition in a familiar framework; most importantly, this formulation will be useful when dealing with Howe's method. To spell out the explicit operational details of the definition, a probabilistic applicative bisimulation can be seen as an equivalence relation* $\mathcal{R} \subseteq \Lambda_\oplus(\emptyset) \times \Lambda_\oplus(\emptyset)$ *such that whenever* $M \mathrel{\mathcal{R}} N$:

1. $[\![M]\!](\mathsf{E} \cap \mathsf{V}\Lambda_\oplus) = [\![N]\!](\mathsf{E} \cap \mathsf{V}\Lambda_\oplus)$, *for any equivalence class* $\mathsf{E}$ *of* $\mathcal{R}$ *(that is, the probability of reaching a value in* $\mathsf{E}$ *is the same for the two terms);*
2. *if* $M$ *and* $N$ *are values, say* $\lambda x.P$ *and* $\lambda x.Q$, *then* $P\{L/x\} \mathrel{\mathcal{R}} Q\{L/x\}$, *for all* $L \in \Lambda_\oplus(\emptyset)$.

*The special treatment of values, in Clause 2., motivates the use of* multisorted *labelled Markov chains in Definition 3.1.*

Terms with the same semantics are indistinguishable:

LEMMA 3.4. *The binary relation* $\mathcal{R} = \{(M,N) \in \Lambda_\oplus(\emptyset) \times \Lambda_\oplus(\emptyset)$ *s.t.* $[\![M]\!] = [\![N]\!]\} \uplus \{(V,V) \in \mathsf{V}\Lambda_\oplus \times \mathsf{V}\Lambda_\oplus\}$ *is a* PAB.

Conversely, knowing that two terms $M$ and $N$ are (bi)similar means knowing quite a lot about their convergence probability:

LEMMA 3.5 (Adequacy of Bisimulation). *If* $M \sim N$, *then* $\sum[\![M]\!] = \sum[\![N]\!]$. *Moreover, if* $M \lesssim N$, *then* $\sum[\![M]\!] \leq \sum[\![N]\!]$.

EXAMPLE 3.6. *The semantics of the terms:*

$$M \stackrel{\text{def}}{=} ((\lambda x.(x \oplus x)) \oplus (\lambda x.x)) \oplus \Omega;$$
$$N \stackrel{\text{def}}{=} \Omega \oplus (\lambda x.Ix);$$

*differ, as for every value* $V$, *we have:*

$$[\![M]\!](V) = \begin{cases} \frac{1}{4} & \text{if } V \text{ is } \lambda x.(x \oplus x) \text{ or } \lambda x.x; \\ 0 & \text{otherwise}; \end{cases}$$
$$[\![N]\!](V) = \begin{cases} \frac{1}{2} & \text{if } V \text{ is } \lambda x.Ix; \\ 0 & \text{otherwise}. \end{cases}$$

*Nonetheless, we can prove* $M \sim N$. *Indeed,* $\nu x.(x \oplus x) \sim \nu x.x \sim \nu x.Ix$ *because, for every* $L \in \Lambda_\oplus(\emptyset)$, *the three terms* $L$, $L \oplus L$ *and* $IL$ *all have the same semantics, i.e.,* $[\![L]\!]$. *Now, consider any equivalence class* $\mathsf{E}$ *of distinguished values modulo* $\sim$. *If* $\mathsf{E}$ *includes the three distinguished values above, then*

$$\mathcal{P}_\oplus(M,\tau,\mathsf{E}) = \sum_{V \in \mathsf{E}} [\![M]\!](V) = \frac{1}{2} = \sum_{V \in \mathsf{E}} [\![N]\!](V) = \mathcal{P}_\oplus(N,\tau,\mathsf{E}).$$

*Otherwise,* $\mathcal{P}_\oplus(M,\tau,\mathsf{E}) = 0 = \mathcal{P}_\oplus(N,\tau,\mathsf{E})$.

### 3.1 Probabilistic Applicative Bisimulation is a Congruence

In this section, we prove that probabilistic applicative bisimulation is indeed a congruence, and that its non-symmetric sibling is a precongruence. The structure of the proof follows Howe [22], so we will not give all the details. The main idea consists in defining a way to turn an arbitrary relation $\mathcal{R}$ on (possibly open) terms to another one, $\mathcal{R}^H$, in such a way that, if $\mathcal{R}$ satisfies a few simple conditions, then $\mathcal{R}^H$ is a (pre)congruence including $\mathcal{R}$. The key step, then, is to prove that $\mathcal{R}^H$ is indeed a (bi)simulation. In view of Proposition 2.9, considering similarity suffices here.

It is here convenient to work with generalizations of relations called $\Lambda_\oplus$-*relations*, i.e. sets of triples in the form $(\overline{x}, M, N)$, where $M, N \in \Lambda_\oplus(\overline{x})$. Thus if a relation has the pair $(M,N)$ with $M, N \in \Lambda_\oplus(\overline{x})$, then the corresponding $\Lambda_\oplus$-relation will include $(\overline{x}, M, N)$. (Recall that applicative (bi)similarity is extended to open terms by considering all closing substitutions.) Given any $\Lambda_\oplus$-relation $\mathcal{R}$, we write $\overline{x} \vdash M \mathrel{\mathcal{R}} N$ if $(\overline{x}, M, N) \in \mathcal{R}$. A $\Lambda_\oplus$-relation $\mathcal{R}$ is said to be *compatible* iff the four conditions below hold:

(Com1) $\forall \overline{x} \in \mathcal{P}_{\mathsf{FIN}}(\mathsf{X}), x \in \overline{x}$: $\overline{x} \vdash x \mathrel{\mathcal{R}} x$,
(Com2) $\forall \overline{x} \in \mathcal{P}_{\mathsf{FIN}}(\mathsf{X}), \forall x \in \mathsf{X} - \overline{x}, \forall M, N \in \Lambda_\oplus(\overline{x} \cup \{x\})$: $\overline{x} \cup \{x\} \vdash M \mathrel{\mathcal{R}} N \Rightarrow \overline{x} \vdash \lambda x.M \mathrel{\mathcal{R}} \lambda x.N$,
(Com3) $\forall \overline{x} \in \mathcal{P}_{\mathsf{FIN}}(\mathsf{X}), \forall M, N, L, P \in \Lambda_\oplus(\overline{x})$: $\overline{x} \vdash M \mathrel{\mathcal{R}} N \wedge \overline{x} \vdash L \mathrel{\mathcal{R}} P \Rightarrow \overline{x} \vdash ML \mathrel{\mathcal{R}} NP$,
(Com4) $\forall \overline{x} \in \mathcal{P}_{\mathsf{FIN}}(\mathsf{X}), \forall M, N, L, P \in \Lambda_\oplus(\overline{x})$: $\overline{x} \vdash M \mathrel{\mathcal{R}} N \wedge \overline{x} \vdash L \mathrel{\mathcal{R}} P \Rightarrow \overline{x} \vdash M \oplus L \mathrel{\mathcal{R}} N \oplus P$.

The notions of an equivalence relation and of a preorder can be straightforwardly generalized to $\Lambda_\oplus$-relations, and any compatible $\Lambda_\oplus$-relation that is an equivalence relation (respectively, a preorder) is said to be a *congruence* (respectively, a *precongruence*).

If bisimilarity is a congruence, then $C[M]$ is bisimilar to $C[N]$ whenever $M \sim N$ and $C$ is a context. In other words, terms can be replaced by equivalent ones in any context. This is a crucial sanity-check any notion of equivalence is expected to pass.

It is well-known that proving bisimulation to be a congruence may be nontrivial when the underlying language contains higher-order functions. This is also the case here. Proving (Com1), (Com2) and (Com4) just by inspecting the operational semantics of the involved terms is indeed possible, but the method fails for (Com3), when the involved contexts contain applications. We thus need to introduce nontrivial technical tools.

Actually, the Howe's lifting of any $\Lambda_\oplus$-relation $\mathcal{R}$ is the relation $\mathcal{R}^H$ defined by the rules in Figure 3. The reader familiar with Howe's method should have a sense of *déjà vu* here: indeed, this is the same definition one finds in the realm of *nondeterministic* $\lambda$-calculi. The language of terms, after all, is the same. This facilitates the first part of the proof. Indeed, one already knows that if $\mathcal{R}$ is a preorder, then $\mathcal{R}^H$ is compatible, closed under term-substitution and includes $\mathcal{R}$, since all these properties are already known (see, e.g. [36]) and only depend on the shape of terms and not on their operational semantics. For the reader's convenience, all these proofs can be found in [10]. Something is missing, however, before we can conclude that $\lesssim^H$ is a precongruence, namely transitivity. We also follow Howe here and consider the transitive closure $(\lesssim^H)^+$, which is a preorder by construction.

This is just the first half of the story: we also need to prove that $(\lesssim^H)^+$ is a simulation. As we already know it is a preorder, the following lemma gives us the missing bit:

LEMMA 3.7 (Key Lemma). *If* $M \lesssim^H N$, *then for every* $X \subseteq \Lambda_\oplus(x)$ *it holds that* $[\![M]\!](\lambda x.X) \leq [\![N]\!](\lambda x.(\lesssim^H(X)))$.

The proof of this lemma is delicate and is discussed in the next section. From the lemma, using a standard argument we derive the needed substitutivity results, and ultimately the most important result of this section.

THEOREM 3.8. *On* $\Lambda_\oplus$-*terms,* $\lesssim$ *is a precongruence and* $\sim$ *is a congruence.*

$$\frac{\overline{x} \vdash x \mathrel{\mathcal{R}} M}{\overline{x} \vdash x \mathrel{\mathcal{R}^H} M}\ (\text{How1}) \qquad \frac{\overline{x} \cup \{x\} \vdash M \mathrel{\mathcal{R}^H} L \qquad \overline{x} \vdash \lambda x.L \mathrel{\mathcal{R}} N \qquad x \notin \overline{x}}{\overline{x} \vdash \lambda x.M \mathrel{\mathcal{R}^H} N}\ (\text{How2})$$

$$\frac{\overline{x} \vdash M \mathrel{\mathcal{R}^H} P \qquad \overline{x} \vdash N \mathrel{\mathcal{R}^H} Q \qquad \overline{x} \vdash PQ \mathrel{\mathcal{R}} L}{\overline{x} \vdash MN \mathrel{\mathcal{R}^H} L}\ (\text{How3}) \qquad \frac{\overline{x} \vdash M \mathrel{\mathcal{R}^H} P \qquad \overline{x} \vdash N \mathrel{\mathcal{R}^H} Q \qquad \overline{x} \vdash P \oplus Q \mathrel{\mathcal{R}} L}{\overline{x} \vdash M \oplus N \mathrel{\mathcal{R}^H} L}\ (\text{How4})$$

**Figure 3.** Howe's Lifting for $\Lambda_{\oplus}$.

### 3.2 Proof of the Key Lemma

Proving the Key Lemma 3.7 turns out to be much more difficult than for deterministic or nondeterministic cases. In particular, the case when $M$ is an application relies on another technical lemma we are now going to give, which itself can be proved by tools from linear programming.

The combinatorial problem we will face while proving the Key Lemma can actually be decontextualized and understood independently. Suppose we have $n = 3$ non-disjoint sets $X_1, X_2, X_3$ whose elements are labelled with real numbers. As an example, we could be in a situation like the one in Figure 4(a) (where for the sake of simplicity only the labels are indicated). We fix three real numbers $p_1 \stackrel{\text{def}}{=} \frac{5}{64}$, $p_2 \stackrel{\text{def}}{=} \frac{3}{16}$, $p_3 \stackrel{\text{def}}{=} \frac{5}{64}$. It is routine to check that for every $I \subseteq \{1, 2, 3\}$ it holds that

$$\sum_{i \in I} p_i \leq ||\bigcup_{i \in I} X_i||,$$

where $||X||$ is the sum of the labels of the elements of $X$. Let us observe that it is of course possible to turn the three sets $X_1, X_2, X_3$ into three disjoint sets $Y_1$, $Y_2$ and $Y_3$ where each $Y_i$ contains (copies of) the elements of $X_i$ whose labels, however, are obtained by splitting the ones of the original elements. Examples of those sets are in Figure 4(b): if you superpose the three sets, you obtain the Venn diagram we started from. Quite remarkably, however, the examples from Figure 4 have an additional property, namely that for every $i \in \{1, 2, 3\}$ it holds that $p_i \leq ||Y_i||$. We now show that finding sets satisfying the properties above is always possible, even when $n$ is arbitrary.

Suppose $p_1, \ldots, p_n \in \mathbb{R}_{[0,1]}$, and suppose that for each $I \subseteq \{1, \ldots, n\}$ a real number $r_I \in \mathbb{R}_{[0,1]}$ is defined such that for every such $I$ it holds that $\sum_{i \in I} p_i \leq \sum_{J \cap I \neq \emptyset} r_J \leq 1$. Then $(\{p_i\}_{1 \leq i \leq n}, \{r_I\}_{I \subseteq \{1,\ldots,n\}})$ is said to be a *probability assignment* for $\{1, \ldots, n\}$. Is it always possible to "disentangle" probability assignments? The answer is positive.

LEMMA 3.9 (Disentangling Probability Assignments). *Let* $\mathbf{P} \stackrel{\text{def}}{=} (\{p_i\}_{1 \leq i \leq n}, \{r_I\}_{I \subseteq \{1,\ldots,n\}})$ *be a probability assignment. Then for every nonempty* $I \subseteq \{1, \ldots, n\}$ *and for every* $k \in I$ *there is* $s_{k,I} \in \mathbb{R}_{[0,1]}$ *such that the following conditions all hold:*

1. *for every* $I$, *it holds that* $\sum_{k \in I} s_{k,I} \leq 1$;
2. *for every* $k \in \{1, \ldots, n\}$, *it holds that* $p_k \leq \sum_{k \in I} s_{k,I} \cdot r_I$.

**Proof.** Any probability assignment $\mathbf{P}$ can be seen as a flow network, where nodes are the nonempty subsets of $\{1, \ldots, n\}$, plus a distinguished source $s$ and target $t$. Edges, then, go from $s$ to each singleton $\{i\}$ (with capacity $p_i$), from every nonempty $I$ to $I \cup \{i\} \subseteq \{1, \ldots, n\}$ whenever $i \notin I$ (with capacity 1) and from every such $I$ to $t$ (with capacity $r_I$). The thesis, then, is easily proved equivalent to showing that such a net supports a flow of value $\sum p_i$. And, indeed, the fact that this is the value of the maximum flow from $s$ to $t$ can be proved via the Max-Flow Min-Cut Theorem. □

REMARK 3.10. *Throughout the following proof we will implicitly use a routine result stating that* $M \lesssim N$ *implies* $[\![M]\!](\lambda x.X) \leq [\![N]\!](\lambda x.{\lesssim}(X))$, *for every* $X \subseteq \Lambda_{\oplus}(x)$. *The property needed by the latter is precisely the reason why we have formulated* $\Lambda_{\oplus}$ *as a multisorted labelled Markov chain:* ${\lesssim}(\nu x.X)$ *consists of distinguished values only, and is nothing but* $\nu x.{\lesssim}(X)$.

**Proof.** [of Lemma 3.7] This is equivalent to proving that if $M \lesssim^H N$, then for every $X \subseteq \Lambda_{\oplus}(x)$ the following implication holds: if $M \Downarrow \mathscr{D}$, then $\mathscr{D}(\lambda x.X) \leq [\![N]\!](\lambda x.(\lesssim^H(X)))$. This is an induction on the structure of the proof of $M \Downarrow \mathscr{D}$. Some interesting cases follow:

- If $M$ is a value $\lambda x.L$ and $\mathscr{D}(\lambda x.L) = 1$, then the proof of $M \lesssim^H N$ necessarily ends as follows:

$$\frac{\{x\} \vdash L \lesssim^H P \qquad \emptyset \vdash \lambda x.P \lesssim N}{\emptyset \vdash \lambda x.L \lesssim^H N}$$

Let $X$ be any subset of $\Lambda_{\oplus}(x)$. Now, if $L \notin X$, then $\mathscr{D}(\lambda x.X) = 0$ and the inequality trivially holds. If, on the contrary, $L \in X$, then $P \in \lesssim^H(X)$. Consider $\lesssim(P)$, the set of terms that are in relation with $P$ via $\lesssim$. We have that for every $Q \in \lesssim(P)$, both $\{x\} \vdash L \lesssim^H P$ and $\{x\} \vdash P \lesssim Q$ hold, and as a consequence $\{x\} \vdash L \lesssim^H Q$ does (this is a consequence of a property of $(\cdot)^H$, see [10]). In other words, $\lesssim(P) \subseteq \lesssim^H(X)$. But then,

$$[\![N]\!](\lambda x.\lesssim^H(X)) \geq [\![N]\!](\lambda x.\lesssim(P)) \geq [\![\lambda x.P]\!](\lambda x.P) = 1.$$

- If $M$ is an application $LP$, then $M \Downarrow \mathscr{D}$ is obtained as follows:

$$\frac{L \Downarrow \mathscr{F} \qquad \{Q\{P/x\} \Downarrow \mathscr{H}_{Q,P}\}_{Q,P}}{LP \Downarrow \sum_Q \mathscr{F}(\lambda x.Q) \cdot \mathscr{H}_{Q,P}}$$

Moreover, the proof of $\emptyset \vdash M \lesssim^H N$ must end as follows:

$$\frac{\emptyset \vdash L \lesssim^H R \qquad \emptyset \vdash P \lesssim^H S \qquad \emptyset \vdash RS \lesssim N}{\emptyset \vdash LP \lesssim^H N}$$

Now, since $L \Downarrow \mathscr{F}$ and $\emptyset \vdash L \lesssim^H R$, by induction hypothesis we get that for every $Y \subseteq \Lambda_{\oplus}(x)$ it holds that $\mathscr{F}(\lambda x.Y) \leq [\![R]\!](\lambda x.\lesssim^H(Y))$. Let us now take a look at the distribution

$$\mathscr{D} = \sum_Q \mathscr{F}(\lambda x.Q) \cdot \mathscr{H}_{Q,P}.$$

Since $\mathscr{F}$ is a *finite* distribution, the sum above is actually the sum of finitely many summands. Let the support $\mathsf{S}(\mathscr{F})$ of $\mathscr{F}$ be $\{\lambda x.Q_1, \ldots, \lambda x.Q_n\}$. It is now time to put the above into a form that is amenable to treatment by Lemma 3.9. Let us consider the $n$ sets $\lesssim^H(Q_1), \ldots, \lesssim^H(Q_n)$; to each term $U$ in them we can associate the probability $[\![R]\!](\lambda x.U)$. We are then in the scope of Lemma 3.9, since by induction hypothesis we know that for every $Y \subseteq \Lambda_{\oplus}(x)$, $\mathscr{F}(\lambda x.Y) \leq [\![R]\!](\lambda x.\lesssim^H(Y))$. We can then conclude that for every

$$U \in \lesssim^H(\{Q_1, \ldots, Q_n\}) = \bigcup_{1 \leq i \leq n} \lesssim^H(Q_i)$$

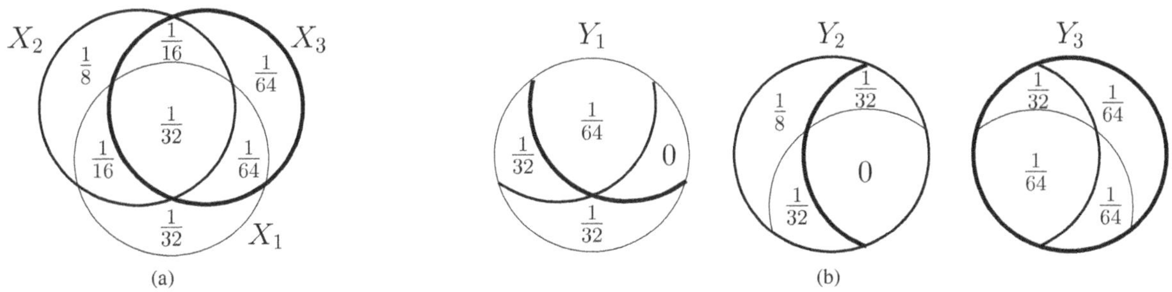


**Figure 4.** Disentangling Sets

there are $n$ real numbers $r_1^{U,R}, \ldots, r_n^{U,R}$ such that:

$$[\![R]\!](\lambda x.U) \geq \sum_{1\leq i\leq n} r_i^{U,R} \qquad \forall U \in \bigcup_{1\leq i\leq n} \lesssim^H(Q_i);$$

$$\mathscr{F}(\lambda x.Q_i) \leq \sum_{U\in\lesssim^H(Q_i)} r_i^{U,R} \qquad \forall 1 \leq i \leq n.$$

So, we can conclude that

$$\mathscr{D} \leq \sum_{1\leq i\leq n}\left(\sum_{U\in\lesssim^H(Q_i)} r_i^{U,R}\right)\cdot \mathscr{H}_{Q_i,P}$$
$$= \sum_{1\leq i\leq n}\sum_{U\in\lesssim^H(Q_i)} r_i^{U,R}\cdot \mathscr{H}_{Q_i,P}.$$

Now, whenever $Q_i \lesssim^H U$ and $P \lesssim^H S$, it follows that $Q_i\{P/x\} \lesssim^H U\{S/x\}$. We can then apply the inductive hypothesis to the $n$ derivations of $Q_i\{P/x\} \Downarrow \mathscr{H}_{Q_i,P}$, obtaining that, for every $X \subseteq \Lambda_\oplus(x)$,

$$\mathscr{D}(\lambda x.X) \leq \sum_{1\leq i\leq n}\sum_{U\in\lesssim^H(Q_i)} r_i^{U,R}\cdot [\![U\{S/x\}]\!](\lambda x.\lesssim^H(X))$$
$$\leq \sum_{1\leq i\leq n}\sum_{U\in\lesssim^H(\{Q_1,\ldots,Q_n\})} r_i^{U,R}\cdot [\![U\{S/x\}]\!](\lambda x.\lesssim^H(X))$$
$$= \sum_{U\in\lesssim^H(\{Q_1,\ldots,Q_n\})}\sum_{1\leq i\leq n} r_i^{U,R}\cdot [\![U\{S/x\}]\!](\lambda x.\lesssim^H(X))$$
$$= \sum_{U\in\lesssim^H(\{Q_1,\ldots,Q_n\})}\left(\sum_{1\leq i\leq n} r_i^{U,R}\right)\cdot [\![U\{S/x\}]\!](\lambda x.\lesssim^H(X))$$
$$\leq \sum_{U\in\lesssim^H(\{Q_1,\ldots,Q_n\})} [\![R]\!](\lambda x.U)\cdot [\![U\{S/x\}]\!](\lambda x.\lesssim^H(X))$$
$$\leq \sum_{U\in\Lambda_\oplus(x)} [\![R]\!](\lambda x.U)\cdot [\![U\{S/x\}]\!](\lambda x.\lesssim^H(X))$$
$$= [\![RS]\!](\lambda x.\lesssim^H(X)) \leq [\![N]\!](\lambda x.\lesssim((\lesssim^H)(X)))$$
$$\leq [\![N]\!](\lambda x.\lesssim^H(X)),$$

which is the thesis.

This concludes the proof. □

### 3.3 Relating Applicative Bisimulation and Context Equivalence

The congruence of applicative bisimilarity yields the inclusion in context equivalence.

THEOREM 3.11. *For all $M, N \in \Lambda_\oplus$, $M \sim N$ implies $M \simeq_\oplus N$.*

The converse inclusion fails. A counterexample is described in the following.

EXAMPLE 3.12. *For $M \stackrel{\text{def}}{=} \lambda x.L \oplus P$ and $N \stackrel{\text{def}}{=} (\lambda x.L) \oplus (\lambda x.P)$ (where $L$ is $\lambda y.\Omega$ and $P$ is $\lambda y.\lambda z.\Omega$), we have $M \not\lesssim N$, hence $M \not\sim N$, but $M \simeq_\oplus N$.*

We prove that the above two terms are context equivalent by means of *CIU-equivalence*. This is a relation that can be shown to coincide with context equivalence by a Context Lemma, itself proved by the Howe's technique. More details are in [10]. See also Section 7.

EXAMPLE 3.13. *We consider again the programs from Example 2.5. Terms* `expone` *and* `exptwo` *only differ because the former performs all probabilistic choices on natural numbers obtained by applying a function to its argument, while in the latter choices are done at the functional level, and the argument to those functions is provided only at a later stage. As a consequence, the two terms are not applicative bisimilar, and the reason is akin to that for the inequality of the terms in Example 3.12. In contrast, the bisimilarity between* `expone` *and* `expthree k`*, where* `k` *is any natural number, intuitively holds because both* `expone` *and* `expthree k` *evaluate to a single term when fed with a function, while they start evolving in a genuinely probabilistic way only after the second argument is provided. At that point, the two functions evolve in very different ways, but their semantics (in the sense of Section 2) is the same (cf., Lemma 3.4). As a bisimulation one can use the equivalence generated by the relation*

$$\left(\bigcup_{\mathtt{k}}\{(\mathtt{expone},\mathtt{expthree\ k})\}\right) \cup \{(M,N) \mid [\![M]\!] = [\![N]\!]\}$$
$$\cup \left(\bigcup_{L}\{(\lambda\mathtt{n}.\mathtt{B}\{L/\mathtt{f}\}, \lambda\mathtt{n}.\mathtt{C}\{L/\mathtt{f}\})\}\right)$$

*using* `B` *and* `C` *for the body of* `expone` *and* `expthree` *respectively.*

## 4. The Discriminating Power of Probabilistic Contexts

We show here that applicative bisimilarity and context equivalence collapse if the tested terms are pure, *deterministic*, $\lambda$-terms. In other words, if the probabilistic choices are brought into the terms only through the inputs supplied to the tested functions, applicative bisimilarity and context equivalence yield exactly the same discriminating power. To show this, we prove that, on pure $\lambda$-terms, both relations coincide with the *Levy-Longo tree equality*, which equates terms with the same Levy-Longo tree (briefly LLT) [14].

LLT's are the lazy variant of Böhm Trees (briefly BT), the most popular tree structure in the $\lambda$-calculus. BT's only correctly express the computational content of $\lambda$-terms in a *strong* regime, while they fail to do so in the lazy one. For instance, the term $\lambda x.\Omega$ and $\Omega$, as both *unsolvable* [4], have identical BT's, but in a lazy regime we would always distinguish between them; hence they have different LLT's. The *Levy-Longo tree* of $M$, $LT(M)$, is coinductively constructed as follows: $LT(M) \stackrel{\text{def}}{=} \lambda x_1.\ldots x_n.\bot$

if $M$ is an unsolvable of order $n$; $LT(M) \stackrel{\text{def}}{=} \top$ if $M$ is an unsolvable of order $\infty$; finally if $M$ has principal head normal form $\lambda x_1 \dots x_n.yM_1 \dots M_m$, then $LT(M)$ is a tree with root $\lambda x_1 \dots x_n.y$ and with $LT(M_1), \dots, LT(M_m)$ as subtrees. Being defined coinductively, LLT's can of course be infinite. We write $M =_{\text{LL}} N$ iff $LT(M) = LT(N)$.

EXAMPLE 4.1. *Let $\Xi$ be an unsolvable of order $\infty$ such as $\Xi \stackrel{\text{def}}{=} (\lambda x.\lambda y.(xx))(\lambda x.\lambda y.(xx))$, and consider the terms*

$$M \stackrel{\text{def}}{=} \lambda x.(x(\lambda y.(x\Xi\Omega y))\Xi); \qquad N \stackrel{\text{def}}{=} \lambda x.(x(x\Xi\Omega)\Xi).$$

*These terms have been used to prove non-full-abstraction results in a canonical model for the lazy $\lambda$-calculus by Abramsky and Ong [2]. For this, they show that in the model the convergence test is definable (this operator, when it receives an argument, would return the identity function if the supplied argument is convergent, and would diverge otherwise). The convergence test, $\nabla$, can distinguish between the two terms, as $M\nabla$ reduces to an abstraction, whereas $N\nabla$ diverges. However, no pure $\lambda$-term can make the same distinction. The two terms also have different LL trees:*

*Although in $\Lambda_\oplus$, as in $\Lambda$, the convergence test operator is not definable, $M$ and $N$ can be separated using probabilities by running them in a context $C$ that would feed $\Omega \oplus \lambda z.\lambda u.z$ as argument; then $C[M]\Downarrow_{\frac{1}{2}}$ whereas $C[N]\Downarrow_{\frac{1}{4}}$.*

EXAMPLE 4.2. *Abramsky's canonical model is itself coarser than LLT equality. For instance, the terms $M \stackrel{\text{def}}{=} \lambda x.xx$ and $N \stackrel{\text{def}}{=} \lambda x.(x\lambda y.(xy))$, have different LLT's but are equal in Abramsky's model (and hence equal for context equivalence in $\Lambda$). They are separated by context equivalence in $\Lambda_\oplus$, for instance using the context $C \stackrel{\text{def}}{=} [\cdot](I \oplus \Omega)$, since $C[M]\Downarrow_{\frac{1}{4}}$ whereas $C[N]\Downarrow_{\frac{1}{2}}$.*

We already know that on full $\Lambda_\oplus$, applicative bisimilarity ($\sim$) implies context equivalence ($\simeq_\oplus$). Hence, to prove that *on pure $\lambda$-terms* the two equivalences collapse to LLT equality ($=_{\text{LL}}$), it suffices to prove that, for those pure terms, $\simeq_\oplus$ implies $=_{\text{LL}}$, and that $=_{\text{LL}}$ implies $\sim$.

The first implication is obtained by a variation on the Böhm-out technique, a powerful methodology for separation results in the $\lambda$-calculus, often employed in proofs about local structure characterisation theorems of $\lambda$-models. For this we exploit an inductive characterisation of LLT equality via stratification approximants. The $n$-approximant (for $n \geq 1$), written $=^n_{\text{LL}}$, is essentially obtained by observing a tree only up-to level $n$. The key Lemma 4.3 shows that any difference on the trees of two $\lambda$-terms within level $n$ can be observed by a suitable context of the probabilistic $\lambda$-calculus.

We write $\uplus M$ as an abbreviation for the term $\Omega \oplus M$. We denote by $Q_n$, $n > 0$, the term $\lambda x_1 \dots \lambda x_n.x_n x_1 x_2 \cdots x_{n-1}$. This is usually called the *Böhm permutator* of degree $n$. Böhm permutators play a key role in the Böhm-out technique. A variant of them, the $\uplus$-permutators, play a pivotal role in Lemma 4.3 below. A term $M \in \Lambda_\oplus$ is a *$\uplus$-permutator of degree $n$* if either $M = Q_n$ or there exists $0 \leq r < n$ such that

$$M = \lambda x_1 \dots \lambda x_r. \uplus \lambda x_{r+1} \cdots \lambda x_n.x_n x_1 \cdots x_{n-1}.$$

A function $f$ from the positive integers to $\lambda$-terms is a *$\uplus$-permutator function* if, for all $n$, $f(n)$ is a $\uplus$-permutator of degree $n$.

LEMMA 4.3. *Suppose $M \neq^n_{\text{LL}} N$ for some $n$, and let $\{x_1, \dots, x_r\}$ be the free variables in $M, N$. Then there are integers $m_{x_1}, \dots, m_{x_r}$ and $k$, and permutator functions $f_{x_1}, \dots, f_{x_r}$ such that, for all $m > k$, there are closed terms $\overline{R_m}$ such that the following holds: if $M\{f_{x_1}(m+m_{x_1})/x_1\}\dots\{f_{x_r}(m+m_{x_r})/x_r\}\overline{R_m}\Downarrow_r$ and $N\{f_{x_1}(m+m_{x_1})/x_1\}\dots\{f_{x_r}(m+m_{x_r})/x_r\}\overline{R_m}\Downarrow_s$ , then $r \neq s$.*

The proof goes by induction on the least $n$ such that $M \neq^n_{\text{LL}} N$.

The fact the Böhm-out technique actually works implies that the discriminating power of probabilistic contexts is at least as strong as the one of LLT's.

COROLLARY 4.4. *For $M, N \in \Lambda$, $M \simeq_\oplus N$ implies $M =_{\text{LL}} N$.*

To show that LLT equality is included in probabilistic applicative bisimilarity, we proceed as follows. First we define a refinement of the latter, essentially one in which we *observe* all probabilistic choices. As a consequence, the underlying bisimulation game may ignore probabilities. The obtained notion of equivalence is strictly finer than probabilistic applicative bisimilarity. The advantage of the refinement is that *both* the inclusion of LLT equality in the refinement, and the inclusion of the latter in probabilistic applicative bisimilarity turn out to be relatively easy to prove. A *direct* proof of the inclusion of LLT equality in probabilistic applicative bisimilarity would have been harder, as it would have required extending the notion of a Levy-Longo tree to $\Lambda_\oplus$, then reasoning on substitution closures of such trees. The definition below relies on two notions of reduction: $M \longrightarrow_p N$ means that $M$ call-by-name reduces to $N$ in one step with probability $p$. (As a matter of fact, $p$ can be either 1 or $\frac{1}{2}$.) Then $\Longrightarrow$ is obtained by composing $\longrightarrow$ zero or more times (and multiplying the corresponding real numbers).

DEFINITION 4.5. *A relation $\mathcal{R} \subseteq \Lambda_\oplus(\emptyset) \times \Lambda_\oplus(\emptyset)$ is a* strict applicative bisimulation *whenever $M \mathrel{\mathcal{R}} N$ implies*

1. *if $M \longrightarrow_1 P$, then $N \Longrightarrow_1 Q$ and $P \mathrel{\mathcal{R}} Q$;*
2. *if $M \longrightarrow_{\frac{1}{2}} P$, then $N \Longrightarrow_{\frac{1}{2}} Q$ and $P \mathrel{\mathcal{R}} Q$;*
3. *if $M = \lambda x.P$, then $N \Longrightarrow_1 \lambda x.Q$ and $P\{L/x\} \mathrel{\mathcal{R}} Q\{L/x\}$ for all $L \in \Lambda_\oplus(\emptyset)$;*
4. *the converse of 1., 2. and 3..*

Strict applicative bisimilarity *is the union of all strict applicative bisimulations.*

If two terms have the same LLT, then passing them the same argument $M \in \Lambda_\oplus$ produces *exactly* the same choice structure: intuitively, whenever the first term finds (a copy of) $M$ in head position, also the second will find $M$.

LEMMA 4.6. *If $M =_{\text{LL}} N$ then $M \mathrel{\mathcal{R}} N$, for some strict applicative bisimulation $\mathcal{R}$.*

Terms which are strict applicative bisimilar cannot be distinguished by applicative bisimilarity proper, since the requirements induced by the latter are less strict than the ones the former imposes:

LEMMA 4.7. *Strict applicative bisimilarity is included in applicative bisimilarity.*

Since we now know that for *pure, deterministic* $\lambda$-terms, $=_{\text{LL}}$ is included in $\sim$ (by Lemma 4.6 and Lemma 4.7), that $\sim$ is included in $\simeq_\oplus$ (by Theorem 3.11) and that the latter is included in $=_{\text{LL}}$ (Corollary 4.4), we can conclude:

COROLLARY 4.8. *The relations $=_{\text{LL}}$, $\sim$, and $\simeq_\oplus$ coincide in $\Lambda$.*

## 5. Coupled Logical Bisimulation

In this section we derive a coinductive characterisation of probabilistic context equivalence on the whole language $\Lambda_\oplus$ (as opposed to the subset of sum-free $\lambda$-terms as in Section 4). For this, we need to

$$\frac{}{M \oplus N \rightsquigarrow \langle M, \frac{1}{2}\rangle + \langle N, \frac{1}{2}\rangle}\ \mathsf{ss}$$

$$\frac{}{\lambda x.M \rightsquigarrow \langle \lambda x.M, 1\rangle}\ \mathsf{sl} \qquad \frac{[\![M_i]\!] = \mathscr{D}_i}{\Sigma_i\langle M_i, p_i\rangle \rightsquigarrow \Sigma_i\langle \mathscr{D}_i, p_i\rangle}\ \mathsf{spc}$$

$$\frac{}{ZM \rightsquigarrow Z \bullet M}\ \mathsf{sp} \qquad \frac{E \rightsquigarrow F}{EM \rightsquigarrow FM}\ \mathsf{sa}$$

**Figure 5.** Reduction Rules for $\Lambda_\oplus^{\mathrm{FS}}$

manipulate formal weighted sums. Thus we work with an extension of $\Lambda_\oplus$ in which such weighted sums may appear in redex position. An advantage of having formal sums is that the transition system on the extended language can be small-step and deterministic — any closed term that is not a value will have exactly one possible internal transition.

This will make it possible to pursue the *logical bisimulation* method, in which the congruence of bisimilarity is proved using a standard induction argument over all contexts. The refinement of the method handling probabilities, called *coupled* logical bisimulation, uses *pairs* of relations, as we need to distinguish between ordinary terms and terms possibly containing formal sums.

We preferred to follow logical bisimulations rather then environmental bisimulations because the former admit a simpler definition (in the latter, each pair of terms is enriched with an environment, that is, an extra set of pairs of terms). Moreover it is unclear what environments should be when one also considers formal sums. We leave this for future work.

Formal sums are a tool for representing the behaviour of running $\Lambda_\oplus$ terms. Thus, on terms with formal sums, only the results for closed terms interest us. However, the characterization of contextual equivalence in $\Lambda_\oplus$ as coupled logical bisimulation also holds on open terms.

### 5.1 Notation and Terminology

We write $\Lambda_\oplus^{\mathrm{FS}}$ for the extension of $\Lambda_\oplus$ in which formal sums may appear in redex position. Terms of $\Lambda_\oplus^{\mathrm{FS}}$ are defined as follows ($M$, $N$ being $\Lambda_\oplus$-terms):

$$E, F ::= EM \;\Big|\; \Sigma_{i\in I}\langle M_i, p_i\rangle \;\Big|\; M \oplus N \;\Big|\; \lambda x.M.$$

In a formal sum $\Sigma_{i\in I}\langle M_i, p_i\rangle$, $I$ is a countable (possibly empty) set of indices such that $\sum_{i\in I} p_i \leq 1$. We use $+$ for binary formal sums. Formal sums are ranged over by metavariables like $H, K$. When each $M_i$ is a value (i.e., an abstraction) then $\Sigma_{i\in I}\langle M_i, p_i\rangle$ is a *(formally summed) value*; such values are ranged over by $Z, Y, X$. If $H = \Sigma_{i\in I}\langle M_i, p_i\rangle$ and $K = \Sigma_{j\in J}\langle M_j, p_j\rangle$ where $I$ and $J$ are disjoint, then $H \oplus K$ abbreviates $\Sigma_{r\in I\cup J}\langle M_r, \frac{p_r}{2}\rangle$. Similarly, if for every $j \in J$ $H_j$ is $\Sigma_{i\in I}\langle M_{i,j}, p_{i,j}\rangle$, then $\Sigma_j\langle H_j, p_j\rangle$ stands for $\Sigma_{(i,j)}\langle M_{i,j}, p_{i,j} \cdot p_j\rangle$. For $H = \Sigma_i\langle M_i, p_i\rangle$ we write $\mathbf{\Sigma}(H)$ for the real number $\sum_i p_i$. If $Z = \Sigma_i\langle \lambda x.M_i, p_i\rangle$, then $Z \bullet N$ stands for $\Sigma_i\langle M_i\{N/x\}, p_i\rangle$. The set of closed terms is $\Lambda_\oplus^{\mathrm{FS}}(\emptyset)$.

Any partial value distribution $\mathscr{D}$ (in the sense of Section 2) can be seen as the formal sum $\Sigma_{V\in \mathsf{V}\Lambda_\oplus}\langle V, \mathscr{D}(V)\rangle$. Similarly, any formal sum $H = \Sigma_{i\in I}\langle M_i, p_i\rangle$ can be mapped to the distribution $\sum_{i\in I} p_i \cdot [\![M_i]\!]$, that we indicate with $[\![H]\!]$.

Reduction between $\Lambda_\oplus^{\mathrm{FS}}$ terms, written $E \rightsquigarrow F$, is defined by the rules in Figure 5; these rules are given on top of the operational semantics for $\Lambda_\oplus$ as defined in Section 2, which is invoked in the premise of rule $\mathsf{spc}$ (if there is a $i$ with $M_i$ not a value). The reduction relation $\rightsquigarrow$ is deterministic and strongly normalizing. We use $\overset{*}{\rightsquigarrow}$ for its reflexive and transitive closure. Lemma 5.1 shows the agreement between the new reduction relation and the original one.

LEMMA 5.1. *For all $M \in \Lambda_\oplus(\emptyset)$ there is a value $Z$ such that $M \overset{*}{\rightsquigarrow} Z$ and $[\![M]\!] = [\![Z]\!]$.*

**Proof.** One first show that for all $E$ there is $n$ such that $E \rightsquigarrow^n Z$. Then one reasons with a double induction: an induction on $n$, and a transition induction, exploiting the determinism of $\rightsquigarrow$. □

### 5.2 Context Equivalence and Bisimulation

In $\Lambda_\oplus^{\mathrm{FS}}$ certain terms (i.e., formal sums) may only appear in redex position; ordinary terms (i.e., terms in $\Lambda_\oplus$), by contrast, may appear in arbitrary position. When extending context equivalence to $\Lambda_\oplus^{\mathrm{FS}}$ we therefore have to distinguish these two cases. Moreover, as our main objective is the characterisation of context equivalence in $\Lambda_\oplus$, we set a somewhat constrained context equivalence in $\Lambda_\oplus^{\mathrm{FS}}$ in which contexts may not contain formal sums (thus the $\Lambda_\oplus^{\mathrm{FS}}$ contexts are the same as the $\Lambda_\oplus$ contexts). We call these *simple* $\Lambda_\oplus^{\mathrm{FS}}$ *contexts*, whereas we call *general* $\Lambda_\oplus^{\mathrm{FS}}$ *context* an unconstrained context, i.e., a $\Lambda_\oplus^{\mathrm{FS}}$ term in which the hole $[\cdot]$ may appear in any places where a term from $\Lambda_\oplus$ was expected — including within a formal sum. (Later we will see that allowing general contexts does not affect the resulting context equivalence.) Terms possibly containing formal sums are tested in evaluation contexts, i.e., contexts of the form $[\cdot]\overline{M}$. We write $E \Downarrow_p$ if $E \overset{*}{\rightsquigarrow} Z$ and $\mathbf{\Sigma}(Z) = p$ (recall that $Z$ is unique, for a given $E$).

DEFINITION 5.2 (Context Equivalence in $\Lambda_\oplus^{\mathrm{FS}}$). *Two $\Lambda_\oplus$-terms $M$ and $N$ are* context equivalent in $\Lambda_\oplus^{\mathrm{FS}}$, *written $M \simeq_\oplus^{\mathrm{FS}} N$, if for all (closing) simple $\Lambda_\oplus^{\mathrm{FS}}$ contexts $C$, we have $C[M]\Downarrow_p$ iff $C[N]\Downarrow_p$. Two $\Lambda_\oplus^{\mathrm{FS}}$-terms $E$ and $F$ are* evaluation-context equivalent, *written $E \approxeq_\oplus^{\mathrm{FS}} F$, if for all (closing) $\Lambda_\oplus^{\mathrm{FS}}$ evaluation contexts $C$, we have $C[E]\Downarrow_p$ iff $C[F]\Downarrow_p$.*

In virtue of Lemma 5.1, context equivalence in $\Lambda_\oplus$ coincides with context equivalence in $\Lambda_\oplus^{\mathrm{FS}}$.

We now introduce a bisimulation that yields a coinductive characterisation of context equivalence (and also of evaluation-context equivalence). A *coupled relation* is a pair $(\mathcal{V}, \mathcal{E})$ where: $\mathcal{V} \subseteq \Lambda_\oplus(\emptyset) \times \Lambda_\oplus(\emptyset)$, $\mathcal{E} \subseteq \Lambda_\oplus^{\mathrm{FS}}(\emptyset) \times \Lambda_\oplus^{\mathrm{FS}}(\emptyset)$, and $\mathcal{V} \subseteq \mathcal{E}$. Intuitively, we place in $\mathcal{V}$ the pairs of terms that should be preserved by all contexts, and in $\mathcal{E}$ those that should be preserved by evaluation contexts. For a coupled relation $\mathcal{R} = (\mathcal{V}, \mathcal{E})$ we write $\mathcal{R}_1$ for $\mathcal{V}$ and $\mathcal{R}_2$ for $\mathcal{E}$. The union of coupled relations is defined componentwise: e.g., if $\mathcal{R}$ and $\mathcal{S}$ are coupled relations, then the coupled relation $\mathcal{R} \cup \mathcal{S}$ has $(\mathcal{R} \cup \mathcal{S})_1 \overset{\mathrm{def}}{=} \mathcal{R}_1 \cup \mathcal{S}_1$ and $(\mathcal{R} \cup \mathcal{S})_2 \overset{\mathrm{def}}{=} \mathcal{R}_2 \cup \mathcal{S}_2$. If $\mathcal{V}$ is a relation on $\Lambda_\oplus$, then $\mathcal{V}^{\mathrm{C}}$ is the context closure of $\mathcal{V}$ in $\Lambda_\oplus$, i.e., the set of all (closed) terms of the form $(C[\overline{M}], C[\overline{N}])$ where $C$ is a multi-hole $\Lambda_\oplus$ context and $\overline{M}\ \mathcal{V}\ \overline{N}$.

DEFINITION 5.3. *A coupled relation $\mathcal{R}$ is a* coupled logical bisimulation *if whenever $E\ \mathcal{R}_2\ F$ we have:*

1. *if $E \rightsquigarrow D$, then $F \overset{*}{\rightsquigarrow} G$, where $D\ \mathcal{R}_2\ G$;*
2. *if $E$ is a formally summed value, then $F \overset{*}{\rightsquigarrow} Y$ with $\mathbf{\Sigma}(E) = \mathbf{\Sigma}(Y)$, and for all $M\ \mathcal{R}_1^{\mathrm{C}}\ N$ we have $(E \bullet M)\ \mathcal{R}_2\ (Y \bullet N)$;*
3. *the converse of 1. and 2..*

Coupled logical bisimilarity, $\approx$, *is the union of all coupled logical bisimulations (hence $\approx_1$ is the union of the first component of all coupled logical bisimulations, and similarly for $\approx_2$).*

In a coupled bisimulation $(\mathcal{R}_1, \mathcal{R}_2)$, the bisimulation game is only played on the pairs in $\mathcal{R}_2$. However, the first relation $\mathcal{R}_1$ is relevant, as inputs for tested functions are built using $\mathcal{R}_1$ (Clause 2. of Definition 5.3). Actually, also the pairs in $\mathcal{R}_1$ are tested, because in any coupled relations it must be $\mathcal{R}_1 \subseteq \mathcal{R}_2$. The values produced by the bisimulation game for coupled bisimulation on $\mathcal{R}_2$ are formal sums (not plain $\lambda$-terms), and this is why we do not require them to be in $\mathcal{R}_1$: formal sums should only appear in redex position, but terms in $\mathcal{R}_1$ can be used as arguments to bisimilar functions and can therefore end up in arbitrary positions.

We will see below another aspect of the relevance of $\mathcal{R}_1$: the proof technique of logical bisimulation only allows us to prove substitutivity of the bisimilarity in arbitrary contexts *for the pairs of terms* in $\mathcal{R}_1$. For pairs in $\mathcal{R}_2$ but not in $\mathcal{R}_1$ the proof technique only allows us to derive preservation in evaluation contexts.

In the proof of congruence of coupled logical bisimilarity we will push "as many terms as possible" into the first relation, i.e., the first relation will be as large as possible. However, in proofs of bisimilarity for concrete terms, the first relation may be very small, possibly a singleton or even empty. Then the bisimulation clauses become similar to those of applicative bisimulation (as inputs of tested function are "almost" identical). Summing up, in coupled logical bisimulation the use of two relations gives us more flexibility than in ordinary logical bisimulation: depending on the needs, we can tune the size of the first relation. It is possible that some of the above aspects of coupled logical bisimilarity be specific to call-by-name, and that the call-by-value version would require non-trivial modifications.

REMARK 5.4. *In a coupled logical bisimulation, the first relation is used to construct the inputs for the tested functions (the formally summed values produced in the bisimulation game for the second relation). Therefore, such first relation may be thought of as a "global" environment— global because it is the same for each pair of terms on which the bisimulation game is played. As a consequence, coupled logical bisimulation remains quite different from environmental bisimulation [42], where the "environment" for constructing inputs is local to each pair of tested terms. Coupled logical bisimulation follows ordinary logical bisimulation [41], in which there is only one global environment; in ordinary logical bisimulation, however, the global environment coincides with the set of tested terms. The similarity with logical bisimulation is also revealed by non-monotonicity of the associated functional (in contrast, the functional associated to environmental bisimulation is monotone); see Remark 5.11.*

As an example of use of coupled logical bisimulation, we revisit the counterexample 3.12 to the completeness of applicative bisimilarity with respect to contextual equivalence.

EXAMPLE 5.5. *We consider the terms of Example 3.12 and show that they are in $\approx_1$, hence also in $\simeq_\oplus$ (contextual equivalence of $\Lambda_\oplus$), by Corollary 5.9 and $\simeq_\oplus^{\mathrm{FS}} = \simeq_\oplus$. Recall that the terms are $M \stackrel{\mathrm{def}}{=} \lambda x.(L \oplus P)$ and $N \stackrel{\mathrm{def}}{=} (\lambda x.L) \oplus (\lambda x.P)$ for $L \stackrel{\mathrm{def}}{=} \lambda z.\Omega$ and $P \stackrel{\mathrm{def}}{=} \lambda y.\lambda z.\Omega$. We set $\mathcal{R}_1$ to contain only $(M, N)$ (this is the pair that interests us), and $R_2$ to contain the pairs $(M, N), (\langle M, 1\rangle, \langle \lambda x.L, \frac{1}{2}\rangle + \langle \lambda x.P, \frac{1}{2}\rangle), (\langle L + P, 1\rangle, \langle L, \frac{1}{2}\rangle + \langle P, \frac{1}{2}\rangle)$, and a set of pairs with identical components, namely $(\langle L, \frac{1}{2}\rangle + \langle P, \frac{1}{2}\rangle, \langle L, \frac{1}{2}\rangle + \langle P, \frac{1}{2}\rangle)$, $(\langle \Omega, \frac{1}{2}\rangle + \langle \lambda u.\Omega, \frac{1}{2}\rangle, \langle \Omega, \frac{1}{2}\rangle + \langle \lambda u.\Omega, \frac{1}{2}\rangle)$, $(\langle \lambda u.\Omega, \frac{1}{2}\rangle, \langle \lambda u.\Omega, \frac{1}{2}\rangle)$, $(\langle \Omega, \frac{1}{2}\rangle, \langle \Omega, \frac{1}{2}\rangle)$, $(\emptyset, \emptyset)$, where $\emptyset$ is the empty formal sum. Thus $(\mathcal{R}_1, \mathcal{R}_2)$ is a coupled logical bisimulation.*

The main challenge towards the goal of relating coupled logical bisimilarity and context equivalence is the substitutivity of bisimulation. We establish the latter exploiting some *up-to techniques* for bisimulation. We only give the definitions of the techniques, omitting the statements about their soundness. The first up-to technique allows us to drop the bisimulation game on silent actions:

DEFINITION 5.6 (Big-Step Bisimulation). *A coupled relation $\mathcal{R}$ is a* big-step coupled logical bisimulation *if whenever $E \;\mathcal{R}_2\; F$, the following holds: if $E \Rrightarrow Z$ then $F \Rrightarrow Y$ with $\mathbf{\Sigma}(Z) = \mathbf{\Sigma}(Y)$, and for all $M \;\mathcal{R}_1^{\mathrm{C}}\; N$ we have $(Z \bullet M) \;\mathcal{R}_2\; (Y \bullet N)$.*

In the reduction $\leadsto$, computation is performed at the level of formal sums; and this is reflected, in coupled bisimulation, by the application of values to formal sums only. The following up-to technique allows computation, and application of input values, also with ordinary terms. In the definition, we extract a formal sum from a term $E$ in $\Lambda_\oplus^{\mathrm{FS}}$ using the function $\mathcal{D}(\cdot)$ inductively as follows:

$$\mathcal{D}(EM) \stackrel{\mathrm{def}}{=} \Sigma_i \langle M_i M, p_i\rangle \text{ whenever } \mathcal{D}(E) = \Sigma_i \langle M_i, p_i\rangle;$$

$$\mathcal{D}(M) \stackrel{\mathrm{def}}{=} \langle M, 1\rangle; \qquad \mathcal{D}(H) \stackrel{\mathrm{def}}{=} H.$$

DEFINITION 5.7. *A coupled relation $\mathcal{R}$ is a* bisimulation up-to formal sums *if, whenever $E \;\mathcal{R}_2\; F$, then either (one of the bisimulation clauses of Definition 5.3 applies), or ($E, F \in \Lambda_\oplus$ and one of the following clauses applies):*

1. *$E \leadsto D$ with $\mathcal{D}(D) = \langle M, \frac{1}{2}\rangle + \langle N, \frac{1}{2}\rangle$, and $F \leadsto G$ with $\mathcal{D}(G) = \langle L, \frac{1}{2}\rangle + \langle P, \frac{1}{2}\rangle$, $M \;\mathcal{R}_2\; L$, and $N \;\mathcal{R}_2\; P$;*
2. *$E = \lambda x.M$ and $F = \lambda x.N$, and for all $P \;\mathcal{R}_1^{\mathrm{C}}\; Q$ we have $M\{P/x\} \;\mathcal{R}_2\; N\{Q/x\}$;*
3. *$E = (\lambda x.M)P\overline{M}$ and $F = (\lambda x.N)Q\overline{N}$, and $M\{P/x\}\overline{M} \;\mathcal{R}_2\; N\{Q/x\}\overline{N}$.*

According to Definition 5.7, in the bisimulation game for a coupled relation, given a pair $(E, F) \in \mathcal{R}_2$, we can either choose to follow the bisimulation game in the original Definition 5.3; or, if $E$ and $F$ do not contain formal sums, we can try one of the new clauses above. The advantage of the first new clause is that it allows us to make a split on the derivatives of the original terms. The advantage of the other two new clauses is that they allow us to directly handle the given $\lambda$-terms, without using the operational rules of Figure 5 and therefore without introducing formal sums. To understand the first clause, suppose $E \stackrel{\mathrm{def}}{=} (M \oplus N)L$ and $F \stackrel{\mathrm{def}}{=} P \oplus Q$. We have $E \leadsto (\langle M, \frac{1}{2}\rangle + \langle N, \frac{1}{2}\rangle)L \stackrel{\mathrm{def}}{=} G$ with $\mathcal{D}(G) = \langle ML, \frac{1}{2}\rangle + \langle NL, \frac{1}{2}\rangle$, and $F \leadsto \langle P, \frac{1}{2}\rangle + \langle Q, \frac{1}{2}\rangle \stackrel{\mathrm{def}}{=} H$, with $\mathcal{D}(H) = H$, and it is sufficient now to ensure $(ML) \;\mathcal{R}_2\; P$, and $(NL) \;\mathcal{R}_2\; Q$.

Using the above proof technique, we can prove the necessary substitutivity property for bisimulation. The use of up-to techniques, and the way bisimulation is defined (in particular the presence of a clause for $\tau$-steps and the possibility of using the pairs in the bisimulation itself to construct inputs for functions), make it possible to use a standard argument by induction over contexts.

LEMMA 5.8. *If $\mathcal{R}$ is a bisimulation then the context closure $\mathcal{S}$ with*

$\mathcal{S}_1 \stackrel{\mathrm{def}}{=} \mathcal{R}_1^{\mathrm{C}}$;

$\mathcal{S}_2 \stackrel{\mathrm{def}}{=} \mathcal{R}_2 \cup \mathcal{R}_1^{\mathrm{C}} \cup \{(E\overline{M}, F\overline{N})$ *s.t.* $E \;\mathcal{R}_2\; F$ *and* $M_i \;\mathcal{R}_1^{\mathrm{C}}\; N_i\}$;

*is a bisimulation up-to formal sums.*

Using Lemma 5.8 we can prove the inclusion in context equivalence.

COROLLARY 5.9. *If $M \approx_1 N$ then $M \simeq_\oplus^{\mathrm{FS}} N$. Moreover, if $E \approx_2 F$ then $E \cong_\oplus^{\mathrm{FS}} F$.*

The converse of Corollary 5.9 is proved exploiting a few simple properties of $\cong_\oplus^{\mathrm{FS}}$ (e.g., its transitivity, the inclusion $\leadsto \subseteq \cong_\oplus^{\mathrm{FS}}$).

THEOREM 5.10. *We have $\simeq_\oplus^{\mathrm{FS}} \subseteq \approx_1$, and $\cong_\oplus^{\mathrm{FS}} \subseteq \approx_2$.*

It also holds that coupled logical bisimilarity is preserved by the formal sum construct; i.e., $M_i \approx_1 N_i$ for each $i \in I$ implies $\Sigma_{i\in I}\langle M_i, p_i\rangle \approx_2 \Sigma_{i\in I}\langle N_i, p_i\rangle$. As a consequence, context equivalence defined on general $\Lambda_\oplus^{\mathrm{FS}}$ contexts is the same as that set on simple contexts (Definition 5.2).

REMARK 5.11. *The functional induced by coupled logical bisimulation is* not monotone. *For instance, if $\mathcal{V} \subseteq \mathcal{W}$, then a pair of terms may satisfy the bisimulation clauses on $(\mathcal{V}, \mathcal{E})$, for some $\mathcal{E}$,* *but not on $(\mathcal{W}, \mathcal{E})$, because the input for functions may be taken from the larger relation $\mathcal{W}$. (Recall that coupled relations are* pairs *of relations. Hence operations on coupled relations, such as union and inclusion, are defined component-wise.) However, Corollary 5.9 and Theorem 5.10 tell us that there is indeed a largest bisimulation, namely the pair $(\simeq_{\oplus}^{\mathrm{FS}}, \approxeq_{\oplus}^{\mathrm{FS}})$.*

With logical (as well as environmental) bisimulations, up-to techniques are particularly important to relieve the burden of proving concrete equalities. A powerful up-to technique in higher-order languages is *up-to contexts*. We present a form of up-to contexts combined with the big-step version of logical bisimilarity. Below, for a relation $\mathcal{R}$ on $\Lambda_{\oplus}$, we write $\mathcal{R}^{\mathrm{CFS}}$ for the closure of the relation under general (closing) $\Lambda_{\oplus}^{\mathrm{FS}}$ contexts.

DEFINITION 5.12. *A coupled relation $\mathcal{R}$ is a* big-step coupled logical bisimulation up-to contexts *if whenever $E\ \mathcal{R}_2\ F$, the following holds: if $E \Rrightarrow Z$ then $F \Rrightarrow Y$ with $\mathbf{\Sigma}(Z) = \mathbf{\Sigma}(Y)$, and for all $M\ \mathcal{R}_1^{\mathrm{C}}\ N$, we have $(Z \bullet M)\ \mathcal{R}_1^{\mathrm{CFS}}\ (Y \bullet N)$.*

For the soundness proof, we first derive the soundness of a small-step up-to context technique, whose proof, in turn, is similar to that of Lemma 5.8 (the up-to-formal-sums technique of Definition 5.7 already allows some context manipulation; we need this technique for the proof of the up-to-contexts technique).

EXAMPLE 5.13. *We have seen that the terms* `expone` *and* `exptwo` *of Example 2.5 are not applicative bisimilar. We can show that they are context equivalent, by proving that they are coupled bisimilar. We sketch a proof of this, in which we employ the up-to technique from Definition 5.12. We use the coupled relation $\mathcal{R}$ in which $\mathcal{R}_1 \stackrel{\text{def}}{=} \{(\texttt{expone}, \texttt{exptwo})\}$, and $\mathcal{R}_2 \stackrel{\text{def}}{=} \mathcal{R}_1 \cup \{(A_M, B_N) \mid M\ \mathcal{R}_1^{\mathrm{C}}\ N\}$ where $A_M \stackrel{\text{def}}{=} \lambda n.((Mn) \oplus (\texttt{expone}\, M\, (n+1)))$, and $B_N \stackrel{\text{def}}{=} (\lambda x.Nx) \oplus (\texttt{exptwo}\, (\lambda x.N(x+1)))$. This is a big-step coupled logical bisimulation up-to contexts. The interesting part is the matching argument for the terms $A_M, B_N$; upon receiving an argument $m$ they yield the summed values $\Sigma_i \langle M(m+1), p_i\rangle$ and $\Sigma_i \langle N(m+1), p_i\rangle$ (for some $p_i$'s), and these are in $\mathcal{R}_1^{\mathrm{CFS}}$.*

## 6. Beyond Call-by-Name Reduction

So far, we have studied the problem of giving sound (and sometime complete) coinductive methods for program equivalence in a probabilistic $\lambda$-calculus endowed with *call-by-name* reduction. One may wonder whether what we have obtained can be adapted to other notions of reduction, and in particular to *call-by-value* reduction (e.g., the call-by-value operational semantics of $\Lambda_{\oplus}$ from [9]).

Since our construction of a labelled Markov chain for $\Lambda_{\oplus}$ is somehow independent on the underlying operational semantics, defining a call-by-value probabilistic applicative bisimulation is effortless. The proofs of congruence of the bisimilarity and its soundness can also be transplanted to call-by-value.

When we restrict our attention to pure $\lambda$-terms, as we do in Section 4, we are strongly relying on call-by-name evaluation: LLT's only reflect term equivalence in a call-by-name lazy regime. We leave the task of generalizing the results to eager evaluation to future work, but we conjecture that, in that setting, probabilistic choice *alone* does not give contexts the same discriminating power as probabilistic bisimulation. Similarly we have not investigated the call-by-value version of coupled logical bisimilarity, as our current proofs rely on the appearance of formal sums only in redex position, a constraint that would probably have to be lifted for call-by-value.

## 7. A Comparison with Nondeterminism

Syntactically, $\Lambda_{\oplus}$ is identical to an eponymous language introduced by de'Liguoro and Piperno [13]. The semantics we present here, however, is quantitative, and this has of course a great impact on context equivalence. While in a nondeterministic setting what one observes is the *possibility* of converging (or of diverging, or both), terms with different convergence probabilities are considered different in an essential way here. Actually, nondeterministic context equivalence and probabilistic context equivalence are incomparable. As an example of terms that are context equivalent in the *must* sense but not probabilistically, we can take $I \oplus (I \oplus \Omega)$ and $I \oplus \Omega$. Conversely, $I$ is probabilistically equivalent to any term $M$ that reduces to $I \oplus M$ (which can be defined using fixed-point combinators), while $I$ and $M$ are not equivalent in the *must* sense, since the latter can diverge (the divergence is irrelevant probabilistically because it has probability zero). *May* context equivalence, in contrast, is coarser than probabilistic context equivalence.

Despite the differences, the two semantics have similarities. Analogously to what happens in nondeterministic $\lambda$-calculi, applicative bisimulation and context equivalence do *not* coincide in the probabilistic setting, at least if call-by-name is considered. The counterexamples to full abstraction are much more complicated in call-by-value $\lambda$-calculi [27], and cannot be easily adapted to the probabilistic setting.

## 8. Conclusions

This is the first paper in which bisimulation techniques for program equivalence are shown to be applicable to probabilistic $\lambda$-calculi.

On the one hand, Abramsky's idea of seeing interaction as application is shown to be amenable to a probabilistic treatment, giving rise to a congruence relation that is sound for context equivalence. Completeness, however, fails: the way probabilistic applicative bisimulation is defined allows one to distinguish terms that are context equivalent, but which behave differently as for *when* choices and interactions are performed. On the other, a notion of coupled logical bisimulation is introduced and proved to precisely characterise context equivalence for $\Lambda_{\oplus}$. Along the way, applicative bisimilarity is proved to coincide with context equivalence on pure $\lambda$-terms, yielding the Levy-Longo tree equality.

The crucial difference between the two main bisimulations studied in the paper is not the style (applicative *vis-à-vis* logical), but rather the fact that while applicative bisimulation insists on relating only individual terms, coupled logical bisimulation is more flexible and allows us to relate formal sums (which we may think as distributions). This also explains why we need distinct reduction rules for the two bisimulations. See examples 3.12 and 5.5. While not complete, applicative bisimulation, as it stands, is simpler to use than coupled logical bisimulation. Moreover it is a natural form of bisimulation, and it should be interesting trying to transport the techniques for handling it onto variants or extensions of the language.

Topics for future work abound — some have already been hinted at in earlier sections. Among the most interesting ones, one can mention the transport of applicative bisimulation onto the language $\Lambda_{\oplus}^{\mathrm{FS}}$. We conjecture that the resulting relation would coincide with coupled logical bisimilarity and context equivalence, but going through Howe's technique seems more difficult than for $\Lambda_{\oplus}$, given the infinitary nature of formal sums and their confinement to redex positions.

Also interesting would be a more *effective* notion of equivalence: even if the two introduced notions of bisimulation avoid universal quantifications over all possible contexts, they refer to an essentially infinitary operational semantics in which the meaning of a term is obtained as the least upper bound of all its finite approximations. Would it be possible to define bisimulation in terms of approximations without getting too fine grained?

Bisimulations in the style of logical bisimulation (or environmental bisimulation) are known to require up-to techniques in order to avoid tedious equality proofs on concrete terms. In the paper we have introduced some up-to techniques for coupled logical bisimilarity, but additional techniques would be useful. Up-to techniques could also be developed for applicative bisimilarity.

More in the long-run, we would like to develop sound operational techniques for so-called *computational indistinguishability*, a key notion in modern cryptography. Computational indistinguishability is defined similarly to context equivalence; the context is however required to work within appropriate resource bounds, while the two terms can have different observable behaviors (although with negligible probability). We see this work as a very first step in this direction: complexity bounds are not yet there, but probabilistic behaviour, an essential ingredient, is correctly taken into account.

## Acknowledgments

The authors would like to thank the anonymous referees for the many interesting comments. This work is partially supported by the ANR project 12IS02001 'PACE', and the project MIUR PRIN 2010LHT4KM 'CINA'.

## References


[1] S. Abramsky. The Lazy λ-Calculus. In D. Turner, editor, *Research Topics in Functional Programming*, pages 65–117. Addison Wesley, 1990.

[2] S. Abramsky and C.-H. L. Ong. Full abstraction in the lazy lambda calculus. *Inf. Comput.*, 105(2):159–267, 1993.

[3] E. Astesiano and G. Costa. Distributive semantics for nondeterministic typed lambda-calculi. *Theor. Comput. Sci.*, 32:121–156, 1984.

[4] H. P. Barendregt. *The Lambda Calculus – Its Syntax and Semantics*, volume 103 of *Studies in Logic and the Foundations of Mathematics*. North-Holland, 1984.

[5] M. Bernardo, R. De Nicola, and M. Loreti. A uniform framework for modeling nondeterministic, probabilistic, stochastic, or mixed processes and their behavioral equivalences. *Inf. Comput.*, 225:29–82, 2013.

[6] G. Boudol. Lambda-calculi for (strict) parallel functions. *Inf. Comput.*, 108(1):51–127, 1994.

[7] G. Boudol and C. Laneve. The discriminating power of the λ-calculus with multiplicities. *Inf. Comput.*, 126(1):83–102, 1996.

[8] D. Comaniciu, V. Ramesh, and P. Meer. Kernel-based object tracking. *IEEE Trans. on Pattern Analysis and Machine Intelligence,*, 25(5): 564–577, 2003.

[9] U. Dal Lago and M. Zorzi. Probabilistic operational semantics for the lambda calculus. *RAIRO - Theor. Inf. and Applic.*, 46(3):413–450, 2012.

[10] U. Dal Lago, D. Sangiorgi, and M. Alberti. On coinductive equivalences for probabilistic higher-order functional programs (long version). Available at `http://arxiv.org/abs/1311.1722`, 2013.

[11] V. Danos and R. Harmer. Probabilistic game semantics. *ACM Trans. Comput. Log.*, 3(3):359–382, 2002.

[12] R. De Nicola and M. Hennessy. Testing equivalences for processes. *Theor. Comput. Sci.*, 34:83–133, 1984.

[13] U. de'Liguoro and A. Piperno. Non deterministic extensions of untyped lambda-calculus. *Inf. Comput.*, 122(2):149–177, 1995.

[14] M. Dezani-Ciancaglini and E. Giovannetti. From bohm's theorem to observational equivalences: an informal account. *Electr. Notes Theor. Comput. Sci.*, 50(2):83–116, 2001.

[15] M. Dezani-Ciancaglini, J. Tiuryn, and P. Urzyczyn. Discrimination by parallel observers: The algorithm. *Inf. Comput.*, 150(2):153–186, 1999.

[16] T. Ehrhard, M. Pagani, and C. Tasson. The computational meaning of probabilistic coherence spaces. In *LICS*, pages 87–96, 2011.

[17] S. Goldwasser and S. Micali. Probabilistic encryption. *J. Comput. Syst. Sci.*, 28(2):270–299, 1984.

[18] N. D. Goodman. The principles and practice of probabilistic programming. In *POPL*, pages 399–402, 2013.

[19] A. D. Gordon. Bisimilarity as a theory of functional programming. *Electr. Notes Theor. Comput. Sci.*, 1:232–252, 1995.

[20] A. D. Gordon, M. Aizatulin, J. Borgström, G. Claret, T. Graepel, A. V. Nori, S. K. Rajamani, and C. V. Russo. A model-learner pattern for bayesian reasoning. In *POPL*, pages 403–416, 2013.

[21] M. Hennessy. Exploring probabilistic bisimulations, part I. *Formal Asp. Comput.*, 24(4-6):749–768, 2012.

[22] D. J. Howe. Proving congruence of bisimulation in functional programming languages. *Inf. Comput.*, 124(2):103–112, 1996.

[23] R. Jagadeesan and P. Panangaden. A domain-theoretic model for a higher-order process calculus. In *ICALP*, pages 181–194, 1990.

[24] C. Jones and G. D. Plotkin. A probabilistic powerdomain of evaluations. In *LICS*, pages 186–195, 1989.

[25] V. Koutavas, P. B. Levy, and E. Sumii. From applicative to environmental bisimulation. *Electr. Notes Theor. Comput. Sci.*, 276: 215–235, 2011.

[26] K. G. Larsen and A. Skou. Bisimulation through probabilistic testing. *Inf. Comput.*, 94(1):1–28, 1991.

[27] S. B. Lassen. *Relational Reasoning about Functions and Nondeterminism*. PhD thesis, University of Aarhus, 1998.

[28] S. Lenglet, A. Schmitt, and J.-B. Stefani. Howe's method for calculi with passivation. In *CONCUR*, pages 448–462, 2009.

[29] C. D. Manning and H. Schütze. *Foundations of statistical natural language processing*, volume 999. MIT Press, 1999.

[30] C.-H. L. Ong. Non-determinism in a functional setting. In *LICS*, pages 275–286, 1993.

[31] P. Panangaden. *Labelled Markov Processes*. Imperial College Press, 2009.

[32] S. Park, F. Pfenning, and S. Thrun. A probabilistic language based on sampling functions. *ACM Trans. Program. Lang. Syst.*, 31(1), 2008.

[33] J. Pearl. *Probabilistic reasoning in intelligent systems: networks of plausible inference*. Morgan Kaufmann, 1988.

[34] A. Pfeffer. IBAL: A probabilistic rational programming language. In *IJCAI*, pages 733–740. Morgan Kaufmann, 2001.

[35] A. M. Pitts. Operationally-based theories of program equivalence. In *Semantics and Logics of Computation*, pages 241–298. Cambridge University Press, 1997.

[36] A. M. Pitts. Howe's method for higher-order languages. In D. Sangiorgi and J. Rutten, editors, *Advanced Topics in Bisimulation and Coinduction*, pages 197–232. Cambridge University Press, 2011.

[37] N. Ramsey and A. Pfeffer. Stochastic lambda calculus and monads of probability distributions. In *POPL*, pages 154–165, 2002.

[38] N. Saheb-Djahromi. Probabilistic LCF. In *MFCS*, volume 64 of *LNCS*, pages 442–451, 1978.

[39] D. Sands. From SOS rules to proof principles: An operational metatheory for functional languages. In *POPL*, pages 428–441, 1997.

[40] D. Sangiorgi and D. Walker. *The pi-Calculus – a theory of mobile processes*. Cambridge University Press, 2001.

[41] D. Sangiorgi, N. Kobayashi, and E. Sumii. Logical bisimulations and functional languages. In *FSEN*, volume 4767 of *LNCS*, pages 364–379, 2007.

[42] D. Sangiorgi, N. Kobayashi, and E. Sumii. Environmental bisimulations for higher-order languages. *ACM Trans. Program. Lang. Syst.*, 33(1):5, 2011.

[43] K. Sieber. Call-by-value and nondeterminism. In *TLCA*, volume 664 of *LNCS*, pages 376–390, 1993.

[44] S. Thrun. Robotic mapping: A survey. *Exploring artificial intelligence in the new millennium*, pages 1–35, 2002.

# Probabilistic Coherence Spaces are Fully Abstract for Probabilistic PCF *

Thomas Ehrhard Christine Tasson

Laboratoire PPS - CNRS - Université Paris Diderot

thomas.ehrhard@pps.univ-paris-diderot.fr

christine.tasson@pps.univ-paris-diderot.fr

Michele Pagani

Laboratoire LIPN - Université Paris 13

michele.pagani@lipn.univ-paris13.fr

## Abstract

Probabilistic coherence spaces (**PCoh**) yield a semantics of higher-order probabilistic computation, interpreting types as convex sets and programs as power series. We prove that the equality of interpretations in **PCoh** characterizes the operational indistinguishability of programs in PCF with a random primitive.

This is the first result of full abstraction for a semantics of probabilistic PCF. The key ingredient relies on the regularity of power series.

Along the way to the theorem, we design a weighted intersection type assignment system giving a logical presentation of **PCoh**.

***Categories and Subject Descriptors*** D.3.1 [*Programming Languages*]: Formal Definitions and Theory - Semantics

***Keywords*** Full Abstraction, Probabilistic PCF

## 1. Introduction

Probabilistic behaviors appear in many places in the study of programing languages, for instance if the environment of a program behaves randomly or if the program uses probabilistic constructs.

To understand how the introduction of probabilities changes the computational landscape, we use *Semantics*. Indeed, in the last decades [24, 27, 30], semantics has succeeded in giving insights on the way programs compute. More precisely, *operational semantics* allows one to formalize a program by the sequence of its execution steps, while *denotational semantics* represents programs by functions in some mathematical space relating the interpretations of inputs and outputs in a compositional way. If this last mathematical representation is correct and accurate enough, then denotational properties lead to computational features. A key example is *full abstraction* [23], stating that operational indistinguishability (i.e. behaving in the same way in any context) is characterized by denotational equivalence (i.e. having the same interpretation). So semantics is useful both to give a precise meaning to syntactical constructs and to separate non-equivalent programs.

Of course, probabilistic semantics have already been investigated. First, the domain-theoretic approach has led to a *probabilistic powerdomain* [19, 29] which is a sibling of the non-deterministic power domain [27]. This approach follows the computational monad method [25]: programs are interpreted as functions from the input domain to the powerdomain of the output domain. Intuitively, a program takes an input and returns a probability distribution on outputs. This line of work has been continued by the continuous random variable construction [15], introducing standard tools of probability theory into semantics. Secondly, the game-theoretic approach [1, 18] has been extended with probabilistic features [5]. Intuitively, probabilistic programs are interpreted as probabilistic strategies, that are stochastic processes on the plays of the games associated with the types of the programs.

*Quantitative semantics* follows another tradition stemming from Linear Logic models [10, 11]. From the very beginning, Linear Logic has been associated with intuitions coming from calculus and linear algebra [7, 8, 12]. Indeed, programs are interpreted as entire series between mathematical spaces or as analytic functors between sets [17], and programs that use their resources only once are interpreted as linear functions. This connection with resource consumption has been fruitful in the last decade with the introduction of differential nets and resource calculus [2, 9]. Recently, quantitative semantics has been explicitly related to the study of quantitative properties such as time or space consumed by a computation [22]. This illustrates a new paradigm where a semiring of scalars allows one to encode non-deterministic or probabilistic computations as opposed to the domain paradigm where monads are used. Another important tenet of Linear Logic is the perfect duality between programs and environments since a program can be seen as the environment of other programs. Therefore, representing probabilistic environments or programs will boil down to the same study. *Probabilistic coherence spaces* provide a quantitative semantics [4, 14] which model probabilistic computations.

The main contribution of the present work is to show that probabilistic coherence spaces provide a fully abstract model of PPCF, a probabilistic extension of the functional programing language PCF [28]. Although the proof follows the general pattern that consists in finding a *definable* context that separates two terms, the key ingredient is based on Calculus (see Lemma 25) since programs are interpreted as power series.

To our knowledge, no known model of probabilistic PCF has yet been proved to be fully abstract. Games semantics provide fully abstract models of standard PCF via an extensional collapse [1, 18]. This technique has been adapted to probabilistic game semantics, providing a fully abstract model of probabilistic idealized ALGOL [5] (an extension of probabilistic PCF with references). Our result characterizes the operational indistinguishability without the

* Partially founded by French ANR project COQUAS (number 12 JS02 006 01) and CNRS chair "Logique linéaire et calcul".



*POPL '14*, January 22–24, 2014, San Diego, CA, USA.



ACM 978-1-4503-2544-8/14/01... $15.00.

http://dx.doi.org/10.1145/2535838.2535865

need of an extensional collapse and deals with a functional probabilistic language with no references.

Section 2 is devoted to an insight on the way programs and data are interpreted in probabilistic coherence spaces. Section 3 is devoted to the syntax and the operational semantics. Next, in Section 4, we describe the key notions of probabilistic coherence spaces that will be useful to prove, in Section 5, full abstraction. Along the way to the theorem, we define an intersection type assignment system (Figure 3) giving a logical presentation to the model. This system has an interest by its own, allowing one to turn a question of computing the semantics of a term (and hence its operational behavior) into a proof search problem. Finally, in Section 6, we show that inequational full abstraction fails, i.e. the semantical order does not coincide with the operational one. For this, we achieve a context lemma for probabilistic PCF (Proposition 31).

**Notation 1.** We write $\mathbb{N}$ for the set of non negative *integers*, $\mathbb{N}^*$ for the set of positive integers ($\mathbb{N}^* \triangleq \mathbb{N}\backslash\{0\}$), $\mathbb{R}_+$ for the set of non negative *real* numbers and $\overline{\mathbb{R}}_+ \triangleq \mathbb{R}_+ \cup \{\infty\}$ for the completed real half line. Let $S$ be a set, $\sharp S$ denotes its cardinality. *Multisets* of elements of $S$ are identified with functions $S \to \mathbb{N}$. If $m$ is such a multiset, $\mathrm{Supp}\,(m)$ denotes its *support* set $\{a \in S \text{ s.t. } m(a) \neq 0\}$. A *finite multiset* is a multiset with a finite support. We write $\mathcal{M}_{\mathrm{f}}\,(S)$ for the set of all finite multisets of elements of $S$. We enumerate $m$ by using $(a, i) \in m$ to denote $a \in \mathrm{Supp}\,(m)$ and $1 \leq i \leq m(a)$. Whenever $(a_1, \dots, a_n) \in S^n$, we write $[a_1, \dots, a_n]$ for the finite multiset: $a \in S \mapsto \sharp\{i \text{ s.t. } a_i = a\}$. The empty multiset is $[\,]$ and $\uplus$ is the multiset union: $(m \uplus p)(a) \triangleq m(a) + p(a)$. A *vector* $v \in \overline{\mathbb{R}}_+^S$ is given by its values $v_a$ on any index $a \in S$. Given a multiset $m \in \mathcal{M}_{\mathrm{f}}\,(S)$, we define the power $v^m \triangleq \prod_{a \in \mathrm{Supp}(m)} v_a^{m(a)}$. For any $a \in S$, let $e_a \in \overline{\mathbb{R}}_+^S$ be the base vector $(e_a)_b \triangleq \delta_{a,b}$, with $\delta_{a,b}$ denoting the Kronecker symbol.

Let us fix our typographic conventions: $a, b, c$ range over web elements and $m, p, q$ over multisets. $v, w, u$ range over vectors, $\phi, \psi, \xi$ over matrices, $\alpha, \beta, \gamma$ over monomials. $A, B, C$ range over simple types, $\mathtt{Int}$ being the integer type. $x, y, z$ range over term variables. $M, N, P$ range over terms. Finally, $\kappa, \mu, \nu$ range over scalars in $\mathbb{R}_+$ and $\vec{\kappa}$ denotes a list of scalars and similarly for the other metavariables.

## 2. Denoting Probabilistic Programing

Probabilistic programs use two levels of randomness: the first one on data (i.e. terms of ground type), the second one on programs (i.e. terms of higher-order type).

A *probabilistic datum* is a random variable whose outcome is given to the program. Thus, a probabilistic datum will be characterized by its law, that will be its *interpretation*. Then, a *probabilistic program* uses random instructions and behaves like a function from probabilistic data to probabilistic data. Moreover, a program can call several times its argument $x$. Each of its occurrences is represented by the outcome of an independent random variable with the same distribution as $x$.

We consider two examples of probabilistic data of type $\mathtt{Int}$. The first one, $\mathtt{Coin}$, is the toss of a $0/1$ fair coin. The second one, $\mathtt{Rand}(n)$, follows the discrete uniform distribution with outcomes between $0$ and $n-1$.

If we are only interested in resulting values, then $\mathtt{Int}$ is interpreted by the set of non negative integers $|\mathtt{Int}| = \mathbb{N}$. First, we consider $\mathtt{Coin}$ and $\mathtt{Rand}(n)$ as non deterministic data, and interpret them by the range of the corresponding random variables:

$$|\mathtt{Coin}| = \{0, 1\} \quad \text{and} \quad |\mathtt{Rand}(n)| = \{0, \dots, n-1\}.$$

Then, to take into account the randomized behavior of the datum, we associate a coefficient to each outcome: its probability to happen. The interpretation of a datum is now given by a sequence of non-negative integers indexed by the possible outcomes:

$$[\![\mathtt{Coin}]\!] = (\tfrac{1}{2}, \tfrac{1}{2}, 0, \dots) \text{ and } [\![\mathtt{Rand}(n)]\!] = (\underbrace{\tfrac{1}{n}, \dots, \tfrac{1}{n}}_{n}, 0 \dots).$$

In general, we will interpret the integer type by subprobability[1] distributions over $\mathbb{N}$:

$$\mathrm{P}\,(\mathtt{Int}) = \left\{(\kappa_n)_{n \in \mathbb{N}} \in \mathbb{R}_+^{\mathbb{N}} \text{ s.t. } \textstyle\sum_{n \in \mathbb{N}} \kappa_n \leq 1\right\}.$$

For probabilistic programs, we follow the same pattern as for probabilistic data. First, their *non deterministic* behavior is described. Then, coefficients are introduced in order to render their *quantitative* behavior.

As an example, let us consider the program $\mathtt{Rand} : \mathtt{Int} \Rightarrow \mathtt{Int}$ that takes an input value $n$, and returns any non negative integer strictly less than $n$ with equal chances and make it interact with probabilistic data (e.g. a probabilistic distribution over $\mathbb{N}$).

Focusing on the association between input and output values, its non deterministic behavior is described as a relation: $|\mathtt{Rand}| \subseteq |\mathtt{Int}| \times |\mathtt{Int}|$

$$|\mathtt{Rand}| = \left\{(n, a) \text{ s.t. } n \in \mathbb{N},\ a \in \{0, \dots, n-1\}\right\}.$$

Then we associate a coefficient to each pair input-output. It represents the quantitative account of getting the given output knowing the input. The interpretation of the program is now turned into a matrix indexed by the values interpreting inputs (column indices) and outputs (raw indices)[2]: $[\![\mathtt{Rand}]\!] \in (\mathbb{R}_+)^{|\mathtt{Int}| \times |\mathtt{Int}|}$

$$[\![\mathtt{Rand}]\!] = \begin{array}{c} \begin{matrix} \overset{0}{\downarrow} & \overset{1}{\downarrow} & \overset{2}{\downarrow} & \cdots & \overset{n}{\downarrow} & \cdots \end{matrix} \\ \begin{pmatrix} 0 & 1 & \frac{1}{2} & \cdots & \frac{1}{n} & \cdots \\ 0 & 0 & \frac{1}{2} & \cdots & \frac{1}{n} & \cdots \\ \vdots & \vdots & 0 & \ddots & \vdots & \\ & & \vdots & 0 & \frac{1}{n} & \\ & & & \vdots & \ddots & \ddots \end{pmatrix} \end{array} \begin{array}{l} \\ \to 0 \\ \to 1 \\ \vdots \\ \to n-1 \\ \vdots \end{array} \tag{1}$$

The interaction between the program $\mathtt{Rand}$ and a probabilistic datum $x$ is then given by the product of the matrix interpreting the program and of the sequence interpreting the datum. Besides, this probabilistic program preserves subprobability distributions.

Actually, this approach is valid only if the program uses exactly once its argument. Indeed, as a side effect of the call-by-name[3] execution strategy, each occurrence of a probabilistic datum behaves as an independent sample of a random variable. So, if a program makes several calls to a given probabilistic datum, then the outcomes of the calls may differ due to the randomized setting.Thus, we gather the input values into a finite multiset: finite, since if the execution of a program terminates, then the number of resources effectively used is finite; multiset rather than a sequence since this model is not accurate enough to distinguish the order of the inputs.

To illustrate this point, we examine the probabilistic programs:

$$\begin{aligned} \mathtt{Once} &\triangleq \lambda x^{\mathtt{Int}}.\mathsf{if}(x, \mathtt{Coin}, \underline{42}), \\ \mathtt{Twice} &\triangleq \lambda x^{\mathtt{Int}}.\mathsf{if}(x, \mathsf{if}(x, \mathtt{Coin}, \underline{42}), \mathsf{if}(x, \underline{42}, \underline{0})), \end{aligned}$$

where $\mathsf{if}(x, \_, \_)$ branches depending whether $x$ evaluates to zero or not. Notice that the two programs uses, among others, probabilistic

[1] Since a call to a datum can fail, the total probability distribution over the possible values may be less than 1.

[2] $[\![\mathtt{Rand}]\!]$ is the transpose of a stochastic matrix and the image of a subprobability distribution is the matrix product $[\![\mathtt{Rand}]\!] \cdot v$.

[3] This phenomenon will also appear in a call-by-value setting, if every probabilistic datum $x$ is replaced by its CPS translation $\lambda a^{\mathtt{Int}}.x$.

instructions and that they call once or twice their input. Their interpretation is given by a matrix indexed by finite multisets (the input) and integers (the output). Coefficients are non zero only if the multiset is of size one or two:

$$[\![\texttt{Once}]\!] : \begin{cases} ([0],\ 0) \mapsto \frac{1}{2} \\ ([0],\ 1) \mapsto \frac{1}{2} \\ ([a], 42) \mapsto 1 \ \text{if}\ a \neq 0 \\ (m,\ a) \mapsto 0 \ \text{otherwise.} \end{cases} \qquad [\![\texttt{Twice}]\!] : \begin{cases} ([0,0],\ 0) \mapsto \frac{1}{2} \\ ([0,0],\ 1) \mapsto \frac{1}{2} \\ ([0,a], 42) \mapsto 2 \ \text{if}\ a \neq 0 \\ ([a,b],\ 0) \mapsto 1 \ \text{if}\ a \neq 0, b \neq 0 \\ (\ m\ ,\ a) \mapsto 0 \ \text{otherwise.} \end{cases}$$

On the second example, two quantitative phenomena are mixed up. The first one is probabilistic: coefficient $\frac{1}{2}$ comes from the use of `coin`. The second one stems from branching construction: two different execution traces are leading to $\underline{42}$, either the two outcomes of the random variable $x$ are first 0, and then $a \neq 0$, or its outcomes are first $a$, and then 0. In our model, these traces are gathered in the same multiset $[0, a]$ and the coefficient 2 is the combinatorial counterpart. This gives a hint of why programs are not represented as random variables.

Now, the interaction of a probabilistic program with a probabilistic data boils down to a matrix product adapted to take into account multiplicities.

Let us consider a probabilistic datum $x$ : `Int` and a program $M$ : `Int` $\Rightarrow$ `Int`. As a reminder, the $a$-th coefficient $[\![x]\!]_a$ is the probability that $a$ is the outcome of $x$. The probability $[\![(M)\, x]\!]_b$, that $(M)\, x$ returns $b$, is given by decomposing the computation in pairwise disjoint events. Each event corresponds to an intermediate multiset $m$ gathering the input values that are effectively used during computation:

$$[\![(M)\, x]\!]_b = \sum_{m \in \mathcal{M}_f(\mathbb{N})} [\![M]\!]_{(m,b)}\, [\![x]\!]^m, \tag{2}$$

(see Notation 1 for $[\![x]\!]^m$) is the probability that independent calls to $x$ returns the values gathered in $m$. In this way, every coefficient $[\![(M)\, x]\!]_b$ is a power series with infinitely many variables, that are the $[\![x]\!]_a$ for $a \in \mathbb{N}$.

Applying Formula (2), we compute the non zero coefficients:

$$[\![(\texttt{Once})\, x]\!]_0 = [\![(\texttt{Once})\, x]\!]_1 = \tfrac{1}{2}\, [\![x]\!]_0 \qquad [\![(\texttt{Once})\, x]\!]_{42} = \sum_{a \geq 1} [\![x]\!]_a$$

$$[\![(\texttt{Twice})\, x]\!]_0 = \tfrac{1}{2}\, [\![x]\!]_0^2 + \sum_{a,b \geq 1} [\![x]\!]_a\, [\![x]\!]_b$$

$$[\![(\texttt{Twice})\, x]\!]_1 = \tfrac{1}{2}\, [\![x]\!]_0^2 \qquad [\![(\texttt{Twice})\, x]\!]_{42} = 2 \sum_{a \geq 1} [\![x]\!]_0\, [\![x]\!]_a$$

Notice that every coefficient of $[\![(\texttt{Once})\, x]\!]$ is a linear function and every coefficient of $[\![(\texttt{Twice})\, x]\!]$ is a polynomial of degree 2. Besides, `Once` and `Twice` preserve subprobability distributions:

$$\sum_b [\![(\texttt{Once})\, x]\!]_b = \tfrac{1}{2}\, [\![x]\!]_0 + \tfrac{1}{2}\, [\![x]\!]_0 + \sum_{a \geq 1} [\![x]\!]_a \leq 1$$

$$\begin{aligned} \sum_b [\![(\texttt{Twice})\, x]\!]_b &= [\![x]\!]_0^2 + 2\, [\![x]\!]_0 \sum_{a \geq 1} [\![x]\!]_a + (\sum_{a \geq 1} [\![x]\!]_a)^2, \\ &= (\sum_{a \geq 0} [\![x]\!]_a)^2 \leq 1. \end{aligned}$$

## 3. Probabilistic PCF

We define the language PPCF in Figure 1. This system is a minor variant with respect to the probabilistic extension of PCF presented in [4] (see Remark 6). The grammar of terms is obtained by adding to standard PCF a random number generator `rand`.The typing rules (Figure 1(b)) are the usual ones, with `rand` of type `Int` $\Rightarrow$ `Int`. From now on, we call *program* a closed term of type `Int`. Figure 1(c) gives the one step *reduction relation* $\xrightarrow{\kappa}$, implementing a weak head-reduction (i.e. a lazy call-by-name strategy). The relation is weighted with a probability $\kappa \in [0, 1]$ equal to 1 except for steps firing a $(\texttt{rand})\, \underline{n}$ redex, reducing to any numeral in $\{\underline{0}, \ldots, \underline{n-1}\}$ with equal probability $\frac{1}{n}$. The probability of a reduction sequence is the product of the weights of all its steps. Some notational conventions are introduced in Figure 1(d) and will be used henceforth.

**Example 2.** Notice (by induction on $n \geq 1$) that the term $\texttt{choose}(M_i)_{i=1}^n$, for $1 \leq i \leq n$ reduces (in several steps) to any $M_i$ with equal probability $\frac{1}{n}$. In general, any reduction sequence has a probability given by a rational number in $[0, 1]$, since $\texttt{rand}\, n$ introduces just fractions.

**Example 3.** The fix-point constructor yields infinite reduction sequences, like the typical loop $\Omega_A \xrightarrow{1} (\lambda x^A.x)\, \Omega_A \xrightarrow{1} \Omega_A$. However, we can have terms with infinite reduction sequences but converging to a normal form with probability 1. Indeed, take $M \triangleq \mathsf{fix}(\lambda x^{\texttt{Int}}.x \oplus \underline{0})$ (see notations in Figure 1(d)) we have:

$$M \xrightarrow{1} (\lambda x^{\texttt{Int}}.x \oplus \underline{0})\, M \xrightarrow{1} M \oplus \underline{0} \xrightarrow{\frac{1}{2}} \underline{0}, \qquad M \oplus \underline{0} \xrightarrow{\frac{1}{2}} M$$

The probability that $M$ reduces to $\underline{0}$ is equal to the sum of the probabilities of all finite reductions sequences from $M$ to $\underline{0}$, which is $\sum_{n=0}^{\infty} \frac{1}{2^{n+1}} = 1$, $n$ being the number of loops taken by a sequence.

A way for precisely defining the probability of convergence of a term to a normal form is by giving the operational semantics as a Markov process over the set of PPCF terms, following [4]. The transition matrix $\textsc{Proba} \in [0,1]^{\text{PPCF} \times \text{PPCF}}$ is defined by:

$$\textsc{Proba}_{M,N} \triangleq \begin{cases} \kappa & \text{if } M \xrightarrow{\kappa} N, \\ 1 & \text{if } M = N \text{ is a normal form,} \\ 0 & \text{otherwise.} \end{cases} \tag{3}$$

Notice that $\textsc{Proba}_{M,N}$ is well-defined since there exists at most one reduction step $M \xrightarrow{\kappa} N$, once fixed $M$ and $N$. $\textsc{Proba}$ is a stochastic matrix (i.e. for all $M$, $\sum_{N \in \text{PPCF}} \textsc{Proba}_{M,N} = 1$). The value of $\textsc{Proba}_{M,N}$ intuitively describes the probability of evolving from the state $M$ to the state $N$ in one step.

A term $M$ is *absorbing* whenever $\textsc{Proba}_{M,M} = 1$: the absorbing states are those which are invariant under the transition matrix. Notice that the normal forms are all absorbing, but the converse is false, e.g. $\Omega$ is an absorbing term.

The $n$-th power $\textsc{Proba}^n$ of the matrix $\textsc{Proba}$ is a stochastic matrix on PPCF (in case $n = 0$, we have the identity matrix on PPCF). Intuitively, the value of $\textsc{Proba}^n_{M,N}$ is the probability of evolving from the state $M$ to the state $N$ in exactly $n$ steps.

**Proposition 4** ([4, Lemma 32]). *Let $M \in$ PPCF and $N$ absorbing, the sequence $\{\textsc{Proba}^n_{M,N}\}_{n \in \mathbb{N}}$ is monotonic.*

We can thus define, for every program $M$ and $n \in \mathbb{N}$:

$$\textsc{Proba}^{\infty}_{M,\underline{n}} \triangleq \sup_{k=0}^{\infty}(\textsc{Proba}^k_{M,\underline{n}}) \tag{4}$$

Intuitively, $\textsc{Proba}^{\infty}_{M,\underline{n}}$ defines the probability that $M$ reaches a numeral $\underline{n}$ in an arbitrary number of steps.

In standard PCF the observational pre-order is defined with respect to the termination of a term in a context of type `Int`. In a probabilistic framework like PPCF, one can refine such a pre-order

Types $A, B, C ::= \texttt{Int} \mid A \Rightarrow B$ Terms $M, N, P ::= x \mid \lambda x^A.M \mid (M)\,N \mid \mathsf{fix}(M) \mid \underline{0} \mid \mathsf{s}(M) \mid \mathsf{p}(M) \mid \mathsf{if}(M, N, P) \mid \texttt{rand}$

(a) Grammar of types and terms. The constant Int is the base type of integers. Given $n \in \mathbb{N}$, $\underline{n}$ will denote its associated *numeral*, defined as $\mathsf{s}^n(\underline{0})$.

$$\frac{}{\Gamma, x : A \vdash x : A} \qquad \frac{\Gamma, x : A \vdash M : B}{\Gamma \vdash \lambda x^A.M : A \Rightarrow B} \qquad \frac{\Gamma \vdash M : A \Rightarrow B \quad \Gamma \vdash N : A}{\Gamma \vdash (M)\,N : B} \qquad \frac{\Gamma \vdash M : A \Rightarrow A}{\Gamma \vdash \mathsf{fix}(M) : A}$$

$$\frac{}{\Gamma \vdash \underline{0} : \texttt{Int}} \qquad \frac{\Gamma \vdash P : \texttt{Int}}{\Gamma \vdash \mathsf{s}(P) : \texttt{Int}} \qquad \frac{\Gamma \vdash P : \texttt{Int}}{\Gamma \vdash \mathsf{p}(P) : \texttt{Int}} \qquad \frac{\Gamma \vdash M : \texttt{Int} \quad \Gamma \vdash N : A \quad \Gamma \vdash P : A}{\Gamma \vdash \mathsf{if}(M, N, P) : A} \qquad \frac{}{\Gamma \vdash \texttt{rand} : \texttt{Int} \Rightarrow \texttt{Int}}$$

(b) Simple type assignment system.

$$\left(\lambda x^A.M\right) N \xrightarrow{1} M\,[N/x] \qquad \mathsf{if}(\underline{0}, N, P) \xrightarrow{1} N \qquad \mathsf{p}(\underline{n+1}) \xrightarrow{1} \underline{n}$$

$$\mathsf{fix}(M) \xrightarrow{1} (M)\,\mathsf{fix}(M) \qquad \mathsf{if}(\underline{n+1}, N, P) \xrightarrow{1} P \qquad (\texttt{rand})\,\underline{n} \xrightarrow{\frac{1}{n}} \underline{k}, \quad \text{for } k < n$$

$$\frac{M \xrightarrow{\kappa} M',\ M \text{ not abstract.}}{(M)\,N \xrightarrow{\kappa} (M')\,N} \qquad \frac{M \xrightarrow{\kappa} M'}{\mathsf{s}(M) \xrightarrow{\kappa} \mathsf{s}(M')} \qquad \frac{M \xrightarrow{\kappa} M'}{\mathsf{p}(M) \xrightarrow{\kappa} \mathsf{p}(M')} \qquad \frac{M \xrightarrow{\kappa} M'}{\mathsf{if}(M, N, P) \xrightarrow{\kappa} \mathsf{if}(M', N, P)} \qquad \frac{M \xrightarrow{\kappa} M'}{(\texttt{rand})\,M \xrightarrow{\kappa} (\texttt{rand})\,M'}$$

(c) Reduction rules. In case $n = 0$, $(\texttt{rand})\,\underline{n}$ is a normal form.

$$\Omega_A \triangleq \mathsf{fix}(\lambda x^A.x) \qquad M \oplus N \triangleq \mathsf{if}((\texttt{rand})\,\underline{2}, M, N)$$

$$\texttt{choose}(\,) \triangleq \Omega_A \qquad \texttt{choose}(M_1, \ldots, M_{n+1}) \triangleq \mathsf{if}((\texttt{rand})\,\underline{n+1}, M_{n+1}, \texttt{choose}(M_1, \ldots, M_n))$$

$$\mathsf{if}(\wedge_{i=1}^{0} M_i, N, P) \triangleq N \qquad \mathsf{if}(\wedge_{i=1}^{n+1} M_i, N, P) \triangleq \mathsf{if}(M_{n+1}, \mathsf{if}(\wedge_{i=1}^{n} M_i, N, P), P)$$

$$\mathsf{if}(M = \underline{0}, N, P) \triangleq \mathsf{if}(M, N, P) \qquad \mathsf{if}(M = \underline{n+1}, N, P) \triangleq \mathsf{if}(\mathsf{p}(M) = \underline{n}, N, P)$$

(d) Notational conventions. Also, we can use $\texttt{choose}(M_i)_{i=1}^{n}$ as a shortcut for $\texttt{choose}(M_1, \ldots, M_n)$.

**Figure 1:** Probabilistic extension of PCF.

by comparing the probability of convergence. Let $\mathcal{C}^{\Gamma,A}$ be the set of contexts $Q$ mapping terms $M$ of type $A$ in the environment $\Gamma$, into programs $Q[M]$, i.e. closed terms of type Int.

**Definition 5** (Observational pre-order). Given $\Gamma \vdash M : A$, and $\Gamma \vdash N : A$, we define[4]:

$$M \sqsubseteq_\Gamma N \ \text{ iff } \ \forall Q \in \mathcal{C}^{\Gamma,A}, \textsc{Proba}^{\infty}_{Q[M],\underline{0}} \leq \textsc{Proba}^{\infty}_{Q[N],\underline{0}}\,.$$

Let $\equiv_\Gamma$ be the equivalence induced by $\sqsubseteq_\Gamma$.

*Remark* 6. There are slightly different probabilistic primitives that can be added to PCF. We have chosen a quite standard one, rand, implementing CAML function Random.int. In [5, 21] it is also considered the more basic $\texttt{Coin} \triangleq (\texttt{rand})\,\underline{2}$. Another possibility is to allow an arbitrary superposition of two terms $M \oplus_\kappa N$, for $\kappa \in [0, 1]$, evaluating to $M$ with probability $\kappa$ and to $N$ with probability $1 - \kappa$, see e.g. [15, 19]. Concerning $n$-ary distributions, there is $\oplus_{i=1}^{n} \kappa_i M_i$, evaluating to any $M_i$ with probability $\kappa_i$ [26]. Finally, [4] allows any probabilistic distribution over the whole set of numerals $(\kappa_n)_{n \in \mathbb{N}}$, evaluating to $\underline{n}$ with probability $\kappa_n$.

Obviously, Coin can be defined as $\oplus_{\frac{1}{2}}$ as well as $(\texttt{rand})\,\underline{2}$. Also, both $\oplus_\kappa$ and rand are definable as $\oplus_{i=1}^{n} \kappa_i M_i$, and the latter as $(\kappa_n)_{n \in \mathbb{N}}$. However, the converses are less trivial. In [5, Figure 6] the authors show how to define rand as a recursive program using just Coin. On the contrary, $\oplus_\kappa$ is strictly more expressive than rand and Coin, since it is not true that all real numbers can be approximated by series of rational numbers generated from PPCF terms (hence recursively enumerable series). One can then wonder whether the observational equivalence on PCF terms depends on the chosen probabilistic primitive. The full abstraction gives a negative answer to the question: all such primitives induce the same observational equivalence on PCF terms, which is in fact the equivalence induced by **Pcoh** (Corollary 28).

[4] The numeral $\underline{0}$ chosen for testing the equality is not significant. Indeed, from a context $Q$ semi-separating two terms $M$, $N$ on a numeral $\underline{n}$, i.e. such that $\textsc{Proba}^{\infty}_{Q[M],\underline{n}} \not\leq \textsc{Proba}^{\infty}_{Q[N],\underline{n}}$, one can get a context semi-separating $M$ and $N$ on another numeral $\underline{m}$ by applying a suitable number of $\mathsf{p}(\,)$ or $\mathsf{s}(\,)$ constructors.

## 4. Probabilistic Coherence Spaces

We present probabilistic coherence spaces [4, 14] and recall the main results needed to state and prove the full abstraction theorem.

The category **PCoh** of *probabilistic coherence spaces* is a model of PPCF. As usual, types are interpreted as objects of the category and programs as maps between the interpretation of the input and output types.

Actually, **PCoh** is underlied by a model of linear logic that we do not make explicit for the sake of brevity, but we refer to [4].

### 4.1 Probabilistic Coherence Spaces

A probabilistic coherence space is a pair $(|\mathcal{A}|, \mathrm{P}(\mathcal{A}))$ of a set $|\mathcal{A}|$ and a set $\mathrm{P}(\mathcal{A})$ of vectors in the module $\mathbb{R}_+^{|\mathcal{A}|}$. Intuitively, the elements in $|\mathcal{A}|$ represent atomic data, while the vectors in $\mathrm{P}(\mathcal{A})$

express probabilistic data. At the ground type, $\mathrm{P}(\texttt{Int})$ is in fact the convex set of the subprobability distributions of the elements in $|\texttt{Int}|$. However, at higher-order types, this intuition is lost[5] and the definition of $\mathrm{P}(\mathcal{A})$ depends on a duality condition describing the probability of having an interaction between a datum of type $A$ (which is a program) and an environment.

Consider a program and an environment interacting on atomic data $a$ included in a set $|\mathcal{A}|$ such that their respective interpretation are positive real vectors: $v, w \in \mathbb{R}_+^{|\mathcal{A}|}$. Their pairing gives a quantitative estimation of the interaction success

$$\langle v, w\rangle \triangleq \sum_{a\in|\mathcal{A}|} v_a\, w_a \in \overline{\mathbb{R}}_+. \tag{5}$$

We say that their interaction is probabilistic whenever $\langle v, w\rangle \leq 1$. We then define a polar operation on sets of vectors $\mathrm{P} \subseteq \mathbb{R}_+^{|\mathcal{A}|}$ as

$$\mathrm{P}^\perp \triangleq \{w \in \mathbb{R}_+^{|\mathcal{A}|} \text{ s.t. } \forall v \in \mathrm{P}\ \langle v, w\rangle \leq 1\}. \tag{6}$$

The probabilistic duality environment/program is then enforced in our model by the closedness condition $P^{\perp\perp} = P$.

**Definition 7** ([4, 14]). A *probabilistic coherence space*, or PCS for short, is a pair $\mathcal{A} = (|\mathcal{A}|, \mathrm{P}(\mathcal{A}))$ where $|\mathcal{A}|$ is a countable set called the *web* of $\mathcal{A}$ and $\mathrm{P}(\mathcal{A})$ is a subset of $\mathbb{R}_+^{|\mathcal{A}|}$ satisfying:

1. $\mathrm{P}(\mathcal{A})^{\perp\perp} = \mathrm{P}(\mathcal{A})$,
2. $\forall a \in |\mathcal{A}|, \exists \kappa > 0, \forall v \in \mathrm{P}(\mathcal{A}), v_a \leq \kappa$,
3. $\forall a \in |\mathcal{A}|, \exists \kappa > 0, \kappa e_a \in \mathrm{P}(\mathcal{A})$.

As a side effect, Condition (1) forces $\mathrm{P}(\mathcal{A})$ to be a convex set. Condition (2) requires the projection of $\mathrm{P}(\mathcal{A})$ in any direction to be bounded, while (3) forces $\mathrm{P}(\mathcal{A})$ to cover every direction.[6]

**Example 8.** The set $\mathrm{P}(\texttt{Int})$ of subprobability distributions over $\mathbb{N}$ yields a PCS. In particular, $\mathrm{P}(\texttt{Int})^{\perp\perp} = \mathrm{P}(\texttt{Int})$, its polar being $\mathrm{P}(\texttt{Int})^\perp = [0, 1]^{\mathbb{N}}$.

### 4.2 The category PCoh

The *objects* of **PCoh** are the PCSs and the set $\mathbf{PCoh}(\mathcal{A}, \mathcal{B})$ of *morphisms from* $\mathcal{A}$ *to* $\mathcal{B}$ is the set of matrices $\phi \in \mathbb{R}_+^{\mathcal{M}_f(|\mathcal{A}|)\times|\mathcal{B}|}$ such that $\forall v \in \mathrm{P}(\mathcal{A})$, $\phi(v) \in \mathrm{P}(\mathcal{B})$, where

$$\forall b \in |\mathcal{B}|,\ (\phi(v))_b \triangleq \sum_{m\in\mathcal{M}_f(|\mathcal{A}|)} \phi_{m,b} \cdot v^m, \tag{7}$$

(see Notation 1 for the definition of $v^m$). Following Section 2, a morphism is presented as a matrix that gathered the coefficients of the power series described by the Equation (7).

The *identity on* $\mathcal{A}$ is given by the matrix

$$\mathrm{Id}^{\mathcal{A}}_{m,a} \triangleq \begin{cases} 1 & \text{if } m = [a], \\ 0 & \text{otherwise.}\end{cases}$$

In fact, we have $\mathrm{Id}^{\mathcal{A}}(v) = v$, for every $v \in \mathrm{P}(\mathcal{A})$.

Let $\phi \in \mathbf{PCoh}(\mathcal{A}, \mathcal{B})$ and $\psi \in \mathbf{PCoh}(\mathcal{B}, \mathcal{C})$, their composition must satisfy: $\forall v \in \mathrm{P}(\mathcal{A})$, $(\psi \circ \phi)(v) = \psi(\phi(v))$. In matricial terms, this comes out as: $\forall c \in |\mathcal{C}|$,

$$\sum_{m\in\mathcal{M}_f(|\mathcal{A}|)} (\psi\circ\phi)_{m,c} \cdot v^m = \sum_{p\in\mathcal{M}_f(|\mathcal{B}|)} \psi_{p,c} \cdot (\phi(v))^p$$
$$= \sum_{p\in\mathcal{M}_f(|\mathcal{B}|)} \psi_{p,c} \cdot \prod_{b\in\mathrm{Supp}(p)} \Big(\sum_{q\in\mathcal{M}_f(|\mathcal{A}|)} \phi_{q,b} \cdot v^q\Big)^{p(b)}.$$

Now, to extract the coefficient of the monomial $v^m$, we distribute product over sum. This amounts to choosing a partition of $m = \biguplus(q_{(b,i)})_{(b,i)\in p}$ matching the enumeration $\{(b, i) \text{ s.t. } b \in \mathrm{Supp}(p), i \leq p(b)\}$ of $p$.

Therefore, the *composition* $\psi \circ \phi$ is defined[7] as the matrix coefficients, for $m \in \mathcal{M}_f(|\mathcal{A}|)$ and $c \in |\mathcal{C}|$:

$$(\psi\circ\phi)_{m,c} \triangleq \sum_{p\in\mathcal{M}_f(|\mathcal{B}|)} \psi_{p,c} \sum_{\substack{(m_{(b,i)})_{(b,i)\in p} \\ \text{s.t.} \\ m=\biguplus(m_{(b,i)})}} \prod_{(b,i)\in p} \phi_{m_{(b,i)},b}. \tag{8}$$

### 4.3 PCoh is Cartesian Closed

The *cartesian product* of any countable family $(\mathcal{A}_i)_{i\in I}$ of PCSs is:

$$|\textstyle\prod_{i\in I} \mathcal{A}_i| \triangleq \bigcup_{i\in I}(\{i\} \times |\mathcal{A}_i|),$$

$$\mathrm{P}\left(\textstyle\prod_{i\in I}\mathcal{A}_i\right) \triangleq \left\{ v \in (\mathbb{R}_+)^{|\prod_{i\in I}\mathcal{A}_i|} \text{ s.t. } \begin{array}{l}\forall i \in I, \\ \pi_i(v) \in \mathrm{P}(\mathcal{A}_i)\end{array} \right\},$$

where $\pi_i(v)$ is the vector in $\mathbb{R}_+^{|\mathcal{A}_i|}$ denoting the $i$-th component of $v$, i.e. $(\pi_i(v))_a \triangleq v_{(i,a)}$.

The $j$*-th projection* $\mathrm{Pr}^j \in \mathbf{PCoh}(\prod_{i\in I}\mathcal{A}_i, \mathcal{A}_j)$ and the *product* $\langle\phi_i\rangle_{i\in I} \in \mathbf{PCoh}(\mathcal{B}, \prod_{i\in I}\mathcal{A}_i)$ are given by:

$$\mathrm{Pr}^j_{m,a} \triangleq \begin{cases} 1 & \text{if } m = [(j, a)], \\ 0 & \text{otherwise.}\end{cases} \qquad (\langle\phi_i\rangle_{i\in I})_{p,(j,a)} = (\phi_j)_{p,a}$$

The *terminal object* $\mathbf{1}$ is given by the empty product $(\emptyset, \{\mathbf{0}\})$. Notice that the set of *points* of a PCS $\mathcal{A}$, i.e. the set $\mathbf{PCoh}(\mathbf{1}, \mathcal{A})$, is isomorphic to the convex set $\mathrm{P}(\mathcal{A})$.

**Notation 9.** We write $\mathcal{A}_1\times\mathcal{A}_2$ for the binary product: in the sequel, we present any $v \in \mathrm{P}(\mathcal{A}_1 \times \mathcal{A}_2)$ as the pair $(\pi_1(v), \pi_2(v)) \in \mathrm{P}(\mathcal{A}_1) \times \mathrm{P}(\mathcal{A}_2)$ of its components.

Notice that the set $\mathcal{M}_f\left(|\prod_{i\in I}\mathcal{A}_i|\right)$ is isomorphic to the set-theoretic cartesian product $\prod_{i\in I}\left(\mathcal{M}_f(|\mathcal{A}_i|)\right)$, via the map associating any $m \in \mathcal{M}_f\left(|\prod_{i\in I}\mathcal{A}_i|\right)$ with the $I$-indexed family $(m_i)_{i\in I}$ defined as $m_i(a) \triangleq m(i, a)$. This means that any morphism $\phi \in \mathbf{PCoh}(\prod_{i\in I}\mathcal{A}_i, \mathcal{B})$ can be presented as a matrix indexed by sequences in $\left(\prod_{i\in I}\mathcal{M}_f(|\mathcal{A}_i|)\right) \times |\mathcal{B}|$.

The *object of morphisms* is defined as

$$|\mathcal{A} \Rightarrow \mathcal{B}| \triangleq \mathcal{M}_f(|\mathcal{A}|) \times |\mathcal{B}|, \qquad \mathrm{P}(\mathcal{A} \Rightarrow \mathcal{B}) \triangleq \mathbf{PCoh}(\mathcal{A}, \mathcal{B}).$$

**PCoh** is then turned into a cartesian closed category by the *evaluation* $\mathrm{Ev} \in \mathbf{PCoh}((\mathcal{A} \Rightarrow \mathcal{B}) \times \mathcal{A}, \mathcal{B})$ and the *curryfication* $\mathrm{Cur}(\phi) \in \mathbf{PCoh}(\mathcal{C}, \mathcal{A} \Rightarrow \mathcal{B})$, for every $\phi \in \mathbf{PCoh}(\mathcal{C} \times \mathcal{A}, \mathcal{B})$, defined as:

$$\mathrm{Ev}_{(m,p),a} \triangleq \begin{cases} 1 & \text{if } m = [(p, v)], \\ 0 & \text{otherwise,}\end{cases} \qquad \mathrm{Cur}(\phi)_{m,(p,b)} \triangleq \phi_{(m,p),b}$$

Notice that the above equations use Notation 9, e.g. representing a multiset in $\mathcal{M}_f(|(\mathcal{A} \Rightarrow \mathcal{B}) \times \mathcal{A}|)$ as a pair $(m, p)$ of multisets in $\mathcal{M}_f(|\mathcal{A} \Rightarrow \mathcal{B}|) \times \mathcal{M}_f(|\mathcal{A}|)$.

Actually, the category **PCoh** is *well-pointed* in the sense that the equality of morphisms is extensional, i.e. given two matrices $\phi, \psi \in \mathbf{PCoh}(\mathcal{A}, \mathcal{B})$, if for every $v \in \mathrm{P}(\mathcal{A})$, $\phi(v) = \psi(v)$, then $\phi = \psi$. To sum up, we have:

[5] $\mathrm{P}(\mathcal{A})$ is not anymore a subset of $[0, 1]^{|\mathcal{A}|}$, see discussion in Section 2.

[6] These conditions are introduced in [4] for keeping finite all the scalars involved, yet they are not explicitly stated in the definition of PCS in [14].

[7] The definition of Equation (8) is due to [17]. On a side note, remark that in [4], the authors use another formulation in which identical summands produced by different partitions are gathered. This gives rise to multinomial coefficients that are hidden in the sums of the present formulation. However, the two definitions give rise to the same matrix.

**Proposition 10** ([4, §1.6]). ***PCoh** is a well pointed cartesian closed category.*

### 4.4 Object of numerals and Cpo-Enrichement

The *object of numerals* of **PCoh** is the PCS $\mathcal{I}nt \triangleq (\mathbb{N}, \mathrm{P}(\mathtt{Int}))$ equipped with the morphisms $\mathrm{z} \in \mathbf{PCoh}(\mathbf{1}, \mathcal{I}nt) \simeq \mathrm{P}(\mathcal{I}nt)$, pred, succ $\in \mathbf{PCoh}(\mathcal{I}nt, \mathcal{I}nt)$, and ifz $\in \mathbf{PCoh}(\mathcal{I}nt \times \mathcal{I}nt \times \mathcal{I}nt, \mathcal{I}nt)$ defined as

$$\mathrm{z}_n = \delta_{0,n}, \qquad \mathrm{pred}_{m,n} = \delta_{m,[n+1]}, \qquad \mathrm{succ}_{m,n+1} = \delta_{m,[n]},$$

$$\mathrm{ifz}_{(m,p,q),n} = \begin{cases} 1 & \text{if } (m,p,q) = ([0],[n],[]), \\ & \text{or } (m,p,q) = ([k+1],[],[n]), \\ 0 & \text{otherwise.} \end{cases}$$

The natural order on $\mathbb{R}_+$ enriches **PCoh** with a *cpo-structure*, defined componentwise on morphisms: i.e., given $\phi, \psi \in \mathbf{PCoh}(\mathcal{A}, \mathcal{B})$

$$\phi \leq \psi \quad \text{iff} \quad \forall m \in \mathcal{M}_{\mathrm{f}}(|\mathcal{A}|), \forall b \in \mathcal{M}_{\mathrm{f}}(|\mathcal{B}|), \phi_{m,b} \leq \psi_{m,b}.$$

The matrix $\mathbf{0}$ is the minimum element and the lub of a directed net $(\phi_d)_{d\in D}$ is then given by

$$\big(\sup_{d\in D}(\phi_d)\big)_{m,b} \triangleq \sup_{d\in D}\big((\phi_d)_{m,b}\big),$$

*Remark* 11. The componentwise order on matrices is not extensional, i.e. there are $\phi, \psi \in \mathbf{PCoh}(\mathcal{A}, \mathcal{B})$ such that $\forall v \in \mathrm{P}(\mathcal{A})$, $\phi(v) \leq \psi(v)$, but $\phi \not\leq \psi$. For example, take $\phi, \psi \in \mathbf{PCoh}(\mathcal{I}nt, \mathcal{I}nt)$:

$$\phi_{m,n} \triangleq \begin{cases} 1 & \text{if } m = [k], n = 0, \\ 0 & \text{otherwise.} \end{cases} \qquad \psi_{m,n} \triangleq \begin{cases} 1 & \text{if } m = [], n = 0, \\ 0 & \text{otherwise.} \end{cases}$$

Although $\phi \not\leq \psi$, for every subprobability distribution of natural numbers $v \in \mathrm{P}(\mathcal{I}nt)$, we get $\phi(v) = (\sum_k v_k, 0, 0, \dots) \leq (1, 0, 0, \dots) = \psi(v)$. In fact, we will use this mismatch for disproving the inequality full abstraction in Section 6.

### 4.5 PCoh is an Adequate Model of PPCF

The model of PPCF is obtained by extending the usual categorical interpretation of PCF to `rand`.

With a type $A$, we associate a PCS $\mathcal{A}$, by induction on the type: $\mathtt{Int} \mapsto \mathcal{I}nt$ and $A \Rightarrow B \mapsto \mathcal{A} \Rightarrow \mathcal{B}$.

Let $\Gamma = x_1 : A_1, \dots, x_n : A_n$. The interpretation of a judgment $\Gamma \vdash M : B$ is a morphism $[\![M]\!]^\Gamma$ of $\mathbf{PCoh}(\prod_{i=1}^n \mathcal{A}_i, \mathcal{B})$, defined in Figure 2 by structural induction on the unique derivation of $\Gamma \vdash M : B$.

The fix-point operator $\mathsf{fix}(M)$ is the lub of its approximants, given by induction by

$$\mathsf{fix}^0\phi \triangleq \mathbf{0}, \qquad \mathsf{fix}^{n+1}\phi \triangleq \mathrm{Ev} \circ \langle \phi, \mathsf{fix}^n\phi \rangle.$$

The operator `rand` is defined by using (a multiset variant of) the matrix `Rand` of Equation (1):

$$[\![\mathtt{rand}]\!]_{m,k} \triangleq \begin{cases} \frac{1}{n} & \text{if } m = [n], k < n, \\ 0 & \text{otherwise.} \end{cases}$$

Together with the categorical interpretation of a term, we describe its action on the vectors in the convex set associated with its input type. Notice that, since the category is well pointed of the category, this action univocally determines the interpretation of the term. Notice also that the matrices interpreting the basic constructs in Figure 2 have 0, 1 coefficients, except for $[\![\mathtt{rand}]\!]$ which is interpreted as the random function that introduces rational numbers in $[0, 1]$. Coefficients greater than 1 may be produced by composition of morphisms (Equation 8).

Thanks to Notation 9, $[\![M]\!]^\Gamma$ can be described as a vector indexed by a tuple $(\vec{m}, b)$ of $\vec{m} \in \mathcal{M}_{\mathrm{f}}(|\Gamma|)$ and a web element $b \in |\mathcal{B}|$. This convention will be used hereafter.

**Example 12.** If `Coin` is identified with $(\mathtt{rand})\ \underline{2}$, then the interpretation of `Once` and `Twice` are the matrices given in Section 2.

Consider the term $\Omega_A \triangleq \mathsf{fix}(\lambda x^A.x)$. Notice that $[\![\lambda x^A.x]\!]$ is different from zero only on the web elements of the form $([a], a)$, so that $\mathsf{fix}^n\ [\![\lambda x^A.x]\!]\ (\mathbf{0}) = \mathbf{0}$ for any natural number $n$. We conclude $[\![\Omega_A]\!] = \mathbf{0}$, as expected.

Consider now the term $P \triangleq \mathsf{fix}(\lambda x^{\mathtt{Int}}.x \oplus \underline{0})$. We have that $[\![\lambda x^{\mathtt{Int}}.x \oplus \underline{0}]\!]_{(m,a)} = \frac{1}{2}[\![x]\!]^m_a + \frac{1}{2}[\![\underline{0}]\!]^m_a$, i.e. it is equal to $\frac{1}{2}$ when $m = [a]$, or when $m = []$ and $a = 0$, otherwise it is equal to 0. This means that $\mathsf{fix}^n\ [\![\lambda x^{\mathtt{Int}}.x \oplus \underline{0}]\!]\ (\mathbf{0}) = \frac{1}{2} + \frac{1}{4} + \dots + \frac{1}{2^n}$, for any $n > 0$. We conclude that $[\![P]\!] \triangleq \sup_n \mathsf{fix}^n\ [\![\lambda x^{\mathtt{Int}}.x \oplus \underline{0}]\!]\ (\mathbf{0}) = 1$.

**Proposition 13** (Soundness [4]). *The semantics is invariant under reduction, i.e. for every $\Gamma \vdash M : B$:*

$$[\![M]\!]^\Gamma = \sum_N \mathrm{PROBA}_{M,N}\, [\![N]\!]^\Gamma.$$

*Proof (Sketch).* The invariance under reduction rules of the standard PCF redexes follows by cartesian closedness and the cpo-enrichement of **PCoh**. The soundness of the reduction of $(\mathtt{rand})\ \underline{n}$ is straight from the definition of $[\![\mathtt{Rand}]\!]$. The soundness of the context rules depends on the fact that the interpretation of a context is linear in the argument associated with the fired redex. For example, the soundness of the context rule associated with application depends on the equality: $\mathrm{Ev} \circ \langle \kappa\phi + \mu\psi, \xi \rangle = \kappa(\mathrm{Ev} \circ \langle \phi, \xi \rangle) + \mu(\mathrm{Ev} \circ \langle \psi, \xi \rangle)$ □

**Theorem 14** (Adequacy [4]). *Let $M$ be a closed term of type `Int`. Then, $[\![M]\!]$ is the sub-probability distribution on $\mathbb{N}$ such that*

$$\forall n \in \mathbb{N},\ [\![M]\!]_n = \mathrm{PROBA}^\infty_{M,\underline{n}}.$$

*Remark* 15. Adequacy allows one to prove that specific primitives are not definable in the language. A noteworthy example is the *parallel or* function [27]. In our setting, this should be a closed term `por` : `Int` ⇒ `Int` ⇒ `Int` such that $\mathrm{PROBA}^\infty_{((\mathtt{por})\underline{0})\underline{0},\underline{0}}$, $\mathrm{PROBA}^\infty_{((\mathtt{por})\underline{1})\Omega,\underline{1}}$ and $\mathrm{PROBA}^\infty_{((\mathtt{por})\Omega)\underline{1},\underline{1}}$ are equal to 1. By adequacy, $[\![\mathtt{por}]\!]\,(e_0)(e_0)_1 = [\![\mathtt{por}]\!]\,(e_1)(\mathbf{0})_0 = [\![\mathtt{por}]\!]\,(\mathbf{0})(e_1)_0 = 1$. By definition of a morphism in **PCoh**, $[\![\mathtt{por}]\!]\,(e_0)(e_0)$ must be a subprobability distribution, hence $[\![\mathtt{por}]\!]\,(e_0)(e_0)_0 = 0$. That implies $[\![\mathtt{por}]\!]_{([],[]),0} = 0$. On the other hand, $[\![\mathtt{por}]\!]\,(e_1)(e_1)_0 \geq [\![\mathtt{por}]\!]\,(e_1)(\mathbf{0})_0 + [\![\mathtt{por}]\!]\,(\mathbf{0})(e_1)_0 - [\![\mathtt{por}]\!]_{[],[],0} = 2$, which contradicts that $[\![\mathtt{por}]\!]\,(e_1)(e_1)$ is a subprobability distribution. We conclude that `por` is not a term of PPCF.

However, let us mention that the *Gustave* function is a valid morphism of **PCoh** (see [13]).

Full abstraction extends to higher-order types the perfect matching syntax / semantics stated by adequacy on `Int`. One direction of full abstraction is indeed a consequence of Theorem 14.

**Corollary 16** (Abstraction). *Given $\Gamma \vdash M : A$, and $\Gamma \vdash N : A$, we have that $[\![M]\!] \leq [\![N]\!]$ implies $M \sqsubseteq_\Gamma N$. In particular, $[\![M]\!] = [\![N]\!]$ implies $M \equiv_\Gamma N$.*

*Proof.* By induction on $C[\,]$, one proves that $[\![M]\!] \leq [\![N]\!]$ implies $[\![C[M]]\!] \leq [\![C[N]]\!]$. Then the result follows from Theorem 14. □

## 5. Full Abstraction

We prove *equational full abstraction* (Theorem 27), that is the converse of the part of Corollary 16 dealing with equality. This is a straightforward consequence of Lemma 26 stating that for any

$$\Gamma \xrightarrow{\mathrm{Pr}^i} A_i \qquad \vec{v} \longmapsto \vec{v}_i \qquad [\![x_i]\!]^\Gamma$$

$$\Gamma \xrightarrow{\mathrm{Cur}([\![M]\!]^{\Gamma,x:B})} A \Rightarrow B \qquad \vec{v} \longmapsto \mathrm{Cur}(u \mapsto \phi(\vec{v},u)) \qquad [\![\lambda x^B.M]\!]^\Gamma, \text{ with } \phi = [\![M]\!]^{\Gamma,x:B}$$

$$\Gamma \xrightarrow{\langle [\![M]\!]^\Gamma, [\![N]\!]^\Gamma \rangle} (A \Rightarrow B) \,\&\, A \xrightarrow{\mathrm{Ev}} B \qquad \vec{v} \longmapsto \phi(\vec{v})(\psi(\vec{v})) \qquad [\![(M)\,N]\!]^\Gamma, \text{ with } \phi = [\![M]\!]^\Gamma, \psi = [\![N]\!]^\Gamma$$

$$\Gamma \xrightarrow{\mathbb{T}} \mathbf{1} \xrightarrow{\mathtt{z}} \mathtt{Int} \qquad \vec{v} \longmapsto (1,0,0,\ldots) \qquad [\![\underline{0}]\!]^\Gamma$$

$$\Gamma \xrightarrow{[\![M]\!]^\Gamma} \mathtt{Int} \xrightarrow{\mathrm{succ}} \mathtt{Int} \qquad \vec{v} \longmapsto (0, w_0, w_1, \ldots) \qquad [\![\mathsf{s}(M)]\!]^\Gamma, \text{ with } w = [\![M]\!]^\Gamma(\vec{v})$$

$$\Gamma \xrightarrow{[\![M]\!]^\Gamma} \mathtt{Int} \xrightarrow{\mathrm{pred}} \mathtt{Int} \qquad \vec{v} \longmapsto (w_1, w_2, \ldots) \qquad [\![\mathsf{p}(M)]\!]^\Gamma, \text{ with } w = [\![M]\!]^\Gamma(\vec{v})$$

$$\Gamma \xrightarrow{\mathbb{T}} \mathbf{1} \xrightarrow{\mathtt{rand}} \mathtt{Int} \Rightarrow \mathtt{Int} \qquad \vec{v} \longmapsto [\![\mathtt{rand}]\!] \qquad [\![\mathtt{rand}]\!]^\Gamma$$

$$\Gamma \xrightarrow{\langle [\![M]\!]^\Gamma, [\![N]\!]^\Gamma, [\![N']\!]^\Gamma \rangle} \mathtt{Int} \times A \times A \xrightarrow{\mathrm{ifz}} \mathtt{Int} \qquad \vec{v} \longmapsto w_0 u + \textstyle\sum_{n=1}^{\infty} w_n u' \qquad [\![\mathsf{if}(M,N,P)]\!]^\Gamma, \text{ with } w = [\![M]\!]^\Gamma(\vec{v}),\ u = [\![N]\!]^\Gamma(\vec{v}),\ u' = [\![N']\!]^\Gamma(\vec{v})$$

$$\Gamma \xrightarrow{\sup_n \mathrm{fix}^n([\![M]\!]^\Gamma)} A \qquad \vec{v} \longmapsto \sup_n \mathrm{fix}^n(w) \qquad [\![\mathsf{fix}(M)]\!]^\Gamma, \text{ with } w = [\![M]\!]^\Gamma(\vec{v})$$

**Figure 2:** The standard semantics of PPCF terms together with its action on $\vec{v} \in \mathrm{P}(\Gamma)$.

closed terms $M$ and $N$ having different interpretations in **Pcoh**, there is a *testing* term $P$ such that $(P)\,M$ and $(P)\,N$ reduce to $\underline{0}$ with different probabilities. Let us outline the path to this result.

With any web element $a$, we associate a testing term $\mathcal{P}(a)$ that is described in Figure 5 and that reminds the contexts used in [3]. $\mathcal{P}(a)$ is not an ordinary term of PPCF since its construction uses a random operator, weighted by a list $\vec{X}$ of *formal parameters*. However, a parameterized term becomes an ordinary PPCF term when we substitute $\vec{X}$ by a list $\vec{\kappa}$ of rationals in $[0,1]$. Following [6], we introduce in Figure 3 an *intersection type system* that defines semantics of parameterized terms. This interpretation is a formal power series over $\vec{X}$ (Definition 21). Moreover, parameterized semantics is compatible with **Pcoh** through substitution of parameters (Lemma 20).

Now, assume that $M$ and $N$ are interpreted by different matrices and pick a web element $a$ such that $[\![M]\!]_a \neq [\![N]\!]_a$. Then, the semantics of the parameterized terms $(\mathcal{P}(a))\,M$ and $(\mathcal{P}(a))\,N$ are distinct formal power series. Indeed, Lemma 24 implies that they differ at least on one coefficient.

Finally, Lemma 25 ensures the existence of a list $\vec{\kappa}$ of rationals in $[0,1]$ on which these power series disagree. So, the substitution of $\vec{X}$ by $\vec{\kappa}$ in $\mathcal{P}(a)$ produces a testing context separating $M$ and $N$.

We first describe *parameterized* PPCF in Subsection 5.1. Then, testing terms are presented in Subsection 5.2. We conclude in Subsection 5.3 with the full abstraction theorem.

### 5.1 Parameterized PPCF

Let $\mathfrak{P}$ be a denumerable set of formal parameters. $X, Y, Z$ range over parameters in $\mathfrak{P}$.

The *grammar* of parameterized PPCF is an extension of PPCF (Figure 1(a)) by multiplication of terms by parameters:

$$\mathrm{PPCF}^{\mathfrak{P}} ::= \cdots \mid X \cdot M, \text{ where } X \in \mathfrak{P}.$$

The *simple type* of $X \cdot M$ under a context $\Gamma$ is $A$ whenever $\Gamma \vdash M : A$ in PPCF (Figure 1(b)).

The *substitution* of parameters by scalars let us recover ordinary terms from parameterized ones. More precisely, let $M \in \mathrm{PPCF}^{\mathfrak{P}}$ and $\frac{n}{m} \in [0,1]$ be a rational number. We define $M\left[\frac{n}{m}/X\right]$ as the term obtained by replacing in $M$ any subterm of shape $X \cdot N$ with

$$\mathtt{choose}(N^n, \Omega^{m-n}) \triangleq \mathtt{choose}(\underbrace{N,\ldots,N}_{n \text{ times}}, \underbrace{\Omega,\ldots,\Omega}_{m-n \text{ times}}) \tag{9}$$

(see Figure 1(d) for $\mathtt{choose}$ definition). Substitution is then generalized to lists $\vec{X}$ of parameters and $\vec{\kappa}$ of rationals as $M\left[\vec{\kappa}/\vec{X}\right]$.

**Fact 17.** *If $\vec{X}$ is the list of all parameters in $M$ and $\vec{\kappa}$ a list of rational numbers in $[0,1]$, then $M\left[\vec{\kappa}/\vec{X}\right]$ is a term of* PPCF.

The *semantics* of $\mathrm{PPCF}^{\mathfrak{P}}$ is a refinement of PPCF semantics taking into account parameters. Yet, for the sake of the full abstraction proof, we give a different presentation and use a *weighted intersection type system*. Roughly speaking, types are *web elements* and with each type derivation $\pi$, we associate a *weight* $\omega(\pi)$ which is a positive *monomial*, i.e. a product of rationals in $[0,1]$ and of finitely many parameters. Then, the interpretation $[\![M]\!]$ of a $\mathrm{PPCF}^{\mathfrak{P}}$ term $M$ is a matrix indexed by web elements. For each web element, there can be several type derivations and the corresponding coefficient is the sum of their weights.

More precisely, Figure 3 describes the rules for constructing a derivation $\pi :: \Gamma^\bullet \vdash_\alpha M : a$ of what we call a *web judgment* $\Gamma^\bullet \vdash_\alpha M : a$. Notice that $\Gamma \vdash M : A$ is a valid simple type judgment, $a \in |\mathcal{A}|$ and $\alpha$ is a monomial. Besides, a *web context* $\Gamma^\bullet$ is defined as a function mapping any typed variable $x^C$ occurring in $\Gamma$ to a finite multiset $m \in \mathcal{M}_{\mathrm{f}}(|\mathcal{C}|)$ of web elements and mapping variables non-appearing in $\Gamma$ to the empty multiset. For instance, for any $\Gamma = x_1 : C_1 \ldots x_n : C_n$ and $\vec{m} \in \mathcal{M}_{\mathrm{f}}(|\Gamma|)$, $\Gamma^{\vec{m}}$ denotes the web context $x_i^{C_i} \mapsto \vec{m}_i$ for $1 \leq i \leq n$. Disjoint unions $\Gamma^\bullet \uplus \Delta^\bullet$ of web contexts are defined pointwise.

**Fact 18.** *If $\Gamma^\bullet \vdash_\alpha M : a$ is derivable and $\Gamma^\bullet(x)$ is a non-empty multiset, then $x$ is free in $M$.*

Rules $\mathtt{app}$ and $\mathtt{fix}$ deserve some comments. Application of $\mathrm{PPCF}^{\mathfrak{P}}$ terms is interpreted following Equation (8) that defines composition. Remark that indices of $\mathtt{app}$ mainly coincide with the indices of the sums in (8), with one more difficulty since we have to split contexts. Now, $\mathtt{fix}$ is derived from the rule $\mathtt{app}$ and from

$$\frac{}{x^A : [a] \vdash_1 x : a}\ \mathtt{var} \qquad \frac{}{\vdash_1 \underline{n} : n}\ \mathtt{nat} \qquad \frac{k < n}{\vdash_{\frac{1}{n}} \mathtt{rand} : ([n], k)}\ \mathtt{rand} \qquad \frac{\Gamma^\bullet, x^A : m \vdash_\alpha M : a}{\Gamma^\bullet \vdash_\alpha \lambda x^A.M : (m, a)}\ \mathtt{abs}$$

$$\frac{\Gamma^{\bullet\prime} \vdash_\alpha M : (m,b) \qquad \forall (a,i) \in m,\quad \Gamma^\bullet_{(a,i)} \vdash_{\beta_{(a,i)}} N : a}{\Gamma^\bullet \vdash_{\alpha \prod_{(a,i)\in m} \beta_{(a,i)}} (M)\, N : b}\ \mathtt{app}_{(m,(\Gamma^\bullet_{(a,i)})_{(a,i)\in m})} \quad \text{s.t.} \begin{cases} m \in \mathcal{M}_{\mathrm{f}}(|\mathcal{A}|) \\ \Gamma^{\bullet\prime} \uplus \biguplus_{(a,i)\in m} \Gamma^\bullet_{(a,i)} = \Gamma^\bullet \end{cases}$$

$$\frac{\Gamma^{\bullet\prime} \vdash_\alpha M : (m,b) \qquad \forall (a,i) \in m,\quad \Gamma^\bullet_{(a,i)} \vdash_{\beta_{(a,i)}} \mathsf{fix}(M) : a}{\Gamma^\bullet \vdash_{\alpha \prod_{(a,i)\in m} \beta_{(a,i)}} \mathsf{fix}(M) : b}\ \mathtt{fix}_{(m,(\Gamma^\bullet_{(a,i)})_{(a,i)\in m})} \quad \text{s.t.} \begin{cases} m \in \mathcal{M}_{\mathrm{f}}(|\mathcal{A}|) \\ \Gamma^{\bullet\prime} \uplus \biguplus_{(a,i)\in m} \Gamma^\bullet_{(a,i)} = \Gamma^\bullet \end{cases}$$

$$\frac{\Gamma^\bullet \vdash_\alpha M : n+1}{\Gamma^\bullet \vdash_\alpha \mathsf{p}(M) : n}\ \mathtt{pred} \qquad \frac{\Gamma^\bullet \vdash_\alpha M : n}{\Gamma^\bullet \vdash_\alpha \mathsf{s}(M) : n+1}\ \mathtt{succ}$$

$$\frac{\Gamma^\bullet \vdash_\beta M : 0 \qquad \Delta^\bullet \vdash_\alpha N : a}{\Gamma^\bullet \uplus \Delta^\bullet \vdash_{\beta\alpha} \mathsf{if}(M, N, P) : a}\ \mathtt{if}_0 \qquad \frac{\Gamma^\bullet \vdash_\beta M : n+1 \qquad \Delta^\bullet \vdash_\alpha P : a}{\Gamma^\bullet \uplus \Delta^\bullet \vdash_{\beta\alpha} \mathsf{if}(M, N, P) : a}\ \mathtt{if}_s \qquad \frac{\Gamma^\bullet \vdash_\alpha M : a}{\Gamma^\bullet \vdash_{\alpha X} X \cdot M : a}\ \mathtt{par}$$

**Figure 3:** Semantics of parameterized PPCF.

$\mathsf{fix}(M) \xrightarrow{1} (M)\,\mathsf{fix}(M)$. To illustrate this point and the followings, we detail Examples 22 and 23 at the end of this subsection.

**Fact 19.** *If $\Gamma \vdash M : A$ then $\sum_{\pi::\Gamma^{\vec m} \vdash M:a} \omega(\pi)$ is a power series with finitely many variables in $\mathfrak{P}$ and non negative coefficients. Thus, for any list $\vec\kappa$ of non negative reals, $\big(\sum_{\pi::\Gamma^{\vec m}\vdash M:a} \omega(\pi)\big)(\vec\kappa)$ is well defined.*

The following fundamental lemma ensures the soundness of the weighted type system that computes the semantics of $\mathrm{PPCF}^{\mathfrak{P}}$.

**Lemma 20** (Soundness). *Let $M$ be a term of $\mathrm{PPCF}^{\mathfrak{P}}$ such that $\Gamma \vdash M : B$ and $\vec X$ lists its parameters. For any $\vec p \in \mathcal{M}_f(|\Gamma|)$, $b \in |\mathcal{B}|$, and any list $\vec\kappa$ of rational numbers in $[0,1]$,*

$$\left[\!\left[ M \left[\vec\kappa/\vec X\right] \right]\!\right]^\Gamma_{\vec p, b} = \Big( \sum_{\pi::\Gamma^{\vec p}\vdash M:b} \omega(\pi) \Big)(\vec\kappa) \tag{10}$$

*Proof.* We prove Equation (10) by structural induction on $M$, using rules of Figure 3 and the definition of the categorical interpretation of a term in PPCF. We consider the term $\mathsf{fix}(M)$ greater than $(M^n)\,y$ for any natural number $n > 0$ and variable $y$. In fact, we are using the induction on the ordinal $\omega^2$.

Most cases follow directly from induction hypothesis. We only detail three cases: (i) multiplication with a parameter, (ii) application, (iii) fix-point.

(i) Assume $M = X_i \cdot N$ and $\kappa_i = \frac{n}{m}$. Then (using Equation (9)) we get: $M\left[\vec\kappa/\vec X\right] = \mathtt{choose}\big(N\left[\vec\kappa/\vec X\right]^n, \Omega^{m-n}\big)$. Besides, $[\![\Omega]\!] = \mathbf{0}$ (Example 12), so $\left[\!\left[M\left[\vec\kappa/\vec X\right]\right]\!\right]^\Gamma_{\vec p,b} = \frac{n}{m}\left[\!\left[N\left[\vec\kappa/\vec X\right]\right]\!\right]^\Gamma_{\vec p,b}$.

Now, any derivation $\tau :: \Gamma^{\vec p} \vdash M\left[\vec\kappa/\vec X\right] : b$ consists of a sequence of $h \le n$ rules $\mathtt{if}_s$ with on top, the rule $\mathtt{if}_0$ with a derivation $\pi :: \Gamma^{\vec p} \vdash N\left[\vec\kappa/\vec X\right] : b$ as right premise. Indeed, the subterm $\Omega$ has no web type (see Example 23). When $\pi$ is fixed, $\omega(\tau) = \frac{\omega(\pi)}{m}$ and there are as many derivations $\tau$ as many choices of $h \in \{1, \dots, n\}$. So, we compute

$$\sum_{\tau::\Gamma^{\vec p}\vdash M:b} \omega(\tau)\left[\vec\kappa/\vec X\right] = \frac{n}{m}\Big( \sum_{\pi::\Gamma^{\vec p}\vdash N:b} \omega(\pi)\left[\vec\kappa/\vec X\right]\Big),$$

which is equal to $\frac{n}{m}\left(\left[\!\left[N\left[\vec\kappa/\vec X\right]\right]\!\right]^\Gamma_{\vec p,b}\right)$ by induction hypothesis. We conclude by gathering the equalities of the two paragraphs.

(ii) Assume $M = (N)\,P$. Thanks to the categorical semantics, $[\![(N)\,P]\!]^\Gamma_{\vec p,b} = \big(\mathrm{Ev} \circ \langle [\![N]\!]^\Gamma, [\![P]\!]^\Gamma \rangle\big)_{\vec p,b}$. Then by definition of composition (Equation (8)) and left linearity of Ev, $[\![(N)\,P]\!]^\Gamma_{\vec p,b}$ is

$$\sum_{\substack{m\in\mathcal{M}_{\mathrm{f}}(|\mathcal{A}|),\\ (\vec p_{(a,i)})_{(a,i)\in m} \text{ s.t.}\\ \biguplus_{(a,i)\in m}\vec p_{(a,i)} \subseteq \vec p}} [\![N]\!]^\Gamma_{\vec p \setminus \biguplus \vec p_{(a,i)}, (m,b)} \prod_{(a,i)\in m} [\![P]\!]^\Gamma_{\vec p_{(a,i)}, a}.$$

By induction hypothesis and distributing product over sum, we get

$$\sum_{\substack{m\in\mathcal{M}_{\mathrm{f}}(|\mathcal{A}|),\\ (\vec p_{(a,i)})_{(a,i)\in m}\\ \text{s.t. } \biguplus \vec p_{(a,i)} \subseteq \vec p}} \ \sum_{\substack{\tau::\vec q\vdash N:(m,b)\\ \text{where}\\ \vec q = \vec p \setminus \biguplus \vec p_{(a,i)}}} \omega(\tau) \sum_{\substack{(\pi_{(a,i)})_{(a,i)\in m}\\ \text{s.t. } \forall (a,i)\in m,\\ \pi_{(a,i)}::\vec p_{(a,i)}\vdash P:a}} \ \prod_{(a,i)\in m} \omega(\pi_{(a,i)})$$

Although the indices of the sums might be frightening, they precisely describe all possible derivations of $\Gamma^{\vec p} \vdash (N)\,P : b$. Namely, the first sum defines the label of the terminal application rule, while the other sums give the choices of the derivations of their premises. The total weight is then the product of premise weights.

(iii) Assume $M = \mathsf{fix}(N)$. Any derivation $\pi :: \Gamma^{\vec p} \vdash \mathsf{fix}(N) : b$ ends with a cluster of $\mathtt{fix}$ rules (see Example 23). For $n \in \mathbb{N}^*$, let $\Pi^n$ be the set of derivations whose cluster height is at most $n$.

Now, remark that a derivation in $\Pi^n$ can be transformed into a derivation $\tau :: \Gamma^{\vec p}, y^B : [\,] \vdash (N^n)\,y : b$ (where $y$ is fresh) by replacing $\mathtt{fix}$ rules with $\mathtt{app}$ rules (keeping labels) and each occurrence of $\mathsf{fix}(N)$ with $(N^h)\,y$ for the suitable $h \le n$. Besides, this transformation preserves weights. Therefore:

$$\sum_{\pi\in\Pi^n} \omega(\pi) = \sum_{\tau::\Gamma^{\vec p}, y^B:[\,]\vdash (N^n)y:b} \omega(\tau)$$

Since $[\![\mathsf{fix}(N)]\!]^{\Gamma}_{\vec{p},b} = \bigvee_{n\in\mathbb{N}} [\![(N^n)\,y]\!]^{\Gamma,y}_{(\vec{p},[]),b}$, and by induction hypothesis: $[\![(N^n)\,y]\!]^{\Gamma,y}_{(\vec{p},[]),b} = \bigvee_{n\in\mathbb{N}} \sum_{\tau::\Gamma^{\vec{p}},y^B:[]\vdash(N^n)y:b} \omega(\tau)$,

$$[\![\mathsf{fix}(N)]\!]^{\Gamma}_{\vec{p},b} = \bigvee_{n\in\mathbb{N}} \sum_{\pi\in\Pi^n} \omega(\pi) = \sum_{\pi\in\bigcup_n \Pi^n} \omega(\pi) = \sum_{\pi::\Gamma^{\vec{p}}\vdash\mathsf{fix}(N):b} \omega(\pi)$$

□

According to this result, we generalize the semantics notation to parameterized PPCF:

**Definition 21.** For any term $M$ in PPCF$^{\mathfrak{P}}$ with $n$ parameters,

$$[\![M]\!]^{\Gamma^\bullet}_a \triangleq \sum_{\pi::\Gamma^\bullet\vdash M:a} \omega(\pi) \tag{11}$$

It is a power series whose domain of convergence contains $[0,1]^n$.

The weighted type assignment system of Figure 3 has an interest by its own. It turns computation of semantics of terms (and hence its observational behavior) into a proof search problem.

The reader can convince himself that this approach is useful by computing the semantics of the following examples by applying directly rules of Figure 2.

**Example 22.** Let $k$ and $k'$ be non negative integers. Let us consider the possible derivations of the application $(M)\,N$ with

$$M \triangleq \lambda x^{\mathtt{Int}}.\mathsf{if}(x, \Omega_{\mathtt{Int}}, \mathsf{if}(x, \Omega_{\mathtt{Int}}, \underline{42})), \qquad N \triangleq \mathsf{if}(y, \underline{k}, \underline{k'}).$$

The derivable judgments on the term $N$ are of the form $y^{\mathtt{Int}} : [\overline{n}] \vdash_1 N : \overline{k}$, with $\overline{k} \in \{k, k'\}$. In fact, once fixed $\overline{n}$, the derivation is unique and is given at the left-hand side of Figure 4. As for the term $M$, the derivable judgments are of the form $y^{\mathtt{Int}} : [\,] \vdash_1 M : ([h,h'], 42)$, with $h, h' > 0$. However, in this case we have two different derivations whenever $h \neq h'$: one derivation is given at the right-hand side of Figure 4, while the other one is obtained by swapping the order between the `var` rules on $h$ and $h'$.

The weight of a derivation of $(M)\,N$ is 1. However, the number of derivation of a fix judgment $y^{\mathtt{Int}} : [n, n'] \vdash_1 (M)\,N : 42$ depends on $n, n', k, k'$ following cases:

- if $k = k'$ and $n = n'$, then there is exactly one derivation;
- if $k = k'$ and $n \neq n'$, then there are two derivations, one ending with the rule $\mathsf{app}_{([k,k],\{(k,1)\mapsto[n],(k,2)\mapsto[n']\})}$ and the other one with the rule $\mathsf{app}_{([k,k],\{(k,1)\mapsto[n'],(k,2)\mapsto[n]\})}$;
- if $k \neq k'$ and $n = n'$, then there are two possible derivations, depending on which is the derivation used for inferring the judgment on $M$; notice that the final rule typing $(M)\,N$ must be $\mathsf{app}_{([k,k'],\{(k,1)\mapsto[n],(k',1)\mapsto[n]\})}$;
- if $k \neq k'$ and $n \neq n'$, then there are four possible derivations, depending on the last rule (i.e. $\mathsf{app}_{([k,k'],\{(k,1)\mapsto[n],(k',1)\mapsto[n']\})}$ or $\mathsf{app}_{([k,k'],\{(k,1)\mapsto[n'],(k',1)\mapsto[n]\})}$) and on the derivation for inferring $M$.

Actually, by Lemma 20, weights of possible derivations sums into $[\![(M)\,N]\!]^y$, i.e.

$$[\![(M)\,N]\!]^y_{m,h} = \begin{cases} 1 & \text{if } h = 42, k = k', m = [n,n], \\ 2 & \text{if } h = 42, k = k', m = [n \neq n'], \\ & \text{or } h = 42, k \neq k', m = [n,n], \\ 4 & \text{if } h = 42, k \neq k', m = [n \neq n'], \\ 0 & \text{otherwise.} \end{cases}$$

**Example 23.** Any derivation of a fix-point term $\mathsf{fix}(M)$ ends with a cluster of `fix` rules, each rule has one premise typing $M$ and a number of premises typing $\mathsf{fix}(M)$ and along which the cluster grows. Since the derivation must be finite, the cluster eventually ends with `fix` rules of label $([\,],())$. They have exactly one premise typing $M$ with a web element of shape $([\,],a)$. As a consequence, the term $\Omega_A = \mathsf{fix}(\lambda x^A.x)$ has no web type, as $\lambda x^A.x$ cannot have a web type of shape $([\,],a)$. We find again $[\![\Omega_A]\!] = \mathbf{0}$.

On the other hand, any derivation of $\mathsf{fix}(\lambda x^{\mathtt{Int}}.x \oplus \underline{0})$ will end with a branch of $n > 0$ `fix` rules: $n-1$ rules labelled by $([0],())$, and the rule at the top of the branch labelled by $([\,],())$ and having as premise the unique derivation of $\vdash_{\frac{1}{2}} \lambda x^{\mathtt{Int}}.x \oplus \underline{0} : ([\,],0)$. The whole derivation has conclusion $\vdash_{\frac{1}{2^n}} \mathsf{fix}(\lambda x^{\mathtt{Int}}.x \oplus \underline{0}) : 0$ and the sum of these weights for $n > 0$ yields $[\![\mathsf{fix}(\lambda x^{\mathtt{Int}}.x \oplus \underline{0})]\!]_0 = 1$. We find again the results of Examples 3 and 12.

$$\begin{aligned} \mathcal{P}(n) &= \lambda x^{\mathtt{Int}}.\mathsf{if}(x = \underline{n}, \underline{0}, \Omega_{\mathtt{Int}}) \\ \mathcal{N}(n) &= \underline{n} \\ \mathcal{P}(a) &= \lambda z^{B\Rightarrow C}.(\mathcal{P}(c))\,((z)\,\mathtt{choose}(X_i \cdot \mathcal{N}(b_i))_{i=1}^n) \\ \mathcal{N}(a) &= \lambda x^B.\mathsf{if}(\wedge_{i=1}^n (\mathcal{P}(b_i))\,x, \mathcal{N}(c), \Omega_C) \end{aligned}$$

**Figure 5:** testing terms. In the higher-order case, i.e. $A = B \Rightarrow C$, we suppose $a = ([b_1,\ldots,b_n],c)$, with $b_i \in |\mathcal{B}|$ and $c \in |\mathcal{C}|$. Subtesting terms are supposed to have disjoint parameters and the $X_i$'s occurring in the definition of $\mathcal{P}(a)$ are assumed to be fresh.

### 5.2 Testing terms

Figure 5 associates with every web element $a \in |\mathcal{A}|$ two closed terms of PPCF$^{\mathfrak{P}}$: one term $\mathcal{P}(a)$ of type $A \Rightarrow \mathtt{Int}$ and one term $\mathcal{N}(a)$ of type $A$, defined by mutual induction on $A$.

$\mathcal{P}(a)$ and $\mathcal{N}(a)$ are named *testing terms*. The parameters occurring in this terms are in a bijective correspondence with the elements of the multisets appearing in $a$ (at all depths).

In the following, we focus on $[\![\mathcal{P}(a)]\!]_{(m,0)}$ and $[\![\mathcal{N}(a)]\!]_{a'}$, for any $m \in \mathcal{M}_f(|\mathcal{A}|)$ and $a' \in \mathcal{A}$, which are formal series in the parameters occurring in the terms (Fact 19). More precisely, we are interested in the coefficient of the monomial having each parameter of the term occurring with degree 1. This monomial is called the *skeleton of* $a$ and is denoted by $\mathtt{sk}(a)$.

**Lemma 24.** *Let $A$ be a type, $a, a' \in |\mathcal{A}|$ and $m \in \mathcal{M}_f(|\mathcal{A}|)$. In the series $[\![\mathcal{P}(a)]\!]_{(m,0)}$ (resp. $[\![\mathcal{N}(a)]\!]_{a'}$), the monomial $\mathtt{sk}(a)$ has a non zero coefficient if and only if $m = [a]$ (resp. $a' = a$).*

*Proof.* By definition, the coefficient of the monomial $\mathtt{sk}(a)$ in $[\![\mathcal{P}(a)]\!]_{(m,0)}$ can be recovered from the sum of the weights of the derivations of shape $P :: \vdash_{\kappa\mathtt{sk}(a)} \mathcal{P}(a) : (m,0)$, and similarly for $[\![\mathcal{N}(a)]\!]_{a'}$. Hence, the statement is equivalent to the following property $\mathtt{IH}(A)$, which will be proved by induction on type $A$:

- ⋆ *For any $a \in |\mathcal{A}|$, there is a derivation of $\vdash_{\kappa\mathtt{sk}(a)} \mathcal{P}(a) : (m,0)$, with $\kappa \neq 0$, if and only if $m = [a]$*
- ⋆ *For any $a \in |\mathcal{A}|$, there is a derivation of $\vdash_{\kappa\mathtt{sk}(a)} \mathcal{N}(a) : a'$, with $\kappa \neq 0$, if and only if $a' = a$.*

For the ground type `Int`, testing terms have no parameters, so that the monomial $\mathtt{sk}(n)$ is the constant term of the series. The derivations of $\mathcal{P}(n)$ and $\mathcal{N}(n)$ are unique and of shape:

$$\dfrac{\dfrac{\dfrac{m = [n]}{x : m \vdash_1 x : n} \quad \dfrac{}{\vdash_1 \underline{0} : 0}}{x : m \vdash_1 \mathsf{if}(x = \underline{n}, 0, \Omega_\iota) : 0}}{\vdash_1 \lambda x^\iota.\mathsf{if}(x = \underline{n}, 0, \Omega_\iota) : (m,0)} \qquad \dfrac{a' = n}{\vdash_1 \underline{n} : a'}$$

$$\dfrac{\dfrac{}{y^{\mathtt{Int}}:[\overline{n}]\vdash_1 y:\overline{n}} \qquad \dfrac{}{y^{\mathtt{Int}}:[\,]\vdash_1 \underline{k}:\overline{k}}}{y^{\mathtt{Int}}:[\overline{n}]\vdash_1 N:\overline{k}} \qquad \dfrac{\dfrac{\dfrac{}{y^{\mathtt{Int}}:[\,],x^{\mathtt{Int}}:[h]\vdash_1 x:h} \qquad \dfrac{\dfrac{}{y^{\mathtt{Int}}:[\,],x^{\mathtt{Int}}:[h']\vdash_1 x:h'} \quad \dfrac{}{y^{\mathtt{Int}}:[\,],x^{\mathtt{Int}}:[\,]\vdash_1 \underline{42}:42}}{y^{\mathtt{Int}}:[\,],x^{\mathtt{Int}}:[h']\vdash_1 \mathsf{if}(x,\Omega_{\mathtt{Int}},\underline{42}):42}}{y^{\mathtt{Int}}:[\,],x^{\mathtt{Int}}:[h,h']\vdash_1 \mathsf{if}(x,\Omega_{\mathtt{Int}},\mathsf{if}(x,\Omega_{\mathtt{Int}},\underline{42})):42}}{y^{\mathtt{Int}}:[\,]\vdash_1 M:([h,h'],42)}$$

**Figure 4:** Weighted derivations discussed in the Example 22

$$\dfrac{\dfrac{\dfrac{\mathtt{IH}(C)\colon q=[c]}{\vdash_\gamma \mathcal{P}(c):(q,0)}③ \qquad \dfrac{\dfrac{\begin{array}{c}m=[(p',c)]\\ p'=[b'_1,\dots,b'_{k'}]\end{array}}{z:m\vdash_1 z:(p',c)}⑤ \qquad \forall j\in\{1,\dots,k'\},\ \dfrac{\dfrac{\dfrac{\mathtt{IH}(B)\colon b_{i_j}=b'_j}{\vdash_{\beta_{i_j}} \mathcal{N}(b_{i_j}):b'_j}⑧}{\vdash_{X_{i_j}\beta_{i_j}} X_{i_j}\cdot\mathcal{N}(b_{i_j}):b'_j}⑦}{\vdash_{\frac{1}{k}X_{i_j}\beta_{i_j}} \mathtt{choose}(X_i\cdot\mathcal{N}(b_i))_{i=1}^k : b'_j}⑥}{z:m\vdash_\beta (z)\,\mathtt{choose}(X_i\cdot\mathcal{N}(b_i))_{i=1}^k : c}④}{z:m\vdash_{\omega(P)} (\mathcal{P}(c))\,(z)\,\mathtt{choose}(X_i\cdot\mathcal{N}(b_i))_{i=1}^k : 0}②}{\vdash_{\omega(P)} \lambda z^{B\Rightarrow C}.(\mathcal{P}(c))\,(z)\,\mathtt{choose}(X_i\cdot\mathcal{N}(b_i))_{i=1}^k : (m,0)}①$$

**Figure 6:** Proof derivation contributing in the $\mathtt{sk}(a)$ monomial in $\mathcal{P}(a)$.

We conclude that the coefficient is non zero iff $m = [n]$ and $a' = n$.

For the inductive case, let us assume that the result holds for type $B$ and $C$ and that $a = ([b_1,\dots,b_k],c) \in |\mathcal{B}\Rightarrow\mathcal{C}|$. Notice that $\mathtt{sk}(a) = \mathtt{sk}(c)\prod_{i=1}^k X_i\mathtt{sk}(b_i)$. A derivation of $\vdash_{\kappa\mathtt{sk}(a)} \mathcal{P}(a) : (m,0)$, with $\kappa \neq 0$, must be as described in Figure 6, as justified below:

① The only possible rule is the abstraction one.

②,③ For using the application rule, we have to choose an intermediate multiset $q \in \mathcal{M}_{\mathrm{f}}(|\mathcal{B}\Rightarrow\mathcal{C}|)$ and a context $\Gamma^{\bullet\prime}$ such that $\Gamma^{\bullet\prime} \vdash_\gamma \mathcal{P}(c) : (q,0)$ is derivable. Since $\mathcal{P}(c)$ is a closed term, by Fact 18, $\Gamma^{\bullet\prime}$ must be empty (i.e. mapping all variables to the empty multiset). Moreover, by definition, the parameters occurring in $\mathcal{P}(c)$ must be different from those occurring in each $X_i\cdot\mathcal{N}(b_i)$. Therefore, $\gamma = \nu\mathtt{sk}(c)$, with $\nu \neq 0$. By induction hypothesis in ③, we infer that $q = [c]$. We then deduce that ② is a binary applicative rule of label $\mathtt{app}_{([c],(z:m))}$. Hence, the right premise is the sequent $z : m \vdash_\beta (z)\,\mathtt{choose}(X_i\cdot\mathcal{N}(b_i))_{i=1}^k : c$, for a $\beta$ of the shape $\mu\prod_{i=1}^k X_i\cdot\mathtt{sk}(b_i)$.

④,⑤ The shape of the term forces us to use the application rule again: let $p' = [b'_1,\dots,b'_{k'}]$ denote the intermediate multiset. Since the left premise is the only one in which $z$ appears, there is only one possible way of separating the context: $\Gamma^{\bullet\prime} = z : m$ and $\Gamma^\bullet_{b'_j} = \emptyset$. Since the only possible rule for ⑤ is the $\mathtt{var}$ rule, we get $m = [(p',c)]$. We conclude that ④ is an applicative rule with $k'+1$ premises, the $k'$ right premises being of shape $\vdash_{\beta_j} \mathtt{choose}(X_i\cdot\mathcal{N}(b_i))_{i=1}^k : b'_j$.

⑥,⑦,⑧ For any $j \in \{1\dots k'\}$, there is a cluster of $h < k$ rules $\mathtt{if}_s$ and at the top of it a rule $\mathtt{if}_0$ with, as right premise, a weighted typing of a summand $X_{i_j}\cdot\mathcal{N}(b_{i_j})$. From that we must apply a $\mathtt{par}$ rule (numbered ⑦) and get as premise a sequent of shape $\vdash_{\beta_{i_j}} \mathcal{N}(b_{i_j}) : b'_j$, for $i_j \in 1\dots k$ and weight $\beta_{i_j}$. Then, notice that the weight of the conclusion of ⑦ is $X_{i_j}\beta_{i_j}$ and that of the conclusion of ⑥ is $\frac{1}{k}X_{i_j}\beta_{i_j}$. On the one hand, the reasoning on ② gives us $\beta = \mu\prod_{i=1}^k X_i\cdot\mathtt{sk}(b_i)$, while the definition of the weight of the conclusion of ④ gives us $\beta = \prod_{j=1}^{k'}\frac{1}{k}X_{i_j}\cdot\beta_{i_j}$. Since by definition no parameter $X_i$ occurs in $\mathcal{N}(b_{i_j})$, hence no $X_i$ appears in $\beta_{i_j}$, we have that the mapping $j \mapsto i_j$ is a bijective correspondence between $\{1,\dots,k'\}$ and $\{1,\dots,k\}$, so $k = k'$. Finally, since the sets of parameters occurring in the $\mathcal{N}(b_{i_j})$ are pairwise disjoint, we deduce that $\beta_{i_j}$ is proportional to $\mathtt{sk}(b_{i_j})$. We can then apply the induction hypothesis on ⑧ and deduce that $b_{i_j} = b_i$, and so $p' = [b_1,\dots,b_k]$.

Combining all these results, we eventually get that $m = [(p',c)] = [([b_1,\dots,b_k],c)] = [a]$. We conclude that there is a derivation of $\vdash_{\kappa\mathtt{sk}(a)} \mathcal{P}(a) : (m,0)$ if and only if $m = [a]$.

Now, let us consider a derivation of $\vdash_{\kappa\mathtt{sk}(a)} \mathcal{N}(a) : a'$, which must have the following form:

$$\dfrac{\dfrac{\vdots}{x : p' \vdash_\alpha \mathsf{if}(\wedge_{i=1}^k (\mathcal{P}(b_i))\,x, \mathcal{N}(c), \Omega_C) : c'}}{\vdash_\alpha \lambda x^B.\mathsf{if}(\wedge_{i=1}^k (\mathcal{P}(b_i))\,x, \mathcal{N}(c), \Omega_C) : (p',c')}$$

We prove by recursion on $k - j$ the property $\mathtt{RH}(j)$:

⋆ *if* $x : p' \vdash_\alpha \mathsf{if}(\wedge_{i=j}^k (\mathcal{P}(b_i))\,x, \mathcal{N}(c), \Omega_C) : c'$ *is derivable, then* $\alpha$ *is proportional to* $\mathtt{sk}(c)\prod_{i=j}^k \mathtt{sk}(b_i)$ *if and only if* $c = c'$ *and* $p' = [b_j,\dots,b_k]$.

The base case ($j = k$) is the induction hypothesis $\mathtt{IH}(C)$. Indeed, if $x : p' \vdash_\alpha \mathcal{N}(c) : c'$ is derivable, then, by Fact 18, $p'$ is empty, so that the weight $\alpha$ is proportional to $\mathtt{sk}(c)$ if and only if $c = c'$. The inductive case is proved accordingly to Figure 7:

① Since $\Omega_C$ has no web type (Example 23), the only possible rule is $\mathtt{if}_0$. The choice of how to partition the context $m_1 \uplus m_2$ will be deduced from the type derivation. Since by definition the set of parameters in $\mathcal{P}(b_j)$ and the set of parameters in $\mathsf{if}(\wedge_{i=j+1}^k (\mathcal{P}(b_i))\,x, \mathcal{N}(c), \Omega_C)$ are disjoint, we have that $\beta$ is proportional to $\mathtt{sk}(b_j)$ and $\gamma$ is proportional to $\prod_{i=j+1}^k \mathtt{sk}(b_i)$.

② For the right premise we can then apply the hypothesis $\mathtt{RH}(j{+}1)$ and deduce that $c = c'$ and $m_2 = [b_{j+1},\dots,b_k]$.

③,④ For the left premise, the only possible rule is $\mathtt{app}$. We have then to choose the intermediate multiset $m'$. As in the previous cases, one can argue that the left premise has empty context

$$\dfrac{\dfrac{\dfrac{\mathtt{IH}(A)\colon m_1=[b_j]}{\vdash_\beta \mathcal{P}(b_j):(m_1,0)}\;\text{④} \qquad \dfrac{}{x:m_1\vdash_1 x:m_1}}{x:m_1\vdash_\beta(\mathcal{P}(b_j))\,x:0}\;\text{③} \qquad \dfrac{\mathtt{RH}(j+1)\colon c=c',\, m_2=[b_{j+1},\dots,b_k]}{x:m_2\vdash_\gamma \mathsf{if}(\wedge_{i=j+1}^k(\mathcal{P}(b_i))\,x,\mathcal{N}(c),\Omega_C):c'}\;\text{②}}{x:m_1\uplus m_2\vdash_{\beta\gamma}\mathsf{if}(\wedge_{i=j}^k(\mathcal{P}(b_i))\,x,\mathcal{N}(c),\Omega_C):c'}\;\text{①}$$

**Figure 7:** Proof derivation contributing in the $\mathtt{sk}(a)$ monomial in $\mathcal{N}(a)$.

since $\mathcal{P}(b_j)$ is closed and then the induction hypothesis $\mathtt{IH}(C)$ gives $m' = [b_j]$. This means that ③ has only one premise at the right-hand side, which is a conclusion of a $\mathtt{var}$ rule, so that $m' = m_1$.

We conclude by combining all these results: we get that the context $m_1 \uplus m_2 = [b_j, \dots, b_k]$ and $c = c'$.

We have proved that $\mathtt{RH}(1)$ holds: $c = c'$ and $p' = [b_1, \dots, b_k]$, hence $a' = a$. $\square$

### 5.3 Main Result

The theory of multi-variables analytic functions can be subtler than single variable ones (for instance zeros of functions are not isolated in general). In the following Lemma 25, we underline that the coefficients of a power series vanishing on a neighborhood of zero have to be null. Indeed, coefficients are computed by successive derivations as limits of difference quotients. We then apply this result to power series with possibly negative coefficients.

**Lemma 25.** *[16] Let $f$ be a power series from $\mathbb{R}^n$ to $\mathbb{R}$ absolutely converging on $[0,1]^n$. If $f$ vanishes on a dense subset of $[0,1]^n$, then the coefficients of the power series $f$ are zero.*

**Lemma 26.** *Let $M$ and $N$ be two closed terms of* PPCF *with the same type $A$. If $[\![M]\!] \neq [\![N]\!]$, then there is a* PPCF *term $P$ of type $A \Rightarrow \mathtt{Int}$ such that* $\text{PROBA}^{\infty}_{(P)M,\underline{0}} \neq \text{PROBA}^{\infty}_{(P)N,\underline{0}}$.

*Proof.* Let $a \in |\mathcal{A}|$ such that $[\![M]\!]_a \neq [\![N]\!]_a$. Consider the testing term $\mathcal{P}(a)$ as defined in Figure 5.

Let $f$ denote the series $[\![(\mathcal{P}(a))\, M]\!]_{\underline{0}}$, which, by Definition 21 is a power series from $[0,1]^n$ to $[0,1]$, where $n$ is the number of parameters in $\mathcal{P}(a)$. Let $\mathtt{cf}(\mathtt{sk}(a), f)$ denote the coefficient of the monomial $\mathtt{sk}(a)$ in $f$. By definition (Equation (11)) this coefficient is given by the sum of the weights of the possible derivations of $\vdash_\alpha (\mathcal{P}(a))\, M : 0$, for $\alpha$ proportional to $\mathtt{sk}(a)$. The last rule of this derivation must be an $\mathtt{app}$ rule of shape:

$$\dfrac{\vdash_\gamma \mathcal{P}(a) : (m, 0) \qquad \forall (a', i) \in m, \quad \vdash_{\beta_{(a',i)}} M : a'}{\vdash_{\gamma \prod_{(a',i)\in m} \beta_{(a',i)}} (\mathcal{P}(a))\, M : 0}$$

Since $M$ has no free parameter (it is a term of PPCF), each $\beta_{(a',i)}$ is a positive real number. Hence, $\alpha = \gamma \prod_{(a',i)\in m} \beta_{(a',i)}$ is proportional to $\mathtt{sk}(a)$ iff $\gamma$ is proportional to $\mathtt{sk}(a)$. We can then apply Lemma 24 and get $m = [a]$. Moreover, by Lemma 20, the sum of the weights of the derivations of $\vdash M : a$ is equal to the scalar $[\![M]\!]_a$. To sum up, we conclude:

$$\mathtt{cf}(\mathtt{sk}(a), f) = \mathtt{cf}(\mathtt{sk}(a), [\![\mathcal{P}(a)]\!]_{([a],0)})\, [\![M]\!]_a$$

with $\mathtt{cf}(\mathtt{sk}(a), [\![\mathcal{P}(a)]\!]_{([a],0)}) \neq 0$. By an analogous reasoning:

$$\mathtt{cf}(\mathtt{sk}(a), g) = \mathtt{cf}(\mathtt{sk}(a), [\![\mathcal{P}(a)]\!]_{([a],0)})\, [\![N]\!]_a$$

where $g$ denotes the power series $[\![(\mathcal{P}(a))\, N]\!]_{\underline{0}}$. We can conclude that $f$ and $g$ have a different coefficient for the monomial $\mathtt{sk}(a)$ as soon as $[\![M]\!]_a \neq [\![N]\!]_a$.

Now, we apply Lemma 25 to the series $f - g$, which is not the zero power series because of the coefficient of $\mathtt{sk}(a)$. Therefore, as rational numbers are dense in $[0,1]$, there is a list $\vec{\kappa}$ of rational numbers in $[0,1]$ such that $f(\vec{\kappa}) \neq g(\vec{\kappa})$. By Lemma 20, this is equivalent to $\left[\!\left[\left(\mathcal{P}(a)\left[\vec{\kappa}/\vec{X}\right]\right) M\right]\!\right]_{\underline{0}} \neq \left[\!\left[\left(\mathcal{P}(a)\left[\vec{\kappa}/\vec{X}\right]\right) N\right]\!\right]_{\underline{0}}$. We conclude by setting $P = \mathcal{P}(a)\left[\vec{\kappa}/\vec{X}\right]$. Actually, $P$ is a well-defined PPCF term by Fact 17. So, by adequacy (Theorem 14), $\text{PROBA}^{\infty}_{(P)M,\underline{0}} = [\![(P)\, M]\!]_0 \neq [\![(P)\, N]\!]_0 = \text{PROBA}^{\infty}_{(P)N,\underline{0}}$. $\square$

**Theorem 27** (Full Abstraction)**.** *Given $\Gamma \vdash M : A$, and $\Gamma \vdash N : A$, we have:*

$$M \equiv_\Gamma N \text{ iff } [\![M]\!]^\Gamma = [\![N]\!]^\Gamma .$$

*Proof.* By Corollary 16 and Lemma 26. $\square$

As a consequence, the observational equivalence does not depend on the chosen probabilistic primitive (recall Remark 6):

**Corollary 28.** *For any* $\mathtt{p} \in \{\mathtt{Coin}, \mathtt{rand}, \oplus_\kappa, \oplus_i \kappa_i, (\kappa_n)_{n\in\mathbb{N}}\}$, *let $\equiv_{\mathtt{p}}$ denote the observational equivalence induced by the extension of* PCF *with the probabilistic primitive* $\mathtt{p}$*. The equivalence $\equiv_{\mathtt{p}}$ coincides with the equality of the interpretations in* **PCoh**. *In particular, $\equiv_{\mathtt{p}}$ gives the same equivalence on* PCF *terms, for any choice of* $\mathtt{p}$.

*Proof (Sketch).* We have that $\equiv_{\mathtt{Coin}} = \equiv_{\mathtt{rand}}$ since the two primitives $\mathtt{Coin}$ and $\mathtt{rand}$ are interdefinable by [5]. Similarly, by the discussion of Remark 6, we have: $\equiv_{\mathtt{rand}} \supseteq \equiv_{\oplus_\kappa} \supseteq \equiv_{\oplus_i \kappa_i} \supseteq \equiv_{(\kappa_n)_{n\in\mathbb{N}}}$ . In [4], the adequacy property of **PCoh** is established for the language containing the the $(\kappa_n)_{n\in\mathbb{N}}$ primitive, hence $\equiv_{(\kappa_n)_{n\in\mathbb{N}}}$ contains the equality $=_{\mathbf{Pcoh}}$ of the interpretations in **PCoh**. Finally, by Theorem 27, we have $=_{\mathbf{Pcoh}} \supseteq \equiv_{\mathtt{rand}}$ and we can conclude. $\square$

## 6. A counter-example to inequational FA

We prove that inequational full abstraction fails for **PCoh**. The proof consists in: (i) showing that the morphisms of Remark 11, that proves the non-extensionality of the **PCoh** order, are definable in PPCF (Equation 12); (ii) achieving a context lemma (Proposition 31) allowing us to infer the observational inequality by just observing the behavior of closed terms in applicative contexts.

If one would like to enrich the language in order to make observable also the componentwise order of **PCoh**, one should add a kind of differential operator to PPCF, in the spirit of [9]. However, such an extension is not trivial, since **PCoh** is known not to be sound for the whole differential $\lambda$-calculus.

Let us define $M_1$ and $M_2$ as follows:

$$M_1 \triangleq \lambda x^{\mathtt{Int}}.\mathsf{if}(x, \underline{0}, \underline{0}), \qquad M_2 \triangleq \lambda x^{\mathtt{Int}}.\underline{0}. \qquad (12)$$

By using rules of Figure 3 and Lemma 20, one can check that the semantics of the two terms is given by the morphisms of Example 11, i.e. $[\![M_1]\!] = \phi$ and $[\![M_2]\!] = \psi$. Hence, the two matrices $[\![M_1]\!]$ and $[\![M_2]\!]$ are incomparable in **Pcoh**.

In order to prove $M_1 \sqsubseteq M_2$, we use a standard reasoning and introduce a logical relation (Definition 29) allowing us to shrink the set of contexts (Proposition 31). We conclude with Corollary 32.

**Definition 29.** By structural induction on a type $A$, we define the binary relation $\lhd_A$ over closed PPCF terms of type $A$, as follows: $N \lhd_{\texttt{Int}} N'$ iff $\forall n \in \mathbb{N}$, $[\![N]\!]_n \leq [\![N']\!]_n$, and $M \lhd_{A \Rightarrow B} M'$ iff $\forall N \lhd_A N'$, $(M)\, N \lhd_B (M')\, N'$.

**Lemma 30.** *Let $M$ be a term of type $x_1 : A_1, \ldots, x_n : A_n \vdash M : A$. If for all $i$, $N_i \lhd_{A_i} N'_i$, then $M\left[\vec{N}/\vec{x}\right] \lhd_A M\left[\vec{N'}/\vec{x}\right]$.*

**Proposition 31.** *Let $M$ and $N$ be closed terms of type $A$. Then, $M \lhd_A N$ iff $M \sqsubseteq_A N$.*

**Corollary 32.** *The terms $M_1$ and $M_2$ of Equation* (12) *are logically related: $M_1 \lhd_{\texttt{Int} \Rightarrow \texttt{Int}} M_2$. Hence, $M_1 \sqsubseteq M_2$.*

## 7. Conclusion

We show that the observational equality over probabilistic programs is faithfully described by **PCoh**, a relatively abstract model based on convex sets and extensional functions. The proof uses innovative tools which might be useful to study probabilistic programing from a semantical viewpoint. In a language with random functions, two programs should be considered different not only when they give different results, but also when they give the same result but with different probabilities. Showing this difference can be much harder than in a deterministic language. Indeed, it requires a sharp control over coefficients expressing probabilities. **PCoh** denotes programs with power series, this allows us to use standard tools of Calculus for handling probabilities.

Although we chose one probabilistic primitive (see Remark 6), Corollary 28 shows that our result does not depend on this choice. Moreover, we focused on PPCF, a call-by-name functional language, but our result might be extended to other frameworks. In fact, **PCoh** comes from a model of linear logic: it is the cokleisli category associated with the exponential comonad, that corresponds to the translation of the functional arrow $A \Rightarrow B$ into the linear logic formula $!A \multimap B$. Call-by-value can be obtained by using the Eilenberg-Moore construction, i.e. translating $A \Rightarrow B$ into $!(A \multimap B)$. Control operators can be introduced considering a polarized fragment of linear logic. Yet, extending this model to concurrent systems or references is certainly more challenging.

A crucial tool in the proof of full abstraction is the use of the type system of Figure 3, which is a kind of intersection type system. In fact, a web element $([a_1, \ldots, a_n], b)$ can be seen as a type $(a_1 \wedge \cdots \wedge a_n) \to b$, where the intersection is non-idempotent. This system is a quantitative refinement of De Carvalho's [6] and yields the first logical presentation of a vectorial based semantics. Clearly, both type inference and type checking are undecidable. However, one can look for interesting restrictions of PPCF where the system becomes decidable, in the spirit of [20].

Last, it should be noticed that, unlike most full abstraction models for PCF, our model has no simple PPCF-definability properties. Our full abstraction proof builds applicative contexts using terms which belong to a very small subset of the domains associated with types. Their discriminating power relies on a strong regularity property of power series (unlike smooth functions, a power series which vanishes on an open set must be equal to 0, see for example to the function defined by $e^{-1/x^2}$ for $x > 0$ and 0 for $x \leq 0$). In contrast, most full abstraction proofs build applicative contexts using terms which belong to a *dense* subset of the corresponding domains.

## References


[1] S. Abramsky, R. Jagadeesan, and P. Malacaria. Full abstraction for PCF. *Information and Computation*, 163(2):409–470, Dec. 2000.

[2] G. Boudol, P.-L. Curien, and C. Lavatelli. A semantics for lambda calculi with resources. *Math. Struct. Comp. Sci.*, 9(4):437–482, 1999.

[3] A. Bucciarelli, A. Carraro, T. Ehrhard, G. Manzonetto, et al. Full abstraction for resource calculus with tests. In *CSL11 – Annual Conference of the EACSL*, volume 12, pages 97–111, 2011.

[4] V. Danos and T. Ehrhard. Probabilistic coherence spaces as a model of higher-order probabilistic computation. *Inf. Comput.*, 209(6):966–991, 2011.

[5] V. Danos and R. Harmer. Probabilistic game semantics. *ACM Transactions on Computational Logic*, 3(3):359–382, July 2002.

[6] D. de Carvalho. Execution Time of λ-Terms via Denotational Semantics and Intersection Types. Preprint, 2009.

[7] T. Ehrhard. On Köthe sequence spaces and linear logic. *Math. Struct. Comput. Sci.*, 12:579–623, 2002.

[8] T. Ehrhard. Finiteness spaces. *Math. Struct. Comput. Sci.*, 15(4):615–646, 2005.

[9] T. Ehrhard and L. Regnier. The Differential Lambda-Calculus. *Theor. Comput. Sci.*, 309(1):1–41, 2003.

[10] J.-Y. Girard. The system F of variable types, fifteen years later. *Theor. Comput. Sci.*, 45:159–192, 1986.

[11] J.-Y. Girard. Linear logic. *Theor. Comput. Sci.*, 50:1–102, 1987.

[12] J.-Y. Girard. Normal functors, power series and lambda-calculus. *Ann. Pure Appl. Logic*, 37(2):129–177, 1988.

[13] J.-Y. Girard. Coherent banach spaces: a continuous denotational semantics. *Theor. Comput. Sci.*, 227:297, 1999.

[14] J.-Y. Girard. Between logic and quantic: a tract. In T. Ehrhard, J.-Y. Girard, P. Ruet, and P. Scott, editors, *Linear Logic in Computer Science*, volume 316 of *London Math. Soc. Lect. Notes Ser.* CUP, 2004.

[15] J. Goubault-Larrecq and D. Varacca. Continuous random variables. In *LICS*, pages 97–106. IEEE Computer Society, 2011.

[16] É. Goursat. *Cours d'analyse mathématique. Tome I.* Gauthier-Villars, 1918.

[17] R. Hasegawa. Two applications of analytic functors. *Theor. Comput. Sci.*, 272(1-2):113–175, 2002.

[18] M. Hyland and L. Ong. On full abstraction for PCF. *Information and Computation*, 163(2):285–408, Dec. 2000.

[19] C. Jones and G. Plotkin. A probabilistic powerdomains of evaluation. In *LICS*. IEEE Computer Society, 1989.

[20] A. J. Kfoury and J. B. Wells. Principality and decidable type inference for finite-rank intersection types. In *POPL*, pages 161–174, 1999.

[21] U. D. Lago and M. Zorzi. Probabilistic operational semantics for the lambda calculus. *RAIRO - Theor. Inf. and Applic.*, 46(3):413–450, 2012.

[22] J. Laird, G. Manzonetto, G. McCusker, and M. Pagani. Weighted relational models of typed lambda-calculi. In *LICS 2013*. IEEE Press, June 2013.

[23] R. Milner. Fully abstract models of typed lambda-calculi. *Theor. Comput. Sci.*, 4:1–22, 1977.

[24] R. Milner and C. Strachey. *A Theory of Programming Language Semantics*. Chapman and Hall, London, 1976.

[25] E. Moggi. Computational lambda-calculus and monads. In *LICS*, pages 14–23. IEEE Computer Society, 1989.

[26] A. D. Pierro, C. Hankin, and H. Wiklicky. Probabilistic lambda-calculus and quantitative program analysis. *J. Log. Comput.*, 15(2): 159–179, 2005.

[27] G. D. Plotkin. A powerdomain construction. *SIAM J. Comput.*, 5(3): 452–487, 1976.

[28] G. D. Plotkin. LCF considered as a programming language. *Theor. Comput. Sci.*, 5(3):225–255, 1977.

[29] N. Saheb-Djahromi. Cpo's of measures for nondeterminism. *Theor. Comput. Sci.*, 12:19–37, 1980.

[30] D. Scott. Continuous lattices. In Lawvere, editor, *Toposes, Algebraic Geometry and Logic*, volume 274 of *Lecture Notes in Math.*, pages 97–136. Springer, 1972.

# Tabular: A Schema-Driven Probabilistic Programming Language


Andrew D. Gordon
Microsoft Research and University of Edinburgh

Thore Graepel
Microsoft Research

Nicolas Rolland
Microsoft Research

Claudio Russo
Microsoft Research

Johannes Borgström
Uppsala University

John Guiver
Microsoft Research



## Abstract

We propose a new kind of probabilistic programming language for machine learning. We write programs simply by annotating existing relational schemas with probabilistic model expressions. We describe a detailed design of our language, Tabular, complete with formal semantics and type system. A rich series of examples illustrates the expressiveness of Tabular. We report an implementation, and show evidence of the succinctness of our notation relative to current best practice. Finally, we describe and verify a transformation of Tabular schemas so as to predict missing values in a concrete database. The ability to query for missing values provides a uniform interface to a wide variety of tasks, including classification, clustering, recommendation, and ranking.



***Categories and Subject Descriptors*** D.3.2 [*Programming Languages*]: Language Classifications—Specialized application languages; I.2.6 [*Artificial Intelligence*]: Learning—Parameter Learning

***Keywords*** Bayesian reasoning; machine learning; model-learner pattern; probabilistic programming; relational data


## 1. Introduction

The core idea of this paper is to write probabilistic models by annotating relational schemas. We illustrate this idea on a database for recording outcomes of a two-player game without draws.

| Players | |
|---|---|
| Name | string |

| Matches | |
|---|---|
| Player1 | link(Players) |
| Player2 | link(Players) |
| Win1 | bool |

In this *concrete schema*, we have a Players table with column Name, and a Matches table, with columns Player1, Player2, and Win1 ("Player 1 wins"). As well as scalar types such as **bool** or **string**, a column may have a type such as **link**(Players), which means the column holds integer foreign keys to the Players table. (For simplicity, we assume that every table has a single-column primary key ID, a common case in practice. We also assume that in a table with $n$ rows the keys are integers normalized to lie in the range $0..n-1$; thus, we omit the primary key column from schemas.)

To illustrate some of the key ideas of Tabular, we consider the TrueSkill model (Herbrich et al. 2006), which is deployed at cloud-scale to make selections of players of roughly equal skill as opponents in online gaming. In this model, each player has an underlying numeric skill Skill, players' performances in a match are noisy copies of their skills, and each match is won by the player with the greater performance.

| Players | | | |
|---|---|---|---|
| Name | string | input | |
| Skill | real | latent | Gaussian(25.0,0.01) |
| **Matches** | | | |
| Player1 | link(Players) | input | |
| Player2 | link(Players) | input | |
| Perf1 | real | latent | Gaussian(Player1.Skill,1.0) |
| Perf2 | real | latent | Gaussian(Player2.Skill,1.0) |
| Win1 | bool | output | Perf1 > Perf2 |

Although its starting point is the underlying concrete schema, a Tabular schema may contain additional *latent columns*, which contain random variables to help model concrete data. In our example, the Players table has a latent column Skill, containing a numeric skill for each player, while the Matches table has latent columns Perf1 and Perf2, containing the performances of the two players in the match.

So that a schema defines a probability distribution over database instances, we annotate columns with probabilistic *model expressions*, which define distributions over entries in the column. Model expressions allow predictions to be made for the values of associated columns. Our example shows three sorts of annotated column:

(1) A concrete column marked as an *output* has a model expression that predicts values of the column. For example, the Win1 column is an output; its model expression indicates the winner is the player with the greater performance. The model expression can be applied to predict a future match outcome based on skills learnt from training data.




*POPL '14*, January 22–24, 2014, San Diego, CA, USA.
Copyright © 2014 ACM 978-1-4503-2544-8/14/01...$15.00.
http://dx.doi.org/10.1145/2535838.2535850

(2) A concrete column marked as an *input* is used to condition the probabilistic model, but has no model expression and cannot be predicted by the model. For example, the Player1 column in the Matches table is an input; it is used to characterize a match but is not considered to be uncertain.

(3) Finally, a column marked as *latent* is an auxiliary column, not present in the concrete database, whose model expression forms part of the model, and can be predicted. For example, the Skill column has a model expression indicating each entry is drawn from a Gaussian distribution with mean 25 and precision 0.01.

A Tabular program divides the columns of the concrete database into input and output columns, and determines a probabilistic model that predicts the output columns given the input columns. If all the cells in a concrete column have values we say the column is *observed*, but otherwise, when there are missing values, we say it is *observable*.

We consider two forms of inference. In both forms, input columns are observed. In *query-by-latent-column*, we assume that output columns are observed—we have data for each cell in the column—and the task is to predict the latent columns. Towards the end of the paper, in Section 7, we also consider *query-by-missing-value*, where output columns are observable, and the task is to predict the missing values in output columns.

***Query-by-Latent-Column*** Given a table of players and a table listing the outcomes of matches between those players, TrueSkill infers a numeric skill for each player, used for matchmaking. Consider the following tables of players and matches.

Players

| ID | Name |
|---|---|
| 0 | "Alice" |
| 1 | "Bob" |
| 2 | "Cynthia" |

Matches

| ID | Player1 | Player2 | Win1 |
|---|---|---|---|
| 0 | 0 | 1 | **false** |
| 1 | 1 | 2 | **false** |

Initially, TrueSkill assigns the same uncertain skill prior to each player. Given data showing that player 0 has been beaten by player 1, who in turn has been beaten by player 2, TrueSkill infers posterior skill distributions reflecting the likely ranking player 0 < player 1 < player 2.

The *query-by-latent-column* problem for Tabular is to determine the probability distribution over latent databases for a given schema, given a concrete database. In theory, the latent database is a joint distribution over all latent columns of the database. In a practical implementation, we consider only the marginals (projections) of each of the variables in the latent database. In particular, for the TrueSkill schema, conditioned on the concrete database above, the marginal representation of the distribution over latent databases consists of the following tables.

PlayersLatent

| ID | Skill |
|---|---|
| 0 | Gaussian(22.51, 1.45) |
| 1 | Gaussian(25.22, 1.53) |
| 2 | Gaussian(27.93, 1.45) |

MatchesLatent

| ID | Perf1 | Perf2 |
|---|---|---|
| 0 | Gaussian(22.49, 1.11) | Gaussian(25.25, 1.14) |
| 1 | Gaussian(25.25, 1.14) | Gaussian(27.96, 1.11) |

The distribution over the latent database can be stored in the same relational store as the original concrete database, joined with the concrete tables. While Tabular is specific to the domain of specifying probabilistic models for relational data, users are free to deploy whatever programming or query notation is appropriate to preprocess the data into relational form and to postprocess the results of inference.

***Query-by-Missing-Value*** In this mode, we use tables with missing values in observed columns as queries. For example, the following amounts to a query asking how likely it is that player 2 would beat player 0, to help decide on placing a bet.

Matches

| ID | Player1 | Player2 | Win1 |
|---|---|---|---|
| 3 | 2 | 0 | ? |

The result of such a query might be the following, indicating there is an 85% chance player 2 will beat player 0.

MatchesQueryLatent

| ID | Win1 |
|---|---|
| 3 | Bernoulli(0.85) |

***A Schema-Driven Recipe for Probabilistic Modelling*** In designing Tabular, we have in mind *data enthusiasts* (Hanrahan 2012), the large class of end users who wish to model and learn from their data, who have some knowledge of probability distributions and database schemas, but who are not necessarily professional programmers.

Tabular supports the following recipe for modelling data.

(1) Start with the schema (such as the Players and Matches tables).

(2) Add latent columns (Skill, Perf1 and Perf2).

(3) Write probabilistic models for latent and observed columns (skills have a prior, performances are noisy copies of skills, the player with the highest performance wins).

(4a) Learn latent columns and table parameters from complete data (we learn players' skills from a dataset of match outcomes).

(4b) Or predict missing values from partially-observed data (we predict a future match outcome based on a row (p1,p2,?)).

There is more to the whole cycle of learning from data—such as gathering and preprocessing data, and visualizing and interpreting results—but the recipe above addresses a crucial component.

***Models as Factor Graphs*** Factor graphs are a standard class of probabilistic graphical models of data, with many applications (Koller and Friedman 2009). Having modelled data with a factor graph, one can apply a range of inference algorithms to infer properties of the data or make predictions. The TrueSkill model was originally expressed as a factor graph such as the one below, in typical "plates and gates" notation.

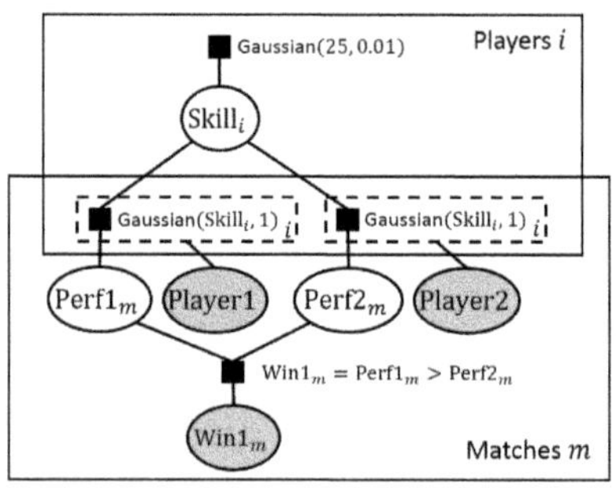


The circular nodes of the graph represent random variables, and the black squares are factors relating random variables. The large enclosing boxes labelled "Players *i*" and "Matches *m*" are known as *plates*, and indicate that the enclosed subgraphs are to be replicated. The two dotted boxes are known as *gates* (Minka and Winn 2008), and indicate choices governed by an incoming edge. The nodes for some random variables are shaded to indicate they are *observed*, while unshaded variables are *latent*. Together with exact factor annotations, factor graphs represent joint probability distributions.

Like many visual notations, factor graphs become awkward as models become complex. Instead, we turn to probabilistic programming languages, where models are code, random variables are program variables, factors are primitive operations, plates are loops, and gates are conditionals or switches. BUGS (Gilks et al. 1994) is the most popular example, and there is much current interest, witness the wiki `probabilistic-programming.org`. In this paper, we create models with a direct interpretation as factor graphs by writing schema annotations in a high-level probabilistic language.

***Innovations in the Design of Tabular*** By using the relational modelling of the data encoded in the concrete schema, we write models succinctly because each table description implicitly defines a loop (a plate) over its rows. Moreover, we save our user the trouble of writing code to transfer data and results between language and database. The main conceptual innovations in Tabular are:

(1) Annotations on a relational schema so as to construct a graphical model, with *input*, *output*, and *latent* columns.

(2) A grammar of model expressions to stipulate the models for latent and output columns, with the semantics of tables and schemas given as models assembled compositionally from the models for individual columns.

(3) *Query-by-latent-column*: infer latent columns from the concrete database, given input columns and fully-observed output columns.

(4) *Query-by-missing-value*: infer missing values in output columns, given input columns and partially-observed output columns.

***Technical Contributions and Evaluations*** We present the detailed syntax and type system of Tabular, and semantics by translation to a core probabilistic calculus, Fun. Theorem 1 (Translation Preserves Typing) asserts that the semantics respects the Tabular type system. Theorem 2 asserts that a certain factor graph, expressed in Fun, correctly implements query-by-latent-column.

We describe an implementation of Tabular using Infer.NET, based on our semantics. To test Tabular in practice, we reimplement a series of factor-graph models for psychometric data first performed using Infer.NET directly (Bachrach et al. 2012), with essentially the same results. Theorem 3 justifies a transformation on Tabular schemas that implements query-by-missing-value in terms of query-by-latent-column.

An extended version of this paper, with additional examples and screenshots, appears as a technical report (Gordon et al. 2013b).

## 2. Fun and the Model-Learner Pattern

***Fun, Probabilistic Programming for Factor Graphs*** We use a version of the core calculus Fun (Borgström et al. 2011) with arrays of deterministic size, but without a conditioning operation (**observe**) within expressions. This version of Fun can be seen as a first-order subset of the stochastic lambda-calculus (Ramsey and Pfeffer 2002); it is akin also to HANSEI (Kiselyov and Shan 2009). Fun expressions have a semantics in the probability monad, but also have a direct interpretation using factor graphs.

We have scalar types **bool**, **int**, and **real**, record types (that are constructed from field typings), and array types. Let **string** = **int**[] and **vector** = **real**[] and **matrix** = **vector**[]. Let $c$ range over the field names, $s$ range over constants of base type, and let $\mathrm{ty}(s) = T$ mean that constant $s$ has type $T$.

**Types and Values (Scalars, Records, Arrays):** $T, V$

| | |
|---|---|
| $S ::= \mathbf{bool} \mid \mathbf{int} \mid \mathbf{real}$ | scalar type |
| $T,U ::= S \mid \{RT\} \mid T[\,]$ | type |
| $RT ::= \varnothing \mid c : T; RT$ | field typings |
| $V ::= s \mid \{c_1 = V_1; \ldots; c_n = V_n\} \mid [V_1, \ldots, V_n]$ | |

**Expressions of Fun:** $E$

| | |
|---|---|
| $E,F ::=$ | expression |
| $x \mid s$ | variable, constant |
| $\mathbf{if}\ E\ \mathbf{then}\ F_1\ \mathbf{else}\ F_2$ | if-then-else |
| $\{R\} \mid E.c$ | record literal, projection |
| $[E_1, \ldots, E_n] \mid E[F]$ | array literal, lookup |
| $[\mathbf{for}\ x < E \rightarrow F]$ | for-loop (scope of index $x$ is $F$) |
| $\mathbf{let}\ x = E\ \mathbf{in}\ F$ | let (scope of $x$ is $F$) |
| $g(E_1, \ldots, E_n)$ | primitive $g$ with arity $n$ |
| $D(E_1, \ldots, E_n)$ | distribution $D$ with arity $n$ |
| $R ::= \varnothing \mid c = E; R$ | field bindings |

We write $\mathrm{fv}(\phi)$ for the set of variables occurring free in a phrase of syntax $\phi$, such as an expression $E$, and identify syntax up to consistent renaming of bound variables. We sometimes use tuples $(E_1, \ldots, E_n)$ and tuple types $T_1 * \cdots * T_n$ below: they stand for the corresponding records and record types with numeric field names $1, 2, \ldots, n$. We write **fst** $E$ for $E.1$ and **snd** $E$ for $E.2$. The *empty record* $\{\}$ represents a void or unit value. We write $\{c_1 : T_1; \ldots; c_n : T_n\}$ for a concrete record type, and thus $\{\}$ for the empty record type; $\{c_1 = E_1; \ldots; c_n = E_n\}$, for a concrete record term; and use the comprehension syntax $\{c_i : T_i\}^{i \in 1..n}$ and $\{c_i = E_i\}^{i \in 1..n}$ to index the components of a record type or term (when ordering matters) or $\{c : T_c\}^{c \in C}$ and $\{c = E_c\}^{c \in C}$ (where $C$ is a *set* of field names) when ordering is irrelevant. Field typings and field bindings are just association lists; we sometimes use $RT_1; RT_2$ to denote the *concatenation* of field typings $RT_1$ and $RT_2$, and $R_1; R_2$ for the concatenation of field bindings. We implicitly identify record types up to re-ordering of field typings. We assume a collection of total deterministic functions $g$, including arithmetic and logical operators. We also assume families $D$ of standard probability distributions, including, for example, the following. (A Gaussian takes a *precision* parameter precision; the *standard deviation* $\sigma$ follows from the identity $\sigma^2 = 1/\mathsf{precision}$.)

**Distributions:** $D : (x_1 : T_1; \ldots; x_n : T_n) \rightarrow T$

$\mathsf{Bernoulli} : (\mathsf{bias} : \mathbf{real}) \rightarrow \mathbf{bool}$
$\mathsf{Gaussian} : (\mathsf{mean} : \mathbf{real}, \mathsf{precision} : \mathbf{real}) \rightarrow \mathbf{real}$
$\mathsf{Beta} : (\mathsf{a} : \mathbf{real}, \mathsf{b} : \mathbf{real}) \rightarrow \mathbf{real}$
$\mathsf{Gamma} : (\mathsf{shape} : \mathbf{real}, \mathsf{scale} : \mathbf{real}) \rightarrow \mathbf{real}$
$\mathsf{DirichletSymmetric} : (\mathsf{length} : \mathbf{int}, \mathsf{alpha} : \mathbf{real}) \rightarrow \mathbf{vector}$
$\mathsf{Discrete} : (\mathsf{probs} : \mathbf{vector}) \rightarrow \mathbf{int}$
$\mathsf{DiscreteUniform} : (\mathsf{range} : \mathbf{int}) \rightarrow \mathbf{int}$

***Semi-Observed Models*** We explain the semantics of Tabular by translating to Bayesian models encoded using Fun expressions. We consider a Bayesian model to be a probabilistic function, from some *input* to some *output*, that is governed by a *parameter*, itself generated probabilistically from a deterministic *hyperparameter*. Our semantics is compositional: the model of a whole schema is assembled from models of tables, which themselves are composed from models of rows, assembled from models of individual cells. This formulation follows Gordon et al. (2013a), with two refinements. First, when we apply a model to data, the model output is *semi-observed*, that is, each output is a pair consisting of an observed component (like a game outcome in TrueSkill) plus an unobserved latent component (like a performance in TrueSkill). Second, the hyperparameter is passed to the sampling distribution $\mathsf{Gen}(h, w, x)$ as well as to the parameter distribution $\mathsf{Prior}(h)$ for convenient model building.

**Notation for Bayesian Models:**

| | | |
|---|---|---|
| Hyper | $E_h$ | default hyperparameter ($E_h$ deterministic) |
| Prior($h$) | $E_w$ | distribution over parameter (given $h$) |
| Gen($h, w, x$) | $E_{yz}$ | distribution over output (given $h$, $w$, and $x$) |

(Hyperparameters and parameters both determine the distribution of outputs given an input; the difference is that we specify our uncertain knowledge of parameters (but not hyperparameters) using the prior distribution, so that our uncertainty about parameters (but not hyperparameters) is reduced by conditioning on data.)

For example, here is a model for linear regression, that is, the task of fitting a straight line to data points. This example illustrates the informal notation for Fun expressions used in Section 3. For instance, we write $a \sim \mathsf{Gaussian}(h.\mu_A, 1)$ to mean that random variable $a$ is distributed according to $\mathsf{Gaussian}(h.\mu_A, 1)$. We write $x := E$ to indicate that $x$ is the value of deterministic expression $E$.

**Linear Regression: (Illustrative of informal notation for Fun)**

| | |
|---|---|
| Hyper | The record $\{\mu_A = 0; \mu_B = 0\}$. |
| Prior($h$) | The record $\{A = a; B = b\}$ where $a \sim \mathsf{Gaussian}(h.\mu_A, 1)$ and $b \sim \mathsf{Gaussian}(h.\mu_B, 1)$. |
| Gen($h, w, x$) | The pair $(y, z)$ where $z := (w.A) * x + w.B$ and $y \sim \mathsf{Gaussian}(z, 1)$. |

In our formal semantics for Tabular, we use a compact notation $P ::= \langle E_h, (h)E_w, (h, w, x)E_{yz} \rangle$ for a model. Our regression example is written in compact notation as follows.

$$\begin{array}{l} \langle \{\mu_A = 0; \mu_B = 0\}, \\ \quad (h)\textbf{let } a = \mathsf{Gaussian}(h.\mu_A, 1) \textbf{ in} \\ \quad\quad \textbf{let } b = \mathsf{Gaussian}(h.\mu_B, 1) \textbf{ in } \{A = a; B = b\}, \\ \quad (h, w, x)\textbf{let } z = (w.A) * x + w.B \textbf{ in let } y = \mathsf{Gaussian}(z, 1) \textbf{ in } (y, z) \rangle \end{array}$$

We use variable $x$ for the input, $y$ for the observed output, $z$ for the latent output, $w$ for the parameter, and $h$ for the hyperparameter.

***Databases as Fun Values*** We view a database as a record $\{t_1 = B_1; \ldots; t_n = B_n\}$ holding (relational) tables $B_1, \ldots, B_n$ named $t_1, \ldots, t_n$. A table $B$ is an array $[r_1, \ldots, r_m]$ of rows, where each row is a record $r_i = \{c_1 = V_1; \ldots; c_n = V_n\}$, where $c_1, \ldots, c_n$ are the columns of the table, and $V_1, \ldots, V_n$ are the items in the column for that row. (We view a table as an array so that a primary key is simply an index into the array, and omit primary keys from rows.)

The column annotations in a Tabular schema partition a whole database into a pair $d = (d_x, d_y)$ where $d_x$ is the *input database*, with the input columns of each table, and $d_y$ is the *observed database*, with the observed columns of each table. (For each table, the numbers of rows in the input and observed databases must match.)

The *latent database* $d_z$ is a database with just the latent columns of the schema, and the *database parameter* $V_w$ is a record holding parameters for each table.

The purpose of *query-by-latent-column* is to predict the database parameter and latent database from the input and observed databases.

***Distributions Induced by a Semi-Observed Model*** In later sections, we define the semantics of a Tabular schema as a model $P$. In general, a model $P$ defines several probability distributions:

- *Prior* $p(w \mid h)$ is $w \sim P.\mathsf{Prior}(h)$.
- *Full sampling* $p(y, z \mid h, w, x)$ is $y, z \sim P.\mathsf{Gen}(h, w, x)$.
- *Sampling distribution* $p(y \mid h, w, x)$ is $\int p(y, z \mid h, w, x) dz$.
- *Predictive distribution* $p(y \mid x, h)$ is $\int p(y \mid h, w, x) p(w \mid h) dw$.

Training data for a model consists of a pair $d = (d_x, d_y)$ where $d_y$ is the observed output given input $d_x$. In our case, $d_x$ is the input database and $d_y$ is the observed database. Conditioned on such data $d = (d_x, d_y)$ we obtain posterior distributions:

- *Posterior* $p(w \mid d, h) = \frac{p(d_y \mid h, w, d_x) p(w \mid h)}{p(d_y \mid d_x, h)}$.
- *Posterior latent* $p(z \mid d, h) = \int \frac{p(d_y, z \mid h, w, d_x)}{p(d_y \mid h, w, d_x)} p(w \mid d, h) dw$.

(The term $p(d_y \mid d_x, h)$ is known as the *evidence* for the model, used later in our comparison of different models on the same dataset).

Given $d = (d_x, d_y)$, the *semantics of query-by-latent-column* is to compute the posterior $p(w \mid d, h)$ on the database parameter, and the posterior latent distribution $p(z \mid d, h)$ on the latent database.

## 3. Tabular, By Example

### 3.1 Tabular and the Generative Process for Tables

A schema $\mathbb{S}$ is an ordered list of tables, named $t_1, \ldots, t_n$, each of which has a table descriptor $\mathbb{T}$, that is itself an ordered list of typed columns, named $c_1, \ldots, c_n$. The key concept of Tabular is to place an annotation $A$ on each column so as to define a probabilistic model for the relational schema.

We present first a core version of Tabular, where the model expressions $M$ on columns are simply Fun expressions $E$.

**Tabular Schemas, Tables and Annotations: $\mathbb{S}$, $\mathbb{T}$, $A$**

| | | |
|---|---|---|
| $\mathbb{S} ::= \varnothing \mid (t \mapsto \mathbb{T})\mathbb{S}$ | | (database) schema |
| $\mathbb{T} ::= \varnothing \mid (c \mapsto A : T)\mathbb{T}$ | | table descriptor |
| $A ::=$ | | annotation |
| **hyper**($E$) | | hyperparameter |
| **param**($M$) | | parameter |
| **input** | | input |
| **output**($M$) | | output |
| **latent**($M$) | | latent |
| $M ::= E$ | (to be completed) | model expression |

The types $T$ on concrete columns are typically scalars, but our semantics allows these types to be arbitrary. The Tabular syntax for types and expressions slightly extends Fun syntax with features to find the sizes of tables and to dereference foreign keys.

**Additional Types and Expressions of Tabular Fun: $T$, $E$**

| | |
|---|---|
| $T ::= \cdots \mid \textbf{link}(t)$ | type |
| $E ::= \cdots \mid \textbf{sizeof}(t) \mid (E : \textbf{link}(t)).c$ | expression |

The expression **sizeof**($t$) returns the number of rows in table $t$. The expression $(E : \textbf{link}(t)).c$ returns the item in column $c$ of the row in table $t$ keyed by the integer $E$. In the common case when $E$ is a column $c_k$ annotated with type **link**($t$), we write $c_k.c$ as a shorthand for $(c_k : \textbf{link}(t)).c$. Values of type **link**($t$) are integers serving as foreign keys to the table $t$. For simplicity, our type system treats each type **link**($t$) as a synonym for **int**.

***Generative Process for Tables*** A table descriptor $\mathbb{T}$ is a function from the concrete table holding the **input** and **output** columns, to the *predictive table*, which additionally holds the **latent** columns. The descriptor defines a generative process to produce (1) the hyperparameters and parameters of the table, and (2) the output and latent columns of the table, by a loop over the rows of the table.

In step (1), outside the loop over the data, we process the annotations in turn to define the hyperparameters and parameters, ignoring the input, output, and latent annotations.

- $c \mapsto$ **hyper**($E$) defines $c$ as the deterministic expression $E$.
- $c \mapsto$ **param**($E$) samples $c$ from probabilistic expression $E$.

In step (2), a loop over each row of the concrete table, we process the annotations in turn to sample independently each row of the predictive table, with items for each of the input, output, and latent columns.

- $c \mapsto$ **input** copies $c$ from the input row.
- $c \mapsto$ **output**$(E)$ samples $c$ from probabilistic expression $E$.
- $c \mapsto$ **latent**$(E)$ samples $c$ from probabilistic expression $E$.

In step (2), inside the data loop, we ignore the hyperparameter and parameter annotations, although expressions may depend on the variables defined in step (1) outside the loop.

A schema $\mathbb{S}$ describes a generative process to produce (1) the hyperparameters and parameters of each table, and (2) the predictive table for each concrete table. Tables and columns are lexically scoped in sequence, although the variables bound in step (1) cannot refer to variables bound later in step (2).

Later on, we formalize the generative processes for tables and schemas using our model notation; step (1) corresponds to the Hyper and Prior parts, while step (2) corresponds to the Gen part.

***Example: Conjugate Bernoulli*** This standard model is used to generate random bits with a probability distribution that is itself random; it is a key ingredient of mixture models.

| CoinFlips | | | |
|---|---|---|---|
| alpha | int | hyper | 1 |
| beta | int | hyper | 1 |
| Bias | real | param | Beta(alpha,beta) |
| Coin | bool | output | Bernoulli(Bias) |

In step (1) of the generative process, we define both alpha and beta as 1, and sample Bias from the distribution Beta(1,1), the uniform distribution on the unit interval. In step (2), we generate each row of the table by sampling the Coin variable from the distribution Bernoulli(Bias) on **bool**, which returns **true** with probability Bias. Overall, we sample the shared parameter Bias, whereas we sample each output Coin independently for each row.

A concrete database for this schema is simply one table with a single column Coin containing Booleans. Inference computes the distribution of the Bias parameter.

***Distributions with Conjugate Priors*** In Bayesian theory, the Beta distribution over the parameter of the Bernoulli distribution is a particular case of a *conjugate prior*. It is convenient for efficient inference to choose a prior that is conjugate to a sampling distribution. Hence, we define *primitive models* for various standard sampling distributions and conjugate priors.

**Library of Primitive Models: $P$**

$P ::= \langle E_h, (h)E_w, (h,w,x)E_y \rangle$ primitive model

$\mathsf{CBernoulli} \triangleq \langle \{\alpha = 1.0; \beta = 1.0\},$
$(h)\mathsf{Beta}(h.\alpha, h.\beta),$
$(h,w,x)\mathsf{Bernoulli}(w)\rangle$

$\mathsf{CGaussian} \triangleq \langle \{\mu = 0.0; \tau = 1.0; \kappa = 1.0; \theta = 2.0\},$
$(h)\{\mu = \mathsf{Gaussian}(h.\mu, h.\tau);$
$\tau = \mathsf{Gamma}(h.\kappa, h.\theta)\}\},$
$(h,w,x)\mathsf{Gaussian}(w.\mu, w.\tau)\rangle$

$\mathsf{CDiscrete} \triangleq \langle \{\mathsf{N} = 2; \alpha = 1.0\},$
$(h)\mathsf{DirichletSymmetric}(h.N, h.\alpha),$
$(h,w,x)\mathsf{Discrete}(w)\rangle$

These models are defined as primitives built from closed Fun expressions. The model CBernoulli is exactly equivalent to our previous example. The concentration $\alpha$ of a CDiscrete determines whether the parameter—a probability vector of length N drawn from the symmetric Dirichlet distribution—is uniformly distributed ($\alpha = 1.0$), biased towards sparse vectors ($\alpha < 1.0$) or dense vectors ($\alpha > 1.0$). Notice that Gaussian is a distribution $D$ that can occur within an expression $E$, while CGaussian is a primitive model that may occur as a model expression $M$ in the full syntax of Tabular.

***Completing Tabular*** We add primitive and indexed model expressions to enable the succinct expression of complex models.

**Completing the Syntax of Model Expressions: $M$**

| | |
|---|---|
| $M ::=$ | model expression |
| $E$ | simple |
| $P(c_1 = E_1, \ldots, c_n = E_n)$ | primitive, with hyperparameters |
| $M[E_{\text{index}} < E_{\text{size}}]$ | indexed |

The semantics of a model expression $M$ for a column $c$ is a model $P$ whose output explains how to generate the entry for $c$ in each row of a table. The model $P$ has a restricted form $P = \langle \{\}, (h)E_w, (h,w,x)E_y \rangle$, with no hyperparameters, and where $h \notin \text{fv}(E_w, E_y)$ and $x \notin \text{fv}(E_y)$. Hence, in our notations below, we omit the bound variables $h$ and $x$.

A simple model $E$ produces its output by running $E$.

**Model for Simple Model Expression $E$:**

| | |
|---|---|
| Hyper | The empty record $\{\}$. |
| Prior() | The empty record $\{\}$. |
| Gen$(w)$ | $y$ where $y \sim E$. |

A primitive model $P(c = E_c{}^{c \in C'})$ acts like the library model $P$, except that when $P$.Hyper $= \{c = F_c{}^{c \in C}\}$ and $C' \subseteq C$, hyperparameter $c$ is set to $E_c$ if $c \in C'$, and otherwise to the default $F_c$.

**Model for $P(c = E_c{}^{c \in C'})$:**

| | |
|---|---|
| Hyper | The empty record $\{\}$. |
| Prior() | $P.\mathsf{Prior}(\{c = E_c{}^{c \in C'}; c = F_c{}^{c \in C \setminus C'}\})$. |
| Gen$(w)$ | $P.\mathsf{Gen}(\{c = E_c{}^{c \in C'}; c = F_c{}^{c \in C \setminus C'}\}, w, \{\})$. |

An indexed model $M[E_{\text{index}} < E_{\text{size}}]$ creates its parameter to be an array of $E_{\text{size}}$ instances of the parameter of $M$, and produces its output like $M$ but using the parameter instance indexed by $E_{\text{index}}$.

**Model for $M[E_{\text{index}} < E_{\text{size}}]$ where $P$ is the model for $M$:**

| | |
|---|---|
| Hyper | The empty record $\{\}$. |
| Prior() | $[w_1, \ldots, w_{E_{size}}]$ where $w_i \sim P.\mathsf{Prior}()$ for $i \leq E_{size}$. |
| Gen$(w)$ | $y \sim P.\mathsf{Gen}(w_i)$ where $i := E_{\text{index}}$. |

***Generative Process for Tables in Full Tabular*** In the full language, the model expression for a column $c$ has both a parameter and an output; we use the variable $c\$$ for the parameter, and the variable $c$ for the output.

In step (1) the generative process, we process the annotations in turn to define the hyperparameters and parameters.

- $c \mapsto$ **hyper**$(E)$ defines $c$ as the deterministic expression $E$.
- $c \mapsto$ **param**$(M)$ samples $c\$$ from $P.\mathsf{Prior}()$ and samples $c$ from $P.\mathsf{Gen}(c\$)$ where $P$ models $M$.
- $c \mapsto$ **input** is ignored.
- $c \mapsto$ **output**$(M)$ samples $c\$$ from $P.\mathsf{Prior}()$ where $P$ models $M$.
- $c \mapsto$ **latent**$(M)$ samples $c\$$ from $P.\mathsf{Prior}()$ where $P$ models $M$.

In step (2), a loop over each row of the input table, we process the annotations in turn to define each row of the predictive table.

- $c \mapsto$ **hyper**$(E)$ is ignored.
- $c \mapsto$ **param**$(M)$ is ignored.
- $c \mapsto$ **input** copies $c$ from the input row.
- $c \mapsto$ **output**$(M)$ samples $c$ from $P.\mathsf{Gen}(c\$)$ where $P$ models $M$.
- $c \mapsto$ **latent**$(M)$ samples $c$ from $P.\mathsf{Gen}(c\$)$ where $P$ models $M$.

The generative process for the core language is a special case, where the \$ suffixed variables are empty records. As before, the variables defined in step (1) are static variables defined once per table, whereas the variables defined in step (2) are defined for each row of the table. The \$ suffixed variables help define the semantics of Tabular, but are not directly available to Tabular programs.

### 3.2 Examples of Models and Queries

A mixture model is a probabilistic choice between two or more other models. We begin with several varieties of mixture model.

***Mixture of Two Gaussians*** Our first mixture model makes use of the library models CBernoulli and CGaussian.

| MoG1 | | | |
|---|---|---|---|
| z | bool | latent | CBernoulli() |
| g1 | real | latent | CGaussian() |
| g2 | real | latent | CGaussian() |
| y | real | output | if z then g1 else g2 |

In step (1) of the generative process, we sample parameters z\$ (containing the bias) from the prior of CBernoulli(), and parameters g1\$, g2\$ (each containing a mean $\mu$ and precision $\tau$) from the prior of CGaussian(). The empty hyperparameter lists in CBernoulli() and CGaussian() indicate that we use the default hyperparameters built into the models, that is, $\{\alpha = 1.0; \beta = 1.0\}$ and $\{\mu = 0.0; \tau = 1.0; \kappa = 1.0; \theta = 2.0\}$.

In step (2), we generate each row of the table by sampling z from the distribution Bernoulli(z\$), g1 and g2 from the distributions Gaussian(g1\$.$\mu$,g1\$.$\tau$) and Gaussian(g2\$.$\mu$,g2\$.$\tau$) and finally defining the output y to be g1 or g2, depending on z.

Given a concrete database for this schema (a column y of random numbers that is expected to be grouped into two clusters around the means of the two Gaussians) inference learns the posterior distributions of the parameters z\$, g1\$, and g2\$, and also fills in the latent columns. The inferred distribution of each z indicates how likely each y is to have been drawn from each of the clusters.

***Mixture of an Array of Gaussians*** To generalize to a many-way mixture, we first decide on a number n of mixture components (clusters); in this case we set n=5. To randomly select a cluster we use the CDiscrete library model, which has an integer hyperparameter N and outputs natural numbers less than N. The default value of N is 2; to define a mixture model with n components we override the default as CDiscrete(N=n). A model CDiscrete(N=2) is akin to a CBernoulli that outputs 0 or 1.

| MoG2 | | | |
|---|---|---|---|
| n | int | hyper | 5 |
| z | int | latent | CDiscrete(N=n) |
| y | real | output | CGaussian()[z < n] |

The indexed model CGaussian()[z < n] denotes a model whose parameter is an array of n parameter records (containing mean $\mu$ and precision $\tau$ fields) for the underlying CGaussian model. The output of the indexed model is obtained by first picking the parameter record at index z, and then getting an output from the CGaussian model with those parameters.

The parameter of column z is a *probability vector* of length N, an array of non-negative real numbers that sum to 1, indicating the chance of each output value. The parameter for the y column is an array of n parameter records for the underlying CGaussian model.

The observed output of each row is determined by first sampling the cluster z from the discrete distribution, and then sampling from CGaussian[z < n]. With n=2 we recover our previous mixture of two Gaussians.

***User/Movie/Rating Schema*** Our final mixture model is a Tabular version of the factor graph in Figure 1 of Singh and Graepel (2012), where it was automatically generated from a relational schema.

| User | | | |
|---|---|---|---|
| z | int | latent | CDiscrete(N=4) |
| Name | string | input | |
| IsMale | bool | output | CBernoulli()[z] |
| Age | int | output | CDiscrete(N=100)[z] |
| **Movie** | | | |
| z | int | latent | CDiscrete(N=4) |
| Title | string | input | |
| Genre | int | output | CDiscrete(N=7)[z] |
| Year | int | output | CDiscrete(N=100)[z] |
| **Rating** | | | |
| u | link(User) | input | |
| m | link(Movie) | input | |
| Score | int | output | CDiscrete(N=5)[u.z,m.z] |

The model for the Score column illustrates a couple of notations regarding indexed models. First, a doubly-indexed model $M[E_1 < F_1, E_2 < F_2]$ is short for $(M[E_1 < F_1])[E_2 < F_2]$. Second, we write $M[E]$ as short for $M[E < n]$ when we know that $E$ is output by CDiscrete(N=$n$).

Each row in the User table belongs to one of four clusters, indexed by the latent variable z which has a CDiscrete model. For each cluster, there is a corresponding distribution over gender (IsMale) and Age. Similarly, each row in the Movie table is modelled by a four-way mixture, indexed by z, with Genre and Year attributes. Finally, each row in the Rating table has links to a user u and to a movie m, and also a Score attribute that is modelled by a discrete distribution indexed by the clusters of the user and the movie, corresponding to a stochastic block model (Nowicki and Snijders 2001).

***Query-by-Latent-Column and TrueSkill*** We illustrate direct use of query-by-latent-column with reference to TrueSkill, and also a programming style where we introduce new *query tables* purely for the purpose of formulating queries.

First, as illustrated in Section 1, given tables of players and matches, inference computes distributions for the latent Skill column; these skills can be used to do matchmaking or to display in leaderboards. It also infers distributions for the Perf1 and Perf2 columns, which may indicate whether a player was on form or not on the occasion of a particular match.

Second, suppose we wish to bet on the outcomes of upcoming matches between members $p$ and $q$ of the Players table. We add a fresh query table Bets, which has the same schema as Matches except that Win1 is latent instead of being an observed output. We place one row in this new table, with $p$ for Player1 and $q$ for Player2, and inference computes distributions for the three latent columns, including a Bernoulli for Win1 indicating the odds of a win. By placing multiple rows in the Bets table we can predict the outcomes of multiple upcoming matches.

| Bets | | | |
|---|---|---|---|
| Player1 | link(Players) | input | |
| Player2 | link(Players) | input | |
| Perf1 | real | latent | Gaussian(Player1.Skill,1.0) |
| Perf2 | real | latent | Gaussian(Player2.Skill,1.0) |
| Win1 | bool | latent | Perf1 > Perf2 |

Third, consider an online situation where there is a large table of players, and a relatively small number of players $q_i$ queuing to begin fresh online games. We may wish to select one of the $q_i$ to play against a new player $p$. To do so, we add the Sim query table below, and fill it with rows $(p, q_i)$ for each $i$. The latent column Similar holds **true** if the two players are close in skill (less than 0.1 units apart). Inference fills this column with Bernoulli distributions which can be used to select a partner close in skill to $p$. Both the means and variances of the skills of players enter into the marginal probability of being Similar, thus making use of the full probabilistic formulation.

| Sim | | | |
|---|---|---|---|
| Player1 | link(Players) | input | |
| Player2 | link(Players) | input | |
| Similar | bool | latent | abs(Player1.Skill−Player2.Skill)<0.1 |

# 4. Formal Semantics of Tabular

## 4.1 Semantics of Fun (Review)

We here recall the semantics of Fun without zero-probability observations (Bhat et al. 2013). We write $\Gamma \vdash E : T$ to mean that in type environment $\Gamma = x_1 : T_1, \ldots, x_n : T_n$ ($x_i$ distinct) expression $E$ has type $T$. Let $\mathrm{Det}(E)$ mean that $E$ contains no occurrence of $D(\ldots)$. The typing rules for Fun are standard for a first-order functional language; some examples follow below.

**Selected Typing Rules of Fun Expressions: $\Gamma \vdash E : T$**

(Fun Random)
$$\frac{D : (x_1 : T_1 * \cdots * x_n : T_n) \to U \quad \Gamma \vdash E_i : T_i \text{ for } i \in 1..n}{\Gamma \vdash D(E_1, \ldots, E_n) : U}$$

(Fun AConst)
$$\frac{\Gamma \vdash E_i : T \text{ for } i \in 1..n}{\Gamma \vdash [E_1, \ldots, E_n] : T[\,]}$$

(Fun Iter)
$$\frac{\Gamma, x : \mathbf{int} \vdash F : T \quad \Gamma \vdash E : \mathbf{int} \quad \mathrm{Det}(E)}{\Gamma \vdash [\mathbf{for}\ x < E \to F] : T[\,]}$$

(Fun Index)
$$\frac{\Gamma \vdash E : T[\,] \quad \Gamma \vdash F : \mathbf{int}}{\Gamma \vdash E[F] : T}$$

The interpretation of a type $T$ is the Borel-measurable set $\mathbf{V}_T$ of closed values of type $T$ (real numbers, integers, records, and so on) using the standard topology. A function $f : T \to U$ is measurable if $f^{-1}(A) \subseteq \mathbf{V}_T$ is measurable for all measurable $A \subseteq \mathbf{V}_U$; all continuous functions are measurable.

A finite measure $\mu$ over $T$ is a function from (Borel-measurable) subsets of $\mathbf{V}_T$ to the non-negative real numbers, that is countably additive, that is, $\mu(\cup_i A_i) = \Sigma_i \mu(A_i)$ if $A_1, A_2, \ldots$ are pair-wise disjoint. The finite measure $\mu$ is called a probability measure if $\mu(\mathbf{V}_T) = 1.0$. If $\mu$ is a probability measure on $T$ and $f : T \to U$ is measurable, we let $f^{-1}\mu(A) \triangleq \mu(f^{-1}(A))$. In this context $f$ is called a *random variable*.

The semantics of a closed Fun expression $E$ is a probability measure $\mathrm{P}_E$ over its return type. It is defined via a semantics of open Fun expressions (Ramsey and Pfeffer 2002) in the probability monad (Giry 1982). We write $\mathrm{P}_E$ for the probability measure corresponding to a closed expression $E$; if $\varnothing \vdash E : T$ then $\mathrm{P}_E$ is a probability measure on $\mathbf{V}_T$. If $\vdash E : T_1 * \cdots * T_n$, and for $i = 1..m$ we have $\vdash V_i : U_i$ and $F_i$ det and $x_1 : T_1, \ldots, x_n : T_n \vdash F_i : U_i$, we write $\mathrm{P}_E[x_1, \ldots, x_n \mid F_1 = V_1 \wedge \cdots \wedge F_m = V_m]$ for (a version of) the conditional probability distribution of $\mathrm{P}_E$ given $f = (V_1, \ldots, V_m)$ where $f(x_1, \ldots, x_n) = (F_1, \ldots, F_m)$.

## 4.2 Semantics of Semi-Observed Models

A model is associated with four types: a hyperparameter type $H$, a parameter type $W$, an input type $X$, and an output type $Y$.

**Model Types and Typing of Models: $Q$, $\vdash P : Q$**

$Q ::= \langle H, W, X, Y \rangle$ quadruple type of model

(Model Prim)
$$\frac{\varnothing \vdash E_h : H \quad \mathrm{Det}(E_h) \quad h : H \vdash E_w : W \quad h : H, w : W, x : X \vdash E_y : Y}{\vdash \langle E_h, (h)E_w, (h,w,x)E_y \rangle : \langle H, W, X, Y \rangle}$$

In a semi-observed model, $Y$ is a pair type, where the second component holds the latent variables of the model. Given a semi-observed model, the standard distributions are obtained as follows.

**Proposition 1.** *Given a model $P = \langle E_h, (h)E_w, (h,w,x)E_{yz} \rangle$ such that $\vdash P : \langle H, W, X, Y * Z \rangle$ the following Fun expressions denote the standard distributions:*

- *Prior:* $\mathbf{let}\ h = E_h\ \mathbf{in}\ E_w$.
- *Full sampling (where $h = V_h$, $w = V_w$, $x = V_x$):* $\mathbf{let}\ h = V_h\ \mathbf{in}\ \mathbf{let}\ w = V_w\ \mathbf{in}\ \mathbf{let}\ x = V_x\ \mathbf{in}\ E_{yz}$.
- *Sampling (where $h = V_h$, $w = V_w$, $x = V_x$):* $\mathbf{let}\ h = V_h\ \mathbf{in}\ \mathbf{let}\ w = V_w\ \mathbf{in}\ \mathbf{let}\ x = V_x\ \mathbf{in}\ \mathbf{fst}\ E_{yz}$.
- *Joint posterior (where $x = V_X$, $y = V_y$):* $\mathrm{P}_E[w, yz \mid \mathbf{fst}\ yz = V_y]$ *where* $E = \mathbf{let}\ h = E_h\ \mathbf{in}\ \mathbf{let}\ w = E_w\ \mathbf{in}\ \mathbf{let}\ x = V_x\ \mathbf{in}\ w, E_{yz}$.
- *Posterior:* $\mathbf{fst}^{-1}\mathrm{P}$ *where* P *is the joint posterior; and*
- *Posterior latent* $(\mathbf{snd} \circ \mathbf{snd})^{-1}\mathrm{P}$ *where* P *is the joint posterior.*

## 4.3 Typing and Translation of Tabular

When typing schemas, we use *binding times* to track the availability of variables. Let $\mathbf{B}$ be the set $\{\mathbf{h}, \mathbf{w}, \mathbf{xyz}\}$ of binding times ordered such that $\bot = \mathbf{h} < \mathbf{w} < \mathbf{xyz} = \top$. Here $\mathbf{h}$ stands for the (deterministic) hyperparameter phase, $\mathbf{w}$ stands for the (non-deterministic) parameter phase, and $\mathbf{xyz}$ stands for the generative phase of the computation. We use metavariables $\ell$ and $pc$ to range over $\mathbf{B}$. Informally, variables declared at one time may only be used in expressions typed at or above that time (the current time $pc$ is maintained as an additional index of the Tabular typing judgments). Binding times are also used to prevent the mention of non-deterministic parameters in expressions used as (necessarily deterministic) hyperparameters, and generative data in the construction of either hyperparameters or parameters. When translating to Fun, binding times ensure that the target program is well-scoped, and deterministic where needed.

**Tabular Levels and Typing Environments: $\ell$, $\Gamma$**

| | |
|---|---|
| $\ell, pc ::= \mathbf{h} \mid \mathbf{w} \mid \mathbf{xyz}$ | binding time |
| $\Gamma ::=$ | environment |
| $\varnothing$ | empty |
| $\Gamma, x :^{\ell} T$ | variable typing |
| $\Gamma, t : \langle\{RT\}\rangle$ | predictive row type for $t$ |

Environments declare variables with their binding time and type, and tables with their predictive row types.

**Judgments of the Tabular Type System:**

| | |
|---|---|
| $\Gamma \vdash \diamond$ | environment $\Gamma$ is well-formed |
| $\Gamma \vdash T$ | in $\Gamma$, type $T$ is well-formed |
| $\Gamma \vdash^{pc} E : T$ | in $\Gamma$ at binding time $pc$, expr. $E$ has type $T$ |
| $\Gamma \vdash^{pc} M : W, T$ | in $\Gamma$ at $pc$, model $M$ has params $W$, returns $T$ |
| $\Gamma \vdash \mathbb{T} : Q$ | in $\Gamma$, table $\mathbb{T}$ has type $Q$ |
| $\Gamma \vdash \mathbb{S} : Q$ | in $\Gamma$, schema $\mathbb{S}$ has type $Q$ |

**Formation Rules for Environments: $\Gamma \vdash \diamond$**

(Env Empty)
$$\frac{}{\varnothing \vdash \diamond}$$

(Env Var)
$$\frac{\Gamma \vdash T \quad x \notin \mathrm{dom}(\Gamma)}{\Gamma, x :^{\ell} T \vdash \diamond}$$

(Env Table)
$$\frac{\Gamma \vdash \{RT\} \quad t \notin \mathrm{dom}(\Gamma)}{\Gamma, t : \langle\{RT\}\rangle \vdash \diamond}$$

**Formation Rules for Types: $\Gamma \vdash T$**

(Type Scalar)
$$\frac{\Gamma \vdash \diamond}{\Gamma \vdash S}$$

(Type Array)
$$\frac{\Gamma \vdash T}{\Gamma \vdash T[\,]}$$

(Type Record)
$$\frac{\Gamma \vdash \diamond \quad \forall c \in C. \Gamma \vdash T_c}{\Gamma \vdash \{c : T_c\}^{c \in C}}$$

The translation of a Tabular schema to a model is performed by four judgments. Though defined relationally, the relations are partial functions on untyped terms and total functions on well-typed Tabular terms.

**Judgments of the Translation:**

| | |
|---|---|
| $E \Downarrow F$ | Tabular expression $E$ translates to Fun expr. $F$ |
| $M \Downarrow \langle E_w, (w)E \rangle$ | model $M$ translates to $\langle E_w, (w)E \rangle$ |
| $\mathbb{T} \Downarrow P$ | marked up table $\mathbb{T}$ translates to prim. model $P$ |
| $\mathbb{S} \Downarrow P$ | marked up schema $\mathbb{S}$ translates to $P$ |

**Lemma 2** (Determinacy). *If* $\mathbb{S} \Downarrow P$ *and* $\mathbb{S} \Downarrow P'$ *then* $P = P'$.

**Theorem 1** (Translation Preserves Typing).
*If* $\varnothing \vdash \mathbb{S} : Q$ *then there exists* $P$ *such that* $\mathbb{S} \Downarrow P$ *and* $\vdash P : Q$.

### 4.4 Expressions

The main subtlety when translating schemas is to support foreign keys. We use the notation $(E : \mathbf{link}(t)).c$ within Fun expressions to stand for the column $c$ of the row in table $t$ indexed by key $E$.

In particular, when constructing the model for a table $t_j$, we may dereference a foreign key of type $\mathbf{link}(t_i)$ to a previous table $t_i$ with $i < j$. For instance, in the TrueSkill schema, there is a reference from $t_2 = \mathsf{Matches}$ to $t_1 = \mathsf{Players}$. To translate such foreign keys, we arrange that for each table $t_i$ there is a global variable named $t_i$ that holds the *predictive table* for $t_i$, that is, the join of the input sub-table $x_i$, the output sub-table $y_i$, and the latent sub-table $z_i$, for each $i$. Hence, an expression $(E : \mathbf{link}(t_i)).c$ means $t_i[E].c$; for example, $(\mathsf{Player1} : \mathbf{link}(\mathsf{Players})).\mathsf{Skill}$ compiles to $\mathsf{Players}[\mathsf{Player1}].\mathsf{Skill}$.

**Typing Rules for Tabular Expressions:** $\Gamma \vdash^{pc} E : T$

(TABULAR VAR)
$$\frac{\Gamma \vdash \diamond \quad \Gamma = \Gamma_1, x :^{\ell} T, \Gamma_2 \quad \ell \leq pc}{\Gamma \vdash^{pc} x : T}$$

(TABULAR SIZEOF)
$$\frac{\Gamma \vdash^{pc} \#t : \mathbf{int} \quad t \in \mathrm{dom}(\Gamma)}{\Gamma \vdash^{pc} \mathbf{sizeof}(t) : \mathbf{int}}$$

(TABULAR DEREF)
$$\frac{\Gamma \vdash^{pc} E : \mathbf{int} \quad \mathbf{xyz} \leq pc \quad \Gamma = \Gamma', t : \langle \{d : T_d\}^{d \in C} \rangle, \Gamma'' \quad c \in C}{\Gamma \vdash^{pc} (E : \mathbf{link}(t)).c : T_c}$$

Rule (TABULAR VAR) allows a reference to $x$ only if $x$ is declared with a binding time $l \leq pc$, where $pc$ is the current binding time.

**Translation Rules for Tabular Expressions:** $E \Downarrow F$

(TRANS VAR)
$$\frac{}{x \Downarrow x}$$

(TRANS SIZEOF)
$$\frac{}{\mathbf{sizeof}(t) \Downarrow \#t}$$

(TRANS DEREF)
$$\frac{E \Downarrow F}{(E : \mathbf{link}(t)).c \Downarrow t[F].c}$$

(the remaining rules are simple homomorphic translations)

### 4.5 Model Expressions

**Typing Rules for Model Expressions:** $\Gamma \vdash^{pc} M : W, T$

(MODEL SIMPLE)
$$\frac{\Gamma \vdash^{pc} E : T}{\Gamma \vdash^{pc} E : \{\}, T}$$

(MODEL PRIM)
$$\frac{\Gamma \vdash \diamond \quad P = \langle \{R\}, (h)E_w, (h, w, x)E_y \rangle \quad \vdash P : \langle \{c : H_c\}^{c \in C}, W, \{\}, Y \rangle \quad \forall c \in C' \subseteq C.\ \ \Gamma \vdash^{\mathbf{h}} E_c : H_c \ \wedge\ \mathrm{Det}(E_c)}{\Gamma \vdash^{pc} P(c = E_c{}^{c \in C'}) : W, Y}$$

(MODEL INDEXED)
$$\frac{\Gamma \vdash^{pc} M : W, T \quad \Gamma \vdash^{pc} E_{\mathrm{index}} : \mathbf{int} \quad \Gamma \vdash^{\mathbf{h}} E_{\mathrm{size}} : \mathbf{int} \quad \mathrm{Det}(E_{\mathrm{size}})}{\Gamma \vdash^{pc} M[E_{\mathrm{index}} < E_{\mathrm{size}}] : W[], T}$$

Primitive models must have void input; we allow to only replace a part $C'$ of their hyperparameters $C$. The upper bound $E_{\mathrm{size}}$ of an indexed model has binding time $\mathbf{h}$, since it must be deterministic and the same for all rows of the table.

**Translation Rules for Model Expressions:** $M \Downarrow P$

(TRANS SIMPLE) ($w \notin \mathrm{fv}(F)$)
$$\frac{E \Downarrow F}{E \Downarrow \langle \{\}, (w)F \rangle}$$

(TRANS PRIM) ($w \notin \mathrm{fv}(E_h)$)
$$\frac{P = \langle \{c = F_c\}^{c \in C}, (h)E_w, (h, w, x)E_y \rangle \quad E_c \Downarrow E'_c\ (c \in C') \quad \hat{E}_c = \text{if } c \in C' \text{ then } E'_c \text{ else } F_c \quad E_h = \{c = \hat{E}_c\}^{c \in C}}{P(c = E_c{}^{c \in C'}) \Downarrow \langle \mathbf{let}\ h = E_h\ \mathbf{in}\ E_w, (w)\mathbf{let}\ h = E_h\ \mathbf{in}\ \mathbf{let}\ x = \{\}\ \mathbf{in}\ E_y \rangle}$$

(TRANS INDEXED) ($w \notin \mathrm{fv}(F_{\mathrm{index}})$)
$$\frac{E_{\mathrm{index}} \Downarrow F_{\mathrm{index}} \quad E_{\mathrm{size}} \Downarrow F_{\mathrm{size}} \quad M \Downarrow \langle E_w, (w)E_y \rangle}{M[E_{\mathrm{index}} < E_{\mathrm{size}}] \Downarrow \langle [\mathbf{for}\ \_ < F_{\mathrm{size}} \to E_w], (w)\mathbf{let}\ w = w[F_{\mathrm{index}}]\ \mathbf{in}\ E_y \rangle}$$

A simple model has no prior. The prior of an indexed model is an array of $F_{\mathrm{size}}$ independent samples of the prior of the underlying model. In the output, we use the prior value at index $F_{\mathrm{index}}$.

### 4.6 Tables

The typing and translation rules for tables are defined inductively and determine the semantics for the shared hyperparameter, shared parameter, and a pair of output and latent columns for a single row of the table.

**Typing Rules for Tables:** $\Gamma \vdash \mathbb{T} : Q$

(TABLE EMPTY)
$$\frac{\Gamma \vdash \diamond}{\Gamma \vdash \varnothing : \langle \{\}, \{\}, \{\}, \{\} * \{\} \rangle}$$

(TABLE HYPER) ($A = \mathbf{hyper}(E)$)
$$\frac{\varnothing \vdash^{\mathbf{h}} E : H \quad \mathrm{Det}(E) \quad \Gamma, c :^{\mathbf{h}} H \vdash \mathbb{T} : \langle \{RH\}, W, X, Y * Z \rangle}{\Gamma \vdash (c \mapsto A : H)\mathbb{T} : \langle \{c : H; RH\}, W, X, Y * Z \rangle}$$

(TABLE PARAM) ($A = \mathbf{param}(M)$)
$$\frac{\Gamma \vdash^{\mathbf{w}} M : W_{\$}, W \quad \Gamma, c :^{\mathbf{w}} W \vdash \mathbb{T} : \langle H, \{RW\}, X, Y * Z \rangle \quad c\$ \notin \mathrm{dom}(\Gamma) \cup \mathrm{dom}(\mathbb{T})}{\Gamma \vdash (c \mapsto A : W)\mathbb{T} : \langle H, \{c\$ : W_{\$}; c : W; RW\}, X, Y * Z \rangle}$$

(TABLE INPUT) ($A = \mathbf{input}$)
$$\frac{\Gamma, c :^{\mathbf{xyz}} X \vdash \mathbb{T} : \langle H, W, \{RX\}, Y * Z \rangle}{\Gamma \vdash (c \mapsto A : X)\mathbb{T} : \langle H, W, \{c : X; RX\}, Y * Z \rangle}$$

(TABLE OUTPUT) ($A = \mathbf{output}(M)$)
$$\frac{\Gamma \vdash^{\mathbf{xyz}} M : W, Y \quad \Gamma, c :^{\mathbf{xyz}} Y \vdash \mathbb{T} : \langle H, \{RW\}, X, Y * Z \rangle}{\Gamma \vdash (c \mapsto A : Y)\mathbb{T} : \langle H, \{c\$ : W; RW\}, X, \{c : Y; RY\} * Z \rangle}$$

(TABLE LATENT) ($A = \mathbf{latent}(M)$)
$$\frac{\Gamma \vdash^{\mathbf{xyz}} M : W, Z \quad \Gamma, c :^{\mathbf{xyz}} Z \vdash \mathbb{T} : \langle H, \{RW\}, X, Y * \{RZ\} \rangle}{\Gamma \vdash (c \mapsto A : Z)\mathbb{T} : \langle H, \{c\$ : W; RW\}, X, Y * \{c : Z; RZ\} \rangle}$$

Rule (TABLE HYPER) ensures that $E$ is deterministic and closed and declares $c$ at binding time $\mathbf{h}$ so it can be referenced at all binding times. Rule (TABLE PARAM) ensures that $M$ is checked at level $\mathbf{w}$ (not $pc$) so that its generative expression has no data dependencies and is safe to use at the parameter level. Rule (TABLE INPUT) extends the context with $c$ declared at $\mathbf{xyz}$. Rule (TABLE OUTPUT) extends the context with $c$ declared at $\mathbf{xyz}$ and records the types of parameter $c\$$ and output $c$ by extending the parameter and output record types of the table. Rule (TABLE LATENT) is symmetric to (TABLE OUTPUT), but instead extends the latent record type.

The translation rules for tables make use of auxiliary *let-contexts*, ranged over by $\mathscr{L}$. These denote a spine of (Fun) **let**-bindings ending in a hole $[]$, and are defined inductively as follows.

**(Core Fun) Let contexts: $\mathscr{L}$**

| | |
|---|---|
| $\mathscr{L} ::=$ | let context |
| $[]$ | hole |
| $\textbf{let } x = E \textbf{ in } \mathscr{L}$ | let binding |

The operation $\mathscr{L}[E]$ plugs the hole of a $\mathscr{L}$ with a body $E$, producing a (Fun) expression.

$$\begin{aligned} [][E] &= E \\ (\textbf{let } x = E' \textbf{ in } \mathscr{L})[E] &= \textbf{let } x = E' \textbf{ in } (\mathscr{L}[E]) \end{aligned}$$

**Translation Rules for Tables: $\mathbb{T} \Downarrow P$**

(TRANS EMPTY)

$$\dfrac{}{\varnothing \Downarrow \langle\{\},(h)\{\},(h,w,x)(\{\},\{\})\rangle}$$

(TRANS HYPER) $(c \notin \{h,w,x\})$

$$\dfrac{E \Downarrow E_h \qquad \mathbb{T} \Downarrow \langle\{R_h\},(h)E_w,(h,w,x)E\rangle}{(c \mapsto \textbf{hyper } E : T_c)\mathbb{T} \Downarrow \langle\{c = E_h, R_h\},(h)\textbf{let } c = h.c \textbf{ in } E_w,(h,w,x)\textbf{let } c = h.c \textbf{ in } E\rangle}$$

(TRANS PARAM) $(h \notin \text{fv}(E_w, E_c, c\$, c) \quad c \notin \{h,w,x\})$

$$\dfrac{M \Downarrow \langle E_w,(w_c)E_c\rangle \qquad \mathbb{T} \Downarrow \langle E_h,(h)\mathscr{L}_w[\{R_w\}],(h,w,x)E\rangle}{\begin{array}{l}(c \mapsto \textbf{param } M : T_c)\mathbb{T} \Downarrow \\ \quad \langle E_h,\ (h)\textbf{let } c\$ = E_w \textbf{ in let } c = E_c \textbf{ in } \mathscr{L}_w[\{c\$ = c\$; c = c; R_w\}], \\ \quad (h,w,x)\textbf{let } c = w.c \textbf{ in } E\rangle\end{array}}$$

(TRANS INPUT)

$$\dfrac{\mathbb{T} \Downarrow \langle E_h,(h)E_w,(h,w,x)E\rangle \qquad c \notin \{h,w,x\}}{(c \mapsto \textbf{input} : T_c)\mathbb{T} \Downarrow \langle E_h,(h)E_w,(h,w,x)\textbf{let } c = x.c \textbf{ in } E\rangle}$$

(TRANS OUTPUT) $(h \notin \text{fv}(E_w) \quad h,w,x \notin \text{fv}(E_c,c)))$

$$\dfrac{M \Downarrow \langle E_w,(w_c)E_c\rangle \quad \mathbb{T} \Downarrow \langle E_h,(h)\mathscr{L}_w[\{R_w\}],(h,w,x)\mathscr{L}_o[(\{R_y\},E_z)]\rangle}{\begin{array}{l}(c \mapsto \textbf{output } M : T_c)\mathbb{T} \Downarrow \\ \quad \langle E_h,\ (h)\textbf{let } c = E_w \textbf{ in } \mathscr{L}_w[\{c\$ = c, R_w\}], \\ \quad (h,w,x)\textbf{let } c = (\textbf{let } w_c = w.c\$ \textbf{ in } E_c) \textbf{ in } \mathscr{L}_o[(\{c = c; R_y\},E_z)]\rangle\end{array}}$$

(TRANS LATENT) $(h \notin \text{fv}(E_w) \quad h,w,x \notin \text{fv}(E_c,c))$

$$\dfrac{M \Downarrow \langle E_w,(w_c)E_c\rangle \quad \mathbb{T} \Downarrow \langle E_h,(h)\mathscr{L}_w[\{R_w\}],(h,w,x)\mathscr{L}_o[(E_y,\{R_z\})]\rangle}{\begin{array}{l}(c \mapsto \textbf{latent } M : T_c)\mathbb{T} \Downarrow \\ \quad \langle E_h,\ (h)\textbf{let } c = E_w \textbf{ in } \mathscr{L}_w[\{c\$ = c, R_w\}], \\ \quad (h,w,x)\textbf{let } c = (\textbf{let } w_c = w.c\$ \textbf{ in } E_c) \textbf{ in } \mathscr{L}_o[(E_z,\{c = c; R_z\})]\rangle\end{array}}$$

Rule (TRANS HYPER) merely extends the hyperparameter record of the remaining table and rebinds $c$ as the projection $h.t$ in the prior and gen of the model. Rule (TRANS PARAM) extends table $\mathbb{T}$'s prior with two fields for the prior and gen of $M$, and rebinds parameter $c$ as the projection $w.c$ in the gen of the row. Rule (TRANS INPUT) just binds $c$ as the projection $x.c$ of input row $x$ in the gen of the table (but does not export $c$ since it is neither output nor latent). Rule (TRANS OUTPUT) just defines $c$ as the gen of its model, whose parameter $w_c$ is obtained from $w.c\$$; $c$ is exported in the output record of the row. Rule (TRANS LATENT) is symmetric to (TRANS OUTPUT), but instead extends the latent record.

For example, here is a single-table schema for linear regression.

| LinearRegression | | | |
|---|---|---|---|
| muA | real | hyper | 0 |
| muB | real | hyper | 0 |
| A | real | param | Gaussian(muA,1) |
| B | real | param | Gaussian(muB,1) |
| X | real | input | |
| Z | real | latent | A∗X + B |
| Y | real | output | Gaussian(Z,1) |

The row semantics of this table is as follows. For readability, we inline some variable definitions. Since this table only uses simple model expressions, the \$ suffixed fields for the parameters of model expressions all contain the empty record. Modulo these redundant fields, we recover the model from Section 2.

**Model for a Row of the LinearRegression Table:**

| | |
|---|---|
| Hyper | {muA = 0; muB = 0} |
| Prior($h$) | {A\$ = {}; A = Gaussian($h$.muA, 1);<br>A\$ = {}; B = Gaussian($h$.muB, 1);<br>Z\$ = {}; Y\$ = {}} |
| Gen($h,w,x$) | **let** Z = w.A∗ x.X + w.B **in**<br>**let** Y = Gaussian(Z,1)} **in**<br>({Y=Y},{Z=Z}) |

### 4.7 Schemas

**Typing Rules for Schemas: $\Gamma \vdash \mathbb{S} : Q$**

(SCHEMA EMPTY)

$$\dfrac{\Gamma \vdash \diamond}{\Gamma \vdash \varnothing : \langle\{\},\{\},\{\},\{\} * \{\}\rangle}$$

(SCHEMA TABLE)

$$\dfrac{\begin{array}{l}\Gamma \vdash \mathbb{T} : \langle H, W, \{RX_t\}, \{RY_t\} * \{RZ_t\}\rangle \\ \Gamma, \#t :^{\mathbf{h}} \textbf{int}, t : \langle\{RX_t; RY_t; RZ_t\}\rangle \vdash \\ \quad \mathbb{S} : \langle\{RH\},\{RW\},\{RX\},\{RY\} * \{RZ\}\rangle \\ H' = \{\#t : \textbf{int}; RH\} \quad W' = \{t : W; RW\} \quad X' = \{t : \{RX_t\}[]; RX\} \\ Y' = \{t : \{RY_t\}[]; RY\} \quad Z' = \{t : \{RZ_t\}[]; RZ\}\end{array}}{\Gamma \vdash (t \mapsto \mathbb{T})\mathbb{S} : \langle H', W', X', Y' * Z'\rangle}$$

Rule (SCHEMA TABLE) uses the model type of the table to extend the context with a declaration of the table's size, $\#t$ at level $\mathbf{h}$, (($\#t$ is used in the translation of **sizeof**(t)) as well as the predictive row type of $t$: this is the union of its input, output, and latent fields. The table's default hyperparameters (of type $H$) are applied in the translation of $t$ and do not appear in the type of the schema. The rule extends the components of the schema's model type with additional fields for the table size; the parameters of the table (as a nested record); the inputs of the table (a nested *array* of records); and the pair of output and latent table records extended with fields for the output and latent *arrays* of records for $t$.

**Translation Rules for Schemas: $\mathbb{S} \Downarrow P$**

(TRANS EMPTY)

$$\dfrac{}{\varnothing \Downarrow (\{\},(h)\{\},(h,w,x)\{\})}$$

(TRANS TABLE)

$$\dfrac{\begin{array}{l}\mathbb{T} \Downarrow \langle E_h,(h_t)E_w,(h_t,w_t,x_i)\mathscr{L}_t[\{R_y\},\{R_z\}]\rangle \\ R_x = \{c = x_i.c \mid c \in \text{inputs}(\mathbb{T})\} \\ \mathbb{S} \Downarrow (\{R_h\},(h)\mathscr{L}_w[R_w],(h,w,x)\mathscr{L}_{yz}[\{S_y\},\{S_z\}] \\ E_t = \textbf{let } h_t = E_h \textbf{ in let } w_t = w.t \textbf{ in} \\ \qquad [\textbf{for } i < \#t \to \textbf{let } x_i = x.t[i] \textbf{ in } \mathscr{L}_t[\{R_x; R_y; R_z\}]] \\ E_y = [\textbf{for } i < \#t \to \{c = t[i].c\}^{c \in \text{dom}(R_y)}] \\ E_z = [\textbf{for } i < \#t \to \{c = t[i].c\}^{c \in \text{dom}(R_z)}] \\ h \notin \text{fv}(\textbf{let } h_t = E_h \textbf{ in } E_w, t, \#t) \quad h,w,x \notin \text{fv}(E_t, t, \#t)\end{array}}{\begin{array}{l}(t \mapsto \mathbb{T})\mathbb{S} \Downarrow \\ \langle\{\#t = 1, R_h\}, \\ (h)\textbf{let } t = \textbf{let } h_t = E_h \textbf{ in } E_w \textbf{ in let } \#t = h.\#t \textbf{ in } \mathscr{L}_w[\{t = t; R_w\}], \\ (h,w,x)\textbf{let } \#t = h.\#t \textbf{ in let } t = E_t \textbf{ in} \\ \qquad \mathscr{L}_{yz}[(\{t = E_y; R_y\},\{t = E_z; R_z\})]\rangle\end{array}}$$

Rule (TRANS TABLE) takes the model for the parameters and a single row of $t$ and constructs a model that draws once from the prior of $t$ then replicates $t$'s output distribution across an array of size $\#t$. The intermediate array, $E_t$, contains the predictive table for $t$, merging the input, output and latent sub-records of $t$ as single records. Expressions $E_y$ and $E_z$ are used to reshuffle the array of merged records into separate arrays of output and latent sub-records. The rule extends $\mathbb{S}$'s hyperparameter record with a default binding for $\#t$ (with arbitrary value 1); table sizes must be consistently overriden before inference.

***Translation examples*** To illustrate our schema translation and our treatment of foreign keys, here is the translation of TrueSkill, rewritten a little for readability: first, the two row models for the two tables, followed by the model of the whole schema.

**Model for a Row of Table** Players: $P_1$

```
Hyper        {}
Prior(h)     {Skill$ = {}}
Gen(h,w,x)   let Skill =Gaussian(25,0.01) in
             ({},{Skill = Skill})
```

**Model for a Row of Table** Matches: $P_2$

```
Hyper        {}
Prior(h)     {Perf1$ = {}; Perf2$ = {}; Win1$ = {}}
Gen(h,w,x)   let Perf1=Gaussian(Players[x.Player1].Skill,1) in
             let Perf2=Gaussian(Players[x.Player2].Skill,1) in
             let Win1= Perf1 > Perf2 in
             ({Win1 = Win1},{Perf1 = Perf1; Perf2 = Perf2})
```

**Model for the TrueSkill Schema:**

```
Hyper        {#Players = 1, #Matches = 1}
Prior(h)     {Players = P1.Prior(P1.Hyper),
              Matches = P2.Prior(P2.Hyper)}
Gen(h,w,x)
let Players = [for i <h.#Players →
    let Skill = Gaussian(25,0.01) in
    {Skill = Skill}]
let Matches = [for i <h.#Matches →
    let Player1 = x.Matches[i].Player1 in
    let Player2 = x.Matches[i].Player2 in
    let Perf1=Gaussian(Players[Player1].Skill,1) in
    let Perf2=Gaussian(Players[Player2].Skill,1) in
    let Win1= Perf1 > Perf2 in
    ({Player1 = Player1; Player2 = Player2;
      Win1 = Win1; Perf1 = Perf1; Perf2 = Perf2}) ]
({ Players = [for i < h.#Players → {}];
   Matches = [for i < h.#Matches →
             {Win1 = Matches[i].Win1}]},
 { Players = [for i < h.#Players → {Skill = Players[i].Skill}];
   Matches = [for i < h.#Matches →
   {Perf1 = Matches[i].Perf1; Perf2 = Matches[i].Perf2}}])
```

### 4.8 A Reference Learner for Query-by-Latent-Column

We conclude with a *learner API*, a programming interface for query-by-latent-column: the API allows a user to accumulate a dataset split into input and observed databases. To perform queries, we bundle a database and a schema into a *learner* $L = (d \mid \mathbb{S})$ where $d = (d_x, d_y)$ and $d_x$ is the input database and $d_y$ is the observed database. (We assume the types of $d$ and $\mathbb{S}$ match, as discussed in the next section.) To pick out the sizes of tables in a database, we let $\#(\{t_1 = B_1; \ldots; t_n = B_n\}) \triangleq \{\#t_1 = |B_1|; \ldots; \#t_n = |B_n|\}$. We support the following functional API.

- Let $L_0(\mathbb{S})$ be the *empty learner*, that is, $\mathbb{S}$ plus a pair of databases with the right table names but no table rows.
- Let $\mathsf{train}(L, (d'_x, d'_y))$ be $L' = ((d_x + d'_x, d_y + d'_y) \mid \mathbb{S})$ where $+$ is concatenation of arrays in records, and $L = ((d_x, d_y) \mid \mathbb{S})$.
- Let $\mathsf{params}(L)$ be the posterior distribution $p(w \mid d, h)$ induced by $P$, where $L = (d \mid \mathbb{S})$, $P$ models $\mathbb{S}$, and $h = \#(d_x)$.
- Let $\mathsf{latents}(L)$ be the posterior latent distribution $p(z \mid d, h)$ induced by $P$, where $L = (d \mid \mathbb{S})$, $P$ models $\mathbb{S}$, and $h = \#(d_x)$.

Compared to the reference learner of Gordon et al. (2013a), this new API can learn latent outputs since it works on semi-observed models. Our current implementation uses Infer.NET Fun to compute approximate marginal forms of the posterior distributions on the database parameter and latent database, and persists them to the relational store. The API allows an incremental implementation, where the abstract state $L$ is represented by a distribution over the parameters and latent variables, computed after each call to train. Our current implementation does not support this optimization, maintains the whole dataset $d$, and does inference from scratch when necessary. The incremental formulation of our learner is consistent with the Algebraic Classifier formulation of Izbicki (2013), which promises reductions in computational complexity for cross-validation and enable efficient online and parallel training algorithms based on the monoidal or group structure of such learners.

Now that we have schema typing and a semantics of schemas as models, we can perform inference as follows. A learner $L = (d_x, d_y \mid \mathbb{S})$ is queryable if $\vdash \mathbb{S} : \langle H, W, X, Y * Z \rangle$ and $\varnothing \vdash d_x : X$ and $\varnothing \vdash d_y : Y$, and for all tables $t_i \in \mathrm{dom}(\mathbb{S})$ we have $|d_x.t_i| = |d_y.t_i| \geq 1$. In particular, the empty learner is not queryable, since it contains empty tables. We can now implement a latent column query.

**Theorem 2.** *If $L = (d_x, d_y \mid \mathbb{S})$ is queryable, there is a closed Fun expression $E(d_x)$ such that if $\mu \triangleq \mathrm{P}_{E(d_x)}\left[w, yz \mid \mathbf{fst}\ yz = d_y\right]$ then*

(1) $\mathsf{params}(L) = \mathbf{fst}^{-1}\mu$; *and*
(2) $\mathsf{latents}(L) = (\mathbf{snd} \circ \mathbf{snd})^{-1}\mu$.

*Proof:* Assume that $\mathbb{S} \Downarrow \langle E_h, (h)E_w, (h,w,x)E_{yz} \rangle$, and let expression $E(d_x) \triangleq \mathbf{let}\ h = \#(d_x)\ \mathbf{in}\ \mathbf{let}\ w = E_w\ \mathbf{in}\ \mathbf{let}\ x = d_x\ \mathbf{in}\ w, E_{yz}$. By Proposition 1, $\mu$ as above yields the sought distributions. ∎

## 5. Outline of Practical Implementation

Our implementation builds on the model-learner pattern of Gordon et al. (2013a), in which models are represented as records of type-indexed F# quotations representing typed Fun expressions. Our initial Tabular implementation generates such strongly-typed models. This target confers two advantages: the quotation fragments are compact yet statically checked for type correctness; the resulting terms are easily JIT-compiled to produce efficient sampling code.

For clarity, the semantics in Section 4 splits compilation into type-checking followed by untyped translation. To create strongly-typed quotations, we need to convince F#'s type checker that our dynamically constructed quotations are composed in a statically safe manner. The most direct way to do so is to re-structure the separate typing and translation judgments as single elaboration judgments that couple type-checking with translation. The F# rendition of this idea is a triple of polymorphic functions that represent the typing contexts as a pair of (nested) tuples. Contexts are extended as required by using polymorphic recursion in recursive calls to elaboration. The output of elaboration is a value of existential type containing both the target type and the target translation of the source term. Since type variables have accurate run-time representations in .NET, we can directly compare the types of generated sub-expressions as needed, avoiding the need to maintain separate type representations.

| | | | |
|---|---|---|---|
| **Participants** | | | |
| Ability | real | latent | Gaussian(0.0,1.0) |
| **Questions** | | | |
| Answer | int | latent | DiscreteUniform(8) |
| Difficulty | real | latent | Gaussian(0.0,1.0) |
| Discrimination | real | latent | Gamma(5.0,0.2) |
| **QuestionsTrain** | | | |
| QuestionID | link(Questions) | input | |
| Answer | int | output | QuestionID.Answer |
| **Responses** | | | |
| ParticipantID | link(Participants) | input | |
| QuestionID | link(Questions) | input | |
| Advantage | real | latent | DB(ParticipantID.Ability − QuestionID.Difficulty,0.2) |
| Know | bool | latent | Probit(Advantage,QuestionID.Discrimination) |
| Guess | int | latent | DiscreteUniform(8) |
| Response | int | latent | if Know then QuestionID.Answer else Guess |
| **ResponsesTrain** | | | |
| ResponseID | link(Responses) | input | |
| Response | int | output | ResponseID.Response |

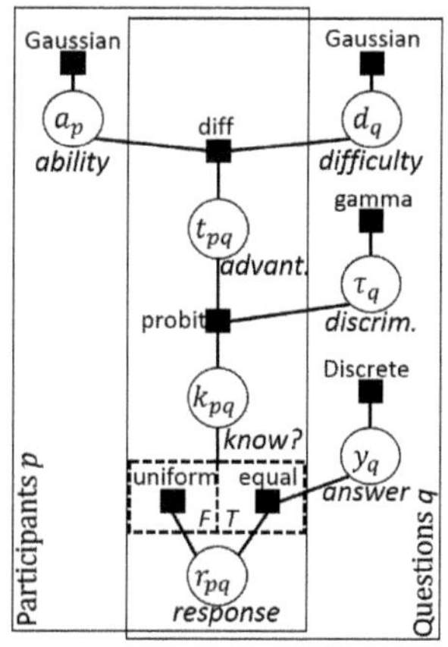


**Figure 1.** The DARE model in Tabular and factor-graph notation. The model is implemented in annotations to the three main tables Participants, Questions, and Responses. Tables QuestionsTrain and ResponsesTrain provide a mechanism for missing data.

## 6. Case Study: Intelligence Testing

Tabular has been designed to make the paradigm of model-based machine learning (Bishop 2013) usable for practitioners who are not machine learning experts. We describe a case study of data analysis using Tabular based on a dataset from intelligence testing.

Our case study relies on models first published by Bachrach et al. (2012) and data provided by the Cambridge Psychometrics Centre, based on testing material by Pearson Assessment. We use a dataset of responses to a standard multiple-choice intelligence test called Raven's Standard Progressive Matrices (SPM). The test consists of sixty questions, each comprising a matrix of shapes with one element missing and eight possible answers, exactly one of which is correct. The sample consists of 121 subjects who filled SPM for its standardization in the British market in 2006. The factor graph for the full Difficulty-Ability-Response (DARE) model is shown in Figure 1. Responses and true answers may or may not be observed.

Figure 1 also depicts the full DARE model in Tabular. Each participant is characterized by a latent Ability. Each question is characterized by a (true) Answer, a Difficulty and a Discrimination parameter. Responses depend on ParticipantID and QuestionID. Under the model, an Advantage variable is calculated as the difference between ability of participant and difficulty of question. The Boolean variable Know, which represents whether the participant knows the answer or not, is modelled as a probit over Advantage with Discrimination as the dispersion parameter. DB returns its first argument, and is a pragma to the underlying inference algorithm, to apply a damping factor for better convergence. Guess represents a random guess from a uniform distribution over all possible responses. The participant's Response is taken to be the question Answer if Know is true and Guess otherwise. The model relies on two sources of observed data: correct answers to the questions and responses provided by students. A subset of correct answers can be provided through the table QuestionsTrain. A subset of given responses can be provided through the table ResponsesTrain.

Note that there are simplified versions of the full DARE model in which a) only the student's ability is modelled (A model) or b) the students' abilities and the questions' difficulties are modelled (DA model). The model is run once to answer two types of queries given a subset of the true answers and a subset of given responses: i) Infer the missing correct answers to questions and ii) Infer the missing responses of students.

Figure 2 shows how the Tabular implementation differs from the Infer.NET implementation on a sample run where 30% of responses and 30% of true answers are unobserved. The data contained 121 participants, 60 questions, 41 training questions, 7260 responses and 5082 training responses. The inference results of Infer.NET and Tabular based implementations are very similar. They differ slightly because of differences in the way our compiler translated the Tabular formulation into Infer.NET code from the direct implementation by an expert. However, the Infer.NET code including the necessary data transformation code is much longer than the succinct and readable Tabular code that was added to the existing data schema to describe the same model. Tabular's excessively high compilation times are not due to the Tabular to Fun translation, which takes less than one second for each model, but to a flaw in the Fun compiler: Fun inlines all data before compiling, a convenient but unnecessary measure avoided by Infer.NET. To demonstrate that the excessive compile times can be reduced, we prototyped a second compiler, Tabular II, that translates Tabular programs directly to Infer.NET. On the DARE case study Tabular II improves compile times by two orders of magnitude, and inference time by up to one order of magnitude, yielding performance that is more competitive with handwritten Infer.NET (Figure 2).

## 7. Query-by-Missing-Value

Inference of latent columns requires that all output columns contain a valid value at each row. However, many real datasets contain missing values. *Query-by-missing-value* infers the posterior probability of missing values in output columns, conditioned on observed values actually present in the database. In a missing-values query, each attribute is either *known*, or *missing*; we use ? to denote missing values.

**Query-by-Missing-Value Database:** $d^?$

| | |
|---|---|
| $V^? ::= ? \mid V$ | missing or known value |
| $r^? ::= \{c_1 = V_1^?, \dots, c_n = V_n^?\}$ | query-by-missing-value row |
| $R^? ::= [r_0^?; \dots; r_n^?]$ | query-by-missing-value table |
| $d^? ::= \{t_1 = R_1^?, \dots, t_n = R_n^?\}$ | query-by-missing-value database |

Let a *missing-values learner* $(d_x, d_y^? \mid \mathbb{S})$ be a learner where $d_x$ is a normal value and $d_y^?$ is a query-by-missing-value database. Such a learner can be queryable (as defined in Section 4.8), where we let $\Gamma \vdash ? : T$ for any $T$ and $\Gamma$.

The result of inference on a queryable missing-values learner is the joint posterior distribution for all the ? entries in $d_y^?$, in addition to the latent columns and the parameters of each table. For a formal

| Model | Language | LOC Data | LOC Model | LOC Inference | LOC total | Compile seconds | Infer seconds | Model log evidence | Avg. (log) prob. test responses. | Avg. (log) prob. test answers. |
|---|---|---|---|---|---|---|---|---|---|---|
| A | Tabular | 0 | 17 | 0 | 17 | 126 | 10 | -7499.74 | (-1.432),0.239 | (-3.435),0.032 |
| A | Tabular II | | | | | 0.41 | 1.47 | -7499.74 | (-1.432),0.239 | (-3.424),0.033 |
| A | Infer.NET | 73 | 45 | 20 | 138 | 0.32 | 0.38 | -7499.74 | (-1.432),0.239 | (-3.425),0.033 |
| DA | Tabular | 0 | 18 | 0 | 18 | 145 | 11 | -5932.80 | (-1.118),0.327 | (-0.699),0.497 |
| DA | Tabular II | | | | | 0.40 | 1.54 | -5933.52 | (-1.118),0.327 | (-0.739),0.478 |
| DA | Infer.NET | 73 | 47 | 21 | 141 | 0.34 | 0.43 | -5933.25 | (-1.118),0.327 | (-0.724),0.485 |
| DARE | Tabular | 0 | 19 | 0 | 19 | 163 | 16 | -5823.01 | (-1.119),0.327 | (-0.551),0.576 |
| DARE | Tabular II | | | | | 0.42 | 6.46 | -5820.40 | (-1.119),0.327 | (-0.528),0.590 |
| DARE | Infer.NET | 73 | 49 | 22 | 144 | 0.37 | 2.8 | -5820.40 | (-1.119),0.327 | (-0.528),0.590 |

**Figure 2.** Comparison of Tabular and Infer.NET implementations of different variants of the DARE model for multiple-choice questionnaires (machine configuration: DELL Precision T3600, Intel(R) Xeon(R) CPU E5-1620 with 16GB RAM, Windows 8 Enterprise and .NET 4.0).

definition, we need to compute the observations of $d_y^?$, that is, the entries in $d_y^?$ present in the database and their values.

**Observations of a missing-values query:** $\mathsf{O}_E(\cdot)$

$$\mathsf{O}_E(?) \triangleq \textbf{true} \qquad \mathsf{O}_E(V) \triangleq E = V$$

$$\begin{aligned} \mathsf{O}_E(\{c_i = V_i^?\}^{i \in 1..n}) &\triangleq \textstyle\bigwedge_{i\in 1..n} \mathsf{O}_{E.c_i}(V_i^?) \\ \mathsf{O}_E([r_i^?]^{i \in 0..n}) &\triangleq \textstyle\bigwedge_{i\in 0..n} \mathsf{O}_{E[i]}(r_i^?) \\ \mathsf{O}_E(\{t_i = R_i^?\}^{i \in 1..n}) &\triangleq \textstyle\bigwedge_{i\in 1..n} \mathsf{O}_{E.c_i}(R_i^?) \end{aligned}$$

If $L(d_x, d_y^? \mid \mathbb{S})$ is a queryable missing-values learner and $\mathbb{S} \Downarrow \langle E_h, (h)E_w, (h,w,x)E_{yz}\rangle$ then the prior distribution of $L$ is given by $\mathrm{P}_E$ where $E = \textbf{let } h = \#(d_x) \textbf{ in let } w = E_w \textbf{ in let } x = d_x \textbf{ in } w, E_{yz}$, and the joint posterior is the conditional probability distribution $\mathrm{P}_E\left[w, yz \mid \mathsf{O}_{\textbf{fst}\ yz}(d_y^?)\right]$.

***Example of Query-by-Missing-Value*** Inferno is an experimental embedding of probabilistic inference in a spreadsheet (`http://research.microsoft.com/inferno/`). Given a probabilistic model for the whole spreadsheet, Inferno can fill in the missing values of empty cells, and also detect outliers: cells whose values are far from what is predicted by the model.

An Inferno spreadsheet can be considered as a queryable learner, where each spreadsheet column is an output but may have missing values, and there is an additional latent column for each row. The Tabular schema below corresponds to the Generalized Gaussian model produced by Inferno on a three-column table. We here consider only real-valued columns; other data types such as Booleans and integers can also be encoded as (vectors of) real numbers with appropriate (probabilistically invertible) link functions.

| GG | | | |
|---|---|---|---|
| V | vector | latent | CVectorGaussian(Ncols=3) |
| X0 | real | output | V[0] |
| X1 | real | output | V[1] |
| X2 | real | output | V[2] |

(The library model CVectorGaussian is akin to CGaussian, but outputs vectors from a multivariate Gaussian distribution with Gaussian and Wishart priors.)

The query is a table *GG* containing the spreadsheet data, with empty cells replaced by ?, such as the following.

GG

| ID | X0 | X1 | X2 |
|---|---|---|---|
| 0 | 1.0 | 2.1 | 2.9 |
| 1 | 2.1 | ? | 6.3 |
| 2 | ? | 2.7 | 3.5 |

Here $\mathsf{O}_y(GG) = y[0].\mathsf{X0} = 1.0 \wedge y[0].\mathsf{X1} = 2.1 \wedge \cdots \wedge y[2].\mathsf{X1} = 2.7 \wedge y[2].\mathsf{X2} = 3.5$.

***Translating Query-by-Missing-Value to Query-by-Latent-Column*** Missing-values queries can be answered by translating them to a latent column query and performing inference on the latter. The key idea is to create a new table for each output column of the original table, that contains just the known values in that column. In the translation of the orginal table, each output column is simply turned into a latent column. For example, the Inferno GG model translates to the following tables.

| GG' | | | |
|---|---|---|---|
| V | vector | latent | CVectorGaussian(Ncols=3) |
| X0 | real | latent | V[0] |
| X1 | real | latent | V[1] |
| X2 | real | latent | V[2] |
| **X0** | | | |
| R | link(GG') | input | |
| V | real | output | R.X0 |
| **X1** | | | |
| R | link(GG') | input | |
| V | real | output | R.X1 |
| **X2** | | | |
| R | link(GG') | input | |
| V | real | output | R.X2 |

Above, the query tables (X0, X1, and X2) each contain a value column V and a reference column R, which denotes the row from which the value came. Since the GG' table contains no input columns, all the data is in the query tables.

X0

| ID | R | V |
|---|---|---|
| 0 | 0 | 1.0 |
| 1 | 1 | 2.1 |

X1

| | R | V |
|---|---|---|
| 0 | 0 | 2.1 |
| 1 | 2 | 2.7 |

X2

| | R | V |
|---|---|---|
| 0 | 0 | 2.9 |
| 1 | 1 | 6.3 |
| 2 | 2 | 3.5 |

***Formal Translation*** We fix a queryable missing-values learner $(d_x, d_y^? \mid \mathbb{S})$ where $\mathbb{S} = (t_j \mapsto \mathbb{T}_j)^{j \in 1..m}$ and each table $\mathbb{T}_j = (c_{ji} \mapsto A_{ji} : T_{ji})^{i \in 1..n_j}$. Let $O_j = \{i \in 1..j \mid A_{ji} = \mathsf{O}(\_)\}$.

We let $[\![\mathsf{Observed}(M)]\!] \triangleq \mathsf{Latent}(M)$, and $[\![A]\!] \triangleq A$ otherwise. We then translate the schema $\mathbb{S}$ as follows.

$$\begin{aligned} \mathbb{T}_{ji} &\triangleq (\mathsf{R} \mapsto \mathsf{Input} : \textbf{int}, \\ &\qquad \mathsf{V} \mapsto \mathsf{Observed}((\mathsf{R} : \textbf{link}(t_j)).c_{ji}) : T_{ji}) \text{ if } i \in O_j \\ \mathbb{T}'_j &\triangleq (c_{ji} \mapsto [\![A_{ji}]\!] : T_{ji})^{i \in 1..n_j} \\ \mathbb{S}' &\triangleq (t_j \mapsto \mathbb{T}'_j, (t_{ji} \mapsto \mathbb{T}_{ji})^{i \in O_j})^{j \in 1..m} \end{aligned}$$

To translate the database, we first translate the observations in $d_y^?$.

$$\begin{aligned} Rx_{ji} &\triangleq [\{\mathsf{R} = k\} \mid d_y^?.t_j[k].c_{ji} \neq ?]^{k \in 0..|d_y^?.t_j|-1} \\ Ry_{ji} &\triangleq [\{\mathsf{V} = d_y^?.t_j[k].c_i\} \mid d_y^?.t_j[k].c_{ji} \neq ?]^{k \in 0..|d_y^?.t_j|-1}. \end{aligned}$$

The translations of the original tables have no observed values.

$$Ry_j \triangleq [\{\}]^{k \in 0..|d_x.t_j|-1}$$

Finally, we can combine these tables into a new database $d'_x, d'_y$.

$$d'_x \triangleq \{t_j \mapsto d_x.t_j; \{t_{ji} \mapsto Rx_{ji}\}^{i \in O_j}\}^{j \in 1..m}$$
$$d'_y \triangleq \{t_j \mapsto Ry_j;\ \{t_{ji} \mapsto Ry_{ji}\}^{i \in O_j}\}^{j \in 1..m}$$

**Lemma 3.** *If $(d_x, d_y^? \mid \mathbb{S})$ is a queryable missing-values learner, then $(d'_x, d'_y \mid \mathbb{S}')$ as defined above is a queryable learner.*

To answer the missing-values query using the results of inference for the translated learner, we need to go from an inferred distribution for the translated schema $\mathbb{S}'$ to a distribution for the original schema $\mathbb{S}$. This is done by the function $I$ defined below.

$$I(w,(\_,z)) = (\{t_j = w.t_j\}^{j \in 1..m},$$
$$(\{t_j = [\{c_{ji} = z.t_j[k].c_{ji}\}^{i \in O_j}]^{k \in 0..|d_y^?.t_j|-1}\}^{j \in 1..m},$$
$$\{t_j = [\{c_{ji} = z.t_j[k].c_{ji}\}^{i \in L_j}]^{k \in 0..|d_y^?.t_j|-1}\}^{j \in 1..m})).$$

We can now show that the translation is correct: it reduces query-by-missing-value to query-by-latent-column.

**Theorem 3.** *Let $L = (d_x, d_y^? \mid \mathbb{S})$ be a queryable missing-values learner. Let $L' = (d'_x, d'_y \mid \mathbb{S}')$ as defined above, and let $\mu$ be the semantics of the latent column query on $L'$ as given in Theorem 2. Then $I^{-1}\mu$ is a version of the joint posterior conditional distribution $\mathrm{P}_E\left[w, yz \mid \mathsf{O}_{\mathbf{fst}\ yz}(d_y^?)\right]$ of $L$.*

*Proof:* (*sketch*) The compilation merely adds deterministic data and copies of random variables, which are then ignored by $I$. ■

As an optimization, an implementation might only translate observed columns where some data is missing in the current database into new tables. In the example above, there are no missing values in column X2 in the database, so it can remain observed in $GG'$, and no new table needs to be created for its contents.

***User/Movie/Rating Recommender*** Recall the User/Movie/Rating Schema of Section 3.2. Given existing tables of users, movies, and ratings, suppose we wish to recommend to user $i$ movies that they are likely to rate with five stars. To do so, we first modify the annotation on the movie column of the Rating table, adding a uniform per-row prior distribution.

| Rating | | | |
|---|---|---|---|
| u | **link**(User) | **input** | |
| m | **link**(Movie) | **output** | DiscreteUniform(SizeOf(Movie)) |
| Score | **int** | **output** | CDiscrete(N=5)[u.z,m.z] |

We then add a single row $\{\mathsf{u} = i;\ \mathsf{m} = ?;\ \mathsf{Score} = 5\}$ to the existing data in the Rating table, denoting that user $i$ has rated an unknown movie with 5 stars. This missing-values query is then translated to a corresponding latent column query in the manner defined above. Inference returns a discrete distribution over movie IDs for the missing value. Finally, high probability IDs can be selected for recommendation to the user.

In a variation of this query, we can weight the results by how many people have seen (that is, rated) each movie. To this end, we add interdependence between rows (a shared frequency prior) by instead using the model CDiscrete(N=SizeOf(Movie)) for the movie column, and then proceed as above.

## 8. Related work

***Probabilistic Programming Languages*** There is by now a number of probabilistic programming languages, that differ in their target audience, expressive power, performance, and philosophy. BUGS (Bayesian Inference using Gibbs sampling) (Gilks et al. 1994) is a simple language for specifying probabilistic models that allows for inference using Gibbs sampling. It is widely used in the Bayesian community, but so far does not scale to large datasets. Microsoft Research's Infer.NET (Minka et al. 2012) achieves better scalabililty through support of deterministic approximate inference algorithms such as expectation propagation and variational message passing. Church (Goodman et al. 2008) is a relatively new probabilistic programming language based on Lisp, which allows for recursion and enables non-parametric Bayesian models through memoization. Furthermore, there are languages like IBAL (Pfeffer 2007) and Figaro (Pfeffer 2009), which incorporate decision-theoretic concepts as well. FACTORIE (McCallum et al. 2009) is an imperative framework for constructing graphical models in the form of factor graphs, used mostly for information extraction. All these languages follow the traditional paradigm of separating the code from the data schema and hence make it necessary to replicate the data schema within the language and to import the data from a database. On the other hand, Tabular is focused on learning from relational data, and does not directly address some of the emerging application areas of probabilistic programming such as vision as inverse graphics (Mansinghka et al. 2013; Wingate et al. 2011), or decision making for security (Mardziel et al. 2011).

***Probabilistic Databases*** Probabilistic databases represent a line of research in which the database community is concerned with the question of how to handle uncertain knowledge in relational databases (see, for example, Dalvi et al. (2009)). Typically, the assumption is made that each tuple is only in the database with a given probability, and that the presence of different tuples are independent events. The resulting probabilistic database can be interpreted in terms of the possible worlds semantics. It is further assumed that the probability values associated with each tuple are provided by the data collector, for example, from knowledge about measuring errors or from probabilistic models outside the probabilistic database. The main technical difficulty is to evaluate queries against probabilistic databases because despite the simplistic independence assumption on the presence of tuples, complex queries involving logical and aggregation operators can lead to difficult inference problems. This is also the main difference to the Tabular approach: whereas probabilistic databases work with concrete probabilities, Tabular works with non-probabilistic database schemas containing simple tuples (possibly with missing values) and allows building probabilistic models based on that data. In contrast to probabilistic database systems Tabular is thus compatible with the vast majority of existing relational datasets.

***Statistical Relational Learning*** Statistical Relational Learning operates in domains that exhibit both uncertainty and relational structure (see Getoor and Taskar (2007) for an excellent overview). Several contributions focus on combining probability and first-order logic, such as Bayesian Logic (BLOG) (Milch et al. 2005) which allows reasoning about unknown objects or Bayesstore (Wang et al. 2008), which bridges the world of probabilistic databases and statistical relational learning. Tabular is more closely related to work that makes direct use of data in a relational database schema such as Getoor et al. (2007), Heckerman et al. (2007), and Neville and Jensen (2007). Tabular is based on directed graphical models, distinguishing it from Markov Logic (Domingos and Richardson 2004). Tabular was also inspired by a concept called PQL (Van Gael 2011) which augments the SQL query language with statements that construct a factor graph aligned with a given database schema. In summary, Tabular can be viewed as a language that enables the construction of statistical relational models directly from a schema, but goes beyond prior work in this field in that it allows the introduction of latent variables and models continuous as well as discrete variables.

Tabular was directly inspired by the question of finding a textual notation for the factor graphs generated by InfernoDB (Singh and Graepel 2012) which constructs a hierarchical mixture-based graphical model in Infer.NET (Minka et al. 2012) from an arbitrary relational schema. CrossCat (Shafto et al. 2006) is a related model, which handles single tables with mixed types (real, integer, bool). With Tabular, these types of model can be implemented in a few lines of code, and we envisage the automatic synthesis of a Tabular program that best models a given relational dataset, similar to the work of Grosse et al. (2012) on matrix decompositions.

## 9. Conclusions

We propose *schema-driven probabilistic programming* as a new principle of programming language design. The idea is to design a probabilistic modelling language by starting with a database schema and enriching it with notations for describing random variables, their probability distributions and interdependencies, how they relate to data matching the schema, and what is to be inferred.

## Acknowledgments

Conversations about this work with Chris Bishop, Lucas Bordeaux, John Bronskill, Tom Minka, and John Winn were invaluable. Misha Aizatulin made many contributions to the Fun system on which this work depends. Marcin Szymczak and Danny Tarlow commented on a draft. We would like to thank John Rust and Michal Kosinski from the Cambridge Psychometrics Centre as well as Pearson Assessments for providing the IQ dataset for research purposes.

## References

Y. Bachrach, T. Graepel, T. Minka, and J. Guiver. How to grade a test without knowing the answers - a Bayesian graphical model for adaptive crowdsourcing and aptitude testing. In Proc. *ICML '12*, Omnipress 2012.

S. Bhat, J. Borgström, A. D. Gordon, and C. V. Russo. Deriving probability density functions from probabilistic functional programs. In Proc. *TACAS '13*, volume 7795 of *LNCS*, pages 508–522. Springer, 2013.

C. M. Bishop. Model-based machine learning. *Philosophical Transactions of the Royal Society A: Mathematical, Physical and Engineering Sciences*, 371(1984), 2013.

J. Borgström, A. D. Gordon, M. Greenberg, J. Margetson, and J. Van Gael. Measure transformer semantics for Bayesian machine learning. In Proc. *ESOP'11*, volume 6602 of *LNCS*, pages 77–96. Springer, 2011. Download available at `http://research.microsoft.com/fun`.

N. N. Dalvi, C. Ré, and D. Suciu. Probabilistic databases: diamonds in the dirt. *Commun. ACM*, 52(7):86–94, 2009.

P. Domingos and M. Richardson. Markov logic: A unifying framework for statistical relational learning. In Proc. *SRL2004*, pages 49–54, 2004.

L. Getoor and B. Taskar, editors. *Introduction to Statistical Relational Learning*. The MIT Press, 2007.

L. Getoor, N. Friedman, D. Koller, A. Pfeffer, and B. Taskar. Probabilistic relational models. In Getoor and Taskar (2007).

W. R. Gilks, A. Thomas, and D. J. Spiegelhalter. A language and program for complex Bayesian modelling. *The Statistician*, 43:169–178, 1994.

M. Giry. A categorical approach to probability theory. In B. Banaschewski, editor, *Categorical Aspects of Topology and Analysis*, volume 915 of *Lecture Notes in Mathematics*, pages 68–85. Springer, 1982.

N. Goodman, V. K. Mansinghka, D. M. Roy, K. Bonawitz, and J. B. Tenenbaum. Church: a language for generative models. In Proc. *UAI'08*, pages 220–229. AUAI Press, 2008.

A. D. Gordon, M. Aizatulin, J. Borgström, G. Claret, T. Graepel, A. Nori, S. Rajamani, and C. Russo. A model-learner pattern for Bayesian reasoning. In Proc. *POPL '13*, pages 403–416, ACM Press, 2013a.

A. D. Gordon, T. Graepel, N. Rolland, C. Russo, J. Borgström, and J. Guiver. Tabular: A schema-driven probabilistic programming language. Technical Report MSR-TR-2013-118, Microsoft Research, 2013b.

R. Grosse, R. Salakhutdinov, W. T. Freeman, and J. B. Tenenbaum. Exploiting compositionality to explore a large space of model structures. In Proc. *UAI '12*, pages 306–315. AUAI Press, 2012.

P. Hanrahan. Analytic database technologies for a new kind of user: the data enthusiast. In Proc. *SIGMOD '12*, pages 577–578. ACM, 2012.

D. Heckerman, C. Meek, and D. Koller. Probabilistic Entity-Relationship Models, PRMs, and Plate Models. In Getoor and Taskar (2007).

R. Herbrich, T. Minka, and T. Graepel. Trueskill$^{tm}$: A Bayesian skill rating system. In Proc. *NIPS'06*, pages 569–576, MIT Press, 2007.

M. Izbicki. Algebraic classifiers: a generic approach to fast cross-validation, online training, and parallel training. In Proc. *ICML 2013*, *JMLR W&CP* 28(3):648-656, 2013.

O. Kiselyov and C. Shan. Embedded probabilistic programming. In Proc. *DSL '09*, volume 5658 of *LNCS*, pages 360–384. Springer, 2009.

D. Koller and N. Friedman. *Probabilistic Graphical Models*. The MIT Press, 2009.

V. K. Mansinghka, T. D. Kulkarni, Y. N. Perov, and J. B. Tenenbaum. Approximate Bayesian image interpretation using generative probabilistic graphics programs. To appear in Proc. *NIPS'13*. Available at `http://arxiv.org/abs/1307.0060`, 2013.

P. Mardziel, S. Magill, M. Hicks, and M. Srivatsa. Dynamic enforcement of knowledge-based security policies. In Proc. *CSF'11*, pages 114–128. IEEE Computer, 2011.

A. McCallum, K. Schultz, and S. Singh. Factorie: Probabilistic programming via imperatively defined factor graphs. In Proc. *NIPS'09*, pages 1249–1257. Curran Associates, 2009.

B. Milch, B. Marthi, S. J. Russell, D. Sontag, D. L. Ong, and A. Kolobov. BLOG: Probabilistic models with unknown objects. In Proc. *Probabilistic, Logical and Relational Learning — A Further Synthesis*, 2005.

T. Minka and J. M. Winn. Gates. In Proc. *NIPS'08*, pages 1073–1080. MIT Press, 2008.

T. Minka, J. Winn, J. Guiver, and D. Knowles. Infer.NET 2.5, 2012. Microsoft Research Cambridge. http://research.microsoft.com/infernet.

J. Neville and D. Jensen. Relational dependency networks. *Journal of Machine Learning Research*, 8(8):653–692, 2007.

K. Nowicki and T. A. B. Snijders. Estimation and prediction for stochastic blockstructures. *J. Amer. Statist. Assoc.*, 96:1077–1087, 2001.

A. Pfeffer. The design and implementation of IBAL: A general-purpose probabilistic language. In Getoor and Taskar (2007).

A. Pfeffer. Figaro: An object-oriented probabilistic programming language. Technical report, Charles River Analytics, 2009.

N. Ramsey and A. Pfeffer. Stochastic lambda calculus and monads of probability distributions. In Proc. *POPL '02*, pages 154–165. ACM, 2002.

P. Shafto, C. Kemp, V. Mansinghka, M. Gordon, and J. B. Tenenbaum. Learning cross-cutting systems of categories. In Proc. *CogSci '06*, pages 2146–2151. Cognitive Science Society, 2006.

S. Singh and T. Graepel. Compiling relational database schemata into probabilistic graphical models. *CoRR*, abs/1212.0967, 2012.

J. Van Gael. PQL—probabilistic query language. Blog post available at `http://jvangael.github.io/2011/05/12/pqla-probabilistic-query-language/`, May 2011.

D. Z. Wang, E. Michelakis, M. Garofalakis, and J. M. Hellerstein. Bayesstore: managing large, uncertain data repositories with probabilistic graphical models. *Proc. VLDB Endow.*, 1(1):340–351, Aug. 2008.

D. Wingate, N. D. Goodman, A. Stuhlmüller, and J. M. Siskind. Nonstandard interpretations of probabilistic programs for efficient inference. In Proc. *NIPS '11*, pages 1152–1160, 2011.

# Modular, Higher-Order Cardinality Analysis in Theory and Practice

Ilya Sergey
IMDEA Software Institute
ilya.sergey@imdea.org

Dimitrios Vytiniotis Simon Peyton Jones
Microsoft Research
{dimitris,simonpj}@microsoft.com

## Abstract

Since the mid '80s, compiler writers for functional languages (especially lazy ones) have been writing papers about identifying and exploiting thunks and lambdas that are used only once. However it has proved difficult to achieve both power and simplicity in practice. We describe a new, modular analysis for a higher-order language, which is both simple and effective, and present measurements of its use in a full-scale, state of the art optimising compiler. The analysis finds many single-entry thunks and one-shot lambdas and enables a number of program optimisations.

***Categories and Subject Descriptors*** D.1.1 [*Programming Techniques*]: Applicative (Functional) Programming; F.3.2 [*Logics and Meanings of Programs*]: Semantics of Programming Languages — Program analysis, Operational semantics

***General Terms*** Languages, Theory, Analysis

***Keywords*** compilers, program optimisation, static analysis, functional programming languages, Haskell, lazy evaluation, thunks, cardinality analysis, types and effects, operational semantics

## 1. Introduction

Consider these definitions, written in a purely functional language like Haskell:

```
wurble1, wurble2 :: (Int -> Int) -> Int
wurble1 k = sum (map k [1..10])
wurble2 k = 2 * k 0

f1 :: [Int] -> Int
f1 xs = let ys = map costly xs
        in  wurble (\n. sum (map (+ n) ys))
```

Here we assume that `costly` is some function that is expensive to compute and `wurble` is either `wurble1` or `wurble2`. If we replace `ys` by its definition, we could transform `f1` into `f2`:

```
f2 xs = wurble (\n. sum (map (+ n) (map costly xs)))
```

A compiler like GHC can now use *short-cut deforestation* to fuse the two `maps` into one, eliminating the intermediate list altogether, and offering a substantial performance win (Gill et al. 1993).


*POPL '14*, January 22–24, 2014, San Diego, CA, USA.

http://dx.doi.org/10.1145/2535838.2535861

Does this transformation make the program run faster or slower? It depends on `wurble`! For example, `wurble1` calls its function argument ten times, so if `wurble` = `wurble1`, function `f2` would compute `costly` ten times for each element of `xs`; whereas `f1` would do so only once. On the other hand if `wurble` = `wurble2`, which calls its argument exactly once, then `f2` is just as efficient as `f1`, and `map/map` fusion can improve it further.

The reverse is also true. If the programmer writes `f2` in the first place, the *full laziness transformation* (Peyton Jones et al. 1996) will float the sub-expression `(map costly xs)` out of the `\n`-expression, so that it can be shared. That would be good for `wurble1` but bad for `wurble2`.

What is needed is an analysis that can provide a sound approximation of how often a function is called – we refer to such an analysis as a *cardinality analysis*. An optimising compiler can then use the results of the analysis to guide its transformations. In this paper we provide just such an analysis:

- We characterise two different, useful forms of cardinality, namely (a) how often a function is called, and (b) how often a thunk is forced in a lazy language (Section 2). Of these, the former is relevant under both call-by-need and call-by-value, while the latter is specific to call-by-need.
- We present a backwards analysis that can soundly and efficiently approximate both forms of cardinality for a non-strict, higher-order language (Section 3). A significant innovation is our use of *call demands* to model the usage of a function; this makes the analysis both powerful and modular.
- We prove that our algorithm is sound; for example if it claims that a function is called at most once, then it really is (Section 4). This proof is not at all straightforward, because it must take account of sharing — that is the whole point! So we cannot use standard denotational techniques, but instead must use an operational semantics that models sharing explicitly.
- We formalise a number of program optimisations enabled by the results of the cardinality analysis, prove them sound and, what is more important, improving (Section 5).
- We have implemented our algorithm by extending the Glasgow Haskell Compiler (GHC), a state of the art optimising compiler for Haskell. Happily, the implementation builds directly on GHC's current strictness and absence analyser, and is both simple and efficient (Section 6).
- We measured how often the analysis finds called-once functions and used-once thunks (Section 7); and how much this knowledge improved the performance of real programs (Sections 7.1–7.2). The analysis proves quite effective in that many one-shot lambdas and single-entry thunks are detected (in the range 0-30%, depending on the program). Improvements in performance are modest but consistent (a few percent): programs already optimised by GHC are a challenging target!

We discuss related work in Section 8. Distinctive features of our work are (a) the notion of call demands, (b) a full implementation measured against a state of the art optimising compiler, and (c) the combination of simplicity with worthwhile performance improvements.

## 2. What is Cardinality Analysis?

Cardinality analysis answers three inter-related questions, in the setting of a non-strict, pure functional language like Haskell:

- How many times is a particular, syntactic lambda-expression *called* (Section 2.1)?
- Which components of a data structure are *never evaluated*; that is, are *absent* (Section 2.3)?
- How many times is a particular, syntactic thunk *evaluated* (Section 2.4)?

### 2.1 Call cardinality

We saw in the introduction an example where it is helpful to know when a function calls its argument at most once. A lambda that is called at most once is called a *one-shot lambda*, and they are extremely common in functional programming: for example a *continuation* is usually one-shot. So cardinality analysis can be a big win when optimising continuation-heavy programs.

Nor is that all. As we saw in the Introduction, inlining under a one-shot lambda (to transform `f1` into `f2`) allows short-cut deforestation to fuse two otherwise-separate calls of `map`. But short-cut deforestation *itself* introduces many calls of of the function `build`:

```
build :: (forall b. (a -> b -> b) -> b -> b) -> [a]
build g = g (:) []
```

You can see that `build` calls its argument exactly once, and inlining `ys` in calls like `(build (\cn. ...ys...))` turns out to be crucial to making short-cut deforestation work in practice. Gill devotes a section of his thesis to elucidating this point (Gill 1996, Chapter 4.3). Gill lacked an analysis for one-shot lambdas, so his implementation (still extant in GHC today) relies on a gross hack: he taught GHC's optimiser to behave specially for `build` itself, and a couple of other functions. No user-defined function will have this good behaviour. Our analysis subsumes the hack, by providing an analysis that deduces the correct one-shot information for `build`, as well as many other functions.

### 2.2 Currying

In a higher order language with curried functions, we need to be careful about the details. For example, consider

```
f3 a = wurble a (\x.let t = costly x in \y. t+y)

wurble1 a g = g 2 a + g 3 a
wurble2 a g = sum (map (g a) [1..1000])
```

If `wurble` was `wurble1`, then in `f3` it would be best to inline `t` at its use site, thus:

```
f4 a = wurble1 a (\x.\y. costly x + y)
```

The transformed `f4` is much better than `f3`: it avoids allocating a thunk for `t`, and avoids allocating a function closure for the `\y`. But if `f3` called `wurble2` instead, such a transformation would be disastrous. Why? Because `wurble2` applies its argument `g` to one argument `a`, and the function thus computed is applied to each of 1000 integers. In `f3` we will compute `(costly a)` once, but `f4` will compute it 1000 times, which is arbitrarily bad.

So our analysis of `wurble2` must be able to report "`wurble2`'s argument `g` is called[1] once (applied to one argument), and the result is called many times". We formalise this by giving a *usage signature* to `wurble`, like this:

$$\begin{array}{lll}\texttt{wurble1} & :: & U \to C^{\omega}(C^1(U)) \to \bullet \\ \texttt{wurble2} & :: & U \to C^1(C^{\omega}(U)) \to \bullet\end{array}$$

The notation $C^{\omega}(C^1(U))$ is a *usage demand*: it describes how a (function) value is used. The demand type $U \to C^{\omega}(C^1(U)) \to \bullet$ describes how a function uses its *arguments*, therefore it gives a usage demand for each argument. (The "$\bullet$" has no significance; we are just used to seeing something after the final arrow!) Informally, the $C^1(d)$ means "this argument is called *once* (applied to one argument), and the result is used with usage $d$", whereas $C^{\omega}(d)$ means "this argument may be called many times, with *each* result used with usage $d$". The $U$ means "is used in some unknown way (or even not used at all)". Note that `wurble1`'s second argument usage is $C^{\omega}(C^1(U))$, *not* $C^{\omega}(C^{\omega}(U))$; that is, in all cases the result of applying `g` to one argument is then called only once.

### 2.3 Absence

Consider this function

```
f x = case x of (p,q) -> <cbody>
```

A strictness analyser can see that `f` is strict in `x`, and so can use call-by-value. Moreover, rather than allocate a pair that is passed to `f`, which immediately takes it apart, GHC uses a worker/wrapper transformation to pass the pieces separately, thus:

```
f x = case x of (p,q) -> fw p q
fw p q = <cbody>
```

Now `f` (the "wrapper") is small, and can be inlined at `f`'s call sites, often eliminating the allocation of the pair; meanwhile `fw` (the "worker") does the actual work. Strictness analysis, and the worker/wrapper transform to exploit its results, are hugely important to generating efficient code for lazy programs (Peyton Jones and Partain 1994; Peyton Jones and Santos 1998).

In general, `f`'s right-hand side often does not have a *syntactically visible* `case` expression. For example, what if `f` simply called another function `g` that was strict in `x`? Fortunately the worker/wrapper transform is easy to generalise. Suppose the right hand side of `f` was just `<fbody>`. Then we would transform to

```
f x = case x of (p,q) -> fw p q
fw p q = let x = (p,q) in <fbody>
```

Now we hope that the binding for `x` will cancel with `case` expressions in `<fbody>`, and indeed it usually proves to be so (Peyton Jones and Santos 1998).

But what if `<fbody>` did not use `q` at all? Then it would be stupid to pass `q` to `fw`. We would rather transform to:

```
f x = case x of (p,q) -> fw p
fw p = let x = (p, error "urk") in <fbody>
```

This turns out to be very important in practice. Programmers seldom write functions with wholly-unused arguments, but they frequently write functions that use only *part* of their argument, and ignoring this point leads to large numbers of unused arguments being passed around in the "optimised" program after the worker-wrapper transformation. Absence analysis has therefore been part of GHC since its earliest days (Peyton Jones and Partain 1994), but it has never been formalised. In the framework of this paper, we give `f` a usage signature like this:

$$\texttt{f} :: U(U, A) \to \bullet$$

The $U(U, A)$ indicates that the argument is a product type; that is, a data type with just one constructor. The $A$ (for "absent") indicates that `f` discards the second component of the product.

[1] We will always use "called" to mean "applied to one argument".

### 2.4 Thunk cardinality

Consider these definitions

```
f :: Int -> Int -> Int
f x c = if x > 0  then c + 1 else
        if x == 0 then 0     else c - 1

g y = f y (costly y)
```

Since `f` is not strict in `c`, `g` must build a thunk for `(costly y)` to pass to `f`. In call-by-need evaluation, thunks are *memoised*. That is, when a thunk is evaluated at run-time, it is overwritten with the value so that if it is evaluated a second time the already-computed value can be returned immediately. But in this case we can see that `f` *never evaluates its second argument more than once*, so the memoisation step is entirely wasted. We call these *single-entry thunks*.

Memoisation is not expensive, but it is certainly not free. Operationally, a pointer to the thunk must be pushed on the stack when evaluation starts, it must be black-holed to avoid space leaks (Jones 1992), and the update involves a memory write. If cardinality analysis can identify single-entry thunks, as well as one-shot lambdas, that would be a Good Thing. And so it can: we give `f` the usage signature:

$$\texttt{f} :: \omega{*}U \to 1{*}U \to \bullet$$

The "$\omega{*}$" modifier says that `f` may evaluate its first argument more than once, while the "$1{*}$" says that it evaluates its second argument at most once.

### 2.5 Call vs evaluation

For functions, there is a difference between being *evaluated* once and *called* once, because of Haskell's `seq` function. For example:

```
f1 g = g `seq` 1     -- f1  ::  1*U -> •
f2 g = g `seq` g 2   -- f2  ::  ω*C¹(U) -> •
f3 g = g 3           -- f3  ::  1*C¹(U) -> •
```

The function `seq` evaluates its first argument (to head-normal form) and returns its second argument. If its first argument is a function, the function is evaluated to a lambda, but not called. Notice that `f2`'s usage type says that `g` is evaluated more than once, but applied only once. For example consider the call

```
f (\x. x + y)
```

How many times is `y` evaluated? For `f` equal to `f1` the answer is zero; for `f2` and `f3` it is one.

## 3. Formalising Cardinality Analysis

We now present our analysis in detail. The syntax of the language we analyse is given in Figure 1. It is quite conventional: just lambda calculus with pairs and (non-recursive) `let`-expressions. Constants $\kappa$ include literals and primitive functions over literals, as well as Haskell's built-in `seq`. We use A-normal form (Sabry and Felleisen 1992) so that the issues concerning thunks show up only for `let` and not also for function arguments.

### 3.1 Usage demands

Our cardinality analysis is a backwards analysis over an abstract domain of *usage demands*. As with any such analysis, the abstract domain embodies a balance between the *cost* of the analysis and its *precision*. Our particular choices are expressed in the syntax of usage demands, given in Figure 1. A usage demand $d$ is one of the following:

- $U(d_1^\dagger, d_2^\dagger)$ applies to pairs. The pair itself is evaluated and its first component is used as described by $d_1^\dagger$ and its second by $d_2^\dagger$.

**Expressions and values**

$$\begin{array}{rcl} e & ::= & x \mid v \mid e\ x \mid \texttt{let}\ x = e_1\ \texttt{in}\ e_2 \\ & & \mid \texttt{case}\ e_1\ \texttt{of}\ (x_1, x_2) \to e_2 \\ v & ::= & \kappa \mid \lambda x\,.\,e \mid (x_1, x_2) \end{array}$$

**Annotated expressions and values**

$$\begin{array}{rcl} \mathsf{e} & ::= & x \mid \mathsf{v} \mid \mathsf{e}\ x \mid \texttt{let}\ x \overset{m}{=} \mathsf{e}_1\ \texttt{in}\ \mathsf{e}_2 \\ & & \mid \texttt{case}\ \mathsf{e}_1\ \texttt{of}\ (x_1, x_2) \to \mathsf{e}_2 \\ \mathsf{v} & ::= & \kappa \mid \lambda^m x\,.\,\mathsf{e} \mid (x_1, x_2) \end{array}$$

**Usage demands and multi-demands**

$$\begin{array}{rcl} d & ::= & C^n(d) \mid U(d_1^\dagger, d_2^\dagger) \mid U \mid HU \\ d^\dagger & ::= & A \mid n{*}d \\ n & ::= & 1 \mid \omega \\ m & ::= & 0 \mid 1 \mid \omega \end{array}$$

**Non-syntactic demand equalities**

$$\begin{array}{rcl} C^\omega(U) & \equiv & U \\ U(\omega{*}U, \omega{*}U) & \equiv & U \\ U(A, A) & \equiv & HU \end{array}$$

**Usage types**

$$\tau \ ::= \ \bullet \mid d^\dagger \to \tau$$

**Usage type expansion**

$$\begin{array}{rcl} d^\dagger \to \tau & \preceq & d^\dagger \to \tau \\ \bullet & \preceq & \omega{*}U \to \bullet \end{array}$$

**Free-variable usage environments (fv-usage)**

$$\varphi \ ::= \ (x{:}d^\dagger), \varphi \mid \epsilon$$

**Auxiliary notation on environments**

$$\begin{array}{rcl} \varphi(x) & = & d^\dagger \text{ when } (x{:}d^\dagger) \in \varphi \\ & & A \text{ otherwise} \end{array}$$

**Usage signatures and signature environments**

$$\begin{array}{rcl} \rho & ::= & \langle k\,;\tau\,;\varphi\rangle \quad k \in \mathbb{Z}_{>0} \\ P & ::= & (x{:}\rho), P \mid \epsilon \end{array}$$

$$\begin{array}{lll} \multicolumn{3}{l}{\mathit{transform}(\langle k\,;\tau\,;\varphi\rangle, d)} \\ = & \langle \tau\,;\varphi\rangle & \text{if } d \sqsubseteq C^1(\ldots k\text{-fold}\ldots C^1(U)) \\ = & \langle \omega{*}\tau\,;\omega{*}\varphi\rangle & \text{otherwise} \end{array}$$

**Figure 1:** Syntax of terms, values, usage types, and environments

- $C^n(d)$ applies to functions. The function is called at most $n$ times, and *on each call* the result is used as described by $d$. Call demands are, to the best of our knowledge, new.
- $U$, or "used", indicating no information; the demand can use the value in an arbitrary way.
- $HU$, or "head-used", is a special case; it is the demand that `seq` places on its first argument: `seq` $:: HU \to U \to \bullet$.

A usage demand $d$ always uses the root of the value exactly once; it cannot express absence or multiple evaluation. That is done by $d^\dagger$, which is either $A$ (absent), or $n{*}d$ indicating that the value is used at most $n$ times in a way described by $d$. In both $C^n(d)$ and $n{*}d$, the multiplicity $n$ is either 1 or $\omega$ (meaning "many"). Notice that a call demand $C^n(d)$ has a $d$ inside it, not a $d^\dagger$: if a function is called, its body is evaluated exactly once. This is different from pairs. For example, if we have

```
let x = (e1, e2) in fst x + fst x
```

then `e1` is evaluated twice.

Both $U$ and $HU$ come with some non-syntactic equalities, denoted by $\equiv$ in Figure 1 and necessary for the proof of well-typedness (Section 4). For example, $U$ is equivalent to a pair demand whose components are used many times, or a many-call-demand where the result is used in an arbitrary way. Similarly, for pairs $HU$ is equivalent to $U(A, A)$, while for functions $HU$ is equivalent to $C^0(A)$, if we had such a thing. In the rest of the paper all definitions

$$\boxed{\mu(d^\dagger) = m}$$

$$\mu(A) = 0 \qquad \mu(n{*}d) = n$$

$$\boxed{d_1^\dagger \,\&\, d_2^\dagger = d_3^\dagger \qquad d_1^\dagger \sqcup d_2^\dagger = d_3^\dagger}$$

$$\begin{array}{rcl}
A \,\&\, d^\dagger &=& d^\dagger \\
d^\dagger \,\&\, A &=& d^\dagger \\
n_1{*}d_1 \,\&\, n_2{*}d_2 &=& \omega{*}(d_1 \,\&\, d_2)
\end{array}$$

$$\begin{array}{rcl}
A \sqcup d^\dagger &=& d^\dagger \\
d^\dagger \sqcup A &=& d^\dagger \\
n_1{*}d_1 \sqcup n_2{*}d_2 &=& (n_1 \sqcup n_2){*}(d_1 \sqcup d_2)
\end{array}$$

$$\boxed{d_1 \,\&\, d_2 = d_3 \qquad d_1 \sqcup d_2 = d_3}$$

$$\begin{array}{rcl}
d \,\&\, U &=& U \\
U \,\&\, d &=& U \\
d \,\&\, HU &=& d \\
HU \,\&\, d &=& d \\
C^{n_1}(d_1) \,\&\, C^{n_2}(d_2) &=& C^{\omega}(d_1 \sqcup d_2) \\
U(d_1^\dagger, d_2^\dagger) \,\&\, U(d_3^\dagger, d_4^\dagger) &=& U(d_1^\dagger \,\&\, d_3^\dagger, d_2^\dagger \,\&\, d_4^\dagger)
\end{array}$$

$$\begin{array}{rcl}
d \sqcup U &=& U \\
U \sqcup d &=& U \\
d \sqcup HU &=& d \\
HU \sqcup d &=& d \\
C^{n_1}(d_1) \sqcup C^{n_2}(d_2) &=& C^{n_1 \sqcup n_2}(d_1 \sqcup d_2) \\
U(d_1^\dagger, d_2^\dagger) \sqcup U(d_3^\dagger, d_4^\dagger) &=& U(d_1^\dagger \sqcup d_3^\dagger, d_2^\dagger \sqcup d_4^\dagger)
\end{array}$$

$$\boxed{\varphi_1 \,\&\, \varphi_2 = \varphi_3 \qquad \varphi_1 \sqcup \varphi_2 = \varphi_3}$$

$$\begin{array}{rcl}
\varphi_1 \,\&\, \varphi_2 &=& \{(x{:}d_1^\dagger \,\&\, d_2^\dagger) \mid \varphi_i(x) = d_i^\dagger\} \\
\varphi_1 \sqcup \varphi_2 &=& \{(x{:}d_1^\dagger \sqcup d_2^\dagger) \mid \varphi_i(x) = d_i^\dagger\}
\end{array}$$

$$\boxed{\tau_1 \sqcup \tau_2 = \tau_3}$$

$$\begin{array}{rcl}
(d_1^\dagger \to \tau_1) \sqcup (d_1^\dagger \to \tau_2) &=& (d_1^\dagger \sqcup d_2^\dagger) \to (\tau_1 \sqcup \tau_2) \\
\tau \sqcup \bullet &=& \bullet
\end{array}$$

$$\boxed{\langle \tau_1 \,;\, \varphi_1 \rangle \sqcup \langle \tau_2 \,;\, \varphi_2 \rangle = \langle \tau_3 \,;\, \varphi_3 \rangle}$$

$$\langle \tau_1 \,;\, \varphi_1 \rangle \sqcup \langle \tau_2 \,;\, \varphi_2 \rangle \quad = \quad \langle \tau_1 \sqcup \tau_2 \,;\, \varphi_1 \sqcup \varphi_2 \rangle$$

$$\boxed{n{*}d_1^\dagger = d_2^\dagger \qquad n{*}\tau_1 = \tau_2 \qquad n{*}\varphi_1 = \varphi_2}$$

$$\begin{array}{rcl}
1{*}d^\dagger &=& d^\dagger \\
\omega{*}d^\dagger &=& d^\dagger \,\&\, d^\dagger \\
n{*}\bullet &=& \bullet \\
n{*}(d^\dagger \to \tau) &=& (n{*}d^\dagger) \to (n{*}\tau) \\
n{*}\varphi &=& \{x : n{*}\varphi(x) \mid x \in dom(\varphi)\}
\end{array}$$

$$\boxed{n_1 \sqcup n_2 = n_3}$$

$$1 \sqcup 1 = 1 \quad \omega \sqcup n = \omega \quad n \sqcup \omega = \omega$$

$$\boxed{a \sqsubseteq b}$$

$$a \sqsubseteq b \quad \Leftrightarrow \quad (a \sqcup b) = b$$

**Figure 2:** Demands and demand operations

$$\boxed{P \Vdash e \downarrow d \Rightarrow \langle \tau \,;\, \varphi \rangle \rightsquigarrow \mathsf{e}}$$

$$\frac{(x : \rho) \in P \quad \langle \tau \,;\, \varphi \rangle = \mathit{transform}(\rho, d)}{P \Vdash x \downarrow d \Rightarrow \langle \tau \,;\, \varphi \,\&\, (x{:}1{*}d) \rangle \rightsquigarrow x}\ \textsc{VarDn}$$

$$\frac{x \notin dom(P)}{P \Vdash x \downarrow d \Rightarrow \langle \bullet \,;\, (x{:}1{*}d) \rangle \rightsquigarrow x}\ \textsc{VarUp}$$

$$\frac{P \Vdash e \downarrow d_e \Rightarrow \langle \tau \,;\, \varphi \rangle \rightsquigarrow \mathsf{e}}{P \Vdash \lambda x\,.\,e \downarrow C^n(d_e) \Rightarrow \langle \varphi(x) \to \tau \,;\, n{*}(\varphi \backslash_x) \rangle \rightsquigarrow \lambda^n x\,.\,\mathsf{e}}\ \textsc{Lam}$$

$$\frac{P \Vdash \lambda x\,.\,e \downarrow C^\omega(U) \Rightarrow \langle \tau \,;\, \varphi \rangle \rightsquigarrow \mathsf{e}'}{P \Vdash \lambda x\,.\,e \downarrow U \Rightarrow \langle \tau \,;\, \varphi \rangle \rightsquigarrow \mathsf{e}'}\ \textsc{LamU}$$

$$\frac{}{P \Vdash \lambda x\,.\,e \downarrow HU \Rightarrow \langle \tau \,;\, \epsilon \rangle \rightsquigarrow \lambda^1 x\,.\,\mathsf{e}}\ \textsc{LamHU}$$

$$\frac{P \Vdash e_1 \downarrow C^1(d) \Rightarrow \langle d_2^\dagger \to \tau_r \,;\, \varphi_1 \rangle \rightsquigarrow \mathsf{e}_1 \quad P \Vdash^{*} y \downarrow d_2^\dagger \Rightarrow \varphi_2}{P \Vdash e_1\ y \downarrow d \Rightarrow \langle \tau_r \,;\, \varphi_1 \,\&\, \varphi_2 \rangle \rightsquigarrow \mathsf{e}_1\ y}\ \textsc{AppA}$$

$$\frac{P \Vdash e_1 \downarrow C^1(d) \Rightarrow \langle \bullet \,;\, \varphi_1 \rangle \rightsquigarrow \mathsf{e}_1 \quad P \Vdash^{*} y \downarrow \omega{*}U \Rightarrow \varphi_2}{P \Vdash e_1\ y \downarrow d \Rightarrow \langle \bullet \,;\, \varphi_1 \,\&\, \varphi_2 \rangle \rightsquigarrow \mathsf{e}_1\ y}\ \textsc{AppB}$$

$$\frac{P \Vdash^{*} x_i \downarrow d_i^\dagger \Rightarrow \varphi_i \quad i \in 1,2}{P \Vdash (x_1, x_2) \downarrow U(d_1^\dagger, d_2^\dagger) \Rightarrow \langle \bullet \,;\, \varphi_1 \,\&\, \varphi_2 \rangle \rightsquigarrow (x_1, x_2)}\ \textsc{Pair}$$

$$\frac{P \Vdash (x_1, x_2) \downarrow U(\omega{*}U, \omega{*}U) \Rightarrow \langle \bullet \,;\, \varphi \rangle \rightsquigarrow \mathsf{e}}{P \Vdash (x_1, x_2) \downarrow U \Rightarrow \langle \bullet \,;\, \varphi \rangle \rightsquigarrow \mathsf{e}}\ \textsc{PairU}$$

$$\frac{}{P \Vdash (x_1, x_2) \downarrow HU \Rightarrow \langle \bullet \,;\, \epsilon \rangle \rightsquigarrow (x_1, x_2)}\ \textsc{PairHU}$$

$$\frac{\begin{array}{c} P \Vdash e_r \downarrow d \Rightarrow \langle \tau \,;\, \varphi_r \rangle \rightsquigarrow \mathsf{e}_r \\ P \Vdash e_s \downarrow U(\varphi_r(x), \varphi_r(y)) \Rightarrow \langle \_ \,;\, \varphi_s \rangle \rightsquigarrow \mathsf{e}_s \end{array}}{\begin{array}{l} P \Vdash \mathtt{case}\ e_s\ \mathtt{of}\ (x, y) \to e_r \downarrow d \Rightarrow \langle \tau \,;\, \varphi_r \backslash_{x,y} \,\&\, \varphi_s \rangle \\ \qquad \rightsquigarrow \mathtt{case}\ \mathsf{e}_s\ \mathtt{of}\ (x, y) \to \mathsf{e}_r \end{array}}\ \textsc{Case}$$

$$\boxed{P \Vdash^{*} x \downarrow d^\dagger \Rightarrow \varphi}$$

$$\frac{}{P \Vdash^{*} x \downarrow A \Rightarrow \epsilon}\ \textsc{Abs} \qquad \frac{P \Vdash x \downarrow d \Rightarrow \langle \tau \,;\, \varphi \rangle \rightsquigarrow x}{P \Vdash^{*} x \downarrow n{*}d \Rightarrow n{*}\varphi}\ \textsc{Multi}$$

**Figure 3:** Algorithmic cardinality analysis specification, part 1.

and metatheory are modulo-$\equiv$ (checking that all our definitions do respect $\equiv$ is routine).

### 3.2 Usage analysis

The analysis itself is shown in Figures 3 and 4. The main judgement form is written thus

$$P \Vdash e \downarrow d \Rightarrow \langle \tau \,;\, \varphi \rangle \rightsquigarrow \mathsf{e}'$$

which should be read thus: *in signature environment $P$, and under usage demand $d$, the term $e$ places demands $\langle \tau \,;\, \varphi \rangle$ on its components, and elaborates to an annotated term $\mathsf{e}'$*. The syntax of each of these components is given in Figure 1, and their roles in the judgement are the following:

- The *signature environment* $P$ maps some of free variables of $e$ to their *usage signatures*, $\rho$ (Section 3.5). Any free variables outside the domain of $P$ have an uninformative signature.
- The *usage demand*, $d$, describes the degree to which $e$ is evaluated, including how many times its sub-components are evaluated or called.
- Using $P$, the judgement transforms the incoming demand $d$ into the demands $\langle\tau\ ;\ \varphi\rangle$ that $e$ places on its *arguments* and *free variables* respectively:
  - The usage that $e$ places on its argument is given by $\tau$, which gives a demand $d^\dagger$ for each argument.
  - The usage that $e$ places on its free variables is given by its free-variable usage (fv-usage), $\varphi$, which is simply a finite mapping from variables to usage demands.
- We will discuss the elaborated expressions $\mathsf{e}'$ in Section 3.7.

For example, consider the expression

$$e = \lambda x\ .\ \texttt{case}\ x\ \texttt{of}\ (p, q) \to (p, f\ \texttt{True})$$

Suppose we place demand $C^1(U)$ on $e$, so that $e$ is called, just once. What demand does it then place on its arguments and free variables?

$$\epsilon \mapsto e \downarrow C^1(U) \Rightarrow \langle 1{*}\,U(\omega{*}\,U, A) \to \bullet\ ;\{f \mapsto 1{*}\,C^1(U)\}\rangle$$

That is, $e$ will use its argument once, its argument's first component perhaps many times, but will ignore its arguments second component (the $A$ in the usage type). Moreover $e$ will call $f$ just once.

In short, we think of the analysis as describing a *demand transformer*, transforming a demand on the result of $e$ into demands on its arguments and free variables.

### 3.3 Pairs and case expressions

With these definitions in mind, we can look at some of the analysis rules in Figure 3. Rule PAIR explains how to analyse a pair under a demand $U(d_1^\dagger, d_2^\dagger)$. We simply analyse the two components, under $d_1^\dagger$ or $d_2^\dagger$ respectively, and combine the results with "&". The auxiliary judgement $\mapsto^*$ (Figure 3) deals with the multiplicity of the argument demands $d_i^\dagger$.

The "&" operator, pronounced "both", is defined in Figure 2, and combines the free-variable usages $\varphi_1$ and $\varphi_2$. For the most part the definition is straightforward, but there is a very important wrinkle for call demands:

$$C^{n_1}(d_1)\ \&\ C^{n_2}(d_2) = C^\omega(d_1 \sqcup d_2)$$

The "$\omega$" part is easy, since $n_1$ and $n_2$ are both at least 1. But note the switch from & to the least upper bound $\sqcup$! To see why, consider what demand this expression places on `f`:

```
f 1 2 + f 3 4
```

Each call gives a usage demand for `f` of $1{*}\,C^1(C^1(U))$, and if we use & to combine that demand with itself we get $\omega{*}\,C^\omega(C^1(U))$. The inner "1" is a consequence of the switch to $\sqcup$, and rightly expresses the fact that no partial application of `f` is called more than once.

The other rules for pairs PAIRU, PAIRHU, and case expressions CASE should now be readily comprehensible ($\varphi_r\backslash_{x,y}$ stands for the removal of $\{x, y\}$ from the domain of $\varphi_r$.).

### 3.4 Lambda and application

Rule LAM for lambdas expects the incoming demand to be a call demand $C^n(d_e)$. Then it analyses the body $e$ with demand $d_e$ to give $\langle\tau\ ;\ \varphi\rangle$. If $n = 1$ the lambda is called at most once, so we can return $\langle\tau\ ;\ \varphi\rangle$; but if $n = \omega$ the lambda may be called more than once, and each call will place a new demand on the free variables. The $n{*}\varphi$ operation on the bottom line accounts for this multiplicity, and is defined in Figure 2. Rule LAMU handles an incoming demand of $U$ by treating it just like $C^\omega(U)$, while LAMHU deals with the head-used demand $HU$, where the lambda is not even called so we do not need to analyse the body, and $\mathsf{e}$ is obtained from $e$ by adding arbitrary annotations. Similarly the return type $\tau$ can be any type, since the $\lambda$-abstraction is not going to be applied, but is only head-used. Dually, given an application $(e\ y)$, rule APPA analyses $e$ with demand $C^1(d)$, reflecting that $e$ is here called once. This returns the demand $\langle d_2^\dagger \to \tau_2\ ;\ \varphi_1\rangle$ on the context. Then we can analyse the argument under demand $d_2^\dagger$, using $\mapsto^*$, yielding $\varphi_2$; and combine $\varphi_1$ and $\varphi_2$. Rule APPB applies when analysing $e_1$ yields the less-informative usage type $\bullet$.

### 3.5 Usage signatures

Suppose we have the term

```
let f = \x.\y. x True  in  f p q
```

We would like to determine the correct demands on `p` and `q`, namely $1{*}C^1(U)$ and $A$ respectively. The gold standard would be to analyse `f`'s right-hand side at every call site; that is, to behave as if `f` were inlined at each call site. But that is not very modular; with deeply nested function definitions, it can be exponentially expensive to analyse each function body afresh at each call site; and it does not work at all for recursive functions. Instead, we want to analyse `f`, summarise its behaviour, and then use that summary at each call site. This summary is called `f`'s *usage signature*. Remember that the main judgement describes how a term transforms a demand for the value into demands on its context. So a usage signature must be a (conservative approximation of this) demand transformer.

There are many ways in which one might approximate `f`'s demand transformer, but rule LETDN (Figure 4) uses a particularly simple one:

- Look at `f`'s right hand side $\lambda y_1 \ldots \lambda y_k\ .\ e_1$, where $e_1$ is not a lambda-expression.
- Analyse $e_1$ in demand $U$, giving $\langle\tau_1\ ;\ \varphi_1\rangle$.
- Record the triple $\langle k\ ; \varphi(\overline{y}) \to \tau_1\ ; \varphi_1\backslash_{\overline{y}}\rangle$ as `f`'s usage signature in the environment $P$ when analysing the body of the `let`.

Now, at a call site of `f`, rule VARDN calls $\mathit{transform}(\rho, d)$ to use the recorded usage signature $\rho$ to transform the demand $d$ for this occurrence of `f`.

What does $\mathit{transform}(\langle k\ ; \tau\ ; \varphi\rangle, d)$ do (Figure 1)? If the demand $d$ on `f` is stronger than $C^1(\ldots C^1(U))$, where the call demands are nested $k$ deep, we can safely unleash $\langle\tau\ ;\ \varphi\rangle$ at the call site. If not, we simply treat the function as if it were called many times, by unleashing $\langle\omega{*}\tau\ ;\omega{*}\varphi\rangle$, multiplying both the demand type $\tau$ and the usage environment $\varphi$ (Figure 2). Rule LETDNABS handles the case when the variable is not used in the body.

### 3.6 Thunks

The LETDN rule unleashes (an approximation to) the demands of the right-hand side at each usage site. This is good if the right hand side is a lambda, but not good otherwise, for two reasons. Consider

```
let x = y + 1  in  x + x
```

How many times is `y` demanded? Just once! The thunk `x` is demanded twice, but `x`'s thunk is memoised, so the `y+1` is evaluated only once. So it is wrong to unleash a demand on `y` at each of `x`'s occurrence sites. Contrast the situation where `x` is a function

```
let x = \v. y + v  in  x 42 + x 239
```

Here `y` really *is* demanded twice, and LETDN does that. Another reason that LETDN would be sub-optimal for thunks is shown here:

$$\frac{\begin{array}{c} P \mapsto e_1 \downarrow U \Rightarrow \langle \tau_1 \,;\, \varphi_1 \rangle \rightsquigarrow \mathtt{e}_1 \\ \tau_f = \varphi_1(\overline{y}) \to \tau_1 \\ P,\, f{:}\langle k \,;\, \tau_f \,;\, \varphi_1 \backslash_{\overline{y}} \rangle \mapsto e_2 \downarrow d \Rightarrow \langle \tau \,;\, \varphi_2 \rangle \rightsquigarrow \mathtt{e}_2 \\ \varphi_2(f) \sqsubseteq n * C^{n_1}(\ldots(C^{n_k}(\ldots)\ldots)) \end{array}}{\begin{array}{r} P \mapsto \texttt{let}\; f = \lambda y_1 \ldots y_k \,.\, e_1 \;\texttt{in}\; e_2 \downarrow d \Rightarrow \langle \tau \,;\, (\varphi_2 \backslash_f) \rangle \\ \rightsquigarrow \texttt{let}\; f \stackrel{n}{=} \lambda^{n_1} y_1 \ldots \lambda^{n_k} y_k \,.\, \mathtt{e}_1 \;\texttt{in}\; \mathtt{e}_2 \end{array}} \;\textsc{LetDn}$$

$$\frac{\begin{array}{c} P \mapsto e_1 \downarrow U \Rightarrow \langle \tau_1 \,;\, \varphi_1 \rangle \rightsquigarrow \mathtt{e}_1 \\ \tau_f = \varphi_1(\overline{y}) \to \tau_1 \quad \varphi_2(f) = A \\ P,\, f{:}\langle k \,;\, \tau_f \,;\, \varphi_1 \backslash_{\overline{y}} \rangle \mapsto e_2 \downarrow d \Rightarrow \langle \tau \,;\, \varphi_2 \rangle \rightsquigarrow \mathtt{e}_2 \end{array}}{\begin{array}{r} P \mapsto \texttt{let}\; f = \lambda y_1 \ldots y_k \,.\, e_1 \;\texttt{in}\; e_2 \downarrow d \Rightarrow \langle \tau \,;\, (\varphi_2 \backslash_f) \rangle \\ \rightsquigarrow \texttt{let}\; f \stackrel{0}{=} \lambda^{1} y_1 \ldots \lambda^{1} y_k \,.\, \mathtt{e}_1 \;\texttt{in}\; \mathtt{e}_2 \end{array}} \;\textsc{LetDnAbs}$$

$$\frac{\begin{array}{c} P \mapsto e_2 \downarrow d \Rightarrow \langle \tau \,;\, \varphi_2 \rangle \rightsquigarrow \mathtt{e}_2 \\ n * d_x = \varphi_2(x) \quad P \mapsto e_1 \downarrow d_x \Rightarrow \langle \_ \,;\, \varphi_1 \rangle \rightsquigarrow \mathtt{e}_1 \end{array}}{\begin{array}{r} P \mapsto \texttt{let}\; x = e_1 \;\texttt{in}\; e_2 \downarrow d \Rightarrow \langle \tau \,;\, \varphi_1 \,\&\, (\varphi_2 \backslash_x) \rangle \\ \rightsquigarrow \texttt{let}\; x \stackrel{n}{=} \mathtt{e}_1 \;\texttt{in}\; \mathtt{e}_2 \end{array}} \;\textsc{LetUp}$$

$$\frac{P \mapsto e_2 \downarrow d \Rightarrow \langle \tau \,;\, \varphi_2 \rangle \rightsquigarrow \mathtt{e}_2 \quad A = \varphi_2(x)}{\begin{array}{r} P \mapsto \texttt{let}\; x = e_1 \;\texttt{in}\; e_2 \downarrow d \Rightarrow \langle \tau \,;\, \varphi_2 \backslash_x \rangle \\ \rightsquigarrow \texttt{let}\; x \stackrel{0}{=} \mathtt{e}_1 \;\texttt{in}\; \mathtt{e}_2 \end{array}} \;\textsc{LetUpAbs}$$

**Figure 4:** Algorithmic cardinality analysis specification, part 2 (`let`-rules).

```
let x = (p,q)  in  case x of (a,b) -> a
```

The body of the `let` places usage demand $1 * U(U, A)$ on `x`, and if we analysed `x`'s right-hand side in that demand we would see that `q` was unused. So we get more information if we wait until we know the aggregated demand on `x`, and use it to analyse its right-hand side.

This idea is embodied in the LETUP rule, used if LETDN does not apply (*i.e.*, the right hand side is not a lambda). Rule LETUP first analyses the body $e_2$ to get the demand $\varphi_2(x)$ on $x$; then analyses the right-hand side $e_1$ using that demand. Notice that the multiplicity $n$ of the demand that $e_2$ places on $x$ is ignored; that is because the thunk is memoised. Otherwise the rule is quite straightforward. Rule LETUPABS deals with the case when the bound variable is unused in the body.

### 3.7 Elaboration

How are we to take advantage of our analysis? We do so by *elaborating* the term during analysis, with annotations of two kinds (see the syntax of annotated expressions in Figure 1):

- `let`-bindings carry an annotation $m \in 0, 1, \omega$, to indicate how often the `let` binding is evaluated.
- Lambdas $\lambda^m x \,.\, e$ carry an annotation $m \in 0, 1, \omega$, to indicate how often the lambda is called. 0 serves as an indicator that the lambda is not supposed to be called at all.

Figure 3 shows the elaborated terms after the "$\rightsquigarrow$". The operational semantics (Section 4) gets stuck if we use a thunk or lambda more often than its claimed usage; and the optimising transformations (Section 5) are guided by the same annotations.

### 3.8 A more realistic language

The language of Figure 1 is stripped to its bare essentials. Our implementation handles all of Haskell, or rather the Core language to which Haskell is translated by GHC. In particular:

- Usage signatures for constants $\kappa$ are predefined.
- All data types with a single constructor (*i.e.*, simple products) are treated analogously to pairs in the analysis.
- Recursive data types with more than one constructor and, correspondingly, `case` expressions with more than one alternative (and hence also conditional statements) are supported. The analysis is more approximate for such types: only usage demands that apply to such types are $U$ and $HU$ not $U(d_1^\dagger, d_2^\dagger)$. Furthermore, `case` expressions with multiple branches give rise to a least upper bound $\sqcup$ combination of usage types, as usual.
- Recursive functions and `let`-bindings are handled, using the standard kind of fixpoint iteration over a finite-height domain.

## 4. Soundness of the Analysis

We establish the soundness of our analysis in a sequence of steps. Soundness means that if the analysis claims that, say, a lambda is one-shot, then that lambda is only called once; and similarly for single-entry thunks. We formalise this property as follows:

- We present an operational semantics, written $\hookrightarrow$, for the annotated language that counts how many times thunks have been evaluated and $\lambda$-abstractions have been applied. The semantics simply gets stuck when these counters reach zero, which will happen only if the claims of the analysis are false (Section 4.1).
- Our goal is to prove that if an expression $e$ is elaborated to $\mathsf{e}$ by the analysis, then $\mathsf{e}$ in the instrumented semantics behaves identically to $e$ in a standard un-instrumented call-by-need semantics (Section 4.3). For reasons of space we omit the rules for the un-instrumented call-by-need semantics which are completely standard (Sestoft 1997), and are identical to the rules of Figure 5 if one simply ignores all the annotations and the multiplicity side-conditions. We refer to this semantics as $\longrightarrow$.
- We prove soundness by giving a type system for the *annotated terms*, and showing that for well-typed terms, the instrumented semantics $\hookrightarrow$ simulates $\longrightarrow$, in a type-preserving way.

### 4.1 Counting operational semantics

We present a simple *counting* operational semantics for *annotated terms* in Figure 5. This is a standard semantics for call-by-need, except for the fact that multiplicity annotations decorate the terms, stacks, and heaps. The syntax for heaps, denoted with $\mathsf{H}$, contains two forms of bindings, one for expressions $[x \stackrel{m}{\mapsto} \texttt{Exp(e)}]$ and one for already evaluated expressions $[x \stackrel{m}{\mapsto} \texttt{Val(v)}]$. The multiplicity $m \in \{0, 1, \omega\}$ denotes how many more times are we allowed to de-reference this particular binding. The stacks, denoted with $\mathsf{S}$, are just lists of frames. The syntax for frames includes *application frames* $(\bullet\ y)$, which store a reference $y$ to an argument, *case-frames* $((x, y) \to \mathsf{e})$, which account for the execution of a `case`-branch, and *update frames* of the form $\#(x, m)$, which take care of updating the heap when the active expression reduces to a value. The first component of an update frame is a name of a variable to be updated, and the second one is its thunk cardinality.

Rule ELET allocates a new binding on the heap. The rules EBETA fires only if the cardinality annotation is non-zero; it de-references an `Exp(e)` binding and emits an update frame. Rules EBETA, EAPP, EPAIR and EPRED are standard. Notice that EBETA also fires only if the $\lambda$'s multiplicity $m$ is non-zero. Note that the analysis does not assign zero-annotations to lambdas, but we need them for the soundness result.

Rule ELKPV de-references a binding for an already-evaluated expression $[x \stackrel{m}{\mapsto} \texttt{Val(v)}]$, and in a standard semantics would return $\mathsf{v}$ leaving the heap unaffected. In our counting semantics however,

**Heaps**

$$\begin{array}{rcl} \mathsf{H} & ::= & \epsilon \\ & \mid & [x \overset{m}{\mapsto} \mathtt{Exp}(\mathsf{e})], \mathsf{H} \\ & \mid & [x \overset{m}{\mapsto} \mathtt{Val}(\mathsf{v})], \mathsf{H} \end{array}$$

**Stacks**

$$\begin{array}{rcl} \mathsf{S} & ::= & \epsilon \mid (\bullet\ y) : \mathsf{S} \\ & \mid & \#(x, m) : \mathsf{S} \\ & \mid & ((x, y) \to \mathsf{e}) : \mathsf{S} \end{array}$$

**Auxiliary definitions**

$$\begin{array}{rcl} \mathit{split}(\lambda^m x\ .\ \mathsf{e}) & = & (\lambda^{m_1} x . \mathsf{e}, \lambda^{m_2} x . \mathsf{e}) \\ & & \text{where } m_1 + m_2 = m \\ \mathit{split}(\mathsf{v}) & = & (\mathsf{v}, \mathsf{v}) \quad \text{otherwise} \end{array}$$

$$\boxed{\langle \mathsf{H}_0 ; \mathsf{e}_0 ; \mathsf{S}_0 \rangle \hookrightarrow \langle \mathsf{H}_1 ; \mathsf{e}_1 ; \mathsf{S}_1 \rangle}$$

$$\begin{array}{llcl}
\text{ELET} & \langle \mathsf{H} ; \mathtt{let}\ x \overset{m}{=} \mathsf{e}_1\ \mathtt{in}\ \mathsf{e}_2 ; \mathsf{S} \rangle & \hookrightarrow & \langle \mathsf{H}, [x \overset{m}{\mapsto} \mathtt{Exp}(\mathsf{e}_1)] ; \mathsf{e}_2 ; \mathsf{S} \rangle \\
\text{ELKPE} & \langle \mathsf{H}, [x \overset{m}{\mapsto} \mathtt{Exp}(\mathsf{e})] ; x ; \mathsf{S} \rangle & \hookrightarrow & \langle \mathsf{H} ; \mathsf{e} ; \#(x, m) : \mathsf{S} \rangle \quad \text{if } m \geq 1 \\
\text{ELKPV} & \langle \mathsf{H}, [x \overset{m+1}{\mapsto} \mathtt{Val}(\mathsf{v})] ; x ; \mathsf{S} \rangle & \hookrightarrow & \langle \mathsf{H}, [x \overset{m}{\mapsto} \mathtt{Val}(\mathsf{v}_1)] ; \mathsf{v}_2 ; \mathsf{S} \rangle \\
 & & & \text{s.t. } \mathit{split}(\mathsf{v}) = (\mathsf{v}_1, \mathsf{v}_2) \\
\text{EUPD} & \langle \mathsf{H} ; \mathsf{v} ; \#(x, m+1) : \mathsf{S} \rangle & \hookrightarrow & \langle \mathsf{H}, [x \overset{m}{\mapsto} \mathtt{Val}(\mathsf{v}_1)] ; \mathsf{v}_2 ; \mathsf{S} \rangle \\
 & & & \text{s.t. } \mathit{split}(\mathsf{v}) = (\mathsf{v}_1, \mathsf{v}_2) \\
\text{EBETA} & \langle \mathsf{H} ; \lambda^m x . \mathsf{e} ; (\bullet\ y) : \mathsf{S} \rangle & \hookrightarrow & \langle \mathsf{H} ; \mathsf{e}[y/x] ; \mathsf{S} \rangle \quad \text{if } m \geq 1 \\
\text{EAPP} & \langle \mathsf{H} ; \mathsf{e}\ y ; \mathsf{S} \rangle & \hookrightarrow & \langle \mathsf{H} ; \mathsf{e} ; (\bullet\ y) : \mathsf{S} \rangle \\
\text{EPAIR} & \langle \mathsf{H} ; \mathtt{case}\ \mathsf{e}_s\ \mathtt{of}\ (x, y) \to \mathsf{e}_r ; \mathsf{S} \rangle & \hookrightarrow & \langle \mathsf{H} ; \mathsf{e}_s ; ((x, y) \to \mathsf{e}_r) : \mathsf{S} \rangle \\
\text{EPRED} & \langle \mathsf{H} ; (x_1, x_2) ; ((y_1, y_2) \to \mathsf{e}_r) : \mathsf{S} \rangle & \hookrightarrow & \langle \mathsf{H} ; \mathsf{e}_r[x_1/y_1, x_2/y_2] ; \mathsf{S} \rangle
\end{array}$$

**Figure 5:** A non-deterministic counting operational semantics. The guards for counting restrictions are highlighted by grey boxes.

we need to account for two things. First, we decrease the multiplicity annotation on the binding (from $m + 1$ to $m$ in rule ELKPV). Moreover, the value v can in the future be used both directly (since it is now the active expression), *and* indirectly through a future de-reference of $x$. We express this by *non-deterministically splitting* the value v, returning two values $\mathsf{v}_1$ and $\mathsf{v}_2$ whose top-level $\lambda$-annotations sum up to the original (see *split* in Figure 5). Our proof needs only ensure that among the non-deterministic choices there *exists* a choice that simulates $\longrightarrow$. Rule EUPD is similar except that the heap gets updated by an update frame.

### 4.2 Checking well-annotated terms

We would like to prove that if we analyse a term $e$, producing an annotated term e, then if $e$ executes for a number of steps in the standard semantics $\longrightarrow$, then execution of e does not get stuck in the instrumented semantics $\hookrightarrow$ of Figure 5. To do this we need to prove preservation and progress lemmas, showing that each step takes a well-annotated term to a well-annotated term, and that well-annotated terms do not get stuck.

Figure 6 says what it means to be "well-annotated", using notation from Figures 1 and 2. The rules look very similar to the analysis rules of Figures 3-4, except that we check an annotated term, rather than producing one. For example, rule TLAM checks that the annotation on a $\lambda$-abstraction $(m)$ is at least as large as the call cardinality we press on this $\lambda$-abstraction $(n)$. As evaluation progresses the situation clarifies, so the annotations may become more conservative than the checker requires, but that is fine.

A more substantial difference is that instead of holding concrete demand transformers $\rho$ as the analysis does (Figure 1), the environment $P$ holds *generalised demand transformers* $\varrho$. A generalised demand transformer is simply a monotone function from a demand to a pair $\langle \tau ; \varphi \rangle$ of a type and a usage environment (Figure 6). In the TLETDN rule, we clairvoyantly choose any such transformer $\varrho$, which is sound for the RHS expression – denoted with $P \models \mathsf{e}_1 : \varrho$. We still check that that $\mathsf{e}_1$ can be type checked with some demand $d_1$ that comes from type-checking the body of the `let` $(\varphi_2(x))$. In rule TVARDN we simply apply the transformer $\varrho$ to get a type and fv-usage environment.

Rule WFTRANS imposes two conditions necessary for the soundness of the transformer. First, it has to be a monotone function on the demand argument. Second, it has to soundly approximate any type and usage environment that we can attribute to the expression. One can easily confirm that the intensional representation used in the analysis satisfies both properties for the $\lambda$-expressions bound with LETDN.

Because these rules conjure up functions $\varrho$ out of thin air, and have universally quantified premises (in WFTRANS), they do not constitute an algorithm. But for the very same reasons they are convenient to reason about in the metatheory, and that is the only reason we need them. In effect, Figure 6 constitutes an elaborate invariant for the operational semantics.

### 4.3 Soundness of the analysis

The first result is almost trivial.

**Lemma 4.1** (Analysis produces well-typed terms). *If* $P \vdash\!\!\blacktriangleright e \downarrow d \Rightarrow \langle \tau ; \varphi \rangle \rightsquigarrow \mathsf{e}$ *then* $P \vdash \mathsf{e} \downarrow d \Rightarrow \langle \tau ; \varphi \rangle$.

We would next like to show that well-typed terms do not get stuck. To present the main result we need some notation first.

**Definition 4.1** (Unannotated heaps and stacks and erasure). We use $H$ and $S$ to refer to an un-instrumented heap and stack respectively. We use $\mathsf{e}^\natural = e$ to mean that the erasure of all annotations from e is $e$, and we define $\mathsf{S}^\natural = S$ and $\mathsf{H}^\natural = H$ analogously.

We can show that annotated terms run for at least as many steps as their erasures would run in the un-instrumented semantics:

**Theorem 4.2** (Safety for annotated terms). *If* $\epsilon \vdash \mathsf{e}_1 \downarrow HU \Rightarrow \langle \tau ; \epsilon \rangle$ *and* $e_1 = \mathsf{e}_1^\natural$ *and* $\langle \epsilon ; e_1 ; \epsilon \rangle \longrightarrow^k \langle H ; e_2 ; S \rangle$ *then there exist* H, $\mathsf{e}_2$ *and* S, *such that* $\langle \epsilon ; \mathsf{e}_1 ; \epsilon \rangle \hookrightarrow^k \langle \mathsf{H} ; \mathsf{e}_2 ; \mathsf{S} \rangle$, $\mathsf{H}^\natural = H$, $\mathsf{S}^\natural = S$ *and* $\mathsf{e}_2^\natural = e_2$.

Unsurprisingly, to prove this theorem we need to generalise the statement to talk about a single-step reduction of a configuration with arbitrary (but well-annotated) heap and stack. Hence we introduce *a well-annotated configuration relation*, denoted $\vdash \langle \mathsf{H} ; \mathsf{e} ; \mathsf{S} \rangle$, that extends the well-annotation invariant of Figure 6 to configurations. For reasons of space, we only give the statement of the theorem below, and defer the details of the well-annotation relation to the extended version of the paper (Sergey et al. 2013).

**Lemma 4.3** (Single-step safety). *Assume that* $\vdash \langle \mathsf{H}_1 ; \mathsf{e}_1 ; \mathsf{S}_1 \rangle$. *If* $\langle \mathsf{H}_1^\natural ; \mathsf{e}_1^\natural ; \mathsf{S}_1^\natural \rangle \longrightarrow \langle H_2 ; e_2 ; S_2 \rangle$ *in the un-instrumented semantics, then there exist* $\mathsf{H}_2$, $\mathsf{e}_2$ *and* $\mathsf{S}_2$, *such that* $\langle \mathsf{H}_1 ; \mathsf{e}_1 ; \mathsf{S}_1 \rangle \hookrightarrow \langle \mathsf{H}_2 ; \mathsf{e}_2 ; \mathsf{S}_2 \rangle$, $\mathsf{H}_2^\natural = H_2$, $\mathsf{e}_2^\natural = e$ *and* $\mathsf{S}_2^\natural = S_2$, *and moreover* $\vdash \langle \mathsf{H}_2 ; \mathsf{e}_2 ; \mathsf{S}_2 \rangle$.

Notice that the counting semantics is non-deterministic, so Lemma 4.3 simply ensures that there *exists* a possible transition in the counting semantics that always results in a well-typed configuration. Lemma 4.3 crucially relies on yet another property, below.

$$P ::= \epsilon \mid P, (x{:}\varrho) \qquad \varrho \in d \mapsto \langle \tau \,;\, \varphi \rangle$$

$$\boxed{P \vdash \mathsf{e} \downarrow d \Rightarrow \langle \tau \,;\, \varphi \rangle}$$

$$\frac{(x : \varrho) \in P \quad \langle \tau \,;\, \varphi \rangle = \varrho(d)}{P \vdash x \downarrow d \Rightarrow \langle \tau \,;\, \varphi \,\&\, (x{:}1{*}d) \rangle}\;\textsc{TVarDn}$$

$$\frac{x \notin dom(P)}{P \vdash x \downarrow d \Rightarrow \langle \bullet \,;\, (x{:}1{*}d) \rangle}\;\textsc{TVarUp}$$

$$\frac{d \sqsubseteq C^n(d_e) \quad m \geq n \quad P \vdash \mathsf{e} \downarrow d_e \Rightarrow \langle \tau \,;\, \varphi \rangle}{P \vdash \lambda^m x\,.\,\mathsf{e} \downarrow d \Rightarrow \langle \varphi(x) \rightarrow \tau \,;\, n{*}(\varphi \backslash_x) \rangle}\;\textsc{TLam}$$

$$\frac{d \sqsubseteq HU}{P \vdash \lambda^m x\,.\,\mathsf{e} \downarrow d \Rightarrow \langle \tau \,;\, \epsilon \rangle}\;\textsc{TLamHU}$$

$$\frac{\begin{array}{c} P \vdash \mathsf{e}_1 \downarrow C^1(d) \Rightarrow \langle \tau_1 \,;\, \varphi_1 \rangle \\ \tau_1 \preceq d_2^\dagger \rightarrow \tau_r \quad P \Vdash^{*} y \downarrow d_2^\dagger \Rightarrow \varphi_2 \end{array}}{P \vdash \mathsf{e}_1\ y \downarrow d \Rightarrow \langle \tau_r \,;\, \varphi_1 \,\&\, \varphi_2 \rangle}\;\textsc{TApp}$$

$$\frac{d \sqsubseteq U(d_1^\dagger, d_2^\dagger) \quad P \Vdash^{*} x_1 \downarrow d_1^\dagger \Rightarrow \varphi_1 \quad P \Vdash^{*} x_2 \downarrow d_2^\dagger \Rightarrow \varphi_2}{P \vdash (x_1, x_2) \downarrow d \Rightarrow \langle \bullet \,;\, \varphi_1 \,\&\, \varphi_2 \rangle}\;\textsc{TPair}$$

$$\frac{\begin{array}{c} P \vdash \mathsf{e}_r \downarrow d \Rightarrow \langle \tau \,;\, \varphi_r \rangle \\ P \vdash \mathsf{e}_s \downarrow U(\varphi_r(x), \varphi_r(y)) \Rightarrow \langle \_ \,;\, \varphi_s \rangle \end{array}}{P \vdash \mathtt{case}\ \mathsf{e}_s\ \mathtt{of}\ (x, y) \rightarrow \mathsf{e}_r \downarrow d \Rightarrow \langle \tau \,;\, \varphi_r \backslash_{x,y} \,\&\, \varphi_s \rangle}\;\textsc{TCase}$$

$$\frac{\begin{array}{c} m \geq \mu(\varphi_2(x)) \quad \varphi_2(x) \sqsubseteq n * d_1 \\ P \vdash \mathsf{e}_1 \downarrow d_1 \Rightarrow \langle \tau_1 \,;\, \varphi_1 \rangle \quad P \Vdash^{\pm} \mathsf{e}_1 : \varrho \\ P, (x{:}\varrho) \vdash \mathsf{e}_2 \downarrow d \Rightarrow \langle \tau \,;\, \varphi_2 \rangle \end{array}}{P \vdash \mathtt{let}\ x \overset{m}{=} \mathsf{e}_1\ \mathtt{in}\ \mathsf{e}_2 \downarrow d \Rightarrow \langle \tau \,;\, (\varphi_2 \backslash_x) \rangle}\;\textsc{TLetDn}$$

$$\frac{\begin{array}{c} m \geq n \quad P \vdash \mathsf{e}_2 \downarrow d \Rightarrow \langle \tau \,;\, \varphi_2 \rangle \\ n{*}d_x = \varphi_2(x) \quad P \vdash \mathsf{e}_1 \downarrow d_x \Rightarrow \langle \_ \,;\, \varphi_1 \rangle \end{array}}{P \vdash \mathtt{let}\ x \overset{m}{=} \mathsf{e}_1\ \mathtt{in}\ \mathsf{e}_2 \downarrow d \Rightarrow \langle \tau \,;\, \varphi_1 \,\&\, (\varphi_2 \backslash_x) \rangle}\;\textsc{TLetUp}$$

$$\frac{P \vdash \mathsf{e}_2 \downarrow d \Rightarrow \langle \tau \,;\, \varphi_2 \rangle \quad A = \varphi_2(x)}{P \vdash \mathtt{let}\ x \overset{m}{=} \mathsf{e}_1\ \mathtt{in}\ \mathsf{e}_2 \downarrow d \Rightarrow \langle \tau \,;\, \varphi_1 \,\&\, (\varphi_2 \backslash_x) \rangle}\;\textsc{TLetUpAbs}$$

$$\boxed{P \Vdash^{*} x \downarrow d^\dagger \Rightarrow \varphi}$$

$$\frac{}{P \Vdash^{*} x \downarrow A \Rightarrow \epsilon}\;\textsc{TAbs} \qquad \frac{P \vdash x \downarrow d \Rightarrow \langle \tau \,;\, \varphi \rangle}{P \Vdash^{*} x \downarrow n{*}d \Rightarrow n{*}\varphi}\;\textsc{TMulti}$$

$$\boxed{P \Vdash^{\pm} \mathsf{e} : \varrho}$$

$$\frac{\begin{array}{l} \forall d_1, d_2\,.\, d_1 \sqsubseteq d_2 \Longrightarrow \varrho(d_1) \sqsubseteq \varrho(d_2) \\ \forall d, \varphi, \tau\,.\,(P \vdash \mathsf{e} \downarrow d \Rightarrow \langle \tau \,;\, \varphi \rangle) \Longrightarrow \langle \tau \,;\, \varphi \rangle \sqsubseteq \varrho(d) \end{array}}{P \Vdash^{\pm} \mathsf{e} : \varrho}\;\textsc{WFTrans}$$

**Figure 6:** Well-annotated terms

**Lemma 4.4** (Value demand splitting). *If* $P \vdash \mathsf{v} \downarrow (d_1 \,\&\, d_2) \Rightarrow \langle \tau \,;\, \varphi \rangle$ *then there exists a split* $split(\mathsf{v}) = (\mathsf{v}_1, \mathsf{v}_2)$ *such that:* $P \vdash \mathsf{v}_1 \downarrow d_1 \Rightarrow \langle \tau_1 \,;\, \varphi_1 \rangle$ *and* $P \vdash \mathsf{v}_2 \downarrow d_2 \Rightarrow \langle \tau_2 \,;\, \varphi_2 \rangle$ *and moreover* $\tau_1 \sqsubseteq \tau$, $\tau_2 \sqsubseteq \tau$ *and* $\varphi_1 \,\&\, \varphi_2 \sqsubseteq \varphi$.

Why is Lemma 4.4 important? Consider the following

```
let x = v  in  case x 3 of (y,z) -> x 4
```

$$\frac{}{\epsilon \propto \epsilon}\;\textsc{HSim1} \qquad \frac{\mathsf{H}_1 \propto \mathsf{H}_2}{\mathsf{H}_1, [x \overset{0}{\mapsto} \mathtt{Exp}(\mathsf{e})] \propto \mathsf{H}_2}\;\textsc{HSim2}$$

$$\frac{n \geq 1 \quad \mathsf{H}_1 \propto \mathsf{H}_2 \quad \mathsf{e}_1 \propto \mathsf{e}_2}{\mathsf{H}_1, [x \overset{n}{\mapsto} \mathtt{Exp}(\mathsf{e}_1)] \propto \mathsf{H}_2, [x \overset{n}{\mapsto} \mathtt{Exp}(\mathsf{e}_2)]}\;\textsc{HSim3}$$

$$\frac{\mathsf{H}_1 \propto \mathsf{H}_2}{\mathsf{H}_1, [x \overset{0}{\mapsto} \mathtt{Val}(\mathsf{v})] \propto \mathsf{H}_2}\;\textsc{HSim4}$$

$$\frac{\mathsf{H}_1 \propto \mathsf{H}_2 \quad \mathsf{v}_1 \propto \mathsf{v}_2}{\mathsf{H}_1, [x \overset{\omega}{\mapsto} \mathtt{Val}(\mathsf{v}_1)] \propto \mathsf{H}_2, [x \overset{\omega}{\mapsto} \mathtt{Val}(\mathsf{v}_2)]}\;\textsc{HSim5}$$

$$\frac{}{\epsilon \propto \epsilon}\;\textsc{SSim1} \qquad \frac{\mathsf{S}_1 \propto \mathsf{S}_2}{(\#(x, 1) : \mathsf{S}_1) \propto \mathsf{S}_2}\;\textsc{SSim2}$$

$$\frac{\mathsf{S}_1 \propto \mathsf{S}_2}{(\#(x, \omega) : \mathsf{S}_1) \propto (\#(x, \omega) : \mathsf{S}_2)}\;\textsc{SSim3}$$

$$\frac{\mathsf{S}_1 \propto \mathsf{S}_2}{(\bullet\ y) : \mathsf{S}_1 \propto (\bullet\ y) : \mathsf{S}_2}\;\textsc{SSim4}$$

$$\frac{\mathsf{e}_1 \propto \mathsf{e}_2 \quad \mathsf{S}_1 \propto \mathsf{S}_2}{((x, y) \rightarrow \mathsf{e}_1) : \mathsf{S}_1 \propto ((x, y) \rightarrow \mathsf{e}_2) : \mathsf{S}_2}\;\textsc{SSim5}$$

**Figure 7:** Auxiliary simulation relation (heaps and stacks)

The demand exercised on `x` from the body of the `let`-binding will be $C^1(U) \,\&\, C^1(U) = C^\omega(U)$ and hence the value `v` will be checked against this demand (using the LETUP rule), unleashing an environment $\varphi$. However, after substituting `v` in the body (which is ultimately what call-by-need will do) we will have checked it against $C^1(U)$ and $C^1(U)$ independently, unleashing $\varphi_1$ and $\varphi_2$ in each call site. Lemma 4.4 ensures that reduction never increases the demand on the free variables of the environment, and hence safety is not compromised. It is precisely the proof of Lemma 4.4 that requires demand transformers to be monotone in the demand arguments, ensured by WFTRANS.

**Theorem 4.5** (Safety of analysis). *If* $\epsilon \Vdash\!\blacktriangleright e_1 \downarrow HU \Rightarrow \langle \tau \,;\, \epsilon \rangle \rightsquigarrow \mathsf{e}_1$ *and* $\langle \epsilon \,;\, e_1 \,;\, \epsilon \rangle \longrightarrow^k \langle H \,;\, e_2 \,;\, S \rangle$*, then there exist* $\mathsf{H}$, $\mathsf{e}_2$ *and* $\mathsf{S}$*, such that* $\langle \epsilon \,;\, \mathsf{e}_1 \,;\, \epsilon \rangle \hookrightarrow^k \langle \mathsf{H} \,;\, \mathsf{e}_2 \,;\, \mathsf{S} \rangle$, $\mathsf{H}^\natural = H$, $\mathsf{S}^\natural = S$ *and* $\mathsf{e}_2^\natural = e_2$.

The proof is just a combination of Lemma 4.1 and Theorem 4.2.

# 5. Optimisations

We discuss next the two optimisations enabled by our analysis.

## 5.1 Optimised allocation for thunks

We show here that for 0-annotated bindings there is no need to allocate an entry in the heap, and for 1-annotated ones we don't have to emit an update frame on the stack. Within the chosen operational model, this optimisation is of *dynamic* flavour so we express this by providing a new, *optimising* small-step machine for the annotated expressions. The new semantics is defined in Figure 8. We will show that programs that can be evaluated via the counting semantics (Figure 5) can be also evaluated via the optimised semantics in a smaller or equal number of steps.

The proof is a simulation proof, hence we define relations between heaps / optimised heaps, and stacks / optimised stacks that are preserved during evaluation.

$$\langle \mathsf{H}_0 \,;\, \mathsf{e}_0 \,;\, \mathsf{S}_0\rangle \Longrightarrow \langle \mathsf{H}_1 \,;\, \mathsf{e}_1 \,;\, \mathsf{S}_1\rangle$$

| | | | |
|---|---|---|---|
| OPT-ELETA | $\langle \mathsf{H} \,;\, \texttt{let}\ x \overset{0}{=} \mathsf{e}_1\ \texttt{in}\ \mathsf{e}_2 \,;\, \mathsf{S}\rangle$ | $\Longrightarrow$ | $\langle \mathsf{H} \,;\, \mathsf{e}_2 \,;\, \mathsf{S}\rangle$ |
| OPT-ELETU | $\langle \mathsf{H} \,;\, \texttt{let}\ x \overset{n}{=} \mathsf{e}_1\ \texttt{in}\ \mathsf{e}_2 \,;\, \mathsf{S}\rangle$ | $\Longrightarrow$ | $\langle \mathsf{H}[x \overset{n}{\mapsto} \mathsf{Exp}(\mathsf{e}_1)] \,;\, \mathsf{e}_2 \,;\, \mathsf{S}\rangle$ where $n \geq 1$ |
| OPT-ELKPEM | $\langle \mathsf{H}, [x \overset{\omega}{\mapsto} \mathsf{Exp}(\mathsf{e})] \,;\, x \,;\, \mathsf{S}\rangle$ | $\Longrightarrow$ | $\langle \mathsf{H} \,;\, \mathsf{e} \,;\, \#(x, \omega) : \mathsf{S}\rangle$ |
| OPT-ELKPEO | $\langle \mathsf{H}, [x \overset{1}{\mapsto} \mathsf{Exp}(\mathsf{e})] \,;\, x \,;\, \mathsf{S}\rangle$ | $\Longrightarrow$ | $\langle \mathsf{H} \,;\, \mathsf{e} \,;\, \mathsf{S}\rangle$ |
| OPT-ELKPV | $\langle \mathsf{H}, [x \overset{\omega}{\mapsto} \texttt{Val}(\mathsf{v})] \,;\, x \,;\, \mathsf{S}\rangle$ | $\Longrightarrow$ | $\langle \mathsf{H}, [x \overset{\omega}{\mapsto} \texttt{Val}(\mathsf{v})] \,;\, \mathsf{v} \,;\, \mathsf{S}\rangle$ |
| OPT-EUPD | $\langle \mathsf{H} \,;\, \mathsf{v} \,;\, \#(x, \omega) : \mathsf{S}\rangle$ | $\Longrightarrow$ | $\langle \mathsf{H}, [x \overset{\omega}{\mapsto} \texttt{Val}(\mathsf{v})] \,;\, \mathsf{v} \,;\, \mathsf{S}\rangle$ |
| OPT-EBETA | $\langle \mathsf{H} \,;\, \lambda^m x.\mathsf{e} \,;\, (\bullet\ y) : \mathsf{S}\rangle$ | $\Longrightarrow$ | $\langle \mathsf{H} \,;\, \mathsf{e}[y/x] \,;\, \mathsf{S}\rangle$ |
| OPT-EAPP | $\langle \mathsf{H} \,;\, \mathsf{e}\ y \,;\, \mathsf{S}\rangle$ | $\Longrightarrow$ | $\langle \mathsf{H} \,;\, \mathsf{e} \,;\, (\bullet\ y) : \mathsf{S}\rangle$ |
| OPT-EPAIR | $\langle \mathsf{H} \,;\, \texttt{case}\ \mathsf{e}_s\ \texttt{of}\ (x, y) \to \mathsf{e}_r \,;\, \mathsf{S}\rangle$ | $\Longrightarrow$ | $\langle \mathsf{H} \,;\, \mathsf{e}_s \,;\, ((x, y) \to \mathsf{e}_r) : \mathsf{S}\rangle$ |
| OPT-EPRED | $\langle \mathsf{H} \,;\, (x_1, x_2) \,;\, ((y_1, y_2) \to \mathsf{e}_r) : \mathsf{S}\rangle$ | $\Longrightarrow$ | $\langle \mathsf{H} \,;\, \mathsf{e}_r[x_1/y_1, x_2/y_2] \,;\, \mathsf{S}\rangle$ |

**Figure 8:** Optimised counting semantics

**Definition 5.1** (Auxiliary $\propto$-relations). We write $\mathsf{e}_1 \propto \mathsf{e}_2$ iff $\mathsf{e}_1$ and $\mathsf{e}_2$ differ only on the $\lambda$-annotations. $\mathsf{H}_1 \propto \mathsf{H}_2$ and $\mathsf{S}_1 \propto \mathsf{S}_2$ are defined in Figure 7.

For this optimisation the annotations on $\lambda$-abstractions play no role, hence we relate *any* expressions that differ only on those.

Figure 7 tells us when a heap $\mathsf{H}$ is related with an *optimised* heap $\mathsf{H}_{opt}$ with the relation $\mathsf{H} \propto \mathsf{H}_{opt}$. As we have described, there are no $\overset{0}{\mapsto}$ bindings in the optimised heap. Moreover notice that there are no bindings of the form $[x \overset{1}{\mapsto} \texttt{Val}(v)]$ in either the optimised or unoptimised heap. It is easy to see why: every heap binding starts life as $[x \overset{m}{\mapsto} \mathsf{Exp}(\mathsf{e})]$. By the time $\mathsf{Exp}(\mathsf{e})$ has become a value $\texttt{Val}(\mathsf{v})$, we have already used $x$ once. Hence, if originally $m = \omega$ then the value binding will also be $\omega$ (in the optimised or unoptimised semantics). If it was $m = 1$ then it can only be 0 in the un-optimised heap and non-existent in the optimised heap. If it was $m = 0$ then no such bindings would have existed in the optimised heap anyway.

The relation between stacks is given with $\mathsf{S} \propto \mathsf{S}_{opt}$. Rule SSIM2 ensures that there are no frames $\#(x, 1)$ in the optimised stack. In fact during evaluation it is easy to observe that there are not going to be any update frames $\#(x, 0)$ in the original or optimised stack.

We can now state the optimisation simulation theorem.

**Theorem 5.1** (Optimised semantics). *If* $\langle \mathsf{H}_1;\mathsf{e}_1;\mathsf{S}_1\rangle \propto \langle \mathsf{H}_2;\mathsf{e}_2;\mathsf{S}_2\rangle$ *and* $\langle \mathsf{H}_1 \,;\, \mathsf{e}_1 \,;\, \mathsf{S}_1\rangle \hookrightarrow \langle \mathsf{H}_1' \,;\, \mathsf{e}_1' \,;\, \mathsf{S}_1'\rangle$ *then there exists* $k \in \{0, 1\}$ *s.t.* $\langle \mathsf{H}_2 \,;\, \mathsf{e}_2 \,;\, \mathsf{S}_2\rangle \Longrightarrow^k \langle \mathsf{H}_2' \,;\, \mathsf{e}_2' \,;\, \mathsf{S}_2'\rangle$ *and* $\langle \mathsf{H}_1' \,;\, \mathsf{e}_1' \,;\, \mathsf{S}_1'\rangle \propto \langle \mathsf{H}_2' \,;\, \mathsf{e}_2' \,;\, \mathsf{S}_2'\rangle$.

Notice that the counting semantics may not be able to take a transition at some point due to the wrong non-deterministic choice but in that case the statement of Theorem 5.1 holds trivially. Finally, we tie together Theorems 5.1 and 4.5 to get the following result.

**Theorem 5.2** (Analysis is safe for optimised semantics). *If* $\Vdash e_1 \downarrow HU \Rightarrow \langle \tau \,;\, \epsilon\rangle \rightsquigarrow \mathsf{e}_1$ *and* $\langle \epsilon \,;\, e_1 \,;\, \epsilon\rangle \longrightarrow^n \langle H \,;\, e_2 \,;\, S\rangle$ *then* $\langle \epsilon \,;\, \mathsf{e}_1 \,;\, \epsilon\rangle \Longrightarrow^m \langle \mathsf{H} \,;\, \mathsf{e}_2 \,;\, \mathsf{S}\rangle$ *s. t.* $\mathsf{e}_2^\natural = e_2$, $m \leq n$, *and there exist* $\mathsf{H}_2$ *and* $\mathsf{S}_2$ *s.t.* $\mathsf{H}_2^\natural = H$ *and* $\mathsf{S}_2^\natural = S$ *and* $\mathsf{H}_2 \propto \mathsf{H}$ *and* $\mathsf{S}_2 \propto \mathsf{S}$.

Theorem 5.2 says that if a program $e_1$ evaluates in n steps to $e_2$ in the reference semantics, then it also evaluates to the same $e_2$ (modulo annotation) in the optimised semantics in $n$ steps or fewer; and the heaps and stacks are consistent. Moreover, the theorem has informative content on infinite sequences. For example it says that for any point in the evaluation in the reference semantics, we will have earlier reached a corresponding intermediate configuration in the optimised semantics with consistent heaps and stacks.

### 5.2 `let`-in floating into one-shot lambdas

As discussed in Section 2, we are interested in the particular case of `let`-floating (Peyton Jones et al. 1996): moving the binder into the body of a lambda-expression. This transformation is trivially *safe*, given obvious syntactic side conditions (Moran and Sands 1999, §4.5), however, in general, it is not *beneficial*. Here we describe the conditions under which `let`-in floating makes things better in terms of the length of the program execution sequence.

We start by defining `let`-in floating in a form of syntactic rewriting:

**Definition 5.2** (`let`-in floating for *one-shot* lambdas).

$$\begin{aligned} & \texttt{let}\ z \overset{m_1}{=} \mathsf{e}_1\ \texttt{in}\ (\texttt{let}\ f \overset{m_2}{=} \lambda^1 x\ .\ \mathsf{e}\ \texttt{in}\ \mathsf{e}_2) \\ \Longrightarrow\ & \texttt{let}\ f \overset{m_2}{=} \lambda^1 x\ .\ (\texttt{let}\ z \overset{m_1}{=} \mathsf{e}_1\ \texttt{in}\ \mathsf{e})\ \texttt{in}\ \mathsf{e}_2, \end{aligned}$$

for any $m_1$, $m_2$ and $z \notin FV(\mathsf{e}_2)$.

Next, we provide a number of definitions necessary to formulate the so called *improvement* result (Moran and Sands 1999). The improvement is formulated for closed, well-formed configurations. For a configuration $\langle \mathsf{H} \,;\, \mathsf{e} \,;\, \mathsf{S}\rangle$ to be *closed*, any free variables in $\mathsf{H}$, $\mathsf{e}$ and $\mathsf{S}$ must be contained in a union $dom(\mathsf{H}) \cup dom(\mathsf{S})$, where $dom(\mathsf{H})$ is a set of variables bound by a heap $\mathsf{H}$, and $dom(\mathsf{S})$ is a set of variables marked for update in a stack $\mathsf{S}$. A configuration is *well-formed* if $dom(\mathsf{H})$ and $dom(\mathsf{S})$ are disjoint.

**Definition 5.3** (Convergence). For a closed configuration $\langle \mathsf{H};\mathsf{e};\mathsf{S}\rangle$,

$$\begin{aligned} \langle \mathsf{H} \,;\, \mathsf{e} \,;\, \mathsf{S}\rangle \Downarrow^N &\overset{\text{def}}{=} \exists \mathsf{H}', \mathsf{v}, N\ .\ \langle \mathsf{H} \,;\, \mathsf{e} \,;\, \mathsf{S}\rangle \hookrightarrow^N \langle \mathsf{H}' \,;\, \mathsf{v} \,;\, \epsilon\rangle \\ \langle \mathsf{H} \,;\, \mathsf{e} \,;\, \mathsf{S}\rangle \Downarrow^{\leq N} &\overset{\text{def}}{=} \exists M\ .\ \langle \mathsf{H} \,;\, \mathsf{e} \,;\, \mathsf{S}\rangle \Downarrow^M\ \text{and}\ M \leq N \end{aligned}$$

The following theorem shows that local let-in floating into the body of a one-shot lambda does not make the execution longer.

**Theorem 5.3** (Let-in float improvement). *For any* $\mathsf{H}$ *and* $\mathsf{S}$, *if*

$$\langle \mathsf{H} \,;\, \texttt{let}\ z \overset{m}{=} \mathsf{e}_1\ \texttt{in}\ (\texttt{let}\ f \overset{m_1}{=} \lambda^1 x\ .\ \mathsf{e}\ \texttt{in}\ \mathsf{e}_2) \,;\, \mathsf{S}\rangle \Downarrow^N$$

*and* $z \notin FV(\mathsf{e}_2)$, *then*

$$\langle \mathsf{H} \,;\, \texttt{let}\ f \overset{m_1}{=} \lambda^1 x\ .\ (\texttt{let}\ z \overset{m}{=} \mathsf{e}_1\ \texttt{in}\ \mathsf{e})\ \texttt{in}\ \mathsf{e}_2 \,;\, \mathsf{S}\rangle \Downarrow^{\leq N}.$$

Even though Theorem 5.3 gives a termination-dependent result, its proof (Sergey et al. 2013) goes via a simulation argument, hence it is possible to state the theorem in a more general way without requiring termination.

We also expect that the improvement result extends to arbitrary program contexts, but have not carried out the exercise.

# 6. Implementation

We have implemented the cardinality analyser by extending the demand analysis machinery of the Glasgow Haskell Compiler, available from its open-source repository.[2] We briefly summarise some implementation specifics in this section.

## 6.1 Analysis

The implementation of the analysis was straightforward, because GHC's existing strictness analyser is already cast as a backwards analysis, exactly like our new cardinality analysis. So the existing analyser worked unchanged; all that was required was to enrich the domains over which the analyser works.[3] In total, the analyser increased from 900 lines of code to 1,140 lines, an extremely modest change.

We run the analysis twice, once in the middle of the optimisation pipeline, and once near the end. The purpose of the first run is to expose one-shot lambdas, which in turn enable a cascade of subsequent transformations (Section 6.3). The second analysis finds the single-entry thunks, which are exploited by the code generator. This second analysis is performed very late in the pipeline (a) so that it sees the result of all previous inlining and optimisation and (b) because the single-entry thunk information is not robust to certain other transformations (Section 6.4).

## 6.2 Absence

GHC exploits absence in the worker/wrapper split, as described in Section 2.3: absent arguments are not passed from the wrapper to the worker.

## 6.3 One-shot lambdas

As shown in Section 5.2, there is no run-time payoff for one-shot lambdas. Rather, the information enables some important compile-time transformations. Specifically, consider

$$\texttt{let}\ x = \texttt{costly}\ v\ \texttt{in}\ \ldots(\lambda y.\ldots x \ldots)\ldots$$

If the $\lambda y$ is a one-shot lambda, the binding for $x$ can be floated inside the lambda, without risk of duplicating the computation of `costly`. Once the binding for $x$ is inside the $\lambda y$, several other improvements may happen:

- It may be inlined at $x$'s use site, perhaps entirely eliminating the allocation of a thunk for $x$.
- It may enable a rewrite rule (eg `foldr/build` fusion) to fire.
- It may allow two lambdas to be replaced by one. For example

$$\begin{array}{ll} & \texttt{f} = \lambda v.\ \texttt{let}\ x = \texttt{costly}\ v\ \texttt{in}\ \lambda y.\ldots x\ldots \\ \Longrightarrow & \texttt{f} = \lambda v.\lambda y.\ldots(\texttt{costly}\ v)\ldots \end{array}$$

  The latter produces one function with two arguments, rather than a curried function that returns a heap-allocated lambda (Marlow and Peyton Jones 2006).

## 6.4 Single-entry thunks

The code that GHC compiles for a thunk begins by pushing an *update frame* on the stack, which includes a pointer to the thunk. Then the code for the thunk is executed. When evaluation is complete, the value is returned, and the update frame overwrites the thunk with an indirection to the values (Peyton Jones 1992). It is easy to modify this mechanism to take advantage of single-entry thunks: *we do not generate the push-update-frame code for single-entry thunks*. There is a modest code size saving (fewer instructions generated) and a modest runtime saving (a few store instructions saved on thunk entry, and a few more when evaluation is complete).

[2] `http://github.com/ghc/ghc`

[3] This claim is true in spirit, but in practice we substantially refactored the existing analyser when adding usage cardinalities.

| Program | Synt. $\lambda^1$ | Synt. Thnk$^1$ | RT Thnk$^1$ |
|---|---|---|---|
| `anna` | 4.0% | 7.2% | 2.9% |
| `bspt` | 5.0% | 15.4% | 1.5% |
| `cacheprof` | 7.6% | 11.9% | 5.1% |
| `calendar` | 5.7% | 0.0% | 0.2% |
| `constraints` | 2.0% | 3.2% | 4.5% |
| `cryptarithm2` | 0.6% | 3.0% | 74.0% |
| `gcd` | 12.5% | 0.0% | 0.0% |
| `gen_regexps` | 5.6% | 0.0% | 0.2% |
| `hpg` | 5.2% | 0.0% | 4.1% |
| `integer` | 8.3% | 0.0% | 0.0% |
| `life` | 3.2% | 0.0% | 1.8% |
| `mkhprog` | 27.4% | 20.8% | 5.8% |
| `nucleic2` | 3.5% | 3.1% | 3.2% |
| `partstof` | 5.8% | 10.7% | 0.1% |
| `sphere` | 7.8% | 6.2% | 20.0% |
| ... and 72 more programs | | | |
| Arithmetic mean | 10.3% | 12.6% | 5.5% |

**Table 1.** Analysis results for **`nofib`**: ratios of *syntactic* one-shot lambdas (Synt. $\lambda^1$), *syntactic* used-once thunks (Synt. Thnk$^1$) and *runtime* entries into single-entry thunks (RT Thnk$^1$).

Take care though! The single-entry property is not robust to program transformation. For example, common sub-expression elimination (CSE) can combine two single-entry thunks into one multiple-entry one, as can this sequence of transformations:

$$\begin{array}{rll} & & \texttt{let}\ y \stackrel{1}{=} e\ \texttt{in}\ \texttt{let}\ x = y + 0\ \texttt{in}\ x * x \\ \text{Identity of } + & \Longrightarrow & \texttt{let}\ y \stackrel{1}{=} e\ \texttt{in}\ \texttt{let}\ x = y\ \texttt{in}\ x * x \\ \text{Inline } x & \Longrightarrow & \texttt{let}\ y \stackrel{1}{=} e\ \texttt{in}\ y * y \qquad \text{Wrong!} \end{array}$$

This does not affect the formal results of the paper, but it is the reason that our second run of the cardinality analysis is immediately before code generation.

# 7. Evaluation

To measure the accuracy of the analysis, we counted the proportion of (a) one-shot lambdas and (b) single-entry thunks. In both cases, these percentages are of the *syntactically occurring* lambdas or thunks respectively, measured over the code of the benchmark program only, not library code. Table 1 shows the results reported by our analysis for programs from the `nofib` benchmark suite (Partain 1993). The numbers are quite encouraging. One-shot lambdas account for 0-30% of all lambdas, while single-entry thunks are 0-23% of all thunks.

The static (syntactic) frequency of single-entry thunks may be very different to their *dynamic frequency* in a program execution, so we instrumented GHC to measure the latter. (We did not measure the dynamic frequency of one-shot lambdas, because they confer no direct performance benefit.) The "RT Thunk" column of Table 1 gives the dynamic frequency of single-entry thunks in the same `nofib` programs. Note that these statistics include single-entry thunks from libraries, as well as the benchmark program code. The results vary widely. Most programs do not appear to use single-entry thunks much, while a few use many, up to 74% for `cryptarithm2`.

## 7.1 Optimising `nofib` programs

In the end, of course, we seek improved runtimes, although the benefits are likely to be modest. One-shot lambdas do not confer

| Program | Allocs | | Runtime | |
|---|---|---|---|---|
| | No hack | Hack | No hack | Hack |
| anna | -2.1% | -0.2% | +0.1% | -0.0% |
| bspt | -2.2% | -0.0% | -0.0% | +0.0% |
| cacheprof | -7.9% | -0.6% | -6.1% | -5.0% |
| calendar | -9.2% | +0.2% | -0.0% | -0.0% |
| constraints | -0.9% | -0.0% | -1.2% | -0.2% |
| cryptarithm2 | -0.3% | -0.3% | -2.3% | -2.1% |
| gcd | -15.5% | -0.0% | -0.0% | +0.0% |
| gen_regexps | -1.0% | -0.1% | -0.0% | -0.0% |
| hpg | -2.0% | -1.0% | -0.1% | -0.0% |
| integer | -0.0% | -0.0% | -8.8% | -6.6% |
| life | -0.8% | -0.0% | -5.9% | -1.8% |
| mkhprog | -11.9% | +0.1% | -0.0% | -0.0% |
| nucleic2 | -14.1% | -10.9% | +0.0% | +0.0% |
| partstof | -95.5% | -0.0% | -0.0% | -0.0% |
| sphere | -1.5% | -1.5% | +0.0% | -0.1% |
| ... and 72 more programs | | | | |
| Min | -95.5% | -10.9% | -28.2% | -12.1% |
| Max | +3.5% | +0.5% | +1.8% | +2.8% |
| Geometric mean | -6.0% | -0.3% | -2.2% | -1.4% |

**Table 2.** Cardinality analysis-enabled optimisations for `nofib`

any performance benefits directly; rather, they remove potential obstacles from other compile-time transformations. Single-entry thunks, on the other hand give an immediate performance benefit, by omitting the push-update-frame code, but it is a small one.

Table 2 summarises the effect of cardinality analysis when running the `nofib` suite. "Allocs" is the change in how much heap was allocated when the program is run and "Runtime" is a change in the actual program execution time.

In Section 2.1 we mentioned a hack, used by Gill in GHC, in which he hard-coded the call-cardinality information for three particular functions: `build`, `foldr` and `runST`. Our analysis renders this hack redundant, as now the same results can be soundly *inferred*. We therefore report two sets of results: relative to an un-hacked baseline, and relative to a hacked baseline. In both cases binary size of the (statically) linked binaries falls slightly but consistently (2.0% average), which is welcome. This may be due to less push-update-frame code being generated.

Considering *allocation*, the numbers relative to the non-hacked baseline are quite encouraging, but relative to the hacked compiler the improvements are modest: the hack was very effective! Otherwise, only one program, `nucleic2` shows a significant (11%) reduction in allocation, which turned out to be because a thunk was floated inside a one-shot lambda and ended up never being allocated, exactly as advertised.[4]

A shortcoming of `nofib` suite is that *runtimes* tend to be short and very noisy: even with the execution key `slow` only 18 programs from the suite run for longer than half second (with a maximum of 2.5 seconds for `constraints`). Among those long-runners the biggest performance improvement is 8.8% (for `integer`), with an average of 2.3%.

[4] One can notice that the new compiler sometimes performs *worse* than the cardinality-unaware versions in a very few benchmarks in `nofib`. In a highly optimising compiler with many passes it is very hard to ensure that every "optimisation" always makes the program run faster; and, even if a pass does improve the program *per se*, to ensure that every subsequent pass will carry out all the optimisations that it did before the earlier improvement was implemented. The data show that we do not always succeed. We leave for the future some detailed forensic work to find out exactly why.

| Program | RT Thnk[1] | No-Opt RT | RT Δ |
|---|---|---|---|
| binary-trees | 49.4% | 66.83 s | -9.2% |
| fannkuch-redux | 0.0% | 158.94 s | -3.7% |
| n-body | 5.7% | 38.41 s | -4.4% |
| pidigits | 8.8% | 41.56 s | -0.3% |
| spectral-norm | 4.6% | 17.83 s | -1.7% |

**Table 3.** Optimisation of the programs from Benchmarks Game

| Library | $\lambda^1$ | Thnk[1] | Benchmark | Alloc Δ |
|---|---|---|---|---|
| attoparsec | 32.8% | 19.3% | benchmarks | -7.1% |
| binary | 16.8% | 0.9% | bench | -0.2% |
| | | | builder | -0.3% |
| | | | get | -4.3% |
| bytestring | 5.3% | 4.3% | boundcheck | -0.5% |
| | | | all | -6.6% |
| cassava | 26.4% | 9.8% | benchmarks | -0.7% |

**Table 4.** Analysis and optimisation results for `hackage` libraries

| Program | LOC | GHC Alloc Δ | | GHC RT Δ | |
|---|---|---|---|---|---|
| | | No hack | Hack | No hack | Hack |
| anna | 5740 | -1.6% | -1.5% | -0.8% | -0.4% |
| cacheprof | 1600 | -1.7% | -0.4% | -2.3% | -1.8% |
| fluid | 1579 | -1.9% | -1.9% | -2.8% | -1.6% |
| gamteb | 1933 | -0.5% | -0.1% | -0.5% | -0.1% |
| parser | 2379 | -0.7% | -0.2% | -2.6% | -0.6% |
| veritas | 4674 | -1.4% | -0.3% | -4.5% | -4.1% |

**Table 5.** Compilation with optimised GHC

For more realistic numbers, we measured the improvement in runtime, relative to the hacked compiler, for several programs from the Computer Language Benchmarks Game.[5] The results are shown in Table 3. All programs were run with the official shootout settings (except `spectral-norm`, to which we gave a bigger input value of 7500) on a 2.7 GHz Intel Core i7 OS X machine with 8 Gb RAM. These are uncharacteristic Haskell programs, optimised to within an inch of their life by dedicated Haskell hackers. There is no easy meat to be had, and indeed the heap-allocation changes are so tiny (usually zero, and -0.2% at the most in the case of `binary-trees`) that we omit them from the table. However, we do get one joyful result: a solid speedup of 9.2% in `binary-trees` due to fewer thunk updates. As you can see, nearly half of its thunks entered at runtime are single-entry.

### 7.2 Real-world programs

To test our analysis and the cardinality-powered optimisations on some real-world programs, we chose four continuation-heavy libraries from the `hackage` repository:[6] `attoparsec`, a fast parser combinator library, `binary`, a lazy binary serialisation library, `bytestring`, a space-efficient implementation of byte-vectors, and `cassava`, a CSV parsing and encoding library.

These libraries come with accompanying benchmark suites, which we ran both for the baseline compiler and the cardinality-powered one. Table 4 contains the ratios of syntactic one-shot lambdas and used-once thunks for the libraries, as well relative improvement in memory allocation for particular benchmarks. Since we were interested only in the absolute improvement against the state of

[5] `http://benchmarksgame.alioth.debian.org/`

[6] `http://hackage.haskell.org/`

the art, we made our comparison with respect to the contemporary version of (hacked) baseline GHC. The encouraging results for `attoparsec` are explained by its relatively high ratio of one-shot lambdas, which is typical for parser combinator libraries.

GHC itself is a very large Haskell program, written in a variety of styles, so we compiled it with and without cardinality-powered optimisations, and measured the allocation and runtime improvement when using the two variants to compile several programs. The results are shown in Table 5. As in the other cases, we get modest but consistent improvements.

## 8. Related Work

### 8.1 Abstract interpretation for usage and absence

The goal of the traditional *usage/absence* analyses is to figure out which parts of the programs are used, and which are not (Peyton Jones and Partain 1994). This question was first studied in the late 80's, when an elegant representation of the usage analysis in terms of *projections* (Hinze 1995) was given by Wadler and Hughes (Wadler and Hughes 1987). Their formulation allows one to define a *backwards* analysis — inferring the usage of *arguments* of a function from the usage of its *result* — an idea that we adopted wholesale. Our work has important differences, notably (a) call demands $C^n(d)$, which appear to be entirely new; and (b) the ability to treat nested lambdas, which requires us to capture the usage of free variables in a usage signature. Moreover our formal underpinning is quite different to their (denotational) approach, because we fundamentally must model *sharing*.

### 8.2 Type-based approaches

The notion of "single-entry" thunks and "one-shot" lambdas is reminiscent of *linear types* (Girard 1995; Turner and Wadler 1999), a similarity that was noticed very early (Launchbury et al. 1993). Linear types *per se* are far too restrictive (see, for example, Wansbrough and Peyton Jones (1999, § 2.2) for details), but the idea of using a *type system* to express usage information inspired a series of "once upon a type" papers[7] (Gustavsson 1998; Turner et al. 1995; Wansbrough 2002; Wansbrough and Peyton Jones 1999).

Alas, a promising idea turned out to lead, step by step, into a deep swamp. Firstly, *subtyping* proved to be essential, so that a function that used its argument once could have a type like $Int^1 \to Int$, but still be applied to an argument $x$ that was used many times and had type $Int^\omega$ (Wansbrough and Peyton Jones 1999). Then *usage polymorphism* proved essential to cope with currying: *"[Using the monomorphic system] in the entirety of the standard libraries, just two thunks were annotated as used-once"* (Wansbrough 2002, 3.7). Gustavsson advocated *bounded* polymorphism to gain greater precision (Gustavsson and Sveningsson 2001), while Wansbrough extended usage polymorphism to data types, sometimes resulting in data types with many tens of usage parameters. The interaction of ordinary type polymorphism with all these usage-type features was far from straightforward. The inference algorithm for a polymorphic type system with bounds and subtyping is extremely complex. And so on. Burdened with these intellectual and implementation complexities, Wansbrough's heroic prototype in GHC (around 2,580 LOC of brand-new code; plus pervasive changes to thousands of lines of code elsewhere) turned out to be unsustainable, and never made it into the main trunk.

Our system sidesteps these difficulties entirely by treating the problem as a backwards analysis like strictness analysis, rather than as a type system. This is what gives the simplicity to our approach, but also prevents it from giving "rich" demand signatures to third- and higher-order functions: our usage types can account uniformly only for the first- and second-order functions, thanks to call demands. For example what type might we attribute to

```
f x g = g x
```

The usage of `x` depends on the particular `g` in the call, so usage polymorphism would be called for. This is indeed more expressive but it is also more complicated. We deliberately limit precision for very higher-order programs, to gain simplicity.

At some level abstract interpretation and type inference can be seen as different sides of the same coin, but there are some interesting differences. For example, our LETDN and LETUP rules are explicit about information flow; in the former, information flows from the definition of a function to its uses, while in the latter the flow is reversed. Type systems use unification variables to allow much richer information flow — but at the cost of generating constraints involving subtyping and bounds that are tricky to solve.

Another intriguing difference is in the handling of free variables:

```
let f = \x. y + x  in  if b then f 1 else y
```

How many times is the free variable `y` evaluated in this expression? Obviously just once, and LETDN discovers this, because we unleash the demand on `y` at `f`'s call site, and lub the two branches of the `if`. But type systems behave like LETUP: compute the demand on `f` (namely, called once) and from that compute the demand on `y`. Then combine the demand on `y` from the body of the `let` (used at most once), and from `f`'s right hand side (used at most once), yielding the result that `y` is used many times. We have lost the fact that the two uses come from different branches of the conditional. The fact that our usage signatures include the $\varphi$ component makes them more expressive than mere types — unless we extend the type system yet further with an *polymorphic effect system* (Hage et al. 2007; Holdermans and Hage 2010). Moreover, the analysis approach deals very naturally with absence, and with product types such as pairs, which are ubiquitous. Type-based approaches do not do so well here.

In short, an analysis-based approach has proved much simpler intellectually than the type-based one, and far easier to implement. One might wonder if a clever type system might give better results in practice, but Wansbrough's results (mostly zero change to allocation; one program allocated 15% more, one 14% less (Wansbrough 2002)) were no more compelling than those we report. Our proof technique does however share much in common with Wansbrough and Gustavsson's work, all three being based on an operational semantics with an explicit heap.

One other prominent type-based usage system is Clean's *uniqueness types* (Barendsen and Smetsers 1996). Clean's notion of uniqueness is, however, fundamentally different to ours. In Clean a unique-typed argument places a restriction on the *caller* (to pass the only copy of the value), whereas for us a single-entry argument is a promise by *callee* (to evaluate the argument at most once).

### 8.3 Other related work

Call demands, introduced in this paper, appear to be related to the notion of *applicativeness*, employed in the recent work on relevance typing (Holdermans and Hage 2010). In particular, applicativeness means that an expression either "guaranteed to be applied to an argument" (S), or "may not be applied to an argument" (L). In this terminology S corresponds to a "strong" version of our demands $C^\omega(d)$, which requires $d \sqsubset U$, and L is similar to our $U$. The `seq`-like evaluation of expressions corresponds to our demand $HU$. However, neither call- nor thunk-cardinality are captured by the concept of applicativeness.

[7] The title, as so often, is due to Wadler.

Abstract *counting* or *sharing* analysis conservatively determines which parts of the program might be used by several components or accessed several times in the course of execution. Early work employed a *forward* abstract interpretation framework (Goldberg 1987; Hudak 1986). Since the forward abstract interpreter makes assumptions about *arguments* of a function it examines, the abstract interpretation can account for multiple combinations of those and may, therefore, be extremely expensive to compute.

Recent development on the systematic construction of abstract interpretation-based static analyses for higher-order programs, known as *abstracted abstract machines* (AAM), makes it straightforward to derive an analyser from an existing small-step operational semantics, rather than come up with an ad-hoc *non-standard* one (Van Horn and Might 2010). This approach also greatly simplifies integration of the counting abstract domain to account for sharing (Might and Shivers 2006). However, the abstract interpreters obtained this way are *whole-program* forward analysers, which makes them non-modular. It would be, however, an interesting future work to build a backwards analysis from AAM.

## 9. Conclusion

Cardinality analysis is simple to implement (it added 250 lines of code to a 140,000 line compiler), and it gives real improvements for serious programs, not just for toy benchmarks; for example, GHC itself (a very large Haskell program) runs 4% faster. In the context of a 20-year-old optimising compiler, a gain of this magnitude is a solid win.

***Acknowledgements*** We are grateful to Johan Tibell for the suggestion to use benchmark-accompanied `hackage` libraries and the `cabal bench` utility for the experiments in Section 7.2. We also thank the POPL'14 reviewers for their useful feedback.

## References

Erik Barendsen and Sjaak Smetsers. Uniqueness typing for functional languages with graph rewriting semantics. *Mathematical Structures in Computer Science*, 6(6):579–612, 1996.

Andy Gill. *Cheap Deforestation for Non-strict Functional Languages*. PhD thesis, University of Glasgow, Department of Computer Schence, 1996.

Andy Gill, John Launchbury, and Simon Peyton Jones. A Short Cut to Deforestation. In *Proceedings of the Sixth ACM Conference on Functional Programming Languages and Computer Architecture*, pages 223–232, 1993.

Jean-Yves Girard. Linear logic: its syntax and semantics. In *Proceedings of the workshop on Advances in linear logic*, pages 1–42. Cambridge University Press, 1995.

Benjamin Goldberg. Detecting sharing of partial applications in functional programs. In *Functional Programming Languages and Computer Architecture*, volume 274 of *LNCS*, pages 408–425. Springer-Verlag, 1987.

Jörgen Gustavsson. A type based sharing analysis for update avoidance and optimisation. In *Proceedings of the Third ACM SIGPLAN International Conference on Functional Programming (ICFP'98)*, pages 39–50. ACM, 1998.

Jörgen Gustavsson and Josef Sveningsson. A usage analysis with bounded usage polymorphism and subtyping. In *Implementation of Functional Languages (IFL 2000), Selected Papers*, volume 2011 of *LNCS*, pages 140–157. Springer, 2001.

Jurriaan Hage, Stefan Holdermans, and Arie Middelkoop. A generic usage analysis with subeffect qualifiers. In *Proceedings of the 12th ACM SIGPLAN International Conference on Functional Programming (ICFP'07)*, pages 235–246. ACM, 2007.

Ralf Hinze. *Projection-based strictness analysis - theoretical and practical aspects*. PhD thesis, Bonn University, 1995.

Stefan Holdermans and Jurriaan Hage. Making "stricternes" more relevant. In *PEPM'10: Proceedings of the 2010 ACM SIGPLAN workshop on Partial evaluation and program manipulation*, pages 121–130. ACM, 2010.

Paul Hudak. A semantic model of reference counting and its abstraction. In *Proceedings of the 1986 ACM Conference on Lisp and Functional Programming*, pages 351–363. ACM, 1986.

Richard Jones. Tail recursion without space leaks. *J. Funct. Program.*, 2 (1):73–79, 1992.

John Launchbury, Andy Gill, John Hughes, Simon Marlow, Simon Peyton Jones, and Philip Wadler. Avoiding unnecessary updates. In *Proceedings of the 1992 Glasgow Workshop on Functional Programming*, Workshops in Computing, pages 144–153. Springer, 1993.

Simon Marlow and Simon Peyton Jones. Making a fast curry: push/enter vs. eval/apply for higher-order languages. *J. Funct. Program.*, 16(4-5): 415–449, 2006.

Matthew Might and Olin Shivers. Improving flow analyses via ΓCFA: abstract garbage collection and counting. In *Proceedings of the Eleventh ACM SIGPLAN International Conference on Functional Programming (ICFP'06)*, pages 13–25. ACM, 2006.

Andrew Moran and David Sands. Improvement in a Lazy Context: An Operational Theory for Call-by-Need. In *POPL'99: Proceedings of the 26th annual ACM SIGPLAN-SIGACT symposium on Principles of programming languages*, pages 43–56. ACM, 1999.

Will Partain. The `nofib` benchmark suite of Haskell programs. In *Proceedings of the 1992 Glasgow Workshop on Functional Programming*, Workshops in Computing, pages 195–202. Springer, 1993.

Simon Peyton Jones. Implementing Lazy Functional Languages on Stock Hardware: The Spineless Tagless G-Machine. *J. Funct. Program.*, 2(2): 127–202, 1992.

Simon Peyton Jones and Will Partain. Measuring the effectiveness of a simple strictness analyser. In *Proceedings of the 1993 Glasgow Workshop on Functional Programming*, pages 201–220. Springer, 1994.

Simon Peyton Jones and André Santos. A transformation-based optimiser for Haskell. *Science of Computer Programming*, 32(1-3):3–47, 1998.

Simon Peyton Jones, Will Partain, and André Santos. Let-floating: Moving Bindings to Give Faster Programs. In *Proceedings of the First ACM SIGPLAN International Conference on Functional Programming (ICFP'96)*, pages 1–12. ACM, 1996.

Amr Sabry and Matthias Felleisen. Reasoning about programs in continuation-passing style. In *Proceedings of the 1992 ACM Conference on Lisp and Functional Programming*, pages 288–298. ACM, 1992.

Ilya Sergey, Dimitrios Vytiniotis, and Simon Peyton Jones. Modular, Higher-Order Cardinality Analysis in Theory and Practice. Extended version. Technical Report MSR-TR-2013-112, Microsoft Research, 2013. Available at `http://research.microsoft.com/apps/pubs/?id=204260`.

Peter Sestoft. Deriving a lazy abstract machine. *J. Funct. Program.*, 7(3): 231–264, 1997.

David N. Turner and Philip Wadler. Operational interpretations of linear logic. *Theor. Comput. Sci.*, 227(1-2):231–248, 1999.

David N. Turner, Philip Wadler, and Christian Mossin. Once upon a type. In *Proceedings of the Seventh ACM Conference on Functional Programming Languages and Computer Architecture*, pages 1–11. ACM, 1995.

David Van Horn and Matthew Might. Abstracting abstract machines. In *Proceedings of the 15th ACM SIGPLAN International Conference on Functional Programming (ICFP'10)*, pages 51–62. ACM, 2010.

Philip Wadler and John Hughes. Projections for strictness analysis. In *Functional Programming Languages and Computer Architecture*, volume 274 of *LNCS*, pages 385–407. Springer-Verlag, 1987.

Keith Wansbrough. *Simple Polymorphic Usage Analysis*. PhD thesis, Computer Laboratory, University of Cambridge, 2002.

Keith Wansbrough and Simon Peyton Jones. Once Upon a Polymorphic Type. In *POPL'99: Proceedings of the 26th annual ACM SIGPLAN-SIGACT symposium on Principles of programming languages*, pages 15–28. ACM, 1999.

# Profiling for Laziness

Stephen Chang
stchang@ccs.neu.edu

PLT at Northeastern University
Boston, MA 02115

Matthias Felleisen
matthias@ccs.neu.edu

## Abstract

While many programmers appreciate the benefits of lazy programming at an abstract level, determining which parts of a concrete program to evaluate lazily poses a significant challenge for most of them. Over the past thirty years, experts have published numerous papers on the problem, but developing this level of expertise requires a significant amount of experience.

We present a profiling-based technique that captures and automates this expertise for the insertion of laziness annotations into strict programs. To make this idea precise, we show how to equip a formal semantics with a metric that measures waste in an evaluation. Then we explain how to implement this metric as a dynamic profiling tool that suggests where to insert laziness into a program. Finally, we present evidence that our profiler's suggestions either match or improve on an expert's use of laziness in a range of real-world applications.

***Categories and Subject Descriptors*** D.3.1 [*Programming Languages*]: Formal Definitions and Theory

***General Terms*** laziness; profiling; code refactoring

## 1. Where To Be Lazy

Experts have extolled the benefits of laziness for decades now. As Hughes explained [12], lazy programming languages enable programmers to design code in a modular way; even earlier, Abelson and Sussman [1] argued that programs in strict languages can profit from laziness. Programmers have learned, however, that the key to deploying laziness is moderation, because laziness severely complicates reasoning about a program's resource consumption [11].

Approaches to taming laziness come from two different directions. From one direction, lazy language researchers have devised strategies for determining when to safely *remove* laziness [4, 6, 16]. Because these methods still tend to leave too much laziness behind, lazy programmers frequently annotate their programs with strictness annotations such as Haskell's `seq` [18]. From the other direction, strict programmers *add* laziness via constructs such as `delay` and `force`, for example to manage large data structures [17], delay possibly unneeded tasks [8], or leverage other lazy design patterns [21]. Though the strict approach is appealing since most programs need only a small amount of laziness [5, 14, 15, 20], finding exactly where to add the laziness can be problematic.



*POPL '14*, January 22–24, 2014, San Diego, CA, USA.

ACM 978-1-4503-2544-8/14/01...$15.00.
http://dx.doi.org/10.1145/2535838.2535887

Consider a programmer who wishes to insert laziness annotations into a finite strict program in order to improve its performance. The problem is that laziness is a flow-oriented, global property of programs. Inserting an annotation in one place tends to require additional annotations at other, distant points in the program. Omitting even one of these annotations can result in the complete loss of the desired benefits. In short, the difficulty in placing laziness in strict programs is a "devastating handicap."[1]

Recently, Chang [3] tackled the problem with a static analysis-based tool. This static analysis assumes that a programmer has partially annotated a program. Based on these annotations and a control-flow analysis, it suggests additional `delay` annotations. Because the tool considers only static information, it merely approximates where laziness is needed and often produces spurious suggestions. The requirement for some initial "seed" annotations contributes additional imprecision. Finally, Chang reports that he occasionally has to run his tool more than once to find expert-level placement but offers no guidance on this issue.

In this paper, we present a dynamic solution that interprets information from an execution to determine which parts of the program to evaluate lazily. Our solution consists of three concrete contributions. First, we show how to equip a call-by-value $\lambda$-calculus semantics with a metric for assessing each expression's *laziness potential*. Roughly, laziness potential represents the amount of "unneeded computation" performed by the evaluation of an expression. It thus predicts the degree to which a program's performance benefits from delaying that expression. Second, we explain how to implement this metric as a dynamic profiler for an untyped scripting language.[2] After profiling a program on a typical input, the tool suggests where to add laziness annotations. Third, we present evidence that our profiler generates advice comparable to that of experts in the literature. For most of the programs we examined, our profiler requests the insertion of `delay`s at the same places as human experts; in a few instances, the profiler's suggestions achieve the same performance benefits with fewer laziness annotations.

The next section presents some motivating examples, and section 3 formally describes the notion of laziness potential. Section 4 presents our prototype profiler implementation, while section 5 demonstrates its effectiveness. Finally, the remaining sections conclude with related and future work.

## 2. Laziness Potential, the Intuition

In some instances, it is easy for a programmer to identify where laziness is beneficial. Other times, trying to find these spots in a program is challenging. In this section, we explain our method for finding such spots with a series of examples.

[1] http://pchiusano.blogspot.com/2009/05/optional-laziness-doesnt-quite-cut-it.html

[2] These languages tend to support laziness annotations natively or with libraries and should benefit most from our work. Our work applies to typed languages as well; see section 5.

### 2.1 Criteria for Laziness

If an expression's result is not used, we should delay its evaluation. Informally, a value is *used* if it reaches a position that requires a specific (kind of) value to continue the evaluation process. Examples of such positions are the operands to primitive functions, the test in a conditional, and the function position in an application. In contrast, positions such as arguments to a programmer's functions and data constructors do not use their values. Thus the underlined argument in the following expression should be delayed:

$$(\lambda x.1)\ \underline{(2+3)}$$

Our initial laziness criterion does not cover the case where a program evaluates an expression more than once, e.g., via recursion, producing multiple values. We could extend our criterion to delay expressions where *none* of its values are used, but obviously this binary classification is useless for practical cases. Consider the following pseudocode, which represents a function definition and its use in a typical strict functional language:

```
(1) def rng n m =
(2)   if n ≥ m then nil
(3)   else n :: rng (n+1) m
(4)
(5) let lst = rng 1 1000
(6) in (second lst) + (third lst)
```

A call to *rng* $n$ $m$ produces the list of integers in $[n, m)$. In this example, the (underlined) recursive call to *rng* is evaluated multiple times and produces multiple values. Although `second` and `third` use two of these values, the program is likely to benefit from delaying the underlined expression because most of the list is unused.

The example suggests a quantitative criterion for the injection of laziness into strict programs. Specifically, it hints that the ratio of the number of used results to the total number of results per expression might pinpoint delayable expressions. In the example, the recursive call to *rng* is evaluated $m - n = 999$ times and two of the values are used, giving it a ratio of $2/999$.

Profiling this example with our tool reports the following:

```
rng (n+1) m [ln 3]: 2/999 values used
```

An expression with such a low ratio seems like a promising candidate for laziness, but as the following (boxed) changes to the example show, this first quantitative criterion is still insufficient:

```
(1) def rng f n m =
(2)   if n ≥ m then nil
(3)   else f n :: rng f (n+1) m
(4)
(5) let lst = rng add1 1 1000
(6) in (second lst) + (third lst)
```

Here is some data returned by our profiler:

```
f n [ln 3]: 2/999 values used
rng f (n+1) m [ln 3]: 2/999 values used
```

The expressions $f\ n$ and $rng\ f\ (n{+}1)\ m$ have equal ratios, seemingly indicating that the program benefits equally from delaying each. A programmer immediately understands, however, that this recommendation is misleading because delaying the call to *rng* would prevent most calls to $f$.

To combine these factors, we focus only on the unused values, and additionally weight them by the number of *child-values* created during the creation of an unused value. Essentially, this *weight* is correlated to the size of the dynamic value-dependency tree whose root is the unused value. The weight of an *expression* then, which we dub its *laziness potential*, is roughly the average of the weights of all its unused values. Our profiler reports this information, too:

```
rng f (n+1) m [ln 3]: 2/999 values used
- delaying 997 unused avoids 2989 subvalues, wgt=2990
f n [ln 3]: 2/999 values used
- delaying 997 unused avoids 0 subvalues, wgt=1
```

A higher weight indicates a greater benefit from laziness. The exact calculation of laziness potential is discussed in section 3 but the important takeaway here is that the profiler now considers delaying the call to *rng* more beneficial than delaying the call to $f$, which aligns with a programmer's intuition.

Laziness potential seems promising as a criterion but the following "generate and filter" example demonstrates another problem:

```
(1)  def rng f n m =
(2)    if n ≥ m then nil
(3)    else f n :: rng f (n+1) m
(4)  def filter p? lst =
(5)    if nil? lst then nil
(6)    else let x = first lst
(7)           in if p? x then x :: filter p? (rest lst)
(8)              else filter p? (rest lst)
(9)
(10) let lst = filter even? (rng add1 1 1000)
(11) in (second lst) + (third lst)
```

Profiling this example reports the following initial data:

```
filter p? (rest lst) [ln 7]: 2/500 used
- delaying 498 unused avoids 2486 subvalues, wgt=2487
```

meaning the profiler proposes delaying only a call to *filter*. Intuitively, the recursive call to *rng* should be delayed as well, but it does not appear in the results because *filter* "uses" the entire list.

In response, our profiler iteratively:

1. simulates delaying the expression with the highest laziness potential, and then
2. recalculates usages to possibly uncover more unused values.

With this refinement, the profiler reports:

```
~~~~~~~~~~~~~~ Profiling Summary: Round 0 ~~~~~~~~~~~~~~
  filter p? (rest lst) [ln 7]: 2/500 values used
  - delaying 498 unused avoids 2486 subvalues, wgt=2487

~~~~~~~~~~~~~~ Profiling Summary: Round 1 ~~~~~~~~~~~~~~
  rng f (n+1) m [ln 3]: 4/999 values used
  - delaying 995 unused avoids 983 subvalues, wgt=2984
  f n [ln 3]: 5/999 values used
  - delaying 994 unused avoids 0 subvalues, wgt=1
```

After round 0, the analysis simulates a delay of the call to *filter* and then recomputes all usages, revealing unused values from the call to *rng* in round 1. This process repeats until there are no more unused expressions. The profiler then reports that delaying both the calls to *filter* and *rng* would benefit program performance.

### 2.2 A Complete Example

This subsection shows how a programmer can use our laziness-potential profiler to solve the $n$-queens problem. We compare our result to Chang's [3], who describes the problem like this:

> The $n$-queens problem makes an illustrative playground for advertising lazy programming. An idiomatic lazy solution to such a puzzle may consist of just two parts: a part that places $n$ queens at arbitrary positions on an $n$ by $n$ chess board, and a part for deciding whether a particular placement is a solution to the puzzle.

Thus, Chang separates the program into two independent components and defines one function to compute a solution:

$$\texttt{def}\ nqueens\ n = \texttt{first}\ (filter\ isValid\ all\_placements)$$

where

$$\begin{array}{l}\texttt{let}\ all\_placements = foldl\ process\_row\ \texttt{[nil]}\ (rng\ n)\\ \texttt{def}\ process\_row\ r\ qss\_so\_far =\\ \quad foldr\ (\lambda(qs\ new\_qss).\\ \qquad\qquad (map\ (\lambda c.(r,c)::qs)\ (rng\ n))\ @\ new\_qss)\\ \qquad\quad \texttt{nil}\ qss\_so\_far\end{array}$$

While $all\_placements$ generates a stream of all possible queen placements, $isValid$ checks whether a placement is valid according to the rules of chess. The solution then composes these functions via *filter* and **first**.

As Chang explains, "the approach cleanly separates two distinct concerns: $all\_placements$ ignore[s] the rules of the puzzle, while $isValid$ enforce[s] them. If the components were large, two different programmers could tackle them in parallel. All they would have to agree on is the representation of queen placements, for which we choose a list of board coordinates $(r, c)$." Accordingly, running $all\_placements\ n$ yields a list of lists of positions:

```
[[(n,1);(n-1,1); ... ;(1,1)];
   ...;
 [(n,n);(n-1,n); ... ;(1,n)]]
```

Each line represents one possible placement.

In a strict language, computing $all\_placements$ generates *all* possible placements. Adding laziness preserves the elegant solution and makes it efficient because it prevents unnecessary evaluation. The question is which parts should be delayed. As Chang [3] reports, naïvely switching all lists to lazy lists does not improve program performance. Chang then presents a static tool to aid programmers with the task of inserting additional laziness. For $n$-queens, with lazy lists as the initial source of laziness, the static analysis makes the key suggestion of adding laziness to *foldr*, which results in a significant speedup.

*Without any such initial hints*, our profiler suggests laziness at the same place in *foldr* and also suggests laziness in *filter*:

```
filter p? (rest lst) [ln 23]: 0/2 values used
- delaying 2 unused avoids 5242 subvalues, wgt=5243
foldr f base (rest lst) [ln 40]: 36/85 vals used
- delaying 49 unused avoids 1939 subvalues, wgt=1507
```

Figure 1 summarizes the running times for the 8-queens program implemented in Racket [9] and varying degrees of laziness. The figure reports that the strict version is slow and that adding the suggestions from Chang's static tool produces roughly a four-fold speedup. However, adding laziness annotations as suggested by our profiler produces a program that is roughly *twenty times faster* than the strict version. Chang's oversight is due to the "seed" laziness required by the static analysis. In order for the static tool to compute its suggestions, Chang recommends first converting lists to lazy lists, as strict programmers looking to add laziness commonly do. It turns out, however, that this inserts *too much laziness*. As evident from our profiler's recommendations, *only filter* needs additional laziness; the other lists should be evaluated eagerly.

| Implementation Description | Time (ms) |
|---|---|
| no laziness | 20245 |
| static tool-based suggestions from [3] | 4874 |
| profiler-based suggestions | 1057 |

**Figure 1.** Running times for an 8-queens program.

## 3. Laziness Potential, the Definition

As our informal presentation suggests, we consider *laziness potential* the key to determining where to insert effective laziness annotations in strict programs. This section formally defines the notion in two stages, using a small model.

### 3.1 Partially-labeled $\lambda$-calculus

Our model starts from a labeled version of the untyped $\lambda$-calculus:

$$\begin{array}{rl} e \in Exp = & x \mid v \mid e\ e \mid {}^{\boldsymbol{\ell}}e \mid {}^{\boldsymbol{\ell}\cdot\ell}e\\ v \in LabVal = & w^{\vec{\ell}}\\ w \in Val = & \lambda x.e\\ x \in Var,\ & \boldsymbol{\ell} \in eLab,\ \ell \in vLab\end{array}$$

The syntax employs two kinds of labels. Static labels $\boldsymbol{\ell}$ (in bold) name a syntactic expression in the source program. Dynamic labels $\ell$ (plain) name a value during evaluation, i.e., the result of one runtime execution of an expression with a particular set of bindings for its free variables. Define a program to be a closed expression $e$ with only static labels. As the grammar indicates, static labels are *optional* decorations. During evaluation, a statically labeled expression may be paired with a dynamic label at the upper left. Evaluation may also tag *values* with any number of dynamic labels, all positioned at the upper right and denoted with $\vec{\ell}$. We use $w$ when we wish to refer to a value without labels.

A program may evaluate an expression multiple times, e.g. via recursion, so a statically $\boldsymbol{\ell}$-labeled expression may be associated with a set of dynamic labels representing the values that this expression produces. Further, we wish to compute *usage* of these values, which requires tracking value flow, so values themselves may accumulate multiple $\ell$ labels to enable identification of the value's source expression(s). In the example $\underline{(\lambda x.x)\ \underline{((\lambda z.z)\ \lambda y.y)}}$, $\lambda y.y$ is the result of evaluating both underlined expressions and thus must have two dynamic labels.

Evaluation contexts [7] specify the order of evaluation in our labeled $\lambda$-calculus. They are the standard by-value evaluation contexts, plus an additional labeled context:

$$E \in ECtx = [\,] \mid E\ e \mid v\ E \mid {}^{\boldsymbol{\ell}\cdot\ell}E$$

These contexts dictate that reductions take place within a labeled expression only if it comes with a static and a dynamic label.

The $\longmapsto$ reduction relation specifies one step of evaluation. It is generated from three basic notions of reduction: $\beta_v$ and two additional reductions that introduce and manipulate value labels:

$$\begin{array}{rcll} E[(\lambda x.e)^{\vec{\ell}}\ v] & \longmapsto & E[e\{x ::= v\}] & (\beta_v)\\ E[{}^{\boldsymbol{\ell}}e] & \longmapsto & E[{}^{\boldsymbol{\ell}\cdot\ell}e],\ \ell \notin E[{}^{\boldsymbol{\ell}}e] & (vstart)\\ E[{}^{\boldsymbol{\ell}\cdot\ell}w^{\vec{\ell}}] & \longmapsto & E[w^{\ell,\vec{\ell}}] & (vend)\end{array}$$

The semantics satisfies a conventional well-definedness theorem.

**Theorem 1** (Well-Definedness). *A program $e$ either reduces to a value $v$ or starts an infinitely long chain of reductions.*

*Proof Sketch.* The $\longmapsto$ relation satisfies unique decomposition, so $e$ is a value or can be partitioned uniquely into an evaluation context and a redex. Using a progress-and-preservation approach [7], we can then show that this property is preserved for all reductions. □

From an extensional perspective, the labeled $\lambda$-calculus reduces programs just like the by-value $\lambda$-calculus [19]. Theorem 2 says that the labeled calculus produces the same result, modulo labels, as the unlabeled by-value semantics generated by $\beta_v$. The $\longmapsto_v$ relation is the by-value standard reduction and $\longmapsto\!\!\!\!\to_v$ is its reflexive, transitive closure. The function $\xi$ strips labels from programs.

**Theorem 2** (Label Non-interference). *For any labeled program $e_1$, if $e_1 \longmapsto\!\!\!\!\rightarrow e_2$, then $\xi(e_1) \longmapsto\!\!\!\!\rightarrow_v \xi(e_2)$.*

*Proof Sketch.* Show, by cases on $\longmapsto$, that if $e_1 \longmapsto e_2$, then either $\xi(e_1) \longmapsto_v \xi(e_2)$ or $\xi(e_1) = \xi(e_2)$. □

From an intensional perspective, labels play a critical role. Expressions may be labeled in three different ways and the two label-related reductions specify transitions between labelings. Suppose a redex is statically labeled with $\boldsymbol{\ell}$. Before it is evaluated, a unique, dynamic label $\ell$ is generated and placed on the upper-left, as indicated by the *vstart* reduction. When such a labeled subexpression is reduced to a value, a *vend* reduction shifts the value label from the left-hand side to the right-hand side and discards the static label.

## 3.2 Labeling a Program

The labeled $\lambda$-calculus does not specify which expressions in a program to label statically. Hence, the calculus is applicable in a variety of scenarios, depending on the specific labeling strategy.

For the purposes of finding candidates for lazy evaluation, we employ a function $\mathcal{L}$ that maps unlabeled expressions to expressions with labels on arguments that are not already values:

$$\boxed{\mathcal{L} : \mathit{Exp} \rightarrow \mathit{Exp}}$$

$$\begin{aligned}
\mathcal{L}[\![x]\!] &= x \\
\mathcal{L}[\![\lambda x.e]\!] &= \lambda x.\mathcal{L}[\![e]\!] \\
\mathcal{L}[\![e_1\ e_2]\!] &= \mathcal{L}[\![e_1]\!]\ \mathcal{L}_{arg}[\![e_2]\!]
\end{aligned}$$

$$\begin{aligned}
\mathcal{L}_{arg}[\![x]\!] &= x \\
\mathcal{L}_{arg}[\![\lambda x.e]\!] &= \lambda x.\mathcal{L}[\![e]\!] \\
\mathcal{L}_{arg}[\![e_1\ e_2]\!] &= {}^{\boldsymbol{\ell}}(\mathcal{L}[\![e_1]\!]\ \mathcal{L}_{arg}[\![e_2]\!])
\end{aligned}$$

The $\mathcal{L}$ function labels only applications because delaying values or variables is pointless. Furthermore, only applications in an argument position receive a label. Again, it is not beneficial to delay applications in a usage context because the created suspension is immediately forced. We also do not label function bodies. We prefer to delay its application to avoid spoiling the proper implementation of tail calls for the execution of annotated programs.

## 3.3 Usage Contexts

To determine whether a particular value is used during evaluation, we define usage contexts $U$:

$$\begin{aligned}
u \in \mathit{uCtx} &= [\,]\ e \\
U \in \mathit{UCtx} &= [\,] \mid E[u]
\end{aligned}$$

Intuitively, a context is a usage context if creating a redex requires a specific (kind of) value placed in the hole. In our core calculus, the function position of an application is the only usage context because it requires a $\lambda$ value. In addition, the top-level context is a usage context and thus a program result is considered "used."

## 3.4 Extending the Model

By design, our model smoothly generalizes to constructs found in practical languages. Almost any evaluation-context-based reduction semantics can easily be extended to an appropriate labeled reduction system. The only requirements are to extend the usage contexts and labeling strategy.

We extend our model with typical features. Specifically, we add constants, let, conditionals, primitive arithmetic and boolean operations, lists and list operations, and `delay` and `force` laziness constructs; see figures 2 and 3. The reductions are conventional [7]:

$$\begin{aligned}
e =\ & \ldots \mid n \mid b \mid \texttt{let}\ x = e\ \texttt{in}\ e \mid \texttt{if}\ e\ \texttt{then}\ e\ \texttt{else}\ e \\
& \mid o\ e\ e \mid \texttt{and}\ e\ e \mid \texttt{or}\ e\ e \mid \texttt{not}\ e \\
& \mid \texttt{cons}\ e\ e \mid \texttt{first}\ e \mid \texttt{rest}\ e \mid \texttt{nil} \mid \texttt{nil?}\ e \\
& \mid \texttt{delay}\ e \mid \texttt{force}\ e \\
o =\ & + \mid - \mid * \mid /,\ n \in \mathbb{N},\ b = \texttt{\#t} \mid \texttt{\#f} \\
w =\ & \ldots \mid n \mid b \mid \texttt{cons}\ v\ v \mid \texttt{nil} \mid \texttt{delay}\ e \\
E =\ & \ldots \mid \texttt{let}\ x = E\ \texttt{in}\ e \mid \texttt{if}\ E\ \texttt{then}\ e\ \texttt{else}\ e \\
& \mid o\ E\ e \mid o\ v\ E \mid \texttt{and}\ E\ e \mid \texttt{and}\ v\ E,\ v \neq \texttt{\#f} \\
& \mid \texttt{or}\ E\ e \mid \texttt{or}\ \texttt{\#f}\ E \mid \texttt{not}\ E \\
& \mid \texttt{cons}\ E\ e \mid \texttt{cons}\ v\ E \mid \texttt{first}\ E \mid \texttt{rest}\ E \mid \texttt{nil?}\ E \\
& \mid \texttt{force}\ E
\end{aligned}$$

**Figure 2.** Syntax for an extended by-value language.

$$\begin{array}{rcll}
E[\texttt{let}\ x = v\ \texttt{in}\ e] & \longmapsto & E[e\{x ::= v\}] & (\mathit{let}) \\
E[\texttt{if}\ \texttt{\#f}\ \texttt{then}\ e_1\ \texttt{else}\ e_2] & \longmapsto & E[e_2] & (\mathit{iff}) \\
E[\texttt{if}\ v\ \texttt{then}\ e_1\ \texttt{else}\ e_2] & \longmapsto & E[e_1],\ v \neq \texttt{\#f} & (\mathit{ift}) \\
E[o\ v_1\ v_2] & \longmapsto & E[\delta\ v_1\ v_2] & (\mathit{prim}) \\
E[\texttt{or}\ v\ e] & \longmapsto & E[v],\ v \neq \texttt{\#f} & (\mathit{ort}) \\
E[\texttt{or}\ \texttt{\#f}\ v] & \longmapsto & E[v] & (\mathit{orf}) \\
E[\texttt{and}\ \texttt{\#f}\ e] & \longmapsto & E[\texttt{\#f}] & (\mathit{andf}) \\
E[\texttt{and}\ v_1\ v_2] & \longmapsto & E[v_2],\ v_1 \neq \texttt{\#f} & (\mathit{andt}) \\
E[\texttt{not}\ \texttt{\#f}] & \longmapsto & E[\texttt{\#t}] & (\mathit{notf}) \\
E[\texttt{not}\ v] & \longmapsto & E[\texttt{\#f}],\ v \neq \texttt{\#f} & (\mathit{nott}) \\
E[\texttt{first}\ (\texttt{cons}\ v_1\ v_2)] & \longmapsto & E[v_1] & (\mathit{fst}) \\
E[\texttt{rest}\ (\texttt{cons}\ v_1\ v_2)] & \longmapsto & E[v_2] & (\mathit{rst}) \\
E[\texttt{nil?}\ \texttt{nil}] & \longmapsto & E[\texttt{\#t}] & (\mathit{nil}) \\
E[\texttt{nil?}\ v] & \longmapsto & E[\texttt{\#f}],\ v \neq \texttt{nil} & (\mathit{nil}) \\
E[\texttt{force}\ (\texttt{delay}\ e)] & \longmapsto & E[\texttt{force}\ e] & (\mathit{frcd}) \\
E[\texttt{force}\ v] & \longmapsto & E[v],\ v \neq \texttt{delay}\ e & (\mathit{frcv})
\end{array}$$

**Figure 3.** Semantics for an extended by-value language.

- The true and false boolean literals are `#t` and `#f`. The semantics treats all non-`#f` values as true, as is standard in untyped (and some typed) languages.
- The `and` and `or` primitives are short-circuiting, meaning that the second argument is only evaluated if necessary. This behavior is reflected in the evaluation contexts for `and` and `or`.
- The `force` form is recursive, specified by the *frcd* rule, meaning that applying a single `force` to a suspension returns the underlying value no matter how many `delay`s it is wrapped in.
- Untyped `force` is idempotent, as seen in the *frcv* rule. Applying `force` to a non-delayed value returns that value.

Here is the extended set of usage contexts:

$$\begin{aligned}
u =\ & \ldots \mid \texttt{if}\ [\,]\ e\ e \mid o\ [\,]\ e \mid o\ v\ [\,] \\
& \mid \texttt{and}\ [\,]\ e \mid \texttt{and}\ v\ [\,],\ v \neq \texttt{\#f} \mid \texttt{or}\ [\,]\ e \mid \texttt{or}\ \texttt{\#f}\ [\,] \\
& \mid \texttt{not}\ [\,] \mid \texttt{first}\ [\,] \mid \texttt{rest}\ [\,] \mid \texttt{nil?}\ [\,] \mid \texttt{force}\ [\,]
\end{aligned}$$

Finally, we extend our labeling function to mark expressions of interest, maintaining the goal of finding expressions to delay. In addition to arguments in a function application, we label the bound expression in a `let` and the arguments to `cons`. The ellipses traverse all other expressions in a homomorphic manner:

$$\mathcal{L}[\![e_1\ e_2]\!] = \mathcal{L}[\![e_1]\!]\ \mathcal{L}_{arg}[\![e_2]\!]$$
$$\mathcal{L}[\![\texttt{let}\ x = e_1\ \texttt{in}\ e_2]\!] = \texttt{let}\ x = \mathcal{L}_{arg}[\![e_1]\!]\ \texttt{in}\ \mathcal{L}[\![e_2]\!]$$
$$\mathcal{L}[\![\texttt{cons}\ e_1\ e_2]\!] = \texttt{cons}\ \mathcal{L}_{arg}[\![e_1]\!]\ \mathcal{L}_{arg}[\![e_2]\!]$$
$$\ldots$$

$$\mathcal{L}_{arg}[\![x]\!] = x$$
$$\mathcal{L}_{arg}[\![v]\!] = \mathcal{L}[\![v]\!]$$
$$\mathcal{L}_{arg}[\![e]\!] = {}^{\boldsymbol{\ell}}(\mathcal{L}[\![e]\!]),\ \text{if } e \neq x \text{ or } v$$

### 3.5 Calculating Laziness Potential

We calculate laziness potential via functions that extract information from the propagation of labels in reduction sequences. Let *Red* be the set of finite reduction sequences. In the following definitions, a comma-separated series of expressions represents an element of *Red*, i.e., a trace. We also use $(\mathbb{T}\ e)$ to denote $e$'s complete trace.

The $\mathbb{V}$ function takes a reduction sequence and a static label $\boldsymbol{\ell}$ and returns a set of dynamic labels representing the values generated by the $\boldsymbol{\ell}$-labeled expression over the course of reduction:

$$\boxed{\mathbb{V} : Red \times eLab \rightarrow \mathcal{P}(vLab)}$$
$$\mathbb{V}\ (e)\ \boldsymbol{\ell} = \emptyset$$
$$\mathbb{V}\ (E[{}^{\boldsymbol{\ell}}e], E[{}^{\boldsymbol{\ell}\cdot\ell}e], e', \ldots)\ \boldsymbol{\ell} = \{\ell\} \cup \mathbb{V}\ (e', \ldots)\ \boldsymbol{\ell}$$
$$\mathbb{V}\ (e, e', \ldots)\ \boldsymbol{\ell} = \mathbb{V}\ (e', \ldots)\ \boldsymbol{\ell},\ \text{if } e \neq E[{}^{\boldsymbol{\ell}}e_0]$$

Intuitively, $\mathbb{V}$ inspects all *vstart* steps. In the last example from section 2.1, call it program $P$, if the recursive call to *filter* has static label $\boldsymbol{\ell}_1$, then a new dynamic label is created every time ${}^{\boldsymbol{\ell}_1}$(*filter p?* (`rest` *lst*)) is a redex and $\mathbb{V}\ (\mathbb{T}\ P)\ \boldsymbol{\ell}_1 = \{\ell_1, \ldots, \ell_{500}\}$.

The $\mathbb{U}$ function counts how many times a specified value is used in a given reduction sequence, as dictated by usage contexts:

$$\boxed{\mathbb{U} : Red \times vLab \rightarrow \mathbb{N}}$$
$$\mathbb{U}\ (w^{\vec{\ell}})\ \ell = 1,\ \text{if } \ell \in \vec{\ell}$$
$$\mathbb{U}\ (e)\ \ell = 0,\ \text{if } e \neq v,\ \text{or } e = w^{\vec{\ell}} \text{ but } \ell \notin \vec{\ell}$$
$$\mathbb{U}\ (U[w^{\vec{\ell}}], e', \ldots)\ \ell = 1 + (\mathbb{U}\ (e', \ldots)\ \ell),\ \text{if } \ell \in \vec{\ell}$$
$$\mathbb{U}\ (e, e', \ldots)\ \ell = \mathbb{U}\ (e', \ldots)\ \ell,$$
$$\text{if } e \neq U[v],\ \text{or } e = U[w^{\vec{\ell}}] \text{ but } \ell \notin \vec{\ell}$$

An $\ell$-labeled value is unused in $(\mathbb{T}\ e)$ if $\mathbb{U}\ (\mathbb{T}\ e)\ \ell = 0$. The **unused** function relies on $\mathbb{U}$ and $\mathbb{V}$ to compute (the labels of) all the unused values produced by a particular expression in $e$:

$$\boxed{\textbf{unused} : Exp \times eLab \rightarrow \mathcal{P}(vLab)}$$
$$\textbf{unused}\ (e, \boldsymbol{\ell}) = \{\ell \mid \ell \in \mathbb{V}\ (\mathbb{T}\ e)\ \boldsymbol{\ell},\ \mathbb{U}\ (\mathbb{T}\ e)\ \ell = 0\}$$

For sample program $P$, if `second` and `third` are desugared to `first`s and `rest`s, then two created values reach a `first` [ ] or `rest` [ ] usage context, so for $\ell_i \in \{\ell_1, \ldots, \ell_{500}\}$, $\mathbb{U}\ (\mathbb{T}\ P)\ \ell_i = 1$ for two values of $i$ and is otherwise 0. Thus, **unused** $(P, \boldsymbol{\ell}_1) = 2$.

The $\mathbb{C}$ function returns the labels of all the child-values that are generated *during* the creation of a given $\ell$-labeled value:

$$\boxed{\mathbb{C} : Red \times vLab \rightarrow \mathcal{P}(vLab)}$$
$$\mathbb{C}\ (e)\ \ell = \emptyset$$
$$\mathbb{C}\ (E[{}^{\boldsymbol{\ell}\cdot\ell}e], e', \ldots)\ \ell = \mathbb{C}'\ (e', \ldots)\ \ell$$
$$\mathbb{C}\ (e, e', \ldots)\ \ell = \mathbb{C}\ (e', \ldots)\ \ell,\ \text{if } e \neq E[{}^{\boldsymbol{\ell}\cdot\ell}e_0]$$

$$\boxed{\mathbb{C}' : Red \times vLab \rightarrow \mathcal{P}(vLab)}$$
$$\mathbb{C}'\ (e)\ \ell = \emptyset$$
$$\mathbb{C}'\ (E[w^{\ell,\vec{\ell}}], e', \ldots)\ \ell = \emptyset$$
$$\mathbb{C}'\ (E[{}^{\boldsymbol{\ell}}e], E[{}^{\boldsymbol{\ell}\cdot\ell'}e], e', \ldots)\ \ell = \{\ell'\} \cup \mathbb{C}'\ (e', \ldots)\ \ell$$
$$\mathbb{C}'\ (e, e', \ldots)\ \ell = \mathbb{C}'\ (e', \ldots)\ \ell,\ \text{if } e \neq E[{}^{\boldsymbol{\ell}}e_0]$$

When the creation of the specified value begins, the $\mathbb{C}$ function dispatches to $\mathbb{C}'$. When this helper function encounters a reduction that creates another value label, it adds it to its results. When evaluation of the specified value completes or the reduction sequence ends, the helper function stops collecting labels.

The **created** function uses $\mathbb{C}$ to compute (the labels of) all child-values generated during the creation of all the unused values of a given $\boldsymbol{\ell}$-labeled expression in $e$:

$$\boxed{\textbf{created} : Exp \times eLab \rightarrow \mathcal{P}(vLab)}$$
$$\textbf{created}\ (e, \boldsymbol{\ell}) = \bigcup_{\ell \in \textbf{unused}\ (e, \boldsymbol{\ell})} \mathbb{C}\ (\mathbb{T}\ e)\ \ell$$

In our running example, **created** $(P, \boldsymbol{\ell}_1)$ tallies the additional values created while evaluating each of $\ell_1, \ldots, \ell_{500}$, about 2,500.

Finally, the **LP** function computes the *laziness potential* of an $\boldsymbol{\ell}$-labeled expression in program $e$. Roughly, the function computes the "average" number of child-values generated during the creation of an unused value of expression $\boldsymbol{\ell}$, if **unused** $(e, \boldsymbol{\ell}) \neq \emptyset$:

$$\boxed{\textbf{LP} : Exp \times eLab \rightarrow \mathbb{R}}$$
$$\textbf{LP}\ (e, \boldsymbol{\ell}) = \frac{|(\textbf{unused}\ (e, \boldsymbol{\ell})) \cup (\textbf{created}\ (e, \boldsymbol{\ell}))|}{|(\textbf{unused}\ (e, \boldsymbol{\ell})) \setminus (\textbf{created}\ (e, \boldsymbol{\ell}))|}$$

The function uses **unused** to compute the (labels of the) unused values created by the specified $\boldsymbol{\ell}$-labeled expression and **created** to compute the (labels of the) child-values. Together, these two sets represent the total number of wasted values for which expression $\boldsymbol{\ell}$ is responsible. The numerator of the calculation uses the union of the two sets to avoid double-counting values, for example when expression $\boldsymbol{\ell}$ is a recursive call. To compute the desired ratio, **LP** divides the total value count by the number of unused values produced by expression $\boldsymbol{\ell}$. The denominator of the calculation additionally subtracts those unused values that are child-values of other unused values. This appropriately gives higher weight to recursive calls, which matches a programmer's intuition.

In the running example, all but one of the 498 unused values are induced by the first recursive call to *filter*. Thus the denominator in the laziness potential for $\boldsymbol{\ell}_1$ is one and **LP** $(P, \boldsymbol{\ell}_1) \approx 2500$.

The **LP** function computes the laziness potential of one particular expression in a program. Delaying the expression with the highest laziness potential should generate the largest possible benefit but doing so may reveal additional opportunities for laziness. Hence, we iteratively define the following series of **LP** functions:

$$\mathbf{LP}_0\ (e, \boldsymbol{\ell}) = \mathbf{LP}\ (e, \boldsymbol{\ell})$$

$$\mathbf{LP}_{i+1}\ (e, \boldsymbol{\ell}) = \mathbf{LP}_i\ (C^{force}[\texttt{delay}\ {}^{\boldsymbol{\ell}^{max}}e_{max}], \boldsymbol{\ell}),$$

$$\text{where } e = C[{}^{\boldsymbol{\ell}^{max}}e_{max}]$$

$$\text{and } \boldsymbol{\ell}^{max} = \underset{\boldsymbol{\ell}' \in e, \textbf{unused}\ (e, \boldsymbol{\ell}') \neq \emptyset}{\arg\max}\ \mathbf{LP}_i\ (e, \boldsymbol{\ell}')$$

An $\mathbf{LP}_{i+1}$ function first `delay`s the subexpression with (according to $\mathbf{LP}_i$) maximal laziness potential and adds appropriate forcing for the used values of that subexpression. It then uses $\mathbf{LP}_i$ on this transformed program to determine the next opportunity for laziness injection. In the definition, $\boldsymbol{\ell}^{max}$ labels $e_{max}$, the expression with the most laziness potential, and $C$ is its context. Since some values produced by $e_{max}$ may still be used, $C^{force}$ is $C$ augmented with `force`s around those usage contexts that require $e_{max}$'s values. Though it is sufficient to simply force every usage context in $C$, a flow analysis like Chang's [3] may compute a more a precise placement of `force`s.

In our running example, assume $\mathbf{LP}_0$ determines that the $\boldsymbol{\ell}_1$-labeled *filter* expression has the highest laziness potential. Then $\mathbf{LP}_1$ first delays $\boldsymbol{\ell}_1$ and inserts `force`s at its use points. $\mathbf{LP}_1$ then re-runs the augmented program and recomputes laziness potential for other expressions. Assume that both arguments to `cons` in *rng* also have static labels. As mentioned in section 2.1, the $\mathbf{LP}_1$ computations would find that the call to both *rng* and $f$ create unused values but that only the unused values of *rng* subsequently induce many more values and thus has higher laziness potential.

**A Non-theorem** An astute reader may wonder whether we can relate the laziness potential of an expression to a formal step-counting cost model. It would show that the suggestions are guaranteed to improve a program's performance. Unfortunately, the predictive capability of a step-counting model depends on how laziness is implemented meaning the desired theorem may hold only for semantic cost models truly close to one specific implementation.

## 4. A Laziness Profiler

An implementation of a laziness profiler cannot use the definition of $\mathbf{LP}_i$ as a blueprint because it is highly impractical to re-run a modified program for every $i$. Instead our profiler creates a value dependence graph in an online fashion during a single execution and uses this graph to perform laziness potential calculations.

### 4.1 Usage Information Gathering

Table 1 describes the collected information. It also lists the analogous mathematical function from section 3.5. The $\mathcal{I}$ function instruments a labeled $\lambda$-calculus program to collect this information:

$$\boxed{\mathcal{I} : \mathit{Exp} \to \mathit{Exp}}$$

$$\mathcal{I}[\![x]\!] = x$$

$$\mathcal{I}[\![\lambda x.e]\!] = \lambda x.\mathcal{I}[\![e]\!]$$

$$\mathcal{I}[\![e_1\ e_2]\!] = \mathcal{U}[\![\mathcal{I}[\![e_1]\!]]\!]\ \mathcal{A}[\![\mathcal{I}[\![e_2]\!]]\!]$$

$\mathcal{I}$ relies on two additional functions, $\mathcal{A}$ and $\mathcal{U}$, to instrument argument and usage positions, respectively. We defined $\mathcal{I}$ only for core $\lambda$-calculus expressions so far but in general the application of $\mathcal{A}$ exactly follows the labeling strategy from the previous section. In other words, a subexpression in a program is only instrumented as an "argument" if it has a static label $\boldsymbol{\ell}$. In addition, a subexpression is instrumented with $\mathcal{U}$ if it resides in a usage context.

Here are $\mathcal{A}$ and $\mathcal{U}$, which inject imperative code fragments that perform the required accounting during program execution:

| Information collected during evaluation | Math function |
|---|---|
| ALL-VNUMS : $\mathcal{P}(vLab)$ | |
| set of labels representing all values created during evaluation | |
| EXPR-VALS : $eLab \to \mathcal{P}(vLab)$ | $\mathbb{V}$ |
| maps an expression label to a set of value labels representing the values created by that expression during evaluation | |
| CHILD-VNUMS : $vLab \to vLab$ | $\mathbb{C}$ |
| maps a value label $\ell$ to a value label $\ell_{hi}$ such that the set of values created while evaluating $\ell$ is the exclusive interval $(\ell, \ell_{hi})$; i.e., the $\ell$-rooted subtree in the value-dependency tree | |
| USES : $vLab \to \mathbb{N}$ | $\mathbb{U}$ |
| the number of times a value is used during evaluation | |
| USES-BY-VNUM : $vLab \to vLab \to \mathbb{N}$ | |
| maps a value label $\ell$ to another map of value labels to counts, representing the value usage while evaluating $\ell$ only; to avoid double-counting uses, a value with label $\ell_{used}$ is considered used while evaluating value $\ell$ only if $\ell$ is the immediate ancestor in the program's value-dependency tree; for example, if value $\ell$ is created while evaluating another value with label $\ell_{parent}$, then $\ell_{used}$ is considered used while evaluating $\ell$ but *not* while evaluating $\ell_{parent}$ | |

**Table 1.** Information collected by the profiler.

```
A[[ℓe]] = let ℓnew = next-vnum () in
          ALL-VNUMS ∪= {ℓnew}
          EXPR-VALS[ℓ] ∪= {ℓnew}
          push-ctxt-vnum ℓnew
          let w^ℓ⃗ = ℓe in
          pop-ctxt-vnum ()
          CHILD-VNUMS[ℓnew] = current-vnum ()
          return w^(ℓnew,ℓ⃗)

U[[e]] = let ℓctxt = top-ctxt-vnum () in
         let w^ℓ⃗ = e in
         for ℓ ∈ ℓ⃗:
           USES[ℓ] += 1
           USES-BY-VNUM[ℓctxt][ℓ] += 1
         return w^ℓ⃗
```

In these definitions, `let` $w^{\vec{\ell}} = e$ is a pattern-matching notation that means evaluate $e$, bind the resulting value to $w$, and bind any resulting value labels to the vector $\vec{\ell}$. The $\mathcal{A}$ and $\mathcal{U}$-instrumented code generates unique dynamic labels from a counter, and it tracks which value is being evaluated via a value stack. The interfaces for the counter and the stack are described in table 2.

| counter | |
|---|---|
| `current-vnum` | returns the current count |
| `next-vnum` | returns then increments current count |
| **stack** | |
| `push-ctxt-vnum` | adds a value label to the top of the stack |
| `pop-ctxt-vnum` | removes top label from the context stack |
| `top-ctxt-vnum` | returns top label but does not pop it |

**Table 2.** Auxiliary functions for instrumenting functions.

### 4.2 Post-Execution Analysis

Before we show the loop that computes $\mathbf{LP}_i$, we introduce functions that use the collected information from table 1:

$$\texttt{unused}\ \boldsymbol{\ell} =$$
$$\{\ell \mid \ell \in \text{EXPR-VALS}[\boldsymbol{\ell}],\ \ell \in \text{ALL-VNUMS},\ \text{USES}[\ell] = 0\}$$
$$\texttt{created}_v\ \ell =$$
$$\{\ell_{sub} \mid \ell < \ell_{sub} < \text{CHILD-VNUMS}[\ell],\ \ell_{sub} \in \text{ALL-VNUMS}\}$$
$$\texttt{created}\ \boldsymbol{\ell} = \bigcup_{\ell \in \texttt{unused}\ \boldsymbol{\ell}} \texttt{created}_v\ \ell$$
$$\texttt{LP}\ \boldsymbol{\ell} = \frac{|(\texttt{unused}\ \boldsymbol{\ell}) \cup (\texttt{created}\ \boldsymbol{\ell})|}{|(\texttt{unused}\ \boldsymbol{\ell}) \setminus (\texttt{created}\ \boldsymbol{\ell})|}$$

For program $e$, the main processing loop then looks like this:

$$\texttt{while}\ (\bigcup_{\boldsymbol{\ell} \in e} \texttt{unused}\ \boldsymbol{\ell}) \neq \emptyset :$$
$$\boldsymbol{\ell} = \underset{\boldsymbol{\ell}' \in e, \texttt{unused}\ \boldsymbol{\ell}' \neq \emptyset}{\arg\max} (\texttt{LP}\ \boldsymbol{\ell}')$$
$$\texttt{for}\ \ell \in (\texttt{unused}\ \boldsymbol{\ell}) : \texttt{erase}\ \ell$$
$$\texttt{record-result}\ \boldsymbol{\ell}$$

The loop performs another iteration as long as some expression in the program has an unused value. If all values are used, i.e., the program cannot benefit from laziness, then the profiler does not report any suggestions. At the start of each iteration, the analysis selects an expression with the currently greatest laziness potential, identified with label $\boldsymbol{\ell}$ above. The analysis then simulates delaying this expression by "erasing" its unused values via `erase`:

$$\texttt{erase}\ \ell =$$
$$\texttt{sub-uses-by-vnum}\ \ell$$
$$\text{ALL-VNUMS} \setminus= \{\ell\}$$
$$\texttt{for}\ \ell_{sub} \in (\texttt{created}_v\ \ell) : \texttt{erase}\ \ell_{sub}$$
$$\texttt{sub-uses-by-vnum}\ \ell =$$
$$\texttt{for}\ (\ell_{used}, n) \in \text{USES-BY-VNUM}[\ell] : \text{USES}[\ell_{used}] \mathrel{-}= n$$

The `erase` function erases a value by (1) subtracting its usage of values from the total usage counts; (2) marking the value as erased by removing it from ALL-VNUMS, so it is not considered in subsequent calculations; and (3) recursively erasing all child-values that were created while evaluating the parameter value.

Finally, at the end of each iteration, the analysis records the delayed expression via `record-result`, so it can present a summary to the programmer after the calculations terminate. The main loop always terminates since each iteration of the loop "erases" at least one unused value.

**Theorem 3.** *The profiler implements the labeled λ-calculus model.*

*Proof Sketch.* The interesting part is showing that our post-execution analysis implements the functions from section 3.5. Specifically, the $i$th iteration of the main loop in this section corresponds to the $\mathbf{LP}_i$ function. In an iteration, both the model and implementation first compute the expression with highest laziness potential. The implementation then "erases" information pertaining to this expression and loops, while the math model inserts `delay`s and `force`s and re-runs the program. Thus the correctness of the implementation hinges on a correspondence between the `erase` function and the `delay` and `force` transformation in $\mathbf{LP}_i$.

Delaying an expression and then forcing the needed thunks eliminates: (1) the unused values produced by that expression, (2) the usages incurred while producing those unused values, and (3) all child-values of those unneeded values and their usages. Similarly, an iteration of the main loop in the implementation calls `erase` to eliminate: (1) all unused values of the highest potential expression by removing them from ALL-VNUMS, the set of all values produced during execution, (2) subtracts the usages incurred by those unused values, as recorded in USES-BY-VNUM, from the total usage counts in USES, and (3) recursively calls `erase` for each (remaining) child-value, as recorded in CHILD-VNUMS.

Note that the theorem does not hold once side-effects as simple as exception handling are added to the language, although our empirical evidence suggests that this is not an issue in practice. □

### 4.3 Implementation

We have implemented a prototype of the profiler described in this section for most of the Racket language [9]. The profiler supports all the language constructs from section 3.4, as well as several other frequently used Racket forms such as pattern matching (`match`), named records (`struct`), sequence iterations and comprehensions (`for`), additional binding forms (`define`, `let*`, etc.), much of the object system, and a large part of the syntax system. We use Racket's syntax system to modify the compiler so that it implements $\mathcal{I}[\![\cdot]\!]$, $\mathcal{U}[\![\cdot]\!]$, and $\mathcal{A}[\![\cdot]\!]$. Using this compiler API greatly simplifies the implementation of our profiler.

**A Note on Performance** Preliminary measurements indicate roughly a two to three order-of-magnitude slowdown when profiling certain degenerate programs. This kind of slowdown is not unreasonable for high-level profilers because programmers are expected to test their code with ***small** representative inputs*. Programs requiring laziness are *especially* suited for this style of testing because they generate lots of excess unused data, but so long as the ratio of unused to used data remains the same, it does not matter to the profiler whether the absolute amount of data is large or small.

## 5. Evaluation

To demonstrate the usefulness of the laziness potential metric, we present the results of profiling a range of real-world examples known to benefit from laziness: some of Okasaki's purely functional data structures, monadic parser combinators, and AI game players. We show that in most cases, the profiler reproduces the knowledge of experts. Secondarily, when our results differ from the experts, we turn to wall-clock measurements to further evaluate our profiler's output.

**General Profiling Issues** In general, profilers produce meaningful results only when given representative programs. For example, it is impossible to demonstrate the effectiveness of a memory profiler using programs without memory leaks. Similarly, we wish to demonstrate our profiler's effectiveness at inserting laziness into strict programs for performance reasons; thus we choose well-known uses of laziness rather than arbitrary programs and use inputs designed to force our test applications to rely on laziness.

Our experiments proceeded as follows:

1. we implemented one of the expert examples as a strict program;
2. we then profiled this strict version in a representative context;
3. and finally, we re-inserted `delay`s according to the profiler's suggestions. We inserted appropriate `force`s by hand, but one could in principle derive the positions automatically [3].

We conducted all experiments in Racket, an untyped language. We ported all implementations verbatim as we found them, except for a few type-related discrepancies. Okasaki points out [17, page 35] that laziness in a typed language occasionally requires extra annotations "to make the types work out". For example, typed languages must delay an empty stream tail, while in an untyped language, this annotation is unneeded since the empty stream is a value. In general, laziness in typed languages requires a pairing of `delay`s and `force`s, while untyped languages are more flexible due to the recursive and idempotent nature of untyped `force`.

| Data Structure | Description | Result |
|---|---|---|
| **Basic Data Structures** | | |
| banker's queue | canonical two-list functional queue with streams | Ⓟ |
| banker's deque | like the banker's queue, but allows inserting and deleting from both ends | Ⓟ |
| binomial heap | stores ordered elements in a series of increasingly sized trees, analogous to the representation of binary numbers; supports constant amortized time insert and log worse-case merge, delete min, and min operations | ⊜ |
| pairing heap | stores ordered elements as a tree where each node consists of a heap element and a list of subheaps; supports constant worst-case time insert, merge, and min operations, and log amortized time delete min operation | ⊜ |
| **Insightful Data Structures** | | |
| physicist's queue | canonical two-list functional queue with a stream front list, an eager front list cache, and a delayed rear list | ⊛ |
| real-time queue | converted banker's queue with an incrementally reversed rear list, with the goal of achieving worst case, rather than amortized, bounds | ⊜ |
| real-time deque | double-ended version of real-time queue | ⊜ |
| bootstrapped queue | improves on banker's queue by eliminating redundancy in append operation. | ⊜ |
| catenable list | lists that support constant amortized time append | ⊜ |
| implicit queue | achieves constant amortized operations via implicit recursive slowdown | Ⓟ |
| implicit deque | double-ended version of implicit queue | Ⓟ |
| **Other Functional Data Structures** | | |
| finger tree | Hinze and Paterson's general purpose data structure (related to implicit queues) | Ⓟ |

Ⓟ = profiler-assisted implementation outperforms Okasaki's implementation

⊜ = profiler suggests the same lazy annotations as Okasaki's implementation

⊛ = mixed results

**Table 3.** Comparison of Okasaki's lazy data structures with analogous profiler-generated data structures.

### 5.1 Purely Functional Data Structures

Okasaki's purely functional data structures make up a well-known library of algorithms that benefit from some degree of laziness in the data representation. At the same time, these data structures do not assume that the underlying language is lazy. Hence they are a nearly ideal test bed for checking the usefulness of our profiler.

The appropriateness of our comparisons depends on the design of a particular data structure. We therefore classify Okasaki's lazy data structures into two categories:

1. The first kind of lazy data structure is derived from an existing strict data structure. Okasaki added laziness to improve performance without making any other changes.
2. The second kind of data structure is either designed with laziness in mind or is converted from an existing strict data structure with changes more significant than simply adding laziness.

The first kind of data structure, dubbed *basic*, is ideal for evaluating our profiler because a straightforward comparison of the laziness annotations is appropriate. For the second kind of data structure, which we refer to as *insightful*, the laziness is possibly integral to its design and removing the laziness may not yield a realistic strict data structure. Hence, any results concerning insightful structures may be less general than basic ones, but enlightening nonetheless.

Table 3 describes several data structures of each kind and presents the results of our comparisons. For most examples, our profiler suggests laziness identical to Okasaki's version. In some cases, however, our profiler suggests what appears to be a better use of laziness, and we present these latter cases in detail.

**Banker's Queue** Our profiler-assisted banker's queue and deque implementations improve on Okasaki's versions. To help readers understand the differences and how they come about, we present the queue experiment in more detail.

```
def enq x (Q f len_f r len_r) = chk f len_f (x::r) (len_r+1)

def chk f len_f r len_r =
  if len_r ≤ len_f then Q f len_f r len_r
  else [Q (f ++ rev r) (len_f + len_r) nil 0]_rotation

def hd (Q nil _ _ _) = error
  | hd (Q (x::f) len_f r len_r) = x
def tl (Q nil _ _ _) = error
  | tl (Q (x::f) len_f r len_r) = chk f (len_f−1) r len_r

def (++) nil lst = lst
  | (++) (x::xs) lst = x::(xs ++ lst)

def rev lst = rev/acc lst nil
def rev/acc nil acc = acc
  | rev/acc (x::xs) acc = rev/acc xs (x::acc)
```

**Figure 4.** Functional queue implementation without laziness.

The canonical functional queue is implemented with two eager lists, a "rear" list onto which elements are added to the queue, and a "front" list from which elements are removed. A record data definition, ($Q$ *front* $len_f$ *rear* $len_r$), represents these queues where $Q$ is the constructor and *front*, $len_f$, *rear*, and $len_r$ are field names. The front and rear lists are *front* and *rear*, respectively, and $len_f$ and $len_r$ are the number of elements in each list.

Figure 4 presents this strict queue implementation in pseudocode. Function definitions in the figure use a pattern-matching syntax to decompose lists and queues, where _ is the wildcard pattern. The *enq* function adds an element to a queue, *hd* returns the

```
def enq x (Q f len_f r len_r) = chk f len_f $(x::r) (len_r+1)

def chk f len_f r len_r =
  if len_r ≤ len_f then Q f len_f r len_r
  else Q (f ++ rev r) (len_f + len_r) nil 0

def hd (Q $nil _ _ _) = error
  | hd (Q $(x::f) len_f r len_r) = x
def tl (Q $nil _ _ _) = error
  | tl (Q $(x::f) len_f r len_r) = chk f (len_f−1) r len_r

def (++) $nil lst = lst
  | (++) $(x::xs) lst = $(x::(xs ++ lst))

def rev lst = $(rev/acc lst nil)
def rev/acc $nil acc = acc
  | rev/acc $(x::xs) acc = rev/acc xs $(x::acc)
```

**Figure 5.** Okasaki's lazy banker's queue.

frontmost element without removing it, and *tl* removes the front element and returns the remaining elements as a new queue. The figure also includes infix list append, ++, and list reverse, *rev*.

When elements are added to *rear* or removed from *front*, a queue maintains the invariant that the size of *front* must be equal to or greater than the size of *rear*. When *rear* is larger than *front*, a *rotation* is performed (figure 4 box), i.e., *rear* is reversed and appended to the end of *front*, and *rear* is reset to empty. The *chk* function checks the queue invariant and performs rotations as needed. Though reversing a list takes time proportional to the size of the list, for any given set of inserted elements, the list containing those elements is only reversed once. Thus a functional queue supports constant amortized time *enq*, *hd*, and *tl* operations.

Rotations are expensive but since the rotated elements are added to the end of *front* and are not needed immediately, laziness might improve the strict queue implementation. Also the constant amortized time bounds of the strict queue do not hold when the queue is used *persistently*. To illustrate this problem, consider a queue with enough elements such that calling *tl* triggers a rotation. Calling *tl* repeatedly on this pre-rotated queue triggers a rotation each time. While the cost of the first rotation is amortized over all the elements, the subsequent rotations require more than constant amortized time because the "savings" are already spent by the first one.

To address these issues, Okasaki adds laziness to the strict queue implementation. The new queue, dubbed the banker's queue,[3] replaces the eager lists with lazy streams and is shown in figure 5. We adopt Okasaki's syntax for laziness, where $ prefixing an expression delays that expression, while $ in a pattern means to force the argument before trying to match the pattern.

Since the banker's queue merely adds laziness to the strict queue, it falls into the *basic* kind of lazy data structure described earlier. To see what laziness annotations our profiler suggests, we need a representative benchmark that uses the strict queue:

```
def build&sum size tosum = sum (build size) tosum
def build n = buildq 0 n
def buildq n n = Q nil 0 nil 0
  | buildq m n = enq m (buildq (m+1) n)
def sum q n = sumq q 0 n
def sumq q n n = 0
  | sumq q m n = (hd q) + (sumq (tl q) (m+1) n)
```

[3] Okasaki uses the banker's method to determine the queue's complexity.

```
def enq x (Q f len_f r len_r) = chk f len_f [(x::r)]_1 (len_r+1)

def chk f len_f r len_r =
  if len_r ≤ len_f then Q f len_f r len_r
  else Q (f ++ [$(rev r)]_2) (len_f + len_r) nil 0

def hd (Q $nil _ _ _) = error
  | hd (Q $(x::f) len_f r len_r) = x
def tl (Q $nil _ _ _) = error
  | tl (Q $(x::f) len_f r len_r) = chk f (len_f−1) r len_r

def (++) $nil lst = lst
  | (++) $(x::xs) lst = x:: [$(xs ++ lst)]_3

def rev lst = [rev/acc lst nil]_1
def rev/acc nil acc = acc
  | rev/acc (x::xs) acc = rev/acc xs [(x::acc)]_1
```

**Figure 6.** Profiler-assisted version of lazy banker's queue.

The *build* function builds a queue of the specified size while *sum* adds up the specified number of elements from the front of the given queue. The *build&sum* function combines *build* and *sum*.

Our representative benchmark should benefit from laziness if we sum only the first few elements of the queue, leaving most of the queue unused. Hence, profiling this benchmark should reveal the places where it is profitable to insert laziness annotations. Specifically, profiling *build&sum* 1024 50 produces the following laziness suggestions:

```
rev r [ln 5]: 8/10 values used
- delaying 2 unused avoids 3848 subvalues, wgt=2564
xs ++ lst [ln 13]: 645/1013 values used
- delaying 368 unused avoids 2204 subvalues, wgt=1870
```

Figure 6 shows a lazy queue that implements these suggestions. Our profiler-assisted lazy queue has fewer and different laziness annotations than Okasaki's. Specifically, the profiler does not recommend inserting laziness in *enq* and *rev* (boxes 1), leaving *rear* as an eager list.[4] This is justified because *rev* is monolithic, i.e., it always traverses its entire argument regardless of whether it is an eager list or a lazy stream. Instead, our profiler suggests a single delay around the call to *rev* in *chk* (box 2). The profiler also differs in its suggestion to delay the tail of the list returned by append (box 3) while Okasaki delays the entire list. Since the first list element is already a value, this difference is trivial.

Since our profiler recommends uses of laziness different from Okasaki, we further compare the queue implementations with empirical experiments. We timed several calls to *build&sum*, varying the number of elements summed. For each run, we used a fixed queue of size $2^{20}$:

$$\texttt{for } i \in [0, 2^{20}] : \texttt{time } (build\&sum\ 2^{20}\ i) \qquad \text{(BUILD\&SUM)}$$

The graph in figure 7 shows that using an eager rear list in the profiler-assisted lazy queue improves performance over Okasaki's queue, which has to build a suspension for each element.

A problem is that the BUILD&SUM benchmark does not test persistence, because the queue is used in a single-threaded manner. To expose persistence-related issues, a representative benchmark must

[4] Okasaki observes in a footnote that the rear list could be left as an eager list but, because of his preference of theoretical simplicity over practical optimizations, he presents the version in figure 5.

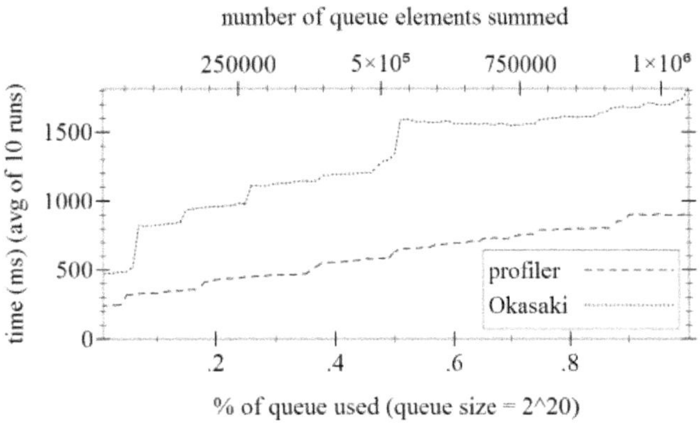


**Figure 7.** Summing elements of a banker's queue (lower is better).

| implementation | test name | subtest | time (ms) |
|---|---|---|---|
| strict | strict | *time1* | 250 |
| strict | strict | *time2* | 250 |
| Okasaki | PERSIST:LAZY | *time1* | 828 |
| Okasaki | PERSIST:LAZY | *time2* | 0 |
| profiler-assisted | PERSIST:LAZY | *time1* | 94 |
| profiler-assisted | PERSIST:LAZY | *time2* | 0 |

**Table 4.** Testing persistence with rotations in the banker's queue.

construct a queue such that a *tl* operation on the queue triggers the rotations suggested by the spikes in the graph of figure 7. For the lazy queues, the rotation operation is delayed, so we must remove a sufficient number of elements before the rotation is forced. Specifically, we build a queue of size $2^n - 1$, right after a delayed rotation is appended to the end of *front*, and then remove $2^{n-1} - 1$ elements from the queue. Removing the next element of the queue forces the rotation. This benchmark uses a *drop* function, which removes some number of elements from a list. We again use $n = 20$ in the persistence benchmark:

```
let q = drop (build (2^20−1)) (2^19−1)        (PERSIST:LAZY)
in time1 = time (tl q); time2 = time (tl q)
```

Table 4 presents timings for the persistence benchmarks. For reference, we additionally include times for a strict queue, which requires the same time on each access because it repeats the rotation each time. In contrast, the lazy queue times verify that both implementations offer truly constant amortized operations, with the profiler-assisted queue outperforming Okasaki's queue.

Though our laziness potential model does not explicitly account for the memoization that enables constant amortized operations for persistently used queues, our profiler is still able to suggest laziness annotations that satisfy the desired behavior, which is a pleasant surprise. This suggests that reasoning with laziness potential possibly suffices to account for both the delaying and the memoization benefits of laziness, which makes intuitive sense because programmers typically do not use laziness for memoization only. This observation warrants further investigation in future work.

**Physicist's Queue** Okasaki's physicist's queue differs from the banker's queue in three ways. First, it employs a plain list for the rear list instead of a stream. Second, the front list is a delayed plain list instead of a stream. Third, the content of the front list is cached into a separate plain list before a rotation, speeding up *hd* accesses. Thus the physicist's queue requires an extra field in

```
def enq x (Qp f' f len_f r len_r) = chk f' f len_f (x::r) (len_r+1)

def chk f' f len_f r len_r =
  if len_r ≤ len_f then chkw f' f len_f r len_r
  else let f'' = force f
       in chkw f'' $(f'' ++ rev r) (len_f + len_r) nil 0

def chkw nil f len_f r len_r = (Qp (force f) f len_f r len_r)
  | chkw f' f len_f r len_r = (Qp f' f len_f r len_r)

def hd (Qp nil _ _ _ _) = error
  | hd (Qp (x::f') f len_f r len_r) = x
def tl (Qp nil _ _ _ _) = error
  | tl (Qp (x::f') f len_f r len_r) =
     chkw f' $(rest (force f)) (len_f−1) r len_r

def (++) nil lst = lst
  | (++) (x::xs) lst = x::(xs ++ lst)

def rev lst = rev/acc lst nil
def rev/acc nil acc = acc
  | rev/acc (x::xs) acc = rev/acc xs (x::acc)
```

**Figure 8.** Okasaki's lazy physicists's queue.

```
def enq x (Qp f' f len_f r len_r) = chk f' f len_f (x::r) (len_r+1)

def chk f' f len_f r len_r =
  if len_r ≤ len_f then chkw f' f len_f r len_r
  else chkw f (f ++ $(rev r)) (len_f + len_r) nil 0

def chkw nil f len_f r len_r = (Qp f f len_f r len_r)
  | chkw f' f len_f r len_r = (Qp f' f len_f r len_r)

def hd (Qp $nil _ _ _ _) = error
  | hd (Qp $(x::f') f len_f r len_r) = x
def tl (Qp $nil _ _ _ _) = error
  | tl (Qp $(x::f') $(y::f) len_f r len_r) =
     chkw f' f (len_f−1) r len_r

def (++) $nil lst = lst
  | (++) $(x::xs) lst = x::$(xs ++ lst)

def rev lst = rev/acc lst nil
def rev/acc nil acc = acc
  | rev/acc (x::xs) acc = rev/acc xs (x::acc)
```

**Figure 9.** Profiler-assisted lazy physicists's queue.

its data definition: ($Q_p$ $front_{cache}$ *front* $len_f$ *rear* $len_r$). Figure 8 shows the implementation for Okasaki's physicist's queue.

Deriving the physicist's queue from the strict queue (in figure 4) involves more than just adding lazy annotations, so it belongs in the *insightful* category of data structure. Nevertheless, we follow the previously described steps to develop the alternative implementation in figure 9. It turns out that laziness potential cannot replicate Okasaki's caching strategy, and the profiler suggests turning *front* and $front_{cache}$ into duplicate lazy streams. The other profiler suggestions are identical to the profiled *banker's* queue: the rear list remains an eager list and is delayed with a single delay in *chk*.

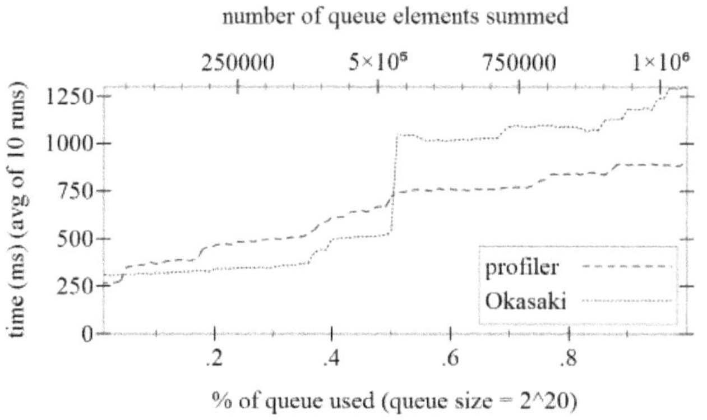


**Figure 10.** Summing physicist's queue elements (lower is better).

Figure 10 shows physicist's queue timings for the BUILD&SUM benchmark. With its caching, Okasaki's physicist's queue is faster than the profiler-assisted implementation, until half the queue is used. After that point, the benefits of caching in the Okasaki's queue are nullified because the entire *front* list must be forced anyways. Also, forcing this last part of *front* takes much longer due to all the extra suspensions created by $tl$, which manifests as a large spike in the graph. Essentially, our profiler-assisted queue forces a little of *front* with each $tl$ call, while Okasaki's version delays all the forcings until the second half of the queue is consumed. Deciding which queue implementation is better depends on the expected use cases.

**Implicit Queues** Implicit queue and deque data structures pose challenging obstacles for both designers and profilers. Hinze and Paterson's finger trees [10] are a related data structure and pose the same problems. This section presents details concerning queues; the cases for deques and finger trees are similar; see table 3.

Implicit queues rely on implicit recursive slowdown [17, Ch. 11], a technique inspired by functional representations of Peano numerals. Thus implicit queues are also an *insightful* kind of data structure. Like explicit queues, implicit queues offer constant amortized time $hd$, $tl$, and $enq$ operations. Essentially, the queue maintains some front elements and some rear elements in two "digit" structures, with the remaining elements residing in a delayed middle queue. Here are the record definitions for implicit queues.

A *digit* is a $(Zero)$ or $(One\ x)$ or $(Two\ x\ y)$

A *queue* is a $(Shallow\ digit)$ or $(Deep\ digit_f\ midQ\ digit_r)$

A "digit" is either a $Zero$, $One$, or $Two$ structure and an implicit queue itself is represented with either a $Shallow$ or a $Deep$ structure. A $Shallow$ queue is comprised of a single digit while a $Deep$ queue has two digits plus a delayed middle queue of element *pairs*.

Figure 11 presents $enq$, $tl$, and $hd$ for implicit queues. The $enq$ function shows the progression of a queue's internal state as more elements are added, with the digits transitioning from $Zero$ to $Two$, and the queue itself from $Shallow$ to $Deep$. These transitions are reversed in $tl$. Finally, the $hd$ function returns the front element by destructuring a queue in a straightforward manner.

While the design of this data structure leverages laziness to support constant amortized operations, it also magnifies the overhead of laziness because every operation must destructure not only the queue, but many fields of the queue as well. These numerous destructuring operations result in a high rate of suspension creation and forcing. In fact, profiling the BUILD&SUM benchmark only finds expressions with low laziness potential, even for queues where most or all of the elements are unused, suggesting that the

```
def enq (Shallow (Zero)) x = Shallow (One x)
  | enq (Shallow (One x)) y =
      Deep (Two x y) nil (Zero)
  | enq (Deep f m (Zero)) x = Deep f m (One x)
  | enq (Deep f m (One x)) y =
      Deep f $(enq (force m) (x, y)) (Zero)

def hd (Shallow (Zero)) = error
  | hd (Shallow (One x)) = x
  | hd (Deep (One x) m r) = x
  | hd (Deep (Two x y) m r) = x

def tl (Shallow (Zero)) = error
  | tl (Shallow (One x)) = Shallow (Zero)
  | tl (Deep (One x) $(Shallow (Zero)) r) = Shallow r
  | tl (Deep (One x) $m r) =
      let (y, z) = hd m in Deep (Two y z) $(tl m) r
  | tl (Deep (Two x y) m r) = Deep (One y) m r
```

**Figure 11.** Implicit queue operations.

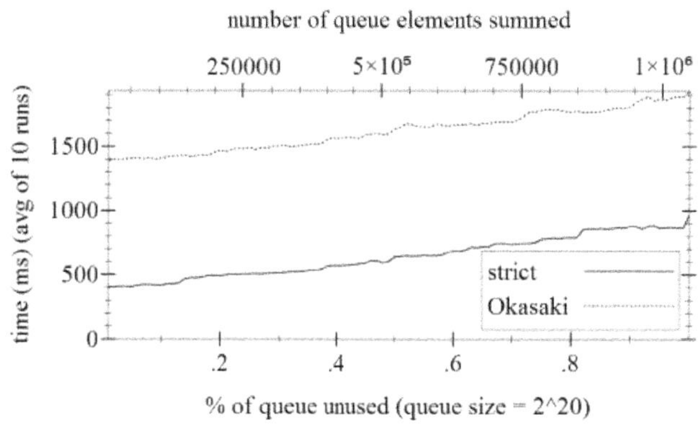


**Figure 12.** Summing elements of a implicit queue (lower is better).

data structure should not use any laziness. This makes intuitive sense since each operation effectively "uses" the entire queue.

To investigate this discrepancy, figure 12 presents BUILD&SUM timing information for a strict queue compared to Okasaki's queue. The chart shows that the high rate of suspension creation and forcing negates any benefits that laziness might provide, no matter how much of the queue is used. Obviously, the laziness overhead is implementation dependent. We implemented suspensions with a lambda and a mutable box. Although direct compiler support for suspensions would likely improve performance of the lazy queue and decrease the gap, the discrepancy is large enough that an implementer should consider omitting laziness.

While BUILD&SUM does not use the queue persistently, the worst-case "expensive" operation for implicit queues is only logarithmic in the size of the queue (as opposed to the linear rotations of the banker's queue). Thus, even when we tested the queues with persistent-usage benchmarks, the strict version still outperformed the lazy one. In conclusion, this experiment further supports omitting laziness from an implicit queue implementation even if it may spoil its theoretical properties.

### 5.2 Monadic Parser Combinators

Our second suite of benchmarks concerns Parsec [13], a monadic parser combinator library. Leijen and Meijer point to one spot in the monadic bind operator where laziness is key, calling it "essential for efficient behavior." Since the library is a higher-order program, we instantiated it for five different scenarios to apply our profiler: a CSV parser, a URL query parser, a JSON parser, and an HTTP request parser.[5] In every case, the profiler suggested adding laziness at the exact spot identified by the Parsec paper.

### 5.3 Manipulating Game Trees

Our final benchmark is an AI game algorithm from Land of Lisp [2], which introduces programmers to functional Lisp via a series of games. One of these games, Dice of Doom, is a turn-based strategy game similar to Risk. After several chapters, a diligent student is rewarded with a full-fledged game, complete with graphical interface and AI players. An AI player generates a game tree of all possible moves to help it determine the next move and utilizes laziness to manage the tree. Without laziness, the AI player analyzes only a small version of the game. Utilizing laziness, however, the AI player scales to a realistic-size game.

The game implementation (some 1,500 lines of code) constitutes a broad-spectrum benchmark for our profiler, not only because it requires laziness, but also because it uses many additional language features such as mutable state, list comprehensions, and GUI libraries. Our profiler is able to instrument the game and collects data as the game is played, returning suggestions when the game concludes. It suggests enough laziness so that playing the full game is possible but with fewer annotations than the Land of Lisp version.

## 6. Related Work

**Strictness Analysis** A concept related to "use" is the denotational notion of strictness [4, 16], which is defined via $\perp$: a function $f$ is strict if $f\ \perp = \perp$. In a lazy language, a strict function's argument does not need to be delayed. In the strict world, however, there is no analogous $\perp$-like value that extensionally indicates when to delay an expression. We must instead consider intensional value flows, which is precisely what "use" captures.

**Low-Utility Data Structures** Xu et al. [22] present a tool that uses an object cost-benefit analysis to help programmers find inefficient parts of Java programs. While they analyze imperative, object-oriented programs instead of functional ones, they have goals similar to ours. However, a key difference lies in their somewhat indirect approach. Their goal is to find problematic spots in the program source, but they compute costs at the level of memory accesses and bytecode instructions, thus requiring an extra final step to interpret the results in terms of the source. It is not clear how the paper achieves this last step, which becomes even more complicated for a higher-order language. Our approach computes laziness potential directly in terms of a high-level semantics, from which the problem spots in a program become apparent.

## 7. Conclusion and Future Work

We introduce the notion of laziness potential, a metric that predicts which program expressions benefit from lazy evaluation. Our Racket profiler implements these calculations and guides programmers with the insertion of laziness annotations. An evaluation of our profiler automatically replicates, and in some cases improves on, the laziness in a range of real-world applications, demonstrating the potential usefulness of our approach.

Though we presented laziness potential for a by-value $\lambda$-calculus and implemented our profiler for a matching language, the idea should be applicable to any language that supports both strict and lazy evaluation. Specifically, our insights may transfer to a lazy language with strictness annotations, such as Haskell. While the maturity of Haskell's strictness analysis already assists programmers with the task of eliminating unnecessary laziness, the approach is intrinsically limited by its static, approximate nature. Hence, books for real-world programmers [18] suggest the insertion of strictness annotations to help the compiler. We conjecture that a *dynamic* profiler, based on the notion of laziness potential, would assist these programmers with the difficult task of locating appropriate positions for these annotations.

[5] We followed Real World Haskell [18] for guidance.

## Acknowledgments

We thank Greg Morrisett for initial inspiration, Asumu Takikawa and J. Ian Johnson for reading drafts, and the reviewers for their suggestions. This work has been partly supported by NSF Infrastructure grant CI-ADDO-EN 0855140.

## References

[1] H. Abelson, G. J. Sussman, and J. Sussman. *Structure and Interpretation of Computer Programs*. MIT Press, 1984.

[2] C. Barski. *Land of Lisp*. No Starch Press, 2011.

[3] S. Chang. Laziness by need. In *Proc. 22nd ESOP*, pages 81–100, 2013.

[4] C. Clack and S. L. Peyton Jones. Strictness analysis — a practical approach. In *Proc. 2nd FPCA*, pages 35–49, 1985.

[5] R. Ennals and S. Peyton Jones. Optimistic evaluation: an adaptive evaluation strategy for non-strict programs. In *Proc. 8th ICFP*, pages 287–298, 2003.

[6] K.-F. Faxén. Cheap eagerness: speculative evaluation in a lazy functional language. In *Proc. 5th ICFP*, pages 150–161, 2000.

[7] M. Felleisen, R. B. Findler, and M. Flatt. *Semantics Engineering with PLT Redex*. MIT Press, 2009.

[8] R. B. Findler, S. Guo, and A. Rogers. Lazy contract checking for immutable data structures. In *Proc. 19th IFL*, pages 111–128, 2007.

[9] M. Flatt and PLT. Reference: Racket. Technical Report PLT-TR-2013-1, PLT Inc., 2013. `http://racket-lang.org/tr1/`.

[10] R. Hinze and R. Paterson. Finger trees: a simple general-purpose data structure. In *J. Funct. Program.*, pages 197–217, 2006.

[11] P. Hudak, J. Hughes, S. P. Jones, and P. Wadler. A history of Haskell: being lazy with class. In *Proc. 3rd HOPL*, pages 12-1–12-55, 2007.

[12] J. Hughes. Why functional programming matters. *Comp. J.*, 32:98–107, 1989.

[13] D. Leijen and E. Meijer. Parsec: direct style monadic parser combinators for the real world. TR UU-CS-2001-35, Utrecht University, 2001.

[14] J.-W. Maessen. Eager Haskell: resource-bounded execution yields efficient iteration. In *Proc. Haskell Workshop*, pages 38–50, 2002.

[15] F. Morandat, B. Hill, L. Osvald, and J. Vitek. Evaluating the design of the R language. In *Proc. 26th ECOOP*, pages 104–131, 2012.

[16] A. Mycroft. *Abstract interpretation and optimising transformations for applicative programs*. PhD thesis, University of Edinburgh, 1981.

[17] C. Okasaki. *Purely Functional Data Structures*. Cambridge University Press, 1998.

[18] B. O'Sullivan, D. Stewart, and J. Goerzen. *Real World Haskell*. O'Reilly Media, 2008.

[19] G. D. Plotkin. Call-by-name, call-by-value and the $\lambda$-calculus. *Theor. Comput. Sci.*, 1:125–159, 1975.

[20] K. E. Schauser and S. C. Goldstein. How much non-strictness do lenient programs require? In *Proc. 7th FPCA*, pages 216–225, 1995.

[21] P. Wadler. How to replace failure by a list of successes. In *Proc. 2nd FPCA*, pages 113–128, 1985.

[22] G. Xu, N. Mitchell, M. Arnold, A. Rountev, E. Schonberg, and G. Sevitsky. Finding low-utility data structures. In *Proc. 31st PLDI*, pages 174–186, 2010.

# Fair Reactive Programming

Andrew Cave Francisco Ferreira Prakash Panangaden Brigitte Pientka

School of Computer Science,
McGill University, Montreal, Canada
{acave1,fferre8,prakash,bpientka}@cs.mcgill.ca

## Abstract

Functional Reactive Programming (FRP) models reactive systems with events and signals, which have previously been observed to correspond to the "eventually" and "always" modalities of linear temporal logic (LTL). In this paper, we define a constructive variant of LTL with least fixed point and greatest fixed point operators in the spirit of the modal mu-calculus, and give it a proofs-as-programs interpretation as a foundational calculus for reactive programs. Previous work emphasized the propositions-as-types part of the correspondence between LTL and FRP; here we emphasize the proofs-as-programs part by employing structural proof theory. We show that the type system is expressive enough to enforce liveness properties such as the fairness of schedulers and the eventual delivery of results. We illustrate programming in this calculus using (co)iteration operators. We prove type preservation of our operational semantics, which guarantees that our programs are causal. We give also a proof of strong normalization which provides justification that our programs are productive and that they satisfy liveness properties derived from their types.

***Categories and Subject Descriptors*** D.1.1 [*Programming Techniques*]: Applicative (Functional) Programming

***Keywords*** temporal logic; propositions-as-types; functional reactive programming; liveness

## 1. Introduction

Reactive programming seeks to model systems which react and respond to input such as games, print and web servers, or user interfaces. Functional reactive programming (FRP) was introduced by Elliott and Hudak [10] to raise the level of abstraction for writing reactive programs, particularly emphasizing higher-order functions. Today FRP has several implementations [7–9, 29]. Many allow one to write unimplementable non-causal functions, where the present output depends on future input, and space leaks are all too common.

Recently there has been a lot of interest in type-theoretic foundations for (functional) reactive programming [14, 17, 22–24] with the intention of overcoming these shortcomings. In particular, Jeffrey [14] and Jeltsch [17] have recently observed that Pnueli's linear temporal logic (LTL) [31] can act as a type system for FRP.

In this paper, we present a novel logical foundation for discrete time FRP with (co)iteration operators which exploits the expressiveness afforded by the proof theory (i.e. the universal properties) for least and greatest fixed points, in the spirit of the modal $\mu$-calculus [21]. The "always", "eventually" and "until" modalities of LTL arise simply as special cases. We do this while still remaining relatively conservative over LTL.

Moreover, we demonstrate that distinguishing between and interleaving of least and greatest fixed points is key to statically guarantee liveness properties, i.e. something will eventually happen, by type checking. To illustrate the power and elegance of this idea, we describe the type of a fair scheduler – any program of this type is guaranteed to be fair, in the sense that each participant is guaranteed that his requests will eventually be served. Notably, this example requires the expressive power of interleaving least fixed points and greatest fixed points (a construction due to Park [30]) which is unique to our system.

Our approach of distinguishing between least and greatest fixed points and allowing for iteration and coiteration is in stark contrast to prior work in this area: Jeffrey's work [15, 16] for example only supports less expressive combinators instead of the primitive (co)recursion our system affords, and only particular instances of our recursive types. Krishnaswami et al. employ a more expressive notion of recursion, which entails *unique* (guarded) fixed points [22–24]. This implies that their type systems are incapable of expressing liveness properties, in constrast to our work. Jeltsch [17, 18] describes denotational settings for FRP, some of which are capable of expressing liveness guarantees. However, the theory of fixed points is largely undeveloped in his setting. Our technical contributions are as follows:

- A type system which, in addition to enforcing causality (as in previous systems [14, 23]), also enables one to enforce liveness properties; fairness being a particularly intriguing example. Moreover, our type system acts as a sound proof system for LTL. While previous work [14] emphasized the propositions-as-types component of the correspondence between LTL and FRP, the present work additionally emphasizes the proof-as-programs part of the correspondence through the lens of structural proof theory.
- A novel operational semantics which provides a reactive intepretation of our programs. One can evaluate the result of a program for the first $n$ time steps, and in the next time step, resume evaluation for the $(n+1)$st result. It allows one to evaluate programs one time step at a time. Moreover, we prove type preservation of our operational semantics. As a consequence, our foundation is *causal*: future inputs do not affect present results.


*POPL '14*, January 22–24, 2014, San Diego, CA, USA.

ACM 978-1-4503-2544-8/14/01...$15.00.
http://dx.doi.org/10.1145/2535838.2535881

- A strong normalization proof using Tait's method of saturated sets which justifies that our programs are productive total functions. It also demonstrates that our programs satisfy liveness properties derived from their types. Notably, our proof tackles the generality of interleaving fixed points, and offers a novel treatment of functoriality.

The paper is organized as follows: To illustrate the main idea, limitations and power of our foundation, we give several examples in Sec. 2. In particular, we elaborate the implementation of two fair schedulers where our foundation statically guarantees that each request will eventually be answered. We then introduce the syntax (Sec. 3) of our calculus which features (co)iteration operators and explicit delay operators together with typing rules (Sec. 4). In Sec. 5 we describe the operational semantics and prove type preservation. In Sec. 6, we outline the proof of strong normalization. In Sec. 7, we discuss consequences of strong normalization and type preservation, namely causality, liveness, and productivity. We conclude with related work.

## 2. Examples

To illustrate the expressive power of our calculus, we first present several motivating examples using an informal ML or Haskell-like syntax. For better readability we use general recursion in our examples, although our foundation only provides (co)iteration operators. However, all the examples can be translated into our foundation straightforwardly and we subsequently illustrate the elaboration in Sec 3.

On the type level, we employ a type constructor ◯ corresponding to the "next" modality of LTL to describe data available in the next time step. On the term level, we use the corresponding introduction form • and elimination form **let** • `x = e` **in** `e'` where `x` is bound to the value of the expression `e` in the next time step.

### 2.1 The "always" modality

Our first example `app` produces a stream of elements of type `B`, given a stream `fs` of functions of type `A` → `B` and a stream `xs` of elements of type `A` by applying the $n$th function in `fs` to the $n$th value in `xs`. Such streams are thought of as values which *vary in time*.

Here we use the □ type of LTL to describe temporal streams, where the $n$th value is available at the $n$th time step. □ `A` can be defined in terms of the ◯ modality as follows using a standard definition as a greatest fixed point (a coinductive datatype).

```
codata □ A = _::_ of A × ◯ □ A
```

□ `A` has one constructor `::` which is declared as an infix operator and takes an `A` now and recursively a □ `A` in the next time step.

The functions `hd` and `tl` can then be defined, the only caveat being that the type of `tl` expresses that the result is only available in the next time step:

```
hd : □ A → A
tl : □ A → ◯ □ A
```

Finally, we can implement the `app` function as follows:

```
app : □ (A → B) → □ A → □ B
app fs xs =
 let • fs' = tl fs
     • xs' = tl xs
 in  ((hd fs) (hd xs)) :: (• (app fs' xs'))
```

We use the ◯ elimination form, **let** • to bind the variables `fs'` and `xs'` to values of the remaining streams in the next time step. Our typing rules will guarantee that `fs'` and `xs'` are only usable underneath a •, which we will explain further in the following examples.

Such a program is interpreted *reactively* as a process which, at each time step, receives a function `A` → `B` and a value `A` and produces a value `B`. More generally, given $n$ functions `A` → `B` and $n$ values `A`, it can compute $n$ values `B`.

### 2.2 The "eventually" modality

A key feature of our calculus is the distinction between least fixed points and greatest fixed points. In other words, the distinction between data and codata. This allows us to make a distinction between events that *may* eventually occur and events that *must* eventually occur. This is a feature not present in the line of work by Krishnaswami and his collaborators, Benton and Hoffman [22–24] – they have *unique* (guarded) fixed points which intuitively correspond to our greatest fixed points.

To illustrate the benefits of having both, least and greatest fixed points, we present here the definition of LTL's ◇ operator (read: "eventually") as a data type, corresponding to a type of events in reactive programming:

```
data ◇ A = Now of A | Later of ◯ ◇ A
```

The function `evapp` below receives an event of type `A` and a time-varying stream of functions `A` → `B`. It produces an event of type `B`. Operationally, `evapp` waits for the `A` to arrive, applies the function available at that time, and fires the resulting `B` event immediately:

```
evapp : ◇ A → □(A → B) → ◇ B
evapp ea fs = case  ea of
| Now x      ⇒ Now ((hd fs) x)
| Later ea' ⇒ let • ea'' = ea'
                  • fs'  = tl fs
              in Later (• (evapp ea'' fs'))
```

This is not the only choice of implementation for this type. Such functions could opt to produce a `B` event before the `A` arrives, or even long after (if `B` is something concrete such as `bool`).

However, all functions with this type (in our system) have the property that *given* that an `A` is eventually provided, it *must* eventually produce a `B`, although perhaps not at the same time. This is our first example of a *liveness property* guaranteed by a type. This is in contrast to the "weak eventually" modality present in other work, which does not guarantee the production of an event.

It is interesting to note that this program (and all the other programs we write) can rightly be considered proofs of their corresponding statements in LTL.

### 2.3 Abstract server

Here we illustrate an abstract example of a server whose type guarantees responses to requests. This example is inspired by a corresponding example in Jeffrey's [16] recent work.

We wish to write a server which responds to two kinds of requests: `Get` and `Put` with possible responses `OK` and `Error`. We represent these:

```
data Req  = Get | Put
data Resp = OK  | Error
```

At each time step, a server specifies how to behave in the future if it did not receive a request, and furthermore, if it receives a request, it specifies how to respond and also how to behave in the future. This is the informal explanation for the following server type, expressed as codata (here, we use coinductive record syntax):

```
codata  Server = {noreq : ◯ Server,
                  some : Req → Resp × ◯ Server}
```

Now we can write the server program which responds to Get with OK and Put with Error:

```
server : Server
server = { noreq = • server,
           some = λr. if  isGet r
                      then  (OK, • server)
                      else  (Error, • server)}
```

Above, we say that if no request is made, we behave the same in the next time step. If some request is made, we check if it is a Get request and respond appropriately. In either case, in the next time step we continue to behave the same way. More generally, we could opt to behave differently in the next time step by e.g. passing along a counter or some memory of previous requests.

It is clear that this type guarantees that every request must immediately result in a response, which Jeffrey calls a liveness guarantee. In our setting, we reserve the term liveness guarantee for something which has the traditional flavor of "eventually something good happens". That is, they are properties which cannot be falsified after any finite amount of time, because the event may still happen. The present property of immediately providing a response does not have this flavor: it can be falsified by a single request which does not immediately receive a response. In our setting, liveness properties arise strictly from uses of inductive types (i.e. data, or $\mu$ types) combined with the temporal $\bigcirc$ modality, which requires something to happen arbitrarily (but finitely!) far into the future.

### 2.4 Causality-violating (and other bad) programs

We wish to disallow programs such as the following, which has the effect of pulling data from the future into the present; it violates a causal interpretation of such programs. Moreover, its type is certainly not a theorem of LTL for arbitrary A!

```
predictor : ○ A → A
predictor x = let • x' = x in  x'
      -- does not typecheck
```

Our typing rules disallow this program roughly by restricting variables bound under a • to only be usable under a •, in much the same way as Krishnaswami [22].

Similarly, the type $\bigcirc(A + B)$ expresses that either an A or a B is available in the next time step, but it is not known yet which one it will be. Hence we disallow programs such as the following by disallowing case analysis on something only available in the future:

```
predictor : ○(A + B) → ○ A + ○ B
predictor x = let • x' = x in
 case  x' of       -- does not typecheck
   | inl  a ⇒ inl  (• a)
   | inr  a ⇒ inr  (• b)
```

Such a program would tell us now whether we will receive an A or a B in the future. Again this violates causality. Due to this interpretation, there is no uniform inhabitant of this type, despite being a theorem of classical LTL. Similarly, $\bigcirc\bot \to \bot$ is uninhabited in our system; one cannot get out of doing work today by citing the end of the world tomorrow.

Although it would be harmless from the perspective of causality, we disallow also the following:

```
import : A → ○ A
import x = • x     -- does not typecheck
```

This is disallowed on the grounds that it is not uniformly a theorem of LTL. Krishnaswami and Benton allow it in [23], but disallow it later in [24] to manage space usage. Syntactically, this is accomplished by removing from scope all variables not bound under a • when moving under a •. However, some concrete instances of this type are inhabited, for example the following program which brings natural numbers into the future:

```
import : Nat → ○ Nat
import Zero = • Zero
import (Succ n) = let • n' = import n
                  in  •(Succ n')
```

Our calculus does *not* have Nakano's guarded recursion [13] `fix : (○ A → A) → A` because it creates for us undesirable inhabitants of certain inductive types (such inductive types collapse into coinductive types). For example, the following would be an undesirable inhabitant of $\lozenge A$ in which the $A$ is never delivered:

```
never : ◇ A
never = fix (λx. Later x)      -- disallowed
```

Finally, the following program which attempts to build a constant stream cannot be elaborated into the foundational calculus. While it is guarded, we must remove all local variables from scope in the bodies of recursive definitions, so the occurrence of x is out of scope.

```
repeat : A → □ A
repeat x = xs
  where  xs = x :: •xs       -- x out  of  scope !
```

This is intentional – the above type is not uniformly a theorem of LTL, so one should not expect it to be inhabited. As Krishnaswami et al. [24] illustrate, this is precisely the kind of program which leads to space leaks.

### 2.5 Fair scheduling

Here we define a type expressing the fair interleavings of two streams, and provide examples of fair schedulers employing this type – this is the central example illustrating the unique power of the presented system. This is enabled by our system's ability to properly distinguish between and interleave least and greatest fixed points (i.e. data and codata). Other systems in the same vein typically collapse least fixed points into greatest fixed points or simply lack the expressiveness of recursive types.

First we require the standard "until" modality of LTL, written A $\mathcal{U}$ B. This is a sequence of As, terminated with a B. In the setting of reactive programming, Jeltsch [18] calls programs of this type *processes* – they behave as time-varying signals which eventually terminate with a value.

```
data  A 𝒰 B = Same of  A × (○ (A 𝒰 B))
            | Switch of  B
```

Notably, since this is an inductive type, the B must eventually occur. The coinductive variant is "weak until"; the B might never happen, in which case the As continue forever.

We remark that without temporal modalities, A $\mathcal{U}$ B is isomorphic to (List A) × B, but because of the $\bigcirc$, it matters when the B happens.

We define also a slightly stronger version of "until" which requires at least one A, which we write A $\hat{\mathcal{U}}$ B.

```
type  A 𝒰̂  B = A × ○ (A 𝒰 B)
```

We characterize the type of fair interleavings of a stream of A s and Bs as some number of As until some number of Bs (at least one), until an A, and the process restarts. This is fair in the sense that it guarantees infinitely many As and infinitely many Bs. As a coinductive type:

```
codata  Fair A B =
 In of  (A 𝒰 (B 𝒰̂ (A × ○(Fair A B))))
```

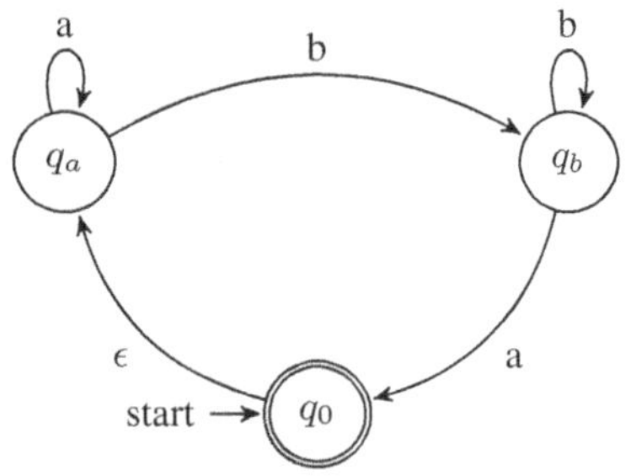


**Figure 1.** Scheduler automaton.

The reader may find it helpful to compare this type to the corresponding Büchi automaton in Figure 1. Jeltsch briefly discusses [18] essentially the same type; here we have the tools necessary to write programs with this type. That is to say, we can write examples of fair schedulers which take a stream of As and a stream of Bs and select from them fairly. Here is the simplest fair scheduler which simply alternates selecting an A and B:

```
sched : □ A → □ B → Fair A B
sched as bs =
let • as' = tl as
    • bs' = tl bs
in
   In  (Switch (hd bs,
     • (Switch (hd as',
     let • as'' = tl as'
         • bs'' = tl bs'
     in  • (sched as'' bs'')))))
```

The reader may notice that this scheduler drops the As at odd position and the Bs at even position. This could be overcome if one has `import` for the corresponding stream types, but at the cost of a space leak.

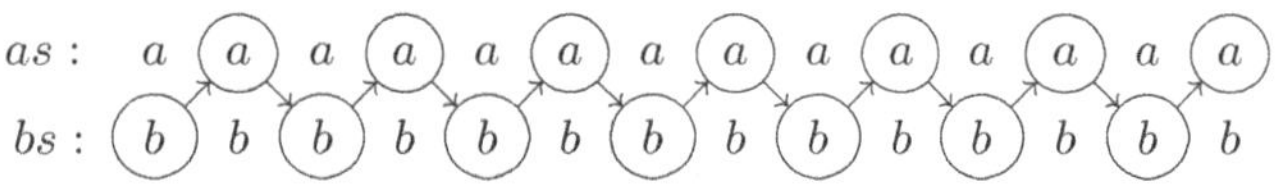


However, this "dropping" behaviour could be viewed positively: in a reactive setting, the source of the A requests could have the option to re-send the same request or even modify the previous request after observing that the scheduler decided to serve a B request instead.

Next we illustrate a more elaborate implementation of a fair scheduler which serves successively more As each time before serving a B. Again the type requires us to eventually serve a B.

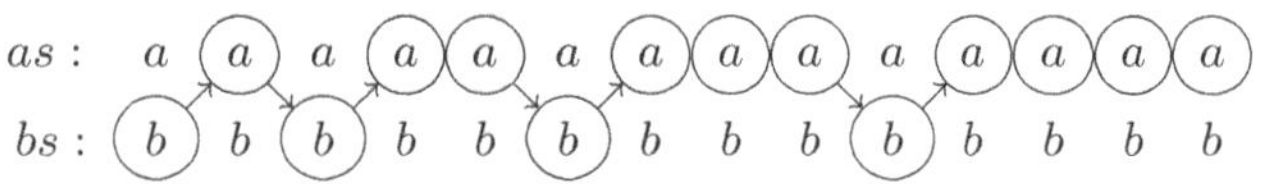


We will need a special notion of "timed natural numbers" to implement the countdown. In the `Succ` case, the predecessor is only available in the next time step:

```
data TNat = Zero | Succ (○ TNat)
```

We can write a function which imports `TNat`s:

```
import : TNat → ○ TNat
```

The scheduler is implemented in Figure 2. It involves two mutually recursive functions: `cnt` is structurally decreasing on a `TNat`, counting down how many As to produce, while the recursive call to `sch2'` is guarded by the necessary `Switch`es to guarantee productivity, and increments the number of As served the next time. `sch2` kicks off the process starting with zero As.

```
mutual
 cnt : TNat → TNat → □ A → □ B
   → (A 𝒰 (B 𝒰̂ (A × ○ (Fair A B))))
 cnt n m as bs =
  let • m'  = import m
      • as' = tl as
      • bs' = tl bs
  in
  case  n of
  | Zero ⇒
   Switch (hd bs, • (Switch (hd as',
   let • m''  = import m'
       • as'' = tl as'
       • bs'' = tl bs'
   in
    • (sch2' (Succ (import m'')) as'' bs'')))
  | Succ p ⇒ let  • n' = p in
   Same (hd as, (• (cnt n' m' as' bs')))
and
  sch2' : TNat → □ A → □ B → Fair A B
  sch2' n as bs = In (cnt n n as bs)

-- Main function
sch2 : □ A → □ B → Fair A B
sch2 as bs = sch2' Zero as bs
```

**Figure 2.** Fair scheduler

To understand why type `TNat` is necessary, we note `cnt` is structurally decreasing on its first argument. This requires the immediate subterm `n'` to be available in the next step, not the current.

The important remark here is that these schedulers can be seen to be fair simply by virtue of typechecking and termination/productivity checking. More precisely, this is seen by elaborating the program to use the (co)iteration operators available in the formal language, which we illustrate in the next section.

## 3. Syntax

The formal syntax for our calculus (Figure 3) includes conventional types such as product types, sum types and function types. Additionally the system has the $\bigcirc A$ modality for values which will have the type $A$ in the next step and least and greatest fixed points, $\mu$ and $\nu$ types. Our convention is to write the letters $A, B, C$ for closed types, and $F, G$ for types which may contain free type variables.

$$
\begin{array}{lll}
\text{Types } A, B, F, G & ::= & 1 \mid F \times G \mid F + G \mid A \to F \mid \\
& & \bigcirc F \mid \mu X.F \mid \nu X.F \mid X \\
\\
\text{Terms } \quad M, N & ::= & x \mid () \mid (M, N) \mid \mathsf{fst}\ M \mid \mathsf{snd}\ M \mid \\
& & \mid \mathsf{inl}\ M \mid \mathsf{inr}\ M \mid \mathsf{case}\ M \ \mathsf{of}\ \mathsf{inl}\ x \mapsto N \mid \mathsf{inr}\ y \mapsto N' \\
& & \mid \lambda x.M \mid M N \mid \bullet M \mid \mathsf{let}\ \bullet x = M \ \mathsf{in}\ N \mid \mathsf{inj}\ M \\
& & \mid \mathsf{iter}_{X.F}\ (x.M)\ N \mid \mathsf{out}\ M \mid \mathsf{coit}_{X.F}\ (x.M)\ N \\
& & \mid \mathsf{map}\ (\Delta.F)\ \eta\ M
\end{array}
$$

$$
\begin{array}{llll}
\text{Contexts} & \Theta, \Gamma & ::= & \cdot \mid \Gamma, x{:}A \\
\text{Kind Contexts} & \Delta & ::= & \cdot \mid \Delta, X : * \\
\text{Type substitutions} & \rho & ::= & \cdot \mid \rho, F/X \\
\text{Morphisms} & \eta & ::= & \cdot \mid \eta, (x.M)/X
\end{array}
$$

**Figure 3.** LTL Syntax

Our term language is mostly standard and we only discuss the terms related to $\bigcirc$ modality and the fixed points, $\mu$ and $\nu$. $\bullet M$ describes a term $M$ which is available in the next time step.

let $\bullet x = M$ in $N$ allows us to use the value of $M$ which is available in the next time step in the body $N$. Our typing rules will guarantee that the variable only occurs under a $\bullet$. Our calculus also includes iteration operator $\mathsf{iter}_{X.F}\ (x.M)\ N$ and coiteration operator $\mathsf{coit}_{X.F}\ (x.M)\ N$. Intuitively, the first argument $x.M$ corresponds to the inductive invariant while $N$ specifies how many times to unroll the fixed point. The introduction form for $\mu$ types is $\mathsf{inj}\ M$, rolling up a term $M$. The elimination form for $\nu$ types is $\mathsf{out}\ M$, unrolling $M$.

We note that the $X.F$ annotations on iter and coit play a key role during runtime, since the operational semantics of map are defined using the structure of $F$ (see Sec. 5). We do not annotate $\lambda$ abstractions with their type because we are primarily interested in the operational behaviour of our language, and not e.g. unique typing. The term $\mathsf{map}\ (\Delta.F)\ \eta\ N$ witnesses that $F$ is a *functor*, and is explained in more detail in the next sections.

Our type language with least and greatest fixed points is expressive enough that we can define the always and eventual modality e.g.:

$$\begin{aligned} \Box A &\equiv \nu X. A \times \bigcirc X \\ \Diamond A &\equiv \mu X. A + \bigcirc X \end{aligned}$$

The definition of $\Box A$ expresses that when we unfold a $\Box A$, we obtain a value of type $A$ (the head of the stream) and another stream in the next time step. The definition of $\Diamond A$ expresses that in each time step, we either have a value of type $A$ now or a postponed promise for a value of type $A$. The use of the least fixed point operator guarantees that the value is only postponed a finite number of times. Using a greatest fixed point would permit always postponing and never providing a value of type $A$.

We can also express the fact that a value of type $A$ occurs infinitely often by using both great and least fixed points. Traditionally one expresses this by combining the always and eventually modalities, i.e. $\Box\Diamond A$. However, there is another way to express this, namely:

$$\mathsf{inf}\ A \equiv \nu X.\mu Y.(A \times \bigcirc X + \bigcirc Y)$$

In this definition, at each step we have the choice of making progress by providing an $A$ or postponing until later. The least fixed point implies that one can only postpone a finite number of times. The two definitions are logically equivalent classically, but have different *constructive content* – they are not isomorphic as types. Intuitively, $\Box\Diamond A$ provides, at each time step, a handle on an $A$ to be delivered at some point in the future. It can potentially deliver several values of type $A$ in the same time step, and the order of the handles may not correspond to the order they are delivered in. On the other hand, $\mathsf{inf} A$ can provide at most one value of type $A$ at each time step. This demonstrates that the inclusion of general $\mu$ and $\nu$ operators in the language (in lieu of a handful of modalities) offers more fine-grained distinctions constructively than it does classically. We show here also the encoding of `Server`, $A\ \mathcal{U}\ B$, $A\ \hat{\mathcal{U}}\ B$ and `Fair` $A\ B$ which we used in the examples in Sec. 2.

$$\begin{aligned} \texttt{Server} &\equiv \nu X. \bigcirc X \times (\texttt{Req} \to \texttt{Resp} \times \bigcirc X) \\ A\ \mathcal{U}\ B &\equiv \mu X.(B + A \times \bigcirc X) \\ A\ \hat{\mathcal{U}}\ B &\equiv A \times \bigcirc (A\ \mathcal{U}\ B) \\ \texttt{Fair}\ A\ B &\equiv \nu X.(A\ \mathcal{U}\ (B\ \hat{\mathcal{U}}\ (A \times \bigcirc X))) \end{aligned}$$

Finally, to illustrate the relationship between our formal language which features (co)iteration operators and the example programs which were written using general recusion, we show here the program *app* in our foundation. Here we need to use the pair of $fs$ and $xs$ as the coinduction invariant:

Well-formedness of types: $\Delta \vdash F : *$

$$\frac{}{\Delta \vdash 1 : *} \quad \frac{\Delta \vdash F : * \quad \Delta \vdash G : *}{\Delta \vdash F \times G : *} \quad \frac{\Delta \vdash F : * \quad \Delta \vdash G : *}{\Delta \vdash F + G : *}$$

$$\frac{\cdot \vdash A : * \quad \Delta \vdash F : *}{\Delta \vdash A \to F : *} \quad \frac{\Delta, X : * \vdash F : *}{\Delta \vdash \mu X.F : *} \quad \frac{\Delta, X : * \vdash F : *}{\Delta \vdash \nu X.F : *}$$

$$\frac{\Delta \vdash F : *}{\Delta \vdash \bigcirc F : *} \quad \frac{(X : *) \in \Delta}{\Delta \vdash X : *}$$

**Figure 4.** Well-formed types

Typing Rules for $\to, \times, +, 1$

$$\frac{\Theta; \Gamma, x{:}A \vdash M{:}B}{\Theta; \Gamma \vdash \lambda x.M{:}A \to B} \quad \frac{\Theta; \Gamma \vdash M{:}A \to B \quad \Theta; \Gamma \vdash N{:}A}{\Theta; \Gamma \vdash M N{:}B}$$

$$\frac{x{:}A \in \Gamma}{\Theta; \Gamma \vdash x{:}A} \quad \frac{}{\Theta; \Gamma \vdash (){:}1} \quad \frac{\Theta; \Gamma \vdash M{:}A \quad \Theta; \Gamma \vdash N{:}B}{\Theta; \Gamma \vdash (M, N){:}A \times B}$$

$$\frac{\Theta; \Gamma \vdash M{:}A \times B}{\Theta; \Gamma \vdash \mathsf{fst}\ M{:}A} \quad \frac{\Theta; \Gamma \vdash M{:}A \times B}{\Theta; \Gamma \vdash \mathsf{snd}\ M{:}B}$$

$$\frac{\Theta; \Gamma \vdash M{:}A}{\Theta; \Gamma \vdash \mathsf{inl}\ M{:}A + B} \quad \frac{\Theta; \Gamma \vdash N{:}B}{\Theta; \Gamma \vdash \mathsf{inr}\ N{:}A + B}$$

$$\frac{\Theta; \Gamma \vdash M{:}A + B \quad \Theta; \Gamma, x{:}A \vdash N_1{:}C \quad \Theta; \Gamma, y{:}B \vdash N_2{:}C}{\Theta; \Gamma \vdash \mathsf{case}\ M\ \mathsf{of}\ \mathsf{inl}\ x \mapsto N_1 \mid \mathsf{inr}\ y \mapsto N_2{:}C}$$

Rules for $\bigcirc$ modality and least and greatest fixed points

$$\frac{\cdot; \Theta \vdash M{:}A}{\Theta; \Gamma \vdash \bullet M{:}\bigcirc A} \quad \frac{\Theta; \Gamma \vdash M{:}\bigcirc A \quad \Theta, x{:}A; \Gamma \vdash N{:}C}{\Theta; \Gamma \vdash \mathsf{let}\ \bullet x = M\ \mathsf{in}\ N{:}C}$$

$$\frac{\Theta; \Gamma \vdash M{:}[\mu X.F/X]F}{\Theta; \Gamma \vdash \mathsf{inj}\ M{:}\mu X.F} \quad \frac{\cdot; x{:}[C/X]F \vdash M{:}C \quad \Theta; \Gamma \vdash N{:}\mu X.F}{\Theta; \Gamma \vdash \mathsf{iter}_{X.F}\ (x.M)\ N{:}C}$$

$$\frac{\cdot; x{:}C \vdash M : [C/X]F \quad \Theta; \Gamma \vdash N{:}C}{\Theta; \Gamma \vdash \mathsf{coit}_{X.F}\ (x.M)\ N{:}\nu X.F} \quad \frac{\Theta; \Gamma \vdash M{:}\nu X.F}{\Theta; \Gamma \vdash \mathsf{out}\ M{:}[\nu X.F/X]F}$$

$$\frac{\Delta \vdash F : * \quad \Theta; \Gamma \vdash M{:}[\rho_1]F \quad \rho_1 \vdash \eta : \rho_2}{\Theta; \Gamma \vdash \mathsf{map}\ (\Delta.F)\ \eta\ M{:}[\rho_2]F}$$

Typing Rules for morphisms: $\rho_1 \vdash \eta : \rho_2$

$$\frac{\rho_1 \vdash \eta{:}\rho_2 \quad \cdot; x : A \vdash M : B}{\rho_1, A/X \vdash \eta, (x.M)/X : \rho_2, B/X} \quad \frac{}{\cdot \vdash \cdot : \cdot}$$

**Figure 5.** Typing Rules

$$\begin{aligned} &app : \Box(A \to B) \to \Box A \to \Box B \\ &app\ fs\ xs \equiv \mathsf{coit}_{X.B \times \bigcirc X}\ (x. \\ &\quad \mathsf{let} \bullet fs' = tl\ (\mathsf{fst}\ x)\ \mathsf{in} \\ &\quad \mathsf{let} \bullet xs' = tl\ (\mathsf{snd}\ x)\ \mathsf{in} \\ &\qquad (\ (hd\ (\mathsf{fst}\ x))\ (hd\ (\mathsf{snd}\ x))\ ,\ \bullet(fs', xs')\ ) \\ &)\ (fs, xs) \end{aligned}$$

## 4. Type System

We define well-formed types in Fig. 4. In particular, we note that free type variables cannot occur to the left of a $\to$. That is to say, we employ a strict positivity restriction, in contrast to Krishnaswami's guardedness condition [22].

We give a type assignment system for our calculus in Fig. 5 where we distinguish between the context $\Theta$ which provides types for variables which will become available in the next time step (i.e.

when going under a •) and the context Γ which provides types for the variables available at the current time. The main typing judgment, $\Theta; \Gamma \vdash M : A$ asserts that $M$ has type $A$ given the context Θ and Γ.

In general, our type system is similar to that of Krishnaswami and collaborators. While in their work, the validity of assumptions at a given time step is indicated either by annotating types with a time [23] or by using different judgments (i.e. now, later, stable) [22], we separate assumptions which are valid currently from the assumptions which are valid in the next time step via two different contexts. Much more importantly, our foundation differs in the treatment of recursive types and recursion.

Most rules are standard. When traversing $\lambda x.M$, the variable is added to the context Γ describing the fact that $x$ is available in the current time step. Similarly, variables in each of the branches of the case-expression, are added to Γ.

The interesting rules are the ones for ◯ modality and fixed points $\mu$ and $\nu$. In the rule $I_{\bigcirc}$, the introduction rule for ◯ with corresponding constructor •, provides a term to be evaluated in the next time step. It is then permitted to use the variables promised in the next time step, so the assumptions in Θ move to the "available" position, while the assumptions in Γ are no longer available. In fact, the variables in Θ remain inaccessible until going under a • – this is how causality is enforced. Our motivation for forgetting about current assumptions Γ and not allowing them to persist is that we wish to obtain a type system which is sound for LTL. Allowing Γ to persist would make the unsound $A \to \bigcirc A$ easily derivable. In the work of Krishnaswami et. al [24], forgetting about current assumptions plays a key role in managing space usage.

The corresponding elimination form let $\bullet\, x = M$ in $N$ simply adds $x{:}A$, the type of values promised by $M$, to the context Θ and we continue to check the body $N$ allowing it to refer to $x$ under a •.

The elimination form for $\mu$ is an iteration operator iter. Examining an instantiation of this rule for $\mathsf{Nat} \equiv \mu X.1 + X$ may help to clarify this rule:

$$\frac{\cdot\,;\, x : 1 + C \vdash M : C \quad \Theta; \Gamma \vdash N : \mu X.1 + X}{\Theta; \Gamma \vdash \mathsf{iter}_{X.1+X}\ (x.M)\ N : C}$$

The term $M$ contains the base case and the step case ($M$ will typically be a case analysis on $x$), while $N$ specifies how many times to iterate the step case of $M$ starting at the base case of $M$. For example, we illustrate here the doubling function on natural numbers written using this iteration operator. We write 0 for the term $\mathsf{inj}\ (\mathsf{inl}\,())$ and $\mathsf{suc}\ m$ for the term $\mathsf{inj}\ (\mathsf{inr}\ m)$.

$$\begin{aligned} db &= \mathsf{iter}_{X.1+X}(x.\mathsf{case}\ x\ \mathsf{of}\ \mathsf{inl}\ y \mapsto 0 \\ &\qquad\qquad\qquad\qquad \mid \mathsf{inr}\ w \mapsto \mathsf{suc}(\mathsf{suc}\ w)) \\ double &= \lambda x{:}\mathsf{Nat}.db\ x \end{aligned}$$

We note that dropping Θ and Γ in the first premise is essential. Intuitively, the bodies of recursive definitions need to be used at arbitrary times, while Γ and Θ are only available for the current and next time steps, respectively. This is easiest to see for the coit rule, where keeping Γ allows a straightforward derivation of $A \to \Box A$ (`repeat`), which is unsound for LTL and easily produces space leaks. Similarly, keeping Γ in the iter rule allows one to derive the unsound $A \to \Diamond B \to A\ \mathcal{U}\ B$ which says that if $A$ holds now, and $B$ eventually holds, then $A$ in fact holds until $B$ holds.

$$\begin{aligned} &unsound : A \to \Diamond B \to A\ \mathcal{U}\ B \\ &unsound \equiv \lambda a.\ \lambda eb.\ \mathsf{iter}_{X.B+\bigcirc X}\ (y. \\ &\quad \mathsf{case}\ y\ \mathsf{of} \\ &\qquad |\mathsf{inl}\ b \mapsto \mathsf{inj}\ (\mathsf{inl}\ b) \\ &\qquad |\mathsf{inr}\ u \mapsto \mathsf{inj}\ (\mathsf{inr}\ (a, u)) - a \text{ out of scope!} \\ &\quad )\ eb \end{aligned}$$

The typing rules for $\mu$ and $\nu$ come directly from the universal properties of initial algebras and terminal coalgebras. The reader may find it clarifying to compare these rules to the universal properties, depicted here:

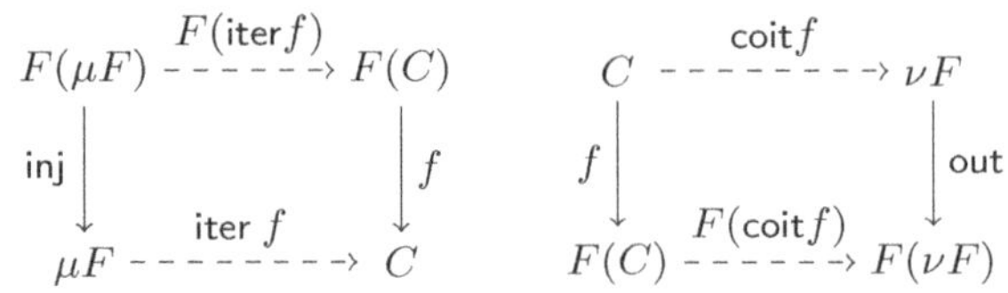


Unsurprisingly, the primitive recursion operator below can be derived from our iteration operator, so we do not lose expressiveness by providing only iteration. Of course, in practice rec is necessary to write efficient programs.

$$\frac{\cdot\,; x{:}[C \times \mu X.F/X]F \vdash M{:}C \quad \Theta; \Gamma \vdash N{:}\mu X.F}{\Theta; \Gamma \vdash \mathsf{rec}_{X.F}\ (x.M)\ N{:}C}$$

The term $\mathsf{map}\ (\Delta.F)\ \eta\ M$ witnesses that $F$ is a *functor*. It has the effect of applying the transformations specified by $\eta$ at the positions in $M$ specified by $F$. It is a *generic program* defined on the structure of $F$. While this term is definable at the meta-level using the other terms in the language, we opt to include it in our syntax, because doing so significantly simplifies the operational semantics and proof of normalization. In this term, Δ binds the free variables of $F$. It is illustrative to consider the case where $F(Y) = \mathsf{list}\ Y = \mu X.1 + Y \times X$. If $y : A \vdash M : B$ and $N : \mathsf{list}\ A$, then $\mathsf{map}\ (Y.\ \mathsf{list}\ Y)\ ((y.\ M)/Y)\ N : \mathsf{list}\ B$. In this case, map implements the standard notion of map on lists! We will sometimes not write the Δ when the intention is clear.

We define two notions of substitution: substitution for a "current" variable, written $[N/x]M$, and substitution for a "next" variable, written $[N/x]^{\bullet}M$. The key case in their definition is the case for $\bullet M$. For current substitution $[N/x](\bullet M)$, in well-scoped terms, $x$ cannot occur in $M$, so we define:

$$[N/x](\bullet M) = \bullet M$$

For next substitution $[N/x]^{\bullet}(\bullet M)$, in the body of $M$, $x$ becomes a current variable, so we can defer to current substitution, defining:

$$[N/x]^{\bullet}(\bullet M) = \bullet([N/x]M)$$

These definitions are motivated by the desire to obtain tight bounds on how substitution interacts with the operational semantics without having to keep typing information to know that terms are well-scoped. These substitutions satisfy the following typing lemma.

**Lemma 1.** *Substitution Typing*

1. *If* $\Theta; \Gamma, x{:}A \vdash M : B$ *and* $\Theta; \Gamma \vdash N : A$ *then* $\Theta; \Gamma \vdash [N/x]M : B$
2. *If* $\Theta, x{:}A; \Gamma \vdash M : B$ *and* $\cdot; \Theta \vdash N : A$ *then* $\Theta; \Gamma \vdash [N/x]^{\bullet}M : B$

## 5. Operational Semantics

Next, we define a small-step operational semantics using evaluation contexts. Since we allow full reductions, a redex can be under a binder and in particular may occur under a ◯ modality. We define evaluation contexts in Fig. 6. We index an evaluation context $\mathcal{E}_k$ by a depth $k$ which indicates how many ◯ modalities we traverse. Intuitively, the depth $k$ tells us how far we have stepped in time - or to put it differently, at our current time, we know that we have

$$
\begin{array}{rcl}
\mathcal{E}_{k+1} & ::= & \bullet\mathcal{E}_k \\
\mathcal{E}_k & ::= & \mathcal{E}_k\ N \mid M\ \mathcal{E}_k \mid \mathsf{fst}\ \mathcal{E}_k \mid \mathsf{snd}\ \mathcal{E}_k \mid (\mathcal{E}_k, M) \mid (M, \mathcal{E}_k) \\
& & \mid \lambda x.\mathcal{E}_k \mid \mathsf{case}\ \mathcal{E}_k\ \mathsf{of\ inl}\ x \mapsto N \mid \mathsf{inr}\ y \mapsto N' \\
& & \mid \mathsf{inl}\ \mathcal{E}_k \mid \mathsf{case}\ M\ \mathsf{of\ inl}\ x \mapsto \mathcal{E}_k \mid \mathsf{inr}\ y \mapsto N \\
& & \mid \mathsf{inr}\ \mathcal{E}_k \mid \mathsf{case}\ M\ \mathsf{of\ inl}\ x \mapsto N \mid \mathsf{inr}\ y \mapsto \mathcal{E}_k \\
& & \mid \mathsf{let}\ \bullet x = \mathcal{E}_k\ \mathsf{in}\ N \mid \mathsf{let}\ \bullet x = M\ \mathsf{in}\ \mathcal{E}_k \mid \mathsf{inj}\ \mathcal{E}_k \\
& & \mid \mathsf{iter}_{X.F}\ (x.M)\ \mathcal{E}_k \mid \mathsf{coit}_{X.F}\ (x.M)\ \mathcal{E}_k \\
& & \mid \mathsf{out}\ \mathcal{E}_k \mid \mathsf{map}\ (\Delta.F)\ \eta\ \mathcal{E}_k \\
\mathcal{E}_0 & ::= & []
\end{array}
$$

**Figure 6.** Evaluation contexts

$$
\begin{array}{lcl}
(\lambda x.M)\ N & \longrightarrow & [N/x]M \\
\mathsf{fst}(M, N) & \longrightarrow & M \\
\mathsf{snd}(M, N) & \longrightarrow & N \\
\mathsf{case}\ (\mathsf{inl}\ M)\ \mathsf{of\ inl}\ x \mapsto N_1 \mid \mathsf{inr}\ y \mapsto N_2 & \longrightarrow & [M/x]N_1 \\
\mathsf{case}\ (\mathsf{inr}\ M)\ \mathsf{of\ inl}\ x \mapsto N_1 \mid \mathsf{inr}\ y \mapsto N_2 & \longrightarrow & [M/y]N_2 \\
\mathsf{let}\ \bullet x = \bullet M\ \mathsf{in}\ N & \longrightarrow & [M/x]^{\bullet}N \\
\mathsf{iter}_{X.F}\ (x.M)\ (\mathsf{inj}\ N) & \longrightarrow & \\
\quad [(\mathsf{map}\ (X.F)\ ((y.\ \mathsf{iter}_{X.F}\ (x.M)\ y)/X)\ N)/x]M & & \\
\mathsf{out}\ (\mathsf{coit}_{X.F}\ (x.M)\ N) & \longrightarrow & \\
\quad \mathsf{map}\ (X.F)\ ((y.\ \mathsf{coit}_{X.F}\ (x.M)\ y)/X)\ ([N/x]M) & &
\end{array}
$$

**Figure 7.** Operational Semantics

taken $k$ time steps and therefore terms under $k$ $\bigcirc$ modalities are available to us now.

Single step reduction is defined on evaluation contexts at a time $\alpha < \omega + 1$ (i.e. either $\alpha \in \mathbb{N}$ or $\alpha = \omega$) and states that we can step $\mathcal{E}_k[M]$ to $\mathcal{E}_k[N]$ where $M$ is a redex occurring at depth $k$ where $k \leq \alpha$ and $M$ reduces to $N$. More precisely, the reduction rule takes the following form:

$$\frac{M \longrightarrow N}{\mathcal{E}_k[M] \rightsquigarrow_\alpha \mathcal{E}_k[N]}\ \text{if } k \leq \alpha$$

If $\alpha = 0$, then we are evaluating all redexes now and do not evaluate terms under a $\bigcirc$ modality. If we advance to $\alpha = 1$, we in addition can contract all redexes at depth 1, i.e. terms occurring under one $\bullet$, and so on. At $\alpha = \omega$, we are contracting all redexes under any number of $\bullet$. We have reached a normal form at time $\alpha$ if for all $k \leq \alpha$ all redexes at depth $k$ have been reduced and no further reduction is possible.

The contraction rules for redexes (see Fig. 7) are mostly straightforward - the only exceptions are the iteration and coiteration rules. If we make an observation about a corecursive value by $(\mathsf{out}\ (\mathsf{coit}_{X.F}\ (x.M)\ N))$, then we need to compute one observation of the resulting object using $M$, and explain how to make more observations at the recursive positions specified by $F$. Dually, if we unroll an iteration $(\mathsf{iter}_{X.F}\ (x.M)\ (\mathsf{inj}\ N))$, we need to continue performing the iteration at the recursive positions of $N$ (the positions are specified by $F$), and reduce the result using $M$.

Performing an operation at the positions specified by $F$ is accomplished with map, which witnesses that $F$ is a functor. The operational semantics of map are presented in Fig. 8. They are driven by the type $F$. Most cases are straightforward and more or less forced by the typing rules. The key cases, and the reason for putting map in the syntax in the first place, are those for $\mu$ and $\nu$. For $\mu$, we reduce $N$ until it is of the form inj $N$. At which point, we can continue applying $\eta$ inside $N$, where now at the recursive positions specified by $Y$ we need to continue recursively applying map. The case for $\nu$ is similar, except it is triggered when we demand an observation with out.

We remark that we do not perform reductions inside the bodies of iter, coit, and map (see Fig. 6), as these are in some sense timeless terms (they will be used at multiple points in time), and it is not clear how our explictly timed notion of operational semantics could interact with these. We sidestep the issue by disallowing reductions inside these bodies.

To illustrate the operational semantics and the use of map, we consider an example of a simple recursive program: doubling a natural number.

***Example*** We revisit here the program *double* which multiplies a given natural number by two given in the previous section. Recall the following abbreviations for natural numbers: $0 = \mathsf{inj}\ (\mathsf{inl}())$, $\mathsf{suc}\ w = \mathsf{inj}\ (\mathsf{inr}\ w)$, $1 = \mathsf{suc}\ 0$, etc.

Let us first compute *double* 0.

$$
\begin{array}{l}
\quad \mathit{double}\ 0 \\
\longrightarrow \mathit{db}\ (\mathsf{inj}\ (\mathsf{inl}\ ())) \\
\longrightarrow \mathsf{case}\ M_0\ \mathsf{of\ inl}\ y \mapsto 0 \mid \mathsf{inr}\ w \mapsto \mathsf{suc}\ (\mathsf{suc}\ w)
\end{array}
$$

where

$$
\begin{array}{rl}
M_0 & = \mathsf{map}\ (1 + X)\ (y.\mathit{db}\ y/X)\ (\mathsf{inl}\ ()) \\
& \longrightarrow^* \mathsf{case}\ (\mathsf{inl}())\ \mathsf{of\ inl}\ v \mapsto \mathsf{inl}() \mid \mathsf{inr}\ u \mapsto \mathsf{inr}(\mathit{db}\ u)
\end{array}
$$

$$
\begin{array}{l}
\longrightarrow^* \mathsf{case}\ (\mathsf{inl}\ ())\ \mathsf{of\ inl}\ y \mapsto 0 \mid \mathsf{inr}\ w \mapsto \mathsf{suc}\ (\mathsf{suc}\ w) \\
\longrightarrow 0
\end{array}
$$

We now compute *double* 1

$$
\begin{array}{l}
\quad \mathit{double}\ 1 \\
\longrightarrow \mathit{db}\ (\mathsf{inj}\ (\mathsf{inr}\ 0)) \\
\longrightarrow \mathsf{case}\ M_1\ \mathsf{of\ inl}\ y \mapsto 0 \mid \mathsf{inr}\ w \mapsto \mathsf{suc}\ (\mathsf{suc}\ w)
\end{array}
$$

where

$$
\begin{array}{rl}
M_1 & = \mathsf{map}\ (1 + X)\ (y.\mathit{db}\ y/X)\ (\mathsf{inr}\ 0) \\
& \longrightarrow^* \mathsf{case}\ (\mathsf{inr}\ 0)\ \mathsf{of\ inl}\ v \mapsto \mathsf{inl}() \mid \mathsf{inr}\ u \mapsto \mathsf{inr}(\mathit{db}\ u)
\end{array}
$$

$$
\begin{array}{l}
\longrightarrow^* \mathsf{case}\ (\mathsf{inr}(\mathit{db}\ 0))\ \mathsf{of\ inl}\ y \mapsto 0 \mid \mathsf{inr}\ w \mapsto \mathsf{suc}\ (\mathsf{suc}\ w) \\
\longrightarrow^* \mathsf{case}\ (\mathsf{inr}\ 0)\ \mathsf{of\ inl}\ y \mapsto 0 \mid \mathsf{inr}\ w \mapsto \mathsf{suc}\ (\mathsf{suc}\ w) \\
\longrightarrow \mathsf{suc}\ (\mathsf{suc}\ 0) = 2
\end{array}
$$

We have the following type soundness result for our operational semantics:

**Theorem 2** (Type Preservation). *For any $\alpha$, if $M \rightsquigarrow_\alpha N$ and $\Theta; \Gamma \vdash M : A$ then $\Theta; \Gamma \vdash N : A$*

Observe that after evaluating $M \rightsquigarrow_n^* N$, where $N$ is in normal form, one can then resume evaluation $N \rightsquigarrow_{n+1}^* N'$ to obtain the cumulative result available at the next time step. One may view this as restarting the computation, aiming to compute the result up to $n + 1$, but with the results up to time $n$ memoized. In practical implementations, one is typically only concerned with $\rightsquigarrow_0$ (see Sec. 7), however considering the general $\rightsquigarrow_\alpha$ gives us the tools to analyze programs from a more global viewpoint, which is important for liveness guarantees.

Our definition of substitution is arranged so that we can prove the following bounds on how substitution interacts with $\rightsquigarrow$, which are important in our proof of strong normalization. Notice that these are independent of any typing assumptions.

**Proposition 3.**

1. *If $N \rightsquigarrow_\alpha N'$ then $[N/x]M \rightsquigarrow_\alpha^* [N'/x]M$*
2. *If $M \rightsquigarrow_\alpha M'$ then $[N/x]M \rightsquigarrow_\alpha [N/x]M'$*
3. *If $N \rightsquigarrow_n N'$ then $[N/x]^{\bullet}M \rightsquigarrow_{n+1}^* [N'/x]^{\bullet}M$*
4. *If $N \rightsquigarrow_\omega N'$ then $[N/x]^{\bullet}M \rightsquigarrow_\omega^* [N'/x]^{\bullet}M$*
5. *If $M \rightsquigarrow_\alpha M'$ then $[N/x]^{\bullet}M \rightsquigarrow_\alpha [N/x]^{\bullet}M'$*

Our central result is a proof of strong normalization for our calculus which we prove in the next section.

$$
\begin{array}{llll}
\text{map} & (\Delta.\, X)\ \eta & N \longrightarrow [N/x]M & \text{if } \eta(X) = x.M \\
\text{map} & (\Delta.\, 1)\ \eta & N \longrightarrow () & \\
\text{map} & (\Delta.\, F \times G)\ \eta & N \longrightarrow (\text{map } (\Delta.\, F)\ \eta\ (\text{fst } N), \text{map } (\Delta.\, G)\ \eta\ (\text{snd } N)) & \\
\text{map} & (\Delta.\, F + G)\ \eta & N \longrightarrow \text{case } N \text{ of inl } y \mapsto \text{inl}(\text{map } (\Delta.\, F)\ \eta\ y) & \\
 & & \qquad \mid \text{inr } z \mapsto \text{inr}(\text{map } (\Delta.\, G)\ \eta\ z) & \\
\text{map} & (\Delta.\, A \to F)\ \eta & N \longrightarrow \lambda y.\text{map } (\Delta.\, F)\ \eta\ (N\ y) & \\
\text{map} & (\Delta.\, \bigcirc F)\ \eta & N \longrightarrow \text{let } \bullet y = N \text{ in } \bullet \text{map } (\Delta.\, F)\ \eta\ y & \\
\text{map} & (\Delta.\, \mu Y.F)\ \eta\ (\text{inj } N) & \longrightarrow \text{inj } (\text{map } (\Delta, Y.\, F)\ (\eta, (x.\ \text{map } (\Delta.\, \mu Y.F)\ \eta\ x)/Y)\ N) & \\
\text{out (map} & (\Delta.\, \nu Y.F)\ \eta & N) \longrightarrow \text{map } (\Delta, Y.\, F)\ (\eta, (x.\ \text{map } (\Delta.\, \nu Y.F)\ \eta\ x)/Y)\ (\text{out } N) &
\end{array}
$$

**Figure 8.** Operational semantics of map

## 6. Strong Normalization

In this section we give a proof of strong normalization for our calculus using the Girard-Tait reducibility method [11, 12, 34]. In our setting, this means we prove that for any $\alpha \leq \omega$, every reduction sequence $M \rightsquigarrow_\alpha \ldots$ is finite, for well-typed terms $M$. This means that one can compute the approximate value of $M$ up to time $\alpha$. In fact, this result actually gives us more: our programs are suitably causal using normalization at 0, and the type of a program gives rise to a liveness property which it satisfies, using normalization at $\omega$. Our logical relation is in fact a degenerate form of Kripke logical relation, as we index it by an $\alpha \leq \omega$ to keep track of how many time steps we are normalizing. It is degenerate in that the partial order we use on $\omega + 1$ is discrete, i.e. $\alpha \leq \beta$ precisely when $\alpha = \beta$. It is not step-indexed because our strict positivity condition on $\mu$ and $\nu$ allows us to interpret them without the aid of step indexing.

This proof is made challenging by the presence of interleaving $\mu$ and $\nu$ types and (co)iteration operators. This has been treated before by Matthes [27] as well as Abel and Altenkirch [1]. Others have considered non-interleaving cases or with other forms of recursion, such as Mendler [28] and Jouannaud and Okada [19]. To our knowledge, ours is the first such proof which treats map as primitive syntax with reduction rules instead of a derivable operation, which we find simplifies the proof substantially as it allows us to consider map independently of iter and coit in the proof.

We use a standard inductive characterization of strongly normalizing terms:

**Definition 4** (Strongly normalizing)**.** *We define sn as the inductive closure of:*

$$\frac{\forall M', M \rightsquigarrow_\alpha M' \Longrightarrow M' \in sn_\alpha}{M \in sn_\alpha}$$

*We say $M$ is* strongly normalizing at $\alpha$ *if $M \in sn_\alpha$.*

It is immediate from this definition that if $M \in sn_\alpha$ and $M \rightsquigarrow_\alpha M'$ then $M' \in sn_\alpha$. Since this is an inductive definition, it affords us a corresponding induction principle: To show that a property $P$ holds of a term $M \in sn_\alpha$, one is allowed to assume that $P$ holds for all $M'$ such that $M \rightsquigarrow_\alpha M'$. One can easily verify by induction that if $M \in sn_\alpha$ then there are no infinite $\rightsquigarrow_\alpha$ reduction sequences rooted at $M$.

For our proof, we use Tait's saturated sets instead of Girard's reducibility candidates, as this allows us to perform the syntactic analysis of redexes separate from the more semantic parts of the proof. This technique has been used by Luo [26], Altenkirch [2], and Matthes [27].

In the following, we will speak of indexed sets, by which we mean a subset of terms for each $\alpha \leq \omega$, i.e. $\mathcal{A} : \omega + 1 \to \mathcal{P}(tm)$, where we write $tm$ for the set of all terms. We overload the notation $\subseteq$, $\cap$, and $\cup$ to mean pointwise inclusion, intersection, and union. That is, if $\mathcal{A}$ and $\mathcal{B}$ are indexed sets, we will write $\mathcal{A} \subseteq \mathcal{B}$ to mean $\mathcal{A}^\alpha \subseteq \mathcal{B}^\alpha$ for all $\alpha$.

**Definition 5.** *We define the following* next step operator *on indexed sets $\mathcal{A} : \omega + 1 \to \mathcal{P}(tm)$:*

$$
\begin{array}{lcl}
(\blacktriangleright \mathcal{A})^0 & \equiv & tm \\
(\blacktriangleright \mathcal{A})^{m+1} & \equiv & \mathcal{A}^m \\
(\blacktriangleright \mathcal{A})^\omega & \equiv & \mathcal{A}^\omega
\end{array}
$$

The motivation for this is that it explains what happens when we go under a $\bullet$ – we are now interested in reducibility under one fewer $\bullet$.

Below, we define a notion of normalizing weak head reduction. We write $M \twoheadrightarrow_\alpha M'$ for a contraction, and $M \rightarrowtriangle_\alpha N$ for a contraction occuring under a weak head context. This is a weak head reduction where every term which may be lost along the way (e.g. by a vacuous substitution) is required to be strongly normalizing. This is a characteristic ingredient of the saturated set method. It is designed this way so as to (backward) preserve strong normalization. The intuition is that weak head redexes are unavoidable – reducing other redexes can only postpone a weak head reduction, not eliminate it. We define below weak head reduction contexts and normalizing weak head reduction. We show only the lambda case. The full definition can be found in the long version of the paper.

$$
\begin{array}{lcl}
\mathcal{H} & ::= & [\,] \mid \text{fst } \mathcal{H} \mid \text{snd } \mathcal{H} \mid \mathcal{H}N \mid \text{iter}_{X.F}\ (x.M)\ \mathcal{H} \\
 & & \mid \text{map } (\Delta.\, \mu X.F)\ \eta\ \mathcal{H} \mid \text{out } \mathcal{H} \mid \text{let } \bullet x = \mathcal{H} \text{ in } N \\
 & & \mid \text{case } \mathcal{H} \text{ of inl } x \mapsto N_1 \mid \text{inr } y \mapsto N_2
\end{array}
$$

$$\frac{M \twoheadrightarrow_\alpha M'}{\mathcal{H}[M] \rightarrowtriangle_\alpha \mathcal{H}[M']} \qquad \frac{N \in sn_\alpha}{(\lambda x.M)\ N \twoheadrightarrow_\alpha [N/x]M}$$

**Lemma 6.** *$sn_\alpha$ is backward closed under normalizing weak head reduction: If $M' \in sn_\alpha$ and $M \rightarrowtriangle_\alpha M'$ then $M \in sn_\alpha$*

We note that in all of our proofs, the subscript $\alpha$ plays little to no role, except of course in the cases pertaining to the next step operator $\bigcirc$. For this reason, we typically highlight the $\bigcirc$ cases of the proofs.

We define the indexed set of terms $sne$ ("strongly normalizing neutral") which are strongly normalizing, but are stuck with a variable in place of a weak head redex.

**Definition 7.** *We define $sne_\alpha = \{\mathcal{H}[x] \in sn_\alpha\}$*

We can now define saturated sets as subsets of strongly normalizing terms. The rest of the proof proceeds by showing that our types can be interpreted as saturated sets, well-typed terms inhabit saturated sets, and hence are strongly normalizing.

**Definition 8** (Saturated sets). *An indexed set* $\mathcal{A} : \omega + 1 \to \mathcal{P}(tm)$ *is* saturated *if*

1. $\mathcal{A} \subseteq sn$
2. *For any* $\alpha, M, M'$, *if* $M \rightharpoonup^*_\alpha M'$ *and* $M' \in \mathcal{A}^\alpha$ *then* $M \in \mathcal{A}^\alpha$ *(*Backward closure under normalizing weak head reduction*)*
3. $sne \subseteq \mathcal{A}$

It is immediate from Lemma 6 that $sn$ is saturated.

**Definition 9.** *For an indexed set* $\mathcal{A} : \omega + 1 \to \mathcal{P}(tm)$, *we define* $\overline{\mathcal{A}}$ *as its closure under conditions 2 and 3. i.e.*

$$\overline{\mathcal{A}}^\alpha \equiv \{M | \exists M'.M \rightharpoonup^*_\alpha M' \wedge (M' \in \mathcal{A}^\alpha \vee M' \in sne_\alpha)\}$$

To interpret least and greatest fixed points, we construct a complete lattice structure on saturated sets:

**Lemma 10.** *Saturated sets form a complete lattice under* $\subseteq$, *with greatest lower bounds and least upper bounds given by:*

$$\bigwedge \mathcal{S} \equiv (\bigcap \mathcal{S}) \cap sn \qquad \bigvee \mathcal{S} \equiv \overline{\bigcup \mathcal{S}}$$

For $\wedge$, we intersect with $sn$ so that the nullary lower bound is $sn$, and hence saturated. For non-empty $\mathcal{S}$, we have $\bigwedge \mathcal{S} = \bigcap \mathcal{S}$. As a consequence, by an instance of the Knaster-Tarski fixed point theorem, we have the following:

**Corollary 11.** *Given* $F$ *which takes predicates to predicates, we define:*

$$\begin{aligned} \mu F &\equiv \bigwedge \{\mathcal{C} \text{ saturated} \mid F(\mathcal{C}) \subseteq \mathcal{C}\} \\ \nu F &\equiv \bigvee \{\mathcal{C} \text{ saturated} \mid \mathcal{C} \subseteq F(\mathcal{C})\} \end{aligned}$$

*If* $F$ *is monotone and takes saturated sets to saturated sets, then* $\mu F$ *(resp.* $\nu F$*) is a least (resp. greatest) fixed point of* $F$ *in the lattice of saturated sets*

The following operator definitions are convenient, as they allow us to reason at a high level of abstraction without having to introduce $\alpha$ at several places in the proof.

**Definition 12.** *We define:*

$$\begin{aligned} (\mathcal{A} \circ f)^\alpha &\equiv \{M | fM \in \mathcal{A}^\alpha\} \\ (\mathcal{A} \star f)^\alpha &\equiv \{fM | M \in \mathcal{A}^\alpha\} \end{aligned}$$

*We will often use these notations for partially applied syntactic forms, e.g.* $\mathcal{A}\star$ *inj*

We are now in a position to define the operators on saturated sets which correspond to the operators in our type language.

**Definition 13.** *We define the following operations on saturated sets:*

$$\begin{aligned} \mathbf{1} &\equiv sn \\ (\mathcal{A} \times \mathcal{B}) &\equiv \overline{(\mathcal{A} \circ \mathsf{fst}) \cap (\mathcal{B} \circ \mathsf{snd})} \\ (\mathcal{A} + \mathcal{B}) &\equiv \overline{(\mathcal{A} \star \mathsf{inl}) \cup (\mathcal{B} \star \mathsf{inr})} \\ (\mathcal{A} \to \mathcal{B})^\alpha &\equiv \overline{\{M | \forall N \in \mathcal{A}^\alpha.(MN) \in \mathcal{B}^\alpha\}} \\ (\bigcirc \mathcal{A}) &\equiv \overline{(\blacktriangleright \mathcal{A}) \star \bullet} \\ \boldsymbol{\mu}\mathcal{F} &\equiv \mu(\mathcal{X} \mapsto \overline{\mathcal{F}(\mathcal{X}) \star \mathsf{inj}}) \\ \boldsymbol{\nu}\mathcal{F} &\equiv \nu(\mathcal{X} \mapsto \mathcal{F}(\mathcal{X}) \circ \mathsf{out}) \end{aligned}$$

Notice that $\boldsymbol{\mu}\mathcal{F}$ is defined regardless of whether $\mathcal{F}$ is monotone, although we only know that $\boldsymbol{\mu}\mathcal{F}$ is actually a least fixed point when $\mathcal{F}$ is monotone. We remark also that our $\to$ definition does not resemble the Kripke-style definition one might expect. That is to say, we are using the discrete partial order on $\omega + 1$. We do not need the monotonicity that the standard ordering would grant us, since our type system does not in general allow carrying data into the future.

**Lemma 14.** *The operators defined in Definition 13 take saturated sets to saturated sets.*

We are now ready to interpret well-formed types as saturated sets. The definition is unsurprising, given the operators defined previously.

**Definition 15.** *Given* $\rho$, *an environment mapping the free variables of* $F$ *to saturated sets, we define the interpretation* $[\![F]\!](\rho)$ *of an open type as a saturated set as follows:*

$$\begin{aligned} [\![X]\!](\rho) &\equiv \rho(X) \\ [\![1]\!](\rho) &\equiv \mathbf{1} \\ [\![F \times G]\!](\rho) &\equiv [\![F]\!](\rho) \times [\![G]\!](\rho) \\ [\![F + G]\!](\rho) &\equiv [\![F]\!](\rho) + [\![G]\!](\rho) \\ [\![A \to F]\!](\rho) &\equiv [\![A]\!](\cdot) \to [\![F]\!](\rho) \\ [\![\bigcirc F]\!](\rho) &\equiv \bigcirc [\![F]\!](\rho) \\ [\![\mu X.F]\!](\rho) &\equiv \boldsymbol{\mu}(\mathcal{X} \mapsto [\![F]\!](\rho, \mathcal{X}/X)) \\ [\![\nu X.F]\!](\rho) &\equiv \boldsymbol{\nu}(\mathcal{X} \mapsto [\![F]\!](\rho, \mathcal{X}/X)) \end{aligned}$$

*Observe that, by lemma 14, every* $[\![F]\!](\rho)$ *is saturated.*

If $\theta = N_1/y_1, ..., N_n/y_n$ and $\sigma = M_1/x_1, ..., M_m/x_m$ are simultaneous substitutions, we write $[\theta; \sigma]M$ to mean substituting the $N_i$ with next substitution $[N_i/y_i]^\bullet(-)$ and the $M_i$ with the current substitution $[M_i/x_i](-)$. We may write this explicitly as follows:

$$[N_1/y_1^\bullet, ..., N_n/y_n^\bullet; M_1/x_1, ..., M_m/x_m]M$$

If $\sigma = M_1/x_1, ..., M_m/x_m$ and $\mathbf{\Gamma} = x_1 : \mathcal{A}_1, ..., x_m : \mathcal{A}_m$, then we write $\sigma \in \mathbf{\Gamma}^\alpha$ to mean $M_i : \mathcal{A}_i^\alpha$ for all $i$, and similarly for $\theta \in \mathbf{\Theta}^\alpha$.

**Definition 16** (Semantic typing). *We write* $\mathbf{\Theta}; \mathbf{\Gamma} \vDash M : \mathcal{C}$, *where the free variables of* $M$ *are bound by* $\mathbf{\Theta}$ *and* $\mathbf{\Gamma}$, *if for any* $\alpha$ *and any substitutions* $\theta \in (\blacktriangleright \mathbf{\Theta})^\alpha$ *and* $\sigma \in \mathbf{\Gamma}^\alpha$, *we have* $[\theta; \sigma]M \in \mathcal{C}^\alpha$

Next we show that the term constructors of our language obey corresponding semantic typing lemmas. We prove the easier cases first (i.e. constructors other than map, iter, and coit), as their results are used in the next lemma pertaining to map. We state only the non-standard cases. For the full statement, see the long version.

**Lemma 17** (Interpretation of term constructors). *The following hold, where we assume* $\mathbf{\Theta}$, $\mathbf{\Gamma}$, $\mathcal{A}$, $\mathcal{B}$, *and* $\mathcal{C}$ *are saturated.*

1. *If* $\cdot; \mathbf{\Theta} \vDash M : \mathcal{A}$ *then* $\mathbf{\Theta}; \mathbf{\Gamma} \vDash \bullet M : \bigcirc \mathcal{A}$
2. *If* $\mathbf{\Theta}; \mathbf{\Gamma} \vDash M : \bigcirc \mathcal{A}$ *and* $\mathbf{\Theta}, x{:}\mathcal{A}; \mathbf{\Gamma} \vDash N : \mathcal{B}$ *then* $\mathbf{\Theta}; \mathbf{\Gamma} \vDash$ let $\bullet x = M$ *in* $N : \mathcal{B}$
3. *If* $\mathcal{F}$ *is a monotone function from saturated sets to saturated sets, and* $\mathbf{\Theta}; \mathbf{\Gamma} \vDash M : \mathcal{F}(\boldsymbol{\mu}\mathcal{F})$ *then* $\mathbf{\Theta}; \mathbf{\Gamma} \vDash$inj $M : \boldsymbol{\mu}\mathcal{F}$
4. *If* $\mathcal{F}$ *is a monotone function from saturated sets to saturated sets, and* $\mathbf{\Theta}; \mathbf{\Gamma} \vDash M : \boldsymbol{\nu}\mathcal{F}$ *then* $\mathbf{\Theta}; \mathbf{\Gamma} \vDash$out $M : \mathcal{F}(\boldsymbol{\nu}\mathcal{F})$

*Proof.* We show only the case for $\bullet$. The rest are straightforward or standard.

1. We are given $\cdot; \mathbf{\Theta} \vDash M : \mathcal{A}$, i.e. for any $\alpha$ and $\theta \in \mathbf{\Theta}^\alpha$, that $[\cdot; \theta]M \in \mathcal{A}^\alpha$.
   Suppose we are given $\alpha$ and $\theta \in (\blacktriangleright \mathbf{\Theta})^\alpha$ and $\sigma \in \mathbf{\Gamma}^\alpha$.
   Case $\alpha = 0$: Then $(\blacktriangleright \mathcal{A})^0 = tm$, so $[\cdot; \theta]M \in (\blacktriangleright \mathcal{A})^0$
   Case $\alpha = m + 1$: Then $(\blacktriangleright \mathcal{A})^{m+1} = \mathcal{A}^m$, and $\theta \in \mathbf{\Theta}^m$. By our assumption, taking $\alpha = m$, we have $[\cdot; \theta]M \in \mathcal{A}^m$
   Case $\alpha = \omega$: Then $(\blacktriangleright \mathcal{A})^\omega = \mathcal{A}^\omega$, and $\theta \in \mathbf{\Theta}^\omega$. By our assumption, $[\cdot; \theta]M \in \mathcal{A}^\omega$
   In any case, we have $[\cdot; \theta]M \in (\blacktriangleright \mathcal{A})^\alpha$.
   Then $[\theta; \sigma](\bullet M) = \bullet([\cdot; \theta]M) \in (\blacktriangleright \mathcal{A} \star \bullet)^\alpha$
   Hence $[\theta; \sigma](\bullet M) \in (\bigcirc \mathcal{A})^\alpha$ as required. □

With this lemma, it remains only to handle map, iter, and coit. Below we show the semantic typing lemma for map. We write $\rho_1 \vDash \eta : \rho_2$ where $\eta = (x.M_1/X_1, ..., x.M_m/X_m)$ and $\rho_1 = \mathcal{A}_1/X_1, ..., \mathcal{A}_m/X_m$ and $\rho_2 = \mathcal{B}_1/X_1, ..., \mathcal{B}_m/X_m$ and the $\mathcal{A}_i$

and $\mathcal{B}_i$ are saturated to mean $x : \mathcal{A}_i \vDash M_i : \mathcal{B}_i$ for each $i$. Notably, because we define map independently of iter and coit, we can prove this directly before tackling iter and coit, offering a simplification of known proofs for interleaving $\mu\nu$. For readability, we write $F$ instead of $(\Delta.F)$.

**Lemma 18** (Semantic typing for map). *If $\rho_1 \vDash \eta : \rho_2$ then $x : [\![F]\!](\rho_1) \vDash \mathsf{map}\ F\ \eta\ x : [\![F]\!](\rho_2)$*

*Proof.* Notice by unrolling the definitions, this is equivalent to showing $[\![F]\!](\rho_1) \subseteq [\![F]\!](\rho_2) \circ (\mathsf{map}\ \ F\ \eta)$. The proof proceeds by induction on $F$. We show only the case for $\mu$. The case for $\nu$ is analogous. The rest are straightforward using Lemma 17 and backward closure. We present the proof in more detail in the long version.

Case $\mu X.F$: This proceeds primarily using the least fixed point property and $\twoheadrightarrow$ closure.

Let $\mathcal{C} = [\![\mu X.F]\!](\rho_2) = \mu(\mathcal{X} \mapsto \overline{[\![F]\!](\rho_2, \mathcal{X}) \star \mathsf{inj}})$
Let $\mathcal{D} = \mathcal{C} \circ (\mathsf{map}(\mu X.F)\eta)$
Let $N = (\mathsf{map}\ F\ (\eta, \mathsf{map}\ (\mu X.F)\ \eta))$

1. $\mathcal{D}$ is saturated
2. $x : \mathcal{D} \vDash \mathsf{map}\ (\mu X.F)\ \eta\ x : \mathcal{C}$ (by definition of $\vDash$, $\mathcal{D}$)
3. $x : [\![F]\!](\rho_1, \mathcal{D}) \vDash \mathsf{map}\ F\ (\eta, \mathsf{map}\ (\mu X.F)\ \eta)\ x : [\![F]\!](\rho_2, \mathcal{C})$ (by I.H.)
4. $[\![F]\!](\rho_1, \mathcal{D}) \subseteq [\![F]\!](\rho_2, \mathcal{C}) \circ (\mathsf{map}\ F\ (\eta, \mathsf{map}\ (\mu X.F)\ \eta))$ (by definition of $\vDash$)
   $\subseteq [\![F]\!](\rho_2, \mathcal{C}) \star \mathsf{inj} \circ \mathsf{inj} \circ N$
   $\subseteq \overline{[\![F]\!](\rho_2, \mathcal{C}) \star \mathsf{inj}} \circ \mathsf{inj} \circ N$ (by mon. of $\circ$)
   $= \mathcal{C} \circ \mathsf{inj} \circ N$ (by rolling fixed point)
   $= \mathcal{C} \circ (\mathsf{inj}(\mathsf{map}\ F\ (\eta, \mathsf{map}\ (\mu X.F)\ \eta) -))$ (by def)
   $\subseteq \mathcal{C} \circ (\mathsf{map}\ (\mu X.F)\ \eta\ (\mathsf{inj}\ -))$ (by $\twoheadrightarrow$ closure)
   $= \mathcal{C} \circ (\mathsf{map}\ (\mu X.F)\ \eta) \circ \mathsf{inj}$
   $= \mathcal{D} \circ \mathsf{inj}$ (by def)
5. $[\![F]\!](\rho_1, \mathcal{D}) \star \mathsf{inj} \subseteq \mathcal{D}$ (by adjunction $\star$)
6. $\overline{[\![F]\!](\rho_1, \mathcal{D}) \star \mathsf{inj}} \subseteq \mathcal{D}$ (by adjunction $\overline{(-)}$)
7. $[\![\mu X.F]\!](\rho_1) \subseteq \mathcal{D}$ (by lfp property)
8. $y : [\![\mu X.F]\!](\rho_1) \vDash \mathsf{map}\ (\mu X.F)\ \eta\ y : [\![\mu X.F]\!](\rho_2)$ (by definitions of $\vDash$, $\mathcal{D}$, $\mathcal{C}$) □

The only term constructors remaining to consider are iter and coit. These are the subject of the next two lemmas, which are proven similarly to the $\mu$ and $\nu$ cases of the map lemma. Namely, they proceed primarily by using the least (greatest) fixed point properties and backward closure under $\twoheadrightarrow$, appealing to the map lemma. The proofs can be found in the long version of the paper.

**Lemma 19.** *If $x : [\![F]\!](\mathcal{C}/X) \vDash M : \mathcal{C}$ where $\mathcal{C}$ is saturated, we have $y : [\![\mu X.F]\!] \vDash \mathsf{iter}_{X.F}\ (x.M)\ y\colon \mathcal{C}$*

**Lemma 20.** *If $x : \mathcal{C} \vDash M : [\![F]\!](\mathcal{C}/X)$ where $\mathcal{C}$ is saturated, we have $y : \mathcal{C} \vDash \mathsf{coit}_{X.F}\ (x.M)\ y\colon [\![\nu X.F]\!]$*

By now we have shown that all of the term constructors can be interpreted, and hence the fundamental theorem is simply an induction on the typing derivation, appealing to the previous lemmas.

**Theorem 21** (Fundamental theorem). *If $\Theta; \Gamma \vdash M : A$, then we have $[\![\Theta]\!]; [\![\Gamma]\!] \vDash M : [\![A]\!]$*

**Corollary 22.** *If $\Theta; \Gamma \vdash M : A$ then for any $\alpha$, $M$ is strongly normalizing at $\alpha$.*

## 7. Causality, Productivity and Liveness

We discuss here some of the consequences of type soundness and strong normalization and explain how our operational semantics enables one to execute programs reactively.

We call a term $M$ a $\alpha$-value if it cannot step further at time $\alpha$. We may write this $M \not\rightsquigarrow_\alpha$. We obtain as a consequence of strong normalization that there is no closed inhabitant of the type $\bot$ (which we define as $\mu X.X$), since there is no closed $\alpha$-value of this type. Perhaps surprisingly, we can also show there is no closed inhabitant of $\bigcirc\bot \to \bot$. For if there was some $\vdash f : \bigcirc\bot \to \bot$, we could evaluate $x : \bot; \cdot \vdash f(\bullet x) : \bot$ at 0 to obtain a 0-value $x : \bot; \cdot \vdash v : \bot$, which by inspection of the possible 0-values, cannot exist!

Similarly, we can demonstrate an interesting property of the type $B \equiv \mu X.\bigcirc X$. First, there is no closed term of type $B \to \bot$. For if there was some $f : B \to \bot$, we could normalize $x : B; \cdot \vdash f(\mathsf{inj}\ \bullet x) : B$ at time 0 to obtain a 0-value $x : B; \cdot \vdash v : \bot$, which cannot exist. Moreover, there is no closed term of type $B$, since there is no closed $\omega$-value of type $B$. That is, $B$ is neither inhabited nor provably uninhabited inside the logic.

To show how our operational semantics and strong normalization give rise to a causal (reactive) interpretation of programs, as well as an explanation of the liveness properties guaranteed by the types, we illustrate here the reactive execution of an example program $x_0 : \Diamond P \vdash M_0 : \Diamond Q$. Such a program can be thought of as waiting for a $P$ event from its environment, and at some point delivering a $Q$ event. For simplicity, we assume that $P$ and $Q$ are pure (non-temporal) types such as $Bool$ or $\mathbb{N}$. We consider sequences of interaction which begin as follows, where we write $\mathsf{now}\ p$ for $\mathsf{inj}\ (\mathsf{inl}\ p)$ and $\mathsf{later} \bullet t$ for $\mathsf{inj}\ (\mathsf{inr}(\bullet t))$.

$$\begin{array}{lcl} [\mathsf{later} \bullet x_1/x_0]M_0 & \rightsquigarrow_0^* & \mathsf{later} \bullet M_1 \\ [\mathsf{later} \bullet x_2/x_1]M_1 & \rightsquigarrow_0^* & \mathsf{later} \bullet M_2 \\ & \vdots & \end{array}$$

Each such step of an interaction corresponds to the environment telling the program that it does not yet have the $P$ event in that time step, and the program responding saying that it has not yet produced a $Q$ event. Essentially, at each stage, we leave a hole $x_i$ standing for input not yet known at this stage, which we will refine further in the next time step. The resulting $M_i$ acts as a continuation, specifying what to compute in the next time step. We note that each $x_i{:}\Diamond P \vdash M_i : \Diamond Q$ by type preservation. Such a sequence may not end, if the environment defers providing a $P$ forever. However, it may end one of two ways. The first is if eventually the environment supplies a closed value $p$ of type $P$:

$$[\mathsf{now}\ p/x_{i+1}]M_{i+1} \quad \rightsquigarrow_\omega^* \quad v \not\rightsquigarrow_\omega$$

In this case, $\vdash [\mathsf{now}\ p/x_{i+1}]M_{i+1} : \Diamond Q$. By type preservation and strong normalization, we can evaluate this completely to $\vdash v : \Diamond Q$. By an inspection of the closed $\omega$-values, $v$ must be of the form $\mathsf{later}(\bullet\mathsf{later}(\bullet \cdots (\mathsf{now}\ q)))$. That is, a $Q$ is eventually delivered in this case.

The second way such an interaction sequence may end is if the program produces a result before the environment has supplied a $P$:

$$\begin{array}{lcl} & \vdots & \\ [\mathsf{later} \bullet x_{i+1}/x_i]M_i & \rightsquigarrow_0^* & \mathsf{now}\ q \end{array}$$

We remark that type preservation of $\rightsquigarrow_0$ provides an explanation of *causality*: since $x_{i+1} : \Diamond P; \cdot \vdash [\mathsf{later} \bullet x_{i+1}/x_i]M_i : \Diamond Q$, if evaluating the term $[\mathsf{later} \bullet x_{i+1}/x_i]M_i$ with $\rightsquigarrow_0$ produces a 0-value $v$, then $x_{i+1} : \Diamond P; \cdot \vdash v : \Diamond Q$ and by an inspection of the 0-values of this type, we see that $v$ must be of the form $\mathsf{later} \bullet M_{i+1}$ or $\mathsf{now}\ p$ – since the variable $x_{i+1}$ is in the next context, it cannot interfere with the part of the value in the present, which means the present component cannot be stuck on $x_{i+1}$. That is, $x_{i+1}$ could only possibly occur in $M_{i+1}$. This illustrates that future inputs do not affect present output – this is precisely what we mean by causality.

We also remark that strong normalization of $\rightsquigarrow_0$ guarantees *reactive productivity*. That is, the evaluation of $[\mathsf{later} \bullet x_{i+1}/x_i]M_i$ is guaranteed to terminate at some 0-value $v$ by strong normalization. As an aside, we note that if we were to use a time-indexed type system such as that of Krishnaswami and Benton [23], one could generalize this kind of argument to reduction at $n$, and normalize terms using $\rightsquigarrow_n$ to obtain $n$-value where $x$ can only occur at time step $n+1$. This gives a more global perspective of reactive execution. However, we use our form of the type system because we find it corresponds better in practice to how one thinks about reactive programs (one step at a time).

Finally, strong normalization of $\rightsquigarrow_\omega$ provides an explanation of *liveness*. When evaluating a closed term $\vdash M : \Diamond Q$ at $\omega$, we arrive at a closed $\omega$-value $v : \Diamond Q$. By inspection of the normal forms, such a value must provide a result after only finitely many delays. This is to say that when running programs reactively, the environment may choose not to satisfy the prequisite liveness requirement (e.g. it may never supply a $P$ event). In which case, the output of the program cannot reasonably be expected to guarantee its liveness property, since it may be waiting for an input event which never comes. However, we have the conditional result that *if* the environment satisfies its liveness requirement (e.g. eventually it delivers a $P$ event) *then* the result of the interaction satisfies its liveness property (e.g. eventually the program will fire a $Q$ event).

## 8. Related Work

Most closely related to our work is the line of work by Krishnaswami and his collaborators [22–24]. Our type systems are similar; in particular our treatment of the $\bigcirc$ modality and causality. The key distinction lies in the treatment of recursion and fixed points. Krishnaswami et al. employ a Nakano-style [13] *guarded* recursion rule which allows some productive programs to be written more conveniently than with our (co)iteration operators. However, their recursion rule has the effect of collapsing least fixed points into greatest fixed points. Both type systems can be seen as proofs-as-programs interpretations of temporal logics; ours has the advantage that it is capable of expressing liveness guarantees (and hence it retains a tighter relationship to LTL). In their recent work [22, 24], they obtain also promising results about space usage, which we have so far ignored in our foundation. In his most recent work, Krishnaswami [22] describes an operational semantics with better sharing behaviour than ours.

Another key distinction between the two lines of work is that where we restrict to fixed points of *strictly positive functors*, Krishnaswami restricts to *guarded* fixed points – type variables always occur under $\bigcirc$; even negative occurrences are permitted. In contrast, our approach allows a unified treatment of typical pure recursive datatypes (e.g. list) and temporal types (e.g. $\Box A$), as well as more exotic "mixed" types such as $\nu X.X + \bigcirc X$. Krishnaswami observes that allowing negative, guarded occurrences enables the definition of guarded recursion. As a consequence, this triggers a collapse of (guarded) $\mu$ and $\nu$, so negative occurrences appear incompatible with our goals.

Also related is the work of Jeffrey [14, 16] and Jeltsch [17], who first observed that LTL propositions correspond to FRP types. Both consider also continuous time, while we focus on discrete time. Here we provide a missing piece of this correspondence: the proofs-as-programs component. Jeffrey writes programs with a set of causal combinators, in contrast to our ML-like foundation. His systems lack general (co)recursive datatypes and as a result, one cannot write practical programs which enforce some liveness properties such as fairness as we do here. In his recent work [16], he illustrates what he calls a liveness guarantee. The key distinction is that our liveness guarantees talk about *some* point in the future, while Jeffrey only illustrates guarantees about *specific* points in time. We illustrated in Sec. 2 that our type system can also provide similar guarantees. We claim that our notion of liveness retains a tighter correspondence to the concept of liveness as it is defined in the temporal logic world.

Jeltsch [17, 18] studies denotational settings for reactive programming, some of which are capable of expressing liveness guarantees. He obtains the result that his Concrete Process Categories (CPCs) can express liveness when the underlying time domain has a greatest element. He does not describe a language for programming in CPCs, and hence it is not clear how to write programs which enforce liveness properties in CPCs, unlike our work. He discusses also least and greatest fixed points, but does not mention the interleaving case in generality, nor does he treat their existence or metatheory as we do here. His CPCs may provide a promising denotational semantics for our calculus.

The classical linear $\mu$-calculus (often called $\nu TL$) forms the inspiration for our calculus. The study of (classical) $\nu TL$ proof systems goes back at least to Lichtenstein [25]. Our work offers a constructive, type-theoretic view on $\nu TL$. Kojima and Igarashi [20] also investigate proof systems for a constructive variant of LTL with many of the same properties as ours (e.g. the non-provability of $\bigcirc\bot \rightarrow \bot$). They do not investigate least/greatest fixed points or modalities other than $\bigcirc$.

Synchronous dataflow languages, such as Esterel [3], Lustre [6], and Lucid Synchrone [32] are also related. Our work contributes to a logical understanding of synchronous dataflow, and in particular our work could possibly be seen as providing a liveness-aware type system for such languages.

Birkedal et al. [5] also use a logical relation indexed by an ordinal larger than $\omega$, in particular to model countable non-determinism (which arises when modeling fairness in concurrent settings). Our $\omega + 1$ is a much smaller ordinal than they require, owing to the fact that we are not concerned with non-determinism in the present work. Severi and de Vries [33] prove normalization results for pure type systems augmented with a "later" modality. Their systems have Nakano style guarded recursion and streams as their only instance of (co)inductive types. For this reason, the connection with liveness is absent from their work.

## 9. Conclusion

We have presented a type-theoretic foundation for reactive programming inspired by a constructive interpretation of linear temporal logic, extended with least and greatest fixed point type constructors, in the spirit of the modal $\mu$-calculus. The distinction of least and greatest fixed points allows us to distinguish between events which may eventually occur or must eventually occur. Our type system acts as a sound proof system for LTL, and hence expands on the Curry-Howard interpretation of LTL. We prove also strong normalization, which, together with type soundness, guarantees causality, productivity, and liveness of our programs.

## 10. Future Work

Our work provides a foundational basis for exploring expressive temporal logics as type systems for FRP. From a practical standpoint, however, our calculus is lacking a few key features. For example, the `import` functions we wrote in Section 2 unnecessarily traverse the entire term. From a foundational perspective, it is interesting to notice that they can be implemented at all. However, in practice, one would like to employ a device such as Krishnaswami's *stability* [22] to allow constant-time import for such types. We believe that our system can provide a solid foundation for exploring such features in the presence of liveness guarantees.

It would also be useful to explore more general forms of recursion with syntactic or typing restrictions such as sized types to guarantee productivity and termination/liveness, which would allow our examples to typecheck as they are instead of by manual elaboration into (co)iteration. Tackling this in the presence of interleaving $\mu$ and $\nu$ is challenging. This is one motivation for using Nakano-style guarded recursion [13]. A promising direction is to explore the introduction of Nakano-style guarded recursion at so-called *complete* types in our type system (by analogy with the complete ultrametric spaces of [23]) – roughly, types where occurrences of $\mu$ are restricted. This would be a step in the direction of unifying the two approaches.

We are in the process of developing a denotational semantics for this calculus in the category of presheaves on $\omega + 1$, inspired by the work of Birkedal et al. [4] who study the presheaves on $\omega$, as well as Jeltsch [18] who studies more general (e.g. continuous) time domains. The idea is that the extra point "at infinity" expresses the *global* behaviour – it expresses our liveness guarantees, which can only be observed from a global perspective on time. The chief challenge in our setting lies in constructing interleaving fixed points. It is expected that such a denotational semantics will provide a crisper explanation of our liveness guarantees.

## References


[1] A. Abel and T. Altenkirch. A predicative strong normalisation proof for a lambda-calculus with interleaving inductive types. In *TYPES*, pages 21–40, 1999.

[2] T. Altenkirch. *Constructions, Inductive Types and Strong Normalization.* PhD thesis, University of Edinburgh, November 1993.

[3] G. Berry and L. Cosserat. The esterel synchronous programming language and its mathematical semantics. In *Seminar on Concurrency, Carnegie-Mellon University*, pages 389–448, London, UK, UK, 1985. Springer-Verlag. ISBN 3-540-15670-4.

[4] L. Birkedal, R. E. Mogelberg, J. Schwinghammer, and K. Stovring. First steps in synthetic guarded domain theory: Step-indexing in the topos of trees. In *Proceedings of the 26th Annual IEEE Symposium on Logic in Computer Science (LICS)*, pages 55 –64. IEEE Computer Society, 2011.

[5] L. Birkedal, A. Bizjak, and J. Schwinghammer. Step-indexed relational reasoning for countable nondeterminism. Submitted, journal version of CSL'11 paper, 2013.

[6] P. Caspi, D. Pilaud, N. Halbwachs, and J. A. Plaice. Lustre: a declarative language for real-time programming. In *Proceedings of the 14th ACM SIGACT-SIGPLAN Symposium on Principles of Programming Languages*, POPL '87, pages 178–188. ACM, 1987.

[7] G. H. Cooper and S. Krishnamurthi. Embedding dynamic dataflow in a call-by-value language. In *Proceedings of the 15th European Conference on Programming Languages and Systems*, ESOP'06, pages 294–308. Springer-Verlag, 2006.

[8] A. Courtney. Frappé functional reactive programming in java. In *Proceedings of the Third International Symposium on Practical Aspects of Declarative Languages*, PADL '01, pages 29–44. Springer-Verlag, 2001.

[9] J. Donham. Functional reactive programming in OCaml. URL `https://github.com/jaked/froc`.

[10] C. Elliott and P. Hudak. Functional reactive animation. In *Proceedings of the second ACM SIGPLAN International Conference on Functional Programming*, pages 263–273. ACM, 1997.

[11] J. Y. Girard. *Interprétation fonctionnelle et elimination des coupures de l'arithmtique d'ordre supérieur.* These d'état, Université de Paris 7, 1972.

[12] J.-Y. Girard, Y. Lafont, and P. Tayor. *Proofs and types.* Cambridge University Press, 1990.

[13] H. Hiroshi Nakano. A modality for recursion. In *Proceedings of the 15th Annual IEEE Symposium on Logic in Computer Science*, pages 255 –266. IEEE Computer Society, 2000.

[14] A. Jeffrey. LTL types FRP: linear-time temporal logic propositions as types, proofs as functional reactive programs. In *Proceedings of the sixth Workshop on Programming Languages meets Program Verification*, pages 49–60. ACM, 2012.

[15] A. Jeffrey. Causality for free! parametricity implies causality for functional reactive programs. In *Proceedings of the seventh Workshop on Programming Languages meets Program Verification*, pages 57–68. ACM, 2013.

[16] A. Jeffrey. Functional reactive programming with liveness guarantees. In *18th International Confernece on Functional Programming*. ACM, 2013.

[17] W. Jeltsch. Towards a common categorical semantics for linear-time temporal logic and functional reactive programming. *Electronic Notes in Theoretical Computer Science*, 286(0):229–242, 2012.

[18] W. Jeltsch. Temporal logic with until: Functional reactive programming with processes and concrete process categories. In *Proceedings of the seventh Workshop on Programming Languages meets Program Verification*, pages 69–78. ACM, 2013.

[19] J.-P. Jouannaud and M. Okada. Abstract data type systems. *Theoretical Computer Science*, 173(2):349 – 391, 1997.

[20] K. Kojima and A. Igarashi. Constructive linear-time temporal logic: Proof systems and kripke semantics. *Information and Computation*, 209(12):1491 – 1503, 2011. ISSN 0890-5401. ¡ce:title¿Intuitionistic Modal Logic and Applications (IMLA 2008)¡/ce:title¿.

[21] D. Kozen. Results on the propositional $\mu$-calculus. *Theoretical Computer Science*, 27(3):333 – 354, 1983.

[22] N. R. Krishnaswami. Higher-order functional reactive programming without spacetime leaks. In *18th International Confernece on Functional Programming*. ACM, 2013.

[23] N. R. Krishnaswami and N. Benton. Ultrametric semantics of reactive programs. In *Proceedings of the 2011 IEEE 26th Annual Symposium on Logic in Computer Science*, pages 257–266. IEEE Computer Society, 2011.

[24] N. R. Krishnaswami, N. Benton, and J. Hoffmann. Higher-order functional reactive programming in bounded space. In *Proceedings of the 39th annual ACM SIGPLAN-SIGACT Symposium on Principles of Programming Languages*, pages 45–58. ACM, 2012.

[25] O. Lichtenstein. *Decidability, Completeness, and Extensions of Linear Time Temporal Logic*. PhD thesis, The Weizmann Institute of Science, 1991.

[26] Z. Luo. *An Extended Calculus of Constructions*. PhD thesis, University of Edinburgh, 1990.

[27] R. Matthes. *Extensions of System F by Iteration and Primitive Recursion on Monotone Inductive Types*. PhD thesis, University of Munich, 1998.

[28] N. P. Mendler. *Inductive Definition in Type Theory*. PhD thesis, Cornell University, 1988.

[29] H. Nilsson, A. Courtney, and J. Peterson. Functional reactive programming, continued. In *Proceedings of the 2002 ACM SIGPLAN workshop on Haskell*, pages 51–64. ACM, 2002.

[30] D. M. R. Park. Concurrency and automata on infinite sequences. In P. Deussen, editor, *Theoretical Computer Science, Proceedings of the 5th GI-Conference*, Lecture Notes in Computer Science (LNCS 104, pages 167–183. Springer, 1981.

[31] A. Pnueli. The temporal logic of programs. In *Proceedings of the 18th Annual Symposium on Foundations of Computer Science*, pages 46–57. IEEE Computer Society, 1977.

[32] M. Pouzet. *Lucid Synchrone, version 3. Tutorial and reference manual.* Université Paris-Sud, LRI, April 2006.

[33] P. G. Severi and F.-J. J. de Vries. Pure type systems with corecursion on streams: from finite to infinitary normalisation. *SIGPLAN Not.*, 47 (9):141–152, Sept. 2012. ISSN 0362-1340.

[34] W. W. Tait. Intensional interpretations of functionals of finite type i. *The Journal of Symbolic Logic*, 32(2):pp. 198–212, 1967.

# Optimal Dynamic Partial Order Reduction

Parosh Abdulla   Stavros Aronis   Bengt Jonsson   Konstantinos Sagonas
Department of Information Technology, Uppsala University, Sweden

## Abstract

Stateless model checking is a powerful technique for program verification, which however suffers from an exponential growth in the number of explored executions. A successful technique for reducing this number, while still maintaining complete coverage, is Dynamic Partial Order Reduction (DPOR). We present a new DPOR algorithm, which is the first to be provably optimal in that it always explores the minimal number of executions. It is based on a novel class of sets, called *source sets*, which replace the role of persistent sets in previous algorithms. First, we show how to modify an existing DPOR algorithm to work with source sets, resulting in an efficient and simple to implement algorithm. Second, we extend this algorithm with a novel mechanism, called *wakeup trees*, that allows to achieve optimality. We have implemented both algorithms in a stateless model checking tool for Erlang programs. Experiments show that source sets significantly increase the performance and that wakeup trees incur only a small overhead in both time and space.

***Categories and Subject Descriptors*** D.2.4 [*Software Engineering*]: Software/Program Verification; D.2.5 [*Software Engineering*]: Testing and Debugging; F.3.1 [*Logics and Meanings of Programs*]: Specifying and Verifying and Reasoning about Programs

***General Terms*** Algorithms, Verification, Reliability

***Keywords*** dynamic partial oder reduction; software model checking; systematic testing; concurrency; source sets; wakeup trees

## 1. Introduction

Verification and testing of concurrent programs is difficult, since one must consider all the different ways in which processes/threads can interact. *Model checking* addresses this problem by systematically exploring the state space of a given program and verifying that each reachable state satisfies a given property. Applying model checking to realistic programs is problematic, however, since it requires to capture and store a large number of global states. *Stateless model checking* [7] avoids this problem by exploring the state space of the program without explicitly storing global states. A special runtime scheduler drives the program execution, making decisions on scheduling whenever such decisions may affect the interaction between processes. Stateless model checking has been successfully implemented in tools, such as VeriSoft [8] and CHESS [20].


*POPL '14*, January 22–24, 2014, San Diego, CA, USA.

ACM 978-1-4503-2544-8/14/01... $15.00.
http://dx.doi.org/10.1145/2535838.2535845

While stateless model checking is applicable to realistic programs, it suffers from combinatorial explosion, as the number of possible interleavings grows exponentially with the length of program execution. There are several approaches that limit the number of explored interleavings, such as depth-bounding and context bounding [19]. Among them, *partial order reduction* (POR) [3, 6, 21, 26] stands out, as it provides full coverage of all behaviours that can occur in *any* interleaving, even though it explores only a representative subset. POR is based on the observation that two interleavings can be regarded as equivalent if one can be obtained from the other by swapping adjacent, non-conflicting (independent) execution steps. In each such equivalence class (called a *Mazurkiewicz trace* [17]), POR explores at least one interleaving. This is sufficient for checking most interesting safety properties, including race freedom, absence of global deadlocks, and absence of assertion violations [3, 6, 26].

Existing POR approaches are essentially based on two techniques, both of which reduce the set of process steps that are explored at each scheduling point:

- The *persistent set* technique, that explores only a provably sufficient subset of the enabled processes. This set is called a *persistent set* [6] (variations are *stubborn sets* [26] and *ample sets* [3]).
- The *sleep set* technique [6], that maintains information about the past exploration in a so-called *sleep set*, which contains processes whose exploration would be provably redundant.

These two techniques are independent and complementary, and can be combined to obtain increased reduction.

The construction of persistent sets is based on information about possible future conflicts between threads. Early approaches analyzed such conflicts statically, leading to over-approximations and therefore limiting the achievable reduction. *Dynamic Partial Order Reduction* (DPOR) [4] improves the precision by recording actually occurring conflicts during the exploration and using this information to construct persistent sets on-the-fly, "by need". DPOR guarantees the exploration of at least one interleaving in each Mazurkiewicz trace when the explored state space is acyclic and finite. This is the case in stateless model checking in which only executions of bounded length are analyzed [4, 8, 20].

***Challenge*** Since DPOR is excellently suited as a reduction technique, several variants, improvements, and adaptations for different computation models have appeared [4, 15, 22, 24, 25]. The obtained reduction can, however, vary significantly depending on several factors, e.g. the order in which processes are explored at each point of scheduling. For a particular implementation of DPOR (with sleep sets) [11], up to an order of magnitude of difference in the number of explored interleavings has been observed, when different strategies are used. For specific communication models, specialized algorithms can achieve better reduction [25]. Heuristics for choosing which next process to explore have also been investigated without conclusive results [14].

Let us explain one fundamental reason for the above variation in obtained reduction. In DPOR, the combination of persistent set and sleep set techniques guarantees to explore at least one complete interleaving in each Mazurkiewicz trace. Moreover, it has already been proven that the use of sleep sets is sufficient to prevent the complete exploration of two different but equivalent interleavings [10]. At first sight, this seems to imply that sleep sets can give optimal reduction. What it actually implies, however, is that when the algorithm tries an interleaving which is equivalent to an already explored one, the exploration will begin but it will be blocked sooner or later by the sleep sets in what we call a *sleep-set blocked* exploration. When only sleep sets are used for reduction, the exploration effort will include an arbitrary number of sleep-set blocked explorations. It is here where persistent sets enter the picture, and limit the number of initiated explorations. Computation of smaller persistent sets, leads to fewer sleep-set blocked explorations. However, as we will show in this paper, persistent sets are not powerful enough to completely prevent sleep-set blocked exploration.

In view of these variations, a fundamental challenge is to develop an *optimal* DPOR algorithm that: (i) always explores the minimum number of interleavings, regardless of scheduling decisions, (ii) can be efficiently implemented and (iii) is applicable to a variety of computation models, including communication via shared variables and message passing.

***Contributions*** In this paper, we present a new DPOR algorithm, called *optimal-DPOR*, which is provably optimal in that it always explores exactly one interleaving per Mazurkiewicz trace, and never initiates any sleep set-blocked exploration. Our optimal algorithm is based on a new theoretical foundation for partial order reduction, in which persistent sets are replaced by a novel class of sets, called *source sets*. Source sets are often smaller than persistent sets and are provably minimal, in the sense that the set of explored processes from some scheduling point must be a source set in order to guarantee exploration of all Mazurkiewicz traces. When a minimal persistent set contains more elements than the corresponding source set, the additional elements will always initiate sleep-set blocked explorations.

We will use a two-step approach to describe our optimal algorithm. In the first step, we develop a simpler DPOR algorithm, called *source-DPOR*, which is based on source sets. It is derived by modifying the classical DPOR algorithm by Flanagan and Godefroid [4] so that persistent sets are replaced by source sets. The power of source sets can already be observed in the algorithm *source-DPOR*: it achieves significantly better reduction in the number of explored interleavings than the classical DPOR algorithm. In fact, *source-DPOR* explores the minimal number of interleavings for a large number of our benchmarks in Section 9.

Although *source-DPOR* often achieves optimal reduction, it may sometimes encounter sleep-set blocked explorations. Therefore, in the second step, we combine source sets with a novel mechanism, called *wakeup trees*, thus deriving the algorithm *optimal-DPOR*. Wakeup trees control the initial steps of future explorations, implying that *optimal-DPOR* never encounters any sleep-set blocked (i.e. redundant) exploration. An important feature of wakeup trees is that they are simple data structures that are constructed from already explored interleavings, hence they do not increase the amount of exploration. On the other hand, they allow to reduce the number of explored executions. In our benchmarks, maintenance of the wakeup trees reduces total exploration time when *source-DPOR* encounters sleep-set blocked explorations and it never requires more than 10% of additional time in the cases where there are none or only a few sleep-set blocked explorations. Memory consumption is practically always the same between the DPOR algorithms and the space cost of maintaining wakeup trees is very small in our experience.

We show the applicability of our algorithms to a wide range of computation models, including shared variables and message passing, by formulating them in a general setting, which only assumes that we can compute a *happens-before* relation (also called a causal ordering) between the events in an execution. For systems with shared variables, the happens-before relation can be based on the variables that are accessed or modified by events. For message passing systems, the happens-before relation can be based on correlating the transmission of a message with the corresponding reception. Our approach allows to make finer distinctions, leading to better reduction, than many other approaches that define a happens-before relation which is based on program statements, possibly taking into account the local state in which they are executed [3, 4, 6, 8, 14, 25, 26]. For instance, we allow a send transition to be dependent with another send transition only if the order in which the two messages are received is significant.

We have implemented both *source-DPOR* and *optimal-DPOR* as extensions for Concuerror [2], a stateless model checking tool for Erlang programs. Erlang's concurrency model focuses primarily on message passing, but it is also possible to write programs which manipulate shared data structures. Our evaluation shows that on a wide selection of benchmarks, including benchmarks from the DPOR literature, but more importantly on real Erlang applications of significant size, we obtain optimal reduction in the number of interleavings even with *source-DPOR*, therefore significantly outperforming the original DPOR algorithm not only in number of interleavings but in total execution time as well.

***Organization*** In the next section, we illustrate the basic new ideas of our technique. We introduce our computational model and formulation of the partial-order framework in Section 3. In Section 4 we introduce source sets. The *source-DPOR* algorithm is described in Section 5. We formalize the concept of wakeup trees in Section 6, before describing the *optimal-DPOR* algorithm in Section 7. Implementation of the algorithms is described in Section 8, and experimental evaluation in Section 9. The paper ends by surveying related work and offering some concluding remarks.

## 2. Basic Ideas

In this section, we give an informal introduction to the concepts of source sets and wakeup trees, and their improvement over existing approaches, using some small examples.

| $p$: | $q$: | $r$: |
|---|---|---|
| `write x; (1)` | `read y;` | `read z;` |
| | `read x; (2)` | `read x; (3)` |

**Example** 1: Writer-readers code excerpt.

***Source Sets*** In Example 1, the three processes $p$, $q$, and $r$ perform dependent accesses to the shared variable x. Two accesses are dependent if they access the same variable and at least one is a write. The accesses to y and z are not dependent with anything else. For this program, there are four Mazurkiewicz traces (i.e. equivalence classes of executions), each characterized by its sequence of accesses to x (three accesses can be ordered in six ways, but two pairs of orderings are equivalent since they differ only in the ordering of adjacent reads, which are not dependent).

Any POR method selects some subset of $\{p, q, r\}$ to perform some first step in the set of explored executions. It is not enough to select only $p$, since then executions where some read access happens before the write access of $p$ will not be explored. In DPOR, assume that the first execution to be explored is $p.q.q.r.r$ (we denote executions by the sequence of scheduled process steps). A DPOR

Initially: `x := y := z := 0`

| p: | r: | s: |
|---|---|---|
| `x := 1; (1)` | `m := y; (3)` | `n := z; (5)` |
| q: | `if m = 0 then` | `l := y; (6)` |
| `y := 1; (2)` | `    z := 1; (4)` | `if n = 1 then` |
| | | `    if l = 0 then` |
| | | `        x := 2; (7)` |

**Example** 2: Program with control flow.

algorithm will detect the dependency between step (1) by $p$ and step (2) by $q$, and note that it seems necessary to explore sequences that start with a step of $q$. The DPOR algorithm will also detect the dependency between (1) and (3) and possibly note that it is necessary to explore sequences that start with a step of $r$.

Existing DPOR methods guarantee that the set of processes explored from the initial state is a *persistent set*. In short, a set $P$ of processes is persistent in the initial state if in any execution from the initial state, the first step that is dependent with the first step of some process in $P$ must be taken by some process in $P$. In this example, the only persistent set which contains $p$ in the initial state is $\{p, q, r\}$. To see this, suppose that, e.g. $r$ is not in the persistent set $P$, i.e. $P = \{p, q\}$. Then the execution $r.r$ contains no step from a process in $P$, but its second step is dependent with the first step of $p$, which is in $P$. In a similar way, one can see that also $q$ must be in $P$.

In contrast, our source set-based algorithms allow $S = \{p, q\}$ as the set of processes explored from the initial state. The set $S$ is sufficient, since any execution that starts with a step of $r$ is equivalent to some execution that starts with the first (local) step of $q$. The set $S$ is not a persistent set, but it is a *source set*. Intuitively, a set $S$ of processes is a source set if for each execution $E$ from the initial state there is some process $proc$ in $S$ such that the first step in $E$ that is dependent with $proc$ is taken by $proc$ itself. To see that $\{p, q\}$ is a source set, note that when $E$ is $r.r$, then we can choose $q$ as $proc$, noting that $r.r$ is not dependent with $q$. Any persistent set is also a source set, but, as shown by this example, the converse is not true.

Our algorithm *source-DPOR* combines source sets with sleep sets, and will explore exactly four interleavings, whereas any algorithm based on persistent sets will explore at least five (if the first explored execution starts with $p$), some of which will be sleep-set blocked if sleep sets are used. If we extend the example to include $n$ reading processes instead of just two, the number of sleep-set blocked explorations increases significantly (see Table 2 in Section 8).

Sleep sets were introduced [6] to prevent redundant exploration. They are manipulated as follows: (i) after exploring interleavings that begin with some process $p$, the process $p$ is added to the sleep set, and (ii) when a process step that is dependent with $p$ is executed, $p$ is removed from the sleep set. The effect is that the algorithm need never explore a step of a process in the sleep set. In Example 1, for instance, after having explored executions starting with $p$, the process $p$ is added to the sleep set. When exploring executions that start with $q$, the process $p$ is still in the sleep set after the first step of $q$, and should not be explored next, since executions that start with $q.p$ are equivalent to executions that start with $p.q$.

***Wakeup Trees*** As mentioned, by utilizing source sets, *source-DPOR* will explore a minimal number of executions for the program of Example 1. There are cases, however, where *source-DPOR* encounters sleep-set blocked exploration.

We illustrate this by Example 2, a program with four processes, $p, q, r, s$. Two events are dependent if they access the same shared

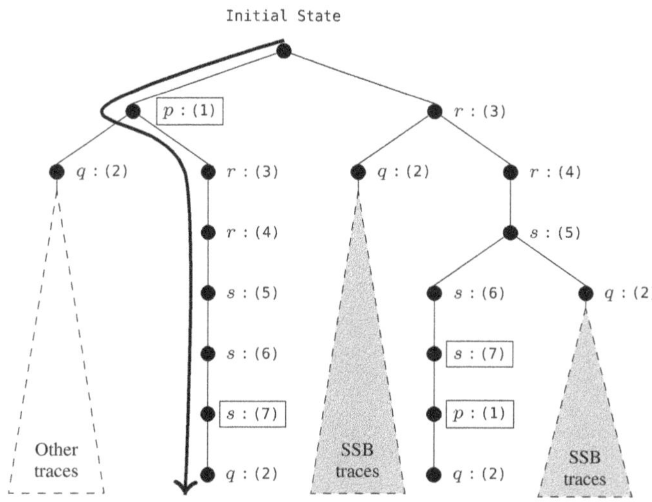


**Figure 1.** Explored interleavings for Example 2.

variable, i.e. x,y or z. Variables m,n,l are local. Each statement accessing a global variable has a unique label; e.g., process $s$ has three such statements labeled (5), (6), and (7). Statements that operate on local variables are assumed to be part of the previous labeled statement. For example, label (6) marks the read of the value of y, together with the assignment on l, and the condition check on n. If the value of n is 1, the condition check on l is also part of (6), which ends just before the assignment on x that has the label (7). Similar assumptions are made for the other local statements.

Consider a DPOR algorithm that starts the exploration with $p$, explores the interleaving $p.r.r.s.s.s$ (marked in Figure 1 with an arrow from top to bottom), and then detects the race between events (1) and (7). It must then explore some interleaving in which the race is reversed, i.e., the event (7) occurs before the event (1). Note that event (7) will occur only if it is preceded by the sequence (3) - (4) - (5) - (6) and not preceded by a step of process $q$. Thus, an interleaving that reverses this race must start with the sequence $r.r.s.s$. Such an interleaving is shown in Figure 1 between the two chunks labeled "SSB traces".

Having detected the race in $p.r.r.s.s.s$, *source-DPOR* adds $r$ to the source set at the initial state. However, it does not "remember" that $r$ must be followed by $r.s.s$ to reverse the race. After exploring $r$, it may therefore continue with $q$. However, after $r.q$ any exploration is doomed to encounter sleep-set blocking, meaning that the exploration reaches a state in which all enabled processes are in the sleep set. To see this, note that $p$ is in the sleep set when exploring $r$, and will remain there forever in any sequence that starts with $r.q$ (as explained above, it is removed only after the sequence $r.r.s.s.s$). This corresponds to the left chunk of "SSB traces" in Figure 1.

Optimal-DPOR solves this problem by replacing the backtrack set with a structure called a *wakeup tree*. This tree contains initial fragments of executions that are guaranteed not to encounter sleep set blocking. In the example, Optimal-DPOR algorithm will handle the race between (1) and (7) by adding the sequence $r.r.s.s.s$ to the wakeup tree. The point is that after $r.r.s.s.s$, the process $p$ has been removed from the sleep set, and so sleep set blocking is avoided.

## 3. Framework

In this section, we introduce the technical background material. First, we present the general model of concurrent systems for which the algorithms are formulated, thereafter the assumptions on the happens-before relation, and finally the notions of independence and races.

### 3.1 Abstract Computation Model

We consider a concurrent system composed of a finite set of *processes* (or threads). Each process executes a deterministic program, whereby statements act on the (global) *state* of the system, which is made up of the local states of each process and the shared state of the system. We assume that the state space does not contain cycles, and that executions have bounded length. We do not restrict to a specific mode of process interaction, allowing instead the use of shared variables, messages, etc.

Let $\Sigma$ be the set of (global) states of the system. The system has a unique *initial state* $s_0 \in \Sigma$. We assume that the program executed by a process $p$ can be represented as a partial function $\mathit{execute}_p : \Sigma \mapsto \Sigma$ which moves the system from one state to a subsequent state. Each such application of the function $\mathit{execute}_p$ represents an atomic *execution step* of process $p$, which may depend on and affect the global state. We let each execution step (or just *step* for short) represent the combined effect of some global statement together with the following finite sequence of local statements (that only access and affect the local state of the process), ending just before the next global statement. This avoids consideration of interleavings of local statements of different processes in the analysis. Such an optimization is common in tools such as VeriSoft [7].

The execution of a process is said to *block* in some state $s$ if the process cannot continue (i.e. $\mathit{execute}_p(s)$ is undefined): for example, trying to receive a message in a state where the message queue is empty. To simplify the presentation, we assume in Sections 3–7 that a process does not disable another process, i.e. if $p$ is enabled and another process $q$ performs a step, then $p$ is still enabled. This assumption is valid for Erlang programs. Note that a process can disable itself, e.g. after a step such that the next statement is a `receive` statement.

An *execution sequence* $E$ of a system is a finite sequence of execution steps of its processes that is performed from the initial state $s_0$. Since each execution step is deterministic, an execution sequence $E$ is uniquely characterized by the sequence of processes that perform steps in $E$. For instance, $p.p.q$ denotes the execution sequence where first $p$ performs two steps, followed by a step of $q$. The sequence of processes that perform steps in $E$ also uniquely determine the (global) state of the system after $E$, which is denoted $s_{[E]}$. For a state $s$, let $\mathit{enabled}(s)$ denote the set of processes $p$ that are enabled in $s$ (i.e., for which $\mathit{execute}_p(s)$ is defined). We use . to denote concatenation of sequences of processes. Thus, if $p$ is not blocked after $E$, then $E.p$ is an execution sequence.

An *event* of $E$ is a particular occurrence of a process in $E$. We use $\langle p, i\rangle$ to denote the $i$th event of process $p$ in the execution sequence $E$. In other words, the event $\langle p, i\rangle$ is the $i$th execution step of process $p$ in the execution sequence $E$. We use $\mathit{dom}(E)$ to denote the set of events $\langle p, i\rangle$ which are in $E$, i.e. $\langle p, i\rangle \in \mathit{dom}(E)$ iff $E$ contains at least $i$ steps of $p$. We will use $e, e', \ldots$ to range over events. We use $\mathit{proc}(e)$ to denote the process $p$ of an event $e = \langle p, i\rangle$. If $E.w$ is an execution sequence, obtained by concatenating $E$ and $w$, then $\mathit{dom}_{[E]}(w)$ denotes $\mathit{dom}(E.w) \setminus \mathit{dom}(E)$, i.e. the events in $E.w$ which are in $w$. As a special case, we use $\mathit{next}_{[E]}(p)$ to denote $\mathit{dom}_{[E]}(p)$.

We use $<_E$ to denote the total order between events in $E$, i.e. $e <_E e'$ denotes that $e$ occurs before $e'$ in $E$. We use $E' \leq E$ to denote that the sequence $E'$ is a prefix of the sequence $E$.

### 3.2 Event Dependencies

A central concept in DPOR algorithms is that of a happens-before relation between events in an execution sequence (also called a *causal relation* [24]). We denote the happens-before relation in the execution sequence $E$ by $\rightarrow_E$. Intuitively, for an execution sequence $E$, and two events $e$ and $e'$ in $\mathit{dom}(E)$, $e \rightarrow_E e'$ means that $e$ "happens before", or "causally precedes" $e'$. For instance, $e$ can be the transmission of a message that is received by $e'$, or $e$ can be a write operation to a shared variable that is accessed by $e'$.

Our algorithms assume a function (called a *happens-before assignment*), which assigns a "happens-before" relation to any execution sequence. In order not to restrict to a specific computation model, we take a general approach, where the happens-before assignment is only required to satisfy a set of natural properties, which are collected in Definition 3.1. As long as it satisfies these properties, its precision can vary. For instance, the happens-before assignment can let any transmission to a certain message buffer be causally related with a reception from the same buffer. However, better reduction can be attained if the assignment does not make the transmission of a message dependent with a reception of a different one.

In practice, the happens-before assignment function is implemented as expected by relating accesses to the same variables, transmissions and receptions of the same messages, etc., typically using *vector clocks* [16]. In Section 8 we describe such an assignment suitable for Erlang programs.

DEFINITION 3.1. A happens-before assignment, which assigns a unique happens-before relation $\rightarrow_E$ to any execution sequence $E$, is *valid* if it satisfies the following properties for all execution sequences $E$.

1. $\rightarrow_E$ is a partial order on $\mathit{dom}(E)$, which is included in $<_E$.
2. The execution steps of each process are totally ordered, i.e. $\langle p, i\rangle \rightarrow_E \langle p, i{+}1\rangle$ whenever $\langle p, i{+}1\rangle \in \mathit{dom}(E)$,
3. If $E'$ is a prefix of $E$, then $\rightarrow_E$ and $\rightarrow_{E'}$ are the same on $\mathit{dom}(E')$.
4. Any linearization $E'$ of $\rightarrow_E$ on $\mathit{dom}(E)$ is an execution sequence which has exactly the same "happens-before" relation $\rightarrow_{E'}$ as $\rightarrow_E$. This means that the relation $\rightarrow_E$ induces a set of equivalent execution sequences, all with the same "happens-before" relation. We use $E \simeq E'$ to denote that $E$ and $E'$ are linearizations of the same "happens-before" relation, and $[E]_{\simeq}$ to denote the equivalence class of $E$.
5. If $E \simeq E'$, then $s_{[E]} = s_{[E']}$.
6. For any sequences $E$, $E'$ and $w$, such that $E.w$ is an execution sequence, we have $E \simeq E'$ if and only if $E.w \simeq E'.w$.
7. If $p$, $q$, and $r$ are different processes, then if $\mathit{next}_{[E]}(p) \rightarrow_{E.p.r} \mathit{next}_{[E.p]}(r)$ and $\mathit{next}_{[E]}(p) \not\rightarrow_{E.p.q} \mathit{next}_{[E.p]}(q)$, then $\mathit{next}_{[E]}(p) \rightarrow_{E.p.q.r} \mathit{next}_{[E.p.q]}(r)$. □

The first six properties should be obvious for any reasonable happens-before relation. The only non-obvious one would be the last. Intuitively, if the next step of $p$ happens before the next step of $r$ after the sequence $E$, then the step of $p$ still happens before the step of $r$ even when some step of another process, which is not dependent with $p$, is inserted between $p$ and $r$. This property holds in any reasonable computation model that we could think of. As examples, one situation is when $p$ and $q$ read a shared variable that is written by $r$. Another situation is that $p$ sends a message that is received by $r$. If an intervening process $q$ is independent with $p$, it cannot affect this message, and so $r$ still receives the same message.

Properties 4 and 5 together imply, as a special case, that if $e$ and $e'$ are two consecutive events in $E$ with $e \not\rightarrow_E e'$, then they can be swapped and the (global) state after the two events remains the same.

### 3.3 Independence and Races

We now define independence between events of a computation. If $E.p$ and $E.w$ are both execution sequences, then $E \models p\Diamond w$ denotes that $E.p.w$ is an execution sequence such that $\mathit{next}_{[E]}(p) \not\rightarrow_{E.p.w} e$ for any $e \in \mathit{dom}_{[E.p]}(w)$. In other words, $E \models p\Diamond w$ states that the next event of $p$ would not "happen before" any event in $w$

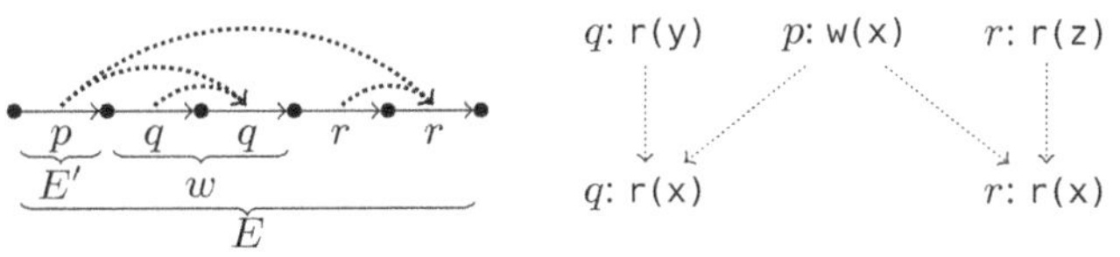


**Figure 2.** A sample run of the program in Example 1 is shown to the left. This run is annotated by a happens-before relation (the dotted arrows). To the right, the happens-before relation is shown as a partial order. Notice that $E' \models q\Diamond r$ since $q$ and $r$ are not happens-before related in $E'.r.q$. We also observe that $I_{[E']}(w) = \{q\}$, as $q$ is the only process occuring in $w$ and its first occurrence has no predecessor in the dotted relation in $w$. Furthermore, $WI_{[E']}(w) = \{q, r\}$, since $r$ is not happens-before related to any event in $w$.

in the execution sequence $E.p.w$. Intuitively, it means that $p$ is independent with $w$ after $E$. In the special case when $w$ contains only one process $q$, then $E \models p\Diamond q$ denotes that the next steps of $p$ and $q$ are independent after $E$. We use $E \not\models p\Diamond w$ to denote that $E \models p\Diamond w$ does not hold.

For a sequence $w$ and $p \in w$, let $w \setminus p$ denote the sequence $w$ with its first occurrence of $p$ removed, and let $w \lceil p$ denote the prefix of $w$ up to but not including the first occurrence of $p$. For an execution sequence $E$ and an event $e \in dom(E)$, let $pre(E, e)$ denote the prefix of $E$ up to, but not including, the event $e$. For an execution sequence $E$ and an event $e \in E$, let $notdep(e, E)$ be the sub-sequence of $E$ consisting of the events that occur after $e$ but do not "happen after" $e$ (i.e. the events $e'$ that occur after $e$ such that $e \not\rightarrow_E e'$).

A central concept in most DPOR algorithms is that of a race. Intuitively, two events, $e$ and $e'$ in an execution sequence $E$, where $e$ occurs before $e'$ in $E$, are in a race if

- $e$ happens-before $e'$ in $E$, and
- $e$ and $e'$ are "concurrent", i.e. there is an equivalent execution sequence $E' \simeq E$ in which $e$ and $e'$ are adjacent.

Formally, let $e \lessdot_E e'$ denote that $proc(e) \neq proc(e')$, that $e \rightarrow_E e'$, and that there is no event $e'' \in dom(E)$, different from $e'$ and $e$, such that $e \rightarrow_E e'' \rightarrow_E e'$.

Whenever a DPOR algorithm detects a race, then it will check whether the events in the race can be executed in the reverse order. Since the events are related by the happens-before relation, this may lead to a different global state: therefore the algorithm must try to explore a corresponding execution sequence. Let $e \precsim_E e'$ denote that $e \lessdot_E e'$, and that the race can be reversed. Formally, if $E' \simeq E$ and $e$ occurs immediately before $e'$ in $E'$, then $proc(e')$ was not blocked before the occurrence of $e$.

In Figure 2, there are two pairs of events $e, e'$ such that $e \lessdot_E e'$, namely $\langle p, 1\rangle, \langle q, 2\rangle$ and $\langle p, 1\rangle, \langle r, 2\rangle$. It also holds for both these pairs that $e \precsim_E e'$ since both $q$ and $r$ are enabled before $\langle p, 1\rangle$. In other words, both the races in the program are reversible.

## 4. Source Sets

In this section, we define the new concept of source sets. Intuitively, source sets contain the processes that can perform "first steps" in the possible future execution sequences. Let us first define two related notions of possible "first steps" in a sequence.

- For an execution sequence $E.w$, let $I_{[E]}(w)$ denote the set of processes that perform events $e$ in $dom_{[E]}(w)$ that have no "happens-before" predecessors in $dom_{[E]}(w)$. More formally, $p \in I_{[E]}(w)$ if $p \in w$ and there is no other event $e \in dom_{[E]}(w)$ with $e \rightarrow_{E.w} next_{[E]}(p)$.
- For an execution sequence $E.w$, define $WI_{[E]}(w)$ as the union of $I_{[E]}(w)$ and the set of processes $p$ such that $p \in enabled(s_{[E]})$ and $E \models p\Diamond w$.

The point of these concepts is that for an execution sequence $E.w$:

- $p \in I_{[E]}(w)$ if and only if there is a sequence $w'$ such that $E.w \simeq E.p.w'$, and
- $p \in WI_{[E]}(w)$ if and only if there are sequences $w'$ and $v$ such that $E.w.v \simeq E.p.w'$.

Definition 4.1 (Source Sets). Let $E$ be an execution sequence, and let $W$ be a set of sequences, such that $E.w$ is an execution sequence for each $w \in W$. A set $P$ of processes is *a source set for $W$ after $E$* if for each $w \in W$ we have $WI_{[E]}(w) \cap P \neq \emptyset$. □

The key property is that if $P$ is a source set for $W$ after $E$, then for each execution sequence of form $E.w$ with $w \in W$, there is a process $p \in P$ and a sequence $w'$ such that $E.p.w' \simeq E.w.v$ for some sequence $v$. Therefore, when an exploration algorithm intends to cover all suffixes in $W$ after $E$, the set of processes that are chosen for exploration from $s_{[E]}$ must be a source set for $W$ after $E$.

**Algorithm 1:** Source-DPOR algorithm

```
1  Initially Explore(⟨⟩, ∅);
2  Explore(E, Sleep) ;
3    if ∃p ∈ (enabled(s_[E]) \ Sleep) then
4      backtrack(E) := {p} ;
5      while ∃p ∈ (backtrack(E) \ Sleep) do
6        foreach e ∈ dom(E) such that(e ≾_{E.p} next_[E](p)) do
7          let E′ = pre(E, e);
8          let v = notdep(e, E).p ;
9          if I_[E′](v) ∩ backtrack(E′) = ∅ then
10           add some q′ ∈ I_[E′](v) to backtrack(E′);
11       let Sleep′ := {q ∈ Sleep | E⊨p◇q} ;
12       Explore(E.p, Sleep′);
13       add p to Sleep ;
```

## 5. Source-DPOR

In this section, we present the *source-DPOR* algorithm. It is shown in Algorithm 1. As mentioned in the introduction, it is the first step towards our optimal algorithm, and is derived from the classical DPOR algorithm [4] by replacing persistent sets with source sets. *Source-DPOR* performs a depth-first search, using the recursive procedure $Explore(E, Sleep)$, where $E$ is the stack, i.e. the past execution sequence explored so far, and *Sleep* is a sleep set, i.e. a set of processes that need not be explored from $s_{[E]}$. The algorithm maintains, for each prefix $E'$ of $E$, a set $backtrack(E')$ of processes that will eventually be explored from $E'$.

$Explore(E, Sleep)$ initializes $backtrack(E)$ to consist of an arbitrary enabled process which is not in *Sleep*. Thereafter, for each process $p$ in $backtrack(E)$ which is not in *Sleep*, the algorithm performs two phases: race detection (lines 6–10) and state exploration (lines 11–13).

In the race detection phase, the algorithm first finds the events $e$ in $E$ that are in a race with the next step of $p$, and where the race can be reversed (line 6). For each such event $e \in dom(E)$, the algorithm must explore an execution sequence in which the race is reversed. Using the notation of the algorithm, such an execution sequence is equivalent to a sequence of form $E'.v.proc(e).z$, where $v$ is obtained by appending $p$ after the sequence $notdep(e, E)$ of events that occur after $e$ in $E.p$, but do not "happen after" $e$, and $z$ is any continuation of the execution. Note that we insert all of $notdep(e, E)$ before $next_{[E]}(p)$, since $notdep(e, E)$ includes all events that follow $e$ in $E$ that "happen before" $next_{[E]}(p)$, which must be performed before $next_{[E]}(p)$ when the race is reversed. The events in $E$ that "happen after" $e$, should still occur after $e$, in the sequence $z$. A sequence equivalent to $E'.v.proc(e).z$ can be performed by taking a step of a process in $I_{[E']}(v)$ immediately after $E'$. The algorithm therefore (at line 9) checks whether some process in $I_{[E']}(v)$ is already in $backtrack(E')$. If not, then a process in $I_{[E']}(v)$ is added to $backtrack(E')$. This ensures that a sequence equivalent to $E'.v.proc(e).z$ has been or will be explored by the algorithm.

In the exploration phase, exploration is started recursively from $E.p$, using an appropriately initialized sleep set. Sleep sets are manipulated as follows: (i) after finishing exploration of $E.p$, the process $p$ is added to sleep set at $E$, and (ii) when the exploration of $E.p$ is started recursively from $E$, the sleep set $Sleep'$ of $E.p$ is initialized to be the set of processes currently in the sleep set of $E$ that are independent with $p$ after $E$ (i.e., $Sleep' = \{q \in Sleep \mid E \models q \diamondsuit p\}$). The effect is that the algorithm need never explore $E.p$ for any process $p \in Sleep$, since that would always lead to a sequence which is equivalent to one that has been explored from a prefix of $E$. For processes $p$ that were added according to Case (i) above, this is obvious. To see why a process $q$ in the initial sleep set $Sleep'$ of $E.p$ need not be explored, note that any execution sequence of form $E.p.q.v$ is equivalent to the execution sequence $E.q.p.v$ (by $E \models q \diamondsuit p$). Since the algorithm guarantees to have explored some sequence in $[E.q.p.v]_{\simeq}$ whenever $q$ is in the sleep set of $E$, it need not explore $E.p.q$.

***Correctness*** Algorithm 1 is correct in the sense that for all maximal execution sequences $E$, the algorithm explores some execution sequence in $[E]_{\simeq}$. For lack of space, the proof is omitted. The main part of the proof establishes that when $Explore(E, Sleep)$ returns, the set $Sleep$ will be a source set for $W$ after $E$, where $W$ is the set of suffixes $w$ such that $E.w$ is an execution sequence.

***On Source Sets and Persistent Sets*** The mechanism by which source-DPOR produces source sets rather than persistent sets is the test at line 9. In persistent set-based DPOR algorithms [4, 14, 22, 23, 25], this test must be stronger, and at least guarantee that $backtrack(E')$ contains a process $q$ such that $q$ performs some event in $v$ which "happens-before" $next_{[E]}(p)$ in $E.p$. Such a test guarantees that the first event in $v$ which is dependent with some process in $backtrack(E')$ is performed by some process in $backtrack(E')$, thus making $backtrack(E')$ a persistent set. In contrast, our test at line 9 does not require the added process to perform an event which "happens-before" $next_{[E]}(p)$ in $E'.v$. Consider, for instance, that $v$ is just the sequence $q.p$, where $q$ is independent with $p$ after $E'$. Then, since the event of $q$ does not "happen-before" the event of $p$, there is an execution sequence $E'.p.q$ in which $p$ is dependent with the process $proc(e)$ in $backtrack(E')$ but need not be in $backtrack(E')$. On the other hand, since $q \in I_{[E']}(p.q)$, the set $backtrack(E')$ (together with the initial sleep set at $E'$) is still a source set for the possible continuations after $E'$.

## 6. Wakeup Trees

As we described earlier, *source-DPOR* may still lead to sleep-set blocked explorations. We therefore present an algorithm, called *optimal-DPOR*, which is provably optimal in that it always explores exactly one interleaving per Mazurkiewicz trace, and never encounters sleep-set blocking. Optimal-DPOR is obtained by combining source sets with a novel mechanism, called *wakeup trees*, which control the initial steps of future explorations.

Wakeup trees can be motivated by looking at lines 7–11 of Algorithm 1. At these lines, it is found that some execution sequence starting with $E'.v$ should be performed in order to reverse the detected race. However, at lines 10–11, only a single process from the sequence $v$ is entered into $backtrack(E')$, thus "forgetting" information about how to reverse the race. Since the new exploration after $E'.q$ does not "remember" this sequence $v$, it may explore a completely different sequence, which could potentially lead to sleep set blocking. To prevent such a situation, we replace the backtrack set by a so-called *wakeup tree*. The wakeup tree contains initial fragments of the sequences that are to be explored after $E'$. Each fragment guarantees that no sleep set blocking will be encountered during the exploration.

To define wakeup trees, we first generalize the relations $p \in I_{[E]}(w)$ and $p \in WI_{[E]}(w)$ to the case when $p$ is a sequence. Let $E$ be an execution sequence and let $v$ and $w$ be sequences of processes.

- Let $v \sqsubseteq_{[E]} w$ denote that there is a sequence $v'$ such that $E.v.v'$ and $E.w$ are execution sequences with $E.v.v' \simeq E.w$. Intuitively, $v \sqsubseteq_{[E]} w$ if, after $E$, the sequence $v$ is a possible way to start an execution that is equivalent to $w$.
- Let $v \sim_{[E]} w$ denote that there are sequences $v'$ and $w'$ such that $E.v.v'$ and $E.w.w'$ are execution sequences with $E.v.v' \simeq E.w.w'$. Intuitively, $v \sim_{[E]} w$ if, after $E$, the sequence $v$ is a possible way to start an execution that is equivalent to an execution sequence of form $E.w.w'$.

As special cases, for a process $p$ we have $p \in I_{[E]}(w)$ iff $p \sqsubseteq_{[E]} w$, and $p \in WI_{[E]}(w)$ iff $p \sim_{[E]} w$.

As examples, in Figure 2, we have $q.r \sqsubseteq_{[E']} q.q.r.r$ but $q.q \not\sqsubseteq_{[E']} r.r$. We also have $q.q \sim_{[E']} r.r$ since $E'.q.q.r.r \simeq E'.r.r.q.q$. Note that $\sim_{[E]}$ is not transitive. The relation $v \sim_{[E]} w$ can be checked using the following recursive definition.

LEMMA 6.1. The relation $v \sim_{[E]} w$ holds if either $v = \langle\rangle$, or $v$ is of form $p.v'$, and either

- $p \in I_{[E]}(w)$ and $v' \sim_{[E.p]} (w \setminus p)$, or
- $E \models p \diamondsuit w$ and $v' \sim_{[E.p]} w$. □

The following lemma states some useful properties.

LEMMA 6.2. Let $E$ be an execution sequence, and let $v$, $w$, and $w'$ be sequences. Then

1. $E.w' \simeq E.w$ implies that (i) $v \sqsubseteq_{[E]} w$ iff $v \sqsubseteq_{[E]} w'$, and (ii) $w \sqsubseteq_{[E]} v$ iff $w' \sqsubseteq_{[E]} v$, and (iii) $v \sim_{[E]} w$ iff $v \sim_{[E]} w'$;
2. $v \sqsubseteq_{[E]} w$ and $w \sim_{[E]} w'$ imply $v \sim_{[E]} w'$;
3. $p \in WI_{[E]}(w)$ and $w' \sqsubseteq_{[E]} w$ imply $p \in WI_{[E]}(w')$;
4. $p \in WI_{[E]}(w)$ and $E \models p \diamondsuit q$ and $E \models q \diamondsuit w$ imply $p \in WI_{[E]}(q.w)$. □

The above properties follow from the definitions.

Let us define an *ordered tree* as a pair $\langle B, \prec\rangle$, where $B$ (the set of *nodes*) is a finite prefix-closed set of sequences of processes, with the empty sequence $\langle\rangle$ being the root. The children of a node $w$, of form $w.p$ for some set of processes $p$, are ordered by the ordering $\prec$. In $\langle B, \prec\rangle$, such an ordering between children has been extended to the total order $\prec$ on $B$ by letting $\prec$ be the induced post-order relation between the nodes in $B$. This means that if the children $w.p_1$ and $w.p_2$ are ordered as $w.p_1 \prec w.p_2$, then $w.p_1 \prec w.p_2 \prec w$ in the induced post-order.

DEFINITION 6.3 (Wakeup Tree). Let $E$ be an execution sequence, and $P$ be a set of processes. A *wakeup tree after* $\langle E, P\rangle$ is an ordered tree $\langle B, \prec\rangle$, such that the following properties hold

1. $WI_{[E]}(w) \cap P = \emptyset$ whenever $w$ is a leaf of $B$;
2. whenever $u.p$ and $u.w$ are nodes in $B$ with $u.p \prec u.w$, and $u.w$ is a leaf, then $p \notin WI_{[E.u]}(w)$. □

Intuitively, a wakeup tree after $\langle E, P \rangle$ is intended to consist of initial fragments of sequences that should be explored after $E$ to avoid sleep set blocking, when $P$ is the current sleep set at $E$. To see this, note that if $q \in P$, then (by the way sleep sets are handled) $q \notin I_{[E]}(w)$ for any sequence $w$ that is explored after $E$. If, in addition, $E \models q \Diamond w$, then $q$ is still in the sleep set at $E.w$. To prevent this, we therefore require $q \notin WI_{[E]}(w)$, which is the same as Property 1, i.e., $WI_{[E]}(w) \cap P = \emptyset$. Property 2 implies that if a process $p$ is added to the sleep set at $E.u$, after exploring $E.u.p$, then by the same reasoning as above, it will have been removed from the sleep set when we reach $E.u.w$.

The *empty* wakeup tree is the tree $\langle \{\langle\rangle\}, \emptyset \rangle$, which consists only of the root $\langle\rangle$. We state a useful property of wakeup trees.

LEMMA 6.4. If $\langle B, \prec \rangle$ is a wakeup tree after $\langle E, P \rangle$ and $w, w' \in B$ and $w$ is a leaf which satisfies $w' \sim_{[E]} w$, then $w \preceq w'$. □

The lemma states that any leaf $w'$ is the smallest (w.r.t. $\prec$) node in the tree which is consistent with $w'$ after $E$.

*Proof:* We prove the lemma by contradiction. Assume $w' \prec w$. Then there are $u, p, v, v'$ such that $w' = u.p.v'$ and $w = u.v$ such that $u.p \prec u.v$. Since $u.v$ is a leaf, we have $p \notin WI_{[E.u]}(v)$ by Property 2 of Definition 6.3. Hence $p \not\sim_{[E.u]} v$, which implies $u.p \not\sim_{[E]} u.v$, which implies $u.p.v' \not\sim_{[E]} u.v$, i.e. $w' \not\sim_{[E]} w$. □

For a wakeup tree $\langle B, \prec \rangle$ and a process $p \in B$, define *subtree*$(\langle B, \prec \rangle, p)$ to denote the subtree of $\langle B, \prec \rangle$ rooted at $p$, i.e. *subtree*$(\langle B, \prec \rangle, p) = \langle B', \prec' \rangle$ where $B' = \{w \mid p.w \in B\}$ and $\prec'$ is the restriction of $\prec$ to $B'$.

Let $\langle B, \prec \rangle$ be a wakeup tree after $\langle E, P \rangle$. For any sequence $w$ such that $E.w$ is an execution sequence with $WI_{[E]}(w) \cap P = \emptyset$, we define the operation $insert_{[E]}(w, \langle B, \prec \rangle)$, with the properties:

1. $insert_{[E]}(w, \langle B, \prec \rangle)$ is also a wakeup tree after $\langle E, P \rangle$,
2. any leaf of $\langle B, \prec \rangle$ remains a leaf of $insert_{[E]}(w, \langle B, \prec \rangle)$, and
3. $insert_{[E]}(w, \langle B, \prec \rangle)$ contains a leaf $u$ with $u \sim_{[E]} w$.

A simple construction of $insert_{[E]}(w, \langle B, \prec \rangle)$ is the following: Let $v$ be the smallest (w.r.t. to $\prec$) sequence $v'$ in $B$ such that $v' \sim_{[E]} w$. If $v$ is a leaf, $insert_{[E]}(w, \langle B, \prec \rangle)$ can be taken as $\langle B, \prec \rangle$ and we are done. Otherwise, let $w'$ be a shortest sequence such that $w \sqsubseteq_{[E]} v.w'$, and add $v.w'$ as a new leaf, which is ordered after all already existing nodes in $B$ of form $v.w''$.

As an illustration, using Example 1, assume that a wakeup tree $\langle B, \prec \rangle$ after $\langle \langle\rangle, \emptyset \rangle$ contains $p$ as the only leaf. Then the operation $insert_{[\langle\rangle]}(q.q, \langle B, \prec \rangle)$ adds $q.q$ as a new leaf with $p \prec q.q$. If we thereafter perform $insert_{[\langle\rangle]}(r.r, \langle B, \prec \rangle)$, then the wakeup tree remains the same, since $q.q \sim_{[\langle\rangle]} r.r$, and $q.q$ is already a leaf.

## 7. Optimal-DPOR

In this section, we present the optimal algorithm, shown in Algorithm 2. The algorithm performs a depth-first search, using the recursive procedure $Explore(E, Sleep, WuT)$, where $E$ and *Sleep* are as in Algorithm 1, and *WuT* is a wakeup tree after $\langle E, Sleep \rangle$, containing extensions of $E$ that are guaranteed to be explored (in order) by $Explore(E, Sleep, WuT)$. If *WuT* is empty, then $Explore(E, Sleep, WuT)$ is free to explore any extension of $E$.

Like Algorithm 1, the algorithm runs in two modes: race detection (lines 3–8) and state exploration (lines 9–22), but it is slightly differently organized. Instead of analyzing races at every invocation of $Explore$, races are analyzed in the entire execution sequence only when a maximal execution sequence has been generated. The reason for this is that the test at line 7 is precise only when the used sequence $v$, which is defined at line 6, includes all events in the entire execution that do not "happen after" $e$, also those that occur after $e'$. Therefore $v$ can be defined only when $E$ is a maximal execution sequence.

**Algorithm 2:** Optimal-DPOR algorithm.

1 **Initially** $Explore(\langle\rangle, \emptyset, \langle \{\langle\rangle\}, \emptyset \rangle)$;
2 $Explore(E, Sleep, WuT)$ ;
3   **if** $enabled(s_{[E]}) = \emptyset$ **then**
4     **foreach** $e, e' \in dom(E)$ **such that** $(e \precsim_E e')$ **do**
5       **let** $E' = pre(E, e)$;
6       **let** $v = (notdep(e, E).proc(e'))$ ;
7       **if** $sleep(E') \cap WI_{[E']}(v) = \emptyset$ **then**
8         $insert_{[E']}(v, wut(E'))$
9   **else**
10     **if** $WuT \neq \langle \{\langle\rangle\}, \emptyset \rangle$ **then**
11       $wut(E) := WuT$ ;
12     **else**
13       **choose** $p \in enabled(s_{[E]})$;
14       $wut(E) := \langle \{p\}, \emptyset \rangle$ ;
15     $sleep(E) := Sleep$ ;
16     **while** $\exists p \in wut(E)$ **do**
17       **let** $p = \min_{\prec} \{p \in wut(E)\}$;
18       **let** $Sleep' = \{q \in sleep(E) \mid E \models p \Diamond q\}$ ;
19       **let** $WuT' = subtree(wut(E), p)$ ;
20       $Explore(E.p, Sleep', WuT')$;
21       add $p$ to $sleep(E)$ ;
22       remove all sequences of form $p.w$ from $wut(E)$ ;

In the race detection phase, Algorithm 2 must be able to access the current sleep set for each prefix $E'$ of the currently explored execution sequence $E$. For each such prefix $E'$, the algorithm therefore maintains a set of processes $sleep(E')$, which is the current sleep set at $E'$. In a similar way, for each prefix $E'$ of $E$, the algorithm maintains $wut(E')$, which is the current wakeup tree at $E'$.

Let us now explain the race detection mode, which is entered whenever the exploration reaches the end of a complete sequence (i.e. $enabled(s_{[E]}) = \emptyset$). In this mode, the algorithm investigates all races that can be reversed in the just explored sequence $E$. Such a race consists of two events $e$ and $e'$ in $E$, such that $e \precsim_E e'$. Let $E' = pre(E, e)$ and let $v = notdep(e, E).proc(e')$, i.e. the subsequence of $E$ consisting of the events that occur after $e$ but do not "happen after" $e$, followed by $proc(e')$ (this notation is introduced at lines 5–6). The reversible race $e \precsim_E e'$ indicates that there is another execution sequence, which performs $v$ after $E'$, and in which the race is reversed, i.e. the event $e'$ happens before the event $e$. Since $E'.v$ is incompatible with the currently explored computation, the algorithm must now make sure that it will be explored if it was not explored previously. If some $p \in sleep(E')$ is in $WI_{[E']}(v)$, then some execution equivalent to one starting with $E'.v$ will have been explored previously. If not, we perform the operation $insert_{[E']}(v, wut(E'))$ to make sure that some execution equivalent to one starting with $E'.v$ will be explored in the future.

In the exploration mode, which is entered if exploration has not reached the end of an execution sequence, first the wakeup tree $wut(E)$ is initialized to *WuT*. If *WuT* is empty, then (as we will state in Lemma 7.2) the sleep set is empty, and an arbitrary enabled process is entered into $wut(E)$. The sleep set $sleep(E)$ is initialized to the sleep set that is passed as argument in this call to $Explore$. Thereafter, each sequence in $wut(E)$ is subject to exploration. We find the first (i.e. minimal) single-process branch $p$ in $wut(E)$ and call $Explore$ recursively for the sequence $E.p$. In this call, the associated sleep set $Sleep'$ is obtained from $sleep(E)$ in the same way as in Algorithm 1. The associated wakeup tree *WuT'* is obtained as the corresponding subtree of $wut(E)$. Thereafter, $Explore$ is called recursively for the sequence $E.p$ with the modified sleep set *Sleep'* and wakeup tree *WuT'*. After $Explore(E.p, Sleep', WuT')$ has returned, the sleep set $sleep(E)$ is extended with $p$, and all sequences beginning with $p$ are removed from $wut(E)$.

### 7.1 Correctness

Let us now prove the correctness of the optimal-DPOR algorithm. Throughout, we assume a particular completed execution of optimal-DPOR. This execution consists of a number of terminated calls to $Explore(E, Sleep, WuT)$ for some values of the parameters $E$, *Sleep*, and *WuT*. Let $\mathcal{E}$ denote the set of execution sequences $E$ that have been explored in some call of form $Explore(E, \cdot, \cdot)$. Define the ordering $\propto$ on $\mathcal{E}$ by letting $E \propto E'$ if $Explore(E, \cdot, \cdot)$ returned before $Explore(E', \cdot, \cdot)$. Intuitively, if one were to draw an ordered tree that shows how the exploration has proceeded, then $\mathcal{E}$ would be the set of nodes in the tree, and $\propto$ would be the post-order between nodes in that tree.

We begin by establishing some useful invariants.

LEMMA 7.1. If $E.p \propto E.w$ then $p \notin I_{[E]}(w)$.

*Proof:* After the call to $Explore(E.p, \cdot, \cdot)$ has returned, we have that $p \in sleep(E)$. It follows from the rules for manipulating sleep sets, that if $E.w \in \mathcal{E}$ and $E.p \propto E.w$ then $p \notin I_{[E]}(w)$. □

LEMMA 7.2. Whenever Algorithm 2 is inside a call of form $Explore(E, Sleep, WuT)$, then

1. $wut(E)$ is a wakeup tree after $\langle E, sleep(E) \rangle$,
2. if *WuT* is empty, then *Sleep* is empty. □

The following lemma captures the relationship between wakeup trees and $\langle \mathcal{E}, \propto \rangle$.

LEMMA 7.3. Let $\langle \mathcal{E}, \propto \rangle$ be the tree of explored execution sequences. Consider some point in the execution, and the wakeup tree $wut(E)$ at that point, for some $E \in \mathcal{E}$.

1. If $w \in wut(E)$ for some $w$, then $E.w \in \mathcal{E}$.
2. If $w \prec w'$ for $w, w' \in wut(E)$ then $E.w \propto E.w'$

*Proof:* The properties follow by noting how the exploration from any $E \in \mathcal{E}$ is controlled by the wakeup tree $wut(E)$ at lines 16 – 22. □

We can now give the proof of correctness for the algorithm:

THEOREM 7.4. Whenever a call to $Explore(E, Sleep, WuT)$ returns during Algorithm 2, then for all maximal execution sequences of form $E.w$, the algorithm has explored some execution sequence $E'$ which is in $[E.w]_{\simeq}$.

Since initially the algorithm is called with $Explore(\langle\rangle, \emptyset, \langle\{\langle\rangle\}, \emptyset\rangle)$, Theorem 7.4 implies that for all maximal execution sequences of form $E$ the algorithm explores some execution sequence $E'$ which is in $[E]_{\simeq}$.

*Proof of Theorem 7.4:* By induction on the set of execution sequences $E$ that are explored during the considered execution, using the ordering $\propto$ (i.e. the order in which the corresponding calls to $Explore$ returned).

*Base Case:* This case is the first sequence $E$ for which the call $Explore(E, \cdot, \cdot)$ returns. By the algorithm, $E$ is already maximal, so the theorem trivially holds.

*Inductive Step:* Consider an arbitrary execution sequence $E \in \mathcal{E}$ that is explored by the algorithm. Let $Final\_sleep(E)$ denote the value of $sleep(E)$ when $Explore(E, Sleep, WuT)$ returns. Let $done(E)$ denote $Final\_sleep(E) \setminus Sleep$, i.e. the set of processes that are explored from $s_{[E]}$. As inductive hypothesis, we assume that the theorem holds for all execution sequences $E'$ with $E' \propto E$.

The inductive step is proven by contradiction. Assume that $E.w$ is a maximal execution sequence such that the algorithm has not explored any execution sequence $E'$ in $[E.w]_{\simeq}$. We first prove that this implies $WI_{[E]}(w) \cap Final\_sleep(E) = \emptyset$. The proof is by contradiction. Assume that there is a $p \in WI_{[E]}(w)$ with $p \in Final\_sleep(E)$, i.e. $p \in sleep(E)$ at some point during the exploration. Let $E'$ be the longest prefix of $E$ such that $E'.p \in \mathcal{E}$, and define $w'$ by $E'.w' = E$. By the handling of sleep sets, we have $E' \models p \diamond w'$. It follows by the definition of $WI_{[E]}(w)$ that there is a $w''$ such that $E.w \simeq E.p.w'' \simeq E'.w'.p.w'' \simeq E'.p.w'.w''$. By the inductive hypothesis applied to $E'.p$, the algorithm has explored some execution sequence in $[E'.p.w'.w'']_{\simeq} = [E.w]_{\simeq}$, which gives a contradiction.

For each process $p \in Final\_sleep(E)$, let $E'_p$ be the prefix of $E$ such that $E'_p.p$ is the last (w.r.t. $\propto$) execution sequence of form $E''_p.p$, with $E''_p$ being a prefix of $E$, that precedes $E$ (w.r.t. $\propto$). (Note that if $p \in done(E)$ then $E'_p = E$, but if $p \in Sleep$ then $E'_p$ is a strict prefix of $E$.) Let $w'_p$ be defined by $E = E'_p.w'_p$ (note that $E'_p \models p \diamond w'_p$). Let $w_p$ be the longest prefix of $w$ such that $E \models p \diamond w_p$, and let $e_p$ be the first event in $dom_{[E]}(w)$ which is not in $w_p$. (Such an event $e_p$ must exist, since otherwise $w_p = w$ which implies $E \models p \diamond w$, which implies $p \in WI_{[E]}(w)$, which contradicts $WI_{[E]}(w) \cap Final\_sleep(E) = \emptyset$.) Let $q \in Final\_sleep(E)$ be such that $w_q$ is a longest prefix among the prefixes $w_p$ for $p \in Final\_sleep(E)$. If there are several processes $p \in Final\_sleep(E)$ such that $w_p$ is the same longest prefix, then let $q$ be the process among these such that $E'_q.q$ is minimal (w.r.t. $\propto$). Let $w_R$ be $w_q.proc(e_q)$.

Consider the exploration of $E'_q.q$, which happens in the call $Explore(E'_q.q, Sleep', \cdot)$ with *Sleep'* as the sleep set argument. Since $E'_q.q$ is an execution sequence, and $E'_q \models q \diamond (w'_q.w_q)$, it follows that $E'_q.w'_q.w_q.q$ is an execution sequence. Since $E'_q.w'_q.w_q.e_q$ is an execution sequence, and $q$ does not disable $e_q$ (since $q$ and $proc(e_q)$ are different), we conclude that $E'_q.w'_q.w_q.q.e_q$ and hence $E'_q.q.w'_q.w_q.e_q = E'_q.q.w'_q.w_R$ is an execution sequence.

We next establish that $WI_{[E'_q.q]}(w'_q.w_R) \cap Sleep' = \emptyset$, using a proof by contradiction, as follows. Assume that some process $p$ is in $WI_{[E'_q.q]}(w'_q.w_R) \cap Sleep'$. By the construction of *Sleep'* at line 18, the process $p$ must be in $sleep(E'_q)$ just before the call to $Explore(E'_q.q, Sleep', \cdot)$, and satisfy $E'_q \models p \diamond q$. From $p \in WI_{[E'_q.q]}(w'_q.w_R)$ and Property 3 of Lemma 6.2, we infer $p \in WI_{[E'_q.q]}(w'_q.w_q)$. From this, $E'_q \models p \diamond q$ and Property 4 of Lemma 6.2, it follows that $p \in WI_{[E'_q]}(q.w'_q.w_q)$, which, using $E'_q.q.w'_q.w_q \simeq E'_q.w'_q.w_q.q$ (which follows from $E'_q \models q \diamond (w'_q.w_q)$), implies $p \in WI_{[E'_q]}(w'_q.w_q.q)$, which by Property 3 of Lemma 6.2 imply $p \in WI_{[E'_q]}(w'_q.w_q)$. From this, and the property that $p \in sleep(E'_q)$ just before the call to $Explore(E'_q.q, Sleep', \cdot)$, we have by the handling of sleep sets that $p \notin I_{[E'_q]}(w'_q.w_q)$, which together with $p \in WI_{[E'_q]}(w'_q.w_q)$ implies $E'_q \models p \diamond w'_q.w_q$. This, and the fact that $p \in sleep(E'_q)$ just before the call to $Explore(E'_q.q, Sleep', \cdot)$, implies that $p \in Final\_sleep(E'_q.w'_q)$, i.e. $p \in Final\_sleep(E)$. Since $E'_q \models p \diamond w'_q.w_q$, we have by construction that $e_p = e_q$. But since among the processes $p$ with $e_p = e_q$ we chose $q$ to be the first one for which a call of form $Explore(E'_q.p, \cdot, \cdot)$ was performed, we have that $p \notin sleep(E'_q)$ just before the call to $Explore(E'_q.q, Sleep', \cdot)$, whence $p \notin Sleep'$. Thus we have a contradiction.

Let $z'$ be any sequence that makes $E'_q.q.w'_q.w_R.z'$ maximal (such a $z'$ can always be found, since $E'_q.q.w'_q.w_R$ is an execution sequence). From $WI_{[E'_q.q]}(w'_q.w_R) \cap Sleep' = \emptyset$ (proven in the preceding paragraph) follows $WI_{[E'_q.q]}(w'_q.w_R.z') \cap Sleep' = \emptyset$. Hence, no execution sequence in $[E'_q.q.w'_q.w_R.z']_\simeq$ was explored before the call to $Explore(E'_q.q, Sleep', \cdot)$ (otherwise, there would be a call $Explore(E''.p, \cdot, \cdot)$ with $E''$ a prefix of $E'_q$ and $p \in Sleep'$, and defining $w''$ by $E''.w'' = E'_q$, we would have $E'' \models p \Diamond w''$ and $p \in WI_{[E'_q.q]}(w'_q.w_R.z')$, thus contradicting $WI_{[E'_q.q]}(w'_q.w_R.z') \cap Sleep' = \emptyset$). By the inductive hypothesis for $E'_q.q$ applied to $w'_q.w_R.z'$, the algorithm then explores some sequence of form $E'_q.q.z$ in $[E'_q.q.w'_q.w_R.z']_\simeq$.

By the construction of $w_R$, we have $next_{[E'_q]}(q) \precsim_{E'_q.q.w'_q.w_R.z'} e_q$. From $E'_q.q.z \simeq E'_q.q.w'_q.w_R.z'$, it follows that the same race between $next_{[E]}(q)$ and $e_q$ will also occur in $E'_q.q.z$, i.e. we have $next_{[E'_q]}(q) \precsim_{E'_q.q.z} e_q$. Since the sequence $E'_q.q.z$ is actually explored by the algorithm, it will encounter the race $next_{[E'_q]}(q) \precsim_{E'_q.q.z} e_q$. When handling it,

- $E$ in the algorithm will correspond to $E'_q.q.z$ in this proof,
- $e$ in the algorithm will correspond to $next_{[E'_q]}(q)$ in this proof, and
- $e'$ in the algorithm will correspond to $e_q$ in this proof.

Let $v = (notdep(next_{[E'_q]}(q), E'_q.q.z).proc(e_q))$ be the sequence $v$ at line 6 in the algorithm. Let $x$ be $notdep(next_{[E'_q]}(q), E'_q.q.z)$ and let $x'$ be $notdep(next_{[E'_q]}(q), E'_q.q.w'_q.w_R.z')$. We note that $w'_q.w_q$ is a prefix of $x'$. From $E'_q.q.z \simeq E'_q.q.w'_q.w_R.z'$ and the definitions of $x$ and $x'$, it follows that $E'_q.x \simeq E'_q.x'$, and hence that $E'_q.x.proc(e_q) \simeq E'_q.x'.proc(e_q)$. Let $x''$ be obtained from $x'$ by adding $proc(e_q)$ just after the prefix $w'_q.w_q$ (i.e., in the same place that it has in $w'_q.w_R.z'$). Since $e_q$ "happens after" $next_{[E'_q]}(q)$ in $E'_q.q.w'_q.w_R.z'$, it follows that no events in $x'$ "happen after" $e_q$ in $E'_q.q.w'_q.w_R.z'$. Hence $E'_q.x'' \simeq E'_q.x'.proc(e_q)$. Since $w'_q.w_R$ is a prefix of $x''$ we have $w'_q.w_R \sqsubseteq_{[E'_q]} x''$, which by $E'_q.x'' \simeq E'_q.x'.proc(e_q)$ implies $w'_q.w_R \sqsubseteq_{[E'_q]} x'.proc(e_q)$, which by $E'_q.x.proc(e_q) \simeq E'_q.x'.proc(e_q)$ implies $w'_q.w_R \sqsubseteq_{[E'_q]} v$. By properties of sleep sets and the construction of $w_R$, it follows that $sleep(E'_q) \cap WI_{[E'_q]}(w'_q.w_R) = \emptyset$. This implies, by $w'_q.w_R \sqsubseteq_{[E'_q]} v$, that $sleep(E'_q) \cap WI_{[E'_q]}(v) = \emptyset$. Thus, the test at line 7 will succeed, and after performing line 8, the wakeup tree $wut(E'_q)$ will (by the specification of *insert*) contain a leaf $y$ such that $y \sim_{[E'_q]} v$. Since at this point $q \in wut(E'_q)$ and $q \notin WI_{[E'_q]}(v)$ we have, by definition of *insert*, that and $E'_q \not\models q \Diamond y$. By Property 1 of Lemma 7.3 we then have $E'_q.y \in \mathcal{E}$.

From $w'_q.w_R \sqsubseteq_{[E'_q]} v$ and $y \sim_{[E'_q]} v$, it follows by Property 2 of Lemma 6.2 that $y \sim_{[E'_q]} w'_q.w_R$. Furthermore, from $E'_q \models q \Diamond w'_q$ (which follows from $E'_q \models q \Diamond w'_q.w_q$) and $E'_q \not\models q \Diamond y$, it follows that $y$ is not a prefix of $w'_q$. Let $u$ be the longest common prefix of $y$ and $w'_q.w_R$. We claim that $w'_q$ is a strict prefix of $u$. Otherwise, there are different processes $p, p'$ and a sequence $v''$ such that $u.p'.v'' = w'_q$ and $u.p$ is a prefix of $y$. From $y \sim_{[E'_q]} w'_q.w_R$ and Property 2 of Lemma 6.2, we infer $y \sim_{[E'_q]} u.p'$. If $u.p' \in wut(E'_q)$ when $y$ is inserted, we infer by Lemma 6.4 and Property 2 of Lemma 7.3 that $E'_q.y \propto E'_q.u.p'$. If $u.p' \notin wut(E'_q)$ when $y$ is inserted, we also infer $E'_q.y \propto E'_q.u.p'$, since then $y$ will be explored before $u.p'$. Thus $E'_q.y \propto E'_q.u.p'$, which implies $E'_q.u.p \propto E'_q.u.p'.v''$, which by handling of sleep sets implies $p \notin I_{[E'_q.u]}(p'.v'')$. By $y \sim_{[E'_q]} w'_q$, implying $u.p \sim_{[E'_q]} u.p'.v''$, we have $p \sim_{[E'_q.u]} p'.v''$, which is the same as $p \in WI_{[E'_q.u]}(p'.v'')$. By $p \notin I_{[E'_q.u]}(p'.v'')$ this implies $E'_q.u \models p \Diamond (p'.v'')$. This implies that $p \in sleep(E'_q.w'_q)$, i.e., $p \in sleep(E)$. Hence by the construction of $w_R$, we have $p \notin WI_{[E'_q.u.p'.v'']}(w_R)$, which together with $E'_q.u \models p \Diamond (p'.v'')$ implies $p \notin WI_{[E'_q.u]}(p'.v''.w_R)$, which implies $u.p \not\sim_{[E'_q]} u.p'.v''.w_R$, which implies $y \not\sim_{[E'_q]} w'_q.w_R$, which contradicts the construction of $y$.

Thus, $w'_q$ is a strict prefix of $u$. Since $E'_q.y$, and hence $E'_q.u$, is explored by the algorithm, we have $E_q.u \propto E_q.w'_q$. Moreover, since $u$ is a prefix of $w'_q.w_R$, we infer that $E'_q.u$ is a prefix of $E'_q.w'_q.w$. This means that there is a sequence $w''$ such that $E'_q.u.w'' \simeq E.w$. It follows by the inductive hypothesis applied to $E'_q.u$ that the algorithm has explored some maximal sequence in $[E'_q.u.w'']_\simeq$ and hence in $[E.w]_\simeq$. This contradicts the assumption at the beginning of the inductive step. This concludes the proof of the inductive step, and the theorem is proven. □

### 7.2 Optimality

In this section, we prove that optimal-DPOR is optimal in the sense that it never explores two different but equivalent execution sequences and never encounters sleep set blocking. The following theorem, which is essentially the same as Theorem 3.2 of Godefroid *et al.* [10] establishes that sleep sets alone are sufficient to prevent exploration of two equivalent *maximal* execution sequences:

THEOREM 7.5. *Optimal-DPOR never explores two maximal execution sequences which are equivalent.*

*Proof:* Assume that $E_1$ and $E_2$ are two equivalent maximal execution sequences, which are explored by the algorithm. Then they are both in $\mathcal{E}$. Assume w.l.o.g. that $E_1 \propto E_2$. Let $E$ be their longest common prefix, and let $E_1 = E.p.v_1$ and $E_2 = E.v_2$. By Lemma 7.1 we have $p \notin I_{[E]}(v_2)$, which contradicts $E_1 \simeq E_2$ and the maximality of $E_1$ and $E_2$. □

We will now prove that Algorithm 2 is optimal in the sense that it never encounters sleep-set blocking. Let us first define this precisely.

DEFINITION 7.6 (Sleep Set Blocking). During the execution of Algorithm 2, a call to $Explore(E, Sleep, WuT)$ is *sleep set blocked* if $enabled(s_{[E]}) \neq \emptyset$ and $enabled(s_{[E]}) \subseteq Sleep$. □

Now let us state and prove the corresponding optimality theorem.

THEOREM 7.7. *During any execution of Algorithm 2, no call to* $Explore(E, Sleep, WuT)$ *is ever sleep set blocked.*

*Proof:* Consider a call $Explore(E, Sleep, WuT)$ during the exploration. Then any sequence in $WuT$ is enabled after $E$. By Lemma 7.2, $WuT$ is a wakeup tree after $\langle E, Sleep\rangle$. Thus, if $Sleep \neq \emptyset$, then $WuT$ contains a sequence $w$ such that $Sleep \cap WI_{[E]}(w) = \emptyset$. Letting $p$ be the first process in $w$, this implies $p \notin Sleep$, implying that $p$ is enabled and thus $enabled(s_{[E]}) \not\subseteq Sleep$. □

## 8. Implementation

In this section we describe our implementation in the context of Concuerror [2], a stateless model checking tool for Erlang.

***Erlang*** Erlang is an industrially relevant programming language based on the actor model of concurrency [1]. In Erlang, actors are realized by language-level processes implemented by the runtime system instead of being directly mapped to OS threads. Each Erlang process has its own private memory area (stack, heap and mailbox) and communicates with other processes via message passing. A call to the `spawn` function creates a new process $P$ and returns a *process identifier* (PID) that can be used to send messages to $P$. Messages are sent *asynchronously* using the `!` (or `send`) function. Messages get placed in the mailbox of the receiving process in the order they arrive. A process can then consume messages using *selective* pattern matching in `receive` expressions, which are *blocking* operations

```
1 -module(readers).
2 -export([readers/1]).
3
4 readers(N) ->
5   ets:new(tab, [public, named_table]),
6   Writer = fun() -> ets:insert(tab, {x, 42}) end,
7   Reader = fun(I) -> ets:lookup(tab, I), ets:lookup(tab, x) end,
8   spawn(Writer),
9   [spawn(fun() -> Reader(I) end) || I <- lists:seq(1, N)],
10  receive after infinity -> deadlock end.
```

**Figure 3.** Writer-readers program in Erlang.

when a process mailbox does not contain any matching message. Optionally, a `receive` may contain an `after` clause which specifies a *timeout* value (either an integer or the special value `infinity`) and a value to be returned if the timeout time (in ms) is exhausted.

Erlang processes do not share any memory by default. Still, the Erlang implementation comes with a key-value store mechanism, called *Erlang Term Storage (ETS)*, that allows processes to create memory areas where terms shared between processes can be inserted, looked up, and updated. Such areas are the ETS tables that are explicitly declared `public`. The runtime system automatically serializes accesses to these tables when this is necessary. Each ETS table is owned by the process that created it and its memory is reclaimed by the runtime system when this process exits.

Erlang has all the ingredients needed for concurrency via message passing and most of the ingredients (e.g. reads and writes to shared data, etc.) needed for concurrent programming using shared memory. Unsurprisingly, Erlang programs are prone to "the usual" errors associated with concurrent execution, although the majority of them revolves around message passing and misuse of built-in primitives implemented in C.

Figure 3 shows Example 1 written in Erlang, generalized to `N` instead of just two readers. A public ETS table shared between `N+1` processes: `N` readers and one writer. The writer inserts a key-value pair, using `x` as a key. Each of the `N` readers tries to read two entries from this table: some entry with a different key in each process (an integer in the range 1..`N`) and the entry keyed by `x`. The `receive` expression on line 10 forces the process executing the `readers` code to get stuck at this point, ensuring that the process owning the table stays alive, which in turn preserves the ETS table.

***Concuerror*** Concuerror [2] is a systematic testing tool for finding concurrency errors in Erlang programs or verifying their absence. Given a program and a test to run, Concuerror uses a stateless search algorithm to systematically explore the execution of the test under conceptually all process interleaving. To achieve this, the tool employs a source-to-source transformation that inserts instrumentation at *preemption points* (i.e. points where a context switch is allowed to occur) in the code under execution. This instrumentation allows Concuerror to take control of the scheduler when the program is run, without having to modify the Erlang VM in any way. In the current VM, a context switch may occur at any function call. Concuerror inserts preemption points only at process actions that interact with (i.e. inspect or update) shared state. Concuerror supports the complete Erlang language and can instrument programs of any size, including any libraries they use. The tool employs two techniques to reduce the number of explored traces: (i) an optimization which avoids exploring traces that involve processes blocking on `receive` expressions [2] and (ii) *context-bounding* [19], a technique that restricts the number of explored traces with respect to a user-supplied parameter, which Concuerror calls *preemption bound*. In this respect, Concuerror is similar to the CHESS tool [20].

***Our implementation*** We extended Concuerror with three DPOR algorithms: (i) the algorithm presented by Flanagan and Godefroid with the sleep set extension [5], (ii) *source-DPOR* and (iii) *optimal-DPOR*. To implement these we had to encode rules for dependencies between operations that constitute preemption points. These rules are shared between all DPOR variants. For lookups and inserts to ETS tables (i.e. reads and writes) the rules are standard (two operations conflict if they act on the same key and at least one is an insert). For sending and receiving operations the "happens before" relation ($\rightarrow_E$) is the following:

- Two `send`s are ordered by $\rightarrow_E$ if they send to the same process, even if the messages are the same. (Note that if we would not order two `send`s that send the same message, then when we reorder them, the corresponding `receive` will not "happen after" the same `send` statement.)
- A `send` "happens before" the `receive` statement that receives the message it sent. A race exists between these statements only if the `receive` has an `after` clause.
- A `receive` which executes its `after` clause "happens before" a subsequent `send` which sends a message that it can consume.

There are also other race-prone primitives in Erlang, but it is beyond the scope of this paper to describe how they interact.

Concuerror uses a *vector clock* [16] for each process at each state, to calculate the happens before relation for any two events. The calculation of the vector clocks uses the ideas presented in the original DPOR paper [4]. The only special case is for the association of a `send` with a `receive`, where we instrument the message itself with the vector clock of the sending process.

## 9. Experiments

We report experimental results that compare the performance of the three DPOR algorithms, which we will refer to as 'classic' (for the algorithm of [5]), 'source' and 'optimal'. We run all benchmarks on a desktop with an i7-3770 CPU (3.40 GHz), 16GB of RAM running Debian Linux 3.2.0-4-amd64. The machine has four physical cores, but presently Concuerror uses only one of them. In all benchmarks, Concuerror was started with the option `-p inf`, which instructs the tool to use an infinite preemption bound, i.e., verify these programs.

***Performance on two "standard" benchmarks*** First, we report performance on the two benchmarks from the DPOR paper [4]: filesystem and indexer. These are benchmarks that have been used to evaluate another DPOR variant (DPOR-CR [22]) and a technique based on unfoldings [11]. As both programs use locks, we had to emulate a locking mechanism using Erlang. To make this translation we used particular language features:

filesystem: This benchmark uses two lock-handling primitives, called `acquire` and `release`. The assumptions made for these primitives are that an `acquire` and a `release` operation on the same lock are never co-enabled and should therefore not tried to be interleaved in a different way than they occur. Thus, `acquire`s are the only operations that can be swapped, if possible, to get a different interleaving.
We implemented the lock objects in Erlang as separate processes. To acquire the lock, a process sends a message with its identifier to the "lock process" and waits for a reply. Upon receiving the message, the lock process uses the identifier to reply and then waits for a `release` message. Other `acquire` messages are left in the lock's mailbox. Upon receiving the `release` message the lock process loops back to the start, retrieving the next `acquire` message and notifying the next process. This behavior can be implemented in Erlang using two selective `receive`s.

| Benchmark | Traces Explored | | | Time | | |
|---|---|---|---|---|---|---|
| | classic | source | optimal | classic | source | optimal |
| filesystem(14) | 4 | 2 | 2 | 0.54s | 0.36s | 0.35s |
| filesystem(16) | 64 | 8 | 8 | 8.13s | 1.82s | 1.78s |
| filesystem(18) | 1024 | 32 | 32 | 2m11s | 8.52s | 8.86s |
| filesystem(19) | 4096 | 64 | 64 | 8m33s | 18.62s | 19.57s |
| indexer(12) | 78 | 8 | 8 | 0.74s | 0.11s | 0.10s |
| indexer(15) | 341832 | 4096 | 4096 | 56m20s | 50.24s | 52.35s |

**Table 1.** Performance of DPOR algorithms on two benchmarks.

indexer: This benchmark uses a CAS primitive instruction to check whether a specific entry in a matrix is 0 and set it to a new value. The "Erlang way" to do this, is to try to execute an `insert_new` operation on an ETS table: if another entry with the same key exists the operation returns `false`; otherwise the operation returns `true` and the table now contains the new entry.

Both benchmarks are parametric on the number of threads they use. For filesystem we used 14, 16, 18 and 19 threads. For indexer we used 12 and 15 threads.

Table 1 shows the number of traces that the algorithms explore as well as the time it takes to explore them. It is clear that our algorithms, which in these benchmarks explore the same (optimal) number of interleavings, beat 'classic' DPOR with sleep sets, by a margin that becomes wider as the number of threads increases. As a sanity check, Kählönen *et al.* [11] report that their unfolding-based method is also able to explore only 8 paths for indexer(12), while their prototype implementation of DPOR extended with sleep sets and support for commutativity of reads and writes explores between 51 and 138 paths (with 85 as median value). The numbers we report (78 for 'classic' DPOR and 8 for our algorithms) are very similar.

***Performance on two synthetic benchmarks*** Next we compare the algorithms on two synthetic benchmarks that expose differences between them. The first is the readers program of Figure 3. The results, for 2, 8 and 13 readers are shown in Table 2. For 'classic' DPOR the number of explored traces is $O(3^{N})$ here, while source- and optimal-DPOR only explore $2^{N}$ traces. Both numbers are exponential in N but, as can be seen in the table, for e.g. $N = 13$ source- and optimal-DPOR finish in about one and a half minute, while the DPOR algorithm with the sleep set extension [5] explores two orders of magnitude more (mostly sleep-set blocked) traces and needs almost one and a half hours to complete.

| Benchmark | Traces Explored | | | Time | | |
|---|---|---|---|---|---|---|
| | classic | source | optimal | classic | source | optimal |
| readers(2) | 5 | 4 | 4 | 0.02s | 0.02s | 0.02s |
| readers(8) | 3281 | 256 | 256 | 13.98s | 1.31s | 1.29s |
| readers(13) | 797162 | 8192 | 8192 | 86m 7s | 1m26s | 1m26s |
| lastzero(5) | 241 | 79 | 64 | 1.08s | 0.38s | 0.32s |
| lastzero(10) | 53198 | 7204 | 3328 | 4m47s | 45.21s | 27.61s |
| lastzero(15) | 9378091 | 302587 | 147456 | 1539m11s | 55m 4s | 30m13s |

**Table 2.** Performance of DPOR algorithms on more benchmarks.

**Variables:** `int array[0..N] := {0,0,...,0}, i;`

**Thread** 0**:** `for (i := N; array[i] != 0; i--);`

**Thread** $j$ ($j \in$ 1..N)**:** `array[`$j$`] := array[`$j$`-1] + 1;`

**Figure 4.** The pseudocode of the `lastzero(N)` benchmark.

| Benchmark | Traces Explored | | | Time | | |
|---|---|---|---|---|---|---|
| | classic | source | optimal | classic | source | optimal |
| dialyzer | 12436 | 3600 | 3600 | 14m46s | 5m17s | 5m46s |
| gproc | 14080 | 8328 | 8104 | 3m 3s | 1m45s | 1m57s |
| poolboy | 6018 | 3120 | 2680 | 3m 2s | 1m28s | 1m20s |
| rushhour | 793375 | 536118 | 528984 | 145m19s | 101m55s | 105m41s |

**Table 3.** Performance of DPOR algorithms on four real programs.

| | filesystem(19) | indexer(15) | gproc | rushhour |
|---|---|---|---|---|
| classic | 92.98 | 245.32 | 557.31 | 24.01 |
| source | 66.07 | 165.23 | 480.96 | 24.01 |
| optimal | 76.17 | 174.60 | 481.07 | 31.07 |

**Table 4.** Memory consumption (in MB) for selected benchmarks.

The second benchmark is the lastzero(N) program whose pseudocode is shown in Figure 4. Its N+1 threads operate on an array of N+1 elements which are all initially zero. In this program, thread 0 searches the array for the zero element with the highest index, while the other N threads read one of the array elements and update the next one. The final state of the program is uniquely defined by the values of `i` and `array[1..N]`. What happens here is that thread 0 has control flow that depends on data that is exposed to races and represents a case when *source-DPOR* may encounter sleep-set blocking, that the *optimal-DPOR* algorithm avoids. As can be seen in Table 2, *source-DPOR* explores about twice as many traces than *optimal-DPOR* and, naturally, even if it uses a cheaper test, takes almost twice as much time to complete.

***Performance on real programs*** Finally, we evaluate the algorithms on four Erlang applications. The programs are: (i) dialyzer: a parallel static code analyzer included in the Erlang distribution; (ii) gproc: an extended process dictionary(iii) poolboy: a worker pool factory[1]; and (iv) rushhour: a program that uses processes and ETS tables to solve the Rush Hour puzzle in parallel. The last program, rushhour, is complex but self-contained (917 lines of code). The first three programs, besides their code, call many modules from the Erlang libraries, which Concuerror also instruments. The total number of lines of instrumented code for testing the first three programs is 44596, 9446 and 79732, respectively.

Table 3 shows the results. Here, the performance differences are not as profound as in synthetic benchmarks. Still, some general conclusions can be drawn: (1) Both source- and optimal-DPOR explore less traces than 'classic' (from 50% up to 3.5 times fewer) and require less time to do so (from 42% up to 2.65 times faster). (2) Even in real programs, the number of sleep-set blocked explorations is significant. (3) Regarding the number of traces explored, *source-DPOR* is quite close to optimal, but manages to completely avoid sleep-set blocked executions in only one program (in dialyzer). (4) *Source-DPOR* is faster overall, but only slightly so compared to *optimal-DPOR* even though it uses a cheaper test. In fact, its maximal performance difference percentage-wise from *optimal-DPOR* is a bit less than 10% (in dialyzer again).

Although, due to space limitations, we do not include a full set of memory consumption measurements, we mention that all algorithms have very similar, and quite low, memory needs. Table 4 shows numbers for gproc, the real program which requires most memory, and for all benchmarks where the difference between source and optimal is more than one MB. From these numbers, it can also be deduced that the size of the wakeup tree is small. In fact, the average size of the wakeup trees for these programs is less than three nodes.

[1] `https://github.com/uwiger/gproc` and `https://github.com/devinus/poolboy`

## 10. Related Work

In early approaches to stateless model checking [8], it was observed that reduction was needed to combat the explosion in number of explored interleavings. Several reduction methods have been proposed including partial order reduction and context bounding [19]. Since early persistent set techniques [3, 6, 26] relied on static analysis, sleep set techniques were used in VeriSoft [7]. It was observed that sleep sets are sufficient to prevent the complete exploration of different but equivalent interleavings [10], but additional techniques were needed to reduce sleep-set blocked exploration.

Dynamic partial order reduction [4] showed how to construct persistent sets on-the-fly "by need", leading to better reduction. Similar techniques have been applied in testing and symbolic execution, e.g., to *concolic testing*, where new test runs are initiated in response to detected races [24]. Several variants, improvements, and adaptations of DPOR for stateless model checking [14, 25] and concolic testing [22, 23] have appeared, all based on persistent sets. Our algorithms can be applied to all these contexts to provide increased or optimal reduction in the number of explored interleavings.

A related area is *reachability testing*, in which test executions of concurrent programs are steered by the test harness. Lei and Carver present a technique for exploring all Mazurkiewicz traces in a setting with a restricted set of primitives (message passing and monitors) for process interaction [15]. The scheduling of new test executions explicitly pairs message transmissions with receptions, and could potentially require significant memory, compared to the more lightweight approach of software model checking. The technique of Lei and Carver guarantees to avoid re-exploration of different but equivalent maximal executions (corresponding to Theorem 7.5), but reports blocked executions.

Kahlon *et al.* [12] present a normal form for executions of concurrent programs and prove that two different normal-form executions are not in the same Mazurkiewicz trace. This normal form can be exploited by SAT- or SMT-based bounded model checkers, but it can *not* be used by stateless model checkers that enumerate the execution sequences by state-space exploration. Kähkönen *et al.* [11] use unfoldings [18], which can also obtain optimal reduction in number of interleavings. However, this technique has significantly larger overhead than DPOR-like techniques, and also needs an additional post-processing step for checking non-local properties such as races and deadlocks. A technique for using transition-based partial order reduction for message-passing programs, without moving to an event-based formulation is to refine the concept of dependency between transitions to that of *conditional dependency* [6, 9, 13].

## 11. Conclusion

We have presented *optimal-DPOR*, a new DPOR algorithm which is the first to be provably optimal in that it is guaranteed both to explore the minimal number of executions and to avoid sleep set blockings. It is based on a novel class of sets, called *source sets*. Source sets make existing DPOR algorithms significantly more efficient, and can be extended with wakeup trees to achieve optimality. In the derivation of the optimal algorithm, we have first presented a simpler algorithm, *source-DPOR*, which maintains less information than the optimal algorithm. On the other hand, the extra overhead of maintaining wakeup trees is very moderate in practice (never more than 10% in our experiments), which is a good trade-off for having an optimality guarantee and the possibility to run arbitrarily faster. We intend to further explore the ideas behind source sets and wakeup trees, not only for verification but also for new ways of testing programs.

## Acknowledgments

This work was carried out within the Linnaeus centre of excellence UPMARC (Uppsala Programming for Multicore Architectures Research Center) and was supported in part by the EU FP7 STREP project RELEASE (287510) and the Swedish Research Council.

## References

[1] J. Armstrong. Erlang. *Comm. of the ACM*, 53(9):68–75, 2010.

[2] M. Christakis, A. Gotovos, and K. Sagonas. Systematic testing for detecting concurrency errors in Erlang programs. In *ICST*, 2013.

[3] E. M. Clarke, O. Grumberg, M. Minea, and D. Peled. State space reduction using partial order techniques. *STTT*, 2:279–287, 1999.

[4] C. Flanagan and P. Godefroid. Dynamic partial-order reduction for model checking software. In *POPL*, pages 110–121. ACM, 2005.

[5] C. Flanagan and P. Godefroid. Addendum to *Dynamic partial-order reduction for model checking software*, 2005. Available at `http://research.microsoft.com/en-us/um/people/pg/`.

[6] P. Godefroid. *Partial-Order Methods for the Verification of Concurrent Systems: An Approach to the State-Explosion Problem*. PhD thesis, University of Liège, 1996. Also, volume 1032 of LNCS, Springer.

[7] P. Godefroid. Model checking for programming languages using VeriSoft. In *POPL*, pages 174–186. ACM Press, 1997.

[8] P. Godefroid. Software model checking: The VeriSoft approach. *Formal Methods in System Design*, 26(2):77–101, 2005.

[9] P. Godefroid and D. Pirottin. Refining dependencies improves partial-order verification methods. In *CAV*, volume 697 of *LNCS*, 1993.

[10] P. Godefroid, G. J. Holzmann, and D. Pirottin. State-space caching revisited. *Formal Methods in System Design*, 7(3):227–241, 1995.

[11] K. Kähkönen, O. Saarikivi, and K. Heljanko. Using unfoldings in automated testing of multithreaded programs. In *ASE*, pages 150–159. ACM, 2012.

[12] V. Kahlon, C. Wang, and A. Gupta. Monotonic partial order reduction: An optimal symbolic partial order reduction technique. In *CAV*, volume 5643 of *LNCS*, pages 398–413. Springer, 2009.

[13] S. Katz and D. Peled. Defining conditional independence using collapses. *Theoretical Computer Science*, 101:337–359, 1992.

[14] S. Lauterburg, R. Karmani, D. Marinov, and G. Agha. Evaluating ordering heuristics for dynamic partial-order reduction techniques. In *FASE*, volume 6013 of *LNCS*, pages 308–322. Springer, 2010.

[15] Y. Lei and R. Carver. Reachability testing of concurrent programs. *IEEE Trans. Softw. Eng.*, 32(6):382–403, 2006.

[16] F. Mattern. Virtual time and global states of distributed systems. In M. Cosnard, editor, *Proc. Workshop on Parallel and Distributed Algorithms*, pages 215–226, Ch. de Bonas, France, 1989. Elsevier.

[17] A. Mazurkiewicz. Trace theory. In *Advances in Petri Nets*, 1986.

[18] K. McMillan. A technique of a state space search based on unfolding. *Formal Methods in System Design*, 6(1):45–65, 1995.

[19] M. Musuvathi and S. Qadeer. Iterative context bounding for systematic testing of multithreaded programs. In *PLDI*, pages 446–455, 2007.

[20] M. Musuvathi, S. Qadeer, T. Ball, G. Basler, P. Nainar, and I. Neamtiu. Finding and reproducing heisenbugs in concurrent programs. In *OSDI*, pages 267–280. USENIX Association, 2008.

[21] D. Peled. All from one, one for all, on model-checking using representatives. In *CAV*, volume 697 of *LNCS*, pages 409–423, 1993.

[22] O. Saarikivi, K. Kähkönen, and K. Heljanko. Improving dynamic partial order reductions for concolic testing. In *ACSD*. IEEE, 2012.

[23] K. Sen and G. Agha. Automated systematic testing of open distributed programs. In *FASE*, volume 3922 of *LNCS*, pages 339–356, 2006.

[24] K. Sen and G. Agha. A race-detection and flipping algorithm for automated testing of multi-threaded programs. In *Haifa Verification Conference*, volume 4383 of *LNCS*, pages 166–182. Springer, 2007.

[25] S. Tasharofi et al. TransDPOR: A novel dynamic partial-order reduction technique for testing actor programs. In *FMOODS/FORTE*, volume 7273 of *LNCS*, pages 219–234. Springer, 2012.

[26] A. Valmari. Stubborn sets for reduced state space generation. In *Advances in Petri Nets*, volume 483 of *LNCS*, pages 491–515, 1990.

# Modular Reasoning about Heap Paths via Effectively Propositional Formulas


Shachar Itzhaky
Tel Aviv University
shachar@tau.ac.il

Anindya Banerjee
IMDEA Software Institute, Madrid, Spain
anindya.banerjee@imdea.org

Neil Immerman
University of Massachusetts, Amherst, USA
immerman@cs.umass.edu

Ori Lahav
Tel Aviv University
orilahav@post.tau.ac.il

Aleksandar Nanevski
IMDEA Software Institute, Madrid, Spain
aleks.nanevski@imdea.org

Mooly Sagiv
Tel Aviv University
msagiv@acm.org



## Abstract

First order logic with transitive closure, and separation logic enable elegant interactive verification of heap-manipulating programs. However, undecidabilty results and high asymptotic complexity of checking validity preclude complete automatic verification of such programs, even when loop invariants and procedure contracts are specified as formulas in these logics. This paper tackles the problem of procedure-modular verification of reachability properties of heap-manipulating programs using efficient decision procedures that are complete: that is, a SAT solver must generate a counterexample whenever a program does not satisfy its specification. By (a) requiring each procedure modifies a fixed set of heap partitions and creates a bounded amount of heap sharing, and (b) restricting program contracts and loop invariants to use only deterministic paths in the heap, we show that heap reachability updates can be described in a simple manner. The restrictions force program specifications and verification conditions to lie within a fragment of first-order logic with transitive closure that is reducible to effectively propositional logic, and hence facilitate sound, complete and efficient verification. We implemented a tool atop Z3 and report on preliminary experiments that establish the correctness of several programs that manipulate linked data structures.



***Categories and Subject Descriptors*** D.3.3 [**Programming Languages**]: Dynamic storage management

***Keywords*** linked list; SMT; verification


## 1. Introduction

This paper shows how to harness existing SAT solvers for proving that a potentially recursive procedure satisfies its specification and for automatically producing counterexamples when it does not. We concentrate on proving safety properties of imperative programs manipulating linked data structures which is challenging since we need to reason about unbounded memory and destructive pointer updates. The tricky part is to identify a logic which is expressive enough to enable the modular verification of interesting procedures and properties and weak enough to enable sound and complete verification using SAT solvers.

Recently it was shown [11] how to employ effectively propositional logic (or BSR logic[1]) for verifying programs manipulating linked lists. It decides the validity of formulas of the form $\forall^*\exists^* q$ using SAT solvers where $q$ is a quantifier free relational formula (or equivalently decides the satisfiability of $\exists^*\forall^* q$ formulas). It has been successfully used in many other contexts [18].

In this paper we show that effectively propositional logic does not suffice to naturally express the effect on the global heap when the local heap of a procedure is accessible via shared nodes from outside. For example, Fig. 1 shows a pre- and post-heap before a list pointed-to by $h$ is reversed. The problem is how to express the change in reachability between nodes such as $z_i$ and list nodes $1, 2, \ldots, 5$: note that, e.g., nodes $3, 4, 5$ are unreachable from $z_1$ in the post-heap.

This paper shows that in many cases, including the above example, reachability can be checked precisely using SAT solvers. Our solution is based on the following principles:

- We follow the standard techniques (e.g., see [2, 14, 25, 29]) by requiring that the programmer defines the set of potentially modified elements.
- The programmer only specifies postconditions on local heaps and ignores the effect of paths from the global heap.
- We provide a general and exact **adaptation rule** for adapting postconditions to the global heap. This adaptation rule is expressible in a generalized version of BSR called $AE^{AR}$. $AE^{AR}$ allows an extra **entry** function symbol which maps each node $u$ in the global heap into the first node accessible from $u$ in the local heap. In Fig. 1, $z_1, z_2$ and $z_3$ are mapped to $2, 3$ and $4$, respectively. The key facts are that $AE^{AR}$ suffices to precisely define the global reachability relationship after each procedure call and yet any $AE^{AR}$ formula can be simulated by a BSR

[1] Due to Bernays, Schönfinkel and Ramsey.




*POPL '14*, January 22–24, 2014, San Diego, CA, USA.



ACM 978-1-4503-2544-8/14/01... $15.00.
http://dx.doi.org/10.1145/2535838.2535854

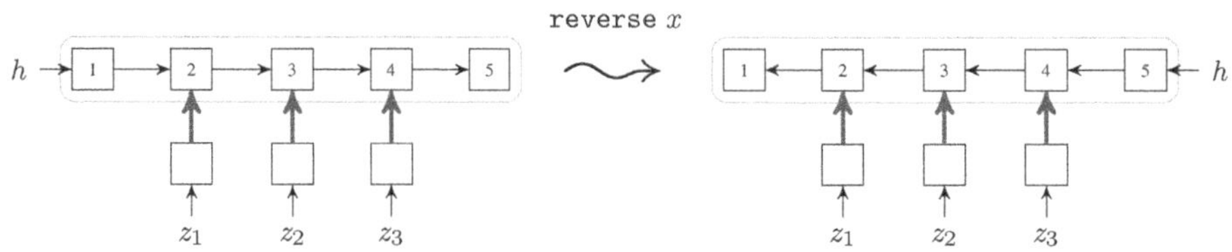


**Figure 1.** Reversing a list pointed to by a head $h$ with many shared nodes accessible from outside the local heap (surrounded by a rounded rectangle).

formula. Thus the automatic methods of [11] still apply to this significantly more general setting.

- We restrict the verified procedures in order to guarantee that the generated verification condition of every procedure remains in $AE^{AR}$. The main restrictions are: type correctness, deterministic paths in the heap, limited number of changed list segments in the local heap (each of which may be unbounded) and limited amount of newly created heap sharing by each procedure call. These restrictions are enforced by the generated verification condition in $AE^{AR}$. This formula is automatically checked by the SAT solver.

### 1.1 Main Results

The results in this paper can be summarized as follows:

- We define a new logic, $AE^{AR}$, which extends BSR with a limited idempotent function and yet is equi-satisfiable with BSR.
- We provide a precise adaptation rule in $AE^{AR}$, which expresses the locality property of the change, and in conjunction with the postcondition on the local heap, precisely updates the reachability relation of the global heap.
- We generate a modular verification formula in $AE^{AR}$ for each procedure, asserting that the procedure satisfies its pre- and post-conditions and the above restrictions. This verification condition is sound and complete, i.e., it is valid if and only if the procedure adheres to the restrictions and satisfies its requirements. We implemented this tool on top of Z3.
- We show that many programs can be modularly verified using our methods. They satisfy our restrictions and their BSR invariants can be naturally expressed.

### 1.2 A Running Example

To make the discussion more clear, we start with an example program. We use the union-find data structure[2], which maintains a forest using a parent pointer at each node (see Fig. 2) [24].

The method `find` requires that the argument $x$ is not null. The formula $\mathrm{tail}_f(x, r_x)$ asserts that the auxiliary variable $r_x$ is equal to the root of $x$. The procedure changes the pointers of some nodes in the closed interval $[x, r_x]_f$ to point directly to $r_x$. Intervals are formally defined later (Definition 5). Intuitively, the closed interval $[a, b]_f$ denotes the set of nodes pointed to by $a$, $a.f$, $a.f.f$ and so on up until $b$ inclusive.

The return value of `find` (denoted by retval) is $r_x$. The postcondition uses the symbol $\underline{f}$ that denotes the value of $f$ before the method was invoked. Since `find` compresses paths from ancestors of $x$ to single edges to $r_x$, this root may be shared via new parent pointers. Fig. 3 depicts a typical run of `find`.

[2] We have simplified `union` by not keeping track of the sizes of sets in order to attach the smaller set to the larger.

@ requires $x \neq \mathrm{null} \wedge \mathrm{tail}_f(x, r_x)$
@ mod $[x, r_x]_f$
@ ensures $\mathrm{retval} = r_x \wedge$ $\forall \alpha, \beta \in \mathrm{mod} : \alpha \langle f^* \rangle \beta \leftrightarrow \alpha = \beta \vee \beta = r_x$

```
Node find(Node x) {
  Node i = x.f;
  if (i != null) {
    i = find(i);
    x.f = i;
  }
  else {
    i = x;
  }
  return i;
}
```

@ requires $x \neq \mathrm{null} \wedge y \neq \mathrm{null} \wedge \mathrm{tail}_f(x, r_x) \wedge \mathrm{tail}_f(y, r_y)$
@ mod $[x, r_x]_f \cup [y, r_y]_f$
@ ensures

$$\forall \alpha, \beta \in \mathrm{mod} : \begin{array}{l} (x \langle \underline{f}^* \rangle \alpha \rightarrow (\alpha \langle f^* \rangle \beta \leftrightarrow \\ \qquad \beta = \alpha \vee \beta = r_x \vee \beta = r_y)) \\ \wedge (y \langle \underline{f}^* \rangle \alpha \rightarrow (\alpha \langle f^* \rangle \beta \leftrightarrow \beta = \alpha \vee \beta = r_y)) \end{array}$$

```
void union(Node x, Node y){
  Node t = find(x); Node s = find(y);
  if (t != s) t.f = s;
}
```

**Figure 2.** An annotated implementation of Union-Find in Java. $f$ is the backbone field denoting the parent of a tree node.

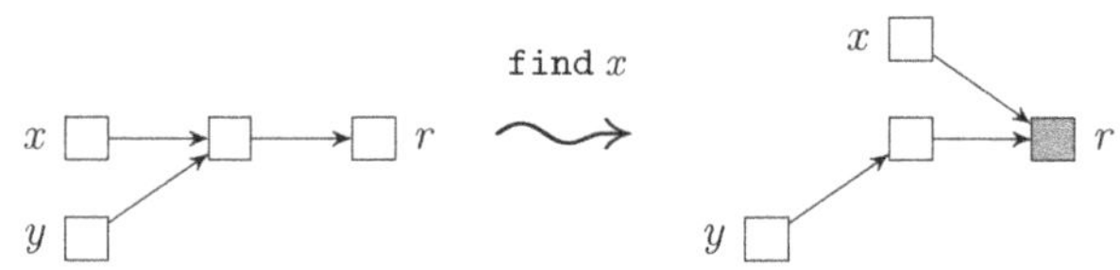


**Figure 3.** An example scenario of running `find` (■ = return value).

The method `union` requires that both its arguments are not null. It potentially modifies the ancestors of $x$ and $y$, i.e., $[x, r_x]_f \cup [y, r_y]_f$. Fig. 4 depicts a typical run of `union`. Notice that we support an unbounded number of cutpoints [21] (see Section 8).

### 1.3 Working Assumptions

**Type correct** The procedure manipulates references to dynamically created objects in a type-safe way. For example, we do not support pointer arithmetic.

**Deterministic Reachability** The specification may use arbitrary uninterpreted relations. It may also use the reachability formula $\alpha \langle f^* \rangle \beta$ meaning that $\beta$ is reachable from $\alpha$ via zero or more

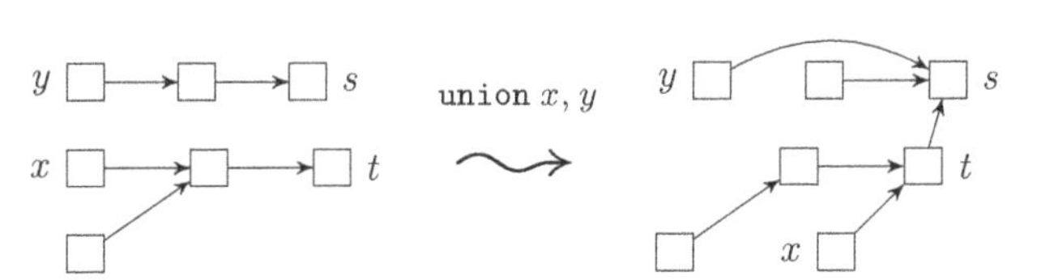


**Figure 4.** An example scenario of running `union`.

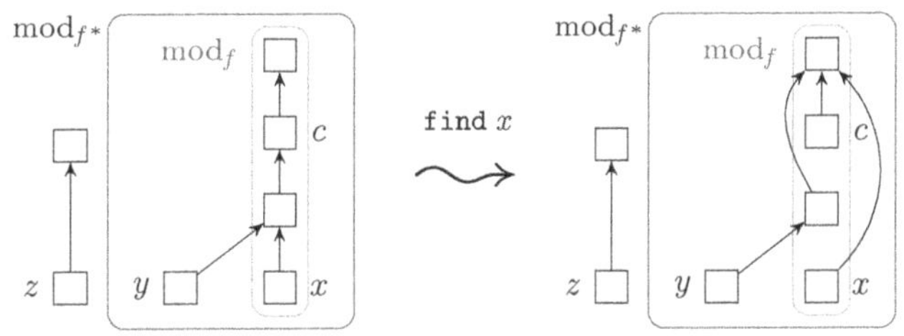


**Figure 5.** A case where changes made by `find` have a non-local effect: $y\langle \underline{f}^*\rangle c$, but $\neg y\langle f^*\rangle c$.

steps along the functional backbone field $f$. It may not use $f$ in any other way. Until Section 6, we require $f$ to be acyclic and we restrict our attention to only one backbone field.

**Precondition** There is a **requires clause** defining the precondition which is written in alternation-free relational first-order logic ($AF^R$) and may use the relation $f^\star$ [11].

**Mod-set** There is a **modifies clause** defining the mod-set ($\text{mod}_f$), which is the set of potentially changed memory locations (We include both source and target of every edge that is added or deleted). The modified set may have an unbounded number of vertices, but we require it to be the union of a bounded number of $f$-intervals, that is chains of vertices through $f$-pointers.

**Postcondition** There is an **ensures clause** which exactly defines the new reachability relation $f^\star$ restricted to $\text{mod}_f$. The ensures clause, written in $AF^R$, may use two vocabularies (employing both $\underline{f}$ and $f$ to refer to the reachability relations before and after.

**Bounded new sharing** All the new shared nodes — nodes pointed to by more than one node — must be pointed to by local variables at the end of the procedure's execution. This requires that only a bounded number of new shared nodes can be introduced by each procedure call. Note that many heap-manipulating programs exhibit limited sharing as noted in the experimental measurements of Mitchell [16]. A similar restriction is also used in shape analysis techniques for device driver programs [27].

**Loop-free** We assume that all code is loop free, with loops replaced by recursive calls.

### 1.4 Outline of the rest of this paper

Section 2 provides a rule for adapting local changes to states containing a global heap. The idea is that the programmer only specifies changes in a small, local area of the heap. Section 3 introduces a new logic called $AE^{AR}$. Section 4 formalizes the requirements for specifying the meaning of commands and procedures. The technique for generating verification conditions is presented in Section 5. Extensions to the frameworks are discussed in Section 6. Our preliminary verification experience appears in Section 7. Section 8 discusses related work and Section 9 concludes. Details of the logical proof are contained in [10, Appendix A].

## 2. Adaptation of Local Effect to the Global Heap

Our goal is to reason modularly about a procedure that modifies a subset of the heap. We wish to automatically update the reachability relation in the entire heap based on the changes to the modified subset. We remark that in this paper we are concerned with reachability between any two nodes in the heap, as opposed to only those pointed to by program variables. When we discuss sharing we mean sharing via pointer fields in the heap as opposed to aliasing from stack variables, which does not concern us in this paper.

### 2.1 Non-Local Effects

Reachability is inherently non-local: a single edge mutation can affect the reachability of an unbounded number of points that are an unbounded distance from the point of change. Fig. 5 contains a typical run of `find`. Two kinds of "frames" are depicted: (i) $\text{mod}_f = [x, r_x)_f$, specified by the programmer, denotes the nodes whose edges can be directly changed by `find`— this is the standard notion of a frame condition; (ii) $\text{mod}_{f^*}$ denotes nodes for which $f^*$, the path relation, has changed. We do not and, in general we cannot, specify $\text{mod}_{f^*}$ in a modular way because it usually depends on variables outside the scope of this function such as $y$ in Fig. 5. In the example shown, there is a path from $y$ to $c$ before the call which does not exist after the call. Furthermore, $\text{mod}_{f^*}$ can be an arbitrarily large set: in particular, it may not be expressible as the union of a bounded set of intervals: for example, when adding a subtree as a child of some node in another tree, $\text{mod}_f$ spans only one edge, whereas $\text{mod}_{f^*}$ is the entire subtree added — which may contain an unbounded number of branches.

The postcondition of `find` is sound (every execution of `find` satisfies it), but incomplete: it does not provide a way to determine information concerning paths outside mod, such as from $y$ to $c$ in Fig. 5. Therefore, this rule is often not enough in order to verify the correctness of programs that invoke `find` in larger contexts.

Notice the difficulty of updating the global heap, especially the part $\text{mod}_{f^*} \setminus \text{mod}_f$. In particular, using only the local specification of `find`, one would not be able to prove that $\neg y\langle f^*\rangle c$. Indeed, the problem is updating the reachability of elements that are **outside** mod; in more complex situations, these elements may be far from the changed interval, and their number may be unbounded.

One possibility to avoid the problem of incompleteness is to specify a postcondition which is specific to the context in which the invocation occurs. However, such a solution requires reasoning per call site and is thus not modular. We wish to develop a rule that will fit in all contexts. Reasoning about all contexts is naturally done by quantification.

### 2.2 An FO(TC) Adaptation Rule

A standard way to modularize specifications is to specify the local effect of a procedure and then to use a general adaptation rule (or frame rule) to derive the global effect. In our case, we know that locations outside mod are not modified. Therefore, for example, after a call to `find`, a new path from node $\sigma$ to node $\tau$ is either an old path from $\sigma$ to $\tau$, or it consists of an old path to a node $\alpha \in \text{mod}$, a new path from $\alpha$ to a node $\beta \in \text{mod}$ and an old path from $\beta$ to $\tau$. We express this below, first letting $q$ denote an old edge that is not inside mod:

$$\begin{array}{lll} \forall \alpha,\beta : \alpha\langle q\rangle\beta & \leftrightarrow & \alpha\langle \underline{f}\rangle\beta \land (\alpha \notin \text{mod} \lor \beta \notin \text{mod}) \\ \forall \sigma,\tau : \sigma\langle f^*\rangle\tau & \leftrightarrow & \sigma\langle \underline{q}^*\rangle\tau \ \lor\ \exists \alpha,\beta \in \text{mod} : \\ & & \sigma\langle q^*\rangle\alpha \ \land\ \alpha\langle f^*\rangle\beta \ \land\ \beta\langle q^*\rangle\tau \end{array} \qquad (1)$$

eq (1) is a completely general adaptation rule: it defines $f^*$ on the global heap assuming we know $f^*$ on the local heap and we also have access to the old path relation $q^*$. The problem with this rule is that it uses a logic that is too expressive and thus hard for automated reasoning: FO(TC) is not decidable (in fact, not even

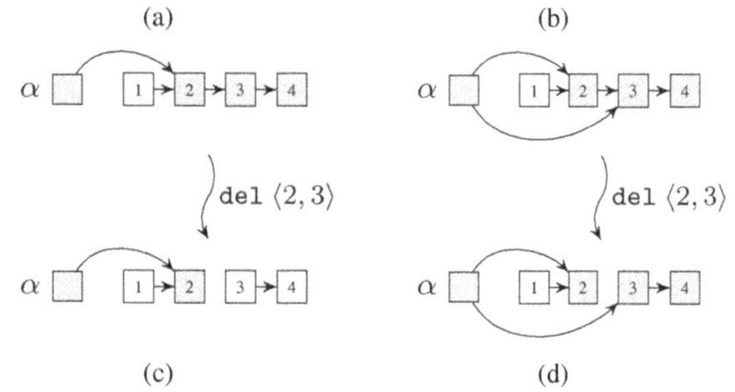


**Figure 6.** Memory states with non-unique pointers where global reasoning about reachability is hard. In the memory state (a), there is one edge from $\alpha$ into the modified-set $\{1,2,3,4\}$, and in memory state (b), there are two edges from $\alpha$ into the same modified-set, $\{1,2,3,4\}$. The two memory states have the same reachability relation and therefore are indistinguishable in terms of reachability. The memory states (c) and (d) are obtained from the memory states (a) and (b), respectively, by deleting the edge $\langle 2,3\rangle$. The reachability in (c) is not the same as in (d), which shows it is impossible to update reachability in general w.r.t. edge deletion, without using the edge relation.

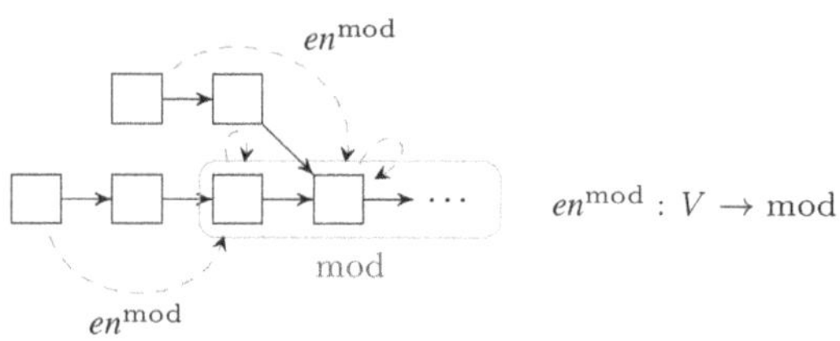


**Figure 7.** The function $en^{\text{mod}}$ maps every node $\sigma$ to the first node in mod reachable from $\sigma$. Notice that for any $\alpha \in \text{mod}$, $en^{\text{mod}}(\alpha) = \alpha$ by definition.

recursively enumerable). The first problem is that the $q^*$ relation is not usually first order expressible and generally requires transitive closure. For example, Fig. 6 shows that in general the adaptation rule is not necessarily definable using only the reachability relation, when there are multiple outgoing edges per node. We avoid this problem by only reasoning about functional fields, $f$.

The second problem with eq (1) is that it contains quantifier alternation. $\alpha$ matches an arbitrary node in mod which may be of arbitrary size. Therefore, it is not completely obvious how to avoid existential quantifications.

### 2.3 An Adaptation Rule in a Restricted Logic

We now present an equivalent adaptation rule in a restricted logic, without transitive closure or extra quantifier-alternations. This is possible due to our assumptions from Section 1.3 and it greatly simplifies reasoning about modified paths in the entire heap. We require a new function symbol, $en^{\text{mod}}$. We call $en^{\text{mod}}(\sigma)$ the **entry point** of $\sigma$ in mod, i.e., the first node on the (unique) path from $\sigma$ that enters mod, and null if no such node exists (see Figure 7).

Note that since transitive closure is only applied to functions, entry points such as $\alpha$ in eq (1) are uniquely determined by $\sigma$, the origin of the path. A key property of $en^{\text{mod}}$ is that on mod itself, $en^{\text{mod}}$ is the identity, and therefore for any $\sigma \in V$ it holds that $en^{\text{mod}}(en^{\text{mod}}(\sigma)) = en^{\text{mod}}(\sigma))$ — that is, the function $en^{\text{mod}}$ is **idempotent**. It is important to note that $en^{\text{mod}}$ does not change as a result of local modifications in mod. Hence, we do not need to

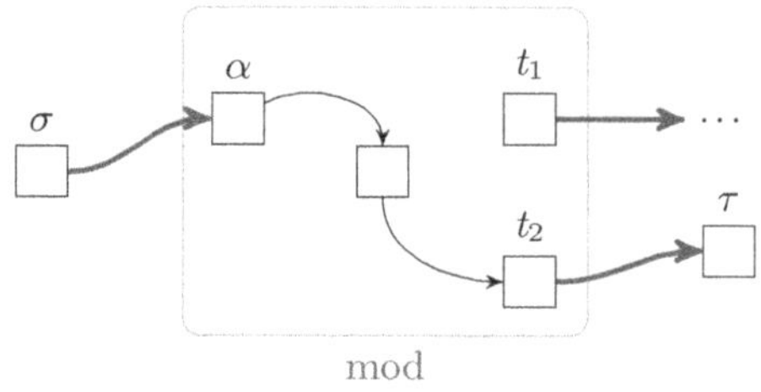


**Figure 8.** This diagram depicts how an arbitrary path from $\sigma \notin \text{mod}$ to $\tau \notin \text{mod}$ is constructed from three segments: $[\sigma,\alpha]_f$, $[\alpha,t_i]_f$, and $[t_i,\tau]_{\underline{f}}$ (here $i = 2$). Arrows in the diagram denote paths; thick arrows entering and exiting the box denote paths that were not modified since they are outside of mod. Here, $\alpha = en^{\text{mod}}(\sigma)$ is an entry-point and $t_1, t_2$ are exit-points.

worry about $en^{\text{mod}}$ in the pre-state as opposed to the post-state. Formally, $en^{\text{mod}}$ is characterized by the following formula:

$$\begin{aligned}\forall\sigma :\ & (en^{\text{mod}}(\sigma) = \text{null} \land \forall\alpha \in \text{mod} : \neg\sigma\langle \underline{f}^*\rangle\alpha) \lor \\ & (\sigma\langle \underline{f}^*\rangle en^{\text{mod}}(\sigma) \land en^{\text{mod}}(\sigma) \in \text{mod} \land \\ & \forall\alpha \in \text{mod} : \sigma\langle \underline{f}^*\rangle\alpha \to en^{\text{mod}}(\sigma)\langle \underline{f}^*\rangle\alpha)\end{aligned} \tag{2}$$

Using $en^{\text{mod}}$ the new adaptation rule adapt[mod] is obtained by considering, for every source and target, the following three cases:

**Out-In:** The source is out of mod; the target is in;
**In-Out:** The source is in mod; the target is out;
**Out-Out:** The source and target are both out of mod.

The full adaptation rule is obtained by taking the conjunction of the formulas for each case (eq (3), eq (4), eq (5)), that are described below, and the formula defining $en^{\text{mod}}$ (eq (2)).

***Out-In Paths*** Using $en^{\text{mod}}$ we can easily handle paths that enter mod. Such paths originate at some $\sigma \notin \text{mod}$ and terminate at some $\tau \in \text{mod}$. Any such path therefore has to go through $en^{\text{mod}}(\sigma)$ as depicted in Fig. 8. Thus, the following simple formula can be used:

$$\forall\sigma \notin \text{mod}, \tau \in \text{mod} : \sigma\langle f^*\rangle\tau \leftrightarrow en^{\text{mod}}(\sigma)\langle f^*\rangle\tau \tag{3}$$

Observe that for any $\beta \in \text{mod}$, the atomic formula used above, $en^{\text{mod}}(\sigma)\langle f^*\rangle\beta$, corresponds to the FO(TC) sub-formula $\exists\alpha \in \text{mod} : \sigma\langle q^*\rangle\alpha \land \alpha\langle f^*\rangle\beta$ from eq (1).

***In-Out Paths*** We now shift attention to paths that exit mod. Exit points, that is, last points on some path that belong to mod, are more subtle since both ends of the path are needed to determine them. The end of the path is not enough since it can be shared, and the origin of the path is not enough since it can exit the set multiple times, because a path may exit mod and enter it again later. Therefore, we cannot define a function in a similar manner to $en^{\text{mod}}$. The fact that transitive closure is only applied to functions is useful here: every interval $[\alpha,\beta]$ has at most one exit $\beta$. We therefore utilize the fact that mod is expressed as a bounded union of intervals — which bounds the potential exit points to a bounded set of terms. We will denote the exit points of mod by $t_i$.

For example, in the procedure `swap` shown in Fig. 9, $\text{mod} = [x, f_x^3]$ and there is one exit point $t_1 = f_x^3$ ($f_x^3$ is a constant set by the precondition to have the value of $f(f(f(x)))$ using the inversion formula eq (6) to be introduced formally in Section 3.1).

Any path that originates in mod and terminates outside mod must leave through a last exit point $t_i$ (see Fig. 10). Notice that the exit points also do not change as a result of modifying edges between nodes in mod. Let $p$ be a path from $\sigma$ to $\tau$ and let $t_i$ be the last exit point along $p$. Note that the part of the path from $t_i$ to

@ requires $E_f(x, f_x^1) \wedge E_f(f_x^1, f_x^2) \wedge E_f(f_x^3, f_x^2) \wedge$
$x \neq \text{null} \wedge f_x^1 \neq \text{null} \wedge f_x^2 \neq \text{null}$
@ mod $[x, f_x^3]$
@ ensures ...

```
void swap(Node x) {
  Node t = x.f;
  x.f = t.f;
  t.f = x.f.f;
  x.f.f = t;
}
```

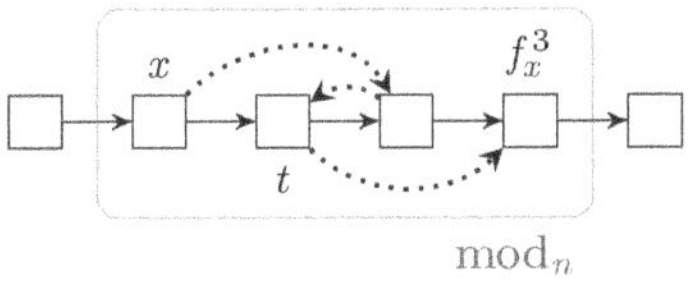


**Figure 9.** A simple function that swaps two adjacent elements following x in a singly-linked list. Dotted lines denote the new state after the swap. The notation e.g. $E_f(x, f_x^1)$ denotes the single edge from $x$ to $f_x^1$ following the $f$ field.

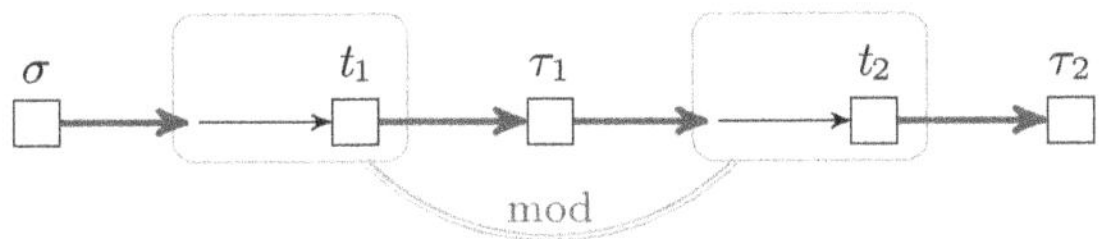


**Figure 10.** A subtle situation occurs when the path from $\sigma$ passes through multiple exit-points. In such a case, the relevant exit-point for $\sigma\langle f^*\rangle\tau_1$ is $t_1$, whereas for $\sigma\langle f^*\rangle\tau_2$ and $\tau_1\langle f^*\rangle\tau_2$ it would be $t_2$.

```
void swap_two(Node a, Node b) {
  swap(a); swap(b);
}
```

**Figure 11.** An example of a procedure where the mod-set is not (essentially) convex.

$\tau$ consists only of unchanged edges — since they are all outside of mod. We can therefore safely use $\underline{f}^*$, rather than $q^*$, to characterize it. The part of the path from $\sigma$ to $t_i$ can be characterized by $f^*$, because $\sigma$ and $t_i$ are both in mod. Therefore the entire path can be expressed as $\sigma\langle f^*\rangle t_i \wedge t_i\langle \underline{f}^*\rangle\tau$. Thus, we obtain the following formula:

$$\begin{aligned}\forall\sigma \in \text{mod}, \tau \notin \text{mod} : \ &\sigma\langle f^*\rangle\tau \ \leftrightarrow \\ &\textstyle\bigvee_{t_i}(\sigma\langle f^*\rangle t_i \wedge t_i\langle \underline{f}^*\rangle\tau \ \wedge \ \bigwedge_{t_j \neq t_i} t_j \notin [t_i, \tau]_{\underline{f}})\end{aligned} \tag{4}$$

Note that eq (4) corresponds the sub-formula $\exists\beta : \alpha\langle f^*\rangle\beta \wedge \beta\langle q^*\rangle\tau$ in eq (1).

***Out-Out Paths*** For paths between $\sigma$ and $\tau$, both outside mod, there are two possible situations:

- The path goes **through** mod (as in Fig. 8). In this case, we can reuse the in-out case, by taking $en^{\text{mod}}(\sigma)$ instead of $\sigma$.
- The path is entirely outside of mod (see Fig. 12).

The corresponding formula in this case is:

$$\begin{aligned}&\forall\sigma \notin \text{mod}, \tau \notin \text{mod} : \ \sigma\langle f^*\rangle\tau \ \leftrightarrow \\ &\textstyle\bigvee_{t_i}(en^{\text{mod}}(\sigma)\langle f^*\rangle t_i \wedge t_i\langle \underline{f}^*\rangle\tau \wedge \bigwedge_{t_j \neq t_i} t_j \notin [t_i, \tau]_{\underline{f}}) \\ &\vee \quad en^{\text{mod}}(\sigma) = en^{\text{mod}}(\tau) \ \wedge \ \sigma\langle \underline{f}^*\rangle\tau\end{aligned} \tag{5}$$

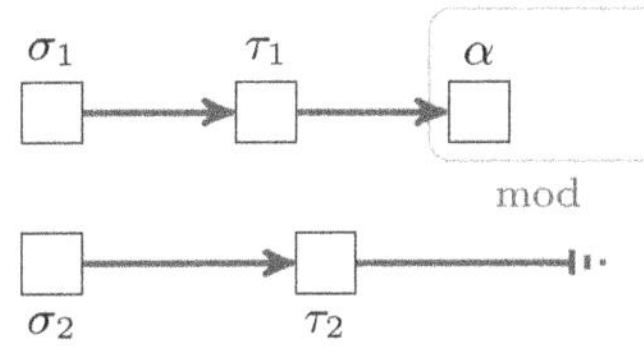


**Figure 12.** Paths that go entirely untouched. $en^{\text{mod}}(\sigma_1) = \alpha$, whereas $en^{\text{mod}}(\sigma_2) = \text{null}$.

Notice that the second disjunct covers the case where there is a path from $\tau$ to mod ($en^{\text{mod}}(\sigma) = en^{\text{mod}}(\tau) \neq \text{null}$) and the case where there is none ($en^{\text{mod}}(\sigma) = en^{\text{mod}}(\tau) = \text{null}$).

In conclusion, our adaptation rule, adapt[mod], is the conjunction of the three formulas in eq (3), eq (4), eq (5), and the formula defining $en^{\text{mod}}$ (eq (2)). We need some more formalism, introduced in the next section, before we show that adapt[mod] meets our needs.

## 3. Adaptable Heap Reachability Logic

In this section we introduce an extension of $AE^R$ from [11], called **adaptable heap reachability logic**, and denoted by $AE^{AR}$. This extension still has the attractive property of $AE^R$, as it is effectively reducible to the function-free $\forall^*\exists^*$-fragment of first-order logic, and thus its validity can be checked by a SAT-solver.

### 3.1 Preliminaries

This section reviews the $AF^R$ (alternation free) and $AE^R$ ($\forall\exists$) logics from [11]. They are decidable for validity since their negation corresponds to the BSR fragment [18]. These logics include the relation $f^*$ (the reflexive transitive closure of $f$) but forbid the explicit use of function symbols including $f$. Until Section 6 we will use at most one designated backbone function ($f$) per formula.

**Definition 1.** A **vocabulary** $\mathcal{V} = \langle \mathcal{C}, \{f\}, \mathcal{R}\rangle$ is a triple of constant symbols, function symbol, relation symbols.
A **term**, $t$, is a variable or constant symbol.
An **atomic formula** is one of the following: (i) $t_1 = t_2$; (ii) $r(t_1, t_2, \ldots, t_a)$ where $r$ is a relation symbol of arity $a$; (iii) $t_1\langle f^*\rangle t_2$.

A **quantifier-free formula** ($QF^R$) is a boolean combination of atomic formulas. A **universal formula** begins with zero or more universal quantifiers followed by a quantifier-free formula. An **alternation-free formula** ($AF^R$) is a boolean combination of universal formulas. $AE^R$ consists of formulas with quantifier-prefix $\forall^*\exists^*$.

In particular, $QF^R \subset AF^R \subset AE^R$. The preconditions and the postconditions in Fig. 2 are all $AF^R$ formulas.

***Decidability and Inversion*** Every $AE^R$ formula can be translated to a first-order $\forall^*\exists^*$ formula via the following steps [11]. (i) Add a new uninterpreted relation $R_f$ which is intended to represent $\langle f^*\rangle$, the reflexive transitive closure of reachability via $f$, (ii) Add the consistency rule $\Gamma_{\text{linOrd}}$ shown in Table 1, which requires that $R_f$ is a total order, i.e., reflexive, transitive, acyclic, and linear, and (iii) Replace all occurrences of $t_1\langle f^*\rangle t_2$ by $R_f(t_1, t_2)$.

**Proposition 1** (Simulation of $AE^R$). *[12, Proposition 3, Appendix A.1] Consider $AE^R$ formula $\varphi$ over vocabulary $\mathcal{V} = \langle \mathcal{C}, \{f\}, \mathcal{R}\rangle$. Let $\varphi' \stackrel{\text{def}}{=} \varphi[R_f(t_1, t_2)/t_1\langle f^*\rangle t_2]$. Then $\varphi'$ is a first-order formula over vocabulary $\mathcal{V}' = \langle \mathcal{C}, \emptyset, \mathcal{R} \cup \{R_f\}\rangle$ and $\Gamma_{\text{linOrd}} \rightarrow \varphi'$ is valid if and only if the original formula $\varphi$ is valid.*

| | |
|---|---|
| $\forall \alpha : R_f(\alpha, \alpha) \quad \wedge$ | reflexivity |
| $\forall \alpha, \beta, \gamma : R_f(\alpha, \beta) \wedge R_f(\beta, \gamma) \rightarrow R_f(\alpha, \gamma) \quad \wedge$ | transitivity |
| $\forall \alpha, \beta : R_f(\alpha, \beta) \wedge R_f(\beta, \alpha) \rightarrow \alpha = \beta \quad \wedge$ | acyclicity |
| $\forall \alpha, \beta, \gamma : R_f(\alpha, \beta) \wedge R_f(\alpha, \gamma) \rightarrow (R_f(\beta, \gamma) \vee R_f(\gamma, \beta))$ | linearity |

**Table 1.** A universal formula $\Gamma_{\text{linOrd}}$ requiring that all points reachable from a given point are linearly ordered.

When the graph of $f$ is acyclic, the relation $E_f$ characterizing the function $f$ can be recovered from its reflexive transitive closure, $f^*$, at the cost of an extra universal quantifier:

$$E_f(\alpha, \beta) \stackrel{\text{def}}{=} \alpha\langle f^+\rangle\beta \wedge \forall\gamma : \alpha\langle f^+\rangle\gamma \rightarrow \beta\langle f^*\rangle\gamma \qquad (6)$$

Here $\alpha\langle f^+\rangle\beta \stackrel{\text{def}}{=} \alpha\langle f^*\rangle\beta \wedge \alpha \neq \beta$.

### 3.2 Adaptable Heap Reachability Logic

The new logic $AE^{AR}$ is obtained by augmenting $AE^R$ with unary function symbols, denoted by $g, h_1, \ldots, h_n$ where:

- $g$ must be interpreted as an idempotent function.
- The images $h_1, \ldots, h_n$ are all bounded by some pre-determined parameter $N$, that is: each $h_i$ takes at most $N$ distinct values.
- Function symbols may not be nested, i.e., all terms involving function symbols have the form $f(z)$, where $z$ is a variable.

We later show that $AE^{AR}$ suffices for expressing the verification conditions of the programs discussed above. In the typical use case, the function $g$ assigns the entry point in the mod-set for every node (called $en^{\text{mod}_f}$ above), and the functions $h_1, \ldots, h_n$ are used for expressing the entry points in inner mod-sets. The main attractive feature of this logic is given in the following theorem.

**Theorem 1.** *Any $AE^{AR}$-formula $\varphi$ can be translated to an equi-valid (first-order) function-free $\forall^*\exists^*$-formula.*

The proof of Theorem 1, given in [10, Appendix A], begins by translating $\varphi$ to a $\forall^*\exists^*$-formula $\varphi'$ as described in Proposition 1, without modifying the function symbols $g, h_1, \ldots, h_n$. The function symbols are then replaced by new relation and constant symbols. We add new universal formulas to express the above semantic restrictions on the functions.

## 4. Modular Specifications of Procedure Behaviours

### 4.1 Notations

**Definition 2.** Let $\mathcal{V} = \langle \mathcal{C}, \{f\}, \mathcal{R}\rangle$ be a vocabulary including the constant symbol null. A **state**, $M$, is a logical structure with domain $|M|$, including null, and $\text{null}^M = \text{null} = f^M(\text{null})$, where $s^M$ is the interpretation of the symbol $s$ in the structure $M$. A state is **appropriate** for an annotated procedure *proc* if its vocabulary includes every symbol occurring in its annotations, and constants corresponding to all of the program variables occurring in *proc*.

The diagrams in this paper denote states. For example Fig. 1 shows a transition between two states.

Below we define the notion of two-vocabulary structures, which are useful to describe relations between pre- and post-states.

**Definition 3** (Two-vocabulary Structure). *For states $\underline{M}$ and $M$ over the same vocabulary $\mathcal{V} = \langle \mathcal{C}, \{f\}, \mathcal{R}\rangle$ and with the same domain ($|\underline{M}| = |M|$), we denote by $\underline{M}/M$ the structure over the two-vocabulary $\mathcal{V}' = \langle \mathcal{C} \cup \underline{\mathcal{C}} \setminus \{\underline{\text{null}}\}, \{f, \underline{f}\}, \mathcal{R} \cup \underline{\mathcal{R}}\rangle$ obtained by combining $\underline{M}, M$ in the following way: $f$ is interpreted as $f^M$ and $\underline{f}$ is interpreted as $f^{\underline{M}}$, and similarly for all the other symbols.*

**Definition 4** (Backbone Differences). *For states $\underline{M}$ and $M$ over the same vocabulary $\mathcal{V} = \langle \mathcal{C}, \{f\}, \mathcal{R}\rangle$ and with the same domain ($|\underline{M}| = |M|$), the set $\underline{M} \oplus M$ consists of the "differences between $\underline{M}$ and $M$ w.r.t. $f$, excluding* null*", i.e. all elements $u$ of $|M|$ such that $f^M(u) \neq f^{\underline{M}}(u)$, as well as their non-*null *images in $f^M$ and $f^{\underline{M}}$.*

For example, in Fig. 3, let $\underline{M}$ be the left structure and $M$ the right structure. Then $M \oplus \underline{M} = \{x, r, \Box\}$, where $\Box$ is the unlabeled node with an edge from $x$ in the left diagram.

### 4.2 Modification Set

We must specify the **mod-set**, mod, containing all the endpoints of edges that are modified. Therefore when adding or deleting an edge $\langle s, t\rangle$, both ends — the source, $s$, and the target, $t$ — are included in mod. Often in programming language semantics, only the source is considered modified. However, thinking of the heap as a graph, it is useful to consider both ends of a modified edge as modified. For example, in the running example program `find` (Fig. 2), since new references to $r_x$ may be introduced as a result of path compression, the root $r_x$ is also considered as part of mod.

Our mod-sets are built from two kinds of intervals:

**Definition 5** (Intervals). The **closed interval** $[a, b]_f$ is

$$[a, b]_f \stackrel{\text{def}}{=} \{\gamma \mid a\langle f^*\rangle\gamma \wedge \gamma\langle f^*\rangle b\}$$

and the **half-open interval** $[a, \text{null})_f$ is:

$$[a, \text{null})_f \stackrel{\text{def}}{=} \{\gamma \mid a\langle f^*\rangle\gamma \wedge \gamma\langle f^+\rangle\text{null}\}$$

(notice that $\gamma\langle f^*\rangle\text{null}$ is always true in acyclic heaps).

**Definition 6** (mod-set). *The mod-set,* mod, *of a procedure is a union $I_1 \cup I_2 \cup \ldots \cup I_k$, where each $I_i$ may be $[s_i, t_i]_f$ or $[s_i, \text{null})_f$, $s_i, t_i$ are parameters of the procedure or constant symbols occurring in the pre-condition.*

In our examples, the mod-sets of `find` and `union` are written above each procedure, preceded by the symbol "@ mod' (Fig. 2). Note that it follows from Definition 6 that $\alpha \in \text{mod}$, is expressible as a quantifier-free formula.

**Definition 7.** *Given an appropriate state $M$ for proc with modset* mod, $\text{mod}^M$ *is the set of all elements in $|M|$ that are in one of the intervals defining* mod *(see Definition 5).*

### 4.3 Pre- and Post-Conditions

The programmer specifies $AF^R$ pre- and post-conditions. Two-vocabulary formulas may be used in the post-conditions where $\underline{f}$ denotes the value of $f$ before the call.

### 4.4 Specifying Atomic Commands

Table 2 provides specification of atomic commands. They describe the memory changed by atomic statements and the changes on the local heap.

***Accessing a pointer field*** The statement `ret = y.f` reads the content of the $f$-field of `y`, into `ret`. It requires that `y` is not `null` and that an auxiliary variable `s` points to the $f$-field of `y` (which may be `null`). It does not modify the heap at all. It sets `ret` to `s`.

| Command | Pre | Mod | Post |
|---|---|---|---|
| `retval = y.f` | $y \neq \text{null} \wedge E_f(y, s)$ | $\emptyset$ | $\text{retval} = s$ |
| `y.f = null` | $y \neq \text{null} \wedge E_f(y, s)$ | $[y, s]_f$ | $\neg y\langle f^*\rangle s \wedge \neg s\langle f^*\rangle y$ |
| `assume y.f==null;` `y.f = x` | $y \neq \text{null} \wedge E_f(y, \text{null}) \wedge \neg x\langle f^*\rangle y$ | $[y, y]_f \cup [x, x]_f$ | $y\langle f^*\rangle x \wedge \neg x\langle f^*\rangle y$ |

**Table 2.** The specifications of atomic commands. $s$ is a local constant denoting the $f$-field of $y$. $E_f$ is the inversion formula defined in eq (6).

It is interesting to note that the postcondition is quantfier free and much simpler than the one provided in [11]. The reason is that we do not need to specify the effect on the whole heap.

***Edge Removals*** The statement `y.f = null` sets the content of the $f$-field of `y`, to `null`. It requires that `y` is not `null` and that an auxiliary variable `s` points to the $f$-field of `y` (which may be `null`). It modifies the node pointed-to by `y` and potentially the node pointed-to by `s`. Notice that the modset includes the elements pointed to by $y$ and $s$, the two end-points of the edge. It removes paths between `y` and `s`. The postcondition asserts that there are no paths from $y$ to $s$. Also, since $s$ is potentially modified, it asserts that there are no paths from $s$ to $y$.

***Edge Additions*** The statement `y.f = x` is specified assuming without loss of generality, that the statement `y.f = null` was applied before it. Thus, it only handles edge additions. It therefore requires that `y` is not `null` and its $f$-field is `null`. It modifies the node pointed-to by `y` and potentially the node pointed-to by `x`. It creates a new path from `y` to `x` and asserts the absence of new paths from `x` back to `y`. Again the absence of back paths (denoted by $\neg x\langle f^*\rangle y$) is needed for completeness. The reason is that both the node pointed-to by `x` and `y` are potentially modified. Since `x` is potentially modified, without this assertion, a post-state in which `x.f == y` will be allowed by the postcondition.

### 4.4.1 Soundness and Completeness

We now formalize the notion of soundness and completeness of modular specifications and assert that the specifications of atomic commands are sound and complete.

**Definition 8** (Soundness and Completeness of Procedure Specification)**.** *Consider a procedure proc with precondition P, modset* mod, *post-condition Q. We say that* $\langle P, \text{mod}, Q\rangle$ ***is sound with respect to*** *proc if for every appropriate pre-state* $\underline{M}$ *such that* $\underline{M} \models P$*, and appropriate post-state* $M$ *which is a potential outcome of the body of proc when executed on* $\underline{M}$*: (i)* $\underline{M} \oplus M \subseteq \text{mod}^{\underline{M}}$*, (ii)* $\underline{M}/M \models Q$*. Such a triple* $\langle P, \text{mod}, Q\rangle$ ***is complete with respect to*** *proc if for every appropriate states* $\underline{M}$*,* $M$ *such that (i)* $\underline{M} \models P$*, (ii)* $\underline{M}/M \models Q$*, and (iii)* $\underline{M} \oplus M \subseteq \text{mod}^{\underline{M}}$*, then there exists an execution of the body of proc on* $\underline{M}$ *whose outcome is* $M$*.*

The following proposition establishes the correctness of atomic statements.

**Proposition 2** (Soundness and Completeness of Atomic Commands)**.** *The specifications of atomic commands given in Table 2 are sound and complete.*

The following lemma establishes the correctness of `find` and `union`, which is interesting since they update an unbounded amount of memory.

**Lemma 1** (Soundness and Completeness of Union-Find)**.** *The specification of* `find` *and* `union` *in Fig. 2 is sound and complete.*

We can now state the following proposition:

**Proposition 3** (Soundness and Completeness of adapt[])**.** *Let* mod *be a mod-set of some procedure proc. Let* $M$ *and* $\underline{M}$ *be two appropriate states for proc. Then,* $\underline{M} \oplus M \subseteq \text{mod}^{\underline{M}}$ *iff* $\underline{M}/M$ *augmented with some interpretation for the function symbol* $en^{\text{mod}}$ *is a model of* adapt[mod].

$$
\begin{aligned}
wp[\![\mathsf{skip}]\!](Q) &\stackrel{\text{def}}{=} Q\\
wp[\![x := y]\!], Q) &\stackrel{\text{def}}{=} Q[y/x]\\
wp[\![S_1 \;;\; S_2]\!](Q) &\stackrel{\text{def}}{=} wp[\![S_1]\!](wp[\![S_2]\!](Q))\\
wp[\![\mathsf{if}\ B\ \mathsf{then}\ S_1\ \mathsf{else}\ S_2]\!](Q) &\stackrel{\text{def}}{=} [\![B]\!] \wedge wp[\![S_1]\!](Q) \vee\\
&\qquad \neg[\![B]\!] \wedge wp[\![S_2]\!](Q)
\end{aligned}
$$

**Table 3.** Standard rules for computing weakest liberal preconditions for loop free code without pointer accesses. $[\![B]\!]$ is the $AF^R$ formula for program conditions and $Q$ is the postcondition expressed as an $AF^R$ formula.

## 5. Generating Verification Condition for Procedure With Sub-calls in $AE^{AR}$

We follow the standard procedures, e.g. [26], which generates a verification condition for a procedure annotated with specification using weakest (liberal) preconditions. Roughly speaking, for a Hoare triple $\{P\}prog\{Q\}$, we generate the usual verification condition $vc[prog] = P \rightarrow wp[\![prog]\!](Q)$.

For the basic commands (assignment, composition, and conditional) we employ the standard definitions, given in Table 3.

### 5.1 Modular Verification Conditions

The modular verification condition would also contain a conjunct for checking that mod affected by the invoked procedure is a subset of the "outer" mod. This way the specified restriction can be checked in $AE^{AR}$ and the SMT solver can therefore be used to enforce it automatically.

### 5.2 Weakest-precondition of Call Statements

As discussed in Section 2, the specification as it appears in the "ensures" clause of a procedure's contract is a local one, and in order to make reasoning complete we need to adapt it in order to handle arbitrary contexts. This is done by conjoining $Q_{proc}$ occurring in the "ensures" clause from the specification of *proc* with the universal adaptation rule adapt[mod], where mod is replaced with the mod-set as specified in the "modifies" clause of *proc*.

Table 4 presents a formula for the weakest-precondition of a statement containing the single procedure call, where the invoked procedure has the specifications as in Fig. 13, where "*proc*" has the formal parameters $\overline{x} = x_1, \ldots, x_k$, and it is used with $\overline{a} = a_1, \ldots, a_k$ (used in the formula) as the actual arguments for a specific procedure call; we assume w.l.g. that each $a_i$ is a local variable of the calling procedure.

In general it is not obvious how to enforce that the set of locations modified by inner calls is a subset of the set of locations declared by the outer procedure. Moreover, this can be tricky to check since it depends on aliasing and paths between nodes pointed

@ requires $P_{proc}$
@ mod $\quad$ $\text{mod}_{proc}$
@ ensures $Q_{proc}$
*return-type proc*$(\overline{x})$ `{ ... }`

**Figure 13.** Specification of *proc* with placeholders.

$$wp[\![r := proc(\overline{a})]\!](Q) \stackrel{\text{def}}{=} P_{proc}[\overline{a}/\overline{x}] \land \forall\alpha : \alpha \in \text{mod}_{proc}[\overline{a}/\overline{x}] \to \alpha \in \text{mod}_{prog} \land \forall\varsigma : Q_{proc}[\overline{a}/\overline{x}, \widehat{f}/f, f/\underline{f}, \varsigma/\text{retval}] \land \text{adapt}\left[\text{mod}_{proc}[f/\underline{f}]\right][\overline{a}/\overline{x}, \widehat{f}/f, f/\underline{f}] \to Q[\widehat{f}/f, \varsigma/r]$$

**Table 4.** Computing the weakest (liberal) precondition for a statement containing a procedure call. $r$ is a local variable that is assigned the return value; $\overline{a}$ are the actual arguments passed. $\widehat{f}$ is a fresh function symbol.

to by different variables. Fortunately, the sub-formula $\forall\alpha : \alpha \in \text{mod}_{proc}[\overline{a}/\overline{x}] \to \alpha \in \text{mod}_{prog}$ captures this property, ensuring that the outer procedure does not exceed its own mod specification, taking advantage of the interval-union structure of the mod. Since all the modifications (even atomic ones) are done by means of procedure calls, this ensures that no edges incident to nodes outside mod are changed.

**Proposition 4.** *The rule for wp*$[\![]\!]$ *of call statements is sound and complete, that is, when proc is a procedure with specification as in Fig. 13, called in the context of prog whose mod-set is* mod*:*

$$\begin{gathered} \underline{M} \models wp[\![r := proc(\overline{a})]\!](Q) \\ \Updownarrow \\ \underline{M} \models P_{proc}[\overline{a}/\overline{x}] \land \text{mod}_{proc}^{\underline{M}} \subseteq \text{mod}^{\underline{M}} \land \\ \forall M : \left(\underline{M}/M \models Q_{proc}[\overline{a}/\overline{x}] \land \underline{M} \oplus M \subseteq \text{mod}_{proc}^{\underline{M}}\right) \\ \Rightarrow M[r \mapsto \text{retval}^M] \models Q \end{gathered} \tag{7}$$

### 5.3 Reducing Function Symbols

Notice that when we apply the adaptation rule for $AE^{AR}$, as discussed above, it introduces a new function symbol $en^{\text{mod}}$ depending on the concrete mod-set of the called procedure. This introduces a complication: the mod-sets of separate procedure calls may differ from the one of the top procedure, hence multiple applications of Table 4 naturally require a separate function symbol $en^{\text{mod}}$ for every such invocation. Consider for example the situation of `union` making two invocations to `find`. In Fig. 14 one can see that the mod of `union` is $[x, r_x]_f \cup [y, r_y]_f$, while the mod of the first call `t := find(x)` is $[x, r_x]_f$, which may be a proper subset of the former. The mod of the second invocation is $[y, r_y]_f$, which may overlap with $[x, r_x]_f$.

To meet the requirement of $AE^{AR}$ concerning the function symbols, we observe that: $(a)$ the amount of sharing any particular function call creates, as well as the entire call, is bounded, and we can pre-determine a bound for it; $(b)$ the modification set of any sub-call must be a subset of the top call, as otherwise it violates the obligation not to change any edge outside mod. These two properties allow us to express the functions $en^{\text{mod}}$ of the sub-calls using $en^{\text{mod}}$ of the top procedure and extra intermediate functions with bounded image. Thus, we replace all of the function symbols $en^S$ introduced by adapt$[S]$ for different $S$'s, with a single (global, idempotent) function symbol together with a set of bounded function symbols.

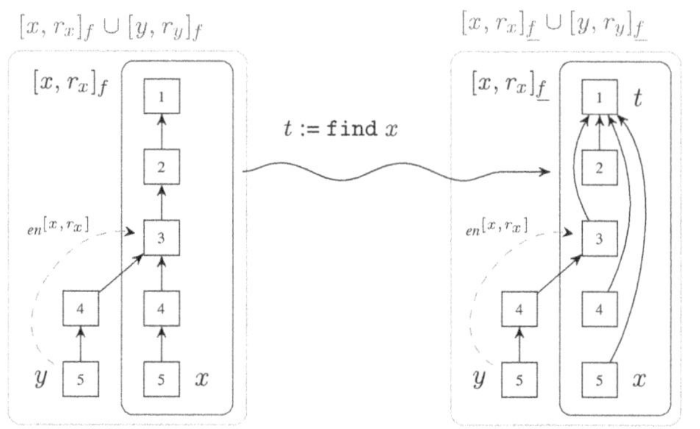


**Figure 14.** An example invocation of `find` inside `union`.

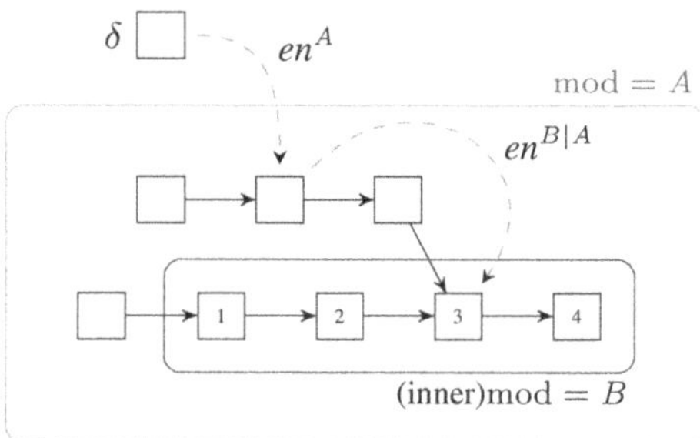


**Figure 15.** The inner $en^{\text{mod}}$ is constructed from the outer one by composing with an auxiliary function $en^{B|A}$.

Consider a statement $r := proc(\overline{a})$ in a procedure *prog*. Let $A$ denote the mod-set of *prog*, and $B$ — the mod-set of *proc*. We show how $en^B$ can be expressed using $en^A$ and one more function, where the latter has a bounded range. We define $en^{B|A} : A \setminus B \to B$ a new function that is the restriction of $en^B$ to the domain $A \setminus B$. $en^{B|A}$ is defined as follows:

$$en^B(\sigma) \stackrel{\text{def}}{=} \begin{cases} en^A(\sigma) & en^A(\sigma) \in B \\ en^{B|A}(en^A(\sigma)) & \text{otherwise} \end{cases} \tag{8}$$

Using equality the nesting of function symbols can be reduced (without affecting the quantifier alternation).

Consult Fig. 15; notice that $en^{B|A}(\sigma)$ is always either:

- The beginning $s_i$ of one of the intervals $[s_i, t_i]_f$ of $B$ (such as [1] in the figure);
- A node that is **shared** by backbone pointers from two nodes in $A$ (such as [3]);
- The value null.

A bound on the number of $s_i$'s is given in the modular specification of *proc*. A bound on the number of shared nodes is given in the next subsection. This bound is effective for all the procedure calls in *prog*; hence $en^{B|A}$ can be used in the restricted logic $AE^{AR}$.

### 5.4 Bounding the Amount of Sharing

We show that under the restrictions of the specification given in Section 2 and Section 4, the number of shared nodes inside mod — that is, nodes in mod that are pointed to by more than one $f$-pointer of other nodes in mod — has a fixed bound throughout the procedure's execution.

Consider a typical loop-free program *prog* containing calls of the form $v_i := proc_i(\overline{a}_i)$. Assume that the mod-set of *prog* is a union of $k$ intervals. We show how to compute a bound on the number of shared nodes inside the mod-set. Since there are $k$ start points, at most $\binom{k}{2}$ elements can be shared when *prog* starts executing. Each sub-procedure invoked from *prog* may introduce, by our restriction, at most as many shared nodes as there are local variables in the sub-procedure. Therefore, by computing the sum over all invocation statements in *prog*, plus $\binom{k}{2}$, we get a fixed bound on the number of shared nodes inside the mod-set.

$$N_{\text{shared}} = k + \binom{k}{2} + \sum_{proc_i} |Pvar_{proc_i}|$$

$Pvar^{proc_i}$ signifies the set of local variables in the procedure $proc_i$. Notice that if the same procedure is invoked twice, it has to be included twice in the sum as well.

### 5.5 Verification Condition for the Entire Procedure

Since every procedure on its own is loop-free, the verification condition is straightforward:

$$vc[prog] = P_{prog} \to wp[\![prog]\!]\big(Q_{prog} \wedge \text{“}shared \subseteq Pvar\text{”}\big)$$

where “*shared* $\subseteq$ *Pvar*” is a shorthand for the $(AE^R)$ formula:

$$\begin{aligned}\forall \alpha, \beta, \gamma \in \text{mod} : E_f(\alpha, \gamma) \wedge E_f(\beta, \gamma) \to \\ \alpha = \beta \vee \textstyle\bigvee_{v \in Pvar} \gamma = v\end{aligned} \tag{9}$$

See eq (6) for the definition of $E_f$. It expresses the obligation mentioned in Section 1.3 that all the shared nodes in mod should be pointed to by local variables, effectively limiting newly introduced sharing to a bounded number of memory locations.

Now $vc[prog]$ is expressed in $AE^{AR}$, and it is valid if-and-only-if the program meets its specification. Its validity can be checked using effectively-propositional logic according to Section 3.

## 6. Extensions

### 6.1 Explicit Memory Management

This section sketches how to handle explicit allocation and reclamation of memory and exemplifies it on simple procedures shown in Fig. 16 and Fig. 17. The procedures `push` and `pushMany` extend a list at the beginning by an unbounded of fresh elements allocated using `new`. The procedure `deleteAll` takes as argument a list that has no foreign pointers into it, and explicitly frees all elements. We verify that the procedures do not introduce dangling pointers.

Table 5 updates the specification of atomic commands (provided in Table 2) to handle explicit memory management operations. For simplicity, we follow Ansii C semantics but do not handle arrays and pointer arithmetic. The allocation statement assigns a freed location denoted by $s$ to retval and sets its value to be non-freed. All accesses to memory locations pointed-to by $y$ in statements `retval = y.f`, `y.f = x`, and `x = y` are required to access non-freed memory. Finally, `free(y)` sets the free predicate to true for the node pointed-to by $y$. As a result, all the nodes reachable from $y$ cannot be accessed.

The adaptation rule needs to be augmented in order to accommodate the change. Since nodes that are about to be allocated do not have names, the mod shall refer only to allocated nodes; free nodes can always be changed and they need not be specified in the mod. Of course, the procedure's post-condition should describe the new structure of the allocated area in terms of reachability, if modular reasoning is desired.

The change would be as follows: whenever there is a reference to some $\sigma \notin$ mod (in eq (3), eq (4), and eq (5)), we would now consider only $\sigma \notin (\text{mod} \cup \underline{free})$. This way the adaptation rule makes no claims regarding the free nodes. Everything else remains just the same.

@ requires $\neg free(h)$
@ mod $[h, h]_f$
@ ensures $\forall \alpha : free(\alpha) \leftrightarrow \underline{free}(\alpha) \wedge \alpha \neq \text{retval}$
$\quad\text{retval}\langle f^* \rangle h \wedge \neg \underline{h\langle f^* \rangle}\text{retval}$

```
Node push(Node h) {
  Node e = new Node();
  e.f = h;
  return e;
}
```

@ requires $\neg free(h)$
@ mod $[h, h]_f$
@ ensures $\forall \alpha : free(\alpha) \to \underline{free}(\alpha)$
$\quad\forall \alpha : \underline{free}(\alpha) \wedge \neg free(\alpha) \to$
$\quad h\langle f^* \rangle \alpha \wedge \alpha \langle f^+ \rangle \underline{h}$

```
Node pushMany(Node h) {
  if (?) {
    h = push(h);
    h = pushMany(h);
  }
  return h;
}
```

**Figure 16.** The procedure `push` allocates a new element and inserts it to the beginning of the list. The procedure `pushMany` calls `push`on the same list an arbitrary number of times.

@ requires $\forall \alpha, \beta : h\langle f^* \rangle \alpha \wedge \beta \langle f^* \rangle \alpha \to h \langle f^* \rangle \beta$ /* *dominance* */
$\quad\forall \alpha : \neg \alpha \langle f^+ \rangle h$
@ mod $[h, \text{null})_f$
@ ensures $\forall \alpha, \beta \in \text{mod} : \neg \alpha \langle f^+ \rangle \beta$
$\quad\forall \alpha : free(\alpha) \leftrightarrow \underline{free}(\alpha) \vee h \langle \underline{f}^* \rangle \alpha$

```
Node deleteAll(Node h) {
  if (h != null) {
    j = h.f;
    h.f = null;
    free(h);
    deleteAll(j);
  }
}
```

**Figure 17.** The procedure `deleteAll` explicitly reclaims the elements of a list dominated by its head, where no other pointers to this list exist.

### 6.2 Cyclic Linked-Lists

For data structures with a single pointer, the acyclicity restriction may be lifted by using an alternative formulation that keeps and maintains more auxiliary information [7, 13]. This can be easily done in $AF^R$, see [11].

### 6.3 Doubly-linked lists

To verify a program that manipulates a doubly-linked list, we need to support two fields $b$ and $f$. $AF^R$ supports this as long as the only atomic formulas used in assertions are $\alpha \langle f^* \rangle \beta$ and $\alpha \langle b^* \rangle \beta$ (and not, for example, $\alpha \langle (b|f)^* \rangle \beta$). In particular, we can specify the doubly-linked list property:

$$\forall \alpha, \beta : h\langle f^* \rangle \alpha \wedge h \langle f^* \rangle \beta \to (\alpha \langle f^* \rangle \beta \leftrightarrow \beta \langle b^* \rangle \alpha).$$

| Command | Pre | Mod | Post |
|---|---|---|---|
| `retval = new()` | $free(s)$ | $\emptyset$ | $\text{retval} = s \land \neg free(s)$ |
| `access y` | $\neg free(y)$ | $\emptyset$ | |
| `free(y)` | $y \neq \text{null} \land \neg free(y)$ | $\emptyset$ | $free(y)$ |

**Table 5.** The specifications of atomic commands for resource allocations in a C like language.

Unfortunately modularity presents another challenge: how the modset should be specified, and how to formulate the adaptation rule. Since there are two pointer fields (forward and backward), the adaptation rule (eq (1)) has to be instantiated twice. However that would require mod to be defined as a union of intervals also according to $b$ in addition to its being defined as such using $f$; otherwise our logical arguments from Section 2.3 no longer hold.

When the input is a valid doubly-linked list this can always be done, since $[\alpha, \beta]_f = [\beta, \alpha]_b$. In cases such where the input is somewhat altered or corrupt (for example [23]), the logic will have to be modified to incorporate the volatile exit points of back-pointers potentially pointing to arbitrary nodes. This extension is out of the current scope.

## 7. Experimental Results

### 7.1 Implementation Details

A VC generator described in Section 5 is implemented in Python, and PLY (Python Lex-Yacc) is employed at the front-end to parse modular recursive procedure specifications as defined in Section 4. The tool checks that the pre and the post-conditions are specified in $AF^R$ and that the modset is defined. SMT-LIB v2 [3] standard notation is used to format the VC and to invoke Z3. The validity of the VC can be checked by providing its negation to Z3. If Z3 exhibits a satisfying assignment then that serves as counterexample for the correctness of the assertions. If no satisfying assignment exists, then the generated VC is valid, and therefore the program satisfies the assertions.

The output model/counterexample (S-Expression), if one is generated, is then also parsed and $f^*$ is evaluated on all pairs of nodes. This structure represents the state of the program either at the input or at the beginning of a loop iteration: running the program from this point will violate one or more invariants. To provide feedback to the user, $f$ is recovered by computing eq (6)), and then the `pygraphviz` tool is used to visualize and present to the user a directed graph, whose vertices are nodes in the heap, and whose edges are the $f$ pointer fields.

### 7.2 Verification Examples

We have written modular specifications for the example procedures shown in Table 7. We are encouraged by the fact that it was not difficult to express assertions in $AF^R$ for these procedures. The annotated examples and the VC generation tool are publicly available with the submission. We only picked examples with interesting cut-points to show the benefits of our approach in contrast to [11].

To give some account of the programs' sizes, we observe the program summary specification given as pre- and postcondition, count the number of atomic formulas in each of them, and note the depth of quantifier nesting; all our samples had only universal quantifiers in the specification. We did the same for the generated VC; naturally, the the VC is much larger than the specification even for small programs. Still, the time required by Z3 to prove that the VC is valid is short.

Thanks to the fact that FOL-based tools, and in particular SAT solvers, permit multiple relation symbols we were able to express

| | |
|---|---|
| UF: find, UF: union | — Implementation of a Union-Find dynamic data structure. |
| SLL: filter | — Takes a linked list and deletes all elements not satisfying some predicate $C$. |
| SLL: quicksort | — Sorts a linked-list in-place using the Quicksort algorithm. |
| SLL: insert-sort | — Creates a new, sorted linked-list from a given list by repeatedly running `insert` on the elements of the input list. |

**Table 6.** Description of some pointer manipulating programs verified by our tool.

| Benchmark | Formula size | | | | | Solving time |
|---|---|---|---|---|---|---|
| | P,Q | | mod | VC | | |
| | # | $\forall$ | # | # | $\forall$ | (Z3) |
| SLL: filter | 7 | 2 | 1 | 217 | 6 | 0.48s |
| SLL: quicksort | 25 | 2 | 1 | 745 | 9 | 1.06s |
| SLL: insert-sort | 21 | 2 | 1 | 284 | 11 | 0.37s |
| UF: find | 13 | 2 | 1 | 203 | 6 | 0.40s |
| UF: union | 20 | 2 | 2 | 188 | 6 | 1.39s |

**Table 7.** Implementation Benchmarks; P,Q — program's specification given as pre- and post-condition, mod— mod-set, VC — verification condition, # — number of atomic formulas/intervals, $\forall$ — quantifier nesting The tests were conducted on a 1.7GHz Intel Core i5 machine with 4GB of RAM, running OS X 10.7.5. The version of Z3 used was 4.2, complied for 64-bit Intel architecture (using `gcc` 4.2, LLVM). The solving time reported is wall clock time of the execution of Z3.

ordering properties in sorted lists, and thus in the sorting routines implementing Quicksort and insertion-sort.

***Checked properties.*** For Table 6, apart from find and union, we also checked full functional correctness of the other examples (filter, quicksort, insertion sort). For filter, we checked that elements remain in the same order and that only the elements satisfying the filtering predicate were removed. For the sorting routines, we checked that the resulting list contains the same elements and is indeed sorted (via an order relation).

### 7.3 Buggy Examples

We also applied the tool to erroneous programs and programs with incorrect assertions. The results, including run-time statistics and formula sizes, are reported in Table 8. The table lists four kinds of deliberately-introduced bugs that were provided as input to the tool. Formula sizes are measured in the same way as in Table 7.

In addition, for every detected bug, our tool generates a concrete counterexample depicting a state of the heap violating some assertion. We measured the size of the model generated, by observing the size of the generated domain — which reflects the number of nodes in the heap. As expected, Z3 was able to produce concrete counterexample of reasonable size, producing output which is readable for the programmer and useful for debugging. In fact, our tool converts Z3 models into directed graph diagrams which facili-

| Benchmark (+ Nature of defect) | Formula size P,Q # | ∀ | VC # | ∀ | Solving time (Z3) | C.e. size (\|L\|) |
|---|---|---|---|---|---|---|
| UF: find<br>Incorrect handling of corner case | 27 | 3 | 201 | 6 | 1.60s | 2 |
| UF: union<br>Incorrect specification | 19 | 2 | 186 | 6 | 0.70s | 8 |
| SLL: filter<br>Uncontrolled sharing | 36 | 4 | 317 | 6 | 0.49s | 14 |
| SLL: insert-sort<br>Unmet call precondition | 21 | 2 | 283 | 9 | 0.88s | 8 |

**Table 8.** Information about benchmarks that demonstrate detection of several kinds of bugs in pointer programs. In addition to the previous measurements, the last column lists the size of the generated counterexample in terms of the number of vertices — linked-list or tree nodes.

tate debugging our assertions. Since the counterexamples are slight variations of the correct programs, size and running time statistics are similar.

# 8. Related Work

## 8.1 Modular Verification

The area of modular procedure specification is heavily studied. Many of these works require that the user declare potential changes similar to the modset (e.g., see [2, 14, 25, 29]). The frame rule of separation logic [9] naturally supports modular reasoning where the separating conjunction combines the local postcondition with the assertion at the call site. Unlike separation, reachability is a higher abstraction which relies on type correctness and naturally abstracts operations such as garbage collection. Nevertheless, in Section 6.1 we show that it can also deal with explicit memory reclamations.

We believe that our work in this paper pioneers the usage of an effectively propositional logic which is a weak logic to perform modular reasoning in a sound and complete way. Our adaptation rule is more complex than the frame rule as it automatically updates reachability. The idea of using the idempotent entry point function to enable local reasoning about list-manipulating programs (including an EPR reduction) has been explored independently by Piskac et al. [19], where it was used to automate the frame rule in separation logic. In this paper we identify a general EPR fragment of assertions for which this idea of the idempotent entry point function is sound and complete.

### 8.1.1 Cutpoints

Rinetzky et al. [21] introduce cutpoint objects which are objects that can reach the area of the heap accessible by the procedure without passing through objects directly pointed-to by parameters. Cutpoints complicate program reasoning. They are used in model checking [1] and static analysis [6, 22]. Examples such as the ones in [23] which include (unbounded) cutpoints from the stack are handled by our method without any changes. These extra cutpoints cannot change the reachabilty and thus have no effect. Interestingly, we can also handle certain programs which manipulate unbounded cutpoints. Instead, we do limit the amount of new sharing in paths which are necessary for the verification. For example, the find procedure shown in Fig. 2 includes unbounded sharing which can be created by the client program. A typical client such as a spanning tree construction algorithm will indeed create unbounded sharing. In the future, we plan to verify such clients by abstracting away the pointers inside the union-find tree.

## 8.2 Decision Procedures

Many decision procedures for reasoning about linked lists have been proposed [4, 15, 17, 28]. All these logics are based on monadic second-order logic on trees which has a non-elementary time (and space) asymptotic complexity. We follow [11] in using a weak logic which permits sound and complete reasoning using off the shelf SAT solvers which are efficient in practice and can be implemented in polynomial space. Indeed our preliminary experimental results reported Section 7 show that Z3 is fast enough and may be even useful for automatically generating abstract interpreters as suggested by [20].

Interestingly, the adaptation rule drastically simplifies the Weakest-Precondition rules given in [11]. Notice the specifications in Table 2 do not use quantifiers at all, whereas in [11] the formulas contain quantifiers with alternations. Indeed the appropriate quantifiers are added in a generic manner by the adaptation rule and weakest-precondition.

## 8.3 Incremental Reachability Update

Formulas for updating transitive closure w.r.t., graph mutations have been developed by various authors (e.g., [5, 7, 8, 13]). These works assume that a single edge is added and deleted. This submission generalizes these results to procedures which perform unbounded mutations. Indeed our adaptation rule generalizes [7, 11, 13]) which provides reachability update formula w.r.t. the removal of a single edge.

# 9. Conclusion

A crucial method for simplifying the reasoning about linked data structures is partitioning them into basic blocks, where each basic block has only one entry point and one exit point. This paper slightly generalizes by reasoning about blocks with a potentially unbounded number of entry points, as demonstrated by `find` and `union`. Notice that this unboundedness supports modularity: even in the case where in every particular call context there is a bounded number of paths (e.g. when there is a bounded number of roots in the heap), the bound is not known in advance, therefore the programmer has to prepare for an unbounded number of cases.

It is important to note that the adaptation rule adds expressive power to verifying programs: it is in general impossible for the programmer to define, in $AF^R$, a modular specification for all the procedures. Generation of a verification condition requires coordination between the separate call sites as mentioned above, in particular taking note of potential sharing. This coordination requires per-call-site instantiation, which, thanks to having the adaptation rule in the framework, is done automatically.

Finally we remark that there is a trade-off between mod and the post-condition: defining a simpler, but larger mod may cause the post-condition to become more complicated, sometimes not even $AF^R$-expressible. Also notice that if mod $= V$ (the entire heap), modular reasoning becomes trivial since it can be done by relational composition, but this puts the burden of writing the most complete post-conditions on the programmer, which sometimes is not even possible in a limited logic.

Therefore, we believe that this paper takes a step towards modular reasoning about reachability in programs that manipulate linked lists. Lifting such reasoning to more complex data structures such as trees and graphs remains future work.

***Acknowledgement.*** Thanks to the anonymous referees for their comments. Itzhaky, Lahav and Sagiv were funded by the European Research Council under the European Union's Seventh Framework Program (FP7/2007-2013) / ERC grant agreement no. [321174-VSSC] and by a grant from the Israel Science Foundation (652/11). Banerjee and Nanevski were partially supported by by Spanish MINECO projects TIN2009-14599-C03-02 Desafios, TIN2010-20639 Paran10, TIN2012-39391-C04-01 Strongsoft, EU NoE Project 256980 Nessos, AMAROUT grant PCOFUND-GA-2008-229599, and Ramon y Cajal grant RYC-2010-0743. Immerman was partially supported by NSF grant CCF 1115448.

## References


[1] M. F. Atig, A. Bouajjani, and S. Qadeer. Context-bounded analysis for concurrent programs with dynamic creation of threads. Logical Methods in Computer Science, 7(4), 2011.

[2] M. Barnett, M. Fähndrich, K. R. M. Leino, P. Müller, W. Schulte, and H. Venter. Specification and verification: the spec# experience. Commun. ACM, 54(6):81–91, 2011.

[3] C. Barrett, A. Stump, , and C. Tinelli. SMTLIB: Satisfiability Modulo Theories Library, 2013. http://smtlib.cs.uiowa.edu/docs.html.

[4] A. Bouajjani, C. Dragoi, C. Enea, and M. Sighireanu. Accurate invariant checking for programs manipulating lists and arrays with infinite data. In ATVA, pages 167–182, 2012.

[5] G. Dong and J. Su. Incremental and decremental evaluation of transitive closure by first-order queries. Inf. & Comput., 120:101–106, 1995.

[6] A. Gotsman, J. Berdine, and B. Cook. Interprocedural shape analysis with separated heap abstractions. In SAS, pages 240–260, 2006.

[7] W. Hesse. Dynamic Computational Complexity. PhD thesis, UMass in Computer Science, June 2003.

[8] N. Immerman. Descriptive complexity. Graduate texts in computer science. Springer, 1999.

[9] S. S. Ishtiaq and P. W. O'Hearn. Bi as an assertion language for mutable data structures. In POPL, pages 14–26, 2001.

[10] S. Itzhaky, A. Banerjee, N. Immerman, O. Lahav, A. Nanevski, and M. Sagiv. Modular reasoning about heap paths via effectively propositional formulas. Technical report, Tel Aviv University, 2013. `http://www.cs.tau.ac.il/~shachar/dl/tr-2013b.pdf`.

[11] S. Itzhaky, A. Banerjee, N. Immerman, A. Nanevski, and M. Sagiv. Effectively-propositional reasoning about reachability in linked data structures. In CAV, pages 756–772, 2013.

[12] S. Itzhaky, A. Banerjee, N. Immerman, A. Nanevski, and M. Sagiv. Effectively-propositional reasoning about reachability in linked data structures. Technical report, Tel Aviv University, 2013. `http://www.cs.tau.ac.il/~shachar/dl/tr-2013.pdf`.

[13] S. K. Lahiri and S. Qadeer. Back to the future: revisiting precise program verification using smt solvers. In POPL, pages 171–182, 2008.

[14] G. T. Leavens, A. L. Baker, and C. Ruby. Preliminary design of JML: a behavioral interface specification language for Java. ACM SIGSOFT Software Engineering Notes, 31(3):1–38, 2006.

[15] P. Madhusudan, G. Parlato, and X. Qiu. Decidable logics combining heap structures and data. In POPL, pages 611–622. ACM, 2011.

[16] N. Mitchell, E. Schonberg, and G. Sevitsky. Making sense of large heaps. In ECOOP, pages 77–97, 2009.

[17] A. Møller and M. I. Schwartzbach. The pointer assertion logic engine. In PLDI, pages 221–231. ACM, 2001.

[18] R. Piskac, L. M. de Moura, and N. Bjørner. Deciding effectively propositional logic using dpll and substitution sets. J. Autom. Reasoning, 44(4):401–424, 2010.

[19] R. Piskac, T. Wies, and D. Zufferey. Automating separation logic using smt. In CAV, pages 773–789, 2013.

[20] T. W. Reps, S. Sagiv, and G. Yorsh. Symbolic implementation of the best transformer. In VMCAI, pages 252–266, 2004.

[21] N. Rinetzky, J. Bauer, T. W. Reps, S. Sagiv, and R. Wilhelm. A semantics for procedure local heaps and its abstractions. In POPL, pages 296–309, 2005.

[22] N. Rinetzky, M. Sagiv, and E. Yahav. Interprocedural shape analysis for cutpoint-free programs. In SAS, pages 284–302, 2005.

[23] X. Rival and B.-Y. E. Chang. Calling context abstraction with shapes. In POPL, pages 173–186, 2011.

[24] R. E. Tarjan. Efficiency of a good but not linear set union algorithm. Journal of the ACM, 22(2):215–225, 1975.

[25] J. Wing. The CMU Larch Project. 1995. URL `http://www.cs.cmu.edu/afs/cs/project/larch/www/home.html`.

[26] G. Winskel. The Formal Semantics of Programming Languages: An Introduction. Foundations of Computing Series. Zone Books, U.S., 1993. ISBN 9780262731034.

[27] H. Yang, O. Lee, J. Berdine, C. Calcagno, B. Cook, D. Distefano, and P. W. O'Hearn. Scalable shape analysis for systems code. In CAV, pages 385–398, 2008.

[28] G. Yorsh, A. M. Rabinovich, M. Sagiv, A. Meyer, and A. Bouajjani. A logic of reachable patterns in linked data-structures. J. Log. Algebr. Program., 73(1-2):111–142, 2007.

[29] K. Zee, V. Kuncak, and M. C. Rinard. Full functional verification of linked data structures. In PLDI, pages 349–361, 2008.

# A Sound and Complete Abstraction for Reasoning about Parallel Prefix Sums *

Nathan Chong Alastair F. Donaldson Jeroen Ketema
Imperial College London
{nyc04,afd,jketema}@imperial.ac.uk

## Abstract

Prefix sums are key building blocks in the implementation of many concurrent software applications, and recently much work has gone into efficiently implementing prefix sums to run on massively parallel graphics processing units (GPUs). Because they lie at the heart of many GPU-accelerated applications, the correctness of prefix sum implementations is of prime importance.

We introduce a novel abstraction, the *interval of summations*, that allows scalable reasoning about implementations of prefix sums. We present this abstraction as a monoid, and prove a soundness and completeness result showing that a generic sequential prefix sum implementation is correct for an array of length $n$ if and only if it computes the correct result for a specific test case when instantiated with the interval of summations monoid. This allows correctness to be established by running a single test where the input and result require $O(n\lg(n))$ space. This improves upon an existing result by Sheeran where the input requires $O(n\lg(n))$ space and the result $O(n^2\lg(n))$ space, and is more feasible for large $n$ than a method by Voigtländer that uses $O(n)$ space for the input and result but requires running $O(n^2)$ tests. We then extend our abstraction and results to the context of data-parallel programs, developing an automated verification method for GPU implementations of prefix sums. Our method uses static verification to prove that a generic prefix sum implementation is data race-free, after which functional correctness of the implementation can be determined by running a single test case under the interval of summations abstraction.

We present an experimental evaluation using four different prefix sum algorithms, showing that our method is highly automatic, scales to large thread counts, and significantly outperforms Voigtländer's method when applied to large arrays.

***Categories and Subject Descriptors*** F.3.1 [*Logics and Meanings of Programs*]: Specifying, Verifying & Reasoning about Programs

***Keywords*** Parallel prefix sum computation; GPUs; abstraction; formal verification.

* This work was supported by the EU FP7 STREP project CARP (project number 287767), the EPSRC PSL project (EP/I006761/1), and an EPSRC First Grant (EP/K011499/1).



*POPL '14*, January 22–24, 2014, San Diego, CA, USA.
Copyright © 2014 ACM 978-1-4503-2544-8/14/01...$15.00.
http://dx.doi.org/10.1145/2535838.2535882

## 1. Introduction

The prefix sum operation, which given an array $A$ computes an array $B$ consisting of all sums of prefixes of $A$, is an important building block in many high performance computing applications. A key example is *stream compaction*: suppose a group of $n$ threads has calculated a number of data items in parallel, each thread $t$ ($1 \leq t \leq n$) having computed $d_t$ items; now the threads must write the resulting items to a shared array `out` in a compact manner, i.e. thread $t$ should write its items to a series of $d_t$ indices of `out` starting from position $d_1 + \cdots + d_{t-1}$. Compacting the data stream by serialising the threads, so that thread 1 writes its results, followed by thread 2, etc., would be slow. Instead, compaction can be performed in parallel via a prefix sum. Each thread $t$ writes its count $d_t$ to an array `count` at position $t$, then the threads perform an exclusive parallel prefix sum (defined formally in Section 2) on `count` to yield an array `index`. The prefix sum sets the elements of `index` to $[0, d_1, d_1+d_2, \ldots, d_1+\cdots+d_{n-1}]$, so that a thread $t$ can write its results to `out` compactly starting from position `index`$[t]$.

Stream compaction is just one example; the prefix sum operation is defined for any binary associative operator, and prefix sums using various operators have found wide application in computationally intensive tasks. A selection of examples are summarised in Table 1. For several decades the design of efficient parallel prefix sums has been an active research area. Parallel prefix sums were first implemented in hardware circuits as logic for propagating carry bits in adders [34]. The design space for these circuits has been explored and important circuits known in the literature are due to Kogge and Stone [21], Ladner and Fischer [22], and Brent and Kung [5]. More recent work by Sheeran [33] has further explored the design space. In software, prefix sum algorithms have been used in the context of evaluating polynomials in parallel [36] and Blelloch [3] has proposed the use of prefix sums as a primitive parallel operation, giving numerous examples of their application [4]. Prefix sums are now primitives in parallel programming models such as MPI [29] and OpenMP [35].

Recently there has been a great deal of interest in implementing efficient prefix sums for acceleration on massively parallel graphics processing units (GPUs) [2, 7, 12, 16, 26, 31], implemented using GPU programming models such as OpenCL [19] and CUDA [27]. The major benchmark suites for general-purpose GPU programming, SHOC [12], Rodinia [7] and Parboil [37] all include a variety of prefix sum implementations. The *thrust*[1] and CUDA Data Parallel Primitives (*cudpp*)[2] libraries implement efficient prefix sum primitives for NVIDIA GPUs.

We present a method for formally verifying that a *generic* parallel prefix sum implementation—designed to work for any data

[1] `http://code.google.com/p/thrust/`

[2] `http://code.google.com/p/cudpp/`

| Prefix sum application | Data-type | Operator |
|---|---|---|
| Stream compaction [2, 16] | Int | $+$ |
| Sorting algorithms [16, 30] | Int | $+$ |
| Polynomial interpolation [13] | Float | $*^a$ |
| Line-of-sight calculation [4] | Int | max |
| Binary addition [22] | pairs-of-bits | carry operator |
| Finite state machine simulation [22] | transition functions | function composition |

[a] Floating point multiplication is not actually associative, but is often treated as such in applications where some error can be tolerated.

**Table 1.** Some applications of parallel prefix sums. Stream compaction requires an exclusive prefix sum; the other applications employ regular prefix sums. The carry operator and functional composition are examples of non-commutative operators.

```
void prefixSum(const T *in, T *out) {
  out[0] = in[0];
  for(unsigned i = 1; i < n; i++)
    out[i] = out[i-1] ⊕ in[i];
}
```

**Figure 1.** A sequential prefix sum for inputs of length $n$

type with an associative operator—is functionally correct. Because prefix sum implementations are at the heart of many parallel applications, the correctness of these implementations is vital. The challenges of concurrent programming make it especially hard to correctly implement prefix sums for modern architectures such as GPUs. This motivates a dedicated verification method.

By observing that a generic prefix sum algorithm may only exploit the property of associativity, we have devised a novel abstraction which we call the *interval of summations* abstraction. For $i \leq j$, the interval of summations abstraction represents a contiguous summation interval of input elements $\texttt{in}[i] \oplus \cdots \oplus \texttt{in}[j]$ (with respect to any data type and associative operator $\oplus$) abstractly as a pair $(i, j)$. Abstract summation intervals can be added together if they 'kiss': the abstract sum of $(i, j)$ and $(k, l)$ is $(i, l)$ if $j+1 = k$; otherwise, the addition results in a special value $\top$ which represents all sums of input elements that are not necessarily contiguous. Summing any monoid element to $\top$ yields $\top$, modelling the fact that, using only the property of associativity, a non-contiguous summation of inputs cannot be made contiguous by adding more inputs. We present the interval of summations abstraction as a monoid, with an identity element representing an empty summation. This makes it possible to run a generic prefix sum implementation with respect to the data type and operator defined by the interval of summations monoid.

Our first main contribution is a theorem showing that a sequential generic prefix sum on $n$ elements is correct for all data types and operators if and only if, when instantiated using the interval of summations monoid and applied to the input sequence $[(0,0), (1,1), \ldots, (n-1, n-1)]$, it computes the correct result sequence: $[(0,0), (0,1), \ldots, (0, n-1)]$. This theorem shows that the interval of summations abstraction is sound and complete: by running a single test we can establish either that the generic prefix sum is correct (if the test passes), or that it is incorrect for one specific data-type/operator pair, namely that of the interval of summations monoid itself (if the test fails). Our result provides a highly scalable method for verifying sequential prefix sums: elements of the interval of summations monoid capable of representing intervals of up to length $n$ can be encoded using $O(\lg(n))$ bits, allowing a generic prefix sum to be verified by running a *single test case* requiring $O(n \lg(n))$ space for both the input and result. This is an improvement on a previous result by Sheeran [33, 38] which allows a sequential program implementing a prefix sum to be verified by running one test case requiring $O(n \lg(n))$ space for the input and $O(n^2 \lg(n))$ space for the result. For large values of $n$, this space requirement becomes infeasible. Our method is also more practically feasible than an alternative approach of Voigtländer [38] that uses only $O(n)$ space for the input and result but requires running $O(n^2)$ tests.

Our second main contribution is an extension of our method and theoretical results to the case of barrier-synchronising data-parallel programs, the programming model of GPU kernels. This is a contribution over previous work on the correctness of parallel prefix sums [33, 38] which applies to synchronous parallel hardware described as sequential HASKELL programs, but not to asynchronous concurrent programs. We show that if a data-parallel program implementing a generic prefix sum can be proved free from data races then correctness of the prefix sum can be established by running a single test case using the interval of summations monoid, as in the sequential case. We use this result to design and implement a highly automatic method for verifying parallel prefix sum implementations at the level of GPU kernel source code, using the GPUVerify tool [1] to prove data race-freedom.

We present a large experimental evaluation using four different prefix sum algorithms implemented as OpenCL kernels. We show that race-freedom of these kernels can be proven efficiently for all power-of-two element sizes up to $2^{31}$, and that verifying the kernels by running a single test is very fast: using two NVIDIA GPUs, two Intel CPUs (for which OpenCL is also supported), and an ARM GPU, prefix sums on vectors of up to length $10^6$ can be checked in a matter of seconds. We argue that, once race-freedom has been established, the method of Voigtländer [38] can also be used to prove correctness of prefix sum implementations using testing, but show that our method dramatically outperforms Voigtländer's approach, which requires running $O(n^2)$ tests.

Because we can efficiently prove data race-freedom of GPU kernels implementing prefix sums for all conceivably useful sizes, and because verification using our method involves running a single test case, taking no longer than using the prefix sum in practice, we claim that we have made a major step towards solving the problem of verifying GPU implementations of generic prefix sums.

## 2. Background on Prefix Sums

We briefly review the definitions of a prefix sum and an exclusive prefix sum, and give examples of sequential and parallel prefix sum implementations.

Given a set $\mathbb{S}$ with an associative binary operation $\oplus$ (i.e., a semigroup), the *prefix sum* of a list $[s_1, s_2, \ldots, s_n]$ of elements of $\mathbb{S}$ is the list:

$$[s_1, s_1 \oplus s_2, \ldots, s_1 \oplus s_2 \oplus \cdots \oplus s_n]$$

consisting of all sums of prefixes, in increasing order of length. For example, if we consider the set of integers under addition, the prefix sum of $[1, 3, 5, 7]$ is $[1, 4, 9, 16]$.

If $(\mathbb{S}, \oplus)$ has an identity element $\mathbf{1}$, so that $(\mathbb{S}, \oplus)$ is a monoid, then the *exclusive prefix sum* of $[s_1, s_2, \ldots, s_n]$ is defined as:

$$[\mathbf{1}, s_1, s_1 \oplus s_2, \ldots, s_1 \oplus s_2 \oplus \cdots \oplus s_{n-1}].$$

For example, if $\mathbb{S}$ is the set of all four-bit binary numbers and $\oplus$ is the *bitwise-or* operator with identity 0000 then the exclusive prefix sum of $[0001, 0010, 0100, 1000]$ is $[0000, 0001, 0011, 0111]$.

It is trivial to implement a sequential prefix sum: the C-like program of Figure 1 computes the prefix sum of `in` into `out`,

```
kernel void koggeStone(const local T *in, local T *out) {
  out[tid] = in[tid];
  barrier();
  for (unsigned offset = 1; offset < n; offset *= 2) {
    T temp;
    if (tid ≥ offset) temp = out[tid-offset];
    barrier();
    if (tid ≥ offset) out[tid] = temp ⊕ out[tid];
    barrier();
  }
}
```

**Figure 2.** Kogge-Stone prefix sum implemented in OpenCL

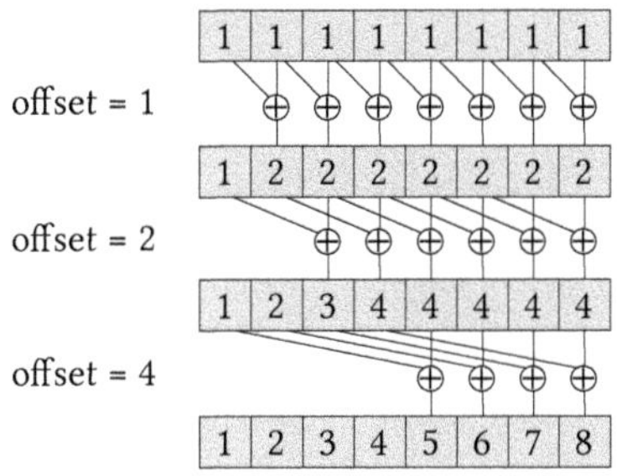


**Figure 3.** Evolution of the `output` array for the Kogge-Stone kernel of Figure 2 with $n = 8$ for an example input

where $T$ is some data type with associative binary operator $\oplus$. An exclusive prefix sum can be implemented similarly.[3]

Figure 2 shows the Kogge-Stone parallel prefix sum implemented in OpenCL and designed to be executed by a single work-group of $n$ threads.[4] The `koggeStone` function is marked `kernel` to indicate that it is the entry point for a GPU kernel, and arrays `in` and `out` have the `local` qualifier to indicate that they are allocated in GPU memory local to the work-group. Threads execute asynchronously, and a thread can use `tid` to access its unique thread identifier, in the range $\{0, \ldots, n-1\}$. Threads synchronise by calling `barrier()`, which causes all threads to wait until every thread reaches the barrier statement. On each iteration of the loop, every thread whose `tid` is greater than or equal to `offset` sums the value it has already computed with the value previously computed by the thread `offset` places to the left. Figure 3 illustrates how the `output` array evolves when the kernel is instantiated using integer addition and applied to the input $[1, 1, 1, 1, 1, 1, 1, 1]$, with $n = 8$.

## 3. Sequential Computational Model

We present a sequential imperative programming language, and define what it means to implement a correct prefix sum in this language. This provides a simple foundation on which to clearly introduce our interval of summations abstraction, which we do in Section 4. We extend our language, abstraction and theoretical results to apply to data-parallel programs (and in particular GPU kernels) in Section 5.

***Syntax and typing*** The syntax for our language is shown in Figure 4, where $c$ ranges over literal values, $v$ and $A$ over scalar and array variable names, respectively, and $op$ over an unspecified set of binary operators. Our presentation can be easily extended to cater for operators of other arities.

[3] For ease of presentation, we assume throughout that the input length $n$ is hard-coded into the program under consideration. In practice, $n$ would be supplied as a parameter.

[4] For readability, we deviate a little from the precise syntax of OpenCL.

| | | |
|---|---|---|
| expr $e$ | $::= c$ | literal |
| | $\mid v$ | variable |
| | $\mid A[e]$ | array element |
| | $\mid e_1 \; op \; e_2$ | operator |
| stmt $s$ | $::= v := e$ | variable assignment |
| | $\mid A[e_1] := e_2$ | array element assignment |
| | $\mid \text{if}\,(e)\,\{ss_1\}\,\text{else}\,\{ss_2\}$ | conditional |
| | $\mid \text{while}\,(e)\,\{ss\}$ | loop |
| stmts $ss$ | $::= \varepsilon$ | empty sequence |
| | $\mid s; ss$ | sequence |

**Figure 4.** Syntax

All variables, arrays and literals are typed (assuming some standard syntax for variable and type declarations, which we omit). Types for scalar variables and literals are drawn from a set of base types $\mathcal{T}$, ranged over by $T$, which includes at least integers and Booleans (denoted Int and Bool respectively)—equipped with the usual literals and operators—and the single-element type Unit. Array variables have type Array($T$) which denotes all maps of type $\mathsf{Int} \to T$. For ease of presentation we assume no out-of-bounds errors occur and we do not allow arrays of arrays. The language also omits features such as pointers, procedures and unstructured control flow. In Section 6 we argue that our technique extends to languages with these features.

The typing rules of the language are straightforward and are depicted in Figure 5. As usual there is a context $\Gamma$ which specifies the types of variables.

***Operational semantics*** Let Var be a set of variables and Arr a set of arrays all of which are assumed to be typed. A *variable store* $\sigma_{\mathrm{v}}$ is a mapping

$$\mathsf{Var} \to \biguplus_{T \in \mathcal{T}} T$$

such that if $v \in \mathsf{Var}$ is of type $T$, then $\sigma_{\mathrm{v}}(v)$ is of type $T$. An *array store* $\sigma_{\mathrm{A}}$ is a mapping

$$\mathsf{Arr} \to \biguplus_{T \in \mathcal{T}} \mathsf{Array}(T)$$

such that if $A$ is of type Array($T$), then $\sigma_{\mathrm{A}}(A)$ is of type Array($T$).

Expressions are evaluated under a variable store and an array store. Denoting the evaluation of an expression $e$ by $[\![e]\!]^{\sigma_{\mathrm{v}}}_{\sigma_{\mathrm{A}}}$, we define:

$$[\![c]\!]^{\sigma_{\mathrm{v}}}_{\sigma_{\mathrm{A}}} = c \qquad [\![A[e]]\!]^{\sigma_{\mathrm{v}}}_{\sigma_{\mathrm{A}}} = \sigma_{\mathrm{A}}(A)([\![e]\!]^{\sigma_{\mathrm{v}}}_{\sigma_{\mathrm{A}}})$$
$$[\![v]\!]^{\sigma_{\mathrm{v}}}_{\sigma_{\mathrm{A}}} = \sigma_{\mathrm{v}}(v) \qquad [\![e_1 \; op \; e_2]\!]^{\sigma_{\mathrm{v}}}_{\sigma_{\mathrm{A}}} = [\![e_1]\!]^{\sigma_{\mathrm{v}}}_{\sigma_{\mathrm{A}}} \; op \; [\![e_2]\!]^{\sigma_{\mathrm{v}}}_{\sigma_{\mathrm{A}}}$$

Figure 6 gives the operational semantics for our language. The semantics is defined over *program states* $\mathcal{S} = (\sigma_{\mathrm{v}}, \sigma_{\mathrm{A}}, ss)$ with $\sigma_{\mathrm{v}}$ a variable store, $\sigma_{\mathrm{A}}$ an array store and $ss$ a sequence of statements. In the figure, $ss_1 \cdot ss_2$ denotes the concatenation of sequences of statements $ss_1$ and $ss_2$. The rules are standard for an imperative language like ours, except that we have both a variable and an array store instead of just a single store. Although this split is not strictly needed here, it eases the extension to data-parallel programs in Section 5 where we shall regard variables as thread-local and arrays as shared among all threads.

Let a *program* $P$ be a sequence of statements. An *initial state of* $P$ is any program state with $P$ as the sequence of statements. Given an initial state $\mathcal{S}_0$ of $P$, an *execution of a program* $P$ is a finite or infinite sequence:

$$\mathcal{S}_0 \to_{\mathrm{s}} \mathcal{S}_1 \cdots \to_{\mathrm{s}} \mathcal{S}_i \to_{\mathrm{s}} \mathcal{S}_{i+1} \to_{\mathrm{s}} \cdots$$

with each $\mathcal{S}_i$ ($i \geq 0$) a program state. An execution is *maximal* if it (a) cannot be extended by applying one of the rules from the

$$\frac{c \text{ of type } T}{\Gamma \vdash c : T}\ (\text{T-LITERAL}) \qquad \frac{v : T \in \Gamma}{\Gamma \vdash v : T}\ (\text{T-VARIABLE}) \qquad \frac{A : \mathsf{Array}(T) \in \Gamma \quad \Gamma \vdash e : \mathsf{Int}}{\Gamma \vdash A[e] : T}\ (\text{T-ARRAY})$$

$$\frac{op \text{ of type } T_1 \times T_2 \to T_3 \quad \Gamma \vdash e_1 : T_1 \quad \Gamma \vdash e_2 : T_2}{\Gamma \vdash e_1\ op\ e_2 : T_3}\ (\text{T-OP})$$

(a) Typing rules for expressions

$$\frac{v : T \in \Gamma \quad \Gamma \vdash e : T}{\Gamma \vdash v := e : \mathsf{Unit}}\ (\text{T-ASSIGN}) \qquad \frac{A : \mathsf{Array}(T) \in \Gamma \quad \Gamma \vdash e_1 : \mathsf{Int} \quad \Gamma \vdash e_2 : T}{A[e_1] := e_2 : \mathsf{Unit}}\ (\text{T-ARRAY-ASSIGN})$$

$$\frac{\Gamma \vdash e : \mathsf{Bool} \quad \Gamma \vdash ss_1 : \mathsf{Unit} \quad \Gamma \vdash ss_2 : \mathsf{Unit}}{\Gamma \vdash \text{if } (e)\ \{ss_1\} \text{ else } \{ss_2\} : \mathsf{Unit}}\ (\text{T-ITE}) \qquad \frac{\Gamma \vdash e : \mathsf{Bool} \quad \Gamma \vdash ss : \mathsf{Unit}}{\Gamma \vdash \text{while } (e)\ \{ss\} : \mathsf{Unit}}\ (\text{T-LOOP})$$

$$\frac{}{\Gamma \vdash \varepsilon : \mathsf{Unit}}\ (\text{T-EMPTY}) \qquad \frac{\Gamma \vdash s : \mathsf{Unit} \quad \Gamma \vdash ss : \mathsf{Unit}}{\Gamma \vdash s; ss : \mathsf{Unit}}\ (\text{T-SEQ})$$

(b) Typing rules for statements

**Figure 5.** Typing rules of our sequential programming language

$$\frac{\sigma'_{\mathrm{V}} = \sigma_{\mathrm{V}}[v \mapsto [\![e]\!]^{\sigma_{\mathrm{V}}}_{\sigma_{\mathrm{A}}}]}{(\sigma_{\mathrm{V}}, \sigma_{\mathrm{A}}, v := e; ss') \to_{\mathrm{s}} (\sigma'_{\mathrm{V}}, \sigma_{\mathrm{A}}, ss')}\ (\text{S-ASSIGN}) \qquad \frac{[\![e_1]\!]^{\sigma_{\mathrm{V}}}_{\sigma_{\mathrm{A}}} = n \quad A' = \sigma_{\mathrm{A}}(A)[n \mapsto [\![e_2]\!]^{\sigma_{\mathrm{V}}}_{\sigma_{\mathrm{A}}}] \quad \sigma'_{\mathrm{A}} = \sigma_{\mathrm{A}}[A \mapsto A']}{(\sigma_{\mathrm{V}}, \sigma_{\mathrm{A}}, A[e_1] := e_2; ss') \to_{\mathrm{s}} (\sigma_{\mathrm{V}}, \sigma'_{\mathrm{A}}, ss')}\ (\text{S-ARRAY})$$

$$\frac{[\![e]\!]^{\sigma_{\mathrm{V}}}_{\sigma_{\mathrm{A}}}}{(\sigma_{\mathrm{V}}, \sigma_{\mathrm{A}}, \text{if } (e)\ \{ss_1\} \text{ else } \{ss_2\}; ss') \to_{\mathrm{s}} (\sigma_{\mathrm{V}}, \sigma_{\mathrm{A}}, ss_1 \cdot ss')}\ (\text{S-ITE-T}) \qquad \frac{\neg[\![e]\!]^{\sigma_{\mathrm{V}}}_{\sigma_{\mathrm{A}}}}{(\sigma_{\mathrm{V}}, \sigma_{\mathrm{A}}, \text{if } (e)\ \{ss_1\} \text{ else } \{ss_2\}; ss') \to_{\mathrm{s}} (\sigma_{\mathrm{V}}, \sigma_{\mathrm{A}}, ss_2 \cdot ss')}\ (\text{S-ITE-F})$$

$$\frac{[\![e]\!]^{\sigma_{\mathrm{V}}}_{\sigma_{\mathrm{A}}}}{(\sigma_{\mathrm{V}}, \sigma_{\mathrm{A}}, \text{while } (e)\ \{ss\}; ss') \to_{\mathrm{s}} (\sigma_{\mathrm{V}}, \sigma_{\mathrm{A}}, ss \cdot \text{while } (e)\ \{ss\}; ss')}\ (\text{S-LOOP-T}) \qquad \frac{\neg[\![e]\!]^{\sigma_{\mathrm{V}}}_{\sigma_{\mathrm{A}}}}{(\sigma_{\mathrm{V}}, \sigma_{\mathrm{A}}, \text{while } (e)\ \{ss\}; ss') \to_{\mathrm{s}} (\sigma_{\mathrm{V}}, \sigma_{\mathrm{A}}, ss')}\ (\text{S-LOOP-F})$$

**Figure 6.** Operational semantics of our sequential programming language

operational semantics or (b) is infinite. We say $P$ *terminates for an initial state* $\mathcal{S}$, if all maximal executions starting from $\mathcal{S}$ are finite. Note that the maximal execution is unique in the current case as execution is deterministic; this will no longer be so in the data-parallel case of Section 5. The proof that our type system and operational semantics satisfy the usual safety property—that types are preserved under execution and progress can always be made unless termination has occurred [28, Section 8.3]—is standard.

***Prefix sum algorithms*** We now define what it means for a program in our language to implement a prefix sum algorithm.

Recall from Section 2 that a prefix sum can be defined with respect to a semigroup, and an exclusive prefix sum with respect to a monoid. Because most prefix sums of interest in practice are over monoids we shall henceforth consider prefix sums over monoids. All the results we present restrict easily to the case of semigroups.

We shall write $M$ to refer to a monoid with elements $\mathbb{S}_M \in \mathcal{T}$, binary operator $\oplus_M$ (which we assume is a programming language operator) and identity $\mathbf{1}_M \in \mathbb{S}_M$. Moreover, we say that a variable $v$, respectively an array $A$, *is read-only in* $P$ if no assignment of the form $v := \ldots$, respectively $A[e] := \ldots$, occurs in $P$.

**Definition 3.1.** Let $M$ be a monoid, $P$ be a program, $n$ a natural number, and `in`, `out` arrays of type $\mathsf{Array}(\mathbb{S}_M)$ such that `in` is read-only in $P$. The program $P$ *computes an* $M$*-prefix sum of length* $n$ *from* `in` *to* `out` *for an initial state* $\mathcal{S}$ if $P$ terminates for $\mathcal{S}$ and for each final array store $\sigma_{\mathrm{A}}$ it holds that $\sigma_{\mathrm{A}}(\mathtt{out})(k) = \bigoplus_{M,\, 0 \le i \le k} \sigma_{\mathrm{A}}(\mathtt{in})(i)$ $(0 \le k < n)$.

The program $P$ *implements an* $M$*-prefix sum of length* $n$ *from* `in` *to* `out` if $P$ computes an $M$-prefix sum of length $n$ from `in` to `out` for every initial state.

Whether a program *computes* a prefix sum for a given input can be established by running the program; determining whether a program *implements* a prefix sum amounts to functional verification. Implementation of an exclusive prefix sum is defined analogously.

Designating the array `in` as read-only is for ease of presentation, making it sufficient to consider only the final array store in the above definition and avoiding the need to relate final and initial array stores.

We observe that Definition 3.1 quantifies over all possible final array stores to be able to cover the data-parallel case of Section 5. In the current sequential case the final array store is unique as execution is deterministic.

Henceforth we shall assume that a prefix sum is always from `in` to `out`, and shall simply talk about a program implementing an $M$-prefix sum of length $n$, or computing an $M$-prefix sum of length $n$ from an initial state.

## 4. The Interval of Summations Abstraction

We now turn our attention to proving the correctness of *generic* prefix sums: prefix sums that are designed to be polymorphic, so that they work for any type and operator that together have the properties of a monoid. We present our main theoretical result, that correctness of a generic prefix sum of length $n$ can be established by showing that the prefix sum is correct for one particular monoid, the *interval of summations monoid*, for one particular input.

***Generic prefix sums*** Let us extend our programming language with a fresh *generic type* $\mathbb{S}_X$, a new operator $\oplus_X : \mathbb{S}_X \times \mathbb{S}_X \to \mathbb{S}_X$, and a distinguished literal value $\mathbf{1}_X$ of type $\mathbb{S}_X$. We intend this generic type to represent an arbitrary monoid $X = (\mathbb{S}_X, \oplus_X)$ with identity $\mathbf{1}_X$.

We call a program that makes use of $\mathbb{S}_X$ a *generic program*. Akin to a generic method in JAVA, a template method in C++, or a function with a type class context in HASKELL, a generic program cannot be directly executed: it must first be instantiated with respect to a specific type.

**Definition 4.1.** Let $P$ be a generic program and $M$ a monoid. We write $P[M]$ to denote the program that is identical to $P$ except that every occurrence of $\mathbb{S}_X$, $\oplus_X$, $\mathbf{1}_X$ is replaced by $\mathbb{S}_M$, $\oplus_M$, $\mathbf{1}_M$, respectively. We refer to the process of obtaining $P[M]$ from $P$ as a *monoid substitution*.

If $M$ already occurs in $P$ then we cannot tell, from $P[M]$ alone, which uses of $M$ were already present in $P$ or originated from uses of $X$. We handle this issue as follows, to simplify our formal treatment: if $M$ occurs in $P$ then we choose a monoid $M'$ isomorphic to $M$ such that $M'$ does not occur in $P$, and we define $P[M]$ to be $P[M']$. For ease of presentation we still refer to the monoid $M'$ as $M$.

It is easy to see that monoid substitution is well-defined, and that if the abstract program $P$ is well-typed according to the rules of Figure 5 then applying a monoid substitution to $P$ leads to a well-typed program.

**Definition 4.2** (Generic prefix sums)**.** Let $P$ be a generic program. Then $P$ *implements a generic prefix sum of length* $n$ if `in` and `out` are of type $\mathsf{Array}(\mathbb{S}_X)$ and, for every monoid $M$, $P[M]$ implements an $M$-prefix sum of length $n$.

***The interval of summations monoid*** The key insight behind our result is the observation that a generic prefix sum can only rely on the properties of a monoid: associativity and the existence of an identity element. Relying on any additional properties specific to a particular operator, such as commutativity, idempotence or distributivity with respect to some other operator, would render the prefix sum inapplicable in general.

Suppose we wish to compute a prefix sum of length $n$ from array `in` into array `out`, with respect to an arbitrary monoid $M$. Thus `in` and `out` have type $\mathsf{Array}(\mathbb{S}_M)$, and the prefix sum operator is $\oplus_M$. If the prefix sum is correctly implemented then at the end of the computation each element of `out` must be the sum of a contiguous sequence of elements of `in`. For example, $\texttt{out}[0]$ should be equal to $\texttt{in}[0]$ and $\texttt{out}[3]$ to $\texttt{in}[0] \oplus_M \texttt{in}[1] \oplus_M \texttt{in}[2] \oplus_M \texttt{in}[3]$. As computation progresses, these contiguous summations are built up using the $\oplus_M$ operator, initially starting with individual elements of `in`.

Consider, for any $0 \leq k < n$, how $\texttt{out}[k]$ could be computed (to give the main intuition in a simple manner we ignore possible uses of the identity element): either (a) the existing value of a variable or array element could be copied into $\texttt{out}[k]$ or (b) $\texttt{out}[k]$ could be derived by summing two values of $\mathbb{S}_M$, $c$ and $d$, say, using $\oplus_M$. In the latter case

- $c$ and $d$ are summations of contiguous elements of `in`: $c = \bigoplus_{M,\, 0 \leq j \leq i_1} \texttt{in}[j]$ and $d = \bigoplus_{M,\, i_2 \leq j \leq k} \texttt{in}[j]$, for some $i_1$ and $i_2$ (where an empty summation is defined to be $\mathbf{1}_M$), and
- the summations $c$ and $d$ must 'kiss': we must have $i_1 + 1 = i_2$.

If $c$ and $d$ did not have these forms then, using only the laws of associativity and identity, it would not be possible to rewrite $c \oplus_M d$ into the form $\bigoplus_{M, 0 \leq j \leq k} \texttt{in}[j]$, the required value for $\texttt{out}[k]$. By a similar argument, if $c$ (similarly $d$) is in turn constructed by summing two values $e$ and $f$ then $e$ and $f$ must both be contiguous summations of elements of `in` that kiss, otherwise it would not be possible, using just the monoid laws, to rearrange $e \oplus_M f$ into the form of $c$. Continuing this argument we can see that a correct generic prefix sum must compute its result by successively summing partial sums of contiguous input elements that kiss; if a non-contiguous sum is ever constructed then this sum *cannot* contribute to the final prefix sum result.

We introduce a monoid, the *interval of summations monoid*, which captures abstractly the notion of contiguous summation intervals, and the operation of summing pairs of kissing intervals.

**Definition 4.3.** The *interval of summations monoid* $I$ (henceforth referred to as the *interval monoid*) has the elements

$$\mathbb{S}_I = \{(i_1, i_2) \in \mathsf{Int} \times \mathsf{Int} \mid i_1 \leq i_2\} \cup \{\mathbf{1}_I, \top\}$$

and a binary operator $\oplus_I$ defined by:

$$\begin{aligned} \mathbf{1}_I \oplus_I x = x \oplus_I \mathbf{1}_I &= x \quad \text{for all } x \in \mathbb{S}_I \\ \top \oplus_I x = x \oplus_I \top &= \top \quad \text{for all } x \in \mathbb{S}_I \\ (i_1, i_2) \oplus_I (i_3, i_4) &= \begin{cases} (i_1, i_4) & \text{if } i_2 + 1 = i_3 \\ \top & \text{otherwise} \end{cases} \end{aligned}$$

It is easily checked that $I$ defines a monoid with identity $\mathbf{1}_I$.

The interval monoid abstractly describes summations of elements of `in` with respect to an arbitrary monoid, say, $M$. A pair $(i_1, i_2)$ abstractly describes the summation $\bigoplus_{M,\, i_1 \leq i \leq i_2} \texttt{in}[i]$. The identity $\mathbf{1}_I$ represents an empty interval of summations, thus is an abstraction of $\mathbf{1}_M$. Finally, the element $\top$ represents all non-empty summations of elements `in` with respect to $\oplus_M$ that are not known to correspond to contiguous summations.

The $\oplus_I$ operator precisely captures the effect of summing two contiguous summations. For $i_1 \leq i_2 < i_3$,

$$\bigoplus_{M,\, i_1 \leq i \leq i_2} \texttt{in}[i] \oplus_M \bigoplus_{M,\, i_2+1 \leq i \leq i_3} \texttt{in}[i] = \bigoplus_{M,\, i_1 \leq i \leq i_3} \texttt{in}[i]$$

and, correspondingly, $(i_1, i_2) \oplus_I (i_2 + 1, i_3) = (i_1, i_3)$. The way $\oplus_I$ treats $\mathbf{1}_I$ expresses the fact that adding an empty summation to either side of a summation interval has no effect. Finally, the treatment of $\top$ by the operator captures the argument above: using only the properties of a monoid, it is not possible to transform a non-contiguous summation into a contiguous one by applying the $\oplus_M$ operator. Notice that $\top$ is an *absorbing element*, or *annihilating element*, of $I$: once a summation has become non-contiguous there can be no return.

Superficially, it may appear that the interval monoid is similar to the abstract domain of intervals that is commonly used in abstract interpretation [11]. The domains are in fact very different: an element $(i, j)$ of our interval of summations domain represents a single concrete value that can be expressed as a summation, whereas an element $[i, j]$ of the traditional domain of intervals represents the set of values $\{i, i+1, \ldots, j\}$.

We now define a condition on initial program stores which, for a given natural number $n$, ensures that the first $n$ elements of `in` are abstracted in the interval monoid by appropriate singleton summation intervals, and that all other array elements and variables of type $\mathbb{S}_I$ have values that are not known to be summation intervals.

**Definition 4.4** (Singleton condition for sequential programs)**.** Let $P$ be a generic program with `in` of type $\mathsf{Array}(\mathbb{S}_X)$. An initial state of $P[I]$ with variable store $\sigma_{\mathrm{v}}$ and array store $\sigma_{\mathrm{A}}$ satisfies the *singleton condition for* $n$ if

1. for all $v$ of type $\mathbb{S}_X$ in $P$, $\sigma_{\mathrm{v}}(v) = \top$;
2. for all $A$ of type $\mathsf{Array}(\mathbb{S}_X)$ in $P$ and $k \in \mathsf{Int}$,

$$\sigma_{\mathrm{A}}(A)(k) = \begin{cases} (k, k) & \text{if } A = \texttt{in} \text{ and } k \in \{0, \ldots, n-1\} \\ \top & \text{otherwise} \end{cases}$$

We can now state our main theorem which shows that, with respect to generic prefix sums, the interval monoid is a sound and complete abstraction: a program implements a generic prefix sum if and only if it implements a prefix sum when instantiated with the interval monoid. In fact, our result is stronger than this: it shows that correctness of a generic prefix sum can be established by considering the interval monoid instantiation only for those initial stores that satisfy the singleton condition.

**Theorem 4.5** (Soundness and completeness)**.** *Let $P$ be a generic program and $n$ a natural number. Then:*

> *$P[I]$ computes an $I$-prefix sum of length $n$ for every initial state satisfying the singleton condition for $n$*
>
> $$\Longleftrightarrow$$
>
> *$P$ implements a generic prefix sum of length $n$.*

Given a generic program $P$, the main proof idea is to simulate the execution of $P[M]$ for any monoid $M$ by $P[I]$, and vice versa, whilst relating the states encountered in the executions. To this end, we first define a reification function.

***Reification*** Let $M$ be a monoid and let $\mathsf{ArrayStore}$ denote the type of array stores. Define $\mathrm{Reify}_M : \mathbb{S}_I \times \mathsf{ArrayStore} \to \mathcal{P}(\mathbb{S}_M)$:

$$\mathrm{Reify}_M((i_1, i_2), \sigma_A) = \{\bigoplus_{M,\, i_1 \le i \le i_2} \sigma_A(\mathtt{in})(i)\}$$
$$\mathrm{Reify}_M(\mathbf{1}_I, \sigma_A) = \{\mathbf{1}_M\}$$
$$\mathrm{Reify}_M(\top, \sigma_A) = \mathbb{S}_M$$

Thus $\mathrm{Reify}_M$ maps a contiguous summation represented abstractly in the interval monoid to the set containing the corresponding concrete summation in the monoid $M$, and maps an unknown summation, represented by $\top$ in the interval monoid, to the full set of elements of $M$.

Let $P$ be a generic program and for a monoid $M$ let $\mathsf{State}_{P[M]}$ denote the set of all program states of $P[M]$. We lift $\mathrm{Reify}_M$ to map states of $P[I]$ to sets of states of $P[M]$. Formally,

$$\mathrm{Reify}_M : \mathsf{State}_{P[I]} \to \mathcal{P}(\mathsf{State}_{P[M]})$$

is defined by $(\sigma'_v, \sigma'_A, ss') \in \mathrm{Reify}_M(\sigma_v, \sigma_A, ss)$ if and only if

- for all $v$ of type $T$ in $P$
$$\sigma'_v(v) = \sigma_v(v) \qquad \text{if } T \neq \mathbb{S}_X$$
$$\sigma'_v(v) \in \mathrm{Reify}_M(\sigma_v(v), \sigma_A) \qquad \text{if } T = \mathbb{S}_X$$
- for all $A$ of type $\mathsf{Array}(T)$ in $P$ and $k \in \mathsf{Int}$
$$\sigma'_A(A)(k) = \sigma_A(A)(k) \qquad \text{if } T \neq \mathbb{S}_X$$
$$\sigma'_A(A)(k) \in \mathrm{Reify}_M(\sigma_A(A)(k), \sigma_A) \qquad \text{if } T = \mathbb{S}_X$$
- there exists a generic program $Q$ such that $ss = Q[I]$ and $ss' = Q[M]$.

Observe that the generic program $Q$ in the final condition is unique even if $I$ or $M$ is used in $P$, due to the discussion following Definition 4.1.

***Simulation*** We can now prove our simulation result.

**Lemma 4.6.** *Let $P$ be a generic program and $M$ a monoid. If $\mathcal{S}_I$ is a program state of $P[I]$ and $\mathcal{S}_M \in \mathrm{Reify}_M(\mathcal{S}_I)$ is a program state of $P[M]$, then*

- *if $\mathcal{S}_I \to_s \mathcal{S}'_I$, there exists a program state $\mathcal{S}'_M \in \mathrm{Reify}_M(\mathcal{S}'_I)$ of $P[M]$ such that $\mathcal{S}_M \to_s \mathcal{S}'_M$, and*
- *if $\mathcal{S}_M \to_s \mathcal{S}'_M$, there exists a program state $\mathcal{S}'_I$ of $P[I]$ such that $\mathcal{S}_I \to_s \mathcal{S}'_I$ and $\mathcal{S}'_M \in \mathrm{Reify}_M(\mathcal{S}'_I)$.*

*Proof.* Let $\mathcal{S}_I$ be a program state of $P[I]$ and $\mathcal{S}_M \in \mathrm{Reify}_M(\mathcal{S}_I)$ be a program state of $P[M]$. Moreover, let $Q$ be the generic program such that $Q[I]$ and $Q[M]$ are the program components of $\mathcal{S}_I$ and $\mathcal{S}_M$, respectively.

Observe that monoid substitution (Definition 4.1) satisfies the following algebraic laws for any monoid $M$:

$$(v := e)[M] \equiv v := (e[M])$$
$$(A[e_1] := e_2)[M] \equiv A[e_1] := (e_2[M])$$
$$(\text{if }(e)\,\{ss_1\}\text{ else }\{ss_2\})[M] \equiv \text{if }(e)\,\{ss_1[M]\}\text{ else }\{ss_2[M]\}$$
$$(\text{while }(e)\,\{ss\})[M] \equiv \text{while }(e)\,\{ss[M]\}$$
$$\varepsilon[M] \equiv \varepsilon$$
$$(s; ss)[M] \equiv s[M]; ss[M]$$

where it is immediate by the typing rules and the definition of generic programs that neither $\oplus_X$ nor $\mathbf{1}_X$ can occur in either the expression $e_1$ of $A[e_1] := e_2$ or the expression $e$ of a conditional or loop. For the same reason, it follows that if the first statement in $Q$ is a loop or conditional with guard $e$, then $e$ will evaluate identically in both $\mathcal{S}_I$ and $\mathcal{S}_M$. Thus, whatever the form of $Q$, the same rule from the operational semantics applies in both $\mathcal{S}_I$ and $\mathcal{S}_M$. Let the resulting program states after application of the rule be $\mathcal{S}'_I$ and $\mathcal{S}'_M$. By the algebraic laws it is now immediate that there exists a unique generic program $Q'$ such that $Q'[I]$ is the sequence of statements of $\mathcal{S}'_I$ and $Q'[M]$ is the sequence of statements of $\mathcal{S}'_M$.

It remains to show that the conditions on the stores of $\mathcal{S}'_I$ and $\mathcal{S}'_M$ are satisfied. If the applied rule was one of S-ITE-T, S-ITE-F, S-LOOP-T, S-LOOP-F, this is immediate, as the stores are identical before and after the steps.

For S-ASSIGN there are two cases to consider. If $v$ is not of type $\mathbb{S}_X$ in $Q$, it is immediate by the typing rules and the genericity of $Q$ that $e$ evaluates identically in both $\mathcal{S}_I$ and $\mathcal{S}_M$. If $v$ is of type $\mathbb{S}_X$ in $Q$, it follows by the typing rules and associativity of $\oplus_X$ that $e$ is an expression of the form $x_0 \oplus_X \cdots \oplus_X x_k$ where for all $x_i$ with $0 \le i \le k$ either (a) the identity element $\mathbf{1}_X$, (b) a variable or (c) an array element. For each $x_i = A[e']$, the expression $e'$ evaluates identically in both $\mathcal{S}_I$ and $\mathcal{S}_M$ by the typing rules and genericity of $Q$. The result is now immediate by the definition of $\oplus_I$ and the fact that (a) for each $x_i = \mathbf{1}_X$ we have $\mathbf{1}_M \in \mathrm{Reify}_M(\mathbf{1}_I, \sigma_A)$, (b) for each variable $v$ among $x_i$ we have by assumption that $\sigma'_v(v) \in \mathrm{Reify}_M(\sigma_v(v), \sigma_A(\mathtt{in}))$, and (c) for each $A[e']$ among $x_i$ we have $\sigma'_A(A)([\![e']\!]^{\sigma'_v}_{\sigma'_A}) \in \mathrm{Reify}_M(\sigma_A(A)([\![e']\!]^{\sigma_v}_{\sigma_A}), \sigma_A(\mathtt{in}))$, where $(\sigma_v, \sigma_A)$ are the stores of $\mathcal{S}_I$ and $(\sigma'_v, \sigma'_A)$ those of $\mathcal{S}'_M$.

For S-ARRAY observe that $e_1$ evaluates identically in both $\mathcal{S}_I$ and $\mathcal{S}_M$ by the typing rules and genericity of $Q$. Hence, the same array element is updated in each application of the rule. There are now two cases to consider, i.e., $A$ is or is not of type $\mathsf{Array}(\mathbb{S}_X)$ in $Q$. These cases are identical to those of S-ASSIGN. ☐

**Lemma 4.7.** *Let $P$ be a generic program, $M$ a monoid, and $n$ a natural number. If $\mathcal{S}_M$ is an initial state of $P[M]$, then there exists an initial state $\mathcal{S}_I$ of $P[I]$ satisfying the singleton condition for $n$ such that $\mathcal{S}_M \in \mathrm{Reify}_M(\mathcal{S}_I)$ and*

- *if $\mathcal{S}_I \to_s^* \mathcal{S}'_I$, there exists a program state $\mathcal{S}'_M \in \mathrm{Reify}_M(\mathcal{S}'_I)$ of $P[M]$ such that $\mathcal{S}_M \to_s^* \mathcal{S}'_M$, and*
- *if $\mathcal{S}_M \to_s^* \mathcal{S}'_M$, there exists a program state $\mathcal{S}'_I$ of $P[I]$ such that $\mathcal{S}_I \to_s^* \mathcal{S}'_I$ and $\mathcal{S}'_M \in \mathrm{Reify}_M(\mathcal{S}'_I)$.*

*Proof.* Let $\mathcal{S}_M$ be an initial state of $P[M]$. The lemma is immediate by induction on the number of steps applying Lemma 4.6 once we show that an initial state $\mathcal{S}_I$ of $P[I]$ exists that satisfies the singleton condition for $n$ such that $\mathcal{S}_M \in \mathrm{Reify}_M(\mathcal{S}_I)$. To this end, write $\mathcal{S}_M$ as $(\sigma'_v, \sigma'_A, P[M])$ and define $\mathcal{S}_I$ as $(\sigma_v, \sigma_A, P[I])$ with

- for all $v$ of type $T$ in $P$
$$\sigma_v(v) = \begin{cases} \sigma'_v(v) & \text{if } T \neq \mathbb{S}_X \\ \top & \text{if } T = \mathbb{S}_X \end{cases}$$

- for all $A$ of type $\mathsf{Array}(T)$ in $P$ and $k \in \mathsf{Int}$

$$\sigma_{\mathrm{A}}(A)(k) = \begin{cases} (k,k) & \text{if } A = \mathtt{in} \text{ and } k \in \{0,...,n-1\} \\ \top & \text{if } A = \mathtt{in} \text{ and } k \notin \{0,...,n-1\} \\ \top & \text{if } A \neq \mathtt{in} \text{ and } T = \mathbb{S}_X \\ \sigma'_{\mathrm{A}}(A)(k) & \text{otherwise} \end{cases}$$

That $\mathcal{S}_I$ satisfies the singleton condition for $n$ and that we have $\mathcal{S}_M \in \mathrm{Reify}_M(\mathcal{S}_I)$ is now immediate. □

*Proof (Theorem 4.5).* The $\Leftarrow$-direction is trivial, as $I$ is a monoid. For the $\Rightarrow$-direction, let $M$ be a monoid and $\mathcal{S}_M$ an initial state of $P[M]$. By Lemma 4.7 there exists an initial state $\mathcal{S}_I$ of $P[I]$ such that $\mathcal{S}_I$ satisfies the singleton condition and $\mathcal{S}_M \in \mathrm{Reify}(\mathcal{S}_I)$. All executions starting from $\mathcal{S}_I$ are terminating because $P[I]$ implements an $I$-prefix sum. By Lemma 4.7, for every terminating execution (and thus *every* execution) $\mathcal{S}_I \rightarrow^*_{\mathrm{s}} \mathcal{S}'_I$ there exists a corresponding terminating execution $\mathcal{S}_M \rightarrow^*_{\mathrm{s}} \mathcal{S}'_M$ such that $\mathcal{S}'_M \in \mathrm{Reify}_M(\mathcal{S}'_I)$. Moreover, these are the only executions of $\mathcal{S}_M$: if there would exist a non-terminating or another terminating execution starting from $\mathcal{S}_M$, then the induction argument from Lemma 4.7 would yield an additional execution starting from $\mathcal{S}_I$. Because $P[I]$ computes an $I$-prefix sum, we have for the array store $\sigma_{\mathrm{A}}$ of $\mathcal{S}'_I$ that $\sigma_{\mathrm{A}}(\mathtt{out})(k) = \bigoplus_{I,\, 0 \le i \le k} \sigma_{\mathrm{A}}(\mathtt{in})(i) = (0,k)$ for all $k \in \{0,\ldots,n-1\}$. Hence, by definition of reification for the array store $\sigma'_{\mathrm{A}}$ of $\mathcal{S}'_M$ we have that $\sigma'_{\mathrm{A}}(\mathtt{out})(k) = \bigoplus_{M,\, 0 \le i \le k} \sigma'_{\mathrm{A}}(\mathtt{in})(i)$ for all $k \in \{0,\ldots,n-1\}$. □

## 5. Extension to Data-Parallel Programs

We next consider data-parallel programs, or *kernels*, in which threads synchronise by means of barriers.

***Syntax, typing and semantics*** We extend the language of Figure 4 with a *barrier synchronisation* statement as follows:

$$\text{stmt } s ::= \ \cdots \mid \text{barrier}$$

The typing rule for barrier is straightforward:

$$\frac{}{\Gamma \vdash \text{barrier} : \mathsf{Unit}} \ (\text{T-BARRIER})$$

The typing rules for expressions and all other statements are as before (see Figure 5).

Given a finite set of thread identifiers $D \subset \mathsf{Int}$, a *kernel (program) state* is a tuple $(\sigma_{\mathrm{A}}, K)$ with $\sigma_{\mathrm{A}}$ an array store and $K$ a map from $D$ to (variable store, sequence of statements)-pairs such that for each $t \in D$ and variable store $\sigma_{\mathrm{v}}$ of $K(t)$ we have $\sigma_{\mathrm{v}}(tid) = t$. The array store $\sigma_{\mathrm{A}}$ represents arrays that are shared among all threads, and $K$ represents the local variables and instruction sequence for each thread. The variable $tid$ represents the identity of a thread, and must occur read-only in every program $P$. Our theoretical presentation does not depend on the existence of $tid$, but the prefix sum implementations we evaluate in Section 7 rely on each thread having a unique identifier.

Figure 7 gives the operational semantics of our kernel programming language, where $\rightarrow_{\mathrm{s}}$ is as defined in Figure 6. The semantics is a standard interleaving semantics (see rule K-STEP) with an additional rule for barrier synchronisation (rule K-BARRIER). Rule K-BARRIER checks whether all threads are either at a barrier or have terminated; the additional condition that at least one thread must be at a barrier ensures that rule K-BARRIER and termination are mutually exclusive.

The semantics assumes that statements are executed atomically, so that for example a thread can execute a shared state update such as $A[i] := A[j] + 1$ in a single step. This assumption is not valid in practice: such a statement would involve issuing separate (and possibly multiple) load and store instructions between which other threads could interleave. Even if we refined the semantics to reflect this, we would still need to account for the weak memory models of modern architectures. However, if a program is free from data races, which we define formally below, the effects of this assumption are not visible. The verification technique for GPU implementations of parallel prefix sums, which we present in Section 6, depends on proving that a GPU kernel is free from data races.

Our rules for barrier synchronisation follow the MPI programming model [14] in which it is valid for parallel processes to synchronise at syntactically distinct barriers. In GPU programming models, such as OpenCL and CUDA the rules for barrier synchronisation are stricter, requiring that all threads synchronise at the same barrier, and that if a barrier is inside a loop all threads must have executed the same number of loop iterations on reaching the barrier [19, 27]; precise semantics for barrier synchronisation in GPU kernels have been formally specified [1, 10]. Our results for the looser barrier synchronisation model of MPI makes our technique more widely applicable. Adding stricter conditions for barrier synchronisation does not affect our theoretical results, and the GPUVerify tool used as part of our verification method checks the stricter conditions required in the GPU setting.

Given a kernel program $P$, an *initial state of* $P$ is any kernel state $(\sigma_{\mathrm{A}}, K)$ where, for every thread $t$, the sequence of statements of $K(t)$ is $P$. An execution of a program $P$ starts from an initial state. Maximal executions and termination for an initial state are defined as for sequential programs. Note that the interleaving nature of the semantics means that there may be multiple maximal executions, contrary to the sequential case.

***Prefix sums and generic prefix sums*** Computation and implementation of a prefix sum is defined as in the sequential case (see Definition 3.1) with $P$ interpreted as a kernel program. A generic kernel program and generic prefix sum are also defined as in the sequential case (Definition 4.1).

***Interval monoid*** Employing the interval monoid as is (Definition 4.3), we extend the definition of the singleton condition to kernel programs, taking into account that there is now a variable store per thread.

**Definition 5.1** (Singleton condition for kernel programs)**.** Let $P$ be a generic program with in of type $\mathsf{Array}(X)$. An initial state $(\sigma_{\mathrm{A}}, K)$ of $P[I]$ satisfies the *singleton condition for* $n$ if

1. for all $t \in D$ and $v$ of type $\mathbb{S}_X$ in $P$, $\sigma_{\mathrm{v}}(v) = \top$ with $\sigma_{\mathrm{v}}$ the variable store of $K(t)$;
2. condition 2 of Definition 4.4 is satisfied

***Soundness and completeness*** Our soundness and completeness theorem for sequential programs, Theorem 4.5, can now be stated identically for kernel programs. The proof strategy is the same, using reification of abstract states to concrete states to set up a simulation, using lemmas analogous to Lemma 4.6 and Lemma 4.7. We explain the notable differences in how the proof is set up.

The $\mathrm{Reify}_M$ function is adapted to map states of kernel programs $P[I]$ to sets of states of kernel programs $P[M]$. The function treats the array store as before, but must take into account the fact that each thread now has its own variable store and program. Thus, while reification of array stores still operates at the level of the whole program state, reification of the variable store and program component now operates at the level of each individual thread. The definition is left unchanged otherwise.

The proof of Lemma 4.6 translates to the case of kernel programs by observing that

$$\text{barrier}[M] \equiv \text{barrier}$$

$$\frac{K(t) = (\sigma_V, ss) \qquad (\sigma_V, \sigma_A, ss) \rightarrow_s (\sigma'_V, \sigma'_A, ss') \qquad K' = K[t \mapsto (\sigma'_V, ss')]}{(\sigma_A, K) \rightarrow_k (\sigma'_A, K')} \text{(K-STEP)}$$

$$\frac{\left(\forall t : \exists \sigma_V : \bigvee \begin{matrix} (\exists ss : K(t) = (\sigma_V, \text{barrier}; ss) \wedge K'(t) = (\sigma_V, ss)) \\ (K(t) = (\sigma_V, \varepsilon) \qquad \wedge K'(t) = (\sigma_V, \varepsilon)) \end{matrix}\right) \qquad \exists t, \sigma_V, ss : K(t) = (\sigma_V, \text{barrier}; ss)}{(\sigma_A, K) \rightarrow_k (\sigma_A, K')} \text{(K-BARRIER)}$$

**Figure 7.** Operational semantics of our kernel programming language, extending the sequential rules of Figure 6

and that by this algebraic law and the algebraic laws from the proof of Lemma 4.6 we have that the same rule will be applied in both the case of $\mathcal{S}_I$ and $\mathcal{S}_M$, where the proof of Lemma 4.6 is embedded in the treatment of the K-STEP case.

In proving Lemma 4.7 for kernel programs, we must relate an initial state $\mathcal{S}_M = (\sigma'_A, K')$ of $P[M]$ to an initial state $\mathcal{S}_I$ of $P[I]$ that satisfies the singleton condition. Otherwise, the proof is identical to that of Lemma 4.7. The definition of the initial state $\mathcal{S}_I$ is easily adapted from the definition in the proof of Lemma 4.7 by applying the definition for the variable store to the variable store of each individual thread; the definition is left unchanged otherwise.

***Data race freedom*** We now define what it means for a kernel program to exhibit a data race. We show that if a kernel program is data race-free then, due to the properties of barrier synchronisation, the program computes a *deterministic* result. The verification technique we present in Section 6 depends on this guarantee of determinism and, as discussed above, establishing race-freedom of a kernel avoids the need to reason about weak memory semantics or the granularity of memory accesses.

Say that we *read from an array element* $A[i]$ in an execution step if $\sigma_A(A)(i)$ is referenced during the evaluation of any of the expressions occurring in the step. Likewise, say that we *write to an array element* $A[i]$ in an execution step if $\sigma_A(A)(i)$ is updated in the step. An *array element* $A[i]$ *is accessed* if it is either read from or written to in the execution step. Observe that an array element can be accessed multiple times in a single execution step, e.g., when evaluating $A[tid] := A[tid] \oplus_M \mathbf{1}_M$.

**Definition 5.2.** Let $\mathcal{S}_0 \rightarrow_k^* \mathcal{S}_n$ be an execution of a kernel program $P$. The execution is said to have a *data race* if there are steps $\mathcal{S}_i \rightarrow_k \mathcal{S}_{i+1}$ and $\mathcal{S}_j \rightarrow_k \mathcal{S}_{j+1}$ along the execution such that:

- distinct threads are responsible for these steps,
- a common array element is accessed in both execution steps,
- at least one of the accesses writes to the array element,
- no application of K-BARRIER occurs in between the accesses.

A program $P$ is *data race-free* if for every initial state $\mathcal{S}_0$ of $P$ and execution starting from $\mathcal{S}_0$ it holds that the execution does not have a data race.

**Theorem 5.3.** *Let $P$ be a generic kernel program and let $M$ be a monoid. Then: $P[M]$ is data race-free $\iff$ $P[M']$ is data race-free for all monoids $M'$.*

*Proof.* The $\Leftarrow$-direction is trivial, as $M$ is a monoid. For the $\Rightarrow$-direction, observe that neither the control-flow nor the array accesses can be influenced by the choice of $M'$ by the typing rules and genericity of $P$. □

We now argue that data race-free kernel programs behave deterministically. Say that *a barrier synchronisation occurs* during execution of a program whenever the K-BARRIER rule of Figure 7 applies. Suppose that a kernel program is race-free, and consider executing the program from an initial state $\mathcal{S}$. Race-freedom means that the execution of one thread cannot depend upon the actions of another until all threads participate in a barrier synchronisation. Thus while the threads may interleave nondeterminstically, their individual execution is deterministic and when the first barrier synchronisation occurs (assuming all threads reach a barrier without diverging), the program state $\mathcal{S}_1$ is deterministic. By a similar argument, individual thread execution until the next barrier synchronisation is deterministic, leading to a deterministic program state $\mathcal{S}_2$ when the second barrier synchronisation occurs. Applying this argument and using induction on program executions, we can prove the following:

**Lemma 5.4.** *Let $P$ be a data race-free kernel program and let $\mathcal{S}$ be an initial state of $P$. If there exists a finite, maximal execution starting from $\mathcal{S}$ with final array store $\sigma_A$, then all executions starting from $\mathcal{S}$ are finite and for all maximal executions the final array store is $\sigma_A$.*

## 6. An Automated Verification Technique

Our theoretical results show that to verify functional correctness of a generic parallel prefix sum of length $n$, implemented as a barrier-synchronising program, it suffices to prove that the program is free from data races and then test that the program behaves correctly with respect to the interval monoid for every initial state with `in` $= [(0, 0), (1, 1), \ldots, (n-1, n-1)]$. In practice, a library routine for computing a prefix sum takes no input except for `in` so that there is just a single input to test.

GPU kernels are barrier synchronising programs that are *required* to be data race-free: the semantics of an OpenCL or CUDA kernel is undefined if the kernel exhibits data races [19, 27]. Thus our results suggest the following method for verifying functional correctness of GPU kernels that claim to implement generic prefix sums with respect to a single input array:

1. Prove that the GPU kernel is data race-free.
2. Run the interval monoid test to check functional correctness.

Steps 1 and 2 can be conducted independently, but the functional correctness guarantee provided by step 2 is conditional on the result of step 1. We now discuss how we have implemented a practical verification method for generic prefix sums written in OpenCL, based on this approach.

***Representing a generic prefix sum*** The OpenCL programming model does not support generic functions directly. However, it is easy to describe a generic prefix sum by writing a kernel that uses a symbol `TYPE` and a macro `OPERATOR` as placeholders for the concrete type and operator with respect to which the prefix sum should be executed. A concrete choice of type and operator can be chosen by including a header file that specifies `TYPE` and `OPERATOR`.

***Race analysis*** Step 1 above can be discharged to any sound verifier for GPU kernels capable of proving race-freedom. For GPU kernels this includes the PUG [24] and GPUVerify [1] tools, which rely on SMT solvers, and the tool described in [23] which performs verification using a combination of dynamic and static analysis. In our experiments (Section 7) we use the GPUVerify tool because it is actively maintained and publicly available, and is the only tool supporting the multi-platform OpenCL programming model, which allows us to evaluate step 2 above on a number of platforms.

By Theorem 5.3, we can prove race-freedom of a generic prefix sum using any choice of `TYPE` and `OPERATOR`. In our experiments we use the interval monoid.

***Running the interval monoid test case*** Step 2 above requires an encoding of the interval monoid. Observe that to check a prefix sum of length $n$ we need only encode elements $(i, j)$ of the interval monoid for $0 \leq i \leq j < n$, as well as the $\mathbf{1}_I$ and $\top$ elements. An element can thus be encoded using $O(\lg(n))$ bits, meaning that $O(n \lg(n))$ space is required for the test input and result. With this encoding, the interval monoid test case can be executed as a regular OpenCL kernel.

***Soundness, completeness and automation*** Our verification strategy is sound due to the guarantees provided by the version of Theorem 4.5 for kernel programs, together with Theorem 5.3 and Lemma 5.4, and the requirement that a sound method for verifying race-freedom is used. As with any dynamic technique, soundness of the testing phase of our approach depends on the probity of the compiler, driver and hardware implementation of the architecture on which the test is executed. In our experiments we guard against this source of unsoundness by testing with respect to multiple, diverse platforms.

Our verification strategy is only *complete* if the technique used to prove race freedom is complete. The GPUVerify method which we employ is not complete: the technique uses both thread abstraction and loop invariant abstraction, which can lead to false positive data race reports.

A small amount of manual effort is required in order to prove race-freedom of prefix sum kernels: GPUVerify tries to perform automatic inference of invariants required to prove race-freedom, but often this inference is not strong enough and manual invariants must be supplied by the programmer. However, these invariants are *checked* by GPUVerify—they are not taken on trust by the tool. In the examples we consider in Section 7 we disabled automatic invariant inference and supplied a small number of relatively simple, non-quantified loop invariants by hand. The dynamic analysis phase of our verification method is fully automatic.

***Handling extended programming language features*** Our sequential language and its data-parallel extension omit real-world language features such as procedures, unstructured control flow, and pointers (with associated aliasing issues). We are confident that our results apply directly in this extended setting under the condition that data of generic type $\mathbb{S}_X$ are never accessed via pointers with different element types. This is important for the testing part of our approach; without this restriction it would be possible to pass our test case by casting the `out` array to a `char` pointer and writing the desired final result for the interval monoid byte-by-byte. Proving race-freedom in the presence of intricate pointer manipulation can be challenging, but is possible with the right invariants and is supported by GPUVerify. Because GPUVerify operates at the level of control flow graphs using the techniques of [10], unstructured control flow is also supported.

Nevertheless, the prefix sum implementations we have seen in practice do *not* manipulate pointers in complex ways, call auxiliary procedures or exhibit unstructured control flow.

As discussed in Section 3, the requirement that the input array `in` be read-only is for ease of presentation only and can be dropped in practice, allowing our technique to be used in verifying prefix sums that operate in place.

| Algorithm | Depth | Size | Fanout |
|---|---|---|---|
| Sequential | $n$ | $n$ | 2 |
| Kogge-Stone | $\lg n$ | $n \lg n - (n-1)$ | 2 |
| Sklansky | $\lg n$ | $(n/2) \lg n$ | $n$ |
| Brent-Kung | $(2 \lg n) - 1$ | $2n - \lg n - 2$ | 2 |
| Blelloch | $2 \lg n$ | $2(n-1)$ | 2 |

**Table 2.** Characteristics of the prefix sum algorithms considered in this paper where $n$ is the number of elements

## 7. Experimental Evaluation

We demonstrate the effectiveness of our method for prefix sum verification in practice by applying it to four different algorithms implemented as OpenCL kernels.

All materials required to reproduce our experimental results, including implementations all kernels, are available online.[5]

***Details of prefix sum kernels*** We evaluate our technique using four different, well-known prefix sum algorithms: Kogge-Stone [21], Sklansky [34], Brent-Kung [5] and Blelloch [4]. The Blelloch algorithm is an exclusive prefix sum.

Figure 8 provides a circuit diagram description for each algorithm. There is a wire for each input and data flows top-down through the circuit. Each node • performs the binary associative operator on its two inputs and produces an output that passes downward and also optionally across the circuit (through a diagonal wire). Table 2 gives a comparison of these algorithms, as well as the straightforward sequential implementation, in terms of circuit characteristics: *depth*, the number of levels; *size*, the number of nodes; and *fanout*, the maximum number of outbound wires per node, as the size of the input (or width) $n$ of the circuit varies. The depth of a circuit indicates how long it takes for the result to propagate through the circuit, and thus dictates the time taken for prefix sum computation. Size indicates how many gates would be required to build the circuit in hardware, while fanout indicates the required driving capacitance of the output gate. A software implementation of a prefix sum is *work efficient* if the number of operations required is within the same order of magnitude as the sequential version. The size column of Figure 2 indicates that Blelloch and Brent-Kung are work-efficient, while Kogge-Stone and Sklansky are not. A more detailed discussion of these characteristics can be found in [16].

Through a survey of several GPU code repositories (the AMD APP SDK,[6] the NVIDIA CUDA SDK,[7] and the SHOC [12], Rodinia [7] and Parboil [37] benchmarks) we found Kogge-Stone to be the most widely used GPU implementation of a prefix sum in practice, Blelloch to be used where an exclusive prefix sum is required, and Brent-Kung employed several times in one large CUDA kernel that computes eigenvalues of a matrix. Sklansky is the oldest prefix sum algorithm we consider; we did not see it used in practical GPU kernels.

***Experimental setup*** As discussed in Section 6, we use the GPUVerify tool [1] to prove that each kernel is free from data races. These experiments were performed on a Linux machine with a 1.15 GHz AMD Phenom 9600B 4 core processor, using a version of GPUVerify downloaded from the tool web page[8] on 26 June 2013.

We then verify functional correctness for each kernel by running the interval of summations test case. We give results for five different platforms: two NVIDIA GPUs – a 1.16 GHz GeForce GTX 570

[5] `http://multicore.doc.ic.ac.uk/tools/GPUVerify/POPL14`

[6] `http://developer.amd.com/tools/heterogeneous-computing/amd-accelerated-parallel-processing-app-sdk/`

[7] `https://developer.nvidia.com/gpu-computing-sdk`

[8] `http://multicore.doc.ic.ac.uk/tools/GPUVerify/`

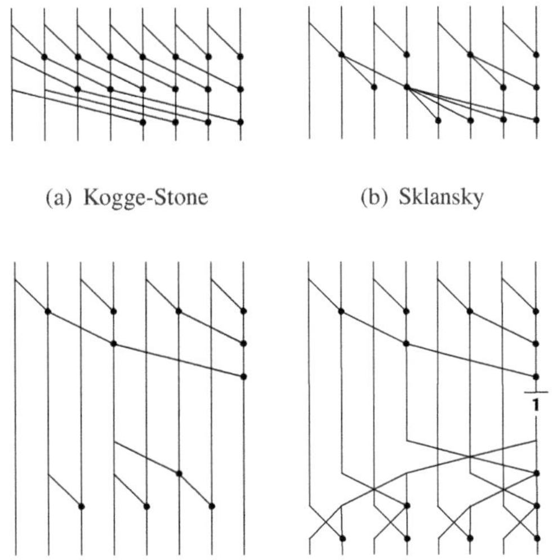


(a) Kogge-Stone (b) Sklansky

(c) Brent-Kung (d) Blelloch

**Figure 8.** Circuit representations of the prefix sum algorithms for $n = 8$ elements

and a 1.15 GHz Tesla M2050; two Intel CPUs – a 2.13 GHz 4 core Xeon E5606 and a 2.67 GHz 6 core Xeon X5650; and one ARM GPU – a 533 MHz 4 core Mali T604. These devices exhibit a range of power and performance characteristics. The NVIDIA GPUs offer a large number of parallel processing elements running at a relatively low clock-rate; the Intel CPUs run at a higher clock-rate but exhibit less parallelism; and the ARM GPU is designed for high power-efficiency. We chose to run on multiple platforms to guard against possible unsound results as a result of a particular compiler, driver or hardware configuration. Each experiment was run with a timeout of 1 hour. All the timing results we present are averages over three runs.

In [38], Voigtländer shows for sequential programs that a generic prefix sum is correct for all input lengths if it can be shown to behave correctly for all input lengths with respect to two binary operators over a set of three elements. He shows further that it is sufficient to consider $O(n^2)$ test inputs: $n(n+1)/2$ tests using the first operator and $n-1$ tests using the second operator. The result of [38] considers *all* possible $n$, but also restricts so that a prefix sum of a specific length $n$ can be shown correct by testing the corresponding set of inputs. Our Lemma 5.4 allows us to lift this method to race-free barrier-synchronising programs. Thus, by way of comparison, we also tried dynamically verifying the prefix sum kernels by running, for each element size, the set of Voigtländer tests. We discuss Voigtländer's paper further in the related work (Section 8).

Verification using the interval of summations test case and the Voigtländer tests both require race-freedom to be established, thus the overhead of race checking applies to both approaches.

***Results for proving race-freedom*** Table 3 presents verification times, in seconds, for proving race-freedom of each of our prefix sum kernels using GPUVerify, for a selection of power-of-two element counts up to $2^{31}$. Times for the power-of-two thread counts not shown are in the same order of magnitude.

The results show that verification time is more-or-less independent of the number of threads executing the kernel. This is because GPUVerify checks race-freedom for a kernel with respect to an arbitrary pair of threads, and reasons about loops using invariants rather than by unrolling. This excellent scalability demonstrates that the data race analysis aspect of our verification method is practical for very large arrays.

As noted in Section 6, we disabled automatic invariant inference in GPUVerify as it did not allow fully automatic verification of our examples. Instead we provided relatively simple, non-quantified loop invariants for each of our kernels in order for verification to succeed. For example, for the loop of the Kogge-Stone kernel shown in Figure 2 we provided the following invariant (no further invariants were necessary):

$$\mathsf{no\_read}(\mathsf{out}) \wedge \mathsf{no\_write}(\mathsf{out})$$

which specifies that no access to the out array is in-flight at the head of the loop. The most intricate invariant we had to specify, for the Blelloch kernel, was:

$$(\mathsf{d}\ \&\ (\mathsf{d}-1)) = 0 \wedge ((\mathsf{offset} = 0 \wedge \mathsf{d} = N) \vee \mathsf{d} * \mathsf{offset} = N)\,.$$

Here, d and offset are loop counters, with d increasing in powers-of-two from 1 to $N$, and offset decreasing in powers-of-two from $N$ to 1, and finally reaching zero. The conjunct $(\mathsf{d}\ \&\ (\mathsf{d}-1)) = 0$ uses the bitwise-and operator, &, to compactly express that $d$ must be a power-of-two or zero.

Counting each top-level conjunct of a loop invariant as a separate invariant, the number of invariants required for verification of each kernel was as follows: (Kogge-Stone, 2); (Sklansky, 1); (Brent-Kung, 4); (Blelloch, 6). The invariants did not have to be tailored for individual thread counts.

***Results for dynamic analysis*** The **I** rows of Table 4 present, for each prefix sum and platform, the time in seconds taken to run the single interval of summations test for power-of-two array sizes from $2^9$ to $2^{14}$ and $2^{18}$ to $2^{20}$ (results in between follow a similar trend). For each array size we also show in the **#Voigtländer tests** row the total number of tests that would need to be run to verify the kernel using Voigtländer's method and the **V** rows show how long these tests took to run. The times are end-to-end, taking into account device initialisation, creation of memory buffers, compilation of the OpenCL kernel,[9] copying data into memory buffers, running the test and validating the result. For the Voigtländer tests we used a wrapper so that device initialisation, creation of memory buffers and kernel compilation is performed only once for each array size. We note that while in theory an array of length $n$ can be processed by $n/2$ concurrent threads (or $n$ threads in the case of Kogge-Stone), it is up to the OpenCL runtime to decide how to schedule threads across hardware resources, and that in practice a large number of threads will be launched in a series of waves.

From the **I** rows it can be seen that running the interval of summations test case is very fast on all platforms, even for arrays of length $2^{20}$. It may seem surprising that the runtime does not increase significantly as the array size increases. This is because (a) computing with the interval monoid is very cheap, requiring only integer equality testing and addition by a constant and (b) the expense of online compilation of the OpenCL kernel, which dominates the runtime of these simple tests.

The **V** rows show that, unsurprisingly, running a quadratic number of tests per array size does not scale well. On all platforms, we found that sizes of $n \geq 2^{14}$ exhausted our time limit of 1 hour, showing that the Voigtländer method will not scale to large arrays.

## 8. Related Work

***Relationship to results by Voigtländer and Sheeran*** The closest work to this paper is work by Voigtländer [38] which proves two interesting results for sequential generic prefix sums.

[9] In the OpenCL model, a kernel is compiled at runtime using an online compiler, so that it need not be pre-compiled for any given device [19].

| $n$ | $2^1$ | $2^2$ | $2^3$ | ... | $2^8$ | $2^9$ | $2^{10}$ | $2^{11}$ | $2^{12}$ | $2^{13}$ | $2^{14}$ | ... | $2^{29}$ | $2^{30}$ | $2^{31}$ |
|---|---|---|---|---|---|---|---|---|---|---|---|---|---|---|---|
| **Kogge-Stone** | 5.7 | 5.8 | 5.9 | | 5.8 | 5.8 | 6.0 | 5.6 | 5.8 | 5.7 | 5.6 | | 6.4 | 6.4 | 6.6 |
| **Sklansky** | 5.6 | 6.1 | 6.5 | | 6.8 | 6.6 | 6.7 | 6.8 | 6.7 | 6.5 | 6.4 | | 7.3 | 8.1 | 7.9 |
| **Brent-Kung** | 5.9 | 6.7 | 7.4 | | 12.3 | 11.4 | 12.9 | 10.2 | 10.3 | 10.7 | 12.6 | | 14.9 | 11.1 | 16.4 |
| **Blelloch** | 6.0 | 7.4 | 9.0 | | 12.4 | 12.6 | 13.8 | 12.0 | 14.1 | 11.6 | 12.3 | | 15.5 | 13.0 | 14.8 |

**Table 3.** Time (in seconds) taken to prove race freedom for prefix sum kernels, for increasing array lengths. An array of length $n$ is processed by $n/2$ threads, except in the case of Kogge-Stone where $n$ threads are used.

| $n$ | | $2^9$ | $2^{10}$ | $2^{11}$ | $2^{12}$ | $2^{13}$ | $2^{14}$ | ... | $2^{18}$ | $2^{19}$ | $2^{20}$ |
|---|---|---|---|---|---|---|---|---|---|---|---|
| **#Voigtländer tests** | | 131,839 | 525,823 | $2.1 \times 10^6$ | $8.4 \times 10^6$ | $3.4 \times 10^7$ | $1.3 \times 10^8$ | ... | $3.4 \times 10^{10}$ | $1.4 \times 10^{11}$ | $5.5 \times 10^{11}$ |
| | | | | | **NVIDIA GeForce GTX 570** | | | | | | |
| **Kogge-Stone** | **V** | 19.2 | 76.2 | 337.6 | 1463.9 | - | - | | - | - | - |
| | **I** | 0.4 | 0.5 | 0.3 | 0.4 | 0.3 | 0.4 | | 0.4 | 0.4 | 0.4 |
| **Sklansky** | **V** | 18.5 | 71.8 | 320.2 | 1438.3 | - | - | | - | - | - |
| | **I** | 0.4 | 0.4 | 0.4 | 0.4 | 0.4 | 0.4 | | 0.4 | 0.4 | 0.4 |
| **Brent-Kung** | **V** | 19.0 | 69.3 | 317.3 | 1454.3 | - | - | | - | - | - |
| | **I** | 0.5 | 0.4 | 0.4 | 0.4 | 0.4 | 0.4 | | 0.4 | 0.4 | 0.4 |
| **Blelloch** | **V** | 19.2 | 75.4 | 324.2 | 1595.3 | - | - | | - | - | - |
| | **I** | 0.5 | 0.4 | 0.4 | 0.4 | 0.4 | 0.4 | | 0.4 | 0.4 | 0.4 |
| | | | | | **NVIDIA Tesla M2050** | | | | | | |
| **Kogge-Stone** | **V** | 14.6 | 36.1 | 160.9 | 653.0 | 2796.8 | - | | - | - | - |
| | **I** | 0.3 | 0.3 | 0.6 | 0.5 | 0.5 | 0.5 | | 0.6 | 0.5 | 0.6 |
| **Sklansky** | **V** | 12.2 | 32.5 | 149.6 | 609.3 | 2601.5 | - | | - | - | - |
| | **I** | 0.3 | 0.3 | 0.5 | 0.5 | 0.5 | 0.5 | | 0.6 | 0.6 | 0.6 |
| **Brent-Kung** | **V** | 10.9 | 35.9 | 165.7 | 678.1 | 2889.2 | - | | - | - | - |
| | **I** | 0.3 | 0.3 | 0.6 | 0.5 | 0.6 | 0.5 | | 0.6 | 0.6 | 0.6 |
| **Blelloch** | **V** | 10.9 | 36.7 | 166.0 | 679.9 | 2931.8 | - | | - | - | - |
| | **I** | 0.3 | 0.3 | 0.5 | 0.6 | 0.6 | 0.6 | | 0.6 | 0.6 | 0.6 |
| | | | | | **Intel Xeon X5650** | | | | | | |
| **Kogge-Stone** | **V** | 21.1 | 109.8 | 660.8 | 3467.1 | - | - | | - | - | - |
| | **I** | 1.3 | 1.3 | 1.3 | 1.3 | 1.3 | 1.3 | | 1.3 | 1.3 | 1.3 |
| **Sklansky** | **V** | 12.2 | 78.4 | 404.8 | 2003.9 | - | - | | - | - | - |
| | **I** | 1.3 | 1.3 | 1.3 | 1.3 | 1.3 | 1.3 | | 1.3 | 1.3 | 1.3 |
| **Brent-Kung** | **V** | 12.6 | 80.4 | 469.9 | 2272.5 | - | - | | - | - | - |
| | **I** | 1.3 | 1.3 | 1.3 | 1.3 | 1.3 | 1.3 | | 1.3 | 1.3 | 1.3 |
| **Blelloch** | **V** | 12.9 | 80.7 | 472.1 | 2332.5 | - | - | | - | - | - |
| | **I** | 1.3 | 1.3 | 1.3 | 1.3 | 1.3 | 1.3 | | 1.3 | 1.4 | 1.3 |
| | | | | | **Intel Xeon E5606** | | | | | | |
| **Kogge-Stone** | **V** | 107.0 | 909.2 | - | - | - | - | | - | - | - |
| | **I** | 1.9 | 1.9 | 2.1 | 2.1 | 2.0 | 2.1 | | 2.4 | 2.7 | 3.2 |
| **Sklansky** | **V** | 38.7 | 266.0 | 1221.5 | - | - | - | | - | - | - |
| | **I** | 1.9 | 1.9 | 2.0 | 2.1 | 2.0 | 2.0 | | 2.2 | 2.3 | 2.4 |
| **Brent-Kung** | **V** | 51.5 | 409.1 | 1793.8 | - | - | - | | - | - | - |
| | **I** | 2.0 | 2.0 | 2.1 | 2.1 | 2.1 | 2.1 | | 2.3 | 2.3 | 2.5 |
| **Blelloch** | **V** | 54.3 | 429.9 | 1900.3 | - | - | - | | - | - | - |
| | **I** | 1.9 | 2.0 | 2.1 | 2.1 | 2.1 | 2.1 | | 2.4 | 2.4 | 2.6 |
| | | | | | **ARM Mali T604** | | | | | | |
| **Kogge-Stone** | **V** | 287.0 | 1166.1 | - | - | - | - | | - | - | - |
| | **I** | 0.3 | 0.3 | 0.3 | 0.3 | 0.3 | 0.3 | | 0.4 | 0.4 | 0.5 |
| **Sklansky** | **V** | 287.2 | 1147.6 | - | - | - | - | | - | - | - |
| | **I** | 0.3 | 0.3 | 0.3 | 0.3 | 0.3 | 0.3 | | 0.4 | 0.4 | 0.5 |
| **Brent-Kung** | **V** | 287.4 | 1108.1 | - | - | - | - | | - | - | - |
| | **I** | 0.4 | 0.4 | 0.4 | 0.4 | 0.4 | 0.4 | | 0.4 | 0.5 | 0.6 |
| **Blelloch** | **V** | 277.0 | 1105.3 | - | - | - | - | | - | - | - |
| | **I** | 0.4 | 0.4 | 0.4 | 0.4 | 0.4 | 0.4 | | 0.4 | 0.5 | 0.6 |

**Table 4.** Time (in seconds) taken to establish correctness of prefix sum implementations, for increasing array lengths, on NVIDIA GPU, Intel CPU and ARM GPU architectures. The number of test cases associated with Voigtländer's method for each array length is also shown.

First Voigtländer shows, using relational parametricity, that a generic prefix sum is correct if and only if it behaves correctly for each length $n$ with respect to integer lists and list concatenation when applied to the input $[[0], [1], \ldots, [n-1]]$, that is, it yields the output $[[0], [0, 1], \ldots, [0, \ldots, n-1]]$. Voigtländer states that this result was inspired by earlier unpublished work by Sheeran; Sheeran confirms this claim when exploiting the result in later work on the design of prefix sum algorithms [33]. We refer to this as the Sheeran result. The result also holds for fixed lengths $n$, which means the result is similar to our result for sequential prefix sums with respect to the interval monoid. However, the Sheeran result cannot be used for practical verification of prefix sums for large $n$, because $O(n^2 \lg(n))$ space is required to represent the result.[10] Our interval of summations monoid avoids this problem by exploiting the fact that, as argued in Section 4, a correct generic prefix sum should *never* compute a non-contiguous summation. The interval of summations abstraction thus allows a contiguous summation to be represented precisely and compactly as an interval $(i, j)$ (or as $\mathbf{1}_I$ in the case of an empty summation), and collapses all other summations into the absorbing element $\top$.

Letting $L$ denote the monoid of integer lists under list concatenation employed by the Sheeran method, there is an obvious homomorphism $\theta : L \to I$ defined by:

$$\theta([x_1, \ldots, x_m]) = \begin{cases} \mathbf{1}_I & \text{if } m = 0 \\ (x_1, x_m) & \text{if } m > 0 \text{ and} \\ & \quad x_{i+1} = x_i + 1 \ (1 \leq i < m) \\ \top & \text{otherwise} \end{cases}$$

This homomorphism discards exactly those summations that cannot contribute to a correct generic prefix sum.

Secondly, Voigtländer presents an elegant proof of the "0-1-2-Principle" for parallel prefix computation. In the spirit of the 0-1-Principle of Knuth [20],[11] the 0-1-2-Principle states that a prefix sum algorithm is correct on all ternary sequences with every associative operator (defined over the ternary set) if and only if it is correct on any input sequence with an associative operator. In fact, carefully tracing his proof, Voigtländer observes that it suffices to consider just two operators and for every length $n$ a particular input set of ternary sequences of size $O(n^2)$ and $O(n)$ for his first and second operator, respectively. As with the Sheeran result, this result also holds for fixed lengths $n$. Voigtländer does not present an experimental evaluation of his method in [38]; we believe that our work is the first to do so. As we demonstrated in the experiments of Section 7, verifying a prefix sum by running Voigtländer's set of tests does not scale to large array sizes.

The focus of [33, 38] is on *sequential* HASKELL programs describing parallel synchronous hardware. In contrast, we have presented a method for verifying prefix sums implemented as asynchronous barrier-synchronising programs, leading to a practical method for verifying GPU kernel implementations. Due to our imperative, data-parallel setting, we present proofs using a direct simulation argument; we are not aware of any work on using relational parametricity to reason about data-parallel programs and believe this would be challenging.

***Correct-by-derivation prefix sums*** An alternative approach by Hinze [17] is to construct prefix sums that are correct by derivation. In Hinze's work, rather than verifying candidate implementations for functional correctness, new prefix sum circuits are built from a set of basic primitives and combinators. The correctness of these circuits is ensured by a set of algebraic laws derived for these combinators. Similar to the work of Sheeran, prefix sums are given as HASKELL programs describing circuit layouts. We are not aware of any work that translates this approach to a data-parallel setting.

***Formal verification of GPU kernels*** Recently a number of techniques for formal or semi-formal analysis of GPU kernels have been proposed [1, 9, 18, 23–25], and formal semantics for GPU kernels have been studied in-depth [10, 15]. The PUG [24] and GPUVerify [1] methods aim to statically prove race-freedom, while the method described in [23] uses a combination of dynamic and static analysis for race-freedom verification. We employed GPUVerify to prove race-freedom of prefix sum kernels in our experimental evaluation (Section 7). The GKLEE [25] and KLEE-CL [9] methods employ dynamic symbolic execution, based on the KLEE tool [6], to find data races and array bounds errors in CUDA and OpenCL kernels, respectively.

A recent technique for functional verification of OpenCL kernels using permission-based separation logic [18] could, in principle, be applied to generic prefix sum kernels. However, tool support for automation of this method is not yet available.

In prior work we introduced *barrier invariants* [8] to enable reasoning about data-dependent GPU kernels, and used barrier invariants to statically prove functional properties of Blelloch, Brent-Kung and Kogge-Stone prefix sum kernels. The challenges in making this approach scale provided insights which ultimately led to the interval of summations abstraction, and we used an early formulation of the abstraction to verify the Kogge-Stone kernel in [8]. The method for prefix sum verification presented here significantly outperforms the technique of [8], but the concept of barrier invariants has wider applicability.

## 9. Conclusions

We have introduced the interval of summations abstraction, investigated theoretical guarantees provided by this abstraction for verifying prefix sum algorithms, and shown that it can be used to design a practical and scalable verification method for GPU kernel implementations of prefix sums. Our experimental results demonstrate that we can prove race-freedom of prefix sum implementations for all conceivably useful array sizes, after which checking functional correctness of a prefix sum boils down to running a single test case, taking no longer than the time required to run the prefix sum in practice. We believe this substantiates our claim that we have made a major step towards solving the problem of functional verification for GPU implementations of generic prefix sums.

Our approach depends on the ability to prove that a data-parallel program behaves deterministically. For models of computation where barriers provide the only means of synchronisation this boils down to proving race-freedom (Lemma 5.4). Our approach thus extends to prefix sums written in programming models such as OpenMP, MPI and pthreads as long as these implementations use barriers exclusively for synchronisation, in favour of locks or atomic operations. Correspondingly, our method cannot be applied to GPU kernel implementations where threads communicate using atomics; in practice we have not seen the use of atomics in prefix sum kernels.

We have considered verification of prefix sums with respect to fixed array sizes. To prove that a prefix sum is correct for *all* array sizes it would be necessary to prove race-freedom for arbitrary array sizes, and also to prove that the prefix sum would compute the correct result for our interval of summations test case for every array size. While the former is beyond the scope of current tools such as GPUVerify, and the latter obviously cannot be achieved through testing, one could attempt to establish both through (manual or partially automated) mathematical proof.

We deliberately designed the interval of summations abstraction to capture the specific case of prefix sums, due to the importance of this class of algorithms. The abstraction can be used to analyse any algorithm that operates over an abstract monoid as long as the results computed by the algorithm are required to be contiguous summations. We are aware of one further class of such algorithms: reduction operations. The reduction of an array $[s_1, s_2, \ldots, s_n]$ is the sum $s_1 \oplus s_2 \oplus \cdots \oplus s_n$. Indeed, a reduction is performed during the first phase of the Blelloch and Brent-Kung prefix sum algorithms.

[10] The space complexity is $O(n^2 \lg(n))$ for correct algorithms; an incorrect algorithm could apply the concatenation operator arbitrarily many times, requiring unbounded space.

[11] If an oblivious sorting algorithm is correct on all Boolean valued input sequences then it is correct on input sequences over any totally ordered set.

A natural question is to ask if there are prefix sum algorithms that gain efficiency by exploiting other properties of operators, such as commutativity or idempotence. We are aware of recent work by Sergeev [32] which investigates prefix sum circuits for the XOR operator, exploiting the fact that this operator satisfies the identity $x \oplus y \oplus y = x$. Beyond prefix sums, there is scope for devising abstractions to allow representation-independent reasoning via a canonical test case in less restricted settings. For example, potentially discontiguous summations of monoid elements can be represented using lists [33, 38], and commutativity can be accommodated by switching to a bag representation. However, these representations lose the space-efficiency afforded by the interval of summations abstraction which allows our approach to scale.

## Acknowledgments

We are grateful to Josh Berdine, Pantazis Deligiannis, Samin Ishtiaq, Alan Mycroft, Jakob Grue Simonsen, John Wickerson and our POPL reviewers for their insightful comments on various drafts of this work, and to Akash Lal for helpful discussion.

We thank Daniel Liew (Imperial College), Anton Lokhmotov (ARM) and Dong Ping Zhang (AMD) for their assistance with our experimental evaluation.

Finally, we thank Mary Sheeran and Janis Voigtländer for their work, which inspired our efforts.

## References

[1] A. Betts, N. Chong, A. F. Donaldson, S. Qadeer, and P. Thomson. GPUVerify: a verifier for GPU kernels. In *OOPSLA*, pages 113–132, 2012.

[2] M. Billeter, O. Olsson, and U. Assarsson. Efficient stream compaction on wide SIMD many-core architectures. In *HPG*, pages 159–166, 2009.

[3] G. E. Blelloch. Scans as primitive parallel operations. *IEEE Trans. Comput.*, 38(11):1526–1538, 1989.

[4] G. E. Blelloch. Prefix sums and their applications. In J. H. Reif, editor, *Synthesis of Parallel Algorithms*. Morgan Kaufmann, 1990.

[5] R. P. Brent and H.-T. Kung. A regular layout for parallel adders. *IEEE Trans. Computers*, 31(3):260–264, 1982.

[6] C. Cadar, D. Dunbar, and D. R. Engler. KLEE: Unassisted and automatic generation of high-coverage tests for complex systems programs. In *OSDI*, pages 209–224, 2008.

[7] S. Che et al. Rodinia: A benchmark suite for heterogeneous computing. In *Workload Characterization*, pages 44–54, 2009.

[8] N. Chong, A. F. Donaldson, P. H. Kelly, J. Ketema, and S. Qadeer. Barrier invariants: A shared state abstraction for the analysis of data-dependent GPU kernels. In *OOPSLA*, pages 605–622, 2013.

[9] P. Collingbourne, , C. Cadar, and P. H. J. Kelly. Symbolic testing of OpenCL code. In *HVC'11*, pages 203–218, 2012.

[10] P. Collingbourne, A. F. Donaldson, J. Ketema, and S. Qadeer. Interleaving and lock-step semantics for analysis and verification of GPU kernels. In *ESOP*, pages 270–289, 2013.

[11] P. Cousot and R. Cousot. Abstract interpretation: A unified lattice model for static analysis of programs by construction or approximation of fixpoints. In *POPL*, pages 238–252, 1977.

[12] A. Danalis et al. The scalable heterogeneous computing (SHOC) benchmark suite. In *GPGPU 2010*, pages 63–74, 2010.

[13] O. Eğecioğlu, E. Gallopoulos, and C. Koç. A parallel method for fast and practical high-order Newton interpolation. *BIT Numerical Mathematics*, 30:268–288, 1990.

[14] W. Gropp, E. Lusk, and A. Skjellum. *Using MPI: Portable Parallel Programming with the Message Passing Interface*. MIT Press, 2nd edition, 1999.

[15] A. Habermaier and A. Knapp. On the correctness of the SIMT execution model of GPUs. In *ESOP*, pages 316–335, 2012.

[16] M. Harris, S. Sengupta, and J. Owens. Parallel prefix sum (scan) with CUDA. In H. Nguyen, editor, *GPU Gems 3*. Addison-Wesley, 2007.

[17] R. Hinze. An algebra of scans. In *MPC*, pages 186–210, 2004.

[18] M. Huisman and M. Mihelčić. Specification and verification of GPGPU programs using permission-based separation logic. In *BYTE-CODE*, 2013.

[19] Khronos OpenCL Working Group. The OpenCL specification, version 1.2, 2012.

[20] D. E. Knuth. *The Art of Computer Programming*, volume 3. Addison-Wesley, 2nd edition, 1998.

[21] P. M. Kogge and H. S. Stone. A parallel algorithm for the efficient solution of a general class of recurrence equations. *IEEE Trans. Computers*, C-22(8):786–793, 1973.

[22] R. E. Ladner and M. J. Fischer. Parallel prefix computation. *J. ACM*, 27(4):831–838, 1980.

[23] A. Leung, M. Gupta, Y. Agarwal, et al. Verifying GPU kernels by test amplification. In *PLDI*, pages 383–394, 2012.

[24] G. Li and G. Gopalakrishnan. Scalable SMT-based verification of GPU kernel functions. In *FSE*, pages 187–196, 2010.

[25] G. Li, P. Li, G. Sawaya, G. Gopalakrishnan, I. Ghosh, and S. P. Rajan. GKLEE: concolic verification and test generation for GPUs. In *PPoPP*, pages 215–224, 2012.

[26] D. Merrill and A. Grimshaw. Parallel scan for stream architectures. Technical Report CX2009-14, Department of Computer Science, University of Virginia, 2009.

[27] NVIDIA. CUDA C programming guide, version 5.0, 2012.

[28] B. C. Pierce. *Types and Programming Languages*. MIT Press, 2002.

[29] P. Sanders and J. L. Träff. Parallel prefix (scan) algorithms for MPI. In *PVM/MPI*, pages 22–29, 2006.

[30] N. Satish, M. Harris, and M. Garland. Designing efficient sorting algorithms for manycore GPUs. In *IPDPS*, pages 1–10, 2009.

[31] S. Sengupta, M. Harris, Y. Zhang, and J. D. Owens. Scan primitives for GPU computing. In *GH*, pages 97–106, 2007.

[32] I. Sergeev. On the complexity of parallel prefix circuits. Technical Report TR13-041, Electronic Colloquium on Computational Complexity, 2013.

[33] M. Sheeran. Functional and dynamic programming in the design of parallel prefix networks. *J. of Funct. Program.*, 21(1):59–114, 2011.

[34] J. Sklansky. Conditional-sum addition logic. *IRE Trans. Electronic Computers*, EC-9:226–231, 1960.

[35] B. So, A. M. Ghuloum, and Y. Wu. Optimizing data parallel operations on many-core platforms. In *In First Workshop on Software Tools for Multi-Core Systems (STMCS)*, 2006.

[36] H. S. Stone. Parallel processing with the perfect shuffle. *IEEE Trans. Comput.*, 20(2):153–161, 1971.

[37] J. Stratton et al. Parboil: A revised benchmark suite for scientific and commercial throughput computing. Technical Report IMPACT-12-01, University of Illinois at Urbana-Champaign, 2012.

[38] J. Voigtländer. Much ado about two (pearl): a pearl on parallel prefix computation. In *POPL*, pages 29–35, 2008.

# Authenticated Data Structures, Generically

Andrew Miller, Michael Hicks, Jonathan Katz, and Elaine Shi

University of Maryland, College Park, USA

## Abstract

An authenticated data structure (ADS) is a data structure whose operations can be carried out by an untrusted *prover*, the results of which a *verifier* can efficiently check as authentic. This is done by having the prover produce a compact proof that the verifier can check along with each operation's result. ADSs thus support outsourcing data maintenance and processing tasks to untrusted servers without loss of integrity. Past work on ADSs has focused on particular data structures (or limited classes of data structures), one at a time, often with support only for particular operations.

This paper presents a generic method, using a simple extension to a ML-like functional programming language we call $\lambda\bullet$ (lambda-auth), with which one can program authenticated operations over any data structure defined by standard type constructors, including recursive types, sums, and products. The programmer writes the data structure largely as usual and it is compiled to code to be run by the prover and verifier. Using a formalization of $\lambda\bullet$ we prove that all well-typed $\lambda\bullet$ programs result in code that is secure under the standard cryptographic assumption of collision-resistant hash functions. We have implemented $\lambda\bullet$ as an extension to the OCaml compiler, and have used it to produce authenticated versions of many interesting data structures including binary search trees, red-black+ trees, skip lists, and more. Performance experiments show that our approach is efficient, giving up little compared to the hand-optimized data structures developed previously.

***Categories and Subject Descriptors*** D.3.3 [*Programming Languages*]: Language Constructs and Features—Data types and structures

***General Terms*** Security, Programming Languages, Cryptography

## 1. Introduction

Suppose data provider would like to allow third parties to mirror its data, providing a query interface over it to clients. The data provider wants to assure clients that the mirrors will answer queries over the data truthfully, even if they (or another party that compromises a mirror) have an incentive to lie. As examples, the data provider might be providing stock market data, a certificate revocation list, the Tor relay list, or the state of the current Bitcoin ledger [22].



*POPL '14*, January 22–24, 2014, San Diego, CA, USA.

ACM 978-1-4503-2544-8/14/01... $15.00.
http://dx.doi.org/10.1145/2535838.2535851

Such a scenario can be supported using *authenticated data structures* (ADS) [5, 24, 31]. ADS computations involve two roles, the *prover* and the *verifier*. The mirror plays the role of the prover, storing the data of interest and answering queries about it. The client plays the role of the verifier, posing queries to the prover and verifying that the returned results are authentic. At any point in time, the verifier holds only a short *digest* that can be viewed as summarizing the current contents of the data; an authentic copy of the digest is provided by the data owner. When the verifier sends the prover a query, the prover computes the result and returns it along with a *proof* that the returned result is correct; both the proof and the time to produce it are linear in the time to compute the query result. The verifier can attempt to verify the proof (in time linear in the size of the proof) using its current digest, and will accept the returned result only if the proof verifies. If the verifier is also the data provider, the verifier may also update its data stored at the prover; in this case, the result is an updated digest and the proof shows that this updated digest was computed correctly. ADS computations have two properties. *Correctness* implies that when both parties execute the protocol correctly, the proofs given by the prover verify correctly and the verifier always receives the correct result. *Security*[1] implies that a computationally bounded, malicious prover cannot fool the verifier into accepting an incorrect result.

Authenticated data structures can be traced back to Merkle [18]; the well-known *Merkle hash tree* can be viewed as providing an authenticated version of a bounded-length array. More recently, authenticated versions of data structures as diverse as sets [23, 27], dictionaries [1, 12], range trees [16], graphs [13], skip lists [11, 12], B-trees [21], hash trees [26], and more [15] have been proposed. In each of these cases, the design of the data structure, the supporting operations, and how they can be proved authentic have been reconsidered from scratch, involving a new, potentially tricky proof of security. Arguably, this state of affairs has hindered the advancement of new data-structure designs as previous ideas are not easily reused or reapplied. We believe that ADSs will make their way into systems more often if they become easier to build.

This paper presents $\lambda\bullet$ (pronounced "lambda auth"), a language for programming authenticated data structures. $\lambda\bullet$ represents the first *generic*, language-based approach to building dynamic authenticated data structures with provable guarantees. The key observation underlying $\lambda\bullet$'s design is that, whatever the data structure or operation, the computations performed by the prover and verifier can be made structurally the same: the prover constructs the proof at key points when executing a query, and the verifier checks a proof by using it to "replay" the query, checking at each key point that the computation is self-consistent.

$\lambda\bullet$ implements this idea using what we call *authenticated types*, written $\bullet\tau$, with coercions $auth$ and $unauth$ for introducing and eliminating values of an authenticated type. Using standard func-

[1] This property is sometimes called *soundness* but we eschew this term to avoid confusion with its standard usage in programming languages.

tional programming features, the programmer writes her ADS's datatype definition and its corresponding operations (e.g., queries and updates) to use authenticated types. For example, as we show later in the paper, the programmer could write an efficient authenticated binary search tree using the (OCaml-style) type definition `type bst = Tip | Bin of •bst × int × •bst` along with essentially standard routines for querying and insertion. Then, given such a program, the λ• compiler produces code for both a prover and a verifier that will produce or confirm, respectively, a proof of the correct execution of the corresponding operation. Proofs consist of a stream of what we call *shallow projections* of the data the prover visits while running its routine: the prover's code adds to this stream at each *unauth* call, while the verifier's code draws from the stream at the corresponding call, checking for consistency. We give a more detailed overview of how this approach works, and how authenticated types are represented, in Section 2. Importantly, as we show in Sections 3 and 4, *any* well-typed program written in λ• compiles to a prover and verifier which are correct and secure, where security holds under the standard cryptographic assumption of *collision-resistant hash functions*.[2]

λ• provides two key benefits over prior work. First, it is extremely *flexible*. We can use λ• to implement any dynamic data structure, both queries and updates, expressible using ML-style data types (involving sums, products, and recursive types). Our theoretical development, though not our implementation, also supports authenticated functions. Previous work by Martel et al. [17] can also be used to build DAG-oriented ADSs, but it supports only queries and not (incremental) updates, requires the data structure have a single root, and does not support authenticated functions. λ•'s flexibility does not compromise its performance. To the best of our knowledge the asymptotic performance of every prior ADS construction from the literature based on collision-resistant hashing can be matched by λ•. We have implemented an optimizing λ• compiler as an extension to the OCaml compiler (described in Section 5), and using it we have implemented Merkle trees, authenticated binary search trees, red-black+ trees, skip lists, and planar separator trees, as well as improvements to standard Bitcoin data structures. Experiments described in Section 6 confirm the expected asymptotic performance of λ• ADSs, show the benefit of the two compiler optimizations we implemented (which exploit space/time tradeoffs), and demonstrate that the performance of λ• ADSs is competitive with hand-rolled versions.

λ•'s second main benefit is *ease of use*. We find that it is relatively simple to construct an ADS using λ•: just write the standard data structure in a purely functional style, and sprinkle in authenticated types; we give a flavor for this in the next section. Pleasantly, there is no need for the ADS designer to prove anything: Assuming the resulting program type checks, the programmer is assured that the produced prover and verifier code enjoy both correctness and security. By contrast, Martel et al. [17] provide no such support; programmers must write and check their implementations manually. λ• ADSs can be freely composed and customized just as one might expect with normal data structures, a fact which we hope will make them more readily deployable. All of this is in contrast to the state of practice with ADSs today, summarized in Section 7, which tends to favor hand-rolled versions that are hard to build, customize, and compose.

In summary, this paper makes the following contributions:

1. We present λ•, a purely functional language in which one can write a rich array of authenticated data structures using a novel feature we call *authenticated types*.

[2] Informally, hash is collision-resistant if it is computationally infeasible to find distinct inputs $x, x'$ such that $\mathsf{hash}(x) = \mathsf{hash}(x')$. We treat this more formally in Section 4.4.

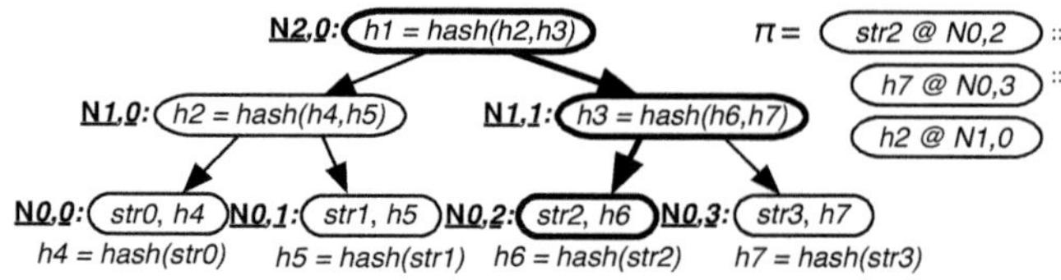


**Figure 1.** A Merkle tree and proof $\pi$ for fetch(2) describing the highlighted path (with bold edge and node outlines).

2. We formalize the semantics and type rules for λ• and prove that all well-typed λ• programs produce ADS protocols that are both correct and secure.
3. We have implemented λ• as an extension to the OCaml compiler[3] and used it to program a variety of existing and new ADSs, showing good asymptotic performance that is competitive with hand-rolled implementations.

## 2. Overview

This section presents an overview of our approach. We begin by describing Merkle trees, the canonical example of an authenticated data structure. Then we give a flavor for λ• by showing how we can use it to implement Merkle trees. We conclude with a discussion of the flexibility and ease-of-use benefits of using λ• to write efficient authenticated data structures.

### 2.1 Background: Merkle trees

The canonical example of an ADS is a *Merkle tree* [19], which is the authenticated version of a full binary tree where data is stored at the leaves but not the interior nodes. A Merkle tree of height $h$ can represent an array of $n = 2^{h-1}$ elements, $x_0, \ldots, x_{n-1}$. Each leaf node is coupled with a *digest* that consists of the hash of the associated element, while each internal node contains a digest that is the hash of the concatenation of the digests of its two children. A depiction of a Merkle tree for $h = 3$ is given in Figure 1. Each leaf is associated with a string $str0$, $str1$, etc. Each node is numbered according to its position in the tree, with $x, y$ indicating $x$ as the row and $y$ as the column.

The canonical Merkle-tree query fetches the value $x_i$ at index $i \in [0, n-1]$. When thus queried, the prover (call it $P$) returns the value $x_i$ along with the set of digests $\pi$ needed to compute the root digest. The verifier (call it $V$) keeps a copy of the root digest itself, and checks the proof by recomputing this digest from the proof to make sure the two match. Figure 1 shows the proof $\pi$ for a fetch at position $i = 2$ (i.e., the leaf at position $N0, 2$). It consists of three elements in sequence, the string $str2$, the hash $h_7$, and the hash $h_2$; these are labeled with the salient nodes of the tree that they relate to. Verification proceeds bottom up: $V$ computes the hash of $str2$, which is $h_6$, and concatenates that with the hash $h_7$ provided in $\pi$. It then concatenates these two and takes the hash to compute what should be the digest for node $N1, 1$, i.e., $h_3$. Then it concatenates $h_2$, the hash for $N1, 0$ provided in $\pi$, with its computed digest for $N1, 1$ and hashes the result. It then confirms that this computed digest equals $h_1$, the digest it stores for the whole tree.

***Performance analysis.*** Because the tree is perfectly balanced, the size of the proof is always $\log_2 n$; additionally the computational cost for each of $P$ and $V$ is $\log_2 n$. The overall size of the data structure stored by $P$ is $O(n)$, whereas $V$ at no point requires more than a constant amount of storage or memory. In particular, $V$ only stores a constant-sized digest of the tree between fetch operations,

[3] The full open-source code for our implementation is available at the following URL: `http://www.cs.umd.edu/~amiller/gpads/`

```
type tree = Tip of string | Bin of •tree × •tree
type bit = L | R
let rec fetch (idx:bit list) (t:•tree) : string =
  match idx, unauth t with
  | [], Tip a → a
  | L :: idx, Bin(l,_) → fetch idx l
  | R :: idx, Bin(_,r) → fetch idx r
```

**Figure 2.** Merkle trees in λ•. The tree is assumed to be complete, i.e., with a power-of-two number of leaves.

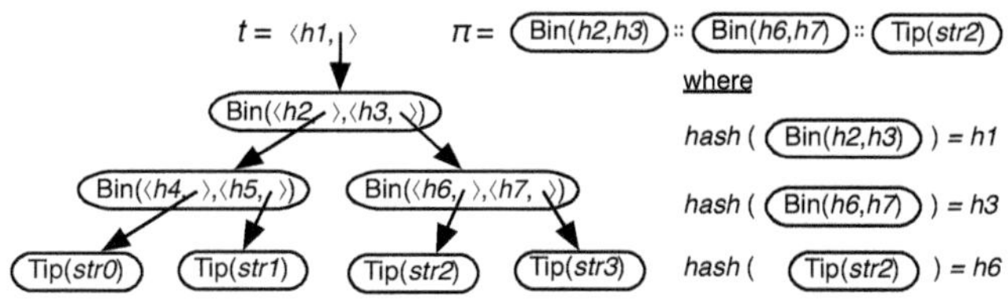


**Figure 3.** A λ• Merkle tree $t$ at the prover (of type •tree from Figure 2) and proof stream $\pi$ for query fetch $t$ [R; L]. Hashes of relevant shallow projections are given in the lower right.

and because $V$ processes each (constant-sized) hash in order, it can discard it immediately after it is read. For this reason, we often refer to $\pi$ as a proof *stream*.

***Security analysis.*** As described in the Introduction, we are interested in two properties of this scheme. *Correctness* says that when $P$ executes a query $f$ over a tree $t$ correctly, then $V$ gets the same result as it would have if it had just computed $f(t)$ normally. The second property, *security*, says that a computationally bounded, cheating prover $P^*$ cannot cause $V$ to accept an incorrect answer. The basis of this property is the use of collision-resistant hashes: we can show that if $P^*$ can cause $V$ to accept an incorrect answer then the proof returned by $P^*$ will yield a collision. We state these properties precisely, in the context of λ•, in Section 4.

### 2.2 Introducing λ•, a language for programming ADSs

The Merkle tree verification procedure was carefully designed with the properties of the underlying data structure in mind. In particular, there can be but one *path* from the root to a given leaf, and from this path we can determine digests sufficient to recompute the root digest. The question is: how might we generalize this approach to arbitrary data structures $t$ involving arbitrary computations $f$? We designed λ• as a solution to this problem.

λ• is a completely standard, purely functional programming language extended with *authenticated types* $\bullet\tau$, along with coercions *auth* and *unauth*, which have type $\forall\alpha.\alpha \rightarrow \bullet\alpha$ (for introducing authenticated values) and type $\forall\alpha.\bullet\alpha \rightarrow \alpha$ (for eliminating authenticated values), respectively. A function $f$ using authenticated types is compiled to variations $f_P$ and $f_V$ for the prover and verifier, respectively. Data of type $\bullet\tau$ stored at the prover is like a normal value of type $\tau$ but augmented with digests, while data of type $\bullet\tau$ stored at the verifier is simply a compact digest. The *auth*/*unauth* coercions at the prover facilitate proof generation, while at the verifier they check a provided proof. In short, λ•'s design exploits the observation that proof generation and proof verification can be made structurally *identical* essentially by piggybacking them on top of the ideal computation of $f(t)$.

***Example.*** As an illustration, Figure 2 shows a version of Merkle trees written in our OCaml-based λ• implementation. The type tree is simply a binary tree with strings stored at the leaves. The fetch function takes an index expressed as a list of bits, which is interpreted as a path through the tree, with L bits directing the traversal to the left, and R bits directing it right. The function returns the string associated with the Tip that is eventually reached. Notice that since the argument t has type •tree, the function must call *unauth* t to coerce it to a tree to be matched against (we give a use of *auth* in Section 2.3).

***Interpretation of authenticated types.*** All standard constructs have the usual semantics in both $f_P$ and $f_V$, but authenticated types are interpreted differently.

**Prover** For $f_P$, values of type $\bullet\tau$ consist of pairs $\langle h, v\rangle$ where $v$ has type $\tau$ and $h$ is its digest, i.e., a hash of the *shallow projection* of $v$. The shallow projection of a value is just the value itself for all values of type $\tau$ that do not consist of any authenticated types $\bullet\tau_0$, while the shallow projection of an authenticated value $\langle h, v\rangle$ is just the digest $h$ (the formal definition is in Figure 9). Looking at the definition of type tree in the figure, we can see that recursive references to the tree in the Bin case are authenticated. As such, the prover's representation is just as described in the previous subsection: each node of the tree has the form Bin$(\langle h_1, v_1\rangle, \langle h_2, v_2\rangle)$, which consists of the left subtree $v_1$ and its digest $h_1$, and the right subtree $v_2$ and its digest $h_2$. Each digest consists of the hash of the shallow projection of its respective tree. So, if $v_1$ was a leaf Tip$(s)$, the shallow projection is just Tip$(s)$ itself, and thus $h_1$ is the hash of Tip$(s)$. On the other hand, suppose $v_1$ was a node Bin$(\langle h_{11}, v_{11}\rangle, \langle h_{12}, v_{12}\rangle)$. Then Bin$(h_{11}, h_{12})$ is this node's shallow projection, and $h_1$ is its digest.

**Verifier** For $f_V$, values of type $\bullet\tau$ consist solely of the digest $h$ of some value of type $\tau$. As such, for our example, while the prover maintains the entire tree data structure, the verifier only keeps the digest of the root. In general, values in $f_V$ are the shallow projections of their corresponding values in $f_P$; we define this notion formally in the next section.

Turning to the coercions, for both the prover and verifier the *auth* $v$ coercion computes the hash $h$ of the shallow projection of $v$; for the prover, this hash is paired with $v$ while the verifier retains only $h$ itself. The interesting part is the semantics of *unauth*. For the prover, *unauth* is called with $\langle h, v\rangle$ and it simply returns $v$. In addition, it computes the shallow projection of $v$ and adds it to the proof $\pi$, which is just a list of such shallow projections. We often refer to $\pi$ as a proof *stream* to emphasize the list structure. For the verifier, *unauth* takes a hash $h$ and compares it to the hash of the element $s$ at the head of the proof stream, which should be a shallow projection of type $\tau$. If all is well, this element is the one the Prover put there and so the hashes will match and the coercion returns $s$. Otherwise there is a problem and verification fails.

***Example Merkle-tree query.*** Figure 3 depicts the prover's version of an object of type •tree corresponding to the Merkle tree from Figure 1. These trees are structurally similar but not identical; in particular, notice that a node's digest is stored with the pointer to that node, rather than at the node itself. Suppose the prover executes the query (fetch [R; L] $t$), which corresponds to the query from Section 2.1. The figure also depicts the proof stream $\pi$ it produces, along with the hashes of shallow projections of relevant tree elements. The first thing the prover will execute is *unauth* $t$, which returns the pointer to the first node, and stores its shallow projection Bin$(h_2,h_3)$ in the proof stream—notice that this is the same as the pointed-to node but the sub-tree pointers have been dropped. Execution continues to the third case of the **match**, which recursively calls (fetch [L] r), where r is bound to the authenticated value $\langle h_3, v\rangle$ such that $v$ is the right subtree. The prover then invokes *unauth* on this pair, returning $v$ and adding Bin$(h_6,h_7)$ to the proof stream. This time we take the second case of the **match**, recursing on $\langle h_6, \mathsf{Tip}(str2)\rangle$, so the call to *unauth* returns Tip($str2$) and adds its shallow projection (Tip($str2$) itself) to the proof stream. Execution concludes with $str2$ as the final result while the final proof stream $\pi$ consists of three elements, representing the three nodes visited.

The verifier begins with the proof stream $\pi$ and just the digest of $t$, which is $h_1$. It then runs (fetch [R; L] $t$) using its version of the code. It first executes *unauth* $h_1$, which compares $h_1$ to the hash of the first element $s_0$ of the proof stream, which is Bin($h_2$,$h_3$). The hashes match, as per the equations given in the lower right of the figure, and thus execution continues using $s_0$. Execution proceeds to the third case of the **match**, recursively calling fetch with [L] and $h_3$. This time, calling *unauth* $h_3$ results in comparing $h_3$ to the hash of the second element in the proof stream, which is Bin($h_6$,$h_7$), and once again the hashes match and the proof stream element is returned. The second branch of the **match** fires, so the recursive call passes [] and $h_6$. Finally, *unauth* $h_6$ compares $h_6$ to the hash of the final element of the proof stream, Tip($str2$), which is returned as the hashes match. Thus execution concludes with the final result as $str2$. As all hash checks succeeded, the verifier has confirmed the prover's execution is correct.

***Analysis.*** λ• Merkle trees are asymptotically as efficient as the originals, and as secure. As before, the verifier maintains only the constant-sized digest between queries, and the size of the fetch proof and the time to generate and verify it is $O(\log_2 n)$: the proof stream consists of one (constant-size) shallow projection for each recursive call to fetch. The argument for security once again rests on collision-resistant hashes, though λ• verification checks the root digest top-down rather than bottom-up. Our proof stream has some redundancy (it contains hashes $h_2$, $h_3$, $h_6$, and $h_7$, whereas in Figure 1 the proof contains only $h_2$ and $h_7$) but this is only a constant factor and can be optimized away (cf. Section 5.2).

### 2.3 Discussion: Benefits of λ•

The primary benefit of writing ADSs in λ• over prior approaches is *flexibility* and *ease of use*. λ• can support essentially any computation over a DAG-oriented data structure that is expressed as a functional program. Moreover, as proved in Section 4, writing an ADS in λ• ensures it is both correct and secure; there is no need for a designer to make a new argument for each new data structure. As far as we are aware, λ• can be used to implement any previously proposed ADS based on collision-resistant hashing. As described in Section 6, so far we have successfully implemented Merkle trees and authenticated versions of binary search trees, red-black+ trees [24], skip lists [29], and variations of the Bitcoin block chain [22], all of which enjoy asymptotically identical, or better, performance than their specially-designed counterparts.

***Support for updates.*** Martel et al. [17] also previously proposed a general-purpose scheme that supports ADSs based on DAGs. In principle, their scheme could also support the above-mentioned data structures, but only for query computations, not updates. By contrast, updates are completely natural in λ•. For example, the function update in Figure 4 updates a Merkle tree. The verifier could submit a request to the prover to run (update [R; L] $t$ $str4$). The prover will produce a proof stream $\pi$ for the operation along with a new authenticated tree $t'$ that contains the modification, and which shares much of the structure of the original tree $t$, as per standard functional programming style. The prover can then update its root to now be $t'$ and then send the verifier the result of the execution, which is the digest portion of $t'$ and the proof stream

```
let rec update (idx:bit list) (t:•tree) (newval:string) : •tree =
  match idx, unauth t with
  | [], Tip _ → auth(Tip newval)
  | L::idx', Bin(l,r) → auth(Bin(update idx' l newval, r))
  | R::idx', Bin(l,r) → auth(Bin(l, update idx' r newval))

let update_cps (idx:bit list) (t:•tree) (newval:string) : •tree =
  let rec _update (k : •(•tree → •tree)) idx t x : •tree =
    match idx, unauth t with
    | [], Tip _ → (unauth k) (auth(Tip x))
    | L :: idx', Bin(l,r) →
      _update (auth(fun t → auth(Bin(t,r)))) idx' l x
    | R :: idx', Bin(l,r) →
      _update (auth(fun t → auth(Bin(l,t)))) idx' r x
  in _update (auth(fun t → t)) idx t newval

type stack = E | SL of •stack × •tree | SR of •stack × •tree
let update_stk (idx:bit list) (t:•tree) (newval:string) : •tree =
  let rec build idx t (s:stack) : •tree × stack =
    match idx, unauth t with
    | [], Tip _ → auth(Tip newval), s
    | L::idx', Bin(l,r) → build idx l (SL(auth s, r))
    | R::idx', Bin(l,r) → build idx r (SL(auth s, l)) in
  let rec apply (child:•tree, s:stack) : •tree =
    match s with
    | E → child
    | SL(s, r) → apply (auth(Bin(child, r)), unauth s)
    | SR(s, l) → apply (auth(Bin(l, child)), unauth s) in
  apply (build idx t E)
```

**Figure 4.** Functions for updating a Merkle tree in λ•.

$\pi$. The verifier can then use $\pi$ in the usual way to verify that (the digest of) $t'$ is indeed the right result and then update its local root.[4]

***Controlling performance.*** The fact that λ• is a general-purpose programming language means that it affords substantial flexibility to the ADS designer in customizing an ADS design to her needs.

As one possible customization, the designer might refactor operations to better control space usage. Consider the update function once again. While the proof stream contributes only a constant space overhead, since the verifier can discard each element after it is read, we observe that executing update will require $O(\log n)$ stack space, since the function is not tail recursive. One way to eliminate this overhead is to rewrite update in continuation-passing style (CPS) such that the continuation itself is authenticated, as for the function update_cps given in the middle of Figure 4. As such, recursive uses of nested continuations will be replaced with a hash, effectively bounding the depth of the stack encoded in the continuation. To the best of our knowledge, no prior work has considered authenticated closures. Another way to achieve the same effect, but perhaps less elegantly, is to use an explicit authenticated stack as is done by update_stk given at the bottom of the figure.

The designer could also tune performance by adjusting the definition of the data structure itself. For example, we could have defined Merkle trees instead as follows:

```
type tree = Tip of string | Bin of •(tree × tree)
```

In this case, we are only hashing nodes, and will never hash tips. This definition makes more sense when the hash of the Tip is larger

[4] In general, the prover will return the shallow projection of the result of a computation back to the verifier; when the result is a normal value the prover will thus return the value itself (as with the result in our (fetch [R; L] $t$) example query).

| | | |
|---|---|---|
| Types $\tau$ | ::= | $1 \mid \tau_1 \to \tau_2 \mid \tau_1 + \tau_2 \mid \tau_1 \times \tau_2 \mid \mu\alpha.\tau \mid \alpha \mid \bullet\tau$ |
| Values $v$ | ::= | $() \mid x \mid \lambda x.e \mid \mathbf{rec}\ x.\lambda y.e$ |
| | $\mid$ | $\mathbf{inj}_1\ v \mid \mathbf{inj}_2\ v \mid (v_1, v_2) \mid \mathbf{roll}\ v$ |
| Exprs $e$ | ::= | $v \mid \mathbf{let}\ x = e_1\ \mathbf{in}\ e_2 \mid v_1\ v_2 \mid \mathbf{case}\ v\ v_0\ v_1$ |
| | $\mid$ | $\mathbf{prj}_1\ v \mid \mathbf{prj}_2\ v \mid \mathbf{unroll}\ v \mid \mathit{auth}\ v \mid \mathit{unauth}\ v$ |

**Figure 5.** Syntax for types and terms

$$\frac{\Gamma \vdash v : \tau_1}{\Gamma \vdash \mathbf{inj}_1\ v : \tau_1 + \tau_2} \qquad \frac{\Gamma \vdash v : \tau_2}{\Gamma \vdash \mathbf{inj}_2\ v : \tau_1 + \tau_2}$$

$$\frac{\Gamma \vdash v : \tau_1 + \tau_2 \qquad \Gamma \vdash v_1 : \tau_1 \to \tau \qquad \Gamma \vdash v_2 : \tau_2 \to \tau}{\Gamma \vdash \mathbf{case}\ v\ v_1\ v_2 : \tau}$$

$$\frac{\Gamma \vdash v : \tau}{\Gamma \vdash \mathit{auth}\ v : \bullet\tau} \qquad \frac{\Gamma \vdash v : \bullet\tau}{\Gamma \vdash \mathit{unauth}\ v : \tau}$$

**Figure 6.** Selected typing rules

than the representation of Tip itself, e.g., if the tree stored integers instead of strings. As another variation, we might imagine defining a tree that only optionally authenticates its children:

```
type tree =
  | Tip of string
  | Bin of tree × tree
  | AuthBin of •(tree × tree)
```

Then the tree might go several levels using Bin before using AuthBin. This design thus increases the constant factor on asymptotic space usage, but may reduce proving/verification time.

All of these customizations are possible, and easy to experiment with, thanks to the fact that λ• is a general-purpose programming language. However, this flexibility cuts both ways: there is nothing (at the moment) stopping the programmer from producing a suboptimal design. As an extreme example, the programmer could write type tree = Tip of string | Bin of tree × tree—i.e., without any use of authenticated types! This design will be secure and correct, as with every λ• program, but will effectively require the verifier to maintain the entire tree, not simply a digest. Fortunately, there is a simple rule of thumb that may have already become evident to the reader by this point: the data-structure type definition should authenticate recursive references, thus aiming for shallow projections to be constant-sized. We leave to interesting future work the task of automating the transformation of a •-free type definition to an efficient authenticated one.

## 3. λ•: A Language with Authenticated Types

This section formalizes λ•, our language for writing computations over authenticated data structures. We present the syntax, typing rules, and operational semantics for λ• programs. The next section proves that λ• computations produce correct and secure results.

### 3.1 Syntax

Figure 5 presents the syntax for λ•. Other than authenticated types $\bullet\tau$, the type language is entirely standard, consisting of the unit type 1, function types $\tau_1 \to \tau_2$, sum types $\tau_1 + \tau_2$, product types $\tau_1 \times \tau_2$, recursive types $\mu\alpha.\tau$, and variable types $\alpha$ arising from these. In this syntax, our authenticated tree type defined in Figure 2 would be written $\mu\alpha.\mathsf{string} + (\bullet\alpha \times \bullet\alpha)$, where string would itself be encoded, e.g., as a list of Peano-style integers. Our formal language does not include parametric polymorphism for simplicity, but adding it would present no difficulties. The language does not support references because mutations would risk invalidating hashes for $\bullet\tau$ values. In particular, given an authenticated value $\langle h, v\rangle$ where $v$ is a reference, a mutation via $v$ may invalidate $h$.

Terms (values $v$ and expressions $e$) are in administrative normal form [7] to keep the semantics simple. In this form, the grammar forces us to write **let** $x = e_1$ **in let** $y = e_2$ **in** $x\ y$ instead of the more familiar $e_1\ e_2$, for example. In addition to variables $x$, the term language includes functions $\lambda x.e$ and function application $v_1\ v_2$; sum-type values $\mathbf{inj}_1\ v$ and $\mathbf{inj}_2\ v$ which are eliminated by **case** $v\ v_0\ v_1$, where $v_0$ and $v_1$ are expected to be functions; products $(v_1, v_2)$ eliminated by expressions $\mathbf{prj}_1\ v$ and $\mathbf{prj}_2\ v$; values of recursive type introduced via **roll** $v$ and eliminated by **unroll** $v$; and finally fixpoints **rec** $x.\lambda y.e$ for defining recursive functions (where inside of $\lambda y.e$ references to $x$ refer to the function itself). Authenticated types $\bullet\tau$ are introduced by coercion $\mathit{auth}$ and eliminated by $\mathit{unauth}$.

### 3.2 Typing

The typing judgment for λ• programs is the usual one, written $\Gamma \vdash e : \tau$. It states that expression $e$ has type $\tau$ under environment $\Gamma$, where $\Gamma$ is a map from variables $x$ to types $\tau$. Typing rules for most constructs are standard. Selected rules are given in Figure 6.

### 3.3 Operational semantics

In practice, our compiler takes a program like the one in Figure 2 and outputs versions to be run by the prover and the verifier. In our formalization, we define distinct semantics for the same program, as determined by an execution mode $m$, where $m = P$ for the prover's execution, and $m = V$ for the verifier's. We also define a mode $I$ for the *Ideal* case, representing a computation that happens in the normal way, ignoring authenticated types; this is needed for stating the security and correctness properties.

We define a small-step operational semantics of the form $\ll \pi, e \gg \to_m \ll \pi', e' \gg$, where $m$ is the mode and $\pi$ is the proof stream, which is a list of shallow projections $s$. This can be read: *An expression e coupled with a proof stream $\pi$ can evaluate one step in mode $m$ to produce an expression $e'$ and an updated proof stream $\pi'$.* We define $\ll \pi, e \gg \to_m^i \ll \pi', e' \gg$ to be the transitive multi-step application of the single-step relation; it states that $e$ *evaluates, in i steps, to $e'$ in mode $m$, starting with proof stream $\pi$ and finishing with $\pi'$*. The proof stream is *produced* in mode $P$, so $\pi$ is a prefix of $\pi'$ in this mode. The stream is *consumed* in mode $V$, and thus $\pi'$ is a suffix of $\pi$. The proof stream is ignored in mode $I$. We use the operator @ to denote the concatenation of two proof streams, treating @ as associative with the empty stream [] as the identity. We write $[s]$ as the singleton stream containing element $s$.

The rules for standard language features are identical in all three modes, and are standard. They are defined in the top portion of Figure 7, and we discuss them briefly in order. The rule for function application, $(\lambda x.e)\ v$, substitutes $v$ for $x$ in $e$—this substitution is written $e[v\backslash x]$. Application of a recursive function is similar: when the function (**rec** $x.\lambda y.e$) is on the left-hand side of an application, we substitute $x$ in the function body $e$ with the recursive function itself. Let-binding is used to sequence computations, either evaluating the bound expression $e_1$ one step or else, if this expression is a value $v_1$, substituting that value for $x$ in the body $e_2$. The semantics of **case** depends on whether it is given $\mathbf{inj}_1\ v$ or $\mathbf{inj}_2\ v$; in the former case we substitute $v$ in the first lambda term (the "true branch"), else we substitute it in the second ("false") one. Projection from a pair $(v_1, v_2)$ produces $v_1$ for $\mathbf{prj}_1$ and $v_2$ for $\mathbf{prj}_2$. Finally, the recursive type coercions **unroll** and **roll** nullify each other.

$$\begin{array}{ll}
\ll \pi, (\lambda x.e)\ v \gg & \rightarrow_m\ \ll \pi, e[v \backslash x] \gg \\
\ll \pi, (\textbf{rec}\ x.\lambda y.e)\ v \gg & \rightarrow_m\ \ll \pi, (\lambda y.e')\ v \gg \\
& \text{where } e' = e[(\textbf{rec}\ x.\lambda y.e) \backslash x] \\
\ll \pi, \textbf{let}\ x = v_1\ \textbf{in}\ e_2 \gg & \rightarrow_m\ \ll \pi, e_2[v_1 \backslash x] \gg \\
\ll \pi, \textbf{case}\ (\textbf{inj}_1\ v)(\lambda x.e_1)(\lambda x.e_2) \gg & \rightarrow_m\ \ll \pi, e_1[v \backslash x] \gg \\
\ll \pi, \textbf{case}\ (\textbf{inj}_2\ v)(\lambda x.e_1)(\lambda x.e_2) \gg & \rightarrow_m\ \ll \pi, e_2[v \backslash x] \gg \\
\ll \pi, \textbf{prj}_1\ (v_1, v_2) \gg & \rightarrow_m\ \ll \pi, v_1 \gg \\
\ll \pi, \textbf{prj}_2\ (v_1, v_2) \gg & \rightarrow_m\ \ll \pi, v_2 \gg \\
\ll \pi, \textbf{unroll}\ (\textbf{roll}\ v) \gg & \rightarrow_m\ \ll \pi, v \gg
\end{array}$$

$$\frac{\ll \pi, e_1 \gg \rightarrow_m \ll \pi', e_1' \gg}{\ll \pi, \textbf{let}\ x = e_1\ \textbf{in}\ e_2 \gg \rightarrow_m \ll \pi', \textbf{let}\ x = e_1'\ \textbf{in}\ e_2 \gg}$$

$$\frac{\ll \pi, e \gg \rightarrow_m^i \ll \pi', e' \gg \quad \ll \pi', e' \gg \rightarrow_m \ll \pi'', e'' \gg}{\ll \pi, e \gg \rightarrow_m^{i+1} \ll \pi'', e'' \gg} \qquad \ll \pi, e \gg \rightarrow_m^0 \ll \pi, e \gg$$

**Figure 7.** Standard single-step and multi-step operational rules

$$\begin{array}{lll}
\ll \pi, \mathit{auth}\ v \gg & \rightarrow_I & \ll \pi, v \gg \\
\ll \pi, \mathit{unauth}\ v \gg & \rightarrow_I & \ll \pi, v \gg \\
\ll \pi, \mathit{auth}\ v \gg & \rightarrow_P & \ll \pi, \langle \mathsf{hash}\ (\![v]\!), v \rangle \gg \\
\ll \pi, \mathit{unauth}\ \langle h, v \rangle \gg & \rightarrow_P & \ll \pi\ @\ [\ (\![v]\!)\ ],\ v \gg \\
\ll \pi, \mathit{auth}\ v \gg & \rightarrow_V & \ll \pi, \mathsf{hash}\ v \gg
\end{array}$$

$$\frac{\mathsf{hash}\ s_0 = h}{\ll [s_0]\ @\ \pi, \mathit{unauth}\ h \gg \rightarrow_V \ll \pi, s_0 \gg}$$

$$\text{where } v ::= \ldots \mid h \mid \langle h, v \rangle$$

**Figure 8.** Operational rules for authenticated values

$$\begin{array}{llll}
(\![()]\!) = () & & (\![x]\!) = x \\
(\![\langle h, v \rangle]\!) = h & & (\![\lambda x.e]\!) = \lambda x.(\![e]\!) \\
(\![\mathit{auth}\ v]\!) = \mathit{auth}\ (\![v]\!) & & (\![\mathit{unauth}\ v]\!) = \mathit{unauth}\ (\![v]\!) \\
(\![(v_1, v_2)]\!) = ((\![v_1]\!), (\![v_2]\!)) & & (\![\textbf{prj}_i\ v]\!) = \textbf{prj}_i\ (\![v]\!) \\
(\![\textbf{roll}\ v]\!) = \textbf{roll}\ (\![v]\!) & & (\![\textbf{unroll}\ v]\!) = \textbf{unroll}\ (\![v]\!) \\
(\![\textbf{rec}\ x.\lambda y.e]\!) = \textbf{rec}\ x.(\![\lambda y.e]\!) & & (\![\textbf{inj}_i\ v]\!) = \textbf{inj}_i\ (\![v]\!)
\end{array}$$

$$(\![\textbf{case}\ v\ v_0\ v_1]\!) = \textbf{case}\ (\![v]\!)\ (\![v_0]\!)\ (\![v_1]\!)$$
$$(\![\textbf{let}\ x = e_1\ \textbf{in}\ e_2]\!) = \textbf{let}\ x = (\![e_1]\!)\ \textbf{in}\ (\![e_2]\!)$$

**Figure 9.** Shallow projection of an expression $e$, written $(\![e]\!)$

The rules for the multi-step relation are given at the bottom of Figure 7, and are also standard.

The operational rules for authenticated values are given in Figure 8. For mode $I$, authenticated values of type $\bullet\tau$ are merely values of type $\tau$ and the $\mathit{auth}/\mathit{unauth}$ operations are no-ops. For mode $P$, values of type $\bullet\tau$ are implemented as a pair $\langle h, v \rangle$ of a hash $h$ and a value $v$ (of type $\tau$). As shown in the $\mathit{auth}$ rule, the hash is computed by applying a hash function hash over the shallow projection of $v$, written $(\![v]\!)$. We do not formalize the semantics of hash explicitly; in practice it can be implemented by serializing the value it is given and hashing that using a collision-resistant hash function.[5] The shallow projection operation is defined in Figure 9. It is essentially a fold over the structure of the term, preserving that structure in every case but that of values $\langle h, v \rangle$: here we simply drop the value $v$ and retain the hash $h$. Another interesting case is functions $\lambda x.e$: we recursively descend into $e$ to translate any $\langle h, v \rangle$ values that appear there. Such values will not appear in source programs, but they can arise via substitution under lambdas. Returning to Figure 8, the mode-$P$ semantics of $\mathit{unauth}\ \langle h, v \rangle$ is to strip off the hash, returning $v$, while adding the shallow projection of $v$ to the end of the proof stream. Finally, for mode $V$ the representation of $\bullet\tau$ is the hash $h$ of a value of type $\tau$. The $\mathit{auth}$ rule constructs this representation, while the $\mathit{unauth}$ rule checks that the hash value matches the shallow projection at the head of the proof stream.

[5] For functions $\lambda x.e$, serialization involves pretty-printing the function's code such that alpha-equivalent functions will have the same hash value. We discuss implementing authenticated functions more in Section 5.3.

## 4. Metatheory

We want to show that well-typed $\lambda\bullet$ programs will (a) produce correct results—that is, results that all three modes agree on—or else (b) a malicious prover has been able to find a hash collision, which by assumption is computationally difficult. We call property (a) *correctness* and property (b) *security*. In this section we state and prove these two properties.

### 4.1 Type Soundness

To begin, we want to prove that $\lambda\bullet$'s design is sensible in that the ideal semantics is sound (and entirely ordinary). We can prove the standard type soundness lemma about the ideal mode's semantics.

**Lemma 1** (Type Soundness). *If $\Gamma \vdash e : \tau$, then either $e$ is a value, or there exists $e'$ and $i > 0$ such that $\ll [], e \gg \rightarrow_I^i \ll [], e' \gg$ and $\Gamma \vdash e' : \tau$.*

*Proof.* The proof is completely standard, using progress and preservation lemmas, and inducting on $\ll [], e \gg \rightarrow_I^i \ll [], e' \gg$. □

### 4.2 Agreement

Now we must define what we mean when we say that the different execution modes "agree" on their results—it cannot be that these results are syntactically equal because each mode interprets authenticated values differently. For example, consider the update function from Figure 4. In the ideal setting, this function will return a normal tree $v$—because $\bullet\tau$ values are the same as those of type $\tau$, the tree $v$ will contain no digests. On the other hand, the prover will return a value $\langle h, v_P \rangle$, where $h$ is the digest of $v_P$. For the same insertion on the same tree, the results $v$ and $\langle h, v_P \rangle$ in $I$ and $P$ modes, respectively, should "agree" without being equal: $v$ will just be a normal tree, while $v_P$ will contain digests—but the elements and sub-trees, excepting the digests, should be the same. And, running the insertion at the verifier will return a digest $h$, which should match the digest in the prover's returned value $\langle h, v_P \rangle$.

We formalize this connection as a three-way type-indexed relation $\Gamma \vdash e\ e_P\ e_V : \tau$, given in Figure 10, which states: *in environment $\Gamma$, ideal expression $e$, prover expression $e_P$, and verifier expression $e_V$ all* agree *at type $\tau$.* In every case but that of authenticated values (the last rule), agreement follows syntactic structure of the terms, and the shape of each rule matches that of the standard type rules. The rule for authenticated values formalizes the intuition given above; it states that $\Gamma \vdash v\ \langle h, v_P \rangle\ h : \bullet\tau$ holds when (a) the digest $h$ of both the prover and verifier is the same; (b) this digest is the hash of the shallow projection of the prover's value $v_P$; (c) the prover's value $v_P$ agrees with the ideal value $v$.

Now we prove some useful facts about terms in agreement.

**Lemma 2** (Agreement). *Suppose $\Gamma \vdash e\ e_P\ e_V : \tau$. Then*

1. $(\![e_P]\!) = e_V$.
2. *$\Gamma \vdash e\ e_P'\ e_V' : \tau$ implies that $e_P' = e_P$ and $e_V = e_V'$.*

$$\Gamma \vdash ()\ ()\ () : 1 \qquad \frac{\Gamma(x) = \tau}{\Gamma \vdash x\ x\ x : \tau} \qquad \frac{\Gamma, x{:}\tau_1 \vdash e\ e_P\ e_V : \tau_2}{\Gamma \vdash (\lambda x.e)\ (\lambda x.e_P)\ (\lambda x.e_V) : \tau_1 \rightarrow \tau_2}$$

$$\frac{\Gamma \vdash v_1\ v_{1P}\ v_{1V} : \tau_1 \rightarrow \tau_2 \qquad \Gamma \vdash v_2\ v_{2P}\ v_{2V} : \tau_1}{\Gamma \vdash (v_1\ v_2)\ (v_{1P}\ v_{2P})\ (v_{1V}\ v_{2V}) : \tau_2}$$

$$\frac{\Gamma \vdash e_1\ e_{1P}\ e_{1V} : \tau_1 \qquad \Gamma, x{:}\tau_1 \vdash e_2\ e_{2P}\ e_{2V} : \tau_2}{\Gamma \vdash (\mathbf{let}\ x = e_1\ \mathbf{in}\ e_2)\ (\mathbf{let}\ x = e_{1P}\ \mathbf{in}\ e_{2P})\ (\mathbf{let}\ x = e_{1V}\ \mathbf{in}\ e_{2V}) : \tau_2} \qquad \frac{\Gamma, x{:}\tau_1 \rightarrow \tau_2 \vdash (\lambda y.e)\ (\lambda y.e_P)\ (\lambda y.e_V) : \tau_1 \rightarrow \tau_2}{\Gamma \vdash (\mathbf{rec}\ x.\lambda y.e)\ (\mathbf{rec}\ x.\lambda y.e_P)\ (\mathbf{rec}\ x.\lambda y.e_V) : \tau_1 \rightarrow \tau_2}$$

$$\frac{\Gamma \vdash v\ v_P\ v_V : \tau_1}{\Gamma \vdash (\mathbf{inj}_1\ v)\ (\mathbf{inj}_1\ v_P)\ (\mathbf{inj}_1\ v_V) : \tau_1 + \tau_2} \qquad \frac{\Gamma \vdash v\ v_P\ v_V : \tau_2}{\Gamma \vdash (\mathbf{inj}_2\ v)\ (\mathbf{inj}_2\ v_P)\ (\mathbf{inj}_2\ v_V) : \tau_1 + \tau_2}$$

$$\frac{\begin{array}{c}\Gamma \vdash v\ v_P\ v_V : \tau_1 + \tau_2 \\ \Gamma \vdash v_P\ v_{1P}\ v_{1V} : \tau_1 \rightarrow \tau \\ \Gamma \vdash v_V\ v_{1V}\ v_{2V} : \tau_2 \rightarrow \tau\end{array}}{\Gamma \vdash (\mathbf{case}\ v\ v_1\ v_2)\ (\mathbf{case}\ v_P\ v_{1P}\ v_{2P})\ (\mathbf{case}\ v_V\ v_{1V}\ v_{2V}) : \tau} \qquad \frac{\Gamma \vdash v_1\ v_{1P}\ v_{1V} : \tau_1 \qquad \Gamma \vdash v_2\ v_{2P}\ v_{2V} : \tau_2}{\Gamma \vdash (v_1, v_2)\ (v_{1P}, v_{2P})\ (v_{1V}, v_{2V}) : \tau_1 \times \tau_2}$$

$$\frac{\Gamma \vdash v\ v_P\ v_V : \tau_1 \times \tau_2}{\Gamma \vdash (\mathbf{prj}_1 v)\ (\mathbf{prj}_1\ v_P)\ (\mathbf{prj}_1\ v_V) : \tau_1} \qquad \frac{\Gamma \vdash v\ v_P\ v_V : \tau_1 \times \tau_2}{\Gamma \vdash (\mathbf{prj}_2\ v)\ (\mathbf{prj}_2\ v_P)\ (\mathbf{prj}_2\ v_V) : \tau_2} \qquad \frac{\Gamma \vdash v\ v_P\ v_V : \tau[\mu\alpha.\tau \backslash \alpha]}{\Gamma \vdash (\mathbf{roll}\ v)\ (\mathbf{roll}\ v_P)\ (\mathbf{roll}\ v_V) : \mu\alpha.\tau}$$

$$\frac{\Gamma \vdash v\ v_P\ v_V : \mu\alpha.\tau}{\Gamma \vdash (\mathbf{unroll}\ v)\ (\mathbf{unroll}\ v_P)\ (\mathbf{unroll}\ v_V) : \tau[\mu\alpha.\tau \backslash \alpha]} \qquad \frac{\Gamma \vdash v\ v_P\ v_V : \tau}{\Gamma \vdash (\mathit{auth}\ v)\ (\mathit{auth}\ v_P)\ (\mathit{auth}\ v_V) : \bullet\tau}$$

$$\frac{\Gamma \vdash v\ v_P\ v_V : \bullet\tau}{\Gamma \vdash (\mathit{unauth}\ v)\ (\mathit{unauth}\ v_P)\ (\mathit{unauth}\ v_V) : \tau} \qquad \frac{\vdash v\ v_P\ (\!|v_P|\!) : \tau \qquad \mathsf{hash}\ (\!|v_P|\!) = h}{\Gamma \vdash v\ \langle h, v_P \rangle\ h : \bullet\tau}$$

**Figure 10.** Agreement relation: defines those expressions that *agree* (i.e., that are morally, if not syntactically, the same) in the Ideal, Prover, and Verifier modes. The most interesting rule is the last one, while the rest are three-way versions of the standard type rules.

*3.* $\Gamma \vdash e : \tau$

*4. Either $e$, $e_P$, and $e_V$ are all values, or none of them are.*

*Proof.* By induction on $\Gamma \vdash e\ e_P\ e_V : \tau$. □

The first part shows the agreement relation is intimately connected to the shallow projection operator—a prover's term only ever agrees with a verifier's term when the latter is the shallow projection of the former. Moreover, we prove for any given ideal term $e$, there is at most one pair of terms $e_P$ and $e_V$ that agree with it under a given environment $\Gamma$ and type $\tau$, that agreement implies $e$ is well-typed, and that values only agree with other values.

***Client and server agree.*** In a client/server application scenario, a query/update sent by the client will reference the data structure stored at the server using a free variable, e.g., the $t$ in the query fetch $t$ 4. To run this query on the server, we substitute the prover's representation for $t$, while to verify the result at the client, we substitute $t$'s digest. These representations should agree. The following lemma states that, given an expression $e$ containing free variables with authenticated types, substituting authenticated values that agree for the free variables of $e$ produces versions $e_I$, $e_P$, and $e_V$ that also agree.

**Lemma 3.** *Given the following:*

*1.* $\Gamma \vdash e : \tau$ *where* $e$ *contains no values of type* $\bullet\tau$

*2. For all* $x_i \in \mathit{domain}(\Gamma)$,

*(a)* $\Gamma(x_i) = \bullet\tau_i$ *for some* $\tau_i$

*(b)* $\vdash v_i\ \langle h_i, v_{Pi} \rangle\ h_i : \bullet\tau_i$ *for some* $\langle h_i, v_i \rangle$ *and* $v_{Pi}$

*3.* $e_P = e[\langle h_1, v_{P1} \rangle \backslash x_1]...[\langle h_n, v_{Pn} \rangle \backslash x_n]$
$e_V = e[h_1 \backslash x_1]...[h_n \backslash x_n]$
$e_I = e[v_1 \backslash x_1]...[v_n \backslash x_n]$

*Then* $\vdash e_I\ e_P\ e_V : \tau$.

The proof of this lemma follows from straightforward application of the following substitution lemma:

**Lemma 4** (Substitution). *If* $\Gamma, x{:}\tau' \vdash e\ e_P\ e_V : \tau$ *and* $\vdash v\ v_P\ v_V : \tau'$, *then* $\Gamma \vdash (e[v \backslash x])\ (e_P[v_P \backslash x])\ (e_V[v_V \backslash x]) : \tau$.

*Proof.* The proof is by induction on $\Gamma, x{:}\tau' \vdash e\ e_P\ e_V : \tau$. The only interesting case is when $\Gamma, x{:}\tau' \vdash v'\ \langle h, v'_P \rangle\ h : \bullet\tau$. The empty environment in the premise $\vdash v'\ v'_P\ (\!|v'_P|\!) : \tau$ ensures that $v'$ and $v'_P$ contain no variables, so the substitution will be the identity and the result follows by assumption. □

### 4.3 Correctness and Security

Now we can state and prove our main theorem, Theorem 1, which encapsulates the two properties of interest, correctness and security. For both properties, we start with the assumption that terms $e$, $e_P$, and $e_V$ agree (which will be the case at the start of evaluating a query/update as per Lemma 3). The ideal-mode evaluation represents the specification of correctness: if $e$ can evaluate to $e'$ in ideal mode in $i$ steps, then the verifier, when consuming the proof stream $\pi$ produced by the prover's evaluation of $e_P$, should evaluate to some $e'_V$ which (along with the prover's resulting term $e'_P$) agrees with $e'$. On the other hand, if the verifier does not consume $\pi$ but rather some other, adversarially chosen stream $\pi_\mathcal{A}$ that does not contain $\pi$ as a prefix (e.g., because the server is behaving maliciously or incorrectly), then the only way the verifier can accept an *incorrect* result is if the adversary has found a *hash collision*. That is, the consumed stream $\pi_\mathcal{A}$ contains an element $s^\dagger$ that corresponds to an element $s$ in $\pi$ such that $s \neq s^\dagger$ but $\mathsf{hash}\ s = \mathsf{hash}\ s^\dagger$.

As discussed further in Section 4.4, this implies the standard cryptographic notion of security for this setting if hash is collision-resistant. Here is the theorem, stated formally:

**Theorem 1.** *Suppose that* $\vdash e\ e_P\ e_V : \tau$.

**Correctness:** *If* $\ll [], e \gg \rightarrow_I^i \ll [], e' \gg$ *then there exist* $e'_P$, $e'_V$, $\pi$ *such that*

- $\ll [], e_P \gg \rightarrow_P^i \ll \pi, e'_P \gg$
- $\ll \pi, e_V \gg \rightarrow_V^i \ll [], e'_V \gg$
- $\vdash e'\ e'_P\ e'_V : \tau$

**Security:** *If* $\ll \pi_{\mathcal{A}}, e_V \gg \rightarrow_V^i \ll \pi', e'_V \gg$ *then*

1. *there exist* $e'$, $e'_P$, $\pi$, *such that*
   - $\ll [], e \gg \rightarrow_I^i \ll [], e' \gg$
   - $\ll [], e_P \gg \rightarrow_P^i \ll [] \mathbin{@} \pi, e'_P \gg$
   - $\pi_{\mathcal{A}} = \pi \mathbin{@} \pi'$
   - $\vdash e'\ e'_P\ e'_V : \tau$
2. *or else there exist* $j \leq i$, $e'_P$, $\pi_0$, $s$ *and* $s^\dagger$ *such that*
   - $\ll [], e_P \gg \rightarrow_P^j \ll [] \mathbin{@} \pi_0 \mathbin{@} [s], e'_P \gg$
   - $\pi_{\mathcal{A}} = \pi_0 \mathbin{@} [s^\dagger] \mathbin{@} \pi'$
   - $s \neq s^\dagger$ *but* $\mathsf{hash}\ s = \mathsf{hash}\ s^\dagger$.

The proof is by induction on the length $i$ of the multi-step derivations, relying on two lemmas about the Correctness and Security of single-step evaluation, which we present next.

**Lemma 5** (Correctness). *If* $\vdash e\ e_P\ e_V : \tau$ *and* $\ll [], e \gg \rightarrow_I \ll [], e' \gg$ *then there exist* $e'_P$, $e'_V$, *and* $\pi$ *such that for all* $\pi'$, $\pi_p$

1. $\vdash e'\ e'_P\ e'_V : \tau$
2. $\ll \pi_p, e_P \gg \rightarrow_P \ll \pi_p \mathbin{@} \pi, e'_P \gg$
3. $\ll \pi \mathbin{@} \pi', e_V \gg \rightarrow_V \ll \pi', e'_V \gg$.

*Proof.* By induction on $\vdash e\ e_P\ e_V : \tau$. Most cases are straightforward, and follow by application of the Substitution lemma. The two interesting cases deal with authenticated computations:

- Suppose $e$, $e_P$, and $e_V$ are $auth\ v$, $auth\ v_P$ and $auth\ v_V$, respectively. Each can take a step in its respective mode, producing $v$, $\langle \mathsf{hash}\,\llparenthesis v_P \rrparenthesis, v_P\rangle$, and $\mathsf{hash}\, v_V$, respectively, leaving the proof stream unchanged (i.e., $\pi = []$). Now we must prove $\vdash v\ \langle \mathsf{hash}\,\llparenthesis v_P \rrparenthesis, v_P\rangle\ \mathsf{hash}\, v_V : \bullet\tau$, which in turn requires proving $\vdash v\ v_P\ \llparenthesis v_P \rrparenthesis : \tau$ and $\mathsf{hash}\,\llparenthesis v_P \rrparenthesis = \mathsf{hash}\, v_V$. Both are the consequence of Lemma 2.1 and $\vdash e\ e_P\ e_V : \tau$.
- Suppose $e$, $e_P$, and $e_V$ are $unauth\ v$, $unauth\ v_P$ and $unauth\ v_V$, respectively. By inversion on $\vdash e\ e_P\ e_V : \tau$ we know that $\vdash v\ \langle h, v_P\rangle\ h : \bullet\tau$ and by inversion on this we know $\vdash v\ v_P\ \llparenthesis v_P \rrparenthesis : \tau$ and $h = \mathsf{hash}\llparenthesis v_P \rrparenthesis$. We can set $\pi = [\llparenthesis v_P \rrparenthesis]$, and then each term can take a step in its respective mode to $v$, $v_P$, and $\llparenthesis v_P \rrparenthesis$, which agree by Lemma 2.1. □

Finally, we demonstrate that a verifier term that begins in agreement and takes a step remains in agreement unless an adversary has managed to find a hash collision.

**Lemma 6** (Security). *Given the following:*

- $\vdash e\ e_P\ e_V : \tau$
- $\ll \pi_{\mathcal{A}}, e_V \gg \rightarrow_V \ll \pi', e'_V \gg$

*then there exist* $e'$, $e'_P$, *and* $\pi$ *such that for all* $\pi_p$,

- $\ll [], e \gg \rightarrow_I \ll [], e' \gg$
- $\ll \pi_p, e_P \gg \rightarrow_P \ll \pi_p \mathbin{@} \pi, e'_P \gg$

*and either*

1. $\vdash e'\ e'_P\ e'_V : \tau$ *and* $\pi_{\mathcal{A}} = \pi \mathbin{@} \pi'$, *or else*
2. *there exists a pair* $s$ *and* $s^\dagger$ *such that* $\pi = [s]$ *and* $\pi_{\mathcal{A}} = [s^\dagger] \mathbin{@} \pi'$ *with* $s \neq s^\dagger$ *but* $\mathsf{hash}\ s = \mathsf{hash}\ s^\dagger$.

*Proof.* By induction on $\vdash e\ e_P\ e_V : \tau$. Since $e_V$ is not a value, we know from Lemma 2.4 that neither are $e$ or $e_P$, so we can always introduce $e'$ and $e'_P$. Most cases are straightforward because evaluation yields $\pi = []$ and $\pi_{\mathcal{A}} = \pi'$, and $\vdash e'\ e'_P\ e'_V : \tau$ can be obtained directly from inversion on $\vdash e\ e_P\ e_V : \tau$. The remaining cases are for let binding and $unauth$. The former follows by induction. For the latter we have $e$, $e_P$, and $e_V$ are $unauth\ v$, $unauth\ v_P$ and $unauth\ v_V$, respectively. Since these terms agree by assumption, we know that $v_P = \langle h, v'_P\rangle$ and $v_V = h = \mathsf{hash}(\llparenthesis v'_P \rrparenthesis)$ for some $v'_P$. From the stepping rule for $\rightarrow_P$, we know $\pi = [\llparenthesis v'_P \rrparenthesis]$. Then there are three possible outcomes depending on $\pi_{\mathcal{A}}$:

1. $\pi_{\mathcal{A}} = []$, or $\pi_{\mathcal{A}} = [s^\dagger] \mathbin{@} \pi'$ and $\mathsf{hash}\ s^\dagger \neq h$, in which case $\ll \pi_{\mathcal{A}}, e_V \gg$ is stuck and we have a contradiction
2. $\pi_{\mathcal{A}} = [\llparenthesis v'_P \rrparenthesis] \mathbin{@} \pi'$ and $e'_V = \llparenthesis v'_P \rrparenthesis$, from which $\vdash e'\ e'_P\ e'_V : \tau$ follows directly
3. $\pi_{\mathcal{A}} = [s^\dagger] \mathbin{@} \pi'$ and $\llparenthesis v'_P \rrparenthesis \neq s^\dagger$, but $\mathsf{hash}\ \llparenthesis v'_P \rrparenthesis = \mathsf{hash}\ s^\dagger$. □

Although the Security property guarantees that the ideal computation can always take as many steps as the verifier (in particular, the verifier cannot run forever if the ideal computation terminates), we would also like to show that ideal computation can take as many steps as the prover.

**Remark 1.** *Suppose* $\vdash e\ e_P\ e_V : \tau$ *and* $\ll \pi_p, e_P \gg \rightarrow_P^i \ll \pi_p \mathbin{@} \pi, e'_P \gg$. *Then there exists* $e'$, $e'_V$ *such that* $\vdash e'\ e'_P\ e'_V : \tau$, $\ll [], e \gg \rightarrow_I^i \ll [], e' \gg$, *and* $\ll \pi, e_V \gg \rightarrow_V^i \ll [], e'_V \gg$.

*Proof.* This follows from straightforward induction on derivation length $i$ and $\vdash e\ e_P\ e_V : \tau$, applying Lemmas 2 and 5.

### 4.4 Cryptographic Security

In the cryptographic security definition for a fixed ADS protocol, (e.g., as per Papamanthou et al. [25]), somewhat informally, there is an attacker who is assumed able to control the interaction between an honest prover and verifier. The attacker may specify a sequence of operations ("queries") $q_1, \ldots, q_t$ that the verifier poses to the prover. For each such query, the prover generates and sends a proof to the verifier; both parties update their local state as appropriate. Finally, the attacker specifies a query $q_{t+1}$ along with an adversarially generated proof string $\pi_{\mathcal{A}}$; the attacker *succeeds* if $\pi_{\mathcal{A}}$ causes the verifier to output an incorrect result for the given query. The ADS is parameterized by a *security parameter* $k$ which we may identify with the output length of the hash function being used. The ADS is *secure* if no attacker running in polynomial time (in $k$) succeeds with non-negligible probability. Security is proven by contradiction with the collision-resistance of an appropriately chosen hash function.

To translate the standard cryptographic notion to our setting, we must address three technicalities. First, we must provide a notion of programs and inputs, such that the ADS is specified by an arbitrary $\lambda\bullet$ program, and the adversary is allowed to choose the inputs. Second, in order to show contradiction with collision-resistance, we must define a specific procedure by which the hash function is instantiated *after* the ADS program and the adversary are fixed. Finally, we must relate the number of reduction steps taken by a $\lambda\bullet$ program to a number of steps taken by a Turing machine. We then claim that the reduction argument in Theorem 1 implies that this security definition holds for every $\lambda\bullet$ program.

***Inputs.*** We can treat the free variables in an open $\lambda\bullet$ expression as program inputs. In our running example, for instance, the expression fetch idx t has idx and t as free variables. The adversary chooses the inputs by computing well-typed and in-agreement values to substitute for each of the free variables.

***Choosing the hash function.*** Our language is parameterized by an arbitrary hash function, which we have assumed is collision-resistant. However, to be precise, collision-resistance is only defined formally for a *family* of hash functions rather than some fixed hash function (see Katz and Lindell [14]). That is, collision-resistance is defined according to the following game: First, take an arbitrary adversary that runs in polynomial-time given a security parameter $k$. Next, choose hash randomly from a family of functions, and give the adversary a description of hash as input. The family of hash functions is *collision-resistant* if the the adversary outputs a collision in hash with negligible probability in $k$.

The following game captures this notion in the context of $\lambda\bullet$:

1. Let $e$ be an arbitrary well-typed $\lambda\bullet$ program specifying the data structure being supported, and let $\mathcal{A}$ be an arbitrary adversary that runs in polynomial-time (in $k$).
2. Choose hash at random from a collision-resistant family of $k$-bit hash functions, and then compile $e_P$ and $e_V$.
3. $\mathcal{A}$ *succeeds* if, given $k$ and hash as input, it outputs in-agreement values to substitute for the free variables of $e$, $e_P$, and $e_V$, and a proof stream $\pi_{\mathcal{A}}$, such that after some polynomial of steps $i$, the verifier outputs an incorrect answer; i.e., a value $e'_V$ such that $\ll \pi_{\mathcal{A}}, e_V \gg \rightarrow^i_V \ll \pi'_{\mathcal{A}}, e'_V \gg$ for some $\pi'_{\mathcal{A}}$, but there is no $e', e'_P$ such that $\ll [], e \gg \rightarrow^i_I \ll [], e' \gg$ and $\vdash e'\ e'_P\ e'_V : \tau$.

Note that the game begins with an arbitrary well-typed $\lambda\bullet$ program $e$, before the hash function has been chosen. Although $\lambda\bullet$ is parameterized by hash, the ideal terms are invariant to the choice of hash function, so we can fix $e$ and $\Gamma \vdash e : \tau$ before choosing hash. However, the prover and verifier terms $e_P$ and $e_V$ may actually contain digests, so we must instantiate hash before compiling $e_P$ and $e_V$.

If $\mathcal{A}$ succeeds, then by Theorem 1 we can evaluate $e_P$ and $e_V$ (on $\pi_{\mathcal{A}}$) for $j \leq i$ steps, and extract the collision $s$ and $s^\dagger$. Thus, it only remains for us to show that evaluation of $e_V$ and $e_P$ also takes polynomial time, and then we can obtain from $\mathcal{A}$ a polynomial-time collision-finding algorithm with the same success probability.

***Polynomial-time execution.*** It is well known that standard lambda-calculus evaluation and Turing-machine execution are polynomially equivalent [4]; that is, a lambda-calculus interpreter implemented as a Turing machine can simulate $i$ lambda-calculus evaluation steps in $O(poly(i))$ Turing-machine steps. The only nonstandard terms in $\lambda\bullet$ are $auth$ and $unauth$, and each involves at most one hash computation during evaluation. The time to compute a hash is proportional to the size of the serialized shallow projection, which depends on the hash output length $k$. Therefore, if an ideal program $e$ takes $i$ steps to reach a value, a Turing machine can simulate the execution of $e$ in $O(poly(i))$ steps and the corresponding $e_P$ and $e_V$ in $O(poly(ik))$ steps. Since we assume $i$ is bounded by $O(poly(k))$, the entire evaluation is $O(poly(k))$.

# 5. Implementation

This section describes our prototype extension to the OCaml compiler for supporting authenticated types. We discuss basic compilation,[6] two optimizations we implement, and current limitations.

[6] Our technique for extending the OCaml compiler is based on a 2012 blog post by Jun Furuse: `https://bitbucket.org/camlspotter/compiler-libs-hack`

## 5.1 Compilation

The compilation process works as follows. The programmer writes an OCaml program $p$ like that of Figure 2 that contains uses of authenticated types. The code will link against the ADS module, whose signature declares $\bullet\alpha$ as abstract[7] and declares the (polymorphic) types of the $auth$ and $unauth$ coercions. Program $p$ is then passed to our extended compiler which, depending on a command-line *mode* flag, replaces each application of $auth$ and $unauth$ it finds with a call to a prover- or verifier-specific implementation; the resulting code is linked with the ADS module.

This module, given in Figure 11, defines type $\bullet\alpha$ as either a digest (just the hash, represented as a string), or as a pair of the hash and a value of type $\alpha$. The next four functions define the prover's and verifier's versions of $auth$ and $unauth$, respectively; the calls to $auth$ and $unauth$ will be replaced by calls to these functions instead. We can see that their code largely matches the operational rules given in Figure 8, where the proof stream from the rules is implemented as OCaml channels, prf_output and prf_input. The one departure is that auth_prover and unauth_prover additionally take a function shallow that is invoked to perform the shallow projection operation. This operation is needed because OCaml does not provide a generic method for folding/mapping over the structure of a term. As such, our compiler generates type-specific shallow projection functions where needed, and includes them in the replaced calls to $auth$ and $unauth$. The type of the shallow projection operator is determined by the concrete type inferred at each $auth/unauth$ call. For example, the $unauth$ in **let** x : int = $unauth$ y is inferred to have type $\bullet$int $\rightarrow$ int. Therefore, we need a shallow projection operation of type int $\rightarrow$ int (which is just the identity). The generated code will refer to the ADS module's shallow_$\bullet$ function, shown at the bottom of the figure, for handling (nested) authenticated values.

Library functions are provided to enable the programmer to manipulate the proof and verification streams, for example by writing/reading to a file or a socket, or performing multiple authenticated operations with separate proofs in a single execution.

Figure 12 shows the result of compiling a variant of authenticated binary search trees. The top of the figure is the code provided by the programmer. Compilation will replace the call to $auth$ with a call to auth_bst1 and the call to $unauth$ with a call to unauth_bst. These functions are defined at the bottom of the figure, and employ the needed, type-specific shallow projection operations.

The hash function referenced in Figure 11 is polymorphic, having type $\forall\alpha.\alpha \rightarrow$ string. It is implemented by first serializing the argument and then hashing it using SHA1 (which is widely used as a collision-resistant hash function).

For serialization, we use OCaml's default serializer implemented in the Marshal module. This choice has an implication for security: the worst-case cost to compute the hash of a malicious string is bounded only by the representation of an integer in OCaml, either 32 or 64 bits, depending on the OS. We used the *no-sharing* option for the Marshal module to guarantee that any two equal objects have equal serializations.[8]

[7] Type $\bullet\alpha$ is written in ASCII as $\alpha$ authtype, but we continue writing $\bullet\alpha$ for consistency.

[8] It may be the case that two terms of different types have equal serializations using Marshal; however, since we only interpret serialized values according to known static types (no polymorphism), it would take a collision *at the same type* to harm security. In our formalism, which is essentially dynamically typed, we assume serialization (encased in the abstract hash function) is bijective.

```
type •α = | Digest of string (* the digest *)
          | Prover of string × α

let auth_prover (shallow: α → α) (v:α) : •α =
  Prover(hash (shallow v), v)

let unauth_prover (shallow: α → α) (v:•α) : α =
  let Prover(_,x) = v in
  to_channel !prf_output (shallow x);
  x

let auth_verifier (v:α) : •α = Digest(hash v)

let unauth_verifier (v:•α) : α =
  let Digest(h) = v in
  let y = from_channel !prf_input in
  assert h = hash y;
  y

let shallow_• (Prover(h,_): •α) : •α = Digest(h)
```

**Figure 11.** The implementation of type constructor • and the Prover and Verifier's *unauth* and *auth* coercions.

```
(* User-provided code *)
type bst = Tip
  | Bin of •bst × int × •bst
  | AuthBin of •(bst × int × bst)
let is_empty (t:•bst) : bool = (unauth t = Tip)
let mk_leaf (x:int) : •bst = AuthBin(auth(Tip, x, Tip))

(* Generated Prover code *)
let rec shallow_bst : bst → bst = function
  | Tip → Tip
  | Bin (x, y, z) → Bin(shallow_• x, y, shallow_• z)
  | AuthBin (x) → AuthBin (shallow_bst1 x)
and shallow_bst1 : bst × int × bst → bst × int × bst
= function (x, y, z) → (shallow_bst x, y, shallow_bst z)

let unauth_bst = unauth_prover shallow_bst
let auth_bst1 = auth_prover shallow_bst1
```

**Figure 12.** Example types and generated code (for prover)

### 5.2 Optimizations

Our compiler implements two optimizations that reduce the size of the proof stream, *reuse buffering*, and *suspended disbelief*.

***Reuse buffering.*** We can reduce the size of the proof stream, and speed up proving/verification, when we anticipate that the same elements may appear in the proof stream more than once. For example, a client may submit a batch of operations to the server that end up re-traversing many of the nodes of the ADS. The client could cache the shallow projections of these elements locally instead of reading them from the proof stream multiple times.

This optimization requires modifying the *unauth* and *auth* functionality; the modification is simlar for both prover and verifier. A counter is incremented each time *auth* or *unauth* is called. Each party maintains two data structures: *LRU-Map*, a mapping from *auth*/*unauth* counter values to shallow projections, indicating the least-recently-used ordering, and *Digest-Map*, a mapping from digests to *auth*/*unauth* counter values; collectively *Digest-Map* and *LRU-Map* are referred to as "the cache," as they contain corresponding elements. When *unauth* is called, if the digest exists in *Digest-Map*, the prover omits (resp., verifier fetches from the cache) the corresponding shallow projection, then updates the counter value associated with it in the cache; otherwise, the prover appends it to (resp., verifier reads it from) the proof stream and adds it to the cache. If the size of the cache exceeds the parameter, then the least recently used element (the smallest key in *LRU-Map*) is removed. The proof generation/checking/size benefits come at the cost of having to store the cache.

***Suspending disbelief.*** This optimization eliminates redundancy in shallow projections that contain hashes computable from nested shallow projections appearing subsequently in the proof stream. This idea is implicit in the verification procedure for Merkle trees (Section 2.1). We can approximate the optimization for arbitrary data structures in λ• by modifying *unauth* (for both the prover and verifier) to use a buffer to "suspend disbelief."

For the prover, the goal is to decide which digests in a shallow projection can safely be omitted, which are those that correspond to nodes that will be visited during subsequent calls to *unauth*. To achieve this, we extend the representation for •α values:

```
type •α = ... | Susp of string × α × bool ref
              | Sentinel
```

Each time *unauth* is called, the shallow projection is computed differently: each immediate child, Prover(d,a), would ordinarily be replaced with Digest(d) but is instead replaced with Susp(d,a,flag), where flag is a fresh mutable flag (initially **false**) that indicates whether the digest can be omitted. When one of these children is accessed by *unauth* the corresponding flag is set. Rather than writing the shallow projection immediately to the proof stream, it is appended to a queue. The queue is flushed when execution reaches a programmer-inserted insist annotation. This is a hint that belief need no longer be suspended; its placement has no effect on security but it is best used at the end of a distinct operation. Before a queue element is added to the proof stream, occurrences of Susp(d,a,flag) are (functionally) replaced with Sentinel when !flag is **true**, and replaced with Digest(d) when !flag is **false**.

When the verifier encounters a shallow projection object in the proof stream containing Sentinel values, its digest cannot be computed immediately so the object is stored in a set referred to as the *suspended-disbelief* buffer. If *unauth* is subsequently called on an immediate child of a node in this buffer, even if the shallow projection is available in the proof stream, the root hash is unknown so it cannot be immediately validated either. Thus we extend the •α representation again with a new tag, Suspension.

```
type •α = ... | Suspension of string ref × (unit → unit)
```

For every object placed in the buffer, each immediate Sentinel is replaced with a Suspension containing a callback closure and a mutable reference (initially empty) optionally containing a hash. When a leaf node is accessed, the Suspension reference is updated with the actual digest of the leaf, and the callback is invoked. The callback encapsulates a pointer to the parent node, and checks if all immediate Suspension children have been populated with digests. If so, the callback removes the node from the buffer, computes the node's digest, and takes one of two actions: if the reference already contains a digest, then the two are compared for equality; if not, then the reference is updated with the computed digest, and the callback closure is invoked. Thus validation propagates upwards from the leaves to the root.

A caveat of this optimization is that it exposes the verifier to potential resource exhaustion attacks, as (potentially infinite) computation is performed on untrusted data before it is validated. A solution would be to bound the number of steps the program should take before the buffer is cleared. Another caveat is that this optimization requires additional storage on the verifier in contrast to the original Merkle tree optimization.

### 5.3 Supporting full OCaml

Our compiler prototype supports authenticating the OCaml equivalent of the type language given in Figure 5 with the exception of function types. This support has been sufficient to program a variety of interesting data structures, as described in the next section.

To implement authenticated functions requires that we be able to perform the shallow projection of a lambda term. Our formalism does this by folding over the syntax of the lambda term's body to find authenticated values $\langle h, v \rangle$ and replace them with values $h$. In an implementation this operation is tantamount to transforming a closure's environment. We could do this quite naturally using Siskind and Pearlmutter's map-closure operator [30], but unfortunately (as they point out) it is not clear how to implement this operator in a statically typed language, since the compiler cannot, in general, know the types of a given closure's environment variables. We could imagine storing type information with the closure (e.g., Crary et al's [3] term representations for types) in support of a generic, run-time shallow projection operation as per the formalism. In the meantime, the most natural use of authenticated closures we have found is to support shallow CPS transformations; we can use an explicit stack to the same effect, as shown in Figure 4.

Among other OCaml features not yet supported, the most desirable is authenticated polymorphic types. Similarly to closure environments, the compiler cannot know types needed to perform shallow projection—if a value given to $auth$ and $unauth$ is polymorphic, then its type is determined by how type variables are instantiated at a particular call-site. Once again, a generic shallow projection operator as per our formalism (and easily implemented in a dynamically typed language) would fit the bill. We could imagine requiring that $auth$ and $unauth$ each take an additional type parameter; in most cases it could be statically determined, but to support polymorphism it could be passed as an argument, e.g., to the polymorphic function containing the $auth/unauth$ call.

## 6. Evaluation

To demonstrate the effectiveness and generality of our language and compiler, we have implemented a variety of ADSs. We analyze their performance and confirm it empirically with benchmarks for selected algorithms. Our benchmarks were conducted using an Amazon EC2 "m1.xlarge" instance (an Intel E5645 2.4GHz processor, with 16GB of RAM). All data structures were stored in RAM. Complete code is given in our extended technical report [20].

***Merkle trees.*** Our version of Merkle trees was given in Figure 2. As Merkle trees are the most common authenticated data structure, and are readily implemented, we compared the running time of our compiled verifier routine to hand-written implementations in OCaml and in C (see Figure 13(c)). The benchmark consists of 10,000 random accesses to trees of height $h$ for $h \in [5, 19]$. Each array element is a 1024 byte string; thus the largest tree contains approximately $250,000$ elements and stores approximately 250 MB of data in total. Compared to the hand-optimized version in C, the program generated by our compiler is slower by only a factor of two; the hand-written OCaml code is about 30% slower than the C program. Profiling with gprof reveals that substantial overhead is due to the Marshal serialization routine used by our compiler; the hand-written OCaml code avoids this serialization by concatenating the child digests directly.

***Red-black+ Trees.*** A red-black+ tree is a self-balancing binary tree—the + indicates that internal nodes only store keys, and the values are stored only in the leaves. This data structure is appropriate for a (updatable) dictionary. We consider authenticated search trees to be the second oldest authenticated data structure, proposed by Naor and Nissim [24] to implement certificate revocation lists. Our results are asymptotically equivalent: the storage cost to the prover for the entire data structure is $O(n)$, while the computation cost per operation for both prover and verifier is $O(log\, n)$; the size of the proof stream is also $O(log\, n)$. Note that we also implement an authenticated version of normal binary search trees, too, and these also have the expected performance.

In Figure 13(a), we show the empirical runtime performance of the authenticated red-black+ tree for both the prover ($P$) and verifier ($V$) modes, as well the ideal mode with the • annotations and $unauth/auth$ commands erased, to show the overall computational overhead of authentication. The benchmark consists of $100,000$ random insertions into a random tree containing $2^k$ elements, for each $k \in [4, 21]$. $P$ runs approximately 25% faster than $V$; this is because $V$ computes a hash during both $unauth$ and $auth$ instructions whereas $P$ only computes a hash during $auth$. According to profiler analysis (using gprof), $V$ spends $55\%$ of its time in the SHA1 hash routine and $30\%$ in (de)serialization routines; $P$ spends $28\%$ of its time computing SHA1, $30\%$ performing serialization and $22\%$ in garbage collection. The overhead of $P$ is approximately a factor of 100 compared to the ordinary data structure. We omit similar benchmarks for our other algorithms as the results are similar.

We measured the largest amount of memory allocated by OCaml during this benchmark as shown in Figure 13(b). This illustrates the key advantage of an authenticated data structure scheme: while $P$ incurs space overhead by a factor of 3 vs the Ideal mode, the space requirement of the $V$ is effectively constant.

Finally, we used this benchmark to evaluate the effectiveness of our two compiler optimizations on proof size (see Figure 13(d)). For a binary tree, the suspended-disbelief buffer results in a proof-size reduction of almost 50%, since only one of the left or right child digests must be transmitted for each node. The reuse cache is most effective when the tree is small and mostly fits in the cache; thus since the cache-size parameter in our benchmark is 1000, the proof is nearly empty up to trees of height 9. However, because the benchmark consists of random queries, the leaves and nodes toward the bottom are accessed almost uniformly at random, so only a constant number of nodes near the root are read from the cache each query. The cache would be more beneficial in applications where some nodes were accessed much more frequently. We only implemented the two optimizations separately; combining the two is left as future work.

***Skip Lists.*** Skip lists [29] are randomized data structures providing similar performance (in expectation) to binary search trees.[9] Our results are asymptotically equivalent to previous work on authenticated skip lists [12]: the storage cost to $P$ for the entire data structure is $O(\log n)$, where $n$ is the number of elements inserted; the expected computational cost to $P$ and $V$ as well as the size of the proof stream is $O(\log n)$, but $O(n)$ in the worst case.

***Planar Separator Trees.*** Planar separator trees (PSTs) are data structures that can be used to efficiently query the distance of the shortest path between two vertices in a planar graph (e.g., many road maps) [6]. A separator of a graph is a collection of vertices inducing a binary partition on the graph, such that any path from a vertex in one partition to a vertex in the other partition must pass through a vertex in the separator. A consequence of the planar separator theorem is that every planar graph has a separator that is *small*

[9] Random algorithms can be used in $\lambda\bullet$ as long as $P$ and $V$ both use the same pseudorandom function and seed.

($O(\sqrt{n})$ where $n$ is the number of vertices) yet induces a balanced partition (both partitions have at least $\frac{n}{3}$ elements); a search structure can be built over the graph by recursively constructing separators for each partition. While the naïve solution of storing the shortest distance between every pair of vertices requires $O(n^2)$ storage, the planar separator tree requires only $O(n^{\frac{3}{2}})$ space. The shortest distance between any two points can be computed in $O(\sqrt{n} \log n)$ time using this data structure. A potential application of an authenticated planar separator tree is for a mobile device user to query a service provider for travel directions, along with a proof that the response is actually the shortest path (rather than, e.g., one that routes the user out of their way past billboards for which the service provider might receive a profit). Using our authenticated compiler, the proof size and computation cost for $P$ and $V$ is also $O(\sqrt{n} \log n)$. We include this primarily as an example of a data structure that has not been treated as an ADS in prior work, but is straightforward to authenticate using our framework.

***Bitcoin.*** Bitcoin [22] is a peer-to-peer network implementing a virtual currency; it features an authenticated data structure called the *blockchain*, which represents a history of transactions. A global ledger can be computed from the blockchain, which, abstractly speaking, contains a set of currently valid coins. A valid transaction removes a past coin from the ledger and adds a new one (assigned to the recipient of the coin).

The current Bitcoin data structure suffers from two drawbacks: 1) a miner (verifier) needs to maintain an entire copy of the global ledger to efficiently perform validation of transactions, which may become unscalable as the number of coins increases; and 2) at install time, a new client needs to download the entire transaction history and perform a linear computation (in the size of the block chain) to construct the ledger even when it trusts the root digest.

These drawbacks can be resolved if we build the ledger (as an authenticated set) into the block chain data structure. We have done this in our language by composing the blockchain data structure with a ledger consisting of our authenticated red-black+ tree, thereby reducing client storage to $O(\log M)$, where $M$ bounds the number of coins in the ledger. Full details are given our supplemental technical report [20].

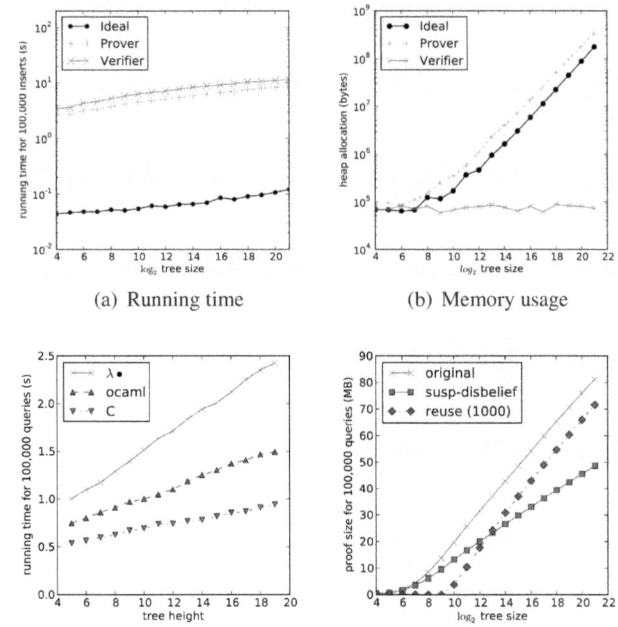


(a) Running time

(b) Memory usage

(c) our λ• compiler vs hand-optimized code

(d) proof size with optional optimizations

**Figure 13.** Empirical performance evaluation results. For 100,000 insertions into a red-black+ tree, (a) running time for Prover, Verifier, and Ideal; (b) memory usage (heap size). (c) Running time for fetch operation in a balanced merkle tree, for the program generated by our compiler, hand-written OCaml code, and hand-written C code; For 100,000 random insertions in a binary search tree, (d) the effect of two optional optimizations on proof stream size, compared with two optional optimizations: a reuse-cache (of size 1000) and the belief-suspension buffer.

## 7. Related Work

As mentioned earlier, authenticated data structure research has had a flurry of results [1, 12, 15, 16, 19, 23] from the cryptography community, proposing authenticated versions of set (non)-membership, dictionaries, range queries, certain graph queries, B-trees, etc.

To the best of our knowledge, no one has offered a general authenticated data structure implementation for generic programs. Those closest work is by Martel *et. al.* [16], which proposes a method for designing authenticated data structures for a class of data structures referred to as "search DAGs." Their model is limited to *static* data structures, i.e., it does not support updates, which are supported by λ•. Our approach is also easier to use, since the programmer writes largely standard (purely functional) implementations of data structures and their operations, and the compiler generates the prover/verifier code; in their approach, the task of designing and implementing ADS still must be done by hand.

Our programmatically generated ADS implementations have performance competitive with known customized ADS constructions based on collision-resistant hashes. We note, however, that while most are, not all known ADS constructions are based on collision resistant hash functions. For example, bilinear-group based ADS constructions exist for set operations [27]. Using alternative algebraic primitives other than collision resistant hashes can sometimes yield asymptotically better ADS constructions.

Beyond the optimizations we have implemented (see Section 5.2), there are other known optimizations that we have not an included. An example is the technique of "commutative hashing" due to Goodrich et al. [12] which reduces the proof size when it is irrelevant which (of possibly several) child nodes are traversed. We believe it is likely that optimizations for specific data structures could be incorporated generally into our compiler. Other optimizations lie further outside our model; an example is a line of work beginning with Merkle's original paper [2, 18] in which the stored data is not arbitrary, but is instead generated algorithmically (e.g., using a pseudo-random number generator). In this case, the prover's storage costs can be significantly reduced by recomputing data on the fly rather than storing it. In our performance evaluation we consider memory usage and running time; however some work in authenticated data structures [16, 21] considers I/O efficiency, another practical characteristic.

Verified computation [9] and succinct non-interactive arguments of knowledge (SNARKs) [10, 28] can also yield asymptotically better protocols for ensuring integrity of outsourced computation (e.g., with $O(1)$ amount of client computation other than reading the input and output). However, while theoretically attractive, known verified computation schemes and SNARKs are orders of magnitude more expensive than constructions based on collision-resistant hashes in practice [28]—partly due to the use of heavyweight cryptographic primitives such as fully homomorphic encryption.

ZQL [8] is a language for writing verified computations over hidden inputs; this is achieved by compiling programs to custom zero-knowledge protocols. Thus, unlike λ•, ZQL provides correctness, security, *and* privacy. However, this comes at the price of a more limited language, e.g., ZQL does not support branching or higher-order functions generally. In addition, ZQL's absolute performance is much worse due to the use of more heavyweight cryptography.

## 8. Conclusions

We have presented λ•, the first programming language for authenticated data structures (ADS). We have formally proven that every well-typed λ• program compiles to a secure protocol, and we have implemented λ• as a simple compiler extension to OCaml so that a programmer can easily derive an authenticated data structure from any ordinary one. The protocols generated by our compiler are competitive with the state-of-the-art in hand-rolled ADSs.

We believe this work is long past-due. ADS are a 30-year-old technique in cryptography, and yet researchers have overlooked the simple connection between ADSs encapsulated in our notion of authenticated types. We plan to extend our language to be more expressive, and to include more efficient techniques based on advanced cryptographic primitives. We hope our work encourages ADS adoption in future secure computing infrastructure.

***Acknowledgments*** We thank Zooko and the Tahoe-LAFS team for several conversations that inspired our approach, and Nikhil Swamy and the anonymous reviewers for invaluable comments on drafts of this paper. This research was sponsored in part by NSF grant CNS-1111599, and by the US Army Research Laboratory and the UK Ministry of Defence under Agreement Number W911NF-06-3-0001. The views and conclusions contained in this document are those of the authors and should not be interpreted as representing the official policies, either expressed or implied, of the US Army Research Laboratory, the U.S. Government, the UK Ministry of Defense, or the UK Government. The US and UK Governments are authorized to reproduce and distribute reprints for Government purposes notwithstanding any copyright notation hereon.

## References

[1] A. Anagnostopoulos, M. T. Goodrich, and R. Tamassia. Persistent authenticated dictionaries and their applications. In *Proc. ISC*, pages 379–393, London, UK, UK, 2001. Springer-Verlag.

[2] P. Berman, M. Karpinski, and Y. Nekrich. Optimal trade-off for Merkle tree traversal. *Theor. Comput. Sci.*, 372(1):26–36, Mar. 2007.

[3] K. Crary, S. Weirich, and G. Morrisett. Intensional polymorphism in type-erasure semantics. *Journal of Functional Programming*, 12(6), 2002.

[4] U. Dal Lago and S. Martini. An invariant cost model for the lambda calculus. In *Logical Approaches to Computational Barriers*, pages 105–114. Springer, 2006.

[5] P. Devanbu, M. Gertz, C. Martel, and S. G. Stubblebine. Authentic third-party data publication. In *Data and Application Security*, pages 101–112. Springer, 2002.

[6] R. Duan. Planar separator theorem and its applications. lecture slides, Advanced Graph Algorithms, Summer 2012. max planck institut informatik. `http://www.mpi-inf.mpg.de/departments/d1/teaching/ss12/AdvancedGraphAlgorithms/Slides10.pdf`.

[7] C. Flanagan, A. Sabry, B. F. Duba, and M. Felleisen. The essence of compiling with continuations. In *Proc. PLDI*, 1993.

[8] C. Fournet, M. Kohlweiss, G. Danezis, and Z. Luo. ZQL: A compiler for privacy-preserving data processing. In *USENIX Security*, 2013.

[9] R. Gennaro, C. Gentry, and B. Parno. Non-interactive verifiable computing: Outsourcing computation to untrusted workers. In *CRYPTO 2010*, pages 465–482. Springer, 2010.

[10] R. Gennaro, C. Gentry, B. Parno, and M. Raykova. Quadratic span programs and succinct NIZKs without PCPs. Cryptology ePrint Archive, Report 2012/215, 2012. `http://eprint.iacr.org/`.

[11] M. T. Goodrich, C. Papamanthou, and R. Tamassia. On the cost of persistence and authentication in skip lists. In *Proc. Intl. Workshop on Experimental Algorithms*, volume 4525 of *LNCS*, pages 94–107. Springer, 2007.

[12] M. T. Goodrich, R. Tamassia, and A. Schwerin. Implementation of an authenticated dictionary with skip lists and commutative hashing. In *Proc. DARPA Information Survivability Conference and Exposition II (DISCEX II)*, pages 68–82, 2001.

[13] M. T. Goodrich, R. Tamassia, and N. Triandopoulos. Efficient authenticated data structures for graph connectivity and geometric search problems. *Algorithmica*, 60(3):505–552, 2011.

[14] J. Katz and Y. Lindell. *Introduction to Modern Cryptography*. Chapman & Hall/CRC Press, 2007.

[15] F. Li, K. Yi, M. Hadjieleftheriou, and G. Kollios. Proof-infused streams: Enabling authentication of sliding window queries on streams. In *VLDB*, pages 147–158, 2007.

[16] C. Martel, G. Nuckolls, P. Devanbu, M. Gertz, A. Kwong, and S. Stubblebine. A general model for authentic data publication, 2001. Available from `http://www.cs.ucdavis.edu/~devanbu/files/model-paper.pdf`.

[17] C. Martel, G. Nuckolls, P. Devanbu, M. Gertz, A. Kwong, and S. G. Stubblebine. A General Model for Authenticated Data Structures. *Algorithmica*, 39(1):21–41, Jan. 2004.

[18] R. C. Merkle. Secure communications over insecure channels. *Communications of the ACM*, 21(4):294–299, Apr. 1978.

[19] R. C. Merkle. A certified digital signature. In G. Brassard, editor, *Proc. CRYPTO '89*, volume 435 of *LNCS*, pages 218–238. Springer-Verlag, 1989.

[20] A. Miller, M. Hicks, J. Katz, and E. Shi. Full version: Authenticated data structures, generically. `http://www.cs.umd.edu/~amiller/gpads-full.pdf`, Jan. 2014.

[21] E. Mykletun, M. Narasimha, and G. Tsudik. Authentication and integrity in outsourced databases. *Trans. Storage*, 2(2):107–138, 2006.

[22] S. Nakamoto. Bitcoin: A peer-to-peer electronic cash system. Technical report, unpublished, 2009.

[23] M. Naor and K. Nissim. Certificate revocation and certificate update. In *Proc. USENIX*, pages 217–228, Berkeley, 1998.

[24] M. Naor and K. Nissim. Certificate revocation and certificate update. *IEEE J. on Sel. Areas Commun.*, 18(4):561–570, 2000.

[25] C. Papamanthou and R. Tamassia. Time and space efficient algorithms for two-party authenticated data structures. In *Information and Communications Security*, pages 1–15. Springer, 2007.

[26] C. Papamanthou, R. Tamassia, and N. Triandopoulos. Authenticated hash tables. In *Proc. ACM Conference on Computer and Communications Security (CCS)*, pages 437–448. ACM, October 2008.

[27] C. Papamanthou, R. Tamassia, and N. Triandopoulos. Optimal verification of operations on dynamic sets. In *CRYPTO*, pages 91–110, 2011.

[28] B. Parno, C. Gentry, J. Howell, and M. Raykova. Pinocchio: Nearly practical verifiable computation. In *Proc. IEEE SSP*, 2013.

[29] W. Pugh. Skip lists: a probabilistic alternative to balanced trees. *Communications of the ACM*, 33(6):668–676, 1990.

[30] J. M. Siskind and B. A. Pearlmutter. First-class nonstandard interpretations by opening closures. In *POPL*, 2007.

[31] R. Tamassia. Authenticated data structures. In *11th Annual European Symposium on Algorithms*, Sept. 2003.

# Gradual Typing Embedded Securely in JavaScript

Nikhil Swamy[1] Cédric Fournet[1] Aseem Rastogi[2] Karthikeyan Bhargavan[3]
Juan Chen[1] Pierre-Yves Strub[4] Gavin Bierman[1]

Microsoft Research[1] University of Maryland[2] INRIA[3] IMDEA Software Institute[4]
{nswamy, fournet, juanchen, gmb}@microsoft.com, aseem@cs.umd.edu, karthikeyan.bhargavan@inria.fr, pierre-yves@strub.nu

## Abstract

JavaScript's flexible semantics makes writing correct code hard and writing secure code extremely difficult. To address the former problem, various forms of gradual typing have been proposed, such as Closure and TypeScript. However, supporting all common programming idioms is not easy; for example, TypeScript deliberately gives up type soundness for programming convenience. In this paper, we propose a gradual type system and implementation techniques that provide important safety and security guarantees.

We present TS$^\star$, a gradual type system and source-to-source compiler for JavaScript. In contrast to prior gradual type systems, TS$^\star$ features full runtime reflection over *three* kinds of types: (1) simple types for higher-order functions, recursive datatypes and dictionary-based extensible records; (2) the type `any`, for dynamically type-safe TS$^\star$ expressions; and (3) the type `un`, for untrusted, potentially malicious JavaScript contexts in which TS$^\star$ is embedded. After type-checking, the compiler instruments the program with various checks to ensure the type safety of TS$^\star$ despite its interactions with arbitrary JavaScript contexts, which are free to use `eval`, stack walks, prototype customizations, and other offensive features. The proof of our main theorem employs a form of type-preserving compilation, wherein we prove all the runtime invariants of the translation of TS$^\star$ to JavaScript by showing that translated programs are well-typed in JS$^\star$, a previously proposed dependently typed language for proving functional correctness of JavaScript programs.

We describe a prototype compiler, a secure runtime, and sample applications for TS$^\star$. Our examples illustrate how web security patterns that developers currently program in JavaScript (with much difficulty and still with dubious results) can instead be programmed naturally in TS$^\star$, retaining a flavor of idiomatic JavaScript, while providing strong safety guarantees by virtue of typing.

***Categories and Subject Descriptors*** D.3.1 [*Programming Languages*]: Formal Definitions and Theory—Semantics; D.4.6 [*Operating Systems*]: Security and Protection—Verification.

***Keywords*** type systems; language-based security; compilers


*POPL '14*, January 22–24, 2014, San Diego, CA, USA.

http://dx.doi.org/10.1145/2535838.2535889

## 1. Introduction

Writing secure JavaScript is notoriously difficult. Even simple functions, which appear safe on the surface, can be easily broken. As an illustration, consider the script below, simplified from actual scripts in the OWASP CSRFGuard (2010) and Facebook API (2013), security-critical JavaScript libraries that aim to impose access controls on the networking APIs provided by web browsers.

```
function send(u,m) {/*Stand-in for XMLHttpRequest*/}
function protect(send) {
  var whitelist={"https://microsoft.com/mail":true,
                 "https://microsoft.com/owa":true};
  return function (url, msg) {
         if (whitelist[url]) send(url, msg);
       };
} send = protect(send);
```

The function call `protect(send)` on the last line returns a function that interposes an access control check on `send`. If this script were to run in isolation, it would achieve its intended functionality. However, JavaScript programs rarely run in isolation—programmers explicitly link their code with third-party frameworks, and, worse, unexpected code fragments can be injected into the web sandbox by cross-site scripting attacks. For example, the following script running in the same sandbox as `protect` could succeed in sending a message to an unintended recipient.

```
Object.prototype["http://evil.com"]=true;
send("http://evil.com", "bypass!");
```

This is just one attack on `protect`; similar attacks are often the consequence of unintended callbacks to untrusted code (caused, for example, by implicit coercions, getters or setters, prototype hacking, and global object overwriting). Experimentally, we found and reported several such security flaws in the OWASP CSRFGuard and Facebook API scripts, suggesting that untrusted callbacks remain difficult both to prevent and to contain.

**1.1 Attacks $\approx$ Type Errors** Arguably, each of these attacks can be blamed on JavaScript's lax notion of dynamic type-safety. Many runtime behaviors that are traditionally viewed as dynamic type errors (e.g., accessing non-existent properties from an object) are not errors in JavaScript. However, almost *any* such error while running a sensitive script can be exploited by a malicious context, as follows. Anticipating that the script will dereference an otherwise undefined property `x`, which in JavaScript would just return the value `undefined`, a hostile context can define

```
Object.defineProperty(Object.prototype,"x",
                      {get:function(){/*exploit*/}});
```

then run the script and, as `x` is dereferenced and triggers the callback, access any argument on the caller stack. Thus, for protecting good scripts from bad ones, silent type errors in JavaScript are just as dangerous as buffer overruns in C. Despite the numerous dynamic checks performed by the JavaScript runtime, some stronger notion of type safety is called for.

Other researchers have made similar observations. For example, Fournet et al. (2013) show several attacks on a similar piece of code and argue that carefully mediating the interaction between a script and its context is essential for security. They show how to compile f*, a statically typed, ML-like source language to JavaScript in a fully abstract way, allowing programmers to write and reason about functions like `protect` in ML, and to let their compiler generate secure JavaScript automatically. This is an attractive design, but the sad truth is that millions of JavaScript programmers are unlikely to switch to ML. Meanwhile, Bhargavan et al. (2013) have developed DJS, a minimal, statically typed, secure core of JavaScript, primarily for writing first-order, string-processing functions using arrays of fixed size. DJS is suitable for writing security-critical code, like cryptographic libraries, and Bhargavan et al. prove that the behavior of programs accepted by the DJS type checker is independent of the JavaScript environment in which they may run. Many others propose analyses for subsets of JavaScript (Chugh et al. 2012; Guarnieri and Livshits 2009; Guha et al. 2011; Hedin and Sabelfeld 2012; Swamy et al. 2013; Taly et al. 2011), although the guarantees provided only hold if the entire environment in which the program runs is also in the subset in question. Efforts like AdSafe (`http://www.adsafe.org`) and Caja (`http://code.google.com/p/google-caja`) address the problem of safely loading untrusted JavaScript into a program's environment after analyzing and rewriting it. However, in order to do this reliably, various JavaScript features are forbidden, e.g., Politz et al. (2011) show that by ruling out many commonly used JavaScript features (e.g., `eval` or explicit prototype manipulation), AdSafe can safely sandbox untrusted code. Although we find the work on JavaScript subsets a promising line to pursue (indeed, even the ECMAScript standard is evolving towards the definition of subsets, such as the strict mode), assumptions about subsetting the environment are hard to validate in the presence of cross-site scripts.

### 1.2 TS★: a gradually type-safe language within JavaScript

This paper presents TS★, a source programming language that retains many of the dynamic programming idioms of JavaScript, while ensuring type-safety even in an untrusted JavaScript environment. TS★ supports writing functions like `protect` exactly as shown, while a compiler from TS★ to JavaScript ensures that the access control check in `protect` cannot be subverted.

Although significantly more flexible than f* or DJS, TS★ still rules out many inherently unsafe features of JavaScript for the code we protect, thereby enforcing a stricter programming discipline and facilitating security code reviews. We intend TS★ to be used to protect security-critical scripts—guarding, for instance, sensitive resources and capabilities—executed on web pages that also include dynamically loaded, untrusted, potentially malicious scripts. By necessity, most of the code running on these pages is provided by third parties; we leave such code unchanged (and unprotected). Nonetheless, by lightly rewriting the security-critical scripts, and gradually typing them (Siek and Taha 2006), we enforce a strong notion of dynamic type-safety. In addition, we protect our scripts using type-directed wrappers to shield them from adversarial JavaScript environments. This places them on a robust type-safe foundation, from which we can reason about their security. In comparison, other gradually typed extensions to JavaScript, like TypeScript (`http://www.typescriptlang.org`) and Closure (`https://developers.google.com/closure/compiler`), aim primarily to increase programmer productivity by using types for documentation and code completion, but provide no safety guarantee.

The concrete syntax of TS★ extends JavaScript with a type-annotation language based on TypeScript. Our implementation works by first using TypeScript to infer types for every sub-term. It then uses the inferred types to type-check the program once again, this time using a more restrictive type system. If this step is successful, the program is compiled to plain JavaScript (instrumented with various runtime checks to enforce type-safety) for execution. The TS★ type system itself has the following prominent features:

***A statically typed core of functions, datatypes and records*** The base type system of TS★ includes primitive types like `bool`, `number` and `string`; higher-order function types; recursive datatypes; and extensible records of fields with optional immutability annotations. Records are equipped with a structural subtyping relation. For example, the type `point` defined below is a subtype of a record that omits some of its fields, and function subtyping is, as usual, contravariant on the arguments and covariant on the results.

```
{x:number; y:number; setX:const (number->unit)}
```

***Dynamically typed fragment*** The type `any` is for dynamically typed TS★ expressions. All the types from the statically typed core are subtypes of `any`, and all TS★ terms whose subterms all have type `any` can always be given the type `any`. In the spirit of JavaScript, in the `any`-fragment, we view records as extensible dictionaries with string-valued keys. TS★ supports the use of computed properties, e.g., in `any`-typed code, expressions like `p["set"+"X"]` or `whitelist[url]` are legal ways to safely project the appropriate field from the underlying object, if it exists. Dynamically typed code and its interactions with statically typed code are instrumented by our compiler for safety. As far as we are aware, ours is the first gradual type system to soundly support dictionary-based mutable records and computed properties.

***Runtime reflection over types*** Case analysis on the runtime type of a value is a common idiom in JavaScript and other dynamically typed languages—Guha et al. (2011) present several typical uses of JavaScript's `typeof` operator. TS★ embraces this idiom and compiles programs with runtime type information (RTTI) to support introspection on *all source types* at runtime, e.g., `isTag<point>p` checks whether the RTTI of `p` is a structural subtype of `point`. In addition to providing an expressive source programming construct, RTTI also forms the basis of an efficient and simple enforcement mechanism for gradual typing, an alternative to prior proposals based on higher-order contracts (Findler and Felleisen 2002).

**un*, the type of the adversary, mediated by wrappers*** Finally, and most distinctively, TS★ provides a *second dynamic type*, **un**. Any JavaScript term which cannot be typed either statically or dynamically can be given the type **un** and simply passes through our compiler without further analysis or modification. As such, **un** is the type of arbitrary, potentially adversarial JavaScript expressions. Our **un** type is reminiscent of types for adversaries, as proposed by Gordon and Jeffrey (2001). However, unlike prior uses of **un** in the context of secure compilers (e.g. Fournet et al. 2013), **un** is a first-class type in TS★: **un** values may be stored in records, used as arguments and results of functions, etc. The type **un** is incomparable to **any** in the subtyping relation and, in contrast with **any**, all operations on **un** values are mediated by wrappers that safely build coercions to and from **un** (as well as other types). The wrappers enforce a strict heap separation between the **un**-context and typed TS★, ensuring that adversarial code cannot break type invariants.

### 1.3 Evaluating TS★: theory and practice

We specify our compiler as a type-directed translation relation (§3). To formalize properties of the translated program, we give TS★ a translation semantics to JS★, a dependently typed model of JavaScript developed by Swamy et al. (2013), which is in turn based on λJS by Guha et al. (2010). Precise monadic refinement types in JS★ allow us to conveniently phrase our metatheory (§4) in terms of type-correctness of JS★, yielding three main properties:

*Memory isolation*: un-typed code (i.e., the adversary) cannot directly call, read, write, or tamper with typed values.

*Static safety*: statically typed code is safely compiled without any runtime checks, even in the presence of type-changing updates.

*Dynamic safety*: runtime type information is sound and at least as precise as the static type.

Experimentally, we evaluate TS⋆ by programming and adapting several security-sensitive JavaScript web libraries (§6). Our examples include a OWASP reference library to protect against cross-site request forgeries (CSRF) (Barth et al. 2008); and an adaptation of secure login and JSON-validation scripts within the Facebook API. In summary, our main contributions include:

(1) a type system and runtime support for safely composing statically typed, dynamically typed, and arbitrary JavaScript; (§3)

(2) a type safety theorem and its proof by translation to JS⋆; (§4)

(3) a prototype implementation, including a protocol to ensure that our runtime support runs first on pages hosting compiled TS⋆, and securely initializes our type invariant; (§5)

(4) security applications, illustrating a series of authorization and access control patterns taken from popular security-sensitive web applications and libraries, motivated by new attacks. (§6)

As such, TS⋆ is the first system to provide a notion of type safety useful for secure programming, while handling *all* of JavaScript.

The latest version of our compiler, programming examples, attacks, sample web-application deployments, and a technical report with the full formalization and proofs are all available from `http://research.microsoft.com/fstar`.

## 2. An overview of TS⋆

We begin by presenting the design of TS⋆ informally, using several small examples for illustration. We use the concrete syntax of TypeScript with minor simplifications; for instance we write function types as `t -> t'` rather than TypeScript's `(x:t) => t'`. We also extend the syntax of TypeScript with datatype declarations and immutability qualifiers.

### 2.1 Gradually securing programs by moving from un to any

While we envisage TS⋆ as the basis of a full-fledged gradually typed web-programming language, we initially consider JavaScript programmers willing to harden safety- and security-critical fragments of their code. They can start by giving their existing JavaScript code the type un in TS⋆, and then gradually migrating selected fragments to (dynamically) type-safe code in TS⋆ using the type any.

This exercise is valuable since any code in TS⋆ enjoys a *memory isolation* property, a robust foundation upon which to build secure sub-systems of a larger program. Memory isolation alone prevents many common attacks. For example, the prototype poisoning attack of §1 occurs because of a failure of memory isolation: the command `whitelist[url]` causes a prototype-chain traversal that ends with reading a field of `Object.prototype` which, unfortunately, is a reference to an object controlled by the adversary. Passing `protect` (unchanged) through the TS⋆ compiler while giving `whitelist` the type `any` produces an instrumented version of `protect` with checks to prevent any property dereferences from `whitelist` from accessing `Object.prototype` (or any other un object), thereby foiling the attack. Specifically, from memory isolation, we can prove that every dereference of a field of any object in TS⋆ will only read the immediate fields of that object, and will never access a prototype controlled by the adversary. This ensures that `whitelist[url]` returns true only if `url` is immediately defined in `whitelist`.

Undecorated TS⋆ programs can generally be given the type any (as long as they are well-scoped). Every function parameter in an unannotated TS⋆ program defaults to the type any; every `var`-bound variable is given the type of its initializer. Under this convention, in the program from §1, the type of `protect` is `any -> (any,any)-> any`, which is a subtype of any. When deploying a TS⋆ program, we assume that the JavaScript global object (the `window` object in most browsers) and all objects reachable from it are under control of the attacker. Thus, it is not safe to simply store `protect(send)` into `window.send`, since that would break memory isolation and leak a value of type `any` to un-safe code—our type system prevents the programmer from doing this by mistake.

Instead, TS⋆ provides wrappers to safely export values to the context. The TS⋆ expression `wrap<un>(protect(send))` wraps the `protect(send)` closure and yields a value of type un, indicating that it is safe to hand to any JavaScript context while preserving memory isolation. Dually, for `e:un`, the expression `wrap<any>(e)` safely imports `e` from the context and gives it the type any.

Providing a JavaScript implementation of `wrap` is non-trivial. We base our implementation on wrappers defined by Fournet et al. (2013). Their wrappers are designed to safely export statically typed values from the translation of an f⋆ program (roughly, a simply typed subset of ML) to its JavaScript context; and to import untyped values from the context into f⋆ at specific types. For example, Fournet et al.'s $\mathtt{down}_{(t*u)}$ exports a pair of translated f⋆ values $(v_1, v_2)$ of type $(t*u)$ to the context, by building a new object with two fields initialized to $\mathtt{down}_t(v_1)$ and $\mathtt{down}_u(v_2)$. A corresponding wrapper $\mathtt{up}_{(t*u)}$ does the converse, safely copying a pair from the context and building a value that is the translation of an f⋆ pair of type $(t*u)$. Fournet et al. provide $\mathtt{up}_t$ and $\mathtt{down}_t$ wrappers for types $t$ including **unit**, **bool**, **string**, **number**, pairs, recursive datatypes, and functions. We extend their constructions to additionally build wrappers to and from the type any, and to handle cyclic data structures that can be constructed using records with mutable fields.

To illustrate wrappers in action, we elaborate on our first example. Suppose we wished to protect `window.send` (a fictitious but simpler stand-in for JavaScript's `XMLHttpRequest` object) with an access control check. To support this, the standard library of TS⋆ provides a facility to read fields from, and write fields to, the global object by including the following safe interface to the `window` object implemented in JavaScript. The `win` object, whose interface is shown partially below, shadows the fields of the `window` object, safely reading and writing it within a wrapper to ensure that the `attacker`-controlled window does not break type safety. Using `win` within a TS⋆ program, we can safely import `window.send`, protect it, and export it back to the context using the following snippet of code, typed in a context where the `win` object has mutable un-typed fields. Of course, the attacker may *a priori* obtain a copy, and even redefine `window.send` before our code has the chance to protect and update it, but this is an orthogonal problem, solved once for all TS⋆programs—§2.3 and §5 present our mechanisms to ensure that our scripts run first on a web page.

```
interface win {send: un; ... }
win.send = wrap<un>(protect(wrap<any>(win.send)));
```

Wrappers are expensive, since they deeply copy the contents of objects back and forth, and—by design—they are not necessarily semantics-preserving. (For instance, they sanitize values, filter out some properties, and prevent some aliasing.) Thus, in an attempt to minimize the amount of copying, we may rewrite `protect`, by adding a few types, as shown below.

```
function protect(send:(string,un) -> un) {
  var whitelist={"http://microsoft.com/mail":true,
                 "http://microsoft.com/owa":true};
  return function (url:string, msg:un) {
          if (whitelist[url]) send(url, msg); };
};
win.send =
  wrap<un>(protect(wrap<(string,un)->un>(win.send)));
```

Intuitively, the msg argument in the closure returned by protect is treated abstractly, that is, our script does not directly access it. Thus, there is no need to import that argument from the context (potentially performing a deep copy). On the other hand, the url argument is not abstract—it is used to project a field from the whitelist, and, as such, it had better be a string. The type system of TS* gives us the flexibility to express exactly what should be imported from the context, helping us find a good balance between security and performance. The explicit use of un and wrap are advances of TS* relative to prior languages such as f* or, for that matter, any prior gradually typed programming language.

### 2.2 Expressing invariants with assertions over runtime types

As can be expected of gradual typing, a TS* program migrated from un to any can then, with some effort, be made increasingly statically typed. Static types can improve runtime safety, robustness of code, modularity, as well as provide better IDE support. Static types in TS* also improve performance relative to any-typed code and, relying on RTTI, can enforce data invariants. This is enabled by *static safety* and *dynamic safety*, two properties (in addition to *memory isolation*) provided by TS*.

***Static safety*** TS* ensures that, at runtime, no failures happen during the execution of statically typed parts of the source program. Since there are no runtime checks in the compiled JavaScript for such parts, as a bonus, the performance of statically typed TS* code will approach that of native JavaScript (and potentially exceed it, if the type information can be communicated to the VM).

***Dynamic safety*** Every TS* value $v : t$ (where $t \neq$ un) is compiled to JavaScript with runtime type information (RTTI) that initially reflects $v$'s static type $t$. TS* ensures that, while $v$'s RTTI may evolve during execution (e.g., as fields are added to an extensible record), it is always (a) a subtype of $v$'s static type $t$, and (b) a sound approximation (supertype) of $v$'s most-precise current type, i.e., the RTTI of $v$ may evolve only monotonically with respect to the subtyping relation. We call this property *dynamic safety*.

As an illustration, consider the example below, which codes up a lightweight form of objects with extensible records and closures in TS*, where point is the type defined in §1.

```
function Point(x, y) {
  var self = {};
  self.x=x;
  self.y=y;
  self.setX=function(d:number) { self.x = d; };
  return setTag<point>(self);
}
```

The function Point creates a new point. It allocates a new empty record and stores it in the local variable self, then it adds three fields x, y, and setX. The static type of self is just the empty record. However, TS* allows us to add more fields to self than those documented in its static type. As such, the static type of a record only describes a subset of the fields in the term, as is usual with width-subtyping. Deleting fields from records is also possible—we discuss this in more detail in §3.

In the last line of Point, setTag<point>(self) checks at runtime if the content of self is compatible with the point type, and fails otherwise. The term setTag<point>(self) has static type point, although the static type of self remains unchanged.

Assertions like setTag allow source programmers to safely update RTTI while maintaining the runtime type invariant. Once a value has been tagged as a point, then it is guaranteed to always remain a point. A programmer may choose to add fields to a point, or to further update its type information (e.g., turning it into a coloredPoint), but it will always contain at least the fields of a point. Any attempt to delete, say, the x field, or to change it in a type-incompatible way (using for instance a dynamically typed alias to the point) will cause a runtime error.

In contrast, statically typed code raises no such errors. TS* infers that function Point has type (any,any)-> point, so the code below is statically type safe and does not require any runtime checks.

```
var o = Point(0,0); o.setX(17);
```

As another example,[1] consider that popular web frameworks, like Dojo, provide implementations of the JSON Schema standard.[2] This allows programmers to validate JSON data, writing verbose schemas for them also as JSON objects. In TS*, data invariants can be expressed and enforced directly using types, rather than via schemas. For example, to check that a JSON string can be parsed into an array of user identities, we can write the TS* code below, assuming that JSON.parse has type string -> any. (See online materials for a TS* implementation of a JSON parser.)

```
type users = {id:number; user:string}[]
function check(j:string) : users {
  var o = JSON.parse(j);
  if (canTag<users>(o)) return setTag<users>(o);
  else return [];
}
```

The schema is captured by the type users. We parse a string j as JSON using JSON.parse, then use the TS* operator canTag<t>(o) to check that o's contents are consistent with t. If the check succeeds, we stamp o as a valid users object and return it.

**2.3 Reliable primitive operations** Since the global window object is shared with the adversary, all objects reachable from window may be compromised. This includes all built-in objects provided by the VM, e.g., Object.prototype, Array.prototype, the default String object, and others. In order to ensure memory isolation, translated TS* programs should never read from any of those objects. This is remarkably difficult to arrange in JavaScript, since several primitive operations, e.g., reading and writing fields, depend on base prototypes, as illustrated in §1. Thus, in the face of attacker-controlled prototypes, even simple manipulations of objects are unreliable.

Thankfully, there is a relatively simple way out. JavaScript (since ECMAScript 5) provides a function Object.create, such that Object.create(arg) creates a new object with its prototype field initialized to arg. As a special case, Object.create(null) creates an object with a null prototype, meaning that the created object *does not* inherit the attacker-controlled Object.prototype. Our compiler uses Object.create(null) to create new objects in the translation of a TS* program, allowing manipulations of object fields simply as o.f=v or o["f"]=v, without worrying that a traversal of o's prototype chain will reach an attacker-controlled object.

There is one exception, however. Function objects cannot be allocated using Object.create—they must inherit from the attacker-controlled Function.prototype. However, by an invariant of the translation, we can ensure that the only field ever accessed of a non-un-typed function f is "rtti". So, as long as Function.prototype contains a safe, immutable rtti field, accessing f.rtti will never trigger adversarial code.

The correctness of our translation then requires a reliable way to call Object.create(null) and to initialize Function.prototype.rtti. To achieve this, compiled TS* programs are linked with a library called boot.js. This library is intended to be the first piece of JavaScript that runs on a page—§5 discusses how to make a script run first, reliably, before any adversarial script. boot.js takes a clean copy of Object.create and stores it in an immutable field. Later, the translated TS* code accesses Object.create from this field, rather than as window.Object.create, which is an attacker-controlled path. We show a fragment of boot.js below, simplified slightly to use

[1] Based on http://davidwalsh.name/json-validation.

[2] http://tools.ietf.org/html/draft-zyp-json-schema-03

field names such as `rtti`, instead of the longer names (less likely to clash with source code) used in our implementation.

```
1  function boot() {
2    var Clean    = Object.create(null);
3    Clean.create = Object.create;
4    Clean.isTag  = function (t,s,x) { ... }; ...
5    Clean.wrap   = function (t,s,x) { ... };
6    Object.freeze(Clean);
7    Object.defineProperty(Function.prototype, "rtti",
8    {value:null, writable:false, configurable:false});
9    Object.defineProperty(window, "Clean",
10   {value:Clean, writable:false, configurable:false});
11 };
12 boot(); boot=undefined;
```

The listing above defines a function `boot` that is run once and then discarded. Within the scope of the function, we construct a `Clean` object in which to maintain pristine copies of functions like `Object.create`, on which our translation relies. Lines 4–5 define functions that implement queries and coercions on runtime types and values—we discuss their implementation in detail in §3. Line 6 calls the JavaScript function `freeze`, to make `Clean` immutable. Line 7 initializes `Function.prototype.rtti` and line 9 registers the `Clean` object at the path `window.Clean`—both use JavaScript's `defineProperty`, to define immutable, non-configurable properties.

**2.4 Embedding TS$^\star$ in JavaScript** The `Clean` object in `boot.js` provides trusted core functionality upon which we can build a secure compiler. In this section, we outline the end-to-end embedding within JavaScript of the `Point` example from §2.2. There are a few broad features of the translation that we focus on:

- Adding runtime-type information to every object and function.
- Checking runtime type information in the any fragment.
- Embedding wrappers to safely export/import values.

The listing below shows the translation of the TS$^\star$ function `Point` to JavaScript. The translated code is placed within a single enclosing function to introduce a fresh local scope. Without this precaution, TS$^\star$ definitions would implicitly leak into the global un-typed object. The type annotations in TS$^\star$ are all erased in JavaScript.

```
1  function () {
2   var Point = function (x,y) {
3     var self  = Clean.create(null);
4     self.rtti = ⦇{}⦈;
5     write(self, "x", x);
6     write(self, "y", y);
7     var tmp   = function(d) {write(self, "x", d);}
8     tmp.rtti  = ⦇number → unit⦈;
9     write(self,"setX", tmp);
10    return Clean.setTag(⦇{}⦈,⦇point⦈,self);
11  }
12  Point.rtti = ⦇(any,any) → point⦈;
13  var o = Point(0,0);
14  o.setX(17);
15 }()
```

Line 3: the source empty record `{}` is compiled to a new null-prototype object. Line 4: we set the `rtti` field of `self` to the translation of a source empty record type. Lines 5 and 6: we use the macro *write* to add two properties to the `self` object. This macro (defined in §3) checks that the RTTI of the assigned field (if any) is compatible with the RTTI of the assignee. In this case, since the `rtti` field of `self` is just the empty record, it does not constrain the contents of any of its fields, so these assignments succeed and the fields are added to `self`. Line 7: we translate `setX` and, line 8: we tag it with an `rtti` field recording its source type. We then add it to `self` using *write*. Line 10: the call to `Clean.setTag` checks whether `self`, whose static type is represented by ⦇{}⦈, contains a valid representation of a source `point`. For this, it examines the representation of the type ⦇`point`⦈; notice that the type requires three fields, `x`, `y`, and `setX`; then it checks that the `self` object contains values in those three fields whose RTTIs are compatible with the requested types `number`, `number`, and `number -> unit`, respectively. Once this check succeeds, `setTag` updates the `rtti` field of `self` to ⦇`point`⦈. An invariant of our translation is that the `rtti` field of every object evolves monotonically with respect to the subtyping relation. That is, `self.rtti` was initially ⦇{}⦈ and evolves to ⦇`point`⦈, where `point <: {}`. The RTTI of `self` may evolve further, but it is guaranteed to always remain a subtype of `point`. Line 12: we add an `rtti` field to the `Point`. Finally, lines 13 and 14: we see the translation of a statically typed fragment of TS$^\star$. Pleasantly, the translation there is just the identity.

As shown, the translated program does not interact with its context at all. However, the programmer can choose to export certain values to the context by writing `export function Point(x,y){...}` instead. This instructs the compiler to wrap and export `Point` to the context by inserting the following code after Line 14.

```
win.Point = Clean.wrap(⦇(any,any) → point⦈, ⦇un⦈,Point);
```

| | | | |
|---|---|---|---|
| *Value* | $v$ | $::=$ | $x \mid$ `true` $\mid$ `false` $\mid \lambda x{:}t.e \mid D\,\overline{v}$ |
| *Expr.* | $e$ | $::=$ | $v \mid \{\overline{f} = \overline{e}\} \mid e.f \mid e.f = e' \mid e[e'] \mid e[e'] = e''$ |
| | | $\mid$ | $\textbf{let}\ x = e\ \textbf{in}\ e' \mid e\ e' \mid D\,\overline{e}$ |
| | | $\mid$ | $\textbf{if}\ e\ \textbf{then}\ e'\ \textbf{else}\ e'' \mid q\langle t\rangle e \mid c\langle t\rangle e$ |
| *Query* | $q$ | $::=$ | *isTag* $\mid$ *canTag* $\mid$ *canWrap* |
| *Coercion* | $c$ | $::=$ | *setTag* $\mid$ *wrap* |
| *Type* | $t,u$ | $::=$ | `bool` $\mid$ `T` $\mid$ `any` $\mid$ `un` $\mid t \to u \mid \{\overline{f} :^{\overline{a}} \overline{t}\}$ |
| *Access* | $a$ | $::=$ | `r` $\mid$ `w` |
| *Sig.* | $S$ | $::=$ | $.\ \mid D{:}\overline{t} \to T \mid S,S'$ |
| *Env.* | $\Gamma$ | $::=$ | $.\ \mid x{:}t \mid \Gamma,\Gamma'$ |

**Figure 1.** Formal syntax of TS$^\star$

## 3. Formalizing TS$^\star$

This section formalizes TS$^\star$ by presenting its type system and type-directed translation to JavaScript. We describe in particular our runtime representation of types and the JavaScript implementations of `Q.wrap`, `Q.setTag` and related functions that manipulate translated terms and their types. We conclude this section with a detailed comparison of TS$^\star$ with prior gradual type systems.

**3.1 Syntax** Figure 1 presents our source syntax. To aid in the readability of the formalization, we employ compact, $\lambda$-calculus style notation, writing for example $\lambda x{:}t.e$ instead of `function(x:t) {return e;}`. We also write $\overline{e}$ for a sequence of expressions $e_1, \ldots, e_n$, $f(\overline{e})$ for the application $f(e_1, \ldots, e_n)$, and so on. Our formal syntax does not cover the un-typed fragment, since its typing and compilation are both trivial, although, of course, our theorems specifically address the composition of compiled TS$^\star$ code with arbitrary JavaScript.

Values $v$ include variables $x$, Booleans, typed $\lambda$-abstractions, and data constructors $D$ applied to a sequence of values. For conciseness, we exclude primitives like numbers and strings, since they can in principle be encoded using data constructors. In practice, our implementation supports JavaScript primitives, and so we use them in our examples. This requires some care, however, since some operations on primitive types can be overwritten by the adversary. In such cases, we cache reliable versions of those primitive operations in the `Clean` object built by `boot.js`

In addition to values, expressions $e$ include record literals, projections of static fields, and assignments to static fields. We also include projections of computed fields $e[e']$ and assignment to computed fields $e[e'] = e''$. It is important to note that records, even records of values, are not values, as in JavaScript evaluating a record returns the heap location where the record value is stored. We have `let`-bindings (corresponding to immutable `var` bindings in our concrete syntax); function application; data constructor appli-

$$\boxed{\Gamma \vdash e : t \leadsto s} \qquad \frac{\Gamma \vdash e : u \leadsto s \quad S \vdash u <: t}{\Gamma \vdash e : t \leadsto s}\ (\text{T-Sub}) \qquad \frac{}{\Gamma \vdash x : \Gamma(x) \leadsto x}\ (\text{T-X}) \qquad \frac{\Gamma \vdash \bar{e} : \bar{t} \leadsto \bar{s} \quad \{\bar{f} :^{\bar{a}} \bar{t}\} = t \uplus u \quad S \vdash \mathsf{unFree}(t)}{\Gamma \vdash \{\overline{f = e}\} : u \leadsto \mathit{record}(\overline{f{:}s}, u)}\ (\text{T-Rec})$$

$$\frac{S(D) = \bar{t} \to T \quad \Gamma \vdash \bar{e} : \bar{t} \leadsto \bar{s}}{\Gamma \vdash D\ \bar{e} : T \leadsto \mathit{data}(D, \bar{s}, T)}\ (\text{T-D}) \qquad \frac{\Gamma, x{:}t \vdash e : t' \leadsto s}{\Gamma \vdash \lambda x{:}t.e : t \to t' \leadsto \mathit{fun}(x, e, s, t \to t')}\ (\text{T-Lam}) \qquad \frac{\Gamma \vdash e : u \uplus \{f :^{\mathsf{w}} t\} \leadsto s \quad \Gamma \vdash e' : t \leadsto s'}{\Gamma \vdash e.f = e' : t \leadsto s.f = s'}\ (\text{T-Wr})$$

$$\frac{\Gamma \vdash e{:}u \uplus \{f :^{a} t\} \leadsto s}{\Gamma \vdash e.f : t \leadsto s.f}\ (\text{T-Rd}) \qquad \frac{\Gamma \vdash e : t_1 \to t_2 \leadsto s \quad \Gamma \vdash e' : t_1 \leadsto s'}{\Gamma \vdash e\ e' : t_2 \leadsto s\ s'}\ (\text{T-App}) \qquad \frac{\Gamma \vdash e : u \leadsto s \quad \Gamma, x{:}u \vdash e' : t \leadsto s'}{\Gamma \vdash \mathbf{let}\ x = e\ \mathbf{in}\ e' : t \leadsto (x = s, s')}\ (\text{T-Let})$$

$$\frac{\Gamma \vdash e : \mathsf{any} \leadsto s \quad \forall i.\Gamma \vdash e_i : t \leadsto s_i}{\Gamma \vdash \mathbf{if}\ e\ \mathbf{then}\ e_1\ \mathbf{else}\ e_2 : t \leadsto \texttt{if}\ (s)\ \{s_1\}\ \texttt{else}\ \{s_2\}}\ (\text{T-If}) \qquad \frac{\Gamma \vdash e : t' \leadsto s \quad t' \sim t}{\Gamma \vdash q\langle t\rangle e : \texttt{bool} \leadsto \texttt{Clean.}q(⦇t'⦈, ⦇t⦈, s)}\ (\text{T-Q}) \qquad \frac{\Gamma \vdash e : t' \leadsto s \quad t' \sim t}{\Gamma \vdash c\langle t\rangle e : t \leadsto \texttt{Clean.}c(⦇t'⦈, ⦇t⦈, s)}\ (\text{A-C})$$

$$\frac{\forall i.\Gamma \vdash e_i : \mathsf{any} \leadsto s_i}{\Gamma \vdash e_1\ e_2 : \mathsf{any} \leadsto \mathit{apply}(s_1, s_2)}\ (\text{A-App}) \qquad \frac{\forall i.\Gamma \vdash e_i : \mathsf{any} \leadsto s_i}{\Gamma \vdash e_1[e_2] : \mathsf{any} \leadsto \mathit{read}(s_1, s_2)}\ (\text{A-Rd}) \qquad \frac{\forall i.\Gamma \vdash e_i : \mathsf{any} \leadsto s_i}{\Gamma \vdash e_1[e_2] = e_3 : \mathsf{any} \leadsto \mathit{write}(s_1, s_2, s_3)}\ (\text{A-Wr})$$

$$\boxed{S \vdash t <: t'} \qquad \frac{}{S \vdash t <: t} \qquad \frac{S \vdash t <: t'' \quad S \vdash t'' <: t'}{S \vdash t <: t'} \qquad \frac{S \vdash t' <: t \quad S \vdash u <: u'}{S \vdash t \to u <: t' \to u'} \qquad \frac{S \vdash t <: t'}{S \vdash \{f :^{\mathsf{r}} t\} \uplus u <: \{f :^{\mathsf{r}} t'\} \uplus u} \qquad \frac{S \vdash \mathsf{unFree}(t)}{S \vdash t <: \mathsf{any}} \qquad \frac{S \vdash \mathsf{unFree}(t)}{S \vdash t \uplus u <: u}$$

$$\boxed{S \vdash \mathsf{unFree}(t)} \qquad \frac{}{S \vdash \mathsf{unFree}(\texttt{bool})} \qquad \frac{}{S \vdash \mathsf{unFree}(\mathsf{any})} \qquad \frac{\forall D{:}\bar{t} \to T \in S[T].S \vdash \mathsf{unFree}(\bar{t})}{S \vdash \mathsf{unFree}(T)} \qquad \frac{\forall i.S \vdash \mathsf{unFree}(t_i)}{S \vdash \mathsf{unFree}(t_1 \to t_2)} \qquad \frac{S \vdash \mathsf{unFree}(\bar{t})}{S \vdash \mathsf{unFree}(\{\bar{f} :^{\bar{a}} \bar{t}\})}$$

$$\boxed{t \sim t'} \qquad \frac{}{t \sim t} \qquad \frac{t' \sim t}{t \sim t'} \qquad \frac{}{\mathsf{any} \sim t} \qquad \frac{}{\mathsf{un} \sim t} \qquad \frac{t \sim t' \quad u \sim u'}{t \to t \sim t' \to u'} \qquad \frac{\mathsf{fields}(u_0) \cap \mathsf{fields}(u_1) = \emptyset \quad \forall j.a_j = a'_j \wedge t_j \sim t'_j}{\{\bar{f} :^{\bar{a}} \bar{t}\} \uplus u_0 \sim \{\bar{f} :^{\bar{a}'} \bar{t}'\} \uplus u_1}$$

where

```
let x = s in s'     ≜  function(x){return s';}(s)
record(f̄:s̄,t)       =  let x=Clean.create(null) in (x.f̄=s̄, x.rtti=⦇t⦈)
data(D,s̄,T)         =  let x=Clean.create(null) in (x[ī]=s̄, x.c=⦇D⦈, x.rtti=⦇T⦈, x)
fun(x,e,s,t → t')   =  let f=function(x){var locals(e); return s;} in (f.rtti=⦇t → t'⦈, f)
apply(s1,s2)        =  let f=s1 in let x=s2 in typeof(x)==="function" ? f(Clean.setTag(⦇any⦈, f.rtti.arg,x)) : Clean.die()
read(s1,s2)         =  let x=s1 in let f=s2 in typeof(x)==="object" && Clean.hasField(x,f) ? x[f] : Clean.die()
write(s1,s2,s3)     =  let x=s1 in let f=s2 in let v=s3 in let t = typeof(x)==="object" ? x.rtti : Clean.die() in
                       Clean.mutable(t, f) ? x[f]=Clean.setTag(⦇any⦈, Clean.hasField(t,f) ? t[f] : Clean.Any(v) : Clean.die()

⦇any⦈  =  Clean.Any          ⦇t → t'⦈   =  Clean.arrow(⦇t⦈, ⦇t'⦈)                                  ⦇un⦈  =  Clean.Un
⦇T⦈    =  Clean.data("T")    ⦇{f̄ :ā t̄}⦈ =  let o = Clean.rec()in Clean.addField(o, f̄, ⦇t̄⦈, ā==="w")
```

**Figure 2.** A type-directed translation of TS$^\star$ to JavaScript

cation; and conditionals. Finally, we have RTTI-based query operations $q\langle t\rangle e$, and coercions $c\langle t\rangle e$.

Types $t, u$ include a number of primitive types (`bool` for boolean values, and any and un for dynamic values), abstract data types ranged over by $T$, and records. Record types are written using the shorthand $\{\bar{f} :^{\bar{a}} \bar{t}\}$ to denote the type $\{f_1 :^{a_1} t_1, \ldots, f_n :^{a_n} t_n\}$ where the $f_i$ are distinct and the $a_i$ are accessibility annotations: r for read-only, and w for mutable. We also write $t \uplus u$ for the record type $\{\bar{f}_1 :^{\bar{a}_1} \bar{t}_1, \bar{f}_2 :^{\bar{a}_2} \bar{t}_2\}$, where $t = \{\bar{f}_1 :^{\bar{a}_1} \bar{t}_1\}$ and $u = \{\bar{f}_2 :^{\bar{a}_2} \bar{t}_2\}$.

The type system is given with respect to a signature $S$ which maps data constructors $D$ to their type signature, written $\bar{t} \to T$. In places we need to refer to *all* the data constructors for a given abstract data type $T$ in the signature $S$. We use the shorthand $S[T]$ which is defined as $\{D : \bar{t} \to T \mid S(D) = \bar{t} \to T\}$. We also have a standard type environment $\Gamma$ binding variables to their types.

Although we have data constructors, pattern matching in TS$^\star$ is not primitive. Instead, it can be encoded in terms of the other constructs, as defined below. Note that we freely use `&&` and other Boolean operators, as well as `===`, physical equality on TS$^\star$ values.

$$\mathbf{match}\ e\ \mathbf{with}\ D_{\bar{t} \to T}\bar{x} \to e_1\ \mathbf{else}\ e_2 \triangleq$$
$$\mathbf{let}\ y = e\ \mathbf{in}\ \mathbf{if}\ (\mathit{isTag}\langle T\rangle y\ \texttt{\&\&}\ y.c === \texttt{"D"})\ \mathbf{then}\ \mathbf{let}\ \bar{x} = \overline{y[\texttt{i}]}\ \mathbf{in}\ e_1\ \mathbf{else}\ e_2$$

**3.2 Type system and translation** Figure 2 defines the judgment $\Gamma \vdash e : t \leadsto s$, which states that in an environment $\Gamma$ (along with an implicit signature $S$), the expression $e$ can be given the type $t$ and be translated to the JavaScript program $s$. We present the type system declaratively. In practice, our type checker analyzes a fully decorated AST produced by the type inference algorithm of TypeScript, so implementing the system in Figure 2 is straightforward. (A precise description of this type inference algorithm is beyond the scope of this paper.)

At a high level, the type system is designed to enforce the following three properties mentioned in §2:

***Static safety*** TS$^\star$ programs have no failing dynamic checks during the execution of statically typed sub-terms. We achieve this via two mechanisms: (a) the rules prefixed by (T-) enforce the static typing discipline and they never insert any runtime checks when compiling the program; (b) when a value $v$:any is passed to a context that expects a precise type, e.g. `point`, the compiler inserts instrumentation to ensure that $v$ is indeed at least a `point`. Instrumentation inserted elsewhere in dynamic code also ensures that $v$ henceforth remains at least a `point`. This protects statically typed code from future modifications to $v$. In the other direction, the type system allows for $v$ :`point` to be passed to any-typed context via subtyping.

***Dynamic safety*** The RTTI of $v{:}t$ is always a subtype of $t$ and a sound approximation of $v$'s most precise type—by two mechanisms: (a) $v$'s RTTI initially reflects $t$ and the *setTag* operation ensures that RTTI always evolves towards the more precise types per subtyping, and (b) the rules prefixed by (A-) instrument the translation of the any-typed parts of the source to enforce that modifications to $v$ respect its RTTI. (We envision that an IDE can highlight uses of (A-) rules to the programmer as potential failure points.)

***Memory isolation*** un-typed code cannot directly access an object reference that TS$^\star$ code may dereference; this is enforced by ensuring that the **un** type is treated abstractly. The only way to manipulate **un** values is via defensive wrappers, which means that typed code never dereferences an **un**-typed memory location, and that **any**-typed references are never be handed directly to the adversary. The subtyping rules are designed to prevent masking the presence of **un**-values in records using width-subtyping or subtyping to **any**.

We now turn to describing each of the rules in detail. The first rule in the judgment, (T-SUB), is a subsumption form which shows that a use of subtyping in TS$^\star$ does not change the translation of a term. The subtyping relation $S \vdash t <: t'$ (also in Figure 2) is mostly standard. Depth subtyping on records is permitted only for immutable fields. The penultimate rule allows all types that do not contain the **un** type to be a subtype of **any**. (The auxiliary predicate unFree detects occurrences of **un** in a type.) Allowing `un <: any` would clearly break our invariants. Allowing `{f:un} <: any` is also problematic, since if a value `v:{f:un}` could be promoted to `v:any`, then `v["f"]` would also have type **any**, even though it produces an untrusted value. The last subtyping rule provides width-subtyping on records, forgetting the fields to weaken $t \uplus u$ to $u$, only so long as $t$ contains no occurrences of **un**.

The rule (T-X) for typing variables is standard. (T-REC) introduces a record at type $u$, such that $u$ includes all the **un**-fields (necessary for compatibility with subtyping). Its compilation allocates a new object, safely sets the fields $\bar{f}$ to $\bar{s}$, and finally adds an `rtti` field containing $(\!|u|\!)$. The rule (T-D) for typing data constructors is similar. The typing of functions with (T-LAM) is standard; however, the translation to JavaScript is a bit subtle: it defines a JavaScript function tagged with an `rtti` field, whose body $s$ is preceded by declarations of all the `let`-bound variables in $e$, the source function body. These (and other) rules use the JavaScript form $(\bar{e})$, which evaluates every $e_i$ in $\bar{e}$ and returns the last one.

The rules (T-WR), (T-RD), and (T-APP) are standard. One slight wrinkle in (T-IF) is that we rely on JavaScript implicitly converting $u$ to a boolean—this implicit conversion is a safe primitive operation. One could imagine a stricter variant of (T-IF) with a runtime check to ensure that $u$ is a boolean, without applying implicit conversions. However, (T-IF) as shown is more idiomatic of JavaScript. On the other hand, our treatment of local variables in (T-LET) deviates from JavaScript's `var`-statements—local variables are always immutable in TS$^\star$. We make this choice since mutability, if desired, can be encoded by boxing the let-bound value in a mutable record field. In contrast, encoding immutable local variables given only mutable ones is impossible (even with immutable record fields).

The rules (T-Q) and (A-C) cover queries $q\langle t\rangle e$ and coercions $c\langle t\rangle e$. In each case, we have an expression $e{:}t'$ compiled to $s$, and we apply $q$ or $c$ at type $t$, so long as $t$ and $t'$ are compatible. Type compatibility is a simple reflexive, symmetric, and *non*-transitive relation, in the spirit of Siek and Taha (2006). We discuss the implementation of these operations in the next subsection.

The remaining (A-) rules instrument the translated programs to ensure safety. In (A-APP), we first check that $s$ is a function. Then, before calling the function, we tag the argument with the type of the function's parameter. (A-RD) simply checks that $s_1$ is an object and that $s_1$ has field $s_2$. (A-WR) checks that $s_1$ is an object. It then checks that $s_1$'s RTTI allows for field $s_2$ to be written. If $s_1$'s RTTI does not contain $s_2$, it is treated as a new property addition—deleting a property if it is not present in the RTTI is also straightforward, although we do not cover it here. Otherwise, it should contain a mutable $s_2$ field, and before writing, $s_3$ is tagged with the type expected by $s_1$'s RTTI.

**3.3 Implementing RTTI-based coercions and wrappers** As described in §2.3, runtime support for compiled TS$^\star$ programs is provided by the immutable `Clean` object installed in the global namespace by the first-starter script `boot.js`. This section discusses in detail the `setTag` and `wrap` operations provided by the runtime.

***Updating RTTI with setTag*** The form $setTag\langle t\rangle(e{:}t')$ is compiled to `Clean.setTag(`$(\!|t'|\!)$`,`$(\!|t|\!)$`,`$s$`)`, where `e` compiles to $s$. In this case, the first argument $(\!|t'|\!)$ is redundant, since it can be recovered from the RTTI of $s$ (which, by dynamic safety, must be a refinement of $t'$)—we keep the first argument for uniformity with wrappers, as discussed below. The call `Clean.setTag(`$(\!|t'|\!)$`,`$(\!|t|\!)$`,s)` boils down to `setTagAux(s,`$(\!|t|\!)$`,false)`, whose implementation is shown in Figure 3 (on the left). This code tries to update the RTTI of `s` to be some subtype of $(\!|t|\!)$ and fails otherwise. There are two main concerns that the code addresses: (1) the code should not diverge if `s` is a cyclic data structure (unless `die` is called); (2) if the tag of `s` is updated, then `s` must represent a value of type $t$ and the new tag must be a subtype of both the old tag and $t$. These two concerns are complementary, since certain types (e.g., non-recursive types or types without mutable fields) specifically require all their values to be acyclic. The main idea of `setTagAux(x,t,b)` is to traverse the objects reachable from `x` in a depth-first manner, at each point checking that each field required by $t$ is present in the object at the expected type (lines 11 and 21). Each object encountered in the traversal is temporarily marked (line 7) as visited by assigning `meet(curTag,t)` to `x.tmp`. The assigned value is the greatest subtype of both `curTag` and `t` (which may not exist, in which case the operation fails by calling `die`). Cycles are only permissible when traversing mutable object references and cycles are detected by looking for a marker in `x.tmp`. If the traversal succeeds, the temporary marker is made permanent by updating `x.rtti` (line 4); if it fails, a fatal error is raised by calling `die`, which exhausts the JavaScript stack. This is drastic but effective; friendlier failure modes are feasible too.

Coercions based on `setTag` can be overly conservative, particularly on higher-order values. For example, trying to coerce the identity function `id : any -> any` to the type `bool -> bool` using `setTag` will fail, since `any` $\not<:$ `bool`. As such, RTTI-based coercions are most effective when working with mutable first-order objects. One way to broaden the scope of RTTI-based coercions is, of course, to enrich the type language, e.g., to include polymorphism, or even refinement types—we plan to explore this in the future. Additionally, we provide operations to query RTTI, $isTag\langle t\rangle e$ and $canTag\langle t\rangle e$, that (respectively) allow programmers to query the current tag of $e$ and to test whether or not a `setTag` operation on $e$ would succeed. When RTTI-based coercions are inapplicable (e.g., on **un**-typed values) or overly conservative (e.g., on functions), the `wrap` form is handy—we describe it next.

***Wrappers*** When $e{:}t'$ compiles to $s$, $wrap\langle t\rangle(e{:}t')$ compiles to `Clean.wrap(`$(\!|t|\!)$`,`$(\!|t'|\!)$`,`$s$`)`—Figure 3 shows part of its implementation (on the right). Line 2 is the case where both $(\!|t|\!)$ and $(\!|t'|\!)$ are function types. As expected, we apply a higher-order cast to $s$, wrapping the argument, applying $s$, and then wrapping the result. Thus, `wrap(`$(\!|$`any` $\to$ `any`$|\!)$`,` $(\!|$`bool` $\to$ `bool`$|\!)$`, id)` succeeds where the corresponding `setTag` fails.

***Securely importing from* un** The more interesting case of `wrap` is when the source type is `un` and the target type is `any` (line 7), which occurs when importing an **un**-typed value from the adversary into the typed fragment of TS$^\star$. At line 8, we use JavaScript's `typeof` operator to examine the simple type of `x`, the `un`-typed value being coerced. If `x` has a primitive type, then the coercion is just the identity. If `x` is an object, we aim to enumerate all its fields, then wrap and copy each of those fields into a newly allocated `any`-typed object. This requires some care, however, since directly enumerating or accessing the fields of an `un`-typed objects causes callbacks to the `un`-typed adversary, potentially breaking memory isolation by leaking `any`-typed objects on the stack to the context. As a defense, we build on an idea from Fournet et al. (2013), as follows. At line 14, we allocate a new object `r` into which we will wrap and copy the fields of `x`. Next, we build a closure (`stub` at line 15) which captures

```
function setTagAux(x, t, cycleok) {
 var curTag = tagOf(x);
 if (tmp in x) { cycleok ? curTag = x.tmp : die(); }
 function ok(){ x.rtti=x.tmp;delete x.tmp;return x; }
 if (subtype(curTag, t)) return x;
 if (typeof x !== "object"||x.tmp) die();
 x.tmp = meet(curTag, t);
 switch (t.t) {
  case "record":
   if (curTag.t!=="record"||curTag.t!=="Any") die();
    foreach(t, function(fld, ft) {
     if (!hasField(x,fld)) die();
     if (hasField(curTag,fld) &&
         ft.mut!==curTag[fld].mut)) die();
     setTagAux(x[fld], ft.typ, ft.mut);
    }); return ok();
  case "data"  :
   if(curTag.t !== "Any") die();
   if(!hasField(x,"c")) die();
   var ct = constructors(t)[x.c];
   foreach (ct, function (ix, arg) {
    if (!hasField(x,ix)) die();
    setTagAux(x[ix],arg,false);
   }); return ok();
  default : die();
}}
```

```
1 function wrap (src, tgt, x) {
2  if (src.t === "arrow" && tgt.t === "arrow") {
3   var f = function (y) { return
4     wrap(src.ret,tgt.ret,x(wrap(tgt.arg,src.arg,y)));
5   }; f.rtti = tgt; return f;
6  } ...
7  else if (src.t === "un" && tgt.t === "any") {
8   switch (typeof x) {
9    case "undefined":
10   case "string":
11   case "number":
12   case "boolean": return x;
13   case "object":
14    var r = Clean.create(null);
15    var stub = function () {
16      foreach(x, function (p, v) {
17       r[p] = wrap(⦇un⦈, ⦇any⦈,v);
18    })};
19    callUn(stub); return r;
20   case "function":
21    var un2any=function (x){return wrap(⦇un⦈,⦇any⦈,x);}
22    var any2un=function (x){return wrap(⦇any⦈,⦇un⦈,x);}
23    var f = upfun(any2un,un2any)(x);
24    f.rtti = ⦇any → any⦈; return f;
25   default: die();
26 }}}
```

**Figure 3.** Implementations of `Clean.setTag(u,t,x)` $\triangleq$ `setTagAux(x,t,false)` and `Clean.wrap` (selected fragments)

`r` and `x`, but otherwise takes no arguments and returns nothing. As such, the `stub` can be viewed as a function from `un` to `un`. In the body of `stub`, we enumerate the fields of `x`, then wrap and copy each of them into `r`. All that remains is to call `stub` and return `r`. The call itself is done using `callUn`, which provides a safe way to call an `un`-typed function without breaking memory isolation. The function `callUn(f)` is defined as `upfun(id,id)(f)(undefined)`, where `id` is the identity function, and `upfun` is the wrapper for importing `un`-typed functions from Fournet et al. (2013) (see Figure 4 in that paper). When `x` is a function (line 20), we again use `upfun`, this time exporting the argument and then importing the result back—the returned value has type `any -> any`.

***Securely exporting to* un** The implementation of `wrap(`$(\!|t|\!)$`,`$(\!|\mathrm{un}|\!)$`)(s)` for $t \neq$ un, exports `s` to the context. This case is somewhat simpler, since `s` is a typed value with RTTI which can be safely probed. If $s$ is a primitive, it can be exported as is. If `s` is an object, `wrap` creates an empty object `x`, enumerates all the fields `f` of `s`, exports them recursively and adds them to `x`. For functions, it uses Fournet et. al.'s `downfun` to export it at type `un -> un`.

**3.4 Discussion and related work on gradual typing** Languages that mix static and dynamic types date back at least to Abadi et al. (1991) and Bracha and Griswold (1993). Gradual typing is a technique first proposed by Siek and Taha (2006), initially for a functional language with references, and subsequently for languages with various other features including objects. Several others have worked in this space. For example, Flanagan (2006) introduces hybrid typing, mixing static, dynamic and refinement types; Wadler and Findler (2009) add *blame* to a gradual type system; Herman et al. (2010) present gradual typing with space-efficient wrappers; Bierman et al. (2010) describe type dynamic in C$^\sharp$; and Ina and Igarashi (2011) add gradual typing to generic Java.

Our system is distinct from all others in that it is the first to consider gradual typing for a language *embedded* within a larger, potentially adversarial environment via the type un. We are also, to the best of our knowledge, the first to consider gradual typing as a means of achieving security.

To compare more closely with other systems, let us set aside un for the moment, and focus on the interaction between any and statically typed TS$^\star$. Previous type systems mediate the interactions between static- and any-typed code by *implicitly* attaching casts to values. Higher order casts may fail at a program point far from the point where it was inserted. To account for such failures, blame calculi identify the cast (with a label to indicate the term or context) that causes the failure—Siek et al. (2009) survey blame calculi based on the errors they detect, points of failures, and casts they blame. In contrast, Interactions between static- and any-typed TS$^\star$is based primarily on RTTI. Casts (wrappers in our terminology) are never inserted implicitly, although they are made available to the programmer. This design has the following advantages.

***Preservation of object identity*** Object identity in JavaScript is a commonly used feature. Since TS$^\star$ does not *implicitly* attach casts to values, it never implicitly breaks object identity in the source during compilation. Previous gradual type systems with implicit casts would always break object identity.

***Space efficiency*** Casts can pile up around a value, making the program inefficient. Herman et al. (2010) introduce a novel cast-reduction semantics to gain space-efficiency. Our approach is also space efficient (there is only one RTTI per object) but does not require cast-reduction machinery.

***Static safety and eager failures*** In contrast to our RTTI-based mechanism, statically typed code in other gradual type systems could fail (although blame would help them ascribe it to the any-typed code). Consider the following TS$^\star$ example.

```
let v:any = {f:true} in (λr:{f:ʷint}. r.f) v
```

Compiling this term using (A-APP) introduces a `setTag` on the argument `v` at type `{f:ʷint}`. The `setTag` operation, at runtime, recursively checks that `v` is a `{f:ʷint}`, and expectedly fails. Thus, the failure happens prior to the application, a failure strategy called *eager* in prior works. Herman et al. (2010) also argue that their system can provide eager failures, but transposed to their notation (with the record replaced by a `ref any`), the failure occurs at the property read within the statically typed $\lambda$-term, breaking static safety. When eager runtime checking seems too strict, TS$^\star$ wrappers provide an escape hatch. Arguably, for our security applications, a predictably uniform eager-failure strategy is a suitable default.

***Dynamic safety and blame*** With no failures inside statically typed code to explain at runtime, blame seems less useful with RTTI-based coercions. However, because we enforce dynamic safety

(RTTI evolves monotonically), failures may now arise in **any**-typed code, as in the following example.

```
let v:any={f:true} in (λr:{f:ʷbool}.r.f) v; v.f="hi"
```

This time, the `setTag` of `v` to `{f:ʷint}` succeeds, and it modifies `v`'s RTTI to be `{f:ʷint}`. But now, the update of `v.f` to `"hi"` fails. This failure in the **any**-typed fragment should be blamed on the `setTag` operation instrumented at the application. We plan to pursue the details of this seemingly new notion of blame as future work.

***Gradual typing for monotonic objects*** Independently, in an unpublished manuscript, Siek et al. (2013) investigate gradual typing for a Python-like language (based on an earlier abstract presented at the STOP workshop in 2012). Like us, they notice that constraining the type of a mutable object to evolve monotonically at runtime enables statically typed code to be compiled without runtime checks, leading to improved performance and safety for that fragment. There are some important differences, however. First, Siek et al. require monotonicity with respect to an intentionally naïve subtyping relation. For example, (transposed to our notation) the type of an object can evolve from $t$ =`{f :ʷ any}` to $t'$ =`{f :ʷ number}`, although $t'$ is not a subtype of $t$. This means that, in their system, writing `o.f = true` can fail at runtime, even if `o` has static type $t$, which is prevented by TS$^\star$. This difference stems perhaps from differing perspectives on static safety: Siek et al. are willing to tolerate runtime errors in code whose typing somewhere employs the type **any**; in our system, runtime errors may occur only when **any**-typed values are eliminated (i.e., in our (A-) rules only). Syntactically localizing errors in this manner does not appear as straightforward with naïve subtyping. Additionally, Siek et al. do not aim to model an adversarial context—there is a single dynamic type, not two (i.e., only **any**, no **un**). Exploring how to adapt our type **un** to defend against adversarial Python contexts would be an interesting line of future work.

## 4. Metatheory

This section formally establishes memory isolation, static safety, and dynamic safety for TS$^\star$ programs translated to JavaScript. Clearly, such a proof requires a formal semantics for JavaScript—we rely on JS$^\star$, a translation semantics for JavaScript developed by Swamy et al. (2013), which is in turn based on λJS (Guha et al. 2010). We provide a brief review of JS$^\star$, define the central invariants of our translation, and describe our main theorem. A full formalism, including all proofs, is available online.

**4.1 A review of JS$^\star$ and our high-level proof strategy** JS$^\star$ is a subset of F$^\star$ (Swamy et al. 2011), a programming language whose type system allows expressing functional-correctness properties of higher-order effectful programs. Prior work defines a semantics for JavaScript via translation to JS$^\star$. The semantics is implemented by a tool, called JS2JS$^\star$, that translates JavaScript concrete syntax to JS$^\star$. This semantics for JavaScript has been used previously both as a means of verifying JavaScript source programs (after translation to JS$^\star$) as well as in Fournet et al.'s proof of full abstraction from f$^\star$ to JavaScript. At its core, JS$^\star$ provides a mechanically verified library called *JSVerify* that tries to faithfully model most security-relevant details of JavaScript, including, for example, its object model and its calling convention. The metatheory of TS$^\star$ is stated in terms of its translation to JS$^\star$, i.e., programs that can be type-checked against the *JSVerify* API. The validity of our theorem depends on JS$^\star$ being a faithful model of JavaScript, an assumption that can be checked separately, e.g., by semantics testing.

To set up the formal machinery, we develop a model of our compiler by transposing the translation judgment in Figure 2 to instead generate JS$^\star$ code. The relationship among these translations is depicted alongside. The translation from TS$^\star$ to JS$^\star$ can be seen as the composition of the translation from TS$^\star$ to JavaScript, and then from JavaScript to JS$^\star$. Our main theorem is stated as a type-preservation result from TS$^\star$ to JS$^\star$, where the types in JS$^\star$ are precise enough to capture our desired invariants, i.e., static safety, dynamic safety, and memory isolation.

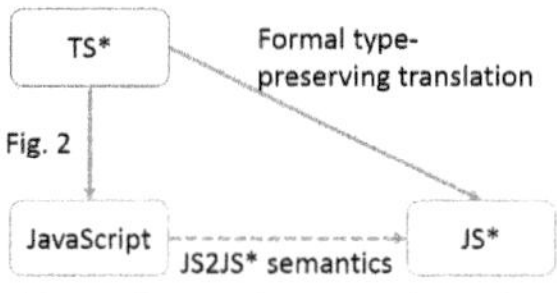

Fig. 2

***Monadic computation types with heap invariants*** All computations in js$^\star$ are typed in a state monad of predicate transformers, *iDST*, which is parametrized by a heap-invariant predicate *HeapInv* and a heap-evolution predicate $\delta$. The type *iDST a WP* is the type of a computation, which for any post-condition *post*, when run in an initial heap $h$, may diverge or else produce a result $v{:}a$ and a final heap $h'$ that satisfy the formula $post\ v\ h' \wedge HeapInv\ h' \wedge \delta\ h\ h'$, so long as $HeapInv\ h \wedge WP\ post\ h$ is valid. Additionally, all intermediate heaps in the computation satisfy *HeapInv*, and every intermediate heap is related to all its successors by $\delta$. That is, in *iDST a WP*, *a* is the result type, and *WP* is a predicate transformer that computes a pre-condition for the computation with respect to *post*, any desired post-condition; *HeapInv* is an invariant on a heap, and $\delta$ is a reflexive and transitive relation constraining how the heap evolves. Our online materials also account for exceptions and fatal errors; however, we gloss over them here for lack of space.

The main idea behind our proof is that a TS$^\star$ term $e{:}t$ is translated to a JS$^\star$ term $e'$ of type $iDST\ dyn\ WP_{[\![t]\!]}$, where

$$WP_{[\![t]\!]} = \Lambda post.\lambda h.\ Ok\ (loc(e))\ h \wedge \forall v\ h'.\ [\![t]\!]\ v\ h' \Longrightarrow post\ v\ h'$$

This ensures that, if $e'$ is run in an initial heap $h$ satisfying $HeapInv\ h$ and $Ok\ (loc(e))\ h$ (meaning that all free-variables of the source-term $e$ are correctly promoted to the heap in JS$^\star$), then either (1) it will terminate with a result $v$ and a final heap $h'$ satisfying $[\![t]\!]\ v\ h'$; or (2) it will diverge. The code may also raise an exception or throw a fatal error, but all the while during the execution of $e'$, *HeapInv* will be true, and the heap will evolve according to $\delta$. This result holds even when $e'$ is linked with arbitrary JavaScript code—adapting the universal typability lemma of Fournet et al. (2013), JavaScript code can always be typed in JS$^\star$ at a type corresponding to **un**.

Our main task then is to carefully define *HeapInv*, $\delta$ and $[\![t]\!]$ such that they capture our desired invariants, and then to prove that translated programs are well-typed in JS$^\star$.

**4.2 Invariants of the translation** To prove memory isolation, JS$^\star$ provides a partitioned heap model. Every object reference $l{:}loc$ carries a tag, $l.tag$, which records the name of the compartment into which the reference points, i.e., each compartment is a disjoint fragment of the domain of the heap. There are six compartments in the heap model. The *Ref* compartment holds objects corresponding to TS$^\star$ records, datatypes, and RTTI; the *Abs* compartment holds function objects; the *Clean* compartment holds the `Clean` object initialized and then frozen by `boot.js`; and the *Un* compartment belongs to the adversary. We focus primarily on properties of these first four compartments. The remaining two compartments, *Inv* and *Stub*, are inherited unchanged from Fournet et al. (2013)—the former is for maintaining local variables, and the latter for tracking function objects used to make safe callbacks to the attacker.

***Refined type dynamic*** All JavaScript values (including the translation of TS$^\star$) are represented as JS$^\star$ values of type *dyn*, defined below. We show only three representative cases. $d{=}Str\ s$ is an injection of $s{:}string$ into type *dyn*, where the refinement $TypeOf\ d{=}string$ recalls the static type. For object references $Obj\ (l{:}loc)$, the refinement is $l$'s tag, i.e., $\{Ref, Abs, Un, Clean\}$. Finally, for functions, $Fun\ o\ f$ builds a value of type *dyn* from a function closure $f$ and the JavaScript object $o$ for that closure. Its refinement is the predicate transformer of $f$.

**type** *dyn* = ...
| *Str*: *string* $\to$ *d*:*dyn*{*TypeOf d*=*string*}
| *Obj*: *l*:*loc* $\to$ *d*:*dyn*{*TypeOf d*=*l.tag*}
| *Fun*: $\forall$*WP*. *o*:*dyn* $\to$ (*this*:*dyn* $\to$ *args*:*dyn* $\to$ *iDST dyn* (*WP o args this*))
$\to$ *d*:*dyn*{*TypeOf d*=*WP*}

***Translation of types*** To recover the precision of TS$^\star$ types in JS$^\star$, we translate source types to predicates on *dyn*-typed values and the heap: $[\![t]\!]\ d\ h$ states that the value *d*:*dyn* is the translation of a source value of type *t* in the heap *h*. The translation of a type is with respect to a heap, since a source value allocated at the type $\{f :^a number\}$, may evolve to become a value of type $\{f :^a number, g :^a number\}$ in some subsequent heap. This is in contrast to, and a significant generalization of, the translation of f$^\star$ to JS$^\star$, where a value's type does not evolve and is not subject to subtyping.

$$
\begin{array}{lcl}
[\![\texttt{string}]\!]\ d\ h & = & \mathit{TypeOf}\ d{=}\mathit{string} \\
[\![\texttt{un}]\!]\ d\ h & = & \mathit{IsUn}\ d \\
[\![t]\!]\ d\ h & = & \exists u <: t.\ \mathit{Tagged}\ u\ d\ h \quad \text{if } t \notin \{\texttt{string},\ \texttt{un}\} \\
\mathit{Tagged}\ u\ d\ h & = & \texttt{"rtti"} \in \mathit{dom}\ h[d] \wedge \mathit{Rep}\ u\ (h[d][\texttt{"rtti"}])\ h \wedge \mathit{Is}\ u\ d\ h \\
\mathit{Is}\ \texttt{any}\ d\ h & = & \mathit{Prim}\ d \vee \mathit{Fun\_is}\ d \vee (\mathit{TypeOf}\ d{=}\mathit{Ref} \wedge \mathit{restAny}\ \{\}\ d\ h) \\
\mathit{Is}\ T\ d\ h & = & \mathit{TypeOf}\ d{=}\mathit{Ref} \wedge \bigvee_{D_{\bar{t}\to T}} h[d][\texttt{"c"}]{=}\mathit{Str}\ \texttt{"D"} \\
& \wedge & \bigwedge_i [\![t_i]\!]\ (h[d][i])\ h \wedge \mathit{restAny}\ \{1..n\}\ d\ h \\
\mathit{Is}\ \{\bar{f} :^{\bar{a}} \bar{t}\}\ d\ h & = & \mathit{TypeOf}\ d{=}\mathit{Ref} \wedge \bar{f} \subseteq \mathit{dom}\ h[d] \\
& \wedge & [\![\bar{t}]\!]\ h[d][\bar{f}]\ h \wedge \mathit{restAny}\ \bar{f}\ d\ h \\
\mathit{Is}\ (t_1 \to t_2)\ d\ h & = & \mathit{TypeOf}\ d = \lambda o\ \mathit{args}\ \mathit{this}.\Lambda p.\lambda h. \\
& & \quad [\![t_1]\!]\ h[\mathit{args}][\texttt{"0"}]\ h \wedge \forall r\ h'.\ [\![t_2]\!]\ r\ h' \Longrightarrow p\ r\ h' \\
\mathit{restAny}\ \mathit{fs}\ d\ h & = & \forall f{\in}\mathit{dom}(h[d])\backslash \mathit{fs}.\ \neg\mathit{Reserved}\ f \Longrightarrow [\![\texttt{any}]\!]\ h[d][f]\ h
\end{array}
$$

Since strings are immutable $[\![\texttt{string}]\!]\ d\ h$ does not depend on *h*. Likewise, an un-typed value always remains un-typed—we define *IsUn* shortly. For other types, $[\![t]\!]\ d\ h$ captures the subtyping relation, stating that there exists a type $u <: t$ such that the value's `rtti` is tagged with the runtime representation of *u* (the predicate $\mathit{Rep}\ u\ (h[d][\texttt{"rtti"}])\ h$), and $\mathit{Is}\ u\ d\ h$, i.e., the value *d* can be typed at *u* in *h*. *Is* any *d h* states that *d* is either a primitive (e.g., a string), a function, or a location in the *Ref* heap where all its non-reserved fields (excluding, e.g., `"rtti"`) are typeable at `any` (*restAny*). For datatypes and records, we require *d* to be a location in the *Ref* heap, with the fields typed as expected, and with all other fields not mentioned in the type being `any`. The case for functions is most interesting. $\mathit{Is}\ (t_1 \to t_2)\ d\ h$ states that *d*'s predicate transformer builds a pre-condition that requires the first argument to satisfy $[\![t_1]\!]$. (All JavaScript functions are variable arity, receiving their arguments in an array; however a non-un-typed TS$^\star$ function will only read the first one.) In return, the predicate transformer ensures that the result *r* (if any) will satisfy $[\![t_2]\!]$ (recall that we are ignoring exceptions here).

***Un values*** The predicate *IsUn v* defines when the value *v* could have been produced by, can be given to, or is accessible by the context. *Un* values include primitives; references to objects in the *Un* heap; or the immutable *Clean* object (which is reachable from the global object). Additionally, *Un* values can be functions whose specification indicates that it takes *Un* arguments to *Un* results.

$$
\begin{array}{l}
\mathit{IsUn}\ x \triangleq \mathit{TypeOf}\ x \in \{\mathit{bool}, \mathit{string}, \mathit{float}, \mathit{Un}, \mathit{Clean}\} \vee \mathit{TypeOf}\ x{=}\mathit{Un2Un} \\
\mathit{Un2Un} \triangleq \lambda o\ \mathit{args}\ \mathit{this}\ \mathit{post}\ h.\ \mathit{IsUn}\ o \wedge \mathit{IsUn}\ \mathit{this} \wedge \mathit{IsUn}\ \mathit{args} \\
\quad \wedge\ (\forall\ r\ h'.\ \mathit{IsUn}\ r \Longrightarrow \mathit{post}\ r\ h')
\end{array}
$$

***HeapInv, the global heap invariant*** Our main heap invariant is a property of every location *x* in the heap. Its full definition contains seven clauses; we show the most important ones.

$$
\begin{array}{lll}
\mathit{HeapInv}\ h \triangleq & \forall x.\ x \in \mathit{dom}\ h \Longrightarrow & \\
(1) & & (x.\mathit{tag}{=}\mathit{Un} \Longrightarrow \forall x \in \mathit{dom}\ h[x].\ \mathit{IsUn}\ h[x]) \\
(2) & \wedge & (x.\mathit{tag}{\in}\{\mathit{Ref},\mathit{Abs}\} \wedge \texttt{"rtti"}{\in}\mathit{dom}\ h[x] \Longrightarrow \exists t.\ \mathit{Tagged}\ t\ d\ h) \\
(3) & \wedge & (x.\mathit{tag}{=}\mathit{Ref} \Longrightarrow \mathit{TypeOf}\ h[x][\texttt{"@proto"}]{=}\mathit{Null}) \\
(4) & \wedge & (x.\mathit{tag}{=}\mathit{Clean} \Longrightarrow \mathit{CleanSpec}\ h[x]\ h)
\end{array}
$$

Clause (1) asserts that all the contents of an *Un* object are also *Un*. Clause (2) asserts that every object in the *Ref* and *Abs* compartment with an `"rtti"` field is tagged properly. Clause (3) additionally specifies that every object in the *Ref* heap has a `null` prototype. Clause (4) asserts that the *Clean* object is specified by *CleanSpec*, which gives a type to each of its fields.

Within this invariant are two key properties of TS$^\star$. The first clause guarantees that the only values reachable from a location in the *Un* heap are themselves un-values. Therein lies our memory isolation property—the adversary can never meddle with TS$^\star$ objects directly, since these reside in the *Ref* and *Abs* heap, which are disjoint from *Un*. The invariant, in its second clause, also captures dynamic safety, i.e., every object in the *Ref* and *Abs* heap, once tagged with RTTI are properly typed according to it.

***$\delta$, the heap evolution invariant*** The full definition of $\delta$ has 4 clauses; we show the main one below: $\delta$ ensures that, for all objects in the *Ref* and *Abs* heaps, their `"rtti"` fields only evolve monotonically downward, according to the subtyping hierarchy.

$$
\begin{array}{l}
\delta\ h0\ h1 \triangleq \forall l \in \mathit{dom}\ h0, t_0, t_1. \\
l.\mathit{tag} \in \{\mathit{Ref},\mathit{Abs}\} \wedge \mathit{Rep}\ t_0\ h0[l][\texttt{"rtti"}]\ h0 \wedge \mathit{Rep}\ t_1\ h1[l][\texttt{"rtti"}]\ h1 \\
\Longrightarrow t_1 <: t_0
\end{array}
$$

A relatively easy lemma derivable from these definitions implies our static safety property. In particular, Lemma 1 guarantees that if a value *v* (potentially a location to a heap-resident record) is typeable at type *t* in some initial heap $h_0$ then as the program's heap evolves according to $\delta$, *v* remains typeable at *t*. This ensures that it is safe for TS$^\star$ to ascribe a value a static type, since that type is an invariant of the value at runtime.

**Lemma 1** (Static safety: $\delta$ preserves the interpretation of types). *For all values v, heaps $h_0$ and $h_1$ such that HeapInv $h_0$, HeapInv $h_1$ and $\delta\ h_0\ h_1$, if for some t we have $[\![t]\!]\ v\ h_0$ then $[\![t]\!]\ v\ h_1$.*

Finally, our main theorem, as promised, is a type preservation result that guarantees memory isolation, dynamic safety and static safety for TS$^\star$ programs translated to JS$^\star$. In the hypothesis, the relation $\Gamma \vdash_f e : t \rightsquigarrow e'$ is the formal translation of TS$^\star$ to JS$^\star$ (the index *f* is the name of the current function object in $e'$; a technical detail). The judgment in the conclusion of the theorem asserts that, in a translated environment, $e'$ has a type that is described by the predicate transformer corresponding to the source type *t*. As explained in §4.1, this ensures that the translated program respects the heap invariants and, if it terminates normally, produces a *t*-typed result.

**Theorem 1** (Type preservation).
*Given a* TS$^\star$ *context* $\Gamma$, *an expression e and a type t,*
*if* $\Gamma \vdash_f e : t \rightsquigarrow e'$ *for some* JS$^\star$ *expression* $e'$ *and function object f, then* $[\![\Gamma]\!], f{:}\mathit{dyn}, \Gamma_{loc(e)} \vdash e' : \mathit{iDST}\ \mathit{dyn}\ \mathit{WP}_{[\![t]\!]}$.

We conclude our formal development with a few remarks on the scope of our theorem and the style of its proof. First, our result is applicable to the translation of TS$^\star$ to JavaScript only inasmuch as JS$^\star$ is an accurate model of all of JavaScript—Fournet et al. (2013) argue for how JS$^\star$ is adequate for all security-relevant features of JavaScript. Regardless, the availability of these semantics together with its program logic is what made our proof feasible. Given an operational semantics, but lacking a program logic, our proof would have been mired in tedious inductions over the operational semantics. With JS$^\star$, we were able to carry out our proof as an induction over the compilation relation, and use the type system of JS$^\star$ to structure and prove our invariants.

Second, our result includes within its trusted computing base the correspondence of `boot.js` to the *CleanSpec* predicate in the last clause of *HeapInv*. While it is perhaps standard for compiler and verification projects to rely on a small amount of trusted code, we would like to do better. In particular, we aim to use the JavaScript verification toolchain developed by Swamy et al. (2013) to verify `boot.js` for compliance with *CleanSpec*—at the time of writing, this was still incomplete. More substantially, we would also like to build a translation validation pipeline for our compiler implementation, reflecting the generated JavaScript back into JS* for verification, i.e., we would like our compiler implementation to be also formally type-preserving.

## 5. Securely deploying TS* programs

The guarantees of TS* depend on `boot.js` being the first script to run on a web page. Many prior works have implicitly assumed that scripts are always executed in the order in which they appear on the page (Jim et al. 2007; Magazinius et al. 2010; Taly et al. 2011), but, as we explain, this is a naïve view. Instead, we develop a standards-based mechanism that ensures that our scripts run first.

**5.1 Securely bootstrapping the TS* runtime** Suppose a script $s$ is lexically the first element in the header of a page located at a URL `U = http://W.com/page.html`; one may expect that it will be guaranteed to run first on any window loaded from `U`. However, this intuition is correct only if the page has not been loaded programmatically from JavaScript by another web page, e.g., within another frame. On a page loaded initially from `U`, the script $s$ will indeed run first. Still, a malicious script running later on the page, or on a different page with the same origin `http://W.com`, may open a window or frame at `U`, and modify all the essential primitives before $s$ begins to run inside the new window frame. This execution order is consistent with the HTML standard (Berjon et al. 2013) and we have confirmed it experimentally on all mainstream browsers.

Hence, any simple first-starter implementation that relies on lexical ordering of script elements will fail if other scripts on the same origin are allowed to open windows or frames. Indeed, the web browser only provides security guarantees at the granularity of an origin (Barth 2011); finer-grained privilege separation between good and bad scripts within the same origin require application-level mechanisms, such as restricting all untrusted scripts to a sublanguage like $\text{SES}_{light}$ (Taly et al. 2011); loading them in sandboxed iframes with few privileges (Akhawe et al. 2012); or modifying the browser to allow the first-starter script to certify all other scripts running on the page (Jim et al. 2007).

Rather than restrict the functionality of untrusted scripts, we propose a mechanism that ensures that our scripts run first. For a given website, we use two distinct origins:

- `http://W.com`, used primarily as the service origin; it does not serve any resource.
- `http://start.W.com`, that serves HTML pages, including scripts compiled from TS*, but where the first two `<script>` elements on every page are as follows:

```
<script src="http://start.W.com/boot.js"></script>
<script>document.domain = "W.com"</script>
```

The crucial step here is that, after `boot.js` has loaded, the page sets `document.domain` to the parent domain `W.com`. This is a standards-based mechanism (Berjon et al. 2013, 5.3.1) by which the page voluntarily gives up its rights to the `http://start.W.com/` origin for client-side same-origin access across frames and windows. Instead, it adopts an *effective script origin* of `http://W.com`.

All subsequent scripts on the page are unrestricted except that they can only read or write into frames or windows that have an effective script origin of `http://W.com`, and hence they cannot tamper with pages on `http://start.W.com`, even if such pages are loaded programmatically into other frames or windows. In all other ways, their functionality is unimpeded, without the need for expensive translations or messaging protocols, as in previous approaches.

More generally, by placing other trusted scripts after `boot.js` and before the assignment to `document.domain`, we can run scripts that grab reliable copies of builtin libraries, such as JSON and `XMLHttpRequest`, for use by subsequent code.

**5.2 Loading scripts with embedded secrets** Our first-starter protocol reliably allows `boot.js` to build a trustworthy environment for our compiled scripts. Conversely, we sometimes need a way for scripts to be able to verify that their environment is trustworthy. This is particularly important when compiled scripts contain secret tokens embedded within them, e.g., to authenticate themselves to other servers. Embedding secrets as constants within program text may seem like an elementary mistake, but this is the predominant way of distributing these tokens in a JavaScript setting. Secrets within scripts must first be protected from malicious websites that may try to load our scripts, and second from malicious scripts on our own website `W.com`. In this threat model, many simple countermeasures one may think of are inadequate.

Even if we require a login cookie for authentication before serving the script, a malicious website that an innocent user visits when logged into `W.com` can make a cross-site script request and obtain the script (an attack sometimes called JavaScript hijacking). If we inline the scripts into our page, malicious scripts can read their source code and obtain the token. Even if they are not inlined but served from `http://start.W.com`, malicious scripts can perform an `XMLHttpRequest` to obtain their source code and then read them. Indeed, these are all methods commonly used by cross-site scripting attacks (e.g., the Samy worm) to break token-based security protections on the web.

To protect our scripts from same-origin attackers, we use a third distinct origin to serve our scripts:

- `https://src.W.com`, the secure source server, only serves GET requests for scripts that may embed secret tokens to be shared between the server and the script. The server refuses cross-origin requests and returns scripts as `text/javascript`, so attackers on `https://start.W.com` can execute these scripts but not read its source, due to the same-origin policy. We recommend the use of HTTPS for any pages that contain secrets, but HTTP is adequate if we exclude network adversaries from our threat model.

To protect our scripts against other websites, we need an additional check. Every script served from `src.W.com` is prefixed by a condition on the current webpage location, that is, before making any use of its secret token, the script checks that `window.location.href` actually begins with `http://start.W.com/`. This ensures that the script has a reliable `Clean` object on that page, introduced by `boot.js`.

Experimentally, we found that checking the current location of a script is quite error-prone. Some scripts try to read `document.domain` (see e.g., OWASP CSRFGuard in §6.1) or `document.location`; others rely on `window.location.href` but then use regular expression or string matching to check it against a target origin. All these techniques lead to attacks because a malicious website could have tampered with its `document` object or with the regular expression libraries. We found and reported such attacks to vendors.

Notably, many browsers allow properties like `document.domain` and `window.location.origin` to be overwritten. Our origin check relies on the `window.location.href` object which is specified as unforgeable in the HTML specification (Berjon et al. 2013, 5.2). In practice, however, we found that some browsers incorrectly allow even supposedly unforgeable objects like `window.document` and `window.location` to be shadowed. We have reported these bugs to various browsers and are in discussions about fixes. If the unforgeability of `window.location.href` turns out to be too strong an assumption, we advocate the use of the origin authentication protocol of Bhargavan et al. (2013).

## 6. Secure web programming with TS*

We have evaluated our compiler by gradually migrating JavaScript sources to TS*, while ensuring that the migrated code (after compilation) exports the same API as the original. We have also written from scratch various utilities like a JSON parser and a reference monitor for HTML5 localStorage. All the code is available online.

We have yet to conduct a thorough performance analysis of our compiler, and to implement further optimizations. But, as mentioned previously, statically typed TS* should incur little, if any, runtime overhead, while un-typed code is unchanged. Understanding and optimizing the performance profile of any-typed code is left as future work.

In this section, we describe how TS* can be used to gradually secure existing access control patterns, as deployed in popular JavaScript APIs. We focus on client-sided, language-based security, relegating most other details to the online materials (notably a description of same-origin policies, protocol- and browser specific security assumptions, and current attacks against them; see also e.g., Bhargavan et al. 2013).

**6.1 OWASP CSRFGuard** We first consider the task of securing client code that performs an `XMLHttpRequest` to the page's server.

***Cross-Site Request Forgeries (CSRF)*** Suppose a website `W` has an API available from JavaScript. Authenticating and authorizing access using cookies ensures that only requests from a logged-in user's browser are accepted. Conversely, if the user has any another websites open in her browser, their scripts also get access to the API, and can thus steal or tamper with the user's data on `W`. Such request forgery attacks are persistently listed in OWASP Top 10 vulnerabilities, and have a serious impact on a variety of websites.

***CSRF Tokens*** As a countermeasure to CSRF, a website `W` can inject a fresh, session-specific, random token into every page it serves, and only accept requests that include this token. Other websites cannot see `W`'s pages (thanks to the same origin policy) hence cannot forge requests. Additionally, cookies and tokens can be protected while in transit by using the HTTPS protocol. OWASP CSRFGuard 3 is the most widely-referenced CSRF protection library. As an advanced feature, it provides a token-injection script that transparently protects AJAX calls by intercepting any `XMLHttpRequest`. (Similar protections exist for frameworks like Django and Ruby-On-Rails.) Crucially, the token must be kept secret from other websites, and also from other scripts loaded on the page; otherwise those scripts may use it to perform arbitrary requests directly, or leak it to some other website.

***Attacks*** The original, unwrapped version of their code relies on `window.location`, `String.startsWith`, and `XMLHttpRequest`, which can be tampered with by a malicious script. We found several such attacks where a malicious website could load the OWASP CSRFGuard script, forge the location, and trick it into releasing the token; we are in discussion with the author towards more robust designs, such as the one proposed here for TS*.

***CSRFGuard in*** **TS*** Following the approach of §2, we migrate to TS* the OWASP proxy that uses the token to provide authentication RPCs to the rest of the library. This small script is typed in TS*, guaranteeing that no malicious script that runs alongside (including the rest of the library) can tamper with its execution.

The TS*proxy, listed below, takes three string arguments: the target URL, the API function name, and the JSON-formatted arguments. It checks that the URL is well-formed and belongs to the current site (to avoid leaking the token to any other site), then it serializes the request as a query string, attaches the token, and makes an AJAX call. Once wrapped, it exports the same interface as before to any (untrusted) scripts loaded on the page. Additionally, it could be directly used by further TS* code.

```
var csrfToken: string = "%GENERATED_TOKEN%"
var targetOrigin: string = "%TARGET_ORIGIN%"
function Rpc(url:string,apifun:string,args:string): any {
  if (String.startsWith(url,String.concat(targetOrigin,"/")) &&
      String.noQueryHash(url)) {
    var m = {method:apifun, args:args, token: csrfToken};
    var request = String.concat("?",QueryString.encode(m));
    var response = xhrGet(String.concat(url,request));}
    return QueryString.decode(response);
  }
  else return "unauthorized URL";
}
```

The first two lines define string literals, inlined by the server as it generates the script—the TS* compilation process ensures, via lexical scoping, that these two strings are private to this script. The `Rpc` function is our secure replacement for `xhrGet`, which performs the actual `XMLHttpRequest`. Compared with the original JavaScript, it includes a few type annotations, and uses either safe copies of builtin libraries, such as `xhrGet` and `String`, or typed TS* libraries, such as `QueryString` (outlined below). Relying on memory isolation and secure loading from TS*, a simple (informal) security review of this script lets us conclude that it does not leak `csrfToken`.

Experimentally, we modified the OWASP library, to isolate and protect the few scripts that directly use the token (such as the proxy above) from the rest of the code, which deals with complex formatting and browser-specific extensions, and is kept unchanged and untrusted. The modified library retains its original interface and functionality, with stronger security guarantees, based on strict, type-based isolation of the token. Its code and sample client- and server-side code are available online. To our knowledge, it is the first CSRF library that provides protection from untrusted scripts.

**6.2 Facebook API** Taking advantage of Cross-Origin Resource Sharing (CORS), Facebook provides a client-side JavaScript API, so that trusted websites may access their personal data—once the user has opted in. Interestingly, Facebook also provides a "debug-mode" library, with systematic dynamic typechecks somewhat similar to those automated by TS*, to help programmers catch client-side errors. We focus on two aspects of their large API: the encoding of strings, and cross-domain messaging.

***QueryString encoding*** We give a TS* implementation of the `QueryString` module (mentioned above) for the REST message format used in the Facebook API.

```
function decode (s:string) : any {
 var res = {};
 if (s === "") return res;
 else {
  var params = String.split(s,"&");
  for (var k in params) {
   var kv = String.split(params[k],"=");
   res[kv["0"]] = kv["1"];
  };
  return res;}
}
```

(The `encode` function is dual.) Our function illustrates support for arrays provided by our compiler,.Importantly, this code may be used to parse untrusted messages; our wrapper for `un` to `string` is straightforward—if the argument is already a string, it is just the identity. Hence, one can write efficient TS* that calls `decode` to parse messages received from the adversary; this coding style is idiomatic in JavaScript, while the checks performed by our type system and runtime prevent many pitfalls.

Another TS*sample illustrates the usage of `Rpc` and our typed JSON library (generalizing `QueryString`) to program a higher-level, statically typed API. It shows, for instance, how to program a client-side proxy for the "/me" method of the Facebook API, which retrieves the user profile; this TS* function has the return type:

```
type profile =
  {id: string; email: string; age_range: {min:number}; ... }
```

***Cross-Domain Messaging*** The Facebook API is meant to run on any website and protects itself from a malicious host by using iframes. For example, if the website calls `FB.login`, the API loads an iframe from `facebook.com` that retrieves the current user's access token and then only sends it to the host website (via `postMessage`) if the host is in a list of authorized origins.

Bhargavan et al. (2013) report attacks on a prior version of this authorization code that were due to typing errors (and have now been patched). We re-implement this code in TS$^\star$ and show how programmers can rely on typing to avoid such attacks.

The `checkOrigins` function below is given the current host origin and verifies it against an array of authorized origins. The `proxyMessage` function uses this check to guard the release of the token to the parent (host) website, using a safe copy of the primitive `postMessage` function.

```
function checkOrigins (given:string,expected:array string):bool{
 for (var k in expected) {
  if(given === expected[k]) return true;}
 return false;}
function proxyMessage(h:string,tok,origins:array string) {
 if(checkOrigins(h,origins)) postMessage('parent',tok,h);}
```

In a previous version of the Facebook API, `proxyMessage` was accidentally called with an `origins` parameter of type `string`, rather than `array string`. This innocuous type error leads to an attack, because the untyped version of the code succeeds with both strings and arrays, but with different results. To see the core problem, consider a call to `checkOrigins` where `given = "h"` and `expected = "http://W.com"`. The `for` loop iterates over each character of `expected`, and hence succeeds, when it should not. In TS$^\star$, iteration is well-typed only for arrays and, unlike JavaScript, this enumerates only the "own" properties of the array. Thus, in our code, this error is caught statically (if the incorrect call to `proxyMessage` is local) or dynamically (if the call is from another iframe); the check fails in both cases and the token is not leaked.

## 7. Conclusions and prospects

This paper aims to broaden the scope of gradual typing: not only it is useful for migrating dynamically type-safe code to more structured statically typed code, it is also useful for moving from unsafe code, vulnerable to security attacks, to a robust mixture of dynamically and statically type-safe code.

Within the context of JavaScript, we have presented TS$^\star$, a language with a gradual type system, a compiler, and runtime support that provides several useful safety and confinement properties. Our preliminary experience suggests that TS$^\star$ is effective in protecting security-critical scripts from attacks—without safety and confinement, such properties are difficult to obtain for JavaScript, and indeed security for such scripts has previously been thought unobtainable in the presence of cross-site scripts.

Even excluding the adversary, TS$^\star$ develops a new point in the design space of gradual typing, using an approach based on runtime type information. This has several useful characteristics, including a simple and uniform failure semantics, and its applicability to a language with extensible objects and object identity.

In the future, we plan to develop TS$^\star$ along several dimensions. On the practical side, we expect to integrate our ideas in an experimental branch of the open source TypeScript compiler, targeting the construction of larger secure libraries. On the theoretical side, we plan to explore the formal certification of our compiler and runtime. We also hope to develop our preliminary ideas on new notions of blame to explain runtime failures in TS$^\star$.

***Acknowledgments*** Many thanks to Martín Abadi, Antoine Delignat-Lavaud, Jeremy Siek, Phil Wadler, and all the anonymous reviewers.

## References

M. Abadi, L. Cardelli, B. Pierce, and G. Plotkin. Dynamic typing in a statically typed language. *ACM ToPLAS*, 13(2):237–268, 1991.

D. Akhawe, P. Saxena, and D. Song. Privilege separation in HTML5 applications. In *Proceedings of USENIX Security*, 2012.

A. Barth. The web origin concept, 2011. IETF RFC6454.

A. Barth, C. Jackson, and J. C. Mitchell. Robust defenses for cross-site request forgery. In *Proceedings of CCS*, 2008.

R. Berjon, T. Leithead, E. Navara, E.D.and O'Conner, and S. Pfeiffer. HTML5. `http://www.w3.org/TR/html5/`, 2013. W3C Cand. Reco.

K. Bhargavan, A. Delignat-Lavaud, and S. Maffeis. Language-based defenses against untrusted browser origins. In *Proceedings of USENIX Security*, 2013.

G. Bierman, E. Meijer, and M. Torgersen. Adding dynamic types to C$^\sharp$. In *Proceedings of ECOOP*, 2010.

G. Bracha and D. Griswold. Strongtalk: Typechecking Smalltalk in a production environment. In *Proceedings of OOPSLA*, 1993.

R. Chugh, D. Herman, and R. Jhala. Dependent types for JavaScript. In *OOPSLA*, 2012.

Facebook API. FB.API, 2013. `http://developers.facebook.com/docs/reference/javascript/`.

R. B. Findler and M. Felleisen. Contracts for higher-order functions. In *Proceedings of ICFP*, 2002.

C. Flanagan. Hybrid type checking. In *Proceedings of POPL*, 2006.

C. Fournet, N. Swamy, J. Chen, P.-E. Dagand, P.-Y. Strub, and B. Livshits. Fully abstract compilation to JavaScript. In *Proceedings of POPL*, 2013.

A. D. Gordon and A. Jeffrey. Authenticity by typing for security protocols. In *Proceedings of CSFW*, 2001.

S. Guarnieri and B. Livshits. Gatekeeper: mostly static enforcement of security and reliability policies for javascript code. In *USENIX security symposium*, SSYM'09. USENIX Association, 2009.

A. Guha, C. Saftoiu, and S. Krishnamurthi. The essence of JavaScript. In *Proceedings of ECOOP*, 2010.

A. Guha, C. Saftoiu, and S. Krishnamurthi. Typing local control and state using flow analysis. In *Proceedings of ESOP*, 2011.

D. Hedin and A. Sabelfeld. Information-flow security for a core of JavaScript. In *Proceedings of CSF*, 2012.

D. Herman, A. Tomb, and C. Flanagan. Space-efficient gradual typing. *Higher Order Symbol. Comput.*, 2010.

L. Ina and A. Igarashi. Gradual typing for generics. In *Proceedings of OOPSLA*, 2011.

T. Jim, N. Swamy, and M. Hicks. Defeating script injection attacks with browser-enforced embedded policies. In *Proceedings of WWW*, 2007.

J. Magazinius, P. H. Phung, and D. Sands. Safe wrappers and sane policies for self protecting JavaScript. In *Proceedings of NordSec*, 2010.

OWASP CSRFGuard. CSRFGuard 3 user manual, 2010. `https://www.owasp.org/index.php/CSRFGuard_3_User_Manual`.

J. G. Politz, S. A. Eliopoulos, A. Guha, and S. Krishnamurthi. Adsafety: type-based verification of javascript sandboxing. In *USENIX Security*, 2011.

J. G. Siek and W. Taha. Gradual typing for functional languages. In *Scheme and Functional Programming Workshop*, 2006.

J. G. Siek, R. Garcia, and W. Taha. Exploring the design space of higher-order casts. In *Proceedings of ESOP*, 2009.

J. G. Siek, M. M. Vitousek, and S. Bharadwaj. Gradual typing for mutable objects. `http://ecee.colorado.edu/~siek/gtmo.pdf`, 2013.

N. Swamy, J. Chen, C. Fournet, P.-Y. Strub, K. Bhargavan, and J. Yang. Secure distributed programming with value-dependent types. In *Proceedings of ICFP*, 2011.

N. Swamy, J. Weinberger, C. Schlesinger, J. Chen, and B. Livshits. Verifying higher-order programs with the Dijkstra monad. In *PLDI*, 2013.

A. Taly, U. Erlingsson, J. C. Mitchell, M. S. Miller, and J. Nagra. Automated analysis of security-critical JavaScript APIs. In *Proceedings of S&P*, 2011.

P. Wadler and R. B. Findler. Well-typed programs can't be blamed. In *Proceedings of ESOP*, 2009.

# Sound Input Filter Generation for Integer Overflow Errors

Fan Long Stelios Sidiroglou-Douskos Deokhwan Kim Martin Rinard
{fanl, stelios, dkim, rinard}@csail.mit.edu
MIT CSAIL

## Abstract

We present a system, SIFT, for generating input filters that nullify integer overflow errors associated with critical program sites such as memory allocation or block copy sites. SIFT uses a static program analysis to generate filters that discard inputs that may trigger integer overflow errors in the computations of the sizes of allocated memory blocks or the number of copied bytes in block copy operations. Unlike all previous techniques of which we are aware, SIFT is sound — if an input passes the filter, it will not trigger an integer overflow error at any analyzed site.

Our results show that SIFT successfully analyzes (and therefore generates sound input filters for) 56 out of 58 memory allocation and block memory copy sites in analyzed input processing modules from five applications (VLC, Dillo, Swfdec, Swftools, and GIMP). These nullified errors include six known integer overflow vulnerabilities. Our results also show that applying these filters to 62895 real-world inputs produces no false positives. The analysis and filter generation times are all less than a second.

***Categories and Subject Descriptors*** F.3.2 [*Semantics of Programming Languages*]: Program Analysis; D.4.6 [*Operating Systems*]: Security and Protection

***General Terms*** Security; Program Analysis

***Keywords*** Integer Overflow; Abstraction; Soundness

## 1. Introduction

Many security exploits target software errors in deployed applications. One approach to nullifying vulnerabilities is to deploy input filters that discard inputs that may trigger the errors.

We present a new static analysis technique and implemented system, SIFT, for automatically generating filters that discard inputs that may trigger integer overflow errors at analyzed memory allocation and block copy sites. We focus on this problem, in part, because of its practical importance. Because integer overflows may enable code injection or other attacks, they are an important source of security vulnerabilities [25, 33, 35].

### 1.1 Previous Filter Generation Systems

Standard filter generation systems start with an input that triggers an error [10–12, 26, 36]. They next use the input to generate an execution trace and discover the path the program takes to the error. They then use a forward symbolic execution on the discovered path (and, in some cases, heuristically related paths) to derive a *vulnerability signature* — a boolean condition that the input must satisfy to follow the same execution path through the program to trigger the same error. The generated filter discards inputs that satisfy the vulnerability signature. Because other unconsidered paths to the error may exist, these techniques are unsound (i.e., the filter may miss inputs that exploit the error).

It is also possible to start with a potentially vulnerable site and use a weakest precondition analysis to obtain an input filter for that site. To the best of our knowledge, the only previous technique that uses this approach [5] is unsound in that 1) it uses loop unrolling to eliminate loops and therefore analyzes only a subset of the possible execution paths and 2) it does not specify a technique for dealing with potentially aliased values. As is standard, the generated filter incorporates *execution path constraints*, i.e., checks from conditional statements along the analyzed execution paths. The goal is to avoid filtering potentially problematic inputs that the program would (because of safety checks at conditionals along the execution path) process correctly. As a result, the generated input filters perform a substantial (between $10^6$ and $10^{10}$) number of operations.

### 1.2 SIFT

SIFT starts with a set of *critical expressions* from memory allocation and block copy sites. These expressions control the sizes of allocated or copied memory blocks at these sites. SIFT then uses an interprocedural, demand-driven, weakest precondition static analysis to propagate the critical expression backwards against the control flow. The result is a symbolic condition that captures all expressions that the application may evaluate (in any execution) to obtain the values of critical expressions. The free variables in the symbolic condition represent the values of input fields. In effect, the symbolic condition captures all of the possible computations that the program may perform on the input fields to obtain the values of critical expressions. Given an input, the generated input filter evaluates this condition over the corresponding input fields to discard inputs that may cause an overflow.

Because SIFT takes all paths to analyzed memory allocation and block copy sites into account, it generates sound filters — if an input passes the filter, it will not trigger an overflow in the evaluation of any critical expression (including the evaluation of intermediate expressions at distant program points that contribute to the value of the critical expression).[1]



*POPL '14*, January 22–24, 2014, San Diego, CA, USA.

ACM 978-1-4503-2544-8/14/01.
http://dx.doi.org/10.1145/2535838.2535888

[1] As is standard in the field, SIFT is designed to work with programs that do not access uninitialized memory. Our analysis therefore comes with the following soundness guarantee. If an input passes the filter for a given critical expression e, the input field annotations are correct (see Section 3.4), and the program has not yet accessed uninitialized memory when the program computes a value of e, then no integer overflow occurs during the evaluation

### 1.3 No Execution Path Constraints

Unlike standard techniques, SIFT incorporates no checks from the program's conditional statements and works only with arithmetic expressions that contribute directly to the values of the critical expressions. This design decision has the following consequences:

- **Sound and Efficient Analysis:** Ignoring execution path constraints improves the efficiency of the analysis because it eliminates the need to track the different constraints that may appear on the many different execution paths to each memory allocation or block copy site. Indeed, this efficiency is critical to the soundness of SIFT's analysis — in general, there may be an intractably large or even statically unbounded number of paths to a given memory allocation or block copy site. Attempting to enumerate all of these different execution paths to derive the complete set of execution path constraints is clearly infeasible and a major source of the unsoundness of previous techniques.
- **Efficient Filters:** Because SIFT ignores checks from conditional statements, it generates much more efficient filters than standard techniques (SIFT's filters perform tens of operations as opposed to tens of thousands or more). Indeed, our experimental results show that, in contrast to standard filters, SIFT's filters spend essentially all of their time reading the input (as opposed to checking if the input may trigger an overflow error).
- **Accurate Filters:** One potential concern is that the program may contain safety checks that enable it to safely process inputs that would otherwise trigger overflows. Ignoring these safety checks may cause the generated filter to discard inputs even though the program can process them safely.

  Our experimental results show that, in practice, ignoring execution path constraints results in no loss of accuracy. Specifically, we tested our generated filters on 62895 real-world inputs for six benchmark applications and found no false positives (incorrectly filtered inputs that the program would have processed correctly). We attribute this potentially counterintuitive result to the fact that standard integer data types usually contain enough bits to represent the memory allocation sizes and block copy lengths that benign inputs typically elicit.

### 1.4 Input Fields With Multiple Instantiations

Input files often contain multiple instantiations of the same input field (for example, when the input file contains repeated components that have the same format). SIFT works with an abstraction in which free variables in the propagated symbolic expressions (and the final symbolic condition) represent *all* instantiations of the corresponding input fields that they reference — i.e., SIFT does not attempt to determine the precise correspondence between variables and different instantiations of the same input field.

This design decision simplifies and extends the range of the analysis. All variables that reference the same input field are interchangeable (because they all represent all possible instantiations of the corresponding input field). SIFT can therefore successfully analyze programs for which it is not possible to statically determine the precise correspondence between variables and different instantiations of the same input field. This design decision also enables SIFT to analyze programs in which a single variable may reference different instantiations of the same input field over the course of the execution. Interchangeability also enables a new expression normalization algorithm that renumbers variables during the analysis of loops to obtain loop invariant expressions (see Section 3.2). These expressions soundly characterize the effect (on the propagated symbolic expression) of loops that may access multiple potentially different instantiations of the same input field.

One final consequence of this design decision is that the generated input filter must check all combinations of input field instantiations when it checks for potential overflows (see Section 3.5). Our experimental results show that, for our benchmark applications, this approach causes, at most, negligible overhead — the generated filters spend essentially all of their time reading the input.

### 1.5 Pointer Analysis and Precondition Generation

SIFT groups pointers into equivalence sets based on an analysis of the potential aliasing relationships between different pointers. To analyze a load statement that loads a value via a pointer, SIFT generates a new variable that represents the loaded value. In the propagated symbolic conditions, each such variable represents *all* values that may be stored via *any* alias of the pointer.

This decision produces an appropriately imprecise abstraction that enables SIFT to successfully analyze programs for which it is not possible to statically determine the precise value that each variable references. It also enables SIFT to work with any sound pointer or alias analysis that provides SIFT with the aliasing information required to soundly update the propagated symbolic condition at statements that access values via pointers (see Section 3.2). To the best of our knowledge, this is the first paper to show how to soundly incorporate an arbitrary off-the-shelf alias or pointer analysis into a precondition generation algorithm.

### 1.6 SIFT Usage Model

SIFT implements the following usage model:

**Module Identification.** Starting with an application that is designed to process inputs presented in one or more input formats, the developer identifies the modules within the application that process inputs of interest. SIFT will analyze these modules to generate an input filter for the inputs that these modules process.

**Input Statement Annotation.** The developer annotates the relevant input statements in the source code of the modules to identify the input field that each input statement reads.

**Critical Site Identification.** SIFT scans the modules to find all *critical sites* (currently, memory allocation and block copy sites). Each critical site has a *critical expression* that determines the size of the allocated or copied block of memory. The generated input filter will discard inputs that may trigger an integer overflow error during the computation of the value of the critical expression.

**Static Analysis.** For each critical expression, SIFT uses a demand-driven backwards static program analysis to automatically derive the corresponding *symbolic condition*. Each conjunct expression in this condition specifies, as a function of the input fields, how the value of the critical expression is computed along one of the program paths to the corresponding critical site.

**Input Parser Acquisition.** The developer obtains (typically from open-source repositories such as Hachoir [1]) a parser for the desired input format. This parser groups the input bit stream into input fields, then makes these fields available via a standard API.

**Filter Generation.** SIFT uses the input parser and symbolic conditions to automatically generate the input filter. When presented with an input, the filter reads the fields of the input and, for each symbolic expression in the conditions, determines if an integer overflow may occur when the expression is evaluated. If so, the filter discards the input. Otherwise, it passes the input along to the application. The generated filters can be deployed anywhere along the path from the input source to the application that ultimately processes the input.

---

of e (including the evaluations of intermediate expressions that contribute to the final value of the critical expression).

### 1.7 Experimental Results

We used SIFT to generate input filters for modules in five real-world applications: VLC 0.8.6h (a network media player), Dillo 2.1 (a lightweight web browser), Swfdec 0.5.5 (a flash video player), Swftools 0.9.1 (SWF manipulation and generation utilities), and GIMP 2.8.0 (an image manipulation application). Together, the analyzed modules contain 58 critical memory allocation and block copy sites. SIFT successfully generated filters for 56 of these 58 critical sites (SIFT's static analysis was unable to derive symbolic conditions for the remaining two critical sites, see Section 5.2 for more details). These applications contain six known integer overflow vulnerabilities at their critical sites. SIFT's filters nullify all of these vulnerabilities.

**Analysis and Filter Generation Times.** We configured SIFT to analyze all critical sites in the analyzed modules, then generate a single, high-performance composite filter that checks for integer overflow errors at all of the sites. The maximum time required to analyze all of the sites and generate the composite filter was less than a second for each benchmark application.

**False Positive Evaluation.** We used a web crawler to obtain a set of at least 6000 real-world inputs for each application (for a total of 62895 input files). We found no false positives — the corresponding composite filters accept all of the input files in this test set.

**Filter Performance.** We measured the composite filter execution time for each of the 62895 input files in our test set. The average time required to read and filter each input was at most 16 milliseconds, with this time dominated by the time required to read in the input file.

### 1.8 Contributions

This paper makes the following contributions:

- **SIFT:** We present SIFT, a sound filter generation system for nullifying integer overflow vulnerabilities. SIFT scans modules to find critical memory allocation and block copy sites, statically analyzes the code to automatically derive symbolic conditions that characterize how the application may compute the sizes of the allocated or copied memory blocks, and generates input filters that discard inputs that may trigger integer overflow errors in the evaluation of these expressions.

  Unlike all previous techniques of which we are aware, SIFT is sound — because it takes all execution paths into consideration, if an input passes the generated filter, it will not trigger an integer overflow error at any analyzed site. Also unlike previous techniques, SIFT generates efficient filters — because SIFT ignores execution path constraints, the generated filters perform tens of operations (as opposed to previous techniques, which incorporate execution path constraints and therefore perform tens of thousands or more operations).

- **Sound and Efficient Static Analysis:** We present a new static analysis that automatically derives symbolic conditions that capture, as a function of the input fields, how the integer values of critical expressions are computed along the various possible execution paths to the corresponding critical site. Unlike standard precondition generation techniques, the SIFT static analysis does not incorporate checks from the program's conditional statements — it instead works only with the arithmetic operations that contribute directly to the values of the critical expressions.

- **Input Fields With Multiple Instantiations:** We present a novel abstraction for input fields with multiple instantiations. This abstraction enables SIFT to analyze programs for which it is impossible to statically determine the precise correspondence between variables and different instantiations of the same input field. With this abstraction, all variables that reference the same input field are interchangable (because they all represent all instantiations of that input field). This interchangability enables a new expression normalization technique that SIFT deploys to automatically obtain invariants for loops that access the values of input fields.

- **Pointer Analysis and Precondition Generation:** We also present a novel abstraction for values that load statements access via pointers. This abstraction enables SIFT to analyze programs for which it is impossible to statically determine the precise value that each pointer references. We believe that this paper is the first to show how to soundly incorporate an arbitrary off-the-shelf alias or pointer analysis into a precondition generation algorithm.

- **Experimental Results:** We present experimental results that illustrate the practical viability of our approach in protecting applications against integer overflow vulnerabilities at memory allocation and block copy sites.

The rest of this paper is organized as follows. Section 2 presents a motivating example that illustrates how SIFT works. Section 3 presents the core SIFT static analysis for C programs. Section 4 presents the formalization of the static analysis and discusses the soundness of the analysis. Section 5 presents the experimental results. Section 6 discusses related work. We conclude in Section 7.

## 2. Example

We next present an example that illustrates how SIFT nullifies an integer overflow vulnerability in Swfdec 0.5.5, an open source shockwave flash player.

Figure 1 presents (simplified) source code from Swfdec. When Swfdec opens an SWF file with embedded JPEG images, it calls `jpeg_decoder_decode()` (line 1 in Figure 1) to decode each JPEG image in the file. This function in turn calls the function `jpeg_decoder_start_of_frame()` (line 7) to read the image metadata and the function `jpeg_decoder_init_decoder()` (line 22) to allocate memory buffers for the JPEG image.

There is an integer overflow vulnerability at lines 43–47 where Swfdec calculates the size of the buffer for a JPEG image as:

```
rowstride * (dec->height_block * 8 * max_v_sample
    / dec->components[i].v_subsample)
```

At this program point, `rowstride` equals:

```
((jpeg_width + 8 * max_h_sample - 1) / (8 * max_h_sample))
    * 8 * max_h_sample / (max_h_sample / h_sample)
```

while the rest of the expression equals

```
((jpeg_height + 8 * max_v_sample - 1) / (8 * max_v_sample))
    * 8 * max_v_sample / (max_v_sample / v_sample)
```

where `jpeg_height` is the 16-bit height input field value that Swfdec reads at line 9 and `jpeg_width` is the 16-bit width input field value that Swfdec reads at line 11. `h_sample` is one of the horizontal sampling factor values that Swfdec reads at line 14, while `max_h_sample` is the maximum horizontal sampling factor value. `v_sample` is one of the vertical sampling factor values that Swfdec reads at line 17, while `max_v_sample` is the maximum vertical sampling factor value. Malicious inputs with specifically crafted values in these input fields can cause the image buffer size calculation to overflow. In this case Swfdec allocates an image buffer that is smaller than required and eventually writes beyond the end of the allocated buffer.

The loop at lines 13–20 reads multiple instantiations of the `h_sample` field and the `v_sample` field. Swfdec computes the

$$C: \quad \mathrm{safe}((((\mathrm{sext}(jpeg\_width^{[16]}, 32) + 8^{[32]} \times \mathrm{sext}(h\_sample\langle 1\rangle^{[4]}, 32) - 1^{[32]})/(8^{[32]} \times \mathrm{sext}(h\_sample\langle 1\rangle^{[4]}, 32)) \\ \times 8^{[32]} \times \mathrm{sext}(h\_sample\langle 1\rangle^{[4]}, 32))/(\mathrm{sext}(h\_sample\langle 1\rangle^{[4]}, 32)/\,\mathrm{sext}(h\_sample\langle 2\rangle^{[4]}, 32))) \\ \times(((\mathrm{sext}(jpeg\_height^{[16]}, 32) + 8^{[32]} \times \mathrm{sext}(v\_sample\langle 1\rangle^{[4]}, 32) - 1^{[32]})/(8^{[32]} \times \mathrm{sext}(v\_sample\langle 1\rangle^{[4]}, 32)) \\ \times 8^{[32]} \times \mathrm{sext}(v\_sample\langle 1\rangle^{[4]}, 32))/(\mathrm{sext}(v\_sample\langle 1\rangle^{[4]}, 32)/\,\mathrm{sext}(v\_sample\langle 2\rangle^{[4]}, 32))))$$

**Figure 2.** The symbolic condition $C$ for the Swfdec example. Subexpressions in $C$ are bit vector expressions. The superscript indicates the bit width of each expression atom. "sext$(v, w)$" is the signed extension operation that transforms the value $v$ to the bit width $w$.

```
1  int jpeg_decoder_decode(JpegDecoder *dec) {
2    ...
3    jpeg_decoder_start_of_frame(dec, ...);
4    jpeg_decoder_init_decoder (dec);
5    ...
6  }
7  void jpeg_decoder_start_of_frame(JpegDecoder*dec){
8    ...
9    dec->height = jpeg_bits_get_u16_be (bits);
10   /* dec->height = SIFT_input("jpeg_height", 16);*/
11   dec->width = jpeg_bits_get_u16_be (bits);
12   /* dec->width = SIFT_input("jpeg_width", 16); */
13   for (i = 0; i < dec->n_components; i++) {
14     dec->components[i].h_sample =getbits(bits, 4);
15     /* dec->components[i].h_sample =
16          SIFT_input("h_sample", 4); */
17     dec->components[i].v_sample =getbits(bits, 4);
18     /* dec->components[i].v_sample =
19          SIFT_input("v_sample", 4); */
20   }
21 }
22 void jpeg_decoder_init_decoder(JpegDecoder*dec){
23   int max_h_sample = 0;
24   int max_v_sample = 0;
25   int i;
26   for (i=0; i < dec->n_components; i++) {
27     max_h_sample = MAX(max_h_sample,
28       dec->components[i].h_sample);
29     max_v_sample = MAX(max_v_sample,
30       dec->components[i].v_sample);
31   }
32   dec->width_blocks=(dec->width+8*max_h_sample-1)
33     / (8*max_h_sample);
34   dec->height_blocks=(dec->height+8*max_v_sample-1)
35     / (8*max_v_sample);
36   for (i = 0; i < dec->n_components; i++) {
37     int rowstride;
38     int image_size;
39     dec->components[i].h_subsample=max_h_sample /
40       dec->components[i].h_sample;
41     dec->components[i].v_subsample=max_v_sample /
42       dec->components[i].v_sample;
43     rowstride=dec->width_blocks * 8 * max_h_sample /
44       dec->components[i].h_subsample;
45     image_size=rowstride * (dec->height_blocks * 8 *
46       max_v_sample / dec->components[i].v_subsample);
47     dec->components[i].image = malloc (image_size);
48   }
49 }
```

**Figure 1.** Simplified Swfdec source code. Input statement annotations appear in comments.

maximum values of these instantiations in the loop at lines 26–31. It then uses these maximum values to compute the size of the allocated buffer at each iteration in the loop (lines 36–48).

**Analysis Challenges:** This example highlights several challenges that SIFT must overcome to successfully analyze and generate a filter for this program. First, the computation of the expression for the size of the buffer uses the `max_h_sample` variable and the `max_v_sample` variable, which correspond to the maximum values of all instantiations of the `h_sample` field and the `v_sample` field. It is impossible to statically determine the precise instantiation that these two variables represent. To overcome this challenge, SIFT uses a novel abstraction in which variables in the propagated symbolic condition represent all instantiations of the corresponding input fields.

Second, the source code snippet contains many load/store statements that access values derived from input fields via pointers. To reason soundly about these load/store statements, SIFT uses an abstraction that enables SIFT to incorporate an off-the-shelf alias analysis [20].

Finally, Swfdec reads the input fields (lines 14 and 17) and computes the size of the allocated memory block (lines 45-46) in the loops at different procedures. SIFT therefore uses an interprocedural analysis that propagates the symbolic conditions across procedure boundaries to obtain precise symbolic conditions. SIFT also deploys a combination of a fixed point analysis and a novel expression normalization technique to obtain loop invariants that successfully characterize the effect of loops on propagated expressions.

We next describe how SIFT generates a sound input filter to nullify this integer overflow error.

**Source Code Annotations:** SIFT provides a declarative specification interface that enables the developer to specify which statements read which input fields. In this example, the developer specifies that the application reads the input fields `jpeg_height`, `jpeg_width`, `h_sample`, and `v_sample` at lines 10, 12, 15–16, and 18–19 in Figure 1. SIFT uses this specification to map the variables `dec->height`, `dec->width`, `dec->components[i].h_sample`, and `dec->components[i].v_sample` at lines 9, 11, 14, and 17 to the corresponding input field values. Note that the input fields `h_sample` and `v_sample` may contain multiple instantiations, which Swfdec reads in the loop at lines 14 and 17.

**Compute Symbolic Condition:** SIFT uses a demand-driven, interprocedural, backward static analysis to compute the symbolic condition $C$ in Figure 2. We use the notation "safe$(e)$" in Figure 2 to denote that overflow errors should not occur in any step of the evaluation of the expression $e$. Subexpressions in $C$ are in *bit vector expression* form so that the expressions accurately reflect the representation of the numbers inside the computer as fixed-length bit vectors as well as the semantics of arithmetic and logical operations as implemented inside the computer on these bit vectors.

In Figure 2, the superscripts indicate the bit width of each expression atom. sext$(v, w)$ is the signed extension operation that transforms the value $v$ to the bit width $w$. SIFT also tracks the sign of each arithmetic operation in $C$. For simplicity, Figure 2 omits this information.

Note that SIFT soundly handles the loops that access the instantiations of the input fields `h_sample` and `v_sample`. In the resulting final symbolic condition $C$, $h\_sample\langle 1\rangle$ represents the instantiation of the input field `h_sample` that corresponds to the program variable `max_h_sample`, while $h\_sample\langle 2\rangle$ represents the instantiation that corresponds to the program variable `dec->components[i].h_sample`. SIFT does not attempt to determine the precise instantiations that $h\_sample\langle 1\rangle$ and $h\_sample\langle 2\rangle$ represent. Instead, SIFT conservatively assumes that

$h\_sample\langle 1\rangle$ and $h\_sample\langle 2\rangle$ may independently represent any instantiation of the field `h_sample`. SIFT handles `v_sample` similarly.

$C$ includes all intermediate expressions evaluated at lines 32–35 and 39–46. In this example, $C$ contains only a single term of the form safe($e$). In general, however, different program paths may compute different values for the critical expression. In this case, the final symbolic condition $C$ will contain multiple conjuncts of the form safe($e$). Each conjuct captures one of the ways that the program computes the value of the critical expression.

**Generate Input Filter:** Starting with the symbolic condition $C$, SIFT generates an input filter that discards any input that violates $C$, i.e., for any term safe($e$) in $C$, the input triggers integer overflow errors when evaluating $e$ (including all subexpressions). The generated filter extracts all instantiations of the input fields `jpeg_height`, `jpeg_width`, `h_sample`, and `v_sample` (these are the input fields that appear in $C$) from an incoming input. It then iterates over all combinations of pairs of the instantiations of the input fields `h_sample` and `v_sample` to consider all possible bindings of $h\_sample\langle 1\rangle$, $h\_sample\langle 2\rangle$, $v\_sample\langle 1\rangle$, and $v\_sample\langle 2\rangle$ in $C$. For each binding, it checks the entire evaluation of $C$ (including the evaluation of all subexpressions) for overflow. If there is no overflow in any evaluation, the filter accepts the input, otherwise it rejects the input.

## 3. Static Analysis

This section presents the SIFT static analysis algorithm. We have implemented our static analysis for C programs using the LLVM Compiler Infrastructure [3].

### 3.1 Core Language and Notation

$$\begin{array}{rcl} s & := & \ell\texttt{:}\ x = \texttt{read(}f\texttt{)} \mid \ell\texttt{:}\ x = c \mid \ell\texttt{:}\ x = y \mid \\ & & \ell\texttt{:}\ x = y\ op\ z \mid \ell\texttt{:}\ x = \texttt{*}p \mid \ell\texttt{:}\ \texttt{*}p = x \mid \\ & & \ell\texttt{:}\ p = \texttt{malloc} \mid \ell\texttt{:}\ \texttt{skip} \mid s'\texttt{;}\ s'' \mid \\ & & \ell\texttt{:}\ \texttt{if}\ (x)\ s'\ \texttt{else}\ s'' \mid \ell\texttt{:}\ \texttt{while}\ (x)\ \{\ s'\ \} \end{array}$$

$$s, s', s'' \in \text{Statement} \qquad f \in \text{InputField}$$
$$x, y, z, p \in \text{Var} \qquad c \in \text{Int} \qquad \ell \in \text{Label}$$

**Figure 3.** The core programming language

Figure 3 presents the core language that we use to present the analysis. The language is modeled on a standard lowered program representation in which 1) nested expressions are converted into sequences of statements of the form $\ell$: $x = y\ op\ z$ (where $x$, $y$, and $z$ are either non-aliased variables or automatically generated temporaries, *op* represents binary arithmetic operations) and 2) all accesses to potentially aliased memory locations occur in load or store statements of the form $\ell$: $x = *p$ or $\ell$: $*p = x$. Each statement contains a unique label $\ell \in$ Label.

A statement of the form "$\ell$: $x$ = `read(`$f$`)`" reads a value from an input field $f$. Because the input may contain multiple instantiations of the field $f$, different executions of the statement may return different values. For example, the loop at lines 14–17 in Figure 1 reads multiple instantiations of the `h_sample` and `v_sample` input fields.

**Labels and Pointer Analysis:** Figure 4 presents four utility functions 1) $\text{first}_S$ : Statement $\to$ Statement, 2) $\text{first}_L$ : Statement $\to$ Label, 3) last : Statement $\to$ Label, and 4) labels : Statement $\to$ Label in our notations. Given a statement $s$, $\text{first}_S(s)$ maps $s$ to the first atomic statement inside $s$, $\text{first}_L(s)$ maps $s$ to the label that corresponds to the first atomic statement inside $s$, last($s$) maps $s$ to the label that corresponds to the last atomic statement inside $s$, and labels($s$) maps $s$ to the set of labels that are inside $s$.

$$\text{first}_S(s) = \begin{cases} \text{first}_S(s') & s = s';\ s'' \\ s & \text{otherwise} \end{cases}$$
$$\text{first}_L(s) = \text{the label of } \text{first}_S(s)$$
$$\text{last}(s) = \begin{cases} \text{last}(s'') & s = s';\ s'' \\ \ell & \text{otherwise, } \ell \text{ is the label of } s \end{cases}$$
$$\text{labels}(s) = \begin{cases} \text{labels}(s') \cup \text{labels}(s'') & s = s';\ s'' \\ \{\ell\} \cup \text{labels}(s') & s = \ell\texttt{: while}\ (x)\ \{\ s'\ \} \\ \{\ell\} \cup \text{labels}(s') \cup \text{labels}(s'') & s = \ell\texttt{: if}\ (x)\ s'\ \texttt{else}\ s'' \\ \{\ell\} & \text{otherwise, } \ell \text{ is the label of } s \end{cases}$$

**Figure 4.** Definitions of $\text{first}_S$, $\text{first}_L$, last, and labels

We use LoadLabel and StoreLabel to denote the set of labels that correspond to load and store statements, respectively. LoadLabel $\subseteq$ Label and StoreLabel $\subseteq$ Label.

Our static analysis uses the DSA pointer analysis [20] in combination with the basic pointer analysis pass in LLVM [2] to disambiguate aliases at load and store statements. Our underlying pointer analysis [2, 20] provides two functions no_alias and must_alias:

$$\text{no\_alias} : (\text{StoreLabel} \times \text{LoadLabel}) \to \text{Bool}$$
$$\text{must\_alias} : (\text{StoreLabel} \times \text{LoadLabel}) \to \text{Bool}$$

We assume that the underlying pointer analysis is sound so that 1) no_alias($\ell_{\text{store}}, \ell_{\text{load}}$) = true only if the load statement at the label $\ell_{\text{load}}$ will *never* retrieve a value stored by the store statement at label $\ell_{\text{store}}$; 2) must_alias($\ell_{\text{store}}, \ell_{\text{load}}$) = true only if the load statement at the label $\ell_{\text{load}}$ will *always* retrieve the last value stored by the store statement at label $\ell_{\text{store}}$ (see Section 4.2 for a formal definition of the soundness requirements that the alias analysis must satisfy).

### 3.2 Intraprocedural Analysis

Because it works with a lowered representation, our static analysis starts with a variable $v$ at a critical program point. It then propagates $v$ backward against the control flow to the program entry point. In this way the analysis computes a symbolic condition that soundly captures how the program, starting with input field values, may compute the value of $v$ at the critical program point. The generated filters use the analysis results to check whether the input may trigger an integer overflow error in any of these computations.

$$\begin{array}{rcl} C & := & C \wedge \text{safe}(e) \mid \text{safe}(e) \\ e & := & e'\ op\ e'' \mid atom \\ atom & := & x \mid c \mid f\langle id\rangle \mid \ell\langle id\rangle \end{array}$$
$$id \in \text{Index} = \{1, 2, \ldots\} \qquad x \in \text{Var} \qquad c \in \text{Int}$$
$$\ell \in \text{LoadLabel} \qquad f \in \text{InputField}$$

**Figure 5.** The condition syntax

**Condition Syntax:** Figure 5 presents the definition of *symbolic conditions* that our analysis manipulates and propagates. A condition $C$ consists of a set of conjuncts of the form safe($e$). Each conjuct safe($e$) requires that the evaluation of the *symbolic expression* $e$ (including all subcomputations in the evaluation, see Section 4.5) should not trigger an overflow.

Symbolic conditions $C$ may contain four kinds of atoms: $c$ represents a constant, $x$ represents the variable `x`, $f\langle id\rangle$ represents a value from the input field $f$, and $\ell\langle id\rangle$ represents a value returned by the load statement with the label $\ell$.

**Abstraction for Input Field Instantiations:** An atom $f\langle id\rangle$ in a symbolic condition $C$ represents the value of an arbitrary instantiation of the input field $f$. The analysis uses the natural number $id$ to distinguish values of potentially different instantiations of $f$. So all occurrences of a given atom $f\langle id\rangle$ in a symbolic condition $C$ represent the same value. If $id_1 \neq id_2$, then $f\langle id_1\rangle$ and $f\langle id_2\rangle$ may

$$
\begin{array}{llll}
F(\ell\texttt{:}\ x = c & ,\ell & ,C) = C[c/x] & \\
F(\ell\texttt{:}\ x = y & ,\ell & ,C) = C[y/x] & \\
F(\ell\texttt{:}\ x = y\ op\ z & ,\ell & ,C) = C[y\ op\ z/x] & \\
F(s'\texttt{;}\ s'' & ,\ell' \in \text{labels}(s') & ,C) = F(s',\ell',C) & \\
F(s'\texttt{;}\ s'' & ,\ell'' \in \text{labels}(s'') & ,C) = F(s',\text{last}(s'),F(s'',\ell'',C)) & \\
F(\ell\texttt{:}\ \texttt{if}\ (v)\ s'\ \texttt{else}\ s'' & ,\ell & ,C) = F(s',\text{last}(s'),C) \wedge F(s'',\text{last}(s''),C) & \\
F(\ell\texttt{:}\ \texttt{if}\ (v)\ s'\ \texttt{else}\ s'' & ,\ell' \in \text{labels}(s') & ,C) = F(s',\ell',C) & \\
F(\ell\texttt{:}\ \texttt{if}\ (v)\ s'\ \texttt{else}\ s'' & ,\ell'' \in \text{labels}(s'') & ,C) = F(s'',\ell'',C) & \\
F(\ell\texttt{:}\ \texttt{while}\ (v)\ \{\ s'\ \} & ,\ell & ,C) = C_{\text{fix}} \wedge C & \text{where } C_{\text{fix}} = \text{norm}(F(s',\text{last}(s'),C_{\text{fix}} \wedge C)) \\
F(\ell\texttt{:}\ \texttt{while}\ (v)\ \{\ s'\ \} & ,\ell' \in \text{labels}(s') & ,C) = F(s,\ell,F(s',\ell',C)) & \\
F(\ell\texttt{:}\ p = \texttt{malloc} & ,\ell & ,C) = C & \\
F(\ell\texttt{:}\ x = \texttt{read}(f) & ,\ell & ,C) = C[f\langle id\rangle/x] & \text{where } id \text{ is fresh} \\
F(\ell\texttt{:}\ x = {*}p & ,\ell & ,C) = C[\ell\langle id\rangle/x] & \text{where } id \text{ is fresh} \\
F(\ell\texttt{:}\ {*}p = x & ,\ell & ,C) = C(\ell_1\langle id_1\rangle,\ell,x)(\ell_2\langle id_2\rangle,\ell,x)\cdots(\ell_n\langle id_n\rangle,\ell,x) & \text{for all } \ell_1\langle id_1\rangle,\cdots,\ell_n\langle id_n\rangle \text{ in } C
\end{array}
$$

$$
\text{where } C(\ell_i\langle id_i\rangle,\ell,x) = \begin{cases} C & \text{if no\_alias}(\ell,\ell_i) \\ C[x/\ell_i\langle id_i\rangle] & \text{if} \neg\,\text{no\_alias}(\ell,\ell_i) \wedge \text{must\_alias}(\ell,\ell_i) \\ C[x/\ell_i\langle id_i\rangle] \wedge C & \text{if} \neg\,\text{no\_alias}(\ell,\ell_i) \wedge \neg\,\text{must\_alias}(\ell,\ell_i) \end{cases}
$$

**Figure 6.** Static analysis rules. The notation $C[e'/e]$ denotes the symbolic condition obtained by replacing every occurrence of $e$ in $C$ with $e'$. $\text{norm}(C)$ is the normalization function that transforms the symbolic condition $C$ to an equivalent normalized condition.

represent different instantiations of $f$ (and may therefore represent different values).

**Abstraction for Values Accessed via Pointers:** An atom $\ell\langle id\rangle$ in a symbolic condition $C$ represents an arbitrary value returned by the load statement at the label $\ell$. The analysis uses the natural number $id$ to distinguish potentially different values loaded at different executions of the load statement. Our analysis materializes atoms of the form $\ell\langle id\rangle$ in the propagated symbolic condition when it analyzes the load statement at the label $\ell$. The analysis will eventually replace these atoms with appropriate expressions based on the aliasing information when it analyzes store statements that may store the corresponding value from the previously analyzed load statement at $\ell$. In our abstraction, $\ell\langle id\rangle$ represents an *arbitrary* value that may be stored via any alias of the pointer dereferenced at $\ell$ during the execution from the starting point of the program to the current program point of the propagated symbolic condition $C$ along any possible execution path (see Section 4.5).

**Analysis Framework:** Given a sequence of statements $s$, a label $\ell$ within $s$ ($\ell \in \text{labels}(s)$), and a symbolic condition $C$ at the program point *after* the corresponding statement at the label $\ell$, our demand-driven backwards analysis computes a symbolic condition $F(s,\ell,C)$. The analysis ensures that if $F(s,\ell,C)$ holds before executing $s$, then $C$ will hold whenever the execution reaches the program point *after* the corresponding statement at the label $\ell$ (see Section 4.6 for the formal definition).

Given a program $s_0$ as a sequence of statements and a variable $v$ at a critical site associated with the label $\ell$, our analysis generates the condition $F(s_0,\ell,\text{safe}(v))$ to create an input filter that checks whether the input may trigger an integer overflow error in the computations that the program performs to obtain the value of $v$ at the critical site.

**Analysis of Assignment, Conditional, and Sequence Statements:** Figure 6 presents the analysis rules for basic program statements. The analysis of assignment statements replaces the assigned variable $x$ with the assigned value ($c$, $y$, $y$ op $z$, or $f\langle id\rangle$, depending on the assignment statement). Here the notation $C[e'/e]$ denotes the new symbolic condition obtained by replacing every occurrence of $e$ in $C$ with $e'$. The analysis rule for the input read statement materializes a new $id$ to represent the read value $f\langle id\rangle$, because the variable $x$ may get the value of a fresh instantiation of the input field $f$ after the statement. This mechanism enables the analysis to correctly distinguish potentially different instantiations of the same input field (because values from potentially different instantiations have different $id$s).

If the label $\ell$ identifies the end of a conditional statement, the analysis of the statement takes the union of the symbolic conditions from the analysis of the true and false branches of the conditional statement. The resulting symbolic condition correctly takes the execution of both branches into account. If the label $\ell$ identifies a program point within one of the branches of a conditional statement, the analysis will propagate the condition from that branch only. The analysis of sequences of statements propagates the symbolic condition backwards through the statements in sequence.

**Analysis of Load and Store Statements:** The analysis of a load statement $x = {*}p$ replaces the assigned variable $x$ with a materialized abstract value $\ell\langle id\rangle$ that represents the loaded value. For input read statements, the analysis uses a newly materialized $id$ to distinguish values read on different executions of the load statement.

The analysis of a store statement ${*}p = x$ uses the alias analysis to appropriately match the stored value $x$ against all loads that may return that value. Specifically, the analysis locates all $\ell\langle id\rangle$ atoms in $C$ that either may or must load a value $v$ that the store statement stores into the location $p$. If the alias analysis determines that the $\ell\langle id\rangle$ expression must load $x$ (i.e., the corresponding load statement will always access the last value that the store statement stored into location $p$), then the analysis of the store statement replaces all occurrences of $\ell\langle id\rangle$ with $x$. If the alias analysis determines that the $\ell\langle id\rangle$ expression may load $x$ (i.e., on some executions the corresponding load statement may load $x$, on others it may not), then the analysis produces two symbolic conditions: one with $\ell\langle id\rangle$ replaced by $x$ (for executions in which the load statement loads $x$) and one that leaves $\ell\langle id\rangle$ in place (for executions in which the load statement loads a value other than $x$).

We note that, if the pointer analysis is imprecise, the symbolic condition may become intractably large. SIFT uses the DSA algorithm [20], a context-sensitive, unification-based pointer analysis. We found that, in practice, this analysis is precise enough to enable SIFT to efficiently analyze our benchmark applications (see Figure 13 in Section 5.2).

**Analysis of Loop Statements:** The analysis uses a fixed-point algorithm to synthesize the loop invariant $C_{\text{fix}}$ required to analyze while loops. Specifically, the analysis of a statement `while (`$x$`)` `{` $s'$ `}` computes a sequence of symbolic conditions $C_i$, where $C_0 = \emptyset$ and $C_i = \text{norm}(F(s',\text{last}(s'),C \wedge C_{i-1}))$. Conceptually,

**Input** : original expression $e_{\text{orig}}$
**Output**: normalized expression $e_{\text{norm}}$

$e_{\text{norm}} \longleftarrow e_{\text{orig}}$
$counter_{\text{field}} \longleftarrow \{\_ \mapsto 0\}$
$counter_{\text{label}} \longleftarrow \{\_ \mapsto 0\}$
**for** $a$ **in** $\text{atoms}(e_{\text{orig}})$ **do**
  **if** *$a$ is in form $f\langle id\rangle$* **then**
    $n' \longleftarrow counter_{\text{field}}(f) + 1$
    $counter_{\text{field}} \longleftarrow counter_{\text{field}}[f \mapsto n']$
    $e_{\text{norm}} \longleftarrow e_{\text{norm}}[*f\langle n'\rangle / f\langle id\rangle]$
  **else if** *$a$ is in form $\ell\langle id\rangle$* **then**
    $n' \longleftarrow counter_{\text{label}}(\ell) + 1$
    $counter_{\text{label}} \longleftarrow counter_{\text{label}}[\ell \mapsto n']$
    $e_{\text{norm}} \longleftarrow e_{\text{norm}}[*\ell\langle n'\rangle / \ell\langle id\rangle]$
**for** $a$ **in** $\text{atoms}(e_{\text{norm}})$ **do**
  **if** *$a$ is in form $*f\langle id\rangle$* **then**
    $e_{\text{norm}} \longleftarrow e_{\text{norm}}[f\langle id\rangle / *f\langle id\rangle]$
  **else if** *$a$ is in form $*\ell\langle id\rangle$* **then**
    $e_{\text{norm}} \longleftarrow e_{\text{norm}}[\ell\langle id\rangle / *\ell\langle id\rangle]$

**Figure 7.** Normalization function norm($e$). atoms($e$) is a list that iterates over the distinct atoms in the expression $e$ from left to right in order. The pseudo-code introduces temporary atoms of the forms "$*f\langle id\rangle$" and "$*\ell\langle id\rangle$" to avoid conflicts with existing original atoms in $e_{\text{norm}}$.

$F(\ell\colon v$ = `call` $proc\ v_1 \cdots v_k, \ell, C)$
  where $proc \equiv proc(a_1, a_2, \cdots, a_k)$ `{` $s$`;` `return` $v_{ret}$ `}` and
    $\ell_1\langle id_1\rangle, \cdots, \ell_n\langle id_n\rangle$ are all atoms of the form $\ell\langle id\rangle$ in $C$
**begin**
  $C' \longleftarrow \emptyset$
  $C_v \longleftarrow F(s, \text{last}(s), \text{safe}(v_{ret}))$
  **for** $e_v$ **in** $\text{exprs}(C_v[v_1/a_1] \cdots [v_k/a_k])$ **do**
    $C_1 \longleftarrow F(s, \text{last}(s), \text{safe}(\ell_1\langle id_1\rangle))$
    **for** $e_1$ **in** $\text{exprs}(C_1[v_1/a_1] \cdots [v_k/a_k])$ **do**
      $\cdots$
      $C_n \longleftarrow F(s, \text{last}(s), \text{safe}(\ell_n\langle id_n\rangle))$
      **for** $e_n$ **in** $\text{exprs}(C_n[v_1/a_1] \cdots [v_k/a_k])$ **do**
        $e'_v \longleftarrow \text{make\_fresh}(e_v, C)$
        $e'_1 \longleftarrow \text{make\_fresh}(e_1, C)$
        $\cdots$
        $e'_n \longleftarrow \text{make\_fresh}(e_n, C)$
        $C' \longleftarrow$
          $C' \wedge C[e'_v/v][e'_1/\ell_1\langle id_1\rangle] \cdots [e'_n/\ell_n\langle id_n\rangle]$
  **return** $C'$

**Figure 8.** Procedure call analysis algorithm. exprs($C$) returns the set of expressions that appear in the conjuncts of $C$. For example, $\text{exprs}(\text{safe}(e_1) \wedge \text{safe}(e_2)) = \{e_1, e_2\}$. make_fresh($e, C$) renumbers *ids* in $e$ so that atoms of the forms $\ell\langle id\rangle$ and $f\langle id\rangle$ will not conflict with existing atoms in $C$.

each successive symbolic condition $C_i$ captures the effect of executing an additional loop iteration. The analysis terminates when it reaches a fixed point (i.e., when it has performed $n$ iterations such that $C_n = C_{n-1}$). Here $C_n$ is the discovered loop invariant. This fixed point correctly summarizes the effect of the loop (regardless of the number of iterations that it may perform).

The loop analysis normalizes the analysis result $F(s', \text{last}(s'), C \wedge C_{i-1})$ after each iteration. For a symbolic condition $C = \text{safe}(e_1) \wedge \cdots \wedge \text{safe}(e_n)$, the normalization of $C$ is $\text{norm}(C) = \text{remove\_dup}(\text{safe}(\text{norm}(e_1)) \wedge \cdots \wedge \text{safe}(\text{norm}(e_n)))$, where $\text{norm}(e_i)$ is the normalization of each individual expression in $C$ (using the algorithm presented in Figure 7) and remove_dup() removes duplicate conjuncts from the condition.

Normalization facilitates loop invariant discovery for loops that read input fields or load values via pointers. Each analysis of the loop body during the fixed point computation produces new materialized values $f\langle id\rangle$ and $\ell\langle id\rangle$ with fresh $id$'s. The materialized $f\langle id\rangle$ represent values of input field instantiations that the current loop iteration reads; the materialized $\ell\langle id\rangle$ represent values that the current loop iteration loads via pointers. The normalization algorithm appropriately renumbers these $id$s in the new symbolic condition so that the first appearance of each $id$ is in lexicographic order. This normalization enables the analysis to recognize loop invariants that show up as equivalent successive analysis results that differ only in the materialized $id$'s that they use to represent input field instantiations and values accessed via pointers.

The normalization algorithm is sound because 1) all occurrences of $f\langle id_1\rangle, ..., f\langle id_k\rangle$ are interchangeable, and 2) the normalization only renumbers the $id_1, ..., id_k$. The normalized condition is therefore equivalent to the original condition (see Section 4.6).

The normalization algorithm will reach a fixed point and terminate if it computes the symbolic condition of a value that depends on at most a statically fixed number of values from the loop iterations. For example, our algorithm is able to compute the symbolic condition of the size parameter value of the memory allocation sites in Figure 1 — the value of this size parameter depends only on the values of `jpeg_width` and `jpeg_height`, the current values of `h_sample` and `v_sample`, and the maximum values of `h_sample` and `v_sample`, each of which comes from one previous iteration of the loop at line 26–31.

Note that the algorithm will not reach a fixed point if it attempts to compute a symbolic condition that contains an unbounded number of values from different loop iterations. For example, the algorithm will not reach a fixed point if it attempts to compute a symbolic condition for the sum of a set of numbers computed within the loop (the sum depends on values from all loop iterations). To ensure termination, our current implemented algorithm terminates the analysis and fails to generate a symbolic condition $C$ if it fails to reach a fixed point after ten iterations.

In practice, we expect that many programs may contain expressions whose values depend on an unbounded number of values from different loop iterations. Our analysis can successfully analyze such programs because it is demand driven — it only attempts to obtain precise symbolic representations of expressions that may contribute to the values of expressions in the analyzed symbolic condition $C$ (which, in our current system, are ultimately derived from expressions that appear at memory allocation and block copy sites). Our experimental results indicate that our approach is, in practice, effective for this set of expressions, specifically because these expressions tend to depend on at most a fixed number of values from loop iterations.

### 3.3 Interprocedural Analysis

**Analyzing Procedure Calls:** Figure 8 presents the interprocedural analysis for procedure call sites. Given a symbolic condition $C$ and a function call statement $\ell\colon v$ = `call` $proc\ v_1 \cdots v_k$ that invokes a procedure $proc(a_1, a_2, \cdots, a_k)$ `{` $s$`;` `return` $v_{ret}$ `}`, the analysis computes $F(\ell\colon v$ = `call` $proc\ v_1 \cdots v_k, \ell, C)$.

Conceptually, the analysis performs two tasks. First, it replaces any occurrences of the procedure return value $v$ in $C$ (the symbolic condition after the procedure call) with symbolic expressions that represent the values that the procedure may return. Second, it transforms $C$ to reflect the effect of any store instructions that the procedure may execute. Specifically, the analysis finds expressions $\ell\langle id\rangle$ in $C$ that represent values that 1) the procedure may store into a location $p$ 2) that the computation following the procedure may access via a load instruction that may access (a potentially aliased version of) $p$. It then replaces occurrences of $\ell\langle id\rangle$ in $C$ with symbolic expressions that represent the corresponding values computed (and stored into $p$) within the procedure.

The analysis examines the invoked procedural body $s$ to obtain the symbolic expressions that corresponds to the return value (see line 6) or the value of $\ell\langle id\rangle$ (see lines 8 and 11). The analysis avoids redundant analysis of the invoked procedure by caching the analysis results $F(s, \text{last}(s), \text{safe}(v_{ret}))$ and $F(s, \text{last}(s), \text{safe}(\ell\langle id\rangle))$ for reuse.

Note that symbolic expressions derived from an analysis of the invoked procedure may contain occurrences of the formal parameters $a_1, ..., a_k$. The interprocedural analysis translates these symbolic expressions into the name space of the caller by replacing occurrences of the formal parameters $a_1, ..., a_k$ with the corresponding actual parameters $v_1, ..., v_k$ from the call site (see lines 7, 9, and 12 in Figure 8).

Also note that the analysis renumbers the $ids$ in the symbolic expressions derived from an analysis of the invoked procedure before the replacements (see lines 13–16). This ensures that the atoms of the forms $f\langle id\rangle$ and $\ell\langle id\rangle$ in the expressions are fresh and will not conflict with existing atoms in $C$ after replacements.

**Propagation to Program Entry:** To derive the final symbolic condition at the start of the program, the analysis propagates the current symbolic condition up the call tree through procedure calls until it reaches the start of the program. When the propagation reaches the entry of the current procedure $proc$, the algorithm uses the procedure call graph to find all call sites that may invoke $proc$.

It then propagates the current symbolic condition $C$ to the callers of $proc$, appropriately translating $C$ into the naming context of the caller by substituting any formal parameters of $proc$ that appear in $C$ with the corresponding actual parameters from the call site. The analysis continues this propagation until it has traced out all paths in the call graph from the initial critical site where the analysis started to the program entry point. The final symbolic condition $C$ is the conjunction of the conditions derived along all of these paths.

### 3.4 Extension to C Programs

We next describe how to extend our analysis to real world C programs to generate input filters.

**Identify Critical Sites:** SIFT transforms the application source code into the LLVM intermediate representation (IR) [3], scans the IR to identify critical values (i.e., size parameters of memory allocation and block copy call sites) inside the developer specified module, and then performs the static analysis for each identified critical value. By default, SIFT recognizes calls to standard C memory allocation routines (such as `malloc`, `calloc`, and `realloc`) and block copy routines (such as `memcpy`) as critical sites. SIFT can also be configured to recognize additional memory allocation and block copy routines (for example, `dMalloc` in Dillo).

**Bit Width and Signedness:** SIFT extends the analysis described above to track the bit width of each expression atom. It also tracks the sign of each expression atom and arithmetic operation and correctly handles extension and truncation operations (i.e., signed extension, unsigned extension, and truncation) that change the width of a bit vector. SIFT therefore faithfully implements the representation of integer values in the C program.

**Function Pointers and Library Calls:** SIFT uses its underlying pointer analysis [20] to disambiguate function pointers. It can analyze programs that invoke functions via function pointers.

The static analysis may encounter procedure calls (for example, calls to standard C library functions) for which the source code of the callee is not available. A standard way to handle this situation is to work with an annotated procedure declaration that gives the static analysis information that it can use to analyze calls to the procedure. SIFT currently contains predefined annotations for a small set of important standard library functions that influence our integer overflow analysis (e.g., `memset`() and `strlen`()).

If both the source code and the annotation for an invoked procedure are not available, by default SIFT currently synthesizes information that indicates that symbolic expressions are not available for the return value or for any values accessible (and therefore potentially stored) via procedure parameters (code following the procedure call may load such values). This information enables the analysis to determine if the return value or values accessible via the procedure parameters may affect the analyzed symbolic condition $C$. If so, SIFT does not generate a filter. Because SIFT is demand-driven, this mechanism enables SIFT to successfully analyze programs with library calls (all of our benchmark programs have such calls) as long as the calls do not affect the analyzed symbolic conditions.

**Command Line Arguments:** At four of the 56 critical sites in our analyzed benchmark modules, the absence of overflow depends, in part, on the lengths of the command line arguments. The generated final symbolic condition that SIFT uses to generate the input filter therefore contains variables that represent these lengths. Our currently implemented system sets these lengths to a specific constant value greater than the maximum length of the command line arguments of all benchmark applications. In production use, we expect SIFT deployments to either 1) check that the command line argument lengths are less than this constant value before launching the application or 2) dynamically extract the command line argument lengths when the application is launched, then provide these lengths to the filter.

**Annotations for Input Read Statements:** SIFT provides a declarative specification language that developers use to indicate which input statements read which input fields. In our current implementation, these statements appear in the source code in comments directly below the C statement that reads the input field. See lines 10, 12, 15-16, and 18-19 in Figure 1 for examples that illustrate the use of the specification language in the Swfdec example. The SIFT annotation generator scans the comments, finds the input specification statements, then inserts new nodes into the LLVM IR that contain the specified information. Formally, this information appears as procedure calls of the following form:

$$\text{v} = \text{SIFT\_Input("field\_name", w)};$$

where `v` is a program variable that holds the value of the input field with the field name `field_name`. The width (in bits) of the input field is `w`. The SIFT static analyzer recognizes such procedure calls as specifying the correspondence between input fields and program variables and applies the appropriate analysis rule for input read statements (see Figure 6).

### 3.5 Input Filter Generation

The SIFT filter generator prunes any conjuncts that contain residual occurrences of abstract materialized values $\ell\langle id\rangle$ in the final symbolic condition $C$. It also replaces every residual occurrence of program variables $v$ with 0. These residual occurrences correspond to initial values in the program state $\overline{\sigma}$ and $\overline{h}$ in the abstract semantics (see Section 4.3). After pruning, the final condition $C_{\text{Inp}}$

contains only input field variables of the form $f\langle id \rangle$ and constant atoms.

In effect, the pruning algorithm eliminates any checks involving uninitialized data from the filter — SIFT filters are not designed to nullify overflow errors that may occur when the program accesses uninitialized data (which, in C, may contain arbitrary values). The SIFT soundness theorem (Theorem 4) reflects this restriction. For languages such as Java which initialize data to specific values, the SIFT filter generator would not prune conjuncts involving references to uninitialized data. It would instead protect against overflows involving uninitialized data by replacing residual occurrences of abstract materialized values and program variables with the corresponding initial values.

The generated filter operates as follows. It first uses an existing parser for the input format to parse the input and extract the input fields used in the input condition $C_{\text{Inp}}$. Open source parsers are available for a wide range of input file formats, including all of the formats in our experimental evaluation [1]. These parsers provide a standard API that enables clients to access the parsed input fields.

The generated filter evaluates each conjunct expression in $C_{\text{Inp}}$ by replacing each symbolic input variable in the expression with the corresponding concrete value from the parsed input. If an integer overflow may occur in the evaluation of any expression in $C_{\text{Inp}}$, the filter discards the input and optionally raises an alarm. For input field arrays such as `h_sample` and `v_sample` in the Swfdec example (see Section 2), the input filter enumerates all possible combinations of concrete values (see Figure 11 for the formal definition of condition evaluation). The filter discards the input if any combination can trigger the integer overflow error.

Given multiple symbolic conditions generated from multiple critical program points, SIFT can create a single efficient filter that first parses the input, then checks the parsed input against all final symbolic conditions in sequence. This approach amortizes the overhead of reading the input (in practice, reading the input consumes essentially all of the time required to execute the filter, see Figure 14) over all of the final symbolic condition checks.

## 4. Soundness of the Static Analysis

We next formalize our static analysis algorithm on the core language in Figure 3 and discuss the soundness of the analysis. We focus on the intraprocedural analysis and omit a discussion of the interprocedural analysis as it uses standard techniques based on summary tables.

### 4.1 Dynamic Semantics of the Core Language

**Program State:** We define the program state $(\sigma, \rho, \varsigma, \varrho, Inp)$ as follows:

$$\sigma\text{: Var} \to (\text{Loc}+\text{Int}+\{\text{undef}\}) \qquad \varsigma\text{: Var} \to \text{Bool}$$
$$\rho\text{: Loc} \to (\text{Loc}+\text{Int}+\{\text{undef}\}) \qquad \varrho\text{: Loc} \to \text{Bool}$$
$$Inp\text{: InputField} \to \mathcal{P}(\text{Int})$$

$\sigma$ and $\rho$ map variables and memory locations to their corresponding values. We use undef to represent uninitialized values. We define that if any operand of an arithmetic operation is undef, the result of the operation is also undef. $Inp(f)$ maps the input field $f$ to the corresponding set of the values of all instantiations of the field $f$ in the input file. $Inp$ therefore represents the input file, which remains unchanged during the execution. $\varsigma$ maps each variable to a boolean flag, which tracks whether the computation that generates the value of the variable (including all subcomputations) generates an overflow. $\varrho$ maps each memory location to a boolean overflow flag similar to $\varsigma$.

In the initial state $(\sigma_0, \rho_0, \varsigma_0, \varrho_0, Inp)$, $\sigma_0$ and $\rho_0$ map all variables and locations to undef. $\varsigma_0$ and $\varrho_0$ map all variables and locations to false. The values of uninitialized variables and memory locations are undefined as per the C language specification standard.

**Small Step Rules:** Figure 9 presents the small step dynamic semantics of the language. Note that in Figure 9, overflow$(a, b, op)$ is a function that returns true if and only if the computation $a\, op\, b$ causes overflow. A main point of departure from standard languages is that we also update $\varsigma$ and $\varrho$ to track overflow errors during each execution step. For example, the binop rule in Figure 9 appropriately updates the overflow flag of $x$ in $\varsigma$ by checking whether the computation that generates the value of $x$ (including the subcomputations that generates the value of $y$ and $z$) results in an overflow condition.

Also note that the rule for the input read statement nondeterministically updates the value of $x$ with an arbitrary element chosen from the set $Inp(f)$, which contains the values of all instantiations of the input field $f$ in the input file. This semantics conservatively models the behavior of input read statements in C programs.

### 4.2 Soundness of the Pointer Analysis

Our analysis uses an underlying pointer analysis [20] to analyze programs that use pointers. The underlying pointer analysis provides two functions no_alias and must_alias to our main analysis. We formally state our assumptions about the soundness of the underlying pointer alias analysis as follows:

**Definition 1** (Soundness of no_alias and must_alias)**.** *Given any execution sequence*

$$\langle s_0, \sigma_0, \rho_0, \varsigma_0, \varrho_0 \rangle \longrightarrow \langle s_1, \sigma_1, \rho_1, \varsigma_1, \varrho_1 \rangle \longrightarrow \dots$$

*and two statements $s_{store}$ ($\ell_{store}$ : *p = $x$) and $s_{load}$ ($\ell_{load}$ : $x'$ = *$p'$), we have:*

$$\text{no\_alias}(\ell_{store}, \ell_{load}) \implies \forall i < j :$$
$$(\text{first}_L(s_i) = \ell_{store} \wedge \text{first}_L(s_j) = \ell_{load}) \to \sigma_i(p) \neq \sigma_j(p')$$

$$\text{must\_alias}(\ell_{store}, \ell_{load}) \implies \forall i < j :$$
$$(\text{first}_L(s_i) = \ell_{store} \wedge \text{first}_L(s_j) = \ell_{load} \wedge (\textstyle\bigwedge_{k \in (i,j)} \text{first}_L(s_k) \neq \ell_{store}))$$
$$\to (\sigma_i(p) = \sigma_j(p'))$$

### 4.3 Abstract Semantics

We next define an abstract semantics that allows us to prove the soundness of our static analysis algorithm. There are two key differences between the abstract and original semantics. First, for if and while statements, the abstract semantics conservatively ignores the condition and nondeterministically executes one of the two control flow branches. Second, the abstract semantics conservatively groups values that load and store statements access via pointers into equivalence classes based on the aliasing information from the underlying pointer or alias analysis. It then conservatively models reads via pointers as nondeterministically returning an arbitrary stored value from the corresponding equivalence class. We adopt this abstract semantics because it more closely reflects how SIFT incorporates the underlying pointer or alias analysis and analyzes if, while, store, and load statements.

**Abstract Program State:** We define the abstract program state $(\overline{\sigma}, \overline{\varsigma}, \overline{h}, Inp)$ as follows:

$$\overline{\sigma}\text{: Var} \to \text{Int} \qquad \overline{\varsigma}\text{: Var} \to \text{Bool}$$
$$\overline{h}\text{: LoadLabel} \to \mathcal{P}(\text{Int} \times \text{Bool})$$

Intuitively, $\overline{\sigma}$ and $\overline{\varsigma}$ are the counterparts of $\sigma$ and $\varsigma$ in the original semantics, but $\overline{\sigma}$ and $\overline{\varsigma}$ only track values and flags for variables that have integer values. $\overline{h}$ maps the label of each load statement to the set of values that the load statement may obtain from the memory.

In the initial state $(\overline{\sigma}_0, \overline{\varsigma}_0, \overline{h}_0, Inp)$, $\overline{\sigma}_0$ and $\overline{\varsigma}_0$ map all variables to 0 and false respectively. $\overline{h}_0$ maps all labels of load statements to the empty set.

$$\text{read}\;\frac{c \in \mathit{Inp}(f) \quad \sigma' = \sigma[x \to c] \quad \varsigma' = \varsigma[x \to \text{false}]}{\langle \ell : x = \texttt{read(}f\texttt{)}, \sigma, \rho, \varsigma, \varrho, \mathit{Inp}\rangle \longrightarrow \langle \text{nil: skip}, \sigma', \rho, \varsigma', \varrho, \mathit{Inp}\rangle}$$

$$\text{const}\;\frac{\sigma' = \sigma[x \to c] \quad \varsigma' = \varsigma[x \to \text{false}]}{\langle \ell : x = c, \sigma, \rho, \varsigma, \varrho, \mathit{Inp}\rangle \longrightarrow \langle \text{nil: skip}, \sigma', \rho, \varsigma', \varrho, \mathit{Inp}\rangle}$$

$$\text{assign}\;\frac{\sigma' = \sigma[x \to \sigma(y)] \quad \varsigma' = \varsigma[x \to \varsigma(y)]}{\langle \ell : x = y, \sigma, \rho, \varsigma, \varrho, \mathit{Inp}\rangle \longrightarrow \langle \text{nil: skip}, \sigma', \rho, \varsigma', \varrho, \mathit{Inp}\rangle}$$

$$\text{malloc}\;\frac{\xi \in \text{Loc} \quad \xi \text{ is fresh} \quad \sigma' = \sigma[p \to \xi] \quad \varsigma' = \varsigma[p \to \text{false}]}{\langle \ell : p = \texttt{malloc}, \sigma, \rho, \varsigma, \varrho, \mathit{Inp}\rangle \longrightarrow \langle \text{nil: skip}, \sigma', \rho, \varsigma', \varrho, \mathit{Inp}\rangle}$$

$$\text{seq-1}\;\frac{}{\langle \text{nil: skip}; s, \sigma, \rho, \varsigma, \varrho, \mathit{Inp}\rangle \longrightarrow \langle s, \sigma, \rho, \varsigma, \varrho, \mathit{Inp}\rangle}$$

$$\text{load}\;\frac{\sigma(p) = \xi \quad \xi \in \text{Loc} \quad \sigma' = \sigma[x \to \rho(\xi)] \quad \varsigma' = \varsigma[x \to \varrho(\xi)]}{\langle \ell : x = *p, \sigma, \rho, \varsigma, \varrho, \mathit{Inp}\rangle \longrightarrow \langle \text{nil: skip}, \sigma', \rho, \varsigma', \varrho, \mathit{Inp}\rangle}$$

$$\text{seq-2}\;\frac{\langle s, \sigma, \rho, \varsigma, \varrho, \mathit{Inp}\rangle \longrightarrow \langle s'', \sigma', \rho', \varsigma', \varrho', \mathit{Inp}\rangle}{\langle s; s', \sigma, \rho, \varsigma, \varrho, \mathit{Inp}\rangle \longrightarrow \langle s''; s', \sigma', \rho', \varsigma', \varrho', \mathit{Inp}\rangle}$$

$$\text{store}\;\frac{\sigma(p) = \xi \quad \xi \in \text{Loc} \quad \rho' = \rho[\xi \to \sigma(x)] \quad \varrho' = \varrho[\xi \to \varsigma(x)]}{\langle \ell : *p = x, \sigma, \rho, \varsigma, \varrho, \mathit{Inp}\rangle \longrightarrow \langle \text{nil: skip}, \sigma, \rho', \varsigma, \varrho', \mathit{Inp}\rangle}$$

$$\text{op}\;\frac{\sigma(y) \notin \text{Loc} \quad \sigma(z) \notin \text{Loc} \quad b = \varsigma(y) \vee \varsigma(z) \vee \text{overflow}(\sigma(y), \sigma(z), op)}{\langle \ell : x = y \; op \; z, \sigma, \rho, \varsigma, \varrho, \mathit{Inp}\rangle \longrightarrow \langle \text{nil: skip}, \sigma[x \to \sigma(y) \; op \, \sigma(z)], \rho, \varsigma[x \to b], \varrho, \mathit{Inp}\rangle}$$

$$\text{if-t}\;\frac{\sigma(x) \neq 0}{\langle \ell : \texttt{if}\ (x)\ s\ \texttt{else}\ s', \sigma, \rho, \varsigma, \varrho, \mathit{Inp}\rangle \longrightarrow \langle s, \sigma, \rho, \varsigma, \varrho, \mathit{Inp}\rangle}$$

$$\text{if-f}\;\frac{\sigma(x) = 0}{\langle \ell : \texttt{if}\ (x)\ s\ \texttt{else}\ s', \sigma, \rho, \varsigma, \varrho, \mathit{Inp}\rangle \longrightarrow \langle s', \sigma, \rho, \varsigma, \varrho, \mathit{Inp}\rangle}$$

$$\text{while-f}\;\frac{\sigma(x) = 0}{\langle \ell : \texttt{while}\ (x)\ \{s\}, \sigma, \rho, \varsigma, \varrho, \mathit{Inp}\rangle \longrightarrow \langle \text{nil: skip}, \sigma, \rho, \varsigma, \varrho, \mathit{Inp}\rangle}$$

$$\text{while-t}\;\frac{\sigma(x) \neq 0 \quad s' = s; \ell : \texttt{while}\ (x)\ \{s\}}{\langle \ell : \texttt{while}\ (x)\ \{s\}, \sigma, \rho, \varsigma, \varrho, \mathit{Inp}\rangle \longrightarrow \langle s', \sigma, \rho, \varsigma, \varrho, \mathit{Inp}\rangle}$$

**Figure 9.** The small step operational semantics of the language. "nil" is a special label reserved by the semantics.

$$\text{if-t}\;\frac{}{\langle \ell : \texttt{if}\ (x)\ s\ \texttt{else}\ s', \overline{\sigma}, \overline{\varsigma}, \overline{h}, \mathit{Inp}\rangle \longrightarrow_a \langle s, \overline{\sigma}, \overline{\varsigma}, \overline{h}, \mathit{Inp}\rangle}$$

$$\text{op}\;\frac{b = \overline{\varsigma}(y) \vee \overline{\varsigma}(z) \vee \text{overflow}(\overline{\sigma}(y), \overline{\sigma}(z), op) \quad \overline{\sigma}' = \overline{\sigma}[x \to \overline{\sigma}(y) \; op \, \overline{\sigma}(z)]}{\langle \ell : x = y \; op \; z, \overline{\sigma}, \overline{\varsigma}, \overline{h}, \mathit{Inp}\rangle \longrightarrow_a \langle \text{nil: skip}, \overline{\sigma}', \overline{\varsigma}[x \to b], \overline{h}, \mathit{Inp}\rangle}$$

$$\text{if-f}\;\frac{}{\langle \ell : \texttt{if}\ (x)\ s\ \texttt{else}\ s', \overline{\sigma}, \overline{\varsigma}, \overline{h}, \mathit{Inp}\rangle \longrightarrow_a \langle s', \overline{\sigma}, \overline{\varsigma}, \overline{h}, \mathit{Inp}\rangle}$$

$$\text{malloc}\;\frac{}{\langle \ell : p = \texttt{malloc}, \overline{\sigma}, \overline{\varsigma}, \overline{h}, \mathit{Inp}\rangle \longrightarrow_a \langle \text{nil: skip}, \overline{\sigma}, \overline{\varsigma}, \overline{h}, \mathit{Inp}\rangle}$$

$$\text{load}\;\frac{\langle c, b\rangle \in \overline{h}(\ell) \quad \overline{\sigma}' = \overline{\sigma}[x \to c] \quad \overline{\varsigma}' = \overline{\varsigma}[x \to b]}{\langle \ell : x = *p, \overline{\sigma}, \overline{\varsigma}, \overline{h}, \mathit{Inp}\rangle \longrightarrow_a \langle \text{nil: skip}, \overline{\sigma}', \overline{\varsigma}', \overline{h}, \mathit{Inp}\rangle}$$

$$\text{store}\;\frac{\overline{h}' \text{ satisfies } (*)}{\langle \ell : *p = x, \overline{\sigma}, \overline{\varsigma}, \overline{h}, \mathit{Inp}\rangle \longrightarrow_a \langle \text{nil: skip}, \overline{\sigma}, \overline{\varsigma}, \overline{h}', \mathit{Inp}\rangle}$$

$$\forall \ell_{\text{load}} \in \text{LoadLabel} : \overline{h}'(\ell_{\text{load}}) = \begin{cases} \overline{h}(\ell_{\text{load}}) & \text{no\_alias}(\ell, \ell_{\text{load}}) \\ \{\langle \overline{\sigma}(x), \overline{\varsigma}(x)\rangle\} & \neg\,\text{no\_alias}(\ell, \ell_{\text{load}}) \wedge \text{must\_alias}(\ell, \ell_{\text{load}}) \\ \{\langle \overline{\sigma}(x), \overline{\varsigma}(x)\rangle\} \cup \overline{h}(\ell_{\text{load}}) & \neg\,\text{no\_alias}(\ell, \ell_{\text{load}}) \wedge \neg\,\text{must\_alias}(\ell, \ell_{\text{load}}) \end{cases} \qquad (*)$$

**Figure 10.** The small step abstract semantics. "nil" is a special label reserved by the semantics.

**Small Step Rules:** Figure 10 presents the small step rules for the abstract semantics. We omit rules for simple assignment statements, while statements, and sequence statements for brevity.

The rules for if, while, malloc, load, and store statements reflect the primary differences between the abstract and original semantics. The rules for if and while statements (if-t, if-f, and the omitted while statement rules) in the abstract semantics conservatively ignore the condition and nondeterministically execute one of the two control flow branches. The rule for store statements maintains the state $\overline{h}$ according to the aliasing information. The rule for load statements nondeterministically returns an element from the corresponding set in $\overline{h}$.

### 4.4 Relationship of the Original and the Abstract Semantics

We formally state the relationship between the original and abstract semantics as follows.

**Theorem 2.** *For any execution trace in the original semantics:*

$$\langle s_0, \sigma_0, \rho_0, \varsigma_0, \varrho_0\rangle \longrightarrow \langle s_1, \sigma_1, \rho_1, \varsigma_1, \varrho_1\rangle \longrightarrow \ldots$$

*there is an execution trace in the abstract semantics:*

$$\langle s_0, \overline{\sigma}_0, \overline{\varsigma}_0, \overline{h}_0\rangle \longrightarrow_a \langle s_1, \overline{\sigma}_1, \overline{\varsigma}_1, \overline{h}_1\rangle \longrightarrow_a \ldots$$

*such that the following conditions hold:*

$$\forall i \forall x \in \mathit{Var} : \sigma_i(x) \notin \mathit{Int} \vee (\sigma_i(x) = \overline{\sigma}_i(x) \wedge \varsigma_i(x) = \overline{\varsigma}_i(x))$$

$$\forall i : \text{first}_S(s_i) = \text{“}\ell : x = *p\text{”} \to$$
$$(\rho_i(\sigma_i(p)) \notin \mathit{Int} \vee \langle \rho_i(\sigma_i(p)), \varrho_i(\sigma_i(p))\rangle \in \overline{h}_i(\ell))$$

The intuition behind the first condition is that $\sigma_i$ and $\overline{\sigma}_i$ as well as $\varsigma_i$ and $\overline{\varsigma}_i$ always agree on the variables holding integer values. The intuition behind the second condition is that $\overline{h}_i(\ell)$ corresponds to the possible values that the corresponding load statement of the label $\ell$ may obtain from the memory. When a load statement executes in the original semantics, the obtained integer value is in the corresponding set in $\overline{h}_i$ in the abstract semantics.

This theorem connects an arbitrary program execution in the original semantics to a corresponding execution in the abstract semantics. An important consequence of this theorem is that the soundness of our analysis in the abstract semantics implies the soundness of the analysis in the original semantics. See our technical report [23] for the proof sketch of this theorem.

### 4.5 Evaluation of the Symbolic Condition

Our static analysis maintains and propagates a symbolic condition $C$. Figure 11 defines the evaluation rules of the symbolic condition $C$ over an abstract program state $(\overline{\sigma}, \overline{\varsigma}, \overline{h}, \mathit{Inp})$ The notation $(\overline{\sigma}, \overline{\varsigma}, \overline{h}, \mathit{Inp}) \models C$ denotes that the abstract program state $(\overline{\sigma}, \overline{\varsigma}, \overline{h}, \mathit{Inp})$ satisfies the condition $C$. The evaluation rule for safe$(e_1 \, op \, e_2)$ checks that no overflow error occurs in any subcomputation that contributes to the final value of $(e_1 \, op \, e_2)$.

In our abstraction, each atom of the form $f\langle id\rangle$ corresponds to the value of an arbitrary instantiation of the input field $f$ – i.e., $f\langle id\rangle$ corresponds to an arbitrary element of the set $\mathit{Inp}(f)$. Each atom of the form $\ell\langle id\rangle$ corresponds to an arbitrary value that may be stored via any alias of the corresponding pointer – i.e., $\ell\langle id\rangle$

$$\frac{\forall c \in Inp(f) : (\overline{\sigma}, \overline{\varsigma}, \overline{h}, Inp) \models C[c/f\langle id\rangle]}{(\overline{\sigma}, \overline{\varsigma}, \overline{h}, Inp) \models C} \qquad \frac{\forall \langle c, b\rangle \in \overline{h}(\ell) : (\overline{\sigma}[tmp \to c], \overline{\varsigma}[tmp \to b], \overline{h}, Inp) \models C[tmp/l\langle id\rangle] \quad tmp \text{ is fresh in } C}{(\overline{\sigma}, \overline{\varsigma}, \overline{h}, Inp) \models C}$$

$$\frac{(\overline{\sigma}, \overline{\varsigma}, \overline{h}, Inp) \models C \quad (\overline{\sigma}, \overline{\varsigma}, \overline{h}, Inp) \models \text{safe}(e)}{(\overline{\sigma}, \overline{\varsigma}, \overline{h}, Inp) \models C \wedge \text{safe}(e)} \qquad \frac{(\overline{\sigma}, \overline{\varsigma}, \overline{h}, Inp) \models \text{safe}(e_1) \wedge \text{safe}(e_2) \quad \text{overflow}([[e_1]](\overline{\sigma}), [[e_2]](\overline{\sigma}), op) = \text{false}}{(\overline{\sigma}, \overline{\varsigma}, \overline{h}, Inp) \models \text{safe}(e_1\, op\, e_2)}$$

$$\frac{\overline{\varsigma}(x) = \text{false}}{(\overline{\sigma}, \overline{\varsigma}, \overline{h}, Inp) \models \text{safe}(x)} \qquad [[c]](\overline{\sigma}) = c \qquad [[x]](\overline{\sigma}) = \overline{\sigma}(x) \qquad [[e_1\, op\, e_2]](\overline{\sigma}) = [[e_1]](\overline{\sigma})\, op\, [[e_2]](\overline{\sigma})$$

**Figure 11.** Symbolic condition evaluation rules.

corresponds to an arbitrary element of the set $\overline{h}(\ell)$. The evaluation rules enumerate all possible bindings of $f\langle id\rangle$ and $\ell\langle id\rangle$ to check that no binding causes an overflow.

The definition of the evaluation rules also ensures that all occurrences of $f\langle id\rangle$ which reference the same input field $f$ and all occurrences of $\ell\langle id\rangle$ materialized from the same load statement $\ell$ are interchangable. This interchangability ensures that the normalization algorithm in Section 3.2 is sound — i.e., that renumbering $ids$ in a symbolic condition $C$ does not change the meaning of the condition. Therefore, given symbolic condition $C$, the normalization algorithm produces an equivalent condition $\text{norm}(C)$.

### 4.6 Soundness of the Analysis

**Soundness of the Analysis over the Abstract Semantics:** We formally state the soundness of our analysis over the abstract semantics as follows.

**Theorem 3.** *Given a series of statements $s_i$, a program point $\ell \in \text{labels}(s_i)$ and a start condition $C$, our analysis generates a condition $F(s_i, \ell, C)$, such that if $(\overline{\sigma}_i, \overline{\varsigma}_i, \overline{h}_i, Inp) \models F(s_i, \ell, C)$, then*

$$\begin{aligned}&((\langle s_i, \overline{\sigma}_i, \overline{\varsigma}_i, \overline{h}_i\rangle \longrightarrow_a^* \\ &\langle s_{j-1}, \overline{\sigma}_{j-1}, \overline{\varsigma}_{j-1}, \overline{h}_{j-1}\rangle \longrightarrow_a \\ &\langle s_j, \overline{\sigma}_j, \overline{\varsigma}_j, \overline{h}_j\rangle) \wedge (\text{first}_L(s_{j-1}) = \ell)) \\ &\implies ((\overline{\sigma}_j, \overline{\varsigma}_j, \overline{h}_j, Inp) \models C)\end{aligned}$$

This theorem guarantees that if the abstract program state before executing $s_i$ satisfies $F(s_i, \ell, C)$, then the abstract program state at the program point after the statement at label $\ell$ will always satisfy $C$ (here the notation " $\longrightarrow_a^*$ " denotes the execution of the program for an arbitrary number of steps in the abstract semantics).

**Soundness of the Analysis over the Original Semantics:** Because of the consistency of the abstract semantics and the original semantics (see Section 4.3), we can derive the following soundness property of our analysis over the original semantics based on the soundness property over the abstract semantics:

**Theorem 4.** *Given a program $s_0$, a program point $\ell \in \text{labels}(s_0)$, and a program variable $v$, our analysis generates a condition $C = F(s_0, \ell, \text{safe}(v))$, such that if $(\overline{\sigma}_0, \overline{\varsigma}_0, \overline{h}_0, Inp) \models C$, then*

$$\begin{aligned}&((\langle s_0, \sigma_0, \rho_0, \varsigma_0, \varrho_0\rangle \longrightarrow^* \\ &\langle s_{n-1}, \sigma_{n-1}, \rho_{n-1}, \varsigma_{n-1}, \varrho_{n-1}\rangle \longrightarrow \\ &\langle s_n, \sigma_n, \rho_n, \varsigma_n, \varrho_n\rangle) \wedge (\text{first}_L(s_{n-1}) = \ell)) \\ &\implies (\sigma_n(v) \notin \text{Int} \vee \varsigma_n(v) = \text{false})\end{aligned}$$

This theorem guarantees that if the input satisfies the generated condition $C$ (note that $(\overline{\sigma}_0, \overline{\varsigma}_0, \overline{h}_0, Inp)$ is the predefined constant initial state in Section 4.3), then for any execution in the original semantics (here the notation " $\longrightarrow^*$ " denotes the execution of the program for an arbitrary number of steps in the original semantics), at the program point after the statement of the label $\ell$, as long as the variable $v$ holds an integer value (not an undefined value due to uninitialized access), the computation history for obtaining this integer value contains no overflow error.

| Application | Distinct Fields | Relevant Fields |
|---|---|---|
| VLC | 25 | 2 |
| Dillo | 47 | 3 |
| Swfdec | 219* | 6 |
| png2swf | 47 | 4 |
| jpeg2swf | 300 | 2 |
| GIMP | 189 | 2 |

**Figure 12.** The number of distinct input fields and the number of relevant input fields for analyzed input formats. (*) For Swfdec the second column shows the number of distinct fields in embedded JPEG images in collected SWF files.

## 5. Experimental Results

We evaluate SIFT on modules from five open source applications: VLC 0.8.6h (a network media player), Dillo 2.1 (a lightweight web browser), Swfdec 0.5.5 (a flash video player), Swftools 0.9.1 (SWF manipulation and generation utilities), and GIMP 2.8.0 (an image manipulation application). Each application uses a publicly available input format specification and contains at least one known integer overflow vulnerability (described in either the CVE database or the Buzzfuzz paper [15]). All experiments were conducted on an Intel Xeon X5363 3.00GHz machine running Ubuntu 12.04.

We focus on media and browser applications (client applications) in our experiments due to the ease of obtaining inputs required to evaluate our system against false positives. Other types of applications (e.g., server applications) would require additional infrastructure (i.e., recording network traffic) to test. By design, SIFT is applicable to a wide range of applications.

### 5.1 Methodology

**Input Format and Module Selection:** For each application, we used SIFT to generate filters for the input format that triggers the known integer overflow vulnerability. We therefore ran SIFT on the module that processes inputs in that format. The generated filters nullify not only the known vulnerabilities, but also any integer overflow vulnerabilities at any of the 56 memory allocation or block copy sites in the modules for which SIFT was able to generate symbolic conditions (recall that there are 58 critical sites in these modules in total).

**Input Statement Annotation:** After selecting each module, we added annotations to identify the input statements that read relevant input fields (i.e., input fields that may affect the values of critical expressions at memory allocation or block copy sites). Figure 12 presents, for each module, the total number of distinct fields in our collected inputs for each format, the number of annotated input statements (in all of the modules the number of relevant fields equals the number of annotated input statements — each relevant field is read by a single input statement). We note that the number

| Application | Module | # of IR | Total | Input Relevant | Inside Loop | Max Condition Size | Analysis Time |
|---|---|---|---|---|---|---|---|
| VLC | demux/wav.c | 1.5k | 5 | 3 | 0 | 2 | <0.1s |
| Dillo | png.c | 39.1k | 4 | 3 | 3 | 410 | 0.8s |
| Swfdec | jpeg/*.c | 8.4k | 22 | 19 | 2 | 144 | 0.2s |
| png2swf | all | 11.0k | 21 | 18 | 18 | 16 | 0.2s |
| jpeg2swf | all | 2.5k | 4 | 4 | 4 | 2 | <0.1s |
| GIMP | file-gif-load.c | 3.2k | 2 | 2 | 2 | 2 | <0.1s |

**Figure 13.** Static analysis and filter generation results

of relevant fields is significantly smaller than the total number of distinct fields (reflecting the fact that typically only a relatively small number of fields in each input format may affect the sizes of allocated or copied memory blocks).

The maximum amount of time required to annotate any module was approximately half an hour (Swfdec). The total annotation time required to annotate all benchmarks, including Swfdec, was less than an hour. This annotation effort reflects the fact that, in each input format, there are only a relatively small number of relevant input fields.

**Filter Generation and Test:** We next used SIFT to generate a single composite input filter for each analyzed module. We then downloaded at least 6000 real-world inputs for each input format and ran all of the downloaded inputs through the generated filters. There were no false positives (the filters accepted all of the inputs).

**Vulnerability and Filter Confirmation:** For each known integer overflow vulnerability, we collected a test input that triggered the integer overflow. We confirmed that each generated composite filter, as expected, discarded the input because it correctly recognized that the input would cause an integer overflow.

### 5.2 Analysis and Filter Evaluation

**Analysis Evaluation:** Figure 13 presents static analysis and filter generation results. This figure contains a row for each analyzed module. The first column (Application) presents the application name, the second column (Module) identifies the analyzed module within the application. The third column (# of IR) presents the number of analyzed statements in the LLVM intermediate representation. This number of statements includes not only statements directly present in the module, but also statements from analyzed code in other modules invoked by the original module.

The fourth column (Total) presents the total number of memory allocation and block copy sites in the analyzed module. The fifth column (Input Relevant) presents the number of memory allocation and block copy sites in which the size of the allocated or copied block depends on the values of input fields. For these modules, the sizes at 49 of the 58 sites depend on the values of input fields. The sizes at the remaining nine sites are unconditionally safe — SIFT verifies that they depend only on constants embedded in the program (and that there is no overflow when the sizes are computed from these constants).

The sixth column (Inside Loop) presents the number of memory allocation and block copy sites in which the size parameter depends on variables that occurred inside loops. The sizes at 29 of the 58 sites depend on values computed inside loops. To generate input filters for these sites, SIFT must therefore compute loop invariants that capture the effect of the loop on the sizes that occur at these sites.

The seventh column (Max Condition Size) presents, for each application module, the maximum number of conjuncts in any symbolic condition that occurs in the analysis of that module. The conditions are reasonably compact (and more than compact enough to enable an efficient analysis) — the maximum condition size over all modules is less than 500.

| Application | Format | # of Input | Average Time |
|---|---|---|---|
| VLC | WAV | 10976 | 3ms (3ms) |
| Dillo | PNG | 18983 | 16ms (16ms) |
| Swfdec | SWF | 7240 | 6ms (5ms) |
| png2swf | PNG | 18983 | 16ms (16ms) |
| jpeg2swf | JPEG | 6049 | 4ms (4ms) |
| GIMP | GIF | 19647 | 9ms (9ms) |

**Figure 14.** Generated filter results.

The final column (Analysis Time) presents the time required to analyze the module and generate a single composite filter for all of the successfully analyzed critical sites. The analysis times for all modules are less than a second.

SIFT is unable to generate symbolic conditions for two of the 58 call sites (one in Swfdec and one in png2swf). The expressions at these two sites contain subexpressions whose values depend on an unbounded number of values computed in loops. To analyze such expressions, our analysis currently requires an upper bound on the number of loop iterations. Such an upper bound could be provided, for example, by additional analysis or developer annotations.

**Filter Evaluation:** For each input format, we used a custom web crawler to locate and download at least 6000 inputs in that format. The web crawler starts from a Google search page for the file extension of the specific input format, then follows links in each search result page to download files in the correct format.

Figure 14 presents, for each generated filter, the number of downloaded input files and the average time required to filter each input. We present the average times in the form Xms (Yms), where Xms is the average time required to filter an input and Yms is the average time required to read in the input (but not apply the integer overflow check). These data show that essentially all of the filter time is spent reading in the input.

### 5.3 Filter Confirmation on Vulnerabilities

Each benchmark application contains a known integer overflow vulnerability. To confirm that the generated filters operate correctly, we obtained, for each vulnerability, a malicious input that triggers the integer overflow error. We confirmed that the filters successfully identified and discarded all of these malicious inputs. We also manually examined the root cause of each vulnerability and confirmed that the generated filters completely nullified the vulnerability — if an input passes the filter, it will not trigger the overflow error that enables the vulnerability. See our technical report [23] for the detailed case study of each vulnerability.

### 5.4 Discussion

The experimental results highlight the combination of properties that, together, enable SIFT to effectively nullify potential integer overflow errors at memory allocation and block copy sites. SIFT is efficient enough to deploy in production on real-world modules (the combined program analysis and filter generation times are always under a second), the analysis is precise enough to successfully generate input filters for the majority of memory allocation and block copy sites, the results provide encouraging evidence that the generated filters are precise enough to have few or even no false positives in practice, and the filters execute efficiently enough to deploy with acceptable filtering overhead.

## 6. Related Work

**Weakest Precondition Analysis:** Madhavan et. al. present an approximate weakest precondition analysis to verify the absence of null dereference errors in Java programs [24]. The goal is to verify that, for each pointer dereference, there are appropriate null checks within the program that guard the dereference to ensure that the program will never execute the dereference with a null pointer value. The analysis tracks only pointer dereferences, pointer assignments, and conditions involving null pointer checks.

SIFT faces different challenges and therefore uses different techniques. Instead of using a finite domain to track dereferenced pointers and pointer assignments, SIFT must track potentially unbounded arithmetic symbolic expressions involving input fields and values accessed via pointers. To successfully analyze loops, SIFT's abstraction and expression normalization algorithms work together to discover invariants for loops that may access a statically unbounded number of input field instantiaions (as long as the value of the analyzed expression depends only on a statically bounded number of input field instantiations).

Flanagan et. al. present a general intraprocedural weakest precondition analysis for generating verification conditions for ESC/JAVA programs [14]. SIFT differs in that it focuses on integer overflow errors. Because of this focus, SIFT can synthesize its own loop invariants (Flanagan et. al. rely on developer-provided invariants). In addition, SIFT is interprocedural and uses the analysis results to generate sound filters that nullify integer overflow errors.

**Anomaly Detection:** Anomaly detection techniques generate (unsound) input filters by empirically learning properties of successfully or unsuccessfully processed inputs [16, 19, 34]. Two key differences are that SIFT statically analyzes the application, not its inputs, and takes all execution paths into account to generate a sound filter.

**Input Rectification:** Input rectification [22, 30] empirically learns input constraints from benign training inputs. It then monitors inputs for violations of the learned constraints. Instead of discarding inputs that violate the learned constraints, input rectification modifies the input so that it satisfies the constraints. The goal is to nullify potential errors while still enabling the program to successfully process as much input data as possible. Because it learns the constraints from examples, this technique is not sound — the generated filter may miss some inputs that target the error. It would be possible to combine SIFT with input rectification to obtain a sound input rectification technique.

**Runtime Repair:** Researchers have developed a range of techniques for dynamically detecting and repairing errors in the program's execution [18, 27–29]. These techniques all purposefully change the program's semantics in an attempt to enable the program to successfully process inputs that it would otherwise be unable to process without error. The goal of SIFT, in contrast, is to nullify errors without changing the program's semantics by discarding inputs that might trigger the errors.

**Static Analysis for Finding Integer Overflow and Sign Errors:** Several static analysis tools have been proposed to find integer overflow and/or sign errors [7, 31, 35]. KINT [35], for example, analyzes individual procedures, with the developer optionally providing procedure specifications that characterize the value ranges of the parameters. KINT also unsoundly avoids the loop invariant synthesis problem by replacing each loop with the loop body (in effect, unrolling the loop once). Despite substantial effort, KINT reports a large number of false positives [35].

SIFT addresses a different problem: it is designed to nullify, not detect, overflow errors. In pursuit of this goal, it uses an interprocedural analysis, synthesizes symbolic loop invariants, and soundly analyzes all execution paths to produce a sound filter.

**Symbolic Bug Finding and Validation:** DART [17] and KLEE [6] use symbolic execution to automatically generate test inputs that systematically exercise different control-flow paths in a program. One goal is to find inputs that expose errors in the program. IntScope [33] and SmartFuzz [25] are symbolic execution systems designed specifically to expose integer overflow and/or sign errors. It would be possible to combine these systems with previous input-driven filter generation techniques to obtain filters that discard inputs that take the discovered path to the error. As discussed previously, SIFT differs in that it considers all possible paths so that its generated filters come with a soundness guarantee that if an input passes the filter, it will not exploit the integer overflow error.

Snugglebug [8] is a backward symbolic analysis engine for error validation — the goal is to generate an input that can trigger a potential error identified by some other means. As with other symbolic execution systems, Snugglebug is designed to enumerate all potential paths that the program may take to reach the error. If the number of paths is large or unbounded (for example, if the program contains loops), it may be infeasible to enumerate all paths. SIFT, in contrast, uses a precondition generation technique that can successfully analyze large programs while soundly taking all paths into consideration.

**Runtime Checks and Library Support:** To alleviate the problem of false positives, several research projects have focused on runtime detection tools that dynamically insert runtime checks before integer operations [4, 9, 13, 37]. Another technique is to use safe integer libraries such as SafeInt [21] and CERT's IntegerLib [32] to perform sanity checks at runtime. Using these libraries requires developers to rewrite existing code to use safe versions of integer operations.

However, the inserted code typically imposes non-negligible overhead. When they detect an error, these techniques typically generate a warning and terminate the execution (effectively turning any integer overflow attack into a denial of service attack). SIFT, in contrast, inserts no code into the application and nullifies integer overflow errors by discarding inputs that trigger such errors.

**Benign Integer Overflows:** In some cases, developers may intentionally write code that contains benign integer overflows [13, 33, 35]. A potential concern is that techniques that nullify overflows may interfere with the intended behavior of such programs [13, 33, 35]. Because SIFT focuses on critical memory allocation and block copy sites that are unlikely to have such intentional integer overflows, it is unlikely to nullify benign integer overflows and therefore unlikely interfere with the intended behavior of the program.

## 7. Conclusion

Integer overflow errors can lead to security vulnerabilities. SIFT analyzes how the application computes integer values that appear at memory allocation and block copy sites to generate input filters that discard inputs that may trigger overflow errors in these computations. Our results show that SIFT can quickly generate sound, efficient, and precise input filters for the vast majority of memory allocation and block copy call sites in our analyzed benchmark modules.


## Acknowledgements

We thank Michael Carbin, Sasa Misailovic, and the anonymous reviewers for their insightful comments. We note our earlier technical report [23]. This research was supported by DARPA (Grant FA8650-11-C-7192).

## References


[1] Hachoir. `http://bitbucket.org/haypo/hachoir/wiki/Home`.

[2] LLVM Basic Alias Analysis Pass. `http://llvm.org/docs/AliasAnalysis.html#the-basicaa-pass`.

[3] The LLVM compiler infrastructure. `http://www.llvm.org/`.

[4] D. Brumley, T. Chiueh, R. Johnson, H. Lin, and D. Song. Rich: Automatically protecting against integer-based vulnerabilities. *Department of Electrical and Computing Engineering*, page 28, 2007.

[5] D. Brumley, H. Wang, S. Jha, and D. Song. Creating vulnerability signatures using weakest preconditions. In *Proceedings of the 20th IEEE Computer Security Foundations Symposium*, CSF '07', pages 311–325, Washington, DC, USA, 2007. IEEE Computer Society.

[6] C. Cadar, D. Dunbar, and D. Engler. Klee: unassisted and automatic generation of high-coverage tests for complex systems programs. In *Proceedings of the 8th USENIX conference on Operating systems design and implementation*, OSDI'08, pages 209–224, Berkeley, CA, USA, 2008. USENIX Association.

[7] E. Ceesay, J. Zhou, M. Gertz, K. Levitt, and M. Bishop. Using type qualifiers to analyze untrusted integers and detecting security flaws in c programs. *Detection of Intrusions and Malware & Vulnerability Assessment*, pages 1–16, 2006.

[8] S. Chandra, S. J. Fink, and M. Sridharan. Snugglebug: a powerful approach to weakest preconditions. In *Proceedings of the 2009 ACM SIGPLAN conference on Programming language design and implementation*, PLDI '09, pages 363–374, New York, NY, USA, 2009. ACM.

[9] R. Chinchani, A. Iyer, B. Jayaraman, and S. Upadhyaya. Archerr: Runtime environment driven program safety. *Computer Security–ESORICS 2004*, pages 385–406, 2004.

[10] M. Costa, M. Castro, L. Zhou, L. Zhang, and M. Peinado. Bouncer: securing software by blocking bad input. In *Proceedings of twenty-first ACM SIGOPS symposium on Operating systems principles*, SOSP '07. ACM, 2007.

[11] M. Costa, J. Crowcroft, M. Castro, A. Rowstron, L. Zhou, L. Zhang, and P. Barham. Vigilante: end-to-end containment of internet worms. In *Proceedings of the twentieth ACM symposium on Operating systems principles*, SOSP '05. ACM, 2005.

[12] W. Cui, M. Peinado, and H. J. Wang. Shieldgen: Automatic data patch generation for unknown vulnerabilities with informed probing. In *Proceedings of 2007 IEEE Symposium on Security and Privacy*. IEEE Computer Society, 2007.

[13] W. Dietz, P. Li, J. Regehr, and V. Adve. Understanding integer overflow in c/c++. In *Proceedings of the 2012 International Conference on Software Engineering*, pages 760–770. IEEE Press, 2012.

[14] C. Flanagan and J. B. Saxe. Avoiding exponential explosion: generating compact verification conditions. In *Proceedings of the 28th ACM SIGPLAN-SIGACT symposium on Principles of programming languages*, POPL '01', pages 193–205, New York, NY, USA, 2001. ACM.

[15] V. Ganesh, T. Leek, and M. Rinard. Taint-based directed whitebox fuzzing. In *ICSE '09: Proceedings of the 31st International Conference on Software Engineering*. IEEE Computer Society, 2009.

[16] D. Gao, M. K. Reiter, and D. Song. On gray-box program tracking for anomaly detection. In *Proceedings of the 13th conference on USENIX Security Symposium - Volume 13*, SSYM'04. USENIX Association, 2004.

[17] P. Godefroid, N. Klarlund, and K. Sen. Dart: directed automated random testing. In *Proceedings of the 2005 ACM SIGPLAN conference on Programming language design and implementation*, PLDI '05, pages 213–223, New York, NY, USA, 2005. ACM.

[18] M. Kling, S. Misailovic, M. Carbin, and M. Rinard. Bolt: on-demand infinite loop escape in unmodified binaries. In *Proceedings of the ACM international conference on Object oriented programming systems languages and applications*, OOPSLA '12', pages 431–450, New York, NY, USA, 2012. ACM.

[19] C. Kruegel and G. Vigna. Anomaly detection of web-based attacks. In *Proceedings of the 10th ACM conference on Computer and communications security*, CCS '03. ACM, 2003.

[20] C. Lattner, A. Lenharth, and V. Adve. Making context-sensitive points-to analysis with heap cloning practical for the real world. In *Proceedings of the 2007 ACM SIGPLAN conference on Programming language design and implementation*, PLDI '07, pages 278–289, New York, NY, USA, 2007. ACM.

[21] D. LeBlanc. Integer handling with the c++ safeint class. *url-http://msdn. microsoft. com/en-us/library/ms972705*, 2004.

[22] F. Long, V. Ganesh, M. Carbin, S. Sidiroglou, and M. Rinard. Automatic input rectification. ICSE '12, 2012.

[23] F. Long, S. Sidiroglou, D. Kim, and M. Rinard. Sound input filter generation for integer overflow errors. MIT-CSAIL-TR-2013-018.

[24] R. Madhavan and R. Komondoor. Null dereference verification via over-approximated weakest pre-conditions analysis. In *Proceedings of the 2011 ACM international conference on Object oriented programming systems languages and applications*, OOPSLA '11, pages 1033–1052, New York, NY, USA, 2011. ACM.

[25] D. Molnar, X. C. Li, and D. A. Wagner. Dynamic test generation to find integer bugs in x86 binary linux programs. Usenix Security'09.

[26] J. Newsome, D. Brumley, and D. X. Song. Vulnerability-specific execution filtering for exploit prevention on commodity software. In *NDSS*, 2006.

[27] G. Novark, E. D. Berger, and B. G. Zorn. Exterminator: Automatically correcting memory errors with high probability. In *In Proceedings of the 2007 ACM SIGPLAN Conference on Programming Language Design and Implementation, ACM*. Press, 2007.

[28] J. H. Perkins, S. Kim, S. Larsen, S. Amarasinghe, J. Bachrach, M. Carbin, C. Pacheco, F. Sherwood, S. Sidiroglou, G. Sullivan, W.-F. Wong, Y. Zibin, M. D. Ernst, and M. Rinard. Automatically patching errors in deployed software. In *Proceedings of the ACM SIGOPS 22nd symposium on Operating systems principles*, SOSP '09, pages 87–102, New York, NY, USA, 2009. ACM.

[29] M. Rinard, C. Cadar, D. Dumitran, D. M. Roy, T. Leu, and W. S. Beebee. Enhancing server availability and security through failure-oblivious computing. In *In Proceedings 6 th Symposium on Operating Systems Design and Implementation (OSDI)*, pages 303–316, 2004.

[30] M. C. Rinard. Living in the comfort zone. In *Proceedings of the 22nd annual ACM SIGPLAN conference on Object-oriented programming systems and applications*, OOPSLA '07. ACM, 2007.

[31] D. Sarkar, M. Jagannathan, J. Thiagarajan, and R. Venkatapathy. Flow-insensitive static analysis for detecting integer anomalies in programs. In *IASTED*, 2007.

[32] R. Seacord. *The CERT C secure coding standard*. Addison-Wesley Professional, 2008.

[33] W. Tielei, W. Tao, L. Zhiqiang, and Z. Wei. IntScope: Automatically Detecting Integer Overflow Vulnerability In X86 Binary Using Symbolic Execution. In *16th Annual Network & Distributed System Security Symposium*, 2009.

[34] K. Wang and S. J. Stolfo. Anomalous payload-based network intrusion detection. In *RAID*, 2004.

[35] X. Wang, H. Chen, Z. Jia, N. Zeldovich, and M. Kaashoek. Improving integer security for systems with kint. In *OSDI*. USENIX Association, 2012.

[36] X. Wang, Z. Li, J. Xu, M. K. Reiter, C. Kil, and J. Y. Choi. Packet vaccine: black-box exploit detection and signature generation. CCS '06. ACM, 2006.

[37] C. Zhang, T. Wang, T. Wei, Y. Chen, and W. Zou. Intpatch: Automatically fix integer-overflow-to-buffer-overflow vulnerability at compile-time. *Computer Security–ESORICS 2010*, pages 71–86, 2010.

# Parametric Completeness for Separation Theories

James Brotherston Jules Villard

Dept. of Computer Science, University College London, UK

## Abstract

In this paper, we close the logical gap between provability in the logic BBI, which is the propositional basis for *separation logic*, and validity in an intended class of *separation models*, as employed in applications of separation logic such as program verification. An intended class of separation models is usually specified by a collection of axioms describing the specific model properties that are expected to hold, which we call a *separation theory*.

Our main contributions are as follows. First, we show that several typical properties of separation theories are not definable in BBI. Second, we show that these properties become definable in a suitable *hybrid extension* of BBI, obtained by adding a theory of *naming* to BBI in the same way that *hybrid logic* extends normal modal logic. The binder-free extension HyBBI captures most of the properties we consider, and the full extension HyBBI(↓) with the usual ↓ binder of hybrid logic covers all these properties. Third, we present an axiomatic proof system for our hybrid logic whose extension with any set of "pure" axioms is sound and complete with respect to the models satisfying those axioms. As a corollary of this general result, we obtain, in a parametric manner, a sound and complete axiomatic proof system for any separation theory from our considered class. To the best of our knowledge, this class includes all separation theories appearing in the published literature.

***Categories and Subject Descriptors*** F.3.1 [*Logics and Meanings of Programs*]: Specifying and Verifying and Reasoning about Programs—Logics of programs; F.4.1 [*Mathematical Logic and Formal Languages*]: Mathematical Logic—Model theory, Proof theory, Modal logic

***General Terms*** Theory, verification

***Keywords*** Bunched logic, separation logic, hybrid logic

## 1. Introduction

Essentially, all models are wrong, but some are useful.

G. E. P. Box and N. R. Draper [3], 1987

In mathematical logic, there is a notable tension between *provability* in a deductive system — which typically captures *validity* in some general class of models of the underlying logic — and *validity in the intended model(s)* of practical or theoretical interest. For example, as famously demonstrated by Gödel [15], there are statements of Peano arithmetic (PA) that hold in its intended model, i.e. the natural numbers $\mathbb{N}$, but not in all of its possible models, and so these statements are not provable in PA. This *incompleteness* of logical proof systems with respect to a particular choice of intended model(s) is unavoidable for sufficiently expressive systems. In other cases, it might happen that a logical system is complete but insufficiently expressive to capture the interesting properties of the intended model; that is, some mathematical property of the model cannot be expressed by any formula of the logical language (in which case we say that the intended models are not *definable* or *axiomatisable* within the system). Thus, when formulating a logical system, there are at least two natural and essentially independent questions: first, whether the language of the system is expressive enough to axiomatise the intended models; and, second, whether the system is complete for validity in these intended models.

In this paper, we consider these questions in the context of *separation logic*, an established formalism for reasoning about heap-manipulating programs [24, 6, 26]. The purely propositional part of separation logic is usually considered to be given by Boolean BI (from now on BBI), which is a particular flavour of *bunched logic* obtained by freely combining the connectives of multiplicative intuitionistic linear logic with those of standard classical logic [18, 23]. Provability in BBI corresponds to validity in the general class of relational commutative monoids [14]. Applications of separation logic, on the other hand, typically deal with *specific* such models, or classes thereof, based on the composition of heaps (see [5] for a survey of the models used in practice). Unsurprisingly, these heap models exhibit various interesting mathematical properties that are not true of all relational commutative monoids, and thus are not captured by provability in BBI. For example, composition of disjoint heaps is a cancellative partial (binary) function, which is a special case of the ternary relation in a relational commutative monoid. Various collections of such properties have been advanced in the literature as abstractions over concrete heap models, suitable for program analysis, under the common name of *separation algebra* [8, 12, 11]. We list the model properties commonly found in the literature in Definition 3.1, and call a given collection of such properties a *separation theory*. Our aim is to obtain logical proof systems in which provability accurately captures (validity in) the class of models determined by a separation theory (and preferably by adding as little extra machinery as possible to BBI).

In this paper, we make three main contributions:

- First, we show in Section 3 that BBI is insufficiently expressive to axiomatise most separation theories. Specifically, we show that several commonly considered model properties are not definable by any BBI-formula (e.g., partial functionality and/or cancellativity of the composition operation). Undefinability of a property means that the logic is fundamentally incapable of distinguishing models with the property from those without it. In particular, we find that none of the three different classes of separation algebras found in the literature [8, 12, 11] are definable in BBI.



*POPL '14*, January 22–24, 2014, San Diego, CA, USA.

ACM 978-1-4503-2544-8/14/01.
http://dx.doi.org/10.1145/2535838.2535844

• Second, we introduce in Section 4 a simple *hybrid* extension HyBBI of BBI, which bears the same relation to BBI as normal hybrid logic does to normal modal logic (see [1, 2] for an overview). That is, HyBBI extends BBI with a theory of *naming*: we introduce a second sort of atoms, called *nominals*, which are interpreted as individual states in a model; and we also add a unary hybrid modality $@_\ell$ (parameterised by the nominal $\ell$), so that the hybrid formula $@_\ell A$ is satisfied at any world in a model just when $A$ is satisfied at the world denoted by the nominal $\ell$.

Despite the simplicity of this extension, which is conservative over standard BBI, the hybrid logic HyBBI is expressive enough to define most of the separation theories we consider, including in particular all three concepts of separation algebras from the literature [8, 12, 11]. However, for more complex model properties such as the *cross-split* property of [12], still more expressivity is required: we show in Section 7 how to gain this expressivity by adding the $\downarrow$ binder of hybrid logic to HyBBI.

• Third, we provide a Hilbert-style axiomatic proof system for HyBBI that is *parametrically* sound and complete with respect to any given separation theory. That is, whenever the proof system is extended with the axioms defining a separation theory, the resulting extension is sound and complete with respect to the class of models determined by that theory. (E.g., by adding the axiom defining cancellativity, we obtain a sound and complete proof theory for cancellative models.) Such axiomatic proof systems provide a useful proof-theoretic characterisation of validity in separation theories which can be used as a baseline for, e.g., tableau or sequent-style proof systems.

We present the axiom system and its soundness result in Section 5, and give the completeness theorem in Section 6. Section 7 extends these results to HyBBI with the $\downarrow$ binder.

***Related work.*** Most of our technical results are obtained by adaptations of techniques from modal and hybrid logic. This should come as no surprise, since bunched logics can quite straightforwardly be seen as modal logics; indeed, this view has been exploited previously in the literature on bunched logic, e.g. to obtain completeness results [7, 4]. However, as far as we know, this paper represents the first explicit introduction of hybrid logic into the setting of (abstract) separation logic. In particular, previous work on hybrid logics has seemingly been confined to modal logic with unary modalities connected by De Morgan duality, whereas in this setting we consider the case of binary modalities connected by residuation.

Interestingly, the key concept from hybrid logic, i.e. the explicit naming of elements in the underlying model, has been used implicitly several times in the literature on the proof theory of BBI. For example, the labelled tableau system for BBI [20], which was recently proven complete for partial functional BBI-models [19], relies on a system of semantic labels which pick out individual model states in much the same way as nominal atoms in hybrid logic. Even more recently, labelled nested [22] and non-nested [17] sequent calculi for BBI have appeared, employing semantic labels in a broadly similar way. While such works add names or labels to proof systems as auxiliary tools for simplifying proof search in standard BBI, here we consider these features to be first-class components of the logic. Indeed, we believe that it should be possible to adapt the labelled proof systems in the literature to yield cut-free proof theories for our hybrid extensions of BBI.

In a similar vein, the explicit naming of heaps arises naturally in several extensions of separation logic as an aid to practical program verification. Reynolds conjectured that referring explicitly to the current heap in specifications would allow one to verify programs that manipulate data structures with sharing, such as graphs [25]. Duck et al. recently vindicated this claim by providing automatic verification techniques for such programs, where specifications are written using a constraint language based on separation logic with explicit heaps [13]. In an independent line of research, David and Chin introduced *immutable specifications* [10], which extend separation logic to support the tagging of certain parts of the heap as *immutable*. This can be viewed as adding a heap label in the precondition of a command, corresponding to the immutable part, and asserting the same heap label in the postcondition. The hybrid logics introduced in this paper can be seen as providing a common formal foundation for adding explicit heap atoms and modalities to separation logic-based verification. Our main focus here is on the precise expressivity of these logics.

## 2. Syntax and semantics of BBI

In this section, we introduce formulas of BBI and their Kripke semantics, given by relational commutative monoids (cf. [14]).

**Definition 2.1** (BBI-formula). Let $\mathcal{V}$ be a countably infinite set of *propositional variables*. BBI-*formulas* are built from propositional variables $P \in \mathcal{V}$ using the usual connectives $(\top, \bot, \neg, \wedge, \vee, \to)$ of classical logic, and the so-called "multiplicative" connectives, consisting of the constant I and binary operators $*$ and $-\!\!*$.

By convention, $\neg$ has the highest precedence, followed by $*$, $\wedge$ and $\vee$, with $\to$ and $-\!\!*$ having lowest precedence.

**Definition 2.2** (BBI frames and models). A BBI-*frame* is a a tuple $\langle W, \circ, E\rangle$, where $W$ is a set (of "worlds"), $\circ : W \times W \to \mathcal{P}(W)$ and $E \subseteq W$. We extend $\circ$ pointwise to $\mathcal{P}(W) \times \mathcal{P}(W) \to \mathcal{P}(W)$:

$$W_1 \circ W_2 \stackrel{\text{def}}{=} \bigcup_{w_1 \in W_1, w_2 \in W_2} w_1 \circ w_2$$

A BBI-frame $\langle W, \circ, E\rangle$ is a BBI-*model* if $\circ$ is commutative and associative, and $w \circ E = \{w\}$ for all $w \in W$ (that is, $w \circ e \subseteq \{w\}$ for all $e \in E$ and $w \circ e = \{w\}$ for some $e \in E$). We call $E$ the set of *units* of the model $\langle W, \circ, E\rangle$.

**Definition 2.3** (BBI-validity). Let $M = \langle W, \circ, E\rangle$ be a BBI-frame. A *valuation* for $M$ is a function $\rho$ that assigns to each propositional variable $P \in \mathcal{V}$ a set $\rho(P) \subseteq W$. Given any valuation $\rho$ for $M$, any $w \in W$ and any BBI-formula $A$, we define the forcing relation $M, w \models_\rho A$ by induction on $A$:

$$\begin{array}{rcl}
M, w \models_\rho P & \Leftrightarrow & w \in \rho(P) \\
M, w \models_\rho \top & & \text{always} \\
M, w \models_\rho \bot & & \text{never} \\
M, w \models_\rho \neg A & \Leftrightarrow & M, w \not\models_\rho A \\
M, w \models_\rho A_1 \wedge A_2 & \Leftrightarrow & M, w \models_\rho A_1 \text{ and } M, w \models_\rho A_2 \\
M, w \models_\rho A_1 \vee A_2 & \Leftrightarrow & M, w \models_\rho A_1 \text{ or } M, w \models_\rho A_2 \\
M, w \models_\rho A_1 \to A_2 & \Leftrightarrow & M, w \models_\rho A_1 \text{ implies } M, w \models_\rho A_2 \\
M, w \models_\rho \mathrm{I} & \Leftrightarrow & w \in E \\
M, w \models_\rho A_1 * A_2 & \Leftrightarrow & \exists w_1, w_2 \in W.\ w \in w_1 \circ w_2 \text{ and} \\
 & & M, w_1 \models_\rho A_1 \text{ and } M, w_2 \models_\rho A_2 \\
M, w \models_\rho A_1 -\!\!* A_2 & \Leftrightarrow & \forall w', w'' \in W. \text{ if } w'' \in w \circ w' \text{ and} \\
 & & M, w' \models_\rho A_1 \text{ then } M, w'' \models_\rho A_2
\end{array}$$

$A$ is said to be *valid in* $M$ if $M, w \models_\rho A$ for all valuations $\rho$ and for all $w \in W$. $A$ is *valid* if it is valid in all BBI-models.

**Definition 2.4.** We define $\mathbf{K}_{\mathrm{BBI}}$ to be the proof system obtained by extending a complete Hilbert system for classical logic with the following axioms and inference rules for $*$, $-\!\!*$ and I (where $A \vdash B$ is syntactic sugar for the formula $A \to B$):

$$A * B \vdash B * A \qquad A * (B * C) \vdash (A * B) * C$$

$$A \vdash A * \mathrm{I} \qquad A * \mathrm{I} \vdash A$$

$$\frac{A_1 \vdash B_1 \quad A_2 \vdash B_2}{A_1 * A_2 \vdash B_1 * B_2} \qquad \frac{A * B \vdash C}{A \vdash B -\!\!* C} \qquad \frac{A \vdash B -\!\!* C}{A * B \vdash C}$$

Galmiche and Larchey-Wendling showed [14] that $\mathbf{K}_{\rm BBI}$ is sound and complete with respect to "single-unit" BBI-models, where the set of units is a singleton (cf. Definition 3.1). The corresponding result for our multi-unit setting is an easy corollary.

**Theorem 2.5.** *A* BBI*-formula is* $\mathbf{K}_{\rm BBI}$*-provable iff it is valid.*

## 3. Definable and undefinable properties in BBI

In this section, we review a number of interesting properties of BBI-models encountered in the literature on separation logic, and examine whether or not these properties can be axiomatised, or *defined*, by formulas of BBI. Specifically, we show that several such properties are *not* definable in BBI, by showing that they are not generally preserved by validity-preserving model constructions.

**Definition 3.1** (Separation theories)**.** Letting $M = \langle W, \circ, E\rangle$ be a BBI-model, we introduce the following properties of interest:

*Partial functionality:* $w, w' \in w_1 \circ w_2$ implies $w = w'$;
*Cancellativity:* $(w \circ w_1) \cap (w \circ w_2) \neq \emptyset$ implies $w_1 = w_2$;
*Single unit:* $|E| = 1$, i.e. $w, w' \in E$ implies $w = w'$;
*Indivisible units:* $(w \circ w') \cap E \neq \emptyset$ implies $w \in E$;
*Disjointness:* $w \circ w \neq \emptyset$ implies $w \in E$;
*Divisibility:* for every $w \notin E$ there are $w_1, w_2 \notin E$ such that $w \in w_1 \circ w_2$;
*Cross-split property:* whenever $(t \circ u) \cap (v \circ w) \neq \emptyset$, there exist $tv, tw, uv, uw$ such that $t \in tv \circ tw$, $u \in uv \circ uw$, $v \in tv \circ uv$ and $w \in tw \circ uw$.

Any given collection of model properties from the above list is called a *separation theory*.

All the above axioms are true of standard heap models with the exception of divisibility, which arises naturally in models with fractional permissions. The significance of the individual properties is explained in more detail in [12] (where disjointness and divisibility are referred to as "positivity" and "splittability" respectively). Various different separation theories have been considered in the literature on separation logic. For example, a BBI-model that is both partial functional and cancellative is called a *separation algebra* in [12], while in [8] the same term defines a BBI-model that is partial functional and cancellative with a single unit, and in the "views" framework of [11] the same term again refers to a BBI-model that is simply partial functional.

***Definability in BBI.*** We now examine which of the characteristics of separation theories are *definable* within BBI. We abuse notation slightly by identifying a property of BBI-models with the class of BBI-models satisfying that property.

**Definition 3.2** (Definability)**.** Given a language $\mathcal{L}$ of formulas, a property $\mathcal{P}$ of BBI-models is said to be $\mathcal{L}$*-definable* if there exists an $\mathcal{L}$-formula $A$ such that for all BBI-models $M$,

$$A \text{ is valid in } M \iff M \in \mathcal{P}.$$

We remark that definability could equally well be defined on BBI-*frames*, not just BBI-models. Note that the property of being a BBI-model, among all frames, is itself BBI-definable: take as the defining formula the conjunction of the top four axioms in Definition 2.4 (which define associativity, commutativity and the unit law $E \circ w = \{w\}$). However, we shall be concerned mainly with the properties of BBI-*models* listed in Definition 3.1.

**Proposition 3.3.** *The indivisible units property and the divisibility property are both* BBI*-definable, as follows:*

$$\textit{Indivisible units:} \quad \mathrm{I} \wedge (A * B) \vdash A \qquad \text{(iu)}$$
$$\textit{Divisibility:} \quad \neg\mathrm{I} \vdash \neg\mathrm{I} * \neg\mathrm{I} \qquad \text{(div)}$$

*Proof.* The case of the indivisible units property is shown in [5]. For the case of divisibility, we proceed as follows:

($\Leftarrow$) Assume that $M$ is divisible, let $\rho$ be a valuation for $M$ and let $w \in W$. To show that (div) is valid, we suppose that $M, w \models_\rho \neg\mathrm{I}$, i.e., that $w \notin E$, and require to show that $M, w \models_\rho \neg\mathrm{I} * \neg\mathrm{I}$. Divisibility gives us $w_1, w_2 \in W \setminus E$ such that $w \in w_1 \circ w_2$; thus, $M, w \models_\rho \neg\mathrm{I} * \neg\mathrm{I}$.

($\Rightarrow$) Assume that (div) is valid in $M$, and suppose that $w \in W \setminus E$. Then, $M, w \models_\rho \neg\mathrm{I}$, hence we have $M, w \models_\rho \neg\mathrm{I} * \neg\mathrm{I}$ by validity of (div). This gives us $w_1, w_2$ such that $w \in w_1 \circ w_2$ where $M, w_1 \models_\rho \neg\mathrm{I}$ and $M, w_2 \models_\rho \neg\mathrm{I}$, i.e. $w_1, w_2 \notin E$ as required. □

***Undefinability in BBI.*** Here we show that four of the properties of Defn. 3.1 are not definable in BBI: partial functionality, cancellativity, disjointness and single unit. First, we introduce the *bounded morphic image* and *disjoint union* constructions for BBI-models and show that they preserve validity in a given model, which mirrors the situation arising from their analogues in modal logic [1]. Our undefinability results follow from the fact that the first three of the above properties are not preserved by bounded morphic images, while the last one is not preserved by disjoint unions.

**Definition 3.4** (Bounded morphic image)**.** Let $M = \langle W, \circ, E\rangle$ and $M' = \langle W', \circ', E'\rangle$ be BBI-models. A *bounded morphism* from $M$ to $M'$ is a function $f : W \to W'$ satisfying the following:

1. $w \in E$ iff $f(w) \in E'$;
2. $w \in w_1 \circ w_2$ implies $f(w) \in f(w_1) \circ' f(w_2)$;
3. $f(w) \in w'_1 \circ' w'_2$ implies $\exists w_1, w_2 \in W.\ w \in w_1 \circ w_2$ and $f(w_1) = w'_1$ and $f(w_2) = w'_2$;
4. $w'_2 \in f(w) \circ' w'_1$ implies $\exists w_1, w_2 \in W.\ w_2 \in w \circ w_1$ and $f(w_1) = w'_1$ and $f(w_2) = w'_2$;

We say $M'$ is a *bounded morphic image* of $M$, written $M \twoheadrightarrow M'$, if there is a surjective bounded morphism from $M$ to $M'$.

**Lemma 3.5.** *Let* $M$ *and* $M'$ *be* BBI*-models with* $M \twoheadrightarrow M'$*. Then any* BBI*-formula valid in* $M$ *is also valid in* $M'$*.*

*Proof.* We write $M = \langle W, \circ, E\rangle$ and $M' = \langle W', \circ', E'\rangle$, and let $f : W \to W'$ be a surjective bounded morphism from $M$ to $M'$. Suppose for contradiction that $A$ is valid in $M$, but not in $M'$. Thus there exists a valuation $\rho'$ for $M'$ and $w' \in W'$ such that $M', w' \not\models_{\rho'} A$. We define a valuation $\rho$ for $M$ as follows:

$$\rho(P) \stackrel{\text{def}}{=} \{w \in W \mid f(w) \in \rho'(P)\}$$

As $f$ is surjective, there is a $w \in W$ such that $w' = f(w)$. To obtain the required contradiction, we claim that $M, w \not\models_\rho A$. To show this claim, we prove by structural induction on $A$ that for all $w \in W$, we have $M, w \models_\rho A$ if and only if $M', f(w) \models_{\rho'} A$. We omit the cases for the classical connectives, as they are straightforward by induction hypothesis.

*Case* $A = P \in \mathcal{V}$. Using the definition of $\rho$, we have as required:

$$\begin{array}{rcl} M, w \models_\rho A & \Leftrightarrow & w \in \rho(P) \\ & \Leftrightarrow & f(w) \in \rho'(P) \\ & \Leftrightarrow & M', f(w) \models_{\rho'} P \end{array}$$

*Case* $A = \mathrm{I}$. Using condition 1 in Defn. 3.4, we have as required:

$$M, w \models_\rho \mathrm{I} \Leftrightarrow w \in E \Leftrightarrow f(w) \in E' \Leftrightarrow M', f(w) \models_{\rho'} \mathrm{I}$$

*Case* $A = B * C$. ($\Rightarrow$) Supposing that $M, w \models_\rho B * C$, we have $w \in w_1 \circ w_2$ with $M, w_1 \models_\rho B$ and $M, w_2 \models_\rho C$. Using condition 2 in Defn. 3.4, we have $f(w) \in f(w_1) \circ' f(w_2)$. Furthermore, by induction hypothesis, $M', f(w_1) \models_{\rho'} B$ and $M', f(w_2) \models_{\rho'} C$. Thus $M', f(w) \models_{\rho'} B * C$ as required.

($\Leftarrow$) Supposing that $M', f(w) \models_{\rho'} B * C$, we have $f(w) \in w'_1 \circ' w'_2$ with $M', w'_1 \models_{\rho'} B$ and $M', w'_2 \models_{\rho'} C$. By condition 3 in Defn. 3.4, there are $w_1, w_2 \in W$ with $w \in w_1 \circ w_2$ and $f(w_1) = w'_1$ and $f(w_2) = w'_2$. Thus, by the induction hypothesis, we have $M, w_1 \models_\rho B$ and $M, w_2 \models_\rho C$. Hence $M, w \models_\rho B * C$.

*Case* $A = B \multimap C$. ($\Rightarrow$) Suppose $M, w \models_\rho B \multimap C$. To show that $M', f(w) \models_{\rho'} B \multimap C$, we assume that $w'_2 \in f(w) \circ' w'_1$ and $M', w'_1 \models_{\rho'} B$, and must show $M', w'_2 \models_{\rho'} C$. By condition 4 in Defn. 3.4, there are $w_1, w_2 \in W$ with $w_2 \in w \circ w_1$ and $f(w_1) = w'_1$ and $f(w_2) = w'_2$. Thus, by the induction hypothesis, $M, w_1 \models_\rho B$. Since $M, w \models_\rho B \multimap C$, we obtain $M, w_2 \models_\rho C$, which yields the required $M', w'_2 \models_{\rho'} C$ by induction hypothesis.

($\Leftarrow$) Suppose $M', f(w) \models_{\rho'} B \multimap C$. To show that $M, w \models_\rho B \multimap C$, we assume that $w_2 \in w \circ w_1$ and $M, w_1 \models_\rho B$, and must show $M, w_2 \models_\rho C$. By condition 2 in Defn. 3.4, we have $f(w_2) \in f(w) \circ f(w_1)$, and by induction hypothesis we have $M', f(w_1) \models_{\rho'} B$. Since $M', f(w) \models_{\rho'} B \multimap C$, we obtain $M', f(w_2) \models_{\rho'} C$, which then yields the required $M, w_2 \models_\rho C$ using the induction hypothesis. This completes all cases. □

**Lemma 3.6.** *Let $\mathcal{P}$ be a property of* BBI*-models, and let $M, M'$ be* BBI*-models such that $M \in \mathcal{P}$, $M' \notin \mathcal{P}$ and $M \twoheadrightarrow M'$. Then $\mathcal{P}$ is not* BBI*-definable.*

*Proof.* Suppose for contradiction that the BBI-formula $A$ is valid in exactly those BBI-models with property $\mathcal{P}$. Then $A$ is valid in $M$. By Lemma 3.5, $A$ must be valid in $M'$, since $M \twoheadrightarrow M'$. Hence $M' \in \mathcal{P}$, contradicting the assumption that $M' \notin \mathcal{P}$. □

In fact, Lemma 3.6 applies to BBI-*frames* as well as BBI-models, and implies that if $M \twoheadrightarrow M'$ and $M$ is a BBI-model, then so is $M'$. Otherwise the class of all BBI-models would not be BBI-definable among all BBI-frames, contradiction.

The following result shows that separation algebras as defined by the "views" framework [11] are not BBI-definable.

**Theorem 3.7.** *Partial functionality is not* BBI*-definable.*

*Proof.* By Lemma 3.6, it suffices to exhibit a pair of BBI-models $M$ and $M'$ such that $M$ is partial functional, $M'$ is not partial functional and $M \twoheadrightarrow M'$. We define BBI-models $M = \langle W, \circ, E \rangle$ and $M' = \langle W', \circ', E' \rangle$ as follows:

$$W \stackrel{\text{def}}{=} \{e, v_1, v_2, x_1, x_2, y, z\} \qquad E \stackrel{\text{def}}{=} \{e\}$$
$$w \circ e = e \circ w \stackrel{\text{def}}{=} \{w\} \text{ for all } w \in W$$
$$x_1 \circ v_1 = v_1 \circ x_1 \stackrel{\text{def}}{=} \{y\} \qquad x_1 \circ v_2 = v_2 \circ x_1 \stackrel{\text{def}}{=} \{y\}$$
$$x_2 \circ v_1 = v_1 \circ x_2 \stackrel{\text{def}}{=} \{z\} \qquad x_2 \circ v_2 = v_2 \circ x_2 \stackrel{\text{def}}{=} \{z\}$$

$$W' \stackrel{\text{def}}{=} \{e, v, x, y, z\} \qquad E' \stackrel{\text{def}}{=} \{e\}$$
$$w \circ' e = e \circ' w \stackrel{\text{def}}{=} \{w\} \text{ for all } w \in W'$$
$$x \circ' v = v \circ' x \stackrel{\text{def}}{=} \{y, z\}$$

with $w_1 \circ w_2 = w_1 \circ' w_2 \stackrel{\text{def}}{=} \emptyset$ for all other $w_1$ and $w_2$.

First, we verify that $M$ and $M'$ are indeed BBI-models. Commutativity and the unit law hold in both models by construction. Associativity of $\circ$ and $\circ'$ is straightforward to check since $w_1 \circ (w_2 \circ w_3)$ and $w_1 \circ' (w_2 \circ' w_3)$ are always empty unless one of $w_1, w_2, w_3$ is $e$.

Next, we note that $M$ is partial functional since $|w_1 \circ w_2| \leq 1$ for all $w_1, w_2 \in W$ by construction, whereas $M'$ is not partial functional since $z, y \in x \circ' v$ but $z \neq y$.

Finally, we claim that $M \twoheadrightarrow M'$, i.e., that there is a surjective bounded morphism from $M$ to $M'$. Define $f : W \to W'$ by:

$$f(v_1) = f(v_2) \stackrel{\text{def}}{=} v \qquad f(x_1) = f(x_2) \stackrel{\text{def}}{=} x$$
$$f(w) \stackrel{\text{def}}{=} w \qquad (w \in \{e, y, z\})$$

Clearly $f$ is surjective, so it just remains to check the four bounded morphism conditions in Definition 3.4:

1. Trivial, since $E = E' = \{e\}$ and $f(e) = e$.
2. We just check that every membership statement in the definition of $\circ$ maps under $f$ to a corresponding membership statement in the definition of $\circ'$. E.g., since $y \in x_1 \circ v_2$, we need to check that $f(y) \in f(x_1) \circ' f(v_2)$, i.e., $y \in x \circ' v$, which is the case.
3. We need to check that every membership statement $f(w) \in w'_1 \circ w'_2$ in the definition of $\circ'$ can be "traced back" under $f$ to a corresponding membership statement in the definition of $\circ$. E.g., since $f(z) \in x \circ' v$, we need $w_1, w_2$ such that $z \in w_1 \circ w_2$ and $f(w_1) = x, f(w_2) = v$. By taking, say, $w_1 = x_2$ and $w_2 = v_2$, we are done.
4. Similar to item 3 above, but for membership statements of the form $w'_2 \in f(w) \circ w'_1$. E.g., since $y \in f(v_2) \circ' x$, we need $w_1, w_2$ such that $w_2 \in v_2 \circ w_1$ and $f(w_1) = x, f(w_2) = y$. By taking $w_1 = x_1, w_2 = y$ we are done. □

We remark that there is no *a priori* connection between definability of a property on the one hand, and the existence of complete proof systems for models having the property on the other. In particular, Theorem 3.7 says nothing about the existence of proof theories for BBI that are complete for partial functional models. In fact, Larchey-Wendling and Galmiche showed in [21] that $\mathbf{K}_{\text{BBI}}$ is incomplete for such models. What Theorem 3.7 shows in addition is that, if one were to add (perhaps infinitely many) axioms to $\mathbf{K}_{\text{BBI}}$ so as to obtain a complete system for partial functional models, then provability in this system still would not exclude all models that are *not* partial functional. One can contrast this situation, e.g., with that of $\mathbf{K}_{\text{BBI}}$'s commutativity axiom $A * B \vdash B * A$, which is easily seen to define commutativity and therefore to exclude all non-commutative models.

**Theorem 3.8.** *Cancellativity is not* BBI*-definable.*

*Proof.* By Lemma 3.6, it suffices to exhibit a pair of BBI-models $M$ and $M'$ such that $M$ is cancellative, $M'$ is not cancellative and $M \twoheadrightarrow M'$. We define BBI-models $M = \langle W, \circ, E \rangle$ and $M' = \langle W', \circ', E' \rangle$ as follows:

$$W \stackrel{\text{def}}{=} \{e, v_1, v_2, x, y, z_1, z_2\} \qquad E \stackrel{\text{def}}{=} \{e\}$$
$$w \circ e = e \circ w \stackrel{\text{def}}{=} \{w\} \text{ for all } w \in W$$
$$x \circ v_1 = v_1 \circ x \stackrel{\text{def}}{=} \{z_1\} \qquad x \circ v_2 = v_2 \circ x \stackrel{\text{def}}{=} \{z_2\}$$
$$y \circ v_1 = v_1 \circ y \stackrel{\text{def}}{=} \{z_2\} \qquad y \circ v_2 = v_2 \circ y \stackrel{\text{def}}{=} \{z_1\}$$

$$W' \stackrel{\text{def}}{=} \{e, x, v, y, z\} \qquad E' \stackrel{\text{def}}{=} \{e\}$$
$$w \circ' e = e \circ' w \stackrel{\text{def}}{=} \{w\} \text{ for all } w \in W'$$
$$v \circ' x = x \circ' v = v \circ' y = y \circ' v \stackrel{\text{def}}{=} \{z\}$$

with $w_1 \circ w_2 = w_1 \circ' w_2 \stackrel{\text{def}}{=} \emptyset$ for all other $w_1$ and $w_2$.

First, it is straightforward to verify that $M$ and $M'$ are indeed BBI-models, with associativity holding because $w_1 \circ (w_2 \circ w_3) \neq \emptyset$ implies one of $w_1, w_2, w_3$ is $e$ (and similarly for $\circ'$).

Next, we note that $M$ is cancellative because, by construction, $w' \in (w \circ w_1) \cap (w \circ w_2)$ implies $w_1 = w_2$. On the other hand, $M'$ is not cancellative, for $z \in (v \circ' x) \cap (v \circ' y)$ but $x \neq y$.

Finally, we need a surjective bounded morphism from $M$ to $M'$. We define a map $f : W \to W'$ by

$$f(v_1) = f(v_2) \stackrel{\text{def}}{=} v \qquad f(z_1) = f(z_2) \stackrel{\text{def}}{=} z$$
$$f(w) \stackrel{\text{def}}{=} w \qquad (w \in \{e, x, y\})$$

The verification that $f$ is indeed a surjective bounded morphism is similar to that in the proof of Theorem 3.7. □

Notice that the proof of Theorem 3.8 in fact maps a model that is both partial functional and cancellative with a single unit to a non-cancellative model. Thus, it also establishes that neither the class of models that are partial functional *and* cancellative (the "separation algebras" of [12]) nor the subclass of such models having a single unit (the "separation algebras" of [8]) are BBI-definable.

**Theorem 3.9.** *Disjointness is not* BBI-*definable.*

*Proof.* By Lemma 3.6, it suffices to exhibit a pair of BBI-models $M$ and $M'$ such that $M$ is disjoint, $M'$ is not and $M \twoheadrightarrow M'$. We define BBI-models $M = \langle W, \circ, E\rangle$ and $M' = \langle W', \circ', E'\rangle$ by:

$$\begin{array}{l} W \stackrel{\text{def}}{=} \{e, x, y\} \qquad E \stackrel{\text{def}}{=} \{e\} \\ w \circ e = e \circ w \stackrel{\text{def}}{=} \{w\} \text{ for all } w \in W \\ x \circ y = y \circ x \stackrel{\text{def}}{=} \{x, y\} \end{array}$$

$$\begin{array}{l} W' \stackrel{\text{def}}{=} \{e, x\} \qquad E' \stackrel{\text{def}}{=} \{e\} \\ w \circ' e = e \circ' w \stackrel{\text{def}}{=} \{w\} \text{ for all } w \in W \\ x \circ' x \stackrel{\text{def}}{=} \{x\} \end{array}$$

with $w_1 \circ w_2 = w_1 \circ' w_2 \stackrel{\text{def}}{=} \emptyset$ for all other $w_1$ and $w_2$.

Similar to the previous Theorems 3.7 and 3.8, we can easily verify that $M$ and $M'$ are indeed BBI-models, with $M$ disjoint by construction, whereas $M'$ is not disjoint since $x \neq e$ and $x \circ' x \neq \emptyset$. We define a surjective bounded morphism $f$ from $M$ to $M'$ by

$$f(e) \stackrel{\text{def}}{=} e \qquad f(x) \stackrel{\text{def}}{=} x \qquad f(y) \stackrel{\text{def}}{=} x$$

It just remains to check the bounded morphism conditions, which is similar to the verifications in Theorems 3.7 and 3.8. □

The fact that the single-unit property is not BBI-definable is a straightforward consequence of existing completeness results. We also present a direct proof for pedagogical interest.

**Theorem 3.10.** *The single-unit property is not* BBI-*definable.*

*Proof.* The result can be deduced from the completeness result for single-unit BBI-models in [14]. Suppose for contradiction that the single-unit property is definable by the formula $A$. Then, by completeness, $A$ is provable in $\mathbf{K}_{\text{BBI}}$. Hence, by soundness (Theorem 2.5), $A$ is valid in *all* BBI-models, some of which fail to have the single-unit property. □

Theorem 3.10 can also be shown more directly: we show that the single-unit property is not preserved under the following *disjoint union* construction, which preserves validity.

**Definition 3.11** (Disjoint union). Let $M_1 = \langle W_1, \circ_1, E_1\rangle$, $M_2 = \langle W_2, \circ_2, E_2\rangle$ be BBI-models, where $W_1$ and $W_2$ are disjoint sets. Then $M_1 \uplus M_2$, the *disjoint union* of $M_1$ and $M_2$ is defined as

$$M_1 \uplus M_2 \stackrel{\text{def}}{=} \langle W_1 \cup W_2, \circ_1 \cup \circ_2, E_1 \cup E_2\rangle$$

where $\circ_1 \cup \circ_2 : (W_1 \cup W_2) \times (W_1 \cup W_2) \to \mathcal{P}(W_1 \cup W_2)$ is defined as $\circ_i$ on $W_i \times W_i$ and undefined on $W_1 \times W_2$ and $W_2 \times W_1$.

**Lemma 3.12.** *Let $M_1$, $M_2$ be* BBI-*models. Then any* BBI-*formula valid in both $M_1$ and $M_2$ is also valid in $M_1 \uplus M_2$.*

*Proof.* We write $M_1 = \langle W_1, \circ_1, E_1\rangle$ and $M_2 = \langle W_2, \circ_2, E_2\rangle$. Suppose for contradiction that $A$ is valid in $M_1$ and $M_2$, but not in $M_1 \uplus M_2$. Thus there exists a valuation $\rho$ and $w \in W_1 \cup W_2$ such that $M_1 \uplus M_2, w \not\models_\rho A$. We show the case where $w \in W_1$; the case $w \in W_2$ is similar. We define a valuation $\rho_1$ for $M_1$ by

$$\rho_1(P) \stackrel{\text{def}}{=} \rho(P) \cap M_1$$

To obtain the required contradiction, we claim that $M_1, w \not\models_{\rho_1} A$ (contradicting the supposition that $A$ is valid in $M_1$). To show this claim, we prove that for all $w \in W_1$, we have $M_1, w \models_{\rho_1} A$ if and only if $M_1 \uplus M_2, w \models_\rho A$. This is easily established by a straightforward structural induction on $A$, which we omit. □

**Lemma 3.13.** *Let $\mathcal{P}$ be a property of* BBI-*models, and suppose that there exist* BBI-*models $M_1$ and $M_2$ such that $M_1, M_2 \in \mathcal{P}$ but $M_1 \uplus M_2 \notin \mathcal{P}$. Then $\mathcal{P}$ is not* BBI-*definable.*

*Proof.* Similar to the proof of Lemma 3.6. □

Note that it is straightforward to show that if $M_1$ and $M_2$ are BBI-models then so is $M_1 \uplus M_2$. (Alternatively, similarly to Lemma 3.6, Lemma 3.13 implies that otherwise BBI-models would be undefinable among all BBI-frames, contradiction.)

*Alternative proof of Theorem 3.10.* Let $M_1 = \langle \mathbb{N}, +, \{0\}\rangle$ and $M_2 = \langle \mathbb{N}', +', \{0'\}\rangle$ be disjoint, isomorphic copies of the monoid of natural numbers under addition. $M_1$ and $M_2$ are both single-unit BBI-models, but $M_1 \uplus M_2$ is not, as its set of units is $\{0, 0'\}$. Thus, by Lemma 3.13, the single-unit property is not BBI-definable. □

We have not yet considered the cross-split property from Definition 3.1. In Section 7, we show that this property is definable in a relatively strong hybrid extension of BBI including a binder (see Proposition 7.3). The complication of expressing the property even in that logic leads us to strongly suspect it is not definable in BBI.

**Conjecture 3.14.** *The cross-split property is not* BBI-*definable.*

Cross-split is seemingly preserved by bounded morphic images, disjoint unions and by *generated submodels* (cf. [1]). We believe it should be possible to show its undefinability in BBI by employing a model construction based on *ultrafilter extensions* (cf. [1]), but that is beyond the scope of the present paper.

## 4. HyBBI: a basic hybrid extension of BBI

In this section, we present an extension of BBI, called HyBBI, based upon a simple fragment of *hybrid logic* [1, 2]. This extension allows us to refer to individual elements of the underlying BBI-model (as opposed to sets of elements, as denoted by BBI-formulas) by introducing a second sort of propositional variables called *nominals*. We also introduce a new modality, $@_\ell$, enabling us to evaluate a formula at the world denoted by the nominal $\ell$. The additional expressivity of HyBBI enables us to define the separation theory properties shown in the previous section to be undefinable in BBI.

**Definition 4.1** (HyBBI-formula). We assume a fixed, denumerably infinite set $\mathcal{N}$ of *nominals*, disjoint from the propositional variables. We write lower case letters $j, k, \ell$ etc. for nominals to distinguish them from propositional variables. A HyBBI-formula is defined as a BBI-formula (Defn. 2.1), except that (a) any nominal $\ell \in \mathcal{N}$ counts as an atomic HyBBI-formula, and (b) if $A$ is a HyBBI-formula and $\ell$ a nominal then $@_\ell A$ is a HyBBI-formula.

A HyBBI-formula is said to be *pure* if it contains no propositional (or formula) variables.

**Definition 4.2** (HyBBI-validity). A *hybrid valuation* $\rho$ for a BBI-model $M = \langle W, \circ, E\rangle$ extends a standard valuation (see Defn. 2.3) by additionally mapping every nominal $\ell \in \mathcal{N}$ to an element $\rho(\ell) \in W$. Given any hybrid valuation $\rho$ for $M$, any $w \in W$ and a HyBBI-formula $A$, we define the forcing relation $M, w \models_\rho A$ by extending the definition of the forcing relation in Defn. 2.3 with the following clauses for nominals and the $@_\ell$ modality:

$$\begin{array}{lcl} M, w \models_\rho \ell & \Leftrightarrow & w = \rho(\ell) \\ M, w \models_\rho @_\ell A & \Leftrightarrow & M, \rho(\ell) \models_\rho A \end{array}$$

$A$ is then said to be *valid in* $M$ if $M, w \models_\rho A$ for all hybrid valuations $\rho$ and all $w \in W$ (and simply *valid* if it is valid in all BBI-models).

We observe that HyBBI is a *conservative extension* of BBI; that is, every BBI-formula $A$ is valid according to Definition 2.3 if and only if it is valid according to Definition 4.2 (because the forcing relations in the two definition coincide on BBI-formulas). Thus every property of BBI-models definable in BBI, in particular those described in Proposition 3.3, is also definable in HyBBI. However, HyBBI is strictly more expressive than BBI: several properties not definable in BBI become definable in HyBBI.

**Theorem 4.3.** *The following properties from Definition 3.1 are* HyBBI*-definable via pure formulas:*

| | | |
|---|---|---|
| *Functionality:* | $@_\ell(j * k) \wedge @_{\ell'}(j * k) \vdash @_\ell \ell'$ | (pfn) |
| *Cancellativity:* | $\ell * j \wedge \ell * k \vdash @_j k$ | (cnc) |
| *Single unit:* | $@_{\ell_1}\mathrm{I} \wedge @_{\ell_2}\mathrm{I} \vdash @_{\ell_1}\ell_2$ | (su) |
| *Indivisible units:* | $\mathrm{I} \wedge (\ell_1 * \ell_2) \vdash \ell_1$ | (iu') |
| *Disjointness:* | $\ell * \ell \vdash \mathrm{I} \wedge \ell$ | (dis) |

*Proof.* We treat each property individually.
*Functionality.* ($\Leftarrow$) Assume $M$ is partial functional, let $\rho$ be a valuation for $M$ and let $w \in W$. To show that (pfn) is valid in $M$, we assume that $M, w \models_\rho @_\ell(j * k) \wedge @_{\ell'}(j * k)$, and must show that $M, w \models_\rho @_\ell \ell'$, i.e., that $\rho(\ell) = \rho(\ell')$. By assumption, we have $\rho(\ell) \in \rho(j) \circ \rho(k)$ and $\rho(\ell') \in \rho(j) \circ \rho(k)$. Hence by partial functionality of $M$ we have $\rho(\ell) = \rho(\ell')$ as required.

($\Rightarrow$) Assume that (pfn) is valid in $M$, and suppose $w', w \in w_1 \circ w_2$. We require to show that $w = w'$. Since (pfn) is valid in $M$, we have $M, w \models_\rho$ (pfn) for all $w \in W$ and for any hybrid valuation $\rho$. We define a hybrid valuation $\rho$ for $M$ as follows:

$$\rho(\ell) = w \qquad \rho(\ell') = w' \qquad \rho(j) = w_1 \qquad \rho(k) = w_2$$

Then, showing that $w = w'$ means showing that $M, \rho(\ell) \models_\rho \ell'$, i.e., that $M, w \models_\rho @_\ell \ell'$. As (pfn) is valid in $M$, it suffices to show that $M, w \models_\rho @_\ell(j * k) \wedge @_{\ell'}(j * k)$. Since $w, w' \in w_1 \circ w_2$ by assumption and $M, w_1 \models_\rho j$ and $M, w_2 \models_\rho k$ by construction, we obtain that $M, w \models_\rho j * k$ and that $M, w' \models_\rho j * k$, from which the result follows.

*Cancellativity.* ($\Leftarrow$) Assume $M$ is cancellative, let $\rho$ be a valuation for $M$ and let $w \in W$. To show that (cnc) is valid in $M$, we suppose that $M, w \models_\rho (\ell * j) \wedge (\ell * k)$, and require to show that $M, w \models_\rho @_j k$, i.e., that $\rho(j) = \rho(k)$. That $M, w \models_\rho (\ell * j) \wedge (\ell * k)$ straightforwardly means that $w \in (\rho(\ell) \circ \rho(j)) \cap (\rho(\ell) \circ \rho(k))$. By cancellativity, we thus immediately get that $\rho(j) = \rho(k)$ as required.

($\Rightarrow$) Assume that (cnc) is valid in $M$, and suppose $w' \in (w \circ w_1) \cap (w \circ w_2)$. We require to show that $w_1 = w_2$. Since (cnc) is valid in $M$, we have $M, w \models_\rho$ (cnc) for all $w \in W$ and hybrid valuations $\rho$. We define a hybrid valuation $\rho$ for $M$ as follows:

$$\rho(\ell) = w \qquad \rho(j) = w_1 \qquad \rho(k) = w_2$$

Then by assumption $M, w' \models_\rho (\ell * j) \wedge (\ell * k)$. By validity of (cnc), we deduce that $M, w' \models_\rho @_j k$, hence that $\rho(j) = \rho(k)$, and by construction that $w_1 = w_2$.

*Single unit.* ($\Leftarrow$) Assume $E = \{e\}$, let $\rho$ be a valuation for $M$ and let $w \in W$. We show (su) is valid. Supposing that $M, w \models_\rho @_{\ell_1}\mathrm{I} \wedge @_{\ell_2}\mathrm{I}$, we have that $\rho(\ell_1), \rho(\ell_2) \in E$. Thus $\rho(\ell_1) = \rho(\ell_2) = e$, which yields $M, w \models_\rho @_{\ell_1}\ell_2$ as required.

($\Rightarrow$) Assume (su) is valid and let $e, e' \in E$. We need to show $e = e'$. Define a valuation $\rho$ for $M$ by $\rho(\ell_1) = e$ and $\rho(\ell_2) = e'$. Thus, to show $e = e'$, it suffices to show $M, w \models_\rho @_{\ell_1}\ell_2$ (for any $w \in W$). Since (su) is valid, it suffices to show that $M, w \models_\rho @_{\ell_1}\mathrm{I} \wedge @_{\ell_2}\mathrm{I}$. This follows from our construction of $\rho$.

*Indivisible units.* The equivalence holds by a straightforward modification of the argument for the formula (iu) (see [5]) in Prop. 3.3.

*Disjointness.* ($\Leftarrow$) Assume the disjointness property, let $\rho$ be a valuation for $M$ and let $w \in W$. To show (dis) is valid, we suppose that $M, w \models_\rho \ell * \ell$ and require to show that $M, w \models_\rho \mathrm{I} \wedge \ell$, i.e., that $w = \rho(\ell)$ and $w \in E$. That $M, w \models_\rho \ell * \ell$ means that $w \in \rho(\ell) \circ \rho(\ell)$. In particular, $\rho(\ell) \circ \rho(\ell) \neq \emptyset$ hence, by disjointness, $\rho(\ell) \in E$. We thus get $w \in \rho(\ell) \circ \rho(\ell) = \{\rho(\ell)\}$ hence $w = \rho(\ell)$ and also $w \in E$ as required.

($\Rightarrow$) Assume that (dis) is valid in $M$, and suppose that $w \circ w \neq \emptyset$. We require to show that $w \in E$. Let $w' \in w \circ w$ and $\rho$ be such that $\rho(\ell) = w$. By construction, we have that $M, w' \models_\rho \ell * \ell$, hence by validity of (dis) we get $M, w' \models_\rho \mathrm{I} \wedge \ell$, i.e., $w' = \rho(\ell) = w$ and $w' \in E$, hence $w \in E$ as required. □

**Corollary 4.4.** *Any separation theory from Def. 3.1 not including the cross-split property is* HyBBI*-definable by pure formulas.*

*Proof.* Follows by taking as the defining formula the conjunction of the relevant formulas from Theorem 4.3 and Proposition 3.3. □

As is also the case for BBI (see Conjecture 3.14), we suspect (but do not know) that the cross-split property is not definable even in HyBBI. This is because a straightforward translation of the property into HyBBI would require some way of binding or existentially quantifying nominals, which is not provided by pure nominals or the $@_\ell$ modality. In Section 7 we add a binder to HyBBI, which enables us to express cross-split.

## 5. An axiomatic proof system for HyBBI

Here, we present a Hilbert-style axiomatic proof system for HyBBI, and show that it is sound with respect to validity in BBI-models; we examine questions of completeness in Section 6.

In the rest of the paper, it will often be convenient to reason in terms of $-\circledast$, the De Morgan dual of $-\!*$ defined as

$$A -\!\circledast\, B \stackrel{\text{def}}{=} \neg(A -\!* \neg B)\ .$$

Unpacking the negations and $-\!*$ yields the following forcing relation for $-\circledast$:

$$M, w \models_\rho A_1 -\!\circledast\, A_2 \iff \exists w', w'' \in W.\ w'' \in w \circ w' \text{ and } M, w' \models_\rho A_1 \text{ and } M, w'' \models_\rho A_2$$

(Using $-\circledast$ rather than $-\!*$ means that we deal exclusively with "diamond-type" modalities with an existential interpretation, which frequently makes life easier in our technical developments.)

**Definition 5.1.** We define $\mathbf{K}_{\mathrm{HyBBI}}$ to be the proof system obtained by extending the proof system $\mathbf{K}_{\mathrm{BBI}}$ (see Definition 2.4) with the axioms and rules for nominals and @ given in Figure 1.

$\mathbf{K}_{\mathrm{HyBBI}}$ is based on the proof system for basic hybrid logic in [1]. We have chosen the axioms and rules so as to make the subsequent completeness proof as simple as possible.

**Proposition 5.2.** *Any* $\mathbf{K}_{\mathrm{HyBBI}}$*-provable formula is valid.*

*Proof.* Let $M = \langle W, \circ, E\rangle$ be a BBI-model. Then, assuming $A$ is $\mathbf{K}_{\mathrm{HyBBI}}$-provable, we must show that $A$ is valid in $M$. It suffices to show that all axioms of $\mathbf{K}_{\mathrm{HyBBI}}$ are valid and that validity

| | | | |
|---|---|---|---|
| ($K_@$) | $@_\ell(A \to B) \vdash @_\ell A \to @_\ell B$ | (Nom) | $@_\ell k \wedge @_k A \vdash @_\ell A$ |
| (Self-dual) | $@_\ell A \vdash \neg @_\ell \neg A$ and $\neg @_\ell \neg A \vdash @_\ell A$ | (Agree) | $@_k @_\ell A \vdash @_\ell A$ and $@_\ell A \vdash @_k @_\ell A$ |
| (@-intro) | $\ell \wedge A \vdash @_\ell A$ | (Bridge $*$) | $@_\ell(k * k') \wedge @_k A \wedge @_{k'} B \vdash @_\ell(A * B)$ |
| (Refl) | $\vdash @_\ell \ell$ | (Bridge $-\circledast$) | $@_\ell(k \mathbin{-\circledast} k') \wedge @_k A \wedge @_{k'} B \vdash @_\ell(A \mathbin{-\circledast} B)$ |
| (Sym) | $@_\ell k \vdash @_k \ell$ | | |

$$\frac{\vdash A}{\vdash A[\theta]}\ (\text{Subst}) \qquad \frac{\vdash A}{\vdash @_\ell A}\ (\text{Gen}) \qquad \frac{@_\ell(k * k') \wedge @_k A \wedge @_{k'} B \vdash C}{@_\ell(A * B) \vdash C}\ \begin{array}{l} k, k' \text{ not in } A, B, C \text{ or } \{\ell\} \\ (\text{Paste } *) \end{array}$$

$$\frac{\ell \vdash A}{\vdash A}\ \ell \text{ not in } A\ (\text{Name}) \qquad \frac{@_\ell(k \mathbin{-\circledast} k') \wedge @_k A \wedge @_{k'} B \vdash C}{@_\ell(A \mathbin{-\circledast} B) \vdash C}\ \begin{array}{l} k, k' \text{ not in } A, B, C \text{ or } \{\ell\} \\ (\text{Paste } -\circledast) \end{array}$$

**Figure 1.** Rules and axioms for nominals in $\mathbf{K}_{\text{HyBBI}}$. Note that $\theta$ in the the rule (Subst) is a substitution of nominals for nominals.

is preserved by every proof rule of $\mathbf{K}_{\text{HyBBI}}$. This is a straightforward verification for all the rules and axioms except the two "bridge" axioms and the two "paste" rules. We just show the cases of (Bridge $*$) and (Paste $-\circledast$) here, as the others are similar.

*Case (Bridge $*$).* Let $\rho$ be a valuation for $M$ and let $w \in W$. Suppose $M, w \models_\rho @_\ell(k * k') \wedge @_k A \wedge @_{k'} B$. Then we have $M, \rho(\ell) \models_\rho k * k'$ and $M, \rho(k) \models_\rho A$ and $M, \rho(k') \models_\rho B$. The first of these means that $\rho(\ell) \in \rho(k) \circ \rho(k')$. Thus $M, \rho(\ell) \models_\rho A * B$, i.e. $M, w \models_\rho @_\ell(A * B)$ as required.

*Case (Paste $-\circledast$).* Let $\rho$ be a valuation for $M$ and let $w \in W$. Supposing the premise of the rule is valid in $M$ and $M, w \models_\rho @_\ell(A \mathbin{-\circledast} B)$, we have to show $M, w \models_\rho C$. We have $M, \rho(\ell) \models_\rho A \mathbin{-\circledast} B$ which means that there exist $w', w'' \in W$ such that $w'' \in \rho(\ell) \circ w'$ and $M, w' \models_\rho A$ and $M, w'' \models_\rho B$. Now define the valuation $\rho' = \rho[k \mapsto w', k' \mapsto w'']$, where $k$ and $k'$ are the fresh nominals appearing in the premise of the rule. By construction, and using the fact that $\rho$ and $\rho'$ agree except possibly on the fresh nominals $k, k'$, we have $\rho'(k') \in \rho'(\ell) \circ \rho'(k)$ and $M, \rho'(k) \models_{\rho'} A$ and $M, \rho'(k') \models_{\rho'} B$. The first of these gives us $M, \rho'(\ell) \models_{\rho'} k \mathbin{-\circledast} k'$. Putting everything together, we obtain

$$M, w \models_{\rho'} @_\ell(k \mathbin{-\circledast} k') \wedge @_k A \wedge @_{k'} B$$

Since the premise of the rule is valid by assumption, we obtain $M, w \models_{\rho'} C$. Again, since $\rho$ and $\rho'$ agree except on $k, k'$, which do not appear in $C$, we thus obtain $M, w \models_\rho C$ as required. □

The following example illustrates how the hybrid axioms and rules are used in practice.

**Example 5.3.** The HyBBI-formula $\top * (\mathrm{I} \wedge (\ell \mathbin{-\circledast} A)) \vdash @_\ell A$ is provable in HyBBI.

(Intuitively, the LHS of this formula says that from the current world $w$ one may find a unit $e$ such that $w \circ e$ is defined and $e \circ \rho(\ell)$ is defined and satisfies $A$. This implies that $\rho(\ell)$ itself satisfies $A$.)

*Proof.* First, we show that the following formula is provable:

$$A * @_\ell B \vdash @_\ell B \qquad (1)$$

Let $j, k, k'$ be fresh nominals not occurring in $A$, $B$ or $\{\ell\}$. We have $@_{k'} @_\ell B \vdash @_\ell B$ an instance of (Agree). By weakening for $\wedge$, we thus obtain

$$@_j(k * k') \wedge @_k A \wedge @_{k'} @_\ell B \vdash @_\ell B$$

Using the fact that $k, k'$ are fresh, we can apply the rule (Paste $*$) to derive $@_j(A * @_\ell B) \vdash @_\ell B$. Since the formula

$$j \wedge (A * @_\ell B) \vdash @_j(A * @_\ell B)$$

is an instance of (@-intro), we obtain $j \wedge (A * @_\ell B) \vdash @_\ell B$ by transitivity, and thus easily we have $j \vdash (A * @_\ell B) \to @_\ell B$. Since $j$ is fresh, we obtain $A * @_\ell B \vdash @_\ell B$ by applying (Name).

Next, we show that the following formula is provable:

$$\mathrm{I} \wedge (\ell \mathbin{-\circledast} A) \vdash @_\ell A \qquad (2)$$

We have $\ell \wedge A \vdash @_\ell A$ an instance of (@-intro), whence by contraposition and use of (Self-dual) we obtain $\ell \wedge @_\ell \neg A \vdash \neg A$. Now, since $\ell * @_\ell \neg A \vdash @_\ell \neg A$ is provable as an instance of (1) above, we obtain $\ell \wedge (\ell * @_\ell \neg A) \vdash \neg A$. By straightforward manipulations of plain BBI we can prove

$$(\mathrm{I} \wedge @_\ell \neg A) * \ell \vdash \ell \wedge (\ell * @_\ell \neg A)$$

Thus, by transitivity, we obtain $(\mathrm{I} \wedge @_\ell \neg A) * \ell \vdash \neg A$. This rearranges to $\mathrm{I} \wedge @_\ell \neg A \vdash \ell \mathbin{-\!*} \neg A$ and then to $\mathrm{I} \wedge (\ell \mathbin{-\circledast} A) \vdash \neg @_\ell \neg A$, which yields the required (2) by using (Self-dual).

Now we can supply the required derivation of the formula in the proposition. We can derive $\top * (\mathrm{I} \wedge (\ell \mathbin{-\circledast} A)) \vdash \top * @_\ell A$ using (2). As $\top * @_\ell A \vdash @_\ell A$ is an instance of (1), we have $\top * (\mathrm{I} \wedge (\ell \mathbin{-\circledast} A)) \vdash @_\ell A$ by transitivity as required. □

Interestingly, the converse of the formula in Example 5.3, that is $@_\ell A \vdash \top * (\mathrm{I} \wedge (\ell \mathbin{-\circledast} A))$, is not generally valid, but is valid in all single-unit models (and thus in such models $@_\ell$ is definable already using plain nominals). This is because, in models with a single unit $e$, the composition $w \circ e$ must be defined for *all* $w \in W$, whereas this might fail in models with multiple units. The $@_\ell$ modality enables us to talk about worlds not accessible from the current world via the I, $*$ and $-\!*$ modalities; but in single-unit models, there are no such worlds.

## 6. Completeness for pure extensions of $\mathbf{K}_{\text{HyBBI}}$

In this section, we show a parametric completeness result: any extension of $\mathbf{K}_{\text{HyBBI}}$ with a set of pure axioms Ax is complete with respect to the class of BBI-models satisfying Ax. In particular, we can obtain complete proof systems for many separation theories simply by adding the axioms defining the theory to $\mathbf{K}_{\text{HyBBI}}$.

We follow the basic structure of the corresponding completeness proof for normal hybrid logic in [1], which shows that any consistent set of formulas has a model based upon "named" maximal consistent sets. Compared to this proof, we encounter two additional difficulties. First, we have to work (at least implicitly) with the residuated binary connectives $*$ and $-\!*$, as opposed to a single diamond modality and its De Morgan dual. Second, we have to show that the model we construct is a BBI-model, as opposed to an unrestricted frame.

**Definition 6.1** (Consistent set). Let $\mathcal{K}$ be any proof system. A set $\Gamma$ of formulas is said to be *$\mathcal{K}$-inconsistent* if there are formulas $A_1, \ldots, A_n \in \Gamma$ such that $A_1 \wedge \ldots \wedge A_n \vdash \bot$ is provable in $\mathcal{K}$. Otherwise $\Gamma$ is called *$\mathcal{K}$-consistent.*

**Definition 6.2** (Maximal consistent set). Let $\mathcal{K}$ be any proof system. A set $\Gamma$ of formulas is *maximal $\mathcal{K}$-consistent* (and we call $\Gamma$ a $\mathcal{K}$-MCS) if $\Gamma$ is $\mathcal{K}$-consistent and any $\Delta \supset \Gamma$ is $\mathcal{K}$-inconsistent.

In the rest of this section, whenever we talk about MCSs, consistency and provability, we *always* mean with reference to a fixed but arbitrary extension $\mathbf{K}_{\mathrm{HyBBI}} + \mathrm{Ax}$ of $\mathbf{K}_{\mathrm{HyBBI}}$ with a finite set Ax of axioms expressed as pure formulas.

We begin by recalling some basic facts about MCSs.

**Lemma 6.3.** *For any MCS $\Gamma$ and formulas $A, B$, we have*

1. *if $A \vdash B$ is provable and $A \in \Gamma$ then $B \in \Gamma$;*
2. *$\top \in \Gamma$ and $\bot \notin \Gamma$;*
3. *either $A \in \Gamma$ or $\neg A \in \Gamma$;*
4. *$A \wedge B \in \Gamma$ iff $A, B \in \Gamma$;*
5. *$A \vee B \in \Gamma$ iff $A \in \Gamma$ or $B \in \Gamma$.*

*Proof.* Standard in all cases. □

In the following, we do not refer explicitly to uses of Lemma 6.3, as we use it so frequently.

**Definition 6.4** (Named / pasted MCS). An MCS $\Gamma$ is said to be *named* if there is at least one nominal $\ell \in \Gamma$; any such $\ell$ is called a *name for* $\Gamma$.

$\Gamma$ is said to be *pasted* if

- $@_\ell(A * B) \in \Gamma$ implies $@_\ell(\ell_1 * \ell_2) \wedge @_{\ell_1} A \wedge @_{\ell_2} B \in \Gamma$ for some $\ell_1, \ell_2$, and
- $@_\ell(A \mathrel{-\!\circledast} B) \in \Gamma$ implies $@_\ell(\ell_1 \mathrel{-\!\circledast} \ell_2) \wedge @_{\ell_1} A \wedge @_{\ell_2} B \in \Gamma$ for some $\ell_1, \ell_2$.

**Lemma 6.5** (Extended Lindenbaum Lemma). *Let $\mathcal{N}'$ be a countably infinite set of nominals disjoint from $\mathcal{N}$. If $\Delta$ is a consistent set of formulas then there is a named, pasted MCS $\Delta^+$ (of formulas in the extended nominal language of $\mathcal{N} \cup \mathcal{N}'$) such that $\Delta \subseteq \Delta^+$.*

*Proof.* Let $k_0, k_1, k_2 \ldots$ be an enumeration of $\mathcal{N}'$, and let $B_1$, $B_2$, $B_3 \ldots$ be an enumeration of all formulas in the extended language given by $\mathcal{N} \cup \mathcal{N}'$. Given a consistent set $\Delta$ of formulas, we define a sequence $(\Delta_i)_{i \geq 0}$ of sets of formulas as follows:

- $\Delta_0 \stackrel{\text{def}}{=} \Delta \cup \{k\}$;
- if $\Delta_i \cup \{B_i\}$ is inconsistent then $\Delta_{i+1} \stackrel{\text{def}}{=} \Delta_i$;
- if $\Delta_i \cup \{B_i\}$ is consistent and the formula $B_i$ is not of the form $@_\ell(A * B)$ or $@_\ell(A \mathrel{-\!\circledast} B)$, then $\Delta_{i+1} \stackrel{\text{def}}{=} \Delta_i \cup \{B_i\}$;
- if $\Delta_i \cup \{B_i\}$ is consistent and $B_i = @_\ell(A * B)$ then
$$\Delta_{i+1} \stackrel{\text{def}}{=} \Delta_i \cup \{B_i\} \cup \{@_\ell(k * k') \wedge @_k A \wedge @_{k'} B\}$$
- if $\Delta_i \cup \{B_i\}$ is consistent and $B_i = @_\ell(A \mathrel{-\!\circledast} B)$ then
$$\Delta_{i+1} \stackrel{\text{def}}{=} \Delta_i \cup \{B_i\} \cup \{@_\ell(k \mathrel{-\!\circledast} k') \wedge @_k A \wedge @_{k'} B\}$$

where $k, k'$ in the first and last two clauses are fresh nominals from our enumeration of $\mathcal{N}'$. We claim that $\Delta^+ \stackrel{\text{def}}{=} \bigcup_{i \geq 0} \Delta_i$ is a named, pasted MCS.

First, to see that $\Delta^+$ is consistent, it suffices to show that $\Delta_i$ is consistent for all $i$. We proceed by induction on $i$. In the case $i = 0$, we must show that $\Delta \cup \{k\}$ is consistent. If not, then there are formulas $A_1, \ldots, A_n \in \Delta$ such that, writing $A = \bigwedge_{1 \leq i \leq n} A_i$, we have $A \wedge k \vdash \bot$ provable. Thus $k \vdash \neg A$ is provable, whence by the rule (Name) we have $\vdash \neg A$ provable and thus $A \vdash \bot$ provable, contradicting the consistency of $\Delta$. Now, assuming that $\Delta_i$ is consistent, we must show that $\Delta_{i+1}$ is consistent. This is immediate by induction hypothesis except in the case that $B_i = @_\ell(A * B)$ or $B_i = @_\ell(A \mathrel{-\!\circledast} B)$. We show the case $B_i = @_\ell(A * B)$. In this case, assume for contradiction that there are $A_1, \ldots, A_n \in \Delta_i$ such that, writing $A = \bigwedge_{1 \leq i \leq n} A_i$, the following is provable:

$$A \wedge @_\ell(A * B) \wedge @_\ell(k * k') \wedge @_k A \wedge @_{k'} B \vdash \bot$$

Thus we can also prove

$$@_\ell(k * k') \wedge @_k A \wedge @_{k'} B \vdash \neg A \vee \neg @_\ell(A * B)$$

Since $k, k'$ are fresh nominals, we obtain by applying (Paste $*$):

$$@_\ell(A * B) \vdash \neg A \vee \neg @_\ell(A * B)$$

Thus we obtain $A \wedge @_\ell(A * B) \vdash \bot$, contradicting the assumed consistency of $\Delta_i \cup \{B_i\}$. The case $B_i = A \mathrel{-\!\circledast} B$ is similar, using the rule (Paste $\mathrel{-\!\circledast}$).

Next, we must show that $\Delta^+$ is maximal. Suppose that for some formula $A$, we have $\Delta^+ \cup \{A\}$ consistent but $A \notin \Delta^+$. Note that $A$ appears in our enumeration as $B_i$ say, so by construction it must be that $\Delta_i \cup \{A\}$ is inconsistent (otherwise $A \in \Delta_{i+1} \subseteq \Delta^+$). But then $\Delta^+ \cup \{A\}$ is inconsistent, contradiction.

Next, to see that $\Delta^+$ is named, observe that $k \in \Delta_0 \subseteq \Delta^+$, for some nominal $k$, by construction.

Finally, we show $\Delta^+$ is pasted. First, suppose $@_\ell(A*B) \in \Delta^+$. Note that $@_\ell(A * B)$ appears as some $B_i$ in our enumeration. Now every finite subset of an MCS is consistent, so $\Delta_i \cup \{B_i\}$ must be consistent. Thus, by construction, we have

$$@_\ell(k * k') \wedge @_k A \wedge @_{k'} B \in \Delta_{i+1} \subseteq \Delta^+$$

as required. For similar reasons, whenever $@_\ell(A \mathrel{-\!\circledast} B) \in \Delta^+$ we have $@_\ell(k \mathrel{-\!\circledast} k') \wedge @_k A \wedge @_{k'} B \in \Delta^+$. □

In the following, we define a *named set yielded by* $\Gamma$ to be any set of formulas $\{A \mid @_\ell A \in \Gamma\}$ for some nominal $\ell$.

**Lemma 6.6.** *Let $\Gamma$ be an MCS, and let $\Delta_\ell \stackrel{\text{def}}{=} \{A \mid @_\ell A \in \Gamma\}$ be the named set yielded by $\Gamma$ for each nominal $\ell$. Then the following hold for all nominals $\ell, k$:*

1. *$\Delta_\ell$ is an MCS containing $\ell$;*
2. *if $\ell \in \Delta_k$ then $\Delta_k = \Delta_\ell$;*
3. *$@_\ell A \in \Delta_k$ iff $@_\ell A \in \Gamma$;*
4. *if $\ell$ is a name for $\Gamma$ then $\Gamma = \Delta_\ell$.*

*Proof.* The proof of the analogous result for normal hybrid logic, stated as Lemma 7.24 in [1], suffices for our setting. □

**Definition 6.7.** A BBI-model $\langle W, \circ, E\rangle$ is *named by* the hybrid valuation $\rho$ if for all $w \in W$ there is an $\ell \in \mathcal{N}$ with $\rho(\ell) = w$.

**Definition 6.8.** Let $\Gamma$ be a named, pasted MCS. Then the *named model yielded by* $\Gamma$ is defined as $M^\Gamma \stackrel{\text{def}}{=} \langle W^\Gamma, \circ^\Gamma, E^\Gamma\rangle$, where:

1. $W^\Gamma$ is the set of all named sets yielded by $\Gamma$;
2. $\Delta_1 \circ^\Gamma \Delta_2 \stackrel{\text{def}}{=} \{\Delta \mid A_1 \in \Delta_1, A_2 \in \Delta_2 \text{ implies } A_1 * A_2 \in \Delta\}$;
3. $E^\Gamma \stackrel{\text{def}}{=} \{\Delta \mid \mathrm{I} \in \Delta\}$.

The *canonical valuation* $\rho^\Gamma$ for $M^\Gamma$ is defined by

$$\begin{array}{rcll} \rho^\Gamma(P) & \stackrel{\text{def}}{=} & \{\Delta \mid P \in \Delta\} & P \text{ a proposition} \\ \rho^\Gamma(\ell) & \stackrel{\text{def}}{=} & \{A \mid @_\ell A \in \Gamma\} & \ell \text{ a nominal} \end{array}$$

We show that $M^\Gamma$ is indeed a BBI-model in Lemma 6.13 (but require for the intermediate results only that $M^\Gamma$ is a BBI-frame). We observe that $M^\Gamma$ is indeed named by $\rho^\Gamma$: for any $\Delta \in W^\Gamma$ we have $\Delta = \{A \mid @_\ell A \in \Gamma\}$ for some $\ell$, whence $\rho^\Gamma(\ell) = \Delta$.

**Lemma 6.9** (Existence Lemma for $*$). *For any $\Delta \in W^\Gamma$, if $A_1 * A_2 \in \Delta$ then there exist $\Delta_1, \Delta_2 \in W^\Gamma$ such that $\Delta \in \Delta_1 \circ^\Gamma \Delta_2$ and $A_1 \in \Delta_1$, $A_2 \in \Delta_2$.*

*Proof.* Let $A_1 * A_2 \in \Delta$. We have $\Delta = \{A \mid @_\ell A \in \Gamma\}$ for some nominal $\ell$. Thus $@_\ell(A_1 * A_2) \in \Gamma$. As $\Gamma$ is pasted, we have nominals $\ell_1, \ell_2$ such that $@_\ell(\ell_1 * \ell_2) \wedge @_{\ell_1} A_1 \wedge @_{\ell_2} A_2 \in \Gamma$. Thus $A_1 \in \Delta_1$ and $A_2 \in \Delta_2$, where $\Delta_1 = \{A \mid @_{\ell_1} A \in \Gamma\}$ and $\Delta_2 = \{A \mid @_{\ell_2} A \in \Gamma\}$ are named sets yielded by $\Gamma$.

It just remains to show that $\Delta \in \Delta_1 \circ^\Gamma \Delta_2$. Let $B_1 \in \Delta_1$, $B_2 \in \Delta_2$. By definition, $@_{\ell_1} B_1 \in \Gamma$ and $@_{\ell_2} B_2 \in \Gamma$. As MCSs are closed under provability and conjunction, we have $@_\ell(\ell_1 * \ell_2) \wedge @_{\ell_1} B_1 \wedge @_{\ell_2} B_2 \in \Gamma$. Thus, using the rule (Bridge $*$), we have $@_\ell(B_1 * B_2) \in \Gamma$. Thus $B_1 * B_2 \in \Delta$ as required. □

**Lemma 6.10.** *$\Delta \in \Delta_1 \circ^\Gamma \Delta_2$ if and only if for all formulas $A$ and $B$, $A \in \Delta_2$ and $B \in \Delta$ implies $A \multimap\!\!\circledast\, B \in \Delta_1$.*

*Proof.* We show each direction separately, making use of the fact that $\Delta, \Delta_1, \Delta_2$ are MCSs by part 1 of Lemma 6.6.

($\Leftarrow$) Assume the right-hand side of the implication and let $A_1 \in \Delta_1$ and $A_2 \in \Delta_2$. We must show $A_1 * A_2 \in \Delta$. Suppose for contradiction that $A_1 * A_2 \notin \Delta$. Since $\Delta$ is an MCS, $\neg(A_1 * A_2) \in \Delta$. By assumption, $A_2 \multimap\!\!\circledast\, \neg(A_1 * A_2) \in \Delta_1$, i.e. $\neg(A_2 \multimap\!\!* \neg\neg(A_1 * A_2)) \in \Delta_1$. As $\Delta_1$ is an MCS, we have $A_1 \wedge \neg(A_2 \multimap\!\!* (A_1 * A_2)) \in \Delta_1$. But $A_1 \vdash A_2 \multimap\!\!* (A_1 * A_2)$ is provable, hence so is $A_1 \wedge \neg(A_2 \multimap\!\!* (A_1 * A_2)) \vdash \bot$. This contradicts the consistency of $\Delta_1$. Hence $A_1 * A_2 \in \Delta$ as required.

($\Rightarrow$) Let $A \in \Delta_2$, $B \in \Delta$ and suppose for contradiction that $A \multimap\!\!\circledast\, B \notin \Delta_1$. As $\Delta_1$ is an MCS, we have $A \multimap\!\!* \neg B \in \Delta_1$, so by the main assumption $(A \multimap\!\!* \neg B) * A \in \Delta$. As $\Delta$ is an MCS and $(A \multimap\!\!* \neg B) * A \vdash \neg B$ is provable, $\neg B \in \Delta$. This contradicts the consistency of $\Delta$, so $A \multimap\!\!\circledast\, B \in \Delta_1$ as required. □

**Lemma 6.11** (Existence Lemma for $\multimap\!\!*$). *For any $\Delta \in W^\Gamma$, if $A_1 \multimap\!\!\circledast\, A_2 \in \Delta$ then there exist $\Delta', \Delta'' \in W^\Gamma$ such that $\Delta'' \in \Delta \circ^\Gamma \Delta'$ and $A_1 \in \Delta'$, $A_2 \in \Delta''$.*

*Proof.* We have $\Delta = \{A \mid @_\ell A \in \Gamma\}$ for some nominal $\ell$. Since $A_1 \multimap\!\!\circledast\, A_2 \in \Delta$ by assumption, $@_\ell(A_1 \multimap\!\!\circledast\, A_2) \in \Gamma$. As $\Gamma$ is pasted, we have $@_\ell(\ell_1 \multimap\!\!\circledast\, \ell_2) \wedge @_{\ell_1} A_1 \wedge @_{\ell_2} A_2 \in \Gamma$ for some $\ell_1, \ell_2$. We obtain named sets $\Delta' = \{A \mid @_{\ell_1} A \in \Gamma\}$ and $\Delta'' = \{A \mid @_{\ell_2} A \in \Gamma\}$ yielded by $\Gamma$ with $A_1 \in \Delta'$ and $A_2 \in \Delta''$.

It remains to show that $\Delta'' \in \Delta \circ^\Gamma \Delta'$. By Lemma 6.10, it suffices to show that $A \in \Delta'$ and $B \in \Delta''$ implies $A \multimap\!\!\circledast\, B \in \Delta$. Supposing $A \in \Delta', B \in \Delta''$, we have $@_{\ell_1} A \in \Gamma$ and $@_{\ell_2} B \in \Gamma$. Thus we obtain $@_\ell(\ell_1 \multimap\!\!\circledast\, \ell_2) \wedge @_{\ell_1} A \wedge @_{\ell_2} B \in \Gamma$. Since $\Gamma$ is an MCS it is closed under the rule (Bridge $\multimap\!\!\circledast$), and it follows that $@_\ell(A \multimap\!\!\circledast\, B) \in \Gamma$. Thus $A \multimap\!\!\circledast\, B \in \Delta$ as required. □

**Lemma 6.12** (Truth Lemma). *For any HyBBI-formula $A$ and $\Delta \in W^\Gamma$, we have $M^\Gamma, \Delta \models_{\rho^\Gamma} A$ if and only if $A \in \Delta$.*

*Proof.* By structural induction on $A$. We omit the cases for the classical connectives, as these are straightforward by induction hypothesis, using the properties of MCSs and the fact that any named set yielded by $\Gamma$ is an MCS (see part 1 of Lemma 6.6).

*Case* $A = P$. Using the definition of $\rho^\Gamma$, we have as required:

$$M^\Gamma, \Delta \models_{\rho^\Gamma} P \Leftrightarrow \Delta \in \rho^\Gamma(P) \Leftrightarrow P \in \Delta$$

*Case* $A = \ell$. Using the definition of $\rho^\Gamma$, we have

$$M^\Gamma, \Delta \models_{\rho^\Gamma} \ell \Leftrightarrow \Delta = \rho^\Gamma(\ell) \Leftrightarrow \Delta = \{A \mid @_\ell A \in \Gamma\}$$

Now, going from left to right, we have $\Delta = \{A \mid @_\ell A \in \Gamma\}$ and thus $\ell \in \Delta$ by part 1 of Lemma 6.6. Conversely, assuming $\ell \in \Delta$, we have that $\Delta = \{A \mid @_k A \in \Gamma\}$ for some $k$, and by part 2 of Lemma 6.6 we obtain $\Delta = \{A \mid @_\ell A \in \Gamma\}$ as required.

*Case* $A = \mathrm{I}$. Using the definition of $E^\Gamma$, we easily have as required:

$$M^\Gamma, \Delta \models_{\rho^\Gamma} \mathrm{I} \Leftrightarrow \Delta \in E^c \Leftrightarrow \mathrm{I} \in \Delta$$

*Case* $A = A_1 * A_2$. Using the induction hypothesis, we have:

$$\begin{aligned} & M^\Gamma, \Delta \models_{\rho^\Gamma} A_1 * A_2 \\ \Leftrightarrow\ & \Delta \in \Delta_1 \circ^\Gamma \Delta_2 \text{ and } M^\Gamma, \Delta_1 \models_{\rho^\Gamma} A_1 \text{ and } M^\Gamma, \Delta_2 \models_{\rho^\Gamma} A_2 \\ \Leftrightarrow\ & \Delta \in \Delta_1 \circ^\Gamma \Delta_2 \text{ and } A_1 \in \Delta_1 \text{ and } A_2 \in \Delta_2 \end{aligned}$$

Going from left to right, we immediately get $A_1 * A_2 \in \Delta$ as required from the definition of $\circ^\Gamma$. Going from right to left, we have $A_1 * A_2 \in \Delta$ and must construct the required named sets $\Delta_1, \Delta_2$ yielded by $\Gamma$ satisfying the statement above. This is precisely guaranteed by our Existence Lemma for $*$ (Lemma 6.9).

*Case* $A = A_1 \multimap\!\!* A_2$. Using the induction hypothesis for $A_1$ and $A_2$, we have:

$$\begin{aligned} & M^\Gamma, \Delta \models_{\rho^\Gamma} A_1 \multimap\!\!* A_2 \\ \Leftrightarrow\ & \forall \Delta', \Delta''.\ \Delta'' \in \Delta \circ^\Gamma \Delta' \text{ and } M^\Gamma, \Delta' \models_{\rho^\Gamma} A_1 \text{ implies} \\ & M^\Gamma, \Delta'' \models_{\rho^\Gamma} A_2 \\ \Leftrightarrow\ & \forall \Delta', \Delta''.\ \Delta'' \in \Delta \circ^\Gamma \Delta' \text{ and } A_1 \in \Delta' \text{ implies } A_2 \in \Delta'' \end{aligned}$$

Going from right to left, assume that $A_1 \multimap\!\!* A_2 \in \Delta$, $A_1 \in \Delta'$ and $\Delta'' \in \Delta \circ^\Gamma \Delta'$. By the definition of $\circ^\Gamma$, we have $(A_1 \multimap\!\!* A_2) * A_1 \in \Delta''$, whence we obtain $A_2 \in \Delta''$ as required by modus ponens.

Going from left to right, we must show that $A_1 \multimap\!\!* A_2 \in \Delta$ given the above implication. We show the contrapositive. Assume that $A_1 \multimap\!\!* A_2 \notin \Delta$, i.e. $\neg(A_1 \multimap\!\!* A_2) \in \Delta$. We must construct named sets $\Delta', \Delta''$ yielded by $\Gamma$, with $\Delta'' \in \Delta \circ^\Gamma \Delta'$ and $A_1 \in \Delta'$ but $A_2 \notin \Delta''$, i.e. $\neg A_2 \in \Delta$. This is provided by our Existence Lemma for $\multimap\!\!*$ (Lemma 6.11).

*Case* $A = @_\ell B$. Using the induction hypothesis for $B$, we have:

$$\begin{aligned} M^\Gamma, \Delta \models_{\rho^\Gamma} @_\ell B & \Leftrightarrow M^\Gamma, \rho^\Gamma(\ell) \models_{\rho^\Gamma} B \\ & \Leftrightarrow B \in \rho^\Gamma(\ell) \\ & \Leftrightarrow B \in \{A \mid @_\ell A \in \Gamma\} \\ & \Leftrightarrow @_\ell B \in \Gamma \end{aligned}$$

Now, using part 3 of Lemma 6.6, we have that $@_\ell B \in \Gamma$ if and only if $@_\ell B \in \Delta$. This completes the case, and the proof. □

**Lemma 6.13.** *Let $M^\Gamma = \langle W^\Gamma, \circ^\Gamma, E^\Gamma \rangle$ be the named model yielded by the named, pasted MCS $\Gamma$. Then $M^\Gamma$ is a BBI-model.*

*Proof.* We must show that $M^\Gamma$ satisfies the axioms in Defn. 2.2.

*Commutativity.* It suffices to show that $\Delta_1 \circ^\Gamma \Delta_2 \subseteq \Delta_2 \circ^\Gamma \Delta_1$. Let $\Delta \in \Delta_1 \circ^\Gamma \Delta_2$, and suppose $A_1 \in \Delta_1, A_2 \in \Delta_2$. To show $\Delta \in \Delta_2 \circ^\Gamma \Delta_1$, we have to show $A_2 * A_1 \in \Delta$. As $\Delta \in \Delta_1 \circ^\Gamma \Delta_2$, we have $A_1 * A_2 \in \Delta$. As MCSs are closed under modus ponens and $A_1 * A_2 \vdash A_2 * A_1$ is provable, we have $A_2 * A_1 \in \Delta$.

*Associativity.* It suffices by commutativity to show $\Delta_1 \circ^\Gamma (\Delta_2 \circ^\Gamma \Delta_3) \subseteq (\Delta_1 \circ^\Gamma \Delta_2) \circ^\Gamma \Delta_3$. Assume that $\Delta \in \Delta_1 \circ^\Gamma (\Delta_2 \circ^\Gamma \Delta_3)$, which means that for some $\Delta' \in \Delta_2 \circ^\Gamma \Delta_3$ we have $\Delta \in \Delta_1 \circ^\Gamma \Delta'$. Using part 1 of Lemma 6.6, we have $\ell_1, \ell_2, \ell_3$ such that $\ell_i \in \Delta_i$ for each $i \in \{1, 2, 3\}$. As $\Delta' \in \Delta_2 \circ^\Gamma \Delta_3$, we have $\ell_2 * \ell_3 \in \Delta'$. Thus, as $\Delta \in \Delta_1 \circ^\Gamma \Delta'$, we have $\ell_1 * (\ell_2 * \ell_3) \in \Delta$. By applying associativity, $\ell_1 * (\ell_2 * \ell_3) \vdash (\ell_1 * \ell_2) * \ell_3$ is provable, so $(\ell_1 * \ell_2) * \ell_3 \in \Delta$. By two applications of the Existence Lemma for $*$ (Lemma 6.9) we obtain named sets $\Sigma_1, \Sigma_2, \Sigma_3, \Delta'' \in W^\Gamma$ such that $\ell_i \in \Sigma_i$ for each $i \in \{1, 2, 3\}$, and $\Delta \in \Delta'' \circ^\Gamma \Sigma_3$

and $\Delta'' \in \Sigma_1 \circ^\Gamma \Sigma_2$. By part 2 of Lemma 6.6, $\Sigma_i = \Delta_i$ for each $i \in \{1,2,3\}$. Hence $\Delta \in (\Delta_1 \circ^\Gamma \Delta_2) \circ^\Gamma \Delta_3$ as required.

*Unit law.* We must show that $E^\Gamma \circ^\Gamma \Delta = \{\Delta\}$ for any $\Delta \in W^\Gamma$. First we show that $E^\Gamma \circ^\Gamma \Delta \subseteq \{\Delta\}$. Suppose $\Delta' \in E^\Gamma \circ^\Gamma \Delta$, i.e. there is a $\Delta_E \in E^\Gamma$ such that $\Delta' \in \Delta_E \circ^\Gamma \Delta$. We need to show $\Delta' = \Delta$. First suppose $A \in \Delta$, and note that $\mathrm{I} \in \Delta_E$ by definition. By definition of $\circ^\Gamma$ we have $\mathrm{I} * A \in \Delta'$, and as $\mathrm{I} * A \vdash A$ is provable we must have $A \in \Delta'$. Thus $\Delta' \supseteq \Delta$. To see that $\Delta' = \Delta$ as required, we just observe that if $\Delta' \supset \Delta$ then, as $\Delta'$ is consistent, $\Delta$ is not maximal, contradiction.

We still need to show that $\Delta \in E^\Gamma \circ^\Gamma \Delta$, i.e. that $\Delta \in \Delta_E \circ^\Gamma \Delta$ for some $\Delta_E \in E^\Gamma$. Using part 1 of Lemma 6.6, we have some $\ell \in \Delta$. Since $\ell \vdash \mathrm{I} * \ell$ is provable, we have $\mathrm{I} * \ell \in \Delta$. Using the Existence Lemma for $*$ (Lemma 6.9) we obtain named sets $\Delta_E, \Delta' \in W^\Gamma$ such that $\Delta \in \Delta_E \circ^\Gamma \Delta'$ and $\mathrm{I} \in \Delta_E$ and $\ell \in \Delta'$. Thus $\Delta_E \in E^\Gamma$ and, by part 2 of Lemma 6.6, $\Delta' = \Delta$. This completes the proof. □

**Lemma 6.14.** *Let $M = \langle W, \circ, E\rangle$ be a* BBI*-model named by $\rho$ and let $A$ be a pure formula. Suppose that $M, w \models_\rho A[\theta]$ for all $w \in W$ and nominal substitutions $\theta$. Then $A$ is valid in $M$.*

*Proof.* Letting $\rho'$ be a hybrid valuation and $w \in W$, we must show that $M, w \models_{\rho'} A$. Since $M$ is named by $\rho$, we have that for any $\ell \in \mathcal{N}$ there is a $k \in \mathcal{N}$ such that $\rho(k) = \rho'(\ell)$. Thus we can define the substitution $\theta$ of nominals for nominals by: $\theta(\ell)$ is the first $k \in \mathcal{N}$ with $\rho(k) = \rho'(\ell)$. By hypothesis, we have that $M, w \models_\rho A[\theta]$ for all $w \in W$.

We now prove by structural induction on $A$ that $M, w \models_{\rho'} A$. In the case that $A$ is a nominal $\ell$, we must show that $\rho'(\ell) = w$, and are done since by assumption $w = \rho(\ell[\theta]) = \rho'(\ell)$. Note that $A$ cannot be a propositional variable since it is assumed pure. The other cases follow by induction hypothesis. □

**Theorem 6.15** (Completeness). *Let Ax be a set of pure* HyBBI*-formulas. Then if a* HyBBI*-formula is valid in the class of* BBI*-models satisfying Ax, then it is provable in $\mathbf{K}_{\mathrm{HyBBI}}$ + Ax.*

*Proof.* Let $\mathcal{C}$ be the class of BBI-models satisfying Ax. Suppose $A$ is valid in all BBI-models $M \in \mathcal{C}$, but not provable in $\mathbf{K}_{\mathrm{HyBBI}}$ + Ax. Then $\{\neg A\}$ is consistent. Using the Extended Lindenbaum Lemma (6.5), we can construct a named, pasted MCS $\Gamma \supseteq \{\neg A\}$. Now let $M^\Gamma = \langle W^\Gamma, \circ^\Gamma, E^\Gamma\rangle$ be the named model yielded by $\Gamma$, and $\rho^\Gamma$ the corresponding canonical valuation. By Lemma 6.13, $M^\Gamma$ is a BBI-model.

Furthermore, for any pure formula $B \in$ Ax and any nominal substitution $\theta$, we have that $\vdash B[\theta]$ is provable (using the rule (Subst)), which means that $B[\theta] \in \Delta$ for all $\Delta \in W^\Gamma$ since MCSs are closed under provability. By the Truth Lemma (6.12), we obtain

$$M^\Gamma, \Delta \models_{\rho^\Gamma} B[\theta] \quad \text{for all } B \in \text{Ax}, \Delta \in W^\Gamma, \text{and substitutions } \theta$$

Thus, by Lemma 6.14, all formulas in Ax are valid in $M^\Gamma$, i.e. $M^\Gamma \in \mathcal{C}$. Thus, by the main assumption, $A$ is valid in $M^\Gamma$.

Since $\Gamma$ is named by construction, we have $\Gamma \in W^\Gamma$ by part 4 of Lemma 6.6. Since $\neg A \in \Gamma$, we have $M^\Gamma, \Gamma \models_{\rho^\Gamma} \neg A$ by the Truth Lemma. That is, $M^\Gamma, \Gamma \not\models_{\rho^\Gamma} A$. Thus $A$ is not valid in $M^\Gamma$, contradiction. We conclude $A$ is provable in $\mathbf{K}_{\mathrm{HyBBI}}$ + Ax. □

**Corollary 6.16.** *Let $\mathcal{S}$ be any separation theory from Definition 3.1 not including the cross-split property, and let Ax be the set of pure* HyBBI *formulas defining $\mathcal{S}$, as given by Corollary 4.4.*

*Then a* HyBBI*-formula is provable in $\mathbf{K}_{\mathrm{HyBBI}}$+Ax if and only if it is valid in the class of* BBI*-models satisfying $\mathcal{S}$.*

*Proof.* Follows from Prop. 5.2, Thm. 6.15 and Cor. 4.4. □

# 7. HyBBI with the $\downarrow$ binder

In this section, we study the extension of HyBBI with the $\downarrow$ binder from hybrid logic [2]. Specifically, we show that the elusive cross-split property from Definition 3.1 is definable in this extension, called HyBBI($\downarrow$), and we show how to extend our soundness and parametric completeness results for HyBBI in the previous sections to the setting of HyBBI($\downarrow$).

## 7.1 Formulas and expressivity

**Definition 7.1** (HyBBI($\downarrow$)-formula)**.** A HyBBI($\downarrow$)-formula is defined as for HyBBI (Defn. 4.1), except that if $A$ is a HyBBI($\downarrow$)-formula and $\ell$ a nominal then $\downarrow\ell.\, A$ is a HyBBI($\downarrow$)-formula.

**Definition 7.2** (HyBBI($\downarrow$)-validity)**.** Given any hybrid valuation $\rho$ for a BBI-model $M = \langle W, \circ, E\rangle$, and any $w \in W$, we extend the forcing relation for HyBBI in Defn. 4.2 by the following clause for the $\downarrow$ binder, which binds the given label to the current world:

$$M, w \models_\rho \downarrow\ell.\, A \quad\Leftrightarrow\quad M, w \models_{\rho[\ell := w]} A$$

where $\rho[\ell := w]$ is notation for the hybrid valuation defined as $\rho$ except that $\rho[\ell := w](\ell) \stackrel{\text{def}}{=} w$. The definition of validity for HyBBI then extends immediately to HyBBI($\downarrow$).

**Proposition 7.3.** *The cross-split property (see Definition 3.1) is definable in* HyBBI($\downarrow$) *via the following pure formula:*

$$\begin{aligned}(a * b) \wedge (c * d) \qquad\qquad\qquad\qquad\qquad\qquad & \text{(cs)}\\ \vdash @_a(\top * \downarrow ac.\, @_a(\top * \downarrow ad.\, @_a(ac * ad) & \\ \wedge\, @_b(\top * \downarrow bc.\, @_b(\top * \downarrow bd.\, @_b(bc * bd) & \\ \wedge\, @_c(ac * bc) \wedge @_d(ad * bd))))) &\end{aligned}$$

*Proof.* We use the following formula abbreviations:

$$\begin{array}{lcl} C & \stackrel{\text{def}}{=} & @_c(ac * bc) \wedge @_d(ad * bd) \\ B & \stackrel{\text{def}}{=} & @_b(\top * \downarrow bc.\, @_b(\top * \downarrow bd.\, @_b(bc * bd) \wedge C)) \\ A & \stackrel{\text{def}}{=} & @_a(\top * \downarrow ac.\, @_a(\top * \downarrow ad.\, @_a(ac * ad) \wedge B)) \end{array}$$

Using the fact that $ac$, $ad$ and $a$ are distinct nominals, we have for any BBI-model $M = \langle W, \circ, E\rangle$, valuation $\rho$ and $w \in W$,

$$\begin{array}{l} M, w \models_\rho A \\ \Leftrightarrow M, \rho(a) \models_\rho \top * \downarrow ac.\, @_a(\top * \downarrow ad.\, @_a(ac * ad) \wedge B) \\ \Leftrightarrow \exists w', w_1.\, \rho(a) \in w' \circ w_1 \text{ and} \\ \qquad M, w_1 \models_\rho \downarrow ac.\, @_a(\top * \downarrow ad.\, @_a(ac * ad) \wedge B) \\ \qquad \Leftrightarrow M, w_1 \models_{\rho[ac:=w_1]} @_a(\top * \downarrow ad.\, @_a(ac * ad) \wedge B) \\ \qquad \Leftrightarrow M, \rho(a) \models_{\rho[ac:=w_1]} \top * \downarrow ad.\, @_a(ac * ad) \wedge B \\ \qquad \Leftrightarrow \exists w'', w_2.\, \rho(a) \in w'' \circ w_2 \text{ and} \\ \qquad\quad M, w_2 \models_{\rho[ac:=w_1]} \downarrow ad.\, @_a(ac * ad) \wedge B \\ \qquad\quad \Leftrightarrow M, w_2 \models_{\rho[ac:=w_1, ad:=w_2]} @_a(ac * ad) \wedge B \\ \qquad\quad \Leftrightarrow M, \rho(a) \models_{\rho[ac:=w_1, ad:=w_2]} (ac * ad) \wedge B \\ \Leftrightarrow \exists w_1, w_2.\, \rho(a) \in w_1 \circ w_2 \text{ and } M, \rho(a) \models_{\rho[ac:=w_1, ad:=w_2]} B \end{array}$$

By a similar chain of reasoning, we have

$$\begin{array}{l} M, \rho(a) \models_{\rho[ac:=w_1, ad:=w_2]} B \\ \Leftrightarrow \exists w_3, w_4.\, \rho(b) \in w_3 \circ w_4 \text{ and} \\ \qquad M, \rho(b) \models_{\rho[ac:=w_1, ad;=w_2, bc:=w_3, bd:=w_4]} C \end{array}$$

Finally, we have

$$\begin{array}{l} M, \rho(b) \models_{\rho[ac:=w_1, ad;=w_2, bc:=w_3, bd:=w_4]} C \\ \Leftrightarrow \rho(c) \in w_1 \circ w_3 \text{ and } \rho(d) \in w_2 \circ w_4 \end{array}$$

Putting everything together, we have

$$\begin{array}{l} M, w \models_\rho A \\ \Leftrightarrow \exists w_1, w_2, w_3, w_4.\, \rho(a) \in w_1 \circ w_2, \rho(b) \in w_3 \circ w_4, \\ \qquad \rho(c) \in w_1 \circ w_3, \rho(d) \in w_2 \circ w_4 \end{array}$$

With the above equivalence for $A$ in place, we can now show that (cs) defines the cross-split property of Definition 3.1.

($\Leftarrow$) Suppose $M$ has the cross-split property. We require to show that the formula (cs) is valid in $M$, i.e. that if $M, w \models_\rho (a * b) \wedge (c * d)$ then $M, w \models_\rho A$. Supposing $M, w \models_\rho (a * b) \wedge (c * d)$, we have $w \in (\rho(a) \circ \rho(b)) \cap (\rho(c) \circ \rho(d))$. By the cross-split property, there then exist $ac, ad, bc, bd \in W$ such that $\rho(a) \in ac \circ ad$, $\rho(b) \in bc \circ bd$, $\rho(c) \in ac \circ bc$ and $\rho(d) \in ad \circ bd$. Thus, by the equivalence above, $M, w \models_\rho A$ as required.

($\Rightarrow$) Suppose the formula (cs) is valid in $M$. We require to show that $M$ has the cross-split property. Suppose $w \in (t \circ u) \cap (v \circ w)$. Define a hybrid valuation $\rho$ for $M$ by

$$\rho(a) = t \qquad \rho(b) = u \qquad \rho(c) = v \qquad \rho(d) = w$$

where $a, b, c, d$ are distinct nominals. We have that $M, w \models_\rho (a * b) \wedge (c * d)$. Thus, as (cs) is valid in $M$, we have $M, w \models_\rho A$. Using the equivalence above, there then exist $tv, tw, uv, uw \in W$ such that $t \in tv \circ tw$, $u \in uv \circ uw$, $v \in tv \circ uv$ and $w \in tw \circ uw$ as required. □

The $\downarrow$ binder of HyBBI($\downarrow$) also allows us to encode the definition of the *overlapping conjunction* $\uplus$ of separation logic, which has been used in specifying and verifying programs manipulating data structures with intrinsic sharing [25, 16, 13]. In these works, $\uplus$ is introduced as an new primitive connective, defined by extending the standard forcing relation for BBI (Definition 2.3) as follows:

$$\begin{array}{l} M, w \models_\rho A_1 \uplus A_2 \\ \Leftrightarrow \exists w_1, w_2, w_3, w', w'' \in W. \\ \quad w' \in w_1 \circ w_2 \text{ and } w'' \in w_2 \circ w_3 \text{ and } w \in w' \circ w_3 \\ \quad \text{and } M, w' \models_\rho A_1 \text{ and } M, w'' \models_\rho A_2 \end{array}$$

We give below an equivalent formulation of $A_1 \uplus A_2$ solely in terms of HyBBI($\downarrow$) connectives. We conjecture that this is not possible in BBI (for arbitrary $A_1$ and $A_2$).

**Proposition 7.4.** *For any* HyBBI($\downarrow$) *formulas $A_1$ and $A_2$, the overlapping conjunction $A_1 \uplus A_2$ is definable via the following* HyBBI($\downarrow$) *formula, where $\ell$ and $\ell_s$ do not occur in $A_1$ or $A_2$:*

$$\downarrow\ell.\, \top * \downarrow\ell_s.\, @_\ell(\ell_s \multimap\!\!\circledast A_1) * (\ell_s \multimap\!\!\circledast A_2) * \ell_s$$

*Proof.* Let $M = \langle W, \circ, E\rangle$ be a BBI-model, $\rho$ a valuation for $M$, and $w \in W$.

$$\begin{array}{l} M, w \models_\rho \downarrow\ell.\, \top * \downarrow\ell_s.\, @_\ell(\ell_s \multimap\!\!\circledast A_1) * (\ell_s \multimap\!\!\circledast A_2) * \ell_s \\ \Leftrightarrow M, w \models_{\rho[\ell:=w]} \top * \downarrow\ell_s.\, @_\ell(\ell_s \multimap\!\!\circledast A_1) * (\ell_s \multimap\!\!\circledast A_2) * \ell_s \\ \Leftrightarrow w \in w_s' \circ w_s \text{ and} \\ \qquad M, w_s \models_{\rho[\ell:=w]} \downarrow\ell_s.\, @_\ell(\ell_s \multimap\!\!\circledast A_1) * (\ell_s \multimap\!\!\circledast A_2) * \ell_s \\ \qquad \Leftrightarrow M, w \models_{\rho[\ell:=w,\ell_s:=w_s]} (\ell_s \multimap\!\!\circledast A_1) * (\ell_s \multimap\!\!\circledast A_2) * \ell_s \\ \Leftrightarrow \exists w_1, w_2, w_3, w'.\, w' \in w_1 \circ w_2 \text{ and } w \in w' \circ w_3 \\ \quad \text{and } M, w_1 \models_{\rho'} \ell_s \multimap\!\!\circledast A_1 \text{ and } M, w_3 \models_{\rho'} \ell_s \multimap\!\!\circledast A_2 \\ \quad \text{and } M, w_2 \models_{\rho'} \ell_s \qquad \text{(letting } \rho' = \rho[\ell := w, \ell_s := w_s]) \end{array}$$

Notice now that

$$\begin{array}{l} M, w_1 \models_{\rho'} \ell_s \multimap\!\!\circledast A_1 \\ \Leftrightarrow \exists w', w_1'.\, w' \in w_1 \circ w_1' \text{ and } M, w_1' \models_{\rho'} \ell_s \text{ and } M, w' \models_{\rho'} A_1 \\ \Leftrightarrow \exists w'.\, w' \in w_1 \circ w_s \text{ and } M, w' \models_{\rho'} A_1 \end{array}$$

Consequently, after applying a similar line of reasoning to $w_3$,

$$\begin{array}{l} M, w \models_\rho \downarrow\ell.\, \top * \downarrow\ell_s.\, @_\ell(\ell_s \multimap\!\!\circledast A_1) * (\ell_s \multimap\!\!\circledast A_2) * \ell_s \\ \Leftrightarrow \exists w_1, w_2, w_3, w', w'' \in W.\, w' \in w_1 \circ w_2 \text{ and } w'' \in w_2 \circ w_3 \\ \quad \text{and } w \in w' \circ w_3 \text{ and } M, w' \models_{\rho'} A_1 \text{ and } M, w'' \models_{\rho'} A_2 \\ \Leftrightarrow M, w \models_{\rho'} A_1 \uplus A_2 \end{array}$$

Since $\ell$ and $\ell_s$ are sufficiently fresh, this is equivalent to $M, w \models_\rho A_1 \uplus A_2$. □

A three-place variant $A_1 \langle \uplus : B \rangle A_2$ of the overlapping conjunction was introduced in [9] to deal with some forms of specified sharing. This variant tags the shared core of $A_1$ and $A_2$ with a formula $B$ that it satisfies. Its satisfaction is defined as follows:

$$\begin{array}{l} M, w \models_\rho A_1 \langle \uplus : B \rangle A_2 \\ \Leftrightarrow \exists w_1, w_2, w_3, w', w'' \in W. \\ \quad w' \in w_1 \circ w_2 \text{ and } w'' \in w_2 \circ w_3 \text{ and } w \in w' \circ w_3 \\ \quad \text{and } M, w' \models_\rho A_1 \text{ and } M, w'' \models_\rho A_2 \text{ and } M, w_2 \models_\rho B \end{array}$$

It is easy to modify the defining HyBBI($\downarrow$)-formula of Proposition 7.4 so as to accommodate this variant:

$$\downarrow\ell.\, \top * \downarrow\ell_s.\, B \wedge @_\ell(\ell_s \multimap\!\!\circledast A_1) * (\ell_s \multimap\!\!\circledast A_2) * \ell_s$$

## 7.2 Proof theory, soundness and completeness

**Definition 7.5.** We define $\mathbf{K}_{\mathrm{HyBBI}(\downarrow)}$ to be the proof system obtained by adding the following axiom schema to $\mathbf{K}_{\mathrm{HyBBI}}$:

$$(\text{Bind}\downarrow) \qquad \vdash @_j(\downarrow\ell.\, B \leftrightarrow B[j/\ell])$$

**Lemma 7.6** (Nominal Substitution Lemma). *We have for any model $M = \langle W, \circ, E\rangle$, hybrid valuation $\rho$,* HyBBI($\downarrow$)*-formula $A$ and nominals $j, \ell$,*

$$M, \rho(j) \models_\rho A[j/\ell] \quad \Leftrightarrow \quad M, \rho(j) \models_{\rho[\ell:=\rho(j)]} A$$

*where $[j/\ell]$ is a (capture-avoiding) nominal substitution.*

*Proof.* By structural induction on $A$. The cases not involving nominals are straightforward. We examine the nominal cases, making use of the identity $\rho[\ell := \rho(j)](k) = \rho(k[j/\ell])$:

*Case $A = k \in \mathcal{N}$.* The required equivalence becomes:

$$\begin{array}{ll} & M, \rho(j) \models_\rho k[j/\ell] \Leftrightarrow M, \rho(j) \models_{\rho[\ell:=\rho(j)]} k \\ \text{i.e.} & \rho(j) = \rho(k[j/\ell]) \Leftrightarrow \rho(j) = \rho[\ell := \rho(j)](k) \end{array}$$

which follows from the identity above.

*Case $A = @_k B$.* We have $(@_k B)[j/\ell] = @_{k[j/\ell]} B[j/\ell]$ (noting that $@$ is not a binder, so the nominal substitution applies to the argument $k$), and proceed as follows:

$$\begin{array}{ll} M, \rho(j) \models_\rho @_{k[j/\ell]} B[j/\ell] & \\ \Leftrightarrow M, \rho(k[j/\ell]) \models_\rho B[j/\ell] & \\ \Leftrightarrow M, \rho[\ell := \rho(j)](k) \models_\rho B[j/\ell] & \text{(by above identity)} \\ \Leftrightarrow M, \rho[\ell := \rho(j)](k) \models_{\rho[\ell:=\rho(j)]} B & \text{(by ind. hyp.)} \\ \Leftrightarrow M, \rho(j) \models_{\rho[\ell:=\rho(j)]} @_k B & \end{array}$$

*Case $A = \downarrow k.\, B$.* Without loss of generality, we can assume that $k \neq \ell$. In this case, we have $(\downarrow k.\, B)[j/\ell] = \downarrow k.\, B[j/\ell]$, and can proceed as follows:

$$\begin{array}{ll} M, \rho(j) \models_\rho \downarrow k.\, B[j/\ell] & \\ \Leftrightarrow M, \rho(j) \models_{\rho[k:=\rho(j)]} B[j/\ell] & \\ \Leftrightarrow M, \rho(j) \models_{\rho[k:=\rho(j)][\ell:=\rho(j)]} B & \text{(by ind. hyp.)} \\ \Leftrightarrow M, \rho(j) \models_{\rho[\ell:=\rho(j)][k:=\rho(j)]} B & \\ \Leftrightarrow M, \rho(j) \models_{\rho[\ell:=\rho(j)]} \downarrow k.\, B & \end{array}$$

This completes all cases. □

**Proposition 7.7.** *Any $\mathbf{K}_{\mathrm{HyBBI}(\downarrow)}$-provable formula is valid.*

*Proof.* Given the soundness of $\mathbf{K}_{\mathrm{HyBBI}}$ (Proposition 5.2), we just need to show that the new axiom (Bind $\downarrow$) is valid in all BBI-models. Let $M = \langle W, \circ, E\rangle$ be a BBI-model, let $\rho$ be a valuation for $M$ and let $w \in W$. We need to show that

$$\begin{array}{ll} & M, w \models_\rho @_j((\downarrow\ell.\, B) \leftrightarrow B[j/\ell]) \\ \text{i.e.} & M, \rho(j) \models_\rho \downarrow\ell.\, B \Leftrightarrow M, \rho(j) \models_\rho B[j/\ell] \\ \text{i.e.} & M, \rho(j) \models_{\rho[\ell:=\rho(j)]} B \Leftrightarrow M, \rho(j) \models_\rho B[j/\ell] \end{array}$$

which is guaranteed by Lemma 7.6. □

We can obtain a parametric completeness result for $\mathbf{K}_{\mathrm{HyBBI}(\downarrow)}$ by repeating the Lindenbaum model construction for $\mathbf{K}_{\mathrm{HyBBI}}$ in Section 6. The only difference is that the crucial Truth Lemma needs to be extended to account for the $\downarrow$ binder case (cf. [2]).

**Lemma 7.8** (Extended Truth Lemma). *For any* HyBBI($\downarrow$)*-formula* $A$ *and* $\Delta \in W^\Gamma$, *we have* $M^\Gamma, \Delta \models_{\rho^\Gamma} A$ *if and only if* $A \in \Delta$.

*Proof.* By induction on the size of $A$, with all cases except $A = \downarrow\ell.\, B$ covered by Lemma 6.12. In this case, using the fact that $\Delta = \{A \mid @_j A \in \Gamma\}$ for some nominal $j$, we proceed as follows:

$$
\begin{aligned}
M^\Gamma, \Delta \models_{\rho^\Gamma} \downarrow\ell.\, B &\Leftrightarrow M^\Gamma, \Delta \models_{\rho^\Gamma[\ell:=\Delta]} B \\
&\Leftrightarrow M^\Gamma, \Delta \models_{\rho^\Gamma[\ell:=\rho^\Gamma(j)]} B \\
&\Leftrightarrow M^\Gamma, \Delta \models_{\rho^\Gamma} B[j/\ell] && \text{(by Lemma 7.6)} \\
&\Leftrightarrow B[j/\ell] \in \Delta && \text{(by ind. hyp.)} \\
&\Leftrightarrow @_j B[j/\ell] \in \Gamma
\end{aligned}
$$

Now since $\Gamma$ is an MCS and thus closed under ($K_@$) and the new axiom (Bind $\downarrow$), we have $@_j B[j/\ell] \in \Gamma$ if and only if $@_j \downarrow\ell.\, B \in \Gamma$ if and only if $\downarrow\ell.\, B \in \Delta$, which completes the case. □

**Theorem 7.9** (Completeness). *Let Ax be any set of pure* HyBBI($\downarrow$)*-formulas. Then if a* HyBBI($\downarrow$)*-formula is valid in the class of* BBI*-models satisfying Ax, then it is provable in* $\mathbf{K}_{\mathrm{HyBBI}(\downarrow)} + Ax$.

*Proof.* Exactly as Theorem 6.15, using the Extended Truth Lemma (Lemma 7.8) for HyBBI($\downarrow$) in place of Lemma 6.12. □

**Corollary 7.10.** *Let $\mathcal{S}$ be any separation theory from Definition 3.1, and let Ax be the set of pure* HyBBI($\downarrow$) *formulas defining the properties $\mathcal{S}$, as given by Corollary 4.4 and Proposition 7.3.*

*Then a* HyBBI($\downarrow$)*-formula is provable in* $\mathbf{K}_{\mathrm{HyBBI}(\downarrow)} + Ax$ *if and only if it is valid in the class of* BBI*-models satisfying $\mathcal{S}$.*

*Proof.* Follows from Props. 7.7, 7.3, Thm. 7.9 and Cor. 4.4. □

## 8. Conclusions and future work

In this paper, we show that many separation theories that arise naturally in applications of separation logic, and in particular the various notions of separation algebras introduced in the literature so far, are not definable in the standard propositional basis for separation logic, namely BBI. To overcome these limitations in expressivity, we introduce new hybrid versions of BBI, obtained by marrying BBI with the machinery of hybrid logic, in which the separation theories are definable. In addition, we show how to obtain axiomatic proof systems for these hybrid logics that are sound and complete for any separation theory obtained by combining properties from a list of those we found in the separation logic literature.

In future work, we plan to explore possible applications of our hybrid logics to program analysis, e.g. by adding support for nominals to separation logic. More broadly, we hope that our introduction of more expressive intermediaries between BBI and full first-order logic will help facilitate the expression and verification of more complex program properties, particularly those involving overlapping data structures.

## Acknowledgments

Many thanks to Hongseok Yang for pointing out to us the need for Lemma 6.10, and to Adam Barwell for crucial typing assistance.

Brotherston was supported by an EPSRC Career Acceleration Fellowship and Villard by the EPSRC grant EP/H008373/2.

## References

[1] P. Blackburn, M. de Rijke, and Y. Venema. *Modal Logic*. Cambridge University Press, 2001.

[2] P. Blackburn and B. ten Cate. Pure extensions, proof rules, and hybrid axiomatics. *Studia Logica*, 84(2), 2006.

[3] G. E. P. Box and N. R. Draper. *Empirical model-building and response surfaces*. Wiley series in probability and mathematical statistics. John Wiley & Sons, Inc., 1987.

[4] J. Brotherston and C. Calcagno. Classical BI: Its semantics and proof theory. *Logical Methods in Computer Science*, 6(3), 2010.

[5] J. Brotherston and M. Kanovich. Undecidability of propositional separation logic and its neighbours. To appear in *Journal of the ACM*.

[6] C. Calcagno, D. Distefano, P. O'Hearn, and H. Yang. Compositional shape analysis by means of bi-abduction. *Journal of the ACM*, 58(6), 2011.

[7] C. Calcagno, P. Gardner, and U. Zarfaty. Context logic as modal logic: Completeness and parametric inexpressivity. In *POPL-34*. ACM, 2007.

[8] C. Calcagno, P. O'Hearn, and H. Yang. Local action and abstract separation logic. In *LICS-22*. IEEE Computer Society, 2007.

[9] R. Cherini and J. O. Blanco. Local reasoning for abstraction and sharing. In *SAC-24*. ACM, 2009.

[10] C. David and W.-N. Chin. Immutable specifications for more concise and precise verification. In *OOPSLA-11*. ACM, 2011.

[11] T. Dinsdale-Young, L. Birkedal, P. Gardner, M. J. Parkinson, and H. Yang. Views: compositional reasoning for concurrent programs. In *POPL-40*. ACM, 2013.

[12] R. Dockins, A. Hobor, and A. W. Appel. A fresh look at separation algebras and share accounting. In *APLAS-7*. Springer, 2009.

[13] G. J. Duck, J. Jaffar, and N. C. H. Koh. Constraint-based program reasoning with heaps and separation. 2013. To appear in *CP-19*.

[14] D. Galmiche and D. Larchey-Wendling. Expressivity properties of Boolean BI through relational models. In *FSTTCS-26*. Springer, 2006.

[15] K. Gödel. On formally undecidable propositions of Principia Mathematica and related systems. 1962. English translation by B. Meltzer.

[16] A. Hobor and J. Villard. The ramifications of sharing in data structures. In *POPL-40*. ACM, 2013.

[17] Z. Hou, A. Tiu, and R. Goré. A labelled sequent calculus for Boolean BI: Proof theory and proof search. To appear in *TABLEAUX-22*, 2013.

[18] S. Ishtiaq and P. W. O'Hearn. BI as an assertion language for mutable data structures. In *POPL-28*. ACM, 2001.

[19] D. Larchey-Wendling. The formal strong completeness of Boolean BI. Submitted, 2012.

[20] D. Larchey-Wendling and D. Galmiche. Exploring the relation between intuitionistic BI and Boolean BI: An unexpected embedding. *Mathematical Structures in Computer Science*, 19(3), 2009.

[21] D. Larchey-Wendling and D. Galmiche. The undecidability of Boolean BI through phase semantics. In *LICS-25*. IEEE Computer Society, 2010.

[22] J. Park, J. Seo, and S. Park. A theorem prover for Boolean BI. In *POPL-40*. ACM, 2013.

[23] D. Pym. *The Semantics and Proof Theory of the Logic of Bunched Implications*. Applied Logic Series. Kluwer, 2002.

[24] J. C. Reynolds. Separation logic: A logic for shared mutable data structures. In *LICS-17*. IEEE Computer Society, 2002.

[25] J. C. Reynolds. A short course on separation logic. `http://www.cs.cmu.edu/afs/cs.cmu.edu/project/fox-19/member/jcr/wwwaac2003/aac.html`, 2003.

[26] H. Yang, O. Lee, J. Berdine, C. Calcagno, B. Cook, D. Distefano, and P. O'Hearn. Scalable shape analysis for systems code. In *CAV-20*. Springer, 2008.

# Proof Search for Propositional Abstract Separation Logics via Labelled Sequents

Zhé Hóu Ranald Clouston Rajeev Goré

Research School of Computer Science
The Australian National University
{zhe.hou,ranald.clouston,rajeev.gore}@anu.edu.au

Alwen Tiu

Research School of Computer Science
The Australian National University &
School of Computer Engineering
Nanyang Technological University
atiu@ntu.edu.sg

## Abstract

Abstract separation logics are a family of extensions of Hoare logic for reasoning about programs that mutate memory. These logics are "abstract" because they are independent of any particular concrete memory model. Their assertion languages, called propositional abstract separation logics, extend the logic of (Boolean) Bunched Implications (BBI) in various ways.

We develop a modular proof theory for various propositional abstract separation logics using cut-free labelled sequent calculi. We first extend the cut-fee labelled sequent calculus for BBI of Hóu et al to handle Calcagno et al's original logic of separation algebras by adding sound rules for partial-determinism and cancellativity, while preserving cut-elimination. We prove the completeness of our calculus via a sound intermediate calculus that enables us to construct counter-models from the failure to find a proof. We then capture other propositional abstract separation logics by adding sound rules for indivisible unit and disjointness, while maintaining completeness and cut-elimination. We present a theorem prover based on our labelled calculus for these logics.

***Categories and Subject Descriptors*** F.3.1 [*Specifying and Verifying and Reasoning about Programs*]: Logics of programs

***General Terms*** Languages, Theory, Verification

***Keywords*** Abstract separation logics, automated reasoning, labelled sequents , counter-model construction, bunched implications

## 1. Introduction

Separation logic (SL) [29] is an extension of Hoare logic for reasoning about programs that explicitly mutate memory. This is achieved via an assertion language that, along with the usual (additive) connectives and predicates for first-order logic with arithmetic, has the multiplicative connectives *separating conjunction* $*$, its unit $\top^*$, and *separating implication*, or *magic wand*, $-\!*$ , from the logic of Bunched Implications (BI) [26], as well as the *points-to* predicate $\mapsto$. The additive connectives may be either intuitionistic, as for BI, or classical, as for the logic of *Boolean* Bunched Implications (BBI). Classical additives are more expressive as they support reasoning about non-monotonic commands such as memory deallocation, and assertions such as "the heap is empty" [17]. In this paper we consider classical additives only.

The assertion language of SL must provide a notion of inference to support precondition strengthening and postcondition weakening, yet little such proof theory exists, despite its link with the proof-theoretically motivated BI. Instead, inference must proceed via reasoning directly about the concrete semantics of *heaps*, or finite partial functions from addresses to values. A heap satisfies $P * Q$ iff it can be partitioned into heaps satisfying $P$ and $Q$ respectively; it satisfies $\top^*$ iff it is empty; it satisfies $P -\!* Q$ iff any extension with a heap that satisfies $P$ must then satisfy $Q$; and it satisfies $E \mapsto E'$ iff it is a singleton map sending the address specified by the expression $E$ to the value specified by the expression $E'$. Such concrete semantics are appropriate for proving the correctness of a specific program in a specific environment, but mean that if a different notion of memory (or more generally, resource) is required then a new logic is also required.

Calcagno et al's Abstract Separation Logic (ASL) [8] introduced the abstract semantics of partial cancellative monoids, or *separation algebras*, to unify notions of resources for heaps, heaps with permissions, Petri nets, and other examples. These semantics allow interpretation of $*$, $\top^*$ and $-\!*$ , although the latter is not considered by Calcagno et al. However $\mapsto$ has no meaning in separation algebras in general, and is therefore not a first class citizen of ASL; it may be introduced as a predicate only if an appropriate concrete separation algebra is fixed. Calcagno et al do not consider proof theory for their assertion language, whose propositional fragment we call Propositional Abstract Separation Logic (PASL), but separation algebras are a restriction of *non-deterministic monoids*, which are known to give sound and complete semantics for BBI [13]. In this sense PASL is a refinement of BBI, differing only by the addition of the semantic properties of *partial-determinism* and *cancellativity*.

This link between BBI and PASL semantics raises the question of whether existing proof theory for BBI can be extended to give a sound and cut-free complete proof system for PASL; we answer this question in the affirmative by extending the labelled sequent calculus $LS_{BBI}$ of Hóu et al [16] by adding explicit rules for partial-determinism and cancellativity. The completeness of $LS_{BBI}$ was demonstrated via the Hilbert axiomatisation of BBI, but this avenue is not open to us as partial-determinism and cancellativity are not axiomatisable in BBI [6]; instead completeness follows via a *counter-model construction* procedure. A novelty of



*POPL '14*, January 22–24, 2014, San Diego, CA, USA.
Copyright © 2014 ACM 978-1-4503-2544-8/14/01 . . . $15.00.
http://dx.doi.org/10.1145/2535838.2535864

our counter-model construction is that it can be modularly extended to handle extensions and sublogics of PASL.

We have also implemented proof search using our calculus (although no decision procedure for PASL is possible [5]). To our knowledge this is the first proof to be presented of the cut-free completeness of a calculus for PASL[1], and our implementation is the first automated theorem prover for PASL.

Just as we have a family of separation logics, ranging across different concrete semantics, we now also have a family of abstract separation logics for different abstract semantics. These abstract semantics are often expressed as extensions of the usual notion of separation algebra; most notably Dockins et al [11] suggested the additional properties of positivity (here called *indivisible unit*), *disjointness*, *cross-split*, and *splittability*[2]. Conversely, the abstract semantics for Fictional Separation Logic [18] generalise separation algebras by dropping cancellativity. Hence there is demand for a modular approach to proof theory and proof search for propositional abstract separation logics. Labelled sequent calculi, with their explicitly semantics-based rules, provide good support for this modularity, as rules for the various properties can be added and removed as required. We investigate which properties can be combined without sacrificing our cut-free completeness result.

While we work with abstract models of separation logics, the reasoning principles behind our proof-theoretic methods should be applicable to concrete models also, so we investigate as further work how concrete predicates such as $\mapsto$ might be integrated into our approach. Proof search strategies that come out of our proof-theoretic analysis could also potentially be applied to guide proof search in various encodings of separation logics [1, 24, 30] in proof assistants, e.g., they can guide the constructions of proof tactics needed to automate the reasoning tasks in those embeddings.

***Acknowledgment.*** This work is partly supported by the Australian Research Council Discovery Grant DP110103173.

## 2. The labelled sequent calculus for PASL

In this section we define the *separation algebra* semantics of Calcagno et al [8] for Propositional Abstract Separation Logic (PASL), and present the labelled sequent calculus $LS_{PASL}$ for this logic, adapting the calculus $LS_{BBI}$ for BBI of Hóu et al [16]. Soundness and cut-elimination are then demonstrated for $LS_{PASL}$.

### 2.1 Propositional abstract separation logic

The formulae of PASL are defined inductively as follows, where $p$ ranges over some set $Var$ of propositional variables:

$$A ::= p \mid \top \mid \bot \mid \neg A \mid A \vee A \mid A \wedge A \mid A \rightarrow A \mid \top^* \mid A * A \mid A \mathrel{-\!\!*} A$$

PASL-formulae are interpreted according to the semantics below.

**Definition 2.1.** A *separation algebra*, or partial cancellative commutative monoid, is a triple $(H, \circ, \epsilon)$ where $H$ is a non-empty set, $\circ$ is a partial binary function $H \times H \rightharpoonup H$ written infix, and $\epsilon \in H$, satisfying the following conditions, where '=' is interpreted as 'both sides undefined, or both sides defined and equal':

**identity:** $\forall h \in H.\, h \circ \epsilon = h$
**commutativity:** $\forall h_1, h_2 \in H.\, h_1 \circ h_2 = h_2 \circ h_1$
**associativity:** $\forall h_1, h_2, h_3 \in H.\, h_1 \circ (h_2 \circ h_3) = (h_1 \circ h_2) \circ h_3$
**cancellativity:** $\forall h_1, h_2, h_3, h_4 \in H.$ if $h_1 \circ h_2 = h_3$ and $h_1 \circ h_4 = h_3$ then $h_2 = h_4$

The paradigmatic example of a separation algebra is the set of *heaps*; here $\circ$ is the combination of two heaps with disjoint domain, and $\epsilon$ is the empty heap.

In the paper we prefer to express PASL semantics in the style of *ternary relations*, to maintain consistency with the earlier work of Hóu et al on BBI [16]; it is easy to see that the definition below is a trivial notational variant of Def. 2.1.

**Definition 2.2.** A *PASL Kripke relational frame* is a triple $(H, R, \epsilon)$, where $H$ is a non-empty set of *worlds*, $R \subseteq H \times H \times H$, and $\epsilon \in H$, satisfying the following conditions for all $h_1, h_2, h_3, h_4, h_5$ in $H$:

**identity:** $R(h_1, \epsilon, h_2)$ iff $h_1 = h_2$
**commutativity:** $R(h_1, h_2, h_3)$ iff $R(h_2, h_1, h_3)$
**associativity:** if $R(h_1, h_5, h_4)$ and $R(h_2, h_3, h_5)$ then there exists $h_6$ such that $R(h_6, h_3, h_4)$ and $R(h_1, h_2, h_6)$
**cancellativity:** if $R(h_1, h_2, h_3)$ and $R(h_1, h_4, h_3)$ then $h_2 = h_4$
**partial-determinism:** if $R(h_1, h_2, h_3)$ and $R(h_1, h_2, h_4)$ then $h_3 = h_4$

A *PASL Kripke relational model* is a tuple $(H, R, \epsilon, \nu)$ of a PASL Kripke relational frame $(H, R, \epsilon)$ and a *valuation* function $\nu : Var \rightarrow \mathcal{P}(H)$, where $\mathcal{P}(H)$ is the power set of $H$. The forcing relation $\Vdash$ between a model $\mathcal{M} = (H, R, \epsilon, \nu)$ and a formula is defined in Table 1, where we write $\mathcal{M}, h \not\Vdash A$ for the negation of $\mathcal{M}, h \Vdash A$. Given a model $\mathcal{M} = (H, R, \epsilon, \nu)$, a formula is *true at (world)* $h$ iff $\mathcal{M}, h \Vdash A$. The formula $A$ is *valid* iff it is true at all worlds of all models.

### 2.2 The labelled sequent calculus $LS_{PASL}$

Let $LVar$ be an infinite set of *label variables*, and let the set $\mathcal{L}$ of *labels* be $LVar \cup \{\epsilon\}$, where $\epsilon$ is a label constant not in $LVar$; here we overload the notation for the identity world in the semantics. Labels will be denoted by lower-case letters such as $a, b, x, y, z$. A *labelled formula* is a pair $a : A$ of a label $a$ and formula $A$. As usual in a labelled sequent calculus one needs to incorporate Kripke relations explicitly into the sequents. This is achieved via the syntactic notion of *relational atoms*, which have the form $(a, b \triangleright c)$, where $a, b, c$ are labels. A *sequent* takes the form

$$\mathcal{G}; \Gamma \vdash \Delta$$

where $\mathcal{G}$ is a set of relational atoms, and $\Gamma$ and $\Delta$ are multisets of labelled formulae. Then, $\Gamma; A$ is the multiset union of $\Gamma$ and $\{A\}$.

As the interpretation of the logical connectives of PASL are the same as those for BBI, we may obtain a labelled sequent calculus for PASL, called $LS_{PASL}$, by adding the rules $P$ (partial-determinism) and $C$ (cancellativity) to $LS_{BBI}$ [16]. The rules for $LS_{PASL}$ are presented in Fig. 1, where $p$ is a propositional variable, $A, B$ are formulae, and $w, x, y, z \in \mathcal{L}$. Note that some rules use *label substitutions*. We write $\Gamma[y/x]$ (resp. $\mathcal{G}[y/x]$) for the set of labelled formulae (resp. relational atoms) for which the label variable $x$ has been uniformly replaced by the label $y$. In each rule, the formula (resp. relational atom) shown explicitly in the conclusion is called the *principal* formula (resp. relational atom). A rule with no premise is called a zero-premise rule. Note that the $\rightarrow L$ rule is the classical implication left rule.

A function $\rho : \mathcal{L} \rightarrow H$ from labels to worlds is a *label mapping* iff it satisfies $\rho(\epsilon) = \epsilon$, mapping the label constant $\epsilon$ to the identity world of $H$. Thus we define an *extended PASL Kripke relational model* $(H, R, \epsilon, \nu, \rho)$ as a model equipped with a label mapping.

**Definition 2.3** (Sequent Falsifiability). A sequent $\mathcal{G}; \Gamma \vdash \Delta$ is *falsifiable in an extended model* $\mathcal{M} = (H, R, \epsilon, \nu, \rho)$ if for every

[1] Larchey-Wendling [20] claims that the tableaux for BBI with partial-determinism in [21] can be extended to cover cancellativity, but the "rather involved" proof has not appeared yet.

[2] Dockins et al [11] also suggest generalising separation algebras to have a *set* of units; it is an easy corollary of [6, Lem. 3.11] that single-unit and multiple-unit separation algebras satisfy the same set of formulae.

| | | | | | |
|---|---|---|---|---|---|
| $\mathcal{M}, h \Vdash p$ | iff | $p \in Var$ and $h \in v(p)$ | $\mathcal{M}, h \Vdash \top$ | iff | always |
| $\mathcal{M}, h \Vdash \bot$ | iff | never | $\mathcal{M}, h \Vdash \neg A$ | iff | $\mathcal{M}, h \not\Vdash A$ |
| $\mathcal{M}, h \Vdash A \wedge B$ | iff | $\mathcal{M}, h \Vdash A$ and $\mathcal{M}, h \Vdash B$ | $\mathcal{M}, h \Vdash A \vee B$ | iff | $\mathcal{M}, h \Vdash A$ or $\mathcal{M}, h \Vdash B$ |
| $\mathcal{M}, h \Vdash A \rightarrow B$ | iff | $\mathcal{M}, h \not\Vdash A$ or $\mathcal{M}, h \Vdash B$ | $\mathcal{M}, h \Vdash \top^*$ | iff | $h = \epsilon$ |

$\mathcal{M}, h \Vdash A * B$ iff $\exists h_1, h_2.(R(h_1, h_2, h)$ and $\mathcal{M}, h_1 \Vdash A$ and $\mathcal{M}, h_2 \Vdash B)$

$\mathcal{M}, h \Vdash A \mathrel{-\!\!*} B$ iff $\forall h_1, h_2.((R(h, h_1, h_2)$ and $\mathcal{M}, h_1 \Vdash A)$ implies $\mathcal{M}, h_2 \Vdash B)$

**Table 1.** Semantics of PASL, where $\mathcal{M} = (H, R, \epsilon, \nu)$.

**Identity and Cut:**

$$\frac{}{\mathcal{G};\Gamma;w:p \vdash w:p;\Delta}\ id \qquad \frac{\mathcal{G};\Gamma \vdash x:A;\Delta \quad \mathcal{G}';\Gamma';x:A \vdash \Delta'}{\mathcal{G};\mathcal{G}';\Gamma;\Gamma' \vdash \Delta;\Delta'}\ cut$$

**Logical Rules:**

$$\frac{}{\mathcal{G};\Gamma;w:\bot \vdash \Delta}\ \bot L \qquad \frac{(\epsilon, w \triangleright \epsilon);\mathcal{G};\Gamma \vdash \Delta}{\mathcal{G};\Gamma;w:\top^* \vdash \Delta}\ \top^* L \qquad \frac{}{\mathcal{G};\Gamma \vdash w:\top;\Delta}\ \top R \qquad \frac{}{\mathcal{G};\Gamma \vdash \epsilon:\top^*;\Delta}\ \top^* R$$

$$\frac{\mathcal{G};\Gamma;w:A;w:B \vdash \Delta}{\mathcal{G};\Gamma;w:A \wedge B \vdash \Delta}\ \wedge L \qquad \frac{\mathcal{G};\Gamma \vdash w:A;\Delta \quad \mathcal{G};\Gamma \vdash w:B;\Delta}{\mathcal{G};\Gamma \vdash w:A \wedge B;\Delta}\ \wedge R$$

$$\frac{\mathcal{G};\Gamma \vdash w:A;\Delta \quad \mathcal{G};\Gamma;w:B \vdash \Delta}{\mathcal{G};\Gamma;w:A \rightarrow B \vdash \Delta}\ \rightarrow L \qquad \frac{\mathcal{G};\Gamma;w:A \vdash w:B;\Delta}{\mathcal{G};\Gamma \vdash w:A \rightarrow B;\Delta}\ \rightarrow R$$

$$\frac{(x, y \triangleright z);\mathcal{G};\Gamma;x:A;y:B \vdash \Delta}{\mathcal{G};\Gamma;z:A * B \vdash \Delta}\ *L \qquad \frac{(x, z \triangleright y);\mathcal{G};\Gamma;x:A \vdash y:B;\Delta}{\mathcal{G};\Gamma \vdash z:A \mathrel{-\!\!*} B;\Delta}\ \mathrel{-\!\!*} R$$

$$\frac{(x, y \triangleright z);\mathcal{G};\Gamma \vdash x:A;z:A * B;\Delta \quad (x, y \triangleright z);\mathcal{G};\Gamma \vdash y:B;z:A * B;\Delta}{(x, y \triangleright z);\mathcal{G};\Gamma \vdash z:A * B;\Delta}\ *R$$

$$\frac{(x, y \triangleright z);\mathcal{G};\Gamma;y:A \mathrel{-\!\!*} B \vdash x:A;\Delta \quad (x, y \triangleright z);\mathcal{G};\Gamma;y:A \mathrel{-\!\!*} B;z:B \vdash \Delta}{(x, y \triangleright z);\mathcal{G};\Gamma;y:A \mathrel{-\!\!*} B \vdash \Delta}\ \mathrel{-\!\!*} L$$

**Structural Rules:**

$$\frac{(y, x \triangleright z);(x, y \triangleright z);\mathcal{G};\Gamma \vdash \Delta}{(x, y \triangleright z);\mathcal{G};\Gamma \vdash \Delta}\ E \qquad \frac{(u, w \triangleright z);(y, v \triangleright w);(x, y \triangleright z);(u, v \triangleright x);\mathcal{G};\Gamma \vdash \Delta}{(x, y \triangleright z);(u, v \triangleright x);\mathcal{G};\Gamma \vdash \Delta}\ A$$

$$\frac{(x, \epsilon \triangleright x);\mathcal{G};\Gamma \vdash \Delta}{\mathcal{G};\Gamma \vdash \Delta}\ U \qquad \frac{(x, w \triangleright x);(y, y \triangleright w);(x, y \triangleright x);\mathcal{G};\Gamma \vdash \Delta}{(x, y \triangleright x);\mathcal{G};\Gamma \vdash \Delta}\ A_C$$

$$\frac{(\epsilon, w' \triangleright w');\mathcal{G}[w'/w];\Gamma[w'/w] \vdash \Delta[w'/w]}{(\epsilon, w \triangleright w');\mathcal{G};\Gamma \vdash \Delta}\ Eq_1 \qquad \frac{(\epsilon, w' \triangleright w');\mathcal{G}[w'/w];\Gamma[w'/w] \vdash \Delta[w'/w]}{(\epsilon, w' \triangleright w);\mathcal{G};\Gamma \vdash \Delta}\ Eq_2$$

$$\frac{(x, y \triangleright z);\mathcal{G}[z/w];\Gamma[z/w] \vdash \Delta[z/w]}{(x, y \triangleright z);(x, y \triangleright w);\mathcal{G};\Gamma \vdash \Delta}\ P \qquad \frac{(x, y \triangleright z);\mathcal{G}[y/w];\Gamma[y/w] \vdash \Delta[y/w]}{(x, y \triangleright z);(x, w \triangleright z);\mathcal{G};\Gamma \vdash \Delta}\ C$$

**Side conditions:**
Only label variables (not $\epsilon$) may be substituted for.
In the rule $A$, $A_C$, the label $w$ does not occur in the conclusion.
In $*L$ and $\mathrel{-\!\!*} R$, the labels $x$ and $y$ do not occur in the conclusion.

**Figure 1.** The labelled sequent calculus $LS_{PASL}$ for Propositional Abstract Separation Logic.

$x : A \in \Gamma$, $(a, b \triangleright c) \in \mathcal{G}$, and for every $y : B \in \Delta$, we have $(\mathcal{M}, \rho(x) \Vdash A)$, $R(\rho(a), \rho(b), \rho(c))$ and $(\mathcal{M}, \rho(y) \not\Vdash B)$. It is *falsifiable* if it is falsifiable in some extended model.

**Theorem 2.1** (Soundness)**.** *For any formula $A$, and for an arbitrary label $w$, if the labelled sequent $\vdash w : A$ is derivable in $LS_{PASL}$ then $A$ is valid.*

*Proof.* We prove that the rules of $LS_{PASL}$ preserve falsifiability upwards. The proof is straightforward so we omit the details; but refer the interested reader to a similar proof for $LS_{BBI}$ [16]. □

### 2.3 Cut-elimination

The only differences between $LS_{PASL}$ and $LS_{BBI}$ [16] are the additions of the structural rules $P$ and $C$, so we may prove cut-elimination by the same route, which in turn follows from the usual cut-elimination procedure for labelled sequent calculi for modal logics [25]. We therefore omit full proof details and simply list the necessary lemmas. We use $ht(\Pi)$ to denote the height of the derivation $\Pi$.

**Lemma 2.2** (Substitution)**.** *If $\Pi$ is an $LS_{PASL}$ derivation for the sequent $\mathcal{G};\Gamma \vdash \Delta$ then there is an $LS_{PASL}$ derivation $\Pi'$ of the sequent $\mathcal{G}[y/x];\Gamma[y/x] \vdash \Delta[y/x]$ such that $ht(\Pi') \leq ht(\Pi)$.*

**Lemma 2.3** (Admissibility of weakening). *If $\mathcal{G};\Gamma \vdash \Delta$ is derivable in $LS_{PASL}$, then for all structures $\mathcal{G},\Gamma'$ and $\Delta'$, the sequent $\mathcal{G};\mathcal{G}';\Gamma;\Gamma' \vdash \Delta;\Delta'$ is derivable with the same height in $LS_{PASL}$.*

**Lemma 2.4** (Invertibility). *If $\Pi$ is a cut-free $LS_{PASL}$ derivation of the conclusion of a rule, then there is a cut-free $LS_{PASL}$ derivation for each premise, with height at most $ht(\Pi)$.*

**Lemma 2.5** (Admissibility of contraction). *If $\mathcal{G};\mathcal{G};\Gamma;\Gamma \vdash \Delta;\Delta$ is derivable in $LS_{PASL}$, then $\mathcal{G};\Gamma \vdash \Delta$ is derivable with the same height in $LS_{PASL}$.*

**Theorem 2.6** (Cut-elimination). *If $\mathcal{G};\Gamma \vdash \Delta$ is derivable in $LS_{PASL}$ then it is derivable without using the cut rule.*

*Proof.* The proof follows the same structure as that for $LS_{BBI}$, utilising the lemmas above. The additional cases we need to consider are those involving the rules $P$ and $C$; their treatment is similar to that for $Eq_1$ in the proof for $LS_{BBI}$ [16]. □

## 3. Completeness of $LS_{PASL}$

We prove the completeness of $LS_{PASL}$ with respect to the Kripke relational semantics by a counter-model construction. A standard way to construct a counter-model for an unprovable sequent is to show that it can be saturated by repeatedly applying all applicable inference rules to reach a limit sequent where a counter-model can be constructed. In adopting such a counter-model construction strategy to $LS_{PASL}$ we encounter difficulty in formulating the saturation conditions for rules involving label substitutions. We therefore adopt the approach of Hóu et al [16], using an intermediate system without explicit use of label substitutions, but where equivalences between labels are captured via an entailment $\vdash_E$.

Let $r$ be an instance of a structural rule in which the substitution used is $\theta$: this is the identity substitution except when $r$ is $Eq_1$, $Eq_2$, $P$ or $C$. We can view $r$ (upwards) as a function that takes a set of relational atoms (in the conclusion of the rule) and outputs another set (in the premise). We write $r(\mathcal{G},\theta)$ for the output relational atoms of an instance of $r$ with substitution $\theta$ and with conclusion containing $\mathcal{G}$. Let $\sigma$ be a sequence of instances of structural rules $[r_1(\mathcal{G}_1,\theta_1);\cdots;r_n(\mathcal{G}_n,\theta_n)]$. Given a set of relational atoms $\mathcal{G}$, the result of the (backward) application of $\sigma$ to $\mathcal{G}$, denoted by $\mathcal{S}(\mathcal{G},\sigma)$, is defined as below, where $^\frown$ is used for sequence concatenation:

$$\mathcal{S}(\mathcal{G},\sigma) = \begin{cases} \mathcal{G} & \text{if } \sigma = [\,] \\ \mathcal{S}(\mathcal{G}\theta \cup r(\mathcal{G}',\theta),\sigma') & \text{if } \mathcal{G}' \subseteq \mathcal{G} \text{ and} \\ & \sigma = [r(\mathcal{G}',\theta)]^\frown\sigma' \\ \text{undefined} & \text{otherwise} \end{cases}$$

Given $\sigma = [r_1(\mathcal{G}_1,\theta_1);\cdots;r_n(\mathcal{G}_n,\theta_n)]$, let $subst(\sigma)$ be the composite substitution $\theta_1 \circ \cdots \circ \theta_n$, where $t(\theta_1 \circ \theta_2)$ means $(t\theta_1)\theta_2$. We write $s \equiv t$ to mean that $s$ and $t$ are syntactically equal.

**Definition 3.1** (Equivalence entailment). Let $\mathcal{G}$ be a set of relational atoms. The entailment relation $\mathcal{G} \vdash_E (a = b)$ holds iff there exists a sequence $\sigma$ of $Eq_1, Eq_2, P, C$ applications such that $\mathcal{S}(\mathcal{G},\sigma)$ is defined, and $a\theta \equiv b\theta$, where $\theta = subst(\sigma)$.

Since substitution is no longer in the calculus, some inference rules that involve matching two equal labels need to be changed. We define the intermediate system $ILS_{PASL}$ as $LS_{PASL}$ minus $\{Eq_1, Eq_2, P, C\}$, with certain rules changed following Fig. 2. Note that the equivalence entailment $\vdash_E$ is not a premise, but rather a condition of the rules.

Given a set of relational atoms $\mathcal{G}$, we define the relation $=_\mathcal{G}$ as follows: $a =_\mathcal{G} b$ iff $\mathcal{G} \vdash_E (a = b)$. We show next that $=_\mathcal{G}$ is in fact an equivalence relation. This equivalence relation will be useful in our counter-model construction later.

**Lemma 3.1.** *Let $\mathcal{G}$ be a set of relational atoms, if $\mathcal{G} \vdash_E (a = b)$ by applying $\sigma_1$ and $\mathcal{G} \vdash_E (c = d)$ by applying $\sigma_2$, then $\exists\sigma_3$ such that $\mathcal{S}(\mathcal{G},\sigma_1) \vdash_E (c\theta = d\theta)$ by $\sigma_3$, where $\theta = subst(\sigma_1)$.*

*Proof.* Note that $\mathcal{S}(\mathcal{G},\sigma_1) = \mathcal{G}\theta$. So essentially we need to show that if $\mathcal{G} \vdash_E (c = d)$, then $\mathcal{G}\theta \vdash_E (c\theta = d\theta)$. This is a consequence of the substitution Lemma 2.2. □

**Lemma 3.2.** *Given a set of relational atoms $\mathcal{G}$, the relation $=_\mathcal{G}$ is an equivalence relation on the set of labels.*

*Proof.* We show that $\vdash_E$ satisfies the following conditions:

**Reflexivity:** for any label $a$ that occurs in $\mathcal{G}$, we have $\mathcal{G} \vdash_E (a = a)$ by applying an empty sequence of $Eq_1, Eq_2, P, C$ rules.

**Symmetry:** if $\mathcal{G} \vdash_E (x = y)$, via a sequence $\sigma$ of $Eq_1, Eq_2, P, C$ applications. Let $\theta = subst(\sigma)$, then by definition $x\theta \equiv y\theta$ in $\mathcal{G}\theta$. Thus $y\theta \equiv x\theta$, and we obtain that $\mathcal{G} \vdash_E (y = x)$.

**Transitivity:** if $\mathcal{G} \vdash_E (x = y)$ and $\mathcal{G} \vdash_E (y = z)$, then by Lemma 3.1 we obtain a sequence $\sigma$ of $Eq_1, Eq_2, P, C$ applications, and let $\theta = subst(\sigma)$, then $x\theta \equiv y\theta \equiv z\theta$. Thus $\mathcal{G} \vdash_E (x = z)$. □

The intermediate system $ILS_{PASL}$ is equivalent to $LS_{PASL}$, i.e., every sequent provable in $ILS_{PASL}$ is also provable in $LS_{PASL}$, and vice versa. This connection is easy to make, as is shown by Hóu et al. [16]. Properties such as contraction admissibility, closure under substitution etc. also hold for $ILS_{PASL}$.

**Lemma 3.3.** *The intermediate labelled calculus $ILS_{PASL}$ is equivalent to $LS_{PASL}$.*

We now give a counter-model construction procedure for $ILS_{PASL}$ which, by Lemma 3.3, applies to $LS_{PASL}$ as well. In the construction, we assume that labelled sequents such as $\mathcal{G};\Gamma \vdash \Delta$ are built from **sets** $\mathcal{G},\Gamma,\Delta$ rather than **multisets**. This is harmless since contraction is admissible in our calculus.

As the counter-model construction involves infinite sets and sequents, we extend the definition of $\vdash_E$ appropriately as below.

**Definition 3.2.** A (possibly infinite) set $\mathcal{G}$ of relational atoms satisfies $\mathcal{G} \vdash_E (x = y)$ iff $\mathcal{G}_f \vdash_E (x = y)$ for some finite $\mathcal{G}_f \subseteq \mathcal{G}$.

Given a set of relational atoms $\mathcal{G}$, the equivalence relation $=_\mathcal{G}$ partitions $\mathcal{L}$ into equivalence classes $[a]_\mathcal{G}$ for each label $a \in \mathcal{L}$:

$$[a]_\mathcal{G} = \{a' \in \mathcal{L} \mid a =_\mathcal{G} a'\}.$$

The counter-model procedure is essentially a procedure to saturate a sequent by applying all applicable rules repeatedly. The aim is to obtain an infinite saturated sequent from which a counter-model can be extracted. We first define a list of desired properties of such an infinite sequent which would allow the counter-model construction. This is given in the following definition.

**Definition 3.3** (Hintikka sequent). A labelled sequent $\mathcal{G};\Gamma \vdash \Delta$ is a *Hintikka sequent* if it satisfies the following conditions for any formulae $A, B$ and any labels $a, a', b, c, d, e, z$:

1. It is not the case that $a : A \in \Gamma$, $b : A \in \Delta$ and $a =_\mathcal{G} b$.
2. If $a : A \wedge B \in \Gamma$ then $a : A \in \Gamma$ and $a : B \in \Gamma$.
3. If $a : A \wedge B \in \Delta$ then $a : A \in \Delta$ or $a : B \in \Delta$.
4. If $a : A \to B \in \Gamma$ then $a : A \in \Delta$ or $a : B \in \Gamma$.
5. If $a : A \to B \in \Delta$ then $a : A \in \Gamma$ and $a : B \in \Delta$.
6. If $a : \top^* \in \Gamma$ then $a =_\mathcal{G} \epsilon$.
7. If $a : \top^* \in \Delta$ then $a \neq_\mathcal{G} \epsilon$.
8. If $z : A * B \in \Gamma$ then $\exists x, y, z'$ such that $(x, y \triangleright z') \in \mathcal{G}$, $z =_\mathcal{G} z'$, $x : A \in \Gamma$ and $y : B \in \Gamma$.
9. If $z : A * B \in \Delta$ then $\forall x, y, z'$ if $(x, y \triangleright z') \in \mathcal{G}$ and $z =_\mathcal{G} z'$ then $x : A \in \Delta$ or $y : B \in \Delta$.

$$\frac{\mathcal{G} \vdash_E (w_1 = w_2)}{\mathcal{G}; \Gamma; w_1 : p \vdash w_2 : p; \Delta}\ id \qquad \frac{\mathcal{G} \vdash_E (w = \epsilon)}{\mathcal{G}; \Gamma \vdash w : \top^*; \Delta}\ \top^* R \qquad \frac{(x, w \triangleright x'); (y, y \triangleright w); (x, y \triangleright x'); \mathcal{G}; \Gamma \vdash \Delta \qquad (x, y \triangleright x'); \mathcal{G} \vdash_E (x = x')}{(x, y \triangleright x'); \mathcal{G}; \Gamma \vdash \Delta}\ A_C$$

$$\frac{(u, w \triangleright z); (y, v \triangleright w); (x, y \triangleright z); (u, v \triangleright x'); \mathcal{G}; \Gamma \vdash \Delta \qquad (x, y \triangleright z); (u, v \triangleright x'); \mathcal{G} \vdash_E (x = x')}{(x, y \triangleright z); (u, v \triangleright x'); \mathcal{G}; \Gamma \vdash \Delta}\ A$$

$$\frac{(x, y \triangleright w'); \mathcal{G}; \Gamma \vdash x : A; w : A * B; \Delta \qquad (x, y \triangleright w'); \mathcal{G}; \Gamma \vdash y : B; w : A * B; \Delta \qquad (x, y \triangleright w'); \mathcal{G} \vdash_E (w = w')}{(x, y \triangleright w'); \mathcal{G}; \Gamma \vdash w : A * B; \Delta}\ *R$$

$$\frac{(x, w' \triangleright z); \mathcal{G}; \Gamma; w : A \multimap B \vdash x : A; \Delta \qquad (x, w' \triangleright z); \mathcal{G}; \Gamma; w : A \multimap B; z : B \vdash \Delta \qquad (x, w' \triangleright z); \mathcal{G} \vdash_E (w = w')}{(x, w' \triangleright z); \mathcal{G}; \Gamma; w : A \multimap B \vdash \Delta}\ \multimap L$$

Side condition: the label $w$ in $A$, $A_C$ does not occur in the conclusion.

**Figure 2.** Changed rules in the intermediate system $ILS_{PASL}$.

10. If $z : A \multimap B \in \Gamma$ then $\forall x, y, z'$ if $(x, z' \triangleright y) \in \mathcal{G}$ and $z =_\mathcal{G} z'$, then $x : A \in \Delta$ or $y : B \in \Gamma$.
11. If $z : A \multimap B \in \Delta$ then $\exists x, y, z'$ such that $(x, z' \triangleright y) \in \mathcal{G}$, $z =_\mathcal{G} z'$, $x : A \in \Gamma$ and $y : B \in \Delta$.
12. For any label $m \in \mathcal{L}$, $(m, \epsilon \triangleright m) \in \mathcal{G}$.
13. If $(a, b \triangleright c) \in \mathcal{G}$ then $(b, a \triangleright c) \in \mathcal{G}$.
14. If $(a, b \triangleright c) \in \mathcal{G}$ and $(d, e \triangleright a') \in \mathcal{G}$ and $a =_\mathcal{G} a'$, then $\exists f, f'$ such that $(d, f \triangleright c) \in \mathcal{G}$, $(b, e \triangleright f') \in \mathcal{G}$ and $f =_\mathcal{G} f'$.
15. $a : \bot \notin \Gamma$ and $a : \top \notin \Delta$.

**Lemma 3.4.** *Every Hintikka sequent is falsifiable.*

*Proof.* Let $\mathcal{G}; \Gamma \vdash \Delta$ be a Hintikka sequent. We construct an extended model $\mathcal{M} = (H, \triangleright_\mathcal{G}, \epsilon_\mathcal{G}, \nu, \rho)$ as follows:

- $H = \{[a]_\mathcal{G} \mid a \in \mathcal{L}\}$
- $\triangleright_\mathcal{G}([a]_\mathcal{G}, [b]_\mathcal{G}, [c]_\mathcal{G})$ iff $\exists a', b', c'.(a', b' \triangleright c') \in \mathcal{G}$, $a =_\mathcal{G} a'$, $b =_\mathcal{G} b'$, $c =_\mathcal{G} c'$
- $\epsilon_\mathcal{G} = [\epsilon]_\mathcal{G}$
- $\nu(p) = \{[a]_\mathcal{G} \mid a : p \in \Gamma\}$ for every $p \in Var$
- $\rho(a) = [a]_\mathcal{G}$ for every $a \in \mathcal{L}$.

To reduce clutter, we shall drop the subscript $\mathcal{G}$ in $[a]_\mathcal{G}$ and write $[a], [b] \triangleright_\mathcal{G} [c]$ instead of $\triangleright_\mathcal{G}([a], [b], [c])$.

We first show that $\mathcal{F} = (H, \triangleright_\mathcal{G}, \epsilon_\mathcal{G})$ is a PASL Kripke relational frame. The identity, commutativity and associativity properties of $\mathcal{F}$ follow immediately from Definition 3.3, clause 12, 13, and 14, respectively. We next show partial-determinism and cancellativity:

**Partial-determinism:** If $[a], [b] \triangleright_\mathcal{G} [c]$ and $[a], [b] \triangleright_\mathcal{G} [d]$ hold, then there exists some $(a', b' \triangleright c') \in \mathcal{G}$ and $(a'', b'' \triangleright d') \in \mathcal{G}$ such that $[a] = [a'] = [a'']$, $[b] = [b'] = [b'']$, $[c] = [c']$, $[d] = [d']$. Then by Lemma 3.1, $\mathcal{G} \vdash_E (c' = d')$ by using rule $P$ to unify $c'$ and $d'$, thus we obtain that $[c] = [c'] = [d] = [d']$.

**Cancellativity:** If $[a], [b] \triangleright_\mathcal{G} [c]$ and $[a], [d] \triangleright_\mathcal{G} [c]$ hold, then we can find some $(a', b' \triangleright c') \in \mathcal{G}$ and $(a'', d' \triangleright c'') \in \mathcal{G}$ such that $[a] = [a'] = [a'']$, $[c] = [c'] = [c'']$, $[b] = [b']$, $[d] = [d']$. Then by Lemma 3.1, $\mathcal{G} \vdash_E (b' = c')$ by using $C$ to unify $b'$ and $c'$, thus we obtain that $[b] = [b'] = [c] = [c']$.

So $\mathcal{M}$ is indeed a model based on a PASL Kripke relational frame. We show next that $\mathcal{G}; \Gamma \vdash \Delta$ is falsifiable in $\mathcal{M}$. We need to show the following (where $\rho(m) = [m]$):

(1) If $(a, b \triangleright c) \in \mathcal{G}$ then $([a], [b] \triangleright_\mathcal{G} [c])$.
(2) If $m : A \in \Gamma$ then $\mathcal{M}, \rho(m) \Vdash A$.
(3) If $m : A \in \Delta$ then $\mathcal{M}, \rho(m) \not\Vdash A$.

Item (1) follows from the definition of $\triangleright_\mathcal{G}$. We prove (2) and (3) simultaneously by induction on the size of $A$. In the following, to simplify presentation, we omit the $\mathcal{M}$ from the forcing relation.

**Base cases:** when $A$ is an atomic proposition $p$.

- If $m : p \in \Gamma$ then $[m] \in \nu(p)$ by definition of $\nu$, so $[m] \Vdash p$.
- Suppose $m : p \in \Delta$, but $[m] \Vdash p$. Then $m' : p \in \Gamma$, for some $m'$ such that $m' =_\mathcal{G} m$. This violates condition 1 in Def. 3.3. Thus $[m] \not\Vdash p$.

**Inductive cases:** when $A$ is a compound formula. We show here the interesting cases involving multiplicative connectives:

- If $m : \top^* \in \Gamma$ then $[m] = [\epsilon]$ by condition 6 in Def. 3.3. Since $[\epsilon] \Vdash \top^*$, we obtain $[m] \Vdash \top^*$.
- If $m : \top^* \in \Delta$, by condition 7 in Def. 3.3, $[m] \neq [\epsilon]$ and then $[m] \not\Vdash \top^*$.
- If $m : A * B \in \Gamma$, by condition 8 in Def. 3.3, $\exists a, b, m'$ such that $(a, b \triangleright m') \in \mathcal{G}$ and $[m] = [m']$ and $a : A \in \Gamma$ and $b : B \in \Gamma$. By the induction hypothesis, $[a] \Vdash A$ and $[b] \Vdash B$. Thus $[a], [b] \triangleright_\mathcal{G} [m]$ holds and $[m] \Vdash A * B$.
- If $m : A * B \in \Delta$, by condition 9 in Def. 3.3, $\forall a, b, m'$ if $(a, b \triangleright m') \in \mathcal{G}$ and $[m] = [m']$, then $a : A \in \Delta$ or $b : B \in \Delta$. By the induction hypothesis, if such $a, b$ exist, then $[a] \not\Vdash A$ or $[b] \not\Vdash B$. For any $[a], [b] \triangleright_\mathcal{G} [m]$, there must be some $(a', b' \triangleright m'') \in \mathcal{G}$ such that $[a] = [a']$, $[b] = [b']$, $[m] = [m'']$. Then $[a] = [a'] \not\Vdash A$ or $[b] = [b'] \not\Vdash B$ therefore $[m] \not\Vdash A * B$.
- If $m : A \multimap B \in \Gamma$, by condition 10 in Def. 3.3, $\forall a, b, m'$ if $(a, m' \triangleright b) \in \mathcal{G}$ and $[m] = [m']$, then $a : A \in \Delta$ or $b : B \in \Gamma$. By the induction hypothesis, if such $a, b$ exists, then $[a] \not\Vdash A$ or $[b] \Vdash B$. Consider any $[a], [m] \triangleright_\mathcal{G} [b]$, there must be some $(a', m'' \triangleright b') \in \mathcal{G}$. So $[a] = [a'] \not\Vdash A$ or $[b] = [b'] \Vdash B$, thus $[m] \Vdash A \multimap B$.
- If $m : A \multimap B \in \Delta$, by condition 11 in Def. 3.3, $\exists a, b, m'$ such that $(a, m' \triangleright b) \in \mathcal{G}$ and $[m] = [m']$ and $a : A \in \Gamma$ and $b : B \in \Delta$. By the induction hypothesis, $[a] \Vdash A$ and $[b] \not\Vdash B$ and $[a], [m] \triangleright_\mathcal{G} [b]$ holds, thus $[m] \not\Vdash A \multimap B$. □

To prove the completeness of $ILS_{PASL}$, we have to show that any given unprovable sequent can be extended to a Hintikka sequent. To do so we need a way to enumerate all possible applicable rules in a fair way so that every rule will be chosen infinitely often. Traditionally, this is achieved via a fair enumeration strategy of every principal formula of every rule. Since our calculus contains structural rules with no principal formulas, we need to include them in the enumeration strategy as well. For this purpose, we define a notion of *extended formulae*, given by the grammar:

$$ExF ::= F \mid \mathbb{U} \mid \mathbb{E} \mid \mathbb{A} \mid \mathbb{A}_C$$

where $F$ is a formula, and $\mathbb{U}, \mathbb{E}, \mathbb{A}, \mathbb{A}_C$ are constants. The intention is that $\mathbb{U}, \mathbb{E}, \mathbb{A}, \mathbb{A}_C$ will be as used as "dummy" principal formulae for the structural rules $U$, $E$, $A$, and $A_C$, respectively. A scheduler then determines the sequence of rule applications to apply.

**Definition 3.4.** A *schedule* is a tuple $(O, m, ExF, R)$, where $O$ is either 0 (left) or 1 (right), $m$ is a label, $ExF$ is an extended formula and $R$ is a set of relational atoms such that $|R| \leq 2$. Let $\mathcal{S}$ denote the set of all schedules. A *scheduler* is a function from the set of natural numbers $\mathcal{N}$ to $\mathcal{S}$. A scheduler $\phi$ is *fair* if for every schedule $S$, the set $\{i \mid \phi(i) = S\}$ is infinite.

**Lemma 3.5.** *There exists a fair scheduler.*

*Proof.* Our proof follows a similar proof in [20]. To adapt their proof, we need to show that the set $\mathcal{S}$ is countable, which follows from the fact that $\mathcal{S}$ is a finite product of countable sets. □

From now on, we shall fix a fair scheduler, which we call $\phi$. We assume that the set of labels $\mathcal{L}$ is totally ordered, and its elements can be enumerated as $a_0, a_1, a_2, \ldots$ where $a_0 = \epsilon$. This indexing is used to select fresh labels in our construction of Hintikka sequents.

We say the formula $F$ is not cut-free provable in $ILS_{PASL}$ if the sequent $\vdash w : F$ is not cut-free derivable in $ILS_{PASL}$ for any label $w \neq \epsilon$. Since we shall be concerned only with cut-free provability, in the following when we mention derivation, we mean cut-free derivation.

**Definition 3.5.** Let $F$ be a formula which is not cut-free provable in $ILS_{PASL}$. We construct a series of finite sequents $\{\mathcal{G}_i; \Gamma_i \vdash \Delta_i\}_{i \in \mathcal{N}}$ from $F$ where $\mathcal{G}_1 = \Gamma_1 = \emptyset$ and $\Delta_1 = a_1 : F$.

Assuming that $\mathcal{G}_i; \Gamma_i \vdash \Delta_i$ has been defined, we define $\mathcal{G}_{i+1}; \Gamma_{i+1} \vdash \Delta_{i+1}$ as follows. Suppose we have the schedule $\phi(i) = (O_i, m_i, ExF_i, R_i)$.

- If $O_i = 0$, $ExF_i$ is a PASL formula $C_i$ and $m_i : C_i \in \Gamma_i$:
  - If $C_i = F_1 \wedge F_2$, then $\mathcal{G}_{i+1} = \mathcal{G}_i$, $\Gamma_{i+1} = \Gamma_i \cup \{m_i : F_1, m_i : F_2\}$, $\Delta_{i+1} = \Delta_i$.
  - If $C_i = F_1 \rightarrow F_2$. If there is no derivation for $\mathcal{G}_i; \Gamma_i \vdash m_i : F_1; \Delta_i$ then $\Gamma_{i+1} = \Gamma_i$, $\Delta_{i+1} = \Delta_i \cup \{m_i : F_1\}$. Otherwise $\Gamma_{i+1} = \Gamma_i \cup \{m_i : F_2\}$, $\Delta_{i+1} = \Delta_i$. In both cases, $\mathcal{G}_{i+1} = \mathcal{G}_i$.
  - If $C_i = \top^*$, then $\mathcal{G}_{i+1} = \mathcal{G}_i \cup \{(\epsilon, m_i \triangleright \epsilon)\}$, $\Gamma_{i+1} = \Gamma_i$, $\Delta_{i+1} = \Delta_i$.
  - If $C_i = F_1 * F_2$, then $\mathcal{G}_{i+1} = \mathcal{G}_i \cup \{(a_{2i}, a_{2i+1} \triangleright m_i)\}$, $\Gamma_{i+1} = \Gamma_i \cup \{a_{2i} : F_1, a_{2i+1} : F_2\}$, $\Delta_{i+1} = \Delta_i$.
  - If $C_i = F_1 \mathrel{-\!\!*} F_2$ and $R_i = \{(x, m \triangleright y)\} \subseteq \mathcal{G}_i$ and $\mathcal{G}_i \vdash_E (m = m_i)$. If $\mathcal{G}_i; \Gamma_i \vdash x : F_1; \Delta_i$ has no derivation, then $\Gamma_{i+1} = \Gamma_i$, $\Delta_{i+1} = \Delta_i \cup \{x : F_1\}$. Otherwise $\Gamma_{i+1} = \Gamma_i \cup \{y : F_2\}$, $\Delta_{i+1} = \Delta_i$. In both cases, $\mathcal{G}_{i+1} = \mathcal{G}_i$.
- If $O_i = 1$, $ExF_i$ is a PASL formula $C_i$, and $m_i : C_i \in \Delta$:
  - If $C_i = F_1 \wedge F_2$. If there is no derivation for $\mathcal{G}_i; \Gamma_i \vdash m_i : F_1; \Delta_i$ then $\Delta_{i+1} = \Delta_i \cup \{m_i : F_1\}$. Otherwise $\Delta_{i+1} = \Delta_i \cup \{m_i : F_2\}$. In both cases, $\mathcal{G}_{i+1} = \mathcal{G}_i$ and $\Gamma_{i+1} = \Gamma_i$.
  - If $C_i = F_1 \rightarrow F_2$, then $\Gamma_{i+1} = \Gamma \cup \{m_i : F_1\}$, $\Delta_{i+1} = \Delta_i \cup \{m_i : F_2\}$, and $\mathcal{G}_{i+1} = \mathcal{G}_i$.
  - $C_i = F_1 * F_2$ and $R_i = \{(x, y \triangleright m)\} \subseteq \mathcal{G}_i$ and $\mathcal{G}_i \vdash_E (m_i = m)$. If $\mathcal{G}_i; \Gamma_i \vdash x : F_1; \Delta_i$ has no derivation, then $\Delta_{i+1} = \Delta_i \cup \{x : F_1\}$. Otherwise $\Delta_{i+1} = \Delta_i \cup \{y : F_2\}$. In both cases, $\mathcal{G}_{i+1} = \mathcal{G}_i$ and $\Gamma_{i+1} = \Gamma_i$.
  - If $C_i = F_1 \mathrel{-\!\!*} F_2$, then $\mathcal{G}_{i+1} = \mathcal{G}_i \cup \{(a_{2i}, m_i \triangleright a_{2i+1})\}$, $\Gamma_{i+1} = \Gamma_i \cup \{a_{2i} : F_1\}$, and $\Delta_{i+1} = \Delta_i \cup \{a_{2i+1} : F_2\}$.
- If $ExF_i \in \{\mathbb{U}, \mathbb{E}, \mathbb{A}, \mathbb{A}_C\}$, we proceed as follows:
  - If $ExF_i = \mathbb{U}$, $R_i = \{(a_n, \epsilon \triangleright a_n)\}$, where $n \leq 2i+1$, then $\mathcal{G}_{i+1} = \mathcal{G}_i \cup \{(a_n, \epsilon \triangleright a_n)\}$, $\Gamma_{i+1} = \Gamma_i$, $\Delta_{i+1} = \Delta_i$.
  - If $ExF_i = \mathbb{E}$, $R_i = \{(x, y \triangleright z)\} \subseteq \mathcal{G}_i$, then $\mathcal{G}_{i+1} = \mathcal{G}_i \cup \{(y, x \triangleright z)\}$, $\Gamma_{i+1} = \Gamma_i$, $\Delta_{i+1} = \Delta_i$.
  - If $ExF_i = \mathbb{A}$, $R_i = \{(x, y \triangleright z); (u, v \triangleright x')\} \subseteq \mathcal{G}_i$ and $\mathcal{G}_i \vdash_E (x = x')$, then $\mathcal{G}_{i+1} = \mathcal{G}_i \cup \{(u, a_{2i} \triangleright z), (y, v \triangleright a_{2i})\}$, $\Gamma_{i+1} = \Gamma_i$, $\Delta_{i+1} = \Delta_i$.
  - If $ExF_i = \mathbb{A}_C$, $R_i = \{(x, y \triangleright x')\} \subseteq \mathcal{G}_i$, and $\mathcal{G}_i \vdash_E (x = x')$ then $\mathcal{G}_{i+1} = \mathcal{G}_i \cup \{(x, a_{2i} \triangleright x), (y, y \triangleright a_{2i})\}$, $\Gamma_{i+1} = \Gamma_i$, $\Delta_{i+1} = \Delta_i$.
- In all other cases, $\mathcal{G}_{i+1} = \mathcal{G}_i$, $\Gamma_{i+1} = \Gamma_i$ and $\Delta_{i+1} = \Delta_i$.

Intuitively, each tuple $(O_i, m_i, ExF_i, R_i)$ corresponds to a potential rule application . If the components of the rule application are in the current sequent, we apply the corresponding rule to these components. The indexing of labels guarantees that the choice of $a_{2i}$ and $a_{2i+1}$ are always fresh for the sequent $\mathcal{G}_i; \Gamma_i \vdash \Delta_i$. The construction in Def. 3.5 non-trivially extends a similar construction of Hintikka CSS due to Larchey-Wendling [20], in addition to which we have to consider the cases for structural rules.

We say $\mathcal{G}'; \Gamma' \vdash \Delta' \subseteq \mathcal{G}; \Gamma \vdash \Delta$ iff $\mathcal{G}' \subseteq \mathcal{G}$, $\Gamma' \subseteq \Gamma$ and $\Delta' \subseteq \Delta$. A labelled sequent $\mathcal{G}; \Gamma \vdash \Delta$ is *finite* if $\mathcal{G}, \Gamma, \Delta$ are finite sets. Define $\mathcal{G}'; \Gamma' \vdash \Delta' \subseteq_f \mathcal{G}; \Gamma \vdash \Delta$ iff $\mathcal{G}'; \Gamma' \vdash \Delta' \subseteq \mathcal{G}; \Gamma \vdash \Delta$ and $\mathcal{G}'; \Gamma' \vdash \Delta'$ is finite. If $\mathcal{G}; \Gamma \vdash \Delta$ is a finite sequent, it is *consistent* iff it does not have a derivation in $ILS_{PASL}$. A (possibly infinite) sequent $\mathcal{G}; \Gamma \vdash \Delta$ is *finitely-consistent* iff every $\mathcal{G}'; \Gamma' \vdash \Delta' \subseteq_f \mathcal{G}; \Gamma \vdash \Delta$ is consistent.

We write $\mathcal{L}_i$ for the set of labels occurring in the sequent $\mathcal{G}_i; \Gamma_i \vdash \Delta_i$. Thus $\mathcal{L}_1 = \{a_1\}$. The following lemma states some obvious properties of the construction of the sequents $\mathcal{G}_i; \Gamma_i \vdash \Delta_i$. This can be proved by a simple induction on $i$.

**Lemma 3.6.** *For any $i \in \mathcal{N}$, the following properties hold:*

1. *$\mathcal{G}_i; \Gamma_i \vdash \Delta_i$ has no derivation*
2. *$\mathcal{L}_i \subseteq \{a_0, a_1, \cdots, a_{2i-1}\}$*
3. *$\mathcal{G}_i; \Gamma_i \vdash \Delta_i \subseteq_f \mathcal{G}_{i+1}; \Gamma_{i+1} \vdash \Delta_{i+1}$*

Given the construction of the series of sequents we have just seen above, we define a notion of a *limit sequent*, as the union of every sequent in the series.

**Definition 3.6** (Limit sequent)**.** Let $F$ be a formula unprovable in $ILS_{PASL}$. The *limit sequent for* $F$ is the sequent $\mathcal{G}^\omega; \Gamma^\omega \vdash \Delta^\omega$ where $\mathcal{G}^\omega = \bigcup_{i \in \mathcal{N}} \mathcal{G}_i$ and $\Gamma^\omega = \bigcup_{i \in \mathcal{N}} \Gamma_i$ and $\Delta^\omega = \bigcup_{i \in \mathcal{N}} \Delta_i$ and where $\mathcal{G}_i; \Gamma_i \vdash \Delta_i$ is as defined in Definition 3.5.

**Lemma 3.7.** *If $F$ is a formula unprovable in $ILS_{PASL}$, then the limit labelled sequent for $F$ is a Hintikka sequent.*

*Proof.* Let $\mathcal{G}^\omega; \Gamma^\omega \vdash \Delta^\omega$ be the limit sequent. First we show that $\mathcal{G}^\omega; \Gamma^\omega \vdash \Delta^\omega$ is finitely-consistent. Consider any $\mathcal{G}; \Gamma \vdash \Delta \subseteq_f \mathcal{G}^\omega; \Gamma^\omega \vdash \Delta^\omega$, we show that $\mathcal{G}; \Gamma \vdash \Delta$ has no derivation. Since $\mathcal{G}, \Gamma, \Delta$ are finite sets, there exists $i \in \mathcal{N}$ s.t. $\mathcal{G} \subseteq \mathcal{G}_i$, $\Gamma \subseteq \Gamma_i$, and $\Delta \subseteq \Delta_i$. Moreover, $\mathcal{G}_i; \Gamma_i \vdash \Delta_i$ is not provable in $ILS_{PASL}$. Since weakening is admissible in $ILS_{PASL}$, $\mathcal{G}; \Gamma \vdash \Delta \subseteq_f \mathcal{G}_i; \Gamma_i \vdash \Delta_i$ cannot be provable either. So condition 1, 7 and 15 in Definition 3.3 hold for the limit sequent, for otherwise we would be able to construct a provable finite labelled sequent from the limit sequent. We show the proofs that the other conditions in Definition 3.3 involving multiplicative connectives and structural rules are also satisfied by the limit sequent; the cases (1-5) and (15) for the additives are straightforward and are therefore omitted here.

6. If $m : \top^* \in \Gamma^\omega$, then $m : \top^* \in \Gamma_i$ for some $i \in \mathcal{N}$ since each labelled formula from $\Gamma^\omega$ must appear somewhere in the sequence. Then there exists $j > i$ such that $\phi(j) = (0, m, \top^*, R)$ where this formula becomes principal. By construction $(\epsilon, m \triangleright \epsilon) \in \mathcal{G}_{j+1} \subseteq \mathcal{G}^\omega$. Then $\mathcal{G}^\omega \vdash_E (m = \epsilon)$ because $\mathcal{G}_{j+1} \vdash_E (m = \epsilon)$. So $m =_{\mathcal{G}^\omega} \epsilon$.
8. If $m : F_1 * F_2 \in \Gamma^\omega$, then it is in some $\Gamma_i$, where $i \in \mathcal{N}$. Then there exists $j > i$ such that $\phi(j) = (0, m, F_1 * F_2, R)$.

By construction $\mathcal{G}_{j+1} = \mathcal{G}_j \cup \{(a_{2j}, a_{2j+1} \triangleright m)\} \subseteq \mathcal{G}^\omega$, and $\Gamma_{j+1} = \Gamma_j \cup \{a_{2j} : F_1, a_{2j+1} : F_2\} \subseteq \Gamma^\omega$.

9. If $m : F_1 * F_2 \in \Delta^\omega$, then it is in some $\Delta_i$, where $i \in \mathcal{N}$. For any $(x, y \triangleright m') \in \mathcal{G}^\omega$ such that $\mathcal{G}^\omega \vdash_E (m = m')$, there exists $j > i$ such that $(x, y \triangleright m') \in \mathcal{G}_j$ and $\mathcal{G}_j \vdash_E (m = m')$. Also, there exists $k > j$ such that $\phi(k) = (1, m, F_1 * F_2, \{(x, y \triangleright m')\})$ where the labelled formula becomes principal. Since $(x, y \triangleright m') \in \mathcal{G}_k$ and $\mathcal{G}_k \vdash (m = m')$, we have either $x : F_1 \in \Delta_{k+1} \subseteq \Delta^\omega$ or $y : F_2 \in \Delta_{k+1} \subseteq \Delta^\omega$.
10. If $m : F_1 \mathrel{-\!\!*} F_2 \in \Gamma^\omega$, similar to case 8.
11. If $m : F_1 \mathrel{-\!\!*} F_2 \in \Delta^\omega$, similar to case 9.
12. For each $a_n \in \mathcal{L}$, there is a $j \geq n$ such that $\phi(j) = (O, m, \mathbb{U}, \{(a_n, \epsilon \triangleright a_n)\})$ where $U$ is applied to $a_n$. Then $\mathcal{G}_{j+1} = \mathcal{G}_j \cup \{(a_n, \epsilon \triangleright a_n)\} \subseteq \mathcal{G}^\omega$, because $n \leq 2j + 1$.
13. If $(x, y \triangleright z) \in \mathcal{G}^\omega$, then it is in some $\mathcal{G}_i$, where $i \in \mathcal{N}$. Then there is a $j > i$ such that $\phi(j) = (O, m, \mathbb{E}, \{(x, y \triangleright z)\})$ where $E$ is applied. Then $\mathcal{G}_{j+1} = \mathcal{G}_j \cup \{(y, x \triangleright z)\} \subseteq \mathcal{G}^\omega$.
14. If $(x, y \triangleright z) \in \mathcal{G}^\omega$, $(u, v \triangleright x') \in \mathcal{G}^\omega$, and $x =_{\mathcal{G}^\omega} x'$, then there is some $\mathcal{G}_i$, $i \in \mathcal{N}$ such that $\{(x, y \triangleright z), (u, v \triangleright x')\} \subseteq \mathcal{G}_i$ and $\mathcal{G}_i \vdash_E (x = x')$. There are two cases to consider, depending on whether $(x, y \triangleright z)$ and $(u, v \triangleright x')$ are the same relational atoms. Suppose they are distinct. Then there must be some $j > i$ such that $\phi(j) = (O, m, \mathbb{A}, \{(x, y \triangleright z), (u, v \triangleright x')\})$. Then $\{(x, y \triangleright z), (u, v \triangleright x')\} \in \mathcal{G}_j$ and $\mathcal{G}_j \vdash_E (x = x')$. By construction we obtain that $\mathcal{G}_{j+1} = \mathcal{G}_j \cup \{(u, a_{2j} \triangleright z), (y, v \triangleright a_{2j})\} \subseteq \mathcal{G}^\omega$. If $(x, y \triangleright z)$ and $(u, v \triangleright x')$ are the same relational atom, then a similar argument can be applied, but in this case the schedule to choose is one which selects $\mathbb{A}_C$ rather than $\mathbb{A}$. □

**Theorem 3.8** (Completeness). *Every formula $F$ unprovable in $ILS_{PASL}$ is not valid (in PASL relational Kripke models).*

*Proof.* We construct a limit sequent $\mathcal{G}^\omega; \Gamma^\omega \vdash \Delta^\omega$ for $F$ following Definition 3.6. By the construction of the limit sequent, we have $a_1 : F \in \Delta^\omega$. By Lemma 3.7, this limit sequent is a Hintikka sequent, and therefore by Lemma 3.4, $\mathcal{G}^\omega; \Gamma^\omega \vdash \Delta^\omega$ is falsifiable. This means there exists a model $(\mathcal{F}, \nu, \rho)$ that satisfies $\mathcal{G}^\omega$ and $\Gamma^\omega$ and falsifies every element of $\Delta^\omega$, including $a_1 : F$, which means that $F$ is false at world $\rho(a_1)$. Thus $F$ is not valid. □

## 4. Extensions of PASL

We now consider some extensions of PASL obtained by imposing additional properties on the semantics, as suggested by Dockins et al [11]. We show that sound rules for *indivisible unit* and the stronger property of *disjointness* can be added to our labelled sequent calculus without jeopardising our completeness proof, but that the more exotic properties of *splittability* and *cross-split* are not fully compatible with our current framework.

***Indivisible unit.*** The unit $\epsilon$ in a commutative monoid $(H, \circ, \epsilon)$ is indivisible iff the following holds for any $h_1, h_2 \in H$:

$$\forall h_1, h_2 \in H. \text{ if } h_1 \circ h_2 = \epsilon \text{ then } h_1 = \epsilon. \quad (1)$$

Relationally, this corresponds to the first-order condition:

$$\forall h_1, h_2 \in H. \text{ if } R(h_1, h_2, \epsilon) \text{ then } h_1 = \epsilon \quad (2)$$

Note that this also means that $h_2 = \epsilon$ whenever $h_1 \circ h_2 = \epsilon$. Most memory models in the literature have indivisible unit [5], so this property seems appropriate for reasoning about concrete applications of separation logic. Indivisible unit can be axiomatised by the following formula [6]:

$$\top^* \wedge (A * B) \rightarrow A$$

We use the following sound rule to capture this property:

$$\frac{(\epsilon, y \triangleright \epsilon); \mathcal{G}[\epsilon/x]; \Gamma[\epsilon/x] \vdash \Delta[\epsilon/x]}{(x, y \triangleright \epsilon); \mathcal{G}; \Gamma \vdash \Delta} \; IU$$

Note that we can then instantiate the label $y$ to $\epsilon$ by applying $Eq_1$ upwards. Recall that the sequent calculus $LS_{BBI}$ [16] is just the sequent calculus $LS_{PASL}$ minus the rules $C$ and $P$.

**Proposition 4.1.** *The formula $\top^* \wedge (A * B) \rightarrow A$ is provable in $LS_{BBI} + IU$. The proof is as shown in Figure 3 (a).*

**Theorem 4.2.** *$LS_{PASL} + IU$ is sound and cut-free complete with respect to the class of PASL Kripke relational frames (and separation algebras) with indivisible unit.*

*Proof.* Soundness is straightforward as the rule $IU$ essentially just encodes the first-order formula (2) into the labelled sequent calculus. Completeness can be proved via the same counter-model construction for $LS_{PASL}$ (Theorem 3.8). That is, we first define an intermediate calculus $ILS_{PASL} + IU$ that is equivalent to $LS_{PASL} + IU$, and do counter-model construction in $ILS_{PASL} + IU$. Since the $IU$ rule contains substitution, the rule will be localised into the entailment relation $\vdash_E$, so the definition of $\vdash_E$ in Definition 3.1 is modified to allowed $IU$ in addition to $Eq_1, Eq_2, P$ and $C$. Thus the rules of $ILS_{PASL} + IU$ are exactly the same as $ILS_{PASL}$, and the only change is in the definition of $\vdash_E$ . The equivalence between $LS_{PASL} + IU$ and $ILS_{PASL} + IU$ can be proved as in Lemma 3.3.

We then show that a Hintikka sequent yields a Kripke relational frame that corresponds to a separation algebra with indivisible unit. No additional clauses are needed in the definition of Hintikka sequent since it is parametric on the entailment relation $\vdash_E$.

For a Hintikka sequent $\mathcal{G}; \Gamma \vdash \Delta$, suppose $(H, \triangleright_\mathcal{G}, [\epsilon])$ is the PASL Kripke relational frame generated by $\mathcal{G}$. Given any $[a], [b] \triangleright_\mathcal{G} [\epsilon]$, we can find a $(a', b' \triangleright c') \in \mathcal{G}$ such that $[a] = [a'], [b] = [b'], [\epsilon] = [c']$. Also, we can use the rule $IU$ to derive $\mathcal{G} \vdash_E (a' = \epsilon)$. Thus by Lemma 3.1, we obtain $[a] = [a'] = [\epsilon]$. So the structure $(H, \triangleright_\mathcal{G}, [\epsilon])$ generated by $\mathcal{G}$ is indeed a PASL Kripke relational frame that obeys indivisible unit.

The saturation with logical and structural rules $\mathbb{E}, \mathbb{U}, \mathbb{A}, \mathbb{A}_C$ is then the same as in Sec. 3. □

***Disjointness.*** The separating conjunction $*$ in separation logic requires that the two combined heaps have disjoint domains [29]. In a separation algebra $(H, \circ, \epsilon)$, disjointness is defined by the following additional requirement:

$$\forall h_1, h_2 \in H. \text{ if } h_1 \circ h_1 = h_2 \text{ then } h_1 = \epsilon \quad (3)$$

Relationally, this corresponds to the first-order condition:

$$\forall h_1, h_2 \in H. \text{ if } R(h_1, h_1, h_2) \text{ then } h_1 = \epsilon \quad (4)$$

The disjointness condition is captured in labelled sequent calculus by the following rule, where $x, y$ are labels.

$$\frac{(\epsilon, \epsilon \triangleright y); \mathcal{G}[\epsilon/x]; \Gamma[\epsilon/x] \vdash \Delta[\epsilon/x]}{(x, x \triangleright y); \mathcal{G}; \Gamma \vdash \Delta} \; D$$

In fact disjointness implies indivisible unit (but not vice versa), as shown by Dockins et al. [11]. Thus we can prove the axiom for indivisible unit by using $LS_{BBI} + D$.

**Proposition 4.3.** *The formula $\top^* \wedge (A * B) \rightarrow A$ is provable in $LS_{BBI} + D$. Figure 3(b) shows the derivation of the formula; we highlight the principal relational atoms where they are not obvious.*

**Theorem 4.4.** *$LS_{PASL} + D$ is sound and cut-free complete with respect to the class of Kripke relational frames (and separation algebras) with disjointness.*

*Proof.* Similar to Theorem 4.2. □

$$\begin{array}{cl}
\hline
(\epsilon, a_2 \rhd \epsilon); \epsilon : A; a_2 : B \vdash \epsilon : A & id \\ \hline
(a_1, a_2 \rhd \epsilon); a_1 : A; a_2 : B \vdash \epsilon : A & IU \\ \hline
(a_1, a_2 \rhd a_0); a_0 : \top^*; a_1 : A; a_2 : B \vdash a_0 : A & \top^* L \\ \hline
; a_0 : \top^*; a_0 : A * B \vdash a_0 : A & *L \\ \hline
; a_0 : \top^* \wedge (A * B) \vdash a_0 : A & \wedge L \\ \hline
; \vdash a_0 : (\top^* \wedge (A * B)) \to A & \to R
\end{array}$$

(a)

$$\begin{array}{cl}
\hline
(\epsilon, \epsilon \rhd \epsilon); \cdots ; \epsilon : A; \epsilon : B \vdash \epsilon : A & id \\ \hline
(\epsilon, a_1 \rhd \epsilon); \cdots ; a_1 : A; \epsilon : B \vdash \epsilon : A & Eq_1 \\ \hline
(a_1, w_2 \rhd w_1);(\epsilon, \epsilon \rhd w_2); \boxed{(a_1, \epsilon \rhd \epsilon)}; \cdots ; a_1 : A; \epsilon : B \vdash \epsilon : A & E \\ \hline
(a_1, w_2 \rhd w_1); \boxed{(a_2, a_2 \rhd w_2)}; (a_1, a_2 \rhd \epsilon); \cdots ; a_1 : A; a_2 : B \vdash \epsilon : A & D \\ \hline
(a_1, w_1 \rhd \epsilon); \boxed{(\epsilon, a_2 \rhd w_1); (a_1, a_2 \rhd \epsilon)}; \cdots ; a_1 : A; a_2 : B \vdash \epsilon : A & A \\ \hline
(\epsilon, \epsilon \rhd \epsilon); (a_1, a_2 \rhd \epsilon); a_1 : A; a_2 : B \vdash \epsilon : A & A \\ \hline
(a_1, a_2 \rhd \epsilon); a_1 : A; a_2 : B \vdash \epsilon : A & U \\ \hline
(a_1, a_2 \rhd a_0); a_0 : \top^*; a_1 : A; a_2 : B \vdash a_0 : A & \top^* L \\ \hline
; a_0 : \top^*; a_0 : A * B \vdash a_0 : A & *L \\ \hline
; a_0 : \top^* \wedge (A * B) \vdash a_0 : A & \wedge L \\ \hline
; \vdash a_0 : \top^* \wedge (A * B) \to A & \to R
\end{array}$$

(b)

**Figure 3.** Derivations of the axiom of indivisible unit in: (a) $LS_{BBI} + IU$ and (b) $LS_{BBI} + D$.

***Splittability and cross-split.*** The property of infinite splittability is sometimes useful when reasoning about the kinds of resource sharing that occur in divide-and-conquer style computations [11]. A monoid $(H, \circ, \epsilon)$ has splittability if for every $h_0 \in H \setminus \{\epsilon\}$, there are $h_1, h_2 \in H \setminus \{\epsilon\}$ such that $h_1 \circ h_2 = h_0$. Relationally, this corresponds to: if $h_0 \neq \epsilon$ then there exist $h_1 \neq \epsilon, h_2 \neq \epsilon$ such that $R(h_1, h_2, h_0)$. This property can be axiomatised as the BBI formula $\neg\top^* \to (\neg\top^* * \neg\top^*)$ [6]. We give the following rule for splittability, where $x, y$ are fresh:

$$\frac{(x, y \rhd z); \mathcal{G}; \Gamma \vdash x : \top^*; y : \top^*; z : \top^* \Delta}{\mathcal{G}; \Gamma \vdash z : \top^*; \Delta} \; S$$

**Proposition 4.5.** *The rule S for splittability is sound.*

*Proof.* Assume the conclusion of $S$ is falsifiable in an extended relational model $(H, R, \epsilon, v, \rho)$; we show that the premise is also falsifiable. So suppose that everything in $\mathcal{G} \cup \Gamma$ is true, and everything in $\{z : \top^*\} \cup \Delta$ is false in the model. Specifically, $z : \top^*$ is false, meaning $\rho(z) \not\Vdash \top^*$, thus $\rho(z) \neq \epsilon$. By splittability, there exist some $h_1, h_2 \in H \setminus \{\epsilon\}$ such that $R(h_1, h_2, \rho(z))$ holds. Let $\rho' = \rho \cup \{x \mapsto h_1, y \mapsto h_2\}$. Then $(x, y \rhd z)$ is true under $\rho'$. Also, since $\rho'(x) \neq \epsilon$ and $\rho'(y) \neq \epsilon$, the labelled formulae $x : \top^*$ and $y : \top^*$ are false under $\rho'$. Thus the model with frame $(H, R, \epsilon)$, valuation $v$, and label mapping $\rho'$ falsifies the premise. □

**Proposition 4.6.** *The axiom $\neg\top^* \to (\neg\top^* * \neg\top^*)$ for splittability is provable in $LS_{BBI} + S$.*

*Proof.* We start from $\neg\top^* \to (\neg\top^* * \neg\top^*)$, and obtain the following derivation backward:

$$\begin{array}{cl}
(a_1, a_2 \rhd a_0); \vdash a_1 : \top^*; a_2 : \top^*; a_0 : \top^*; a_0 : \neg\top^* * \neg\top^* & \\ \hline
; \vdash a_0 : \top^*; a_0 : \neg\top^* * \neg\top^* & S \\ \hline
; a_0 : \neg\top^* \vdash a_0 : \neg\top^* * \neg\top^* & \neg L \\ \hline
; \vdash a_0 : \neg\top^* \to (\neg\top^* * \neg\top^*) & \to R
\end{array}$$

Then we can apply $*R$ (backwards) on the top sequent using the relational atom $(a_1, a_2 \rhd a_0)$ to obtain the premises $S_L$ and $S_R$. The left premise $S_L$ can be proved as follows:

$$\begin{array}{cl}
\hline
(\epsilon, a_2 \rhd a_0); \vdash \epsilon : \top^*; \cdots & \top^* R \\ \hline
(a_1, a_2 \rhd a_0); a_1 : \top^* \vdash a_1 : \top^*; \cdots & \top^* L \\ \hline
(a_1, a_2 \rhd a_0); \vdash a_1 : \neg\top^*; a_1 : \top^*; \cdots & \neg R
\end{array}$$

The right premise $S_R$ can be proved similarly. □

Note that the rule $S$ creates new labels in the premise, as the rule $A$ does. However, it also has a principal formula, so it is not a structural rule. Unlike the rules $IU$ and $D$, the rule $S$ cannot simply be localised into the entailment relation $\vdash_E$, so we have to extend the notion of a Hintikka sequent to add a condition corresponding to splittability. The counter-model construction then has to ensure that this condition is satisfied by the limit sequent by ensuring that the rule $S$ is applied in a fair way. We therefore leave the details of this completeness proof for $LS_{PASL} + S$ to future work.

Cross-split is a rather complicated property. It specifies that if a heap can be split in two different ways, then there should be intersections of these splittings. Formally, in a monoid $(H, \circ, \epsilon)$, if $h_1 \circ h_2 = h_0$ and $h_3 \circ h_4 = h_0$, then there should be four elements $h_{13}, h_{14}, h_{23}, h_{24}$, informally representing the intersections $h_1 \cap h_3$, $h_1 \cap h_4$, $h_2 \cap h_3$ and $h_2 \cap h_4$ respectively, such that $h_{13} \circ h_{14} = h_1$, $h_{23} \circ h_{24} = h_2$, $h_{13} \circ h_{23} = h_3$, and $h_{14} \circ h_{24} = h_4$. The corresponding condition on Kripke relational frames is obvious. The following sound rule naturally captures cross-split, where $p, q, s, t, u, v, x, y, z$ are labels:

$$\frac{R; (x, y \rhd z); (u, v \rhd z); \mathcal{G}; \Gamma \vdash \Delta}{(x, y \rhd z); (u, v \rhd z); \mathcal{G}; \Gamma \vdash \Delta} \; CS$$

where $R := (p, q \rhd x); (p, s \rhd u); (s, t \rhd y); (q, t \rhd v)$

and $p, q, s, t$ do not occur in the conclusion

We conjecture that this rule can be handled in the counter-model construction by treating it similarly to the rule $A$. We then need to change the indexing of labels when constructing the limit sequent. Let the rule $A$ choose $a_{4i}$, the rules $*L$ and $-\!\!* R$ choose $a_{4i}, a_{4i+1}$, and the rule $CS$ choose $a_{4i}, a_{4i+1}, a_{4i+2}, a_{4i+3}$ as new labels. Further, let the rule $U$ create the identity relational atom $(a_n, \epsilon \rhd a_n)$ only when $n \leq 4i + 3$. Then each $L_i$ is a subset of $\{a_1, \cdots, a_{4i-1}\}$.

Splittability and cross-split are not as frequently used in separation logic as the other conditions, and they require non-trivial modifications in our current proofs. We note that Reynolds' heap model [29] falsifies splittability, as heaps are finite objects that only non-trivially split finitely often. On the other hand cross-split is true in the heap model; however we are not aware of any formulae whose proof requires this property. For these reasons we omit these from our modular framework of proof systems for PASL.

## 5. Tailoring the labelled calculus

We now consider various labelled calculi obtained by extending $LS_{BBI}$ with one or more structural rules that correspond to partial-determinism ($P$), cancellativity ($C$), indivisible unit (IU), and disjointness ($D$). Most of the results in this section either directly follow from the proofs in previous sections, or are easy adaptations. As those conditions for monoids are often given in a modular way, e.g., in [6, 11], it is not surprising that our structural rules can also be added modularly to $LS_{BBI}$, since they just simulate those conditions directly and individually in the labelled sequent calculus.

***Calculi without cancellativity.*** Some notions of separation logic omit cancellativity [18], so dropping the rule $C$ in $LS_{PASL}$ gives an interesting system. The proofs in Sec. 3 still work if we just insist on a partial commutative monoid, and drop $C$ in $\vdash_E$.

**Theorem 5.1.** *The labelled sequent calculus $LS_{BBI}+P$ is sound and cut-free complete with respect to the partial commutative monoidal semantics for BBI.*

As a result, it is easy to obtain the following sound and complete labelled calculi for the corresponding semantics: $LS_{BBI}+P+IU$ and $LS_{BBI}+P+D$. The proofs are similar to that for Theorem 4.2.

***Calculi without partial-determinism.*** Similar to above, dropping partial-determinism gives another sound and complete labelled calculus $LS_{BBI}+C$, although we are not aware of any concrete models in separation logic that employ this framework.

**Theorem 5.2.** *The labelled sequent calculus $LS_{BBI}+C$ is sound and cut-free complete with respect to the cancellative commutative monoidal semantics for BBI.*

Again, using a similar argument as in Theorem. 4.2, we can obtain sound and complete labelled calculi $LS_{BBI}+C+IU$ and $LS_{BBI}+C+D$.

***Calculi without partial-determinism and cancellativity.*** The labelled calculus $LS_{BBI}+IU$ is sound and complete by Prop. 4.1, and cut-elimination holds.

**Theorem 5.3.** *The labelled sequent calculus $LS_{BBI}+IU$ is sound and cut-free complete with respect to the commutative monoidal semantics for BBI with indivisible unit.*

To prove the completeness of the calculus $LS_{BBI}+D$, we need to go through the counter-model construction proof, since disjointness is not axiomatisable. It is easy to check that the proofs in Section 3 do not break when we define $\vdash_E$ by using $Eq_1, Eq_2, D$ only, and the Hintikka sequent then gives the BBI Kripke relational frame that obeys disjointness. The other proofs remain the same.

**Theorem 5.4.** *The labelled sequent calculus $LS_{BBI}+D$ is sound and cut-free complete with respect to the commutative monoidal semantics for BBI with disjointness.*

To summarise, our approach offers a sound and cut-free calculus for the extension of BBI with every combination of the properties $P, C, IU, D$. The case where none of the properties hold, i.e. regular BBI, have already been solved [16, 27]. Omitting the cases covered by the implication of $IU$ by $D$, this provides us with the following eleven labelled calculi:

| | | |
|---|---|---|
| $LS_{BBI}+IU$ | $LS_{BBI}+C$ | $LS_{BBI}+D$ |
| $LS_{BBI}+P$ | $LS_{PASL}(=LS_{BBI}+P+C)$ | |
| $LS_{BBI}+P+IU$ | $LS_{BBI}+C+IU$ | $LS_{PASL}+IU$ |
| $LS_{BBI}+P+D$ | $LS_{BBI}+C+D$ | $LS_{PASL}+D$ |

## 6. Implementation and experiment

We discuss here an implementation of the proof system $LS_{PASL}+D$. It turns out that the $A_C$ rule is admissible in this system; in fact it is admissible in the subsystem $LS_{BBI}+C$, as shown next, so we do not implement the $A_C$ rule.

**Proposition 6.1.** *The $A_C$ rule is admissible in $LS_{BBI}+C$.*

*Proof.* We show that every derivation in $LS_{BBI}+C$ can be transformed into one with no applications of $A_C$. It is sufficient to show that we can eliminate a single application of $A_C$; then we can eliminate all $A_C$ in a derivation successively starting from the topmost applications in that derivation. So suppose we have a derivation in $LS_{BBI}+C$ of the form:

$$\dfrac{\begin{matrix}\Pi\\ (x,w\rhd x);(y,y\rhd w);(x,y\rhd x);\mathcal{G};\Gamma\vdash\Delta\end{matrix}}{(x,y\rhd x);\mathcal{G};\Gamma\vdash\Delta}\;A_C$$

where $w$ is a new label not in the root sequent. This is transformed into the following derivation:

$$\dfrac{\dfrac{\dfrac{\begin{matrix}\Pi'\\ (x,\epsilon\rhd x);(\epsilon,\epsilon\rhd\epsilon);\mathcal{G}[\epsilon/y];\Gamma[\epsilon/y]\vdash\Delta[\epsilon/y]\end{matrix}}{(x,\epsilon\rhd x);\mathcal{G}[\epsilon/y];\Gamma[\epsilon/y]\vdash\Delta[\epsilon/y]}\;U}{(x,\epsilon\rhd x);(x,y\rhd x);\mathcal{G};\Gamma\vdash\Delta}\;C}{(x,y\rhd x);\mathcal{G};\Gamma\vdash\Delta}\;U$$

where $\Pi'$ is obtained by applying the substitutions $[\epsilon/x]$ and $[\epsilon/w]$ to $\Pi$ (Lemma 2.2). Note that since $w$ does not occur in the root sequent, $\mathcal{G}[\epsilon/x][\epsilon/w]=\mathcal{G}[\epsilon/x]$, $\Gamma[\epsilon/x][\epsilon/w]=\Gamma[\epsilon/x]$ and $\Delta[\epsilon/x][\epsilon/w]=\Delta[\epsilon/x]$. These substitutions do not introduce new instances of $A_C$. □

Our implementation uses the following strategy when applying rules on a sequent:

1. Try to close the branch by rules $id, \bot L, \top^* R, \top^* R$.
2. If (1) not applicable, apply all possible $Eq_1, Eq_2, P, C, IU, D$ rules to unify labels[3].
3. If (1-2) not applicable, apply invertible rules $\wedge L, \wedge R, \to L, \to R, *L, -\!\!* R, \top^* L$ in all possible ways.
4. If (1-3) not applicable, try rules $*R$ or $-\!\!* L$ by choosing existing relational atoms.
5. If none of the existing relational atoms are applicable, or all combinations of $*R, -\!\!* L$ formulae and relational atoms are already applied in (4), apply structural rules on the set $\mathcal{G}_0$ of relational atoms in the sequent as follows.
   (a) Use $E$ to generate all commutative variants of existing relational atoms in $\mathcal{G}_0$, giving a set $\mathcal{G}_1$.
   (b) Apply $A$ for each applicable pair in $\mathcal{G}_1$, generating a set $\mathcal{G}_2$.
   (c) Use $U$ to generate all identity relational atoms for each label in $\mathcal{G}_2$, giving the set $\mathcal{G}_3$.
6. If none of above is applicable, fail.

Step (2) is terminating, because each substitution eliminates a label, and we only have finitely many labels. Step (5) is not applicable when $\mathcal{G}_3=\mathcal{G}_0$. It is also clear that step (5) is terminating. We forbid applications of the rule $A$ to the pair $\{(x,y\rhd z),(u,v\rhd x)\}$ when $\{(u,w\rhd z),(y,v\rhd w)\}$, for some label $w$, (or any commutative variants of this pair, e.g., $\{(w,u\rhd z);(v,y\rhd w)\}$) is already in the sequent. This is because the created relational atoms in such an $A$ application can be unified to existing ones by using rules $P$,$C$.

We view $\Gamma,\Delta$ in a sequent $\mathcal{G};\Gamma\vdash\Delta$ as lists, and each time a logical rule is applied, we place the subformulae in the front of the list. Thus our proof search has a "focusing flavour", that

[3] Although $IU$ is admissible, we keep it because it simplifies proof search.

| | Formula | BBeye (opt) | $FVLS_{BBI}$ (heuristic) | Separata |
|---|---|---|---|---|
| (1) | $(a \mathbin{-\!\!*} b) \wedge (\top * (\top^* \wedge a)) \rightarrow b$ | 0.076 | 0.002 | 0.002 |
| (2) | $(\top^* \mathbin{-\!\!*} \neg(\neg a * \top^*)) \rightarrow a$ | 0.080 | 0.004 | 0.002 |
| (3) | $\neg((a \mathbin{-\!\!*} \neg(a * b)) \wedge ((\neg a \mathbin{-\!\!*} \neg b) \wedge b))$ | 0.064 | 0.003 | 0.002 |
| (4) | $\top^* \rightarrow ((a \mathbin{-\!\!*} (b \mathbin{-\!\!*} c)) \mathbin{-\!\!*} ((a * b) \mathbin{-\!\!*} c))$ | 0.060 | 0.003 | 0.002 |
| (5) | $\top^* \rightarrow ((a * (b * c)) \mathbin{-\!\!*} ((a * b) * c))$ | 0.071 | 0.002 | 0.004 |
| (6) | $\top^* \rightarrow ((a * ((b \mathbin{-\!\!*} e) * c)) \mathbin{-\!\!*} ((a * (b \mathbin{-\!\!*} e)) * c))$ | 0.107 | 0.004 | 0.008 |
| (7) | $\neg((a \mathbin{-\!\!*} \neg(\neg(d \mathbin{-\!\!*} \neg(a * (c * b))) * a)) \wedge c * (d \wedge (a * b)))$ | 0.058 | 0.002 | 0.006 |
| (8) | $\neg((c * (d * e)) \wedge B)$ where $B := ((a \mathbin{-\!\!*} \neg(\neg(b \mathbin{-\!\!*} \neg(d * (e * c))) * a)) * (b \wedge (a * \top)))$ | 0.047 | 0.002 | 0.013 |
| (9) | $\neg(C * (d \wedge (a * (b * e))))$ where $C := ((a \mathbin{-\!\!*} \neg(\neg(d \mathbin{-\!\!*} \neg((c * e) * (b * a))) * a)) \wedge c)$ | 94.230 | 0.003 | 0.053 |
| (10) | $(a * (b * (c * d))) \rightarrow (d * (c * (b * a)))$ | 0.030 | 0.004 | 0.002 |
| (11) | $(a * (b * (c * d))) \rightarrow (d * (b * (c * a)))$ | 0.173 | 0.002 | 0.002 |
| (12) | $(a * (b * (c * (d * e)))) \rightarrow (e * (d * (a * (b * c))))$ | 1.810 | 0.003 | 0.002 |
| (13) | $(a * (b * (c * (d * e)))) \rightarrow (e * (b * (a * (c * d))))$ | 144.802 | 0.003 | 0.002 |
| (14) | $\top^* \rightarrow (a * ((b \mathbin{-\!\!*} e) * (c * d)) \mathbin{-\!\!*} ((a * d) * (c * (b \mathbin{-\!\!*} e))))$ | 6.445 | 0.003 | 0.044 |
| (15) | $\neg(\top^* \wedge (a \wedge (b * \neg(c \mathbin{-\!\!*} (\top^* \rightarrow a)))))$ | timeout(1000s) | 0.003 | 0.003 |
| (16) | $((D \rightarrow (E \mathbin{-\!\!*} (D * E))) \rightarrow (b \mathbin{-\!\!*} ((D \rightarrow (E \mathbin{-\!\!*} ((D * a) * a))) * b)))$, where $D := \top^* \rightarrow a$ and $E := a * a$ | 0.039 | 0.005 | 8.772 |
| (17) | $((\top^* \rightarrow (a \mathbin{-\!\!*} (((a * (a \mathbin{-\!\!*} b)) * \neg b) \mathbin{-\!\!*} (a * (a * ((a \mathbin{-\!\!*} b) * \neg b)))))) \rightarrow ((((\top^* * a) * (a * ((a \mathbin{-\!\!*} b) * \neg b))) \rightarrow (((a * a) * (a \mathbin{-\!\!*} b)) * \neg b)) * \top^*))$ | timeout(1000s) | fail | 49.584 |
| (18) | $(F * F) \rightarrow F$, where $F := \neg(\top \mathbin{-\!\!*} \neg\top^*)$ | invalid | invalid | 0.004 |
| (19) | $(\top^* \wedge (a * b)) \rightarrow a$ | invalid | invalid | 0.003 |

**Table 2.** Experimental results from the prover Separata.

always tries to decompose the subformulae of a principal formula if possible. To guarantee completeness, each time we apply a $*R$ or $\mathbin{-\!\!*} L$ rule, the principal formula is moved to the end of the list, so that each principal formula for non-determinism rules $*R$, $\mathbin{-\!\!*} L$ is considered fairly, i.e. applied in turn.

We incorporate a number of optimisations in the proof search. (1) Back-jumping [2] is used to collect the "unsatisfiable core" along each branch. When one premise of a binary rule has a derivation, we try to derive the other premise only when the unsatisfiable core is not included in that premise. (2) A search strategy discussed by Park et al [27] is also adopted. For $*R$ and $\mathbin{-\!\!*} L$ applications, we forbid the search to consider applying the rule twice with the same pair of principal formula and principal relational atom, since the effect is the same as contraction, which is admissible. (3) Previous work on theorem proving for BBI has shown that associativity of $*$ is a source of inefficiency in proof search [16, 27]. We borrow the idea of the heuristic method presented in [16] to quickly solve certain associativity instances. When we detect $z : A * B$ on the right hand side of a sequent, we try to search for possible worlds (labels) for the subformulae of $A, B$ in the sequent, and construct a binary tree using these labels. For example, if we can find $x : A$ and $y : B$ in the sequent, we will take $x, y$ as the children of $z$. When we can build such a binary tree of labels, the corresponding relational atoms given by the binary tree will be used (if they are in the sequent) as the prioritised ones when decomposing $z : A * B$ and its subformulae. Of course, without a free-variable system, our handling of this heuristic method is just a special case of the original one, but this approach can speed up the search in certain cases.

The experiments in this paper are conducted on a Dell Optiplex 790 desktop with Intel CORE i7 2600 @ 3.4 GHz CPU and 8GB memory, running Ubuntu 13.04. The theorem provers are written in Ocaml.

We test our prover Separata for $LS_{PASL} + D$ on the formulae listed in Table 2; the times displayed are in seconds. We compare the results with provers for BBI, BBeye [27] and the incomplete heuristic-based $FVLS_{BBI}$ [16], when the formula is valid in BBI. We run BBeye in an iterative deepening way, and the time counted for BBeye is the total time it spends. Formulae (1-14) are used by Park et al. to test their prover BBeye for BBI [27]. We can see that for formulae (1-14) the performance of Separata is comparable with the heuristic based prover for $FVLS_{BBI}$. Both provers are generally faster than BBeye. Formula (15) is one that BBeye had trouble with [16], but Separata handles it trivially. However, there are cases where BBeye is faster than Separata. We found the example formula (16) from a set of testings on randomly generated BBI theorems. Formula (17) is a converse example where a randomly generated BBI theorem causes BBeye to time out and $FVLS_{BBI}$ with heuristics to terminate within the timeout but without finding a proof due to its incompleteness. Formula (18) is valid only when the monoid is partial [22], and formula (19) is the axiom of indivisible unit. Some interesting cases for disjointness will be shown later. We do not investigate the details in the performances between these provers because they are for different logics. We leave further optimisations for Separata as future work.

## 7. Future work

In this paper we have focused on *propositional* inference, but the assertion language of separation logic is generally taken to include first-order logic, usually extended with arithmetic, or at least equality. More importantly, this language is interpreted only with respect to some *concrete* semantics, the most well-known of which is the original heap model of Reynolds [29]. We refer readers to that paper for a more careful description of this model; for the purposes of this section we will remark that *values* range across the integers, and *addresses* across some specified subset of the integers; that *heaps* are finite partial functions from addresses to values; and that *expressions* are built up from variables (evaluated with respect to some store), values, and the usual arithmetic operations.

The advantage of this model is that it supports the interpretation of the *points-to* predicate $\mapsto$, which allows direct reference to the contents of the heap: $E \mapsto E'$ is satisfied by a heap iff it is a singleton map sending the address specified by the expression $E$ to the value specified by the expression $E'$.

The question for future research is whether our labelled sequent calculus and implementation could be extended to reason about such concrete predicates; this section presents preliminary work in this direction. While the full power of pointer arithmetic is an important subject for future work, for the purpose of this work we set arithmetic aside and let expressions range across store variables $e, e_1, e_2, \ldots$ only, as is done for example by Berdine et al [3]. The rules for quantifiers are straightforward, e.g.:

$$\frac{\mathcal{G}; \Gamma; h : F[e/x] \vdash \Delta}{\mathcal{G}; \Gamma; h : \exists x.F \vdash \Delta} \exists L \qquad \frac{\mathcal{G}; \Gamma \vdash h : F[e/x]; \Delta}{\mathcal{G}; \Gamma \vdash h : \exists x.F; \Delta} \exists R$$

where $e$ does not appear free in the conclusion of $\exists L$.

Equality between variables simply requires that they are assigned by the store to the same value, giving rise to the rules

$$\frac{\mathcal{G}; \Gamma[e_2/e_1] \vdash \Delta[e_2/e_1]}{\mathcal{G}; \Gamma; h : e_1 = e_2 \vdash \Delta} = L \qquad \frac{}{\mathcal{G}; \Gamma \vdash h : e = e; \Delta} = R$$

Points-to poses a more complex problem as it involves direct interaction with the contents of heaps; Fig. 4 presents putative labelled sequent rules for this predicate. The semantics of $e_1 \mapsto e_2$ first require that the heap be a singleton, which is a spatial property that can be captured by abstract semantics: a 'singleton' world is not equal to the identity world $\epsilon$, and cannot be split into two non-$\epsilon$ worlds. This motivates rules $\mapsto L_1$ and $\mapsto L_2$. The rules $\mapsto L_3$ and $\mapsto L_4$ address the content of heaps: $\mapsto L_3$ says that two heaps with the same address (value of $e_1$) must be the same heap, and $\mapsto L_4$ says that a singleton heap makes a unique assignment.

Our implementation of the calculus defined by adding these rules to $LS_{PASL} + D$ is not complete w.r.t. Reynolds' semantics: for example it is unable to prove the formula below, which is based on a property for septraction due to Vafeiadis and Parkinson [32], and is valid in the heap model:

$$\top^* \to \neg((e_1 \mapsto e_2) \mathrel{-\!\!*} \neg(e_1 \mapsto e_2)) \qquad (5)$$

This formula essentially asserts that a heap satisfying $e_1 \mapsto e_2$ is possible to construct, but our prover does not support explicit heap construction. Nevertheless this incomplete calculus does support strikingly elegant proofs of non-trivial separation logic inferences, such as the DISJOINT axiom of Parkinson [28, Cha. 5.3]:

$$\dfrac{\dfrac{\dfrac{\dfrac{\dfrac{}{(\epsilon, \epsilon \triangleright a_0); \epsilon : (e_1 \mapsto e_2) \vdash a_0 : \bot} \mapsto L1}{(a_1, a_1 \triangleright a_0); a_1 : (e_1 \mapsto e_2) \vdash a_0 : \bot} D}{(a_1, a_2 \triangleright a_0); a_1 : (e_1 \mapsto e_2); a_2 : (e_1 \mapsto e_2) \vdash a_0 : \bot} \mapsto L3}{; a_0 : (e_1 \mapsto e_2) * (e_1 \mapsto e_2) \vdash a_0 : \bot} *L}{; \vdash a_0 : ((e_1 \mapsto e_2) * (e_1 \mapsto e_2)) \to \bot} \to R$$

Our experimental prover Separata+, extending $LS_{PASL} + D$ with the rules of this section, has proved a number of tested SL formulae very rapidly; see Table 3 for some examples. Formulae (1-3) are taken from Galmiche and Méry [14]; in particular, the first is the DISJOINT axiom proved above. Formulae (4-6) are taken from Vafeiadis and Parkinson's study of magic wand's De Morgan dual *septraction*, $\neg(A \mathrel{-\!\!*} \neg B)$ [32]. These results present encouraging evidence that the work of this paper may form the basis of practical theorem proving for the assertion language of separation logic.

Dealing with splittability and cross-split in our labelled calculi is one of our next goals. We are also interested in extending the techniques of this paper to concrete semantics other than Reynolds' heap models, such as those surveyed by Calcagno et al [8] and Jensen and Birkedal [18].

## 8. Related work

There are many more automated tools, formalisations, and logical embeddings for separation logic than can reasonably be surveyed within the scope of this conference paper. Almost all are not directly comparable to this paper because they deal with separation logic for some *concrete* semantics.

One exception to this concrete approach is Holfoot [31], a HOL mechanisation with support for automated reasoning about the 'shape' of SL specifications – exactly those aspects captured by abstract separation logic. However, unlike Separata, Holfoot does not support magic wand. This is a common restriction when automating any notion of SL, because $\mathrel{-\!\!*}$ is a source of undecidability [4]. Conversely, the mechanisations and embeddings that do incorporate magic wand tend to give little thought to (semi-) decision procedures. An important exception to this is the tableaux of Galmiche and Méry [14], which are designed for the decidable fragment of the assertion language of concrete separation logic with $\mathrel{-\!\!*}$ identified by Calcagno et al [7], but may also be extendable to the full assertion language. These methods have not been implemented, and given the difficulty of the development we expect that practical implementation would be non-trivial. Another partial exception to the trend to omit $\mathrel{-\!\!*}$ is SmallfootRG [9], which supports automation yet includes *septraction* [32], the De Morgan dual of $\mathrel{-\!\!*}$. However SmallfootRG does not support additive negation nor implication, and so $\mathrel{-\!\!*}$ cannot be recovered; indeed in this setting septraction is mere 'syntactic sugar' that can be eliminated.

The denigration of magic wand is not without cost, as the connective, while surely less useful than $*$, has found application. A non-exhaustive list follows: generating weakest preconditions via backwards reasoning [17]; specifying iterators [15, 19, 28]; reasoning about parallelism [12]; and various applications of septraction, such as the specification of iterators and buffers [10]. For a particularly deeply developed example, see the correctness proof for the Schorr-Waite Graph Marking Algorithm of Yang [33], which involves non-trivial inferences involving $\mathrel{-\!\!*}$ (Lems. 78 and 79). These examples provide ample motivation to build proof calculi and tool support that include magic wand. Undecidability, which in any case is pervasive in program proof, should not deter us from seeking practically useful automation.

Our work builds upon the labelled sequent calculi for BBI of Hóu et al [16]. Their prover $FVLS_{BBI}$ implements a free-variable calculus for BBI but is incomplete. Our extensions to Hóu et al involves two main advances: first, a counter-model construction necessary to prove completeness; second, our prover deals with labelled sequents directly and (given certain fairness assumptions) is a complete semi-decision procedure for PASL and its variants. The link between BBI and SL is also emphasised as motivation by Park et al [27], whose BBI prover BBeye was used for comparisons in Sec. 6. This work was recently refined by Lee and Park [23], in work independent to our own, to a labelled sequent calculus for Reynolds' heap model. Their calculus, like ours, cannot prove the formula (5)[4] and so is not complete for these semantics. Also related, but so far not implemented, are the tableaux for partial-deterministic BBI of Larchey-Wendling and Galmiche [20, 21], which, as mentioned in the introduction to this paper, are claimed to be extendable with cancellativity to attain PASL via a "rather involved" proof. In contrast, the relative ease with which certain properties can be added or removed from labelled sequent calculi is an important benefit of our approach; this advantage comes from structural rules which directly capture the conditions on Kripke relational frames, and handle the equality of worlds by explicit global substitutions.

Finally we note that the counter-model construction of this paper was necessary to prove completeness because many of the properties we are interested in are not BBI-axiomatisable, as proved by Brotherston and Villard [6]; that paper goes on to give a sound and complete Hilbert axiomatisation of these properties by extending BBI with techniques from hybrid logic. Sequent calculus and proof search in this setting is another promising future direction.

[4] Confirmed by private communications with authors.

$$\frac{}{\mathcal{G};\Gamma;\epsilon : e_1 \mapsto e_2 \vdash \Delta} \mapsto L_1 \qquad \frac{\begin{array}{c}(\epsilon, h_0 \rhd h_0);\mathcal{G}[\epsilon/h_1][h_0/h_2];\Gamma[\epsilon/h_1][h_0/h_2];h_0 : e_1 \mapsto e_2 \vdash \Delta[\epsilon/h_1][h_0/h_2] \\ (h_0, \epsilon \rhd h_0);\mathcal{G}[\epsilon/h_2][h_0/h_1];\Gamma[\epsilon/h_2][h_0/h_1];h_0 : e_1 \mapsto e_2 \vdash \Delta[\epsilon/h_2][h_0/h_1]\end{array}}{(h_1, h_2 \rhd h_0);\mathcal{G};\Gamma;h_0 : e_1 \mapsto e_2 \vdash \Delta} \mapsto L_2$$

$$\frac{\mathcal{G}[h/h'];\Gamma[h/h'];h : e_1 \mapsto e_2;h : e_1 \mapsto e_3 \vdash \Delta[h/h']}{\mathcal{G};\Gamma;h : e_1 \mapsto e_2;h' : e_1 \mapsto e_3 \vdash \Delta} \mapsto L_3 \qquad \frac{\mathcal{G};\Gamma[e_1/e_3][e_2/e_4];h : e_1 \mapsto e_2 \vdash \Delta[e_1/e_3][e_2/e_4]}{\mathcal{G};\Gamma;h : e_1 \mapsto e_2;h : e_3 \mapsto e_4 \vdash \Delta} \mapsto L_4$$

**Figure 4.** Some rules for the predicate $\mapsto$ in separation logic.

| | Formula | Separata+ |
|---|---|---|
| (1) | $((e_1 \mapsto e_2) * (e_1 \mapsto e_2)) \to \bot$ | 0.004 |
| (2) | $(((e1 \mapsto e2) * (e3 \mapsto e4)) \wedge ((e1 \mapsto e2) * (e5 \mapsto e6))) \to ((e3 \mapsto e6) * \top)$ | 0.002 |
| (3) | $(\exists x3x2x1.(((x3 \mapsto x2) * (x1 \mapsto e)) \wedge (x2 = x1))) \to (\exists x4x5.((x4 \mapsto x5) * (x5 \mapsto e)))$ | 0.001 |
| (4) | $\neg((e1 \mapsto e2) -\!\!* \neg(e3 \mapsto e4)) \to ((e1 = e3) \wedge ((e2 = e4) \wedge \top^*))$ | 0.004 |
| (5) | $\neg(((e1 \mapsto p) * (e2 \mapsto q)) -\!\!* \neg(e3 \mapsto r)) \to \neg(((e1 \mapsto p) -\!\!* \neg(\neg((e2 \mapsto q) -\!\!* \neg(e3 \mapsto r)))))$ | 0.002 |
| (6) | $\neg((e1 \mapsto p) -\!\!* \neg(e2 \mapsto q)) \to \neg((e1 \mapsto p) -\!\!* \neg((e2 \mapsto q) \wedge ((e1 \mapsto p) * \top)))$ | 0.003 |

**Table 3.** Experimental results from the prover Separata+.

# References


[1] A. W. Appel. Tactics for separation logic. Unpublished, 2006.

[2] F. Baader. *The Description Logic Handbook: Theory, Implementation, and Applications*. Cambridge University Press, 2003.

[3] J. Berdine, C. Calcagno, and P. W. OHearn. Symbolic execution with separation logic. In *APLAS*, volume 3780 of *LNCS*, pages 52–68, 2005.

[4] R. Brochenin, S. Demria, and E. Lozes. On the almighty wand. *Inform. and Comput.*, 211:106–137, 2012.

[5] J. Brotherston and M. Kanovich. Undecidability of propositional separation logic and its neighbours. In *LICS*, pages 130–139. IEEE, 2010.

[6] J. Brotherston and J. Villard. Parametric completeness for separation theories. Technical Report RN/13/11, UCL, 2013.

[7] C. Calcagno, H. Yang, and P. W. OHearn. Computability and complexity results for a spatial assertion language for data structures. In *FSTTCS*, volume 2245 of *LNCS*, pages 108–119, 2001.

[8] C. Calcagno, P. W. O'Hearn, and H. Yang. Local action and abstract separation logic. In *LICS*, pages 366–378. IEEE, 2007.

[9] C. Calcagno, M. Parkinson, and V. Vafeiadis. Modular safety checking for fine-grained concurrency. In *SAS*, volume 4634 of *LNCS*, 2007.

[10] R. Cherini and J. O. Blanco. Local reasoning for abstraction and sharing. In *SAC*, pages 552–557. ACM, 2009.

[11] R. Dockins, A. Hobor, and A. W. Appel. A fresh look at separation algebras and share accounting. In *APLAS*, volume 5904 of *LNCS*, pages 161–177, 2009.

[12] M. Dodds, S. Jagannathan, and M. J. Parkinson. Modular reasoning for deterministic parallelism. In *POPL*, pages 259–270. ACM, 2011.

[13] D. Galmiche and D. Larchey-Wendling. Expressivity properties of boolean BI through relational models. In *FSTTCS*, volume 4337 of *LNCS*, pages 357–368, 2006.

[14] D. Galmiche and D. Méry. Tableaux and resource graphs for separation logic. *J. Logic Comput.*, 20(1):189–231, 2007.

[15] C. Haack and C. Hurlin. Resource usage protocols for iterators. *J. Object Tech.*, 8(4):55–83, 2009.

[16] Z. Hóu, A. Tiu, and R. Goré. A labelled sequent calculus for BBI: Proof theory and proof search. In *Tableaux*, LNCS, 2013. page 172-187; extended version at arXiv:1302.4783.

[17] S. Ishtiaq and P. W. O'Hearn. BI as an assertion language for mutable data structures. In *POPL*, pages 14–26. ACM, 2001.

[18] J. B. Jensen and L. Birkedal. Fictional separation logic. In *ESOP*, volume 7211 of *LNCS*, pages 377–396, 2012.

[19] N. R. Krishnaswami. Reasoning about iterators with separation logic. In *SAVCBS*, pages 83–86. ACM, 2006.

[20] D. Larchey-Wendling. The formal strong completeness of partial monoidal boolean BI. To appear in J. Logic. Comput., 2013.

[21] D. Larchey-Wendling and D. Galmiche. Exploring the relation between intuitionistic BI and boolean BI: An unexpected embedding. *Math. Structures Comput. Sci.*, 19(3):435–500, 2009.

[22] D. Larchey-Wendling and D. Galmiche. The undecidability of boolean BI through phase semantics. In *LICS*, pages 140–149. IEEE, 2010.

[23] W. Lee and S. Park. A proof system for separation logic with magic wand. Technical Report CSE-2013-7, POSTECH, 2013.

[24] A. McCreight. Practical tactics for separation logic. In *TPHOLs*, volume 5674 of *Lecture Notes in Computer Science*, pages 343–358. Springer, 2009.

[25] S. Negri and J. von Plato. *Structural Proof Theory*. Cambridge University Press, 2001.

[26] P. W. O'Hearn and D. J. Pym. The logic of bunched implications. *Bull. Symbolic Logic*, 5(2):215–244, 1999.

[27] J. Park, J. Seo, and S. Park. A theorem prover for boolean BI. In *POPL*, pages 219–232. ACM, 2013.

[28] M. Parkinson. *Local Reasoning for Java*. PhD thesis, Cambridge, 2005.

[29] J. C. Reynolds. Separation logic: A logic for shared mutable data structures. In *LICS*, pages 55–74. IEEE, 2002.

[30] H. Tuch, G. Klein, and M. Norrish. Types, bytes, and separation logic. In *POPL*, pages 97–108. ACM, 2007.

[31] T. Tuerk. A formalisation of smallfoot in HOL. In *TPHOLs*, volume 5674 of *LNCS*, 2009.

[32] V. Vafeiadis and M. Parkinson. A marriage of rely/guarantee and separation logic. In *CONCUR*, volume 4703 of *LNCS*, pages 256–271, 2007.

[33] H. Yang. *Local Reasoning for Stateful Programs*. PhD thesis, Illinois at Urbana-Champaign, 2001.

# A Proof System for Separation Logic with Magic Wand

Wonyeol Lee Sungwoo Park

Department of Computer Science and Engineering
Pohang University of Science and Technology (POSTECH)
Republic of Korea
{leewy,gla}@postech.ac.kr

## Abstract

Separation logic is an extension of Hoare logic which is acknowledged as an enabling technology for large-scale program verification. It features two new logical connectives, separating conjunction and separating implication, but most of the applications of separation logic have exploited only separating conjunction without considering separating implication. Nevertheless the power of separating implication has been well recognized and there is a growing interest in its use for program verification. This paper develops a proof system for full separation logic which supports not only separating conjunction but also separating implication. The proof system is developed in the style of sequent calculus and satisfies the admissibility of cut. The key challenge in the development is to devise a set of inference rules for manipulating heap structures that ensure the completeness of the proof system with respect to separation logic. We show that our proof of completeness directly translates to a proof search strategy.

***Categories and Subject Descriptors*** F.4.1 [*Mathematical Logic*]: Mechanical theorem proving, Proof theory

***General Terms*** Verification

***Keywords*** Separation logic; Proof system; Theorem prover

## 1. Introduction

Separation logic [28] is an extension of Hoare logic designed to simplify reasoning about programs manipulating mutable data structures with potential pointer aliasing. It features two new logical connectives, separating conjunction $\star$ and separating implication $-\!\!\star$, whose semantics directly assumes memory heaps structured as a monoid. Separating conjunction allows us to describe properties of two disjoint heaps with a single logical formula: $A \star B$ means that a given heap can be divided into two disjoint heaps satisfying $A$ and $B$ respectively. Separating implication, commonly known as magic wand, allows us to reason about hypothetical heaps extending a given heap: $A -\!\!\star B$ means that if a given heap is extended with a disjoint heap satisfying $A$, the resultant heap satisfies $B$. The use of the two separating connectives naturally leads to local reasoning in program verification in that we only need to reason locally about those heaps directly affected by the program.

So far, most of the applications of separation logic have exploited only separating conjunction. For example, all existing verification tools based on separation logic, such as Smallfoot [3], Space Invader [11], THOR [23], SLAyer [1], HIP [25], jStar [12], Xisa [10], VeriFast [19], Infer [7], and Predator [14], use a decidable fragment by Berdine *et al.* [2] or its extension which provides only separating conjunction. By virtue of the principle of local reasoning, however, these tools are highly successful in their individual verification domains despite not using separating implication at all.

Although separating implication is not discussed as extensively as separating conjunction in the literature, its power in program verification has nevertheless been well recognized. Just around the inception of separation logic, Yang [29] already gives an elegant proof of the correctness of the Schorr-Waite algorithm which relies crucially on the use of separating implication in the main loop invariant. Krishnaswami [20] shows how to reason abstractly about an iterator protocol with separation logic by exploiting separating implication in the specification of iterators. Maeda *et al.* [22] adopt the idea of separating implication in extending an alias type system in order to express tail-recursive operations on recursive data structures. Recently Hobor and Villard [17] give a concise proof of the correctness of Cheney's garbage collector in a proof system based on the ramify rule, a cousin of the frame rule of separation logic, whose premise checks a logical entailment involving separating implication. These promising results arguably suggest that introducing separating implication alone raises the level of technology for program verification as much as separation logic only with separating conjunction improves on Hoare logic.

Despite the potential benefit of separating implication in program verification, however, there is still no practical theorem prover for full separation logic. The state-of-the-art theorem provers for separation logic such as SeLoger [16] and SLP [24] support only separating conjunction, and the labelled tableau calculus by Galmiche and Méry [15] does not directly give rise to a proof search strategy. Because of the unavailability of such a theorem prover, all proofs exploiting separating implication should be manually checked, which can be time-consuming even with the help of lemmas provided by the proof system (as in [17]). Another consequence is that no existing verification tools based on separation logic can fully support backward reasoning by weakest precondition generation, which requires separating implication whenever verifying heap assignments (see Ishtiaq and O'Hearn [18]).

This paper develops a proof system $\mathbf{P_{SL}}$ for full separation logic which supports not only separating conjunction but also separating implication. Its design is based on the principle of proof by contradiction from classical logic, and we develop its inference rules in the style of sequent calculus. $\mathbf{P_{SL}}$ uses a new form of sequent,



*POPL '14*, January 22–24, 2014, San Diego, CA, USA.

http://dx.doi.org/10.1145/2535838.2535871

called *world sequent*, in order to give a complete description of the world of heaps, and its use of world sequents allows us to treat separating implication in the same way that it treats separating conjunction. The key challenge in the development of $\mathbf{P_{SL}}$ is to devise a set of inference rules for manipulating heap structures so as to correctly analyze separating conjunction and separating implication. We show that $\mathbf{P_{SL}}$ satisfies the admissibility of cut and that it is sound and complete with respect to separation logic. The proof of completeness directly translates to a proof search strategy, which is the basis for our prototype implementation of $\mathbf{P_{SL}}$. We show that it is easy to extend $\mathbf{P_{SL}}$ with new logical connectives and predicates, such as an overlapping conjunction $A \uplus B$ by Hobor and Villard [17].

Separating implication has been commonly considered to be much harder to reason about than separating conjunction, as partially evidenced by lack of theorem provers supporting separating implication and abundance of verification systems supporting separating conjunction. Our development of $\mathbf{P_{SL}}$, however, suggests that a proof system designed in a principled way can support both logical connectives in a coherent way without requiring distinct treatments. Our prototype implementation of $\mathbf{P_{SL}}$ also suggests that such a proof system can develop into a practical theorem prover for separation logic. To the best of our knowledge, $\mathbf{P_{SL}}$ is the first proof system for full separation logic that satisfies the admissibility of cut and provides a concrete proof search strategy.

This paper is organized as follows. Section 2 gives preliminaries on separation logic. Section 3 develops our proof system $\mathbf{P_{SL}}$ and Section 4 gives three examples of proving world sequents. Section 6 proves the soundness and completeness of $\mathbf{P_{SL}}$ with respect to separation logic and Section 7 discusses the implementation and extension of $\mathbf{P_{SL}}$. Section 8 discusses related work and Section 9 concludes.

## 2. Semantics of separation logic

Separation logic extends classical first-order logic with multiplicative formulas from intuitionistic linear logic:

$$
\begin{array}{rlcl}
\text{formula} & A, B, C & ::= & P \mid \bot \mid \neg A \mid A \vee A \mid \\
 & & & \mathsf{I} \mid A \star A \mid A \mathrel{-\!\!\star} A \mid \exists a.A \\
\text{primitive formula} & P & ::= & [l \mapsto E] \mid E = E \mid \cdots \\
\text{expression} & E & ::= & x \mid a \mid \mathsf{L} \mid \cdots \\
\text{location expression} & l & ::= & x \mid a \mid \mathsf{L} \\
\text{value} & V & ::= & \mathsf{L} \mid \cdots \\
\text{location} & & & \mathsf{L}_1, \mathsf{L}_2, \mathsf{L}_3, \cdots \\
\text{stack variable} & & & x, y, z \\
\text{local variable} & & & a, b, c
\end{array}
$$

$\bot$, $\neg A$, $A \vee B$, and $\exists a.A$ are from classical first-order logic. $\mathsf{I}$ is the multiplicative unit. $A \star B$ is a separating conjunction and $A \mathrel{-\!\!\star} B$ is a separating implication. We define $\top$ as $\neg\bot$, $A \wedge B$ as $\neg(\neg A \vee \neg B)$, and $A \supset B$ as $\neg A \vee B$. We use conventional precedence rules for logical connectives: $\neg > \star > \vee > \mathrel{-\!\!\star} > \exists$. In this work, we do not consider inductively defined predicates.

Primitive formulas include a points-to relation $[l \mapsto E]$ for describing a singleton heap. All other primitive formulas describe relations between expressions; for simplicity, we consider only an equality relation $E = E'$. Expressions denote values which include locations $\mathsf{L}$. Location expressions are a special class of expressions that denote locations. In the present work, we allow only locations as values, but it should be straightforward to introduce additional forms of expressions for new types of values such as booleans and integers. We syntactically distinguish between stack variables which originate from the program being verified (and thus may be called global variables instead) and local variables which are introduced by existential quantifiers (and thus can never appear outside corresponding existential formulas).

We specify the semantics of separation logic with respect to a stack and a heap. A stack $S$ is a finite partial mapping $Var \rightharpoonup Val$ from stack variables to values where $Var$ denotes the set of stack variables and $Val$ denotes the set of values. Given a stack $S$, we can determine a unique value for every expression $E$, which we write as $[\![E]\!]_S$. A heap $H$ is a finite partial mapping $Loc \rightharpoonup Val$ from locations to values where $Loc$ denotes the set of locations. We write $H_1 \# H_2$ to mean that heaps $H_1$ and $H_2$ are disjoint, *i.e.*, $dom(H_1) \cap dom(H_2) = \varnothing$. We write $H_1 \circ H_2$ for the union of disjoint heaps $H_1$ and $H_2$ where $H_1 \# H_2$ is assumed, and $\epsilon$ for an empty heap. Heaps form a commutative cancellative monoid with $\circ$ as the associative operation and $\epsilon$ as the identity:

$$
\begin{array}{rl}
\text{(neutrality)} & H \circ \epsilon = H \\
\text{(commutativity)} & H_1 \circ H_2 = H_2 \circ H_1 \\
\text{(associativity)} & H_1 \circ (H_2 \circ H_3) = (H_1 \circ H_2) \circ H_3 \\
\text{(cancellativity)} & H \circ H_1 = H \circ H_2 \text{ implies } H_1 = H_2.
\end{array}
$$

Given a stack $S$ and a heap $H$, we obtain the semantics of separation logic from the satisfaction relation $(S, H) \models A$ for formulas defined as follows:

- $(S, H) \models [l \mapsto E]$ iff. $H = \langle [\![l]\!]_S \mapsto [\![E]\!]_S \rangle$, *i.e.*, $H$ is a singleton heap mapping $[\![l]\!]_S$ to $[\![E]\!]_S$.
- $(S, H) \models E = E'$ iff. $[\![E]\!]_S = [\![E']\!]_S$.
- $(S, H) \models \bot$ iff. never.
- $(S, H) \models \neg A$ iff. $(S, H) \not\models A$.
- $(S, H) \models A \vee B$ iff. $(S, H) \models A$ or $(S, H) \models B$.
- $(S, H) \models \mathsf{I}$ iff. $dom(H) = \varnothing$, *i.e.*, $H = \epsilon$.
- $(S, H) \models A \star B$ iff. $H = H_1 \circ H_2$ and $(S, H_1) \models A$ and $(S, H_2) \models B$ for some heaps $H_1$ and $H_2$.
- $(S, H) \models A \mathrel{-\!\!\star} B$ iff. $H_2 = H \circ H_1$ implies $(S, H_1) \not\models A$ or $(S, H_2) \models B$ for any heaps $H_1$ and $H_2$.
- $(S, H) \models \exists a.A$ iff. $(S, H) \models [V/a]A$ for some value $V$.

Note that the definition of $(S, H) \models \exists a.A$ directly substitutes value $V$ for local variable $a$ in formula $A$ (in $[V/a]A$) without extending stack $S$ because we syntactically distinguish between stack variables and local variables.

Although the satisfaction relation $(S, H) \models A$ is enough for specifying the semantics of separation logic, we deliberately derive the definition of its negation $(S, H) \not\models A$, which plays an equally important role in the development of our proof system:

- $(S, H) \not\models [l \mapsto E]$ iff. $H \neq \langle [\![l]\!]_S \mapsto [\![E]\!]_S \rangle$, *i.e.*, $dom(H) \neq \{[\![l]\!]_S\}$ or $H([\![l]\!]_S) \neq [\![E]\!]_S$.
- $(S, H) \not\models E = E'$ iff. $[\![E]\!]_S \neq [\![E']\!]_S$.
- $(S, H) \not\models \bot$ iff. always.
- $(S, H) \not\models \neg A$ iff. $(S, H) \models A$.
- $(S, H) \not\models A \vee B$ iff. $(S, H) \not\models A$ and $(S, H) \not\models B$.
- $(S, H) \not\models \mathsf{I}$ iff. $dom(H) \neq \varnothing$, *i.e.*, $H \neq \epsilon$.
- $(S, H) \not\models A \star B$ iff. $H = H_1 \circ H_2$ implies $(S, H_1) \not\models A$ or $(S, H_2) \not\models B$ for any heaps $H_1$ and $H_2$.
- $(S, H) \not\models A \mathrel{-\!\!\star} B$ iff. $H_2 = H \circ H_1$ and $(S, H_1) \models A$ and $(S, H_2) \not\models B$ for some heaps $H_1$ and $H_2$.
- $(S, H) \not\models \exists a.A$ iff. $(S, H) \not\models [V/a]A$ for any value $V$.

We observe that the definition for separating implication is symmetric to the definition for separating conjunction:

- $(S, H) \models A \star B$ should find a certain pair of heaps whereas $(S, H) \not\models A \star B$ should analyze an unspecified pair of heaps.
- $(S, H) \models A \mathrel{-\!\!\star} B$ should analyze an unspecified pair of heaps whereas $(S, H) \not\models A \mathrel{-\!\!\star} B$ should find a certain pair of heaps.

This symmetry suggests that we can incorporate separating implication into the proof system in an analogous way to separating conjunction.

A formula $A$ is valid, written $\models A$, if $(S, H) \models A$ holds for every stack $S$ and heap $H$. Our proof system $\mathbf{P_{SL}}$ can check the validity of every formula in separation logic.

# 3. Proof system $\mathbf{P_{SL}}$ for separation logic

This section presents the proof system $\mathbf{P_{SL}}$ for separation logic which is developed in the style of sequent calculus. We first explain *world sequents*, the main judgment in $\mathbf{P_{SL}}$, and then present the inference rules.

## 3.1 World sequents

The design of $\mathbf{P_{SL}}$ is based on the principle of proof by contradiction from classical logic. We describe the state of each heap with a set of true formulas and another set of false formulas. A world sequent in $\mathbf{P_{SL}}$ gives a description of the entire world of heaps, and a derivation of it means that the description is self-contradictory. Hence, in order to check the validity of a formula in separation logic, we use it as a false formula about an arbitrary heap $w$ (about which nothing is known) and attempt to produce a logical contradiction by proving a world sequent consisting solely of heap $w$. The definition of world sequents and the principle of proof by contradiction are inherited from the nested sequent calculus for Boolean BI by Park *et al.* [26].

Since $\mathbf{P_{SL}}$ is designed to check the validity of a formula, it assumes an arbitrary stack, which implies that every stack variable denotes an arbitrary value. This in turn implies that in a derivation of a world sequent, we may use a fresh stack variable to denote an arbitrary value. We exploit this interpretation of stack variables in an inference rule for first-order formulas.

A world sequent consists of expression relations $\Theta$, heap relations $\Sigma$, and heap sequents $\Pi$:

| | | | |
|---|---|---|---|
| expression relation | $\theta$ | $::=$ | $E = E' \mid E \neq E'$ |
| expression relations | $\Theta$ | $=$ | $\theta_1, \cdots, \theta_n$ |
| heap variable | $w, u, v$ | | |
| heap relation | $\sigma$ | $::=$ | $w \doteq \epsilon \mid w \not\doteq \epsilon \mid$ $w \doteq [l \mapsto E] \mid w \not\doteq [l \mapsto E] \mid$ $w \doteq w_1 \circ w_2$ |
| heap relations | $\Sigma$ | $=$ | $\sigma_1, \cdots, \sigma_n$ |
| truth context | $\Gamma$ | $::=$ | $\cdot \mid \Gamma, A$ |
| falsehood context | $\Delta$ | $::=$ | $\cdot \mid \Delta, A$ |
| heap sequent | $\pi$ | $::=$ | $[\Gamma \Longrightarrow \Delta]^w$ |
| heap sequents | $\Pi$ | $=$ | $\pi_1, \cdots, \pi_n$ |
| world sequent | $\Theta; \Sigma \parallel \Pi$ | | |

- An expression relation $\theta$ is an equality or inequality between two expressions. If we introduce new forms of primitive formulas (*e.g.*, $E < E'$), we should introduce corresponding forms of expression relations.
- We assign a heap variable to each heap, and a heap relation $\sigma$ relates a heap to an empty heap ($w \doteq \epsilon$ and $w \not\doteq \epsilon$), a singleton heap ($w \doteq [l \mapsto E]$ and $w \not\doteq [l \mapsto E]$), or the union of two disjoint heaps ($w \doteq w_1 \circ w_2$). We refer to those heap relation involving an empty heap or a singleton heap as *atomic heap relations*. As heaps form a commutative (cancellative) monoid, we assume commutativity of $\circ$ and use $w_1 \circ w_2$ and $w_2 \circ w_1$ interchangeably.
- A heap sequent $[\Gamma \Longrightarrow \Delta]^w$ describes heap $w$ with truth context $\Gamma$ and falsehood context $\Delta$ which contain true formulas and false formulas, respectively, about heap $w$.

In this way, a world sequent $\Theta; \Sigma \parallel \Pi$ gives a complete description of the world of heaps. We require that no local variable appear in expression relations and heap relations, and that a world sequent contain a unique heap sequent for each heap variable.

A world sequent represents a graph of heaps induced by heap relations. Given a heap relation $w \doteq w_1 \circ w_2$, we say that parent heap $w$ has two child heaps $w_1$ and $w_2$ which are sibling heaps to each other. We can also extend parent-child relations to derive ancestor-descendant relations. If a heap has no pair of child heaps, we call it a terminal heap (where we ignore such a heap relation as $w \doteq w \circ w_\epsilon$ with $w_\epsilon \doteq \epsilon$); otherwise we call it a non-terminal heap. Note that a heap relation $w \doteq \epsilon$ or $w \doteq [l \mapsto E]$ does not immediately mean that $w$ is a terminal heap because we may have another heap relation $w \doteq w_1 \circ w_2$. $\mathbf{P_{SL}}$, however, allows us to normalize all heap relations and turn $w$ into a terminal heap.

$\mathbf{P_{SL}}$ also uses an expression contradiction judgment $\Theta \vdash \bot$ which is an abbreviation of a particular form of a world sequent $\Theta; \cdot \parallel \cdot$ and means that expression relations $\Theta$ produce a logical contradiction. Since the definition of expression relations is extensible, we do not give inference rules for the expression contradiction judgment and just assume a decidable system for it. For simplicity, we write $\Theta \vdash E = E'$ for $\Theta, E \neq E' \vdash \bot$, and $\Theta \vdash E \neq E'$ for $\Theta, E = E' \vdash \bot$. We write $\Theta \vdash [l \mapsto E] = [l' \mapsto E']$ for $\Theta \vdash l = l'$ and $\Theta \vdash E = E'$, and $\Theta \vdash [l \mapsto E] \neq [l' \mapsto E']$ for $\Theta \vdash l \neq l'$ or $\Theta \vdash E \neq E'$.

$\mathbf{P_{SL}}$ consists of logical rules in Figure 1, structural rules in Figure 2, and heap contradiction rules in Figure 3. The logical rules deal with formulas in heap sequents $\Pi$, the structural rules reorganize graphs of heaps induced by heap relations $\Sigma$, and the heap contradiction rules detect logical contradictions in heap relations $\Sigma$, or *heap contradictions*. $\mathbf{P_{SL}}$ shares the logical rules (for propositional and multiplicative formulas) with the nested sequent calculus for Boolean BI in [26], but the structural rules and the heap contradiction rules are specific to separation logic. We read every inference rule from the conclusion to the premise, and the derivation of a world sequent always terminates with a proof of a logical contradiction. Hence, in order to show the validity of a formula $A$, we try to prove a world sequent $\cdot; \cdot \parallel [\cdot \Longrightarrow A]^w$.

## 3.2 Logical rules of $\mathbf{P_{SL}}$

Figure 1 shows the logical rules of $\mathbf{P_{SL}}$. Except for the rule ExpCont, a logical rule focuses on a principal formula in a heap sequent and either produces a logical contradiction (in the rule $\bot$L) or rewrites the world sequent of the conclusion according to the semantics of separation logic in Section 2. For each type of formulas, $\mathbf{P_{SL}}$ has both a left rule, which analyzes a true formula about a heap, and a right rule, which analyzes a false formula about a heap, as in a typical sequent calculus. The rules for points-to relations introduce a corresponding heap relation. The rules for propositional and first-order formulas are from first-order classical logic. In the rule $\exists$L, the fresh stack variable $x$ denotes an arbitrary value. In the rules $\exists$L and $\exists$R, we write $[E/a]A$ for substituting expression $E$ for local variable $a$ in formula $A$. The rules =L and =R are the only rules that add expression relations, and the rule ExpCont checks if expression relations $\Theta$ produce a logical contradiction.

The rules IL and IR use the fact the I is true only at an empty heap. The rules $\star$L and $\star$R are based on the following interpretation of multiplicative conjunction $\star$ which closely matches the semantics of separation logic in Section 2:

- $A \star B$ is true at heap $w$ iff. $w \doteq w_1 \circ w_2$ and $A$ is true at heap $w_1$ and $B$ is true at heap $w_2$ for *some* heaps $w_1$ and $w_2$.
- $A \star B$ is false at heap $w$ iff. $w \doteq w_1 \circ w_2$ implies that $A$ is false at heap $w_1$ or that $B$ is false at heap $w_2$ for *any* heaps $w_1$ and $w_2$.

Hence the rule $\star$L creates (*some*) fresh child heaps $w_1$ and $w_2$, whereas the rule $\star$R chooses (*any*) existing child heaps $w_1$ and

Rules for points-to relations:

$$\frac{\Theta;\Sigma, w \doteq [l \mapsto E] \parallel \Pi, [\Gamma \Longrightarrow \Delta]^{w}}{\Theta;\Sigma \parallel \Pi, [\Gamma, [l \mapsto E] \Longrightarrow \Delta]^{w}}\ {\mapsto}\mathsf{L} \qquad \frac{\Theta;\Sigma, w \not\doteq [l \mapsto E] \parallel \Pi, [\Gamma \Longrightarrow \Delta]^{w}}{\Theta;\Sigma \parallel \Pi, [\Gamma \Longrightarrow \Delta, [l \mapsto E]]^{w}}\ {\mapsto}\mathsf{R}$$

Rules for propositional formulas:

$$\frac{}{\Theta;\Sigma \parallel \Pi, [\Gamma, \bot \Longrightarrow \Delta]^{w}}\ \bot\mathsf{L} \qquad \frac{\Theta;\Sigma \parallel \Pi, [\Gamma \Longrightarrow \Delta, A]^{w}}{\Theta;\Sigma \parallel \Pi, [\Gamma, \neg A \Longrightarrow \Delta]^{w}}\ \neg\mathsf{L} \qquad \frac{\Theta;\Sigma \parallel \Pi, [\Gamma, A \Longrightarrow \Delta]^{w}}{\Theta;\Sigma \parallel \Pi, [\Gamma \Longrightarrow \Delta, \neg A]^{w}}\ \neg\mathsf{R}$$

$$\frac{\Theta;\Sigma \parallel \Pi, [\Gamma, A \Longrightarrow \Delta]^{w} \quad \Theta;\Sigma \parallel \Pi, [\Gamma, B \Longrightarrow \Delta]^{w}}{\Theta;\Sigma \parallel \Pi, [\Gamma, A \vee B \Longrightarrow \Delta]^{w}}\ \vee\mathsf{L} \qquad \frac{\Theta;\Sigma \parallel \Pi, [\Gamma \Longrightarrow \Delta, A, B]^{w}}{\Theta;\Sigma \parallel \Pi, [\Gamma \Longrightarrow \Delta, A \vee B]^{w}}\ \vee\mathsf{R}$$

Rules for multiplicative formulas:

$$\frac{\Theta;\Sigma, w \doteq \epsilon \parallel \Pi, [\Gamma \Longrightarrow \Delta]^{w}}{\Theta;\Sigma \parallel \Pi, [\Gamma, \mathsf{I} \Longrightarrow \Delta]^{w}}\ \mathsf{IL} \qquad \frac{\Theta;\Sigma, w \not\doteq \epsilon \parallel \Pi, [\Gamma \Longrightarrow \Delta]^{w}}{\Theta;\Sigma \parallel \Pi, [\Gamma \Longrightarrow \Delta, \mathsf{I}]^{w}}\ \mathsf{IR}$$

$$\frac{\textit{fresh } w_1, w_2 \quad \Theta;\Sigma, w \doteq w_1 \circ w_2 \parallel \Pi, [\Gamma \Longrightarrow \Delta]^{w}, [A \Longrightarrow \cdot]^{w_1}, [B \Longrightarrow \cdot]^{w_2}}{\Theta;\Sigma \parallel \Pi, [\Gamma, A \star B \Longrightarrow \Delta]^{w}}\ \star\mathsf{L}$$

$$\frac{w \doteq w_1 \circ w_2 \in \Sigma \quad \begin{array}{l} \Theta;\Sigma \parallel \Pi, [\Gamma \Longrightarrow \Delta, A \star B]^{w}, [\Gamma_1 \Longrightarrow \Delta_1, A]^{w_1}, [\Gamma_2 \Longrightarrow \Delta_2]^{w_2} \\ \Theta;\Sigma \parallel \Pi, [\Gamma \Longrightarrow \Delta, A \star B]^{w}, [\Gamma_1 \Longrightarrow \Delta_1]^{w_1}, [\Gamma_2 \Longrightarrow \Delta_2, B]^{w_2} \end{array}}{\Theta;\Sigma \parallel \Pi, [\Gamma \Longrightarrow \Delta, A \star B]^{w}, [\Gamma_1 \Longrightarrow \Delta_1]^{w_1}, [\Gamma_2 \Longrightarrow \Delta_2]^{w_2}}\ \star\mathsf{R}$$

$$\frac{w_2 \doteq w \circ w_1 \in \Sigma \quad \begin{array}{l} \Theta;\Sigma \parallel \Pi, [\Gamma, A \mathrel{-\!\!\star} B \Longrightarrow \Delta]^{w}, [\Gamma_1 \Longrightarrow \Delta_1, A]^{w_1}, [\Gamma_2 \Longrightarrow \Delta_2]^{w_2} \\ \Theta;\Sigma \parallel \Pi, [\Gamma, A \mathrel{-\!\!\star} B \Longrightarrow \Delta]^{w}, [\Gamma_1 \Longrightarrow \Delta_1]^{w_1}, [\Gamma_2, B \Longrightarrow \Delta_2]^{w_2} \end{array}}{\Theta;\Sigma \parallel \Pi, [\Gamma, A \mathrel{-\!\!\star} B \Longrightarrow \Delta]^{w}, [\Gamma_1 \Longrightarrow \Delta_1]^{w_1}, [\Gamma_2 \Longrightarrow \Delta_2]^{w_2}}\ {\mathrel{-\!\!\star}}\mathsf{L}$$

$$\frac{\textit{fresh } w_1, w_2 \quad \Theta;\Sigma, w_2 \doteq w \circ w_1 \parallel \Pi, [\Gamma \Longrightarrow \Delta]^{w}, [A \Longrightarrow \cdot]^{w_1}, [\cdot \Longrightarrow B]^{w_2}}{\Theta;\Sigma \parallel \Pi, [\Gamma \Longrightarrow \Delta, A \mathrel{-\!\!\star} B]^{w}}\ {\mathrel{-\!\!\star}}\mathsf{R}$$

Rules for first-order formulas:

$$\frac{\textit{fresh } x \quad \Theta;\Sigma \parallel \Pi, [\Gamma, [x/a]A \Longrightarrow \Delta]^{w}}{\Theta;\Sigma \parallel \Pi, [\Gamma, \exists a.A \Longrightarrow \Delta]^{w}}\ \exists\mathsf{L} \qquad \frac{\Theta;\Sigma \parallel \Pi, [\Gamma \Longrightarrow \Delta, [E/a]A, \exists a.A]^{w}}{\Theta;\Sigma \parallel \Pi, [\Gamma \Longrightarrow \Delta, \exists a.A]^{w}}\ \exists\mathsf{R}$$

Rules for primitive formulas for expressions:

$$\frac{\Theta, E = E';\Sigma \parallel \Pi, [\Gamma \Longrightarrow \Delta]^{w}}{\Theta;\Sigma \parallel \Pi, [\Gamma, E = E' \Longrightarrow \Delta]^{w}}\ {=}\mathsf{L} \qquad \frac{\Theta, E \neq E';\Sigma \parallel \Pi, [\Gamma \Longrightarrow \Delta]^{w}}{\Theta;\Sigma \parallel \Pi, [\Gamma \Longrightarrow \Delta, E = E']^{w}}\ {=}\mathsf{R} \qquad \frac{\Theta \vdash \bot}{\Theta;\Sigma \parallel \Pi}\ \mathsf{ExpCont}$$

**Figure 1.** Logical rules in the proof system $\mathbf{P_{SL}}$ for separation logic

$w_2$. Similarly the rules ${\mathrel{-\!\!\star}}\mathsf{L}$ and ${\mathrel{-\!\!\star}}\mathsf{R}$ are based on the following interpretation of multiplicative implication $\mathrel{-\!\!\star}$:

- $A \mathrel{-\!\!\star} B$ is true at heap $w$ iff. $w_2 \doteq w \circ w_1$ implies that $A$ is false at heap $w_1$ or that $B$ is true at heap $w_2$ for *any* heaps $w_1$ and $w_2$.
- $A \mathrel{-\!\!\star} B$ is false at heap $w$ iff. $w_2 \doteq w \circ w_1$ and $A$ is true at heap $w_1$ and $B$ is false at heap $w_2$ for *some* heaps $w_1$ and $w_2$.

Hence the rule ${\mathrel{-\!\!\star}}\mathsf{L}$ chooses (*any*) existing sibling heap $w_1$ and parent heap $w_2$, whereas as the rule ${\mathrel{-\!\!\star}}\mathsf{R}$ creates (*some*) fresh sibling heap $w_1$ and parent heap $w_2$. The rules $\star\mathsf{L}$ and ${\mathrel{-\!\!\star}}\mathsf{R}$ are the only logical rules that add parent-child heap relations to extend the graph of heaps, and introduce fresh heap variables $w_1$ and $w_2$ that are not found in the world sequent in the conclusion. The rules $\star\mathsf{R}$ and ${\mathrel{-\!\!\star}}\mathsf{L}$ are the only logical rules that replicate the principal formula into world sequents in the premise.

In the rules $\star\mathsf{R}$ and ${\mathrel{-\!\!\star}}\mathsf{L}$, we allow equalities between heap variables $w_1$, $w_2$, and $w$. Since an equality between these heap variables invalidates the requirement that a world sequent contain a unique heap sequent for each heap variable, we interpret heap sequents for the same heap variable in the rules $\star\mathsf{R}$ and ${\mathrel{-\!\!\star}}\mathsf{L}$ as follows:

- In the conclusion, we implicitly replicate the same heap sequent as necessary.
- In the premise, we combine all changes made to individual heap sequents for the same heap variable to produce a single heap sequent.

For example, an equality $w = w_1$ in the rule $\star\mathsf{R}$ yields the following special instance:

$$\frac{w \doteq w \circ w_2 \in \Sigma \quad \begin{array}{l} \Theta;\Sigma \parallel \Pi, [\Gamma \Longrightarrow \Delta, A \star B, A]^{w}, [\Gamma_2 \Longrightarrow \Delta_2]^{w_2} \\ \Theta;\Sigma \parallel \Pi, [\Gamma \Longrightarrow \Delta, A \star B]^{w}, [\Gamma_2 \Longrightarrow \Delta_2, B]^{w_2} \end{array}}{\Theta;\Sigma \parallel \Pi, [\Gamma \Longrightarrow \Delta, A \star B]^{w}, [\Gamma_2 \Longrightarrow \Delta_2]^{w_2}}$$

The rule $\star\mathsf{R}$ has two more special instances (corresponding to heap relations $w \doteq w_1 \circ w_1$ and $w \doteq w \circ w$), and similarly the rule ${\mathrel{-\!\!\star}}\mathsf{L}$ has a total of three special instances.

Now we can decompose each individual formula by applying its corresponding logical rule, thus accumulating expression relations and heap relations and creating fresh heaps. When expression relations become self-contradictory, we apply the rule $\mathsf{ExpCont}$ to complete the proof search. In order to obtain a complete proof search strategy, however, we should also be able to: 1) enumerate all heap relations $w \doteq w_1 \circ w_2$ and $w_2 \doteq w \circ w_1$ for a given heap $w$ for the rules $\star\mathsf{R}$ and ${\mathrel{-\!\!\star}}\mathsf{L}$; 2) produce heap contradictions, for example, from $w \doteq \epsilon$ and $w \doteq [l \mapsto E]$. (We assume that we can make a correct guess on expression $E$ in the rule $\exists\mathsf{R}$.) The remaining challenge is to devise a set of structural rules and another set of heap contradiction rules satisfying these two requirements, which would enable us to enumerate all feasible heap relations from those

Rules for disambiguating heap relations and leaving only disjoint terminal heaps:

$$\frac{\{w \doteq u_1 \circ u_2, w \doteq v_1 \circ v_2\} \subset \Sigma \quad \textit{fresh}\ w_1, w_2, w_3, w_4 \quad \Theta; \Sigma, \begin{array}{l} u_1 \doteq w_1 \circ w_2, \\ u_2 \doteq w_3 \circ w_4, \\ v_1 \doteq w_1 \circ w_3, \\ v_2 \doteq w_2 \circ w_4 \end{array} \parallel \Pi, \begin{array}{l} [\cdot \Longrightarrow \cdot]^{w_1}, \\ [\cdot \Longrightarrow \cdot]^{w_2}, \\ [\cdot \Longrightarrow \cdot]^{w_3}, \\ [\cdot \Longrightarrow \cdot]^{w_4} \end{array}}{\Theta; \Sigma \parallel \Pi}\ \mathsf{Disj}\star$$

$$\frac{\{w_1 \doteq u_1 \circ u_2, w_2 \doteq u_2 \circ u_3\} \subset \Sigma \quad \textit{fresh}\ w, v_1, v_2, v_3 \quad \Theta; \Sigma, \begin{array}{l} w \doteq w_1 \circ v_3, \\ w \doteq v_1 \circ w_2, \\ u_1 \doteq v_1 \circ v_2, \\ u_3 \doteq v_2 \circ v_3 \end{array} \parallel \Pi, \begin{array}{l} [\cdot \Longrightarrow \cdot]^{w}, \\ [\cdot \Longrightarrow \cdot]^{v_1}, \\ [\cdot \Longrightarrow \cdot]^{v_2}, \\ [\cdot \Longrightarrow \cdot]^{v_3} \end{array}}{\Theta; \Sigma \parallel \Pi}\ \mathsf{Disj}{-\!\!\star}$$

Rules for applying associativity of the union of disjoint heaps.

$$\frac{\{w \doteq u \circ v, u \doteq u_1 \circ u_2\} \subset \Sigma \quad \textit{fresh}\ u' \quad \Theta; \Sigma, u' \doteq u_2 \circ v, w \doteq u_1 \circ u' \parallel \Pi, [\cdot \Longrightarrow \cdot]^{u'}}{\Theta; \Sigma \parallel \Pi}\ \mathsf{Assoc}$$

Rules for propagating atomic heap relations:

$$\frac{\{w \doteq \epsilon, w \doteq w_1 \circ w_2\} \subset \Sigma \quad \Theta; \Sigma, w_1 \doteq \epsilon, w_2 \doteq \epsilon \parallel \Pi}{\Theta; \Sigma \parallel \Pi}\ \mathsf{Prop}\epsilon$$

$$\frac{\{w \doteq [l \mapsto E], w \doteq w_1 \circ w_2\} \subset \Sigma \quad \Theta; \Sigma, w_1 \doteq [l \mapsto E], w_2 \doteq \epsilon \parallel \Pi \quad \Theta; \Sigma, w_1 \doteq \epsilon, w_2 \doteq [l \mapsto E] \parallel \Pi}{\Theta; \Sigma \parallel \Pi}\ \mathsf{Prop}{\mapsto}$$

$$\frac{\{w \dot{\neq} \epsilon, w \doteq w_1 \circ w_2\} \subset \Sigma \quad \Theta; \Sigma, w_1 \dot{\neq} \epsilon \parallel \Pi \quad \Theta; \Sigma, w_2 \dot{\neq} \epsilon \parallel \Pi}{\Theta; \Sigma \parallel \Pi}\ \mathsf{Prop}\epsilon\dot{\neq}$$

$$\frac{\{w \dot{\neq} [l \mapsto E], w \doteq w_1 \circ w_2\} \subset \Sigma \quad \begin{array}{l} \Theta; \Sigma, w_1 \dot{\neq} \epsilon, w_1 \dot{\neq} [l \mapsto E] \parallel \Pi \\ \Theta; \Sigma, w_1 \dot{\neq} \epsilon, w_2 \dot{\neq} \epsilon \parallel \Pi \end{array} \quad \begin{array}{l} \Theta; \Sigma, w_1 \dot{\neq} [l \mapsto E], w_2 \dot{\neq} [l \mapsto E] \parallel \Pi \\ \Theta; \Sigma, w_2 \dot{\neq} \epsilon, w_2 \dot{\neq} [l \mapsto E] \parallel \Pi \end{array}}{\Theta; \Sigma \parallel \Pi}\ \mathsf{Prop}{\mapsto}\dot{\neq}$$

Rules for normalizing heap relations:

$$\frac{\Theta; [w/w']\Sigma, w \doteq u \circ v \parallel \Pi, [\Gamma, \Gamma' \Longrightarrow \Delta, \Delta']^{w}}{\Theta; \Sigma, w \doteq u \circ v, w' \doteq u \circ v \parallel \Pi, [\Gamma \Longrightarrow \Delta]^{w}, [\Gamma' \Longrightarrow \Delta']^{w'}}\ \mathsf{NormEq}$$

$$\frac{\Theta; [w/u]\Sigma, v \doteq \epsilon \parallel \Pi, [\Gamma, \Gamma' \Longrightarrow \Delta, \Delta']^{w}}{\Theta; \Sigma, w \doteq u \circ v, v \doteq \epsilon \parallel \Pi, [\Gamma \Longrightarrow \Delta]^{w}, [\Gamma' \Longrightarrow \Delta']^{u}}\ \mathsf{NormPC} \qquad \frac{\Theta; [w/u]\Sigma, w \doteq \epsilon \parallel \Pi, [\Gamma, \Gamma' \Longrightarrow \Delta, \Delta']^{w}}{\Theta; \Sigma, w \doteq \epsilon, u \doteq \epsilon \parallel \Pi, [\Gamma \Longrightarrow \Delta]^{w}, [\Gamma' \Longrightarrow \Delta']^{u}}\ \mathsf{NormEmpty}$$

Rules for creating an empty heap and applying the monoid laws for empty heaps:

$$\frac{\textit{fresh}\ w_\epsilon \quad \Theta; \Sigma, w_\epsilon \doteq \epsilon \parallel \Pi, [\cdot \Longrightarrow \cdot]^{w_\epsilon}}{\Theta; \Sigma \parallel \Pi}\ \mathsf{ENew} \qquad \frac{w_\epsilon \doteq \epsilon \in \Sigma \quad \Theta; \Sigma, w \doteq w \circ w_\epsilon \parallel \Pi}{\Theta; \Sigma \parallel \Pi}\ \mathsf{EJoin} \qquad \frac{w \doteq w \circ u \in \Sigma \quad \Theta; \Sigma, u \doteq \epsilon \parallel \Pi}{\Theta; \Sigma \parallel \Pi}\ \mathsf{ECancel}$$

**Figure 2.** Structural rules in the proof system $\mathbf{P_{SL}}$ for separation logic

generated by the logical rules and detect all types of heap contradictions.

### 3.3 Structural rules of $\mathbf{P_{SL}}$

The structural rules of $\mathbf{P_{SL}}$ are divided into five groups according to their roles in reorganizing graphs of heaps represented by world sequents. The order of the structural rules in Figure 2 roughly follows their use in the proof of the completeness of $\mathbf{P_{SL}}$ with respect to separation logic (Theorem 6.4). In a certain sense, we design the structural rules so as to obtain a complete proof search strategy for separation logic when the logical rules are already given as in Figure 1. Below we informally discuss the key properties of the structural rules, which we formally present as part of the proof of the completeness of $\mathbf{P_{SL}}$ in Section 6.2.

#### 3.3.1 Rules for disambiguating heap relations

The rules Disj★ and Disj—★ disambiguate heap relations in order to leave only disjoint terminal heaps. Roughly speaking, two heaps are disjoint if they share a common ancestor which has a heap relation separating them.

In the premise of the rule Disj★, child heaps $u_i$ and $v_j$ $(i, j = 1, 2)$ share a common parent heap $w$, but their exact relations are unknown. For example, heap $u_1$ may completely subsume, partially overlap with, or be disjoint from heap $v_1$. In general, each pair of child heaps $u_i$ and $v_j$ are allowed to share a common child heap, so the rule Disj★ disambiguates their relations by introducing four fresh terminal heaps, $w_1$ to $w_4$, which are all disjoint from each other:

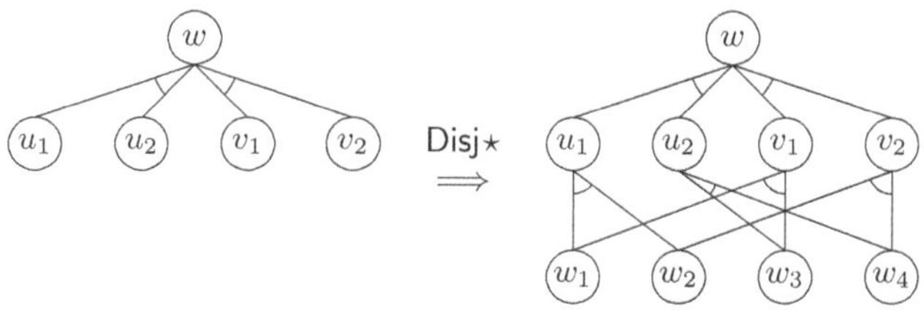


Now, for example, we may assume that the intersection of heaps $u_1$ and $v_1$ is represented by heap $w_1$. Note that if heap $u_i$ or $v_j$ is not a terminal heap, the rule Disj★ gives rise to unknown relations between the existing child heaps of $u_i$ or $v_j$ and two of the fresh terminal heaps. The rule Disj$\star$ corresponds to the cross-split axiom for separation algebras [13].

The rule Disj$-\star$ disambiguates relations between two sibling heaps $u_1$ and $u_3$ of heap $u_2$ by introducing three fresh terminal heaps, $v_1$ to $v_3$, which are all disjoint from each other:

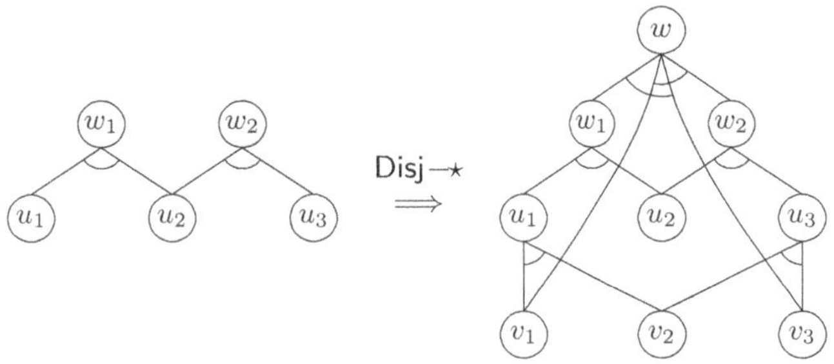


Similarly to the rule Disj$\star$, the rule Disj$-\star$ may give rise to new unknown relations involving heap $w_1$, $w_2$, $u_1$, or $u_3$. Unlike the rule Disj$\star$, however, it also creates a common ancestor $w$ of all heaps. Otherwise the fresh terminal heaps themselves come to have unknown relations, thereby defeating the purpose of applying the rule Disj$-\star$.

Thus the rule Disj$\star$ eliminates unknown relations between child heaps and the rule Disj$-\star$ eliminates unknown relations between sibling heaps of a certain heap, both potentially creating similar unknown relations. By repeatedly applying these rules, we can eventually obtain a graph of heaps such that: *1) there exists a root heap that is an ancestor of all other heaps; 2) all terminal heaps in the graph are disjoint.*

#### 3.3.2 Rule for applying associativity of $\circ$

The rule Assoc creates new heap relations according to associativity of the union of disjoint heaps. Suppose that we have two heap relations $w \doteq u \circ v$ and $u \doteq u_1 \circ u_2$. The rule Assoc introduces a fresh heap $u'$ in order to associate two heaps $u_2$ and $v$ which are known to be disjoint but do not have a common parent heap yet; it also assigns heap $w$ as the common parent heap of heaps $u_1$ and $u'$:

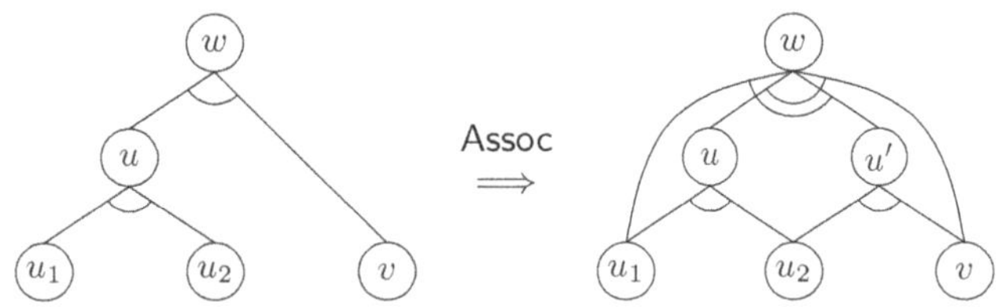


Note that unlike the rules Disj$\star$ and Disj$-\star$, the rule Assoc creates no fresh terminal heaps.

The rule Assoc is crucial for enumerating all heap relations involving a particular heap. The basic observation is that by repeatedly applying the rule Assoc to a graph of heaps, we can eventually obtain another graph of heaps with the same set of terminal heaps such that *for each combination of terminal heaps, there is at least one heap subsuming exactly these terminal heaps and no others.* By starting with a graph of heaps obtained by repeatedly applying the rules Disj$\star$ and Disj$-\star$, then, we can enumerate all feasible heap relations $w \doteq w_1 \circ w_2$ and $w_2 \doteq w \circ w_1$ for a particular heap $w$ where we assume that heaps $w_1$ and $w_2$ are in the graph. For the case that $w_1$ or $w_2$ is an empty heap, however, we need another set of structural rules for dealing with empty heaps. We should also combine heap sequents for the same heap. (Hence we have not yet accomplished the first requirement for obtaining a complete proof search strategy.)

#### 3.3.3 Rules for propagating atomic heap relations

The rules for propagating atomic heap relations, or propagation rules, are designed to propagate all atomic heap relations ($w \doteq \epsilon$, $w \not\doteq \epsilon$, $w \doteq [l \mapsto E]$, $w \not\doteq [l \mapsto E]$) from non-terminal heaps to terminal heaps. A propagation rule converts an atomic heap relation for a heap $w$ into semantically equivalent heap relations for its child heaps $w_1$ and $w_2$ (with $w \doteq w_1 \circ w_2$). It rewrites world sequents according to the following fact on atomic heap relations where we assume $w \doteq w_1 \circ w_2$:

- $w \doteq \epsilon$ iff. $w_1 \doteq \epsilon$ and $w_2 \doteq \epsilon$ (for the rules Prop$\epsilon$ and Prop$\epsilon\not\doteq$ ).
- $w \doteq [l \mapsto E]$ iff. either $w_1 \doteq [l \mapsto E]$ and $w_2 \doteq \epsilon$, or $w_1 \doteq \epsilon$ and $w_2 \doteq [l \mapsto E]$ (for the rules Prop$\mapsto$ and Prop$\mapsto\not\doteq$ ).

For example, we negate the second clause to derive the rule Prop$\mapsto\not\doteq$ which has four world sequents in the premise:

- $w \not\doteq [l \mapsto E]$ iff. 1) $w_1 \not\doteq [l \mapsto E]$ and $w_1 \not\doteq \epsilon$; 2) $w_1 \not\doteq [l \mapsto E]$ and $w_2 \not\doteq [l \mapsto E]$; 3) $w_2 \not\doteq \epsilon$ and $w_1 \not\doteq \epsilon$; or 4) $w_2 \not\doteq \epsilon$ and $w_2 \not\doteq [l \mapsto E]$.

Note that although the new heap relations for the child heaps $w_1$ and $w_2$ collectively imply the original heap relation $\sigma$, we have to preserve $\sigma$ in every world sequent of the premise because it may still interact with another pair of child heaps $w'_1$ and $w'_2$ (with $w \doteq w'_1 \circ w'_2$). After considering all such interactions, however, we may safely discard $\sigma$ (by the rule Weaken to be introduced in Section 6.2).

The propagation rules are the first step toward a complete procedure for producing heap contradictions (which detect all types of heap contradictions). Suppose that we repeatedly apply the propagation rules until no more new heap relations arise from atomic heap relations. After discarding atomic heap relations for non-terminal heaps, we obtain a set of graphs of heaps (with the same structure as the original graph) in which *atomic heap relations reside only for terminal heaps.* Now, in order to produce heap contradictions from atomic heap relations, we need to inspect only terminal heaps of these graphs, which makes it much easier to develop a complete procedure for producing heap contradictions.

#### 3.3.4 Rules for normalizing heap relations

The rules for normalizing heap relations, or normalization rules, merge two identical heaps and isolate empty heaps while simultaneously shrinking the graph of heaps. In the rule NormEq, heaps $w$ and $w'$ are identical and we merge the two heaps by combining their heap sequents. Here we write $[w/w']\Sigma$ for substituting $w$ for $w'$ in every heap relation in $\Sigma$. Note that the rule NormEq implies that $\circ$ is (partial) deterministic. In the rule NormPC, $v \doteq \epsilon$ implies that heaps $w$ and $u$ are identical. Hence we merge the two heaps by combining their heap sequents and isolate the empty heap $v$ from the graph of heaps. Similarly the rule NormEmpty merges two empty heaps $w$ and $u$ by combining their heap sequents. In effect, it allows us to collect all empty heaps, which do not need to be distinguished for the purpose of proof search, into a single empty heap. Note that the rule NormEmpty implies the existence of a single unit of $\circ$. By repeatedly applying the normalization rules to a graph of heaps, we can eventually obtain an equivalent graph which maintains a unique world sequent for each heap and possibly a unique empty heap isolated from the graph.

It is important that the normalization rules shrink the graph of heaps, but preserve all the properties established by the previous structural rules. For example, if the graph satisfies the property that all terminal heaps are disjoint (established by the rules Disj$\star$ and Disj$-\star$), it continues to satisfy the same property after an application of any normalization rule. Hence it is safe to aggressively apply the normalization rules after applying the previous structural rules.

$$\dfrac{}{\Theta; \Sigma, w \doteq \epsilon, w \doteq [l \mapsto E] \parallel \Pi}\,\mathsf{Cont}\epsilon{\mapsto} \qquad \dfrac{}{\Theta; \Sigma, w \doteq \epsilon, w \not\doteq \epsilon \parallel \Pi}\,\mathsf{Cont}\epsilon{\not\doteq} \qquad \dfrac{\Theta \vdash [l \mapsto E] \neq [l' \mapsto E']}{\Theta; \Sigma, w \doteq [l \mapsto E], w \doteq [l' \mapsto E'] \parallel \Pi}\,\mathsf{Cont}{\mapsto}{\doteq}$$

$$\dfrac{\Theta \vdash [l \mapsto E] = [l' \mapsto E']}{\Theta; \Sigma, w \doteq [l \mapsto E], w \not\doteq [l' \mapsto E'] \parallel \Pi}\,\mathsf{Cont}{\mapsto}{\not\doteq} \qquad \dfrac{\Theta \vdash l_1 = l_2}{\Theta; \Sigma, w \doteq w_1 \circ w_2, w_1 \doteq [l_1 \mapsto E_1], w_2 \doteq [l_2 \mapsto E_2] \parallel \Pi}\,\mathsf{Cont}\circ{\mapsto}$$

**Figure 3.** Heap contradiction rules in the proof system $\mathbf{P_{SL}}$ for separation logic

### 3.3.5 Rules for dealing with empty heaps

The last group of structural rules create an empty heap and apply the monoid laws for empty heaps. We use the rule ENew when no rule can directly produce an empty heap. The rule EJoin, which is based on neutrality of $\epsilon$, is sound because extending a heap with an empty heap makes no change. The rule ECancel creates an empty heap when a heap is shown to be a child heap of itself. It is based on cancellativity of $\circ$: we can always generate $w \doteq w \circ w_\epsilon$ and $w_\epsilon \doteq \epsilon$ by the rules ENew and EJoin, and $w \doteq w \circ u$ and $w \doteq w \circ w_\epsilon$ imply $u \doteq \epsilon$ by cancellativity of $\circ$. (Similarly the rule NormPC is based on cancellativity of $\circ$: we can always generate $w \doteq w \circ v$ by the rule EJoin, and $w \doteq u \circ v$ and $w \doteq w \circ v$ imply $w = u$.) It turns out that we need the rule ECancel for the proof of admissibility of cut (Theorem 5.1), but not for the proof of the completeness of $\mathbf{P_{SL}}$ (Theorem 6.4).

Now we can accomplish the first requirement for obtaining a complete proof search strategy. In order to enumerate all heap relations $w \doteq w_1 \circ w_2$ and $w_2 \doteq w \circ w_1$ for a heap $w$, we first analyze the graph of heaps obtained by repeatedly applying the previous structural rules. This produces all such heap relations that involve only non-empty heaps. Then we apply the rule EJoin as necessary to produce all such heap relations that involve empty heaps.

We may think of the rule EJoin as extending heap relations for heap $w$ with a pair of child heaps $w$ and $w_\epsilon$, or a pair of sibling heap $w_\epsilon$ and parent heap $w$. It is the only rule in $\mathbf{P_{SL}}$ that is capable of creating new heap relations for an arbitrary heap. Thus, whenever an arbitrary heap with no heap relation needs a pair of child heaps or a pair of sibling and parent heaps, we should apply the rule EJoin which inevitably reuses an existing empty heap. For example, we prove the validity of $\top \star \top$ as follows:

$$\dfrac{\dfrac{\dfrac{\dfrac{\dfrac{}{\cdot; w_\epsilon \doteq \epsilon, w \doteq w \circ w_\epsilon \parallel [\bot \Longrightarrow \top \star \top]^w, [\cdot \Longrightarrow \cdot]^{w_\epsilon}}\,\bot\mathsf{L}}{\cdot; w_\epsilon \doteq \epsilon, w \doteq w \circ w_\epsilon \parallel [\cdot \Longrightarrow \top \star \top, \top]^w, [\cdot \Longrightarrow \cdot]^{w_\epsilon}}\,\neg\mathsf{R} \quad \vdots}{\cdot; w_\epsilon \doteq \epsilon, w \doteq w \circ w_\epsilon \parallel [\cdot \Longrightarrow \top \star \top]^w, [\cdot \Longrightarrow \cdot]^{w_\epsilon}}\,\star\mathsf{R}}{\cdot; w_\epsilon \doteq \epsilon \parallel [\cdot \Longrightarrow \top \star \top]^w, [\cdot \Longrightarrow \cdot]^{w_\epsilon}}\,\mathsf{EJoin}}{\cdot; \cdot \parallel [\cdot \Longrightarrow \top \star \top]^w}\,\mathsf{ENew}$$

Note that there is no need to create fresh child heaps $w_1$ and $w_2$ with $w \doteq w_1 \circ w_2$: if we can prove the world sequent using fresh child heaps about which nothing is known, we should be able to prove it equally by reusing an existing empty heap. Similarly we prove the validity of $\neg(\top \mathrel{-\!\!\star} \bot)$ as follows:

$$\dfrac{\dfrac{\dfrac{\dfrac{\vdots \quad \dfrac{}{\cdot; w_\epsilon \doteq \epsilon, w \doteq w \circ w_\epsilon \parallel [\top \mathrel{-\!\!\star} \bot, \bot \Longrightarrow \cdot]^w, [\cdot \Longrightarrow \cdot]^{w_\epsilon}}\,\bot\mathsf{L}}{\cdot; w_\epsilon \doteq \epsilon, w \doteq w \circ w_\epsilon \parallel [\top \mathrel{-\!\!\star} \bot \Longrightarrow \cdot]^w, [\cdot \Longrightarrow \cdot]^{w_\epsilon}}\,{-\!\!\star}\mathsf{L}}{\cdot; w_\epsilon \doteq \epsilon \parallel [\top \mathrel{-\!\!\star} \bot \Longrightarrow \cdot]^w, [\cdot \Longrightarrow \cdot]^{w_\epsilon}}\,\mathsf{EJoin}}{\cdot; \cdot \parallel [\top \mathrel{-\!\!\star} \bot \Longrightarrow \cdot]^w}\,\mathsf{ENew}}{\cdot; \cdot \parallel [\cdot \Longrightarrow \neg(\top \mathrel{-\!\!\star} \bot)]^w}\,\neg\mathsf{R}$$

Again we do not create fresh sibling and parent heaps and instead reuse an existing empty heap.

## 3.4 Heap contradiction rules of $\mathbf{P_{SL}}$

The proof system $\mathbf{P_{SL}}$ has five rules, $\mathsf{Cont}\epsilon{\not\doteq}$ to $\mathsf{Cont}\circ{\mapsto}$, for producing heap contradictions. In conjunction with the structural rules, these rules enable us to detect all types of heap contradictions, thereby accomplishing the second requirement for obtaining a complete proof strategy.

To see why, assume a world sequent $\Theta; \Sigma \parallel \Pi$. By repeatedly applying the structural rules in the same order as presented above, we can obtain a semantically equivalent set of world sequents $\Theta; \Sigma_i \parallel \Pi_i$ $(i = 1, \cdots, n)$ such that: 1) $\Sigma_i$ induces a graph of heaps in which all terminal heaps are disjoint; 2) atomic heap relations reside only for terminal heaps and we need to consider only terminal heaps to detect heap contradictions. For an empty heap, we use the rules $\mathsf{Cont}\epsilon{\not\doteq}$ and $\mathsf{Cont}\epsilon{\mapsto}$ which express the only ways to produce heap contradictions from an empty heap with $w \doteq \epsilon$. Note that $w \doteq \epsilon$ and $w \not\doteq [l \mapsto E]$ do not produce a heap contradiction because the former implies the latter. For a terminal singleton heap, we use the rules $\mathsf{Cont}{\mapsto}{\doteq}$ and $\mathsf{Cont}{\mapsto}{\not\doteq}$ which express the only ways to produce heap contradictions from a terminal singleton heap with $w \doteq [l \mapsto E]$. Note that $w \doteq [l \mapsto E]$ implies $w \not\doteq \epsilon$ always and $w \not\doteq [l' \mapsto E']$ if $\Theta \vdash [l \mapsto E] \neq [l' \mapsto E']$ holds. We do not need to consider other forms of terminal heaps, for example, those with no atomic heap relations. Finally the rule $\mathsf{Cont}\circ{\mapsto}$ expresses the only way to produce heap contradictions from two disjoint terminal singleton heaps with $w_1 \doteq [l_1 \mapsto E_1]$ and $w_2 \doteq [l_2 \mapsto E_2]$. This is because if $\Theta \vdash l_1 \neq l_2$ holds, the two heap relations are consistent with $w \doteq w_1 \circ w_2$ and we cannot produce a heap contradiction. In this way, we can detect all types of heap contradictions in heap relations.

# 4. Examples of proving world sequents

This section presents three examples of proving world sequents in $\mathbf{P_{SL}}$. We write $[l \mapsto \cdot]$ to denote $[l \mapsto E]$ for some expression $E$ and assume two distinct location expressions $l$ and $l'$ $(l \neq l')$.

### 4.1 $\neg(([l \mapsto \cdot] \star [l' \mapsto \cdot]) \wedge ([l \mapsto \cdot] \star \neg[l' \mapsto \cdot]))$

The goal formula implies that given a fragment of a heap, we can uniquely determine the remaining fragment. Its proof illustrates that the rule Disj$\star$ indirectly applies cancellativity of $\circ$ to two pairs of child heaps.

We begin with a world sequent $\cdot; \cdot \parallel [\cdot \Longrightarrow C]^w$ where $C$ is the goal formula. After applying the logical rules, we obtain the following graph of heaps where heap relations are displayed for child heaps:

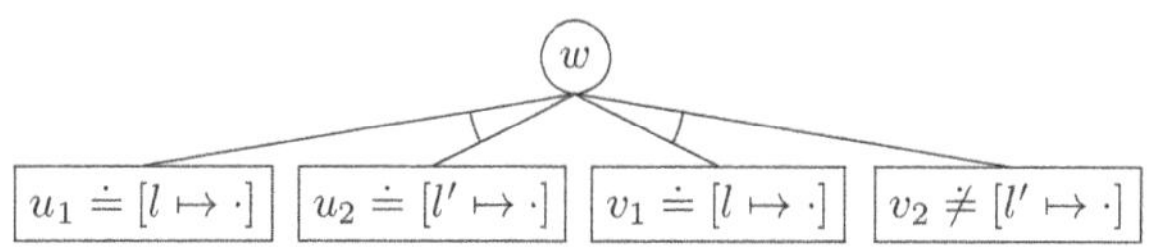


Then we apply the rule Disj$\star$ and the propagation rules Prop$\mapsto$ and Prop${\mapsto}{\not\doteq}$ to generate $2 \times 2 \times 2 \times 4 = 32$ different world sequents as new goals. All these new goals are immediately provable by the rules $\mathsf{Cont}\epsilon{\mapsto}$, $\mathsf{Cont}\epsilon{\not\doteq}$, and $\mathsf{Cont}{\mapsto}{\not\doteq}$. An example of such a world sequent has heap relations $w_4 \doteq [l' \mapsto \cdot]$, originating from heap $u_2$ by the rule Prop$\mapsto$, and $w_4 \not\doteq [l' \mapsto \cdot]$, originating from heap $v_2$ by the rule Prop$\mapsto\not\doteq$ :

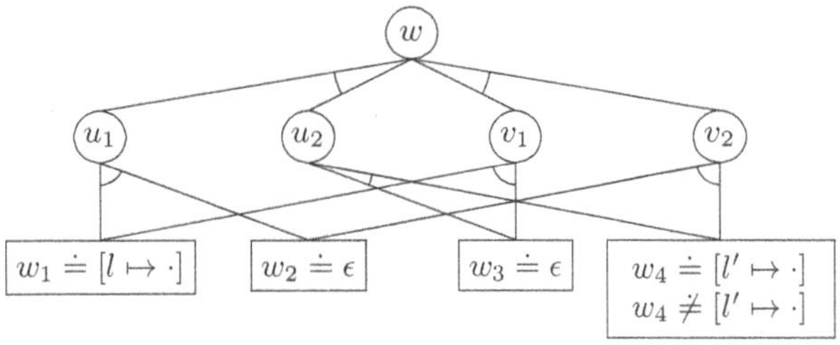


By applying the rule Cont$\mapsto\not\doteq$ to heap $w_4$, we complete the proof.

### 4.2 $A \star A \supset A$ where $A = \neg(\top \mathrel{-\!\!\star} \neg\mathsf{I})$

The goal formula is valid in separation logic because heaps form a partial deterministic monoid: $H_1 \circ H_2$ may be undefined (when $H_1 \# H_2$ does not hold), but if it is defined, the result is unique. In contrast, the same formula is not valid in Boolean BI, the underlying theory of separation logic, which assumes a non-deterministic monoid [21].

The proof illustrates the use of the rule EJoin in proving a non-trivial formula. After applying the logical rules to a world sequent $\cdot;\cdot \parallel [\cdot \Longrightarrow A \star A \supset A]^w$, we obtain the following graph of heaps:

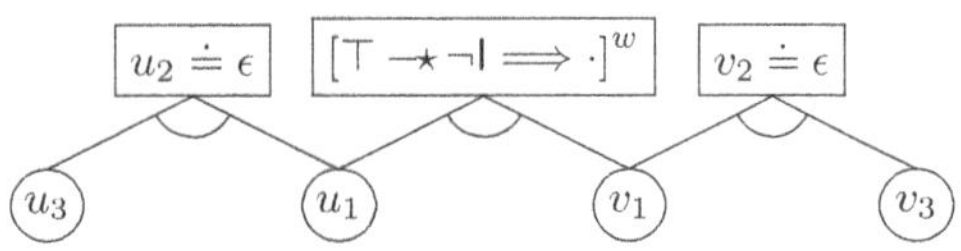


Since heap $w$ has no sibling and parent heaps, we cannot apply the rule $\mathrel{-\!\!\star}$L to $\top \mathrel{-\!\!\star} \neg\mathsf{I}$ at this point. To make further progress, we apply either the rule Disj$\mathrel{-\!\!\star}$ or the rule EJoin after creating an empty heap. If we apply the rule EJoin, we obtain the following graph:

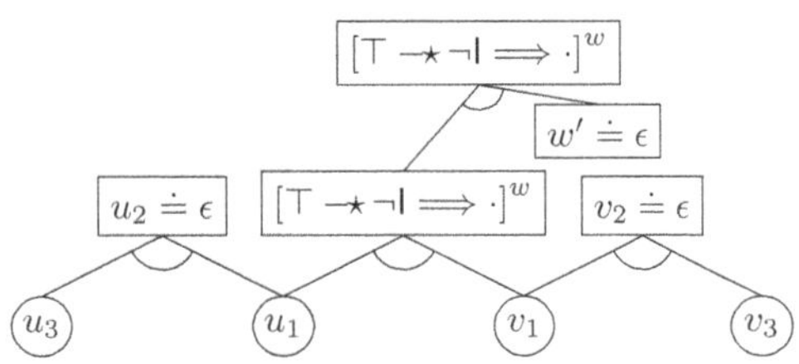


An application of the rule $\mathrel{-\!\!\star}$L to $\top \mathrel{-\!\!\star} \neg\mathsf{I}$ at heap $w$ generates two new goals, and the interesting case produces $\neg\mathsf{I}$ as a true formula at the same heap (where we omit $\top \mathrel{-\!\!\star} \neg\mathsf{I}$):

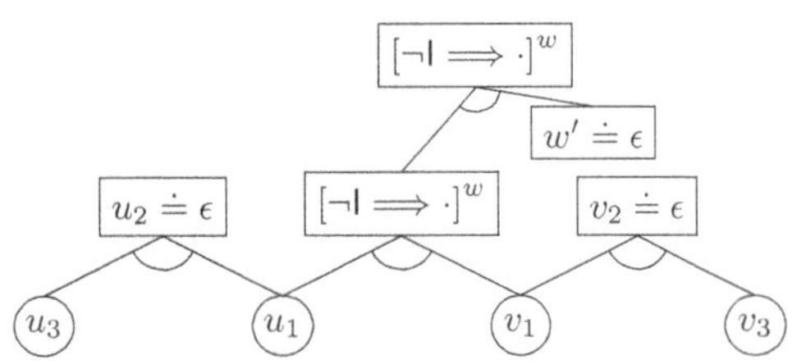


By applying the logical rules to heap $w$ and the propagation rule Prop$\epsilon$, we obtain the following graph:

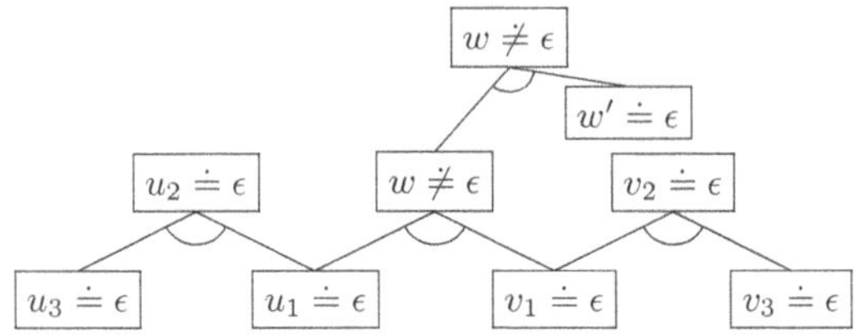


Now we can either apply the propagation rule Prop$\epsilon\not\doteq$ to heap $w$ or use the rule NormPC to complete the proof.

### 4.3 $\neg(([l' \mapsto \cdot] \mathrel{-\!\!\star} \bot) \wedge ([l \mapsto \cdot] \star \neg([l \mapsto \cdot] \mathrel{-\!\!\star} ([l' \mapsto \cdot] \mathrel{-\!\!\star} \bot))))$

The goal formula is an example of a formula that cannot be proven without an application of the rule Disj$\mathrel{-\!\!\star}$. After applying the logical rules to a world sequent $\cdot;\cdot \parallel [\cdot \Longrightarrow C]^{w_1}$ where $C$ is the goal formula, we obtain the following graph:

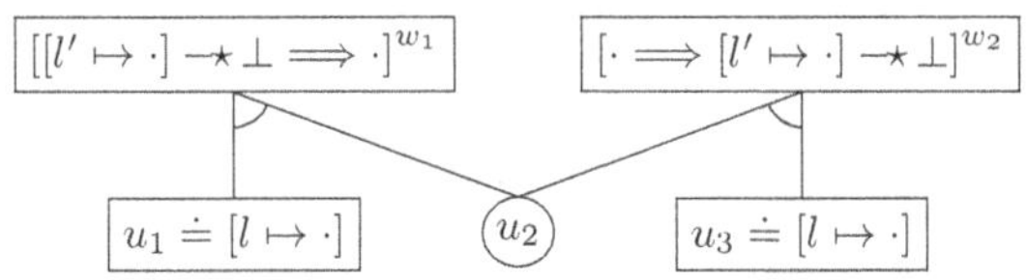


We wish to identify heaps $w_1$ and $w_2$ (because heaps $u_1$ and $u_3$ are identical), but there is no way to make further progress toward identifying $w_1$ and $w_2$ without applying the rule Disj$\mathrel{-\!\!\star}$. Hence we apply the rule Disj$\mathrel{-\!\!\star}$ and the propagation rule Prop$\mapsto$ to heaps $u_1$ and $u_3$. After eliminating three new goals that are immediately provable, we obtain the following graph:

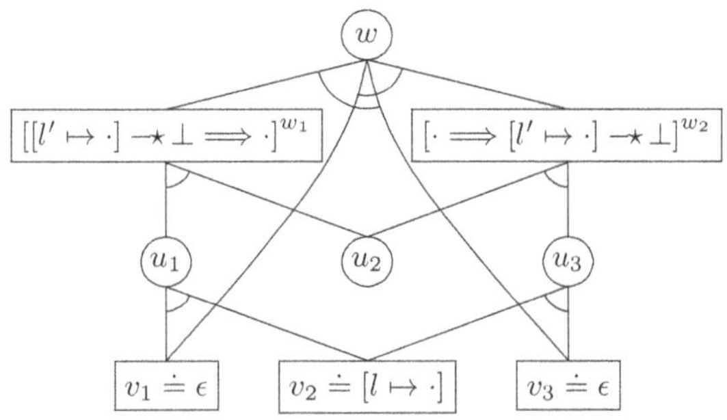


By applying the rule NormPC to merge heaps $w_1$ and $w_2$, we obtain a heap sequent $[[l' \mapsto \cdot] \mathrel{-\!\!\star} \bot \Longrightarrow [l' \mapsto \cdot] \mathrel{-\!\!\star} \bot]^w$, which is easily provable.

## 5. Admissibility of cut

We state the admissibility of cut in $\mathbf{P_{SL}}$ as follows:

**Theorem 5.1** (Admissibility of cut). *If* $\Theta; \Sigma \parallel \Pi, [\Gamma \Longrightarrow \Delta, C]^w$ *and* $\Theta; \Sigma \parallel \Pi, [\Gamma, C \Longrightarrow \Delta]^w$, *then* $\Theta; \Sigma \parallel \Pi, [\Gamma \Longrightarrow \Delta]^w$.

Theorem 5.1 assumes a few properties, such as weakening and contraction, of the expression contradiction judgment $\Theta \vdash \bot$ (for which we do not provide inference rules). In particular, we assume its own admissibility of cut (where $\neg\theta$ denotes the negation of $\theta$): $\Theta_1, \theta \vdash \bot$ and $\Theta_2, \neg\theta \vdash \bot$ imply $\Theta_1, \Theta_2 \vdash \bot$.

The first step in the proof of Theorem 5.1 is to show that it is safe to merge two arbitrary heap sequents:

**Lemma 5.2.** *If* $\Theta; \Sigma \parallel \Pi, [\Gamma_1 \Longrightarrow \Delta_1]^u, [\Gamma_2 \Longrightarrow \Delta_2]^v$, *then* $\Theta; [u/v]\Sigma \parallel \Pi, [\Gamma_1, \Gamma_2 \Longrightarrow \Delta_1, \Delta_2]^u$.

Intuitively the second world sequent inherits every heap relation from the first world sequent, so we should be able to prove the second by the same sequence of rules in the proof of the first or its subsequence.

Next we prove the contraction property for heap relations:

**Proposition 5.3.** *If* $\Theta; \Sigma, \sigma, \sigma \parallel \Pi$, *then* $\Theta; \Sigma, \sigma \parallel \Pi$.

The statement in Proposition 5.3 implicitly assumes that we may apply the rules Disj$\star$, Disj$-\!\!\star$, and Assoc to the same heap relation. For the rules Disj$\star$ and Disj$-\!\!\star$, the proof for such an application, which essentially has no effect, requires the rules ENew and EJoin, which are necessary for the completeness of $\mathbf{P_{SL}}$ anyway. For the rule Assoc, however, the proof for such an application requires the rule ECancel, which is unnecessary for the completeness of $\mathbf{P_{SL}}$. Hence, if we never apply the rule Assoc to the same heap relation, we may discard the rule ECancel.

To prove Theorem 5.1, we generalize its statement as follows:

**Lemma 5.4.** *If* $\Theta_1; \Sigma_1 \parallel \Pi_1, [\Gamma_1 \Longrightarrow \Delta_1, C]^w$ *and* $\Theta_2; \Sigma_2 \parallel \Pi_2, [\Gamma_2, C \Longrightarrow \Delta_2]^w$, *then* $\Theta_1, \Theta_2; \Sigma_1, \Sigma_2 \parallel \Pi_1 \uplus \Pi_2, [\Gamma_1, \Gamma_2 \Longrightarrow \Delta_1, \Delta_2]^w$.

Here $\Pi_1 \uplus \Pi_2$ denotes the result of combining heap sequents for the same heap variable. In conjunction with the contraction property for formulas, Lemma 5.4 implies Theorem 5.1.

# 6. Soundness and completeness of $\mathbf{P_{SL}}$

This section proves the soundness and completeness of the proof system $\mathbf{P_{SL}}$ with respect to separation logic. The proof of soundness is straightforward, whereas the proof of completeness uses several subtle properties of graphs of heaps represented by world sequents. In this section, metavariable $W$ denotes world sequents and heap variables directly refer to heaps. For simplicity, we do not consider first-order formulas.

## 6.1 Soundness

The soundness property states that a derivation of a world sequent means that its semantic interpretation is self-contradictory. As a special case, we obtain Theorem 6.1:

**Theorem 6.1** (Soundness). *If* $\cdot; \cdot \parallel [\cdot \Longrightarrow A]^w$, *then* $\models A$.

The key step in the proof of soundness is to show that in any inference rule of $\mathbf{P_{SL}}$, the world sequent in the conclusion is either self-contradictory in itself or semantically implies the disjunction of all world sequents in the premise. Given a stack $S$, let us write $[\![W]\!]_S$ for the interpretation of world sequent $W$ according to the semantics of separation logic (which is formally defined below). We wish to prove that a derivation of $W$ implies $\neg[\![W]\!]_S$, *i.e.*, $[\![W]\!]_S$ is self-contradictory, for any stack $S$. Suppose that the last inference rule in the derivation of $W$ is not an axiom and has world sequents $W_1, \cdots, W_n$ in its premise ($n \geq 1$). By induction hypothesis, we have $\neg[\![W_1]\!]_S, \cdots, \neg[\![W_n]\!]_S$, or equivalently, $\bigwedge_{i=1,\cdots,n} \neg[\![W_i]\!]_S$. Then, by proving that $[\![W]\!]_S$ implies $\bigvee_{i=1,\cdots,n} [\![W_i]\!]_S$, we prove that $\bigwedge_{i=1,\cdots,n} \neg[\![W_i]\!]_S$ implies $\neg[\![W]\!]_S$. Now $\neg[\![W]\!]_S$ immediately follows.

Formally we define $[\![W]\!]_S$ using three auxiliary semantic functions $[\![\theta]\!]_S$, $[\![\sigma]\!]_S$, and $[\![\pi]\!]_S$, all of which follow our intuition on world sequents given in Section 3.1:

$$\begin{array}{rcl}
[\![E = E']\!]_S &=& [\![E]\!]_S = [\![E']\!]_S \\
[\![E \neq E']\!]_S &=& [\![E]\!]_S \neq [\![E']\!]_S \\
[\![w \doteq \epsilon]\!]_S &=& w = \epsilon \\
[\![w \not\doteq \epsilon]\!]_S &=& w \neq \epsilon \\
[\![w \doteq [l \mapsto E]]\!]_S &=& w = \langle [\![l]\!]_S \mapsto [\![E]\!]_S \rangle \\
[\![w \not\doteq [l \mapsto E]]\!]_S &=& w \neq \langle [\![l]\!]_S \mapsto [\![E]\!]_S \rangle \\
[\![w \doteq w_1 \circ w_2]\!]_S &=& w = w_1 \circ w_2 \\
[\![[\Gamma \Longrightarrow \Delta]^w]\!]_S &=& \bigwedge_{A \in \Gamma} (S, w) \models A \wedge \bigwedge_{B \in \Delta} (S, w) \not\models B \\
[\![\Theta; \Sigma \parallel \Pi]\!]_S &=& \bigwedge_{\theta \in \Theta} [\![\theta]\!]_S \wedge \bigwedge_{\sigma \in \Sigma} [\![\sigma]\!]_S \wedge \bigwedge_{\pi \in \Pi} [\![\pi]\!]_S
\end{array}$$

Now we prove the key step in the proof of soundness:

**Lemma 6.2.** *For every inference rule with the conclusion* $W$ *and the premise consisting of* $W_1, \cdots, W_n$, *it holds that* $[\![W]\!]_S$ *implies* $\bigvee_{i=1,\cdots,n} [\![W_i]\!]_S$ *for any stack* $S$. *If* $n = 0$, *we have* $\neg[\![W]\!]_S$.

As a corollary, we prove that a derivation of a world sequent means that its semantic interpretation is self-contradictory.

**Corollary 6.3.** *If there is a derivation of a world sequent* $W$ *in* $\mathbf{P_{SL}}$, *then* $\neg[\![W]\!]_S$ *holds for any stack* $S$. *For the rule* ExpCont, *we assume that* $\Theta \vdash \bot$ *implies* $\neg[\![\Theta \vdash \bot]\!]_S$.

Then a derivation of $\cdot; \cdot \parallel [\cdot \Longrightarrow A]^w$ implies $(S, w) \models A$:

$$\neg[\![\cdot; \cdot \parallel [\cdot \Longrightarrow A]^w]\!]_S \;=\; \neg(S, w) \not\models A \;=\; (S, w) \models A$$

Since $w$ denotes an arbitrary heap, we have $\models A$ and Theorem 6.1 follows.

## 6.2 Completeness

The completeness property states that a valid formula in separation logic has a proof of its negation in $\mathbf{P_{SL}}$:

**Theorem 6.4** (Completeness). *If* $\models A$, *then* $\cdot; \cdot \parallel [\cdot \Longrightarrow A]^w$.

For the proof of completeness, we weaken the rules $\star$R and $-\!\!\star$L by discarding their principal formula in the premise. The original rules are invertible and useless applications with wrong heap relations are safe, but only because the principal formula survives in the premise and we can always try different heap relations without having to backtrack. This is, however, inadequate for the proof of completeness, which must show how to actually find a right heap relation. Hence we weaken the rules $\star$R and $-\!\!\star$L to directly reflect the semantics of $\star$ and $-\!\!\star$, but also present a scheme for computing the complete set of heap relations for a given heap. We also introduce an explicit weakening rule for eliminating an atomic heap relation (which is admissible) as a new structural rule:

$$\frac{\sigma \text{ is an atomic heap relation} \quad \Theta; \Sigma \parallel \Pi}{\Theta; \Sigma, \sigma \parallel \Pi}\ \mathsf{Weaken}$$

We use the rule Weaken to eliminate all atomic heap relations at non-terminal heaps when the propagation rules can produce no more new heap relations. As explained in Section 5, we do not use the rule ECancel.

Our proof of Theorem 6.4 uses three new concepts: *canonical world sequents*, *disjunctive derivation states*, and *conjunctive proof goals*.

A canonical world sequent $Z$ is a special form of a world sequent such that if $\neg[\![Z]\!]_S$ holds for any stack $S$, we can construct its derivation using only the rules $\bot$L, ExpCont, and the heap contradiction rules. (In Proposition 6.12, we introduce a class of world sequents that are shown to be canonical.)

A disjunctive derivation state $\Psi$ for a world sequent $W$ is a set of world sequents that constitute all the leaves in a partial derivation of $W$. That is, a disjunctive derivation state $\Psi = \{W_1, \cdots, W_n\}$ for a world sequent $W$ means that there is a partial derivation of the following form:

$$\frac{W_1 \quad \cdots \quad W_n}{\vdots}{W}$$

We use a reduction judgment $\Psi \overset{R}{\mapsto} \Psi'$ to mean that such a partial derivation expands to another partial derivation with disjunctive derivation state $\Psi'$ by an application of the logical or structural rule $R$ to some world sequent $W_i$ ($1 \leq i \leq n$). That is, we have $\Psi' = \Psi - \{W_i\} \cup \{W_i^1, \cdots, W_i^m\}$ with:

$$\begin{array}{c} \dfrac{W_i^1 \quad \cdots \quad W_i^m}{W_1 \quad \cdots \quad W_i \quad \cdots \quad W_n}\,R \\ \vdots \\ \overline{W} \end{array}$$

We write $\Psi \mapsto^* \Psi'$ for the reflexive and transitive closure of $\mapsto$. For a stack $S$, we define the interpretation $[\![\Psi]\!]_S = \bigvee_{W_i \in \Psi} [\![W_i]\!]_S$.

A conjunctive proof goal $\Omega$ is a set of disjunctive derivation states for a common world sequent. Given a logical or structural rule $R$, we use a reduction judgment $\Omega \overset{R}{\leadsto} \Omega'$ to mean that we can generate $\Omega'$ by applying the rule $R$ to some disjunctive derivation state $\Psi$ in $\Omega$. That is, we have $\Omega' = \Omega - \{\Psi\} \cup \{\Psi'_1, \cdots, \Psi'_n\}$ and $\Psi \overset{R}{\mapsto} \Psi'_i$ for $i = 1, \cdots, n$. If $R$ is the rule $\star$R or $-\!\!\star$L, we have $n \geq 1$ and produce each $\Psi'_i$ by focusing on the same formula in the same heap sequent in the same world sequent in $\Psi$. For all the other rules, we have $n = 1$ and replace $\Psi$ by $\Psi'_1$. We write $\Omega \leadsto^* \Omega'$ for the reflexive and transitive closure of $\leadsto$. For a stack $S$, we define the interpretation $[\![\Omega]\!]_S = \bigwedge_{\Psi_i \in \Omega} [\![\Psi_i]\!]_S$.

In order to prove Theorem 6.4, assume a goal formula $A$ such that $\models A$. We aim to build a sequence of conjunctive proof goals $\Omega^1, \cdots, \Omega^N$ such that:

- $\Omega^1 = \{\{W\}\}$ where $W = \cdot; \cdot \parallel [\cdot \Longrightarrow A]^w$.
- $\Omega^i \overset{R_i}{\leadsto} \Omega^{i+1}$ for $i = 1, \cdots, N-1$ where $R_i$ is a logical or structural rule.
- $[\![\Omega^{i+1}]\!]_S$ implies $[\![\Omega^i]\!]_S$ for $i = 1, \cdots, N-1$ and any stack $S$.
- $\Omega^N$ contains only canonical world sequents.

With such a sequence of conjunctive proof goals, we can build a derivation of $W$ as follows:

- Since we have $\models A$, we have
$$(S, w) \models A = \neg(S, w) \not\models A = \neg[\![W]\!]_S = \neg[\![\Omega^1]\!]_S$$
for any stack $S$.
- Since $[\![\Omega^N]\!]_S$ implies $[\![\Omega^1]\!]_S$, we have $\neg[\![\Omega^N]\!]_S$.
- Since every disjunctive derivation state in $\Omega^N$ contains only canonical world sequents, we may write $\Omega^N = \bigcup_j \Psi_j$ and $\Psi_j = \bigcup_k Z_k^j$.
- Since we have $\neg[\![\Omega^N]\!]_S = \neg \bigwedge_j [\![\Psi_j]\!]_S = \bigvee_j \neg[\![\Psi_j]\!]_S$, there exists a disjunctive derivation state $\Psi_j$ such that $\neg[\![\Psi_j]\!]_S$ holds.
- Since we have $\neg[\![\Psi_j]\!]_S = \neg \bigvee_k [\![Z_k^j]\!]_S = \bigwedge_k \neg[\![Z_k^j]\!]_S$, we have $\neg[\![Z_k^j]\!]_S$ for each $k$.
- Since $\Omega^1 \leadsto^* \Omega^N$, we have $\{W\} \mapsto^* \Psi_j$.
- Since we have $\neg[\![Z_k^j]\!]_S$ for each $k$, there is a derivation of $Z_k^j$ for each $k$ by the definition of canonical world sequents.
- By combining $\{W\} \mapsto^* \Psi_j$ and the derivation of $Z_k^j$ for each $k$, we obtain a derivation of $W$.

Below we explain how to build such a sequence of conjunctive proof goals.

### 6.2.1 Completeness of the invertible rules

Suppose that a world sequent in $\Omega^i$ contains a formula to which we can apply a rule $R$ other than $\bot$L, $\star$R, and $-\!\!\star$L. By applying the rule $R$, we obtain $\Omega^i \overset{R}{\leadsto} \Omega^{i+1}$. By Corollary 6.6, $[\![\Omega^{i+1}]\!]_S$ implies $[\![\Omega^i]\!]_S$ for any stack $S$. In this way, we can eliminate all such formulas without losing completeness.

**Proposition 6.5.** *Except for the rules* $\bot$L, ExpCont, $\star$R, $-\!\!\star$L, *and* Weaken, *every logical or structural rule with the conclusion* $W$ *and the premise consisting of* $W_1, \cdots, W_n$ *is invertible in that* $\bigvee_{i=1,\cdots,n} [\![W_i]\!]_S$ *implies* $[\![W]\!]_S$ *for any stack* $S$.

**Corollary 6.6** (Completeness of the invertible rules)**.** *For such an invertible rule* $R$ *and any stack* $S$,

*if* $\{W\} \overset{R}{\mapsto} \Psi$, *then* $[\![\Psi]\!]_S$ *implies* $[\![\{W\}]\!]_S$.

### 6.2.2 Completeness of the rules $\star$R, $-\!\!\star$L, and Weaken

We now show how to recover the completeness of the rules $\star$R and $-\!\!\star$L. We introduce several notations in order to concisely describe properties of graphs of heaps:

- $w \nearrow u$ means that there is a sequence of zero or more child-parent relations from heap $w$ to heap $u$ in the graph: $w = w_0$, $w_1 \doteq w_0 \circ w'_0$, $\cdots$, $w_n \doteq w_{n-1} \circ w'_{n-1}$, and $w_n = u$ for $n \geq 0$. Hence, if $w \neq u$, heap $w$ is a descendant of heap $u$, or equivalently, heap $u$ is an ancestor of heap $w$. Note that we allow $w \nearrow w$.
- $w\uparrow$ means that $w$ is a terminal heap, *i.e.*, there is no heap relation $w \doteq u \circ v$.
- $T(w)$ denotes the set of terminal descendants of heap $w$, *i.e.*, $T(w) = \{v \mid v\uparrow \text{ and } v \nearrow w\}$.

We assume that heap relations in every world sequent induce not only a graph of heaps but also a special empty heap $w_\epsilon$ with heap relation $w_\epsilon \doteq \epsilon$ that is separate from the graph. This assumption is safe because we can always generate such a special empty heap with the rule ENew if there is none, and combine multiple empty heaps with the rule NormEmpty if there are many. We classify world sequents according to the property of graphs of heaps induced by their heap relations (without considering its special empty heap $w_\epsilon$) as follows:

1. Elementary: if $w \doteq w_1 \circ w_2$, then $T(w_1) \cap T(w_2) = \varnothing$.
2. Rooted: elementary and there is a root heap $w$ such that $v \nearrow w$ for every heap $v$.
3. Consistent: rooted and if $w \doteq u_1 \circ u_2$ and $w \doteq v_1 \circ v_2$, then $T(u_1) \cup T(u_2) = T(v_1) \cup T(v_2)$.
4. Full: consistent and for any non-empty set $S$ of terminal heaps, there exists at least one heap $w$ with $T(w) = S$.
5. $\star$-ready for heap $w$: full and for any pair of non-empty sets $S_1$ and $S_2$ of terminal heaps such that $S_1 \cap S_2 = \varnothing$ and $S_1 \cup S_2 = T(w)$, there exist heaps $w_1$ and $w_2$ such that $w \doteq w_1 \circ w_2$ with $T(w_1) = S_1$ and $T(w_2) = S_2$.
6. $-\!\!\star$-ready for heap $w$: full and for any pair of non-empty sets $S_1$ and $S_2$ of terminal heaps such that $T(w) \cap S_1 = \varnothing$ and $T(w) \cup S_1 = S_2$, there exist heaps $w_1$ and $w_2$ such that $w_2 \doteq w \circ w_1$ with $T(w_1) = S_1$ and $T(w_2) = S_2$.
7. Saturated: full and applications of the propagation rules produce no more new heap relations.
8. Sanitized: full and non-terminal heaps have no atomic heap relations.
9. Normalized: sanitized with no empty heaps and for any non-empty set $S$ of terminal heaps, there exists a unique heap $w$ with $T(w) = S$.
10. Expanded: obtained by applying only the logical rules except $\star$R and $-\!\!\star$L to some consistent world sequent.

Suppose that a world sequent in $\Omega^i$ contains a false formula $A \star B$ or a true formula $A -\!\!\star B$ about heap $w$. By converting it into normalized world sequents that are also $\star$-ready or $-\!\!\star$-ready for heap $w$ according to Corollary 6.10, we obtain $\Omega^i \leadsto^* \Omega^{i+1}$ such that $[\![\Omega^{i+1}]\!]_S$ implies $[\![\Omega^i]\!]_S$ for any stack $S$. By Proposition 6.11, we can apply the rule $\star$R or $-\!\!\star$L to obtain $\Omega^{i+2}$ with $\Omega^{i+1} \overset{\star\mathsf{R}}{\leadsto} \Omega^{i+2}$ or $\Omega^{i+1} \overset{-\!\star\mathsf{L}}{\leadsto} \Omega^{i+2}$ such that $[\![\Omega^{i+2}]\!]_S$ implies $[\![\Omega^{i+1}]\!]_S$ for any stack $S$. In this way, we can eliminate every false formula $A \star B$ or true formula $A \multimap\!\!\star\, B$ without losing completeness.

**Lemma 6.7.** *For a world sequent $W$ of a particular kind, there exists a world sequent $W'$ of another kind such that:*
*1) $\{W\} \mapsto^* \{W'\}$ by applying only the structural rules;*
*2) $[\![\{W'\}]\!]_S$ implies $[\![\{W\}]\!]_S$ for any stack $S$,*
*where one of the following holds:*
*1. $W$ is expanded and $W'$ is rooted;*
*2. $W$ is rooted (generated in step 1) and $W'$ is consistent;*
*3. $W$ is consistent and $W'$ is full;*
*4. $W$ is full and $W'$ is $\star$-ready for a given heap $w$;*
*4'. $W$ is full and $W'$ is $-\!\star$-ready for a given heap $w$;*
*8. $W$ is sanitized and $\star$-ready ( $-\!\star$-ready) for a given heap $w$, and $W'$ is normalized and $\star$-ready ( $-\!\star$-ready) for heap $w$.*

**Lemma 6.8.** *For a world sequent $W$ of a particular kind, there exists a disjunctive derivation state $\Psi$ such that:*
*1) $\{W\} \mapsto^* \Psi$ by applying only the propagation rules;*
*2) $[\![\Psi]\!]_S$ implies $[\![\{W\}]\!]_S$ for any stack $S$,*
*where one of the following holds:*
*5. $W$ is $\star$-ready for a given heap $w$, and every world sequent in $\Psi$ is saturated as well as $\star$-ready for heap $w$.*
*6. $W$ is $-\!\star$-ready for a given heap $w$, and every world sequent in $\Psi$ is saturated as well as $-\!\star$-ready for heap $w$.*

**Lemma 6.9** (Completeness of the rule Weaken). *For any saturated world sequent $W$, there exists a sanitized world sequent $W'$ such that:*
*1) $\{W\} \mapsto^* \{W'\}$ by applying only the rule* Weaken*;*
*2) $[\![\{W'\}]\!]_S$ implies $[\![\{W\}]\!]_S$ for any stack $S$.*

**Corollary 6.10.** *For any expanded world sequent $W$ and heap $w$, there exists a disjunctive derivation state $\Psi$ such that:*
*1) $\{W\} \mapsto^* \Psi$ by applying only the structural rules;*
*2) $\Psi$ contains only normalized world sequents that are also $\star$-ready or $-\!\star$-ready for heap $w$;*
*3) $[\![\Psi]\!]_S$ implies $[\![\{W\}]\!]_S$ for any stack $S$.*

**Proposition 6.11** (Completeness of the rules $\star$R and $-\!\star$L).
*Consider a normalized world sequent $W$ that is also $\star$-ready for heap $w$. Suppose that we obtain $\{W\} \overset{\star R}{\mapsto} \Psi_i$ by applying the rule $\star$R to a false formula $A \star B$ about heap $w$ for each heap relation $w \doteq w_i \circ w_i'$ $(i = 1, \cdots, n)$, and $\{W\} \overset{\star R}{\mapsto} \Psi_\epsilon$ by applying the rule $\star$R to the same formula for another heap relation $w \doteq w \circ w_\epsilon$. Then a conjunctive proof goal $\Omega = \{\Psi_1, \cdots, \Psi_n, \Psi_\epsilon\}$ satisfies:*
*1) $\{\{W\}\} \overset{\star R}{\leadsto} \Omega$;*
*2) $[\![\Omega]\!]_S$ implies $[\![\{\{W\}\}]\!]_S$ for any stack $S$;*
*3) No world sequent in $\Omega$ contains the false formula $A \star B$ about heap $w$;*
*4) Every world sequent in $\Omega$ is still normalized and thus consistent.*
*Similarly for the rule $-\!\star$L where we use each heap relation $w_i \doteq w \circ w_i'$.*

### 6.2.3 Completeness of the heap contradiction rules

Suppose that after eliminating all formulas other than $\bot$, we obtain a conjunctive proof goal $\Omega^i$ which contains only expanded world sequents. By Corollary 6.10, we can obtain $\Omega^i \leadsto^* \Omega^{i+1}$ such that every world sequent in $\Omega^{i+1}$ is normalized and $[\![\Omega^{i+1}]\!]_S$ implies $[\![\Omega^i]\!]_S$ for any stack $S$. Proposition 6.12 shows that $\Omega^{i+1}$ contains only canonical world sequents.

**Proposition 6.12** (Completeness of the heap contradiction rules).
*A normalized world sequent $W$ with no formulas other than $\bot$ is canonical. That is, if $\neg[\![W]\!]_S$ holds for any stack $S$, we can construct its derivation using only the rules $\bot$L,* ExpCont*, and the heap contradiction rules. For the rule* ExpCont*, we assume that $\neg[\![\Theta \vdash \bot]\!]_S$ implies $\Theta \vdash \bot$.*

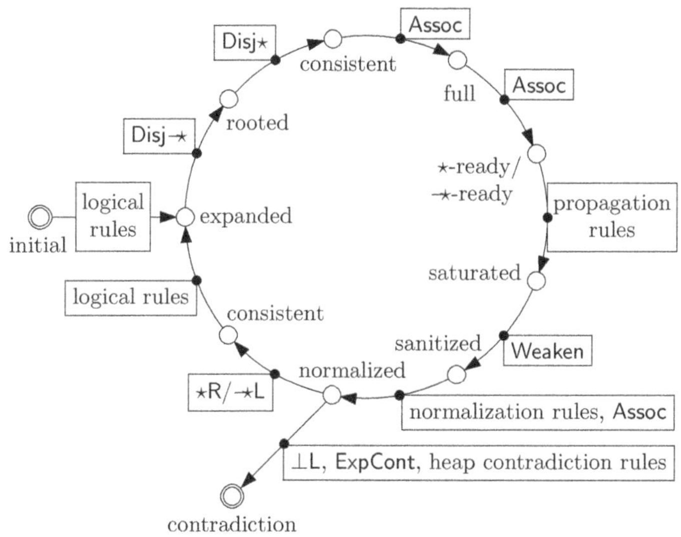


**Figure 4.** Proof search strategy based on the proof of Theorem 6.4

Thus we conclude the proof of Theorem 6.4.

### 6.3 Proof search strategy

Figure 4 shows the proof search strategy based on the proof of Theorem 6.4. Given a world sequent of the form $\cdot; \cdot \parallel [\cdot \Longrightarrow A]^w$, we repeatedly apply the logical rules other than the rules $\star$R and $-\!\star$L to obtain expanded world sequents according to Corollary 6.6 (from initial to expanded). Then we apply a series of structural rules to obtain normalized world sequents according to Corollary 6.10 (from expanded to normalized). If no formulas other than $\bot$ remain, we attempt to generate a logical contradiction according to Proposition 6.12 (from normalized to contradiction). Otherwise we apply the rule $\star$R or $-\!\star$L to obtain consistent world sequents according to Proposition 6.11 (from normalized to consistent). By repeatedly applying the logical rules other than the rules $\star$R and $-\!\star$L again, we obtain another set of expanded world sequents according to Corollary 6.6 (from consistent to expanded). In this way, we can eventually decompose all formulas other than $\bot$ and complete the proof search.

As it directly translates to a proof search strategy, the proof of Theorem 6.4 agrees with the result that propositional separation logic is decidable [9]. Since first-order separation logic is undecidable [5], the proof system $\mathbf{P_{SL}}$ becomes undecidable in the presence of the rule $\exists$R. We also remark that in the presence of propositional variables, even propositional separation logic is undecidable [6].

### 6.4 Validity of formulas in $\mathbf{P_{SL}}$

As established by Theorems 6.1 and 6.4, the notion of validity in $\mathbf{P_{SL}}$ means that a formula is true (or an assumption of its falsehood leads to a logical contradiction) at an arbitrary heap about which nothing is known. An important implication of assuming such an arbitrary heap is that we in effect assume *an arbitrary world of heaps*, since even the relationship with an external heap can be thought of as a property of the arbitrary heap, which is assumed to be unknown. In particular, we may not assume the existence of a singleton heap with location L even if the goal formula contains a points-to relation $[\mathsf{L} \mapsto E]$.

As an example, consider a formula

$$A = \mathsf{I} \supset \neg([\mathsf{L} \mapsto E] \mathrel{-\!\!\star} \neg[\mathsf{L} \mapsto E])$$

which states that an empty heap combined with a heap satisfying $[\mathsf{L} \mapsto E]$ cannot be a heap where $[\mathsf{L} \mapsto E]$ is false. According to the semantics of separation logic in Section 2, this formula is valid *but only provided that a singleton heap satisfying* $[\mathsf{L} \mapsto E]$ *is known to exist.* The existence of such a singleton heap, however, is an assumption that can be justified only by inspecting the formula at the meta-logical level. Since $\mathbf{P_{SL}}$ assumes an arbitrary world of heaps without knowing the existence of such a singleton heap, it fails to prove the above formula.

If we are to show the validity of a formula by exploiting prior knowledge on the world of heaps, we should prove an extended formula that incorporates its meta-logical property as well. For example, in order to show the validity of the above formula $A$ when the existence of a singleton heap satisfying $[\mathsf{L} \mapsto E]$ is already known, we should instead prove an extended formula

$$[\mathsf{L} \mapsto E] \star \top \supset \neg(\neg A \star \top)$$

which states that if the world of heaps contains a heap satisfying $[\mathsf{L} \mapsto E]$, there cannot exist a heap where $A$ is false, *i.e.*, $A$ is true at any heap. An attempt to prove the extended formula produces a world sequent

$$\cdot;\ \begin{array}{l} w \doteq u_1 \circ u_2, \\ w \doteq v_1 \circ v_2 \end{array} \ \|\ \begin{array}{l} [\cdot \Longrightarrow \cdot]^{w}, \\ [[\mathsf{L} \mapsto E] \Longrightarrow \cdot]^{u_1}, \\ [\top \Longrightarrow \cdot]^{u_2}, \\ [\cdot \Longrightarrow A]^{v_1}, \\ [\top \Longrightarrow \cdot]^{v_2} \end{array}$$

which essentially expresses that formula $A$ is false at an arbitrary heap when there exists a heap satisfying $[\mathsf{L} \mapsto E]$. A proof of this world sequent complies with the validity of formula $A$ in separation logic.

## 7. Discussion

Our prototype implementation of $\mathbf{P_{SL}}$ (without first-order formulas) is based on the proof of Theorem 6.4, but with a few changes. In particular, it internally uses a different type of normalized world sequents which maintain a unique heap corresponding to each non-empty set of terminal heaps, but permit unknown relations between heaps. The decision is based on the observation that it is the rules $\mathsf{Disj}\star$ and $\mathsf{Disj}\mathrel{-\!\!\star}$ (for eliminating unknown relations between heaps) that contributes the most to the complexity of graphs of heaps. Thus it selectively applies the rules $\mathsf{Disj}\star$ and $\mathsf{Disj}\mathrel{-\!\!\star}$ only when it cannot complete the proof search otherwise.

Our experience with the prototype implementation of $\mathbf{P_{SL}}$ shows that it allows us to incorporate new logical connectives and predicates in a principled way without having to introduce additional structural rules. As an example, consider an overlapping conjunction $A \uplus B$ by Hobor and Villard [17] which can be defined in the framework of $\mathbf{P_{SL}}$ as follows:

- $A \uplus B$ is true at heap $w$ iff. $w \doteq w_1 \circ v_2$, $w \doteq v_1 \circ w_2$, $w_1 \doteq v_1 \circ u$, $w_2 \doteq u \circ v_2$, and $A$ is true at heap $w_1$ and $B$ is true at heap $w_2$ for *some* heaps $w_1, w_2, v_1, v_2$, and $u$.
- $A \uplus B$ is false at heap $w$ iff. $w \doteq w_1 \circ v_2$, $w \doteq v_1 \circ w_2$, $w_1 \doteq v_1 \circ u$, and $w_2 \doteq u \circ v_2$ implies that $A$ is false at heap $w_1$ or that $B$ is false at heap $w_2$ for *any* heaps $w_1, w_2, v_1, v_2$, and $u$.

We directly translate this definition into two inference rules for $\uplus$:

$$\frac{\textit{fresh } w_1, w_2, v_1, v_2, u \qquad \Theta; \Sigma,\ \begin{array}{l} w \doteq w_1 \circ v_2, \\ w \doteq v_1 \circ w_2, \\ w_1 \doteq v_1 \circ u, \\ w_2 \doteq u \circ v_2 \end{array} \ \|\ \Pi, [\Gamma \Longrightarrow \Delta]^w,\ \begin{array}{l} [A \Longrightarrow \cdot]^{w_1}, \\ [B \Longrightarrow \cdot]^{w_2}, \\ [\cdot \Longrightarrow \cdot]^{v_1}, \\ [\cdot \Longrightarrow \cdot]^{v_2}, \\ [\cdot \Longrightarrow \cdot]^{u} \end{array}}{\Theta; \Sigma \ \|\ \Pi, [\Gamma, A \uplus B \Longrightarrow \Delta]^w}\ \uplus\mathsf{L}$$

$$\frac{\begin{array}{l} w \doteq w_1 \circ v_2, \\ w \doteq v_1 \circ w_2, \\ w_1 \doteq v_1 \circ u, \\ \{\, w_2 \doteq u \circ v_2 \,\} \subset \Sigma \end{array} \quad \begin{array}{l} \Theta; \Sigma \ \|\ \Pi,\ \begin{array}{l} [\Gamma \Longrightarrow \Delta, A \uplus B]^w, \\ [\Gamma_1 \Longrightarrow \Delta_1, A]^{w_1}, \\ [\Gamma_2 \Longrightarrow \Delta_2]^{w_2} \end{array} \\ \Theta; \Sigma \ \|\ \Pi,\ \begin{array}{l} [\Gamma \Longrightarrow \Delta, A \uplus B]^w, \\ [\Gamma_1 \Longrightarrow \Delta_1]^{w_1}, \\ [\Gamma_2 \Longrightarrow \Delta_2, B]^{w_2} \end{array} \end{array}}{\Theta; \Sigma \ \|\ \Pi,\ \begin{array}{l} [\Gamma \Longrightarrow \Delta, A \uplus B]^w, \\ [\Gamma_1 \Longrightarrow \Delta_1]^{w_1}, \\ [\Gamma_2 \Longrightarrow \Delta_2]^{w_2} \end{array}}\ \uplus\mathsf{R}$$

Note that we obtain the rules $\uplus\mathsf{L}$ and $\uplus\mathsf{R}$ exactly in the same way that we derive the rules $\star\mathsf{L}$ and $\star\mathsf{R}$ from the interpretation of multiplicative conjunction $\star$. The only difference is that we create five fresh heaps in the rule $\uplus\mathsf{L}$ and try to detect a subgraph consisting of six existing heaps in the rule $\uplus\mathsf{R}$. Equally important is that we need no additional structural or heap contradiction rules because overlapping conjunction does not require new forms of heap relations. Thus, in principle, it is relatively easy to incorporate overlapping conjunction into our prototype implementation of $\mathbf{P_{SL}}$. Overall we may think of $\mathbf{P_{SL}}$ as a highly extensible proof system for separation logic.

## 8. Related work

### 8.1 Automated verification tools based on separation logic

Separation logic has been the basis for a number of automated verification tools targeting programs using mutable data structures. The first such tool is Smallfoot by Berdine *et al.* [3] which aims to test the feasibility of automated verification using separation logic. To achieve full automation, it permits no pointer arithmetic and verifies only shape properties of linked lists and trees. Space Invader by Distefano *et al.* [11] permits pointer arithmetic by integrating the abstract interpretation method into the symbolic execution method in [4]. THOR by Magill *et al.* [23] is an extension of Space Invader which is capable of tracking the length of linked lists. SLAyer by Berdine *et al.* [1] is another extension of Space Invader which uses higher-order predicates to express common properties of nodes in linked lists. The use of higher-order predicates enables SLAyer to verify shape properties of composite linked lists such as linked lists of circular linked lists.

There are also several tools supporting arbitrary data structures. HIP by Nguyen and Chin [25] allows users to specify invariants on arbitrary data structures in terms of inductive predicates. Since checking these invariants usually relies on basic properties of inductive predicates that are easy to prove but difficult to discover automatically, HIP requires users to explicitly state such properties in the form of lemmas, which are automatically proven and then applied as necessary. Similarly to HIP, VeriFast by Jacobs *et al.* [19] relies on user-supplied inductive predicates and lemmas. Unlike HIP, however, VeriFast requires users to provide proofs of these lemmas and specify when to apply them. jStar by Distefano and Parkinson [12] is an extension of Space Invader which exploits user-supplied abstraction rules in order to support arbitrary data structures. Its distinguishing feature is the ability to infer loop invariants automatically. Xisa by Chang and Rival [10] takes a different approach by indirectly specifying invariants on data structures with validation code. Xisa analyzes validation code to extract inductive predicates for describing invariants as well as lemmas for describing their basic properties. Since validation code can be written in common programming languages, users of Xisa do not need the expertise to specify invariants of interest in terms of inductive predicates.

All these tools use as their logical foundation not full separation logic but only its decidable fragment by Berdine *et al.* [2], which does not include separating implication $-\!\!\star$. As shown by Ishtiaq and O'Hearn [18], lack of separating implication implies no support for backward reasoning by weakest precondition generation for those programs performing heap assignments or allocation. As a result, these tools allow only forward reasoning based on symbolic execution as in [4] and do not demonstrate the full potential of separation logic in program verification.

### 8.2 Proof search in full separation logic

Despite the practical importance of separating implication, proof search in full separation logic has not drawn much attention from researchers. Calcagno *et al.* [8] present a translation from propositional separation logic to first-order logic (with only propositional connectives and no multiplicative connectives) for which a decision procedure already exists. The labelled tableau calculus for separation logic by Galmiche and Méry [15] supports both separating conjunction and separating implication. Similarly to our proof system $\mathbf{P_{SL}}$, their calculus combines both syntactic (tableau) and semantic (labelled) formulations and uses labels to directly refer to heaps. Although it is shown to be sound and complete, their calculus does not give rise to a proof search strategy. Specifically, in order to check that all branches in a tableau are logically or structurally inconsistent, we need two semantic functions, a measure and an interpretation, for each branch. Their calculus, however, does not explain how to construct such semantic functions for each branch and it is not clear how to extract a concrete proof search strategy.

The closest proof system to ours is the nested sequent calculus $\mathbf{S_{BBI}}$ for Boolean BI by Park *et al.* [26], which inspired the overall design of $\mathbf{P_{SL}}$. Similarly to world sequents in $\mathbf{P_{SL}}$, sequents in $\mathbf{S_{BBI}}$ use a truth context consisting of true formulas and a falsehood context consisting of false formulas, and both systems are based on the principle of proof by contradiction. Because of the similarity in syntactic formulations, their approach to dealing with separating conjunction and separating implication in $\mathbf{S_{BBI}}$ equally applies to our setting for $\mathbf{P_{SL}}$, which is not surprising considering that separation logic is just an instance of Boolean BI with additional restrictions on the semantic structure. The structural rules of $\mathbf{P_{SL}}$, however, are specific to separation logic and are designed independently of $\mathbf{S_{BBI}}$. Since $\mathbf{S_{BBI}}$ allows propositional variables, we may use its theorem prover as a supplementary system for our implementation of $\mathbf{P_{SL}}$.

For theorem provers based on the decidable fragment of separation logic by Berdine *et al.* [2] (without separating implication), see, for example, SeLoger [16] and SLP [24]. For an isomorphism between (intuitionistic) separation logic and implicit dynamic frames, see [27].

## 9. Conclusion

We have presented a proof system $\mathbf{P_{SL}}$ for full separation logic with separating implication. Considering the potential benefit of separating implication, we envision that program verification systems in the future will provide separating implication and support backward reasoning by weakest precondition generation for their scalability in program verification. We also envision that proof assistants can interface with theorem provers for separation logic and provide a powerful automation tactic for dealing with logical connectives from separation logic. When extended with inductively defined predicates, $\mathbf{P_{SL}}$ may serve as a practical foundation for such systems.

## Acknowledgments

We are grateful to the anonymous reviewers for their helpful comments and Zhé Hóu for a comment on the completeness of $\mathbf{P_{SL}}$ that led to the discussion in Section 6.4. This work was supported by the Engineering Research Center of Excellence Program of Korea Ministry of Science, ICT & Future Planning (MSIP)/National Research Foundation of Korea (NRF) (Grant NRF-2008-0062609) and Mid-career Researcher Program through NRF funded by the MEST (2010-0022061).

## References

[1] Josh Berdine, Cristiano Calcagno, Byron Cook, Dino Distefano, Peter W. O'Hearn, Thomas Wies, and Hongseok Yang. Shape analysis for composite data structures. In *Proc. CAV*, pages 178–192, 2007.

[2] Josh Berdine, Cristiano Calcagno, and Peter W. O'Hearn. A decidable fragment of separation logic. In *Proc. FSTTCS*, pages 97–109, 2004.

[3] Josh Berdine, Cristiano Calcagno, and Peter W. O'Hearn. Smallfoot: Modular automatic assertion checking with separation logic. In *Proc. FMCO*, pages 115–137, 2005.

[4] Josh Berdine, Cristiano Calcagno, and Peter W. O'Hearn. Symbolic execution with separation logic. In *Proc. APLAS*, pages 52–68, 2005.

[5] Rémi Brochenin, Stéphane Demri, and Etienne Lozes. On the almighty wand. *Information and Computation*, 211:106–137, 2012.

[6] James Brotherston and Max Kanovich. Undecidability of propositional separation logic and its neighbours. In *Proc. LICS*, pages 130–139, 2010.

[7] Cristiano Calcagno and Dino Distefano. Infer: an automatic program verifier for memory safety of C programs. In *Proceedings of the Third international conference on NASA Formal methods*, pages 459–465, 2011.

[8] Cristiano Calcagno, Philippa Gardner, and Matthew Hague. From separation logic to first-order logic. In *Proc. FOSSACS*, pages 395–409, 2005.

[9] Cristiano Calcagno, Hongseok Yang, and Peter W. O'Hearn. Computability and complexity results for a spatial assertion language for data structures. In *Proceedings of the 21st Conference on Foundations of Software Technology and Theoretical Computer Science*, pages 108–119, 2001.

[10] Bor-Yuh Evan Chang and Xavier Rival. Relational inductive shape analysis. In *Proc. POPL*, pages 247–260, 2008.

[11] Dino Distefano, Peter W. O'Hearn, and Hongseok Yang. A local shape analysis based on separation logic. In *Proc. TACAS*, pages 287–302, 2006.

[12] Dino Distefano and Matthew J. Parkinson. jStar: towards practical verification for Java. In *Proc. OOPSLA*, pages 213–226, 2008.

[13] Robert Dockins, Aquinas Hobor, and Andrew W. Appel. A fresh look at separation algebras and share accounting. In *Proc. APLAS*, pages 161–177, 2009.

[14] Kamil Dudka, Petr Müller, Petr Peringer, and Tomáš Vojnar. Predator: a tool for verification of low-level list manipulation. In *Proc. TACAS*, pages 627–629, 2013.

[15] Didier Galmiche and Daniel Méry. Tableaux and resource graphs for separation logic. *Journal of Logic and Computation*, 20:189–231, 2010.

[16] Christoph Haase, Samin Ishtiaq, Joël Ouaknine, and Matthew J. Parkinson. SeLoger: A tool for graph-based reasoning in separation logic. In *Proc. CAV*, pages 790–795, 2013.

[17] Aquinas Hobor and Jules Villard. The ramifications of sharing in data structures. In *Proc. POPL*, pages 523–536, 2013.

[18] Samin S. Ishtiaq and Peter W. O'Hearn. BI as an assertion language for mutable data structures. In *Proc. POPL*, pages 14–26, 2001.

[19] Bart Jacobs, Jan Smans, and Frank Piessens. VeriFast: Imperative programs as proofs. In *Proc. VSTTE*, pages 59–68, 2010.

[20] Neelakantan R. Krishnaswami. Reasoning about iterators with separation logic. In *Proc. SAVCBS*, pages 83–86, 2006.

[21] Dominique Larchey-Wendling and Didier Galmiche. The undecidability of boolean BI through phase semantics. In *Proc. LICS*, pages 140–149, 2010.

[22] Toshiyuki Maeda, Haruki Sato, and Akinori Yonezawa. Extended alias type system using separating implication. In *Proc. TLDI*, pages 29–42, 2011.

[23] Stephen Magill, Josh Berdine, Edmund M. Clarke, and Byron Cook. Arithmetic strengthening for shape analysis. In *Proc. SAS*, pages 419–436, 2007.

[24] Juan Antonio Navarro Pérez and Andrey Rybalchenko. Separation logic + superposition calculus = heap theorem prover. In *Proc. PLDI*, pages 556–566, 2011.

[25] Huu Hai Nguyen and Wei-Ngan Chin. Enhancing program verification with lemmas. In *Proc. CAV*, pages 355–369, 2008.

[26] Jonghyun Park, Jeongbong Seo, and Sungwoo Park. A theorem prover for Boolean BI. In *Proc. POPL*, pages 219–232, 2013.

[27] Matthew J. Parkinson and Alexander J. Summers. The relationship between separation logic and implicit dynamic frames. In *Proc. ESOP*, pages 439–458, 2011.

[28] John C. Reynolds. Separation logic: A logic for shared mutable data structures. In *Proc. LICS*, pages 55–74, 2002.

[29] Hongseok Yang. An example of local reasoning in BI pointer logic: the Schorr-Waite graph marking algorithm. In *Proceedings of the 1st Workshop on Semantics, Program Analysis, and Computing Environments for Memory Management*, pages 41–68, 2001.

# From Parametricity to Conservation Laws, via Noether's Theorem

Robert Atkey

bob.atkey@gmail.com

## Abstract

Invariance is of paramount importance in programming languages and in physics. In programming languages, John Reynolds' theory of relational parametricity demonstrates that parametric polymorphic programs are invariant under change of data representation, a property that yields "free" theorems about programs just from their types. In physics, Emmy Noether showed that if the action of a physical system is invariant under change of coordinates, then the physical system has a conserved quantity: a quantity that remains constant for all time. Knowledge of conserved quantities can reveal deep properties of physical systems. For example, the conservation of energy is by Noether's theorem a consequence of a system's invariance under time-shifting.

In this paper, we link Reynolds' relational parametricity with Noether's theorem for deriving conserved quantities. We propose an extension of System F$\omega$ with new kinds, types and term constants for writing programs that describe classical mechanical systems in terms of their Lagrangians. We show, by constructing a relationally parametric model of our extension of F$\omega$, that relational parametricity is enough to satisfy the hypotheses of Noether's theorem, and so to derive conserved quantities for free, directly from the polymorphic types of Lagrangians expressed in our system.

***Categories and Subject Descriptors*** D.3.1 [*Programming Languages*]: Formal Definitions and Theory; J.2 [*Physical Sciences and Engineering*]: Physics

***General Terms*** Languages, Theory, Types, Physics

***Keywords*** classical mechanics; relational parametricity; higher-kinded types; invariance; conservation laws

## 1. Introduction

Reynolds' theory of relational parametricity [18] tells us that parametrically polymorphic programs automatically satisfy invariance properties. Such invariance properties are often called *Free Theorems*, after Wadler [22], since they follow "for free" from the types of programs, rather than through detailed study of the program text. An illustrative example is the free theorem for programs $f$ with the following type:

$$f : \forall\alpha.\ \mathsf{List}\ \alpha \to \mathsf{Nat}$$



*POPL '14*, January 22–24, 2014, San Diego, CA, USA.

ACM 978-1-4503-2544-8/14/01...$15.00.
http://dx.doi.org/10.1145/2535838.2535867

Such programs take lists of $\alpha$s, for any type $\alpha$, and return natural numbers. Using Reynolds' theory of relational parametricity, Wadler showed that *any* $f$ with this type satisfies the following property:

$$\forall\alpha,\beta,g:\alpha\to\beta,l:\mathsf{List}\ \alpha.\ f\ [\alpha]\ l = f\ [\beta]\ (\mathrm{map}\ g\ l)$$

Thus, any $f$ with the type given above is invariant under mapping some arbitrary function $g$ over its input. Thinking in terms of abstract data types and change of data representation, this free theorem states that $f$ is invariant under change of data representation from an arbitrary type $\alpha$ to another arbitrary type $\beta$, via $g$.

The use of invariance under change to derive useful consequences is a technique much older than programming languages. In physics, *Noether's theorem* [14] provides a general way to derive conservation laws for physical systems from invariance properties. Informally speaking, Noether's theorem states that every continuous symmetry of a physical system implies the existence of a corresponding conserved quantity. A conserved quantity is a function of the state of the system that is constant for all time. We illustrate the use of Noether's theorem with a simple example of a classical system consisting of two particles of equal mass $m$ connected by a spring with spring constant $k$, such that the particles are constrained to move one-dimensionally.

Noether's theorem applies to systems described in terms of *Lagrangians*. For classical mechanics, a Lagrangian is a function of time and the positions and velocities of all the particles in the system, to the difference between the kinetic energy and the potential energy of the system. For our system with two particles at positions $x_1$ and $x_2$ with velocities $\dot{x_1}$ and $\dot{x_2}$ the Lagrangian is:

$$L(t,x_1,x_2,\dot{x_1},\dot{x_2}) = \frac{1}{2}m(\dot{x_1}^2+\dot{x_2}^2) - \frac{1}{2}k(x_1-x_2)^2 \quad (1)$$

The first summand represents the total kinetic energy of the system in terms of the mass and velocities, while the second summand represents the potential energy contained within the spring due to the distance between the particles.

From the Lagrangian (1), using the *principle of stationary action*, we can derive the following two equations of motion for this system. (We describe the principle of stationary action, and the process for deriving the equations of motion fully in Section 2.) For this system, the equations of motion are a pair of ordinary differential equations (ODEs) that describe how the positions and velocities of the particles evolve over time (the second derivative with respect to time, $\ddot{x_i}$, denotes the acceleration of the $i$th particle):

$$m\ddot{x_1} = -k(x_1-x_2) \qquad m\ddot{x_2} = -k(x_2-x_1)$$

We could now proceed to solve these ODEs to further analyse the behaviour of this system. However, Noether's theorem gives us a powerful way of gaining insight into properties of these ODEs "for free", without necessarily having to find solutions to them. This is accomplished by finding invariance properties of the Lagrangian.

The Lagrangian (1) does not refer to any fixed point in space; only the relative distance between the two particles, along with their velocities, is relevant. Therefore, the Lagrangian (1) is invariant under translation in space by some arbitrary displacement $y$:

$$L(t, x_1, x_2, \dot{x_1}, \dot{x_2}) = L(t, x_1 + y, x_2 + y, \dot{x_1}, \dot{x_2}) \tag{2}$$

By Noether's theorem, invariance under spatial translation implies that the linear momentum of the whole system is constant for all time. For this system, conservation of linear momentum is stated mathematically as the vanishing of the derivative with respect to time of the total linear momentum of the system:

$$\frac{d}{dt} m(\dot{x}_1 + \dot{x_2}) = 0 \tag{3}$$

In general, Noether's theorem gives us a way of deriving conserved properties like (3) from invariance properties like (2). In this case, we have used invariance under translation in space to derive conservation of linear momentum. Other common examples include invariance under translation in time, yielding conservation of energy, and invariance under rotation, yielding conservation of angular momentum. We will see examples of each of these kinds of invariance, and their consequent conservation laws, in Section 5.

The invariance property stated in Equation (2) is highly reminiscent of the free theorem we stated for the polymorphic program at the start of this introduction. A change in representation in the input, whether a change in data representation from a type $\alpha$ to a type $\beta$, or a change in where time zero is counted from, results in no change in the output. Since Reynolds' relational parametricity allowed us to derive the invariance properties for the program $f$ just by looking at its type, we ask the following question:

**Question:** *Is it possible to use Reynolds' theory of relational parametricity to derive the invariance properties of Lagrangians required for Noether's theorem to derive conservation laws?*

In this paper, we answer this question positively. We show that it is indeed the case that we can use a generalised version of Reynolds' theory of relational parametricity to prove the geometric invariance properties required for the hypotheses of Noether's theorem. We construct an extension of System F$\omega$ suitable for writing invariant Lagrangians, with a relationally parametric model that allows us to prove invariance properties as free theorems. In our system, the Lagrangian (1) we gave above for describing a system of two particles coupled by a spring will have the type:

$$\forall y{:}\mathsf{T}(1).$$
$$C^\infty(\mathbb{R}\langle 1,0\rangle \times \mathbb{R}\langle 1,y\rangle \times \mathbb{R}\langle 1,y\rangle \times \mathbb{R}\langle 1,0\rangle \times \mathbb{R}\langle 1,0\rangle, \mathbb{R}\langle 1,0\rangle)$$

We explain this type by breaking it down from left to right. The quantifier $\forall y{:}\mathsf{T}(1)$ indicates that we are quantifying over all translations $y$ in one-dimensional space, just as we did implicitly in Equation (2). The notation $C^\infty(-,-)$ denotes the type of *smooth* functions between spaces. (A smooth function is a function that is infinitely differentiable.) All the functions that we wish to use as Lagrangians must be smooth (at least up to second order) for the theory to work. The type $\mathbb{R}\langle g, x\rangle$ denotes real numbers that vary with some linear transformation $g$ and translation $x$. In this case, all the linear transformations are 1, indicating no transformation. Likewise, when the translation component is 0, there is no translation. Thus a value of type $\mathbb{R}\langle 1,0\rangle$ is invariant, but a value of type $\mathbb{R}\langle 1,y\rangle$ varies with the translation $y$. In the smooth function type above, the domain space consists of vectors of five real numbers: the time, the two particle positions, which vary with the translation $y$, and the two particle velocities.

Atkey, Johann and Kennedy [5], building on work by Kennedy [11], have already presented a polymorphic type system for expressing geometric invariance properties similar to the translation invariance property in Equation (2). In the present work, we extend their type system by embedding it within System F$\omega$. The benefits of this embedding are twofold. Firstly, by using the richer type-level structure of System F$\omega$, we can easily add useful indexed types like length indexed vectors and smooth function types, both of which would have required special treatment in the special purpose type system presented by Atkey *et al.*. Secondly, by using System F$\omega$ as our base, we are able to reuse the reflexive graph-based relationally parametric semantics presented by Atkey [3], extending it as appropriate for our geometric setting.

***Contributions*** Our core contributions are threefold:

1. We reformulate the type system for geometric invariance of Atkey, Johann and Kennedy [5] as an extension of System F$\omega$. This shows that the special status of the group-indexed types in Atkey *et al.*'s work can be incorporated into a standard framework for indexed types.
2. We present a relationally parametric semantics of our extension of System F$\omega$. In this model, following Atkey's model for basic System F$\omega$ [3], each kind is interpreted as a reflexive graph. Our key technical contribution is to note that the many geometric groups that we wish to incorporate are expressible as groupoids, and hence as reflexive graphs. We therefore show that Reynolds' theory of relational parametricity, suitably generalised to indexed types by considering reflexive graphs, already accommodates geometric invariance properties.
3. Finally, we connect the free theorems derivable from our relationally parametric semantics with Noether's theorem for deriving conservation laws. We present many examples of invariant Lagrangians expressible in our type system, along with the consequent conservation laws for physical systems. In each case, the necessary invariance property is derived from the type of the Lagrangian.

***Outline***

- In the next section, Section 2, we describe the necessary background to understand Noether's theorem and the conservation laws it generates. We briefly introduce the Lagrangian formulation of classical mechanics, define precisely what it means for a physical system to be invariant under transformations, and state Noether's theorem.
- Having shown how invariance generates conservation laws in Section 2, in Section 3 we show how to derive invariance properties from indexed types. We present a relationally parametric semantics for System F$\omega$, and show how geometric invariance properties can be accomodated within this semantics.
- In Section 4 we construct a type system for classical mechanics by extending System F$\omega$ with the necessary constants for smooth function types and combinators for constructing smooth functions. Programming directly with our combinators in raw System F$\omega$ is awkward, due to the point-free style required, so in Section 4.2 we define a surface syntax for defining smooth functions that is translated into our applied System F$\omega$.
- In Section 5 we present several examples of using our extension of System F$\omega$ for writing invariant Lagrangians that describe physical systems.
- Section 6 concludes, and offers directions for further work.

## 2. Conservation Laws from Invariance

Noether's theorem applies to systems described using the formalism of Lagrangian mechanics, a reformulation of Newtonian classical mechanics. In this section we can only offer a very brief introduction to the concepts of Lagrangian mechanics. The reader is referred to other sources, such as Landau and Lifschitz [12] or Arnol'd [2] for the necessary background in the mathematical theory of classical mechanics. Lagrangian mechanics, and Noether's theorem, make crucial use of the Calculus of Variations. Gelfand and Fomin [7] provide a good introduction to this topic.

In this section, we will endeavour to keep the presentation relatively elementary. However, some knowledge of differential and integral calculus will be required. Knowledge of basic Newtonian mechanics will also be helpful. We will use standard notation from physics and mathematics for integrals and (partial) derivatives. In particular, when discussing derivatives with respect to time, we use dot notation: $\dot{x}$ for the first derivative of $x$ with respect to time, and $\ddot{x}$ for the second derivative.

### 2.1 Lagrangian Mechanics

Lagrangian mechanics is a branch of analytical mechanics, along with Hamiltonian mechanics [2, 12]. Analytical mechanics seeks to discover the underlying structure of Newtonian classical mechanics by reformulating it in different terms.

***Lagrangian and Action*** For Lagrangian mechanics, classical mechanical systems are described in terms of *Lagrangians* $L = T - V$, where $T$ is the total kinetic energy of the system, and $V$ is the total potential energy. The Lagrangian is a function of time, the positions of all the particles in the system, and their velocities. This is usually written like so, with abuse of notation for $\dot{q}$ which is a variable here, not the derivative of a function:

$$L(t, q, \dot{q}) = T - V$$

In this expression, $q$ and $\dot{q}$ are actually vectors containing the components of the position and velocity vectors for each particle. A key feature of Lagrangian mechanics is that the coordinate system used to describe the system need not necessarily be the usual cartesian coordinates. For example, one of the components of $q$ might be the angle of swing of a pendulum. This use of generalised coordinates is one of the advantages of Lagrangian mechanics over the Newtonian presentation in terms of positions and forces.

The Lagrangian for a particular system is used to define the *action* of that system. For a particular path $q : \mathbb{R} \to \mathbb{R}^n$ and endpoints $a < b$ in time, the action of the Lagrangian $L$ over this path is defined by the following integral:

$$\mathcal{S}[q; a; b] = \int_a^b L(t, q(t), \dot{q}(t))\, dt$$

Below, we will use the principle of stationary action to select the physically realisable paths from all the possible paths $q : \mathbb{R} \to \mathbb{R}^n$.

**Example 1.** We have already seen an example of a Lagrangian, in the introduction, describing a system of two particles coupled by a spring. Another example of a Lagrangian describes a system consisting of a single particle of mass $m$ acted upon by a constant downward gravitational field with gravitational potential $g$:

$$L(t, x, y, \dot{x}, \dot{y}) = \frac{1}{2}m(\dot{x}^2 + \dot{y}^2) - mgy \qquad (4)$$

Again, the left summand represents the kinetic energy of the system in terms of the mass and horizontal and vertical velocities of the particle. The right summand represents the potential energy of the system due to the gravitational field's strength determined by the particle's distance from a fixed baseline at $y = 0$.

***The Principle of Stationary Action*** The *principle of stationary action* states that the physically realisable paths $q$ are the paths that yield stationary points (i.e., either minima or maxima) of the action $\mathcal{S}[q; a; b]$, for all $a$ and $b$. Defining what is exactly meant by a stationary point of the action is beyond the scope of this paper, and can be found in standard references on the calculus of variations, such as Gelfand and Fomin [7]. The key point for our purposes is that a path $q$ satisfies the principle of stationary action if and only if it satisfies a system of ODEs derived from the Lagrangian $L$, called the Euler-Lagrange equations:

$$\frac{d}{dt}\frac{\partial L}{\partial \dot{q}_i} - \frac{\partial L}{\partial q_i} = 0 \qquad (5)$$

The ODEs derived from the Lagrangian for a classical mechanical system are called the *equations of motion* for the system.

The notation in the Euler-Lagrange equation, while standard, is not exactly clear, especially to a programming language theorist used to a more careful treatment of variables. The two partial derivatives $\frac{\partial L}{\partial \dot{q}_i}$ and $\frac{\partial L}{\partial q_i}$ take partial derivatives of $L$ with respect to $\dot{q}_i$ and $q_i$ *as variables*. The derivative with respect to time, $\frac{d}{dt}$, then treats $\dot{q}_i$ as a function of time, hence the appearance of the second derivatives $\ddot{q}_i$ in the equations of motion. Sussman and Wisdom [20] criticise the standard presentation of Lagrangian mechanics for this kind of confusing notation, and define a clearer notation based on the Scheme programming language. We elect to stick with the standard notation as used in physics textbooks just for familiarity.

**Example 2.** Computing the Euler-Lagrange equations for the Lagrangian (4), above, yields a pair of ODEs, one each for the $x$ and $y$ coordinates of the single particle of the system:

$$m\ddot{x} = 0 \qquad\qquad m\ddot{y} = -mg$$

Note that both these ODEs have the form $F = m\ddot{x}$, just as in Newton's second law. Lagrangian mechanics allows, from the principle of stationary action, the derivation of Newton's second law, instead of postulating it as an axiom.

### 2.2 Noether's Theorem

As we described in the introduction, Noether's theorem provides us with deep insights into the properties of the solutions of the Euler-Lagrange equations. Formally, Noether's theorem requires the invariance of the action $\mathcal{S}$, rather than invariance of the Lagrangian itself. We therefore first define what is meant by invariance of the action, and then state Noether's theorem.

***Invariance of the Action*** Let

$$\mathcal{S}[q; a; b] = \int_a^b L(t, q(t), \dot{q}(t))\, dt$$

be the action of some physical system described by the Lagrangian $L$. Assume a differentiable invertible function $\Phi : \mathbb{R} \to \mathbb{R}$ that transforms time in some way and a function $\Psi : \mathbb{R}^n \to \mathbb{R}^n$ that transforms the vector of generalised coordinates $\vec{q}$ to another vector of generalised coordinates $\Psi(\vec{q})$.

The action $\mathcal{S}$ is *invariant* between the endpoints $a$ and $b$, under the transformations $\Phi$ and $\Psi$, if it is the case that for all paths $q$:

$$\int_a^b L(t, q(t), \dot{q}(t))\, dt = \int_{\Phi(a)}^{\Phi(b)} L(s, q^*(s), \frac{dq^*}{ds}(s))\, ds \qquad (6)$$

where $q^*(s) = (\Psi \circ q \circ \Phi^{-1})(s)$ is the path $q$ transformed by $\Phi$ and $\Psi$. By change of variables, the right hand integral in the above equation is equal to the following integral:

$$\int_a^b L(\Phi(t), q^*(\Phi(t)), \frac{dq^*}{ds}(\Phi(t))) \cdot |\dot{\Phi}(t)|\, dt$$

For our application to classical mechanics, the endpoints $a$ and $b$ are arbitrary, so we can rewrite Equation (6) to the following equation between applications of the Lagrangian:

$$L(t, q(t), \dot{q}(t)) = L(\Phi(t), q^*(\Phi(t)), \frac{dq^*}{ds}(\Phi(t))) \cdot |\dot{\Phi}(t)| \qquad (7)$$

For most examples, it will be the case that $\Phi$ has the form $\Phi(t) = t + t'$ and $\Psi$ is an affine transformation $\Psi(q) = Gq + x$, where $G$ is an $n \times n$ real matrix and $x \in \mathbb{R}^n$. In this case, Equation (7) simplifies further, using the definition of $q^*$ and the chain rule of differentiation, to:

$$L(t, q(t), \dot{q}(t)) = L(t + t', Gq(t) + x, G\dot{q}(t)) \qquad (8)$$

Equation (8) is obviously implied by the following equation, where we treat $q$ and $\dot{q}$ as universally quantified variables, instead of as functions of time:

$$L(t, q, \dot{q}) = L(t + t', Gq + x, G\dot{q}) \qquad (9)$$

Equation (9) is the form of invariance that the free theorems we derive from the types of our typed language for classical mechanics will usually take. We define our type system for classical mechanics in Sections 3 and 4 below.

**Example 3.** In the introduction, we stated that the Lagrangian (1) describing the spring-coupled system is invariant under translation in space. Our running example in this section, the Lagrangian (4) for the single particle under gravity, is not invariant under all spatial translations, due to the reference in the potential energy term to the distance from the fixed baseline at $y = 0$. It is invariant under translations along the $x$-axis, however. Both Lagrangians are also invariant under translations in time, a special case of Equation (9):

$$L(t, q, \dot{q}) = L(t + t', q, \dot{q})$$

This invariance property is simply a consequence of the fact that neither Lagrangian explicitly mentions the time $t$.

***Noether's Theorem*** Noether's theorem applies to actions that are *continuously* invariant. Being continuously invariant means that, instead of having fixed transformations $\Phi$ and $\Psi$, we have two families of transformations, $\Phi_\epsilon$ and $\Psi_\epsilon$, differentiably indexed by a real parameter $\epsilon$, such that $\Phi_0$ and $\Psi_0$ are the identity function.

**Theorem 1** (Noether). *If the action*

$$\mathcal{S}[q; a; b] = \int_a^b L(t, q(t), \dot{q}(t))\, dt$$

*is invariant under $\epsilon$-indexed families of transformations $\Phi_\epsilon$ and $\Psi_\epsilon$, then the equation*

$$\frac{d}{dt}\left(\sum_{i=1}^{n} \frac{\partial L}{\partial \dot{q}_i}\psi_i + \left(L - \sum_{i=1}^{n} \dot{q}_i \frac{\partial L}{\partial \dot{q}_i}\right)\phi\right) = 0 \qquad (10)$$

*holds for all paths $q$ satisfying the Euler-Lagrange equations (5), where $\psi = \frac{\partial \Psi}{\partial \epsilon}\big|_{\epsilon=0}$ and $\phi = \frac{\partial \Phi}{\partial \epsilon}\big|_{\epsilon=0}$.*

*Proof.* E.g., Gelfand and Fomin [7], Section 20. □

**Example 4.** In Example 3, we noted that the Lagrangians (1) and (4) are both invariant under arbitrary translations in time. In terms of continuous invariance, their corresponding actions are invariant under the families $\Phi_\epsilon(t) = t + \epsilon$ and $\Psi_\epsilon(q) = q$. Plugging these definitions into Equation (10), we learn that, for these systems:

$$\frac{d}{dt}\left(L - \sum_{i=1}^{2} \dot{q}_i \frac{\partial L}{\partial \dot{q}_i}\right) = 0$$

For the spring-coupled particles Lagrangian, (1), we obtain:

$$\frac{d}{dt}\left(\frac{1}{2}m(\dot{x}_1{}^2 + \dot{x}_2{}^2) + \frac{1}{2}k(x_1 - x_2)^2\right) = 0$$

and for the single particle under gravity Lagrangian (4), we obtain:

$$\frac{d}{dt}\left(\frac{1}{2}m(\dot{x}^2 + \dot{y}^2) + mgy\right) = 0$$

In both cases, we have discovered that, as a consequence of invariance under translation in time, the total energy of the system is conserved (note that the $-$ signs in the original Lagrangians have turned into $+$s). In general, invariance under translation in time implies, via Noether's theorem, conservation of energy.

This finishes our short introduction to Lagrangian mechanics and Noether's theorem. We have shown how Noether's theorem can be used to derive conservation laws from invariance properties. We now go on to showing how suitable invariance properties can be derived from types, building towards Section 4, where we construct a type system for writing Lagrangians that expresses invariance properties directly in the types. In Section 5, we give examples of invariant Lagrangians and their consequent conservation laws.

## 3. Invariance from Types

We derive invariance properties from types by constructing a relationally parametric model of System F$\omega$, which we then extend with suitable kind-, type-, and term-level constants for writing invariant Lagrangians. Our relationally parametric model is based on the reflexive graph model presented by Atkey [3] (based on previous work on reflexive graph models of relational parametricity by Robinson and Rosolini [19] and Hasegawa [9]). In reflexive graph models of relational parametricity, the kinds of System F$\omega$ are interpreted as reflexive graphs, while types are interpreted as morphisms of reflexive graphs. As demonstrated by Atkey, uniformly interpreting kinds as reflexive graphs allows for a straightforward interpretation of higher kinds like $* \to *$. In the present setting, reflexive graphs will allow us to accomodate arbitrary groupoids as kinds (Section 3.3). Groupoid kinds are the key technical tool that we need to derive the kinds of geometric invariance properties we need for Noether's theorem.

### 3.1 System F$\omega$: Syntax and Relationally Parametric Model

We now present the syntax and relationally parametric semantics of System F$\omega$. Since we will incrementally extend the syntax of the system throughout this section and the next, we do not state a final triple of theorems stating that we have correctly interpreted kinds, types and terms. Rather, we state the necessary properties of the interpretation as three separate properties (Properties 1, 2, and 3, below), and maintain them as we extend the system.

We deviate from the standard presentation of System F$\omega$ in that we distinguish between large and small kinds, and only allow quantification over small kinds. In particular, the kind of types $*$ is *not* small. The reason for this choice is that we desire a simple set-theoretic model. However, requiring that we have a set of sets closed under large products, in order to interpret quantification over the kind $*$, would force us to use an intuitionistic metatheory [17]. The basic results of the Calculus of Variations that we are relying on, such as the derivation of the Euler-Lagrange equations, use excluded middle in their proofs, so an intuitionistic metatheory is not an option. We therefore just assume that we have a set of "small" sets, which includes the real numbers and is closed under subsets, products, function spaces and set comprehensions.

***Syntax*** The kinds of System F$\omega$ include at least the base kind of types, $*$, and function and product kinds, as generated by the following grammar:

$$\kappa ::= * \mid \kappa_1 \to \kappa_2 \mid \kappa_1 \times \kappa_2 \mid \cdots$$

We will extend the collection of kinds in Section 3.2 with type-level natural numbers, and in Section 3.3 with groupoid kinds.

We use the judgement $\kappa$ small to denote when the kind $\kappa$ will be interpreted by a small reflexive graph (to be defined below). The kind $*$ is not small, but the construction of function and product

$$\frac{\alpha : \kappa \in \Theta}{\Theta \vdash \alpha : \kappa} \qquad \frac{\Theta, \alpha : \kappa_1 \vdash A : \kappa_2}{\Theta \vdash \lambda\alpha : \kappa_1.\, A : \kappa_1 \to \kappa_2}$$

$$\frac{\Theta \vdash F : \kappa_1 \to \kappa_2 \qquad \Theta \vdash A : \kappa_1}{\Theta \vdash FA : \kappa_2}$$

$$\frac{\Theta \vdash A : \kappa_1 \qquad \Theta \vdash B : \kappa_2}{\Theta \vdash \langle A, B\rangle : \kappa_1 \times \kappa_2} \qquad \frac{\Theta \vdash A : \kappa_1 \times \kappa_2}{\Theta \vdash \pi_i\, A : \kappa_i}\; i \in \{1,2\}$$

$$\frac{\Theta \vdash A : * \qquad \Theta \vdash B : *}{\Theta \vdash A \times B : *} \qquad \frac{\Theta \vdash A : * \qquad \Theta \vdash B : *}{\Theta \vdash A \to B : *}$$

$$\frac{\Theta, \alpha : \kappa \vdash A : * \qquad \kappa \text{ small}}{\Theta \vdash \forall \alpha{:}\kappa.\, A : *}$$

**Figure 1.** Types and their Kinds

$$\frac{\Theta, \alpha : \kappa_1 \vdash A : \kappa_2 \qquad \Theta \vdash B : \kappa_1}{\Theta \vdash (\lambda\alpha : \kappa_1.A)\, B \equiv A\{B/\alpha\} : \kappa_2}\,\beta$$

$$\frac{\Theta \vdash A : \kappa_1 \to \kappa_2}{\Theta \vdash (\lambda\alpha : \kappa_1.A\ \alpha) \equiv A : \kappa_1 \to \kappa_2}\,\eta$$

$$\frac{\Theta \vdash A_1 : \kappa_1 \qquad \Theta \vdash A_2 : \kappa_2}{\Theta \vdash \pi_i\, \langle A_1, A_2\rangle \equiv A_i : \kappa_i}\,\beta$$

$$\frac{\Theta \vdash A : \kappa_1 \times \kappa_2}{\Theta \vdash \langle \pi_1 A, \pi_2 A\rangle \equiv A : \kappa_1 \times \kappa_2}\,\eta$$

plus: reflexivity, symmetry, transitivity and congruence

**Figure 2.** Type equality

kinds preserves smallness:

$$\frac{\kappa_1 \text{ small} \qquad \kappa_2 \text{ small}}{\kappa_1 \to \kappa_2 \text{ small}} \qquad \frac{\kappa_1 \text{ small} \qquad \kappa_2 \text{ small}}{\kappa_1 \times \kappa_2 \text{ small}}$$

The additional kinds we introduce below will all be small.

The well-kinded types, type equalities, and well-typed terms of System F$\omega$ are shown in Figures 1, 2 and 3, respectively. Kinding contexts $\alpha_1 : \kappa_1, ..., \alpha_n : \kappa_n$ are denoted by $\Theta$ and typing contexts $x_1 : A_1, ..., x_n : A_n$ are denoted by $\Gamma$. Note that typing contexts $\Gamma$ only contain well-kinded types of kind $*$. Terms also have an equational theory, with $\beta\eta$-laws for functions, products, and universal quantification, which we omit. Our presentation of System F$\omega$ is entirely standard (see, e.g., Pierce [16]), except for the restriction to small kinds in the formation of universal kinds $\forall\alpha{:}\kappa.A$. As is the case for kinds, we will extend the types, type equalities, and terms in Sections 3.2, 3.3 and 4, below.

***Reflexive Graphs and the Interpretation of Kinds*** We will interpret every kind $\kappa$ as a reflexive graph, which we now define. A *reflexive graph* is a triple $(O, R, \mathrm{id})$, where $O$ is a large set of objects, $R : O \times O \to \mathsf{Set}$ assigns a small set of directed 'edges' to each pair of objects, and $\mathrm{id} : \Pi o \in O.\ R(o, o)$ assigns a distinguished 'identity' edge from every object to itself. We think of the edges of a reflexive graph as abstract "relations" between the objects. Indeed, in the interpretation of the kind of types, $*$, below, the edges will be exactly relations.

$$\frac{x : A \in \Gamma}{\Theta \mid \Gamma \vdash x : A} \qquad \frac{\Theta \mid \Gamma \vdash e : A \qquad \Theta \vdash A \equiv B : *}{\Theta \mid \Gamma \vdash e : B}$$

$$\frac{\Theta \mid \Gamma \vdash e_1 : A_1 \quad \Theta \mid \Gamma \vdash e_2 : A_2}{\Theta \mid \Gamma \vdash (e_1, e_2) : A_1 \times A_2} \qquad \frac{\Theta \mid \Gamma \vdash e : A_1 \times A_2}{\Theta \mid \Gamma \vdash \pi_i e : A_i}\; i \in \{1,2\}$$

$$\frac{\Theta \mid \Gamma, x : A \vdash e : B}{\Theta \mid \Gamma \vdash \lambda x : A.\, e : A \to B}$$

$$\frac{\Theta \mid \Gamma \vdash e_1 : A \to B \qquad \Theta \mid \Gamma \vdash e_2 : A}{\Theta \mid \Gamma \vdash e_1 e_2 : B}$$

$$\frac{\Theta, \alpha : \kappa \mid \Gamma \vdash e : A \qquad \alpha \notin \mathit{fv}(\Gamma)}{\Theta \mid \Gamma \vdash \Lambda\alpha{:}\kappa.\, e : \forall\alpha{:}\kappa.A}$$

$$\frac{\Theta \mid \Gamma \vdash e : \forall\alpha{:}\kappa.A \qquad \Theta \vdash B : \kappa}{\Theta \mid \Gamma \vdash e\,[B] : A\{B/\alpha\}}$$

**Figure 3.** Terms and their Types

A *small* reflexive graph is a reflexive graph $(O, R, \mathrm{id})$ where $O$ is a small set of objects. We use small reflexive graphs as the semantic interpretation of small kinds.

The interpretation of kinds as reflexive graphs, and small kinds as small reflexive graphs is a key property of our semantics that we will maintain as we add additional kinds in Sections 3.2 and 3.3, below. We state this as Property 1 of our semantics:

**Property 1.** *Each kind $\kappa$ is interpreted as a reflexive graph $[\![\kappa]\!]$. If $\kappa$ small, then $[\![\kappa]\!]$ is a small reflexive graph.*

An appealing interpretation of reflexive graphs is as "categories without composition". Following this intuition, we define morphisms of reflexive graphs as "functors", without the preservation of composition condition. A *morphism of reflexive graphs* $(O_1, R_1, \mathrm{id}_1)$ and $(O_2, R_2, \mathrm{id}_2)$ is a pair of mappings $f : O_1 \to O_2$ and $r : \forall o, o' \in O_1.\ R_1(o, o') \to R_2(f\,o, f\,o')$ such that identities are preserved: $r\ o\ o\ (\mathrm{id}_1\ o) = \mathrm{id}_2\ (f\ o)$. We use morphisms of reflexive graphs below to interpret well-kinded types.

We will use the notation $-^O$, $-^R$ and $-^{\mathrm{id}}$ for the first, second and third projections out of tuples representing reflexive graphs. Similarly, we use $-^f$ and $-^r$ for the first and second projections out of tuples representing reflexive graph morphisms.

We now define the interpretations of the basic kinds of System F$\omega$ we defined above, making sure that we maintain Property 1. At base kind, the collection of objects is simply the (large) set of all small sets; edges between $A$ and $B$ are binary relations on $A$ and $B$ (i.e., subsets of $A \times B$); and the distinguished identity edge is exactly the equality relation:

$$[\![*]\!] = (\mathsf{Set}, \mathsf{Rel}, \equiv)$$

The reflexive graph $[\![*]\!]$ is not small, due to the collection of all small sets $\mathsf{Set}$ not forming a small set.

For higher kinds $\kappa_1 \to \kappa_2$, the collection of objects consists of reflexive graph morphisms from the interpretation of $\kappa_1$ to the interpretation of $\kappa_2$; the edges between morphisms $(f, r)$ and $(f', r')$ are edge transformers; and the distinguished identity relation for $(f, r)$ is just $r$:

$$\begin{array}{l}[\![\kappa_1 \to \kappa_2]\!] = \\ \quad (\{(f,r) \mid (f,r) : [\![\kappa_1]\!] \to [\![\kappa_2]\!]\}, \\ \quad ((f,r),(f',r')) \mapsto \Pi o, o'.[\![\kappa_1]\!]^R(o,o') \to [\![\kappa_2]\!]^R(f\ o, f'\ o'), \\ \quad (f,r) \mapsto r\ )\end{array}$$

By the assumption that our collection of small sets is closed under the formation of function spaces and set comprehension, if $[\![\kappa_1]\!]$ and $[\![\kappa_2]\!]$ are small reflexive graphs, then so is $[\![\kappa_1 \to \kappa_2]\!]$.

Product kinds are interpreted by taking the product of their interpretations as reflexive graphs:

$$\begin{array}{l}[\![\kappa_1 \times \kappa_2]\!] = \\ \quad ([\![\kappa_1]\!]^O \times [\![\kappa_2]\!]^O, \\ \quad\; ((o_1,o_2),(o_1',o_2')) \mapsto [\![\kappa_1]\!]^R(o_1,o_1') \times [\![\kappa_2]\!]^R(o_2,o_2'), \\ \quad\; (o_1,o_2) \mapsto ([\![\kappa_1]\!]^{\mathrm{id}}(o_1), [\![\kappa_2]\!]^{\mathrm{id}}(o_2)))\end{array}$$

The collection of objects of the interpretation of a product kind is the product of the underlying collections of objects of the two parts, and the relational component is simply the product of the relational components. This naturally leads to the identity component being defined as the tuple of the identity components of the two parts. Again, by assumption that our collection of small sets is closed under products, if $[\![\kappa_1]\!]$ and $[\![\kappa_2]\!]$ are small reflexive graphs, then so is $[\![\kappa_1 \times \kappa_2]\!]$. Product kinds generalise to the interpretation of kinding contexts $\Theta = \alpha_1 : \kappa_1, ..., \alpha_n : \kappa_n$, which are interpreted as the product of the reflexive graph interpretations of $\kappa_1, ..., \kappa_n$:

$$\begin{array}{l}[\![\alpha_1 : \kappa_1, ..., \alpha_n : \kappa_n]\!] = \\ \quad ([\![\kappa_1]\!]^O \times ... \times [\![\kappa_n]\!]^O, \\ \quad\; (\theta,\theta') \mapsto [\![\kappa_1]\!]^R(\pi_1\theta, \pi_1\theta') \times ... \times [\![\kappa_n]\!]^R(\pi_n\theta, \pi_n\theta'), \\ \quad\; \theta \mapsto ([\![\kappa_1]\!]^{\mathrm{id}}(\pi_1\theta), ..., [\![\kappa_n]\!]^{\mathrm{id}}(\pi_n\theta)))\end{array}$$

In Sections 3.2 and 3.3 below, we will extend System F$\omega$ with additional kinds, and assign them reflexive graph interpretations, making sure that we maintain Property 1.

***Interpretation of Types*** Well-kinded types $\Theta \vdash A : \kappa$ from Figure 1 are interpreted as reflexive graph morphisms $[\![A]\!] : [\![\Theta]\!] \to [\![\kappa]\!]$. We sum this up as a property of our semantics:

**Property 2.** *Each well-kinded type $\Theta \vdash A : \kappa$ is interpreted as a reflexive graph morphism $[\![A]\!] : [\![\Theta]\!] \to [\![\kappa]\!]$, such that if $\Theta \vdash A \equiv B : \kappa$ then $[\![A]\!] = [\![B]\!]$.*

The interpretation of the $\lambda$-calculus fragment (i.e., variables, $\lambda$-abstraction and application, and products) of the language of well-kinded types is displayed in Figure 4. The interpretations are unsurprising given the reflexive graph interpretation of the kinds $\kappa_1 \to \kappa_2$ and $\kappa_1 \times \kappa_2$ we gave above.

Figure 5 shows the interpretations of the basic type constructors for function and product types, and of universal quantification. Each of these constructs builds an object of kind $*$, so the object-level interpretation is a small set in Set, and the relation-level interpretation is an actual relation. In the cases of the function and product types, the object-level interpretation is just as set-theoretic function and product respectively, and the relation-level interpretation uses the standard logical relations interpretations of these type constructors. Universal quantification, $\forall\alpha{:}\kappa.\ A$, is interpreted at the object level by taking the dependent product over the objects of the interpretation of $\kappa$ (this product exists because we have stipulated that $\kappa$ must be small), and then restricting to those elements of the dependent product that preserve relations. This restriction is required for this interpretation to preserve identity edges, and so be a reflexive graph morphism. The relation-level interpretation of universal quantification is the standard relational interpretation of such types, albeit here generalised to kinds interpreted as arbitrary reflexive graphs.

Well-kinded typing contexts $\Theta \vdash \Gamma$ are interpreted as reflexive graph morphisms $[\![\Gamma]\!] : [\![\Theta]\!] \to [\![*]\!]$ by taking the product of the interpretations of their constituent types, similar to the interpretation of the product types $A \times B$.

We will extend basic System F$\omega$ with additional types and type equalities in Sections 3.2, 3.3, and 4, below. These new types will also be assigned interpretations as reflexive graph morphisms, and we will ensure that Property 2 is maintained.

***Interpretation of Terms*** We omit the straightforward and relatively uninteresting interpretation of well-typed terms $\Theta \mid \Gamma \vdash e : A$, and just state that there is a well-defined function interpreting each well-typed term, with the property that it takes related environments to related results; this is the fundamental theorem of logical relations for System F$\omega$:

**Property 3.** *For all well-typed terms $\Theta \mid \Gamma \vdash e : A$ there is a function $[\![e]\!] \in (\forall\theta \in [\![\Theta]\!]^O.\ [\![\Gamma]\!]^f\theta \to [\![A]\!]^f\theta)$, such that, for all $\theta, \theta' \in [\![\Theta]\!]^O$, $\rho \in [\![\Theta]\!]^R(\theta,\theta')$, $\gamma \in [\![\Gamma]\!]^f\theta$ and $\gamma' \in [\![\Gamma]\!]^f\theta'$, if $(\gamma,\gamma') \in [\![\Gamma]\!]^r\theta\theta'\rho$ then $([\![e]\!]\theta\gamma, [\![e]\!]\theta'\gamma') \in [\![A]\!]^r\theta\theta'\rho$. Moreover, this interpretation is sound for the $\beta\eta$ equational theory of terms.*

### 3.2 Discrete Kinds

In Section 3.1, we only had a single base kind: the kind $*$ of proper types, with a specific interpretation as the reflexive graph of sets and relations. We now describe two families of base kinds with interpretations that are particular sorts of reflexive graph. In this section, we look at discrete kinds; kinds whose reflexive graph interpretations are such that the reflexive edges are the only edges between objects. In the following section (Section 3.3), we look at groupoid kinds, where edges are composable and invertible.

Discrete kinds can be seen as the natural way of lifting types up to the kind level. For our purposes, we will only require a kind of natural numbers, which we will use for constructing $n$-ary vectors of positions and velocities when we use our type system for writing Lagrangians in Section 4. The kind of natural numbers is small:

$$\kappa ::= \cdots \mid \mathsf{nat} \qquad\qquad \frac{}{\mathsf{nat\ small}}$$

The interpretation of this kind as a reflexive graph goes as follows:

$$[\![\mathsf{nat}]\!] = (\mathbb{N}, (n_1,n_2) \mapsto \{* \mid n_1 = n_2\}, n \mapsto *)$$

The collection of objects of this reflexive graph is simply the set of natural numbers. The only edges in the graph are unique edges between equal numbers. Since we have assumed that our collection of small sets contains the natural numbers, we have clearly maintained Property 1 of our semantics.

We add new type-level constructs for the kind Nat of natural numbers, representing zero and successor, and a kind-generic recursion operator:

$$\frac{}{\Theta \vdash \mathit{zero} : \mathsf{nat}} \qquad \frac{\Theta \vdash A : \mathsf{nat}}{\Theta \vdash \mathit{succ}\ A : \mathsf{nat}}$$

$$\frac{\Theta \vdash A : \mathsf{nat} \qquad \Theta \vdash B : \kappa \qquad \Theta \vdash C : \kappa \to \kappa}{\Theta \vdash \mathit{natrec}_\kappa\ A\ B\ C : \kappa}$$

These three constructs all have the evident interpretations in terms of the inductive structure of the natural numbers, and satisfy the following $\beta$-laws, maintaining Property 2 of our semantics:

$$\begin{array}{ll}\mathit{natrec}_\kappa\ \mathit{zero}\ B\ C & \equiv B \\ \mathit{natrec}_\kappa\ (\mathit{succ}\ A)\ B\ C & \equiv C\ (\mathit{natrec}_\kappa\ A\ B\ C)\end{array}$$

### 3.3 Groupoid Kinds

Discrete kinds are useful for lifting types up to the kind level, but they do not really exploit the flexibility of reflexive graphs. Moreover, they do not provide us with the invariance properties we require to apply Noether's theorem. By considering kinds whose interpretations are groupoids, we will be able to derive the invariance properties that we need.

Recall that a groupoid is a category in which all morphisms have inverses [15]. Functors between categories always preserve

$$\begin{aligned}
\llbracket\Theta \vdash \alpha_i : \kappa_i\rrbracket^f \theta &= \pi_i \theta \\
\llbracket\Theta \vdash \alpha_i : \kappa_i\rrbracket^r \theta\theta'\rho &= \pi_i \rho \\[1em]
\llbracket\Theta \vdash \lambda\alpha{:}\kappa_1.\, A : \kappa_1 \to \kappa_2\rrbracket^f \theta &= (\lambda o \in \llbracket\kappa_1\rrbracket^O.\, \llbracket A\rrbracket^f(\theta, o), \lambda o, o' \in \llbracket\kappa_1\rrbracket^O, r \in \llbracket\kappa_1\rrbracket^R(o, o').\, \llbracket A\rrbracket^r(\theta, o)(\theta, o')(\llbracket\Theta\rrbracket^{\mathrm{id}}\theta, r)) \\
\llbracket\Theta \vdash \lambda\alpha{:}\kappa_1.\, A : \kappa_1 \to \kappa_2\rrbracket^r \theta\theta'\rho &= \lambda o, o' \in \llbracket\kappa_1\rrbracket^O, r \in \llbracket\kappa_1\rrbracket^R(o, o').\, \llbracket A\rrbracket^r(\theta, o)(\theta', o')(\rho, r) \\[1em]
\llbracket\Theta \vdash FA : \kappa_2\rrbracket^f \theta &= \pi_1(\llbracket F\rrbracket^f\, \theta)\, (\llbracket A\rrbracket^f\, \theta) \\
\llbracket\Theta \vdash FA : \kappa_2\rrbracket^r \theta\theta'\rho &= \llbracket F\rrbracket^r \theta\theta'\rho\, (\llbracket A\rrbracket^f \theta)(\llbracket A\rrbracket^f \theta')(\llbracket A\rrbracket^r \theta\theta'\rho) \\[1em]
\llbracket\Theta \vdash \langle A, B\rangle : \kappa_1 \times \kappa_2\rrbracket^f \theta &= (\llbracket A\rrbracket^f \theta, \llbracket B\rrbracket^f \theta) \\
\llbracket\Theta \vdash \langle A, B\rangle : \kappa_1 \times \kappa_2\rrbracket^r \theta\theta'\rho &= (\llbracket A\rrbracket^r \theta\theta'\rho, \llbracket B\rrbracket^r \theta\theta'\rho) \\[1em]
\llbracket\Theta \vdash \pi_i A : \kappa_i\rrbracket^f \theta &= \pi_i(\llbracket A\rrbracket^f \theta) \\
\llbracket\Theta \vdash \pi_i A : \kappa_i\rrbracket^r \theta\theta'\rho &= \pi_i(\llbracket A\rrbracket^r \theta\theta'\rho)
\end{aligned}$$

**Figure 4.** Interpretation of type-level $\lambda$-calculus as reflexive graph morphisms

$$\begin{aligned}
\llbracket\Theta \vdash A \to B : *\rrbracket^f \theta &= \llbracket A\rrbracket^f \theta \to \llbracket B\rrbracket^f \theta \\
\llbracket\Theta \vdash A \to B : *\rrbracket^r \theta\theta'\rho &= \{(f, f') \mid \forall (a, a') \in \llbracket A\rrbracket^r \theta\theta'\rho.\, (f\ a, f'\ a') \in \llbracket B\rrbracket^r \theta\theta'\rho\} \\[1em]
\llbracket\Theta \vdash A \times B : *\rrbracket^f \theta &= \llbracket A\rrbracket^f \theta \times \llbracket B\rrbracket^f \theta \\
\llbracket\Theta \vdash A \times B : *\rrbracket^r \theta\theta'\rho &= \{((a, b), (a', b')) \mid (a, a') \in \llbracket A\rrbracket^r \theta\theta'\rho, (b, b') \in \llbracket B\rrbracket^r \theta\theta'\rho\} \\[1em]
\llbracket\Theta \vdash \forall\alpha{:}\kappa.\, A : *\rrbracket^f \theta &= \{x \in (\forall o \in \llbracket\kappa\rrbracket^O.\, \llbracket A\rrbracket^f(\theta, o)) \mid \forall o, o', r \in \llbracket\kappa\rrbracket^R(o, o').\, (x\ o, x\ o') \in \llbracket A\rrbracket^r(\theta, o)(\theta, o')(\llbracket\Theta\rrbracket^{\mathrm{id}}\theta, r)\} \\
\llbracket\Theta \vdash \forall\alpha{:}\kappa.\, A : *\rrbracket^r \theta\theta'\rho &= \{(x, x') \mid \forall o, o', r \in \llbracket\kappa\rrbracket^R(o, o').\, (x\ o, x'\ o') \in \llbracket A\rrbracket^r(\theta, o)(\theta', o')(\rho, r)\}
\end{aligned}$$

**Figure 5.** Interpretation of basic types as reflexive graph morphisms

isomorphisms, so morphisms of groupoids are just functors. Every group is a groupoid with one object, and a morphism from this object to itself for every element of the group: composition is the group operation, inverses are given by the group inverses, and the identity morphism is given by the group unit. Homomorphisms between groups are in one-to-one correspondence with functors between the corresponding groupoids. An example of a groupoid that is not a group is given by the collection of cartesian spaces (i.e., $\mathbb{R}^n$ for some $n$), with all diffeomorphisms (smooth functions with smooth inverses) as the morphisms.

Trivially, every groupoid is a reflexive graph, simply by forgetting the composition and inverses. Likewise, every functor between groupoids is a morphism of reflexive graphs, by forgetting the preservation of composition. Therefore, given any groupoid, we can add a new kind to System F$\omega$ that is interpreted by that groupoid, and given any functor $f : \llbracket \mathsf{G}_1 \rrbracket \to \llbracket \mathsf{G}_2 \rrbracket$ between groupoids interpreting kinds $\mathsf{G}_1$ and $\mathsf{G}_2$, we obtain a type constant of kind $\mathsf{G}_1 \to \mathsf{G}_2$, with interpretation $f$.

***Integers*** Our first groupoid kind is $\mathsf{Z}$, interpreted by additive group of integers. We will use this kind to state the types of the trigonometric functions sin and cos in Section 4.1, which are periodic with period $2\pi$. The kind $\mathsf{Z}$ is small:

$$\kappa ::= \cdots \mid \mathsf{Z} \qquad\qquad \frac{}{\mathsf{Z}\ \text{small}}$$

The kind $\mathsf{Z}$ has the following interpretation as a reflexive graph:

$$\llbracket \mathsf{Z} \rrbracket = (\{*\}, \lambda(*, *).\, \mathbb{Z}, \lambda *.\, 0)$$

Note the difference between this interpretation and the interpretation of the kind $\mathsf{Nat}$ in the previous section. In the interpretation of $\mathsf{Nat}$, the objects were complex and the relations were trivial. The reflexive graph interpreting $\mathsf{Z}$ has a trivial collection of objects, but a rich structure at the relation level, given by the group of integers.

This structure means that we can add the following type-level constants to our system:

$$\frac{}{\Theta \vdash 0 : \mathsf{Z}} \qquad \frac{\Theta \vdash A : \mathsf{Z} \quad \Theta \vdash B : \mathsf{Z}}{\Theta \vdash A + B : \mathsf{Z}} \qquad \frac{\Theta \vdash A : \mathsf{Z}}{\Theta \vdash -A : \mathsf{Z}}$$

Each of these constants has a trivial object-level interpretation, due to the trivial collection of objects in the reflexive graph $\llbracket \mathsf{Z} \rrbracket$. At the relation-level, the interpretations are simply given using the group structure of the integers. These interpretations satisfy the abelian group axioms, so we add these axioms to the type-level equations.

***Translation and Linear Transformation Groups*** The group of integers is not suitable for stating the invariance properties we require to apply Noether's theorem. To do so, we require groups of translations and invertible linear transformations. We extend our type system with small kinds representing $n$-dimensional ($n \geq 0$) translations, invertible linear transformations, and orthogonal transformations:

$$\kappa ::= \cdots \mid \mathsf{T}(n) \mid \mathsf{GL}(n) \mid \mathsf{O}(n) \qquad \frac{}{\mathsf{T}(n), \mathsf{GL}(n), \mathsf{O}(n)\ \text{small}}$$

The interpretations of these kinds follow the same pattern as for the kind $\mathsf{Z}$ above. Each interpretation is a reflexive graph with a trivial collection of objects, and relations taken from the appropriate group:

$$\begin{aligned}
\llbracket \mathsf{T}(n) \rrbracket &= (\{*\}, \lambda(*, *).\, \mathbb{R}^n, \lambda *.\, \vec{0}) \\
\llbracket \mathsf{GL}(n) \rrbracket &= (\{*\}, \lambda(*, *).\, \mathrm{GL}(n), \lambda *. I) \\
\llbracket \mathsf{O}(n) \rrbracket &= (\{*\}, \lambda(*, *).\, \mathrm{O}(n), \lambda *. I)
\end{aligned}$$

Here, we take $\mathrm{GL}(n)$ to be exactly the group of invertible real $n \times n$ matricies, and $\mathrm{O}(n)$ to be the group of $n \times n$ orthogonal matricies (recall that an orthogonal matrix is one whose transpose is equal to its inverse). We add the group operations and group axioms for each of these groupoid kinds in the same way as we did for the kind $\mathsf{Z}$ above, except that we use multiplicative notation for the kinds $\mathsf{GL}(n)$ and $\mathsf{O}(n)$. Note that, except for $\mathsf{GL}(0)$, $\mathsf{GL}(1)$, $\mathsf{O}(0)$ and $\mathsf{O}(1)$, the groups $\mathsf{GL}(n)$ and $\mathsf{O}(n)$ are not abelian.

We also extend our type system with the following type-level constants. Each of these is interpreted by the correspondingly named homomorphism between the groups involved. For example, $scale_n$ is interpreted by the homomorphism $\mathrm{GL}(1) \to \mathrm{GL}(n)$ that takes a non-zero real number $s$ to the matrix with $s$s along the diagonal and zeros elsewhere.

$$\begin{aligned} &exp &&: \mathsf{T}(1) \to \mathsf{GL}(1) \\ &ortho_n &&: \mathsf{O}(n) \to \mathsf{GL}(n) \\ &scale_n &&: \mathsf{GL}(1) \to \mathsf{GL}(n) \\ &\underline{c} * - &&: \mathsf{Z} \to \mathsf{T}(1) \end{aligned}$$

In the last of these $\underline{c}$ stands for an arbitrary real constant. Since each of these is interpreted by a group homomorphism, we are justified in adding the group homomorphism laws as axioms to our type-level equational theory, maintaining Property 2.

***The Groupoid of Cartesian Spaces*** Finally in this section, we introduce the groupoid kind of cartesian spaces, which we will use for the configuration spaces of the classical mechanical systems we describe in our system. As we noted above, the collection of cartesian spaces is a groupoid with a non-trivial collection of objects. We extend our system with a kind of cartesian spaces:

$$\kappa ::= \cdots \mid \mathsf{CartSp}$$

with the following interpretation:

$$\begin{aligned} &[\![\mathsf{CartSp}]\!] = \\ &\quad (\mathbb{N}, \lambda m, n.\ \{f : \mathbb{R}^m \to \mathbb{R}^n \mid f \text{ a diffeomorphism}\}, \lambda n.\ \mathrm{id}_{\mathbb{R}^n}) \end{aligned}$$

We have chosen to represent cartesian spaces of dimension $n$ just as the natural number $n$. This gives us a canonical representation of $n$-dimensional space for each $n$, avoiding tricky problems with isomorphic constructions of the same space.

Cartesian spaces are closed under products:

$$\frac{\Theta \vdash X : \mathsf{CartSp} \qquad \Theta \vdash Y : \mathsf{CartSp}}{\Theta \vdash X \times Y : \mathsf{CartSp}}$$

with the following interpretation, where the cartesian product of cartesian spaces adds their dimensions, and composes diffeomorphisms "in parallel":

$$\begin{aligned} &[\![X \times Y]\!]^f \theta &&= [\![X]\!]^f \theta + [\![Y]\!]^f \theta \\ &[\![X \times Y]\!]^r \theta\theta'\rho &&= \lambda(\vec{x}, \vec{y}).\ ([\![X]\!]^r \theta\theta'\rho\vec{x}, [\![Y]\!]^r \theta\theta'\rho\vec{y}) \end{aligned}$$

Cartesian spaces are generated by the following construct that yields the $n$-dimensional cartesian space ($n \geq 0$) that varies with the given invertible linear transformation and translation:

$$\frac{\Theta \vdash G : \mathsf{GL}(n) \qquad \Theta \vdash T : \mathsf{T}(n)}{\Theta \vdash \mathbb{R}^n\langle G, T\rangle : \mathsf{CartSp}}$$

As a notational convenience, we write $\mathbb{R}^1\langle G, T\rangle$ as just $\mathbb{R}\langle G, T\rangle$ and $\mathbb{R}^0\langle G, T\rangle$ as just $\mathbb{R}^0$.

The type $\mathbb{R}^n\langle G, T\rangle$ has the following interpretation as a reflexive graph morphism:

$$\begin{aligned} &[\![\mathbb{R}^n\langle G, T\rangle]\!]^f \theta &&= n \\ &[\![\mathbb{R}^n\langle G, T\rangle]\!]^r \theta\theta'\rho &&= \lambda\vec{x}.\ ([\![G]\!]^r \theta\theta'\rho)\vec{x} + [\![T]\!]^r \theta\theta'\rho \end{aligned}$$

Note that $[\![\mathbb{R}^n\langle G, T\rangle]\!]^r \theta\theta'([\![\Theta]\!]^{\mathrm{id}}\theta)$ is the identity diffeomorphism, so this interpretation preserves identity edges, exactly as required in the definition of reflexive graph morphisms. Consequently, the interpretation of $\mathbb{R}^n\langle G, T\rangle$, and also the interpretation for products of cartesian spaces, preserves Property 2.

Using the type-level natural numbers and their recursion operator, we can define a type of $n$-ary products of a cartesian space:

$$vec = \lambda n{:}\mathsf{Nat}, X{:}\mathsf{CartSp}.\ natrec\ n\ \mathbb{R}^0\ (\lambda x.\ X \times x)$$

$n$-ary products of cartesian spaces will be useful in Section 5 when we define Lagrangians describing systems that are generic in the number of particles involved.

Finally, we include an operator that takes any cartesian space to its corresponding proper type:

$$\frac{\Theta \vdash X : \mathsf{CartSp}}{\Theta \vdash \wr X \int : *}$$

with the following straightforward interpretation:

$$\begin{aligned} &[\![\wr X \int]\!]^f \theta &&= \mathbb{R}^{[\![X]\!]^f \theta} \\ &[\![\wr X \int]\!]^r \theta\theta'\rho &&= \{(\vec{x}, \vec{x'}) \mid ([\![X]\!]^r \theta\theta'\rho)\vec{x} = \vec{x'}\} \end{aligned}$$

## 4. A Type System for Classical Mechanics

In the previous section we constructed a way to derive invariance properties from types. In Section 2, we saw that Noether's theorem is a method for deriving conservation laws for classical mechanical systems from their invariance properties. In this section, we construct a type system for constructing invariant Lagrangians. In the following section, Section 5, we present several uses of our type system for defining invariant Lagrangians that describe many different kinds of classical mechanical systems.

### 4.1 Extending System F$\omega$ with Smooth Functions

***The Type of Smooth Functions*** Given a pair of cartesian spaces $X$ and $Y$ we provide a way to construct the type of smooth invariant smooth functions from $X$ to $Y$:

$$\frac{\Theta \vdash X : \mathsf{CartSp} \qquad \Theta \vdash Y : \mathsf{CartSp}}{\Theta \vdash C^\infty(X, Y) : *}$$

with the following interpretation. Since $C^\infty(X, Y)$ is a proper type, the relational interpretation in this case is a genuine relation. We relate functions that are invariant under the diffeomorphism interpretations of $X$ and $Y$ in the current relational context $\rho$:

$$\begin{aligned} &[\![C^\infty(X, Y)]\!]^f \theta &&= \{f : \mathbb{R}^{[\![X]\!]^f \theta} \to \mathbb{R}^{[\![Y]\!]^f \theta} \mid f \text{ smooth}\} \\ &[\![C^\infty(X, Y)]\!]^f \theta\theta'\rho &&= \{(f, f') \mid \forall \vec{x} \in \mathbb{R}^{[\![X]\!]^f \theta}. \\ & &&\qquad ([\![Y]\!]^r \theta\theta'\rho)(f\ \vec{x}) = f'\ ([\![X]\!]^r \theta\theta'\rho\vec{x})\} \end{aligned}$$

***An Example Free Theorem*** We are now in a position to formally show how we can use the relationally parametric model we have defined to derive invariance properties. Consider a closed term with the following type:

$$e : \forall o : \mathsf{O}(n).\ C^\infty(\mathbb{R}^n\langle ortho_n(o), 0\rangle, \mathbb{R}\langle 1, 0\rangle)$$

We can deduce, from Property 3 and the relational interpretations of all the types involved, that the denotation of $e$ satisfies the following free theorem:

$$\forall O \in \mathrm{O}(n).\ \forall \vec{x} \in \mathbb{R}^n.\ [\![e]\!](O\vec{x}) = [\![e]\!](\vec{x})$$

This free theorem is exactly the kind of invariance property we require to apply Noether's theorem. Compare the form of the statement here, with the mildly more general statement of Equation 9, back in Section 2. Moreover, $[\![e]\!]$ is a smooth function from $\mathbb{R}^n$ to $\mathbb{R}$, just as we require for Lagrangian mechanics.

***Combinators for Smooth Functions*** Of course, such free theorems are pointless without ways to build elements of the smooth function spaces. We now extend our type system, for the last time, with a set of term-level constants for constructing smooth functions, invariant under linear transformations and translations.

Our first set of combinators constructs constant and identity smooth functions, and composes smooth functions between cartesian spaces. We also have combinators for pairing and projection for the product of cartesian spaces.

$$\begin{array}{ll} \mathrm{const} & : \wr Y \int \to C^\infty(X, Y) \\ \mathrm{id} & : C^\infty(X, X) \\ (\ggg) & : C^\infty(X, Y) \to C^\infty(Y, Z) \to C^\infty(X, Z) \\ \mathrm{pair} & : C^\infty(X, Y) \to C^\infty(X, Z) \to C^\infty(X, Y \times Z) \\ \mathrm{proj}_1 & : C^\infty(X \times Y, X) \\ \mathrm{proj}_2 & : C^\infty(X \times Y, Y) \end{array}$$

Next, we include combinators for constant, invariant, vectors, the zero vector, vector addition, subtraction and scaling. We also include the Euclidean dot product of vectors. The type dot product operation is where the orthogonal group kind $\mathsf{O}(n)$ is used: the dot product of vectors is invariant under orthogonal transformations.

$$\begin{array}{ll} \vec{c} & : \wr \mathbb{R}^n\langle 1, 0\rangle \int \\ 0 & : \forall g{:}\mathsf{GL}(n).\ \wr\, \mathbb{R}^n\langle g, 0\rangle \int \\ (+) & : \forall g{:}\mathsf{GL}(n), t_1, t_2{:}\mathsf{T}(n). \\ & \qquad C^\infty(\mathbb{R}^n\langle g, t_1\rangle \times \mathbb{R}^n\langle g, t_2\rangle, \mathbb{R}^n\langle g, t_1 + t_2\rangle) \\ (-) & : \forall g{:}\mathsf{GL}(n), t_1, t_2{:}\mathsf{T}(n). \\ & \qquad C^\infty(\mathbb{R}^n\langle g, t_1\rangle \times \mathbb{R}^n\langle g, t_2\rangle, \mathbb{R}^n\langle g, t_1 - t_2\rangle) \\ (*) & : \forall g_1{:}\mathsf{GL}(1), g_2{:}\mathsf{GL}(n). \\ & \qquad C^\infty(\mathbb{R}\langle g_1, 0\rangle \times \mathbb{R}^n\langle g_2, 0\rangle, \mathbb{R}^n\langle \mathit{scale}_n(g_1)g_2, 0\rangle) \\ (\cdot) & : \forall g{:}\mathsf{GL}(1), o{:}\mathsf{O}(n). \\ & \quad C^\infty(\mathbb{R}^n\langle(\mathit{scale}_n\ g)(\mathit{ortho}_n\ o), 0\rangle \times \\ & \qquad \mathbb{R}^n\langle(\mathit{scale}_n\ g)(\mathit{ortho}_n\ o), 0\rangle, \mathbb{R}\langle(\mathit{scale}_n\ g)^2, 0\rangle) \end{array}$$

Each of these combinators has a straightforward interpretation as a smooth function, and the proof that the fundamental theorem of logical relations is maintained for our system (i.e., that Property 3 is maintained) follows directly from elementary facts about linear algebra.

It will be useful for our examples to have the following trigonometric functions, exponential function and division operation. The types of each of these functions describes some of their invariance properties, such as the periodicity of the sin and cos functions. A technical problem with our current system is that we do not account for the non-definedness of division at 0, nor do we account for the square root of negative numbers. However, division and square root will be useful in our examples in Section 5, so we take a pragmatic approach, in common with most physics textbooks, and informally treat them as total functions.

$$\begin{array}{ll} \sin & : \forall z{:}\mathsf{Z}.\ C^\infty(\mathbb{R}\langle 1, \underline{2\pi} * z\rangle, \mathbb{R}\langle 1, 0\rangle) \\ \cos & : \forall z{:}\mathsf{Z}.\ C^\infty(\mathbb{R}\langle 1, \underline{2\pi} * z\rangle, \mathbb{R}\langle 1, 0\rangle) \\ \exp & : \forall t{:}\mathsf{T}(1).\ C^\infty(\mathbb{R}\langle 1, t\rangle, \mathbb{R}\langle \mathit{exp}\ t, 0\rangle) \\ (/) & : \forall g_1, g_2{:}\mathsf{GL}(1).\ C^\infty(\mathbb{R}\langle g_1, 0\rangle \times \mathbb{R}\langle g_2, 0\rangle, \mathbb{R}\langle g_1 g_2^{-1}, 0\rangle) \\ \mathrm{sqrt} & : \forall g{:}\mathsf{GL}(1).\ C^\infty(\mathbb{R}\langle g \cdot g, 0\rangle, \mathbb{R}\langle g, 0\rangle) \end{array}$$

Finally, we include three primitive combinators for dealing with $n$-ary products of vectors. These combinators will be useful when defining Lagrangians that are generic in the number of particles.

$$\begin{array}{ll} \mathrm{sum} & : \forall n{:}\mathsf{Nat}, g{:}\mathsf{GL}(1). C^\infty(\mathit{vec}\ n\ (\mathbb{R}\langle g, 0\rangle), \mathbb{R}\langle g, 0\rangle) \\ \mathrm{map} & : \forall n{:}\mathsf{Nat}. C^\infty(Z \times X, Y) \to C^\infty(Z \times \mathrm{vec}\ n\ X, \mathrm{vec}\ n\ Y) \\ \mathrm{cross} & : \forall m, n{:}\mathsf{Nat}. \\ & \qquad C^\infty(\mathit{vec}\ m\ X \times \mathit{vec}\ n\ Y, \mathit{vec}\ (m * n)\ (X \times Y)) \end{array}$$

The combinator sum sums the list of real numbers it is given, while cross takes the cartesian product of two vectors of elements of cartesian spaces, and map maps the given smooth function over a vector. The multiplication of natural numbers $m * n$ is straightforwardly defined in terms of the *natrec* recursion operator. We will use cross in Section 5 to define Lagrangians in terms of the interactions between systems of particles.

$$\begin{array}{ll} \lfloor z \rfloor_\Delta & = \mathrm{const}\ z \\ \lfloor x \rfloor_\Delta & = \underline{\mathrm{project}_\Delta}(x) \\ \lfloor \mathrm{let}\ \vec{x} = e_1\ \mathrm{in}\ e_2 \rfloor_\Delta & = \mathrm{pair\ id}\ \lfloor e_1 \rfloor_\Delta \ggg \lfloor e_2 \rfloor_{\Delta, \vec{x}} \\ \lfloor (e_1, ..., e_n) \rfloor_\Delta & = \underline{\mathrm{pair}_n}(\lfloor e_1 \rfloor_\Delta, ..., \lfloor e_n \rfloor_\Delta) \\ \lfloor e_1(e_2) \rfloor_\Delta & = \lfloor e_2 \rfloor_\Delta \ggg e_1 \\ \lfloor \vec{c} \rfloor_\Delta & = \mathrm{const}\ \vec{c} \\ \lfloor 0 \rfloor_\Delta & = \mathrm{const}\ 0 \\ \lfloor e_1 + e_2 \rfloor_\Delta & = \mathrm{pair}\ \lfloor e_1 \rfloor_\Delta\ \lfloor e_2 \rfloor_\Delta \ggg (+) \\ \lfloor e_1 - e_2 \rfloor_\Delta & = \mathrm{pair}\ \lfloor e_1 \rfloor_\Delta\ \lfloor e_2 \rfloor_\Delta \ggg (-) \\ \lfloor e_1 e_2 \rfloor_\Delta & = \mathrm{pair}\ \lfloor e_1 \rfloor_\Delta\ \lfloor e_2 \rfloor_\Delta \ggg (*) \\ \lfloor e_1 \cdot e_2 \rfloor_\Delta & = \mathrm{pair}\ \lfloor e_1 \rfloor_\Delta\ \lfloor e_2 \rfloor_\Delta \ggg (\cdot) \\ \lfloor \sin e \rfloor_\Delta & = \lfloor e \rfloor_\Delta \ggg \sin \\ \lfloor \cos e \rfloor_\Delta & = \lfloor e \rfloor_\Delta \ggg \cos \\ \lfloor \exp e \rfloor_\Delta & = \lfloor e \rfloor_\Delta \ggg \exp \\ \lfloor e_1 / e_2 \rfloor_\Delta & = \mathrm{pair}\ \lfloor e_1 \rfloor_\Delta\ \lfloor e_2 \rfloor_\Delta \ggg (/) \\ \lfloor \mathrm{sqrt}\ e \rfloor_\Delta & = \lfloor e \rfloor_\Delta \ggg \mathrm{sqrt} \\ \lfloor \mathrm{sum}\ e \rfloor_\Delta & = \lfloor e \rfloor_\Delta \ggg \mathrm{sum} \\ \lfloor \mathrm{map}\ (x.\ e_1)\ e_2 \rfloor_\Delta & = \mathrm{pair\ id}\ \lfloor e_2 \rfloor_\Delta \ggg (\mathrm{map}\ \lfloor e_1 \rfloor_{\Delta, x}) \\ \lfloor \mathrm{cross}\ e_1\ e_2 \rfloor_\Delta & = \mathrm{pair}\ \lfloor e_1 \rfloor_\Delta\ \lfloor e_2 \rfloor_\Delta \ggg \mathrm{cross} \end{array}$$

**Figure 7.** Desugaring of the surface syntax

### 4.2 A Surface Syntax for Smooth Functions

The combinators we have presented allow the construction of smooth invariant functions, but doing so is painful due to the point-free style that they force. In order to be able to actually define readable Lagrangians in our calculus, we define a surface syntax for writing smooth functions that is desugared into our extended version of System F$\omega$.

We define a typing judgement of smooth terms $\Theta \mid \Gamma; \Delta \vdash e : X$ by the rules in Figure 6, where $\Theta$ and $\Gamma$ are the kinding and typing contexts of our extension of F$\omega$, and $\Delta = x_1 : X_1, ..., x_n : X_n$ is a context of cartesian spaces. That is, for each $x : X$ in $\Delta$, we have $\Theta \vdash X : \mathsf{CartSp}$.

The desugaring of smooth function terms into our extension of System F$\omega$ is via the operation $\lfloor - \rfloor_\Delta$, defined in Figure 7. In this definition, we make use of two derived combinators for projection and pairing:

$$\begin{array}{ll} \underline{\mathrm{project}_{x:X,\Delta}}(x) & = \mathrm{proj}_1 \\ \underline{\mathrm{project}_{y:Y,\Delta}}(x) & = \mathrm{proj}_2 \ggg \underline{\mathrm{project}_\Delta}(x) \quad (x \neq y) \end{array}$$

and

$$\begin{array}{ll} \underline{\mathrm{pair}_1}(e) & = e \\ \underline{\mathrm{pair}_{n+1}}(e, \vec{e}) & = \mathrm{pair}\ e\ (\underline{\mathrm{pair}_n}(\vec{e})) \end{array}$$

The following theorem follows easily by induction on the typing derivations of smooth terms, where $\lfloor \Delta \rfloor = \lfloor x_1 : X_1, ..., x_n : X_n \rfloor = X_1 \times ... \times X_n$:

**Theorem 2.** *If* $\Theta|\Gamma; \Delta \vdash e : X$ *then* $\Theta|\Gamma \vdash \lfloor e \rfloor_\Delta : C^\infty(\lfloor \Delta \rfloor, X)$.

## 5. Examples of Conservation Laws from Types

We now present a number of examples of classical mechanical systems expressible in the type system we constructed in the previous section, and derive the free theorems and consequent conserved properties for each one. These examples are all standard examples demonstrating the application of Lagrangian mechanics (see, for example, Landau and Lifschitz [12]). Our contribution here is to express them in a type system that makes clear their invariance properties.

**Administrative rules**

$$\frac{z : \{\!|X|\!\} \in \Gamma}{\Theta \mid \Gamma; \Delta \vdash z : X} \qquad \frac{x : X \in \Delta}{\Theta \mid \Gamma; \Delta \vdash x : X} \qquad \frac{\Theta \mid \Gamma; \Delta \vdash e_1 : X_1 \times \ldots \times X_n \qquad \Theta \mid \Gamma; \Delta, x_1 : X_1, \ldots, x_n : X_n \vdash e_2 : Y}{\Theta \mid \Gamma; \Delta \vdash \text{let } x_1, \ldots, x_n = e_1 \text{ in } e_2 : Y}$$

$$\frac{\begin{array}{c}\Theta \mid \Gamma \vdash e_1 : C^\infty(X, Y) \\ \Theta \mid \Gamma; \Delta \vdash e_2 : X\end{array}}{\Theta \mid \Gamma; \Delta \vdash e_1(e_2) : Y} \qquad \frac{\Theta \mid \Gamma; \Delta \vdash e_1 : X \quad \ldots \quad \Theta \mid \Gamma; \Delta \vdash e_n : X_n}{\Theta \mid \Gamma; \Delta \vdash (e_1, \ldots, e_n) : X_1 \times \ldots \times X_n}$$

**Vector space operations, and dot product**

$$\frac{\vec{c} \in \mathbb{R}^n}{\Theta \mid \Gamma; \Delta \vdash \vec{c} : \mathbb{R}^n\langle 1, 0\rangle} \qquad \frac{\Theta \vdash G : \mathsf{GL}(n)}{\Theta \mid \Gamma; \Delta \vdash 0 : \mathbb{R}^n\langle G, 0\rangle} \qquad \frac{\Theta \mid \Gamma; \Delta \vdash e_1 : \mathbb{R}^n\langle G, T_1\rangle \qquad \Theta \mid \Gamma; \Delta \vdash e_2 : \mathbb{R}^n\langle G, T_2\rangle}{\Theta \mid \Gamma; \Delta \vdash e_1 + e_2 : \mathbb{R}^n\langle G, T_1 + T_2\rangle}$$

$$\frac{\Theta \mid \Gamma; \Delta \vdash e_1 : \mathbb{R}^n\langle G, T_1\rangle \qquad \Theta \mid \Gamma; \Delta \vdash e_2 : \mathbb{R}^n\langle G, T_2\rangle}{\Theta \mid \Gamma; \Delta \vdash e_1 - e_2 : \mathbb{R}^n\langle G, T_1 - T_2\rangle} \qquad \frac{\Theta \mid \Gamma; \Delta \vdash e_1 : \mathbb{R}\langle G_1, 0\rangle \qquad \Theta \mid \Gamma; \Delta \vdash e_2 : \mathbb{R}^n\langle G_2, 0\rangle}{\Theta \mid \Gamma; \Delta \vdash e_1 e_2 : \mathbb{R}^n\langle \mathit{scale}_n(G_1) G_2, 0\rangle}$$

$$\frac{\Theta \mid \Gamma; \Delta \vdash e_1 : \mathbb{R}^n\langle \mathit{scale}_n(G)\mathit{ortho}_n(O), 0\rangle \qquad \Theta \mid \Gamma; \Delta \vdash e_2 : \mathbb{R}^n\langle \mathit{scale}_n(G)\mathit{ortho}_n(O), 0\rangle}{\Theta \mid \Gamma; \Delta \vdash e_1 \cdot e_2 : \mathbb{R}\langle \mathit{scale}_n(G)^2, 0\rangle}$$

**Transcendental functions**

$$\frac{\Theta \mid \Gamma; \Delta \vdash e : \mathbb{R}\langle 1, T\rangle}{\Theta \mid \Gamma; \Delta \vdash \exp e : \mathbb{R}\langle \mathit{exp}\, T, 0\rangle} \qquad \frac{\Theta \mid \Gamma; \Delta \vdash e : \mathbb{R}\langle 1, \underline{2\pi} * Z\rangle}{\Theta \mid \Gamma; \Delta \vdash \sin e : \mathbb{R}\langle 1, 0\rangle} \qquad \frac{\Theta \mid \Gamma; \Delta \vdash e : \mathbb{R}\langle 1, \underline{2\pi} * Z\rangle}{\Theta \mid \Gamma; \Delta \vdash \cos e : \mathbb{R}\langle 1, 0\rangle}$$

**Division, square root, sum, and cross**

$$\frac{\Theta \mid \Gamma; \Delta \vdash e_1 : \mathbb{R}\langle G_1, 0\rangle \qquad \Theta \mid \Gamma; \Delta \vdash e_2 : \mathbb{R}\langle G_2, 0\rangle}{\Theta \mid \Gamma; \Delta \vdash \dfrac{e_1}{e_2} : \mathbb{R}\langle G_1 G_2^{-1}, 0\rangle} \qquad \frac{\Theta \mid \Gamma; \Delta \vdash e : \mathbb{R}\langle G^2, 0\rangle}{\Theta \mid \Gamma; \Delta \vdash \text{sqrt } e : \mathbb{R}\langle G, 0\rangle} \qquad \frac{\Theta \mid \Gamma; \Delta \vdash e : \mathit{vec}\ N\ (\mathbb{R}\langle G, 0\rangle)}{\Theta \mid \Gamma; \Delta \vdash \text{sum } e : \mathbb{R}\langle G, 0\rangle}$$

$$\frac{\Theta \mid \Gamma; \Delta, x : X \vdash e_1 : Y \qquad \Theta \mid \Gamma; \Delta \vdash e_2 : \mathit{vec}\ N\ X}{\Theta \mid \Gamma; \Delta \vdash \text{map } (x.\ e_1)\ e_2 : \mathit{vec}\ N\ Y} \qquad \frac{\Theta \mid \Gamma; \Delta \vdash e_1 : \mathit{vec}\ M\ X \qquad \Theta \mid \Gamma; \Delta \vdash e_2 : \mathit{vec}\ N\ Y}{\Theta \mid \Gamma; \Delta \vdash \text{cross } e_1\ e_2 : \mathit{vec}\ (M * N)\ (X \times Y)}$$

**Figure 6.** A surface syntax for smooth functions

### 5.1 Single Particles

***Free Particle*** Our first example is of a simple Lagrangian for a single free particle in 3-dimensional space, with no external forces. We define the Lagrangian using the syntax for smooth terms we defined in the previous section, in the following kinding, typing and cartesian space contexts:

$$\begin{aligned} \Theta &= t_t : \mathsf{T}(1), t_x : \mathsf{T}(3), o : \mathsf{O}(3) \\ \Gamma &= m : \{\!|\mathbb{R}\langle 1, 0\rangle|\!\} \\ \Delta &= t : \mathbb{R}\langle 1, t_t\rangle, x : \mathbb{R}^3\langle \mathit{ortho}_3(o), t_x\rangle, \dot{x} : \mathbb{R}^3\langle \mathit{ortho}_3(o), 0\rangle \end{aligned}$$

where $o$ represents an arbitrary orthogonal transformation of the space, $t_t$ represents a translation in time, $t_x$ represents a 3-dimensional translation in space, $m$ is the constant mass of the free particle, $t$ is the current time, $x$ is the current position of the particle, and $\dot{x}$ is the current velocity.

We write the Lagrangian like so, which in the absence of external forces just consists of the kinetic energy term:

$$L = \frac{1}{2} m(\dot{x} \cdot \dot{x}) : \mathbb{R}\langle 1, 0\rangle$$

By the fundamental theorem of logical relations for our calculus (Property 3), we can derive the following free theorems, one each for the three group parameters $t_t$, $t_x$ and $o$. Quantifying over translations in time, $t_t$, gives us invariance under translation in time:

$$\forall t_t \in \mathbb{R}.\ [\![L]\!](t + t_t, \vec{x}, \dot{\vec{x}}) = [\![L]\!](t, \vec{x}, \dot{\vec{x}})$$

As we saw in Example 4, Noether's theorem tells us that invariance under translation in time yields conservation of energy. Likewise, quantifying over translations in space, $t_x$, gives us invariance under translation in space:

$$\forall \vec{t_x} \in \mathbb{R}^3.\ [\![L]\!](t, \vec{x} + \vec{t_x}, \dot{\vec{x}}) = [\![L]\!](t, \vec{x}, \dot{\vec{x}})$$

Similar to the example of the spring-coupled particles in the introduction, invariance under translations in space yields conservation of linear momentum.

Quantification over orthogonal transformations $o : \mathsf{O}(3)$ yields the following free theorem, which states that the Lagrangian is invariant under modification of the positions and velocities by arbitrary orthogonal transformations $O$:

$$\forall O \in \mathsf{O}(3).\ [\![L]\!](t, O\vec{x}, O\dot{\vec{x}}) = [\![L]\!](t, \vec{x}, \dot{\vec{x}})$$

We are particularly interested in the orthogonal transformations derived from rotations, since these will give us the continuous transformations we need to apply Noether's theorem. For example, rotation by an angle $\epsilon$ around the $x_3$-axis is given by the following $\epsilon$-indexed family of orthogonal matricies:

$$O_\epsilon = \begin{pmatrix} \cos\epsilon & \sin\epsilon & 0 \\ -\sin\epsilon & \cos\epsilon & 0 \\ 0 & 0 & 1 \end{pmatrix}$$

This leads to the following $\epsilon$-indexed family of transformations, suitable for Noether's theorem:

$$\Psi_\epsilon \begin{pmatrix} x_1 \\ x_2 \\ x_3 \end{pmatrix} = O_\epsilon \begin{pmatrix} x_1 \\ x_2 \\ x_3 \end{pmatrix} = \begin{pmatrix} x_1 \cos\epsilon + x_2 \sin\epsilon \\ -x_1 \sin\epsilon + x_2 \cos\epsilon \\ x_3 \end{pmatrix}$$

Plugging this into Equation 10, and using the definition of $L$ above, we obtain the following conservation law:

$$\frac{d}{dt}(m\dot{x}x_2 - m\dot{x}x_1) = 0$$

This is exactly conservation of angular momentum around the $x_3$-axis [12]. By considering the families of orthogonal matrices for rotation around other axes, we can also derive conservation laws for angular momentum around arbitrary axes.

***Particle in a Potential Field*** If we now extend the typing context of our example with an arbitrary potential energy function $V$, depending on the position of the particle, we can define the Lagrangian for a single particle acted upon by a potential field that depends on the position of the particle. The invariance properties of the whole system will depend upon the invariance properties of the potential field. If we assume the following contexts:

$$\begin{aligned}
\Theta &= t_t : \mathsf{T}(1), o : \mathsf{O}(3)\\
\Gamma &= m : ⟅\mathbb{R}\langle 1, 0\rangle⟆,\\
&\quad V : \forall o{:}\mathsf{O}(3).\ C^\infty(\mathbb{R}^3\langle ortho_3(o), 0\rangle, \mathbb{R}\langle 1, 0\rangle)\\
\Delta &= t : \mathbb{R}\langle 1, t_t\rangle, x : \mathbb{R}^3\langle ortho_3(o), 0\rangle, \dot{x} : \mathbb{R}^3\langle ortho_3(o), 0\rangle
\end{aligned}$$

where everything is as in the previous example, except for the addition of the polymophic potential energy function $V$. We incorporate this into our Lagrangian like so:

$$L = \frac{1}{2}m(\dot{x}\cdot\dot{x}) - V(x) : \mathbb{R}\langle 1, 0\rangle$$

Even though $V$ is left abstract, the types of $t$, $x$, $\dot{x}$ and $L$ tell us that this Lagrangian is invariant under translations in time and also under all orthogonal transformations. Hence, by Noether's theorem, the system this Lagrangian describes has energy and angular momentum as conserved quantities.

### 5.2 The $n$-Body Problem

Using the constructs of our calculus for dealing with $n$-ary vectors of positions and velocities, we can compactly write Lagrangians that describe systems of $n$ particles interacting through Newtonian gravitational attraction. We use the following kinding, typing and cartesian space contexts, where the type-level parameter $n$ represents the number of particles that we are considering. For simplicity, we assume that all the bodies involved in the system have equal mass $m$.

$$\begin{aligned}
\Theta &= n : \mathsf{Nat}, t_t : \mathsf{T}(1), t_x : \mathsf{T}(3), o : \mathsf{O}(3)\\
\Gamma &= m : ⟅\mathbb{R}\langle 1, 0\rangle⟆\\
\Delta &= t : \mathbb{R}\langle 1, t_t\rangle,\\
&\quad x : vec\ n\ (\mathbb{R}^3\langle ortho_3(o), t_x\rangle),\\
&\quad \dot{x} : vec\ n\ (\mathbb{R}^3\langle ortho_3(o), 0\rangle)
\end{aligned}$$

The Lagrangian for this system is defined as follows in our surface syntax for smooth terms. The kinetic energy component is the sum of the kinetic energies of all the particles in the system. The potential energy components sums up all the gravitational potential energies due to the interactions between each pair of bodies, where $G$ is the gravitational constant.

$$\begin{aligned}
L = {}& \tfrac{1}{2}m(\text{sum (map } (\dot{x_i}.\ \dot{x_i}\cdot\dot{x_i}))\ \dot{x}) -\\
& \text{sum (map } ((x_i, x_j).\ Gm^2/|x_i - x_j|)\ (\text{cross } x\ x)) : \mathbb{R}\langle 1, 0\rangle
\end{aligned}$$

We have used the notation $|e|$ as shorthand for sqrt $(e \cdot e)$, i.e., the norm of the vector $e$.

Again, just by looking at the types of $t$, $x$, $\dot{x}$, and $L$, we can determine via free theorems that this Lagrangian is invariant under translation in time and space, and under all orthogonal transformations. Hence, by Noether's theorem, this system has energy and linear and angular momentum as conserved quantities.

### 5.3 Pendulum

All our examples above have used rectangular coordinate systems. Part of the power of the Lagrangian formulation of classical mechanics is the ability to use appropriate generalised coordinates to describe systems in simple terms. A standard example is that of a pendulum, where we take the angle $\theta$ of swing from the vertical as the coordinate.

We use the following kinding, typing and cartesian space contexts:

$$\begin{aligned}
\Theta &= t_t : \mathsf{T}(1), z : \mathsf{Z}\\
\Gamma &= m : ⟅\mathbb{R}\langle 1, 0\rangle⟆, l : ⟅\mathbb{R}\langle 1, 0\rangle⟆\\
\Delta &= t : \mathbb{R}\langle 1, t_t\rangle, \theta : \mathbb{R}\langle 1, \underline{2\pi} * z\rangle, \dot{\theta} : \mathbb{R}\langle 1, 0\rangle
\end{aligned}$$

where $m$ is the mass at the end of the pendulum (we assume the rod of the pendulum to be massless), $l$ is the length of the pendulum, $\theta$ is the angle of swing and $\dot{\theta}$ is the current rate of change of the angle of swing.

Defining the Lagrangian for this system is a matter of simple trigonometry and differential calculus:

$$\begin{aligned}
L = {}& \text{let } y = l\sin\theta \text{ in}\\
& \text{let } \dot{x} = l\dot{\theta}\cos\theta \text{ in}\\
& \text{let } \dot{y} = -l\dot{\theta}\sin\theta \text{ in}\\
& \quad \tfrac{1}{2}m(\dot{x}^2 + \dot{y}^2) - mgy : \mathbb{R}\langle 1, 0\rangle
\end{aligned}$$

From the type of $t$, we can easily determine that this Lagrangian is invariant under translation in time, and hence the total energy is a conserved quantity of this system. We can also derive another free theorem due to the quantification over the group of integers via the variable $z$. However, this does not yield a continuous invariance of the Lagrangian, and hence no conserved quantity via Noether's theorem.

### 5.4 Oscillators

***Coupled Particles*** Our first example of a Lagrangian in the introduction was of a pair of particles of equal mass coupled by a spring, for which we derived conservation of linear momentum and energy. In terms of our type system, we have the following kinding, typing and cartesian space contexts, where $m$ is the individual mass of the two particles, and $k$ is the spring constant:

$$\begin{aligned}
\Theta &= t_t : \mathsf{T}(1), t_x : \mathsf{T}(1)\\
\Gamma &= m : ⟅\mathbb{R}\langle 1, 0\rangle⟆, k : ⟅\mathbb{R}\langle 1, 0\rangle⟆\\
\Delta &= t : \mathbb{R}\langle 1, t_t\rangle, x_1 : \mathbb{R}\langle 1, t_x\rangle, x_2 : \mathbb{R}\langle 1, t_x\rangle,\\
&\quad \dot{x_1} : \mathbb{R}\langle 1, 0\rangle, \dot{x_2} : \mathbb{R}\langle 1, 0\rangle
\end{aligned}$$

In our surface syntax for smooth terms, the Lagrangian is written just as it was in the introduction:

$$L = \frac{1}{2}m(\dot{x_1}^2 + \dot{x_2}^2) - \frac{1}{2}k^2(x_1 - x_2)^2 : \mathbb{R}\langle 1, 0\rangle$$

The free theorems for this term state the invariance in time and space translation:

$$\begin{aligned}
&\forall t_t : \mathbb{R}.\ [\![L]\!](t + t_t, x_1, x_2, \dot{x_1}, \dot{x_2}) = [\![L]\!](t, x_1, x_2, \dot{x_1}, \dot{x_2})\\
&\forall t_x : \mathbb{R}.\ [\![L]\!](t, x_1 + t_x, x_2 + t_x, \dot{x_1}, \dot{x_2}) = [\![L]\!](t, x_1, x_2, \dot{x_1}, \dot{x_2})
\end{aligned}$$

As we saw in Section 2, these invariance properties allow us to deduce conservation of energy and linear momentum for this system.

***Damped Oscillator*** All of the example Lagrangians we have looked at so far have had no dependence on time, and so they have all described systems with total energy as a conserved quantity. A system with a single particle attached to a damped spring (whose other endpoint is fixed at position 0) provides an example of system that does not have energy as a conserved quantity. This example is taken from Neuenschwander's book [13]. We use the following kinding, typing and cartesian space contexts:

$$\Theta = t_t : \mathsf{T}(1)$$
$$\Gamma = k : \wr \mathbb{R}\langle 1, 0 \rangle \int$$
$$\Delta = t : \mathbb{R}\langle 1, t_t + t_t \rangle, x : \mathbb{R}\langle exp(-t_t), 0 \rangle, \dot{x} : \mathbb{R}\langle exp(-t_t), 0 \rangle$$

Here, the position and velocity of the single particle *scale* with the exponential of the translation in time. This will account for the exponential damping we apply to the system. For simplicity, we assume that the mass of the particle and the spring constant are both 1. The Lagrangian for this system looks similar to the coupled pair above, except for an additional damping factor:

$$L = \left( \frac{1}{2}\dot{x}^2 - \frac{1}{2}x^2 \right) \exp(t) : \mathbb{R}\langle 1, 0 \rangle$$

From the types of $t$, $x$ and $\dot{x}$, we learn that this system is invariant under the families of transformations $\Phi_\epsilon(t) = t + 2\epsilon$ and $\Psi_\epsilon(x) = e^\epsilon x$. This leads to the following conservation law for this system, linking energy and linear momentum:

$$\frac{d}{dt}\left[ \left( \frac{1}{2}x\dot{x} + \frac{1}{2}\dot{x}^2 + \frac{1}{2}x^2 \right) e^t \right] = 0$$

## 6. Conclusions

We have presented a type system for writing invariant Langrangians, with a relationally parametric semantics that allows the derivation of free theorems that can be used with Noether's theorem to discover conservation laws for classical mechanical systems. Our key technical contribution has been the observation that relationally parametric models of System F$\omega$ admit kinds that are interpreted as groupoids, allowing geometric invariance properties to be integrated directly into the model.

***Related Work*** We are not aware of any other work linking type systems or relational parametricity with invariance properties for classical mechanics, or with Noether's theorem. We have already mentioned the work of Atkey, Johann and Kennedy [5] that uses relational parametricity with a specialised type system to derive geometric invariance properties, albeit in a setting without smooth functions, and without an application to Noether's theorem. In this paper, we have placed Atkey *et al.*'s work in a more general setting by framing it as an extension of System F$\omega$, which allows us to (a) incorporate type-level computation, as we used to define the $n$-ary vectors of coordinates; and (b) to reuse previous work on relationally parametric models of System F$\omega$ by Atkey [3].

Sussman and Wisdom [20] reformulate Lagrangian and Hamiltonian mechanics in a more programming language style so that it can be implemented within the programming language Scheme. In doing so, they clear up some of the ambiguous syntax common in the standard presentations of classical mechanics. However, they do not attempt to incorporate invariance properties into types, as we have done here.

There has been prior work on programming languages inspired by theoretical physics. Quantum programming languages, which hope to exploit the properties of quantum computation in an understandable way, have been the subject of study for several years now. We cite Abramsky [1] as an introduction to this field.

***Future Work*** We have barely scratched the surface of the applicability of Noether's theorem to theoretical physics. Conservation laws for classical and quantum field theories are derivable from the much more general theorem that Noether originally proved [14]. Neuenschwander's book [13] describes in an easy to read way how Noether's theorem applies to field theories, allowing for relativistic and quantum systems to be studied, and how it naturally leads to the notion of Gauge invariance, an important principle in modern theories of particle physics.

From the type system point of view, it seems clear that greater precision in the types will be required in order to accomodate more detailed physical theories. Study of relational parametricity for dependent types, as done for example by Bernardy *et al.* [6] and Atkey *et al.* [4] may be useful here. Also, recent work on homotopy type theory and, in particular $\infty$-groupoid models of type theory is almost certainly relevant [21].

For each of the examples in Section 5, we computed the necessary typing derivations by hand. Type inference for the system was have presented here, or some variant of it, is a key item of future work. Ideally, the user would enter the description of a Lagrangian, and the system would be able to tell them the free theorems, and consequent conservation laws that hold. Kennedy [10] and Gundry [8] have studied type inference for the related, but simpler, setting of dimension types.

## References


[1] S. Abramsky. High-Level Methods for Quantum Computation and Information. Proceedings, LICS, 2004.

[2] V. I. Arnol'd. *Mathematical Methods of Classical Mechanics*. Springer, 1989.

[3] R. Atkey. Relational Parametricity for Higher Kinds. Proceedings, CSL, 2012.

[4] R. Atkey, N. Ghani, and P. Johann. A Relationally Parametric Model of Dependent Type Theory. Proceedings, POPL, 2014.

[5] R. Atkey, P. Johann, and A. J. Kennedy. Abstraction and Invariance for Algebraically Indexed Types. Proceedings, POPL, 2013.

[6] J.-P. Bernardy, P. Jansson, R. Paterson. Proofs for Free: Parametricity for Dependent Types. *Journal of Functional Programming* 22(2), pp. 107-152, 2012.

[7] I. M. Gelfand and S. V. Fomin, R. A. Silverman (ed.). *Calculus of Variations*. Dover Publications, 2000.

[8] A. Gundry. Type Inference for Units of Measure. Technical Report, University of Strathclyde, 2011.

[9] R. Hasegawa. Relational Limits in General Polymorphism. *Publications of the Research Institute for Mathematical Sciences* 30, pp. 535–576, 1994.

[10] A. J. Kennedy. Dimension Types. Proceedings, ESOP, 1994.

[11] A. J. Kennedy. Relational Parametricity and Units of Measure. Proceedings, POPL, pp. 442-455, 1997.

[12] L. D. Landau and E. M. Lifschitz. *Mechanics*. Pergamon Press. 1967.

[13] D. E. Neuenschwander. *Emmy Noether's Wonderful Theorem*. The John Hopkins University Press, 2011.

[14] E. Noether, M. Tavel (translator). Invariant Variation Problems. *Transport Theory and Statistical Physics* 1(3), pp. 186-207, 1971. Original in *Gott. Nachr.*, 1918:235-257, 1918.

[15] S. Mac Lane. *Categories for the Working Mathematician*, 2nd edition. Springer, 1998.

[16] B. Pierce. *Types and Programming Languages*. MIT Press, 2002.

[17] A. M. Pitts. Polymorphism is Set Theoretic, Constructively. *Proc., Category Theory and Computer Science*, pp. 12–39, 1987.

[18] J. C. Reynolds. Types, Abstraction and Parametric Polymorphism. *Information Processing* 83, pp. 513-523, 1983.

[19] E. Robinson and G. Rosolini. Reflexive Graphs and Parametric Polymorphism. *Proc., Logic in Computer Science*, pp. 364–371, 1994.

[20] G. J. Sussman and J. Wisdom. Structure and Interpretation of Classical Mechanics. MIT Press, 2001

[21] The Univalent Foundations Program. *Homotopy Type Theory*. Institute for Advanced Study, 2013.

[22] P. Wadler. Theorems for Free!. Proceedings, FPCA, pp. 347-359, 1989.

# A Relationally Parametric Model of Dependent Type Theory


Robert Atkey
bob.atkey@gmail.com

Neil Ghani
University of Strathclyde
neil.ghani@strath.ac.uk

Patricia Johann
Appalachian State University
johannp@appstate.edu



## Abstract

Reynolds' theory of relational parametricity captures the invariance of polymorphically typed programs under change of data representation. Reynolds' original work exploited the typing discipline of the polymorphically typed $\lambda$-calculus System F, but there is now considerable interest in extending relational parametricity to type systems that are richer and more expressive than that of System F.

This paper constructs parametric models of predicative and impredicative dependent type theory. The significance of our models is twofold. Firstly, in the impredicative variant we are able to deduce the existence of initial algebras for all *indexed* functors. To our knowledge, ours is the first account of parametricity for dependent types that is able to lift the useful deduction of the existence of initial algebras in parametric models of System F to the dependently typed setting. Secondly, our models offer conceptual clarity by uniformly expressing relational parametricity for dependent types in terms of reflexive graphs, which allows us to unify the interpretations of types and kinds, instead of taking the relational interpretation of types as a primitive notion. Expressing our model in terms of reflexive graphs ensures that it has canonical choices for the interpretations of the standard type constructors of dependent type theory, except for the interpretation of the universe of small types, where we formulate a refined interpretation tailored for relational parametricity. Moreover, our reflexive graph model opens the door to generalisations of relational parametricity, for example to higher-dimensional relational parametricity.



***Categories and Subject Descriptors*** D.3.1 [*Programming Languages*]: Formal Definitions and Theory; D.1.1 [*Programming techniques*]: Applicative (functional) programming

***General Terms*** Languages, Theory, Types

***Keywords*** relational parametricity, dependent type theory


## 1. Introduction

Reynolds' theory of relational parametricity captures the invariance of polymorphically typed programs under change of data representation [28]. Relational parametricity has been shown to yield a wide range of useful and surprising consequences, including free theorems [35], data type representations [13], optimisation of recursive programs [18], and geometric invariance properties [3]. Reynolds' original work exploited the typing discipline of the polymorphically typed $\lambda$-calculus System F, but there is now considerable interest in extending relational parametricity to type systems that are richer and more expressive than that of System F.

Relational parametricity for systems with type-level computation — of which System F$\omega$ is the prototypical example — has been studied by Vytiniotis and Weirich [33] and by Atkey [2]. The latter builds on earlier work by Hasegawa [14], who gives general requirements a model must satisfy in order to interpret System $F\omega$. The extra expressive power of System F$\omega$ allows for Church Encodings of *indexed* types. For example, the standard example of a Generalised Algebraic Datatype (GADT) [7] for typed expressions containing constants and pairing can be represented by the following System F$\omega$ type:

$$\lambda\tau.\forall\alpha{:}{*}{\to}{*}.(\forall\sigma.\sigma{\to}\alpha\,\sigma){\to}(\forall\sigma,\sigma'.\alpha\,\sigma{\to}\alpha\,\sigma'{\to}\alpha(\sigma{\times}\sigma')){\to}\alpha\,\tau$$

Relational parametricity can be used to show that this type enjoys an *initiality* property [2], showing that it is isomorphic to the normal GADT of typed expressions.

By introducing a kind of natural numbers, it is also possible to encode in System F$\omega$ interesting indexed types like length-indexed vectors. However, due to the rigid separation of types and terms in System F$\omega$, type-level and term-level naturals are not the same thing, which leads to duplication and loss of expressivity. Dependent type theories weaken the distinction between types and terms, allowing terms to appear in types. It is therefore natural to ask whether or not relational parametricity extends to systems with type dependency, and whether or not the consequences of relational parametricity (suitably generalised) carry over as well.

In this paper, we answer both these questions in the affirmative. We build a model of dependent type theory (in predicative and impredicative variants) that naturally extends Reynolds' original relationally parametric model. We also show that, within the impredicative model, every indexed functor $F$ has an initial algebra, given by the dependently typed Church encoding:

$$\lambda x : X.\, \Pi A : X \to \mathsf{U}.\, (\Pi x : X.\mathsf{T}(FAx) \to \mathsf{T}(Ax)) \to \mathsf{T}(A\ x)$$

(The symbol $\mathsf{U}$ stands for the universe of small types, and $\mathsf{T}$ transforms a small type into a proper type; we define the syntax of dependent types in Section 3.) To our knowledge the model we present in this paper is the first parametric model, syntactic *or* semantic, of dependent type theory to establish this key theorem.

The question of the existence of relationally parametric models of dependent type theory has already been established as relevant for applications: Chlipala [8] assumes relational parametricity for representing higher-order abstract syntax, and Nanevski *et al.* [23] assumes properties of type abstraction for enforcing security properties. In this paper we demonstrate that relationally parametric models of dependent type theory do exist, though we leave questions about potential applications to future work.

***Approaches to Understanding Relational Parametricity*** Since Reynolds' original model-theoretic formulation, relational para-




*POPL '14*, January 22–24, 2014, San Diego, CA, USA.



ACM 978-1-4503-2544-8/14/01...$15.00.
http://dx.doi.org/10.1145/2535838.2535852

metricity has been studied in a number of settings. Reynolds' original model was elucidated by Bainbridge *et al.* [4], who also moved to a PER-based interpretation of types to handle foundational set-theoretic problems, caused by impredicativity, with Reynolds' original formulation. Robinson and Rosolini [30] studied Reynolds' model from the point of view of internal categories, again to work around foundational problems with the semantics of impredicativity. More usefully for us, Robinson and Rosolini reformulated Reynolds' original model in terms of reflexive graphs. Reflexive graphs capture the essence of relationally parametric models: types are simultaneously interpreted as sets and as relations between sets, with a distinguished reflexive relation, called the "equality relation", from any set to itself, and open types are interpreted as morphisms between reflexive graphs. The model of dependent type theory that we construct in this paper is built on the category of reflexive graphs and reflexive graph morphisms that Robinson and Rosolini used to interpret the types of System F. Reflexive graph models of parametricity have also appeared implicitly in the work of Hasegawa [13, 14], and explicitly in the work of Dunphy and Reddy [11], both in settings without type dependency.

Other approaches to understanding parametricity include Pitts' operational models of programming languages with polymorphic types and recursion [24]; Plotkin and Abadi's logic for parametricity [26]; and Wadler's translation of System F into second-order predicate logic [34].

The study of relational parametricity for systems with dependent types originates with Takeuti [31] and has recently been taken up by Bernardy *et al.* [5] and Krishnaswami and Dreyer [19]. Both Takeuti and Bernardy *et al.* study relational parametricity for dependent types via syntactic translations from one type theory to another. Krishnaswami and Dreyer construct a realizability model of the Calculus of Constructions, using Quasi-PERs to simultaneously define the underlying and relational interpretations of types. They demonstrate the adequacy of the Church encoding of the non-indexed initial algebra representing the natural numbers, but do not mention the Church encodings of indexed initial algebras that we consider in this paper.

The distinguishing feature of the parametric model of dependent types developed in this paper is that we follow Robinson and Rosolini in taking the interpretation of types as *reflexive graphs* as primitive, rather than explicitly seeking a relational interpretation of dependent types, as was done in the work of Takeuti, Bernardy *et al.* and Krishnaswami and Dreyer. In order to capture relational parametricity, our model interprets the universe U of small types in terms of sets and relations, so that we recover a relational interpretation of types *within* the setting of reflexive graphs (Section 4.3). By taking reflexive graphs as primitive, we can offer the following two significant contributions:

- At a results level, as we have mentioned above, we are able to show that the impredicative variant of our reflexive graph model contains initial algebras for all indexed functors (Section 5.4). The *reflexive* property of reflexive graphs plays a crucial role in the proof, being the appropriate generalisation of the key identity extension property of relationally parametric models of System F. Our models for both the predicative and impredicative variants also validate free theorems about polymorphic terms (Section 5.1), in the style of Wadler [35].
- At a conceptual level, reflexive graphs offer both canonical choices when building parametric models, and insight into the structure of relational parametricity. Robinson and Rosolini used reflexive graphs to bring clarity to relationally parametric models of System F, and here we use reflexive graphs to bring clarity to relationally parametric models of dependent type theory. Since reflexive graph models are presheaf models, we are provided with canonical choices of much of the structure of dependent types: for example, there is a canonical choice of interpretation of Π-types, up to isomorphism. For the interpretation of the universe of small types there is no canonical choice. The obvious choice is to capture a semantic notion of smallness, using a construction due to Hofmann and Streicher. However, we demonstrate that smallness by itself is inadequate for relational parametricity, and we identify two further semantic properties, discreteness and proof-irrelevance, that must be captured by our interpretation of a universe of small types (Section 4.3).

***Structure of the Paper***

- In Section 2 we trace a path from the original relationally parametric model of Reynolds, with its explicit use of relations, through to the reflexive graph formulation of parametricity, originally due to Robinson and Rosolini and, separately, Hasegawa. Since most presentations of relational parametricity for System F are explicitly formulated in terms of relations (e.g., Wadler's "Theorems for Free"), we carefully demonstrate that, at the level of System F, the relational and reflexive graph formulations are equivalent. This gives us the necessary foundation on which to build a parametric model of dependent types.
- Section 3 recalls necessary syntactic and semantic background. We set out the precise variants of Martin-Löf Type Theory (predicative and impredicative) that we will model. We also recall the definition of Categories with Families (CwFs), a sound and complete class of categorical models of dependent type theory.
- We construct our parametric models of dependent types in Section 4 by showing that the category of reflexive graphs forms a CwF. The key feature of our models, apart from our use of reflexive graphs, is in our interpretation of the universe U of small types. We examine the necessary features that the interpretation of U must capture (namely smallness, discreteness, and proof-irrelevance) and build them into the model.
- With our parametric models in hand, we demonstrate several consequences of it in Section 5. We show that our model supports simple free theorems, as well as the construction of initial algebras for arbitrary indexed functors.
- Section 6 concludes and offers directions for future work.

## 2. Relational Parametricity and Reflexive Graphs

In this section we introduce the semantic structures used to construct our parametric model of dependent types. To this end, we first recall in Section 2.1 the "direct" method for building relationally parametric models of System F, as originally proposed by Reynolds [28] and elucidated by Bainbridge *et al.* [4]. We then show in Section 2.2 how to reformulate this model in terms of reflexive graphs, following Robinson and Rosolini [30].

Any model of System F, or any extension of it, must confront the issue of modelling impredicative type quantification. Reynolds showed that classical set-theoretic models of impredicative polymorphism cannot exist [27]. To overcome this problem, we build our models of impredicative type theories in an impredicative meta-theory. Specifically, we use the Calculus of Inductive Constructions with the predicative Type universe hierarchy, an impredicative universe Set, a (disjoint) impredicative universe Prop, and axioms for functional extensionality, and proof irrelevance and propositional extensionality in Prop. This theory is implemented in the Coq proof assistant [9] with the `-impredicative-set` option, and the three axioms postulated. We work informally within this meta-theory, using set-theoretic notation. By taking this synthetic approach, we can dispense with the technicalities of constructing a model within

$$\frac{(\alpha : *) \in \Gamma}{\Gamma \vdash \alpha : *} \qquad \frac{\Gamma \vdash A : * \qquad \Gamma \vdash B : *}{\Gamma \vdash A \to B : *} \qquad \frac{\Gamma, \alpha : * \vdash A : *}{\Gamma \vdash \forall \alpha{:}*.\, A : *}$$

**Figure 1.** Well-kinded Types in System F

classical set theory using PERs or internal categories. A fully formalised relationally parametric model of System F has been constructed in this setting by Atkey [1].

### 2.1 Relational Models of Parametricity for System F

The well-kinded types of System F are shown in Figure 1. By these rules, well-kinded types are either type variables, function types, or universally quantified types. Kinding contexts $\Gamma$ are lists of type variable/kind pairs $\alpha : *$ that do not contain duplicate type variable names. In System F, there is only the base kind $*$ of types.

***Interpretation of Types*** In the model presented by Bainbridge *et al.* [4], each well-kinded type $\Gamma \vdash A : *$ is assigned two interpretations: an *underlying interpretation* $[\![\Gamma \vdash A : *]\!]_o$ that interprets a type as a function on the universe $\mathcal{U}$ of small sets, and a *relational interpretation* $[\![\Gamma \vdash A : *]\!]_r$ that interprets a type as a transformer of relations between underlying interpretations. If, for any two sets $X, Y \in \mathcal{U}$, $\mathrm{Rel}(X,Y)$ denotes the set of binary relations between $X$ and $Y$, and if $|\Gamma|$ stands for the number of members of $\Gamma$, then the underlying interpretation and the relational interpretation of $\Gamma \vdash A : *$ have the following meta-theoretic types:

$$[\![\Gamma \vdash A : *]\!]_o \in \mathcal{U}^{|\Gamma|} \to \mathcal{U}$$

$$[\![\Gamma \vdash A : *]\!]_r \in \forall \gamma_1, \gamma_2 \in \mathcal{U}^{|\Gamma|}.\ \mathrm{Rel}^{|\Gamma|}(\gamma_1, \gamma_2) \to \mathrm{Rel}([\![\Gamma \vdash A : *]\!]_o \gamma_1, [\![\Gamma \vdash A : *]\!]_o \gamma_2)$$

The underlying interpretation and the relational interpretation of $\Gamma \vdash A : *$ are explicitly linked by the appearance of the underlying interpretation in the type of the relational interpretation. The two interpretations are also linked by the *identity extension* property, which states that the relational interpretation of any type $\Gamma \vdash A : *$ preserves equality:

$$\forall \gamma \in \mathcal{U}^{|\Gamma|}.\ [\![\Gamma \vdash A : *]\!]_r\ \gamma\ \gamma\ \mathrm{Eq}_\gamma = \mathrm{Eq}_{[\![\Gamma \vdash A:*]\!]_o \gamma}$$

Here, $\mathrm{Eq}_X$ is the equality relation on the set $X$, and $\mathrm{Eq}_\gamma$ for a tuple of sets $\gamma = (X_1, ..., X_{|\Gamma|})$ is the tuple $(\mathrm{Eq}_{X_1}, ..., \mathrm{Eq}_{X_{|\Gamma|}})$.

Identity extension is the key property that makes a model *relationally parametric*, rather than just logical relations over an existing model. We can read it as saying that every element of the interpretation of a closed type is related to itself by the relational interpretation of that type. Therefore, identity extension is similar to the abstraction theorem (see *Interpretation of Terms* at the end of this subsection), except that it applies to *all* elements of the denotation of a type, not just the denotations of terms. Consequently, we are able to use the relational interpretation of types to reason about arbitrary elements of the denotations of those types, not just elements that are the interpretations of terms.

As we shall see when we construct the interpretation of the type-theoretic universe of small types in Section 4.3 below, our model of dependent types will satisfy the (suitably generalised) identity extension property for this universe. Identity extension is essential in our proof of the existence of initial algebras in Section 5.4.

A consequence of requiring identity extension is that the underlying interpretation and the relational interpretation must be defined simultaneously. This is due to the interpretation of types of the form $\Gamma \vdash \forall \alpha{:}*.A : *$. Indeed, if we do not cut down the underlying interpretations of universal types to include only the "parametric" elements, then we will be unable to prove the identity extension property. This cutting down is shown in Bainbridge *et al.*'s definitions of the underlying interpretations and relational interpretations for universal types, here adapted to our setting:

$$\begin{aligned}
&[\![\Gamma \vdash \forall \alpha{:}*.A : *]\!]_o \gamma = \\
&\quad \{x : \forall X \in \mathcal{U}.\ [\![\Gamma, \alpha : * \vdash A : *]\!]_o(\gamma, X) \mid \\
&\qquad \forall X, Y, R \in \mathrm{Rel}(X,Y). \\
&\qquad\quad (x\ X, x\ Y) \in [\![\Gamma, \alpha : * \vdash A : *]\!]_r(\gamma, X)(\gamma, Y)(\mathrm{Eq}_\gamma, R)\}
\end{aligned}$$

$$\begin{aligned}
&[\![\Gamma \vdash \forall \alpha{:}*.A : *]\!]_r \gamma_1 \gamma_2 \rho = \\
&\quad \{(x, y) \mid \forall X, Y, R \in \mathrm{Rel}(X,Y). \\
&\qquad (x\ X, y\ Y) \in [\![\Gamma, \alpha : * \vdash A : *]\!]_r(\gamma_1, X)(\gamma_2, Y)(\rho, R)\}
\end{aligned}$$

We will refer back to this definition when we construct the interpretation of dependent products ($\Pi$-types) in our relationally parametric model of dependent types in Section 4.4.

***Interpretation of Terms*** A well-typed term of System F is determined by the typing judgement $\Gamma; \Theta \vdash M : A$ where $\Gamma$ is a kinding context, $\Theta$ is a typing context consisting of variable name/type pairs $x_i : A_i$ where each $A_i$ is well-kinded with respect to $\Gamma$, and $A$ is also well-kinded with respect to $\Gamma$. We write $\Gamma \vdash \Theta$ to indicate when all the types in the typing context $\Theta$ are well-kinded with respect to the kinding context $\Gamma$. We omit the (entirely standard) typing rules that generate the judgement $\Gamma; \Theta \vdash M : A$.

The interpretation of types that we sketched above is extended to an interpretation of typing contexts $\Theta$ by tupling together the interpretations of the constituent types and using the standard logical relations interpretation of product types. Each well-typed term $\Gamma; \Theta \vdash M : A$ is interpreted as a family $[\![\Gamma; \Theta \vdash M : A]\!]_o$ of functions from the underlying interpretation of the typing context $\Theta$ to the underlying interpretation of the type $A$, indexed by the underlying interpretations of the free type variables:

$$[\![\Gamma; \Theta \vdash M : A]\!]_o : \forall \gamma \in \mathcal{U}^{|\Gamma|}.\ [\![\Gamma \vdash \Theta]\!]_o \gamma \to [\![\Gamma \vdash A : *]\!]_o \gamma$$

Because the underlying interpretations and relational interpretations of types are mutually defined, we must simultaneously define $[\![\Gamma; \Theta \vdash M : A]\!]_o$ and prove the following property, which states that the relational interpretations of $\Theta$ and $A$ are preserved:

$$\begin{aligned}
&\forall \gamma_1, \gamma_2 \in \mathcal{U}^{|\Gamma|}, \rho \in \mathrm{Rel}^{|\Gamma|}(\gamma_1, \gamma_2), \\
&\quad \theta_1 \in [\![\Gamma \vdash \Theta]\!]_o \gamma_1, \theta_2 \in [\![\Gamma \vdash \Theta]\!]_o \gamma_2. \\
&\qquad (\theta_1, \theta_2) \in [\![\Gamma \vdash \Theta]\!]_r \gamma_1 \gamma_2 \rho \Rightarrow \\
&\qquad\quad ([\![\Gamma; \Theta \vdash M : A]\!]_o\ \gamma_1\ \theta_1, [\![\Gamma; \Theta \vdash M : A]\!]_o\ \gamma_2\ \theta_2) \in \\
&\qquad\qquad [\![\Gamma \vdash A : *]\!]_r \gamma_1 \gamma_2 \rho
\end{aligned}$$

This preservation of relations property has been variously called Reynolds' Abstraction Theorem [28], the Fundamental Theorem of Logical Relations [25], and the Parametricity Theorem [21].

### 2.2 Reflexive Graph Models of Parametricity for System F

The two-level approach of the Reynolds/Bainbridge *et al.* model, in which types are assigned an underlying interpretation and a relational interpretation, works well for the relatively simple setting of System F. However, it is difficult to see how to extend this approach to allow for more complex features such as higher kinds, which allow function kinds such as $* \to *$, and type-level computation, as is found in dependent type theories. The primary difficulty lies in extending the definition of the identity extension property. When we only considered the base kind $*$, interpreted as the collection of sets $X \in \mathcal{U}$, there was an obvious notion of "equality relation". But it is not so obvious what "equality relation" should mean when interpreting higher kinds. One complication is that, no matter what our notion of "equality relation" ends up being, an equality relation for a higher-kinded type must actually be a relation transformer. This complication is further compounded when attempting to interpret a dependent type theory in which types may depend on terms as well as types. Fortunately, by using reflexive graphs, as introduced by

Robinson and Rosolini [30], we can construct a parametric model of System F that naturally extends to dependent types.

**Definition 1.** *A* reflexive graph *is a 5-tuple* $(\Gamma_O, \Gamma_R, \Gamma_{refl}, \Gamma_{src}, \Gamma_{tgt})$ *comprising a pair of sets* $\Gamma_O$ *and* $\Gamma_R$*, together with three functions*

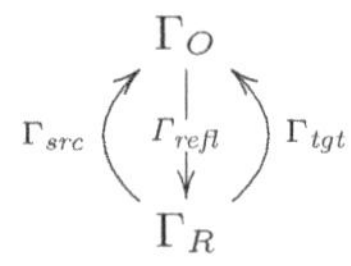


*such that* $\Gamma_{src} \circ \Gamma_{refl} = \mathrm{id}_{\Gamma_O} = \Gamma_{tgt} \circ \Gamma_{refl}$. *A* morphism $f$ *between reflexive graphs* $\Gamma$ *and* $\Delta$ *is a pair of functions* $(f_o, f_r)$ *that makes every square the following diagram commute:*

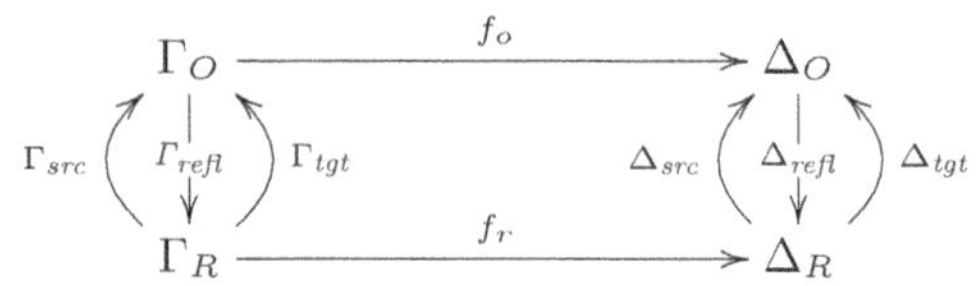


The set $\Gamma_O$ is called the set of *objects*, and $\Gamma_R$ is called the set of *relations*, of the reflexive graph.

We use reflexive graphs for two purposes: to model collections of types, and to model specific types. The first use takes $\Gamma_O$ to be a set of *sets* and $\Gamma_R$ to be a set of *relations* over those sets. Each relation $\gamma_r \in \Gamma_R$ is thus a relation between $\Gamma_{src}(\gamma_r)$, and $\Gamma_{tgt}(\gamma_r)$ and each set $\gamma_o \in \Gamma_O$ has a distinguished relation $\Gamma_{refl}(\gamma_o)$ relating $\gamma_o$ to itself. This intuition underlies the following example.

**Example 1.** *If* $\mathcal{U}$ *is a universe of small sets, then the kind* $*$ *of types can be interpreted as a reflexive graph (also called* $*$*) as follows:*

$$*_O = \mathcal{U} \qquad *_R = \{(X, Y, R) \mid X, Y \in \mathcal{U}, R \in \mathrm{Rel}(X, Y)\}$$

$$*_{refl}(X) = (X, X, \mathrm{Eq}_X) \quad *_{src}(X, Y, R) = X \quad *_{tgt}(X, Y, R) = Y$$

*The objects of this reflexive graph are thus small sets from* $\mathcal{U}$*, and its relations are ordinary binary relations between such sets. For each* $X \in \mathcal{U}$*, the function* $*_{refl}$ *takes the equality relation to be the distinguished binary relation on* $X$*. For this choice of relation the identity extension property is a straightforward consequence of the definition of a reflexive graph morphism.*

Our second use of reflexive graphs takes $\Gamma_O$ to be a specific set and $\Gamma_R$ to be a reflexive relation on that set, represented as a (multi-)set of pairs of elements that are related. Then $\Gamma_{refl}$ ensures that $\Gamma_R$ is reflexive, while $\Gamma_{src}$ and $\Gamma_{tgt}$ map each pair of related elements to the component elements that are so related. This intuition underlies the following example, which forms the basis of the interpretation of the natural number type we present in Section 4.4.

**Example 2.** *A reflexive graph can be built from the set of natural numbers as follows:*

$$\begin{array}{ll} nat_O = \mathbb{N} & nat_{refl}(n) = n \\ nat_R = \mathbb{N} & nat_{src}(n) = n \\ & nat_{tgt}(n) = n \end{array}$$

*The objects of this reflexive graph are just the natural numbers. For any* $n \in nat_R$*, we have* $nat_{src}(n) = nat_{tgt}(n) = n$*, so two natural numbers are related if and only if they are equal. Generalising the construction of nat, for any set* $X$ *there is a reflexive graph* $(X, X, \mathrm{id}_X, \mathrm{id}_X, \mathrm{id}_X)$ *that has* $X$ *as its set of objects and relates objects in* $X$ *if and only if they are equal. In particular, if* $1$ *is a terminal object in the category of sets, then* $(1, 1, \mathrm{id}_1, \mathrm{id}_1, \mathrm{id}_1)$ *is terminal in the category of reflexive graphs.*

Reflexive graphs can be equivalently defined as covariant presheaves over the category $\mathrm{RG} = \bullet \overset{src}{\underset{tgt}{\leftleftarrows}} \!\!\xrightarrow{refl}\! \bullet$ where $src \circ refl = \mathrm{id} = tgt \circ refl$. Morphisms between reflexive graphs are exactly natural transformations between presheaves in $\mathrm{Set}^{\mathrm{RG}}$. Viewing reflexive graphs as presheaves ensures that the following well-known properties of categories of presheaves hold for categories of reflexive graphs as well. Firstly, categories of presheaves are always cartesian, so we can use the finite product structure to interpret kinding contexts. Secondly, categories of presheaves are always cartesian closed, which allows for the interpretation of higher kinds [2]. Finally, presheaf categories always form a (non-parametric) model of dependent type theory [15], a fact that will help us construct the *parametric* model we present in Section 4.

***Interpretation of Types*** A well-kinded type $\Gamma \vdash A : *$ is interpreted as a reflexive graph morphism from the $|\Gamma|$-fold product of the reflexive graph $*$ from Example 1 to $*$ itself. Just as we did in Example 1, we identify a context with its reflexive graph interpretation and use the same notation for both. Unfolding the definitions shows that a reflexive graph morphism is nothing more than a pair comprised of an underlying interpretation and a relational interpretation satisfying the identity extension property, exactly as in the two-level semantics in Section 2.1. For any reflexive graph $\Gamma$, we think of the homset $\mathrm{Set}^{\mathrm{RG}}(\Gamma, *)$ as providing interpretations of types over $\Gamma$.

***Interpretation of Terms*** Just as in Section 2.1, the interpretation of types can be extended to an interpretation of typing contexts by tupling in the current setting. A well-kinded typing context $\Gamma$ is therefore also interpreted as an object of $\mathrm{Set}^{\mathrm{RG}}(\Gamma, *)$. In the reflexive graph model, a well-typed term $\Gamma; \Theta \vdash M : A$ is then interpreted, as before, as a morphism from the interpretation of the typing context $\Theta$ to the interpretation of the type $A$, i.e., as a morphism in the category $\mathrm{Set}^{\mathrm{RG}}(\Gamma, *)$:

**Definition 2.** *Let* $A, B \in \mathrm{Set}^{\mathrm{RG}}(\Gamma, *)$*. A morphism from* $A$ *to* $B$ *is a function* $M : \forall \gamma_o \in \Gamma_O.\ A_o(\gamma_o) \to B_o(\gamma_o)$ *such that for all* $\gamma_r \in \Gamma_R$*, if* $A_r(\gamma_r) = (A_1, A_2, R_A \subseteq A_1 \times A_2)$ *and* $B_r(\gamma_r) = (B_1, B_2, R_B \subseteq B_1 \times B_2)$ *then for all* $(a_1, a_2) \in R_A$*,* $(M\ (\Gamma_{src}(\gamma_r))\ a_1, M\ (\Gamma_{tgt}(\gamma_r))\ a_2) \in R_B$*. This definition makes each homset* $\mathrm{Set}^{\mathrm{RG}}(\Gamma, *)$ *into a category.*

Note that the fundamental theorem of logical relations stated at the very end of Section 2.1 is identical to the condition in Definition 2, up to the reformulation of types as reflexive graph morphisms.

## 3. Martin-Löf Type Theory with a Universe: Syntax and Categorical Semantics

The reflexive graph model of parametricity we present in Section 4 is defined with respect to the specific formulation of dependent type theory that we set out in this section. The type theory we consider is a standard variant of Martin-Löf type theory [22] with a natural number type $\mathsf{nat}$, dependent product types $\Pi x{:}A.B$, and a Tarski-style universe $\mathsf{U}$ closed under natural numbers and dependent products. Our default assumption is that the universe $\mathsf{U}$ is predicative, but we will also consider an impredicative universe in order to more closely relate our results with (impredicative) System F. Our type theory includes $\beta$- and $\eta$-equality rules for dependent product types, as well as $\beta$-equality rules for the natural numbers. Since our universe is Tarski-style, we have an explicit "decoder" type former $\mathsf{T}$ to take terms of type $\mathsf{U}$ to actual types.

The type theories we present in this section are close to the theories underlying the Agda [6] and Coq [9] systems. Our predicative theory is close to Agda, except that we only have one inductive type (the natural numbers), and we only have one universe, with an explicit universe decoder. The impredicative variant is close to the Calculus of Constructions (the theory underlying the impredicative variant of Coq), except with a natural number type, and an explicit universe decoder. Our use of an explicit universe decoder

| Judgement | Intuitive meaning |
|---|---|
| $\Gamma$ ctxt | $\Gamma$ is a well-formed context |
| $\Gamma \vdash A$ type | $A$ is a well-formed type in the context $\Gamma$ |
| $\Gamma \vdash M : A$ | the term $M$ has type $A$ in the context $\Gamma$ |
| $\Gamma \vdash A = B$ type | $A$ and $B$ are equal types in the context $\Gamma$ |
| $\Gamma \vdash M = N : A$ | the terms $M$ and $N$ are equal at the type $A$ in the context $\Gamma$ |

**Figure 2.** Judgement forms

is a technical device that means we do not have to deal with coherence issues arising from multiple typing derivations of the same term. Moving to an implicit universe decoder with our models does not present any problems that do not already arise when defining models of dependent types with a universe.

### 3.1 Syntax and Typing

The raw contexts, types, and terms are defined as follows:

$$\begin{array}{lcl} \Gamma & ::= & \diamond \mid \Gamma, x : A \\ A, B, C & ::= & \Pi x{:}A.B \mid \mathsf{Nat} \mid \mathsf{U} \mid \mathsf{T}\, M \\ M, N, P & ::= & x \mid \lambda x.M \mid MN \mid \mathsf{ze} \mid \mathsf{su}\, M \mid \\ & & \mathsf{Nrec}(x.A, M^z, x\, p.M^s, N) \mid \mathsf{nat} \mid \pi x{:}M.N \end{array}$$

We will write $A \to B$ for the type $\Pi x{:}A.B$ when $x$ does not appear free in $B$, and similarly write $M \to N$ for the term $\pi x{:}M.N$ when $x$ does not appear free in $N$. Capture avoiding substitution of terms for variables in pre-syntax types ($A[N/x]$) and terms ($M[N/x]$) is defined in the usual way. In the term $\mathsf{Nrec}(x.A, M^z, x\, p.M^s, N)$, the variable $x$ is considered bound in $A$, and the variables $x$ and $p$ are considered bound in $M^s$.

The well-formed types and well-typed terms are defined using a collection of five mutually inductively defined judgements. The five different judgements and their intuitive meanings are given in Figure 2. The first three judgements define subsets of the raw syntax that are to be considered "well-formed" under some assumptions. The remaining two judgements define when two types or terms are considered as equal for the purposes of the theory. The rules generating the judgements are given in Figure 3 and type rules for type equality judgements are given in Figure 4. The rules for term equality judgements, that is $\beta$- and $\eta$-equality for $\Pi$-types and $\beta$-equality for $\mathsf{Nat}$ are displayed in Figure 4. The type and term equality judgements are also understood to include the reflexivity, symmetry, transitivity and congruence rules. Note that, due to the type former $\mathsf{T}$, the congruence rules make type equality depend on term equality. Further discussion about these rules, and close relatives of them, can be found in Hofmann's survey of the syntax and semantics of dependent type theories [15].

***Impredicativity*** The additional rules for considering an impredicative universe are given in Figure 5. These rules replace the rules U-$\pi$ in Figure 3 and $\beta$-U-$\pi$ in Figure 4 describing the U-former $\pi x{:}M.N$. Impredicativity allows the construction of types in $\mathsf{U}$ (i.e., of small types) by quantification over some large type $A$, which may, in fact, be $\mathsf{U}$ itself. We can therefore construct a universe $\mathsf{U}$ — for example, such that $\pi a{:}\mathsf{U}.\ a \to a : \mathsf{U}$ — that is not permitted in the predicative theory. When $\mathsf{U}$ is impredicative, our type theory is equivalent to a variant of Coquand and Huet's Calculus of Constructions [10].

### 3.2 Categories with Families

The syntax of Martin-Löf Type Theory is a complex system of mutually inductive definitions. The mutual dependencies between well-formed types, equality, and well-typed terms severely complicate directly defining and proving sound a semantics for type theory. We address this issue by formulating our reflexive graph model

**Context formation** ($\Gamma$ ctxt)

$$\frac{}{\diamond\ \text{ctxt}}\ (\textsc{Emp}) \qquad \frac{\Gamma\ \text{ctxt} \qquad \Gamma \vdash A\ \text{type}}{\Gamma, x : A\ \text{ctxt}}\ (\textsc{Ext})$$

**Type Formers** ($\Gamma \vdash A$ type)

$$\frac{\Gamma \vdash A\ \text{type} \qquad \Gamma, x : A \vdash B\ \text{type}}{\Gamma \vdash \Pi x{:}A.\ B\ \text{type}}\ (\textsc{Ty-}\Pi)$$

$$\frac{}{\Gamma \vdash \mathsf{Nat}\ \text{type}}\ (\textsc{Ty-Nat}) \qquad \frac{}{\Gamma \vdash \mathsf{U}\ \text{type}}\ (\textsc{Ty-U})$$

$$\frac{\Gamma \vdash M : \mathsf{U}}{\Gamma \vdash \mathsf{T}M\ \text{type}}\ (\textsc{Ty-T})$$

**Typing Rules** ($\Gamma \vdash M : A$)

$$\frac{\Gamma, x : A, \Gamma'\ \text{ctxt}}{\Gamma, x : A, \Gamma' \vdash x : A}\ (\textsc{Var})$$

$$\frac{\Gamma \vdash M : A \qquad \Gamma \vdash A = B\ \text{type}}{\Gamma \vdash M : B}\ (\textsc{Conv})$$

$$\frac{\Gamma, x : A \vdash M : B}{\Gamma \vdash \lambda x{:}A.M : \Pi x{:}A.B}\ (\textsc{Lam})$$

$$\frac{\Gamma \vdash M : \Pi x{:}A.B \qquad \Gamma \vdash N : A}{\Gamma \vdash MN : B[N/x]}\ (\textsc{App})$$

$$\frac{}{\Gamma \vdash \mathsf{ze} : \mathsf{Nat}}\ (\textsc{Ze}) \qquad \frac{\Gamma \vdash n : \mathsf{Nat}}{\Gamma \vdash \mathsf{su}\ n : \mathsf{Nat}}\ (\textsc{Su})$$

$$\frac{\begin{array}{c}\Gamma, x : \mathsf{Nat} \vdash A\ \text{type} \\ \Gamma \vdash M^z : A[\mathsf{ze}/x] \\ \Gamma, n : \mathsf{Nat}, p : A[n/x] \vdash M^s : A[\mathsf{su}\ n/x] \\ \Gamma \vdash n : \mathsf{Nat}\end{array}}{\Gamma \vdash \mathsf{Nrec}(x.\ A, M^z, n\, p.\ M^s, n) : A[n/x]}\ (\textsc{Nrec})$$

$$\frac{}{\Gamma \vdash \mathsf{nat} : \mathsf{U}}\ (\textsc{U-nat})$$

$$\frac{\Gamma \vdash M : \mathsf{U} \qquad \Gamma, x : \mathsf{T}M \vdash N : \mathsf{U}}{\Gamma \vdash \pi x{:}M.N : \mathsf{U}}\ (\textsc{U-}\pi)$$

**Figure 3.** Typing Rules of Martin-Löf Type Theory with Universe

$$\frac{\Gamma \vdash A\ \text{type} \qquad \Gamma, x : A \vdash M : \mathsf{U}}{\Gamma \vdash \pi x{:}A.M : \mathsf{U}}\ (\textsc{U-}\pi')$$

$$\frac{\Gamma \vdash A\ \text{type} \qquad \Gamma, x : A \vdash M : \mathsf{U}}{\Gamma \vdash \mathsf{T}(\pi x{:}A.\ M) = \Pi x{:}A.\ \mathsf{T}M\ \text{type}}\ (\beta\textsc{-U-}\pi')$$

**Figure 5.** Rules for Impredicative Quantification

**Type Equality Rules** ($\Gamma \vdash A = B$ type)

$$\frac{}{\Gamma \vdash \mathsf{T}\ \mathsf{nat} = \mathsf{Nat}\ \text{type}}\ (\beta\text{-U-NAT}) \qquad \frac{\Gamma \vdash M : \mathsf{U} \qquad \Gamma, x : \mathsf{T}M \vdash N : \mathsf{U}}{\Gamma \vdash \mathsf{T}(\pi x{:}M.N) = \Pi x{:}\mathsf{T}M.\ \mathsf{T}N\ \text{type}}\ (\beta\text{-U-}\pi)$$

*elided:* type equality is an equivalence relation and a congruence with respect to all type formers.

**Term Equality Rules** ($\Gamma \vdash M = N : A$)

$$\frac{\Gamma, x : A \vdash M : B \qquad \Gamma \vdash N : A}{\Gamma \vdash (\lambda x{:}A.\ M)N = M[N/x] : B[N/x]}\ (\Pi\text{-}\beta) \qquad \frac{\Gamma \vdash M : \Pi x{:}A.B}{\Gamma \vdash (\lambda x{:}A.\ Mx) = M : \Pi x{:}A.B}\ (\Pi\text{-}\eta)$$

$$\frac{\Gamma, x : \mathsf{Nat} \vdash A\ \text{type} \qquad \Gamma \vdash M^z : A[\mathsf{ze}/x] \qquad \Gamma, n : \mathsf{Nat}, p : A[n/x] \vdash M^s : A[\mathsf{su}\ n/x]}{\Gamma \vdash \mathsf{Nrec}(x.A, M^z, n\, p.M^s, \mathsf{ze}) = M^z : A[\mathsf{ze}/x]}\ (\beta\text{-ZE})$$

$$\frac{\Gamma, x : \mathsf{Nat} \vdash A\ \text{type} \qquad \Gamma \vdash M^z : A[\mathsf{ze}/x] \qquad \Gamma, n : \mathsf{Nat}, p : A[n/x] \vdash M^s : A[\mathsf{su}\ n/x] \qquad \Gamma \vdash n : \mathsf{Nat}}{\Gamma \vdash \begin{array}{l}\mathsf{Nrec}(x.\ A, M^z, n\, p.\ M^s, \mathsf{su}\ n) \\ \quad = M^s[n/n, \mathsf{Nrec}(x.A, M^z, n\, p.M^s, n)/p]\end{array} : P[\mathsf{su}\ n/x]}\ (\beta\text{-SU})$$

*elided:* term equality is an equivalence relation and a congruence with respect to all term formers.

**Figure 4.** Type and Term Equality Judgements

in terms of *categories with families* (CwFs), a notion originally due to Dybjer [12]. CwFs form a sound and complete class of categorical models of many variants of dependent type theory, as explained by Hofmann [15]. Therefore, by demonstrating that the category of reflexive graphs forms a CwF with the appropriate additional structure needed for the type formers we have chosen, we are guaranteed to have soundly modelled the syntax of the type theory presented in the previous section.

We present the definition of a CwF (Definition 3), and then present the extra structure required for dependent products (Definition 4), a natural number type (Definition 5), and a universe of small types (Definition 6). We loosely follow Hofmann's presentation [15], except that we specialise for our particular type theory.

***The Basic Structure*** CwFs provide enough structure to interpret the contexts, types, and terms of a type theory, along with simultaneous substitutions and their action on types and terms. Judgemental equality on types and terms is modelled directly as equality in the model; in particular, there is no semantic structure corresponding to the rule CONV. Here, we define comprehension in terms of a bijection between sets of morphisms and semantic terms. This is equivalent to Hofmann's definition of comprehension in terms of projections and weakening. We treat projection and weakening as derived structure, as described after the following definition.

**Definition 3.** *A* Category with Families *(CwF) consists of:*

1. *A category $\mathcal{C}$, whose objects are intended as the semantic interpretations of contexts and whose morphisms are intended as the interpretations of simultaneous substitutions;*
2. *For each $\Gamma \in \mathrm{Ob}(\mathcal{C})$, a collection $\mathrm{Ty}(\Gamma)$ of* semantic types*;*
3. *For each $\Gamma \in \mathrm{Ob}(\mathcal{C})$ and semantic type $A \in \mathrm{Ty}(\Gamma)$, a collection $\mathrm{Tm}(\Gamma, A)$ of* semantic terms*;*
4. *For every morphism $f : \Gamma \to \Delta$ in $\mathcal{C}$, a function*
$$-\{f\} : \mathrm{Ty}(\Delta) \to \mathrm{Ty}(\Gamma)$$
*interpreting type substitution, and for every $A \in \mathrm{Ty}(\Delta)$, a function*
$$-\{f\} : \mathrm{Tm}(\Delta, A) \to \mathrm{Tm}(\Gamma, A\{f\})$$
*interpreting term substitution, such that the following hold:*
$$A\{\mathrm{id}_\Gamma\} = A \qquad (1)$$
$$A\{f\}\{g\} = A\{f \circ g\} \qquad (2)$$
$$M\{\mathrm{id}_\Gamma\} = M \qquad (3)$$
$$M\{f\}\{g\} = M\{f \circ g\} \qquad (4)$$
*Equations 3 and 4 are well-typed by virtue of Equations 1 and 2, respectively.*
5. *A chosen terminal object 1 in $\mathcal{C}$, interpreting the empty context;*
6. *For each $\Gamma \in \mathrm{Ob}(\mathcal{C})$ and $A \in \mathrm{Ty}(\Gamma)$ an object $\Gamma.A \in \mathrm{Ob}(\mathcal{C})$ (called the* comprehension of *$A$) such that there is a bijection*
$$\mathcal{C}(\Delta, \Gamma.A) \cong \{(f, M) \mid f : \Delta \to \Gamma, M \in \mathrm{Tm}(\Delta, A\{f\})\}$$
*that is natural in $\Delta$.*

An alternative presentation of points (1) to (4) of Definition 3 is as a functor $\mathcal{C}^{\mathrm{op}} \to \mathrm{Fam(SET)}$, where SET is the category of large sets (which includes the category Set as an object).

Given $f : \Delta \to \Gamma$ and $M \in \mathrm{Tm}(\Delta, A\{f\})$, we write $\langle f, M\rangle$ for the associated morphism $\Delta \to \Gamma.A$ in $\mathcal{C}$ given by the isomorphism in point (6) of Definition 3. Conversely, given a morphism $f : \Delta \to \Gamma.A$ in $\mathcal{C}$, we write $f^{\#1} : \Delta \to \Gamma$ and $f^{\#2} \in \mathrm{Tm}(\Delta, A\{f^{\#1}\})$ for the associated morphism and semantic term. The following definitions derive projection and weakening structure from Definition 3, and also define the semantic counterpart of a simultaneous substitution of a term for a variable.

1. For any $\Gamma \in \mathrm{Ob}(\mathcal{C})$ and $A \in \mathrm{Ty}(\Gamma)$, the *first projection* morphism $\mathrm{p}^\Gamma_A : \Gamma.A \to \Gamma$ is defined as $p^\Gamma_A = \mathrm{id}^{\#1}_{\Gamma.A}$. This is used to interpret weakening by discarding a single variable.
2. For any $\Gamma \in \mathrm{Ob}(\mathcal{C})$ and $A \in \mathrm{Ty}(\Gamma)$, the *second projection* $\mathrm{q}^\Gamma_A \in \mathrm{Tm}(\Gamma.A, A\{p^\Gamma_A\})$ is defined as $q^\Gamma_A = \mathrm{id}^{\#2}_{\Gamma.A}$. This is used to interpret the rule VAR.
3. For any $\Gamma, \Delta \in \mathrm{Ob}(\mathcal{C})$, $A \in \mathrm{Ty}(\Gamma)$ and morphism $f : \Delta \to \Gamma$, the *weakening* of $f$ by $A$, $\mathrm{wk}_A f : \Delta.A\{f\} \to \Gamma.A$ is defined as $\mathrm{wk}_A f = \langle f \circ \mathrm{p}^\Delta_{A\{f\}}, \mathrm{q}^\Delta_{A\{f\}}\rangle$. This is used to lift simultaneous substitutions to work in larger contexts.
4. For any $\Gamma \in \mathrm{Ob}(\mathcal{C})$, $A \in \mathrm{Ty}(\Gamma)$ and $M \in \mathrm{Tm}(\Gamma, A)$, we define the morphism $\overline{M} : \Gamma \to \Gamma.A$ as $\overline{M} = \langle \mathrm{id}_\Gamma, M\rangle$. Mor-

phisms built from semantic terms are used to build simultaneous substitutions that substitute (semantic) terms for variables.

***Dependent Products*** Hofmann's presentation of the structure for interpreting dependent product types in a CwF admits the possibility of not supporting the $\eta$-rule. But since the type theory we consider in this paper does include the $\eta$-rule $\Pi$-$\eta$, we can use the following compact definition to describe the requirements ensuring that a CwF supports dependent products.

**Definition 4.** *A CwF $\mathcal{C}$* supports dependent products *if for all semantic contexts $\Gamma \in \mathrm{Ob}(\mathcal{C})$ and semantic types $A \in \mathrm{Ty}(\Gamma)$ and $B \in \mathrm{Ty}(\Gamma.A)$ there exists a semantic type $\Pi AB \in \mathrm{Ty}(\Gamma)$, natural in $\Gamma$, such that there is a bijection $\Lambda : \mathrm{Tm}(\Gamma.A, B) \cong \mathrm{Tm}(\Gamma, \Pi AB)$, natural in $\Gamma$.*

Definition 4 gives a semantic counterpart of the abstraction rule LAM. We define the following semantic counterpart of the application rule APP. For $\Gamma$, $A$ and $B$ as in Definition 4, and $M \in \mathrm{Tm}(\Gamma, \Pi AB)$ and $N \in \mathrm{Tm}(\Gamma, A)$, we define $\mathrm{App}^{\Gamma}_{A,B}(M, N) \in \mathrm{Tm}(\Gamma, B\{\overline{N}\})$ by $\mathrm{App}^{\Gamma}_{A,B} = (\Lambda^{-1}(M))\{\overline{N}\}$.

***The Natural Number Type*** The structure required to model the type of natural numbers directly follows the syntactic structure we presented in Section 3, modulo the more explicit presentation of substitution inherent in the CwF formalism. The following definition gives semantic counterparts to the rules ZE, SU, and NREC.

**Definition 5.** *A CwF $\mathcal{C}$* supports natural numbers *if, for all $\Gamma \in \mathrm{Ob}(\mathcal{C})$, there is a semantic type $Nat^{\Gamma} \in \mathrm{Ty}(\Gamma)$ (we usually omit the superscript $\Gamma$), semantic terms $zero \in \mathrm{Tm}(\Gamma, Nat)$ and $succ \in \mathrm{Tm}(\Gamma.Nat, Nat)$, and, for each $A \in \mathrm{Ty}(\Gamma.Nat)$, a function on semantic terms $Nrec_A$ of type $\mathrm{Tm}(\Gamma, A\{\overline{zero}\}) \times \mathrm{Tm}(\Gamma.Nat.A, A\{\mathrm{wk}_{Nat}\, \mathrm{p}^{\Gamma}_{Nat} \circ \overline{succ} \circ \mathrm{p}^{\Gamma.Nat}_{A}\}) \to \mathrm{Tm}(\Gamma.Nat, A)$ such that Nat, zero, succ and Nrec are natural in $\Gamma$, and the following two equations hold:*

$$Nrec_A(M^z, M^s)\{\overline{zero}\} = M^z \tag{5}$$

$$Nrec_A(M^z, M^s)\{\mathrm{wk}_{Nat}\, \mathrm{p}^{\Gamma}_{Nat} \circ \overline{succ}\} = M^s\{\overline{Nrec_A(M^z, M^s)}\} \tag{6}$$

***Universe*** The CwF interpretation of the universe U is just the translation of the syntactic structure into the CwF framework. The following definitions are semantic counterparts to U-NAT, U-$\pi$, and U-$\pi$'. We treat the predicative and impredicative cases separately.

**Definition 6.** *A CwF $\mathcal{C}$* supports a predicative universe closed under natural numbers and dependent product *if (a) for all $\Gamma \in \mathrm{Ob}(\mathcal{C})$ there exist semantic types $U \in \mathrm{Ty}(\Gamma)$ and $T \in \mathrm{Ty}(\Gamma.U)$, both natural in $\Gamma$; (b) there exists a semantic term $nat \in \mathrm{Tm}(\Gamma, U)$, natural in $\Gamma$ such that $T\{\overline{nat}\} = Nat$; and (c) for all $M \in \mathrm{Tm}(\Gamma, U)$ and $N \in \mathrm{Tm}(\Gamma.T\{\overline{M}\}, U)$ there exists a semantic term $\pi MN \in \mathrm{Tm}(\Gamma, U)$, natural in $\Gamma$; such that $T\{\overline{\pi MN}\} = \Pi(T\{\overline{M}\})(T\{\overline{N}\})$.*

**Definition 7.** *A CwF $\mathcal{C}$* supports an impredicative universe closed under natural numbers and dependent product *if there are $U$, $T$, and $nat$ as in Definition 6, and for all $A \in \mathrm{Ty}(\Gamma)$ and $M \in \mathrm{Tm}(\Gamma.A, U)$ there exists a semantic term $\pi AM \in \mathrm{Tm}(\Gamma, U)$, natural in $\Gamma$, such that: $T\{\overline{\pi AM}\} = \Pi A(T\{\overline{M}\})$.*

# 4. The Reflexive Graph Model of Type Theory

Constructing our reflexive graph model of type theory is now a matter of showing that the category of reflexive graphs from Section 2 has the structure of a category with families. The essential tasks are to (a) establish what a family of reflexive graphs over a reflexive graph is, in order to model types (Sections 4.1 and 4.2); and (b) to determine the interpretation of the universe type U (Section 4.3). Once we have done the former, the interpretations of $\Pi$-types and the natural number type are determined up to isomorphism (Section 4.4). As an intuitive guide for determining the correct definition of a family of reflexive graphs, we use standard results about fibrational models of dependent types. Knowledge of fibrations is not required to understand our final definitions.

## 4.1 Families of Reflexive Graphs

A standard way to model the dependency of types on terms is to use the *families fibration* $p : \mathrm{Fam(Set)} \to \mathrm{Set}$, where the category $\mathrm{Fam(Set)}$ has as objects pairs $(X, P)$, where $X \in \mathrm{Set}$ and $P : X \to \mathrm{Set}$, and the functor $p$ projects out the first element. The basic idea of the families fibration is that a pair $(X, P)$ represents a context $X$ and a collection $P$ of types indexed by the elements of $X$. However, in a reflexive graph model of parametricity we want to index not by sets, but by reflexive graphs in $\mathrm{Set}^{\mathrm{RG}}$. Fortunately, there is a natural way to do this. By standard results about fibrations (see Exercise 1.8.8 in Jacobs [17]), the functor $p^{\mathrm{RG}} : \mathrm{Fam(Set)}^{\mathrm{RG}} \to \mathrm{Set}^{\mathrm{RG}}$, defined as $p^{\mathrm{RG}}(F) = p \circ F$, is also a fibration. This hints that objects of $\mathrm{Fam(Set)}^{\mathrm{RG}}$ are the natural interpretations of dependent types in a reflexive graph model of parametricity, and that the functor $p^{\mathrm{RG}}$ should send each such object to the reflexive graph interpreting the context over which the type that object interprets is indexed.

Unpacking the definition of $\mathrm{Fam(Set)}^{\mathrm{RG}}$, we see that an object of $\mathrm{Fam(Set)}^{\mathrm{RG}}$ is equivalent to a pair $(\Gamma, A)$ of a reflexive graph $\Gamma$, together with a family $A$ of reflexive graphs that is *over* $\Gamma$, in the following sense:

**Definition 8.** *Let $\Gamma$ be a reflexive graph. A* family of reflexive graphs over $\Gamma$ *is a 5-tuple $A = (A_O, A_R, A_{refl}, A_{src}, A_{tgt})$, where:*

$$\begin{aligned}
A_O &: \Gamma_O \to \mathrm{Set}\\
A_R &: \Gamma_R \to \mathrm{Set}\\
A_{refl} &: \forall \gamma_o \in \Gamma_O.\ A_O(\gamma_o) \to A_R(\Gamma_{refl}(\gamma_o))\\
A_{src} &: \forall \gamma_r \in \Gamma_R.\ A_R(\gamma_r) \to A_O(\Gamma_{src}(\gamma_r))\\
A_{tgt} &: \forall \gamma_r \in \Gamma_R.\ A_R(\gamma_r) \to A_O(\Gamma_{tgt}(\gamma_r))
\end{aligned}$$

*such that the following equations hold:*

$$\forall \gamma_o \in \Gamma_O.\ A_{src}(\Gamma_{refl}(\gamma_o)) \circ A_{refl}(\gamma_o) = \mathrm{id} \tag{7}$$

$$\forall \gamma_o \in \Gamma_O.\ A_{tgt}(\Gamma_{refl}(\gamma_o)) \circ A_{refl}(\gamma_o) = \mathrm{id} \tag{8}$$

Morphisms between pairs of families of reflexive graphs over the same reflexive graph are derived from the morphisms of $\mathrm{Fam(Set)}^{\mathrm{RG}}$. This yields the following definition:

**Definition 9.** *Let $\Gamma$ be a reflexive graph and let $A$ and $B$ be families of reflexive graphs over $\Gamma$. A* morphism $M$ from $A$ to $B$ *consists of a pair of functions*

$$\begin{aligned}
M_o &: \forall \gamma_o \in \Gamma_O.\ A_O(\gamma_o) \to B_O(\gamma_o)\\
M_r &: \forall \gamma_r \in \Gamma_R.\ A_R(\gamma_r) \to B_R(\gamma_r)
\end{aligned}$$

*such that*

$$\begin{aligned}
&\forall \gamma_o \in \Gamma_o, a_o \in A_O(\gamma_o).\\
&\qquad B_{refl}(\gamma_o)(M_o\ \gamma_o\ a_o) = M_r\ (\Gamma_{refl}(\gamma_o))\ (A_{refl}(\gamma_o)(a_o))\\
&\forall \gamma_r \in \Gamma_R, a_r \in A_R(\gamma_r).\\
&\qquad B_{src}(\gamma_r)(M_r\ \gamma_r\ a_r) = M_o\ (\Gamma_{src}(\gamma_r))\ (A_{src}(\gamma_r)(a_r))\\
&\forall \gamma_r \in \Gamma_R, a_r \in A_R(\gamma_r).\\
&\qquad B_{tgt}(\gamma_r)(M_r\ \gamma_r\ a_r) = M_o\ (\Gamma_{tgt}(\gamma_r))\ (A_{tgt}(\gamma_r)(a_r))
\end{aligned}$$

Families of reflexive graphs over a reflexive graph $\Gamma$ and morphisms between them form a category $\mathrm{RG\text{-}Fam}(\Gamma)$.

## 4.2 Reflexive Graphs as a Category with Families

We define a CwF structure on the category of reflexive graphs as follows. For each reflexive graph $\Gamma$, we define the collection of *semantic types* $\mathrm{Ty}(\Gamma)$ to be the collection of families of reflexive graphs over $\Gamma$ as defined in Definition 8. Given a reflexive graph $\Gamma$ and a family $A$ of reflexive graphs over $\Gamma$, we define the collection of *semantic terms* $\mathrm{Tm}(\Gamma, A)$ to be the collection of morphisms from the terminal family $(\lambda\gamma_o \in \Gamma_O.*, \lambda\gamma_r \in \Gamma_R.*, \lambda\gamma_o \in \Gamma_O.\mathrm{id}_*, \lambda\gamma_r \in \Gamma_R.\mathrm{id}_*, \lambda\gamma_r \in \Gamma_R.\mathrm{id}_*)$ of reflexive graphs over $\Gamma$ to $A$, as in Definition 9. Spelling this definition out, suppressing the contribution of the terminal family, a semantic term $M \in \mathrm{Tm}(\Gamma, A)$ is defined as a pair of functions $(M_o, M_r)$:

$$M_o : \forall\gamma_o \in \Gamma_O.\ A_O(\gamma_o) \qquad M_r : \forall\gamma_r \in \Gamma_R.\ A_R(\gamma_r)$$

such that

$$\forall\gamma_o \in \Gamma_O.\ A_{\mathit{refl}}(\gamma_o)(M_o(\gamma_o)) = M_r(\Gamma_{\mathit{refl}}(\gamma_o)) \quad (9)$$

$$\forall\gamma_r \in \Gamma_R.\ A_{\mathit{src}}(\gamma_r)(M_r(\gamma_r)) = M_o(\Gamma_{\mathit{src}}(\gamma_r)) \quad (10)$$

$$\forall\gamma_r \in \Gamma_R.\ A_{\mathit{tgt}}(\gamma_r)(M_r(\gamma_r)) = M_o(\Gamma_{\mathit{tgt}}(\gamma_r)) \quad (11)$$

For each reflexive graph morphism $f : \Delta \to \Gamma$, substitution $A\{f\}$ in semantic types $A$ and substitution $M\{f\}$ in semantic terms are both defined by pre-composition. Comprehension structure is given by the following definition, which can be seen as the dependent version of the cartesian product of reflexive graphs used in Section 2.2 to interpret the non-dependent kinding and typing contexts of System F.

**Definition 10.** *Let $\Gamma$ be a reflexive graph, and let $A \in \mathrm{Ty}(\Gamma)$ be a semantic type. Define the* comprehension $\Gamma.A$ *as the following reflexive graph:*

$$\begin{array}{ll} (\Gamma.A)_O & = \{(\gamma_o, a_o) \mid \gamma_o \in \Gamma_O, a_o \in A_O(\gamma_o)\} \\ (\Gamma.A)_R & = \{(\gamma_r, a_r) \mid \gamma_r \in \Gamma_R, a_r \in A_R(\gamma_r)\} \\ (\Gamma.A)_{\mathit{refl}}(\gamma_o, a_o) & = (\Gamma_{\mathit{refl}}(\gamma_o), A_{\mathit{refl}}(\gamma_o)(a_o)) \\ (\Gamma.A)_{\mathit{src}}(\gamma_r, a_r) & = (\Gamma_{\mathit{src}}(\gamma_r), A_{\mathit{src}}(\gamma_r)(a_r)) \\ (\Gamma.A)_{\mathit{tgt}}(\gamma_r, a_r) & = (\Gamma_{\mathit{tgt}}(\gamma_r), A_{\mathit{tgt}}(\gamma_r)(a_r)) \end{array}$$

*Given $f : \Delta \to \Gamma$ and $M \in \mathrm{Tm}(\Delta, A\{f\})$, define $\langle f, M\rangle : \Delta \to \Gamma.A$ as follows:*

$$\langle f, M\rangle_o(\delta_o) = (f_o(\delta_o), M_o(f_o(\delta_o)))$$
$$\langle f, M\rangle_r(\delta_r) = (f_r(\delta_r), M_r(f_r(\delta_r)))$$

*Given $f : \Delta \to \Gamma.A$, define $f^{\#1} : \Delta \to \Gamma$ and $f^{\#2} \in \mathrm{Tm}(\Delta, A\{f^{\#1}\})$ as follows:*

$$(f^{\#1})_o(\delta_o) = \text{let } (\gamma_o, a_o) = f_o(\delta_o) \text{ in } \gamma_o$$
$$(f^{\#1})_r(\delta_r) = \text{let } (\gamma_r, a_r) = f_r(\delta_r) \text{ in } \gamma_r$$
$$(f^{\#2})_o(\delta_o) = \text{let } (\gamma_o, a_o) = f_o(\delta_o) \text{ in } a_o$$
$$(f^{\#2})_r(\delta_r) = \text{let } (\gamma_r, a_r) = f_r(\delta_r) \text{ in } a_r$$

The next proposition follows by mechanical checking of the requirements in Definition 3.

**Proposition 1.** *The category of reflexive graphs has the structure of a CwF, where the collection of semantic types $\mathrm{Ty}(\Gamma)$ is the collection of families of reflexive graphs over $\Gamma$, and the collection of semantic terms $\mathrm{Tm}(\Gamma, A)$ is the collection of morphisms from the terminal family of reflexive graphs over $\Gamma$ to $A$.*

### 4.3 Interpreting the Universe of Small Types

By Definition 6, the basic structure we require to interpret the type-theoretic universe comprises semantic types $U \in \mathrm{Ty}(\Gamma)$ and $T \in \mathrm{Ty}(\Gamma.U)$. So $T$ takes elements of $U$ to semantic types. But which semantic types (i.e., families of reflexive graphs) ought to be elements of $U$? Unlike in the case of $\Pi$-types and the natural number type, where we are constrained in our interpretation up to isomorphism by the equations of the calculus (Section 4.4), we are free to select any collection of semantic types, as long as it contains the natural number type and is closed under $\Pi$-types.

Since the reflexive graph model is a covariant presheaf model over the reflexive graph category RG (Section 2.2), a plausible choice would be to use Hofmann and Streicher's general definition of the interpretation of a type-theoretic universe in presheaf models given some set-theoretic universe $\mathcal{U}$ [16]. Spelling out their construction in the setting of reflexive graphs yields:

$$\begin{array}{l} U^{\mathrm{HS}}_O(\gamma_o) = \text{the set of small reflexive graphs} \\ U^{\mathrm{HS}}_R(\gamma_r) = \{(A, B, R \in \mathcal{U}, R_{\mathit{src}} : R \to A_O, R_{\mathrm{tgt}} : R \to B_O) \mid \\ \qquad\qquad A, B \text{ are small reflexive graphs}\} \end{array}$$

Thus, the objects of $U^{\mathrm{HS}}$ are small reflexive graphs, and the relations are spans between small reflexive graphs. As Hofmann and Streicher show, this definition exactly captures the *small* families of reflexive graphs: families of reflexive graphs where the sets of objects and sets of relations are always taken from the universe $\mathcal{U}$. Put mathematically, if we write RG-Fam$_s(\Gamma)$ for the subcategory of small families of reflexive graphs over some reflexive graph $\Gamma$, then we have $\mathrm{Tm}(\Gamma, U^{\mathrm{HS}}) \cong \mathrm{Ob}(\text{RG-Fam}_s(\Gamma))$.

However, despite precisely capturing smallness, Hofmann and Streicher's universe is too big for our purposes. We want to lift the consequences of relational parametricity from System F to the setting of dependent types. To do this, we need to accurately replicate the salient features of the kind $*$ of System F types in our interpretation of the type-theoretic universe U.

Recall the definition of the reflexive graph $*$ representing the System F kind of types from Example 1. This reflexive graph has the following three properties, only the first of which is captured by the Hofmann-Streicher universe. Firstly, the sets of objects and relations are *small*, in the sense of belonging to the universe $\mathcal{U}$ of small sets. Secondly, the reflexive structure of $*$ indicates that the equality relation is distinguished amongst all possible binary relations on sets; this is the essential identity extension property. As we saw in Example 2, reflexive graphs in which only equal objects are related can be modelled by taking the sets of objects and relations to be equal. Thirdly, the relations between sets are *proof-irrelevant*: since a relation $R$ from $X$ to $Y$ is a subset of $X \times Y$, and since each pair $(x, y)$ is either in the subset or not, there is at most one way that $x$ and $y$ can be related. Proof-irrelevance is essential for reasoning using a relationally parametric model: we use the relational level to reason about equality at the object level, but we have nothing to reason about the relational level with, so proof-irrelevance is needed to make sure that equality at this level is trivial. This insight is formalised in Lemma 2 below, and heavily used in Section 5. We note in passing that thinking along these lines motivates the formulation of $\infty$-reflexive graphs (a.k.a., reflexive globular sets), where there is always another level to reason about the one below.

The three properties just discussed motivate this definition:

**Definition 11.** *Let $\Gamma$ be a reflexive graph. A family $A$ of reflexive graphs over $\Gamma$ is:*

1. small *if, for all $\gamma_o \in \Gamma_O$, $A_O(\gamma_o) \in \mathcal{U}$ and for all $\gamma_r \in \Gamma_R$, $A_R(\gamma_r) \in \mathcal{U}$;*
2. discrete *if, for all $\gamma_o \in \Gamma_O$, the reflexive graph on the left of the following diagram is isomorphic to a reflexive graph generated by a set (on the right of the diagram):*

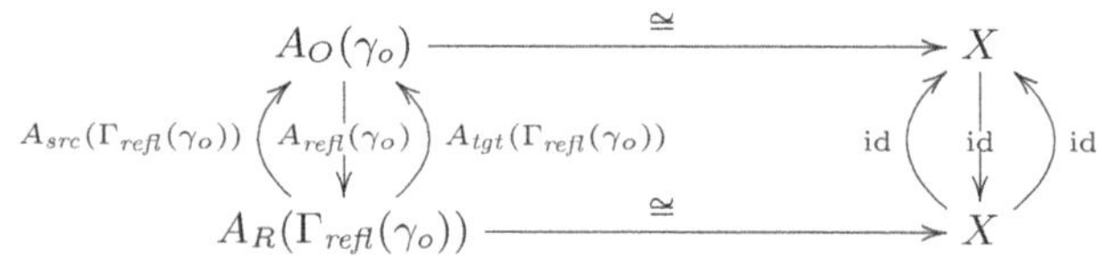


3. proof-irrelevant *if, for all $\gamma_r \in \Gamma_R$, $\langle A_{\mathit{src}}(\gamma_r), A_{\mathit{tgt}}(\gamma_r)\rangle : A_R(\gamma_r) \to A_O(\Gamma_{\mathit{src}}(\gamma_r)) \times A_O(\Gamma_{\mathit{tgt}}(\gamma_r))$ is injective.*

*We write RG-Fam$_{\mathrm{sdpi}}(\Gamma)$ for the full subcategory of RG-Fam$(\Gamma)$ consisting of small, discrete, proof-irrelevant reflexive graphs.*

In parts (2) and (3) of this definition, we have chosen to enforce the conditions of discreteness and proof-irrelevance only up to isomorphism. This laxness will be important when showing that the interpretation of the type-theoretic universe of small types is closed under dependent products in Section 4.4. Definition 11 is justified by the following representation result:

**Proposition 2.** *Let* $\Gamma$ *be a reflexive graph. There is an equivalence of categories:* $\mathrm{Set}^{\mathrm{RG}}(\Gamma, *) \simeq \text{RG-Fam}_{\mathrm{sdpi}}(\Gamma)$.

Proposition 2 shows that the reflexive graph model of dependent types can internally represent the semantic System F types and terms, up to isomorphism. This suggests that we can use the reflexive graph $*$ as the basis of our interpretation of U. However, the equivalence of categories in Proposition 2 is too weak to soundly model the type *equalities* we required for the universe decoder type operator T in Figure 4 (specifically, the semantic counterparts of these equalities in Definitions 6 and 7). We now remedy this by refining the definition of our reflexive graph $*$ to provide an interpretation for U with the required properties.

***A Small, Discrete, Proof Irrelevant Universe*** For any reflexive graph $\Gamma$ we define semantic types $U \in \mathrm{Ty}(\Gamma)$ and $T \in \mathrm{Ty}(\Gamma.U)$:

$$\begin{aligned} U_O(\gamma_o) &= \text{the set of small discrete reflexive graphs} \\ U_R(\gamma_r) &= \{(A, B, R \in \mathcal{U}, R_{src} : R \to A_O, R_{tgt} : R \to B_O \mid \\ &\qquad A, B \text{ are small discrete reflexive graphs}, \\ &\qquad \langle R_{src}, R_{tgt}\rangle : R \to A_O \times B_O \text{ is injective}\} \end{aligned}$$

$$\begin{aligned} U_{refl}(\gamma_o)(A) &= (A, A, A_R, A_{src}, A_{tgt}) \\ U_{src}(\gamma_r)(A, B, R, R_{src}, R_{tgt}) &= A \\ U_{tgt}(\gamma_r)(A, B, R, R_{src}, R_{tgt}) &= B \end{aligned}$$

If $A$ is a discrete reflexive graph, then $\langle A_{src}, A_{tgt}\rangle : A_R \to A_O \times A_O$ is necessarily injective, so the definition of $U_{refl}$ makes sense. We define the semantic types $T \in \mathrm{Ty}(\Gamma.U)$ as follows:

$$\begin{aligned} T_O(\gamma_o, A) &= A_O \\ T_R(\gamma_r, (A, B, R, R_{src}, R_{tgt})) &= R \\ T_{refl}(\gamma_o, A) &= A_{refl} \\ T_{src}(\gamma_r, (A, B, R, R_{src}, R_{tgt})) &= R_{src} \\ T_{tgt}(\gamma_r, (A, B, R, R_{src}, R_{tgt})) &= R_{tgt} \end{aligned}$$

The definitions of $U$ and $T$ we have just presented fulfil part (a) of Definition 6. The following lemma states that we have successfully internalised the subcategories $\text{RG-Fam}_{\mathrm{sdpi}}(\Gamma)$.

**Lemma 1.** *For any* $M \in \mathrm{Tm}(\Gamma, U)$, *the family* $T\{\overline{M}\}$ *is small, discrete, and proof-irrelevant and this mapping forms a bijection of sets:* $T\{-\} : \mathrm{Tm}(\Gamma, U) \cong \mathrm{Ob}(\text{RG-Fam}_{\mathrm{sdpi}}(\Gamma))$, *natural in* $\Gamma$.

The fact that this lemma gives us a bijection is useful because it means that to show that the universe $U$ is closed under some semantic type former, we need only show that the semantic type former is closed under the condition of being a small, discrete, and proof-irrelevant family of reflexive graphs. Below, we define the small counterparts of dependent products and the natural number type – parts (b) and (c) of Definition 6 – using the right-to-left direction of this bijection to obtain a representation in $U$ of a small, discrete, proof-irrelevant family, which we write as $repr : \mathrm{Ob}(\text{RG-Fam}_{\mathrm{sdpi}}(\Gamma)) \to \mathrm{Tm}(\Gamma, U)$.

We note the following crucial property of proof-irrelevant families. By proof-irrelevance, there is exactly one way that any two object-level elements can be related. Therefore, for any two terms of proof-irrelevant type, if the object-level interpretations are equal then so are the relation-level interpretations. This lemma plays an important role in showing that the interpretation of the type-theoretic universe we have defined is closed under dependent products (Lemma 3, below), and also in the applications of relational parametricity that we describe in Section 5.

**Lemma 2.** *Let* $\Gamma$ *be a reflexive graph and let* $A \in \mathrm{Ty}(\Gamma)$ *be a proof-irrelevant family of reflexive graphs. For any pair of semantic terms* $M, N \in \mathrm{Tm}(\Gamma, A)$, $M_o = N_o$ *implies* $M_r = N_r$.

*Proof.* Since $M$ and $N$ are semantic terms, and $M_o = N_o$, we have, for all $\gamma_r \in \Gamma_R$, $A_{src}(\gamma_r)(M_r(\gamma_r)) = M_o(\Gamma_{src}(\gamma_r)) = N_o(\Gamma_{src}(\gamma_r)) = A_{src}(\gamma_r)(N_r(\gamma_r))$. Similarly, we have $A_{tgt}(\gamma_r)(M_r(\gamma_r)) = A_{tgt}(\gamma_r)(N_r(\gamma_r))$, for all $\gamma_r \in \Gamma_R$. By proof-irrelevance of $A$, the function $\langle A_{src}(\gamma_r), A_{tgt}(\gamma_r)\rangle$ formed by pairing is injective, hence $M_r = N_r$. □

### 4.4 Interpreting Dependent Products and Natural Numbers

To complete our reflexive graph model of type theory, it remains to provide the interpretations of Π-types and the natural number type. Due to the $\beta\eta$-rules we have chosen for Π-types we actually have no choice, up to isomorphism, in how to interpret these types. We spell out the details here to demonstrate the way that type constructors are interpreted in the reflexive graph model.

***Dependent Products*** The interpretation of Π-types directly generalises the interpretation of System F ∀-types that we presented in Section 2.1, the additional complication coming from the fact that we need to consider relation *transformers* rather than just relation preservation (see also Atkey's relationally parametric model of System F$\omega$ [2], which also deals with relation transformers). In the interpretation of Π-types, the object level consists of a pair of an object-level function and a relation-level function, connected by three coherence axioms, similar to the definition of semantic terms in Section 4.2. The relation level consists of a pair of object-level interpretations and a relation transformer relating them. Written out in full, the definition is a little daunting, remember that, up to isomorphism, we are essentially forced into this definition.

**Definition 12.** *Let* $\Gamma$ *be a reflexive graph, and* $A \in \mathrm{Ty}(\Gamma)$ *and* $B \in \mathrm{Ty}(\Gamma.A)$ *be semantic types in the reflexive graph CwF. Define the semantic type* $\Pi AB \in \mathrm{Ty}(\Gamma)$ *as follows:*

$$\begin{aligned} &(\Pi AB)_O(\gamma_o) = \\ &\quad \{\, (f_o, f_r) \mid \\ &\qquad f_o : \forall a_o \in A_O(\gamma_o).\ B_O(\gamma_o, a_o), \\ &\qquad f_r : \forall a_r \in A_R(\Gamma_{refl}(\gamma_o)).\ B_R(\Gamma_{refl}(\gamma_o), a_r), \\ &\qquad \forall a_r \in A_R(\Gamma_{refl}(\gamma_o)).\ B_{src}(\Gamma_{refl}(\gamma_o), a_r)(f_r\ a_r) = \\ &\qquad\qquad f_o(A_{src}(\Gamma_{refl}(\gamma_o))(a_r)), \\ &\qquad \forall a_r \in A_R(\Gamma_{refl}(\gamma_o)).\ B_{tgt}(\Gamma_{refl}(\gamma_o), a_r)(f_r\ a_r) = \\ &\qquad\qquad f_o(A_{tgt}(\Gamma_{refl}(\gamma_o))(a_r)), \\ &\qquad \forall a_o \in A_O(\gamma_o).\ B_{refl}(\gamma_o, a_o)(f_o\ a_o) = f_r(A_{refl}(\gamma_o)(a_o)) \,\} \end{aligned}$$

$$\begin{aligned} &(\Pi AB)_R(\gamma_r) = \\ &\quad \{\, ((f_o^{src}, f_r^{src}), (f_o^{tgt}, f_r^{tgt}), r) \mid \\ &\qquad (f_o^{src}, f_r^{src}) \in (\Pi AB)_O(\Gamma_{src}(\gamma_r)), \\ &\qquad (f_o^{tgt}, f_r^{tgt}) \in (\Pi AB)_O(\Gamma_{tgt}(\gamma_r)), \\ &\qquad r : \forall a_r \in A_R(\gamma_r).\ B_R(\gamma_r, a_r), \\ &\qquad \forall a_r \in A_R(\gamma_r).\ B_{src}(\gamma_r, a_r)(r\ a_r) = f_o^{src}(A_{src}(\gamma_r)(a_r)), \\ &\qquad \forall a_r \in A_R(\gamma_r).\ B_{tgt}(\gamma_r, a_r)(r\ a_r) = f_o^{tgt}(A_{tgt}(\gamma_r)(a_r)) \,\} \end{aligned}$$

$$\begin{aligned} (\Pi AB)_{refl}(\gamma_o)(f_o, f_r) &= ((f_o, f_r), (f_o, f_r), f_r) \\ (\Pi AB)_{src}(\gamma_r)(f^{src}, f^{tgt}, r) &= f^{src} \\ (\Pi AB)_{tgt}(\gamma_r)(f^{src}, f^{tgt}, r) &= f^{tgt} \end{aligned}$$

*Given a semantic term* $M \in \mathrm{Tm}(\Gamma.A, B)$, *we define* $(\Lambda M) \in \mathrm{Tm}(\Gamma, \Pi AB)$ *as follows:*

$$\begin{aligned} &(\Lambda M)_o(\gamma_o) = (\lambda a_o.\ M_o(\gamma_o, a_o), \lambda a_r.\ M_r(\Gamma_{refl}(\gamma_o), a_r)) \\ &(\Lambda M)_r(\gamma_r) = \\ &\qquad ((\Lambda M)_o(\Gamma_{src}(\gamma_r)), (\Lambda M)_o(\Gamma_{tgt}(\gamma_r)), \lambda a_r.\ M_r(\gamma_r, a_r)) \end{aligned}$$

*and, conversely, given* $N \in \mathrm{Tm}(\Gamma, \Pi AB)$ *, we define* $(\Lambda^{-1}N) \in \mathrm{Tm}(\Gamma.A, B)$ *as follows:*

$$(\Lambda^{-1}N)_o(\gamma_o, a_o) = \mathit{let}\ (f_o, f_r) = N_o(\gamma_o)\ \mathit{in}\ f_o(a_o)$$
$$(\Lambda^{-1}N)_r(\gamma_r, a_r) = \mathit{let}\ (f^{src}, f^{tgt}, r) = N_r(\gamma_r)\ \mathit{in}\ r(a_r)$$

**Proposition 3.** *The reflexive graph CwF supports dependent products (Definition 4), using the structure defined in Definition 12.*

If the families $A \in \mathrm{Ty}(\Gamma)$ and $B \in \mathrm{Ty}(\Gamma.A)$ are small, then so is the family $\Pi AB \in \mathrm{Ty}(\Gamma)$. This is a consequence of assuming that the set-theoretic universe $\mathcal{U}$ is a universe of small sets, and so is closed under dependent products and tupling. It is straightforward to check that for closure under discreteness and proof-irrelevance, only the family $B$ need be discrete and proof-irrelevant:

**Lemma 3.** *Let* $A \in \mathrm{Ty}(\Gamma)$ *and* $B \in \mathrm{Ty}(\Gamma.A)$*. If* $B$ *is discrete and proof-irrelevant, then so is* $\Pi AB \in \mathrm{Ty}(\Gamma)$*.*

**Proposition 4.** *Part (c) of Definition 6 is fulfilled by the definition* $\pi MN = \mathit{repr}(\Pi(T\{\overline{M}\})(T\{\overline{N}\}))$*.*

If we further assume that our collection of small sets $\mathcal{U}$ is closed under large products, then we also have an interpretation of an impredicative type-theoretic universe. By Lemma 3, only the codomain type $B$ need be discrete and proof-irrelevant for $\Pi AB$ to be discrete and proof-irrelevant. Therefore, if $\mathcal{U}$ is closed under large products, then $U$ is closed under impredicative quantification.

**Proposition 5.** *Under the assumption of an impredicative universe* $\mathcal{U}$*, Definition 7 is fulfilled by* $\pi AM = \mathit{repr}(\Pi A(T\{\overline{M}\}))$*.*

***The Natural Number Type*** For each reflexive graph $\Gamma$, we define a semantic type $\mathit{Nat} \in \mathrm{Ty}(\Gamma)$ as follows, reusing the definition of the reflexive graph of natural numbers from Example 2:

$$\mathit{Nat}_O(\gamma_o) = \mathbb{N} \qquad \mathit{Nat}_{\mathit{refl}}(\gamma_o)(n) = n$$
$$\mathit{Nat}_R(\gamma_r) = \mathbb{N} \qquad \mathit{Nat}_{src}(\gamma_r)(n) = n$$
$$\mathit{Nat}_{tgt}(\gamma_r)(n) = n$$

Since the family $\mathit{Nat}$ does not actually depend on its argument, this definition is trivially natural in $\Gamma$.

The zero and successor semantic terms $\mathit{zero} \in \mathrm{Tm}(\Gamma, \mathit{Nat})$ and $\mathit{succ} \in \mathrm{Tm}(\Gamma.\mathit{Nat}, \mathit{Nat})$ are defined using the corresponding structure of the natural numbers:

$$\mathit{zero}_o(\gamma_o) = 0 \qquad \mathit{succ}_o(\gamma_o, n) = n + 1$$
$$\mathit{zero}_r(\gamma_r) = 0 \qquad \mathit{succ}_r(\gamma_r, n) = n + 1$$

It is almost immediate that these are well-defined semantic terms, given the trivial structure of the semantic type $\mathit{Nat}$. Likewise, naturality in $\Gamma$ is trivial.

The natural number recursor $\mathit{Nrec}$ is given, for $A \in \mathrm{Ty}(\Gamma.\mathit{Nat})$, $M^z \in \mathrm{Tm}(\Gamma, A\{\overline{\mathit{zero}}\})$, and $M^s \in \mathrm{Tm}(\Gamma.\mathit{Nat}.A, A\{\mathrm{wk}_{\mathit{Nat}}\, \mathrm{p}^{\Gamma}_{\mathit{Nat}} \circ \overline{\mathit{succ}} \circ \mathrm{p}^{\Gamma.\mathit{Nat}}_{A}\})$, by recursion on the natural number argument:

$$(\mathit{Nrec}_A(M^z, M^s))_o(\gamma_o, 0) = M^z_o(\gamma_o)$$
$$(\mathit{Nrec}_A(M^z, M^s))_r(\gamma_r, 0) = M^z_r(\gamma_r)$$
$$(\mathit{Nrec}_A(M^z, M^s))_o(\gamma_o, n+1) = M^s_o(\gamma_o, n, (\mathit{Nrec}_A(M^z, M^s))_o(\gamma_o, n))$$
$$(\mathit{Nrec}_A(M^z, M^s))_r(\gamma_r, n+1) = M^s_r(\gamma_r, n, (\mathit{Nrec}_A(M^z, M^s))_r(\gamma_r, n))$$

Equations (5) and (6) specifying the interaction between $\mathit{Nrec}$ and $\mathit{zero}$ and $\mathit{succ}$ hold almost by definition. Naturality in $\Gamma$ is proved by induction on the natural number argument.

**Proposition 6.** *The CwF formed from the category of reflexive graphs supports natural numbers (Definition 5). Moreover, the families* $\mathit{Nat} \in \mathrm{Ty}(\Gamma)$ *are small, discrete and proof irrelevant, so part (b) of Definition 6 is fulfilled by* $nat = \mathit{repr}(\mathit{Nat})$*.*

### 4.5 Main Theorem

By the results of the preceding subsections, we have shown that:

**Theorem 1.** *The category of reflexive graphs can be given the structure of a CwF that supports dependent products and natural numbers. Assuming the existence of a universe* $\mathcal{U}$ *of small sets, the category of reflexive graphs supports a predicative universe closed under natural numbers and dependent products, and if* $\mathcal{U}$ *is closed under large products then the CwF supports an impredicative universe closed under natural numbers and dependent products.*

As we argued in the paragraph before Definition 11, our interpretation of the type-theoretic universe U supports the identity extension property we identified in Section 2.1 as crucial for relationally parametric models. Thus, we are justified in referring to the model we have constructed here as relationally parametric.

## 5. Consequences of Parametricity

Having built our parametric model of dependent type theory, we now investigate some of the consequences of our construction. Our careful construction of the interpretation of the type-theoretic universe U as capturing the small, discrete, and proof-irrelevant families now bears fruit: we recover many of the interesting consequences of relationally parametricity that have been observed in the non-dependently typed settings of System F and System F$\omega$.

As a practical matter, calculating directly within the model we have constructed in the previous section is complicated by the "projection-based" presentation of relational interpretations forced by the reflexive graph formalism. We therefore use the following notational shorthands when reasoning within the model:

1. If $A \in \mathrm{Ty}(\Gamma)$ is a proof-irrelevant family of reflexive graphs, we write $(a, a') \in A_R(\gamma_r)$ if there exists $a_r \in A_R(\gamma_r)$ such that $A_{src}(\gamma_r)(a_r) = a$ and $A_{src}(\gamma_r)(a_r) = a'$. By proof-irrelevance the pair $(a, a')$ completely determines $a_r$ if it exists.
2. If $f \in (\Pi AB)_O(\gamma_o)$, we identify $f$ with its first component, so we can treat it as a function $\forall a_o \in A_O(\gamma_o).\ B_O(\gamma_o, a_o)$. Similarly, if $f \in (\Pi AB)_R(\gamma_r)$ we identify $f$ with its relation transformer component, which has type $\forall a_r \in A_R(\gamma_r).\ B_R(\gamma_r, a_r)$.
3. We will be liberal in confusing the curried and uncurried versions of the semantic interpretations of inhabitants of dependent products. This decreases the number of parentheses required.

We first prove a simple free theorem, in order to demonstrate reasoning within the model, and the utility of the construction of our interpretation of the type-theoretic universe as only containing *proof-irrelevant* families. We then go on to adapt Atkey's proof of the existence of higher-kinded initial algebras [2] to the impredicative dependently typed setting. This proof also relies on proof-irrelevance, and also makes essential use of the discreteness of members of $U$ in Lemma 7.

### 5.1 A Free Theorem

We begin by proving a simple free theorem in the style of Wadler [35]. This example shows that the ordinary consequences of relational parametricity are preserved when moving from polymorphic calculi to the richer world of dependent type theory with a universe.

**Theorem 2.** *If* $\Gamma \vdash M : \Pi a : \mathsf{U}.\ \mathsf{T}a \to \mathsf{T}a$ *then, for any* $\Gamma \vdash X : \mathsf{U}$, $\Gamma \vdash Y : \mathsf{U}$, $\Gamma \vdash f : \mathsf{T}X \to \mathsf{T}Y$*, and* $\Gamma \vdash x : \mathsf{T}X$*, the equation* $\Gamma \vdash f\ (M\ X\ x) = M\ Y\ (f\ x) : \mathsf{T}Y$ *is sound when interpreted in the models constructed in Section 4.*

*Proof.* Unwinding the definitions, we see that we must establish the following two equations, in which we have reused the letters $\Gamma$, $M$, $X$, $Y$, $f$ and $x$ to stand for the semantic interpretations of the corresponding syntactic objects, we have applied currying where convenient, and we have identified the small types $X$ and $Y$ with their decodings via $\mathsf{T}$:

$$\forall \gamma_o \in \Gamma_O.\ f_o(\gamma_o, M_o(\gamma_o, X_o(\gamma_o), x_o(\gamma_o))) = M_o(\gamma_o, Y_o(\gamma_o), f_o(\gamma_o, x_o(\gamma_o)))$$

$$\forall \gamma_r \in \Gamma_R.\ f_r(\gamma_r, M_r(\gamma_r, X_r(\gamma_r), x_r(\gamma_r))) = M_r(\gamma_r, Y_r(\gamma_r), f_r(\gamma_r, x_r(\gamma_r)))$$

The interpretation of the type $\mathsf{T}Y$ is a proof-irrelevant family, so by Lemma 2 we only need to prove the first of the above equations, from which the second necessarily follows. For a given $\gamma_o$, we use the relational interpretation $M_r$ of $M$, instantiated at $\Gamma_{refl}(\gamma_o)$:

$$M_r(\Gamma_{refl}(\gamma_o), -, -) : \forall R \in U_R(\Gamma_{refl}(\gamma_o)).\ T_R(\Gamma_{refl}(\gamma_o), R) \to T_R(\Gamma_{refl}(\gamma_o), R)$$

Again unwinding the definitions, and using the fact that $M_r$ is connected to $M_o$ via the equations for sources and targets of relations in (10) and (11), we have the following property:

$$\forall A, A' \in U_O(\gamma_o), R \subseteq A_O \times A'_O, (a, a') \in R.\ (M_o(\gamma_o, A, a), M_o(\gamma_o, A', a')) \in R$$

We instantiate $A$ and $A'$ with the small discrete reflexive graphs $X$ and $Y$, respectively, at $\gamma_o$. We take $R = \{(x, y) \mid f_o(\gamma_o, x) = y\}$. Then $(x_o(\gamma_o), f_o(\gamma_o, x_o(\gamma_o))) \in R$, so $(M_o(\gamma_o, X_O(\gamma_o), x_o(\gamma_o)), M_o(\gamma_o, Y_O(\gamma_o), f_o(\gamma_o, x_o(\gamma_o)))) \in R$, and the desired equation holds thus by definition of $R$. □

### 5.2 Categories of Indexed Types and Indexed Functors

We now start on our proof that the relationally parametric model that we have constructed supports initial algebras for all indexed functors. To this end, we first define the appropriate category of indexed small types where the carriers of indexed initial algebras reside. The construction of our category of indexed small types is carried out with respect to some fixed context $\Gamma$. For each judgement $\Gamma \vdash X$ type, we define the category of $X$-indexed small types to have as objects terms $\Gamma \vdash A : X \to \mathsf{U}$, and define morphisms between objects $\Gamma \vdash A : X \to \mathsf{U}$ and $\Gamma \vdash B : X \to \mathsf{U}$ to be terms $\Gamma \vdash f : \Pi x{:}X.\ \mathsf{T}(A\ x) \to \mathsf{T}(B\ x)$. Identities and composition are defined in the obvious way. Composition is associative due to the $\eta$-rule for dependent products.

We write $A \Rightarrow B$ to stand for the type $\Pi x{:}X.\ \mathsf{T}(A\ x) \to \mathsf{T}(B\ x)$. We will also use the type $\Gamma, a : X \to \mathsf{U}, b : X \to \mathsf{U} \vdash \Pi x{:}X.\ \mathsf{T}(a\ x) \to \mathsf{T}(b\ x)$ type, i.e., the type of morphisms where the domain and codomain are abstracted as variables. As a notational convenience, we write "morph" as shorthand for this type, and similarly for its semantic interpretation $\mathrm{morph} \in \mathrm{Ty}(\Gamma.\Pi XU.\Pi XU)$.

Morphisms in the category of $X$-indexed small types induce relations between their domain and codomain objects, as given by the following definition. This definition is the $X$-indexed generalisation of the functional relation from the free theorem in Section 5.1.

**Definition 13.** *Let $\Gamma \vdash A : X \to \mathsf{U}$ and $\Gamma \vdash B : X \to \mathsf{U}$. Given a morphism $\Gamma \vdash f : A \Rightarrow B$, we define $\langle f \rangle$, called the* graph relation *of $f$, to be the following element of $(\Pi XU)_R$:*

$$\lambda \gamma_r \in \Gamma_R.\ (A_o(\Gamma_{src}(\gamma_r)), B_o(\Gamma_{tgt}(\gamma_r)), \lambda x_r \in X_R(\gamma_r).\ (A_o(\Gamma_{src}(\gamma_r))(X_{src}(\gamma_r)(x_r)), B_o(\Gamma_{tgt}(\gamma_r))(X_{tgt}(\gamma_r)(x_r)), \{(a, b) \mid (f_o(\Gamma_{src}(\gamma_r), X_{src}(\gamma_r)(x_r), a), b) \in B_r(\gamma_r)(x_r)\}))$$

The following lemma is a direct consequence of Definition 13.

**Lemma 4.** *Let $\Gamma \vdash A : X \to \mathsf{U}$, $\Gamma \vdash B : X \to \mathsf{U}$, and $\Gamma \vdash f : A \Rightarrow B$. Then for all $\gamma_o \in \Gamma_O$, $(f_o(\gamma_o), \mathrm{id}) \in \mathrm{morph}_R(\Gamma_{refl}(\gamma_o), \langle f \rangle(\Gamma_{refl}(\gamma_o)), B_r(\Gamma_{refl}(\gamma_o)))$.*

***Indexed Functors*** $X$-indexed initial algebras are defined in terms of $X$-indexed functors, which we now define. An $X$-indexed functor is a pair $(F, \mathit{Fmap})$ of terms

$$\Gamma \vdash F : (X \to \mathsf{U}) \to (X \to \mathsf{U})$$
$$\Gamma \vdash \mathit{Fmap} : \Pi A, B{:}X \to \mathsf{U}.\ (A \Rightarrow B) \to (FA \Rightarrow FB)$$

where $\mathit{Fmap}$ preserves the identities and composition of the category of $X$-indexed small types when interpretated in the reflexive graph model. Indexed functors interact nicely with graph relations, as captured by the following *Graph Lemma*:

**Lemma 5.** *Let $\Gamma \vdash f : A \Rightarrow B$. For all $\gamma_o \in \Gamma_O$ and $x_r \in X_R(\Gamma_{refl}(\gamma_o))$, if $(a, b) \in F_r(\Gamma_{refl}(\gamma_o), \langle f \rangle(\Gamma_{refl}(\gamma_o)))(x_r)$ then $(a, b) \in \langle \mathit{Fmap}\ A\ B\ f \rangle(\Gamma_{refl}(\gamma_o))(x_r)$.*

### 5.3 The Category of $F$-algebras

For an $X$-indexed functor $(F, \mathit{Fmap})$, initial $F$-algebras are initial objects in the category of $F$-algebras, which we now define. Fix an $X$-indexed functor $(F, \mathit{Fmap})$. The objects of the category of $F$-algebras are pairs of terms $(A, k^A)$ where $\Gamma \vdash A : X \to \mathsf{U}$ and $\Gamma \vdash k^A : FA \Rightarrow A$. Morphisms between $(A, k^A)$ and $(B, k^B)$ are terms $\Gamma \vdash h : A \Rightarrow B$ such that, if $\circ$ is the composition of the category of $X$-indexed small types, then

$$\Gamma \vdash k^B \circ \mathit{Fmap}\ A\ B\ h = h \circ k^A : FA \Rightarrow B$$

An *initial $F$-algebra* is an initial object in the category of $F$-algebras, i.e., an $F$-algebra $(\mu F, \mathrm{in})$ such that there exists a term

$$\Gamma \vdash \mathit{fold} : \Pi A : X \to \mathsf{U}.\ (FA \Rightarrow A) \to (\mu F \Rightarrow A)$$

such that the following two equations hold. The first equation states that *fold* always yields $F$-algebra morphisms:

$$\frac{\Gamma \vdash A : X \to \mathsf{U} \qquad \Gamma \vdash k^A : FA \Rightarrow A \qquad \Gamma \vdash x : X \qquad \Gamma \vdash M : \mathsf{T}(\mu F\ x)}{\Gamma \vdash \mathit{fold}\ A\ k^A\ x\ (\mathrm{in}\ x\ M) = k^A\ x\ (\mathit{Fmap}\ \mu F\ A\ (\mathit{fold}\ A\ k^A)\ x\ M : \mathsf{T}(A\ x)}$$

The second equation states that the $F$-algebra morphisms generated by *fold* are unique, as required by initiality:

$$\frac{\Gamma \vdash A : X \to \mathsf{U} \qquad \Gamma \vdash k^A : FA \Rightarrow A \qquad \Gamma \vdash h : \mu F \Rightarrow A \qquad h \text{ is an } F\text{-algebra morphism}}{\Gamma \vdash h = \mathit{fold}\ A\ k^A : \mu F \Rightarrow A}$$

Morphisms between $F$-algebras have the following relational property in terms of their graph relations. This property will be useful when we prove that initial $F$-algebras always exist.

**Lemma 6.** *Let $(A, k^A)$ and $(B, k^B)$ be $F$-algebras. If $h$ is an $F$-algebra morphism from $(A, k^A)$ to $(B, k^B)$, then for all $\gamma_o \in \Gamma_O$,*

$$(k_o^A(\gamma_o), k_o^B(\gamma_o)) \in \mathrm{morph}_R(\Gamma_{refl}(\gamma_o), F_r(\Gamma_{refl}(\gamma_o), \langle h \rangle(\Gamma_{refl}(\gamma_o))), \langle h \rangle(\Gamma_{refl}(\gamma_o)))$$

### 5.4 Construction of Initial $F$-algebras

Having defined all the necessary background, we now show that, within the impredicative version of our relationally parametric model of dependent types, initial $F$-algebras exist for all $X$-indexed functors $(F, \mathit{Fmap})$. Given an $X$-indexed functor

$(F, Fmap)$, we make the following definitions:

$$\mu F = \lambda x : X.\ \Pi A : X \to \mathsf{U}.\ (FA \Rightarrow A) \to \mathsf{T}(A\ x)$$
$$fold = \lambda A{:}X \to \mathsf{U}.\ \lambda k^A{:}(FA \Rightarrow A).\ \lambda x{:}X.\ \lambda e{:}\mathsf{T}(\mu F\ x).\ e\ A\ k^A$$
$$\begin{aligned} \mathrm{in} = \lambda x : X.\ \lambda e : \mathsf{T}(F(\mu F)x).\ \lambda A : X \to \mathsf{U}.\ \lambda k^A : (FA \Rightarrow A). \\ k^A\ x\ (Fmap\ \mu F\ A\ (fold\ A\ k^A)\ x\ e) \end{aligned}$$

Note that, up to notational changes induced by our presentation of the universe U, and the more general setting, these definitions are identical to those given by Atkey [2] for constructing higher-kinded initial algebras in a relationally parametric model of System F$\omega$.

The proof that these definitions actually give an initial $F$-algebra follows from two applications of the following lemma:

**Lemma 7.** *The following equation holds when interpreted in the reflexive graph model:*

$$\frac{\begin{array}{cc} \Gamma \vdash A : X \to \mathsf{U} & \Gamma \vdash k^A : FA \Rightarrow A \\ \Gamma \vdash B : X \to \mathsf{U} & \Gamma \vdash k^B : FB \Rightarrow B \\ \Gamma \vdash h : A \Rightarrow B & h \text{ is an } F\text{-algebra homomorphism} \\ \Gamma \vdash x : X & \Gamma \vdash M : \mathsf{T}(\mu F\ x) \end{array}}{\Gamma \vdash h\ x\ (M\ A\ k^A) = M\ B\ k^B : \mathsf{T}(B\ x)}$$

*Proof.* By Lemma 2 we need only prove the object-level part of the equation. Given $\gamma_o \in \Gamma_O$, we instantiate $M_r$ with $\Gamma_{\mathit{refl}}(\gamma_o)$, the graph relation $\langle h\rangle(\Gamma_{\mathit{refl}}(\gamma_o))$, and the pair $(k_o^A(\gamma_o), k_o^B(\gamma_o))$, by Lemma 6, to obtain

$$\begin{aligned} (M_o(\gamma_o, A_o(\gamma_o), k_o^A(\gamma_o)), M_o(\gamma_o, B_o(\gamma_o), k_o^B(\gamma_o))) \in \\ \langle h\rangle(\Gamma_{\mathit{refl}}(\gamma_o))(X_{\mathit{refl}}(\gamma_o)(x_o(\gamma_o))) \end{aligned}$$

Unfolding the graph relation, this statement is equivalent to:

$$\begin{aligned} &(h_o(\gamma_o, x_o(\gamma_o), M_o(\gamma_o, A_o(\gamma_o), k_o^A(\gamma_o))), M_o(\gamma_o, B_o(\gamma_o), k_o^B(\gamma_o))) \\ &\in B_r(\Gamma_{\mathit{refl}}(\gamma_o), X_{\mathit{refl}}(\gamma_o)(x_o(\gamma_o))) \end{aligned}$$

Now, by the identity extension property that is built into the reflexive graph model, the relation $B_r(\Gamma_{\mathit{refl}}(\gamma_o), X_{\mathit{refl}}(\gamma_o)(x_o(\gamma_o)))$ is equal to $U_{\mathit{refl}}(\gamma_o, x_o(\gamma_o))(B_o(\gamma_o, x_o(\gamma_o)))$. By the discreteness of elements of the universe $U$, this relation is, up to isomorphism, the equality relation on the small set $B_o(\gamma_o, x_o(\gamma_o))$. We thus have

$$\begin{aligned} & h_o(\gamma_o, x_o(\gamma_o), M_o(\gamma_o, A_o(\gamma_o), k_o^A(\gamma_o))) \\ = \quad & M_o(\gamma_o, B_o(\gamma_o), k_o^B(\gamma_o)) \quad \square \end{aligned}$$

We can now state the following key property of our model.

**Theorem 3.** *Any $X$-indexed functor $(F, Fmap)$ has an initial $F$-algebra.*

*Proof.* We must verify that the two equations in Section 5.3 hold. The first equation, stating that *fold* always generates $F$-algebra morphisms, follows directly by using the $\beta$-reduction rules of the type theory. The second equation requires relational parametricity. Expanding the definitions, we see that we need to prove that $h\ x\ M = M\ A\ k^A$. By Lemma 7, together with the fact that $h$ is an $F$-algebra morphism, we have that $h\ x\ (M\ \mu F\ \mathrm{in}) = M\ A\ k^A$. Using Lemma 7 again, this time with an arbitrary $F$-algebra $(B, k^B)$, and setting $h = \mathrm{fold}\ B\ k^B$ yields $M\ \mu F\ \mathrm{in}\ B\ k^B = M\ B\ k^B$. Extensionality therefore gives $M\ \mu F\ \mathrm{in} = M$, and thus $h\ x\ M = M\ A\ k^A$, as required. □

Despite the considerably more general setting, the above proof is almost identical to that given by Atkey for higher-kinded initial algebras in a relationally parametric model of System F$\omega$. The proofs of other results presented by Atkey — e.g., the existence of an extensional equality type and existentials — also translate to the impredicative dependently typed setting with little change.

## 6. Conclusion and Directions for Future Work

We have presented a parametric model of dependent types that has two significant features. First, our model is based on reflexive graphs, which naturally generalise existing relationally parametric models of System F: just as the construction of a parametric model for System F can be seen as moving from a model based on Set to a model based on $\mathrm{Set}^{\mathrm{RG}}$, so our parametric model of dependent types can be seen as moving from a fibration $p : \mathrm{Fam}(\mathrm{Set}) \to \mathrm{Set}$ to a fibration $p^{\mathrm{RG}} : \mathrm{Fam}(\mathrm{Set})^{\mathrm{RG}} \to \mathrm{Set}^{\mathrm{RG}}$. Second, our model supports the derivation of key results, such as the existence of initial algebras. We believe ours is the first parametric model, syntactic *or* semantic, to establish the dependently-typed generalisation of this key property of relationally parametric models of System F.

The most exciting avenue for future work is in comparing the reflexive graph model we have presented here with the strikingly similar groupoid and $\infty$-groupoid models of type theory [32]. Reflexive graphs can be seen as "categories without composition", whereas groupoids are categories with inverses. In light of the many useful results derivable from relational parametricity, further investigation of the reduced amount of structure of reflexive graphs looks promising (Robinson has already investigated "Parametricity as Isomorphism": parametricity where types are interpreted as groupoids [29]). In particular, Voevodsky's univalence axiom states that isomorphic types are actually equal. But Reynolds' relational parametricity reveals that often types need only be *related*, not isomorphic, for them to be indistinguishable to programs. Is there a Reynoldsian version of univalence waiting to be formulated?

## References


[1] R. Atkey. A Deep Embedding of Parametric Polymorphism in Coq. *Proc., Workshop on Mechanising Metatheory*, 2009.

[2] R. Atkey. Relational Parametricity for Higher Kinds. *Proc., Computer Science Logic*, pp. 46–61, 2012.

[3] R. Atkey, P. Johann, and A. Kennedy. Abstraction and Invariance for Algebraically Indexed Types. *Proc., Principles of Programming Languages*, pp. 87–100, 2013.

[4] E. S. Bainbridge, P. J. Freyd, A. Scedrov, and P. J. Scott. Functorial Polymorphism. *Theoretical Computer Science* 70(1), pp. 35–64, 1990.

[5] J.-P. Bernardy, P. Jansson, and R. Paterson. Proofs for Free - Parametricity for Dependent Types. *Journal of Functional Programming* 22(2), pp. 107–152, 2012.

[6] A. Bove, P. Dybjer, and U. Norell. A Brief Overview of Agda – A Functional Language with Dependent Types. *Proc., Theorem Proving in Higher Order Logics*, 2009.

[7] J. Cheney and R. Hinze. A lightweight implementation of generics and dynamics. *Proc., Workshop on Haskell*, pp. 90–104, 2002.

[8] A. Chlipala. Parametric higher-order abstract syntax for mechanized semantics. *Proc., International Conference on Functional Programming*, pp. 143–156, 2008.

[9] The Coq Development Team. The Coq proof assistant reference manual. *LogiCal Project*, Version 8.0, 2004.

[10] T. Coquand and G. P. Huet. The Calculus of Constructions. *Information and Computation* 76(2/3), pp. 95–120, 1988.

[11] B. Dunphy and U. S. Reddy. Parametric Limits. *Proc., Logic in Computer Science*, pp. 242–251, 2004.

[12] P. Dybjer. Internal Type Theory. *Proc., Types for Proofs and Programs*, pp. 120–134, 1996.

[13] R. Hasegawa. Categorical Data Types in Parametric Polymorphism. *Mathematical Structures in Computer Science* 4(1), pp. 71–109, 1994.

[14] R. Hasegawa. Relational Limits in General Polymorphism. *Publications of the Research Institute for Mathematical Sciences* 30, pp. 535–576, 1994.

[15] M. Hofmann. Syntax and Semantics of Dependent Types. In *Semantics and Logics of Computation*, Cambridge University Press, pp. 79–130, 1997.

[16] M. Hofmann and T. Streicher. Lifting Grothendieck Universes. Unpublished manuscript. 199?

[17] B. Jacobs. *Categorical Logic and Type Theory*. Elsevier, 1999.

[18] P. Johann. Short Cut Fusion: Proved and Improved. *Proc., Semantics, Application, and Implementation of Program Generation*, pp. 47–71, 2001.

[19] N. Krishnaswami and D. Dreyer. Internalizing Relational Parametricity in the Extensional Calculus of Constructions. *Proc., Computer Science Logic*, 2013.

[20] S. Mac Lane. *Categories for the Working Mathematician, Second Edition.* Springer-Verlag, 1998.

[21] H. G. Mairson. Outline of a Proof Theory of Parametricity. *Proc., Functional Programming Languages and Computer Architecture*, pp. 313–327, 1991.

[22] P. Martin-Löf. *Intuitionistic Type Theory*. Bibliopolis, 1984.

[23] A. Nanevski, A. Banerjee, D. Garg. Dependent Type Theory for Verification of Information Flow and Access Control Policies. *ACM Transactions on Programming Languages and Systems* 35(2), pp. 6:1–6:41, 2013.

[24] A. M. Pitts. Parametric Polymorphism and Operational Equivalence. *Mathematical Structures in Computer Science* 10, pp. 321–359, 2000.

[25] G. D. Plotkin. Lambda Definability and Logical Relations. Technical Report, University of Edinburgh, 1973.

[26] G. D. Plotkin and M. Abadi. A Logic for Parametric Polymorphism. *Proc., Typed Lambda Calculi and Applications*, pp. 361–375, 1993.

[27] J. C. Reynolds. Polymorphism is Not Set-Theoretic. *Proc., Semantics of Data Types*, pp. 145–156, 1984.

[28] J. C. Reynolds. Types, Abstraction and Parametric Polymorphism. *Information Processing* 83, pp. 513–523, 1983.

[29] E. Robinson. Parametricity as Isomorphism. *Theoretical Computer Science* 136, pp. 163–181, 1994.

[30] E. Robinson and G. Rosolini. Reflexive Graphs and Parametric Polymorphism. *Proc., Logic in Computer Science*, pp. 364–371, 1994.

[31] I. Takeuti. The Theory of Parametricity in the Lambda Cube. Technical Report 1217, Kyoto University, 2001.

[32] The Univalent Foundations Program. *Homotopy Type Theory*. Institute for Advanced Study, 2013.

[33] D. Vytiniotis and S. Weirich Parametricity, Type Equality, and Higher-Order Polymorphism. *Journal of Functional Programming* 20(2), pp. 175–201, 2010.

[34] P. Wadler. The Girard-Reynolds Isomorphism (second edition). *Theoretical Computer Science* 375(1-3), pp. 201–226, 2007.

[35] P. Wadler. Theorems for Free! *Proc., Functional Programming Languages and Computer Architecture*, pp. 347–359, 1989.

# Game Semantics for Interface Middleweight Java *

Andrzej S. Murawski
DIMAP and Department of Computer Science
University of Warwick

Nikos Tzevelekos
School of Electronic Engineering and Computer Science
Queen Mary, University of London

## Abstract

We consider an object calculus in which open terms interact with the environment through interfaces. The calculus is intended to capture the essence of contextual interactions of Middleweight Java code. Using game semantics, we provide fully abstract models for the induced notions of contextual approximation and equivalence. These are the first denotational models of this kind.

***Categories and Subject Descriptors*** D.3.1 [*Formal Definitions and Theory*]: Semantics; F.3.2 [*Semantics of Programming Languages*]: Denotational semantics

***Keywords*** Full Abstraction, Game Semantics, Contextual Equivalence, Java

## 1. Introduction

Denotational semantics is charged with the construction of mathematical universes (denotations) that capture program behaviour. It concentrates on compositional, syntax-independent modelling with the aim of illuminating the structure of computation and facilitating reasoning about programs. Many developments in denotational semantics have been driven by the quest for full abstraction [21]: a model is *fully abstract* if the interpretations of two programs are the same precisely when the programs behave in the same way (i.e. are contextually equivalent). A faithful correspondence like this opens the path to a broad range of applications, such as compiler optimisation and program transformation, in which the preservation of semantics is of paramount importance.

Recent years have seen *game semantics* emerge as a robust denotational paradigm [4, 6, 12]. It has been used to construct the first fully abstract models for a wide spectrum of programming languages, previously out of reach of denotational semantics. Game semantics models computation as an exchange of moves between two players, representing respectively the program and its computational environment. Accordingly, a program is interpreted as a strategy in a game corresponding to its type. Intuitively, the plays that game semantics generates constitute the observable patterns that a program produces when interacting with its environment, and this is what underlies the full abstraction results. Game semantics is compositional: the strategy corresponding to a compound program phrase is obtained by canonical combinations of those corresponding to its sub-phrases. An important advance in game semantics was the development of nominal games [3, 17, 26], which underpinned full abstraction results for languages with dynamic generative behaviours, such as the $\nu$-calculus [3], higher-order concurrency [18] and ML references [24]. A distinctive feature of nominal game models is the presence of names (e.g. memory locations, references names) in game moves, often along with some abstraction of the store.

The aim of the present paper is to extend the range of the game approach towards real-life programming languages, by focussing on Java-style objects. To that end, we define an imperative object calculus, called Interface Middleweight Java (IMJ), intended to capture contextual interactions of code written in Middleweight Java (MJ) [9], as specified by interfaces with inheritance. We present both equational (contextual equivalence) and inequational (contextual approximation) full abstraction results for the language. To the best of our knowledge, these are the first denotational models of this kind.

***Related Work*** While the operational semantics of Java has been researched extensively [7], there have been relatively few results regarding its denotational semantics. More generally, most existing models of object-oriented languages, such as [8, 15], have been based on global state and consequently could not be fully abstract.

On the other hand, contextual equivalence in Java-like languages has been studied successfully using operational approaches such as trace semantics [2, 13, 14] and environmental bisimulation [16]. The trace-based approaches are closest to ours and the three papers listed also provide characterizations of contextual equivalence. The main difference is that traces are derived operationally through a carefully designed labelled transition system and, thus, do not admit an immediate compositional description in the style of denotational semantics.

However, similarities between traces and plays in game semantics indicate a deeper correspondence between the two areas, which also manifested itself in other cases, e.g. [20] vs [19]. At the time of writing, there is no general methodology for moving smoothly between the two approaches, but we believe that there is scope for unifying the two fields in the not so distant future.

In comparison to other game models, ours has quite lightweight structure. For the most part, playing consists of calling the opponent's methods and returning results to calls made by the opponent. In particular, there are no justification pointers between moves. This can be attributed to the fact that Java does not feature first-class higher-order functions and that methods in Java objects cannot be updated. On the other hand, the absence of pointers makes definitions of simple notions, such as well-bracketing, less direct, since the dependencies between moves are not given explicitly any

* Research supported by the Engineering and Physical Sciences Research Council (EP/J019577/1) and a Royal Academy of Engineering Research Fellowship (Tzevelekos).


*POPL'14*, January 22–24, 2014, San Diego, CA, USA.

ACM 978-1-4503-2544-8/14/01... $15.00.
http://dx.doi.org/10.1145/2535838

$$\frac{}{\Delta|\Gamma \vdash x : \theta}\,(x{:}\theta)\in\Gamma \qquad \frac{}{\Delta|\Gamma \vdash a : \mathcal{I}}\,(a{:}\mathcal{I})\in\Gamma \qquad \frac{}{\Delta|\Gamma \vdash \mathsf{skip} : \mathsf{void}} \qquad \frac{}{\Delta|\Gamma \vdash \mathsf{null} : \mathcal{I}}\,\mathcal{I}\in\mathsf{dom}(\Delta) \qquad \frac{}{\Delta|\Gamma \vdash i : \mathsf{int}}$$

$$\frac{\Delta|\Gamma \vdash M : \mathsf{int} \quad \Delta|\Gamma \vdash M' : \mathsf{int}}{\Delta|\Gamma \vdash M \oplus M' : \mathsf{int}} \qquad \frac{\Delta|\Gamma, x:\theta' \vdash M : \theta \quad \Delta|\Gamma \vdash M' : \theta'}{\Delta|\Gamma \vdash \mathsf{let}\, x = M' \,\mathsf{in}\, M : \theta} \qquad \frac{\Delta|\Gamma \vdash M : \mathcal{I} \quad \Delta|\Gamma \vdash M' : \mathcal{I}}{\Delta|\Gamma \vdash M = M' : \mathsf{int}} \qquad \frac{\Delta|\Gamma \vdash M : \mathcal{I}'}{\Delta|\Gamma \vdash (\mathcal{I})M : \mathcal{I}}\,\Delta\vdash\mathcal{I}\leq\mathcal{I}' \vee \Delta\vdash\mathcal{I}'\leq\mathcal{I}$$

$$\frac{\Delta|\Gamma \vdash M : \mathsf{int} \quad \Delta|\Gamma \vdash M', M'' : \theta}{\Delta|\Gamma \vdash \mathsf{if}\, M \,\mathsf{then}\, M' \,\mathsf{else}\, M'' : \theta} \qquad \frac{\Delta|\Gamma, x:\mathcal{I} \vdash \mathcal{M} : \Theta}{\Delta|\Gamma \vdash \mathsf{new}(x : \mathcal{I}; \mathcal{M}) : \mathcal{I}}\,\Delta(\mathcal{I})\restriction \mathit{Meths}=\Theta \qquad \frac{\Delta|\Gamma \vdash M : \mathcal{I} \quad \Delta|\Gamma \vdash M' : \theta}{\Delta|\Gamma \vdash M.\mathsf{f} := M' : \mathsf{void}}\,\Delta(\mathcal{I}).\mathsf{f}=\theta$$

$$\frac{\Delta|\Gamma \vdash M : \mathcal{I}}{\Delta|\Gamma \vdash M.\mathsf{f} : \theta}\,\Delta(\mathcal{I}).\mathsf{f}=\theta \qquad \frac{\Delta|\Gamma \vdash M : \mathcal{I} \quad \bigwedge_{i=1}^{n}(\Delta|\Gamma \vdash M_i : \theta_i)}{\Delta|\Gamma \vdash M.\mathsf{m}(M_1, \cdots, M_n) : \theta}\,\Delta(\mathcal{I}).\mathsf{m}=\vec{\theta}\to\theta \qquad \frac{\bigwedge_{i=1}^{n}(\Delta|\Gamma \uplus \{\vec{x}_i : \vec{\theta}_i\} \vdash M_i : \theta_i)}{\Delta|\Gamma \vdash \mathcal{M} : \Theta}\,\begin{array}{l}\Theta=\{\mathsf{m}_i{:}\vec{\theta}_i\to\theta_i \mid 1\leq i\leq n\}\\ \mathcal{M}=\{\mathsf{m}_i{:}\lambda\vec{x}_i.M_i \mid 1\leq i\leq n\}\end{array}$$

**Figure 1.** Typing rules for IMJ terms and method-set implementations

more and need to be inferred from plays. The latter renders strategy composition non-standard. Because it is impossible to determine statically to which arena a move belongs, the switching conditions (cf. [6]) governing interactions become crucial for determining the strategy responsible for each move. Finally, it is worth noting that traditional copycat links are by definition excluded from our setting: a call/return move for a given object cannot be copycatted by the other player, as the move has a fixed polarity, determined by the ownership of the object. In fact, identity strategies contain plays of length at most two!

***Further Directions*** In future work, we would like to look for automata-theoretic representations of fragments of our model in order to use them as a foundation for a program verification tool for Java programs. Our aim is to take advantage of the latest developments in automata theory over infinite alphabets [10], and fresh-register automata in particular [23, 27], to account for the nominal features of the model.

## 2. The language IMJ

We introduce an imperative object calculus, called Interface Middleweight Java (IMJ), in which objects are typed using interfaces. The calculus is a stripped down version of Middleweight Java (MJ), expressive enough to expose the interactions of MJ-style objects with the environment.

*Definition* 1. Let *Ints*, *Flds* and *Meths* be sets of *interface*, *field* and *method* identifiers. We range over them respectively by $\mathcal{I}$, f, m and variants. The ***types*** $\theta$ of IMJ are given below, where $\vec{\theta}$ stands for a sequence $\theta_1, ..., \theta_n$ of types (for any $n$). An ***interface definition*** $\Theta$ is a finite set of typed fields and methods. An ***interface table*** $\Delta$ is a finite assignment of interface definitions to interface identifiers.

$$\begin{aligned} \mathit{Types} \ni \theta &::= \mathsf{void} \mid \mathsf{int} \mid \mathcal{I} \\ \mathit{IDfns} \ni \Theta &::= \emptyset \mid (\mathsf{f} : \theta), \Theta \mid (\mathsf{m} : \vec{\theta} \to \theta), \Theta \\ \mathit{ITbls} \ni \Delta &::= \emptyset \mid (\mathcal{I} : \Theta), \Delta \mid (\mathcal{I}\langle\mathcal{I}\rangle : \Theta), \Delta \end{aligned}$$

We write $\mathcal{I}\langle\mathcal{I}'\rangle : \Theta$ for *interface extension*: interface $\mathcal{I}$ extends $\mathcal{I}'$ with fields and methods from $\Theta$. We stipulate that the extension relation must not lead to circular dependencies. Moreover, each identifier f, m can appear at most once in each $\Theta$, and each $\mathcal{I}$ can be defined at most once in $\Delta$ (i.e. there is at most one element of $\Delta$ of the form $\mathcal{I} : \Theta$ or $\mathcal{I}\langle\mathcal{I}'\rangle : \Theta$). Thus, each $\Theta$ can be seen as a finite partial function $\Theta : (\mathit{Flds} \cup \mathit{Meths}) \rightharpoonup \mathit{Types}^*$. We write $\Theta.\mathsf{f}$ for $\Theta(\mathsf{f})$ and $\Theta.\mathsf{m}$ for $\Theta(\mathsf{m})$. Similarly, $\Delta$ defines a partial function $\Delta : \mathit{Ints} \rightharpoonup \mathit{IDfns}$ given by

$$\Delta(\mathcal{I}) = \begin{cases} \Theta & (\mathcal{I} : \Theta) \in \Delta \\ \Delta(\mathcal{I}') \cup \Theta & (\mathcal{I}\langle\mathcal{I}'\rangle : \Theta) \in \Delta \\ \text{undefined} & \text{otherwise} \end{cases}$$

An interface table $\Delta$ is ***well-formed*** if, for all interface types $\mathcal{I}, \mathcal{I}'$:

- if $\mathcal{I}'$ appears in $\Delta(\mathcal{I})$ then $\mathcal{I}' \in \mathsf{dom}(\Delta)$,
- if $(\mathcal{I}\langle\mathcal{I}'\rangle : \Theta) \in \Delta$ then $\mathsf{dom}(\Delta(\mathcal{I}')) \cap \mathsf{dom}(\Theta) = \emptyset$.

Henceforth we assume that interface tables are well-formed. Interface extensions yield a subtyping relation. Given a table $\Delta$, we define $\Delta \vdash \theta_1 \leq \theta_2$ by the following rules.

$$\frac{}{(\mathcal{I}\langle\mathcal{I}'\rangle : \Theta), \Delta \vdash \mathcal{I} \leq \mathcal{I}'}$$

$$\frac{}{\Delta \vdash \theta \leq \theta} \qquad \frac{\Delta \vdash \theta_1 \leq \theta_2 \quad \Delta \vdash \theta_2 \leq \theta_3}{\Delta \vdash \theta_1 \leq \theta_3}$$

We might omit $\Delta$ from subtyping judgements for economy.

*Definition* 2. Let $\mathbb{A}$ be a countably infinite set of ***object names***, which we range over by $a$ and variants. IMJ ***terms*** are listed below, where we let $x$ range over a set of *variables* *Vars*, and $i$ over $\mathbb{Z}$. Moreover, $\oplus$ is selected from some set of binary numeric operations. $\mathcal{M}$ is a ***method-set implementation***. Again, we stipulate that each m appear in each $\mathcal{M}$ at most once.

$$\begin{aligned} M ::= {} & x \mid a \mid \mathsf{skip} \mid \mathsf{null} \mid i \mid M \oplus M \mid \mathsf{let}\, x = M \,\mathsf{in}\, M \\ & \mid M = M \mid \mathsf{if}\, M \,\mathsf{then}\, M \,\mathsf{else}\, M \mid (\mathcal{I})M \mid \mathsf{new}(x : \mathcal{I}; \mathcal{M}) \\ & \mid M.\mathsf{f} \mid M.\mathsf{f} := M \mid M.\mathsf{m}(\vec{M}) \end{aligned}$$

$$\mathit{MImps} \ni \mathcal{M} ::= \emptyset \mid (\mathsf{m} : \lambda\vec{x}.M), \mathcal{M}$$

The terms are typed in contexts comprising an interface table $\Delta$ and a variable context $\Gamma = \{x_1 : \theta_1, \cdots, x_n : \theta_n\} \cup \{a_1 : \mathcal{I}_1, \cdots, a_m : \mathcal{I}_m\}$ such that any interface in $\Gamma$ occurs in $\mathsf{dom}(\Delta)$. The typing rules are given in Figure 1.

For the operational semantics, we define the sets of ***term values***, ***heap configurations*** and ***states*** by:

$$\begin{aligned} \mathit{TVals} \ni v &::= \mathsf{skip} \mid i \mid \mathsf{null} \mid a \\ \mathit{HCnfs} \ni V &::= \emptyset \mid (\mathsf{f} : v), V \\ \mathit{States} \ni S &: \mathbb{A} \rightharpoonup \mathit{Ints} \times (\mathit{HCnfs} \times \mathit{MImps}) \end{aligned}$$

If $S(a) = (\mathcal{I}, (V, \mathcal{M}))$ then we write $S(a) : \mathcal{I}$, while $S(a).\mathsf{f}$ and $S(a).\mathsf{m}$ stand for $V.\mathsf{f}$ and $\mathcal{M}.\mathsf{m}$ respectively, for each f and m.

Given an interface table $\Delta$ such that $\mathcal{I} \in \mathsf{dom}(\Delta)$, we let the default heap configuration of type $\mathcal{I}$ be

$$V_{\mathcal{I}} = \{\mathsf{f} : v_\theta \mid \Delta(\mathcal{I}).\mathsf{f} = \theta\},$$

where $v_{\mathsf{void}} = \mathsf{skip}$, $v_{\mathsf{int}} = 0$ and $v_{\mathcal{I}} = \mathsf{null}$. The operational semantics of IMJ is given by means of a small-step transition relation

$(S, i \oplus i') \longrightarrow (S, j)$, if $j = i \oplus i'$ $\quad (S, \mathsf{let}\, x = v \,\mathsf{in}\, M) \longrightarrow (S, M[v/x]) \quad (S, (\mathcal{I})\mathsf{null}) \longrightarrow (S, \mathsf{null})$

$(S, \mathsf{if}\, 0 \,\mathsf{then}\, M \,\mathsf{else}\, M') \longrightarrow (S, M') \quad (S, \mathsf{if}\, 1 \,\mathsf{then}\, M \,\mathsf{else}\, M') \longrightarrow (S, M) \quad (S, a = a) \longrightarrow (S, 1)$

$(S, (\mathcal{I})a) \longrightarrow (S, a)$, if $S(a) : \mathcal{I}' \wedge \mathcal{I}' \leq \mathcal{I} \quad (S, a = a') \longrightarrow (S, 0)$, if $a \neq a' \quad (S, a.\mathsf{f}) \longrightarrow (S, S(a).\mathsf{f})$

$(S, \mathsf{new}(x : \mathcal{I}; \mathcal{M})) \longrightarrow (S \uplus \{(a, \mathcal{I}, (V_{\mathcal{I}}, \mathcal{M}[a/x]))\}, a) \quad (S, a.\mathsf{m}(\vec{v})) \longrightarrow (S, M[\vec{v}/\vec{x}])$, if $S(a).\mathsf{m} = \lambda\vec{x}.M$

$(S, a.\mathsf{f} := v) \longrightarrow (S[a \mapsto (\mathcal{I}, (V[\mathsf{f} \mapsto v], \mathcal{M})], \mathsf{skip})$, if $S(a) = (\mathcal{I}, (V, \mathcal{M}))$

$(S, E[M]) \longrightarrow (S', E[M'])$, if $(S, M) \longrightarrow (S', M')$

**Figure 2.** Operational semantics of IMJ.

between terms-in-state, presented in Figure 2. The transition relation uses *evaluation contexts* $E$ that are defined as follows.

$$\begin{aligned} E ::= &\ \mathsf{let}\, x = \_ \,\mathsf{in}\, M \mid \_ \oplus M \mid i \oplus \_ \mid \_ = M \mid a = \_ \\ &\mid \mathsf{if}\, \_ \,\mathsf{then}\, M \,\mathsf{else}\, M' \mid (\mathcal{I})\_ \mid \_.\mathsf{f} \mid \_.\mathsf{f} := M \mid a.\mathsf{f} := \_ \\ &\mid \_.\mathsf{m}(\vec{M}) \mid a.\mathsf{m}(v_1, \cdots, v_i, \_, M_{i+2}, \cdots, M_n) \end{aligned}$$

Given $\Delta|\emptyset \vdash M : \mathsf{void}$, we write $M \Downarrow$ if there exists $S$ such that $(\emptyset, M) \longrightarrow^* (S, \mathsf{skip})$.

*Definition* 3. Given $\Delta|\Gamma \vdash M_i : \theta$ $(i = 1, 2)$, we shall say that $\Delta|\Gamma \vdash M_1 : \theta$ ***contextually approximates*** $\Delta|\Gamma \vdash M_2 : \theta$ if, for all $\Delta' \supseteq \Delta$ and all contexts $C$ such that $\Delta'|\emptyset \vdash C[M_i] : \mathsf{void}$, if $C[M_1] \Downarrow$ then $C[M_2] \Downarrow$. We then write $\Delta|\Gamma \vdash M_1 \lesssim M_2 : \theta$. Two terms are ***contextually equivalent*** (written $\Delta|\Gamma \vdash M_1 \cong M_2 : \theta$) if they approximate each other.

For technical convenience, IMJ features the let construct, even though it is definable: given $\Delta|\Gamma, x : \theta' \vdash M : \theta$ and $\Delta|\Gamma \vdash M' : \theta'$, consider $\mathsf{new}(\, x : \mathcal{I}; \mathsf{m} : \lambda x.M\,).\mathsf{m}(M')$, where $\mathcal{I}$ is a fresh interface with a single method $\mathsf{m} : \theta \rightarrow \theta'$. As usual, we write $M; M'$ for $\mathsf{let}\, x = M \,\mathsf{in}\, M'$, where $x$ is not free in $M'$.

Although IMJ does not have explicit local variables, they could easily be introduced by taking $\mathsf{let}\,(x = \mathsf{new}(y : \mathcal{I}_\theta;))\,\mathsf{in} \cdots$, where $\mathcal{I}_\theta$ has a single field of type $\theta$. In the same manner, one can define variables and methods that are *private* to objects, and invisible to the environment through interfaces.

*Example* 1 ([16]). Let $\Delta = \{\mathsf{Empty} : \emptyset, \mathsf{Cell} : (\mathsf{get} : \mathsf{void} \rightarrow \mathsf{Empty}, \mathsf{set} : \mathsf{Empty} \rightarrow \mathsf{void}), \mathsf{Var}_E : (\mathsf{val} : \mathsf{Empty}), \mathsf{Var}_I : (\mathsf{val} : \mathsf{int})\}$ and consider the terms $\Delta|\emptyset \vdash M_i : \mathsf{Cell}$ $(i = 1, 2)$ defined by

$$\begin{aligned} M_1 \equiv &\ \mathsf{let}\, v = \mathsf{new}(x : \mathsf{Var}_E;)\,\mathsf{in}\ \mathsf{new}(x : \mathsf{Cell}; \mathcal{M}_1) \\ M_2 \equiv &\ \mathsf{let}\, b = \mathsf{new}(x : \mathsf{Var}_I;)\,\mathsf{in} \\ &\ \mathsf{let}\, v_1 = \mathsf{new}(x : \mathsf{Var}_E;)\,\mathsf{in} \\ &\ \mathsf{let}\, v_2 = \mathsf{new}(x : \mathsf{Var}_E;)\,\mathsf{in}\ \mathsf{new}(x : \mathsf{Cell}; \mathcal{M}_2) \end{aligned}$$

with

$$\begin{aligned} \mathcal{M}_1 = &\ (\mathsf{get} : \lambda().v.\mathsf{val}, \\ &\ \ \mathsf{set} : \lambda y.(v.\mathsf{val} := y)) \\ \mathcal{M}_2 = &\ (\mathsf{get} : \lambda().\mathsf{if}\,(b.\mathsf{val})\,\mathsf{then}\,(b.\mathsf{val} := 0; v_1.\mathsf{val}) \\ &\ \qquad\qquad\qquad \mathsf{else}\,(b.\mathsf{val} := 1; v_2.\mathsf{val}), \\ &\ \ \mathsf{set} : \lambda y.(v_1.\mathsf{val} := y;\ v_2.\mathsf{val} := y)). \end{aligned}$$

We have $\Delta|\emptyset \vdash M_1 \cong M_2 : \mathsf{Cell}$. Intuitively, each of the two implementations of Cell corresponds to recording a single value of type Empty (using set) and providing access to it via get. The difference lies in the way the value is stored: a single private variable is used in $M_1$, while two variables are used in $M_2$. However, in the latter case the variables always hold the same value, so it does not matter which of the variables is used to return the value.

The game semantics of the two terms will turn out to consist of plays of the shape $*^{\emptyset}\, n^{\Sigma_0}\, G_0^*\, S_1\, G_1^* \cdots S_k\, G_k^*$, where

$$\begin{aligned} G_i &= \begin{cases} \mathsf{call}\, n.\mathsf{get}(*)^{\Sigma_0}\ \mathsf{ret}\, n.\mathsf{get}(\mathtt{nul})^{\Sigma_0} & i = 0 \\ \mathsf{call}\, n.\mathsf{get}(*)^{\Sigma_i}\ \mathsf{ret}\, n.\mathsf{get}(n_i)^{\Sigma_i} & i > 0 \end{cases} \\ S_i &= \mathsf{call}\, n.\mathsf{set}(n_i)^{\Sigma_i}\ \mathsf{ret}\, n.\mathsf{set}(*)^{\Sigma_i} \end{aligned}$$

and $\Sigma_i = \{n \mapsto (\mathsf{Cell}, \emptyset)\} \cup \{n_j \mapsto (\mathsf{Empty}, \emptyset) \mid 0 < j \leq i\}$. Intuitively, the plays describe all possible interactions of a Cell object. The first two moves $*^{\emptyset}\, n^{\Sigma_0}$ correspond to object creation. After that, the $G_i$ segments represent the environment reading the current content (initially having null value), while the $S_i$ segments correspond to updating the content with a reference name provided by the environment. The stores $\Sigma_i$ attached to moves consist of all names that have been introduced during the interaction so far.

It is worth noting that, because IMJ has explicit casting, a context can always guess the actual interface of an object and extract any information we may want to hide through casting.

*Example* 2. Let $\Delta = \{\mathsf{Empty} : \emptyset, \mathsf{Point}\langle\mathsf{Empty}\rangle : (\mathsf{x} : \mathsf{int}, \mathsf{y} : \mathsf{int})\}$ and consider the terms $\Delta|\emptyset \vdash M_i : \mathsf{Empty}$ $(i = 1, 2)$ defined by:

$$\begin{aligned} M_1 \equiv &\ \mathsf{new}(x : \mathsf{Empty};), \\ M_2 \equiv &\ \mathsf{let}\, p = \mathsf{new}(x : \mathsf{Point};)\,\mathsf{in}\ p.\mathsf{x} := 0; p.\mathsf{y} := 1; (\mathsf{Empty})p. \end{aligned}$$

In our model they will be interpreted by the strategies $\sigma_1 = \{\epsilon, *^{\emptyset}\, n^{\{n \mapsto (\mathsf{Empty}, \emptyset)\}}\}$ and $\sigma_2 = \{\epsilon, *^{\emptyset}\, n^{\{n \mapsto (\mathsf{Point}, \{\mathsf{x} \mapsto 0, \mathsf{y} \mapsto 1\})\}}\}$ respectively. Using e.g. the casting context $C \equiv (\mathsf{Point})\_; \mathsf{skip}$, we can see that $\Delta|\emptyset \vdash M_2 \not\lesssim M_1 : \mathsf{Empty}$. On the other hand, Theorem 20 will imply $\Delta|\emptyset \vdash M_1 \lesssim M_2 : \mathsf{Empty}$.

On the whole, IMJ is a compact calculus that strips down Middleweight Java to the essentials needed for interface-based interaction. Accordingly, we suppressed the introduction of explicit class hierarchy, as it would remain invisible to the environment anyway and any class-based internal computations can be represented using standard object encodings [1].

At the moment the calculus allows for single inheritance for interfaces only, but extending it to multiple inheritance is not problematic. The following semantic developments only rely on the assumption that $\leq$ must not give rise to circularities.

## 3. The game model

In our discussion below we assume a fixed interface table $\Delta$.

The game model will be constructed using mathematical objects (moves, plays, strategies) that feature names drawn from the set $\mathbb{A}$. Although names underpin various elements of our model, we do not want to delve into the precise nature of the sets containing them. Hence, all of our definitions preserve name-invariance, i.e. our objects are (strong) *nominal sets* [11, 26]. Note that we do not need the full power of the theory but mainly the basic notion of name-permutation. For an element $x$ belonging to a (nominal) set $X$ we write $\nu(x)$ for its name-support, which is the set of names occurring in $x$. Moreover, for any $x, y \in X$, we write $x \sim y$ if there is a permutation $\pi$ such that $x = \pi \cdot y$.

We proceed to define a category of games. The objects of our category will be ***arenas***, which are nominal sets carrying specific type information.

*Definition* 4. An ***arena*** is a pair $A = (M_A, \xi_A)$ where:

- $M_A$ is a nominal set of ***moves***;
- $\xi_A : M_A \to (\mathbb{A} \rightharpoonup \mathit{Ints})$ is a nominal *typing function*;

such that, for all $m \in M_A$, $\mathsf{dom}(\xi_A(m)) = \nu(m)$.

We start by defining the following basic arenas,

$$1 = (\{*\}, \{(*, \emptyset)\}, \quad \mathbb{Z} = (\mathbb{Z}, \{(i, \emptyset)\},$$
$$\mathcal{I} = (\mathbb{A} \cup \{\mathtt{nul}\}, \{(\mathtt{nul}, \emptyset)\} \cup \{(a, a, \mathcal{I})\}),$$

for all interfaces $\mathcal{I}$. Given arenas $A$ and $B$, we can form the arena $A \times B$ by:

$$M_{A\times B} = \{(m,n) \in M_A \times M_B \mid a \in \nu(m) \cap \nu(n) \implies \xi_A(m,a) \leq \xi_B(n,a) \vee \xi_B(n,a) \leq \xi_A(m,a)\}$$

$$\xi_{A\times B}((m,n),a) = \begin{cases} \xi_A(m,a) & \text{if } a \notin \nu(n) \vee \xi_A(m,a) \leq \xi_B(n,a) \\ \xi_B(n,a) & \text{otherwise} \end{cases}$$

Another important arena is $\#(\mathcal{I}_1, \cdots, \mathcal{I}_n)$, with:

$$M_{\#(\vec{\mathcal{I}})} = \{(a_1, \cdots, a_n) \in \mathbb{A}^n \mid a_i\text{'s distinct}\}$$
$$\xi_{\#(\vec{\mathcal{I}})}((a_1, \cdots, a_n), a_i) = \mathcal{I}_i$$

for all $n \in \mathbb{N}$. In particular, $\mathbb{A}^{\#0} = 1$.

For each type $\theta$, we set $\mathit{Val}_\theta$ to be the set of *semantic values* of type $\theta$, given by:

$$\mathit{Val}_{\mathsf{void}} = M_1, \quad \mathit{Val}_{\mathsf{int}} = M_{\mathbb{Z}}, \quad \mathit{Val}_{\mathcal{I}} = M_{\mathcal{I}}.$$

For each type sequence $\vec{\theta} = \theta_1, \cdots, \theta_n$, we set $\mathit{Val}_{\vec{\theta}} = \mathit{Val}_{\theta_1} \times \cdots \times \mathit{Val}_{\theta_n}$.

We let a ***store*** $\Sigma$ be a type-preserving finite partial function from names to object types and field assignments, that is, $\Sigma : \mathbb{A} \rightharpoonup \mathit{Ints} \times (\mathit{Flds} \rightharpoonup \mathit{Val})$ such that $|\Sigma|$ is finite and

$$\Sigma(a) : \mathcal{I} \wedge \Delta(\mathcal{I}).\mathsf{f} = \theta \implies \Sigma(a).\mathsf{f} = v \wedge \Sigma \vdash v \leq \theta,$$

where the new notation is explained below. First, assuming $\Sigma(a) = (\mathcal{I}', \phi)$, the judgement $\Sigma(a) : \mathcal{I}$ holds iff $\mathcal{I} = \mathcal{I}'$ and $\Sigma(a).\mathsf{f}$ stands for $\phi(\mathsf{f})$. Next we define typing rules for values in store contexts:

$$\frac{v \in \mathit{Val}_{\mathsf{void}}}{\Sigma \vdash v : \mathsf{void}} \qquad \frac{v \in \mathit{Val}_{\mathsf{int}}}{\Sigma \vdash v : \mathsf{int}} \qquad \frac{\Sigma(v) : \mathcal{I} \vee v = \mathtt{nul}}{\Sigma \vdash v : \mathcal{I}}$$

and write $\Sigma \vdash v \leq \theta$ for $\Sigma \vdash v : \theta \vee (\Sigma \vdash v : \mathcal{I}' \wedge \mathcal{I}' \leq \theta)$.

We let $\mathit{Sto}$ be the set of all stores. We write $\mathsf{dom}(\Sigma(a))$ for the set of all $\mathsf{f}$ such that $\Sigma(a).\mathsf{f}$ is defined. We let $\mathit{Sto}_0$ contain all stores $\Sigma$ such that:

$$\forall a \in \mathsf{dom}(\Sigma), \mathsf{f} \in \mathsf{dom}(\Sigma(a)).\ \Sigma(a).\mathsf{f} \in \{*, 0, \mathtt{nul}\}$$

and we call such a $\Sigma$ a *default store*.

Given arenas $A$ and $B$, plays in $AB$ will consist of sequences of moves (with store) which will be either moves from $M_A \cup M_B$, or moves representing method calls and returns. Formally, we define:

$$M_{AB} = M_A \cup M_B \cup \mathit{Calls} \cup \mathit{Retns}$$

where we set $\mathit{Calls} = \{\mathsf{call}\ a.\mathsf{m}(\vec{v}) \mid a \in \mathbb{A} \wedge \vec{v} \in \mathit{Val}^*\}$ and $\mathit{Retns} = \{\mathsf{ret}\ a.\mathsf{m}(v) \mid a \in \mathbb{A} \wedge v \in \mathit{Val}\}$.

*Definition* 5. A ***legal sequence*** in $AB$ is a sequence of moves from $M_{AB}$ that adheres to the following grammar (*Well-Bracketing*), where $m_A$ and $m_B$ range over $M_A$ and $M_B$ respectively.

$$L_{AB} ::= \epsilon \mid m_A X \mid m_A Y m_B X$$
$$X ::= Y \mid Y\,(\mathsf{call}\ a.\mathsf{m}(\vec{v}))\,X$$
$$Y ::= \epsilon \mid YY \mid (\mathsf{call}\ a.\mathsf{m}(\vec{v}))\,Y\,(\mathsf{ret}\ a.\mathsf{m}(v))$$

We write $L_{AB}$ for the set of legal sequences in $AB$. In the last clause above, we say that $\mathsf{call}\ a.\mathsf{m}(\vec{v})$ ***justifies*** $\mathsf{ret}\ a.\mathsf{m}(v)$.

To each $s \in L_{AB}$ we assign a ***polarity*** function $p$ from move occurrences in $s$ to the set $\mathit{Pol}_1 = \{O, P\}$. Polarities represent the two players in our game reading of programs: O is the *Opponent* and P is the *Proponent* in the game. The latter corresponds to the modelled program, while the former models the possible computational environments surrounding the program. Polarities are complemented via $\overline{O} = \{P\}$ and $\overline{P} = \{O\}$. In addition, the polarity function must satisfy the condition:

- For all $m_X \in M_X$ ($X = A, B$) occurring in $s$ we have $p(m_A) = O$ and $p(m_B) = P$; (*O-starting*)
- If $mn$ are consecutive moves in $s$ then $p(n) \in \overline{p(m)}$. (*Alternation*)

It follows that there is a unique $p$ for each legal sequence $s$, namely the one which assigns $O$ precisely to those moves appearing in odd positions in $s$.

A ***move-with-store*** in $AB$ is a pair $m^\Sigma$ with $\Sigma \in \mathit{Sto}$ and $m \in M_{AB}$. For each sequence $s$ of moves-with-store we define the set of *available names* of $s$ by:

$$\mathsf{Av}(\epsilon) = \emptyset, \quad \mathsf{Av}(sm^\Sigma) = \Sigma^*(\mathsf{Av}(s) \cup \nu(m))$$

where, for each $X \subseteq \mathbb{A}$, we let $\Sigma^*(X) = \bigcup_i \Sigma^i(X)$, with

$$\Sigma^0(X) = X, \quad \Sigma^{i+1}(X) = \nu(\Sigma(\Sigma^i(X))).$$

That is, a name is available in $s$ just if it appears inside a move in $s$, or it can be reached from an available name through some store in $s$. We write $\underline{s}$ for the underlying sequence of moves of $s$ (i.e. $\pi_1(s)$), and let $\sqsubseteq$ denote the prefix relation between sequences. If $s'm^\Sigma \sqsubseteq s$ and $a \in \nu(m^\Sigma) \setminus \nu(s')$ then we say $a$ ***is introduced*** by $m^\Sigma$ in $s$.[1] In such a case, we define the *owner* of the name $a$ in $s$, written $o(a)$, to be $p(m)$ (where $p$ is the polarity associated with $\underline{s}$). For each polarity $X \in \{O, P\}$ we let

$$X(s) = \{a \in \nu(s) \mid o(a) = X\}$$

be the set of names in $s$ owned by $X$.

*Definition* 6. A ***play*** in $AB$ is a sequence of moves-with-store $s$ such that $\underline{s}$ is a legal sequence and, moreover, for all $s'm^\Sigma \sqsubseteq s$:

- It holds that $\mathsf{dom}(\Sigma) = \mathsf{Av}(s'm^\Sigma)$. (*Frugality*)
- If $a \in \mathsf{dom}(\Sigma)$ with $\Sigma(a) : \mathcal{I}$ then:
  - if $m \in M_X$, for $X \in \{A, B\}$, then $\mathcal{I} \leq \xi_X(m, a)$;
  - for all $n^T$ in $s'$, if $a \in \mathsf{dom}(T)$ then $T(a) : \mathcal{I}$;
  - if $\Delta(\mathcal{I}).\mathsf{m} = \vec{\theta} \to \theta$ then:
    - if $m = \mathsf{call}\ a.\mathsf{m}(\vec{v})$ then $\Sigma \vdash \vec{v} : \vec{\theta'}$ for some $\vec{\theta'} \leq \vec{\theta}$,
    - if $m = \mathsf{ret}\ a.\mathsf{m}(v)$ then $\Sigma \vdash v : \theta'$ for some $\theta' \leq \theta$.

  (*Well-classing*)
- If $m = \mathsf{call}\ a.\mathsf{m}(\vec{v})$ then $o(a) \in \overline{p(m)}$. (*Well-calling*)

We write $P_{AB}$ for the set of plays in $AB$.

[1] By abuse of notation, we frequently write instead "$a$ is introduced by $m$ in $s$". Recall also that $\nu(s)$ collects all names appearing in $s$; in particular, $\nu(m_1^{\Sigma_1} \cdots m_i^{\Sigma_i}) = \nu(m_1) \cup \nu(\Sigma_1) \cup \cdots \cup \nu(m_i) \cup \nu(\Sigma_i)$.

Note above that, because of well-bracketing and alternation, if $m = \mathsf{ret}\, a.\mathsf{m}(v)$ then well-calling implies $o(a) = p(m)$. Thus, the frugality condition stipulates that names cannot appear in a play in unreachable parts of a store (cf. [17]). Moreover, well-classing ensures that the typing information in stores is consistent and adheres to the constraints imposed by $\Delta$ and the underlying arenas. Finally, well-calling implements the specification that each player need only call the other player's methods. This is because calls to each player's own methods cannot in general be observed and so should not be accounted for in plays.

Given arenas $A, B, C$, next we define interaction sequences, which show how plays from $AB$ and $BC$ can interact to produce a play in $AC$. The sequences will rely on moves with stores, where the moves come from the set:

$$M_{ABC} = M_A \cup M_B \cup M_C \cup \mathit{Calls} \cup \mathit{Retns}\,.$$

The moves will be assigned polarities from the set:

$$\mathit{Pol}_2 = \{\, O_L, P_L, O_L P_R, P_L O_R, O_R, P_R \,\}\,.$$

The index $L$ stands for "left", while $R$ means "right". The indices indicate which part of the interaction ($A$, $B$ or $C$) a move comes from, and what polarity it has therein. We also consider an auxiliary notion of *pseudo-polarities*:

$$OO = \{O_L, O_R\}, \quad PO = \{P_L, P_L O_R\}, \quad OP = \{P_R, O_L P_R\}.$$

Each polarity has an opposite pseudo-polarity determined by:

$$\overline{O_L} = \overline{O_L P_R} = PO, \quad \overline{O_R} = \overline{P_L O_R} = OP, \quad \overline{P_L} = \overline{P_R} = OO.$$

Finally, each $X \in \{AB, BC, AC\}$ has a designated set of polarities given by:

$$p(AB) = \{O_L, P_L, O_L P_R, P_L O_R\},$$
$$p(BC) = \{O_R, P_R, O_L P_R, P_L O_R\},$$
$$p(AC) = \{O_L, P_L, O_R, P_R\}.$$

Note the slight abuse of notation with $p$, as it is also used for move polarities.

Suppose $X \in \{AB, BC, AC\}$. Consider a sequence $s$ of moves-with-store from $ABC$ (i.e. a sequence with elements $m^\Sigma$ with $m \in M_{ABC}$) along with an assignment $p$ of polarities from $\mathit{Pol}_2$ to moves of $s$. Let $s \upharpoonright X$ be the subsequence of $s$ containing those moves-with-store $m^\Sigma$ of $s$ for which $p(m) \in p(X)$. Additionally, we define $s \upharpoonright_\gamma X$ to be $\gamma(s \upharpoonright X)$, where the function $\gamma$ acts on moves-with-store by restricting the domains of stores to available names:

$$\gamma(\epsilon) = \epsilon, \quad \gamma(sm^\Sigma) = \gamma(s)\, m^{\Sigma \upharpoonright \mathsf{Av}(sm^\Sigma)}.$$

*Definition* 7. An ***interaction sequence*** in $ABC$ is a sequence $s$ of moves-with-store in $ABC$ satisfying the following conditions.

- For each $s'm^\Sigma \sqsubseteq s$, $\mathsf{dom}(\Sigma) = \mathsf{Av}(s'm^\Sigma)$. (*Frugality*)
- If $s'm^\Sigma \sqsubseteq s$ and $a \in \mathsf{dom}(\Sigma)$ with $\Sigma(a) : \mathcal{I}$ then:
  - if $m \in M_X$, for $X \in \{A, B, C\}$, then $\mathcal{I} \leq \xi_X(m, a)$;
  - for all $n^T$ in $s'$, if $a \in \mathsf{dom}(T)$ then $T(a) : \mathcal{I}$;
  - if $\Delta(\mathcal{I}).\mathsf{m} = \vec{\theta} \to \theta$ then:
    - if $m = \mathsf{call}\, a.\mathsf{m}(\vec{v})$ then $\Sigma \vdash \vec{v} : \vec{\theta'}$ for some $\vec{\theta'} \leq \vec{\theta}$,
    - if $m = \mathsf{ret}\, a.\mathsf{m}(v)$ then $\Sigma \vdash v : \theta'$ for some $\theta' \leq \theta$.

  (*Well-classing*)
- There is a polarity function $p$ from move occurrences in $\underline{s}$ to $\mathit{Pol}_2$ such that:
  - For all $m_X \in M_X$ ($X = A, B, C$) occurring in $\underline{s}$ we have $p(m_A) = O_L$, $p(m_B) = P_L O_R$ and $p(m_C) = \overline{P_R}$;
  - If $mn$ are consecutive moves in $\underline{s}$ then $p(n) \in \overline{p(m)}$.

  (*Alternation*)
- If $s'm^\Sigma \sqsubseteq s$ then $m = \mathsf{call}\, a.\mathsf{m}(\vec{v})$ implies $o(a) \in \overline{p(m)}$. (*Well-calling*)
- For each $X \in \{AB, BC, AC\}$, $\underline{s \upharpoonright X} \in L_X$. (*Projecting*)
- If $s'm^\Sigma \sqsubseteq s$ and $m = \mathsf{ret}\, a.\mathsf{m}(v)$ then there is a move $n^T$ in $s'$ such that, for all $X$ such that $p(m) \in p(X)$, $n$ is the justifier of $m$ in $\underline{s \upharpoonright X}$. (*Well-returning*)
- *Laird's conditions* [17]:
  - $P(s \upharpoonright_\gamma AB) \cap P(s \upharpoonright_\gamma BC) = \emptyset$;
  - $(P(s \upharpoonright_\gamma AB) \cup P(s \upharpoonright_\gamma BC)) \cap O(s \upharpoonright_\gamma AC) = \emptyset$;
  - For each $s' \sqsubseteq s$ ending in $m^\Sigma n^T$ and each $a \in \mathsf{dom}(T)$, if
    - $p(m) \in PO$ and $a \notin \nu(s' \upharpoonright_\gamma AB)$,
    - or $p(m) \in OP$ and $a \notin \nu(s' \upharpoonright_\gamma BC)$,
    - or $p(m) \in OO$ and $a \notin \nu(s' \upharpoonright_\gamma AC)$,

    then $\Sigma(a) = T(a)$.

We write $\mathit{Int}(ABC)$ for the set of interaction sequences in $ABC$.

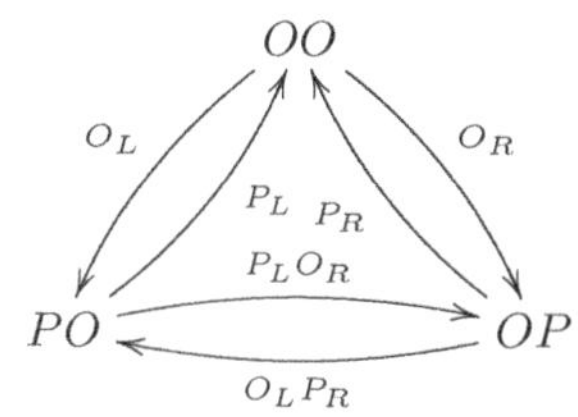


**Figure 3.** Interaction diagram for $\mathit{Int}(ABC)$. The diagram specifies the alternation of polarities in interaction sequences. Transitions are labelled by move polarities, while $OO$ is the initial state.

Note that, by projecting and well-returning, each return move in $s$ has a unique justifier. Next we show that the polarities of moves inside an interaction sequence are uniquely determined by the ***interaction diagram*** of Figure 3. The diagram can be seen as an automaton accepting $\underline{s}$, for each $s \in \mathit{Int}(ABC)$. The edges represent moves by their polarities, while the labels of vertices specify the polarity of the next (outgoing) move. For example, from $OO$ we can only have a move $m$ with $p(m) \in \{O_L, O_R\}$, for any $p$.

**Lemma 1.** *Each $s \in \mathit{Int}(ABC)$ has a unique polarity function $p$.*

*Proof.* Suppose $s \in \mathit{Int}(ABC)$. We claim that the alternation, well-calling, projecting and well-returning conditions uniquely specify $p$. Consider the interaction diagram of Figure 3, which we read as an automaton accepting $\underline{s}$, call it $\mathcal{A}$. The edges represent moves by their polarities, while the labels of vertices specify the polarity of the next (outgoing) move. By projecting we obtain that the first element of $\underline{s}$ is some $m_A$ and, by alternation, its polarity is $O_L$. Thus, $OO$ is the initial state.
We now use induction on $|s|$ to show that $\mathcal{A}$ has a unique run on $\underline{s}$. The base case is trivial, so suppose $\underline{s} = s'm$. By induction hypothesis, $\mathcal{A}$ has a unique run on $s'$, which reaches some state $X$. We do a case analysis on $m$. If $m \in M_A \cup M_B \cup M_C$ then there is a unique edge accepting $m$ and, by alternation, this edge must depart from $X$. If, on the other hand, $m = \mathsf{call}\, a.\mathsf{m}(\vec{v})$ then the fact that $o(a) \in \overline{p(m)}$ gives two possible edges for accepting $m$. But observe that no combination of such edges can depart from $X$. Finally, let $m = \mathsf{ret}\, a.\mathsf{m}(v)$ be justified by some $n$ in $s'$. Then, by well-bracketing, $n$ is the justifier of $m$ in all projections, and hence the edge accepting $m$ must be the opposite of the one accepting $n$ (e.g. if $m$ is accepted by $O_L$ then $n$ is accepted by $P_L$). ☐

Next we show that interaction sequences project to plays. The projection of interaction sequences in $ABC$ on $AB$, $BC$ and $AC$

leads to the following definition of projections of polarities,

$$\pi_{AB}(X_L) = X \qquad \pi_{AB}(X_L Y_R) = X \qquad \pi_{AB}(Y_R) = \text{undef.}$$
$$\pi_{BC}(X_L) = \text{undef.} \qquad \pi_{BC}(X_L Y_R) = Y \qquad \pi_{BC}(Y_R) = Y$$
$$\pi_{AC}(X_L) = X \qquad \pi_{AC}(X_L Y_R) = \text{undef.} \qquad \pi_{AC}(Y_R) = Y$$

where $X, Y \in \{O, P\}$. We can now show the following.

**Lemma 2.** *Let $s \in Int(ABC)$. Then, for each $X \in \{AB, BC, AC\}$ and each $m^\Sigma$ in $s$, if $p(m) \in p(X)$ then $\pi_X(p(m)) = p_X(m)$, where $p_X$ is the polarity function of $s \upharpoonright X$.*

*Proof.* We show this for $X = AB$, the other cases are proven similarly, by induction on $|s| \geq 0$; the base case is trivial. For the inductive case, if $m$ is the first move in $s$ with polarity in $p(AB)$ then, by projecting, $m \in M_A$ and therefore $p(m) = O_L$ and $p_{AB}(m) = O$, as required. Otherwise, let $n$ be the last move in $s$ with polarity in $p(AB)$ before $m$. By IH, $p_{AB}(n) = \pi_{AB}(p(n))$. Now, by projecting, $p_{AB}(m) = p_{AB}(n)$ and observe that, for all $X \in p(n)$, $\pi_{AB}(X) = \pi_{AB}(p(n))$, so in particular $\pi_{AB}(p(m)) = \pi_{AB}(p(n)) = p_{AB}(n) = p_{AB}(m)$. □

The following lemma formulates a taxonomy on names appearing in interaction sequences.

**Lemma 3.** *Let $s \in Int(ABC)$. Then,*

*1. $\nu(s) = O(s \upharpoonright_\gamma AC) \uplus P(s \upharpoonright_\gamma AB) \uplus P(s \upharpoonright_\gamma BC)$;*

*2. if $s = tm^\Sigma$ and:*
- *$p(m) \in OO$ and $s \upharpoonright_\gamma AC = t'm^{\Sigma'}$,*
- *or $p(m) \in PO$ and $s \upharpoonright_\gamma AB = t'm^{\Sigma'}$,*
- *or $p(m) \in OP$ and $s \upharpoonright_\gamma BC = t'm^{\Sigma'}$,*

*then $\nu(t) \cap \nu(m^{\Sigma'}) \subseteq \nu(t')$ and, in particular, if $m$ introduces name $a$ in $t'm^{\Sigma'}$ then $m$ introduces $a$ in $s$.*

*Proof.* For 1, by definition of interactions we have that these sets are disjoint. It therefore suffices to show the left-to-right inclusion. Suppose that $a \in \nu(s)$ is introduced in some $m^\Sigma$ in $s$, with $p(m) \in PO$, and let $s \upharpoonright_\gamma AB = \cdots m^{\Sigma'} \cdots$. If $a \in \nu(m^{\Sigma'})$ then $a \in P(s \upharpoonright_\gamma AB)$, as required. Otherwise, by Laird's last set of conditions, $a$ is copied from the store of the move preceding $m^\Sigma$ in $s$, a contradiction to its being introduced at $m^\Sigma$. Similarly if $p(m) \in OP$. Finally, if $p(m) \in OO$ then we work similarly, considering $O(s \upharpoonright_\gamma AC)$.
For 2, we show the first case, and the other cases are similar. It suffices to show that $(\nu(m^{\Sigma'}) \setminus \nu(t')) \cap \nu(t) = \emptyset$. So suppose $a \in \nu(m^{\Sigma'}) \setminus \nu(t')$, therefore $a \in O(s \upharpoonright_\gamma AC)$. But then we cannot have $a \in \nu(t)$ as the latter, by item 1, would imply $a \in P(s \upharpoonright_\gamma AB) \cup P(s \upharpoonright_\gamma BC)$. □

**Proposition 4.** *For all $s \in Int(ABC)$, the projections $s \upharpoonright_\gamma AB$, $s \upharpoonright_\gamma BC$ and $s \upharpoonright_\gamma AC$ are plays in $AB$, $BC$ and $AC$ respectively.*

*Proof.* By frugality of $s$ and application of $\gamma$, all projections satisfy frugality. Moreover, well-classing is preserved by projections. For well-calling, let $m = \mathsf{call}\, a.\mathsf{m}(\vec{v})$ be a move in $s$ and let $n^T$ be the move introducing $a$ in $s$. Suppose $p(m) \in p(AB)$ and let us assume $p_{AB}(m) = O$. We need to show that $o_{AB}(m) = P$. By $p_{AB}(m) = O$ we obtain that $p(m) \in \{O_L, O_L P_R\}$ and, by well-calling of $s$, we have that $o(a) \in PO$. Thus, $p(n) \in PO$ and, by Lemma 3, $n$ introduces $a$ in $s \upharpoonright_\gamma AB$ and therefore $o_{AB}(n) = P$, as required. If, on the other hand, $p_{AB}(m) = P$ then we obtain $p(n) \in OO \cup OP$ and therefore, by Lemma 3, $a \in P(s \upharpoonright_\gamma BC) \cup O(s \upharpoonright_\gamma AC)$. Thus, by the same lemma, $a \notin P(s \upharpoonright_\gamma AB)$ and hence $o_{AB}(a) = O$. The cases for the other projections are shown similarly. □

In our setting programs will be represented by *strategies* between arenas. We shall introduce them next after a few auxiliary definitions. Intuitively, strategies capture the observable computational patterns produced by a program.

Let us define the following notion of subtyping between stores. For $\Sigma, \Sigma' \in Sto$, $\Sigma \leq \Sigma'$ holds if, for all names $a$,

$$\Sigma'(a) : \mathcal{I}' \implies \Sigma(a) \leq \mathcal{I}' \wedge \forall \mathsf{f} \in \mathsf{dom}(\Sigma'(a)).\Sigma(a).\mathsf{f} = \Sigma'(a).\mathsf{f}$$

In particular, if $a$ is in the domain of $\Sigma'$, $\Sigma$ may contain more information about $a$ because of assigning to $a$ a larger interface. Accordingly, for plays $s, s' \in P_{AB}$, we say that $s$ is an ***O-extension*** of $s'$ if $s$ and $s'$ agree on their underlying sequences, while their stores may differ due to subtyping related to O-names. Where such subtyping leads to $s$ having stores with more fields than those in $s'$, P is assumed to copy the values of those fields. Formally, $s \leq_O s'$ is defined by the rules:

$$\frac{}{\epsilon \leq_O \epsilon} \qquad \frac{s \leq_O s' \quad \Sigma \leq \Sigma' \quad \Sigma \upharpoonright P(sm^\Sigma) \subseteq \Sigma'}{sm^\Sigma \leq_O s'm^{\Sigma'}}\ {\scriptstyle p(m)=O}$$

$$\frac{sn^T \leq_O s' \quad \Sigma \leq \Sigma' \quad \Sigma \text{ extends } \Sigma' \text{ by } T}{sn^T m^\Sigma \leq_O s'm^{\Sigma'}}\ {\scriptstyle p(m)=P}$$

where $\Sigma$ extends $\Sigma'$ by $T$ if:

- for all $a \in \mathsf{dom}(\Sigma) \setminus \mathsf{dom}(\Sigma')$, $\Sigma(a) = T(a)$;
- for all $a$ and $\mathsf{f} \in \mathsf{dom}(\Sigma(a)) \setminus \mathsf{dom}(\Sigma'(a))$, $\Sigma(a).\mathsf{f} = T(a).\mathsf{f}$.

The utility of O-extension is to express semantically the fact that the environment of a program may use up-casting to inject in its objects additional fields (and methods) not accessible to the program.

*Definition* 8. A ***strategy*** $\sigma$ in $AB$ is a non-empty set of even-length plays from $P_{AB}$ satisfying the conditions:

- If $sm^\Sigma n^T \in \sigma$ then $s \in \sigma$. (*Even-prefix closure*)
- If $sm^\Sigma, sn^T \in \sigma$ then $sm^\Sigma \sim sn^T$. (*Determinacy*)
- If $s \in \sigma$ and $s \sim t$ then $t \in \sigma$. (*Equivariance*)[2]
- If $s \in \sigma$ and $t \leq_O s$ then $t \in \sigma$. (*O-extension*)

We write $\sigma : A \to B$ when $\sigma$ is a strategy in $AB$. If $\sigma : A \to B$ and $\tau : B \to C$, we define their ***composition*** $\sigma;\tau$ by:

$$\sigma;\tau = \{s \upharpoonright_\gamma AC \mid s \in \sigma \| \tau\}$$

where $\sigma \| \tau = \{s \in Int(ABC) \mid s \upharpoonright_\gamma AB \in \sigma \wedge s \upharpoonright_\gamma BC \in \tau\}$.

In definitions of strategies we may often leave the presence of the empty sequence implicit, as the latter is a member of every strategy. For example, for each arena $A$, we define the strategy:

$$\mathtt{id}_A : A \to A = \{m_A^\Sigma m_A^\Sigma \in P_{AA}\}$$

The next series of lemmata allow us to show that strategy composition is well defined.

**Lemma 5.** *If $sm^\Sigma, sn^T \in \sigma \| \tau$ with $p(m) \notin OO$ then $sm^\Sigma \sim sn^T$. Hence, if $s_1 m^\Sigma, s_2 n^T \in \sigma \| \tau$ with $p(m) \notin OO$ and $s_1 \sim s_2$ then $s_1 m^\Sigma \sim s_2 n^T$.*

*Proof.* For the latter part, if $s_1 = \pi \cdot s_2$ then, since $\pi \cdot (s_2 n^T) \in \sigma \| \tau$, by former part of the claim we have $s_1 m^\Sigma \sim \pi \cdot (s_2 n^T)$ so $s_1 m^\Sigma \sim s_2 n^T$.
Now, for the former part, suppose WLOG that $p(m) \in PO$. Then, by the interaction diagram, we also have $p(n) \in PO$. As $sm^\Sigma, sn^T \upharpoonright_\gamma AB \in \sigma$, by determinacy of $\sigma$ we get $s'm^{\Sigma'} \sim s'n^{T'}$,

[2] Recall that, for any nominal set $X$ and $x, y \in X$, we write $x \sim y$ just if there is a permutation $\pi$ such that $x = \pi \cdot y$.

with $s'm^{\Sigma'} = sm^{\Sigma} \restriction_\gamma AB$ and $s'n^{T'} = sn^{T} \restriction_\gamma AB$. We therefore have $(s', m^{\Sigma'}) \sim (s', n^{T})$ and, trivially, $(s, s') \sim (s, s')$. Moreover, by Lemma 3, $\nu(m^{\Sigma'}) \cap \nu(s) \subseteq \nu(s')$ and $\nu(n^{T'}) \cap \nu(s) \subseteq \nu(s')$ hence, by Strong Support Lemma [26], $sm^{\Sigma'} \sim sn^{T'}$. By Laird's last set of conditions, the remaining values of $\Sigma, T$ are determined by the last store in $s$, hence $sm^{\Sigma} \sim sn^{T}$. □

**Lemma 6.** *If $s_1, s_2 \in \sigma \| \tau$ end in moves with polarities in $p(AC)$ and $s_1 \restriction_\gamma AC = s_2 \restriction_\gamma AC$ then $s_1 \sim s_2$.*

*Proof.* By induction on $|s_1 \restriction_\gamma AC| > 0$. The base case is encompassed in $s_i = s_i' m^{\Sigma_i}$ with $p(m) \in OO$, $i = 1, 2$, where note that by IH $m$ will have the same polarity in $s_1, s_2$. Then, by IH we get $s_1' = \pi \cdot s_2'$, for some $\pi$. Let $s_i'' m^{\Sigma'} = s_i \restriction_\gamma AC$, for $i = 1, 2$, so in particular $s_1'' = \pi \cdot s_2''$ and therefore $(s_1', s_1'') \sim (s_2', s_2'')$. Moreover, by hypothesis, we trivially have $(m^{\Sigma'}, s_1'') \sim (m^{\Sigma'}, s_2'')$ and hence, by Lemma 3 and Strong Support Lemma [26], we obtain $s_1' m^{\Sigma'} \sim s_2' m^{\Sigma'}$ which implies $s_1 \sim s_2$ by Laird's conditions. Suppose now $s_i = s_i' s_i'' m^{\Sigma_i}$, $i = 1, 2$, with $p(m) \in P(AC) \setminus OO$ and the last move in $s_i'$ being the last move in $s_i' s_i''$ having polarity in $p(AC)$. By IH, $s_1' \sim s_2'$. Then, by consecutive applications of Lemma 5, we obtain $s_1 \sim s_2$. □

**Proposition 7.** *If $\sigma : A \to B$ and $\tau : B \to C$ then $\sigma; \tau : A \to C$.*

*Proof.* We show that $\sigma; \tau$ is a strategy. Even-prefix closure and equivariance are clear. Moreover, since each $s \in \sigma \| \tau$ has even-length projections in $AB$ and $BC$, we can show that its projection in $AC$ is even-length too. For O-extension, if $s \in \sigma; \tau$ and $t \leq_O s$ with $s = u \restriction_\gamma AC$ and $u \in \sigma \| \tau$, we can construct $v \in Int(ABC)$ such that $t = v \restriction_\gamma AC$ and $v \leq_O u$, where $\leq_O$ is defined for interaction sequences in an analogous way as for plays (with condition $p(m) = O$ replaced by $p(m) \in OO$, and $p(m) = P$ by $p(m) \in PO \cup OP$). Moreover, $v \restriction_\gamma AB \leq_O u \restriction_\gamma AB$ and $v \restriction_\gamma BC \leq_O u \restriction_\gamma BC$, so $t \in \sigma; \tau$. Finally, for determinacy, let $sm^{\Sigma}, sn^{T} \in \sigma; \tau$ be due to $s_1 s_1' m^{\Sigma'}, s_2 s_2' n^{T'} \in \sigma \| \tau$ respectively, where $s_1, s_2$ both end in the last move of $s$. By Lemma 6, we have $s_1 \sim s_2$ and thus, by consecutive applications of Lemma 5, we get $s_1 s_1' m^{\Sigma'} \sim s_2 s_2' n^{T'}$, so $sm^{\Sigma} \sim sn^{T}$. □

The above result shows that strategies are closed under composition. We can prove that composition is associative and, consequently, obtain a category of games.

**Proposition 8.** *For all $\rho : A \to B$, $\sigma : B \to C$ and $\tau : C \to D$, $(\rho; \sigma); \tau = \rho; (\sigma; \tau)$.*

*Definition* 9. Given a class table $\Delta$, we define the category $\mathcal{G}_\Delta$ having arenas as objects and strategies as morphisms. Identity morphisms are given by $\mathtt{id}_A$, for each arena $A$.

Note that neutrality of identity strategies easily follows from the definitions and, hence, $\mathcal{G}_\Delta$ is well defined. In the sequel, when $\Delta$ can be inferred from the context, we shall write $\mathcal{G}_\Delta$ simply as $\mathcal{G}$. As a final note, for class tables $\Delta \subseteq \Delta'$, we can define a functor

$$\Delta/\Delta' : \mathcal{G}_\Delta \to \mathcal{G}_{\Delta'}$$

which acts as the identity map on arenas, and sends each $\sigma : A \to B$ of $\mathcal{G}_\Delta$ to:

$$(\Delta/\Delta')(\sigma) = \{s \in P_{AB}^{\Delta'} \mid \exists t \in \sigma.\, s \leq_O t\}$$

where $P_{AB}^{\Delta'}$ refers to plays in $\mathcal{G}_{\Delta'}$. In the other direction, we can define a strategy transformation:

$$(\Delta'/\Delta)(\sigma) = \sigma \cap P_{AB}^{\Delta}$$

which satisfies $\Delta'/\Delta(\Delta/\Delta'(\sigma)) = \sigma$.

## 4. Soundness

Here we introduce constructions that will allow us to build a model of IMJ. We begin by defining a special class of strategies. A strategy $\sigma : A \to B$ is called ***evaluated*** if there is a function $f_\sigma : M_A \to M_B$ such that:

$$\sigma = \{m_A^{\Sigma} m_B^{\Sigma} \in P_{AB} \mid m_B = f_\sigma(m_A)\}.$$

Note that equivariance of $\sigma$ implies that, for all $m_A \in M_A$ and permutations $\pi$, it holds that $\pi \cdot f_\sigma(m_A) = f_\sigma(\pi \cdot m_A)$. Thus, in particular, $\nu(f_\sigma(m_A)) \subseteq \nu(m_A)$.

Recall that, for arenas $A$ and $B$, we can construct a product arena $A \times B$. We can also define projection strategies:

$$\pi_1 : A \times B \to A = \{(m_A, m_B)^{\Sigma} m_A^{\Sigma} \in P_{(A \times B)A}\}$$

and, analogously, $\pi_2 : A \times B \to B$. Note that the projections are evaluated. Moreover, for each object $A$,

$$!_A = \{m_A^{\Sigma} *^{\Sigma} \mid m_A^{\Sigma} \in P_{A1}\}$$

is the unique evaluated strategy of type $A \to 1$.

Given strategies $\sigma : A \to B$ and $\tau : A \to C$, with $\tau$ evaluated, we define:

$$\langle \sigma, \tau \rangle : A \to B \times C = \{m_A^{\Sigma} s[(m_B, f_\tau(m_A))/m_B] \mid m_A^{\Sigma} s \in \sigma\}$$

where we write $s[m'/m_B]$ for the sequence obtained from $s$ by replacing any occurrences of $m_B$ in it by $m'$ (note that there can be at most one occurrence of $m_B$ in $s$).

The above structure yields products for evaluated strategies.

**Lemma 9.** *Evaluated strategies form a wide subcategory of $\mathcal{G}$ which has finite products, given by the above constructions. Moreover, for all $\sigma : A \to B$ and $\tau : A \to C$ with $\tau$ evaluated, $\langle \sigma, \tau \rangle; \pi_1 = \sigma$ and $\langle \sigma, \tau \rangle = \langle \sigma, \mathtt{id}_A \rangle; \langle \pi_1, \pi_2; \tau \rangle$.*

Using the above result, we can extend pairings to general $\sigma : A \to B$ and $\tau : A \to C$ by:

$$\langle \sigma, \tau \rangle \;=\; A \xrightarrow{\langle \sigma, \mathtt{id}_A \rangle} B \times A \xrightarrow{\langle \pi_2; \tau, \pi_1 \rangle} C \times B \xrightarrow{\cong} B \times C$$

where $\cong$ is the isomorphism $\langle \pi_2, \pi_1 \rangle$. The above represents a notion of *left-pairing* of $\sigma$ and $\tau$, where the effects of $\sigma$ precede those of $\tau$. We can also define a *left-tensor* between strategies:

$$\sigma \times \tau \;=\; A \times B \xrightarrow{\langle \pi_1; \sigma, \pi_2 \rangle} A' \times B \xrightarrow{\langle \pi_1, \pi_2; \tau \rangle} A' \times B'$$

for any $\sigma : A \to A'$ and $\tau : B \to B'$.

**Lemma 10.** *Let $\tau' : A' \to A$, $\sigma : A \to B_1$, $\tau : A \to B_2$, $\sigma_1 : B_1 \times B_2 \to C_1$ and $\sigma_2 : B_2 \to C_2$, with $\tau$ and $\tau'$ evaluated. Then $\tau'; \langle \sigma, \tau \rangle; \langle \sigma_1, \pi_2; \sigma_2 \rangle = \langle \tau'; \langle \sigma, \tau \rangle; \sigma_1, \tau'; \tau; \sigma_2 \rangle$.*

*Proof.* The result follows from the simpler statements:

$$\tau; \langle \sigma, \mathtt{id} \rangle = \langle \tau; \sigma, \tau \rangle, \quad \langle \sigma, \mathtt{id} \rangle; \langle \sigma', \pi_2 \rangle = \langle \langle \sigma; \mathtt{id} \rangle; \sigma', \mathtt{id} \rangle,$$

for all appropriately typed $\sigma, \sigma', \tau$, with $\tau$ evaluated, and Lemma 9. □

An immediate consequence of the above is:

$$A \xrightarrow{\langle \sigma; \tau \rangle} B_1 \times B_2 \xrightarrow{\sigma_1 \times \sigma_2} C_1 \times C_2 \;=\; A \xrightarrow{\langle \sigma; \sigma_1, \tau; \sigma_2 \rangle} C_1 \times C_2$$

More generally, Lemma 10 provides us with naturality conditions similar to those present in *Freyd categories* [25] or, equivalently, categories with monadic products [22].

We also introduce the following weak notion of coproduct. Given strategies $\sigma, \tau : A \to B$, we define:

$$[\sigma, \tau] : \mathbb{Z} \times A \to B = \{(1, m_A)^{\Sigma} s \mid m_A^{\Sigma} s \in \sigma\} \cup \{(0, m_A)^{\Sigma} s \mid m_A^{\Sigma} s \in \tau\}$$

Setting $\hat{i} : 1 \to \mathbb{Z} = \{*i\}$, for each $i \in \mathbb{Z}$, we can show the following.

**Lemma 11.** *For all strategies $\sigma' : A' \to A$ and $\sigma, \tau : A \to B$,*

- $\langle !; \hat{0}, \mathtt{id}\rangle; [\sigma, \tau] = \tau$ *and* $\langle !; \hat{1}, \mathtt{id}\rangle; [\sigma, \tau] = \sigma$;
- *if $\sigma'$ is evaluated then* $(\mathtt{id}_{\mathbb{Z}} \times \sigma'); [\sigma, \tau] = [\sigma'; \sigma, \sigma'; \tau]$.

Method definitions in IMJ induce a form of exponentiation:

$$\frac{\bigwedge_{i=1}^{n}(\Delta|\Gamma \uplus \{\vec{x}_i : \vec{\theta}_i\} \vdash M_i : \theta_i)}{\Delta|\Gamma \vdash \mathcal{M} : \Theta} \quad {\scriptstyle \Theta=\{\mathsf{m}_i:\vec{\theta}_i\to\theta_i \mid 1\leq i\leq n\} \atop \scriptstyle \wedge \mathcal{M}=\{\mathsf{m}_i:\lambda\vec{x}_i.M_i \mid 1\leq i\leq n\}}$$

the modelling of which requires some extra semantic machinery. Traditionally, in call-by-value game models, exponentiation leads to 'effectless' strategies, corresponding to higher-order value terms. In our case, higher-order values are methods, manifesting themselves via the objects they may inhabit. Hence, exponentiation necessarily passes through generation of fresh object names containing these values. These considerations give rise to two classes of strategies introduced below.

We say that an even-length play $s \in P_{AB}$ is ***total*** if it is either empty or $s = m_A^{\Sigma} m_B^{\Sigma \uplus T} s'$ and:

- $T \in \mathit{Sto}_0$ and $\nu(m_B) \cap \nu(\Sigma) \subseteq \nu(m_A)$,
- if $s' = s'' m^{\Sigma'} n^{T'}$ and $a \in \mathsf{dom}(\Sigma) \setminus \nu(\gamma(m_A^{\Sigma_0} m_B^{\Sigma_0 \uplus T} s'))$, for $\Sigma_0 \in \mathit{Sto}_0$ such that $\gamma(m_A^{\Sigma_0} m_B^{\Sigma_0 \uplus T} s') \in P_{AB}$, then $a \notin \nu(n)$ and $T'(a) = \Sigma'(a)$.

We write $P_{AB}^{\mathrm{t}}$ for the set of total plays in $AB$. Thus, in total plays, the initial move $m_A$ is immediately followed by a move $m_B$, and the initial store $\Sigma$ is *invisible* to P in the sense that P cannot use its names nor their values. A strategy $\phi : A \to B$ is called ***single-threaded*** if it consists of total plays and satisfies the conditions:[3]

- for all $m_A^{\Sigma} \in P_{AB}$ there is $m_A^{\Sigma} m_B^{T} \in \phi$;
- if $m_A^{\Sigma} m_B^{\Sigma \uplus T} s \in \phi$ then $\gamma(m_A^{\Sigma_0} m_B^{\Sigma_0 \uplus T} s) \in \phi$, for $\Sigma_0 \in \mathit{Sto}_0$;
- if $m_A^{\Sigma} m_B^{\Sigma \uplus T} s\, \mathsf{call}\, a.\mathsf{m}(\vec{v})^{\Sigma'} s' \in \phi$ and $a \in \nu(T)$ then $s = \epsilon$.

Thus, single-threaded strategies reply to every initial move $m_A^{\Sigma}$ with a move $m_B^{T}$ which depends only on $m_A$ (i.e. P does not *read* before playing). Moreover, $m_B^{T}$ does not change the values of $\Sigma$ (P does not *write*) and may introduce some fresh objects, albeit with default values. Finally, plays of single-threaded strategies consist of just one *thread*, where a thread is a total play in which there can be at most one call to names introduced by its second move.

Conversely, given a total play starting with $m_A^{\Sigma} m_B^{\Sigma \uplus T}$, we can extract its threads by tracing back for each move in $s$ the method call of the object $a \in \nu(T)$ it is related to. Formally, for each total play $s = m_A^{\Sigma} m_B^{\Sigma \uplus T} s'$ with $|s'| > 0$, the *threader* move of $s$, written $\mathsf{thrr}(s)$, is given by induction:

- $\mathsf{thrr}(s' m^{\Sigma'}) = \mathsf{thrr}(s')$, if $p(m) = P$;
- $\mathsf{thrr}(s' \mathsf{call}\, a.\mathsf{m}(\vec{v})^{\Sigma'}) = \mathsf{call}\, a.\mathsf{m}(\vec{v})^{\Sigma'}$, if $a \in \nu(T)$;
- $\mathsf{thrr}(s' n^{T} s'' \mathsf{call}\, a.\mathsf{m}(\vec{v})^{\Sigma'}) = \mathsf{thrr}(s' n^{T})$, if $a \in P(s) \setminus \nu(T)$ and $n$ introduces $a$.
- $\mathsf{thrr}(s' n^{T} s'' m^{\Sigma'}) = \mathsf{thrr}(s' n^{T})$, if $p(m) = O$ and $n$ justifies $m$.

If $s = s' n^{T'} s''$ with $|s'| \geq 2$, we set $\mathsf{thrr}(n^{T'}) = \mathsf{thrr}(s' n^{T'})$. Then, the ***current thread*** of $s$ is the subsequence of $s$ containing only moves with the same threader move as $s$, that is, if $\mathsf{thrr}(s) = m^{\Sigma'}$ and $s = m_A^{\Sigma} m_B^{\Sigma \uplus T} s'$ then

$$\lceil s \rceil = m_A^{\Sigma} m_B^{\Sigma \uplus T} (s' \upharpoonright m^{\Sigma'})$$

[3] Note that the use of the term "thread" here is internal to game semantics parlance and in particular should not be confused with Java threads.

where the restriction retains only those moves $n^{T'}$ of $s'$ such that $\mathsf{thrr}(n^{T'}) = m^{\Sigma'}$. We extend this to the case of $|s| \leq 2$ by setting $\lceil s \rceil = s$. Finally, we call a total play $s \in P_{AB}$ ***thread-independent*** if for all $s' m^{\Sigma'} \sqsubseteq^{even} s$ with $|s'| > 2$:

- if $\gamma(\lceil s' m^{\Sigma'} \rceil) = s'' m^{\Sigma''}$ then $\nu(\Sigma'') \cap \nu(s') \subseteq \nu(s'')$;
- if $s'$ ends in some $n^{T'}$ and $a \in \mathsf{dom}(\Sigma') \setminus \nu(\gamma(\lceil s' m^{\Sigma'} \rceil))$ then $\Sigma'(a) = T'(a)$.

We write $P_{AB}^{\mathrm{ti}}$ for the set of thread-independent plays in $AB$.

We can now define strategies which occur as interleavings of single-threaded ones. Let $\phi : A \to B$ be a single-threaded strategy. We define: $\phi^{\dagger} = \{s \in P_{AB}^{\mathrm{ti}} \mid \forall s' \sqsubseteq^{even} s.\ \gamma(\lceil s' \rceil) \in \phi\}$.

**Lemma 12.** *$\phi^{\dagger}$ is a strategy, for each single-threaded $\phi$.*

*Proof.* Equivariance, Even-prefix closure and O-extension follow from the corresponding conditions on $\phi$. For determinacy, if $sm^{\Sigma}, sn^{T} \in \phi^{\dagger}$ with $|s| > 0$ then, using determinacy of $\phi$ and the fact that P-moves do not change the current thread, nor do they modify or use names from other threads, we can show that $sm^{\Sigma} \sim sn^{T}$. □

We say that a strategy $\sigma$ is ***thread-independent*** if $\sigma = \tau^{\dagger}$ for some single-threaded strategy $\tau$. Thus, thread-independent strategies do not depend on initial stores and behave in each of their threads in an independent manner. Note in particular that evaluated strategies are thread-independent (and single-threaded).

**Lemma 13.** *Let $\sigma : A \to B$ and $\tau : A \to C$ be strategies with $\tau$ thread-independent. Then, $\langle \sigma, \tau \rangle; \pi_1 = \sigma$ and:*

$$\langle \sigma, \tau \rangle \;=\; A \xrightarrow{\langle \tau, \sigma \rangle} C \times B \xrightarrow{\cong} B \times C\,.$$

*Proof.* The former claim is straightforward. For the latter, we observe that the initial effects of $\sigma$ and $\tau$ commute: on initial move $m_A^{\Sigma}$, $\tau$ does not read the store updates that $\sigma$ includes in its response $m_B^{\Sigma'}$, while $\sigma$ cannot access the names created by $\tau$ in its second move $m_C^{\Sigma' \uplus T}$. □

It is worth noting that the above lemma does not suffice for obtaining categorical products. Allowing thread-independent strategies to create fresh names in their second move breaks universality of pairings. Considering, for example, the strategy:

$$\sigma : 1 \to \mathcal{I} \times \mathcal{I} = \{* \, (a,a)^{\Sigma} \in P_{1(\mathcal{I} \times \mathcal{I})} \mid \Sigma \in \mathit{Sto}_0\}$$

we can see that $\sigma \neq \langle \sigma; \pi_1, \sigma; \pi_2 \rangle$, as the right-hand-side contains plays of the form $* \, (a,b)^{T}$ with $a \neq b$.

We can now define an appropriate notion of exponential for our games. Let us assume a translation assigning an arena $[\![\vec{\theta}]\!]$ to each type sequence $\vec{\theta}$. Moreover, let $\mathcal{I}$ be an interface such that

$$\Delta(\mathcal{I}) \upharpoonright \mathit{Meths} = \{\mathsf{m}_1 : \vec{\theta}_1 \to \theta_1, \cdots, \mathsf{m}_n : \vec{\theta}_n \to \theta_n\}$$

where $\vec{\theta}_i = \theta_{i1}, \cdots, \theta_{im_i}$, for each $i$. For any arena $A$, given single-threaded strategies $\phi_1, \cdots, \phi_n : A \to \mathcal{I}$ such that, for each $i$, if $m_A^{\Sigma} a^{\Sigma \uplus T} s \in \phi_i$ then

$$a \notin \nu(\Sigma) \wedge T(a) : \mathcal{I} \wedge (\mathsf{call}\, a.\mathsf{m}(\vec{v}) \in s \implies \mathsf{m} = \mathsf{m}_i),$$

we can group them into one single-threaded strategy:

$$\langle\langle \phi_1, \ldots, \phi_n \rangle\rangle : A \to \mathcal{I} = \bigcup_{i=1}^{n} \phi_i\,.$$

Note that the $a$ above is fresh for each $m_A^{\Sigma}$ (i.e. $a \notin \nu(m_A^{\Sigma})$).

Let now $\sigma_1, \cdots, \sigma_n$ be strategies with $\sigma_i : A \times [\![\vec{\theta_i}]\!] \to [\![\theta_i]\!]$. For each $i$, we define the single-threaded strategy $\Lambda(\sigma_i) : A \to \mathcal{I}$:

$$\Lambda(\sigma_i) = \{m_A^\Sigma a^{\Sigma \uplus T} \mathsf{call}\, a.m_i(\vec{v})^{\Sigma'} s \in P_{A\mathcal{I}}^{\mathsf{t}} \mid \gamma((m_A, \vec{v})^{\Sigma'} s) \in \sigma_i\}$$
$$\cup \{m_A^\Sigma a^{\Sigma \uplus T} \mathsf{call}\, a.m_i(\vec{v})^{\Sigma'} s\ \mathsf{ret}\, a.\mathsf{m}_i(v)^{T'} s' \in P_{A\mathcal{I}}^{\mathsf{t}} \mid$$
$$\gamma((m_A, \vec{v})^{\Sigma'} s\, v^{T'} s') \in \sigma_i\} \cup \{m_A^\Sigma a^{\Sigma \uplus T} \in P_{A\mathcal{I}}^{\mathsf{t}}\}$$

where $a \notin \nu(\Sigma, \vec{v}, v, s, s', \Sigma', T')$ and $T(a) : \mathcal{I}$. By definition, $\Lambda(\sigma_i)$ is single-threaded. Therefore, setting

$$\Lambda(\sigma_1, \ldots, \sigma_n) = \langle\langle \Lambda(\sigma_1), \ldots, \Lambda(\sigma_n) \rangle\rangle^\dagger : A \to \mathcal{I},$$

we obtain a thread-independent strategy implementing a simultaneous currying of $\sigma_1, \cdots, \sigma_n$. In particular, given translations $[\![M_i]\!]$ for each method in a method-set implementation $\mathcal{M}$, we can construct:

$$[\![\mathcal{M}]\!] : [\![\Gamma]\!] \to \mathcal{I} = \Lambda([\![M_1]\!], \cdots, [\![M_n]\!]).$$

Finally, we define *evaluation strategies* $\mathtt{ev}_{\mathsf{m}_i} : \mathcal{I} \times [\![\vec{\theta_i}]\!] \to [\![\theta_i]\!]$ by (taking even-length prefixes of):

$$\mathtt{ev}_{\mathsf{m}_i} = \{(a, \vec{v})^\Sigma \mathsf{call}\, a.\mathsf{m}_i(\vec{v})^\Sigma \mathsf{ret}\, a.\mathsf{m}_i(v)^T v^T \in P_{A_i} \mid \Sigma(a) \leq \mathcal{I}\}$$

where $A_i = (\mathcal{I} \times [\![\vec{\theta_i}]\!])[\![\theta_i]\!]$. We can now show the following natural mapping from groups of strategies in $A \times [\![\vec{\theta_i}]\!] \to [\![\theta_i]\!]$ to thread-independent ones in $A \to \mathcal{I}$.

**Lemma 14.** *Let $\sigma_1, \cdots, \sigma_n$ be as above, and let $\tau : A' \to A$ be evaluated. Then,*

- $\Lambda(\sigma_1, \ldots, \sigma_n) \times \mathtt{id}; \mathtt{ev}_{\mathsf{m}_i} = \sigma_i$,
- $\tau; \Lambda(\sigma_1, \ldots, \sigma_n) = \Lambda((\tau \times \mathtt{id}); \sigma_1, \ldots, (\tau \times \mathtt{id}); \sigma_n)$.

Apart from dealing with exponentials, in order to complete our translation we need also to address the appearance of $x : \mathcal{I}$ in the rule[4]

$$\frac{\Gamma, x : \mathcal{I}, \Delta \vdash \mathcal{M} : \Theta}{\Gamma, \Delta \vdash \mathsf{new}(x : \mathcal{I}; \mathcal{M}) : \mathcal{I}}\ \Delta(\mathcal{I}) \restriction \mathit{Meths} = \Theta.$$

Recall that

$$[\![\mathcal{M}]\!] : [\![\Gamma]\!] \times \mathcal{I} \to \mathcal{I} \tag{1}$$

is obtained using exponentiation. Thus, the second move of $[\![\mathcal{M}]\!]$ will appear in the right-hand-side $\mathcal{I}$ above and will be a fresh name $b$ which will serve as a handle to the methods of $\mathcal{M}$: in order to invoke $\mathsf{m} : \lambda\vec{x}.M$ on input $\vec{v}$, the Opponent would have to call $b.\mathsf{m}(\vec{v})$. The remaining challenge is to merge the two occurrences of $\mathcal{I}$ in (1). We achieve this as follows. Let us assume a well-formed extension $\Delta'$ of $\Delta$:

$$\Delta' = (\mathcal{I}' : (\mathsf{f}' : \mathcal{I})), \Delta$$

that is, $\mathcal{I}'$ contains a single field $\mathsf{f}'$ of type $\mathcal{I}$. We next define the strategy $\kappa_\mathcal{I} : 1 \to \mathcal{I}' \times \mathcal{I}$ of $\mathcal{G}_{\Delta'}$:

$$\kappa_\mathcal{I} = \{* (a', a)^{\Sigma_0} \mathsf{call}\, a.\mathsf{m}(\vec{v})^\Sigma \mathsf{call}\, b.\mathsf{m}(\vec{v})^\Sigma \mathsf{ret}\, b.\mathsf{m}(v)^T \mathsf{ret}\, a.\mathsf{m}(v)^T\}^\dagger$$

where $\mathsf{m} \in \mathsf{dom}(\Delta(\mathcal{I}))$, $b = \Sigma(a').\mathsf{f}'$, and $\Sigma_0 \in \mathit{Sto}_0$ is such that $\Sigma_0(a) : \mathcal{I}$ and $\Sigma_0(a') : \mathcal{I}'$. We let $[\![\mathsf{new}(x : \mathcal{I}; \mathcal{M})]\!]$ be the strategy:[5]

$$[\![\Gamma]\!] \xrightarrow{\langle \mathtt{id}, !; \kappa_\mathcal{I} \rangle; \cong} \mathcal{I}' \times [\![\Gamma]\!] \times \mathcal{I} \xrightarrow{\mathtt{id} \times \langle [\![\mathcal{M}]\!], \pi_2 \rangle} \mathcal{I}' \times \mathcal{I} \times \mathcal{I} \xrightarrow{(\mathtt{asn}_{\mathsf{f}'} \times \mathtt{id}); \pi_2} \mathcal{I}$$

and $\mathtt{asn}_\mathsf{f}$ is the assignment strategy:

$$\mathtt{asn}_\mathsf{f} : \mathcal{I} \times [\![\theta]\!] \to 1 = \{(a, v)^\Sigma *^{\Sigma[a.\mathsf{f} \mapsto v]} \in P_{(\mathcal{I} \times [\![\theta]\!])1}\},$$

for each field $\mathsf{f}$. Thus, object creation involves creating a pair of names $(a', a)$ with $a : \mathcal{I}$ and $a' : \mathcal{I}'$, where $a$ is the name of the object we want to return. The name $a'$ serves as a store where the handle of the method implementations, that is, the name created by the second move of $[\![\mathcal{M}]\!]$, will be passed. The strategy $\kappa_\mathcal{I}$, upon receiving a request $\mathsf{call}\, a.\mathsf{m}(\vec{v})^\Sigma$, simply forwards it to the respective method of $a'.\mathsf{f}'$ and, once it receives a return value, copies it back as the return value of the original call.

Let $\#(\vec{\mathcal{I}}) : \vec{\mathcal{I}} \to \#(\vec{\mathcal{I}}) = \{\vec{a}^\Sigma \vec{a}^\Sigma \mid a_i\text{s distinct}\}$, for each sequence of interfaces $\vec{\mathcal{I}}$. The latter has a right inverse $\#(\vec{\mathcal{I}})^{-r} : \#(\vec{\mathcal{I}}) \to \vec{\mathcal{I}}$ with the same plays. We can now define the semantic translation of terms.

*Definition* 10. The semantic translation is given as follows.

- Contexts $\Gamma = \{x_1 : \theta_1, \cdots, x_n : \theta_n\} \cup \{a_1 : \mathcal{I}_1, \cdots, a_m : \mathcal{I}_m\}$ are translated into arenas by
$$[\![\Gamma]\!] = [\![\theta_1]\!] \times \cdots \times [\![\theta_n]\!] \times \#(\mathcal{I}_1, \cdots, \mathcal{I}_m),$$
where $[\![\mathsf{void}]\!] = 1$, $[\![\mathsf{int}]\!] = \mathbb{Z}$ and $[\![\mathcal{I}]\!] = \mathcal{I}$.
- Terms are translated as in Figure 4 (top part).

In order to prove that the semantics is sound, we will also need to interpret terms inside state contexts. Let $\Gamma \vdash M : \theta$, with $\Gamma = \Gamma_1 \cup \Gamma_2$, where $\Gamma_1$ contains only variables and $\mathsf{dom}(\Gamma_2) = \mathsf{dom}(S)$. A term-in-state-context $(S, M)$ is translated into the strategy:

$$[\![\Gamma_1 \vdash (S, M)]\!] = [\![\Gamma_1]\!] \xrightarrow{[\![S]\!]} [\![\Gamma_1]\!] \times \vec{\mathcal{I}} \xrightarrow{\mathtt{id} \times \#(\vec{\mathcal{I}})} [\![\Gamma]\!] \xrightarrow{[\![M]\!]} [\![\theta]\!].$$

The semantic translation of states (Figure 4, lower part), comprises two stages:

$$[\![\Gamma_1 \vdash S]\!] = [\![\Gamma_1]\!] \xrightarrow{[\![S]\!]_1} [\![\Gamma_1]\!] \times \vec{\mathcal{I}} \xrightarrow{[\![S]\!]_2} [\![\Gamma_1]\!] \times \vec{\mathcal{I}}.$$

The first stage, $[\![S]\!]_1$, creates the objects in $\mathsf{dom}(S)$ and implements their methods. The second stage of the translation, $[\![S]\!]_2$, initialises the fields of the newly created objects.

In the rest of this section we show soundness of the semantics. Let us call NEW, FIELDUP, FIELDAC and METHODCL respectively the transition rules in Figure 2 which involve state. Given a rule $\mathtt{r}$, we write $(S, M) \xrightarrow{\mathtt{r}} (S', M')$ if the transition $(S, M) \longrightarrow (S', M')$ involves applying $\mathtt{r}$ and context rules.

**Proposition 15** (Correctness). *Let $(S, M)$ be a term-in-state-context and suppose $(S, M) \xrightarrow{\mathtt{r}} (S', M')$.*

1. *If the transition $\mathtt{r}$ is not stateful then $[\![M]\!] = [\![M']\!]$.*
2. *If $\mathtt{r}$ is one of* FIELDAC *or* FIELDUP *then $[\![S]\!]_2; (\mathtt{id} \times \#(\vec{\mathcal{I}})); [\![M]\!] = [\![S']\!]_2; (\mathtt{id} \times \#(\vec{\mathcal{I}})); [\![M']\!]$.*
3. *If $\mathtt{r}$ is one of* METHODCL *or* NEW *then $[\![(S, M)]\!] = [\![(S', M')]\!]$.*

*Thus, in every case, $[\![(S, M)]\!] = [\![(S', M')]\!]$.*

*Proof.* Claim 1 is proved by using the naturality results of this section. For the $\mathsf{let}$ construct, we show by induction on $M$ that $[\![M[v/x]]\!] = \langle \mathtt{id}, [\![v]\!] \rangle; [\![M]\!]$. For 2 we use the following properties of field assignment and access:

$$\langle \mathtt{asn}_\mathsf{f}, \pi_1 \rangle; \pi_2; \mathtt{drf}_\mathsf{f} = \langle \mathtt{asn}_\mathsf{f}, \pi_2 \rangle; \pi_2 : \mathcal{I} \times [\![\theta]\!] \to [\![\theta]\!]$$
$$\langle \mathtt{asn}_\mathsf{f}, \pi_1 \rangle \times \mathtt{id}; \pi_2; \mathtt{asn}_\mathsf{f} = \mathtt{id} \times \pi_2; \mathtt{asn}_\mathsf{f} : \mathcal{I} \times [\![\theta]\!] \times [\![\theta]\!] \to 1$$

which are easily verifiable (the former one states that assigning a field value and accessing it returns the same value; the latter that two assignments in a row have the same effect as just the last one). The final claim follows by showing that the diagrams below

[4] Note that $x$ may appear free in $\mathcal{M}$; it stands for the keyword this of Java.

[5] Here we omit wrapping $[\![\mathcal{M}]\!]$ inside $\Delta/\Delta'$, as well as wrapping the whole $[\![\mathsf{new}(x : \mathcal{I}; \mathcal{M})]\!]$ in $\Delta'/\Delta$, for conciseness.

- $\llbracket\Gamma\vdash x_i:\theta_i\rrbracket=\llbracket\Gamma\rrbracket\xrightarrow{\pi_i}\llbracket\theta_i\rrbracket$;
- $\llbracket\Gamma\vdash a_i:\mathcal{I}_i\rrbracket=\llbracket\Gamma\rrbracket\xrightarrow{\pi_{n+1}}\#(\overrightarrow{\mathcal{I}})\xrightarrow{\#(\overrightarrow{\mathcal{I}})^{-r}}\overrightarrow{\mathcal{I}}\xrightarrow{\pi_i}\mathcal{I}_i$;
- $\llbracket\Gamma\vdash\mathsf{skip}:\mathsf{void}\rrbracket=\llbracket\Gamma\rrbracket\xrightarrow{!}1$;
- $\llbracket\Gamma\vdash\mathsf{null}:\mathcal{I}\rrbracket=\llbracket\Gamma\rrbracket\xrightarrow{!;\hat{\mathtt{nul}}}\mathcal{I}$, where $\hat{\mathtt{nul}}:1\to\mathcal{I}=\{*\,\mathtt{nul}\}$;
- $\llbracket\Gamma\vdash i:\mathsf{int}\rrbracket=\llbracket\Gamma\rrbracket\xrightarrow{!;\hat{i}}\mathbb{Z}$;
- $\llbracket\Gamma\vdash\mathsf{let}\,x=M'\,\mathsf{in}\,M:\theta\rrbracket=\llbracket\Gamma\rrbracket\xrightarrow{\langle\mathtt{id},\llbracket M'\rrbracket\rangle}\llbracket\Gamma\rrbracket\times\llbracket\theta'\rrbracket\xrightarrow{\llbracket M\rrbracket}\llbracket\theta\rrbracket$;
- $\llbracket\Gamma\vdash(\mathcal{I})M:\mathcal{I}\rrbracket=\llbracket\Gamma\rrbracket\xrightarrow{\llbracket M\rrbracket}\mathcal{I}'\xrightarrow{\mathtt{stp}_{\mathcal{I}'\mathcal{I}}}\mathcal{I}$, where $\mathtt{stp}_{\mathcal{I}'\mathcal{I}}:\mathcal{I}'\to\mathcal{I}=\{\mathtt{nul}\,\mathtt{nul}\}\cup\{a^{\Sigma}a^{\Sigma}\in P_{\mathcal{I}'\mathcal{I}}\mid\Sigma(a)\le\mathcal{I}\}$;
- $\llbracket\Gamma\vdash M\oplus M':\mathsf{int}\rrbracket=\llbracket\Gamma\rrbracket\xrightarrow{\langle\llbracket M\rrbracket,\llbracket M'\rrbracket\rangle}\mathbb{Z}\times\mathbb{Z}\xrightarrow{\oplus}\mathbb{Z}$, where $\oplus:\mathbb{Z}\times\mathbb{Z}\to\mathbb{Z}=\{(i,j)\,(i\oplus j)\}$;
- $\llbracket\Gamma\vdash M=M':\mathsf{int}\rrbracket=\llbracket\Gamma\rrbracket\xrightarrow{\langle\llbracket M\rrbracket,\llbracket M'\rrbracket\rangle}\mathcal{I}\times\mathcal{I}\xrightarrow{\mathsf{eq}}\mathbb{Z}$, where $\mathsf{eq}=\{(a,a)^{\Sigma}\,1^{\Sigma}\in P_{(\mathcal{I}\times\mathcal{I})\mathbb{Z}}\}\cup\{(a,b)^{\Sigma}\,0^{\Sigma}\in P_{(\mathcal{I}\times\mathcal{I})\mathbb{Z}}\mid a\neq b\}$;
- $\llbracket\Gamma\vdash\mathsf{if}\,M\,\mathsf{then}\,M'\,\mathsf{else}\,M'':\theta\rrbracket=\llbracket\Gamma\rrbracket\xrightarrow{\langle\llbracket M\rrbracket,\mathtt{id}\rangle}\mathbb{Z}\times\llbracket\Gamma\rrbracket\xrightarrow{[\llbracket M'\rrbracket,\llbracket M''\rrbracket]}\llbracket\theta\rrbracket$;
- $\llbracket\Gamma\vdash\mathsf{new}(x{:}\mathcal{I};\mathcal{M}):\mathcal{I}\rrbracket=\llbracket\Gamma\rrbracket\xrightarrow{\langle\mathtt{id},!;\kappa_{\mathcal{I}}\rangle;\cong}\mathcal{I}'\times\llbracket\Gamma\rrbracket\times\mathcal{I}\xrightarrow{\mathtt{id}\times\langle\llbracket\mathcal{M}\rrbracket,\pi_2\rangle}\mathcal{I}'\times\mathcal{I}\times\mathcal{I}\xrightarrow{\mathtt{asn}_{f'}\times\mathtt{id}}1\times\mathcal{I}\xrightarrow{\pi_2}\mathcal{I}$,
  where $\llbracket\mathcal{M}\rrbracket=\llbracket\Gamma\rrbracket\times\mathcal{I}\xrightarrow{\Lambda(\llbracket M_1\rrbracket,\dots,\llbracket M_n\rrbracket)}\mathcal{I}$ if $\mathcal{M}=\{\mathsf{m}_1:\lambda\vec{x}_1.M_1,\cdots,\mathsf{m}_n:\lambda\vec{x}_n.M_n\}$;
- $\llbracket\Gamma\vdash M.\mathsf{f}:=M':\mathsf{void}\rrbracket=\llbracket\Gamma\rrbracket\xrightarrow{\langle\llbracket M\rrbracket,\llbracket M'\rrbracket\rangle}\mathcal{I}\times\llbracket\theta\rrbracket\xrightarrow{\mathtt{asn_f}}1$;
- $\llbracket\Gamma\vdash M.\mathsf{f}:\theta\rrbracket=\llbracket\Gamma\rrbracket\xrightarrow{\llbracket M\rrbracket}\mathcal{I}\xrightarrow{\mathtt{drf_f}}\llbracket\theta\rrbracket$, where $\mathtt{drf_f}:\mathcal{I}\to\llbracket\theta\rrbracket=\{a^{\Sigma}v^{\Sigma}\in P_{\mathcal{I}\llbracket\theta\rrbracket}\mid\Sigma(a).\mathsf{f}=v\}$;
- $\llbracket\Gamma\vdash M.\mathsf{m}(\vec{M}):\theta\rrbracket=\llbracket\Gamma\rrbracket\xrightarrow{\langle\llbracket M\rrbracket,\llbracket\vec{M}\rrbracket\rangle}\mathcal{I}\times\llbracket\vec{\theta}\rrbracket\xrightarrow{\mathsf{ev_m}}\llbracket\theta\rrbracket$, where $\llbracket\vec{M}\rrbracket=\langle\langle\langle\llbracket M_1\rrbracket,\llbracket M_2\rrbracket\rangle,\cdots\rangle,\llbracket M_n\rrbracket\rangle$.

---

- $\llbracket\Gamma_1\vdash S\rrbracket=\llbracket\Gamma_1\rrbracket\xrightarrow{\langle\mathtt{id},\overrightarrow{\kappa_{\mathcal{I}}}\rangle}\llbracket\Gamma_1\rrbracket\times\overrightarrow{(\mathcal{I}'\times\mathcal{I})}\xrightarrow{\cong}\overrightarrow{\mathcal{I}'}\times(\llbracket\Gamma_1\rrbracket\times\overrightarrow{\mathcal{I}})\xrightarrow{\mathtt{id}\times\langle\pi_2;\llbracket\overrightarrow{\mathcal{M}}\rrbracket,\mathtt{id}\rangle}\overrightarrow{\mathcal{I}'}\times\overrightarrow{\mathcal{I}}\times(\llbracket\Gamma_1\rrbracket\times\overrightarrow{\mathcal{I}})\xrightarrow{\cong\times\mathtt{id}}\overrightarrow{(\mathcal{I}'\times\mathcal{I})}\times(\llbracket\Gamma_1\rrbracket\times\overrightarrow{\mathcal{I}})$
  $\xrightarrow{(\overrightarrow{\mathtt{asn}_{f'}}\times\mathtt{id});\pi_2}\llbracket\Gamma_1\rrbracket\times\overrightarrow{\mathcal{I}}\xrightarrow{\langle\mathtt{id},\langle\overrightarrow{\mathtt{id}},\llbracket\vec{V}\rrbracket\rangle\rangle}(\llbracket\Gamma_1\rrbracket\times\overrightarrow{\mathcal{I}})\times\overrightarrow{\overrightarrow{\mathcal{I}}}\times\overrightarrow{\overrightarrow{\llbracket\theta\rrbracket}}\xrightarrow{\mathtt{id}\times\cong}(\llbracket\Gamma_1\rrbracket\times\overrightarrow{\mathcal{I}})\times\overrightarrow{\overrightarrow{(\mathcal{I}\times\llbracket\theta\rrbracket)}}\xrightarrow{(\mathtt{id}\times\overrightarrow{\mathtt{asn_f}});\pi_1}\llbracket\Gamma_1\rrbracket\times\overrightarrow{\mathcal{I}}$,

  where $\mathsf{dom}(S)=\{a_1,\cdots,a_n\}$, $\overrightarrow{\kappa_{\mathcal{I}}}=\langle\kappa_{\mathcal{I}_1},\cdots,\kappa_{\mathcal{I}_n}\rangle$, $S(a_i):\mathcal{I}_i$, $\overrightarrow{\mathcal{I}'}=\mathcal{I}'_1\times\cdots\times\mathcal{I}'_n$, $\overrightarrow{\mathcal{I}}=\mathcal{I}_1\times\cdots\times\mathcal{I}_n$, $\overrightarrow{\mathcal{M}}=(\mathcal{M}_1,\cdots,\mathcal{M}_n)$, $\mathcal{M}_i=S(a_i)\restriction\mathit{MImps}$, $\llbracket\overrightarrow{\mathcal{M}}\rrbracket=\langle\llbracket\mathcal{M}_1\rrbracket,\cdots,\llbracket\mathcal{M}_n\rrbracket\rangle$, $\mathtt{asn}_{f'}=\mathtt{asn}_{f'_1}\times\cdots\times\mathtt{asn}_{f'_n}$, $\vec{V}=(V_1,\cdots,V_n)$, $V_i=S(a_i)\restriction\mathit{HCnfs}$, $\llbracket\vec{V}\rrbracket=\langle\llbracket V_1\rrbracket,\cdots,\llbracket V_n\rrbracket\rangle$, $V_i=(\mathsf{f}_i^1:v_i^1,\cdots,\mathsf{f}_i^{n_i}:v_i^{n_i})$, $\llbracket V_i\rrbracket=\langle\llbracket v_i^1\rrbracket,\cdots,\llbracket v_i^{n_i}\rrbracket\rangle$, $\overrightarrow{\mathtt{asn_f}}=\mathtt{asn}_{\mathsf{f}_i}\times\cdots\times\mathtt{asn}_{\mathsf{f}_n}$, $\mathtt{asn}_{\mathsf{f}_i}=\mathtt{asn}_{\mathsf{f}_i^1}\times\cdots\times\mathtt{asn}_{\mathsf{f}_i^{n_i}}$.

---

**Figure 4.** The semantic translation of IMJ.

commute (we write $A$ for $\llbracket\Gamma\rrbracket\times\overrightarrow{\mathcal{I}}$),

$$\begin{array}{ccccc}
\overrightarrow{\mathcal{I}'}\times A\times\llbracket\vec{\theta}\rrbracket & \xrightarrow{\mathtt{id}\times\llbracket\overrightarrow{\mathcal{M}}\rrbracket\times\mathtt{id}} & \overrightarrow{\mathcal{I}'}\times\overrightarrow{\mathcal{I}}\times\llbracket\vec{\theta}\rrbracket & \xrightarrow{\langle\cong,\pi_2;\pi_i\rangle\times\mathtt{id}} & \overrightarrow{(\mathcal{I}'\times\mathcal{I})}\times\mathcal{I}_i\times\llbracket\vec{\theta}\rrbracket \\
\Big\downarrow{\scriptstyle\mathtt{id}\times\langle\llbracket\overrightarrow{\mathcal{M}}\rrbracket,\llbracket\mathcal{M}_i\rrbracket\rangle\times\mathtt{id}} & & & & \Big\downarrow{\scriptstyle(\overrightarrow{\mathtt{asn}_{f'}}\times\mathtt{ev_m});\pi_2} \\
\overrightarrow{\mathcal{I}'}\times\overrightarrow{\mathcal{I}}\times\mathcal{I}_i\times\llbracket\vec{\theta}\rrbracket & \xrightarrow{\cong\times\mathtt{id}} & \overrightarrow{(\mathcal{I}'\times\mathcal{I})}\times\mathcal{I}_i\times\llbracket\vec{\theta}\rrbracket & \xrightarrow{(\overrightarrow{\mathtt{asn}_{f'}}\times\mathtt{ev_m});\pi_2} & \llbracket\theta\rrbracket
\end{array}$$

$$\begin{array}{ccccc}
\llbracket\Gamma_1\rrbracket & & & & \\
\Big\downarrow{\scriptstyle\chi} & & & & \\
\overrightarrow{\mathcal{I}'}\times A\times A & \xrightarrow{\mathtt{id}\times\langle\pi_2;\pi_i,\sigma'\rangle} & \overrightarrow{\mathcal{I}'}\times A\times\mathcal{I}_i\times\llbracket\vec{\theta}\rrbracket & \xrightarrow{\mathtt{id}\times\llbracket\overrightarrow{\mathcal{M}}\rrbracket\times\mathtt{id}} & \overrightarrow{\mathcal{I}'}\times\overrightarrow{\mathcal{I}}\times\mathcal{I}_i\times\llbracket\vec{\theta}\rrbracket \\
\Big\downarrow{\scriptstyle\mathtt{id}\times\sigma'} & & & & \Big\downarrow{\scriptstyle\cong\times\mathtt{id}} \\
\overrightarrow{\mathcal{I}'}\times A\times\llbracket\vec{\theta}\rrbracket & & & & \overrightarrow{(\mathcal{I}'\times\mathcal{I})}\times\mathcal{I}_i\times\llbracket\vec{\theta}\rrbracket \\
\Big\downarrow{\scriptstyle\mathtt{id}\times\llbracket\overrightarrow{\mathcal{M}}\rrbracket\times\mathtt{id}} & & & & \Big\downarrow{\scriptstyle(\overrightarrow{\mathtt{asn}_{f'}}\times\mathtt{ev_m});\pi_2} \\
\overrightarrow{\mathcal{I}'}\times\overrightarrow{\mathcal{I}}\times\llbracket\vec{\theta}\rrbracket & \xrightarrow{\langle\cong,\pi_2;\pi_i\rangle\times\mathtt{id}} & \overrightarrow{(\mathcal{I}'\times\mathcal{I})}\times\mathcal{I}_i\times\llbracket\vec{\theta}\rrbracket & \xrightarrow{(\overrightarrow{\mathtt{asn}_{f'}}\times\mathtt{ev_m});\pi_2} & \llbracket\theta\rrbracket
\end{array}$$

where $\sigma':A\to\llbracket\vec{\theta}\rrbracket$ a combination of values and assignments, and

$$\chi=\llbracket\Gamma_1\rrbracket\xrightarrow{\langle\mathtt{id},\overrightarrow{\kappa_{\mathcal{I}}}\rangle}\llbracket\Gamma_1\rrbracket\times\overrightarrow{\mathcal{I}'}\times\overrightarrow{\mathcal{I}}\xrightarrow{(\delta\times\mathtt{id}\times\delta);\cong}\overrightarrow{\mathcal{I}'}\times A\times A$$

with $\delta=\langle\mathtt{id},\mathtt{id}\rangle$. The former diagram says that, assigning method implementations $\overrightarrow{\mathcal{M}}$ to object stores $\vec{a}'$ and calling $\mathcal{M}_i$ on some method $\mathsf{m}$ is the same as assigning $\overrightarrow{\mathcal{M}}$ to $\vec{a}'$ and evaluating instead a new copy of $\mathcal{M}_i$ on $\mathsf{m}$. The reason the diagram commutes is that the copy of $\mathcal{M}_i$ differs from the original just in the handle name (the one returned in the codomain of $\llbracket\mathcal{M}_i\rrbracket$), but the latter is hidden via composition with $\mathsf{ev_m}$. The latter diagram stipulates that if we create $\vec{a}$ with methods $\overrightarrow{\mathcal{M}}$, then calling $a_i$ on $\mathsf{m}$ is the same as calling $\mathcal{M}_i$ on $\mathsf{m}$. The latter holds because of the way that $\kappa_{\mathcal{I}_i}$ manipulates calls inside the interaction, by delegating calls to methods of $a_i$ to $\mathcal{M}_i$. □

**Proposition 16** (Computational Soundness). *For all* $\vdash M:\mathsf{void}$, *if* $M\Downarrow$ *then* $\llbracket M\rrbracket=\{**\}$ *(i.e.* $\llbracket M\rrbracket=\llbracket\mathsf{skip}\rrbracket$*).*

*Proof.* This directly follows from Correctness. □

**Proposition 17** (Computational Adequacy). *For all* $\vdash M:\mathsf{void}$, *if* $\llbracket M\rrbracket=\{**\}$ *then* $M\Downarrow$.

*Proof.* Suppose, for the sake of contradiction, that $\llbracket M\rrbracket=\{**\}$ and $M\not\Downarrow$. We notice that, by definition of the translation for blocking constructs (castings and conditionals may block) and due to Correctness, if $M\not\Downarrow$ were due to some reduction step being blocked then the semantics would also block. Thus, $M\not\Downarrow$ must be due to divergence. Now, the reduction relation restricted to all rules but METHODCL is strongly normalising, as each transition decreases the size of the term. Hence, if $M$ diverges then it must involve infinitely many METHODCL reductions and our argument below shows that the latter would imply $\llbracket M\rrbracket=\{\epsilon\}$.
For any term $\Gamma\vdash N:\theta$ and $a\in\mathbb{A}\setminus\mathsf{dom}(\Gamma)$, construct $\Gamma_a\vdash N_a$, where $\Gamma_a=\Gamma\uplus\{a:\mathsf{Var}_I\}$, by recursively replacing each subterm of $N$ of the shape $N'.\mathsf{m}(\vec{N})$ with $a.\mathsf{f}:=(a.\mathsf{f}+1);N'.\mathsf{m}(\vec{N})$.

$\mathsf{Var}_I$ is an interface with a sole field $\mathsf{f}$ : int. Observe that each $s \in [\![\Gamma \vdash N]\!]$ induces some $s' \in [\![\Gamma_a \vdash N_a]\!]$ such that $a$ appears in $s'$ only in stores (and in a single place in the initial move) and O never changes the value of $a.\mathsf{f}$, while P never decreases the value of $a.\mathsf{f}$. We write $[\![\Gamma_a \vdash N_a]\!]_a$ for the subset of $[\![\Gamma_a \vdash N_a]\!]$ containing precisely these plays. Then, take $M_0$ to be the term $\mathsf{let}\, x = \mathsf{new}(x : \mathsf{Var}_I;)\, \mathsf{in}\, (M_a[x/a]; x.\mathsf{f})$, where $x$ a fresh variable. Because $** \in [\![M]\!]$, we get $*j \in [\![M_0]\!]$ for some $j \in \mathbb{Z}$. Consider now the infinite reduction sequence of $(\emptyset, M)$. It must have infinitely many METHODCL steps, so suppose $(\emptyset, M) \longrightarrow^* (S, M')$ contains $j+1$ such steps. Then, we obtain $(\emptyset, M_0) \longrightarrow^* (S_a, (M')_a; a.\mathsf{f})$, with $S_a(a).\mathsf{f} = j+1$. By Correctness, we have that $*j \in [\![S_a, (M')_a; a.\mathsf{f}]\!] = [\![S_a]\!]; (\mathtt{idx}\#); [\![(M')_a; a.\mathsf{f}]\!]_a$. Since in $[\![(M')_a]\!]_a$ the value of $a$ cannot decrease, and its initial value is $j+1$ (as stipulated by $S_a$), we reach a contradiction. □

## 5. Full Abstraction

Recall that, given plays $s, s'$, we call $s$ an O-extension of $s'$ (written $s \le_O s'$) if $s, s'$ are identical except the type information regarding O-names present in stores: the types of O-names in $s$ may be subtypes of those in $s'$. We shall write $s \le_P s'$ for the dual notion involving P-names, i.e., $s \le_P s'$ if $s, s'$ are the same, but the types of P-names in $s'$ may be subtypes of those in $s$. Then, given $X \in \{O, P\}$ and fixed $A, B$, let us define $\mathsf{cl}_X(s) = \{s' \in P_{AB} \mid s' \le_X s\}$ and $\mathsf{cl}_X(\sigma) = \bigcup_{s\in\sigma} \mathsf{cl}_X(s)$. We write $P_{\Delta|\Gamma\vdash\theta}$ for $P_{[\![\Gamma]\!][\![\theta]\!]}$. A play will be called *complete* if it is of the form $m_A Y m_B Y$.

Next we establish a definability result stating that any complete play (together with other plays implied by O-closure) originates from a term.

**Lemma 18** (Definability). *Let $s \in P_{\Delta|\Gamma\vdash\theta}$ be a complete play. There exists $\Delta' \supseteq \Delta$ and $\Delta'|\Gamma \vdash M : \theta$ such that $[\![\Delta'|\Gamma \vdash M : \theta]\!] = \mathsf{cl}_O(s)$.*

*Proof.* The argument proceeds by induction on $|s|$. For $s = \epsilon$, any divergent term suffices. For example, one can take $\Delta' = \Delta \oplus \{\mathsf{Div} \mapsto (\mathsf{m} : \mathsf{void} \to \mathsf{void})\}$, and pre-compose any term of type $\theta$ with $\mathsf{new}(x : \mathsf{Div};\ \mathsf{m} : \lambda().\mathsf{m}()\,).\mathsf{m}()$.

Suppose $s \neq \epsilon$. Then the second move can be a question or an answer. We first show how to reduce the former case to the latter, so that only the latter needs to be attacked directly.

Suppose

$$s = q^{\Sigma_q}\ \mathsf{call}\, o.\mathsf{m}(\vec{u})^{\Sigma_1}\ s_1\ \mathsf{ret}\, o.\mathsf{m}(v)^{\Sigma_2}\ s_2\ w^{\Sigma_3}\ s_3,$$

where $o : \mathcal{I}'$ and $\Delta(\mathcal{I}')(\mathsf{m}) : \overrightarrow{\mathcal{I}_L} \to \mathcal{I}_R$. Consider $\Delta' = \Delta \oplus \{\mathcal{I}'' \mapsto (\overrightarrow{\mathsf{f}' : \mathcal{I}_L},\ \mathsf{m}' : \mathcal{I}_R \to \theta)\}$ and the following play from $P_{\Delta'|\Gamma\vdash\mathcal{I}''}$:

$$s' = q^{\Sigma_q}\ p^{\Sigma_1'}\ s_1'\ \mathsf{call}\, p.\mathsf{m}'(v)^{\Sigma_2'}\ s_2'\ \mathsf{ret}\, p.\mathsf{m}'(v)^{\Sigma_3'}\ s_3',$$

where $p \notin \nu(s)$, $\Sigma_i' = \Sigma_i \oplus \Sigma$, $\Sigma = \{p \mapsto (\mathcal{I}'', \overrightarrow{f' \mapsto u})\}$ and $s_j'$ is the same as $s_j$ except that each store is extended by $\Sigma$. If $\Delta'|\Gamma \vdash M' : \mathcal{I}'$ satisfies the Lemma for $s'$ then, for $s$, one can take $\mathsf{let}\, x_p = M'\ \mathsf{in}\, x_p.\mathsf{m}'(y.\mathsf{m}(\overrightarrow{x_p.f'}))$, where $y$ refers to $o$, i.e., $y$ is of the shape $x.\vec{f}$, where $x \in \mathsf{dom}\,\Gamma$ and $\vec{f}$ is a sequence of fields that points at $o$ in $\Sigma_q$.

Thanks to the reduction given above we can now assume that $s \in P_{\Delta|\Gamma\vdash\theta}$ is non-empty and

$$s = q^{\Sigma_q}\ m_0^{\Sigma_0}\ m_1^{\Sigma_1} \cdots m_{2k}^{\Sigma_{2k}},$$

where $m_0$ is an answer. We are going to enrich $s$ in two ways so that it is easier to decompose. Ultimately, the decomposition of $s$ will be based on the observation that the $m_1^{\Sigma_1} \cdots m_{2k}^{\Sigma_{2k}}$ segment can be viewed as an interleaving of threads, each of which is started by a move of the form $\mathsf{call}\, p$ for some P-name $p$. A thread consists of the starting move and is generated according to the following two rules: $m_{2i}$ belongs to the thread of $m_{2i-1}$ and every answer-move belongs to the same thread as the corresponding question-move.

- The first transformation of $s$ brings forward the point of P-name creation to the second move. In this way, threads will never create objects and, consequently, it will be possible to compose them without facing the problem of object fusion.
  Suppose $P(s) = \vec{p_i}$ and $p_i : \mathcal{I}_{p_i}$. Let $\Delta' = \Delta \oplus \{\mathcal{I}_P \mapsto \overrightarrow{f_i : \mathcal{I}_{p_i}}\}$. Consider $s' = (n, q)^{\Sigma_q'}\ m_0^{\Sigma_0'}\ m_1^{\Sigma_1'} \cdots m_{2k}^{\Sigma_{2k}'}$, where $\Sigma_q' = \Sigma_q \oplus \{n \mapsto (\mathcal{I}_P, \overrightarrow{\mathsf{null}})\}$ and $\Sigma_i' = \Sigma_i \oplus \{n \mapsto (\mathcal{I}_P, \vec{p_i})\} \oplus \{p_i \mapsto (\mathcal{I}_{p_i}, \overrightarrow{\mathsf{null}}) \mid \Sigma_i(p_i) \text{ undefined},\ p_i \in P(s)\}$. Let $\Gamma' = \{x_n : \mathcal{I}_P\} \oplus \Gamma$. Observe that $s' \in P_{\Delta'|\Gamma'\vdash\theta}$.
- The second transformation consists in storing the unfolding play in a global variable. It should be clear that the recursive structure of types along with the ability to store names is sufficient to store plays in objects. Let $\mathcal{I}_{play}$ be a signature that makes this possible. This will be used to enforce the intended interleaving of threads after their composition (in the style of Innocent Factorization [5]). Let $\Delta'' = \Delta' \oplus \{\mathsf{History} \mapsto \mathsf{play} : I_{play}\}$ and $\Gamma'' = \{x_h : \mathsf{History}\} \oplus \Gamma$. Consider

  $$s'' = (h, n, q)^{\Sigma_q''}\ m_0^{\Sigma_0''}\ m_1^{\Sigma_1''} \cdots m_{2k}^{\Sigma_{2k}''}$$

  with

  $$\begin{aligned} \Sigma_q'' &= \Sigma_q' \oplus \{h \mapsto (\mathsf{History}, \mathsf{play} \mapsto \mathsf{null})\}, \\ \Sigma_{2i}'' &= \Sigma_{2i}' \oplus \{h \mapsto (\mathsf{History}, \mathsf{play} \mapsto s'_{\le m_{2i}})\}, \\ \Sigma_{2i+1}'' &= \Sigma_{2i+1}' \oplus \{h \mapsto (\mathsf{History}, \mathsf{play} \mapsto s'_{\le m_{2i}})\}. \end{aligned}$$

  Observe that $s'' \in P_{\Delta''|\Gamma'\vdash\theta}$.

Now we shall decompose $m_1^{\Sigma_1''} \cdots m_{2k}^{\Sigma_{2k}''}$ into threads. Recall that each of them is a subsequence of $s''$ of the form

$$\mathsf{call}\, p.\mathsf{m}(\vec{u})^{\Sigma_c}\quad t\quad \mathsf{ret}\, p.\mathsf{m}(v)^{\Sigma_r}$$

where the segment $t$ contains moves of the form $\mathsf{call}\, o$ or $\mathsf{ret}\, o$ for some $o \in O(s)$. We would now like to invoke the IH for each thread but, since a thread is not a play, we do so for the closely related play $(h, n, q, \vec{u})^{\Sigma_c}\ t'\ v^{\Sigma_r}$. Let us call the resultant term $M_{p,\mathsf{m},\vec{u},\Sigma_c}$. Next we combine terms related to the same $p : \mathcal{I}_p$ into an object definition by

$$M_p \equiv \mathsf{new}(x : \mathcal{I}_p;\ \mathsf{m} : \lambda\vec{u}.\mathsf{case}(\vec{u}, \Sigma_c)[M_{p,\mathsf{m},\vec{u},\Sigma_c}]).$$

The case statement, which can be implemented in IMJ using nested if's, is needed to recognize instances of $\vec{u}$ and $\Sigma_c$ that really occur in threads related to $p$. In such cases the corresponding term $M_{p,\mathsf{m},\vec{u},\Sigma_c}$ will be run. Otherwise, the statement leads to divergence.

The term $M$ for $s$ can now be obtained by taking

$\mathsf{let}\, x_n = \mathsf{new}(x : \mathcal{I}_P;)\ \mathsf{in}$
$\mathsf{let}\, x_h = \mathsf{new}(x : \mathsf{History};)\ \mathsf{in}$
$\mathsf{let}\, \overrightarrow{x_{p_i} = M_{p_i}}\ \mathsf{in}$
$\quad \mathsf{assert}(q^{\Sigma_q}); \overrightarrow{x_n.f_i = x_{p_i}}; \mathsf{make}(\Sigma_0''); \mathsf{play}(m_0)$

where $\overrightarrow{x_{p_i} = M_{p_i}}$ represents a series of bindings (one for each P-name $p_i \in P(s)$), $\mathsf{assert}((h, n, q)^{\Sigma_q''})$ is a conditional that converges if and only if the initial values of free $\Gamma$ identifiers as well as values accessible through them are consistent with $q$ and $\Sigma_q$ respectively, $\mathsf{make}(\Sigma_0'')$ is a sequence of assignments that set values to those specified in $\Sigma_0''$ (up-casts need to be performed to ensure typability) and $\mathsf{play}(m_0)$ is skip, $i$, null or, if $m_0$ is a name, it is a term of the form $(\theta)y.\vec{f}$, where $y$ is $x_n$ or $(x : I_x) \in \Gamma$ such that $y.\vec{f}$ gives an access path to $m_0$ in $\Sigma_0''$. □

We conclude with full abstraction results both in inequational and equational forms. For technical convenience, we shall use a modified (but equivalent) definition of contextual approximation.

**Lemma 19.** *Let* $\Gamma = \{x_1 : \mathcal{I}_1, \cdots, x_k : \mathcal{I}_k\}$, $\Delta|\Gamma \vdash M_i : \theta$ $(i = 1, 2)$, *and* $\Delta' = \Delta \cup \{\mathsf{Wrap}_{\Gamma,\mathcal{I}} \mapsto (f : (\mathcal{I}_1, \cdots, \mathcal{I}_k) \to \theta)\}$. *Then* $\Delta|\Gamma \vdash M_1 \sqsubseteq M_2$ *if and only if, for all* $\Delta'' \supseteq \Delta'$ *and* $\Delta'', z : \mathsf{Wrap}_{\Gamma,\mathcal{I}} \vdash \mathsf{test} : \mathsf{void}$, *if* $C_{\mathsf{test}}[M_1] \Downarrow$ *then* $C_{\mathsf{test}}[M_2] \Downarrow$, *where* $C_{\mathsf{test}}[-] \equiv \mathsf{let}\ z = \mathsf{new}(x : \mathsf{Wrap}_{\Gamma,\mathcal{I}}; f : \lambda\vec{x_i}.[-])\ \mathsf{in\ test}$.

*Proof.* The Lemma holds because, on the one hand, it relies on contexts of a specific shape and, on the other hand, any closing context $C[-]$ for $M_i$ can be presented in the above form with $\mathsf{test} \equiv C[z.f(x_1, \cdots, x_k)]$. □

Given a term $\Delta|\Gamma \vdash M : \theta$, let us write $[\![\Delta|\Gamma \vdash M : \theta]\!]_{comp}$ for the set of complete plays from $[\![\Delta|\Gamma \vdash M : \theta]\!]$. In what follows, we shall often omit $\Delta|\Gamma, \vdash$ for brevity.

**Theorem 20** (Inequational full abstraction). *Given* $\Delta|\Gamma \vdash M_i : \theta$ $(i = 1, 2)$, *we have* $\Delta|\Gamma \vdash M_1 \sqsubseteq M_2 : \theta$ *if and only if*

$$\mathsf{cl}_P([\![\Delta|\Gamma \vdash M_1 : \theta]\!]_{comp}) \subseteq \mathsf{cl}_P([\![\Delta|\Gamma \vdash M_2 : \theta]\!]_{comp}).$$

*Proof.* The proof uses the following play transformation. Given $t = q^{\Sigma_q} s_1 a^{\Sigma_a} s_2 \in P_{\Delta|\Gamma\vdash\theta}$, we define $\bar{t} \in P_{\Delta',\mathsf{Wrap}_{\Gamma,\mathcal{I}}\vdash\mathsf{void}}$ as

$$n^{\Sigma_n}\ \mathsf{call}\, n.f(q)^{\Sigma_q \oplus \Sigma_n}\ s_1^{\oplus\Sigma_n}\ \mathsf{ret}\, n.f(a)^{\Sigma_a \oplus \Sigma_n}\ s_2^{\oplus\Sigma_n}\ *^{\Sigma\oplus\Sigma_n},$$

where $\Delta', \mathsf{Wrap}_{\Gamma,\mathcal{I}}$ are the same as in the above Lemma, $\Sigma_n = \{n \mapsto (\mathsf{Wrap}_{\Gamma,\mathcal{I}}, \emptyset)\}$, $s^{\oplus\Sigma_n}$ stands for $s$ in which each store was augmented by $\Sigma_n$ and $\Sigma$ is the store of the last move in $t$. Intuitively, $\bar{t}$ is the play that $C_{\mathsf{test}}[-]$ needs to provide for a terminating interaction with $t$.

($\Rightarrow$) Let $s \in \mathsf{cl}_P([\![M_1]\!]_{comp})$. Then there exists $s' \in [\![M_1]\!]_{comp}$ with $s \in \mathsf{cl}_P(s')$. Apply Definability to $\overline{s'}$ to obtain $\Delta'', z : \mathsf{Wrap}_{\Gamma,\mathcal{I}} \vdash \mathsf{test} : \mathsf{void}$ such that $[\![\mathsf{test}]\!] = \mathsf{cl}_O(\overline{s'})$. Because $s' \in [\![M_1]\!]_{comp}$ and Adequacy holds, we must have $C_{\mathsf{test}}[M_1] \Downarrow$. From $M_1 \sqsubseteq M_2$ we obtain $C_{\mathsf{test}}[M_2] \Downarrow$. Hence, because of Soundness, there exists $s'' \in [\![M_2]\!]_{comp}$ such that $\overline{s''} \in [\![\mathsf{test}]\!]$. Since $[\![\mathsf{test}]\!] = \mathsf{cl}_O(\overline{s'})$, it follows that $\overline{s''} \in \mathsf{cl}_O(\overline{s'})$ and, consequently, $s' \in \mathsf{cl}_P(s'')$. Thus, $s \in \mathsf{cl}_P(s')$ and $s' \in \mathsf{cl}_P(s'')$. Hence, $s \in \mathsf{cl}_P(s'')$ and, because $s'' \in [\![M_2]\!]_{comp}$, we can conclude $s \in \mathsf{cl}_P([\![M_2]\!]_{comp})$.

($\Leftarrow$) Let $C_{\mathsf{test}}[-]$ be such that $C_{\mathsf{test}}[M_1] \Downarrow$. By Soundness, there exists $s \in [\![M_1]\!]_{comp}$ such that $\bar{s} \in [\![\mathsf{test}]\!]$. Because $[\![M_1]\!]_{comp} \subseteq \mathsf{cl}_P([\![M_1]\!]_{comp})$ and $\mathsf{cl}_P([\![M_1]\!]_{comp}) \subseteq \mathsf{cl}_P([\![M_2]\!]_{comp})$, we also have $s \in \mathsf{cl}_P([\![M_2]\!]_{comp})$. Thus, there exists $s' \in [\![M_2]\!]_{comp}$ such that $s \in \mathsf{cl}_P(s')$. Consequently, $\overline{s'} \in \mathsf{cl}_O(\bar{s})$. Since $\bar{s} \in [\![\mathsf{test}]\!]$, we also have $\overline{s'} \in [\![\mathsf{test}]\!]$. Because $s' \in [\![M_2]\!]_{comp}$ and $\overline{s'} \in [\![\mathsf{test}]\!]$, by Adequacy, we can conclude that $C_{\mathsf{test}}[M_2] \Downarrow$. □

*Example* 3. Let us revisit Example 2. We have $\mathsf{cl}_P(\sigma_1) = \sigma_1$ and $\mathsf{cl}_P(\sigma_2) = \sigma_2 \cup \{*^{\emptyset}, n^{\{n\mapsto(\mathsf{Empty},\emptyset)\}}\}$, i.e. $\mathsf{cl}_P(\sigma_1) \subsetneq \mathsf{cl}_P(\sigma_2)$. Thus, it follows from Theorem 20 that $\Delta|\emptyset \vdash M_1 \sqsubseteq M_2$ and $\Delta|\emptyset \vdash M_1 \not\cong M_2$.

**Theorem 21** (Equational full abstraction). *Given* $\Delta|\Gamma \vdash M_i : \theta$ $(i = 1, 2)$, $\Delta|\Gamma \vdash M_1 \cong M_2 : \theta$ *if and only if*

$$[\![\Delta|\Gamma \vdash M_1 : \theta]\!]_{comp} = [\![\Delta|\Gamma \vdash M_2 : \theta]\!]_{comp}.$$

*Proof.* The preceding result implies that $M_1 \cong M_2$ if and only if $\mathsf{cl}_P([\![M_1]\!]_{comp}) = \mathsf{cl}_P([\![M_2]\!]_{comp})$. We show that this implies $[\![M_1]\!]_{comp} = [\![M_2]\!]_{comp}$. Let $s \in [\![M_1]\!]_{comp}$. By $\mathsf{cl}_P([\![M_1]\!]_{comp}) = \mathsf{cl}_P([\![M_2]\!]_{comp})$, it must be the case that $s \in \mathsf{cl}_P([\![M_2]\!]_{comp})$, i.e., there exists $s' \in [\![M_2]\!]_{comp}$ such that $s \in \mathsf{cl}_P(s')$. Again, by $\mathsf{cl}_P([\![M_1]\!]_{comp}) = \mathsf{cl}_P([\![M_2]\!]_{comp})$, it follows that $s' \in \mathsf{cl}_P([\![M_1]\!]_{comp})$, i.e., there exists $s'' \in [\![M_1]\!]_{comp}$ such that $s' \in \mathsf{cl}_P(s'')$. So, we have $s \in \mathsf{cl}_P(s')$ and $s' \in \mathsf{cl}_P(s'')$, which implies $s \in \mathsf{cl}_P(s'')$. However, $s, s'' \in [\![M_1]\!]_{comp}$, so $s \in \mathsf{cl}_P(s'')$ entails $s = s''$. Hence, $s \in \mathsf{cl}_P(s')$ and $s' \in \mathsf{cl}_P(s)$, and $s = s'$ follows. Because $s' \in [\![M_2]\!]_{comp}$, we showed $s \in [\![M_2]\!]_{comp}$. The other inclusion is derived analogously. □

## References


[1] M. Abadi and L. Cardelli. *A theory of objects*. Springer Verlag, 1996.

[2] E. Ábraham, M. M. Bonsangue, F. S. de Boer, A. Gruener, and M. Steffen. Observability, connectivity, and replay in a sequential calculus of classes. In Proceedings of *FMCO*, 2004.

[3] S. Abramsky, D. R. Ghica, A. S. Murawski, C.-H. L. Ong, and I. D. B. Stark. Nominal games and full abstraction for the nu-calculus. In Proceedings of *LICS*, 2004.

[4] S. Abramsky, R. Jagadeesan, and P. Malacaria. Full abstraction for PCF. *Information and Computation*, 163:409–470, 2000.

[5] S. Abramsky and G. McCusker. Linearity, sharing and state: a fully abstract game semantics for Idealized Algol with active expressions. In *Algol-like languages*, pages 297–329. Birkhaüser, 1997.

[6] S. Abramsky and G. McCusker. Game semantics. In *Logic and Computation: Marktoberdorf Proceedings*. Springer-Verlag, 1998.

[7] J. Alves-Foss, editor. *Formal Syntax and Semantics of Java*, volume 1523 of *Lecture Notes in Computer Science*. Springer, 1999.

[8] J. Alves-Foss and F. S. Lam. Dynamic denotational semantics of Java. In *Formal Syntax and Semantics of Java*, pages 201–240. 1999.

[9] G.M. Bierman, M.J. Parkinson, and A.M. Pitts. MJ: An imperative core calculus for Java and Java with effects. Technical Report 563, Computer Laboratory, University of Cambridge, 2002.

[10] H. Björklund and T. Schwentick. On notions of regularity for data languages. *Theor. Comput. Sci.*, 411(4-5):702–715, 2010.

[11] M. J. Gabbay and A. M. Pitts. A new approach to abstract syntax with variable binding. *Formal Aspects of Computing*, 13:341–363, 2002.

[12] J. M. E. Hyland and C.-H. L. Ong. On Full Abstraction for PCF. *Information and Computation*, 163(2):285–408, 2000.

[13] A. Jeffrey and J. Rathke. Java Jr: Fully abstract trace semantics for a core Java language. In Proceedings of *ESOP*, 2003.

[14] A. Jeffrey and J. Rathke. A fully abstract may testing semantics for concurrent objects. *Theor. Comput. Sci.*, 338(1-3):17–63, 2005.

[15] S. N. Kamin and U. S. Reddy. Two semantic models of object-oriented languages. In *Theoretical Aspects of Object Oriented Programming*, pages 463–495. MIT Press, 1994.

[16] V. Koutavas and M. Wand. Reasoning about class behavior. In Proceedings of *FOOL/WOOD*, 2007.

[17] J. Laird. A game semantics of local names and good variables. In *Proceedings of FOSSACS*, 2004.

[18] J. Laird. Game semantics for higher-order concurrency. In Proceedings of *FSTTCS*, 2006.

[19] J. Laird. Game semantics for call-by-value polymorphism. In *Proceedings of ICALP*, 2010.

[20] S. B. Lassen and P. B. Levy. Typed normal form bisimulation for parametric polymorphism. In *Proceedings of LICS*, 2008.

[21] R. Milner. Fully abstract models of typed lambda-calculi. *Theoretical Computer Science*, 4(1):1–22, 1977.

[22] E. Moggi. Computational lambda-calculus and monads. In *Proceedings of LICS*, 1989.

[23] A. S. Murawski and N. Tzevelekos. Algorithmic nominal game semantics. In *Proceedings of ESOP*, 2011.

[24] A. S. Murawski and N. Tzevelekos. Game semantics for good general references. In *Proceedings of LICS*, 2011.

[25] J. Power and E. Robinson. Premonoidal categories and notions of computation. *Math. Struct. in Comput. Sci.*, 7:453–468, 1997.

[26] N. Tzevelekos. Full abstraction for nominal general references. *Logical Methods in Computer Science*, 5(3), 2009.

[27] N. Tzevelekos. Fresh-register automata. In *Proc. of POPL*, 2011.

# Abstract Acceleration of General Linear Loops

Bertrand Jeannet
INRIA
bertrand.jeannet@inria.fr

Peter Schrammel *
University of Oxford
peter.schrammel@cs.ox.ac.uk

Sriram Sankaranarayanan †
University of Colorado, Boulder
srirams@colorado.edu

## Abstract

We present abstract acceleration techniques for computing loop invariants for numerical programs with linear assignments and conditionals. Whereas abstract interpretation techniques typically over-approximate the set of reachable states iteratively, abstract acceleration captures the effect of the loop with a single, non-iterative transfer function applied to the initial states at the loop head. In contrast to previous acceleration techniques, our approach applies to any linear loop without restrictions. Its novelty lies in the use of the *Jordan normal form* decomposition of the loop body to derive symbolic expressions for the entries of the matrix modeling the effect of $n \geq 0$ iterations of the loop. The entries of such a matrix depend on $n$ through complex polynomial, exponential and trigonometric functions. Therefore, we introduces an *abstract domain for matrices* that captures the linear inequality relations between these complex expressions. This results in an abstract matrix for describing the fixpoint semantics of the loop.

Our approach integrates smoothly into standard abstract interpreters and can handle programs with nested loops and loops containing conditional branches. We evaluate it over small but complex loops that are commonly found in control software, comparing it with other tools for computing linear loop invariants. The loops in our benchmarks typically exhibit polynomial, exponential and oscillatory behaviors that present challenges to existing approaches. Our approach finds non-trivial invariants to prove useful bounds on the values of variables for such loops, clearly outperforming the existing approaches in terms of precision while exhibiting good performance.

## 1. Introduction

We present a simple yet effective way of inferring accurate loop invariants of *linear loops*, *i.e.* loops containing linear assignments and guards, as exemplified by the programs shown in Figs. 1 and 2. Such loops are particularly common in control and digital signal processing software due to the presence of components such as filters, integrators, iterative loops for equation solving that compute square roots, cube roots and loops that interpolate complex functions using splines. Static analysis of such programs using standard abstract interpretation theory over polyhedral abstract domains often incurs a significant loss of precision due to the use of extrapolation techniques (widening) to force termination of the analysis. However, widening is well-known to be too imprecise for such loops. In fact, specialized domains such as ellipsoids and arithmetic-geometric progressions were proposed to deal with two frequently occurring patterns that are encountered in control loops [12, 13]. These domains enable static analyzers for control systems, *e.g.*, ASTRÉE, to find the strong loop invariants that can establish bounds on the variables or the absence of run-time errors [10].

```
          real x,y,z,t;
          assume(-2<=x<=2 and -2<=y<=2 and -2<=z<=2);
loop      t := 0;
head -->  •
          while (x+y <= 30) <---------- loop guard
            { x := x+y; y := y+z; z := z+1;
loop          t := t+1; }
exit -->  •
```

**Figure 1.** Linear loop having a cubic behavior.

In this paper, we present a promising alternative approach to such loops by capturing the effect of a linear loop by means of a so-called *meta-transition* [5] that maps an initial set of states to an invariant at the loop head. This process is commonly termed *acceleration*. The idea of accelerations was first studied for communicating finite-state machines [5] and counter automata [14]. Such accelerations can be either *exact* (see [3] for a survey), or *abstract* [18]. Abstract acceleration seeks to devise a transformer that maps initial sets of states to the best correct over-approximation of the invariant at the loop head for a given abstract domain, typically the convex polyhedra domain. Abstract acceleration enables static analyzers to avoid widening for the innermost loops of the program by replacing them by meta-transitions. As discussed in [39] and observed experimentally in [38], abstract acceleration presents the following benefits w.r.t. widening:

(i) It is locally *more precise* because it takes into account the loop body in the extrapolation it performs, whereas widening considers only sequences of invariants.
(ii) It performs *more predictable* approximations because it is monotonic (unlike widening).
(iii) It makes the analysis *more efficient* by speeding up convergence to a fixed point. For programs without nested loops, our acceleration renders the program loop-free.

Apart from abstract interpretation, techniques such as symbolic execution and bounded model-checking, that are especially efficient over loop-free systems, can benefit from loop acceleration.

In this paper we present a novel approach to computing abstract accelerations. Our approach is *non-iterative*, avoiding widening. We focus on the linear transformation induced by a linear loop body

* Supported by the ARTEMIS VeTeSS project and ERC project 280053.

† Supported by the US National Science Foundation (NSF) under Grant No. 0953941. All opinions involved are those of the authors and not necessarily of the US National Science Foundation.



*POPL '14*, January 22–24, 2014, San Diego, CA, USA.

http://dx.doi.org/10.1145/2535838.2535843

modeled by a square matrix $A$. We seek to approximate the set of matrices $\{I, A, A^2, \ldots\}$, which represent the possible linear transformations that can be applied to the initial state of the program to obtain the current state. This set could be defined as fixed point equations on matrices and solved iteratively on a suitable abstract domain for matrices. However, such an approach does not avoid widening and suffers from efficiency issues, because a matrix for a program with $n$ variables has $n^2$ entries, thus requiring a matrix abstract domain with $n^2$ different dimensions.

***Contributions.*** The overall contribution of this paper is an abstract acceleration technique for computing the precise effect of any linear loop on an input predicate. It relies on the computation of the Jordan normal form of the square matrix $A$ for the loop body. Being based on abstract acceleration, it integrates smoothly into an abstract interpretation-based analyzer and can be exploited for the analysis of general programs with nested loops and conditionals by transforming them into multiple loops around a program location.

The first technical contribution is an abstract acceleration method for computing, non-iteratively, an approximation of the set $\{I, A, A^2, \ldots\}$ in an *abstract domain for matrices*. It enables the analysis of any infinite, non-guarded linear loop. The main idea is to consider the Jordan normal form $J$ of the transformation matrix $A$. Indeed, the particular structure of the Jordan normal form $J$ has two advantages:

(i) It results in closed-form expressions for the coefficients of $J^n$, on which asymptotic analysis techniques can be applied that remove the need for widening,

(ii) It reduces the number of different coefficients of $J^n$ to at most the dimension of the vector space (efficiency issue).

This first contribution involves a conceptually simple but technically involved derivation that we omit in this paper and which can be found in the extended version [23].

The second technical contribution addresses loops with guards that are conjunctions of linear inequalities. We present an original technique for bounding the number of loop iterations. Once again, we utilize the Jordan normal form. These two techniques together make our approach more powerful than ellipsoidal methods (*e.g.* [34]) that are restricted to stable loops, because the guard is only weakly taken into account.

We evaluate our approach by comparing efficiency and the precision of the invariants produced with other invariant synthesis approaches, including abstract interpreters and constraint-based approaches. The evaluation is carried out over a series of simple loops, alone or inside outer loops (such as in Fig. 2), exhibiting behaviors such as polynomial, stable and unstable exponentials, and inward spirals (damped oscillators). We show the ability of our approach to *discover polyhedral invariants* that are sound over-approximations of the reachable state space. For such systems, any inductive reasoning *in* a linear domain as performed by, *e.g.*, standard abstract interpretation with Kleene iteration and widening is often unable to find a linear invariant other than *true*. In contrast, our approach is shown to find useful bounds for many of the program variables that appear in such loops. To our knowledge, our method is the first one able to bound the variables in the *convoyCar* example of Sankaranarayanan et al. [36].

***Outline.*** We introduce some basic notions in §2. §3 gives an overview of the ideas of this paper. §§4 to 6 explain the contributions in detail. §7 summarizes our experimental results and §8 discusses related work before §9 concludes.

## 2. Preliminaries

In this section, we recall the notions of linear assertions and convex polyhedra, and we define the model of linear loops for which we will propose acceleration methods.

```
real t,te,time;
assume(te=14 and 16<=t and t<=17);
while true {
  time := 0; -- timer measuring duration in each
mode
  while (t<=22) { -- heating mode
    t := 15/16*t-1/16*te+1; time++;
  }
  time := 0;
  while (t>=18){ -- cooling mode
    t := 15/16*t-1/16*te; time++;
  }
}
```

**Figure 2.** A thermostat system, composed of two simple loops inside a outer loop.

### 2.1 Linear assertions and convex polyhedra

Let $x_1, \ldots, x_p$ be real-valued variables, collectively forming a $p \times 1$ column vector $\vec{x}$. A linear expression is written as an inner product $\vec{c} \cdot \vec{x}$, wherein $\vec{c} \in \mathbb{R}^p$. A linear inequality is of the form $\vec{c} \cdot \vec{x} \leq d$ with $d \in \mathbb{R}$. A *linear assertion* is a conjunction of linear inequalities: $\varphi(\vec{x}) : \bigwedge_{i=1}^{q} \vec{c}_i \cdot \vec{x} \leq d_i$. The assertion $\varphi$ is succinctly written as $C\vec{x} \leq \vec{d}$, where $C$ is an $q \times p$ matrix whose $i^{\text{th}}$ row is $\vec{c}_i$. Likewise, $\vec{d}$ is an $q \times 1$ column vector whose $j^{\text{th}}$ coefficient is $d_j$. The linear assertion consisting of the single inequality $0 \leq 0$ represents the assertion *true* while the assertion $1 \leq 0$ represents the assertion *false*.

Given a linear assertion $\varphi$, the set $[\![\varphi]\!] = \{\vec{x} \in \mathbb{R}^p \mid \varphi(\vec{x})\}$ is a convex polyhedron. The set of all convex polyhedra contained in $\mathbb{R}^p$ is denoted by $\mathcal{CP}(\mathbb{R}^p)$. We recall that a convex polyhedron $P \in \mathcal{CP}(\mathbb{R}^p)$ can be represented in two ways:

(a) The *constraint representation* $C\vec{x} \leq \vec{d}$ with matrix $C$ and vector $\vec{d}$.

(b) The *generator representation* with a set of vertices $V = \{\vec{v}_1, \ldots, \vec{v}_k\}$ and rays $R = \{\vec{r}_1, \ldots, \vec{r}_l\}$, wherein $\vec{x} \in P$ iff

$$\vec{x} = \sum_{i=1}^{k} \lambda_i \vec{v}_i + \sum_{j=1}^{l} \mu_j \vec{r}_j \text{ with } \lambda_i, \mu_j \geq 0 \text{ and } \textstyle\sum_i \lambda_i = 1$$

### 2.2 Linear loops

We consider *linear loops* consisting of a while loop, the body of which is a set of assignments without tests and the condition is a linear assertion.

DEFINITION 1 (Linear loop). *A linear loop $(G, \vec{h}, A, \vec{b})$ is a program fragment of the form*

$$\mathsf{while}(G\vec{x} \leq \vec{h})\ \vec{x} := A\vec{x} + \vec{b};$$

*where $\varphi : G\vec{x} \leq \vec{h}$ is a linear assertion over the state variables $\vec{x}$ representing the loop condition and $(A, \vec{b})$ is the linear transformation associated with the loop body.*

Figure 1 shows an example of a linear loop with a guard that computes $y = x(x+1)/2$ by the successive difference method. We give another example below.

EXAMPLE 1 (Thermostat). *Figure 2 models the operation of a thermostat that switches between the heating and cooling modes over time. The variables* `t`, `te` *model the room and outside temperatures, respectively. We wish to show that the value of* `t` *remains within some bounds that are close to the switch points* 18, 22 *units.*

Any linear loop $(G, \vec{h}, A, \vec{b})$ can be *homogenized* by introducing a new variable $\xi$ that is a place holder for the constant 1 to a loop of the form

$$\text{while}\left(\begin{pmatrix}G & \vec{h}\end{pmatrix}\begin{pmatrix}\vec{x}\\ \xi\end{pmatrix} \le \vec{0}\right)\left\{ \begin{pmatrix}\vec{x}\\ \xi\end{pmatrix} := \begin{pmatrix}A & \vec{b}\\ 0 & 1\end{pmatrix}\begin{pmatrix}\vec{x}\\ \xi\end{pmatrix}; \right\}$$

Henceforth, we will use the notation $(G \to A)$ to denote the *homogenized linear loop* while $(G\vec{x} \le \vec{0})\{\ \vec{x}' := A\vec{x};\ \}$.

DEFINITION 2 (Semantic function). *The semantic function of a linear loop $(G \to A)$ over sets of states is the functional*

$$(G \to A)(X) \triangleq A(X \cap [\![G\vec{x} \le 0]\!]) \quad , \quad X \subseteq \mathbb{R}^p$$

*where $A(Y)$ denotes the image of a set $Y$ by the transformation $A$.*

### 2.3 Convex and template polyhedra abstract domains

The set of convex polyhedra $\mathcal{CP}(\mathbb{R}^p)$ ordered by inclusion is a lattice with the greatest lower bound $\sqcap$ being the set intersection and the least upper bound $\sqcup$ being the convex hull. The definition of the domain includes an abstraction function $\alpha$ that maps sets of states to a polyhedral abstraction and a corresponding concretization function $\gamma$. We refer the reader to the original work of Cousot and Halbwachs for a complete description [9].

It is well-known that the abstract domain operations such as join and transfer function across non-invertible assignments are computationally expensive. As a result, many *weakly-relational* domains such as octagons and templates have been proposed [29, 37]. Given a matrix $T \in \mathbb{R}^{q\times p}$ of $q$ linear expressions, $\mathcal{CP}_T(\mathbb{R}^p) \subsetneq \mathcal{CP}(\mathbb{R}^p)$ denotes the set of *template polyhedra* on $T$:

$$\mathcal{CP}_T(\mathbb{R}^n) = \left\{P \in \mathcal{CP}(\mathbb{R}^p) \mid \exists \vec{u} \in \bar{\mathbb{R}}^q : P = \{\vec{x} \mid T\vec{x} \le \vec{u}\}\right\}$$

where $\bar{\mathbb{R}}$ denotes $\mathbb{R} \cup \{\infty\}$. A template polyhedron will be denoted by $(T, \vec{u})$. If $T$ is is fixed, it is uniquely defined by the vector $\vec{u}$. $\mathcal{CP}_T(\mathbb{R}^p)$ ordered by inclusion is a complete lattice. The abstraction $\alpha_T$ and concretization $\gamma_T$ are defined elsewhere [37].

## 3. Overview

This section provides a general overview of the ideas in this paper, starting with abstract acceleration techniques.

***Abstract Acceleration*** Given a set of initial states $X_0$ and a loop with the semantic function $\tau$, the smallest loop invariant $X$ containing $X_0$ can be formally written as

$$X = \tau^*(X_0) \triangleq \bigcup_{n\ge 0} \tau^n(X_0)$$

Abstract acceleration seeks an "optimal" approximation of $\tau^*$ in a given abstract domain with abstraction function $\alpha$ [18]. Whereas the standard abstract interpretation approach seeks to solve the fix point equation $Y' = \alpha(X_0) \sqcup \alpha(\tau(Y'))$ by iteratively computing

$$Y = (\alpha \circ \tau)^*(\alpha(X_0)) \qquad (1)$$

the abstract acceleration approach uses $\tau^*$ to compute

$$Z = \alpha \circ \tau^*(\alpha(X_0)) \qquad (2)$$

Classically, Eqn. (1) is known as the minimal fixed point (MFP) solution of the reachability problem whereas Eqn. (2) is called the Merge-Over-All-Paths (MOP) solution. The latter is known to yield more precise results [24].

The technical challenge of abstract acceleration is thus to obtain a closed-form approximation of $\alpha \circ \tau^*$ that avoids both inductive reasoning in the abstract domain and the use of widening.

***Abstract acceleration without guards using matrix abstract domains*** We now present an overview for linear loop without guards, with semantic function $\tau = (\mathit{true} \to A)$. For any set $X$, we have

$$\tau^*(X) = \bigcup_{n\ge 0} \tau^n(X) = \bigcup_{n\ge 0} A^n X$$

Our approach computes a finitely representable approximation $\mathcal{M}$ of the countably infinite set of matrices $\bigcup_{n\ge 0} A^n$. Thereafter, abstract acceleration simply applies $\mathcal{M}$ to $X$.

The following example illustrates the first step.

EXAMPLE 2 (Exponential 1/4). *We consider the program*

```
while(true){ x=1.5*x; y=y+1 }
```

*of which Fig. 3 depicts some trajectories. After homogenization, the loop's semantic function is*

$$G = \begin{pmatrix}0 & 0 & 0\end{pmatrix} \to A = \begin{pmatrix}1.5 & 0 & 0\\ 0 & 1 & 1\\ 0 & 0 & 1\end{pmatrix}$$

*Here, it is easy to obtain a closed-form symbolic expression of $A^n$:*

$$A^n = \begin{pmatrix}1.5^n & 0 & 0\\ 0 & 1 & n\\ 0 & 0 & 1\end{pmatrix}$$

*The idea for approximating $\bigcup_{n\ge 0} A^n$ is to consider a set of matrices of the form*

$$\mathcal{M} = \left\{\begin{pmatrix}m_1 & 0 & 0\\ 0 & 1 & m_2\\ 0 & 0 & 1\end{pmatrix} \mid \varphi_{\mathcal{M}}(m_1, m_2)\right\}$$

*with $\varphi_{\mathcal{M}}$ a linear assertion in a template domain such that $\forall n \ge 0 : A^n \subseteq \mathcal{M}$. Using an octagonal template, for instance, the following assertion satisfies the condition above:*

$$\varphi_{\mathcal{M}} : \begin{cases} m_1 \in [1, +\infty] = [\inf_{n\ge 0} 1.5^n, \sup_{n\ge 0} 1.5^n] \\ m_2 \in [0, +\infty] = [\inf_{n\ge 0} n, \sup_{n\ge 0} n] \\ m_1 + m_2 \in [1, +\infty] = [\inf_{n\ge 0}(1.5^n + n), \sup_{n\ge 0}(1.5^n + n)] \\ m_1 - m_2 \in [0.25, +\infty] = [\inf_{n\ge 0}(1.5^n - n), \sup_{n\ge 0}(1.5^n - n)] \end{cases}$$

*These constraints actually define the smallest octagon on entries $m_1, m_2$ that makes $\mathcal{M}$ an overapproximation of $A^* = \{A^n \mid n \ge 0\}$. It is depicted in Fig. 3. The technique to evaluate the non-linear* inf *and* sup *expressions above is described in §5.2.*

This is the first important idea of the paper. §4 formalizes the notion of abstract matrices, whereas §5 will exploit the Jordan normal form of $A$ to effectively compute $\alpha(A^*)$ for any matrix $A$, *i.e.* to accelerate the loop body.

***Applying the abstraction to acceleration*** The next step is to apply the matrix abstraction $\mathcal{M} = \alpha(A^*)$ to an abstract element $X$. For illustration, assume that both $\mathcal{M}$ and $X$ are defined by linear assertions $\varphi_{\mathcal{M}}$ and $\varphi_X$ from the polyhedral domain or some sub-polyhedral domains. Applying the set of matrices $\mathcal{M}$ to $X$ amounts to computing (an approximation of)

$$\left\{\begin{pmatrix}m_1 & 0 & 0\\ 0 & 1 & m_2\\ 0 & 0 & 1\end{pmatrix}\begin{pmatrix}x\\ y\\ 1\end{pmatrix} \;\middle|\; \begin{matrix}\varphi_{\mathcal{M}}(m_1, m_2) \wedge \\ \varphi_X(x, y)\end{matrix}\right\} \qquad (3)$$

This is not trivial, as the matrix multiplication generates bilinear expressions. §4 proposes a general approach for performing the abstract multiplication. The result of the procedure is illustrated by the example that follows:

EXAMPLE 3 (Exponential 2/4). *Assume that in Ex. 2 and Eqn. (3), $\varphi_X = (x \in [1, 3] \wedge y \in [1, 2])$. We compute the abstract matrix multiplication*

$$\mathcal{M}X = \left\{\begin{pmatrix}m_1 \cdot x\\ 1 + m_2 \cdot y\\ 1\end{pmatrix} \;\middle|\; \begin{matrix}1 \le x \le 3 \wedge 0 \le y \le 2 & \wedge\\ m_1 \ge 1 \wedge m_2 \ge 0 & \wedge\\ m_1 - m_2 \ge 0.25 & \end{matrix}\right\}$$

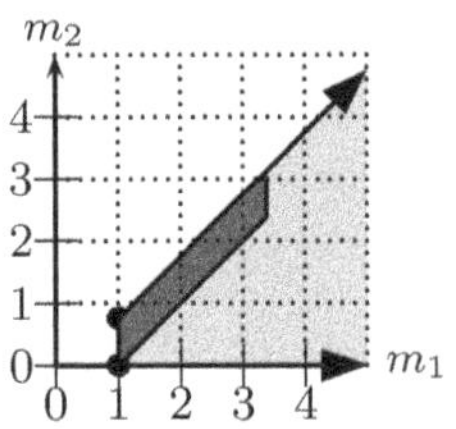


**Figure 3.** Octagons defined by $\varphi_{\mathcal{M}}$ in Example 2 (light gray), and by $\varphi_{\mathcal{M}'}$ in Ex. 5 (dark gray).

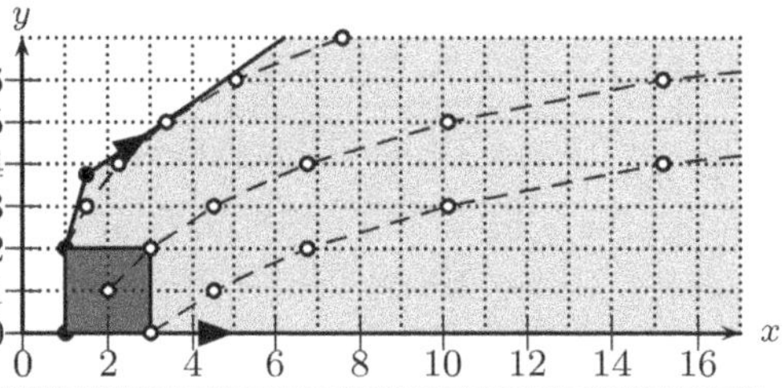


**Figure 4.** Trajectories (dashed) starting from $(1,2)$, $(2,1)$ and $(3,0)$ in Ex. 2, initial set of states $X$ (dark gray), and invariant $Y$ approximating $A^*X$ (light gray) in Ex. 3.

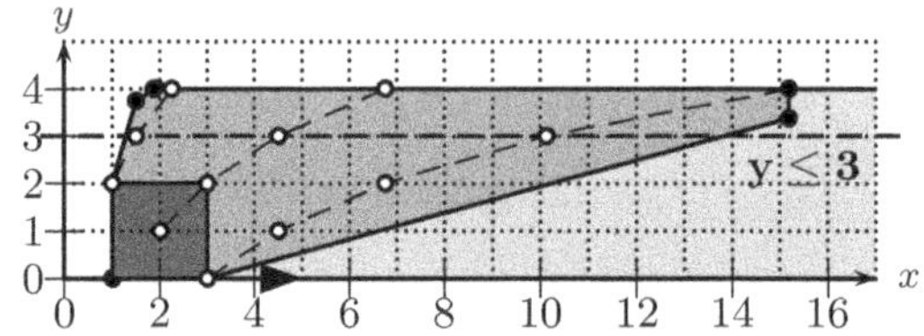


**Figure 5.** Initial set of states $X$ (dark gray), invariant $Y$ approximating $(G \to A)^*(X)$ in Ex. 4 (light gray), and the better invariant $Z$ (medium gray) discovered in Ex. 5 by exploiting the number of iterations.

$$\subseteq \left\{ \begin{pmatrix} x' \\ y' \\ 1 \end{pmatrix} \;\middle|\; \begin{array}{ll} x' \geq 1 \wedge y' \geq 0 & \wedge \\ x' - 1.5y' \geq -4.125 & \wedge \\ 3.5x' - y' \geq 1.5 & \end{array} \right\} = Y$$

*where $Y$ is the result obtained by the method described in §4 and is depicted in Fig. 4.*

***Handling Guards*** We consider loops of the form $\tau = G \to A$ and illustrate how the loop condition (guard) $G$ is handled. A simple approach takes the guard into account after the fixpoint of the loop without guard is computed:

$$(G \to A)^*(X) \subseteq X \cup (G \to A) \circ (G \to A^*)(X)$$

which is then abstracted with $X \sqcup (G \to A) \circ (G \to \alpha(A^*))(X)$. However, such an approach is often unsatisfactory.

EXAMPLE 4 (Exponential 3/4). *We add the guard $y \leq 3$ to our running Ex. 2. Using the approximation above with $X$ as in Ex. 3, we obtain the invariant $Y$ depicted in Fig. 5. In this result $y$ is bounded but $x$ remains unbounded.*

Our idea is based on the observation that the bound on $y$ induced by the guard implies a bound $N$ on the maximum number of iterations for any initial state in $X$. Once this bound is known, we can exploit the knowledge $\tau^*(X) = \bigcup_{n=0}^{N} \tau^n(X)$ and consider the better approximation

$$(G \to A)^*(X) \subseteq X \sqcup (G \to A) \circ \left( G \to \alpha\left( \bigcup_{n=0}^{N-1} A^n \right) \right)(X)$$

The set of matrices $\bigcup_{n=0}^{N-1} A^n$ is then approximated in the same way as $A^*$ in §3. We could perform an iterative computation for small $N$, however, a polyhedral analysis without widening operator is intractably expensive for hundreds or thousands iterations, while our method is both, precise and efficient.

EXAMPLE 5 (Exponential 4/4). *In our running example, it is easy to see that the initial condition $y_0 \in [0,2]$ together with the guard $y \leq 3$ implies that the maximum number of iteration is $N = 4$. Thus, we can consider the set of matrices $\mathcal{M}' = \alpha(\bigcup_{n=0}^{N-1} A^n)$ defined by the following assertion satisfies the condition $\varphi_{\mathcal{M}'}$ above:*

$$\begin{cases} m_1 \in [1, 3.375] = [\inf_{0 \leq n \leq 3} 1.5^n,\ \sup_{0 \leq n \leq 3} 1.5^n] \\ m_2 \in [0,3] = [\inf_{0 \leq n \leq 3} n,\ \sup_{0 \leq n \leq 3} n] \\ m_1 + m_2 \in [1, 6.375] = [\inf_{0 \leq n \leq 3} (1.5^n + n),\ \sup_{0 \leq n \leq 3} (1.5^n + n)] \\ m_1 - m_2 \in [0.25, 1] = [\inf_{0 \leq n \leq 3} (1.5^n - n),\ \sup_{0 \leq n \leq 3} (1.5^n - n)] \end{cases}$$

*which is depicted in Fig. 3. Using the formula above, we obtain the invariant $Z$ depicted in Fig. 5, which is much more precise than the invariant $Y$ discovered with the simple technique.*

§6 presents the technique for over-approximating the number of iterations of a loop where the guard $G$ is a general linear assertion, $A$ is any matrix and $X$ any polyhedron. This is the third main contribution of the paper.

***An Illustrative Comparison*** The capability of our method to compute over-approximations of the reachable state space goes beyond state-of-the-art invariant inference techniques. The following table lists the bounds obtained on the variables of the thermostat of Ex. 1, Fig. 2 for some competing techniques:

| INTERPROC [22] | ASTRÉE [4] | STING [7, 36] | this paper |
|---|---|---|---|
| heating: | | | |
| $16 \leq t$<br>$0 \leq time$ | $16 \leq t \leq 22.5$<br>$0 \leq time$ | $16 \leq t \leq 22.5$<br>$0 \leq time \leq 13$ | $16 \leq t \leq 22.5$<br>$0 \leq time \leq 9.76$ |
| cooling: | | | |
| $t \leq 22.5$<br>$0 \leq time$ | $17.75 \leq t \leq 22.5$<br>$0 \leq time$ | $17.75 \leq t \leq 22.5$<br>$0 \leq time \leq 19$ | $17.75 \leq t \leq 22.5$<br>$0 \leq time \leq 12.79$ |

There are many other invariant generation techniques and tools for linear systems (see §8). Many approaches sacrifice precision for speed, and therefore are inaccurate on the type of linear loops considered here. Other, more specialized approaches require conditions such as Lyapunov-stability, diagonalizability of the matrix, polynomial behavior (nilpotency or monoidal property), or handle only integer loops.

***Outline of the rest of the paper*** The rest of the paper develops the ideas illustrated in this section. §4 formalizes the notion of matrix abstract domains and presents a technique for the abstract matrix multiplication operation. §5 shows how to approximate the set of matrices $A^* = \bigcup_{n \geq 0} A^n$ for any square matrix $A$ in order to accelerate loops without guards. §6 presents a technique for taking the guard of loops into account by approximating $N$, the maximum number of iterations possible from a given set of initial states. §7 presents the experimental evaluation on various kinds of linear loops, possibly embedded into outer loops. §8 discusses related work and §9 concludes.

## 4. Matrix abstract domains

In this section we present abstract domains for matrices. We will use abstract matrices to represent the accelerated abstract transformer of a linear loop. Hence, the main operation on abstract matrices we use in this paper is abstract matrix multiplication (§4.2).

### 4.1 Extending abstract domains from vectors to matrices

We abstract sets of square matrices in $\mathbb{R}^{p \times p}$ by viewing them as vectors in $\mathbb{R}^{p^2}$ and by reusing known abstract domains over vectors. However, since the concrete matrices we will be dealing with belong to subspaces of $\mathbb{R}^{p \times p}$, we first introduce *matrix shapes* that allow us to reduce the number of entries in abstract matrices.

DEFINITION 3 (Matrix shape). *A matrix shape $\Psi : \mathbb{R}^m \to \mathbb{R}^{p\times p}$ is a bijective, linear map from $m$-dimensional vectors to $p \times p$ square matrices. Intuitively, matrix shapes represent matrices whose entries are linear (or affine) combinations of $m > 0$ entries.*

EXAMPLE 6. *In Ex. 2, we implicitly considered the matrix shape*

$$\Psi: \quad \mathbb{R}^2 \quad \to \quad Mat_\Psi \quad \subseteq \mathbb{R}^{3\times 3}$$
$$\begin{pmatrix} m_1 \\ m_2 \end{pmatrix} \mapsto \begin{pmatrix} m_1 & 0 & 0 \\ 0 & 1 & m_2 \\ 0 & 0 & 1 \end{pmatrix}$$

The set $Mat_\Psi = \{\Psi(\vec{m}) \mid \vec{m} \in \mathbb{R}^m\}$ represents all possible matrices that can be formed by any vector $\vec{m}$. It represents a subspace of the vector space of all matrices.

A matrix shape $\Psi$ induces an isomorphism between $\mathbb{R}^m$ and $Mat_\Psi$: $\Psi(a_1\vec{m}_1 + a_2\vec{m}_2) = a_1\Psi(\vec{m}_1) + a_2\Psi(\vec{m}_2)$.

Abstract domain for matrices are constructed by (a) choosing an abstract domain for vectors $\vec{m}$ and (b) specifying a matrix shape $\Psi$. Given an abstract domain $A$ for vectors $\vec{m}$ (eg, the polyhedral domain) and a shape $\Psi$, the corresponding matrix abstract domain defines a domain over subsets of $Mat_\Psi$.

EXAMPLE 7. *Recall the matrix shape $\Psi : \mathbb{R}^2 \to Mat_\Psi \subseteq \mathbb{R}^{3\times 3}$ from Ex. 6. Consider the octagon $P = (m_1 \geq 1 \wedge m_2 \geq 0 \wedge m_1 + m_2 \geq 1 \wedge m_1 - m_2 \geq 0.25) \in Oct(\mathbb{R}^2)$. Together they represent an abstract matrix $(P, \Psi)$ which represents the set of matrices:*

$$\left\{ \begin{pmatrix} m_1 & 0 & 0 \\ 0 & 1 & m_2 \\ 0 & 0 & 1 \end{pmatrix} \middle| \begin{array}{c} m_1 \geq 1, m_2 \geq 0, \\ m_1 + m_2 \geq 1, \\ m_1 - m_2 \geq 0.25 \end{array} \right\}.$$

DEFINITION 4 (Abstract domain for matrices induced by $\Psi$). *Let $A \subseteq \wp(\mathbb{R}^m)$ be an abstract domain for $m$-dimensional vectors ordered by set inclusion and with the abstraction function $\alpha_A : \wp(\mathbb{R}^m) \to A$. Then, $\Psi(A)$ ordered by set inclusion is an abstract domain for $\wp(Mat_\Psi)$ with the abstraction function*

$$\alpha_{\Psi(A)}(\mathcal{M}) = \Psi \circ \alpha_A \circ \Psi^{-1}(\mathcal{M}).$$

Note that since $\Psi$ is an isomorphism: the lattices $A$ and $\Psi(A)$ can be shown to be isomorphic. For generality, the *base domain* $A$ can be an arbitrary abstract domain for the data type of the matrix entries. In our examples, we specifically discuss common numerical domains such as convex polyhedra, intervals, octagons and templates.

## 4.2 Abstract matrix multiplication

We investigate now the problem of convex polyhedra matrix multiplication, motivated by the need for applying an acceleration $\alpha(A^*)$ to an abstract property $X$ as shown in §3.

***The problem.*** We consider two convex polyhedra matrices $\mathcal{M}_s = \Psi_s(P_s)$. We aim at computing an approximation of

$$\mathcal{M} = \mathcal{M}_1\mathcal{M}_2 = \{M_1 M_2 \mid M_1 \in \mathcal{M}_1 \wedge M_2 \in \mathcal{M}_2\} \qquad (4)$$

under the form of a convex polyhedron on the coefficients of the resulting matrix. Observe that $\mathcal{M}$ may be non-convex as shown by the following example.

EXAMPLE 8. *Consider the two abstract matrices*

$$\mathcal{M}_1 = \left\{ \begin{pmatrix} 1-m & 0 \\ 0 & m \end{pmatrix} \middle| m \in [0,1] \right\} \quad \mathcal{M}_2 = \left\{ \begin{pmatrix} 1-n \\ n \end{pmatrix} \middle| n \in [0,1] \right\}$$

*We have*

$$\mathcal{M}_1\mathcal{M}_2 = \left\{ \begin{pmatrix} (1-m)(1-n) \\ mn \end{pmatrix} \middle| m \in [0,1] \wedge n \in [0,1] \right\}$$

*This corresponds to the well-known non-convex set of points $x \in [0,1] \wedge y \in [0,1] \wedge (x-y)^2 + 1 \geq 2(x+y)$, depicted to the right.*

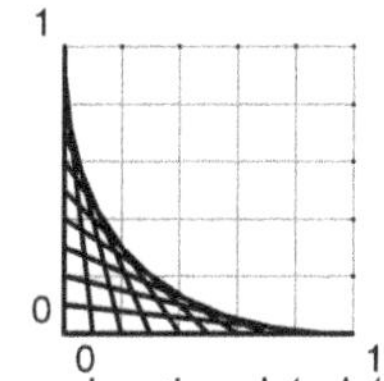


We may follow at least two approaches for approximating $\mathcal{M}_1\mathcal{M}_2$:

- Either we consider the constraint representations of $\mathcal{M}_1$ and $\mathcal{M}_2$, and we resort to optimization techniques to obtain a template polyhedra approximation of the product;
- Or we consider their generator representations to obtain a convex polyhedron approximating the product.

We opted in this paper for the second, *i.e.* the *generator* approach, which leads to more accurate results:

– it delivers general convex polyhedra, more expressive than template polyhedra obtained by optimization;
– it computes the best correct approximation in the convex polyhedra domain for bounded matrices (Thm. 1 below), whereas in the constraint approach the exact optimization problem involves bilinear expressions (see Eqn. (3) or Ex. 8) and must be relaxed in practice.

***Multiplying abstract matrices using generators.*** Given two finite sets of matrices $X = \{X_1, \ldots, X_m\}$ and $Y = \{Y_1, \ldots, Y_k\}$ we write $X \otimes Y$ to denote the set

$$X \otimes Y = \{X_i Y_j \mid X_i \in X,\ Y_j \in Y\}$$

If $\mathcal{M}_s$ is expressed as a system of matrix vertices $V_s = (V_{s,i_s})$ and matrix rays $R_s = (R_{s,j_s})$, $s = 1, 2$, then

$$\mathcal{M}_s = \left\{ \textstyle\sum_{i_s} \lambda_{i_s} V_{s,i_s} + \sum_{j_s} \mu_{j_s} R_{s,j_s} \;\middle|\; \begin{array}{c} \lambda_{i_s}, \mu_{j_s} \geq 0 \\ \sum_{i_s} \lambda_{i_s} = 1 \end{array} \right\}$$

and Eqn. (4) can be rewritten

$$\mathcal{M} = \mathcal{M}_1\mathcal{M}_2 =$$
$$\left\{ \begin{array}{l} \sum_{i_1,i_2} \lambda_{1,i_1}\lambda_{2,i_2} V_{1,i_1} V_{2,i_2} \\ + \sum_{i_1,j_2} \lambda_{1,i_1}\mu_{2,j_2} V_{1,i_1} R_{2,j_2} \\ + \sum_{i_2,j_1} \mu_{1,j_1}\lambda_{2,i_2} R_{1,j_1} V_{2,i_2} \\ + \sum_{j_1,j_2} \mu_{1,j_1}\mu_{2,j_2} R_{1,j_1} R_{2,j_2} \end{array} \middle| \begin{array}{l} \lambda_{1,i_1}, \mu_{1,j_1} \geq 0 \\ \lambda_{2,i_2}, \mu_{2,j_2} \geq 0 \\ \sum_{i_1} \lambda_{1,i_1} = 1 \\ \sum_{i_2} \lambda_{2,i_2} = 1 \end{array} \right\} \qquad (5)$$

We obtain the following result:

THEOREM 1. *Let $\mathcal{M}_1$ and $\mathcal{M}_2$ be two abstract matrices expressed as a system of vertices and rays: $V_1, R_1$ for $\mathcal{M}_1$ and $V_2, R_2$ for $\mathcal{M}_2$. The matrix polyhedron $\widetilde{\mathcal{M}}$ defined by the set of vertices*
$$V = V_1 \otimes V_2$$
*and the set of rays*
$$R = (V_1 \otimes R_2) \cup (R_1 \otimes V_2) \cup (R_1 \otimes R_2)$$
*is an overapproximation of $\mathcal{M} = \mathcal{M}_1\mathcal{M}_2$.*

*Moreover, if $\mathcal{M}_1$ and $\mathcal{M}_2$ are bounded, i.e. if $R_1 = R_2 = \emptyset$, then $\widetilde{\mathcal{M}}$ is the smallest polyhedron matrix containing $\mathcal{M}$.*

PROOF. *For the first part of the theorem, we observe that in Eqn. (5), $\sum_{i_1,i_2} \lambda_{1,i_1}\lambda_{2,i_2} = 1$ and the other similar sums are positive and unbounded. Hence*

$$\mathcal{M} \subseteq \widetilde{\mathcal{M}} = \left\{ \begin{array}{l} \sum_{i_1,i_2} \lambda'_{i_1,i_2} V_{1,i_1} V_{2,i_2} \\ + \sum_{i_1,j_2} \mu'_{i_1,j_2} V_{1,i_1} R_{2,j_2} \\ + \sum_{i_2,j_1} \mu''_{j_1,i_2} R_{1,j_1} V_{2,i_2} \\ + \sum_{j_1,j_2} \mu'''_{j_1,j_2} R_{1,j_1} R_{2,j_2} \end{array} \middle| \begin{array}{l} \lambda'_{i_1,i_2} \geq 0 \\ \mu'_{i_1,j_2} \geq 0 \\ \mu''_{j_1,i_2}, \mu'''_{j_1,j_2} \geq 0 \\ \sum_{i_1,i_2} \lambda'_{i_1,i_2} = 1 \end{array} \right\}$$

*which proves the first statement. Now assume that $R_1 = R_2 = \emptyset$, which means that both $\mathcal{M}_1$ and $\mathcal{M}_2$ are bounded and that $R = \emptyset$. We will show that all the generator vertices of $\widetilde{\mathcal{M}}$ belong to $\mathcal{M}$, hence any of their convex combination (i.e. any element of $\widetilde{\mathcal{M}}$) belongs to the convex closure of $\mathcal{M}$: Consider the generator vertex*

$V_{1,i_1}V_{2,i_2} \in V$ *of* $\widetilde{\mathcal{M}}$. *By taking in Eqn. (5)* $\lambda_{s,i_s} = 1$ *and* $i'_s \neq i_s \implies \lambda_{s,i'_s} = 0$ *for* $s = 1, 2$, *we obtain that* $V \in \mathcal{M}$. □

EXAMPLE 9. *In Ex. 3, we multiplied the unbounded set of matrices* $\mathcal{M}$ *depicted in Fig. 3 and defined by 2 vertices and 2 rays by the bounded set of vectors* $X$ *depicted in Fig. 4 and generated by 4 vertices, which resulted in the convex polyhedra* $Y$ *depicted in Fig. 4 which is generated by 3 vertices and 2 rays (we omit redundant generators).*

Regarding complexity, this operation is quadratic w.r.t. the number of generators, which is itself exponential in the worst-case w.r.t. the number of constraints. In practice, we did not face complexity problems in our experiments, apart from the high-dimensional *convoyCar3* example described in §7.

Observe that by using generators and applying Thm. 1, we lose information about matrix shapes. In our case, we will perform only abstract matrix-vector multiplication, hence the number of entries of the product matrix (actually a vector) will be the dimension of the space $\mathbb{R}^p$. The multiplication of an abstract matrix $\mathcal{M}$ and a concrete matrix $R$ ($\mathcal{M}R$ or $R\mathcal{M}$) can be computed exactly by considering the generators of $\mathcal{M}$.

## 5. Abstract acceleration of loops without guards

In this section, we consider loops of the form

$$\mathsf{while(true)}\{\vec{x} := A\vec{x}\}$$

Given an initial set of states $X$ at the loop head, the least inductive invariant at loop head is

$$A^*X = \{A^n X \mid n \geq 0, n \in \mathbb{Z}\}\,.$$

Our goal is to compute a template polyhedra matrix $\mathcal{M}$ such that

$$\alpha_T(A^*) \sqsubseteq \mathcal{M}$$

given a template $T$ on the coefficients of the matrices $M \in A^*$.

The key observation underlying our approach uses a well-known result from matrix algebra. Any square matrix $A$ can be written in a special form known as the Jordan normal form using a change of basis transformation $R$:

$$A = R^{-1}JR \text{ and } J = RAR^{-1}$$

such that for any $n$

$$A^n = R^{-1}J^nR \text{ and } J^n = RA^nR^{-1}\,.$$

As a result, instead of computing an abstraction of the set

$$A^* = \{I, A, A^2, A^3, \ldots\}$$

we will abstract the set

$$J^* = \{I, J, J^2, J^3, \ldots\}\,.$$

1. The block diagonal structure of $J$ allows us to *symbolically* compute the coefficients of $J^n$ as a function of $n$. §5.1 presents details on the Jordan form and the symbolic representation of $J^n$.
2. The form of $J$ immediately dictates the matrix shape $\Psi(\vec{m})$ and the matrix subspace $Mat_\Psi$ containing $J^*$.
3. We then consider a fixed set $T$ of *linear template expressions* over $\vec{m}$. We use asymptotic analysis to compute bounds on each expression in the template. §5.2 explains how this is computed.
4. Once we have computed an abstraction $\mathcal{M} \sqsupseteq \alpha(J^*)$, we will return into the original basis by computing $R^{-1}\mathcal{M}R$ to obtain an abstraction for $A^*$, which is the desired loop acceleration.

In this section, we assume arbitrary precision numerical computations. The use of finite precision computations is addressed in §7.

### 5.1 The real Jordan normal form of a matrix

A classical linear algebra result is that any matrix $A \in \mathbb{R}^{p\times p}$ can be transformed in a *real Jordan normal form* by considering an appropriate basis [28]:

$$A = R^{-1}\overbrace{\begin{pmatrix} J_1 & & \\ & \ddots & \\ & & J_r \end{pmatrix}}^{J = \mathrm{Diag}[J_1 \ldots J_r]}R\;,\; J_s \triangleq \begin{pmatrix} \overset{0}{\Lambda_s} & \overset{1}{I} & & \overset{p_s-1}{} \\ & \ddots & \ddots & \\ & & \Lambda_s & I \\ & & & \Lambda_s \end{pmatrix}$$

with $\Lambda_s = \lambda_s$ and $I = 1$

if $\lambda_s$ is a real eigenvalue of $M$,

or $\Lambda_s = \begin{pmatrix} \lambda_s\cos\theta_s & -\lambda_s\sin\theta_s \\ \lambda_s\sin\theta_s & \lambda_s\cos\theta_s \end{pmatrix}$ and $I = \begin{pmatrix} 1 & 0 \\ 0 & 1 \end{pmatrix}$

if $\lambda_s e^{i\theta_s}$ and $\lambda_s e^{-i\theta_s}$ are complex conjugate eigenvalues of $M$, with $\lambda_s > 0$ and $\theta_s \in [0, \pi[$.

The Jordan form is useful because we can write a closed-form expression for its $n^{\text{th}}$ power $J^n = \mathrm{Diag}[J_1^n \ldots J_r^n]$. Each block $J_s^n$ is given by

$$J_s^n = \begin{pmatrix} \Lambda_s^n & \binom{n}{1}\Lambda_s^{n-1} & \cdots\cdots\cdots & \binom{n}{p_s-1}\Lambda_s^{n-p_s+1} \\ & \Lambda_s^n & \binom{n}{1}\Lambda_s^{n-1} & \vdots \\ & & \ddots & \binom{n}{1}\Lambda_s^{n-1} \\ & & & \Lambda_s^n \end{pmatrix} \tag{6}$$

$$\text{and } \Lambda_s^n = \lambda_s^n\,(1) \quad \text{or} \quad \lambda_s^n\begin{pmatrix} \cos n\theta_s & -\sin n\theta_s \\ \sin n\theta_s & \cos n\theta_s \end{pmatrix}$$

with the convention that $\binom{n}{k}\lambda_s^{n-k} = 0$ for $k > n$.

Hence, coefficients of $J_s^n$ have the general form

$$\varphi[\lambda, \theta, r, k](n) = \binom{n}{k}\lambda^{n-k}\cos((n-k)\theta - r\tfrac{\pi}{2}) \tag{7}$$

with $\lambda \geq 0$, $\theta \in [0, \pi]$, $r \in \{0, 1\}$ and $k \geq 0$, in which $r = 1$ enables converting the cosine into a sine. The precise expressions for $\lambda, \theta, r, k$ as functions of the position $i, j$ in the matrix $J$ are omitted here to preserve the clarity of presentation.

Next, we observe that the closed form $J_s^n$ specifies the required shape $\Psi_s(\vec{m}_s)$ for abstracting $J_s^n$ for all $n \geq 0$. For instance, if $\lambda_s$ is a real eigenvalue, we have

$$\Psi_s : \begin{pmatrix} m_0 \\ \vdots \\ m_{p_s-1} \end{pmatrix} \mapsto \begin{pmatrix} m_0 & m_1 & \ldots & m_{p_s} - 1 \\ & m_0 & m_1 & \vdots \\ & & \ddots & m_1 \\ & & & m_0 \end{pmatrix}$$

Likewise, $\Psi(\vec{m})$ for the entire matrix $J^n$ is obtained by the union of the parameters for each individual $J_s^n$.

PROPOSITION 1. *Given the structure of the real Jordan normal form* $J$*, we may fix a matrix shape* $\Psi(\vec{m})$ *such that* $J^* = \{I, J, J^2, \ldots\} \subseteq Mat_\Psi$ *and* $\vec{m} \in \mathbb{R}^m$ *with* $m \leq p$*, where* $p$ *is the dimension of the square matrix* $J$.

Hence, we will work in a matrix subspace, the dimension of which is less than or equal to the number of variables in the loop. This reduction of dimensions using matrix shapes is absolutely essential for our technique to be useful in practice.

### 5.2 Abstracting $J^*$ within template polyhedron matrices

***The principle.*** Let us fix a template expression matrix $T \in \mathbb{R}^{q\times m}$ composed of linear expressions $\{T_1, \ldots, T_q\}$ on parameters $\vec{m}$. Knowing the symbolic form of each $J^n$, we obtain a symbolic form $\vec{m}(n) = \Psi^{-1}(J^n)$ for parameters $\vec{m}$, hence a symbolic form for linear expressions $e_j(n) = T_j \cdot \vec{m}(n)$ . By deriving an upper bound

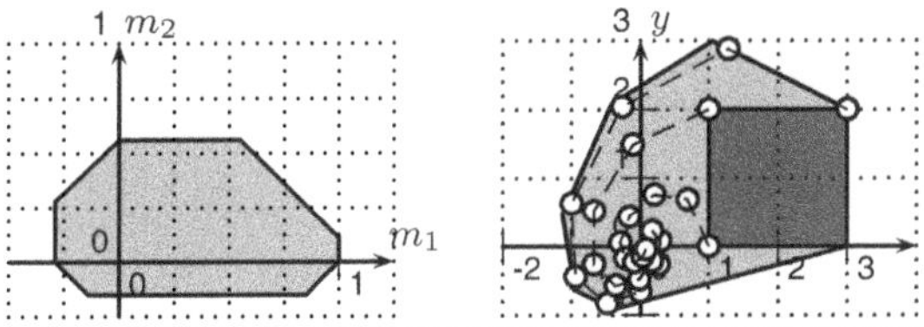


**Figure 6.** On the left-hand side, the octagon on the two non-constant coefficients of the matrices $A^n, n \geq 0$ of Ex. 10, that defines the approximation $\mathcal{M} \supseteq \{A^n \mid n \geq 0\}$. On the right-hand side, the image $\alpha(\mathcal{M}X)$ in light gray of the box $X$ in dark gray by the set $\mathcal{M}$ using the method of §4.2.

$u_j$ for each $e_j(n), n \geq 0$, we obtain a sound approximation of the set $\{\vec{m}(n) \mid n \geq 0\}$, and hence of $J^*$.

THEOREM 2 (Abstracting $J^*$ in template polyhedron matrices). *The template polyhedron matrix*

$$\alpha_T(J^*) \triangleq \Psi([\![T\vec{m} \leq \vec{u}]\!]) \text{ with } \vec{u} = \sup_{n \geq 0} T\vec{m}(n)$$

*is the best correct overapproximation of $J^*$ in the template polyhedra matrix domain defined by T. Moreover, any $\vec{u}' \geq \vec{u}$ defines a correct approximation of $J^*$.*

PROOF. $J^* = \bigcup_{n \geq 0} J^n = \bigcup_{n \geq 0} \Psi(\vec{m}(n)) = \Psi(\{\vec{m}(n) \mid n \geq 0\})$. *Considering the matrix $T$ and referring to §2.3,*

$$\alpha_T(\{\vec{m}(n) \mid n \geq 0\}) = \{\vec{m} \mid T\vec{m} \leq \sup_{\vec{m} \in \{\vec{m}(n) \mid n \geq 0\}} T\vec{m}\}$$
$$= \{\vec{m} \mid T\vec{m} \leq \sup_{n \geq 0} T\vec{m}(n)\} = \{\vec{m} \mid T\vec{m} \leq \vec{u}\}$$

□

The approximation of the set of matrices $J^*$ reduces thus to the computation of an upper bound for the expressions $e_j(n)$.

***Computing upper bounds.*** To simplify the analysis, we restrict template expressions $T_j$ to involve at most 2 parameters from $\vec{m}$. As each parameter/coefficient $m_k$ in matrix $J^n$ is of the form of Eqn. (7), we have to compute an upper bound for expressions of the form

$$\mu_1 \binom{n}{k_1} \lambda_1^{n-k_1} \cos((n-k_1)\theta_1 - r_1\tfrac{\pi}{2}) + \mu_2 \binom{n}{k_2} \lambda_2^{n-k_2} \cos((n-k_2)\theta_2 - r_2\tfrac{\pi}{2}) \quad (8)$$

with $\mu_1, \mu_2 \in \mathbb{R} \wedge \mu_1 \neq 0$. Computing bounds on this expression is at the heart of our technique. However, the actual derivations are tedious and do not contribute to the main insights of our approach. Hence we omit the detailed derivations, and refer to the extended version [23] for details. The main properties of the technique we implemented are that it computes

- exact bounds if the two involved eigenvalues are real ($\theta_1, \theta_2 \in \{0, \pi\}$);
- exact bounds *in reals* if $\theta_1 = \theta_2 \wedge k_1 = k_2 = 0 \vee \mu_2 = 0$, and "reasonable" bounds if $k_1 = k_2 = 0$ is replaced by $k_1 > 0 \vee k_2 > 0$;
- no interesting bounds otherwise (because they are just the linear combination of the bounds found for each term).

Concerning the choice of template expressions in our implementation, we fix a parameter $\ell$ and we consider all the expressions of the form (cf. "logahedra" [20])

$$\pm\alpha m_i \pm (1-\alpha) m_j \text{ with } \alpha = \frac{k}{2^\ell}, 0 \leq k \leq 2^\ell, \quad (9)$$

The choice of $\ell = 1$ corresponds to octagonal expressions.

***Examples.*** In Ex. 3 and Fig. 3 we showed the approximation of a set $A^*$ using octagonal template expression, with the matrix $A$ being a Jordan normal form with real eigenvalues 1.5 and 1. For instance, consider the expression $m_2 - m_1 = n - 1.5^n$ in Example 2, which falls in the first case above. We look at the derivative of the function $f(x) = x - 1.5^x$, we infer that $\forall x \geq 3.6 : f'(x) < 0$ by linearizing appropriately $f'(t)$, hence we can compute the least upper bound as $\max\{f(n) \mid 0 \leq n \leq 4\}$.

Next, we give another example with complex eigenvalues.

EXAMPLE 10. *Take $a = 0.8\cos\theta$ and $b = 0.8\sin\theta$ with $\theta = \pi/6$. and consider the loop* `while(true){x'=a*x-b*y; y=a*x+b*y; x=x'}`. *The trajectories (see Fig. 6 (right)) of this loop follow an inward spiral. The loop body transformation is*
$$A = \begin{pmatrix} 0.8\cos\theta & -0.8\sin\theta & 0 \\ 0.8\sin\theta & 0.8\cos\theta & 0 \\ 0 & 0 & 1 \end{pmatrix}$$
*with A already in real Jordan normal form. The matrix subspace containing $A^*$ is of the form $M = \begin{pmatrix} m_1 & -m_2 & 0 \\ m_2 & m_1 & 0 \\ 0 & 0 & 1 \end{pmatrix}$. We have $m_1(n) = 0.8^n \cos n\theta$ and $m_2(n) = 0.8^n \sin n\theta$; applying our bounding technique on octagonal template constraints on $\vec{m}$, we obtain an approximation $\mathcal{M}$ of $A^*$ defined by the constraints*
$$\begin{cases} m_1 \in [-0.29, 1.00] & m_1 + m_2 \in [-0.29, 1.12] \\ m_2 \in [-0.15, 0.56] & m_1 - m_2 \in [-0.57, 1.00] \end{cases}$$
*Consider, for example, the expression $m_1 + m_2 = 0.8^n(\cos n\theta + \sin n\theta)$ in Example 10 below, which falls into the second case above ($\theta_1 = \theta_2 \wedge k_1 = k_2 = 0 \vee \mu_2 = 0$). We first rewrite it as $f(x) = 0.8^x\sqrt{2}\sin(x\theta + \frac{\pi}{4})$. The term $0.8^x$ being decreasing, the least upper bound of $f$* in reals *is in the range $x \in [0, \pi/4\theta]$. Hence we can consider the upper bound* $\max\{f(n) \mid 0 \leq n \leq \lceil \pi/4\theta \rceil\}$.

*The possible values $(m_1, m_2)$ are plotted in Fig. 6 (right). Assuming an initial set $X : x \in [1,3] \wedge y \in [0,2]$, we compute $\alpha(\mathcal{M}X)$ to be the polyhedron depicted in Fig. 6 (right).*

In this section, we have described the computation of a correct approximation $\mathcal{M}$ of $J^*$ in the template polyhedron domain, from which we can deduce a correct approximation $R^{-1}\mathcal{M}R$ of $A^* = R^{-1}J^*R$. Applying Thm. 1, we are thus able to approximate the set $A^*X$ of reachable states at the head of a linear loop while(true){$\vec{x} := A\vec{x}$} with the expression $(R^{-1}\mathcal{M}R) \otimes X$, where $X$ is a convex polyhedron describing the initial states.

## 6. Abstract acceleration of loops with guards

In this section, we consider loops of the form

$$\text{while}(G\vec{x} \leq 0)\{\vec{x} := A\vec{x}\}$$

modeled by the semantic function $G \to A$, as explained in §2. Given an initial set of states $X$, we compute an over-approximation of $Y = (G \to A)^*(X)$ using a convex polyhedral domain, which after unfolding is expressed as

$$Y = X \cup \bigcup_{n \geq 1} \Big( \Big( \bigwedge_{0 \leq k \leq n-1} GA^k \Big) \to A^n \Big)(X) \quad (10)$$

The unfolding effectively computes the pre-condition of the guard $G$ on the initial state $X$ as $GA^k$.

### 6.1 The simple technique

The expression $(G \to A)^*$ unfolded in Eqn. (10) is too complex to be accelerated precisely. A simple technique to approximate it safely is to exploit the following inclusion:

PROPOSITION 2. *For any set X and linear transformation $G \to A$,*

$$(G \to A)^* \subseteq id \cup \Big( \underbrace{(G \to A)}_{\text{finally, take into account the guard}} \circ (G \to \underbrace{A^*}_{\text{acceleration without guard}}) \Big) \quad (11)$$

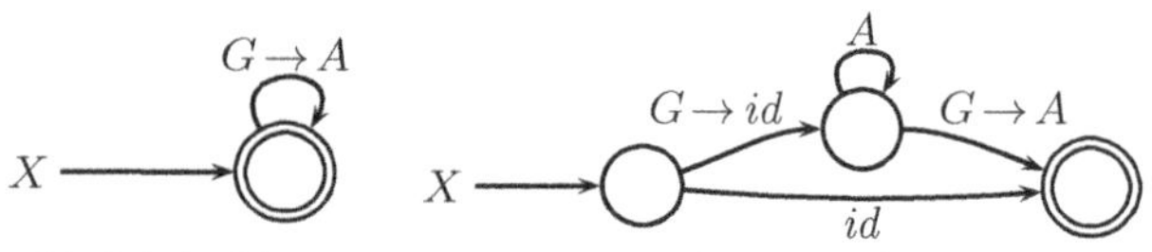


**Figure 7.** Original loop and approximation in term of invariant in accepting (double-lined) location, illustrating Prop. 2.

Fig. 7 illustrates graphically Prop. 2: the invariant attached to the accepting location of Fig. 7(a) is included in the invariant attached to the accepting location of Fig. 7(b). It is interesting to point out the fact that the abstract acceleration techniques described in [18, 39] make assumptions on the matrix $A$ and exploit convexity arguments so that the inclusion (11) becomes an equality. The idea behind Prop. 2 is applied to matrix abstract domains to yield Prop. 3:

PROPOSITION 3. *Let $A = R^{-1}JR$ with $J$ a real Jordan normal form, $T$ a template expression matrix, $\mathcal{M} = R^{-1}\alpha_T(J^*)R$ and $X$ a convex polyhedron, then $(G \to A)^*(X)$ can be approximated by the convex polyhedron*

$$X \sqcup (G \to A)\big(\mathcal{M} \otimes (X \sqcap G)\big) \tag{12}$$

This approach essentially consists of partially unfolding the loop, as illustrated by Fig. 7(b), and reusing abstract acceleration without guard. However, since the guard is only taken into account *after* the actual acceleration, precision is lost regarding the variables that are not constrained by the guard. Ex. 4 and Figures 4 and 5 in §3 illustrate this weakness: $y$ is constrained by the guard, whereas $x$ remains unbounded.

### 6.2 Computing and exploiting bounds on the number of iterations.

To overcome the above issue, we propose a solution based on finding the maximal number of iterations $N$ of the loop for any initial state in $X$, and then to abstract the set of matrices $\{A^0, \dots, A^N\}$ instead of the set $A^*$. The basic idea is that if there exists $N \geq 0$ such that $A^N X \cap G = \emptyset$, then $N$ is an upper bound on the number of iterations of the loop for any initial state in $X$. Bounding the number of iterations is a classical problem in termination analysis, to which our general approach provides a new, original solution.

The following theorem formalizes this idea: We assume now a guarded linear transformation $G \to J$ where $J$ is already a Jordan normal form.

THEOREM 3. *Given a set of states $X$, a template expression matrix $T$ and the set of matrix $\mathcal{M} = \alpha_T(J^*)$, we define*

$$\mathcal{G} = \mathcal{M} \cap \{M \mid \exists \vec{x} \in (X \cap G) \;:\; GM\vec{x} \leq 0\}$$
$$N = \min\{n \mid J^n \notin \mathcal{G}\}$$

*with the convention $\min \emptyset = \infty$.*
*$\mathcal{G}$ is the set of matrices $M \subseteq \mathcal{M}$ of which the image of at least one input state $\vec{x} \in X$ satisfies $G$. If $N$ is bounded, then*

$$(G \to J)^*(X) = \bigcup_{n=0}^{N} (G \to J)^n(X)$$

PROOF. *As $J^N \in \mathcal{M} \setminus \mathcal{G}$, we have $\forall \vec{x} \in (X \cap G) \;:\; GJ^N\vec{x} > 0$, or in other words $(J^N X) \cap G = \emptyset$. This implies that $\big((G \to J)^N X\big) \cap G = \emptyset$ and $(G \to J)^{N+1} X = \emptyset$.* □

The definition of $\mathcal{G}$ and $N$ in Thm. 3 can be transposed in the space of vectors using the matrix shape $\Psi$:

THEOREM 4. *Under the assumption of Thm. 3, and considering $\vec{m}(n) = \Psi^{-1}(J^n)$, we have*

$$\Psi^{-1}(\mathcal{G}) = \left\{ \begin{array}{l} \Psi^{-1}(\mathcal{M}) \cap \\ \{\vec{m} \mid \exists \vec{x} : \vec{x} \in X \cap G : G\Psi(\vec{m})\vec{x} \leq 0\} \end{array} \right. \tag{13}$$

$$N = \min\{n \mid \vec{m}(n) \notin \Psi^{-1}(\mathcal{G})\} \tag{14}$$

Our approach to take into the guard is thus to compute a finite bound $N$ with Eqns. (13) and (14) and to replace in Eqn. (12)

$$\mathcal{M} = R^{-1} \cdot \alpha_T(J^*) \cdot R$$

with $\mathcal{M}' = R^{-1} \cdot \alpha_T(\{J^n \mid 0 \leq n \leq N-1\}) \cdot R$ and $R$ the basis transformation matrix (see Prop. 3).

EXAMPLE 11. *In our Examples 2-5, we had $\vec{m}(n) = \Psi^{-1}(J^n) = \begin{pmatrix} 1.5^n \\ n \end{pmatrix}$, $\Psi^{-1}(\mathcal{M}) = (m_1 \geq 1 \wedge m_2 \geq 0 \wedge m_1 + m_2 \geq 1 \wedge m_1 - m_2 \geq 0.25)$, see Fig. 3 (light gray), $X = (x \in [1,3] \wedge y \in [0,2])$, see Fig. 5 (dark gray), and $G = (y \leq 3)$. The second term of the intersection in Eqn. (13) evaluates to $m_2 \leq 3$, thus $\Psi^{-1}(\mathcal{G}) = (m_1 \geq 1 \wedge 0 \leq m_2 \leq 3 \wedge m_1 + m_2 \geq 1 \wedge m_1 - m_2 \geq 0.25)$. This gives us through Eqn. (14) the bound $N = 4$ on the number of loop iterations. The abstraction $\mathcal{M}' = \alpha_T(\{J^n \mid 0 \leq n \leq 3\})$, depicted on Fig. 3 (dark gray), removes those matrices from $\mathcal{M}$ that do not contribute to the acceleration result due to the guard. Finally, we accelerate using $\mathcal{M}'$ and obtain the result shown in Fig. 5 (medium gray).*

More details about these computations are given in the next section.

### 6.3 Technical issues

Applying Thms. 3 and 4 requires many steps. First, we approximate $\Psi^{-1}(\mathcal{G})$ (see Eqn. (13)), and then as a second step we can approximate the maximum number of iterations $N$ according to Eqn. (14). Finally, we have to compute $\alpha_T\{J^n \mid 0 \leq n \leq N-1\}$.

***Approximating*** $\Psi^{-1}(\mathcal{G})$. Let us denote $Q = \Psi^{-1}(\mathcal{G})$ and $P = \Psi^{-1}(\mathcal{M})$. $Q$ is defined in Eqn. (13) by the conjunction of quadratic constraints on $\vec{x}$ and $\vec{m}$ followed by an elimination of $\vec{x}$. Exact solutions exist for this problem, but they are costly. The alternative adopted in this paper is to approximate $Q$ by quantifying $\vec{x}$ on the bounding box of $X \cap G$ instead of quantifying it on $X \cap G$. Let us denote the bounding box of a polyhedron $Z$ with the vector of intervals $[\underline{Z}, \overline{Z}]$. We have

$$\begin{array}{rl} Q & \subseteq P \cap \{\vec{m} \mid \exists \vec{x} : \vec{x} \in [\underline{X \cap G}, \overline{X \cap G}] \wedge G\Psi(\vec{m})\vec{x} \leq 0\} \\ & = \\ & P \cap \{\vec{m} \mid G\Psi(\vec{m})[\underline{X \cap G}, \overline{X \cap G}] \leq 0\} \triangleq Q' \end{array} \tag{15}$$

$Q'$ is defined by intersecting $P$ with *interval-linear constraints* on $\vec{m}$ and it is much easier to compute than $Q$: one can use

- algorithms for interval linear constraints [6], in particular interval linear programming [33], or
- the linearization techniques of [30] that are effective if the vectors $\vec{m}$ are "well-constrained" by $P$.

In this paper, we exploit the last method which is implemented in the APRON library [21].

EXAMPLE 12. *Coming back to our running Examples 2-5 and 11, we have*

$$G\Psi(\vec{m})[\underline{X \cap G}, \overline{X \cap G}] = (0\;1\;-3)\begin{pmatrix} m_1 & 0 & 0 \\ 0 & 1 & m_2 \\ 0 & 0 & 1 \end{pmatrix}\begin{pmatrix} [1,3] \\ [0,2] \\ 1 \end{pmatrix}$$

$$= (0\;1\;-3)\begin{pmatrix} [1,3]m_1 \\ [0,2] + m_2 \\ 1 \end{pmatrix} = m_2 + [-3,-1]$$

*Hence $Q' = P \cap [\![m_2 + [-3,-1] \leq 0]\!] = P \cap [\![m_2 \leq 3]\!]$*

***Approximating the maximum number of iterations* $N$.** Computing $N$ as defined in Eqn. (14) is not easy either, because the components of vector $\vec{m}(n)$ are functions of defined by Eqn. (7). Our approach is to exploit a matrix of template expressions.

PROPOSITION 4. *Under the assumption of Thm. 4, for any polyhedron $Q' \supseteq Q$ and template expression matrix $T'$,*

$$N \leq \min\Big\{n \mid \exists j : T'_j \cdot \vec{m}(n) > \sup_{\vec{m}\in Q'} T'_j \cdot \vec{m}\Big\} \qquad (16)$$

PROOF. *We have $Q \subseteq Q' \subseteq \alpha_{T'}(Q')$. From $Q \subseteq \alpha_{T'}(Q')$, it follows $\vec{m}(n) \notin \alpha_{T'}(Q') \Rightarrow \vec{m}(n) \notin Q$, and $\min\{n \mid \vec{m}(n) \notin \alpha_{T'}(Q')\} \geq \min\{n \mid \vec{m}(n) \notin Q\} = N$. $\vec{m}(n) \notin \alpha_{T'}(Q')$ is equivalent to $\exists j : T'_j \cdot \vec{m}(n) > \sup_{\vec{m}\in\alpha_{T'}(Q')} T'_j \cdot \vec{m}$ and $\sup_{\vec{m}\in Q'} T'_j \cdot \vec{m} = \sup_{\vec{m}\in\alpha_{T'}(Q')} T'_j \cdot \vec{m}$, hence we get the result.* □

In our implementation we compute such a $Q'$ as described in the previous paragraph and we choose for $T'$ the template matrix $T$ considered in §5.2, to which we may add the constraints of $Q'$.

The computation of such minima ultimately relies on the Newton-Raphson method for solving equations. Our implementation deals with the same cases as those mentioned in §5.2 and in other cases safely returns $N_j = \infty$. We refer to the extended version [23] for details.

EXAMPLE 13. *Coming back to Examples 2-5 and 11-12, and considering $T_j = (0\ 1)$, we have*

$$T_j \cdot \vec{m}(n) = (0\ 1) \cdot \begin{pmatrix} 1.5^n \\ n \end{pmatrix} = n,\ e_j = \sup_{\vec{m}\in Q'} T_j \cdot \vec{m} = \sup_{\vec{m}\in Q'} m_2 = 3$$

*and $N_j = \min\{n \mid T_j \cdot \vec{m}(n) > e_j\} = 4$, which proves that 4 is an upper bound on the maximum number of iterations of the loop, as claimed in Ex. 5.*

***Computing* $\alpha_T\{J^n \mid 0 \leq n \leq N-1\}$.** If no finite upper bound $N$ is obtained with Prop. 4 (given an input polyhedron $X$), then we apply the method of §6.1. Otherwise, we replace in Eqn. (12) the set $\mathcal{M} = \alpha_T(A^*)$ with $\mathcal{M}' = \alpha_T(\{J^n \mid 0 \leq n \leq N-1\})$. This set $\mathcal{M}'$ can be computed using the same technique as those mentioned in §5.2 and detailed in [23], or even by enumeration if $N$ is small. Ex. 5 and Figs. 3-5 illustrate the invariant we obtain this way on our running example.

EXAMPLE 14 (Running example with more complex guard). *Coming back to Examples 2-5, we consider the same loop but with the guard $x + 2y \leq 100$ represented by the matrix $(1\ \ 2\ \ -100)$. Compared to Ex. 12 we have now $G\Psi(\vec{m})[\underline{X \sqcap G}, \overline{X \sqcap G}] = [1,3]m_1 + [0,4] + 2m_2 - 100$, hence, if $P$ is defined by $\varphi_{\mathcal{M}}$ as in Ex. 2,*

$$\begin{aligned} Q' &= P \sqcap [\![ [1,3]m_1 + 2m_2 \leq [96,100] ]\!] \\ &\subseteq P \sqcap [\![ m_1 + 2 + 2m_2 \leq 100 ]\!] \\ &\quad \textit{linearization based on } P \Rightarrow m_1 \geq 1 \Rightarrow m_1 + 2 \leq [1,3]m_1 \end{aligned}$$

*Using $Q'$ to bound the number of iterations according to Eqn. (16) leads to $N = 11$ (obtained with the template expression $T_j = (1\ 2)$ tasken from the guard). At last we obtain the invariant $Z$ depicted in Fig. 8. If instead of octagonal template expressions with $\ell = 1$ in Eqn. (9), we choose $\ell = 3$, we do not improve the bound $N = 11$ but we still obtain the better invariant $Z'$ on Fig. 8.*

### 6.4 Summary

We summarize now our method in the general case:

Given a guarded linear transformation $G \to A$, with $J = RAR^{-1}$ the (real) Jordan normal form of $A$, its associated matrix shape $\Psi$, a template expression matrix $T$ and a convex polyhedron $X$ representing a set of states, we compute an overapproximation $(G \to A)^*(X)$ with

$$X \sqcup (G \to A)\big((R^{-1}\mathcal{M}) \otimes Y\big)$$

where
1. $Y = R(X \sqcap G)$,
2. $P = \alpha_T(\Psi^{-1}(J^*))$,
3. $Q' = P \sqcap \{GR^{-1}\Psi(\vec{m})[\underline{Y}, \overline{Y}] \leq 0\}$,
4. $N$ approximated by some $N'$ using Prop. 4,
5. $\mathcal{M} = \begin{cases} \alpha_T(J^*) & \text{if } N' = \infty \\ \alpha_T(\{J^n \mid 0 \leq n \leq N'-1\}) & \text{otherwise} \end{cases}$

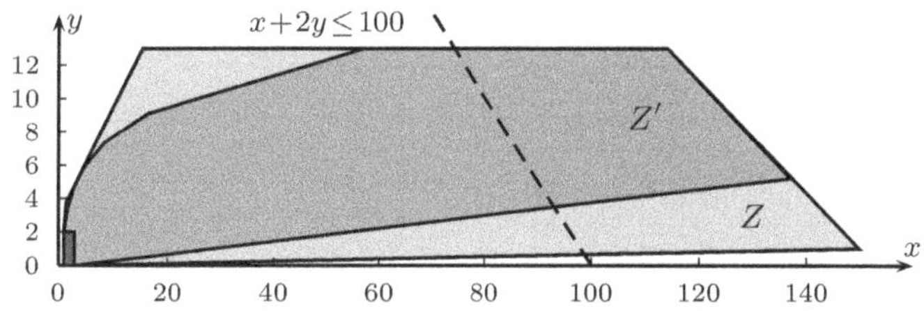


**Figure 8.** Initial set of states $X$ (dark gray), loop invariants $Z$ (light gray) and $Z'$ (medium gray) obtained in Ex. 14.

## 7. Implementation and Experiments

We implemented the presented approach in a prototype tool, evaluated over a series of benchmark examples with various kinds of linear loops, possibly embedded into outer loops, and compared it to state-of-the-art invariant generators.

### 7.1 Implementation

We integrated our method in an abstract interpeter based on the APRON library [21]. We detail below some of the issues involved.

***Computation of the Jordan normal form*** To ensure soundness, we have taken a symbolic approach using the computer algebra software SAGE[1] for computing the Jordan normal forms and transformation matrices over the field of algebraic numbers. The matrices are then approximated by safe enclosing interval matrices.

***Loops with conditionals*** Loops of which the body contains conditionals like *while($G$){ if ($C$) $\vec{x}' = A_1\vec{x}$ else $\vec{x}' = A_2\vec{x}$}* can be transformed into two self-loops $\tau_1, \tau_2$ around a "head" location that are executed in non-deterministic order: We iteratively accel-

erate each self-loop separately $(\tau_1^{\otimes} \circ \tau_2^{\otimes})^*$. Since convergence of the outer loop $(\cdot)^*$ is not guaranteed in general, we might have to use widening. Yet, practical experience shows that in many cases a fixed point is reached after a few iterations.

***Nested loops*** We could use a similar trick to transform nested loops *while($G_1$){while($G_2$){$\vec{x}' = A_2\vec{x}$}; $\vec{x}' = A_1\vec{x}$}* into multiple linear self-loops $\tau_1, \tau_2, \tau_3$ by adding a variable $y$ (initialized to 0) to encode the control flow:

$$\begin{aligned} \tau_1 &: \ (G_1\vec{x} \leq 0 \wedge y = 0) \to (\vec{x}' = \vec{x} \wedge y' = 1) \\ \tau_2 &: \ (G_2\vec{x} \leq 0 \wedge y = 1) \to (\vec{x}' = A_2\vec{x} \wedge y' = 1) \\ \tau_3 &: \ (G_2\vec{x} > 0 \wedge y = 1) \to (\vec{x}' = A_1\vec{x} \wedge y' = 0) \end{aligned}$$

However, the encoding of the control flow in an integer variable is ineffective because of the convex approximation of the polyhedral

[1] www.sagemath.org

| | characteristics | | | | inferred bounds | | | | | analysis time (sec) | | | | |
|---|---|---|---|---|---|---|---|---|---|---|---|---|---|---|
| name | type | $s_{max}$ | #var | #bds | IProc | Sti | J | J vs IProc | J vs Sti | IProc | Sti | J | JSage | JAna |
| Examples with single loops | | | | | | | | | | | | | | |
| parabola_i1 | $\neg s,\neg c,g$ | 3 | 3 | 60 | 46 | 38 | 54 | +8,+17 | +16, +12 | 0.007 | 237 | 2.509 | 2.494 | 0.015 |
| parabola_i2 | $\neg s,\neg c,g$ | 3 | 3 | 60 | 36 | 32 | 54 | +18, +6 | +22, +13 | 0.008 | 289 | 2.509 | 2.494 | 0.015 |
| cubic_i1 | $\neg s,\neg c,g$ | 4 | 4 | 80 | 54 | 34 | 72 | +18,+26 | +38, +12 | 0.015 | 704 | 2.474 | 2.393 | 0.081 |
| cubic_i2 | $\neg s,\neg c,g$ | 4 | 4 | 80 | 34 | 28 | 72 | +38, +9, -2 | +44, +11 | 0.018 | 699 | 2.487 | 2.393 | 0.094 |
| exp_div | $\neg s,\neg c,g$ | 2 | 2 | 32 | 24 | 21 | 28 | +4, +6, -2 | +7, +7 | 0.004 | 31.6 | 2.308 | 2.299 | 0.009 |
| oscillator_i0 | $s,c,\neg g$ | 1 | 2 | 28 | 1 | 0 | 24 | +23, +0, -1 | +24, +0 | 0.004 | 0.99 | 2.532 | 2.519 | 0.013 |
| oscillator_i1 | $s,c,\neg g$ | 1 | 2 | 28 | 0 | 0 | 24 | +24, +0 | +24, +0 | 0.004 | 1.06 | 2.532 | 2.519 | 0.013 |
| inv_pendulum | $s,c,\neg g$ | 1 | 4 | 8 | 0 | 0 | 8 | +8, +0 | +8, +0 | 0.009 | 0.920 | 65.78 | 65.24 | 0.542 |
| convoyCar2_i0 | $s,c,\neg g$ | 2 | 5 | 20 | 3 | 4 | 9 | +6, +0 | +5, +1 | 0.007 | 0.160 | 5.461 | 4.685 | 0.776 |
| convoyCar3_i0 | $s,c,\neg g$ | 3 | 8 | 32 | 3 | 3 | 15 | +12, +0 | +12, +0 | 0.010 | 0.235 | 24.62 | 11.98 | 12.64 |
| convoyCar3_i1 | $s,c,\neg g$ | 3 | 8 | 32 | 3 | 3 | 15 | +12, +0 | +12, +0 | 0.024 | 0.237 | 23.92 | 11.98 | 11.94 |
| convoyCar3_i2 | $s,c,\neg g$ | 3 | 8 | 32 | 3 | 3 | 15 | +12, +0 | +12, +0 | 0.663 | 0.271 | 1717 | 11.98 | 1705 |
| convoyCar3_i3 | $s,c,\neg g$ | 3 | 8 | 32 | 3 | 3 | 15 | +12, +0 | +12, +0 | 0.122 | 0.283 | 1569 | 11.98 | 1557 |
| Examples with nested loops | | | | | | | | | | | | | | |
| thermostat | $s,\neg c,g$ | 2 | 3 | 24 | 18 | 24 | 24 | +6, +1, -1 | +0, +6 | 0.004 | 0.404 | 4.391 | 4.379 | 0.012 |
| oscillator2_16 | $\neg s,c,g$ | 1 | 2 | 48 | 9 | t.o. | 48 | +27, +0 | t.o. | 0.003 | t.o. | 4.622 | 4.478 | 0.144 |
| oscillator2_32 | $\neg s,c,g$ | 1 | 2 | 48 | 9 | t.o. | 48 | +39, +0 | t.o. | 0.003 | t.o. | 4.855 | 4.490 | 0.365 |

"$s/\neg s$": stable/unstable loop; "$c/\neg c$": has complex eigenvalues or not; "$g/\neg g$": loops with/without guard; $s_{max}$: size of largest Jordan block(s); **"#var"**: nb. of variables; **"#bds"**: nb. of bounds to be inferred at all control points; **"IProc","Sti","J"**: nb. of finite bounds inferred by INTERPROC, STING, and our method ("J"); **"J vs IProc","J vs Sti"**: **"+x,+y,[-z]"**: nb. of infinite bounds becoming finite, nb. of improved finite bounds[, nb. of less precise finite bounds (omitted if 0)] obtained with our method over INTERPROC, STING; **"analysis time"**: running times (seconds), with **"JSage","JAna"** corresponding to computation of the Jordan normal form using SAGE and the analysis itself, and **"J"** being the sum of these two times. "t.o." means time out after one hour.

**Table 1.** Experimental results.

abstract domain, this transformation causes an inacceptable loss of precision. For this reason, we accelerate only inner loops in nested loops situations. Our experimental comparison shows that computing precise over-approximations of inner loops greatly improves the analysis of nested loops, even if widening is applied to outer loops.

### 7.2 Evaluation

***Benchmarks*** Our benchmarks listed in Table 1 include various examples of linear loops as commonly found in control software. They contain filters and integrators that correspond to various cases of linear transformations (real or complex eigenvalues, size of Jordan blocks). *parabola* and *cubic* are loops with polynomial behavior (similar to Fig. 1), *exp_div* is Ex. 5 and *thermostat* is Ex. 1. *inv_pendulum* is the classical model of a pendulum balanced in upright position by movements of the cart it is mounted on. *oscillator* is a damped oscillator, and *oscillator2* models a pendulum that is only damped in a range around its lowest position, as if it was grazing the ground, for example. This is modeled using several modes. In *ConvoyCar* [36], a leading car is followed by one or more cars, trying to maintain their position at 50m from each other:

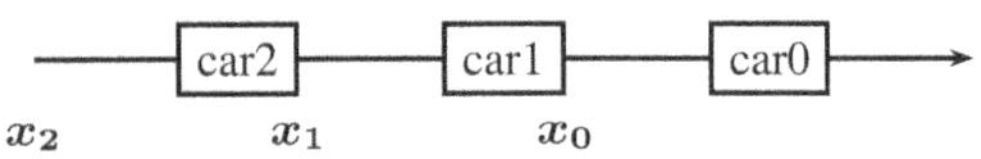


The equations for $N-1$ following cars are:

$$\text{for all } i \in [1, N-1] : \ddot{x}_i = c(\dot{x}_{i-1} - \dot{x}_i) + d(x_{i-1} - x_i - 50)$$

We analyzed a discretized version of this example to show that there is no collision, and to compute bounds on the relative positions and speeds of the cars. This example is particularily interesting because the real Jordan form of the loop body has blocks associated to complex eigenvalues of size $N-1$.

All benchmarks have non-deterministic initial states (typically bounding boxes). Some benchmarks where analyzed for different sets of initial states (indicated by suffix $\_ix$).

***Comparison*** Existing tools can only handle subsets of these examples with reasonable precision. We compared our method with

- INTERPROC [22] that implements standard polyhedral analysis with widening [8];
- STING that implements the method of [7, 36].

A comparison with the ASTRÉE tool on the *thermostat* example has been given in Section 3. A detailed *qualitative* comparison between various methods described in §8 is shown in Table 2.

***Results*** Table 1 lists our experimental results.[2] We compared the tools based on the number of *finite* bounds inferred for the program variables in each control point. Where applicable, we report the number of bounds more/less precise finite bounds inferred by our tool in comparison to the other tools.

We note that our analysis dramatically improves the accuracy over the two competing techniques. On all the benchmarks considered, it generally provides strictly stronger invariants and is practically able to infer finite variable bounds whenever they exist. For instance, for the *thermostat* example (Fig. 2), we infer that at least 6.28 and at most 9.76 seconds are continuously spent in heating mode and 10.72 to 12.79 seconds in cooling mode. INTERPROC just reports that time is non-negative and STING is able to find the much weaker bounds [0.88, 13.0] and [0.94, 19.0]. On the *convoyCar* examples, our method is the only one that is able to obtain non-trivial bounds on distances, speeds and accelerations.

Yet, this comes at the price of increased computation times in general. INTERPROC is significantly faster on all examples; STING is faster on half of the benchmarks and significantly slower on the other half: for two examples, STING does not terminate within the given timeout of one hour, whereas our tool gives precise bounds after a few seconds. It must be noted that part of the higher computation time of our tool is a "one-time" investment for computing loop accelerations that can pay off for multiple applications in the course of a deployment of our approach in a tool such as ASTRÉE. In all but two of the examples (the exceptions being `convoyCar3_i[2|3]`), the one-time cost dominates the overall

[2] A detailed account of the benchmarks and the obtained invariants can be found on `http://www.cs.ox.ac.uk/people/peter.schrammel/acceleration/jordan/`.

| type of linear transformation | illustrating examples | this paper | linear abstr. accel. [2, 18] | ellipsoids [13, 31, 34] | relational abstraction [27, 32, 35, 41] | ALIGATOR [26] | STING [7, 36] |
|---|---|---|---|---|---|---|---|
| translations/resets $\lambda_i=1 \wedge s_k \leq 2 \vee \lambda_i=0$ | | yes | yes | no | yes | yes | yes |
| polynomials $\lambda_i \in \{0,1\}$ | parabola, cubic | yes | no | no | no | yes | no |
| exponentials $\lambda_i \in \mathbb{R}^+ \wedge s_k=1$ | exp_div | yes | no | no | if $\|\lambda_i\|<1$ | no | if $\|\lambda_i\|<1$ |
| rotations $\lambda_i \in \mathbb{C} \wedge s_k=1$ | oscillator, oscillator2, inv_pendulum | yes | no | if $\|\lambda_i\|<1$ | no | no | no |
| non-diagonalizable & non-polynomial $s_k \geq 2 \wedge \lambda_i \notin \{0,1\}$ | thermostat, convoyCar | yes | no | no | no | no | if $\|\lambda_i\|<1$ |
| unstable & non-polynomial $\|\lambda_i\|>1$ | exp_div, oscillator2 | yes | no | no | no | no | no |
| loop guard handling | parabola, cubic, exp_div, thermostat, oscillator2 | yes | yes | partially | yes | no | yes |
| inputs/noise | | no | yes | yes | yes | no | yes |
| abstract domain | | polyhedra | polyhedra | ellipsoids | template polyhedra | polynomial equalities | polyhedra |

$s_k$ is the size of a Jordan block and $\lambda_i$ its associated eigenvalue.

**Table 2.** Classification of linear loops and the capabilities of various analysis methods to infer precise invariants

cost of our analysis. All in all, computation times remain reasonable in the view of the tremendous gain in precision.

## 8. Related work

***Invariants of linear loops.*** The original *abstract acceleration* technique of Gonnord et al [11, 18] precisely abstracts linear loops performing translations, translations/resets and some other special cases. The *affine derivative closure* method [2] approximates any loop by a translation; hence it can handle any linear transformation, but it is only precise for translations. The tool INVGEN [19] uses template-based constraint solving techniques for property-directed invariant generation, but it is restricted to integer programs.

Methods from linear filter analysis target *stable* linear systems in the sense of Lyapunov stability. These techniques consider *ellipsoidal domains*. Unlike our method, they are able to handle inputs, but they do not deal with guards. Feret [12, 13] designs specialized domains for first and second order filters. These methods are implemented in the ASTRÉE tool [4]. Monniaux [31] computes interval bounds for composed filters. Roux et al [34] present a method based on semidefinite programming that infers both shape and ratio of an ellipsoid that is an invariant of the system. In contrast, our method does not impose any stability requirement.

Colon et al [7, 36] describe a method, implemented in the tool STING, for computing single inductive, polyhedral invariants for loops based on non-linear constraint solvers. It is a computationally expensive method and in contrast, our approach is able to infer sound polyhedral over-approximations for loops where the only *inductive polyhedral* invariant is true.

*Relational abstraction* methods [27, 35, 41] aim at finding a relation between the initial state $\vec{x}$ and any future state $\vec{x}'$ in continuous linear systems $d\vec{x}(t)/dt = A\vec{x}(t)$, which is a problem similar to the acceleration of discrete linear loops. The invariants are computed based on off-the-shelf quantifier elimination methods over real arithmetic. In contrast to our method, they handle only diagonalizable matrices $A$. [32] proposes a similar approach for discrete loops. All these works compute a (template) polyhedral relation between input and output states, and do not take into account the actual input states. Hence, in contrast to our method, they are unable to capture accurately unstable and rotating behavior.

*Strategy iteration* methods [15–17] compute best inductive invariants *in the abstract domain* with the help of mathematical programming. They are not restricted to simple loops and they are able to compute the invariant of a whole program at once. However, they are restricted to template domains, *e.g.* template polyhedra and quadratic templates, and hence, unlike our method, they are unable to *infer* the shape of invariants.

The ALIGATOR tool [26] infers loop invariants that are polynomial *equalities* by *solving the recurrence equations* representing the loop body in closed form. The class of programs that can be handled by Aligator is incomparable to that considered in this paper. Whereas Aligator handles a subset of non-linear polynomial assignments our work is currently restricted to linear assignments. In contrast, we take into account linear inequality loop conditions, and can compute inequality invariants.

***Bounding loop iterations.*** Many papers have investigated the problem of bounding the number of iterations of a loop, either for computing widening thresholds [40] by linear extrapolation, termination analysis [1] using ranking functions or for WCET analysis [25] based on solving recurrence equations. Yazarel and Pappas [42] propose a method for computing time intervals where a linear continuous system fulfills a given safety property. Their method can handle complex eigenvalues by performing the analysis in the polar coordinate space. However, they can only deal with diagonalizable systems.

All these methods assume certain restrictions on the form of the (linear) loop, whereas our approach applies to any linear loop.

## 9. Conclusion

We presented a novel abstract acceleration method for discovering polyhedral invariants of loops with general linear transformations. It is based on abstracting the transformation matrices induced by any number of iterations, polyhedral matrix multiplication, and a method for estimating the number of loop iterations that also works in case of exponential and oscillating behavior. Our experiments show that we are able to infer invariants that are out of the reach of existing methods. The precise analysis of linear loops is an essential feature of static analyzers for control programs. Precise loop invariants are equally important for alternative verification methods based on model checking, for example. Further possible applications include termination proofs and deriving complexity bounds of algorithms.

***Ongoing work.*** In this paper, we considered only closed systems, *i.e.* without inputs. However, important classes of programs that we want to analyze, *e.g.* digital filters, have inputs. Hence, we are extending our methods to loops of the form $G\vec{x}+H\vec{\xi} \leq 0 \rightarrow \vec{x}' = A\vec{x} + B\vec{\xi}$ with inputs $\vec{\xi}$ (similar to [39]). Moreover, our method easily generalizes to linear continuous systems $d\vec{x}(t)/dt = A\vec{x}(t)$, *e.g.* representing the modes of a hybrid automaton, by considering their analytical solution $\vec{x}(t) = e^{At}\vec{x}(0)$.

## References


[1] C. Alias, A. Darte, P. Feautrier, and L. Gonnord. Multi-dimensional rankings, program termination, and complexity bounds of flowchart programs. In *SAS*, volume 6337 of *LNCS*, pages 117–133, 2010.

[2] C. Ancourt, F. Coelho, and F. Irigoin. A modular static analysis approach to affine loop invariants detection. In *NSAD*, volume 267 of *ENTCS*, pages 3–16. Elsevier, 2010.

[3] S. Bardin, A. Finkel, J. Leroux, and L. Petrucci. Fast: acceleration from theory to practice. *STTT*, 10(5):401–424, 2008.

[4] B. Blanchet, P. Cousot, R. Cousot, J. Feret, L. Mauborgne, A. Miné, D. Monniaux, and X. Rival. A static analyzer for large safety-critical software. In *PLDI*, pages 196–207. ACM, 2003.

[5] B. Boigelot and P. Godefroid. Symbolic verification of communication protocols with infinite state spaces using QDDs. In *CAV*, volume 1102 of *LNCS*, July 1996.

[6] L. Chen, A. Miné, J. Wang, and P. Cousot. An abstract domain to discover interval linear equalities. In *VMCAI*, volume 5944 of *LNCS*, 2010.

[7] M. Colón, S. Sankaranarayanan, and H. Sipma. Linear invariant generation using non-linear constraint solving. In *Computer Aided Verification, CAV'03*, volume 2725, 2003.

[8] P. Cousot and N. Halbwachs. Automatic discovery of linear restraints among variables of a program. In *Symposium on Principles of programming languages, POPL'78*, pages 84–96, 1978. .

[9] P. Cousot and N. Halbwachs. Automatic discovery of linear restraints among the variables of a program. In *POPL*, pages 84–97, 1978.

[10] P. Cousot, R. Cousot, J. Feret, L. Mauborgne, A. Miné, and X. Rival. Why does Astrée scale up? *FMSD*, 35(3), 2009.

[11] P. Feautrier and L. Gonnord. Accelerated invariant generation for C programs with Aspic and C2fsm. *ENTCS*, 267(2):3–13, 2010.

[12] J. Feret. Static analysis of digital filters. In *ESOP*, volume 2986 of *LNCS*, pages 33–48, 2004.

[13] J. Feret. Numerical abstract domains for digital filters. In *Numerical and Symbolic Abstract Domains*, 2005.

[14] A. Finkel and J. Leroux. How to compose Presburger-accelerations: Applications to broadcast protocols. In *FSTTCS*, volume 2556 of *LNCS*, pages 145–156, 2002.

[15] S. Gaubert, E. Goubault, A. Taly, and S. Zennou. Static analysis by policy iteration on relational domains. In *ESOP*, volume 4421 of *LNCS*, 2007.

[16] T. M. Gawlitza and H. Seidl. Precise relational invariants through strategy iteration. In *Computer Science Logic*, volume 4646 of *LNCS*, pages 23–40. Springer, 2007.

[17] T. M. Gawlitza, H. Seidl, A. Adjé, S. Gaubert, and É. Goubault. Abstract interpretation meets convex optimization. *Journal of Symbolic Computation*, 47(12):1512–1532, 2012.

[18] L. Gonnord and N. Halbwachs. Combining widening and acceleration in linear relation analysis. In *SAS*, volume 4218 of *LNCS*, 2006.

[19] A. Gupta and A. Rybalchenko. InvGen: an efficient invariant generator. In *CAV*, volume 5643 of *LNCS*, pages 634–640, 2009.

[20] J. M. Howe and A. King. Logahedra: A new weakly relational domain. In *Automated Technology for Verification and Analysis, ATVA'09*, volume 5799 of *LNCS*, pages 306–320. Springer, 2009.

[21] B. Jeannet and A. Miné. APRON: A library of numerical abstract domains for static analysis. In *CAV*, volume 5643 of *LNCS*, pages 661–667, 2009. `http://apron.cri.ensmp.fr/library/`.

[22] B. Jeannet, M. Argoud, and G. Lalire. The INTERPROC interprocedural analyzer. `http://pop-art.inrialpes.fr/interproc/interprocweb.cgi`.

[23] B. Jeannet, P. Schrammel, and S. Sankaranarayanan. Abstract acceleration of general linear loops. *CoRR*, abs/1311.768, 2013.

[24] J. B. Kam and J. D. Ullman. Monotone data flow analysis frameworks. *Acta Informatica*, 7:305–317, 1977.

[25] J. Knoop, L. Kovács, and J. Zwirchmayr. Symbolic loop bound computation for wcet analysis. In *Perspectives of Systems Informatics*, volume 7162 of *LNCS*, pages 227–242. Springer, 2011.

[26] L. Kovács. Invariant generation for p-solvable loops with assignments. In *CSR*, volume 5010 of *LNCS*, pages 349–359, 2008.

[27] G. Lafferriere, G. J. Pappas, and S. Yovine. Symbolic reachability computation for families of linear vector fields. *JSC*, 32(3):231–253, 2001.

[28] P. Lancaster and M. Tismenetsky. *The Theory of Matrices (2nd edition)*. Academic Press, 1984.

[29] A. Miné. The octagon abstract domain. In *AST 2001 in WCRE 2001*, IEEE, pages 310–319. IEEE CS Press, October 2001.

[30] A. Miné. Symbolic methods to enhance the precision of numerical abstract domains. In *VMCAI*, volume 3855 of *LNCS*, pages 348–363, 2006.

[31] D. Monniaux. Compositional analysis of floating-point linear numerical filters. In *CAV*, volume 3576 of *LNCS*, pages 199–212, 2005.

[32] D. Monniaux. Automatic modular abstractions for linear constraints. In *POPL*. ACM, 2009.

[33] J. Rohn. Solvability of systems of interval linear equations and inequalities. In *Linear Optimization Problems with Inexact Data*, pages 35–77, 2006.

[34] P. Roux, R. Jobredeaux, P.-L. Garoche, and E. Feron. A generic ellipsoid abstract domain for linear time invariant systems. In *HSCC*, pages 105–114. ACM, 2012.

[35] S. Sankaranarayanan and A. Tiwari. Relational abstractions for continuous and hybrid systems. In *CAV*, volume 6806 of *LNCS*, pages 686–702. Springer, 2011.

[36] S. Sankaranarayanan, H. B. Sipma, and Z. Manna. Constraint-based linear-relations analysis. In *SAS*, volume 3148 of *LNCS*, pages 53–68, 2004.

[37] S. Sankaranarayanan, H. B. Sipma, and Z. Manna. Scalable analysis of linear systems using mathematical programming. In *VMCAI*, volume 3385 of *LNCS*, 2005.

[38] P. Schrammel and B. Jeannet. Logico-numerical abstract acceleration and application to the verification of data-flow programs. In *SAS*, volume 6887 of *LNCS*, pages 233–248, 2011.

[39] P. Schrammel and B. Jeannet. Applying abstract acceleration to (co-)reachability analysis of reactive programs. *Journal of Symbolic Computation*, 47(12):1512–1532, 2012.

[40] A. Simon and A. King. Widening polyhedra with landmarks. In *Prog. Languages and Systems, APLAS'06*, volume 4279 of *LNCS*, 2006.

[41] A. Tiwari. Approximate reachability for linear systems. In *HSCC*, volume 2623 of *LNCS*, pages 514–525. Springer, 2003.

[42] H. Yazarel and G. J. Pappas. Geometric programming relaxations for linear system reachability. In *American Control Conference*, pages 553–559, 2004.

# Minimization of Symbolic Automata

Loris D'Antoni
University of Pennsylvania
lorisdan@cis.upenn.edu

Margus Veanes
Microsoft Research
margus@microsoft.com

## Abstract

Symbolic Automata extend classical automata by using symbolic alphabets instead of finite ones. Most of the classical automata algorithms rely on the alphabet being finite, and generalizing them to the symbolic setting is not a trivial task. In this paper we study the problem of minimizing symbolic automata. We formally define and prove the basic properties of minimality in the symbolic setting, and lift classical minimization algorithms (Huffman-Moore's and Hopcroft's algorithms) to symbolic automata. While Hopcroft's algorithm is the fastest known algorithm for DFA minimization, we show how, in the presence of symbolic alphabets, it can incur an exponential blowup. To address this issue, we introduce a new algorithm that fully benefits from the symbolic representation of the alphabet and does not suffer from the exponential blowup. We provide comprehensive performance evaluation of all the algorithms over large benchmarks and against existing state-of-the-art implementations. The experiments show how the new symbolic algorithm is faster than previous implementations.

***Categories and Subject Descriptors*** F.2.2 [*Theory of Computation*]: Automata over infinite objects, Regular languages

***Keywords*** Minimization, Symbolic Automata

## 1. Introduction

Classical automata theory builds on two basic assumptions: there is a *finite state space*; and there is a *finite alphabet*. The topic of this paper is along the line of work challenging the second assumption. *Symbolic finite automata* (SFAs) are finite state automata in which the alphabet is given by a *Boolean algebra* that may have an infinite domain, and transitions are labeled with predicates over such algebra. Symbolic automata originated from the intent to support regular expressions in the context of static and dynamic program analysis [43]. Lately, they were also used for supporting regular expressions (modulo label theories) in the context of modern logical inference engines [9, 42].

Most classical automata algorithms view the size $k$ of the alphabet as a constant and use specialized data structures that are optimized for this view [7]. Therefore, it is not clear if or how such algorithms would work when the alphabet is infinite. Understanding how operations over the finite alphabet lift to the symbolic setting is a challenging task. Some classical automata constructions are extended to SFAs in [26]. For example, the *product* (intersection) $M_1 \times M_2$ of two symbolic automata $M_1$ and $M_2$ is computed by building product transitions of the form $\langle p_1, p_2\rangle \xrightarrow{\varphi_1\wedge\varphi_2} \langle q_1, q_2\rangle$ from transitions $p_1 \xrightarrow{\varphi_1} q_1$, $p_2 \xrightarrow{\varphi_2} q_2$, in $M_1, M_2$, where the guards $\varphi_1$ and $\varphi_2$ are composed using *conjunction* and pruned when *unsatisfiable*. The complexity of such constructions clearly depends on the complexity of checking satisfiability in the label theory. In this particular case, constructing the product has complexity $\mathcal{O}(f(\ell)m^2)$, where $m$ is the number of transitions, $f(l)$ is the cost of checking satisfiability of predicates of size $l$ in the label theory, and $\ell$ is the size of the biggest predicate in $M_1$ and $M_2$.

This paper focuses on the problem of minimizing automata over symbolic alphabets and, to the best of our knowledge, it is the first paper that investigates this problem. Minimizing *deterministic finite automata* (DFAs) is one of the fundamental concepts in automata theory. It occurs in numerous areas, such as programming languages, text processing, computational linguistics, graphics, etc.

Before looking for an algorithm for minimizing SFAs we first need to answer a fundamental question: what does it mean for an SFA to be minimal? Intuitively, any two distinct states $p$ and $q$ of a minimal SFA must be *distinguishable*, where two states $p$ and $q$ are distinguishable if there exists an input sequence $s$ that starting from $p$ leads to a final (non-final) state and starting from $q$ leads to a non-final (final) state. This notion is similar to DFA minimality.

The original algorithms for minimizing DFAs were given by Huffman [29], Moore [34], and Hopcroft [27]. Since, all such algorithms use iterations over the finite alphabet, they do not immediately extend to the symbolic setting. In the following paragraphs we briefly describe how we extended the classical algorithms to SFAs, and how we designed a new minimization algorithm that fully takes advantage of the symbolic representation of the alphabet.

Our first algorithm is called $Min^{\mathbf{M}}_{\text{SFA}}$ and takes inspiration from a reformulation of Moore's (Huffman's) algorithm described in [28]. The key idea from the algorithm in [28] is the following:

> if two states $p$ and $q$ are distinguishable, and there exists a character $a$, and transitions $\delta(a, p') = p$ and $\delta(a, q') = q$, then $p'$ and $q'$ are distinguishable.

This idea nicely translates to the symbolic setting as:

> if two states $p$ and $q$ are distinguishable, and there exist transitions $p' \xrightarrow{\varphi} p$ and $q' \xrightarrow{\psi} q$ such that $\varphi\wedge\psi$ is satisfiable, then $p'$ and $q'$ are distinguishable.

Starting with the fact that final and non-final states are distinguishable, we can use a fixpoint computation for grouping states into groups of indistinguishable states. This procedure uses a number of iterations that is quadratic in the number of states. Moreover, each iteration is linear in the number of transitions.

Unfortunately, $Min^{\mathbf{M}}_{\text{SFA}}$ does not scale in the case of a performance critical application described in Section 7.1, where SFAs



*POPL '14*, January 22–24, 2014, San Diego, CA, USA.

http://dx.doi.org/10.1145/2535838.2535849

| | $Min^{\mathbf{M}}_{\text{SFA}}$ | $Min^{\mathbf{H}}_{\text{SFA}}$ | $Min^{\mathbf{N}}_{\text{SFA}}$ |
|---|---|---|---|
| *Satisfiability checking*, $\wedge$, $\vee$ | ✓ | ✓ | ✓ |
| *Predicate negation* | | ✓ | ✓ |
| *Minterm generation* | | ✓ | |

**Table 1.** Summary of operations needed over a given label theory in the respective minimization algorithms.

end up having thousands of states, and the complexity of $Min^{\mathbf{M}}_{\text{SFA}}$ was not acceptable. To this end, we studied a generalization of Hopcrofts algorithm, called $Min^{\mathbf{H}}_{\text{SFA}}$. Hopcroft's algorithm is based on a technique called partition refinement of states, and, with worst case complexity $O(kn \log n)$ ($n$ = number of states, and $k$ = number of alphabet symbols), it is the most efficient algorithm for minimizing DFAs. The main idea behind $Min^{\mathbf{H}}_{\text{SFA}}$ is to subdivide all the labels in the SFA into non-overlapping predicates called minterms. Such minterms can then be seen as atomic characters in the sense of classical DFAs, allowing us to use the classical Hopcroft's algorithm over the finite set of minterms. Even though $Min^{\mathbf{H}}_{\text{SFA}}$ performs well in the aforementioned application, it suffers from another problem: in the worst case, the number of minterms can be exponential in the number of edges of the SFA. Moreover, our experiments showed that this factor can indeed be observed when considering more complex label theories, such as the theory of pairs over $string \times int$ (§ 6.4).

This leads to our main algorithmic contribution in the paper. We designed $Min^{\mathbf{N}}_{\text{SFA}}$, a new algorithm for SFA minimization which takes full advantage of the symbolic representation of the input alphabet. $Min^{\mathbf{N}}_{\text{SFA}}$ is inspired by the idea of refining the partition of the state space used by Hopcroft's algorithm, but does not require the pre-computation of minterms as in $Min^{\mathbf{H}}_{\text{SFA}}$. The key observation is that the set of relevant predicates can be computed locally, rather than using all the transitions of the SFA. While $Min^{\mathbf{N}}_{\text{SFA}}$ is similar to $Min^{\mathbf{H}}_{\text{SFA}}$ in terms of state complexity, it does not suffer from the exponential complexity related to the minterm computation. In fact, in all our experiments, both $Min^{\mathbf{H}}_{\text{SFA}}$ and $Min^{\mathbf{M}}_{\text{SFA}}$ are outperformed by $Min^{\mathbf{N}}_{\text{SFA}}$.

Table 1 presents a summary of the minimization algorithms, illustrating their dependency on operations over the label theory.

We compared the performance of the three algorithms using: 1) the benchmark of randomly generated DFAs presented in [3], 2) the SFAs generated by common regular expressions taken from the web, 3) a set of SFAs aimed at showing the exponential minterm explosion, 4) a randomly generated set of SFAs over a complex alphabet theory, and 5) the SFAs generated during the transformation from Monadic Second Order logic to DFAs [38]. In experiments 2 and 3 we also compared the performance of our implementation of $Min^{\mathbf{H}}_{\text{SFA}}$ against the implementation of Hopcroft's algorithm in [3] and in the `brics.automaton` [1] library, and we observed similar performance characteristics that validated our implementation. In the fifth experiment we compared our results against Mona [22], the state of the art tool for deciding Monadic Second Order logic.

***Contributions.*** In summary, our contributions are:

- a formal study of the notion of minimality of SFAs (§2);
- two algorithms for minimizing SFAs based on classical DFA algorithms (§3 and §4);
- a completely new algorithm for minimizing SFAs together with a proof of its correctness (§5);
- a comprehensive evaluation of the algorithms using a variety of different benchmarks (§6); and
- a description of several concrete applications of such minimization algorithms (§7).

## 2. Effective Boolean algebras and SFAs

We first formally define the notion of effective Boolean algebra and symbolic finite automata. Next, we develop a theory which explains what it means for a symbolic finite automata to be minimal.

An *effective Boolean algebra* $\mathcal{A}$ has components $(\mathfrak{D}, \Psi, [\![\_]\!], \bot, \top, \vee, \wedge, \neg)$. $\mathfrak{D}$ is an r.e. (recursively enumerable) set of *domain elements*. $\Psi$ is an r.e. set of *predicates* closed under the Boolean connectives and $\bot, \top \in \Psi$. The *denotation function* $[\![\_]\!] : \Psi \to 2^{\mathfrak{D}}$ is r.e. and is such that, $[\![\bot]\!] = \emptyset$, $[\![\top]\!] = \mathfrak{D}$, for all $\varphi, \psi \in \Psi$, $[\![\varphi \vee \psi]\!] = [\![\varphi]\!] \cup [\![\psi]\!]$, $[\![\varphi \wedge \psi]\!] = [\![\varphi]\!] \cap [\![\psi]\!]$, and $[\![\neg\varphi]\!] = \mathfrak{D} \setminus [\![\varphi]\!]$. For $\varphi \in \Psi$, we write $IsSat(\varphi)$ when $[\![\varphi]\!] \neq \emptyset$ and say that $\varphi$ is *satisfiable*. $\mathcal{A}$ is *decidable* if $IsSat$ is decidable.

The intuition is that such an algebra is represented programmatically as an API with corresponding methods implementing the Boolean operations and the denotation function. We are primarily going to use the following two effective Boolean algebras in the examples, but the techniques in the paper are fully generic.

$\mathbf{2}^{\text{BV}k}$ is the powerset algebra whose domain is the finite set $\text{BV}k$, for some $k > 0$, consisting of all nonnegative integers smaller than $2^k$, or equivalently, all $k$-bit bit-vectors. A predicate is represented by a BDD of depth $k$.[1] The Boolean operations correspond directly to the BDD operations, $\bot$ is the BDD representing the empty set. The denotation $[\![\beta]\!]$ of a BDD $\beta$ is the set of all integers $n$ such that a binary representation of $n$ corresponds to a solution of $\beta$.

$\text{SMT}^{\sigma}$ is the decision procedure for a theory over some sort $\sigma$, say integers, such as the theory of integer linear arithmetic. This algebra can be implemented through an interface to an SMT solver. $\Psi$ contains in this case the set of all formulas $\varphi(x)$ in that theory with one fixed free integer variable $x$. For example, a formula $(x \bmod k) = 0$, say $div_k$, denotes the set of all numbers divisible by $k$. Then $div_2 \wedge div_3$ denotes the set of numbers divisible by six.

We can now define symbolic finite automata. Intuitively, a symbolic finite automaton is a finite automaton over a symbolic alphabet, where edge labels are replaced by predicates. In order to preserve the classical closure operations (intersection, complement, etc.), the predicates must form an effective Boolean algebra.

**Definition 1.** A *symbolic finite automaton* (*SFA*) $M$ is a tuple $(\mathcal{A}, Q, q^0, F, \Delta)$ where $\mathcal{A}$ is an effective Boolean algebra, called the *alphabet*, $Q$ is a finite set of *states*, $q^0 \in Q$ is the *initial state*, $F \subseteq Q$ is the set of *final states*, and $\Delta \subseteq Q \times \Psi_{\mathcal{A}} \times Q$ is a finite set of *moves* or *transitions*. ⊠

Elements of $\mathfrak{D}_{\mathcal{A}}$ are called *characters* and finite sequences of characters, elements of $\mathfrak{D}_{\mathcal{A}}^*$, are called *words*; $\epsilon$ denotes the empty word. A move $\rho = (p, \varphi, q) \in \Delta$ is also denoted by $p \xrightarrow{\varphi}_M q$ (or $p \xrightarrow{\varphi} q$ when $M$ is clear), where $p$ is the *source* state, denoted $Src(\rho)$, $q$ is the *target* state, denoted $Tgt(\rho)$, and $\varphi$ is the *guard* or *predicate* of the move, denoted $Grd(\rho)$. A move is *feasible* if its guard is satisfiable. Given a character $a \in \mathfrak{D}_{\mathcal{A}}$, an *a-move* of $M$ is a move $p \xrightarrow{\varphi} q$ such that $a \in [\![\varphi]\!]$, also denoted $p \xrightarrow{a}_M q$ (or $p \xrightarrow{a} q$ when $M$ is clear). In the following let $M = (\mathcal{A}, Q, q^0, F, \Delta)$ be an SFA.

**Definition 2.** A word $w = a_1 a_2 \cdots a_k \in \mathfrak{D}_{\mathcal{A}}^*$, is *accepted at state p of M*, denoted $w \in \mathscr{L}_p(M)$, if there exist $p_{i-1} \xrightarrow{a_i}_M p_i$ for $1 \leq i \leq k$, such that $p_0 = p$, and $p_k \in F$. The *language accepted by M* is $\mathscr{L}(M) \stackrel{\text{def}}{=} \mathscr{L}_{q^0}(M)$. ⊠

[1] The variable order of the BDD is the reverse bit order of the binary representation of a number, in particular, the most significant bit has the lowest ordinal.

Given a state $q \in Q$, we use the following definitions for the set transitions from and to $q$:

$$\overrightarrow{\Delta}(q) \stackrel{\text{def}}{=} \{\rho \in \Delta \mid Src(\rho) = q\}, \quad \overleftarrow{\Delta}(q) \stackrel{\text{def}}{=} \{\rho \in \Delta \mid Tgt(\rho) = q\}.$$

The definitions are lifted to sets in the usual manner. The following terminology is used to characterize various key properties of $M$. A state $p$ of $M$ is called *partial* if there exists a character $a$ for which there exist no $a$-move with source state $p$.

- $M$ is *deterministic*: for all $p \xrightarrow{\varphi} q, p \xrightarrow{\varphi'} q' \in \Delta$, if $IsSat(\varphi \wedge \varphi')$ then $q = q'$.
- $M$ is *complete*: there are no partial states.
- $M$ is *clean*: for all $p \xrightarrow{\varphi} q \in \Delta$, $p$ is reachable from $q^0$ and $IsSat(\varphi)$,
- $M$ is *normalized*: for all $p, q \in Q$, there is at most one move from $p$ to $q$.
- $M$ is *minimal*: $M$ is deterministic, complete, clean, normalized, and for all $p, q \in Q$, $p = q$ if and only if $\mathscr{L}_p(M) = \mathscr{L}_q(M)$.[2]

For the special case in which $M$ is *deterministic and complete*, we denote the transition function using the function $\delta_M : \mathfrak{D}_\mathcal{A} \times Q \to Q$, such that for all $a \in \mathfrak{D}_\mathcal{A}$ and $p \in Q$, $\delta_M(a,p) \stackrel{\text{def}}{=} q$, where $q$ is the state such that $p \xrightarrow{a}_M q$. Observe that, because of determinism, if $p \xrightarrow{\varphi_1}_M q_1$, $p \xrightarrow{\varphi_2}_M q_2$, and $a \in [\![\varphi_1 \wedge \varphi_2]\!]$, then $q_1 = q_2$. Moreover, due to completeness, there exists some $q$ and $\varphi$ such that $p \xrightarrow{\varphi}_M q$ and $a \in [\![\varphi]\!]$.

Determinization of SFAs is always possible and is studied in [42]. Completion is straightforward: if $M$ is not complete then add a new state $q_\emptyset$ and the self-loop $q_\emptyset \xrightarrow{\top} q_\emptyset$, and for each partial state $q$ add the move $(q, \bigwedge_{\rho \in \overrightarrow{\Delta}(q)} \neg Grd(\rho), q_\emptyset)$. Observe that completion requires negation of predicates.

Normalization is obvious: if there exist states $p$ and $q$ and two distinct transitions $p \xrightarrow{\varphi} q$ and $p \xrightarrow{\psi} q$, then replace these transitions with the single transition $p \xrightarrow{\varphi \vee \psi} q$. This does not affect $\mathscr{L}_p(M)$ for any $p$.

We always assume that $M$ is clean. Cleaning amounts to running a standard forward reachability algorithm that keeps only reachable states, and eliminates infeasible moves. Observe that infeasible moves $p \xrightarrow{\perp} q$ do not add expressiveness and might cause unnecessary state space explosion.

It is important to show that minimality of SFAs is in fact well-defined in the sense that minimal SFAs are unique up to renaming of states and equivalence of predicates. To do so we use the following construction.

Assume $M = (\mathcal{A}, Q, q^0, F, \Delta)$ to be deterministic and complete. Let $\Sigma_\mathcal{A}$ denote the *first-order language* that contains the *unary relation symbol* $\bar{F}$ and the *unary function symbol* $\bar{a}$ for each $a \in \mathfrak{D}_\mathcal{A}$. We define the *$\Sigma_\mathcal{A}$-structure of* $M$, denoted by $\mathfrak{M}$, to have the universe $Q$, and the interpretation function:

$$\bar{F}^\mathfrak{M} \stackrel{\text{def}}{=} F, \quad \forall \bar{a} \in \Sigma_\mathcal{A}, p \in Q\, (\bar{a}^\mathfrak{M}(p) \stackrel{\text{def}}{=} \delta_M(a,p)).$$

Also, let

$$\begin{aligned} M(\epsilon) &\stackrel{\text{def}}{=} q^0, \\ M(w \cdot a) &\stackrel{\text{def}}{=} \delta_M(a, M(w)) \qquad \text{for } a \in \mathfrak{D}_\mathcal{A} \text{ and } w \in \mathfrak{D}_\mathcal{A}^*. \end{aligned}$$

In other words, $M(w)$ is the state reached in $M$ for the word $w \in \mathfrak{D}_\mathcal{A}^*$. Recall that two $\Sigma$-structures are *isomorphic* if there exists a bijective mapping between their universes that preserves the meaning of all symbols in $\Sigma$.

**THEOREM** 1. *If $M$ and $N$ are minimal SFAs over the same alphabet $\mathcal{A}$ such that $\mathscr{L}(M) = \mathscr{L}(N)$, then $\mathfrak{M}$ and $\mathfrak{N}$ are isomorphic $\Sigma_\mathcal{A}$-structures.*

*Proof*: Assume $M$ and $N$ to be minimal SFAs over $\mathcal{A}$ such that $\mathscr{L}(M) = \mathscr{L}(N)$. We define $\imath : \mathfrak{M} \cong \mathfrak{N}$ as follows:

$$\forall w \in \mathfrak{D}_\mathcal{A}^* (\imath(M(w)) \stackrel{\text{def}}{=} N(w)).$$

To show that $\imath$ is well-defined as a function, observe first that all states of $M$ correspond to some $w$ because $M$ is clean. Second, we prove that for all words $v$ and $w$, if $M(v) = M(w)$ then $N(v) = N(w)$. Fix $v, w \in \mathfrak{D}_\mathcal{A}^*$ such that $M(v) = M(w)$. Then, for all $u \in \mathfrak{D}_\mathcal{A}^*$,

$$\begin{aligned} u \in \mathscr{L}_{N(v)}(N) &\Leftrightarrow v \cdot u \in \mathscr{L}(N) \\ &\overset{(\text{by } \mathscr{L}(M)=\mathscr{L}(N))}{\Leftrightarrow} v \cdot u \in \mathscr{L}(M) \\ &\Leftrightarrow u \in \mathscr{L}_{M(v)}(M) \\ &\overset{(\text{by } M(w)=M(v))}{\Leftrightarrow} u \in \mathscr{L}_{M(w)}(M) \\ &\Leftrightarrow w \cdot u \in \mathscr{L}(M) \\ &\overset{(\text{by } \mathscr{L}(M)=\mathscr{L}(N))}{\Leftrightarrow} w \cdot u \in \mathscr{L}(N) \\ &\Leftrightarrow u \in \mathscr{L}_{N(w)}(N) \end{aligned}$$

So, $\mathscr{L}_{N(v)}(N) = \mathscr{L}_{N(w)}(N)$, and thus $N(v) = N(w)$ by minimality of $N$. So, $\imath$ is well-defined as a function. By switching the roles of $M$ and $N$ we also get the opposite direction. Thus,

$$(*) \qquad \forall v, w \in \mathfrak{D}_\mathcal{A}^* (M(v) = M(w) \Leftrightarrow N(v) = N(w))$$

Next, we show that $\imath$ is an isomorphism.

First, we show that $\imath$ is bijective: $\imath$ is onto because $N$ is clean, i.e., each state of $N$ corresponds to $N(w)$ for some word $w$; $\imath$ is into because if $M(v) \neq M(w)$ then, by $(*)$, $\imath(M(v)) = N(v) \neq N(w) = \imath(M(w))$.

Finally, we show that $\imath$ is an embedding of $\mathfrak{M}$ into $\mathfrak{N}$, i.e., that $\imath$ preserves all the functions and the relations: for all $p \in Q_M$, $p \in \bar{F}^\mathfrak{M} \Leftrightarrow \imath(p) \in \bar{F}^\mathfrak{N}$, and for all $p \in Q_M$ and $a \in \mathfrak{D}_\mathcal{A}$, $\imath(\bar{a}^\mathfrak{M}(p)) = \bar{a}^\mathfrak{N}(\imath(p))$.

Let $p \in Q_M$. Let $w$ be any word such that $p = M(w)$. Then

$$\begin{aligned} p \in \bar{F}^\mathfrak{M} &\Leftrightarrow M(w) \in \bar{F}^\mathfrak{M} \Leftrightarrow w \in \mathscr{L}(M) \Leftrightarrow w \in \mathscr{L}(N) \\ &\Leftrightarrow N(w) \in \bar{F}^\mathfrak{N} \Leftrightarrow \imath(M(w)) \in \bar{F}^\mathfrak{N} \Leftrightarrow \imath(p) \in \bar{F}^\mathfrak{N}. \end{aligned}$$

and, for any $a \in \mathfrak{D}_\mathcal{A}$,

$$\begin{aligned} \imath(\bar{a}^\mathfrak{M}(p)) &= \imath(\bar{a}^\mathfrak{M}(M(w))) = \imath(\delta_M(a, M(w))) \\ &= \imath(M(w \cdot a)) = N(w \cdot a) = \delta_N(a, N(w)) \\ &= \bar{a}^\mathfrak{N}(N(w)) = \bar{a}^\mathfrak{N}(\imath(M(w))) = \bar{a}^\mathfrak{N}(\imath(p)) \end{aligned}$$

Thus $\mathfrak{M}$ and $\mathfrak{N}$ are isomorphic. ⊠

The theorem implies that minimal SFAs are unique up to renaming of states and up to equivalence of predicates due to normalization.

**DEFINITION** 3. Two states $p, q \in Q$ are *$M$-equivalent*, $p \equiv_M q$, when $\mathscr{L}_p(M) = \mathscr{L}_q(M)$. ⊠

We have that $\equiv_M$ is an equivalence relation. If $\equiv$ is an equivalence relation over $Q$, then for $q \in Q$, $q_{/\equiv}$ denotes the equivalence class containing $q$, for $X \subseteq Q$, $X_{/\equiv}$ denotes $\{q_{/\equiv} \mid q \in X\}$, and $M_{/\equiv}$ denotes the SFA $M_{/\equiv} \stackrel{\text{def}}{=} (\mathcal{A}, Q_{/\equiv}, q^0_{/\equiv}, F_{/\equiv}, \Delta_{/\equiv})$ where:

$$\Delta_{/\equiv} \stackrel{\text{def}}{=} \{(p_{/\equiv}, \bigvee_{(p,\varphi,q) \in \Delta} \varphi, q_{/\equiv}) \mid p, q \in Q, \exists \varphi((p, \varphi, q) \in \Delta)\}$$

[2] It is sometimes convenient to define minimality over incomplete SFAs, in which case the *dead-end* state $q$ ($q \neq q^0$ and $\mathscr{L}_q(M) = \emptyset$) is eliminated if it is present.

Observe that $M_{/\equiv}$ is normalized by construction. We need the following theorem that shows that minimization of SFAs preserves their intended semantics.

**THEOREM** 2. *Let $M$ be a clean, complete and deterministic SFA. Then $M_{/\equiv_M}$ is minimal and $\mathscr{L}(M) = \mathscr{L}(M_{/\equiv_M})$.*

*Proof*: Let $\equiv$ be $\equiv_M$. Clearly, $M_{/\equiv}$ is clean and complete because $M$ is clean and complete. To show determinism, let $\mathbf{p} \xrightarrow{a}_{M_{/\equiv}} \mathbf{q}_1$, and $\mathbf{p} \xrightarrow{a}_{M_{/\equiv}} \mathbf{q}_2$. Take $p_1, p_2 \in \mathbf{p}$, $q_1 \in \mathbf{q}_1$ and $q_2 \in \mathbf{q}_2$ such that $p_1 \xrightarrow{a}_M q_1$ and $p_2 \xrightarrow{a}_M q_2$. Since $\mathscr{L}_{p_1}(M) = \mathscr{L}_{p_2}(M)$, and $M$ is deterministic, it follows that $\mathscr{L}_{q_1}(M) = \mathscr{L}_{q_2}(M)$ i.e., $\mathbf{q}_1 = \mathbf{q}_2$. Thus,

$$(*) \qquad \forall a \in \mathfrak{D}_{\mathcal{A}}, p \in Q_M(\delta_{M_{/\equiv}}(a, p_{/\equiv}) = \delta_M(a,p)_{/\equiv}).$$

Minimality of $M_{/\equiv}$ follows from the definition. Next, we show by induction over the length of $w$ that

$$(\star) \qquad \forall w \in \mathfrak{D}_{\mathcal{A}}^*(M(w)_{/\equiv} = M_{/\equiv}(w))$$

For $w = \epsilon$ we have that $M(\epsilon) = q_M^0$, $M_{/\equiv}(\epsilon) = q_{M_{/\equiv}}^0$, and $q_{M_{/\equiv}}^0 = (q_M^0)_{/\equiv}$.

For $w = v \cdot a$, where $a \in \mathfrak{D}_{\mathcal{A}}$ and $v \in \mathfrak{D}_{\mathcal{A}}^*$, we have that

$$\begin{aligned} M(v \cdot a)_{/\equiv} &= \delta_M(a, M(v))_{/\equiv} \stackrel{\text{(by }(*))}{=} \delta_{M_{/\equiv}}(a, M(v)_{/\equiv}) \\ &\stackrel{\text{(by IH)}}{=} \delta_{M_{/\equiv}}(a, M_{/\equiv}(v)) = M_{/\equiv}(v \cdot a). \end{aligned}$$

It follows that, for all words $w \in \mathfrak{D}_{\mathcal{A}}^*$, $w \in \mathscr{L}(M)$ iff $M(w) \in F_M$ iff $M(w)_{/\equiv} \in F_{M_{/\equiv}}$ iff (by $(\star)$) $M_{/\equiv}(w) \in F_{M_{/\equiv}}$ iff $w \in \mathscr{L}(M_{/\equiv})$. Thus $\mathscr{L}(M) = \mathscr{L}(M_{/\equiv})$. ⊠

Theorems 1 and 2 are classical theorems lifted to arbitrary (possibly infinite) alphabets. Theorem 2 implies that SFAs have equivalent minimal forms that, by Theorem 1, are unique up to relabeling of states, and modulo equivalence of predicates in $\mathcal{A}$. In particular, since for all $Q$ and all equivalence relations $E$ over $Q$, $|Q_{/E}| \leq |Q|$, each equivalent form has minimal number of states.

## 3. Moore's algorithm over symbolic alphabets

Moore's minimization algorithm [34] of DFAs (also due to Huffman [29]) is commonly known as the *standard* algorithm. Even though the classical version of Moore's algorithm depends on the alphabet being finite, the general idea can be lifted to SFAs as follows. Given an SFA $M$, initially, let $D$ be the binary relation $(F \times F^c) \cup (F^c \times F)$, where $F^c$ is $Q \setminus F$. Compute the fixpoint of $D$ as follows: if $\langle p, q\rangle \in D$ and there exist moves $(p', \varphi, p)$ and $(q', \psi, q)$ where $\varphi \wedge \psi$ *is satisfiable*[3] then add $\langle p', q'\rangle$ to $D$. This process clearly terminates. Upon termination, $E = (Q \times Q) \setminus D$ is the equivalence relation $\equiv_M$, and the SFA $M_{/E}$ is therefore minimal. We refer to this algorithm as $Min^{\mathrm{M}}_{\mathrm{SFA}}$. Observe that $Min^{\mathrm{M}}_{\mathrm{SFA}}$ checks only *satisfiability of conjunctions* of conditions and does not depend on the full power of the alphabet algebra, in particular it does not require the ability to complement predicates (assuming the initial completion of $M$ is viewed as a separate preprocessing step). This is in contrast with the generalization of Hopcroft's algorithm discussed in the next section.

***Complexity.*** In the finite alphabet case Moore's algorithm can be implemented in $\mathcal{O}(kn\log n)$ (using the approach described in [10]), where $n$ is the number of states of the DFA, and $k$ the number of characters in the input alphabet. However, such implementation relies on the alphabet being finite.

[3] In a concrete implementation a dictionary can be used to maintain $D$ similar to the case of DFAs [28, Section 3.4].

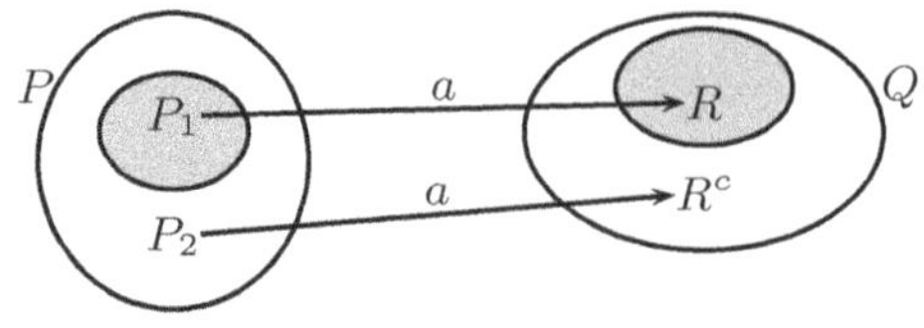


**Figure 1.** The idea behind an $(a, R)$-split of a part $P$.

Our implementation of the version of Moore's algorithm presented above has the following complexity. Given an SFA $A$, let $n$ be the number of states of $A$, $m$ the number of moves of $A$, and $\ell$ the size of the largest guard appearing in a transition of $A$ (the biggest predicate). If the complexity of the alphabet theory for instances of size $l$ is $f(l)$, then $Min^{\mathrm{M}}_{\mathrm{SFA}}$ has complexity $\mathcal{O}(m^2 f(\ell))$, which is $\mathcal{O}(n^4 f(\ell))$ assuming normalized $A$ where $m$ is $\mathcal{O}(n^2)$.

## 4. Hopcroft's algorithm over symbolic alphabets

Hopcroft's algorithm [27] for minimizing DFAs is based on a technique called *partition refinement* of states. The symbolic version of Hopcroft's algorithm is given in Figure 3. Initially the set of states is partitioned into two sets: *final* states and *non-final* states, i.e., $\mathcal{P} = \{F, Q \setminus F\}$. Here we assume that the SFA $M$ is complete and nontrivial, so that both $F$ and $Q \setminus F$ are nonempty. The partition $\mathcal{P}$ induces the equivalence relation $\equiv_{\mathcal{P}}$ (or $\equiv$ when $\mathcal{P}$ is clear from the context) over $Q$, such that $Q_{/\equiv} = \mathcal{P}$. At a high level, $\mathcal{P}$ is refined as follows: suppose there exist parts $P, R \in \mathcal{P}$ and a character $a \in \mathfrak{D}_{\mathcal{A}}$ such that some $a$-move from $P$ goes into $R$, and some $a$-move from $P$ goes into $R^c$ ($Q \setminus R$). Then the $(a, R)$-*split of* $P$ is the set $\{P_1, P_2\}$, where $P_1$ (resp. $P_2$) is the set of all $p \in P$ from which there is an $a$-move into $R$ (resp. $R^c$). $P$ is then replaced in $\mathcal{P}$ by $P_1$ and $P_2$. See Figure 1. The $(a, R)$-split of $P$ is well-defined by determinism and completeness of $M$. The following invariant is maintained by splitting.

**LEMMA** 1. *After each refinement step of $\mathcal{P}$, for all $p, q \in Q$, if $p \not\equiv q$ then $\mathscr{L}_p(M) \neq \mathscr{L}_q(M)$.*

*Proof*: Initially, for $p_1 \in F$: $\epsilon \in \mathscr{L}_{p_1}(M)$ , and $p_2 \in Q \setminus F$: $\epsilon \notin \mathscr{L}_{p_2}(M)$. So, the statement holds for step $i = 0$. To see that the statement holds after step $i+1$, fix $P, R \in \mathcal{P}_i$ and $a \in \mathfrak{D}_{\mathcal{A}}$ such that $(P_1, P_2)$ is the $(a, R)$-split of $P$. It is enough to show that, for all $p_1 \in P_1, p_2 \in P_2$, $\mathscr{L}_{p_1}(M) \neq \mathscr{L}_{p_2}(M)$. Consider $p_1 \xrightarrow{a} q_1$ and $p_2 \xrightarrow{a} q_2$. Since $q_1$ and $q_2$ belong to distinct parts of $\mathcal{P}_i$, by IH, there exists a word $w$ such that $w \in \mathscr{L}_{q_1}(M)$ iff $w \notin \mathscr{L}_{q_2}(M)$. Moreover, by determinism of $M$, we have $a \cdot w \in \mathscr{L}_{p_j}(M)$ iff $w \in \mathscr{L}_{q_j}(M)$ for $j \in \{1, 2\}$. So, $a \cdot w \in \mathscr{L}_{p_1}(M)$ iff $a \cdot w \notin \mathscr{L}_{p_2}(M)$, and thus $\mathscr{L}_{p_1}(M) \neq \mathscr{L}_{p_2}(M)$. ⊠

Assuming a simple iterative refinement loop of $\mathcal{P}$, splitting is repeated until no further splits are possible, i.e., until $\mathcal{P}$ is *finest*, at which point the following property holds.

**LEMMA** 2. *Upon termination of refinement of $\mathcal{P}$, for all $p, q \in Q$, if $p \equiv q$ then $\mathscr{L}_p(M) = \mathscr{L}_q(M)$.*

*Proof*: By way of contradiction. Suppose

$(*)$ there exists a word $x$ and states $p_1 \equiv p_2$, such that $x \in \mathscr{L}_{p_1}(M) \Leftrightarrow x \notin \mathscr{L}_{p_2}(M)$.

Choose $w$ to be a *shortest* such $x$. Since $w$ cannot be $\epsilon$ (because $\{p_1, p_2\} \subseteq F$ or $\{p_1, p_2\} \subseteq Q \setminus F$), there are $a$ and $v$ such that $a \cdot v = w$, and moves $p_1 \xrightarrow{\varphi_1} q_1$ and $p_2 \xrightarrow{\varphi_2} q_2$ such that $a \in [\![\varphi_1]\!]$ and $a \in [\![\varphi_2]\!]$. The choice of $q_1$ and $q_2$ is unique for given $a$ by determinism, thus $w \in \mathscr{L}_{p_i}(M) \Leftrightarrow v \in \mathscr{L}_{q_i}(M)$ for $i \in \{1, 2\}$. So, by $(*)$, $v \in \mathscr{L}_{q_1}(M) \Leftrightarrow v \notin \mathscr{L}_{q_2}(M)$.

```
1  Minterms_A(ψ̄) ≝
2    tree := new Tree(⊤_A, null, null);
3    foreach (ψ in ψ̄) tree.Refine(ψ);
4      return Leaves(tree); //return the set of all the leaf predicates
5  class Tree
6    Predicate φ; Tree left; Tree right;
7    Refine(ψ) ≝
8      if (IsSat_A(φ ∧_A ψ) and IsSat_A(φ ∧_A ¬_A ψ))
9        if (left = null) //if the tree is a leaf then split φ into two parts
10         left := new Tree(φ ∧_A ψ,null,null); //[[φ]] ∩ [[ψ]]
11         right := new Tree(φ ∧_A ¬_A ψ,null,null); //[[φ]] \ [[ψ]]
12       else left.Refine(ψ); right.Refine(ψ); //refine subtrees recursively
```

**Figure 2.** Minterm generation for $\bar{\psi} \subseteq \Psi_{\mathcal{A}}$ modulo $\mathcal{A}$.

We now have the following contradiction. There are two cases: 1) if $q_1 \not\equiv q_2$, say $q_1 \in R$ and $q_2 \in R^c$ for some part $R$, then $\mathcal{P}$ *is not finest* because we can split the part $P \in \mathcal{P}$ such that $p_1, p_2 \in P$ using the $(a, R)$-split of $P$. 2) if $q_1 \equiv q_2$ then, because $|v| < |w|$ and $(*)$ holds for $x = v$ and $q_1, q_2$ in place of $p_1, p_2$, it follows that *$w$ is not the shortest $x$ such that $(*)$ holds* ↯. ⊠

In addition to the state partition refinement, in the symbolic case, we also use *predicate refinement*. Predicate refinement builds a set of *minterms*. A minterm is a minimal satisfiable Boolean combinations of all guards that occur in the SFA. The algorithm is shown in Figure 2. It uses a binary tree whose leaves define the partition. Initially the tree is the leaf $\top$. Each time a predicate $\psi$ is used to refine the tree it may cause splitting of its leaves into finer predicates. The following example illustrates such minterm generation.

**Example 1.** Consider the alphabet algebra $\mathbf{2}^{\mathrm{BV}7}$ (ASCII characters). We use standard regex notation for character classes. Suppose that the following two guards occur in the given SFA: `\w` ($[\![$`\w`$]\!] = [\![$`[a-zA-Z0-9_]`$]\!]$), and `\d` ($[\![$`\d`$]\!] = [\![$`[0-9]`$]\!]$). Then, the value of *tree* in $\mathit{Minterms}_{\mathbf{2}^{\mathrm{BV}7}}(\{$`\w`, `\d`$\})$ in line 4 in Figure 2 is either the first of the two trees below if `\w` is selected first in the loop of line 3, or else the second tree (note that $[\![$`\d`$]\!] \subsetneq [\![$`\w`$]\!]$ so $[\![$`\d` $\wedge$ `\w`$]\!] = [\![$`\d`$]\!]$):

The minterms are the leaves `\d`, `\w` $\wedge \neg$`\d` and $\neg$`\w`. ⊠

Next, we analyze a property of the set of minterms. Given a predicate $\psi \in \Psi_{\mathcal{A}}$ and a state $p \in Q$, define:

$$\boldsymbol{\delta}(\psi, p) \stackrel{\text{def}}{=} \{\mathit{Tgt}(\rho) \mid \rho \in \overrightarrow{\Delta}(p),\ \mathit{IsSat}(\mathit{Grd}(\rho) \wedge \psi)\}$$

$$\boldsymbol{\delta}^{-1}(\psi, p) \stackrel{\text{def}}{=} \{\mathit{Src}(\rho) \mid \rho \in \overleftarrow{\Delta}(p),\ \mathit{IsSat}(\mathit{Grd}(\rho) \wedge \psi)\}$$

$$\boldsymbol{\delta}^{-1}(\psi, P) \stackrel{\text{def}}{=} \bigcup_{p \in P} \boldsymbol{\delta}^{-1}(\psi, p) \quad (\text{for } P \subseteq Q)$$

Let $\mathit{Minterms}(M) \stackrel{\text{def}}{=} \mathit{Minterms}_{\mathcal{A}}(\bigcup_{\rho \in \Delta} \mathit{Grd}(\rho))$. The following proposition implies that all characters that occur in one minterm are indistinguishable.

**Proposition 1.** *Let $M$ be deterministic and complete. For all $\psi \in \mathit{Minterms}(M)$ and $p \in Q$, $|\boldsymbol{\delta}(\psi, p)| = 1$.*

We can therefore treat $\boldsymbol{\delta}$ as a *function* from $\mathit{Minterms} \times Q$ to $Q$ and reduce minimization of the SFA to minimization of the DFA with alphabet $\mathit{Minterms}$ and transition function $\boldsymbol{\delta}$. In particular, we can use Hopcroft's algorithm. We refer to the resulting algorithm by $\mathit{Min}^{\mathbf{H}}_{\mathrm{SFA}}$. Such an algorithm is shown in Figure 3.

```
Min^H_SFA(M = (A, Q, q^0, F, Δ)) ≝
  P := {F, Q \ F}; //initial partition
  W := {if (|F| ≤ |Q \ F|) then F else Q \ F};
  Ψ := Minterms_A({Grd(ρ) | ρ ∈ Δ}); //compute the minterms
  while (W ≠ ∅) //iterate over unvisited parts
    R := choose(W); W := W \ {R};
    foreach (ψ in Ψ) //iterate over all minterms
      S := δ^{-1}(ψ, R); //all states leading into R for given minterm
      while (exists (P in P) where P ∩ S ≠ ∅ and P \ S ≠ ∅)
        ⟨P, W⟩ := Split_{P,W}(P, P ∩ S, P \ S); //split P
  return M/≡_P;
Split_{P,W}(P, P1, P2) ≝ ⟨P', W'⟩ where
  P' = (P \ {P}) ∪ {P1, P2} //refine P
  W' = if (P ∈ W) then (W \ {P}) ∪ {P1, P2} //both parts
       else W ∪ {if (|P1| ≤ |P2|) then P1 else P2} //smaller part
```

**Figure 3.** Hopcroft's minimization algorithm lifted to deterministic SFAs. $M$ is assumed to be clean, complete, and nontrivial ($F \neq \emptyset$ and $Q \setminus F \neq \emptyset$).

Lifting the transition relation to be over *minterms* is a powerful hammer that can be used to adapt most classical automata algorithms to the symbolic setting. However, one drawback of minterm generation is that, in the worst case, the number of minterms of an SFA is exponential in the number of guards occurring in the SFA. The following example illustrates a worst case scenario in which, due to such a problem, $\mathit{Min}^{\mathbf{H}}_{\mathrm{SFA}}$ runs in exponential time.

**Example 2.** Let the character domain be nonnegative integers $< 2^k$. Suppose $\beta_i(x)$ is a predicate that is true for $x$ iff the $i$'th bit of the binary representation of $x$ is 1, e.g. $\beta_3(8)$ is true and $\beta_3(7)$ is false. Predicate $\beta_3$ can be defined as $\neg((x\&8) = 0)$, provided that, besides equality, the bitwise-and operator $\&$ is a built-in function symbol of $\Psi_{\mathcal{A}}$ (e.g., consider the bit-vector theory of an SMT solver). Similarly, we may also use the algebra $\mathbf{2}^{\mathrm{BV}k}$, where the size of the concrete BDD representation for $\beta_i$ is linear in $k$, it has one node that is labeled by $i$ and whose left child (case bit is 0) is false and whose right child (case bit is 1) is true. The point is that predicates are small (essentially constant) in size. Consider the following SFA $M_k$ with such an alphabet $\mathcal{A}$.

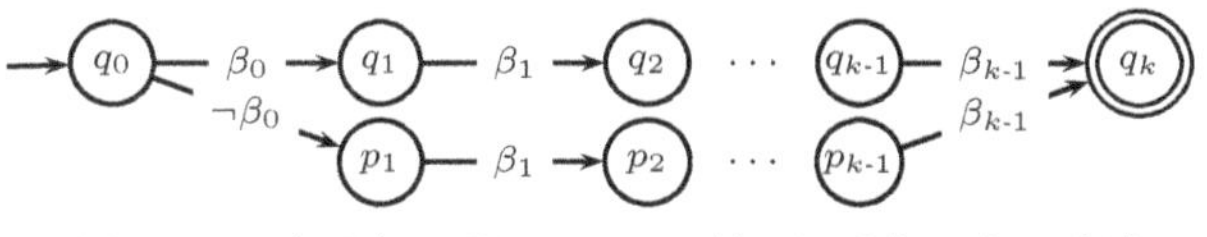


Then $\mathit{Minterms}(M_k) = \mathit{Minterms}_{\mathcal{A}}(\{\neg\beta_i, \beta_i\}_{i<k}) = \{\hat{n}\}_{n<2^k}$ has $2^k$ elements, where $[\![\hat{n}]\!] = \{n\}$. For example, suppose $k = 3$, then $[\![\beta_2 \wedge \neg\beta_1 \wedge \beta_0]\!] = \{5\}$. The minimal automaton is

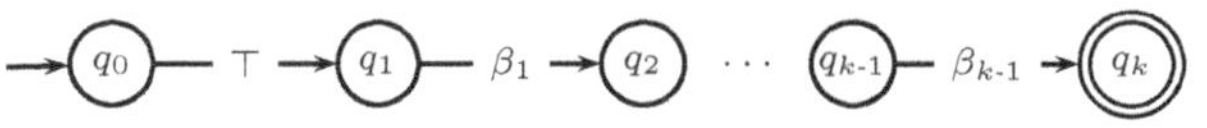


The dead-end state $q_\emptyset$ necessary for completion is implicit. ⊠

***Complexity.*** In the finite alphabet case, Hopcroft's algorithm has complexity $\mathcal{O}(kn \log n)$, where $n$ is the number of states of the DFA and $k$ is the number of characters in the input alphabet [27], assuming $k$ is treated as a constant. It is shown in [31] that if $k$ is $\mathcal{O}(n)$ then the complexity of the algorithm presented in [27] is

1 $Min^{\mathbf{N}}_{\text{SFA}}(M = (\mathcal{A}, Q, q^0, F, \Delta)) \stackrel{\text{def}}{=}$

2 $\quad \mathcal{P} := \{F, Q \setminus F\};$ *//initial partition*

3 $\quad W := \{$**if** $(|F| \leq |Q \setminus F|)$ **then** $F$ **else** $Q \setminus F\};$

4 $\quad$**while** $(W \neq \emptyset)$ *//main loop*

5 $\quad\quad R :=$ **choose**$(W);\ W := W \setminus \{R\};$

6 $\quad\quad S := \{Src(\tau) \mid \tau \in \overleftarrow{\Delta}(R)\};$ *//all states leading into $R$*

$\quad\quad$ *//$\Gamma(p)$ denotes the set of all characters leading from $p \in S$ into $R$*

7 $\quad\quad \Gamma := \{p \mapsto \bigvee_{\tau \in \overleftarrow{\Delta}(R), Src(\tau)=p} Grd(\tau) \mid p \in S\};$

8 $\quad\quad$**while** (**exists** ($P$ **in** $\mathcal{P}$) **where** $P \cap S \neq \emptyset$ **and** $P \setminus S \neq \emptyset$)

9 $\quad\quad\quad \langle \mathcal{P}, W \rangle := Split_{\mathcal{P},W}(P, P \cap S, P \setminus S);$ *//($\_$, $R$)-split*

10 $\quad\quad$**while** (**exists** ($P$ **in** $\mathcal{P}$) **where** $P \cap S \neq \emptyset$ **and**

11 $\quad\quad\quad\quad$**exists** $(p_1, p_2$ **in** $P)$ **where** $IsSat(\neg(\Gamma(p_1) \Leftrightarrow \Gamma(p_2))))$

12 $\quad\quad\quad a :=$ **choose**$([\![\neg(\Gamma(p_1) \Leftrightarrow \Gamma(p_2))]\!]);$

13 $\quad\quad\quad P_1 := \{p \in P \mid a \in [\![\Gamma(p)]\!]\};$

14 $\quad\quad\quad \langle \mathcal{P}, W \rangle := Split_{\mathcal{P},W}(P, P_1, P \setminus P_1);$ *//($a$, $R$)-split*

15 $\quad$**return** $M_{/\equiv_{\mathcal{P}}};$

**Figure 4.** Minimization of deterministic SFAs. $M$ is assumed to be clean, complete and nontrivial. $Split_{\mathcal{P},W}$ is defined in Figure 3.

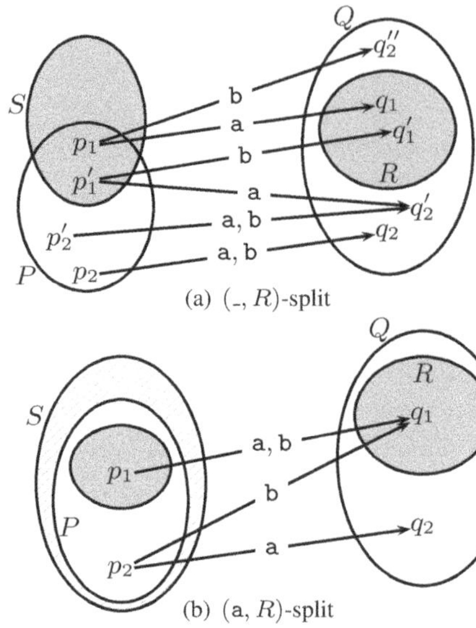


**Figure 5.** Split cases of $P$ in $Min^{\mathbf{N}}_{\text{SFA}}$. Suppose $\mathfrak{D}_{\mathcal{A}} = \{\mathtt{a}, \mathtt{b}\}$.

$O(n^3)$, but it is also shown that $\mathcal{O}(kn \log n)$ complexity can be maintained with a more careful implementation.

Given an SFA, let $n$ be the number of states, let $m$ be the number of moves, and let $\ell$ be the size of the largest label (guard) of a move. In a normalized SFA there are at most $n^2$ moves. Let $\mu$ be the number of minterms of the SFA; $\mu$ is bounded by $2^m$. Each minterm is of the form $\phi_1 \wedge \ldots \wedge \phi_m$, where each $\phi_i$ is a guard or a negated guard, and thus minterms have size $O(m\ell)$. The computation of minterms is $\mathcal{O}(2^m f(m\ell))$ where $f$ is the complexity to decide satisfiability of formulas of given size. The rest of the algorithm (after line 4) can be seen as a standard implementation of Hopcroft's algorithm, where the SFA is first transformed into a DFA with an alphabet of minterm identifiers where each SFA label has been replaced by identifiers of all relevant minterms. Then $\Psi$ is viewed as a concrete alphabet (of such minterm identifiers). In the final result, the identifiers are mapped back to minterms and the resulting SFA is normalized. The overall complexity is then $\mathcal{O}(2^m f(m\ell) + 2^m n \log n)$.

## 5. Minimization without minterm generation

When inspecting the worst case complexity of $Min^{\mathbf{H}}_{\text{SFA}}$, the factor that stands out the most is the exponential blowup caused by the predicate refinement (minterm generation). In this section we investigate a new technique which is based on the symbolic representation of the alphabet, and that avoids minterm generation. Figure 4 shows $Min^{\mathbf{N}}_{\text{SFA}}$, a new minimization algorithm, that does not require predicate refinement.

The intuition behind $Min^{\mathbf{N}}_{\text{SFA}}$ is the following: when splitting a partition's part, it is not necessary to provide the exact witness that defines the split, instead it is enough to check if some witness (or witness set) exists. The main steps are the two inner while loops in Figure 4, they both refine the partition $\mathcal{P}$ with respect to $R$. In the first loop (lines 8–9) a part $P$ is split into $P \cap S$ and $P \setminus S$ without using a fixed witness (see Figure 5(a) where $\{\{p_1, p'_1\}, \{p_2, p'_2\}\}$ is a ($\_$, $R$)-split of $P$, but it is neither an ($\mathtt{a}$, $R$)-split nor a ($\mathtt{b}$, $R$)-split of $P$). The second loop (lines 10–14) splits $P$ if there *exists* some $a$ that produces an $(a, R)$-split of $P$. Such an element $a$ must somehow distinguish at least two states $p_1$ and $p_2$ of $P$, (see Figure 5(b)), so that the split is indeed proper and guarantees progress.

The first loop (lines 8–9) is an optimization that can be omitted without sacrificing correctness, provided that for $p \notin S$ we let $\Gamma(p) \stackrel{\text{def}}{=} \perp$. The conditions $P \setminus S \neq \emptyset$ and $P \cap S \neq \emptyset$ together imply that there exist $p_1 \in P \cap S$ and $p_2 \in P \setminus S$ and thus $[\![\Gamma(p_1)]\!] \neq \emptyset$ but $[\![\Gamma(p_2)]\!] = \emptyset$, so $\neg(\Gamma(p_1) \Leftrightarrow \Gamma(p_2))$ is satisfiable.

The concrete implementation is shown in Figure 6. It differs from the abstract algorithm in that it computes local minterms, and does not compute any concrete witnesses (the element $a$ is not computed) in the second loop. In the concrete implementation it is important to keep the first loop for the following reasons. One is efficiency, the first loop is cheaper. Second is simplicity, it is useful to work with $\Gamma$ as a dictionary or array whose index set is $S$, and it is practical to assume that the invariant $P \subseteq S$ holds during the second loop.

Next, we formally prove the correctness of $Min^{\mathbf{N}}_{\text{SFA}}$. The proof provides more intuition on how the algorithm works. We then provide more details on how the concrete implementation works.

**THEOREM 3.** *$Min^{\mathbf{N}}_{\text{SFA}}(M)$ is minimal, and $\mathscr{L}(Min^{\mathbf{N}}_{\text{SFA}}(M)) = \mathscr{L}(M)$.*

*Proof*: We show first that the invariant of Lemma 1 holds. The invariant clearly holds initially. We show that it is preserved by each split (lines 8–9, and lines 10–14).

First, consider the first splitting loop in Figure 4. Fix $R \in \mathcal{P}$ and let $S = \{Src(\tau) \mid \tau \in \overleftarrow{\Delta}(R)\}$, and choose $P \in \mathcal{P}$ such that $P_1 = P \cap S \neq \emptyset$ and $P_2 = P \setminus S \neq \emptyset$. Fix $p_1 \in P_1$ and $p_2 \in P_2$. Then, there is a move $p_1 \xrightarrow{\varphi_1} q_1$ for some $q_1 \in R$. Let $a \in [\![\varphi_1]\!]$. Since $p_2 \notin S$ and $M$ is complete, for some $q_2 \in R^c$ there exist a move $p_2 \xrightarrow{\varphi_2} q_2$ such that $a \in [\![\varphi_2]\!]$. The situation is illustrated in Figure 5(a). By using the invariant, $\mathscr{L}_{q_1}(M) \neq \mathscr{L}_{q_2}(M)$, there is a word $w$ such that $w \in \mathscr{L}_{q_1}(M) \Leftrightarrow w \notin \mathscr{L}_{q_2}(M)$. Thus, by using the fact that $M$ is deterministic, $a \cdot w \in \mathscr{L}_{p_1}(M) \Leftrightarrow a \cdot w \notin \mathscr{L}_{p_2}(M)$. Therefore, $\mathscr{L}_{p_1}(M) \neq \mathscr{L}_{p_2}(M)$.

Second, consider the second splitting loop. Fix $P$ and $p_1, p_2 \in P$ that satisfy the loop condition. All parts in $\mathcal{P}$ that intersect with $S$ must be subsets of $S$ due to the first splitting loop, so, since $M$ is clean, $P \subseteq S$, $IsSat(\Gamma(p_1))$ and $IsSat(\Gamma(p_2))$. The condi-

```
MinSFA(Automaton<S> fa)
{
  var fB  = new Block(fa.GetFinalStates());
  var nfB = new Block(fa.GetNonFinalStates());
  var blocks = new Dictionary<int, Block>();
  foreach (var q in fa.GetFinalStates()) blocks[q] = fB;
  foreach (var q in fa.GetNonFinalStates()) blocks[q] = nfB;
  var W = new BlockStack();
  if (nfB.Count < fB.Count) W.Push(nfB); else W.Push(fB);

  while (!W.IsEmpty) {
    var R = W.Pop();
    var G = ... //Γ in Figure 4
    var S = G.Keys;
    var relevant = ... //blocks intersecting with S
    foreach (var P in relevant){  //lines 8-9 in Figure 4
      var P1 = ...  //P∩S
      if (P1.Count < P.Count) {  //(_,R)-split of P
        foreach (var p in P1) { P.Remove(p); blocks[p] = P1;}
        if (W.Contains(P)) W.Push(P1);
        else if (P.Count <= P1.Count) W.Push(P);
        else W.Push(P1);
    }}
    bool iterate = true;
    while (iterate) {  //lines 10-14 in Figure 4
      iterate = false;
      relevant = ... //blocks intersecting with S
      foreach (var P in relevant) {
        var P1 = new Block();
        var psi = G[P.Current];  //start with some element of P
        bool splitterFound = false;
        P1.Add(P.Current);

        while (P.MoveNext()) {
          var q = P.Current;
          var phi = G[q];
          if (splitterFound) {
            if (IsSat(psi & phi)) { P1.Add(q); psi = psi & phi;}
          } else {
            if (IsSat(psi & !phi)) {
              psi = psi & !phi;     //refine the local minterm
              splitterFound = true;
            } else {  //psi implies phi
              if (IsSat(phi & !psi)) {
                P1.Clear(); P1.Add(q);   //set P1 to {q}
                psi = phi & !psi;   //swap the local minterm
                splitterFound = true;
              } else P1.Add(q);   //psi is equivalent to phi
        }}}
        if (P1.Count < P.Count) {  //(a,R)-split of P for some a
          iterate = (iterate || (P.Count > 2));
          foreach (var p in P1) { P.Remove(p); blocks[p] = P1; }
          if (W.Contains(P)) W.Push(P1);
          else if (P.Count <= P1.Count) W.Push(P);
          else W.Push(P1);
  }}}}
  ...   //construct the result using blocks and normalize it
}
```

**Figure 6.** Concrete implementation of $Min^{\mathbf{N}}_{\text{SFA}}$.

tion $IsSat(\neg(\Gamma(p_1) \Leftrightarrow \Gamma(p_2)))$ means that either $IsSat(\Gamma(p_1) \wedge \neg\Gamma(p_2))$ or $IsSat(\Gamma(p_2) \wedge \neg\Gamma(p_1))$. Assume the former case and choose $a \in [\![\Gamma(p_1) \wedge \neg\Gamma(p_2)]\!]$. By definition of $\Gamma$, we know that there is a move $p_1 \xrightarrow{\varphi_1} q_1$ where $q_1 \in R$ such that $a \in [\![\varphi_1]\!]$. Moreover, since $a \notin [\![\Gamma(p_2)]\!]$, and $\Gamma(p_2)$ covers *all* the characters that lead from $p_2$ to $R$, there must be (by completeness and determinism of $M$) a move $p_2 \xrightarrow{\varphi_2} q_2$ where $q_2 \in R^c$ and $a \in [\![\varphi_2]\!]$. See Figure 5(b). It follows as above, by using $\mathscr{L}_{q_1}(M) \neq \mathscr{L}_{q_2}(M)$, that $\mathscr{L}_{p_1}(M) \neq \mathscr{L}_{p_2}(M)$. Since each step properly refines the partition, Lemma 1 follows.

We now show that Lemma 2 holds. The proof is by way of contradiction.

(*) Assume there exists a word $x$, a part $P \in \mathcal{P}$, and two states $p_1, p_2 \in P$ such that $x \in \mathscr{L}_{p_1}(M) \Leftrightarrow x \notin \mathscr{L}_{p_2}(M)$.

Let $w$ be *shortest* such $x$. Since $w$ cannot be $\epsilon$, there exist $a$ and $v$ such that $w = a \cdot v$. So, there are, by determinism and completeness of $M$, unique $q_1$ and $q_2$ such that $p_1 \xrightarrow{a} q_1$ and $p_2 \xrightarrow{a} q_2$. It follows that $v \in \mathscr{L}_{q_1}(M) \Leftrightarrow v \notin \mathscr{L}_{q_2}(M)$. So $q_1 \not\equiv q_2$ or else $v$ satisfies (*) and $v$ is shorter that $w$.

Consider any fixed computation of $Min^{\mathbf{N}}_{\text{SFA}}$. It follows from the definition of $Split_{\mathcal{P},W}$, that $W$ is always a subset of $\mathcal{P}$ and (due to the first condition of the update to $W$), if $W$ ever contains a part containing a state $q$, then $W$ will keep containing a part that contains $q$ until such a part is removed from $W$ in line 5.

Next, we show that the following $W$-*invariant* must hold at all times: for all $R \in W$, $q_1 \in R \Leftrightarrow q_2 \in R$. Let $\{\iota, \hat{\iota}\} = \{1, 2\}$. Suppose, by way of contradiction, that at some point in line 5 a part $R$ is chosen from $W$ such that $q_\iota \in R$, and $q_{\hat{\iota}} \notin R$. So, $p_\iota \in S$, with $S$ as in line 6. We then have two following cases.

1. If $p_{\hat{\iota}} \notin S$, then $p_\iota$ and $p_{\hat{\iota}}$ are split apart in the first splitting loop. This contradicts the fact that $p_1 \equiv p_2$.
2. Assume $p_{\hat{\iota}} \in S$ and consider the second splitting loop. By choice of the character $a$ above, we know that there exist moves $p_\iota \xrightarrow{\varphi_\iota} q_\iota$ and $p_{\hat{\iota}} \xrightarrow{\varphi_{\hat{\iota}}} q_{\hat{\iota}}$ where $a \in [\![\varphi_\iota]\!]$ and $a \in [\![\varphi_{\hat{\iota}}]\!]$. It follows that $a \notin [\![\Gamma(p_{\hat{\iota}})]\!]$ (because $M$ is deterministic and $q_{\hat{\iota}} \notin R$) while $a \in [\![\Gamma(p_\iota)]\!]$. So $a \in [\![\Gamma(p_\iota)]\!] \setminus [\![\Gamma(p_{\hat{\iota}})]\!]$, or, in other words, $a \in [\![\Gamma(p_\iota) \wedge \neg\Gamma(p_{\hat{\iota}})]\!]$, and therefore $IsSat(\neg(\Gamma(p_\iota) \Leftrightarrow \Gamma(p_{\hat{\iota}})))$ holds. Consequently, $p_\iota$ and $p_{\hat{\iota}}$ end up in distinct parts upon termination of the second splitting loop. This again contradicts the fact that $p_1 \equiv p_2$.

So, initially $q_1 \in F \Leftrightarrow q_2 \in F$, or else the initial part of $W$ violates the invariant. But now consider the point when the part containing both $q_1$ and $q_2$ is split into two parts containing $q_1$ and $q_2$ respectively. But at this point, at least one of those parts will be added to $W$ by definition of $Split_{\mathcal{P},W}$. Thus, we have reached the desired contradiction, because the $W$-invariant is violated at that point.

We have shown that, upon termination of $Min^{\mathbf{N}}_{\text{SFA}}(M)$, $\equiv_{\mathcal{P}}$ coincides with $\equiv_M$. It follows from Theorem 2 that $M_{/\equiv_{\mathcal{P}}}$ is minimal and accepts $\mathscr{L}(M)$. ⊠

***Implementation.*** A simplified version of our concrete C# implementation of $Min^{\mathbf{N}}_{\text{SFA}}$ is shown in Figure 6. Parts of a state partition are represented by mutable sets called *blocks*, i.e., objects of type `Block`, and states are represented by integers. Each block contains a `HashSet` of states. The search frontier $W$ is maintained as a stack of blocks, and the partition $\mathcal{P}$ is an array of blocks, called `blocks`, that is indexed by states.

The first inner while loop (lines 8–9 in Figure 4) is implemented by iterating over all blocks `P` that intersect with `S`. The content of block `P1` becomes `P` ∩ `S`, while the content of block `P` is updated to `P` \ `S`. Observe that blocks are objects (pointers), thus if `W` contains `P`, after the (_, `R`)-split it will still contain `P` as well as the new block `P1`.

The second inner while loop (lines 10–14 in Figure 4) is implemented by en efficient encoding of the search for $p_1$ and $p_2$ in line 11 of Figure 4. Moreover, no concrete witness $a$ is computed. Instead, a "local minterm" (called `psi` or $\psi$ in Figure 6), is computed using $\Gamma$. This avoids the use of *model generation* that is more expensive than satisfiability checking (i.e. checking if there *exists* a model).[4] Thus, the implementation does not rely on model generation. Observe also that the second inner while loop relies on the fact that all remaining (`relevant`) blocks that intersect with $S$ must be *contained* in $S$ due to the first inner loop. The split of $P$

[4] Although $IsSat_{\mathcal{A}}(\varphi)$ is formally defined as $[\![\varphi]\!]_{\mathcal{A}} \neq \emptyset$, satisfiability checking is a more lightweight operation than actual model generation, in particular, in the context of SMT solvers.

then happens with respect to $\psi$, which, by construction, is a member of $Minterms(\{\Gamma(p) \mid p \in P\})$, so some member $a$ of $[\![\psi]\!]$ would have produced the same split.

***Relation to classical techniques.*** Implementation of Hopcroft's algorithm is discussed in detail in [7]. In the classical setting, the notions of blocks and $(a, R)$-splits are standard, the pair $(R, a)$ is called a *splitter* in classical algorithms, where it plays a key role. The idea of splitting a block into two and keeping only the smaller block in the waiting set $W$ is a core classical feature. In the case of *partial* DFAs, the algorithms are similar except that $W$ must be initialized with both $F$ and $F^c$ [40].

In classical implementations the waiting set $W$ consists of *splitters* rather than blocks, where characters have been *preselected*. The same is true for partial DFAs except that only those characters that are relevant for a given block are being used, which is beneficial for DFAs with sparse transition graphs. In the symbolic setting the character selection is indirect and achieved only through the satisfiability checks using local minterms during the second loop. The alphabet algebra may be infinite in the case of SFAs, this is not possible in the classical setting. As far as we know, the idea behind the first inner loop of $Min^{\mathbf{N}}_{\mathrm{SFA}}$ and the notion of $(\_, R)$-splits (recall Figure 5), say *free splitters* $(R, \_)$, have not been studied in the classical setting.

***Complexity.*** The complexity of $Min^{\mathbf{N}}_{\mathrm{SFA}}$ depends on several factors, most importantly on the representation of predicates and the concrete representation of the partition refinement data structure, that is explained above.

First of all, observe that each $\Gamma(p)$ has size at most $\mathcal{O}(n\ell)$, and the total size of $\Gamma$ is $\mathcal{O}(n^2\ell)$. Since the split operator always adds to $W$ only the smallest partition, the outer loop is run at most $\log n$ times. The two internal loops have different running times:

- the first loop is run at most $n$ times, with an internal complexity of $\mathcal{O}(n)$, due to the split operation, and
- the second loop is run at most $n$ times, and if the complexity of the label theory for instances of size $l$ is $f(l)$, the complexity of each iteration is at most $\mathcal{O}(nf(n\ell))$. This is due to the $n$ internal iterations over the current part P. We also notice that each iteration calls the solver on a predicate of size at most $\mathcal{O}(n\ell)$.

We can conclude that $Min^{\mathbf{N}}_{\mathrm{SFA}}$ has complexity $\mathcal{O}(n^2 \log n \cdot f(n\ell))$. As we will observe in the next section, the quadratic behavior is not observed in practice.

# 6. Evaluation

We evaluate the performance of $Min^{\mathbf{N}}_{\mathrm{SFA}}$, $Min^{\mathbf{H}}_{\mathrm{SFA}}$, and $Min^{\mathbf{M}}_{\mathrm{SFA}}$ with the following experiments:

1. We minimize the randomly generated DFAs from the benchmark presented in [3]. This experiment analyzes the performance in the presence of small finite alphabets and allows us to validate our implementation of $Min^{\mathbf{H}}_{\mathrm{SFA}}$ against the results shown in [3];
2. We minimize the SFAs generated by common regular expressions taken from the web. This experiment measures performance in the case of typical character alphabets (Unicode);
3. We minimize the SFAs $M_k$ from Example 2 to show the worst case exponential behavior of $Min^{\mathbf{H}}_{\mathrm{SFA}}$. In this experiment we also compare against the `brics` library, a state-of-the-art automata library that uses character ranges as a symbolic representations of finite alphabets;

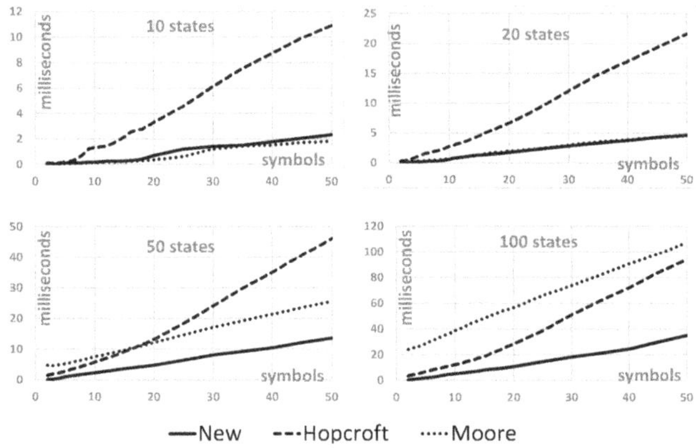


**Figure 7.** Running times on benchmark of randomly generated DFAs. The corresponding SFAs are over the theory of bitvectors and each set of input symbols is represented as a predicate using a binary decision diagram (BDD).

4. We minimize randomly generated SFAs over the theory of pairs of integers and strings. Here, we analyze the performance in the case in which the alphabet is infinite; and
5. We implemented the classical procedure for transforming Monadic Second Order (MSO) logic formulae into DFAs [38] and measure how the running time of such transformation is affected by different minimization algorithms. This last test aims at understanding the performance in the case of very large alphabets. We also compare our implementation against the tool Mona [22], the state of the art library for deciding MSO formulae.

All the experiments are run on a 64 bits Intel(R) Xeon(R) 3.60GHz processor with 8 GB of RAM memory.

## 6.1 Small randomly generated DFAs

In [3] the performance of several minimization algorithms are compared against a set of randomly generated DFAs. Such benchmark contains 5 million DFAs with number of states ranging between 5 and 1000, and alphabet sizes ranging between 2 and 50. The set of DFAs in [3] is uniformly generated at random, and therefore it offers good statistical coverage of the set of all possible DFAs with such number of states and alphabet sizes.

We run $Min^{\mathbf{N}}_{\mathrm{SFA}}$, $Min^{\mathbf{M}}_{\mathrm{SFA}}$ and $Min^{\mathbf{H}}_{\mathrm{SFA}}$ on such set of DFAs. Figure 7 shows the results. For simplicity we only plot the results for DFAs with 10, 20, 50, and 100 states. Each plot contains the running time for each algorithm, where the $x$ axis represents the number of symbols in the alphabet. In [3], Moore's algorithm is not considered and we weren't therefore able to validate the accuracy of our implementation of $Min^{\mathbf{M}}_{\mathrm{SFA}}$. However, we were able to replicate the behavior of Hopcroft's algorithm shown [3] using $Min^{\mathbf{H}}_{\mathrm{SFA}}$.

Figure 7 shows how the complexity of $Min^{\mathbf{M}}_{\mathrm{SFA}}$ highly depends on the number of states, while the complexity of $Min^{\mathbf{H}}_{\mathrm{SFA}}$ is mainly affected by the number of input alphabets. We can indeed see that, already for 100 states, $Min^{\mathbf{M}}_{\mathrm{SFA}}$ performs worse than $Min^{\mathbf{H}}_{\mathrm{SFA}}$. In this experiment, for most of the input DFAs the number of minterms was the same as the number of input symbols.

It is not a surprise that $Min^{\mathbf{N}}_{\mathrm{SFA}}$ is much faster than both $Min^{\mathbf{M}}_{\mathrm{SFA}}$ and $Min^{\mathbf{H}}_{\mathrm{SFA}}$. Indeed, $Min^{\mathbf{N}}_{\mathrm{SFA}}$'s performance seems to be resistant to both bigger state space and bigger alphabets. Moreover, for no single input $Min^{\mathbf{N}}_{\mathrm{SFA}}$ is slower than $Min^{\mathbf{M}}_{\mathrm{SFA}}$ or $Min^{\mathbf{H}}_{\mathrm{SFA}}$.

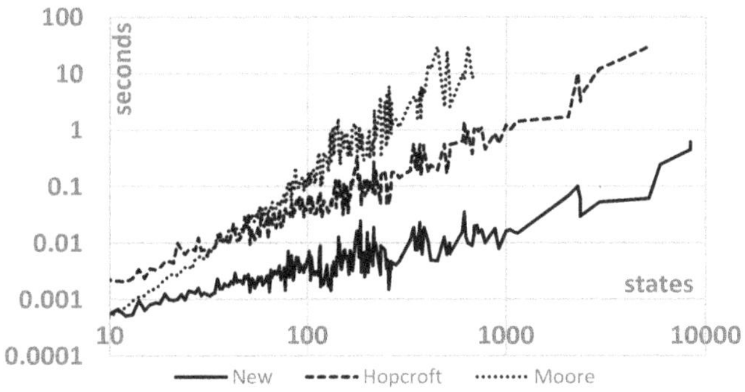


**Figure 8.** Running times on regexes from regexlib. Both axes are in log-scale.

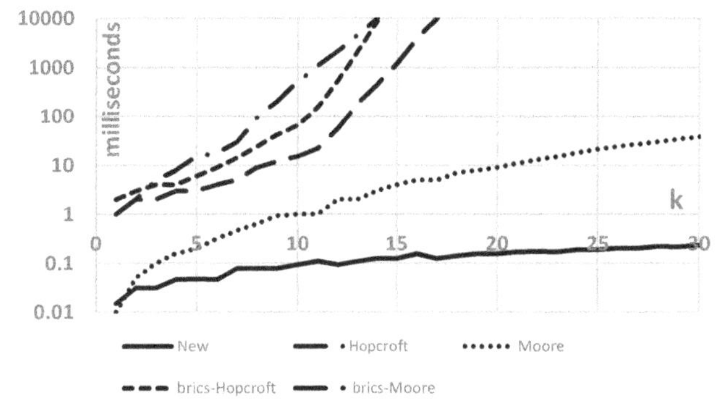


**Figure 9.** Running times on the $M_k$ SFAs of Example 2. The $y$-axis is in log-scale.

### 6.2 Unicode regular expressions

Next, we compared the performance of different minimization algorithms over a sample set of 1850 SFAs over the alphabet $\mathbf{2}^{\text{BV16}}$ (of Unicode characters) constructed from typical regexes (taken from a public web-site[5] of popular regexes). Figure 8 shows the running times. The figure clearly shows how $Min^{\mathbf{N}}_{\text{SFA}}$ is faster than both $Min^{\mathbf{H}}_{\text{SFA}}$ and $Min^{\mathbf{M}}_{\text{SFA}}$ for every input instance. Moreover, it can be appreciated how for bigger state sizes (70-80 states) $Min^{\mathbf{H}}_{\text{SFA}}$ starts outperforming $Min^{\mathbf{M}}_{\text{SFA}}$.

In all cases, the number of minterms turned out to be *smaller* (by a factor between 2 and 3) than the total number of predicates, and the exponential blowup of minterms never occurred. The size of the generated SFAs ranged from 2 states to 15800 states with an average of 100 states. After the minimization each SFA was 32% smaller (number of states) than the original SFA.

The following is a typical regex from the sample set:

```
[NS]\d{1,}(\:[0-5]\d){2}.{0,1}\d{0,},[EW]\d{1,}(\:[0-5]\d){2}
```

The generated SFA uses 16 predicates (such as `\d`)[6] while there are only 7 minterms (such as `[:]`). For this regex, the determinized SFA has 47 states and the minimized SFA has 23 states.

Since the number of minterms does not blowup, is there a performance incentive in using $Min^{\mathbf{N}}_{\text{SFA}}$ in this context? The answer is yes since the total time used to minimize all 1700 SFAs was 20 seconds when using $Min^{\mathbf{H}}_{\text{SFA}}$, and only 0.8 seconds when using $Min^{\mathbf{N}}_{\text{SFA}}$, thus showing a 24x speedup.

We also measured the performance of the minimization algorithm implemented in the `brics.automaton` library (version 1.11-8) that uses *symbolic integer ranges* to represent Unicode characters, but does not implement them as a Boolean algebra (since ranges are not closed under complement and union). We observed that the `brics` implementation of Hopcroft's algorithms is comparable to our implementation of $Min^{\mathbf{H}}_{\text{SFA}}$, and for 95% of the regexes the running times of `brics` Hopcroft's algorithm and $Min^{\mathbf{H}}_{\text{SFA}}$ were at most 5% apart. The trend of $Min^{\mathbf{H}}_{\text{SFA}}$ in Figure 8 is very similar to that of the Hopcroft's implementation in the `brics` library. We decided not to include the latter in the plot for the following reasons: 1) `brics` is implemented in Java, while our implementations are all in C#, and 2) in `brics`, the code corresponding to the minterm computation is not part of the minimization algorithm, therefore the comparison would not be completely fair (especially for big instances).

[5] `http://regexlib.com/`

[6] We use standard regex character class notation for character predicates.

### 6.3 Alphabet corner cases

The next experiment shows the importance of avoiding the minterm generation used by $Min^{\mathbf{H}}_{\text{SFA}}$. We consider the SFAs $M_k$ from Example 2, for values of $k$ ranging between 1 and 31, over the alphabet $\mathbf{2}^{\text{BV32}}$ of 32-bit bit-vectors. Figure 9 shows the running times for $Min^{\mathbf{N}}_{\text{SFA}}$, $Min^{\mathbf{H}}_{\text{SFA}}$, and $Min^{\mathbf{M}}_{\text{SFA}}$.

As expected, the performance of $Min^{\mathbf{H}}_{\text{SFA}}$ degrades exponentially. Already for $k = 11$, minimizing the SFA using $Min^{\mathbf{H}}_{\text{SFA}}$ took 1 second due to minterm generation, while both $Min^{\mathbf{M}}_{\text{SFA}}$ and $Min^{\mathbf{N}}_{\text{SFA}}$ took less than 1ms. For $Min^{\mathbf{M}}_{\text{SFA}}$ the time increased from 1ms to .1sec with $k = 31$, while for $Min^{\mathbf{N}}_{\text{SFA}}$ the time remained below 1ms for all the values of $k$.

Similarly to the previous experiment, we also compared the running time of the sample set against Hopcroft's and Moore's minimization algorithm in the `brics.autmaton` library (version 1.11-8). For this experiment, we decided to show the `brics` performance in order to appreciate how this particular example causes the number of ranges to grow exponentially, causing Hopcroft's algorithm to be very slow. It is interesting to notice that the `brics` implementation of Moore's algorithm is also slow. This is again due to the alphabet's blowup caused by the ranges algebra.

### 6.4 Complex theories

We compare the performance of $Min^{\mathbf{N}}_{\text{SFA}}$, $Min^{\mathbf{H}}_{\text{SFA}}$ and $Min^{\mathbf{M}}_{\text{SFA}}$ over a sample set of 220 randomly generated SFAs over the theory of pairs over $string \times int$. The guards of each SFAs are conjunctions of simple predicates over strings and integers. In the theory of strings we only allow comparison against a constant string, while for integers we generate unary predicates containing $+, -, <, =$ and integer constants. The set of generated SFAs is created as follows. We first generated a set $S$ of 10 SFAs with at most 10 states. For each SFA $a \in S$ we also compute the complement, and for every pair $a, b \in S$ we compute the union, intersection, and difference of $a$ and $b$.

Figure 10 shows the running time of each algorithm for different numbers of states. We first observe how the performance of $Min^{\mathbf{H}}_{\text{SFA}}$ quickly degrades when increasing the number of states. This is mainly due to the large number of minterms. Since the predicates are randomly generated, many overlaps are possible and the number of minterms grows quickly. Next, we can see how the performance of $Min^{\mathbf{M}}_{\text{SFA}}$ is affected by the increasing number of states. Finally, $Min^{\mathbf{N}}_{\text{SFA}}$ can quickly minimize SFAs with up to 96 states in less than 1.5 seconds. This experiment shows how $Min^{\mathbf{N}}_{\text{SFA}}$ is not affected by complex theories, while $Min^{\mathbf{H}}_{\text{SFA}}$ and $Min^{\mathbf{M}}_{\text{SFA}}$ are both impractical in this setting.

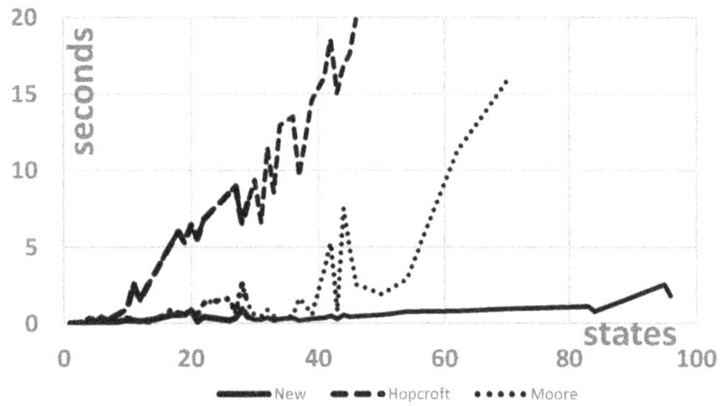


**Figure 10.** Running times for SFAs over the theory $String \times Int$ with 20 seconds timeout.

### 6.5 From Monadic Second-Order logic predicates to DFAs

The relation between regular languages and logic has been extensively investigated in the past [38]. Particularly, every regular language can be expressed as a formula in Monadic Second-Order logic (MSO) over strings, and vice versa. In the rest of the section we assume the alphabet to be a finite set $\Sigma$, say $\{a, b\}$. The following is an example of an MSO formula: $\phi = \exists x.\hat{a}(x)$ where $\hat{a}$ is a unary relation symbol. A string $s \in \Sigma^*$ is a model of $\phi$, iff there exists a *position* $x$ in the string with label $a$. Transforming MSO formulas to automata gives us an algorithm for deciding satisfiability of MSO formulas.

The procedure for converting an MSO formula into a DFA inductively transforms each sub-formula into the corresponding DFA and then combines such DFAs using classical regular language operations. The complexity arises from the presence of free variables, that range over positions. For example, in the formula $\hat{a}(x)$, $x$ occurs free. In order to represent such a language, the alphabet $\Sigma$ is extended with one extra bit to $\Sigma \times \{0, 1\}$. The string $\langle a, 0\rangle\langle b, 0\rangle\langle a, 1\rangle$ over the extended alphabet will then represent that the third position of the string $aba$ is assigned to variable $x$. Following this intuition, every sub-formula $\psi$ is compiled into a DFA over the alphabet $\Sigma \times \{0, 1\}^n$ where $n$ is the number of quantified variables around $\psi$. For each existential quantification a projection is performed which leads to a non-deterministic automaton that must be determinized when a negation on it is performed. This means that each quantifier alternation might therefore lead to an exponential blowup, and in general the procedure has non-elementary complexity.

Despite the non-elementary complexity, practical algorithms that can translate non-trivial MSO formulas are presented in [22]. The tool implementing such algorithms is called Mona. The two key-features of such algorithms are:

1. determinizing and minimizing the intermediate DFA at every step in the transformation, and
2. using BDDs for representing the lifted bit-vector alphabets.

We implemented the same transformation using the BDD solver in our library, and compared the performance using different minimization algorithms.

Figure 11 shows the performance of the transformation for different MSO formulas. The running time for Mona are also shown. The four sub-figures depict the running time for the MSO to DFA transformation for the following formulas:

a) $\exists x_1, \ldots, x_k.\ x_1 < \ldots < x_k$, for $k$ between 2 and 40,

b) $\exists x_1, \ldots, x_k.\ x_1 < \ldots < x_k \wedge a(x_1) \wedge \ldots \wedge a(x_k)$, for $k$ between 2 and 40,

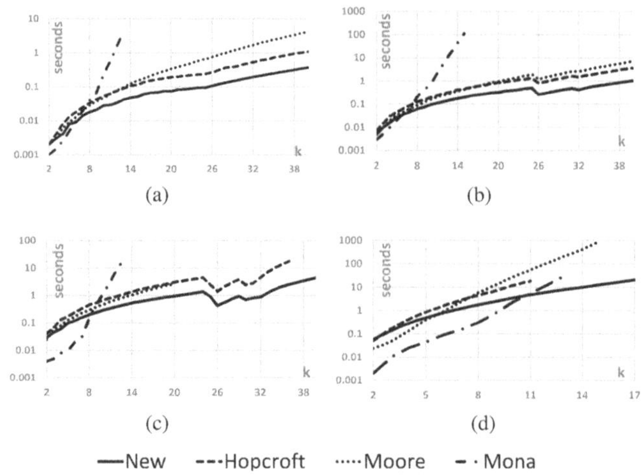


**Figure 11.** MSO to DFA running times. The $y$-axes are in log-scale.

c) $(\exists x_1, \ldots, x_k.\ x_1 < \ldots < x_k \wedge a(x_1) \wedge \ldots \wedge a(x_k)) \vee \exists y.c(y)$, for $k$ between 2 and 40,

d) $\exists x_1, \ldots, x_k.\ f_k$ where $f_2 = (x_1 < x_2 \wedge a(x_1)) \vee c(x_1)$, and for $n > 2$, $f_n = f_{n-1} \wedge ((x_{n-1} < x_n \wedge a(x_{n-1})) \vee c(x_{n-1}))$, for $k$ between 2 and 17.

All the values missing from the graphs are due to the algorithms running out of memory. The figure shows the following behaviors:

- for all of the four classes of formulas, the transformation based on $Min^{\mathbf{N}}_{\text{SFA}}$ is able to create the DFAs for higher values of $k$ (number of nested variables) than those supported by Mona;
- for small instances Mona is faster than our implementation. However for higher values of $k$ our implementation is faster, even when using $Min^{\mathbf{H}}_{\text{SFA}}$ or $Min^{\mathbf{M}}_{\text{SFA}}$;
- while Mona immediately shows an exponential behavior (very steep slope), we couldn't observe such trend in our implementation; and
- $Min^{\mathbf{N}}_{\text{SFA}}$ is faster than $Min^{\mathbf{H}}_{\text{SFA}}$ and $Min^{\mathbf{M}}_{\text{SFA}}$, and it is also less memory intensive (it runs out of memory for higher $k$).

Even though such formulas are only a small benchmark, they are quite representative of the kind of inputs that cause Mona's transformation to be impractical. We believe that the performance improvement of our implementation with respect to Mona is primarily due to a better use of the BDD solver, rather than due to the minimization algorithm.

## 7. Applications

The development of the theory of symbolic automata, including use of minimization, is motivated by several concrete practical problems. Here we discuss three such applications. In each case we illustrate what kind of character theory we are working with, the role of minimization, and focus on the benefits of the symbolic representation.

### 7.1 Regex processing

Practical applications of regular expressions or *regexes* is ubiquitous. Practical regexes differ from schoolbook regular expressions in the following aspects:

- they support, besides non-regular features that go beyond capabilities of finite state automata representations, constructs such as *bounded quantifiers* and *character classes*, that make them more appealing (more succinct) than their classical counterparts, and

- the size of the alphabet is $2^{16}$ due to the widely adopted UTF16 standard of Unicode characters.

As a somewhat unusual example, the regex `^[\uFF10-\uFF19]$` matches the set of digits in the so-called Wide Latin range of Unicode. We let the alphabet algebra be $\mathbf{2}^{\mathrm{BV16}}$. Let the BDD $\beta_w^7$ represent all ASCII word characters as the set of character codes {'0',...,'9','A',...,'Z','_','a',...,'z'}. We write '0' for the code 48, 'a' for the code 97, etc. Let also $\beta_d^7$ represent the set of all decimal digits {'0',...,'9'} and let $\beta_\_$ represent underscore {'_'}. By using the Boolean operations, e.g., $\beta_w^7 \wedge \neg(\beta_d^7 \vee \beta_\_)$ represents the set of all upper- and lowercase ASCII letters. As a regex character class it is expressible as `[\w-[\d_\x7F-\uFFFF]]`.

Regexes are used in many different contexts. A common use of regexes is as a constraint language over strings for *checking* presence or absence of different patterns, e.g., for *security validation* of packet headers in network protocols. Another application, is the use of regexes for *generating* strings that match certain criteria, e.g., for *fuzz testing* applications. As another application consider the *password generation* problem based on constraints given in form of regexes. Here is a concrete set of constraints adopted in password generation:[7]

1. Length is $k$ and characters are in visible ASCII range: `^[\x21-\x7E]{`$k$`}$`
2. There are at least two letters: `[a-zA-Z].*[a-zA-Z]`
3. There is at least one digit: `\d`
4. There is at least one non-word character: `\W`

The smallest feasible value for $k$ is obviously 4. Consider SFAs $A_1, A_2, A_3$, and $A_4$ for each case and let $A$ be their product. For $k = 4$ the minimized version of $A$ has 12 states, and minimizing $A$ with any of $Min^{\mathbf{N}}_{\mathrm{SFA}}$, $Min^{\mathbf{H}}_{\mathrm{SFA}}$, or $Min^{\mathbf{M}}_{\mathrm{SFA}}$ takes a few ms. When $k$ is increased to 40,[8] the number of states increases to 444 and minimizing using $Min^{\mathbf{N}}_{\mathrm{SFA}}$ or $Min^{\mathbf{H}}_{\mathrm{SFA}}$ takes respectively 15 and 90 ms, while $Min^{\mathbf{M}}_{\mathrm{SFA}}$ becomes impractical, taking more than 43 sec (450x slower).

The minimal (canonical) form of $A$ plays an important role here. Together with finiteness of the language accepted by $A$, minimality is used to guarantee a *uniform distribution* of the passwords generated from $A$. Uniformity is achieved by using the canonical form of the state graph together with the canonical form of the guards. While uniform sampling of $a \in [\![\varphi]\!]$ is not possible for arbitrary alphabet theories, it is a well-known feature of BDDs.

### 7.2 Sanitizer analysis

Sanitizers are string transformation routines (special purpose encoders) that are extensively used in web applications, in particular as the first line of defense against cross site scripting (XSS) attacks. There are at least three, semantically very different, string sanitizers involved in a single web page: CssEncoder, UrlEncoder, and HtmlEncoder. A large class of sanitizers (including all the ones mentioned above) can be described and analyzed using *symbolic finite state transducers* (SFTs) [25]. SFAs are used in that context for certain operations over SFTs, for example for checking domain equivalence of SFTs [44]. Since several basic operations are quadratic in the number of states (product, union), minimization comes in handy as a tool for reducing the state space size,

In this setting we choose a different character theory. We use integer linear modular arithmetic (or bit-vector arithmetic of an SMT solver, in our case Z3 [19]) in place of BDDs. The main advantage of this choice is that it makes it possible to seamlessly combine the guards over characters with expressions over *yields*, i.e. the *symbolic outputs* of SFT moves. A concrete example of a yield is the following transformation that takes a character and encodes it as a sequence of five other characters:

$$f: \quad \lambda x.[\texttt{'\&'},\ \texttt{'\#'},\quad (((x \div 10) \bmod 10) + 48),\\ ((x \bmod 10) + 48),\ \texttt{';'}]$$

In general, a yield denotes a function from $\mathfrak{D}_{\mathcal{A}}$ to $\mathfrak{D}_{\mathcal{A}}^*$ (or to $\mathfrak{D}_{\mathcal{B}}$ when the output alphabet $\mathcal{B}$ is different from the input alphabet $\mathcal{A}$). In the yield above, for example, $f$('a') is the sequence ['&','#','9','7',';'] (or the string "a"). Given $f$ as above, a typical SFT move $\rho$ looks like:

$$\rho: \quad q \xrightarrow{(\lambda x.0<x<32)/\lambda x.f(x)} q$$

This specific rule happens to be an HtmlEncoder rule for encoding control characters in state $q$ and remaining in that state. What is the connection with SFAs and the theory mentioned above? For analyzing the idempotence of an encoder with such rules, the encoder is sequentially composed with itself. As a result, this leads to an SFT with more complex guards and outputs (SFTs are closed under composition). When composing the move $\rho$ with itself (i.e., roughly speaking, feeding the five output characters as its inputs again five times in a row), the guard of the composed rule will have sub-conditions such as $0 < (((x \div 10) \bmod 10) + 48) < 32$, which may involve nontrivial arithmetic operations (in this particular case the guard of the composed move will be infeasible). One of the operations performed during *idempotence* analysis is checking whether the original SFT and the composed one have the same *domain*. This reduces to *language equivalence* of SFAs for which the guards involve arithmetic operations of the above kind, that are not readily expressible using the earlier BDD based approach. Domain equivalence of two SFTs checks that both the SFTs accept/reject the same input sequences. Maintaining the SFAs minimal speeds up the equivalence check, and in general provides a better understanding of the structure of the domain language.

In general, the alphabet theory may be a Boolean combination of other decidable theories that are available for example in state-of-the-art SMT solvers. In the context of sanitizers, encoders, and decoders, the alphabet theory is a combination of lists, tuples, bit-vectors and integer linear arithmetic. Lists are used for example to represent composite characters or characters that represent "lookahead" [17]. We demonstrated in the evaluation section that, when the alphabet theory is complex the algorithm $Min^{\mathbf{N}}_{\mathrm{SFA}}$ outperforms both $Min^{\mathbf{H}}_{\mathrm{SFA}}$ and $Min^{\mathbf{M}}_{\mathrm{SFA}}$ by several orders of magnitude enabling analysis of bigger sanitizers/encoders.

### 7.3 Solving Monadic Second Order logic

We already anticipated in Section 6.5 how Monadic Second Order (MSO) logic predicates can be transformed into equivalent DFAs using a non-elementary algorithm. Such algorithm also provides a decision procedure for MSO.

We already discussed how several techniques have been introduced by the tool Mona [22] in order to make such transformation practical. Keeping the DFA minimal at any step in the transformation is one of the key techniques. We gave experimental evidence of the fact that the new algorithm presented in this paper, and in general the use of symbolic automata, can further move the barrier of solvable MSO formulas, in terms of both formula's size (number of nested quantifiers) and running times.

[7] Recall the standard convention: a regex without the start-anchor ^ matches any prefix and a regex without the end-anchor $ matches any suffix.

[8] Relevant values of $k$ in the above scenario depend on the concrete context, but range between 4 and 128

## 8. Related work

***DFA Minimization:*** The classical algorithms for DFA minimization have been studied and analyzed extensively in several different aspects. In particular, Moore's algorithm is studied in [10] where it is shown that, by a clever change of data structures, its complexity can be reduced from $O(kn^2)$ to $O(kn \log n)$. The bound $O(kn \log n)$ has been shown to be tight for Hopcroft's algorithm [6, 8]. Brzozowski [13] observed that a DFA can be minimized by reversing its transitions, then determinizing, then reversing its transitions again, and finally determinizing again. However, due to the determinization steps, this procedure is exponential and we decided not to consider it in this paper. Linear time algorithms have been studied for minimizing acyclic automata [32, 36] and automata containing only simple cycles [2]. The book chapter [7] provides an in-depth study of the state-of-the-art techniques for automata minimization, including the approaches mentioned above and several other ones. Watson [45] also provides an elegant classification of the classical minimization algorithms based on their structural properties.

In the case of DFAs, it matters whether the DFA to be minimized is partial (incomplete), because it may be useful to avoid completion of DFAs with sparse transition graphs. Minimization of partial DFAs is studied in [5, 39, 40]. In this setting the complexity of the algorithm depends on the number of transitions rather than on the size of the alphabet, however, in the case of DFAs these two quantities are generally related. In contrast, in a normalized SFA the number of transitions is independent of the alphabet size, and it is at most $n^2$ where $n$ is the number of states. One concrete difference between the minimization algorithms of complete DFAs versus partial DFAs is that the initial value of the waiting set $W$ (see Figure 3) for the partial case must contain both the sets $F$ and $F^c$ [40]. We believe that similar modifications may be applied to $Min^{\mathbf{N}}_{\text{SFA}}$, even though we expect that in the case of SFAs the benefit of using partiality might not be as visible. In fact, a complete SFA has at most $n$ transitions more than a partial one. Moreover, in the case of SFAs, there are different ways for completing an SFA, e.g., one can effectively restrict the alphabet to only those characters that are mentioned in the trimmed SFA (SFA without dead-end states) prior to completion.

***Different Notions of Minimization:*** A notion of incremental minimization is investigated in [47]. An incremental minimization algorithm can be halted at any point and produce a partially minimal DFA which is equivalent to the starting DFA, and has less or equal number of states. If the algorithm runs till completion, a minimal DFA is computed. In this paper we did not address incremental computation, however it would be interesting to identify variants of the presented algorithms with such a property. A similar idea, based on intermediate computation results, is used for a modular minimization algorithm in [14]. An algorithm for building a minimal DFA accepting a given finite set of strings is presented in [15]. The same paper investigates the problem of "maintaining" a minimal DFA when applying modification such as node, edge, or string deletion and insertion to an already minimal DFA. This class of problems is called dynamic minimization.

A parallel version of Moore's algorithm is presented in [37]. We are not aware of a parallel version of Hopcroft's algorithm. We leave as an open problem identifying parallel algorithms corresponding to $Min^{\mathbf{H}}_{\text{SFA}}$ and $Min^{\mathbf{N}}_{\text{SFA}}$.

A variant of minimization called hyper-minimization is investigated in [24]. Given an input DFA $A$, a DFA $A'$ is hyper minimal with respect to $A$ if it is the smallest DFA that differs from $A$ only on a finite number of strings. In the case of symbolic automata, this definition doesn't extend naturally due to potentially infinite alphabet. A less restrictive notion called $k$-minimization is studied in [21]. Given an input DFA $A$, a DFA $A'$ is $k$-minimal with respect to $A$ if it is the smallest DFA that differs from $A$ only on strings of length smaller or equal than $k$. This second restriction naturally extends to symbolic automata. A more general notion is that of minimization up to $E$-equivalence, where given a regular language $E$, the DFA $A'$ is allowed to differ from $A$ on a set of strings $L \subseteq E$ [23]. Extending the results of [21, 23] to symbolic automata is an interesting open research direction. Relationships between minimality and selection of final states are studied in [35] where *uniform* minimality is defined as minimality for any choice of final states.

***Automata with Predicates:*** The concept of automata with predicates instead of concrete symbols was first mentioned in [46] and was first discussed in [41] in the context of natural language processing. A symbolic generalization of Moore's algorithm was first discussed in [43]. To the best of our knowledge, no other minimization algorithms have been studied for SFAs. The MONA implementation [22] provides decision procedures for monadic second-order logic, and it relies on a highly-optimized BDD-based representation for automata which has seen extensive engineering effort [30]. Therefore, the use of BDDs in the context of automata is not new, but is used here as an example of a Boolean algebra that seems particularly well suited for working with Unicode alphabets.

***Minimization of Other Automata:*** The problem of automata minimization has been investigated in several other settings. A new approach for minimizing *nondeterministic* automata and nondeterministic Büchi automata has been studied in [33]. The problem of minimizing weighted automata (automata computing functions from strings to a semi-ring) is studied in [20]. Classical minimization algorithms are used in this setting, and we hope that the results shown in this paper can extend to such domain. The minimization problem has also been studied for timed automata [11] and register automata [16]. These models are able to represent infinite domains, but not arbitrary theories. An orthogonal direction is to extend the techniques presented in this paper to minimization of symbolic *tree* automata [18].

***Other Applications:*** The problem of learning of symbolic transducers has recently been studied in [12]. Classical automata learning is based on Angluin's algorithm [4], which fundamentally relies on DFA minimality. An almost unexplored topic is whether such learning techniques can be extended to SFAs.

## 9. Conclusions

We presented three algorithms for minimizing Symbolic Finite Automata (SFAs). We first extended Moore's algorithm and Hopcroft's algorithm to the symbolic setting. We then show that, while in the classical setting Hopcroft's algorithm is the fastest known minimization algorithm, in the presence of symbolic alphabets, it might incur in an exponential blowup. To address this issue, we introduced a new minimization algorithm that fully benefits from the symbolic representation of the alphabet and does not suffer from the exponential blowup. The new algorithm is a refinement of Hopcroft's one in which splits are computed locally without having to consider the entire input alphabet. The new algorithm can also be adopted in the classical setting. Finally, we implemented all the algorithms and provided experimental evidence that the new minimization algorithm is the most efficient one in practice.

***Acknowledgments.*** We thank Marco Almeida for helping us accessing his benchmark of randomly generated DFAs. Loris D'Antoni was supported by the NSF Expeditions in Computing award CCF 1138996, and this work was done as part of an internship at Microsoft Research. We also thank the anonymous reviewers for their insightful comments.

## References


[1] BRICS finite state automata utilities. http://www.brics.dk/automaton/.

[2] J. Almeida and M. Zeitoun. Description and analysis of a bottom-up DFA minimization algorithm. *Information Processing Letters*, 107(2):52–59, 2008.

[3] M. Almeida, N. Moreira, and R. Reis. On the performance of automata minimization algorithms. Technical Report DCC-2007-03, University of Porto, 2007.

[4] D. Angluin. Learning regular sets from queries and counterexamples. *Inf. Comput.*, 75(2):87–106, 1987.

[5] M.-P. Béal and M. Crochemore. Minimizing incomplete automata. In *Finite-State Methods and Natural Language Processing, 7th International Workshop*, pages 9–16, 2008.

[6] J. Berstel, L. Boasson, and O. Carton. Hopcroft's automaton minimization algorithm and Sturmian words. In *DMTCS'2008*, pages 355–366, 2008.

[7] J. Berstel, L. Boasson, O. Carton, and I. Fagnot. Minimization of automata. To appear in Handbook of Automata, 2011.

[8] J. Berstel and O. Carton. On the complexity of Hopcroft's state minimization algorithm. In *CIAA'2004*, volume 3317, pages 35–44, 2004.

[9] N. Bjørner, V. Ganesh, R. Michel, and M. Veanes. An SMT-LIB format for sequences and regular expressions. In P. Fontaine and A. Goel, editors, *SMT'12*, pages 76–86, 2012.

[10] N. Blum. An $0(n \log n)$ implementation of the standard method for minimizing $n$-state finite automata. *Information Processing Letters*, 57:65–69, 1996.

[11] M. Bojaczyk and S. Lasota. A machine-independent characterization of timed languages. In A. Czumaj, K. Mehlhorn, A. Pitts, and R. Wattenhofer, editors, *Automata, Languages, and Programming*, volume 7392 of *LNCS*, pages 92–103. Springer Berlin Heidelberg, 2012.

[12] M. Botinčan and D. Babić. Sigma*: symbolic learning of input-output specifications. In *POPL '13*, pages 443–456, New York, NY, USA, 2013. ACM.

[13] J. A. Brzozowski. Canonical regular expressions and minimal state graphs for definite events. In *Proc. Sympos. Math. Theory of Automata*, pages 529–561, New York, 1963.

[14] D. Bustan. Modular minimization of deterministic finite-state machines. In *In 6th International Workshop on Formal Methods for Industrial Critical Systems*, pages 163–178, 2001.

[15] R. C. Carrasco and M. L. Forcada. Incremental construction and maintenance of minimal finite-state automata. *Comput. Linguist.*, 28(2):207–216, June 2002.

[16] S. Cassel, B. Jonsson, F. Howar, and B. Steffen. A succinct canonical register automaton model for data domains with binary relations. In S. Chakraborty and M. Mukund, editors, *ATVA 2012*, volume 7561 of *LNCS*, pages 57–71. Springer, 2012.

[17] L. D'Antoni and M. Veanes. Equivalence of extended symbolic finite transducers. In N. Sharygina and H. Veith, editors, *CAV 2013*, volume 8044 of *LNCS*, pages 624–639. Springer, 2013.

[18] L. D'Antoni, M. Veanes, B. Livshits, and D. Molnar. Fast: A transducer-based language for tree manipulation. Technical Report MSR-TR-2012-123, Microsoft Research, November 2012.

[19] L. de Moura and N. Bjørner. Z3: An Efficient SMT Solver. In *TACAS'08*, LNCS. Springer, 2008.

[20] M. Droste, W. Kuich, and H. Vogler. *Handbook of Weighted Automata*. Springer Publishing Company, Incorporated, 1st edition, 2009.

[21] P. Gawrychowski, A. Jež, and A. Maletti. On minimising automata with errors. In *MFCS'11*, pages 327–338, Berlin, Heidelberg, 2011. Springer.

[22] J. Henriksen, J. Jensen, M. Jørgensen, N. Klarlund, B. Paige, T. Rauhe, and A. Sandholm. Mona: Monadic second-order logic in practice. In *TACAS '95*, volume 1019 of *LNCS*. Springer, 1995.

[23] M. Holzer and S. Jakobi. From equivalence to almost-equivalence, and beyond – minimizing automata with errors. In H.-C. Yen and O. Ibarra, editors, *Developments in Language Theory*, volume 7410 of *LNCS*, pages 190–201. Springer, 2012.

[24] M. Holzer and A. Maletti. An nlogn algorithm for hyper-minimizing a (minimized) deterministic automaton. *Theor. Comput. Sci.*, 411(38-39):3404–3413, 2010.

[25] P. Hooimeijer, B. Livshits, D. Molnar, P. Saxena, and M. Veanes. Fast and precise sanitizer analysis with Bek. In *USENIX Security*, August 2011.

[26] P. Hooimeijer and M. Veanes. An evaluation of automata algorithms for string analysis. In *VMCAI'11*, volume 6538 of *LNCS*, pages 248–262. Springer, 2011.

[27] J. Hopcroft. An $n \log n$ algorithm for minimizing states in a finite automaton. In Z. Kohavi, editor, *Theory of machines and computations, Proc. Internat. Sympos., Technion, Haifa, 1971*, pages 189–196, New York, 1971. Academic Press.

[28] J. E. Hopcroft and J. D. Ullman. *Introduction to Automata Theory, Languages, and Computation*. Addison Wesley, 1979.

[29] D. Huffman. The synthesis of sequential switching circuits. *Journal of the Franklin Institute*, 257(3–4):161–190,275–303, 1954.

[30] N. Klarlund, A. Møller, and M. I. Schwartzbach. MONA implementation secrets. *International Journal of Foundations of Computer Science*, 13(4):571–586, 2002.

[31] T. Knuutila. Re-describing an algorithm by Hopcroft. *Theor. Comput. Sci.*, 250(1-2):333–363, 2001.

[32] S. L. Krivol. Algorithms for minimization of finite acyclic automata and pattern matching in terms. *Cybernetics*, 27:324–331, 1991.

[33] R. Mayr and L. Clemente. Advanced automata minimization. In *POPL'13*, pages 63–74, 2013.

[34] E. F. Moore. Gedanken-experiments on sequential machines. *Automata studies, Annals of mathematics studies*, (34):129–153, 1956.

[35] A. Restivo and R. Vaglica. Some remarks on automata minimality. In G. Mauri and A. Leporati, editors, *DLT'2011*, volume 6795 of *LNCS*, pages 15–27. Springer, 2011.

[36] D. Revuz. Minimisation of acyclic deterministic automata in linear time. *Theoret. Comput. Sci.*, 92:181–189, 1992.

[37] A. Tewari, U. Srivastava, and P. Gupta. A parallel DFA minimization algorithm. In *HiPC 2002*, volume 2552 of *LNCS*, pages 34–40. Springer, 2002.

[38] W. Thomas. Languages, automata, and logic. In *Handbook of Formal Languages*, pages 389–455. Springer, 1996.

[39] A. Valmari. Fast brief practical DFA minimization. *Information Processing Letters*, 112:213–217, 2012.

[40] A. Valmari and P. Lehtinen. Efficient minimization of DFAs with partial transition functions. In S. Albers and P. Weil, editors, *STACS 2008*, pages 645–656, Dagstuhl, 2008.

[41] G. van Noord and D. Gerdemann. Finite state transducers with predicates and identities. *Grammars*, 4(3):263–286, 2001.

[42] M. Veanes, N. Bjørner, and L. de Moura. Symbolic automata constraint solving. In C. Fermüller and A. Voronkov, editors, *LPAR-17*, volume 6397 of *LNCS/ARCoSS*, pages 640–654. Springer, 2010.

[43] M. Veanes, P. de Halleux, and N. Tillmann. Rex: Symbolic regular expression explorer. In *ICST'10*, pages 498–507. IEEE, 2010.

[44] M. Veanes, P. Hooimeijer, B. Livshits, D. Molnar, and N. Bjørner. Symbolic finite state transducers: Algorithms and applications. In *POPL'12*, pages 137–150, 2012.

[45] B. W. Watson. A taxonomy of finite automata minimization algorithms. Computing Science Report 93/44, Eindhoven University of Technology, January 1995.

[46] B. W. Watson. Implementing and using finite automata toolkits. In *Extended finite state models of language*, pages 19–36, New York, NY, USA, 1999. Cambridge University Press.

[47] B. W. Watson and J. Daciuk. An efficient incremental DFA minimization algorithm. *Nat. Lang. Eng.*, 9(1):49–64, Mar. 2003.

# Consistency Analysis of Decision-Making Programs *

Swarat Chaudhuri
Rice University
swarat@rice.edu

Azadeh Farzan
University of Toronto
azadeh@cs.toronto.edu

Zachary Kincaid
University of Toronto
zkincaid@cs.toronto.edu

## Abstract

Applications in many areas of computing make discrete decisions under *uncertainty*, for reasons such as limited numerical precision in calculations and errors in sensor-derived inputs. As a result, individual decisions made by such programs may be nondeterministic, and lead to contradictory decisions at different points of an execution. This means that an otherwise correct program may execute along paths, that it would not follow under its ideal semantics, violating essential program invariants on the way. A program is said to be *consistent* if it does not suffer from this problem despite uncertainty in decisions.

In this paper, we present a sound, automatic program analysis for verifying that a program is consistent in this sense. Our analysis proves that each decision made along a program execution is consistent with the decisions made earlier in the execution. The proof is done by generating an invariant that abstracts the set of all decisions made along executions that end at a program location $l$, then verifying, using a fixpoint constraint-solver, that no contradiction can be derived when these decisions are combined with new decisions made at $l$.

We evaluate our analysis on a collection of programs implementing algorithms in *computational geometry*. Consistency is known to be a critical, frequently-violated, and thoroughly studied correctness property in geometry, but ours is the first attempt at automated verification of consistency of geometric algorithms. Our benchmark suite consists of implementations of convex hull computation, triangulation, and point location algorithms. On almost all examples that are not consistent (with two exceptions), our analysis is able to verify consistency within a few minutes.

***Categories and Subject Descriptors*** D.2.4 [*Software/Program Verification*]: Correctness proofs; F.3.2 [*Semantics of Programming Languages*]: Program analysis; F.2.2 [*Computational Geometry and Object Modelling*]: Geometric algorithms, languages, and systems; G.4 [*Mathematical Software*]: Reliability and robustness

***Keywords*** Program Analysis; Uncertainty; Consistency; Geometry; Robustness

* This research was partially supported by NSF Award #1156059 and an NSERC Discover Grant.



*POPL '14*, January 22–24, 2014, San Diego, CA, USA.
Copyright © 2014 ACM 978-1-4503-2544-8/14/01...$15.00.
http://dx.doi.org/10.1145/2535838.2535858

**if** ($\texttt{Left}(p,q)$) **then** $L_1$ **else** $L_4$;
**if** ($\texttt{Left}(q,r)$) **then** $L_2$ **else** $L_5$;
**if** ($\texttt{Left}(p,r)$) **then** $L_3$ **else** $L_6$

**Figure 1.** A possibly-inconsistent code snippet

## 1. Introduction

The problem of making decisions under uncertainty has fascinated computer scientists for a long time [13]. Abstractly, a decision-making process is a program that gathers information about an external world using a set of queries, and based on this information, makes changes to its discrete internal state. An issue with such programs is that the information that they gather from the world may be *uncertain*, and this uncertainty may affect program's decisions. Even a single "wrong" decision may lead the program down code paths that were never meant to be followed, leading to unforeseen errors.

For example, consider a program that queries the world for the relative positions of three points $p$, $q$, and $r$ on a line. Let $\texttt{Left}(u,v)$ denote the *decision* by the program that $u$ lies to the left of $v$, and $\mathit{Left}(u,v)$ the *fact* that $u$ is actually to the left of $v$. Now suppose the program makes the decisions $\texttt{Left}(p,q)$ and $\texttt{Left}(q,r)$. In this case, the program should also decide that $\texttt{Left}(p,r)$, as the laws of geometry demand that

$$(\mathit{Left}(p,q) \wedge \mathit{Left}(q,r)) \implies \mathit{Left}(p,r). \quad (1)$$

However, uncertainty creates a difference between what ought to be and what is. Different queries to the world can be independently uncertain, and if $p$, $q$ and $r$ are close enough to be within the margin of error, the program may very well decide from the final query that "not $\texttt{Left}(p,r)$" holds. Suppose now that the program in question looks like the one in Fig. 1. Then, in the above scenario, it will execute the code $\texttt{L}_1;\texttt{L}_2;\texttt{L}_6$, a sequence that would not be executed *under any input* in the program's ideal semantics, where the laws of geometry hold. Since algorithm design often does not consider this scenario, the consequence could be a serious error.

A decision-making program is *consistent* if it is immune from errors like the one described above. Abstractly, let $\mathcal{R}$ be an axiomatic specification of the "laws" that we know to hold in a world $\Theta$ (e.g. Eqn. 1). A program is consistent if it does not contradict any axioms in $\mathcal{R}$ no matter what answers it receives as the result of its queries to the world $\Theta$.

Consistency is an essential concern in applications where programs make boolean decisions under uncertainty. It is, for example, a thoroughly studied problem in computational geometry [7, 15, 16, 21, 26], where programs make decisions about relative positions of objects in continuous geometric spaces[1]. Often, these positions can

[1] In the geometry literature, consistency is known as *robustness*. We avoid the latter term given its recent use [4, 5, 19] in the program verification literature to denote an entirely different concept.

```
if Left(p, q)
    then L1;
        if Left(q, r)
            then L2; L3
            else L5; if Left(p, r) then L3 else L6
    else
        L4;
        if Left(q, r)
            then L2; if Left(p, r) then L3 else L6
            else L5; L6
```

**Figure 2.** Consistent variant of code in Fig. 1.

only be known with limited degree of certainty and up to a limited level of accuracy. For instance, a robot doing geometric reasoning to detect collisions with other objects must base its discrete decisions on uncertain sensor data. Even on a standalone computer, the outcomes of discrete queries about geometric datasets are typically uncertain due to numerical inaccuracies [22]. It is well-known that inconsistency between such decisions can cause everyday geometric algorithms to crash, go into infinite loops, and violate essential postconditions [21].

At the same time, consistency in our sense is not easily enforced through usual software engineering practices. It is difficult to *test* a program for consistency since, by definition, errors due to uncertainty may not be reproducible. Furthermore, as software is typically designed without uncertainty in mind, consistency is usually outside the scope of manual reasoning about algorithms. For example, most algorithm designers *assume* the axioms of geometry to hold to reason about correctness of their designs, and would not imagine situations where they might break down when these axioms are contradicted. Finally, reasoning about consistency requires one to relate decisions made at different points in a program execution to each other. Most programmers find this type of global reasoning about programs to be inherently difficult.

Given all this, the problem of *automatic formal verification* of the consistency of a decision-making program seems to be important. Intriguingly, there is very little prior work on this problem. Researchers in application areas like computational geometry have traditionally steered clear of static reasoning about consistency, instead focusing on dynamic approaches [21]. While there is an emerging literature on quantitative reasoning about uncertain programs [4, 5, 19] in the formal methods community, to our knowledge there has been no prior work on verifying that a program makes sequences of discrete decisions consistently. In this paper, we present a sound, automatic program analysis to address this verification problem.

Our analysis applies to infinite-state programs that query a world consisting of an arbitrary number of abstractly defined data objects. A *decision* is the outcome of a query. We model uncertainty using nondeterminism, assuming that each query by the program can return either true or false. To see how a program can be consistent under such a model, consider the code in Fig. 2, which is equivalent to the program in Fig. 1 in the absence of uncertainty (i.e., when $\texttt{Left}(x, y)$ if and only if $\mathit{Left}(x, y)$). However, even if the `Left` queries resolve nondeterministically due to uncertainty, this code is still guaranteed to satisfy the axiom in Eqn. (1). The subtle difference between the two codes is that the one in Fig. 1 does not query a fact when, from the context and the set of axioms, the only non-contradictory answer to the query is known.

To automatically prove the consistency of programs like the one in Fig. 1, we must track the path-sensitive dependencies between different decisions made by the program. This is especially challenging when the program manipulates an unbounded number of objects. For example, suppose that a program decides, by repeatedly querying the world, that

$$\texttt{Left}(p_1, p_2), \texttt{Left}(p_2, p_3), \ldots, \texttt{Left}(p_{n-1}, p_n)$$

for objects $p_1, \ldots, p_n$. If the program now also queries for the relative positions of $p_1$ and $p_n$, we may have a consistency violation. This is because we have $\texttt{Left}(p_1, p_n)$ as a logical consequence of the program's decisions by Eqn. 1 while due to uncertainty the result of this query may very well be "not $\texttt{Left}(p_1, p_n)$." To prove consistency, we must be able to reason that this type of violations, namely those that are derived through *unbounded trees* of reasoning, cannot occur.

Our approach to the automation of such proofs is based on an inductive argument. First, for each program location $l$, we compute an invariant $\mathcal{H}_l$ — called the *history invariant* — that abstracts the set of all decisions made along all possible executions leading to $l$. Inductively, we assume the decisions in $\mathcal{H}_l$ to be mutually consistent. Next we compute a *current-decision invariant* $d_l$ that abstracts the set of *new* decisions that may be made at $l$. Consistency verification now amounts to establishing that no decision in the set represented by $d_l$, taken together with a subset of decisions in $\mathcal{H}_l$, can violate an axiom. We show that this check can be accomplished using a standard fixpoint constraint solver [14]. Decisions taken during the execution of a program, over a collection of input objects, are abstracted by tuples of integers (where integers stand for object identifiers); e.g. $\langle 1, 2 \rangle$ may stand for the decision $\texttt{Left}(p_1, p2)$. This then accommodates the abstraction of decision invariants (as defined above) by integer linear arithmetic formulae.

We evaluate our analysis by applying it to a suite of programs from the domain of computational geometry [7, 21], including implementations of standard algorithms for convex hull computations, triangulation, and point location algorithms. While small in size, programs like these are at the heart of geometric libraries used by large real-world systems such as CAD, Geographical Information Systems, Computer Graphics, and various Scientific Computing applications. These examples are also complex: the reasons why they satisfy consistency or fail to do so are often subtle, and small, innocent-looking changes to the code can turn a consistent algorithm into an inconsistent one, or vice versa. However, in almost all of the programs that are actually consistent, our analysis is able to prove consistency automatically and efficiently.

We summarize the contributions of this paper as follows:

- We formulate the problem of verifying the consistency of infinite-state decision-making programs (Sec. 2), and give a sound, automatic program analysis to solve it. (Sec. 4).
- We identify an application domain for our analysis where consistency is a critical correctness property, and where program analysis has not been tried before (Sec. 3).
- We provide a prototype implementation of our system, and evaluate the practical utility of the system using a comprehensive suite of convex hull and triangulation algorithms. (Sec. 5).

## 2. Formalizing consistency

In this section, we formalize the property of consistency for decision-making programs. We start by defining the "worlds" that are queried by our programs. These queries are answered with uncertainty, and it is this uncertainty that may cause a violation of consistency.

### 2.1 Modelling the world

A world consists of a set of typed objects together with a set of predicates that are used to query various relationships between these objects. Formally, a *world* is a tuple $\Theta = \langle \mathit{Base}, O, \mathcal{Q}, \mathcal{R} \rangle$, where $Base$ is a set of base types, $O$ is universe of *objects* with types ranging over $Base$, $\mathcal{Q}$ is a set of *predicate symbols* whose arguments have types in $Base$, and $\mathcal{R}$ is a finite set of *axioms*, where an axiom is a *universally quantified* first-order formula over the predicates in $\mathcal{Q}$.

Intuitively, the predicates in $\mathcal{Q}$ form the "interface" between programs and the world $\Theta$. We assume for easier exposition that each $A \in \mathcal{Q}$ has the same arity $m$. The axioms $\mathcal{R}$ codify the laws of the world — e.g., the laws of geometry. Since the understanding of nontrivial worlds is often partial, we do not expect our axioms to be complete in a mathematical sense.

*Example* 1. Let $\Theta_{tc} = \langle\{\texttt{1DPoint}\}, O, \mathcal{Q}_{tc}, \mathcal{R}_{tc}\rangle$ be a world in which `1DPoint` is the type of points arranged on a line, $O$ is a set of such points, and $\mathcal{Q}_{tc}$ consists of a single predicate *Left*. The predicate $Left(u, v)$ holds for `1DPoints` $u$ and $v$ iff $u$ lies to the left of $v$—i.e., if $u.x < v.x$, where $u.x$ and $v.x$ are respectively the coordinates of $u$ and $v$ with respect to a fixed origin. A sensible set of axioms $\mathcal{R}_{tc}$ for $\Theta_{tc}$ is as follows:

1. The transitivity axiom used in the introduction:
$$\forall y_1, y_2, y_3 : \\ y_1 \neq y_2 \wedge y_2 \neq y_3 \wedge y_3 \neq y_1 \implies \\ (Left(y_1, y_2) \wedge Left(y_2, y_3) \implies Left(y_1, y_3)).$$
2. An axiom that asserts that *Left* is "complete" — i.e., any two distinct points on the line are related by *Left*:
$$\forall y_1, y_2 : y_1 \neq y_2 \implies (Left(y_1, y_2) \vee Left(y_2, y_1)). \quad \square$$

To reduce notation, we adopt two simple syntactic conventions while writing down axioms. First, we drop the explicit universal quantifiers over the axiom variables. Second, without loss of generality, we use distinct variable names in the axioms to represent distinct objects in models of the theory. For example, the first axiom in the above example is written simply as
$$Left(y_1, y_2) \wedge Left(y_2, y_3) \implies Left(y_1, y_3),$$
the assumptions $(y_1 \neq y_2)$, $(y_2 \neq y_3)$, and $(y_1 \neq y_3)$ following from the fact that $y_1$ and $y_2$ are different symbols. It is acceptable, however, to write the axiom $R(x, x)$ to state that a predicate $R$ is reflexive.

### 2.2 Programs

Next we define a core language DMP of decision-making programs. Programs in this language are a symbolic transition systems that can manipulate both individual objects and *lists* of objects.

There is a key modelling question in the definition of DMP: how do we model the uncertainty in a program's queries about the world? Our definition does this via nondeterminism: we assume that *every* call of a program to a world predicate may return an incorrect answer.

This model may appear too conservative at first sight, given that we do not model uncertainty quantitatively. However, it has several advantages. The first and foremost is its *generality*: the model is equally applicable to settings where uncertainty is the result of sensing errors as it is to the settings where floating-point error is the source of uncertainty. Any reasonable quantitative model of uncertainty, on the other hand, would have to be domain-specific, and perhaps consider low-level details of the hardware used for sensing or computation.

Second, our model is simpler and therefore more amenable to automated reasoning than quantitative models. Indeed, given the highly challenging nature of the consistency analysis problem, this model offers a "sweet spot" for static analysis.

Finally, our empirical experience with the model is satisfactory. We ran some experiments with our benchmark examples from Sec. 5 for the case when uncertainty is only due to numerical error. For the examples that are inconsistent under our model, it was always possible to produce a concrete input that forces the program to violate basic invariants under floating-point semantics. In other words, these examples would be inconsistent under any other reasonable definition of consistency.

***Program syntax.*** Let us fix a world $\Theta = \langle Base, O, \mathcal{Q}, \mathcal{R}\rangle$ and a universe of *variables*. Each variable represents either an object in $O$ or a list of such objects. Variables of base types are denoted by $x, x_1, x_2, \ldots$, and variables of list types (representing collections of objects) are denoted by $X, X_1, X_2, \ldots$.

We assume an alphabet[2] $\mathtt{Q}$ of symbols whose members have a one-to-one correspondence with the predicates in $\mathcal{Q}$. For $A \in \mathcal{Q}$, we denote the corresponding symbol in $\mathtt{Q}$ by $\mathtt{A}$. Also, we define a symbol $\bar{\mathtt{A}}$ for each $\mathtt{A} \in \mathtt{Q}$ and let $\bar{\mathtt{Q}}$ be the set of such symbols. It is assumed that $\mathtt{Q}$ and $\bar{\mathtt{Q}}$ do not have any overlap with each other or with $\mathcal{Q}$. Intuitively, for objects $p_1, \ldots, p_m$, the notation $\mathtt{A}(p_1, \ldots, p_m)$ represents the decision made by the program that the fact $A(p_1, \ldots, p_m)$ holds, and $\bar{\mathtt{A}}(p_1, \ldots, p_m)$ represents the decision that the fact $\neg A(p_1, \ldots, p_m)$ holds.

We allow a program to test and manipulate its local variables using the following primitives:

- We allow boolean expressions that test whether a list is empty: $X = \emptyset$ and $X \neq \emptyset$.
- We allow the following kinds of assignments to variables:
  1. $x_1 := x_2$. An assignment where an object-valued variable $x_1$ is set to the value of another object-valued variable $x_2$.
  2. $x := first(X)$ and $x := last(X)$. Respectively set $x$ to the value of the first and last element of the list $X$. The list $X$ is not updated.
  3. $x := next(X)$ and $x := pop(X)$. Respectively remove the first and last elements of the list $X$, and set $x$ to the value of this element.
  4. $X := \emptyset$. Sets $X$ to the empty list.
  5. $X_1 := X_2$. Sets the list $X_1$ to the value of the list $X_2$.
  6. $prepend(x, X)$. Adds the object $x$ to the front of the list $X$.
  7. $append(x, X)$. Adds the object $x$ to the end of the list $X$.

The syntax of DMP programs is now given as follows:

**Definition 1** (Programs). *A program over a world $\Theta$ is a tuple $P = \langle Loc, l_0, \mathcal{T}\rangle$, where $Loc$ is a finite set of* locations, *$l_0 \in Loc$ is the* initial location, *and $\mathcal{T}$ is a set of* transitions. *A transition $\langle l \,|\, T \,|\, l'\rangle$ from a location $l$ to a location $l'$ is of one of the following forms:*

*1.* $\langle l \,|\, \mathtt{A}(x_1, \ldots, x_m) \,|\, l'\rangle$
*2.* $\langle l \,|\, \bar{\mathtt{A}}(x_1, \ldots, x_m) \,|\, l'\rangle$
*3.* $\langle l \,|\, assume(b) \,|\, l'\rangle$
*4.* $\langle l \,|\, U \,|\, l'\rangle$

*where $\mathtt{A} \in \mathtt{Q}$; $\bar{\mathtt{A}} \in \bar{\mathtt{Q}}$; $x_i \in Var$; $b$ is a boolean expression; and each $U$ is an assignment of one the forms above.*

Each transition $\langle l \mid T \mid l'\rangle$ takes the program from location $l$ to location $l'$. Transitions of forms (1) and (2) represent queries to the world and decisions made on basis of those queries. A transition of form (1) is taken when a call to $\mathtt{A} \in \mathtt{Q}$ returns $true$, and one of form (2) is taken when it returns $false$. Transitions of form (3) are local tests on program variables while those of form (4) are updates to variables. For instance, the transition $\langle l \mid x := first(X) \mid l'\rangle$ is executed when control is at $l$, sets $x$ to the first element of $X$ (without updating $X$), and moves the control to $l'$.

[2] Note the typewriter font used for $\mathtt{Q}$, which distinguishes this set from $\mathcal{Q}$.

The sets of locations and variables of $P$ are respectively denoted by $Loc(P)$ and $Var(P)$. Note that a location may have multiple outgoing or incoming transitions. However, we assume, without loss of generality, that whenever $P$ has a query transition $\langle l \mid \alpha(\ldots) \mid l' \rangle$, then it has no other outgoing transition at $l$. We denote by $Loc_P^{\alpha}$ the set of locations in $P$ that have an outgoing transition of the above form. Collectively, locations like this are known as *query locations*.

We assume all predicates in $P$ to be well-typed: if a transition is guarded by $\mathtt{A}(x_1, \ldots, x_m)$ and $x_i$ is of type $\tau_i$, then the type of $\mathtt{A}$ is $(\tau_1 \times \cdots \times \tau_m)$.

***Uncertain Semantics.*** Now we sketch the semantics of programs under uncertainty. Let a *state* of $P$ be a pair $s = (l, \sigma)$, where $l$ is a location and $\sigma$ is a function that maps variables $x_i$ and $X_i$ to appropriately typed values. The set of states of $P$ is denoted by $\Sigma(P)$.

The semantics of $P$ is defined using a labelled transition system $\langle \Sigma, \rightharpoonup, \Sigma_{in} \rangle$, where $\rightharpoonup$ is a set of *semantic transitions* and $\Sigma_{in}$ is a set of *initial states*. An initial state of $P$ is a state of the form $(l_0, \sigma)$ for some $\sigma$, and where each object $o$ appears at most once in at most one list in the domain of $\sigma$ (i.e., initially the contents of the lists are repetition-free and pairwise disjoint).

The set $\rightharpoonup$ is the least relation such that for all transitions $t = \langle l \,|\, T \,|\, l' \rangle$ in $P$,

- If $T$ is a query $\alpha(x_1, \ldots, x_m)$ (for $\alpha \in \mathtt{Q} \cup \overline{\mathtt{Q}}$), then we have $(l, \sigma) \stackrel{t}{\rightharpoonup} (l', \sigma)$ for all $\sigma$.
- If $T$ is an assignment $x := e$ or $X := E$, then for each state $(l, \sigma)$, we have $(l, \sigma) \stackrel{t}{\rightharpoonup} (l', \sigma')$, where $\sigma'$ is obtained by updating the variables of $P$ according to the semantics of assignments sketched earlier.
- If $T$ is a test $assume(b)$ and $(l, \sigma)$ is a state that satisfies $b$, then we have $(l, \sigma) \stackrel{t}{\rightharpoonup} (l', \sigma)$.

We define an *(uncertain) execution* of $P$ as a finite sequence $\rho = (l_0, \sigma_0) \stackrel{t_0}{\rightharpoonup} (l_1, \sigma_1) \cdots (l_n, \sigma_n)$ such that $(l_0, \sigma_0) \in \Sigma_{in}$ and for all $i$, $(l_i, \sigma_i) \stackrel{t_i}{\rightharpoonup} (l_{i+1}, \sigma_{i+1})$. For each location $l$, the set of executions ending at a state $(l, \sigma)$ (for some $\sigma$) is denoted by $Exec(l)$. The set of all executions of $P$ is denoted by $Exec(P)$.

It seems intuitive to define a semantics of programs in *absence of uncertainty* where queries obtain true information about the world — e.g., a query transition $\langle l \mid \mathtt{A}(x_1, \ldots, x_m) \mid l' \rangle$ is enabled at a state where $x_i$ has value $p_i$ if and only if the relation $A(p_1, \ldots, p_m)$ holds in the world. However, such an ideal semantics is of no use to our analysis where the core concern is the effect of uncertainty, and therefore, we do not develop this semantics.

### 2.3 Consistency

An uncertain execution of a DMP program $P$, may issue a sequence of queries whose answers, taken together, violate $\mathcal{R}$. We say that $P$ is consistent if this cannot happen in any uncertain execution.

To formalize this notion of consistency we need a formal definition for decisions: a *decision* in the world $\Theta$ is a literal $\delta = \alpha(p_1, \ldots, p_m)$, where $\alpha \in (\mathtt{Q} \cup \overline{\mathtt{Q}})$, $p_1, \ldots, p_m \in O$, and the type of $p_i$ matches the expected type of the $i$-th input to $\mathcal{Q}$. We denote the set of decisions over $\Theta$ by $Dec(\Theta)$ or simply $Dec$. For a decision $\delta$, $[\![\delta]\!]$ denotes the literal $A(p_1, \ldots, p_m)$ when $\delta$ equals $\mathtt{A}(p_1, \ldots, p_m)$, and $\neg A(p_1, \ldots, p_m)$ when $\delta$ equals $\overline{\mathtt{A}}(p_1, \ldots, p_m)$.

Now let $\rho = (l_0, \sigma_0) \stackrel{t_0}{\rightharpoonup} (l_1, \sigma_1) \cdots \stackrel{t_n}{\rightharpoonup} (l_{n+1}, \sigma_{n+1})$ be an execution of $P$. We define a *decision of* $\rho$ to be any decision $\delta = \alpha(p_1, \ldots, p_m) \in Dec$ such that for some $i$, we have:

1. $t_i = \langle l_i \,|\, \alpha(x_1, \ldots, x_m) \mid l_{i+1} \rangle$
2. for all $j \in \{1, ..., m\}$, $p_j = \sigma_i(x_j)$.

The set of decisions of $\rho$ is denoted by $Dec(\rho)$.

One can collectively represent the decisions made during an execution $\rho$ of $P$ using a logical formula, which we call the *decision formula* of that execution, which is defined as:

$$\Psi(\rho) = \bigwedge_{\delta \in Dec(\rho)} [\![\delta]\!].$$

Consistency of $P$ is now defined as follows:

**Definition 2** (Consistency). *The program $P$ is* consistent *(with respect to the world $\Theta$) if for all executions $\rho \in Exec(P)$, the formula $\Psi(\rho) \wedge (\bigwedge_{R \in \mathcal{R}} R)$ is satisfiable.*

Thus our goal is to verify that a given program $P$ is consistent under the above definition.

*Example* 2. Let us consider the code in Fig. 2 once again. It is easy to translate this code to a DMP program over the world $\Theta_{tc}$ from Example 1 (we assume $L_1$-$L_6$ are simple assignments). This program manipulates a bounded number of objects and has a bounded number of executions; by enumerating these executions, we find that it is consistent.

Now let us consider a more involved program, also over $\Theta_{tc}$, that issues queries over an unbounded number of objects. As with the previous example, we write the program in a more readable structured syntax which can be easily translated into DMP:

1 $x_1 := next(X);\;\; x_2 := next(X)$
2 **while** $X \neq \emptyset$
3 **do if** $\mathtt{Left}(x_1, x_2)$ **then skip else skip**
4 $x_1 := x_2;\;\; x_2 := next(X)$

In our model, the test in Line 3 can always evaluate incorrectly. However, we can argue that this program is consistent nonetheless.

Let the objects in the input list $X$ have identifiers 1 to $n$. Consider the execution $\rho$ that takes the $true$-branch of the code in all iterations. The decision formula for $\rho$ is

$$\Psi(\rho) = Left(1, 2) \wedge Left(2, 3) \wedge Left(3, 4) \ldots Left(n-1, n).$$

Now note that $(\Psi(\rho) \wedge R)$, where $R$ is the conjunction of the axioms in Example 1, is satisfiable. It is not hard to see that for *every* execution $\rho'$ of $P_{tc}$, $(\Psi(\rho') \wedge R)$ is satisfiable. Therefore, the program is consistent. On the other hand, if the program made an extra decision $\mathtt{Left}(n, 1)$ somewhere in the execution, then the conjunct $Left(n, 1)$ would be added to $\Psi(\rho)$, and the above property would no longer hold.

## 3. Consistency in geometric programs

In this section, we show how the notion of consistency plays out in the context of computational geometry. We do so using two examples. Both are algorithms for computing a convex hull for a set of points in two dimensions (2D); one of the algorithms is not consistent, while the other is. As before, we describe the algorithms using a more readable, structured syntax rather than that of DMP.

### 3.1 The world

Any convex hull algorithm queries a geometric space about positions of points in it — this space $\Theta_{ch}$ is our world. Formally, we let $\Theta_{ch} = \langle \{\mathtt{2DPoint}\}, O, \mathcal{Q}_{ch}, \mathcal{R}_{ch} \rangle$, where $\mathtt{2DPoint}$ is the type of points on the 2D plane, $O$ is the set of all 2D points, and $\mathcal{Q}_{ch}$ consists of a single *orientation predicate* $Lturn(u, v, w)$. The semantics of this predicate is that $Lturn(u, v, w)$ is true when $w$ is to the left of the infinite directed line $\overrightarrow{uv}$. For example, in Fig. 6(a), we have $Lturn(p_1, p_2, p_3)$. Under the ideal semantics of reals, this

1. **Cyclic symmetry:** $Lturn(x, y, z) \implies Lturn(y, z, x)$.
2. **Antisymmetry:** $Lturn(x, y, z) \implies \neg Lturn(x, z, y)$.
3. **Nondegeneracy:** $Lturn(x, y, z) \vee Lturn(x, z, y)$.
4. **Interiority:** $Lturn(x, y, t) \wedge Lturn(y, z, t) \wedge Lturn(z, x, t) \implies Lturn(x, y, z)$.
5. **Transitivity:** $Lturn(x, y, z) \wedge Lturn(x, y, t) \wedge Lturn(y, z, t) \wedge Lturn(y, z, w) \wedge Lturn(t, y, w) \implies Lturn(x, y, w)$.

**Figure 3.** Knuth's axioms for convex hull algorithms

predicate can be defined as

$$(v.x - u.x)(w.y - u.y) - (v.y - u.y)(w.x - u.x) > 0$$

where $u.x$ and $u.y$ are respectively the $x$- and $y$-coordinates of $u$.

We define $\mathcal{R}_{ch}$ using an axiomatization of convex hull predicates (Fig. 3) by Knuth [17]. Consider Fig. 6(a) again, and note that $Lturn(p_1, p_2, p_3)$. Axiom 1 says that this implies the facts $Lturn(p_3, p_1, p_2)$ and $Lturn(p_2, p_3, p_1)$; Axiom 2 says that we cannot have $Lturn(p_1, p_3, p_2)$ in this case. Axiom 3 is an *assumption* that no three input points are collinear (collinear points form a degenerate case for convex hull algorithms).

Axiom 4 says that (Fig. 4 (a)) if $p_2$ is to the left of $\overrightarrow{p_1p_2}$, $\overrightarrow{p_2p_3}$ and $\overrightarrow{p_3p_1}$, then $p_4$ is *inside* the triangle $\triangle p_1p_2p_3$, and more over the triangle is oriented counter clockwise, or $p_3$ is to the left of $\overrightarrow{p_1p_2}$. Axiom 5 defines a transitivity property of *Lturn*: to understand its geometric intuition, consider Fig. 4(b) with $x = p_1$, $y = p_2$, $z = p_3$, $t = p_4$, and $w = p_5$. In this case, we have $Lturn(p_1, p_2, p_3)$, $Lturn(p_1, p_2, p_4)$, $Lturn(p_2, p_3, p_4)$, $Lturn(p_2, p_3, p_5)$, $Lturn(p_4, p_2, p_5)$. The axiom demands that we also have $Lturn(p_1, p_2, p_5)$, which is indeed true here.

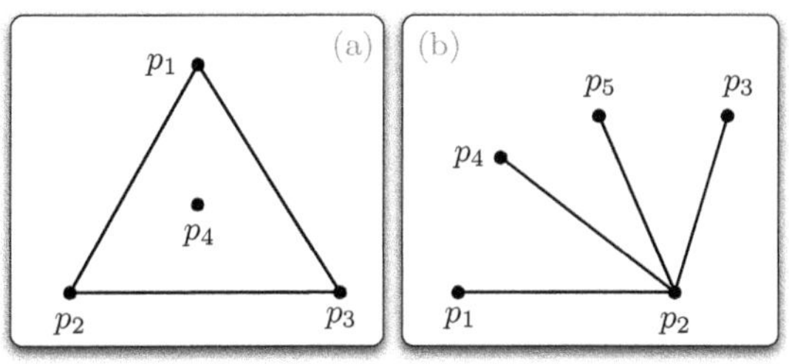


**Figure 4.** Interiority and transitivity axioms

Axioms 1–5 are easily seen to be consistent with Euclidean geometry. In [17], Knuth argues that if the results of all *Lturn* predicate checks for a set of points satisfy these axioms, then a convex hull always exists. While the above axioms are specific to convex hulls, similar axiomatizations are known for other classes of geometric computations.

### 3.2 Inconsistent convex hull

Consider the algorithm SIMPLECONVEXHULL [7] in Fig. 5, which is a naive (and slow) algorithm for computing the convex hull of a set of points $S$. Note that it is standard for convex hulls to have a counterclockwise orientation. Following the convention developed earlier, we use $\overline{\texttt{Lturn}}(u, v, w)$ to denote the *decision* made by the algorithm that $\neg Lturn(u, v, w)$. The algorithm iterates over all pairs of points $(u, v)$ (as potential convex hull edges); if there exists a point $w$ such that the decision $\overline{\texttt{Lturn}}(u, v, w)$ is made, then $(u, v)$ is removed from the set of edges forming the convex hull (since if $(u, v)$ is an edge of the convex hull (in the counter-clockwise direction), then every other point must lie to the left of $(u, v)$). It is easy to see that if the algorithm is implemented using

```
Input: A set S of points in the 2D plane.
Output: A list E containing the edges of the convex hull
SIMPLECONVEXHULL(S)
E := ∅
for all ordered pairs (u, v) ∈ S × S with u ≠ v
    do valid := true
        for all w ∈ S with u ≠ w and v ≠ w
            do if ¬Lturn(u, v, w)
                then valid := false
        if valid
          then add the directed edge (u, v) to E
```

**Figure 5.** Inconsistent convex hull

ideal reals, without any uncertainty, then SIMPLECONVEXHULL in fact computes a convex hull.

On the other hand, under uncertainty (for example, due to floating-point error), the decision $\overline{\texttt{Lturn}}(u, v, w)$ can evaluate non-deterministically. Consider the input set in Fig. 6 where the correct hull is illustrated in (a). $Lturn(p_1, p_2, p_3)$ is true, but the points $p_1, p_2, p_3$ are *nearly* collinear. First, note that the algorithm may evaluate $\texttt{Lturn}$ for all permutations of the three points $p_1$, $p_2$, and $p_3$. If, *due to numerical uncertainty*, the program decides that $\overline{\texttt{Lturn}}(p_1, p_2, p_3)$, $\overline{\texttt{Lturn}}(p_2, p_3, p_1)$, and $\overline{\texttt{Lturn}}(p_1, p_3, p_2)$, then none of the three edges $(p_1, p_2)$, $(p_2, p_3)$, and $(p_1, p_3)$ will belong to the convex hull, and the resulting hull will be as illustrated in (b), which is not even a closed curve. Similarly, we could have a scenario where all three edges end up in the convex hull, where all the three queries return true, and the result will be as in (c); again, completely wrong, since it has two cycles.

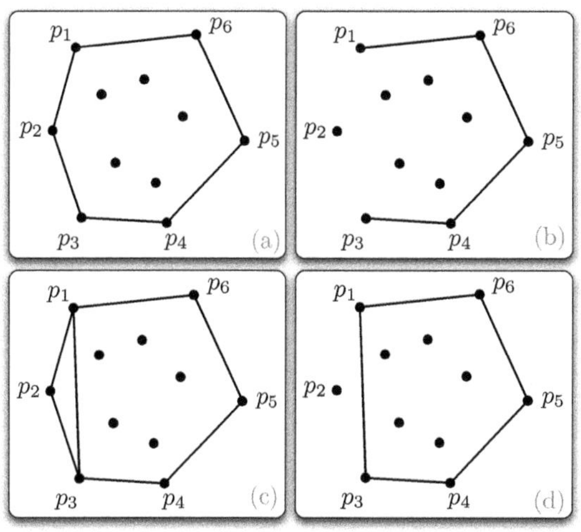


**Figure 6.** Inconsistency in convex hull

The main problem is that, for both cases (b) and (c), where decisions $\overline{\texttt{Lturn}}(p_1, p_2, p_3)$ and $\overline{\texttt{Lturn}}(p_1, p_3, p_2)$ are both taken, there is an inconsistency with the antisymmetry axiom of Fig. 3. The *consistent* executions of this program result in either (a) or (d). The convex hull in (d) is obtained from deciding that $\overline{\texttt{Lturn}}(p_1, p_2, p_3)$, $\overline{\texttt{Lturn}}(p_2, p_3, p_1)$, and $\texttt{Lturn}(p_1, p_3, p_2)$; these decisions are not all correct, but they are consistent. Consequently, while Figure (d) is slightly different from the ideal answer, it is structurally a convex hull: an output that would be produced by the ideal real-number algorithm on *some* input (this is an input in which $p_2$ is perturbed to move to the left of line $\overrightarrow{p_1p_3}$ ). In contrast, (b) and (c) are outputs that the ideal algorithm could never produce.

To see why this difference is substantial, consider a procedure that iterates over the "hull" computed by the convex hull routine, starting with $p_2$ and terminating when it comes back to $p_2$ again. In case (d), it will terminate as usual. In case (b), it will not be able to proceed past $p_2$. In (c), it could get stuck in an infinite loop.

The inconsistency of the above algorithm is by no means a rare anomaly. Many everyday implementations of convex hulls (and other geometric computations) are inconsistent. The crashes, infinite loops, and other errors that inconsistency can lead to are well-documented. We refer the reader to [21] for an in depth discussion of the consequences of inconsistent geometric computations.

### 3.3 Consistent convex hull: Graham Scan [12]

*Graham scan* [12] (Fig. 8) is an example of a consistent convex hull algorithm.

The point $p_0$, which we know belongs to $H$, is our "sentinel". In the main loop, we check if the last two points $u$ and $v$ of $H$ together with a new point $w$ from $S$ make a left turn (this test is encoded using the `Lturn` predicate). If so, then we *speculatively* assume that these points belong to the hull and add $w$ to $H$. If not, then $v$ cannot belong to the convex hull of $S$ (since both edges adjacent to $v$ have a point to the right of them, and therefore, they cannot be convex hull edges), and we *delete* it from $H$. For example, upon considering $\langle p_1, p_2, p_3 \rangle$ in the figure, $p_2$ is deleted from $H$. In general, we keep deleting until the last two points in $H$ together with $w$ make a left turn. Note that there is no bound on the number of points that may be deleted during this step.

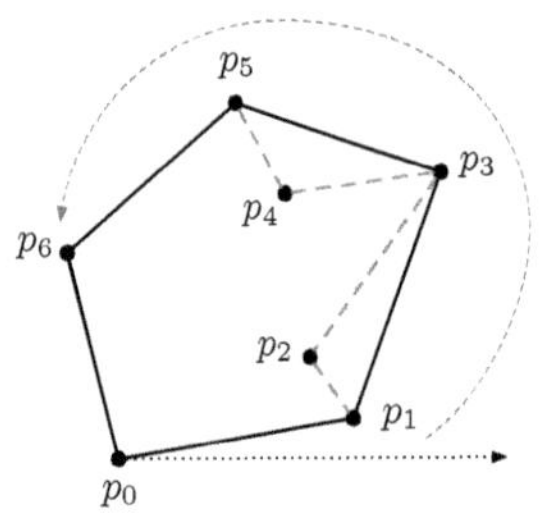


**Figure 7.** Graham Scan

The Graham Scan algorithm, unlike the naive algorithm, is consistent (we discuss why in Sec. 5). It is very difficult to reason about consistency of this algorithm manually. One needs to reason about all program paths containing unboundedly many facts (dependent on the size of input) and argue that none contains an inconsistency with respect to the axioms. An expert user may be able to argue why none of the first 3 axioms (in Fig. 3) can ever be falsified by this algorithm. The algorithm progresses in a way that, for every three points $p$, $q$, and $r$, it evaluates the $Lturn(p, q, r)$ predicate exactly once (the last point $r$ is always a fresh new point). Therefore, it is not possible to find two predicate evaluations that are not consistent with any of the first three axioms (which all need two different evaluations of the predicate on two different permutations of the same 3 points). But, extending this reasoning to axioms 4 and 5 manually is difficult. In the next section, we present an analysis that is able to easily verify the consistency of the above algorithm.

We note that the assumption that the input points are sorted on basis of their polar angle from $p_0$ is needed for the algorithm's functional correctness. However, it is irrelevant to the program's consistency: even if the input points were ordered arbitrarily, the decisions made in an execution of the algorithm would not violate Knuth's axioms, and structurally, the output would still be a simple closed cycle. Our analysis chooses to ignore the assumption that the input list is sorted in this way (this information is lost in abstraction), and still discovers an automated proof that the algorithm is consistent.

## 4. Verifying consistency

In this section, we describe our method for algorithmic verification of consistency. Let us fix a world $\Theta = (Base, O, \mathcal{Q}, \mathcal{R})$ and a program $P$. The broad idea of our algorithm is to prove $P$

**Input**: A point $p_0$ (right-most bottom-most point in the set) and (non-empty) list of $S$ of points. The points in $S$ are assumed to be sorted on basis of increasing polar angle from $p_0$.

**Output**: List $H$ containing the points forming the convex hull, also sorted on basis of their polar angle from $p_0$

```
GRAHAMSCAN(p0, S)
if |S| < 3 then return [p0; S]
H := [next(S); next(S)]
for w := next(S)
    do
        v := last(H); u := secondLast(H)
        while ¬ Lturn(u, v, w)
            do pop(H)
                if |H| ≥ 2
                    then v := last(H) ; u := secondLast(H)
                    else break
        Append w to H
w := p0; v := last(H); u := secondLast(H)
while ¬ Lturn(u, v, w)
    do pop(H)
        if |H| ≥ 2
        then v := last(H) ; u := secondLast(H)
        else break
Append p0 to H
return H
```

**Figure 8.** Consistent Convex Hull Algorithm: Graham Scan. The operation *secondLast* returns the second last element of the list, without modifying the list.

consistent by an inductive argument: each time a new decision is made, we assume that the set of decisions that have already been made are consistent and prove that the new decision does not violate consistency (in combination with past decisions). We automate this reasoning in two phases as follows.

In the first phase, we approximate the sets of decisions that can be made by executions of $P$ by constructing an integer abstraction $\Pi$ of $P$ and then computing numerical invariants for $\Pi$. Example 2 illustrates the idea behind the integer abstraction, which models objects as integer identifiers, and sets of decisions with sets of integer tuples. We analyze $\Pi$ with an abstract interpreter to compute for each query location $l$ of $P$:

1. A *current-decision invariant* $d_l$ that symbolically represents the set of decisions that can be made at $l$.
2. A *history invariant* $\mathcal{H}_l$ that symbolically represents the set of all decisions made along executions that end at location $l$.

Our representation of a set of decisions by a numerical invariant makes use of a set of integer auxiliary variables which represent the arguments of queries (recalling that our encoding represents objects as integer identifiers). A set of decisions (i.e., a set of tuples of objects) is represented by an arithmetic formula over the program variables as well as the auxiliary variables. The set of models of such a formula can be interpreted as a set of decisions (or more accurately, as a function mapping program states to a set of decisions).

For example, let us revisit the program of Example 2 (reproduced here for convenience).

```
x1 := next(X);  x2 := next(X)
while X ≠ ∅
    do if Left(x1, x2) then skip else skip
        x1 := x2;  x2 := next(X)
```

Let us assume that the objects in the list have strictly increasing IDs (e.g. the first point on the list has ID 1, the second ID 2, and so on), and let us use auxiliary variables $\#^1_{\texttt{Left}}$ and $\#^2_{\texttt{Left}}$ to respectively represent the IDs of the first and second arguments of the call to `Left`. At line 3, we have the invariant $x_1 < x_2$, and we have outgoing query transitions $\texttt{A}(x_1, x_2)$ and $\bar{\texttt{A}}(x_1, x_2)$. The current-decision invariant at this location is:

$$d_l : \#^1_{\texttt{Left}} = x_1 < x_2 = \#^2_{\texttt{Left}}.$$

On the other hand, in a history invariant, $\#^1_{\texttt{Left}}$ and $\#^2_{\texttt{Left}}$ refer to the IDs of the arguments of an arbitrarily selected *past call* to `Left`, while $x_1$ and $x_2$ refer to the *current* program variables. Since the program processes list elements in order of increasing IDs, the following history invariant holds at Line 3:

$$\mathcal{H}_l : \#^1_{\texttt{Left}} < \#^2_{\texttt{Left}} \leq x_1 < x_2$$

In the second phase of the algorithm, we verify that for each query location $l$ in the program $P$, there is a model of the world that is consistent with the decisions $d_l$ and $\mathcal{H}_l$ (i.e., $d_l$, $\mathcal{H}_l$, and the world axioms $\mathcal{R}$ together cannot derive *false*). The challenge here is that there may be no obvious inconsistency between $d_l$ and $\mathcal{H}_l$, but *false* may be derived using the axioms in $\mathcal{R}$ (and there is no *a priori* bound on the size of such a proof).

To overcome this challenge, we generate a logic program from the world axioms $\mathcal{R}$ that, given a current-decision invariant $d_l$ and a history invariant $\mathcal{H}_l$, generates every decision that can follow from the decisions in $d_l$ and $\mathcal{H}_l$. The problem now reduces to verifying that this system cannot possibly derive a contradiction. This task can be solved automatically using existing fixpoint constraint solvers, such as $\mu$Z [14]. Next, we describe the two phases of the algorithm in detail.

### 4.1 Generating history and current-decision invariants

To generate the history and current-decision invariants used by our consistency verification procedure, we first abstract $P$ by a program $\Pi$ over the integers. In $\Pi$, each object accessed by $P$ is modelled as a integer ID.[3] In addition to simulating the execution of $P$, $\Pi$ records the decisions it makes using a set of auxiliary variables (denoted by $\#$).

#### Constructing $\Pi$

We abstract lists $\lambda$ by pairs consisting of the IDs of the first and last element of $\lambda$. The challenge in this list abstraction is to maintain information about a list $\lambda$ as objects are added to it or removed from it. Our approach to doing so is to maintain the invariant that the objects in $\lambda$ appear in an order *sorted* by their IDs (note that there is no relation between these IDs and any values associated with the objects themselves; we just assign the IDs to the elements of the list in order in which they appear on the list). For instance, let $X^0$ and $X^1$ respectively denote the IDs of the first and last items in a list $X$. Assuming that our sortedness invariant holds, the integer abstraction of $next(X)$ returns the value of $X^0$ and sets $X^0$ to a nondeterministically chosen value between the current values of $X^0$ and $X^1$. Note that since the abstraction assigns the integer IDs (they are not part of original object information), all the input lists to the program are initially assumed to satisfy this invariant (based on the precondition about the disjointness of the lists and the elements on each list that we already mentioned in Section 2.2).

Of course, the sortedness invariant can be violated when the program tries to insert an item $x$ into a list $X$. We detect such violations by comparing the ID of $x$ with the value $X^1$; if sortedness is violated, we conservatively flag the program as inconsistent.

[3] Our analysis can be generalized to one where object IDs are not integers but tuples of integers, or even more generally, elements of a partially ordered set. For simplicity, we stick to integer IDs in this paper.

We now present the construction of $\Pi$ formally. To avoid introducing more notation, we describe the program $\Pi$ in a DMP-like syntax. An integer program is a tuple $\langle Loc, Var, l_0, \mathcal{T}\rangle$, where $Loc$ is a set of locations, $Var$ is a set of variables ranging over the integers and booleans, $l_0 \in Loc$ is an initial location, and $\mathcal{T}$ is a set of transitions. Transitions between locations $l$ and $l'$ have the following forms:

- Test transitions $\langle l \mid assume(b) \mid l'\rangle$, where $b$ is a linear arithmetic formula,
- $\langle l \mid havoc(x) \mid l'\rangle$, which changes the value of the variable, $x$ to an arbitrary integer value,
- $\langle l \mid x := e \mid l'\rangle$, an assignment to variable $x$, and
- $\langle l \mid assert(b) \mid l'\rangle$, which asserts that a property $b$ (expressed as a linear arithmetic formula) holds.

We do not give a detailed semantics for these transitions as they are standard. For simplicity, we sometimes write sequential compositions of transitions as a single transition—e.g., the syntax $\langle l \mid x := e; havoc(x) \mid l'\rangle$ is abbreviation for a pair of transitions $\langle l \mid x := e \mid l''\rangle$ and $\langle l'' \mid havoc(x) \mid l'\rangle$, where $l''$ is a location that is not used anywhere else in the program.

Now, let $P = \langle Loc_P, Var_P, l_{0,P}, \mathcal{T}_P\rangle$. We construct the program $\Pi = \langle Loc_\Pi, Var_\Pi, l_{0,\Pi}, \mathcal{T}_\Pi\rangle$ as follows:

- The initial location $l_{0,\Pi}$ of $\Pi$ is a fresh location, not in $Loc_P$. $Loc_\Pi$ contains $Loc_P$ and $l_{0,\Pi}$, and also a number of auxiliary locations introduced in the translation of transitions (Fig. 9). $\Pi$ inherits a notion of query locations from $P$: for all $\alpha \in \texttt{Q} \cup \bar{\texttt{Q}}$, we define $Loc^\alpha_\Pi = Loc^\alpha_P$.
- $Var_\Pi$ is the least set such that:
  1. For each object-valued variable $x$ in $P$, $Var_\Pi$ contains an integer-valued variable that tracks the ID of $x$. Abusing notation, we call this variable $x$ as well.
  2. For every list-valued variable $X$ in $P$, $Var_\Pi$ contains two integer-valued variables $X^0$ and $X^1$ that track the IDs of the first and last elements of $X$.
  3. For each $\texttt{A} \in \texttt{Q}$ and each $1 \leq i \leq m$, $Var_\Pi$ has an integer-valued variable $\#^i_{\texttt{A}}$ ranging over the integers. These variables are used to record A-decisions.
  4. $Var_\Pi$ contains a special boolean-valued variable $flag_{\texttt{A}}$ for each $\texttt{A} \in \texttt{Q}$. This variable is set to *true* when the $\#^i_{\texttt{A}}$ variables are initialized — i.e., the arguments of some query is assigned to them. Initially, each $flag_{\texttt{A}}$ variable is *false*.
- The set of transitions $\mathcal{T}_\Pi$ of $\Pi$ is defined by the rules in Fig. 9. Here, the rule INIT captures the fact that the $\#^i_{\texttt{A}}$s are uninitialized at the beginning of program executions. The two rules QUERY-1 and QUERY-2 abstract query transitions. One of them sets the $\#_{\texttt{A}}$ variables while the other does nothing — together, they model a nondeterministic choice to save the arguments of a decision in the $\#_{\texttt{A}}$ variables. The remaining rules are integer abstractions of updates to and tests of object and list-valued variables.

#### Current-decision and History Invariants

Having constructed an integer program abstraction $\Pi$ of $P$, we may use standard techniques to generate for each location $l \in Loc_\Pi$ a (numerical) *history invariant* $\mathcal{H}_l$. Our implementation employs an abstract interpreter over a domain of partitioned octagons, which we describe further in Sec. 5.1. Each $\mathcal{H}_l$ is a linear arithmetic formula over the variables $Var_\Pi$, which includes the variables which correspond to object-valued variables of $P$ as well as the auxiliary # and *flag*variables.

$$\text{(Init)}\ \frac{\mathtt{Q} = \{\mathtt{A}_1, \ldots, \mathtt{A}_{|\mathtt{Q}|}\}}{\langle l_{0,\Pi} \,|\, \mathit{flag}_{\mathtt{A}_1} := \mathit{false}; \ldots; \mathit{flag}_{\mathtt{A}_{|\mathtt{Q}|}} := \mathit{false} \,|\, l_0\rangle \in \mathcal{T}_\Pi} \qquad \text{(Asgn)}\ \frac{\langle l \mid x_1 := x_2 \mid l'\rangle \in \mathcal{T}_P}{\langle l \mid x_1 := x_2 \mid l'\rangle \in \mathcal{T}_\Pi}$$

$$\text{(Test-empty)}\ \frac{\langle l \mid assume(X = \emptyset) \mid l'\rangle \in \mathcal{T}_P}{\langle l \mid assume(X^0 > X^1) \mid l'\rangle \in \mathcal{T}_\Pi} \qquad \text{(Test-not-empty)}\ \frac{\langle l \mid assume(X \neq \emptyset) \mid l'\rangle \in \mathcal{T}_P}{\langle l \mid assume(X^0 \leq X^1) \mid l'\rangle \in \mathcal{T}_\Pi}$$

$$\text{(Query-1)}\ \frac{\langle l \,|\, \alpha(x_1, \ldots, x_m) \,|\, l'\rangle \in \mathcal{T}_P \quad \alpha \in \{\mathtt{A}\} \cup \{\bar{\mathtt{A}}\}}{\langle l \mid \#^1_{\mathtt{A}} := x_1; \ldots; \#^m_{\mathtt{A}} := x_m; \mathit{flag}_{\mathtt{A}} := true \mid l'\rangle \in \mathcal{T}_\Pi} \qquad \text{(Query-2)}\ \frac{\langle l \,|\, \alpha(x_1, \ldots, x_m) \,|\, l'\rangle \in \mathcal{T}_P \quad \alpha \in \{\mathtt{A}\} \cup \{\bar{\mathtt{A}}\}}{\langle l \mid assume(true) \mid l'\rangle \in \mathcal{T}_\Pi}$$

$$\text{(First)}\ \frac{\langle l \mid x := \mathit{first}(X) \mid l'\rangle \in \mathcal{T}_P}{\langle l \mid assert(X^0 \leq X^1); x := X^0 \mid l'\rangle \in \mathcal{T}_\Pi} \qquad \text{(Next)}\ \frac{\langle l \mid x := next(X) \mid l'\rangle \in \mathcal{T}_P}{\langle l \,|\, x := X^0; havoc(X^0); assume(x < X^0 \leq max(X^1, X^0 + 1) \,|\, l'\rangle \in \mathcal{T}_\Pi}$$

$$\text{(Last)}\ \frac{\langle l \mid x := last(X) \mid l'\rangle \in \mathcal{T}_P}{\langle l \mid assert(X^0 \leq X^1); x := X^1 \mid l'\rangle \in \mathcal{T}_\Pi} \qquad \text{(TL)}\ \frac{\langle l \mid x := pop(X) \mid l'\rangle \in \mathcal{T}_P}{\langle l \,|\, x := X^1; havoc(X^1); assume(min(X^0, X^1 - 1) \leq X^1 < x) \,|\, l'\rangle \in \mathcal{T}_\Pi}$$

$$\text{(LA)}\ \frac{\langle l \mid X_1 := X_2 \mid l'\rangle \in \mathcal{T}_P}{\langle l \mid X^0_1 := X^0_2; X^1_1 := X^1_2 \mid l'\rangle \in \mathcal{T}_\Pi} \qquad \text{(Empty)}\ \frac{\langle l \,|\, X := \emptyset \,|\, l'\rangle \in \mathcal{T}_P}{\langle l \,|\, havoc(X^0); havoc(X^1); assume(X^0 > X^1) \,|\, l'\rangle \in \mathcal{T}_\Pi}$$

$$\text{(App)}\ \frac{\langle l \mid append(x, X) \mid l'\rangle \in \mathcal{T}_P}{\begin{array}{l}\langle l \,|\, assume(X^0 > X^1); X^0 := x; X^1 := x \,|\, l'\rangle \in \mathcal{T}_\Pi \\ \langle l \,|\, assume(X^0 \leq X^1); assert(x > X^1); X^1 := x \,|\, l'\rangle \in \mathcal{T}_\Pi.\end{array}} \qquad \text{(AF)}\ \frac{\langle l \mid prepend(x, X) \mid l'\rangle \in \mathcal{T}_P}{\begin{array}{l}\langle l \,|\, assume(X^0 > X^1); X^0 := x; X^1 := x \,|\, l'\rangle \\ \langle l \,|\, assume(X^0 \leq X^1); assert(x < X^0); X^0 := x \,|\, l'\rangle\end{array}}$$

**Figure 9.** Construction of the transitions $\mathcal{T}_\Pi$ of $\Pi$ from $P = \langle Loc_P, Var_P, l_{0,P}, \mathcal{T}_P\rangle$

Our construction of $\Pi$ ensures that any such formula $\mathcal{H}_l$ can be interpreted as a mapping from traces to sets of decisions made along those traces. The intuition behind this interpretation is as follows. Let $\rho$ be a program trace, which ends in a state $(l, \sigma)$. For any A, consider the set of models of $\mathcal{H}_l$ which send each variable to its value in $\sigma$ and in which the $\#_{\mathtt{A}}$ variables have been initialized ($\mathit{flag}_{\mathtt{A}}$ is true). Each such model $M$ corresponds to an A-decision, namely, the decision $\mathtt{A}(M(\#^1_{\mathtt{A}}), \ldots, M(\#^m_{\mathtt{A}}))$ (where $M(\#^i_{\mathtt{A}})$ denotes $M$'s interpretation of the variable $\#^i_{\mathtt{A}}$). The set of decisions obtained from models of $\mathcal{H}_l$ in this way is a superset of the set of decisions made along $\rho$. The precise statement of this interpretation of $\mathcal{H}_l$ is the following lemma.

**Lemma 1.** *Suppose that $\rho$ is an execution of $P$, ending in a state $(l, \sigma)$. Let id be any mapping from the objects accessed in $\rho$ to integer IDs such that IDs increase along every list in the initial state of $\rho$. Let $\mathtt{A} \in \mathtt{Q}$, and let $V$ be the set of all variables in $Var_\Pi$ except the $\#_{\mathtt{A}}$ variables. Define*

$$H_{l,\mathtt{A}} = \exists V. \Big(\mathcal{H}_l \wedge \mathit{flag}_{\mathtt{A}} = true \wedge \bigwedge_{x \in Var_P} x = id(\sigma(x))\Big).$$

*Then for any $\mathtt{A}(p_1, \ldots, p_m) \in Dec(\rho)$, the model $M$ that sends each $\#^i_{\mathtt{A}}$ to $p_i$ is a model of $H_{l,\mathtt{A}}$ (and similarly for any $\bar{\mathtt{A}}(p_1, \ldots, p_m) \in Dec(\rho)$).*

*Proof.* Let $\rho = (l_0, \sigma_0) \xrightarrow{t_0} (l_1, \sigma_1) \cdots (l_n, \sigma_n)$, with $l_n = l$. Let $\alpha(p_1, \ldots, p_m) \in Dec(\rho)$. Then there is some $i$ such that

- $t_i = \langle l_i \,|\, \alpha(x_1, \ldots, x_m) \,|\, l_{i+1}\rangle$
- for all $j \in \{1, \ldots, m\}$, $p_j = \sigma_i(x_j)$.

With the exception of query, append, and prepend transitions, for any transition of $P$, there is a unique sequence of corresponding transitions in $\Pi$, given in Fig. 9. For append and prepend transitions, there are two corresponding transitions, but their guards are disjoint so there is a unique choice for the translation of these transitions when the pre-state is fixed. For query transitions there are two corresponding transition sequences given by the (Query-1) and (Query-2) rules. Consider the execution $\rho_\Pi$ of $\Pi$ which executes the sequence of transitions corresponding to $\rho$, using the (Query-1) rule for the query transition $t_i$ and (Query-2) for all other query transitions along $\rho$, (and which chooses the "correct" non-deterministic updates to the list variables to make the executions $\rho$ and $\rho_\Pi$ agree).

Let $(l, \sigma_\Pi)$ be the final state of $\rho_\Pi$. Then $\sigma_\Pi$ sends each object-valued variable $x$ to $id(\sigma(x))$, sends each $\#^i_{\mathtt{A}}$ to $id(p_i)$, and sends $\mathit{flag}_{\mathtt{A}}$ to $true$. Since $\mathcal{H}_l$ is an invariant at location $l$, we must have $\sigma_\Pi \models \mathcal{H}_l$. It follows that $M$, the restriction of $\sigma_\Pi$ to the $\#^i_{\mathtt{A}}$ variables, is a model of $H_{l,\mathtt{A}}$. □

Now we describe how to compute current-decision invariants. Consider a query location $l$ with an outgoing query transition $\langle l \mid \alpha(x_1, \ldots, x_m) \mid l'\rangle$, where $\alpha \in \{\mathtt{A}, \bar{\mathtt{A}}\}$ for some $\mathtt{A} \in \mathtt{Q}$. By the syntactic assumptions laid out in Sec. 2, $l$ has no other outgoing transition. The current-decision invariant at $l$ can be computed from $\mathcal{H}_l$ as:

$$d_l = (\exists\#.\mathcal{H}_l) \wedge \left(\bigwedge_{i=1}^{m} (x_i = \#^i_{\mathtt{A}})\right)$$

where $\exists\#$ denotes the existential quantification of each #-variable. Intuitively, $d_l$ constrains the relationships between the program variables and the objects involved in the "new" decision made at $l$.

### 4.2 Proving Consistency of Decisions

Once the history ($\mathcal{H}_l$) and current-decision ($d_l$) invariants have been generated for each query location $l$, consistency verification can be reduced to the problem of proving *false* cannot be derived from the combination of $\mathcal{H}_l$, $d_l$, and the world axioms $\mathcal{R}$. Our reduction makes use of our inductive assumption that there is no derivation of *false* using only decisions from $\mathcal{H}_l$.

Now we show how to automate this proof obligation.

#### Decision proof systems

For expository purposes, we will begin by defining *decision proof systems*, a Datalog-like normal form for the world axioms $\mathcal{R}$. After, we proceed to the construction of a logic program that can be used to verify consistency of the program $P$.

Normalized axioms can be of two forms:

- *Generators:* These rules derive new decisions that are logical consequences of decisions taken by the program. Formally, a generator is a rule of the form

$$\alpha(y_1,\ldots,y_m) \leftarrow \alpha_1(y_{11},\ldots,y_{1m})\wedge\cdots\wedge\alpha_k(y_{k1},\ldots,y_{km})$$

where $\alpha, \alpha_i$ are in $(\mathtt{Q}\cup\overline{\mathtt{Q}})$, and the $y_{ij}$'s range over objects.

- *Violators:* These rules identify direct contradictions between decisions that have either been made by the program or derived by the generators. Such a rule has the form

$$\bot \leftarrow \mathtt{A}_i(y_1,\ldots,y_m) \wedge \overline{\mathtt{A}_i}(y_1,\ldots,y_m).$$

where $\bot$ is a special symbol (intuitively indicating *false*), $\mathtt{A}\in\mathtt{Q}$ and the $y_i$'s range over objects.

We interpret the relations in the above rules as sets of decisions, and the rule as a way to derive new decisions or derive contradictions.

Now we describe how to construct a decision proof system $\mathcal{M}_\mathcal{R}$ from a set of axioms $\mathcal{R}$. First, we construct the formula $\bigwedge_{R\in\mathcal{R}} R$ and convert it into the conjunctive normal form (per our current notation, we assume that the initial quantifiers are omitted from formulas in $\mathcal{R}$). Let the resultant formula have clauses $C_1,\ldots,C_n$.

Now consider any clause $C_j = t_1 \vee\cdots\vee t_k$ of the formula constructed in the previous step. Here, each $t_i$ is either of the form $A_i(y_{i1},\ldots,y_{im_1})$ or of the form $\neg A_i(y_{i1},\ldots,y_{im})$. We define two literals $\mathtt{t_i}$ and $\overline{\mathtt{t_i}}$ for each $t_i$. If $t_i = A_i(y_{i1},\ldots,y_{im})$, then we have

$$\mathtt{t_i} = \mathtt{A}_i(y_{i1},\ldots,y_{im}) \qquad \overline{\mathtt{t_i}} = \overline{\mathtt{A}_i}(y_{i1},\ldots,y_{im}).$$

If $t_i = \neg A_i(y_{i1},\ldots,y_{im})$, then we have

$$\mathtt{t_i} = \overline{\mathtt{A}_i}(y_{i1},\ldots,y_{im}) \qquad \overline{\mathtt{t_i}} = \mathtt{A}_i(y_{i1},\ldots,y_{im}).$$

$\mathcal{M}_\mathcal{R}$ is defined to be the least set of rules such that:

1. For each clause $C_j = t_1\vee\cdots\vee t_k$ and each $r\in\{1,...,k\}$, $\mathcal{M}_\mathcal{R}$ has the generator

$$\mathtt{t}_r \leftarrow \overline{\mathtt{t_1}}\wedge\cdots\wedge\overline{\mathtt{t}_{r-1}}\wedge\overline{\mathtt{t}_{r+1}}\wedge\cdots\wedge\overline{\mathtt{t}_k}.$$

2. For each predicate $\mathtt{A}\in\mathtt{Q}$, $\mathcal{M}_\mathcal{R}$ has the violator

$$\bot \leftarrow \mathtt{A}(y_1,...,y_m)\wedge\overline{\mathtt{A}}(y_1,...,y_m).$$

*Example* 3. Consider once again the world $\Theta_{tc}$ of Example 1, which supports the predicate *Left* over 1-D points. The following decision proof system $\mathcal{M}_{\mathcal{R}_{tc}}$ is obtained from the axioms of $\Theta_{tc}$:

$$\begin{aligned}
\overline{\mathtt{Left}}(y_1,y_2) &\leftarrow \mathtt{Left}(y_2,y_1)\\
\mathtt{Left}(y_1,y_2) &\leftarrow \overline{\mathtt{Left}}(y_2,y_1)\\
\mathtt{Left}(y_1,y_3) &\leftarrow \mathtt{Left}(y_1,y_2)\wedge\mathtt{Left}(y_2,y_3)\\
\overline{\mathtt{Left}}(y_2,y_3) &\leftarrow \mathtt{Left}(y_1,y_2)\wedge\overline{\mathtt{Left}}(y_1,y_3)\\
\overline{\mathtt{Left}}(y_1,y_2) &\leftarrow \mathtt{Left}(y_2,y_3)\wedge\overline{\mathtt{Left}}(y_1,y_3)\\
\bot &\leftarrow \mathtt{Left}(y_1,y_2)\wedge\overline{\mathtt{Left}}(y_1,y_2) \quad \square
\end{aligned}$$

**Proving consistency**

We now show how to construct (from the current-decision invariants, and history invariants, and the decision proof system) a logic program which derives the symbol $\bot$ if $P$ is inconsistent. If this logic program *cannot* derive $\bot$, this proves that $P$ is consistent.

First, we provide some intuition. Let $l$ be a query location. We compute for each predicate $\mathtt{A}\in\mathtt{Q}$ a relation $Hist_{l,\mathtt{A}}$ which relates the final states of program executions that end at $l$ to the decisions of the form $\mathtt{A}(...)$ or $\overline{\mathtt{A}}(...)$ which are logical consequences of the decisions made along those executions.[4] We also compute for each $\alpha\in\mathtt{Q}\cup\overline{\mathtt{Q}}$ a relation $New_{l,\alpha}$, which is similar to $Hist_{l,\mathtt{A}}$ except that it includes the decision made at $l$, but not necessarily the decisions which are consequences of decisions in $Hist_{l,\mathtt{A}}$.

The sets $Hist_{l,\mathtt{A}}$ and $New_{l,\alpha}$ can be described using a set of Datalog-style rules, given in the following. We use $\vec{x} = \langle x_1,\ldots,x_n\rangle$ to denote the list of the variables corresponding to object-valued variables of $P$. These variables will be "threaded through" each of the inference rules, so they may be thought of as symbolic constants that help to mediate relationships between the current decision and previous decisions. Alternately, they may be thought of as a way of adding a degree of path-sensitivity to our analysis: we may think of each valuation of the variables $\vec{x}$ as a "universe", and threading $\vec{x}$ through each inference rule as a way of keeping universes separate.

We begin with rules that "initialize" $Hist_{l,\mathtt{A}}$ and $New_{l,\alpha}$ using the history and current-decision invariants:

$$\begin{aligned}
Hist_{l,\mathtt{A}}(y_1,\ldots,y_m,\vec{x}) &\leftarrow \mathcal{H}_l[\#^1_\mathtt{A}\mapsto y_1;\ldots;\#^m_\mathtt{A}\mapsto y_m]\\
&\qquad \wedge flag_\mathtt{A}\\
New_{l,\alpha}(y_1,\ldots,y_m,\vec{x}) &\leftarrow d_l[\#^1_\mathtt{A}\mapsto y_1;\ldots;\#^m_\mathtt{A}\mapsto y_m]\\
&\qquad \text{if } l\in Loc^\alpha_\Pi \text{ and } \alpha\in\{\mathtt{A},\overline{\mathtt{A}}\}\\
New_{l,\alpha}(y_1,\ldots,y_m,\vec{x}) &\leftarrow \emptyset \qquad \text{otherwise}
\end{aligned}$$

Now we give rules to derive the consequences of decisions in $d_l$ taken together with decisions in $\mathcal{H}_l$. For each generator $R_g\in\mathcal{M}_\mathcal{R}$ of the form

$$\alpha(y_1,\ldots,y_m) \leftarrow \alpha_1(y_{11},\ldots,y_{1m})\wedge\cdots\wedge\alpha_k(y_{k1},\ldots,y_{km}),$$

where $\alpha\in\{\mathtt{A},\overline{\mathtt{A}}\}$ and for all $i$, $\alpha_i\in\{\mathtt{A_i},\overline{\mathtt{A_i}}\}$, we add:

$$\begin{aligned}
Hist_{l,\mathtt{A}}(y_1,\ldots,y_m,\vec{x}) &\leftarrow Hist_{l,\mathtt{A}_1}(y_{11},\ldots,y_{1m},\vec{x})\wedge\ldots\\
&\qquad \wedge Hist_{l,\mathtt{A}_k}(y_{k1},\ldots,y_{km},\vec{x})\\
New_{l,\alpha}(y_1,\ldots,y_m,\vec{x}) &\leftarrow \Omega_{l,\alpha_1}(y_{11},\ldots,y_{1m},\vec{x})\wedge\ldots\\
&\qquad \wedge\Omega_{l,\alpha_k}(y_{k1},\ldots,y_{km},\vec{x})
\end{aligned}$$

where $\Omega_{l,\alpha_i}\in\{New_{l,\alpha_i}, Hist_{l,\mathtt{A}_i}\}$ and such that at least one of the $\Omega_{l,\alpha_i}$'s is $New_{l,\alpha_i}$. The requirement that at least one of the $\Omega_{l,\alpha_i}$'s is $New_{l,\alpha_i}$ ensures that $New_{l,\alpha}$ does not include decisions that are *solely* derived from decisions in $\mathcal{H}_l$. This is used to encode our inductive assumption that there are no inconsistencies in $\mathcal{H}_l$.

Finally, for each predicate $\mathtt{A}\in\mathtt{Q}$, we generate three violator rules that detect direct contradictions:

$$\begin{aligned}
\bot &\leftarrow New_{l,\mathtt{A}}(y_1,...,y_m,\vec{x})\wedge Hist_{l,\mathtt{A}}(y_1,...,y_m,\vec{x})\\
\bot &\leftarrow New_{l,\overline{\mathtt{A}}}(y_1,...,y_m,\vec{x})\wedge Hist_{l,\mathtt{A}}(y_1,...,y_m,\vec{x})\\
\bot &\leftarrow New_{l,\mathtt{A}}(y_1,...,y_m,\vec{x})\wedge New_{l,\overline{\mathtt{A}}}(y_1,...,y_m,\vec{x})
\end{aligned}$$

Let $\mathcal{M}_{\Pi,\mathcal{R}}$ be the system of all rules constructed as above. We have the following lemma:

**Lemma 2.** *Suppose that program $P$ is inconsistent. Then $\bot$ belongs to the least fixpoint of $\mathcal{M}_{\Pi,\mathcal{R}}$.*

*Proof.* Let $\rho = (l_0,\sigma_0)\xrightarrow{t_0}(l_1,\sigma_1)\cdots(l_n,\sigma_n)$ be an execution of the program $P$ such that $\mathcal{M}_\mathcal{R}$ can derive $\bot$ from $Dec(\rho)$. Without loss of generality, we may assume no proper prefix of $\rho$ satisfies this property. It follows that $t_{n-1}$, the last transition of $\rho$, must be a decision transition $\langle l_{n-1}\mid\alpha(z_1,...,z_m)\mid l_n\rangle$ for some $\alpha, z_1,\ldots,z_m$. For notational convenience, we use $l$ to denote $l_{n-1}$, and use $\rho'$ to denote the trace $\rho$ with its last action omitted. Let $id$ be any mapping form the object accessed in $\rho$ to integer IDs such that IDs increase along every list in the initial state $\sigma_0$. Let $\vec{x}$ be the vector of the object-valued variables of $P$, and define

$$\vec{p} = \langle id(\sigma_{n-1}(x_1)),...,id(\sigma_{n-1}(x_n))\rangle$$

Let $T$ be a derivation tree for $\bot$ using the inference rules in $\mathcal{M}_\mathcal{R}$, with the elements of $Dec(\rho)$ taken as axioms.

[4] Note that since the outcome of decisions are uncertain, we need not compute a corresponding $Hist_{l,\overline{\mathtt{A}}}$ relations, because it would be they would be identical to the $Hist_{l,\mathtt{A}}$ relations.

**Initialization**:

$$New_{\texttt{Left}}(y_1, y_2, x_1, x_2) \leftarrow x_1 = y_1 < y_2 = x_2$$
$$New_{\overline{\texttt{Left}}}(y_1, y_2, x_1, x_2) \leftarrow x_1 = y_1 < y_2 = x_2$$
$$Hist_{\texttt{Left}}(y_1, y_2, x_1, x_2) \leftarrow y_1 < y_2 \leq x_1 < x_2$$

**Totality**:

$$Hist_{\overline{\texttt{Left}}}(y_1, y_2, x_1, x_2) \leftarrow Hist_{\texttt{Left}}(y_2, y_1, x_1, x_2)$$
$$Hist_{\texttt{Left}}(y_1, y_2, x_1, x_2) \leftarrow Hist_{\overline{\texttt{Left}}}(y_2, y_1, x_1, x_2)$$
$$New_{\overline{\texttt{Left}}}(y_1, y_2, x_1, x_2) \leftarrow New_{\texttt{Left}}(y_2, y_1, x_1, x_2)$$
$$New_{\texttt{Left}}(y_1, y_2, x_1, x_2) \leftarrow New_{\overline{\texttt{Left}}}(y_2, y_1, x_1, x_2)$$

**Violators**:

$$\bot \leftarrow Hist_{\texttt{Left}}(y_1, y_2, x_1, x_2) \wedge New_{\overline{\texttt{Left}}}(y_1, y_2, x_1, x_2)$$
$$\bot \leftarrow New_{\texttt{Left}}(y_1, y_2, x_1, x_2) \wedge Hist_{\overline{\texttt{Left}}}(y_1, y_2, x_1, x_2)$$
$$\bot \leftarrow New_{\texttt{Left}}(y_1, y_2, x_1, x_2) \wedge New_{\overline{\texttt{Left}}}(y_1, y_2, x_1, x_2)$$

**Transitivity**:

$$Hist_{\texttt{Left}}(y_1, y_3, x_1, x_2) \leftarrow Hist_{\texttt{Left}}(y_1, y_2, x_1, x_2) \wedge Hist_{\texttt{Left}}(y_2, y_3, x_1, x_2)$$
$$Hist_{\overline{\texttt{Left}}}(y_2, y_3, x_1, x_2) \leftarrow Hist_{\texttt{Left}}(y_1, y_2, x_1, x_2) \wedge Hist_{\overline{\texttt{Left}}}(y_1, y_3, x_1, x_2)$$
$$Hist_{\overline{\texttt{Left}}}(y_1, y_2, x_1, x_2) \leftarrow Hist_{\texttt{Left}}(y_1, y_2, x_1, x_2) \wedge Hist_{\overline{\texttt{Left}}}(y_1, y_3, x_1, x_2)$$
$$New_{\texttt{Left}}(y_1, y_3, x_1, x_2) \leftarrow New_{\texttt{Left}}(y_1, y_2, x_1, x_2) \wedge New_{\texttt{Left}}(y_2, y_3, x_1, x_2)$$
$$New_{\texttt{Left}}(y_1, y_3, x_1, x_2) \leftarrow Hist_{\texttt{Left}}(y_1, y_2, x_1, x_2) \wedge New_{\texttt{Left}}(y_2, y_3, x_1, x_2)$$
$$New_{\texttt{Left}}(y_1, y_3, x_1, x_2) \leftarrow New_{\texttt{Left}}(y_1, y_2, x_1, x_2) \wedge Hist_{\texttt{Left}}(y_2, y_3, x_1, x_2)$$
$$New_{\overline{\texttt{Left}}}(y_2, y_3, x_1, x_2) \leftarrow New_{\texttt{Left}}(y_1, y_2, x_1, x_2) \wedge New_{\overline{\texttt{Left}}}(y_1, y_3, x_1, x_2)$$
$$New_{\overline{\texttt{Left}}}(y_2, y_3, x_1, x_2) \leftarrow Hist_{\texttt{Left}}(y_1, y_2, x_1, x_2) \wedge New_{\overline{\texttt{Left}}}(y_1, y_3, x_1, x_2)$$
$$New_{\overline{\texttt{Left}}}(y_2, y_3, x_1, x_2) \leftarrow New_{\texttt{Left}}(y_1, y_2, x_1, x_2) \wedge Hist_{\overline{\texttt{Left}}}(y_1, y_3, x_1, x_2)$$
$$New_{\overline{\texttt{Left}}}(y_1, y_2, x_1, x_2) \leftarrow New_{\texttt{Left}}(y_1, y_2, x_1, x_2) \wedge New_{\overline{\texttt{Left}}}(y_1, y_3, x_1, x_2)$$
$$New_{\overline{\texttt{Left}}}(y_1, y_2, x_1, x_2) \leftarrow Hist_{\texttt{Left}}(y_1, y_2, x_1, x_2) \wedge New_{\overline{\texttt{Left}}}(y_1, y_3, x_1, x_2)$$
$$New_{\overline{\texttt{Left}}}(y_1, y_2, x_1, x_2) \leftarrow New_{\texttt{Left}}(y_1, y_2, x_1, x_2) \wedge Hist_{\overline{\texttt{Left}}}(y_1, y_3, x_1, x_2)$$

**Figure 10.** $\mathcal{M}_{\Pi,\mathcal{R}_{tc}}$ for the program in Example 2.

For any subtree $T'$ of $T$, we say that $T'$ is *new* if one of its axioms is $\alpha(\sigma_{n-1}(z_1), ..., \sigma_{n-1}(z_m))$; otherwise, we say $T'$ is *old*. We first prove that for any *old* subtree $T'$ of $T$ with root $\alpha'(q_1, ..., q_m)$, we have

$$\langle id(\sigma_{n-1}(z_1)), ..., id(\sigma_{n-1}(z_m)), \vec{p}\rangle \in Hist_{l,\texttt{A}}$$

(where $\alpha' \in \{\texttt{A}, \overline{\texttt{A}}\}$).

- Base case: $T'$ is an axiom, so we must have

$$\alpha'(p_1, ..., p_m) \in Dec(\rho')$$

It follows from Lemma 1 and the fact that $Hist_{l,\texttt{A}}$ is closed under the following inference rule:

$$Hist_{l,\texttt{A}}(y_1, \ldots, y_m, \vec{x}) \leftarrow \mathcal{H}_l[\#_1^{\texttt{A}} \mapsto y_1; \ldots; \#_m^{\texttt{A}} \mapsto y_m] \wedge flag_{\texttt{A}}$$

that $\langle p_1, \ldots, p_m, \vec{p}\rangle \in Hist_{l,\texttt{A}}$.
- Inductive step: $T'$ ends with the application of a generator rule $R_g \in \mathcal{M}_{\mathcal{R}}$, say

$$\begin{aligned}\alpha(q_1, \ldots, q_m) \leftarrow\ & \alpha_1(q_{11}, \ldots, q_{1m}) \\ & \wedge \cdots \\ & \wedge\ \alpha_k(q_{k1}, \ldots, q_{km})\end{aligned}$$

(where $\alpha \in \{\texttt{A}, \overline{\texttt{A}}\}$ and $\alpha_i \in \{\texttt{A}_i, \overline{\texttt{A}_i}\}$). Let $T_1, \ldots, T_k$ be the subtrees of $T$ corresponding to the premises of $R_g$. Since each of $T_1, \ldots, T_k$ is a proper subtree of $T$, we have $\langle q_{i1}, ..., q_{im}, \vec{p}\rangle \in Hist_{l,\texttt{A}_i}$ for each $i$ by our inductive hypothesis. Since $Hist_{l,\texttt{A}}$ is closed under the following inference rule: $Hist_{l,\texttt{A}}(y_1, \ldots, y_m, \vec{x}) \leftarrow Hist_{l,\texttt{A}_1}(y_{11}, \ldots, y_{1m}, \vec{x}) \wedge \cdots \wedge Hist_{l,\texttt{A}_k}(y_{k1}, \ldots, y_{km}, \vec{x})$ we have that $\langle q_1, \ldots, q_m, \vec{p}\rangle \in Hist_{l,\texttt{A}}$.

We can use a similar argument to show that for any *new* subtree $T'$ of $T$ with root $\alpha'(q_1, ..., q_m)$, we have $\langle q_1, ..., q_m, \vec{p}\rangle \in New_{l,\alpha'}$.

The final inference rule used in $T$ must be the application of a violator rule. At least one of the immediate subtrees of $T$ must be *new*, since if they are all old, the axioms of $T$ are contained in $Dec(\rho')$ which violates our minimality assumption. It follows that we may use one of the violator rules to derive $\bot$, and therefore $\bot$ belongs to the least fixpoint of $\mathcal{M}_{\Pi,\mathcal{R}}$. □

*Example* 4. The logic program $\mathcal{M}_{\Pi,\mathcal{R}_{tc}}$ constructed for the program program $P_{tc}$ in Example 2 (with respect to the specification of the world $\Theta_{tc}$) is given in Figure 10. Since the only query location is Line 3 of the program, we omit location subscripts in this figure. $\mu$Z is able to determine that this program cannot derive $\bot$, so the program $P_{tc}$ is certified consistent.

Summarizing, our algorithm CHECK-CONSISTENCY for verifying the consistency of $P$ is as follows. First we construct an integer abstraction $\Pi$ and generate numerical invariants using an abstract interpreter. We check that each assertion in the program is safe according to the invariants produced by the abstract interpreter; if a assertion violation is found (indicating a violation of our sorted list abstraction), we report $P$ to be possibly inconsistent. Second, we construct the logic program $\mathcal{M}_{\Pi,\mathcal{R}}$ and check if $\mathcal{M}_{\Pi,\mathcal{R}}$ can derive $\bot$. If it can, we report $P$ to be possibly inconsistent, otherwise we report $P$ to be consistent.

By Lemma 2, we immediately have:

**Theorem 1.** *If the algorithm* CHECK-CONSISTENCY *certifies a program $P$ to be consistent, then $P$ is consistent.*

### 4.3 Limitations

Our algorithm is sound but incomplete. There are several possible sources of loss of precision here: (1) the abstraction of lists by pairs of integers, which require to maintain the invariant that the lists are sorted by IDs; (2) the limitations of the abstract interpretation used to compute the history and current-decision invariants; and (3) the incompleteness of $\mu$Z. In our empirical experience so far, these inaccuracies have not mattered much. The only substantial source of imprecision has been the abstraction of lists by pairs, but as elaborated in the next section, only in two of our benchmark examples does this pose a problem. Also, one could presumably eliminate this issue with a more sophisticated list abstraction.

## 5. Implementation and evaluation

We have implemented our approach and experimented with a collection of standard geometric algorithms. In this section, we report on the results. It is important to bear in mind that (1) it is very difficult to declare an algorithm consistent/inconsistent by a light inspection (even by an expert user), and (2) it is even more difficult to manually prove it is consistent.

### 5.1 Implementation

Our tool is implemented in OCaml on top of a CIL [23] frontend. In addition to taking a C file as input, the tool requires the user to supply a proof system $\mathcal{M}$ (in the form of a set of rules; see Fig. 3). The tool operates in three phases. First, an integer C program is generated from the original program. Then, numerical invariants are generated for the integer program using an abstract domain we will describe below. Then, for each control point in the program at which a decision is made, two Datalog programs are generated (using the invariants from the first phase and the decision proof system $\mathcal{M}$): one Datalog program for the case that the new decision is positive, and one for the case that its negative. Lastly, we use $\mu$Z [14] to check whether a query in any of these Datalog programs succeeds; if all queries fail, then the input program is consistent.

The abstract domain we use to generate numerical invariants is a partitioned octagon domain. Partitioning is a technique used to reduce the precision lost in an abstract domain due to an imprecise join operator [3]. An element of this domain is a partial function $f$ from a finite set of *cells* to octagons. The cells form a covering of the state space, and we require that for every cell $c$, the concretization of the octagon $f(c)$ lies inside $c$; such a function represents a finite disjunction of octagons, where each octagon belongs to a different cell. In our partitioning scheme, the cells corresponds to sets of program variable equalities. We built our partitioned octagon domain on top of the octagon domain implemented in APRON [2].

### 5.2 Benchmarks

We collected a set of geometric algorithms from computational geometry textbooks [8, 9]. These include several convex hull algorithms, a few point location algorithms, and a few triangulation algorithms. Algorithms like this are the core building blocks of geometric libraries such as CGAL [1].

The algorithms are presented in the books as pseudocode, and therefore, there is occasionally more than one way of implementing them. Note that we are not referring to implementation details such as choice of data structures; we included more than one version of the same algorithm whenever there was an algorithmic choice about list traversal strategies and other similar notions that can make a difference in the outcome of our verification algorithm. Below, we provide a high level summary of the benchmarks.

***Convex Hulls.*** We have already discussed two convex hull algorithms: SIMPLECONVEXHULL and GRAHAMSCAN in Sec. 3. The former is not consistent. We discuss the details of the consistency check for the latter in the following. The set of benchmarks consists of three other convex hull algorithms: the Gift Wrapping algorithm, the Incremental Hull algorithm, and Fortune's algorithm. For the Gift Wrapping algorithm, we present two different variations on how the point set is traversed. The incremental hull is a recursive algorithm which has three variations on how the recursive step is performed. Fortune's algorithm uses a major subroutine that computes a half of a convex hull (which is effectively called twice); we include this subroutine as a separate benchmark. Note that Fortune's consistency is not trivially implied by the consistency of this subroutine. In [8], a slight variation of Fortune's original algorithm [10] was presented which is inconsistent (in contrast to the original algorithm being designed specifically to be consistent). Since all other examples were collected from textbooks, we included this version in the set of benchmarks as well.

***Triangulation.*** A *triangulation* of a planar point set $P$ is a subdivision of the plane determined by a maximal set of non-crossing edges whose vertex set is $P$. The word maximal in the definition indicates that any edge not in triangulation must intersect the interior of at least one of the edges in the triangulation.

(Rule G1) $\texttt{Lturn}(y, z, x) \leftarrow \texttt{Lturn}(x, y, z)$

(Rule G2) $\texttt{Lturn}(y, x, z) \leftarrow \overline{\texttt{Lturn}}(x, y, z)$

(Rule G4) $\texttt{Lturn}(x, y, z) \leftarrow \texttt{Lturn}(x, y, s) \wedge \texttt{Lturn}(y, z, s) \wedge \texttt{Lturn}(z, x, s)$

(Rule G5) $\texttt{Lturn}(x, y, t) \leftarrow \texttt{Lturn}(x, y, z) \wedge \texttt{Lturn}(x, y, s) \wedge \texttt{Lturn}(y, z, s) \wedge \texttt{Lturn}(y, z, t) \wedge \texttt{Lturn}(s, y, t)$

(Rule V1) $\bot \leftarrow \texttt{Lturn}(x, y, z) \wedge \overline{\texttt{Lturn}}(x, y, z)$

**Figure 11.** Decision proof system for the $Lturn$ predicate.

In our benchmarks we have Triangle Splitting, Incremental triangulation, and Delaunay triangulation. Triangle Splitting makes use of a *point location* algorithm (see below), and therefore, its consistency depends on the consistency of the underlying point location algorithm (i.e., if the latter is inconsistent, then the former is also inconsistent). Since we have two different *point location* algorithms in our benchmarks, we have two versions of the Triangle Splitting algorithm respectively. Incremental triangulation is algorithmically similar to the incremental convex hull and we similarly included three versions of it depending on the recursing strategy. Both Triangle Splitting and Incremental triangulation algorithms use the same `Lturn` predicate that is used by the convex hull algorithms.

Delaunay triangulation is a specific type of triangulation that has special uses in many areas, e.g. in terrain reconstruction. These algorithms use an operation called *flipping* to turn an arbitrary triangulation into a Delaunay one or to construct a Delaunay triangulation incrementally. Flipping relies on a new predicate called `InCircle` that tests if a given point lies within a given circle. The predicate comes with its own complete set of axioms [17] — for brevity, we omit the definition of this new predicate and its corresponding axioms here and refer the interested reader to [17]. Unfortunately, all textbook Delaunay triangulation algorithms are inconsistent, and this inconsistency leads to nontermination under some inputs.

***Point Location.*** In a *point location* algorithm, the input is usually a triangulation (of a point set) and a point $p$, and the goal is to find the particular triangle that contains $p$. Point location queries arise in various settings, such as finding one's location on a map and computer graphics (it is an essential part of ray-tracing algorithms). In the example that we now consider, the location is a target triangle. There are various inconsistent point location algorithms; Fortune [10] proposed a consistent algorithm for point location. We included Fortune's algorithm and a standard inconsistent algorithm that is routinely used in ray tracer implementations.

***Axioms and decision proof system.*** All our benchmarks use the $Lturn$ predicate introduced earlier; we assume an axiomatization as in Fig. 3 for this predicate. Fig. 11 offers a sketch of the decision proof system derived from these axioms. Here, Rules G1 and G2 represent the nondegeneracy case of axiom 3 in Fig. 3. Rules G1 corresponds to the cyclic symmetry and antisymmetry axioms, while rules G4 and G5 represent the interiority and transitivity axioms. Rule V1 is the violator rule for the `Lturn` predicate.

### 5.3 Experimental Results

Table 1 presents the result of the experiments carried out using our tool. The upper, middle, and the lower part of the table respectively show the results for a variety of convex hull, point location, and triangulation algorithms.

The first two columns (after the benchmark names) indicate whether the benchmark is consistent and whether our tool managed to prove it consistent. A "NO" answer by the tool means that a counterexample was found for the consistency of the *integer* C

| Benchmark | Consistent? | Proved Consistent? | Invariant Generation Time | Consistency Analysis Time | Invariant Size |
|---|---|---|---|---|---|
| SlowHull | NO | NO | 14s | 2s | 780 (2) |
| Graham Scan | YES | YES | 22s | 38s | 4188 (4) |
| Gift Wrapping v1 | NO | NO | 24s | 2s | 1494 (2) |
| Gift Wrapping v2 | NO | NO | — | — | — |
| Incremental Hull v1 | YES | YES | 1m5s | 44s | 4454 (2) |
| Incremental Hull v2 | YES | YES | 1m1s | 2m23s | 5904 (2) |
| Incremental Hull v3 | YES | NO | 1m35s | 22s | 22658 (4) |
| Fortune (half) Hull | YES | YES | 10s | 13s | 774 (2) |
| Fortune Hull | YES | YES | 2m43s | 5m17s | 30088 (8) |
| Fortune Hull (t) | NO | NO | 48s | 10s | 10440 (6) |
| Point Location v1 | YES | YES | 25s | 2m28s | 2608 (4) |
| Point Location v2 | NO | NO | 1m26s | 2s | 566 (6) |
| Hull Triangle Location | NO | NO | 1m38s | 4s | 2202 (6) |
| Incremental Triangulation v1 | YES | YES | 1m12s | 44s | 4454 (2) |
| Incremental Triangulation v2 | YES | YES | 1m8s | 2m23s | 5904 (2) |
| Incremental Triangulation v3 | YES | NO | 1m38s | 31s | 22658 (2) |
| Triangle Splitting v1.1 | YES | YES | 40s | 2m28s | 2608 (4) |
| Triangle Splitting v1.2 | NO | NO | 1m45s | 2s | 566 (6) |
| Triangle Splitting v2 | NO | NO | — | — | — |
| Delaunay Triangulation v1 | NO | NO | 6s | 0s | 152 (2) |
| Delaunay Triangulation v2 | NO | NO | — | — | — |

**Table 1.** Automated Consistency Verification Results. Invariant Generation Time refers to the time that it takes for the invariants to be generated for the integer program. Consistency Analysis time refers to the time that it takes $\mu$Z to prove the consistency claims. Invariant Size refers to the size of the invariants (in number of conjuncts); where there is more than one decision location in the program, we add the invariants up into a total number, but indicate the number of claims within parentheses.

program. However, since this integer program is an overapproximation of the behaviour of the original C program, the counterexample may not be a real one. Note that since our tool is *sound*, a NO/YES combination is not a possibility for these two columns. And, since it is not complete, a YES/NO option is a possibility.

For some of the benchmarks, no times are reported. This is because the benchmark was declared inconsistent in the integer program generation phase, since the proper ordering constraints were not followed while manipulating lists in the program. Interestingly, in all such cases, the program is indeed inconsistent.

***Summary of Results.*** Out of the 21 benchmarks, 9 are consistent. There are 3 inconsistent benchmarks that are declared inconsistent when the integer program generation fails to generate a meaningful program. Note that the $\mu$Z terminates much faster in the case where an inconsistency is found since it finds a satisfiable assignment relatively quickly in these cases, whereas for the consistent cases, it has to effectively prove the lack of a satisfiable assignment.

For almost all (except two) benchmarks, if the program is consistent, our tool succeeds to prove it. For a variation of Incremental convex hull (v3) and the corresponding incremental triangulation algorithm (v3), the list abstraction is too coarse to prove the example consistent. The reason for inconsistency is that in the *integer* program, the program is practically making repeat queries. In our uncertain semantics, we assume that repeat queries may get different result from the original ones. If we drop this assumption, then the tool can be easily tuned to prove these two benchmarks consistent as well. The fact that we can prove almost all consistent examples correct using our tool suggests that our proposed abstraction technique is powerful despite its simplicity.

### 5.4 Detailed Discussion of Graham Scan

We discussed the Graham Scan algorithm as an example in Sec. 3. Here we provide a more detailed consistency argument, to provide some intuition why our tool succeeds in proving it consistent.

First, an integer program is generated from this program. Here, we assume that the points in $S$ are assigned integer IDs in the order that they are fetched from the input list (from 1 to $|S|$). The point $p_0$ has an ID 0. As stated earlier, we ignore the assumption that the input points are sorted according to their polar angle. From this point on, we just refer to the points by their numeric identifiers.

Now consider line 6 of the Graham Scan code (Fig. 8), where the query $\texttt{Lturn}(u, v, w)$ is made. We note that $u < v < w$ is an invariant here, and from this observation, we can deduce the following history invariant for this location:

$$\mathcal{H}(\#_1, \#_2, \#_3, u, v, w, p_0) \equiv p_0 < \#_1 < \#_2 < \#_3.$$

Now consider the new decision that is about to be made at line 6: $Lturn(u, v, w)$. Invariant generation provides us with the following facts about values of $u$,$v$, and $w$:

$$d_{\overline{\texttt{Lturn}}}(\#_1, \#_2, \#_3, u, v, w, p_0) \equiv u < v < w \wedge w > \#_3 \wedge p_0 < \#_1 < \#_2 < \#_3$$

Note that the actual invariant generated by our tool contains many more conjuncts and variables. Here, we are stripping it to the essential core to demonstrate the reasoning. Also, this is a specific case where the outcome of the query was false. There will be a similar case where the outcome of the query is true,

$$d_{\texttt{Lturn}}(\#_1, \#_2, \#_3, u, v, w, p_0) \equiv u < v < w \wedge w > \#_3 \wedge p_0 < \#_1 < \#_2 < \#_3$$

but the reasoning below will be the same (though done separately for each of) the two cases.

Combining the information for the history and the current decision, it is easy to argue that if the history is already consistent, then the new decision added will not create any new inconsistencies with respect to any of the rules in Fig. 11. Since the third argument $w$ is (provably) strictly greater than the arguments $\#_1, \#_2, \#_3$ which characterize all past decisions, it is easy to see why this is the case. Each argument of the $Lturn$ predicate appears at least twice among the premises of every single rule in Fig. 11; therefore, any decision with fresh new point $w$ cannot be involved in generating any new facts or causing a violation. The actual reasoning for this is done by $\mu$Z in our implementation.

Now consider the decision at line 14. Here, $w$ never changes and always points to $p_0$ (i.e. $id_w = 0$). Naturally, the history for line 6 is also part of the history for line 14. But the history for line 14 also includes the decisions made previously in the same loop.

Our analysis produces the following history invariant:

$$\mathcal{H}(\#_1, \#_2, \#_3, u, v, w, p_0) \equiv (p_0 < \#_1 < \#_2 < \#_3) \vee (p_0 < \#_1 < \#_2 \wedge \#_3 = p_0)$$

where the first disjunct refers to the history based on the decisions made at line 6 and the second disjunct refers to the history based on the decisions made at line 14. The current decision invariant is:

$$d_{\overline{\texttt{Lturn}}}(\#_1, \#_2, \#_3, u, v, w, p_0) \equiv ((u < v) \wedge w = p_0 \wedge (p_0 < \#_1 < \#_2 < \#_3)) \vee ((u < v) \wedge (w = p_0) \wedge (v > \#_2) \wedge (p_0 < \#_1 < \#_2) \wedge \#_3 = p_0))$$

and, similar to above, there is a positive version of this decision. It is a bit harder to *manually* reason about this case. Intuitively, it is easy to reason that the decision, where the last argument is always a fresh new value 0, cannot generate any new facts or violations when considered together with the history decisions that are generated at line 6 (in which 0 never appears).

The argument about why no new violations are created as a result of combining the new decision with the part of history that comes from line 14 is similar to the case of line 6.

## 6. Related work

The problem of consistency has been studied in depth in the computational geometry literature [15, 16, 21, 26]. This literature has developed several subtly different notions of consistency for geometric programs; our definition coincides with a definition used by, among others, Fortune [10]. However, so far as we know, there is no prior work on static verification of consistency in this area: to the extent that verification is mentioned at all, it is stated to be "too difficult to be realistic" [20]. Instead, existing approaches focus on dynamic techniques that are often based on high-precision library operations. The inherent limitation of such approaches is that they do not reason globally about uncertain decisions made at different program points, and hence do not give end-to-end guarantees of consistency. The only work on formal verification of geometric programs that we know of comes from the theorem proving community [24], and this work does not study consistency.

There is an emerging body of work on reasoning about program behaviour in the presence of uncertainty [4, 5, 18, 19, 25]. However, none of these analyses can reason about the notion of consistency considered in this paper; instead, they focus on quantitative differences in a program's behaviour due to uncertainty. Also not applicable are abstract-interpretation-based techniques for quantifying numerical errors in programs [6, 11], as none of these methods reason about divergence in control flow caused by uncertainty. In contrast, uncertain control flow is perhaps the most central aspect of the geometric programs studied here.

## 7. Conclusion

We have introduced the problem of automatically verifying the consistency of programs that make decisions under uncertainty, and taken the first steps towards solving the problem. Our solution can automatically verify the consistency of a comprehensive set of algorithms for computing convex hulls and triangulations.

While this paper focused on finding *proofs* of robustness, the dual problem of finding inputs that cause a geometric program to violate robustness is also of interest. Also, we restricted ourselves in this paper to a model of uncertainty where *every* predicate can evaluate nondeterministically. As we showed, even under this highly adversarial execution model, many everyday computations are consistent. However, future work should also study less hostile models of numerical uncertainty. There are several ways to account for this fact. For instance, a possibility is to consider quantitative models of uncertainty properties where a query "flips" with a certain probability, or under certain conditions on the inputs.

## References


[1] CGAL, Computational Geometry Algorithms Library. http://www.cgal.org.

[2] J. Bertrand and A. Miné. Apron: A library of numerical abstract domains for static analysis. In *CAV*, pages 661–667, 2009.

[3] François Bourdoncle. Abstract interpretation by dynamic partitioning. *Journal of Functional Programming*, 2(04):407–435, 1992.

[4] S. Chaudhuri, S. Gulwani, and R. Lublinerman. Continuity analysis of programs. In *POPL*, pages 57–70, 2010.

[5] S. Chaudhuri, S. Gulwani, and R. Lublinerman. Continuity and robustness s of programs. *Commun. ACM*, 55(8):107–115, 2012.

[6] L. Chen, A. Miné, J. Wang, and P. Cousot. Interval polyhedra: An abstract domain to infer interval linear relationships. In *SAS*, 2009.

[7] M. De Berg, O. Cheong, and M. Van Kreveld. *Computational geometry: algorithms and applications*. Springer-Verlag, 2008.

[8] Mark de Berg, Marc van Kreveld, Mark Overmars, and Otfried Schwarzkopf. *Computational Geometry: Algorithms and Applications*. Springer-Verlag, 2000.

[9] S. Devadoss and J. O'Rourke. *Discrete and Computational Geometry*. Princeton University Press, 2011.

[10] S. Fortune. Stable maintenance of point set triangulations in two dimensions. In *FOCS*, pages 494–499, 1989.

[11] E. Goubault. Static analyses of the precision of floating-point operations. In *SAS*, pages 234–259, 2001.

[12] Ronald L. Graham. An efficient algorithm for determining the convex hull of a finite planar set. *Inf. Process. Lett.*, 1(4):132–133, 1972.

[13] J. Halpern. *Reasoning about uncertainty*. The MIT Press, 2003.

[14] K. Hoder, N. Bjørner, and L. de Moura. $\mu$Z - an efficient engine for fixed points with constraints. In *CAV*, 2011.

[15] C. Hoffmann, J. Hopcroft, and M. Karasick. Towards implementing robust geometric computations. In *SoCG*, pages 106–117, 1988.

[16] C.M. Hoffmann. The problems of accuracy and robustness in geometric computation. *Computer*, 22(3):31–39, 1989.

[17] D.E. Knuth. *Axioms and Hulls (LNCS #606)*. Springer-Verlag, 1992.

[18] R. Majumdar, E. Render, and P. Tabuada. A theory of robust software synthesis. *CoRR*, abs/1108.3540, 2011.

[19] R. Majumdar and I. Saha. Symbolic robustness analysis. *Real-Time Systems Symposium, IEEE International*, 0:355–363, 2009.

[20] K. Mehlhorn. *The reliable algorithmic software challenge RASC*, pages 255–263. 2003.

[21] K. Mehlhorn and C. Yap. *Robust geometric computation*. `http://cs.nyu.edu/~yap/book/egc`, 2011.

[22] D. Monniaux. The pitfalls of verifying floating-point computations. *ACM Trans. Program. Lang. Syst.*, 30(3), 2008.

[23] George C. Necula, Scott McPeak, Shree Prakash Rahul, and Westley Weimer. CIL: Intermediate language and tools for analysis and transformation of C programs. In *CC*, pages 213–228, 2002.

[24] D. Pichardie and Y. Bertot. Formalizing convex hull algorithms. In *TPHOLs*, volume 2152 of *LNCS*, pages 346–361. Springer, 2001.

[25] J. Reed and B. Pierce. Distance makes the types grow stronger: A calculus for differential privacy. In *ICFP*, 2010.

[26] R. Shewchuk. Adaptive precision floating-point arithmetic and fast robust geometric predicates. *Discrete & Computational Geometry*, 18(3):305–363, 1997.

# Toward General Diagnosis of Static Errors

Danfeng Zhang Andrew C. Myers
Department of Computer Science
Cornell University
Ithaca, NY, 14853
zhangdf@cs.cornell.edu andru@cs.cornell.edu

## Abstract

We introduce a general way to locate programmer mistakes that are detected by static analyses such as type checking. The program analysis is expressed in a constraint language in which mistakes result in unsatisfiable constraints. Given an unsatisfiable system of constraints, both satisfiable and unsatisfiable constraints are analyzed, to identify the program expressions most likely to be the cause of unsatisfiability. The likelihood of different error explanations is evaluated under the assumption that the programmer's code is mostly correct, so the simplest explanations are chosen, following Bayesian principles. For analyses that rely on programmer-stated assumptions, the diagnosis also identifies assumptions likely to have been omitted. The new error diagnosis approach has been implemented for two very different program analyses: type inference in OCaml and information flow checking in Jif. The effectiveness of the approach is evaluated using previously collected programs containing errors. The results show that when compared to existing compilers and other tools, the general technique identifies the location of programmer errors significantly more accurately.

***Categories and Subject Descriptors*** D.2.5 [*Testing and Debugging*]: Diagnostics; D.4.6 [*Security and Protection*]: Information flow controls; F.3.2 [*Semantics of Programming Languages*]: Program analysis.

***Keywords*** Error diagnosis; static program analysis; type inference; information flow

## 1. Introduction

Sophisticated type systems and other program analyses enable verification of complex, important properties of software. Advances in type inference, dataflow analysis, and constraint solving have made these verification methods more practical by reducing both analysis time and annotation burden. However, the impact on industrial practice is disappointing.

We posit that a key barrier to adoption of sophisticated analyses is that debugging is difficult when the analysis reports an error. When deep, non-local software properties are being checked, the analysis may detect an inconsistency in a part of the program far from the actual error, resulting in a misleading error message. Determining from this message where the true error lies can require an unreasonably complete understanding of how the analysis works.

We are motivated to study this problem based on experience with two programming languages: ML, whose unification-based type inference algorithm sometimes generates complex, even misleading error messages [35], and Jif [30], a version of Java that statically analyzes the security of information flow within programs but whose error messages also confuse programmers [19]. Prior work has explored a variety of methods for improving error reporting in each of these languages. Although these methods are usually specialized to a single language and analysis, they still frequently fail to identify the location of programmer mistakes.

In this work, we take a more general approach. Most program analyses, including type systems and type inference algorithms, can be expressed as systems of constraints over variables. In the case of ML type inference, variables stand for types, constraints are equalities between different type expressions, and type inference succeeds when the corresponding system of constraints is satisfiable.

When constraints are unsatisfiable, the question is how to report the failure indicating an error by the programmer. The standard practice is to report the failed constraint along with the program point that generated it. Unfortunately, this simple approach often results in misleading error messages—the actual error may be far from that program point. Another approach is to report all expressions that might contribute to the error (e.g., [7, 14, 34, 35]). But such reports are often verbose and hard to understand [16].

Our insight is that when the constraint system is unsatisfiable, a more holistic approach should be taken. Rather than looking at a failed constraint in isolation, the structure of the constraint system as a whole should be considered. The constraint system defines paths along which information propagates; both satisfiable and unsatisfiable paths can help locate the error. An expression involved in many unsatisfiable paths is more likely to be erroneous; an expression that lies on many satisfiable paths is more likely correct. This approach can be justified on Bayesian grounds, under the assumption, captured as a prior distribution, that code is mostly correct.

In some languages, the satisfiability of constraint systems depends on environmental assumptions, which we call hypotheses. The same general approach can also be used to identify hypotheses likely to be missing: a small, weak set of hypotheses that makes constraints satisfiable is more likely than a large, strong set.

***Contributions*** This paper presents the following contributions:

1. A general constraint language that can express a broad range of program analyses. We show that it can encode both ML type inference and Jif information flow analysis, as well as other analyses, including many dataflow analyses (Section 3).
2. A general algorithm for identifying likely program errors, based on the analysis of a constraint system extracted from the pro-


*POPL '14*, January 22–24, 2014, San Diego, CA, USA.

http://dx.doi.org/10.1145/2535838.2535870

```
1  let f(lst: move list): (float*float) list =
2    ...
3    let rec loop lst x y dir acc =
4      if lst = [] then
5        acc
6      else
7        print_string "foo"
8    in
9    List.rev (loop lst 0.0 0.0 0.0 [(0.0,0.0)])
```

**Figure 1.** OCaml example. Line 9 is blamed for a mistake at line 7.

```
1  public final byte[{}]{this} encText;
2  ...
3  public void m(FileOutputStream[{this}]{this}
4      encFos) throws (IOException) {
5    try {
6      for (int i=0; i<encText.length; i++)
7        encFos.write(encText[i]);
8    } catch (IOException e) {}
9  }
```

**Figure 2.** Jif example. Line 3 is blamed for a mistake at line 1.

gram. Using a Bayesian posterior distribution [13], the algorithm suggests program expressions that are likely errors and offers hypotheses that the programmer is likely to have omitted (Sections 4 and 5).

3. An evaluation of this new error diagnosis algorithm on two different sets of programs written in OCaml and Jif. As part of this evaluation we use a large set of programs collected from students using OCaml to do programming assignments [22] (Section 6). Appealingly, high-quality results do not rely on language-specific tuning.

## 2. Approach

Our general approach to diagnosing errors can be illustrated through examples from two languages: ML and Jif.

### 2.1 ML type inference

The power of type inference is that programmers may omit types. But when type inference fails, the resulting error messages can be confusing. Consider Figure 1, containing (simplified) OCaml code written by a student working on a programming assignment [22]. The OCaml compiler reports that the expression `[(0.0, 0.0)]` at line 9 is a list, but is used with type `unit`. However, the programmer's actual fix shows that the error is the `print_string` expression at line 7.

The misleading report arises because currently prevalent error reporting methods (e.g., in OCaml [31], SML [28], and Haskell [17]) unify types according to type constraints or typing rules, and report the last expression considered, the one on which unification fails. However, the first failed expression can be far from the actual error, since early unification using an erroneous expression may lead type inference down a garden path of incorrect inferences.

In our example, the inference algorithm unifies (i.e., equates) the types of the four highlighted expressions, in a particular order built into the compiler. One of those expressions, `[(0.0, 0.0)]`, is blamed because the inconsistency is detected when unifying its type.

Prior work has attempted to address this problem by reporting either the complete *slice* of the program relating to a type inference failure, or a smaller subset of unsatisfiable constraints [7, 14, 34, 35]. Unfortunately, both variants of this approach can still require considerable manual effort to identify the actual error within the program slice, especially when the slice is large.

### 2.2 Jif label checking

Confusing error messages are not unique to traditional type inference. The analysis of information flow security, which checks a different kind of nonlocal code property, can also generate confusing messages when security cannot be verified.

Jif [30] is a Java-like language whose static analysis of information flow often generates confusing error messages [19]. Figure 2 shows a simplified version of code written by a Jif programmer. Jif programs are similar to Java programs except that they specify security labels, shadowed in the example. Omitted labels (such as the label of `i` at line 6) are inferred automatically. However, Jif label inference works differently from ML type inference algorithms: the type checker generates constraints on labels, creating a system of inequalities that are then solved iteratively. For instance, the compiler generates a constraint $\{\} \leq$ `{this}` for line 7, bounding the label of the argument `encText[i]` by that on the formal parameter to `write()`, which is `{this}` because of `encFos`'s type.

Jif error messages are a product of the iterative process used to solve these constraints. The solver uses a two-pass process that involves both raising lower bounds and lowering upper bounds on labels to be solved for. Errors are reported when the lower bound on a label cannot be bounded by its upper bound.

As with ML, early processing of an incorrect constraint may cause the solver to detect an inconsistency later at the wrong location. In this example, Jif reports that a constraint at line 3 is wrong, but the actual programmer mistake is the label $\{\}$ at line 1.

Jif permits programmers to specify assumptions, capturing trust relationships that are expected to hold in the environment in which the program is run. A common reason why label checking fails in Jif is that the programmer has gotten these assumptions wrong (sharing constraints on ML functor parameters are also assumptions, but are simpler and less central to ML programming).

For instance, an assignment from a memory location labeled with a patient's security label to another location with a doctor's label might fail to label-check because the crucial assumption is missing that the doctor acts for the patient. That assumption would imply that an information flow from patient to doctor is secure.

In this paper, we propose a unified way to infer both program expressions likely to be wrong and assumptions likely to be missing.

### 2.3 Overview of the approach

As a basis for a general way to diagnose errors, we define an expressive constraint language that can encode a large class of program analyses, including not only ML type inference and Jif label checking, but also dataflow analyses.

Constraints in this language assert partial orderings on constraint elements. These constraints are then converted into a representation as a directed graph. In that graph, a node represents a constraint element, and a directed edge represents an ordering between the two elements it connects.

For example, Figure 3 is part of the constraint graph generated from the OCaml code of Figure 1. Each node represents either the type of a program expression or a declared type; in the figure, nodes are annotated with the line numbers of that expression or declaration. Each solid edge represents one constraint generated by an OCaml typing rule. For example, the leftmost node represents the type of the result of `print_string`, which is `unit`. Since function `loop` can return this result, the leftmost node is connected by edges to the node representing the result type of `loop` (at line 9).

Type inference fails if there is at least one unsatisfiable path within the constraint graph, indicating a sequence of unifications that generate a contradiction. Consider, for example, the three paths $P_1$, $P_2$, and $P_3$ in the figure. The end nodes of each path must

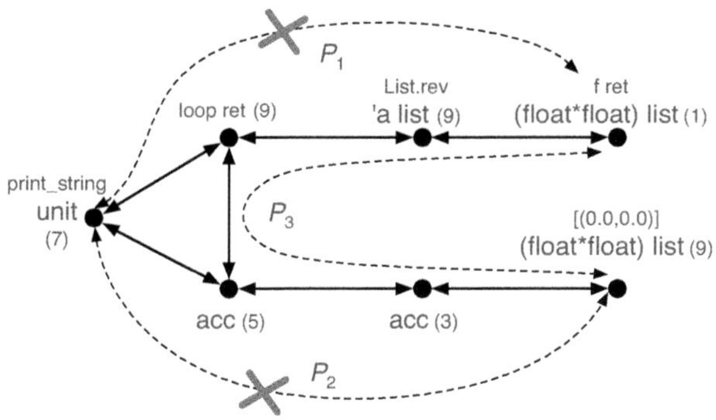


**Figure 3.** Part of the constraint graph for the OCaml example

represent the same types. Other such inferred paths exist, such as between the node for `unit` and the node for variable $acc_{(3)}$, but these paths are not shown since a path with at least one variable on an end node is trivially satisfiable. We call paths that are not trivially satisfiable, such as $P_1$, $P_2$, and $P_3$, the *informative* paths.

In this example, the paths $P_1$ and $P_2$ are unsatisfiable because the types at their endpoints are different. Note that path $P_2$ corresponds to the expressions highlighted in the OCaml code. By contrast, path $P_3$ is satisfiable.

The constraints along unsatisfiable paths form a complete explanation of the error, but one that is often too verbose. Our goal is to be more useful by pinpointing where along the path the error occurs. The key insight is to analyze both satisfiable and unsatisfiable paths.

In Figure 3, the strongest candidate for the real source of the error is the leftmost node of type `unit`, rather than the lower-right expression of type `(float*float) list` that features in the misleading error report produced by OCaml. Two general heuristics help us identify `unit` as the culprit:

1. All else equal, an explanation for unsatisfiability in which programmers have made fewer mistakes is more likely. This is an application of Occam's Razor. In this case, the minimum explanation is a single expression (the `unit` node) which appears on both unsatisfiable paths.
2. The `unit` node appears only on unsatisfiable informative paths, but not on the informative, satisfiable path $P_3$. Since erroneous nodes are less likely to appear in satisfiable paths, the `unit` node is a better error explanation than any node lying on path $P_3$.

Appealingly, these two heuristics rely only on graph structure, and are oblivious to the language and program being diagnosed. The same generic approach can therefore be applied to very different program analyses: our tool correctly and precisely points out the actual error in both the OCaml and Jif examples above.

In addition to helping identify incorrect expressions, the constraint graph also provides enough information to identify assumptions that are likely to be missing.

## 3. Constraint language

Central to our approach is a general core constraint language that can be used to capture a large class of program analyses. In this constraint language, constraints are inequalities using an ordering $\leq$ that corresponds to a flow of information through a program. The constraint language also has constructors and destructors corresponding to computation on that information.

### 3.1 Syntax

The syntax of the constraint language is formalized in Figure 4.

$$G ::= G_1 \wedge G_2 \mid A \qquad\qquad A ::= C_1 \vdash C_2$$
$$C ::= I_1 \wedge \ldots \wedge I_n \;\; {}^{(n\geq 0)} \qquad\qquad I ::= E_1 \leq E_2$$
$$E ::= \alpha \mid c(E_1, \ldots, E_{a(c)}) \mid \overline{c}^{i}(E) \mid E_1 \sqcup E_2 \mid E_1 \sqcap E_2 \mid \bot \mid \top$$

**Figure 4.** Syntax of constraints

The top-level goal $G$ to be solved is a conjunction of assertions $A$, each with the form $C_1 \vdash C_2$, where constraint $C_1$ is the hypothesis (that is, assumption) and constraint $C_2$ is a conclusion to be satisfied.

A constraint $C$, serving either as the hypothesis or as the conclusion of an assertion, is a possibly empty conjunction of inequalities $I$ over elements from $E$, based on the ordering $\leq$. We denote an empty conjunction as $\emptyset$, and abbreviate $\emptyset \vdash C_2$ as $\vdash C_2$.

An element $E$ may be a variable $\alpha \in \mathbf{Var}$ whose value is to be solved for, an application of constructor $c \in \mathbf{Con}$ or the $i$-th argument to a constructor application, represented by $\overline{c}^{i}(E)$. The arity of constructor $c$ is represented as $a(c)$. Constants $c$ are nullary constructors, with arity 0.

The ordering $\leq$ is treated abstractly, but it must define a lattice with the usual join ($\sqcup$) and meet ($\sqcap$) operators, which can be used as syntax. The bottom and top of the element ordering are $\bot$ and $\top$.

***Example*** To model ML type inference, we can represent the type `int->bool` as a constructor application $\mathsf{fn}(\mathsf{int}, \mathsf{bool})$, where $\mathsf{int}$ and $\mathsf{bool}$ are constants. Its first projection $\overline{\mathsf{fn}}^{1}(\mathsf{fn}(\mathsf{int}, \mathsf{bool}))$ is $\mathsf{int}$.

Consider the expressions `acc` (line 5) and `print_string` (line 7) in Figure 1. These are branches of an `if` statement, so one assertion is generated to enforce that they have the same type: $\vdash acc_{(5)} \leq \mathsf{unit} \wedge \mathsf{unit} \leq acc_{(5)}$. Section 3.4.1 describes in more detail how assertions are generated for ML.

### 3.2 Interpretation of constraints

The partial ordering on two applications of the same constructor is determined by the variances of that constructor's arguments. For each argument, the ordering of the applications is either covariant with respect to that argument (denoted by +), contravariant with respect to that argument (−), or invariant with respect to it.

More general partial ordering rules on constructors (e.g., a rule $c_1(x, y) \leq c_2(y, x)$ can also be handled by our inference algorithm in 4.3 in a manner similar to the handling of $\sqcap$ and $\sqcup$, though with increased complexity.

With these abstract definitions, the *validity* of variable-free constraints can be defined in a natural way. A variable-free goal $G$ is valid if all assertions it contains are valid. An assertion $C_1 \vdash C_2$ is valid if the partial orderings in $C_2$ are entailed from $C_1$, using just the lattice properties of the relation $\leq$ and the variances of the various constructor arguments.

***Example*** Let $A, B, C$ be three distinct constants. Then $A \leq B \wedge B \leq C \vdash A \leq C$ is valid by the transitivity of $\leq$. Assertion $\vdash A \leq A \sqcup B$ is valid by the definition of join. Assertion $\vdash A \leq B$ is invalid: the empty assumption does not entail the conclusion.

### 3.3 Satisfiability

Validity as defined so far works for constraints without variables. When constraints mention variables, they are satisfiable if there exists a valuation of all variables such that the goal after value substitution is valid.

Satisfiability depends on the *ground terms* $\mathcal{T}$ that a variable can map into. Let $\mathcal{T}$ be the greatest fixed point of the following rules:

- All constants are in $\mathcal{T}$.
- $c(t_1, \ldots, t_{a(c)}) \in \mathcal{T}$ if $\forall_{i \in \{1,\ldots,a(c)\}}\, t_i \in \mathcal{T}$ and $c \in \mathbf{Con}$.

Notice that ground terms may be infinite. This feature is essential for modeling recursive types.

A valuation $\Phi : \mathbf{Var} \rightarrow \mathcal{T}$ is a function from variables to ground terms. A goal is *satisfiable* when there exists a valuation $\Phi$ such that the goal is valid after substitution using $\Phi$.

***Example*** Let $\alpha \in \mathbf{Var}$, $A, B, C \in \mathcal{T}$. Then $\vdash \alpha \leq A$ is trivially satisfiable by the valuation $\Phi(\alpha) = A$ or $\Phi(\alpha) = \bot$. However, $\vdash \alpha \leq A \wedge B \leq \alpha$ is unsatisfiable since otherwise, $B \leq A$ by the transitivity of $\leq$, yet this ordering on $A$ and $B$ is not entailed.

### 3.4 Expressiveness

The constraint language is the interface between various program analyses and our diagnostic tool. To use this tool, the program analysis implementer must instrument the compiler or analysis to express a given program analysis as a set of constraints in the constraint language.

As we now show, the constraint language is expressive enough to capture a variety of different program analyses. Of course, the constraint language is not intended to express *all* program analyses, such as analyses that involve arithmetic. We leave incorporating a larger class of analyses into our framework as future work.

#### 3.4.1 ML type inference

ML type inference maps naturally into constraint solving, since typing rules are usually equality constraints on types. Numerous efforts have been made in this direction (e.g., [2, 14, 16, 26, 36]).

Most of these formalizations are similar, so we discuss how Damas's Algorithm T [8] can be recast into our constraint language, extending the approach of Haack and Wells [14]. We follow that approach since it supports let-polymorphism. Further, our evaluation builds on an implementation of that approach.

For simplicity, we only discuss the subset of ML whose syntax is shown in Figure 5. However, our implementation does support a much larger set of language features, including `match` expressions and user-defined data types.

In this language subset, expressions can be variables ($x$), integers ($n$), binary operations ($+$), functions abstractions $\texttt{fn}\ x \rightarrow e$, function applications ($e_1\ e_2$), or let bindings ($\texttt{let}\ x = e_1\ \texttt{in}\ e_2$). Notice that let-polymorphism is allowed, such as an expression ($\texttt{let}\ id = \texttt{fn}\ x \rightarrow x\ \texttt{in}\ id\ 2$)

The typing rules that generate constraints are shown in Figure 5. Types $t$ can be type variables to be inferred ($\alpha$), the predefined integer type $\mathsf{int}$, and function types constructed by $\rightarrow$.

The typing rules have the form $e : \langle \Gamma, t, C \rangle$. $\Gamma$ is a typing environment that maps a variable $x$ to a set of types. Intuitively, $\Gamma$ tracks a set of types with which $x$ must be consistent. Let $[\,]$ be an environment that maps all variables to $\emptyset$, and $\Gamma\{x \mapsto T\}$ be a map identical to $\Gamma$ except for variable $x$. $\Gamma_1 \cup \Gamma_2$ is a pointwise union for all type variables: $\forall x.(\Gamma_1 \cup \Gamma_2)(x) = \Gamma_1(x) \cup \Gamma_2(x)$. As before, $C$ is a constraint in our language. It captures the type equalities that must be true in order to give $e$ the type $t$. Note that a type equality $t = t'$ is just a shorthand for the assertion $\vdash t \leq t' \wedge t' \leq t$.

Most of the typing rules are straightforward. To type-check $\texttt{fn}\ x \rightarrow e$, we ensure that the type of $x$ is consistent with all appearances in $e$, which is done by requiring $\alpha_x = t'$ for all $t' \in \Gamma(T)$. The mapping $\Gamma(x)$ is cleared since $x$ is bound only in the function definition. The rule for let-bindings is more complicated. Because of let-polymorphism, the inferred type of $e_1$ ($t_1$) may contain free type variables. To support let-polymorphism, we generate a fresh variant of $\langle \Gamma_1, t_1, C_1 \rangle$, where free type variables are replaced by fresh ones, for each use of $x$ in $e_2$. These fresh variants are then required to be equal to the corresponding uses of $x$.

Creating one variant for each use in the rule for let-bindings may increase the size of generated constraints, and hence make our error diagnosis algorithm more expensive. However, we find performance is still reasonable with this approach. One way to avoid this limitation is to add polymorphically constrained types, as in [12]. We leave that as future work.

$$e ::= x \mid n \mid e_1 + e_2 \mid \texttt{fn}\ x \rightarrow e \mid e_1\ e_2 \mid \texttt{let}\ x = e_1\ \texttt{in}\ e_2$$
$$t ::= \alpha \mid \mathsf{int} \mid t \rightarrow t$$

$$\frac{}{x : \langle [\,]\{x \mapsto \{\alpha_x\}\}, \alpha, \alpha_x = \alpha \rangle} \qquad \frac{}{n : \langle [\,], \alpha, \mathsf{int} = \alpha \rangle}$$

$$\frac{e_1 : \langle \Gamma_1, t_1, C_1 \rangle \qquad e_2 : \langle \Gamma_2, t_2, C_2 \rangle}{e_1 + e_2 : \langle \Gamma_1 \cup \Gamma_2, \alpha, \mathsf{int} = t_1 \wedge \mathsf{int} = t_2 \wedge \mathsf{int} = \alpha \wedge C_1 \wedge C_2 \rangle}$$

$$\frac{e : \langle \Gamma, t, C \rangle \qquad \Gamma(x) = T}{\texttt{fn}\ x \rightarrow e : \langle \Gamma\{x \mapsto \emptyset\}, \alpha, \bigwedge\{\alpha_x = t' \mid t' \in T\} \wedge \alpha = \alpha_x \rightarrow t \wedge C \rangle}$$

$$\frac{e_1 : \langle \Gamma_1, t_1, C_1 \rangle \qquad e_2 : \langle \Gamma_2, t_2, C_2 \rangle}{e_1\ e_2 : \langle \Gamma_1 \cup \Gamma_2, \alpha, t_1 = t_2 \rightarrow \alpha \wedge C_1 \wedge C_2 \rangle}$$

$$\frac{e_1 : \langle \Gamma_1, t_1, C_1 \rangle \qquad e_2 : \langle \Gamma_2, t_2, C_2 \rangle \qquad \Gamma_2(x) = \{t'_1, \ldots, t'_n\}}{\texttt{let}\ x = e_1\ \texttt{in}\ e_2 : \langle \Gamma'_1 \cup \Gamma_2\{x \mapsto \emptyset\}, \alpha, \alpha = t_2 \wedge C \wedge C'_1 \wedge C_2 \rangle}$$

where $\langle \Gamma_{1,1}, t_{1,1}, C_{1,1} \rangle \ldots \langle \Gamma_{1,k}, t_{1,k}, C_{1,k} \rangle$, $k = \max(1, n)$, are fresh variants of $\langle \Gamma_1, t_1, C_1 \rangle$, $\Gamma'_1 = \bigcup_{1 \leq i \leq k} \Gamma_{1,i}$, $C'_1 = \bigwedge_{1 \leq i \leq k} C_{1,i}$ and $C = \{t_{1,1} = t'_1, \ldots, t_{1,n} = t'_n\}$

**Figure 5.** Constraint generation for a subset of ML. $\alpha$ and $\alpha_x$ are fresh variables in typing rules.

#### 3.4.2 Information-flow control

In information-flow control systems, information is tagged with security labels, such as "unclassified" or "top secret". Such security labels naturally form a lattice [9], and the goal of such systems is to ensure that all information flows upward in the lattice.

To demonstrate the expressiveness of our core constraint language, we show that it can express the information flow checking in the Jif language [30]. To the best of our knowledge, ours is the first general constraint language expressive enough to model the challenging features of Jif.

***Label inference and checking*** Jif [30] statically analyzes the security of information flow within programs. All types are annotated with security labels drawn from the decentralized label model (DLM) [29].

Information flow is checked by the Jif compiler using constraint solving. For instance, given an assignment $x := y$, the compiler generates a constraint $L(y) \leq L(x)$, meaning that the label of $x$ must be at least as restrictive as that of $y$.

The programmer can omit some security labels and let the compiler generate them. For instance, when the label of $x$ is not specified, assignment $x := y$ generates a constraint $L(y) \leq \alpha_x$, where $\alpha_x$ is a label variable to be inferred.

Hence, Jif constraints are broadly similar in structure to our general constraint language. However, some features of Jif are challenging to model.

***Label model*** The basic building block of the DLM is a set of *principals* representing users and other authority entities. Principals are structured as a lattice with respect to a relation *actsfor*. The proposition $A$ *actsfor* $B$ means $A$ is at least as privileged as $B$.

Security policies on information are expressed as *labels* that mention these principals. For example, the confidentiality label {patient → doctor} means that the principal patient permits the principal doctor to learn the labeled information. Principals can be used to construct integrity labels as well.

For example, consider the following Jif code:

```
int {patient→ ⊤} x;
int y = x;
int {doctor→ ⊤} z;
if (doctor actsfor patient) z = y;
```

The two assignments generate two satisfiable assertions:

$$\vdash \mathsf{conf}(\mathsf{patient}, \top) \leq \alpha_y$$
$$\wedge \quad \mathsf{patient} \leq \mathsf{doctor} \vdash \alpha_y \leq \mathsf{conf}(\mathsf{doctor}, \top)$$

The principals patient and doctor are constants, and the covariant constructor $\mathsf{conf}(p_1, p_2)$ represents confidentiality labels.

A DLM confidentiality policy can be treated as a covariant constructor on principals. Integrity policies are dual to confidentiality policies, so they can be treated as contravariant constructors on principals. The proof can be found in the associated technical report [38].

***Label polymorphism*** Label polymorphism makes it possible to write reusable code that is not tied to any specific security policy. For instance, consider a function foo with the signature `int foo(bool{A→A} b)`. Instead of requiring the parameter b to have exactly the label {A→A}, the label serves as an upper bound on the label of the actual parameter.

Modeling label polymorphism is straightforward, using hypotheses. The constraint $C_{\mathtt{b}} \leq \{\mathtt{A} \rightarrow \mathtt{A}\}$ is added to the hypotheses of all constraints generated by the method body, where the constant $C_{\mathtt{b}}$ represents the label of variable b.

***Method constraints*** Methods in Jif may contain "where clauses", explicitly stating constraints assumed to hold true during the execution of the method body. The compiler type-checks the method body under these assumptions and ensures that the assumptions are true at all method call sites. In the constraint language, method constraints are modeled as hypotheses.

#### 3.4.3 Dataflow analysis

Dataflow analysis is used not only to optimize code but also to check for common errors such as uninitialized variables and unreachable code. Classic instances of dataflow analysis include reaching definitions, live variable analysis and constant propagation.

Aiken [1] showed how to formalize dataflow analysis algorithms as the solution of a set of constraints with equalities over the following elements (a subclass of the more general *set constraints* in [1]):

$$E ::= A_1 \mid \ldots \mid A_n \mid \alpha \mid E_1 \cup E_2 \mid E_1 \cap E_2 \mid \neg E$$

where $A_1, \ldots, A_n$ are constants, $\alpha$ is a constraint variable, elements represents sets of constants, and $\cup, \cap, \neg$ are the usual set operators.

Consider live variable analysis. Let $\mathsf{S_{def}}$ and $\mathsf{S_{use}}$ be the set of program variables that are defined and used in a statement $S$, and let $succ(S)$ be the statement executed immediately after $S$. Two constraints are generated for statement $S$:

$$S_{in} = \mathsf{S_{use}} \cup (S_{out} \cap \neg \mathsf{S_{def}})$$
$$S_{out} = \bigcup_{X \in succ(S)} X_{in}$$

where $S_{in}, S_{out}, X_{in}$ are constraint variables.

Our constraint language is expressive enough to formalize common dataflow analyses since the constraint language above is nearly a subset of ours: set inclusion is a partial order, and negation can be eliminated by preprocessing in the common case where the number of constants is finite (e.g., $\neg \mathsf{S_{def}}$ is finite).

### 3.5 Errors and explanations

Recall that the goal of this work is to diagnose the cause of errors. Therefore we are interested not just in the satisfiability of a set of assertions, but also in finding the best explanation for why they are not satisfiable. Failures can be caused by both incorrect constraints and missing hypotheses.

***Incorrect constraints*** One cause of unsatisfiability is the existence of incorrect constraints appearing in the conclusions of assertions. Constraints are generated from program expressions, so the presence of an incorrect constraint means the programmer wrote the wrong expression.

***Missing hypotheses*** A second cause of unsatisfiability is the absence of constraints in the hypothesis. The absence of necessary hypotheses means the programmer omitted needed assumptions.

In our approach, an *explanation* for unsatisfiability may consist of both incorrect constraints and missing hypotheses. To find good explanations, we proceed in two steps. The system of constraints is first converted into a representation as a constraint graph (Section 4). This graph is then analyzed using Bayesian principles to identify the explanations most likely to be correct (Section 5).

## 4. Constraint graph

The core constraint language has a natural graph representation that enables analyses of the system of constraints. In particular, the satisfiability of the constraints can be tested via context-free-language reachability in the graph.

### 4.1 Running example

We use the following example throughout this section to illustrate the key ideas behind the constraint graph representation.

***Example*** Consider the following set of constraints.

$$\vdash \alpha \leq \mathsf{fn}(\mathtt{ty1}, \mathtt{bool}) \wedge \mathtt{ty1} \leq \mathtt{ty2} \vdash \beta \leq \alpha \wedge \vdash \mathsf{fn}(\mathtt{ty2}, \mathtt{int}) \leq \beta$$

We interpret $\leq$ here as the subtyping relation. The constructor $\mathsf{fn}(E_1, E_2)$ represents the function type $E_1 \rightarrow E_2$. Note that the constructor fn is contravariant in its first argument and covariant in its second. The identifiers ty1, ty2, bool, int are distinct constants and $\alpha, \beta$ are type variables to be inferred.

The first assertion claims that $\alpha$ is a subtype of $\mathsf{fn}(\mathtt{ty1}, \mathtt{bool})$, with no hypotheses. The third assertion is similar. The second assertion says that $\beta$ is a subtype of $\alpha$ under the assumption that ty1 is a subtype of ty2.

To determine whether this goal is satisfiable, we construct a constraint graph to infer partial orderings that must hold based on these constraints and the built-in, language-independent inference rules associated with the relation $\leq$, the constructors used, and the operators $\sqcup$ and $\sqcap$.

### 4.2 Constraint graph construction

The graph contains a node for each distinct element in the constraint system. For each partial ordering $E_1 \leq E_2$ appearing in assertion conclusions, a directed edge exists from $E_1$ to $E_2$, representing the legal flow of information. We call this edge an LEQ edge.

Hypotheses of assertions are recorded on the LEQ edges generated by the corresponding conclusions. We denote an edge annotated by hypothesis $H$ as $\mathsf{LEQ}\{H\}$. For instance, the second constraint in our running example, $\mathtt{ty1} \leq \mathtt{ty2} \vdash \beta \leq \alpha$, generates an edge $\mathsf{LEQ}\{\mathtt{ty1} \leq \mathtt{ty2}\}$ from node $\beta$ to node $\alpha$.

Additional *constructor edges* in the constraint graph represent the action of constructors. Constructor edges connect the constructor's arguments to the element representing its result. For example,

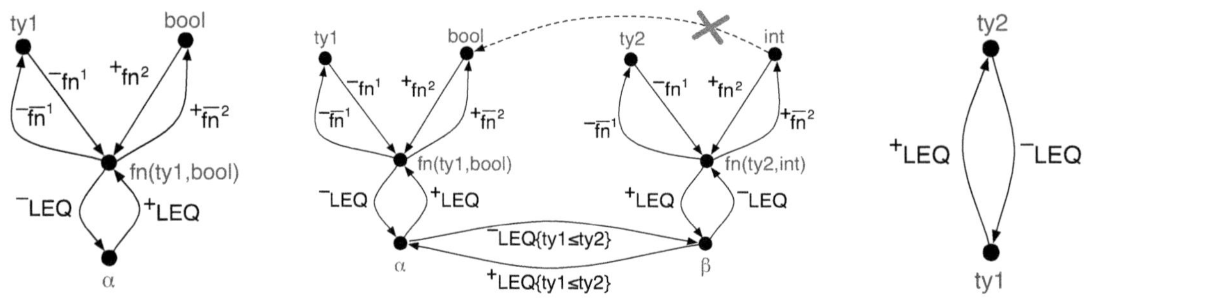


(a) Constructor edges (b) Full constraint graph (c) Hypothesis graph

**Figure 6.** Constraint graph generated from unsatisfiable constraints

there would be a constructor edge to the node representing the element fn(ty1, bool) from each of the nodes for ty1 and bool, as illustrated in Figure 6(a).

Constructor edges include the following annotations: the constructor name, the argument position, and the *variance* of the parameter (covariant, contravariant or invariant). For instance, the edge labeled $(^{-}\mathsf{fn}^1)$ connects the first argument to the constructor application. For each constructor edge there is also a dual decomposition edge that connects the constructor application back to its arguments. It is distinguished by an overline above the constructor name in the graph, and has the same variance: for example, $(^{-}\overline{\mathsf{fn}}^1)$.

To simplify reasoning about the graph, LEQ edges are also duplicated in the reverse direction, with negative variance. Thus, the first assertion in the example, $\vdash \alpha \leq$ fn(ty1, bool), generates a $(^{+}\mathsf{LEQ})$ edge from $\alpha$ to fn(ty1, bool), and a $(^{-}\mathsf{LEQ})$ edge in the other direction, as illustrated in Figure 6(a).

The constraint graph generated using all three assertions from the example is shown in Figure 6(b), excluding the dotted arrow.

***Formal construction of the constraint graph*** Figure 7 formally presents a function $\mathcal{A}$ that translates a set of assertions $A_1 \wedge \ldots \wedge A_n$ into a constraint graph with annotated edges. The graph is represented in the translation as a set of edges defined by the set **Edge**. The nodes of the constructed graph are implicitly defined by their connecting edges. Nodes are drawn from the set **Node**, which consists of the legal elements $E$ modulo the least equivalence relation $\sim$ that satisfies the commutativity of the operations $\sqcup$ and $\sqcap$ and that is preserved by the productions in Figure 4.

As shown, there are three kinds of edges. The LEQ edges, annotated with hypotheses, are generated by the translation rule for $\mathcal{A}[\![C \vdash E_1 \leq E_2]\!]$ and by the rules for meets and joins. Constructor edges are generated by the rules $\mathcal{E}[\![\mathit{cons}(E_1, \ldots, E_n)]\!]C$ and $\mathcal{E}[\![\overline{\mathit{cons}}^i(E)]\!]C$, which connect a constructor application to its arguments. Invariant arguments generate edges as though they were both covariant and contravariant, so twice as many edges are generated.

### 4.3 Inferring node orderings

The constraint graph facilitates inferring all $\leq$ relationships that can be proved using the corresponding constraints. The idea is to construct a context-free grammar, shown in Figure 8, whose productions correspond to inference rules for "$\leq$" relationships.

To perform inference, each production is interpreted as a reduction rule that replaces the right-hand side with the single LEQ edge appearing on the left-hand side. For instance, the transitivity of $\leq$ is expressed by the first grammar production, which derives $(^{p}\mathsf{LEQ}\{H_1 \wedge H_2\})$ from consecutive LEQ edges $(^{p}\mathsf{LEQ}\{H_1\})$ and $(^{p}\mathsf{LEQ}\{H_2\})$, where $p$ is some variance. The inferred LEQ edge has hypotheses $H_1$ and $H_2$ since the inferred partial ordering is valid only when both $H_1$ and $H_2$ hold.

$$n : \textbf{Node} \qquad\qquad (\textbf{Node} = \textbf{Element}/\!\sim)$$
$$e : \textbf{Edge} ::= (^{p}\mathsf{LEQ})\{C\}(n_1 \mapsto n_2) \mid (^{p_i}\mathit{cons}^i)(n_1 \mapsto n_2) \mid (^{p_i}\overline{\mathit{cons}}^i)(n_1 \mapsto n_2)$$
$$\textbf{Graph} = \wp(\textbf{Edge}) \qquad \mathcal{A}[\![G]\!] : \textbf{Graph} \qquad \mathcal{E}[\![E]\!]C : \textbf{Graph}$$

$$\mathcal{A}[\![A_1 \wedge \ldots \wedge A_n]\!] = \bigcup_{i \in 1..n} \mathcal{A}[\![A_i]\!]$$
$$\mathcal{A}[\![C \vdash I_1 \wedge \ldots \wedge I_n]\!] = \bigcup_{i \in 1..n} \mathcal{A}[\![C \vdash I_i]\!]$$
$$\mathcal{A}[\![C \vdash E_1 \leq E_2]\!] = \mathcal{E}[\![E_1]\!]C \cup \mathcal{E}[\![E_2]\!]C \cup \{(^{+}\mathsf{LEQ})\{C\}(E_1 \mapsto E_2), (^{-}\mathsf{LEQ})\{C\}(E_2 \mapsto E_1)\}$$
$$\mathcal{E}[\![\alpha]\!]C = \mathcal{E}[\![c]\!]C = \mathcal{E}[\![\bot]\!]C = \mathcal{E}[\![\top]\!]C = \emptyset$$
$$\mathcal{E}[\![\mathit{cons}(E_1, \ldots, E_n)]\!]C = \bigcup_{i \in 1..n} \Big(\{(^{p_i}\mathit{cons}^i)(E_i \mapsto \mathit{cons}(E_1, \ldots, E_n))\} \cup \{(^{p_i}\overline{\mathit{cons}}^i)(\mathit{cons}(E_1, \ldots, E_n) \mapsto E_i)\} \cup \mathcal{E}[\![E_i]\!]C\Big)$$
$$\mathcal{E}[\![\overline{\mathit{cons}}^i(E)]\!]C = \{(^{p_i}\mathit{cons}^i)(\overline{\mathit{cons}}^i(E) \mapsto E)\} \cup \{(^{p_i}\overline{\mathit{cons}}^i)(E \mapsto \overline{\mathit{cons}}^i(E))\} \cup \mathcal{E}[\![E]\!]C$$
(where $p_i$ is the variance of argument $i$ to constructor *cons*)
$$\mathcal{E}[\![E_1 \sqcup E_2]\!]C = \bigcup_{i \in 1..2} \Big(\{(^{+}\mathsf{LEQ})\{C\}(E_i \mapsto E_1 \sqcup E_2)\} \cup \{(^{-}\mathsf{LEQ})\{C\}(E_1 \sqcup E_2 \mapsto E_i)\} \cup \mathcal{E}[\![E_i]\!]C\Big)$$
$$\mathcal{E}[\![E_1 \sqcap E_2]\!]C = \bigcup_{i \in 1..2} \Big(\{(^{+}\mathsf{LEQ})\{C\}(E_1 \sqcap E_2 \mapsto E_i)\} \cup \{(^{-}\mathsf{LEQ})\{C\}(E_i \mapsto E_1 \sqcap E_2)\} \cup \mathcal{E}[\![E_i]\!]C\Big)$$

**Figure 7.** Construction of the constraint graph

$$(^{p}\mathsf{LEQ}\{H_1 \wedge H_2\}) ::= (^{p}\mathsf{LEQ}\{H_1\})\ (^{p}\mathsf{LEQ}\{H_2\})$$
$$(^{+}\mathsf{LEQ}\{H\}) ::= (^{p}c^i)\ (^{p}\mathsf{LEQ}\{H\})\ (^{p}\overline{c}^i)$$
$$(^{-}\mathsf{LEQ}\{H\}) ::= (^{p}c^i)\ (^{\overline{p}}\mathsf{LEQ}\{H\})\ (^{p}\overline{c}^i)$$
where $c \in \textbf{Con}$, $1 \leq i \leq a(c)$, $p \in \{+, -\}$, $\overline{+} = -$ and $\overline{-} = +$

**Figure 8.** Context-free grammar for $(^{+}\mathsf{LEQ})$ inference

The power of context-free grammars is needed in order to handle reasoning about constructors. In the running example, applying transitivity to the constraints yields ty1 $\leq$ ty2 $\vdash$ fn(ty2, int) $\leq$ fn(ty1, bool). Then, because fn is contravariant in its first argument, we derive $\texttt{ty1} \leq \texttt{ty2}$. Similarly, we can derive $\texttt{int} \leq \texttt{bool}$, the dotted arrow in Figure 6(b).

To capture this kind of reasoning, we use the first two productions in Figure 8. In our example of Figure 6(b), the path from ty1 to ty2 has the following edges: $(^-\mathsf{fn}^1)$ $(^-\mathsf{LEQ})$ $(^-\mathsf{LEQ}\{\texttt{ty1} \leq \texttt{ty2}\})$ $(^-\mathsf{LEQ})$ $(^-\overline{\mathsf{fn}}^1)$. These edges reduce via the first and then the second production to an edge $(^+\mathsf{LEQ}\{\texttt{ty1} \leq \texttt{ty2}\})$ from ty1 to ty2. Note that the variance is flipped because the first constructor argument is contravariant. Similarly, we can infer another $(^+\mathsf{LEQ}\{\texttt{ty1} \leq \texttt{ty2}\})$ edge from int to bool.

The third grammar production in Figure 8 is the dual of the second production, ensuring the invariant that each $(^+\mathsf{LEQ})$ edge has an inverse $(^-\mathsf{LEQ})$ edge. In our example of Figure 6(b), there is also an edge $(^-\mathsf{LEQ}\{\texttt{ty1} \leq \texttt{ty2}\})$ from ty2 to ty1, derived from the following edges: $(^-\mathsf{fn}^1)$ $(^+\mathsf{LEQ})$ $(^+\mathsf{LEQ}\{\texttt{ty1} \leq \texttt{ty2}\})$ $(^+\mathsf{LEQ})$ $(^-\overline{\mathsf{fn}}^1)$. These edges reduce via the first and then the third production to an edge $(^-\mathsf{LEQ}\{\texttt{ty1} \leq \texttt{ty2}\})$ from ty2 to ty1.

Computing all inferable $(^+\mathsf{LEQ})$ edges according to the context-free grammar in Figure 8 is an instance of *context-free-language reachability*, which is well-studied in the literature [5, 27] and has been used for a number of program-analysis applications [33]. We adapt the dynamic programming algorithm of Barrett et al. [5] to find shortest $(^+\mathsf{LEQ})$ paths. We call such paths *supporting paths* since the hypotheses along these paths justify the inferred $(^+\mathsf{LEQ})$ edges. We extend this algorithm to also handle join and meet nodes.

Take join nodes, for instance (meet is handled dually). The rule $E_1 \sqcup E_2 \leq E \iff E_1 \leq E \ \wedge \ E_2 \leq E$ can be used in two directions. The direction from left to right is already handled when we construct edges for join elements (Figure 7).

To use the rule in the other direction, we use the following procedure when a new edge $(^+\mathsf{LEQ})\{C\}(n_1 \mapsto n_2)$ is processed: for each join element $E$ where $n_1$ is an argument of the $\sqcup$ operator, we add an edge from $E$ to $n_2$ if all arguments of the $\sqcup$ operator have a $(^+\mathsf{LEQ})$ edge to $n_2$.

### 4.4 Checking the satisfiability of $(^+\mathsf{LEQ})$ edges

A $(^+\mathsf{LEQ})$ edge, whether inferred or specified directly in an assertion, is added to the graph only when the corresponding $\leq$ ordering is entailed by the constraints along the supporting path. Hence, the constraints along the path must be unsatisfiable if the partial ordering on the end nodes is unsatisfiable.

When either end node of a $(^+\mathsf{LEQ})$ edge is a variable or a $\sqcup(\sqcap)$ node where at least one argument of $\sqcup(\sqcap)$ is a variable, the edge is trivially satisfiable and hence not informative for error diagnosis. For simplicity, we ignore such edges and refer subsequently only to informative $(^+\mathsf{LEQ})$ edges. Two informative $(^+\mathsf{LEQ})$ edges can be inferred in Figure 6(b). These edges are $\texttt{int} \mapsto \texttt{bool}$ and $\texttt{ty1} \mapsto \texttt{ty2}$, though only the first is shown.

A $(^+\mathsf{LEQ})$ edge holds only if all hypotheses on the edge hold too. Therefore, the satisfiability of an edge $(^+\mathsf{LEQ})\{C\}(n_1 \mapsto n_2)$ is equivalent to the satisfiability of the assertion $C \vdash n_1 \leq n_2$. In our running example, the combined hypotheses along both informative edges are $\texttt{ty1} \leq \texttt{ty2}$. Therefore, satisfiability of the constraint system reduces to satisfiability of these assertions:

$$\texttt{ty1} \leq \texttt{ty2} \vdash \texttt{int} \leq \texttt{bool} \qquad \texttt{ty1} \leq \texttt{ty2} \vdash \texttt{ty1} \leq \texttt{ty2}$$

To check the satisfiability of these assertions, we test if the conclusion can be proved from all constraints in the hypothesis. Recall that a constraint graph facilitates the inference of all provable partial ordering given a set of constraints. Therefore, a *hypothesis graph* is constructed in exactly the same way as the constraint graph to find all provable $\leq$ relations.

Specifically, to test if an edge $(^+\mathsf{LEQ})\{C\}(n_1 \mapsto n_2)$ is satisfiable, we construct a hypothesis graph using $C$ as described in Section 4.2 and find all inferable $(^+\mathsf{LEQ})$ edges as described in Section 4.3. Edge $(^+\mathsf{LEQ})\{C\}(n_1 \mapsto n_2)$ is unsatisfiable if the relationship $(^+\mathsf{LEQ})(n_1 \mapsto n_2)$ cannot be inferred from the hypothesis graph using $C$.

For our running example, the hypothesis graphs for both informative edges are the same. From this graph, shown in Figure 6(c), $\texttt{int} \leq \texttt{bool}$ is not provable. The constraints along the supporting path from int to bool form a proof of unsatisfiability.

***Satisfiable and unsatisfiable paths*** When the partial ordering on the end nodes of a path is invalid, we say that the path is *end-to-end unsatisfiable*. End-to-end unsatisfiable paths are helpful because the constraints along the path explain why the inconsistency occurs.

Also useful for error diagnosis is the set of *satisfiable* paths: paths where there is a valid partial ordering on any two nodes on the path for which a $(^+\mathsf{LEQ})$ relationship can be inferred.

Any remaining paths are ignored in our error diagnosis algorithm, since by definition they must contain at least one end-to-end unsatisfiable subpath. For brevity, we subsequently use the term *unsatisfiable path* to mean a path that is *end-to-end* unsatisfiable.

## 5. Ranking explanations

The algorithm in Section 4 identifies unsatisfiable paths in the constraint graph, which correspond to sets of unsatisfiable constraints expressed by our constraint language.

Although the information along unsatisfiable paths already captures why the goal is unsatisfiable, reporting all constraints along a path may give more information than the programmer can digest. Our approach is to use Bayesian reasoning to identify programmer errors more precisely.

### 5.1 A Bayesian interpretation

The cause of errors can be wrong constraints, missing hypotheses, or both. To keep our diagnostic method as general as possible, we avoid building in domain-specific knowledge about mistakes programmers tend to make. However, the framework does permit adding such knowledge in a straightforward way.

The language-level entity about which errors are reported can be specific to the language. OCaml reports typing errors in expressions, whereas Jif reports errors in information-flow constraints. To make our diagnosis approach general, we treat entities as an abstract set $\Omega$ and assume a mapping $\Phi$ from entities to constraints. We assume a prior distribution on entities $P_\Omega$, defining the probability that an entity is wrong. Similarly, we assume a prior distribution $P_\Psi$ on hypotheses $\Psi$, defining the probability that a hypothesis is missing.

Given entities $E \subseteq \Omega$ and hypotheses $H \subseteq \Psi$, we are interested in the probability that $E$ and $H$ are the cause of the error observed. In this case, the observation $o$ is the satisfiability of informative paths within the program. We denote the observation as $o = (o_1, o_2, \ldots, o_n)$, where $o_i \in \{\texttt{unsat}, \texttt{sat}\}$ represents unsatisfiability or satisfiability of the corresponding path. The observation follows some unknown distribution $P_O$.

We are interested in finding a subset $E$ of entities $\Omega$ and a subset $H$ of hypotheses $\Psi$ for which the posterior probability $P(E, H|o)$ is large, meaning that $E$ and $H$ are likely causes of the given observation $o$. In particular, a *maximum a priori* estimate is a pair $(E, H)$ at which the posterior probability takes its maximum value; that is, at $\arg\max_{E\subseteq\Omega, H\subseteq\Psi} P(E, H|o)$.

By Bayes' theorem, $P(E, H|o)$ is equal to

$$P_{\Omega\times\Psi}(E, H)P(o|E, H)/P_O(o)$$

The factor $P_O(o)$ does not vary in the variables $E$ and $H$, so it can be ignored. Assuming the prior distributions on $\Omega$ and $\Psi$ are independent, a simplified term can be used:

$$P_\Omega(E)P_\Psi(H)P(o|E, H)$$

$P_\Omega(E)$ is the prior knowledge of the probability that a set of entities $E$ is wrong. In principle, this term might be estimated by learning from a large corpus of buggy programs or using language-specific heuristics. For simplicity and generality, we assume that each entity is equally likely to be wrong; we leave the incorporation of language-specific knowledge to future work.

We also assume the probability of each entity being the cause is independent.[1] Hence, $P_\Omega(E)$ is estimated by $P_1^{|E|}$, where $P_1$ is a constant representing the likelihood that a single entity is wrong.

$P_\Psi(H)$ is the prior knowledge of the probability that hypotheses $H$ are missing. Of course, not all hypotheses are equally likely to be wrong. For example, the hypothesis $\top \leq \perp$ is too strong to be useful: it makes all constraints succeed. The likely missing hypothesis is both weak and small. Our general heuristics for obtaining this term are discussed in Section 5.3.

$P(o|E, H)$ is the probability of observing the constraint graph, given that entities $E$ are wrong and hypotheses $H$ are missing. To estimate this factor, we assume that the satisfiability of the remaining paths is independent. This allows us to write $P(o|E, H) = \prod_i P(o_i|E, H)$. The term $P(o_i|E, H)$ is calculated using two heuristics:

1. For an unsatisfiable path, either something along the path is wrong, or adding $H$ to the hypotheses on the path makes the partial ordering on end nodes valid. So $P(o_i = \texttt{unsat}|E, H)$ is equal to 1 in this case, and is otherwise 0.
2. A satisfiable path is unlikely (with some constant probability $P_2 < 0.5$) to contain a wrong entity. Since adding or removing $H$ does not affect a path that is already satisfiable, $P(o_i = \texttt{sat}|E, H)$ is not affected by $H$. Hence, we have $P(o_i = \texttt{sat}|E, H) = P_2$ if path $p_i$ contains a constraint generated by some entity in $E$. Otherwise, $P(o_i = \texttt{sat}|E, H) = 1 - P_2$.

The first heuristic suggests we only need to consider the entities and hypotheses that explain all unsatisfiable paths (otherwise $P(o_i|E, H) = 0$ for some $o_i = \texttt{unsat}$ by heuristic 1). We denote this set by $\mathcal{G}$. Suppose nsat (a constant) paths are satisfiable, and entities $E$ appear on $k_E$ of them. Then, based on the simplifying assumptions made, we have

$$\begin{aligned}
&\arg\max_{E\subseteq\Omega, H\subseteq\Psi} P_\Omega(E)P_\Psi(H)P(o|E,H) \\
&= \arg\max_{E\subseteq\Omega, H\subseteq\Psi} P_1^{|E|}P_\Psi(H)P_2^{k_E}(1-P_2)^{\texttt{nsat}-k_E}\Pi_{i:o_i=\text{unsat}}P(o_i|E) \\
&= \arg\max_{(E,H)\in\mathcal{G}} P_1^{|E|}(P_2/(1-P_2))^{k_E}P_\Psi(H)
\end{aligned}$$

An intuitive understanding of this estimation is that the cause must explain all unsatisfiable paths; the wrong entities are likely to be small ($|E|$ is small) and not used often on satisfiable paths (since $P_2 < 1 - P_2$ by heuristic 2); the missing hypothesis is likely to be weak and small, as defined in Section 5.3, which maximizes the term $P_\Psi(H)$.

Although this estimation is affected by the values of $P_1$ and $P_2$, empirical study suggests that the diagnosis result is insensitive to their values across a broad range (see Section 6.2.1).

### 5.2 Inferring likely wrong entities

The term $P_1^{|E|}(P_2/(1-P_2))^{k_E}$ can be used to calculate the likelihood that a subset of entities is the cause. However, its computation for all possible sets of entities can be impractical. Therefore, we propose an instance of A* search [15], based on novel heuristics, to calculate optimal solutions in a practical way.

[1] It seems likely that the precision of our approach could be improved by refining this assumption, since the (rare) missed locations in our evaluation usually occur when the programmer makes a similar error multiple times.

A* search is a heuristic search algorithm for finding minimum-cost solution nodes in a graph of search nodes. In our instance of the algorithm, each search node $n$ represents a set of entities deemed wrong, denoted $E_n$. A solution node is one that explains all unsatisfiable paths—the corresponding entities appear in all unsatisfiable paths. An edge corresponds to adding a new entity to the current set.

The key to making A* search effective is a good cost function $f(n)$. The cost function is the sum of two terms: $g(n)$, the cost to reach node $n$, and $h(n)$, a *heuristic function* estimating the cost from $n$ to a solution.

Before defining the cost function $f(n)$, we note that maximizing the likelihood $P_1^{|E|}(P_2/(1-P_2))^{k_E}$ is equivalent to minimizing $C_1|E| + C_2k_E$, where $C_1 = -\log P_1$ and $C_2 = -\log(P_2/(1-P_2))$ are both positive constants because $0 < P_1 < 1$ and $0 < P_2 < 0.5$. Hence, the cost of reaching $n$ is

$$g(n) = C_1|E_n| + C_2k_{E_n}$$

To obtain a good estimate of the remaining cost—that is, the heuristic function $h(n)$—our insight is to use the number of entities required to cover the remaining unsatisfiable paths, denoted as $\mathcal{P}_{\texttt{rm}}$, since $C_1$ is usually larger than $C_2$. More specifically, $h(n) = 0$ if $\mathcal{P}_{\texttt{rm}} = \emptyset$. Otherwise, $h(n) = C_1$ if $\mathcal{P}_{\texttt{rm}}$ is covered by one single entity; $h(n) = 2C_1$ otherwise.

An important property of the heuristic function is its optimality: all and only the most likely wrong subsets of entities are returned. The proof is included in the associated technical report [38]. The heuristic search algorithm is also efficient in practice: on current hardware, it takes about 10 seconds when the search space is over $2^{1000}$. More performance details are given in Section 6.

Since the remaining part of our instance of A* search is largely standard, we leave the details in the accompanied technical report [38]. The only nonstandard feature is that the search stops when a suboptimal suggestion is found, rather than when the first suggestion is found, since we are interested in all top-ranked suggestions.

### 5.3 Inferring missing hypotheses

Another factor in the Bayesian interpretation is the likelihood that hypotheses (assumptions) are missing. Recall that a path from element $E_1$ to $E_2$ in a constraint graph is unsatisfiable if the conjunction of hypotheses along the path is insufficient to prove the partial ordering $E_1 \leq E_2$. So we are interested in inferring a set of missing hypotheses that are sufficient to repair unsatisfiable paths in a constraint graph.

#### 5.3.1 Motivating example

Consider the following assertions:

$$\begin{aligned}
&(\texttt{Bob} \leq \texttt{Carol} \vdash \texttt{Alice} \leq \texttt{Bob}) \\
\wedge&(\texttt{Bob} \leq \texttt{Carol} \vdash \texttt{Alice} \leq \texttt{Carol}) \\
\wedge&(\texttt{Bob} \leq \texttt{Carol} \vdash \texttt{Alice} \leq \texttt{Carol} \sqcup \perp)
\end{aligned}$$

Since the only hypothesis we have is $\texttt{Bob} \leq \texttt{Carol}$ (meaning Carol is more privileged than Bob), none of the three constraints in the conclusion holds. One trivial solution is to add all invalid conclusions to the hypothesis. This approach would add $\texttt{Alice} \leq \texttt{Bob} \wedge \texttt{Alice} \leq \texttt{Carol} \wedge \texttt{Alice} \leq \texttt{Carol} \sqcup \perp$ to the hypotheses. However, this naive approach is undesirable for two reasons:

1. An invalid hypothesis may invalidate the program analysis. For instance, adding an insecure information flow to the hypotheses can violate security. The programmer has the time-consuming, error-prone task of checking the correctness of every hypothesis.
2. A program analysis may combine static and dynamic approaches. For instance, although most Jif label checking is static, some hypotheses are checked dynamically. So a large hypothesis may also hurt run-time performance.

It may also be tempting to select the minimal missing hypothesis, but this approach does not work well either: a single assumption $\top \leq \bot$ is always a minimal missing hypothesis for all unsatisfiable paths. Given $\top \leq \bot$, any partial order $E_1 \leq E_2$ can be proved since $E_1 \leq \top \leq \bot \leq E_2$. However, this assumption is obviously too strong to be useful.

Intuitively, we are interested in a solution that is both *weakest* and *minimal*. In the example above, our tool returns a hypothesis with only one constraint `Alice` $\leq$ `Bob`: both weakest and minimal.

We now formalize the *minimal weakest missing hypothesis*, and give an algorithm for finding this missing hypothesis.

#### 5.3.2 Missing hypothesis

Consider an unsatisfiable path $P$ that supports an ($^+$LEQ) edge $e = (^+\mathsf{LEQ})\{C\}(n_1 \mapsto n_2)$. For simplicity, we denote the hypothesis of $P$ as $\mathcal{H}(P) = C$, and the conclusion $\mathcal{C}(P) = n_1 \leq n_2$.

We define a *missing hypothesis* as follows:

DEFINITION 1. *Given unsatisfiable paths $\mathcal{P} = \{P_1, P_2, \ldots, P_n\}$, a set of inequalities $S$ is a missing hypothesis for $\mathcal{P}$ iff $\forall P_i \in \mathcal{P} \,.\, \mathcal{H}(P_i) \wedge \bigwedge_{I \in S} I \vdash \mathcal{C}(P_i)$.*

Intuitively, adding all inequalities in the missing hypothesis to the assertions' hypotheses removes all unsatisfiable paths in the constraint graph.[2]

***Example*** Returning to the example in Section 5.3.1, it is easy to verify that `Alice` $\leq$ `Bob` is a missing hypothesis that makes all of the assertions valid.

#### 5.3.3 Finding a minimal weakest hypothesis

We are not interested in all missing hypotheses; instead, we want to find one that is both *minimal* and as *weak* as possible.

To simplify the notation, we further define the conclusion set of unsatisfiable paths $\mathcal{P}$ as the union of all conclusions: $\mathcal{C}(\mathcal{P}) = \bigcup\{\mathcal{C}(P_i) \mid P_i \in \mathcal{P}\}$.

The first insight is that the inferred missing hypothesis should not be too *strong*.

DEFINITION 2. *For a set of unsatisfiable paths $\mathcal{P}$, a missing hypothesis $S$ is no weaker than $S'$ iff*

$$\forall I' \in S' \,.\, \exists P \in \mathcal{P} \,.\, \mathcal{H}(P) \wedge \bigwedge_{I \in S} I \vdash I'$$

That is, $S$ is no weaker than $S'$ if all inequalities in $S'$ can be proved from $S$, using at most one existing hypothesis.

Given this definition, the first property we show is that every subset of $\mathcal{C}(\mathcal{P})$ that forms a missing hypothesis is maximally weak:

LEMMA 1. *$\forall S \subseteq \mathcal{C}(\mathcal{P})$. $S$ is a missing hypothesis $\implies$ no missing hypothesis is strictly weaker than $S$.*

**Proof**. Suppose there exists a strictly weaker missing hypothesis $S'$. Since $S'$ is a missing hypothesis, $\mathcal{H}(P_i) \wedge \bigwedge_{I' \in S'} I' \vdash \mathcal{C}(P_i)$ for all $i$. Since $S \subseteq \mathcal{C}(\mathcal{P})$, $\forall I \in S \,.\, \mathcal{H}(P_i) \wedge \bigwedge_{I' \in S'} I' \vdash I$. So $S'$ is no weaker than $S$. Contradiction. □

The lemma above suggests that subsets of $\mathcal{C}(\mathcal{P})$ may be good candidates for a weak missing hypothesis. However, they are not necessarily minimal. For instance, the entire set $\mathcal{C}(\mathcal{P})$ is a maximally weak missing hypothesis.

To remove the redundancy in this weakest hypothesis, we observe that some of the conclusions are subsumed by others. To be more specific, we say a conclusion $c_i$ ***subsumes*** another conclusion $c_j = \mathcal{C}(P_j)$ if $c_i \wedge \mathcal{H}(P_j) \vdash c_j$. Intuitively, if $c_i$ subsumes $c_j$, then adding $c_i$ to the hypothesis of $P_j$ makes $P_j$ satisfiable.

***Example*** Return to the example in Section 5.3.1. The missing hypothesis `Alice` $\leq$ `Bob` is both the weakest and minimal.

Based on Lemma 1 and the definition above, finding a minimal weakest missing hypothesis in $\mathcal{C}(\mathcal{P})$ is equivalent to finding the minimum subset of $\mathcal{C}(\mathcal{P})$ which subsumes all $c \in \mathcal{C}(\mathcal{P})$. This gives us the following algorithm:

***Algorithm*** Given a set of unsatisfiable paths $\mathcal{P} = \{P_1, P_2, \ldots, P_n\}$:

1. Construct the set $\mathcal{C}(\mathcal{P})$ from the unsatisfiable paths.
2. For all $c_i, c_j$ in $\mathcal{C}(\mathcal{P})$, add $c_j$ to set $S_i$, the set of conclusions subsumed by $c_i$, if $c_i$ subsumes $c_j$.
3. Find the minimum cover $M$ of $\mathcal{C}(\mathcal{P})$, where $\mathcal{S} = \{S_1, \ldots, S_n\}$ and $M \subseteq \mathcal{S}$.
4. Return $\{c_i \mid S_i \in M\}$.

A brute force algorithm for finding the minimal weakest missing hypothesis may check all possible hypotheses. That is on the order of $2^{N^2}$ (the number of all subsets of $\leq$ orderings on elements) where $N$ is the total number of elements used in the constraints. While the complexity of our algorithm is exponential in the number of unsatisfiable paths in the constraint graph, this number is usually small in practice. So the computation is still feasible.

## 6. Evaluation

### 6.1 Implementation

We implemented our general error diagnostic tool in Java. The implementation includes about 5,500 lines of source code, excluding comments and blank lines.

As input, the diagnostic tool reads in constraints following the syntax of Figure 4. The program analyses to be diagnosed must be modified to emit those constraints.

To evaluate our error diagnostic tool on real-world program analyses, we modified the Jif compiler and an extension to the OCaml compiler, EasyOCaml [11], to generate constraints in our constraint language format. EasyOCaml is an extension of OCaml 3.10.2 that generates the labeled constraints defined in [14].

Generating constraints in our language format involved only modest effort. Changes to the Jif compiler include about 300 LoC (lines of code) above more than 45,000 LoC in the Jif compiler. Changes to EasyOCaml include about 500 LoC above the 9,000 LoC of the EasyOCaml extension. Slightly more effort is required for EasyOCaml because that compiler did not track the locations of type variables; this functionality had to be added to trace constraints back to the corresponding source code.

### 6.2 Case study: OCaml error reporting

To evaluate the quality of our ranking algorithm, we used a corpus of previously collected OCaml programs containing errors, collected by Lerner et al. [22]. The data were collected from a graduate-level programming-language course for part-time students with at least two years professional software development experience. The data came from 5 homework assignments and 10 students participating in the class. Each assignment requires students to write 100–200 lines of code.

From the data, we analyzed only type mismatch errors, which correspond to unsatisfiable constraints. Errors such as unbound values or too many arguments to a constructor are more easily localized and are not our focus.

[2] A more general form of missing hypothesis might infer individual hypotheses for each path. But it is less feasible to do so.

We also exclude programs using features not supported by Easy-OCaml and files where the user's fix is unclear. After excluding these files, 336 samples remain.

***Analysis*** Analyzing a file and the quality of error report message manually can be inherently subjective. We made the following efforts to make our analysis less subjective:

1. Instead of judging which error message is more useful, we judged whether the error locations the tools reported were correct.
2. To locate the actual error in the program, we use the user's changes with larger timestamps as a reference. Files where the error location is unclear are excluded in our evaluation.

To ensure the tools return precisely the actual error, a returned location is judged as correct only when it is a subset of the actual error locations.

One subtlety of judging correctness is that multiple locations can be good suggestions, because of let-bindings. For instance, consider a simple OCaml program:

```
let x = true in x + 1
```

Even if the programmer later changed `true` to be some integer, the error suggestion of the let-binding of `x` and the use of `x` are still considered to be correct since they bind to the same expression as the fix. However, the operation `+` and the integer `1` are not since the fix is not related.

Since the OCaml error message reports an expression that appears to have the wrong type, to make the reports comparable, we use expressions as the program entities on which we run our inference algorithm—our tool reports likely wrong expressions in evaluation. Recall that our tool can also generate reports of why an expression has a wrong type, corresponding to unsatisfiable paths in the constraint graph. Using such extra information might improve the error message, but we do not use that capability in the evaluation.

Another mismatch is that our tool inherently reports a small set of program entities (expressions in this case) with the same estimated quality, whereas OCaml reports one error at one time. To make the comparison fair, we make the following efforts:

1. For cases where we report a better result (our tools finds the error location that OCaml misses), we ensure that all locations returned are correct.
2. For other cases, we ensure that the majority of the suggestions are correct.

Moreover, the average top rank suggestion size is smaller than 2. Therefore, our evaluation results should not be affected much by the fact that our tool can offer multiple suggestions.

### 6.2.1 Sensitivity

Recall that maximizing the likelihood of entities $E$ being an error is equivalent to minimizing the term $C_1|E| + C_2 k_E$, where $C_1 = -\log P_1$ and $C_2 = -\log(P_2/(1-P_2))$ (see, Section 5.2). Hence, the ranking is only affected by the ratio between $C_1$ and $C_2$.

To test how sensitive our tool is to the choice of $P_1$ and $P_2$, we collect two important statistics for a wide range of $P_1$ and $P_2$ values: 1) the number of programs where the actual error is missing in top rank suggestions (among 336 programs), 2) the average number of suggestions in the top rank. The result is summarized in Table 1.

We arrange the columns in Table 1 such that for any $0 < P_2 < 0.5$, $P_1$ decreases exponentially from left to right. The last column corresponds to the special case when $P_2 = 0.5$.

Empirically, the overall suggestion quality is best when $P_1 = P_2'^3$, where $P_2' = P_2/1 - P_2$. However, the quality of the suggestions is close for any $P_1$ and $P_2$ s.t. $P_2'^2 \le P_1 \le P_2'^6$; the results are not very sensitive to the choice of these parameters.

If satisfiable paths are ignored ($P_2 = 0.5$, that is, $C_2 = 0$), the top-rank suggestion size is much larger, and more errors are missing. Hence, using satisfiable paths is important to suggestion quality.

The quality of the error report is also considerably worse when $P_1$ is very large relative to $P_2$ ($P_1 = P_2'$). This result shows that unsuccessful paths are more important than successful paths, but that ascribing too importance to the unsuccessful paths (e.g., at $P_1 = P_2'^{10}$) also hurts the quality of the error report.

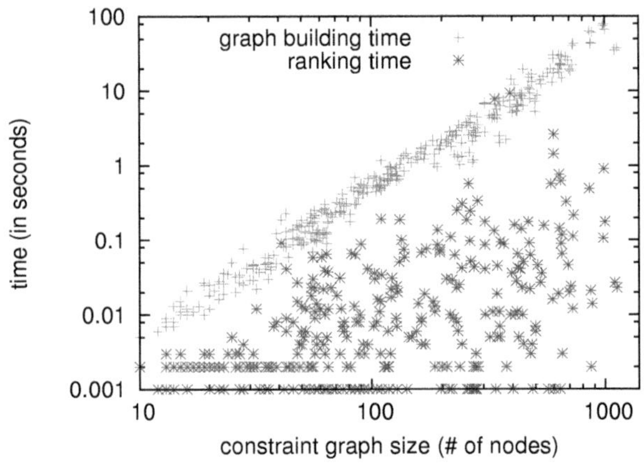


**Figure 10.** Performance

### 6.2.2 Comparison with OCaml and Seminal

For each file we analyze, we consider both the error location reported by OCaml and the top-ranked suggestion of our tool (based on the setting $P_1 = (P_2/1 - P_2)^3$). We reused the data offered by the authors of the Seminal tool [22], who labeled the correctness of Seminal's error location report.

We classify the files into one of the following five categories and summarize the results in Figure 9:

1. Our approach suggests an error location that matches the programmer's fix, but the other tool's location misses the error.
2. Our approach reports multiple correct error locations that match the programmer's fix, but the other tool only reports one of them.
3. Both approaches find error locations corresponding to the programmer's fix.
4. Both approaches miss the error locations corresponding to the programmer's fix.
5. Our tool misses the error location but the other tool captures it.

The result shows that OCaml's reports find about 75% of the error locations but miss the rest. Seminal's reports on error locations are slightly better, finding about 80% of the error locations.

Compared with both OCaml and Seminal, our tool consistently identifies a higher percentage of error locations across all homeworks, with an average of 96%.

In about 10% of cases, our tool identifies multiple errors in programs. According to the data, the programmers usually fixed these errors one by one since the OCaml compiler only reports one at a time. Reporting multiple errors at once may be more helpful.

***Limitations*** Of course, our tool sometimes misses errors. We studied programs where our tool missed the error location, finding that in each case it involved multiple interacting errors. In some cases

| | $P_1 = P_2'$ | $P_1 = P_2'^2$ | $P_1 = P_2'^3$ | $P_1 = P_2'^4$ | $P_1 = P_2'^5$ | $P_1 = P_2'^6$ | $P_1 = P_2'^{10}$ | $P_2 = 0.5$ |
|---|---|---|---|---|---|---|---|---|
| Missed Error | 21 | 15 | 14 | 17 | 17 | 16 | 22 | 23 |
| Avg. Sugg. Size | 1.86 | 1.80 | 1.72 | 1.69 | 1.70 | 1.69 | 1.67 | 5.58 |

**Table 1.** The quality of top-ranked suggestions with various values of $P_1$ and $P_2$, where $P_2' = P_2/1 - P_2$.

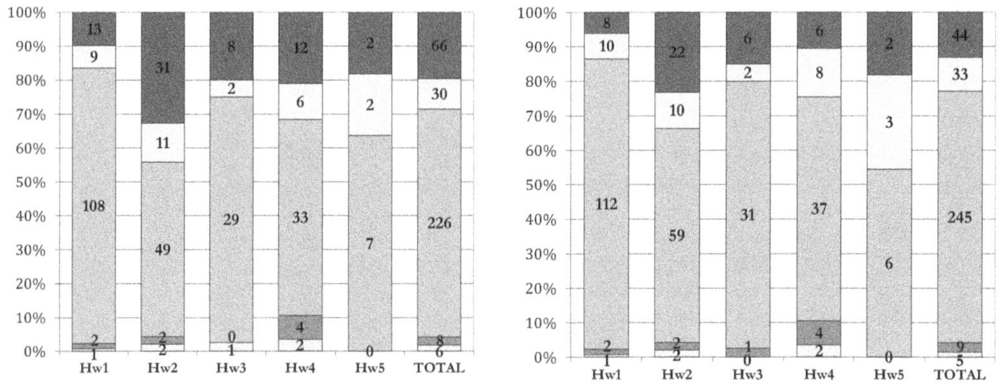


(a) Comparison with the OCaml compiler

(b) Comparison with Seminal

**Figure 9.** Results organized by homework assignment. From top to bottom, columns represent programs where (1) our tool finds a correct error location that the other tool misses. (2) both approaches report the correct error location, but our tool reports multiple (correct) error locations; (3) both approaches report the correct error location; (4) both approaches miss the error location; (5) our tool misses the error location while the other tool identifies one of them. For every assignment, our tool does the best job of locating the error.

the programmer made a similar error multiple times. Our tool fails to identify such errors because they violate the assumption of error independence. As our result suggests, this situation is rare.

The comparison between the tools is not completely apples-to-apples. We only collect type mismatch errors in the evaluation. OCaml is very effective at finding other kinds of errors such as unbound variables or wrong numbers of arguments, and Seminal not only finds errors but also proposes fixes.

#### 6.2.3 Performance

We measured the performance of our tool on a Ubuntu 11.04 system using a dual core at 2.93GHz with 4G memory. Results are shown in Figure 10. We separate the time spent generating and inferring LEQ edges in the graph from that spent computing rankings.

The results show how the running time of both graph building time and ranking time scale with increasing constraint graph size. Interestingly, graph building, including the inference of ($^+$LEQ) relationships, dominates and is in practice quadratic in the graph size. The graph size has less impact on the running time of our ranking algorithm. We suspect the reason is that the running time of our ranking algorithm is dominated by the number of unsatisfiable paths, which is not strongly related to total graph size.

Considering graph construction time, all programs finish in 79 seconds, and over 95% are done within 20 seconds. Ranking is more efficient: all programs finish in 10 seconds. Considering the human cost to identify error locations, the performance seems acceptable.

### 6.3 Case study: Jif hypothesis inference

We also evaluated how helpful our hypothesis inference algorithm is for Jif. In our experience with using Jif, we have found missing hypotheses to be a common source of errors.

A corpus of buggy programs was harder to find for Jif than for OCaml. We obtained application code developed for other, earlier projects using either Jif or Fabric (a Jif extension). These applications are interesting since they deal with real-world security concerns.

| | Secure | Tie | Better | Worse | Total |
|---|---|---|---|---|---|
| Number | 12 | 17 | 11 | 0 | 40 |
| Percentage | 30% | 42.5% | 27.5% | 0% | 100% |

**Table 2.** Hypothesis inference result

To mimic potential errors programmer would meet while writing the application, we randomly removed hypotheses from these programs, generating, in total, 40 files missing 1–5 hypotheses. The frequency of occurrence of each application in these 40 files corresponds roughly to the size of the application.

For all files generated in this way, we classified each file into one of four categories, with the results summarized in Table 2:

1. The program passed Jif/Fabric label checking after removing the hypotheses: the programmer made unneeded assumptions.
2. The generated missing hypotheses matched the one we removed.
3. The generated missing hypotheses provides an assumption that removes the error, but that is weaker than the one we removed (in other words, an improvement).
4. Our tool fails to find a suggestion better than the one removed.

The number of redundant assumptions in these applications is considerable (30%). We suspect the reason is that the security models in these applications are nontrivial, so programmers have difficulty formulating their security assumptions. This observation suggests that the ability to automatically infer missing hypotheses could be very useful to programmers.

All the automatically inferred hypotheses had at least the same quality as manually written ones. This preliminary result suggests that our hypothesis inference algorithm is very effective and should be useful to programmers.

| | Errors | Separate | Combined | Interactive |
|---|---|---|---|---|
| Missing hypothesis | 11 | 10 | 7 | 11 |
| Wrong expression | 5 | 4 | 4 | 4 |
| Total | 16 | 14 | 11 | 15 |
| Percentage | 100% | 87.5% | 68.75% | 93.75% |

**Table 3.** Jif case study result. (1) Separate: top rank of both separately computed hypothesis and expression suggestions (2) Combined: top rank combined result only (3) Interactive approach

### 6.4 Case study: combined errors

To see how useful our diagnostic tool is for Jif errors that occur in practice, we used a corpus of buggy Fabric programs that a developer collected earlier during the development of the "FriendMap" application [3]. As errors were reported by the compiler, the programmer also clearly marked the nature and true location of the error. This application is interesting for our evaluation purposes since it is complex—it was developed over the course of six weeks by two developers—and it contains both types of errors: missing hypotheses and wrong expressions.

The corpus contains 24 buggy Fabric programs. One difficulty in working on these programs directly was that 9 files contained many errors. This happened because the buggy code was commented out earlier by the programmer to better localize the errors reported by the Fabric compiler. We posit that this can be avoided if a better error diagnostic tool, like ours, is used. For these files, we reproduced the errors the programmer pointed out in the notes when possible and ignored the rest. Redundancy—programs producing the same errors—was also removed. Result for the remaining 16 programs are shown in Table 3.

Most files contain multiple errors. We used the errors recorded in the note as actual errors, and an error is counted as being identified only when the actual error is suggested among top rank suggestions.

The first approach (Separate) measures errors identified if the error type is known ahead, or both hypothesis and expression suggestions separately computed are used. The result is comparable to the result in Sections 6.2 and 6.3, where error types are known ahead.

Providing a concise and correct error report when multiple errors interact can be more challenging. We evaluated the performance of two approaches providing combined suggestions. The combined approach simply ranks the combined suggestions by size. Despite its simplicity, the result is still useful since this approach is automatic.

The interactive approach calculates missing hypotheses and requires a programmer to mark the correctness of these hypotheses. Then, correct hypotheses are used and wrong entities are suggested to explain the remaining errors. We think this is the most promising approach, since it involves limited manual effort: hypotheses are usually facts of properties to be checked, such as "is a flow from `Alice` to `Bob` secure?". We leave a more comprehensive study of this approach to future work.

## 7. Related work

***Program analyses, constraints and graph representations*** Modeling program analyses via constraint solving is not a new idea. The most related work is on set constraint-based program analysis [1, 2] and type qualifiers [12]. However, these constraint languages do not model hypotheses, which are important for some program analyses, such as information flow.

Program slicing, shape analysis, and flow-insensitive points-to analysis are expressible using graph-reachability [33]. Melski and Reps [27] show the interchangeability between context-free-language reachability (CFL-reachability) and a subset of set constraints [1]. But only a small set of constraints—in fact, a single variable—may appear on the right hand side of a partial order. Moreover, no error diagnostic approach is proposed for the graphs.

***Error diagnoses for type inference and information-flow control*** Dissatisfaction with error reports has led to earlier work on improving the error messages of both ML-like languages and Jif.

Efforts on improving type-error messages in ML-like languages can be traced to the early work of Wand [35] and of Johnson and Walz [18]. These two pieces of work represent two directions in improving error messages: the former traces *everything* that contributes to the error, whereas the latter attempts to infer the *most likely* cause. We only discuss the most related among them, but Heeren's summary [16] provides more details.

In the first direction, several efforts [7, 12, 14, 32, 34] improve the basic idea of Wand [35] in various ways. Despite the attractiveness of feeding a full explanation to the programmer, the reports are usually verbose and hard to follow [16].

In the second direction, one approach is to alter the order of type unification [21, 25]. But since the error location may be used anywhere during the unification procedure, any specific order fails in some circumstance. Some prior work [16, 18] builds a type graph from a more limited constraint language and infers error locations based on heuristics mostly tailored for type inference. Though the "weighted options" heuristic in [18] uses successful type unifications to distinguish abnormal types from normal ones, information about satisfiable paths is leveraged with finer-granularity in our approach, to distinguish the *constraints* that caused errors. This is shown to be effective in Section 6.2.1.

A third approach is to generate fixes for errors by searching for similar programs [22, 26] or type substitutions [6] that do type-check. Unfortunately, we cannot obtain a common corpus to perform direct comparison with some of this prior work [6, 26]. It is worth noting that the ranking heuristics used in [6] are language-specific: there is no obvious way to extend them to information flow, for instance. We are able to compare directly with the work of Lerner et al. [22]; the results of Section 6.2 suggest that our approach finds error locations more accurately. In fact, by pinpointing where searches for fixes are likely to be productive, our approach ought to be complementary.

For information-flow control, King et al. [19] propose to generate a trace explaining the information-flow violation. Although this approach also constructs a diagnosis from a dependency graph, only a subset of the DLM model is handled. As in type-error slicing, reporting whole paths can yield very verbose error reports. Recent work by Weijers et al. [37] diagnoses information-flow violations in a higher-order, polymorphic language. But the mechanism is based on tailored heuristics and a more limited constraint language. Moreover, the algorithm in [37] diagnoses a single unsatisfiable path, while our algorithm diagnoses multiple errors.

***Probabilistic inference*** Applying probabilistic inference to program analysis has appeared in earlier work, particularly on specification inference [20, 24]. Our contribution is to apply probabilistic inference to a general class of static analyses, allowing errors to be localized without language-specific tuning. Also related is work on statistical methods for diagnosing dynamic errors (e.g., [23, 39]). These algorithms rely on a different principle—statistical interpretation—and do not handle important features for static analysis, such as constructors and hypotheses.

The work of Ball et al. on diagnosing errors detected by model checking has exploited a similar insight by using information about traces for both correct execution and for errors to localize error causes [4]. Beyond differences in context, that work differs in not actually using probabilistic inference; each error trace is considered in isolation, and transitions are not flagged as causes if they lie on *any* correct trace.

***Missing hypothesis inference*** The most related work on inferring likely missing hypotheses is the recent work by Dillig et al. on error diagnosis using abductive inference [10]. This work computes small, relevant queries presented to a user that capture exactly the information a program analysis is missing to either discharge or validate the error. It does not attempt to identify incorrect constraints.

With regard to hypothesis inference, the algorithm in [10] infers missing hypotheses for a single assertion, while our tool finds missing hypotheses that satisfy a *set* of assertions. Further, the algorithm of [10] infers additional invariants on *variables* (e.g., $x \leq 3$ for a constraint variable $x$), while our algorithm also infers missing partial orderings on *constructors* (e.g., `Alice` $\leq$ `Bob` in Section 5.3.1).

## 8. Conclusion

Better tools for helping programmers locate the errors detected by program analysis should make them more willing to use the many powerful program analyses that have been developed. The science of diagnosing programmer errors is still rather primitive, but this paper takes a step towards improving the situation. Our analysis of program constraint graphs offers a general, principled way to identify both incorrect expressions and missing assumptions. Results on two very different languages, OCaml and Jif, with little language-specific customization, suggest this approach is promising and broadly applicable.

There are many interesting directions to take this work. Though we have shown that the technique works well on two very different type systems, it would likely be fruitful to apply these ideas to other type systems and program analyses, and to explore more sophisticated ways to estimate the likelihood of different error explanations.

## Acknowledgments

Nate Foster, Mike George, Chinawat Isradisaikul, Jean-Baptiste Jeannin, Vincent Rahli, Robert Soulé and Ross Tate gave many useful comments on this presentation. We also thank Ben Lerner and Dan Grossman for making available the excellent data set they used for their work on Seminal, Dexter Kozen for pointing out the similarity between our constraints and set constraints, and Mike George for a well-organized and labeled set of Jif test cases.

This work was supported by two grants from the Office of Naval Research, N00014-09-1-0652 and N00014-13-1-0089, by MURI grant FA9550-12-1-0400, by a grant from the National Science Foundation (CCF-09644909), and by a grant administered by the Air Force Research Laboratory.

## References

[1] A. Aiken. Introduction to set constraint-based program analysis. *Science of Computer Programming*, 35:79–111, 1999.

[2] A. Aiken and E. L. Wimmers. Type inclusion constraints and type inference. In *Conf. Functional Programming Languages and Computer Architecture*, pp. 31–41, 1993.

[3] O. Arden, M. D. George, J. Liu, K. Vikram, A. Askarov, and A. C. Myers. Sharing mobile code securely with information flow control. In *Proc. IEEE Symp. on Security and Privacy*, pp. 191–205, May 2012.

[4] T. Ball, M. Naik, and S. Rajamani. From symptom to cause: Localizing errors in counterexample traces. In *POPL 30*, pp. 97–105, Jan. 2003.

[5] C. Barrett, R. Jacob, and M. Marathe. Formal-language-constrained path problems. *SIAM Journal on Computing*, 30:809–837, 2000.

[6] S. Chen and M. Erwig. Counter-factual typing for debugging type errors. In *POPL 41*, Jan. 2014.

[7] V. Choppella and C. T. Haynes. Diagnosis of ill-typed programs. Technical report, Indiana University, December 1995.

[8] L. M. M. Damas. *Type assignment in programming languages*. PhD thesis, Department of Computer Science, University of Edinburgh, 1985.

[9] D. E. Denning. A lattice model of secure information flow. *Comm. of the ACM*, 19(5):236–243, 1976.

[10] I. Dillig, T. Dillig, and A. Aiken. Automated error diagnosis using abductive inference. In *PLDI'12*, pp. 181–192, 2012.

[11] EasyOCaml. http://easyocaml.forge.ocamlcore.org.

[12] J. S. Foster, R. Johnson, J. Kodumal, and A. Aiken. Flow-insensitive type qualifiers. *ACM Trans. Prog. Lang. Syst.*, 28(6):1035–1087, Nov. 2006.

[13] A. Gelman, J. B. Carlin, H. S. Stern, and D. B. Rubin. *Bayesian Data Analysis*. Chapman & Hall/CRC, 2nd edition, 2004.

[14] C. Haack and J. B. Wells. Type error slicing in implicitly typed higher-order languages. *Science of Computer Programming*, 50(1–3):189–224, 2004.

[15] P. Hart, N. Nilsson, and B. Raphael. A formal basis for the heuristic determination of minimum cost paths. *Systems Science and Cybernetics, IEEE Transactions on*, 4(2):100–107, 1968.

[16] B. J. Heeren. *Top Quality Type Error Messages*. PhD thesis, Universiteit Utrecht, The Netherlands, Sept. 2005.

[17] P. Hudak, S. P. Jones, and P. Wadler. Report on the programming language Haskell. *SIGPLAN Notices*, 27(5), May 1992.

[18] G. F. Johnson and J. A. Walz. A maximum flow approach to anomaly isolation in unification-based incremental type inference. In *POPL 13*, pp. 44–57, 1986.

[19] D. King, T. Jaeger, S. Jha, and S. A. Seshia. Effective blame for information-flow violations. In *Int'l Symp. on Foundations of Software Engineering*, pp. 250–260, 2008.

[20] T. Kremenek, P. Twohey, G. Back, A. Ng, and D. Engler. From uncertainty to belief: inferring the specification within. In *OSDI'06*, pp. 161–176, 2006.

[21] O. Lee and K. Yi. Proofs about a folklore let-polymorphic type inference algorithm. *ACM Trans. Prog. Lang. Syst.*, 20(4):707–723, 1998.

[22] B. S. Lerner, M. Flower, D. Grossman, and C. Chambers. Searching for type-error messages. In *PLDI'07*, pp. 425–434, 2007.

[23] B. Liblit, M. Naik, A. X. Zheng, A. Aiken, and M. I. Jordan. Scalable statistical bug isolation. In *PLDI'05*, pp. 15–26, 2005.

[24] B. Livshits, A. V. Nori, S. K. Rajamani, and A. Banerjee. Merlin: specification inference for explicit information flow problems. In *PLDI'09*, pp. 75–86, 2009.

[25] B. J. McAdam. On the unification of substitutions in type inference. In *Implementation of Functional Languages*, pp. 139–154, 1998.

[26] B. J. McAdam. *Repairing Type Errors in Functional Programs*. PhD thesis, Laboratory for Foundations of Computer Science, The University of Edinburgh, 2001.

[27] D. Melski and T. Reps. Interconvertibility of a class of set constraints and context-free language reachability. *Theoretical Computer Science*, 248(1–2):29–98, 2000.

[28] R. Milner, M. Tofte, and R. Harper. *The Definition of Standard ML*. MIT Press, Cambridge, MA, 1990.

[29] A. C. Myers and B. Liskov. A decentralized model for information flow control. In *SOSP'97*, pp. 129–142, 1997.

[30] A. C. Myers, L. Zheng, S. Zdancewic, S. Chong, and N. Nystrom. Jif 3.0: Java information flow. Software release, `www.cs.cornell.edu/jif`, July 2006.

[31] OCaml programming language. http://ocaml.org.

[32] V. Rahli, J. B. Wells, and F. Kamareddine. A constraint system for a SML type error slicer. Technical Report HW-MACS-TR-0079, Heriot-Watt university, 2010.

[33] T. Reps. Program analysis via graph reachability. *Information and Software Technology*, 40(11–12):701–726, 1998.

[34] F. Tip and T. B. Dinesh. A slicing-based approach for locating type errors. *ACM Trans. on Software Engineering and Methodology*, 10(1):5–55, 2001.

[35] M. Wand. Finding the source of type errors. In *POPL 13*, 1986.

[36] M. Wand. A simple algorithm and proof for type inference. *Fundamenta Informaticae*, 10:115–122, 1987.

[37] J. Weijers, J. Hage, and S. Holdermans. Security type error diagnosis for higher-order, polymorphic languages. In *ACM SIGPLAN workshop on Partial evaluation and program manipulation*, pp. 3–12, 2013.

[38] D. Zhang and A. C. Myers. Toward general diagnosis of static errors: Technical report. Technical Report http://hdl.handle.net/1813/33742, Cornell University, Aug. 2014.

[39] A. X. Zheng, B. Liblit, and M. Naik. Statistical debugging: simultaneous identification of multiple bugs. In *ICML'06*, pp. 1105–1112, 2006.

# Counter-Factual Typing for Debugging Type Errors *

Sheng Chen
School of EECS, Oregon State University
chensh@eecs.oregonstate.edu

Martin Erwig
School of EECS, Oregon State University
erwig@eecs.oregonstate.edu

## Abstract

Changing a program in response to a type error plays an important part in modern software development. However, the generation of good type error messages remains a problem for highly expressive type systems. Existing approaches often suffer from a lack of precision in locating errors and proposing remedies. Specifically, they either fail to locate the source of the type error consistently, or they report too many potential error locations. Moreover, the change suggestions offered are often incorrect. This makes the debugging process tedious and ineffective.

We present an approach to the problem of type debugging that is based on generating and filtering a comprehensive set of type-change suggestions. Specifically, we generate *all* (program-structure-preserving) type changes that can possibly fix the type error. These suggestions will be ranked and presented to the programmer in an iterative fashion. In some cases we also produce suggestions to change the program. In most situations, this strategy delivers the correct change suggestions quickly, and at the same time never misses any rare suggestions. The computation of the potentially huge set of type-change suggestions is efficient since it is based on a variational type inference algorithm that type checks a program with variations only once, efficiently reusing type information for shared parts.

We have evaluated our method and compared it with previous approaches. Based on a large set of examples drawn from the literature, we have found that our method outperforms other approaches and provides a viable alternative.

***Categories and Subject Descriptors*** F.3.3 [*Logics and Meanings of Programs*]: Studies of Program Constructs–Functional constructs,Type structure; D.3.2 [*Programming Languages*]: Language Classifications–Applicative (functional) languages; D.2.5 [*Software Engineering*]: Testing and Debugging

***General Terms*** Languages, Theory

***Keywords*** Type inference, error localization, type error messages, choice types, change suggestions, type-error debugging

* This work is supported by the National Science Foundation under the grants CCF-0917092, CCF-1219165, and IIS-1314384.


*POPL '14*, January 22–24, 2014, San Diego, CA, USA.
ACM 978-1-4503-2544-8/14/01...$15.00. Copyright is held by the owner/author(s). Publication rights licensed to ACM.
http://dx.doi.org/10.1145/2535838.2535863.

## 1. Introduction

Generating informative and helpful type error messages remains a challenge for implementing type inference algorithms. Soon after the algorithm $\mathcal{W}$ [8] had been developed, this problem was recognized [15, 26]. It has since prompted numerous research efforts [7, 12, 14, 16–18, 20, 21, 23, 25, 27, 29]. Although considerable progress has been made, there is still no single method that consistently produces satisfactory results. Most of the existing approaches perform poorly in certain cases.

As an example, consider the following Haskell function `palin`, which checks whether a list is a palindrome [24]. The first equation for `fold` contains a type error and should return `z` instead of `[z]`.

```
fold f z []     = [z]
fold f z (x:xs) = fold f (f z x) xs
flip f x y = f y x
rev = fold (flip (:)) []
palin xs = rev xs == xs
```

Existing tools have difficulties in finding this error. For example, the Glasgow Haskell Compiler (GHC) 7.6[1] produces the following error message.[2]

```
Occurs check: cannot construct the infinite type: t0 = [t0]
Expected type: [[t0]]
  Actual type: [t0]
In the second argument of '(==)', namely 'xs'
In the expression: rev xs == xs
```

While technically accurate, the error message doesn't directly point to the source of the error, and it doesn't tell the user how it could be fixed either. The use of compiler jargon makes the error message difficult to understand for many programmers. While giving reasons for the failure of unification might be useful for experienced programmers and type system experts, such error messages still require some effort to manually reconstruct some of the types and solve unification problems. (Hugs98[3] produces a similar error message and suffers from the same problems.)

One of the problems of the approach taken in GHC is that it commits to a *single* error location, because in some cases the program text does not contain enough information to confidently make the right decision about the correct error location. This has led to a number of program slicing approaches that try to identify a *set* of possible error locations instead.

The basic idea is to find *all* program positions that contribute to a type error and exclude those that do not. For example, the Skalpel[4] type error slicer for SML [12] produces the following

[1] `www.haskell.org/ghc/`

[2] For presentation purposes, we have slightly edited the outputs of some tools by changing their indentation and line breaks.

[3] `www.haskell.org/hugs/`

[4] `www.macs.hw.ac.uk/ultra/skalpel/`

result. (We have translated the program into ML for Skalpel to work.)

```
fun fold f z  []        = [z] ;
  | fold f z  (x::xs) = fold f  (f (z,x)) xs ;
fun flip f (x,y) = f (y, x) ;
fun rev xs = fold ( (flip op ::)) [] xs ;
fun palin  xs = rev xs = xs  ;
```

Showing too many program locations involved in the type error diminishes the value of the slicing approach because of the cognitive burden put on the programmer to work through all marked code and to single out the proper error location. To address this problem, techniques have been developed that try to minimize the possible locations contributing to a type error. An example is the Chameleon Type Debugger,[5] which produces the following output.

```
fold f z []     = [z] ;
fold f z (x:xs)= fold f (f z x) xs ;
flip f x y = f y x ;
rev = fold (flip (:)) [] ;
palin xs = rev xs = xs ;
```

Chameleon is based on constraint solving and identifies a minimal set of unsatisfiable constraints, from which the corresponding places in the program contributing to the type error are derived. While Chameleon is a clear improvement over other slicing approaches in reporting fewer potential error locations, a programmer still has to work through several code parts to find the type error. In particular, figuring out which types should be used at specific locations can be quite time consuming.

On the other end of the single-vs.-many location spectrum we find approaches that, like GHC or Hugs, follow Johnson and Walz's idea of finding the most likely erroneous location and try to add explanations or suggestions for how to correct the error. One example is the Helium compiler[6], which was developed to support the teaching of typed functional programming languages. A declared focus of Helium is to generate good error messages [14]. For our example, it produces the following message.

```
(5,19): Type error in infix application
 expression        : rev xs == xs
 operator          : ==
   type            : a      -> a    -> Bool
   does not match  : [[b]] -> [b] -> c
 because           : unification would give infinite type
```

Unfortunately, Helium doesn't perform much better than GHC or Hugs on this example and provides feedback only in terms of internal representations used by the compiler.

Seminal[7] is a tool for type checking ML programs that also produces change suggestions [18, 19]. Seminal blames the type error on the function `palin` and suggests the following corrective change.

```
File "Palin.ml", line 8, characters 21-27:
This expression has type 'a list list but is
here used with type 'a list
Relevant code: rev xs
-----------------------------------------------
File "Palin.ml", line 8, characters 15-17:
Try replacing
    xs == (rev xs)
with
    ( == ) (xs, (rev xs))
of type
    'b list * 'b list list -> bool
within context
    let palin xs = ( == ) (xs, (rev xs)) ;;
```

Unfortunately, the suggested error location is not correct (according to [24]), and although the suggested change will eliminate the type error, it changes the wrong code (the suggested change of partially applying `==` to the pair of differently typed lists turns `palin`'s type into `'a list -> 'a list * 'a list list -> Bool`.)

Offering change suggestions is a double-edged sword: While it can be very helpful in simplifying the task of fixing type errors, it can also be sometimes very misleading, and frustrating when the suggested change doesn't work. In the shown example, both change-suggesting tools fail to correctly locate the error location.

The tasks of debugging type errors seems to be an inherently ambiguous undertaking, because in some situations there is just not enough information present in the program to generate a correct change suggestion. Consider, for example, the expression `not 1`. The error in this expression is either `not` or `1`,[8] but without any additional knowledge about the purpose of the expression, there is no way to decide whether to replace the function or the argument. This is why it is generally impossible to isolate one point in the program as the source of a type error. This fact provides a strong justification for slicing approaches that try to provide an unbiased account of error situations. On the other hand, in many cases some locations are more likely than others, and specifically in larger programs, information about the context of an erroneous expression can go a long way of isolating a single location for a type error.

Thus, a reasonable compromise between slicing and single-error-reporting approaches could be a method to principally compute *all* possible type error locations (together with possible change suggestions) and present them ranked and in small portions to the programmer. At the core of such an approach has to be a type checker that produces a complete set of type changes that would make the program type correct.

In this paper we present a method for *counter-factual change inference*, whose core is a technique to answer the question "What type should a particular subexpression have to remove type errors in a program". We have also implemented and evaluated a prototype for a type checker that is based on this technique.

To keep the complexity manageable we only produce so-called *atomic* type changes, that is, type changes for the leaves of the program's abstract syntax tree. This helps avoid the introduction of too exotic or too extreme changes. Consider, for example, the non-atomic type change suggested by Seminal for the `palin` program, which seems to be not realistic. Or consider changing a whole program to a value of type `Bool` or `Int`, which always works but is hardly ever correct.

However, errors that are best fixed by non-atomic expression changes are quite common. Examples are the swapping of function arguments or the addition of missing function arguments. The identification of such non-atomic program changes is not ruled out by

[5] `ww2.cs.mu.oz.au/~sulzmann/chameleon/`. Since Chameleon doesn't offer a type diagnosis option anymore, the result is reproduced directly from [24].

[6] `www.cs.uu.nl/wiki/bin/view/Helium/WebHome`

[7] `cs.brown.edu/~blerner/papers/seminal_prototype.html`

[8] It could also be the case that the whole expression is incorrect and should be replaced by something else, but we ignore this case for now.

| Rank | Loc | Code | Change code of type/expression | To new type/expression | Result type |
|---|---|---|---|---|---|
| 1 | (1,19) | `(:)`[9] | `a -> [a] -> [a]` | `a -> [b] -> a` | `[a] -> Bool` |
| | | | `[z]` | `z` | |
| 2 | (5,22) | `xs` | `[a]` | `[[a]]` | `[a] -> Bool` |
| 3 | (5,12) | `rev` | `[a] -> [[a]]` | `[a] -> [a]` | `[a] -> Bool` |
| 4 | (5,19) | `(==)` | `[a] -> [a] -> Bool` | `[[a]] -> [a] -> b` | `[a] -> b` |
| 5 | (4,7) | `fold` | `(a -> b -> a) -> a -> [b] -> [a]` | `([a] -> a -> [a]) -> [b] -> [a] -> [a]` | `[a] -> Bool` |

Figure 1: Ranked list of single-location type and expression change suggestions inferred for the `palin` example.

the approach taken and can actually often be achieved by deducing expression changes from type changes.

Returning to the `palin` example, Figure 1 shows a ranked list of all (single-location) type changes, computed by our prototype, that can fix the type error. The correct change ranks first in our method. Note that this is not a representation intended to be given to end users. We rather envision an integration into a user interface in which locations are underlined and hovering over those locations with the mouse will pop up windows with individual change suggestions. In this paper we focus on the technical foundation to compute the information required for implementing such a user interface.

Each suggestion is essentially represented by the expression that requires a change together with the inferred actual and expected type of that expression. (Since we are only considering atomic type changes, this expression will always be a constant or variable in case of a type change, but it can be a more complicated expression in case of deduced expression change.) We also show the position of the code in the program[10] and the result types of the program if the corresponding change is adopted. This information is meant as an additional guide for programmers to select among suggestions.

The list of shown suggestions is produced in several steps. First, we generate (lazily) all possible type changes, that is, even those that involve several locations. Note that sometimes the suggested types are unexpected. For example, the suggested type for `fold` is `([a] -> a -> [a]) -> [b] -> [a] -> [a]` although `(a -> b -> a) -> a -> [b] -> a` would be preferable. This phenomenon can be generally attributed to the context of the expression. On the one hand, the given context can be too restrictive and coerce the inferred type to be more specific than it has to be, just as in this example the first argument `flip (:)` forces `fold` to have `[a] -> a -> [a]` as the type of its first argument. On the other hand, the context could also be too unrestrictive. There is no information about how `fold` is related to `[]` in the fourth line of the program. Thus, the type of the second argument of `fold` is inferred as `[b]`. This imprecision can't be remedied by exploiting type information of the program.

Second, we filter out those type changes that involve only one location. We present those first to the programmer since these are generally easier to understand and to adopt than multi-location change suggestions. Should the programmer reject all these single-location suggestions, two-location suggestions will be presented next, and so on.

Third, in addition to type-change suggestions, we also try to infer some non-atomic expression changes from type changes. In general, only the programmer who wrote the program knows how to translate required type changes into expression changes. However, there are a number of common programming mistakes, such as swapping or forgetting arguments, that are indicated by type-change suggestions. Similar to Seminal, our prototype identifies these kind of changes that are mechanical and do not require a deep understanding of the program semantics. In our example, we infer the replacement of `[z]` by `z`, because the expected type requires that the return type be the same as the first argument type. We thus suggest to use the first argument, that is `z`, to replace the application `(:) z []`.

Note however, that we don't infer a similar change for the fifth type change because `fold` is partially applied in the definition, and we have no access to the third argument of `fold`. Had the `rev` function been implemented using an eta-expanded list argument, say `xs`, we would have also inferred the suggestion to change `fold (flip (:)) [] xs` to `xs`.

Note also that we do not supplement type-change suggestions with atomic expression changes. For example, in the second suggestion, we do *not* suggest to replace `xs` by `[xs]`. There are two reasons for this. On the one hand, we believe that, given the very specific term to change, the inferred type, and the expected type, the corresponding required expression change is often easy to deduce for a programmer. On the other hand, suggesting specific expression changes requires knowledge about program semantics that is in many cases not readily available in the program. Thus, such suggestions can often be misleading.

Finally, all the type-change suggestions are ranked according to a few simple, but effective complexity heuristics.

At the core of the proposed method is a type system for inferring a set of type-change suggestions. This type system is described in detail in Section 4. We show that the type system generates a complete and correct set of atomic type change suggestions.

The type system is based on a systematic variation of the types of atomic expressions in a program. Therefore, some background information on how to represent variation in expressions and types, how to make use of it for the purpose of type inference, and what technical challenges this poses, is provided in Section 2. Equipped with the necessary technical background, the rationale behind variation-based type-change inference can then be explained on a high level in Section 3.

The algorithmic aspects of type inference and some measures for controlling runtime complexity are discussed in Section 5. We also briefly describe a set of heuristics that we use for ranking change suggestions. The method of deducing expression changes from type changes is discussed in Section 6. We have evaluated our prototype implementation by comparing it with three closely related tools and found that counter-factual typing can generate correct change suggestions more often than the other approaches. The evaluation is described in Section 7. Related work is discussed in Section 8, and conclusions presented in Section 9 complete this paper.

## 2. Variation-Based Typing

The idea of variation-based type change inference is to explicitly represent and reason about discrepancies between inferred and expected types that are detected by the type checker. This idea can be realized in different ways, and the counter-factual (CF) type

[9] Our prototype represents `[z]` as `(:) z []`.

[10] We have added the line and column numbers by hand since our prototype currently works on abstract syntax and doesn't have access to the information from the parser.

inference presented in this paper is just one incarnation of this more general strategy. In this section we will introduce the idea of variation-based typing, and gather some technical machinery that will then be employed to formalize counter-factual type change inference.

First, the goal of CF type inference is to generate suggestions for how to change types and expressions in a program to fix a type error. Both kinds of changes will be represented using the generic choice representation of the choice calculus that was introduced in [11]. The first application of this representation in the context of type checking was to extend type inference to program families (that is, a set of related programs) [5]. We will introduce the concept of *choices*, *variational expressions* and *types*, and some related concepts in Section 2.1.

Second, when type checking a program family, it is important to obtain the types of some programs (family members) even if the typing of other programs fails. This leads to the notion of *partial types*, *typing patterns*, and an associate method for *partial unification*. The application rule will be further generalized to accommodate partial types. We will explain these concepts in Section 2.2.

### 2.1 Variational Expressions and Variational Types

The Choice Calculus [11] provides a disciplined way of representing variation in software. The most important concept is the named choice, which can be used to represent variation points in both expressions and types. For example, the variational expression $e = \texttt{not}\ A\langle\texttt{1},\texttt{True}\rangle$ contains the named choice $A$ that represents a choice between the two constants `1` and `True` as the argument to `not` .

The process of eliminating a variation point is called *selection*. Selection takes a selector of the form $D.i$, where $D$ is the name of the variation point, traverses the expression and replaces all the variation points named $D$ with its corresponding $i$th alternative. In this paper, we are only concerned with binary choices, that is, $i$ will be either 1 or 2. For example, selecting $A.1$ from $e$ yields the plain expression `not 1`. Plain expressions are obtained after all choices are eliminated from a variational expression. Note that variation points with different names vary independently of one another, and only those with the same name are synchronized during selection. For example, the variational expression $A\langle\texttt{odd},\texttt{not}\rangle\ A\langle\texttt{1},\texttt{True}\rangle$ represents only the two expressions `odd 1` and `not True`, while $A\langle\texttt{odd},\texttt{not}\rangle\ B\langle\texttt{1},\texttt{True}\rangle$ represents the four expressions `odd 1`, `odd True`, `not 1`, and `not True`.

Through the use of independent choices, variational programs can very quickly encode a huge number of programs that differ only slightly. Ensuring the type correctness of all selectable plain programs is challenging because the brute-force approach of generating and checking each variant individually is generally infeasible. Variational typing [5] solves this problem by introducing variational types and a method for typing variational programs in one run. The result of type checking a variational program is a variational type, from which the types for individual program variants can be obtained with the same selection as the program is derived.

The syntax of variational types is shown below where $\alpha$ ranges over type variables, and $\gamma$ ranges over type constants.

$$\phi \quad ::= \quad \gamma \mid \alpha \mid \phi \to \phi \mid D\langle\phi,\phi\rangle \mid \bot$$

The type $\bot$ is used to denote the occurrences of type errors and will be discussed shortly in Section 2.2.

Under variational typing, the expression $A\langle\texttt{odd},\texttt{not}\rangle$ has the type $A\langle\texttt{Int} \to \texttt{Bool},\texttt{Bool} \to \texttt{Bool}\rangle$. The most important property of variational typing is that the type for each plain expression selected from the variational expression can be obtained through the same selections from the corresponding variational type. For example, selecting $A.2$ from both the variational expression and type, the expression `not` has the type $\texttt{Bool} \to \texttt{Bool}$.

$$\text{Typing patterns} \quad \pi \quad ::= \quad \bot \mid \top \mid D\langle\pi,\pi\rangle$$

$$\boxed{\uparrow\ : \phi \to \phi}$$

$$\begin{aligned}
\uparrow(\phi_1 \to \phi_2) &= \phi_1 \to \phi_2 \\
\uparrow(D\langle\phi_1 \to \phi_1', \phi_2 \to \phi_2'\rangle) &= D\langle\phi_1,\phi_2\rangle \to D\langle\phi_1',\phi_2'\rangle \\
\uparrow(D\langle\phi_1,\phi_2\rangle) &= \uparrow(D\langle\uparrow(\phi_1),\uparrow(\phi_2)\rangle) \\
\uparrow(\phi) &= \bot \to \bot \qquad \text{(otherwise)}
\end{aligned}$$

$$\boxed{\bowtie\ : \phi \times \phi \to \pi}$$

$$\begin{aligned}
\phi \bowtie \phi &= \top & D\langle\overline{\phi_1}\rangle \bowtie D\langle\overline{\phi_2}\rangle &= D\langle\overline{\phi_1 \bowtie \phi_2}\rangle \\
\bot \bowtie \phi &= \bot & D\langle\overline{\phi}\rangle \bowtie \phi' &= D\langle\overline{\phi \bowtie \phi'}\rangle \\
\phi \bowtie \bot &= \bot & \phi' \bowtie D\langle\overline{\phi}\rangle &= D\langle\overline{\phi' \bowtie \phi}\rangle \\
\phi \bowtie \phi' &= \bot & \phi_1 \to \phi_2 \bowtie \phi_1' \to \phi_2' &= (\phi_1 \bowtie \phi_1') \otimes (\phi_2 \bowtie \phi_2')
\end{aligned}$$

$$\boxed{\lhd : \pi \times \phi \to \phi} \qquad \boxed{\otimes : \pi \times \pi \to \pi}$$

$$\begin{aligned}
\bot \lhd \phi &= \bot & \top \otimes \pi &= \pi \\
\top \lhd \phi &= \phi & \bot \otimes \pi &= \bot \\
D\langle\overline{\pi}\rangle \lhd \phi &= D\langle\overline{\pi \lhd \phi}\rangle & D\langle\overline{\phi}\rangle \otimes \phi' &= D\langle\overline{\phi \otimes \phi'}\rangle
\end{aligned}$$

Figure 2: Operations for typing applications

An important technical part of variational typing is the fact that the equivalence of choices is not merely syntactical, but governed by a set of equivalence rules, originally described in [11]. For example, $A\langle\texttt{Int},\texttt{Int}\rangle$ is equivalent to `Int`, written as $A\langle\texttt{Int},\texttt{Int}\rangle \equiv \texttt{Int}$, since either decision in $A$ yields `Int`. The equivalence relationship plays an important part in, and poses a challenge to, the unification of variational types. For details we refer to [5].

A shortcoming of the variational typing approach is that it can succeed only if all variants are well typed, that is, it is impossible to assign a type to the variational expression $A\langle\texttt{odd},\texttt{not}\rangle\ \texttt{1}$, even though one of its variants is type correct. Error-tolerant variational typing addresses this issue.

### 2.2 Error-Tolerant Variational Typing

The idea of error-tolerant typing [4] is to assign the type $\bot$ to program variants that contain type errors. The explicit representation of type errors via $\bot$ as normal types supports the continuation of the typing process in the presence of type errors. Moreover, each variational program can be typed, and the resulting variational type contains $\bot$ for all variants that are type incorrect and a plain type for all type-correct variants. For example, $A\langle\texttt{odd},\texttt{not}\rangle\ \texttt{1}$ has the type $A\langle\texttt{Bool},\bot\rangle$, which encodes exactly the types that we obtain if we generate and type each expression separately.

The most challenging part of the error-tolerant type system is the handling of function applications because type errors can be introduced in different ways. For example, the function might not have an arrow type, or the type of the argument might not match the argument type of the function. Moreover, we have to consider the case of partial matching, that is, in the case of variational types, the argument type of the function and the type of the argument might be compatible for some variants only. Deciding in such a case that the whole application is of type $\bot$ would be too restrictive. This challenge is addressed by the following typing rule [4].

$$\frac{\Gamma \vdash e_1 : \phi_1 \qquad \Gamma \vdash e_2 : \phi_2 \qquad \phi_2' \to \phi' = \uparrow(\phi_1) \qquad \pi = \phi_2' \bowtie \phi_2 \qquad \phi = \pi \lhd \phi'}{\Gamma \vdash e_1\ e_2 : \phi}$$

The first two premises retrieve the types for the function and argument. Unlike in the traditional application rule, however, we do not require $\phi_1$ to be a function type. Instead, the third premise tries to lift $\phi_1$ into an arrow type using a function $\uparrow$ that is defined at the top of Figure 2. Lifting specifically accounts for the case in which $\phi_1$ is a choice between arrow types, as in $\uparrow(A\langle \texttt{Bool} \rightarrow \texttt{Bool}, \texttt{Int} \rightarrow \texttt{Bool}\rangle) = A\langle \texttt{Bool}, \texttt{Int}\rangle \rightarrow A\langle \texttt{Bool}, \texttt{Bool}\rangle$, and it also deals with, and introduces if necessary, error types. For example, $\uparrow(A\langle \texttt{Int} \rightarrow \texttt{Bool}, \texttt{Int}\rangle)$ can succeed only by introducing an error type and thus yields $A\langle \texttt{Int}, \bot\rangle \rightarrow A\langle \texttt{Bool}, \bot\rangle$.

The fourth premise computes a typing pattern $\pi$ that records to what degree (that is, in which variants) the type of $e_2$ matches the argument type of the (partial) arrow type obtained for $e_1$. As can be seen in Figure 2, a typing pattern is a (possibly deeply nested) choice of the two values $\bot$ (type error) and typing success ($\top$). The computation of a typing pattern proceeds by induction over the type structure of its arguments. Note that the definition given in Figure 2 contains overlapping patterns and assumes that more specific cases are applied before more general ones. When two rules are equally applicable, the computed result is equivalent modulo the $\equiv$ relation [4]. Note also that we employ the abbreviating notation $\bar{x}$ for a sequence of alternatives $x_1, \ldots, x_n$ (types or expressions) used within choices. (In Figure 2, this applies only to the case $n = 2$.)

For two plain types, matching reduces to checking equality. For example, $\texttt{Int} \bowtie \texttt{Int} = \top$ and $\texttt{Int} \bowtie \texttt{Bool} = \bot$. On the other hand, matching a plain type with a variational type results in a choice pattern. For example, $\texttt{Int} \bowtie D\langle \texttt{Int}, \texttt{Bool}\rangle = D\langle \top, \bot\rangle$.

Note that for two arrow types to be matched successfully, both their corresponding argument types and return types have to be matched successfully. There is no partial matching for function types. We define the operation $\otimes$ to achieve this, which is also presented in Figure 2. We can essentially view it as the logical "and" operation if we treat $\top$ as true and $\bot$ as false. For example, when computing $\texttt{Int} \rightarrow A\langle \texttt{Bool}, \texttt{Int}\rangle \bowtie B\langle \texttt{Int}, \bot\rangle \rightarrow \texttt{Bool}$, we first obtain $B\langle \top, \bot\rangle$ and $A\langle \bot, \top\rangle$ for matching the argument types and return types, respectively. Next, we use $\otimes$ to derive the final result as $A\langle \bot, B\langle \top, \bot\rangle\rangle$.

In the fifth and final premise, the typing pattern is used to preserve the type errors that the fourth premise has potentially produced. This is done by "masking" the return type with the typing pattern. The masking operation essentially replaces all the $\top$s in the typing pattern with the variants in the return type and leaves all $\bot$s unchanged, denoting the occurrences of type errors.

To see the application rule in action, consider the expression $A\langle \texttt{not}, \texttt{odd}\rangle\ B\langle \texttt{1}, \texttt{True}\rangle$. The first two premises produce the following typing judgments.

$$A\langle \texttt{not}, \texttt{odd}\rangle : A\langle \texttt{Bool} \rightarrow \texttt{Bool}, \texttt{Int} \rightarrow \texttt{Bool}\rangle$$
$$B\langle \texttt{1}, \texttt{True}\rangle : B\langle \texttt{Int}, \texttt{Bool}\rangle$$

Lifting transforms the type of the function into $A\langle \texttt{Bool}, \texttt{Int}\rangle \rightarrow A\langle \texttt{Bool}, \texttt{Bool}\rangle$, which is equivalent to $A\langle \texttt{Bool}, \texttt{Int}\rangle \rightarrow \texttt{Bool}$. The computation of $A\langle \texttt{Bool}, \texttt{Int}\rangle \bowtie B\langle \texttt{Int}, \texttt{Bool}\rangle$ yields $\pi = A\langle B\langle \bot, \top\rangle, B\langle \top, \bot\rangle\rangle$, and masking the return type of the function, $\texttt{Bool}$, with $\pi$ yields $A\langle B\langle \bot, \texttt{Bool}\rangle, B\langle \texttt{Bool}, \bot\rangle\rangle$.

## 3. Counter-Factual Typing

The main idea behind counter-factual typing is to systematically vary parts of the ill-typed program to find changes that can eliminate the corresponding type error(s) from the program. It is infeasible to apply this strategy directly on the expression level since there are generally infinitely many changes that one could consider. Therefore, we perform the variation on the type level. Basically, we ask for each atomic expression $e$ the counter-factual question: *What type should e have to make the program well typed?*

The counter-factual reasoning is built into the type checking process in the following way. To determine the type of an expression $e$ we first infer $e$'s type, say $\phi$. But then, instead of fixing this type, we leave the decision open and assume $e$ to have the type $D\langle \phi, \alpha\rangle$, where $D$ is a fresh name and $\alpha$ is a fresh type variable. By leaving the type of $e$ open to revision we account for the fact that $e$ may, in fact, be the source of a type error. By choosing a fresh type variable for $e$'s alternative type, we enable type information to flow from the context of $e$ to forge an alternative type $\phi'$ that fits into the context in case $\phi$ doesn't. If $\phi$ does fit the context, it is unifiable with $\phi'$, and the choice could in principle be removed. However, this is not really necessary (and we, in fact, don't do this) since in case of a type-correct program, we can find the type at the end of the typing process by simply selecting the first option from all generated choices.

Let us illustrate this idea with a simple example. Consider the expression $e = \texttt{not 1}$. If we vary the types of both `not` and `1`, we obtain the following typing judgments.

$$\texttt{not} : A\langle \texttt{Bool} \rightarrow \texttt{Bool}, \alpha_1\rangle$$
$$\texttt{1} : B\langle \texttt{Int}, \alpha_2\rangle$$

where $\alpha_1$ and $\alpha_2$ represent the expected types of `not` and `1` according to their respective contexts. To find the types $\alpha_1$ and $\alpha_2$, we have to solve the following unification problem.

$$A\langle \texttt{Bool} \rightarrow \texttt{Bool}, \alpha_1\rangle \equiv^? B\langle \texttt{Int}, \alpha_2\rangle \rightarrow \alpha_3$$

where $\alpha_3$ denotes the result type of the application and $\equiv^?$ denotes that the unification problem is solved modulo the type equivalence relation mentioned in Section 2.1 rather than the usual syntactical identity.

Another subtlety of the unification problem is that two types may not be unifiable. In that case a solution to the unification problem consists of a so-called *partial unifier*, which is both most general and introduces as few errors as possible. The unification algorithm developed in [4] achieves both these goals.

For the above unification problem, the following unifier is computed. The generality introduced by $\alpha_6$ and $\alpha_7$ ensures that only the second alternatives of choices $A$ and $B$ are constrained [5].

$$\{\alpha_1 \mapsto A\langle \alpha_6, B\langle \texttt{Int}, \alpha_4\rangle \rightarrow \alpha_5\rangle,$$
$$\alpha_2 \mapsto B\langle \alpha_7, A\langle \texttt{Bool}, \alpha_4\rangle\rangle,$$
$$\alpha_3 \mapsto A\langle \texttt{Bool}, \alpha_5\rangle\}$$

Additionally, the unification algorithm returns a typing pattern that characterizes all the viable variants and helps to compute the result type of the varied expression. In this case we obtain $A\langle B\langle \bot, \top\rangle, \top\rangle$. Based on the unifier and the typing pattern, we can compute that the result type of the varied expression of `not 1` is $\phi = A\langle B\langle \bot, \texttt{Bool}\rangle, \alpha_5\rangle$. From the result type and the unifier, we can draw the following conclusions.

- If we don't change $e$, that is, we select $A.1$ and $B.1$ from the varied expression, the type of the expression is $\bot$ (the variant corresponds to $A.1$ and $B.1$ in the result type), which reflects the fact that the original expression is ill typed.
- If we vary `not` to some other expression $f$, that is, if we select variant $A.2$ and $B.1$ from the variational result type, the result type will be $\alpha_5$. Moreover, the type of $f$ is obtained by selecting $A.2$ and $B.1$ from the type that $\alpha_1$ is mapped to, which yields $\texttt{Int} \rightarrow \alpha_5$. In other words, by changing `not` to an expression of type $\texttt{Int} \rightarrow \alpha_5$, `not 1` becomes well typed. In the larger context, $\alpha_5$ may be further constrained to have some other type.
- If we vary `1` to some expression $g$, that is, if we select $A.1$ and $B.2$ from the variational type, then the result type becomes `Bool`.
- If we vary both `not` to $f$ and `1` to $g$, which means to select $A.2$ and $B.2$, the result type is $\alpha_5$. Moreover, from the unifier we know that $f$ and $g$ should have the types $\alpha_4 \rightarrow \alpha_5$ and $\alpha_4$, respectively.

| | | | |
|---|---|---|---|
| Term variables | $x, y, z$ | Value constants | $c$ |
| Type variables | $\alpha, \beta$ | Type constants | $\gamma$ |

| | | | |
|---|---|---|---|
| Expressions | $e, f$ | $::=$ | $c \mid x \mid \lambda x.e \mid e\ e \mid \texttt{let}\ x = e\ \texttt{in}\ e \mid \texttt{if}\ e\ \texttt{then}\ e\ \texttt{else}\ e$ |

| | | | |
|---|---|---|---|
| Monotypes | $\tau$ | $::=$ | $\gamma \mid \alpha \mid \tau \to \tau$ |
| Variational types | $\phi$ | $::=$ | $\tau \mid \bot \mid D\langle\phi,\phi\rangle \mid \phi \to \phi$ |
| Type schemas | $\sigma$ | $::=$ | $\phi \mid \forall\overline{\alpha}.\phi$ |
| Selectors | $s$ | $::=$ | $D.i$ |

| | | | |
|---|---|---|---|
| Type environments | $\Gamma$ | $::=$ | $\varnothing \mid \Gamma, x \mapsto \sigma$ |
| Substitutions | $\eta, \theta$ | $::=$ | $\varnothing \mid \eta, \alpha \mapsto \phi$ |
| Choice environments | $\Delta$ | $::=$ | $\varnothing \mid \Delta, (l, D\langle\phi,\phi\rangle)$ |

Figure 3: Syntax of expressions, types, and environments

This gives us all atomic type changes for the expression `not 1`. The combination of creating variations at the type level and variational typing provides an efficient way of finding all possible type changes.

## 4. Type-Change Inference

This section presents the type system that generates a complete set of atomic corrective type changes. After defining the syntax for expressions and types in Section 4.1, we present the typing rules for type-change inference in Section 4.2. In Section 4.3 we investigate some important properties of the type-change inference system.

### 4.1 Syntax

We consider a type checker for lambda calculus with let-polymorphism. Figure 3 shows the syntax for the expressions, types, and meta environments for the type system. We extend the bar notation to other sequences of elements, such as bindings. Both the definitions of expressions and types are conventional, except for variational types, which introduce choice types and the error type.

We use $l$ to denote program locations, in particular, leaves in ASTs. We assume that there is a function $\ell_e(f)$ that returns $l$ for $f$ in $e$. For presentation purposes, we assume that $f$ uniquely determines a location. We may omit the subscript $e$ when the context is clear. The exact definition of $\ell(\cdot)$ does not matter.

As usual, $\Gamma$ binds type variables to type schemas for storing typing assumptions. We use $\eta$ to denote type substitutions that map type variables to variational types. The metavariable $\theta$ ranges over type substitutions that are unifiers for unifiable types or partial unifiers for nonunifiable types. Finally, we use the choice environment $\Delta$ to associate choice types that were generated during the typing process with the corresponding location in the program. Operations on types can be lifted to $\Delta$ by applying them to the types in $\Delta$.

We stipulate the conventional definition of $FV$ that computes the free type variables in types, type schemas, and type environments. We write $\eta_{/S}$ for $\{\alpha \mapsto \phi \in \eta \mid \alpha \notin S\}$.

The application of a type substitution to a type schema is written as $\eta(\sigma)$ and replaces free type variables in $\sigma$ by the corresponding images in $\eta$. The definition is as follows.

$$\eta(\bot) = \bot \qquad \eta(\phi_1 \to \phi_2) = \eta(\phi_1) \to \eta(\phi_2)$$
$$\eta(\forall\overline{\alpha}.\phi) = \forall\overline{\alpha}.\eta_{/\overline{\alpha}}(\phi) \qquad \eta(\alpha) = \begin{cases} \alpha & \text{if } \alpha \notin dom(\eta) \\ \phi & \text{if } \alpha \mapsto \phi \in \eta \end{cases}$$
$$\eta(D\langle\overline{\phi}\rangle) = D\langle\overline{\eta(\phi)}\rangle$$

Note that we do not consider variational polymorphic types. This is not a problem since we can always lift quantifiers out of choices. For instance, $D\langle\forall\alpha.\phi_1, \forall\beta.\phi_2\rangle$ can be transformed to $\forall\alpha_1\beta_1.D\langle\phi_1', \phi_2'\rangle$ with $\alpha_1 \notin FV(\phi_1)$ and $\beta_1 \notin FV(\phi_2)$, and $\phi_1' = \{\alpha \mapsto \alpha_1\}(\phi_1)$ and $\phi_2' = \{\beta \mapsto \beta_1\}(\phi_2)$.

$$\boxed{\Gamma \vdash e : \phi|\Delta}$$

CON
$$\frac{c \text{ is of type } \gamma \qquad D \text{ fresh}}{\Gamma \vdash c : D\langle\gamma,\phi\rangle|\{(\ell(c), D\langle\gamma,\phi\rangle)\}}$$

VAR
$$\frac{\Gamma(x) = \forall\overline{\alpha}.\phi_1 \qquad D \text{ fresh} \qquad \phi = \{\overline{\alpha \mapsto \phi'}\}(\phi_1)}{\Gamma \vdash x : D\langle\phi,\phi_2\rangle|\{(\ell(x), D\langle\phi,\phi_2\rangle)\}}$$

UNBOUND
$$\frac{x \notin dom(\Gamma) \qquad D \text{ fresh}}{\Gamma \vdash x : D\langle\bot,\phi\rangle|\{(\ell(x), D\langle\bot,\phi\rangle)\}}$$

ABS
$$\frac{\Gamma, x \mapsto \phi \vdash e : \phi'|\Delta}{\Gamma \vdash \lambda x.e : \phi \to \phi'|\Delta}$$

LET
$$\frac{\Gamma, x \mapsto \phi \vdash e : \phi|\Delta \qquad \overline{\alpha} = FV(\phi) - FV(\Gamma) \qquad \Gamma, x \mapsto \forall\overline{\alpha}.\phi \vdash e' : \phi'|\Delta'}{\Gamma \vdash \texttt{let}\ x = e\ \texttt{in}\ e' : \phi'|\Delta \cup \Delta'}$$

APP
$$\frac{\Gamma \vdash e_1 : \phi_1|\Delta_1 \qquad \Gamma \vdash e_2 : \phi_2|\Delta_2 \qquad \phi_2' \to \phi' = \uparrow(\phi_1) \qquad \pi = \phi_2' \bowtie \phi_2 \qquad \phi = \pi \lhd \phi'}{\Gamma \vdash e_1\ e_2 : \phi|\Delta_1 \cup \Delta_2}$$

IF
$$\frac{(\Gamma \vdash e_i : \phi_i|\Delta_i)^{i:1..3} \qquad \pi_1 = \phi_1 \bowtie \texttt{Bool} \qquad \pi_2 = \phi_2 \bowtie \phi_3 \qquad \phi = \pi_1 \lhd (\pi_2 \lhd \phi_2)}{\Gamma \vdash \texttt{if}\ e_1\ \texttt{then}\ e_2\ \texttt{else}\ e_3 : \phi|\Delta_1 \cup \Delta_2 \cup \Delta_3}$$

Figure 4: Rules for type-change inference

### 4.2 Typing Rules

Figure 4 presents the typing rules for inferring type changes. The typing judgment is of the form $\Gamma \vdash e : \phi|\Delta$ and produces as a result a variational type $\phi$ that represents all the typing "potential" for $e$ plus a set of type changes $\Delta$ for the atomic subexpressions of $e$ that will lead to the types in $\phi$.

Since we are only interested in atomic changes during this phase, we only vary the leaves in the AST of programs, which are constants and variable references. This is reflected in the typing rules as we generate fresh choices in rules CON, VAR, and UNBOUND. In each case, we place the actual type in the first alternative and an arbitrary type in the second alternative of the choice. When an unbound variable is accessed, it causes a type error. We thus put $\bot$ in the first alternative of the choice.

The rules ABS and LET for abstractions and let-expressions are very similar to those in other type systems except that variables are bound to variational types. The rule APP for typing applications is very similar to the application rule discussed in Section 2.2. The only difference is that the rule here keeps track of the information for $\Delta$.

The IF rule employs the same machinery as the APP rule for the potential introduction of type errors and partially correct types. In particular, the condition $e_1$ is not strictly required to have the type `Bool`. However, only the variants that are equivalent to `Bool` are type correct. Likewise, only the variants in which both branches are equivalent are type correct.

$$\boxed{\Delta \Downarrow \Delta'}$$

$$\varnothing \Downarrow \varnothing \qquad \frac{\Delta \Downarrow \Delta' \qquad \exists \tau\colon D\langle\overline{\phi}\rangle \equiv \tau}{\Delta, (l, D\langle\overline{\phi}\rangle) \Downarrow \Delta'} \qquad \frac{\Delta \Downarrow \Delta' \qquad \neg\exists \tau\colon D\langle\overline{\phi}\rangle \equiv \tau}{\Delta, (l, D\langle\overline{\phi}\rangle) \Downarrow \Delta', (l, D\langle\overline{\phi}\rangle)}$$

$$\boxed{\lfloor \_ \rfloor_{\_} : \phi \times s \to \phi}$$

$$\lfloor \tau \rfloor_s = \tau \qquad \lfloor \phi_1 \to \phi_2 \rfloor_s = \lfloor \phi_1 \rfloor_s \to \lfloor \phi_2 \rfloor_s$$

$$\lfloor \bot \rfloor_s = \bot \qquad \lfloor B\langle\overline{\phi}\rangle \rfloor_{A.i} = B\langle\overline{\lfloor \phi \rfloor_{A.i}}\rangle \quad \text{if } A \neq B$$

$$\lfloor B\langle\overline{\phi}\rangle \rfloor_{B.i} = \lfloor \phi_i \rfloor_{B.i}$$

Figure 5: Simplifications and selection

### 4.3 Properties

In this section we investigate some important properties of the type-change inference system. We show that it is consistent in the sense that any type selected from the result variational type can be obtained by applying the changes as indicated by that selection. We also show that the type-change inference is complete in finding all corrective atomic type changes. Based on this result we also show that the type-change inference system is a conservative extension of the Hindley-Milner type system (HM).

We start with the observation that type-change inference always succeeds in deriving a type for any given expression and type environment.

LEMMA 1. *Given e and* $\Gamma$, *there exist* $\phi$ *and* $\Delta$ *such that* $\Gamma \vdash e : \phi|\Delta$.

The proof of this lemma is obvious because for any construct in the language, even for unbound variables, there is a corresponding typing rule in Figure 4 that is applicable and returns a type.

Next, we need to simplify $\Delta$ in the judgment $\Gamma \vdash e : \phi|\Delta$ to investigate the properties of the type system. Specifically, we define a simplification relation $\Downarrow$ in Figure 5 that eliminates idempotent choices from $\Delta$. Note that the sole purpose of simplification is to eliminate choice types that are equivalent to monotypes, or equivalently, remove all positions that don't contribute to type errors. Thus, there is no need to simplify types nested in choice $D$ in Figure 5. Also, we formally define the selection operation $\lfloor \phi \rfloor_s$ in Figure 5. Selection extends naturally to lists of selectors in the following way: $\lfloor \phi \rfloor_{s'\overline{s}} = \lfloor \lfloor \phi \rfloor_{s'} \rfloor_{\overline{s}}$.

Next we want to establish the correctness of the inferred type changes. Formally, a *type update* is a mapping from program locations to monotypes. The intended meaning of one particular type update $l \mapsto \tau$ is to change the expression at $l$ to an expression of type $\tau$. We use $\delta$ to range over type updates. A type update is given by the locations and the second component of the corresponding choice types in the choice environment. We use $\downarrow\cdot$ to extract that mapping from $\Delta$. The definition is $\downarrow\Delta = \{l \mapsto \tau_2 \mid (l, D\langle\tau_1, \tau_2\rangle) \in \Delta\}$. (For the time being we assume that all the alternatives of choices in $\Delta$ are monotypes; we will lift this restriction later.) For example, with $\Delta = \{(l, A\langle \texttt{Int}, \texttt{Bool}\rangle)\}$ we have $\downarrow\Delta = \{l \mapsto \texttt{Bool}\}$.

The application of a type update is part of a *type update system* that is defined by the set of typing rules shown in Figure 6. These typing rules are identical to an ordinary Hindley-Milner type system, except that they allow to "override" the types of atomic expressions according to a type update $\delta$ that is a parameter for the rules. We only show the rules for constants, variables, and applications since those for abstractions and let-expressions are obtained from the HM ones in the same way as the application rule by simply adding the $\delta$ parameter. We write more shortly $\delta(e)$ for $\delta(\ell(e))$, and we use the "orelse" notation $\delta(e)||\tau$ to pick the type $\delta(e)$ if $\delta(e)$ is defined and $\tau$ otherwise.

CON-C
$$\frac{c \text{ is of type } \gamma}{\Gamma; \delta \vdash c : \delta(c)||\gamma}$$

VAR-C
$$\Gamma; \delta \vdash x : \delta(x)||\{\overline{\alpha \mapsto \tau}\}(\Gamma(x))$$

APP-C
$$\frac{\Gamma; \delta \vdash e_1 : \tau_1 \to \tau \qquad \Gamma; \delta \vdash e_2 : \tau_1}{\Gamma; \delta \vdash e_1\ e_2 : \tau}$$

Figure 6: Rules for the type-update system

The rules CON-C and VAR-C employ a type update if it exists. Otherwise, the usual typing rules apply. Rule APP-C delegates the application of change updates to subexpressions since we are considering atomic change suggestions only.

We can now show that by applying any of the inferred type changes (using the rules in Figure 6), we obtain the same types that are encoded in the variational type potential computed by type-change inference. We employ the following additional notation. We write $\Delta.2$ for the list of selectors $D.2$ for each choice $D\langle\rangle$ in $\Delta$. For example, $\{(\ell_1, A\langle\texttt{Int},\texttt{Bool}\rangle), (\ell_2, B\langle\texttt{Bool},\texttt{Int}\rangle)\}.2 = [A.2, B.2]$. Formally, we have the following result. (We assume that $\Delta$ has been simplified by $\Downarrow$ in Figure 5 and the alternatives of choices in $\Delta$ are plain, as mentioned before.)

THEOREM 1 (Type-change inference is consistent). *For any given e and* $\Gamma$, *if* $\Gamma \vdash e : \phi|\Delta$ *and there is some* $\tau$ *such that* $\lfloor \phi \rfloor_{\Delta.2} = \tau$, *then* $\Gamma; \downarrow\Delta \vdash e : \tau$.

Moreover, the type-change inference is complete since it can generate a set of type changes for any desired type.

THEOREM 2 (Type-change inference is complete). *For any e,* $\Gamma$ *and* $\delta$, *if* $\Gamma; \delta \vdash e : \tau$, *then there exist* $\phi$, $\Delta$, *and a typing derivation for* $\Gamma \vdash e : \phi|\Delta$ *such that* $\downarrow\Delta = \delta$ *and* $\lfloor \phi \rfloor_{\Delta.2} = \tau$.

The proofs for these two theorems can be constructed through an induction over the typing derivations of both type systems. In particular, note that constants and variable reference have the same type in these two systems, regardless of whether or not they are changed.

The introduction of arbitrary alternative types in rules CON, VAR, and UNBOUND are the reason that type-change inference is highly non-deterministic, that is, for any expression $e$ we can generate an arbitrary number of type derivations with different type potentials and corresponding type changes.

Many of those derivations don't make much sense. For example, we can derive $\Gamma \vdash \texttt{5} : A\langle\texttt{Int},\texttt{Bool}\rangle|\Delta$ where $\Delta = \{(\ell_5(\texttt{5}), A\langle\texttt{Int},\texttt{Bool}\rangle)\}$. However, since the expression `5` is type correct, it doesn't make sense to suggest a change for it.

On the other hand, the ill-typed expression $e =$ `not (succ 5)` can be typed in two different ways that can correct the error, yielding two different type potentials and type changes. We can either suggest to change `succ` to an expression of type $\texttt{Int} \to \texttt{Bool}$, or we can suggest to change `not` into something of type $\texttt{Int} \to \alpha_1$. The first suggestion is obtained by a derivation for $\Gamma \vdash e : A\langle\bot, \alpha_1\rangle|\Delta_1$ with $\Delta_1 = \{(\ell_e(\texttt{not}), A\langle\texttt{Bool} \to \texttt{Bool}, \texttt{Int} \to \alpha_1\rangle)\}$. The second suggestion is obtained by a derivation for $\Gamma \vdash e : B\langle\bot, \texttt{Bool}\rangle|\Delta_2$ with $\Delta_2 = \{(\ell_e(\texttt{succ}), B\langle\texttt{Int} \to \texttt{Int}, \texttt{Int} \to \texttt{Bool}\rangle)\}$.

Interestingly, we can combine both suggestions by deriving a more general typing statement, that is, we can derive the judgment $\Gamma \vdash e : A\langle B\langle\bot, \texttt{Bool}\rangle, B\langle\alpha_1, \alpha_2\rangle\rangle|\Delta_3$ where

$$\Delta_3 = \{(\ell_e(\texttt{not}), A\langle\texttt{Bool} \to \texttt{Bool}, B\langle\texttt{Int} \to \alpha_1, \alpha_3 \to \alpha_2\rangle\rangle), \\ (\ell_e(\texttt{succ}), B\langle\texttt{Int} \to \texttt{Int}, A\langle\texttt{Int} \to \texttt{Bool}, \texttt{Int} \to \alpha_3\rangle\rangle)\}$$

We can show that the third typing is better than the first two in the sense that its result type (a) contains fewer type errors than either of the result types and (b) is more general. For example, by selecting $[A.1, B.2]$ from both result types, we obtain $\bot$ and `Bool`, respectively. Making the same selection into the third result type, we obtain `Bool`. Likewise, when we select with $[A.2, B.1]$, we get the types $\alpha_1$, $\bot$, and $\alpha_1$, respectively. For each selection, the third result type is better than either one of the first two.

In the following we show that this is not an accident, but that we can, in fact, always find a most general change suggestion from which all other suggestions can be instantiated.

First, we extend the function $\downarrow$ to take as an additional parameter a list of selectors $\bar{s}$. We also extend the definition to work with general variational types (and not just monotypes).

$$\downarrow_{\bar{s}}\Delta = \{l \mapsto \lfloor\phi_2\rfloor_{\bar{s}} \mid (l, D\langle\phi_1,\phi_2\rangle) \in \Delta \wedge D.2 \in \bar{s}\}$$

Intuitively, we consider all the locations for which the second alternative of the corresponding choices are chosen. We need to apply the selection $\lfloor\phi_2\rfloor_{\bar{s}}$ because each variational type may include other choice types that are subject to selection by $\bar{s}$.

Next we will show that type-change inference produces most general type changes from which any individual type change can be instantiated. We observe that type potentials and type changes can be compared in principally two different ways. First, the result of type-change inference $\phi|\Delta$ can be *more defined* than another result $\phi'|\Delta'$, which means that for any $\bar{s}$ for which $\lfloor\phi'\rfloor_{\bar{s}}$ yields a monotype then so does $\lfloor\phi\rfloor_{\bar{s}}$. Second, a result $\phi|\Delta$ can be *more general* than another result $\phi'|\Delta'$, written as $\phi \le \phi'$, if there is some type substitution $\eta$ such that $\phi' = \eta(\phi)$. (Similarly, we call a type update $\delta_1$ more general than another type update $\delta_2$, written as $\delta_1 \le \delta_2$, if $dom(\delta_1) = dom(\delta_2)$ and there is some $\eta$ such that for all $l$ $\delta_2(l) = \eta(\delta_1(l))$.

Since we have these two different relationships between type changes, we have to show the generality of type-change inference in several steps.

First, we show that we can generalize any type change that produces a type error in the resulting variational type for a particular selection when there is another type change that does not produce a type error for the same selection.

LEMMA 2 (Most defined type changes). *Given $e$ and $\Gamma$ and two typings $\Gamma \vdash e : \phi_1|\Delta_1$ and $\Gamma \vdash e : \phi_2|\Delta_2$, if $\lfloor\phi_1\rfloor_{\bar{s}} = \bot$ and $\lfloor\phi_2\rfloor_{\bar{s}} = \tau$, then there is a typing $\Gamma \vdash e : \phi_3|\Delta_3$ such that*

- $\lfloor\phi_3\rfloor_{\bar{s}} = \lfloor\phi_2\rfloor_{\bar{s}}$ *and for all other* $\bar{s}'$ $\lfloor\phi_3\rfloor_{\bar{s}'} = \lfloor\phi_1\rfloor_{\bar{s}'}$.
- $\downarrow_{\bar{s}}\Delta_3 = \downarrow_{\bar{s}}\Delta_2$ *and* $\downarrow_{\bar{s}'}\Delta_3 = \downarrow_{\bar{s}'}\Delta_2$ *for all other* $\bar{s}'$.

Next we show that given any two type changes, we can always find a type change that generalizes the two.

LEMMA 3 (Generalizability of type changes). *For any two typings $\Gamma \vdash e : \phi_1|\Delta_1$ and $\Gamma \vdash e : \phi_2|\Delta_2$, if neither $\lfloor\phi_1\rfloor_{\bar{s}} \le \lfloor\phi_2\rfloor_{\bar{s}}$ nor $\lfloor\phi_2\rfloor_{\bar{s}} \le \lfloor\phi_1\rfloor_{\bar{s}}$ holds, there is a typing $\Gamma \vdash e : \phi_3|\Delta_3$ such that*

- $\lfloor\phi_3\rfloor_{\bar{s}} \le \lfloor\phi_1\rfloor_{\bar{s}}$, $\lfloor\phi_3\rfloor_{\bar{s}} \le \lfloor\phi_2\rfloor_{\bar{s}}$ *and for all other* $\bar{s}'$, $\lfloor\phi_3\rfloor_{\bar{s}'} = \lfloor\phi_1\rfloor_{\bar{s}'}$.
- $\downarrow_{\bar{s}}\Delta_3 \le \downarrow_{\bar{s}}\Delta_1$, $\downarrow_{\bar{s}}\Delta_3 \le \downarrow_{\bar{s}}\Delta_2$ *and for all other* $\bar{s}'$, $\downarrow_{\bar{s}'}\Delta_3 = \downarrow_{\bar{s}'}\Delta_1$.

We can now combine and generalize Lemmas 2 and 3 and see that type-change inference can always produce maximally error-free and general results at the same time. This is an important result, captured in the following theorem.

THEOREM 3 (Most general and error-free type changes). *Given $e$ and $\Gamma$ and two typings $\Gamma \vdash e : \phi_1|\Delta_1$ and $\Gamma \vdash e : \phi_2|\Delta_2$, there is a typing $\Gamma \vdash e : \phi_3|\Delta_3$ such that for any $\bar{s}$,*

- *if* $\lfloor\phi_1\rfloor_{\bar{s}} = \bot$ *and* $\lfloor\phi_2\rfloor_{\bar{s}} = \tau$, *then* $\lfloor\phi_3\rfloor_{\bar{s}} = \tau$ *and* $\downarrow_{\bar{s}}\Delta_3 = \downarrow_{\bar{s}}\Delta_2$.
- *if* $\lfloor\phi_2\rfloor_{\bar{s}} = \bot$ *and* $\lfloor\phi_1\rfloor_{\bar{s}} = \tau$, *then* $\lfloor\phi_3\rfloor_{\bar{s}} = \tau$ *and* $\downarrow_{\bar{s}}\Delta_3 = \downarrow_{\bar{s}}\Delta_1$.
- *if* $\lfloor\phi_1\rfloor_{\bar{s}} = \tau_1$ *and* $\lfloor\phi_2\rfloor_{\bar{s}} = \tau_2$, *then* $\lfloor\phi_3\rfloor_{\bar{s}} \le \tau_1$ *and* $\lfloor\phi_3\rfloor_{\bar{s}} \le \tau_2$. *Moreover,* $\downarrow_{\bar{s}}\Delta_3 \le \downarrow_{\bar{s}}\Delta_1$ *and* $\downarrow_{\bar{s}}\Delta_3 \le \downarrow_{\bar{s}}\Delta_2$.

The proofs for Lemma 2, Lemma 3 and Theorem 3 can be established by showing that in each derivation step, the result types from two derivations can always be combined into the result type for a third derivation such that the new result type is both more general and contains fewer errors. The key ingredient we need is that given a variational type, we can change the type for a specific variant and leave all other variants unchanged.

From Theorems 3 and 2 it follows that there is a typing for complete and principal type changes. We express this in the following theorem.

THEOREM 4 (Complete and principal type changes). *Given $e$ and $\Gamma$, there is a typing $\Gamma \vdash e : \phi|\Delta$ such that for any $\delta$ if $\Gamma; \delta \vdash e : \tau$, then there is some $\bar{s}$ such that $\lfloor\phi\rfloor_{\bar{s}} \le \tau$ and $\downarrow_{\bar{s}}\Delta \le \delta$.*

Finally, there is a close relationship between type-change inference and the HM type system. When type-change inference succeeds with an empty set of type changes, it produces a non-variational type that is identical to the one derived by HM. This result is captured in the following theorem, where we write $\Gamma \vdash e : \tau$ to express that expression $e$ has the type $\tau$ under $\Gamma$ in the HM type system.

THEOREM 5. *For any given $e$ and $\Gamma$, $\Gamma; \varnothing \vdash e : \tau \Longleftrightarrow \Gamma \vdash e : \tau$.*

Based on Theorem 1, Theorem 2, Theorem 5 and the fact that $\downarrow\varnothing = \varnothing$, we can infer that when a program is well typed, the type change-inference system and the HM system produce the same result.

THEOREM 6. $\Gamma \vdash e : \tau|\varnothing$ *if and only if* $\Gamma \vdash e : \tau$.

Note that $\Gamma \vdash e : \tau|\varnothing$ implies that $\Gamma \vdash e : \phi|\Delta$, $\phi \equiv \tau$, and $\Delta \Downarrow \varnothing$. This theorem also implies that type-change inference will never assign a monotype to a type-incorrect program.

## 5. A Change Inference Algorithm

This section presents an algorithm for inferring type changes. We will discuss properties of the algorithm as well as strategies to bound its complexity.

Given the partial type unification algorithm presented in [4], the inference algorithm is obtained by a straightforward translation of the typing rules presented in Figure 4. The cases for variable reference and `if` statements are shown below. Function application is very similar to `if` statements, and the cases for abstractions and let-expressions can be derived from $\mathcal{W}$ by simply adding the threading of $\Delta$.

$infer : \Gamma \times e \to \theta \times \phi \times \Delta$
$infer(\Gamma, x) =$
  $\phi' \leftarrow inst(\Gamma(x))$ — *returns $\bot$ when $x$ is unbound*
  $\phi \leftarrow D\langle\phi',\alpha\rangle$ — *$D$ and $\alpha$ are fresh*
  return $(\varnothing, \phi, \{(\ell(x), \phi)\})$

$infer(\Gamma,$ `if` $e_1$ `then` $e_2$ `else` $e_3) =$
  $(\theta_1, \phi_1, \Delta_1) \leftarrow infer(\Gamma, e_1)$
  $(\theta', \pi') \leftarrow vunify(\phi_1,$ `Bool`$)$
  $(\theta_2, \phi_2, \Delta_2) \leftarrow infer(\theta'\theta_1(\Gamma), e_2)$
  $(\theta_3, \phi_3, \Delta_3) \leftarrow infer(\theta_2\theta'\theta_1(\Gamma), e_3)$
  $(\theta_4, \pi_4) \leftarrow vunify(\theta_3(\phi_2), \phi_3,)$
  $\theta \leftarrow \theta_4\theta_3\theta_2\theta'\theta_1$
  return $(\theta, \pi' \lhd (\pi_4 \lhd \theta_4(\phi_3)), \theta(\Delta_1 \cup \Delta_2 \cup \Delta_3))$

For variable reference, the algorithm first tries to find the type of the variable in $\Gamma$ and either instantiates the found type schema with fresh type variables or returns $\bot$ if the variable is unbound. After that, a fresh choice containing a fresh type variable is returned. The variable then has the returned choice type with the inferred type in the first alternative and the type variable in the second.

For typing `if` statements, we use an algorithm *vunify*$(\phi_1, \phi_2)$ for partial unification [4]. In addition to a partial unifier a typing pattern is generated to describe which variants are unified successfully and which aren't (see Section 3). Otherwise, the algorithm follows in a straightforward way the usual strategy for type inference.

We can prove that the algorithm *infer* correctly implements the typing rules in Figure 4, as expressed in the following theorems.

THEOREM 7 (Type-change inference is sound). *Given any $e$ and $\Gamma$, if infer$(\Gamma, e) = (\theta, \phi, \Delta)$, then $\theta(\Gamma) \vdash e : \phi|\Delta$.*

At the same time, the type inference is complete and principal. We use the auxiliary relation $\phi_1 \preceq \phi_2$ to express that for any $\bar{s}$, either $\lfloor\phi_2\rfloor_{\bar{s}} = \bot$ or $\lfloor\phi_1\rfloor_{\bar{s}} \leq \lfloor\phi_2\rfloor_{\bar{s}}$. Intuitively, this expresses that either the corresponding variant in $\phi_1$ is more general or more correct. We also define $\Delta_1 \preceq \Delta_2$ if for any $(l, \phi_1) \in \Delta_1$ and $(l, \phi_2) \in \Delta_2$ the condition $\phi_1 \leq \phi_2$ holds.

THEOREM 8 (Type-change inference is complete and principal). *If $\theta(\Gamma) \vdash e : \phi|\Delta$, then infer$(\Gamma, e) = (\theta_1, \phi_1, \Delta_1)$ such that $\theta = \eta_1\theta_1$ for some $\eta_1$, $\Delta_1 \preceq \Delta$, and $\phi_1 \preceq \phi$.*

From Theorems 3 and 8 it follows that our type-change inference algorithm correctly computes all type changes for a given expression in one single run.

During the type-change inference process, choice types can become deeply nested and the size of types can become exponential in the nesting levels. Fortunately, this occurs only with deep nestings of function applications where each argument type is required to be the same. For example, the function $f : \alpha \to \alpha \to \ldots \to \alpha$ is more likely to cause this problem than the functions $g : \alpha_1 \to \alpha_2 \to \ldots \to \alpha_n$ and $h : \gamma \to \gamma \to \ldots \to \gamma$ because only the function $f$ requires all argument types to be unified, which causes choice nesting to happen.

To keep the run-time complexity of our inference algorithm under control, we eliminate choices beyond an adjustable nesting level that satisfy one of the following conditions: (A) choices whose alternatives are unifiable, and (B) choices whose alternatives contain errors in the same places. These two conditions ensure that the eliminated choices are unlikely to contribute to type errors. There are cases in which this strategy fails to eliminate choices, but this happens only when there are already too many type errors in the program, and we therefore stop the inference process and report type errors and change suggestions found so far.

This strategy allows us to maintain choices whose corresponding locations are likely sources of type errors and discard those that aren't. Note, however, that this strategy sacrifices the completeness property captured in Theorem 8. We have evaluated the running time and the precision of error diagnosis against the choice nesting levels (see Section 7). We observed that only in very rare cases will the choice nesting level reach 17, a value that variational typing is able to deal with decently [5].

Finally, we briefly describe a set of simple heuristics that define the ranking of type and expression changes. (1) We prefer places that have deduced expression changes (see Section 6) because these changes reflect common editing mistakes [18]. (2) We favor changes that are lower in the abstract syntax trees because changes at those places have least effect on the context and are least likely to introduce exotic results. (3) We prefer changes that have minimal shape difference between the inferred type and the expected type. For example, a change that doesn't influence the arities of function types is ranked higher than a change that does change arities.

## 6. Deducing Expression Changes

While it is generally impossible to deduce expression changes from type changes, there are several idiosyncratic situations in which type changes do point to likely expression changes. These situations can be identified by unifying both types of a type change where the unification is performed modulo a set of axioms that represent the pattern inherent in the expression change.

As an example, consider the following expression.[11]

```
zipWith (\(x,y) -> x+y) [1,2] [3,4]
```

Our type change inference suggests to change `zipWith` from its original type `(a -> b -> c) -> [a] -> [b] -> [c]` to something of type `((Int,Int) -> Int) -> [Int] -> [Int] -> d`. Given these two types, we can deduce to curry the first argument to the function `zipWith` to remove the type error. (At the same time, we substitute `d` in the result type with `Int`.)

By employing unification modulo different theories, McAdam [21] has developed a theory and an algorithm to systematically deduce changes of this sort. We have adopted this approach (and extended it slightly) for deducing expression changes, such as swapping the arguments of function calls, currying and uncurrying of functions, or adding and removing arguments of function calls.

The extension is based on a simple form of identifying non-arity-preserving type changes. Such a change is used to modify the types, then McAdam's approach is applied, and the result is then interpreted in light of the non-arity-preserving type change as a new form of expression change. As an example, here is the method of identifying the addition or removal of arguments to function calls. In this case, the differences in the two types to be unified will lead to a second-level type change that pads one of the types with an extra type variable. For example, given the inferred type $\tau_1 \to \tau_3$ and the expected type $\tau_1 \to \tau_2 \to \tau_3$, we turn the first type into $\alpha \to \tau_1 \to \tau_3$. The application of McAdam's approach suggests to swap the arguments. Also, $\alpha$ is mapped to $\tau_2$. Interpreting the swapping suggestion through the second-level type change of padding, we deduce the removal of the second argument.

Besides these systematic change deductions, we also support some ad-hoc expression changes. Specifically, we infer changes by inspecting the expected type only. For example, if the inferred type for `f` in `f g e` is `b -> c` while the expected type is `(a -> b) -> a -> c`, we suggest to change `f g e` to `f (g e)`.

Another example are situations in which the result type of an expected type matches exactly one of its (several) argument types. In that case we suggest to replace the whole expression with the corresponding argument. This case applies, in fact, to the `palin` example, where the type change for `(:)` is to replace `a -> [a] -> [a]` by `a -> [b] -> a`. We therefore infer to replace `(:) z []`, which is `[z]`, by `z` because the first argument type is the same as the return type. Another case is when in expression `f g h` the expected type for `f` is `(a -> b) -> a -> b`. Then we suggest to remove `f` from the expression. There are more such ad-hoc changes that are useful in some situations, but we will not discuss them here.

In Section 8 we will compare our method with McAdam's original. Here we only note that the success of the method in our prototype depends to a large degree on the additional information provided by type-change inference, specifically, the more precise and less biased expected types that are used for the unification.

## 7. Evaluation

To evaluate the usefulness and efficiency of the counter-factual typing approach, we have implemented a prototype of type-change inference and expression-change deduction in Haskell. (In addition

[11] This example is adapted from [18], where `zipWith` is called `map2`.

| | 86 examples with Oracle | | | | | 35 ambiguous examples | | |
|---|---|---|---|---|---|---|---|---|
| | 1 | 2 | 3 | $\geq 4$ | never | complete | partial | incorrect |
| CF typing | 67.4 | 80.2 | 88.4 | 91.9 | 8.1 | 100.0 | 0.0 | 0.0 |
| Seminal | 47.7 | 54.7 | 58.1 | 59.3 | 40.7 | 40.0 | 25.7 | 34.3 |
| Helium | 61.6 | - | - | 61.6 | 38.4 | 0.0 | 100.0 | 0.0 |
| GHC | 17.4 | - | - | 17.4 | 82.6 | 0.0 | 34.3 | 65.7 |

Figure 7: Evaluation results for different approaches over 121 collected examples (in %).

to the constructs shown in Section 4 the prototype also supports some minor, straightforward extensions, such as data types and case expressions.) We compare the results produced by our CF typing tool to Seminal [18, 19], Helium [13, 14], and GHC. There are several reasons for selecting this group of tools. First, they provide currently running implementations. Second, these tools provide a similar functionality as CF typing, namely, locating type errors and presenting change suggestions, both at the type and the expression level. We have deliberately excluded slicing tools from the comparison because they only show all possible locations, and don't suggest changes.[12]

For evaluating the applicability and accuracy of the tools we have gathered a collection of 121 examples from 22 publications about type-error diagnosis. These papers include recent Ph.D. theses [14, 21, 27, 29] and papers that represent most recent and older work [15, 18, 23]. These papers cover many different perspectives of the type-error debugging problem, including error slicing, explanation systems, reordering of unification, automatic repairing, and interactive debugging. Since the examples presented in each paper have been carefully chosen or designed to illustrate important problem cases for type-error debugging, we have included them all, except for examples that involve type classes since our tool (as well as Seminal) doesn't currently support type classes. This exclusion did not have a significant effect. We gathered 8 unique examples regarding type classes involved in type errors discussed in [24, 24, 27]. Both GHC and Helium were able to produce a helpful error message in only 1 case. Otherwise, the examples range from very simple, such as `test = map [1,10] even` to very complex ones, such as the `plot` example introduced in [27].

We have grouped the examples into two categories. The first group ("with Oracle") contains 86 examples for which the correct version is known (because it either is mentioned in the paper or is obvious from the context). The other group ("ambiguous") contains the remaining 35 examples that can be reasonably fixed by several different single-location changes. For the examples in the "with Oracle" group, we have recorded how many correct suggestions each tool can find with at most *n* attempts. For the examples in the "ambiguous" group, we have determined how often a tool produces a complete, partial, or incorrect set of suggestions. For example, for the expression `\f g a -> (f a, f 1, g a, g True)`, which is given in [2], Helium suggests to change `True` to something of type `Int`. While this is correct, there are also other changes possible, for example, changing `f 1` to `f True`. Since these are not mentioned, the result is categorized as partial.

Figure 7 presents the results for the different tools and examples with unconstrained choice nesting level for CF typing. Note that GHC's output is considered correct only when it points to the correct location and produces an error message that is not simply reporting a unification failure or some other compiler-centric point of view. We have included GHC only as a baseline since it is widely known. The comparison of effectiveness is meant to be between CF typing, Seminal, and Helium.

[12] There are a few interactive approaches that have been proposed [6, 24], but they do currently not provide running implementations. Moreover, Chameleon [27] has evolved to focus on typing extensions of the Haskell type system. Since the tool has switched off its type-debugging facilities, it is not a viable candidate for comparison.

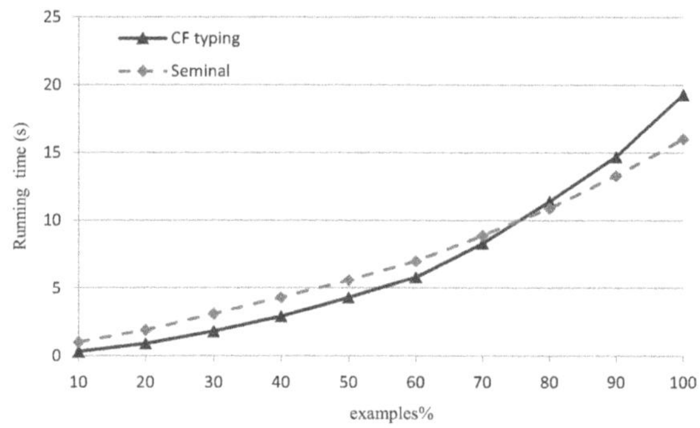


Figure 8: Running time for typing $x\%$ of the examples 10 times.

The numbers show that CF typing performs overall best. Even if we only consider the first change suggestion, it outperforms Helium which comes in second. Taking into account second and third suggestions, Seminal catches up, but CF typing performs even better.

In cases where Helium produces multiple suggestions, all suggestions are wrong. For CF typing 21 out of the 58 correct suggestions (that is, 36%) are expression changes. For Seminal the numbers are 20 out of 41 (or 51%), and for Helium it is 15 out of 52 (or 29%). This shows that Seminal produces a higher rate of expression change suggestions at a lower overall correctness rate.

Most of Helium and Seminal's failures are due to incorrectly identified change locations. Another main reason for Seminal's incorrect suggestions is that it introduces too extreme changes. In several cases, Seminal's change suggestion doesn't fix the type error.

Most cases for which CF typing fails are caused by missing parentheses. For example, for the expression `print "a" ++ "b"` [18], our approach suggests to change `print` from the inferred type `a -> IO ()` to the type `String -> String` or change `(++)` from the expected type `[a] -> [a] -> [a]` to the inferred type `IO () -> String -> String`. Neither of the suggestions allows us to deduce the regrouping of the expression.

To summarize, since the examples that we used have been designed to test very specific cases, the numbers do not tell much about how the systems would perform in everyday practice. They provide more like a stress test for the tools, but the direct comparison shows that CF typing performs very well compared with other tools and thus presents a viable alternative to type debugging.

With the help of variational typing, we can generate all the potential changes very efficiently. The running time for all the collected examples is within 2 seconds. Figure 8 shows the running time for both our approach and Seminal for processing the reported examples. For each point $(x, y)$ on the curve, it means that $x\%$ of all examples are processed with $y$ seconds. The running time for our approach is measured on a laptop with a 2.8GHz dual core processor and 3GB RAM running Windows XP and GHC 7.0.2. The running time for Seminal is measured on the same machine with Cygwin 5.1. The purpose of the graph is simply to demonstrate the feasibility of our approach.

Second, we have evaluated how increasing levels of choice nestings affect the efficiency of the inference algorithm and how putting a limit on maximum nesting levels as described in Section 5 can regain efficiency at the cost of precision. For this purpose, we have automatically generated large examples, and we use functions of types like $\alpha \to \alpha \to \ldots \to \alpha$ to trigger the choice elimination s-

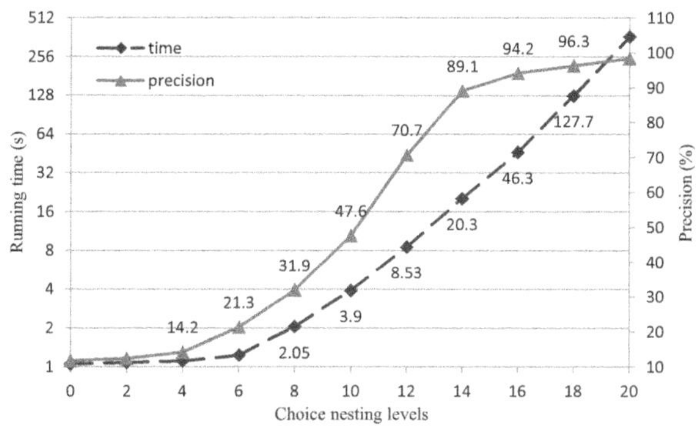


Figure 9: Limits on choice nesting trade efficiency for precision.

trategies discussed in Section 5. We first generated 200 type correct examples and then introduced one or two type errors in each example by changing the leaves, swapping arguments and so on. Each example contains about 60000 nodes in its tree representation.

Figure 9 presents the running time and precision against choice nesting levels for these generated examples. A change suggestion is considered correct if it fixes a type error and appears among the first four changes for that example. Precision is measured by dividing the number of examples that have correct change suggestions over the number of all examples. From the figure we observe that a nesting level cut-off between 12 and 18 achieves both high precision and efficiency.

## 8. Related Work

We have grouped our discussion of related work according to major features shared by the different approaches.

***Reporting single locations*** Most of the single-error-location approaches are based on some variant of the algorithm $\mathcal{W}$ and report an error as soon as the algorithm fails. Since the original algorithm $\mathcal{W}$ is biased in the order in which unification problems are solved (which has a negative impact on locating errors), many approaches have tried to eliminate this bias. Examples are algorithms $\mathcal{M}$ [17], $\mathcal{G}$ [10], $\mathcal{W}^{SYM}$ and $\mathcal{M}^{SYM}$ [20], and $\mathcal{UAE}$ and $\mathcal{IEI}$ [30]. All these algorithms interpret the place of unification failure as the source of the type error. In contrast, Johnson and Walz [15] and the Helium tool [13, 14] use heuristics to select the most likely error location from a set of potential places. Although heuristics often work well and lead to more accurate locations, they can still get confused due to the single-location constraint. In contrast, we explore all potential changes and rank them from most to least likely.

In deducing expression changes from type changes, we have used (an extension of) McAdam's technique [21]. Since his approach is based on the algorithm $\mathcal{W}$, it suffers from the bias of error locating mentioned above. Moreover, his approach doesn't have access to the precise expected type, which helps in our approach to ensure that deduced expression changes will not have an impact on the program as a whole.

***Explaining type conflicts*** Some approaches have focused on identifying and explaining the causes of type conflicts. Wand [26] records each unification step so that they can be tracked back to the failure point. Duggan and Bent [9] on the other hand record the reason for each unification that is being performed. Beaven and Stansifer [1] and Yang [28] produce textual explanation for the cause of the type errors.

While these techniques can be useful in many cases, there are also potential downsides. First, the explanation can become quite verbose and repetitive, and the size grows rapidly as the program size increases. Second, the explanation is inherently coupled to the underlying algorithm that performs the inference. Thus, knowledge about how the algorithms work is often needed to understand the produced messages. Third, the explanations usually lead to the failure point, which is often the result of biased unification and not the true cause of the type error. Finally, although a potential fix for the type error may lurk in the middle of the explanation chain, it's not always clear about how to exploit it and change the program.

***Interactive debugging*** While many tools attempt to improve the static presentation of type error information, interactive approaches give users a better understanding about the type error or why certain types have been inferred for certain expressions. Consequently, several approaches to interactive type debugging have been pursued.

The ability to infer types for unbound variables enable a type debugging paradigm that is based on the idea of replacing a suspicious program snippet by a fresh variable [2]. If such replacement leads to a type correct program, then the error location has been identified. However, the original system proposed by Berstein and Stark requires users to do these steps manually. Later, Braßel [3] automated this process by systematically commenting out parts of the program and running the type checker iteratively. Since type changing is based on unification, it can again introduce the bias problem. Also, it is unclear how to handle programs that contain more than one type error.

Through employing a number of different techniques, Chitil [6], Neubauer and Thiemann [22], and Stuckey [24, 27] have developed tools that allow users to explore a program and inspect the types for any subexpression. Chameleon [24, 27] also allows users to query how the types for specific expressions are inferred. All these approaches provide a mechanism for users to explore a program and view the type information. However, none of them provides direct support for finding or fixing type errors.

***Error slicing*** The main advantage of slicing approaches [12, 23, 25] is that they return all locations related to type errors. The downside is that they cover too many locations. Recent improvements in Chameleon [27] have helped to reduce the number of locations, but the problem still persists (recall the example in the Introduction). Moreover, slicing tools do not provide suggestions of how to get rid of the type error.

Like error slicing approaches, our CF typing approach is complete in not missing any potential change. However, the changes we presented to users involve fewer locations. Usually, users have to focus on only one location and its suggestions for type changes.

***Embracing type uncertainty*** Similar to choice types, sum types can also encode many types. Neubauer and Thiemann [22] developed a type system based on discriminative sum types to record the causes of type errors. Specifically, they place two non-unifiable types into a sum type. Technically, named choice types provide more fine-grained control over variations in types than discriminative sum types. While sum types are unified component-wise, this is only the case for choice types of the same name. Each alternative in a choice type is unified with all the alternatives in other choices with different names. Also, their system returns a set of sources related to type errors. Thus, it can be viewed as an error slicing approach. However, compared to other slicing approaches, it is not guaranteed that the returned set of locations is minimal. Moreover, the approach doesn't provide specific change locations or change suggestions.

***Typing by searching*** CF typing and Seminal [18, 19] could both be called "search based", although the search happens at different levels. While CF typing explores changes on the type level, Seminal works on the expression level directly, which makes it impossible for Seminal to generate a complete set of type-change suggestions. Given an ill-typed program, Seminal first has to decide where the type error is. Seminal uses a binary search to locate the erroneous place. This way of searching causes Seminal to make mistakes in locating errors when the first part of the program itself doesn't contain a type error but actually triggers type errors because it's too constrained. For example, the cause of the type error in the `palin` example discussed in Section 1 is the `fold` function, which is itself well typed. As a result, Seminal fails to find a correct suggestion.

Once the problematic expression is found, Seminal searches for a type-corrected program by creating mutations of the original program. For example, by swapping the arguments to functions, currying or uncurrying function calls, and so on. Compared to our change deduction approach, this has both advantages and disadvantages. In some cases, it can find a correct change while our approach fails to do so, as, for example, in the missing-parentheses problem discussed in Section 7. On the other hand, its power to generate arbitrarily complicated changes can lead to bizarre suggestions, such as the suggestion to change `xs == (rev xs)` to `(==) (xs,(rev xs))`.

## 9. Conclusions

We have presented a new method for debugging type errors. The approach is based on the notion of counter-factual typing, which is the idea of systematically varying the types of all atomic program elements to generate a typing potential for the erroneous program that can be explored and reasoned about. We have exploited this typing potential and the associated set of type changes to create a ranked list of type-change and expression-change suggestions that can eliminate type errors from programs. A comparison of a prototype implementation with other tools has demonstrated that the approach works very well and, in fact, outperforms its competitors.

In future work, we plan to investigate other uses of typing potentials and type changes. For example, the integrated choice-based representation provides opportunities for defining type queries that can be used to examine programs and also form the basis for sophisticated user interfaces to support more interactive forms of type debugging. We also plan to investigate how well the approach works for the debugging of type errors in richer type systems.

## References


[1] M. Beaven and R. Stansifer. Explaining type errors in polymorphic languages. *ACM Letters on Programming Languages and Systems*, 2:17–30, 1994.

[2] K. L. Bernstein and E. W. Stark. Debugging type errors. Technical report, State University of New York at Stony Brook, 1995.

[3] B. Braßel. Typehope: There is hope for your type errors. In *Int. Workshop on Implementation of Functional Languages*, 2004.

[4] S. Chen, M. Erwig, and E. Walkingshaw. An Error-Tolerant Type System for Variational Lambda Calculus. In *ACM Int. Conf. on Functional Programming*, pages 29–40, 2012.

[5] S. Chen, M. Erwig, and E. Walkingshaw. Extending Type Inference to Variational Programs. *ACM Trans. on Programming Languages and Systems*, 2013. To appear.

[6] O. Chitil. Compositional explanation of types and algorithmic debugging of type errors. In *ACM Int. Conf. on Functional Programming*, pages 193–204, September 2001.

[7] V. Choppella. *Unification Source-Tracking with Application To Diagnosis of Type Inference*. PhD thesis, Indiana University, 2002.

[8] L. Damas and R. Milner. Principal type-schemes for functional programs. In *ACM Symp. on Principles of Programming Languages*, pages 207–212, 1982.

[9] D. Duggan and F. Bent. Explaining type inference. In *Science of Computer Programming*, pages 37–83, 1995.

[10] H. Eo, O. Lee, and K. Yi. Proofs of a set of hybrid let-polymorphic type inference algorithms. *New Generation Computing*, 22(1):1–36, 2004.

[11] M. Erwig and E. Walkingshaw. The Choice Calculus: A Representation for Software Variation. *ACM Trans. on Software Engineering and Methodology*, 21(1):6:1–6:27, 2011.

[12] C. Haack and J. B. Wells. Type error slicing in implicitly typed higher-order languages. In *European Symposium on Programming*, pages 284–301, 2003.

[13] B. Heeren, D. Leijen, and A. van IJzendoorn. Helium, for learning haskell. In *Proceedings of the 2003 ACM SIGPLAN workshop on Haskell*, Haskell '03, pages 62–71, New York, NY, USA, 2003. ACM.

[14] B. J. Heeren. *Top Quality Type Error Messages*. PhD thesis, Universiteit Utrecht, The Netherlands, Sept. 2005.

[15] G. F. Johnson and J. A. Walz. A maximum-flow approach to anomaly isolation in unification-based incremental type inference. In *ACM Symp. on Principles of Programming Languages*, pages 44–57, 1986.

[16] O. Lee and K. Yi. Proofs about a folklore let-polymorphic type inference algorithm. *ACM Trans. on Programming Languages and Systems*, 20(4):707–723, July 1998.

[17] O. Lee and K. Yi. A generalized let-polymorphic type inference algorithm. Technical report, Technical Memorandum ROPAS-2000-5, Research on Program Analysis System, Korea Advanced Institute of Science and Technology, 2000.

[18] B. Lerner, M. Flower, D. Grossman, and C. Chambers. Searching for type-error messages. In *ACM Int. Conf. on Programming Language Design and Implementation*, pages 425–434, 2007.

[19] B. Lerner, D. Grossman, and C. Chambers. Seminal: searching for ml type-error messages. In *Workshop on ML*, pages 63–73, 2006.

[20] B. J. McAdam. *Repairing type errors in functional programs*. PhD thesis, University of Edinburgh. College of Science and Engineering. School of Informatics., 2002.

[21] B. J. McAdam. *Reporting Type Errors in Functional Programs*. PhD thesis, Larboratory for Foundations of Computer Science, The University of Edinburgh, 2002.

[22] M. Neubauer and P. Thiemann. Discriminative sum types locate the source of type errors. In *ACM Int. Conf. on Functional Programming*, pages 15–26, 2003.

[23] T. Schilling. Constraint-free type error slicing. In *Trends in Functional Programming*, pages 1–16. Springer, 2012.

[24] P. J. Stuckey, M. Sulzmann, and J. Wazny. Interactive type debugging in haskell. In *ACM SIGPLAN Workshop on Haskell*, pages 72–83, 2003.

[25] F. Tip and T. B. Dinesh. A slicing-based approach for locating type errors. *ACM Trans. on Software Engineering and Methodology*, 10(1):5–55, Jan. 2001.

[26] M. Wand. Finding the source of type errors. In *ACM Symp. on Principles of Programming Languages*, pages 38–43, 1986.

[27] J. R. Wazny. *Type inference and type error diagnosis for Hindley/Milner with extensions*. PhD thesis, The University of Melbourne, January 2006.

[28] J. Yang. Explaining type errors by finding the source of a type conflict. In *Trends in Functional Programming*, pages 58–66. Intellect Books, 2000.

[29] J. Yang. *Improving Polymorphic Type Explanations*. PhD thesis, Heriot-Watt University, May 2001.

[30] J. Yang, G. Michaelson, P. Trinder, and J. B. Wells. Improved type error reporting. In *Int. Workshop on Implementation of Functional Languages*, pages 71–86, 2000.

# Battery Transition Systems *

Udi Boker
The Interdisciplinary Center, Herzliya, Israel

Thomas A. Henzinger
IST Austria, Klosterneuburg, Austria

Arjun Radhakrishna
IST Austria, Klosterneuburg, Austria

## Abstract

The analysis of the energy consumption of software is an important goal for quantitative formal methods. Current methods, using weighted transition systems or energy games, model the energy source as an ideal resource whose status is characterized by one number, namely the amount of remaining energy. Real batteries, however, exhibit behaviors that can deviate substantially from an ideal energy resource. Based on a discretization of a standard continuous battery model, we introduce *battery transition systems*. In this model, a battery is viewed as consisting of two parts – the available-charge tank and the bound-charge tank. Any charge or discharge is applied to the available-charge tank. Over time, the energy from each tank diffuses to the other tank.

Battery transition systems are infinite state systems that, being not well-structured, fall into no decidable class that is known to us. Nonetheless, we are able to prove that the $\omega$-regular model-checking problem is decidable for battery transition systems. We also present a case study on the verification of control programs for energy-constrained semi-autonomous robots.

***Categories and Subject Descriptors*** Theory of computation [*Logic*]: Verification by model checking

***General Terms*** Theory, Verification

***Keywords*** Battery, Transition systems, energy, model checking

## 1. Introduction

Systems with limited energy resources, such as mobile devices or electric cars, have become ubiquitous in everyday life. In accordance, there is a growing attention to the formal modeling of such systems and the analysis of their behavior. These systems are commonly modeled as weighted transition systems, where the states of the transition system represent the system configurations, the transitions represent the possible operations, and the weights on the transitions correspond to the energy consumed (negative value) or added (positive value) during the operation. In recent literature (for example, [7, 8, 19]), weighted transition systems have been analyzed with respect to various problems, such as finite-automaton emptiness problem (starting from a given initial energy, can a specific configuration be reached while keeping the energy positive in all intermediate steps?), and Büchi emptiness problem (can a specific configuration be visited repeatedly, while keeping the energy positive?).

In all these works, the energy-resource is idealized. In particular, it is assumed that its status can be completely characterized by one number, namely the amount of remaining energy. However, physical systems with energy restrictions often use batteries, which are far from an ideal-energy source. One such non-ideal behavior of a battery behavior is the "recovery effect", where the available energy at certain times is smaller than the sum of energies consumed and charged. Intuitively, the recovery effect is a result of the fact that energy is consumed from the edge of the battery, while the total charge is spread across the entire battery. When the consumption is high, additional time may be required until the charge diffuses from the inside of the battery to its edge, during which period there is no available energy, possibly failing the required operation.

The recovery effect is often noticed in our daily usage of battery-powered systems, for example mobile phones – a phone might shutdown due to an "out of power" condition, but then become live again after an idle period.

We aim to formally model such energy systems with non-ideal resources. We define a "battery transition system" (BTS), where the system is viewed as a weighted transition system, as is standard. However, the semantics of its possible traces is specified differently, to capture non-ideal behaviors. The semantics we specify for BTSs correspond to a discretization of a well-known battery model – the kinetic battery model (KiBaM) [20]. There are various battery models in the literature, admitting various accuracies and complexities, among which the KiBaM model is a good choice for the purpose of properly analyzing systems with the recovery effect [17]. We elaborate, in Section 2, on various battery models, and explain the derivation of BTS semantics from the KiBaM model.

**Semantics**. The status of the battery in a BTS is a pair $(x, y)$, where $x$ represents the *available charge* (available for immediate usage) and $y$ the *bound charge* (internal charge in a battery that is not immediately available). During each transition, some amount of charge diffuses between $x$ and $y$. The weight of the transition (say $w$) affects only $x$ in the current step. The diffusion rate depends on the difference between $x$ and $y$, and on two constants of the battery: a *width constant* $c \in \mathbb{R}$ with $0 < c < 1$, and a *diffusion constant* $k \in \mathbb{R}$ with $0 < k < c(1-c)$. Formally, making a transition of weight $w$ from a battery status $(x, y)$, results in the battery status $(x', y')$, where $x' = x - k \cdot (\frac{x}{c} - \frac{y}{1-c}) + w$ and $y' = y + k \cdot (\frac{x}{c} - \frac{y}{1-c})$. The value $k \cdot (\frac{x}{c} - \frac{y}{1-c})$ represents the amount of charge diffused between $x$ and $y$. The above transition is legal if the available charge $x$ remains positive after the transition.

* This work was supported in part by the Austrian Science Fund NFN RiSE (Rigorous Systems Engineering), and by the ERC Advanced Grant QUAREM (Quantitative Reactive Modeling).



*POPL'14*, January 22–24, 2014, San Diego, CA, USA.

http://dx.doi.org/10.1145/2535838.2535875

The diffusion constant $k = \frac{1}{8}$; The width constant $c = \frac{1}{2}$.

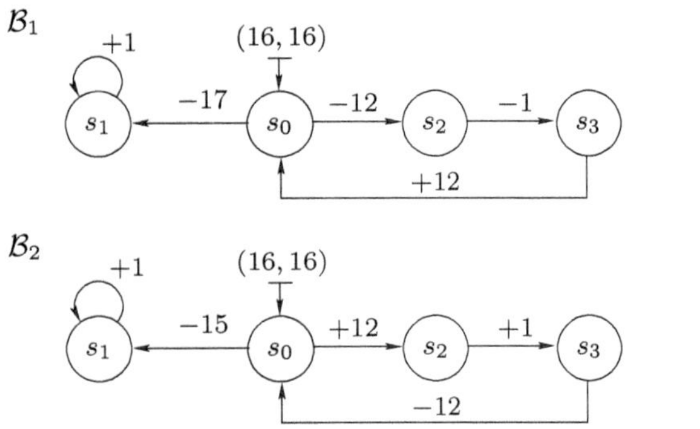


**Figure 1.** In the battery system $\mathcal{B}_1$, a trace reaching the state $s_1$ must make a cycle with total negative energy. In $\mathcal{B}_2$, an illegal trace must make different choices at different visits in $s_0$.

The mathematical properties of a BTS are shown to be inherently different from those of a simple-energy transition system (where only the value of $x+y$ is considered), as illustrated in Fig. 1: Considering the system $\mathcal{B}_1$ as a simple-energy system, where only the total energy should remain positive, $s_1$ is directly reachable from $s_0$, and the cycle $s_0 \to s_2 \to s_3 \to s_0$ is completely useless. On the other hand, viewing $\mathcal{B}_1$ as a BTS, in order to go from state $s_0$ to $s_1$, counterintuitively, a legal trace must first take the cycle through $s_2$ and $s_3$. Though decreasing the total energy, the cycle temporarily increases the available energy, allowing the transition to $s_1$. Furthermore, it is known that a simple-energy system (even with multi-dimension energies) admits an illegal trace if and only if it admits a memoryless illegal trace (always making the same choice at each state) [8]. However, an illegal trace in the system $\mathcal{B}_2$ of Fig. 1 must make different choices at different visits in state $s_0$ (Theorem 3).

**Model checking**. We consider the finite-automaton, Büchi, and Streett emptiness problems for a BTS; these problems are central to the model checking of systems with no fairness constraints, weak fairness constraints, and strong fairness constraints, respectively.

As BTSs are infinite-state systems, it is natural to ask if they fall into a known, tractable, class of infinite state systems. For example, standard model-checking algorithms exist for well-structured transition systems (e.g., lossy channel systems, timed automata [2], etc), where a well-quasi ordering can be defined on the states of the infinite systems, and this ordering is compatible with the transition relation of the system. However, for BTSs, we can show that the infinite sequence $(1,1), (\frac{3}{4}, 1\frac{1}{4}), (\frac{11}{16}, 1\frac{5}{16}), (\frac{43}{64}, 1\frac{21}{64}), \ldots$ of battery statuses is monotonically decreasing with respect to any ordering that is compatible with transitions. Intuitively, this sequence contains battery statuses that have equal total charge, but strictly decreasing available charge. This implies that model-checking algorithms from the domain of well-structured transitions systems do not apply directly to BTS.

We solve the finite-automaton emptiness problem by building a forward reachability tree, along the lines of the Karp-Miller tree for Petri nets [11]. There, using the well-structured properties of Petri-nets, the Karp-Miller tree is shown to be a finite summarization of all reachable states, despite there being infinitely-many reachable states. A BTS is not well-structured, yet we are able to generate a finite "summary tree", having all the reachability data, by proving the following key observations: 1. Once the total energy in a battery status is high-enough, the problem can be reduced to simple-energy reachability; 2. Considering some characteristic properties of battery statuses allows to define a simulation-compatible total ordering between statuses having the same total energy; and 3. Repeating a cycle whose total energy sums to 0 makes the battery status converge monotonically to a limit value independent of the initial status. Despite the fact that the above ordering is not well-founded, i.e., there may be infinite chains, the last observation lets us take limits of infinite chains while constructing the reachability tree.

In simple-energy systems, extending the finite automaton emptiness algorithm to a Büchi emptiness algorithm is straightforward – checking whether there is a reachable Büchi state that has a cycle back to itself, such that the sum of weights on the cycle is non-negative. In a BTS, such a simple solution does not work – a cycle that does not decrease the total energy might still fail the process after finitely many iterations, as the available charge can slightly decreases on every iteration. A simple modification, seeking cycles that do not decrease both the total and the available energies is too restrictive, as the available charge may still converge to a positive value. We solve the Büchi emptiness problem by showing that if there exists an accepted trace, there also exists a lasso-shaped accepted trace having one of two special forms. These forms concern the way that the available charge changes along the cycle. By a delicate analysis of the reachability tree, we then solve the question of whether the transition system allows for a trace in one of these special forms. The Streett emptiness problem is solved similarly, by using a small extension of the Büchi emptiness algorithm.

We show that our algorithms for the finite-automaton, Büchi, and Streett emptiness problems are in PSPACE with respect to the number of states in the transition system and a unary representation of the weights. If weights are represented in binary, or if the battery constants are arbitrarily small and represented in binary, the space complexity grows exponentially.

**Case study: Robot control**. We examine a semi-autonomous robot control in an energy-constrained environment. We present a small programming language for robot-controllers and define quantitative battery-based semantics for controllers written in that language. We solve the $\omega$-regular model-checking problem for programs written in this language, using our results on battery transition systems. We demonstrate the inadequacy of standard quantitative verification techniques, where the battery is viewed as an ideal energy resource – they might affirm, for example, that the robot can reach some target locations, while taking into account the non-ideal behavior of its battery, it cannot.

**Related work**. Batteries are involved devices, exhibiting various different phenomena. Accordingly, there are many different works considering these aspects, for example scheduling the load among several batteries [4, 9, 16, 18], optimizing the lifetime of a battery with respect to the "cycle aging effect" [1], analyzing the thermal effects, and more.

To the best of our knowledge, this is the first work to formally analyze an energy system with a non-ideal energy source. Previous work has either considered ideal energy sources (for example, [8]) or provides approximations for the battery life-time with respect to various discharge scenarios (for example, [16, 17]).

Our finite-automaton emptiness algorithm follows the approach taken in the Karp-Miller tree [11] which can be used in general for well-structured transition systems [12]. However, our systems are not well-structured and a naive application of this technique does not entail termination of algorithms. We use ideas from flattable systems [3] and additional analysis of BTSs to produce a terminating version of these algorithms. In particular, we also use an intricate analysis of BTSs to get an algorithm for deciding Büchi and Streett properties. This kind of analysis is not possible for general flattable systems.

## 2. Battery Models

We provide a short description of how batteries are modeled in the literature, and explain how we derive our formal model of a battery.

A battery consists of one or more electrochemical cells, each of which contain a negative electrode (anode), a positive electrode (cathode), and a separator between them. During discharge and recharge, electrons move through the external circuit, while chemical reaction produces or consumes chemical energy inside the battery. For example, during discharge in lithium-ion (Li-ion) batteries, positive lithium ions move from the anode to the cathode, while the reverse occurs during recharge (see Fig. 2).

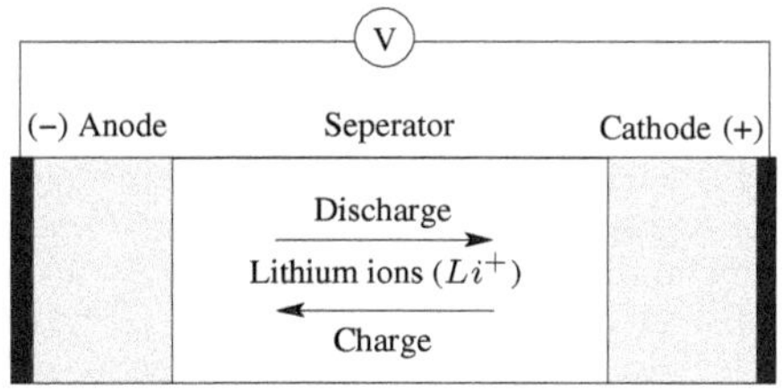


**Figure 2.** Schematic of a lithium-ion (Li-ion) battery.

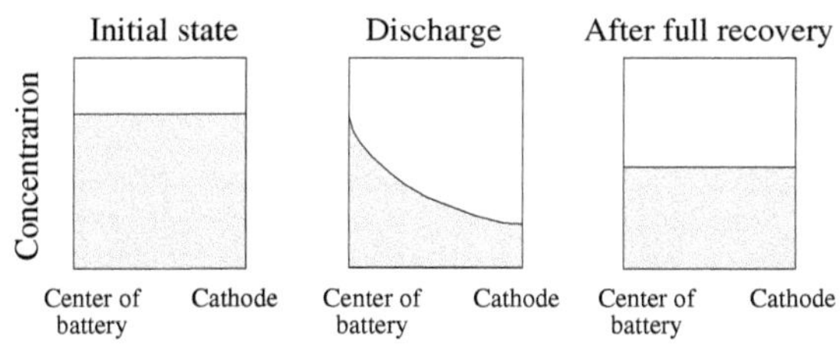


**Figure 3.** Concentration of electroactive species along the battery, following a discharge and a recovery phase.

Batteries of all types have a "recovery effect", meaning that the chemical reaction inside the battery does not keep up with the rate of the external activity. Internally, in Li-ion batteries, the concentration of the electroactive species near the electrodes becomes smaller than their concentration in the interior of the battery. When the battery has low load for some time, the ions have enough time to diffuse to the electrodes, and charge recovery takes place (see Fig. 3). The well-known symptom of this is that a battery might be "empty" after some usage, but then becomes "charged" after an idle period.

There are many battery models modeling various aspects of a real battery. The most accurate ones model the electrochemical reactions in detail [5, 10, 13, 21]. Though highly accurate, they require configuration of many (usually around 50) parameters, making them difficult to analyze. Another approach taken is to model the electrical properties of the battery using voltage sources, resistors, and other elements [14, 15]. These approximate battery voltage behavior well, but their modeling of the available battery capacity is inaccurate. A third class consists of the analytical models that describe the battery at a high abstraction level, modeling only its major properties by means of a few equations. The dominant models of this class are the kinetic battery model [20], and the diffusion model [22]. A detailed description of the various models can be found in [16, 17].

The possibly simplest, yet useful, model that handles the recovery effect is the kinetic battery model (KiBaM) [20]. While being originally developed for Lead-Acid batteries to model both battery capacity and battery voltage, its capacity modeling was found to be a good approximation even for more modern batteries such as the Li-ion battery. In [16, 17], it was theoretically shown that KiBaM

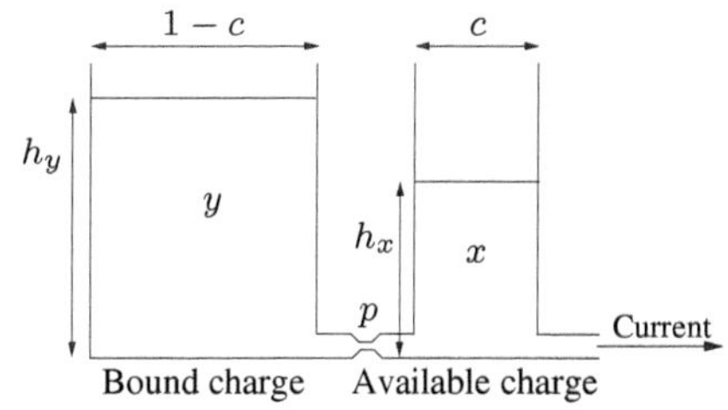


**Figure 4.** Kinetic battery model (KiBaM).

is a first order approximation of the diffusion model, which was designed for Li-ion batteries. In addition, their experimental results show that it has up to 7 percent deviation from the accurate electrochemical models.

We concentrate on a battery's available capacity, and hence, adopt the KiBaM model. In this model, the battery charge is distributed over two tanks: the available-charge tank, denoted $x$, of width $c \in (0, 1)$, and the bound-charge tank, denoted $y$, of width $1 - c$ (see Fig. 4). The external current gets electrons only from the available-charge tank, whereas electrons from the bound-charge tank flow to the available-charge tank. When recharging, the reverse process occurs, electrons are added directly to the available-charge tank, from there they flows to the bound-charge tank. The charge flows between the tanks through a "valve" with a fixed conductance $p$. The parameter $p$ has the dimension 1/time and influences the rate at which the charge can flow between the two tanks. This rate is also proportional to the height difference between the two tanks. If the heights are given by $h_x = x/c$ and $h_y = y/(1 - c)$, and the current load by $w(t)$, the charge in the tank over time behaves according to the following system of differential equations [20]:

$$\frac{dx}{dt} = -w(t) - p(h_x - h_y); \qquad \frac{dy}{dt} = p(h_x - h_y) \quad (1)$$

with initial conditions $x(0) = c \cdot C$ and $y(0) = (1 - c) \cdot C$, where $C$ is the total battery capacity. The battery cannot supply charge when there is no charge left in the available-charge tank.

We are interested in calculating the battery status along a discrete-time transition system, thus consider the equations (1) for fixed time steps. We get the following equations:

$$x_{i+1} = x_i - w_i - k(h_{x_i} - h_{y_i}); \qquad y_{i+1} = y_i + k(h_{x_i} - h_{y_i}) \quad (2)$$

where $x_i$ and $y_i$ are the values of $x$ and $y$ before the time step $i$, respectively, $w_i$ is the total load on the battery at time step $i$, and $k = p \times$ (length of a time step). The smaller the time steps are, the smaller $k$ is, and the more accurate the discretization is.

We further need to ensure that the discretization does not introduce undesirable behaviours. In Eq. 1 if $h_x > h_y$ and $w(t)$ is 0, the relation $h_x > h_y$ keeps holding. We should ensure this in the discrete model, i.e., if $h_{x_i} > h_{y_i}$ and $w_i = 0$, then it cannot be that $h_{x_{i+1}} \leq h_{y_{i+1}}$.

Formalizing the above requirement, we have

$$h_{x_{i+1}} = \frac{x_{i+1}}{c} = \frac{x_i - 0 - k(h_{x_i} - h_{y_i})}{c} = h_{x_i} - \frac{k(h_{x_i} - h_{y_i})}{c};$$

$$h_{y_{i+1}} = \frac{y_{i+1}}{1-c} = \frac{y_i + k(h_{x_i} - h_{y_i})}{1-c} = h_{y_i} + \frac{k(h_{x_i} - h_{y_i})}{1-c}.$$

Hence, $h_{x_{i+1}} - h_{y_{i+1}} = (h_{x_i} - h_{y_i})(1 - k(\frac{1}{c(1-c)}))$.

Therefore, the parameter $k$ is acceptable if $k(\frac{1}{c(1-c)}) < 1$, leading to the conclusion that

$$k < c(1 - c) \quad (3)$$

## 3. Battery Transition Systems

We incorporate the discrete battery model from Equation 2 into a weighted transition system. The system consists of finitely many control-states and weighted transitions between them, where the weights denote the amount of energy recharged/consumed at each operation.

### 3.1 Weighted Transition Systems and Battery Semantics

A *transition system* is a tuple $\langle S, \Delta, s_\iota \rangle$ where $S$ is a (possibly infinite) set of control states, $s_\iota \in S$ is the initial control state, and $\Delta \subseteq S \times S$ is a set of transitions. A *weighted transition system* (WTS) is a tuple $\mathcal{S} = \langle S, \Delta, s_\iota, \nu \rangle$ where $\langle S, \Delta, s_\iota \rangle$ is a transition system, and $\nu : \Delta \to \mathbb{Z}$ is a weight function labeling transitions with integer weights[1].

A *battery transition system* (BTS or *battery system*, for short) is a tuple $\mathcal{B} = \langle \langle S, \Delta, s_\iota, \nu \rangle, c, k \rangle$ where $\langle S, \Delta, s_\iota, \nu \rangle$ is a WTS with a finite number of control states (i.e., $|S| < \infty$), $c \in \mathbb{R}$ is a *width constant* with $0 < c < 1$, and $k \in \mathbb{R}$ is a *diffusion constant* with $0 < k < c(1-c)$.

**Semantics**. Given a BTS $\mathcal{B} = \langle \mathcal{S}, c, k \rangle$, a *battery status* $(x, y) \in \mathbb{R}^2_{>0}$ represents the current configuration of the battery. Intuitively, the values $x$ and $y$ represent the charge in the available-charge tank and the bound-charge tank of the battery, respectively (see Figure 4).

If the current battery status is $(x, y)$, on a transition of weight $w$, we define the change in the battery status using a function $\texttt{Post} : \mathbb{R}^2 \times \mathbb{Z} \to \mathbb{R}^2$, letting the battery status after the transition $(x', y') = \texttt{Post}((x, y), w)$. Here, we follow the standard convention of energy transition systems and consider a positive (resp. negative) weight as adding (resp. drawing) a charge to (resp. from) the battery. In matrix notation, we have the following.

$$\texttt{Post}((x,y),w) = \left[\mathcal{A}_\mathcal{B} \cdot \begin{pmatrix} x \\ y \end{pmatrix}\right]^\top + \begin{pmatrix} w \\ 0 \end{pmatrix}^\top, \text{ where}$$

$$\mathcal{A}_\mathcal{B} = \begin{pmatrix} 1 - \frac{k}{c} & \frac{k}{1-c} \\ \frac{k}{c} & 1 - \frac{k}{1-c} \end{pmatrix}$$

The matrix $\mathcal{A}_\mathcal{B}$ is called the *diffusion matrix*. Note that the $\texttt{Post}$ function indeed follows Equation 2 except for the change in the sign of $w$. The values $\frac{k}{c} \cdot x$ and $\frac{k}{1-c} \cdot y$ denote the heights $h_x$ and $h_y$ of the two tanks, and hence, we get that $x' = x - k \cdot (h_x - h_y) + w$ and $y' = y + k \cdot (h_x - h_y)$. We abuse notation by defining $\texttt{Post}(\mathbf{t}, w_1 w_2 \dots w_m)$ inductively as $\texttt{Post}(\texttt{Post}(\mathbf{t}, w_1), w_2 \dots w_m)$ where each $w_i \in \mathbb{Z}$.

Given an *initial battery status* $\mathbf{t}_\iota \in \mathbb{R}^2_{>0}$, the *semantics* of a BTS $\mathcal{B} = \langle \langle S, \Delta, s_\iota, \nu \rangle, c, k \rangle$ is given by a (possibly infinite) transition system $\langle E, \to, e_\iota \rangle$ where $E = S \times \mathbb{R}^2_{>0}$ is the set of states, $\to \subseteq E \times E$ is the transition relation, and $e_\iota = (s_\iota, \mathbf{t}_\iota)$ is the initial state.

- We call each $(s, \mathbf{t}) \in E$ an *extended state* with $s \in S$ being its control state, and $\mathbf{t} \in \mathbb{R}^2_{>0}$ being its battery status [2].
- We have $((s, \mathbf{t}), (s', \mathbf{t}')) \in \to$ if and only if $\texttt{Post}(\mathbf{t}, w) = \mathbf{t}'$ and $(s, s') \in \Delta \wedge \nu((s, s')) = w$. We write $(s, \mathbf{t}) \to (s', \mathbf{t}')$ instead of $((s, \mathbf{t}), (s', \mathbf{t}')) \in \to$.

A weight $w$ (and by extension, a transition with weight $w$) is *feasible* from battery status $\mathbf{t}$ if $\texttt{Post}(\mathbf{t}, w) \in \mathbb{R}^2_{>0}$, namely if $\texttt{Post}(\mathbf{t}, w)$ is a valid battery status. Similarly, a sequence of weights $w_0 w_1 \dots w_n$ is feasible from $\mathbf{t}$ iff $w_0$ is feasible from $\mathbf{t}$ and each $w_i$ is feasible from $\texttt{Post}(\mathbf{t}, w_0 \dots w_{i-1})$. Extending the nomenclature, we call every $\mathbf{t} \in \mathbb{R}^2 \setminus \mathbb{R}^2_{>0}$ *infeasible*.

The *traces* of a BTS $\mathcal{B}$, denoted $\Pi(\mathcal{B})$, are given by (infinite or finite) paths of the form $\pi = (s_0, \mathbf{t_0})(s_1, \mathbf{t_1}) \dots$ where $s_0 = s_\iota$ and $\mathbf{t_0} = \mathbf{t}_\iota$ and for every $i \geq 1$, we have $(s_{i-1}, \mathbf{t_{i-1}}) \to (s_i, \mathbf{t_i})$. The corresponding *control trace* is given by $\theta = \texttt{control}(\pi) = s_0 s_1 \dots$, and the set of control traces by $\Theta(\mathcal{B}) = \{\texttt{control}(\pi) \mid \pi \in \Pi(\mathcal{B})\}$. We say that a (finite or infinite) sequence of control states $s_0 s_1 \dots$ is feasible from a battery status $\mathbf{t}$ iff the weight sequence $w_0 w_1 \dots$ is feasible from $\mathbf{t}$, where $(s_i, s_{i+1}) \in \Delta \wedge \nu((s_i, s_{i+1})) = w_i$.

**Energy feasibility**. We define an alternate set of semantics corresponding to the classical notion of ideal-energy systems. We say that $(x, y) \in \mathbb{R}^2$ is *energy-feasible* if $x + y > 0$. As for the term "feasible", we further extend the notion of energy-feasible as follows: 1. A sequence of weights $w_0 \dots w_n$ is energy-feasible from $(x, y)$ iff $\texttt{Post}((x, y), w_0 \dots w_i)$ is energy-feasible for all $0 \leq i \leq n$; and 2. A sequence of control states $s_0 s_1 \dots$ is energy-feasible from $(x, y)$ iff $w_0 w_1 \dots$ is energy-feasible from $(x, y)$ where $w_i = \nu(s_i, s_{i+1})$.

***Characteristic functions.*** For mathematical simplicity, we follow the approach taken in [20] and use an alternate representation for battery statuses. We represent $(x, y)$ using two other numbers, denoting it $[\mathsf{e}; \mathsf{d}]$, where $\mathsf{e}$ and $\mathsf{d}$ are defined by the following *energy* and *deviation* functions.

- $\mathsf{e} = \texttt{energy}((x, y)) = x + y$; and
- $\mathsf{d} = \texttt{deviation}((x, y)) = x - y \cdot \dfrac{c}{1-c}$.

Intuitively, $\mathsf{e}$ is the total energy in the battery and $\mathsf{d}$ is the difference between the heights of the two tanks multiplied by the factor $c$. The mathematical simplicity in using *energy* and *deviation* stems from the fact that they correspond to the eigenvectors of the diffusion matrix. Given $\mathsf{e} = \texttt{energy}(\mathbf{t})$ and $\mathsf{d} = \texttt{deviation}(\mathbf{t})$, the battery status $\mathbf{t} = (x, y)$ is uniquely determined: $x = c\mathsf{e} + (1-c)\mathsf{d}$ and $y = \mathsf{e} - x$. Hence, we use the notations $[\mathsf{e}; \mathsf{d}]$ and $(x, y)$ interchangeably.

**Proposition 1.** *For any battery status* $[\mathsf{e}; \mathsf{d}]$ *and* $w \in \mathbb{N}$, *we have that* $\texttt{Post}([\mathsf{e}; \mathsf{d}], w) = [\mathsf{e} + w; \lambda \cdot \mathsf{d} + w]$ *where* $\lambda = 1 - \frac{k}{1-c} - \frac{k}{c}$.

The above proposition is a translation of the $\texttt{Post}$ function to the $[\mathsf{e}; \mathsf{d}]$ notation. Intuitively, the energy is increased by the weight $w$ as expected, while the difference in the tank heights is first reduced by a constant factor of $\lambda$ and then increased due to the charge $w$ added to the first column. The factor $\lambda$ turns out to be the central parameter of the battery, playing a key role in how BTSs behaves. The following lemma formalizes the intuition that the bound-charge tank ($y$) cannot get empty before the available-charge tank ($x$) does.

**Lemma 2.** *Suppose battery status* $(x, y)$ *is feasible, and let* $\texttt{Post}((x, y), w) = (x', y')$. *We have* $[\mathsf{e}'; \mathsf{d}'] = (x', y')$ *is feasible iff* $x' > 0$, *and, equivalently, if and only if* $c\mathsf{e}' + (1-c)\mathsf{d}' > 0$.

*Proof.* The *only if* implication is obvious. As for the *if*, we have $x' = (1 - \frac{k}{c})x + \frac{k}{1-c}y + w$ and $y' = \frac{k}{c}x + (1 - \frac{k}{1-c})y$. Assuming $x > 0$ and $y > 0$, it easily follows that $y' > 0$. Hence, $(x', y')$ is infeasible if and only if $x' \leq 0$ or equivalently, if $x' = c\mathsf{e}' + (1-c)\mathsf{d}' \leq 0$ □

***Model checking.*** The problems we consider ask for the existence of a control trace $\theta$ in the semantics of a BTS $\mathcal{B}$ with control states $S$ given an initial battery status $\mathbf{t}$, such that $\theta \in \Phi$ for some given *objective set* $\Phi \subseteq S^* \cup S^\omega$. Specifically, we consider the following objective sets $\Phi$:

[1] The weights in a weighted transition system are often rational numbers rather than integers. All of our results equally hold for rational weights, by simply multiplying all weights by the product of all denominators.

[2] All of our results equally hold for the case that the element values should be non-negative, rather than strictly positive, but the proofs are marginally simpler in the strictly positive case.

- **Finite-automaton emptiness.** Asking if there exists a feasible trace to a set of target control states. Formally, given target control states $T \subseteq S$, we have $\Phi = \texttt{Reach}(T) = \{s_0 s_1 \ldots \mid \exists i : s_i \in T\}$, i.e., $\Phi$ is the set of control traces which visit $T$ at least once.
- **Büchi emptiness.** Asking if there exists a feasible trace which visits a set of target Büchi states infinitely often. Formally, given Büchi control states $L \subseteq S$, we have $\Phi = \texttt{Büchi}(L) = \{s_0 s_1 \ldots \mid \forall j \exists i > j : s_i \in L\}$.
- **Streett emptiness.** The objective is specified by a set of request-grant pairs $\langle R_i, G_i \rangle$ (where each pair consists of a set $R_i \subseteq S$ of *request* control states and a set $G_i$ of *grant* control states). The objective asks if there exists a feasible trace in the system such that for every request-grant pair, either $G_i$ is visited infinitely often or $R_i$ is visited finitely often. Formally, given a set of Streett pairs $P = \{\langle R_0, G_0 \rangle, \langle R_1, G_1 \rangle, \ldots, \langle R_m, G_m \rangle\}$, we have $\Phi = \texttt{Streett}(P) = \{s_0 s_1 \ldots \mid \forall 0 \leq i \leq m : [(\forall p \exists q > p : s_q \in G_i) \vee (\exists p \forall q > p : s_q \notin R_i)]\}$.

We call the traces which satisfy the finite-automaton, Büchi, and Streett conditions, accepting, Büchi, and Streett traces, respectively.

### 3.2 (Battery VS. Ideal-Energy) Transition Systems

Due to the recovery effect, BTSs behave qualitatively differently from a simple-energy transition systems. Nevertheless, in the domain where the energy in the battery is high, they do behave similarly. This lets us solve problems related to unlimited initial credit (referred to as "unknown initial credit") by reducing them to the simple-energy system problems.

**Different Behavior**. The BTS $\mathcal{B}_1$ of Fig. 1 demonstrates a key difference from a simple-energy system – the total energy in the initial state is 32, while a transition of weight $(-17)$ cannot be taken, since the available energy is only 16. Yet, taking the cycle through states $s_2$ and $s_3$ reduces the total energy, but allows the $(-17)$-transition. After the cycle, the battery status is $(19\frac{3}{4}, 11\frac{1}{4})$, which becomes $(\frac{5}{8}, 13\frac{3}{8})$ following a $(-17)$-transition.

We formalize the difference in the theorem below. It is known that if an ideal-energy system contains an infeasible trace, it contains a memoryless infeasible trace [8]. A memoryless trace is one where a control state is always followed by the same control state. However, an infeasible trace in the system $\mathcal{B}_2$ of Fig. 1 must make different choices at different visits in state $s_0$.

**Theorem 3.** *A battery transition system may have feasible (resp. infeasible) traces without having any memoryless feasible (resp. infeasible) traces.*

*Proof.* Consider the BTS $\mathcal{B}_1$ in Figure 1. There is a trace for reaching $s_1$, as well as an infinite trace, however both traces make non-uniform choices at different visits in $s_0$. Analogously, an infeasible trace in the system $\mathcal{B}_2$ of Figure 1 must make different choices at $s_0$. We prove below the claim for $\mathcal{B}_2$. Analogous arguments and calculations can be made with respect to $\mathcal{B}_1$.

The only nondeterminism in $\mathcal{B}_2$ is in state $s_0$, allowing transitions to states $s_1$ and $s_2$. A trace that first chooses $s_1$ is legal, since the $(-15)$-transition is feasible from the initial status, after which there are only positive-weight transitions. The other memoryless option, of always choosing $s_2$, is also legal: Let $(x, y)$ be the battery status when first reaching $s_2$. It can be shown that the first few cycles $s_2 \rightarrow s_3 \rightarrow s_0 \rightarrow s_2$ are feasible, after which the battery status will be $(x', y')$, such that $x' > x$ and $y' > y$. By the monotonicity of the $\texttt{Post}$ function, it follows that the cycle can be repeated forever.

On the other hand, first choosing $s_2$ and then choosing $s_1$ makes an illegal trace: The battery status when returning to $s_0$ is $(12\frac{3}{4}, 20\frac{1}{4})$, which changes to $(-\frac{5}{8}, 18\frac{3}{8})$ after the $(-15)$-transition. □

**High energy domain and unknown initial credit problems**. In energy systems, one often considers "unknown-initial-credit problems", asking if there is some initial energy that allows accomplishing a task. It is clear that every control state of a battery system can be reached, at least once, if there is a path leading to it and enough initial energy to start with. This is formalized in the following lemma (which will also serve us in Theorem 5 and in Section 4).

**Lemma 4.** *Consider a BTS $\mathcal{B} = \langle\langle S, \Delta, s_\iota, \nu\rangle, k, c\rangle$. There exist constants $\texttt{HighEnergyConstant}(\mathcal{B}, i)$ for every $i \in \mathbb{N}$ such that for every feasible extended state $(s_0, [\mathsf{e}; \mathsf{d}])$ with $\mathsf{e} > \texttt{HighEnergyConstant}(\mathcal{B}, i)$, every weight sequence $w_0 w_1 \ldots w_{i-1}$ of length $i$ is feasible from $(s_0, [\mathsf{e}; \mathsf{d}])$.*

*Proof.* We define the constants inductively as follows:
(a) $\texttt{HighEnergyConstant}(\mathcal{B}, 0) = 0$ if $i = 0$; and
(b) $\texttt{HighEnergyConstant}(\mathcal{B}, i) =$
$\max\left(\texttt{HighEnergyConstant}(\mathcal{B}, i-1) + W, \frac{W}{c(1-\lambda)}\right)$ otherwise. Here, $W = \max_{(s,s') \in \Delta} |\nu((s, s'))|$.

We prove the theorem by induction. When $i = 0$, the weight sequence is empty and there is nothing to prove.

For the induction case, assume that we have shown the result up to $i - 1$. Let $\texttt{Post}([\mathsf{e}; \mathsf{d}], w) = [\mathsf{e}'; \mathsf{d}']$. From Proposition 1, we get that $\mathsf{e}' = \mathsf{e} + w$ and $\mathsf{d}' = \lambda \mathsf{d} + w$. If $[\mathsf{e}'; \mathsf{d}']$ is feasible and $\mathsf{e}' \geq \texttt{HighEnergyConstant}(\mathcal{B}, i-1)$, we can apply the induction hypothesis on the weight sequence $w_1 \ldots w_{i-1}$ to prove the result. We show these facts below.

- We have $\mathsf{e}' = \mathsf{e} + w > \texttt{HighEnergyConstant}(\mathcal{B}, i) + w \geq \texttt{HighEnergyConstant}(\mathcal{B}, i-1) + W + w$. As $w \geq -W$, we have that $\mathsf{e}' > \texttt{HighEnergyConstant}(\mathcal{B}, i-1) \geq 0$.
- Further, we have that $c\mathsf{e}' + (1-c)\mathsf{d}' = c\mathsf{e} + cw + (1-c)\lambda\mathsf{d} + (1-c)w$ or, equivalently, $c\mathsf{e}' + (1-c)\mathsf{d}' = (1-\lambda)c\mathsf{e} + w + \lambda(c\mathsf{e} + (1-c)\mathsf{d})$. As $[\mathsf{e}; \mathsf{d}]$ is feasible, by Proposition 1, $c\mathsf{e} + (1-c)\mathsf{d} > 0$. Further, $\mathsf{e} > \texttt{HighEnergyConstant}(\mathcal{B}, i) \geq \frac{W}{c(1-\lambda)}$. Using these, we get $c\mathsf{e}' + (1-c)\mathsf{d}' > -W + w \geq 0$. By Lemma 2, $[\mathsf{e}'; \mathsf{d}']$ is feasible, completing the proof.

□

The following theorem states that the emptiness problems for battery systems reduce to the corresponding problems for energy systems if the initial energy is large enough.

**Theorem 5.** *Let $\mathcal{B} = \langle\langle S, \Delta, s_\iota, \nu\rangle, k, c\rangle$ be a BTS, $W = \max_{(s,s') \in \Delta} |\nu((s, s'))|$, and $T$, $L$ and $\{\langle R_0, G_0\rangle, \ldots, \langle R_n, G_n\rangle\}$ be a set of target states, a set of Büchi states, and a set of Streett pairs, respectively. There exist constants $M_R = \texttt{HighEnergyConstant}(\mathcal{B}, |S|)$, $M_B = \texttt{HighEnergyConstant}(\mathcal{B}, 3|S| + 2W|S|^2)$, and $M_S = \texttt{HighEnergyConstant}(\mathcal{B}, |S| + |S|^2 + W|S|^2 + W|S|^3)$ such that for any extended state $(s, [\mathsf{e}; \mathsf{d}])$: if $\mathsf{e} > M_R$ (resp. $\mathsf{e} > M_B$ and $\mathsf{e} > M_S$), a feasible accepting (resp. Büchi and Streett) trace starting from $(s, [\mathsf{e}; \mathsf{d}])$ exists iff an energy-feasible accepting (resp. Büchi and Streett) trace exists.*

*Proof of theorem 5.* In all three parts, the existence of an energy feasible trace is directly implied by the existence of a feasible trace. Therefore, we only deal with showing that the existence of an energy feasible trace implies the existence of a feasible trace.

The first part (finite-automaton emptiness) follows directly from Lemma 4. If there exists a path from $s$ to the target set

$T$, there exists a path of length at most $|S|$. Taking $M_R$ = HighEnergyConstant($\mathcal{B}, |S|$) is sufficient to give us the result.

For the second part (Büchi emptiness), the existence of an energy feasible trace implies that there exists a reachable cycle which visits a Büchi state and has non-negative total weight. It can be shown that the length of such a cycle can be bounded by $2|S| + 2W|S|^2$. Now, if $\mathtt{e} >$ HighEnergyConstant($\mathcal{B}, |S| + 2|S| + 2W|S|^2$), we can show, using Lemma 4, that there is a feasible path from $(s, [\mathtt{e}; \mathtt{d}])$ to some $(s', [\mathtt{e}'; \mathtt{d}'])$ where $s'$ is on the cycle and $\mathtt{e}' >$ HighEnergyConstant($\mathcal{B}, 2|S| + 2W|S|^2$). Now, the cycle is feasible from $(s', [\mathtt{e}'; \mathtt{d}'])$ and further, on returning to $s'$, the energy is at least $\mathtt{e}'$ (as the total weight of the cycle is non-negative). Using such reasoning, it is easy to see that the cycle is repeatedly feasible from $(s', [\mathtt{e}'; \mathtt{d}'])$. Hence, a value of $M_B$ = HighEnergyConstant($\mathcal{B}, |S| + 2|S| + 2W|S|^2$) is sufficient.

The proof for the third part is very similar to the proof of the second part except for the bound on the length of the cycle. □

A straightforward consequence of the above theorem is that the unknown initial credit problems for BTSs are decidable. Furthermore, using the above theorem, it is easy to show that these BTS problems are equivalent to the corresponding energy-systems problems, which can be solved in polynomial time [6].

**Corollary 6.** *Given a BTS $\mathcal{B}$ and a finite-automaton, Büchi, or Streett condition, the problem of whether there is an initial battery status $[\mathtt{e}; \mathtt{d}]$, such that there exists a feasible trace in $\mathcal{B}$ satisfying the condition is decidable in polynomial time.*

## 4. The Bounded-Energy Reachability Tree

Our algorithms for solving the emptiness problems are based on representing the infinite tree of all the possible traces in the BTS in a finite tree that summarizes all required information. The construction of the tree uses a "high-energy constant" – exploration from states whose energy is above the constant is stopped, as they can be further handled by a reduction to a simple-energy system using Theorem 5. Hence, the tree summarizes bounded-energy reachability, and we denote it BERT. As in Theorem 5, the value of the high-energy constant depends on the problem to be solved. We describe how we construct the tree, taking the high-energy constant as a parameter. We start with some basic lemmata about a total order among battery statuses of equal energy. Then, we present the 0-cycle saturation lemma, which helps summarize unbounded iterations of cycles in a finite manner.

**Feasibility order for battery statuses**. The following lemma shows that there exists a total order on the set of battery statuses with the same energy such that every weight sequence feasible from a lower battery status is also feasible from a higher battery status.

**Lemma 7.** *Given two battery statuses $[\mathtt{e}; \mathtt{d}]$ and $[\mathtt{e}; \mathtt{d}']$ with $\mathtt{d} > \mathtt{d}'$, every weight sequence $w_0 w_1 \ldots w_{n-1}$ feasible from $[\mathtt{e}; \mathtt{d}']$ is also feasible from $[\mathtt{e}; \mathtt{d}]$. Furthermore, if $\mathtt{Post}([\mathtt{e}; \mathtt{d}], w_0 \ldots w_{n-1}) = [\mathtt{e}''; \mathtt{d}'']$ and $\mathtt{Post}([\mathtt{e}; \mathtt{d}'], w_0 \ldots w_{n-1}) = [\mathtt{e}''; \mathtt{d}''']$, we have $\mathtt{d}'' > \mathtt{d}'''$.*

*Proof.* We prove the result by induction. For the base case, we let the weight sequence be of length 1, i.e., $w_0$. From Proposition 1, we know that $\mathtt{Post}([\mathtt{e}, \mathtt{d}], w_0) = [\mathtt{e} + w_0, \lambda\mathtt{d} + w_0]$ and $\mathtt{Post}([\mathtt{e}, \mathtt{d}'], w_0) = [\mathtt{e} + w_0, \lambda\mathtt{d}' + w_0]$. Hence, $\mathtt{d}'' = \lambda\mathtt{d} + w_0$ and $\mathtt{d}''' = \lambda\mathtt{d}' + w_0$. As $\mathtt{d} > \mathtt{d}'$, we get that $\lambda\mathtt{d} + w_0 > \lambda\mathtt{d}' + w_0$ and $\mathtt{d}'' > \mathtt{d}'''$.

Now, assume that $[\mathtt{e} + w_0; \lambda\mathtt{d}' + w_0]$ is feasible. By Lemma 2, we get that $c(\mathtt{e}+w_0)+(1-c)(\lambda\mathtt{d}'+w_0) > 0$. As $d > d'$, we have $c(\mathtt{e}+w_0)+(1-c)(\lambda\mathtt{d}+w_0) > 0$ and $c(\mathtt{e}+w_0)+(1-c)\mathtt{d}'' > 0$. This gives us that $[\mathtt{e} + w_0; \mathtt{d}'']$ is feasible, hence completing the proof for the base case.

Now, assume that the required result holds for every weight sequence of length $n - 1$. Applying the induction hypothesis on the battery statuses $[\mathtt{e} + w_0; \lambda\mathtt{d} + w_0]$ and $[\mathtt{e} + w_0; \lambda\mathtt{d}' + w_0]$ and the weight sequence $w_1 \ldots w_{n-1}$ gives us the required result. □

Guided by Lemma 7 above, we define a partial order on the set of battery statuses as follows: $[\mathtt{e}'; \mathtt{d}'] \sqsubseteq [\mathtt{e}; \mathtt{d}]$ if $\mathtt{e} = \mathtt{e}'$ and $\mathtt{d}' \leq \mathtt{d}$, in which case we say that $[\mathtt{e}; \mathtt{d}]$ *subsumes* $[\mathtt{e}'; \mathtt{d}']$. We extend the partial order $\sqsubseteq$ to extended states (with both control states and battery statuses) by letting $(s', [\mathtt{e}'; \mathtt{d}']) \sqsubseteq (s, [\mathtt{e}; \mathtt{d}])$ if $s = s'$ and $[\mathtt{e}'; \mathtt{d}'] \sqsubseteq [\mathtt{e}; \mathtt{d}]$. Lemma 7 can now be restated as follows: *If $(s', [\mathtt{e}'; \mathtt{d}']) \sqsubseteq (s, [\mathtt{e}; \mathtt{d}])$, every control path feasible from $(s', [\mathtt{e}'; \mathtt{d}'])$ is also feasible from $(s, [\mathtt{e}; \mathtt{d}])$.*

**Zero-cycle saturation**. We formalize below the key observation that 0-energy cycles can be finitely summarized: an infinite run along such a cycle monotonically converges to a fixed battery status. Moreover, the deviation in the limit is independent of the initial status.

**Lemma 8** (Zero-cycle saturation)**.** *Let $w_0 \ldots w_{n-1}$ be a sequence of weights such that $\sum_{i=0}^{n-1} w_i = 0$ and let $\mathbf{t_0}, \mathbf{t_1}, \ldots$ be a sequence of tuples in $\mathbb{R}^2$, such that $\mathbf{t_{i+1}} = \mathtt{Post}(\mathbf{t_i}, \mathbf{w_0} \ldots \mathbf{w_{n-1}})$. We have the following:*

1. *The sequence $\mathbf{t_0}, \mathbf{t_1}, \ldots$ converges (say to $\mathbf{t}^* = [\mathtt{e}^*; \mathtt{d}^*]$). In other words, $\forall \epsilon \geq 0. \exists m \in \mathbb{N} : |\mathbf{t}^* - \mathbf{t_m}|_1 \leq \epsilon$ where $|.|_1$ denotes the maximum absolute component in a vector.*
2. *We have $\forall i \in \mathbb{N} : \mathbf{t}^* \sqsubseteq \mathbf{t_i} \sqsubseteq \mathbf{t_0}$ or $\forall i \in \mathbb{N} : \mathbf{t_0} \sqsubseteq \mathbf{t_i} \sqsubseteq \mathbf{t}^*$. In the latter case, if $w_0 \ldots w_{n-1}$ is feasible from $\mathbf{t_0}$ it is feasible from each $\mathbf{t_i}$.*

*Proof.* Let $\mathbf{t_i} = [\mathtt{e}_i; \mathtt{d}_i]$. Obviously, $\forall i. \mathtt{e}_i = \mathtt{e}^*$. By repeated application of Proposition 1 on the weights $w_0 w_1 \ldots w_{n-1}$, starting with $\mathbf{t_i}$, we have $\mathtt{d}_{i+1} = \mathtt{d}_i \cdot \lambda^n + \sum_{p=0}^{n-1} w_p \cdot \lambda^{n-1-p}$. Hence, for all $i \in \mathbb{N}$, $\mathtt{d}_i = \mathtt{d}_0 \cdot \lambda^{i \cdot n} + \sum_{q=0}^{i-1} L \cdot \lambda^{n \cdot q}$, where $L = \sum_{p=0}^{n-1} w_p \cdot \lambda^{n-1-p}$. From this, it follows that the sequence $\mathbf{d_i}$ converges to $\mathbf{d}^* = \sum_{q=0}^{\infty} L \cdot \lambda^{q \cdot n} = L \cdot \frac{1}{1-\lambda^n}$. Further,

$$
\begin{aligned}
\mathtt{d}_{(i+1)} &= \mathtt{d}_0 \cdot \lambda^{i \cdot n + n} + L \cdot \sum_{q=0}^{i} \lambda^{n \cdot q} \\
&= \mathtt{d}_0 \cdot \lambda^{i \cdot n} + L \cdot \sum_{q=0}^{i-1} \lambda^{n \cdot q} + \mathtt{d}_0 \cdot [\lambda^{i \cdot n + n} - \lambda^{i \cdot n}] + L \cdot \lambda^{i \cdot n} \\
&= \mathtt{d}_i + \mathtt{d}_0 \cdot [\lambda^{i \cdot n + n} - \lambda^{i \cdot n}] + L \cdot \lambda^{i \cdot n} \\
&= \mathtt{d}_i + \lambda^{i \cdot n}(1 - \lambda^n) \cdot [\frac{L}{1 - \lambda^n} - \mathtt{d}_0] \\
&= \mathtt{d}_i + \lambda^{i \cdot n}(1 - \lambda^n) \cdot [d^* - \mathtt{d}_0]
\end{aligned}
$$

Since $\forall i. \lambda^{i \cdot n}(1 - \lambda^n)$ is positive, it follows that $d_{i+1}$ is bigger, or not, than $d_i$ based on whether $d^* < \mathtt{d}_0$ or not. If $d^* < \mathtt{d}_0$, we get $\mathtt{d}_0 > \mathtt{d}_1 > \ldots > d^*$, or, equivalently, $\mathbf{t_0} \sqsupseteq \mathbf{t_1} \sqsupseteq \ldots \sqsupseteq \mathbf{t}^*$. Similarly, if $d^* \geq \mathtt{d}_0$, we get $\mathtt{d}_0 \leq \mathtt{d}_1 \leq \ldots \leq d^*$, or, equivalently, $\mathbf{t_0} \sqsubseteq \mathbf{t_1} \sqsubseteq \ldots \sqsubseteq \mathbf{t}^*$. The feasibility of $w_0 \ldots w_n$ from each $\mathbf{t_i}$ follows from Lemma 7 and $\mathbf{t_i} \sqsupseteq \mathbf{t_0}$. □

We denote the limit deviation $\mathbf{d}^*$ as $\mathtt{Saturate}(w_0 w_1 \ldots w_{n-1})$, i.e., $\mathtt{Saturate}(w_0 w_1 \ldots w_{n-1}) = \frac{1}{1-\lambda^n} \cdot \left(\sum_{p=0}^{n-1} w_p \cdot \lambda^{n-1-p}\right)$. Note that this deviation does not depend on the initial battery status $\mathbf{t_0}$. Accordingly, we extend the definition of the function Saturate to battery statuses as $\texttt{Saturate}([\mathsf{e};\mathsf{d}], w_0 w_1 \ldots w_{n-1}) = [\mathsf{e}; \texttt{Saturate}(w_0 w_1 \ldots w_n)]$.

**Constructing the tree**. For generating a finite tree with all the relevant bounded energy reachability information, we explore the feasible states and transitions starting from the initial state. However,

1. Extended states with high-enough energies are not explored further, and
2. If an extended state $\mathbf{q}$ that has an ancestor $\mathbf{q}'$ with the same control state and the same energy (but possibly a different deviation) is reached, we check the feasibility order, i.e., if $\mathbf{q} \sqsubseteq \mathbf{q}'$ or $\mathbf{q}' \sqsubseteq \mathbf{q}$. If $\mathbf{q} \sqsubseteq \mathbf{q}'$ we stop exploration from $\mathbf{q}$; otherwise, we saturate this 0-energy cycle from $\mathbf{q}'$ to $\mathbf{q}$, i.e., calculate the fixed battery status $\mathbf{t}^*$ to which an infinite run on that cycle will monotonically converge to (see Lemma 8). Then, we replace the battery status in $\mathbf{q}'$ with the maximum between battery status in $\mathbf{q}$ and $\mathbf{t}^*$.

The procedure `ComputeBERT` (Algorithm 1) computes the bounded-energy reachability tree `BERT`, given a BTM $\mathcal{B}$, an initial battery status $\mathbf{t}$, and an energy bound $M$. It is a rooted tree where each node is labelled with an extended state. During the procedure's execution, each node in the tree is either open (in `OpenNodes`) or closed, and exploration will only continue from open nodes. In addition, each node contains a Boolean field $star$, marking whether its label is a result of saturation. Initially, the root of `BERT` is labelled with the initial extended state $(s_\iota, \mathbf{t})$ and the root node is added to the set of `OpenNodes`.

In each step, one open node (`currNode`) is picked and removed from the set of `OpenNodes`. Let $\texttt{currNode}.label = (s, [\mathsf{e};\mathsf{d}])$. By default, we append to `currNode` children labelled by all feasible successors of $(s, [\mathsf{e};\mathsf{d}])$ (we call this an exploration step). If one of the following holds, we do not perform the exploration step.

- In case the energy (i.e., $\mathsf{e}$) of `currNode` is greater than the given bound $M$, we stop exploration from it.
- In case an ancestor `ancestor` (with label $(s, [\mathsf{e};\mathsf{d}'])$) of `currNode` has the same control state and energy as `currNode`:
  - If $[\mathsf{e};\mathsf{d}] \sqsubseteq [\mathsf{e};\mathsf{d}']$ we stop exploration from `currNode`.
  - If $[\mathsf{e};\mathsf{d}'] \sqsubset [\mathsf{e};\mathsf{d}]$ we i) delete all the descendants of `ancestor`; and ii) replace the battery status in the label of `ancestor` with the $\sqsubset$-maximum between $[\mathsf{e};\mathsf{d}]$ and the zero-cycle saturation of $[\mathsf{e};\mathsf{d}']$, where $\mathsf{d}'$ is the 0-cycle saturation of the the weight sequence from `ancestor` to `currNode`. Note that if the weight sequence from `ancestor` to `currNode` is infeasible from $[\mathsf{e};\mathsf{d}']$ (which can happen if there is a saturation of another cycle between the `ancestor` and `currNode`), we replace $[\mathsf{e};\mathsf{d}']$ by $[\mathsf{e};\mathsf{d}]$ and not the maximum.

When no open nodes are left, the procedure stops and returns `BERT`. We prove in a series of lemmata the properties of the procedure `ComputeBERT` and of the returned tree.

**Termination**. We prove that Algorithm 1 terminates for every input, by showing a bound on both the number of possible nodes in `BERT` and the number of node deletions in an execution. The latter bound follows from (i) every deletion event strictly increases a deviation value; and (ii) the number of possible values that a deviation can get in a deletion event is bounded. Note that this is in contradiction to the unbounded number of deviations that may occur in a trace of the BTS $\mathcal{B}$.

**Lemma 9.** *Algorithm 1 terminates on all inputs.*

*Proof.* Termination follows from a bound on both the number of possible nodes in `BERT` and the number of node deletions in an execution.

The number of nodes in a tree depends on the fanout of the nodes and the length of the branches. The fanout of every node in

**Algorithm 1** `ComputeBERT`: Computing the bounded-energy reachability tree

**Require:** Battery system $\mathcal{B} = \langle\langle S, \Delta, s_\iota, \nu\rangle, k, c\rangle$, initial battery status $\mathbf{t}$, energy bound $M$
1: `BERT` $\leftarrow$ `EmptyTree`
2: $\texttt{BERT}.root.label \leftarrow (s_\iota, \mathbf{t})$; $\texttt{BERT}.root.star \leftarrow$ **false**
3: `OpenNodes` $\leftarrow \{\texttt{BERT}.root\}$
4: **while** `OpenNodes` $\neq \emptyset$ **do**
5: Pick and remove `currNode` from `OpenNodes`
6: $(s_0, [\mathsf{e};\mathsf{d}]) \leftarrow \texttt{currNode}.label$
7: // If we found a good cycle, saturate that cycle
8: **if** `currNode` has an ancestor `ancestor` with label $(s_0, [\mathsf{e};\mathsf{d}'])$ **then**
9: **if** $\mathsf{d} > \mathsf{d}'$ **then**
10: $s_0 \ldots s_n s_0 \leftarrow$ control state sequence in node labels from `ancestor` to `currNode`
11: $w_0 \ldots w_n \leftarrow \nu((s_0, s_1))\nu((s_1, s_2)) \ldots \nu((s_n, s_0))$
12: **if** $w_0 w_1 \ldots w_n$ is feasible from $[e; d']$ and $\texttt{Saturate}(w_0 \ldots w_n) > \mathsf{d}$ **then**
13: $\texttt{ancestor}.label \leftarrow (s_0, [\mathsf{e}; \texttt{Saturate}(w_0 \ldots w_n)])$;
14: $\texttt{ancestor}.star \leftarrow$ **true**
15: **else** {There was another cycle saturation between `ancestor` and `currNode`}
16: $ancestor.label \leftarrow [\mathsf{e};\mathsf{d}]$
17: $\texttt{BERT}.delete$(all descendants of `ancestor`)
18: `OpenNodes` $\leftarrow$ `OpenNodes` $\cup$ {`ancestor`} $\setminus$ all descendants of `ancestor`
19: **continue;** // If $\mathsf{d} < \mathsf{d}'$ there is no further exploration from the current node
20: **else** {Explore one step further}
21: **for all** $(s_0, s') \in \Delta$ **do**
22: **if** $\texttt{Post}([\mathsf{e};\mathsf{d}], \nu(s_0, s'))$ is feasible **then**
23: `newNode` $\leftarrow$ new child of `currNode`
24: $\texttt{newNode}.label \leftarrow (s', \texttt{Post}([\mathsf{e};\mathsf{d}], \nu(s_0, s')))$;
25: $\texttt{newNode}.star \leftarrow$ **false**
26: **if** $\texttt{energy}(\texttt{Post}([\mathsf{e};\mathsf{d}], \nu(s_0, s'))) \leq M$ **then**
27: `OpenNodes` $\leftarrow$ `OpenNodes` $\cup$ `newNode`
28: **return** `BERT`

`BERT` is bounded by the number of states in the BTS $\mathcal{B}$. As for the branches, the control state and energy of each node in a path is unique, except for the leaf, giving a bound of $|S| \times M + 1$ to the length of a path.

The bound on the number of deletions follows from (i) every deletion event strictly increases a deviation value; and (ii) the number of possible values that a deviation can get in a deletion event is bounded. Note that this is in contradiction to the unbounded number of deviations that may occur in a trace of the BTS $\mathcal{B}$.

Consider a node-deletion event in the execution of Algorithm 1, and a new deviation value set to $\texttt{ancestor}.label$.

(i) The new value is either $\texttt{Saturate}(w_0 \ldots w_n)$ or $\mathsf{d}$, set in Line 14 or Line 16, which are in the scope of "if $\texttt{Saturate}(w_0 \ldots w_n) > \mathsf{d} > \mathsf{d}'$" or "if $\mathsf{d} > \mathsf{d}'$", respectively, while the old value is $\mathsf{d}'$.

(ii) The new value is uniquely determined by the following:

- The value of $\texttt{Saturate}(w_0 \ldots w_n)$, where $w_0 \ldots w_n$ is the sequence of weights from `ancestor` to `currNode`; or
- The label of the last saturated (i.e., starred) node between `ancestor` and `currNode`, and the suffix $w_i \ldots w_n$ of $w_0 \ldots w_n$ corresponding to the segment from the last starred node to `currNode`, otherwise.

In the first case, resulting from Line 14, the new value only depends on $w_0 \ldots w_n$, which in turn is determined by $s_0 s_1 \ldots s_n s_0$. In the second case, resulting from Line 16, let $(s_i, [\mathsf{e}^{(i)}; \mathsf{d}^{(i)}])$ be the label of the last starred node. By Lemma 8, $[e^{(i)}; d^{(i)}]$ only depends on the sequence of weights in a simple cycle of the BTS $\mathcal{B}$, thus may take a bounded number of possible values. The new value is then calculated by $\texttt{Post}([e^{(i)}; d^{(i)}], w_i \dots w_n)$, which only depends on $[e^{(i)}; d^{(i)}]$ and the sequence $w_i \dots w_n$. □

**Correctness**. We now prove that BERT is a summarization of all extended states reachable through states of low-energy. Let $\texttt{Reach}(M)$ be the set of extended states reachable from the initial state of the BTS $\mathcal{B}$ through paths containing only extended states of energy less than $M$. In the lemmata below, we prove the following:

- *Soundness.* For every node node in BERT and for all $\epsilon > 0$, there is an extended state $\mathbf{q} \in \texttt{Reach}(M)$ such that $\mathbf{q} \sqsubseteq$ node.*label* and the difference between the deviations of $\mathbf{q}$ and node.*label* is smaller than $\epsilon$.
- *Completeness.* For every extended state $\mathbf{q} \in \texttt{Reach}(M)$, there exists a node node in BERT such that $\mathbf{q} \sqsubseteq$ node.*label*.

**Lemma 10** (Soundness). *For every node* node *with label* $(s, [e; d])$ *encountered in an execution of Algorithm 1 and* $\epsilon > 0$, *there exists an extended state* $(s, [e; d - \delta])$ *reachable from* $(s_\iota, \mathbf{t})$ *with* $0 \le \delta < \epsilon$.

*Proof.* The claim can be proved by looking at all the points in the algorithm where a new label is created (lines 10, 14, and 25). The claim is trivially true for the initial label of the root. Assume as induction hypothesis that the claim holds for every label encountered upto the current point of the execution. Fix $\epsilon \ge 0$.

*Saturation.* Let the new label be created during a deletion event, in line 10 or line 14. In the case the label of currNode is copied to the label of ancestor, the proof follows immediately as we are just copying an existing label. Otherwise, we are taking the Saturate value, and the proof is based on Lemma 8. By iterating the path from ancestor to currNode a sufficient number of times, we can get as close as necessary (i.e., within $\epsilon$) to the limit of the zero-weight cycle saturation. Lemma 8 also gives us that every iteration is feasible.

*Exploration.* Let $(s', [e'; d'])$ be a new node label created in line 25. Choosing $\epsilon' < \min(\frac{\epsilon}{\lambda}, ce' + (1-c)d')$, by the induction hypothesis, there is a feasible path from $(s_\iota, \mathbf{t})$ to $(s, [e; d - \delta'])$ with $0 \le \delta' < \epsilon'$.

Now, we have $[e'; d'] = \texttt{Post}([e; d], w) = [e + w; \lambda d + w]$ and $\texttt{Post}([e; d - \delta'], w) = [e'; d' - \lambda \cdot \delta']$. Letting $\delta = \lambda\delta'$, we get $0 \le \delta = \lambda\delta' < \lambda\epsilon' \le \epsilon$. If we prove that $[e'; d' - \delta]$ is feasible, we are done as we have shown that the path from $(s_\iota, \mathbf{t})$ to $(s, [e; d - \delta'])$ followed by the feasible transition from $(s, [e; d - \delta'])$ to $(s', [e'; d' - \delta])$ is a path from $(s_\iota, \mathbf{t})$ to $(s', [e'; d' - \delta])$.

As $[e'; d']$ is feasible, we get that $ce' + (1-c)d' > 0$. As we chose that $\epsilon' < ce' + (1-c)d'$, we get that $ce' + (1-c)d' - \delta = ce' + (1-c)d' - \lambda\delta' > ce' + (1-c)d' - \lambda\epsilon' > ce' + (1-c)d' - \lambda(ce' + d') > (1-\lambda)(ce' + (1-c)d') > 0$. This completes the proof for this case. □

**Lemma 11** (Completeness). *Let* $(s, [e; d])$ *be an extended state with* $e < M$ *that is reachable from* $(s_\iota, \mathbf{t})$ *through extended states with energy less than* $M$. *Then, there exists a node with label* $(s, [e; d'])$ *in* BERT *with* $d' \ge d$.

*Proof.* We prove the lemma by induction on the length of the path from $(s_\iota, \mathbf{t})$ to $(s, [e; d])$. For paths of length 0, it is trivial as $(s_\iota, \mathbf{t})$ is the initial label of the root. Suppose we have proven the claim for paths upto the length $n - 1$.

It is easy to induct to length $n$. Suppose the path of length $n - 1$ ending with $(s, [e; d])$ is extended to length $n$ by adding $(s^\sharp, [e^\sharp; d^\sharp])$. The proof has two cases:

- If the node labelled with $(s, [e; d'])$ is a non-leaf node, then it has a successor labelled $(s^\sharp, [e^\sharp; d^{\sharp\prime}])$, with $d^{\sharp\prime} > d^\sharp$, which is the required node. This follows from lines 21–27 of Algo. 1.
- If the BERT node labelled with $(s, [e; d'])$ is a leaf node, it will have an ancestor labelled $(s, [e; d''])$ with $d'' \ge d$. This follows from line 19 of Algorithm 1. Since the latter node is not a leaf, we comply with the previous case, and we are done.

□

## 5. Model Checking

We are now ready to tackle the finite-automaton, Büchi, and Streett emptiness problems for BTSs. We show that the problems are decidable and give suitable algorithms. The algorithms are based on Theorem 5 and analysis of the bounded-energy reachability tree, as constructed in Section 4.

### 5.1 Finite-Automaton Emptiness

Combining the results from the previous section on bounded energy reachability tree and Theorem 5, we can obtain a complete algorithm for the finite-automaton emptiness problem in a battery system. Given a BTS $\mathcal{B}$ with states $S$, an initial battery status $\mathbf{t}$, the algorithm works as follows:

- Build a bounded-energy reachability tree $\texttt{BERT} = \texttt{ComputeBERT}(\mathcal{B}, (s_\iota, \mathbf{t}), M)$, where $M = \texttt{HighEnergyConstant}(\mathcal{B}, |S|)$;
- If there is a node label $(s, [e; d])$ in BERT where $s$ is in the target set $T$, return **true**;
- If there is a node label $(s, [e; d])$ in BERT where $e > M$, and some node in the target set is reachable from $(s, [e; d])$ through an energy-feasible path, return **true**;
- Otherwise, return **false**.

The correctness proof of the algorithm follows from Lemma 4 and the soundness and completeness of the bounded-energy reachability tree (Lemmas 10–11). The following theorem states that this algorithm can be implemented in polynomial space in the inputs.

**Theorem 12.** *The finite-automaton emptiness problem for BTSs is decidable in polynomial space with respect to the number of control states in the BTS and a unary encoding of weights.*

*Proof.* The major part of the algorithm is the construction of the bounded-energy reachability tree. For a given energy bound $M$, this tree can contain an exponential number of nodes in $M$. However, using standard on-the-fly techniques, we can reduce the space complexity, only storing the current branch of the tree being explored. The corresponding space is the product of the number of nodes in each branch and the bits required for storing a node's label.

By the proof of Lemma 9, the length of each branch in the tree is bounded by $|S| \times M + 1$, where $S$ are the states of the given BTS $\mathcal{B}$. For the finite-automaton emptiness algorithm, we use $M = \texttt{HighEnergyConstant}(\mathcal{B}, |S|)$ and by the proof of Lemma 4, we have $M \le |S|W + \frac{W}{c(1-\lambda)}$, where $W$ is the maximal negative weight in the BTS. With a unary encoding of the constants, $M$ is polynomial in the size of the input.

To complete the proof, we need to show that all the labels created in BERT can be represented in polynomial space in the energy bound $M$.

A label contains a control state, an energy, and a deviation. There are $|S| < M$ control states and up to $M$ different energies.

As for the deviations, they are generated by a sequence of operations, involving two functions: Post (defined in Section 3) and Saturate (defined in Lemma 8). By Lemma 8, the value of Saturate is independent of the deviation value before saturation. Hence, the deviation at each node in BERT is a result of the last Saturate operation in the branch of BERT leading to the node, followed by some Post operations. By the proof of Lemma 9, the length of each branch in the tree is polynomial in $M$, implying up to $M$ applications of Post. Hence, it is left to show that the Saturate function generates a deviation that can be stored in space polynomial in $M$, and that each application of the Post function adds up to $b$ bits, where $b$ is polynomial in $M$.

By Lemma 8, given a sequence $w_0 w_1 \dots w_{n-1}$ of weights, $\texttt{Saturate}(w_0 w_1 \dots w_{n-1}) = \frac{1}{1-\lambda^n} \cdot \left(\sum_{p=0}^{n-1} w_p \cdot \lambda^{n-1-p}\right)$. The space required to store this value is polynomial in the constant $\lambda$ and $n$, where $n \leq |S| < M$. In each application of Post on a battery status $[\mathtt{e};\mathtt{d}]$ and weight $w$, we have, by Proposition 1, that $\texttt{Post}([\mathtt{e};\mathtt{d}], w) = [\mathtt{e}';\mathtt{d}']$, with $d' = \lambda \cdot \mathtt{d} + w$. Hence, storing $\mathtt{d}'$ requires up to $b$ bits more than storing $\mathtt{d}$, where $b$ is polynomial in the constant $\lambda$ and $|w| < M$. □

### 5.2 Büchi and Streett Emptiness

Suppose we are given a BTS $\mathcal{B} = \langle\langle S, \Delta, s_\iota, \nu\rangle, k, c\rangle$ and a Büchi condition given by a set of Büchi states $B \subseteq S$. Our approach to Büchi emptiness consists of two major parts. If there exists a Büchi trace containing an extended state with energy more than $M_B = 3|S| + 2W|S|^2$, the problem can be reduced to the Büchi problem for simple-energy systems (Theorem 5). Therefore, we concentrate on the case where the energy of states is bounded by $M_B$. Here, the key idea is that if the energies of the extended states are bounded, then a BTS has a Büchi trace if and only if it has a Büchi trace of a special form.

First, we define the notion of an energy-unique path: we call a control trace $s_0 s_1 \dots s_n$ *energy-unique* if we have $\sum_{i=0}^{p} \nu((s_i, s_{i+1})) \neq \sum_{i=0}^{q} \nu((s_i, s_{i+1})) \vee s_p \neq s_q$ for $p \neq q$. Intuitively, $s_0 s_1 \dots s_n$ is energy-unique if no trace whose corresponding control trace is $s_0 \dots s_n$ has two extended states with the same control state and equal energy. Similarly, $s_0 s_1 \dots s_n$ is an *energy-unique* 0*-energy cycle* if $s_0 s_1 \dots s_n$ is energy-unique and $\sum_{i=0}^{n-1} \nu((s_i, s_{i+1})) + \nu((s_n, s_0)) = 0$.

The following theorem intuitively states that if there exists a bounded-energy Büchi trace in $\mathcal{B}$, then there exists a lasso-shaped bounded-energy Büchi trace where the first state of the cycle in the lasso is a Büchi state and the cycle in the lasso has one of the two following forms:

- the cycle is an energy-unique 0-energy cycle $s_0^l \dots s_n^l s_0^l$, such that the sequence $s_0^l s_1^l \dots s_n^l s_0^l$ is feasible from $s_0^l$ with the battery status $\texttt{Saturate}(w_0 w_1 \dots w_n)$, where $w_i = \nu((s_i^l, s_{i+1}^l))$ for $i < n$ and $w_n = \nu((s_n^l, s_0^l))$; or
- the cycle is an energy-unique 0-energy cycle composed of an alternating sequence of energy-unique paths and energy-unique 0-energy cycles. Here, every energy-unique 0-energy cycle in the sequence is unique.

**Theorem 13.** *Suppose a BTS $\mathcal{B}$ has a Büchi trace such that every extended state has energy less than some constant $M$. Then, $\mathcal{B}$ has a Büchi trace $\pi$ such that the corresponding control trace $\theta$ has one of the following two forms:*

*Form 1* $\theta = \theta_h (s_0^l s_1^l \dots s_n^l)^\omega$ *where $s_0^l$ is a Büchi state, and $s_0^l s_1^l \dots s_n^l s_0^l$ is an energy-unique 0-energy cycle.*

*Form 2* $\theta = \theta_h (\theta_l)^\omega$, *where* $\theta_h, \theta_l \in S^*$ *and* $\theta_l = (s_0^0 \dots s_{k_0}^0)(\theta_{l0})^{r_0} \dots (s_0^n \dots s_{k_1}^n) \dots (\theta_{ln})^{r_n} (s_0^{n+1} \dots s_{k_{n+1}}^{n+1})$ *and (a) each $\theta_{li}$ is a distinct energy-unique 0-energy cycle; (b) each $s_0^i \dots s_{k_i}^i$ is a energy-unique path; (c) $\theta_l$ is a 0-energy cycle; and (d) $s_0^0$ is a Büchi state.*

We omit the proof of Theorem 13 due to lack of space. The proof proceeds by taking a witness Büchi trace and reducing it to one of the two forms by deleting parts of the trace where the initial and final energies and control states are the same, while the final deviation is less than the initial deviation.

**The algorithm**. The Büchi-emptiness algorithm intuitively consists of two separate parts: (a) searching for high energy Büchi traces (where some extended state has energy more than $M_B = \texttt{HighEnergyConstant}(\mathcal{B}, 3|S| + 2W|S|^2)$); and (b) searching for low energy fair traces (where every extended state has energy less than $M_B$). The algorithm first constructs $\texttt{BERT} = \texttt{ComputeBERT}(\mathcal{B}, (s_\iota, \mathtt{t}), M_B)$.

*High energy.* For every node label $(s, [\mathtt{e};\mathtt{d}])$ in the BERT where $\mathtt{e} > M_B$, we check (using techniques of [6]) whether there exists an energy-feasible fair trace from it.

*Form 1 low energy.* For every node label $(s, [\mathtt{e};\mathtt{d}])$ in BERT with $\mathtt{e} \leq M_B$ and $s \in B$, we check if there exists a fair trace of Form 1 starting from $(s, [\mathtt{e};\mathtt{d}])$. Performing this check entails constructing energy-unique 0-energy cycles $\theta_l$ starting from $s$ and examining if $\theta_l$ is feasible from $\texttt{Saturate}((s, [\mathtt{e};\mathtt{d}]), \theta_l)$.

*Form 2 low energy.* For every $s \in B$ and $\mathtt{e} < M_B$, we run Algorithm 2 with initial state $s$ and initial battery status $[\mathtt{e};\mathtt{d}]$ to check if there exists a fair trace of Form 2. Here, $\mathtt{d}$ is the maximum deviation of a node label which has control state $s$ and energy $\mathtt{e}$.

**Algorithm 2** Finding form 2 low energy fair traces

**Require:** Battery system $\mathcal{B} = \langle\langle S, \Delta, s_\iota, \nu\rangle, k, c\rangle$, Energy bound $M \in \mathbb{N}$, Control state $s$, Initial battery status $[\mathtt{e};\mathtt{d}]$

```
d* ← d
while true do
    BERT ← ComputeBERT(⟨⟨S, Δ, s, ν⟩, k, c⟩, [e; d*], M)
    P ← {leaf.label | BERT leaf leaf has label (s, [e; d']) ∧
        leaf has a starred ancestor }
    if P = ∅ then
        return false
    else if d* = max{d' | (s, [e; d']) ∈ P} then
        return true
    else
        d* ← max{d' | (s, [e; d']) ∈ P}
```

**Lemma 14.** *Algorithm 2 returns* `true` *if $\mathcal{B}$ contains a Büchi trace of Form 2, and* `false` *otherwise.*

Intuitively, Algorithm 2 works by finding some deviation $\mathtt{d}^*$ such that $(s, [\mathtt{e};\mathtt{d}^*])$ is feasibly reachable from itself through some number of 0-energy cycle saturations (represented by starred nodes). In every iteration of the while-loop, it decreases the possible value for $\mathtt{d}^*$ to the largest deviation for control-state $s$ and energy $\mathtt{e}$ reachable from the previous value of $\mathtt{d}^*$ through some starred nodes. If $\mathtt{d}^*$ becomes so low that we are not able to saturate any 0-energy cycle starting from $(s, [\mathtt{e};\mathtt{d}^*])$, then we return false.

**Theorem 15.** *Büchi emptiness for battery transition systems is decidable in polynomial space with respect to the number of states and a unary encoding of weights and constants.*

Equipped with Theorem 13, the proof of Theorem 15 follows in a similar fashion as in Theorem 12.

Using similar techniques, we can construct an algorithm for Streett emptiness. In this case, also keeping track of the set of states visited along each branch of the reachability tree.

**Theorem 16.** *Street emptiness for battery transition systems is decidable in polynomial space with respect to the number of states and a unary encoding of weights and constants.*

### 5.3 $\omega$-Regular Model Checking

Equipped with a procedure for checking Büchi emptiness (Theorem 15), one can check whether a given BTS $\mathcal{B}$ satisfies any $\omega$-

regular constraint $\varphi$ that is defined with respect to $\mathcal{B}$'s states. Such a constraint can be formalized, for example, by a linear temporal logic (LTL) formula, whose atomic propositions are the names of the states in $\mathcal{B}$. Indeed, any $\omega$-regular constraint $\varphi$ can be translated to a Büchi automaton $\mathcal{A}$, such that $\mathcal{A}$'s language is equivalent to the language of $\varphi$ (or to the language of its negation, as is the common practice in the case of an LTL formula) [24]. Now, one can take the product of $\mathcal{A}$ and $\mathcal{B}$, defined in the usual way, getting a BTS $\mathcal{C}$ with a Büchi emptiness problem.

As Streett emptiness is a special case of $\omega$-regular model checking, one may wonder why we bothered to have Theorem 16. The reason lies in the complexity – In Theorem 16, we show that Streett emptiness can be solved in the same complexity class as the one for Büchi emptiness, while translating a Streett automaton into a Büchi automaton might involve an exponential state blowup [23].

## 6. Case Study

We conclude this paper with a case study relating to controlling an energy-constrained robot. We first define a toy language for programming the robot controller, inspired by various real languages for programming robots, and define how the different constructs interact with the environment.

***The setting.*** We model a semi-autonomous robot that operates in an *arena* $D_L$ where each $l \in D_L$ is a possible location of the robot. For example, a location can be an $(x, y)$ vector, providing the position of the robot in a plane of $1,000 \times 1,000$ squares.

We model the *environment* of the robot as a function that gives attributes to each location in the arena. Formally, the environment is $\mathcal{E} : D_L \to \langle D_{E_1}, D_{E_2}, \ldots, D_{E_m} \rangle$ where each $D_{E_i}$ is a finite domain of some property. For example, the environment may define the terrain of each location and whether it lies in the sun or in the shade, in which case $\mathcal{E}(3,5) = \langle$"smooth terrain", "sun"$\rangle$ means that the location $(3,5)$ is a sunny place with a smooth terrain. Note that, in this case study, the environment is time invariant.

The actions of the robot are governed by its *control program*. In each time step, denoted by a 'tick', the control program computes *output actions* based on some *external inputs*, *sensor values*, and the values of the robot's *internal variables*.

The external input is given by *input variables* $\langle I_1, \ldots, I_k \rangle$, each over a finite domain $D_{I_i}$, and it comes from an external independent agent. The sensor values, given by *sensor variables* $\langle S_1, \ldots, S_r \rangle$, over the finite domains $D_{S_1}, \ldots, D_{S_r}$, are computed automatically based on the environment of the robot and its current location. Formally, for each sensor variable $S_i$ there is a function $\xi_i : \mathcal{E} \times D_L \to D_{S_i}$. The robot also has some *internal variables*, $\langle N_1, \ldots, N_g \rangle$, over the finite domains $D_{N_1}, \ldots, D_{N_g}$, used for putting a logic in its behavior. The output actions are given by *output variables* $\langle A_1, \ldots, A_l \rangle$, over the finite domains $D_{A_1}, \ldots, D_{A_l}$. Upon performing the actions, the current location, given in the variable $L$, is automatically computed based on the previous location and the actions; formally, by a function $\eta : D_L \times D_{A_1} \times \ldots \times D_{A_l} \to D_L$.

The *state* of the robot, $\mathcal{V}$, encapsulates the values of all the above variables. There is a *cost function* Energy which gives the energy gain (positive) or consumption (negative) of actions in the given environment, i.e., Energy is of type $D_{E_1} \times \ldots \times D_{E_m} \times D_{A_1} \times \ldots \times D_{A_l} \to \mathbb{Z}$. For the functions $\eta$, $\xi_i$, and Energy, we use the short-hand of applying the function to the whole state instead of the relevant variables. For example, instead of writing "$\xi_i(l) = v$ and value of $L$ in state $\sigma$ is $l$", we write "$\xi_i(\sigma) = v$".

***The controller language.*** The language of the robot-control program is defined by the syntax shown in Figure 5. Most of the constructs in this language are standard, and will not be explained in detail. Note that the program cannot directly write to the location variables and sensor variables, but can only write to the internal variables and action variables. The most interesting construct in the syntax is the `tick` statement. Intuitively, the `tick` statement performs the actions described by the output variables (i.e., changes the location using the $\eta$ function) and reads new values into the sensor variables (based on the environment and the current state, using the $\xi_i$ functions) and into the input variables (nondeterministically). The formal semantics of the `tick` statement is described in the next paragraph.

```
program := statements

statements := statement | statement; statements
statement := (label : tick) | action_var = expr
        | internal_var = expr | skip
        | if (expr == 0) statements else statements
        | while (expr == 0) statements
expr := sensor_var | input_var | internal_var
        | expr + expr | constant | expr * expr
        | (expr == 0) ? expr : expr
```

**Figure 5.** Syntax of the robot-control language

We provide in Example 17 a simple setting of an environment, a control program, and the finite domains of the various variables.

**Example 17.**

**The environment (arena).**

| $x \backslash y$ | *1* | *2* | *3* | *4* |
|---|---|---|---|---|
| *1* | - | - | × | - |
| *2* | × | / | × | - |
| *3* | - | / | / | / |
| *4* | - | × | / | / |

Legends.
□ : *Sun* ; ▒ : *Shade*
- : *hard* ; / : *soft* ; ×: *obstacle*

**The robot variables.**

Location. $D_L = \{(1,1), (1,2), \ldots, (4,4)\}$

Inputs. $D_{I_1} = \{Move, None\}$
$D_{I_2} = \{Front, Back, Left, Right\}$

Sensors. $D_{S_1} = \{InTheSun, InTheShade\}$
$D_{S_2} = \{SunOnFront, NoSunOnFront\}$
*... Sensors for sun and obstacles all around*
$D_{S_9} = \{ObstacleOnRight, NoObstacleOnRight\}$

Actions. $D_{A_1} = \{Move, None\}$
$D_{A_2} = \{Front, Back, Left, Right\}$

Internal. $D_{N_1} = \{InTheSun, InTheShade\}$
$D_{N_2} = \{WasInTheSun, WasInTheShade\}$
$D_{N_3} = \{Was^2InTheSun, Was^2InTheShade\}$

**The cost function.** *(The direction does not matter.)*
Energy$(Sun, Hard/Soft, None) = +12$
Energy$(Sun, Hard, Move) = +1$
Energy$(Sun, Soft, Move) = -1$
Energy$(Shade, Hard/Soft, None) = -5$
Energy$(Shade, Hard, Move) = -12$
Energy$(Shade, Soft, Move) = -15$

**The robot-control program.**
*The program, intuitively, defines the following behavior.*

- *Obey the external input, whenever it is legal. Otherwise, do nothing, if legal, or else check for a legal action.*
- *The constraints for a legal action:*
  - *Do not go into an obstacle. (A location out of the arena is considered as an obstacle.)*

- *Do not stay in the sun for more than two consecutive steps.*
- *Whenever staying for two consecutive steps in the sun, avoid the sun for at least two consecutive steps.*

*The code is straightforward; we give below some of its fragments.*

```
while(1) {
// Check if the input is legal
  // Moving into an obstacle?
  if (I1 = Move &&
        (  I2 = Front && S6 = ObstacleOnFront
        || I2 = Back && S7 = ObstacleOnBack
        || I2 = Left && S8 = ObstacleOnLeft
        || I2 = Right && S9 = ObstacleOnRight )
     )
      A1 := None
  // Too much in the sun?
  if (N2 = WasInTheSun
      && (N1 = InTheSun || N3 = Was^2InTheSun) && ...
     )
     // Choose a legal action
     if (N1 = InTheShadow)
        A1 := None
     else if (S2=NoSunOnFront && S6=NoObstacleOnFront)
        A1 := Move; A2 := Front
     ...
  label1 : tick;
  N3 := (N2=WasInTheSun)? Was^2InTheSun:Was^2InTheShade
  N2 := (N1=InTheSun)? WasInTheSun : WasInTheShade
  N1 := S1
}
```

***Semantics.*** Consider a robot-control program $P$, and fix diffusion constant $k$ and a width constant $c$ for a battery. We define the semantics of $P$ in the standard small-step operational style. We summarize the state of the program as $(\sigma, \mathbf{t})$ where $\sigma$ is a valuation of the variables, and $\mathbf{t}$ is a battery status. Therefore, the small-step semantics is given by a relation $\Rightarrow$ where intuitively, $(P, (\sigma, \mathbf{t})) \Rightarrow (P', (\sigma', \mathbf{t}'))$ holds if executing the first step from the program fragment $P$ at state $(\sigma, \mathbf{t})$ leads to $(\sigma', \mathbf{t}')$ and the remaining program fragment is $P'$.

We assume that all the constructs except `tick` are executed instantaneously, and without any consumption of power; hence, the only construct that updates the battery status in the summary is the `tick`. Therefore, for all the other constructs, we do not explicitly present the semantics, but point out that the semantics are similar to a standard while-language. For the `tick` construct, we define the semantics using the proof rules from Figure 6.

Intuitively, on executing a `tick`, the effects of the output actions are performed, the sensor variables are updated based on the new location and environment, the next valuation of the input variables is given, and then the battery status is updated based on the cost of the actions in the current environment.

***Problem statement.*** We consider model-checking problems; that is, asking whether a given model satisfies a given specification. The model, in our case, is a robot and its environment; namely, a robot-control program, battery constants, an initial battery status, an environment with locations $D_L$, and an initial location. The specification is a regular or $\omega$-regular language over the (finite or infinite) sequences of locations in $D_L$. The model-checking problem is affirmatively answered if the robot has a path, in the given setting, such that the sequence of locations along the path belongs to the language of the specification.

Consider, for example, the setting of Example 17 together with an initial location $(1, 1)$, a battery width constant $\frac{1}{2}$, a battery diffusion constant $\frac{1}{8}$, and an initial battery status $(16, 16)$. A regular specification can ask, for instance, whether the robot has a finite path reaching the location $(3, 2)$. An $\omega$-regular specification can ask, say, whether the robot has an infinite path visiting the location $(1, 4)$ infinitely often, while avoiding the locations $(3, 1)$ and $(4, 4)$.

***Model-checking algorithm.*** Given a control-program $P$, an environment $\mathcal{E}$, a battery width constant $c$, a battery diffusion constant $k$, an initial battery status $\mathbf{t}_\iota$, and an initial variable valuation $\sigma_\iota$, we define the equivalent battery transition system $\mathsf{BTS}[\![P, \mathcal{E}, c, k, \mathbf{t}_\iota, \sigma_\iota]\!] = \langle\langle S, \Delta, s_\iota, \nu\rangle, c, k\rangle$ as follows.

Let $L$ be the set of labels of the `tick` statements in the program.

- A state in the BTS is a pair $(l, \sigma)$ where $l \in L$ is a label, and $\sigma$ is a valuation of all the variables in the program.
- There exists a transition from $(l_1, \sigma_1)$ to $(l_2, \sigma_2)$ on weight $w$ if for some program fragments $P_1$ and $P_2$:
  - there exist battery statuses $\mathbf{t_1}$ and $\mathbf{t_2}$ and a proof that $((\mathtt{l_1} : \mathtt{tick}); P_1, (\mathbf{t_1}, \sigma_1)) \Rightarrow ((\mathtt{l_2} : \mathtt{tick}); P_2, (\mathbf{t_2}, \sigma_2))$ where the $Tick$ rule is applied exactly once; and
  - there exist battery statuses $\mathbf{t_1}$ and $\mathbf{t_2}$, such that there is a proof $(P, (\sigma_\iota, \mathbf{t_1})) \Rightarrow ((\mathtt{l_1} : \mathtt{tick}); P_1, (\sigma_1, \mathbf{t_2}))$.
- The cost of a transition from $(l, \sigma)$ is $w$ if applying the *cost* function on the valuation of the environment and action variables in $\sigma$ is $w$.
- The initial state $s_\iota$ is given by $(l, \sigma)$ such that there exists a program fragment $P_1$ and a battery status $\mathbf{t}$ such that there is a proof of $(P, (\sigma_\iota, \mathbf{t})) \Rightarrow (((\mathtt{l} : \mathtt{tick}); P_1), (\sigma, \mathbf{t}))$ containing no applications of the $Tick$ rule. Due to the determinism of our language, it is guaranteed that there exists only one such $(l, \sigma)$.

A part of the BTS corresponding to Example 17 is given in Figure 7.

The battery diffusion constant $k = \frac{1}{8}$ and its width constant $c = \frac{1}{2}$.

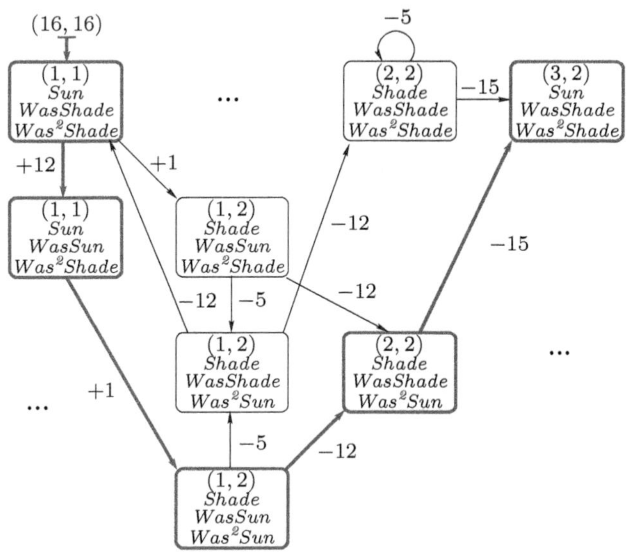


**Figure 7.** A part of the BTS that corresponds to the robot and its environment, as described in Example 17. The best path to location $(3, 2)$ appears in boldface blue. This path is infeasible by the BTS semantics, while feasible by models that are based on an ideal-energy resource.

We have the following theorem.

**Theorem 18.** *Consider a robot model-checking problem consisting of a control-program $P$, an environment $\mathcal{E}$ with locations $D_L$, a battery width constant $c$, a battery diffusion constant $k$, an initial*

$$\frac{}{(\texttt{label}:\texttt{tick},(\sigma,\mathbf{t}))\Rightarrow(\texttt{effects};\texttt{sensors};\texttt{inputs};\texttt{battery},(\sigma,\mathbf{t}))}\ \text{Tick}$$

$$\frac{cost(\sigma)=w \quad \texttt{Post}(\mathbf{t},w)=\mathbf{t}'}{(\texttt{battery},(\sigma,\mathbf{t}))\Rightarrow(\texttt{skip},(\sigma,\mathbf{t}'))}\ \text{Battery} \qquad \frac{v_1\in D_{I_1} \quad \ldots \quad v_l\in D_{I_l}}{(\texttt{inputs},(\sigma,\mathbf{t}))\Rightarrow(\texttt{skip},(\sigma[\forall k: I_k:=v_k],\mathbf{t}'))}\ \text{Inputs}$$

$$\frac{v_1=\xi_1(\sigma) \quad \ldots \quad v_r=\xi_r(\sigma)}{(\texttt{sensors},(\sigma,\mathbf{t}))\Rightarrow(\texttt{skip},(\sigma[\forall k: S_k:=v_k],\mathbf{t}'))}\ \text{Sensors} \qquad \frac{v=\eta(\sigma)}{(\texttt{effects},(\sigma,\mathbf{t}))\Rightarrow(\texttt{skip},(\sigma[\forall k: L:=v],\mathbf{t}'))}\ \text{Effects}$$

**Figure 6.** Semantics of `tick`

*battery status* $\mathbf{t}_\iota$*, an initial variable valuation* $\sigma_\iota$*, and a regular or* $\omega$*-regular language* $\phi$ *over the sequences of locations in* $D_L$*.*

*Let* $\mathcal{B} = \mathsf{BTS}[\![P,\mathcal{E},c,k,\mathbf{t}_\iota,\sigma_\iota]\!]$*. For a control state* $b \in \mathcal{B}$*, let* $\mathsf{Location}(b)$ *be the valuation of the robot location variable in* $b$*. Let* $\phi'$ *be a regular or* $\omega$*-regular language over sequences of control locations in* $\mathcal{B}$*, such that a sequence* $b_0, b_1, \ldots \in \Phi'$ *iff* $\mathsf{Location}(b_0), \mathsf{Location}(b_1), \ldots \in \Phi$*.*

*Then, the robot model-checking problem is equivalent to the BTS model-checking of* $\mathcal{B}$ *and* $\phi'$*.*

***Battery vs. ideal energy.*** Model-checking the robot behavior, taking into account the non-ideal aspects of the energy resource, is inherently different from considering the battery as an ideal energy resource, as demonstrated in Example 17. There, the robot cannot go with an initial battery status of $(16, 16)$ from location $(1, 1)$ to $(3, 2)$ (cf., Theorem 3.) On the other hand, it is possible to go from location $(4, 4)$ to $(3, 4)$, starting with the same initial battery status. Note that such a situation is impossible with a model that is based on an ideal-energy resource, as the energy loss going from location $(4, 4)$ to $(3, 4)$ is 15, while from location $(1, 1)$ to $(3, 2)$ it is only 14! (The reason, as elaborated on in Sections 2–3, lies in the influence of the energy changes along the path on the available charge of the battery.)

## 7. Conclusions and Future Work

We presented the first discrete formal model of battery systems and showed that the standard automaton emptiness problems for this model are decidable. Further, these battery transition systems do not fall into the large class of well-structured transition systems.

In terms of future work, a natural direction is to explore standard program analysis and program synthesis questions for systems that use batteries. For example, to begin with, one could define an extension to standard imperative languages to allow programs to branch based on the status of the battery. For programs written in such a language, one could attempt to compute invariants about the combined program- and battery-state through abstract interpretation. Also, one could attempt battery-aware partial-program synthesis for such a language. This would be a generalization of the battery-aware scheduling problem studied in [18]. Another direction to explore is the possibility of solving two-player games for battery transition system, leading to battery-aware algorithms for synthesis of reactive systems.

## References


[1] R. Adany and T. Tamir. Online algorithm for battery utilization in electric vehicles. In *FedCSIS*, pages 349–356, 2012.

[2] R. Alur, C. Courcoubetis, and D. L. Dill. Model-checking for real-time systems. In *LICS*, pages 414–425, 1990.

[3] S. Bardin, A. Finkel, J. Leroux, and P. Schnoebelen. Flat acceleration in symbolic model checking. In *ATVA*, volume 3707 of *LNCS*, pages 474–488, 2005.

[4] L. Benini, G. Castelli, A. Macii, E. Macii, M. Poncino, and R. Scarsi. Extending lifetime of portable systems by battery scheduling. In *DATE*, pages 197–203, 2001.

[5] G. G. Botte, V. R. Subramanian, and R. White. Mathematical modeling of secondary lithium batteries. *Electrochimica Acta*, 45(15):2595–2609, 2000.

[6] A. Chakrabarti, L. de Alfaro, T. Henzinger, and M. Stoelinga. Resource interfaces. In *EMSOFT*, volume 2855 of *LNCS*, pages 117–133, 2003.

[7] K. Chatterjee and L. Doyen. Energy parity games. *Theor. Comput. Sci.*, 458:49–60, 2012.

[8] K. Chatterjee, L. Doyen, T. A. Henzinger, and J. F. Raskin. Generalized mean-payoff and energy games. In *FSTTCS*, volume 8 of *LIPIcs*, pages 505–516, 2010.

[9] C. Chiasserini and R. Rao. Energy efficient battery management. *J. on Selected Areas in Communications*, 19(7):1235–1245, 2001.

[10] M. Doyle, T. F. Fuller, and J. Newman. Modeling of galvanostatic charge and discharge of the lithium/polymer/insertion cell. *J. of the Electrochemical Society*, 140(6):1993, 1526–1533.

[11] A. Finkel and P. Schnoebelen. Parallel program schemata. *J. of Computer and System Sciences*, 3(2):147–195, 1969.

[12] A. Finkel and P. Schnoebelen. Well-structured transition systems everywhere! *Theor. Comput. Sci.*, 256(1–2):63–92, 2001.

[13] T. F. Fuller, M. Doyle, and J. Newman. Relaxation phenomena in lithiumion-insertion cells. *J. of the Electrochemical Society*, 141(4): 982–990, 1994.

[14] S. Gold. A PSPICE macromodel for lithium-ion batteries. In *Annual Battery Conference on Applications and Advances*, pages 215–222, 1997.

[15] S. C. Hageman. Simple PSPICE models let you simulate common battery types. *Electronic Design News*, 38(22):117–129, 1993.

[16] M. R. Jongerden. *Model-based energy analysis of battery powered systems*. PhD thesis, University of Twente, 2010.

[17] M. R. Jongerden and B. R. Haverkort. Which battery model to use? *IET Software*, 3(6):445–457, 2009.

[18] M. R. Jongerden, A. Mereacre, H. C. Bohnenkamp, B. R. Haverkort, and J.-P. Katoen. Computing optimal schedules for battery usage in embedded systems. *IEEE Trans. Industrial Informatics*, 6(3):276–286, 2010.

[19] K. G. Larsen, S. Laursen, and J. Srba. Action investment energy games. In *MEMICS*, volume 7721 of *LNCS*, pages 155–167, 2012.

[20] J. Manwell and J. McGowan. Lead acid battery storage model for hybrid energy systems. *Solar Energy*, 50(5):399–405, 1993.

[21] E. Podlaha and H. Cheh. Modeling of cylindrical alkaline cells. *J. of the Electrochemical Society*, 14(1):15–27, 1994.

[22] D. Rakhmatov and S. Vrudhula. An analytical high-level battery model for use in energy management of portable electronic systems. In *International Conference on Computer Aided Design (ICCAD)*, pages 488–493, 2001.

[23] S. Safra and M. Vardi. On $\omega$-automata and temporal logic. In *STOC*, pages 127–137, 1989.

[24] M. Vardi. An automata-theoretic approach to linear temporal logic. In *Logics for Concurrency: Structure versus Automata*, volume 1043 of *LNCS*, pages 238–266, 1996.

# Symbolic Optimization with SMT Solvers


Yi Li
University of Toronto
liyi@cs.toronto.edu

Aws Albarghouthi
University of Toronto
aws@cs.toronto.edu

Zachary Kincaid
University of Toronto
zkincaid@cs.toronto.edu

Arie Gurfinkel
Software Engineering Institute, CMU
arie@cmu.edu

Marsha Chechik
University of Toronto
chechik@cs.toronto.edu



## Abstract

The rise in efficiency of Satisfiability Modulo Theories (SMT) solvers has created numerous uses for them in software verification, program synthesis, functional programming, refinement types, etc. In all of these applications, SMT solvers are used for generating satisfying assignments (e.g., a witness for a bug) or proving unsatisfiability/validity (e.g., proving that a subtyping relation holds). We are often interested in finding not just an arbitrary satisfying assignment, but one that optimizes (minimizes/maximizes) certain criteria. For example, we might be interested in detecting program executions that maximize energy usage (performance bugs), or synthesizing short programs that do not make expensive API calls. Unfortunately, none of the available SMT solvers offer such optimization capabilities.

In this paper, we present SYMBA, an efficient SMT-based optimization algorithm for *objective functions* in the theory of linear real arithmetic (LRA). Given a formula $\varphi$ and an objective function $t$, SYMBA finds a satisfying assignment of $\varphi$ that maximizes the value of $t$. SYMBA utilizes efficient SMT solvers as black boxes. As a result, it is easy to implement and it directly benefits from future advances in SMT solvers. Moreover, SYMBA can optimize a set of objective functions, reusing information between them to speed up the analysis. We have implemented SYMBA and evaluated it on a large number of optimization benchmarks drawn from program analysis tasks. Our results indicate the power and efficiency of SYMBA in comparison with competing approaches, and highlight the importance of its multi-objective-function feature.



***Categories and Subject Descriptors*** G.1.6 [*Optimization*]: Constrained optimization; F.3.1 [*Specifying and Verifying and Reasoning about Programs*]: Invariants

***Keywords*** optimization; satisfiability modulo theories; invariant generation; symbolic abstraction; program analysis





*POPL '14*, January 22–24, 2014, San Diego, CA, USA.



http://dx.doi.org/10.1145/2535838.2535857


## 1. Introduction

Over the past decade or so, we have witnessed an incredible improvement in the performance of *Satisfiability Modulo Theories* (SMT) solvers [10] and the range of logical theories they support. These advances made SMT solvers (e.g., Z3 [22], MathSAT [18], CVC [9], etc.) household names in the programming languages and verification communities, creating an explosion in the range of applications in which they are deployed, and paving the way for innovations that would not have been possible otherwise.

To mention a few, in *verification*, SMT solvers have been used for device driver verification [7, 35], checking complex verification conditions [23, 39, 49], and improving precision of invariant generation [34, 46]; in *testing and bug finding*, they have been instrumental in making symbolic execution [15, 27], fuzzing [28], and bounded model checking techniques [19, 25] practical; in *program synthesis*, they have been used to search for programs satisfying a given specification [31, 59]; in *functional programming*, they have been used to support strong typing guarantees with refinement types [13, 53].

In all of the aforementioned applications, SMT solvers are used for (1) generating satisfying assignments (e.g., a witness for a bug) or (2) proving unsatisfiability/validity (e.g., proving that a subtyping relation holds). To the best of our knowledge, none of the available SMT solvers support finding *optimal* satisfying assignments, i.e., satisfying assignments that minimize (or maximize) a given *objective function*. In this paper, we present SYMBA, an efficient SMT-based optimization algorithm for objective functions in the theory of *linear real arithmetic* (LRA). Given a formula $\varphi$ and an objective function $t$, e.g., $x + y$, SYMBA computes the smallest constant $k$ such that $\varphi \Rightarrow t \leqslant k$ [1]. Specifically, SYMBA finds a satisfying assignment of $\varphi$ that exhibits the least upper bound $k$ (maximum value) of an objective function $t$. In what follows, we start by arguing that such an algorithm has a wide array of applications in verification, bug finding, synthesis, and others. We then highlight SYMBA's salient features and describe its high-level operation.

***Applications of Optimization*** We start by describing potential applications of SYMBA in the following domains:

- *Numerical invariant generation:* Numerical abstract domains, e.g., intervals [20] and octagons [42], are often used to generate numerical program invariants. The main ingredient in such an analysis is the *abstract transformer*: an operator that takes a set of initial states and an instruction (or a basic block), and com-

[1] Note that $k$ is $\infty$ if $t$ is unbounded in $\varphi$, and $-\infty$ if $\varphi$ is unsatisfiable

putes a set of reachable states, often using convex optimization techniques. Since SYMBA can optimize over arbitrary LRA formulas (*non-convex optimization*), it can precisely compute abstract transformers over loop-free program fragments (encoded as formulas), without losing precision due to join or multiple applications of the transformer. This problem is known in the literature as *symbolic abstraction* and has been studied for a number of domains [45, 46, 52, 60, 61]. By designing optimization algorithms that exploit the power of SMT solvers, we enable efficient implementations of precise abstract transformers for a variety of numerical domains [55]. We discuss this application in more detail in Sec. 4, where we generate our benchmark suite from symbolic abstraction queries made by a program analysis tool [5].

A similar approach can be used for solving systems of Horn-like clauses in LRA [30, 32], which capture a large number of sequential and concurrent program verification tasks. Since Horn clauses are represented symbolically in SMT-LIB [14], applying traditional numerical abstract domains for solving them is not a straightforward endeavour, but SYMBA can be easily used to build a fixpoint solver for such clauses.

- *Counterexample generation:* In symbolic execution and bounded model checking, program executions are encoded succinctly as a formula. An SMT solver is then used to find a satisfying assignment of this formula that acts as a witness of an erroneous execution. By augmenting the encoding with arithmetic cost functions, we can use SYMBA to find counterexamples that maximize or minimize certain criteria. For example, we might be interested in finding performance bugs, e.g., execution traces with the highest energy or memory consumption. By assigning costs to program instructions and API calls, we can detect such executions using an optimizing SMT solver.
- *Program synthesis:* Program synthesis involves generating a program that satisfies a given specification. For example, in [31, 37], non-trivial bit-manipulating program snippets are synthesized from specifications by using SMT solvers to search through all possible combinations of bit-level operations (instructions). Similar to the counterexample generation described above, the goal is often to synthesize the shortest programs, or ones with the smallest cost. For example, when the synthesized snippet is part of a performance-critical code (e.g., as in superoptimization [41]), the size of the synthesized snippet and the operations it performs are crucial. By augmenting formulas given to the SMT solver with costs, we can instruct it to synthesize programs that minimize a given criterion.
- *Constraint programming:* In recent work [38], Köksal et al. proposed incorporating an SMT solver into an extension of Scala, allowing constraint manipulation as part of the language. One of the important constructs in their language is min/max, which returns the minimum/maximum satisfying assignment of a constraint w.r.t to an objective function, and enables elegant implementations of algorithms for problems like knapsack. Due to the unavailability of off-the-shelf solvers with an optimization feature, the authors use a simple binary search optimization algorithm restricted to bounded discrete domains. The authors of [38] also comment on the state-of-the-art of SMT solvers by saying: "*...we found that a number of features, if natively supported by solvers, could directly bring benefits to constraint programming. These include 1) support for enumeration of theory models and 2) solving constraints while minimizing/maximizing a given term.*" SYMBA is thus an answer to point 2 for LRA terms (objective functions).
- *Interpolant generation:* Craig interpolation has proved to be a powerful technique for software verification based on predicate abstraction [36]. Interpolants are generated from unsatisfiability proofs. For linear real arithmetic, this can be performed by constructing a system of constraints whose solution is a proof of unsatisfiability (and an interpolant) [54]. As recently shown [4], the simplicity of the proof can be crucial to discovering the predicates required for a safe inductive invariant. Finding simple proofs boils down to finding an optimal solution of the system of constraints. Using SYMBA, this can be automated, without the need for the heuristics employed in [4].

***Symbolic Optimization with* SYMBA** Given a formula $\varphi$ and a set of objective functions (*objectives* for short) $T = \{t_1, \ldots, t_n\}$, SYMBA computes the strongest formula

$$\mathsf{opt}_T(\varphi) \equiv t_1 \leqslant k_1 \wedge \ldots \wedge t_n \leqslant k_n,$$

such that $\varphi \Rightarrow \mathsf{opt}_T(\varphi)$, where $k_i \in \mathbb{R} \cup \{\infty, -\infty\}$. We call $\mathsf{opt}_T(\varphi)$ the *optimal solution* of $T$ w.r.t. $\varphi$. In other words, SYMBA computes the least upper bound (maximum value) $k_i$ of each objective $t_i$ w.r.t. the satisfying assignments of $\varphi$.[2]

Note that we are optimizing a *set* of objective functions, as opposed to a single function as in traditional optimization problems. This allows SYMBA to reuse information computed for one objective in order to speed up the optimization of other objectives. This feature allows *incremental* implementations of SYMBA, where we can continuously ask for optimizing different objectives without losing previously computed information (in a style similar to the `push/pop` interface implemented by most SMT solvers). The incremental interface is useful, for example, when computing an abstract transformer for the intervals domain, where we need to find the maximum and minimum values of each live variable.

SYMBA maintains both an *under-* and an *over-approximation* of the optimal solution $\mathsf{opt}_T(\varphi)$. It works by sampling points (models) in $\varphi$ in a systematic manner, using an SMT solver, and adding the points to the under-approximation in order to extend it. The process continues until the under-approximation is equal to the optimal solution. The key insight underlying SYMBA is how to carry out the sampling process in an *infinite space* of satisfying assignments, while ensuring convergence to least upper bounds and discovery of *unbounded* objectives.

SYMBA also maintains an over-approximation of $\mathsf{opt}_T(\varphi)$ (when it terminates, the two approximations are equivalent). Maintaining an over-approximation allows us to halt SYMBA at any point and still compute an over-approximation of the optimal solution (e.g., an over-approximation of the best abstract transformer). This makes SYMBA resilient to SMT solver failures and resource (e.g., time) depletion.

Another important feature of SYMBA is that it treats the underlying SMT solver as a black-box, using it to generate models and check validity. This makes SYMBA easy to implement, allowing us to take advantage of the existing highly-optimized SMT solvers without having to dive into their intricate implementations, and directly benefiting from future advances in SMT solving.

Our implementation of SYMBA uses the Z3 SMT solver. We have performed a thorough evaluation of SYMBA on a large set of realistic benchmarks drawn from program analysis tasks. We have also compared SYMBA against [57], which is, to the best of our knowledge, the only other proposed SMT-based optimization technique. The technique of [57] optimizes a single objective function, and is built into the MATHSAT SMT solver. For a fairer compari-

[2] Note that our goal is to find an optimal value for each objective independently (using a different satisfying assignment of $\varphi$), as opposed to a *pareto-optimal* satisfying assignment, i.e., a single assignment that optimizes all objective functions and cannot be improved upon.

son against SYMBA, we have also implemented a multi-objective-function extension of the approach in [57] in the Z3 SMT solver (using its available source code [3]) and experimented with various configurations. Our results demonstrate the efficiency and robustness of SYMBA against competing approaches, and highlight the effectiveness of its multi-objective-function feature and our proposed implementation optimizations.

***Contributions*** We summarize our contributions as follows:

- SYMBA: a novel SMT-based optimization algorithm for objective functions in linear real arithmetic, with wide-ranging applications in program analysis, synthesis, etc. SYMBA utilizes efficient SMT solvers as black boxes. Thus, it is easy to implement and it directly benefits from future advances in SMT solving. Moreover, SYMBA can optimize a set of objective functions, reusing information between them to speed up the optimization task.
- An extensive evaluation of SYMBA against other proposed techniques in the literature on a large set of program analysis benchmarks. Our results indicate the power and efficiency of SYMBA in comparison with competing approaches, and highlight the importance of its multi-objective-function feature.
- An implementation of SYMBA, multiple implementations of the approach in [57], and a large set of optimization benchmarks drawn from program analysis tasks. Our source code, binaries, and benchmarks are available at:

  `http://bitbucket.org/arieg/ufo`

***Organization*** In Sec. 2, we demonstrate the operation of SYMBA on simple examples. In Sec. 3, we formalize SYMBA and prove its correctness. In Sec. 4, we describe our implementation and experimental evaluation. In Sec. 5 and 6, we compare SYMBA to related work and conclude the paper, respectively.

## 2. SYMBA by Example

In this section, we illustrate the operation of SYMBA on two formulas, a 2-dimensional and a 3-dimensional one.

### 2.1 A 2-dimensional Example

Consider the LRA formula

$$\varphi \equiv 1 \leqslant y \leqslant 3 \wedge (1 \leqslant x \leqslant 3 \vee x \geqslant 4)$$

containing the real variables $x$ and $y$ and represented pictorially by the black boxes in Fig. 1. Suppose that our set of objectives is $T = \{y, x+y\}$. That is, we would like to find the least upper bound for $y$ and $x + y$ in $\varphi$. (Note that if we want to find the minimum value for $y$, we can simply add $-y$ as an objective to $T$.) In this example, the optimal solution is

$$\mathsf{opt}_T(\varphi) \equiv y \leqslant 3 \wedge x + y \leqslant \infty,$$

since $x + y$ is unbounded in $\varphi$. Formulas of the form $t \leqslant \infty$ are treated as *true*, and $t \leqslant -\infty$ as *false*.

Initially, the under-approximation of $\mathsf{opt}_T(\varphi)$ is

$$U \equiv y \leqslant -\infty \wedge x + y \leqslant -\infty \equiv \mathit{false},$$

and the over-approximation is

$$O \equiv y \leqslant \infty \wedge x + y \leqslant \infty \equiv \mathit{true}.$$

SYMBA maintains the invariant $U \Rightarrow \mathsf{opt}_T(\varphi) \Rightarrow O$ (note that $U$ is an under approximation of $\mathsf{opt}_T(\varphi)$, not necessarily $\varphi$, and similarly with $O$). SYMBA alternates between two main operations: GLOBALPUSH, which is used to grow the under-approximation by sampling points (models) of $\varphi$ that lie outside the under-approximation; and UNBOUNDED, which is used to detect unbounded objectives. In this example, 3 is the upper bound for $y$, and $x + y$ is unbounded.

***First* GLOBALPUSH** SYMBA starts with a GLOBALPUSH by querying an SMT solver for a model of $\varphi$ that is not a model of $U$ (i.e., lies outside the under-approximation). Suppose the solver returns the point $\mathsf{p}_1 = (2, 2)$. The under-approximation $U$ is the strongest formula of the form $t_1 \leqslant k_1 \wedge \ldots \wedge t_n \leqslant k_n$ that contains the set of points found by the solver (i.e., a *convex hull* expressed in terms of the objectives). So, the under-approximation is updated to $U \equiv y \leqslant 2 \wedge x + y \leqslant 4$ (since the maximum values of $y$ and $x + y$ seen so far are 2 and 4, respectively). This is shown as the shaded region $U_1$ in Fig. 1.

**UNBOUNDED** $(\mathsf{p}_1, y)$ SYMBA now tries to prove that $y$ is unbounded. First, we categorize points into boundary classes as follows: Let $\mathcal{E}(\varphi) = \{l = k \mid l \leqslant k \in \varphi\}$, i.e., $\mathcal{E}(\varphi)$ is the set of all atomic formulas appearing in $\varphi$ with the inequalities replaced by equalities. In our example, $\mathcal{E}(\varphi) = \{x = 1, x = 3, x = 4, y = 1, y = 3\}$. Informally, $\mathcal{E}(\varphi)$ represents the set of edges (boundaries) appearing in Fig. 1. The boundary class $[\mathsf{p}]$ of a point $\mathsf{p}$ is $\{e \in \mathcal{E}(\varphi) \mid \mathsf{p} \models e\}$, i.e., the set of equalities in $\mathcal{E}(\varphi)$ satisfied by $\mathsf{p}$. For $\mathsf{p}_1$, $[\mathsf{p}_1] = \emptyset$, since $\mathsf{p}_1$ does not lie on any of the boundaries. The intuition underlying UNBOUNDED is finding a ray $r$ from a point $\mathsf{p}$ in $\varphi$ such that a given objective $t$ is increasing along $r$, and $r$ never hits any boundaries of $\varphi$ (i.e., completely contained in $\varphi$).

UNBOUNDED queries the SMT solver for a point $\mathsf{p}'$ s.t. $[\mathsf{p}'] = [\mathsf{p}_1]$ and $y(\mathsf{p}_1) < y(\mathsf{p}')$, where $y(\mathsf{p}')$ is the valuation of $y$ at point $\mathsf{p}'$. The point $\mathsf{p}' = (2, 2.5)$ satisfies this condition. Then UNBOUNDED queries for a point $\mathsf{p}''$ s.t. $[\mathsf{p}'] \subset [\mathsf{p}'']$ and $y(\mathsf{p}') \leqslant y(\mathsf{p}'')$. If no such $\mathsf{p}''$ exists, then we know that $y$ is unbounded. Intuitively, we are asking whether we can keep increasing the value of $y$ from $\mathsf{p}'$ without *touching* a point $\mathsf{p}''$ on one of the boundaries in $\mathcal{E}(\varphi)$. In this case, such a $\mathsf{p}''$ exists, so it is added to the under-approximation as $\mathsf{p}_2 = (3, 3)$ in Fig. 1. Note that $\mathsf{p}_2$ exhibits the upper bound of $y$; SYMBA detects that and strengthens the over-approximation $O$ to $y \leqslant 3$. After witnessing the point $\mathsf{p}_2$, $U$ is updated to become $y \leqslant 3 \wedge x+y \leqslant 6$ (see region $U_2$ in the figure).

***Second* GLOBALPUSH** Suppose that SYMBA calls GLOBALPUSH. The result is a point in $\varphi$ but not in $U$. Let $\mathsf{p}_3 = (5, 3)$ be the point found by GLOBALPUSH. As a result, $U$ is updated to $y \leqslant 3 \wedge x + y \leqslant 8$ (see region $U_3$).

**UNBOUNDED** $(\mathsf{p}_3, x + y)$ SYMBA now applies UNBOUNDED to check if $x+y$ is unbounded. Suppose UNBOUNDED picks the point $\mathsf{p}_3$. First, it finds a point $\mathsf{p}' = (6, 3)$ which increases $x + y$ and is in the same boundary class as $\mathsf{p}_3$. Then, it tries to find a point $\mathsf{p}''$ that has a boundary class $[\mathsf{p}'] \subset [\mathsf{p}'']$ and has a greater (or equal) valuation of $x + y$ than $\mathsf{p}'$. Since no such point $\mathsf{p}''$ exists, SYMBA concludes that $x + y$ is unbounded. Intuitively, SYMBA discovers that it is possible to keep finding points along the boundary $y = 3$ that increase $x + y$ without encountering any other boundary, thus concluding that $x+y$ is unbounded. We formally specify and prove the correctness of UNBOUNDED in Sec. 3.

The under-approximation $U$ is now updated to become $y \leqslant 3$ (region $U_4$), by dropping the upper bound for $x + y$. At this point, $U \equiv O$, so SYMBA terminates with the optimal solution $y \leqslant 3$.

### 2.2 A 3-dimensional Example

We now illustrate the operation of SYMBA on the formula

$$\varphi \equiv 0 \leqslant x \leqslant 3 \wedge 0 \leqslant z \leqslant 2 \wedge (2y \leqslant -x + 4 \vee 4y = 3x + 3),$$

containing the variables $x$, $y$, and $z$ and depicted in Fig. 2. Suppose, for simplicity, that we would like to find the least upper bound only for $y$, i.e., $T = \{y\}$.

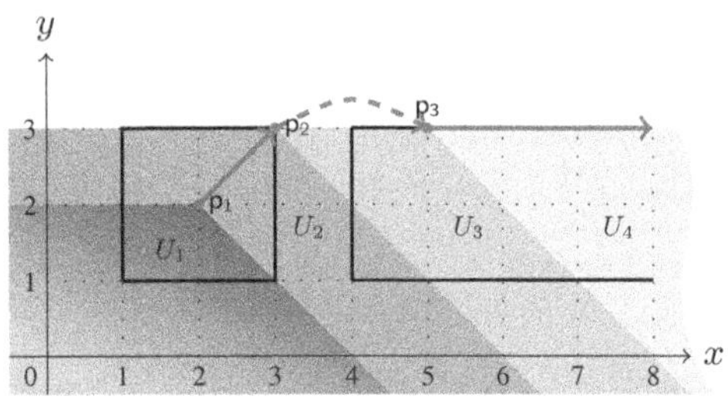


**Figure 1.** Illustration of SYMBA on a 2-D example.

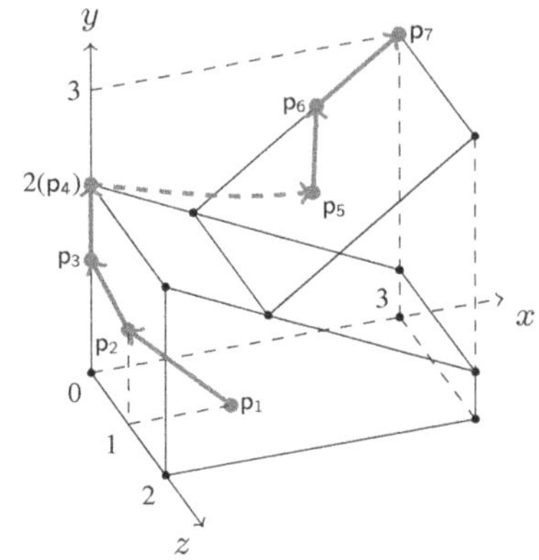


**Figure 2.** Illustration of SYMBA on a 3-D example.

***First* GLOBALPUSH** Similar to our previous example, SYMBA starts with $U \equiv$ *false* and $O \equiv$ *true* and uses GLOBALPUSH to find the initial point. Suppose the SMT solver returns the point $p_1 = (1, 0, 1)$ denoting values of $(x, y, z)$. Thus, $U \equiv y \leqslant 0$.

**UNBOUNDED $(p_1, y)$** To check if $y$ is unbounded, SYMBA applies UNBOUNDED starting from $p_1$. Since it cannot prove that $y$ is unbounded, it finds the point $p_2 = (0, 1, 1)$, where $[p_1] \subset [p_2]$ and $y(p_1) < y(p_2)$, i.e., a point showing that increasing the value of $y$ from $p_1$ can hit a boundary. After applying UNBOUNDED to $p_2$, SYMBA can get the point $p_3$, and then point $p_4$ (after applying UNBOUNDED to $p_3$). As a result, $U \equiv y \leqslant 2$. From point $p_4$, SYMBA cannot apply UNBOUNDED, since there does not exist a point $p'$ where $[p'] = [p_4]$ that increases the value of $y$. Intuitively, $p_4$ represents a local maximum.

***Second* GLOBALPUSH** To escape the local maximum, SYMBA uses GLOBALPUSH to query the SMT solver for a point outside $U$. In this case, it might find the point $p_5 = (1.8, 2.1, 1)$, and thus $U$ becomes $y \leqslant 2.1$.

**UNBOUNDED $(p_5, y)$** SYMBA continues trying to prove that $y$ is unbounded by performing UNBOUNDED from $p_5$, leading to $p_6$ and then $p_7$. SYMBA detects that $p_7$ represents the maximum value of $y$ in $\varphi$ and terminates with the optimal solution $y \leqslant 3$.

We have illustrated the workings of SYMBA on two formulas representing non-convex shapes, and showed how it utilizes an SMT solver to find least upper bounds and detect unboundedness of arbitrary linear expressions (objective functions). In the following sections, we describe SYMBA formally and discuss our implementation and experimental results.

## 3. SYMBA: The Symbolic Optimization Algorithm

In this section, we provide definitions required for the rest of the paper and formalize SYMBA as a set of inference rules.

### 3.1 Definitions

***Formulas*** Let $\mathcal{L}$ be a topologically-closed (i.e., all atoms are non-strict inequalities) subset of Quantifier Free Linear Real Arithmetic (QF_LRA), defined as follows:

$$\begin{array}{rcll} \varphi \in \mathcal{L} & ::= & \mathit{true} \mid \mathit{false} \mid P \wedge P' \mid P \vee P' & \\ P, P' \in \mathit{Atoms} & ::= & c_1x_1 + \cdots + c_nx_n \leqslant k, & n \in \mathbb{N} \\ x_i \in \mathit{Vars} & ::= & \{x_1, \ldots, x_n\}, & \end{array}$$

where $c_i, k \in \mathbb{R}$.

We use $[\![\varphi]\!]$ to denote the set of all satisfying assignments (models) of $\varphi$. A *model* $p$ : *Vars* $\rightarrow \mathbb{R}$ of $\varphi$, denoted $p \models \varphi$, is a valuation of the variables of $\varphi$ such that $\varphi(p) \equiv$ *true*, where $\varphi(p)$ is $\varphi$ with every occurrence of a variable $x$ replaced by $p(x)$. Geometrically, $p$ is a point in $\mathbb{R}^n$, and in what follows, we use the terms *model* and *point* to refer to $p$ interchangeably. We use *Atoms*$(\varphi)$ to denote the set of all *Atoms* appearing in $\varphi$, and *Vars*$(\varphi)$ to denote the set of all *Vars* appearing in $\varphi$.

***Optimal Solutions*** Let $\varphi$ be a formula in $\mathcal{L}$. Let $T = \{t_1, \ldots, t_n\}$ be a set of linear expressions, *objective functions*, where each $t_i$ is of the form $c_1x_1 + \cdots + c_mx_m$, where $c_i \in \mathbb{R}$ and *Vars*$(\varphi) = \{x_1, \ldots, x_m\}$. The goal of SYMBA is to compute a vector $(k_1, \ldots, k_n)$, where each $k_i \in \mathbb{R} \cup \{\infty, -\infty\}$, such that for each $t_i$, $\varphi \Rightarrow t_i \leqslant k_i$ and there does not exist $k'_i < k_i$ where $\varphi \Rightarrow t_i \leqslant k'_i$. We say that $(k_1, \ldots, k_n)$ is the *optimal solution* of $T$ w.r.t. $\varphi$, and denote it as $\mathsf{opt}_T(\varphi)$. We call each value $k_i$ the *optimal value* (or the least upper bound) of $t_i$ in $\varphi$.

Given such a vector $V = (k_1, \ldots, k_n)$, where $n = |T|$, we use $\mathsf{form}_T(V)$ to denote the formula $\bigwedge_{i \in [1,n]} t_i \leqslant k_i$. Given a model $p$ of $\varphi$, we use $p^T$ to denote the vector $(t_1(p), \ldots, t_{|T|}(p))$.

Given two vectors $V_1$ and $V_2$ of equal length, we use $\mathsf{min}(V_1, V_2)$ and $\mathsf{max}(V_1, V_2)$ to denote the pointwise minimum and maximum of the two vectors, respectively. We say $V_1 \leqslant V_2$ if each element of $V_1$ is less than or equal to its corresponding element in $V_2$, or if there exists a $-\infty$ in $V_1$. Intuitively, $V_1 \leqslant V_2$ *iff* $\mathsf{form}_T(V_1) \Rightarrow \mathsf{form}_T(V_2)$. Therefore, we say that $V_2$ is *weaker* than $V_1$ if $V_1 < V_2$ (or $V_1$ is *stronger* than $V_2$).

***Combinations of Theories*** For clarity of presentation, we restrict ourselves to applying SYMBA to formulas in $\mathcal{L}$. It is important to note, however, that SYMBA is applicable to quantifier-free formulas over any combination of theories $\mathcal{T} \cup \mathcal{LRA}^{\leqslant}$, where $\mathcal{T}$ is an arbitrary combination of theories, and $\mathcal{LRA}^{\leqslant}$ is linear real arithmetic restricted to non-strict inequalities. The only restriction we require is that $\mathcal{T}$ and $\mathcal{LRA}^{\leqslant}$ have disjoint signatures. In other words, atomic formulas should be over $\mathcal{T}$ or $\mathcal{LRA}^{\leqslant}$, exclusively. For example, $\mathcal{T}$ can be the combination of the theories of bitvectors and arrays (perhaps for modelling program executions). The rest of our presentation can apply directly to SMT formulas over $\mathcal{T} \cup \mathcal{LRA}^{\leqslant}$ without any modification.

### 3.2 SYMBA Formalized

We now formalize the symbolic optimization algorithm SYMBA as a set of inference rules shown in Fig. 3.

Given a set of objectives $T = \{t_1, \ldots, t_n\}$ and a formula $\varphi$ in $\mathcal{L}$, SYMBA computes $\mathsf{opt}_T(\varphi)$. The *state* of SYMBA is a tuple $\langle M, U, O \rangle$, where $M$ is a set of models of $\varphi$; $U$ is an under-approximation of $\mathsf{opt}_T(\varphi)$ (i.e., $U \leqslant \mathsf{opt}_T(\varphi)$ is invariant); and $O$ is an over-approximation of $\mathsf{opt}_T(\varphi)$ (i.e., $\mathsf{opt}_T(\varphi) \leqslant O$ is

$$\frac{}{\langle \emptyset, (-\infty, \ldots, -\infty), (\infty, \ldots, \infty)\rangle}\ \textsc{Init} \qquad \frac{p \models \varphi \wedge \neg \mathsf{form}_T(U)}{\langle M, U, O\rangle \rightarrow \langle M \cup \{p\}, \mathsf{max}(U, p^T), O\rangle}\ \textsc{GlobalPush}$$

$$\frac{\begin{array}{c} U = (k_1, \ldots, k_n) \quad p_2 \models \varphi \quad [p_2] = [p_1] \quad t_i(p_1) < t_i(p_2) \\ \nexists p_3 \models \varphi \cdot t_i(p_2) \leqslant t_i(p_3) \wedge [p_2] \subset [p_3] \end{array}}{\langle M, U, O\rangle \rightarrow \langle M, \mathsf{max}(U, (k_1, \ldots, k_{i-1}, \infty, k_{i+1}, \ldots, k_n)), O\rangle}\ \textsc{Unbounded}(p_1 \in M, t_i \in T)$$

$$\frac{p_2, p_3 \models \varphi \quad t_i(p_1) < t_i(p_2) \leqslant t_i(p_3) \quad [p_1] = [p_2] \subset [p_3]}{\langle M, U, O\rangle \rightarrow \langle M \cup \{p_3\}, \mathsf{max}(U, p_3^T), O\rangle}\ \textsc{Unbounded-Fail}(p_1 \in M, t_i \in T)$$

$$\frac{O = (k_1, \ldots, k_n) \quad m = \max\{t_i(p') \mid p' \in M\} \quad \varphi \Rightarrow t_i \leqslant m}{\langle M, U, O\rangle \rightarrow \langle M, U, \mathsf{min}(O, (k_1, \ldots, k_{i-1}, m, k_{i+1}, \ldots, k_n))\rangle}\ \textsc{Bounded}(t_i \in T)$$

**Figure 3.** Inference rules used by SYMBA.

invariant). Note that for clarity of presentation, we treated $\mathsf{opt}_T(\varphi)$, $U$, and $O$ as formulas in Sec. 2, whereas here we treat them as vectors and use $\mathsf{form}_T(V)$ to convert a vector $V$ to the formula it represents.

When SYMBA terminates, we know that $U = O = \mathsf{opt}_T(\varphi)$. Initially, as defined by the rule INIT, $M = \emptyset, U = (-\infty, \ldots, -\infty)$, and $O = (\infty, \ldots, \infty)$. The rules GLOBALPUSH, UNBOUNDED, and UNBOUNDED-FAIL are used to weaken $U$ until it is equal to $\mathsf{opt}_T(\varphi)$, whereas BOUNDED strengthens $O$ until it is equal to $\mathsf{opt}_T(\varphi)$.

GLOBALPUSH finds a model of $\varphi$ that is not captured by $\mathsf{form}_T(U)$ (i.e., lies outside the under-approximation) and adds it to $U$ to weaken it (using max). When the rule GLOBALPUSH no longer applies, we know that $U = \mathsf{opt}_T(\varphi)$. Note that applying this rule alone does not guarantee that $U$ eventually reaches $\mathsf{opt}_T(\varphi)$ for two reasons:

1. Since we are dealing with real variables, GLOBALPUSH might keep finding models that approach the upper bound of one of the objectives asymptotically.
2. GLOBALPUSH cannot detect whether an objective is unbounded, so it will keep finding models that increase the value of the unbounded objective indefinitely.

To that end, the rules UNBOUNDED and UNBOUNDED-FAIL are used to detect unbounded objectives and help GLOBALPUSH avoid asymptotic behavior. UNBOUNDED takes as parameters a model $p_1 \in M$ and an objective $t_i \in T$ and attempts to prove that $t_i$ is unbounded as follows: First, it tries to find a point $p_2 \models \varphi$ such that $[p_1] = [p_2]$ and $t(p_1) < t(p_2)$. Then, it looks for a point $p_3$ such that $p_3 \models \varphi$, $[p_2] \subset [p_3]$ and $t(p_2) \leqslant t(p_3)$. If no such $p_3$ exists, then $t$ is unbounded in $\varphi$. Otherwise, UNBOUNDED-FAIL adds $p_3$ to $M$. The intuition here is as follows: If we can find a model $p_2$, then we know that $t$ can increase along the hyperplanes in $\mathcal{E}(\varphi)$. If no point $p_3$ exists, then we know that we can keep increasing $t$ indefinitely without encountering any of the boundaries in $\mathcal{E}(\varphi)$ that are not in $[p_2]$, thus showing that $t$ is unbounded. This is analogous to the technique used by the simplex method for showing that a dimension is unbounded in a convex polyhedron. We further discuss the intuition underlying UNBOUNDED and prove its correctness in Sec. 3.3.

In addition to the aforementioned rules, the rule BOUNDED detects whether a model $p \in M$ exhibits the least upper bound of some objective $t$, and strengthens the over-approximation accordingly. Note that the over-approximation is not required for the correctness of SYMBA, but its availability allows us to guarantee that SYMBA maintains a *sound approximation* $O$ of $\mathsf{opt}_T(\varphi)$ at every point of its execution. This makes SYMBA resilient to SMT solver failures and allows us to limit resource consumption when desired. That is, by prematurely terminating SYMBA during its execution, we can recover optimal values of some of the objective functions, as maintained by the over-approximation.

***Example*** We illustrate the applications of the rules on the 2-D example from Sec. 2.1 and shown in Fig. 1. Assume that after the initial call to GLOBALPUSH, $M = \{\mathsf{p}_1 = (2,2)\}$, $\mathsf{form}_T(U) \equiv y \leqslant 2 \wedge x + y \leqslant 4$, and $\mathsf{form}_T(O) \equiv \mathit{true}$.

Applying UNBOUNDED-FAIL to $\mathsf{p}_1 \in M$ and $y \in T$ adds $\mathsf{p}_2 = (3,3)$ to $M$. Next, BOUNDED is used to detect that $\mathsf{p}_2$ exhibits the least upper bound of $y$, and updates $O$ so that $\mathsf{form}_T(O) \equiv y \leqslant 3$.

Assume that the second application of GLOBALPUSH adds point $\mathsf{p}_3 = (5,3)$ to $M$. Applying UNBOUNDED$(\mathsf{p}_3, x+y)$ detects that $x + y$ is unbounded. At this point, $\mathsf{form}_T(U)$ becomes $y \leqslant 3$, making GLOBALPUSH inapplicable. Therefore, $\varphi \Rightarrow \mathsf{form}_T(U)$, and $U = O = \mathsf{opt}_T(\varphi)$.

In what follows, we discuss and prove soundness of SYMBA, and define terminating sequences of rule applications.

### 3.3 Soundness

We start by showing soundness of the UNBOUNDED rule.

A necessary and sufficient condition for proving that a given objective $t$ is unbounded within $\varphi$ is the existence of a convex polyhedron $\varphi_c$, e.g., a ray, such that $t$ is unbounded in $\varphi_c$ and $\varphi_c \Rightarrow \varphi$. Our solution addresses two problems:

1. How to restrict the space from which $\varphi_c$ is drawn while maintaining completeness, i.e., ensuring that $\varphi_c$ is found whenever $t$ is unbounded in $\varphi$.
2. How to check that $\varphi_c \Rightarrow \varphi$.

The idea we use here is to restrict $\varphi_c$ to formulas of the form

$$\bigwedge E \wedge t \geqslant k,$$

where $E \subseteq \mathcal{E}(\varphi)$ and $k \in \mathbb{R}$. This space of convex polyhedra is sufficient for completeness. For instance, consider the example from Fig. 1. To prove that the $x+y$ direction is unbounded, we find a point $\mathsf{p}_3 = (5,3)$ that lies on the boundary $y = 3 \in \mathcal{E}(\varphi)$ and ask whether $\varphi_c \equiv y = 3 \wedge x + y \geqslant 8$ is contained in $\varphi$. Furthermore, we perform the containment check implicitly by checking whether there is a point in $\varphi_c$, along any direction that increases $x + y$, that intersects a boundary of $\varphi$. In our running example, such a point does not exist (see Fig. 1). Thus, $x + y$ is unbounded. For another example, consider the point $p_1 = (2, 2)$. Since $p_1$ does not lie on any boundary, to check if $x + y$ is unbounded we ask whether $\varphi_c \equiv x + y \geqslant 4$ is contained in $\varphi$ (i.e., we check whether increasing $x + y$ in $\varphi_c$ does not encounter boundaries in $\varphi$). This is not the case, and the counterexample is the point $p_2$, shown in Fig. 1, that lies on the boundaries $x = 3$ and $y = 3$.

Thm. 1 formalizes this construction using boundary classes and states its correctness for proving that an objective is unbounded in $\varphi$.

**Theorem 1** (Soundness of UNBOUNDED). *Given a formula $\varphi$ in $\mathcal{L}$ and a linear expression $t$ over the variables of $\varphi$, then $\nexists k \in \mathbb{R} \cdot \varphi \Rightarrow t \leqslant k$ (i.e., $t$ is unbounded) if and only if there exist $p_1, p_2 \models \varphi$ such that*

1. $t(p_1) < t(p_2)$
2. $[p_1] = [p_2]$
3. $\nexists p_3 \models \varphi \cdot t(p_2) \leqslant t(p_3) \wedge [p_2] \subset [p_3]$

*Proof.* Proofs are available in the appendix. □

In other words, if the UNBOUNDED rule was applied, then $\varphi_c \equiv [p_2] \wedge t \geqslant t(p_2)$ is contained in $\varphi$. In the theorem, conditions 1 and 2 imply that $t$ is unbounded within $\varphi_c$, and condition 3 implies that increasing $t$ in $\varphi_c$ does not encounter any boundaries of $\varphi$, i.e., $[p_2] \wedge t \geqslant t(p_2)$ is subsumed by $\varphi$. It follows from this theorem that UNBOUNDED maintains the invariant $U \leqslant \mathsf{opt}_T(\varphi)$, since the optimal solution cannot have a least upper bound for $t$ if it is unbounded (i.e., the least upper bound of $t$ is $\infty$).

**Theorem 2** (Soundness of SYMBA). *If* GLOBALPUSH *does not apply, i.e., $\varphi \wedge \neg\mathsf{form}_T(U) \Rightarrow false$, then $U = \mathsf{opt}_T(\varphi)$.*

*Proof.* Follows trivially from the invariant $U \leqslant \mathsf{opt}_T(\varphi)$. □

### 3.4 Termination

We now discuss sufficient conditions for ensuring termination of SYMBA. For simplicity of presentation, we assume that $T$ contains a single objective $t$. We start by defining a *fairness* condition on the scheduling of SYMBA's rules that ensures termination.

A *fair scheduling* is an infinite sequence of actions $a_1, a_2, \ldots$, where $a_i \in \{$GLOBALPUSH, UNBOUNDED, UNBOUNDED-FAIL$\}$, and the following conditions apply:

1. GLOBALPUSH appears infinitely often, and
2. if a point $p$ is added to $M$ along the execution sequence, then both UNBOUNDED($p, t$) and UNBOUNDED-FAIL($p, t$) eventually appear.

Condition 1 ensures that SYMBA does not get stuck in a local maximum. Condition 2 ensures that we visit every local maximum by visiting every boundary class, thus guaranteeing that either the least upper bound of $t$ is found or it is proved unbounded. Recall the 3-D example from Sec. 2, where $T = \{y\}$. Suppose our execution only applies the GLOBALPUSH rule. Then $U$ might grow asymptotically towards the least upper bound of $y$, e.g., $y \leqslant 2, y \leqslant 2.1, y \leqslant 2.11$, etc., never reaching $y \leqslant 3$. Condition 2 forces computing models that lie on one or more of the boundaries $\mathcal{E}(\varphi)$, thus avoiding this asymptotic behaviour. But applying UNBOUNDED and UNBOUNDED-FAIL alone without applying GLOBALPUSH might get us stuck in local maxima. For example, on point $p_4$ in Fig. 2, UNBOUNDED(-FAIL) are inapplicable. Condition 1 ensures that we eventually find a model outside the current under-approximation (see $p_5$), thus escaping the local maximum.

A *k-sequence* for an objective $t$ is a sequence of points $p_1, \ldots, p_k$, where $\forall i \geqslant 1 \cdot p_i \models \varphi \wedge ([p_i] \subset [p_{i+1}]) \wedge t(p_i) \leqslant t(p_{i+1})$, and UNOUNDED-FAIL($p_k, t$) fails to apply. For example, in Fig. 2, $p_1, p_2, p_3, p_4$ is a $k$-sequence.

Since $[p_i]$ for a $k$-sequence strictly grows in size and the largest boundary class has size at most $|Atoms(\varphi)|$, a $k$-sequence is of length at most $k = |Atoms(\varphi)|$. Lemma 1 states that the last model $p_k$ of a $k$-sequence always exhibits the largest value of $t$ in its boundary class $[p_k]$.

**Lemma 1.** *Let $\varphi$ be a formula, and $t$ be an objective bounded in $\varphi$. Then, in every execution of* SYMBA, *the last element $p_k$ in every $k$-sequence for $t$ satisfies $t(p_k) = \max\{t(p) \mid p \models \varphi \wedge [p_k]\}$.*

*Proof.* According to the definition of a $k$-sequence, UNBOUNDED-FAIL($p_k, t$) does not apply. Since $t$ is bounded, premises of UNBOUNDED do not hold either. Combining premises of the two rules, there does not exist $p'_k \models \varphi \wedge [p_k]$ such that $t(p_k) < t(p'_k)$. Thus, $t(p_k) = \max\{t(p) \mid p \models \varphi \wedge [p_k]\}$. □

We are now ready to prove termination of any fair execution of SYMBA. We assume that SYMBA terminates when GLOBALPUSH is no longer applicable, i.e., $\varphi \Rightarrow \mathsf{form}_T(U)$.

**Theorem 3.** SYMBA *terminates after a finite number of actions in any fair execution.*

*Proof.* We split the proof into two cases as follows:

*Case 1: $t$ is bounded within $\varphi$.* Suppose SYMBA is non-terminating. Then, in any fair scheduling, infinitely many GLOBALPUSH creates infinitely many $k$-sequences. Following Lemma 1, there are infinitely many models $p$ in the execution sequence such that $p \models \varphi$ and $t(p) = \max\{t(p') \mid p' \models \varphi \wedge [p]\}$. We denote the set of such points by $P$. In any fair execution, GLOBALPUSH must appear after $p$ is added to $M$. Therefore, there exists a point $p' \in P$ such that $t(p) < t(p')$. As a result, there is a sequence of points $p_1, p_2, \ldots$ in $P$ such $t(p_1) < t(p_2) < t(p_3) < \cdots$. Hence, $\forall i, j \cdot i \neq j \Rightarrow [p_i] \neq [p_j]$. Since the number of boundary classes is finite, SYMBA eventually finds the least upper bound of $t$ and terminates.

*Case 2: $t$ is unbounded.* Using the same argument as above, SYMBA eventually finds a point in an unbounded boundary class (due to the finite number of boundary classes) such that the three conditions in Thm. 1 hold. After that, GLOBALPUSH becomes inapplicable. □

## 4. Implementation and Evaluation

### 4.1 Implementation

We have implemented SYMBA in C++, using the Z3 SMT solver [22] for satisfiability queries. Our implementation accepts a formula $\varphi$ and a set of objectives $T$ written in the standard SMT-LIB2 [8] format. It then computes the optimal solution $\mathsf{opt}_T(\varphi)$ and returns the result. We have made available the executable and benchmarks online.

***Detecting Unbounded Objectives*** Our implementation of UNBOUNDED and UNBOUNDED-FAIL exploits the incremental (PUSH/POP) interface that most SMT solvers supply. Moreover, instead of implementing the BOUNDED rule explicitly, we show how to update the over-approximation for *free*, as a side effect of applying the UNBOUNDED rules.

Fig. 4 shows the procedure UNBOUNDEDIMPL: our implementation of the UNBOUNDED rules. We assume that there is a global SMT *context* in which the formula $\varphi$ has been asserted. An active boundary class $c$ and a objective $t_i$ are passed in as parameters. $U[t_i]$ and $O[t_i]$ refer to the $i$-th element of the vectors $U$ and $O$, respectively. SAT and UNSAT refer to the current state of the SMT context, and GETMODEL() returns a model satisfying the current

1: **function** UNBOUNDIMPL($c \in \mathcal{P}(\mathcal{E}(\varphi)), t_i \in T$)
2: PUSH()
3: ASSERT($t_i > U[t_i]$)
4: **if** UNSAT **then**
5: $O[t_i] \leftarrow U[t_i]$; POP(); **return**
6: ASSERT($\bigwedge c$)
7: **if** UNSAT **then**
8: POP(); **return**
9: ASSERT($\bigvee(\mathcal{E}(\varphi) \setminus c)$))
10: **if** SAT **then** ▷ UNBOUNDED-FAIL
11: POP(); **return** GETMODEL()
12: **else** ▷ UNBOUNDED
13: $U[t_i] \leftarrow \infty$
14: POP(); **return**

**Figure 4.** Implementation of UNBOUNDED(-FAIL).

state of the context if one exists. PUSH() and POP() are used to store and restore the state of the context, respectively.

We start by incrementally asserting the conditions of UNBOUNDED implicitly. Given $c$ and $t_i$, we know that there is a previously sampled point $p_1 \models c$ such that $t_i(p_1) \leqslant U[t_i]$. First, in lines 3-8, we check if there exists a model $p_2 \models \varphi$ such that $t_i(p_2) > t_i(p_1)$ and $[p_2] = [p_1]$. We do this in two stages. We first check if there exists $p_2$ such that $t_i(p_2) > t_i(p_1)$. If not, we can update the over-approximation $O$ accordingly (line 5). Otherwise, we check if there exists $p_2'$ in the same boundary class as $p_1$ (line 6). If no such $p_2'$ exists, then neither UNBOUNDED nor UNBOUNDED-FAIL applies. Given that $p_2'$ exists, we check for the existence of $p_3$ in a stronger boundary class (lines 9-13). If $p_3$ exists, we apply UNBOUNDED-FAIL; otherwise, we apply UNBOUNDED.

***Scheduling Policy*** Our implementation is a scheduling of SYMBA's rules (Fig. 3) that satisfies the fairness conditions (in Sec. 3.4).

We start by applying the GLOBALPUSH rule to obtain an initial point $p$. We generate a $k$-sequence starting at $p$ (for each $t \in T$) by applying UNBOUNDED(-FAIL) until either UNBOUNDED is applicable (in which case the objective is unbounded) or UNBOUNDED-FAIL is not applicable (in which case we apply GLOBALPUSH to obtain a new initial point and start the process again). It is easy to check that this is a fair sequence, and therefore this process always terminates.

To evaluate variations of the scheduling policy described above, we instrumented our implementation with a parameter *balance* $\in (0, 100]$ which ensures that UNBOUNDEDIMPL does not take more than *balance*% of the total execution time. Specifically, during execution, if UNBOUNDEDIMPL has taken more than *balance*% of the elapsed time, SYMBA switches to applying the GLOBALPUSH rule until the time taken by UNBOUNDEDIMPL so far is less than *balance*% of the elapsed time. Intuitively, when *balance* is 100, the deterministic schedule described above is in effect.

***Optimizations*** Another effective optimization is to limit $\mathcal{E}(\varphi)$ to a "relevant" subset when applying the UNBOUNDED rule. In our experiments, we noticed that the set $\mathcal{E}(\varphi)$ of equality constraints can be quite large, which burdens the SMT solver. Removing irrelevant equality constraints decreases the size of the SMT queries. To find the set of "relevant" constraints, we define a relation $\propto$: $Atoms(\varphi) \times Atoms(\varphi)$ as follows: $P \propto P'$ if and only if

1. $Vars(P) \cap Vars(P') \neq \emptyset$, or
2. $\exists P'' \in Atoms(\varphi) \cdot P \propto P'' \wedge P'' \propto P'$,

where $Vars(P)$ is the set of variables appearing in $P$.

We then define *the boundary class of p w.r.t. t* as $[p]_t = \{a \in \mathcal{E}(\varphi) \mid p \models a \wedge t \propto a\}$. Removing constraints that are not $\propto$-related to $t$ corresponds to carrying out our algorithm on the projection of $\varphi$ onto a lower-dimensional space, where the projection is guaranteed to have the same maximum value for $t$ as $\varphi$; thus correctness is not affected.

| STATISTIC | AVG. | MAX. | MIN. | STD. |
|---|---|---|---|---|
| # of Variables | 882 | 19,170 | 40 | 1,647 |
| # of Objectives | 56 | 386 | 20 | 15 |
| # of Nodes in DAG | 7,278 | 127,987 | 1,121 | 10,619 |

**Table 1.** Aggregate statistics of our 1,065 benchmarks.

## 4.2 Experimental Evaluation

Our experimental evaluation is designed to compare SYMBA against other symbolic optimization techniques, and to assess the effectiveness of our different implementation heuristics.

We conducted two classes of experiments: (1) a comparison with existing SMT-based optimization techniques [57]; and (2) an evaluation of the effects of different implementation heuristics, as well as information reuse among multiple objectives, on the efficiency of SYMBA. We describe these in detail below.

***Benchmarks*** As discussed in Sec. 1, one possible application of optimization is computing abstract transformers for numerical abstract domains. We have incorporated SYMBA into the UFO program analysis and verification framework [5] and used it as an abstract transformer (abstract post operator) for the family of *Template Constraint Matrix* (TCM) domains [55]. A TCM domain is parameterized by a set of *templates* $T = \{t_1, \ldots, t_n\}$, which are linear expressions over program variables. Given an abstract state $\varphi_{pre}$ describing a set of initial (pre) states and a loop-free program fragment encoded as a formula $\varphi_{lf}$, the best (most precise) abstract transformer for a TCM domain computes the strongest formula $\bigwedge t_i \leqslant k_i$ that is implied by $\varphi_{pre} \wedge \varphi_{lf}$. Thus, we can use SYMBA to compute the best abstract transformer by simply computing $\mathsf{opt}_T(\varphi_{pre} \wedge \varphi_{lf})$. Note that the TCM domains subsume a number of popular domains, including intervals, octagons, octahedra, etc. For instance, by setting $T$ to all live variables and their negation at the destination program location, then we get an intervals domain, since the result of SYMBA can be interpreted as the minimum and maximum value of each program variable after executing the program fragment denoted by $\varphi_{lf}$.

We generated our benchmarks from a set of C programs used in the 2013 Software Verification Competition (SV-COMP) [1]. The programs cover a range of software, from Linux and Windows device drivers to models of SSH and sequentialized concurrent SystemC programs.[3] We narrowed the set down to 604 C programs that were not trivially discharged (proved correct or incorrect) by UFO. We instrumented UFO to record abstract post queries in SMT-LIB2 format, and collected 10K+ queries made by UFO on these C programs.

Each abstract post query is represented by a formula encoding a set of initial states and a program fragment between two cutpoints (as in *large block encoding* [12, 33]). For the set of objectives, we used all variables (as well as their negation) that are in scope at the destination cutpoint (i.e., an intervals domain). From the generated queries, we selected the hardest 1,065 benchmarks for evaluation (which took SYMBA more than 0.5s to process). Table 1 shows the average, maximum, minimum, and standard deviation, of the number of variables, objective functions, and nodes in the DAG representation of the formulas in our benchmarks. We conducted all of our experiments on a machine running Linux with an Intel i5 3.1GHz processor and 4GB of RAM.

[3] We drew 2,000+ programs from the following SV-COMP categories: `ControlFlowIntegers`, `SystemC`, `ProductLines`, and `DeviceDrivers64`.

***Comparing with Existing Tools*** To the best of our knowledge, the work of Sebastiani and Tomasi [57] is the only other SMT technique that addresses the problem of finding optimal assignments for LRA objective functions. At a high level, the technique works as follows:

**A** Sample a satisfiable disjunct $\varphi_d$ from a given formula $\varphi$ using an SMT solver.

**B** Since $\varphi_d$ is a conjunction of atoms, the linear arithmetic atoms in $\varphi_d$ represent a convex polyhedron. So, use any *linear programming* (LP) solver to find the optimal value of a given objective function within the given disjunct.

**C** Check, using an SMT solver, whether the result is optimal for all of $\varphi$. If not, go back to step **A** and sample a new disjunct. The process is guaranteed to terminate since there are finitely many disjuncts.

We have acquired a binary of the implementation described in [57] from the authors. Their tool is called OPT-MATHSAT, as it is built in the MATHSAT SMT solver [18]. There are two issues threatening the validity of a direct comparison between SYMBA and OPT-MATHSAT: (1) OPT-MATHSAT accepts a single objective function, meaning that we have to call it multiple times per benchmark, each time with a different objective. Since we do not have access to its source code, we cannot tell if multiple calls to OPT-MATHSAT incur significant pre-processing overhead. (2) Our implementation of SYMBA uses Z3 as its underlying SMT solver, whereas OPT-MATHSAT uses MATHSAT.

In order to avoid these issues and establish a fairer comparison, we have implemented two versions of the *linear search* (LS) algorithm proposed in [57] and implemented in OPT-MATHSAT:

1. LS(OPT-Z3): By accessing the available Z3 source code [3], we modified the linear arithmetic solver of Z3 to allow optimization of LRA objectives in the satisfying assignments. A DPLL($T$) [26] solver like Z3 lazily finds propositionally satisfiable disjuncts (conjunctions of atoms) from a given formula $\varphi$, and uses a (theory) $T$-solver to decide the satisfiability of the atoms (in our case linear constraints) [24]. We instrumented Z3's linear arithmetic solver such that it does not terminate immediately after the first satisfying assignment is found, but finds an optimal satisfying assignment for a given objective function. This was implemented using the standard incremental simplex solving procedure under exact (rational) representation. We call the modified tool OPT-Z3. LS(OPT-Z3) is an implementation of LS in Z3 that uses OPT-Z3 as its LP solver. This is analogous to the implementation described in [57], where a modified version of MATHSAT's linear arithmetic solver is used as the LP solver.
2. LS(LP) uses an off-the-shelf LP solver as its convex optimization engine. We have chosen two well-known open source LP libraries: the GNU Linear Programming Kit (GLPK) [40] and the Sequential Object-oriented Simplex (SOPLEX) [62] [4].

Both versions of LS use Z3 for sampling disjuncts and checking optimality (i.e., steps **A** and **C** above), but different LP solvers for finding optimal values (step **B**). Unlike OPT-MATHSAT, both LS(OPT-Z3) and LS(LP) accept multiple objective functions, and optimize them simultaneously. Specifically, in step **B**, they make multiple calls to the LP solver to find an optimal value for each objective function.

[4] We used GLPK v4.51 custom-built. The solver implements the primal two-phase simplex method based on floating point arithmetic. We used SOPLEX v1.7.1, which uses floating point arithmetic.

**SYMBA *Configurations*** We use the following SYMBA configurations:

1. SYMBA($X$): SYMBA with different scheduling policies, where $X$ specifies the value of *balance*.
2. SYMBAONEOBJ: Same as SYMBA(100), but optimizes a single objective at a time. That is, execution is restarted from scratch for each objective function.
3. SYMBA$(X)^{\text{OPT-Z3}}$: Same as SYMBA($X$), but uses Z3 with the modified linear arithmetic solver OPT-Z3 (we describe this in more detail below).

***Results:* SYMBA *vs. Other Techniques*** Fig. 5(a) shows the results of running SYMBA(100) vs. OPT-MATHSAT on the 1,065 SMT-LIB2 benchmarks with a timeout of 100 seconds per benchmark. Each point on the graph represents a benchmark. The axes correspond to the CPU time (measured in seconds—log scale) taken by SYMBA(100) ($x$-axis) and OPT-MATHSAT ($y$-axis). The points above the diagonal represent problems where SYMBA is faster. Points at the top right corner are cases where both OPT-MATHSAT and SYMBA(100) cannot complete the benchmark in the allotted 100 seconds[5]. OPT-MATHSAT has 13 timeouts vs. 19 timeouts by SYMBA(100). Our results clearly show that SYMBA(100) outperforms OPT-MATHSAT on our set of benchmarks in most cases. The average and maximum speed up of SYMBA(100) vs. OPT-MATHSAT are 2.2x and 10.4x, respectively.

We now compare SYMBA against our multi-objective-function implementation of the linear search algorithm employed by OPT-MATHSAT. Fig. 5(b) compares the execution times of SYMBA(100) vs. LS(OPT-Z3). The results clearly demonstrate the superior performance of LS(OPT-Z3): most benchmarks are solved in less time by LS(OPT-Z3), often by an order of magnitude. LS(OPT-Z3) has 7 timeouts.

To understand the reasons behind these performance differences, we took a closer look at the benchmarks where SYMBA(100) is significantly slower than LS(OPT-Z3). We noticed two recurring problems for SYMBA on these benchmarks: (1) the majority of the time is spent in the UNBOUNDEDIMPL function, indicating the expensive nature of UNBOUNDEDIMPL calls and ineffectiveness of our scheduling strategy when *balance*=100; (2) applications of GLOBALPUSH make very small expansions to the under-approximation $U$, indicating that we prefer *guided* applications of GLOBALPUSH. To address point (1), we ensured that UNBOUNDEDIMPL does not take more than 40% of the execution time by setting *balance* to 40. To address point (2), we considered applying GLOBALPUSH using OPT-Z3 (described above) instead of Z3. That is, instead of GLOBALPUSH asking Z3 for a point that lies outside the under-approximation $U$, we made GLOBALPUSH supply OPT-Z3 with one of the objective functions, and whenever the Z3's DPLL($T$) solver finds a satisfiable disjunct with a point outside the under-approximation, it finds a satisfying assignment that maximizes that objective function within that disjunct. This causes the GLOBALPUSH rule to produce models that are *farther away* from the current under-approximation, expediting convergence. We call this configuration SYMBA$(40)^{\text{OPT-Z3}}$.

Fig. 5(c) compares the execution times of SYMBA$(40)^{\text{OPT-Z3}}$ vs. LS(OPT-Z3). The results now show that SYMBA$(40)^{\text{OPT-Z3}}$ outperforms LS(OPT-Z3) on 81% of the benchmarks, with a 5.0x maximum speedup and a 1.4x average speedup per benchmark. Moreover, SYMBA$(40)^{\text{OPT-Z3}}$ solves all 1,065 benchmarks without timing out. We have also run the two other configurations of lin-

[5] Since OPT-MATHSAT accepts a single objective at a time, we invoked it multiple times per benchmark, giving it a timeout of 100 seconds per objective. If the total time (for all objectives) taken for a benchmark is more than 100 seconds, OPT-MATHSAT is considered to have timed out.

ear search, LS(GLPK) and LS(SoPLEX). They exhibit similar behaviour to LS(OPT-Z3), but are slightly slower. We cross-checked all results produced by different tools (when they do not timeout) and all of them match.

***Results:* SYMBA*'s Configurations*** Table 2 summarizes the results of running all the aforementioned algorithms and configurations on the same set of benchmarks with a timeout of 100 seconds per benchmark. The results of running SYMBA(100) are summarized in row 1 of Table 2. SYMBA(100) was able to solve 1,046 out of 1,065 benchmarks in 3,841 seconds. In the process, it made ~395K SMT queries using 24,387 invocations of GLOBALPUSH and 164,156 invocations of UNBOUNDEDIMPL.

Rows 2-3 capture the results of running SYMBA($X$), where $X$ is 60 and 20, respectively. When $X$ is 60 (time spent in UNBOUNDEDIMPL is restricted to 60% of the total time) the number of GLOBALPUSH calls goes up by about 400%. Time is spent in making unguided discovery rather than big leap towards the goal. This even affects UNBOUNDEDIMPL, the number of calls slightly increases since more points are sampled. When $X$ is 20, it was only able to solve 766 benchmarks, for which the number of calls to GLOBALPUSH goes above 130K while the number of calls to UNBOUNDEDIMPL drops to ~42K. Our experiments show that 100 is the best value for *balance* when running SYMBA($X$)[6]. Conversely, when running SYMBA$(X)^{\text{OPT-Z3}}$, we found that we greatly benefit from a lower *balance* value (*balance*=40 gives us best performance), since there the GLOBALPUSH rule can discover unbounded objectives, alleviating the pressure on UNBOUNDEDIMPL.

SYMBAONEOBJ (see Row 4 of Table 2) was able to solve 1,045 problems in 6,867 seconds. SYMBAONEOBJ uses the same configuration as SYMBA(100) except that it finds solutions for multiple objectives independently, without reusing models amongst different objectives (as SYMBA does). Using SYMBAONEOBJ causes the number of SMT queries to go up by 15% and the number of GLOBALPUSH calls to increase by 300%. Optimizing multiple objective functions simultaneously ensures that all objectives benefit from the sampled models and potentially avoids repeating expensive SMT calls.

***Summary*** The experiments compare our proposed SMT-based symbolic optimization algorithm with existing techniques and highlight the effectiveness of various implementation heuristics and optimizations. We compared SYMBA with OPT-MATHSAT as well as two LP based implementations of its algorithm on a large set of benchmarks generated from program analysis tasks. The results demonstrate the power of SYMBA's approach. A configuration that employs both efficient scheduling policy and convex optimization outperforms them all and solves all the benchmarks. Our experiments also demonstrate the importance of SYMBA's multi-objective-function capability.

## 5. Related Work

Our work intersects with different areas of research. In this section, we compare SYMBA with (1) other optimization techniques in SAT and SMT solvers; (2) optimization techniques employed within the context of abstract interpretation [21]; (3) linear programming techniques; and (4) classification techniques from the machine learning community.

***Optimization in SAT/SMT*** Within the SMT and SAT solving arena, numerous forms of optimization have been proposed (e.g., MAX-SAT/SMT in Yices [2]). The closest to SYMBA is the recent of work of Sebastiani and Tomasi [57]. Similar to SYMBA, they propose an SMT-based solution for optimizing objective functions in LRA, and to the best of our knowledge, this is the only other work that addresses this problem. As explained in Sec. 4, this approach works by sampling a satisfiable disjunct (convex polyhedron) from a given formula using the SMT solver as a black box. Then, using any LP solver, it finds the optimal value of an objective function in that disjunct. It then checks if the optimal value is globally optimal (again, using the SMT solver); otherwise, more disjuncts are sampled. Effectively, this approach lazily builds the DNF of a formula until the disjunct with the optimal value of a given objective function is found. Compared to [57], SYMBA does not require an off-the-shelf LP solver (or access to a modified theory solver within the SMT solver [57]) Instead, SYMBA offers a simple and elegant optimization algorithm that can be easily implemented on top of existing SMT solvers, without using any external tools. Moreover, SYMBA can simultaneously optimize multiple objective functions. SYMBA also maintains an over-approximation of the optimal solution, allowing us to prematurely terminate it and still retrieve optimal values for a subset of the objective functions. As we show in Sec. 4, the multi-objective-function feature can also be implemented within the approach of [57]. Both SYMBA and [57] can apply to formulas over mixed theories.

In [17], Cimatti et al. proposed a theory of *costs* for augmenting an SMT solver with pseudo-boolean (PB) constraints [11]. At a high level, their theory allows associating a cost with individual Boolean constraints. The goal then is to find a satisfying assignment that minimizes/maximizes the total cost. Thus, the theory of costs enables encoding *weighted MAX-SAT/SMT* problems – in fact, the two problems are equivalent. It is easy to see that SYMBA subsumes the weighted MAX-SMT problem. For example, we can associate with each Boolean constraint $B_i$ a cost $c_i$, and add a constraint $\mathsf{ite}(B_i, c_i = k_i, c_i = 0)$, where $k_i \in \mathbb{R}$. Then, our objective is to minimize or maximize the sum of all costs $c_1 + \ldots + c_n$.

Another form of optimization in the SMT framework is that of Nieuwenhuis and Oliveras [47]. Their optimization technique extends the traditional DPLL($T$) algorithm for SMT solving with extra rules for strengthening the theory $T$ midway during execution, e.g., a theory solver for linear arithmetic might be strengthened to find only assignments with values less than 10. This allows guiding the solver towards satisfying assignments that maximize or minimize certain objective functions. The authors show how to implement weighted MAX-SMT in their general framework. It is unclear to us if their theory strengthening approach can be used to implement an optimization procedure for LRA objective functions (as in this paper). Moreover, unlike SYMBA, their approach is not easily implementable, as it requires deep modifications to an SMT solver.

In more recent work [16], Chaganty et al. consider the problem of finding *most likely* satisfying assignments in the presence of probabilistic constraints. There, an SMT solver is used to handle axioms, i.e., constraints with 0 or 1 probabilities, and a *relational solver* (e.g., [48]) is used to handle other probabilistic constraints. It is important to note that the relational solver can be replaced by a weighted MAX-SMT solver (as noted in [16]). Thus, SYMBA can be directly applicable to solving such problems. We leave this interesting direction for future work.

***Optimization in Abstract Interpretation*** Numerical abstract domains have been an active subject of research due to their importance in different program analyses. As discussed earlier, an important operation in such domains is the abstract transformer (post), which can often be phrased as an optimization problem over formulas in LRA. As a result, optimization has been a subject of interest within the program analysis community.

For example, Monniaux [44] proposed an algorithm for computing best abstract transformers of *Template Constraint Matrix* (TCM) domains [55] over loop-free code. As discussed in Sec. 4,

[6] We omit SYMBA(40) and SYMBA(80) from the table as they exhibit similar performance to SYMBA(60).

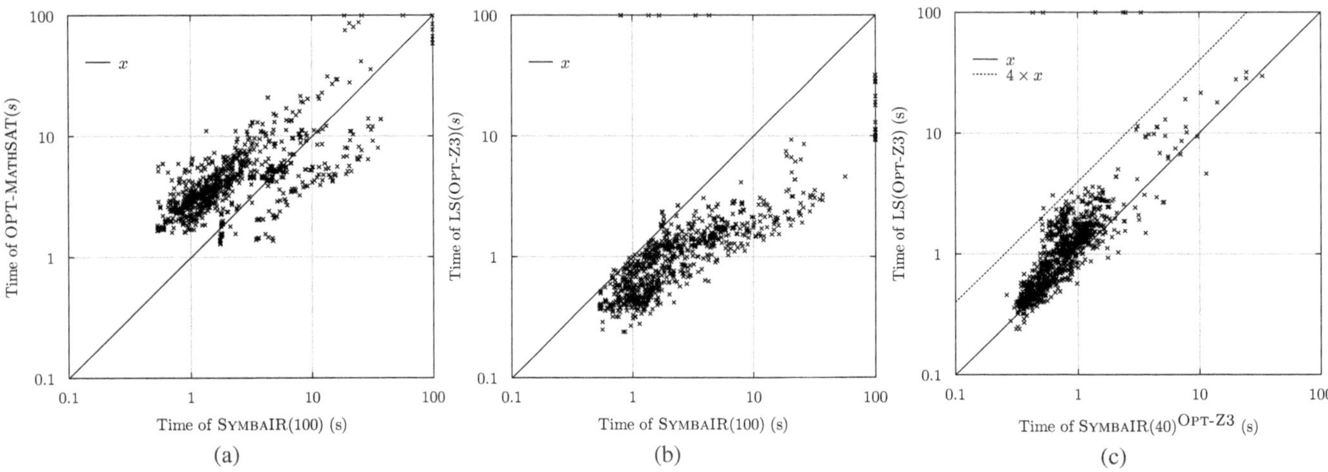


**Figure 5.** Performance comparison between (a) SYMBA(100) vs. OPT-MATHSAT, (b) SYMBA(100) vs. LS(OPT-Z3), and (c) SYMBA(40)$^{\text{OPT-Z3}}$ vs LS(OPT-Z3).

| | CONFIGURATION | TOTAL TIME(S) | # SMT QUERIES | # SOLVED | # GLOBALPUSH | # UNBOUNDEDIMPL |
|---|---|---|---|---|---|---|
| 1 | SYMBA(100) | 3,841 | 394,579 | 1,046 | 24,387 | 164,156 |
| 2 | SYMBA(60) | 5,720 | 577,068 | 1,015 | 120,112 | 179,278 |
| 3 | SYMBA(20) | 2,716 | 231,906 | 766 | 132,051 | 42,227 |
| 4 | SYMBAONEOBJ | 6,867 | 445,181 | 1,045 | 83,421 | 162,796 |
| 5 | SYMBA(40)$^{\text{OPT-Z3}}$ | 1,087 | 84,814 | 1,065 | 7,007 | 51,898 |
| 6 | OPT-MATHSAT | 5,992 | - | 1,052 | - | - |
| 7 | LS(OPT-Z3) | 1,521 | 20,829 [a] | 1,058 | - | - |
| 8 | LS(GLPK) | 3,098 | 20,854 | 1,063 | - | - |
| 9 | LS(SOPLEX) | 2,791 | 20,920 | 1,065 | - | - |

[a] We do not count calls to LP solver (including OPT-Z3) in step **B**.

**Table 2.** Overall results for different SYMBA and LS configurations, as well as OPT-MATHSAT, on the 1065 SMT-LIB2 benchmarks.

TCM domains are parameterized by a set of templates $T$, or objective functions. Loop-free program segments, along with a set of initial states, can be encoded as a formula $\varphi$ in LRA. Then, the problem of computing the *best* abstract transformer becomes that of computing $\mathsf{opt}_T(\varphi)$. This problem is known in the program analysis community as *symbolic abstraction*. The approach in [44] uses quantifier elimination, which is admissible in LRA. In later work, Monniaux and Gonnord [46] attack the problem from a different angle, using an SMT solver to sample disjuncts $\varphi_d$ of $\varphi$, and, using off-the-shelf solvers, to find the optimal solution $\mathsf{opt}_T(\varphi_d)$ of each disjunct. Surprisingly, this is done in the same manner as proposed by Sebastiani and Tomassi [57] for LRA optimization in SMT (discussed above).

Recently, Thakur and Reps [60] proposed a generalization of Stålmarck's SAT solving method [58] to richer logics. The algorithm attempts to prove a formula $\varphi$ unsatisfiable by iteratively refining an over-approximation of $\varphi$ starting from *true* until arriving at *false*. They showed how the algorithm can be instantiated with abstract domains, such as polyhedra, and used to compute best abstractions of formulas in LRA within the given abstract domain. Thus, by instantiating their algorithm with a TCM domain, we can compute $\mathsf{opt}_T(\varphi)$ for $\varphi$ in LRA. Their approach is a general framework for symbolic abstraction that is applicable to a wide range of logics and abstract domains.

In contrast to these techniques, our goal with SYMBA is to bring LRA optimization to an SMT setting, leveraging the power and generality of SMT solvers, and making optimization directly usable by researchers who are already familiar with, and actively using, SMT solvers. Additionally, with SYMBA, we do not only find the optimal value of a given objective function, but also the satisfying assignment that results in such a value (found in the set of models $M$). This is a crucial requirement when, e.g., searching for optimal counterexample witnesses, where we need a trace of the counterexample (i.e., an optimal satisfying assignment) and not the optimal value of the given objective function.

***Linear Programming*** In the field of linear programming, the optimization problem over conjunctions and disjunctions of convex polyhedra (as in our setting) has been known as *Linear Disjunctive Programming* (LDP) [6]. Later, *Linear Generalized Disjunctive Programming* (LGDP) [51] was proposed; there, Boolean variables are used to explicitly model discrete decisions. LDP and LGDP are equivalent to SYMBA when it is applied to formulas over LRA and propositional variables. Most notable approaches for solving LGDP problems carefully convert the problem to a *Mixed Integer Linear Programming* (MILP) problem, e.g., [56], and use existing MILP solvers to solve it. In comparison to such techniques, SYMBA can handle formulas over arbitrary theories (in combination with LRA), and can simultaneously optimize multiple objective functions. Additionally, SYMBA uses infinite precision rational arithmetic employed by SMT solvers, whereas LGDP solvers tend to use floating point arithmetic, potentially losing precision.

***Classification and Machine Learning*** A fundamental problem in machine learning is *classification*: given a set of positive and negative examples, find a classifier that predicts whether a given example is positive or negative. For example, using Support Vector Machines (SVMs) [50], one can compute linear inequalities separating positive and negative points in some space $\mathbb{R}^n$.

SYMBA can be viewed as a sophisticated classification algorithm, where positive and negative examples are models of $\varphi$ and $\neg\varphi$, respectively. The goal is to find the best classifier, represented by a conjunction of linear inequalities (objective functions), that does not misclassify any of the positive examples (i.e., is implied by $\varphi$). SYMBA only samples positive examples (from $\varphi$) and keeps weakening a classifier (the under-approximation $U$) until it encompasses all positive examples. As Reps et al. point out in [52], weakening an under-approximation by sampling more points is analogous to the approach of the simple learning algorithm Find-S [43]. Find-S gradually weakens a classifier, starting from *false*, by iteratively taking into account more and more positive examples.

## 6. Conclusions and Future Work

We proposed SYMBA, an efficient SMT-based optimization algorithm for objective functions stated in the theory of linear real arithmetic. SYMBA utilizes efficient SMT solvers as black boxes, making it easy to implement without requiring modifications to existing intricate SMT solver implementations, and enabling it to directly benefit from future advances in SMT solving. We have evaluated SYMBA on benchmarks drawn from abstract transformer computations for numerical abstract domains. Our thorough experimental evaluation indicates the advantages of our approach over other proposed techniques.

We see many avenues for future work. First, the most natural next step is extending SYMBA to integer arithmetic objective functions. We believe this can be done by augmenting SYMBA's rules with new ones that introduce Gomory cuts (cutting planes) [29] in order to prune infeasible solutions. Another interesting direction is handling non-linear objective functions, in order to model complex cost functions. From an engineering perspective, we would also like to study efficient parallel implementations of SYMBA's rules.

## References


[1] Competition On Software Verification - (SV-COMP). `http://sv-comp.sosy-lab.org`.

[2] Yices SMT Solver. `http://yices.csl.sri.com`.

[3] Z3 Source Code Repository. `http://z3.codeplex.com/`.

[4] A. Albarghouthi and K. L. McMillan. Beautiful Interpolants. In *Proc. of CAV'13*, pages 313–329, 2013.

[5] A. Albarghouthi, A. Gurfinkel, and M. Chechik. UFO: A Framework for Abstraction- and Interpolation-Based Software Verification. In *Proc. of CAV'12*, pages 672–678, 2012.

[6] E. Balas. Disjunctive programming: Properties of the convex hull of feasible points. *Discrete Applied Mathematics*, 89(1–3):3 - 44, 1998.

[7] T. Ball and S. Rajamani. The SLAM Toolkit. In *Proc. of CAV'01*, volume 2102 of *LNCS*, pages 260–264, 2001.

[8] C. Barrett, A. Stump, and C. Tinelli. The SMT-LIB Standard: Version 2.0. Technical report, Department of Computer Science, The University of Iowa, 2010. Available at `www.SMT-LIB.org`.

[9] C. Barrett, C. Conway, M. Deters, L. Hadarean, D. Jovanović, T. King, A. Reynolds, and C. Tinelli. CVC4. In *Proc. of CAV'11*, pages 171–177, 2011.

[10] C. W. Barrett, R. Sebastiani, S. A. Seshia, and C. Tinelli. Satisfiability modulo theories. In *Handbook of Satisfiability*, pages 825–885. 2009.

[11] P. Barth. A Davis-Putnam based enumeration algorithm for linear pseudo-Boolean optimization. Technical Report MPI-I-95-2-003, Max-Planck-Institute für Informatik, 1995.

[12] D. Beyer, A. Cimatti, A. Griggio, M. E. Keremoglu, and R. Sebastiani. Software Model Checking via Large-Block Encoding. In *Proc. of FMCAD'09*, pages 25–32, 2009.

[13] G. M. Bierman, A. D. Gordon, C. Hritcu, and D. E. Langworthy. Semantic Subtyping with an SMT Solver. *J. Funct. Program.*, 22(1): 31–105, 2012.

[14] N. Bjorner, K. McMillan, and A. Rybalchenko. Program Verification as Satisfiability Modulo Theories. In *Proc. of SMT'12*, 2012.

[15] C. Cadar, D. Dunbar, and D. R. Engler. KLEE: Unassisted and Automatic Generation of High-Coverage Tests for Complex Systems Programs. In *Proc. of OSDI'08*, pages 209–224, 2008.

[16] A. Chaganty, A. Lal, A. Nori, and S. Rajamani. Combining Relational Learning with SMT Solvers using CEGAR. In *Proc. of CAV'13*, pages 447–462, 2013.

[17] A. Cimatti, A. Franzén, A. Griggio, R. Sebastiani, and C. Stenico. Satisfiability Modulo the Theory of Costs: Foundations and Applications. In *Proc. of TACAS'10*, pages 99–113, 2010.

[18] A. Cimatti, A. Griggio, B. J. Schaafsma, and R. Sebastiani. The MathSAT5 SMT Solver. In *Proc. of TACAS'13*, pages 93–107, 2013.

[19] E. Clarke, D. Kroening, and F. Lerda. A Tool for Checking ANSI-C Programs. In *Proc. of TACAS'04*, volume 2988 of *LNCS*, pages 168–176, March 2004.

[20] P. Cousot and R. Cousot. Static Determination of Dynamic Properties of Programs. In *Proc. of the Colloque sur la Programmation*, 1976.

[21] P. Cousot and R. Cousot. Abstract Interpretation: A Unified Lattice Model For Static Analysis of Programs by Construction or Approximation of Fixpoints. In *Proc. of POPL'77*, pages 238–252, 1977.

[22] L. de Moura and N. Bjørner. Z3: An Efficient SMT Solver. In *Proc. of TACAS'08*, LNCS, pages 337–340, 2008.

[23] R. DeLine and K. R. M. Leino. BoogiePL: A Typed Procedural Language for Checking Object-oriented Programs. Technical report, Microsoft Research, 2005.

[24] B. Dutertre and L. de Moura. A Fast Linear-Arithmetic Solver for DPLL(T). In *Proc. of CAV'06*, pages 81–94, 2006.

[25] S. Falke, F. Merz, and C. Sinz. LLBMC: Improved Bounded Model Checking of C Programs Using LLVM. In *Proc. of TACAS'13*, pages 623–626, 2013.

[26] H. Ganzinger, G. Hagen, R. Nieuwenhuis, A. Oliveras, and C. Tinelli. DPLL(T): Fast Decision Procedures. In *Proc. of CAV'04*, LNCS, pages 175–188, 2004.

[27] P. Godefroid, N. Klarlund, and K. Sen. DART: Directed Automated Random Testing. In *Proc. of PLDI'05*, pages 213–223, 2005.

[28] P. Godefroid, M. Y. Levin, and D. A. Molnar. SAGE: Whitebox Fuzzing for Security Testing. *Commun. ACM*, 55(3):40–44, 2012.

[29] R. E. Gomory. Outline of an Algorithm for Integer Solutions to Linear Programs. *Bull. Amer. Math. Soc.*, 64(5):275–278, 1958.

[30] S. Grebenshchikov, N. P. Lopes, C. Popeea, and A. Rybalchenko. Synthesizing Software Verifiers from Proof Rules. In *Proc. of PLDI'12*, pages 405–416, 2012.

[31] S. Gulwani, S. Jha, A. Tiwari, and R. Venkatesan. Synthesis of Loop-Free Programs. In *Proc. of PLDI'11*, pages 62–73, 2011.

[32] A. Gupta, C. Popeea, and A. Rybalchenko. Solving Recursion-Free Horn Clauses over LI+UIF. In *Proc. of APLAS'11*, pages 188–203, 2011.

[33] A. Gurfinkel, S. Chaki, and S. Sapra. Efficient Predicate Abstraction of Program Summaries. In *Proc. of NFM'11*, volume 6617 of *LNCS*, pages 131–145, 2011.

[34] W. R. Harris, S. Sankaranarayanan, F. Ivancic, and A. Gupta. Program Analysis via Satisfiability Modulo Path Programs. In *Proc. of POPL'10*, pages 71–82, 2010.

[35] T. Henzinger, R. Jhala, R. Majumdar, and G. Sutre. Lazy Abstraction. In *Proc. of POPL'02*, pages 58–70, 2002.

[36] T. A. Henzinger, R. Jhala, R. Majumdar, and K. L. McMillan. Abstractions from Proofs. In *Proc. of POPL'04*, pages 232–244, 2004.

[37] S. Jha, S. Gulwani, S. A. Seshia, and A. Tiwari. Oracle-Guided Component-Based Program Synthesis. In *Proc. of ICSE'10*, pages 215–224, 2010.

[38] A. S. Köksal, V. Kuncak, and P. Suter. Constraints as Control. In *Proc. of POPL'12*, pages 151–164, 2012.

[39] K. R. M. Leino. Dafny: An Automatic Program Verifier for Functional Correctness. In *Proc. of LPAR'10*, pages 348–370, 2010.

[40] A. Makhorin. The GNU Linear Programming Kit. http://www.gnu.org/software/glpk/, 2000.

[41] H. Massalin. Superoptimizer: a Look at the Smallest Program. *SIGARCH Comput. Archit. News*, 15(5):122–126, Oct. 1987.

[42] A. Miné. The Octagon Abstract Domain. *J. Higher-Order and Symbolic Computation*, 19(1):31–100, 2006.

[43] T. M. Mitchell. *Machine Learning*. McGraw-Hill, Inc., New York, NY, USA, 1997.

[44] D. Monniaux. Automatic Modular Abstractions for Linear Constraints. In *Proc. of POPL'09*, pages 140–151, 2009.

[45] D. Monniaux. Automatic Modular Abstractions for Template Numerical Constraints. *Logical Methods in Computer Science*, 6(3), 2010.

[46] D. Monniaux and L. Gonnord. Using Bounded Model Checking to Focus Fixpoint Iterations. In *Proc. of SAS'11*, pages 369–385, 2011.

[47] R. Nieuwenhuis and A. Oliveras. On SAT Modulo Theories and Optimization Problems. In *Proc. of SAT'06*, pages 156–169, 2006.

[48] F. Niu, C. Ré, A. Doan, and J. Shavlik. Tuffy: Scaling Up Statistical Inference in Markov Logic Networks Using an RDBMS. *Proc. of VLDB'11*, pages 373–384, 2011.

[49] R. Piskac, T. Wies, and D. Zufferey. Automating Separation Logic using SMT. In *Proc. of CAV'13*, 2013.

[50] J. C. Platt. Fast Training of Support Vector Machines Using Sequential Minimal Optimization. In *Advances in Kernel Methods*, pages 185–208. MIT Press, 1999.

[51] R. Raman and I. Grossmann. Modelling and Computational Techniques for Logic Based Integer Programming. *Computers and Chemical Engineering*, 18(7):563 - 578, 1994.

[52] T. Reps, M. Sagiv, and G. Yorsh. Symbolic Implementation of the Best Transformer. In *Proc. of VMCAI'04*, volume 2937 of *LNCS*, 2004.

[53] P. M. Rondon, M. Kawaguchi, and R. Jhala. Liquid Types. In *Proc. of PLDI'08*, pages 159–169, 2008.

[54] A. Rybalchenko and V. Sofronie-Stokkermans. Constraint Solving for Interpolation. *J. Symb. Comput.*, 45(11):1212–1233, 2010.

[55] S. Sankaranarayanan, H. B. Sipma, and Z. Manna. Scalable Analysis of Linear Systems using Mathematical Programming. In *Proc. of VMCAI'05*, pages 25–41, 2005.

[56] N. W. Sawaya and I. E. Grossmann. A Cutting Plane Method for Solving Linear Generalized Disjunctive Programming Problems. *Computers And Chemical Engineering*, 29(9):1891 - 1913, 2005.

[57] R. Sebastiani and S. Tomasi. Optimization in SMT with $\mathcal{LA}(\mathbb{Q})$ Cost Functions. In *Proc. of IJCAR'12*, pages 484–498, 2012.

[58] M. Sheeran and G. Stålmarck. A Tutorial on Stålmarck's Proof Procedure for Propositional Logic. *FMSD*, 16:23–58, 2000.

[59] A. Solar-Lezama, L. Tancau, R. Bodík, S. A. Seshia, and V. A. Saraswat. Combinatorial Sketching for Finite Programs. In *Proc. of ASPLOS'06*, pages 404–415, 2006.

[60] A. V. Thakur and T. W. Reps. A Method for Symbolic Computation of Abstract Operations. In *Proc. of CAV'12*, pages 174–192, 2012.

[61] A. V. Thakur, M. Elder, and T. W. Reps. Bilateral Algorithms for Symbolic Abstraction. In *Proc. of SAS'12*, pages 111–128, 2012.

[62] R. Wunderling. *Paralleler und Objekt-orientierter Simplex-Algorithmus*. PhD thesis, Technische Universität Berlin, 1996.

## 7. Appendix

**Lemma 2.** *Given an $\mathcal{L}$ formula $\varphi_c$ defining a convex polyhedron (conjunction of linear constraints), if $p \models \varphi_c$, $[p] \subseteq [p']$, $t(p) \leqslant t(p')$ and $\nexists p'' \models \varphi_c \cdot t(p) \leqslant t(p'') \wedge [p] \subset [p'']$, then $p' \models \varphi_c$.*

*Proof.* Formula $\varphi_c \wedge [p]$ can be written as a system of linear inequalities as follows:

$$\mathbf{A}\vec{x} = \vec{b} \tag{1a}$$

$$\mathbf{C}\vec{x} \geqslant \vec{d} \tag{1b}$$

By definition, $p$ satisfies the system and Eq. 1a is a subset of $[p]$ according to the definition of boundary class. Because $[p] \subseteq [p']$, $p'$ must satisfy Eq. 1a. Suppose $p' \not\models \varphi_c$. Then there exists some $k$ such that $\vec{c_k} \cdot \vec{p} > d_k$ and $\vec{c_k} \cdot \vec{p'} < d_k$

Note that $\vec{c_k} \cdot \vec{p} \neq d_k$ since $\vec{c_k} \cdot \vec{p'} \neq d_k$ and $[p] \subseteq [p']$. We now show that there exists a point $\vec{p_k} = \alpha\vec{p} + (1-\alpha)\vec{p'}$ $(0 < \alpha < 1)$ in the convex hull of $p$ and $p'$ s.t. $\vec{c_k} \cdot \vec{p_k} = d_k$. Since $t(p) \leqslant t(p')$, it is easy to show that $t(p) \leqslant t(p_k)$. Let $\vec{c_k} \cdot \vec{p} = d_k + \delta_1$, $\vec{c_k} \cdot \vec{p'} = d_k - \delta_2$ (where $\delta_1 > 0$ and $\delta_2 > 0$), and $\alpha = \frac{\delta_2}{\delta_1 + \delta_2}$. We have $\vec{c_k} \cdot \vec{p_k} = d_k$. We know that $[p] \subset [p_k]$ because $p_k$ is in the convex hull of $p$ and $p'$ and $\{\vec{c_k} \cdot \vec{x} = d_k\} \notin [p] \wedge \{\vec{c_k} \cdot \vec{x} = d_k\} \in [p_k]$.

Suppose $p_k \not\models \varphi_c$, i.e., there exists $j$ s.t. $\vec{c_j} \cdot \vec{p_k} < d_j$, we then repeat the above process. Each point $p_i$ found satisfies $t(p) \leqslant t(p_i) \wedge [p] \subset [p_i]$. We are guaranteed to find a point $p''$ in the convex hull s.t. it is also within $\varphi_c$, because in each step we satisfy at least one more inequality. This contradicts the condition $\nexists p'' \models \varphi_c \cdot t(p) \leqslant t(p'') \wedge [p] \subset [p'']$. Therefore, $p' \models \varphi_c$. □

***Proof of Thm. 1*** ($\Leftarrow$) We prove this direction by contradiction. First, let $p_1, p_2 \models \varphi$ be two models satisfying the three conditions of the theorem. Suppose there is a point $p^* \models \varphi$ s.t. $t(p^*)$ is the upper bound for $t$ in $\varphi$. We show that there is always a point $p_2' \models \varphi$ s.t. $t(p_2') > t(p^*)$.

Pick a point $p_2'$ s.t. $\vec{p_2'} = \vec{p_2} + \lambda(\vec{p_2} - \vec{p_1})$. It follows that $t(p_2') > t(p^*)$ when $\lambda > \frac{(\vec{p^*} - \vec{p_2}) \cdot \vec{t}}{(\vec{p_2} - \vec{p_1}) \cdot \vec{t}}$. The notation $\vec{p}$ denotes the vector representation $(p(x_1), \ldots, p(x_n))$ of the model $p : Vars \to \mathbb{R}$, where $Vars = \{x_1, \ldots, x_n\}$.

Let the formula $\varphi'$ define a convex polyhedron s.t. $p_2 \models \varphi'$ and $\varphi' \Rightarrow \varphi$. Let $\varphi_c \equiv \varphi' \wedge \bigwedge[p_2]$. We know the following:

1. $\varphi_c$ defines a convex polyhedron (by its definition).
2. $\nexists p_2'' \models \varphi_c \cdot t(p_2) \leqslant t(p_2'') \wedge [p_2] \subset [p_2'']$ (by condition 3 of the theorem).
3. $[p_2] \subseteq [p_2']$ (since $p_2'$ is in the affine set of $p_1$ and $p_2$).
4. $t(p_2) \leqslant t(p_2')$ (since $\lambda \geqslant 0$).

Following the result of Lemma 2, $p_2'$ is in $\varphi_c$ which is also in $\varphi$. This contradicts the assumption that $t(p^*)$ is the least upper bound for $t$. Therefore, term $t$ is unbounded in $\varphi$.

($\Rightarrow$) Given that $t$ is unbounded in $\varphi$, we look for two models $p_1, p_2 \models \varphi$ that satisfy the required conditions. Pick $p_1, p_2 \models \varphi$ s.t. $[p_1] = [p_2]$, $t(p_2) > t(p_1)$, and $[p_1]$ is the most restrictive boundary class within which $t$ is unbounded (i.e., $t$ is unbounded in $\varphi \wedge \bigwedge[p_1]$, and there does not exist a boundary class $c \supset [p_1]$ s.t. $t$ is unbounded in $\varphi \wedge \bigwedge c$). We know that such a class exists because $t$ is unbounded in $\varphi$ (otherwise $t$ is bounded in every boundary class and $\varphi$ is bounded). In other words, since (1) there are infinitely many models of $\varphi$ with increasing values of $t$ and (2) finitely many boundary classes, there has to be a boundary class $[p_1]$ s.t. $t$ is unbounded in $\varphi \wedge \bigwedge[p_1]$ and there doesn't exist a class $c \supset [p_1]$ where $t$ is unbounded in $\varphi \wedge \bigwedge c$.

If there are no classes $c \supset [p_1]$, or for every $c \supset [p_1]$, $\varphi \wedge \bigwedge c \Rightarrow$ *false*, then $p_1$ and $p_2$ satisfy the three conditions of the theorem. Otherwise, let $m = \max_{p \models \varphi \wedge \psi} t(p)$, where $\psi \equiv \bigvee_{c \supset [p_1]} \bigwedge c$ (i.e., all classes stronger than $[p_1]$). We know that $m$ is defined (i.e., not $\infty$) because of our assumption on the class $[p_1]$. If $m < t(p_2)$, then $p_1$ and $p_2$ satisfy the three conditions of the theorem. Otherwise, since $t$ is unbounded in $\varphi \wedge \bigwedge[p_1]$, we can find two models $p_1', p_2' \models \varphi$ s.t. $m < t(p_1') < t(p_2')$ and $[p_1] = [p_1'] = [p_2']$. As a result, $p_1'$ and $p_2'$ satisfy the three conditions in the theorem. □

# Abstract Effects and Proof-Relevant Logical Relations


Nick Benton
Microsoft Research, Cambridge, UK
nick@microsoft.com

Martin Hofmann
LMU, Munich, Germany
hofmann@ifi.lmu.de

Vivek Nigam
UFPB, João Pessoa, Brazil
vivek.nigam@gmail.com



## Abstract

We give a denotational semantics for a region-based effect system that supports type abstraction in the sense that only externally visible effects need to be tracked: non-observable internal modifications, such as the reorganisation of a search tree or lazy initialisation, can count as 'pure' or 'read only'. This 'fictional purity' allows clients of a module to validate soundly more effect-based program equivalences than would be possible with previous semantics. Our semantics uses a novel variant of logical relations that maps types not merely to partial equivalence relations on values, as is commonly done, but rather to a proof-relevant generalisation thereof, namely setoids. The objects of a setoid establish that values inhabit semantic types, whilst its morphisms are understood as proofs of semantic equivalence. The transition to proof-relevance solves two awkward problems caused by naïve use of existential quantification in Kripke logical relations, namely failure of admissibility and spurious functional dependencies.



***Categories and Subject Descriptors*** D.3.3 [*Programming Languages*]: Language Constructs and Features – Dynamic storage management; F.3.2 [*Logic and Meanings of Programs*]: Semantics of Programming Languages – Denotational semantics, Program analysis; F.3.2 [*Logic and Meanings of Programs*]: Studies of Program Constructs – Type structure

***General Terms*** Languages, Theory

***Keywords*** Type and effect systems, region analysis, logical relations, parametricity, program transformation


## 1. Introduction

The last decade has witnessed significant progress in modelling and reasoning about the tricky combination of effects and higher-order language features (first-class functions, modules, classes). The object of study may be ML-like, Java-like, or assembly-like, but the common source of trickiness is the way effectful operations may be *partially* encapsulated behind higher-order abstractions. Several closely-related problems have been addressed using common techniques that include separation, Kripke logical relations and step-indexing. One is to devise models and reasoning principles for establishing contextual (in)equivalences [18, 36]. A second is to establish equivalence between high-level and low-level code fragments, *e.g.*, for compiler correctness [5, 23]. A third is to define Hoare-style logics for showing programs satisfy assertions [38]. A fourth, which we address here, is to study type systems and analyses that can characterize particular *classes* of behavior (such as purity) and be used to justify equivalences more generically.

Effect systems [22] refine conventional types by adding information capturing an upper bound on the effects expressions may have. Several recent papers [3, 6, 7, 26, 41], have explored the semantics of effect systems, with a focus not merely on showing correctness of analyses, but on providing a rigorous account of the conditions under which effect-dependent optimizations and refactorings are sound. An example is the commutation of stateful computations $M$ and $N$, subject to the condition that the sets of storage locations potentially written by $M$ and $N$ are disjoint, and that neither potentially reads a location that the other writes.

We seek interpretations of effect-refined types (over an unrefined model) that can justify such equivalences. Indeed, it is the interpretations, rather than rules for assigning such types to terms, that we regard as primary. Types provide a common interface language that can be used by clients in modular reasoning about rewrites; types can be assigned to particular terms by a mixture of more or less sophisticated inference systems, or by deeper semantic reasoning about particular implementations.

A key notion in reasoning about encapsulated state is that of *separation*: invariants depending upon mutually disjoint parts of the store. Intuitively, if each function with direct access to a part preserves the corresponding invariant, then all the invariants will be preserved by any composition of functions. Disjointness is naïvely understood in terms of sets of heap locations. A memory allocator, for example, guarantees that its own private data structures, memory previously handed out to clients, and any freshly-allocated block inhabit mutually disjoint sets of locations. Since the introduction of fractional permissions, work on separation logic often goes beyond this simple model, introducing resources that are combined with a separating conjunction, but which are not literally interpreted as predicates on disjoint locations. Research on 'domain-specific' [28], 'fictional' [17, 25], 'subjective' [30], or 'superficial' [29] separation logics and type theories aims to allow custom notions of separable resource to be introduced and combined modularly. This paper presents a semantics for effect systems supporting fictional, or 'abstract', notions of both effects and separation.

We have previously interpreted effect-refined types for stateful computations as binary relations, defined via preservation of particular sets of store relations [7]. This already provides some abstraction. The semantics is extensional so, for example, a function that reads a reference cell but doesn't produce observably different results depending on the value read can soundly be counted as pure (contrasting with, for example, models of permissions that instrument the concrete semantics). Such a semantics can also interpret the 'masking' rule, allowing certain non-observable effects not to appear in annotations [6]. But here we go further, generalizing the interpretation of regions to, intuitively, partial equiva-




*POPL '14*, January 22–24, 2014, San Diego, CA, USA.
Copyright © 2014 ACM 978-1-4503-2544-8/14/01...$15.00.
http://dx.doi.org/10.1145/2535838.2535869

lence relations. This allows, for example, a lookup function for a set ADT to be assigned a read-but-not-write effect, even though the concrete implementation may involve non-observable writes to rebalance an internal datastructure. Moving to PERs in this way requires us to revisit the notion of separation, allowing types to involve distinct regions whose concrete implementations overlap, albeit non-observably, in memory.

Earlier models of dynamic allocation [6] have used Kripke logical relations in which worlds are finite partial bijections between locations, with region-colored links. Two computations $c, c' : \mathbb{H} \rightharpoonup \mathbb{H} \times \mathbb{V}$, where $\mathbb{H}, \mathbb{V}$ are sets of (partial) heaps and values, respectively, are in the computation relation $T_\varepsilon[\![A]\!]\mathsf{w}$, for world $\mathsf{w}$, effect $\varepsilon$ and result type $A$ when $\forall \mathsf{h}, \mathsf{h}', \mathsf{h}_1, \mathsf{h}'_1.\ \mathsf{h}, \mathsf{h}' \models \mathsf{w} \Rightarrow \exists \mathsf{w}_1 \geq \mathsf{w}.\ \mathsf{h}_1, \mathsf{h}'_1 \models \mathsf{w}_1 \wedge (\mathsf{h}, \mathsf{h}_1, \mathsf{h}', \mathsf{h}'_1, \mathsf{w}, \mathsf{w}_1) \in [\![\varepsilon]\!] \wedge (v, v') \in [\![A]\!]\mathsf{w}_1$ where $c\,\mathsf{h} = (\mathsf{h}_1, v)$ and $c'\,\mathsf{h}' = (\mathsf{h}'_1, v')$. Here, $[\![A]\!]\mathsf{w}_1$ is the (world-dependent) logical relation at the result type and $[\![\varepsilon]\!]$ the interpretation of the effect, which can be given in various ways, *e.g.*, in terms of binary relations on stores to be preserved. The notation $\mathsf{h}, \mathsf{h}' \models \mathsf{w}$ means that for each link $(\mathsf{l}, \mathsf{l}') \in \mathsf{w}$, $\mathsf{l} \in \mathrm{dom}(\mathsf{h})$, $\mathsf{l}' \in \mathrm{dom}(\mathsf{h}')$.

However, generalizing such a logical relation from bijections to PERs is surprisingly difficult. The problematic part is the existential quantification over world extensions: $\exists \mathsf{w}_1 \geq \mathsf{w}$. This says that $c$ and $c'$ are related at world $\mathsf{w}$ if there is *some* future world $\mathsf{w}_1$, allowing for the computations to perform allocations, at which the respective final states and values are related. This pattern of quantification occurs in many accounts of generativity, but the dependence of $\mathsf{w}_1$ on both $\mathsf{h}$ and $\mathsf{h}'$ creates a difficulty when one generalizes from bijections to PERs and tries to prove equivalences. Roughly, one has to consider varying the initial heap in which one computation, say $c'$, is started; the existential then supplies one with a *different* extension that is not at all related, even on the side of $c$ where the heap stays the same, to the one with which one started. In the case of bijections, the fact that $\mathsf{h}_1$ depends only on $\mathsf{h}$ (not on $\mathsf{h}'$) allows one to deduce sufficient information about the domain of $\mathsf{w}_1$ from the clause $\mathsf{h}_1, \mathsf{h}'_1 \models \mathsf{w}_1$, but this breaks down in the more abstract setting.

To fix this problem, we will essentially replace the existential quantifier in the logical relation by appropriate Skolem functions, explicitly enforcing the correct dependencies. In the language of type theory, this amounts to replacing the existential with a $\Sigma$-type. A statement like $(c, c') \in T_\varepsilon[\![A]\!]$ is no longer just a proposition, but we rather have a "set of proofs" $(p : c \sim c') \in T_\varepsilon[\![A]\!]$, and our constructions will explicitly maps proofs to proofs.

We have previously shown [4] how the formalism of *setoids* can be used to make such intuitions both rigorous and more general. That work, dealing with a version of Pitts and Stark's $\nu$-calculus, used proof-relevant setoids to solve another problem associated with the use of existential quantification: that it fails to preserve admissibility of predicates and relations and so interacts badly with general recursion. Here we show how that technology scales to a much richer language and type system.

## 2. Motivating Examples

We will assign effect-refined types to terms in a fairly conventional monadically-structured untyped metalanguage with higher-order functions and dynamically allocated references to flat data. The language is defined formally later on, but the following examples of the kind of equivalences and typings we will be able to justify should be comprehensible.

***Memoisation*** Let *memo* be the function

$$\begin{array}{l}\lambda f.\mathtt{let}\ x \Leftarrow \mathtt{ref}(\underline{0})\ \mathtt{in}\ \mathtt{let}\ y \Leftarrow \mathtt{ref}(f\ \underline{0})\ \mathtt{in} \\ \quad \lambda a.\mathtt{if}\ a\ = !x\ \mathtt{then}\ !y\ \mathtt{else}\ \mathtt{let}\ r \Leftarrow f\ a\ \mathtt{in}\ x := a; y := r; r\end{array}$$

where $t_1; t_2\ =\ \mathtt{let}\ \_ \Leftarrow t_1\ \mathtt{in}\ t_2$ is sequential composition and $=$ is equality on storable values. So, *memo* returns a memoized version of its argument. Unlike previous models of effects, our model justifies the typing $memo : (int \xrightarrow{\emptyset} int) \xrightarrow{\emptyset} (int \xrightarrow{\emptyset} int)$, saying that if $f$ is observationally pure, $memo\,f$, is too, and so can participate in any program equivalence relying on purity. For example, a client can deduce the observational equivalence of the programs below purely on the basis of typing:

$$\lambda y.\mathtt{let} g \Leftarrow memo\,(\lambda x.x + 1)\mathtt{in}\, e \equiv \mathtt{let} g \Leftarrow memo\,(\lambda x.x + 1)\mathtt{in}\,\lambda y.e$$

***Overlapping references*** Let $p, p^{-1}$ implement a bijection $\mathbb{Z} \to \mathbb{Z} \times \mathbb{Z}$, then

$$\begin{array}{rl} v_{or} := \lambda\_.\mathtt{let}\ r \Leftarrow \mathtt{ref}(\underline{0})\ \mathtt{in}\,( & \!\!\lambda\_.(p(!r)).1,\ \lambda\_.(p(!r)).2, \\ & \lambda n.\mathtt{let}\,(x, y) \Leftarrow p(!r)\ \mathtt{in}\ r := p^{-1}(n, y), \\ & \lambda n.\mathtt{let}\,(x, y) \Leftarrow p(!r)\ \mathtt{in}\ r := p^{-1}(x, n)) \end{array}$$

which multiplexes two abstract integer references onto a single concrete one, can be given the type

$$\begin{array}{rl}\tau_{or} := & unit \xrightarrow{al_{\mathsf{r1}}, al_{\mathsf{r2}}} (unit \xrightarrow{rd_{\mathsf{r1}}} int) \times (unit \xrightarrow{rd_{\mathsf{r2}}} int) \times \\ & (int \xrightarrow{wr_{\mathsf{r1}}} unit) \times (int \xrightarrow{wr_{\mathsf{r2}}} unit)\end{array}$$

expressing that it allocates in two regions, r1 and r2, and returns a tuple of functions, each of which reads or writes just one region. This typing justifies, for example, permuting writes to the two abstract references.

***Set factory*** A more realistic example, for which we do not give concrete code, is a function *setfactory* that generates mutable integer sets. Calling *setfactory* allocates a new reference cell pointing to a linked list of integers (initially empty) and returns a triple of functions (*mem*, *add*, *rem*) for testing membership of the represented set, adding a new integer to the set and removing an integer from the set. The implementation of *mem* searches for its integer argument in the linked list, but at the same time mutates the list by removing duplicates and, just for fun, potentially relocating some of the nodes. The other operations can potentially perform similar optimizations.

We can justify the following semantic typing for *setfactory*:

$$setfactory : \forall \mathsf{r}.unit \xrightarrow{al_{\mathsf{r}}} (int \xrightarrow{rd_{\mathsf{r}}} bool) \times (int \xrightarrow{rd_{\mathsf{r}}, wr_{\mathsf{r}}} unit) \times (int \xrightarrow{rd_{\mathsf{r}}, wr_{\mathsf{r}}} unit)$$

which expresses that *setfactory* allocates in some (possibly fresh) region r and returns operations that, observably, only read r (the first one) and/or write in r (the second and third one) even though, physically, all three functions may read, write, and allocate concrete locations.

Thus, these functions can participate in corresponding effect-dependent program equivalences. For example, *mem* operations may be swapped and duplicated.

***Lazy Initialization*** The following definitions illustrate an 'allocate-on-write' form of lazy initialization:

$$\begin{array}{lcl} make & = & \lambda\_.\mathtt{ref}(\underline{0}) \\ getx & = & \lambda p.\mathtt{if}\ !p = \underline{0}\ \mathtt{then}\ \underline{0}\ \mathtt{else}\ !(!p.1) \\ gety & = & \lambda p.\mathtt{if}\ !p = \underline{0}\ \mathtt{then}\ \underline{0}\ \mathtt{else}\ !(!p.2) \\ setx & = & \lambda p.\lambda n.\mathtt{if}\ !p = \underline{0}\ \mathtt{then}\ p := (\mathtt{ref}(n), \mathtt{ref}(\underline{0}))\ \mathtt{else}\ !p.1 := n \\ sety & = & \lambda p.\lambda n.\mathtt{if}\ !p = \underline{0}\ \mathtt{then}\ p := (\mathtt{ref}(\underline{0}), \mathtt{ref}(n))\ \mathtt{else}\ !p.2 := n \end{array}$$

We can introduce a new abstract type $point_{\mathsf{r1},\mathsf{r2}}$ for which the following typings can be semantically justified:

$$\begin{array}{ll} make : unit \xrightarrow{al_{\mathsf{r2}}} point_{\mathsf{r1},\mathsf{r2}} & \\ getx : point_{\mathsf{r1},\mathsf{r2}} \xrightarrow{rd_{\mathsf{r1}}} int & gety : point_{\mathsf{r1},\mathsf{r2}} \xrightarrow{rd_{\mathsf{r2}}} int \\ setx : point_{\mathsf{r1},\mathsf{r2}} \xrightarrow{\emptyset} int \xrightarrow{wr_{\mathsf{r1}}} unit & setx : point_{\mathsf{r1},\mathsf{r2}} \xrightarrow{\emptyset} int \xrightarrow{wr_{\mathsf{r2}}} unit \end{array}$$

Observe that the allocation effects are flagged in the *make* function, even though the physical allocations happen on demand, in the *set* functions. Note also that semantic reasoning is necessary to justify that these definitions are well-typed at all, as a *point* holds different kinds of value at different times.

## 3. Syntax and Semantics

In this section we define the syntax and denotational semantics of our untyped metalanguage for stateful computations. We also give an effect-refined type system for this language that is parameterized by semantically-justified axioms. We omit the standard details of interpreting CBV languages via the metalanguage and of adequacy, relating the operationally induced observational equivalence to equality in the model.

***Denotational Model*** A *predomain* is an $\omega$-cpo, *i.e.*, a partial order with suprema of ascending chains. A *domain* is a predomain with a least element, $\bot$. Recall that $f : A \to A'$ is *continuous* if it is monotone $x \le y \Rightarrow f(x) \le f(y)$ and preserves suprema of chains, *i.e.*, $f(\sup_i x_i) = \sup_i f(x_i)$. Any set is a predomain with the discrete order. If $X$ is a set and $A$ a predomain then any $f : X \to A$ is continuous. A subset $U$ of a predomain $A$ is *admissible* if whenever $(a_i)_i$ is an ascending chain in $A$ such that $a_i \in U$ for all $i$, then $\sup_i a_i \in U$, too. If $f : X \times A \to A$ is continuous and $A$ is a domain then one defines $f^\dagger(x) = \sup_i f_x^i(\bot)$ with $f_x(a) = f(x,a)$. One has, $f(x, f^\dagger(x)) = f^\dagger(x)$ and if $U \subseteq A$ is admissible and $f : X \times U \to U$ then $f^\dagger : X \to U$, too. We denote a partial (continuous) function from set (predomain) $A$ to set (predomain) $B$ by $f : A \rightharpoonup B$.

We assume two sets $\mathbb{L}$ and $\mathbb{V}_b$ modelling concrete locations, and the R-values that can be stored in locations. We assume that R-values include integers, written $int(n)$ for some $n \in \mathbb{Z}$, booleans, written $bool(b)$ for $b \in \mathbb{B}$, locations $loc(\mathsf{l})$ for some $\mathsf{l} \in \mathbb{L}$, and tuples of R-values, written $(v_1, \ldots, v_n)$. We assume that it is possible to tell whether a value is of that form and in this case to retrieve the components. Heaps $\mathsf{h} \in \mathbb{H}$ are *finite maps* from $\mathbb{L} \to \mathbb{V}_b$. The domain of a heap $\mathsf{h}$ is $\mathrm{dom}(\mathsf{h}) \subseteq \mathbb{L}$. We write $\emptyset \in \mathbb{H}$ for the empty heap. If $v \in \mathbb{V}_b, \mathsf{l} \in \mathrm{dom}(\mathsf{h})$ then $\mathsf{h}[\mathsf{l} \mapsto v]$ is the heap that updates $\mathsf{l}$ to contain $v$; $new(\mathsf{h}, v)$ yields a pair $(\mathsf{l}, \mathsf{h}')$ where $\mathsf{l} \in \mathbb{L}$ and $\mathsf{h}' \in \mathbb{H}$.

The following properties hold: $\mathrm{dom}(\emptyset) = \emptyset$, $\mathrm{dom}(\mathsf{h}[\mathsf{l} \mapsto v]) = \mathrm{dom}(\mathsf{h})$, $(\mathsf{h}[\mathsf{l} \mapsto v])(\mathsf{l}') = \mathit{if}\ \mathsf{l} = \mathsf{l}'\ \mathit{then}\ v\ \mathit{else}\ \mathsf{h}(\mathsf{l}')$, and if $new(\mathsf{h}, v) = (\mathsf{l}, \mathsf{h}')$ then $\mathrm{dom}(\mathsf{h}') = \mathrm{dom}(\mathsf{h}) \cup \{\mathsf{l}\}$ and $\mathsf{l} \notin \mathrm{dom}(\mathsf{h})$ and $\mathsf{h}'(\mathsf{l}) = v$.

Note that heaps and R-values are discrete predomains; we do not here model higher-order store (storing objects with nontrivial order, such as functions). Our stores are 'flat', like those of object-oriented languages.

We define the predomain of values $\mathbb{V}$ and the domain of computations $\mathbb{C}$ simultaneously as follows: $\mathbb{C} = \mathbb{H} \rightharpoonup \mathbb{H} \times \mathbb{V}$ are partial continuous functions from $\mathbb{H}$ to $\mathbb{H} \times \mathbb{V}$, the bottom element being the everywhere undefined function. Values are defined as either R-values, tuples of values or continuous functions from values to computations: $\mathbb{V} \simeq \mathbb{V}_b + \mathit{fun}(\mathbb{V} \to \mathbb{C}) + \mathbb{V}^*$. Such domain equations can be solved by standard methods.

***Syntax*** The syntax of untyped values and computations is:

$$\begin{array}{lll} v & ::= & x \mid () \mid c \mid (v_1, v_2) \mid v.1 \mid v.2 \mid \mathtt{rec}\ f\ x = t \\ t & ::= & v \mid \mathtt{let}\ x \Leftarrow t_1\ \mathtt{in}\ t_2 \mid v_1\ v_2 \mid \mathtt{if}\ v\ \mathtt{then}\ t_1\ \mathtt{else}\ t_2 \\ & & !v \mid v_1 := v_2 \mid \mathtt{ref}(v) \end{array}$$

Here, $x$ ranges over variables and constants $c$ over constant symbols, each of which has an associated interpretation $[\![c]\!] \in \mathbb{V}$; these include numerals $\underline{n}$ with $[\![\underline{n}]\!] = int(n)$, booleans, arithmetic operations, test functions to tell whether a value is an integer, a function, a pair, or a reference, equality test for R-values, etc. $\mathtt{rec}\ f\ x = t$ defines a recursive function with body $e$ and recursive calls made via $f$; we use $\lambda x.t$ as syntactic sugar in the case when $f \notin fv(t)$. Finally, $!v$ (reading) returns the contents of location $v$, $v_1 := v_2$ (writing) updates location $v_1$ with value $v_2$, and $\mathtt{ref}(v)$ (allocating) returns a fresh location initialized with $v$. The metatheory is simplified by using "let-normal form", in which the only elimination for computations is let, though we sometimes nest computations as shorthand for let-expanded versions in examples.

The untyped denotational semantics of values $[\![v]\!] \in \mathbb{V} \to \mathbb{V}$ and terms $[\![t]\!] \in \mathbb{V} \to \mathbb{C}$ is defined in usual way by inductive clauses, which we omit here.

Types are given by the grammar

$$\tau ::= \mathtt{unit} \mid \mathtt{int} \mid \mathtt{bool} \mid A \mid \tau_1 \times \tau_2 \mid \tau_1 \xrightarrow{\varepsilon} \tau_2$$

where $A$ ranges over user-specified abstract types. They will typically include region-indexed reference types such as $\mathtt{intref}_r$ and also types like lists, sets, and even objects, again possibly refined by regions. The metavariable $\varepsilon$ represents an *effect*, that is a subset of some fixed set of elementary effects about which we say more later. The core typing rules for values and computations are shown in Figure 1. The side condition on rule Dead requires us to ascertain that $t_1$ terminates for all inputs and heaps satisfying the contracts specified in $\Gamma, \varepsilon$.

We assume an ambient set of *typing axioms* each having the form $(v, \tau)$ where $v$ is a value in the metalanguage and $\tau$ is a type meaning that $v$ is claimed to be of type $\tau$ and that this will be proved "manually" using the semantics rather than using the typing rules.

We also assume an ambient set of *equality axioms* each having the form $(v, v', \tau)$ and asserting semantic equality of $v$ and $v'$ at type $\tau$, again to be justified "manually". We assume that whenever $(v, v', \tau)$ is an axiom so are $(v, \tau)$ and $(v', \tau)$.

The equational theory can be classified in three different categories: basic, congruence and effect-dependent. An extract of the basic and congruence equations are depicted in Figure 2. The theory also includes all the usual beta and eta laws and commuting conversions for conditionals as well as for `let`. We will give a semantic interpretation of typed equality judgments which is sound for observational equivalence.

As with typings, further equations involving effectful computations may be justified semantically in a particular model and added to the theory. In particular, we can justify the soundness of four effect-based equations, namely, dead, duplicated and commuting computation, and pure lambda hoist also shown in Figure 2. The core theory then allows one to deduce new semantic equalities from already proven ones.

## 4. Abstract Locations

We now define the concept of an *abstract location* which generalizes physical locations in that it models a portion of the store that can be read from and updated. Such portion may comprise a fixed set of physical locations or a varying such set (as in the case of a linked list with some given root). It may also reside in just a part of a physical location, *e.g.*, comprise the two low order bits of an integer value stored in a physical location. Furthermore, the equality on such abstract location may be coarser than physical equality, *e.g.*, two linked lists might be considered equal when they hold the same set of elements, and there may be an invariant, *e.g.*, the linked list should contain integer entries and be neither circular nor aliased with other parts of the heap. This then prompts us to model an abstract location as a partial equivalence relation (PER) on heaps together with two more components that describe how modifications of the abstract location interact with the heap as a whole. Thus, next to a PER, an abstract location also contains a reflexive transitive relation ("guarantee") modelling its evolution by way of modifying actions.

We will define a notion of when abstract locations are independent, generalizing the traditional notion of separation. However, there is some extra complexity due to the fact that whatever custom notions of equality and separation we introduce, we would like them all to interact well with the underlying built-in allocator. A

$$\frac{}{\Gamma \vdash \texttt{true} : \texttt{bool}} \qquad \frac{}{\Gamma \vdash \texttt{false} : \texttt{bool}} \qquad \frac{}{\Gamma \vdash \underline{n} : \texttt{int}} \qquad \frac{(v,\tau) \text{ a type axiom}}{\Gamma \vdash v : \tau} \qquad \frac{}{\Gamma, x : \tau \vdash x : \tau} \qquad \frac{\Gamma \vdash v : \tau}{\Gamma \vdash v : \tau \,\&\, \emptyset}$$

$$\frac{\Gamma \vdash v : \tau_1 \times \tau_2}{\Gamma \vdash v.i : \tau_i} \qquad \frac{\Gamma \vdash v_1 : \tau_1 \quad \Gamma \vdash v_2 : \tau_2}{\Gamma \vdash (v_1, v_2) : \tau_1 \times \tau_2} \qquad \frac{\Gamma \vdash v_1 : \tau_1 \xrightarrow{\varepsilon} \tau_2 \quad \Gamma \vdash v_2 : \tau_1}{\Gamma \vdash v_1\, v_2 : \tau_2 \,\&\, \varepsilon} \qquad \frac{\Gamma, f{:}\tau_1 \xrightarrow{\varepsilon} \tau_2, x{:}\tau_1 \vdash e : \tau_2 \,\&\, \varepsilon}{\Gamma \vdash \texttt{rec}\, f\, x = e : \tau_1 \xrightarrow{\varepsilon} \tau_2} \qquad \frac{\Gamma \vdash e : \tau \,\&\, \varepsilon_1 \quad \varepsilon_1 \subseteq \varepsilon_2}{\Gamma \vdash e : \tau \,\&\, \varepsilon_2}$$

$$\frac{\Gamma \vdash v : \texttt{int} \quad \Gamma \vdash e_1 : \tau \,\&\, \varepsilon \quad \Gamma \vdash e_2 : \tau \,\&\, \varepsilon}{\Gamma \vdash \texttt{if}\, v\, \texttt{then}\, e_1\, \texttt{else}\, e_2 : \tau \,\&\, \varepsilon} \qquad \frac{\Gamma \vdash e_1 : \tau_1 \,\&\, \varepsilon \quad \Gamma, x{:}\tau_1 \vdash e_2 : \tau_2 \,\&\, \varepsilon}{\Gamma \vdash \texttt{let}\, x \Leftarrow e_1\, \texttt{in}\, e_2 : \tau_2 \,\&\, \varepsilon} \qquad \frac{\Gamma \vdash t : \tau \,\&\, \varepsilon \quad \mathsf{r} \notin \mathrm{regs}(\Gamma) \cup \mathrm{regs}(\tau)}{\Gamma \vdash t : \tau \,\&\, \varepsilon \setminus \{rd_{\mathsf{r}}, wr_{\mathsf{r}}, al_{\mathsf{r}}\}}\ \text{Masking}$$

**Figure 1.** Core rules for effect typing

Basic Equations (Extract)

$$\frac{\Gamma \vdash t : \tau \,\&\, \varepsilon}{\Gamma \vdash t = t : \tau \,\&\, \varepsilon} \qquad \frac{\Gamma \vdash t = t' : \tau \,\&\, \varepsilon}{\Gamma \vdash t' = t : \tau \,\&\, \varepsilon} \qquad \frac{\Gamma \vdash t = t' : \tau \,\&\, \varepsilon \quad \Gamma \vdash t' = t'' : \tau \,\&\, \varepsilon}{\Gamma \vdash t = t'' : \tau \,\&\, \varepsilon} \qquad \frac{\Gamma \vdash v = v' : \tau}{\Gamma \vdash v = v' : \tau \,\&\, \emptyset} \qquad \frac{\Gamma, \vdash v : \tau_1 \times \tau_2}{\Gamma \vdash v = (v.1, v.2) : \tau_1 \times \tau_2}$$

$$\frac{\Gamma \vdash v_1 : \tau_1 \quad \Gamma \vdash v_2 : \tau_2}{\Gamma \vdash (v_1, v_2).i = v_i : \tau_i} \qquad \frac{\Gamma, f : \tau_1 \xrightarrow{\varepsilon} \tau_2, x{:}\tau_1 \vdash t = t' : \tau_2 \,\&\, \varepsilon}{\Gamma \vdash (\texttt{rec}\, f\, x = t) = (\texttt{rec}\, f\, x = t') : \tau_1 \xrightarrow{\varepsilon} \tau_2} \qquad \frac{\Gamma, f : \tau_1 \xrightarrow{\varepsilon} \tau_2, x{:}\tau_1 \vdash t : \tau_2 \,\&\, \varepsilon \quad \Gamma \vdash v : \tau_1}{\Gamma \vdash (\texttt{rec}\, f\, x = t)\, v = t[v/x, (\texttt{rec}\, f\, x = t)/f] : \tau_2 \,\&\, \varepsilon}$$

$$\frac{\Gamma \vdash v : \tau_1 \,\&\, \varepsilon \quad \Gamma, x : \tau_1 \vdash t : \tau_2 \,\&\, \varepsilon}{\Gamma \vdash \texttt{let}\, x \Leftarrow v\, \texttt{in}\, t = t[v/x] : \tau_2 \,\&\, \varepsilon} \qquad \frac{\Gamma \vdash t_1 : \tau_1 \,\&\, \varepsilon \quad \Gamma \vdash t_2 : \tau_2 \,\&\, \varepsilon \quad \Gamma, x : \tau_2, y : \tau_1 \vdash t_3 : \tau_3 \,\&\, \varepsilon}{\Gamma \vdash \texttt{let}\, x \Leftarrow (\texttt{let}\, y \Leftarrow t_1\, \texttt{in}\, t_2)\, \texttt{in}\, t_3 = \texttt{let}\, y \Leftarrow t_1\, \texttt{in}\, \texttt{let}\, x \Leftarrow t_2\, \texttt{in}\, t_3 : \tau_3 \,\&\, \varepsilon} \qquad \frac{(v, v', \tau) \text{ an equality axiom}}{\Gamma \vdash v = v' : \tau}$$

Congruence Equations (Extract)

$$\frac{\Gamma \vdash v = v' : \tau_1 \times \tau_2}{\Gamma \vdash v.i = v'.i : \tau_i} \qquad \frac{\Gamma \vdash v = v' : \texttt{bool} \,\&\, \emptyset \quad \Gamma \vdash t_1 = t_1' : \tau \,\&\, \varepsilon \quad \Gamma \vdash t_1 = t_1' : \tau \,\&\, \varepsilon}{\Gamma \vdash \texttt{if}\, v\, \texttt{then}\, t_1\, \texttt{else}\, t_2 = \texttt{if}\, v'\, \texttt{then}\, t_1'\, \texttt{else}\, t_2' : \tau \,\&\, \varepsilon}$$

Effect Based Equations

$$\frac{\Gamma \vdash t_1 : \tau_1 \,\&\, \varepsilon_1 \quad \Gamma \vdash t : \tau \,\&\, \varepsilon \quad \mathrm{wrs}(\varepsilon_1) = \emptyset}{\Gamma \vdash (\texttt{let}\, x \Leftarrow t_1\, \texttt{in}\, t) = t : \tau \,\&\, \varepsilon}\ \text{Dead, provided } t_1 \text{ terminates}$$

$$\frac{\Gamma \vdash t_1 : \tau_1 \,\&\, \emptyset \quad \Gamma, x : X, y : \tau_1 \vdash t : \tau \,\&\, \varepsilon}{\Gamma \vdash (\lambda x.\texttt{let}\, y \Leftarrow t_1\, \texttt{in}\, t) = (\texttt{let}\, y \Leftarrow t_1\, \texttt{in}\, \lambda x.t) : (X \xrightarrow{\varepsilon} \tau) \,\&\, \emptyset}\ \text{Pure Lambda Hoist}$$

$$\frac{\Gamma \vdash t_1 : \tau_1 \,\&\, \varepsilon_1 \quad \Gamma, x : \tau_1, y : \tau_1 \vdash t : \tau \,\&\, \varepsilon \quad \mathrm{wrs}(\varepsilon_1) \cap \mathrm{rds}(\varepsilon_1) = \mathrm{als}(\varepsilon_1) = \emptyset}{\Gamma \vdash (\texttt{let}\, x \Leftarrow t_1\, \texttt{in}\, \texttt{let}\, y \Leftarrow t_1\, \texttt{in}\, t) = (\texttt{let}\, x \Leftarrow t_1\, \texttt{in}\, t) : \tau \,\&\, \varepsilon \cup \varepsilon_1}\ \text{Duplicated}$$

$$\frac{\begin{array}{c}\Gamma \vdash t_1 : \tau_1 \,\&\, \varepsilon_1 \quad \Gamma \vdash t_2 : \tau_2 \,\&\, \varepsilon_2 \quad \Gamma, x : \tau_1, y : \tau_2 \vdash t : \tau \,\&\, \varepsilon \\ \mathrm{rds}(\varepsilon_1) \cap \mathrm{wrs}(\varepsilon_2) = \mathrm{rds}(\varepsilon_2) \cap \mathrm{wrs}(\varepsilon_1) = \mathrm{wrs}(\varepsilon_1) \cap \mathrm{wrs}(\varepsilon_2) = \emptyset\end{array}}{\Gamma \vdash (\texttt{let}\, x \Leftarrow t_1\, \texttt{in}\, \texttt{let}\, y \Leftarrow t_2\, \texttt{in}\, t) = (\texttt{let}\, y \Leftarrow t_2\, \texttt{in}\, \texttt{let}\, x \Leftarrow t_1\, \texttt{in}\, t) : \tau \,\&\, \varepsilon_1 \cup \varepsilon_2 \cup \varepsilon}\ \text{Commuting}$$

**Figure 2.** Basic, congruence, and effect based equational theory

$$\begin{array}{ll}
\pi \cdot \mathsf{l} = \pi(\mathsf{l}) & \pi \cdot (a_1, a_2) = (\pi \cdot a_1, \pi \cdot a_2) \\
\pi \cdot (L \subseteq \mathbb{L}) = \{\pi(\mathsf{l}) \mid \mathsf{l} \in L\} & \mathrm{dom}(\pi \cdot \mathsf{h}) = \pi \cdot (\mathrm{dom}(\mathsf{h})) \\
(\pi \cdot \mathsf{h})(\mathsf{l}) = \pi \cdot (\mathsf{h}(\pi^{-1}(\mathsf{l}))) & \pi \cdot R = \{\vec{\mathsf{h}} \mid \pi^{-1} \cdot \vec{\mathsf{h}} \in R\} \\
\pi \cdot (\mathsf{h}_1, \ldots, \mathsf{h}_n) = (\pi \cdot \mathsf{h}_1, \ldots, \pi \cdot \mathsf{h}_n) &
\end{array}$$

**Figure 3.** Action of permutations

freshly allocated concrete cell should be independent of any existing abstract locations, for example, and abstract locations should not be sensitive to the behaviour of the underlying allocator. Were we working in a lower-level language (in which the allocator is just another piece of code to be verified), we would hope that concrete locations could be treated as a special case of abstract ones, but this seems to require a notion of when one notion of location is an abstraction of another (Jensen and Birkedal have taken some steps along such a path [25]). Instead, we here bake in compatibility with the underlying allocator using nominal ideas

Following Gabbay and Pitts [21], we write *perm*($\mathbb{L}$) for the group of permutations of $\mathbb{L}$ and define an action $\pi \cdot -$ of permutations $\pi \in perm(\mathbb{L})$ for values, stores, sets of locations, and relation on stores. Table 3 contains the most important cases: Note that permutations act differently on sets of locations and on sets / relations on heaps. In the sequel we call "object" anything that the permutations act on, *i.e.* locations, values, stores, etc. For example, a list of heaps $\vec{\mathsf{h}}$ is in the relation $\pi \cdot R$ iff the list of heaps obtained by undoing the permutation $(\pi^{-1} \cdot \vec{\mathsf{h}})$ is in the relation $R$. We define the set of fixpoints of a permutation $\pi$ as $\mathrm{fix}(\pi) = \{\mathsf{l} \mid \pi(\mathsf{l}) = \mathsf{l}\}$. For an object $x$, a support of $x$ is a set of locations $L$ such that $\mathrm{fix}(\pi) \supseteq L \Rightarrow \pi \cdot x = x$. Gabbay and Pitts show [21] that if an object has *a* finite support then it has a (unique) *least* support, which we write $supp(x)$.

It is clear that stores, values, and finite sets of locations always have a finite support. A store relation having a finite support is called finitely supported. For example, the predicate $P$ on stores asserting that there is a linked list starting at location $X$ has support $\{X\}$. Note that although a linked list in $\mathsf{h}$ witnessing that $\mathsf{h} \in P$ may have a large 'footprint', the support still is just $\{X\}$ because the internal nodes of such a linked list will be consistently renamed by the permutation action.

**Definition 4.1** (Abstract Location). *An* abstract location $\mathfrak{l}$ *(on the chosen set $\mathbb{H}$) consists of the following data:*

- *a non-empty, finitely supported, partial equivalence relation (PER) $\mathfrak{l}^R$ on $\mathbb{H}$ modelling the "semantic equality" on the bits of the store that $\mathfrak{l}$ uses (a "rely-condition");*
- *a finitely supported transitive relation $\mathfrak{l}^G$ modelling what bits of the store "writes to $\mathfrak{l}$" leave intact (a "guarantee condition").*

*That is, if* $(\mathsf{h}, \mathsf{h}_1) \in \mathfrak{l}^G$ *then* $\mathsf{h}_1$ *might arise by writing to* $\mathfrak{l}$ *in* $\mathsf{h}$ *and all possible writes are specified by* $\mathfrak{l}^G$*;*

*subject to the conditions, where* $\pi$ *is a permutation and* $\mathsf{h} : \mathfrak{l}^R$ *is shorthand for* $(\mathsf{h}, \mathsf{h}) \in \mathfrak{l}^R$*:*

1. *if* $\mathrm{fix}(\pi) \supseteq supp(\mathfrak{l}^R)$ *then* $\mathsf{h} : \mathfrak{l}^R \Rightarrow (\mathsf{h}, \pi \cdot \mathsf{h}) \in \mathfrak{l}^R$.
2. *if* $\mathsf{h} : \mathfrak{l}^R$ *then* $(\mathsf{h}, \mathsf{h}) \in \mathfrak{l}^G$*;*
3. *if* $(\mathsf{h}, \mathsf{h}_1) \in \mathfrak{l}^G$ *then* $\mathsf{h} : \mathfrak{l}^R$ *and* $\mathsf{h}_1 : \mathfrak{l}^R$*;*
4. $\mathfrak{l}^R; \mathfrak{l}^G \subseteq \mathfrak{l}^G; \mathfrak{l}^R$*, that is, if* $(\mathsf{h}, \mathsf{h}') \in \mathfrak{l}^R$ *and* $(\mathsf{h}, \mathsf{h}_1) \in \mathfrak{l}^G$*, then there exists* $\mathsf{h}'_1$ *such that* $(\mathsf{h}', \mathsf{h}'_1) \in \mathfrak{l}^G$ *and* $(\mathsf{h}_1, \mathsf{h}'_1) \in \mathfrak{l}^R$.
5. *if* $\mathsf{h} : \mathfrak{l}^R$ *and* $\mathsf{h}_1 \supseteq \mathsf{h}$ *then* $(\mathsf{h}_1, \mathsf{h}) \in \mathfrak{l}^R$ *thus* $\mathfrak{l}^R$ *"looks" no further than the currently allocated portion of the heap.*
6. *if* $\mathsf{h} : \mathfrak{l}^R$ *and* $(\mathsf{h} \uplus \mathsf{h}', \mathsf{h}'_1) \in \mathfrak{l}^G$*, then* $\exists \mathsf{h}_1.(\mathsf{h}, \mathsf{h}_1) \in \mathfrak{l}^G \wedge \mathsf{h}'_1 = \mathsf{h}_1 \uplus \mathsf{h}'$.

Condition 1 asserts that semantic equality is closed under relocation. It rules out relations that stipulate equality of internal pointers (not to fixed ones which would enlarge the support, but between h and h′). Conditions 5 and 6 ensure that relies and guarantees interact well with future extensions of the heap, preserving and being independent of fresh locations.

We write $\mathsf{h} \overset{\mathfrak{l}}{\sim} \mathsf{h}'$ to denote $(\mathsf{h}, \mathsf{h}') \in \mathfrak{l}^R$; $\mathsf{h} \overset{\mathfrak{l}}{\rightarrow} \mathsf{h}_1$ to denote $(\mathsf{h}, \mathsf{h}_1) \in \mathfrak{l}^G$. We also use the notation $supp(\mathfrak{l})$ for $supp(\mathfrak{l}^R) \cup supp(\mathfrak{l}^G)$.

If $\pi$ is a permutation we define $\pi \cdot \mathfrak{l} = (\pi \cdot \mathfrak{l}^R, \pi \cdot \mathfrak{l}^G)$; it is easy to see that $\pi \cdot \mathfrak{l}$ is an abstract location and $\mathrm{fix}(\pi) \supseteq supp(\mathfrak{l}) \Rightarrow \pi \cdot \mathfrak{l} = \mathfrak{l}$.

Furthermore, for any $\pi$ and $\pi'$ such that $\pi|_{supp(\mathfrak{l})} = \pi'|_{supp(\mathfrak{l})}$, one has $\pi \cdot \mathfrak{l} = \pi' \cdot \mathfrak{l}$. This makes the following definition possible:

**Definition 4.2** (relocation of abstract locations)**.** *Let* $\mathfrak{l}$ *be an abstract location and* $u : supp(\mathfrak{l}) \rightarrow \mathbb{L}$ *be injective. Then* $u \cdot \mathfrak{l}$ *is defined as* $\pi \cdot \mathfrak{l}$ *for some* $\pi$ *extending* $u$*. We have* $supp(u \cdot \mathfrak{l}) = u(supp(\mathfrak{l}))$.

For an example, consider the following abstract location $\mathfrak{set}_X$, with support $\{X\}$, implementing the set example introduced above:

$$\begin{aligned}\mathfrak{set}_X^R = \; & \{(\mathsf{h}, \mathsf{h}') \mid \text{If h and h}' \text{ contain a linked list starting from } X \\ & \text{and these lists contain the same set of integers.}\}\\ \mathfrak{set}_X^G = \; & \{(\mathsf{h}, \mathsf{h}_1) \mid \mathsf{h} : \mathfrak{l}_X^R, \mathsf{h}_1 : \mathfrak{l}_X^R \text{ and } \forall \mathsf{l}.\mathsf{l} \in \mathrm{dom}(\mathsf{h}) \setminus F(\mathsf{h}, X) \Rightarrow \mathsf{h}(\mathsf{l}) = \mathsf{h}_1(\mathsf{l})\}\end{aligned}$$

where $F(\mathsf{h}, X)$ is the set of the locations in h reached by the linked list starting from $X$. The rely set, $\mathfrak{set}_X^R$, specifies that two heaps are equivalent when linked lists denote the same set of integers. The guarantee, $\mathfrak{set}_X^G$, specifies that a write to this abstract location may not change concrete locations not in the linked list.

Note, in particular, how this example validates condition Definition 4.1(1): We can relocate one of the two linked lists without compromising relatedness in $\mathfrak{set}_X^R$ provided we leave the entry point $X$ fixed. If one tried to modify our abstract location to relate linked lists with the exact same footprint, then property 1 would fail.

**Definition 4.3** (Separated Heap)**.** *Let* $\mathfrak{l}_1, \mathfrak{l}_2, \ldots, \mathfrak{l}_n$ *be abstract locations. A heap* $\mathsf{h}$ *is separated with respect to* $\mathfrak{l}_1, \mathfrak{l}_2, \ldots, \mathfrak{l}_n$*, written* $\mathrm{sep}(\mathsf{h}, \{\mathfrak{l}_1, \mathfrak{l}_2, \ldots, \mathfrak{l}_n\})$*, iff for all* $1 \leq i \leq n$. $\mathsf{h} : \mathfrak{l}_i^R$ *and for all* $j \neq i$ *and for any heap* $\mathsf{h}_1$ *such that* $\mathsf{h} \overset{\mathfrak{l}_j}{\rightarrow} \mathsf{h}_1$*, we have* $\mathsf{h} \overset{\mathfrak{l}_i}{\sim} \mathsf{h}_1$ *and, coinductively,* $\mathrm{sep}(\mathsf{h}_1, \{\mathfrak{l}_1, \mathfrak{l}_2, \ldots, \mathfrak{l}_n\})$.

**Definition 4.4** (Independence)**.** *Abstract locations* $\mathfrak{l}_1, \mathfrak{l}_2, \ldots, \mathfrak{l}_n$ *are independent, written* $\perp(\{\mathfrak{l}_1, \mathfrak{l}_2, \ldots, \mathfrak{l}_n\})$*, if* $\mathsf{h}_1 : \mathfrak{l}_1, \ldots, \mathsf{h}_n : \mathfrak{l}_n$*, then there exists* $\mathsf{h}$*, where* $\mathrm{sep}(\mathsf{h}, \{\mathfrak{l}_1, \mathfrak{l}_2, \ldots, \mathfrak{l}_n\})$ *and* $\mathsf{h} \overset{\mathfrak{l}_i}{\sim} \mathsf{h}_i$ *for* $1 \leq i \leq n$.

The definition of independence implies that quotienting by the intersection of the PERs yields a product of the individual quotients. As the separated heap h as defined above is unique up to $\sim$ (with respect to $\mathfrak{l}_1, \ldots, \mathfrak{l}_n$), we use the notation $\mathsf{h}_1 \oplus \mathsf{h}_2 \oplus \cdots \oplus \mathsf{h}_n$ to denote a canonical separated heap.

Returning to the *setfactory* example, consider two sets $\mathfrak{set}_X$ and $\mathfrak{set}_Y$, where $X$ and $Y$ are the concrete locations where the linked lists implementing, respectively, $\mathfrak{set}_X$ and $\mathfrak{set}_Y$ start. If $X$ and $Y$ are different, we use coinduction to show $\mathfrak{set}_X$ and $\mathfrak{set}_Y$ are independent, using the following set as the witnessing co-inductive hypothesis for the separated heaps requirement:

$$\begin{aligned}P_{set} = \; & \{\mathsf{h} \mid \exists \mathsf{h}_1, \mathsf{h}_2.(\mathsf{h} = \mathsf{h}_1 \uplus \mathsf{h}_2) \wedge \\ & ([X \mapsto nil] \overset{\mathfrak{set}_X}{\longrightarrow} \mathsf{h}_1) \wedge ([Y \mapsto nil] \overset{\mathfrak{set}_Y}{\longrightarrow} \mathsf{h}_2)\}.\end{aligned}$$

This set contains the disjoint unions of any evolution of the linked lists pointed by the concrete locations $X$ and $Y$.

The following lemma will be helpful for relocating abstract locations and asserting independence.

**Lemma 4.5.** *If* $supp(\mathfrak{l}_1) \cap supp(\mathfrak{l}_2) = \emptyset$*, then* $\mathfrak{l}_1 \perp \mathfrak{l}_2$.

**Proof** Let $\mathsf{h}_1 : \mathfrak{l}_1$ and $\mathsf{h}_2 : \mathfrak{l}_2$. Let $L_1 = \mathrm{dom}(\mathsf{h}_1)$ and $L_2 = \mathrm{dom}(\mathsf{h}_2)$. Choose permutations $\pi_1$ and $\pi_2$ such that $\pi_1 \cdot L_1 \cap \pi_2 \cdot L_2 = \emptyset$ and $\mathrm{fix}(\pi_i) \supseteq supp(\mathfrak{l}_i^R)$. Define the pasted heap $\mathsf{h}_1 \oplus \mathsf{h}_2$ by

$$(\mathsf{h}_1 \oplus \mathsf{h}_2)(\mathsf{l}) = \begin{cases} (\pi_1 \cdot \mathsf{h}_1)(\mathsf{l}), \text{ if } \mathsf{l} \in \pi_1 \cdot L_1 \\ (\pi_2 \cdot \mathsf{h}_2)(\mathsf{l}), \text{ if } \mathsf{l} \in \pi_2 \cdot L_2 \\ \text{undefined otherwise} \end{cases}$$

Thus, in particular, $\mathrm{dom}(\mathsf{h}_1 \oplus \mathsf{h}_2) = \pi_1 \cdot L_1 \uplus \pi_2 \cdot L_2$.

From Def. 4.1(1) we know $(\mathsf{h}_1, \pi_1 \cdot \mathsf{h}_1) \in \mathfrak{l}_1^R$. We also have $(\mathsf{h}_1, \pi_1^{-1} \cdot (\mathsf{h}_1 \oplus \mathsf{h}_2)) \in \mathfrak{l}_1^R$ by Def. 4.1(5), thus $(\pi_1 \cdot \mathsf{h}_1, \mathsf{h}_1 \oplus \mathsf{h}_2) \in \mathfrak{l}_1^R$ so we can conclude by transitivity. The remaining properties are left to the reader. □

**Definition 4.6.** *If* $\mathfrak{l}_1, \mathfrak{l}_2$ *are independent, we form a joint location* $\mathfrak{l}_1 \otimes \mathfrak{l}_2$ *specified as follows:*

- $(\mathfrak{l}_1 \otimes \mathfrak{l}_2)^R = \{(\mathsf{h}, \mathsf{h}') \mid (\mathsf{h}, \mathsf{h}') \in \mathfrak{l}_1^R \cap \mathfrak{l}_2^R$ *and* $\mathrm{sep}(\mathsf{h}, \{\mathfrak{l}_1, \mathfrak{l}_2\})$ *and* $\mathrm{sep}(\mathsf{h}', \{\mathfrak{l}_1, \mathfrak{l}_2\})\}$
- $(\mathfrak{l}_1 \otimes \mathfrak{l}_2)^G = (\mathfrak{l}_1^G \cup \mathfrak{l}_2^G)^*$ *restricted to* $(\mathfrak{l}_1 \otimes \mathfrak{l}_2)^R$*;*

**Lemma 4.7.** *If* $\mathfrak{l}_1$ *and* $\mathfrak{l}_2$ *are independent abstract locations, then the joint location* $\mathfrak{l}_1 \otimes \mathfrak{l}_2$ *is an abstract location.*

**Lemma 4.8.** *Let* $\mathfrak{l}_1$ *and* $\mathfrak{l}_2$ *be independent abstract locations. Then* $(\mathfrak{l}_1 \otimes \mathfrak{l}_2)^G \subseteq \mathfrak{l}_1^G; \mathfrak{l}_2^G; (\mathfrak{l}_1 \otimes \mathfrak{l}_2)^R$.

**Lemma 4.9.** $\perp(\{\mathfrak{l}_1, \mathfrak{l}_2, \mathfrak{l}_3\})$ *if and only if* $\mathfrak{l}_2 \perp \mathfrak{l}_3$ *and* $\mathfrak{l}_1 \perp (\mathfrak{l}_2 \otimes \mathfrak{l}_3)$.

**Definition 4.10.** *Let* $\mathbf{1}$ *be the abstract location as follows,* $\mathbf{1}^R = \mathbb{H} \times \mathbb{H}$ *and* $(\mathsf{h}, \mathsf{h}') \in \mathbf{1}^G$ *if and only if* $\mathsf{h} = \mathsf{h}'$*. Notice that* $supp(\mathbf{1}) = \emptyset$.

**Lemma 4.11.** $\mathfrak{l}_1 \perp \mathfrak{l}_2$ *if and only if and* $\mathfrak{l}_2 \perp \mathfrak{l}_1$*. Moreover,* $\mathbf{1} \otimes \mathfrak{l} = \mathfrak{l}$.

**Remark 4.12.** *Motivated by the axioms of separation algebras [13] one might conjecture that* $\otimes$ *is cancellative, i.e. that* $\mathfrak{l}_1 \otimes \mathfrak{l} = \mathfrak{l}_2 \otimes \mathfrak{l}$ *implies* $\mathfrak{l}_1 = \mathfrak{l}_2$*. However, for the above definitions, this does not generally hold.*

### 4.1 Examples of Abstract Locations

Besides abstraction locations for sets of integers used above, we illustrate other instances of abstract locations:

***Single Integer*** For our simplest example, consider an abstract location $\mathfrak{l}_X$, parametric with respect to $X$ as follows:

$$\begin{aligned}\mathfrak{int}_X^R &= \{(\mathsf{h}, \mathsf{h}') \mid \mathsf{h}(X) = n \wedge \mathsf{h}'(X) = n' \Rightarrow int(n) = int(n')\}\\ \mathfrak{int}_X^G &= \{(\mathsf{h}, \mathsf{h}_1) \mid \mathsf{h} : \mathfrak{int}_X^R, \mathsf{h}_1 : \mathfrak{int}_X^R \text{ and } \forall \mathsf{l} \in \mathbb{L}.\mathsf{l} \neq X \Rightarrow \mathsf{h}(\mathsf{l}) = \mathsf{h}_1(\mathsf{l})\}\end{aligned}$$

Two heaps are in its rely relation if the values stored in $X$ are the same; and its guarantee is to leave all other concrete locations alone.

It is also the case that $\mathfrak{int}_X$ and $\mathfrak{int}_Y$ are independent, *i.e.*, $\mathfrak{int}_X \perp \mathfrak{int}_Y$. This is witnessed by the following co-inductive hypothesis to show the separateness condition of heaps with respect to these locations, similar to the one used before for the showing the independence of $\mathfrak{set}_X$ and $\mathfrak{set}_Y$

$$P_{int} = \{\mathsf{h} \mid \exists \mathsf{h}_1, \mathsf{h}_2.(\mathsf{h} = \mathsf{h}_1 \uplus \mathsf{h}_2) \wedge ([X \mapsto 0] \overset{\mathfrak{int}_X}{\longrightarrow} \mathsf{h}_1) \wedge ([Y \mapsto 0] \overset{\mathfrak{int}_Y}{\longrightarrow} \mathsf{h}_2)\}.$$

***Overlapping references*** Recall the overlapping references example introduced earlier. Let $X$ be the concrete location encoding a pair of values. We define abstract locations $\mathfrak{fst}_X$ and $\mathfrak{snd}_X$ by:

$$\begin{aligned}
\mathfrak{fst}_X^R = \quad & \{(\mathsf{h}, \mathsf{h}') \mid \mathsf{h}(X) = (a_1, a_2) \wedge \mathsf{h}'(X) = (a_1', a_2') \wedge a_1 = a_1'\} \\
\mathfrak{snd}_X^R = \quad & \{(\mathsf{h}, \mathsf{h}') \mid \mathsf{h}(X) = (a_1, a_2) \wedge \mathsf{h}'(X) = (a_1', a_2') \wedge a_2 = a_2'\} \\
\mathfrak{fst}_X^G = \quad & \{(\mathsf{h}, \mathsf{h}_1) \mid \mathsf{h} : \mathfrak{fst}_X^R, \mathsf{h}_1 : \mathfrak{fst}_X^R \text{ and} \\
& \quad \forall \mathsf{l} \in \mathbb{L}. \mathsf{l} \neq X \wedge \mathsf{h}(X) = (a_1, a_2) \wedge \mathsf{h}_1(X) = (a_1', a_2') \Rightarrow \\
& \quad \quad \mathsf{h}(\mathsf{l}) = \mathsf{h}_1(\mathsf{l}) \wedge a_2 = a_2'\} \\
\mathfrak{snd}_X^G = \quad & \{(\mathsf{h}, \mathsf{h}_1) \mid \mathsf{h} : \mathfrak{snd}_X^R, \mathsf{h}_1 : \mathfrak{snd}_X^R \text{ and} \\
& \quad \forall \mathsf{l} \in \mathbb{L}. \mathsf{l} \neq X \wedge \mathsf{h}(X) = (a_1, a_2) \wedge \mathsf{h}_1(X) = (a_1', a_2') \Rightarrow \\
& \quad \quad \mathsf{h}(\mathsf{l}) = \mathsf{h}_1(\mathsf{l}) \wedge a_1 = a_1'\}
\end{aligned}$$

The rely of $\mathfrak{fst}_X$ (respectively, $\mathfrak{snd}_X$) specifies that two heaps $\mathsf{h}$ and $\mathsf{h}'$ are equivalent whenever they both store a pair of values in $X$ and the first projections (respectively, second projection) of these pairs are the same. The guarantee of $\mathfrak{fst}_X$ (respectively, $\mathfrak{snd}_X$) specifies that it keeps all other locations alone and does not change the second projection (respectively, first projection) of the pair stored at location $X$.

By using a coinduction hypothesis for separated heaps similar to the ones used above, it is straightforward to verify that $\mathfrak{fst}_X$ and $\mathfrak{snd}_X$ are independent, although they share the concrete location $X$.

***Lazy Initialization*** Recall the Lazy Initialization example introduced earlier. Let $X$ be the concrete location used to store the data that is initialized. We define the following abstract location parametric on $i \in \{1, 2\}$:

$$\begin{aligned}
\mathfrak{lazy}(i)_X^R = \quad & \{(\mathsf{h}, \mathsf{h}') \mid \mathsf{h}(X) = 0 \Rightarrow \mathit{initial}(\mathsf{h}', X) \text{ and} \\
& \quad \mathsf{h}'(X) = 0 \Rightarrow \mathit{initial}(\mathsf{h}, X) \text{ and} \\
& \quad \mathsf{h}(X) = (a_1, a_2) \wedge \mathsf{h}'(X) = (a_1', a_2') \Rightarrow \mathsf{h}(a_i) = \mathsf{h}'(a_i')\} \\
\mathfrak{lazy}(i)_X^G = \quad & \{(\mathsf{h}, \mathsf{h}_1) \mid \mathsf{h} : \mathfrak{l}_X^R, \mathsf{h}_1 : \mathfrak{l}_X^R \text{ and } \mathsf{h}_1(X) = 0 \Rightarrow \mathsf{h}(X) = 0 \text{ and} \\
& \quad \mathsf{h}(X) = (a_1, a_2) \wedge \mathsf{h}_1(X) = (a_1', a_2') \Rightarrow \\
& \quad \quad \forall \mathsf{l}. \mathsf{l} \notin \{X, a_i, a_i'\} \Rightarrow \mathsf{h}(\mathsf{l}) = \mathsf{h}_1(\mathsf{l})\}
\end{aligned}$$

where $\mathit{initial}(\mathsf{h}, X)$ is the predicate $\mathsf{h}(X) = 0 \vee (\mathsf{h}(X) = (\mathsf{a}_1, \mathsf{a}_2) \wedge \mathsf{h}(\mathsf{a}_1) = 0 = \mathsf{h}(\mathsf{a}_2))$.

The rely specifies that two heaps are equivalent when either $X$ is in the initial, uninitialized, state in both of them, as specified by the predicate *initial*, or $X$ in both heaps points to a pair of references, the $i$-th of which also contain the same values. The guarantee condition specifies that $X$ in an updated heap is 0 only if it was so before, and moreover all locations not used in the rely are left unchanged.

## 5. Setoids

Abstract locations capture the invariants that we will use to build our model. The 'big picture' is that types are modelled as functors from a category of worlds into a category of setoids, with terms being interpreted as natural transformations. Worlds will comprise independent abstract locations, whilst setoids are predomains augmented with a proof-relevant notion of equality. In this section, we define the category of setoids more precisely. Section 6 then explains the structure of the category of worlds and setoid-valued functors.

While we assume that the reader is familiar with some notions of category theory, such as functor, natural transformation, and cartesian closure [31], we review some basic concepts and notation here. We compose morphisms in the usual applicative order, thus, if $f : A \to B$ and $g : B \to C$ then $gf : A \to C$. A morphism $u$ in a category $C$ is a monomorphism if $ux = ux'$ implies $x = x'$ for all morphisms $x, x'$.

A commuting square $xu = x'u'$ of morphisms is a pullback if whenever $xv = x'v'$ there is unique $t$ such that $v = ut$ and $v' = u't$. A pair of morphisms $u, u'$ with common domain is a span, a pair of morphisms $x, x'$ with common codomain is a co-span. A category has pullbacks if every co-span can be completed to a pullback square.

We define the *category of setoids* as the exact completion of the category of predomains, see [10, 14]. We recall here the elementary description using the language of dependent types given in an earlier paper *et al.* [4].

**Definition 5.1.** *A* setoid *A consists of a predomain $|A|$ and for any two $x, y \in |A|$ a set $A(x, y)$ of "proofs" (that x and y are equal). The set of triples $\{(x, y, p) \mid p \in A(x, y)\}$ must itself be a predomain and the first and second projections must be continuous. Furthermore, there are continuous functions $r_A : \Pi x \in |A|.A(x, x)$ and $s_A : \Pi x, y \in |A|.A(x, y) \to A(y, x)$ and $t_A : \Pi x, y, z.A(x, y) \times A(y, z) \to A(x, z)$, witnessing reflexivity, symmetry and transitivity; note that no equations between these are imposed.*

In the above definition, continuity of a dependent function such as $t(-, -)$ means the following: If $(x_i)_i$ and $(y_i)_i$ and $(z_i)_i$ are ascending chains in $A$ with suprema $x, y, z$, and $p_i \in A(x_i, y_i)$ and $q_i \in A(y_i, z_i)$ are proofs such that $(x_i, y_i, p_i)_i$ and $(y_i, z_i, q_i)_i$ are also ascending chains, with suprema $(x, y, p)$ and $(y, z, q)$, then $(x_i, z_i, t(p_i, q_i))$ is an ascending chain of proofs (by monotonicity of $t(-, -)$) and its supremum is $(x, z, t(p, q))$.

If $p \in A(x, y)$ we may write $p : x \sim y$ or simply $x \sim y$. We also omit $| - |$ wherever appropriate.

Setoids based on types rather than predomains have been used to provide extensional equality in intuitionistic type theory [2].

**Definition 5.2.** *A morphism from setoid A to setoid B is an equivalence class of pairs $f = (f_0, f_1)$ of continuous functions where $f_0 : |A| \to |B|$ and $f_1 : \Pi x, y \in |A|.A(x, y) \to B(f_0(x), f_0(y))$. Two such pairs $f, g : A \to B$ are* identified *if there exists a continuous function $\mu : \Pi a \in |A|.B(f(a), g(a))$.*

Morphisms are composed in the obvious way to form the category of setoids. In the sequel we tend to omit $|-|$ and 0, 1-subscripts where appropriate, thus writing $x(a)$ for $x_0(a)$ or $a \in A$ or even $a : A$ for $a \in |A|$ etc.

We remark that one could also choose not to identify $\sim$-equal morphisms. We decided to make the identification because standard category-theoretic concepts like cartesian closure, pullbacks, etc. then apply directly, rather than only holding up to $\sim$.

The following is folklore, see also [10].

**Proposition 5.3.** *The category of setoids is cartesian-closed. The cartesian product $A \times B$ of setoids $A, B$ has components $|A \times B| = |A| \times |B|$ and $(A \times B)((a, b), (a', b')) = A(a, a') \times B(b, b')$. The ordering is given component-wise.*

*The underlying predomain of the function space of $A \Rightarrow B$ of setoids $A, B$ is given by the set of* representatives *$(f_0, f_1)$ of morphisms from A to B ordered component- and point-wise. Given two such elements $f = (f_0, f_1)$ and $g = (g_0, g_1)$ a proof $\mu : f \sim g$ in $A \Rightarrow B$ is a continuous function establishing equality of f and g qua morphisms from A to B as in Definition 5.2.*

**Proof** The verification of the cartesian product is straightforward. The application morphism $ap$ from $(A \Rightarrow B) \times A$ to $B$ has components given by $ap_0((f_0, f_1), a) = f_0(a)$ and $ap_1(\mu, p) = f_1(p); \mu(a')$ where $\mu : f \sim g$ and $p : a \sim a'$. Note that we have $f_1(p) : f_0(a) \sim f_0(a')$ and $\mu(a') : f_0(a') \sim g_0(a')$.

Conversely, if $h : C \times A \to B$ is a morphism represented by $(h_0, h_1)$ we define $\lambda(h) : C \to A \Rightarrow B$ by $(\lambda h)_0(c) = (f_0, f_1)$ where $f_0(a) = h_0(c, a)$ and $f_1(p) = h_1(r_C(c), p)$. We also put $(\lambda h)_1(p : c \sim c')(a) = h_1(p, r_A(a))$. If $(h_0', h_1')$ is another representative of $h$ witnessed by a proof $\mu$ then $\lambda c.\lambda a.\mu(c, a)$ witnesses equality of the so constructed abstraction. The remaining verifications are direct. □

**Proposition 5.4.** *The category of setoids has pullbacks.*

**Proof** To construct a pullback of $x : A \to B$ and $x' : A' \to B$ pick representatives $(x_0, x_1)$ and $(x_0', x_1')$ and take the low point of the pullback $U$ to be given by $|U| = \{(a, a', p) \mid a \in A, a' \in A', p \in B(x(a), x'(a'))\}$ and then $U((a, a', p), (a_1, a'_1, p_1)) = A(a, a_1) \times A(a', a'_1)$. The ordering is component wise. The morphism $u : U \to A$ is defined by $u_0(a, a', q) = a$ and $u_1(p, p') = p$. The remaining definitions and verifications are straightforward. Note, however, that when proving the uniqueness of fill-ins to establish the pullback property we make use of the fact that pointwise $\sim$-equal morphisms are identified. □

**Definition 5.5.** *A setoid $D$ has a least element if $|D|$ has a least element $\bot$ and there is also a least proof $\bot \in D(\bot, \bot)$.*

**Proposition 5.6.** *For each $D$ with least element there is a morphism $Y_D : (D \Rightarrow D) \to D$ such that the following hold:*

- *$Y_D = ap\langle id_{D\Rightarrow D}, Y_D\rangle$ (so $Y_D(f)$ is a fixpoint of $f$).*
- *Suppose that both $D, D'$ have least elements and $u : D \to D'$ satisfy $u_0(\bot) = \bot$. Let $D{\Rightarrow}D \leftarrow^{g} X \rightarrow^{g'} D'{\Rightarrow}D'$ be the pullback of $u(-) : D{\Rightarrow}D \to D{\Rightarrow}D'$ and $u(-) : D'{\Rightarrow}D' \to D{\Rightarrow}D'$. So, intuitively, $X$ contains pairs $(f, f')$ with $f : D \Rightarrow D$, $f' : D' \Rightarrow D'$ and $uf = f'u$. Then $uY_D g = Y_{D'} g'$. Intuitively, this means that if $uf = f'u$ and $u(\bot) = \bot$ then $u(Y_D(f)) = Y_{D'}(f')$.*

**Proof** Given $f \in D \Rightarrow D$ construct the least fixpoint of $f_0$ as $\sup_i f_0^i(\bot)$. The passage from $f$ to the least fixpoint being continuous this defines the first part of $Y_D$, i.e., $(Y_D)_0(f) = \sup_i f_0^i(\bot)$. As for the proof component assume that $p : f \sim f'$. By repeatedly invoking $p$ we then get a family of proofs $p_i : f_0^i(\bot) \sim f_0'^i(\bot)$. Using the fact that $r(\bot)$ is the least proof we can then show by induction on $i$ that this family of proofs is increasing and its supremum satisfies $\sup_i p_i : Y_D(f) \sim Y_D(f')$. Thus, we put $(Y_D)_1(p) = \sup_i p_i$ which again is continuous.

It is obvious from the construction as a least fixpoint that the required fixpoint equation is indeed satisfied. As for the second one pick $u : D \Rightarrow D'$and assume $f : D \Rightarrow D$ and $f' : D' \Rightarrow D'$ and a proof $p : uf \sim f'u$. Now, by repeatedly invoking $p$ we get an increasing family of proofs $p_i : uf^i(\bot) \sim f'(u(\bot)) = f'(\bot)$ whose supremum witnesses $u(Y_D(f)) \sim Y_{D'}(f')$. This establishes the claim. □

## 6. Worlds and Setoid-Valued Functors

We now organize abstract locations into a category that will index the meanings of types and terms in a functor category semantics [33, 39]. Our category is morally similar to that of finite sets and injections, which has been used in other work [6, 39]. The difference is that objects are now sets of mutually independent abstract locations and morphisms are slightly more complicated in that they allow relocation of abstract locations. Furthermore, locations are grouped into regions allowing one to approximate them statically.

We begin with some more notational preliminaries. Write ${}^{x}_{u}\diamond^{x'}_{u'}$ or $\mathsf{w}{}^{x}_{u}\diamond^{x'}_{u'}\mathsf{w}'$ (when $\mathsf{w}^{(\prime)} = \mathrm{dom}(x^{(\prime)})$) for a pullback square with morphisms $x, u, x', u'$. We call the common codomain of $x$ and $x'$ the *apex* of the pullback written $\overline{\mathsf{w}}$, while the common domain of $u, u'$, the *low point* of the square, is written $\underline{\mathsf{w}}$. A pair of morphisms $u, u'$ with common domain is a span, a pair of morphisms $x, x'$ with common codomain is a co-span. A category has pullbacks if every co-span can be completed to a pullback square. A pullback square $\mathsf{w}{}^{x}_{u}\diamond^{x'}_{u'}\mathsf{w}'$ with apex $\overline{\mathsf{w}}$ is *minimal* if whenever there is another pullback $\mathsf{w}{}^{x_1}_{u}\diamond^{x'_1}_{u'}\mathsf{w}'$ over the same span and with apex $\overline{\mathsf{w}_1}$, then there is a unique morphism $t : \overline{\mathsf{w}} \to \overline{\mathsf{w}_1}$ such that $x_1 = tx$ and $x'_1 = tx'$.

**Lemma 6.1.** *If a category* **C** *has pullbacks and $\mathsf{w}{}^{x}_{u}\diamond^{x'}_{u'}\mathsf{w}'$ with apex $\overline{\mathsf{w}}$ is a* minimal *pullback then the morphisms $x$ and $x'$ are* jointly epic, *that is, if $fx = gx$ and $fx' = gx'$ then $f = g$.*

For illustration purposes, we notice that the category of finite sets and injections has pullbacks and in it every span can be completed to a minimal pullback. Indeed, if $u : U \to A$ and $u' : U \to A'$ then the apex of the minimal pullback can be chosen as $A \setminus \mathrm{Img}(u) + A'$ with $+$ denoting disjoint union.

**Definition 6.2** (Category of worlds). *Assume given an infinite set Regs of* region names. *The* category of worlds **W** *is defined as follows:*

- *An object (written $\mathsf{w}$ and called a world) comprises a finite set of mutually independent abstract locations written $\mathrm{dom}(\mathsf{w})$ and a function tagging each abstract location in $\mathsf{w}$ with a region from Regs; we write $\mathsf{w}(\mathsf{r})$ for the set of abstract locations in $\mathsf{w}$ tagged with $\mathsf{r}$. We define $supp(\mathsf{w}) = \bigcup_{\mathfrak{l}\in\mathrm{dom}(\mathsf{w})} supp(\mathfrak{l})$.*
- *Let $\mathsf{w}$ and $\mathsf{w}'$ be two worlds. A morphism from $\mathsf{w}$ to $\mathsf{w}'$ is given by an injective function $u : supp(\mathsf{w}) \to supp(\mathsf{w}')$ such that for each $\mathfrak{l} \in \mathrm{dom}(\mathsf{w})$ we have $u \cdot \mathfrak{l} \in \mathrm{dom}(\mathsf{w}')$ (cf. Def. 4.2) and moreover, if $\mathfrak{l} \in \mathsf{w}(\mathsf{r})$ then $u \cdot \mathfrak{l} \in \mathsf{w}'(\mathsf{r})$.*
- *We write $\mathcal{I}(\mathsf{w}, \mathsf{w}')$ for the set of morphisms $u \colon \mathsf{w} \to \mathsf{w}'$ that are set-theoretic inclusions. Note that $u \cdot \mathfrak{l} = \mathfrak{l}$ in this case.*
- *The empty world is denoted $\emptyset$, i.e. $\mathrm{dom}(\emptyset) = \emptyset$.*

For example, a morphism between $\{\mathfrak{int}_X\} \to \{\mathfrak{int}_Y, \mathfrak{set}_Z\}$ (region tags omitted) is given by the injective function that simply maps the concrete location $X$ to the concrete location $Y$.

The abstract locations grouped together in one region represent all the stateful components, be they physical locations or more complex updatable data structures, that belong to that region. Static effect annotations amalgamate possible side effects on any of those components as effects on the region.

The notion of morphism presented here is the simplest possible one that allows us to justify interesting effect-dependent equivalences. There are more general notions of morphism that allow one to justify equivalences relying on representation independence, e.g. ones resulting from replacing $\mathfrak{int}_X$ by $\mathfrak{snd}_Y$ in a program.

It is also possible to define the category of worlds differently by combining all the abstract locations contained in a given region using the $\otimes$-operation. A world then becomes a function assigning to each region a single 'large' abstract location, possibly the trivial one. The presence of a morphism from one world to another then has to imply that the abstract locations attached to a region grow properly, *i.e.*, go from $\mathfrak{l}$ to an abstract region isomorphic to $\mathfrak{l} \otimes \mathfrak{l}'$, which can be elegantly captured by adapting Oles's [33] idea of morphisms between store shapes, which has later been popularized as *lenses* in the context of bidirectional synchronization [20].

We reluctantly decided, for reasons of space and simplicity, against using these more general notions of worlds and morphisms here, but plan to discuss them in an extended version of the paper.

The following is proved just as in the case of finite sets and injections.

**Proposition 6.3.** *In the category* **W** *all morphisms are monomorphisms;* **W** *has pullbacks and all spans in* **W** *can be completed to minimal pullbacks.*

*Moreover, these pullbacks and minimal pullbacks can be chosen in such a way that if one of the two given maps is an inclusion then the one parallel to it is also an inclusion.*

*If $u : \mathsf{w} \to \mathsf{w}_1$ and $x : \mathsf{w}_1 \to \mathsf{w}_2$ then we can find $\mathsf{w}'_1$ and $u' : \mathsf{w} \to \mathsf{w}'_1$ and $x' : \mathsf{w}'_1 \to \mathsf{w}_2$ so that $\mathsf{w}_1{}^{x}_{u}\diamond^{x'}_{u'}\mathsf{w}'_1$ is a minimal pullback and if one of $u, x$ is an inclusion then the opposite morphism can be chosen as an inclusion as well.*

The world $\mathsf{w}'_1$ in the last clause comprises the locations in $\mathsf{w}$ and those in $\mathsf{w}_2$ that are not in $\mathsf{w}_1$. Intuitively, if $\mathsf{w} = A$, $\mathsf{w}_1 = A + B$, $\mathsf{w}_2 = A + B + C$ then $\mathsf{w}'_1 = A + C$.

### 6.1 Setoid-valued functors

A functor $A$ from a category of worlds **W** to the category of setoids comprises as usual for each $\mathsf{w} \in \mathbf{W}$ a setoid $A\mathsf{w}$ and for each $u : \mathsf{w} \to \mathsf{w}'$ a morphism of setoids $Au : A\mathsf{w} \to A\mathsf{w}'$ preserving identities and composition. If $u : \mathsf{w} \to \mathsf{w}'$ and $\mathsf{a} \in A\mathsf{w}$ we may write $u.\mathsf{a}$ or even $u\mathsf{a}$ for $Au(\mathsf{a})$ and likewise for proofs in $A\mathsf{w}$. Note that $(uv).\mathsf{a} = u.(v.\mathsf{a})$.

**Definition 6.4.** *We call a functor $A$* pullback-preserving *(p.p.f.) if for every pullback square $\mathsf{w}\,{}^{x}_{u}\!\diamond^{x'}_{u'}\,\mathsf{w}'$ with apex $\overline{\mathsf{w}}$ and low point $\underline{\mathsf{w}}$ the diagram below is a pullback in the category of setoids.*

$$\begin{array}{ccccc} & & A\overline{\mathsf{w}} & & \\ & \nearrow & & \nwarrow & \\ A\mathsf{w} & & & & A\mathsf{w}' \\ & \nwarrow & & \nearrow & \\ & & A\underline{\mathsf{w}} & & \end{array}$$

Given our characterization of pullbacks in the category of setoids (Prop. 5.4), this condition is equivalent to the existence of a continuous function of type

$$\begin{aligned}&\Pi\mathsf{a} \in A\mathsf{w}.\Pi\mathsf{a}' \in A\mathsf{w}'.A\overline{\mathsf{w}}(x.\mathsf{a}, x'.\mathsf{a}') \to \\ &\qquad \Sigma\underline{\mathsf{a}} \in A\underline{\mathsf{w}}.A\mathsf{w}(u.\underline{\mathsf{a}}, \mathsf{a}) \times A\mathsf{w}'(u'.\underline{\mathsf{a}}, \mathsf{a}')\end{aligned}$$

which amounts to saying that if two values $\mathsf{a} \in A\mathsf{w}$ and $\mathsf{a}' \in A\mathsf{w}'$ are equal in a common world $\overline{\mathsf{w}}$, then this can only be the case because there is a value in the "intersection world" $\underline{\mathsf{w}}$ from which both $\mathsf{a}$ and $\mathsf{a}'$ arise. The witness $\underline{\mathsf{a}}$ is unique up to $\sim$. More importantly, even, two values cannot suddenly become equal just because we move to another world. Even though pullback preservation is not formally needed in the proofs of any of the subsequent results it simplifies the intuition considerably.

**Lemma 6.5.** *If $A$ is a p.p.f. and $u : \mathsf{w} \to \mathsf{w}'$ and $\mathsf{a}, \mathsf{a}' \in A\mathsf{w}$ then there is a continuous function $A\mathsf{w}'(u.\mathsf{a}, u.\mathsf{a}') \to A\mathsf{w}(\mathsf{a}, \mathsf{a}')$. (There is also a continuous function in the other direction just by functoriality.)*

Note that the ordering on worlds and world morphisms is discrete so that continuity only refers to the $A\mathsf{w}'(u.\mathsf{a}, u.\mathsf{a}')$ argument.

**Definition 6.6** (Morphism of functors). *If $A, B$ are p.p.fs., a morphism from $A$ to $B$ is a natural transformation from $A$ to $B$. Thus, concretely, a morphism is an equivalence class of pairs $e = (e_0, e_1)$ of continuous functions where $e_0 \colon \Pi\mathsf{w}.A\mathsf{w} \to B\mathsf{w}$ and*

$$\begin{aligned}e_1 \colon \Pi\mathsf{w}.\Pi\mathsf{w}'.\Pi x \colon \mathsf{w} \to \mathsf{w}'.\Pi a \in A\mathsf{w}.\Pi a' \in A\mathsf{w}'.\\ A\mathsf{w}'(x.\mathsf{a}, \mathsf{a}') \to B\mathsf{w}'(x.e_0(\mathsf{a}), e_0(\mathsf{a}')).\end{aligned}$$

*Two such morphisms $e, e'$ are equal if there exists a continuous function $\mu \colon \Pi\mathsf{w}.\Pi a \in A\mathsf{w}.B\mathsf{w}(e(\mathsf{a}), e'(\mathsf{a}))$.*

These morphisms compose in the obvious way and so the p.p.f.s and morphisms between them form a category.

**Theorem 6.7.** *The category of p.p.f.s is cartesian-closed and has pullbacks. If $A, B$ are p.p.f. then $(A \times B)\mathsf{w} = A\mathsf{w} \times B\mathsf{w}$ and $|(A \Rightarrow B)\mathsf{w}|$ contains pairs $(f_0, f_1)$ as follows: $f_0(u) \in |A\mathsf{w}_1 \Rightarrow B\mathsf{w}_1|$ for each $\mathsf{w}_1$ and $u : \mathsf{w} \to \mathsf{w}_1$. If $u : \mathsf{w} \to \mathsf{w}_1$ and $v : \mathsf{w}_1 \to \mathsf{w}_2$ then*

$$f_1(u, v) \in (A\mathsf{w}_1 \Rightarrow B\mathsf{w}_2)([Av \Rightarrow B\mathsf{w}_2]\ f_0(vu), [A\mathsf{w}_1 \Rightarrow Bv]\ f_0(u))$$

*where*

$$\begin{aligned}[Av \Rightarrow B\mathsf{w}_2] &: (A\mathsf{w}_2 \Rightarrow B\mathsf{w}_2) \to (A\mathsf{w}_1 \Rightarrow B\mathsf{w}_2)\\ [A\mathsf{w}_1 \Rightarrow Bv] &: (A\mathsf{w}_1 \Rightarrow B\mathsf{w}_1) \to (A\mathsf{w}_1 \Rightarrow B\mathsf{w}_2)\end{aligned}$$

*are the obvious composition morphisms.*

*A proof in $(A \Rightarrow B)\mathsf{w}((f_0, f_1), (f_0', f_1'))$ is a function $g$ that for each $u : \mathsf{w} \to \mathsf{w}_1$ yields a proof $g(u) \in (A\mathsf{w}_1 \Rightarrow B\mathsf{w}_1)(f_0(u), f_0'(u))$.*

*The order on objects and proofs is pointwise as usual.*

*Moreover, if $D$ is a p.p.f. with the property that $D\mathsf{w}$ has a least element $\bot_{\mathsf{w}}$ for each $\mathsf{w}$ and whenever $u : \mathsf{w} \to \mathsf{w}_1$ then $u.\bot_{\mathsf{w}} = \bot_{\mathsf{w}_1}$ then there is a morphism $Y_D : (D \Rightarrow D) \to D$ satisfying the same properties as those asserted in Prop. 5.6.*

**Proof** This is a special case of the construction of a functor category with respect to an internal category (here the category of worlds viewed as discrete setoids, thus internal to the category of setoids). One mimics the standard constructions for set-valued functors taking care to keep representatives of morphisms distinct as we did in the construction of the function space of setoids.

The existence of the fixpoint operator does not seem to be known but follows by applying the same method. The rather fine-grained specification of the fixpoint operator on the level of setoids is needed here so that we can assure naturality of $Y_D$ and $Y_D(f)$. □

***Heaps as a setoid*** We will now equip heaps with a world-dependent setoid structure singling out the separated ones (for a particular world) and setting equality to be induced by the ambient rely relations.

**Definition 6.8.** *If $\mathsf{w}$ is a world then the setoid $\mathfrak{S}\mathsf{w}$ is defined by $|\mathfrak{S}\mathsf{w}| = \{\mathsf{h} \in \mathbb{H} \mid \forall\mathsf{l} \in \mathsf{w}.\mathsf{h} : \mathsf{l}^R \wedge \mathrm{sep}(\mathsf{h}, \mathrm{dom}(\mathsf{w}))\}$ and $\mathfrak{S}\mathsf{w}(\mathsf{h}, \mathsf{h}') = \{\star\} \iff \forall\mathsf{l} \in \mathsf{w}.\mathsf{h} \overset{\mathsf{l}}{\sim} \mathsf{h}'$ and $\mathfrak{S}\mathsf{w}(\mathsf{h}, \mathsf{h}') = \emptyset$ otherwise, where $\mathrm{sep}(\mathsf{h}, \mathrm{dom}(\mathsf{w}))$ is the separated heap with respect to the locations in $\mathrm{dom}(\mathsf{w})$ (see Definition 4.3).*

*If $u : \mathsf{w} \to \mathsf{w}'$ and $\mathsf{h} \in \mathfrak{S}\mathsf{w}'$, then we define $\mathsf{h}.u \in \mathfrak{S}\mathsf{w}$ to be $\pi^{-1} \cdot \mathsf{h}$ for some $\pi$ extending $u$. This is well-defined up to $\sim$.*

In this way, $\mathfrak{S}$ becomes a contravariant functor from the category of worlds to the category of setoids.

**Lemma 6.9** (Pasting Lemma). *Let $\mathsf{w}\,{}^{x}_{u}\!\diamond^{x'}_{u'}\,\mathsf{w}'$ be a minimal pullback with apex $\overline{\mathsf{w}}$. Let $\mathsf{h} \in \mathfrak{S}\mathsf{w}$ and $\mathsf{h}' \in \mathfrak{S}\mathsf{w}'$ such that $\mathsf{h}.u \sim \mathsf{h}'.u'$. Then there exists a heap $\mathsf{h}_1 \in \mathfrak{S}\overline{\mathsf{w}}$, unique up to $\sim$, such that $\mathsf{h}_1.x \sim \mathsf{h}$ and $\mathsf{h}_1.x' \sim \mathsf{h}'$.*

**Corollary 6.10.** *Let $u : \mathsf{w} \to \mathsf{w}'$ be a morphism and $\mathsf{h} \in \mathfrak{S}\mathsf{w}$ and $\mathsf{h}' \in \mathfrak{S}\mathsf{w}'$. There exists $\mathsf{h}_1$ unique up to $\sim$ such that $\mathsf{h}_1.u \sim \mathsf{h}$ and $\mathsf{h}_1.u' \sim \mathsf{h}'.u'$ where $\mathsf{w}\,{}^{u}_{0}\!\diamond^{0}_{u'}\,\mathsf{w}_1$ is a minimal pullback with low point $\emptyset$, the empty world.*

Intuitively, $\mathsf{h}_1$ is obtained by overwriting the $\mathsf{w}$-part of $\mathsf{h}'$ according to $\mathsf{h}$.

***Heap Relations***

**Definition 6.11.** *A* relation *$R$ on $\mathfrak{S}$ consists of a subset $R\mathsf{w} \subseteq \mathfrak{S}\mathsf{w} \times \mathfrak{S}\mathsf{w}$ for each $\mathsf{w}$, such that if $(\mathsf{h}, \mathsf{h}') \in R\mathsf{w}$ and $u : \mathsf{w}_0 \to \mathsf{w}$ then $(\mathsf{h}.u, \mathsf{h}'.u) \in R\mathsf{w}_0$, and if $p : \mathsf{h} \sim \mathsf{h}_1$ and $p' : \mathsf{h}' \sim \mathsf{h}_1'$ then $(\mathsf{h}_1, \mathsf{h}_1') \in R\mathsf{w}$, as well.*

The elementary effects track reading, writing, and allocating at the level of regions and are as follows: $wr_{\mathsf{r}}$ (writing within region $\mathsf{r}$), $rd_{\mathsf{r}}$ (reading from within region $\mathsf{r}$), and $al_{\mathsf{r}}$ (allocating within region $\mathsf{r}$). Each elementary effect $\epsilon$ is associated with a set $\mathcal{R}(\epsilon)$ of relations on $\mathfrak{S}$ as follows:

$$\begin{aligned}
R \in \mathcal{R}(rd_{\mathsf{r}}) &\iff (\mathsf{h}, \mathsf{h}') \in R\mathsf{w} \Rightarrow \forall\mathsf{l} \in \mathsf{w}(\mathsf{r}).\mathsf{h} \overset{\mathsf{l}}{\sim} \mathsf{h}'\\
R \in \mathcal{R}(wr_{\mathsf{r}}) &\iff (\mathsf{h}, \mathsf{h}') \in R\mathsf{w} \Rightarrow \forall\mathsf{l} \in \mathsf{w}(\mathsf{r}).\forall\mathsf{h}_1, \mathsf{h}_1'.\mathsf{h}_1 \overset{\mathsf{l}}{\sim} \mathsf{h}_1' \Rightarrow\\
&\qquad \mathsf{h} \overset{\mathsf{l}}{\to} \mathsf{h}_1 \wedge \mathsf{h}' \overset{\mathsf{l}}{\to} \mathsf{h}_1' \Rightarrow (\mathsf{h}_1, \mathsf{h}_1') \in R\mathsf{w}\\
R \in \mathcal{R}(al_{\mathsf{r}}) &\iff (\mathsf{h}, \mathsf{h}') \in R\mathsf{w} \Rightarrow\\
&\qquad \forall\mathsf{w}_1.\forall u \in \mathcal{I}(\mathsf{w}, \mathsf{w}_1).(\mathsf{w}_1 \setminus \mathsf{w}) \subseteq \mathsf{w}_1(\mathsf{r}) \Rightarrow\\
&\qquad\quad \forall\mathsf{h}_1, \mathsf{h}_1' \in \mathfrak{S}\mathsf{w}_1.[\mathsf{h}_1.u \sim \mathsf{h} \wedge \mathsf{h}_1'.u \sim \mathsf{h}' \wedge\\
&\qquad\quad (\mathsf{h}_1, \mathsf{h}_1') \in \textstyle\bigcap_{\mathsf{l} \in \mathsf{w}_1 \setminus \mathsf{w}} \mathsf{l}^R] \Rightarrow (\mathsf{h}_1, \mathsf{h}_1') \in R\mathsf{w}_1
\end{aligned}$$

Thus, $\mathcal{R}(rd_{\mathsf{r}})$ is the set of relations $R$ for which $R$-related heaps contain "equal" (in the sense of $\mathsf{l}^R$) values for all abstract locations in region $\mathsf{r}$; a relation $R \in \mathcal{R}(wr_{\mathsf{r}})$ is oblivious to (preserved by) "equal" writes to any abstract location in $\mathsf{r}$; and a relation $R \in \mathcal{R}(al_{\mathsf{r}})$ is oblivious to extensions of the current world provided that they only add abstract locations in region $\mathsf{r}$, that the initial contents of these newly allocated locations are "equal" in the sense of $(-)^R$, and that nothing else is changed.

Finally, $\mathcal{R}(\varepsilon)$ for a set of effects $\varepsilon$ is defined as follows:

$$\mathcal{R}(\varepsilon) = \bigcap_{\epsilon \in \varepsilon} \mathcal{R}(\epsilon).$$

As in our earlier work [7], the key idea is that computations with effect $\varepsilon$ will preserve all the heap relations that are preserved by all the operations allowed by $\varepsilon$. The larger the set of operations, the fewer relations need be preserved.

**Definition 6.12** (Monad). *Let $A$ be a p.p.f. and $\varepsilon$ an effect. A p.p.f. $T_\varepsilon A$ is defined as follows:*

- *(Objects) Elements of $(T_\varepsilon A)\mathsf{w}$ are pairs $(\mathsf{c}_0, \mathsf{c}_1)$ of partial functions where*

$$\mathsf{c}_0 : \quad \mathfrak{S}\mathsf{w} \rightharpoonup \Sigma \mathsf{w}_1.\mathcal{I}(\mathsf{w}, \mathsf{w}_1) \times \mathfrak{S}\mathsf{w}_1 \times A\mathsf{w}_1$$

*and $\mathsf{c}_1$ is as follows. If $R \in \mathcal{R}(\varepsilon)$ and $(\mathsf{h}, \mathsf{h}') \in R\mathsf{w}$ then $\mathsf{c}_1(R, \mathsf{h}, \mathsf{h}')$ either is undefined and $\mathsf{c}_0(\mathsf{h})$ and $\mathsf{c}_0(\mathsf{h}')$ are both undefined or else $c_1(R, \mathsf{h}, \mathsf{h}')$ is defined and then $\mathsf{c}_0(\mathsf{h})$ and $\mathsf{c}_0'(\mathsf{h}')$ are both defined, say $\mathsf{c}_0(\mathsf{h}) = (\mathsf{w}_1, u, \mathsf{h}_1, \mathsf{a})$ and $\mathsf{c}_0(\mathsf{h}') = (\mathsf{w}_1', u', \mathsf{h}_1', \mathsf{a}')$. In this case, $\mathsf{c}_1(R, \mathsf{h}, \mathsf{h}')$ returns a pair $({}_{v}^{x}\!\Diamond_{v'}^{x'}, p)$ where $\mathsf{w}_1 {}_{v}^{x}\!\Diamond_{v'}^{x'} \mathsf{w}_1'$ such that $xu = x'u'$. Furthermore, $p \in A\overline{\mathsf{w}}(x.\mathsf{a}, x'.\mathsf{a}')$ and, finally, $(\mathsf{h}_1.v, \mathsf{h}_1'.v') \in R\underline{\mathsf{w}}$ where $\underline{\mathsf{w}}$ and $\overline{\mathsf{w}}$ are low point and apex of ${}_{v}^{x}\!\Diamond_{v'}^{x'}$.*
- *(Proofs) Proofs only look at the $(-)_0$ components. Let $\mathsf{c} = (\mathsf{c}_0, \_) \in T_\varepsilon A\mathsf{w}$ and $\mathsf{c}' = (\mathsf{c}_0', \_) \in T_\varepsilon A\mathsf{w}$, then a proof in $(T_\varepsilon A)\mathsf{w}(\mathsf{c}, \mathsf{c}')$ is a partial (continuous) function $\mu$, such that for a given $\mathsf{h} \in \mathfrak{S}\mathsf{w}$:*
  1. *if $\mu(\mathsf{h})$ is undefined, then $\mathsf{c}_0(\mathsf{h})$ and $\mathsf{c}_0'(\mathsf{h})$ are both undefined;*
  2. *if $\mu(\mathsf{h})$ is defined, then $\mathsf{c}_0(\mathsf{h}) = (\mathsf{w}_1, u, \mathsf{h}_1, \mathsf{a})$ and $\mathsf{c}_0'(\mathsf{h}) = (\mathsf{w}_1', u', \mathsf{h}_1', \mathsf{a}')$ are both defined. In this case, $\mu(\mathsf{h})$ returns a tuple $({}_{v}^{x}\!\Diamond_{v'}^{x'}, q)$ satisfying $xu = x'u'$, $q \in A\overline{\mathsf{w}}(x.\mathsf{a}, x'.\mathsf{a}')$ and $\mathsf{h}_1.v \sim \mathsf{h}_1.v'$ in $\mathfrak{S}\underline{\mathsf{w}}$, with $\overline{\mathsf{w}}$ and $\underline{\mathsf{w}}$ apex and low point of ${}_{v}^{x}\!\Diamond_{v'}^{x'}$.*
- *(Order) The order between computations is given point-wise: $(\mathsf{c}_0, \mathsf{c}_1) \leq (\mathsf{c}_0', \mathsf{c}_1')$ if and only if for any $\mathsf{h} \in \mathfrak{S}\mathsf{w}$ we have $\mathsf{c}_0(\mathsf{h}) \leq \mathsf{c}_0'(\mathsf{h})$, which is defined as follows: for all $\mathsf{h} \in \mathfrak{S}\mathsf{w}$ if $\mathsf{c}_0(\mathsf{h})$ is defined so is $\mathsf{c}_0'(\mathsf{h})$. Moreover, if both $\mathsf{c}_0(\mathsf{h})$ and $\mathsf{c}_0'(\mathsf{h})$ are defined as $\mathsf{c}_0(\mathsf{h}) = (\mathsf{w}_1, u_1, \mathsf{h}_1, \mathsf{a}_1)$ and $\mathsf{c}_0'(\mathsf{h}) = (\mathsf{w}_1', u_1', \mathsf{h}_1', \mathsf{a}_1')$, then $\mathsf{w}_1 = \mathsf{w}_1'$, $u_1 = u_1'$, $\mathsf{h}_1 = \mathsf{h}_1'$ and $\mathsf{a}_1 \leq \mathsf{a}_1'$. Finally, if $\mathsf{c}_1(R, \mathsf{h}, \mathsf{h}')$ and $\mathsf{c}_1'(R, \mathsf{h}, \mathsf{h}')$ are defined returning $({}_{v_1}^{x_1}\!\Diamond_{v_1'}^{x_1'}, q)$ and $({}_{v_2}^{x_2}\!\Diamond_{v_2'}^{x_2'}, q')$, then ${}_{v_1}^{x_1}\!\Diamond_{v_1'}^{x_1'} = {}_{v_2}^{x_2}\!\Diamond_{v_2'}^{x_2'}$ and $q \leq q'$.*[1]
- *(Morphism part) Let $x : \mathsf{w} \to \mathsf{w}'$ be a morphism and $\mathsf{c} = (\mathsf{c}_0, \mathsf{c}_1) \in T_\varepsilon A\mathsf{w}$. We are going to describe the first component of $(\mathsf{c}_0', \_) = T_\varepsilon Ax(\mathsf{c})$. Given $\mathsf{h} \in \mathfrak{S}\mathsf{w}'$ write $\mathsf{c}_0(\mathsf{h}.x) = (\mathsf{w}_1, u, \mathsf{h}_1, \mathsf{a})$. Should this application be undefined so is $\mathsf{c}_0'(\mathsf{h})$. Now, using Proposition 6.3, complete $u, x$ to a minimal pullback square ${}_{u}^{x'}\!\Diamond_{x}^{u'}$ with $u' : \mathsf{w}' \to \mathsf{w}_1'$ where $\mathsf{w}_1'$ is the apex of this pullback.*

  *Now, obtain $\mathsf{h}' \in \mathfrak{S}\mathsf{w}'$ from $\mathsf{h}$ by overwriting with $\mathsf{h}_1.u$ using Corollary 6.10. Then paste $\mathsf{h}_1$ and $\mathsf{h}'$ (note that $\mathsf{h}_1.u \sim \mathsf{h}'.u$ by construction) using Lemma 6.9 to yield the desired heap $\mathsf{h}_1' \in \mathfrak{S}\mathsf{w}_1'$. We then put $\mathsf{c}_0(\mathsf{h}) = (\mathsf{w}_1', u', \mathsf{h}_1', x'.\mathsf{a})$.*

  *We omit the remaining components and verifications.*

The proof of the following is tedious but straightforward and will be given in an extended version of this paper.

**Theorem 6.13.** *$T_\varepsilon$ is the functor part of an effect-indexed strong monad [8, 43].*

This theorem means in particular, that each $T_\varepsilon$ is a monad on the category of p.p.f. *i.e.*, for each $A$ there are natural transformation $\eta_A : A \to T_\varepsilon A$ and $\mu_A : T_\varepsilon T_\varepsilon A \to T_\varepsilon A$ subject to the usual laws and whenever $\varepsilon_1 \subseteq \varepsilon_2$ then there is a morphism $T_{\varepsilon_1} A \to T_{\varepsilon_2} A$ which interacts with the monad data in the expected sense.

***Illustration*** Assume an initial heap $\mathsf{h}$, where $\mathsf{h}(X) \mapsto [1, 2, 3]$ and $\mathsf{h}(Y) \mapsto [3, 2, 1]$, that is, $\mathsf{h}$ points to the lists $[1, 2, 3]$ and $[3, 2, 1]$ from concrete locations $X$ and $Y$, respectively. Moreover, let $\mathsf{c}(\mathsf{h}) = (\mathsf{w}_1, u, \mathsf{h}_1, (3, Y))$ and $\mathsf{c}'(\mathsf{h}) = (\mathsf{w}_1', u', \mathsf{h}_1', (3, Z))$, where $\mathsf{h}_1(X) \mapsto [1, 2, 3, 4]$; $\mathsf{h}_1(Y) \mapsto [3, 2, 1, 0]$; and $\mathsf{h}_1(Z) = [4, 2]$, while $\mathsf{h}_1'(X) \mapsto [4, 3, 2, 1]$; $\mathsf{h}_1'(Z) \mapsto [3, 2, 1, 3, 2, 1, 0]$; and $\mathsf{h}_1'(W) = [0, 0]$. We can show that $\mathsf{c}$ and $\mathsf{c}'$ are equal when given $\mathsf{h}$. The proof is illustrated by the diagram below, where an arrow labeled with $\subseteq$ denotes an inclusion and an arrow labeled with a mapping, *e.g.*, $Z \mapsto Y$, denotes the corresponding renaming.

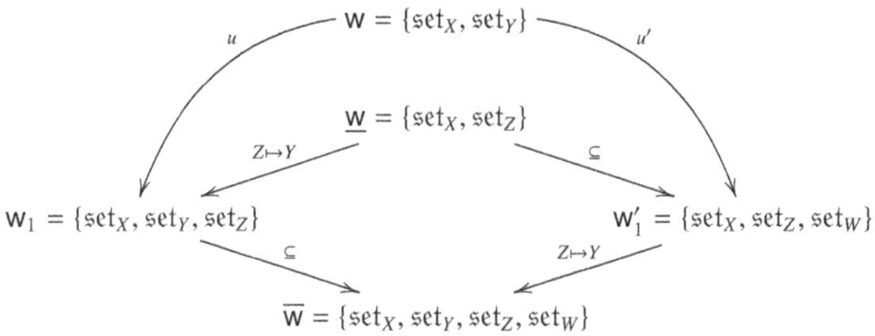


Here, it is easy to check that $\mathsf{h}_1$ and $\mathsf{h}_1'$ are equal when taken to the world $\underline{\mathsf{w}}$, as the concrete locations $X$ in $\mathsf{h}_1$ and $\mathsf{h}_1'$ and $Y$ in $\mathsf{h}_1$ and $Z$ in $\mathsf{h}_1'$ point to lists containing the same set of elements: $\{1, 2, 3, 4\}$ and $\{0, 1, 2, 3\}$, respectively. Notice that the abstract locations $\mathit{set}_Z \in \mathsf{w}_1$ and $\mathit{set}_W \in \mathsf{w}_1'$ are not taken into account. Moreover, the value $(3, Y)$ is also equivalent to $(3, Z)$ when taken to the world $\overline{\mathsf{w}}$, as the morphism $\mathsf{w}_1' \to \overline{\mathsf{w}}$ renames $Z$ to $Y$, while the morphism $\mathsf{w}_1 \to \overline{\mathsf{w}}$ is an inclusion.

We see here that the use of setoids rather than plain sets or predomains is crucial. The proofs in $T_\varepsilon A$ are clearly relevant as they explain in what way the abstract locations correspond to each other. Likewise, the elements of $|T_\varepsilon A|$ contain more information that the mere computation, i.e., the evolution of the heap. Namely, the world extension $\mathsf{w}_1$ will typically contain new abstract locations with new contracts that can be arbitrarily complicated. Thus, it would not be possible to replace $T_\varepsilon A$ with a simple logical predicate on actual computations.

## 7. Proof-relevant Logical Relations

The structure identified so far allows us to interpret our effect type system and the equational theory in the category of p.p.f.

**Definition 7.1** (type interpretation). *A type interpretation consists of an assignment of a p.p.f. $[\![A]\!]$ to each basic type $A$.*

Given a type interpretation we can then assign a p.p.f. $[\![\tau]\!]$ to each type the essential clause being $[\![\tau_1 \xrightarrow{\varepsilon} \tau_2]\!] = [\![\tau_1]\!] \Rightarrow T_\varepsilon \tau_2$. We also interpret a typing context $\Gamma$ as the cartesian product over its bindings: $[\![\Gamma]\!] = \prod_{x \in \mathrm{dom}(\Gamma)} [\![\Gamma(x)]\!]$.

**Lemma 7.2** (masking). *Let $\mathsf{r}$ be a region. For world $\mathsf{w}$ define $\mathsf{w}{-}\mathsf{r}$ by removing all locations in $\mathsf{r}$. If type $\tau$ does not contain $\mathsf{r}$ then for each world $\mathsf{w}$ the morphism $u.(-) : [\![\tau]\!]\mathsf{w}{-}\mathsf{r} \to [\![\tau]\!]\mathsf{w}$ where $u : \mathsf{w}{-}\mathsf{r} \to \mathsf{w}$ is the obvious inclusion is an isomorphism.*

**Definition 7.3** (axiom interpretation). *An axiom interpretation consists of an element $x_{(v,\tau)} \in |[\![\tau]\!]\emptyset|$ (empty world) for each type axiom $(v, \tau)$ and of an element $p_{(v,v',\tau)} \in [\![\tau]\!]\emptyset(x_{(v,\tau)}, x_{(v',\tau)})$ for each equality axiom $(v, v', \tau)$.*

Given an axiom interpretation (and a type interpretation) and a well-typed term $\Gamma \vdash e : \tau \,\&\, \varepsilon$ we define a morphism

$$[\![\Gamma \vdash e : \tau \,\&\, \varepsilon]\!] : [\![\Gamma]\!] \to T_\varepsilon [\![\tau]\!]$$

using the fact that all the typing rules are reflected in the semantics: cartesian closure takes care of application and abstraction and variable management. The fixpoint morphism $Y_D$ takes care of recursive definitions; the indexed monadicity of $T_\varepsilon$ takes care of the rules associated with "let" and effect propagation. Lemma 7.2, fi-

[1] Strictly speaking, $q \leq q'$ needs to be a tuple with the objects they are proving the equality of.

nally, takes care of the masking rule. If $\Gamma \vdash v : \tau$ because of the axiom $(v, \tau)$ then we put $[\![\Gamma \vdash v : \tau]\!](\gamma) = x_{(v,\tau)}$ (constant morphism).

***Effects*** Given a set of effects $\varepsilon$, we write $\text{rds}(\varepsilon) = \{\mathsf{r} \mid rd_{\mathsf{r}} \in \varepsilon\}$, $\text{wrs}(\varepsilon) = \{\mathsf{r} \mid wr_{\mathsf{r}} \in \varepsilon\}$, $\text{als}(\varepsilon) = \{\mathsf{r} \mid al_{\mathsf{r}} \in \varepsilon\}$ and $\text{regs}(\varepsilon) = \text{rds}(\varepsilon) \cup \text{wrs}(\varepsilon) \cup \text{als}(\varepsilon)$. Moreover, the set $nwrs(\varepsilon) = \text{regs}(\varepsilon) \setminus \text{wrs}(\varepsilon)$. We also introduce the following piece of notation for $\mathsf{h}, \mathsf{h}' \in \mathfrak{S}\mathsf{w}$:

$$\mathsf{h} \sim_{\text{rds}(\varepsilon,\mathsf{w})} \mathsf{h}' \iff \forall \mathsf{l} \in \mathsf{w}(\text{rds}(\varepsilon)).\mathsf{h} \overset{\mathsf{l}}{\sim} \mathsf{h}'$$

$$\mathsf{h} \sim_{nwrs(\varepsilon,\mathsf{w})} \mathsf{h}' \iff \forall \mathsf{l} \in \mathsf{w}(nwrs(\varepsilon)).\mathsf{h} \overset{\mathsf{l}}{\sim} \mathsf{h}'$$

which specifies that the heaps $\mathsf{h}$ and $\mathsf{h}'$ are equivalent on all the abstract locations $\mathsf{l}$ in regions associated to read effects in $\varepsilon$ and on the not write locations, respectively.

**Lemma 7.4.** *Let $\Gamma \vdash e : \tau \;\&\; \varepsilon$. Let $\mathsf{w}{}^{x}_{v}\!\Diamond^{x'}_{v'}\mathsf{w}'$ be a pullback square, $\gamma \in [\![\Gamma]\!]\mathsf{w}, \gamma' \in [\![\Gamma]\!]\mathsf{w}'$ be contexts, such that $\mu_\gamma : x.\gamma \sim x.\gamma$ and $\mathsf{c} = [\![\Gamma \vdash e : \tau \;\&\; \varepsilon]\!]\mathsf{w}(\gamma) \in T_\varepsilon A\mathsf{w}$ and $\mathsf{c}' = [\![\Gamma \vdash e : \tau \;\&\; \varepsilon]\!]\mathsf{w}'(\gamma') \in T_\varepsilon A\mathsf{w}'$ be computations, such that $\mu : x.\mathsf{c} \sim x'.\mathsf{c}'$. Let $\mathsf{h} \in \mathfrak{S}\mathsf{w}, \mathsf{h}' \in \mathfrak{S}\mathsf{w}'$ be heaps, such that $\mathsf{h}.v \sim_{\text{rds}(\varepsilon,\underline{\mathsf{w}})} \mathsf{h}'.v'$. Then $\mathsf{c}(\mathsf{h})$ and $\mathsf{c}'(\mathsf{h}')$ co-terminate. Moreover, if they do terminate and $\mathsf{c}(\mathsf{h}) = (\mathsf{w}_1, u_1, \mathsf{h}_1, \mathsf{a}_1)$ and $\mathsf{c}'(\mathsf{h}') = (\mathsf{w}'_1, u'_1, \mathsf{h}'_1, \mathsf{a}'_1)$, then the following diagram exists, in particular, the dashed arrows, where the following is satisfied*

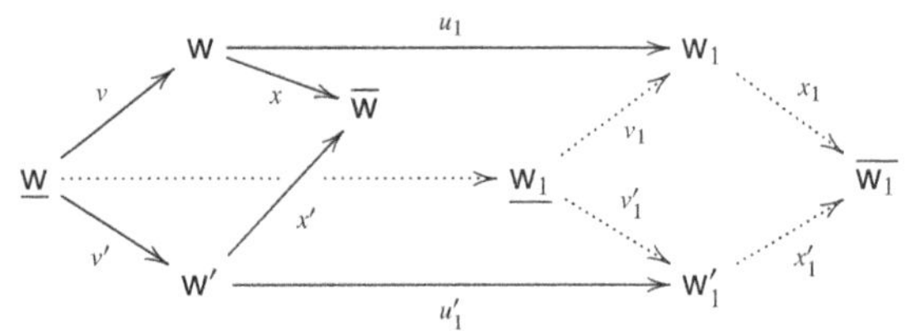


1. $x_1.\mathsf{a} \sim x'_1.\mathsf{a}'$, $\mathsf{w} \cong \underline{\mathsf{w}} \otimes \mathsf{q}$, $\mathsf{w}' \cong \underline{\mathsf{w}} \otimes \mathsf{q}'$, $\mathsf{w}_1 \cong \underline{\mathsf{w}} \otimes \mathsf{q} \otimes \mathsf{q}_1$, $\mathsf{w}'_1 \cong \underline{\mathsf{w}} \otimes \mathsf{q}' \otimes \mathsf{q}'_1$, *for some* $\mathsf{q}_1$ *and* $\mathsf{q}'_1$;
2. *for all* $\mathsf{l} \in \underline{\mathsf{w}}$, *we have either:* $\mathsf{h}.v \overset{\mathsf{l}}{\sim} \mathsf{h}_1.u_1.v$ *and* $\mathsf{h}'.v' \overset{\mathsf{l}}{\sim} \mathsf{h}'_1.u'_1.v'$ *(remain equivalent) or* $\mathsf{h}_1.u_1.v_1 \overset{\mathsf{l}}{\sim} \mathsf{h}'_1.u'_1.v'$ *(equally modified);*
3. *if* $\mathsf{l} \in \underline{\mathsf{w}}(nwrs(\varepsilon))$, *then* $\mathsf{h}.v \overset{\mathsf{l}}{\sim} \mathsf{h}_1.u_1.v$ *and* $\mathsf{h}'.v' \overset{\mathsf{l}}{\sim} \mathsf{h}'_1.u'_1.v'$.
4. *if* $\text{als}(\varepsilon) = \emptyset$, *then there exists a morphism* $\mathsf{c}_\star \in [\![\Gamma]\!] \to T_\varepsilon[\![\tau]\!]$, *such that* $\mathsf{c}_\star \sim \mathsf{c}$ *and if* $\mathsf{c}_\star(\mathsf{w})(\gamma)\mathsf{h} = (\mathsf{w}_\star, u_\star, \mathsf{h}_\star, \mathsf{a}_\star)$ *then* $\mathsf{w}_\star \cong \mathsf{w}$ *(no world extension is needed);*
5. $\underline{\mathsf{w}}\mathsf{w}\underline{\mathsf{w}_1}\mathsf{w}_1$ *and* $\underline{\mathsf{w}}\mathsf{w}'\underline{\mathsf{w}_1}\mathsf{w}'_1$ *are pullbacks.*

**Proof** The proof that the values are equal in $\overline{\mathsf{w}_1}$ follows directly from the definition of computations and effects.

For the item 2, we use the following relation $R$ defined as follows for all worlds $\mathsf{w}_1$, such that $u : \underline{\mathsf{w}} \to \mathsf{w}_1$:

$$\{(\mathsf{h}_1, \mathsf{h}'_1) \mid \mathsf{h}_1.u \sim_{\text{rds}(\varepsilon,\underline{\mathsf{w}})} \mathsf{h}'_1.u \wedge \forall \mathsf{l} \in \underline{\mathsf{w}}.(\mathsf{h}_1.u \overset{\mathsf{l}}{\sim} \mathsf{h} \wedge \mathsf{h}'_1.u \overset{\mathsf{l}}{\sim} \mathsf{h}') \vee \mathsf{h}_1.u \overset{\mathsf{l}}{\sim} \mathsf{h}'_1.u\}$$

Otherwise, for the worlds $\mathsf{w}_2$ not reachable from $\underline{\mathsf{w}}$, the relation $R\mathsf{w}_2$ is the trivial set. Notice that $R \in \mathcal{R}(\varepsilon)$ and it is contravariant. The claim then follows directly by using the morphism from $\underline{\mathsf{w}} \to \underline{\mathsf{w}_1}$.

The proof of item 3 follows in a similar fashion, but we use the following relation:

$$\{(\mathsf{h}_1, \mathsf{h}'_1) \mid \mathsf{h}_1.u \sim_{\text{rds}(\varepsilon,\underline{\mathsf{w}})} \mathsf{h}'_1.u \wedge \mathsf{h}_1.u \sim_{nwrs(\varepsilon,\underline{\mathsf{w}})} \mathsf{h}\}$$

And we use a similar relation for showing that $\mathsf{h}'$ and $\mathsf{h}'_1.u'$ agree on the not written locations $\underline{\mathsf{w}}(nwrs(\varepsilon))$.

For item 4, first, we show that $\mathsf{w}(\mathsf{r})$ and $\underline{\mathsf{w}}(\mathsf{r})$ are equal up to renaming for all regions $\mathsf{r} \notin \text{als}(\mathsf{r})$ by using the following relation $R\mathsf{q}$ for some world $\mathsf{q}$:

$$\{(\mathsf{h}_1, \mathsf{h}'_1) \mid \mathsf{h}_1 \sim \mathsf{h}'_1 \wedge \forall \mathsf{r} \notin \text{als}(\varepsilon).\#_{\mathsf{r}}(\mathsf{q}) \leq \#_{\mathsf{r}}(\mathsf{w})\}$$

where $\#_{\mathsf{r}}$ denotes the number of abstract locations colored with $\mathsf{r}$. Clearly, $R \in \mathcal{R}(\varepsilon)$ as $\varepsilon$ does not contain any allocation effects. Thus, the number of locations in $\mathsf{w}_\star$ is the same as the locations in $\mathsf{w}$, by using the pullback $\mathsf{w}_1{}^{1}_{v}\!\Diamond^{x}_{1}\mathsf{w}_\star$. This gives us one direction, while the other direction is obtained by the universal property of pullbacks. Given this property, one can easily construct the function $\mathsf{c}_\star$. □

**Theorem 7.5** (Equational soundness)**.** *Assume an ambient interpretation of types and axioms. If $\Gamma \vdash e = e' : \tau \;\&\; \varepsilon$ then the morphisms $[\![\Gamma \vdash e : \tau \;\&\; \varepsilon]\!]$ and $[\![\Gamma \vdash e' : \tau \;\&\; \varepsilon]\!]$ are equal morphisms.*

**Proof** By induction on derivations. The core rules are direct from the category-theoretic structure identified so far. The effect-specific rules are nontrivial; however given Lemma 7.4, their proofs follow essentially the same reasoning as in existing literature [6, 41]. As for the axiom rule we argue as follows.

If $\Gamma \vdash v = v' : \tau$ using the axiom $(v, v', \tau)$ then we have $[\![\Gamma \vdash v : \tau]\!](\gamma) = x_{(v,\tau)}$ and $[\![\Gamma \vdash v' : \tau]\!](\gamma) = x_{(v',\tau)}$ and the constant function $\lambda\gamma.p_{(v,v',\tau)}$ is continuous and thus establishes the desired equality. □

## 8. Observational equivalence

We will now relate semantic equality to observational equivalence. So far, a trivial model that identifies everything could also have been used to "justify" our rules. Doing this, however, requires a loose relationship between the setoid interpretation and the computational meanings of raw terms which will be given by a realizability relation.

**Definition 8.1.** *For each type $\tau$, effect $\varepsilon$, and world $\mathsf{w}$ we define admissible relations $\Vdash^{\tau}_{\mathbf{W}} \subseteq \mathbb{V} \times |[\![\tau]\!]\mathbf{W}|$ and $\Vdash^{\tau\&\varepsilon}_{\mathbf{W}} \subseteq \mathbb{C} \times |T_\varepsilon[\![\tau]\!]\mathbf{W}|$ as follows:*

- *If $c \in \mathbb{C}$ then $c \Vdash^{\tau\&\varepsilon}_{\mathsf{w}} (\mathsf{c}_0, \mathsf{c}_1)$ means that for each $\mathsf{h} \in \mathfrak{S}\mathsf{w}$ one has $c(\mathsf{h})$ defined iff $\mathsf{c}_0(\mathsf{h})$ defined and if $c(\mathsf{h}) = (\mathsf{h}_1, a)$ then $\mathsf{c}_0(\mathsf{h}) = (\mathsf{w}_1, u, \mathsf{h}_1, \mathsf{a})$ (same $\mathsf{h}_1$) and $\mathsf{h}_1 \in \mathfrak{S}\mathsf{w}_1$ and $a \Vdash^{\tau}_{\mathsf{w}_1} \mathsf{a}$.*
- *If $fun(f) \in \mathbb{V}$ and $(f_0, f_1) \in |[\![\tau_1 \xrightarrow{\varepsilon} \tau_2]\!]\mathsf{w}|$ then $f \Vdash^{\tau_1 \xrightarrow{\varepsilon} \tau_2}_{\mathsf{w}} (f_0, f_1)$ iff whenever $u : \mathsf{w} \to \mathsf{w}_1$ is an inclusion and $a \Vdash^{\tau_1}_{\mathsf{w}_1} x$ then $f(a) \Vdash^{\tau_2\&\varepsilon}_{\mathsf{w}_1} f_0(x)$.*
- *$\eta \Vdash^{\Gamma}_{\mathsf{w}} \gamma \iff \eta(x) \Vdash^{\Gamma(x)}_{\mathsf{w}} \gamma(x)$ for all $x \in \text{dom}(\Gamma)$.*

**Lemma 8.2.** *The $\Vdash$ relations are indeed admissible and are stable under inclusion; that is whenever $v \Vdash^{X}_{\mathsf{w}} x$ and $u : \mathsf{w} \to \mathsf{w}'$ is an inclusion then $v \Vdash^{X}_{\mathsf{w}_1} u.x$ holds.*

The following soundness property of $\Vdash$ is proved by straightforward induction on typing derivations.

**Theorem 8.3** (Fundamental Lemma)**.** *Assume that the interpretation of types and axioms is chosen such that for all type axioms $(v, \tau)$ one has $v \Vdash^{\tau}_{\emptyset} x_{(v,\tau)}$. Whenever $\Gamma \vdash e : \tau \;\&\; \varepsilon$ and $\eta \Vdash^{\Gamma}_{\mathsf{w}} \gamma$ then $[\![e]\!]\eta \Vdash^{\tau\&\varepsilon}_{\mathsf{w}} [\![\Gamma \vdash e : \tau]\!]_{\mathsf{w}}(\gamma)$.*

**Definition 8.4** (Observational equivalence)**.** *Two value expressions $v, v'$ where $\vdash v : \tau$ and $\vdash v' : \tau$ are observationally equivalent at type $\tau$ if for all $f$ such that $\vdash f : \tau \xrightarrow{\varepsilon}$ `unit` ("observations") it is the case that $[\![f\ v]\!]\emptyset$ is defined iff $[\![f\ v']\!]\emptyset$ is defined. ($\emptyset$ stands for empty heap and environment).*

It is easy to extend this definition to open terms and computation expressions by closing up with lambda abstractions. Intuitively, observationally equivalent expressions, can be replaced by one another in any context without compromising observable behavior. To see this, one can build observations $f$ from such a context by first $\lambda$-abstracting its hole and then adding at the end a wrapper function that tests for some observable feature of the end result signaling failure of the test by nontermination.

**Theorem 8.5** (main result)**.** *If $\vdash v = v' : \tau$ then $v$ and $v'$ are observationally equivalent.*

**Proof** If $f$ is an observation then by the congruence rules we get $\vdash f\ v = f\ v' : \tau$ so, by Theorem 7.5 we find $[\![\vdash f\ v]\!] = [\![\vdash f\ v']\!]$, thus in particular $[\![\vdash f\ v]\!]_\emptyset\emptyset$ (empty world, empty heap) is defined iff $[\![\vdash f\ v']\!]_\emptyset\emptyset$ is defined. Now, if $[\![f\ v]\!]\emptyset$ is defined then by Theorem 8.3 and the definition of $\Vdash$ we can conclude that $[\![\vdash f\ v]\!]_\emptyset\emptyset$

is defined so, using Theorem 8.3 again we get that $[\![f\ v']\!]\emptyset$ is defined. □

## 9. Applications

In this section we give some concrete instantiations of our framework in the form of axioms and their semantic justifications. We do so in more detail for the Overlapping References example shown in Section 2, and in less detail for the other examples.

***Overlapping References*** Recall value $v_{or}$ and type $\tau_{or}$ from Section 2 (two overlapping references). In order to justify the axiom $(v_{or}, \tau_{or})$ we have to construct a semantic object $x_{or} \in [\![\tau_{or}]\!]$ such that $v_{or} \Vdash_{\emptyset}^{\tau_{or}} x_{or}$ which we will now do.

Given world $\mathsf{w}$ we put $x_{or}(\mathsf{w})(\star) = (\mathsf{c}_0, \mathsf{c}_1)$, where $\mathsf{c}_0$ and $\mathsf{c}_1$ are defined as follows ($\star \in [\![\mathtt{unit}]\!]\mathsf{w}$):

$$\mathsf{c}_0(\mathsf{h}) = (u : \mathsf{w} \to \mathsf{w}_1, \mathsf{h}_1, (\mathsf{g}_1, \mathsf{g}_2, \mathsf{s}_1, \mathsf{s}_2))$$

where $new(\mathsf{h}, 0) = (X, \mathsf{h}_1)$, that is, $\mathsf{h}_1$ is obtained from $\mathsf{h}$ by allocating a concrete location $X$; $\mathsf{w}_1$ is the world obtained by extending $\mathsf{w}$ with the abstract locations $\mathfrak{fst}_X$ and $\mathfrak{snd}_X$ defined in Section 4.1, where the former is marked with region r1 and the latter with region r2; finally, $(\mathsf{g}_1, \mathsf{g}_2, \mathsf{s}_1, \mathsf{s}_2)$ are the corresponding semantic objects that get and set values to the projections of pairs stored in $X$, *e.g.*, $\mathsf{g}_1 \in [\![(unit \xrightarrow{rd_{r1}} int)]\!]\mathsf{w}_1$ is the semantic counter part of the function getting the first projection of the pair stored in $X$, defined in a similar way as we do for $x_{or}$.

Note that $v_{or} \Vdash_{\emptyset}^{\tau_{or}} x_{or}$ in particular requires that the new heap returned by $\mathsf{c}_0$ agrees with the one returned by $v_{or}$ and, more generally, we are forced to follow the computational behavior of $v_{or}$ in $x_{or}$. We are free, though to choose the semantic components such as world extensions and, later, pullbacks.

The object $\mathsf{c}_1$, now, is defined as follows: Assume that $R \in \mathcal{R}(\{al_{r1}, al_{r2}\})$ is a heap relation and two heaps $\mathsf{h}, \mathsf{h}' \in \mathfrak{S}\mathsf{w}$ that are related, *i.e.*, $(\mathsf{h}, \mathsf{h}') \in R$. Moreover, assume that $\mathsf{c}_0(\mathsf{h}) = (u : \mathsf{w} \to \mathsf{w} \otimes \mathfrak{fst}_X \otimes \mathfrak{snd}_X, \mathsf{h}_1, (\mathsf{g}_1, \mathsf{g}_2, \mathsf{s}_1, \mathsf{s}_2))$ and $\mathsf{c}_0(\mathsf{h}') = (u : \mathsf{w} \to \mathsf{w} \otimes \mathfrak{fst}_{X'} \otimes \mathfrak{snd}_{X'}, \mathsf{h}'_1, (\mathsf{g}'_1, \mathsf{g}'_2, \mathsf{s}'_1, \mathsf{s}'_2))$, where the former allocates $X$, while the latter allocates $X'$. Note that everything terminates in this example. Now $\mathsf{c}_1(R, \mathsf{h}, \mathsf{h}')$ returns the pullback $\mathsf{w}_1 {}^{X\mapsto X'}{}_1\!\diamond^1_{X\mapsto X'} \mathsf{w}'_1$, where $X$ is mapped to $X'$. It is easy to check that $\mathsf{h}_1$ and $\mathsf{h}'_1$ are related in $R$ when taken to the pullback's low point and that $(\mathsf{g}_1, \mathsf{g}_2, \mathsf{s}_1, \mathsf{s}_2)$ and $(\mathsf{g}'_1, \mathsf{g}'_2, \mathsf{s}'_1, \mathsf{s}'_2)$ are equal in its apex.

Note that once this typing has been justified all equations derivable from it are automatically sound for observational equivalence. Thus, in particular, writes to the two "overlapping reference" commute.

***Set factory*** Let $\mathsf{w}$ be a world and $\mathsf{h} \in \mathfrak{S}\mathsf{w}$. Suppose that $\mathsf{h}_1$ arises from $\mathsf{h}$ by allocating a fresh set data structure, *e.g.*, a linked list, with entry point $X$. Let $\mathfrak{set}_X$ be the abstract location describing this fresh data structure.

Now for any chosen region r we can add $\mathfrak{set}_X$ to r to yield a new world $\mathsf{w}_1$. The function $setfactory_0(\mathsf{w})(\mathsf{h})$ then returns $\mathsf{w}_1$ and a tuple of semantic functions for reading, membership, removal of which we only sketch reading here: If $u : \mathsf{w}_1 \to \mathsf{w}_2$ and $\mathsf{h}_1 \in \mathfrak{S}\mathsf{w}_1$ and $i \in \mathbb{Z}$ then the reading function looks up $i$ in the data structure starting at the entry points $X$ in $\mathsf{h}_1$ (note that $\mathsf{h}_1 \in \mathfrak{S}\mathsf{w}$ asserts that this data structure exists and is well-formed. The returned (abstract) store $\mathsf{h}_2$ might not be the same as $\mathsf{h}$ because internal reorganizations, *e.g.*, removal of duplicates, might have occurred, but no world extension is needed and $\mathsf{h}_1 \sim \mathsf{h}_2$ holds. This together with the fact that the outcome only depends on the $\mathfrak{set}_X^R$ equivalence class (in the proof-relevant sense) justifies a read-only typing for reading.

***Memoization*** For the simple *memo* functional from Section 2 we produce just as in the previous example a fresh abstract location $\mathfrak{l}$ whose specification looks only at the two newly allocated concrete locations, say $\mathsf{l}_x, \mathsf{l}_y$, where the first stores the argument value $i$ and the second the integer value $f(i)$ where $f$ is the pure function to be memoised. The location's $\mathfrak{l}$ rely specifies that two heaps are equivalent when the values stored in $\mathsf{l}_x$ and $\mathsf{l}_y$ are the same: $(\mathsf{h}, \mathsf{h}') \in \mathfrak{l}^R \iff \mathsf{h}(\mathsf{l}_x), \mathsf{h}'(\mathsf{l}_x) \wedge \mathsf{h}(\mathsf{l}_y), \mathsf{h}'(\mathsf{l}_y)$. We see in Lemma 7.4 that if a function is semantically pure (empty effect) then there is a world- and heap-independent function describing its action. Thus the *memo* functional may be considered pure.

### 9.1 State Dependent Abstract Data Types

Although our focus is on effect-dependent equivalences that can be derived from refined typings using our equational rules, we are able to justify some of the well-known tricky examples from the literature on proving equivalences in ML-like languages without effect annotations. Our guarantee conditions here act like the transition system components of the worlds used by Ahmed *et al.* [1, 19].

***Awkward Example*** The first example is the classic *awkward example* [34]. Consider the following two programs:

$e_1 = \mathtt{let}\,x{\Leftarrow}\mathtt{ref}(0)\,\mathtt{in}\,\lambda f.x := 1; f(); !x$ and $e_2 = \lambda f.f(); 1$.

Intuitively, $e_1$ and $e_2$ are equivalent as they both return the value 1, although $e_1$ uses a fresh location to do so. We can formally prove the equivalence as follows: Assign the region where $x$ is allocated as r. If $f$ has the type $\mathtt{unit} \xrightarrow{\varepsilon} \mathtt{unit}$ with effects $\varepsilon$, then $e_1$ has type $(\mathtt{unit} \xrightarrow{\varepsilon} \mathtt{unit}) \xrightarrow{rd_r, wr_r} \mathtt{int}\ \&\ \varepsilon, al_r$, while $e_2$ has type $(\mathtt{unit} \xrightarrow{\varepsilon} \mathtt{unit}) \to \mathtt{int}\ \&\ \varepsilon$. Notice that $\varepsilon$ may contain $rd_r$ or $wr_r$ or both. Moreover, assume that an abstract location in region r looks at a single concrete location $\mathsf{l}$:

$\mathfrak{l}^R = \{(\mathsf{h}, \mathsf{h}') \mid \mathsf{h}(\mathsf{l}) = \mathsf{h}'(\mathsf{l})\}$

$\mathfrak{l}^G = \{(\mathsf{h}, \mathsf{h}_1) \mid \mathsf{h}_1(\mathsf{l}) = 1 \wedge \forall \mathsf{l}' \neq \mathsf{l}.\mathsf{h}(\mathsf{l}') = \mathsf{h}_1(\mathsf{l}')\}$

Notice that it is correct to assign $e_1$ a write effect in region r, as it writes the value 1 to the location assigned to $x$.

For proving the equivalence of $e_1$ and $e_2$, assume a world $\mathsf{w}$ and a heap $\mathsf{h}$. Let $[\![e_1]\!]\mathsf{wh} = (\mathsf{w} \uplus \mathsf{w}_1 \uplus \mathsf{w}_r, u_1, \mathsf{h}_1, \mathsf{a}_1)$ and $[\![e_2]\!]\mathsf{wh} = (\mathsf{w} \uplus \mathsf{w}_1, u_1, \mathsf{h}_2, \mathsf{a}_2)$. We construct a pullback square $\mathsf{w} \uplus \mathsf{w}_1 \uplus \mathsf{w}_r \diamond \mathsf{w} \uplus \mathsf{w}_1$ such that the values $\mathsf{a}_1$ and $\mathsf{a}_2$ are equal in its apex and $\mathsf{h}_1$ and $\mathsf{h}_2$ are equal in its low point. Since $wr_r$ is in the effects of $e_1$, we have that $\mathsf{a}_1 = 1$. We also have $\mathsf{a}_2 = 1$ trivially. Hence $\mathsf{a}_1$ and $\mathsf{a}_2$ are equal in the apex of the pullback square $\mathsf{w} \uplus \mathsf{w}_1 \uplus \mathsf{w}_r \diamond \mathsf{w} \uplus \mathsf{w}_1$. Similarly, $\mathsf{h}_1$ when taken to the low point of the square, that is, where the locations in $\mathsf{w}_r$ are forgotten, the resulting heap is equivalent to $\mathsf{h}_2$.

***Modified Awkward Example*** Consider now the following variant [1, 19] of the awkward example:

$e_1 = \mathtt{let}\ x{\Leftarrow}\mathtt{ref}(0)\ \mathtt{in}\ \lambda f.x := 0; f(); x := 1; f(); !x$

$e_2 = \lambda f.f(); f(); 1.$

The difference is that in the first program $x$ is first assigned 0 and the call-back function is used twice. Interestingly, however, our solution for the Awkward example still works just fine. We can prove semantically that the type of the program $e_1$ has the same type as before in the Awkward example, where the only writes allowed on the abstract location assigned for $x$ is to write the concrete location to one. Then the reasoning follows in a similar way.

***Callback with Lock Example*** We prove the equivalence of the following programs [1, 19]:

$e_1 = \mathtt{let}\ b{\Leftarrow}\mathtt{ref(true)}\ \mathtt{in}\ \mathtt{let}\ x{\Leftarrow}\mathtt{ref}(0)\ \mathtt{in}$
$\quad\langle\lambda f.\mathtt{if}\ !b\ \mathtt{then}\ (b := \mathtt{false};$
$\qquad f(); x := !x + 1; b := \mathtt{true})\ \mathtt{else}\ (), \lambda\_.!x\rangle$

$e_2 = \mathtt{let}\ b{\Leftarrow}\mathtt{ref(true)}\ \mathtt{in}\ \mathtt{let}\ x{\Leftarrow}\mathtt{ref}(0)\ \mathtt{in}$
$\quad\langle\lambda f.\mathtt{if}\ !b\ \mathtt{then}\ (b := \mathtt{false};$
$\qquad \mathtt{let}\ n{\Leftarrow}!x\ \mathtt{in}\ f(); x := n + 1; b := \mathtt{true})\ \mathtt{else}\ (), \lambda\_.!x\rangle.$

Both programs produce a pair of functions, one that increments the value stored in $x$ and the second that returns the value stored in $x$. They use the boolean reference $b$ as lock in the incrementing function. In particular, once this function is called the value in $b$ is set to `false` and only after the call-back is called and the value in $x$ is incremented is $b$ set again to `true`. However, the implementation of the increment function is different. While $e_1$ invokes the call-back $f()$ and then increments the value in $x$, $e_2$ remembers (in $n$) the value of $x$ before the call-back and then uses $n$ to update the value stored in $x$.

Assume that $x$ and $b$ are allocated in the same location ($\mathfrak{l}$) in the region $\mathsf{r}$. We show that these programs are equivalent in the type $((\mathtt{unit} \xrightarrow{\varepsilon} \mathtt{unit}) \xrightarrow{\varepsilon, wr_{\mathsf{r}}, rd_{\mathsf{r}}} \mathtt{unit}) \times (\mathtt{unit} \xrightarrow{rd_{\mathsf{r}}} \mathtt{unit})\ \&\ al_{\mathsf{r}}$, where $\varepsilon$ may contain the effects $wr_{\mathsf{r}}, rd_{\mathsf{r}}$. In particular, the location $\mathfrak{l}$ looks at two concrete locations $\mathsf{l}_b$ and $\mathsf{l}_x$ (storing $x$ and $b$):

$$\mathfrak{l}^R = \{(\mathsf{h}, \mathsf{h}') \mid \mathsf{h}(\mathsf{l}_b) = \mathsf{h}'(\mathsf{l}_b) \wedge \mathsf{h}(\mathsf{l}_x) = \mathsf{h}'(\mathsf{l}_x)\}$$
$$\mathfrak{l}^G = \{(\mathsf{h}, \mathsf{h}_1) \mid \mathsf{h}(\mathsf{l}_b) = \mathtt{false} \Rightarrow \mathsf{h}_1 = \mathsf{h} \text{ and}$$
$$(\mathsf{h}(\mathsf{l}_b) = \mathtt{true} \wedge \mathsf{h}_1(\mathsf{l}_x) = i \wedge \mathsf{h}_1(\mathsf{l}_x) = j) \Rightarrow$$
$$[(\mathsf{h}_1(\mathsf{l}_b) = \mathtt{true}) \wedge (j \leq i) \wedge (\forall \mathsf{l}' \notin \{\mathsf{l}_x, \mathsf{l}_b\}.\mathsf{h}(\mathsf{l}') = \mathsf{h}_1(\mathsf{l}'))]\}$$

First, notice that indeed the two programs above have the effect $wr_{\mathsf{r}}$. The increment of $x$ is allowed by $\mathfrak{l}^G$, as $b$ is initially `true`. To show that the two programs above are equivalent, we show that the value stored in $x$ before and after the call back is called remains the same. This is the case, as even if the callback function has a write effect in the region $\mathsf{r}$, *i.e.*, $wr_{\mathsf{r}} \in \varepsilon$, it cannot change the value of $x$. This is because when the function is called, the value stored in $b$ is `false`, meaning that the heap remains the same.

Despite the above, the model as presented here does not directly justify equivalences involving representation independence, *e.g.*, that our overlapping references $v_{or}$ are observationally equivalent to an implementation that really allocates two integer references. Generalizing world morphisms as discussed after Def. 6.2 does allow many such equivalences to be proved, though a parametric variant, along the lines of that described by Stark [39], would be more powerful still.

## 10. Related and Future Work

We have shown Proof-Relevant Logical Relations, introduced in our previous work [4], can be used to justify nontrivial effect-dependent program equivalences. For the first time it was possible to combine effect-dependent program equivalences with hidden invariants allowing "silent modifications" that do not count towards the ascription of an effect. Earlier accounts of effect-dependent program equivalences [3, 6, 7, 26, 41] do not provide such possibilities.

***Bisimulation*** An alternative approach to proving 'difficult' contextual equivalences is to use techniques based on bisimulation [27]. While bisimulation has been applied to typed calculi [24, 40] the strength of the method lies in being able to deal with fancy computation rules and fairly simple types and contracts rather than well-understood computation rules (call-by-value lambda calculus in our case) and fancy types and contracts. Indeed, we believe that something like our abstract locations and the proof-relevant world extensions would also suggest itself in a bisimulation-based approach to the equivalences studied here.

***Model Variables*** Proof-relevant logical relations or rather the sets $|A\mathsf{w}|$ where $A$ is a semantic type bear a vague relationship with the *model variables* [15] from "design by contract" [32] and more generally data refinement [16]. The commonality is that we track the semantic behavior of a program part with abstract functions on some abstracted set of data that may contain additional information (the "model"). The difference is that we do not focus on particular proof methods or specification formalisms but that we provide a general, sound semantic model for observational equivalence and program transformation and not merely for functional correctness. This is possible by the additional, also proof-relevant part of the semantic equality proofs between the elements of the models. We also note that our account rigorously supports higher-order functions, recursion, and dynamic allocation.

***Separation Logic*** Our abstract locations draw upon several ideas from separation logic [37], in particular the conditions on rely/guarantee assumptions from [42]. Intriguingly, we did not need something resembling the "frame rule" although perhaps the $\Pi$-quantification over larger worlds in function spaces plays its role.

Our use of pullback-preserving functors is motivated by FM-sets [21] or rather the *Schanuel topos* to which they are equivalent. Pitts's [35] gives a comprehensive account. The way in which we work with both permutation actions and functors has some precedent [9], but does feel slightly awkward: it really ought to be possible to combine the two structures into one.

We would like to define a stylized format that allows one to discharge semantic proof obligations in some cases without having to go down to the low-level semantic definitions. We noted that *private transitions* [1] serve a similar purpose and might perhaps suggest a possible approach in our case, too.

We would also like to be able to store values with proof-relevant equality, which would allow a stratified form of higher-order store [12]. Unrestricted higher-order store requires circular definitions of worlds, which has previously been addressed using, for example, metric spaces [11].

***Acknowledgments*** We thank Lennart Beringer and Andrew Kennedy for fruitful discussions. Nigam was supported by CAPES / CNPq and DAAD.

## References

[1] A. Ahmed, D. Dreyer, and A. Rossberg. State-dependent representation independence. In *POPL*, 2009.

[2] G. Barthe, V. Capretta, and O. Pons. Setoids in type theory. *J. Funct. Program.*, 13(2):261–293, 2003.

[3] N. Benton, L. Beringer, M. Hofmann, and A. Kennedy. Relational semantics for effect-based program transformations: higher-order store. In *PPDP*, 2009.

[4] N. Benton, M. Hofmann, and V. Nigam. Proof-relevant logical relations for name generation. In *TLCA*, 2013.

[5] N. Benton and C.-K. Hur. Biorthogonality, step-indexing and compiler correctness. In *ICFP*, 2009.

[6] N. Benton, A. Kennedy, L. Beringer, and M. Hofmann. Relational semantics for effect-based program transformations with dynamic allocation. In *PPDP*, 2007.

[7] N. Benton, A. Kennedy, M. Hofmann, and L. Beringer. Reading, writing and relations. In *APLAS*, volume 4279 of *LNCS*, 2006.

[8] N. Benton, A. Kennedy, and G. Russell. Compiling Standard ML to Java bytecodes. In *ICFP*, 1998.

[9] N. Benton and B. Leperchey. Relational reasoning in a nominal semantics for storage. In *TLCA*, volume 3461 of *LNCS*, 2005.

[10] L. Birkedal, A. Carboni, G. Rosolini, and D. S. Scott. Type theory via exact categories. In *LICS*, 1998.

[11] L. Birkedal, K. Stovring, and J. Thamsborg. The category-theoretic solution of recursive metric-space equations. *Theor. Comp. Sci.*, 411:4102–4122, 2010.

[12] G. Boudol. Typing termination in a higher-order concurrent imperative language. *Inf. Comput.*, 208(6), 2010.

[13] C. Calcagno, P. W. O'Hearn, and H. Yang. Local action and abstract separation logic. In *LICS*, pages 366–378, 2007.

[14] A. Carboni, P. J. Freyd, and A. Scedrov. A categorical approach to realizability and polymorphic types. In *MFPS, LNCS 298*, 1987.

[15] Y. Cheon, G. T. Leavens, M. Sitaraman, and S. H. Edwards. Model variables: cleanly supporting abstraction in design by contract. *Softw., Pract. Exper.*, 35(6):583–599, 2005.

[16] W. P. de Roever and K. Engelhardt. *Data Refinement: Model-oriented Proof Theories and their Comparison*. Cambridge University Press, 1998.

[17] T. Dinsdale-Young, P. Gardner, and M. J. Wheelhouse. Abstraction and refinement for local reasoning. In *VSTTE*, volume 6217 of *LNCS*, 2010.

[18] D. Dreyer, A. Ahmed, and L. Birkedal. Logical step-indexed logical relations. *Logical Methods in Computer Science*, 7(2), 2011.

[19] D. Dreyer, G. Neis, and L. Birkedal. The impact of higher-order state and control effects on local relational reasoning. In *Proc. ICFP, ACM*, pages 143–156, 2010.

[20] J. N. Foster, M. B. Greenwald, J. T. Moore, B. C. Pierce, and A. Schmitt. Combinators for bi-directional tree transformations: a linguistic approach to the view update problem. In *POPL*, pages 233–246, 2005.

[21] M. Gabbay and A. M. Pitts. A new approach to abstract syntax with variable binding. *Formal Asp. Comput.*, 13(3-5):341–363, 2002.

[22] D. K. Gifford and J. M. Lucassen. Integrating functional and imperative programming. In *LISP and Functional Programming*, 1986.

[23] C.-K. Hur and D. Dreyer. A Kripke logical relation between ML and assembly. In *POPL*, 2011.

[24] C.-K. Hur, D. Dreyer, G. Neis, and V. Vafeiadis. The marriage of bisimulations and kripke logical relations. In J. Field and M. Hicks, editors, *POPL*, pages 59–72. ACM, 2012.

[25] J. B. Jensen and L. Birkedal. Fictional separation logic. In *ESOP*, volume 7211 of *LNCS*, 2012.

[26] O. Kammar and G. D. Plotkin. Algebraic foundations for effect-dependent optimisations. In *POPL*, 2012.

[27] V. Koutavas and M. Wand. Small bisimulations for reasoning about higher-order imperative programs. In *POPL*, 2006.

[28] N. Krishnaswami, L. Birkedal, and J. Aldrich. Verifying event-driven programs using ramified frame properties. In *TLDI*, 2010.

[29] N. Krishnaswami, A. Turon, D. Dreyer, and D. Garg. Superficially substructural types. In *ICFP*, 2012.

[30] R. Ley-Wild and A. Nanevski. Subjective auxiliary state for coarse-grained concurrency. In *POPL*, 2013.

[31] S. Mac Lane. *Categories for the Working Mathematician*. Graduate Texts in Mathematics. Springer, 2nd edition, Sept. 1998.

[32] B. Meyer. Applying "design by contract". *IEEE Computer*, 25(10):40–51, 1992.

[33] F. Oles. *A Category-Theoretic Approach to the Semantics of Programming Languages*. PhD thesis, CMU, 1982.

[34] A. Pitts and I. Stark. Operational reasoning for functions with local state. In *Higher order operational techniques in semantics*, pages 227–273. Cambridge University Press, 1998.

[35] A. M. Pitts. *Nominal Sets: Names and Symmetry in Computer Science*, volume 57 of *Cambridge Tracts in Theoretical Computer Science*. Cambridge University Press, 2013.

[36] A. M. Pitts and I. D. B. Stark. Observable properties of higher-order functions that dynamically create local names, or what's new? In *MFCS*, volume 711 of *LNCS*, 1993.

[37] J. C. Reynolds. Separation logic: A logic for shared mutable data structures. In *LICS*, 2002.

[38] J. Schwinghammer, L. Birkedal, B. Reus, and H. Yang. Nested Hoare triples and framè rules for higher-order store. *Logical Methods in Computer Science*, 7(3), 2011.

[39] I. Stark. *Names and Higher-Order Functions*. PhD thesis, U. Cambridge, 1994.

[40] E. Sumii and B. C. Pierce. A bisimulation for type abstraction and recursion. In *POPL*, 2005.

[41] J. Thamsborg and L. Birkedal. A Kripke logical relation for effect-based program transformations. In *ICFP*, 2011.

[42] V. Vafeiadis and M. J. Parkinson. A marriage of rely/guarantee and separation logic. In *CONCUR*, volume 4703 of *LNCS*, 2007.

[43] P. Wadler and P. Thiemann. The marriage of effects and monads. *ACM Trans. Comput. Log.*, 4(1):1–32, 2003.

# Parametric Effect Monads and Semantics of Effect Systems

Shin-ya Katsumata

Research Institute for Mathematical Sciences, Kyoto University, Kyoto, Japan

sinya@kurims.kyoto-u.ac.jp

## Abstract

We study fundamental properties of a generalisation of monad called *parametric effect monad*, and apply it to the interpretation of general effect systems whose effects have sequential composition operators. We show that parametric effect monads admit analogues of the structures and concepts that exist for monads, such as Kleisli triples, the state monad and the continuation monad, Plotkin and Power's algebraic operations, and the categorical ⊤⊤-lifting. We also show a systematic method to generate both effects and a parametric effect monad from a monad morphism. Finally, we introduce two effect systems with explicit and implicit subeffecting, and discuss their denotational semantics and the soundness of effect systems.

***Categories and Subject Descriptors*** D.3.1 [*Programming Languages*]: Formal Definitions and Theory—Semantics; F.3.3 [*Logics and Meanings of Programs*]: Studies of Program Constructs—Type structure

***Keywords*** algebrac operation; computational effect; effect system; lax monoidal functor; monad; parametric effect monad

## 1. Introduction

*Effect system* is a type-based approach to statically estimate computational effects caused by programs. The basic idea of effect system is to add to each typing judgement $\Gamma \vdash M : \tau$ an expression $e$ that estimates the scope of $M$'s computational effect. The expression $e$ is called *effect*. The definition of effects depends on the computational effect that the programming language supports, and also the property we would like to know about the computational effect. For instance,

- Various effect systems and their semantics are studied for the analysis of memory usage during the execution of programs [6, 7, 22, 32, 34, 37]. Effects are defined to be sets of atoms $rd_\rho, wr_\rho, init_\rho$ tagged with regions.
- In [27], an effect system for concurrent ML (an extension of ML with communication primitives) is designed to analyse the communication behaviour of programs. There, effects are expressions of a process calculus.
- In [13], Kammar and Plotkin designs an effect system that estimates the set of algebraic operations invoked during the execution of programs.



*POPL '14*, January 22–24, 2014, San Diego, CA, USA.

ACM 978-1-4503-2544-8/14/01... $15.00.
http://dx.doi.org/10.1145/2535838.2535846

Statically estimating properties of computational effects brings various benefits to the analysis and transformation of programs. The main purpose of the pioneering work by Lucassen and Gifford [22] was to design the effect system that assists safe scheduling of expressions in parallel computing. Since then, many effect systems have been designed for analysing the behaviour of programs. For instance, control flow analysis can be concisely captured as an effect system [28]. The region-based memory management in functional languages is developed based on the idea of effect system [35]. A series of papers [6–8, 34] study a semantic foundation for some aggressive program transformations that depend on the result of effect analysis. Kammar and Plotkin gave a general algebraic account of the effect-dependent optimisations based on the property of algebraic theories [13].

In the seminal paper [37, 38], Wadler integrated the effect annotation and Moggi's monadic interpretation of computational effects into *effect-annotated monadic type* $T(e, \tau)$. He then posed a question: "What is the denotational semantics of the effect-annotated monadic type?" The main theme of this paper is to propose an answer to this problem.

***Semantic Structures for Effect-Annotated Monadic Types*** An answer to Wadler's question consists of 1) a formulation of the concept of effect, and 2) a mathematical structure corresponding to the effect-annotated monadic type.

One type of solution formulates effects as *join semilattices*, and use the join operator to compute the effect of let expressions. In this solution, each effect represents a set of *events*, and an effect-annotated monadic type $T(e, \tau)$ is given to the programs that cause the computational effects (regarded as events) in $e$. The typing rule for let expressions is:

$$\frac{\Gamma \vdash M : T(e,\tau) \quad \Gamma, x : \tau \vdash N : T(e',\sigma)}{\Gamma \vdash \mathsf{let}\ x\ \mathsf{be}\ M\ \mathsf{in}\ N : T(e \vee e', \sigma).} \qquad (1)$$

This type of solutions captures well the feature of the effect systems for memory usage analysis in [6, 7, 22, 32, 34, 37]. One of the earliest solutions of this type is Filliâtre's *generalised monad* [10].

However, using the join operator to compute the effect of let expressions is not always satisfactory. Here are some examples:

1. Let us consider an effect system that estimates exceptions raised by programs (we ignore exception handlers). We define an effect to be a set of exceptions. Then effects form a join semilattice by the set union. An instance of the typing rule (1) is the following derivation:

$$\frac{\Gamma \vdash \mathsf{raise}^{E_1}_\tau : T(\{E_1\},\tau) \quad \Gamma, x : \tau \vdash \mathsf{raise}^{E_2}_\sigma : T(\{E_2\},\sigma)}{\Gamma \vdash \mathsf{let}\ x\ \mathsf{be}\ \mathsf{raise}^{E_1}_\tau\ \mathsf{in}\ \mathsf{raise}^{E_2}_\sigma : T(\{E_1\} \cup \{E_2\},\sigma)}$$

The union of exceptions in the second line is sound, but not precise, because $E_2$ will never be raised.

2. Let us consider an effect system that estimates output strings of programs. A natural definition of an effect is thus a set of strings. Although effects form a join semilattice by the set union, it is inadequate to use the join operator in the typing rule (1) to compute the output strings of let expressions. Rather, we should use the language concatenation $\{l@l' \mid l \in e, l' \in e'\}$.

**Problem 1.1** To compute the effect of let expressions, what kind of a structure shall we assume on effects ?

**Problem 1.2** When the structure on effects is given in the answer to Problem 1.1, what is an appropriate semantic structure for the effect-annotated monadic type?

**Problem 1.3** How do we construct the structures proposed as a solution to Problem 1.2?

***Algebraic Operations with Effects*** The operations that manipulate computational effects, such as raise for exception raising, read / write for store access, etc., are important ingredients to make programming languages rich and expressive. To represent such operations in the monadic semantics of programming languages, Plotkin and Power introduced *algebraic operations* [30].

**Problem 1.4** How do we extend algebraic operations to the semantic structure given as an answer to Problem 1.2?

***The Meaning of Delimiting Monads by Effects*** Wadler pointed out the essence of effects as follows: "*effects delimit the scope of computational effects*" [37, 38]. [1] To elaborate this, suppose that we have a programming language $L$ with computational effects, and a denotational semantics of $L$ using a monad $T_0$. An effect system designed for $L$ introduces an effect-annotated monadic type $T(e, \tau)$, and it is given to the terms whose computational effects is within $e$. This suggests that we may see $T(e, \tau)$ as a *predicate* on $T_0[\![\tau]\!]$.

**Problem 1.5** How do we denotationally formulate that "effects delimit the scope of computational effects"?

Another issue is the *soundness of effect system*. When the effect system asserts that a program $M$ of a base type $b$ has an effect $e$, then we expect that the execution of $M$ causes the computational effect within the scope denoted by $e$. We formulate this as follows. We first specify the scope of computational effects of an effect $e$ by a predicate $S_b e$ on $T_0[\![b]\!]$. Then we consider whether for all judgements $M : T(e, b)$ in the effect system, we have $[\![M]\!] \in S_b e$. If this holds, then we say that the effect system is *sound* with respect to the specifications of effects.

**Problem 1.6** How do we establish the soundness of effect systems with respect to given specifications of effects?

### 1.1 Contributions of this Paper

This paper proposes the following solutions to the above problems. Especially, solutions to Problem 1.3-1.6 are the technical contributions of this paper.

***Solution to Problem 1.1*** We postulate that effects form a *preordered monoid.* The monoid structure is to compute the effect of let expressions, and the preorder is to compare the scope of effects. The typing rule (1) for let expressions is refined to

$$\frac{\Gamma \vdash M : T(e, \tau) \quad \Gamma, x : \tau \vdash N : T(e', \sigma)}{\Gamma \vdash \mathsf{let}\ x\ \mathsf{be}\ M\ \mathsf{in}\ N : T(e \cdot e', \sigma)}. \tag{2}$$

Actually, this typing rule had already appeared in [3] to sketch the idea of effect system, but its semantic account was not given there.

[1] In this paper, the word "delimit" is irrelevant to the *delimited continuation.*

***Solution to Problem 1.2*** Corresponding to the above solution, for a preordered monoid $\mathbb{E} = (E, \lesssim, 1, \cdot)$ of effects, we employ the following triple (plus a strength, which we omit here):

$$T : \mathbb{E} \to [\mathbb{C}, \mathbb{C}], \quad T_1 : \mathrm{Id} \to T1, \quad T_{e,e'} : Te \circ Te' \to T(e \cdot e')$$

satisfying the axioms of *lax monoidal functor* as a semantic structure for interpreting the effect-annotated monadic type. The morphisms $T_1$ and $T_{e,e'}$ replace the unit and multiplication of monad. The axioms of monad become the following commuting diagrams:

$$\begin{array}{ccc} Te & \xrightarrow{T_1 \circ Te} & T1 \circ Te \\ {\scriptstyle Te \circ T_1}\downarrow & \searrow\!\!\!= & \downarrow{\scriptstyle T_{1,e}} \\ Te \circ T1 & \xrightarrow[T_{e,1}]{} & Te \end{array} \qquad \begin{array}{ccc} Te \circ Te' \circ Te'' & \xrightarrow{Te \circ T_{e',e''}} & Te \circ T(e' \cdot e'') \\ {\scriptstyle T_{e,e'} \circ Te''}\downarrow & & \downarrow{\scriptstyle T_{e,e' \cdot e''}} \\ T(e \cdot e') \circ Te'' & \xrightarrow[T_{e \cdot e', e''}]{} & T(e \cdot e' \cdot e'') \end{array}$$

Such a structure is called a *parametric monad* by Melliès [25], and is introduced as an underlying categorical structure for establishing a bridge between linear logic and the theory of strong monads. In this paper, we consider it as a direct counterpart of the effect-annotated monadic type, and study it from the viewpoint of effect system. As we focus on the parametric monads whose parameter categories are preordered monoids of effects, we call them *parametric effect monads* to emphasise the restriction.

We show that there are parametric analogues of the concepts that exist in the theory of monad, such as Kleisli triples, the state monad, the continuation monad, algebraic operations [30], and the categorical $\top\top$-lifting [14]. This situation suggests that parametric effect monads are a natural generalisation of monads. Moreover, preordered monoids and lax monoidal functors are standard concepts in the theory of monoidal category. Therefore, the tools and results on monoidal categories are available for them (e.g. [24, 25]).

We mention the recent work [33] by Tate, where he introduces respectively *effectors* and *productors* as a solution to Problem 1.1 and 1.2. They are more expressive than parametric effect monads (see Section 6.1). Yet, the aforementioned features of parametric effect monad shows that they have rich structures to be studied.

***Solution to Problem 1.3*** We give a systematic method to construct *both* a preordered monoid $\mathbb{E}$ of effects and a parametric $\mathbb{E}$-monad on **Set** from a monad morphism $\alpha : \mathsf{T} \to (\mathsf{S}, \sqsubseteq)$; its codomain is a *preordered monad* [16]. We then extend this construction to domain-theoretic setting. Compared to giving effects and parametric effect monads by hand, it is relatively easy to give effect observations. We demonstrate this method with the case where $\mathsf{T}$ is the writer monad, exception monad, free algebra monad and probabilistic writer monad, deriving parametric effect versions of these monads.

***Solution to Problem 1.4*** We extend algebraic operations to parametric effect monads in two ways. One way is to add to the arity of an algebraic operation an effect $e$ that describes its computational effect. An extended algebraic operation has a triple $(I, J, e)$ as its arity, and it is a natural transformation:

$$\alpha_{e',K} : J \Rightarrow Te'K \to I \Rightarrow T(e \cdot e', K)$$

satisfying certain equational axioms. It bijectively corresponds to a morphism of type $I \to TeJ$.

However, when using an algebraic operation of the above type, we have to align the effect of all the arguments to $e'$. This constraint decreases the accuracy of the estimation of effects in some situations. To remedy this problem, we introduce another way to extend algebraic operations with effects. We allow algebraic operations to have different effects in their argument positions, and describe their effect by an *effect function* $\epsilon$. Then an algebraic operation extended in this way has a tuple $(n, \epsilon)$ as its arity, and it is a certain natural transformation:

$$\alpha_{e_1,\cdots,e_n,I} : Te_1I \times \cdots \times Te_nI \to T(\epsilon(e_1,\cdots,e_n))I.$$

***Solution to Problem 1.5*** Our solution takes two steps. First, we introduce the effect system EFi that is designed as a *refinement type system* over Moggi's computational metalanguage ($\lambda_{\mathrm{ML}}$ for short). Each EFi-type $\tau$ refines its effect erasure $|\tau|$, which is always a $\lambda_{\mathrm{ML}}$-type. We next give a denotational semantics of EFi in a *faithful functor* $p : \mathbb{P} \to \mathbb{C}$ with certain structures. We regard $\mathbb{P}$ as a category of predicates on objects in $\mathbb{C}$, and an object $X$ in $\mathbb{P}$ as a *predicate* on the object $pX$ in $\mathbb{C}$. We then interpret each refinement type $\tau$ as an object $\langle\tau\rangle$ in $\mathbb{P}$ and its effect erasure as an object $[\![|\tau|]\!]$ in $\mathbb{C}$, so that we have $p\langle\tau\rangle = [\![|\tau|]\!]$, that is, the denotation of a refinement type gives a predicate on the denotation of its erasure. To express that effects delimit the computational effects modelled by a monad $\mathsf{T}$ on $\mathbb{C}$, we interpret effect-annotated types by an parametric effect monad $\dot{T}$ on $\mathbb{P}$ such that $p(\dot{T}(e, X)) = \mathrm{T}(pX)$.

***Solution to Problem 1.6*** After categorically formulating the effect soundness, we give a sufficient conditions for the effect system EFi to be sound with respect to a given specification of effects. This sufficient condition is natural and applicable to any monad, preordered monoid of effects, effect specification and algebraic operation. The proof employs an parametric effect version of *categorical* $\top\top$*-lifting* [14].

## Preliminaries

***Notation*** We write $l@l'$ for the concatenation of two sequences $l$ and $l'$. We write $\mathbf{1}$ for 1) the one-point set $\{*\}$, 2) a terminal object in a category, and 3) a trivial category whose unique object is $*$. The disjoint union of sets $I_1,\cdots,I_n$ tagged with $l_1,\cdots,l_n$ is denoted by $l_1(I_1)+\cdots+l_n(I_n)$ .

***Category Theory*** A *thin* category is the one whose homsets have cardinality at most 1. Thin small categories are exactly preordered sets. In this paper, by a bi-CCC we mean a category with chosen finite products, finite coproducts and exponentials.

We write $\omega\mathbf{CPO}$ for the category of all $\omega$-complete posets (which may not contain the least element) and continuous functions between them. We also write **Pre** for the cartesian monoidal category of preordered sets and monotone functions between them.

We use $\bullet$ for the vertical composition and $*$ for the horizontal composition of natural transformations; see [23, Section XII-3] for these operations. For a natural transformation $\alpha$ and a functor $F$, we write $\alpha \circ F$ for $\alpha * \mathrm{id}_F$ and $F \circ \alpha$ for $\mathrm{id}_F * \alpha$, respectively.

***Monad*** We use sans-serif capital letters $\mathsf{T}, \mathsf{S}, \cdots$ to denote monads. Its functor part is referred by Roman capital letters $\mathrm{T}, \mathrm{S}, \cdots$. For a monad $\mathsf{T} = (\mathrm{T}, \eta^{\mathsf{T}}, \mu^{\mathsf{T}})$ and a morphism $f : I \to \mathrm{T}J$, by $f^{\#\mathsf{T}}$ (or $f^{\#}$ if $\mathsf{T}$ is obvious from the context) we mean the *Kleisli lifting* $\mu^{\mathsf{T}}_J \circ \mathrm{T}f$ of $f$. The monads used in this paper are defined in Table 1.

***Computational Metalanguage*** In this paper, by *computational metalanguage* ($\lambda_{\mathrm{ML}}$ for short) we mean the simply typed lambda calculus with products, coproducts, monadic types and algebraic operations; see [26, 30]. The set $\mathrm{Typ}_{\mathrm{ML}}(B)$ of $\lambda_{\mathrm{ML}}$-types generated from a set $B$ is defined by the following BNF:

$$\tau ::= b \mid \textstyle\prod(\tau,\cdots,\tau) \mid \coprod(\tau,\cdots,\tau) \mid \tau \Rightarrow \tau \mid T\tau \quad (b \in B).$$

We specify a $\lambda_{\mathrm{ML}}$ by a $\lambda_{\mathrm{ML}}$*-signature* $\Delta = (B, O, s)$, where $B$ and $O$ are sets of base types and operator symbols respectively, and $s : O \to H(\mathrm{GTyp}(B)^2) + I(\mathbf{N})$ is a function assigning an arity to each operator symbol $o \in O$; here $\mathrm{GTyp}(B)$ is the subset of $\mathrm{Typ}_{\mathrm{ML}}(B)$ consisting only of base types, product types and coproduct types. See Section 4 for the distinction on arities. A semantics of $\lambda_{\mathrm{ML}}(\Delta)$ is specified by a $\lambda_{\mathrm{ML}}(\Delta)$-structure: a tuple $(\mathbb{C}, \mathsf{T}, [\![-]\!])$ where $\mathbb{C}$ is a bi-CCC, $\mathsf{T}$ is a strong monad on $\mathbb{C}$ and $[\![-]\!]$ assigns:

| Category | Symbol | Definition of functor (object part) |
|---|---|---|
| Powerset monad / non-empty powerset monad | | |
| **Set** | $\mathsf{P}/\mathsf{P}^{+}$ | $\mathrm{P}I = 2^I$, $\mathrm{P}^{+}I = 2^I \backslash \{\emptyset\}$ |
| Writer monad | | |
| **Set** | $\mathsf{Wr}(\Sigma)$ | $\mathrm{Wr}(\Sigma)(I) = \Sigma^* \times I$ |
| Exception monad | | |
| **Set** | $\mathsf{Ex}(E)$ | $\mathrm{Ex}(E)(I) = Er(E) + Ok(I)$ |
| Distribution monad | | |
| **Set** | $\mathsf{Ds}$ | $\mathrm{Ds}I = \{f : I \to [0,1] \mid \mathrm{supp}(f) : \text{finite}, \sum_{i\in I} f(i) = 1\}$ |
| Lifting monad | | |
| $\omega\mathbf{CPO}$ | $\mathsf{L}$ | $\mathrm{L}I = I_{\perp}$ |

**Table 1.** Definition of Monads

1. an object $[\![b]\!] \in \mathbb{C}$ to each $b \in B$ (we extend this to $\mathrm{GTyp}(B)$ using the bi-cartesian structure of $\mathbb{C}$),
2. a $([\![\beta]\!], [\![\beta']\!])$-ary algebraic operation $[\![o]\!]$ for $\mathsf{T}$ to each $o \in O$ such that $s(o) = H(\beta, \beta')$, and
3. an $n$-ary algebraic operation $[\![o]\!]$ for $\mathsf{T}$ to each $o \in O$ such that $s(o) = I(n)$.

***Monoidal category*** A monoidal category consists of a category $\mathbb{C}$, an object $\mathbf{I} \in \mathbb{C}$ called the *tensor unit*, a bifunctor $\otimes \in \mathbb{C}^2 \to \mathbb{C}$ called the *tensor product*, and natural isomorphisms $l, r, a$ satisfying coherence axioms; see [23, Section XI-1]. A monoidal category is *strict* if $l, r, a$ are all identities. For every category $\mathbb{C}$, the functor category $[\mathbb{C}, \mathbb{C}]$ together with the identity functor $\mathrm{Id}_{\mathbb{C}}$ and the functor composition forms a *strict monoidal category* [23, Exercise XI-3.1]. We use this strict monoidal structure as the default one on $[\mathbb{C}, \mathbb{C}]$.

A *lax monoidal functor* ("lax" is dropped in [23, Section XI-2]) between monoidal categories $\mathbb{C}, \mathbb{D}$ consists of a functor $F : \mathbb{C} \to \mathbb{D}$, a morphism $F_{\mathbf{I}} : \mathbf{I} \to F\mathbf{I}$ and a natural transformation $F_{I,J} : FI \otimes FJ \to F(I \otimes J)$ satisfying certain conditions. When $F_{\mathbf{I}}$ and $F_{I,J}$ are identities, we replace "lax" with "strict". We write **LaxMonCAT** (resp. **StrictMonCAT**) for the super-large category of strict monoidal categories and lax (resp. strict) monoidal functors between them.

## 2. Parametric Effect Monads

### 2.1 Preordered Monoids as Effects

The role of effects in various effect systems is to represent scopes of computational effects caused by programs. As we stated in Section 1, we adopt the following abstract formalisation of the concept of effect.

**Postulate 2.1** Effects form a *preordered monoid*.

A preordered monoid is exactly a monoid object in the cartesian monoidal category **Pre**; it consists of a preorder $(E, \lesssim)$, an element $1 \in E$ and a monotone function $(\cdot) : (E, \lesssim)^2 \to (E, \lesssim)$ that satisfy the axioms of monoid. Below, by $e \sim e'$ we mean $(e \lesssim e') \wedge (e' \lesssim e)$. To save space, by the juxtaposition of $e$ and $e'$ we mean $e \cdot e'$. A *partially ordered monoid* is a preordered monoid such that $e \sim e' \iff e = e'$. By *join semilattice* we mean a partially ordered monoid whose monoid structure is given by the join operator. We identify preordered monoids and strict monoidal thin small categories.

### 2.2 Parametric Effect Monads

We introduce the main subject of this paper, *parametric effect monad*.

**Definition 2.2** Let $\mathbb{E}$ be a preordered monoid. A *parametric $\mathbb{E}$-monad* on a category $\mathbb{C}$ is a lax monoidal functor

$$T : \mathbb{E} \to [\mathbb{C}, \mathbb{C}].$$

This is expanded to the following elementary definition:

**Definition 2.2-bis** Let $\mathbb{E} = (E, \lesssim, 1, \cdot)$ be a preordered monoid. A parametric $\mathbb{E}$-monad consists of the following data.

1. An endofunctor $Te : \mathbb{C} \to \mathbb{C}$ for every $e \in E$.
2. A natural transformation $T(e \lesssim e') : Te \to Te'$ for every $e \lesssim e'$. This satisfies:
$$T(e \lesssim e) = \mathrm{id}_{Te}, \quad T(e' \lesssim e'') \bullet T(e \lesssim e') = T(e \lesssim e'').$$
3. A natural transformation $T_1 : \mathrm{Id} \to T1$.
4. A natural transformation $T_{e,e'} : Te \circ Te' \to T(ee')$ for every $e, e' \in E$.

These data make the following diagrams commute:

$$\begin{array}{ccc} Te_1 \circ Te'_1 & \xrightarrow{T_{e_1,e'_1}} & T(e_1e'_1) \\ \downarrow{\scriptstyle T(e_1\lesssim e_2)*T(e'_1\lesssim e'_2)} & & \downarrow{\scriptstyle T(e_1e'_1\lesssim e_2e'_2)} \\ Te_2 \circ Te'_2 & \xrightarrow[T_{e_2,e'_2}]{} & T(e_2e'_2) \end{array}$$

$$\begin{array}{ccc} Te & \xrightarrow{T_1 \circ Te} & T1 \circ Te \\ \downarrow{\scriptstyle Te \circ T_1} & \searrow\!\!\searrow & \downarrow{\scriptstyle T_{1,e}} \\ Te \circ T1 & \xrightarrow[T_{e,1}]{} & Te \end{array} \qquad \begin{array}{ccc} Te \circ Te' \circ Te'' & \xrightarrow{Te \circ T_{e',e''}} & Te \circ T(e'e'') \\ \downarrow{\scriptstyle T_{e,e'} \circ Te''} & & \downarrow{\scriptstyle T_{e,e'e''}} \\ T(ee') \circ Te'' & \xrightarrow[T_{ee',e''}]{} & T(ee'e'') \end{array}$$

Parametric effect monads can be equivalently presented in the form of Kleisli triple.

**Definition 2.3** Let $\mathbb{E} = (E, \lesssim, 1, \cdot)$ be a preordered monoid. An *parametric $\mathbb{E}$-Kleisli triple* on a category $\mathbb{C}$ consists of the following data.

1. A functor $T - I : \mathbb{E} \to \mathbb{C}$ for every $I \in \mathbb{C}$.
2. A morphism $\eta_I : I \to T1I$ for every $I \in \mathbb{C}$.
3. A mapping $(-)^{e\#e'} : \mathbb{C}(I, Te'J) \to \mathbb{C}(TeI, T(ee')J)$ for every $I, J \in \mathbb{C}$ and $e, e' \in E$. We call this mapping *Kleisli lifting*.

These data satisfy (below $f : I \to TeJ$ and $g : J \to Te'K$)

$$\begin{array}{rcl} (T(e \lesssim e'')J \circ f)^{e'\#e''} & = & T(e'e \lesssim e'e'')J \circ f^{e'\#e} \\ f^{e'\#e} \circ T(e'' \lesssim e')I & = & T(e''e \lesssim e'e)J \circ f^{e''\#e} \\ f^{1\#e} \circ \eta_I & = & f \\ (\eta_I)^{e\#1} & = & \mathrm{id}_{TeI} \\ (g^{e\#e'} \circ f)^{e''\#(ee')} & = & g^{(e''e)\#e'} \circ f^{e''\#e}. \end{array}$$

**Proposition 2.4** *Let $\mathbb{E}$ be a preordered monoid. Then parametric $\mathbb{E}$-monads on a category $\mathbb{C}$ bijectively correspond to parametric $\mathbb{E}$ Kleisli triples on $\mathbb{C}$.*

Parametric effect monads are yet insufficient to interpret the typing rule (2). We need *tensorial strengths* on them so that we can add an extra parameter to the Kleisli lifting:

$$(-)^{e\#e'} : \mathbb{C}(I \times J, TeK) \to \mathbb{C}(I \times Te'J, T(e'e)K).$$

We derive the concept of strong parametric effect monad as follows. For a category $\mathbb{C}$ with finite products, we write $[\mathbb{C}, \mathbb{C}]_s$ for the category of *strong endofunctors* and *strong natural transformations* between them [18]. We then equip it with the strict monoidal structure given by the identity functor and the composition of strong endofunctors.

**Definition 2.5** Let $\mathbb{C}$ be category with finite products and $\mathbb{E}$ be a preordered monoid. A *strong parametric $\mathbb{E}$-monad* is a lax monoidal functor

$$T : \mathbb{E} \to [\mathbb{C}, \mathbb{C}]_s.$$

We can alternatively define the tensorial strength as a *commutator* between a parametric effect monad $T$ and the action of $\mathbb{C}$ to itself; see [25, Section 4]. We note that $[\mathbf{Set}, \mathbf{Set}]_s$ is isomorphic to $[\mathbf{Set}, \mathbf{Set}]$, thus there is no difference between parametric $\mathbb{E}$-monads and strong ones on **Set**.

### 2.3 Maps from Parametric Effect Monads to Monads

We introduce a particular type of morphism for parametric effect monads. This will be used in Section 5.2 to express the situation that a parametric effect monad specifies predicates on the underlying monad.f

**Definition 2.6** Let $p : \mathbb{C} \to \mathbb{D}$ be a functor, $T$ be a parametric effect monad on $\mathbb{C}$ and $\mathsf{S} = (\mathsf{S}, \eta, \mu)$ be a monad on $\mathbb{D}$. We say that *$p$ maps $T$ to* $\mathsf{S}$ if

$$p(TeX) = \mathsf{S}(pX), \quad p((T_1)_X) = \eta_{pX}, \quad p((T_{e,e'})_X) = \mu_{pX}.$$

Though we omit the detail, there are other variations of morphism for parametric effect monads. They are analogues of the morphisms for monads studied in e.g. [19].

### 2.4 Examples of Parametric Effect Monads

**Example 2.7 (Monads)** Parametric effect monads subsume monads. Let us write $\mathbf{1}$ for the trivial, one-point preordered monoid. Then parametric $\mathbf{1}$-monads on a category $\mathbb{C}$ bijectively correspond to monads on $\mathbb{C}$. This is an instance of the fact that monoids in a monoidal category $\mathbb{V}$ bijectively correspond to lax monoidal functors of type $\mathbf{1} \to \mathbb{V}$.

**Example 2.8 (Parametric Writer Monad)** This example shows the writer monad whose output strings are delimited by a given language. Let $\Sigma$ be a set of alphabets. We consider the following partially ordered monoid $\mathbb{E}$ of languages over $\Sigma$:

$$\mathbb{E} = (\mathrm{P}(\Sigma^*), \subseteq, \{\epsilon\}, \cdot) \quad \text{where} \quad e \cdot e' = \{l@l' \mid l \in e, l' \in e'\}.$$

Then the following data:

$$TeI = e \times I, \quad (T_1)_I(i) = (\epsilon, i), \quad (T_{e,e'})_I(l, (l', i)) = (l@l', i)$$

give a parametric $\mathbb{E}$-monad on **Set**. Although $T$ inherits the structure from the writer monad $\mathsf{Wr}(\Sigma)$, each $Te$ is *not* a monad.

**Example 2.9 (Totality Types)** This is the semantic analogue of *totality types* by Nielsen et al. [31]. We consider the partially ordered monoid $\mathbb{E} = (\{tot, par, bot\}, \leq, tot, \cdot)$ whose order and multiplication are defined as follows:

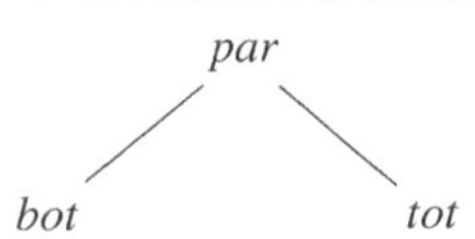


$$x \cdot y = \begin{cases} bot & (x = bot \lor y = bot) \\ tot & (x = tot \land y = tot) \\ par & (\text{otherwise}) \end{cases}$$

The functor $T : \mathbb{E} \to [\omega\mathbf{CPO}, \omega\mathbf{CPO}]$ mapping the above Hasse diagram to the following diagram in $[\omega\mathbf{CPO}, \omega\mathbf{CPO}]$:

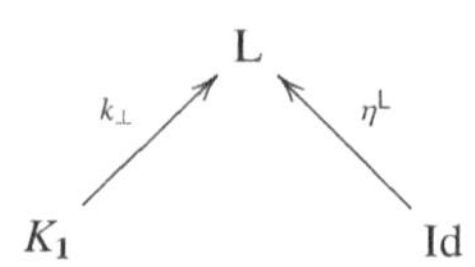


$$\begin{cases} K_1 I & = & \mathbf{1} \\ (k_\bot)_I(*) & = & \bot \end{cases}$$

extends to a parametric $\mathbb{E}$-monad on $\omega\mathbf{CPO}$.

We next give parametric effect versions of the state monad and the continuation monad. For this, we employ a categorical construction called *end* [23, Section IX-5]. Let $\mathbb{E} = (E, \lesssim)$ be a preordered set. The *end* of a functor $F : \mathbb{E}^{op} \times \mathbb{E} \to \mathbf{Set}$ is denoted by $\int_{e\in\mathbb{E}} F(e,e)$, and consists of the tuples $\alpha \in \prod_{e\in E} F(e,e)$ such that

$$\forall e, e' \in E \,.\, e \lesssim e' \Rightarrow F(e \lesssim e', e')(\alpha_{e'}) = F(e, e \lesssim e')(\alpha_e).$$

**Example 2.10 (Parametric State Monad)** Let $\mathbb{E} = (E, \lesssim, 1, \cdot)$ be a preordered monoid and $S : \mathbb{E} \to \mathbf{Set}$ be a (mere) functor. Then the following end

$$TeI = \int_{d\in\mathbb{E}} Sd \Rightarrow (I \times S(de))$$

extends to a parametric $\mathbb{E}$-monad. This end collects the state transformers that take a state of type $Sd$, and update it to a state of type $S(de)$. The effect $e$ abstractly represents what state transformers perform on states. It is added after $d$ because $e$ is the latest action performed on the state.

**Example 2.11 (Parametric Continuation Monad)** We continue using $\mathbb{E}$ and $S$ in the above example. The following end:

$$TeI = \int_{d\in\mathbb{E}} (I \Rightarrow Sd) \Rightarrow S(ed)$$

extends to a parametric $\mathbb{E}$-monad. An element in $TeI$ is a computation $c$ that takes a continuation $k$ of type $I \Rightarrow Sd$, and computes a value in the return type $S(ed)$. The effect $e$ abstractly represents what $c$ performs on the return type. As continuations are invoked after the main computation of $c$, $d$ is added after $e$.

### 2.5 Monads Indexed by Join-Semilattices

Let $\mathbb{E}$ be a poset. Let us call a functor of type $\mathbb{E} \to \mathbf{Mnd}(\mathbb{C})$ an $\mathbb{E}$-*indexed monad*, where $\mathbf{Mnd}(\mathbb{C})$ is the category of monads on $\mathbb{C}$ and monad morphisms between them. It is employed to model the layered structure of computational effects in Filinski's multi-monadic meta language M3L [9]. The typing rule for let expressions in M3L:

$$\frac{\Gamma \vdash M : T(e,\sigma) \quad \Gamma, x : \sigma \vdash N : T(e',\tau) \quad e \le e'}{\Gamma \vdash \mathsf{let}\ x\ \mathsf{be}\ M\ \mathsf{in}\ N : T(e',\tau)}$$

is reminiscent to the one in general effect system. Indeed, when $\mathbb{E}$ is a join semilattice, the general typing scheme (2) augmented with the side condition $e \le e'$ yields the above rule, because $T(e \vee e', \tau) = T(e', \tau)$. We can say more than this syntactic relationship.

**Theorem 2.12** *Let $\mathbb{E}$ be a join semilattice. Then $\mathbb{E}$-indexed monads bijectively correspond to parametric $\mathbb{E}$-monads.*

This theorem is an analogue of [33, Theorem 3], which is stated within effector / productor framework. Filliâtre's *generalized monads* [10] also determine join-semilattice indexed monads that map the least element to the identity monad. There are many examples of monads indexed by join semilattices; see e.g. [13, 33].

## 3. Parametric Effect Monads via Effect Observations

We next introduce a construction of both a preordered monoid $\mathbb{E}$ and a parametric $\mathbb{E}$-monad on **Set** from *effect observations*. This construction is based on the following nature of effects.

1. *Effects are expressions of an ordered algebra.* This point becomes clear when moving to an elaborated effect system, such as the one for behaviour analysis of concurrent ML programs [27]. There, effects are process algebra expressions ordered by their behaviour.

   We capture an ordered algebra structures on effects by a *preordered monad* $(\mathsf{S}, \sqsubseteq)$ on **Set** [16]. It is a pair of a monad $\mathsf{S}$ on **Set** and an assignment $\sqsubseteq$ of a preorder $\sqsubseteq_I$ on $\mathsf{S}I$ to each set $I$ satisfying:

   **(substitutivity)** for every function $f : I \to \mathsf{S}J$, $f^\#$ is a monotone function of type $(\mathsf{S}I, \sqsubseteq_I) \to (\mathsf{S}J, \sqsubseteq_J)$ and

   **(congruence)** for every function $f, g : I \to \mathsf{S}J$, $f \sqsubseteq_J g$ implies $f^\# \sqsubseteq_J g^\#$ (here $\sqsubseteq_J$ is extended to the pointwise order for functions).

   The assignment $\sqsubseteq$ bijectively corresponds to a pointwise **Pre**-enrichment on $\mathbf{Set}_\mathsf{S}$; see [16] for the detail.

2. *Effects are abstractions of computational effects.* Each effect abstractly expresses some aspects of actual computational effects caused by programs.

   We capture this situation by considering a monad $\mathsf{T}$ that models programming language's computational effects, and a *monad morphism* $\alpha : \mathsf{T} \to \mathsf{S}$ that observes computational effects and gives their abstract representations (i.e. effects).

We package the above data into an *effect observation*.

**Definition 3.1** An *effect observation* of a monad $\mathsf{T}$ on **Set** consists of the following data:

1. A preordered monad $(\mathsf{S}, \sqsubseteq)$ on **Set**.
2. A monad morphism $\alpha : \mathsf{T} \to \mathsf{S}$.

The notation for an effect observation (of $\mathsf{T}$) is $\alpha : \mathsf{T} \to (\mathsf{S}, \sqsubseteq)$.

First, from an effect observation we construct a preordered monoid of effects. Let us write $\mathrm{Th}_\mathsf{S}$ for the algebraic theory corresponding to $\mathsf{S}$. We then define an effect to be a $\mathrm{Th}_\mathsf{S}$-polynomial in one variable $*$; in other words, an element in $\mathbf{S1}$. Such polynomials carry the canonical monoid structure given by the variable substitution: the monoid unit 1 is the variable $*$ itself, and the multiplication $\cdot$ is the substitution $e \cdot e' = e[e'/*]$ of $e'$ into $*$ in $e$. We express this monoid structure in terms of $\mathsf{S}$:

**Definition 3.2** Let $(\mathsf{S}, \sqsubseteq)$ be a preordered monad on **Set**. We define the preordered monoid $(\mathbf{S1}, \sqsubseteq_\mathbf{1}, 1, \cdot)$ by

$$1 = \eta^\mathsf{S}_\mathbf{1}(*), \quad e \cdot e' = (\lambda x \in \mathbf{1} \,.\, e')^{\#S}(e). \tag{3}$$

We denote this by $\mathbf{S1}$.

Next, we construct a parametric $\mathbf{S1}$-monad. Let $e \in \mathbf{S1}$ be an effect. We consider the composite function $v_I = \alpha_\mathbf{1} \circ \mathsf{T}!_I : \mathsf{T}I \to \mathbf{S1}$. It first extracts the computation part of $x \in \mathsf{T}I$ by replacing all the values inside $x$ to $*$ $(\in \mathbf{1})$. Then the monad morphism $\alpha_\mathbf{1}$ gives its abstract representation as an effect. We then express that "the computational effect of $x$ is included in the scope of $e$" by the inequality $v_I(x) \sqsubseteq_\mathbf{1} e$, which we use to delimit $\mathsf{T}I$ by effects.

**Theorem 3.3** *Let $\alpha : \mathsf{T} \to (\mathsf{S}, \sqsubseteq)$ be an effect observation of a monad $\mathsf{T}$ on* **Set**. *We define the following assignment $D$ of sets:*

$$DeI = \{x \in \mathsf{T}I \mid \alpha_\mathbf{1} \circ \mathsf{T}!_I(x) \sqsubseteq_\mathbf{1} e\} \quad (e \in \mathbf{S1}, I \in \mathbf{Set})$$

*together with the inclusion function $i_I : DeI \subseteq \mathsf{T}I$. Then:*

1. *The unit $\eta^\mathsf{T}_I$ restricts to a function of type $I \to D1I$.*
2. *For all function $f : I \to De'J$, $(i_J \circ f)^{\#\mathsf{T}}$ restricts to a function of type $DeI \to D(ee')J$.*
3. *The tuple of $D, \eta^\mathsf{T}$ and $(f)^{e\#e'} = (i \circ f)^{\#\mathsf{T}}$ is a parametric* $\mathbf{S1}$-*Kleisli triple.*

When giving an effect system, it is desirable to have the join operator on effects (apart from a monoid structure), because we can use it to unify the effects given to different branches of case expressions. The following examples mainly observe a **Set**-monad $\mathsf{T}$ that models computational effects by means of another monad $\mathsf{S}$ whose preorder admits the join operator, so that $\mathbf{S1}$ also admits the join operator. In some cases S is given as the extension of T with the join operator.

**Example 3.4** We construct a parametric effect monad that is suitable for estimating exceptions raised by programs. There is a distributive law $\mathrm{Ex}(E) \circ \mathsf{P}^+ \to \mathsf{P}^+ \circ \mathrm{Ex}(E)$, and from this we obtain an effect observation of $\mathsf{Ex}(E)$:

$$\eta^{\mathsf{P}^+} \circ \mathsf{Ex}(E) : \mathsf{Ex}(E) \to (\mathsf{P}^+ \circ \mathsf{Ex}(E), \subseteq).$$

Definition 3.2 gives the following partially ordered monoid:

$$(\mathrm{P}^+(\mathrm{Ex}\,\mathbf{1}), \subseteq, \{Ok(*)\}, \cdot),$$

whose monoidal product is given by

$$e \cdot e' = \begin{cases} e & Ok(*) \notin e \\ (e \backslash \{Ok(*)\}) \cup e' & Ok(*) \in e. \end{cases}$$

The parametric $\mathrm{P}^+(\mathrm{Ex}\,\mathbf{1})$-monad $D$ induced by Theorem 3.3 is

$$DeI = \{Er(a) \mid Er(a) \in e\} \cup \{Ok(v) \mid v \in I, Ok(*) \in e\}.$$

We illustrate how effects in $\mathrm{P}^+(\mathrm{Ex}\,\mathbf{1})$ and the parametric effect monad $D$ describes computational effects.

- $c_1 \in D\{Ok(*)\}I$ is a computation that terminates normally, without raising any exception.
- $c_2 \in D\{Er(a), Ok(*)\}I$ is a computation that either terminates normally or may raise an exception $a$, but no other exception will be raised.
- $c_3 \in D\{Er(b), Er(c)\}I$ is a computation that will raise either an exception $b$ or $c$, but do nothing else, including normal termination.

The monoid structure of $\mathrm{P}^+(\mathrm{Ex}\,\mathbf{1})$ appropriately captures the fact that the exception raising cancels the rest of the computation. For instance, consider the sequential execution of the computation $c_3$ followed by $c_2$. As $c_3$ never terminates normally, we will not observe the computational effect caused by $c_2$. The monoid multiplication of $\mathrm{P}^+(\mathrm{Ex}\,\mathbf{1})$ gives the following effect to the sequential execution $c_3; c_2$:

$$\{Er(b), Er(c)\} \cdot \{Er(a), Ok(*)\} = \{Er(b), Er(c)\},$$

which correctly captures the computational effect of $c_3; c_2$.

**Example 3.5** Generalising the previous example, let $\Sigma$ be a first-order single-sorted signature (without equational axioms) and $O$ be the set of symbols defined in $\Sigma$. We write $\mathsf{T}_\Sigma$ for the monad of free-$\Sigma$ algebra, and aim to design the parametric effect monad that estimates the occurrences of operators in $t \in \mathrm{T}_\Sigma I$, and also the closedness of $t$.

The monad morphism we use to observe $T_\Sigma$ is the following $|-| : \mathsf{T}_\Sigma \to \mathsf{P}(Op(O) + Var(-))$:

$$|x| = \{Var(x)\}, \qquad |o(t_1, \cdots, t_n)| = \{Op(o)\} \cup |t_1| \cup \cdots \cup |t_n|$$

It collects the operator symbols and variables occurring in $t$. The partially ordered monoid derived from the effect observation $|-| : \mathsf{T}_\Sigma \to (\mathsf{P}(Op(O) + Var(-)), \subseteq)$ is

$$(\mathrm{P}(Op(O) + Var(\mathbf{1})), \subseteq, \{Var(*)\}, \cdot),$$

whose multiplication is given by

$$e \cdot e' = \begin{cases} e & Var(*) \notin e \\ (e \backslash \{Var(*)\}) \cup e' & Var(*) \in e. \end{cases}$$

The parametric $\mathrm{P}(Op(O) + Var\mathbf{1})$-monad $D$ derived by Theorem 3.3 is

$$DeI = \{t \in T_\Sigma I \mid |t[*/i]| \subseteq e\}.$$

We illustrate how this parametric effect monad estimates occurrences of operator symbols and closedness of $\Sigma$-terms.

- $t \in D\{Op(s), Op(z), Var(*)\}I$ is a $\Sigma$-term consisting of operator symbols $s, z$ and variables. It may be closed. No other operator occurs in $t$.
- $t \in D\{Op(c), Op(f)\}I$ is a closed $\Sigma$-term consisting of the operator symbols $f, c$ only.

**Example 3.6** We derive Example 2.8 by Theorem 3.3. We consider the writer monad $\mathsf{Wr}(\Sigma)$. There is a distributive law $\mathrm{Wr}(\Sigma) \circ \mathrm{P} \to \mathrm{P} \circ \mathrm{Wr}(\Sigma)$, and from this we obtain an effect observation of $\mathsf{Wr}(\Sigma)$:

$$\eta^{\mathsf{P}} \circ \mathrm{Wr}(\Sigma) : \mathsf{Wr}(\Sigma) \to (\mathsf{P} \circ \mathsf{Wr}(\Sigma), \subseteq)$$

Definition 3.2 yields the partially ordered monoid of languages over $\Sigma$, and Theorem 3.3 yields the parametric effect monad that is (isomorphic to) the one in Example 2.8.

**Example 3.7** We consider modelling the programming language that has a character output operator $out_c$ and a binary probabilistic choice operator $- \oplus_p -$, which chooses the left computation with probability $p$ or the right one with probability $1 - p$. We model these computational effects by the composite monad $\mathsf{Ds} \circ \mathrm{Wr}(\Sigma)$ of the distribution monad and the writer monad.

We first derive a parametric effect monad that estimates output strings of programs, ignoring their output probability. For this, we use the monad morphism $\mathrm{supp} : \mathsf{Ds} \to \mathsf{P}^+$ that computes the *support* of a given distribution:

$$\mathrm{supp}_I(d) = \{i \in I \mid d(i) \neq 0\}.$$

By composing the writer monad, we obtain the following effect observation of $\mathsf{Ds} \circ \mathsf{Wr}(\Sigma)$:

$$\mathrm{supp} \circ \mathrm{Wr}(\Sigma) : \mathsf{Ds} \circ \mathsf{Wr}(\Sigma) \to (\mathsf{P}^+ \circ \mathsf{Wr}(\Sigma), \subseteq).$$

We apply Theorem 3.3 to this situation. It yields the partially ordered monoid of non-empty languages $\mathrm{P}^+(\Sigma^*)$ over $\Sigma$ (c.f. Example 2.8). The parametric $\mathrm{P}^+(\Sigma^*)$-monad is then given as

$$\begin{aligned} DeI &= \{d \in \mathrm{Ds}(\mathrm{Wr}(\Sigma)(I)) \mid \mathrm{supp}_{\mathrm{Wr}(1)} \circ \mathrm{Ds}(\mathrm{Wr}(\Sigma)(!_I))(d) \subseteq e\} \\ &= \{d \in \mathrm{Ds}(\Sigma^* \times I) \mid \forall l \in \Sigma^*, i \in I \,.\, d(l, i) \neq 0 \implies l \in e\}. \end{aligned}$$

**Example 3.8** (Continued from the above example) We next derive another parametric effect monad that takes it into account the probability of output strings. Following the pattern of Example 3.4 and 2.8, we extend the (algebraic theory of) distribution monad $\mathsf{Ds}$ with the join operator, then use the embedding of $\mathsf{Ds}$ to the extended monad as an effect observation. The extension of $\mathsf{Ds}$ with the join operator is known to yield the monad that collects *convex subsets of distributions* [12, 36], which we explain below.

Let $X \subseteq \mathrm{Ds}\, I$ be a subset of probability distributions over $I$. The *convex closure* of $X$ collects all the probabilistic combinations of distributions in $X$:

$$CX = \bigcup_{n=0}^{\infty} \left\{ \bigoplus_{i=1}^{n} t(i) \cdot d_i \mid t \in \mathrm{Ds}\{1, \cdots, n\}, d : X^n \right\}.$$

When $CX = X$, we call $X$ *convex*. The monad $\mathsf{Cv}$ of *convex subsets of distributions* then collects all the finitely generated non-empty convex subsets of $\mathrm{Ds}\, I$:

$$\mathrm{Cv}\, I = \{CX \mid \emptyset \subsetneq X \subseteq_{\mathrm{fin}} \mathrm{Ds}\, I\}.$$

The inclusion relation between convex subsets gives a preorder on $\mathsf{Cv}$. We write $\boxplus_{p,I} : (\mathrm{Cv}\, I)^2 \to \mathrm{Cv}\, I$ for the probabilistic summation of two convex subsets:

$$X \boxplus_{p,I} Y = \{d \oplus_p d' \mid d \in X, d' \in Y\}.$$

The singleton set function $\{-\}_I : \mathrm{Ds}\, I \to \mathrm{Cv}\, I$ is a monad morphism, hence we obtain an effect observation

$$\{-\} \circ \mathrm{Wr}(\Sigma) : \mathsf{Ds} \circ \mathsf{Wr}(\Sigma) \to (\mathsf{Cv} \circ \mathsf{Wr}(\Sigma), \subseteq).$$

By applying Theorem 3.3, we obtain the partially ordered monoid $(\mathrm{Cv}(\Sigma^*), \subseteq, \{\{\epsilon : 1\}\}, \cdot)$, and a parametric $\mathrm{Cv}(\Sigma^*)$-monad:

$$DeI = \{d \in \mathrm{Ds}(\Sigma^* \times I) \mid \{\overline{d}\} \in e\},$$

where $\overline{d} \in \mathrm{Ds}(\Sigma^*)$ is the distribution given by $\overline{d}(l) = \sum_{i \in I} d(l, i)$.

We see the role of the convexity in effects. Consider the following conditional expression.

$$M = \text{if } N \text{ then } out_a() \text{ else } out_b().$$

This is a *deterministic* program that outputs either $a$ or $b$. The summary of the side effect is thus "$M$ outputs $a$ with probability 1 or $b$ with probability 1", but it is yet unclear what is the probability of choosing "then" branch and "else" branch by the conditional expression. The monad $\mathsf{Cv}$ handles this situation by taking the convex closure:

$$C(\{\{a : 1\}, \{b : 1\}\}) = \{\{a : p, b : (1 - p)\} \mid p \in [0, 1]\}$$

to give the overall probability of the output strings of $M$.

### 3.1 Effect Observations in an Order-Enriched Setting

We next give an analogue of Theorem 3.3 in a **Pre**-enriched category $\mathbb{C}$. We assume that $\mathbb{C}$ has a terminal object $\mathbf{1}$, and that $\mathbb{C}$ has chosen comma objects of the following form:

$$\begin{array}{ccc} f \downarrow j & \xrightarrow{!} & \mathbf{1} \\ {\scriptstyle \pi_{f,j}} \downarrow & \leq & \downarrow {\scriptstyle j} \\ I & \xrightarrow[f]{} & J \end{array} \qquad (4)$$

An informal way to see the comma object $f \downarrow j$ is that it is the pullback of the inclusion of the downset $\downarrow j \hookrightarrow J$ along $f$.

Below we write $\mathbb{C}_0$ for the underlying ordinary (i.e. **Set**-enriched) category of $\mathbb{C}$. An *effect observation* of a monad $\mathsf{T}$ on $\mathbb{C}_0$ by a **Pre**-enriched monad $\mathsf{S}$ on $\mathbb{C}$ is a monad morphism $\alpha : \mathsf{T} \to \mathsf{S}_0$, where $\mathsf{S}_0$ is the underlying ordinary monad on $\mathbb{C}_0$.

**Theorem 3.9** *Under the above* $\mathbb{C}$ *and an effect observation* $\alpha : \mathsf{T} \to \mathsf{S}_0$*, the following* $\mathbb{E}$ *is a preordered monoid, and* $D$ *is a parametric* $\mathbb{E}$*-monad on* $\mathbb{C}_0$.

$$\begin{array}{rcl} \mathbb{E} & = & (\mathbb{C}(\mathbf{1}, \mathsf{S}\mathbf{1}), \ \leq_{\mathbf{1},\mathsf{S}\mathbf{1}}, \ \eta^{\mathsf{S}}_{\mathbf{1}}, \ \lambda fg\,.\,g^{\#\mathsf{S}} \circ f) \\ DeI & = & (\alpha_{\mathbf{1}} \circ \mathsf{T}!_I) \downarrow e \end{array}$$

**Example 3.10** We derive a parametric effect monad whose effects can capture the behaviour of non-terminating programs. We consider the computational effect of divergence and bell ringing, and represent it by a monad on **ADCPO**, the category of algebraic DCPOs and all continuous functions between them. This category is **Pos**-enriched, has a terminal object 1 and has the comma object of the form (4). It is also closed under the lower powerdomain construction (see e.g. [1]).

We use the lazy counter monad, which is denoted by $\mathsf{B}$ in this example, to represent divergence and bell ringing. The ADCPO $\mathsf{B}I$ is given as the least solution of the recursive domain equation $X \simeq (I + X)_\perp$, and its Hasse diagram is depicted below (in the diagram, $i$ ranges over $I$, and $x \to y$ means $x \leq y$):

$$\begin{array}{lccccccc} & (0,i) & & (1,i) & & (2,i) & & \cdots \\ \mathsf{B}I = \mu Y.(I + Y)_\perp & \uparrow & & \uparrow & & \uparrow & & \\ & 0\perp & \longrightarrow & 1\perp & \longrightarrow & 2\perp & \longrightarrow \cdots \longrightarrow & \infty\perp \end{array}$$

Each element in $\mathsf{B}I$ denotes a phenomenon that may happen by executing a program.

- An element $x\perp$ ($x \in \mathbf{N}$) stands for the phenomenon that "the program rings the bell $x$ times and it is still running".
- The element $\infty\perp$ stands for the phenomenon that "$x\perp$ holds for all $x \in \mathbf{N}$". Thus the program rings the bell forever.
- The element $(x, i)$ stands for the phenomenon that "the program rings the bell $x$ times, then it terminates and returns a value $i$". Especially, when $I = \mathbf{1}$, the element $(x, *)$ stands for that "the program rings the bell $x$ times and terminates".

The order $\leq$ on these elements captures the implication relation between corresponding phenomena.

- The order $(x, i) \geq x\perp$ reflects that if a program terminates after ringing the bell $x$ times, then the program *is* indeed running right after the $x$-th bell.
- The order $x\perp \geq (x - 1)\perp$ reflects that if the phenomenon $x\perp$ happens then $(x - 1)\perp$ also happens before the $x$-th bell.
- The phenomenon $0\perp$ always happens for any program because there is a silent moment right after the program starts. Thus $0\perp$ is the least element.

We next consider the composite functor $\mathsf{P}_l \circ \mathsf{B}$, where $\mathsf{P}_l$ is the lower powerdomain construction. The composite extends to a **Pos**-(i.e. locally monotone) monad over the **Pos**-category **ADCPO**. We then obtain a monad morphism

$$\eta^{\mathsf{P}_l} \circ \mathsf{B} : \mathsf{B} \to \mathsf{P}_l \circ \mathsf{B},$$

to which we can apply Theorem 3.9.

The carrier set of the partially ordered monoid $\mathsf{P}_l(\mathsf{B}\mathbf{1})$ given by Theorem 3.9 is isomorphic to the full-sub poset $C$ of $(\mathbb{N} \cup \{\infty\}, \leq) \times (P(\mathbb{N}), \subseteq)$ consisting of pairs $(k, X)$ such that $\bigsqcup X \leq k$. Each pair $(k, X)$ encodes the following subset of $\mathsf{B}\mathbf{1}$ (below $\downarrow x$ denotes the downset of $x$):

$$\Phi(k, X) = \downarrow (k\perp) \cup \bigcup_{x \in X} \downarrow (x, *),$$

and an effect $(k, X)$ means that one of the phenomena in $\Phi(k, X)$ happens. We note that $(k, \emptyset) \in C$ expresses the behaviour of programs that never terminate.

The unit of $\mathbb{E}$ is $(0, \{0\})$, and the multiplication is

$$(k, X) \cdot (l, Y) = \left(k \sqcup \left(\bigsqcup_{x \in X} (x + l)\right), \{x + y \mid x \in X, y \in Y\}\right).$$

We especially have $(k, \emptyset) \cdot (l, Y) = (k, \emptyset)$, corresponding to that when the first expression of the sequential composition never terminates, the second expression will never be executed, thus its effect will be discarded.

The parametric $\mathsf{P}_l(\mathsf{B}\mathbf{1})$-monad by Theorem 3.9 is the following. With the helper function $\varphi : \mathsf{B}I \to \mathsf{P}_l(\mathsf{B}\mathbf{1})$ defined by:

$$\varphi(x, i) = (x, \{x\}), \quad \varphi(x\perp) = (x, \emptyset)$$

the parametric $\mathsf{P}_l(\mathsf{B}\mathbf{1})$-monad $D$ is given by

$$DeI = \{x \in \mathsf{B}I \mid \varphi(x) \in \Phi(e)\}.$$

## 4. Algebraic Operations for Parametric Effect Monads

We extend Plotkin and Power's *algebraic operations* introduced in [30] to strong parametric effect monads. A straightforward extension is the following:

**Definition 4.1** Let $\mathbb{E}$ be a preordered monoid and $T$ be an strong parametric $\mathbb{E}$-monad on a CCC $\mathbb{C}$. For $I, J \in \mathbb{C}$ and $e \in \mathbb{E}$, an $(I, J, e)$-ary *algebraic operation* for $T$ is a family of morphisms $a_{e',K} : J \Rightarrow Te'K \to I \Rightarrow T(ee')K$, natural on $e'$, such that for any $f : L \times K \to Te''M$, the following square commute:

$$\begin{array}{ccccc} L \times (J \Rightarrow Te'K) & \xrightarrow{c} & J \Rightarrow (L \times Te'K) & \xrightarrow{J \Rightarrow f^{\#}} & J \Rightarrow T(e'e'')M \\ {\scriptstyle L \times a_{e,K}} \downarrow & & & & \downarrow {\scriptstyle a_{e,M}} \\ L \times (I \Rightarrow T(ee')K) & \xrightarrow[c]{} & I \Rightarrow (L \times T(ee')K) & \xrightarrow[I \Rightarrow f^{\#}]{} & I \Rightarrow T(ee'e'')M \end{array}$$

For $n \in \mathbf{N}$ and $e \in \mathbb{E}$, an $(n, e)$-ary algebraic operation is similarly defined by replacing $J \Rightarrow -$ with $(-)^n$ and $I \Rightarrow -$ with Id in the above diagram.

An easy calculation shows that $(I, J, e)$-ary algebraic operations for $T$ bijectively correspond to morphisms of type $I \to TeJ$. This is an analogue of the correspondence between algebraic operations and *generic effects* stated in [30].

### 4.1 Algebraic Operations with Different Effect Arguments

The above extension of algebraic operations is natural, but not satisfactory in some situations. The reason is twofold: 1) a single effect $e$ may not be precise enough to capture the effect of an algebraic operation, and 2) the arguments of an algebraic operation has to have the same effect.

Let us see these problems with the parametric $\mathrm{Cv}(\Sigma^*)$-monad $D$ over the distribution monad $\mathsf{Ds}$ in Example 3.8. We consider restricting the domain and the codomain of $\oplus_p$ to obtain a $(2, e')$-ary algebraic operation for $D$. Following Definition 4.1, it is a certain family of functions of the following type:

$$\oplus_{p,I} : DeI \times DeI \to D(e'e)I.$$

What is an appropriate choice for $e'$? Actually $1 = \{\{\epsilon : 1\}\}$ is the the best. Since the choice operator itself does not output any string, if $e'$ contains some output strings with non-zero probability, then it introduces garbage to the estimation of output strings. We then realise that the effect 1 does not describe the behaviour of the computational effect $\oplus_p$.

Even if we accept $e' = 1$, we have another unsatisfactory point in using the algebraic operation of the above type. When supplying two computations $c_1 \in De_1I$ and $c_2 \in De_2I$ having different effects to $\oplus_{p,I}$, we first need to align their effects to, for example, $c_1, c_2 \in D(e_1 \vee e_2)I$. Then the probabilistic choice of them yields the computation $c_1 \oplus_{p,I} c_2 \in D(e_1 \vee e_2)I$, but this is too rough; for instance even when $p = 0$ (i.e. discarding the left argument) the effect of the left computation survives after the probabilistic choice.

Our solution to these problems is to allow the effects in the argument position of algebraic operations to be different with each other. For instance, in the context of Example 3.8, we give the following domain and codomain to $\oplus_p$:

$$(\oplus_p)_{e_1,e_2,I} : De_1I \times De_2I \to D(e_1 \boxplus_{p,\Sigma^*} e_2)I \tag{5}$$

so that the effect can say more precisely how argument effects are processed by the algebraic operation. We formalise this idea below.

**Definition 4.2** Let $\mathbb{E} = (E, \lesssim, 1, \cdot)$ be a preordered monoid and $T$ be an strong parametric $\mathbb{E}$-monad on a category $\mathbb{C}$ with finite products.

1. An $n$-ary *effect function* on $\mathbb{E}$ is a functor $\epsilon : \mathbb{E}^n \to \mathbb{E}$ such that
$$\epsilon(e_1, \cdots, e_n) \cdot e' = \epsilon(e_1e', \cdots, e_ne').$$
Below we abbreviate the sequence $e_1e', \cdots, e_ne'$ to $\vec{e}e'$.
2. Let $\epsilon$ be an $n$-ary effect function on $\mathbb{E}$. An *$(n, \epsilon)$-ary algebraic operation* for $T$ is a family of morphisms
$$a_{e_1,\cdots,e_n,I} : Te_1I \times \cdots \times Te_nI \to T(\epsilon(e_1, \cdots, e_n))I,$$
which is natural on $e_1, \cdots, e_n \in E$, such that for any $f : K \times I \to Te'J$, the following diagram commute:
$$\begin{array}{ccccc} K \times \prod Te_iI & \xrightarrow{\langle K \times \pi_i \rangle_{i=1}^n} & \prod (K \times Te_iI) & \xrightarrow{\prod f^{e_i \# e'}} & \prod T(e_ie')J \\ {\scriptstyle K \times a_{\vec{e},I}} \downarrow & & & & \downarrow {\scriptstyle a_{\vec{e}e',J}} \\ K \times T(\epsilon(\vec{e}))I & \xrightarrow[f^{\epsilon(\vec{e}) \# e'}]{} & T(\epsilon(\vec{e})e')J & = & T(\epsilon(\vec{e}e'))J \end{array}$$
In the above diagram, $f^{e \# e'} : K \times TeI \to T(ee')J$ is the parametrised Kleisli lifting of $f$ using the strength of $T$.

Currently, it is not clear how to extend the arity in the above definition to arbitrary objects in $\mathbb{C}$. This technical limitation also affects the design of effect systems in Section 5; there, algebraic operations in effect systems are classified into two groups, one corresponding to Definition 4.1 and the other corresponding to the above definition.

We gave a construction of the parametric effect monad $D$ from an effect observation $\alpha : \mathsf{T} \to (\mathsf{S}, \sqsubseteq)$ in Theorem 3.3. We next show that every $n$-ary algebraic operation $a$ for $\mathsf{T}$ can be restricted to an $(n, \epsilon)$-ary algebraic operation for $D$, where $\epsilon$ is constructed from $a$ and $\alpha$. Recall that the monad morphism $\alpha$ maps the $n$-ary algebraic operation $a$ for $\mathsf{T}$ to the one for $\mathsf{S}$. We denote it by $\overline{\alpha}(a)$.

**Theorem 4.3** *Let $\alpha : \mathsf{T} \to (\mathsf{S}, \sqsubseteq)$ be an effect observation of a monad $\mathsf{T}$ on* **Set**, *and $a$ be an $n$-ary algebraic operation for $\mathsf{T}$. We write $D$ for the parametric effect monad derived from the effect observation $\alpha$ by Theorem 3.3.*

1. *Function $\overline{\alpha}(a)_{\mathbf{1}} : (\mathsf{S}\mathbf{1})^n \to \mathsf{S}\mathbf{1}$ is an $n$-ary effect function on* $\mathsf{S}\mathbf{1}$.
2. *Each $a_I$ restricts to a function of the following type:*
$$a_I : De_1I \times \cdots De_nI \to D(\overline{\alpha}(a)_{\mathbf{1}}(e_1, \cdots, e_n))I,$$
*and this is an $(n, \overline{\alpha}(a)_{\mathbf{1}})$-ary algebraic operation for $D$.*

**Example 4.4** (Continued from Example 3.8) From Theorem 4.3, the binary algebraic operation $\oplus_p$ for $\mathsf{Ds} \circ \mathsf{Wr}$ restricts to an $(2, \boxplus_{p,\Sigma^*})$-ary algebraic operation for the parametric effect monad in Example 3.8.

**Example 4.5** Let $\Sigma$ be a first-order single-sorted signature (without equational axioms) and $\mathsf{T}_\Sigma$ be the monad of free $\Sigma$-algebra. There always exists a distributive law $\mathsf{T}_\Sigma \circ \mathsf{P} \to \mathsf{P} \circ \mathsf{T}_\Sigma$, and we obtain the effect observation

$$\eta : \mathsf{T}_\Sigma \to (\mathsf{P} \circ \mathsf{T}_\Sigma, \subseteq).$$

Definition 3.2 applied to this situation yields the preordered monoid $\mathsf{P}(\mathsf{T}_\Sigma(\mathbf{1}))$. The parametric $\mathsf{P}(\mathsf{T}_\Sigma(\mathbf{1}))$-monad $D$ of Theorem 3.3 is

$$DeI = \{t \in \mathsf{T}_\Sigma I \mid t[*/i]_{i \in I} \in e\}.$$

Each term $t \in \mathsf{T}_\Sigma\{1, \cdots, n\}$ gives the following $n$-ary algebraic operation $a_t$ for $\mathsf{T}_\Sigma$:

$$(a_t)_I(t_1, .., t_n) = t[t_i/i]_{i=1}^n.$$

Theorem 4.3 associates to this algebraic operation the following effect function on $\mathsf{P}(\mathsf{T}_\Sigma(\mathbf{1}))$:

$$\overline{\alpha}(a_t)_{\mathbf{1}}(e_1, \cdots, e_n) = \{t[t_i/i]_{i=1}^n \mid t_i \in e_i\}$$

and $a_t$ restricts to the following $(n, \overline{\alpha}(a_t)_{\mathbf{1}})$-ary algebraic operation for $D$:

$$(a_t)_I : De_1I \times \cdots \times De_nI \to D\{t[t_i/i]_{i=1}^n \mid t_i \in e_i\}I.$$

## 5. EFe/EFi: Simply-Typed Monomorphic Effect Systems with Effect Subtyping

We introduce two simply typed monomorphic effect systems, EFe and EFi. These two systems differ in handling effect subtyping. Both styles are adopted in many works. For instance,

- The calculus EFe adopts *explicit subeffecting* by effect coercion operators $T^{e \lesssim e'}$. This language is close to the one considered in Fillinski's M3L [9], where the point we can up-cast effect-annotated types is limited to let expressions. Another example of the effect system that adopts explicit subeffecting is [13].
- The calculus EFi adopts *implicit subeffecting*. Subjects of EFi judgements are $\lambda_{\mathrm{ML}}$-terms, and the subeffecting rule does not change subjects of judgements. Each type of EFi is a *refinement* of its underlying $\lambda_{\mathrm{ML}}$-type. See e.g. [4, 8].

These systems are specified by an EF-signature. We define the set $\mathrm{GTyp}(B)$ of ground types generated from $B$ by the following BNF:

$$\mathrm{GTyp}(B) \ni \beta ::= b \mid \prod(\beta, \cdots, \beta) \mid \coprod(\beta, \cdots, \beta) \quad (b \in B).$$

We write $\mathbf{1}$ for $\prod()$ and $\overline{n}$ for $\coprod(\overbrace{\mathbf{1}, \cdots, \mathbf{1}}^{n})$.

**Definition 5.1** An EF-signature $\Sigma$ consists of the following data:

1. A preordered monoid $\mathbb{E} = (E, \lesssim, 1, \cdot)$.
2. A set $B$ of base types.
3. A set $O$ of symbols for algebraic operations.
4. A function giving arities to algebraic operation symbols:

$$\begin{aligned} s : O \quad \to \quad & H(\mathrm{GTyp}(B)^2 \times E) \\ + \quad & I\{(n, \epsilon) \mid n \in \mathbf{N}, \epsilon : n\text{-ary effect function on } \mathbb{E}\}. \end{aligned}$$

The arity $H(\beta, \beta', e)$ and $I(n, \epsilon)$ are given to the algebraic operations in the style of Definition 4.1 and 4.2, respectively. Every EF-signature $\Sigma = (\mathbb{E}, B, O, s)$ determines an $\lambda_{\mathrm{ML}}$-signature $\Sigma_0 = (B, O, s')$ by discarding the effect information from $s$.

Throughout this section, we use a fixed EF-signature $\Sigma = (\mathbb{E}, B, O, s)$ with $\mathbb{E} = (E, \lesssim, 1, \cdot)$. Both calculi EFe($\Sigma$) and EFi($\Sigma$) share the same set $\mathrm{Typ}_{\mathrm{EF}}(\Sigma)$ of types defined as follows:

$$\begin{aligned} \mathrm{Typ}_{\mathrm{EF}}(\Sigma) \ni \tau \quad ::= \quad & b \mid \prod(\tau, \cdots, \tau) \mid \coprod(\tau, \cdots, \tau) \mid \tau \Rightarrow \tau \mid T(e, \tau) \\ & (b \in B, e \in \mathbb{E}). \end{aligned}$$

We define the *erasure function* $|-| : \mathrm{Typ}_{\mathrm{EF}}(\Sigma) \to \mathrm{Typ}_{\mathrm{ML}}(\Sigma_0)$ by the one that recursively replaces $T(e, \tau)$ by $T|\tau|$. We extend $|-|$ to typing contexts in the canonical way.

### 5.1 Explicit Subeffecting Calculus EFe($\Sigma$)

The calculus EFe($\Sigma$) extends the simply typed lambda calculus with products and coproducts with the following raw terms:

$$[M], \quad \mathsf{let}^{e,e'}\ x^{\tau}\ \mathsf{be}\ M\ \mathsf{in}\ N, \quad T^{e \lesssim e'} M, \quad o(M), \quad o(M, \cdots, M)$$

The first two are parametric analogues of pure-computation constructors and let expressions in $\lambda_{\mathrm{ML}}$. The third one is the (effect) coercion operator. The last two are the syntax for algebraic operations.

The typing rules are displayed in Figure 1. The equational theory of EFe($\Sigma$) extends the $\beta\eta$-equational theory for the simply typed lambda calculus with products and coproducts by the equational axioms displayed in Figure 2. The axioms (6) and (7) guarantee the functoriality of $T(-, \tau)$. The axioms (8)-(12) are a syntax representation of the axioms of parametric effect Kleisli triple (Definition 2.3). The axioms (13) and (14) guarantee that each $o \in O$ behave as an algebraic operation for $T$. The axiom (13) is for the symbol $o \in O$ such that $s(o) = H(\beta, \beta', e)$, while (14) is for $o \in O$ such that $s(o) = I(n, \epsilon)$.

The semantics of EFe($\Sigma$) is specified by an EFe($\Sigma$)-structure.

**Definition 5.2** An EFe($\Sigma$)-*structure* consists of the following data.

1. A bi-CCC $\mathbb{C}$ and an strong parametric $\mathbb{E}$-monad $T$ on $\mathbb{C}$.
2. An object $[\![b]\!] \in \mathbb{C}$ for each $b \in B$. We extend this assignment of $\mathbb{C}$-objects to base types to ground types $\mathrm{GTyp}(B)$ (see Preliminaries section) using the bi-cartesian structure on $\mathbb{C}$ in the canonical way.
3. A $([\![\beta]\!], [\![\beta']\!], e)$-ary algebraic operation $[\![o]\!]$ for $T$, for each $o \in O$ such that $s(o) = H(\beta, \beta', e)$.
4. An $(n, \epsilon)$-ary algebraic operation $[\![o]\!]$ for $T$, for each $o \in O$ such that $s(o) = I(n, \epsilon)$.

Interpretations of EFe($\Sigma$)-types and terms are straightforward.

**Theorem 5.3** *Let* $(\mathbb{C}, T, [\![-]\!])$ *be an* EFe($\Sigma$)*-structure. For every* EFe($\Sigma$)*-judgements* $\Gamma \vdash M, N : \tau$*, if* $M = N$ *holds in the equational theory of* EFe($\Sigma$)*, then we have* $[\![M]\!] = [\![N]\!]$.

### 5.2 Implicit Subeffecting Calculus EFi($\Sigma$)

The implicit subeffecting calculus EFi($\Sigma$) is designed to be a refinement type system for the computational metalanguage $\lambda_{\mathrm{ML}}(\Sigma_0)$. The subject $M$ of an EFi($\Sigma$)-judgement $\Gamma \vdash M : \tau$ is an $\lambda_{\mathrm{ML}}(\Sigma_0)$-term. Thus raw terms do not contain coercion operators $T^{e \lesssim e'}$, and effect annotations on let expressions are removed. Variable binders are also annotated with $\lambda_{\mathrm{ML}}(\Sigma_0)$-types instead of EFi($\Sigma$)-types.

**Proposition 5.4** *If* $\Gamma \vdash M : \tau$ *then* $|\Gamma| \vdash_{\mathrm{ML}} M : |\tau|$.

We move to the semantics of EFi($\Sigma$). The basic idea of refinement type is that each refinement type $\tau$ specifies a certain part, or a *predicate*, of its underlying type $|\tau|$. To model this idea, we employ a categorical setting that provides the concept of predicate on objects in a category.

A simple setting to talk about predicates on objects in a category $\mathbb{C}$ is to consider a *faithful functor* $p : \mathbb{P} \to \mathbb{C}$. We then regard:

- $\mathbb{P}$ as the category of *predicates* on objects in $\mathbb{C}$,
- $pX = I$ as "$X \in \mathbb{P}$ is a predicate over $I \in \mathbb{C}$",
- $p(\dot{f} : X \to Y) = f : I \to J$ as "$f$-image of $X$ is included by $Y$", and the morphism $\dot{f}$ as the unique witness of this statement.

Below, for objects $X, Y \in \mathbb{P}$ and a morphism $f : pX \to pY$ in $\mathbb{C}$, by $f : X \dot{\to} Y$ we mean the statement "there exists a unique $\dot{f} : X \to Y$ in $\mathbb{P}$ such that $p\dot{f} = f$". From the above viewpoint, $\mathrm{id}_I : X \dot{\to} Y$ corresponds to "$X$ implies $Y$" for predicates $X, Y$ over $I \in \mathbb{C}$. Thus the category consisting of objects $X$ such that $pX = I$ and morphisms $\dot{f}$ such that $p(\dot{f}) = \mathrm{id}_I$ may be seen as the preorder of predicates on $I$. We name this category $\mathbb{P}_I$, and call it the *fibre category* over $I$.

Besides, there are products, coproducts, arrow types and effect-annotated monadic types on refinement types; we thus assume that $\mathbb{P}$ is a bi-CCC, and that a parametric effect monad $\dot{T}$ is given on $\mathbb{P}$. The introduction and elimination of these type structures are synchronised with those of the underlying $\lambda_{\mathrm{ML}}$-types. We capture this situation by that $p$ strictly preserves the bi-CC structure on $\mathbb{P}$, and maps $\dot{T}$ to $\mathsf{T}$ (see Definition 2.6). The following two definitions summarises the above discussion.

**Definition 5.5** Let $\Delta$ be a $\lambda_{\mathrm{ML}}$-signature. An $\lambda_{\mathrm{ML}}(\Delta)$-*structure with predicates* consists of the following data.

1. A $\lambda_{\mathrm{ML}}(\Delta)$-structure $(\mathbb{C}, \mathsf{T}, [\![-]\!])$.
2. A bi-CCC $\mathbb{P}$. We denote the bi-CC structure with a dot, like $\dot{\times}, \dot{+}, \dot{\Rightarrow}, \dot{\pi}, \cdots$.
3. A faithful functor $p : \mathbb{P} \to \mathbb{C}$ such that $p$ strictly preserves the bi-CC structure, and each $\mathbb{P}_I$ has the largest element $\top_I$.

The common typing rules for EFe(Σ) and EFi(Σ) (in EFi(Σ) the type annotation $x^\tau$ at a variable binder is replaced by $x^{|\tau|}$)

$$\frac{\Gamma \vdash M_i : \tau_i \quad 1 \le i \le n}{\Gamma \vdash \langle M_1, \cdots, M_n \rangle : \prod(\tau_1, \cdots, \tau_n)} \quad \frac{\Gamma \vdash M : \prod(\tau_1, \cdots, \tau_n) \quad 1 \le i \le n}{\Gamma \vdash \pi_i\, M : \tau_i}$$

$$\frac{\Gamma \vdash M : \tau_i \quad 1 \le i \le n}{\Gamma \vdash \iota_i\, M : \coprod(\tau_1, \cdots, \tau_n)} \quad \frac{\Gamma \vdash M : \coprod(\tau_1, \cdots, \tau_n) \quad \Gamma, x_i : \tau_i \vdash M_i : \tau \quad 1 \le i \le n}{\Gamma \vdash \text{case } M \text{ with } \iota_1\, x_1^{\tau_1} \,.\, M_1, \cdots, \iota_n\, x_n^{\tau_n} \,.\, M_n : \tau}$$

$$\frac{\Gamma, x : \tau \vdash M : \tau'}{\Gamma \vdash \lambda x^\tau \,.\, M : \tau \Rightarrow \tau'} \quad \frac{\Gamma \vdash M : \tau \Rightarrow \tau' \quad \Gamma \vdash N : \tau}{\Gamma \vdash MN : \tau'}$$

$$\frac{\Gamma \vdash M : \beta' \Rightarrow T(e', \tau) \quad s(o) = H(\beta, \beta', e)}{\Gamma \vdash o(M) : \beta \Rightarrow T(ee', \tau)} \quad \frac{\Gamma \vdash M_1 : T(e_1, \tau) \quad \cdots \quad \Gamma \vdash M_n : T(e_n, \tau) \quad s(o) = I(n, \epsilon)}{\Gamma \vdash o(M_1, \cdots, M_n) : T(\epsilon(e_1, \cdots, e_n), \tau)} \quad \frac{}{\Gamma \vdash [M] : T(1, \tau)}$$

Typing rules specific to EFe(Σ)

$$\frac{\Gamma \vdash M : T(e, \tau) \quad e \le e'}{\Gamma \vdash T^{e \le e'}\, M : T(e', \tau)} \quad \frac{\Gamma \vdash M : T(e, \tau) \quad \Gamma, x : \tau \vdash N : T(e', \tau')}{\Gamma \vdash \mathsf{let}^{e,e'}\, x^\tau \mathsf{\ be\ } M \mathsf{\ in\ } N : T(e \cdot e', \tau')}$$

Typing rules specific to EFi(Σ)

$$\frac{\Gamma \vdash M : T(e, \tau) \quad e \le e'}{\Gamma \vdash M : T(e', \tau)} \quad \frac{\Gamma \vdash M : T(e, \tau) \quad \Gamma, x : \tau \vdash N : T(e', \tau')}{\Gamma \vdash \mathsf{let}\, x^{|\tau|} \mathsf{\ be\ } M \mathsf{\ in\ } N : T(e \cdot e', \tau')}$$

**Figure 1.** Typing Rules of EFe(Σ) and EFi(Σ)

$$\begin{aligned}
T^{e \lesssim e}\, M &= M && (6)\\
T^{e' \lesssim e''}\, (T^{e \lesssim e'}\, M) &= T^{e \lesssim e''}\, M && (7)\\
\mathsf{let}^{e',e''}\, x^\tau \mathsf{\ be\ } T^{e \lesssim e'}\, M \mathsf{\ in\ } N &= T^{ee'' \lesssim e'e''}(\mathsf{let}^{e,e''}\, x^\tau \mathsf{\ be\ } M \mathsf{\ in\ } N) && (8)\\
\mathsf{let}^{e'',e'}\, x^\tau \mathsf{\ be\ } M \mathsf{\ in\ } T^{e \lesssim e'}\, N &= T^{e''e \lesssim e''e'}(\mathsf{let}^{e'',e}\, x^\tau \mathsf{\ be\ } M \mathsf{\ in\ } N) && (9)\\
\mathsf{let}^{1,e}\, x^\tau \mathsf{\ be\ } [M] \mathsf{\ in\ } N &= N[M/x] && (10)\\
\mathsf{let}^{e,1}\, x^\tau \mathsf{\ be\ } M \mathsf{\ in\ } [x] &= M && (11)\\
\mathsf{let}^{e,e'e''}\, x^\tau \mathsf{\ be\ } M \mathsf{\ in\ let}^{e',e''}\, y^\sigma \mathsf{\ be\ } N \mathsf{\ in\ } L &= \mathsf{let}^{ee',e''}\, y^\sigma \mathsf{\ be\ } (\mathsf{let}^{e,e'}\, x^\tau \mathsf{\ be\ } M \mathsf{\ in\ } N) \mathsf{\ in\ } L && (12)\\
\mathsf{let}^{ee',e''}\, x^\tau \mathsf{\ be\ } o(M)\, N \mathsf{\ in\ } L &= o(\lambda y^\beta \,.\, \mathsf{let}^{e',e''}\, x^\tau \mathsf{\ be\ } M\, y \mathsf{\ in\ } L)\, N \quad (s(o) = H(\beta, \beta', e)) && (13)\\
\mathsf{let}^{\epsilon(e_1, \cdots, e_n),e'}\, x^\tau \mathsf{\ be\ } o(M_1, \cdots, M_n) \mathsf{\ in\ } N &= o(\mathsf{let}^{e_1,e'}\, x^\tau \mathsf{\ be\ } M_1 \mathsf{\ in\ } N, \cdots, \mathsf{let}^{e_n,e'}\, x^\tau \mathsf{\ be\ } M_n \mathsf{\ in\ } N) \quad (s(o) = I(n, \epsilon)) && (14)
\end{aligned}$$

**Figure 2.** Equational Axioms for EFe(Σ)

The notation for a $\lambda_{\mathrm{ML}}(\Delta)$-structure with predicates is $p : \mathbb{P} \to (\mathbb{C}, \mathsf{T}, [\![-]\!])$.

We note that the largest element $\top_I$ in the fibre $\mathbb{P}_I$ corresponds to $I$ itself in $\mathbb{P}$, or the predicate *true*.

**Definition 5.6** An EFi(Σ)-*structure* is a pair of a $\lambda_{\mathrm{ML}}(\Sigma_0)$-structure $p : \mathbb{P} \to (\mathbb{C}, \mathsf{T}, [\![-]\!])$ with predicates and a strong parametric $\mathbb{E}$-monad $\dot{T}$ on $\mathbb{P}$ such that

1. The functor $p$ maps $\dot{T}$ to $\mathsf{T}$ (see Definition 2.6).
2. For each $o \in O$ such that $s(o) = H(\beta, \beta', e)$, the $([\![\beta]\!], [\![\beta']\!])$-ary algebraic operation $[\![o]\!]$ for $\mathsf{T}$ satisfies: for all $e' \in \mathbb{E}, X \in \mathbb{P}$,

$$[\![o]\!]_{pX} : \top_{[\![\beta']\!]} \dot{\Rightarrow} \dot{T}e'X \dot{\to} \top_{[\![\beta]\!]} \dot{\Rightarrow} \dot{T}(ee')X.$$

3. For each $o \in O$ such that $s(o) = I(n, \epsilon)$, the $n$-ary algebraic operation $[\![o]\!]$ for $\mathsf{T}$ satisfies: for all $e_1, \cdots, e_n \in \mathbb{E}, X \in \mathbb{P}$,

$$[\![o]\!]_{pX} : \dot{T}e_1X \dot{\times} \cdots \dot{\times} \dot{T}e_nX \dot{\to} \dot{T}(\epsilon(e_1, \cdots, e_n))X.$$

The notation for an EFi(Σ)-structure is $p : (\mathbb{P}, \dot{T}) \to (\mathbb{C}, T, [\![-]\!])$.

Given an EFi(Σ)-structure $p : (\mathbb{P}, \dot{T}) \to (\mathbb{C}, \mathsf{T}, [\![-]\!])$, we interpret the calculus EFi(Σ) as follows. We interpret each type $\tau \in \mathrm{Typ}_{\mathrm{EF}}(\Sigma)$ by an object $\langle \tau \rangle \in \mathbb{P}$:

$$\begin{aligned}
\langle b \rangle &= \top_{[\![b]\!]}\\
\langle \prod(\tau_1, \cdots, \tau_n) \rangle &= \dot{\prod}(\langle \tau_1 \rangle, \cdots, \langle \tau_n \rangle)\\
\langle \coprod(\tau_1, \cdots, \tau_n) \rangle &= \dot{\coprod}(\langle \tau_1 \rangle, \cdots, \langle \tau_n \rangle)\\
\langle \tau \Rightarrow \tau' \rangle &= \langle \tau \rangle \dot{\Rightarrow} \langle \tau' \rangle\\
\langle Te\tau \rangle &= \dot{T}e\langle \tau \rangle.
\end{aligned}$$

We have $p\langle \tau \rangle = [\![|\tau|]\!]$, thus refinement types are indeed interpreted by a predicate over $[\![|\tau|]\!]$. We then show that the interpretation of the underlying $\lambda_{\mathrm{ML}}(\Sigma_0)$-judgement of an EFi(Σ)-judgement respects the predicates given by refinement types.

**Theorem 5.7** *Let $p : (\mathbb{P}, \dot{T}) \to (\mathbb{C}, \mathsf{T}, [\![-]\!])$ be an* EFi(Σ)*-structure. For all* EFi(Σ)*-judgements $x : \tau_1, \cdots, x_n : \tau_n \vdash M : \tau$, the interpretation of the $\lambda_{\mathrm{ML}}(\Sigma_0)$-judgement $x : |\tau_1|, \cdots, x_n : |\tau_n| \vdash M : |\tau|$ (which is derivable by Proposition 5.4) in the $\lambda_{\mathrm{ML}}(\Sigma_0)$-structure $(\mathbb{C}, \mathsf{T}, [\![-]\!])$ satisfies:*

$$[\![M]\!] : \langle \tau_1 \rangle \dot{\times} \cdots \dot{\times} \langle \tau_n \rangle \dot{\to} \langle \tau \rangle.$$

### 5.3 Soundness of EFi to Effect Specifications

We next discuss the soundness of EFi with respect to *effect specifications*. Recall that the primary purpose of effect system is to statically estimate computational effects caused by programs. To show the soundness of the estimation, we first need to specify the *meaning*, that is, the scope of computational effects, of each effect. Then the soundness of an effect system is that for every program $M$ having an effect $e$, the computational effect of $M$ is included in the scope assigned to $e$.

In our semantic framework, this discussion is roughly formulated as follows. Let $p : \mathbb{P} \to (\mathbb{C}, \mathsf{T}, [\![-]\!])$ be a $\lambda_{\mathrm{ML}}(\Sigma_0)$-structure with predicates. We specify the meaning of each effect $e$ as a $\mathbb{P}$-object $S_b e$ above $\mathsf{T}[\![b]\!]$; here $b$ is a base type. We then say that $\mathrm{EFi}(\Sigma)$ is sound with respect to the specification $S$ of effects if for all judgements $M : T(e, b)$ in EFi, $[\![M]\!] \in S_b e$. We actually allow certain type of free variables to occur in $M$.

**Definition 5.8** Let $p : \mathbb{P} \to (\mathbb{C}, \mathsf{T}, [\![-]\!])$ be a $\lambda_{\mathrm{ML}}(\Sigma_0)$-structure with predicates. An *effect specification* of $\Sigma$ in $p$ is just a family of functors (i.e. monotone mappings) $\{S_b : \mathbb{E} \to \mathbb{P}_{\mathsf{T}[\![b]\!]}\}_{b \in B}$.

**Definition 5.9** Let $p : \mathbb{P} \to (\mathbb{C}, \mathsf{T}, [\![-]\!])$ be a $\lambda_{\mathrm{ML}}(\Sigma_0)$-structure with predicates and $S$ be an effect specification of $\Sigma$ in $p$. We say that $\mathrm{EFi}(\Sigma)$ is:

1. *rank-0 sound with respect to $S$* if for all $\mathrm{EFi}(\Sigma)$-judgements
$$x_1 : b_1, \cdots, x_n : b_n \vdash M : T(e, b),$$
the interpretation $[\![M]\!]$ of its $\lambda_{\mathrm{ML}}(\Sigma_0)$-judgement in $(\mathbb{C}, \mathsf{T}, [\![-]\!])$ satisfies
$$[\![M]\!] : \mathsf{T}_{[\![b_1]\!]} \dot{\times} \cdots \dot{\times} \mathsf{T}_{[\![b_n]\!]} \dot{\to} S_b e.$$
2. *rank-1 sound with respect to $S$* if for all $\mathrm{EFi}(\Sigma)$-judgements
$$x_1 : \beta_1 \Rightarrow T(e_1, b_1), \cdots, x_n : \beta_n \Rightarrow T(e_n, b_n) \vdash M : \beta \Rightarrow T(e, b),$$
the interpretation $[\![M]\!]$ of its $\lambda_{\mathrm{ML}}(\Sigma_0)$-judgement satisfies
$$[\![M]\!] : \dot{\prod}_{i=1}^{n} (\mathsf{T}_{[\![\beta_i]\!]} \dot{\Rightarrow} S_{b_i} e_i) \dot{\to} (\mathsf{T}_{[\![\beta]\!]} \dot{\Rightarrow} S_b e).$$

Below, by imposing a mild condition on the faithful functor $p : \mathbb{P} \to \mathbb{C}$ of a $\lambda_{\mathrm{ML}}$-structure with predicates, we show that the soundness of EFi is derivable from (a combination of) the following closure properties on effect specifications.

**Definition 5.10** (Continued from Definition 5.8) We say that:

- $S$ is *closed under algebraic operations in* $\Sigma$ if it satisfies the following two sub-conditions:
A) For each $o \in O$ such that $s(o) = H(\beta, \beta', e)$, the $([\![\beta]\!], [\![\beta']\!])$-ary algebraic operation $[\![o]\!]$ for $\mathsf{T}$ satisfies: for all $e' \in \mathbb{E}, b \in B$,
$$[\![o]\!]_{[\![b]\!]} : \mathsf{T}_{[\![\beta']\!]} \dot{\Rightarrow} S_b e' \dot{\to} \mathsf{T}_{[\![\beta]\!]} \dot{\Rightarrow} S_b(ee').$$
B) For each $o \in O$ such that $s(o) = I(n, \epsilon)$, the $n$-ary algebraic operation $[\![o]\!]$ for $\mathsf{T}$ satisfies: for all $e_1, \cdots, e_n \in \mathbb{E}, b \in B$,
$$[\![o]\!]_{[\![b]\!]} : \dot{\prod}_{i=1}^{n} S_b e_i \dot{\to} S_b(\epsilon(e_1, \cdots, e_n)).$$
- $S$ *contains values* if for all $b \in B$, $\eta_{[\![b]\!]} : \mathsf{T}_{[\![b]\!]} \dot{\to} S_b 1$.
- $S$ is *closed under lifting* if the unit
$$\sigma_I^{\mathsf{T},R} : \mathrm{T}I \to (I \Rightarrow \mathrm{T}R) \Rightarrow \mathrm{T}R$$
of the continuation monad transformer [5] satisfies: for all $e, e' \in \mathbb{E}, b, b' \in B$,
$$\sigma_{[\![b]\!]}^{\mathsf{T},[\![b']\!]} : S_b e \dot{\to} (\mathsf{T}_{[\![b]\!]} \dot{\Rightarrow} S_{b'} e') \dot{\Rightarrow} S_{b'}(ee').$$

The condition we impose on $p$ is that: $p$ is a *fibration with fibred small products*. Such fibrations are often used in the categorical formulation of logical relations; see [11, 15]. Under this condition, we can *construct* a strong parametric $\mathbb{E}$-monad on $\mathbb{P}$ from effect specifications. It is a variation of the categorical $\top\top$-lifting in [14].

The construction proceeds as follows. Let $p : \mathbb{P} \to (\mathbb{C}, \mathsf{T}, [\![-]\!])$ be a $\lambda_{\mathrm{ML}}(\Sigma_0)$-structure with predicates such that $p : \mathbb{P} \to \mathbb{C}$ is a fibration with fibred small products. Also, let $S$ be an effect specification of $\Sigma$ in $p$. For each $X \in \mathbb{P}$, we first define an auxiliary $\mathbb{P}$-object $\dot{T}^{e',b}eX$ ($e, e' \in \mathbb{E}, b \in B$) by the following inverse image in the fibration $p$:

$$\begin{array}{ccccc}
\dot{T}^{e',b}eX & \cdots\cdots\rightarrow & (X \dot{\Rightarrow} S_b e') \dot{\Rightarrow} S_b(ee') & & \mathbb{P} \\
 & & & & \downarrow p \\
\mathrm{T}(pX) & \xrightarrow[\sigma_{pX}^{\mathsf{T},[\![b]\!]}]{} & (pX \Rightarrow \mathrm{T}[\![b]\!]) \Rightarrow \mathrm{T}[\![b]\!] & & \mathbb{C}
\end{array}$$

(see also Example 2.11). We then define $\dot{T}^S eX$ to be the following small product (i.e. meet) in the fibre category $\mathbb{P}_{\mathrm{T}(pX)}$:
$$\dot{T}^S eX = \bigwedge_{e' \in \mathbb{E}, b \in B} \dot{T}^{e',b}eX.$$

**Theorem 5.11** *Let $p : \mathbb{P} \to (\mathbb{C}, \mathsf{T}, [\![-]\!])$ be a $\lambda_{\mathrm{ML}}(\Sigma_0)$-structure with predicates such that $p$ is a fibration with fibred small products. Also, let $S$ be an effect specification of $\Sigma$ in $p$.*

1. *$\dot{T}^S$ is a strong parametric $\mathbb{E}$-monad on $\mathbb{P}$, and $p$ maps $\dot{T}^S$ to $\mathsf{T}$.*
2. *If $S$ is closed under algebraic operations, then we have an $\mathrm{EFi}(\Sigma)$-structure $p : (\mathbb{P}, \dot{T}^S) \to (\mathbb{C}, \mathsf{T}, [\![-]\!])$.*
3. *If $S$ is closed under algebraic operations and contains values, then $\mathrm{EFi}(\Sigma)$ is rank-0 sound with respect to $S$.*
4. *$S$ is closed under algebraic operations, contains values and is closed under lifting if and only if $\mathrm{EFi}(\Sigma)$ is rank-1 sound with respect to $S$.*

Theorem 5.11-3 is a parametric analogue of [15, Theorem 7].

**Example 5.12** Let $\Delta = (B, O, s)$ be a $\lambda_{\mathrm{ML}}$-signature, $(\mathbf{Set}, \mathsf{T}, [\![-]\!])$ be a $\lambda_{\mathrm{ML}}(\Delta)$-structure and $\alpha : \mathsf{T} \to (\mathsf{S}, \sqsubseteq)$ be an effect observation. We assume that $\Delta$ contains only natural number-ary algebraic operations. The subobject fibration $p : \mathbf{Sub}(\mathbf{Set}) \to \mathbf{Set}$ (see[11, Chapter 0]) provides the data 2 and 3 of Definition 5.5, and has fibred small products. Therefore $p : \mathbf{Sub}(\mathbf{Set}) \to (\mathbf{Set}, T, [\![-]\!])$ is a $\lambda_{\mathrm{ML}}(\Delta)$-structure with predicates.

We next derive an EF-signature $\Sigma_\Delta = (\mathbf{S1}, B, O, s')$ where $s'$ is defined by
$$s'(o) = (n, \overline{\alpha}([\![o]\!])_1) \quad (s(o) = I(n)).$$
This $s'$ assigns the effect function to each operator symbol in $O$ by Theorem 4.3-1.

We give an effect specification $S$ of $\Sigma_\Delta$ in $p$ by means of the parametric effect monad $D$ derived by Theorem 3.3: $S_b e = (De[\![b]\!] \subseteq \mathsf{T}[\![b]\!])$. This is closed under algebraic operations in $\Sigma_\Delta$ thanks to Theorem 4.3-2, and moreover $S$ contains values and is closed under lifting because $D$ is a parametric effect monad. By Theorem 5.11-4, $\mathrm{EFi}(\Sigma)$ is rank-1 sound with respect to $S$, that is, for every $\mathrm{EFi}(\Sigma_\Delta)$-judgement
$$x_1 : \beta_1 \Rightarrow T(e_1, b_1), \cdots, x_n : \beta_n \Rightarrow T(e_n, b_n) \vdash M : \beta \Rightarrow T(e, b),$$
the interpretation $[\![M]\!]$ of its $\lambda_{\mathrm{ML}}(\Delta)$-judgement in $(\mathbf{Set}, \mathsf{T}, [\![-]\!])$ satisfies: for all functions $f_i : [\![\beta_i]\!] \to De_i[\![b_i]\!]$ and $x \in [\![\beta']\!]$, we have
$$[\![M]\!]\{x_1 : f_1, \cdots, x_n : f_n\}(x) \in De'[\![b']\!].$$

## 6. Related Work

### 6.1 Effectors and Productors

Tate introduced a semantic structure called *effectors* and *productors* in [33] as a solution to Problem 1.1 and 1.2. Through a characterisation of effectors / productors in terms of *multicategory theory*, we show that parametric effect monads are *productors on total principalled effectoids*. A good reference for multicategory theory is [20].

Let us write **MultCAT** for the (super-large) category of multicategories and maps between them. There is an adjunction relating multicategories and strict monoidal categories [20, Section 2.3]:

$$\mathbf{StrictMonCAT} \underset{F}{\overset{U}{\underset{\leftarrow}{\overset{\rightarrow}{\top}}}} \mathbf{MultCAT}$$

The right adjoint $U$ maps a strict monoidal category $(\mathbb{C}, \mathbf{I}, \otimes)$ to its *underlying multicategory* $U\mathbb{C}$ [20, Example 2.1.3]. It has the same objects as $\mathbb{C}$, and its homsets are defined by

$$(U\mathbb{C})([I_1, \cdots, I_n], J) = \mathbb{C}(I_1 \otimes \cdots \otimes I_n, J).$$

The functor $U$ preserves thinness. We also mention a relationship between lax monoidal functors and maps for multicategories, stated as Example 2.1.10 in [20]. For each strict monoidal category $\mathbb{B}$ and $\mathbb{D}$, we have the following bijection:

$$\mathbf{LaxMonCAT}(\mathbb{B}, \mathbb{D}) \simeq \mathbf{MultCAT}(U\mathbb{B}, U\mathbb{D}). \quad (15)$$

We omit the definition of effectors and productors; see [33, Section 5 & 6]. We give the following multicategorical characterisation of effectors and productors:

**Theorem 6.1** *1. [33, Section 9] Effectors bijectively correspond to thin small multicategories. (Below we identify these two concepts.)*

*2. Let $\mathbb{F}$ be an effector. Then $\mathbb{F}$-productors bijectively correspond to maps (for multicategories) of type $\mathbb{F} \to U[\mathbb{C}, \mathbb{C}]$.*

For a preordered monoid $\mathbb{E}$, $U\mathbb{E}$ is an effector called *total principalled effectoid* [33, Section 9]. The following proposition is a consequence of (15):

**Proposition 6.2** *Let $\mathbb{E}$ be a preordered monoid. Then parametric $\mathbb{E}$-monads on a category $\mathbb{C}$ bijectively correspond to $U\mathbb{E}$-productors on $\mathbb{C}$.*

We end this section with the discussion about the unification of productors and parametric effect monads. Let $\mathbb{F}$ be an effector. Using the adjunction $F \dashv U$ and the inclusion of categories **StrictMonCAT** $\subseteq$ **LaxMonCAT**, we obtain

$$\begin{aligned} \mathbf{MultiCAT}(\mathbb{F}, U[\mathbb{C}, \mathbb{C}]) &\simeq \mathbf{StrictMonCAT}(F\mathbb{F}, [\mathbb{C}, \mathbb{C}]) \\ &\subseteq \mathbf{LaxMonCAT}(F\mathbb{F}, [\mathbb{C}, \mathbb{C}]). \end{aligned}$$

We note that $F\mathbb{F}$ is not thin in general. This suggests that productors can be encoded by general parametric monads [25].

### 6.2 Actions of Monoidal Categories

Parametric effect monads are an instance of the broader concept of *action of monoidal categories*. Depending on the degree of the preservation of monoidal structure, there are several variations of this concept, each of which corresponds to *strong*, *lax* and *oplax* monoidal functors of type $\mathbb{M} \to [\mathbb{C}, \mathbb{C}]$.

In mathematics, a category equipped with a strong action of a monoidal category is sometimes called an *actegory* (not a typo!), and studied in e.g. [17]. In Levy's *call-by-push-value*, a strong action of a category with finite products is used as a part of a CBPV value / producer model [21].

Parametric effect monads are exactly lax actions of preordered monoids. Lax actions of general monoidal categories are called *parametric monads* in [25] and *negative $\mathbb{M}$-categories* in [24]. They are introduced to give a unified account of the *tensorial strength* of the continuation monad and the *weak distributive law* in linear logic. The categorical analysis of parametric monads in [24, 25] are readily applicable to parametric effect monads. Especially, the concept of *commutator* for parametric monads in [25] will provide a method to synthesise parametric effect monads, hence effect systems as well. Compared to [24, 25], this paper provides new examples and constructions of parametric (effect) monads arising from the study of a semantics of effect system. We note that parametric effect Kleisli triples and the parametric state / continuation monad can be defined for general monoidal categories.

Recently, Petricek et al. study oplax actions of monoids to categories under the name *indexed comonad* [29, Definition 2]. Although they are the dual of parametric effect monads, the spirit of their work is very close to this work. It is interesting to see whether we can dualise the construction of parametric effect monads using effect observations.

We finally mention a possible generalisation of parametric (effect) monads. A monoidal category $\mathbb{M}$ and a lax monoidal functor of type $\mathbb{M} \to [\mathbb{C}, \mathbb{C}]$ bijectively corresponds to the one-object bicategory $\mathbf{B}\mathbb{M}$ and a lax functor of type $\mathbf{B}\mathbb{M} \to \mathbf{B}[\mathbb{C}, \mathbb{C}]$, respectively. This shift to the bicategory theory suggests us to take a bicategory $\mathbb{E}$ and a lax functor of type $\mathbb{E} \to \mathbf{B}[\mathbb{C}, \mathbb{C}]$ as a generalisation of the monoid structure on effects and the parametric effect monad. An effect is now a *1-cell* $e : X \to Y$ in $\mathbb{E}$, and a parametric effect monad is indexed by the domain and codomain of $e$, like $T_{X,Y}(e)$. A future work is to examine whether we can extend the techniques developed in this paper to bicategorical parametric monads.

### 6.3 Parameterised Moands

Atkey's parameterised monads [2] are another generalisation of monads. They seem to be fundamentally different from parametric effect monads. To exhibit this difference, we recall that one-object $[\mathbb{C}, \mathbb{C}]$-enriched categories are monads on $\mathbb{C}$. Thus $[\mathbb{C}, \mathbb{C}]$-enriched categories are a generalisation of monads; they correspond to *discretely parameterised monads*. Parameterised monads are a further generalisation of such enriched categories. Tate shows an encoding of preorder-parameterised monads as productors [33, Section 7]. At this moment we do not know if it is possible to directly encode parameterised monads as parametric effect monads.

### 6.4 Denotational Semantics of Effect Systems

The implicit subeffecting system and its denotational semantics are used in the study of effect-dependent program optimisation [4, 6–8]. The semantic framework we introduced in Definition 5.5 and 5.6 is influenced by these works, which use PER-like categories as the categories of predicates. They manually construct the denotation of effect-annotated monadic types on the category of predicates, while in this paper we give a mechanical method to construct parametric effect monads by a variant of the semantic $\top\top$-lifting.

## 7. Conclusion

Under the formulation of preordered monoids as a structure on effects and parametric effect monads as a semantic structure for the effect-annotated monadic type, we studied their properties, constructions and applications to the semantics of effect systems. Parametric effect monads admit various analogues of the structures that exist in the theory of monad. We gave a construction of parametric effect monads from effect observations, and semantics of implicit subeffecting calculus EFi. We then discussed the soundness of EFi with respect to a given specification of effects.

A future work is to extend the arity of Definition 4.2 to arbitrary objects so that we can handle fresh name creations and local stores. It is also interesting to extend the construction in Theorem 3.3 to the one over a general category $\mathbb{C}$.

## Acknowledgment

Thanks to Masahito Hasegawa, Susumu Nishimura, Paul-André Melliès, Marco Gaboardi and anonymous reviewers for their helpful comments and suggestions on this paper. Additionally, thanks to Kohei Suenaga for an insightful discussion in Tanakaya. This work was supported by JSPS KAKENHI Grant Number 24700012.

## References


[1] R. M. Amadio and P.-L. Curien. *Domains and lambda-calculi*. Cambridge University Press, New York, NY, USA, 1998.

[2] R. Atkey. Parameterised notions of computation. *J. Funct. Program.*, 19(3-4):335–376, 2009.

[3] G. Barthe, P. Dybjer, L. Pinto, and J. Saraiva, editors. *Applied Semantics, International Summer School, APPSEM 2000, Caminha, Portugal, September 9-15, 2000, Advanced Lectures*, volume 2395 of *LNCS*. Springer, 2002.

[4] N. Benton and P. Buchlovsky. Semantics of an effect analysis for exceptions. In *Proceedings of 2007 ACM SIGPLAN International Workshop on Types in Languages Design and Implementation*, pages 15–26. ACM, 2007.

[5] N. Benton, J. Hughes, and E. Moggi. Monads and effects. In Barthe et al. [3], pages 42–122.

[6] N. Benton, A. Kennedy, L. Beringer, and M. Hofmann. Relational semantics for effect-based program transformations with dynamic allocation. In *Proceedings of the 9th International ACM SIGPLAN Conference on Principles and Practice of Declarative Programming*, pages 87–96. ACM, 2007.

[7] N. Benton, A. Kennedy, L. Beringer, and M. Hofmann. Relational semantics for effect-based program transformations: higher-order store. In *Proceedings of the 11th International ACM SIGPLAN Conference on Principles and Practice of Declarative Programming*, pages 301–312. ACM, 2009.

[8] N. Benton, A. Kennedy, M. Hofmann, and L. Beringer. Reading, writing and relations. In *Programming Languages and Systems, 4th Asian Symposium, APLAS 2006, Proceedings*, volume 4279 of *LNCS*, pages 114–130. Springer, 2006.

[9] A. Filinski. Representing layered monads. In *Proc. POPL 1999*, pages 175–188, 1999.

[10] J.-C. Filliâtre. A theory of monads parameterized by effects. Research Report 1367, LRI, Université Paris Sud, November 1999.

[11] B. Jacobs. *Categorical Logic and Type Theory*. Elsevier, 1999.

[12] B. Jacobs. Coalgebraic trace semantics for combined possibilitistic and probabilistic systems. *Electr. Notes Theor. Comput. Sci.*, 203(5):131–152, 2008.

[13] O. Kammar and G. D. Plotkin. Algebraic foundations for effect-dependent optimisations. In *Proceedings of the 39th ACM SIGPLAN-SIGACT Symposium on Principles of Programming Languages*, pages 349–360. ACM, 2012.

[14] S. Katsumata. A semantic formulation of $\top\top$-lifting and logical predicates for computational metalanguage. In *Proc. CSL '05*, volume 3634 of *LNCS*, pages 87–102. Springer, 2005.

[15] S. Katsumata. Relating computational effects by $\top\top$-lifting. *Inf. Comput.*, 222:228–246, 2013.

[16] S. Katsumata and T. Sato. Preorders on monads and coalgebraic simulations. In *Foundations of Software Science and Computation Structures - 16th International Conference, Proceedings*, volume 7794 of *LNCS*, pages 145–160. Springer, 2013.

[17] G.M. Kelly and G. Janelidze. A note on actions of a monoidal category. *Theory and Applications of Categories*, 9(4):61–91, 2001.

[18] A. Kock. Strong functors and monoidal monads. *Archiv der Mathematik*, 23(1):113–120, 1972.

[19] S. Lack and R. Street. The formal theory of monads ii. *Journal of Pure and Applied Algebra*, 175(1-3):243 – 265, 2002.

[20] T. Leinster. *Higher Operads, Higher Categories*. London Mathematical Society Lecture Note Series. Cambridge University Press, 2004.

[21] P. B. Levy. *Call-by-Push-Value A Functional/Imperative Synthesis*. Springer, 2004.

[22] J. M. Lucassen and D. K. Gifford. Polymorphic effect systems. In *Proceedings of the 15th ACM SIGPLAN-SIGACT symposium on Principles of programming languages*, pages 47–57. ACM, 1988.

[23] S. MacLane. *Categories for the Working Mathematician (Second Edition)*, volume 5 of *Graduate Texts in Mathematics*. Springer, 1998.

[24] P.-A. Mellies. Parametric monads and enriched adjunctions. Manuscript.

[25] P.-A. Mellies. The parametric continuation monad. *Mathematical Structures in Computer Science*, Festschrift in honor of Corrado Böhm for his 90th birthday, 2013.

[26] E. Moggi. Notions of computation and monads. *Inf. Comput.*, 93(1):55–92, 1991.

[27] F. Nielson and H. R. Nielson. From CML to its process algebra. *Theor. Comput. Sci.*, 155:179–219, February 1996.

[28] F. Nielson, H. R. Nielson, and C. Hankin. *Principles of program analysis (2. corr. print)*. Springer, 2005.

[29] T. Petricek, D. A. Orchard, and A. Mycroft. Coeffects: Unified static analysis of context-dependence. In *Automata, Languages, and Programming - 40th International Colloquium, Proceedings*, volume 7966 of *LNCS*, pages 385–397. Springer, 2013.

[30] G. Plotkin and J. Power. Algebraic operations and generic effects. *Applied Categorical Structures*, 11(1):69–94, 2003.

[31] L. Solberg, H. R. Nielson, and F. Nielson. Strictness and totality analysis. In *Static Analysis*, volume 864 of *LNCS*, pages 408–422. Springer Berlin Heidelberg, 1994.

[32] J.-P. Talpin and P. Jouvelot. The type and effect discipline. *Inf. Comput.*, 111(2):245–296, 1994.

[33] R. Tate. The sequential semantics of producer effect systems. In *The 40th Annual ACM SIGPLAN-SIGACT Symposium on Principles of Programming Languages*, pages 15–26. ACM, 2013.

[34] J. Thamsborg and L. Birkedal. A kripke logical relation for effect-based program transformations. In *Proceeding of the 16th ACM SIGPLAN International Conference on Functional Programming*, pages 445–456. ACM, 2011.

[35] M. Tofte and J.-P. Talpin. Implementation of the typed call-by-value lambda-calculus using a stack of regions. In *Proceedings of the 21st ACM SIGPLAN-SIGACT Symposium on Principles of Programming Languages*, pages 188–201, 1994.

[36] D. Varacca and G. Winskel. Distributing probability over non-determinism. *Mathematical Structures in Computer Science*, 16(1):87–113, 2006.

[37] P. Wadler. The marriage of effects and monads. In *Proceedings of the third ACM SIGPLAN International Conference on Functional Programming (ICFP '98)*, pages 63–74. ACM, 1998.

[38] P. Wadler and P. Thiemann. The marriage of effects and monads. *ACM Trans. Comput. Log.*, 4(1):1–32, 2003.

# Applying Quantitative Semantics to Higher-Order Quantum Computing *

Michele Pagani
Université Paris 13, Sorbonne Paris Cité
Villetaneuse, France
michele.pagani@lipn.univ-paris13.fr

Peter Selinger
Dalhousie University
Halifax, Canada
selinger@mathstat.dal.ca

Benoît Valiron
CIS Dept, University of Pennsylvania
Philadelphia, U.S.A.
benoit.valiron@monoidal.net

## Abstract

Finding a denotational semantics for higher order quantum computation is a long-standing problem in the semantics of quantum programming languages. Most past approaches to this problem fell short in one way or another, either limiting the language to an unusably small finitary fragment, or giving up important features of quantum physics such as entanglement. In this paper, we propose a denotational semantics for a quantum lambda calculus with recursion and an infinite data type, using constructions from quantitative semantics of linear logic.

***Categories and Subject Descriptors*** F.3.2 [*Semantics of Programming Languages*]: Denotational semantics

***Keywords*** higher-order; quantum computation; functional programming; completely positive maps; categorical model

## 1. Introduction

Type theory and denotational semantics have been successfully used to model, design, and reason about programming languages for almost half a century. The application of such methods to quantum computing is much more recent, going back only about 10 years [18].

An important problem in the semantics of quantum computing is how to combine quantum computing with higher-order functions, or in other words, how to design a functional quantum programming language. A syntactic answer to this question was arguably given with the design of the quantum lambda calculus [20, 23]. The quantum lambda calculus has a well-defined syntax and operational semantics, with a strong type system and a practical type inference algorithm. However, the question of how to give a *denotational* semantics to the quantum lambda calculus turned out to be difficult, and has remained open for many years [19, 22]. One reason that designing such a semantics is difficult is that quantum computation is inherently defined on *finite dimensional* Hilbert spaces, whereas the semantics of higher-order functional programming languages, including such features as infinite data types and recursion, is inherently infinitary.

In recent years, a number of solutions have been proposed to the problem of finding a denotational semantics of higher-order quantum computation, with varying degrees of success. The first approach [21] was to restrict the language to strict linearity, meaning that each function had to use each argument exactly once, in the spirit of linear logic. In this way, all infinitary concepts (such as infinite types and recursion) were eliminated from the language. Not surprisingly, the resulting finitary language permitted a fully abstract semantics in terms of finite dimensional spaces; this was hardly an acceptable solution to the general problem. The second approach [14] was to construct a semantics of higher-order quantum computation by methods from category theory; specifically, by applying a presheaf construction to a model of first-order quantum computation. This indeed succeeds in yielding a model of the full quantum lambda calculus, albeit without recursion. The main drawbacks of the presheaf model are the absence of recursion, and the fact that such models are relatively difficult to reason about. The third approach [6] was based on the Geometry of Interaction. Starting from a traced monoidal category of basic quantum operations, Hasuo and Hoshino applied a sequence of categorical constructions, which eventually yielded a model of higher-order quantum computation. The problem with this approach is that the tensor product constructed from the geometry-of-interaction construction does not coincide with the tensor product of the underlying physical data types. Therefore, the model drops the possibility of entangled states, and thereby fails to model one of the defining features of quantum computation.

**Our contribution.** In this paper, we give a novel denotational semantics of higher-order quantum computation, based on methods from *quantitative semantics*. Quantitative semantics refers to a family of semantics of linear logic that interpret proofs as linear mappings between vector spaces (or more generally, modules), and standard lambda terms as power series. The original idea comes from Girard's normal functor semantics [4]. More recently, quantitative semantics has been used to give a solid, denotational semantics for various algebraic extensions of lambda calculus, such as probabilistic and differential lambda calculi (e.g. [1], [2]).

One feature of our model is that it can represent *infinite dimensional* structures, and is expressive enough to describe recursive types, such as lists of qubits, and to model recursion. This is achieved by providing an exponential structure *à la* linear logic. Unlike the Hasuo-Hoshino model, our model permits general entanglement. We interpret (a minor variant of) the quantum lambda calculus in this model. Our main result is the adequacy of the model with respect to the operational semantics.

* Partially founded by French ANR project COQUAS (number 12 JS02 006 01) and CNRS chair "Logique linéaire et calcul".



*POPL '14*, January 22–24, 2014, San Diego, CA, USA.

ACM 978-1-4503-2544-8/14/01... $15.00.
http://dx.doi.org/10.1145/2535838.2535879

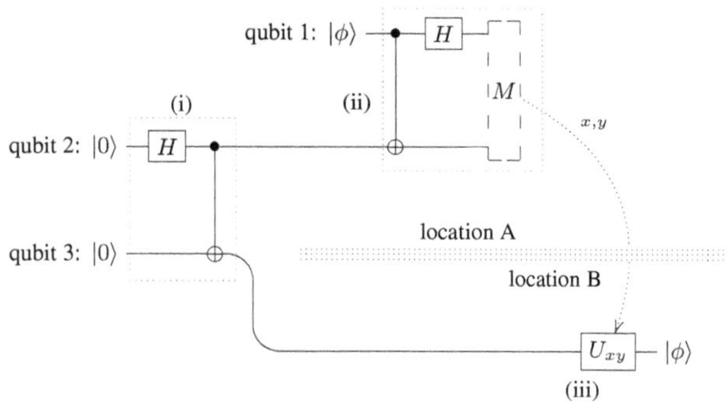


Figure 1: The quantum teleportation protocol.

The model is the juxtaposition of a simple, finite-dimensional model of quantum computation together with a canonical completion yielding the structures of linear logic. Our model demonstrates that the quantum and the classical "universes" work well together, but also – surprisingly – that they do not mix too much, even at higher order types.

**Outline.** In Section 2, we briefly review some background. Section 3 presents the version of the quantum lambda calculus that we use in this paper, including its operational semantics. Section 4 presents the denotational semantics of the quantum lambda calculus, and Section 5 proves the adequacy theorem. Section 6 concludes with some properties of the representable elements.

## 2. Background

### 2.1 Quantum computation in a nutshell

Quantum computation is a computational paradigm based on the laws of quantum physics. We briefly recall some basic notions; please see [17] for a more complete treatment. The basic unit of information in quantum computation is a *quantum bit* or *qubit*, whose state is given by a normalized vector in the two-dimensional Hilbert space $\mathbb{C}^2$. It is customary to write the canonical basis of $\mathbb{C}^2$ as $\{|0\rangle, |1\rangle\}$, and to identify these basis vectors with the booleans false and true, respectively. The state of a qubit can therefore be thought of as a complex linear combination $\alpha|0\rangle + \beta|1\rangle$ of booleans, called a *quantum superposition*. More generally, the state of $n$ qubits is an element of the $n$-fold tensor product $\mathbb{C}^2\otimes\ldots\otimes\mathbb{C}^2$.

There are three kinds of basic operations on quantum data: initializations, unitary maps and measurements. Initialization prepares a new qubit in state $|0\rangle$ or $|1\rangle$. A unitary map, or *gate*, is an invertible linear map $U$ such that $U^* = U^{-1}$; here $U^*$ denotes the complex conjugate transpose of $U$. Finally, the operation of measurement consumes a qubit and returns a classical bit. If $n$ qubits are in state $\alpha|0\rangle\otimes\phi_0+\beta|1\rangle\otimes\phi_1$, where $\phi_0$ and $\phi_1$ are normalized states of $n-1$ qubits, then measuring the leftmost qubit yields false with probability $|\alpha|^2$, leaving the remaining qubits in state $\phi_0$, and true with probability $|\beta|^2$, leaving the remaining qubits in state $\phi_1$.

**Example 1.** A small algorithm is the simulation of an unbiased coin toss: initialize one quantum bit to $|0\rangle$, apply the Hadamard gate sending $|0\rangle$ to $\frac{1}{\sqrt{2}}(|0\rangle+|1\rangle)$ and $|1\rangle$ to $\frac{1}{\sqrt{2}}(|0\rangle-|1\rangle)$, then measure. The result is true with probability $\frac{1}{2}$ and false with probability $\frac{1}{2}$.

**Example 2.** A slightly more involved algorithm is the *quantum teleportation algorithm* (see [17] for details). The procedure is summarized in Figure 1. Wires represent the path of quantum bits in the computation, and time flows from left to right. The gate $\boxed{H}$ stands for an application of the Hadamard gate, whereas the gate $\overset{\bullet}{\oplus}$ is a controlled-not: it negates the bottom qubit if the upper one is in state $|1\rangle$. The box $M$ is a measurement. The unitaries $U_{xy}$ are

$$U_{00} = \left(\begin{smallmatrix}1&0\\0&1\end{smallmatrix}\right),\ U_{01} = \left(\begin{smallmatrix}0&1\\1&0\end{smallmatrix}\right),\ U_{10} = \left(\begin{smallmatrix}1&0\\0&-1\end{smallmatrix}\right),\ U_{11} = \left(\begin{smallmatrix}0&1\\-1&0\end{smallmatrix}\right).$$

The goal is to send a quantum bit in an unknown state $|\phi\rangle$ from Location A to Location B using two classical bits. The procedure can be reversed to send two classical bits using a quantum bit. In this case it is called the *dense coding algorithm* [17].

The algorithm consists of three parts. In (i), two quantum bits (qubits 2 and 3) are entangled in state $\frac{1}{\sqrt{2}}(|00\rangle + |11\rangle)$. In (ii), the input qubit 1 in state $|\phi\rangle$ is entangled with qubit 2, then both are measured. The result is sent over location B, where in (iii) an correction $U_{xy}$ is applied on qubit 3, setting it to state $|\phi\rangle$.

### 2.2 Density matrices and completely positive maps

If we identify $|0\rangle$ and $|1\rangle$ with the standard basis vectors $\left(\begin{smallmatrix}1\\0\end{smallmatrix}\right)$ and $\left(\begin{smallmatrix}0\\1\end{smallmatrix}\right)$, the state of a qubit can be expressed as a two-dimensional vector $v = \alpha|0\rangle + \beta|1\rangle = \left(\begin{smallmatrix}\alpha\\\beta\end{smallmatrix}\right)$. Similarly, the state of an $n$-qubit system can be expressed as an $2^n$-dimensional column vector. Often, it is necessary to consider *probability distributions* on quantum states; these are also known as *mixed states*. Consider a quantum system that is in one of several states $v_1, \ldots, v_k$ with probabilities $p_1, \ldots, p_k$, respectively. The *density matrix* of this mixed state is defined to be $A = \sum_i p_i v_i v_i^*$, where $(-)^*$ denotes the adjoint operator. By a theorem of Von Neumann, the density matrix is a good representation of mixed states, in the following sense: two mixed states are indistinguishable by any physical experiment if and only if they have the same density matrix [17]. Note that $\operatorname{tr} A = p_1 + \ldots + p_k$. For our purposes, it is often convenient to permit sub-probability distributions, so that $p_1 + \ldots + p_k \leqslant 1$.

Let us write $\mathbb{C}^{n\times n}$ for the space of $n \times n$-matrices. Recall that a matrix $A \in \mathbb{C}^{n\times n}$ is called *positive* if $v^*Av \geqslant 0$ for all $v \in \mathbb{C}^n$. Given $A, B \in \mathbb{C}^{n\times n}$, we write $A \sqsubseteq B$ iff $B - A$ is positive; this is the so-called *Löwner partial order*. A linear map $F : \mathbb{C}^{n\times n} \to \mathbb{C}^{m\times m}$ is called *positive* if $A \sqsupseteq 0$ implies $F(A) \sqsupseteq 0$, and *completely positive* if $F \otimes \mathrm{id}_k$ is positive for all $k$, where $\mathrm{id}_k$ is the identity function on $\mathbb{C}^{k\times k}$. If $F$ moreover satisfies $\operatorname{tr}(F(A)) \leqslant \operatorname{tr} A$ for all positive $A$, then it is called a *superoperator*. The density matrices are precisely the positive matrices $A$ of trace $\leqslant 1$. Moreover, the superoperators correspond precisely to those functions from mixed states to mixed states that are physically possible [17, 18].

### 2.3 The category CPM

The category $\mathbf{CPM}_s$ is defined as follows: the objects are natural numbers, and a morphism $F : n \to m$ is a completely positive map $F : \mathbb{C}^{n\times n} \to \mathbb{C}^{m\times m}$. Let **CPM** be the free completion of $\mathbf{CPM}_s$ under finite biproducts; specifically, the objects of **CPM** are sequences $\vec{n} = (n_1, \ldots, n_k)$ of natural numbers, and a morphism $F : \vec{n} \to \vec{m}$ is a matrix $(F_{ij})$ of morphisms $F_{ij} : n_j \to m_i$ of $\mathbf{CPM}_s$. The categories $\mathbf{CPM}_s$ and **CPM** are symmetric monoidal, and in fact, compact closed [18].

### 2.4 Limitations of CPM as a model

The category **CPM** can serve as a fully abstract model for a simple, strictly linear, finitary quantum lambda calculus [21]. For example, the type **bit** is interpreted as $(1, 1)$, and the type **qubit** is interpreted as $(2)$. Measurement, as a map from **qubit** to **bit**, sends $\left(\begin{smallmatrix}a&b\\c&d\end{smallmatrix}\right)$ to $(a, d)$. The coin toss is a map $(1) \to (1, 1)$ sending $(p)$ to $(\frac{p}{2}, \frac{p}{2})$. Function spaces are interpreted via the compact closed structure.

As mentioned in the introduction, the semantics of [21] is extremely limited, because it is completely finitary. Thus recursion, infinite data types, and non-linear functions (i.e., those that can use their argument more than once) had to be completely removed from

*Terms* $M, N, P$ ::=

$x \mid \lambda x^A.M \mid MN \mid \texttt{skip} \mid M;N \mid$
$M \otimes N \mid \texttt{let}\ x^A \otimes y^B = M\ \texttt{in}\ N \mid$
$\texttt{in}_\ell\ M \mid \texttt{in}_r\ M \mid \texttt{match}\ P\ \texttt{with}\ (x^A : M \mid y^B : N) \mid$
$\texttt{split}^A \mid \texttt{letrec}\ f^{A\multimap B}x = M\ \texttt{in}\ N \mid \texttt{meas} \mid \texttt{new} \mid U$

*Values* $V, W$ ::=

$x \mid c \mid \lambda x^A.M \mid V \otimes W \mid \texttt{in}_\ell\ V \mid \texttt{in}_r\ W$

*Types* $A, B, C$ ::=

$\mathbf{qubit} \mid A \multimap B \mid !(A \multimap B) \mid 1 \mid A \otimes B \mid A \oplus B \mid A^\ell.$

Table 1: Grammars of terms, values and types.

the language in order to fit the model. For example, even the simple squaring function $f \mapsto \lambda x.f(f\,x)$ is not representable in **CPM**.

The purpose of the present paper is to remove all of these restrictions. As an example, consider the following pseudo-code (in ML-style):

```
val qlist : qubit -> qubit list
let rec qlist q = if (cointoss) then [q]
            else let (x,y) = entangle q in x::(qlist y)
```

Here, `cointoss` is a fair coin toss, and the function `entangle` sends $\alpha|0\rangle + \beta|1\rangle$ to $\alpha|00\rangle + \beta|11\rangle$.

So if the function **qlist** is applied to a qubit $\alpha|0\rangle + \beta|1\rangle$, the output is $\alpha|0\rangle + \beta|1\rangle$ with probability $\frac{1}{2}$, $\alpha|00\rangle + \beta|11\rangle$ with probability $\frac{1}{4}$, $\alpha|000\rangle + \beta|111\rangle$ with probability $\frac{1}{8}$, and so on. Its semantics should be of type $2 \to (2, 4, 8, \ldots)$, mapping

$$\left(\begin{smallmatrix} a & b \\ c & d \end{smallmatrix}\right) \mapsto \left(\frac{1}{2}\left(\begin{smallmatrix} a & b \\ c & d \end{smallmatrix}\right), \frac{1}{4}\left(\begin{smallmatrix} a&0&0&b \\ 0&0&0&0 \\ 0&0&0&0 \\ c&0&0&d \end{smallmatrix}\right), \ldots\right).$$

The category **CPM** is "almost" capable of handling this case, but not quite, because it cannot express infinite tuples of matrices. The model we propose in this paper is essentially an extension of **CPM** to infinite biproducts, using methods developed in [5, 11, 12, 16].

## 3. A quantum lambda calculus

We define a variant of the typed quantum lambda calculus of [22]. The main difference is that the language in this present paper is a true extension of linear logic (see the type assignment system of Table 2). In particular, in contrast with [22], $!(A \otimes B) \multimap\ !A \otimes !B$ is not provable and there is no need for a subtyping relation. The operational semantics implements a call-by-value strategy. An untyped call-by-name variant has been studied in [10].

The classes of *terms*, *values* and *types* are defined in Table 1. The symbol $c$ ranges over the set of term constants $\{\texttt{skip}, \texttt{split}^A, \texttt{meas}, \texttt{new}, U\}$. The constant $U$ ranges over a set of elementary unitary transformations on quantum bits. In the examples below, we will be using the Hadamard gate $H$ and the controlled-not gate $N_c$, defined as follows [17]:

$$H = \frac{1}{\sqrt{2}}\left(\begin{smallmatrix} 1 & 1 \\ 1 & -1 \end{smallmatrix}\right) \qquad N_c = \left(\begin{smallmatrix} 1&0&0&0 \\ 0&1&0&0 \\ 0&0&0&1 \\ 0&0&1&0 \end{smallmatrix}\right) \tag{1}$$

Notice that bound variables are given in Church style, i.e., with a type annotation. This enables Proposition 4, and simplifies the semantic interpretation of the typed terms. We omit such annotations in the sequel if uninteresting or obvious.

We have two kinds of arrows: the linear arrow $A \multimap B$, and the intuitionistic arrow $!(A \multimap B)$, which is obtained by the call-by-value translation of the intuitionistic implication into linear logic [3]. Intuitively, only the terms of type $!(A \multimap B)$ represent functions that can be used repeatedly, whereas terms of type $A \multimap B$ must be used exactly once. A type of the form $!A$ is called a *!-type* or *non-linear* type, and all other types are called *linear*. The distinction between linear and non-linear types is crucial for allowing the type system to enforce the no-cloning property of quantum physics.

By convention, $\multimap$ is associative to the right, while application and tensor are associative to the left. We use the notation $A^{\otimes n}$ for $A$ tensored $n$ times. The type $A^\ell$ denotes finite lists of type $A$. When doing structural induction on types, we assume that $A^\ell$ is greater than $A^{\otimes n}$, for any $n \in \mathbb{N}$.

The set of terms and types is somewhat spartan; however it can be easily extended by introducing syntactic sugar. Note that, for technical convenience, we have only allowed types of the form $!A$ when $A$ is an arrow type. However, for an arbitrary type $A$, the type $!A$ can be simulated by using $!(1 \multimap A)$ instead.

**Notation 3.** We write $\mathbf{bit} = 1 \oplus 1$, $\texttt{tt} = \texttt{in}_r\ \texttt{skip}$, $\texttt{ff} = \texttt{in}_\ell\ \texttt{skip}$, $\texttt{nil} = \texttt{in}_\ell\ \texttt{skip}$ and $M :: N = \texttt{in}_r\ (M \otimes N)$. We write $\lambda\texttt{skip}.M$ for the term $\lambda z^1.(z;M)$, where $z$ is a fresh variable, and $\texttt{if}\ P\ \texttt{then}\ M\ \texttt{else}\ N$ for $\texttt{match}\ P\ \texttt{with}\ (x^1 : N \mid y^1 : M)$.

A *context* $\Delta$ is a function from a finite set of variables to types. We denote the domain of $\Delta$ by $|\Delta|$, and we write $\Delta = x_1 : A_1, \ldots, x_n : A_n$ whenever $|\Delta| = \{x_1, \ldots, x_n\}$ and $\Delta(x_i) = A_i$. We call $\Delta$ *exponential* (resp. *linear*) whenever all $A_i$ are !-types (resp. no $A_i$ is a !-type). We write $!\Delta$ for a context that is exponential. The notation $\Gamma, \Sigma$ refers to the union of the two contexts $\Gamma$ and $\Sigma$ and assumes that $|\Gamma|$ and $|\Sigma|$ are disjoint.

A *judgement* is a triple $\Gamma \vdash M : A$ of a context $\Gamma$, a term $M$ and a type $A$. A judgement is called *valid* if it can be inferred from the typing rules in Figure 2, using the convention that the contexts $\Gamma$ and $\Sigma$ are linear.

**Proposition 4.** *There is at most one derivation inferring a given typing judgement* $\Gamma \vdash M : A$. □

**Example 5.** In Section 2.4, we wrote the informal program **qlist**. Our language is expressive enough to represent it. The term `cointoss` can be defined as $\texttt{meas}(H(\texttt{new}\,\texttt{tt}))$, and it has type **bit**. The term `entangle` is $\lambda x^{\mathbf{qubit}}.N_c(x \otimes (\texttt{new}\,\texttt{ff}))$, which has type **qubit** $\multimap$ **qubit** $\otimes$ **qubit**. Then, **qlist** is

$$\begin{array}{l} \texttt{letrec}\ f^{\mathbf{qubit}\multimap\mathbf{qubit}^\ell}\,q = \\ \quad \texttt{if cointoss then}\ q :: \texttt{nil} \\ \quad \texttt{else let}\ x^{\mathbf{qubit}} \otimes y^{\mathbf{qubit}} = \texttt{entangle}\ q\ \texttt{in}\ x :: fy \end{array}$$

which has type **qubit** $\multimap$ $\mathbf{qubit}^\ell$. In Examples 9 and 28 we discuss its operational and denotational semantics, respectively.

**Example 6.** In Example 2 and Figure 1, we sketched the quantum teleportation algorithm. We said that the algorithm can be decomposed into 3 parts. Each of these parts can be described and typed in the quantum lambda calculus, yielding a higher-order term. This is an adaptation of an example provided in [20].

(i) generates an EPR pair of entangled quantum bits. Its type is therefore $1 \multimap$ **qubit** $\otimes$ **qubit**. The corresponding term is

$$\mathbf{EPR} = \lambda\texttt{skip}.N_c\left((H(\texttt{new}\,\texttt{ff})) \otimes (\texttt{new}\,\texttt{ff})\right).$$

(ii) performs a Bell measurement on two quantum bits and outputs two classical bits $x, y$. Its type is thus **qubit** $\multimap$ **qubit** $\multimap$ **bit** $\otimes$ **bit**, and the term **BellMeasure** is defined as

$$\lambda q_1.\lambda q_2.\left(\begin{array}{l} \texttt{let}\ x \otimes y = N_c\,(q_1 \otimes q_2) \\ \texttt{in}\ (\texttt{meas}\ (H\ x)) \otimes (\texttt{meas}\ y) \end{array}\right).$$

$$\frac{A \text{ linear}}{!\Delta, x : A \vdash x : A}\ ax \qquad \frac{}{!\Delta, x : !(A \multimap B) \vdash x : A \multimap B}\ axd \qquad \frac{!\Delta \vdash V : A \multimap B \quad V \text{ value}}{!\Delta \vdash V : !(A \multimap B)}\ p \qquad \frac{}{!\Delta \vdash \mathtt{skip} : 1}\ 1_I$$

$$\frac{\Delta, x : A \vdash M : B}{\Delta \vdash \lambda x^A.M : A \multimap B}\ \multimap_I \qquad \frac{!\Delta, \Gamma \vdash M : A \multimap B \quad !\Delta, \Sigma \vdash N : A}{!\Delta, \Gamma, \Sigma \vdash MN : B}\ \multimap_E \qquad \frac{!\Delta, \Gamma \vdash M : 1 \quad !\Delta, \Sigma \vdash N : A}{!\Delta, \Gamma, \Sigma \vdash M;N : A}\ 1_E$$

$$\frac{!\Delta, \Gamma \vdash M : A \quad !\Delta, \Sigma \vdash N : B}{!\Delta, \Gamma, \Sigma \vdash M \otimes N : A \otimes B}\ \otimes_I \qquad \frac{!\Delta, \Gamma \vdash M : A \otimes B \quad !\Delta, \Sigma, x : A, y : B \vdash N : C}{!\Delta, \Gamma, \Sigma \vdash \mathtt{let}\ x^A \otimes y^B = M \ \mathtt{in}\ N : C}\ \otimes_E$$

$$\frac{!\Delta, \Gamma \vdash M : A}{!\Delta, \Gamma \vdash \mathtt{in}_\ell\ M : A \oplus B}\ \oplus_I^\ell \qquad \frac{!\Delta, \Gamma \vdash M : B}{!\Delta, \Gamma \vdash \mathtt{in}_r\ M : A \oplus B}\ \oplus_I^r \qquad \frac{\begin{array}{c} !\Delta, \Sigma, x : A \vdash M : C \\ !\Delta, \Gamma \vdash P : A \oplus B \quad !\Delta, \Sigma, y : B \vdash N : C \end{array}}{!\Delta, \Gamma, \Sigma \vdash \mathtt{match}\ P\ \mathtt{with}\ (x^A : M \mid y^B : N) : C}\ \oplus_E$$

$$\frac{!\Delta, \Gamma \vdash M : 1 \oplus (A \otimes A^\ell)}{!\Delta, \Gamma \vdash M : A^\ell}\ -_I^\ell \qquad \frac{}{!\Delta \vdash \mathtt{split}^A : A^\ell \multimap 1 \oplus (A \otimes A^\ell)}\ \mathtt{split} \qquad \frac{!\Delta, f : !(A \multimap B), x : A \vdash M : B \quad !\Delta, \Gamma, f : !(A \multimap B) \vdash N : C}{!\Delta, \Gamma \vdash \mathtt{letrec}\ f^{A \multimap B}\ x = M\ \mathtt{in}\ N : C}\ \mathtt{rec}$$

$$\frac{}{!\Delta \vdash \mathtt{meas} : \mathbf{qubit} \multimap \mathbf{bit}}\ \mathtt{meas} \qquad \frac{}{!\Delta \vdash \mathtt{new} : \mathbf{bit} \multimap \mathbf{qubit}}\ \mathtt{new} \qquad \frac{U \text{ of arity } n}{!\Delta \vdash U : \mathbf{qubit}^{\otimes n} \multimap \mathbf{qubit}^{\otimes n}}\ U$$

Table 2: Typing rules. The contexts $\Gamma$ and $\Sigma$ are assumed to be linear.

(iii) performs a correction. It takes one quantum bit, two classical bits, and outputs a quantum bit. It has a type of the form $\mathbf{qubit} \multimap \mathbf{bit} \otimes \mathbf{bit} \multimap \mathbf{qubit}$. The term is

$$\begin{aligned} \mathbf{U} = \lambda q.\lambda x \otimes y.\mathtt{if}\ x\ \mathtt{then}\ (\mathtt{if}\ y\ \mathtt{then}\ U_{11}\ q\ \mathtt{else}\ U_{10}\ q) \\ \mathtt{else}\ (\mathtt{if}\ y\ \mathtt{then}\ U_{01}\ q\ \mathtt{else}\ U_{00}\ q). \end{aligned}$$

We can now write the term

$$\begin{aligned} \mathbf{telep} = \quad & \lambda \mathtt{skip}.\mathtt{let}\ x \otimes y = \mathbf{EPR}\ \mathtt{skip}\ \mathtt{in} \\ & \quad \mathtt{let}\ f \quad = \mathbf{BellMeasure}\ x\ \mathtt{in} \\ & \quad \mathtt{let}\ g \quad = \mathbf{U}\ y \\ & \quad \mathtt{in}\ f \otimes g. \end{aligned}$$

It can then be shown that

$$\vdash \mathbf{telep} : !(1 \multimap (\mathbf{qubit} \multimap \mathbf{bit} \otimes \mathbf{bit}) \otimes (\mathbf{bit} \otimes \mathbf{bit} \multimap \mathbf{qubit}))$$

is a valid typing judgement. In other words, the teleportation algorithm produces a pair of entangled functions $f : \mathbf{qubit} \to \mathbf{bit} \otimes \mathbf{bit}$ and $g : \mathbf{bit} \otimes \mathbf{bit} \to \mathbf{qubit}$. These functions have the property that $g(f(|\phi\rangle)) = |\phi\rangle$ for all qubits $|\phi\rangle$, and $f(g(x \otimes y)) = (x \otimes y)$ for all booleans $x$ and $y$. These two functions are each other's inverse, but because they contain an embedded qubit each, they can only be used once. They can be said to form a "single-use isomorphism" between the (otherwise non-isomorphic) types $\mathbf{qubit}$ and $\mathbf{bit} \otimes \mathbf{bit}$. However, the whole procedure is duplicable: one can generate as many one-time-use isomorphism pairs as desired.

### 3.1 Operational semantics

The operational semantics is defined in terms of an abstract machine simulating the behavior of Knill's QRAM model [8]. It is similar to the semantics given in [22].

**Definition 7.** A *quantum closure* is a triple $[q, \ell, M]$ where

- $q$ is a normalized vector of $\mathbb{C}^{2^n}$, for some integer $n \geqslant 0$. The vector $q$ is called the *quantum state*;
- $M$ is a term, not necessarily closed;
- $\ell$ is a one-to-one map from the set of free variables of $M$ to the set $\{1, \ldots, n\}$. It is called the *linking function.*

We write $|\ell|$ for the domain of $\ell$. By abuse of language we may call a closure $[q, \ell, V]$ a *value* when the term $V$ is a value. We denote the set of quantum closures by Cl and the set of quantum closures that are values by Val. We write $\ell|_M$ for the linking function whose domain is restricted to the set of free variables of $M$. We say that the quantum closure $[q, \ell, M]$ is *total* when $|\ell|$ has cardinality $n$, the size of the quantum state. In that case, if $|\ell| = \{x_1, \ldots, x_n\}$ and $\ell(x_i) = i$, we write $\ell$ as $|x_1, \ldots, x_n\rangle$. A quantum closure $[q, |x_1, \ldots, x_n\rangle, M]$ *has a type* $A$, whenever $x_1 : \mathbf{qubit}, \ldots, x_n : \mathbf{qubit} \vdash M : A$. In case $\ell = |x_1, \ldots, x_n\rangle$ we can also write $\ell \vdash M : A$.

The purpose of a quantum closure is to provide a mechanism to talk about terms with embedded quantum data. The idea is that a variable $y \in \mathrm{FV}(M)$ is bound in the closure $[q, \ell, M]$ to qubit number $\ell(y)$ of the quantum state $q$. So for example, the quantum closure $[\frac{1}{\sqrt{2}}(|00\rangle + |11\rangle), |x_1, x_2\rangle, \lambda y^A.y x_1 x_2]$ denotes a term $\lambda y^A.y x_1 x_2$ with two embedded qubits $x_1, x_2$ in the entangled state $|x_1 x_2\rangle = \frac{1}{\sqrt{2}}(|00\rangle + |11\rangle)$.

The notion of $\alpha$-equivalence extends naturally to quantum closures, for instance, the states $[q, |x\rangle, \lambda y^A.x]$ and $[q, |z\rangle, \lambda y^A.z]$ are equivalent. From now on, we tacitly identify quantum closures up to renaming of bound variables.

The evaluation of a term is defined as a probabilistic rewriting procedure on quantum closures, using a call-by-value reduction strategy. We use the notation $[q, \ell, M] \xrightarrow{p} [q', \ell', M']$ to mean that the left-hand side closure reduces in one step to the right-hand side with probability $p \in [0, 1]$.

**Definition 8.** The reduction rules are shown in Table 3. The rules split into three categories: (a) rules handling the classical part of the calculus; (b) rules dealing with quantum data; and (c) congruence rules for the call-by-value strategy. Note that in the statement of the rules, $V$ and $W$ refer to values.

In the rules in Table 3(b), the quantum state $q$ has size $n$. The quantum state $q'$ in the first rule is obtained by applying the $k$-ary unitary gate $U$ to the qubits $\ell(x_1), \ldots, \ell(x_k)$. Precisely, $q' = (\sigma \circ (U \otimes \mathrm{id}) \circ \sigma^{-1})(q)$, where $\sigma$ is the action on $\mathbb{C}^{2^n}$ of any permutation over $\{1, \ldots, n\}$ such that $\sigma(i) = \ell(x_i)$ whenever $i \leqslant k$. In the rules about measurements, we assume that if $q_0$ and $q_1$ are normalized quantum states of the form

$$\textstyle\sum_j \alpha_j |\phi_j\rangle \otimes |0\rangle \otimes |\psi_j\rangle, \quad \sum_j \beta_j |\phi_j\rangle \otimes |1\rangle \otimes |\psi_j\rangle, \qquad (2)$$

then $q_0'$ and $q_1'$ are respectively

$$\textstyle\sum_j \alpha_j |\phi_j\rangle \otimes |\psi_j\rangle, \quad \sum_j \beta_j |\phi_j\rangle \otimes |\psi_j\rangle, \qquad (3)$$

$$[q,\ell,(\lambda x^A.M)\,V] \xrightarrow{1} [q,\ell,M\{V/x\}] \qquad [q,\ell,\texttt{let}\ x^A \otimes y^B \ = V \otimes W\ \texttt{in}\ N] \xrightarrow{1} [q,\ell,N\{V/x,W/y\}]$$

$$[q,\ell,\texttt{skip};N] \xrightarrow{1} [q,\ell,N] \qquad [q,\ell,\texttt{match}\ (\texttt{in}_\ell\ V)\ \texttt{with}\ (x^A : M \mid y^B : N)] \xrightarrow{1} [q,\ell,M\{V/x\}]$$

$$[q,\ell,\texttt{split}V] \xrightarrow{1} [q,\ell,V] \qquad [q,\ell,\texttt{match}\ (\texttt{in}_r\ V)\ \texttt{with}\ (x^A : M \mid y^B : N)] \xrightarrow{1} [q,\ell,N\{V/y\}]$$

$$[q,\ell,\texttt{letrec}\ f^{A\multimap B}\ x = M\ \texttt{in}\ N] \xrightarrow{1} [q,\ell,N\{(\lambda x^A.\texttt{letrec}\ f^{A\multimap B}\ x = M\ \texttt{in}\ M)/f\}]$$

(a) Classical control.

$$[q,\ell,U(x_1\otimes\cdots\otimes x_k)] \xrightarrow{1} [q',\ell,x_1\otimes\cdots\otimes x_k]$$

$$[q,\emptyset,\texttt{new ff}] \xrightarrow{1} [q\otimes|0\rangle,\{y\mapsto n+1\},y] \qquad [\alpha q_0+\beta q_1,\{x\mapsto i\},\texttt{meas}\ x] \xrightarrow{|\beta|^2} [q_1',\emptyset,\texttt{tt}]$$

$$[q,\emptyset,\texttt{new tt}] \xrightarrow{1} [q\otimes|1\rangle,\{y\mapsto n+1\},y] \qquad [\alpha q_0+\beta q_1,\{x\mapsto i\},\texttt{meas}\ x] \xrightarrow{|\alpha|^2} [q_0',\emptyset,\texttt{ff}]$$

(b) Quantum data. The variable $y$ is fresh. The decomposition of the quantum array in the case of $\texttt{meas}\ x$ is explained in Definition 8.

$$[q,\ell,MN] \xrightarrow{p} [q',\ell',M'N] \qquad [q,\ell,M\otimes N] \xrightarrow{p} [q',\ell',M'\otimes N] \qquad [q,\ell,\texttt{in}_\ell\ M] \xrightarrow{p} [q',\ell',\texttt{in}_\ell\ M']$$

$$[q,\ell,VM] \xrightarrow{p} [q',\ell',VM'] \qquad [q,\ell,V\otimes M] \xrightarrow{p} [q',\ell',V\otimes M'] \qquad [q,\ell,\texttt{in}_r\ M] \xrightarrow{p} [q',\ell',\texttt{in}_r\ M']$$

$$[q,\ell,M;N] \xrightarrow{p} [q',\ell',M';N] \qquad [q,\ell,\texttt{let}\ x^A\otimes y^B \ = M\ \texttt{in}\ N] \xrightarrow{p} [q',\ell',\texttt{let}\ x^A\otimes y^B \ = M'\ \texttt{in}\ N]$$

$$[q,\ell,\texttt{match}\ M\ \texttt{with}\ (x^A : P \mid y^B : N)] \xrightarrow{p} [q',\ell',\texttt{match}\ M'\ \texttt{with}\ (x^A : P \mid y^B : N)]$$

(c) Congruence rules, under the hypothesis that for some $\ell_0$ we have $\ell = \ell_0 \uplus \ell|_M$, $\ell' = \ell_0 \uplus \ell'|_{M'}$ and $[q,\ell|_M,M]\xrightarrow{p}[q',\ell'|_{M'},M']$.

Table 3: Reduction rules on closures.

where the vectors $\phi_j$ have dimension $\ell(x)-1$ (so that the measured qubit is $\ell(x)$).

In summary, the quantum state acts as a shared global store that is updated destructively by the various quantum operations.

Note that the only probabilistic reduction step is the one corresponding to measurement. Also, we underline that the hypothesis associated with a congruence rule $[q,\ell,C[M]]\xrightarrow{p}[q',\ell',C[M']]$ takes into account the whole quantum states $q$ and $q'$. In fact, because of the entanglement, the evaluation of $[q,\ell|_M,M]$ may have a side-effect on the state of the qubits pointed to by the variables occurring in the context $C[\,]$.

The rules assume that the involved closures are well-defined. In particular, whenever $[q,\ell,M] \xrightarrow{p} [q,\ell,M']$, the two terms $M$ and $M'$ have the same free variables. For example, the closure $[|00\rangle,|yz\rangle,(\lambda x.y)z]$ cannot reduce and it represents an error: it would reduce to the erroneous quantum closure $[|00\rangle,|yz\rangle,z]$, where the domain of the linking function is not the set of free variables, as specified by Definition 7. The type system will prevent such an error as proven in Proposition 12.

**Example 9.** Recall Example 5. We have $[|\rangle,|\rangle,\texttt{cointoss}] \xrightarrow{1} [|1\rangle,|x\rangle,\texttt{meas}(Hx)] \xrightarrow{1} [\frac{1}{\sqrt{2}}(|0\rangle+|1\rangle),|x\rangle,\texttt{meas}\ x]$, the latter reducing to either $[|\rangle,|\rangle,\texttt{tt}]$ or $[|\rangle,|\rangle,\texttt{ff}]$, with equal probability $\frac{1}{2}$. As for $\texttt{entangle}$, we have that

$$\begin{aligned} & [\alpha|0\rangle+\beta|1\rangle,|x\rangle,\texttt{entangle}\ x] \\ \xrightarrow{1}\ & [\alpha|0\rangle+\beta|1\rangle,|x\rangle,N_c(x\otimes(\texttt{new ff}))] \\ \xrightarrow{1}\ & [\alpha|00\rangle+\beta|10\rangle,|xy\rangle,N_c(x\otimes y)] \\ \xrightarrow{1}\ & [\alpha|00\rangle+\beta|11\rangle,|xy\rangle,x\otimes y]. \end{aligned}$$

Similarly, one can check that $[\alpha|0\rangle+\beta|1\rangle,|q\rangle,\texttt{qlist}\ q]$ behaves as described in Section 2.4, reducing to $[\alpha|0\rangle+\beta|1\rangle,|q\rangle,q::\texttt{nil}]$ with probability $\frac{1}{2}$, to $[\alpha|00\rangle+\beta|11\rangle,|qq'\rangle,q'::q::\texttt{nil}]$ with probability $\frac{1}{4}$, etc. In particular, notice that in any single reduction sequence the variable $q$ has not been duplicated, as correctly asserted by the type of $\texttt{qlist}$.

**Lemma 10** (Substitution). *Suppose $!\Delta,\Gamma,x : A \vdash M : B$ and $!\Delta,\Sigma \vdash V : A$, where $\Gamma$ and $\Sigma$ are linear contexts with disjoint domain. Then $!\Delta,\Gamma,\Sigma \vdash M\{V/x\} : B$.* □

**Proposition 11** (Subject reduction). *When $[q,|y_1\ldots y_n\rangle,M] \xrightarrow{p} [q',|x_1\ldots x_{n'}\rangle,M']$ and $y_1 : \mathbf{qubit},\ldots,y_n : \mathbf{qubit} \vdash M : A$, then $x_1 : \mathbf{qubit},\ldots,x_{n'} : \mathbf{qubit} \vdash M' : A$.* □

**Proposition 12** (Type safety). *If $[q,\ell,M]$ is typable then either $M$ is a value or there is a closure $[q',\ell',M']$ such that $[q,\ell,M] \xrightarrow{p} [q',\ell',M']$. Moreover, if $M$ is not a value, the total probability of all possible single-step reductions from $[q,\ell,M]$ is 1.* □

**Lemma 13** (Totality). *If $[q,\ell,M] \xrightarrow{p} [q',\ell',M']$ and $[q,\ell,M]$ is total, then $[q',\ell',M']$ is total too.*

*Proof.* By induction on a derivation of $[q,\ell,M] \xrightarrow{p} [q',\ell',M']$, one proves that $\dim(q') = \dim(q)+\dim(\ell')-\dim(\ell)$ where $\dim(q)$ is the size of the quantum state $q$ and $\dim(\ell)$ is the cardinality of the domain set of the linking function $\ell$. Then, one gets the statement, since $[q,\ell,M]$ is total iff $\dim(q)=\dim(\ell)$. □

**Notation 14.** The reduction relation $\to$ defines the probability that a closure reduces to another one in a single step. We extend this relation to an arbitrary large (but finite) number of reduction steps with the notation $\mathrm{Red}^n_{[q,\ell,M],[q',\ell',V]}$: it is the total probability of $[q,\ell,M]$ reducing to a value $[q',\ell',V]$. It is defined as the sum of all $\prod_{i=1}^m p_i$, where $[q,\ell,M] \xrightarrow{p_1} [q_1,\ell_1,M_1]\cdots \xrightarrow{p_m} [q,\ell',V]$ is a finite reduction sequence of $m \leqslant n$ steps. We write $\mathrm{Red}^\infty_{[q,\ell,M],[q',\ell',V]}$ for the sup over $n$ of $\mathrm{Red}^n_{[q,\ell,M],[q',\ell',V]}$. Finally, we define the *total probability* $\mathrm{Halt}_{[q,\ell,M]}$ of $[q,\ell,M]$ converging to any value as $\sum_{[q',\ell',V]\in\mathrm{Val}} \mathrm{Red}^\infty_{[q,\ell,M],[q',\ell',V]}$.

## 4. Denotational semantics

We interpret the quantum lambda calculus in a suitable extension $\overline{\mathbf{CPMs}}^\oplus$ of the category **CPM** described in Section 2. What **CPM** essentially misses is the linear logic exponential $!A$, and our plan is to introduce it via the equation

$$!A := \bigoplus_{k=0}^{\infty} A^{\odot k}, \tag{4}$$

where $\bigoplus_{k=0}^{\infty}$ is the infinite biproduct of the family $\{A^{\odot k}\}_k$, each $A^{\odot k}$ being the symmetric $k$-fold tensor power of $A$, i.e., the equalizer of the $k!$ symmetries of the $k$-ary tensor $A^{\otimes k} := A \otimes \cdots \otimes A$.

The category **CPM** cannot express this equation because it lacks both infinite biproducts and a convenient definition of symmetric tensor powers. The category $\overline{\textbf{CPMs}}^{\oplus}$ is in some sense the minimal extension of **CPM** having these two missing ingredients.

The plan of the section is as follows. Section 4.1 presents some preliminary material. Section 4.2 defines $\overline{\textbf{CPMs}}^{\oplus}$ and Section 4.3 develops the categorical structure allowing us to interpret the quantum lambda calculus. Section 4.4 sketches the proof of the soundness of the model with respect to the operational semantics. Finally, Section 4.5 discusses the denotations of the programs **qlist** and **teleport**.

### 4.1 Preliminaries: from CPM to $\overline{\textbf{CPMs}}$

***Permutation groups.*** Let $S_n$ be the symmetric group of degree $n$, i.e., the group of permutations of $n = \{0, \ldots, n-1\}$. Any permutation $g \in S_n$ gives rise to a matrix $P_g \in \mathbb{C}^{n \times n}$, defined by $P_g(e_i) = e_{g(i)}$, where $e_i$ is the $i$th standard basis vector. We define an action of $g$ on $\mathbb{C}^{n\times n}$ by $g \cdot M := P_g M P_g^{-1}$. Moreover, for a subgroup $G \subseteq S_n$, we define

$$G \cdot M := \frac{1}{\#G} \sum_{g \in G} g \cdot M, \tag{5}$$

where $\#G$ is the number of elements of $G$.

**Lemma 15.** *Given a subgroup $G \subseteq S_n$, its action on $\mathbb{C}^{n\times n}$ is idempotent (i.e., $G \cdot G \cdot M = G \cdot M$ for all $M$) and completely positive.*

*Proof.* For the idempotence, notice that for every $g \in G$, $gG = G$, therefore: $G \cdot G \cdot M = \frac{1}{\#G} \sum_{g\in G} gG \cdot M = G \cdot M$. The complete positivity of $G$ is derived from the complete positivity of each map $M \mapsto g \cdot M = P_g M P_g^{-1}$. □

In the sequel, we use the notation $G$ both for a subgroup of $S_n$ and for the completely positive map defined by it. The above Lemma allows us to define the set of completely positive maps from $\mathbb{C}^{n\times n}$ to $\mathbb{C}^{m\times m}$ invariant under the actions of two subgroups $G \subseteq S_n$, $H \subseteq S_m$ by

$$\textbf{CPMs}(G, H) := \{f \in \textbf{CPM}(n, m) \mid G \,;\, f \,;\, H = f\},$$

where $f; g$ is the diagrammatic composition $(f; g)(x) = g(f(x))$, and $\textbf{CPM}(n, m)$ is the set of completely positive maps from $\mathbb{C}^{n\times n}$ to $\mathbb{C}^{m\times m}$.

***Completion of the Löwner positive cone.*** The set $\textbf{CPMs}(G, H)$ is a module over the semi-ring $\mathbb{R}^+$ of the non-negative real numbers. The Löwner order $\sqsubseteq$ on completely positive maps [18] endows this module with the structure of a *bounded* directed complete partial order (bdcpo), i.e., there is a minimum element (the zero function $\mathbf{0}$), and any directed set $D$ that is bounded (i.e., such that there exists $f \in \textbf{CPMs}(G, H)$ such that for all $g \in D$, $g \sqsubseteq f$) has a least upper bound $\bigvee D \in \textbf{CPMs}(G, H)$. However there exist unbounded directed subsets in $\textbf{CPMs}(G, H)$. We therefore need to complete $\textbf{CPMs}(G, H)$ to a dcpo.

The relevant construction is the *D-completion* of [24], which we briefly recall. Given any poset $P$, say that a subset $X$ is *Scott-closed* if it is down-closed and for every directed $I \subseteq S$, if the least upper bound $\bigvee I$ exists in $P$, then $\bigvee I \in S$. We say that a monotone function between posets $f : P \to Q$ is *Scott-continuous* if it preserves all *existing* least upper bounds of directed subsets. Let $\Gamma(P)$ be the set of Scott-closed subsets of $P$; this forms a dcpo under the subset ordering. The *D-completion* $c(P)$ is defined to be the smallest sub-dcpo of $\Gamma(P)$ containing all sets of the form $\downarrow x$. Then $c(P)$ is a dcpo, and there is a canonical injective Scott-continuous map $\iota : P \to c(P)$, defined by $\iota(x) = \downarrow x$, which allows us to regard $P$ as a subset of $c(P)$. The D-completion preserves all existing least upper bounds of directed sets, is idempotent, and satisfies the following universal property: given any other dcpo $E$ and Scott-continuous map $f : P \to E$, there exists a unique Scott-continuous $g : c(P) \to E$ such that $f = \iota \,;\, g$. It follows that the D-completion is functorial. Moreover, if $P$ is a bounded directed complete partial order, then $P$ is an initial subset of $c(P)$, i.e., the only new elements added by the completion are "at infinity". We call these the *infinite* elements of $c(P)$.

The homset $\textbf{CPMs}(G, H)$ is then extended by D-completion, namely, $\overline{\textbf{CPMs}}(G, H) := c(\textbf{CPMs}(G, H))$. The categorical operations are extended in the unique Scott-continuous way, using the universal property of D-completion. This allows us to define indexed sums over $\overline{\textbf{CPMs}}(G, H)$, as follows. If $\{f_i\}_{i\in I} \subseteq \overline{\textbf{CPMs}}(G, H)$ is a (possibly infinite) indexed family, $\sum_{i\in I} f_i$ is defined as $\bigvee_{F \subseteq_{\text{fin}} I} (\sum_{i\in F} f_i)$. Indeed, the set $\{\sum_{i\in F} f_i \;;\; F \subseteq_{\text{fin}} I\}$ is always directed, so has a least upper bound in the order completion $\overline{\textbf{CPMs}}(G, H)$ of $\textbf{CPMs}(G, H)$.

### 4.2 The category $\overline{\textbf{CPMs}}^{\oplus}$

Given a set $A$ and $a, a' \in A$, define the *Kronecker symbol* $\delta_{a,a'} \in \mathbb{N}$ which takes value 1 if $a = a'$ and 0 if $a \neq a'$.

**Objects** are given by indexed families $\mathfrak{A} = \{(d_a^{\mathfrak{A}}, G_a^{\mathfrak{A}})\}_{a\in|\mathfrak{A}|}$, where the index set $|\mathfrak{A}|$ is called the *web* of $\mathfrak{A}$ and, for every $a \in |\mathfrak{A}|$, $d_a^{\mathfrak{A}}$ is a natural non-negative integer, and $G_a^{\mathfrak{A}}$ a subgroup of permutations of degree $d_a^{\mathfrak{A}}$, called respectively the *dimension* and the *permutation group* of $\mathfrak{A}_a$.

**Morphisms** from $\mathfrak{A}$ to $\mathfrak{B}$ are matrices $\phi$ indexed by $|\mathfrak{A}| \times |\mathfrak{B}|$ and such that $\phi_{a,b} \in \overline{\textbf{CPMs}}(G_a^{\mathfrak{A}}, G_b^{\mathfrak{B}})$.

**Composition** of $\phi \in \overline{\textbf{CPMs}}^{\oplus}(\mathfrak{A}, \mathfrak{B})$ and $\psi \in \overline{\textbf{CPMs}}^{\oplus}(\mathfrak{B}, \mathfrak{C})$ is the matrix $\phi \,;\, \psi$ defined by, for $a \in |\mathfrak{A}|$ and $c \in |\mathfrak{C}|$, $(\phi \,;\, \psi)_{a,c} := \sum_{b\in|\mathfrak{B}|} \phi_{a,b} \,;\, \psi_{b,c}$.

**Identity** is the diagonal matrix built with the symmetries of $\mathfrak{A}$, i.e., for $a, a' \in |\mathfrak{A}|$, $\mathrm{id}^{\mathfrak{A}}_{a,a'} := \delta_{a,a'} G_a^{\mathfrak{A}}$.

The description of the objects and the morphisms as indexed families is crucial for inferring the structure of a compact closed Lafont category (Section 4.3). However, it is worthwhile to notice that $\overline{\textbf{CPMs}}^{\oplus}$ can also be presented as a concrete category of modules and linear maps between modules. Let us sketch such an alternative presentation.

Let $\mathfrak{A}$ be an object of $\overline{\textbf{CPMs}}^{\oplus}$. We define a module $\mathrm{Pos}(\mathfrak{A})$ over $\overline{\mathbb{R}^+} = \mathbb{R}^+ \cup \{\infty\}$ as follows. For every $a$ in $|\mathfrak{A}|$, let us write $\mathrm{Pos}(a)$ for the cone of the positive matrices in $G_a^{\mathfrak{A}}(\mathbb{C}^{d_a^{\mathfrak{A}} \times d_a^{\mathfrak{A}}})$, this latter being the subspace of the matrices in $\mathbb{C}^{d_a^{\mathfrak{A}} \times d_a^{\mathfrak{A}}}$ invariant under $G_a^{\mathfrak{A}}$. This positive cone $\mathrm{Pos}(a)$ is an $\mathbb{R}^+$-module. We then define:

$$\mathrm{Pos}(\mathfrak{A}) := \bigoplus_{a\in|\mathfrak{A}|} (c(\mathrm{Pos}(a))\}). \tag{6}$$

In fact, we have that $\mathrm{Pos}(a) \simeq \textbf{CPMs}(S_1, G_a^{\mathfrak{A}})$ and $\mathrm{Pos}(\mathfrak{A}) \simeq \bigoplus_{a\in|\mathfrak{A}|} \overline{\textbf{CPMs}}(S_1, G_a^{\mathfrak{A}})$. Hence, $\mathrm{Pos}(\mathfrak{A})$ is a continuous module over $\overline{\mathbb{R}^+}$: addition and scalar multiplication are defined pointwise and are continuous operations with respect to the Löwner order.

$$[\![\mathtt{meas}]\!]^{!\Delta\vdash\mathbf{qubit}\multimap\mathbf{bit}}_{\vec{m},(*,b)} = \left(\begin{smallmatrix}\alpha & \beta\\ \gamma & \delta\end{smallmatrix}\right) \mapsto \begin{cases}\alpha & \text{if } \vec{m} = \vec{[]} \text{ and } b = \mathtt{ff},\\ \delta & \text{if } \vec{m} = \vec{[]} \text{ and } b = \mathtt{tt},\\ 0 & \text{otherwise.}\end{cases}$$

$$[\![\mathtt{new}]\!]^{!\Delta\vdash\mathbf{bit}\multimap\mathbf{qubit}}_{\vec{m},(b,*)} = \alpha \mapsto \begin{cases}\left(\begin{smallmatrix}\alpha & 0\\ 0 & 0\end{smallmatrix}\right) & \text{if } \vec{m} = \vec{[]} \text{ and } b = \mathtt{ff},\\ \left(\begin{smallmatrix}0 & 0\\ 0 & \alpha\end{smallmatrix}\right) & \text{if } \vec{m} = \vec{[]} \text{ and } b = \mathtt{tt},\\ \mathbf{0} & \text{otherwise.}\end{cases}$$

$$[\![U]\!]^{!\Delta\vdash\mathbf{qubit}^{\otimes n}\multimap\mathbf{qubit}^{\otimes n}}_{\vec{m},(\vec{*},\vec{*})} = M \mapsto \begin{cases}UMU^{-1} & \text{if } \vec{m} = \vec{[]},\\ \mathbf{0} & \text{otherwise.}\end{cases}$$

Table 4: Interpretation of the quantum constants. The writing $\vec{m}$ stands for a sequence of multisets in $|[\![!\Delta]\!]|$, the equality $\vec{m} = \vec{[]}$ meaning that each of these multisets is empty. $U$ and $M$ have the same dimension $\mathbb{C}^{2^n\times 2^n}$, $U$ being unitary.

Let $f : \mathrm{Pos}(\mathfrak{A}) \to \mathrm{Pos}(\mathfrak{B})$ be a continuous module homomorphism. We say that $f$ is *completely positive* if all the module homomorphisms $f_{a,b} = \iota^a \,;\, f \,;\, \pi^b$ are completely positive maps, for all $a \in |\mathfrak{A}|$ and $b \in |\mathfrak{B}|$. (Indeed, since the positive matrices span the complex vector space of square matrices (of corresponding size), one can canonically extend the definition of complete positivity to module homomorphisms $\mathrm{Pos}(a) \to \mathrm{Pos}(b)$).

**Proposition 16.** *There is an isomorphism between the homset* $\overline{\mathbf{CPMs}}^{\oplus}(\mathfrak{A},\mathfrak{B})$ *and the continuous module homomorphisms from* $\mathrm{Pos}(\mathfrak{A})$ *to* $\mathrm{Pos}(\mathfrak{B})$ *that are completely positive.* □

### 4.3 $\overline{\mathbf{CPMs}}^{\oplus}$ as a model of the quantum lambda calculus

A compact closed category is a special case of symmetric monoidal closed category. A symmetric monoidal closed category with finite products, such that each object has a corresponding free commutative comonoid, is called a *Lafont category*, which is known to be a model of intuitionistic linear logic [9, 15]. The category $\overline{\mathbf{CPMs}}^{\oplus}$ can be endowed with such a structure, as we will show in Sections 4.3.1–4.3.4 below. We can therefore interpret the quantum lambda calculus in $\overline{\mathbf{CPMs}}^{\oplus}$.

The denotation $[\![A]\!]$ of a type $A$ is an object of $\overline{\mathbf{CPMs}}^{\oplus}$. In case $A$ is the ground type (i.e., $1$, **qubit**), its denotation is:

$$|[\![\mathbf{qubit}]\!]| := \{\star\}, \quad d^{[\![\mathbf{qubit}]\!]}_{\star} := 2, \quad G^{[\![\mathbf{qubit}]\!]}_{\star} := \{\mathrm{id}\},$$
$$|[\![1]\!]| := \{\star\}, \quad d^{[\![1]\!]}_{\star} := 1, \quad G^{[\![1]\!]}_{\star} := \{\mathrm{id}\}.$$

The denotation of the other types is given by structural induction, following the compact closed Lafont structure of $\overline{\mathbf{CPMs}}^{\oplus}$. We note in particular that the permutation groups play a role only when interpreting !-formulas.

Let $\Gamma = x_1{:}A_1, \ldots, x_n{:}A_n$. The denotation of a typing judgement $\Gamma \vdash M : A$ is a morphism $[\![M]\!]^{\Gamma\vdash A} : [\![A_1 \otimes \cdots \otimes A_n]\!] \to [\![A]\!]$. The definition is by structural induction on the unique type derivation $\pi$ of $\Gamma \vdash M : A$ (see Proposition 4). The denotations of the constants `meas`, `new` and the unitary transformations are given in Table 4. Table 5 briefly recalls the denotation of the usual linear logic rules. Here, the morphisms $\phi, \psi, \phi_A, \phi_B$ refer to the denotation of the premises of the last rule of $\pi$, which are uniquely defined given $\Gamma \vdash M : A$.

In the interpretation of the `letrec` constructor, the fixed point operator Y is defined as follows. Let $\phi$ be a morphism in the set $\overline{\mathbf{CPMs}}^{\oplus}(!C \otimes !A, !A)$. By induction on $n$, we define the morphism $\phi^n \in \overline{\mathbf{CPMs}}^{\oplus}(!C, !A)$: $\phi^0 := !C \xrightarrow{\mathtt{w};!0} !A$, $\phi^{n+1} := !C \xrightarrow{\mathtt{c}} !C \otimes !C \xrightarrow{\mathrm{id}\otimes\phi^n} !C \otimes !A \xrightarrow{\phi} !A$. Since $\phi$ can be regarded as a continuous module homomorphism (in particular it is monotone), the set $\{\phi^n\}$ is directed complete. We define $\mathrm{Y}(\phi)$ as its least upper bound.

#### 4.3.1 Biproduct ($\mathfrak{A} \oplus \mathfrak{B}$)

Let $I$ be a (possibly infinite) set of indexes. The biproduct $\bigoplus_{i\in I}\mathfrak{A}_i$ of a family $\{\mathfrak{A}_i\}_{i\in I}$ of objects in $\overline{\mathbf{CPMs}}^{\oplus}$ is defined by

$$|\bigoplus_{i\in I}\mathfrak{A}_i| := \bigcup_{i\in I}\{i\} \times |\mathfrak{A}_i|, \quad d^{\bigoplus_{i\in I}\mathfrak{A}_i}_{(j,a)} := d^{\mathfrak{A}_j}_a, \quad G^{\bigoplus_{i\in I}\mathfrak{A}_i}_{(j,a)} := G^{\mathfrak{A}_j}_a.$$

The corresponding projections and injections are denoted respectively by $\pi^j$ and $\iota^j$ and defined as:

$$\pi^j_{(i,a),a'} := \iota^j_{a',(i,a)} := \delta_{j,i}\delta_{a,a'}G^{\mathfrak{A}_i}_a.$$

The tupling $\langle\phi_i\rangle_{i\in I}$ (resp. (co)-tupling $[\psi_i]_{i\in I}$) of a family of morphisms $\phi_i$ elements of $\overline{\mathbf{CPMs}}^{\oplus}(\mathfrak{A},\mathfrak{B}_i)$ (resp. $\psi_i$ elements of $\overline{\mathbf{CPMs}}^{\oplus}(\mathfrak{A}_i,\mathfrak{B})$) is defined by $(\langle\phi_i\rangle_{i\in I})_{a,(j,b)} := (\phi_j)_{a,b}$ (resp. $([\psi_i]_{i\in I})_{(j,a),b} := (\psi_j)_{a,b}$).

**Example 17.** Recall that in Notation 3, the type **bit** is interpreted as the biproduct $[\![1]\!] \oplus [\![1]\!]$, which is the two-element family $\{(1,\{\mathrm{id}\})_{\mathtt{tt}}, (1,\{\mathrm{id}\})_{\mathtt{ff}}\}$. The positive cones associated with 1 and **bit** are: $\mathrm{Pos}([\![1]\!]) = \overline{\mathbb{R}^+}$ and $\mathrm{Pos}([\![\mathbf{bit}]\!]) = \overline{\mathbb{R}^+}^2$.

The typing judgement $\vdash \mathtt{tt} : \mathbf{bit}$ is interpreted as the right injection, which can be seen both as a family of two completely positive maps from $\mathbb{C}$ to $\mathbb{C}$ (i.e., $[\![\mathtt{tt}]\!]^{\vdash\mathbf{bit}}_{\star,\mathtt{tt}} = p \mapsto p$ and $[\![\mathtt{tt}]\!]^{\vdash\mathbf{bit}}_{\star,\mathtt{ff}} = p \mapsto 0$) and as a quantum compatible and completely positive map sending $p \in \overline{\mathbb{R}^+}$ to $(0,p) \in \overline{\mathbb{R}^+}^2$. Symmetrically, $[\![\mathtt{ff}]\!]^{\vdash\mathbf{bit}}$ is the map $p \mapsto (p,0)$.

As an example of a term with free variables, consider $\mathtt{Neg}_x :=$ $\mathtt{if}\ x\ \mathtt{then\ ff\ else\ tt}$. The denotation of $x : \mathbf{bit} \vdash \mathtt{Neg}_x : \mathbf{bit}$ can be seen both as a family of four constant maps $[\![\mathtt{Neg}_x]\!]^{\mathbf{bit}\vdash\mathbf{bit}}_{b,b'}$ from $\mathbb{C}$ to $\mathbb{C}$ of value 1 if $b \neq b'$ and 0 otherwise, and as a single map from $\overline{\mathbb{R}^+}^2$ to $\overline{\mathbb{R}^+}^2$ sending $(p,p')$ to $(p',p)$.

#### 4.3.2 Symmetric monoidal structure ($\mathfrak{A} \otimes \mathfrak{B}$, 1 and $\mathfrak{A}^{\ell}$)

The bifunctor $\otimes : \overline{\mathbf{CPMs}}^{\oplus} \times \overline{\mathbf{CPMs}}^{\oplus} \to \overline{\mathbf{CPMs}}^{\oplus}$ is defined on objects $\mathfrak{A}, \mathfrak{B}$ by:

$$|\mathfrak{A}\otimes\mathfrak{B}| := |\mathfrak{A}| \times |\mathfrak{B}|, \qquad d^{\mathfrak{A}\otimes\mathfrak{B}}_{(a,b)} := d^{\mathfrak{A}}_a \times d^{\mathfrak{B}}_b,$$
$$G^{\mathfrak{A}\otimes\mathfrak{B}}_{(a,b)} := \{(g,h)\ ;\ g \in G^{\mathfrak{A}}_a, h \in G^{\mathfrak{B}}_b\},$$

where $d^{\mathfrak{A}}_a \times d^{\mathfrak{B}}_b$ is the multiplication of the two numbers $d^{\mathfrak{A}}_a$ and $d^{\mathfrak{B}}_b$, which can be seen as the lexicographically ordered set of pairs $(i,j)$, for $i < d^{\mathfrak{A}}_a$, $j < d^{\mathfrak{B}}_b$. Hence, the action of a permutation $(g,h) \in G^{\mathfrak{A}\otimes\mathfrak{B}}_{(a,b)}$ on $d^{\mathfrak{A}}_a \times d^{\mathfrak{B}}_b$ can be described as $(i,j) \mapsto (g(i),h(j))$.

The bifunctor $\otimes$ on morphisms is defined componentwise, using the standard tensor of the category **CPM** extended to the infinite elements by the universal property of the D-completion (Section 4.1). The tensor unit is the object $[\![1]\!]$ interpreting the unit type.

The associativity, unit, and symmetry isomorphisms are defined componentwise from the corresponding isomorphisms in **CPM**, composed with the actions of the groups of the objects. E.g., the symmetry is $\sigma^{\mathfrak{A},\mathfrak{B}}_{(a,b),(b',a')} := \delta_{a,a'}\delta_{b,b'}G^{\mathfrak{A}\otimes\mathfrak{B}}_{(a,b)}\ ;\ \sigma^{d^{\mathfrak{A}}_a,d^{\mathfrak{B}}_b}$, where $\sigma^{d^{\mathfrak{A}}_a,d^{\mathfrak{B}}_b}$ is the symmetry in **CPM** between $\mathbb{C}^{d^{\mathfrak{A}}_a\times d^{\mathfrak{A}}_a} \otimes \mathbb{C}^{d^{\mathfrak{B}}_b\times d^{\mathfrak{B}}_b}$ and $\mathbb{C}^{d^{\mathfrak{B}}_b\times d^{\mathfrak{B}}_b} \otimes \mathbb{C}^{d^{\mathfrak{A}}_a\times d^{\mathfrak{A}}_a}$. Notice that it is sufficient to pre-compose $\sigma^{d^{\mathfrak{A}}_a,d^{\mathfrak{B}}_b}$ with $G^{\mathfrak{A}\otimes\mathfrak{B}}_{(a,b)}$ (or, symmetrically, post-compose with $G^{\mathfrak{B}\otimes\mathfrak{A}}_{(b,a)}$), in order to have a map invariant under both the permutation groups $G^{\mathfrak{A}\otimes\mathfrak{B}}_{(a,b)}$ and $G^{\mathfrak{B}\otimes\mathfrak{A}}_{(b,a)}$. This is because $G^{\mathfrak{A}\otimes\mathfrak{B}}_{(a,b)}\ ;\ \sigma^{d^{\mathfrak{A}}_a,d^{\mathfrak{B}}_b} = G^{\mathfrak{A}}_a \otimes G^{\mathfrak{B}}_b\ ;\ \sigma^{d^{\mathfrak{A}}_a,d^{\mathfrak{B}}_b} = \sigma^{d^{\mathfrak{A}}_a,d^{\mathfrak{B}}_b}\ ;\ G^{\mathfrak{B}}_b \otimes G^{\mathfrak{A}}_a =$

$$!\Delta \otimes A \xrightarrow{\mathtt{w}\otimes\mathrm{id}} 1 \otimes A \simeq A$$
(a) $!\Delta, x : A \vdash x : A$

$$!\Delta \otimes !A \xrightarrow{\mathtt{w}\otimes\mathtt{d}} 1 \otimes A \simeq A$$
(b) $!\Delta, x : !A \vdash x : A$

$$!\Delta \xrightarrow{\mathtt{dig}} !!\Delta \xrightarrow{\mathtt{m}} !(!\Delta) \xrightarrow{!\phi} !A$$
(c) $!\Delta, \vdash V : !A$

$$!\Delta \otimes \Gamma \xrightarrow{\Lambda(\phi)} A \multimap B$$
(d) $!\Delta, \Gamma \vdash \lambda x^A.M : A \multimap B$

$$!\Delta \otimes \Gamma \otimes \Sigma \xrightarrow{\mathtt{c}\otimes\mathrm{id}} !\Delta \otimes \Gamma \otimes !\Delta \otimes \Sigma \xrightarrow{\phi\otimes\psi} A \otimes A \multimap B \xrightarrow{\mathrm{eval}} B$$
(e) $!\Delta, \Gamma, \Sigma \vdash MN : B$

$$!\Delta \xrightarrow{\mathtt{w}} 1$$
(f) $!\Delta \vdash \mathtt{skip} : 1$

$$!\Delta \otimes \Gamma \otimes \Sigma \xrightarrow{\mathtt{c}\otimes\mathrm{id}} !\Delta \otimes \Gamma \otimes !\Delta \otimes \Sigma \xrightarrow{\phi\otimes\mathrm{id}} 1 \otimes !\Delta \otimes \Sigma \simeq !\Delta \otimes \Sigma \xrightarrow{\psi} A$$
(g) $!\Delta, \Gamma, \Sigma \vdash M;N : A$

$$!\Delta \otimes \Gamma \otimes \Sigma \xrightarrow{\mathtt{c}\otimes\mathrm{id}} !\Delta \otimes \Gamma \otimes !\Delta \otimes \Sigma \xrightarrow{\phi\otimes\psi} A \otimes B$$
(h) $!\Delta, \Gamma, \Sigma \vdash M \otimes N : A \otimes B$

$$!\Delta \otimes \Gamma \otimes \Sigma \xrightarrow{\mathtt{c}\otimes\mathrm{id}} !\Delta \otimes \Gamma \otimes !\Delta \otimes \Sigma \xrightarrow{\phi\otimes\mathrm{id}} A \otimes B \otimes !\Delta \otimes \Sigma \xrightarrow{\psi} C$$
(i) $!\Delta, \Gamma, \Sigma \vdash \mathtt{let}\ x^A \otimes y^B = M\ \mathtt{in}\ N : C$

$$!\Delta \otimes \Gamma \xrightarrow{\phi} A \xrightarrow{\iota^\ell} A \oplus B$$
(j) $!\Delta, \Gamma \vdash \mathtt{in}_\ell\ M : A \oplus B$

$$!\Delta \otimes \Gamma \xrightarrow{\phi} B \xrightarrow{\iota^r} A \oplus B$$
(k) $!\Delta, \Gamma \vdash \mathtt{in}_r\ M : A \oplus B$

$$!\Delta \otimes \Gamma \otimes \Sigma \xrightarrow{\mathtt{c}\otimes\mathrm{id}} !\Delta \otimes \Gamma \otimes !\Delta \otimes \Sigma \xrightarrow{\psi\otimes\mathrm{id}} (A \oplus B) \otimes !\Delta \otimes \Sigma \xrightarrow{\mathtt{distr}} (A \otimes !\Delta \otimes \Sigma) \oplus (B \otimes !\Delta \otimes \Sigma) \xrightarrow{\phi_A \oplus \phi_B} C$$
(l) $!\Delta, \Gamma, \Sigma \vdash \mathtt{match}\ M\ \mathtt{with}\ (x^A : N \mid y^B : L) : C$

$$!\Delta \otimes \Gamma \xrightarrow{\phi} 1 \oplus (A \otimes A^\ell) \xrightarrow{\mathrm{id}\oplus\mathtt{distr}} 1 \oplus (\textstyle\bigoplus_{n=1}^{\infty} A^{\otimes n}) = A^\ell$$
(m) $!\Delta, \Gamma \vdash M : A^\ell$

$$!\Delta \otimes \Gamma \xrightarrow{\mathtt{c}} !\Delta \otimes \Gamma \otimes !\Delta \xrightarrow{\mathrm{id}\otimes \mathrm{Y}(\mathtt{dig};\mathtt{m};!(\Lambda\phi))} !\Delta \otimes \Gamma \otimes !(A \multimap B) \xrightarrow{\psi} C$$
(n) $!\Delta, \Gamma \vdash \mathtt{letrec}\ f\,x = M\ \mathtt{in}\ N : C$

Table 5: Sketch of the interpretation of the typing judgements, using the Lafont structure of $\overline{\mathbf{CPMs}}^{\oplus}$ defined in Section 4.3. The morphisms $\phi$, $\psi$, $\phi_A$, $\phi_B$ refer to the denotation of the premises of the unique derivation concluding a typing judgement. In (c) and (n), the morphism $\mathtt{m}$ stands for $\mathtt{m}^1$ or the suitable sequence of $\mathtt{m}^{\otimes}$, depending on the context $!!\Delta$.

$\sigma^{d_a^{\mathfrak{A}}, d_b^{\mathfrak{B}}}$ ; $G_{(b,a)}^{\mathfrak{B}\otimes\mathfrak{A}}$. Similar simplifications will be done henceforth without explicitly mentioning it.

**Example 18.** The denotation of **qubit** $\otimes$ **qubit** is the singleton web family $\{(4, \{\mathrm{id}\})_\star\}$. This object is associated with the cone of positive matrices of dimension $4 \times 4$ plus the infinite elements needed to complete the Löwner order. The denotation of **bit** $\otimes$ **bit** instead has a web of cardinality 4, i.e., $\{(\mathtt{ff},\mathtt{ff}), (\mathtt{ff},\mathtt{tt}), (\mathtt{tt},\mathtt{ff}), (\mathtt{ff},\mathtt{ff})\}$, and, for each index $b \in |[\![\mathbf{bit} \otimes \mathbf{bit}]\!]|$, we have $d_b^{[\![\mathbf{bit}\otimes\mathbf{bit}]\!]} = 1$ and $G_b^{[\![\mathbf{bit}\otimes\mathbf{bit}]\!]} = \{\mathrm{id}\}$. This object is associated with the biproduct $\overline{\mathbb{R}^+} \oplus \overline{\mathbb{R}^+} \oplus \overline{\mathbb{R}^+} \oplus \overline{\mathbb{R}^+}$.

Notice that in the above example the tensor product distributes over the biproducts: $[\![\mathbf{bit} \otimes \mathbf{bit}]\!] = [\![(1 \oplus 1) \otimes (1 \oplus 1)]\!] = [\![1 \oplus 1 \oplus 1 \oplus 1]\!]$. This is true in general: the isomorphism between $\mathfrak{A} \otimes (\bigoplus_{i\in I} \mathfrak{B}_i)$ and $\bigoplus_{i\in I}(\mathfrak{A} \otimes \mathfrak{B}_i)$ is

$$\mathtt{distr}_{(a,(i,b)),(i',(a',b'))} := \delta_{i,i'}\delta_{a,a'}\delta_{b,b'}G_{(a,b)}^{\mathfrak{A}\otimes\mathfrak{B}_i}.$$

This isomorphism allows us to define the list constructor as the infinite biproduct of tensor powers $\mathfrak{A}^\ell := \bigoplus_{n=0}^{\infty} \mathfrak{A}^{\otimes n}$. In fact, we have $\mathfrak{A}^\ell \simeq \mathbf{1} \oplus (\mathfrak{A} \otimes \mathfrak{A}^\ell)$.

**Example 19.** The denotation of the unit type list is: $|[\![\mathbf{1}^\ell]\!]| = \mathbb{N}$ and, for every $n \in \mathbb{N}$, $d_n^{[\![\mathbf{1}^\ell]\!]} = 1$, $G_n^{[\![\mathbf{1}^\ell]\!]} = \{\mathrm{id}\}$. This object can be associated with the module $\overline{\mathbb{R}^+}^{\mathbb{N}}$ and is suitable for denoting the numerals in unary notation. Indeed, writing $\underline{n}$ for the list $\mathtt{skip} :: \ldots \mathtt{skip} :: \mathtt{nil}$ of length $n$, we have $[\![\underline{n}]\!]^{\vdash \mathbf{1}^\ell} = p \mapsto (\underbrace{0, \ldots, 0}_{n-1 \text{ times}}, p, 0, \ldots)$.

### 4.3.3 Compact closure ($\mathfrak{A}^\perp$, $\mathfrak{A} \multimap B$)

Dual objects coincide: we have $\mathfrak{A}^\perp := \mathfrak{A}$. The unit $\eta^{\mathfrak{A}} \in \overline{\mathbf{CPMs}}^{\oplus}(\mathbf{1}, \mathfrak{A}^\perp \otimes \mathfrak{A})$ and co-unit $\epsilon^{\mathfrak{A}} \in \overline{\mathbf{CPMs}}^{\oplus}(\mathfrak{A} \otimes \mathfrak{A}^\perp, \mathbf{1})$ are defined componentwise composing the unit and co-unit of **CPM** with the correspondent permutation group. Writing $E_{i,j}$ for the matrix that has 0 everywhere except 1 at $(i,j)$, we have:

$$\eta^{\mathfrak{A}}_{\star,(a,a')} := 1 \mapsto \sum_{i,j<d^{\mathfrak{A}}} G_a^{\mathfrak{A}}(E_{i,j}) \otimes G_a^{\mathfrak{A}}(E_{i,j})$$

$$\epsilon^{\mathfrak{A}}_{(a,a'),\star} := (E_{i,j} \otimes E_{i',j'}) \mapsto \sum_{g,g' \in G_a^{\mathfrak{A}}} \frac{1}{\# G_a^{\mathfrak{A}}} \delta_{g(i),g'(i')}\delta_{g(j),g'(j')}.$$

Compact closed categories are monoidal closed. Let us recall the monoidal closure structure, which is needed to model the abstraction and the application of the quantum lambda calculus. The internal hom object is defined as $\mathfrak{A} \multimap \mathfrak{B} := (\mathfrak{A}^\perp \otimes \mathfrak{B}) = \mathfrak{A} \otimes \mathfrak{B}$. The evaluation morphism $\mathrm{Eval}^{\mathfrak{A},\mathfrak{B}} : \overline{\mathbf{CPMs}}^{\oplus}((\mathfrak{A} \multimap \mathfrak{B}) \otimes \mathfrak{A}, \mathfrak{B})$ and the currying isomorphism $\Lambda(-)$ from $\overline{\mathbf{CPMs}}^{\oplus}(\mathfrak{C} \otimes \mathfrak{A}, \mathfrak{B})$ to $\overline{\mathbf{CPMs}}^{\oplus}(\mathfrak{C}, \mathfrak{A} \multimap \mathfrak{B})$ are,

$$\mathrm{Eval}^{\mathfrak{A},\mathfrak{B}} := \sigma;\alpha;(\epsilon\otimes\mathrm{id});\lambda,\ \ \Lambda(\phi) := \lambda^{-1};(\eta\otimes\mathrm{id});\alpha^{-1};(\mathrm{id}\otimes(\sigma;\phi)),$$

where $\alpha$, $\lambda$, and $\sigma$ are the associative, left unit and symmetric isomorphisms associated with $\otimes$.

**Example 20.** Let us consider the abstraction $\lambda x.\mathtt{Neg}_x$ of the term $\mathtt{Neg}_x$ discussed in Example 17. The denotation $[\![\lambda x.\mathtt{Neg}_x]\!]^{\vdash \mathbf{bit} \multimap \mathbf{bit}}$ is obtained from $[\![\mathtt{Neg}_x]\!]^{x:\mathbf{bit} \vdash \mathbf{bit}}$ just by shifting the matrix indexes: $[\![\lambda x.\mathtt{Neg}_x]\!]^{\vdash \mathbf{bit} \multimap \mathbf{bit}}_{\star,(b,b')} = [\![\mathtt{Neg}_x]\!]^{x:\mathbf{bit} \vdash \mathbf{bit}}_{b,b'}$. Looking at this matrix as a module homomorphism, the map $[\![\lambda x.\mathtt{Neg}_x]\!]^{\vdash \mathbf{bit} \multimap \mathbf{bit}}$ is $p \mapsto (0, p, p, 0)$, which is a map from $\overline{\mathbb{R}^+}$ to $\overline{\mathbb{R}^+}_{(\mathtt{ff},\mathtt{ff})} \oplus \overline{\mathbb{R}^+}_{(\mathtt{ff},\mathtt{tt})} \oplus \overline{\mathbb{R}^+}_{(\mathtt{tt},\mathtt{ff})} \oplus \overline{\mathbb{R}^+}_{(\mathtt{tt},\mathtt{tt})}$, where we make explicit the correspondence between the web elements of $[\![\mathbf{bit} \multimap \mathbf{bit}]\!]$ and the components of the biproduct associated with.

Application corresponds basically to matrix multiplication. For example, $[\![(\lambda x.\mathtt{Neg}_x)(\mathtt{meas}\ y)]\!]^{y:\mathbf{qubit} \vdash \mathbf{bit}}_{\star,b}$ is the function defined as $\sum_{b' \in \{\mathtt{tt},\mathtt{ff}\}} [\![\lambda x.\mathtt{Neg}_x]\!]^{\vdash \mathbf{bit} \multimap \mathbf{bit}}_{\star,(b',b)} [\![\mathtt{meas}\ y]\!]^{y:\mathbf{qubit} \vdash \mathbf{bit}}_{\star,b'}$, which is sending $\left(\begin{smallmatrix}\alpha & \beta \\ \gamma & \delta\end{smallmatrix}\right)$ to $\delta$ if $b = \mathtt{ff}$, $\alpha$ if $b = \mathtt{tt}$, and 0 otherwise.

### 4.3.4 Free commutative comonoids ($\mathfrak{A}^{\odot k}$, $!\mathfrak{A}$)

Let us now focus on the crucial structure modeling the linear logic modality !. We first define the notion of $k$-th symmetric power of an object and then we show how the biproduct of all such symmetric powers yields an exponential structure.

**Notation 21.** Given a set $X$, a *multiset* $\mu$ over $X$ is a function $X \mapsto \mathbb{N}$. The *support* of $\mu$ is the set $|\mu| = \{a \mid \mu(a) \neq 0\} \subseteq X$, the *disjoint union* is $(\mu \uplus \nu)(a) = \mu(a) + \nu(a)$, and the *empty multiset* is the zero constant function. The *cardinality* of $\mu$ is $\sum_{a \in X} \mu(a) \in \mathbb{N} \cup \{\infty\}$. A multiset is finite if it has finite cardinality. $\mathcal{M}_k(X)$ (resp. $\mathcal{M}_f(X)$) is the set of the multisets over $X$ with cardinality $k$ (resp. finite). Finite multisets can be denoted by listing the occurrences of their elements between square brackets, i.e., $\mu = [a, a, b]$ is $\mu(a) = 2$, $\mu(b) = 1$ and zero on the other elements, and $[\,]$ is the empty multiset.

In a symmetric monoidal category, given a natural number $k$, the *k-th symmetric power* of an object $\mathfrak{A}$ is a pair $(\mathfrak{A}^{\odot k}, eq^{\mathfrak{A}^{\odot k}})$ of an object $\mathfrak{A}^{\odot k}$ and a morphism $eq^{\mathfrak{A}^{\odot k}}$ from $\mathfrak{A}^{\odot k}$ to $\mathfrak{A}^{\otimes k}$, which is an equalizer of the $k!$ symmetries of the $k$-ary tensor $\mathfrak{A}^{\otimes k}$. Such equalizers do not exist in general, but they do exist in $\overline{\mathbf{CPMs}}^{\oplus}$ and can be concretely represented using the multisets notation, as follows:

$$|\mathfrak{A}^{\odot k}| := \mathcal{M}_k(|\mathfrak{A}|), \quad d_\mu^{\mathfrak{A}^{\odot k}} := \prod_{a \in |\mu|} (d_a^{\mathfrak{A}})^{\mu(a)},$$

$$G_\mu^{\mathfrak{A}^{\odot k}} := \{(h_a, g_a^1, \ldots, g_a^{\mu(a)})_{a \in |\mu|} \; ; \; h_a \in S_{\mu(a)}, g_a^i \in G_a^{\mathfrak{A}}\},$$

where $(h_a, g_a^1, \ldots, g_a^{\mu(a)})_{a \in |\mu|}$ is a $|\mu|$-indexed family of sequences of permutations and $G_\mu^{\mathfrak{A}^{\odot k}}$ is a group (composition being defined componentwise) whose action on $\mathbb{C}^{d_\mu^{\mathfrak{A}^{\odot k}} \times d_\mu^{\mathfrak{A}^{\odot k}}}$ can be described by seeing $d_\mu^{\mathfrak{A}^{\odot k}}$ as the set of families of sequences of the form $(i_a^1, \ldots, i_a^{\mu(a)})_{a \in |\mu|}$, with $i_a^j < d_a^{\mathfrak{A}}$ for every $j \leqslant \mu(a)$. Then, the action of $(h_a, g_a^1, \ldots, g_a^{\mu(a)})_{a \in |\mu|}$ on such families is:

$$(i_a^1, \ldots, i_a^{\mu(a)})_{a \in |\mu|} \mapsto (g_a^1(i_a^{h_a(1)}), \ldots, g_a^{\mu(a)}(i_a^{h_a(\mu(a))}))_{a \in |\mu|}.$$

The morphism $eq^{\mathfrak{A}^{\odot k}}$ is given by

$$eq^{\mathfrak{A}^{\odot k}}{}_{\mu,(a_1,\ldots,a_k)} := \begin{cases} G_\mu^{\mathfrak{A}^{\odot k}} & \text{if } \mu = [a_1, \ldots, a_k], \\ \mathbf{0} & \text{otherwise.} \end{cases}$$

**Remark 22.** The object $[\![A]\!]^{\odot k}$ describes $k$ *unordered* uses of an element of type $A$. The fact that our model uses the symmetric tensor power $\mathfrak{A}^{\odot k}$ instead of the $k$-fold tensor $\mathfrak{A}^{\otimes k}$ means operationally that the behavior of a program calling its input $k$ times does not depend on the order of the calls.

**Example 23.** In Example 18, we have seen that $[\![\mathbf{qubit}]\!]^{\otimes 2} = \{(4, \{\text{id}\})_\star\}$. The symmetric 2-power $[\![\mathbf{qubit}]\!]^{\odot 2}$ is instead the singleton web family $\{(4, \{\text{id}, \sigma\})_\star\}$, where 4 is represented as the lexicographically ordered set $\{(0,0), (0,1), (1,0), (1,1)\}$ and the permutation $\sigma$ acts on it by $(b, b') \mapsto (b', b)$. The group of permutations $\{\text{id}, \sigma\}$ shrinks the set of possible morphisms to or from $[\![\mathbf{qubit}]\!]^{\odot 2}$. For example, the matrix $N_c$ associated with the controlled-not gate (Equation (1)) defines a complete positive endo-map of $\mathbb{C}^{4\times 4}$, which is an endo-morphism of $[\![\mathbf{qubit}]\!]^{\otimes 2}$ but not of $[\![\mathbf{qubit}]\!]^{\odot 2}$, because $N_c$ is not invariant under the action of $\{\text{id}, \sigma\}$:

$$\{\text{id}, \sigma\}(N_c) = \frac{1}{2}(\text{id}(N_c) + \sigma(N_c)) = \frac{1}{2}\begin{pmatrix} 2&0&0&0 \\ 0&1&0&1 \\ 0&0&1&1 \\ 0&1&1&0 \end{pmatrix} \neq N_c.$$

Concerning the module associated with symmetric tensor powers, $\text{Pos}([\![\mathbf{qubit}]\!]^{\odot 2})$ is the D-completion of

$$\left\{ \begin{pmatrix} \alpha_1 & \alpha_2 & \alpha_2 & \alpha_3 \\ \alpha_4 & \alpha_5 & \alpha_6 & \alpha_7 \\ \alpha_4 & \alpha_6 & \alpha_5 & \alpha_7 \\ \alpha_8 & \alpha_9 & \alpha_9 & \alpha_{10} \end{pmatrix} \text{ positive} \; ; \; \forall i, \alpha_i \in \mathbb{C} \right\}$$

which is a subcone of the positive cone of $\mathbb{C}^{4\times 4}$ of dimension 10.

Concerning biproducts, the denotation of $\mathbf{qubit} \oplus \mathbf{qubit}$ is given by $\{(2, \{\text{id}\})_{\texttt{tt}}, (2, \{\text{id}\})_{\texttt{ff}}\}$, while its symmetric tensor power $[\![\mathbf{qubit} \oplus \mathbf{qubit}]\!]^{\odot 2}$ is given by the three-element family $\{(4, \{\text{id}, \sigma\})_{[\texttt{tt},\texttt{tt}]}, (4, \{\text{id}\})_{[\texttt{tt},\texttt{ff}]}, (4, \{\text{id}, \sigma\})_{[\texttt{ff},\texttt{ff}]}\}$. Notice the difference between the pair $(4, \{\text{id}\})$ associated with $[\texttt{tt}, \texttt{ff}]$ and the pair $(4, \{\text{id}, \sigma\})$ associated with the two multisets of singleton support.

The biproduct $!\mathfrak{A} := \bigoplus_{k=0}^{\infty} \mathfrak{A}^{\odot k}$ of all symmetric powers of $\mathfrak{A}$ can be defined as

$$|!\mathfrak{A}| = \mathcal{M}_f(|\mathfrak{A}|), \quad d_\mu^{!\mathfrak{A}} = d_\mu^{\mathfrak{A}^{\odot k}}, \quad G_\mu^{!\mathfrak{A}} = G_\mu^{\mathfrak{A}^{\odot k}} \quad (\mu \in \mathcal{M}_k(|\mathfrak{A}|))$$

This object yields a concrete representation of the free commutative comonoid generated by $\mathfrak{A}$. The counit (also called *weakening*) $\mathtt{w} \in \overline{\mathbf{CPMs}}^{\oplus}(!\mathfrak{A}, \mathbf{1})$ and the comultiplication (or *contraction*) $\mathtt{c} \in \overline{\mathbf{CPMs}}^{\oplus}(!\mathfrak{A}, !\mathfrak{A} \otimes !\mathfrak{A})$ are:

$$\mathtt{w}_{\mu,\star} := \delta_{\mu,[\,]} G_{[\,]}^{!\mathfrak{A}}, \qquad \mathtt{c}_{\mu,(\mu',\mu'')} := \delta_{\mu,\mu'+\mu''} G_\mu^{!\mathfrak{A}}.$$

The freeness of the comonoid gives the structure of exponential comonad. The functorial promotion maps an object $\mathfrak{A}$ to $!\mathfrak{A}$ and a morphism $\phi \in \overline{\mathbf{CPMs}}^{\oplus}(\mathfrak{A}, \mathfrak{B})$ to $!\phi \in \overline{\mathbf{CPMs}}^{\oplus}(!\mathfrak{A}, !\mathfrak{B})$ defined by, for $\mu \in \mathcal{M}_f(|\mathfrak{A}|)$ and $\nu = [b_1, \ldots, b_k] \in \mathcal{M}_f(|\mathfrak{B}|)$,

$$!\phi_{\mu,\nu} := \sum_{\substack{(a_1,\ldots,a_k),\text{ st} \\ [a_1,\ldots,a_k]=\mu}} G_\mu^{!\mathfrak{A}} \; ; \bigotimes_{i=1}^{k} \phi_{a_i,b_i} \; ; G_\nu^{!\mathfrak{B}}.$$

The counit of the comonad (or *dereliction*) $\mathtt{d} \in \overline{\mathbf{CPMs}}^{\oplus}(!\mathfrak{A}, \mathfrak{A})$ and the comultiplication (or *digging*) $\mathtt{dig} \in \overline{\mathbf{CPMs}}^{\oplus}(!\mathfrak{A}, !!\mathfrak{A})$ are

$$\mathtt{d}_{\mu,a} := \delta_{\mu,[a]} G_a^{\mathfrak{A}}, \qquad \mathtt{dig}_{\mu,M} := \delta_{\mu,\sum M} G_\mu^{!\mathfrak{A}},$$

where $M \in |!!\mathfrak{A}|$ is a multiset of multisets $\nu$ over $|\mathfrak{A}|$ and $\sum M \in |!\mathfrak{A}|$ is the multiset union of such $\nu$'s, i.e., for every $a \in |\mathfrak{A}|$, $\sum M(a) = \sum_{\nu \in |M|} \nu(a)^{M(\nu)}$.

Finally, the last two morphisms that are essential to interpret our calculus are Bierman's $\mathtt{m}^{\otimes} \in \overline{\mathbf{CPMs}}^{\oplus}(!\mathfrak{A} \otimes !\mathfrak{B}, !(\mathfrak{A} \otimes \mathfrak{B}))$ and $\mathtt{m}^{\mathbf{1}} \in \overline{\mathbf{CPMs}}^{\oplus}(\mathbf{1}, !\mathbf{1})$, given by $\mathtt{m}^{\otimes}_{(\mu,\nu),\eta} := \delta_{\eta,\mu\times\nu} G_\eta^{!(\mathfrak{A}\otimes\mathfrak{B})}$ and $\mathtt{m}^{\mathbf{1}}_{\star,\mu} := \delta_{\mu,[\star]} G_\mu^{\mathbf{1}}$, where $\mu \times \nu$ is the multiset in $|!(\mathfrak{A} \otimes \mathfrak{B})|$ defined by, $\mu \times \nu(a, b) := \mu(a)\nu(b)$.

**Example 24.** Using the isomorphism between $\mathcal{M}_f(\{\star\})$ and the set $\mathbb{N}$, and between $\mathcal{M}_f(\{\texttt{tt}, \texttt{ff}\})$ and $\mathbb{N} \times \mathbb{N}$, the free commutative comonoids associated with $[\![1]\!]$ and $[\![\mathbf{bit}]\!]$ are $![\![1]\!] = \{(1, \{\text{id}\})_n\}_{n\in\mathbb{N}}$, and $![\![\mathbf{bit}]\!] = \{(1, \{\text{id}\})_{(n,m)}\}_{n,m\in\mathbb{N}}$. In general, notice that all constructions of the Lafont category preserve the underlying pair $(1, \{\text{id}\})$ and act only at the level of webs. For more involved examples, one should look for objects with larger dimension, like $[\![\mathbf{qubit}]\!]$. For example, $![\![\mathbf{qubit}]\!] = \{(2^n, S_n)_n\}_{n\in\mathbb{N}}$. Notice that $!1$, $!\mathbf{bit}$ and $!\mathbf{qubit}$ are not allowed by our type grammar. In fact, $!\mathbf{qubit}$ is meaningless because of the no-cloning constraint on quantum bits. However, such spaces should exist in the model since they are isomorphic to the denotations of legal types, like $!(1 \multimap 1)$, $!(1 \multimap \mathbf{bit})$ and $!(1 \multimap \mathbf{qubit})$.

### 4.4 The soundness theorem

The soundness of $\overline{\mathbf{CPMs}}^{\oplus}$ with respect to the operational semantics given in Figure 3 is an easy consequence of the fact that the category gives a (dcpo-enriched) model of linear logic. In fact, the operational semantics is a trivial extension of a head-reduction strategy of linear logic cut-elimination.

**Proposition 25.** *The category $\overline{\mathbf{CPMs}}^{\oplus}$ is a dcpo-enriched compact closed Lafont category, hence $\overline{\mathbf{CPMs}}^{\oplus}$ is a model of linear logic.*

*Proof (Sketch).* This basically amounts to showing that $\overline{\mathbf{CPMs}}^{\oplus}$ is the result of a categorical construction applied to $\mathbf{CPM}_s$ which is known to give, under certain circumstances, a dcpo-enriched Lafont category and to preserve the compact closed structure of $\mathbf{CPM}_s$. This construction was sketched in [5] and detailed in [11, 12, 16]. It consists in moving: (i) from $\mathbf{CPM}_s$ to a category $\mathbf{CPMs}$ with symmetric tensors, which is actually a full sub-category of the Karoubi envelope of $\mathbf{CPM}_s$; (ii) to a dcpo-enriched category

$\overline{\mathbf{CPMs}}$ using the D-completion defined in [7, 24]; and, finally, (iii) constructing the free biproduct completion $\overline{\mathbf{CPMs}}^{\oplus}$ of $\overline{\mathbf{CPMs}}$ and applying Equation (4). □

Given a linking $\ell = |y_1, \ldots, y_m\rangle$, we write $\ell \vdash M : A$ for the judgement $y_1 : \mathbf{qubit}, \ldots, y_m : \mathbf{qubit} \vdash M : A$.

**Proposition 26** (Invariance of the interpretation). *Let $\ell$ be the linking $|y_1, \ldots, y_m\rangle$, and assume $\ell \vdash M : A$. If $M$ is not a value, then for all quantum states $q \in \mathbb{C}^{2^m}$,*

$$[\![M]\!]^{\ell \vdash A}(qq^*) = \sum_{[q,\ell,M] \xrightarrow{p} [q',\ell',N]} p \cdot [\![N]\!]^{\ell' \vdash A}(q'q'^*). \quad (7)$$

*Proof.* By hypothesis, $[q, \ell, M]$ is a typable total closure, and so, by Proposition 11 and Lemma 13, all of its reducts $[q', \ell', N]$ are typable total closures, so that $[\![N]\!]^{\ell' \vdash A}(q'q'^*)$ is well-defined.

Equation 7 is proven by cases, depending on the rule applied to $[q, \ell, M]$. The cases of Table 3(a) follows from the fact that $\overline{\mathbf{CPMs}}^{\oplus}$ is a dcpo-enriched model of linear logic. The quantum rules (Table 3(b)) are trivial consequences of Table 4, and the congruence rules of Table 3(c) are done by induction on $M$, using the fact that the category $\overline{\mathbf{CPMs}}^{\oplus}$ is linear. □

**Corollary 27.** *We have $[\![M]\!]_*^{\vdash 1} \geqslant \mathrm{Halt}_{[|\rangle,|\rangle,M]}$.*

*Proof.* By induction on $n$ and using Proposition 7 we can show that $[\![M]\!]_*^{\ell \vdash 1}(qq^*)$ is greater or equal to $\sum_{[q',\ell',V]} \mathrm{Red}^n_{[\ell,q,M],[q',\ell',V]}$. Then $[\![M]\!]_*^{\ell \vdash 1}(qq^*) \geqslant \mathrm{Halt}_{[q,\ell,M]}$ follows by taking the limit as $n \to \infty$,and invoking the monotonicity of $\{\mathrm{Red}^n\}_n$. □

### 4.5 The denotations of qlist and teleport

**Example 28.** Recall the terms of Example 5. The web of $[\![\mathbf{qubit}^\ell]\!]$ is $\mathbb{N}$, while $[\![\mathbf{qubit}^\ell]\!]_n = (2^n, \{\mathrm{id}\})$. Note that $\mathrm{Pos}([\![\mathbf{qubit}^\ell]\!])$ is equivalent to the D-completion of $\bigoplus_n P(\mathbb{C}^{2^n \times 2^n})$ where the set $P(\mathbb{C}^{2^n \times 2^n})$ is the cone of $2^n \times 2^n$ positive matrices. The denotation of the term **qlist** is a morphism in $\overline{\mathbf{CPMs}}^{\oplus}(\mathbf{qubit}, \mathbf{qubit}^\ell)$, that is, a map sending a $2 \times 2$ positive matrix onto $\bigoplus_n P(\mathbb{C}^{2^n \times 2^n})$. The program **qlist** is defined using recursion: its semantics is the limit of the morphisms $f_n$ sending $\left(\begin{smallmatrix} a & b \\ c & d \end{smallmatrix}\right)$ to the infinite sequence $(\mathbf{0}, \frac{1}{2}e_1, \ldots, \frac{1}{2^n}e_n, \mathbf{0}, \mathbf{0}, \ldots)$ where $e_i$ is the $2^i \times 2^i$ positive matrix $\left(\begin{smallmatrix} a & 0 & \cdots & 0 & b \\ 0 & 0 & \cdots & 0 & 0 \\ \vdots & \vdots & \ddots & \vdots & \vdots \\ 0 & 0 & \cdots & 0 & 0 \\ c & 0 & \cdots & 0 & d \end{smallmatrix}\right)$.

This limit is the map sending $\left(\begin{smallmatrix} a & b \\ c & d \end{smallmatrix}\right)$ to the sequence of infinitely increasing matrices $(\mathbf{0}, \frac{1}{2}e_1, \ldots, \frac{1}{2^n}e_n, \ldots)$. Note that the first element of the sequence is $\mathbf{0}$, as the program **qlist** never return the empty list. Also note that all the positive matrices in the sequence represent *entangled states of arbitrary sizes*. Our semantics is the first one to be able to account for such a case: in [6], only fixed sizes were allowed for entangled states.

**Example 29.** We claim in the introduction that the model is expressive enough to describe entanglement at higher-order types. As we discuss in Example 6, the encoding of the quantum teleportation algorithm produces two entangled, mutually inverse functions: $f : \mathbf{qubit} \multimap \mathbf{bit} \otimes \mathbf{bit}$ and $g : \mathbf{bit} \otimes \mathbf{bit} \multimap \mathbf{qubit}$.

The term (**teleport** `skip`) of type $(\mathbf{qubit} \multimap \mathbf{bit} \otimes \mathbf{bit}) \otimes (\mathbf{bit} \otimes \mathbf{bit} \multimap \mathbf{qubit})$ is one instance of such a pair of functions. Its denotation is a finite sequence of 16 square matrices of size $4 \times 4$. Using a lexicographic convention, we can lay them out as in Fig. 6. Because of the convention, morally each row corresponds to an element of type $\mathbf{bit} \otimes \mathbf{bit} \multimap \mathbf{qubit}$ whereas each column corresponds to an element of type $\mathbf{qubit} \multimap \mathbf{bit} \otimes \mathbf{bit}$. Picking a row, i.e., a choice of two left-sided booleans, amounts to choosing the two booleans that will be passed to the function $g$. Picking a column, i.e., a choice of two right-sided booleans, amounts to deciding on the probabilistic result we get from the function $f$. The intersection of a column and a row is therefore the representation of a map $\mathbf{qubit} \multimap \mathbf{qubit}$. This map is a description of a possible path in the control flow of the algorithm.

The matrices on the diagonal correspond to a run of the algorithm as it was intended: applying $g$ to the result of $f$. Since they are supposed to be the identity on **qubit**, we can therefore deduce that the matrices $A_{00,00}$, $A_{01,01}$, $A_{10,10}$ and $A_{11,11}$ are all equal to $\left(\begin{smallmatrix} 1 & 0 & 0 & 1 \\ 0 & 0 & 0 & 0 \\ 0 & 0 & 0 & 0 \\ 1 & 0 & 0 & 1 \end{smallmatrix}\right)$. Since this matrix cannot be written as the tensor of two $2 \times 2$ matrices, we conclude that the denotation $A$ of (**teleport** `skip`) is indeed entangled.

We can compute the other matrices $A_{xy,zt}$ using the same argument: in general, $A_{xy,zt}$ is a composition of $f$ and $g$, except that instead of applying $g$ to $(x, y)$, we apply it to $(z, t)$. We therefore get a function $\mathbf{qubit} \to \mathbf{qubit}$ constructed out of the $U_{--}$ that might (if $xy = zt$) or might not be the identity. In general, the matrix $A_{xy,zt}$ is the denotation of the unitary $U_{zt}U^*_{xy}$. The denotation $A$ is given in full detail in Table 6.

**Remark 30.** Example 29 is a good illustration of what we claimed in the introduction: the model reflects the juxtaposition of quantum and classical structures, even at higher-order types. Here, the control-flow is handled by the biproduct structure, and the quantum part of the algorithm is split across the list of $4 \times 4$ matrices.

## 5. Adequacy

In the following, we prove the adequacy of $\overline{\mathbf{CPMs}}^{\oplus}$ (Theorem 38). This amounts to achieving the converse inequality of Corollary 27. The proof uses a syntactic approach, following [6]. We introduce a bounded $\mathtt{letrec}^n$, which can be unfolded at most $n$ times. On the one hand, the language allowing only bounded `letrec` is strongly normalizing (Lemma 33), hence the adequacy for it can be easily achieved by induction on the longest reduction sequence of a term (Corollary 34). On the other hand, the unbounded `letrec` can be expressed as the supremum of its bounded approximants, both semantically (Lemma 36) and syntactically (Lemma 37). We then conclude the adequacy for the whole quantum lambda calculus by continuity.

**Definition 31.** Let us extend the grammar of terms (Table 1) by adding: (i) a new term $\Omega^A$; (ii) a family of new term constructs $\mathtt{letrec}^n\ f^{A \multimap B}\ x = M\ \mathtt{in}\ N$ indexed by natural numbers $n \geqslant 0$.

The typing rules for these new constructs are

$$\frac{}{!\Delta \vdash \Omega^A : A} \qquad \frac{!\Delta, f : !(A \multimap B), x : A \vdash M : B \qquad !\Delta, \Gamma, f : !(A \multimap B) \vdash N : C}{!\Delta, \Gamma \vdash \mathtt{letrec}^n\ f^{A \multimap B}\ x = M\ \mathtt{in}\ N : C}$$

Their denotations are given, respectively, by the map $\mathbf{0}$ and the family of maps

$$!\Delta \otimes \Gamma \xrightarrow{c} !\Delta \otimes \Gamma \otimes !\Delta \xrightarrow{\mathrm{id} \otimes (\mathtt{dig};\mathtt{m};!(\Lambda\phi))^n} !\Delta \otimes \Gamma \otimes !(A \multimap B) \xrightarrow{\psi} C,$$

where $\phi \in \overline{\mathbf{CPMs}}^{\oplus}(!\Delta \otimes !(A \multimap B) \otimes A, B)$ and $\psi \in \overline{\mathbf{CPMs}}^{\oplus}(!\Delta \otimes \Gamma \otimes !(A \multimap B), C)$ are the denotations of the premises and $(\mathtt{dig};\mathtt{m};!(\Lambda\phi))^n \in \overline{\mathbf{CPMs}}^{\oplus}(!\Delta, !(A \multimap B))$ is defined in a similar fashion as in Table 5.

The reduction rules are updated as follows.

$$[q, \ell, \mathtt{letrec}^0\ f^{A \multimap B}\ x = M\ \mathtt{in}\ N] \xrightarrow{1} [q, \ell, N\{(\lambda x^A.\Omega^B)/f\}]$$

$$[q, \ell, \mathtt{letrec}^{n+1}\ f^{A \multimap B}\ x = M\ \mathtt{in}\ N]$$
$$\xrightarrow{1} [q, \ell, N\{(\lambda x^A.\mathtt{letrec}^n\ f^{A \multimap B}\ x = M\ \mathtt{in}\ M)/f\}].$$

$$
A = \frac{1}{4}\left(
\begin{array}{llll}
A_{00,00} = \begin{pmatrix} 1&0&0&1\\0&0&0&0\\0&0&0&0\\1&0&0&1 \end{pmatrix}, &
A_{00,01} = \begin{pmatrix} 0&0&0&0\\0&1&1&0\\0&1&1&0\\0&0&0&0 \end{pmatrix}, &
A_{00,10} = \begin{pmatrix} 1&0&0&-1\\0&0&0&0\\0&0&0&0\\-1&0&0&1 \end{pmatrix}, &
A_{00,11} = \begin{pmatrix} 0&0&0&0\\0&1&-1&0\\0&-1&1&0\\0&0&0&0 \end{pmatrix}, \\
A_{01,00} = \begin{pmatrix} 0&0&0&0\\0&1&1&0\\0&1&1&0\\0&0&0&0 \end{pmatrix}, &
A_{01,01} = \begin{pmatrix} 1&0&0&1\\0&0&0&0\\0&0&0&0\\1&0&0&1 \end{pmatrix}, &
A_{01,10} = \begin{pmatrix} 0&0&0&0\\0&1&-1&0\\0&-1&1&0\\0&0&0&0 \end{pmatrix}, &
A_{01,11} = \begin{pmatrix} 1&0&0&-1\\0&0&0&0\\0&0&0&0\\-1&0&0&1 \end{pmatrix}, \\
A_{10,00} = \begin{pmatrix} 1&0&0&-1\\0&0&0&0\\0&0&0&0\\-1&0&0&1 \end{pmatrix}, &
A_{10,01} = \begin{pmatrix} 0&0&0&0\\0&1&-1&0\\0&-1&1&0\\0&0&0&0 \end{pmatrix}, &
A_{10,10} = \begin{pmatrix} 1&0&0&1\\0&0&0&0\\0&0&0&0\\1&0&0&1 \end{pmatrix}, &
A_{10,11} = \begin{pmatrix} 0&0&0&0\\0&1&1&0\\0&1&1&0\\0&0&0&0 \end{pmatrix}, \\
A_{11,00} = \begin{pmatrix} 0&0&0&0\\0&1&-1&0\\0&-1&1&0\\0&0&0&0 \end{pmatrix}, &
A_{11,01} = \begin{pmatrix} 1&0&0&-1\\0&0&0&0\\0&0&0&0\\-1&0&0&1 \end{pmatrix}, &
A_{11,10} = \begin{pmatrix} 0&0&0&0\\0&1&1&0\\0&1&1&0\\0&0&0&0 \end{pmatrix}, &
A_{11,11} = \begin{pmatrix} 1&0&0&1\\0&0&0&0\\0&0&0&0\\1&0&0&1 \end{pmatrix}
\end{array}
\right).
$$

Table 6: The denotation of the quantum teleportation algorithm.

The additions to the language do not modify the properties of the language: subject reduction (Proposition 11) and totality (Lemma 13) hold as they are stated, while type safety (Proposition 12) and soundness (Proposition 26) are satisfied, with the proviso of considering the set of normal forms to consist of the set of values *and* the set of terms containing $\Omega$ in evaluating position.

**Definition 32.** A term is called *finitary* when it does not contain any occurrence of the un-indexed `letrec` construct. It can however contain $\Omega$ and any of the indexed $\texttt{letrec}^n$. We call a closure *finitary* when its term is finitary.

**Lemma 33** (Strong normalization)**.** *If* $[q_1, \ell_1, M_1]$ *is finitary and typable, then every reduction sequence of the form* $[q_1, \ell_1, M_1] \xrightarrow{p_1} [q_2, \ell_2, M_2] \xrightarrow{p_2} [q_3, \ell_3, M_3] \xrightarrow{p_3} \cdots$ *is finite.*

*Proof (Sketch).* We reduce the finitary quantum lambda calculus to a simply typed non-deterministic language without quantum states, for which a standard proof technique can be used. The terms of this language are the terms of the extended quantum lambda calculus, minus the `letrec` construct. The operational semantics is obtained from Table 3 and the rules for $\texttt{letrec}^n$ by replacing closures with the respective terms and the rules of Table 3b by dummy reduction rules: like $U(\bullet\otimes\cdots\otimes\bullet) \to \bullet\otimes\cdots\otimes\bullet$, or $\texttt{new}\,\texttt{ff} \to \bullet$. The symbol $\bullet$ denotes a distinct term variable, which, by convention, it is never bound by an abstraction. Clearly, the strong normalization of this language implies that of the finitary quantum lambda calculus. □

**Corollary 34** (Finitary adequacy)**.** *Let $M$ be a closed finitary term of unit type. Then* $[\![M]\!]_*^{\vdash 1} = \mathrm{Halt}_{[|\,\rangle,|\,\rangle,M]}$ .

*Proof (Sketch).* We prove that, for any total finitary quantum closure of unit type $[q, \ell, M]$ we have $[\![M]\!]^{\ell\vdash 1}(qq^*) = \mathrm{Halt}_{[q,\ell,M]}$. In fact, by Lemma 33, there exists $m \in \mathbb{N}$ such that $\mathrm{Halt}_{[q,\ell,M]} = \sum_{[q',\ell',V]} \mathrm{Red}^m_{[q,\ell,M],[q',\ell',V]}$. We conclude by induction on $m$. □

**Definition 35.** Let $\lhd$ be a relation between finitary terms and general terms defined as the smallest congruence relation on terms satisfying, for every $M \lhd M'$ and $N \lhd N'$:

$$N\{(\lambda x^A.\Omega^B)/f\} \lhd (\texttt{letrec}\ f\,x = M'\ \texttt{in}\ N'),$$
$$(\texttt{letrec}^n\ f\,x = M\ \texttt{in}\ N) \lhd (\texttt{letrec}\ f\,x = M'\ \texttt{in}\ N').$$

**Lemma 36.** *If* $\Gamma \vdash M : A$, *then* $[\![M]\!]^{\Gamma\vdash A} = \bigvee_{\substack{M' \lhd M \\ M' \text{ finitary}}} [\![M']\!]^{\Gamma\vdash A}$. □

**Lemma 37.** *If* $M \lhd M'$, *then* $\mathrm{Halt}_{[q,\ell,M]} \leqslant \mathrm{Halt}_{[q,\ell,M']}$.

*Proof (Sketch).* By induction on $n$, one proves the inequality: $\sum_{[q',\ell',V]} \mathrm{Red}^n_{[q,\ell,M],[q',\ell',V]} \leqslant \sum_{[q',\ell',V]} \mathrm{Red}^n_{[q,\ell,M'],[q',\ell',V]}$, from which the statement follows trivially. □

**Theorem 38.** *Let $M$ be a program, i.e., a closed term of unit type. Then* $[\![M]\!]_*^{\vdash 1} = \mathrm{Halt}_{[|\,\rangle,|\,\rangle,M]}$ .

*Proof.* By Corollary 27 we have $[\![M]\!]_*^{\vdash 1} \geqslant \mathrm{Halt}_{[|\,\rangle,|\,\rangle,M]}$. Conversely, by Lemma 36, $[\![M]\!]_*^{\vdash 1} = \bigvee_{M' \lhd M} [\![M']\!]_*^{\vdash 1}$, which is equal to $\bigvee_{M' \lhd M} \mathrm{Halt}_{[|\,\rangle,|\,\rangle,M']}$ by Corollary 34, which is less or equal to $\mathrm{Halt}_{[|\,\rangle,|\,\rangle,M]}$ by Lemma 37. □

## 6. Structure of the sets of representable elements

We conclude this paper with an analysis of some of the properties of the denotation of terms. Recall that a morphism in $\overline{\mathbf{CPMs}}^{\oplus}$ is an indexed family of either completely positive maps, or infinite elements added during D-completion. We show that (1) all types have a non-zero inhabitant; (2) provided that the term constant $U$ ranges over arbitrary unitary matrices, the representable elements of a given homset form a convex set including $\mathbf{0}$; and (3) infinite elements are not part of any representable map.

We first need two auxiliary definitions.

**Definition 39.** We define two type-indexed families of terms $\overline{\omega}_A$ and $\omega_A$ by mutual induction in Table 7. The term $\mathbf{c}$ represents the fair coin toss $\texttt{meas}\,(H\,(\texttt{new}\,\texttt{ff}))$ (recall Example 1) and the notation $\mu f x.M$ stands for $\texttt{letrec}\ f\,x = M\ \texttt{in}\ f$.

**Lemma 40.** *For all types $A$, we have* $\vdash \omega_A : 1 \multimap A$ *and* $\vdash \overline{\omega}_A : A \multimap 1$. *Moreover, the morphisms* $[\![\omega_A]\!]^{\vdash 1\multimap A}$ *and* $[\![\overline{\omega}_A]\!]^{\vdash A\multimap 1}$, *seen as indexed families, do not contain the zero map.* □

**Corollary 41.** *All types are inhabited by at least one closed value of non-null denotation.*

*Proof.* Immediate with Lemma 40: for a given type $A$, choose the term $(\omega_A\ \texttt{skip})$. □

**Proposition 42.** *Given a type $A$ and a context $\Gamma$, the denotations* $[\![M]\!]^{\Gamma\vdash A}$ *of valid typing judgements* $\Gamma \vdash M : A$ *form a convex set including* $\mathbf{0}$.

*Proof.* Suppose that $\Gamma$ is $x_1 : A_1, \ldots, x_n : A_n$. A term $M$ mapping to $\mathbf{0}$ is $(\overline{\omega}_{A_1} x_1; \ldots; \overline{\omega}_{A_n} x_n; \mathbf{\Omega})$ where the term $\mathbf{\Omega}$ is a shortcut for $\texttt{letrec}\ f\,x = f\,x\ \texttt{in}\ f\ \texttt{skip}$, of denotation $\mathbf{0}$.

Now, suppose that $f = [\![M_1]\!]^{\Gamma\vdash A}$ and $g = [\![M_2]\!]^{\Gamma\vdash A}$, and choose two non-negative real numbers $\rho_1$, $\rho_2$ such that $\rho_1 + \rho_2 = 1$. There exists an angle $\phi$ such that $(\cos\phi)^2 = \rho_1$ and that $(\sin\phi)^2 = \rho_2$. As the term constants $U$ range over arbitrary unitaries, the unitary matrix $V_\phi = \left(\begin{smallmatrix} \cos\phi & -\sin\phi \\ \sin\phi & \cos\phi \end{smallmatrix}\right)$ is representable in the quantum lambda calculus. The term $\mathbf{c}' = \texttt{meas}\,(V_\phi\,(\texttt{new}\,\texttt{ff}))$ has denotation $(\rho_1, \rho_2)$. We then conclude that the term $\texttt{if}\ \mathbf{c}'\ \texttt{then}\ M_1\ \texttt{else}\ M_2$ has denotation $\rho_1 f + \rho_2 g$. □

**Proposition 43.** *If* $\Gamma \vdash M : A$ *is valid, then no infinite element is part of the denotation* $[\![M]\!]^{\Gamma\vdash A}$ *of $M$.*

*Proof.* Suppose that one of the infinite elements of the D-completion were to be found in the interpretation of $x_1 : A_1, \ldots, x_n :$

$$
\begin{array}{ll|ll}
\omega_{\mathbf{qubit}} & = \lambda\mathtt{skip}.\mathtt{new\,ff} & \overline{\omega}_{\mathbf{qubit}} & = \lambda x^{\mathbf{qubit}}.\mathtt{if\ meas}\ x\ \mathtt{then\ skip\ else\ skip} \\
\omega_{A\multimap B} & = \lambda\mathtt{skip}.\lambda x^{A}.(\overline{\omega}_A\, x);(\omega_B\, \mathtt{skip}) & \overline{\omega}_{A\multimap B} & = \lambda f^{A\multimap B}.\overline{\omega}_B\,(f\,(\omega_A\, \mathtt{skip})) \\
\omega_{!(A\multimap B)} & = \lambda\mathtt{skip}.\lambda x^{A}.(\omega_{A\multimap B}\, \mathtt{skip})\, x & \overline{\omega}_{!(A\multimap B)} & = \mu g f^{!(A\multimap B)}.\mathtt{if\ c\ then\ skip\ else}\ (\overline{\omega}_{A\multimap B}\, f);(g\, f) \\
\omega_{1} & = \lambda\mathtt{skip}.\mathtt{skip} & \overline{\omega}_{1} & = \lambda\mathtt{skip}.\mathtt{skip} \\
\omega_{A\otimes B} & = \lambda\mathtt{skip}.(\omega_A\, \mathtt{skip}) \otimes (\omega_B\, \mathtt{skip}) & \overline{\omega}_{A\otimes B} & = \lambda x^{A\otimes B}.\mathtt{let}\ z_1 \otimes z_2 \ =\ x\ \mathtt{in}\ (\overline{\omega}_A\, z_1);(\overline{\omega}_B\, z_2) \\
\omega_{A\oplus B} & = \lambda\mathtt{skip}.\mathtt{if\ c\ then}\ (\omega_A\, \mathtt{skip})\ \mathtt{else}\ (\omega_B\, \mathtt{skip}) & \overline{\omega}_{A\oplus B} & = \lambda x^{A\oplus B}.\mathtt{match}\ x\ \mathtt{with}\ (z_1^A : \overline{\omega}_A\, z_1 \mid z_2^B : \overline{\omega}_B\, z_2) \\
\omega_{A^\ell} & = \mu f\mathtt{skip}.\mathtt{if\ c\ then}\ (\mathtt{skip})\ \mathtt{else}\ (\omega_A\, \mathtt{skip}) :: (f\, \mathtt{skip}) & \overline{\omega}_{A^\ell} & = \mu f x^{A^\ell}.\mathtt{match\ split}\ x\ \mathtt{with} \\
 & & & \quad (\ z_1^1\ :\ z_1 \mid z_2^{A\otimes A^\ell}\ :\ \mathtt{let}\ y_1 \otimes y_2 = z_2\ \mathtt{in}\ (\overline{\omega}_A\, y_1);(f\, y_2))
\end{array}
$$

Table 7: Two mutually recursive families of terms

$A_n \vdash M : A$. Then the closed term

$$(\lambda x_1 \ldots x_n.\overline{\omega}_A\, M)(\omega_{A_1}\mathtt{skip}) \ldots (\omega_{A_n}\mathtt{skip})$$

of type 1 has infinite denotation, contradicting Theorem 38. □

This last proposition indicates that infinite elements introduced during the D-completion are really an artifact only needed for the categorical construction. The representable elements in the model are only built out of families of completely positive maps.

## 7. Conclusion

We presented a higher-order lambda calculus for quantum computation featuring classical and quantum data, duplication, recursion, and an infinite parametric type for lists. We then answered a long-standing open question: the description of a model for the full quantum lambda calculus. The model we propose is a free construction based on the known model of completely positive maps, but nevertheless has a concrete presentation.

One thing that this model explains and illustrates is the distinction between the quantum and classical parts of the language. The quantum part is described by completely positive maps (finite dimension), whereas the classical control is given by the Lafont category (i.e., linear logic). The model demonstrates that the two "universes" work well together, but also – surprisingly – that they do not mix too much, even at higher order types (we always have an *infinite* list of *finite* dimensional CPMs). The control flow is completely handled by the biproduct completion, and not by the CPM structure. The adequacy result, moreover, validates that the model is a "good" representation of the language.

One should also note that the product and the coproduct coincide in our model. For example, the model has morphisms that correspond to a program returning true with probability 1 and false with probability 1. We would like to point out that our interpretation is not *surjective*. For example, there are also morphisms in the model corresponding to "probability 2". (Incidentally, adding terms with such behavior makes it possible to build a term whose denotation is $\infty$ – so the fact that this provably does not happen somehow captures the sanity of the model). Interpretations in denotational models are often not surjective. In fact, it is an open problem to give a non-syntactic characterization of the image of our interpretation. Similarly, the problem of full-abstraction is still open.

## References


[1] V. Danos and T. Ehrhard. Probabilistic coherence spaces as a model of higher-order probabilistic computation. *Inform. Comput.*, 2011.

[2] T. Ehrhard. Finiteness spaces. *MSCS*, 15(4):615–646, 2005.

[3] J.-Y. Girard. Linear logic. *Th. Comp. Sc.*, 50:1–102, 1987.

[4] J.-Y. Girard. Normal functors, power series and lambda-calculus. *Ann. Pure Appl. Logic*, 37(2):129–177, 1988.

[5] J.-Y. Girard. Coherent Banach spaces: a continuous denotational semantics. *Theoretical Computer Science*, 227:297, 1999.

[6] I. Hasuo and N. Hoshino. Semantics of higher-order quantum computation via geometry of interaction. In *Proceedings of LICS*, pages 237–246, 2011.

[7] K. Keimel and J. D. Lawson. D-completions and the *d*-topology. *Annals of Pure and Applied Logic*, 159(3):292 – 306, 2009.

[8] E. H. Knill. Conventions for quantum pseudocode. Technical Report LAUR-96-2724, Los Alamos National Laboratory, 1996.

[9] Y. Lafont. *Logiques, catégories et machines.* PhD thesis, Université Paris 7, 1988.

[10] U. D. Lago, A. Masini, and M. Zorzi. Confluence results for a quantum lambda calculus with measurements. *Electr. Notes Theor. Comput. Sci.*, 270(2):251–261, 2011.

[11] J. Laird, G. Manzonetto, and G. McCusker. Constructing differential categories and deconstructing categories of games. *Information and Computation*, 222:247–264, 2013.

[12] J. Laird, G. McCusker, G. Manzonetto, and M. Pagani. Weighted relational models of typed lambda-calculi. In *LICS'13*, 2013.

[13] S. Mac Lane. *Categories for the Working Mathematician.* Springer, 2nd edition, Sept. 1998.

[14] O. Malherbe. *Categorical models of computation: partially traced categories and presheaf models of quantum computation.* PhD thesis, University of Ottawa, 2010.

[15] P.-A. Melliès. Categorical semantics of linear logic. *Panoramas et Synthèses*, 12, 2009.

[16] P.-A. Melliès, N. Tabareau, and C. Tasson. An explicit formula for the free exponential modality of linear logic. In *ICALP'09 (2)*, pages 247–260, 2009.

[17] M. A. Nielsen and I. L. Chuang. *Quantum Computation and Quantum Information.* Cambridge University Press, 2002.

[18] P. Selinger. Towards a quantum programming language. *Mathematical Structures in Computer Science*, 14(4):527–586, 2004.

[19] P. Selinger. Towards a semantics for higher-order quantum computation. In *QPL'04*, TUCS Gen. Publi. No 33, pages 127–143, 2004.

[20] P. Selinger and B. Valiron. A lambda calculus for quantum computation with classical control. *Mathematical Structures in Computer Science*, 16(3):527–552, 2006.

[21] P. Selinger and B. Valiron. On a fully abstract model for a quantum linear functional language. In *QPL'06*, 2008.

[22] P. Selinger and B. Valiron. Quantum lambda calculus. In S. Gay and I. Mackie, editors, *Semantic Techniques in Quantum Computation*, chapter 9, pages 135–172. Cambridge University Press, 2009.

[23] B. Valiron. *Semantics for a higher-order functional programming language for quantum computation.* PhD thesis, Univ. of Ottawa, 2008.

[24] D. Zhao and T. Fan. Dcpo-completion of posets. *Th. Comp. Sc.*, 411 (22–24):2167–2173, 2010.

# A Nonstandard Standardization Theorem

Beniamino Accattoli
Carnegie Mellon University
United States

Eduardo Bonelli
Univ. Nac. de Quilmes and CONICET
Argentina

Delia Kesner
Univ. Paris-Diderot, SPC, PPS, CNRS
France

Carlos Lombardi
Univ. Nac. de Quilmes and Univ. de Buenos Aires
Univ. Paris-Diderot, SPC, PPS, CNRS
Argentina and France

## Abstract

Standardization is a fundamental notion for connecting programming languages and rewriting calculi. Since both programming languages and calculi rely on substitution for defining their dynamics, *explicit substitutions* (ES) help further close the gap between theory and practice.

This paper focuses on standardization for the *linear substitution calculus*, a calculus with ES capable of mimicking reduction in $\lambda$-calculus and linear logic *proof-nets*. For the latter, proof-nets can be formalized by means of a simple *equational theory* over the linear substitution calculus.

Contrary to other extant calculi with ES, our system can be equipped with a *residual theory* in the sense of Lévy, which is used to prove a left-to-right standardization theorem for the calculus with ES but without the equational theory. Such a theorem, however, does not lift from the calculus with ES to proof-nets, because the notion of left-to-right derivation is not preserved by the equational theory. We then relax the notion of left-to-right standard derivation, based on a *total order* on redexes, to a more liberal notion of standard derivation based on *partial orders*.

Our proofs rely on Gonthier, Lévy, and Melliès' axiomatic theory for standardization. However, we go beyond merely applying their framework, revisiting some of its key concepts: we obtain uniqueness (modulo) of standard derivations in an abstract way and we provide a coinductive characterization of their key abstract notion of *external redex*. This last point is then used to give a simple proof that *linear head reduction*—a *nondeterministic* strategy having a central role in the theory of linear logic—is standard.

***Categories and Subject Descriptors*** F.3.2 [*Logics and Meanings of Programs*]: Semantics of Programming Languages - Operational semantics; F.4.1 [*Mathematical Logic and Formal Languages*]: Mathematical Logic - Lambda calculus and related systems; I.1.3 [*Symbolic and Algebraic Manipulation*]: Languages and Systems - evaluation strategies

***General Terms*** Theory, Languages.

***Keywords*** Lambda-calculus, Standardization, Residuals, Explicit Substitutions, Linear Logic, Proof-Nets.

## 1. Introduction

In his seminal paper [35] Plotkin introduced the idea of relating a calculus (given by means of an equational theory induced by a rewriting relation) and a programming language (specified as an abstract machine) via a *standardization* theorem: the programming language implements the standard strategy associated to the calculus. Let us recall what standardization is about. The idea is to identify a class of derivations, called standard, that is *complete*: whenever $t \twoheadrightarrow u$ then there is a standard derivation from $t$ to $u$. Often, it is possible to describe a reduction strategy that produces standard derivations only (the leftmost-outermost strategy in the $\lambda$-calculus), and for which the normalization property holds as a corollary of the standardization theorem: if $t$ has a normal form then the standard strategy will reach this normal form. Completeness and normalization are the justifications for Plotkin's approach.

Another approach to close the gap between calculi and programming languages is to resort to *explicit substitutions* (ES), that are refinements of $\lambda$-calculus where evaluation is decomposed into small steps, and that can be thought as a framework in which to specify abstract machines as strategies.

It would be natural to expect calculi with ES to enjoy standardization theorems whose induced standard strategies justify abstract machines. Surprisingly, the literature does not present any such relationship. This is due to some inherent difficulties. Calculi with ES are complex and fragile rewriting systems for which already studying normalization is technically demanding. Standardization—that mixes confluence and termination arguments—generally is simply out of scope. In particular, ES calculi present *critical pairs* and thus lack *orthogonality*, a basic syntactic property enjoyed by the $\lambda$-calculus and on which most standardization techniques rely on.

This paper makes significant progress on standardization for ES. The starting point is a recent advance in the field of ES. A new generation of calculi with ES *at a distance*, having very simple meta-theories and conceived as *behaviorally equivalent copies* of graphical languages such as linear logic proof-nets, have recently been introduced by Accattoli and Kesner in [6] (see also [2, 3, 5]).


*POPL '14*, January 22–24, 2014, San Diego, CA, USA.

ACM 978-1-4503-2544-8/14/01...$15.00.
http://dx.doi.org/10.1145/2535838.2535886

Traditional calculi with ES implement the ordinary substitution by percolating ES through the term structure until they reach variable occurrences, on which they finally substitute or get garbage collected. The key feature of distance calculi is that the *percolating process* is factored out from the computational process. Indeed, ES at a distance do not move: their dynamics is defined using contexts (*i.e.* terms with holes) that allows them to act directly on single variable occurrences (via a context isolating the occurrence), without any need to commute with the other constructors in between.

***The Framework.*** In this paper we focus on a specific calculus at a distance, *the linear substitution calculus* $\lambda_{\mathtt{lsub}}$, that is both a slight generalization of a calculus by Robin Milner [33] (related to bigraphs), from which it inherits the *substitution rules* at a distance, and a slight modification of the structural $\lambda$-calculus by Accattoli and Kesner [6] (related to proof nets). Such a calculus has some relevant features:

1. *Linear logic and concurrency*: it is tightly connected with the translations of $\lambda$-calculus into linear logic [4] and the $\pi$-calculus [3]. In particular, reduction rules for ES act as exponential cut-elimination rules in linear logic (resp. replication in the $\pi$-calculus).
2. *Linear head reduction (LHR)*: given the deep connection between $\lambda_{\mathtt{lsub}}$ and proof-nets [4], our calculus naturally expresses *linear head reduction*, a notion of evaluation for proof nets that is connected with other fundamental models [3, 5, 14, 15, 17, 29]. Notably, LHR is a strategy for $\lambda_{\mathtt{lsub}}$, while it *cannot* be expressed as a strategy in $\lambda$-calculus.
3. *Simplicity* and *expressiveness*: the calculus is simple (only 3 rewriting rules) and it enjoys numerous desirable properties including: a tight correspondence with the lambda calculus (simulating $\beta$-reduction), confluence on terms and metaterms, preservation of strong $\beta$-normalisation and—as we will show—a theory of residuals.

The linear substitution calculus—as do all other extant calculi with ES—presents critical pairs, and so standardization is non-trivial. However, $\lambda_{\mathtt{lsub}}$ enjoys a unique property, that we call *semantical orthogonality*.

***Orthogonality.*** Orthogonal (first and higher-order) term rewriting systems are defined as left-linear systems without critical pairs. They are the most studied class of rewriting systems, including in particular the $\lambda$-calculus. This notion of *syntactic orthogonality* is handy and simple, but it has the drawback of being too restrictive. Fortunately, orthogonality can be defined in a more abstract way, as the fact that residuals—a standard concept in rewriting theory (see Section 3)—are sufficient to close local confluence diagrams. This form of *semantical orthogonality* is a particular property of syntactic orthogonality, but it is of a behavioral nature and more general. The crucial point is that $\lambda_{\mathtt{lsub}}$ is not syntactically orthogonal but—in contrast to any other calculus with ES—is semantically orthogonal, as we prove in this paper. In this sense $\lambda_{\mathtt{lsub}}$ is the first calculus with ES that conservatively refines $\lambda$-calculus, preserving its orthogonality. Unfortunately, most techniques for standardization rely on syntactical orthogonality. An exception is the abstract theory of standardization developed by Gonthier, Lévy, and Melliès (GLM) [19], and later refined by Melliès [30, 32]. Such a theory can cope even with non semantically orthogonal calculi as the $\lambda\sigma$-calculus, but it takes a much simpler form in presence of semantical orthogonality.

***Left-to-Right Standardization and Beyond.*** Two first contributions of this paper are 1) a theory of residuals for $\lambda_{\mathtt{lsub}}$ and 2) a proof of the axioms of GLM's theory. These technical results allow us to obtain a *left-to-right*[1] standardization theorem generalizing the well-known standardization theorem for $\lambda$-calculus, and capturing the *deterministic* weak (*i.e.* not reducing under abstractions) variant of LHR—that is the variant that actually matches evaluation in the Krivine Abstract Machine and the $\pi$-calculus—as a standard strategy. It is pleasing that the properties of left-to-right derivations extend naturally to $\lambda_{\mathtt{lsub}}$. However, such a standardization theorem is not fully satisfying.

A first reason is that LHR (without the weak restriction) is a nondeterministic strategy whose sequences are not necessarily left-to-right standard. However, the nondeterminism of LHR does not affect the final result nor the length of evaluation sequences (technically, LHR enjoys the diamond property). It is then disappointing that LHR is not left-to-right standard, because LHR is a crucial notion in the theory of linear logic.

A second reason for not being satisfied with the left-to-right standardization theorem concerns the close relationship between the linear substitution calculus and linear logic proof-nets, the model behind its inception. Terms and proof-nets are behaviorally equivalent in a strong sense: every term $t$ maps to a proof-net $P_t$, and every evaluation *step* on $t$ or $P_t$ maps to an evaluation *step* on the other. Additionally, the redexes are in bijection and so concepts such as residuals transfer from terms to proof-nets and viceversa. The interest of proof-nets is that they provide a quotient of terms; remarkably, this quotient can be explicitly characterized by a simple *equational theory* $\sim$ (in the style of [6, 23], and here generated by 3 equations only) turning the behavioral equivalence with linear logic proof-nets into a true isomorphism: for every proof-net $P$ there is a $\sim$-class containing all and only the terms behaviorally equivalent to $P$. Consequently, any notion or result that is stable by equivalence $\sim$ immediately lifts to proof-nets. Unfortunately, left-to-right derivations in the linear substitution calculus are not stable by $\sim$, because $\sim$ swaps some constructors, inverting the relative position of some redexes. Thus, our left-to-right standardization theorem does not hold for proof-nets. This is quite disappointing because proof nets provide an *operational model*, and one would like to have a notion of standard derivation that can be freely transported from the language to the model and viceversa. We then refine our left-to-right standardization theorem.

***Partial Standardization Orders.*** Standard derivations are defined as those reductions that respect a certain order on redexes, for instance the left-to-right order. In GLM's theory such a total order is replaced by a *partial* order, providing a more general but also subtler setting. To achieve a notion of standard derivation that is stable by $\sim$ we are forced to relax the total left-to-right order into a partial order. In the setting of total orders, given a derivation $\rho : t \twoheadrightarrow u$ there is a *unique* standard derivation $\rho'$ to which $\rho$ standardizes, and moreover a deterministic and normalizing standard strategy can be easily obtained by selecting the *minimum* redex according to the order. When the order is partial, instead, there can be many standard derivations to which a derivation standardizes, *i.e.* uniqueness is lost: a standard derivation is an ordered derivation but only up to swaps of $\prec$-disjoint steps. Moreover, although GLM's theory does support partial orders, it requires a number of axioms to hold, some of which are not enjoyed by $\lambda_{\mathtt{lsub}}$ modulo $\sim$. So we shall switch to the axiomatics of Melliès' PhD thesis [32], which is more general and allows us to prove existence of standard derivations for a suitable partial order. However, alas, $\lambda_{\mathtt{lsub}}$ modulo $\sim$ does not even satisfy the axioms of [32] required to obtain uniqueness of stan-

[1] We distinguish between the *leftmost strategy* (that repeatedly reduces the leftmost redex) from *left-to-right* standardization that re-arranges redexes (not necessarily involving the leftmost redex) from left to right. We also use *leftmost* (considering terms as strings of symbols) for what is sometimes called *leftmost-outermost* (that is relative to terms seen as trees).

dard derivations. Nor does it supply us with the guarantee that reducing *external* redexes—the generalization to partial orders of the notion of minimum redexes in the setting of total orders—leads to normal forms. We circumvent these inadequacies of the axiomatic framework by exploiting the embedding of a partial order into a total order, thus proving uniqueness (modulo swappings) of standard derivations and the normalization of a (specific) external strategy.

***Main Contributions.*** A summary of our results follows:

1. **The Standardization Theorem**. We identify a partial order $\prec_{\mathtt{B}}$ that is related to the concept of exponential box in linear logic proof-nets, and that is stable by $\sim$. We show that Melliès' axioms for existence of a standard derivation hold for $\prec_{\mathtt{B}}$, obtaining a standardization theorem for $\lambda_{\mathtt{lsub}}$ modulo $\sim$.
2. **Uniqueness Modulo**. For partial orders, GLM's theory has some additional axioms that ensures uniqueness modulo independent swaps (see Section 8) but one of these axioms *does not hold* for $\lambda_{\mathtt{lsub}}$. Nonetheless, we prove uniqueness in an abstract way, relying on the embedding of the partial box order into the total left-to-right order.
3. **Coinductive External Redexes**. In GLM's theory external redexes are defined somewhat indirectly, via an extraction process [32]. We clarify this concept by providing a direct and simple *coinductive* characterization: an external redex is a minimal redex that is *persistently minimal*, *i.e.* whose (unique) residual after any other redex is still external.
4. **Applications**. We use the coinductive characterization of external redexes to obtain a *normalization theorem* for the leftmost strategy and to give a concise proof by coinduction of the fact that LHR is a standard strategy.

The *nonstandard* character of our standardization result comes at least from the following facts: highlight of the first semantical orthogonal calculus with ES being isomorphic to linear logic proof-nets and enjoying standardization; use of a partial (vs total) order on redexes being stable by equivalence classes; proof of uniqueness (modulo) of standard derivations by means of simple arguments and an original application of GLM's theory to a non-syntactical orthogonal case.

***Abstract Machines.*** As mentioned before, we will show that weak LHR is a standard strategy. In parallel, Accattoli, Barenbaum and Mazza [7] studied the relationship between abstract machines and calculi at a distance obtaining that weak LHR is the strategy implemented by the Krivine Abstract Machine, up to a certain notion of structural equivalence. This result refines a similar one by Danos and Regnier [14], and completes the lifting of Plotkins's approach (relating the SECD machine with a standard strategy in the call-by-value $\lambda$-calculus) to the granularity of explicit substitutions. Moreover, [7] contains similar correspondences between machines for call-by-value (the CEK and Leroy's ZINC) and call-by-need (Sestoft's machine) and some variations over weak LHR. We are confident that the new understanding of standardization for ES provided by our work will lead to analogous standardization theorems for call-by-value and call-by-need variant of the linear substitution calculus, completing the picture.

***Related Work.*** A brief history of standardization may be found in [30]. Standardization was introduced in 1958 by Curry and Feys [13] for the lambda calculus. Lévy [27] strengthens this result by defining the notion of permutation equivalence and showing that every derivation has a unique standard derivation in each equivalence class. Huet and Lévy [21] extend these ideas to first-order term rewriting without critical pairs and also show that one must abandon the left-to-right order for more general orders in these systems. Klop gives the first abstract proof of standardization and applies these ideas to higher-order rewriting [26]. Boudol [10] extends Huet and Lévy's work to term rewriting systems with critical pairs. Clark and Kennaway [12], Khasidashvili and Glauert [25], Paolini and Ronchi Della Rocca [34], and Xi [41] provide further generalizations along various axes. Gonthier, Lévy and Melliès [19] introduce an axiomatic approach to standardization, later refined by Melliès [30, 32], that has turned out to be convenient to deal with our case, due to its abstract nature. Indeed, simple techniques such as Plotkin's inductive reasoning in [35] or the *proof terms* technique by van Oostrom and De Vrijer [40]—extended to the higher-order case by Bruggink [11]—are not easily adaptable to our equational setting. Takahashi's technique [37] does not apply either. There is no relationship between our results and standardization by levels for linear logic proof-nets[2]: both approaches use partial orders, but such orders are incomparable. This is a further reason to consider our result as nonstandard.

***Plan of the Paper.*** The next section introduces the linear substitution calculus. Section 3 defines residuals and Section 4 shows that residuals are compatible with the equivalence $\sim$ in a very strong sense. Section 5 explains the ideas behind the abstract approach to standardization and Section 6 proves the left-to-right standardization theorem. Section 7 explains how the left-to-right order can be relaxed to cope with the equational theory and Section 8 proves our equational standardization theorem. Section 9 provides uniqueness of standard derivations. Section 10 presents a coinductive characterization of external redexes and Section 11 proves the normalization theorem and the fact that (weak) linear head reduction is standard.

## 2. The Linear Substitution Calculus

The set of terms of the *linear substitution calculus*, denoted by $\mathcal{T}$, is generated by the following grammar:

$$t ::= x \mid tt \mid \lambda x.t \mid t[x/t]$$

A term $x$ is called a **variable**, $tu$ an **application**, $\lambda x.t$ an **abstraction** and $t[x/u]$ an **explicit substitution**. The notions of free and bound variables are defined as usual plus $\mathtt{fv}(t[x/u]) := \mathtt{fv}(t) \setminus \{x\} \cup \mathtt{fv}(u)$. We work with the standard notion of $\alpha$-conversion (*i.e.* renaming of bound variables for abstractions and substitutions). We use $C$ to denote a **context** w.r.t. the previous grammar (*i.e.* a term with a unique occurrence of a designated symbol $\Box$ called the *hole*). We write $C[t]$ for the term obtained by replacing the hole of $C$ by the term $t$. We write $C[\![u]\!]$ when the free variables of $u$ are not captured by the context $C$, *i.e.* there are no abstractions or explicit substitutions in $C$ that bind the variables of $\mathtt{fv}(u)$.

The $\lambda_{\mathtt{lsub}}$**-calculus** is given by the set of terms $\mathcal{T}$ and by the **reduction relation** $\rightarrow_{\lambda_{\mathtt{lsub}}}$ defined as the union of $\rightarrow_{\mathtt{dB}}$, $\rightarrow_{\mathtt{ls}}$, and $\rightarrow_{\mathtt{gc}}$, which are the closure by contexts $C$ of the following rewriting rules, where $\mathtt{L}$ denotes a (possibly empty) list of substitutions $[x_1/t_1]\ldots[x_k/t_k]$:

$$\begin{array}{llll} (\lambda x.t)\mathtt{L}u & \mapsto_{\mathtt{db}} & t[x/u]\mathtt{L} & \\ C[\![x]\!][x/u] & \mapsto_{\mathtt{ls}} & C[\![u]\!][x/u] & \\ t[x/u] & \mapsto_{\mathtt{gc}} & t & \text{if } x \notin \mathtt{fv}(t) \end{array}$$

The names $\mathtt{db}$, $\mathtt{ls}$, and $\mathtt{gc}$ stand for *distant beta*, *linear substitution*, and *garbage collection*, respectively. Rule $\mapsto_{\mathtt{db}}$ (resp. $\mapsto_{\mathtt{ls}}$) comes from the structural $\lambda$-calculus [6] (resp. Milner's calculus [33]), while $\mapsto_{\mathtt{gc}}$ belongs to both calculi. In $\mathtt{db}$ we may assume w.l.o.g. that $\bigcup_{i=1}^{k}\{x_i\} \cap \mathtt{fv}(u) = \emptyset$ and $x \notin \mathtt{fv}(u) \cup \bigcup_{i=1}^{k} \mathtt{fv}(t_i)$.

Note that the meta-notation $\mathtt{L} = [x_1/t_1]\ldots[x_k/t_k]$ can also be seen as a context $\Box[x_1/t_1]\ldots[x_k/t_k]$. This fact, together with

[2] Such a standardization theorem is folklore in the linear logic community. See [2, 16] for details.

the use of a context $C$ in the second rule, and the global side condition in the third rule, justify the idea of rewriting rules *at a distance*. The substitution context in rule db is motivated by its encoding in proof-nets, where explicit substitutions are partially free to float (*i.e.* to traverse some term constructors). Such *freedom* is formalized by the forthcoming graphical equivalence and by the study of its properties in Section 4.

The linear substitution calculus enjoys all the properties required of calculi with ES (including simulation of $\beta$-reduction, preservation of strong normalisation, confluence on terms and metaterms and full composition), whose proofs are simple and omitted, as they are minor variations over those for Milner's calculus [24], or those of the structural $\lambda$-calculus [6].

In order to study residuals we need to fix a precise terminology about redexes. A **redex occurrence** in a term $t$ is either a tuple $\langle D, r\rangle$ where $t = D[r]$ and $r = (\lambda x.s)\mathtt{L}u$ (a **dB-redex**) or a tuple $\langle D, r, C\rangle$ where $t = D[r]$ and $r = C[\![x]\!][x/u]$ (a **ls-redex**), or a tuple $\langle D, r\rangle$ where $t = D[r]$, $r = s[x/u]$ and $x \notin \mathtt{fv}(s)$ (a **gc-redex**). For example, the term $t = (xx)[x/y]$ has two different redex occurrences, namely $\langle D_1, r_1, C_1\rangle = \langle\Box, (xx)[x/y], \Box x\rangle$ and $\langle D_2, r_2, C_2\rangle = \langle\Box, (xx)[x/y], x\Box\rangle$. The **pattern** of a redex is $r$, the second component of the tuple; the **box**[3] of the redex is the subterm of the pattern noted $u$, and the **context** of the redex is $D$, the first component of the tuple. We use $A, B, \ldots$ for redexes occurrences and $\mathtt{Red}(t)$ for the set of all redex occurrences of $t$. Given a redex occurrence $A \in \mathtt{Red}(s)$ we write $s \overset{A}{\to} t$ for the **reduction step** obtained by contracting $A$ in $s$.

The **graphical equivalence** $\sim$ is given by the contextual, transitive, symmetric and reflexive closure of $\alpha$-conversion (*i.e.* renaming of bound variables) and the following axioms:

$$\begin{array}{llll} t[x/u][y/v] & \approx_{\mathtt{CS}} & t[y/v][x/u] & x \notin \mathtt{fv}(v)\ \&\ y \notin \mathtt{fv}(u) \\ (\lambda y.t)[x/u] & \approx_{\sigma_1} & \lambda y.t[x/u] & y \notin \mathtt{fv}(u) \\ (tv)[x/u] & \approx_{\sigma_2} & t[x/u]v & x \notin \mathtt{fv}(v) \end{array}$$

This equivalence characterizes exactly the representation of terms as proof-nets, in the sense that $t \sim u$ iff $t$ and $u$ map to the same proof-net [4].

The $\lambda_{\mathtt{lsub}}^{\sim}$**-calculus** is given by the set of terms $\mathcal{T}$ and by the **reduction relation** $\to_{\lambda_{\mathtt{lsub}}^{\sim}}$, defined by the rewriting rules $\{\mathtt{db}, \mathtt{gc}, \mathtt{ls}\}$ modulo the equations $\{\mathtt{CS}, \sigma_1, \sigma_2\}$, *i.e.* , $t \to_{\lambda_{\mathtt{lsub}}^{\sim}} u$ iff $t \sim t' \to_{\lambda_{\mathtt{lsub}}} u' \sim u$. Thus in particular $t \to_{\lambda_{\mathtt{lsub}}} t'$ implies $t \to_{\lambda_{\mathtt{lsub}}^{\sim}} t'$.

Given any reduction relation $\mathcal{R}$, an $\mathcal{R}$**-derivation** is a (possibly empty) sequence of reduction steps having the form $s = t_0 \to_{\mathcal{R}} t_1 \to_{\mathcal{R}} \ldots$. An $\mathcal{R}$-derivation is **finite** iff the associated sequence is finite. We write $d, e, \ldots$ for derivations and $d : s \twoheadrightarrow_{\mathcal{R}} t$ when we stress the **source** $s$ and **target** $t$ of the (finite) derivation. We write $\epsilon$ for the empty derivation and $A; d : s \twoheadrightarrow t$ for the derivation composing $s \overset{A}{\to} u$ to the left of $d : u \twoheadrightarrow t$. A reduction relation $\mathcal{R}$ is said to be **terminating** iff every $\mathcal{R}$-derivation is finite. An element $t$ is said to be in $\mathcal{R}$**-normal form** iff there is no $u$ such that $t \to_{\mathcal{R}} u$.

## 3. Residuals

The residuals of a redex $A$ after a reduction step $t \overset{B}{\to} u$ are the traces of the redex $A$ that appear in the target term $u$. The crucial property that residuals need to satisfy is that any local confluence diagram $u_1 \overset{A_1}{\leftarrow} t \overset{A_2}{\to} u_2$ can be closed by reducing in $u_1$ (resp. $u_2$) all and only the residuals of the redex $A_2$ after $A_1$ (resp. of $A_1$ after $A_2$). When this happens for every possible local confluence diagram we say that the system is **semantically orthogonal**. The subtlety in the study of residuals is that redexes may be duplicated or erased along the way and duplication may even nest two residuals of the same redex. For further references the reader may consult [20, 27, 31, 38].

[3] When terms are represented as linear logic proof-nets, what we call *box* corresponds exactly to the exponential box.

Another simpler notion of orthogonality is *syntactical orthogonality* [21], and happens when the system is left-linear and has no critical pairs. Syntactical orthogonality implies semantic orthogonality but the converse does not hold. In particular, the $\lambda_{\mathtt{lsub}}$-calculus is not syntactically orthogonal but, as we will show in Section 6, it turns out to be semantically orthogonal, a property that no other calculus with ES enjoys. In order to give an intuition on such a phenomenon let us consider a calculus with ES such as $\lambda\sigma$ [1] or $\lambda\mathtt{x}$ [9] containing at least the following reduction rules:

$$\begin{array}{lll} (\lambda x.t)u & \to_{\mathtt{b}} & t[x/u] \\ (tu)[x/v] & \to_{@} & t[x/v]u[x/v] \end{array}$$

The following critical pair arises:

$$(\lambda x.t)[y/v]u[y/v] \;{}_{@}\!\leftarrow ((\lambda x.t)u)[y/v] \to_{\mathtt{b}} t[x/u][y/v]$$

However, the @-step has no residual after the b-step. The b-step also has no residual (note how it would have a residual if the rule were *at a distance*). The diagram can be closed, but only reducing *created* redexes, and so the calculus is not semantically orthogonal.

The formal development of residuals is based on a notion of (well-)labeled term to be introduced next. Note that since $\lambda_{\mathtt{lsub}}$ is not syntactically orthogonal the technique of underlining the redex pattern [26] cannot be applied, *e.g.* in $\underline{(xx)[x/s]}$ the underlining does not distinguish between the two occurrences of the ls redexes.

***Labels.*** In order to follow redexes along a derivation we mark them with special symbols called **labels**, denoted $\alpha, \beta, \gamma, \ldots$. The obtained set of labeled terms, denoted by $\mathcal{T}_{\mathcal{L}}$, is generated by the following grammar.

$$t ::= x \mid x^{\alpha} \mid tt \mid \lambda x.t \mid \lambda x^{\alpha}.t \mid t[x/t] \mid t[x^{\alpha}/t]$$

The notations $x^{(\alpha)}$, $\lambda x^{(\alpha)}.t$ and $t[x^{(\alpha)}/t]$ mean that $x$ may or may not be labeled. We write $\mathtt{Lab}(t)$ to denote the **set of all the labels** of $t$ and $t^{\circ}$ to denote the term obtained from $t$ by **removing all its labels**. Thus for example $((x^{\alpha}y^{\beta})[y/\lambda z^{\gamma}.z])^{\circ} = (xy)[y/\lambda z.z]$.

We extend the meta-notation L to lists of possibly labeled substitutions, and $C$ to possibly labeled contexts. Similarly, the notions of free and bound variables are extended to labeled terms as expected together with their corresponding notion of $\alpha$-conversion. We use $\mathtt{flv}(t)$ to denote the subset of $\mathtt{fv}(t)$ having at least one labeled occurrence, *e.g.* $\mathtt{flv}(x^{\alpha}y^{\beta}[y/z]) = \{x\}$.

**Labeled reduction** $\overset{\alpha}{\to}$ on labeled terms is defined as the contextual closure of the following rewriting rules:

$$\begin{array}{llll} (\lambda x^{\alpha}.t)\mathtt{L}u & \overset{\alpha}{\mapsto}_{\mathtt{dB}} & t[x/u]\mathtt{L} & \\ C[\![x^{\alpha}]\!][x/u] & \overset{\alpha}{\mapsto}_{\mathtt{ls}} & C[\![u]\!][x/u] & \\ t[x^{\alpha}/u] & \overset{\alpha}{\mapsto}_{\mathtt{gc}} & t & x \notin \mathtt{fv}(t) \end{array}$$

Definition of redexes for terms naturally extends to labeled ones. A **labeled redex** $A$ is a redex having a pattern of the form $(\lambda x^{\alpha}.t)\mathtt{L}u$, $C[\![x^{\alpha}]\!][x/u]$ or $t[x^{\alpha}/u]$, and $\alpha$ is called the **label of the redex** $A$. The **anchor** of a redex (labeled or not) is the variable possibly carrying its label. We will usually associate the labels $\alpha$, $\beta$ and $\gamma$ to the redex names $A$, $B$ and $C$ respectively; occasionally we will write $A_{\alpha}$ to emphasize that $\alpha$ is the label of the redex $A$. We write $\mathtt{Red}_{\alpha}(t)$ for all the redexes of $t$ labeled with $\alpha$.

In order to show some key properties required by the axiomatic approach (*cfr.* Section 6) we will work with a subset of labeled terms, written $\mathcal{T}_{\mathcal{WL}}$, called **well-labeled terms**, and defined by:

- $x \in \mathcal{T}_{\mathcal{WL}}$ and $x^{\alpha} \in \mathcal{T}_{\mathcal{WL}}$

- If $t \in \mathcal{T}_{\mathcal{WL}}$ and $x \notin \mathtt{flv}(t)$ then $\lambda x.t \in \mathcal{T}_{\mathcal{WL}}$
- If $t, u \in \mathcal{T}_{\mathcal{WL}}$, then $tu \in \mathcal{T}_{\mathcal{WL}}$
- If $(\lambda x.t)\mathtt{L}, u \in \mathcal{T}_{\mathcal{WL}}$, then $(\lambda x^{\alpha}.t)\mathtt{L}u \in \mathcal{T}_{\mathcal{WL}}$
- If $t, u \in \mathcal{T}_{\mathcal{WL}}$, then $t[x/u] \in \mathcal{T}_{\mathcal{WL}}$
- If $t, u \in \mathcal{T}_{\mathcal{WL}}$ and $x \notin \mathtt{fv}(t)$, then $t[x^{\alpha}/u] \in \mathcal{T}_{\mathcal{WL}}$.

Note that $\lambda x^{\alpha}.x$, $\lambda x.x^{\alpha}$ and $x[x^{\alpha}/u]$ are not in $\mathcal{T}_{\mathcal{WL}}$. Note also that subterms of well-labeled terms are not necessarily well-labeled (*e.g.* the abstraction of a labeled db-redex). Well-labeled terms are stable by reduction and graphical equivalence:

LEMMA 1. *Let $t \in \mathcal{T}_{\mathcal{WL}}$. If $t \xrightarrow{\alpha} u$ or $t \sim u$, then $u \in \mathcal{T}_{\mathcal{WL}}$.*

***Residuals.*** Here we define residuals for the reduction relation $\lambda_{\mathtt{lsub}}$. In Section 4 we will extend them to the $\lambda^{\sim}_{\mathtt{lsub}}$.

A term $t$ can be labeled in different ways, leading to different variants of $t$. More precisely, we say that $t$ is a **variant** of $u$ iff $t^{\circ} = u^{\circ}$. Thus in particular, $t$ is a variant of itself. If $t$ is a variant of $u$, then we will consider the *obvious bijection* between the sets of redexes of $t$ and $u$; sometimes, we will even identify some particular redexes of them which are related by this bijection.

To define the residuals of a redex $A \in \mathtt{Red}(t)$ after a step $t \xrightarrow{B} u$, we consider the **$\alpha$-lift of $t$ *w.r.t.* $A$ by $\alpha$**, written $\mathtt{lift}(t, A, \alpha)$, which is a particular variant of $t$ obtained as follows. Let $\alpha$ be a fresh symbol, *i.e.* $\alpha \notin \mathtt{Lab}(t)$. If the redex $A$ is already labeled in $t$, then change the label of $A$ to $\alpha$, otherwise, if $A$ is not already labeled, assign $\alpha$ to $A$. Let us write $\mathtt{lift}(t, A, \alpha) \xrightarrow{B} u$ for the induced associated reduction step. Then, the **set of residuals of $A$ after** $B$ is given by $A\langle B\rangle := \{\mathtt{Red}_{\alpha}(u) \mid \mathtt{lift}(t, A, \alpha) \xrightarrow{B} u\}$.

It is clear that this definition is completely *independent* from the variant used to lift the term $t$. We write $A\langle B\rangle A'$ for $A' \in A\langle B\rangle$, and $\mathcal{A}\langle B\rangle$ for $\bigcup_{A\in\mathcal{A}} A\langle B\rangle$. For example, taking $v = (x^{\beta}x^{\beta}x^{\beta})[x/y]$, $B = \langle\Box, v, x^{\beta}\Box x^{\beta}\rangle$ (so that $v \xrightarrow{B} (x^{\beta}yx^{\beta})[x/y] = v'$) and $\mathcal{A} = \mathtt{Red}_{\beta}(v) \setminus B$, we have $\mathcal{A}\langle B\rangle = \{B', B''\}$, where $B' = \langle\Box, v', \Box yx^{\beta}\rangle$ and $B'' = \langle\Box, v', x^{\beta}y\Box\rangle$.

***Creation.*** Given a reduction step $t \to_{\lambda_{\mathtt{lsub}}} u$, the set of redexes in $u$ that are not residuals of redexes in $t$ are said to be **created**. While there are only 3 possible ways to create redexes in $\lambda$-calculus [27], in the $\lambda_{\mathtt{lsub}}$-calculus redexes may be created in one of 6 possible ways, we just show below one example for each case, where the reduced redex has label $\alpha$ and the *created* redex is underlined:

| | | | |
|---|---|---|---|
| db creates db: | $((\lambda x^{\alpha}.(\lambda y.s))u)\,v$ | $\to_{\mathtt{dB}}$ | $\underline{(\lambda y.s)[x/u]v}$ |
| db creates ls: | $(\lambda x^{\alpha}.x)u$ | $\to_{\mathtt{dB}}$ | $\underline{x[x/u]}$ |
| db creates gc: | $(\lambda x^{\alpha}.y)u$ | $\to_{\mathtt{dB}}$ | $\underline{y[x/u]}$ |
| ls creates db: | $x^{\alpha}[x/\lambda y.s]u$ | $\to_{\mathtt{ls}}$ | $\underline{(\lambda y.s)[x/\lambda y.s]u}$ |
| ls creates gc: | $x^{\alpha}[x/y]$ | $\to_{\mathtt{ls}}$ | $\underline{y[x/y]}$ |
| gc creates gc: | $z[y^{\alpha}/x][x/u]$ | $\to_{\mathtt{gc}}$ | $\underline{z[x/u]}$ |

Note that dB-steps can create every kind of redex, ls-steps can create $\{\mathtt{dB}, \mathtt{gc}\}$-redexes, and gc-redexes can only create other gc-redexes. Note also that whenever a labeled redex creates a redex $A$, then $A$ is not labeled.

***Developments.*** Labels are particularly useful to study *developments*, *i.e.* derivations in which only residuals of an initial set of redexes are contracted. For that, we first extend the concept of residual to finite derivations as follows: $\mathcal{A}\langle\epsilon\rangle := \mathcal{A}$, $\mathcal{A}\langle B; d\rangle := (\mathcal{A}\langle B\rangle)\langle d\rangle$.

Given $\mathcal{A} \subseteq \mathtt{Red}(t)$, a (possibly infinite) derivation $t = t_0 \xrightarrow{A_1} t_1 \xrightarrow{A_2} t_2 \ldots$ is a **development** of $\mathcal{A}$ iff $A_i \in \mathcal{A}\langle A_1; \ldots; A_{i-1}\rangle$ for all $i$. For example, in the $\lambda_{\mathtt{lsub}}$-calculus, $t_0 = (xx)[x/I] \to (xI)[x/I] \to (II)[x/I]$ is a development of the set containing the two ls-redexes of $t_0$. In the sequel, $\mathcal{A}_1; \ldots; \mathcal{A}_n$ denotes any derivation $d_1; \ldots; d_n$ such that $d_i$ is a development of the set of redexes $\mathcal{A}_i$ for all $i$. The *finite developments (FD)* property states that given a term $t$ and a set of redexes $\mathcal{A} \subseteq \mathtt{Red}(t)$, any development of $\mathcal{A}$ starting at $t$ terminates. This property (proved in Section 6) is one of the key requirements for the axiomatic theory of standardization that we are going to apply. The residual of a derivation over a set of redexes $\mathcal{A}$ is defined as follows: $\epsilon\langle\mathcal{A}\rangle = \epsilon$ and $(B; d)\langle\mathcal{A}\rangle = B\langle e\rangle; d\langle\mathcal{A}\langle B\rangle\rangle$, where $e$ is any development of $\mathcal{A}$.

## 4. Working with Equivalence Classes

In this section we first define the notion of residual of a redex along an equation, so that we will be able to trace redexes along $\lambda^{\sim}_{\mathtt{lsub}}$-derivations. We then show that the notion of residual defined in Section 3 is well-defined w.r.t equivalence classes, *i.e.* 1) the residual relation yields a unique bijection between two redexes in the same $\sim$-equivalence class and 2) residuals of rewriting steps lift to $\sim$-equivalence classes.

The **labeled graphical equivalence**[4] $\sim$ on *labeled terms* is given by the contextual, transitive, symmetric and reflexive closure of $\alpha$-conversion and the following axioms:

| | | | |
|---|---|---|---|
| $t[x^{(\alpha)}/u][y^{(\beta)}/v]$ | $\approx_{\mathtt{CS}}$ | $t[y^{(\beta)}/v][x^{(\alpha)}/u]$ | $x \notin \mathtt{fv}(v)$ & $y \notin \mathtt{fv}(u)$ |
| $(\lambda y^{(\beta)}.t)[x^{(\alpha)}/u]$ | $\approx_{\sigma_1}$ | $\lambda y^{(\beta)}.t[x^{(\alpha)}/u]$ | $y \notin \mathtt{fv}(u)$ |
| $(tv)[x^{(\alpha)}/u]$ | $\approx_{\sigma_2}$ | $t[x^{(\alpha)}/u]v$ | $x \notin \mathtt{fv}(v)$ |

The axioms are to be understood in such a way that each label occurs either in both sides of the axiom or in none of them. An equational proof of $t \sim u$ is a **derivation tree** ending in $t \sim u$ which uses $\alpha$-conversion, the axioms $\approx_{\mathtt{CS}}, \approx_{\sigma_1}$ and $\approx_{\sigma_2}$ and the standard inference schemes expressing compatibility of $\sim$ w.r.t. all term constructors and transitivity, symmetry and reflexivity of $\sim$.

***Residuals Along Equations.*** We now propose a notion of trace of a redex along an equational proof which is similar to that used for derivations. Although the intuitive idea is quite natural, one needs to guarantee that this notion is independent from the particular syntactic proof used to show that a term $t$ is equivalent to another term $u$, a property that we call *well-definedness*.

Given $t \sim u$, $A \in \mathtt{Red}(t)$ and $\alpha \notin \mathtt{Lab}(t)$, we consider the labeled equation $\mathtt{lift}(t, A, \alpha) \sim u$. The **set of residuals of $A$ after** $t \sim u$, is given by $A\langle t \sim u\rangle := \{\mathtt{Red}_{\alpha}(u) \mid \mathtt{lift}(t, A, \alpha) \sim u\}$. Again, this definition is *independent* from the variant used to lift the term $t$. We write $A\langle t \sim u\rangle A'$ iff $A' \in A\langle t \sim u\rangle$ and we extend this notion to sets of redexes as expected, in which case we write $\mathcal{A}\langle t \sim u\rangle\mathcal{A}'$, where $\mathcal{A} \subseteq \mathtt{Red}(t)$ and $\mathcal{A}' \subseteq \mathtt{Red}(u)$. For example, given $v = (x^{\alpha}x^{\alpha})[x/y][x'/y'] \sim (z^{\alpha}[x'/y']z^{\alpha})[z/y] = v'$ and $B = \langle\Box[x'/y'], (x^{\alpha}x^{\alpha})[x/y], \Box x^{\alpha}\rangle$, we have $B\langle v \sim v'\rangle = \{\langle\Box, v', \Box[x'/y']z^{\alpha}\rangle\}$.

***Well-Definedness.*** Despite the simplicity of the equivalence relation $\sim$, the result of well-definedness is not as straightforward as it may seem. In principle, it could be shown by introducing proof-nets and showing that the proof nets corresponding to two $\sim$-equivalent terms $s$ and $t$ are identical: thus there is a bijection between redexes in $s$ and redexes in $t$, since there is a bijection between redexes in $s$ (resp $t$) and redexes in their proof-net representation. We prefer, however, to avoid introducing proof-nets here: on one hand because they are only apparently simpler than terms, on the other hand, to resort to a unique formalism, namely terms, to develop our ideas.

Note that our equations do not duplicate/erase/rename labels, so that any redex has a unique residual along the equivalence. Then well-definedness can be stated as the fact that every equational proof of $t \sim u$ induces the same bijection of redexes. The proof

[4] By abuse of notation we use the same symbol both for the equivalence relation on labeled and unlabeled terms.

of this property is based on the identification of three structural invariants of labeled redexes with respect to the equivalence $\sim$, it is omitted for lack of space.

LEMMA 2 (**Well-Definedness**). *Let $t, u \in \mathcal{T}_{\mathcal{WL}}$ s.t. $t \sim u$. Then there is unique bijection $\phi : \mathtt{Red}(t) \mapsto \mathtt{Red}(u)$ s.t. $\phi(A) = A'$ iff $A\langle t \sim u\rangle A'$.*

Note that uniqueness guarantees that if $t \overset{d_1}{\sim} u$ and $t \overset{d_2}{\sim} u$ are two derivation trees of $t \sim u$, then $A\langle t \overset{d_1}{\sim} u\rangle A'$ iff $A\langle t \overset{d_2}{\sim} u\rangle A'$.

The last result concerns preservation of residuals by means of $\sim$-equivalence classes, where below we write $t \sim_\phi u$ to emphasize that $\phi$ is the (unique) bijection given by Lemma 2.

LEMMA 3. *Let $t \sim_\phi u$. Consider $A, B \in \mathtt{Red}(t)$. If $t \xrightarrow{A} t'$, then:*

1. **Simulation**: *$\exists u'$ s.t. $u \xrightarrow{\phi(A)} u'$ and*
2. **Same equivalence target**: *$t' \sim u'$, i.e. $\exists \xi$ s.t. $t' \sim_\xi u'$, and*
3. **Preservation of residuals**: *if $B\langle A\rangle B'$, then $\phi(B)\langle\phi(A)\rangle\xi(B')$.*

## 5. Abstract Standardization

A *standard* derivation is a *canonical* element of a class of derivations, where canonicity is expressed by means of *completeness*: whenever $t \twoheadrightarrow u$ then there is a standard derivation from $t$ to $u$. In $\lambda$-calculus, a derivation is standard if redexes are selected from *left-to-right*. It is easy to see that the *right-to-left* order, instead, does not provide completeness. Consider the derivation $t = (\lambda x.xx)(II) \rightarrow_\beta (II)(II) \rightarrow_\beta I(II)$: it reduces both redexes in $t$, but it can only be obtained by reducing these redexes according to a left-to-right order, as the right-to-left order would instead give $(\lambda x.xx)(II) \rightarrow_\beta (\lambda x.xx)I \rightarrow_\beta II$. The left-to-right orientation is specific to the $\lambda$-calculus and may not be appropriate for other term rewriting systems, as for example the first-order TRS containing the unique rewriting rule $f(x, a) \rightarrow x$. The abstract theory of standardization then replaces the left-to-right order with an abstract order $\prec$, capturing what we call *the action principle*.

***The Action Principle.*** Let us introduce two crucial concepts. Firstly, reduction of a redex $A$ may **directly act** on another redex $B$ (*i.e.* duplicate/erase it). For example in $\lambda$-calculus, if $t = (\lambda x.xx)(II) \rightarrow_\beta (II)(II)$, then reduction of the leftmost redex $A$ in $t$ duplicates the redex $B = II$. Secondly, reduction of a redex $A$ may **indirectly act** on a redex $B$ by 1) *creating* a new redex $C$ that may directly (or indirectly act) on (a residual of) $B$, or 2) changing the set of redexes that can act on $B$ or on which $B$ can act. An example of the first case: if $t = (\lambda x.x(II))M \rightarrow_\beta M(II)$, where $M = \lambda x.xx$, then reduction of the leftmost redex $A$ in $t$ indirectly acts on the redex $B = II$ by creating the redex $M(II)$ which can duplicate (the residual of) $B$. An example of the second case will be given at the end of Section 8.

Standard derivations are defined abstractly according to the **action principle**: for every redex $A$, reduction of $A$ forbids future reductions of redexes which *may have acted (directly or indirectly) on $A$* before. The nesting order $\prec$ essentially has to induce this principle by capturing as much action as possible (we will see that $\prec$ has to capture direct action, while in general it might capture only some cases of indirect action). The abstract theory of standardization re-organizes derivations according to the action principle, relying on some axioms about the interaction between the nesting order and residuals. Then, whenever the axioms are satisfied, the standardization theorem follows: an abstract reasoning proves that $\prec$-ordered derivations are complete [19, 30, 32].

***Total and Partial Orders.*** The left-to-right order has a fundamental property, it is a *total* order, *i.e.* given two coinitial different redexes $A$ and $B$, then either $A \prec B$ or $B \prec A$. In such a case the abstract theory is quite simple.

Total orders have a limited descriptive power, though. Consider a head-normal form $t = xuv$. The left-to-right order forces the redexes in $u$ to be reduced before those in $v$. However, it is clear that $u$ and $v$ cannot inter*act* in any way, and consequently they could be reduced in parallel even if this parallelism is not captured by the left-to-right order. In other words, the left-to-right order captures more than the action principle. Standardization can then be refined by switching to a *partial* order. For instance, the partial *tree order* $\prec_{tree}$, where $A \prec_{tree} B$ if $B$ is a sub-term of $A$ (so that $A$ and $B$ are unrelated if $B$ is to the right of $A$), captures the parallelism of redexes in $t$ and admits a standardization theorem [30, 32]. The abstract theory of standardization for partial orders is more sophisticated, so for the moment we stay with total orders and shall return to partial orders in Section 7.

In the rest of this section we introduce the necessary notions to deal with the abstract standardization theorem for total orders. In Section 6 we will adapt the left-to-right order to the $\lambda_{\mathtt{lsub}}$-calculus and obtain a left-to-right standardization theorem. From Section 7 to the end of the paper, we will motivate and study a relaxed variant of this order, introducing the framework for partial orders and prove a more general standardization theorem for the $\lambda_{\mathtt{lsub}}^{\sim}$-calculus.

***The Abstract Theory.*** In this paper we resort to the abstract framework developed by Gonthier, Lévy, and Melliès in [19], but we adopt the more general formulation given by Melliès in his PhD thesis [32], as the axioms in [19] will not work when we shall later relax the left-to-right order. The framework is based on *Abstract Rewrite Systems* (ARS), a general formalism encompassing first and higher-order rewriting, plus a *residual relation* $\_\langle\_\rangle\_$ and a *partial order* $\prec$ on redexes, verifying some axioms. The axioms are divided into two groups: The *basic axioms*, which guarantee a well-behaved theory of residuals, and the *standardization axioms*, which concern the interaction of the order with the residual relation.

To formally define the axioms we introduce the following notion. An **Abstract Rewrite System (ARS)** is a tuple of the form $(\mathcal{O}, \mathcal{R}, Src(\_), Tgt(\_), \_\langle\_\rangle\_, \_ \prec \_)$ where $\mathcal{O}$ is called the set of **objects**, $\mathcal{R}$ is called the set of **redexes** , $Src(\_)$ and $Tgt(\_)$ are functions from redexes to objects that we call **source** and **target** functions (resp.), $\_\langle\_\rangle\_$ is a family of binary relations indexed by the set of redexes that we call the **residual relation** and $\prec$ is a partial order on redexes. We say that two redexes $A$ and $B$ are **coinitial** if $Src(A) = t = Src(B)$ for some term $t$. Note that the $\lambda_{\mathtt{lsub}}$-calculus may be seen as an ARS where $\mathcal{O}$ is the set of terms $\mathcal{T}$ defined in Section 2, whereas the $\lambda_{\mathtt{lsub}}^{\sim}$-calculus is an ARS where $\mathcal{O}$ is the set of $\sim$-equivalence classes generated by $\mathcal{T}$ modulo the graphical equivalence $\sim$. The basic axioms are[5]:

- **Autoerasure (AE)**. For any redex $A$, $A\langle A\rangle = \emptyset$.
- **Finite residuals (FR)**. Let $A, B$ be coinitial redexes. Then the set $\{C \mid A\langle B\rangle C\}$ is finite.
- **Uniqueness of ancestors (UA)**. Let $A, B, C$ be coinitial redexes. Then, $B\langle A\rangle B'$ and $C\langle A\rangle C'$ and $B' = C'$ imply $B = C$.
- **Finite Developments (FD)**. Let $\mathcal{A}$ be a set of coinitial redexes. Then any development of $\mathcal{A}$ terminates.
- **Semantic Orthogonality (SO)**. Let $A, B$ be coinitial redexes. Then $Tgt(B\langle A\rangle) = Tgt(A\langle B\rangle)$ and the relations $\langle A; B\langle A\rangle\rangle$ and $\langle B; A\langle B\rangle\rangle$ are exactly the same, where $A; B\langle A\rangle$

[5] In [32] **Autoerasure** is called **A**, **Finite residuals** is called **B**, **Uniqueness of ancestors** is called **D**, and **Semantic Orthogonality** is called **PERM**.

is the derivation that contracts $A$ and then develops $B\langle A\rangle$; likewise for $B; A\langle B\rangle$ (cf. end of Sec. 3).

We consider two standardization axioms:

- **Linearity**. Let $A$ and $B$ be coinitial redexes s.t. $A \not\preceq B$. Then $\exists! B'$ s.t. $B\langle A\rangle B'$.
- **Context-freeness**. Let $A, B, C$ be coinitial redexes s.t. $B\langle A\rangle B'$ and $C\langle A\rangle C'$. If $A \not\prec C$ then $(B \prec C \Leftrightarrow B' \prec C')$.

The linearity axiom captures *direct action*: if $A$ does not nest $B$ then it cannot directly act (*i.e.* duplicate/erase) on $B$, and so $B$ has exactly one residual after $A$. The context-freeness axiom forbids a form of *indirect action* of the second kind: whenever $A$ cannot act on $C$ (*i.e.* $A \not\prec C$) then it cannot grant or remove the power to act on $C$ to any other coinitial redex.

A derivation $d : t \twoheadrightarrow u$ is said to be obtained from a derivation $e : t \twoheadrightarrow u$ by a **standardizing permutation**, written $e \rightsquigarrow d$ (noted $d\angle e$ in [32]), if $d$ is obtained from $e$ by swapping two consecutive redexes which form an inversion w.r.t. $\prec$ in $d$; more precisely, $e \rightsquigarrow d$ if $e = f; B; A'; g$ and $d = f; A; h; g$, and $A \prec B$, where $A\langle B\rangle A'$ and $h$ develops $B\langle A\rangle$. We also say that $d$ is **more standard** than $e$. The classic notion of Lévy's permutation equivalence on derivations, adapted to total orders, can be seen as the equivalence generated by standardization, indeed $d : t \twoheadrightarrow u$ is **permutation equivalent** to $e : t \twoheadrightarrow u$, written $d \equiv e$, iff $d(\rightsquigarrow \cup \rightsquigarrow^{-1})^* e$. In the sequel we write $\equiv_\prec$ when we wish to emphasize the underlying order $\prec$.

A derivation $d$ is **standard** if it is a $\rightsquigarrow$-normal form. The standardization theorem then follows by specializing Thm. 4.7 in [32] to total orders:

THEOREM 1 (**Abstract Total Standardization).** *Consider any ARS equipped with a total order $\prec$ and satisfying the basic and the standardization axioms. Then for any derivation $d : t \twoheadrightarrow u$ there exists a standard derivation $e : t \twoheadrightarrow u$ such that $d \rightsquigarrow^* e$.*

## 6. The Left-to-Right Standardization Theorem

In this section we prove a standardization theorem for the $\lambda_{\mathtt{lsub}}$-calculus relative to a total order. This result is an extension of the left-to-right standardization theorem for $\lambda$-calculus.

***The Left-to-Right Order.*** Given two redexes $A$ and $B$ in $t$ we say that $A$ **is left-to-right nesting** or **on the left of** $B$, written $A \prec_{\mathrm{L}} B$, if the anchor of $A$ is to the left of the anchor of $B$ (looking at $t$ as a string of symbols). Clearly, $\prec_{\mathrm{L}}$ is a total order so that $A \not\prec_{\mathrm{L}} B$ and $A \neq B$ imply $B \prec_{\mathrm{L}} A$.

In order to prove standardization for the $\lambda_{\mathtt{lsub}}$-calculus by means of Theorem 1 we need to verify the basic and the standardization axioms.

***Basic Axioms.*** The first three basic axioms are trivially true. By using (well-)labeled terms to trace residuals we can prove the finite development axiom.

PROPOSITION 1 (**FD).** *Let $t \in \mathcal{T}$ and let $\mathcal{A} \subseteq \mathtt{Red}(t)$. Then any $\lambda_{\mathtt{lsub}}$-development of $\mathcal{A}$ terminates.*

*Proof.* Consider any $t \in \mathcal{T}$ and *lift* every redex in $\mathcal{A} \subseteq \mathtt{Red}(t)$ with a different label belonging to some arbitrary set $\mathbb{L}$. It is clear that the resulting term is a *well-labeled* term. Now, let us consider the labeled reduction relation $\rightarrow_{\mathbb{L}} := \bigcup_{\alpha \in \mathbb{L}} \xrightarrow{\alpha}$. To prove the **(FD)** property it is sufficient to show that the reduction relation $\rightarrow_{\mathbb{L}}$ terminates on well-labeled terms. Termination is proved by means of a measure that strictly decreases with every reduction step (similar to that one used in the proof of Lemma 2 in [6]).

The next proposition proves the semantical orthogonality property for $\lambda_{\mathtt{lsub}}$, that is expressed as a form of local confluence for the labeled system. Again we resort to well-labeled terms.

PROPOSITION 2 (**SO).** *The $\lambda_{\mathtt{lsub}}$-calculus endowed with the left-to-right order satisfies* **Semantic Orthogonality**.

*Proof.* The proof uses well-labeled terms to trace residuals in such a way that axiom (SO) can be reformulated as follows:

*The reduction relations $\xrightarrow{\alpha}$ and $\xrightarrow{\gamma}$ locally commute,* i.e. *if $t, u_1, u_2 \in \mathcal{T}_{\mathcal{WL}}$, $t \xrightarrow{\alpha} u_1$ and $t \xrightarrow{\gamma} u_2$ then there exists $v$ s.t. $u_1 \overset{\gamma}{\twoheadrightarrow} v$ and $u_2 \overset{\alpha}{\twoheadrightarrow} v$.*

This alternative statement can be proved by induction on the relations $\xrightarrow{\alpha}$ and $\xrightarrow{\gamma}$.

***Standardization Axioms.*** Totality of the order $\prec_{\mathrm{L}}$ provides very simple proofs of these axioms:

PROPOSITION 3. *The $\lambda_{\mathtt{lsub}}$-calculus endowed with the left-to-right order satisfies* **Linearity** *and* **Context-freeness**.

*Proof.* **Linearity**. By totality of $\prec_{\mathrm{L}}$, we have to show that if $B \prec_{\mathrm{L}} A$ in $t$ then $\exists! B'$ s.t. $B\langle A\rangle B'$. Now, if $A$ is a $\mathtt{db}$-redex this is obvious, as no redex is duplicated/erased by a $\mathtt{db}$-step. If $A$ is a $\{\mathtt{gc}, \mathtt{ls}\}$-redex then it can only act on redexes whose anchor is in its box, *i.e.* on redexes on its right, and thus not on $B$.
**Context-freeness**. If $A \not\prec_{\mathrm{L}} C$ then $C \prec_{\mathrm{L}} A$. Assume $B \prec_{\mathrm{L}} C$ (and so $B \prec_{\mathrm{L}} C \prec_{\mathrm{L}} A$). Then, $A$ is on the right of both $B$ and $C$. It is easily seen that $A$ can only change the order between redexes on its right; consequently $B' \prec_{\mathrm{L}} C'$. The other direction is by contraposition. Assume $B \not\prec_{\mathrm{L}} C$, that is $C \prec_{\mathrm{L}} B$. We have to prove that $B' \not\prec_{\mathrm{L}} C'$, *i.e.* $C' \prec_{\mathrm{L}} B'$. There are two cases. If $C \prec_{\mathrm{L}} B \prec_{\mathrm{L}} A$ then we reason as in the previous direction, getting $C' \prec_{\mathrm{L}} B'$. Otherwise, we have $C \prec_{\mathrm{L}} A \prec_{\mathrm{L}} B$. Now, the only case that is not immediate is when $A$ is a $\mathtt{ls}$-step. It is enough to observe that a $\mathtt{ls}$-step can only move the redexes in its box at most where the step itself was; hence, $B'$ can at most be where $A$ was (while the position of $C$ is left unchanged), and so $C' \prec_{\mathrm{L}} B'$.

We can then conclude with our first standardization theorem:

COROLLARY 1 (**Left-to-right Standardization for $\lambda_{\mathtt{lsub}}$).** *If $t \twoheadrightarrow_{\lambda_{\mathtt{lsub}}} u$ then there is a $\prec_{\mathrm{L}}$-standard $\lambda_{\mathtt{lsub}}$-derivation from $t$ to $u$.*

*Proof.* It follows from Theorem 1, whose hypothesis are given by Propositions 2, 1, and 3 (the first three basic axioms are immediately seen to hold).

## 7. Towards Equational Standardization

***Proof-Nets.*** The linear substitution calculus has been designed to mimic the representation of $\lambda$-calculus in linear logic proof-nets [18], where $\beta$-reduction is decomposed into small steps. The relationship between the two formalisms occurs at the static and the dynamic levels: every term can be mapped to a proof-net, and every proof-net can be mapped to an $\sim$-equivalence class of terms, as defined in Section 2. Moreover, there is a bijection $\phi$ between the redexes of a term $t$ and the redexes of its corresponding proof-net $PN_t$ which induces a *strong bisimulation* between terms and proof-nets: if $t \rightarrow_{\lambda_{\mathtt{lsub}}} u$ by reducing a redex $A$, then $PN_t \rightarrow_{PN} PN_u$ by reducing $\phi(A)$, and if $PN_t \rightarrow_{PN} R$ then there exists a term $u$ s.t. $t \rightarrow u$ and $R = PN_u$.

The graphical equivalence $\sim$ introduced in Section 2 then inherits a remarkably strong property: it is a *strong bisimulation* between $\lambda_{\mathtt{lsub}}$ and itself, *i.e.* $t \sim u \rightarrow v$ implies that $\exists\, r$ s.t. $t \rightarrow r \sim v$ (the proof is similar to that of the structural $\lambda$-calculus [6]). It, moreover, induces a bijection of redexes, and so it is possible to mimic derivations via $\sim$ as follows: given a derivation $d : t \rightarrow^n u$ and a term $t' \sim t$ we can unambiguously refer to the projection $d' : t' \rightarrow^n u'$ (with $u' \sim u$) of $d$ on $t'$. Since $d$ and $d'$ essentially reduce the same redexes at each step, one expects any reasonable notion of standardization to apply without distinction to both derivations in the sense that either both are standard or none of them is. This would imply, in particular, that our standardization theorem for $\lambda_{\mathtt{lsub}}$ (Corollary 1) also applies to proof-nets. Unfortunately, the left-to-right order does not meet this requirement. Indeed, a left-to-right derivation for $t[x/u][y/v]$ (where $y \notin \mathtt{fv}(u)$) does not project to a left-to-right derivation for $t[y/v][x/u]$, obtained by applying the equation $t[x/u][y/v] \sim_{\mathrm{CS}} t[x/u][y/v]$.

***Relaxing the Order.*** We are therefore going to relax the total left-to-right order $\prec_{\mathrm{L}}$ to a partial order $\prec_{\mathrm{B}}$ that will be stable by $\sim$. The definition of $\prec_{\mathrm{B}}$ shall be guided by the action principle. Because of the linearity axiom, it is mandatory that $\prec_{\mathrm{B}}$ captures direct action between redexes. For that, a simple diagrammatic intuition, due to Klop [26] and then explored by Melliès [30], turns out to be extremely helpful. The idea relies on the analysis of local confluence diagrams. Whenever a redex is duplicated (resp. erased), then the standard derivation should be the longest (resp. shortest) side of the diagram. Consider for example the diagram in Fig.1-*a*. The *standard* way to get from the source to the sink of the diagram is the longest (*i.e.* down-below) side, because the $\mathtt{ls}$-redex *acts on* (*i.e. nests*) the redexes in $s$ [6]. The standard derivation associated to the diagram in Fig.1-*b* —which is an erasing case— is instead the shortest side, because the erasing redex *acts on* the redexes in $s$.

The previous two cases are just reformulations of similar cases in $\lambda$-calculus, and amount to what can be described as *nesting as subterms*. The novelty of $\lambda_{\mathtt{lsub}}$ is that *direct action* (and then nesting of redexes) can also happen *at a distance*. Consider now the example of the diagram in Fig.1-*c*. The duplicated $\mathtt{ls}$-redex on $y$ is not syntactically contained in the acting $\mathtt{ls}$-redex on $x$. Worse, the same diagram applies to terms like $(x[x/y]yz)[y/z]$, where $[x/y]$ and $[y/z]$ are no longer next to each other. According to the action principle, our order has to impose that the $\mathtt{ls}$-redex on $x$ nests the $\mathtt{ls}$-redex on $y$ so that the standard side of the diagram is the longest one. Diagram in Fig.1-*d* is the version at a distance of the erasing diagram, requiring the same notion of nesting at a distance. All these intuitions lead to the partial order of the next section, that will be used in Section 8 to show standardization of the $\lambda^{\sim}_{\mathtt{lsub}}$-calculus.

## 8. The Box Standardization Theorem

We now generalize the notions introduced in Section 5 to the partial **box order**, and then prove the standardization theorem for the $\lambda^{\sim}_{\mathtt{lsub}}$-calculus with respect to this order.

***The Box Order.*** Let $A, B \in \mathtt{Red}(t)$. Then,

- $A$ **immediately boxes** $B$, noted $A \prec^1_{\mathrm{B}} B$ if the anchor of $B$ (*i.e.* the variable possibly carrying a label) is in the box of $A$, *i.e.* if the pattern of $A$ is any of $(\lambda x.t)\mathtt{L}u$, $C[\![x]\!][x/u]$ or $t[x/u]$, then the anchor of $B$ appears in $u$.
- $A$ **boxes** $B$, noted $A \prec_{\mathrm{B}} B$ if $A(\prec^1_{\mathrm{B}})^+B$ (we use $A \preceq_{\mathrm{B}} B$ for $A(\prec^1_{\mathrm{B}})^*B$);
- $A$ **and** $B$ **are disjoint**, noted $A \parallel B$, if $A \not\preceq_{\mathrm{B}} B$ and $B \not\preceq_{\mathrm{B}} A$.

[6] Remark that otherwise one would lose completeness, as there would not be any standard derivation from $C[\![x]\!][x/s]$ to the term $C[\![s']\!][x/s]$, which is the intermediate term in the sequence $C[\![x]\!][x/s] \twoheadrightarrow C[\![s']\!][x/s']$

Note that $A \prec_{\mathrm{B}} B$ implies $A \prec_{\mathrm{L}} B$. Additionally, note the transitive closure in the definition of $\prec_{\mathrm{B}}$—unnecessary for $\prec_{\mathrm{L}}$—which impacts on the proofs of the standardization axioms for $\prec_{\mathrm{B}}$.

The key property of the box order is that it is stable by the equivalence $\sim$. For example, for $t[x/u][y/v]$ with $y \notin \mathtt{fv}(u)$ the redexes in $u$ and the redexes in $v$ are not related by $\prec_{\mathrm{B}}$, so that $\prec_{\mathrm{B}}$ is stable by the permuting axiom $t[y/v][x/u] \sim_{\mathrm{CS}} t[x/u][y/v]$ (where $y \notin \mathtt{fv}(u)$ & $x \notin \mathtt{fv}(v)$). More precisely, given $s \sim t$, the bijection between $\mathtt{Red}(s)$ and $\mathtt{Red}(t)$ defined in Section 4 is order-preserving. To show this property it is sufficient to remark that symbols inside boxes never go in/out these boxes by means of the equivalence relation. Thus, we get:

LEMMA 4 (**Preservation of the Box Order by Equivalence**). *Let $t, u \in \mathcal{T}$ s.t. $t \sim_\phi u$, where $\phi$ is the bijection specified in Lemma 2. Then, $\phi$ commutes with $\prec_{\mathrm{B}}$,* i.e. $A \prec_{\mathrm{B}} B$ *iff* $\phi(A) \prec_{\mathrm{B}} \phi(B)$.

Several remarks on $\prec_{\mathrm{B}}$ are in order:

1. *Disjoint redexes may superpose*: $A \parallel B$ does not necessarily imply that $A$ and $B$ are syntactically disjoint. Examples: the redexes $A_\alpha$ and $B_\beta$ are disjoint but 1) syntactically superposed in $(x^\alpha\, x^\beta)[x/y]$, and 2) syntactically nested in $(\lambda z^\alpha.x^\beta[x/z])y$. However, disjoint redexes always strongly locally commute in the following sense: if $t_0 \xrightarrow{\alpha} t_1$ and $t_0 \xrightarrow{\gamma} t_2$ then there exists $t_3$ s.t. $t_1 \xrightarrow{\gamma} t_3$ and $t_2 \xrightarrow{\alpha} t_3$. Note that this is just a particular case of axiom **(SO)** where the diagram can be closed by using just one reduction step from $t_i$ to $t_3$.
2. *Indirect action*: the box order fails to capture indirect action, in the sense that $A \parallel B$ implies that $A$ cannot directly act on $B$ but it can still indirectly act on it (and viceversa). For example, in the following derivation $A_\alpha \parallel B_\beta$ and $A_\alpha$ creates a redex that can act on $B_\beta$:
$$x^\alpha[x/\lambda y.y]((\lambda z^\beta.z)u) \xrightarrow{\alpha}_{\mathtt{ls}} (\lambda y.y)[x/\lambda y.y]((\lambda z^\beta.z)u)$$
This apparently odd fact—that is not specific to the box order—will not forbid the standardization theorem. Its consequences, and an easy way to deal with them, will be discussed in Section 10. Note that by definition the box order is the *minimum standardization order*, in the sense that it is the transitive closure of the relation capturing direct action only.
3. *The order on $\lambda$-terms*: in [30] (pp. 74-75) Melliès considers three orders on $\lambda$-terms, the *left-to-right* order plus two refinements called the *tree* and the *argument* order. When restricted to $\lambda$-terms, our order coincides with the argument order.
4. *Linear logic interpretation*: we explained that there are two kinds of nesting in $\lambda_{\mathtt{lsub}}$, namely, *subterm nesting* and *nesting at a distance*. In the definition of the box order they are both captured by the notion of *immediately boxes*. In terms of proof-nets, however, they have different interpretations, despite they are both related to the concept of exponential box[7].

***Standardization Up to Square Equivalence.*** A consequence of switching to partial orders is that the notion of standard derivation has to be refined. In fact, partial orders force to work *modulo* the exchanges of disjoint redexes, even to simply define what is an ordered (*i.e.* standard) sequence; this is why abstract standardization is a form of rewriting modulo.

Standardizing permutations are defined as in Section 5. However, to deal with disjoint redexes and adequately represent their

[7] $A$ subterm nests $B$ when $B$ is contained in the !-box of $A$, while $A$ nests $B$ at a distance when the cut corresponding to $B$ crosses an auxiliary conclusion of the box of $A$.

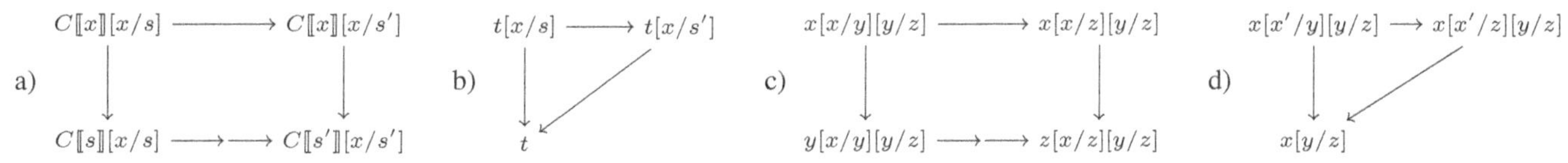

**Figure 1.** Some standardization diagrams.

parallelism induced by the partial order, a new concept is necessary. A derivation $d$ is said to be obtained from a derivation $e$ by **square permutation**, written $d \Diamond^1 e$, if $d = f; A; B'; g$ and $e = f; B; A'; g$ and $A \parallel B$, where $A\langle B\rangle A'$ and $B\langle A\rangle B'$. We write $\Diamond$ for the equivalence relation generated by $\Diamond^1$, and call it **square equivalence**. We use $\rightsquigarrow_{\Diamond}$ for the relation $\rightsquigarrow$ modulo $\Diamond$ and we generalize the permutation equivalence relation $\equiv_{\prec}$ as $(\rightsquigarrow_{\Diamond} \cup \rightsquigarrow_{\Diamond}^{-1})^*$.

A derivation $d$ is **standard** if it is a $\rightsquigarrow$-normal form modulo $\Diamond$. The standardization theorem (Thm. 4.7 in [32]) then follows:

THEOREM 2 (**Abstract Partial Standardization).** *Consider any ARS equipped with a partial order that enjoys the basic and the standardization axioms. Then for every derivation d there exists a standard derivation e s.t.* $d \rightsquigarrow_{\Diamond}^{*} e$.

***Results.*** Our goal is to prove a standardization theorem for $\lambda_{\widetilde{\mathtt{lsub}}}$ relative to $\prec_{\mathtt{B}}$. The proof consists in first obtaining the theorem for $\lambda_{\mathtt{lsub}}$ and then lifting it to $\lambda_{\widetilde{\mathtt{lsub}}}$.

The basic axioms do not mention the order, and thus they still hold for $\lambda_{\mathtt{lsub}}$. The standardization axioms are proved by the following proposition:

PROPOSITION 4. *The $\lambda_{\mathtt{lsub}}$-calculus endowed with the box order $\prec_{\mathtt{B}}$ satisfies* **Linearity** *and* **Context-freeness**.

*Proof.* **Linearity** is easy, by just remarking that a redex $B$ can be duplicated or erased by $A$ only if its anchor is in the box of $A$, case in which $A \prec_{\mathtt{B}} B$. **Context-freeness** requires a detailed study of the interaction between the box order $\prec_{\mathtt{B}}$ and the reduction relation. In particular the proof is involved due to the transitive clause defining the box order, and it is omitted for lack of space.

Then, the previous proposition and Theorem 2 give:

COROLLARY 2 (**Box Standardization for $\lambda_{\mathtt{lsub}}$).** *If $t \twoheadrightarrow_{\lambda_{\mathtt{lsub}}} u$ then there exists a $\prec_{\mathtt{B}}$-standard $\lambda_{\mathtt{lsub}}$-derivation from $t$ to $u$.*

In order to lift the previous result to $\lambda_{\widetilde{\mathtt{lsub}}}$ we use the results on equivalence classes developed in Section 4.

PROPOSITION 5. *The $\lambda_{\widetilde{\mathtt{lsub}}}$-calculus endowed with the box order $\prec_{\mathtt{B}}$ satisfies the basic and the standardization axioms.*

*Proof.* By Lemma 3 and Lemma 4 the notion of residual and the box order lift to $\sim$-equivalence classes preserving their properties. Moreover, the **FD** axiom can be shown exactly as done for $\lambda_{\mathtt{lsub}}$ in Proposition 1, by means of a measure that strictly decreases with every reduction step and remains equal for every pair of equivalent pairs. Therefore, all axioms hold for $\lambda_{\widetilde{\mathtt{lsub}}}$ and we can conclude.

Proposition 5 allows to apply Theorem 2 again and finally obtain our *nonstandard*, equational standardization theorem.

COROLLARY 3 (**Box Standardization for $\lambda_{\widetilde{\mathtt{lsub}}}$).** *If $t \twoheadrightarrow_{\lambda_{\widetilde{\mathtt{lsub}}}} u$ then there is a $\prec_{\mathtt{B}}$-standard $\lambda_{\widetilde{\mathtt{lsub}}}$-derivation from $t$ to $u$.*

The next section will strengthen the result by showing uniqueness (modulo $\Diamond$) of the obtained standard derivation. We conclude this section with a remark.

| | Redex Order | Existence | Uniqueness |
|---|---|---|---|
| $\lambda_{\mathtt{lsub}}$ | Total, left-to-right (Sec. 6) | Thm. 1 | Thm. 3 |
| $\lambda_{\mathtt{lsub}}$ | Partial, box (Sec. 8) | Cor. 2 | Thm. 4 |
| $\lambda_{\widetilde{\mathtt{lsub}}}$ | Partial, box (Sec. 8) | Cor. 3 | Thm. 5 |

**Figure 2.** Summary of results on standardization

***Variation on the Context-Freeness Axiom.*** We use in this paper **Context-freeness** as it appears in Melliès's thesis [32]. In GLM's theory [19], however, the axiom appears in a stronger, symmetric form which does not hold for $\lambda_{\mathtt{lsub}}$. Indeed,

- **Strong context-freeness**. Let $A, B, C$ be coinitial redexes s.t. $B\langle A\rangle B'$ and $C\langle A\rangle C'$. If $A \not\prec C$ then $((B \prec C \Leftrightarrow B' \prec C')$ and $(C \prec B \Leftrightarrow C' \prec B'))$.

Consider $t = (\lambda x^{\alpha}.y^{\gamma}[y/x])(z^{\beta}[z/u])$, where $A_{\alpha} \parallel C_{\gamma}$, $C_{\gamma} \parallel B_{\beta}$, and $A_{\alpha} \prec_{\mathtt{B}} B_{\beta}$. The reduction step of the redex $A_{\alpha}$ yields the term $y^{\gamma}[y/x][x/(z^{\beta}[z/u]]$, where $C'_{\gamma} \prec_{\mathtt{B}} B'_{\beta}$, contradicting the strong form of the axiom (but not the weaker one we use) and providing an example of the second kind of indirect action, as $A_{\alpha}$ changes who can act on (the residual of) $B_{\beta}$.

## 9. Uniqueness

The standardization results obtained up to now concern the *existence* of a standard derivation. In this section the theorems are strengthened by proving *uniqueness* of such derivations. We first discuss the simple case of the left-to-right order, and then provide an original proof of uniqueness (modulo) for the box order.

The axiomatic theory in Mellies' thesis provides uniqueness of standard derivations when two further axioms, **Enclave** and **Stability**, hold (Theorem 4.5 in [32]).

Axiom **Enclave** has two parts. Let $A, B, B'$ be coinitial redexes s.t. $B\langle A\rangle B'$.

1. **Creation**: If $B \prec A$ and $A$ creates a redex $C$, then $B' \prec C$.
2. **Nesting**: Let $C, C'$ be redexes. If $B \prec A \prec C$ and $C\langle A\rangle C'$, then $B' \prec C'$.

In terms of the action principle **Enclave** forbids yet another form of indirect action: if $B$ can directly act on $A$ then $A$ cannot indirectly act on $B$. Consider the *creation* part: if $C \prec B'$ or $C \parallel B'$ then $C$ may act on $B'$, and so $A$ would indirectly act on $B$ ; similarly for the *nesting* part.

PROPOSITION 6. *The $\lambda_{\mathtt{lsub}}$-calculus endowed with the left-to-right order $\prec_{\mathtt{L}}$ satisfies* **Enclave**.

*Proof. Creation*: a simple inspection of the cases of creation (Section 3) shows that a redex $A$ can create a redex $C$ only on its right or at most where it was, so that $C$ cannot nest any redex that was on the left of $A$. *Nesting*: similarly, it is easily seen that $A$ can only move redexes on its right and at most where it was.

In the case of a total standardization order the axiom **Stability** disappears, because its statement (see [32]) assumes two $\prec$-disjoint redexes. Thus, by applying Melliès' theorem we obtain:

THEOREM 3 (**Uniqueness for $\lambda_{\mathtt{lsub}}$**). *If $t \twoheadrightarrow_{\lambda_{\mathtt{lsub}}} u$ then there exists a unique $\prec_{\mathtt{L}}$-standard $\lambda_{\mathtt{lsub}}$-derivation from t to u.*

Switching to partial orders, uniqueness is necessarily relaxed to uniqueness modulo $\Diamond$ (as standard derivations are defined up to $\Diamond$).

Interestingly, for the partial box order both points of **Enclave** fail for $\lambda_{\mathtt{lsub}}$. For *creation* consider the step:

$$s = ((\lambda x^{\beta}.x)(y[z^{\alpha}/z']))[z'/u] \xrightarrow{\alpha} ((\lambda x^{\beta}.x)y)[z'/u] = t$$

Let us call $A_\alpha$ and $B_\beta$ the two labeled redexes in $s$, and $B'_\beta$ (resp. $C$) the residual of $B_\beta$ (resp. the created gc-redex on $z'$) in $t$. We have $B_\beta \prec_{\mathtt{B}} A_\alpha$ but $B'_\beta \not\prec_{\mathtt{B}} C$. For *nesting* it is enough to consider a redex $C$ inside $u$ in the counter-example for *creation*.

So the box order does not capture the indirect action expressed by **Enclave**, and Mellies' axiomatics cannot provide uniqueness modulo $\Diamond$ for $\lambda_{\widetilde{\mathtt{lsub}}}$. However, we can obtain it via another argument. In particular, our alternative proof shows that **Enclave** (together with **Stability**) is a sufficient but by no means necessary condition for uniqueness. We first show uniqueness modulo $\Diamond$ for $\lambda_{\mathtt{lsub}}$, and then lift this result to $\lambda_{\widetilde{\mathtt{lsub}}}$.

THEOREM 4 (**Uniqueness Modulo for $\lambda_{\mathtt{lsub}}$**). *If $t \twoheadrightarrow_{\lambda_{\mathtt{lsub}}} u$ then there exists a $\prec_{\mathtt{B}}$-standard $\lambda_{\mathtt{lsub}}$-derivation from t to u that is unique modulo $\Diamond$.*

*Proof.* (Sketch) Let $e$ be the $\prec_{\mathtt{B}}$-standard $\lambda_{\mathtt{lsub}}$-derivation given by Corollary 2 and $f$ be the unique $\prec_{\mathtt{L}}$-standard derivation given by Corollary 1. We prove that $e\Diamond f$, from which the statement follows. Consider the leftmost contracted redex $C$ in $e = B_1;\ldots;B_n$ (*i.e.* the leftmost redex in $\{A \in \mathtt{Red}(t) \mid A\langle B_1;\ldots;B_i\rangle B_{i+1}, 0 \leq i < n\}$) and let $e'$ be $C;e_1;e_2$ where $e_1 = (B_1;\ldots;B_i)\langle C\rangle$ and $C\langle B_1;\ldots;B_i\rangle B_{i+1}$ and $e_2 = B_{i+2};\ldots;B_n$. It is not difficult to prove, given that $e$ is $\prec_{\mathtt{B}}$-standard, that $e'\Diamond e$, $|e_1| = i$ and so $|e_1;e_2| = |e| - 1$, where $|e|$ denotes the number of steps in $e$. By induction hypothesis we obtain a $\prec_{\mathtt{L}}$-standard derivation $f'$ s.t. $f'\Diamond(e_1;e_2)$. Therefore $C;f'$ is also $\prec_{\mathtt{L}}$-standard and moreover $(C;f')\Diamond(C;e_1;e_2)\Diamond e$. Thm. 3 implies $C;f' = f$.

Note that the proof does not depend concretely on $\lambda_{\widetilde{\mathtt{lsub}}}$, but only on the fact that $\prec_{\mathtt{B}}$ can be embedded in a total order admitting a standardization theorem, which is a fully *abstract* argument.

By exploiting again the results on equivalence classes, we obtain the strongest result of the paper:

THEOREM 5 (**Uniqueness Modulo for $\lambda_{\widetilde{\mathtt{lsub}}}$**). *If $t \twoheadrightarrow_{\lambda_{\widetilde{\mathtt{lsub}}}} u$ then there exists a $\prec_{\mathtt{B}}$-standard $\lambda_{\widetilde{\mathtt{lsub}}}$-derivation from t to u that is unique modulo $\Diamond$.*

*Proof.* By Lemma 3 and Theorem 4 using the stability of the $\prec_{\mathtt{B}}$-order by the equivalence $\sim$ given by Lemma 4.

## 10. External Redexes, Coinductively

When the nesting order $\prec$ is total, standardization is relatively easy, because a derivation $d : t \twoheadrightarrow u$ may be standardized by simply selecting the minimum redex $A$ among the redexes in $t$ that are reduced in $d$ and then repeating the process for the residual of this derivation after $A$. However, when the order is partial—as our box order, and more generally in Gonthier-Levy-Melliès' approach—there may be many $\prec$-minimal redexes among the redexes in $t$ that are reduced in $d$; and randomly selecting one of them does not necessarily produce a standard derivation. This is due to the fact that the partial box order—as it is usually the case with partial orders—fails to properly capture indirect action. Indeed, even if two minimal redexes $A$ and $B$ are necessarily disjoint, $A$ may *create* a redex which will nest (a residual of) $B$.

We illustrate this situation in the simpler setting of the $\lambda$-calculus using the box order (called argument order by Melliès in [30]). Let $I^\alpha$ stand for $\lambda x^\alpha.x$ and $A_\alpha$ for $I^\alpha\, I$ (and similarly for $B_\beta$). Consider the derivation:

$$(I^\alpha\, I)\,(I^\beta\, I) \quad \xrightarrow{\beta}_\beta \quad (I^\alpha\, I)\, I \quad \xrightarrow{\alpha}_\beta \quad I\, I \quad \rightarrow_\beta \quad I$$

Note that both $A_\alpha$ and $B_\beta$ are minimal in the initial term, and the derivation picks at every step a minimal redex. However, the derivation $d$ is not standard. This can be seen by permuting $A_\alpha$ and $B_\beta$, which yields the following $\Diamond$-equivalent derivation, where the two last steps form an inversion for the box order:

$$(I^\alpha\, I)\,(I^\beta\, I) \quad \xrightarrow{\alpha}_\beta I\,(I^\beta\, I) \quad \xrightarrow{\beta}_\beta I\, I \quad \rightarrow_\beta \quad I$$

A standardizing permutation swapping them produces the following standard derivation:

$$(I^\alpha\, I)\,(I^\beta\, I) \quad \xrightarrow{\alpha}_\beta I\,(I^\beta\, I) \quad \rightarrow_\beta (I^\beta\, I) \quad \xrightarrow{\beta}_\beta \quad I$$

This example shows that selecting mimimal redexes does not necessarily give standard derivations when the order is partial. A similar example in $\lambda_{\mathtt{lsub}}$ is obtained by considering the derivations of $x^\alpha[x/\lambda y.y]((\lambda z^\beta.z)u)$.

The solution to this problem is to select an *external* redex [8, 10, 19, 21, 28, 32, 38, 39], *i.e.* a minimal one on which no other redex can indirectly act. The definition of *external redex for a derivation* in GLM's theory is given via an extraction process. In particular, the definition mentions the nesting order only indirectly. Alternatively, external redexes can be defined coinductively as *persistently* minimal redexes, as hinted in [38], *i.e.* the minimal redexes whose (unique) residual after any other redex is still persistently minimal.

We first recall the definition of external redex from [32], that requires two preliminary definitions. A redex $A$ **traverses** a coinitial derivation $d$ becoming $B$, written $A \overset{d}{\longmapsto} B$, iff:

- For $d = \epsilon$, $A \overset{\epsilon}{\longmapsto} B$ iff $B = A$.
- For $d = C;e$, $A \overset{C;e}{\longmapsto} B$ iff $C \not\preceq A$ and $A' \overset{e}{\longmapsto} B$, where $A\langle C\rangle A'$.

A redex $A$ in $t$ can be **extracted** from a derivation $d : t \twoheadrightarrow u$, written $A \curvearrowleft d$, if there exist $d_1, d_2$ s.t. $d = d_1;A';d_2$ and $A \overset{d_1}{\longmapsto} A'$. A redex $A$ in $t$ is **external for** $d : t \twoheadrightarrow u$ if $A \in \mathit{Ext}_\prec(d) := \{B \mid \forall e \equiv_\prec d\,.\, B \curvearrowleft e\}$.

The following result corresponds to Lemma 4.36 in [32].

LEMMA 5 (**External Gives Standard**). *Consider any ARS equipped with a partial order $\prec$ that enjoys the basic and the standardization axioms. If $d = A_1;\ldots;A_n$ and $A_i \in \mathit{Ext}_\prec(A_i;\ldots;A_n)$ $(1 \leq i \leq n)$, then d is $\prec$-standard.*

External redexes generalize leftmost redexes in $\lambda$-calculus, whose key properties are 1) no other redex can act on it, and 2) its unique residual after any other redex is still the leftmost redex. This suggests to define external redexes coinductively as follows.

Let $d : t \twoheadrightarrow u$ be a derivation. The **set of starting redexes** of $d$ is $d^1 := \{B \mid \exists e \text{ s.t. } d \equiv_\prec B;e\}$. A redex $A$ in $t$ is **$\prec$-external for** $d$ if $d$ is not empty and:

1. *Minimality*: $A$ is minimal in $d^1$, and
2. *Persistency*: whenever $d \equiv_\prec B;e$ and $A\langle B\rangle A'$ ($A'$ is unique by minimality), then $A'$ is $\prec$-external in $e$.

The next two technical lemmas are used to relate the two notions of externality. Their proofs are easy:

LEMMA 6. *Let A be $\prec$-external for d. Then:*

*1. $A \curvearrowleft d$, and*
*2. If $e \equiv_\prec d$ then $e^1 = d^1$ and A is $\prec$-external for e.*

LEMMA 7. *Let $A \curvearrowleft d$, i.e. $d = e;A';f$ and $A \overset{e}{\longmapsto} A'$. Then:*

1. *There exists g s.t.* $d \equiv_{\prec} A; g$.
2. *If* $d = B; d'$ *(with* $B \neq A$*) then* $B \not\preceq A$ *and if* $A\langle B\rangle A''$ *then* $A'' \curvearrowleft d'$.

We conclude the section with the equivalence of the two notions of external redex.

PROPOSITION 7. *A is* $\prec$*-external for d iff* $A \in Ext_{\prec}(d)$.

*Proof.* $\Rightarrow$) Let $e \equiv_{\prec} d$. Lemma 6.2 implies that $A$ is $\prec$-external for $e$, and Lemma 6.1 gives $A \curvearrowleft e$, *i.e.* $A \in Ext_{\prec}(d)$. $\Leftarrow$) By coinduction on the definition of $\prec$-external. $A \in Ext_{\prec}(d)$ implies $A \curvearrowleft d$ so that Lemma 7.1 gives $A \in d^1$. Let $B \in d^1$ so that $d \equiv_{\prec} B; e$ and $A \curvearrowleft B; e$. If $B \neq A$ then Lemma 7.2 gives $B \not\preceq A$, that implies $A$ minimal in $d^1$, and $A'' \curvearrowleft e$ if $A\langle B\rangle A''$. Thus, $A'' \in Ext_{\prec}(e)$. By the coinductive hypothesis $A''$ is $\prec$-external for $e$, and thus $A$ is $\prec$-external for $d$.

## 11. Applications

In this section we apply the new characterization of external redexes to obtain a normalization theorem, and to prove that (weak) linear head reduction is standard.

***A Normalizing Strategy for*** $\lambda_{\mathtt{lsub}}$ ***and*** $\lambda_{\mathtt{lsub}}^{\sim}$. Using the coinductive reformulation of external redexes, we can now provide an easy proof that the leftmost strategy, which always reduces the leftmost redex, is normalizing for $\lambda_{\mathtt{lsub}}$ and $\lambda_{\mathtt{lsub}}^{\sim}$, *i.e.* it reaches a normal form, if any. Let us say that a redex $A$ is **universally** $\prec$**-external**, *i.e.* external with respect to any reduction step (and thus wrt any derivation), when the following holds:

1. *Universal minimality*: $A$ is $\prec$-minimal in $\mathtt{Red}(t)$.
2. *Universal persistency*: for any $B \in \mathtt{Red}(t)$, if $A\langle B\rangle A'$ then $A'$ is universally $\prec$-external.

THEOREM 6 (**Normalization**).

1. *The leftmost redex is universally* $\prec_{\mathrm{L}}$*-external* $\lambda_{\mathtt{lsub}}$.
2. *The leftmost strategy is normalizing for* $\lambda_{\mathtt{lsub}}$ *and* $\lambda_{\mathtt{lsub}}^{\sim}$.

*Proof.* 1) By coinduction. *Left-to-right order*: the leftmost redex is $\prec_{\mathrm{L}}$-minimum and by the **Enclave** axiom for $\prec_{\mathrm{L}}$ (Proposition 6) its residual after any other redex is still minimum and thus leftmost. We conclude using the coinductive hypothesis. 2) For $\lambda_{\mathtt{lsub}}$ it follows by Theorem 5.2 in Mellies' thesis [32] (p. 137, formulating abstractly an argument by Huet and Lévy [22]), stating that any strategy reducing $\prec_{\mathrm{L}}$-external redexes is normalizing. For $\lambda_{\mathtt{lsub}}^{\sim}$, let $t$ be a term having an $\lambda_{\mathtt{lsub}}^{\sim}$-normal form. Since $\sim$ can be postponed (*cfr.* Lemma 3) and it is the identity on normal forms, then $t$ has also a normal form in $\lambda_{\mathtt{lsub}}$. The leftmost strategy $\lambda_{\mathtt{lsub}}$-normalizes $t$. Since $\lambda_{\mathtt{lsub}} \subseteq \lambda_{\mathtt{lsub}}^{\sim}$, then the leftmost strategy also $\lambda_{\mathtt{lsub}}^{\sim}$-normalizes $t$.

***Weak Linear Head Reduction is Standard.*** The leftmost strategy captures a relevant strategy in the theory of linear logic, the *weak* (*i.e.* not under abstractions) variant of *linear head reduction*.

To introduce such a notion let us first define weak head contexts by the grammar $W ::= \Box \mid Wt \mid W[x/t]$. **Weak linear head reduction** (WLHR) $\rightarrow_W$ is defined as the closure under *weak head contexts* of the rewriting rules $\{\mapsto_{\mathtt{db}}, \mapsto_{\mathtt{Wls}}\}$, where $\mapsto_{\mathtt{Wls}}$ is the following variation on $\mapsto_{\mathtt{ls}}$:

$$W[\![x]\!][x/u] \mapsto_{\mathtt{Wls}} W[\![u]\!][x/u]$$

Alternatively, $\rightarrow_W$ can be defined as the rewriting relation reducing only the $\{\mathtt{dB}, \mathtt{ls}\}$-redexes whose anchor is in a weak head context.

This notion of reduction is deterministic and tightly related to the $\pi$-calculus [3] and Krivine Abstract Machine [7, 14].

PROPOSITION 8 (**Weak Linear Head Reduction is Standard).**

1. *Every term* $t \in \mathcal{T}$ *has at most one* $\rightarrow_W$ *redex, and if it does then it is the leftmost redex of t.*
2. $\rightarrow_W$*-derivations are* $\prec_{\mathrm{L}}$*-standard (and thus also* $\prec_{\mathrm{B}}$*-standard).*

*Proof.* 1) By induction on $t$. 2) By Lemma 5 and Theorem 6.

***Linear Head Reduction is Standard.*** The head strategy for $\lambda_{\mathtt{lsub}}$ historically arose as a special proof-nets strategy[8] [29]. Given the behavioral equivalence between $\lambda_{\mathtt{lsub}}$ and proof-nets, it can be easily expressed in our setting. For that, let us introduce the set of **head contexts**, that are generated by the grammar $H ::= \Box \mid \lambda x.H \mid H\,t \mid H[x/t]$. **Linear head reduction** (LHR) $\rightarrow_H$ is defined as the closure under *head contexts* of the rewriting rules $\{\mapsto_{\mathtt{db}}, \mapsto_{\mathtt{Hls}}\}$, where $\mapsto_{\mathtt{Hls}}$ is the following variation of the rewriting rule $\mapsto_{\mathtt{ls}}$:

$$H[\![x]\!][x/u] \mapsto_{\mathtt{Hls}} H[\![u]\!][x/u]$$

Alternatively, $\rightarrow_H$ can be defined as the rewriting relation reducing only the $\{\mathtt{dB}, \mathtt{ls}\}$-redexes whose anchor is inside a head context.

Historically, linear head reduction has been defined on ordinary $\lambda$-terms (*i.e.* without explicit substitutions) [14, 29] by using a notion of *virtual redex* (equivalent to a head-redex up to $\sigma$-equivalence [36]). The alternative approach used here, already in use in [2, 3, 5], improves the original presentation in several aspects: there is no need to work with virtual redexes, there is a one-to-one correspondence between LHR in proof-nets and LHR in $\lambda_{\mathtt{lsub}}$, and LHR can be seen as a strategy of $\lambda_{\mathtt{lsub}}$ although it is not a strategy of $\beta$-reduction. Moreover, this presentation of LHR admits a factorization theorem, and can be easily generalized to take place inside arguments of terms [2].

Linear head reduction is another motivation for considering the partial box order on redexes, as we now explain. A crucial point of our definition is that that $\rightarrow_H$—in contrast to $\rightarrow_W$—is nondeterministic, for instance we have both $(\lambda x.y[y/w])z \rightarrow_H (\lambda x.w[y/w])z$ and $(\lambda x.y[y/w])z \rightarrow_H y[y/w][x/z]$. This fact is not a drawback, rather a plus, as it faithfully mimicks the parallelism of cut-elimination in proof-nets. A simple case analysis shows that LHR enjoys the diamond property, *i.e.* any two steps commute and no duplication/erasure is involved. Therefore, the nondeterminism is harmless. In particular, all maximal LHR derivations (if any) have the same length. Concerning standardization, however, not all LHR derivations are standard with respect to the left-to-right order $\prec_{\mathrm{L}}$, consider:

$$(\lambda x.y[y/w])z \rightarrow_H (\lambda x.w[y/w])z \rightarrow_H w[y/w][x/z]$$

This fact is disappointing because the nondeterminism of LHR is only apparent, and so one would like to consider LHR sequences as standard, without having to re-organize them. The box order turns LHR into a standard strategy, giving to the presentation of LHR with explicit substitutions a solid status.

THEOREM 7 (**Linear Head Reduction is Standard).**

1. *Linear head redexes are universally* $\prec_{\mathrm{B}}$*-external.*
2. *Linear head reduction is* $\prec_{\mathrm{B}}$*-standard.*

*Proof.* 1) By coinduction on the definition of universally $\prec$-external. *Universal minimality*: the anchor of $\rightarrow_H$-redexes is out of all boxes, so they can never be nested by another redex. *Universal persistency*: it is easily seen that no redex can move the anchor of a $\rightarrow_H$-redex inside a box. So the residual of a $\rightarrow_H$-redex is a $\rightarrow_H$-redex and we conclude by the coinductive hypothesis. 2) A

[8] The one reducing only cuts out of all !-boxes that do not involve the auxiliary conclusion of any box.

universally external redex is easily seen to be external for every coinitial derivation. Then we conclude applying Lemma 5.

## 12. Conclusions

We study standardization for the linear substitution calculus, a calculus with explicit substitutions, that is not syntactically orthogonal and that it is equipped with an equational theory that makes it isomorphic to linear logic proof-nets. Our main result is a standardization theorem, *nonstandard* because it is based on a partial rather than a total order, it lifts to equivalence classes (*i.e.* proof-nets), and it provides a notion of standard derivation which departs from the one *by levels* in the linear logic literature.

Along the way, we provided other results: 1) a theory of residuals lifting to equivalence classes; 2) a simple left-to-right standardization theorem; 3) a coinductive characterization of the notion of external redex; 4) a normalization theorem; 5) a simple proof that (weak) linear head reduction is standard.

Last, we believe that a further contribution of this paper is the fine analysis of Gonthier, Lévy, and Melliès' axiomatic framework, which gives new intuitions on their complex notions.

## Acknowledgments

We are grateful to Paul-André Melliès for fruitful discussions. This work was partially funded by the French-Argentinian Laboratory in Computer Science **INFINIS** (`www.infinis.org`) and by the Qatar National Research Fund under grant NPRP 09-1107-1-168.

## References

[1] M. Abadi, L. Cardelli, P. L. Curien, and J.-J. Lévy. Explicit substitutions. *Journal of Functional Programming*, 4(1):375–416, 1991.

[2] B. Accattoli. An abstract factorization theorem for explicit substitutions. In *RTA*, pages 6–21, 2012.

[3] B. Accattoli. Evaluating functions as processes. In *TERMGRAPH*, pages 41–55, 2013.

[4] B. Accattoli. *Jumping around the box: graphical and operational studies on λ-calculus and Linear Logic*. PhD thesis, *La Sapienza* University of Rome, february 2011.

[5] B. Accattoli and U. Dal Lago. On the invariance of the unitary cost model for head reduction. In *RTA*, pages 22–37, 2012.

[6] B. Accattoli and D. Kesner. The structural λ-calculus. In *CSL*, pages 381–395, 2010.

[7] B. Accattoli, P. Barenbaum, and D. Mazza. Distilling abstract machines. Submitted, 2013. `https://sites.google.com/site/beniaminoaccattoli/machines.pdf?attredirects=0`.

[8] H. P. Barendregt, R. Kennaway, J. W. Klop, and M. R. Sleep. Needed reduction and spine strategies for the lambda calculus. *Information and Computation*, 75(3):191–231, 1987.

[9] R. Bloo and K. Rose. Preservation of strong normalization in named lambda calculi with explicit substitution and garbage collection. In *Computing Science in the Netherlands*, pages 62–72. Netherlands Computer Science Research Foundation, 1995.

[10] G. Boudol. Computational semantics of term rewriting systems. In *Algebraic methods in semantics*, pages 169–236. Cambridge University Press, 1986.

[11] H. S. Bruggink. *Equivalence of reductions in higher-order rewriting*. PhD thesis, Utrecht University, 2008.

[12] D. Clark and R. Kennaway. Some properties of non-orthogonal term graph rewriting systems. In *SEGRAGRA*, volume 2 of *ENTCS*, pages 36–45, 1995.

[13] H. Curry and R. Feys. *Combinatory Logic*. Number Vol. 1 in Studies in logic and the foundations of mathematics. North-Holland, 1958.

[14] V. Danos and L. Regnier. Head linear reduction, 2003. `http://iml.univ-mrs.fr/~regnier/articles/pam.ps.gz`.

[15] V. Danos, H. Herbelin, and L. Regnier. Game semantics & abstract machines. In *LICS*, pages 394–405, 1996.

[16] D. de Carvalho, M. Pagani, and L. Tortora de Falco. A semantic measure of the execution time in linear logic. *Theor. Comput. Sci.*, 412(20):1884–1902, 2011.

[17] T. Ehrhard and L. Regnier. Böhm trees, krivine's machine and the taylor expansion of lambda-terms. In *CiE*, pages 186–197, 2006.

[18] J.-Y. Girard. Linear logic. *Theoretical Computer Science*, 50(1):1–101, 1987.

[19] G. Gonthier, J.-J. Lévy, and P.-A. Melliès. An abstract standardisation theorem. In *LICS*, pages 72–81, 1992.

[20] G. Huet. Residual theory in λ-calculus: A formal development. *Journal of Functional Programming*, 4(3):371–394, 1994.

[21] G. Huet and J.-J. Lévy. Computations in orthogonal rewriting systems, I and II. In *Computational Logic - Essays in Honor of Alan Robinson*, pages 395–414, 1991.

[22] G. Huet and J.-J. Lévy. Call by Need computations in non-ambiguous linear term rewriting systems. Technical Report 359, INRIA, 1979.

[23] D. Kesner and S. Lengrand. Resource operators for lambda-calculus. *Information and Computation*, 205(4):419–473, 2007.

[24] D. Kesner and S. Ó Conchúir. Milner's lambda calculus with partial substitutions, 2008. `http://www.pps.univ-paris-diderot.fr/~kesner/papers/shortpartial.pdf`.

[25] Z. Khasidashvili and J. R. W. Glauert. Discrete normalization and standardization in deterministic residual structures. In *ALP*, pages 135–149, 1996.

[26] J. W. Klop. *Combinatory Reduction Systems*. Phd thesis, Utrecht University, 1980.

[27] J.-J. Lévy. Réductions correctes et optimales dans le lambda-calcul. Thése d'Etat, Univ. Paris VII, France, 1978.

[28] L. Maranget. Optimal derivations in weak lambda-calculi and in orthogonal terms rewriting systems. In *POPL*, pages 255–269, 1991.

[29] G. Mascari and M. Pedicini. Head linear reduction and pure proof net extraction. *Theoretical Computer Science*, 135(1):111–137, 1994.

[30] P.-A. Melliès. Axiomatic rewriting theory I: A diagrammatic standardization theorem. In *Processes, Terms and Cycles: Steps on the Road to Infinity*, volume 3838 of *LNCS*, pages 554–638. Springer, 2005.

[31] P.-A. Melliès. Axiomatic rewriting theory VI: Residual theory revisited. In *RTA*, pages 24–50, 2002.

[32] P.-A. Melliès. *Description Abstraite de système de réécriture*. PhD thesis, Paris 7 University, 1996.

[33] R. Milner. Local bigraphs and confluence: Two conjectures. *ENTCS*, 175(3):65–73, 2007.

[34] L. Paolini and S. Ronchi Della Rocca. Parametric parameter passing lambda-calculus. *Information and Computation*, 189(1):87–106, 2004.

[35] G. D. Plotkin. Call-by-name, call-by-value and the lambda-calculus. *Theoretical Computer Science*, 1(2):125–159, 1975.

[36] L. Regnier. Une équivalence sur les lambda-termes. *Theoretical Computer Science*, 2(126):281–292, 1994.

[37] M. Takahashi. Parallel reductions in λ-calculus. *Inf. Comput.*, 118(1):120–127, 1995.

[38] Terese. *Term Rewriting Systems*, volume 55 of *Cambridge Tracts in Theoretical Computer Science*. Cambridge University Press, 2003.

[39] V. van Oostrom. Normalisation in weakly orthogonal rewriting. In *RTA*, pages 60–74, 1999.

[40] V. van Oostrom and R. C. de Vrijer. Four equivalent equivalences of reductions. *ENTCS*, 70(6):21–61, 2002.

[41] H. Xi. Upper bounds for standardizations and an application. *Journal of Symbolic Logic*, 64(1):291–303, 1999.

# Closed Type Families with Overlapping Equations

Richard A. Eisenberg
University of Pennsylvania
eir@cis.upenn.edu

Dimitrios Vytiniotis
Simon Peyton Jones
Microsoft Research Cambridge
{dimitris,simonpj}@microsoft.com

Stephanie Weirich
University of Pennsylvania
sweirich@cis.upenn.edu

## Abstract

Open, type-level functions are a recent innovation in Haskell that move Haskell towards the expressiveness of dependent types, while retaining the look and feel of a practical programming language. This paper shows how to increase expressiveness still further, by adding closed type functions whose equations may overlap, and may have non-linear patterns over an open type universe. Although practically useful and simple to implement, these features go *beyond* conventional dependent type theory in some respects, and have a subtle metatheory.

***Categories and Subject Descriptors*** F.3.3 [*Logics and Meanings of Programs*]: Studies of Program Constructs—type structure; D.3.3 [*Programming Languages*]: Language Constructs and Features; F.4.2 [*Mathematical Logic and Formal Languages*]: Grammars and Other Rewriting Systems—parallel rewriting systems

***General Terms*** Design, Languages, Theory

***Keywords*** Type families; Type-level computation; Haskell; System FC

## 1. Introduction

Type families are a relatively recent extension to Haskell that allows the programmer to express type-level computation (Chakravarty et al. 2005). For example, one can say

```
type family Elt (a :: ⋆) :: ⋆
type instance Elt ByteString = Word8
type instance Elt [b] = b
```

The first line declares the type family *Elt* and gives its kind; the second and third are two independent declarations that give two equations for *Elt*. Now the types (*Elt ByteString*) and *Word8* are considered equivalent by the type inference engine, and likewise (*Elt* [*Int*]) and *Int*. Type families have proved to be a popular feature in Haskell, dovetailing particularly nicely with Haskell's type classes. Type families are naturally *partial* and *open*. For example, there is no equation for *Elt Char* above, so *Elt Char* will never be equal to any other type. On the other hand, the author of a new library is free to add a new instance, such as this one:

```
type instance Elt (Set b) = b
```

However, not *all* type-level functions can be defined by open type families. An important example is the equality function, which determines whether two types can be shown equal at compile-time:[1]

```
type family Equal a b :: Bool
type instance Equal a a = True    -- Instance (A)
type instance Equal a b = False   -- Instance (B)
```

The programmer intends these equations to be read top-to-bottom, like a term-level function definition in Haskell. However, because GHC's current type families are open, they must be defined by independent, un-ordered **type instance** equations. The two equations overlap, so they are rightly rejected lest they be used to deduce unsound type equalities. For example, we could reduce the type *Equal Int Int* to both *True* and *False*, since both patterns match.

Yet equality *is* a well-defined function, and a useful one too, as we discuss in Section 2. To fix this omission we introduce *closed type families* with ordered equations, thus:

```
type family Equal a b :: Bool where
  Equal a a = True
  Equal a b = False
```

Now all the equations for the type family are given together, and can be read top-to-bottom. However, behind this simple idea lie a number of complexities. In this paper we describe these pitfalls and their sometimes non-obvious solutions. We make the following contributions:

- We introduce closed type families with overlapping equations, and show how they can readily express programs that were previously inexpressible or required indirect encodings (Section 2).
- Our system supports *non-linear left-hand sides*, such as that for *Equal* above, where the variable *a* is repeated in the first equation. It also supports *coincident overlap*, which allows some lightweight theorem-proving capability to be incorporated in the definitional equality of types (Section 3.4).
- We give the subtle rules that govern type family simplification, including those that determine when a pattern *cannot* be matched by a type (Section 3).
- We describe a typed core language that includes both open and closed type families (Section 4), and prove that it is type-safe, assuming that type families terminate (Section 5). We do that by establishing a *consistency* property of the type equations induced by type families.

[1] Here we use *datatype promotion*, allowing data types like *Bool*, and lists, to be used as kinds (Yorgey et al. 2012).



*POPL '14*, January 22–24, 2014, San Diego, CA, USA.
Copyright © 2014 ACM 978-1-4503-2544-8/14/01...$15.00.
http://dx.doi.org/10.1145/2535838.2535856

- We identify the complications for consistency that arise from non-terminating type families and we expose a subtle oversight in GHC's current rules for open type families in Section 6.
- We have implemented closed type families in GHC as well as a number of case studies, such as the `units` package, an extensible framework for dimensional analysis, presented in the extended version of this paper (Eisenberg et al. 2013). Closed type families are available now in GHC 7.8.

In short, the programmer sees a simple, intuitive language feature, but the design space (and its metatheory) is subtle. Although type families resemble the type-level computation and "large eliminations" found in full-spectrum dependently-typed languages like Coq and Agda, there are important semantic and practical differences. We discuss these in Section 8.

## 2. Closed type families

Haskell (in its implementation in GHC) has supported *type families* for several years. They were introduced to support *associated types*, a feature that Garcia et al.'s (2003) comparison between C++, Haskell, and ML, noted as a C++'s main superiority for generic programming.

Type families were designed to dovetail smoothly with type classes. For example, the type function[2] *Elt* above could be used to specify the element type in a container class:

```
class Container c where
  empty :: c
  member :: Elt c → c → Bool
instance Container [a] where ...
instance Container ByteString where ...
```

New instances for *Container* can be defined as new types are introduced, often in different modules, and correspondingly new equations for *Elt* must be added too. Hence *Elt* must be *open* (that is, can be extended in modules that import it), and *distributed* (can be scattered over many different modules). This contrasts with term-level functions where we are required to define the function all in one place.

The open, distributed nature of type families, typically associated with classes, requires strong restrictions on overlap to maintain soundness. Consider

```
type family F a b :: ⋆
type instance F Int a    = Bool
type instance F a   Bool = Char
```

Now consider the type (*F Int Bool*). Using the first equation, this type is equal to *Bool*, but using the second it is equal to *Char*. So if we are not careful, we could pass a *Bool* to a function expecting a *Char*, which would be embarrassing.

GHC therefore brutally insists that the left-hand sides of two **type instance** equations must not overlap (unify). (At least, unless the right-hand sides would then coincide; see Section 3.4.)

### 2.1 Closed families: the basic idea

As we saw in the Introduction, disallowing overlap means that useful, well-defined type-level functions, such as type level equality, cannot be expressed. Since openness is the root of the overlap problem, it can be solved by defining the equations for the type family *all in one place*. We call this a *closed type family* and define it using a **where** clause on the function's original declaration. The equations may overlap, and are matched top-to-bottom. For example:

[2] We use "type family" and "type function" interchangeably.

```
type family And (a :: Bool) (b :: Bool) :: Bool where
  And True True = True
  And a    b    = False
```

Since the domain of *And* is closed and finite, it is natural to write all its equations in one place. Doing so directly expresses the fact that no further equations are expected.

Although we have used overlap in this example, one can always write functions over *finite* domains without overlap:

```
type family And' (a :: Bool) (b :: Bool) :: Bool where
  And' True  True  = True
  And' False True  = False
  And' True  False = False
  And' False False = False
```

Nevertheless, overlap is convenient for the programmer, mirrors what happens at the term level, avoids a polynomial blowup in program size, and is more efficient (for the type checker) to execute. Furthermore, when defined over an *open* kind, such as $\star$, closed type families allow a programmer to express relationships (such as inequality of types—see Section 2.4) that are otherwise out of reach.

### 2.2 Non-linear patterns

Let us return to our equality function, which can now be defined thus:

```
type family Equal (a :: ⋆) (b :: ⋆) :: Bool where
  Equal a a = True
  Equal a b = False
```

This declaration introduces the type function *Equal*, gives its kind and, in the **where** clause, specifies all its equations. The first equation has a non-linear pattern, in which *a* is repeated, and it overlaps with the second equation. If the domain were finite we could avoid both features by writing out all the equations exhaustively, but new types can be introduced at any time, so we cannot do that here. The issue becomes even clearer when we use *kind polymorphism* (Yorgey et al. 2012), thus:

```
type family Equal (a :: κ) (b :: κ) :: Bool where
  Equal a a = True
  Equal a b = False
```

For example, (*Equal Maybe List*) should evaluate to *False*. It may seem unusual to define a function to compute equality even over types of *function kind* ($\star \to \star$). After all, there is no construct that can compare functions at the term level.

At the type level, however, the type checker decides equality at function kinds all the time! In the world of Haskell types there exist no anonymous type-level functions, nor can type families appear partially applied, so this equality test—which checks for *definitional* equality, in type theory jargon—is straightforward. All *Equal* does is reify the (non-extensional) equality test of the type checker.

In fact, Haskell programmers are used to this kind of equality matching on types; for example, even in Haskell 98 one can write

```
instance Num a ⇒ Num (T a a) where ...
```

Because the type inference engine already supports decidable equality, it is very straightforward to implement non-linear patterns for type functions as well as type classes. Non-linear patterns are convenient for the programmer, expected by Haskell users, and add useful expressiveness. They do make the metatheory much harder, as we shall see, but that is a problem that has to be solved only once.

### 2.3 Type structure matching

In our experience, most cases where closed type families with overlapping equations are useful involve a variation on type equality. However, sometimes we would like to determine whether a type matches a specific top-level structure.

For example, we might want to look at a function type of the form $\mathit{Int} \to (\mathit{Bool} \to \mathit{Char}) \to \mathit{Int} \to \mathit{Bool}$ and determine that this is a function of three arguments.

```
data Nat = Zero | Succ Nat
type family CountArgs (f :: ⋆) :: Nat where
  CountArgs (a → b) = Succ (CountArgs b)
  CountArgs result  = Zero
```

Because the equations are tried in order, any function type will trigger the first equation and any ground non-function type (that is, a type that is not a type variable or an arrow type) will trigger the second. Thus, the type family effectively counts the number of parameters a function requires.

When might this be useful? We have used this type family to write a variable-arity *zipWith* function that infers the correct arity, assuming that the result type is not a function type. Other approaches that we are aware of (Fridlender and Indrika 2000; McBride 2002; Weirich and Casinghino 2010) require some encoding of the desired arity to be passed explicitly. A full presentation of the variable-arity *zipWith* is presented in the extended version of this paper. To achieve the same functionality in a typical dependently typed language like Agda or Coq, we must pattern-match over some inductive universe of codes that can be interpreted into types.

### 2.4 Observing inequality

Type families such as *Equal* allow programmers to observe when types *do not* match. In other words, *Equal Int Bool* automatically reduces to *False*, via the second equation. With open type families, we could only add a *finite number* of reductions of un-equal types to *False*.

However, the ability to observe inequality is extremely useful for expressing failure in compile-time search algorithms. This search could be a simple linear search, such as finding an element in a list. Such search underlies the HList library and its encoding of heterogeneous lists and extensible records (Kiselyov et al. 2004). It also supports Swierstra's solution to the expression problem via extensible datatypes (Swierstra 2008). Both of these proposals use the extension `-XOverlappingInstances` to implement a compile-time equality function.[3]

Type families can directly encode more sophisticated search algorithms than linear list searching, including those requiring backtracking, simply by writing a functional program. For example, the following closed type family determines whether a given element is present in a tree.

```
data Tree a = Leaf a | Branch (Tree a) (Tree a)
type family TMember (e :: κ) (set :: Tree κ) :: Bool where
  TMember e (Leaf x)            = Equal e x
  TMember e (Branch left right) =
    Or (TMember e left) (TMember e right)
```

Implementing this search using overlapping type classes, which do not support backtracking, requires an intricate encoding with explicit stack manipulation.

[3] This extension allows class instances, but not type family instances, to overlap. If the type inference engine chooses the wrong class instance, a program may have incoherent behavior, but it is believed that type safety is not compromised. See Morris and Jones (2010) for relevant discussion.

| | |
|---|---|
| $\tau, \sigma$ | Types |
| $\rho$ | Type patterns (no type families) |
| $F$ | Type families |
| $\Omega$ | Substitutions from type variables to types |

**Figure 1.** Grammar of Haskell metavariables

### 2.5 Summary

Type-level computation is a powerful idea: it allows a programmer to express application-specific compile-time reasoning in the type system. Closed type families fill in a missing piece in the design space, making type families more expressive, convenient, and more uniform with term-level functional programming.

## 3. Simplifying closed family applications

We have shown in the previous sections how type family reduction can be used to equate types. For example, a function requiring an argument of type *T True* can take an argument of type *T (And True True)*, because the latter reduces to the former.

Because the definition of type equality is determined by type family reduction, the static semantics must precisely define what reductions are allowed to occur. That definition turns out to be quite subtle, so this section develops an increasingly refined notion of type family reduction, motivated by a series of examples. The presentation gives a number of definitions, using the vocabulary of Figure 1, but we eschew full formality until Section 4. We use the term *"target"* to designate the type-function application that we are trying to simplify. We say that a type $\tau_1$ *"simplifies"* or *"reduces"* to another type $\tau_2$ if we can rewrite the $\tau_1$ to $\tau_2$ using a (potentially empty) sequence of left-to-right applications of type family equations. We also use the notation $\tau_1 \rightsquigarrow \tau_2$ to denote exactly one application of a type family equation and $\tau_1 \rightsquigarrow^* \tau_2$ to denote an arbitrary number of reductions. Type equality is defined to be roughly the reflexive, symmetric, transitive, congruent closure of type reduction; details are in Section 4.3.

We frequently refer to the example in the introduction, repeated below, with the variables renamed to aid in understanding:

```
type family Equal (a :: κ) (b :: κ) :: Bool where
  Equal a a = True    -- Eqn (A)
  Equal b c = False   -- Eqn (B)
```

### 3.1 No functions on the LHS

If we wish to simplify *Equal Int Int*, equation (A) of the definition matches, so we can safely "fire" the equation (A) to simplify the application to *True*.

Even here we must take a little care. What happens if try this?

```
type family F (a :: Bool) where
  F False       = False
  F True        = True
  F (Equal x y) = True
```

Then *F (Equal Int Bool)* superficially appears to match only the third equation. But of course, if we simplify the argument of *F* in the target, it would become *F False*, which matches the first equation.

The solution here is quite standard: in type family definitions (both open and closed) we do not allow functions in the argument types on the LHS. In terms of Figure 1, the LHS of a function axiom must be a *pattern* $\rho$. This is directly analogous to allowing only constructor patterns in term-level function definitions, and is already required for Haskell's existing open type families.

We then propose the following first attempt at a reduction strategy:

**Candidate Rule 1** (Closed type family simplification). *An equation for a closed type family $F$ can be used to simplify a target $(F\ \overline{\tau})$ if (a) the target matches the LHS of the equation, and (b) no LHS of an* earlier *equation for $F$ matches the target.*

The formal definition of matching follows:

**Definition 1** (Matching). *A pattern $\rho$* matches *a type $\tau$, written* $\mathsf{match}(\rho, \tau)$, *when there is a well-kinded substitution $\Omega$ such that $\Omega(\rho) = \tau$. The domain of $\Omega$ must be a subset of the set of free variables of the pattern $\rho$.*

### 3.2 Avoiding premature matches with apartness

Suppose we want to simplify $\mathit{Equal\ Bool\ d}$. Equation (A) above fails to match, but (B) matches with a substitution $\Omega = [b \mapsto \mathit{Bool}, c \mapsto d]$. But it would be a mistake to simplify $\mathit{Equal\ Bool\ d}$ to $\mathit{False}$. Consider the following code:

```
type family FunIf (b :: Bool) :: ⋆ where
  FunIf True = Int → Int
  FunIf False = ()
bad :: d → FunIf (Equal Bool d)
bad _ = ()
segFault :: Int
segFault = bad True 5
```

If we do simplify the type $\mathit{Equal\ Bool\ d}$ to $\mathit{False}$ then we can show that $\mathit{bad}$ is well typed, since $\mathit{FunIf\ False}$ is $()$. But then $\mathit{segFault}$ calls $\mathit{bad}$ with $d$ instantiated to $\mathit{Bool}$. So $\mathit{segFault}$ expects $\mathit{bad\ True}$ to return a result of type $\mathit{FunIf\ (Equal\ Bool\ Bool)}$, which reduces to $\mathit{Int} \to \mathit{Int}$, so the call in $\mathit{segFault}$ type-checks too. Result: we apply $()$ as a function to 5, and crash.

The error, of course, is that we wrongly simplified the type $(\mathit{Equal\ Bool\ d})$ to $\mathit{False}$; wrongly because the choice of which equation to match depends on how $d$ is instantiated. While the target $(\mathit{Equal\ Bool\ d})$ does not match the earlier equation, *there is a substitution* for $d$ that causes it to match the earlier equation. Our Candidate Rule 1 is insufficient to ensure type soundness. We need a stronger notion of *apartness* between a (target) type and a pattern, which we write as $\mathsf{apart}(\rho, \tau)$ in what follows.

**Candidate Rule 2** (Closed type family simplification). *An equation for a closed type family $F$ can be used to simplify a target $(F\ \overline{\tau})$ if (a) the target matches the LHS of the equation, and (b) every LHS $\overline{\rho}$ of an* earlier *equation for $F$ is apart from the target; that is,* $\mathsf{apart}(\overline{\rho}, \overline{\tau})$.

As a notational convention, $\mathsf{apart}(\overline{\rho}, \overline{\tau})$ considers the lists $\overline{\rho}$ and $\overline{\tau}$ as tuples of types; the apartness check does *not* go element-by-element. We similarly treat uses of $\mathsf{match}$ and $\mathsf{unify}$ (defined shortly) when applied to lists.

To rule out our counterexample to type soundness, apartness must at the very least satisfy the following property:

**Property 2** (Apartness through substitution). *If* $\mathsf{apart}(\rho, \tau)$ *then there exists no $\Omega$ such that* $\mathsf{match}(\rho, \Omega(\tau))$.

An appealing implementation of $\mathsf{apart}(\rho, \tau)$ that satisfies Property 2 is to check that the target $\tau$ and the pattern $\rho$ are *not unifiable*, under the following definition:

**Definition 3** (Unification). *A type $\tau_1$* unifies *with a type $\tau_2$ when there is a well-kinded substitution $\Omega$ such that $\Omega(\tau_1) = \Omega(\tau_2)$. We write* $\mathsf{unify}(\tau_1, \tau_2) = \Omega$ *for the most general such unifier if it exists.*[4]

However this test is not sufficient for type soundness. Consider the type $\mathit{Equal\ Int\ (G\ Bool)}$, where $G$ is a type family. This type does not match equation (A), nor does it *unify* with (A), but it *does* match (B). So according to our rule, we can use (B) to simplify $\mathit{Equal\ Int\ (G\ Bool)}$ to $\mathit{False}$. But, if $G$ were a type function with equation

**type instance** $\mathit{G\ Bool} = \mathit{Int}$

then we could use this equation to rewrite the type to $\mathit{Equal\ Int\ Int}$, which patently *does* match (A) and simplifies to $\mathit{True}$!

In our check of previous equations of a closed family, we wish to ensure that no previous equation can *ever* apply to a given application. Simply checking for unification of a previous pattern and the target is not enough. To rule out this counterexample we need yet another property from the $\mathsf{apart}(\rho, \tau)$ check, which ensures that the target cannot match a pattern of an earlier equation through arbitrary reduction too.

**Property 4** (Apartness through reduction). *If* $\mathsf{apart}(\rho, \tau)$, *then for any $\tau'$ such that $\tau \rightsquigarrow^* \tau'$:* $\neg\mathsf{match}(\rho, \tau')$.

### 3.3 A definition of apartness

We have so far sketched *necessary* properties that the apartness check must satisfy—otherwise, our type system surely is not sound. We have also described why a simple unification-based test does not meet these conditions, but we have not yet given a concrete definition of this check.

Note that we cannot use Property 4 to *define* $\mathsf{apart}(\rho, \tau)$ because it would not be well founded. We need $\mathsf{apart}(\rho, \tau)$ to define how type families should reduce, but Property 4 itself refers to type family reduction. Furthermore, even if this were acceptable, it seems hard to implement. We have to ensure that, for any substitution, no reducts of a target can possibly match a pattern; there can be exponentially many reducts in the size of the type and the substitution.

Hence we seek a conservative but cheap test. Let us consider again why unification is not sufficient. In the example from the previous section, we showed that type $\mathit{Equal\ Int\ (G\ Bool)}$ does not match equation (A), nor does it *unify* with (A). However, $\mathit{Equal\ Int\ (G\ Bool)}$ can simplify to $\mathit{Equal\ Int\ Int}$ and now equation (A) does match the reduct.

To take the behavior of type families into account, we first *flatten* any type family applications in the arguments of the target (i.e., the types $\overline{\tau}$ in a target $F\ \overline{\tau}$) to fresh variables. Only then do we check that the new target is not unifiable with the pattern. This captures the notion that a type family can potentially reduce to any type—anything more refined would require advance knowledge of all type families, impossible in a modular system. In our example, we must check $\mathsf{apart}((a, a), (\mathit{Int}, \mathit{G\ Bool}))$ when trying to use the second equation of $\mathit{Equal}$ to simplify $\mathit{Equal\ Int\ (G\ Bool)}$. We first flatten $(\mathit{Int}, \mathit{G\ Bool})$ into $(\mathit{Int}, x)$ (for some fresh variable $x$). Then we check whether $(a, a)$ cannot be unified with $(\mathit{Int}, x)$. We quickly discover that these types *can* be unified. Thus, $(a, a)$ and $(\mathit{Int}, \mathit{G\ Bool})$ are *not* apart and simplifying $\mathit{Equal\ Int\ (G\ Bool)}$ to $\mathit{False}$ is prohibited.

What if two type family applications in the target type are syntactically identical? Consider the type family $F$ below:

[4] For instance, the implementation of $\mathsf{unify}$ can be the standard first-order unification algorithm of Robinson.

```
type family F a b where
  F Int Bool = Char
  F a   a    = Bool
```

Should the type $F\ (G\ \mathit{Int})\ (G\ \mathit{Int})$ be apart from the left-hand-side $F\ \mathit{Int}\ \mathit{Bool}$? If we flatten to two distinct type variables then it is not apart; if we flatten using a common type variable then it becomes apart. How can we choose if flattening should preserve sharing or not? Let us consider the type $F\ b\ b$, which matches the second equation. It is definitely apart from $F\ \mathit{Int}\ \mathit{Bool}$ and can indeed be simplified by the second equation. What happens, though, if we substitute $G\ \mathit{Int}$ for $b$ in $F\ b\ b$? If flattening did not take sharing into account, $(G\ \mathit{Int}, G\ \mathit{Int})$ would *not* be apart from $(\mathit{Int}, \mathit{Bool})$, and $F\ (G\ \mathit{Int})\ (G\ \mathit{Int})$ wouldn't reduce. Hence, the ability to simplify would not be stable under substitution. This, in turn, threatens the preservation theorem.

Thus, we must identify repeated type family applications and flatten these to the *same* variable. In this way, $F\ (G\ \mathit{Int})\ (G\ \mathit{Int})$ is flattened to $F\ x\ x$ (never $F\ x\ y$), will be apart from the first equation, and will be able to simplify to $\mathit{Bool}$, as desired.

With these considerations in mind, we can now give our implementation of the apartness check:

**Definition 5** (Flattening). *To flatten a type $\tau$ into $\tau'$, written $\tau' = \mathsf{flatten}(\tau)$, process the type $\tau$ in a top-down fashion, replacing every type family application with a type variable. Two or more syntactically identical type family applications are flattened to the same variable; distinct type family applications are flattened to distinct fresh variables.*

**Definition 6** (Apartness). *To test for* $\mathsf{apart}(\rho, \tau)$, *let* $\tau' = \mathsf{flatten}(\tau)$ *and check* $\mathsf{unify}(\rho, \tau')$. *If this unification fails, then $\rho$ and $\tau$ are* apart. *More succinctly:* $\mathsf{apart}(\rho, \tau) = \neg\mathsf{unify}(\rho, \mathsf{flatten}(\tau))$.

We can show that this definition does indeed satisfy the identified necessary properties from Section 3.2. In Section 5.1 we will also identify the *sufficient* conditions for type soundness for *any* possible type-safe implementation of apartness, show that these conditions imply the properties identified in the previous section (a useful sanity check!) and prove that the definition of apartness that we just proposed meets these sufficient conditions.

### 3.4 Allowing more reductions with compatibility

Checking for apartness in previous equations might be unnecessarily restrictive. Consider this code, which uses the function $\mathit{And}$ from Section 2.1:

```
f  :: T a → T b → T (And a b)
tt :: T True

g :: T a → T a
g x = f x tt
```

Will the definition of $g$ type-check? Alas no: the call $(f\ x\ \mathit{tt})$ returns a result of type $T\ (\mathit{And}\ a\ \mathit{True})$, and that matches neither of the equations for $\mathit{And}$. Perhaps we can fix this by adding an equation to the definition of $\mathit{And}$, thus:

```
type family And (a :: Bool) (b :: Bool) :: Bool where
  And True True = True   -- (1)
  And a    True = a      -- (2)
  And a    b    = False  -- (3)
```

But that does not work either: the target $(\mathit{And}\ a\ \mathit{True})$ matches (2) *but is not apart from (1)*, so (2) cannot fire. And yet we would *like* to be able to simplify $(\mathit{And}\ a\ \mathit{True})$ to $a$, as Eqn (2) suggests. Why should this be sound? Because anything that matches both (1) and (2) will reduce to $\mathit{True}$ using either equation. We say that the two equations *coincide* on these arguments. When such a coincidence happens, the apartness check is not needed.

We can easily formalize this intuition. Let us say that two equations are *compatible* when any type that matches both left-hand sides would be rewritten by both equations to the same result, eliminating non-convergent critical pairs in the induced rewriting system:

**Definition 7** (Compatibility). *Two type-family equations $p$ and $q$ are* compatible *iff* $\Omega_1(\mathit{lhs}_p) = \Omega_2(\mathit{lhs}_q)$ *implies* $\Omega_1(\mathit{rhs}_p) = \Omega_2(\mathit{rhs}_q)$.

For example, (1) and (2) are compatible because a type, such as $\mathit{And}\ \mathit{True}\ \mathit{True}$, would be rewritten by both to the same type, namely $\mathit{True}$. It is easy to test for compatibility:

**Definition 8** (Compatibility implementation). *The test for compatibility, written* $\mathsf{compat}(p, q)$, *checks that* $\mathsf{unify}(\mathit{lhs}_p, \mathit{lhs}_q) = \Omega$ *implies* $\Omega(\mathit{rhs}_p) = \Omega(\mathit{rhs}_q)$. *If* $\mathsf{unify}(\mathit{lhs}_p, \mathit{lhs}_q)$ *fails,* $\mathsf{compat}(p, q)$ *holds vacuously.*

The proof that $\mathsf{compat}(p, q)$ implies that $p$ and $q$ are compatible appears in the extended version of this paper and is straightforward. We can now state our final simplification rule for closed type families:

**Rule 9** (Closed type family simplification). *An equation $q$ of a closed type family can be used to simplify a target application $F\ \overline{\tau}$ if the following conditions hold:*

1. *The target $\overline{\tau}$ matches the type pattern $\mathit{lhs}_q$.*
2. *For each earlier equation p, either* $\mathsf{compat}(p, q)$ *or* $\mathsf{apart}(\mathit{lhs}_p, \overline{\tau})$.

For example, we can fire equation (2) on a target that is not apart from (1), because (1) and (2) are compatible. We show that Rule 9 is sufficient for establishing type soundness in Section 5.

Through this use of compatibility, we allow for a limited form of theorem proving within a closed type family definition. The fact that equation (2) is compatible with (1) essentially means that the rewrite rule for (2) is admissible given that for (1). By being able to write such equations in the closed type family definition, we can expand Haskell's definitional equality to relate more types.

### 3.5 Optimized matching

In our original Candidate Rule 2 above, when simplifying a target $F\ \overline{\tau}$ with an equation $q$, we are obliged to check $\mathsf{apart}(\mathit{lhs}_p, \overline{\tau})$, *for every earlier equation p*. But much of this checking is wasted duplication. For example, consider

```
type family F a where
  F Int  = Char   -- (1)
  F Bool = Bool   -- (2)
  F x    = Int    -- (3)
```

If a target matches (2) there is really no point in checking its apartness from (1), because *anything* that matches (2) will be apart from (1). We need only check that the target is apart from any preceding equations that could possibly match the same target.

Happily, this intuition is already embodied in our new simplification Rule 9. This rule checks $\mathsf{compat}(p, q) \lor \mathsf{apart}(\mathit{lhs}_p, \overline{\tau})$ for each preceding equation $p$. But we can *precompute* $\mathsf{compat}(p, q)$ (since it is independent of the target), and in the simplification rule we need check apartness only for the pre-computed list of earlier incompatible equations. In our example, equations (1) and (2) are vacuously compatible, since their left-hand sides do not unify, and hence no type can match both. Thus, there is no need to check for apartness from (1) of a target matching (2).

### 3.6 Compatibility for open families

As discussed in the introduction, **type instance** declarations for open type families must not overlap. With our definition of compatibility, however, we can treat open and closed families more uniformly by insisting that any two instances of the same open type family are compatible:

**Definition 10** (Open type family overlap check). *Every pair of equations $p$ and $q$ for an open type family F must satisfy* $\mathsf{compat}(p, q)$.

Notice that this definition also allows for coincident right-hand sides (as in the case for closed type families, Section 3.4). For example, these declarations are legal:

```
type family Coincide a b
type instance Coincide Int b    = Int
type instance Coincide a   Bool = a
```

These equations overlap, but in the region of overlap they always produce the same result, and so they should be allowed. (GHC already allowed this prior to our extensions.)

### 3.7 Type inference for closed type families

Given the difficulty of type inference for open type families (Chakravarty et al. 2005; Schrijvers et al. 2008), how do we deal with closed ones? Thankfully, this turns out to be remarkably easy: we simply use Rule 9 to simplify closed families in exactly the same stage of type inference that we would simplify an open one. The implementation in GHC is accordingly quite straightforward.

Despite the ease of implementation, there are perhaps complex new possibilities opened by the use of closed families—these are explored in Section 7.6.

## 4. System µFC: formalizing the problem

Thus far we have argued informally. In this section we formalize our design and show that it satisfies the usual desirable properties of type preservation and progress, assuming termination of type family reduction. It is too hard to formulate these proofs for all of Haskell, so instead we formalize µFC, a small, explicitly-typed lambda calculus. This is more than a theoretical exercise: GHC really does elaborate all of Haskell into System FC (Sulzmann et al. 2007a; Weirich et al. 2013), of which µFC is a large subset that omits some details of FC—such as kind polymorphism (Yorgey et al. 2012)—that are irrelevant here.

### 4.1 System µFC

System µFC is an extension of System F, including kinds and explicit equality coercions. Its syntax is presented in Figure 2. This syntax is very similar to recent treatments of System FC (Weirich et al. 2013). We omit from the presentation the choice of ground types and their constructors and destructors, as they are irrelevant for our purposes.

There are a few points to note about type families, all visible in Figure 2. A type family has a particular arity, and always appears saturated in types. That explains the first-order notation $F(\overline{\kappa}){:}\kappa'$ in ground contexts $\Sigma$, and $F(\overline{\tau})$ in types.

A closed type family appears in µFC as a kind signature $F(\overline{\kappa}){:}\kappa'$, and a single *axiom* $C{:}\Psi$, both in the top-level ground context $\Sigma$. The "type" $\Psi$ of the axiom is a list of equations, each of form $[\overline{\alpha{:}\kappa}].\ F(\overline{\tau}) \sim \sigma$, just as we have seen before except that the quantification is explicit. For example, the axiom for *Equal* (restricted for simplicity to kind $\star$) looks like this:

$$\begin{aligned} \mathit{axiomEq} :\quad & [\alpha{:}\star].(\mathit{Equal}\ \alpha\ \alpha) \sim \mathit{True}\ ; \\ & [\alpha{:}\star, \beta{:}\star].(\mathit{Equal}\ \alpha\ \beta) \sim \mathit{False} \end{aligned}$$

Although our notation for lists does not make it apparent, we restrict the form of the equations to require that $F$ refers to only one type family—that is, there are no independent $F_i$. We use subscripts on metavariables to denote which equation they refer to, and we refer to the types $\overline{\rho_i}$ as the *type patterns* of the $i$'th equation. We assume that the variables $\overline{\alpha}$ bound in each equation are distinct from the variables bound in other equations.

An open type family appears as a kind signature and zero or more separate axioms, each with one equation.

| | | | |
|---|---|---|---|
| *Expressions:* | | | |
| $e$ | $::=$ | $x \mid \lambda x{:}\tau.e \mid e_1\ e_2 \mid \Lambda\alpha{:}\kappa.e \mid e\ \tau$ | |
| | $\mid$ | $e \triangleright \gamma$ | Cast |
| | $\mid$ | $\ldots$ | Constructors and destructors of datatypes |
| *Types:* | | | |
| $\tau, \sigma, \psi, \upsilon$ | $::=$ | $\alpha \mid \tau_1 \to \tau_2 \mid \forall\alpha{:}\kappa.\tau$ | |
| | $\mid$ | $\tau_1\ \tau_2$ | Application |
| | $\mid$ | $F(\overline{\tau})$ | Saturated type family |
| | $\mid$ | $H$ | Datatype, such as *Int* |
| $\rho$ denotes a type pattern (with no type families) | | | |
| $\kappa$ | $::=$ | $\star \mid \kappa_1 \to \kappa_2$ | Kinds |
| *Propositions:* | | | |
| $\phi$ | $::=$ | $\tau_1 \sim \tau_2$ | Equality propositions |
| $\Phi$ | $::=$ | $[\overline{\alpha{:}\kappa}].\ F(\overline{\rho}) \sim \sigma$ | Axiom equations |
| $\Psi$ | $::=$ | $\overline{\Phi}$ | List of axiom eqns. (axiom types) |
| *Coercions:* | | | |
| $\gamma, \eta$ | $::=$ | $\gamma_1 \to \gamma_2 \mid \forall\alpha{:}\kappa.\gamma \mid \gamma_1\ \gamma_2 \mid F(\overline{\gamma})$ | |
| | $\mid$ | $\langle\tau\rangle$ | Reflexivity |
| | $\mid$ | $\mathbf{sym}\ \gamma$ | Symmetry |
| | $\mid$ | $\gamma_1 \fatsemi \gamma_2$ | Transitivity |
| | $\mid$ | $\mathbf{left}\ \gamma$ | Left decomposition |
| | $\mid$ | $\mathbf{right}\ \gamma$ | Right decomposition |
| | $\mid$ | $C[i]\ \overline{\tau}$ | Axiom application |

*Contexts:*
Ground: $\Sigma ::= \cdot \mid \Sigma, H{:}\overline{\kappa} \to \star \mid \Sigma, F(\overline{\kappa}){:}\kappa' \mid \Sigma, C{:}\Psi$
Variables: $\Delta ::= \cdot \mid \Delta, x{:}\tau \mid \Delta, \alpha{:}\kappa$
Combined: $\Gamma ::= \Sigma; \Delta$

Substitutions: $\Omega ::= [\overline{\alpha \mapsto \tau}]$

**Figure 2.** The grammar of System µFC

| | |
|---|---|
| $\Gamma \vdash_{\mathsf{tm}} e : \tau$ | Expression typing |
| $\Gamma \vdash_{\mathsf{ty}} \tau : \kappa$ | Type kinding |
| $\Gamma \vdash_{\mathsf{co}} \gamma : \phi$ | Coercion typing |
| $\vdash_{\mathsf{gnd}} \Sigma$ | Ground context validity |
| $\Sigma \vdash_{\mathsf{var}} \Delta$ | Variables context validity |
| $\vdash_{\mathsf{ctx}} \Gamma$ | Context validity |

**Figure 3.** Typing judgments for System µFC

### 4.2 Static semantics

Typing in µFC is given by the judgments in Figure 3. Most of the rules are uninteresting and are thus presented in the extended version of this paper. The typing rules for expressions are entirely straightforward. The only noteworthy rule is the one for casting, which gives the raison d'être for coercions:

$$\frac{\Gamma \vdash_{\mathsf{co}} \gamma : \tau_1 \sim \tau_2 \qquad \Gamma \vdash_{\mathsf{tm}} e : \tau_1}{\Gamma \vdash_{\mathsf{tm}} e \triangleright \gamma : \tau_2}\ \textsc{Tm\_Cast}$$

Here, we see that a cast by a coercion changes the type of an expression. This is what we mean by saying that a coercion witnesses the equality of two types—if there is a coercion between $\tau_1$ and $\tau_2$, then any expression of type $\tau_1$ can be cast into one of type $\tau_2$.

The rules for deriving the kind of a type are straightforward and are omitted from this presentation.

### 4.3 Coercions and axiom application

Coercions are less familiar, so we present the coercion typing rules in full, in Figure 4. The first four rules say that equality is *congruent*—that is, types can be considered equal when they are formed of components that are considered equal. The following three rules assert that coercibility is a proper equivalence relation. The CO_LEFT and CO_RIGHT rules assert that we can decompose complex equalities to simpler ones. These formation rules are incomplete with respect to some unspecified notion of *semantic* equality—that is, we can imagine writing down two types that we "know" are equal, but for which no coercion is derivable. For example, there is no way to use induction over a data structure to prove equality. However, recall that these coercions must all be inferred from a source program, and it is unclear how we would reliably infer inductive coercions.

The last rule of coercion formation, CO_AXIOM, is the one that we are most interested in. The coercion $C[i]\,\overline{\tau}$ witnesses the equality obtained by instantiating the $i$'th equation of axiom $C$ with the types $\overline{\tau}$. For example,

$$\mathit{axiomEq}[0]\ \mathit{Int} : \mathit{Equal\ Int\ Int} \sim \mathit{True}$$

This says that if we pick the first equation of *axiomEq* (we index from 0), and instantiate it at *Int*, we have a witness for *Equal Int Int* $\sim$ *True*.

Notice that the coercion $C[i]\,\overline{\tau}$ specifies exactly which equation is picked (the $i$'th one); µFC is a fully-explicit language. However, the typing rules for µFC must reject unsound coercions like

$$\mathit{axiomEq}[1]\ \mathit{Int}\ \mathit{Int} : \mathit{Equal\ Int\ Int} \sim \mathit{False}$$

and that is expressed by rule CO_AXIOM. The premises of the rule check to ensure that $\Sigma;\Delta$ is a valid context and that all the types $\overline{\tau}$ are of appropriate kinds to be applied in the $i$'th equation. The last premise implements Rule 9 (Section 3.4), by checking no_conflict for each preceding equation $j$. The no_conflict judgment simply checks that *either* (NC_COMPATIBLE) the $i$'th and $j$'th equation for $C$ are compatible, *or* (NC_APART) that the target is apart from the LHS of the $j$'th equation, just as in Rule 9.

In NC_COMPATIBLE, note that the compat judgment does not take the types $\overline{\tau}$: compatibility is a property of equations, and is independent of the specific arguments at an application site. The two rules for compat are exactly equivalent to Definition 8.

These judgments refer to algorithms apart and unify. We assume a correct implementation of unify and propose sufficient properties of apart in Section 5.1. We then show that our chosen algorithm for apart (Definition 6) satisfies these properties.

As a final note, the rules do not check the closed type family axioms for exhaustiveness. A type-family application that matches no axiom simply does not reduce. Adding an exhaustiveness check based on the kind of the arguments of the type family might be a useful, but orthogonal, feature.

## 5. Metatheory

A summary of the structure of the type safety proof, highlighting the parts that are considered in this paper, is in Figure 5. Our main goals are to prove (i) the substitution lemma of types into coercions (Section 5.2), and (ii) a consistency property that ensures we never equate two types such as *Int* and *Bool* (Section 5.3). The substitution and consistency lemmas lead to the preservation and progress theorems respectively, which together ensure type safety. We omit the operational semantics of µFC as well as the other

$\boxed{\Gamma \vdash_{\mathsf{co}} \gamma : \phi}$ Coercion typing

$$\frac{\Gamma \vdash_{\mathsf{co}} \gamma_1 : \tau_1 \sim \tau_1' \qquad \Gamma \vdash_{\mathsf{co}} \gamma_2 : \tau_2 \sim \tau_2' \qquad \Gamma \vdash_{\mathsf{ty}} \tau_1 \to \tau_2 : \star}{\Gamma \vdash_{\mathsf{co}} \gamma_1 \to \gamma_2 : (\tau_1 \to \tau_2) \sim (\tau_1' \to \tau_2')}\ \textsc{Co\_Arrow}$$

$$\frac{\Gamma, \alpha{:}\kappa \vdash_{\mathsf{co}} \gamma : \tau_1 \sim \tau_2 \qquad \Gamma \vdash_{\mathsf{ty}} \forall\,\alpha{:}\kappa.\tau_1 : \star}{\Gamma \vdash_{\mathsf{co}} \forall\,\alpha{:}\kappa.\gamma : (\forall\,\alpha{:}\kappa.\tau_1) \sim (\forall\,\alpha{:}\kappa.\tau_2)}\ \textsc{Co\_Forall}$$

$$\frac{\Gamma \vdash_{\mathsf{co}} \gamma_1 : \tau_1 \sim \sigma_1 \qquad \Gamma \vdash_{\mathsf{co}} \gamma_2 : \tau_2 \sim \sigma_2 \qquad \Gamma \vdash_{\mathsf{ty}} \tau_1\,\tau_2 : \kappa}{\Gamma \vdash_{\mathsf{co}} \gamma_1\,\gamma_2 : (\tau_1\,\tau_2) \sim (\sigma_1\,\sigma_2)}\ \textsc{Co\_App}$$

$$\frac{\overline{\Gamma \vdash_{\mathsf{co}} \gamma : \tau_1 \sim \tau_2} \qquad \Gamma \vdash_{\mathsf{ty}} F(\overline{\tau_1}) : \kappa}{\Gamma \vdash_{\mathsf{co}} F(\overline{\gamma}) : F(\overline{\tau_1}) \sim F(\overline{\tau_2})}\ \textsc{Co\_TyFam}$$

$$\frac{\Gamma \vdash_{\mathsf{ty}} \tau : \kappa}{\Gamma \vdash_{\mathsf{co}} \langle\tau\rangle : \tau \sim \tau}\ \textsc{Co\_Refl}$$

$$\frac{\Gamma \vdash_{\mathsf{co}} \gamma : \tau_1 \sim \tau_2}{\Gamma \vdash_{\mathsf{co}} \mathbf{sym}\,\gamma : \tau_2 \sim \tau_1}\ \textsc{Co\_Sym}$$

$$\frac{\Gamma \vdash_{\mathsf{co}} \gamma_1 : \tau_1 \sim \tau_2 \qquad \Gamma \vdash_{\mathsf{co}} \gamma_2 : \tau_2 \sim \tau_3}{\Gamma \vdash_{\mathsf{co}} \gamma_1 \mathbin{\text{⨾}} \gamma_2 : \tau_1 \sim \tau_3}\ \textsc{Co\_Trans}$$

$$\frac{\Gamma \vdash_{\mathsf{co}} \gamma : \tau_1\,\tau_2 \sim \sigma_1\,\sigma_2 \qquad \Gamma \vdash_{\mathsf{ty}} \tau_1 : \kappa \qquad \Gamma \vdash_{\mathsf{ty}} \sigma_1 : \kappa}{\Gamma \vdash_{\mathsf{co}} \mathbf{left}\,\gamma : \tau_1 \sim \sigma_1}\ \textsc{Co\_Left}$$

$$\frac{\Gamma \vdash_{\mathsf{co}} \gamma : \tau_1\,\tau_2 \sim \sigma_1\,\sigma_2 \qquad \Gamma \vdash_{\mathsf{ty}} \tau_2 : \kappa \qquad \Gamma \vdash_{\mathsf{ty}} \sigma_2 : \kappa}{\Gamma \vdash_{\mathsf{co}} \mathbf{right}\,\gamma : \tau_2 \sim \sigma_2}\ \textsc{Co\_Right}$$

$$\frac{C{:}\Psi \in \Sigma \qquad \Psi = \overline{[\overline{\alpha{:}\kappa}].\ F(\overline{\rho}) \sim \upsilon} \qquad \overline{\Sigma;\Delta \vdash_{\mathsf{ty}} \tau : \kappa_i} \qquad \vdash_{\mathsf{ctx}} \Sigma;\Delta \qquad \forall j < i, \mathsf{no\_conflict}(\Psi, i, \overline{\tau}, j)}{\Sigma;\Delta \vdash_{\mathsf{co}} C[i]\,\overline{\tau} : F(\overline{\rho_i[\overline{\tau/\alpha_i}]}) \sim \upsilon_i[\overline{\tau/\alpha_i}]}\ \textsc{Co\_Axiom}$$

$\boxed{\mathsf{no\_conflict}(\Psi, i, \overline{\tau}, j)}$ Check for equation conflicts

$$\frac{\Psi = \overline{[\overline{\alpha{:}\kappa}].\ F(\overline{\rho}) \sim \upsilon} \qquad \mathsf{apart}(\overline{\rho_j}, \overline{\rho_i[\overline{\tau/\alpha_i}]})}{\mathsf{no\_conflict}(\Psi, i, \overline{\tau}, j)}\ \textsc{NC\_Apart}$$

$$\frac{\mathsf{compat}(\Psi[i], \Psi[j])}{\mathsf{no\_conflict}(\Psi, i, \overline{\tau}, j)}\ \textsc{NC\_Compatible}$$

$\boxed{\mathsf{compat}(\Phi_1, \Phi_2)}$ Equation compatibility

$$\frac{\Phi_1 = [\overline{\alpha_1{:}\kappa_1}].\ F(\overline{\rho_1}) \sim \upsilon_1 \qquad \Phi_2 = [\overline{\alpha_2{:}\kappa_2}].\ F(\overline{\rho_2}) \sim \upsilon_2 \qquad \mathsf{unify}(\overline{\rho_1}, \overline{\rho_2}) = \Omega \qquad \Omega(\upsilon_1) = \Omega(\upsilon_2)}{\mathsf{compat}(\Phi_1, \Phi_2)}\ \textsc{Compat\_Coincident}$$

$$\frac{\Phi_1 = [\overline{\alpha_1{:}\kappa_1}].\ F(\overline{\rho_1}) \sim \upsilon_1 \qquad \Phi_2 = [\overline{\alpha_2{:}\kappa_2}].\ F(\overline{\rho_2}) \sim \upsilon_2 \qquad \mathsf{unify}(\overline{\rho_1}, \overline{\rho_2})\ \text{fails}}{\mathsf{compat}(\Phi_1, \Phi_2)}\ \textsc{Compat\_Distinct}$$

**Figure 4.** Coercion formation rules

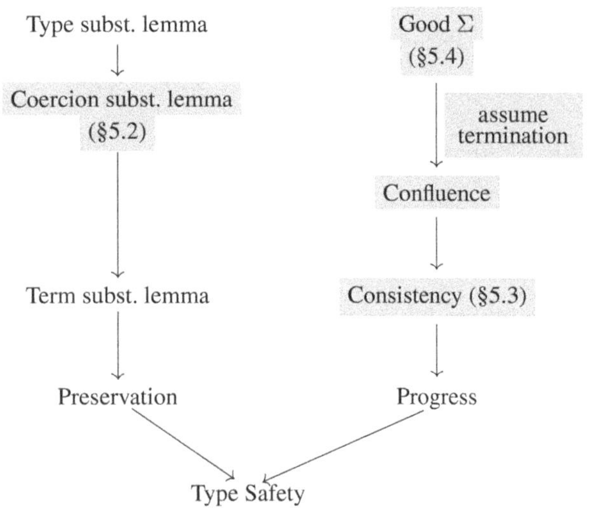


**Figure 5.** Structure of type safety proof. The arrows represent implications. The nodes highlighted in gray are the parts considered in the present work.

lemmas in the main proofs of preservation and progress, because these are all direct adaptations from previous work (Weirich et al. 2011; Sulzmann et al. 2007a).

We stress that, as Figure 5 indicates, we have proved type safety only for *terminating* type families. What exactly does that mean? We formally define the rewrite relation, now written $\Sigma \vdash \cdot \rightsquigarrow \cdot$ to explicit mention the set of axioms, with the following rule:

$$\frac{\begin{array}{ll} C{:}\Psi \in \Sigma & \Psi = \overline{[\alpha{:}\kappa]}.\ F(\overline{\rho}) \sim \upsilon \\ \vdash_{\mathsf{gnd}} \Sigma \quad \overline{\tau} = \rho_i[\overline{\psi/\alpha_i}] & \tau' = \upsilon_i[\overline{\psi/\alpha_i}] \\ \forall j < i, \mathsf{no\_conflict}(\Psi, i, \overline{\psi}, j) & \end{array}}{\Sigma \vdash \mathcal{C}[F(\overline{\tau})] \rightsquigarrow \mathcal{C}[\tau']}\ \textsc{Red}$$

In the conclusion of this rule, $\mathcal{C}[\cdot]$ denotes a type context with exactly one hole. Its use in the rule means that a type family can simplify *anywhere* within a type. Note that the no_conflict premise of this rule is identical to that of the Co_Axiom rule. By "terminating type families" we mean that the $\Sigma \vdash \cdot \rightsquigarrow \cdot$ relation cannot have infinite chains. We discuss non-terminating type families in Section 6.

As a notational convention, we extend the relation to lists of types by using $\Sigma \vdash \overline{\tau_1} \rightsquigarrow \overline{\tau_2}$ to mean that exactly one of the types in $\overline{\tau_1}$ steps to the corresponding type in $\overline{\tau_2}$; in all other positions $\overline{\tau_1}$ and $\overline{\tau_2}$ are identical.

### 5.1 Preliminaries: properties of unification and apartness

In order to prove properties about no_conflict, we must assume the correctness of the unification algorithm:

**Property 11** (unify correct). *If there exists a substitution $\Omega$ such that $\Omega(\overline{\sigma}) = \Omega(\overline{\tau})$, then* unify$(\overline{\sigma}, \overline{\tau})$ *succeeds. If* unify$(\overline{\sigma}, \overline{\tau}) = \Omega$ *then $\Omega$ is a most general unifier of $\overline{\sigma}$ and $\overline{\tau}$.*

In Section 3.2, we gave some *necessary* properties of apart, namely Properties 2 and 4. To prove type soundness we need *sufficient* properties, such as the following three. *Any* implementation of apart that has these three properties would lead to type safety. We prove (in the extended version of this paper) that the given algorithm for apart (Definition 6) satisfies these properties. Due to flattening in the definition of apart, this proof is non-trivial. As a sanity check, we also prove that the sufficient properties imply the necessary ones of Section 3.2.

**Property 12** (Apartness is stable under type substitution). *If* apart$(\overline{\rho}, \overline{\tau})$*, then for all substitutions $\Omega$,* apart$(\overline{\rho}, \Omega(\overline{\tau}))$.

**Property 13** (No unifiers for apart types). *If* apart$(\overline{\rho}, \overline{\tau})$*, then there exists no substitution $\Omega$ such that $\Omega(\overline{\rho}) = \Omega(\overline{\tau})$.*

The final property of the apartness check is the most complex. It ensures that, if an equation can fire for a given target and that target steps, then it is possible to simplify the reduct even further so that the same equation can fire on the final reduct.

**Property 14** (Apartness can be regained after reduction). *If $\overline{\tau} = \Omega(\overline{\rho})$ and $\Sigma \vdash \overline{\tau} \rightsquigarrow \overline{\tau'}$, then there exists a $\overline{\tau''}$ such that*

1. *$\Sigma \vdash \overline{\tau'} \rightsquigarrow^* \overline{\tau''}$,*
2. *$\overline{\tau''} = \Omega'(\overline{\rho})$ for some $\Omega'$, and*
3. *for every $\overline{\rho'}$ such that* apart$(\overline{\rho'}, \overline{\tau})$*:* apart$(\overline{\rho'}, \overline{\tau''})$.

Here is an example of Property 14 in action. Consider the following type families $F$ and $G$:

```
type family F a where
  F (Int, Bool) = Char   -- (A)
  F (a,   a)    = Bool   -- (B)
type family G x where G Int = Double
```

Suppose that our target is $F$ $(G$ $Int, G$ $Int)$, and that our particular implementation of apart allows equation (B) to fire; that is, apart$((Int, Bool), (G\ Int, G\ Int))$. Now, suppose that instead of firing (B) we chose to reduce the first $G$ $Int$ argument to $Double$. The new target is now $F$ $(Double, G$ $Int)$. Now (B) cannot fire, because the new target simply does not match (B) any more. Property 14 ensures that there exist further reductions on the new target that make (B) firable again—in this case, stepping the second $G$ $Int$ to $Double$ does the job. Conditions (2) and (3) of Property 14 formalize the notion "make (B) firable again".

### 5.2 Type substitution in coercions

System μFC enjoys a standard term substitution lemma. This lemma is required to prove the preservation theorem. As shown in Figure 5, the term substitution lemma depends on the substitution lemma for coercions. We consider only the case of interest here, that of substitution in the rule Co_Axiom.

**Lemma 15** (Co_Axiom Substitution). *If $\Sigma; \Delta, \beta{:}\kappa, \Delta' \vdash_{\mathsf{co}} C[i]\ \overline{\tau} : F(\rho_i[\overline{\tau/\alpha_i}]) \sim \upsilon_i[\overline{\tau/\alpha_i}]$ and $\Sigma; \Delta \vdash_{\mathsf{ty}} \sigma : \kappa$, then $\Sigma; \Delta, \Delta'[\sigma/\beta] \vdash_{\mathsf{co}} C[i]\ \overline{\tau[\sigma/\beta]} : F(\rho_i[\overline{\tau/\alpha_i}][\sigma/\beta]) \sim \upsilon_i[\overline{\tau/\alpha_i}][\sigma/\beta]$.*

The proof of this lemma, presented in the extended version of this paper, proceeds by case analysis on the no_conflict judgment. It requires the use of the (standard) type substitution lemma and Property 12, but is otherwise unremarkable.

### 5.3 Consistency

As discussed at the beginning of this section, to establish progress we must show *consistency*. Consistency ensures that we can never deduce equalities between distinct *value types*, denoted with $\xi$:

$$\xi \quad ::= \quad H\,\overline{\tau} \mid \tau_1 \to \tau_2 \mid \forall \alpha{:}\kappa.\tau$$

For example, $Int$, $Bool$, and $\forall \alpha{:}\star.\alpha \to \alpha$ are all value types. A set of axioms is consistent if we cannot deduce bogus equalities like $Int \sim Bool$ or $Int \sim \forall \alpha{:}\star.\alpha \to \alpha$:

**Definition 16** (Consistent contexts). *A ground context* $\Sigma$ *is consistent if, for all coercions* $\gamma$ *such that* $\Sigma; \cdot \vdash_{co} \gamma : \xi_1 \sim \xi_2$*:*

1. *if* $\xi_1 = H\,\overline{\tau_1}$*, then* $\xi_2 = H\,\overline{\tau_2}$*,*
2. *if* $\xi_1 = \tau_1 \to \tau_1'$*, then* $\xi_2 = \tau_2 \to \tau_2'$*, and*
3. *if* $\xi_1 = \forall\,\alpha{:}\kappa.\tau_1$*, then* $\xi_2 = \forall\,\beta{:}\kappa.\tau_2$*.*

How can we check whether an axiom set is consistent? It is extremely hard to do so in general, so instead, following previous work (Weirich et al. 2011), we place syntactic restrictions on the axioms that conservatively guarantee consistency. A set of axioms that pass this check are said to be **Good**. We then prove the consistency lemma:

**Lemma 17** (Consistency). *If* **Good** $\Sigma$*, then* $\Sigma$ *is consistent.*

Following previous proofs, we show that if **Good** $\Sigma$ and $\Sigma; \cdot \vdash_{co} \gamma : \sigma_1 \sim \sigma_2$, then $\sigma_1$ and $\sigma_2$ have a common reduct in the $\rightsquigarrow$ relation. Because the simplification relation preserves type constructors on the heads of types, we may conclude that $\Sigma$ is consistent.

However, one of the cases in this argument is transitivity: the joinability relation must be transitive. That is, if $\tau_1$ and $\tau_2$ have a common reduct $\sigma_1$, and if $\tau_2$ and $\tau_3$ have a common reduct $\sigma_2$, then $\tau_1$ and $\tau_3$ must have a common reduct (they are *joinable*). To show transitivity of joinability, we must show confluence of the rewrite relation, in order to find the common reduct of $\sigma_1$ and $\sigma_2$ (which share $\tau_2$ as an ancestor).

Our approach to this problem is to show *local confluence* (see Figure 6) and then use Newman's Lemma (1942) to get full confluence. Newman's Lemma requires that the rewrite system is terminating—this is where the assumption of termination is used.

The full, detailed proof appears in the extended version of this paper (Eisenberg et al. 2013).

### 5.4 Good contexts

What sort of checks should be in our syntactic conditions, **Good**? We would like **Good** to be a small set of common-sense conditions for a type reduction system, such as the following:

**Definition 18** (**Good** contexts). *We have* **Good** $\Sigma$ *whenever the following four conditions hold:*

1. *For all* $C{:}\Psi \in \Sigma$*:* $\Psi$ *is of the form* $\overline{[\overline{\alpha{:}\kappa}].\ F(\overline{\rho}) \sim v}$ *where all of the* $F_i$ *are the same type family* $F$ *and all of the type patterns* $\overline{\rho_i}$ *do not mention any type families.*
2. *For all* $C{:}\Psi \in \Sigma$ *and equations* $[\overline{\alpha{:}\kappa}].\ F(\overline{\rho}) \sim v$ *in* $\Psi$*: the variables* $\overline{\alpha}$ *all appear free at least once in* $\overline{\rho}$*.*
3. *For all* $C{:}\Psi \in \Sigma$*: if* $\Psi$ *defines an axiom over a type family* $F$ *and has multiple equations, then no other axiom* $C'{:}\Psi' \in \Sigma$ *defines an axiom over* $F$*. That is, all type families with ordered equations are closed.*
4. *For all* $C_1{:}\Phi_1 \in \Sigma$ *and* $C_2{:}\Phi_2 \in \Sigma$ *(each with only one equation),* $\mathsf{compat}(\Phi_1, \Phi_2)$*. That is, among open type families, the patterns of distinct equations do not overlap.*

The clauses of the definition of **Good** are straightforward syntactic checks. In fact, these conditions are exactly what GHC checks for when compiling type family instances. This definition of **Good** leads to the proof of Lemma 17, as described above.

## 6. Non-terminating type families

By default GHC checks every type family for termination, to guarantee that the type checker will never loop. Any such check is necessarily conservative; indeed, GHC rejects the *TMember* function of Section 2.4 (Schrijvers et al. 2008). Although GHC's test could readily be improved, any conservative check limits expressiveness or convenience, so GHC allows the programmer to disable

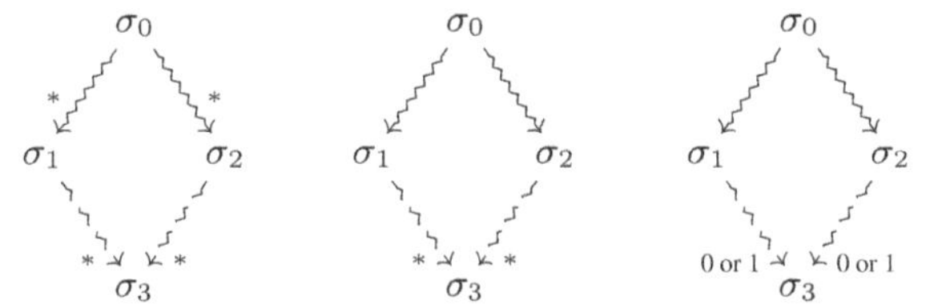


(a) Confluence (b) Local confluence (c) Local diamond

**Figure 6.** Graphical representation of confluence properties. A solid line is a universally quantified input, and a dashed line is an existentially quantified output.

the check. This may make the type checker loop, but *it should not threaten soundness*.

However, the soundness result of Section 5 covers only terminating type families. Surprisingly (to us) non-termination really does lead to a soundness problem (Section 6.1). We propose a solution that (we believe) rules out this problem (Section 6.2), but explain why the main result of this paper is difficult to generalize to non-terminating type families, leaving an open problem for further work.

### 6.1 The problem with infinity

Consider this type family, adapted from Huet (1980):

```
type family D x where
  D ([b], b) = Bool
  D (c,   c) = Int
```

We wish to simplify the target $D\ (a, a)$. The type $(a, a)$ matches the second pattern $(c, c)$, but is it apart from the first pattern $([b], b)$? Definition 6 asserts that they *are* apart since they do not unify: unification fails with an occurs check error. Accordingly, Rule 9 would simplify $D\ (a, a)$ to $Int$. But consider the following definitions, where type family $Loop$ is a nullary (0-argument) type family:

```
type family Loop
type instance Loop = [Loop]
```

If we instantiate $a$ with $Loop$ we get $(Loop, Loop)$ which *can* simplify to $([Loop], Loop)$. The latter *does match* the pattern $([b], b)$, violating Property 4, a necessary condition for soundness.

So, in a non-terminating system our apartness check is unsound. Concretely, using our apartness implementation from Definition 6, we can equate types $Int$ and $Bool$, thus:

$$Int \sim D\ (Loop, Loop) \sim D\ ([Loop], Loop) \sim Bool$$

Conclusion: we must not treat $(a, a)$ as apart from the pattern $([b], b)$, *even though they do not unify*. In some ways this is not so surprising. In our earlier examples, apartness was based on an explicit contradiction ("a $Bool$ cannot be an $Int$"), but here unification fails only because of an occurs check. As the $Loop$ example shows, allowing non-terminating type-family definitions amounts to introducing infinite types, and if we were to allow infinite types, then $(a, a)$ *does* unify with $([b], b)$!

### 6.2 Fixing the problem

The problem with the current apartness check is that finite unification fails too often. We need to replace the unification test in the definition of apartness with unification over *infinite types*:

**type instance** $A = C\ A$
**type instance** $C\ x = D\ x\ (C\ x)$
**type instance** $D\ x\ x = Int$

$$\begin{array}{ll}(1) & A \leadsto C\ A \leadsto D\ A\ (C\ A) \leadsto D\ (C\ A)\ (C\ A) \leadsto Int \\ (2) & A \leadsto C\ A \leadsto^{*}_{\text{by (1)}} C\ Int\end{array}$$

$Int$ and $C\ Int$ have no common reduct.

**Figure 7.** Counter-example to confluence

**Definition 19** (Infinite unification). *Two types* $\tau_1, \tau_2$ *are infinitely unifiable, written* $\text{unify}_\infty(\tau_1, \tau_2)$*, if there exists a substitution* $\omega$ *whose range may include* infinite *types, such that* $\omega(\tau_1) = \omega(\tau_2)$*.*

For example types $(a, a)$ and $([b], b)$ are unifiable with a substitution $\omega = [a \mapsto [[[...]]], b \mapsto [[[...]]]]$. Efficient algorithms to decide unification over infinite types (and compute most general unifiers) have existed for some time and are based on well-established theory (Huet 1976; Courcelle 1983). See Jaffar (1984) for such an algorithm, and Knight (1989) for a general survey.

We conjecture that replacing all uses of unify with $\text{unify}_\infty$ in our definitions guarantees soundness, even in the presence of non-terminating family equations. Alas, this conjecture turns out to be very hard to prove, and touches on open problems in the term-rewriting literature. For example, a rewrite system that has (a) infinite rewrite sequences and (b) non-left-linear patterns, *does not necessarily guarantee confluence*, even if its patterns do not overlap. Figure 7 gives an example, from Klop (1993).

Notice that replacing unify with $\text{unify}_\infty$ may change the reduction relation. For example, a target which is apart from a pattern with a unify-based apartness check may no longer be apart from the same pattern with the more conservative $\text{unify}_\infty$-based apartness check. Yet, type safety (for terminating axiom sets) is not compromised since Property 11 carries over to unification algorithms over infinite types (Huet 1976).

### 6.3 Ramifications for open families

We pause briefly to consider the implications for GHC's existing *open* type families. GHC allows the following definition for an open type family $D'$:

**type family** $D'\ x\ y$
**type instance** $D'\ [b]\ b = Bool$
**type instance** $D'\ c\ \ c = Int$

As described in Section 2, the **type instance** equations of an open type family are required to have non-overlapping left-hand sides, and GHC 7.6 believes that the two equations do not overlap because they do not unify. But, using certain flags, GHC also accepts the definition of $Loop$, and the target $(D'\ Loop\ Loop)$ demonstrates that the combination is unsound precisely as described above.[5]

Happily, if the conjecture of Section 6.2 holds true, we can apply the same fix for open families as we did for closed families: simply use $\text{unify}_\infty$ instead of unify when checking for overlap. Indeed, this is exactly how we have corrected this oversight in GHC 7.8.

## 7. Discussion and Future Work

The study of closed type families opens up a wide array of related issues. This section discusses some of the more interesting points we came across in our work.

[5] Akio Takano has posted an example of how this can cause a program to fail, at `http://ghc.haskell.org/trac/ghc/ticket/8162`.

### 7.1 Denotational techniques for consistency

We do not have a proof of consistency for a system with non-terminating, non-left-linear axioms (even when using $\text{unify}_\infty$ instead of unify). We have seen that confluence is false, and hence cannot be used as a means to show consistency.

A possible alternative approach to proving consistency—side-stepping confluence—is via a denotational semantics for types. We would have to show that if we can build a coercion $\gamma$ such that $\Gamma \vdash \gamma : \tau \sim \sigma$, then $[\![\tau]\!] = [\![\sigma]\!]$, for some interpretation of types into a semantic domain. The "obvious" domain for such a semantics, in the presence of non-terminating computations, is the domain that includes $\bot$ as well as finite and infinite trees. Typically in denotational semantics, recursive type families would be interpreted as the limit of approximations of continuous functions. However, the "obvious" interpretation of type families in this simple domain is not monotone. Consider this type family:

**type family** $F\ a\ b$ **where**
  $F\ x\ \ x \qquad\quad = Int$
  $F\ [x]\ (Maybe\ x) = Char$

It is the case that $(\bot \sqsubseteq [\bot])$ and $(\bot \sqsubseteq Maybe\ \bot)$, but the semantic interpretation of $F$, call it $f$, should satisfy $f(\bot, \bot) = Int$ and $f([\bot], Maybe\ \bot) = Char$. Hence, monotonicity breaks. The lack of monotonicity means that limits of chains of approximations do not exist, and thus that interpretations of functions, such as $f$, are ill-defined.

An alternate definition would give $f(\bot, \bot) = \bot$, but then substitutivity breaks. Indeed, the proof theory can deduce that $F\ x\ x$ is equal to $Int$ for *any* type $x$, even those that have denotation $\bot$.

Alternatively to these approaches, one might want to explore different domains to host the interpretation of types.

### 7.2 Conservativity of apartness

We note in Section 3.3 that our implementation of apartness is conservative. This conservativity is unavoidable—it is possible for open type families to have instances scattered across modules, and thus the apartness check cannot adequately simplify the types involved in every case. However, the current check considers *none* of the type family axioms available, even if one would inform the apartness check. For example, consider

**type family** $G\ a$ **where**
  $G\ Int = Bool$
  $G\ [a] = Char$

and we wish to simplify target $Equal\ Double\ (G\ b)$. It is clear that an application of $G$ can never simplify to $Double$, so we could imagine a more refined apartness check that could reduce this target to $False$. We leave the details of such a check to future work.

### 7.3 Conservativity of coincident overlap: partial knowledge

It is worth noting that the compatibility check (Definition 8) is somewhat conservative. For example, take the type family

**type family** $F\ a\ b$ **where**
  $F\ Bool\ c = Int$
  $F\ d\ \quad e = e$

Consider a target $F\ g\ Int$. The target matches the second equation, but not the first. But, the simplification rule does not allow us to fire the second equation—the two equations are not compatible, and the target is not apart from the first equation. Yet it clearly *would* be safe to fire the second equation in this case, because even if $g$ turns out to be $Bool$, the first equation would give the same result.

It would, however, be easy to modify $F$ to allow the desired simplification: just add a new second equation $F\ a\ Int = Int$. This new equation would be compatible with the first one and therefore would allow the simplification of $F\ g\ Int$.

### 7.4 Conservativity of coincident overlap: requiring syntactic equality

The compatibility check is conservative in a different dimension: it requires syntactic equality of the RHSs after substitution. Consider this tantalizing example:

```
type family Plus a b where
  Plus Zero     a        = a                   -- (A)
  Plus (Succ b) c        = Succ (Plus b c)     -- (B)
  Plus d        Zero     = d                   -- (C)
  Plus e        (Succ f) = Succ (Plus e f)     -- (D)
```

If this type family worked as one would naively expect, it would simplify an addition once *either* argument's top-level constructor were known. (In other dependently typed languages, definitions like this are not possible and require auxiliary lemmas to reduce when the second argument's structure only is known.) Alas, it does not work as well as we would hope. The problem is that not all the equations are compatible. Let's look at (B) and (C). To check if these are compatible, we unify $((Succ\ b), c)$ with $(d, Zero)$ to get $[c \mapsto Zero, d \mapsto Succ\ b]$. The right-hand sides under this substitution are $Succ\ (Plus\ b\ Zero)$ and $Succ\ b$. However, these are not syntactically identical, so equations (B) and (C) are not compatible, and a target such as $Plus\ g\ Zero$ is stuck.

Why not just allow reduction in the RHSs before checking for compatibility? Because doing so is not obviously well-founded! Reducing the $Succ\ (Plus\ b\ Zero)$ type that occurred during the compatibility check above requires knowing that equations (B) and (C) are compatible, which is exactly what we're trying to establish. So, we require syntactic equality to support compatibility, and leave the more general check for future work.

### 7.5 Lack of inequality evidence

One drawback of closed type families is that they sometimes do not compose well with generalized algebraic datatypes (GADTs). Consider the following sensible-looking example:

```
data X a where
  XInt  :: X Int
  XBool :: X Bool
  XChar :: X Char

type family Collapse a where
  Collapse Int = Int
  Collapse x   = Char

collapse :: X a → X (Collapse a)
collapse XInt = XInt
collapse _    = XChar
```

The type function $Collapse$ takes $Int$ to itself and every other type to $Char$. Note the type of the term-level function $collapse$. Its implementation is to match $XInt$—the only constructor of $X$ parameterized by $Int$—and return $XInt$; all other constructors become $XChar$. The structure of $collapse$ exactly mimics that of $Collapse$. Yet, this code does not compile.

The problem is that the type system has no evidence that, in the second equation for $collapse$, the type variable $a$ cannot be $Int$. So, when type-checking the right-hand side $XChar$, it is not type-safe to equate $Collapse\ a$ with $Char$. The source of this problem is that the type system has no notion of *inequality*. If the **case** construct were enhanced to track inequality evidence and axiom application could consider such evidence, it is conceivable that the example above could be made to type-check. Such a notion of inequality has not yet been considered in depth, and we leave it as future work.

### 7.6 Type inference

The addition of closed type families to Haskell opens up new possibilities in type inference. By definition, the full behavior of a closed type family is known all at once. This closed-world assumption allows the type inference engine to perform more improvement on types than would otherwise be possible. Consider the following type family:

```
type family Inj a where
  Inj Int  = Bool
  Inj Bool = Char
  Inj Char = Double
```

Type inference can discover in this case that $Inj$ is indeed an injective type function. When trying to solve a constraint of the form $Inj\ Int \sim Inj\ q$ the type inference engine can deduce that $q$ *must be* equal to $Int$ for the constraint to have a solution. By contrast, if $Inj$ were not identified as injective, we would be left with an unsolved constraint as in principle there could be multiple other types for $q$ that could satisfy $Inj\ Int \sim Inj\ q$.

Along similar lines, we can imagine improving the connection between $Equal$ and $(\sim)$. Currently, if a proof $a \sim b$ is available, type inference will replace all occurrences of $a$ with $b$, after which $Equal\ a\ b$ will reduce to $True$. However, the other direction does not work: if the inference engine knows $Equal\ a\ b \sim True$, it will not deduce $a \sim b$. Given the closed definition of $Equal$, though, it seems possible to enhance the inference engine to be able to go both ways.

These deductions are not currently implemented, but remain as compelling future work.

## 8. Related work

### 8.1 Previous work on System FC

The proof of type soundness presented in this paper depends heavily on previous work for System FC, first presented by Sulzmann et al. (2007a). That work proves consistency only for terminating type families, as we do here.

In a non-terminating system, local confluence does not imply confluence. Therefore, previous work (Weirich et al. 2011) showed confluence of the rewrite system induced by the (potentially non-terminating) axiom set by establishing a *local diamond* property (see Figure 6). However, the proof took a shortcut: the requirements for good contexts effectively limited all axioms to be left-linear. The local diamond proof relies on the fact that, in a system with linear patterns, matching is preserved under reduction. For instance, consider these axioms:

```
type instance F a b = H a
type instance G Int = Bool
```

The type $F\ (G\ Int)\ (G\ Int)$ matches the equation for $F$ and can potentially simplify to $F\ (G\ Int)\ Bool$ or to $F\ Bool\ (G\ Int)$ or even to $F\ Bool\ Bool$. But, in all cases the reduct *also* matches the very same pattern for $F$, allowing local diamond property to be true.[6]

What is necessary to support a local diamond property in a system with *closed* type families, still restricted to linear patterns? We need this property: If $F\ \overline{\tau}$ can reduce by some equation $q$, and $\overline{\tau} \rightsquigarrow \overline{\tau'}$, then $F\ \overline{\tau'}$ can reduce by that same equation $q$. With only open families, this property means that matching must be preserved by reduction. With closed families, however, both matching and *apartness* must be preserved by reduction. Consider the definition for $F'$ below (where $H$ is some other type family):

[6] Actually, under *parallel* reduction; see (Weirich et al. 2011).

$$
\begin{array}{l}
\textbf{type family } F' \; a \; b \textbf{ where} \\
\quad F' \; Int \; Bool = Char \\
\quad F' \; a \quad b \quad\;\; = H \; a
\end{array}
$$

We know that $F' \; (G \; Int) \; (G \; Int)$ matches the second equation and is apart (Definition 6) from the first equation. The reduct $F' \; (G \; Int) \; Bool$ also matches the second equation but is *not* apart from the first equation. Hence, $F' \; (G \; Int) \; Bool$ cannot simplify by either equation for $F'$, and the local diamond property does not hold. Put simply, our apartness implementation is not preserved by reduction.

In a terminating system, we are able to get away with the *weaker* Property 14 for apart (where apartness is not directly preserved under reduction), which our implementation does satisfy. We have designed an implementation of apart which *is* provably stable under reduction, but it is more conservative and less intuitive for programmers. Given that this alternative definition of apart brought a proof of type safety only for potentially non-terminating but *linear* patterns (prohibiting our canonical example *Equal*), and that it often led to stuck targets where a reduction naively seemed possible, we have dismissed it as being impractical. We thus seek out a proof of type safety in the presence of non-terminating, non-left-linear axiom sets.

### 8.2 Type families vs. functional dependencies

Functional dependencies (Jones 2000) (further formalized by Sulzmann et al. (2007b)) allow a programmer to specify a dependency between two or more parameters of a type class. For example, Kiselyov et al. (2004) use this class for their type-level equality function:[7]

$$
\begin{array}{l}
\textbf{class } HEq \; x \; y \; (b :: Bool) \mid x \; y \rightarrow b \\
\textbf{instance } HEq \; x \; x \; True \\
\textbf{instance } (b \sim False) \Rightarrow HEq \; x \; y \; b
\end{array}
$$

The annotation $x \; y \rightarrow b$ in the class header declares a functional dependency from $x$ and $y$ to $b$. In other words, given $x$ and $y$, we can always find $b$.

Functional dependencies have no analogue in GHC's internal language, System FC; indeed they predate it. Rather, functional dependencies simply add extra unification constraints that guide type inference. This can lead to very compact and convenient code, especially when there are multiple class parameters and bi-directional functional dependencies. However, functional dependencies do not generate coercions witnessing the equality between two types. Hence they interact poorly with GADTs and, more generally, with local type equalities. For example, consider the following:

$$
\begin{array}{l}
\textbf{class } Same \; a \; b \mid a \rightarrow b \\
\textbf{instance } Same \; Int \; Int \\[4pt]
\textbf{data } T \; a \textbf{ where} \\
\quad T1 :: T \; Int \\
\quad T2 :: T \; a \\
\textbf{data } S \; a \textbf{ where} \\
\quad MkS :: Same \; a \; b \Rightarrow b \rightarrow S \; a \\[4pt]
f :: T \; a \rightarrow S \; a \rightarrow Int \\
f \; T1 \; (MkS \; b) = b \\
f \; T2 \; s \qquad\;\; = 3
\end{array}
$$

In the $T1$ branch of $f$ we know that $a$ is $Int$, and hence (via the functional dependency and the $Same \; Int \; Int$ instance declaration) the existentially-quantified $b$ must also be $Int$, and the definition should type-check. But GHC rejects $f$, because it cannot produce a well-typed FC term equivalent to it. Could we fix this, by producing evidence in System FC for functional dependencies? Yes; indeed, one can regard functional dependencies as a convenient syntactic sugar for a program using type families. For example we could translate the example like this:

$$
\begin{array}{l}
\textbf{class } F \; a \sim b \Rightarrow Same \; a \; b \textbf{ where} \\
\quad \textbf{type } F \; a \\
\textbf{instance } Same \; Int \; Int \textbf{ where} \\
\quad \textbf{type } F \; Int = Int
\end{array}
$$

Now the (unchanged) definition of $f$ type-checks.

A stylistic difference is that functional dependencies and type classes encourage *logic* programming in the type system, whereas type families encourage *functional* programming.

### 8.3 Controlling overlap

Morris and Jones (2010) introduce *instance chains*, which obviate the need for overlapping instances by introducing a syntax for ordered overlap among instances. Their ideas are quite similar to the ones we present here, with a careful check to make sure that one instance is impossible before moving onto the next. However, the proof burden for their work is lower than ours—a flaw in instance selection may lead to incoherent behavior (e.g., different instances selected for the same code in different modules), but it cannot violate type safety. This is because class instances are compiled solely into term-level constructs (dictionaries), not type-level constructs. In particular, no equalities between different types are created as part of instance compilation.

### 8.4 Full-spectrum dependently typed languages

Type families resemble the type-level computation supported by dependently typed languages. Languages such as Coq (Coq development team 2004) and Agda (Norell 2007) allow ordinary functions to return *types*. As in Haskell, type equality in these languages is defined to include $\beta$-reduction of function application and $\iota$-reduction of pattern matching.

However, there are several significant differences between these type-level functions and type families. The first is that Coq and Agda do not allow the elimination of their equivalents of kind $\star$. There is no way to write a Coq/Agda function analogous to the closed type family below, which returns *True* for function types and *False* otherwise.

$$
\begin{array}{l}
\textbf{type family } IsArrow \; (a :: \star) :: Bool \textbf{ where} \\
\quad IsArrow \; (a \rightarrow b) = True \\
\quad IsArrow \; a \qquad\quad\;\; = False
\end{array}
$$

Instead, pattern matching is only available for *inductive* datatypes. The consistency of these languages prohibits the elimination of non-inductive types such as $\star$ (or *Set*, *Prop*, and *Type*).

Furthermore, pattern matching in Coq and Agda does not support non-linear patterns. As we discussed above, non-linear patterns allow computation to observe whether two types are equal. However, the equational theory of full spectrum languages is much more expressive than that of Haskell. Because these languages allow unsaturated functions in types, it must define when two functions are equal. This comparison is intensional, and allowing computation to observe intensional equality is somewhat suspicious. However, in Haskell, where all type functions must always appear saturated, this issue does not arise.

Due to the lack of non-linear patterns, Coq and Agda programmers must define individual functions for every type that supports decidable equality. (Coq provides a tactic—`decide equality`—to automate this definition.) Furthermore, these definitions do not immediately imply that equality is reflexive; this result must be proved separately and manually applied. In contrast, the closed type family $Equal \; a \; a$ immediately reduces to *True*.

[7] Available from `http://okmij.org/ftp/Haskell/types.html#HList`.

Similarly, functions in Coq and Agda do not support coincident overlap at definition time. Again, these identities can be proven as lemmas, but must be manually applied.

### 8.5 Other functional programming languages

Is our work on closed type families translatable to other functional programming languages with rich type-level programming? We think so. Though the presentation in this paper is tied closely to Haskell, we believe that the notion of apartness would be quite similar (if not the same) in another programming language. Accordingly, the analysis of Section 3 would carry over without much change. The one caveat is that, as mentioned above, non-linear pattern matching depends on the saturation of all type-level functions. If this criterion is met, however, we believe that other languages could adopt the surface syntax and behavior of closed type families as presented here without much change.

## 9. Conclusions

Closed type families improve the usability of type-level computation, and make programming at the type level more reminiscent of ordinary term-level programming. At the same time, closed families allow for the definition of manifestly-reflexive, decidable equality on types of any kind. They allow automatic reductions of types with free variables and allow the user to specify multiple, potentially overlapping but coherent reduction strategies (such as the equations for the *And* example).

On the theoretical side, the question of consistency for non-terminating non-left-linear rewrite systems is an interesting research problem in its own right, quite independent of Haskell or type families, and we offer it as a challenge problem to the reader.

## Acknowledgments

We particularly thank Conor McBride, Joxan Jaffar, and Stefan Kahrs for helping us navigate the literature on term rewriting, and on unification over infinite types. Stefan Kahrs provided the counter-example to confluence. Thanks also to José Pedro Magalhães for detailed and helpful feedback on the paper.

This material is partly supported by the National Science Foundation under Grant Nos. 1116620 and 1319880.

## References

M. Chakravarty, G. Keller, and S. Peyton Jones. Associated type synonyms. In *ACM SIGPLAN International Conference on Functional Programming (ICFP'05)*, Tallinn, Estonia, 2005.

Coq development team. *The Coq proof assistant reference manual*. LogiCal Project, 2004. URL http://coq.inria.fr. Version 8.0.

B. Courcelle. Fundamental properties of infinite trees. *Theoretical computer science*, 25(2):95–169, 1983.

R. A. Eisenberg, D. Vytiniotis, S. Peyton Jones, and S. Weirich. Closed type families with overlapping equations (extended version). Technical report, University of Pennsylvania, 2013.

D. Fridlender and M. Indrika. Functional pearl: Do we need dependent types? *Journal of functional programming*, 10(4):409–415, 2000.

R. Garcia, J. Jarvi, A. Lumsdaine, J. G. Siek, and J. Willcock. A comparative study of language support for generic programming. In *Proceedings of the 18th annual ACM SIGPLAN conference on Object-oriented programing, systems, languages, and applications*, OOPSLA '03, pages 115–134, New York, NY, USA, 2003. ACM. ISBN 1-58113-712-5. . URL http://doi.acm.org/10.1145/949305.949317.

G. Huet. *Résolution d'équations dans les langages d'ordre* $1, 2, \ldots, \omega$. PhD thesis, Université de Paris VII, 1976.

G. Huet. Confluent reductions: Abstract properties and applications to term rewriting systems. *J. ACM*, 27(4):797–821, Oct. 1980. ISSN 0004-5411. . URL http://doi.acm.org/10.1145/322217.322230.

J. Jaffar. Efficient unification over infinite terms. *New Generation Computing*, 2(3):207–219, 1984. ISSN 0288-3635. . URL http://dx.doi.org/10.1007/BF03037057.

M. P. Jones. Type classes with functional dependencies. In G. Smolka, editor, *ESOP*, volume 1782 of *Lecture Notes in Computer Science*, pages 230–244. Springer, 2000. ISBN 3-540-67262-1.

O. Kiselyov, R. Lämmel, and K. Schupke. Strongly typed heterogeneous collections. In *Proc. 2004 ACM SIGPLAN Workshop on Haskell*, Haskell '04, pages 96–107. ACM, 2004.

J. Klop. Term rewriting systems. In *Handbook of logic in computer science (vol. 2)*, pages 1–116. Oxford University Press, Inc., 1993.

K. Knight. Unification: a multidisciplinary survey. *ACM Comput. Surv.*, 21 (1):93–124, Mar. 1989. ISSN 0360-0300. . URL http://doi.acm.org/10.1145/62029.62030.

C. McBride. Faking it: Simulating dependent types in Haskell. *J. Funct. Program.*, 12(5):375–392, July 2002.

J. G. Morris and M. P. Jones. Instance chains: type class programming without overlapping instances. In *Proceedings of the 15th ACM SIGPLAN international conference on Functional programming*, ICFP '10, pages 375–386, New York, NY, USA, 2010. ACM. ISBN 978-1-60558-794-3. . URL http://doi.acm.org/10.1145/1863543.1863596.

M. H. A. Newman. On theories with a combinatorial definition of "equivalence". *Annals of Mathematics*, 43(2):pp. 223–243, 1942. ISSN 0003486X. URL http://www.jstor.org/stable/1968867.

U. Norell. *Towards a practical programming language based on dependent type theory*. PhD thesis, Department of Computer Science and Engineering, Chalmers University of Technology, SE-412 96 Göteborg, Sweden, September 2007.

T. Schrijvers, S. Peyton Jones, M. Chakravarty, and M. Sulzmann. Type checking with open type functions. In *Proceedings of the 13th ACM SIGPLAN international conference on Functional programming*, ICFP '08, pages 51–62, New York, NY, USA, 2008. ACM. ISBN 978-1-59593-919-7. . URL http://doi.acm.org/10.1145/1411204.1411215.

M. Sulzmann, M. M. T. Chakravarty, S. Peyton Jones, and K. Donnelly. System F with type equality coercions. In *Proceedings of the 2007 ACM SIGPLAN international workshop on Types in languages design and implementation*, TLDI '07, pages 53–66, New York, NY, USA, 2007a. ACM.

M. Sulzmann, G. Duck, S. Peyton Jones, and P. Stuckey. Understanding functional dependencies via constraint handling rules. *Journal of Functional Programming*, 17:83–130, Jan. 2007b.

W. Swierstra. Data types à la carte. *J. Funct. Program.*, 18(4):423–436, July 2008. ISSN 0956-7968. . URL http://dx.doi.org/10.1017/S0956796808006758.

S. Weirich and C. Casinghino. Arity-generic datatype-generic programming. In *Proceedings of the 4th ACM SIGPLAN workshop on Programming languages meets program verification*, PLPV '10, pages 15–26, New York, NY, USA, 2010. ACM. ISBN 978-1-60558-890-2. . URL http://doi.acm.org/10.1145/1707790.1707799.

S. Weirich, D. Vytiniotis, S. Peyton Jones, and S. Zdancewic. Generative type abstraction and type-level computation. In *Proceedings of the 38th annual ACM SIGPLAN-SIGACT symposium on Principles of programming languages*, POPL '11, pages 227–240, New York, NY, USA, 2011. ACM.

S. Weirich, J. Hsu, and R. A. Eisenberg. Towards dependently typed Haskell: System FC with kind equality. In *Proceedings of the 18th ACM SIGPLAN International Conference on Functional Programming, ICFP '13, Boston, MA, USA*, New York, NY, USA, 2013. ACM. To appear.

B. A. Yorgey, S. Weirich, J. Cretin, S. Peyton Jones, D. Vytiniotis, and J. P. Magalhães. Giving Haskell a promotion. In *Proc. 8th ACM SIGPLAN workshop on Types in Language Design and Implementation*, TLDI '12, pages 53–66. ACM, 2012.

# Author Index

www.ingramcontent.com/pod-product-compliance
Ingram Content Group UK Ltd.
Pitfield, Milton Keynes, MK11 3LW, UK
UKHW051419290926
15471UKWH00009B/1686